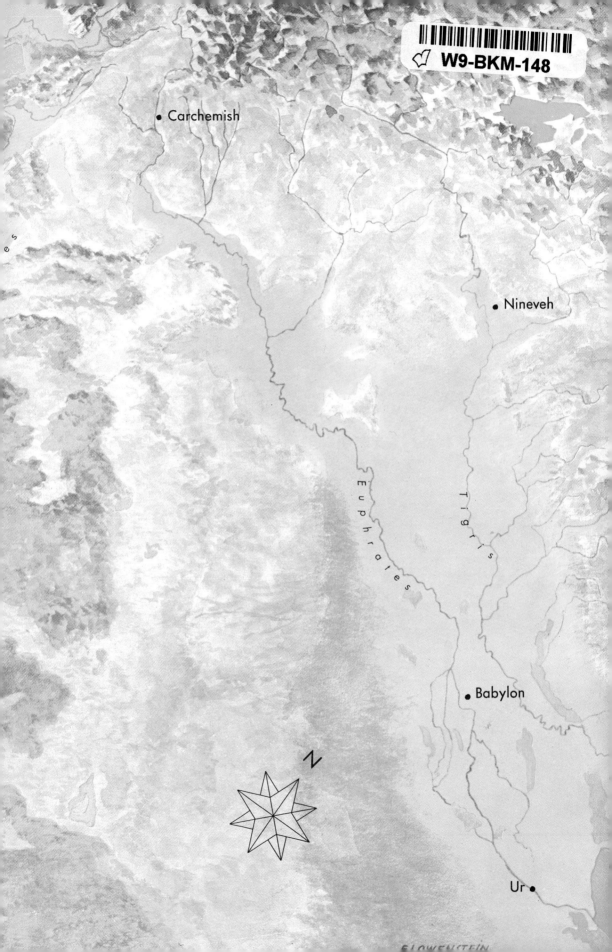

Carchemish

Nineveh

Euphrates

Tigris

Babylon

N

Ur

THE INTERPRETER'S BIBLE

THE INTERPRETER'S BIBLE

IN TWELVE VOLUMES

VOLUME III

THE FIRST AND SECOND BOOKS OF
KINGS

THE FIRST AND SECOND BOOKS OF
CHRONICLES

THE BOOK OF
EZRA

THE BOOK OF
NEHEMIAH

THE BOOK OF
ESTHER

THE BOOK OF
JOB

THE
INTERPRETER'S BIBLE

—

The Holy Scriptures

IN THE KING JAMES AND REVISED STANDARD VERSIONS

WITH GENERAL ARTICLES AND

INTRODUCTION, EXEGESIS, EXPOSITION

FOR EACH BOOK OF THE BIBLE

IN TWELVE VOLUMES

VOLUME
III

דבר־אלהינו יקום לעולם

NEW YORK *Abingdon Press* NASHVILLE

ISBN 0-687-19209-9
Library of Congress Catalog Card Number: 51-12276

Q
SET UP, PRINTED, AND BOUND BY THE
PARTHENON PRESS, AT NASHVILLE,
TENNESSEE, UNITED STATES OF AMERICA

ABBREVIATIONS AND EXPLANATIONS

ABBREVIATIONS

Canonical books and bibliographical terms are abbreviated according to common usage

Amer. Trans. — *The Bible, An American Translation*, Old Testament, ed. J. M. P. Smith

Apoc.—Apocrypha

Aq.—Aquila

ASV—American Standard Version (1901)

Barn.—Epistle of Barnabas

Clem.—Clement

C.T.—Consonantal Text

Did.—Didache

Ecclus.—Ecclesiasticus

ERV—English Revised Version (1881-85)

Exeg.—Exegesis

Expos.—Exposition

Goodspeed—*The Bible, An American Translation*, New Testament and Apocrypha, tr. Edgar J. Goodspeed

Herm. Vis., etc.—The Shepherd of Hermas: Visions, Mandates, Similitudes

Ign. Eph., etc.—Epistles of Ignatius to the Ephesians, Magnesians, Trallians, Romans, Philadelphians, Smyrnaeans, and Polycarp

KJV—King James Version (1611)

LXX—Septuagint

Macc.—Maccabees

Moffatt—*The Bible, A New Translation*, by James Moffatt

M.T.—Masoretic Text

N.T.—New Testament

O.T.—Old Testament

Polyc. Phil.—Epistle of Polycarp to the Philippians

Pseudep. — Pseudepigrapha

Pss. Sol.—Psalms of Solomon

RSV—Revised Standard Version (1946-52)

Samar.—Samaritan recension

Symm.—Symmachus

Targ.—Targum

Test. Reuben, etc.—Testament of Reuben, and others of the Twelve Patriarchs

Theod.—Theodotion

Tob.—Tobit

Vulg.—Vulgate

Weymouth—*The New Testament in Modern Speech*, by Richard Francis Weymouth

Wisd. Sol.—Wisdom of Solomon

QUOTATIONS AND REFERENCES

Boldface type in Exegesis and Exposition indicates a quotation from either the King James or the Revised Standard Version of the passage under discussion. The two versions are distinguished only when attention is called to a difference between them. Readings of other versions are not in boldface type and are regularly identified.

In scripture references a letter (*a, b,* etc.) appended to a verse number indicates a clause within the verse; an additional Greek letter indicates a subdivision within the clause. When no book is named, the book under discussion is understood.

Arabic numbers connected by colons, as in scripture references, indicate chapters and verses in deuterocanonical and noncanonical works. For other ancient writings roman numbers indicate major divisions, arabic numbers subdivisions, these being connected by periods. For modern works a roman number and an arabic number connected by a comma indicate volume and page. Bibliographical data on a contemporary work cited by a writer may be found by consulting the first reference to the work by that writer (or the bibliography, if the writer has included one).

GREEK TRANSLITERATIONS

α = a	ε = e	ι = i	ν = n	ρ = r	φ = ph
β = b	ζ = z	κ = k	ξ = x	σ(ς) = s	χ = ch
γ = g	η = ē	λ = l	ο = o	τ = t	ψ = ps
δ = d	θ = th	μ = m	π = p	υ = u, y	ω = ō

HEBREW AND ARAMAIC TRANSLITERATIONS

I. HEBREW ALPHABET

א = '	ה = h	ט = ṭ	מ(ם) = m	פ(ף) = p, ph	שׁ = s, sh
ב = b, bh	ו = w	י = y	נ(ן) = n	צ(ץ) = ç	תּ = t, th
ג = g, gh	ז = z	כ(ך) = k, kh	ס = ṣ	ק = q	
ד = d, dh	ח = ḥ	ל = l	ע = '	ר = r	

II. MASORETIC POINTING

Pure-long	Tone-long	Short	Composite *sheʷa*
ָ = â	ַ = ā	ַ = a	ֲ = ᵃ
.. = ê	.. = ē	.. = e	ֳ = ᵒ
or ִ = î		ִ = i	
ֹ *or* ' = ô	' = ō	ָ = o	ֱ = ᵉ
ּ = û		= u	

NOTE: (*a*) The *páthaḥ* furtive is transliterated as a *haṭeph-páthaḥ*. (*b*) The simple *sheʷa*, when vocal, is transliterated ᵉ. (*c*) The tonic accent, which is indicated only when it occurs on a syllable other than the last, is transliterated by an acute accent over the vowel.

TABLE OF CONTENTS

VOLUME III

THE FIRST AND SECOND BOOKS OF KINGS

THE FIRST AND SECOND BOOKS OF CHRONICLES

THE INTERPRETER'S BIBLE

THE BOOK OF EZRA AND THE BOOK OF NEHEMIAH

THE BOOK OF ESTHER

THE BOOK OF JOB

*By special arrangement with Abingdon Press the author used the substance of his Exposition of Job as his James A. Gray lectures delivered at Duke University in 1951 prior to the publication of this volume of *The Interpreter's Bible*.

TABLE OF CONTENTS

MAPS

The First and Second Books of

KINGS

Introduction and Exegesis by NORMAN H. SNAITH
Exposition I Kings by RALPH W. SOCKMAN
Exposition II Kings by RAYMOND CALKINS

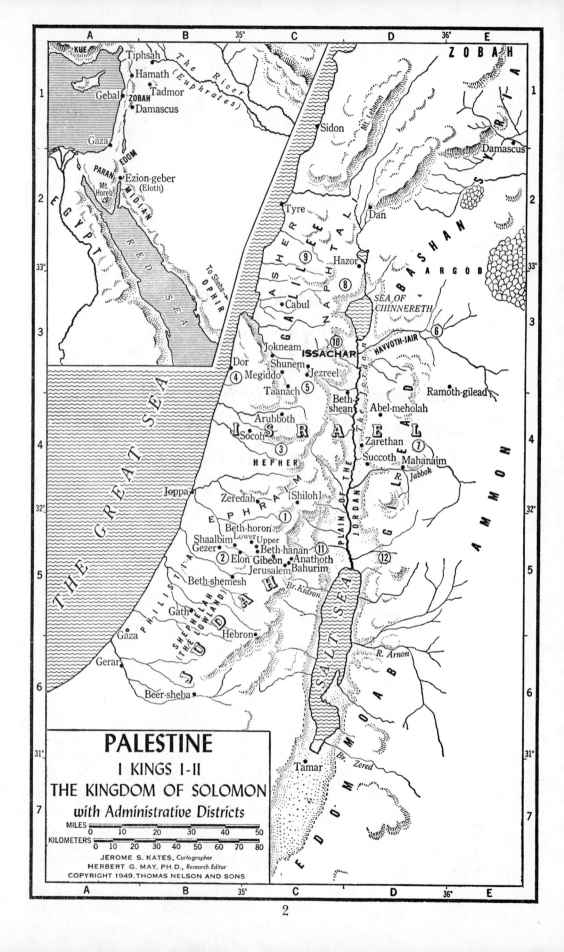

PALESTINE

I KINGS I-II
THE KINGDOM OF SOLOMON
with Administrative Districts

MILES

0   10   20   30   40   50

KILOMETERS

0   10   20   30   40   50   60   70   80

JEROME S. KATES, *Cartographer*

HERBERT G. MAY, PH.D., *Research Editor*

COPYRIGHT 1949, THOMAS NELSON AND SONS

I AND II KINGS

INTRODUCTION

The two books now known as I and II Kings formed originally a single work, and they were the fourth and last book in that section of the Hebrew Bible which is known as the Former Prophets. The division into two books was first made in the Septuagint, probably as a matter of convenience rather than of deliberate design. We know that the books of Jeremiah and Ezekiel were both bisected for convenience in translation, and there are indications that this custom was followed on other occasions also.[1]

In the Septuagint the two books are known as Third and Fourth Kingdoms, and this ancient nomenclature is preserved in part in the Vulgate in its customary compromise between the Hebrew and the Greek in the matter of titles. In the Vulgate, I and II Kings are called III and IV "of Kings." Origen[2] testifies that the Jews regarded them as one book, while the Greeks of his day regarded them as two. In this he is supported by Cyril of Jerusalem[3] and Jerome.[4]

The internal evidence for one original book is to be found in Greek manuscripts, chiefly in the Septuagint Codex Vaticanus and in Lucian's version, but also in other Septuagint manuscripts. In Codex Vaticanus, for instance, the first verse of IV Kingdoms (i.e., II Kings) is found also at the end of III Kingdoms (i.e., I Kings), while the Lucian text repeats the second verse also as far as the end of the first sentence, that is, as far as the word ἠρρώστησεν.

Such an overlap is actually found at the end of II Chronicles in all Bibles, ancient and modern, whatever the language. In the Hebrew Bible, and therefore in every other, the first two verses of Ezra-Nehemiah and the major part of the third verse have been repeated at the end of II Chronicles. The break comes right in the middle of a sentence. Ezra 1:3 states that the devout exiles were not merely to "go up," as the end of II Chronicles says, but that they were to "go up to Jerusalem." The same phenomenon is found in Septuagint manuscripts, not only at the end of III Kingdoms (I Kings), but also at the end of I Kingdoms (I Samuel) and I Chronicles. It was indeed a regular custom of ancient copyists in the case of a single work which had to be written on more than one scroll, and the custom arose "so that the reader could find correctly what should follow."[5]

The first indication of a division in Hebrew Bibles appears in the First Rabbinic Bible of 1517, printed by Daniel Bomberg at his Hebrew printing office in Venice, and edited by Felix Pratensis. There is indeed a complete break in this Bible between I and II Samuel, but an asterisk appears between I and II Kings with a note in the margin which says, "Here the foreigners[6] begin the Fourth Book of Kings."

I. Author

The generally accepted opinion is that the author of the books of Kings completed his

---

[1] H. St. John Thackeray, *The Septuagint and Jewish Worship* (London: British Academy, 1921), pp. 116-36.
[2] According to Eusebius *Church History* VI. 25. 2.
[3] *Catechetical Lectures* IV. 33.
[4] *Preface to the Books of Samuel and Kings.*

[5] Alfred Rahlfs, ed., *Septuaginta* (Stuttgart: Württembergische Bibelanstalt, 1935), I, 564 n.
[6] The word is תלועים, used in the Jerusalem Talmud, Megilla II 73a, of Greek-speaking Jews reading the roll of Esther in Greek and not in Hebrew.

work about 600 B.C., soon after the death of King Josiah, but before the glamour of those days had died away.[7] There was a thorough revision under strong Deuteronomic influence about 550 B.C., and other still later additions, mostly under the influence of the Priestly Code. These successive revisions will be discussed later; meanwhile it is necessary to consider the original author and his aims.

The death of Ashurbanipal in 626 B.C., and the immediately consequent breakup of the Assyrian Empire, gave Josiah of Judah the opportunity to restore the national fortunes in general and the national religion in particular. By 621 B.C. he was busy restoring the temple. One day Hilkiah the priest produced a scroll which he said he had found during the renovations. Perhaps he was astonished to find it; perhaps he knew where to look—that problem will probably never be solved, but the scroll is generally agreed to have been the nucleus of the present book of Deuteronomy.[8] When King Josiah heard Shaphan the secretary read what was written on the scroll, he was so appalled at the terrible threats of disaster as a requital for the idolatries of the past that he forthwith instituted wide and far-reaching reforms. He removed the idols and the idolatrous cult objects which former apostate kings had introduced into the temple (II Kings 23:11-12); he rendered the age-old sites in the environs of Jerusalem unfit for religious use by filling them with dead men's bones (II Kings 23:10, 13-14); he destroyed all the upcountry shrines (II Kings 23:19) so as to centralize the worship in Jerusalem; and he cleared the land of wizards and witches in a determined effort to do away with all forms of necromancy (II Kings 23:24).

With all these reforms the author of the books of Kings was in full-throated agreement. He was a most ardent admirer of King Josiah. Judah never had a king like him, and in II Kings 23:25 he sings his praises in language saturated with Deuteronomic phrases. The writer was certainly full of unbounded zeal for all these reforms. C. F. Burney[9] gives a list of fifty-one Deuteronomic phrases that are characteristic of the style which is dominant throughout the books. Indeed, the whole work is written to demonstrate the soundness, both in theory and practice, of the Deuteronomic theory of

life, with Josiah as the greatest example and proof of its pragmatic value. Our author made everything pass through the Deuteronomic sieve. It is probable that he omitted such material as was not suitable for his didactic purpose; it is possible that he made occasional adjustments in his treatment of the material he used; it is certain that in the result everything has been fitted into the Deuteronomic scheme.

II. Sources

There are three sources mentioned by name, and probably four others. The three which are mentioned are: (a) The Acts of Solomon; (b) The Book of the Chronicles of the Kings of Israel; (c) The Book of the Chronicles of the Kings of Judah. The other four sources of the books of Kings were concerned with the four outstanding figures of the ninth and eighth centuries—Ahab, Elijah, Elisha of the North, and Isaiah of the South. The author-compiler of Josiah's time used the three sources which are mentioned by name and also the Isaiah narratives, but not the other four, which bear many indications of having been inserted at later periods.

A. The Acts of Solomon.—This work is mentioned specifically in I Kings 11:41; it was a biographical rather than a historical document, being designed primarily to set forth the wisdom, the riches, and the general magnificence of King Solomon. The two verses I Kings 3:12-13 might very well stand as a text-introduction for the biography as a whole: "Behold, I give you a wise and discerning mind, so that none like you has been before you and none like you shall arise after you. I give you also what you have not asked, both riches and honor, so that no other king shall compare with you, all your days." The biography seems to have been compiled from the royal annals and from official temple records, but it contained such folk tales as the story of Solomon's judgment in I Kings 3:16-28. Some scholars are of the opinion that the author of the books of Kings found and used the temple records independently of the biography,[10] but it is better on the whole to assume that Solomon's biographer had already incorporated the nucleus of them (there having been very considerable later expansion) to the greater glory of Solomon.

It is from this laudatory biography of Solomon that we get the notice of Solomon's Egyptian marriage (I Kings 3:1), and also the nucleus of the dream at Gibeon. This latter account, as it now stands in I Kings 3:3-15, bears many traces of the author-compiler's own handiwork. Vs. 3 is his, inserted as a preface to the whole story to explain why the king ever

[7] Robert H. Pfeiffer, *Introduction to the Old Testament* (New York: Harper & Bros., 1941), p. 379; also pp. 410, 412.

[8] Deut. 4:44–8:20; 10:12–11:25; 12:1–26:19; 28:1-24, 43-46; 29:1.

[9] *Notes on the Hebrew Text of the Books of Kings* (Oxford: Clarendon Press, 1903), pp. xiii-xiv; see also S. R. Driver, *An Introduction to the Literature of the Old Testament* (rev. ed.; New York: Charles Scribner's Sons, 1913), pp. 200-3.

[10] Pfeiffer, *op. cit.*, pp. 386, 409.

went to Gibeon at all in face of plain Deuteronomic commands to the contrary. The narrative of the dream, as the author found it in his source, was probably very close to what is found in the Chronicler's parallel (II Chr. 1:7-13), where the obviously Deuteronomic elements are almost entirely absent.

The account of Solomon's well-known judgment of the case of the two mothers and the one child is in substantially the form in which the author found it in his source. In the following chapter there are lists of Solomon's chief princes (I Kings 4:1-6) and of the twelve administrators whom he put in charge of the districts into which he divided the country when he apparently sought to break up the local tribal loyalties (I Kings 4:7-19). These lists were doubtless originally in the royal records, but had been incorporated into the biography as evidence of Solomon's power and magnificence. The remainder of I Kings 4 gives further details of Solomon's wealth and splendor and wisdom. Most of the details are from the biography, but vss. 20-21 and 24-25 are later elements, since they are not found in either the Septuagint or Lucian's version.

I Kings 5–8 (English versions, but 5:15–8:66 in the Hebrew) deals with the building of the temple—that is, the preparations, the actual building operations, and the dedication of the completed building. The nucleus was originally in the temple archives, and perhaps after that in the biography, but the whole section has been considerably expanded by the author, himself neither builder nor architect, and it has been worked over more than once during succeeding centuries, especially by scribes who were thoroughly familiar with the layout and the furniture of the postexilic temple.

Other passages which the author found in his source are Solomon's final settlement of accounts with Hiram king of Tyre (I Kings 9:11-14); the building of Millo (I Kings 9:23-25); and the reference to Solomon's ventures in overseas trade (I Kings 9:26-28). There was also in the Acts of Solomon an account of the visit of the queen of Sheba (I Kings 10:1-10, 13, vs. 9 being the author's own addition). The author also found many details concerning Solomon's fabulous wealth. How accurate these figures are may be judged from the statement that in taxation alone Solomon received 666 gold talents annually, that is, about twenty-five million dollars (I Kings 10:14). This material has been partly woven into the story of the queen of Sheba (I Kings 10:11-12), as if to impress her as well as us, and it is continued in the other parts of the chapter. In I Kings 11 there are some original verses from the biography (vss. 1a, 3a, 4a, 7-8), but the rest of vss. 1-8 is due to the author who

saw in these foreign wives the cause of Solomon's departure from the proper Deuteronomic standards of life and the resultant disasters which ensued. Finally comes the author's concluding formula (I Kings 11:41-43).

B. The Book of the Chronicles of the Kings of Israel.—This source is mentioned seventeen times in all, the first time being I Kings 14:19. Here, as before, the author refers the reader to his source if further information is required. The only two northern kings for whom this source is not cited are Jehoram son of Ahab, and Hoshea. Scholars generally agree that the source book came to an end before the reign of Hoshea, since it is not mentioned in connection with him. The omission in the case of Jehoram renders this unlikely. The more probable reason for the omissions is that in neither case did the actual course of the narrative allow the customary notice concerning the death and burial of the king. This notice invariably precedes the author's reference to his source. It may therefore be held that the source did include details from Hoshea's reign, though probably not the story of the final collapse. The source, as a whole, dates from about 725 B.C. The material from this source has been almost invariably embedded in a Deuteronomic framework, for the author used it boldly by way of illustrating his Deuteronomic theme.

C. The Book of the Chronicles of the Kings of Judah.—This source is first mentioned in I Kings 14:29, and fifteen times altogether. The reader is referred to it for further information in the cases of all the kings of Judah, except for Ahaziah and three of the last four kings—Jehoahaz, Jehoiachin, and Zedekiah. In addition, there is no reference in the case of Athaliah, who seized the throne at the death of her son Ahaziah and held it for seven years (II Kings 11:1, 4). The reason for the omission of any reference to the source in the case of Jehoram of Israel may be that the narrative gave the author no opportunity to insert his regular formulas of death, burial place, and source of further information. Exactly the same situation confronted him in the case of Ahaziah of Judah, that other king whom Jehu slew. It is noticeable that the cases of Jehoahaz, Jehoiachin, and Zedekiah are similar to that of Hoshea, for in none of these cases are the death and the place of burial recorded. Like Hoshea, they all three ceased to reign before they died. Particularly are these omissions noteworthy, since the source is actually mentioned in the case of Jehoiakim (II Kings 24:5-6), who died in his bed, and whose death is recorded. We cannot therefore say, as some do, that the Chronicles of the Kings of Judah ceased to be written up in the days of Josiah. As in the parallel chronicle of the northern kings, it may well have included all but the closing scenes of the life of Zedekiah, the last of the Judean kings. The final date of it may therefore be as late as about 590 B.C. Once again, the material taken from this source has been regularly embedded in a Deuteronomic framework, since the author used this material also in bold illustration of his theme.

III. Method

The author's method is most clear in the second section of his work—the period of the two kingdoms—where he had to deal with two separate lines of kings (I Kings 12:1–II Kings 17:41). He goes through the lists steadily, mentioning every successive king in the proper historical order, giving a place even to Zimri, who can scarcely be said to have reigned at all. His attempt to seize the throne at the death of Elah succeeded only to the extent of the elimination of all Elah's kindred, and the occupation of Tirzah, the capital, for seven days (I Kings 16:8-20).

The author does his best to deal with both kingdoms contemporaneously. He does this by dealing with the whole story of one king from accession to death, and then going back to deal with all the kings of the other kingdom who began to reign after his succession. This has the disadvantage of mentioning on occasion a king of the other kingdom whose accession has not yet been recorded, but some anomalies were bound to arise whatever scheme had been adopted. The author's scheme is as good as any, and indeed better than most. He begins this second section of the book by telling the story of Rehoboam's accession with its immediate consequence in the revolt of the northern tribes and the activity of Jeroboam son of Nebat. Having thus mentioned the setting up of the Northern Kingdom of Israel and Jeroboam's establishment of himself as king, the author continues the story of this monarch's reign, records his death, and gives the name of his successor (I Kings 14:20). By this time Rehoboam has been succeeded in the Southern Kingdom by Abijam, and Abijam by Asa, so the author now turns to Judah to give an account of these three reigns. This brings the story of the south down to the end of Asa's reign, an over-all period of sixty-one years. He then goes back to Nadab, Jeroboam's successor in the north, and gives an account of all the kings of Israel who came to the throne while Asa was reigning in the south, Nadab having become king in Asa's second year. This involves the reigns of five northern kings—Baasha, Elah, Zimri, Omri, and Ahab. Because of Asa's long reign the author mentions nothing, except acci-

dentally, about the Southern Kingdom from I Kings 15:25 to I Kings 22:41, the gap having been made even more pronounced by the later interpolation of the Elijah stories and some of the stories of Ahab.

After the death of Ahab we turn back again to his fourth year, when Jehoshaphat of Judah began to reign, but at I Kings 22:51 we return to the north, for Jehoshaphat is dead. With Ahaziah of Israel dying within the year from injuries received through a fall from an upstairs window, Jehoram of Israel soon becomes king. Here the author has to break with the regularity of his scheme because he cannot tell the story of this king's death until he has told the story of Jehu's revolt. He therefore leaves the story of Jehoram of Israel in his fifth year (II Kings 8:15) in order to give an account of the seven years of Jehoram of Judah and of the reign of Ahaziah of Judah up to the time when Ahaziah went to visit his cousin Jehoram, who was lying ill in Jezreel. He is forced to bring the southern story up to this point because he has to tell how Jehu slew two kings in one day. The account of Jehu's revolt therefore necessarily follows the reference to Ahaziah's visit to Jezreel (II Kings 8:29). The author's scheme incidentally is further disrupted by the later insertion of II Kings 2:1–7:20, the first two chapters of which may have belonged to the Elisha narratives, and the last four of which certainly did.

After his account of Jehu's reign, which concludes at II Kings 10:34-36, the author is able to resume his regular scheme. This he now maintains without variation till the Northern Kingdom ceases to exist (II Kings 17:6; the rest of this chapter is by other and later writers). Thereafter, there being now but one kingdom, the author is able to complete the third and last section of his book, which begins at II Kings 18:1, by going straight ahead with the successive kings of Judah until he has brought the history down to his own time. The whole scheme is marked out most clearly by the formulas which the author used, both for the introduction of the successive kings and at the conclusion of the story of their reigns.

His chief difficulty consisted in the dating of the whole period. He did this by giving the year of the reign of the corresponding king in the other kingdom. Actually he had no other method of fixing a date than by such a synchronization, since in his day there was no dating event from which the counting of years could be made. There are discrepancies, three years one way from Jeroboam to Jehu, and twenty-one years the other way from Jehu to the fall of Samaria. Perhaps the errors were in the author's sources, but it is more likely that the miscalculations were his. In any case, it is more than probable that the difficulties of calculating a correct synchronization were well-nigh insurmountable. When, for instance, did Hezekiah actually become king of Judah? Was it 727 B.C., or 725, or 720, or 715? There is some justification for each date, and in this case the confusion certainly belongs in part to the sources. The whole problem of the chronology of the regal period is most complicated, and there is considerable literature on the subject.[11]

IV. Purpose

The author's aim was quite definitely and deliberately religious, and his textbook was the original Deuteronomic nucleus, that is, the scroll which was found in the temple in 621 B.C., the basis of the reformation under King Josiah. He has written the whole history to show how sound the Deuteronomic teaching is, and ultimately to put forward King Josiah as the perfect example of what a Deuteronomic king should do.

The Deuteronomic scroll which Hilkiah found in the temple is a crystallization of the teachings of the great eighth-century prophets, Amos, Hosea, Isaiah, and Micah. The reform of Josiah was actually an attempt to establish their teaching as the official, national religion of the kingdom of Judah. With this there is associated the promise of the continuity of the Davidic dynasty, conditional always upon the proper observance of the Deuteronomic teaching (cf. II Sam. 7:12-16). The author's aim is set down in his account of David's final charge to Solomon (I Kings 2:2-4), a passage which is full of characteristic Deuteronomic phraseology. His purpose is to place before both king and people the injunction: "Keep the charge of the LORD thy God, to walk in his ways, to keep his statutes, and his commandments, and his judgments, and his testimonies, as it is written in the law of Moses, that thou mayest prosper in all that thou doest, and whithersoever thou turnest thyself." Then in vs. 4 comes the particular promise concerning the Davidic dynasty.

The basis of the teaching is to be read in Amos 3:2, with its statement of God's special choice of Israel to be his people out of all the families of the earth. This special choice involved the exclusive right of God to the worship and wholehearted allegiance of Israel. For Israel, "the LORD is our God, the LORD alone" (Deut. 6:4). The nucleus of Deuteronomy does not involve a full doctrine of monotheism, a

[11] See the discussion in W. O. E. Oesterley and T. H. Robinson, *A History of Israel* (Oxford: Clarendon Press, 1932), I, 454-64. See also Edwin R. Thiele, *The Mysterious Numbers of the Hebrew Kings* (Chicago: University of Chicago Press, 1951).

doctrine which became explicit during the Exile, and is actually embodied in the later strata of Deuteronomy (e.g., 4:28, 35, 39). The first stratum of the Deuteronomic teaching, that which forms the basis of the work of the original author of the books of Kings, insists that Israel shall have nothing at all to do with any other gods. "Ye shall not go after other gods, of the gods of the people which are round about you" (Deut. 6:14). The Lord is a jealous God; he is a God who brooks no rival. There must be no slightest acknowledgment in any shape or form, no slightest tolerance for any other god within Israel. The Lord alone may be worshiped, and this by all, whether native Israelite or resident alien. Thus Solomon is severely criticized (I Kings 11:1-8) because he built shrines for the national deities of his many wives and concubines, and the various troubles of his reign are put down to this cause. Three foreign deities are listed as having their worship countenanced by Solomon: the Zidonian Astarte, the Ammonite Melek (Milcom, Molech), and the Moabite Chemosh. Later (I Kings 15:13) Asa of Judah is commended on the ground that he removed his mother Maacah from the position of head of the women's household because she had set up an Asherah idol in Jerusalem. Coupled with this demand for the exclusive worship of the Lord, the author has also taken over the Deuteronomic idea of rigid retribution. Whoever fulfills the Deuteronomic law will assuredly prosper; whoever does not fulfill this law will undoubtedly meet with disaster. The whole history of the kings of both north and south is written to show the workings of this principle.

The author's insistence upon the exclusive worship of the Lord God of Israel works out in two ways. The first is that there shall be one place and one place alone where the one God may be worshiped. This place is Jerusalem, and in particular that temple which David proposed to build, but which his son Solomon actually built. It is difficult to see how the policy of one central sanctuary could have been at all practicable before the fall of Samaria in 722 B.C., since before that time the distances would have been too great, especially before the northern provinces of Israel were detached by the Assyrians in 734 B.C. But in the seventh century the territory of Judah was much circumscribed, and even Beer-sheba in the south was only fifty miles from the northerly border of Judah, which ran in a northwesterly direction close by Jerusalem itself. In any case, such a policy of centralization was essential in any approach toward a true monotheism, or even toward the establishment of the national worship of one God alone. Local shrines meant local loyalties, and unity was essential in the time of national revival which followed the fall of the Assyrian power. Further, the people had been accustomed from time immemorial to the idea of a multiplicity of shrines, each shrine with its own traditions, its own cult, and a special name for the god who was worshiped there. The history of religion shows that such differences lead almost inevitably to polytheism, and it is doubtful whether such ideas could ever be eradicated from the minds of the people, whatever had been said, and however forcefully, by the eighth-century prophets. Any king, therefore, who encouraged any worship, even of the Lord himself, at any shrine other than that at Jerusalem was held by the author to be a bad king and is condemned by him. This forthrightness and rigidness is to be seen at its clearest in the author's condemnation of Jehu (II Kings 10:31). The king undoubtedly believed himself to be a true worshiper of the Lord, so much so that he could make boast of his zeal for the Lord even to the strict and orthodox Jehonadab son of Rechab (II Kings 10:16). The author himself says that "Jehu destroyed Baal out of Israel," but in spite of this he adds that "Jehu was not careful to walk in the law of the LORD the God of Israel with all his heart" (II Kings 10:31). This adverse judgment is due to the fact that Jehu "departed not from the sins of Jeroboam" (vs. 31) and continued the worship at Bethel and the local shrines of the north. No king of Israel thus escapes condemnation, not even the king who followed the dictates of Elijah and Elisha and wiped out the idolatrous house of Omri.

The second result of the author's adherence to the Deuteronomic teaching is his utter abhorrence of everything associated with the local shrines. He is severe against every form of idolatry. He commends every reform which involves the abolition of idols (I Kings 15:12). The climax of the extreme wickedness which made Ahab worse than all his predecessors was his making an idol (I Kings 16:33). Hezekiah is praised because of the clean sweep which he made of idolatrous objects, even including the bronze serpent which tradition associated with Moses. On the other hand, Manasseh did everything which he ought not to have done, and broke every law which the Deuteronomists had laid down. "He made his son to pass through the fire, and practised augury, and used enchantments, and dealt with them that had familiar spirits, and with wizards" (II Kings 21:6 ASV); all this in addition to his restoration of the apostasies of Ahab of Israel and his introduction of the star-gods of Assyria and their cults.

The doctrine of retribution is worked out precisely according to Deuteronomic theory. The difficulties of Solomon are ascribed to the fact that he countenanced the setting up of shrines for his wives. This is why Edom revolted from him under Hadad, and Syria under Rezon. Solomon's apostasy and his troubles are all put by the author at the end of his reign. In this the author was probably influenced by his theories of retribution, not being able to admit that these troubles overtook Solomon the builder of the temple while the king was still faithful to the trust which his father had imposed upon him. But the retribution is nevertheless severe. God is unwilling to destroy the Davidic line in spite of Solomon's sins, but he did raise up Jeroboam to punish the Davidic dynasty by rending away all but one tribe (I Kings 11:32). But although Jeroboam is raised up by God to punish the apostasy of Solomon, yet Jeroboam and his house do not escape judgment because he and his successors did not follow the Davidic model (I Kings 14:7-10). The adherence of the author to the strict Deuteronomic ideas of retributive justice is to be seen particularly in Amaziah's punishment of his father's murderers. He executed the murderers themselves, but he did not put their children to death as the ancient custom demanded. The author states that in doing this Amaziah was acting "according to what is written in the book of the law of Moses" (II Kings 14:6). This law is apparently Deut. 24:16. Another instance of the author's loyalty to the Deuteronomic doctrine of retribution is his comment on Zimri, who managed to seize the throne of Israel for seven days. He can scarcely be said to have reigned at all, but what he did is most important from the author's point of view because it was he who executed the proper retribution on the house of Baasha in that they had continued in the religious separatism of Jeroboam (I Kings 16:12-15).

The author of the books of Kings has not a very great deal to say in line with the humanitarian doctrines of Deuteronomy, nor does he deal with the social crimes of bribery and corruption in the courts and oppression of the poor generally. Such details, important as they are, were outside his immediate purview. He was dealing with the history of the people as a whole. He painted on a broad canvas and with a large brush. Nevertheless he never lost an opportunity of condemning the immoralities which were associated with Canaanite worship, and commended those kings who abolished sacred prostitution, whether it involved males or females (I Kings 14:24; II Kings 23:7).

V. Formulas of the Framework

The author shows his adherence to Deuteronomic principles clearly in the framework into which he has set his material. He has standardized, mostly in Deuteronomic phraseology, his introductions to the reigns of the kings, and equally he has standardized his conclusions.

A. Introductions to the Reigns of the Kings of Judah.—There are four items: 1. The date of the king's accession is given in terms of the year of the reigning king of Israel: "Now in the eighteenth year of King Jeroboam the son of Nebat, Abijam began to reign over Judah" (I Kings 15:1). The same formula is found for every king of Judah from Abijam to Hezekiah, with slight variations in the cases of Jehoshaphat (I Kings 22:41) and Jehoash (II Kings 12:1). After Hezekiah this formula was necessarily abandoned, since in his day there ceased to be a king in Israel.

2. The age of the king at his accession: "Rehoboam was forty-one years old when he began to reign" (I Kings 14:21). This type of note is found for every king from Rehoboam to Zedekiah, though in the case of the boy Jehoash it comes first instead of second, doubtless because of the way in which the whole series of events is wrapped up with his exceeding youthfulness.

3. The name of the queen mother: of Rehoboam son of Solomon, "His mother's name was Naamah the Ammonitess" (I Kings 14:21). This information, necessary in times of plural marriages, is given for every king from Rehoboam to Zedekiah, except for Jehoram and for Ahaz. There seems to be no particular reason for the omission in either case. In the case of Rehoboam the information is given twice, once in the usual position in I Kings 14:21, and again in the Masoretic Text at I Kings 14:31, after the notice of his death; but since this repetition is not found either in the Septuagint or in the parallel text of II Chronicles, it is safe to assume that it is an interpolation into the original text.

4. A brief summary of the king's attitude to the Deuteronomic laws with a definite comparison with "David his father." It is in respect of this last item that the author's didactic purpose is most clearly seen.

Only two kings earned the author's unqualified approbation, Hezekiah and Josiah (II Kings 18:3; 22:2). In each case the detailed account of his reforms, short in the case of Hezekiah but very long in the case of Josiah, is followed by the statement that there never was such a king either before or after (II Kings 18:5; 23:25). There is increased emphasis concerning Josiah, both in respect of the initial approbation and the final summary. In the cases of six other kings the author's praise is modified. This is true even in the case of Asa, who evidently was a great reformer and was responsible for greatly increasing the temple treasures.

The modification is that although "the heart of Asa was wholly true to the LORD all his days" (I Kings 15:14), yet "the high places [i.e., the provincial, upcountry shrines] were not taken away." The five kings, apart from Asa, were Jehoshaphat, Jehoash, Amaziah, Azariah-Uzziah, and Jotham. Each of these kings "did that which was right in the eyes of the LORD," as his father had done before him, "yet the high places were not taken away, and the people still sacrificed and burned incense on the high places" (I Kings 22:43; II Kings 12:2-3; 14:3-4; 15:3-4, 34-35).

The remaining ten kings are all severely criticized in that they "did what was evil in the sight of the LORD" (II Kings 8:18, 27; 21:2, 20; 23:32, 37; 24:9, 19), with modifications in the formula in the cases of Abijam (I Kings 15:3) and Ahaz (II Kings 16:2). The author here shows his abhorrence of any worship at any shrine other than the temple at Jerusalem. The existence of the separate Northern Kingdom was a source of great concern to him because it weaned men away from Jerusalem and encouraged that worship at the local shrines which the author, as a good Deuteronomist, so thoroughly detested. His comments on the wickedness of all the kings of Israel (see below) epitomize this attitude. This is particularly evident in the cases of Jeroboam son of Nebat, and later, Ahab son of Omri. His intense dislike of Jeroboam is concerned with that king's institution of the rival worship of the north, especially the cultus at Bethel, while his hatred of Ahab is concerned more with the sacrifices at the high places than with his condonation of the worship of the Tyrian Baal. The Elijah stories are no part of the original book. Our estimate therefore of Ahab is largely governed by material which the Deuteronomic editor did not use. Three southern kings are severely criticized for doing as Ahab and the kings of Israel had done. These are Ahab's son-in-law Ahaziah (II Kings 8:27), Ahaz (II Kings 16:3) and Manasseh (II Kings 21:3). The main ground of this complaint is that they "sacrificed and burned incense on the high places, and on the hills, and under every green tree" (II Kings 16:4). Manasseh now becomes the type of wicked king (II Kings 21:20). After this the basis of criticism changes somewhat. Jehoahaz and Jehoiakim are condemned because they did as "their fathers" (II Kings 23:32, 37), and Jehoiachin and Zedekiah because they did as Jehoiakim had done (II Kings 24:9, 19). These comments are the work not of the original Deuteronomic author, but of the later Deuteronomic editor of about 550 B.C.

B. Introductions to the Reigns of the Kings of Israel.—Here there are four items: 1. The date of the king's accession is given in terms of the corresponding year of the reigning king of Judah: "In the third year of Asa king of Judah, Baasha the son of Ahijah began to reign over all Israel" (I Kings 15:33).

2. The name of the capital from which he reigned: This was part of the king's offense, since it involved a revolt from David's line reigning in Jerusalem, the only place where, according to the author, either religion or state could properly find its center of loyalty. The capital is mentioned in every case from Baasha onward, first Tirzah until Omri built Samaria, and then Samaria from the time of Ahab until the end of the kingdom of Israel.

3. The length of the king's reign: This is generally in the introduction, but the regular scheme is necessarily varied in the cases of Jeroboam son of Nebat and of Jehu.

4. A brief verdict on the king's character, always condemning him in that "he did what was evil in the sight of the LORD, and walked in the way of Jeroboam and in his sin which he made Israel to sin" (I Kings 15:34). The latter part of this condemnation varies slightly, and Shallum (II Kings 15:13), who reigned but a month, escapes criticism altogether. In the cases of Elah and his murderer, Zimri, the condemnation is found in the concluding formulas, and the reference in the former case does not include Jeroboam. This regular condemnation applies, as we have seen, even to Jehu, who was full of zeal for the Lord and destroyed Baal out of Israel. Even Jehu did not depart from the sins of Jeroboam wherewith he made Israel to sin, though the author does not say that "he did evil in the sight of the LORD," but rather that he "was not careful to walk in the law of the LORD the God of Israel with all his heart" (II Kings 10:31).

The concluding formulas for the kings of both kingdoms have no particular didactic purpose. They refer the reader to the "book of the chronicles of the kings of Judah [Israel]," record the king's death and the place of his burial, and give the name of his son. The formulas are omitted in particular cases where, for instance, the king's reign was cut short by deposition (Jehoahaz, Jehoiachin, Zedekiah in the south, and Hoshea in the north), or by assassination, as in the cases of Joram of Israel and Ahaziah of Judah, the two kings whom Jehu slew in one day. There are necessarily further variations when the successor was a usurper (this for the north only, since David's line was unbroken in the south apart from the interregnum of Athaliah), and when the manner of the king's death was unusual.

We thus see that the whole framework of the author's account of the reigns of the kings depends upon his Deuteronomic principles.

There never ought to have been any breakaway from the south, and there never ought to have been any worship except only in Jerusalem. The worship at any high place was illegitimate, and the cult of the golden calves was wickedness almost beyond words. It combined idolatry with the vice of separation from Jerusalem.

VI. The Two Deuteronomic Editors

The generally accepted opinion is that the author of the books of Kings finished his work about 600 B.C., soon after the death of King Josiah, and that there was a further and thorough Deuteronomic revision about 550 B.C., which was part of a general revision of all the national traditions from Genesis to Kings. It was the time when the two earlier strata of the Pentateuch, known as J and E, were combined with the Deuteronomic material. Thus the editor who created JED as a combined work was also the Deuteronomic editor of the other historical books, Joshua, Judges, and Samuel. His framework for the book of Judges is generally agreed to be modeled on that of his predecessor, the original author of Kings. The Deuteronomic principles, as this second editor of Kings envisaged them, are set out in full in Judg. 2:11-23. The concluding chapters of the books of Kings belong to the same outlook.

A. First Editor (ca. 610 B.C.).—Opinion varies as to the exact date of the original author, that is, the man who used the three main sources which we have discussed—the Acts of Solomon and the Books of the Chronicles of the Kings of Israel and of Judah. Gustav Hölscher [12] maintained that there was a pre-Deuteronomic book of Kings, just as in the case of Samuel. This suggestion has been favored by Otto Eissfeldt,[13] and has gained some ground. Hölscher, however, does not admit that the centralization of the worship belonged to Josiah's reign, but that this king's reforms were on the basis of E. Thus Hölscher's date for his pre-Deuteronomic book of Kings is not materially different from the generally accepted date. He would date his original book near the end of Josiah's reign, and would then say that the re-editing of the book was part of the general revision of all the extant books, about 550 B.C. Most scholars, however, believe that Josiah's reformation did include the idea of centralization of the worship at Jerusalem.

But assuming that the original author of the books of Kings worked under the spell of good King Josiah's glorious days, should one also

[12] "Das Buch der Könige, seine Quellen und seine Redaktion," in Hans Schmidt, ed., ΕΥΧΑΡΙΣΤΗΡΙΟΝ (Göttingen: Vandenhoeck & Ruprecht, 1923), I, 158-213.

[13] *Einleitung in das Alte Testament* (Tübingen: J. C. B. Mohr, 1934), pp. 335-37.

maintain that he wrote after the death of Josiah at Megiddo in 609 B.C.? If so, then the author deliberately ignored the king's untimely death. Such an assumption involves a great deal more than is generally realized, because this disaster beyond question would destroy his whole thesis that those who obey the Deuteronomic laws live long and prosper. Such nevertheless is the position held by Pfeiffer [14] and other scholars generally. They hold that the original book ended at II Kings 23:28, but did not include the last phrase of vs. 25, nor vss. 26-27. It is a much more satisfactory solution of the problem to assume that the original Deuteronomic author concluded his work before the year of Josiah's death, and so was active rather toward the end of the period between 621 and 609 B.C. There is every indication that the collapse after Josiah's death was sudden and complete. The death of Josiah meant the end of Judah's independence, since Necho deposed Jehoahaz and made his pro-Egyptian brother Eliakim-Jehoiachim king in his stead. It is most difficult to see how the author could have done his work in the face of such an obvious denial of the truth of the position he was writing to demonstrate. Every shred of evidence was against him.

The later editor (ca. 550 B.C.) had therefore to meet the difficulty of Josiah's untoward death and thus to maintain the Deuteronomic principles. This he was in a position to do because he had seen in his own time a change in the fortune of the captive Jehoiachin away in exile (II Kings 25:27-30). Apparently a case could be put up for the Deuteronomic theory of life. In spite of the Exile and all its attendant woes, everything still was going to work out correctly according to the Deuteronomic pattern. The disaster which had fallen upon Josiah could still be explained. It was "because of all the provocations with which Manasseh had provoked" God (II Kings 23:26). These idolatries and all his abominations had created such a dead weight of sin that even the superlatively pious Josiah was not able to avoid the inevitable penalty of such flagrant violation of Deuteronomic principles. Therefore the reference to the thirty-one years of Josiah's reign (II Kings 22:1) appears to be an insertion by the later editor, whose conclusion to the original work begins with the "neither" of II Kings 23:25.[15] Thus the incident of II Kings 22:12-20 should be ascribed to the later editor.

The fact that the reader is referred to the Book of the Chronicles of the Kings of Judah for further information concerning Josiah (II Kings 23:28) is no evidence that the author completed his work after the death of King Josiah and before the destruction of the city in 586 B.C. If the later editor could add a similar reference to his story of the reign of Jehoiakim, who died in 597 B.C. (II Kings 24:5), then he could equally have added the reference in connection with the death of Josiah. We find ourselves, therefore, driven to assume that the original author completed his work before the death of Josiah at a time when all was still well and when Judah was still independent. This acquits the author of falsifying the history of the death of Josiah.

B. Second Editor (ca. 550 B.C.).—The second Deuteronomic editor must have been active later than 561 B.C., since he knew of the exaltation of the exiled Jehoiachin (II Kings 25:27-30). He must, however, have finished his work well before 538 B.C., the year when Cyrus captured Babylon, for in that case he would certainly have reflected something of the exuberant enthusiasm of Second Isaiah (Isa. 40–55). The original author was chiefly concerned with the worship at the high places and with the fact that the Northern Kingdom had broken away from the south. The later editor was more concerned with the idolatries. In this he reflects the concern of the exiled Jews, as can be seen from the emphasis placed on this by Second Isaiah. His insertions are also characterized by a less venomous attitude to the Northern Kingdom of Israel. By his time Judah had gone the way of Israel, and both kingdoms had been equally guilty of apostasy. Judah was in no position to preen herself on a favor from God which had been denied to Israel. This is the period when Jeremiah and Ezekiel were looking forward to a restoration of both kingdoms under a single king of the line of David.

There is evidence that the later editor shared this point of view. One passage which is likely to come from him is I Kings 4:20-26. Vs. 27 follows on naturally from vs. 19, so that the intervening verses are easily seen to be an interpolation. They were written in some locality to the east of the Euphrates, for the Hebrew of vs. 24 says "beyond the river" (see ASV mg.), meaning to the "west of the Euphrates," according to the rendering of the Revised Standard Version. In vss. 20, 25 we have a picture of idyllic bliss in a united kingdom such as could scarcely have been envisaged by the earlier author. Another passage which is probably due to this later editorial activity is the supplement to the life of Solomon which is found in I Kings 11:14-40. The introductory verse is reminiscent of the ideas set forth by the editor of Judges, who thought of God as delivering or selling the wayward children of Israel into the power of

[14] *Intro. to O.T.*, p. 379.
[15] Cf. Julius A. Bewer, *The Literature of the Old Testament in Its Historical Development* (rev. ed.; New York: Columbia University Press, 1933), p. 225.

their oppressors (e.g., Judg. 4:2; 6:1). Further, there is an expectation of a united kingdom (I Kings 11:38-39), which may be safely ascribed to the later editor. The whole section is much confused, so that Hugo Winckler,[16] using the variant story of the Septuagint, claimed to find in it two distinct narratives: one told of a boy Hadad of the royal line of Edom, saved by one of his father's servants when David conquered the country, carried into Egypt, brought up there by Pharaoh's queen, who was to return to Edom at David's death and there to rule while Solomon reigned in Judah; and the other narrative concerned a Midianite prince named Adad who fled to Egypt in David's time and was protected there by Pharaoh who gave him his queen's sister as wife. To this combined story there is added the account of Rezon of Damascus and his activities (I Kings 11:23-25). These three mischances, all of them unfavorable to Solomon's prestige, belong to the earlier part of Solomon's reign, not to the end, as is suggested by their present position.

The story of Jeroboam's revolt in I Kings 12:1-24 bears marks of later editing under Deuteronomic influence. Vs. 15 presupposes 11:31, and the story of vss. 21-24 is at variance with the plain statement of 14:30, which says that there was continual war between Rehoboam and Jeroboam. The reference to Shemaiah and his oracle would thus appear to be of later origin, showing traces of the less hostile attitude of the second editor. There are two passages which show a friendly concern for the north unknown to the original author (II Kings 13:22-25; 14:25-27). The attitude of the later editor to both kingdoms is also shown in II Kings 17:7-20; 21:13-14. It is equally probable that he made considerable interpolations into Solomon's dedicatory prayer in I Kings 8.

VII. Tales of the North

The original book of Kings (ca. 610 B.C.) consisted of I Kings 2:1-12, and then ran from I Kings 3:1 to II Kings 23:25a. Into this book there have been interpolated numerous narratives which undoubtedly originated in the Northern Kingdom of Israel. They come from three of the four unnamed sources which have provided the basis of the material used in the completed books of Kings. These three sources were composed of stories which collected around the outstanding figures of the north—Elijah, Elisha, and Ahab. There is considerable difference of opinion among scholars as to the precise allocation of these stories to the various sources, and as to the exact relation between the different narratives. Perhaps the best allocation is

the following: (a) Elijah narratives (I Kings 17-19; II Kings 1:1-18 and I Kings 21; II Kings 9:1-10:31); (b) Elisha narratives (II Kings 2:1-6, 7-15, 16-18, 19-22, 23-25; 4:1-7, 8-37, 38-41, 42-44; 5:1-27; 6:1-7; 8:1-6, 7-15; 13:14-19, 20-21); (c) Ahab narratives (I Kings 20:1-43; 22:1-38 and II Kings 3:4-27; 6:8-23; 6:24–7:20). There is also the narrative of II Kings 14:8-14.

The northern origin of these stories is plain from more than one consideration. The references to Beer-sheba and to Beth-shemesh as "belonging to Judah" (I Kings 19:3; II Kings 14:11) suggest an Israelitish origin. The stories of Amaziah of Judah's impudent challenge to Jehoash of Israel (II Kings 14:8-14) could hardly have been written by a southerner. Further, nothing is said anywhere in these stories against the calf worship of Bethel, nor is there any condemnation of the practice of worshiping and sacrificing at the high places. Indeed, on the contrary, Elijah is virtually commended in that he "repaired the altar of the LORD that had been thrown down" on Mount Carmel (I Kings 18:30). The work of Elijah and his successor is directed almost wholly to the destruction out of Israel of the cult of the Tyrian Baal imported into the country by Ahab's Tyrian wife, Jezebel. The only exception is a similar protest against the practice of seeking oracles from Baal-zebub of Ekron (II Kings 1:1-8), a god which can now be identified with Baal-zebul, the life-god of the Ras Shamra tablets.[17] Yet again, Burney has given a list of peculiarities of diction which portray affinities with what we know of the dialect of northern Palestine.[18]

The Elijah narrative from I Kings 17:1 to 19:21 forms a continuous story. The threat of the dreadful famine produced by the long drought is followed by the story of the straits to which Elijah himself was reduced. His struggle for survival and Ahab's search for fodder provide a most impressive picture of the plight of the country. The effect which the author of these chapters produces by his choice of illustration, his vividness in description, and his complete mastery of language is superb. They mark him as the equal in skill of any Old Testament writer. There are a few interpolations and editorial additions, some of them in the Deuteronomic style and therefore presumably due to the later editor. The most obvious of these interpolations is found in I Kings 19:9b-11a, where the repetition of what really belongs to vss. 13-14 robs the story of the vision of much of its native dramatic excellence.

The remainder of the Elijah narratives have

16 Alttestamentliche Untersuchungen (Leipzig: Eduard Pfeiffer, 1892), pp. 1-15.

17 J. W. Jack, The Ras Shamra Tablets (Edinburgh: T. & T. Clark, 1935), p. 19.
18 Notes on Hebrew Text of Kings, pp. 208-9.

to be separated from the Carmel-Horeb sequence. The story of Naboth's vineyard, as many scholars have maintained, might very well belong to the author of I Kings 17–18. The Septuagint and Lucian place the chapter immediately after the Carmel-Horeb story, and there is much to be said for this order, since ch. 21 has closer affinities with chs. 17–19 than with chs. 20 and 22, and it certainly interrupts the sequence of these two chapters. Pfeiffer holds that ch. 21 was inserted by the original author of 610 B.C., and there are indeed evident traces of Deuteronomic style, especially in vss. 20b-24. On the other hand, there is considerable dramatic power in the telling of the story of Naboth's vineyard, so much so that it is difficult to resist the conclusion that the author of chs. 17–19 is also the author of ch. 21. This brings II Kings 9:1–10:31 into the same cycle, since this passage is the sequel to ch. 21. However, many scholars maintain that the author of II Kings 9:1–10:31 is also the author of I Kings 20; 22; II Kings 3:4-27; 6:8-23; 6:24–7:20, and there are indeed a number of coincidences, although these are of limited significance.

There is also a measure of disagreement concerning the exact limits of the Elisha cycle. Burney [19] has noted a number of similarities of expression in the Elijah stories on the one hand, especially I Kings 17–19, and in II Kings 2:1-18 and 4:1-37 on the other, so that he is inclined to suppose a common authorship. He would add, though tentatively, II Kings 5 and, more uncertainly still, II Kings 8:7-15; 13:14-19. A more adequate explanation of the similarities of expression is that the Elisha stories were written by a less competent author in imitation of the Elijah cycle. They certainly do not show the same dramatic power in spite of the similarities of expression. The prophet Elisha played a decisive part in the shaping of the events of his time, in many respects more outstanding than that played by his illustrious predecessor. Perhaps it was this knowledge of the political importance of Elisha's work which led his biographer to write up the traditions which had gathered around him, beginning with the claim that he was the true successor of Elijah. This claim is given in II Kings 2:9 and 15 in the statement that Elisha received the double portion, that is, the heir's portion of Elijah's spirit. Following this commissioning of the prophet Elisha comes a series of stories, some of which are reflections of incidents in the life of Elijah, for example, the sustenance of the widow (II Kings 4:1-7) and the resurrection of a hostess's son (4:8-37). To these must be added the story of II Kings 8:1-6, where Elisha calls for a famine of seven years as against Elijah's three, a

narrative which is connected with the woman whose son Elisha revived from death. There is one story, much longer than the rest, which approaches in excellence the literary standards of the Elijah cycle: that of Naaman the leper and the Israelitish maid. It nevertheless belongs rather to the wonder-story group of the Elisha cycle, all of which is told to enhance the more-than-human power of the miracle-working man of God, and is not as much concerned with the religious work of the prophet as is the case in the Elijah cycle. The powers of Elisha are superhuman. They partake of the quality of that mana which is constantly met with in the study of primitive religion. Any cavalier treatment of this holy man meets with sudden and awful disaster, even to small boys who laugh at his baldness (II Kings 2:23-25). This magical mana power is still present even in his dead body (II Kings 13:21).

The Elisha narratives may be later than the Elijah cycle, but were necessarily written before the end of the Northern Kingdom. The date for the Elijah cycle is perhaps about 800 B.C., and that of the Elisha cycle about 750 B.C. It may very well be that the author of the Elisha cycle added the Elijah stories to his own collection, so as to make one complete collection dealing with prophetic activity in the north. Neither author saw anything wrong with the Yahweh worship of the north so long as it was not contaminated by foreign cults such as that of Jezebel's Tyrian Baal. The work was probably incorporated by the later Deuteronomic editor of about 550 B.C.: it is unlikely that stories in any way favorable to the north could have been introduced either much before his time or after the trouble which arose over the building of the second temple in Zerubbabel's time (Ezra 4:3).

It seems likely that the Ahab narratives had a different origin from that of the Elijah-Elisha cycles and that they formed part of an independent story of the life of Ahab, who was a great builder and one of the most successful kings the north ever had. It has often been pointed out that in I Kings 20 and 22:1-39 there is hostility not to Ahab but to Syria—a fact which scarcely agrees with the partiality of Elisha for anyone who would destroy the house of Omri. On the other hand, there is no marked antagonism to Ahab in the prophetic narratives as a whole. The hostility is against Jezebel rather than against Ahab, and later against Jehoram, Ahab's son. After all, it was not until the twelfth year of Jehoram's reign that the prophetic revolution took place which set Jehu on the throne. There would therefore appear to be some justification for assuming that all the undated incidents in the Elisha cycle occurred

[19] *Ibid.*, pp. 214-15.

13

during the reign of Jehoram son of Ahab (852-843 B.C.). Every such story can be placed between Jehoram's accession (II Kings 1:17) and his assassination (II Kings 9:24), except for two short narratives which are definitely fixed by their contents in the reign of Joash son of Jehoahaz (800-785 B.C.). The other story of the "impudent" Amaziah is necessarily to be placed within the story of Amaziah's reign. It is alleged that the insertion of all these stories into the reign of Jehoram has caused a certain amount of confusion and discrepancy. However, the discrepancies are not as pronounced as some critics have maintained. The state of peace which is presumed in the Naaman story (II Kings 5) is actually one of complete Israelite subjection to Syria, and this may well be part and parcel of the disastrous atmosphere set forth in II Kings 8:12. Further, Elisha may well have preserved enough friendship with the king to allow for the offer of II Kings 4:13, and also for the state of affairs in II Kings 5 and elsewhere. As has been said already, the revolution did not take place until Jehoram had reigned for over eleven years.

In view both of the many similarities, and also of the many differences which have been noted in all these northern narratives, it seems best to assume three separate origins for the three different cycles, but an interweaving of all three prior to their incorporation by the second Deuteronomic editor.

VIII. Tales of the South

The southern narratives are those which are found in II Kings 18:13–20:19. They comprise the story of Sennacherib's attack on Judah and Jerusalem (18:13–19:37), the account of Hezekiah's sickness (20:1-11), and the narrative of Merodach-baladan's embassy (20:12-19).

The story of Sennacherib's attack contains three distinct elements; first, 18:13 (except for the date) together with 18:17–19:8, 36-37; second, 18:14-16; and third, 19:9b-35. The second of these (18:14-16) is not found in the parallel Isa. 36:1-22, and it is certainly the most clearly historical of the three stories. It shows marked agreements with Sennacherib's own account of the campaign as found on the Taylor Cylinder, especially in respect of the "thirty talents of gold." [20] These three verses are from the Chronicles of the Kings of Judah and belong to the first edition of the books of the Kings, about 610 B.C. The date given in 18:13, however, is difficult, both for this annalistic record itself and for the other two narratives. If Samaria did indeed fall in Hezekiah's sixth year as 18:10

maintains, then Sennacherib's expedition of 701 B.C. was not in Hezekiah's fourteenth year. There are two alternatives. Either the embassy was immediately prior to Sennacherib's expedition and "the fourteenth year" is wrong, or "the fourteenth year" is right and the embassy was about 714 B.C. In this case "the fourteenth year" refers to the events of ch. 20, Hezekiah's sickness, and Merodach-baladan's embassy. Both dates are sound for such activity on the part of this Mesopotamian firebrand. He had set himself up as king in Babylon from 720-710 B.C., and again, though insecurely, for about three months in 702 B.C.

The story of the Rabshakeh and his threats (18:17–19:9, 36-37) is compatible with the story of Hezekiah's submission to the Assyrian king and his payment of tribute on the assumption that in the end the Assyrian Sennacherib was not satisfied with anything less than the occupation of Jerusalem and the deportation of its inhabitants. Especially is this possible since the tribute appears not to have been paid at the time, but sent afterwards to Nineveh (see the Taylor Cylinder [21]). According to the Assyrian account, Sennacherib did actually invest Jerusalem, but there is no record of his having captured it. The explanation given in II Kings 19:7 is that he heard a rumor and forthwith lifted the siege to hurry back to Nineveh. According to 19:9a this rumor was concerned with the advance of a certain Tirhakah, king of Ethiopia. The statement presents considerable difficulty since this king probably did not commence his reign until 691 B.C. Further, even if his advance should be the one mentioned in the Taylor Cylinder,[22] the reference is still difficult because we know that this Egyptian attempt to relieve Jerusalem was ignominiously defeated by the Babylonians, and it certainly did not cause Sennacherib to raise the siege and hurry home. This actual defeat would account very satisfactorily for Hezekiah's abject submission (II Kings 18:14-16), since it would then be clear to him that all hope of help had gone. It is better therefore to assume that the reference to Tirhakah of Ethiopia is a mistake, and that the rumor which sent Sennacherib home so quickly was a rumor of an incipient rebellion by a certain Bel-ibni, whom Sennacherib had placed on the throne of Babylon as vassal king in place of the restless Merodach-baladan.

The third account of the deliverance of Jerusalem from the might of the Assyrian king consisted originally of II Kings 19:9b-20, 32-34, since the "therefore" of vs. 32 follows quite naturally on vs. 20. Into this there has been

---

[20] Col. 3, 1. 34. For a translation, see Burney, op. cit., pp. 377-79.

[21] Col. 3, ll. 39-41.
[22] Col. 2, ll. 73-83.

interpolated, perhaps by the original author, what purports to be a genuine oracle of Isaiah of Jerusalem given in the well-known *qînāh* (lamentation) 3:2 measure, followed with a prose account of one of those signs which formed a feature of Israel's method. There is no particular reason why the main body of this account should not have been inserted by the original author. It is noteworthy that the story does not involve a tremendous slaughter of the Assyrian army. It promises that the king of Assyria "shall not come to this city or shoot an arrow there, or come before it with a shield or cast up a mound against it. By the way that he came, by the same he shall return, and he shall not come into this city" (II Kings 19:32-33). The story of the miraculous destruction of the whole of the Assyrian army depends wholly on vs. 35, a verse which has no connection at all with what precedes and none with what follows it, since the next verses belong to the first of the three accounts of these incidents. It is possible that this particular verse was inserted by some later editor who did not think that the deliverance was spectacular enough, and was influenced by some such writings as Pss. 46 and 91.

The two narratives in ch. 20 probably belong to the fourteenth year of King Hezekiah, that is, 714 B.C. (II Kings 18:13), some thirteen years before the attack of Sennacherib, which is told in detail in II Kings 18–19. The first narrative concerns Hezekiah's sickness and, except for vs. 6, was taken from the Isaiah biography by the original author of 610 B.C. Vs. 6 is probably his insertion, based in part on a calculation subtracting fourteen years of the king's reign from a total of twenty-nine years (II Kings 18:2), and for the rest acting as a connecting link between the account of the sickness and the siege of Jerusalem by Sennacherib, the two incidents having been wrongly made contemporaneous.

The second narrative (II Kings 20:12-19) concerns the embassy of Merodach-baladan, who was seeking to stir up trouble throughout the Assyrian Empire (*ca.* 714 B.C.). There is no reason to suppose that this story came from anywhere other than the Isaiah biography, except that vss. 16-18 must have been worked over by a later editor who knew the story of the destruction and spoliation of Jerusalem in 586 B.C. and of the Exile. They are probably the work of the later editor, who displaced an original conclusion to the story.

In addition to these last-mentioned narratives which have been drawn from the biography of Isaiah, there are also a number of glosses and insertions from later times. Some of these were unknown to the Chronicler (*ca.* 250 B.C.) who used the books of the Kings as his major source for his history of the whole period of the kingdoms. Others of them were not even known to the translators of the Septuagint (*ca.* 200-150 B.C.).

Many of these glosses are due to the influence of the compilers of the Priestly Code, and deal with details of the temple. Such glosses are to be found particularly in I Kings 8 and in the quotation from Gen. 35:10 which is given in I Kings 18:31. The small section in I Kings 6:11-14 is not found at all in the Septuagint, while I Kings 8:1-11 has been worked over by Priestly Code editors so that it now presents a Masoretic text materially different from that in the Septuagint. Other passages which may have been considerably worked over in the earlier part of the second century B.C. are I Kings 4:20–5:14; 5:15–7:51.

In conclusion, the earliest document which is embodied in the present books of Kings dates from the tenth century B.C.—the biography of Solomon's grandeur, including the account of his accession to the throne. The main work was formed toward the end of the seventh century (*ca.* 610 B.C.), not long before the death of good King Josiah. There was further considerable editorial work about the middle of the sixth century B.C., while other editors added their quotas for another four centuries, making an over-all total of some eight hundred years.

IX. Modern Significance

Part of the message of the completed books of Kings belongs to its own day, namely the localization of the worship of God in one particular place. Israel now, equally with other peoples, knows that God is not a respecter of places any more than of persons. This fact is already recognized in Solomon's dedicatory prayer: "But will God indeed dwell on the earth? Behold, heaven and the highest heaven cannot contain thee; how much less this house which I have built!" (I Kings 8:27). The passing years have made this more and more plain, for there is no place at all where a man can go and be away from God (cf. Ps. 139:7-12).

The perennial religious significance of the books of Kings is to be found in the full recognition of monotheism, which is evident in the work of the later editors, and in the stern opposition to all those things in worship which detract from the highest and purest conception of morality. The authors will not countenance in the least any thought of any other deity. This is because they know that the God of Israel is different from any other god. It is possible and it is permitted, for instance, to associate prostitution with the worship of other gods. This is neither possible nor permissible in connection with the worship of the God of Israel. He is not that sort of god. If any king introduces such behavior into the temple at Jerusalem, then he is desecrating the temple and there is no worship of the one true God. A man may "pass his children through the fire" to another god (though, as the later editors would say, they are not gods), but he cannot do this in sacrifice to the one true God. Images of other so-called deities may be found in other lands, but they are not permitted in Yahweh's land. Certainly he cannot be worshiped through such media. Once again, he is not that sort of god. None of the furniture which has association with any of these things can be permitted, for this heritage is too precious ever to be subjected to the risk of contamination and debasement which such things inevitably involve.

The later editor (ca. 550 B.C.) has learned also that this God is ready to pardon and to forgive. The experiences of the Exile had taught that. The earlier editor knew something of this in the partial way which his limited experience had taught him. For every man who sins against his neighbor and repents, in time of national defeat, and in every time of famine, plague, and disaster, this God will hear and forgive. The later editor (I Kings 8:44-61) knew that wherever God's people are scattered, God forgives those who turn to him "with all their mind and with all their heart" (vs. 48). This God, too, is not willing that any should be oppressed. Such an attitude is plain in the northern narrative of Naboth and his vineyard. The conduct of Jezebel is a definite contradiction of those principles which are right and proper in Yahweh's land. He is strong against oppression and injustice of every kind, and this both to condemn the guilty and to exalt the righteous.

But most of all this justice of God shows itself in his stern and rigorous condemnation of sin. No man can sin without setting in motion an inevitable train of consequences. The dire results of sin in sorrow and trouble and death are bound to come. Further, a king like Jeroboam son of Nebat or like Manasseh of Judah can bring his people to disaster and to a doom from which there is no escape. The Deuteronomic teaching is in many ways a stepping-stone to other and deeper truth. This much—the inevitable doom which sin brings in its train—stands for all ages. With it there is the promise shining through at the very end of the books of Kings, a promise of a new beginning when the price has been paid. Out of the sorrows of the Exile there dawns a new hope. The exiled king is restored to some measure of freedom, an earnest of better things to come.

X. Outline of Contents

XI. Selected Bibliography

BARNES, W. E. The First Book of the Kings ("The Cambridge Bible"). Cambridge: Cambridge University Press, 1911.

BENZINGER, IMMANUEL. Die Bücher der Könige ("Kurzer Hand-Commentar zum Alten Testament"). Tübingen: J. C. B. Mohr, 1899.

BURNEY, C. F. Notes on the Hebrew Text of the Books of Kings. Oxford: Clarendon Press, 1903.

KITTEL, RUDOLF. Die Bücher der Könige ("Handkommentar zum Alten Testament"). Göttingen: Vandenhoeck & Ruprecht, 1900.

MONTGOMERY, J. A., and GEHMAN, H. S. A Critical and Exegetical Commentary on the Books of Kings ("International Critical Commentary"). Edinburgh: T. & T. Clark, 1951.

SKINNER, JOHN. Kings ("The New-Century Bible"). New York: Oxford University Press, 1904.

I KINGS

TEXT, EXEGESIS, AND EXPOSITION

1 Now king David was old *and* stricken in years; and they covered him with clothes, but he gat no heat.

1 Now King David was old and advanced in years; and although they covered him with clothes, he could not get warm.

I. THE LAST DAYS OF DAVID (1:1–2:46)

These first two chapters form one section. They were originally the continuation of II Sam. 9–20, but were detached so as to provide a suitable introduction to the story of Solomon's reign. They are thoroughly lively in style and well written. The author evidently had access to firsthand information of the inner life of the court with its plots and counterplots. So clearly is this the case that we may safely assume that he used a court narrative as his source. Nothing of these two chapters is found in Chronicles. Presumably the Chronicler did not wish to perpetuate the memory of any suggestion of difficulty or doubt concerning Solomon's accession to the throne.

The First Book of Kings.—This book is not commonly considered a very fertile field for cultivation. The quarrels between cliques of a court on the way to dissolution, the petty acts of kings who left no lasting footprints, the elaborate description of a temple and a royal palace whose traces have been erased by centuries of war and change—all these seem irrelevant to enduring spiritual values.

But along what at first glance may appear to be a desert road are discovered some oases (see Intro., pp. 15-16). Also one can see the pits of primitive ethics from which the Hebrew-Christian tradition has dug some of its foundation stones of personal conduct and public policy. Amid the interplay of the secular and the spiritual may be seen emerging some regulative principles in the ever-fresh problem of the re-

2 Wherefore his servants said unto him, Let there be sought for my lord the king a young virgin: and let her stand before the king, and let her cherish him, and let her lie in thy bosom, that my lord the king may get heat.

3 So they sought for a fair damsel throughout all the coasts of Israel, and found Abishag a Shunammite, and brought her to the king.

2 Therefore his servants said to him, "Let a young maiden be sought for my lord the king, and let her wait upon the king, and be his nurse; let her lie in your bosom, that my lord the king may be warm." 3 So they sought for a beautiful maiden throughout all the territory of Israel, and found Ab′-ishag the Shu′nammite, and brought her to

The Deuteronomic editor has interpolated two short passages into this court story: 2:2b-4, 10-12. The first of these represents David's deathbed charge to his successor, and it is couched in language which bears an unmistakable Deuteronomic character in every phrase. The second passage contains the obituary notice by the editor, together with the usual information concerning the new king. It may well be that 2:27 also is due to the Deuteronomic editor since it depends upon I Sam. 2:27-36, a passage which he largely rewrote in his own words.

A. RIVALS FOR THE THRONE (1:1-53)

It is evident that according to popular expectation Adonijah was the legitimate heir. He was the eldest surviving son, and while this in itself by no means settled the matter his claim was supported by the great majority of the court party, including Abiathar and Joab, the two men who had been most loyal to David through the years and most intimate in his counsels. Adonijah was ousted from the throne by means of a plot conceived in the first place by Nathan the prophet and Bathsheba, Solomon's mother—the woman who had originally been the wife of Uriah the Hittite. The most that can be said for their nominee is that David may have made a secret promise to the mother that Solomon should succeed to the throne. Even of this there is legitimate doubt, and it is most likely that Bathsheba's statement in vs. 13 was a deliberate fabrication invented to impose upon the aged king. The position of queen mother was one of considerable prestige and influence, and was well worthy of the efforts of an ambitious woman (cf. 15:13).

1. DAVID'S INCAPACITY (1:1-4)

1:1-4. David, aged now approximately seventy years, has become impotent. Every step is taken to rejuvenate him, but without avail. He therefore must cease to be king, and make way for a successor.

Most commentators take these verses to refer to the collapse of the aged king's strength through senile decay. It is assumed that it was a general loss of bodily vigor which led to the necessity for his abdication. But these verses are most valuable in that they provide evidence of "the hole of the pit" whence Israel was dug. They show that in the early days the Hebrews had ideas in common with the peoples by whom they were surrounded. Just as David thought that he could not worship Israel's God except on Israel's soil (I Sam. 26:19; cf. II Kings 5:17-18), so it was believed that the fertility of

lations between church and state. Amid the bloody milieu of intrigue and ruthlessness the roots of prophecy take hold.

As the record begins, the reins of government are slipping from the feeble fingers of the senile David. When the ruling power shifts, the fundamental principles of a nation's government are tested. The strength of the American democratic constitution was never better demonstrated than

when in 1945 it survived the death of a powerful president during the conduct of a great war. But the crude little kingdom which Saul and David had fashioned from Israel's tribes was not yet familiar with even the simplest forms of free government.

1:1-15. *Weakness in the Strong.*—The hero David is here shown in his weakness. This unveiling of one whose name is synonymous

4 And the damsel *was* very fair, and cherished the king, and ministered to him: but the king knew her not.

5 ¶ Then Adonijah the son of Haggith exalted himself, saying, I will be king: and he prepared him chariots and horsemen, and fifty men to run before him.

the king. 4 The maiden was very beautiful; and she became the king's nurse and ministered to him; but the king knew her not.

5 Now Adoni'jah the son of Haggith exalted himself, saying, "I will be king"; and he prepared for himself chariots and horsemen, and fifty men to run before him.

---

the soil and the general prosperity of the people were bound up with the fertility of the king. David by this time is old and decrepit and his sexual vigor is in question. Attempts are made to remedy the situation. The first cure is to heap clothes upon his bed in order to secure such physical heat as might render him capable. When this fails a search is made for the most beautiful young woman in the land. Great emphasis is placed on her charms. The LXX supports this by translating in vs. 2, "and let her excite him and lie with him" (cf. the use of θάλπω in Aeschylus, *Prometheus Bound*, 1. 590). The fact that the king had no intercourse with her is decisive in the story and not a mere interesting addendum. If David was impotent he could no longer be king. Further, there is no point in the story of 2:12-25 unless Abishag the Shunammite had been more than an old man's nurse. She must have been reckoned as David's wife or Solomon would never have interpreted Adonijah's request as a bid for the throne. Also, why should a king be expected to abdicate because he cannot keep warm in bed even when clothes are piled upon him?

This explanation, dependent upon the necessity of the physical vigor of the king, is in line with the ideas of primitive peoples generally, and indeed finds present-day support in the Near East. There was an occasion when the authority of Ibn Saud over his Arabs actually depended on such a factor (H. C. Armstrong, *Lord of Arabia* [Harmondsworth: Penguin Books, 1938], p. 106). A number of instances have been collected by James G. Frazer of the killing of the king when his bodily vigor fails, for "the fertility of men, of cattle, and of the crops is believed to depend sympathetically on the generative power of the king" (*The Golden Bough* [Abridged ed.; London: Macmillan & Co., 1923], pp. 264-83, especially p. 269). There is no need to assume the existence in old Israel of the ritual of the sacred marriage, annually performed in the Mesopotamian cults, since it is clear from the story that the search for the ravishing young woman is exceptional. It is possible, nevertheless, to see here some evidence of primitive ideas among the Hebrews at the beginning of the first millennium B.C.

2. ADONIJAH IS PROCLAIMED KING (1:5-10)

Adonijah had already taken steps to forward his claim to the throne by providing himself with chariot and charioteers, together with fifty outrunners to run in front of his chariot. This conduct was closely similar to that of Absalom when he had sought to establish his claim to the throne (II Sam. 15:1). David allowed Absalom to do this

---

with valor and strength reveals the stark realism of the O.T. record. The writers did not glamorize their heroes at the expense of truth.

5. The Right to Rule.—The writer implies that Adonijah had grown up an undisciplined and ambitious youth whose handsome physique gave him a certain popular appeal. He either used one of the court factions to further his designs on the throne, or allowed himself to be used as a pawn by the designing courtiers. He **exalted himself, saying, I will be king.** Aligning himself with Joab the soldier and Abiathar the

priest, Adonijah staged a religious festival, thus adopting a method common to political usurpers, that of enlisting both the army and the church in support of dynastic designs.

The twentieth century still witnesses the overthrow of governmental rules according to the pattern of Adonijah. But the world's conscience has at least so improved that political aspirants feel obliged to offer a more adequate reason than did David's son, when he said, **I will be king.** Candidates for governmental office must claim that their motive is to serve, and our

| 6 And his father had not displeased him at any time in saying, Why hast thou done so? and he also *was* a very goodly man; and *his mother* bare him after Absalom. | 6 His father had never at any time displeased him by asking, "Why have you done thus and so?" He was also a very handsome man; and he was born next after |

for four years (II Sam. 15:7 [Syriac, Lucian]), and he similarly acquiesced in Adonijah's conduct. It is hard to resist the conclusion that David did regard Absalom as his heir until the latter's death, and that later this choice was transferred to Adonijah. Two additional reasons for his suitability as heir are given in vs. 6. He was the eldest surviving son, and **a very handsome man.** Evidently both Absalom and Adonijah had their father's good looks and attractive ways. Adonijah and his friends held a sacrificial feast, at which apparently (vss. 9, 13) Adonijah was proclaimed king.

officials are called public servants. Yet while there are those who honestly seek power in order to serve the people, in general the game of politics is played on the principle that "to the victors belong the spoils." [1]

So deeply ingrained is the assumption that power is for rule rather than for service that men have difficulty in comprehending the kingship of the Son of man who "came not to be ministered unto, but to minister" (Mark 10:45). But in the long process of history it begins to be recognized increasingly that power must be "of the people, by the people, and for the people." In the thwarting of Adonijah's self-interested scheme is seen another instance that the sovereign God recognizes the right to rule only when it is based on the desire to serve.

6. A Father's Failure.—Had David been so engrossed in public affairs that he neglected the nurture of his son, and **never at any time displeased him by asking, "Why have you done thus and so?"** Was he too doting a father to discipline the boy? Whatever the answer, the parental relationship had failed to fit Adonijah for his future social adjustments.

A university dean once declared that the modern "child-centered" home was creating a more difficult problem for school and college than was made by the old-fashioned home. In earlier days the family operated more as a unit, and the child was geared into the group action; but the modern trend has been to make the individual the center, with the home providing the accessories for his development. Undoubtedly some of the old unenlightened disciplines and regimentation have thus been corrected; but the child who does not learn to subordinate his interests at some points to a larger loyalty is left like Adonijah, ill-prepared for life. The school and the community cannot successfully provide the discipline which the home fails to give.

More correct would it be to say that this dangerous lack of discipline stems not from making the home too "child-centered" but too "individual-centered." Parents in their busy absorption leave home life at loose ends. Children grow up without having learned restraint and co-operation, then transfer their undisciplined individualism to new homes of their own, and the vicious circle continues to mutilate lives and multiply divorces.

Jesus laid down a basic law of stewardship which homes neglect at their peril: "If ye have not been faithful in that which is another man's, who shall give you that which is your own?" (Luke 16:12.) The family is the first training ground in trusteeship. By being guardians of others' interests, the members fit themselves for receiving that which the family is designed to give them. Children or parents, husbands or wives, never get from a home what really belongs to them until they act as if they belonged to it.

The true home is a partnership of free minds wherein the experiences of the elders supplement the experiments of the youngsters. Think what David could have done for Adonijah if he had shared with him the memories of his own spiritually sensitive youth, if he had asked the lad, **Why have you done thus and so?** and then helped to interpret the answers in the light of his own rich experience. John R. Mott has told of an orphaned lad who was reared with such painstaking care by an uncle that when it came time for college, the uncle laid his hands on the boy's shoulders and said, "My boy, do what you have a mind to do." The guardian knew the lad's mind to be so disciplined that his tastes could be trusted.

And now that radio brings the news of the world, the music of all nations, and contributions of thought from all sectors of opinion, the home can be made the magic circle which fits the members of the family to become intelligent and responsive citizens in life's largest relationship, transcending the barriers of provincialism and prejudice.

[1] William Learned Marcy, Speech in U. S. Senate, Jan., 1832.

7 And he conferred with Joab the son of Zeruiah, and with Abiathar the priest: and they following Adonijah helped *him*.

8 But Zadok the priest, and Benaiah the son of Jehoiada, and Nathan the prophet, and Shimei, and Rei, and the mighty men which *belonged* to David, were not with Adonijah.

9 And Adonijah slew sheep and oxen and fat cattle by the stone of Zoheleth, which *is* by En-rogel, and called all his brethren the king's sons, and all the men of Judah the king's servants:

Ab'salom. 7 He conferred with Jo'ab the son of Zeru'iah and with Abi'athar the priest; and they followed Adoni'jah and helped him. 8 But Zadok the priest, and Benai'ah the son of Jehoi'ada, and Nathan the prophet, and Shim'e-i, and Re'i, and David's mighty men were not with Adoni'jah.

9 Adoni'jah sacrificed sheep, oxen, and fatlings by the Serpent's Stone, which is beside En-ro'gel, and he invited all his brothers, the king's sons, and all the royal officials

---

7. Joab was David's nephew, being a son of David's sister, Zeruiah. He was also David's "captain of the host," i.e., commander of the militia, the army in the field which consisted of every able-bodied man called up for the campaign. The small standing army was under the command of Benaiah, captain of the king's bodyguard of foreign mercenaries. Thus Adonijah had no armed force to support his claim at short notice, whereas Solomon had a body of disciplined seasoned troops at his immediate call under the command of Benaiah. This was the decisive factor when the time came for action.

Abiathar the priest was the sole survivor of the massacre by Saul of the house of Eli, the hereditary priests of the ark of Shiloh from the beginning (I Sam. 2:27-28; 22:20). He shared all David's early vicissitudes, and when David came to his kingdom was installed as copriest with Zadok. This Zadok was probably of the original Jebusite priesthood of Jerusalem (H. H. Rowley, *The Re-Discovery of the Old Testament* [Philadelphia: Westminster Press, 1946], p. 73). His descendants were priests at Jerusalem as long as any temple existed. Even when, after the Exile, the priests were called "the priests the sons of Aaron," two thirds of them were Zadokites (I Chr. 24:4).

8. Nathan the prophet had considerable influence at court. He had been in a sufficiently strong position to prevent David from building the temple (II Sam. 7:5-17) and to reprove him in the matter of Uriah the Hittite (II Sam. 12:1-15). He had been particularly interested in Solomon from babyhood, and it was through Nathan that the child was called Jedidiah, "Beloved of Yah" (II Sam. 12:25). It will be seen that Solomon actually had the backing of those who had grown to be strong at court during David's reign, rather than of those who had been David's early comrades.

9. The coronation feast was celebrated hard by the sacred spring of **En-rogel**. This is probably Job's Well (Bîr Ayyûb), and not the modern Virgin's Spring, which was Gihon, where Solomon's coronation feast was held (vs. 33). Gihon was nearer the city, out of sight from Job's Well, though not out of hearing.

7-31. *The Value of Vows.*—In the counterplot to check Adonijah's *coup d'état*, Nathan the prophet resorts to the religious appeal. He sends Bathsheba to remind the aged king of his royal vow before the Lord that Solomon should succeed him on the throne. There is no record of such a vow (cf. Exeg. on vs. 13); and the staging of Bathsheba's visit, with the timing of Nathan's appearance while she was in the king's presence, appears a little too clever to be convincing. But however truth may have been tampered with by his attendants, David's conscience is sensitive to the divine approach, **And the king swore, saying, "As the LORD lives, who has re-**

deemed my soul out of every adversity, as I swore to you by the LORD, the God of Israel, saying, 'Solomon your son shall reign after me, and he shall sit upon my throne in my stead'; even so will I do this day" (vss. 29-30).

Here we see how a vow made to the Lord serves to buttress the human will. If we always lived at our highest levels, if we could always be sure of ourselves, there might be no need of vows and oaths. But we are not always at our best. Knowing the weakness of our wills in the face of irksome or shattering temptations, we do well in moments of moral insight to pledge ourselves to the side of goodness against those

10 But Nathan the prophet, and Benaiah, and the mighty men, and Solomon his brother, he called not.

11 ¶ Wherefore Nathan spake unto Bathsheba the mother of Solomon, saying, Hast thou not heard that Adonijah the son of Haggith doth reign, and David our lord knoweth *it* not?

12 Now therefore come, let me, I pray thee, give thee counsel, that thou mayest save thine own life, and the life of thy son Solomon.

13 Go and get thee in unto king David, and say unto him, Didst not thou, my lord, O king, swear unto thine handmaid, saying, Assuredly Solomon thy son shall reign after me, and he shall sit upon my throne? why then doth Adonijah reign?

14 Behold, while thou yet talkest there with the king, I also will come in after thee, and confirm thy words.

15 ¶ And Bath-sheba went in unto the king into the chamber: and the king was very old; and Abishag the Shunammite ministered unto the king.

of Judah, 10 but he did not invite Nathan the prophet or Benai'ah or the mighty men or Solomon his brother.

11 Then Nathan said to Bathshe'ba the mother of Solomon, "Have you not heard that Adoni'jah the son of Haggith has become king and David our lord does not know it? 12 Now therefore come, let me give you counsel, that you may save your own life and the life of your son Solomon. 13 Go in at once to King David, and say to him, 'Did you not, my lord the king, swear to your maidservant, saying, "Solomon your son shall reign after me, and he shall sit upon my throne"? Why then is Adoni'jah king?' 14 Then while you are still speaking with the king, I also will come in after you and confirm your words."

15 So Bathshe'ba went to the king into his chamber (now the king was very old, and Ab'ishag the Shu'nammite was minis-

3. The Plot in Favor of Solomon (1:11-14)

Nathan and Bathsheba hatch a plot to supersede the generally expected heir in favor of the younger Solomon. It may be asked whether they were reminding David of an ancient promise or were inventing the whole story and palming it off for true on the aged king.

12. The success of Adonijah would certainly involve the execution, sooner or later, of the rival claimant and his known supporters. In the end both Adonijah and Joab lost their lives, and this would have been Abiathar's fate also had he not been a priest and therefore inviolate as a sacred person.

4. Bathsheba Before David (1:15-21)

The two conspirators begin to put their plans into practice with Bathsheba making the first approach. She alleges that David has made a promise in respect of her son

hours when judgment is dimmed by desire. What husband does not know the surge of moral power which has come to his aid when in some hour of temptation he recalled the vows made at the marriage altar? Or perhaps a father has been called back from laxity of living by remembering that day when his little daughter's life was spared, and in gratitude he made his vow of obedience before God. The memory of the vow behind us is often as reinforcing to the will as the vision of the goal before us.

In making a vow to the Lord a man undergirds himself with himself and with God. To break that vow is to go back on oneself and to play false with God. It undoes something in

human character, as the dropping of a spool of thread unrolls what has been wound up. Vows, if thoughtfully kept, help to stiffen vague ideals into sturdy standards. In common use we make a difference between ideals and standards. An ideal is something we hold before ourselves; a standard is something we hold ourselves to. Our lofty ideals and noble sentiments need the strengthening which our godly ancestors got from their fixed moral rules, their settled religious habits, their sense of obligation to a covenant-keeping God.

Vows serve to combine a gentleman's code of honor with a Christian's sensitive conscience. That is a desirable combination, for religious

16 And Bath-sheba bowed, and did obeisance unto the king. And the king said, What wouldest thou?

17 And she said unto him, My lord, thou swarest by the LORD thy God unto thine handmaid, *saying,* Assuredly Solomon thy son shall reign after me, and he shall sit upon my throne.

18 And now, behold, Adonijah reigneth; and now, my lord the king, thou knowest *it* not:

19 And he hath slain oxen and fat cattle and sheep in abundance, and hath called all the sons of the king, and Abiathar the priest, and Joab the captain of the host: but Solomon thy servant hath he not called.

20 And thou, my lord, O king, the eyes of all Israel *are* upon thee, that thou shouldest tell them who shall sit on the throne of my lord the king after him.

21 Otherwise it shall come to pass, when my lord the king shall sleep with his fathers, that I and my son Solomon shall be counted offenders.

tering to the king). **16** Bathshe′ba bowed and did obeisance to the king, and the king said, "What do you desire?" **17** She said to him, "My lord, you swore to your maidservant by the LORD your God, saying, 'Solomon your son shall reign after me, and he shall sit upon my throne.' **18** And now, behold, Adoni′jah is king, although you, my lord the king, do not know it. **19** He has sacrificed oxen, fatlings, and sheep in abundance, and has invited all the sons of the king, Abi′athar the priest, and Jo′ab the commander of the army; but Solomon your servant he has not invited. **20** And now, my lord the king, the eyes of all Israel are upon you, to tell them who shall sit on the throne of my lord the king after him. **21** Otherwise it will come to pass, when my lord the king sleeps with his fathers, that I and my son Solomon will be counted offenders."

Solomon, tells him that Adonijah has already been made king, asks the king to declare his promise publicly, because it is a matter of life and death for her and her son.

21. Sleeps with his fathers: This phrase is in line with the earliest Hebrew ideas of what happens after death. The idea of Sheol is a later development. "Sheol is the land of ghosts, . . . weak and helpless, with no life in themselves." It did not form the basis of the later growth of a belief in a resurrected life after death. That came "primarily from the firm belief that God was still the Saviour of his people," however disastrous their fate might seem to be (N. H. Snaith, "Life after Death: The Biblical Doctrine of Immortality," *Interpretation* I [1947], 309-24, especially pp. 317-18; see also H. Wheeler Robinson, *Inspiration and Revelation in the Old Testament* [Oxford: Clarendon Press, 1946], pp. 94-105). The only passages which by common agreement refer to life beyond the grave are Isa. 26:19 and Dan. 12:2.

Counted offenders: The Hebrew is חטאים, usually translated "sinners." Both the KJV and the RSV are interpreting, neither quite adequately. Early Hebrew ideas of sin, before the rise of the eighth-century prophets, were practical rather than ethical. Here the word has no ethical significance, but means that they will find themselves on

impulses need to be strengthened with a sense of honor as truly as our gentlemanly codes need to be sensitized with godliness. A Christian must be all that becomes a gentleman, and more. There is a value too in the public making of vows. The psalmist adds force to his position when he declares, "I will pay my vows unto the LORD now in the presence of all his people" (Ps. 116:14). Cultured persons are prone to think of religion as a very intimate affair. They do not wish to parade their deep personal feelings. They see the point of A. N. Whitehead's contention that "religion is what the individual

does with his solitariness." [2] But just how private can a person's religious attitudes and convictions be?

Jesus said, "Let your light so shine before men, that they may see your good works, and glorify your Father which is in heaven" (Matt. 5:16). Our faith is not meant to be hidden under a bushel or locked in a closet. Love is meaningless in solitude. What is joy without someone to share it? Courage requires the presence of others to test it and preserve it. With

[2] *Religion in the Making* (New York: The Macmillan Co., 1926), p. 16.

22 ¶ And, lo, while she yet talked with the king, Nathan the prophet also came in.

23 And they told the king, saying, Behold Nathan the prophet. And when he was come in before the king, he bowed himself before the king with his face to the ground.

24 And Nathan said, My lord, O king, hast thou said, Adonijah shall reign after me, and he shall sit upon my throne?

25 For he is gone down this day, and hath slain oxen and fat cattle and sheep in abundance, and hath called all the king's sons, and the captains of the host, and Abiathar the priest; and, behold, they eat and drink before him, and say, God save king Adonijah.

26 But me, *even* me thy servant, and Zadok the priest, and Benaiah the son of Jehoiada, and thy servant Solomon, hath he not called.

27 Is this thing done by my lord the king, and thou hast not showed *it* unto thy servant, who should sit on the throne of my lord the king after him?

22 While she was still speaking with the king, Nathan the prophet came in. 23 And they told the king, "Here is Nathan the prophet." And when he came in before the king, he bowed before the king, with his face to the ground. 24 And Nathan said, "My lord the king, have you said, 'Adoni'jah shall reign after me, and he shall sit upon my throne'? 25 For he has gone down this day, and has sacrificed oxen, fatlings, and sheep in abundance, and has invited all the king's sons, Jo'ab the commander*a* of the army, and Abi'athar the priest; and behold, they are eating and drinking before him, and saying, 'Long live King Adoni'jah!' 26 But me, your servant, and Zadok the priest, and Benai'ah the son of Jehoi'ada, and your servant Solomon, he has not invited. 27 Has this thing been brought about by my lord the king and you have not told your servants who should sit on the throne of my lord the king after him?"

a Gk: Heb *commanders*

---

the losing side, suffering the death penalty for having supported the unsuccessful aspirant; cf. Gen. 43:9, where the KJV rightly has "let me bear the blame for ever," but the Hebrew is, "Then will I be a sinner [וחטאתי] to thee all my days." A similar example is Exod. 9:27, where Pharaoh says, "The LORD is righteous [צדיק], and I and my people are wicked [רשעים]," the meaning being that God has won and Pharaoh has lost. There is no question here of ethics. The rightness of the action is judged solely by the consequences, not by any preconceived moral code. This judgment by results needs to be remembered generally in connection with the words for "sin" and the doctrine of the Atonement. The words can be used, and are often used, not only for the wrong act itself, but also for the consequences of it in suffering, condemnation, and death.

5. THE PLOT DEVELOPS (1:22-27)

22-27. Nathan the prophet is announced as seeking audience of the king. The woman retires according to custom. Nathan's approach is different from that of Bathsheba. He pretends to assume that David has given secret instructions for the coronation of Adonijah, thereby putting Nathan himself and his friends in imminent peril of death. It is evident not only from this, but also from vs. 10, that Solomon had a following even before the climax came when it was imperative that a successor to David should be enthroned.

---

all respect for those secret vows which men keep hidden in their hearts, nevertheless, a pledge gains tremendous support when given in the presence of others. A public vow to the Lord shows where the maker stands. It acknowledges his dependence on God and helps to achieve his independence from the godless crowd. Moreover, the making of a public religious vow strengthens the maker with the comradeship of fellow believers. There are times when we crave

to be alone with God. But there are other situations, such as the threat of public perils, when we get tremendous help from the presence of other God-seekers. As we shall see later in the case of Elijah, we often need to be reminded how many there are whose knees "have not bowed to Baal" (19:18).

David's respect for his vow to the Lord, however his aged mind may have been played upon by clever courtiers, reveals a foundation stone in

28 ¶ Then king David answered and said, Call me Bath-sheba. And she came into the king's presence, and stood before the king.

29 And the king sware, and said, *As* the LORD liveth, that hath redeemed my soul out of all distress,

30 Even as I sware unto thee by the LORD God of Israel, saying, Assuredly Solomon thy son shall reign after me, and he shall sit upon my throne in my stead; even so will I certainly do this day.

31 Then Bath-sheba bowed with *her* face to the earth, and did reverence to the king, and said, Let my lord king David live for ever.

32 ¶ And king David said, Call me Zadok the priest, and Nathan the prophet, and Benaiah the son of Jehoiada. And they came before the king.

33 The king also said unto them, Take with you the servants of your lord, and cause Solomon my son to ride upon mine own mule, and bring him down to Gihon:

34 And let Zadok the priest and Nathan the prophet anoint him there king over Israel: and blow ye with the trumpet, and say, God save king Solomon.

28 Then King David answered, "Call Bathshe'ba to me." So she came into the king's presence, and stood before the king. 29 And the king swore, saying, "As the LORD lives, who has redeemed my soul out of every adversity, 30 as I swore to you by the LORD, the God of Israel, saying, 'Solomon your son shall reign after me, and he shall sit upon my throne in my stead'; even so will I do this day." 31 Then Bathshe'ba bowed with her face to the ground, and did obeisance to the king, and said, "May my lord King David live for ever!"

32 King David said, "Call to me Zadok the priest, Nathan the prophet, and Benai'ah the son of Jehoi'ada." So they came before the king. 33 And the king said to them, "Take with you the servants of your lord, and cause Solomon my son to ride on my own mule, and bring him down to Gihon; 34 and let Zadok the priest and Nathan the prophet there anoint him king over Israel; then blow the trumpet, and say,

6. DAVID TAKES DECISIVE ACTION (1:28-40)

David confirms the oath which Bathsheba and Nathan claimed he had made long before. He then calls for Solomon's supporters, bids them mount Solomon on his own royal mule, escort him to Gihon, and there establish him as king with all proper formalities.

33. My own mule: The mule was the proper riding beast for the king and his sons (II Sam. 13:29; 18:9). Horses were introduced from Egypt in the time of Solomon, and then for driving rather than for riding. Ordinary people rode asses.

34. Anoint him king: Every anointed person (Hebrew, *māshîaḥ;* English, "Messiah") was sacred, regarded as having been chosen by God for a particular purpose, the king to rule God's people, the nation to be his chosen people, and even Cyrus (Isa. 45:1) to set the people of God free from exile, until finally Messiah is the one chosen to usher in the kingdom of God. There is no evidence of any priest being anointed until the high priest of postexilic times—a civil ruler as well as priest. Priests were consecrated but not anointed.

Blow the trumpet: The Hebrew word for **blow** strictly means "thrust," "smite," and it is used regularly for thrusting with a weapon. The reference here is thus to the

the Hebrew-Christian tradition which undergirds civil law with regard for divine sovereignty.

32-40. *Ally or Master?*—In David's court we discover the desire to use God rather than to be used of him. For some men, the concept of Yahweh was still on the level of a tribal deity,

defender and champion of his chosen people. After David has declared his intention of keeping his vow, and has set in motion the program to put Solomon on the throne, Benaiah cries out his hope that the Lord himself will confirm the words of the king. **As the LORD has been with my lord the king, even so may he be with**

35 Then ye shall come up after him, that he may come and sit upon my throne; for he shall be king in my stead: and I have appointed him to be ruler over Israel and over Judah.

36 And Benaiah the son of Jehoiada answered the king, and said, Amen: the LORD God of my lord the king say so *too*.

37 As the LORD hath been with my lord the king, even so be he with Solomon, and make his throne greater than the throne of my lord king David.

38 So Zadok the priest, and Nathan the prophet, and Benaiah the son of Jehoiada, and the Cherethites, and the Pelethites, went down, and caused Solomon to ride upon king David's mule, and brought him to Gihon.

39 And Zadok the priest took a horn of oil out of the tabernacle, and anointed Solomon. And they blew the trumpet; and all the people said, God save king Solomon.

40 And all the people came up after him, and the people piped with pipes, and rejoiced with great joy, so that the earth rent with the sound of them.

'Long live King Solomon!' **35** You shall then come up after him, and he shall come and sit upon my throne; for he shall be king in my stead; and I have appointed him to be ruler over Israel and over Judah." **36** And Benai'ah the son of Jehoi'ada answered the king, "Amen! May the LORD, the God of my lord the king, say so. **37** As the LORD has been with my lord the king, even so may he be with Solomon, and make his throne greater than the throne of my lord King David."

38 So Zadok the priest, Nathan the prophet, and Benai'ah the son of Jehoi'ada, and the Cher'ethites and the Pel'ethites, went down and caused Solomon to ride on King David's mule, and brought him to Gihon. **39** There Zadok the priest took the horn of oil from the tent, and anointed Solomon. Then they blew the trumpet; and all the people said, "Long live King Solomon!" **40** And all the people went up after him, playing on pipes, and rejoicing with great joy, so that the earth was split by their noise.

---

suddenness of the blast of the coronation fanfare, even to this day a unique and shattering sound. Among the Hebrews this fanfare was blown on the shophar, a curved trumpet made from a ram's horn. This horn was also blown as an alarm (Amos 3:6), for rallying in battle (Zeph. 1:16), and in later O.T. times on special religious occasions (Lev. 25:9).

40. Playing on pipes: The ancient versions speak of a great variety of musical instruments, from organs (O.L.), sistra (Syriac), to harps (Targ.) and choruses and melodies (second rendering of O.L.). Whatever instruments they used, they certainly made a great deal of noise. The Hebrew says **that the earth was split by it.**

Solomon, and make his throne greater than the throne of my lord King David (vs. 37).

While fuller revelation has lifted our sights and insights until we see God as sovereign of the universe, we have not outgrown the primitive and selfish desire to use him as the servant of our purposes rather than to submit our programs to his will. Like Benaiah, we pray for the Lord's confirmation of the plans we make. In this tendency C. S. Lewis finds

the real snag in all this drawing up of blue prints for a Christian society. Most of us are not really approaching the subject in order to find out what Christianity says: we are approaching it in the hope of finding support from Christianity for the views of our own party. We are looking for an ally where we are offered either a Master or—a Judge.[3]

[3] *Christian Behavior* (New York: The Macmillan Co., 1944), p. 17.

One of the most popular perversions of Christianity is the presentation of God as a caterer to man-made wants and religious faith as a way of fulfilling human desires. The contemporary pulpit in its effort to draw crowds stresses the satisfactions to be derived from religion—peace of mind, health of body, social acceptability, freedom from tension, financial prosperity, even military success. Preachers try to "sell religion" on the principle of "the public be pleased." They preach to men's desires rather than to their needs. They portray God as a sort of divine Santa Claus coming down to fill our stockings with whatever we may ask in his name. All this some preachers do because they know that people would rather feel good than be good. But they forget that God in Christ came to save rather than to satisfy. Our willful and misguided world needs a Master, not an ally.

41 ¶ And Adonijah and all the guests that *were* with him heard *it* as they had made an end of eating. And when Joab heard the sound of the trumpet, he said, Wherefore *is this* noise of the city being in an uproar?

42 And while he yet spake, behold, Jonathan the son of Abiathar the priest came: and Adonijah said unto him, Come in; for thou *art* a valiant man, and bringest good tidings.

43 And Jonathan answered and said to Adonijah, Verily our lord king David hath made Solomon king.

44 And the king hath sent with him Zadok the priest, and Nathan the prophet, and Benaiah the son of Jehoiada, and the Cherethites, and the Pelethites, and they have caused him to ride upon the king's mule:

41 Adoni'jah and all the guests who were with him heard it as they finished feasting. And when Jo'ab heard the sound of the trumpet, he said, "What does this uproar in the city mean?" 42 While he was still speaking, behold, Jonathan the son of Abi'athar the priest came; and Adoni'jah said, "Come in, for you are a worthy man and bring good news." 43 Jonathan answered Adoni'jah, "No, for our lord King David has made Solomon king; 44 and the king has sent with him Zadok the priest, Nathan the prophet, and Benai'ah the son of Jehoi'ada, and the Cher'ethites and the Pel'ethites; and they have caused him to ride on the

7. Adonijah's Cause Collapses (1:41-53)

The bad news of what has been happening at Gihon soon reaches Adonijah and his supporters at En-rogel. The movement forthwith collapses and every man flees for his life. Adonijah himself seeks sanctuary and his life is spared conditionally upon his future good behavior.

42. Jonathan son of Abiathar the priest shares with Ahimaaz son of Zadok the other priest the reputation of being a long-distance runner. They both appear in the stories of David's reign as runners of repute (II Sam. 15:27; 17:17; 18:27).

Health, peace, and other blessings do come as by-products of Christianity, but only to those who lose themselves in serving the Lord.

41-49. When the Fearful Forsake.—The news of Solomon's coronation reached Adonijah's cohorts while they were at the sacrificial feast which the pretender had prepared for them. At first they could not believe the report. Then consternation set in. And the record is **all the guests of Adonijah trembled, and rose, and each went his own way** (vs. 49).

Consider first why Adonijah's men came together. No doubt different members of the party had differing reasons for being there. One motive in the minds of some must have been a sincere desire to save the kingdom from civil war. The country could not continue strong while divided between two rival claimants. Others very likely were attracted by loyalty to the person of Adonijah, for the report is that he was handsome (cf. vs. 6). Another motive on the part of some was undoubtedly a desire to share in the perquisites of office. If Adonijah came to power there would be royal commissions, offices, special privileges, and profits. And of course some of them had come together out

of fear, for they knew that if the other party succeeded they would suffer. Very probably several of these motives may have been mixed in the mind of each individual, for most of us form our associations from mixed motives. Consider the family itself. It is hardly accurate to say that our family life is motivated purely by love. Family ties are woven of several strands— love, comfort, convenience, security, fear. The English novelist, A. S. M. Hutchinson, in his book *This Freedom*,[4] interpreted a wife as feeling that her husband had married for a home where he could find his comforts and possessions, a place he could step into and call his. The husband on his part felt that his wife had married to have a place which she could step out of, into a security not possessed by her unmarried women competitors in the career field.

And what are the motives which lead to the formation of friendships? Some persons we almost instinctively like. Others are persons with whom we like to be seen. Some of our companions we choose because we can help them, some because they can help us. The golden bonds of friendship contain much alloy.

[4] Boston: Little, Brown & Co., 1922.

45 And Zadok the priest and Nathan the prophet have anointed him king in Gihon; and they are come up from thence rejoicing, so that the city rang again. This *is* the noise that ye have heard.

46 And also Solomon sitteth on the throne of the kingdom.

47 And moreover the king's servants came to bless our lord king David, saying, God make the name of Solomon better than thy name, and make his throne greater than thy throne. And the king bowed himself upon the bed.

48 And also thus said the king, Blessed *be* the LORD God of Israel, which hath given *one* to sit on my throne this day, mine eyes even seeing *it*.

49 And all the guests that *were* with Adonijah were afraid, and rose up, and went every man his way.

50 ¶ And Adonijah feared because of Solomon, and arose, and went, and caught hold on the horns of the altar.

king's mule; 45 and Zadok the priest and Nathan the prophet have anointed him king at Gihon; and they have gone up from there rejoicing, so that the city is in an uproar. This is the noise that you have heard. 46 Solomon sits upon the royal throne. 47 Moreover the king's servants came to congratulate our lord King David, saying, 'Your God make the name of Solomon more famous than yours, and make his throne greater than your throne.' And the king bowed himself upon the bed. 48 And the king also said, 'Blessed be the LORD, the God of Israel, who has granted one of my offspring[b] to sit on my throne this day, my own eyes seeing it.' "

49 Then all the guests of Adoni'jah trembled, and rose, and each went his own way. 50 And Adoni'jah feared Solomon; and he arose, and went, and caught hold of the

[b] Gk: Heb *one*

---

50. The horns of the altar: These were originally bull's horns and represented the strength of deity. They were the most sacred parts of the altar. Here Hebrew ideas

---

Or why do we come together in community associations? Again our motives are mixed. Most of us have an instinct for neighborliness. We join in neighborhood activities in order to escape loneliness, to find recreation, to support welfare organizations. Often we organize in our communities to protect property values, to keep out bad influence, and sometimes to keep out undesirable neighbors.

And while we are considering the motives which prompted Adonijah's partisans, we might examine the reasons for our political party affiliations. We believe that party government is essential to preserve free society. We are supposed to join political parties which help express our convictions. But we have to admit that many are moved not by sincere desire or what is best for the country as a whole but by what promises to serve best the interests of their own group or class. Many merely vote for the party to which their families and friends belong.

Granted, then, that our associations and alliances are formed from mixed motives, let us note what happens when danger threatens. Adonijah's partisans were terrified and they fled. Danger tests and sifts the motives which prompt our associations. In the case of Adonijah's party, danger revealed a fear based on self-interest. Darkening peril produced dominant fear which led to disintegration.

Fear has a legitimate function in life. Like pain, fear is a sentinel which warns of danger. But when fear moves in to the seat of command and becomes chief of staff it heightens the danger. Fear makes men so self-conscious that they cannot see objectively. Fear cows the conscience and perverts moral judgments. Fear weakens efficiency, enervates the body and when it verges toward panic, paralyzes the will. Fear may bring men together in alliances, but it does not hold them together. In the face of common danger during war, racial, religious, and industrial differences within a nation tend to be overlooked. But with the cessation of strife abroad, conflicts and suspicions revive at home. In the face of Nazi terror the United States and the Soviet Union linked arms as allies; but when Hitler was removed, the alliance turned to distrust. Fear makes strange bedfellows, but it does not make lasting comrades.

In the formation and fall of Adonijah's party we see how danger tests the purity of motives. Self-interest, however "enlightened," is not a sufficient bond of unity. Mutual fear is not an adequate foundation for a family of nations. Nothing less than love can hold men together during long peril and strain. And abiding love must be fed from above.

50-53. *A Coward's Castle.*—Adonijah and his followers were seized with panic. In his fear of

51 And it was told Solomon, saying, Behold, Adonijah feareth king Solomon: for, lo, he hath caught hold on the horns of the altar, saying, Let king Solomon swear unto me to-day that he will not slay his servant with the sword.

52 And Solomon said, If he will show himself a worthy man, there shall not a hair of him fall to the earth: but if wickedness shall be found in him, he shall die.

53 So king Solomon sent, and they brought him down from the altar. And he came and bowed himself to king Solomon: and Solomon said unto him, Go to thine house.

2 Now the days of David drew nigh that he should die; and he charged Solomon his son, saying,

2 I go the way of all the earth: be thou strong therefore, and show thyself a man;

horns of the altar. 51 And it was told Solomon, "Behold, Adoni'jah fears King Solomon; for, lo, he has laid hold of the horns of the altar, saying, 'Let King Solomon swear to me first that he will not slay his servant with the sword.'" 52 And Solomon said, "If he prove to be a worthy man, not one of his hairs shall fall to the earth; but if wickedness is found in him, he shall die." 53 So King Solomon sent, and they brought him down from the altar. And he came and did obeisance to King Solomon; and Solomon said to him, "Go to your house."

2 When David's time to die drew near, he charged Solomon his son, saying, 2 "I am about to go the way of all the earth.

once more are in line with heathen custom generally. There were bronze horns on the top of the ziggurat (temple-pyramid) of Babylon, and also on that at Nineveh. All primitive altars had horns, though in many Palestinian altars which have been excavated the horns have been formalized into knobs (S. A. Cook, The Religion of Ancient Palestine in the Light of Archaeology [London: British Academy, 1930], pp. 28-31).

53. Go to your house, i.e., retire from public life. This clemency extended by Solomon is unusual. Possibly he was loath to execute his defeated rival because he had actually been anointed and so might be regarded as a sacred person. David was most scrupulous in this respect concerning "the Lord's anointed." In any case, Solomon's action should be remembered to him for righteousness.

B. David's Last Words (2:1-12)

The dying charge of David to Solomon is composed of two distinct sections. They are very different in temper and in style, the first giving sound advice of the orthodox seventh-century type, the second giving practical counsel after the fashion of an earlier and more brutal age.

1. A Charge to Piety (2:2-4)

This section is full of Deuteronomic phrases. It was inserted by the editor (ca. 610 b.c.) to act as a preface to his whole history of the kings in order to suggest that David was a model Deuteronomic king. The kings who follow are to be judged according to the way in which they obeyed or disobeyed these commands of David (cf. 15:3; etc.). The theme is that the man who obeys the Deuteronomic law with full zeal will prosper in all he does. He must worship God faithfully and in Jerusalem. He must abhor all

Solomon's possible revenge, Adonijah fled to the sanctuary and claimed the protection accorded by the horns of the altar. He sought the same shelter that Joab was to seek (2:28). The horns of the altar were an asylum originally planned for unintentional manslayers. But later they appear to have been made use of by those who feared punishment by death. Adonijah's flight to this sanctuary could well be interpreted

as a confession of guilt. Solomon's act of clemency was a sign of his magnanimity. It enhanced his popularity. It was one more sign of promise which heightened the people's expectancy of their new king.

2:1-4, 12. The Gospel of Success.—When the dying David charged Solomon to keep the statutes as written in the law of Moses, he offered this incentive: that you may prosper in

3 And keep the charge of the LORD thy God, to walk in his ways, to keep his statutes, and his commandments, and his judgments, and his testimonies, as it is written in the law of Moses, that thou mayest prosper in all that thou doest, and whithersoever thou turnest thyself:

4 That the LORD may continue his word which he spake concerning me, saying, If thy children take heed to their way, to walk before me in truth with all their heart and with all their soul, there shall not fail thee (said he) a man on the throne of Israel.

Be strong, and show yourself a man, 3 and keep the charge of the LORD your God, walking in his ways and keeping his statutes, his commandments, his ordinances, and his testimonies, as it is written in the law of Moses, that you may prosper in all that you do and wherever you turn; 4 that the LORD may establish his word which he spoke concerning me, saying, 'If your sons take heed to their way, to walk before me in faithfulness with all their heart and with all their soul, there shall not fail you a man on the throne of Israel.'

immoral cults and have nothing at all to do with any foreign gods. He must care for the poor and the unprivileged in order that God's justice may be established in his land. Further, so long as the kings do this there will always be an heir of David's line to rule in Jerusalem.

2:4. With all their soul: Better, "with all their self," since neither in the O.T. nor in the N.T. does the word **soul** refer to an immortal part of man's nature. In the O.T. it stands for שׁפנ, and in the N.T. for ψυχή, both of which belong to this present life and cease at death. Whatever lives after death is expressed by "spirit," πνεῦμα, and this is a gift of God, not man's either by nature or by merit (cf. I Cor. 15:43-50; etc.).

all that you do and wherever you turn. In assuming that prosperity is the reward of obedience to God, David is in line with much O.T. teaching. The Genesis account of Joseph is one of the greatest success stories in all literature. The psalmists reiterate that the favor of God is revealed in the prosperity of the righteous. To be sure, Jeremiah becomes puzzled at the way justice is meted out, and exclaims, "Wherefore doth the way of the wicked prosper?" (Jer. 12:1). Ecclesiastes was perplexed when he observed that the race is not always "to the swift, . . . nor yet riches to men of understanding, nor yet favor to men of skill" (Eccl. 9:11). The great poetic drama of Job deals with the inexplicable calamities which can befall a godly man; but the poem ends with Job's prosperity restored. When we turn to the N.T., we find Jesus rejected because he did not fit the prevailing success patterns of his people. Yet although Jesus seemed a failure when judged by current measurements, he puts into his Beatitudes the promise of rewards, and he talks about what shall profit men. When we read the letters of Paul, we catch such words as these: "Know ye not that they which run in a race run all, but one receiveth the prize? So run, that ye may obtain" (I Cor. 9:24).

How can the biblical promises of prosperity and reward be reconciled with the basic Christian principles of unselfishness and sacrifice? For one thing, Christ enlarges the popular success patterns. The urge to amount to something is part of our native normal equipment. The child without ambition is like a watch with a broken spring. But the desire to succeed must be made to include more than the self. Personal self-assertiveness must be cured by the process of outgrowing it into larger loyalties. The child grows up within the life of the family and then the welfare of the whole household should become his interest. Later, school and college loyalty should expand the success patterns of the individual to include the larger group. This does not always happen. An educator said that secular education is much concerned with the verbs "to know," "to do," and "to get," while Christian education is concerned primarily with the verbs "to be," "to obey," "to serve," and "to dedicate." Christ enlarges the self to include the interests of the family, the school, the community, the nation, and the world.

Moreover, Jesus in his life and teachings spiritualizes the popular conception of success. We live so within the shadow of the market place that money colors almost all our estimates of success. As we say, "money talks"; but only so long as people listen. And when people become intelligent enough to look for true values, then money ceases to talk so convincingly. Jesus recognized that money has a place in life. He referred to it often in the Gospels. But he put money in its proper and secondary place. Recall the occasion when a man accosted our Lord, asking him to bid his brother divide the family inheritance with him. Jesus refused to serve as

5 Moreover thou knowest also what Joab the son of Zeruiah did to me, *and* what he did to the two captains of the hosts of Israel, unto Abner the son of Ner, and unto Amasa

5 "Moreover you know also what Jo'ab the son of Zeru'iah did to me, how he dealt with the two commanders of the armies of Israel, Abner the son of Ner, and Ama'sa

---

2. DAVID'S LEGACY OF EVIL (2:5-12)

The second section of David's last charge to Solomon (vss. 5-9) is very different from vss. 2-4. Some scholars (e.g., Pfeiffer) hold that these also are the work of the editor, but others (e.g., Skinner, Burney) believe that they belong to the court source, in common with most of the rest of chs. 1–2. The latter alternative is much the more likely. There are no Deuteronomic elements to be found here, either in phrase or in theme. The character of David is not at all idealized as in the previous verses. These commands are wholly consistent with a tenth-century B.C. origin. He was in many respects a man of his own time, and he thought and acted in ways which to us seem both cruel and ruthless. If David's line was to be firmly established, then the bloodguilt which was upon that house must be removed. Both Abner and Amasa were under David's safe conduct when Joab murdered them. Shimei's curse still rested upon David's house, though David himself could do nothing to remove it because of his oath to Shimei. David therefore left these two curses for Solomon to remove, and bade him also remember the oath of good will sworn to the house of the aged Barzillai. There is no need to ascribe the contents of these verses to treachery on David's part or to an unseemly desire for revenge. David's action had been perfectly proper in his lifetime according to the ethics of his day. His charge to Solomon was to take advantage of the opportunity when it comes in order to remove the doom which would prevent the secure establishment of the dynasty.

5. **Putting innocent blood upon the girdle about my loins:** It is best to follow the ancient versions, as the RSV does. The reference to the **girdle** is explained from Jer.

---

judge or divider and warned the man to beware of covetousness. Then he told the parable of the rich farmer whose fields brought forth so bountifully that he decided to build larger barns. Suddenly in the midst of his preparations the man died and the title to his possessions passed from him. Then Jesus added, "So is he that layeth up treasure for himself, and is not rich toward God" (Luke 12:21). To be rich toward God is Jesus' idea of success. And what constitutes such riches? When a person can look around him and see values which he helped to create; work well done, however humble, which leaves the world better off; lives made brighter because he has lived beside them; children whose strength of character has been inherited or caught from him; a community more wholesome because of his residence there; good causes furthered by his service and sacrifice—all this is something of what it is to be rich toward God. Measured by popular standards the career of Jesus was a series of failures. He lost his home, he lost his following, he lost his life. But it was not long after his death that men began to write of "the grace of our Lord Jesus Christ, that, though he was rich, yet for your sakes he became poor, that ye through his poverty might be rich" (II Cor. 8:9).

If we take our measurements from "the low world's level stand," David's promise of prosperity as the reward of obedience to God is not worthy in motive or trustworthy in practice. Christianity is not a gospel of success. But if our tastes are properly trained until virtue begins to be enjoyed as its own reward; if our insights are sharpened to see that the creation of values is better than the collection of profits; if we are unselfish enough to be more concerned with the prosperity of the cause we serve than with our personal prestige; if we are patient to hear what the centuries have to say against the hours, then we are justified in cherishing and trusting the promise that God "is a rewarder of them that diligently seek him" (Heb. 11:6). The rewards of God are not to be bargained for in calculating fashion. The kingdom of heaven is not a factory wherein wage agreements are all signed in advance; but, as Jesus pictured it in his parable of the workers, it is a vineyard in which those who trust fare better than those who bargain (Matt. 20:1-16). The followers of Jesus are his fellow workers, not as hirelings putting in time for a wage, but as friends putting in life for love.

5-9, 13-34. *The Vicious Circle of Vengeance.*
—The record of Joab throws light in several

the son of Jether, whom he slew, and shed the blood of war in peace, and put the blood of war upon his girdle that *was* about his loins, and in his shoes that *were* on his feet.

6 Do therefore according to thy wisdom, and let not his hoar head go down to the grave in peace.

7 But show kindness unto the sons of Barzillai the Gileadite, and let them be of those that eat at thy table: for so they came to me when I fled because of Absalom thy brother.

8 And, behold, *thou hast* with thee Shimei the son of Gera, a Benjamite of Bahurim, which cursed me with a grievous curse in the day when I went to Mahanaim: but he came down to meet me at Jordan, and I sware to him by the LORD, saying, I will not put thee to death with the sword.

9 Now therefore hold him not guiltless: for thou *art* a wise man, and knowest what thou oughtest to do unto him; but his hoar head bring thou down to the grave with blood.

the son of Jether, whom he murdered, avenging[c] in time of peace blood which had been shed in war, and putting innocent blood[d] upon the girdle about my[e] loins, and upon the sandals on my[e] feet. 6 Act therefore according to your wisdom, but do not let his head go down to Sheol in peace. 7 But deal loyally with the sons of Barzil'lai the Gileadite, and let them be among those who eat at your table; for with such loyalty they met me when I fled from Absalom your brother. 8 And there is also with you Shim'e-i the son of Gera, the Benjaminite from Bahu'rim who cursed me with a grievous curse on the day when I went to Mahana'im; but when he came down to meet me at the Jordan, I swore to him by the LORD, saying, 'I will not put you to death with the sword.' 9 Now therefore hold him not guiltless, for you are a wise man; you will know what you ought to do to him, and you shall bring his head down with blood to the grave."

[c] Gk: Heb *placing*
[d] Gk: Heb *blood of war*
[e] Gk: Heb *his*

13:11 as that which clings most closely to a man, and the following figure of **sandals** as that which is bound firmly onto a man. Joab had made David responsible for the blood of Abner and Amasa. David's very protests show by their vigor that he realized his responsibility. Solomon must use his wits (**Act . . . according to** [his] **wisdom,** cf. vs. 6) and see to it that Joab's blood atones for that of Abner and Amasa.

7. **Show kindness:** Lit., "make ḥéṣedh," i.e., keep the agreement which David made with Barzillai (II Sam. 17:27-29; 19:31-39) when he took Barzillai's son to live at court. The word ḥéṣedh comes to be used mainly as a covenant word, and properly denotes the faithfulness with which each party ought to keep the terms of the covenant between them. When the word is used of God it comes to stand for God's mercy toward his people Israel. This is due to Israel's continued apostasy, as a result of which God needs to exercise continual mercy and forbearance toward Israel if anything of the covenant is to survive. Miles Coverdale invented the word "lovingkindness," and he used it in the Psalms for the word ḥéṣedh whenever it stood for God's attitude to his covenant

---

directions. It serves to reveal the bloody feuds begotten by love of power in a time when force was the only arbiter. Joab had chosen the weaker side in the struggle between Adonijah and Solomon. He gambled for glory and lost his life.

Joab also paid the penalty of his ruthlessness. Having shed the blood of Abner and Amasa, he knew what to expect when Solomon came to the throne. He fled in fear to the horns of the altar. But that did not save him. Solomon gave orders for his death, declaring, **The LORD will bring back his bloody deeds upon his own head** (vs. 32). Solomon was ascribing to God the

vengeance he himself was determined to inflict. Such is the custom of conquerors. They take vengeance into their own hands and then pose as the agents of divine justice. Thus the vicious circle goes on. Bloody deeds do come back on the heads of blood-seekers. The old principle of "an eye for an eye, and a tooth for a tooth" is a losing game. Joab is just another illustration of the truth, "All they that take the sword shall perish with the sword" (Matt. 26:52). And the story of the death of Adonijah (vss. 13-25) underlines the same lesson of the nemesis that may come to ambition and to the pride of attempted power.

10 So David slept with his fathers, and was buried in the city of David.

11 And the days that David reigned over Israel *were* forty years: seven years reigned he in Hebron, and thirty and three years reigned he in Jerusalem.

12 ¶ Then sat Solomon upon the throne of David his father; and his kingdom was established greatly.

13 ¶ And Adonijah the son of Haggith came to Bath-sheba the mother of Solomon. And she said, Comest thou peaceably? And he said, Peaceably.

14 He said moreover, I have somewhat to say unto thee. And she said, Say on.

15 And he said, Thou knowest that the kingdom was mine, and *that* all Israel set their faces on me, that I should reign: howbeit the kingdom is turned about, and is become my brother's: for it was his from the LORD.

16 And now I ask one petition of thee, deny me not. And she said unto him, Say on.

17 And he said, Speak, I pray thee, unto Solomon the king, (for he will not say thee nay,) that he give me Abishag the Shunammite to wife.

18 And Bath-sheba said, Well; I will speak for thee unto the king.

19 ¶ Bath-sheba therefore went unto king Solomon, to speak unto him for Adonijah. And the king rose up to meet her, and

10 Then David slept with his fathers, and was buried in the city of David. 11 And the time that David reigned over Israel was forty years; he reigned seven years in Hebron, and thirty-three years in Jerusalem. 12 So Solomon sat upon the throne of David his father; and his kingdom was firmly established.

13 Then Adoni'jah the son of Haggith came to Bathshe'ba the mother of Solomon. And she said, "Do you come peaceably?" He said, "Peaceably." 14 Then he said, "I have something to say to you." She said, "Say on." 15 He said, "You know that the kingdom was mine, and that all Israel fully expected me to reign; however the kingdom has turned about and become my brother's, for it was his from the LORD. 16 And now I have one request to make of you; do not refuse me." She said to him, "Say on." 17 And he said, "Pray ask King Solomon — he will not refuse you — to give me Ab'ishag the Shu'nammite as my wife." 18 Bathshe'ba said, "Very well; I will speak for you to the king."

19 So Bathshe'ba went to King Solomon,

---

people. Elsewhere he followed the LXX (ἔλεος) and the Vulg. (*misericordia*), and translated "mercy" (N. H. Snaith, *The Distinctive Ideas of the Old Testament* [Philadelphia: Westminster Press, 1946], pp. 118-46, 156).

10-12. A chronological insertion by the editor to mark the close of David's reign, containing as much as the circumstances will allow of his regular obituary notice.

C. SOLOMON REMOVES THE CURSES (2:13-46)

Solomon uses his wisdom and removes in turn the three threats to the continued prosperity of the house of David. He makes full use of the opportunities given him by the three men whom he must destroy if he and his heirs would be safe and prosperous.

1. ADONIJAH'S REQUEST (2:13-25)

Adonijah seeks to take Abishag as his wife. He proffers this request through the queen mother who, as head of the harem, holds a dominant place at court. Solomon greets his mother with all proper respect, but interprets the request as a renewed attempt of Adonijah to secure that kingdom which had only just eluded his grasp. It was an ancient Semitic custom that the man who inherited the women of the dead king was his successor (cf. II Sam. 3:7; 12:8; 16:20-23). Solomon takes advantage of Adonijah's folly and sends the captain of his bodyguard to execute him forthwith. The rashness of the request allows Solomon to execute a man who had been anointed king.

19. The seat was indeed a **throne.** The word כסא is rarely used of any ordinary seat,

bowed himself unto her, and sat down on his throne, and caused a seat to be set for the king's mother; and she sat on his right hand.

20 Then she said, I desire one small petition of thee; *I pray thee,* say me not nay. And the king said unto her, Ask on, my mother; for I will not say thee nay.

21 And she said, Let Abishag the Shunammite be given to Adonijah thy brother to wife.

22 And king Solomon answered and said unto his mother, And why dost thou ask Abishag the Shunammite for Adonijah? ask for him the kingdom also; for he *is* mine elder brother; even for him, and for Abiathar the priest, and for Joab the son of Zeruiah.

23 Then king Solomon sware by the LORD, saying, God do so to me, and more also, if Adonijah have not spoken this word against his own life.

24 Now therefore, *as* the LORD liveth, which hath established me, and set me on the throne of David my father, and who hath made me a house, as he promised, Adonijah shall be put to death this day.

25 And king Solomon sent by the hand of Benaiah the son of Jehoiada; and he fell upon him that he died.

26 ¶ And unto Abiathar the priest said the king, Get thee to Anathoth, unto thine own fields; for thou *art* worthy of death: but I will not at this time put thee to death, because thou barest the ark of the Lord GOD before David my father, and because thou hast been afflicted in all wherein my father was afflicted.

27 So Solomon thrust out Abiathar from to speak to him on behalf of Adoni'jah. And the king rose to meet her, and bowed down to her; then he sat on his throne, and had a seat brought for the king's mother; and she sat on his right. 20 Then she said, "I have one small request to make of you; do not refuse me." And the king said to her, "Make your request, my mother; for I will not refuse you." 21 She said, "Let Ab'ishag the Shu'nammite be given to Adoni'jah your brother as his wife." 22 King Solomon answered his mother, "And why do you ask Ab'ishag the Shu'nammite for Adoni'jah? Ask for him the kingdom also; for he is my elder brother, and on his side are Abi'athar[f] the priest and Jo'ab the son of Zeru'iah." 23 Then King Solomon swore by the LORD, saying, "God do so to me and more also if this word does not cost Adoni'jah his life! 24 Now therefore as the LORD lives, who has established me, and placed me on the throne of David my father, and who has made me a house, as he promised, Adoni'jah shall be put to death this day." 25 So King Solomon sent Benai'ah the son of Jehoi'ada; and he struck him down, and he died.

26 And to Abi'athar the priest the king said, "Go to An'athoth, to your estate; for you deserve death. But I will not at this time put you to death, because you bore the ark of the Lord GOD before David my father, and because you shared in all the affliction of my father." 27 So Solomon expelled Abi'athar from being priest to the LORD,

f Gk Syr-Vg: Heb *and for him and for Abiathar*

---

but usually of a seat of high distinction and honor; to sit on the right hand of the king is to sit in the place of power and authority (cf. Acts 7:56; Heb. 1:13, of the risen and ascended Christ).

2. ABIATHAR IS BANISHED (2:26-27)

Solomon now turns to deal with Adonijah's former allies. He cannot execute Abiathar, who is a priest and therefore beyond Solomon's jurisdiction, i.e., so far as matters of life and death are concerned. What Solomon can do, he does. He exiles Abiathar from the royal shrine and from court circles, bids him return to his ancestral property at Anathoth and stay there. This village was some two and a half miles north of Jerusalem, just beyond Nob, where Saul had massacred the house of Eli. Jeremiah the prophet was descended from the priests of Anathoth (Jer. 1:1; 32:7).

27. This verse is due to the Deuteronomic editor, who thus emphasizes the authority of the Zadokite priesthood of Jerusalem.

being priest unto the Lord; that he might fulfil the word of the Lord, which he spake concerning the house of Eli in Shiloh.

28 ¶ Then tidings came to Joab: for Joab had turned after Adonijah, though he turned not after Absalom. And Joab fled unto the tabernacle of the Lord, and caught hold on the horns of the altar.

29 And it was told king Solomon that Joab was fled unto the tabernacle of the Lord; and, behold, *he is* by the altar. Then Solomon sent Benaiah the son of Jehoiada, saying, Go, fall upon him.

30 And Benaiah came to the tabernacle of the Lord, and said unto him, Thus saith the king, Come forth. And he said, Nay; but I will die here. And Benaiah brought the king word again, saying, Thus said Joab, and thus he answered me.

31 And the king said unto him, Do as he hath said, and fall upon him, and bury him; that thou mayest take away the innocent blood, which Joab shed, from me, and from the house of my father.

32 And the Lord shall return his blood upon his own head, who fell upon two men more righteous and better than he, and slew them with the sword, my father David not knowing *thereof, to wit,* Abner the son of Ner, captain of the host of Israel, and Amasa the son of Jether, captain of the host of Judah.

33 Their blood shall therefore return upon the head of Joab, and upon the head of his seed for ever: but upon David, and upon his seed, and upon his house, and upon his throne, shall there be peace for ever from the Lord.

34 So Benaiah the son of Jehoiada went up, and fell upon him, and slew him: and he was buried in his own house in the wilderness.

thus fulfilling the word of the Lord which he had spoken concerning the house of Eli in Shiloh.

28 When the news came to Jo'ab — for Jo'ab had supported Adoni'jah although he had not supported Absalom — Jo'ab fled to the tent of the Lord and caught hold of the horns of the altar. **29** And when it was told King Solomon, "Jo'ab has fled to the tent of the Lord, and behold, he is beside the altar," Solomon sent Benai'ah the son of Jehoi'ada, saying, "Go, strike him down." **30** So Benai'ah came to the tent of the Lord, and said to him, "The king commands, 'Come forth.'" But he said, "No, I will die here." Then Benai'ah brought the king word again, saying, "Thus said Jo'ab, and thus he answered me." **31** The king replied to him, "Do as he has said, strike him down and bury him; and thus take away from me and from my father's house the guilt for the blood which Jo'ab shed without cause. **32** The Lord will bring back his bloody deeds upon his own head, because, without the knowledge of my father David, he attacked and slew with the sword two men more righteous and better than himself, Abner the son of Ner, commander of the army of Israel, and Ama'sa the son of Jether, commander of the army of Judah. **33** So shall their blood come back upon the head of Jo'ab and upon the head of his descendants for ever; but to David, and to his descendants, and to his house, and to his throne, there shall be peace from the Lord for evermore." **34** Then Benai'ah the son of Jehoi'ada went up, and struck him down and killed him; and he was buried in his

---

3. The End of Joab (2:28-34)

David's former commander in chief hears what has happened to Adonijah and Abiathar, his two companions of other days, and flees for sanctuary to grasp the horns of the altar. Solomon interprets this act as a confession of new guilt, and sends Benaiah to execute him. Benaiah dares not do this when he finds Joab on holy ground, but returns to the king for new instructions. The command comes in the form of fulfilling Joab's own words, **I will die here.**

32. The bloodguilt for the murders of Abner and Amasa can be removed from David's house only by the blood of him who was responsible for the murders, i.e., of Joab, who had actually done the deeds, or of David and his kin, who were ultimately responsible. When the RSV translates **his bloody deeds,** it is interpreting according to

35 ¶ And the king put Benaiah the son of Jehoiada in his room over the host: and Zadok the priest did the king put in the room of Abiathar.

36 ¶ And the king sent and called for Shimei, and said unto him, Build thee a house in Jerusalem, and dwell there, and go not forth thence any whither.

37 For it shall be, *that* on the day thou goest out, and passest over the brook Kidron, thou shalt know for certain that thou shalt surely die: thy blood shall be upon thine own head.

38 And Shimei said unto the king, The saying *is* good: as my lord the king hath said, so will thy servant do. And Shimei dwelt in Jerusalem many days.

39 And it came to pass at the end of three years, that two of the servants of Shimei ran away unto Achish son of Maachah king of Gath. And they told Shimei, saying, Behold, thy servants *be* in Gath.

40 And Shimei arose, and saddled his ass, and went to Gath to Achish to seek his servants: and Shimei went, and brought his servants from Gath.

41 And it was told Solomon that Shimei had gone from Jerusalem to Gath, and was come again.

42 And the king sent and called for Shimei, and said unto him, Did I not make thee to swear by the LORD, and protested unto thee, saying, Know for a certain, on the day thou goest out, and walkest abroad own house in the wilderness. 35 The king put Benai'ah the son of Jehoi'ada over the army in place of Jo'ab, and the king put Zadok the priest in the place of Abi'athar.

36 Then the king sent and summoned Shim'e-i, and said to him, "Build yourself a house in Jerusalem, and dwell there, and do not go forth from there to any place whatever. 37 For on the day you go forth, and cross the brook Kidron, know for certain that you shall die; your blood shall be upon your own head." 38 And Shim'e-i said to the king, "What you say is good; as my lord the king has said, so will your servant do." So Shim'e-i dwelt in Jerusalem many days.

39 But it happened at the end of three years that two of Shim'e-i's slaves ran away to Achish, son of Ma'acah, king of Gath. And when it was told Shim'e-i, "Behold, your slaves are in Gath," 40 Shim'e-i arose and saddled an ass, and went to Gath to Achish, to seek his slaves; Shim'e-i went and brought his slaves from Gath. 41 And when Solomon was told that Shim'e-i had gone from Jerusalem to Gath and returned, 42 the king sent and summoned Shim'e-i, and said to him, "Did I not make you swear by the LORD, and solemnly admonish you,

---

modern ideas. It is truer to Hebrew ideas to retain **his blood.** The blood that has been shed calls for vengeance till it has been covered with other blood. Joab dies and the account is closed, there being no bloodguilt incurred for the shedding of Joab's blood, justly slain, especially since he had told Benaiah that he would die there at the altar.

35. This is a short historical note concerning the successors of Joab and Zadok as army chief and priest respectively.

4. THE END OF SHIMEI (2:36-46)

One curse still remains, that uttered by Shimei. Solomon warns Shimei, and bids him dwell in Jerusalem under the modern "open arrest." The king makes it quite clear

---

36-46. When a Man Presumes Too Far.—In this grim story the king is ruthless, but the man upon whom his anger fell had no right to complain. According to his deserts, Shimei might have come to his death long before. David, with great magnanimity, had spared him in spite of his insulting and treacherous hostility (II Sam. 16:5-13; 19:21-23). Solomon had let him continue to live in Jerusalem, but upon the express condition that he stay there, and with the stark warning that if he left the city it was on peril of his life. But when Shimei thought his interests required it, he presumed to go out of the city all the same. He was like a man on parole who violated it, and the judgment on him was already rendered. Always there may be others who need, as Shimei did, to understand that life has conditions that may be

any whither, that thou shalt surely die? and thou saidst unto me, The word *that* I have heard *is* good.

43 Why then hast thou not kept the oath of the LORD, and the commandment that I have charged thee with?

44 The king said moreover to Shimei, Thou knowest all the wickedness which thine heart is privy to, that thou didst to David my father; therefore the LORD shall return thy wickedness upon thine own head:

45 And king Solomon *shall be* blessed, and the throne of David shall be established before the LORD for ever.

46 So the king commanded Benaiah the son of Jehoiada; which went out, and fell upon him, that he died. And the kingdom was established in the hand of Solomon.

3 And Solomon made affinity with Pharaoh king of Egypt, and took Pharaoh's daughter, and brought her into the city of David, until he had made an end of build-

saying, 'Know for certain that on the day you go forth and go to any place whatever, you shall die'? And you said to me, 'What you say is good; I obey.' 43 Why then have you not kept your oath to the LORD and the commandment with which I charged you?" 44 The king also said to Shim'e-i, "You know in your own heart all the evil that you did to David my father; so the LORD will bring back your evil upon your own head. 45 But King Solomon shall be blessed, and the throne of David shall be established before the LORD for ever." 46 Then the king commanded Benai'ah the son of Jehoi'ada; and he went out and struck him down, and he died.

So the kingdom was established in the hand of Solomon.

3 Solomon made a marriage alliance with Pharaoh king of Egypt; he took Phar-

---

that if he leaves Jerusalem on any pretext whatever, it will mean death. Three years afterward Shimei goes to Gath to bring back two runaway slaves. Solomon is now free from all taboos concerning Shimei, so he sends for him on his return and executes him without compunction.

44. Most of the English versions have **the wickedness**; the Hebrew means not any evil designs which were in Shimei's heart and mind, but the actual **evil** brought into being by his curse (II Sam. 16:5-10). The Hebrews of old held that both blessings and curses, once uttered, had a life of their own and were destined inevitably to be fulfilled in the fate of the person, or his kin, against whom they were uttered. Only special action could prevent this (cf. Judg. 17:3). Otherwise nothing that a man does can alter the incidence of the curse or blessing. Isaac's blessing must come true over Jacob because it was uttered over Jacob. The fact that the old man thought he was blessing Esau has nothing to do with it (Gen. 27:35-40). The whole point of the present story is that Shimei placed himself in the wrong by not keeping the oath which Solomon had put upon him (vs. 43). This error gives Solomon the opportunity of dealing with Shimei and at last of removing the curse which all this time had been hanging over his head. Shimei was executed because he had broken a solemn oath in leaving Jerusalem. To have taken action against Shimei before Shimei had committed some such fault as this would have been equivalent to interfering with the action of God.

46. The **kingdom** is indeed now firmly established. Solomon has removed the bloodguilt which rested on his house and has managed by his wisdom to neutralize the curse which Shimei had uttered in days gone by.

II. THE REIGN OF SOLOMON (3:1–11:43)

These nine chapters as they stand tell the story of a king who was wholly devoted to God for the major part of a long and prosperous reign. He was rewarded with honor,

---

inexorable, and that punishment for old sins will no longer be remitted when mercy is flouted by contemptuous carelessness.

3:1-4. Political Expediency.—After Solomon had established his regime by removal of his enemies he sought to strengthen it by a family

ing his own house, and the house of the LORD, and the wall of Jerusalem round about.

2 Only the people sacrificed in high

aoh's daughter, and brought her into the city of David, until he had finished building his own house and the house of the LORD and the wall around Jerusalem. 2 The people were sacrificing at the high places,

---

glory, power, and wisdom. For eight chapters we read of splendor and success. The king who is faithful to the Deuteronomic teaching receives the Deuteronomic rewards. Especially does the king who built the temple at Jerusalem receive the fullest rewards of wealth and honor. In point of fact, Solomon's reign was marred by successful rebellions in Edom and Damascus. Both these kingdoms became independent and did great harm to Solomon, and Rezon of Damascus in particular "was an adversary of Israel all the days of Solomon" (11:25). It is clear from ch. 11 also that the seeds of revolt within Israel had already been sown during the time when Solomon was busy with his grandiose building schemes. The editor has relegated all this material to the last chapter of his account of Solomon's reign, and has ascribed these troubles to the way in which Solomon's many foreign wives entangled him into admitting the worship of foreign gods. That Solomon did this is beyond question, but the editor is manipulating his sources when he ascribes such conduct to Solomon's old age.

A. Solomon's Wisdom and Splendor (3:1–4:30)

1. Solomon's Choice (3:1-15)

The story of Solomon's visit to Gibeon, the vision he saw there, and the choice he made, is contained in vss. 4-15. God offers Solomon in a dream any request he may ask. Solomon asks for wisdom to govern wisely and well according to the pattern of a true and righteous king. His request for this wisdom in government, rather than for wealth and military success, brings him wealth and honor also. This material has proved most useful to the Deuteronomic editor, who needs to add little more than a sentence or so here and there in order to point out the Deuteronomic moral. The nucleus of the paragraph comes from the biography, but there are many editorial additions which are not found in the parallel story of II Chr. 1:3-13, though the Chronicler has additions of his own, notably in his transcript of vss. 3-6.

This story of the vision at Gibeon has been prefaced with the notice of Solomon's marriage to an Egyptian princess, taken from the first of the editor's main sources, The Acts of Solomon (I Kings 11:41). In the LXX vs. 1 is joined with 9:16 and both are inserted after 4:34 (M.T., 5:14). The LXX here probably preserves the order of the editor. The reason for the change in the M.T. may be that a later scribe thought some further explanation was needed to account for Solomon's going to Gibeon and sacrificing there, when the whole book and all later practice and theory held that Jerusalem alone was the legitimate place for such things. Even the addition here of vs. 1 did not satisfy a still later scribe. He thereupon added vs. 2 as a marginal note to justify the statement that Solomon sacrificed elsewhere than at Jerusalem.

3:2. The high places: Sacrifices at these local hill shrines were regarded as legitimate until the Deuteronomic reforms in Josiah's time (cf. 18:32, where Elijah is represented

---

alliance with Egypt. The use of marriage bonds as political aids has been a practice of ruling monarchs down the centuries. Egypt was the nearest, and after David's victories the most powerful of Israel's neighbors.

The politician in Solomon showed not only in his marriage but in his religious practices. While the Chronicler asserts Solomon's love of the Lord, he describes his deviation from devotion by sacrificing at the high places. Perhaps

Solomon justified his use of the pagan shrines by the fact that the ark of Yahweh had not yet been set up. In our time when a Christian congregation has lost its place of worship through fire or flood, it is considered an act of generous comradeship for a Hindu to place his temple at the Christians' disposal. But one can almost read between the lines and discern the motive of political expediency in Solomon's use of the high places. With a non-Hebrew wife and

places, because there was no house built unto the name of the LORD, until those days.

3 And Solomon loved the LORD, walking in the statutes of David his father: only he sacrificed and burnt incense in high places.

4 And the king went to Gibeon to sacrifice there; for that *was* the great high place: a thousand burnt offerings did Solomon offer upon that altar.

5 ¶ In Gibeon the LORD appeared to Solomon in a dream by night: and God said, Ask what I shall give thee.

however, because no house had yet been built for the name of the LORD.

3 Solomon loved the LORD, walking in the statutes of David his father; only, he sacrificed and burnt incense at the high places. **4** And the king went to Gibeon to sacrifice there, for that was the great high place; Solomon used to offer a thousand burnt offerings upon that altar. **5** At Gibeon the LORD appeared to Solomon in a dream by night; and God said, "Ask what I shall

---

as doing a praiseworthy deed in rebuilding the altar on Mount Carmel; cf. also Judg. 6:26; I Sam. 9:10-14). In all the early history of the Hebrews the existence of the hill shrines is assumed as a matter of course. They were the original Canaanite shrines, local models of the great mountain of the gods away to the north, taken over by the invading Israelites, generally with most of the original ritual. Sacred sites are not invented; they are older than history itself. The name of the god may change with the changing of the worshipers, but the site retains its sacredness; cf. the site of Kadesh Naphtali, where a third-century Semitic altar has been found, with traces underneath of an ancient pagan temple of a much earlier date (Cook, *Religion of Ancient Palestine in Light of Archaeology,* pp. 196-97).

3. Sacrificed and burnt incense: All the English versions have this, including the RSV. The Hebrew קטר did not mean "burn incense" until postexilic times. It is better therefore to translate "slaughtered and burned sacrifices," taking the root זבח in its earlier sense of slaughter and the root קטר in its original sense of "causing to smoke," i.e., burning on an altar.

4. Possibly the number **a thousand** represents the total number of offerings he made there from first to last. If this is so, then the frequentative of the RSV is correct, though **used to offer** does not make the matter much more clear than **did . . . offer.** A better translation would be "offered, first and last."

The burnt offering (עולה) is properly a whole offering, all of it burned upon the altar and none of it eaten either by worshiper or by priest. It was entirely a gift to God.

The **altar** (מזבח) was originally a "place of slaughter," as the etymology of the word shows, from an original custom whereby the animal was slain upon a stone (cf. I Sam. 14:33-35). Every slaughter (זבח) was both a sacrifice and a meal in the early nomad days and in the first days of Canaan also.

5. The idea of a god speaking to men in dreams is common in the general religious beliefs of men (cf. Walter Pater, *Marius the Epicurean* [New York: The Macmillan Co., 1926], ch. iii, where the healing dream is a feature of the cult of Asclepius).

---

a non-Hebrew constituency to placate, the young king is being loosened a bit from the faith of his fathers. It is one thing to tolerate other religions within a nation's borders; it is another thing to adopt a politician's practice of patting them all on the back as if they were equally good. At this stage it is too early to condemn Solomon, but reading back from later developments, we can see the first beginnings of religious compromise.

5-15. *A Model Prayer.*—Notwithstanding Solomon's personal imperfections, the prayer ascribed to him is so appropriate for one who

has just assumed a place of public power and responsibility that it has served as a model for rulers since his day. Americans will remember that when the death of Franklin D. Roosevelt placed the burdens of the presidential office on the shoulders of Harry S. Truman, the new executive offered Solomon's petition as his own prayer for guidance. His act enlisted the sympathy of his fellow citizens.

Solomon's prayer breathes the spirit of humility, **I am but a little child; I do not know how to go out or come in.** Measuring himself by the stature of his father, the young sovereign felt

6 And Solomon said, Thou hast showed unto thy servant David my father great mercy, according as he walked before thee in truth, and in righteousness, and in uprightness of heart with thee; and thou hast kept for him this great kindness, that thou hast given him a son to sit on his throne, as *it is* this day.

7 And now, O LORD my God, thou hast made thy servant king instead of David my father: and I *am but* a little child: I know not *how* to go out or come in.

8 And thy servant *is* in the midst of thy people which thou hast chosen, a great people, that cannot be numbered nor counted for multitude.

9 Give therefore thy servant an understanding heart to judge thy people, that I may discern between good and bad: for who is able to judge this thy so great a people?

give you." 6 And Solomon said, "Thou hast shown great and steadfast love to thy servant David my father, because he walked before thee in faithfulness, in righteousness, and in uprightness of heart toward thee; and thou hast kept for him this great and steadfast love, and hast given him a son to sit on his throne this day. 7 And now, O LORD my God, thou hast made thy servant king in place of David my father, although I am but a little child; I do not know how to go out or come in. 8 And thy servant is in the midst of thy people whom thou hast chosen, a great people, that cannot be numbered or counted for multitude. 9 Give thy servant therefore an understanding mind to govern thy people, that I may discern between good and evil; for who is able to govern this thy great people?"

---

6. Great kindness: The Hebrew word is *ḥẹṣedh,* and the reference is to the "great bounty," which God has shown to his chosen king. Thus, in the view of the Deuteronomic editor, both God and David have kept the covenant, David by his faithfulness and uprightness of heart, and God by prospering the king and establishing the heir upon the throne (II Sam. 7:12).

7. Jeremiah speaks of himself as a child in his account of his call (Jer. 1:6), and Solomon similarly refers to himself as **a little child.** The phrase is intended partly to denote the humility of inexperience, but partly also to emphasize Solomon's sense of a divine call to a more-than-human task. Ancient commentators tended to take the statement literally. The LXX (2:12) reckons Solomon to have been twelve years old at his accession, while Josephus (*Antiquities* VIII. 7. 8) makes him out to be fourteen years, and gives him a reign of eighty years. In any case Solomon can scarcely have been more than twenty years old, since he was born about the time of the Ammonite war (II Sam. 12:24), which is unlikely to have been in the earlier half of David's reign.

9. An understanding mind: This is a sound modern translation. The M.T. reads "a hearing heart" (ASV mg.), the root שמע being used in the sense of "hear and obey," as regularly in Deuteronomic passages. The heart is often said to have been regarded by the Hebrews as the seat of the intellect, but the meaning of the word is in fact much wider. It stands for the inner core of a man's being, and thus can be used as the seat of the intellect, the will, the emotions, or whatever aspect of man's nature is involved basically at the time. Thus here it means that Solomon desired "in his heart of hearts,"

---

his littleness and his need. He became "poor in spirit," and poverty of spirit is the opposite of pride. Pride is the first of the deadly sins because it shuts the doors of the mind and heart. It takes away the key to the gates of understanding and fellowship. And just as pride comes first in the list of deadly sins, so Matthew in reporting the Beatitudes puts poverty of spirit as the first of the lively virtues. Emptied of self-importance and self-righteousness, the humble person is prepared to receive the blessings of the kingdom of heaven.

Solomon, though no longer a child in years, revealed the childlike spirit which Jesus said is an essential prerequisite for entrance into the kingdom. Open of mind, he sought to see the truth; and obedient in spirit, he seemed ready to follow where the facts might lead. However dark and confused the problems in any situation, the seeker after truth can and should always clean from the lens of his own mind the befogging preconceptions and presumptions so that he can catch whatever light may break. This is the preparation which Pilate, for ex-

10 And the speech pleased the Lord, that Solomon had asked this thing.

11 And God said unto him, Because thou hast asked this thing, and hast not asked for thyself long life; neither hast asked riches for thyself, nor hast asked the life of thine enemies; but hast asked for thyself understanding to discern judgment;

12 Behold, I have done according to thy word: lo, I have given thee a wise and an understanding heart; so that there was none like thee before thee, neither after thee shall any arise like unto thee.

13 And I have also given thee that which thou hast not asked, both riches, and honor: so that there shall not be any among the kings like unto thee all thy days.

14 And if thou wilt walk in my ways, to keep my statutes and my commandments, as thy father David did walk, then I will lengthen thy days.

10 It pleased the Lord that Solomon had asked this. 11 And God said to him, "Because you have asked this, and have not asked for yourself long life or riches or the life of your enemies, but have asked for yourself understanding to discern what is right, 12 behold, I now do according to your word. Behold, I give you a wise and discerning mind, so that none like you has been before you and none like you shall arise after you. 13 I give you also what you have not asked, both riches and honor, so that no other king shall compare with you, all your days. 14 And if you will walk in my ways, keeping my statutes and my commandments, as your father David walked, then I will lengthen your days."

as we say, to be wholly and completely obedient to the will of God so that he could govern God's people wisely and well. He longed to be the perfect Deuteronomic king.

11. To discern what is right: This is an interpretation rather than a translation. The Hebrew reads "to hear [and obey] *mishpāṭ.*" In a strict sense this latter word is untranslatable. In so far as it means **judgment** it means "judgment according to precedent." But there is always a religious atmosphere about the word. In early times when any matter of faith or practice came up for decision, it was customary to seek a ruling from God at the shrine. The cult official sought this on behalf of the inquirer. If the official was a priest, he sought the answer by casting the sacred lot or by the examination of the entrails of bird or beast. If he was a prophet, it would be in a vision or dream, or else in an ecstasy. This word which thus came straight from God was called a *tôrāh,* probably from the ancient custom of "casting" (*yārāh*) the sacred lot. But when the same question came again, there was already a precedent. The same answer was given as before, but it was then a *mishpāṭ.* The king always governed by *mishpāṭ* ("custom," "precedent"), but if any matter cropped up of any particular difficulty, he would send to the shrine for a new ruling (*tôrāh;* cf. II Kings 19:1-2, 14). Solomon therefore asked for discernment so that he might understand the will of God and obey it, whether as declared in the first place by *tôrāh* or as known in human experience by *mishpāṭ.*

14. This verse is thoroughly Deuteronomic in every detail.

ample, failed to make when he was examining Jesus. The Roman governor asked his prisoner: "Art thou a king then? Jesus answered. Thou sayest that I am a king. To this end was I born, and for this cause came I into the world, that I should bear witness unto the truth. Every one that is of the truth heareth my voice. Pilate saith unto him, What is truth?" (John 18:37-38.) According to the record, Jesus made no answer. There was little use in trying to explain truth to Pilate, who was not sufficiently "of the truth" to wait to learn what it might be and to follow it when presented. Pilate was motivated by expediency, and the God of truth dwells only "with him who is of a contrite and humble spirit" (Isa. 57:15).

Solomon in his humility prayed: **Give thy servant . . . an understanding mind to govern thy people.** Note how frequently the word "understanding" occurs in Proverbs, which popular thought associates with Solomon and his advisers. Understanding is more than information. It is intellectual apprehension, and when applied to human values it includes imaginative comprehension. An **understanding mind** is one able to put itself in the place of others. We may

15 And Solomon awoke; and, behold, *it was* a dream. And he came to Jerusalem, and stood before the ark of the covenant of the LORD, and offered up burnt offerings, and offered peace offerings, and made a feast to all his servants.

16 ¶ Then came there two women, *that were* harlots, unto the king, and stood before him.

17 And the one woman said, O my lord, I and this woman dwell in one house; and I was delivered of a child with her in the house.

15 And Solomon awoke, and behold, it was a dream. Then he came to Jerusalem, and stood before the ark of the covenant of the LORD, and offered up burnt offerings and peace offerings, and made a feast for all his servants.

16 Then two harlots came to the king, and stood before him. 17 The one woman said, "Oh, my lord, this woman and I dwell in the same house; and I gave birth to a

---

15. Thus, according to Deuteronomic standards, Solomon regularizes his action in going to Gibeon. Being unable to sacrifice in a temple which was not yet built, he does the next best thing and sacrifices on the site of the future central sanctuary. The LXX says that he offered sacrifices on an altar before the ark. He offered **burnt offerings and peace offerings,** the former a gift wholly given to God (cf. vs. 4), the latter providing the sacred meal, the **feast for all his servants.** The M.T. has *shelāmîm,* short for *zebhaḥ shelāmîm,* "the shared meal." Opinion differs as to the significance and meaning of *shelāmîm.* Some say the word has to do with "peace," and others with the "fulfillment of vows." The aim was probably to secure *shālôm,* which means not only "peace" but "good fortune," "health," prosperity," these being secured by participating in what had been consecrated, and therefore was divine food.

2. THE JUDGMENT OF SOLOMON (3:16-28)

16-28. This story is given as an example of that wisdom in judgment which was promised at Gibeon. Solomon decides a difficult case with great acuteness. Two women, prostitutes living in the same house, dispute as to whose child is dead and whose child is alive. Both claim the living child. Solomon decides by commanding that the living child be cut into two pieces and shared between the two women. One woman refuses and

---

know the external facts about other persons, other races, other nations, and yet not have imagination enough to get on the inside of their viewpoints and feelings. If our world which has now been reduced to a neighborhood is ever to become a brotherhood, it will be thus transformed by the cultivation of imagination more than by the collection of information.

In our curtained-off world we can look up to God, the Father of all men, and pray for his other children whom he has made of one blood with us. By such repeated praying we can sensitize our imaginations until we approach the understanding sympathy of Jesus, who felt whatever was done to the least of his brethren as having been done to himself (Matt. 25:31-46).

In his search for understanding adequate to the governing of his people Solomon looked up to God first. From a level gaze people do not look very lovable. We must try to see human beings as God sees them. Only as we catch the family atmosphere of our heavenly Father can we cultivate and safeguard reverence for per-

sonality. Divine help is needed to purge the dross of possessiveness from our intimacies, to put charitableness into our charities, to keep our kindnesses from being condescending, to generate sympathy for strangers, and to beget prayers for those who despitefully use us. Without the sympathy nurtured by communion with God, our social attitudes tend toward cynicism; and without the strengthening standards of divine law, our so-called reverence for personality deteriorates toward a pliable sentimentality which is all things to all men. Solomon started on the only plane where rule can give promise of redemption, for "the fear of the LORD is the beginning of wisdom: and the knowledge of the Holy is understanding" (Prov. 9:10).

16-28. *Wisdom and Justice.*—The story of the two harlots is a dramatic demonstration of Solomon's wisdom at work. When the case became noised abroad it aroused admiration for the young ruler's astuteness. The public regard went deeper: **They stood in awe of the king,**

18 And it came to pass the third day after that I was delivered, that this woman was delivered also: and we *were* together; *there was* no stranger with us in the house, save we two in the house.

19 And this woman's child died in the night; because she overlaid it.

20 And she arose at midnight, and took my son from beside me, while thine handmaid slept, and laid it in her bosom, and laid her dead child in my bosom.

21 And when I rose in the morning to give my child suck, behold, it was dead: but when I had considered it in the morning, behold, it was not my son, which I did bear.

22 And the other woman said, Nay; but the living *is* my son, and the dead *is* thy son. And this said, No; but the dead *is* thy son, and the living *is* my son. Thus they spake before the king.

23 Then said the king, The one saith, This *is* my son that liveth, and thy son *is* the dead: and the other saith, Nay; but thy son *is* the dead, and my son *is* the living.

24 And the king said, Bring me a sword. And they brought a sword before the king.

25 And the king said, Divide the living child in two, and give half to the one, and half to the other.

26 Then spake the woman whose the living child *was* unto the king, for her bowels yearned upon her son, and she said, O my lord, give her the living child, and in no wise slay it. But the other said, Let it be neither mine nor thine, *but* divide *it*.

child while she was in the house. **18** Then on the third day after I was delivered, this woman also gave birth; and we were alone; there was no one else with us in the house, only we two were in the house. **19** And this woman's son died in the night, because she lay on it. **20** And she arose at midnight, and took my son from beside me, while your maidservant slept, and laid it in her bosom, and laid her dead son in my bosom. **21** When I rose in the morning to nurse my child, behold, it was dead; but when I looked at it closely in the morning, behold, it was not the child that I had borne." **22** But the other woman said, "No, the living child is mine, and the dead child is yours." The first said, "No, the dead child is yours, and the living child is mine." Thus they spoke before the king. **23** Then the king said, "The one says, 'This is my son that is alive, and your son is dead'; and the other says, 'No; but your son is dead, and my son is the living one.' " **24** And the king said, "Bring me a sword." So a sword was brought before the king. **25** And the king said, "Divide the living child in two, and give half to the one, and half to the other." **26** Then the woman whose son was alive said to the king, because her heart yearned for her son, "Oh, my lord, give her the living child, and by no means slay it." But the other said, "It shall be neither mine nor yours; divide it."

---

offers to let the other have the child. She is the mother. Otto Thenius (*Die Bücher der Könige* [Leipzig: S. Hirzel, 1873], p. 28) quotes a similar case of a Thracian king who had to choose among three men, all of whom claimed to be the son and heir of the dead Cimmerian king. He ordered them to pierce the dead king's body with a spear. One refused. He was the son. The incident of the two women is from the biography, and may very well be, as some allege, an adaptation of a common folklore tale for the greater glory of Solomon. It is a typical example of that Oriental wisdom which is con-

---

because they perceived that the wisdom of God was in him, to render justice (vs. 28). Solomon's shrewd way of deciding the maternity of the child by offering to cut it in two did show an element of divine wisdom in that it sought truth through the test of love. The common saying that love is blind is a misleading half-truth. To be sure, love does dull the vision to some defects, but it also quickens the insight in ways essential to discovering truth and dispensing justice. In the case before Solomon the love of

the real mother had its reward. Likewise, love always wins the verdict before the divine Judge.

When the record asserts of Solomon that the wisdom of God was in him, to render justice, it raises in the reader's mind the relation of wisdom to justice. The classic symbol of justice is that of a blindfolded woman with a scales in her hand, the implication being that the essence of justice is the weighing of the facts in hand with an impartiality which might be lost if the judge were to see the parties involved.

27 Then the king answered and said, Give her the living child, and in no wise slay it: she *is* the mother thereof.

28 And all Israel heard of the judgment which the king had judged; and they feared the king: for they saw that the wisdom of God *was* in him to do judgment.

4 So king Solomon was king over all Israel.

2 And these *were* the princes which he had; Azariah the son of Zadok the priest,

3 Elihoreph and Ahiah, the sons of Shisha, scribes; Jehoshaphat the son of Ahilud, the recorder.

4 And Benaiah the son of Jehoiada *was* over the host: and Zadok and Abiathar *were* the priests:

5 And Azariah the son of Nathan *was* over the officers: and Zabud the son of Nathan *was* principal officer, *and* the king's friend:

27 Then the king answered and said, "Give the living child to the first woman, and by no means slay it; she is its mother." 28 And all Israel heard of the judgment which the king had rendered; and they stood in awe of the king, because they perceived that the wisdom of God was in him, to render justice.

4 King Solomon was king over all Israel, 2 and these were his high officials: Azari'ah the son of Zadok was the priest; 3 Elihor'eph and Ahi'jah the sons of Shisha were secretaries; Jehosh'aphat the son of Ahi'lud was recorder; 4 Benai'ah the son of Jehoi'ada was in command of the army; Zadok and Abi'athar were priests; 5 Azari'ah the son of Nathan was over the officers; Zabud the son of Nathan was priest and

cerned with the actual business of living rather than with abstractions. The Hebrews valued particularly that astuteness which reveals a thorough knowledge of human character both in strength and in weakness. It is a type of wisdom which often becomes a very worldly wisdom.

3. Solomon's Court Officials (4:1-6)

This list of high officials comes with the rest of the chapter from the biography. It illustrates the greatness of Solomon. The biographer has taken extracts from the court annals and has added comments of his own throughout the chapter. The LXX has another list included in the long addition which follows 2:26. Some of the differences between the two lists are extremely perplexing and no satisfactory explanation has been offered. The suggestion that the LXX list refers to the end of the reign and the present list, with its LXX equivalent, to the beginning, does not solve the problem.

4:5. The LXX and Lucian omit the reference to the priest in connection with Zabud son of Nathan. The English versions insert **and** in order to "correct" the syntax. Probably the word ought to be omitted as a mistaken gloss. The word *kōhēn* (**priest**) may have had a wider significance than is generally supposed (cf. II Sam. 8:18, which has never been satisfactorily explained). The duties of **the king's friend** are unknown, but Hushai filled this position in David's time (II Sam. 15:37; 16:16), and the title is mentioned in the Tell el-Amarna letters as a regular official in petty Palestinian court circles of the fourteenth century B.C.

But such a portrayal is hardly adequate. The blindfold should be removed. If we would weigh a situation justly, we must see the background of those involved in it; e.g., the delinquent boy whose home has been a slum and whose playmates have been the gashouse gang cannot be judged justly on the same basis as the boy who has enjoyed every advantage of a good home and Christian culture. And in school that lad whose mind is a place of sharp tensions and

brilliant powers is not to be disciplined on the same basis as the boy whose nature flows along smoothly and placidly. What parent or teacher can do justice to the merits of the different temperaments committed to his care unless he has the insight and imagination to look into the hearts and backgrounds of those whom he must judge?

Divine justice is dispensed by the infinitely wise and understanding Father-God. He looks

6 And Ahishar *was* over the household: and Adoniram the son of Abda *was* over the tribute.

7 ¶ And Solomon had twelve officers over all Israel, which provided victuals for the king and his household: each man his month in a year made provision.

8 And these *are* their names: The son of Hur, in mount Ephraim:

9 The son of Dekar, in Makaz, and in Shaalbim, and Beth-shemesh, and Elon-beth-hanan:

10 The son of Hesed, in Aruboth; to him *pertained* Sochoh, and all the land of Hepher:

11 The son of Abinadab, in all the region of Dor; which had Taphath the daughter of Solomon to wife:

12 Baana the son of Ahilud; *to him pertained* Taanach and Megiddo, and all Beth-shean, which *is* by Zartanah beneath Jezreel, from Beth-shean to Abel-meholah, *even* unto *the place that is* beyond Jokneam:

13 The son of Geber, in Ramoth-gilead; to him *pertained* the towns of Jair the son of Manasseh, which *are* in Gilead; to him *also pertained* the region of Argob, which *is* in Bashan, threescore great cities with walls and brazen bars:

king's friend; 6 Ahi'shar was in charge of the palace; and Adoni'ram the son of Abda was in charge of the forced labor.

7 Solomon had twelve officers over all Israel, who provided food for the king and his household; each man had to make provision for one month in the year. 8 These were their names: Ben-hur, in the hill country of E'phraim; 9 Ben-deker, in Makaz, Sha-al'bim, Beth-shemesh, and E'lonbeth-ha'nan; 10 Ben-hesed, in Arub'both (to him belonged Soco and all the land of Hepher); 11 Ben-abin'adab, in all Naphath-dor (he had Taphath the daughter of Solomon as his wife); 12 Ba'ana the son of Ahi'lud, in Ta'anach, Megid'do, and all Beth-she'an which is beside Zarethan below Jezreel, and from Beth-she'an to A'bel-meho'lah, as far as the other side of Jok'-meam; 13 Ben-geber, in Ramoth-gilead (he had the villages of Ja'ir the son of Manas'-seh, which are in Gilead, and he had the region of Argob, which is in Bashan, sixty great cities with walls and bronze bars);

---

6. Adoniram (Adoram) had been in charge of the forced labor in David's time (II Sam. 20:24), and Solomon developed the system for his building projects.

4. SOLOMON'S PROVINCIAL GOVERNORS (4:7-19)

7-19. This list gives the names of twelve administrative officers and their districts. Each governor provided supplies for Solomon's establishment for one month in the year. The list is important for two reasons. First, the boundaries are not equivalent to the old tribal boundaries. This has been thought to be part of Solomon's deliberate policy, whereby he sought to break up the old tribal loyalties so as to consolidate his own royal rule. If this is so, then we have here one of the causes of the disruption of the united kingdom at Solomon's death. Second, there is no governor over any part of Judah.

---

upon the heart. He sees "the purposes unsure, the instincts immature." He comprehends the meshwork of influences in which each erring child is caught. He is aware that our sins flow together as waters mingle in a stream. Our little finite minds cannot comprehend the fullness of divine compassion, but we sing in faith with Frederick W. Faber:

There's a wideness in God's mercy,
Like the wideness of the sea;
There's a kindness in his justice,
Which is more than liberty.

And we agree with Portia that

Earthly power doth then show likest God's,
When mercy seasons justice.[5]

Mercy is an integral part of true justice. It is not a sentimental forgiveness, not a condescending pity. Mercy is that insight which sees how life looks through the other person's eyes. It is that kindness which gives the benefit of the doubt and days of grace to our debtors. The seer of Patmos comprehended the blending of

[5] Shakespeare, *The Merchant of Venice*, Act IV, scene 1.

14 Ahinadab the son of Iddo *had* Mahanaim:

15 Ahimaaz *was* in Naphtali; he also took Basmath the daughter of Solomon to wife:

16 Baanah the son of Hushai *was* in Asher and in Aloth:

17 Jehoshaphat the son of Paruah, in Issachar:

18 Shimei the son of Elah, in Benjamin:

19 Geber the son of Uri *was* in the country of Gilead, *in* the country of Sihon king of the Amorites, and of Og king of Bashan; and *he was* the only officer which *was* in the land.

20 ¶ Judah and Israel *were* many, as the sand which *is* by the sea in multitude, eating and drinking, and making merry.

14 Ahin'adab the son of Iddo, in Mahana'im; 15 Ahi'ma-az, in Naph'tali (he had taken Bas'emath the daughter of Solomon as his wife); 16 Ba'ana the son of Hushai, in Asher and Bealoth; 17 Jehosh'aphat the son of Paru'ah, in Is'sachar; 18 Shim'e-i the son of Ela, in Benjamin; 19 Geber the son of Uri, in the land of Gilead, the country of Sihon king of the Amorites and of Og king of Bashan. And there was one officer in the land of Judah.

20 Judah and Israel were as many as the sand by the sea; they ate and drank and

This is significant since the chief duty of the governor toward the king was to provide supplies for the court and the standing army of chariots and horses (vss. 22-23, 27-28). Judah was apparently exempt from this levy and was thus favored against the rest of the country. When we realize also that Judah was not liable to labor conscription, we can see that the so-called united kingdom of Judah and Israel was largely a domination of Israel by Judah.

5. THE SPLENDOR OF SOLOMON (4:20-28)

These verses give a picture of idyllic happiness throughout the whole kingdom. In addition we have details of Solomon's magnificence, telling of the size of his establishment and the quantity of provisions necessary for its upkeep.

The LXX and Lucian order of the verses is different from that of the M.T. Vss. 20, 21, 25, and 26 are in the long LXX interpolation which is found after 2:46. The LXX order is probably original, for the details there are much less confused. It is evident that some editor has been busy, apparently in the postexilic period (see vs. 24). He was desirous to extol the greatness of Solomon and to paint an impressive picture of general happiness extending throughout north and south under his rule. Probably the editor who is responsible for these changes is the man who moved the note about the marriage with Pharaoh's daughter to the beginning of ch. 3. Otherwise the rest of this chapter contains material drawn from the annals, though the figures may easily have grown in the telling. It exalts King Solomon, his wealth and splendor and wisdom, all of it according to the pattern set out in the dream at Gibeon.

mercy with justice when in his vision he saw that "there was a rainbow round about the throne" (Rev. 4:3). God rules from a "throne of grace." Solomon was far from such a divine principle of rule, but he had prayed for an understanding heart, and his early career gave promise that **the wisdom of God was in him, to render justice.**

4:20-34. When God Prospers.—The "glory of Solomon" has become proverbial. The reflection of his splendor lingers on the pages of the N.T. The Chronicler not only takes pride in recounting the magnificence of Solomon's court but interprets it as proof of God's favor. The

danger of riches is compounded by the assumption that they are the reward of righteousness. To be sure, our Hebrew-Christian faith does instill the qualities of industry, integrity, and thrift, which tend toward material success. But our faith has not been so effective in controlling the wealth it has helped to create. It was so in Solomon's case.

If there is truth in the proverb that "the love of money is the root of all evil" (I Tim. 6:10), it is certainly not true that the accumulation of money is the fruit of all righteousness. The idea that material prosperity is evidence of divine favor has had devilish results. Jesus sought to

21 And Solomon reigned over all kingdoms from the river unto the land of the Philistines, and unto the border of Egypt: they brought presents, and served Solomon all the days of his life.

22 ¶ And Solomon's provision for one day was thirty measures of fine flour, and threescore measures of meal,

23 Ten fat oxen, and twenty oxen out of the pastures, and a hundred sheep, besides harts, and roebucks, and fallow deer, and fatted fowl.

24 For he had dominion over all *the region* on this side the river, from Tiphsah even to Azzah, over all the kings on this side the river: and he had peace on all sides round about him.

25 And Judah and Israel dwelt safely, every man under his vine and under his fig tree, from Dan even to Beer-sheba, all the days of Solomon.

26 ¶ And Solomon had forty thousand stalls of horses for his chariots, and twelve thousand horsemen.

27 And those officers provided victuals for king Solomon, and for all that came

were happy. 21g Solomon ruled over all the kingdoms from the Eu-phra'tes to the land of the Philistines and to the border of Egypt; they brought tribute and served Solomon all the days of his life.

22 Solomon's provision for one day was thirty measures of fine flour, and sixty measures of meal, 23 ten fat oxen, and twenty pasture-fed cattle, a hundred sheep, besides harts, gazelles, roebucks, and fatted fowl. 24 For he had dominion over all the region west of the Eu-phra'tes from Tiphsah to Gaza, over all the kings west of the Eu-phra'tes; and he had peace on all sides round about him. 25 And Judah and Israel dwelt in safety, from Dan even to Beer-sheba, every man under his vine and under his fig tree, all the days of Solomon. 26 Solomon also had forty thousand stalls of horses for his chariots, and twelve thousand horsemen. 27 And those officers supplied provisions for King Solomon, and for all who

g Heb 5. 1

21. The claim is that the kingdom stretched **from the river** [i.e., **the Euphrates**] . . . **unto the border of Egypt** [i.e., the Wadi el-'Arîsh, approximately half way between Gaza and the Isthmus of Suez], apart from the Philistine country. These are the ideal boundaries, east and west, of Israel's territory. Actually Solomon lost control over Edom (11:22 [LXX]) and over Syria-Damascus (11:24-25).

The RSV correctly translates the word *minḥāh* by **tribute.** This is the original meaning of the word prior to its special use as a sacrificial term. In pre-exilic days the *minḥāh* was a gift to God, being tribute paid to him as owner and lord of the land. This is the meaning in Gen. 4:3 ("offering"). After the Exile the word came to be used for the cereal offering which accompanied every flesh offering (Lev. 23:18; etc.). There is confusion concerning this because the rendering of the KJV is invariably "meat offering." The explanation is that in seventeenth-century English "meat" meant food in general and not flesh in particular (cf. Lev. 6:14-18, where it is obvious that a cereal offering is involved).

22. Altogether a thousand bushels per day of groats and meal were needed apart from the flesh, by no means excessive if Solomon kept forty thousand horses and twelve thousand riders.

24. "Beyond the River" would be a true rendering of the M.T., but **west of the Euphrates** is meant. The translation **on this side** (KJV) is not misleading, though strictly less accurate. The author of this verse evidently lived east of the Euphrates, so that here is clear evidence of the work of an exilic editor.

25. The idyllic picture of Palestinian ease is **every man under his vine and under his fig tree.** He does not want the land "developed," either then or now (cf. Marmaduke Pickthall, *Said the Fisherman* [London: Methuen & Co., 1903], p. 1).

27. There was a time when this verse followed directly after vs. 19. The Hebrew has "these officers," but the usual English rendering is **those officers,** a change made necessary because of the interpolation of the intervening verses.

unto king Solomon's table, every man in his month: they lacked nothing.

28 Barley also and straw for the horses and dromedaries brought they unto the place where *the officers* were, every man according to his charge.

29 ¶ And God gave Solomon wisdom and understanding exceeding much, and largeness of heart, even as the sand that *is* on the seashore.

30 And Solomon's wisdom excelled the wisdom of all the children of the east country, and all the wisdom of Egypt.

31 For he was wiser than all men; than Ethan the Ezrahite, and Heman, and Chalcol, and Darda, the sons of Mahol: and his fame was in all nations round about.

32 And he spake three thousand proverbs: and his songs were a thousand and five.

33 And he spake of trees, from the cedar tree that *is* in Lebanon even unto the hyssop that springeth out of the wall: he spake also of beasts, and of fowl, and of creeping things, and of fishes.

34 And there came of all people to hear the wisdom of Solomon, from all kings of the earth, which had heard of his wisdom.

5 And Hiram king of Tyre sent his servants unto Solomon; for he had heard that they had anointed him king in the

came to King Solomon's table, each one in his month; they let nothing be lacking. 28 Barley also and straw for the horses and swift steeds they brought to the place where it was required, each according to his charge.

29 And God gave Solomon wisdom and understanding beyond measure, and largeness of mind like the sand on the seashore, 30 so that Solomon's wisdom surpassed the wisdom of all the people of the east, and all the wisdom of Egypt. 31 For he was wiser than all other men, wiser than Ethan the Ez'rahite, and Heman, Calcol, and Darda, the sons of Mahol; and his fame was in all the nations round about. 32 He also uttered three thousand proverbs; and his songs were a thousand and five. 33 He spoke of trees, from the cedar that is in Lebanon to the hyssop that grows out of the wall; he spoke also of beasts, and of birds, and of reptiles, and of fish. 34 And men came from all peoples to hear the wisdom of Solomon, and from all the kings of the earth, who had heard of his wisdom.

5 *h* Now Hiram king of Tyre sent his servants to Solomon, when he heard that

h Heb 5. 15

---

6. SOLOMON'S SURPASSING WISDOM (4:29-34)

God more than fulfills the promises of Gibeon. Solomon becomes the wisest of men, and all the world comes to hear him. His wise sayings cover the whole realm of the natural world.

30. The people of the east: In Hebrew the *Benê Qédhem* are the Arabian-Edomite tribes to the southeast of the Dead Sea. Arabia-Edom is the traditional home of that type of epigrammatic wisdom which the Hebrews admired; cf. Job 1:3, where "the people of the east" are the lords of the Arabian desert.

B. ERECTION OF THE TEMPLE (5:1–7:51)
1. PREPARATIONS FOR BUILDING THE TEMPLE (5:1-18)

Solomon arranges with Hiram of Tyre for the delivery of cedar and cypress timber. Hiram contracts to float the timber down the coast in rafts and to break up the rafts at the agreed place. Hiram's men are to do the felling, but Solomon is to provide the unskilled labor. Solomon contracts to pay large quantities annually of wheat and oil.

---

turn the thoughts of greedy men from the feverish search for wealth by pointing them toward the fowls of the air and the flowers of the field, and reminding them that "even Solomon in all his glory was not arrayed like one of these" (Matt. 6:10). There is a competitive wealth

which men like Solomon can fence in and draw others to admire; there is a noncompetitive wealth which gains by sharing.

5:1-18. *The Value of the Home Touch.*— Solomon showed his wisdom not only in dispensing justice but also in the handling of his

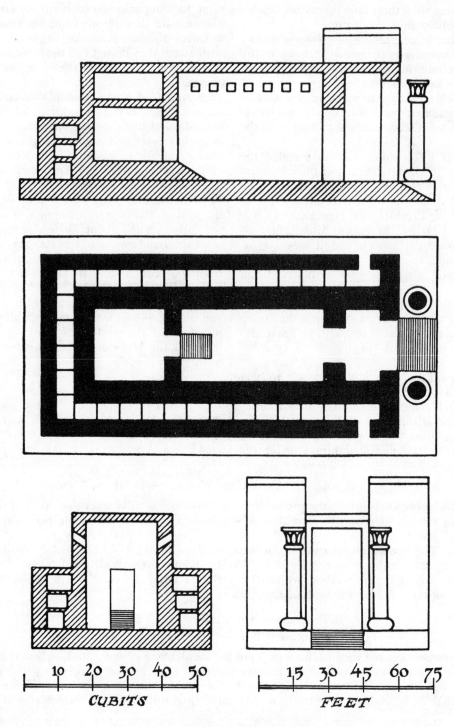

PLAN OF SOLOMON'S TEMPLE

(Adapted from Carl Watzinger, *Denkmäler Palästinas* [Leipzig: J. C. Hinrichs, 1933],
Vol. I, Table 16. Used by permission.)

room of his father: for Hiram was ever a lover of David.

2 And Solomon sent to Hiram, saying,

3 Thou knowest how that David my father could not build a house unto the name of the LORD his God, for the wars which were about him on every side, until the LORD put them under the soles of his feet.

they had anointed him king in place of his father; for Hiram always loved David.

2 And Solomon sent word to Hiram, 3 "You know that David my father could not build a house for the name of the LORD his God because of the warfare with which his enemies surrounded him, until the LORD put

---

Solomon arranges for the stone himself, quarrying it in the hill country of Ephraim, with hired Phoenician stonemasons to do the actual cutting. These experts are from Gebel, i.e., Byblos, twenty miles north of Beyrouth.

The material for this chapter is from the biography, except for vss. 3-6, which are a Deuteronomic interlude.

5:1. The spelling of the name varies, but **Hiram** is correct, being a shortened form of אחירם (*'aḥîrām*), "brother of Ram [the lofty one]."

The name **Tyre** means "rock," and the city was originally built on a rocky islet half a mile from the shore. This rock was a mile long by three quarters of a mile broad. Its double harbor, north and south, made it a famous port, since one harbor or the other was generally accessible in any weather. This was important because the whole coast line was most difficult for sailing ships, being a sandy lee shore with few harbors, and the ships were unable to do much more than sail before the wind, since tacking was an unknown art. Alexander the Great built a causeway sixty yards wide and thus captured the city which had successfully resisted many sieges, even that by the Babylonians. Since that time sand has drifted up from the south, and now the site of ancient Tyre is joined to the mainland by an isthmus half a mile broad.

The LXX and Lucian have here a curious variant, according to which Hiram sent his servants to anoint Solomon. This custom is vouched for in the Tell el-Amarna tablets as a ceremony by which the suzerain confirmed the appointment of his vassal. Winckler suggested that the gifts mentioned in vs. 11 were actually a permanent tribute paid annually to the Tyrian king (Eberhard Schrader, *Die Keilschriften und das Alte Testament,* ed. H. Zimmern and H. Winckler [3rd ed.; Berlin: Reuther & Reichard, 1902-3], I, 237-38).

3-6. The Deuteronomic explanation for David's not having built the temple is that David was too busy establishing the kingdom. The explanation given in II Sam. 7

---

workmen. When he contracted with King Hiram of Tyre for the materials with which to build the temple, he raised a levy of forced labor and dispatched his men into Hiram's country to prepare the timber for shipment. **And he sent them to Lebanon, ten thousand a month in relays; they would be a month in Lebanon and two months at home (vs. 14).** Solomon was wise enough to see that the keeping of home contacts is essential to the morale of men abroad. The nature of man demands some place where he can feel "at home." Home is the spot where our spirits in the presence of love relax from the strain put upon us by the pressure of work. Home is the circle where listening ears allow us to unpack our hearts with words, knowing that understanding sympathy will keep what is worth while and throw away the waste. Home is the environ-

ment where little ones lean on us and look up to us, thereby causing us to stand a bit more firmly and feel a bit taller. Home is the place where we are appraised not in terms of market price but on the basis of what we are, where a Bob Cratchit is a hero to Tiny Tim, however he may be scorned as an underling at the office.

How morale deteriorates when home life is disrupted is shown in time of war. Absentee husbands and fathers, working mothers, uprooted families transplanted by war's emergencies—these are factors which bear fruit in sexual irregularities, multiplied divorces, juvenile delinquency, and many other ills. The prolonged absence of the Hebrew workmen in a foreign land would have tended to weaken both their family ties and their national loyalty. Perhaps we should not read too much into the record here. How much Solomon had his eye on pre-

4 But now the LORD my God hath given me rest on every side, *so that there is* neither adversary nor evil occurrent.

5 And, behold, I purpose to build a house unto the name of the LORD my God, as the LORD spake unto David my father, saying, Thy son, whom I will set upon thy throne in thy room, he shall build a house unto my name.

6 Now therefore command thou that they hew me cedar trees out of Lebanon; and my servants shall be with thy servants: and unto thee will I give hire for thy servants according to all that thou shalt appoint: for thou knowest that *there is* not among us any that can skill to hew timber like unto the Sidonians.

7 ¶ And it came to pass, when Hiram heard the words of Solomon, that he rejoiced greatly, and said, Blessed *be* the LORD this day, which hath given unto David a wise son over this great people.

them under the soles of his feet. 4 But now the LORD my God has given me rest on every side; there is neither adversary nor misfortune. 5 And so I purpose to build a house for the name of the LORD my God, as the LORD said to David my father, 'Your son, whom I will set upon your throne in your place, shall build the house for my name.' 6 Now therefore command that cedars of Lebanon be cut for me; and my servants will join your servants, and I will pay you for your servants such wages as you set; for you know that there is no one among us who knows how to cut timber like the Sido'nians."

7 When Hiram heard the words of Solomon, he rejoiced greatly, and said, "Blessed be the LORD this day, who has given to David a wise son to be over this great peo-

---

is that such a building is contrary to the true and primitive worship of the God of the Hebrews, which should involve a tent. The explanation given in I Chr. 22:8 is that David was a man of blood and therefore not fit to build the temple.

4. The Hebrew *sāṭān* (**adversary**) is used in its original sense of any human agent. In Job, Satan is one of God's heavenly court. His particular duty is to travel to and fro in the earth to see if men are actually as good as they claim to be. If they are not, his duty is to accuse them before the throne of God. Later the word becomes a proper name, and already in I Chr. 21:1 (cf. II Sam. 24:1) Satan is the enemy of God. In the N.T. he is the prince of the kingdom of evil.

6. The **cedars of Lebanon** were famous from antiquity, their wood being hard and therefore proof against dry rot and insects. According to Pliny the cedar roof of the temple of Diana at Ephesus lasted for four hundred years. The wood is close-grained and therefore admirably suitable for carving. Its fragrance is most marked. Cedars at one time covered the whole of the Lebanon, the Anti-Lebanon, and thence north and west into the Taurus Mountains. They were in great demand throughout the Near East, large parts of which have always been treeless country. The Assyrian advances toward the Mediterranean from the twelfth century B.C. onward had in part these cedars as their objective.

6. The skill of the **Sidonians** (Phoenicians) in crafts of every kind was well known in the ancient world; cf. the embroidered robes of Andromache and the silver bowl of Achilles (Homer *Iliad* VI. 290; XXIII. 741-44) .

---

serving family circles and how much he was concerned merely to keep his men in the homeland, we do not know. But in the Hebrew tradition family loyalty has furnished the tough fiber which holds the nation together. Totalitarian states in modern times have minimized the family unit in their development of national strength. The Nazi experiment in weakening home ties for the sake of strengthening the state did not prove successful. The home is

the primary training ground for promoting community and national welfare. And unless the individual learns the squad movements of social action in the family circle, he is ill-fitted to move up to the front line problems of citizenship. Unless we learn to live worthily in our little worlds, we shall not be worth much as workers in the large world.

"The eyes of a fool are in the ends of the earth" (Prov. 17:24) . This bit of Hebrew

8 And Hiram sent to Solomon, saying, I have considered the things which thou sentest to me for: *and* I will do all thy desire concerning timber of cedar, and concerning timber of fir.

9 My servants shall bring *them* down from Lebanon unto the sea; and I will convey them by sea in floats unto the place that thou shalt appoint me, and will cause them to be discharged there, and thou shalt receive *them:* and thou shalt accomplish my desire, in giving food for my household.

10 So Hiram gave Solomon cedar trees and fir trees *according to* all his desire.

11 And Solomon gave Hiram twenty thousand measures of wheat *for* food to his household, and twenty measures of pure oil: thus gave Solomon to Hiram year by year.

12 And the LORD gave Solomon wisdom, as he promised him: and there was peace between Hiram and Solomon; and they two made a league together.

13 ¶ And king Solomon raised a levy out of all Israel; and the levy was thirty thousand men.

ple." **8** And Hiram sent to Solomon, saying, "I have heard the message which you have sent to me; I am ready to do all you desire in the matter of cedar and cypress timber. **9** My servants shall bring it down to the sea from Lebanon; and I will make it into rafts to go by sea to the place you direct, and I will have them broken up there, and you shall receive it; and you shall meet my wishes by providing food for my household." **10** So Hiram supplied Solomon with all the timber of cedar and cypress that he desired, **11** while Solomon gave Hiram twenty thousand cors of wheat as food for his household, and twenty thousand*i* cors of beaten oil. Solomon gave this to Hiram year by year. **12** And the LORD gave Solomon wisdom, as he promised him; and there was peace between Hiram and Solomon; and the two of them made a treaty.

13 King Solomon raised a levy of forced labor out of all Israel; and the levy num-

i Gk: Heb *twenty*

---

11. Twenty thousand is correct, following the LXX, Lucian, Syriac, and II Chr. 2:10, as against the "twenty" of the M.T. The total quantities amount to 220,000 bushels of wheat and 180,000 gallons of best olive oil. **Beaten oil** is the purest oil, obtained by pounding the olives in a mortar instead of the normal procedure of treading them in the press.

12. The Hebrew idiom is "cut a treaty." The custom was common among the Greeks also. Tyndareus, father of Helen, cut a boar in pieces and made all the Greek princes pass between them to confirm the oath to abide by Helen's choice of a husband. The Romans "smote a treaty" (cf. Livy's description of the treaty between the Romans and the Albans, when the priest of Jupiter smote the boar pig with a flint knife [I. 24]). The Roman idea was that Jupiter should smite the offender just as his priest smote the boar pig. The Hebrew idea was that of both parties becoming partakers of the same life, both identifying themselves with the life of the animal sacrificed (cf. Gen. 15:9-21 concerning God's covenant with Abraham, and especially Jer. 34:18, where a covenant is ratified by the cutting of a calf into two pieces; see James G. Frazer, *Folk-lore in the Old Testament* [London: Macmillan & Co., 1919], I, 391-428).

---

wisdom is embedded in the race's culture. When a person spends his time gazing at distant problems and vague generalities he is foolish and futile. We must combine large outlooks with local loyalties and applications. John Henry Jowett once likened Paul's mind to a skylark in its motion. The skylark flies high but keeps its nest on the ground. Similarly, Paul was an ethereal minstrel-pilgrim of the sky, songfully surveying the world. He flew high and far, but he always kept his local nesting places. When we read his letters, we note the intimate

personal touches interspersing his legal discussions and large observations. The homing instinct is a God-given equipment. Jesus revealed the poignancy of his personal longing for a home when he said to the impulsive new convert who wanted to pick up and follow him at once, "Foxes have holes, and birds of the air have nests; but the Son of man hath not where to lay his head" (Luke 9:58). Although Jesus was misunderstood in his own home and maligned by his neighbors in Nazareth, the family remained for him the pattern of relationship

14 And he sent them to Lebanon, ten thousand a month by courses: a month they were in Lebanon, *and* two months at home: and Adoniram *was* over the levy.

15 And Solomon had threescore and ten thousand that bare burdens, and fourscore thousand hewers in the mountains;

16 Besides the chief of Solomon's officers which *were* over the work, three thousand and three hundred, which ruled over the people that wrought in the work.

17 And the king commanded, and they brought great stones, costly stones, *and* hewed stones, to lay the foundation of the house.

18 And Solomon's builders and Hiram's builders did hew *them,* and the stonesquarers: so they prepared timber and stones to build the house.

6 And it came to pass in the four hundred and eightieth year after the children of Israel were come out of the land of Egypt, in the fourth year of Solomon's reign over

---

bered thirty thousand men. 14 And he sent them to Lebanon, ten thousand a month in relays; they would be a month in Lebanon and two months at home; Adoni'ram was in charge of the levy. 15 Solomon also had seventy thousand burden-bearers and eighty thousand hewers of stone in the hill country, 16 besides Solomon's three thousand three hundred chief officers who were over the work, who had charge of the people who carried on the work. 17 At the king's command, they quarried out great, costly stones in order to lay the foundation of the house with dressed stones. 18 So Solomon's builders and Hiram's builders and the men of Gebal did the hewing and prepared the timber and the stone to build the house.

6 In the four hundred and eightieth year after the people of Israel came out of the

---

14. **Relays** is more intelligible today than **courses.** The Hebrew word *ḥaliphôth* means "exchanges." (Cf. the caliph, who is the successor of Mohammed; also Isa. 40:31, "they shall exchange strength," i.e., they shall change their human strength, which is of no avail, and in its place, as its successor, they shall receive the strength of God.)

2. THE TEMPLE EDIFICES (6:1-38)

The building of the temple marks a definite development in Hebrew religion, involving the worship of a settled community as against that of a nomad people. Ancient Hebrew tradition favored a tent as against "a house of cedar" (II Sam. 7:7). The details of the layout of the temple have been taken in the first place from a temple document which was embodied in the biography, but the whole description has been worked over by successive editors. They thought in terms of the second temple, that which was built after the return from exile. The result is that the original scheme is hard to isolate.

The temple was set on the hill, as was reckoned to be proper for temples. This was not because it was thus nearest to the sky, but because it represented the great mountain of the gods away to the north. It was impossible for man actually to appear in the true abode of the gods, but they were gracious enough to be found in such a model of their real home. The entrance to the temple itself was from the east, between two great pillars, and thence through a vestibule (Hebrew, *'ûlām*) which ran the whole width of the edifice, just over thirty feet wide (twenty cubits). The vestibule was ten cubits deep (over fifteen feet) and led into the holy place (Hebrew, *hêkhāl,* Akkadian, *egalu,* properly "palace"), which was forty cubits long (nearly sixty feet) by twenty wide by thirty high, with rafters across at a height of twenty cubits. Beyond this to the

---

between God and men. In building the house of God, Solomon wisely sought to preserve among the builders the homes of men.

6:1–7:1. *A Tale of Two Houses.*—Ch. 6 gives the long and detailed description of the temple which Solomon built, ending with this state-

---

ment, **He was seven years in building it** (vs. 38). Ch. 7 opens immediately with these words, **Solomon was building his own house thirteen years.** Seven years for the house of God; thirteen years for his own palace. Is there significance in the fact that the king spent almost twice as

Israel, in the month Zif, which *is* the second month, that he began to build the house of the Lord.

2 And the house which king Solomon built for the Lord, the length thereof *was* threescore cubits, and the breadth thereof twenty *cubits,* and the height thereof thirty cubits.

3 And the porch before the temple of the house, twenty cubits *was* the length thereof, according to the breadth of the house; *and* ten cubits *was* the breadth thereof before the house.

land of Egypt, in the fourth year of Solomon's reign over Israel, in the month of Ziv, which is the second month, he began to build the house of the Lord. **2** The house which King Solomon built for the Lord was sixty cubits long, twenty cubits wide, and thirty cubits high. **3** The vestibule in front of the nave of the house was twenty cubits long, equal to the width of the house, and ten cubits deep in front of the house.

---

west was the shrine itself (Hebrew, *debhîr*), twenty cubits by twenty by twenty. This was completely dark, there being no external lighting of any kind. On every side of the edifice except the east, where the whole side was taken up by the vestibule, there were three stories of small rooms, the lowest being five cubits wide, the next six, and the uppermost seven. This arrangement provided half a cubit on each side of the lower room to form a resting place for the ceiling beams. The total height of the three stories was fifteen cubits, half the height of the main building as seen from the front (east). The entrance to the small rooms was on the south, and there were staircases from story to story.

6:1. In the LXX this verse is inserted two verses earlier, and vss. 37-38*a* are found here. The verse is a postexilic addition, a different word for month (חדש) being used from that which is found in the rest of the chapter (ירח). **Ziv** was the eighth month of the pre-exilic calendar and the (approximately) second month of the postexilic calendar. The figure of 480 years is actually obtained by adding 50 years of the Babylonian exile to the total number of years assigned by the Deuteronomic editor to the kings of Judah (430 years). The suggestion is that an editor of the Priestly Code period has been busy creating a regular pattern for the history after the exact numerical fashion usual in that school of writers. He has thus made the time from the Exodus to the building of the temple exactly equal to the time from the building of the first temple to the first beginnings of the building of the second temple according to Ezra 5:16. If this verse is indeed late and is due to such a calculation, then there is no longer any main internal support for the earlier date of the invasion of Canaan under Joshua (*ca.* 1407 B.C.).

During the Exile the Jews adopted the Babylonian calendar (of Nippur) and began to reckon their months from the spring new moon. This makes Ziv the second month. It is probable, however, that before the Exile the month began with the full moon, and only after the Exile with the new moon (N. H. Snaith, *The Jewish New Year Festival* [London: Society for Promoting Christian Knowledge, 1947] pp. 96-103). If this is the case, then the new month day of Ziv was equivalent to the fifteenth day of Iyar, the postexilic name for the second month of the Babylonian year.

---

much time on his own house as on the temple of God? We should not read between the lines, but the bare statement would seem to betoken that the secular was beginning to overshadow the spiritual in Solomon's court.

The young king by his prayers and deeds had given evidence that he had what Paul calls "a sense of what is vital in religion" (Rom. 2:18 Moffatt). He had asked for wisdom and under-

standing. Within four years after his coronation he began to build the temple which David had dreamed. But worldly power and luxury were going to Solomon's head and heart. The service of the Lord was losing its priority in his life. If the godly virtues begin to grow in a person's life, they set forces at work which give him strength. God comes to a person who is enslaved by his appetites and makes him master of them.

4 And for the house he made windows of narrow lights.

5 ¶ And against the wall of the house he built chambers round about, *against* the walls of the house round about, *both* of the temple and of the oracle: and he made chambers round about.

6 The nethermost chamber *was* five cubits broad, and the middle *was* six cubits broad, and the third *was* seven cubits broad: for without *in the wall* of the house he made narrowed rests round about, that *the beams* should not be fastened in the walls of the house.

7 And the house, when it was in building, was built of stone made ready before it was brought thither: so that there was neither hammer nor axe *nor* any tool of iron heard in the house, while it was in building.

8 The door for the middle chamber *was* in the right side of the house: and they went up with winding stairs into the middle *chamber,* and out of the middle into the third.

4 And he made for the house windows with recessed frames. 5 He also built a structure against the wall of the house, running round the walls of the house, both the nave and the inner sanctuary; and he made side chambers all around. 6 The lowest story*j* was five cubits broad, the middle one was six cubits broad, and the third was seven cubits broad; for around the outside of the house he made offsets on the wall in order that the supporting beams should not be inserted into the walls of the house.

7 When the house was built, it was with stone prepared at the quarry; so that neither hammer nor axe nor any tool of iron was heard in the temple, while it was being built.

8 The entrance for the lowest*k* story was on the south side of the house; and one went up by stairs to the middle story, and

j Gk: Heb *structure*
k Gk Tg: Heb *middle*

---

4. Recessed frames or **narrow lights:** The Hebrew word is uncertain; the reference is probably to openings wide inside, but narrowing to a slit outside, similar to the windows of the medieval castles of western Europe, made for shooting arrows and for securing light with the minimum of dangers from archers who might be attacking the castle.

5. The Hebrew once more is uncertain, and the ancient translators were puzzled. Possibly the reference is to a continuous buttress built to support the outside walls—an embankment. The Targ. apparently thought of the whole block of side buildings, the three stories of chambers which covered three sides of the main building. These chambers were perhaps designed for family feasts (I Sam. 1:18 [LXX]; 9:22). In the second temple similar chambers were store chambers (I Chr. 9:26; Ezra 8:29; Neh. 10:38).

7. This verse interrupts the description of the small chambers, and is probably a late insertion by a postexilic editor whose activities are the cause of many difficulties both in this chapter and in the next. He evidently knew that no hewing of stone took place on the temple site. Apparently he thought that this was so that there should be no noise during the actual building. It is likely that the original intention is connected with the early custom whereby altars had to be made of unhewn stone. The earliest altar (lit., "place of slaughter") was probably the actual stone in which the god was supposed to be. He thus drank the blood which bathed and soaked into the stone. The stone must not be hewn lest the god should be damaged. When the development of shrines into permanent stone buildings took place, all stone brought onto the site

---

He takes a man who is shiftless and makes him industrious. He transforms the fellow who is dishonest into the reliable and trustworthy employee. He stirs the sluggish spirit and makes it alert. Thereupon these traits of industry, sobriety, honesty, and alertness begin to enlarge their possessor's place in society. That is what

seemed to be happening at first with Solomon. That is what happened to the early Christians in the Roman Empire. They became such good craftsmen that they attracted the attention of Emperor Constantine, who made their religion legal, and in a century or so the once-despised Christians had become the social leaders of the

9 So he built the house, and finished it; and covered the house with beams and boards of cedar.

10 And *then* he built chambers against all the house, five cubits high: and they rested on the house with timber of cedar.

11 ¶ And the word of the LORD came to Solomon, saying,

12 *Concerning* this house which thou art in building, if thou wilt walk in my statutes, and execute my judgments, and keep all my commandments to walk in them; then will I perform my word with thee, which I spake unto David thy father:

13 And I will dwell among the children of Israel, and will not forsake my people Israel.

14 So Solomon built the house, and finished it.

15 And he built the walls of the house within with boards of cedar, both the floor of the house, and the walls of the ceiling: *and* he covered *them* on the inside with wood, and covered the floor of the house with planks of fir.

16 And he built twenty cubits on the sides of the house, both the floor and the walls with boards of cedar: he even built *them* for it within, *even* for the oracle, *even* for the most holy *place*.

from the middle story to the third. 9 So he built the house, and finished it; and he made the ceiling of the house of beams and planks of cedar. 10 He built the structure against the whole house, each story*l* five cubits high, and it was joined to the house with timbers of cedar.

11 Now the word of the LORD came to Solomon, 12 "Concerning this house which you are building, if you will walk in my statutes and obey my ordinances and keep all my commandments and walk in them, then I will establish my word with you, which I spoke to David your father. 13 And I will dwell among the children of Israel, and will not forsake my people Israel."

14 So Solomon built the house, and finished it. 15 He lined the walls of the house on the inside with boards of cedar; from the floor of the house to the rafters*m* of the ceiling, he covered them on the inside with wood; and he covered the floor of the house with boards of cypress. 16 He built twenty cubits of the rear of the house with boards of cedar from the floor to the rafters,*m* and he built this within as an inner sanctuary,

l Heb lacks *each story*
m Gk: Heb *walls*

would thereby be made sacred, so that whatever squaring and shaping of the stone was done would have to be done before transport.

9. This verse makes a break between vss. 8 and 10, where no break ought to be, and it should follow vs. 10 as in the LXX and Lucian; its last phrase contains two difficult and uncertain words, **beams and planks.** Ewald's suggestion (*History of Israel* [London: Longmans, Green & Co., 1871], III, 238-39) is that there was "an ornamental ceiling in squares, with small pieces of cedar wood as dividing beams."

11-14. A late insertion by a priestly editor, too late to find a place in the LXX. He repeated vs. 9*a* in order to dovetail his insertion into the narrative.

16. A Priestly Code editor has inserted **as the most holy place.** This is the first of a series of insertions by which this editor sought to identify the second temple with Solomon's temple. The **most holy place** (lit., "holy of holies") was the inner shrine of the second temple and, apart from store chambers and living quarters, etc., was the only covered place in the main block of buildings.

waning empire. This same story of transformation was repeated in the case of the English Puritans. The sober industriousness inculcated by piety made the followers of Cromwell the founders of England's financial leadership. It is no accident that the Western culture which developed in the wake of Hebrew-Christian expansion is more dynamic than the Oriental civilizations. The prophets of Israel and the evangelists of Christianity teach that man has a fighting chance and is not chained in fatalism, that he shall seek the truth and the truth will make him free. These are among the factors which gave rise to the science, the inventions, the spirit of material progress of our Western world.

17 And the house, that *is,* the temple before it, was forty cubits *long.*

18 And the cedar of the house within *was* carved with knops and open flowers: all *was* cedar; there was no stone seen.

19 And the oracle he prepared in the house within, to set there the ark of the covenant of the LORD.

20 And the oracle in the forepart *was* twenty cubits in length, and twenty cubits in breadth, and twenty cubits in the height thereof: and he overlaid it with pure gold; and *so* covered the altar *which was of* cedar.

21 So Solomon overlaid the house within with pure gold: and he made a partition by the chains of gold before the oracle; and he overlaid it with gold.

22 And the whole house he overlaid with gold, until he had finished all the house: also the whole altar that *was* by the oracle he overlaid with gold.

23 ¶ And within the oracle he made two cherubim *of* olive tree, *each* ten cubits high.

24 And five cubits *was* the one wing of the cherub, and five cubits the other wing

as the most holy place. 17 The house, that is, the nave in front of the inner sanctuary, was forty cubits long. 18 The cedar within the house was carved in the form of gourds and open flowers; all was cedar, no stone was seen. 19 The inner sanctuary he prepared in the innermost part of the house, to set there the ark of the covenant of the LORD. 20 The inner sanctuary[n] was twenty cubits long, twenty cubits wide, and twenty cubits high; and he overlaid it with pure gold. He also made[o] an altar of cedar. 21 And Solomon overlaid the inside of the house with pure gold, and he drew chains of gold across, in front of the inner sanctuary, and overlaid it with gold. 22 And he overlaid the whole house with gold, until all the house was finished. Also the whole altar that belonged to the inner sanctuary he overlaid with gold.

23 In the inner sanctuary he made two cherubim of olivewood, each ten cubits high. 24 Five cubits was the length of one

[n] Vg: Heb *and before the inner sanctuary*
[o] Gk: Heb *covered*

17-22. These verses have been worked over at least twice, once by a Deuteronomic editor (probably the second, *ca.* 550 B.C.), and later by the editor who tried to equate the two temples. The original seems to have consisted of vs. 17, omitting **that is, the nave,** and vs. 20, omitting the reference to the **gold.** Into this the Deuteronomic editor inserted **vs. 19,** thus giving a text close to that of the LXX. The remainder of the verses are still later additions, not in the LXX, describing the decorations of the second temple. In the LXX the reference to the gold plating refers to the altar also. According to both the M.T. and the LXX the whole of the inside of the building, both outer house (temple) and inner shrine, was covered with gold. This would involve a very considerable amount of gold, and no mention is made of it in the stories of the successive plunderings of the temple. Either the mention of the gold is due to the embroidering of tradition, or it was only a thin gilding with liquid gold (C. F. Burney, *Notes on the Hebrew Text of the Books of Kings* [Oxford: Clarendon Press, 1903], pp. 73-74).

21. And he drew chains of gold across: This phrase, in common with the earlier part of this verse, is not in the LXX. A comparison with II Chr. 3:14 suggests that the phrase is a remnant, not easily translated (cf. **and he made a partition by the chains of gold**), of a priestly editor's insertion which involved a reference to the veil which was before the holy of holies of the second temple, as being drawn across with golden chains.

23-28. These verses are original, except that vs. 26 would be better inserted in vs. 23 to follow **olivewood.** There are two types of cherubs in Hebrew lore. There was the

---

But how often it happens that those who have risen through the power of religion fail to give it recognition when they reach the top. Christ finds room at the bottom of the social scale, in the lowly mangers; but there is no room for him at the top. The palatial homes which have been made possible through the labor and laws

inspired by the Christian religion keep no place in their crowded schedule for its worship. The giant businesses which have grown on soil fertilized by Christian faith and hope scorn the little churches which crouch under the shadows of their skyscrapers. Governments which rest upon the integrity and justice inculcated by

of the cherub: from the uttermost part of the one wing unto the uttermost part of the other *were* ten cubits.

25 And the other cherub *was* ten cubits: both the cherubim *were* of one measure and one size.

26 The height of the one cherub *was* ten cubits, and so *was it* of the other cherub.

27 And he set the cherubim within the inner house: and they stretched forth the wings of the cherubim, so that the wing of the one touched the *one* wall, and the wing of the other cherub touched the other wall; and their wings touched one another in the midst of the house.

28 And he overlaid the cherubim with gold.

29 And he carved all the walls of the house round about with carved figures of cherubim and palm trees and open flowers, within and without.

30 And the floor of the house he overlaid with gold, within and without.

wing of the cherub, and five cubits the length of the other wing of the cherub; it was ten cubits from the tip of one wing to the tip of the other. **25** The other cherub also measured ten cubits; both cherubim had the same measure and the same form. **26** The height of one cherub was ten cubits, and so was that of the other cherub. **27** He put the cherubim in the innermost part of the house; and the wings of the cherubim were spread out so that a wing of one touched the one wall, and a wing of the other cherub touched the other wall; their other wings touched each other in the middle of the house. **28** And he overlaid the cherubim with gold.

29 He carved all the walls of the house round about with carved figures of cherubim and palm trees and open flowers, in the inner and outer rooms. **30** The floor of the house he overlaid with gold in the inner and outer rooms.

cherub, one or more than one, who was a guardian of sacred places (cf. Gen. 3:24; Ezek. 28:14) and certainly of Mesopotamian origin. There were also pairs of cherubs. These are personifications of the twin spirits of the thunderstorm (cf. Castor and Pollux in the Roman myths, and the general association of twins with thunder). In this case the pair of cherubs which were in the inner sanctuary are a survival of the descriptions of the Lord as the storm-god, riding on the thunderclouds from the deserts of the south (Hab. 3; Ps. 18:10-17).

29-30. Both verses are in the LXX and Lucian, except for the reference to **open flowers**. Vs. 29 is due to the interpolator who was thinking in terms either of the second temple or of the proposals of Ezek. 41:18. The phrase translated **open flowers** is found in vss. 18, 29, 32, 35—all of them due to this late editor. The word פטורי is difficult, but means "outspread," and so is more likely to be describing "garlands of flowers" (so Skinner and others). The original significance of the **palm trees** is fertility. Such representations were common in ancient temples, and there is ample evidence that Solomon's temple conformed largely to the general pattern (cf. 7:15-37).

The history of worship is largely the story of the continuation of ancient patterns and forms, combined with a continual endeavor to reinterpret them in accordance with new religious ideas. Originally temples were mostly associated with sun worship, and the center line was directed toward the rising sun. The center line of the Jerusalem temple followed this tradition, and it may be that in the earliest days there was some recognized association with a cult of the rising sun. Later custom and tradition involved a deliberate denial of any sun worship, especially when the priests at the feast of Tabernacles marched toward the east gate of the temple and deliberately turned their

Christianity pay only formal and empty tributes to it. The general attitude of so-called Christian society toward Christ is similar to the treatment that might be accorded to one who has transferred the management of his property to his heirs. He is given a place at the table. He is

shown a certain deference. But he is outside the main currents of the ongoing activities. The real business is conducted without him.

The Lord had lifted Israel out of bondage. David in his abounding gratitude felt remorse that his redeeming Lord had no house com-

31 ¶ And for the entering of the oracle he made doors *of* olive tree: the lintel *and* side posts *were* a fifth part *of the wall.*

32 The two doors also *were of* olive tree; and he carved upon them carvings of cherubim and palm trees and open flowers, and overlaid *them* with gold, and spread gold upon the cherubim, and upon the palm trees.

33 So also made he for the door of the temple posts *of* olive tree, a fourth part *of the wall.*

34 And the two doors *were of* fir tree: the two leaves of the one door *were* folding, and the two leaves of the other door *were* folding.

35 And he carved *thereon* cherubim and palm trees and open flowers: and covered *them* with gold fitted upon the carved work.

36 ¶ And he built the inner court with three rows of hewed stone, and a row of cedar beams.

37 ¶ In the fourth year was the foundation of the house of the LORD laid, in the month Zif:

38 And in the eleventh year, in the month Bul, which *is* the eighth month, was the house finished throughout all the parts thereof, and according to all the fashion of it. So was he seven years in building it.

7 But Solomon was building his own house thirteen years, and he finished all his house.

31 For the entrance to the inner sanctuary he made doors of olivewood; the lintel and the doorposts formed a pentagon.*ᵖ*

32 He covered the two doors of olivewood with carvings of cherubim, palm trees, and open flowers; he overlaid them with gold, and spread gold upon the cherubim and upon the palm trees.

33 So also he made for the entrance to the nave doorposts of olivewood, in the form of a square, 34 and two doors of cypress wood; the two leaves of the one door were folding, and the two leaves of the other door were folding. 35 On them he carved cherubim and palm trees and open flowers; and he overlaid them with gold evenly applied upon the carved work. 36 He built the inner court with three courses of hewn stone and one course of cedar beams.

37 In the fourth year the foundation of the house of the LORD was laid, in the month of Ziv. 38 And in the eleventh year, in the month of Bul, which is the eighth month, the house was finished in all its parts, and according to all its specifications. He was seven years in building it.

7 Solomon was building his own house thirteen years, and he finished his entire house.

ᵖ Heb obscure

---

backs to the rising sun and bowed toward the altar. Similarly all the fertility decorations, date palms, pomegranates, etc., had original pagan associations with fertility cults. It was originally believed that the very representation itself constituted an effective prayer to the deity and itself ensured fertility, just as it was believed that the actual ceremonies themselves were efficacious. This "magical" idea dies hard.

31-36. These verses contain details of the doorways, with vss. 32 and 35 as later additions.

37. Here is the original statement concerning the date of the commencement of the building of the temple, of which a later expansion is found in vs. 1.

38. The temple took seven and a half years to build, and it was finished in the autumn, a month too late for the great autumnal feast of Ingathering, which was celebrated at the fullness of the harvest moon. **Bul** was the second month of the pre-exilic calendar, roughly equivalent to the eighth month, Heshvan, of the postexilic calendar.

3. THE PALACE BUILDINGS (7:1-12)

7:1-12. The temple was part of a larger scheme which involved twenty years' work in all (cf. 9:10). The whole set of buildings was enclosed within a great court surrounded by three courses of hewn stones and one course of cedar beams. The temple court was on the north side. To the south of the temple court was the palace court, containing

2 ¶ He built also the house of the forest of Lebanon; the length thereof *was* a hundred cubits, and the breadth thereof fifty cubits, and the height thereof thirty cubits, upon four rows of cedar pillars, with cedar beams upon the pillars.

3 And *it was* covered with cedar above upon the beams, that *lay* on forty-five pillars, fifteen *in* a row.

4 And *there were* windows *in* three rows, and light *was* against light *in* three ranks.

5 And all the doors and posts *were* square, with the windows: and light *was* against light *in* three ranks.

6 ¶ And he made a porch of pillars; the length thereof *was* fifty cubits, and the breadth thereof thirty cubits: and the porch *was* before them: and the *other* pillars and the thick beam *were* before them.

7 ¶ Then he made a porch for the throne where he might judge, *even* the porch of judgment: and *it was* covered with cedar from one side of the floor to the other.

8 ¶ And his house where he dwelt *had* another court within the porch, *which* was of the like work. Solomon made also a house for Pharaoh's daughter, whom he had taken *to wife*, like unto this porch.

9 All these *were of* costly stones, according to the measures of hewed stones, sawed with saws, within and without, even from the foundation unto the coping, and *so on* the outside toward the great court.

10 And the foundation *was of* costly stones, *even* great stones, stones of ten cubits, and stones of eight cubits.

11 And above *were* costly stones, after the measures of hewed stones, and cedars.

12 And the great court round about *was* with three rows of hewed stones, and a row of cedar beams, both for the inner court of

2 He built the House of the Forest of Lebanon; its length was a hundred cubits, and its breadth fifty cubits, and its height thirty cubits, and it was built upon three*q* rows of cedar pillars, with cedar beams upon the pillars. **3** And it was covered with cedar above the chambers that were upon the forty-five pillars, fifteen in each row. **4** There were window frames in three rows, and window opposite window in three tiers. **5** All the doorways and windows*r* had square frames, and window was opposite window in three tiers.

6 And he made the Hall of Pillars; its length was fifty cubits, and its breadth thirty cubits; there was a porch in front with pillars, and a canopy before them.

7 And he made the Hall of the Throne where he was to pronounce judgment, even the Hall of Judgment; it was finished with cedar from floor to rafters.*s*

8 His own house where he was to dwell, in the other court back of the hall, was of like workmanship. Solomon also made a house like this hall for Pharaoh's daughter whom he had taken in marriage.

9 All these were made of costly stones, hewn according to measure, sawed with saws, back and front, even from the foundation to the coping, and from the court of the house of the LORD*t* to the great court. **10** The foundation was of costly stones, huge stones, stones of eight and ten cubits. **11** And above were costly stones, hewn according to measurement, and cedar. **12** The great court had three courses of hewn stone round about, and a course of cedar beams;

q Gk: Heb *four*
r Gk: Heb *posts*
s Syr Vg: Heb *floor*
t With 7. 12. Heb *from the outside*

---

the royal palace with the house of Pharaoh's daughter immediately behind it in the northwest corner. To the south of the palace court there was the throne hall, with an entrance through the hall of pillars on the south side. South again, and standing by itself, separate from all the rest, was **the House of the Forest of Lebanon.** The foundations of all the buildings were of huge stones, with walls of hewn stones, paneled with cedar

---

parable to the king's dwelling. Calling in Nathan the prophet, David said: "See now, I dwell in a house of cedar, but the ark of God dwelleth within curtains. And Nathan said to the king, Go, do all that is in thine heart; for the LORD is with thee" (II Sam. 7:2-3). When Solomon fulfilled his father's dream of building the house

of the Lord, he spent seven years on it, and then thirteen years on his own house. The Lord did not hold as large place in the heart of the son as in that of the father. The spiritual eclipse had begun.

7:2-51. *The Best for the Highest.*—It was Solomon's conviction that altar and throne

the house of the LORD, and for the porch of the house.

13 ¶ And king Solomon sent and fetched Hiram out of Tyre.

14 He *was* a widow's son of the tribe of Naphtali, and his father *was* a man of Tyre, a worker in brass: and he was filled with wisdom, and understanding, and cunning to work all works in brass. And he came to king Solomon, and wrought all his work.

15 For he cast two pillars of brass, of eighteen cubits high apiece: and a line of twelve cubits did compass either of them about.

16 And he made two chapiters *of* molten brass, to set upon the tops of the pillars: the height of the one chapiter *was* five cubits, and the height of the other chapiter *was* five cubits:

so had the inner court of the house of the LORD, and the vestibule of the house.

13 And King Solomon sent and brought Hiram from Tyre. 14 He was the son of a widow of the tribe of Naph'tali, and his father was a man of Tyre, a worker in bronze; and he was full of wisdom, understanding, and skill, for making any work in bronze. He came to King Solomon, and did all his work.

15 He cast two pillars of bronze. Eighteen cubits was the height of one pillar, and a line of twelve cubits measured its circumference; it was hollow, and its thickness was four fingers; the second pillar was the same.*u* 16 He also made two capitals of molten bronze, to set upon the tops of the pillars; the height of the one capital was five cubits, and the height of the other

u Cn Compare Gk and Jer 52. 51: Heb and a line of twelve cubits measured the circumference of the second pillar

inside from floor to roof, with cedar columns in the house of pillars and three rows of fifteen columns each in the house of the forest of Lebanon.

4. HIRAM THE TYRIAN CRAFTSMAN (7:13-14)

13-14. Solomon brings from Tyre a skilled craftsman by the name of **Hiram.** He was a worker in bronze, and he made the bronze furniture for the temple, both the massive fixtures and the implements for use in worship. The craftsman's name was probably *Ḥûrām-'ābhî* (i.e., "Huram is my father"; cf. II Chr. 2:13; 4:16). In II Chr. 2:14 it is stated that his mother was a Danite, but there is nothing there about her being a widow. Possibly the reference to Hiram's widowed mother is to suggest that he was of pure Israelitish descent—a sound Deuteronomic principle.

5. THE TWO BRONZE PILLARS (7:15-22)

Such a pair of pillars was customary at the entrance of temples, not erected within the vestibule, but detached and separate. There have been many suggestions as to their significance—phallic emblems, sun obelisks, representations of deities male and female, etc. The most probable explanation is that they represented the two mountains which flanked the path to the mountain of the gods away to the north, according to the ancient myth. They are called "the sides of the north" (Ps. 48:2; Isa. 14:13; Ezek. 38:6, 15). Similar pillars have been found at the entrances to temples at Tyre, Shechem, Byblos (*ca.* 1500 B.C.), Hierapolis, Paphos, Sardis, Khorsabad, and generally in the East from Asia Minor through to Babylonia (R. B. Y. Scott, "The Pillars Jachin and Boaz," *Journal of Biblical Literature,* LVIII [1939], 143-49). The original significance of the pillars consisted in their symbolism of the approach to the house of God. Whoever would approach the actual dwelling place of the god must pass between the two mountains which flanked the way. The worshiper similarly entered the localized home of the god by passing between the symbolic mountains. It is not easy to say to what extent the twin pillars at Jerusalem had been conventionalized and were there simply because that was the proper traditional way to build entrances to temples. Possibly the names **Jachin** and **Boaz** indicate that a measure of reinterpretation had already taken place. The LXX regarded them as proper names here, but in II Chr. 3:17 translated them "setting-right" and "strength." R. B. Y. Scott suggests (*ibid.,* p. 148) that

17 *And* nets of checkerwork, and wreaths of chainwork, for the chapiters which *were* upon the top of the pillars; seven for the one chapiter, and seven for the other chapiter.

18 And he made the pillars, and two rows round about upon the one network, to cover the chapiters that *were* upon the top, with pomegranates: and so did he for the other chapiter.

19 And the chapiters that *were* upon the top of the pillars *were* of lily work in the porch, four cubits.

20 And the chapiters upon the two pillars *had pomegranates* also above, over against the belly which *was* by the network: and the pomegranates *were* two hundred in rows round about upon the other chapiter.

21 And he set up the pillars in the porch of the temple: and he set up the right pillar, and called the name thereof Jachin: and he set up the left pillar, and called the name thereof Boaz.

capital was five cubits. 17 Then he made two[v] nets of checker work with wreaths of chain work for the capitals upon the tops of the pillars; a net[w] for the one capital, and a net[w] for the other capital. 18 Likewise he made pomegranates;[x] in two rows round about upon the one network, to cover the capital that was upon the top of the pillar; and he did the same with the other capital. 19 Now the capitals that were upon the tops of the pillars in the vestibule were of lily-work, four cubits. 20 The capitals were upon the two pillars and also above the rounded projection which was beside the network; there were two hundred pomegranates, in two rows round about; and so with the other capital. 21 He set up the pillars at the vestibule of the temple; he set up the pillar on the south and called its name Jachin; and he set up the pillar on

[v] Gk: Heb lacks *he made two*
[w] Gk: Heb *seven*
[x] With 2 Mss Compare Gk: Heb *pillars*

they are the first words of two sentences: "He will establish the throne of David and his kingdom forever," and "In the strength of the Lord shall the king rejoice," or some such similar phrase. The pillars were made of נחשת, a word which is used of copper ore (Deut. 8:9; Job 28:2) hardened with tin to form an alloy which we now call **bronze**. Formerly any alloy of copper, especially if it contained tin, was called **brass**, but in modern times brass is an alloy of copper and zinc. The pillars were twenty feet in circumference (i.e., nearly six and a half feet in diameter) and thirty feet high. The suggestions that the pillars represent deities, male or male and female, rest upon misapprehensions. A single pillar usually represented a god, and many pillars represented many gods, unless some of them were altars. If the pillars represented gods, it is not easy to see why there were two only, or why they were situated in front of the vestibule. If the pillars represented male and female (i.e., Baal and Astarte), one would probably have been made of stone and the other of wood.

17. The reading **net** is correct; so the LXX and Lucian. The M.T. differs by one letter, reading שבעה (**seven**) for שבכה.

18. It is clear from vs. 20 that the translation **pomegranates** (RSV) is correct, especially since the rendering **pillars** (KJV) makes no sense. They are emblems of fertility because of the extraordinary number of pips which they contain.

19-22. In the LXX and in Lucian vss. 19-20 follow vs. 21, and vs. 22 is missing altogether. A postexilic editor has been assimilating the text to make it coincide with

stand or fall together. Each sustained the other. If the sign of Solomon's worldliness appears in the fact that he spent thirteen years on his own house and only seven years on the house of the Lord, there is something to counteract this weakness in the quality of work given to both buildings. There is a religious quality in work well done. And Solomon was satisfied with nothing less than the best. Hiram was sum-

moned from Tyre because there was a dearth of distinguished craftsmanship in Israel. Since Hiram's mother was an Israelite, it may be supposed that he was acquainted with Israel's God and did his work in a devout spirit. While art is here brought into the service of religion, it is not lowered to the status of a handmaid. Beauty is not sacrificed to piety. Beauty is an ultimate value along with truth and goodness.

22 And upon the top of the pillars *was* lily work: so was the work of the pillars finished.

23 ¶ And he made a molten sea, ten cubits from the one brim to the other: *it was* round all about, and his height *was* five cubits: and a line of thirty cubits did compass it round about.

24 And under the brim of it round about *there were* knops compassing it, ten in a cubit, compassing the sea round about: the knops *were* cast in two rows, when it was cast.

25 It stood upon twelve oxen, three looking toward the north, and three looking toward the west, and three looking toward the south, and three looking toward the east: and the sea *was set* above upon them, and all their hinder parts *were* inward.

26 And it *was* a handbreadth thick, and the brim thereof was wrought like the brim of a cup, with flowers of lilies: it contained two thousand baths.

the north and called its name Bo'az. 22 And upon the tops of the pillars was lily-work. Thus the work of the pillars was finished.

23 Then he made the molten sea; it was round, ten cubits from brim to brim, and five cubits high, and a line of thirty cubits measured its circumference. 24 Under its brim were gourds, for thirty*y* cubits, compassing the sea round about; the gourds were in two rows, cast with it when it was cast. 25 It stood upon twelve oxen, three facing north, three facing west, three facing south, and three facing east; the sea was set upon them, and all their hinder parts were inward. 26 Its thickness was a handbreadth; and its brim was made like the brim of a cup, like the flower of a lily; it held two thousand baths.

y Heb *ten*

---

what he knew of the second temple. Judging by Jer. 52:23, the wreaths were two to each column, each wreath made of a hundred pomegranates, and festooned so that four were fastened and ninety-six were hanging free. On the top of each column there was a bronze collar, and above this a many-petaled bronze flower open to the sky.

6. The Bronze Sea (7:23-26)

The bronze sea was a huge basin, some seven feet in diameter and just over three feet deep. Around the rim there was a double row of gourds similar to those which were a feature of the carving of the second temple (6:18). They were cast in the same mold as the bronze basin itself, a very clever piece of craftsmanship. The thickness of the casting was **a handbreadth**, i.e., about three inches, the same thickness as the casting of the two bronze columns outside the vestibule. The bronze sea was a representation of the primeval ocean of the Mesopotamian creation myth. Before the world began, or ever the earth and the heavens were formed, there was a great fight between the hero-god and the sea monster of Chaos. The Hebrews took primitive pagan material and used it for their own religious purposes. They made this ancient myth tell the story of the great fight between God and the powers of evil. Still more important, they wove the story into their history so that it became the story of the work of the Savior-God. The overthrow of every oppressor was a repetition in history of what God had been doing since before the beginning of time. They identified the enemy of God with Rahab the dragon, so that Egypt is Rahab (Isa. 30:7), Pharaoh (Ezek. 29:3-6; 32:2-8), Nebuchadrezzar (Jer. 51:34; cf. Jonah). See especially Isa. 51:9-11, where the defeat of the primeval Rahab is connected first with the crossing of the Red Sea and then with the rescue from Babylon. Finally the dragon is antichrist, the beast that rises from the sea (Rev. 13:1; cf. Amos 9:3), and at last he will be overthrown, nevermore to rise (for further details see Hermann Gunkel, *Schöpfung und Chaos in Urzeit und Endzeit* [2nd ed.; Göttingen: Vandenhoeck & Ruprecht, 1921]; N. H. Snaith, *Studies in the Psalter* [London: Epworth Press, 1934], pp. 94-109).

25. The bronze sea was supported by twelve bulls, in four groups of three, pointing toward the four points of the compass. The bull is the ancient symbol of fertility, and

27 ¶ And he made ten bases of brass; four cubits *was* the length of one base, and four cubits the breadth thereof, and three cubits the height of it.

28 And the work of the bases *was* on this *manner:* they had borders, and the borders *were* between the ledges:

29 And on the borders that *were* between the ledges *were* lions, oxen, and cherubim: and upon the ledges *there was* a base above: and beneath the lions and oxen *were* certain additions made of thin work.

30 And every base had four brazen wheels, and plates of brass: and the four corners thereof had undersetters: under the laver *were* undersetters molten, at the side of every addition.

31 And the mouth of it within the chapiter and above *was* a cubit: but the mouth thereof *was* round *after* the work of the base, a cubit and a half: and also upon the mouth of it *were* gravings with their borders, foursquare, not round.

32 And under the borders *were* four wheels; and the axletrees of the wheels *were joined* to the base: and the height of a wheel *was* a cubit and half a cubit.

33 And the work of the wheels *was* like the work of a chariot wheel: their axletrees, and their naves, and their felloes, and their spokes, *were* all molten.

34 And *there were* four undersetters to the four corners of one base: *and* the undersetters *were* of the very base itself.

35 And in the top of the base *was there* a round compass of half a cubit high: and on the top of the base the ledges thereof and the borders thereof *were* of the same.

27 He also made the ten stands of bronze; each stand was four cubits long, four cubits wide, and three cubits high. 28 This was the construction of the stands: they had panels, and the panels were set in the frames 29 and on the panels that were set in the frames were lions, oxen, and cherubim. Upon the frames, both above and below the lions and oxen, there were wreaths of beveled work. 30 Moreover each stand had four bronze wheels and axles of bronze; and at the four corners were supports for a laver. The supports were cast, with wreaths at the side of each. 31 Its opening was within a crown which projected upward one cubit; its opening was round, as a pedestal is made, a cubit and a half deep. At its opening there were carvings; and its panels were square, not round. 32 And the four wheels were underneath the panels; the axles of the wheels were of one piece with the stands; and the height of a wheel was a cubit and a half. 33 The wheels were made like a chariot wheel; their axles, their rims, their spokes, and their hubs, were all cast. 34 There were four supports at the four corners of each stand; the supports were of one piece with the stands. 35 And on the top of the stand there was a round band half a cubit high; and on the top of the stand its stays and its panels

---

the God of the Hebrews was worshiped at Bethel and at Dan in the image of a bull. The cult goes back to the desert days, and Jeroboam's establishment of the bull worship at Bethel was a revival of the worship of the golden calf (cf. 12:28; Exod. 32:4, 8). There is no connection with the Apis bull worship of Egypt. The cult is of general Semitic association.

7. The Ten Bronze Lavers on Wheels (7:27-39)

27-39. This section is complicated because there are two interwoven accounts in which the details differ. A bronze stand of late Mycenaean workmanship has been discovered at Larnaka in Cyprus, and it is evidently a small scale reproduction of such bronze wheeled stands as are described here. The trolley laver from Cyprus is fifteen inches high by nine inches square. Those in Solomon's temple were four feet six inches high by six feet square (Burney, *Notes on Hebrew Text of Kings,* Pl. I; see also Pl. II, a photograph of a wheelless laver stand from Enkomi, Cyprus). They were used, according to II Chr. 4:6, for washing "such things as they offered for the burnt offering,"

36 For on the plates of the ledges thereof, and on the borders thereof, he graved cherubim, lions, and palm trees, according to the proportion of every one, and additions round about.

37 After this *manner* he made the ten bases: all of them had one casting, one measure, *and* one size.

38 ¶ Then made he ten lavers of brass: one laver contained forty baths: *and* every laver was four cubits: *and* upon every one of the ten bases one laver.

39 And he put five bases on the right side of the house, and five on the left side of the house: and he set the sea on the right side of the house eastward, over against the south.

40 ¶ And Hiram made the lavers, and the shovels, and the basins. So Hiram made an end of doing all the work that he made king Solomon for the house of the Lord:

41 The two pillars, and the *two* bowls of the chapiters that *were* on the top of the two pillars; and the two networks, to cover the two bowls of the chapiters which *were* upon the top of the pillars;

42 And four hundred pomegranates for the two networks, *even* two rows of pomegranates for one network, to cover the two bowls of the chapiters that *were* upon the pillars;

43 And the ten bases, and ten lavers on the bases;

44 And one sea, and twelve oxen under the sea;

45 And the pots, and the shovels, and the basins: and all these vessels, which Hiram made to king Solomon for the house of the Lord, *were of* bright brass.

were of one piece with it. 36 And on the surfaces of its stays and on its panels, he carved cherubim, lions, and palm trees, according to the space of each, with wreaths round about. 37 After this manner he made the ten stands; all of them were cast alike, of the same measure and the same form.

38 And he made ten lavers of bronze; each laver held forty baths, each laver measured four cubits, and there was a laver for each of the ten stands. 39 And he set the stands, five on the south side of the house, and five on the north side of the house; and he set the sea on the southeast corner of the house.

40 Hiram also made the pots, the shovels, and the basins. So Hiram finished all the work that he did for King Solomon on the house of the Lord: 41 the two pillars, the two bowls of the capitals that were on the tops of the pillars, and the two networks to cover the two bowls of the capitals that were on the tops of the pillars; 42 and the four hundred pomegranates for the two networks, two rows of pomegranates for each network, to cover the two bowls of the capitals that were upon the pillars; 43 the ten stands, and the ten lavers upon the stands; 44 and the one sea, and the twelve oxen underneath the sea.

45 Now the pots, the shovels, and the basins, all these vessels in the house of the Lord, which Hiram made for King Solo-

---

but this statement must be accepted with reserve, for the same verse continues by saying that the bronze sea "was for the priests to wash in." This can scarcely have been the original significance of the great bronze sea in Solomon's temple, though it is possible that the Chronicler was right so far as the second temple is concerned. The ancient symbols may easily have been reinterpreted in the postexilic period, and we know that it was the Chronicler's custom generally to invest the events of other days with the garments of his own times.

8. The Bronze Objects (7:40-47)

40-47. A summary of all the bronze objects which Hiram cast for the temple and its services. The LXX has an addition in vs. 45 referring to forty-eight pillars partly for the king's house and partly for the temple. As there is no reference elsewhere to these objects, their function and location are unknown. The actual casting was done in the Jordan Valley, the nearest site where there was any considerable clay deposit (George

46 In the plain of Jordan did the king cast them, in the clay ground between Succoth and Zarthan.

47 And Solomon left all the vessels *unweighed,* because they were exceeding many: neither was the weight of the brass found out.

48 And Solomon made all the vessels that *pertained* unto the house of the LORD: the altar of gold, and the table of gold, whereupon the showbread *was,*

49 And the candlesticks of pure gold, five on the right *side,* and five on the left, before the oracle, with the flowers, and the lamps, and the tongs *of* gold,

50 And the bowls, and the snuffers, and the basins, and the spoons, and the censers *of* pure gold; and the hinges *of* gold, *both* for the doors of the inner house, the most holy *place, and* for the doors of the house, *to wit,* of the temple.

mon, were of burnished bronze. 46 In the plain of the Jordan the king cast them, in the clay ground between Succoth and Zarethan. 47 And Solomon left all the vessels unweighed, because there were so many of them; the weight of the bronze was not found out.

48 So Solomon made all the vessels that were in the house of the LORD: the golden altar, the golden table for the bread of the Presence, 49 the lampstands of pure gold, five on the south side and five on the north, before the inner sanctuary; the flowers, the lamps, and the tongs, of gold; 50 the cups, snuffers, basins, dishes for incense, and firepans, of pure gold; and the sockets of gold, for the doors of the innermost part of the house, the most holy place, and for the doors of the nave of the temple.

Adam Smith, *The Historical Geography of the Holy Land* [25th ed.; London: Hodder & Stoughton, 1931], p. 488).

9. THE GOLDEN OBJECTS (7:48-51)

48-51. A summary of all the golden objects which were made for the temple and its services. There are considerable variations in this section between the M.T., the LXX, and Lucian. According to Lucian vs. 48a says, "And Solomon placed the vessels in the house of the Lord," but he has the rest of vss. 48-50 substantially as in the M.T. Similarly for the LXX. Probably these three verses come from a late postexilic addition, since the golden altar was not known even in the first days of the second temple. The original text, as it left the hand of the earlier editor, comprised vss. 48a, 51.

The golden altar was the altar of incense, mentioned first in Exod. 30:27, by no means the earliest stratum of the Priestly Code. The burning of incense was a postexilic development belonging to the more elaborate ritual of later days and due to the influence of Babylonian religion. Originally the incense consisted of frankincense, the sweet-smelling resin of an Indian tree, imported into Palestine through Arabia. According to Exod. 30:34, four other spices were added, each in equal quantities, but in the first century A.D. there were thirteen ingredients (Josephus *Jewish War* V. 5. 5; VI. 8. 3). The reason for the use of incense is rooted in the Oriental's pleasure in fragrances. In the Mesopotamian flood story the gods are pictured as delighting in the fragrance of the sacrificial smoke: "The gods smelled the savor, The gods smelled the goodly savor, The gods gathered like flies over the sacrifice" (Gilgamesh Epic, Tablet XI, ll. 160-62). Such primitive notions are not found in Hebrew story, for much of the anthropomorphic crudeness has been refined away. The idea nevertheless is that the savor of the sacrifices is well pleasing to God. In course of time the burning of incense was regarded as having atoning effectiveness, an idea which became attached more and more to the whole of the sacrificial system. Propitiation tends to replace reconciliation.

The golden table for the bread of the Presence, i.e., for **the showbread,** belonged to the second temple also, but the custom of placing bread before the deity is at least as old as I Sam. 21:6, and was doubtless an ancient and general custom. The original pagan idea was that of providing food for the deity. Among the Hebrews the rite came to stand for Israel's acknowledgment of her continual dependence upon God. In

51 So was ended all the work that king Solomon made for the house of the LORD. And Solomon brought in the things which David his father had dedicated; *even* the silver, and the gold, and the vessels, did he put among the treasures of the house of the LORD.

8 Then Solomon assembled the elders of Israel, and all the heads of the tribes, the chief of the fathers of the children of Israel, unto king Solomon in Jerusalem, that they might bring up the ark of the covenant of the LORD out of the city of David, which *is* Zion.

2 And all the men of Israel assembled themselves unto king Solomon at the feast

51 Thus all the work that King Solomon did on the house of the LORD was finished. And Solomon brought in the things which David his father had dedicated, the silver, the gold, and the vessels, and stored them in the treasuries of the house of the LORD.

8 Then Solomon assembled the elders of Israel and all the heads of the tribes, the leaders of the fathers' houses of the people of Israel, before King Solomon in Jerusalem, to bring up the ark of the covenant of the LORD out of the city of David, which is Zion. 2 And all the men of Israel assem-

postexilic times the twelve loaves (for the twelve tribes) were arranged in two piles. By the time of the Chronicler the tradition had developed to the extent of ten tables, five on each side of the temple (II Chr. 4:8). The ten **lampstands** are mentioned elsewhere only in Jer. 52:19 and in the Chronicler's parallel (II Chr. 4:7, 20). Presumably the tradition of the ten lampstands, in two groups of five before the inner shrine, is a genuine tradition of the first temple; it gave rise to the other tradition of the ten tables for the showbread. The usual reference is to the seven-branched candlestick, which definitely belonged to the second temple, as is witnessed by the Arch of Titus in Rome.

C. DEDICATION OF THE TEMPLE (8:1-66)

This chapter contains an account of the dedication of the temple by Solomon, but it is very far from being in its original state. Vss. 1-13 have been heavily glossed and are found in the LXX in a much shorter form. Vss. 14-61, which form the speeches and prayers made by the king, are thoroughly Deuteronomic in ideas and phrases. Vss. 14-43 date from *ca.* 610 B.C., and are from the first editor, but vss. 44-61 presuppose the Exile, and must be allocated to the later editor. Vss. 62-66 form the original ending to the narrative of vss. 1-13, but they too have been worked over.

1. THE ARK COMES HOME AT LAST (8:1-13)

Now that the temple is completed, Solomon brings the sacred ark into it. The priests carry the ark into the inner shrine, and when they come out the holy cloud fills the temple. God has taken up his abode in his new home, there to remain forever.

8:1-2. The LXX has these two verses in a shorter and original form: "Then King Solomon assembled all the elders of Israel in Zion to bring up the ark of the covenant of the Lord from the city of David, which is Zion, in the month Ethanim." The phrases **the heads of the tribes** and **the leaders of the fathers' houses** are insertions by an editor under the influence of the Priestly Code, with its love for all proper divisions and categories.

8:1-10. *The Ark of the Covenant.*—It remained to put the keystone in the arch of Solomon's building. What could give strength to all this splendor? It was the ark of the covenant. The Israelites were ever to be kept mindful of ther covenant relationship with the Lord, who had brought them out of Egypt. In their dealings with God he was the party of the first

part. God had given the terms of the covenant on Sinai. The ark containing the Sinaitic code was placed in the Holy of Holies.

Ralph Adams Cram, the eminent American architect, used to say that the house of God should become more beautiful the farther in one goes. So often builders begin with an elaborate exterior or façade and then, as their re-

in the month Ethanim, which *is* the seventh month.

3 And all the elders of Israel came, and the priests took up the ark.

4 And they brought up the ark of the LORD, and the tabernacle of the congregation, and all the holy vessels that *were* in the tabernacle, even those did the priests and the Levites bring up.

5 And king Solomon, and all the congregation of Israel, that were assembled unto him, *were* with him before the ark, sacrificing sheep and oxen, that could not be told nor numbered for multitude.

6 And the priests brought in the ark of the covenant of the LORD unto his place, into the oracle of the house, to the most holy *place, even* under the wings of the cherubim.

bled to King Solomon at the feast in the month Eth'anim, which is the seventh month. **3** And all the elders of Israel came, and the priests took up the ark. **4** And they brought up the ark of the LORD, the tent of meeting, and all the holy vessels that were in the tent; the priests and the Levites brought them up. **5** And King Solomon and all the congregation of Israel, who had assembled before him, were with him before the ark, sacrificing so many sheep and oxen that they could not be counted or numbered. **6** Then the priests brought the ark of the covenant of the LORD to its place, in the inner sanctuary of the house, in the most holy place, underneath the wings of

---

Ethanim is the month of the ever-flowing streams, i.e., when all seasonal streams have dried up in the summer drought. It was the first month of the pre-exilic year, beginning with the harvest moon. The identification of it with the seventh month is due to the postexilic change of calendar.

At the feast in the month Ethanim: This was known as the feast of Ingathering (*'āṣîph*), the great harvest feast which began on the night of the harvest full moon. It marked the end of one agricultural year and the beginning of the next. It was the most important of the three great pilgrimage (Hebrew, חג; Arabic, *ḥajj*) feasts of Canaanite religion, all three of which the Hebrews took over when they entered the land. At each of these feasts the people journeyed to their local or favorite shrine to offer their first fruits. These were barley at the feast of Mazzoth (Unleavened Cakes), wheat at the feast of Shabuoth (Weeks), and the vintage at *'āṣîph* (Ingathering). It was not until the time of the Deuteronomic reforms that all men had to appear at the Jerusalem temple. After the Exile, the feast of Ingathering was split into three parts. The main feast, now called Sukkoth (Booths, Tabernacles), was kept on the full moon, now the fifteenth of Tishri, and other elements gravitated to the first of Tishri (festival of Trumpets) and to the tenth of Tishri (day of Atonement). Even when the Passover became very popular during the last years of the second temple, on account of messianic expectations (cf. Jer. 31:8 LXX), the feast of Tabernacles was still "by far the greatest and holiest feast" (Josephus *Antiquities* VIII. 4. 1). Some scholars have been puzzled by the fact that although the temple was finished in the month of Bul, Solomon did not dedicate it until eleven months later. This need occasion no difficulty. He celebrated the opening at the New Year feast. "In Mesopotamia the New Year's festival appears as the confluence of every current of religious thought" (Henri Frankfort, *Kingship and the Gods* [Chicago: University of Chicago Press, 1948], p. 313). What was true of Mesopotamia was probably true of Palestine. He dedicated the temple not when he would, but when he must. This was the high festival of the whole year, and there was no other proper time for such a pre-eminent occasion.

3-4. The LXX says, "The priests carried up the ark and the tent of meeting and the holy vessels which were in the tent of meeting." If these phrases are taken out of the M.T. we get, "And all the elders of Israel brought up the ark of the Lord," which looks very like the original, with the reading of the LXX as an addition to express the postexilic point of view, according to which only the priests might carry the ark. The phrase at the end of vs. 4, **the priests and the Levites brought them up** (i.e., the holy

7 For the cherubim spread forth *their* two wings over the place of the ark, and the cherubim covered the ark and the staves thereof above.

8 And they drew out the staves, that the ends of the staves were seen out in the holy *place* before the oracle, and they were not seen without: and there they are unto this day.

9 *There was* nothing in the ark save the two tables of stone, which Moses put there at Horeb, when the LORD made *a covenant* with the children of Israel, when they came out of the land of Egypt.

10 And it came to pass, when the priests were come out of the holy *place,* that the cloud filled the house of the LORD,

11 So that the priests could not stand to minister because of the cloud: for the glory of the LORD had filled the house of the LORD.

the cherubim. 7 For the cherubim spread out their wings over the place of the ark, so that the cherubim made a covering above the ark and its poles. 8 And the poles were so long that the ends of the poles were seen from the holy place before the inner sanctuary; but they could not be seen from outside; and they are there to this day. 9 There was nothing in the ark except the two tables of stone which Moses put there at Horeb, where the LORD made a covenant with the people of Israel, when they came out of the land of Egypt. 10 And when the priests came out of the holy place, a cloud filled the house of the LORD, 11 so that the priests could not stand to minister because of the cloud; for the glory of the LORD filled the house of the LORD.

---

vessels), is a typical Priestly Code addition. **The priests and the Levites** is a phrase belonging to the time of the latest development of the priesthood. The true Priestly Code phrase for the priests is "the priests, the sons of Aaron"; in Deuteronomy the phrase is "the priests, the Levites." In the earliest days of the settlement in Canaan any man could be a priest if he was properly consecrated, but it was better to have a Levite (Judg. 17–18). Up to the time of the reforms under King Josiah under Deuteronomic influence (621 B.C.), the general situation was: Levites at the southern shrines generally, but Zadokites at Jerusalem; non-Levitical priests at the northern shrines generally, but the sons of Moses at Dan in the far north (Judg. 18:30), and probably the sons of Aaron at Bethel. Josiah attempted to bring all the Levite priests to share in the service of the Jerusalem altar, but the Zadokites resisted (II Kings 23:9), with the result that the Levites in the end had to be content with the inferior offices in the temple. After the Exile the only legitimate priests were known as "the sons of Aaron," even though two thirds of them were Zadokites. The distinction between the priests and the Levites was rigidly maintained, and it was not until the last days of Herod's temple, in the time of Herod Agrippa II, that the Levites were permitted to wear the white robes which distinguished the priesthood (N. H. Snaith, "Worship," in *Record and Revelation,* ed. H. Wheeler Robinson [Oxford: Clarendon Press, 1938], pp. 263-74).

10-11. The **cloud** was that which was believed to shroud the presence of God. In ancient days the presence of the Lord had been manifested in the pillar of cloud which

---

sources become limited, cheapen the interior. Cram's contention was that the genuineness of a church is symbolized by making the interior richer than the exterior. Solomon was therefore religiously correct in making the ark the focal point of the temple. In it was the pledge of the Lord's presence with them and the purpose of their building for him.

11. *The Glory of the Lord.*—The great day of dedication had come. The priests brought the ark of the covenant to its place in the inner shrine of the house. When the carriers of the ark **came out of the holy place, a cloud filled**

the house of the LORD, so that the priests could not stand to minister because of the cloud; for the glory of the LORD filled the house of the LORD.

How a modern newsman would have reported the event we cannot say. Smoke as the symbol of the divine presence is recorded by Isaiah in his vision (Isa. 6:4). The Lord made his appearance to Ezekiel accompanied by fire (Ezek. 1:27). But let not puzzlement over the symbolism distract us from the central fact that the worshipers felt the glory of the Lord filling the temple. G. A. Johnston Ross used to tell his

12 ¶ Then spake Solomon, The LORD said that he would dwell in the thick darkness.	12 Then Solomon said, "The LORD has set the sun in the heavens, but[z] has said that he would dwell in thick darkness.

[z] Gk: Heb lacks *has set the sun in the heavens, but*

protected the marching Israelites (Exod. 14:19-20), or in the cloud which came down and remained by the door of the tent when God spoke with Moses (Exod. 33:9). Similar occasions are the smoke which filled the temple at the time of Isaiah's vision (Isa. 6:4) and the luminous cloud of the Transfiguration (Mark 9:7). At other times the presence of the Deity is manifested in a brightness of burning fire. This is to be noted in the story of the bush (Exod. 3:2), the fire which surrounded the figure in Ezekiel's vision (Ezek. 1:27), and the Shekinah of the rabbis. The luminous haze is generally supposed to have its origin in the brightness which marks the center of the thunderstorm. Allied with this theme is the variant picture of the God that is hidden in darkness because of the awful dread of his majesty (cf. vs. 12).

12-13. The original dedication by Solomon was in the form of an ancient song which the LXX says was taken from the Book of Jashar ("upright"), the early saga of Israel's wars from Egypt to Canaan (Josh. 10:13; II Sam. 1:18). The first half of the first line is missing in the M.T., but has been supplied in the RSV from the LXX.

In thick darkness (RSV): **In the thick darkness** (KJV) is a more accurate translation of the M.T. The reference is not to thick darkness generally but to the particular thick darkness, the heavy cloud (Hebrew, *ʿarāphel*) in which God dwells (Exod. 20:18; Deut. 4:11; etc.). The ark, which was the visible sign of the Lord's presence in the midst of his people, was placed in the shrine (*debhîr*) in complete darkness, so that Solomon did actually build a place of thick, impenetrable darkness in which God could, according to the ideas of the time, happily dwell.

Solomon declares that he has built a house in which the Lord will be able to dwell forever. This verse has received additional meaning from material found at Ras Shamra (the ancient Ugarit). The particular texts involved are V AB (see Charles Virolleaud,

students at Union Theological Seminary that the primary aim of every religious service is to help the worshiper to become conscious of the presence of God. Religious instruction and moral exhortation fall short of the goal, which is to feel that the Lord is near. The purpose of the meetinghouse is to meet God.

The glory of the LORD is an expression which has been carried in our ecclesiastical vocabularies so long that, like a coin worn smooth, it has lost its identification marks. We tend to avoid its use in realistic religious discussion because the word "glory" is regarded by most of us as an emotional word, empty of thought content. At the camp meetings which used to be—and in some areas still are—held each summer, in the heat of the revivalism persons would often break out with shouts of "Glory" or "Hallelujah." Such effervescent expressions could hardly be analyzed. But the fact that a feeling is unanalyzable is not sufficient reason to discard it. After James Russell Lowell heard Ralph Waldo Emerson deliver the Phi Beta Kappa address at Harvard in 1867, he wrote: "Emerson's oration . . . began nowhere

and ended everywhere, and yet, as always with that divine man, it left you feeling that something beautiful had passed that way—something more beautiful than anything else, like the rising and setting of stars." [6] So is it with the glory of God. His majesty "disturbs us with the joy of elevated thoughts"; his mercy starts songs of gratitude singing in the back of our minds; his love lifts us out of our littleness; our feelings outrun our logic; and our hearts leap up to join the angelic chorus, shouting, "Glory to God in the highest."

A little boy, bubbling with questions, looked up at his grandfather and asked, "What is the wind?" The grandparent replied, "I cannot tell you, my lad, what the wind is, but I know how to hoist a sail." **The glory of the LORD** defies adequate definition, but no minister who has not felt it, and cannot help others feel it, will move a congregation in the right direction.

12-21. The Fruit of Frustration.—Why David was denied the privilege of building the temple of his dreams has been the subject of much

[6] *Letters of James Russell Lowell*, ed. Charles Eliot Norton (New York: Harper & Bros., 1894), I, 393.

13 I have surely built thee a house to dwell in, a settled place for thee to abide in for ever.	13 I have built thee an exalted house, a place for thee to dwell in for ever."

La déesse 'Anat [Paris: Paul Geuthner, 1938; "Mission de Ras Shamra"]; also W. F. Albright, "Recent Progress in North-Canaanite Research," *Bulletin of the American Schools of Oriental Research,* No. 70 [1938], pp. 18-24) and II AB (Virolleaud, "Un nouveau chant du poème d'Aleïn Baal," *Syria,* XIII [1932], 113-63; also Albright, "New Light on Early Canaanite Language and Literature," and "More Light on the Canaanite Epic of Aleyân Baal and Môt," *Bulletin of American Schools of Oriental Research,* No. 46 [1932], pp. 15-20; No. 50 [1933], pp. 13-20; Cyrus H. Gordon, *Ugaritic Literature* [Roma: Pontificium Institutum Biblicum, 1949], pp. 28-38). Both these texts, particularly the first, have to do with the building of a house for Baal. The text II AB opens with a lament that Baal has no temple, and both texts have to do with the building of this temple. There is difference of opinion as to the significance of the Ugaritic parallels. Ivan Engnell (*Studies in Divine Kingship in the Ancient Near East* [Uppsala: Almqvist & Wiksells, 1943], p. 114) connects the Ras Shamra texts with the death and resurrection of the god, thus bringing them into line with his general theories of divine kingship and fertility cults. On the other hand Julian Obermann (*Ugaritic Mythology* [New Haven: Yale University Press, 1948], pp. 83-87) thinks that the texts have to do with the changing of the supreme authority over the pantheon from El to Baal. His view is that other Ras Shamra texts have this same motive, e.g., VI AB and the new fragment of III AB published by Virolleaud (*ibid.,* p. 15; Virolleaud, "Fragments mythologiques de Ras-Shamra," *Syria,* XXIV [1944], 1-12). Possibly both theories are right, and the triumph of Baal comes to be the story of an annual liturgy, but the texts clearly state that the building of the house on earth for Baal is a counterpart to Baal's establishment with authority in the Mountain of the Gods.

> Ba'al ascends the Heights of the North,
> Goes up to his house (V AB, A, ll. 21-22).

Further, when Baal sits enthroned in his house, he says:

> I have now been made king,
> I have been brought as king,
> The earth of my realm has rest (II AB, col. 7, ll. 43-44).

Then

> Thou shalt take thy eternal kingdom,
> Thy dominion for generation after generation (III AB, A, 12-13).

So far as Solomon's building of the temple in Jerusalem is concerned, the inference from the Ras Shamra texts is that he is establishing the Lord as supreme god of all,

discussion. The record here does not reveal the reason but does commend the dream. Solomon in his address at the dedication declared: "The LORD said to David my father, 'Whereas it was in your heart to build a house for my name, you did well that it was in your heart; nevertheless you shall not build the house, but your son who shall be born to you shall build the house for my name.'"

Roughly speaking, David had four great aims in his royal career. He desired to win his na-tion's wars, to secure its independence, to build its capital city, and to crown that capital with a fitting temple to Yahweh. May it not be that he did better the first three things because there was a fourth which was beyond his grasp? It sometimes seems to be a fact that our best work is done when we are driven by the urge to accomplish the apparently insuperable. At the time of the preparations for Queen Victoria's second jubilee, Rudyard Kipling promised the *Times* a poem for that great event. He could

14 And the king turned his face about, and blessed all the congregation of Israel: and all the congregation of Israel stood;

15 And he said, Blessed *be* the LORD God of Israel, which spake with his mouth unto David my father, and hath with his hand fulfilled *it*, saying,

14 Then the king faced about, and blessed all the assembly of Israel, while all the assembly of Israel stood. 15 And he said, "Blessed be the LORD, the God of Israel, who with his hand has fulfilled what he promised with his mouth to David my

---

not only in an earthly house, but also in the great Mountain of the North, the home of the gods. He is proclaiming, in fact, that the Lord alone is lord of heaven and earth, making for him **an exalted house, a place for** [him] **to dwell in for ever,** and this not only on earth, but also in some sense in the "eternal" home of the Deity.

The establishment of Jerusalem alone as the one abode on earth for the Lord created difficulties when the fate of exile befell the people. How could they worship their God if Jerusalem was the only place where he could be worshiped, when they were far away in Babylon? The answer was provided by Ezekiel, who saw in a vision that the throne of God was not fixed and firm, immovable, as Isaiah had seen it (Isa. 6), but that it was a chariot, both wheeled and winged, the wheels being wheels within wheels so that they could run north and south, east and west, and the wings so that no distance or intervening mountain could act as barrier. This chariot of the Lord appears to his people in exile (Ezek. 1), since wherever God's people are and need him, there he is to be found. God's love for his house on Mount Zion is shown in the stages by which he leaves his home which Solomon had built, as though he could scarce prevail upon himself to depart from it (Ezek. 10:4 [as far as the threshold]; 10:19 [as far as the east gate of the house]; 11:23 [as far as the Mount of Olives to the east of the city]), till at last he arrives in Babylon by the river Chebar among the captives (1:1; 10:20).

2. SOLOMON'S SPEECH TO THE PEOPLE (8:14-21)

The king tells the people that at first God chose no city for his temple, but chose David to rule the people. David was minded to build a temple for God, but it was God's will and promise that David's son should build such a house of God. This speech and the prayer which follows it give the full Deuteronomic interpretation and expansion

---

write nothing that he liked. The *Times* sent letters, then telegrams, asking for the promised poem. So Kipling shut himself in his room, searched through his notes, found only one phrase he liked, "Lest we forget." Around those words he composed the "Recessional." "That poem," he said, "gave me more trouble than anything I ever wrote." [7]

The lure of the rock that is too high for us enables us to do better the tasks on our reachable level. When we are tempted toward impossible perfections we are helped to perfect the possible. "Be ye therefore perfect, even as your Father which is in heaven is perfect" (Matt. 5:48). This counsel of the Christ is pregnant with practical power—a truth which much of our popular and so-called "practical" preaching fails to grasp. In trying to make Christianity appealing we too often pick out the parts of Christ's gospel which seem sensible to the hardheaded businessman; we seek to show

how "practical" are the principles of Jesus in promoting sales, winning friends, and influencing people. In thus lowering the Master of life to a servant of what we call successful living, we lose "the power from on high." To be sure, there are perfectionists who are so impatient with imperfect instruments and intermediate steps that they become stalled in futility. But the failures of Christian perfectionists are few in comparison with the lowered standards of the gospel revisionists.

All great living is inspired by the vista of the unattained. When Justice Oliver Wendell Holmes reached his ninetieth birthday, rich in honors, still in possession of life's enjoyments, he received many tributes. Of him Chief Justice Charles Evans Hughes said that he had attained the most beautiful and rarest thing in the world, a complete life. Yet despite the seeming completeness of such a well-rounded life, Justice Holmes a year later wrote a letter to the Federal Bar Association in which he said: "Life seems to me like a Japanese picture which our imagi-

[7] Cecil Charles, *Rudyard Kipling: His Life and Works* (London: J. Hewetson & Son, 1912), pp. 43-45.

16 Since the day that I brought forth my people Israel out of Egypt, I chose no city out of all the tribes of Israel to build a house, that my name might be therein; but I chose David to be over my people Israel.

17 And it was in the heart of David my father to build a house for the name of the LORD God of Israel.

18 And the LORD said unto David my father, Whereas it was in thine heart to build a house unto my name, thou didst well that it was in thine heart.

19 Nevertheless thou shalt not build the house; but thy son that shall come forth out of thy loins, he shall build the house unto my name.

20 And the LORD hath performed his word that he spake, and I am risen up in the room of David my father, and sit on the throne of Israel, as the LORD promised, and have built a house for the name of the LORD God of Israel.

21 And I have set there a place for the ark, wherein is the covenant of the LORD, which he made with our fathers, when he brought them out of the land of Egypt.

father, saying, 16 'Since the day that I brought my people Israel out of Egypt, I chose no city in all the tribes of Israel in which to build a house, that my name might be there; but I chose David to be over my people Israel.' 17 Now it was in the heart of David my father to build a house for the name of the LORD, the God of Israel. 18 But the LORD said to David my father, 'Whereas it was in your heart to build a house for my name, you did well that it was in your heart; 19 nevertheless you shall not build the house, but your son who shall be born to you shall build the house for my name.' 20 Now the LORD has fulfilled his promise which he made; for I have risen in the place of David my father, and sit on the throne of Israel, as the LORD promised, and I have built the house for the name of the LORD, the God of Israel. 21 And there I have provided a place for the ark, in which is the covenant of the LORD which he made with our fathers, when he brought them out of the land of Egypt."

---

of II Sam. 7. Why has not David built a temple? The reason there given is that God prefers the ancient tent with its curtains (II Sam. 7:6-7), but here the explanation is that God prefers to wait until he has chosen Jerusalem (so more precisely LXX in vs. 16 and in the parallel II Chr. 6:6) and David to rule over Israel.

16. The phrase **my name** is a reverent circumlocution for "I" (of God). This custom developed steadily through the centuries until in N.T. times we find the Palestinian Gospel using the phrase "the kingdom of heaven" (Matt. 5:3), whereas the Greek-speaking Luke has "the kingdom of God." Other similar substitutions are the Holy One, the Place, and always in the M.T. the Lord for the divine Name.

21. According to vs. 9, "There was nothing in the ark except the two tables of stone which Moses put there at Horeb," to which the LXX adds "the tables of the covenant . . . which the Lord made with the sons of Israel when they went forth out

---

nation does not allow to end with the margin. We aim at the infinite and when our arrow falls to earth it is in flames." [8]

However long or full a life may be, it faces frustration at some points. When we set out seriously to challenge the things that thwart us, and when we summon the aid of "him that is able to do exceeding abundantly above all that we ask or think, according to the power that worketh in us" (Eph. 3:20), it is almost impossible to set a limit to what we can do. The testimony of experience attests the number of those heroic personalities who refused to sur-

[8] Francis Biddle, *Mr. Justice Holmes* (New York: Charles Scribner's Sons, 1942), p. 200.

render to the seemingly inevitable and as a result achieved the seemingly incredible. One such lies buried in an English churchyard and the headstone bears this epitaph, "She hath done what she couldn't." Nevertheless, like David, the best of persons must leave some things undone. Of them it is said, "These all died in faith, not having received the promises" (Heb. 11:13). Yet those who go on working with God in faith come to accept some of their frustrations not only with fortitude but even with gratitude, for what seems to be frustration often serves as a time lock on life's great treasure vault. On the small safe in a man's office may be a combination lock which he can open

22 ¶ And Solomon stood before the altar of the Lord in the presence of all the congregation of Israel, and spread forth his hands toward heaven:

22 Then Solomon stood before the altar of the Lord in the presence of all the assembly of Israel, and spread forth his hands

---

of the land of Egypt." The reference therefore is to the tables of stone. The later tradition (Exod. 16:33; Num. 17:10; Heb. 9:4) is that the ark also contained "a golden urn holding the manna, and Aaron's rod that budded."

3. Solomon's Prayer (8:22-53)

Solomon first offers thanks that God has kept the covenant with David and raised up an heir of David to rule in his place (vss. 23-24). He prays that the promise may be confirmed forever of the establishment of David's line conditional upon the fulfillment of the Deuteronomic way of life (vss. 25-26). Next Solomon prays that the temple may always be the place to which Israel may turn for forgiveness (vss. 27-30). The remainder of the prayer consists of particular instances of intercession which may arise, dealings between man and man (vss. 31-32), defeat in battle (vss. 33-34), drought (vss. 35-36), famine and plagues of every kind (vss. 37-40). Then there comes a plea for the foreigner, that his prayer also may be heard and answered (vss. 41-43), and this is followed by a prayer for victory in war (vss. 44-45). The concluding section presupposes the Exile and therefore presumably is an addition by the exilic editor of *ca.* 550 B.C., unless, as is perhaps more likely, it presupposes the Diaspora rather than the Babylonian exile, and must therefore be placed at a much later date.

22. Solomon stood . . . and spread forth his hands toward heaven: This is the attitude adopted universally in olden time for prayer (cf. Exod. 9:29; II Macc. 3:20).

---

at any time, but down in the large city banks the vaults are equipped with time locks which open only when the appointed time has arrived. Similarly in life, we have little treasure chests of desire from which we can get what we want when we want it. But for opening the great, deep, lasting satisfactions of life, there are time locks which God has set to go off in his own good time. Often when we have to wait for God's hour of opening we feel frustrated, we complain that our prayers are not answered, that if there is a God he is no friend of ours. Must we not confess that many times if we had got what we wanted it would have proved a curse rather than a blessing? What looks like defeat may prove only a divine delay, designed for our good.

. Furthermore, if our lives and purposes are headed toward great ends they outrun the span of a single generation. The frustration of the parents may prove the opportunity of the children. So it was in the case of David. And so runs the perfecting principle: "These all, having obtained a good report through faith, received not the promise: God having provided some better thing for us, that they without us should not be made perfect" (Heb. 11:39-40). When power is pointed toward a loving and righteous purpose it is like a stream headed for the sea. It may be dammed up or diverted, but sooner or later it reaches water level. Christlike power

may be thwarted and crucified, but it is headed Godward and eventually it gets home.

22-26. *Enlarging Religious Understanding.*— Solomon's prayer at the dedication of the temple reveals a stage in the growing conception of God. **O Lord, God of Israel, there is no God like thee, in heaven above or on earth beneath, keeping covenant and showing steadfast love to thy servants who walk before thee with all their heart.** Yahweh is here regarded as more than merely one of the tribal deities, having claims upon Israel equivalent to those of other gods upon their chosen clans (Judg. 11:24). In this second stage of revelation Yahweh is seen as superior to all other gods.

Solomon's concept of God is similar to that voiced on what might be called "Israel's V-E Day," when a song was sung to commemorate the triumph over the pursuing Egyptians at the Red Sea. "I will sing unto the Lord, for he hath triumphed gloriously: the horse and his rider hath he thrown into the sea. . . . Thy right hand, O Lord, is become glorious in power. . . . Who is like unto thee, O Lord, among the gods?" (Exod. 15:1, 6, 11.) The Israelites saw their victories under Moses and David as the work of Yahweh. He was their patron, and they were his people. He had entered into covenant relations with them whereby he would fight for them if they would be faithful to him. They were to show their loyalty to him by having no

23 And he said, LORD God of Israel, *there is* no God like thee, in heaven above, or on earth beneath, who keepest covenant and mercy with thy servants that walk before thee with all their heart:

24 Who hast kept with thy servant David my father that thou promisedst him: thou spakest also with thy mouth, and hast fulfilled *it* with thine hand, as *it is* this day.

toward heaven; 23 and said, "O LORD, God of Israel, there is no God like thee, in heaven above or on earth beneath, keeping covenant and showing steadfast love to thy servants who walk before thee with all their heart; 24 who hast kept with thy servant David my father what thou didst declare to him; yea, thou didst speak with thy mouth, and with thy hand hast fulfilled it this day.

---

23. The statement **there is no God like thee** marks a definite stage in the development of monotheism, i.e., the belief that there is but one God and none other. The belief of the early days of the occupation of Palestine is reflected in Judg. 11:24, where Chemosh of Moab is regarded as having rights over Moab similar to those which the Lord had over Israel. The next stage is seen in Exod. 15:11; Deut. 3:24; and here, where the claim is that there is no god to be compared with the God of Israel, neither in the heavens above nor on the earth beneath. The statement is that the Lord is unique among the gods. It is not denied that there are other gods. This denial is found explicitly in the writings of the Exile, especially in Isa. 40–55; e.g., Isa. 44:6; 46:9, and frequently in ch. 45 (Millar Burrows, *An Outline of Biblical Theology* [Philadelphia: Westminster Press, 1946], pp. 54-60; A. B. Davidson, *The Theology of the Old Testament* [New York: Charles Scribner's Sons, 1931], pp. 58-67) .

The rendering **who keepest covenant and mercy** is preferable to **keeping covenant and showing steadfast love.** The word translated **mercy, steadfast love** is *ḥeṣedh,* and it is used here particularly and definitely of God's faithfulness in his covenant with Israel. The insertion of **showing** in particular tends to make the phrase suggest general affability, especially when it is allied with the words **steadfast love.** Anything that tends toward this identification is to be deprecated. This matter is important because in this word *ḥeṣedh* we have the roots of the N.T. doctrine of grace. The grace of God is not general benevolence showered upon all and sundry, but that particular care which Christians know. It is true that God "maketh his sun to rise on the evil and on the good, and sendeth rain on the just and on the unjust" (Matt. 5:45) . This is his providence, and all creatures live by it, whether they are conscious of it or not. In the case of man, they live by it even when they deny his existence. But grace is concerned with that consciousness of being right with God which none can know except those who have definitely been chosen to love him with all the heart and to do his will. They then become conscious of a personal relationship with God, which on God's part involves an utter self-giving, arising out of a love that is completely and absolutely unselfish. This is the love that is manifested on the Cross, and when we speak of "the grace of our Lord Jesus Christ" we mean this utter self-giving, not merely that general providence which is the basis of any life at all on this earth. Providence is concerned with ordinary physical life.

---

other gods before him, by obeying his laws and offering their sacrifices. Their relationship to him was a neat and simple covenant, attested by special and visible providences.

Life, however, is too complex to leave people long content with such a naïve concept. Religious faith cannot rest safely on special providences and spectacular interventions. When British troops were trapped at Dunkerque in 1940 and escaped across the channel, many persons, even preachers, pointed to the calmness of the water at that particular time as proof of God's intervention on behalf of the English

against the German aggressors. But shortly afterward two large British battleships were sunk off Singapore by some Japanese planes which swept out of a concealing cloud bank. If we attribute the calmness of the channel to God's special concern for the English forces, what are we to say about the clouds at Singapore?

The habit of looking for divine favor in special good fortune, and of seeing God's displeasure in our defeats, leads to confusion and doubt. Hence, as the Hebrew people grew more mature, they rose to a higher conception of the divine relationship. The drama of Job shattered

25 Therefore now, LORD God of Israel, keep with thy servant David my father that thou promisedst him, saying, There shall not fail thee a man in my sight to sit on the throne of Israel; so that thy children take heed to their way, that they walk before me as thou hast walked before me.

26 And now, O God of Israel, let thy word, I pray thee, be verified, which thou spakest unto thy servant David my father.

27 But will God indeed dwell on the earth? behold, the heaven and heaven of heavens cannot contain thee; how much less this house that I have builded?

25 Now therefore, O LORD, God of Israel, keep with thy servant David my father what thou hast promised him, saying, 'There shall never fail you a man before me to sit upon the throne of Israel, if only your sons take heed to their way, to walk before me as you have walked before me.' 26 Now therefore, O God of Israel, let thy word be confirmed, which thou hast spoken to thy servant David my father.

27 "But will God indeed dwell on the earth? Behold, heaven and the highest heaven cannot contain thee; how much less

Grace is concerned with that life which is of the spirit. Providence is concerned with all who are "born of the flesh," but grace with all who are "born of the Spirit" (John 3:6). The difference comes at the point when a man enters a new relationship with God. In the O.T. this relationship was the covenant first sealed at Sinai, and the proper relationship within that covenant is described as ḥeṣedh. On God's part it involved a faithfulness that nothing can destroy, and mercy and forgiveness which seemed always to be necessary because of Israel's continued apostasy. In Christ "the middle wall of partition" is broken down, and the condition of being within the covenant is no longer one of race or of the fulfillment of the law. It is primarily of faith, complete and utter trust, and secondarily of the implementation of that faith by those good works which are the outcome of that faith in God.

25. The condition of the continued favor of God is made quite plain. The sons of David must **take heed to their way,** to walk as David walked. Here we get the idealizing of David into the perfect Deuteronomic king; cf. the standard in the Deuteronomic formula whereby the kings of Judah are judged (15:11).

27. Cf. this verse with vss. 12-13. In that ancient couplet we have little more than the appreciation of the *mysterium tremendum* of the numinous, with its elements of awfulness, overpoweringness, and energy or urgency (Rudolph Otto, *The Idea of the*

the neat little patterns of special providence. The voice out of the whirlwind summoned the stricken Job to consider the vastness of a creation in which the faithfulness of the Lord is to be seen in his infinite and creative providence rather than in his special interventions. Job discovers that the Lord is not a mere Yahweh, greater than all other gods in heaven or on earth, but the Lord of heaven and earth. And the more deeply the Hebrew people lived their way into the power of God, the more confident they became of a divine purpose running through all creation. God's ways are higher than man's ways, as the heavens are high above the earth; but the great Hebrew prophets who lived on the moral mountaintops became convinced that they could trace the divine directions. With eyes undimmed by defeat but washed bright by tears of exile, a prophet confidently asserts, "Behold, the Lord GOD will come with strong hand, and his arm shall rule for him" (Isa. 40:10). To God "the nations are as a drop of a

bucket, and are counted as the small dust of the balance: behold, he taketh up the isles as a very little thing" (Isa. 40:15).

The insight into God's nature continues to grow. After Isaiah declares that the Lord's mighty arm shall be revealed in the ruling of the nations, he immediately asserts: "He shall feed his flock like a shepherd: he shall gather the lambs with his arm, and carry them in his bosom, and shall gently lead those that are with young" (Isa. 40:11). Combined with the majesty and power of God are tenderness and grace. The more mature men become the more clearly they recognize the gentleness of true gianthood. When the Hebrew prophetic mind rose to this conception of God it was being prepared for the supreme revelation in Christ, for it could understand the majesty of power which can fit the measurement of a manger.

27-29. *The Trysting Place of the Spirit.*—At first reading Solomon's words seem to negate the purpose of building the temple. They seem to

28 Yet have thou respect unto the prayer of thy servant, and to his supplication, O LORD my God, to hearken unto the cry and to the prayer, which thy servant prayeth before thee to-day:

this house which I have built! 28 Yet have regard to the prayer of thy servant and to his supplication, O LORD my God, hearkening to the cry and to the prayer which thy

---

Holy, tr. J. W. Harvey [London: Oxford University Press, 1923], pp. 5-30). Here, in vs. 27, we have a conception of God approximating to the idea of omnipresence, a god who is above the limitations of nature—so great that the whole heavens are too small to be his dwelling place. The translation **the highest heaven** is an excellent rendering of the Hebrew, which is, lit., the **heaven of heavens.** This construction is a Hebrew idiom used to express that which is superlative to an exceptional degree, e.g., "the most holy place" (vs. 6), or "the most excellent song of all" (lit., "the song of songs"); and especially Gen. 9:25, where the original is "servant of servants," and the meaning "lowest of servants" (E. F. Kautzsch, ed., *Gesenius' Hebrew Grammar,* tr. A. E. Cowley [2nd English ed.; Oxford: The Clarendon Press, 1910], p. 431, sec. 133 *i*). The actual phrase **heaven of heavens** is here a reminiscence of Deut. 10:14 and is found elsewhere five times only, including the Chronicler's parallel (II Chr. 6:18).

---

parallel the position of those numerous persons who claim to find God better outside the church. **But will God indeed dwell on the earth? Behold, heaven and the highest heaven cannot contain thee; how much less this house which I have built!** Why try to coop the omnipresent God in the cubicles of a man-made shrine, and why hamper the Holy Spirit with parish organizations? Verily, God is too great for spatial limitation. With Wordsworth, we feel his presence as of one

Whose dwelling is the light of setting suns,
And the round ocean and the living air,
And the blue sky, and in the mind of man;
A motion and a spirit, that impels
All thinking things, all objects of all thought,
And rolls through all things.[9]

Jesus himself sought to correct the conceptions which limited the worship of God to institutions and buildings. "God is a Spirit: and they that worship him must worship him in spirit and in truth" (John 4:24).

Yet it is the very illimitableness of God which makes shrines of worship necessary. The infinite must be brought within reach of man's finite mind. Our souls need trysting places with the eternal and the invisible. Solomon's prayer reveals this fact: **That thy eyes may be open night and day toward this house, the place of which thou hast said, "My name shall be there," that thou mayest hearken to the prayer which thy servant offers toward this place.** Spirit with spirit can meet, but their meeting is aided by symbols and places. Our spirits are so dependent on our senses for impression that visual aids are of value if, like Moses, we are

to endure "as seeing him who is invisible" (Heb. 11:27). And unless our spirits find expression through verbal vehicles, the commerce of the soul is halted. A husband may love and respect his wife, but if he never gives voice or visibility to his affection, the romance does not remain. Words without love become sounding brass and tinkling cymbal; but love without words can lose its music too. Some ritual of affection is needed to keep love alive between persons, and also between man and God. We are affected by the power of suggestion, sympathy, and imitation. The sight of others praising God strengthens our feeling that God is praiseworthy. The architectural symbols with their eloquent silence, the rhythmic surge of religious music, the historic ritual of the church reminding us that a great procession of persons like ourselves has walked the same paths of experience, the sermon which at least stirs the conscience if it does not always feed the mind—all these combine to lift our spirits Godward. A worshiping soul in the house of God is lifted as a ship is lifted in the locks of a canal. When one sluice gate of the mind is closed on things secular and another is opened on things invisible and eternal, then the influences of symbol and ritual, of prayer and message, become the "means of grace," flowing under the human spirit and lifting it to a higher level whence it sails away, better able to carry its cargo of personal and public responsibilities.

To be sure, this lifting power of spiritual communion may be felt by souls in solitude. And it may often seem that one can come closer to God in the secrecy of his closet or under the spell of nature's loveliness than in a church with its crowd and commotion. But Evelyn

[9] "Lines Composed a Few Miles Above Tintern Abbey."

29 That thine eyes may be open toward this house night and day, *even* toward the place of which thou hast said, My name shall be there: that thou mayest hearken unto the prayer which thy servant shall make toward this place.

30 And hearken thou to the supplication of thy servant, and of thy people Israel, when they shall pray toward this place: and hear thou in heaven thy dwelling place: and when thou hearest, forgive.

servant prays before thee this day; 29 that thy eyes may be open night and day toward this house, the place of which thou hast said, 'My name shall be there,' that thou mayest hearken to the prayer which thy servant offers toward this place. 30 And hearken thou to the supplication of thy servant and of thy people Israel, when they pray toward this place; yea, hear thou in heaven thy dwelling place; and when thou hearest, forgive.

---

29. My name shall be there: It is most probable that we have here something more than the reverent circumlocution of vs. 16. The connection of "the Name" with the Jerusalem sanctuary is especially characteristic of Deuteronomy (cf. 12:5; etc.). It is a development of the ancient idea that the mention of the true name has in itself effective power. This idea is very clear in Gen. 32:29, and to a lesser extent in Judg. 13:6. The knowledge of the Name would have given power to a mortal over the divine one. The idea of hiding the real name of a person is common among primitive peoples the world over (Frazer, *Folk-lore in the O.T.*, III, 170-72, 191, etc.; also E. F. Kautzsch, "Religion of Israel," in James Hastings, ed., *A Dictionary of the Bible* [New York: Charles Scribner's Sons, 1904], Extra Vol., p. 640), because of the power which can then be exercised over that person when the name is known and spoken. The magical spells of N.T. times consisted largely in the rapid recitation of a number of powerful names until the most effective name caused the expulsion of the demon. When the Deuteronomists said that

---

Underhill in her books reminds us that in the long run the mystical power of common worship has proved more effective than that of private devotion. David and Solomon had a sure sense of spiritual direction in building the temple as the central trysting place, for unless men worship together they tend to neglect their private devotions. The devout soul's direct experience of God is like the artist's intense appreciation of beauty or the poet's inspired glimpse of truth. But these lovely flashes of luminous insight do not give a sufficiently steady light to live by, any more than flashes of lightning furnish adequate light for the motorist to drive by. Left to ourselves, our moods fluctuate. There come hours of exultant faith wherein we feel convinced of God's goodness. There come moments of mystic insight when the atmosphere clears and the very foothills of heaven are visible. But we also have low moods which send us to the basements of our natures. We have cynical hours when we impugn the motives of others and lose faith in noble causes. These high and low tides of the spirit come to us, and in the handling of them we need the help of others. Knowing that Christianity's new converts from Judaism would feel this ebb and flow of religious enthusiasm, the writer of the Epistle to the Hebrews exhorts them: "Let us hold fast the profession of our faith without wavering; . . . and let us consider one another to provoke unto love and to good

works; not forsaking the assembling of ourselves together" (Heb. 10:23-25). The presence of fellow seekers helps to make God more real, not only because we catch the contagion of their faith but also because we must discipline ourselves to their differences. One value of going to church is that we worship with people whom we may not naturally like and in ways which may not be entirely congenial. A good spiritual exercise is to do some unpleasant duty each day just to stretch one's soul; for if we do only what we like to do, and mingle only with the people we like to meet, our range of pleasures shortens and our circle of friends shrinks.

God is a Spirit, and when we ascend to the plane of pure spirit our communion with the heavenly Father will need no material aids. In his vision of the new Jerusalem, John "saw no temple therein: for the Lord God Almighty and the Lamb are the temple of it" (Rev. 21:22). But the Jerusalem of Solomon's day needed a temple, for man's finite nature must have its trysting places with the Infinite.

30, 34, 36, 39, 50. *The Strands of Forgiveness.*
—The recurring motif of Solomon's prayer is **when thou hearest, forgive.** As a study in eloquent and effective praying, the repetition of this plea is worthy of note.

Sir Oliver Lodge said that modern man is too busy to think about the forgiveness of sin. However we bright little modern folk may dull

31 ¶ If any man trespass against his neighbor, and an oath be laid upon him to cause him to swear, and the oath come before thine altar in this house:

32 Then hear thou in heaven, and do, and judge thy servants, condemning the wicked, to bring his way upon his head; and justifying the righteous, to give him according to his righteousness.

33 ¶ When thy people Israel be smitten down before the enemy, because they have sinned against thee, and shall turn again to thee, and confess thy name, and pray, and make supplication unto thee in this house:

34 Then hear thou in heaven, and forgive the sin of thy people Israel, and bring them again unto the land which thou gavest unto their fathers.

31 "If a man sins against his neighbor and is made to take an oath, and comes and swears his oath before thine altar in this house, 32 then hear thou in heaven, and act, and judge thy servants, condemning the guilty by bringing his conduct upon his own head, and vindicating the righteous by rewarding him according to his righteousness.

33 "When thy people Israel are defeated before the enemy because they have sinned against thee, if they turn again to thee, and acknowledge thy name, and pray and make supplication to thee in this house; 34 then hear thou in heaven, and forgive the sin of thy people Israel, and bring them again to the land which thou gavest to their fathers.

God would put his Name in the sanctuary at Jerusalem, they meant not only that prayers made in that place would be effective, but also that Yahweh would there reveal his will in a special manner. The ultimate prayer must always be "Thy will, not mine, be done."

31-32. These verses deal with the case of a charge made against a man when there is no evidence. Everything, therefore, in such a case depends upon the statement of the accused, since there are no witnesses whereby his word can be substantiated or otherwise. He is brought before the altar and there is made to swear an oath. The prayer is that God will ensure that this trial by oath will settle the matter (cf. the trial by ordeal in Num. 5:14-30).

Vs. 32 shows the Deuteronomic system at work. The theory was that the wicked man was rewarded in this life with misfortune according to his wickedness, while the innocent man was rewarded with good fortune according to his innocence. The Deuteronomists were quite sure that this is a moral world in which morality brings prosperity. They were sure also that they ought to see it working, but the experience of the generations taught them that this principle did not work in so far as the life of the individual is concerned, nor in the case of the nation.

33-34. The military defeat of the nation is judged to be due to sin and apostasy from God. Equally, when the people repent and turn back again to God, defeat will be turned to victory and all will once more be well. The word translated **turn again** is שׁוּב, "turn back" (cf. Isa. 7:3, where the name of Isaiah's son, Shear-jashub, does not mean "a remnant shall return" from exile, but "a remnant shall repent"; cf. also Isa. 10:21).

---

the sensitivity of our consciences by dashing about, the stubborn fact of sin remains, and the search for its forgiveness has been the burden of weightiest thought from Greek dramatists and Hebrew prophets down to Eugene O'Neill. As Luther saw, the forgiveness of sin is a knot which needs God's help to unravel. If I trespass against another, he may forgive me; but can I forgive myself? Or suppose I sin against society by not doing my duty as a citizen; can I not make it up later by extra service? Suppose I am a wastrel until I am forty, and then settle down and do unusually good work; does that not

balance up? Or even if I sin so flagrantly that my transgression is called a crime, can I not atone for my offense by paying a fine or serving a term in prison? Why bring God into the matter at all?

The reason is that sin has at least three aspects. For one thing, there is the record. However kind a man may be now, the fact remains that he once cruelly hurt someone. However law-abiding the man is now, he once was in prison. And along with the record is a second aspect of sin, the habit. Evil imaginings and desires, wishes unfulfilled as well as deeds done.

35 ¶ When heaven is shut up, and there is no rain, because they have sinned against thee; if they pray toward this place, and confess thy name, and turn from their sin, when thou afflictest them:

36 Then hear thou in heaven, and forgive the sin of thy servants, and of thy people Israel, that thou teach them the good way wherein they should walk, and give rain upon thy land, which thou hast given to thy people for an inheritance.

37 ¶ If there be in the land famine, if there be pestilence, blasting, mildew, locust, *or* if there be caterpillar; if their enemy be-

35 "When heaven is shut up and there is no rain because they have sinned against thee, if they pray toward this place, and acknowledge thy name, and turn from their sin, when thou dost afflict them, 36 then hear thou in heaven, and forgive the sin of thy servants, thy people Israel, when thou dost teach them the good way in which they should walk; and grant rain upon thy land, which thou hast given to thy people as an inheritance.

37 "If there is famine in the land, if there is pestilence or blight or mildew or

---

The last phrase **and bring them again to the land . . . fathers** suggests a knowledge of the Exile. It is an addition to the work of the original Deuteronomic editor and belongs to the work of the later editor (*ca.* 550 B.C.).

35-36. Drought, with its consequent famine and pestilence, is regarded in the O.T. as a mark of the divine disfavor because of sin. Palestine was a land where the failure of the seasonal rains meant starvation. Prayers for a good autumn rain formed a regular feature of the autumnal feast, both of the pre-exilic feast of Ingathering and of the postexilic feast of Tabernacles. This was especially the case since the "former rain" was due to fall so very soon after the conclusion of the feast. If this October rain did not fall, the ground, baked hard as iron by the long summer drought, could not be plowed. The concern for rain at this feast may be seen in Zech. 14:16-17, and the tragedy of the delayed rains is depicted in Jer. 8:20. See also the Mishnah, Taanith 1:1–3:8, where there is a description of the ceremonies performed to ensure the fall of the seasonal rains if they were long delayed after the end of the feast (Snaith, *Jewish New Year Festival,* pp. 64, 174-76). The conditions for the divine gift of rain in its season are prayer and repentance, but with forgiveness always dependent upon the good will of God. This insistence upon the sovereignty of God is essential to an understanding of the effectiveness of ritual acts (see G. B. Gray, *Sacrifice in the Old Testament* [Oxford: Clarendon Press, 1925], pp. 316-17).

37-40. This paragraph bears indications of the work of a Priestly Code writer: see the literary style of the opening phrases, where the Hebrew noun comes before the conjunction, and the catalogue of woes which follow in the train of famine.

---

are buried in our subconscious and may erupt like smoldering volcanoes. Moreover, sin has its influence as well as its record and habit. The influence of an evil deed has gone forth into the atmosphere of a situation, and the doer can no more recall it than he can recapture his breath. The strands of sin cannot be untangled by merely shaking hands all round and letting bygones be bygones. When Peer Gynt found himself among the trolls, the devilish spirits of Scandinavian folklore, he asked what was the basic difference between trolls and men. He was told that whereas among men the motto was "To thyself be true," among the trolls the motto was "To thyself be enough."[1] Peer, not liking the rigid requirements of being true to himself, welcomed the new principle of

[1] Henrik Ibsen, *Peer Gynt,* Act II, scene 6.

self-sufficiency and pursued it to the point of self-strangulation.

Solomon's prayer not only recognizes the all-pervasiveness of sin—**for there is no man who does not sin** (vs. 46) —but also the divine involvement of sin. The correction of sin cannot be kept on the human level because the conception of sin is as of a divine-human affair: **If they sin against thee . . . and thou art angry with them, and dost give them to an enemy . . . far off or near** (vs. 46). The divine motives and methods are conceived in primitive, concrete, and direct terms; but the prayer makes clear that the strands of sin cannot be unwound by man's self-sufficiency.

The sinning people must **repent with all their mind and with all their heart** (vs. 48). And repentance is shown when **they turn again to**

siege them in the land of their cities; whatsoever plague, whatsoever sickness *there be;*

38 What prayer and supplication soever
be *made* by any man, *or* by all thy people
Israel, which shall know every man the
plague of his own heart, and spread forth
his hands toward this house:

locust or caterpillar; if their enemy besieges
them in any*a* of their cities; whatever
plague, whatever sickness there is; **38** whatever prayer, whatever supplication is made
by any man or by all thy people Israel, each
knowing the affliction of his own heart and
stretching out his hands toward this house;

a Gk Syr: Heb *the land*

---

38. The phrase **the plague of his own heart,** thus following the Hebrew exactly,
is unique. It is an admirable example of the way in which the Hebrew word לבב ("heart")
is used to denote the very inner core of a man's being. The paraphrase **each knowing
the affliction of his own heart** is sound, but the meaning seems to be "when the plague
strikes right home to each man." The hope involved in such phrases is that God will,
through plague and sickness, awaken in man's heart the consciousness of sin, in order
that man may repent and turn in penitence to God. The Hebrew ideas of punishment
for sin are often said to be penal, and undoubtedly this element is strong, especially in
the Deuteronomic writings. On the other hand, such a passage as this shows that beyond
even penal, retributive punishment there can be a redemptive aim. In Ezek. 18 the
idea of exact justice is put forward and worked out with all the rigidity that the most
impersonal idea of justice could demand. And yet, this very chapter concludes with
one of the most impassioned pleas for repentance that is to be found anywhere. The
doctrine of exact retribution (here in vs. 39; cf. also Jer. 17:10; Ezek. 18:20-32) received
steady emphasis from Deuteronomic times onward. It created difficulties later when
the problem of undeserved suffering came to the fore (cf. Isa. 53:8-10; Job and several
psalms). It was seen in the end that retribution could not be restricted to the individual,
nor could it be confined to this life alone. Out of this dilemma there grew ultimately
on the one hand the idea of vicarious suffering so far as this world is concerned, and on
the other hand the idea of a resurrected life after death, so far as the next world is
concerned. No man lives to himself alone, and human destiny cannot be dealt with on
the level of this world only.

---

thee, and acknowledge thy name, and pray
and make supplication to thee in this house
(vs. 33). Sin is not merely a wrong done to
one's neighbor, or a violation of one's own
nature: it is a transgression against a covenant-
keeping God, an act of base ingratitude to the
Lord who has maintained their cause. If sin is
to be forgiven the sinner must first see the deed
as something so ugly and repulsive that he turns
to a new outlook and attitude. Sin must be
shown up by being set in the light of God's
covenant. Solomon's portrayal of the sinned-
against God is not to be compared with the
ineffable appeal of the heavenly Father whom
Jesus shows yearning for his prodigal sons.
Nevertheless, the note of repentance is clear
and recurrent.

Also emphasized is the truth that repentance
is authenticated by reparation. When two persons who have been at odds "make up," as we
say, there follows a desire on the part of each
to "make it up." The truly repentant person
feels that he wants to make up wherein he has
done wrong. And he is not niggardly in his

calculations. He is like Zacchaeus, who was so
mellowed and repentant after Jesus' dinner
conversation that he declared, "The half of my
goods I give to the poor; and if I have taken
any thing from any man by false accusation, I
restore him fourfold" (Luke 19:8). However
sorry we may be for our sins, if we want to retain the profit gained from them we are not
truly repentant. Listen to the king's soliloquy
in *Hamlet:*

> My fault is past. But O, what form of prayer
> Can serve my turn? Forgive me my foul murder!—
> That cannot be; since I am still possess'd
> Of those effects for which I did the murder,—
> My crown, mine own ambition, and my queen.
> May one be pardon'd and retain the offence? [2]

To that last question of the king there is an
ingrained sense of justice which answers, "No."
Solomon's prayer reveals it. Jesus made it clear:
"If thou bring thy gift to the altar, and there
rememberest that thy brother hath aught
against; leave there thy gift before the altar, and

[2] Act III, scene 3.

39 Then hear thou in heaven thy dwelling place, and forgive, and do, and give to every man according to his ways, whose heart thou knowest; (for thou, *even* thou only, knowest the hearts of all the children of men;)

40 That they may fear thee all the days that they live in the land which thou gavest unto our fathers.

41 Moreover concerning a stranger, that *is* not of thy people Israel, but cometh out of a far country for thy name's sake;

---

39 then hear thou in heaven thy dwelling place, and forgive, and act, and render to each whose heart thou knowest, according to all his ways (for thou, thou only, knowest the hearts of all the children of men);

40 that they may fear thee all the days that they live in the land which thou gavest to our fathers.

41 "Likewise when a foreigner, who is not of thy people Israel, comes from a far

---

39. The idea that God knows **the hearts of all the children of men,** and that he judges according to these inmost thoughts, is a definite milestone in the growth of man's knowledge of the nature and the ways of God. The earliest tendency was to think of God as judging by actions independent of true intentions. This notion appears clearly in the story of the fate of Uzzah, who put out his hand apparently with the best of intentions in order to steady the ark and prevent it from falling and being damaged when the oxen bolted. According to the historian (II Sam. 6:6-7), Uzzah was forthwith smitten dead for this action. But with the prophets the emphasis came more and more to be placed on the motive that lies behind the action, so that intention counts for more than the actual deed. Writers in the priestly tradition were more conservative (e.g., II Chr. 26:18-19), and there was always a party among the scribes who thought in terms of deeds rather than of motives. Yet the idea that God judges by the heart rather than by the outward appearance is as old as I Sam. 16:7, where Samuel is at first attracted by the features and the height of Eliab, David's eldest brother. The classical exposition of the prime importance of motive is Mark 7:21.

41-43. This paragraph belongs to that strand of Jewish religion which welcomed the foreigner who sought to worship the God of the Jews. There were many such among

---

go thy way; first be reconciled to thy brother, and then come and offer thy gift" (Matt. 5: 23-24).

But when we set out to make reparation, we discover our inadequacy. On the human level it is impossible to repair all the damage. When we think of the blessings God has given us. and the poor use to which we have put them; when we think of our wasted hours and forfeited opportunities; when we think of the sacrifices made for us by those we have never fully thanked; when we consider the heartaches we have caused those now beyond the reach of our hands and voices, we realize that we cannot make full reparation. Hence repentance and reparation must be supplemented by reconciliation if the strands of sin are to be untangled. We cannot justify ourselves by our works. We can be justified only by faith, the faith which we have in God as our father and the faith which he has in us as his children. The seeds of this conception are found in Solomon's prayer. **Whatever prayer, whatever supplication is made by any man or by all thy people Israel, each knowing the affliction of his own heart and stretching out his hands toward this house;**

---

then hear thou in heaven thy dwelling place, and forgive, and act, and render to each whose heart thou knowest, according to all his ways (for thou, thou only, knowest the hearts of all the children of men). This ancient prayer is reaching toward the infinite understanding of God. It is on the road toward the later revelation of a heavenly Father's compassion. If there is too much seeming search for escape from the consequences of sin rather than from the sin itself, it should be noted that entire exemption from just punishment is not asked. A man killed his wife in a fit of passion. He was sentenced for life. Later he was converted and became a model prisoner. After some years friends suggested that he appeal for a pardon. "No," he replied, "this is the only way I can show God and my Mary that I am truly sorry for what I did to her."

Solomon's prayer is hardly within hailing distance of the doctrine of forgiveness revealed in Christ's atoning death; nevertheless it does contain the "three R's" of the divine schooling—repentance, reparation, and reconciliation.

41-43. *Missionary Motives.*—Compare the motives of Solomon's prayer **for . . . the foreigner**

42 (For they shall hear of thy great name, and of thy strong hand, and of thy stretched out arm;) when he shall come and pray toward this house:

43 Hear thou in heaven thy dwelling place, and do according to all that the stranger calleth to thee for: that all people of the earth may know thy name, to fear thee, as *do* thy people Israel; and that they may know that this house, which I have builded, is called by thy name.

44 ¶ If thy people go out to battle against their enemy, whithersoever thou shalt send them, and shall pray unto the LORD toward the city which thou hast chosen, and *toward* the house that I have built for thy name:

45 Then hear thou in heaven their prayer and their supplication, and maintain their cause.

46 If they sin against thee, (for *there is* no man that sinneth not,) and thou be

country for thy name's sake 42 (for they shall hear of thy great name, and thy mighty hand, and of thy outstretched arm), when he comes and prays toward this house, 43 hear thou in heaven thy dwelling place, and do according to all for which the foreigner calls to thee; in order that all the peoples of the earth may know thy name and fear thee, as do thy people Israel, and that they may know that this house which I have built is called by thy name.

44 "If thy people go out to battle against their enemy, by whatever way thou shalt send them, and they pray to the LORD toward the city which thou hast chosen and the house which I have built for thy name, 45 then hear thou in heaven their prayer and their supplication, and maintain their cause.

46 "If they sin against thee — for there

---

the Dispersion in the time of the apostle Paul, the "devout persons" whom he found in the cities of Asia Minor. The paragraph finds its counterpart in the conclusion of Isa. 2:1-4, especially when this is compared with the conclusion of the parallel passage in Mic. 4:1-5. It is to be seen also in such missionary tracts as Ruth and Jonah. The contrast is found in Deut. 23:3-5 and Neh. 13:1-3. Josephus (*Antiquities* VIII. 4. 3) makes the most he can of this passage in his eagerness to commend his people to the Romans. He claims that the Jews of his day were "not unnatural nor hostile to strangers," as was indeed alleged, for instance, somewhat later by Tacitus (*History* V. 5), who said that "toward the rest of mankind they nourish a sullen and inveterate hatred."

42. The word יד **(hand)** is regularly used to denote authority, power, control (cf. Josh. 8:20, which reads, lit., "there was not in them pairs of hands to flee"). The phrase containing **hand** is earlier than Deuteronomy, but the following phrase, **thy outstretched arm,** is found first in Deut. 4:34, and thereafter five times by itself, apart from its usual use in the present combination.

44-45. This paragraph, as its language and style show, is exilic, as also is the next. It is a prayer for success in battle. It is a characteristic of all peoples that they pray to their god for success in war; such prayers are no criterion of primitive civilization.

46-53. A prayer for all exiles, whether far or near, not only for those captive in Babylonia, but for all such in whatever place or time.

46. Here we find the statement that **there is no man who does not sin.** It is true that "the idea of total depravity . . . is . . . unsupported by the Bible," but it is nevertheless "an observed and undeniable fact that all men are sinners" (Burrows, *Outline of Biblical Theology*, pp. 170, 172). See also Pss. 130:3; 143:2—passages which, together with this verse, have to be taken into account in any comprehensive study of the extent

---

with Christ's great commission (Matt. 28:19-20). This early petitioner feels no compulsion to seek out the foreigner or to send the message of Yahweh to him. Help is asked only for those who come to the temple as seekers. **When he comes and prays toward this house, hear thou, . . . and do according to all for which the foreigner calls to thee; in order that all the**

peoples of the earth may know thy name and fear thee.

When did Israel awaken to a spiritual concern for the peoples beyond her borders? Has Judaism a missionary passion today? How does this prayer's desire to impress the foreigner with the Lord's greatness compare with Jesus' counsel, "Let your light so shine before men,

angry with them, and deliver them to the enemy, so that they carry them away captives unto the land of the enemy, far or near;

47 *Yet* if they shall bethink themselves in the land whither they were carried captives, and repent, and make supplication unto thee in the land of them that carried them captives, saying, We have sinned, and have done perversely, we have committed wickedness;

48 And *so* return unto thee with all their heart, and with all their soul, in the land of their enemies, which led them away captive, and pray unto thee toward their land, which thou gavest unto their fathers, the city which thou hast chosen, and the house which I have built for thy name:

49 Then hear thou their prayer and their supplication in heaven thy dwelling place, and maintain their cause,

is no man who does not sin — and thou art angry with them, and dost give them to an enemy, so that they are carried away captive to the land of the enemy, far off or near; **47** yet if they lay it to heart in the land to which they have been carried captive, and repent, and make supplication to thee in the land of their captors, saying, 'We have sinned, and have acted perversely and wickedly'; **48** if they repent with all their mind and with all their heart in the land of their enemies, who carried them captive, and pray to thee toward their land, which thou gavest to their fathers, the city which thou hast chosen, and the house which I have built for thy name; **49** then hear thou in heaven thy dwelling place their prayer and their supplication, and maintain their cause

---

and the prevalence of sin. All three passages are late and belong to the time of the Diaspora.

47. This verse contains three words for "sin," and they are translated **We have sinned, and have acted perversely and wickedly.** Etymologically the three words used stand for three different conceptions of sin. The first word is *ḥāṭā'*, which properly means "miss the goal." The verb is used in this sense in Prov. 19:2. In Judg. 20:16 it is used of men slinging stones at a hair and not "missing." From this point of view, therefore, the conception of sin is that of aiming at what is right, and failing. The second word is *'āwāh*. The corresponding verb in Arabic means "to err from the way," but in Hebrew the noun and its derivatives are used of "iniquity" rather than of "error," as though the result of deliberate action and not of failure through weakness or lack of knowledge. The third word is *rāsha'*. It is used in Arabic of being loose in the limbs and thus disjointed, irregulated, abnormal. In this way sin refers to being out of the straight, not conforming to what is right and true, in contrast to *çedhāqāh* ("righteousness").

48. Repent with all their mind and . . . heart: The Hebrew actually is "with all their לבב [lit., **heart**] and with all their נפש [lit., "life," soul]." The meaning is not necessarily, as the RSV suggests, "with all their thinking and emotional powers," although both these are certainly involved, but with the whole of their being, right down to the very roots of it. It is the Hebrew idiom for expressing the idea that the repentance must be thorough and complete.

---

that they may see your good works, and glorify your Father which is in heaven" (Matt. 5:16)? Is the primary motive to promote the glory of God or the welfare of the foreigner, and what is the relation between these two objectives? How far is Solomon's interest in the outsider from the good Samaritanism of Jesus? In convincing the foreigner of Yahweh's power, was there an underlying desire to demonstrate Israel's strength? Have Christian missions been purged of all nationalism and imperialism? Such are some of the seed questions embedded

in the soil of Solomon's prayer. They could be fruitfully cultivated in current thought.

When the Nobile expedition made its ill-fated flight over the North Pole in 1928, the report came back via Leningrad that a Swedish scientist had been left to die in the snow by two of his comrades when he was unable to keep up the trek. A considerable outcry was raised by the Russians at the inhumanity of such an act. Yet at just about that time representatives of an American church were in Russia distributing food supplies to relieve the starvation due to

50 And forgive thy people that have sinned against thee, and all their transgressions wherein they have transgressed against thee, and give them compassion before them who carried them captive, that they may have compassion on them:

51 For they *be* thy people, and thine inheritance, which thou broughtest forth out of Egypt, from the midst of the furnace of iron:

52 That thine eyes may be open unto the supplication of thy servant, and unto the supplication of thy people Israel, to hearken unto them in all that they call for unto thee.

53 For thou didst separate them from among all the people of the earth, *to be* thine inheritance, as thou spakest by the hand of Moses thy servant, when thou broughtest our fathers out of Egypt, O Lord God.

50 and forgive thy people who have sinned against thee, and all their transgressions which they have committed against thee; and grant them compassion in the sight of those who carried them captive, that they may have compassion on them 51 (for they are thy people, and thy heritage, which thou didst bring out of Egypt, from the midst of the iron furnace). 52 Let thy eyes be open to the supplication of thy servant, and to the supplication of thy people Israel, giving ear to them whenever they call to thee. 53 For thou didst separate them from among all the peoples of the earth, to be thy heritage, as thou didst declare through Moses, thy servant, when thou didst bring our fathers out of Egypt, O Lord God."

50. Transgressions: The Hebrew פשע means "rebellion," and this certainly ought to be the translation here. The difference between the two renderings is considerable. To use the word "transgression" involves thinking of sin as transgressing a law, but to use the word "rebellion" involves thinking of sin as a revolt against a person. This is the general attitude of the prophets, so that the expression of Isa. 53:6, "We have turned every one to his own way," is truly characteristic of the prophetic attitude. At root the difference involves two ways of thinking about religion: one presupposes a set of rules or laws which must be obeyed, the other involves a particular attitude to a person. It is because the prophetic attitude to God is primarily that of loyalty to a Person that the ethical standards of the Bible grow to be far higher and deeper than any human standard could ever demand.

53. Israel's special claim upon God is his special choice of Israel, wholly undeserved. The Deuteronomic writers are continually emphasizing this idea (Deut. 7:7-8; 9:4-5; 23:5). This belief of special choice is to be found throughout the Bible; indeed the

crop failure. A Soviet commissar came to one of the church workers and asked, "Why are you over here? What are you trying to get out of us anyway?" The Soviet mentality could understand why one should not leave a comrade to die at his feet, but it could not understand why one should go halfway around the world to save people who were dying. The first is humanity; the second is Christianity.

53. *A Chosen People.*—There is no truer test of character than the attitude a man takes toward his inheritance. To a person of high sensibility what is bequeathed to him becomes a sacred trust. It is a matter of honor to keep faith with the dead who no longer are present to reward or restrain. Solomon therefore closes his dedicatory prayer on a strategic note by reference to Israel's heritage. **For thou didst separate them from among all the peoples of the earth, to be thy heritage, as thou didst declare through**

Moses, thy servant, when thou didst bring our fathers out of Egypt, O Lord God (cf. Deut. 7:6). Charles W. Eliot of Harvard used to say that the strongest appeal he could make to a wayward student was to remind him of parental sacrifices and expectations. But while we may feel a sense of honor sufficient to keep faith with our own parents and to preserve our personal inheritance, many do not have the same regard for their social and national heritage. What is everybody's business is often nobody's business. The Deuteronomic writer foresaw that prosperity would tend to beget individualism and warned against wasting Israel's national inheritance (Deut. 9:26). From Moses on, the recurring emphasis on Israel's divine heritage and mission proved of immeasurable value in sustaining morale through suffering and exile.

In so far as the consciousness of our inheritance keeps us humbly grateful, it is wholesome.

54 And it was *so*, that when Solomon had made an end of praying all this prayer and supplication unto the LORD, he arose from before the altar of the LORD, from kneeling on his knees with his hands spread up to heaven.

55 And he stood, and blessed all the congregation of Israel with a loud voice, saying,

56 Blessed *be* the LORD, that hath given rest unto his people Israel, according to all that he promised: there hath not failed one word of all his good promise, which he promised by the hand of Moses his servant.

57 The LORD our God be with us, as he was with our fathers: let him not leave us, nor forsake us:

58 That he may incline our hearts unto him, to walk in all his ways, and to keep his commandments, and his statutes, and his judgments, which he commanded our fathers.

54 Now as Solomon finished offering all this prayer and supplication to the LORD, he arose from before the altar of the LORD, where he had knelt with hands outstretched toward heaven; 55 and he stood, and blessed all the assembly of Israel with a loud voice, saying, 56 "Blessed be the LORD who has given rest to his people Israel, according to all that he promised; not one word has failed of all his good promise, which he uttered by Moses his servant. 57 The LORD our God be with us, as he was with our fathers; may he not leave us or forsake us; 58 that he may incline our hearts to him, to walk in all his ways, and to keep his commandments, his statutes, and his ordinances, which he commanded our fathers.

Bible is written with this fundamental motif. The emphasis of the prophets is always that the choice was due wholly to God's free and unconditioned love, i.e., not conditioned by Israel's deserving or by anything at all outside his nature. It was wholly and entirely his own unfettered choice, and all of grace. The idea of Israel as a nation separate from the rest of the peoples becomes articulate in Amos 3:2, and from that time there is a steady development in the Deuteronomic writings, becoming rigorously exclusive in the postexilic period.

4. SOLOMON'S BLESSING (8:54-61)

Solomon blesses the people, and prays that God's ancient promise shall be fulfilled in them. To that end he prays that God will so incline their hearts that they will keep the Deuteronomic laws with full zeal.

54. The attitude of kneeling during prayer was not common, though it is mentioned some seven times altogether (cf. 19:18). The usual attitude was that of standing with **hands outstretched** (cf. vs. 22).

56. The faithfulness of God in fulfilling his promises is a recurrent theme throughout the Bible. It comes to its full fruition in the Epistle to the Hebrews, where "faith" largely is that which enables men to live and die "not having received what was promised, but having seen it and greeted it from afar" (Heb. 11:13).

58. The writer recognizes that if men are to do the will of God then it must be because he is pleased to **incline our hearts to him**. This idea presents a contradiction which the human mind cannot solve. It is true that every man has a free choice either

---

It gives both the background of memory and the foreground of hope as the proper spiritual setting of our minds. We speak of self-made men, but in giving credit to their resourcefulness we must remember the social resources on which they have drawn. The freedom of opportunity, the stability of laws, the sanctity of contracts by which a person is enabled to conduct his business or career—whence come these? In 1784 a twenty-year-old youth landed in New York. He was the son of a German butcher. His first job was that of peddling cakes. He worked his way up to become a successful fur trader. He bought real estate on Manhattan Island, and the city's growth pyramided its value. His fortune grew until in 1929 the estate founded by John Jacob Astor was estimated at $500,000,000. Giving full credit to the intelligence, industry, and foresight of the individual, we have to admit that much of the mounting

59 And let these my words, wherewith I have made supplication before the Lord, be nigh unto the Lord our God day and night, that he maintain the cause of his servant, and the cause of his people Israel at all times, as the matter shall require:

60 That all the people of the earth may know that the Lord *is* God, *and that there is* none else.

61 Let your heart therefore be perfect with the Lord our God, to walk in his statutes, and to keep his commandments, as at this day.

62 ¶ And the king, and all Israel with him, offered sacrifice before the Lord.

63 And Solomon offered a sacrifice of peace offerings, which he offered unto the Lord, two and twenty thousand oxen, and a hundred and twenty thousand sheep. So the king and all the children of Israel dedicated the house of the Lord.

64 The same day did the king hallow the middle of the court that *was* before the house of the Lord: for there he offered

59 Let these words of mine, wherewith I have made supplication before the Lord, be near to the Lord our God day and night, and may he maintain the cause of his servant, and the cause of his people Israel, as each day requires; 60 that all the peoples of the earth may know that the Lord is God; there is no other. 61 Let your heart therefore be wholly true to the Lord our God, walking in his statutes and keeping his commandments, as at this day."

62 Then the king, and all Israel with him, offered sacrifice before the Lord. 63 Solomon offered as peace offerings to the Lord twenty-two thousand oxen and a hundred and twenty thousand sheep. So the king and all the people of Israel dedicated the house of the Lord. 64 The same day the king consecrated the middle of the court that was before the house of the Lord; for there he offered the burnt offering and the cereal offering and the fat pieces of the

---

to do God's will or to refuse. It is also true that even those first stirrings in the human heart which bring men to him are the work of the Holy Spirit. The degree of emphasis on this point is a safe criterion of the depth of Christian experience.

5. The Sacrifices and the Feast (8:62-66)

Solomon offers an enormous number of animals for the sacred feast. He dedicates the temple by inaugurating the regular daily sacrifice. All this took place at the great autumnal harvest new-year feast which began with the full moon known to us as the harvest moon. The feast lasted seven days and the people all returned home on the eighth day.

63. The LXX omits all reference to the slaughtering of the **sheep**, recording only the slaughter of the **twenty-two thousand oxen.** Josephus mentions twelve thousand sheep, and his figures rarely err on the low side. It is possible that the numbers of the M.T. have grown with the years, but these beasts were slain for the eating of the worshipers, and large numbers of animals would certainly be needed.

64. This is the first mention of **the bronze altar.** There is no evidence that there was such an altar in Solomon's temple. It belonged to the second temple. The verse

---

value was "unearned increment." When we consider the unearned increment of social values which we enjoy we feel ourselves in debt far beyond our power to repay. Only a debtor complex can keep us humbly serving (cf. Rom. 1:14-15). When we are ever mindful that our blessings were bought with a price, that the element of sacrifice runs through the linked generations as the red strand runs through the rope of the British navy to show that it belongs to the crown, then we dedicate ourselves to the task of leaving a world better than we found it.

To waste the privilege for which our fathers paid so dearly is to betray the dead, cheat our children, and dishonor the God who prepared our people to be his heritage. Society is a compact between the living, the dead, and the yet unborn, to use Edmund Burke's formula. Moreover, to Israel it was a covenant between God and his chosen people.

But what is it to be a chosen people? At this point enters the pride which perverts humble gratitude into national preening. It is one thing to be chosen for a special mission; it is another

burnt offerings, and meat offerings, and the fat of the peace offerings: because the brazen altar that *was* before the LORD *was* too little to receive the burnt offerings, and meat offerings, and the fat of the peace offerings.

65 And at that time Solomon held a feast, and all Israel with him, a great congregation, from the entering in of Hamath unto the river of Egypt, before the LORD our God, seven days and seven days, *even* fourteen days.

66 On the eighth day he sent the people away: and they blessed the king, and went unto their tents joyful and glad of heart for all the goodness that the LORD had done for David his servant, and for Israel his people.

peace offerings, because the bronze altar that was before the LORD was too small to receive the burnt offering and the cereal offering and the fat pieces of the peace offerings.

65 So Solomon held the feast at that time, and all Israel with him, a great assembly, from the entrance of Hamath to the Brook of Egypt, before the LORD our God, seven days.[b] 66 On the eighth day he sent the people away; and they blessed the king, and went to their homes joyful and glad of heart for all the goodness that the LORD had shown to David his servant and to Israel his people.

[b] Gk: Heb *seven days and seven days, fourteen days*

---

shows definite traces of editing under the influence of the Priestly Code. This is especially evident in the fact that the word מנחה, **cereal offering,** is used in its postexilic sense of the cereal offering which accompanied every meat offering consumed on the altar (cf. Exeg. on 4:21). The king here is said to be instituting the regular daily offering which was customary in the postexilic temple. This fact is clear in the RSV, with its reference **to the burnt offering and the cereal offering,** both words being in the singular. It is obscured in the KJV because the words there are in the plural, as though he made a multiplicity of offerings because of the very special and unique nature of the occasion. **The peace offerings** were for the great feast in which all the worshipers shared. It was only the fat of these slaughtered beasts which was consumed on the altar. In any case, the tradition is that the beasts were so many that the fat from them was burned in **the middle of the court,** not on any altar which may have been there.

65. From the entrance of Hamath to the Brook of Egypt is the ideal extent of the Holy Land from north to south. The **entrance of Hamath** is the pass between Hermon and the Lebanon, due north of the Sea of Galilee and in latitude 33° 30', the same latitude as both Sidon and Damascus. **Seven days** was the period of the pre-exilic feast of Ingathering. According to Deut. 16:13, 15, the people made ready to go back home on the eighth day (cf. vs. 66). This is the custom described here. The postexilic custom was to hold an עצרת, i.e., "a closing assembly" on the eighth day (cf. the parallel and postexilic account in II Chr. 7:8-10). The addition in the M.T., **and seven days, even fourteen days,** is due to the mistaken enthusiasm of a scribe who thought that the dedication feast and the normal seven-day feast were separate and distinct.

Seven is the sacred number in all areas which were subject to Mesopotamian influence.

---

to be set apart for special favors. The first concept gives a sense of dedication and direction which imparts strength; the second sows the seeds of presumption and truculence. This latter has borne bitter fruit. Napoleon following his star of destiny across the corpses of his countrymen; Fichte asserting that the superiority of German civilization is rooted in the external order; expansionist politicians seeking popular votes by prating about the United States' "manifest destiny"—thus men draw blueprints of their own desires and try to conceal their autographs under the initials of divinity. Their efforts

have resulted in those theories of racial and national superiority which foment wars.

Nations and races that see themselves as the special wards of God must learn the lesson which Peter gained from his vision on the housetop at Joppa, "that God is no respecter of persons" (Acts 10:34). The Father of all mankind plays no favorites. But when the concept of a chosen people is purged of selfish pride, Israel is justified in taking it to itself. The career of the little nation which Moses led out of Egypt, which David welded into a unity, which under the tutelage of the prophets pursued the search

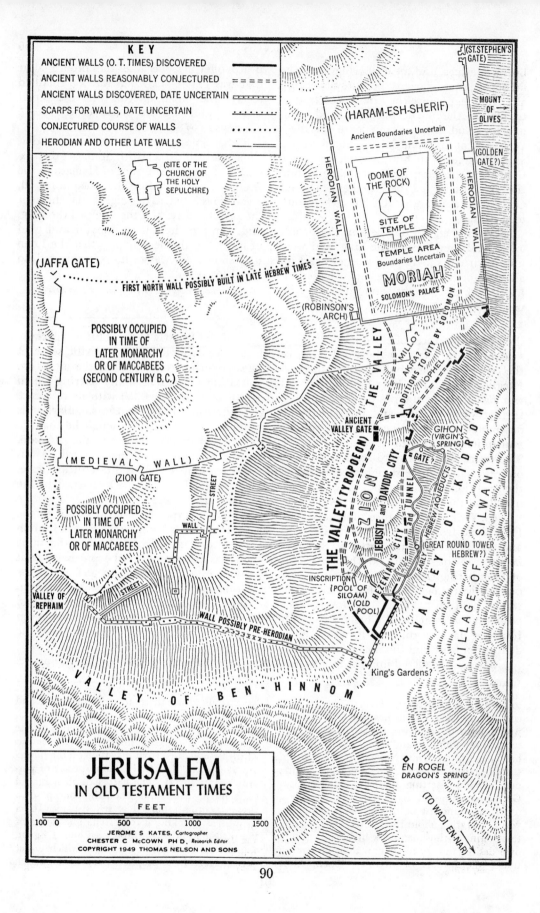

KEY

ANCIENT WALLS (O. T. TIMES) DISCOVERED ─────

ANCIENT WALLS REASONABLY CONJECTURED ═════

ANCIENT WALLS DISCOVERED, DATE UNCERTAIN ┄┄┄┄

SCARPS FOR WALLS, DATE UNCERTAIN ┅┅┅┅

CONJECTURED COURSE OF WALLS ●●●●●

HERODIAN AND OTHER LATE WALLS ─ ─ ─

(SITE OF THE CHURCH OF THE HOLY SEPULCHRE)

(HARAM-ESH-SHERIF)

Ancient Boundaries Uncertain

(DOME OF THE ROCK)

SITE OF TEMPLE

TEMPLE AREA Boundaries Uncertain

MORIAH

SOLOMON'S PALACE?

HERODIAN WALL

HERODIAN WALL

(ST. STEPHEN'S GATE)

MOUNT OF OLIVES →

(GOLDEN GATE?)

(JAFFA GATE)

FIRST NORTH WALL POSSIBLY BUILT IN LATE HEBREW TIMES

(ROBINSON'S ARCH)

POSSIBLY OCCUPIED IN TIME OF LATER MONARCHY OR OF MACCABEES (SECOND CENTURY B.C.)

MILLO?

AKRA?

ADDITIONS TO CITY BY SOLOMON

OPHEL

ANCIENT VALLEY GATE

THE VALLEY

ZION

THE VALLEY (TYROPOEON)

GATE?

GIHON (VIRGIN'S SPRING)

(MEDIEVAL WALL)

(ZION GATE)

STREET

POSSIBLY OCCUPIED IN TIME OF LATER MONARCHY OR OF MACCABEES

WALL

STREET

JEBUSITE and DAVIDIC CITY

HEZEKIAH'S TUNNEL

EARLY HEBREW AQUEDUCTS

2nd

VALLEY OF KIDRON

(VILLAGE OF SILWAN)

(GREAT ROUND TOWER HEBREW?)

INSCRIPTION (POOL OF SILOAM) (OLD POOL)

VALLEY OF REPHAIM

WALL POSSIBLY PRE-HERODIAN

King's Gardens?

VALLEY OF BEN-HINNOM

EN ROGEL DRAGON'S SPRING

JERUSALEM
IN OLD TESTAMENT TIMES
FEET

100 0   500   1000   1500

JEROME S KATES, Cartographer
CHESTER C McCOWN PH D, Research Editor
COPYRIGHT 1949 THOMAS NELSON AND SONS

(TO WADI EN-NAR)

9 And it came to pass, when Solomon had finished the building of the house of the LORD, and the king's house, and all Solomon's desire which he was pleased to do,

2 That the LORD appeared to Solomon the second time, as he had appeared unto him at Gibeon.

3 And the LORD said unto him, I have heard thy prayer and thy supplication, that thou hast made before me: I have hallowed this house, which thou hast built, to put my name there for ever; and mine eyes and mine heart shall be there perpetually.

4 And if thou wilt walk before me, as David thy father walked, in integrity of heart, and in uprightness, to do according to all that I have commanded thee, *and* wilt keep my statutes and my judgments;

5 Then I will establish the throne of thy kingdom upon Israel for ever, as I promised to David thy father, saying, There shall not fail thee a man upon the throne of Israel.

6 *But* if ye shall at all turn from following me, ye or your children, and will not keep my commandments *and* my statutes which I have set before you, but go and serve other gods, and worship them;

9 When Solomon had finished building the house of the LORD and the king's house and all that Solomon desired to build, 2 the LORD appeared to Solomon a second time, as he had appeared to him at Gibeon. 3 And the LORD said to him, "I have heard your prayer and your supplication, which you have made before me; I have consecrated this house which you have built, and put my name there for ever; my eyes and my heart will be there for all time. 4 And as for you, if you will walk before me, as David your father walked, with integrity of heart and uprightness, doing according to all that I have commanded you, and keeping my statutes and my ordinances, 5 then I will establish your royal throne over Israel for ever, as I promised David your father, saying, 'There shall not fail you a man upon the throne of Israel.' 6 But if you turn aside from following me, you or your children, and do not keep my commandments and my statutes which I have set before you, but go and serve other gods

---

D. SOLOMON'S APOGEE AND DECLINE (9:1–11:43)
1. SOLOMON'S SECOND VISION (9:1-9)

The king receives a confirmation at Jerusalem of his first vision at Gibeon and an assurance that his dedicatory prayer has been heard and will be answered. Everything is conditional upon the proper observance of the Deuteronomic principles. The whole section is Deuteronomic, the first five verses from the earlier editor (*ca.* 610 B.C.), the last four from the later editor (*ca.* 550 B.C.). The change of person at vs. 6 (preserved in the KJV but hidden in the RSV) and the fact that vss. 6-9 envisage apostasy from God and speak (cf. O.L. and Syriac) of the temple as a heap of ruins support the

---

for the knowledge of God until it rose to monotheism, which preserved a saving remnant through exile, despair, and dismemberment, and established a moral law which "was our schoolmaster to bring us unto Christ" (Gal. 3:24)—such a nation may well claim the title of a chosen people, which the Lord God **didst separate . . . from among all the peoples of the earth, to be thy heritage.** God has a mission for every individual life which he brings into the world. Horace Bushnell's historic sermon, "Every Man's Life a Plan of God," [3] was to the point. But can we ascribe a divine mission to every nation? Some so-called nations are mere artificial political creations in which it is hard

[3] *Sermons for the New Life* (New York: Charles Scribner's Sons, 1876), pp. 1-28.

to see any hand of destiny. If, however, nations are to be judged by their fruits, Israel was chosen of God.

9:1-9. Treason to Ourselves.—The warning given to Solomon may seem at first to smack of the bartering spirit, present in the primitive interpretation of Yahweh's dealings with his people. The promise is that if Solomon will walk in the way of the Lord as did his father David, he and his nation shall prosper. But if they leave the path of obedience to follow other gods, **Israel will become a proverb and a byword among all peoples** (vs. 7). The beholders of the temple ruins will hiss and ask, **Why has the LORD done thus to this land and to this house?** (vs. 8). The answer will be: **Because they forsook the LORD their God who brought**

7 Then will I cut off Israel out of the land which I have given them; and this house, which I have hallowed for my name, will I cast out of my sight; and Israel shall be a proverb and a byword among all people:

8 And at this house, *which* is high, every one that passeth by it shall be astonished, and shall hiss; and they shall say, Why hath the LORD done thus unto this land, and to this house?

9 And they shall answer, Because they forsook the LORD their God, who brought forth their fathers out of the land of Egypt, and have taken hold upon other gods, and have worshipped them, and served them: therefore hath the LORD brought upon them all this evil.

10 ¶ And it came to pass at the end of twenty years, when Solomon had built the

and worship them, 7 then I will cut off Israel from the land which I have given them; and the house which I have consecrated for my name I will cast out of my sight; and Israel will become a proverb and a byword among all peoples. 8 And this house will become a heap of ruins;[c] everyone passing by it will be astonished, and will hiss; and they will say, 'Why has the LORD done thus to this land and to this house?' 9 Then they will say, 'Because they forsook the LORD their God who brought their fathers out of the land of Egypt, and laid hold on other gods, and worshiped them and served them; therefore the LORD has brought all this evil upon them.' "

10 At the end of twenty years, in which

[c] Syr Old Latin: Heb *high*

contention that the last part only of the section is postexilic (so Burney against the majority of scholars).

9:8. The true reading of the M.T. is "and this house shall be high" (ASV mg.). In the KJV the smoothed reading of the parallel II Chr. 7:21 has been adopted, **this house, which is high,** but the O.L. and Syriac are correct with **will become a heap of ruins.** The alteration may well have been deliberate in the M.T. on the ground that God could scarcely say that the temple would be a heap of ruins.

2. FURTHER DETAILS OF SOLOMON'S MAGNIFICENCE AND WISDOM (9:10–10:29)

This section concludes the editor's story of the splendor of Solomon, and ch. 11 tells the story of his sins and troubles. The section contains a series of extracts from the

their fathers out of the land of Egypt, and laid hold on other gods, and worshiped them and served them; therefore the LORD has brought all this evil upon them (vs. 9). The early Hebrew seers here glimpse the basic truth of retribution for sin, although they have not yet lifted the principle from the low level of give-and-take between Yahweh and his subjects. Modern experience through social and psychological laboratories confirms the evil consequences of wrongdoing, even when no intervening deity is cited to explain them. Twentieth-century writers may not use the words which Isaiah interprets the Lord as speaking to Sennacherib, "Therefore will I put . . . my bridle in thy lips, and I will turn thee back by the way by which thou camest" (Isa. 37:29); but they cannot gainsay the fact that "pride goeth before destruction, and a haughty spirit before a fall" (Prov. 16:18), that power is lost through abuse, and that the way of the transgressor becomes harder and narrower (Prov. 13:15). As a disillusioned youth once said, "We

took what we wanted until we no longer wanted what we took." The dictator who takes law into his own hands finally discovers laws which he cannot handle, and he goes the way of the Napoleons and the Hitlers.

As Jesus looked around the table at the Last Supper he said, "Woe to that man by whom the Son of man is betrayed!" (Mark 14:21). Who punished Judas? Not the company of Jesus whose confidences he had betrayed. Not the Jewish people whose noblest Son he had turned over to the hostile Roman government. No outside agency was called in to condemn Judas. He punished himself. This is the significant thing about playing false to the divine principles. It proves to be playing false to oneself. As Francis Thompson heard the Hound of Heaven say, "All things betray thee, who betrayest Me." Disobedience toward God makes us traitors to ourselves. Solomon was to learn this truth the hard way.

10-28. The Pay-Off.—Splendor such as Solomon's can be bought only at a high price. And

two houses, the house of the LORD, and the king's house,

11 (Now Hiram the king of Tyre had furnished Solomon with cedar trees and fir trees, and with gold, according to all his desire,) that then king Solomon gave Hiram twenty cities in the land of Galilee.

12 And Hiram came out from Tyre to see the cities which Solomon had given him; and they pleased him not.

13 And he said, What cities are these which thou hast given me, my brother? And he called them the land of Cabul unto this day.

Solomon had built the two houses, the house of the LORD and the king's house, 11 and Hiram king of Tyre had supplied Solomon with cedar and cypress timber and gold, as much as he desired, King Solomon gave to Hiram twenty cities in the land of Galilee. 12 But when Hiram came from Tyre to see the cities which Solomon had given him, they did not please him. 13 Therefore he said, "What kind of cities are these which you have given me, my brother?" So they are called the land of

---

biography, short statements for the most part. There has also been some considerable editorial activity. The order in the LXX is quite different, but is no improvement. The reconstruction proposed by Burney (*Notes on Hebrew Text of Kings*, p. 133), partly on the basis of the LXX, is the probable original order in the biography. So far as ch. 9 is concerned, this order is vss. 10, 17-19, 15, 20-23. This arrangement gives first the full list of Solomon's building operations and then the details of the conscripted labor with which he carried out his schemes. Into this description is dovetailed the story of Solomon's sale to Hiram of Tyre of twenty cities in Galilee (vss. 11-14). The amount of gold received was equivalent to nearly one and a half million dollars.

a) SALE OF GALILEAN TERRITORY (9:10-14)

Hiram, having paid the money, comes to inspect the territory and is dissatisfied with the bargain. The story accounts for a popular explanation of the name Galilee as being "as good as nothing."

11. The original statement from the biography began with the mention of the **twenty cities.** The **timber** which Hiram had sent to Solomon had nothing to do with this financial transaction, since Solomon had already paid for that (cf. 5:11). Solomon was short of ready money and had to cede territory in order to get it. This is disguised by the introduction of the parenthesis, necessarily so because the editor's theory is that all went well until toward the end of the reign when Solomon allowed the worship of foreign deities through pressure from his many foreign wives. But the troubles of ch. 11 belong to a much earlier period of the reign than is suggested there, and the loss of Edom and Damascus must have created financial difficulties for Solomon, so that his grandiose building schemes were more expensive than he could actually afford. In the Chronicler's parallel (II Chr. 8:2) the whole transaction is reversed, and Hiram cedes territory to Solomon.

13. Cabul: Ewald's explanation, "like nothing," is probably correct, but represents a popular rather than accurate etymology. The explanation "displeasing" is found in Josephus (*Antiquities* VIII. 5. 3).

---

now it begins to appear that what the exalted monarch had paid was to give him trouble. The twenty cities in Galilee which he gave to Hiram for his services did not please the latter; how Hiram was eventually placated we are not told. Also the forced labor which Solomon levied on his subjects was to prove the seed of a future bitter harvest. He spared his own people of Israel this slave labor. He made them soldiers, officials, commanders, and placed them over the Amorites, the Hittites, and the other subject peoples within his borders. But all this weakened the national structure and unity, for a nation is not safe when half slave and half free.

Then instead of giving himself to the righting of wrongs and the spreading of liberty and justice to all, Solomon went on in his greed for glory. He built a fleet to bring the gold of Ophir for further enrichment of his splendor. Thus ambition weaves the familiar and fatal pattern.

14 And Hiram sent to the king sixscore talents of gold.

15 ¶ And this *is* the reason of the levy which king Solomon raised; for to build the house of the LORD, and his own house, and Millo, and the wall of Jerusalem, and Hazor, and Megiddo, and Gezer.

16 *For* Pharaoh king of Egypt had gone up, and taken Gezer, and burnt it with fire, and slain the Canaanites that dwelt in the city, and given it *for* a present unto his daughter, Solomon's wife.

17 And Solomon built Gezer, and Bethhoron the nether.

18 And Baalath, and Tadmor in the wilderness, in the land,

19 And all the cities of store that Solomon had, and cities for his chariots, and cities for his horsemen, and that which Solomon desired to build in Jerusalem, and in Lebanon, and in all the land of his dominion.

20 *And* all the people *that were* left of the Amorites, Hittites, Perizzites, Hivites, and Jebusites, which *were* not of the children of Israel,

21 Their children that were left after them in the land, whom the children of Israel also were not able utterly to destroy, upon those did Solomon levy a tribute of bondservice unto this day.

22 But of the children of Israel did Solo-

Cabul to this day. 14 Hiram had sent to the king one hundred and twenty talents of gold.

15 And this is the account of the forced labor which King Solomon levied to build the house of the LORD and his own house and the Millo and the wall of Jerusalem and Hazor and Megid'do and Gezer 16 (Pharaoh king of Egypt had gone up and captured Gezer and burnt it with fire, and had slain the Canaanites who dwelt in the city, and had given it as dowry to his daughter, Solomon's wife; 17 so Solomon rebuilt Gezer) and Bethhor'on the lower 18 and Ba'alath and Tamar in the wilderness, in the land of Judah,[d] 19 and all the store-cities that Solomon had, and the cities for his chariots, and the cities for his horsemen, and whatever Solomon desired to build in Jerusalem, in Lebanon, and in all the land of his dominion. 20 All the people who were left of the Amorites, the Hittites, the Per'izzites, the Hivites, and the Jeb'usites, who were not of the people of Israel — 21 their descendants who were left after them in the land, whom the people of Israel were unable to destroy utterly — these Solomon made a forced levy of slaves, and so they are to this day. 22 But of the people of Israel

[d] Heb lacks *of Judah*

---

b) FORCED LABOR LEVY (9:15-23)

Solomon accomplished his huge building program by labor gangs levied on the Northern Kingdom of Israel. The original account seems to have consisted of vss. 15a, 20-23, and into this has been interpolated an account of all the buildings which Solomon erected by means of the *corvée* system. Yet again, vs. 16 is another interpolation, explaining how it came about that Gezer, the dowry of Pharaoh's daughter, had to be rebuilt by Solomon. This verse really belongs to 3:1.

15. The Millo was part of the fortifications of the old Jebusite city of Jerusalem. It was apparently a tower, particularly strong and especially needed there because of the natural weakness of the place on the north side. The word is usually explained as being of Canaanite origin, meaning "that which is filled up."

21. Destroy utterly: Both this and the similar phrase in the KJV are inadequate as a translation of the Hebrew. The verb means "put to the ban." The noun (*ḥērem*) describes that which is sacred to a god other than the Lord and must therefore be utterly destroyed. The same root is used with the same significance on the Moabite stone (l. 17) of the complete destruction of the altar hearth (?) of the Lord which was captured by Mesha of Moab and dragged before the Moabite god Chemosh and utterly destroyed. In Arabic the root is the normal root for "holy," e.g., the modern name for the ancient temple area at Jerusalem is Haram esh-Sherîf.

22. His captains is a conjectural translation. In II Chr. 8:9 the word is combined with the previous word to read "the chiefs of his [?] captains."

mon make no bondmen: but they *were* men of war, and his servants, and his princes, and his captains, and rulers of his chariots, and his horsemen.

23 These *were* the chief of the officers that *were* over Solomon's work, five hundred and fifty, which bare rule over the people that wrought in the work.

24 ¶ But Pharaoh's daughter came up out of the city of David unto her house which *Solomon* had built for her: then did he build Millo.

25 ¶ And three times in a year did Solomon offer burnt offerings and peace offerings upon the altar which he built unto the LORD, and he burnt incense upon the altar that *was* before the LORD. So he finished the house.

26 ¶ And king Solomon made a navy of ships in Ezion-geber, which *is* beside Eloth, on the shore of the Red sea, in the land of Edom.

27 And Hiram sent in the navy his servants, shipmen that had knowledge of the sea, with the servants of Solomon.

28 And they came to Ophir, and fetched

Solomon made no slaves; they were the soldiers, they were his officials, his commanders, his captains, his chariot commanders and his horsemen.

23 These were the chief officers who were over Solomon's work: five hundred and fifty, who had charge of the people who carried on the work.

24 But Pharaoh's daughter went up from the city of David to her own house which Solomon had built for her; then he built the Millo.

25 Three times a year Solomon used to offer up burnt offerings and peace offerings upon the altar which he built to the LORD, burning incense[e] before the LORD. So he finished the house.

26 King Solomon built a fleet of ships at E'zion-ge'ber, which is near Eloth on the shore of the Red Sea, in the land of Edom. 27 And Hiram sent with the fleet his servants, seamen who were familiar with the sea, together with the servants of Solomon; 28 and they went to Ophir, and brought from there gold, to the amount of four hun-

e Gk: Heb *burning incense with it which*

---

c) PHARAOH'S DAUGHTER TAKES UP HER RESIDENCE (9:24)

24. This statement is found elsewhere in the LXX, in vs. 9 and also in the long interpolation after 2:35. The intrusion of this note here gives what may well be an exaggerated emphasis to the incident.

d) SOLOMON'S SACRIFICES (9:25)

25. Solomon used to offer sacrifices **three times a year.** These are probably the three harvest festivals of the pre-exilic period, the feast of Unleavened Bread (the barley harvest festival), the feast of Weeks (the wheat harvest festival), and the feast of Ingathering (vintage and autumn fruits). All three were the occasion of pilgrimages—already established in Canaan when the Hebrews settled in the land. Solomon offered the two types of sacrifice, the **burnt offerings,** wholly burned on the altar as a gift to God, and the so-called **peace offerings,** largely eaten by the worshipers. The last two phrases of the verse are obscure. The easiest solution is that both phrases are postexilic additions, the one to say that Solomon also offered **incense** after the postexilic custom, the other to say that he did everything necessary to complete the temple and secure adequate custom and ritual in it.

e) SOLOMON'S OVERSEAS TRADE (9:26-28)

Solomon sends a trading venture to far-off Ophir from his port on the Gulf of Aqabah, on the northeast arm of the Red Sea (see Nelson Glueck, *The Other Side of the Jordan* [New Haven: American Schools of Oriental Research, 1940], pp. 89-113). His ships were manned by Phoenician seamen. The venture was the forerunner of regular three-year voyages (10:22). The M.T. says that the first voyage brought back 420 talents of gold (ten million dollars), though the LXX states that the amount was only 120 talents.

28. Ophir: There is considerable difference of opinion as to the whereabouts of this El Dorado of ancient times. The three chief suggestions are: first, southeastern Arabia;

from thence gold, four hundred and twenty talents, and brought it to king Solomon.

10 And when the queen of Sheba heard of the fame of Solomon concerning the name of the LORD, she came to prove him with hard questions.

2 And she came to Jerusalem with a very great train, with camels that bare spices, and very much gold, and precious stones: and when she was come to Solomon, she communed with him of all that was in her heart.

3 And Solomon told her all her questions: there was not *any* thing hid from the king, which he told her not.

dred and twenty talents; and they brought it to King Solomon.

10 Now when the queen of Sheba heard of the fame of Solomon concerning the name of the LORD, she came to test him with hard questions. 2 She came to Jerusalem with a very great retinue, with camels bearing spices, and very much gold, and precious stones; and when she came to Solomon, she told him all that was on her mind. 3 And Solomon answered all her questions; there was nothing hidden from the king which he could not explain to her.

second, the Ethiopian coast of the Red Sea, known to the Egyptians as Punt; third, Mashonaland, the ruins of Zimbabwe between the Zambezi and Limpopo rivers. The last is an attractive suggestion, especially since it is known that there were Phoenician settlements along the east coast of Africa. The second is too near for a three-year voyage. The first is the most likely, since the area was famous for its gold in ancient times and was on the regular trade routes to South India, both the overland Arabian route and the Red Sea water route. The words used in 10:22 for "apes," "sandalwood" and perhaps "peacocks" are of Sanskrit origin and still in use to this day on the Malabar Coast.

f) VISIT OF THE QUEEN OF SHEBA (10:1-13)

This story is told to illustrate the surpassing wisdom of Solomon, so great that it spread throughout Arabia among those very tribes which were famous for their wisdom from ancient times. Both Solomon and the queen of Sheba are prominent in Eastern legends. The Arabs called her Bilkis, but in Ethiopian legends her name is Makeda. Sheba was the great trading community of southwestern Arabia, and at this period controlled the overland trade routes.

10:1. There is general agreement that **hard questions** is the best rendering of the Hebrew חידות, partly on the ground that the kind of riddle which is found in the Samson story (Judg. 14:12, 14, 18) is too futile. But Josephus (*Antiquities* VIII. 5. 3)

10:1-13. Not Won by Wonder.—Solomon had prayed that the glory of the temple might turn the minds of foreign visitors to "know thy name and fear thee" (8:43). A test of the temple's power was given in the case of the queen of Sheba. She came to Jerusalem, beheld its splendors, and admitted that Solomon surpassed in wisdom and prosperity all that had been told her (vss. 6-7). In her enthusiasm she cried, **Blessed be the LORD your God, who has delighted in you and set you on the throne of Israel!** But the record of the queen's visit closes thus: **King Solomon gave to the queen of Sheba all that she desired, whatever she asked besides what was given her by the bounty of King Solomon. So she turned and went back to her own land, with her servants.** There is no mention that the queen sought any further knowledge of Solomon's God or came to share the king's faith. The temple had aroused her won-

der, but it had not won a new convert. She had been impressed with what the Lord had done for Israel, but she did not bring him home to herself.

We are familiar with the expression, "bringing a thing home to ourselves." We mean thereby taking it into those vital centers of interest where we really live, so that it affects our daily conduct and stabs us broad awake or, to use an American colloquialism, "gets under the skin." This personal penetration of one's inmost being by the Lord is what the queen of Sheba apparently failed to experience. Men praise the Lord. They build shrines in his name. They make offerings at his altar. But they do not bring him home to themselves.

With the institutional growth of a religion its externalism and formalism tend to increase. In the early pioneering days of a religious movement the emotional experience of its fol-

4 And when the queen of Sheba had seen all Solomon's wisdom, and the house that he had built,

5 And the meat of his table, and the sitting of his servants, and the attendance of his ministers, and their apparel, and his cupbearers, and his ascent by which he went up unto the house of the LORD; there was no more spirit in her.

6 And she said to the king, It was a true report that I heard in mine own land of thy acts and of thy wisdom.

7 Howbeit I believed not the words, until I came, and mine eyes had seen *it;* and, behold, the half was not told me: thy wisdom and prosperity exceedeth the fame which I heard.

8 Happy *are* thy men, happy *are* these thy servants, which stand continually before thee, *and* that hear thy wisdom.

4 And when the queen of Sheba had seen all the wisdom of Solomon, the house that he had built, 5 the food of his table, the seating of his officials, and the attendance of his servants, their clothing, his cupbearers, and his burnt offerings which he offered at the house of the LORD, there was no more spirit in her.

6 And she said to the king, "The report was true which I heard in my own land of your affairs and of your wisdom, 7 but I did not believe the reports until I came and my own eyes had seen it; and, behold, the half was not told me; your wisdom and prosperity surpass the report which I heard. 8 Happy are your wives!*f* Happy are these your servants, who continually stand before

f Gk Syr: Heb *men*

---

says that Hiram and Solomon indulged in such a contest of wits. Similarly, in modern times Charles M. Doughty tells how he spent the evenings with the old man Nejm and his fellow Arabs and when he himself propounded the ancient riddle of the Sphinx, they were all delighted with the homely interpretation. He says, "This kind of parabolical wisdom falls to the Semitic humour and is very pleasant to the Arabs" (*Travels in Arabia Deserta* [New York: Random House, 1946], p. 237).

5. She had no courage left wherewith to continue to compete with him in the interchange of wise and hidden sayings. The Hebrew רוח (**spirit**) normally carries the idea of power, so that as a psychological term it denotes the dominant impulse or characteristic disposition of the individual. It stands for that energy and determination which is the mainspring of action, and this is its significance here.

---

lowers pours forth like the hot lava of a volcano, to be transformed by time into traditions and institutions as rigid and lifeless as the encrustation of a once-active crater. Spectators wonder at the power which once was there, but they do not feel it. To David the simple ark of the covenant was a source of life; to Sheba's queen the magnificent temple was only a spectacle for a momentary thrill.

Organization is as necessary in the religious realm as in other spheres of human activity. We can no more channel the currents of complex social life Godward without the aid of ecclesiastical institutions than we can carry the modern world's commerce in canoes. But as groups and organizations grow, the individual tends to shrink. How preserve the personal from the dwarfing pressure of numbers and the stifling formalism of institutions? The vast cathedrals, the throng of worshipers, the national and world councils of churches impress us with God's greatness; but all this must be supplemented by a sense of his nearness. Im-

pressions can become the food of our souls; but as George Tyrrell reminded us, if they are to become so, we must ruminate them, as cows do their food. To take the inspiration gained from a great service of worship and meditate on it until it becomes the motive power of personal action; to catch world outlooks from the church at large and then to translate these into racial sympathies sweetening the church in the local community; to join with others in common prayer and lofty liturgy and then to transpose these into the first person singular of "my sin," "my Lord," "my faith"—these are among the tasks involved in bringing religion home from the temple. And if in earlier days it was a matter of great difficulty to fix the attention of men on the world within them, because "the largest part of mankind are nowhere greater strangers than at home," [4] it is even more difficult as machine culture tends to make meditation a lost art.

Furthermore, the family has an indispensable

[4] Coleridge, *Table Talk.*

9 Blessed be the LORD thy God, which delighted in thee, to set thee on the throne of Israel: because the LORD loved Israel for ever, therefore made he thee king, to do judgment and justice.

10 And she gave the king a hundred and twenty talents of gold, and of spices very great store, and precious stones: there came no more such abundance of spices as these which the queen of Sheba gave to king Solomon.

11 And the navy also of Hiram, that brought gold from Ophir, brought in from Ophir great plenty of almug trees, and precious stones.

12 And the king made of the almug trees pillars for the house of the LORD, and for the king's house, harps also and psalteries for singers: there came no such almug trees, nor were seen unto this day.

13 And king Solomon gave unto the queen of Sheba all her desire, whatsoever she asked, besides *that* which Solomon gave her of his royal bounty. So she turned and went to her own country, she and her servants.

you and hear your wisdom! **9** Blessed be the LORD your God, who has delighted in you and set you on the throne of Israel! Because the LORD loved Israel for ever, he has made you king, that you may execute justice and righteousness." **10** Then she gave the king a hundred and twenty talents of gold, and a very great quantity of spices, and precious stones; never again came such an abundance of spices as these which the queen of Sheba gave to King Solomon.

11 Moreover the fleet of Hiram, which brought gold from Ophir, brought from Ophir a very great amount of almug wood and precious stones. **12** And the king made of the almug wood supports for the house of the LORD, and for the king's house, lyres also and harps for the singers; no such almug wood has come or been seen, to this day.

13 And King Solomon gave to the queen of Sheba all that she desired, whatever she asked besides what was given her by the bounty of King Solomon. So she turned and went back to her own land, with her servants.

---

9. The queen of Sheba ascribes praise to God for the wisdom of Solomon. God has fulfilled the promise of the dream of Gibeon. The blessing takes a Deuteronomic turn in that God has shown his love for Israel in establishing Solomon upon the throne as a king who shall fulfill the Deuteronomic ideals of **justice and righteousness.**

11-12. The references to the spices and precious stones in vs. 10 have led to the insertion, from 9:26-28, of these two verses in order to complete the tale of the exotic wares which Solomon received by land and sea. The **almug trees** are now generally held to be logs of sandalwood, bright red in color, heavy, and close-grained, and therefore admirably suitable for decorative carving and for the fashioning of musical instruments. On the other hand, Josephus (*Antiquities* VIII. 7. 1) was careful to explain that the almug tree was like pine wood, "but whiter, and [it] glistens more."

13. The bounty probably refers to Solomon's hospitality in general, but he far and away exceeded this in his generosity to the Arabian queen.

---

function in bringing religious faith down from its formal and public manifestations to its personal realization and application. George Santayana, the Spaniard who taught so long and brilliantly at Harvard, became the master of exquisite English, but he confessed that the roots of the language never quite reached the center of his soul, because he did not imbibe in childhood its homely cadences and ditties. Religious faith, like language, is brought home to us in the home. When God in Christ is made head of the house he imparts a lifting purpose which lightens the load of housekeeping. He lessens the frictions which so frequently take the luster off marital love. He infuses the inti-

mate adjustments of home living with the grace of sympathetic understanding. He gives that charitable reasonableness which disarms hasty tempers. He enriches the comradeship of husband and wife with those spiritual insights that do not dim with the fading of passion but deepen with time.

And if we are to bring the Lord home from the temple so that he changes life, we must get him into our circles of work. An English writer once whimsically said that the American businessman goes home to his office every morning. Unless the daily consciousness of God gets into our shops and offices, he does not affect us where we really live. We can pass church resolu-

14 ¶ Now the weight of gold that came to Solomon in one year was six hundred threescore and six talents of gold,

15 Besides *that he had* of the merchantmen, and of the traffic of the spice merchants, and of all the kings of Arabia, and of the governors of the country.

16 ¶ And king Solomon made two hundred targets *of* beaten gold: six hundred *shekels* of gold went to one target.

17 And *he made* three hundred shields *of* beaten gold; three pounds of gold went to one shield: and the king put them in the house of the forest of Lebanon.

18 ¶ Moreover, the king made a great throne of ivory, and overlaid it with the best gold.

19 The throne had six steps, and the top of the throne *was* round behind: and *there*

14 Now the weight of gold that came to Solomon in one year was six hundred and sixty-six talents of gold, 15 besides that which came from the traders and from the traffic of the merchants, and from all the kings of Arabia and from the governors of the land. 16 King Solomon made two hundred large shields of beaten gold; six hundred shekels of gold went into each shield. 17 And he made three hundred shields of beaten gold; three minas of gold went in to each shield; and the king put them in the House of the Forest of Lebanon. 18 The king also made a great ivory throne, and overlaid it with the finest gold. 19 The throne had six steps, and at the back of the

g) CLIMAX OF SOLOMON'S SPLENDOR (10:14-29)

These verses contain miscellaneous details, taken doubtless from the biography of Solomon, all to demonstrate that God more than fulfilled the promises he had made to the young king.

14. **Six hundred and sixty-six talents of gold** were the equivalent of about sixteen and a quarter million dollars, and this does not include the taxes he levied on traders. The figure seems to be very high, especially in view of the purchasing power of gold, which was considerably higher than even the pre-1914 level. On the other hand, it is small in comparison with modern expenditure, and the items detailed in vss. 16-21, together with the cost of the standing army of chariotry, both purchase and maintenance, would demand an enormous income.

15. The **governors** were vassal princes who paid tribute to Solomon and were allowed to exercise their authority subject to his will. It is unlikely that the reference is to Solomon's administrative officers (4:7-19), since the context deals with foreigners. Further, the word פחה is an Assyrian loan word meaning "viceroy."

16. The larger **shields** were oblong and were made to cover the whole body like the Roman *scutum*, weighing about twenty pounds. The smaller shields were round, like the Roman *clipeus*, weighing about five pounds. They were used by the royal bodyguard on ceremonial occasions (cf. 14:26-28).

tions about Christianizing industry, but broad generalizations are not enough. Each employer must look at his relations with his men in the light of Christ's teachings to see if he is out primarily to make profits or to develop persons, to see if he puts property values above human values. The employee must look at his pay envelope in the light of Christ's principles to see if he is giving a just return for wages received. Individuals cannot delegate their relations with God to a corporation or a labor union. To the Christian Christ should ever be a personal influence in his place of work, as F. W. Robertson, the beloved minister of Brighton, was to a certain shopkeeper in that city. The man kept a

picture of Robertson in a room back of his little shop, and he said that when he was tempted to do something mean, to take advantage of a customer, or to be unkind, he would step back and look at Robertson's face. From the temple to the closet, the home, the office; from general praise to particular situations; from obeisance to obedience—such are some of the steps by which God becomes a reality to individuals. Solomon's temple impressed the queen of Sheba, but she went back to her own land and her own gods.

10:14–11:3. *The Gold Tarnishes.*—Solomon's reign received more scriptural publicity than that of any other monarch. The detail into

were stays on either side on the place of the seat, and two lions stood beside the stays.

20 And twelve lions stood there on the one side and on the other upon the six steps: there was not the like made in any kingdom.

21 ¶ And all king Solomon's drinking vessels *were of* gold, and all the vessels of the house of the forest of Lebanon *were of* pure gold; none *were of* silver: it was nothing accounted of in the days of Solomon.

22 For the king had at sea a navy of Tharshish with the navy of Hiram: once in three years came the navy of Tharshish, bringing gold, and silver, ivory, and apes, and peacocks.

23 So king Solomon exceeded all the kings of the earth for riches and for wisdom.

24 ¶ And all the earth sought to Solomon, to hear his wisdom, which God had put in his heart.

25 And they brought every man his present, vessels of silver, and vessels of gold, and garments, and armor, and spices, horses, and mules, a rate year by year.

26 ¶ And Solomon gathered together chariots and horsemen: and he had a thousand and four hundred chariots, and twelve thousand horsemen, whom he bestowed in the cities for chariots, and with the king at Jerusalem.

27 And the king made silver *to be* in Jerusalem as stones, and cedars made he *to be* as the sycamore trees that *are* in the vale, for abundance.

28 ¶ And Solomon had horses brought out of Egypt, and linen yarn: the king's merchants received the linen yarn at a price.

throne was a calf's head, and on each side of the seat were arm rests and two lions standing beside the arm rests, **20** while twelve lions stood there, one on each end of a step on the six steps. The like of it was never made in any kingdom. **21** All King Solomon's drinking vessels were of gold, and all the vessels of the House of the Forest of Lebanon were of pure gold; none were of silver, it was not considered as anything in the days of Solomon. **22** For the king had a fleet of ships of Tarshish at sea with the fleet of Hiram. Once every three years the fleet of ships of Tarshish used to come bringing gold, silver, ivory, apes, and peacocks.*g*

23 Thus King Solomon excelled all the kings of the earth in riches and in wisdom. **24** And the whole earth sought the presence of Solomon to hear his wisdom, which God had put into his mind. **25** Every one of them brought his present, articles of silver and gold, garments, myrrh, spices, horses, and mules, so much year by year.

26 And Solomon gathered together chariots and horsemen; he had fourteen hundred chariots and twelve thousand horsemen, whom he stationed in the chariot cities and with the king in Jerusalem. **27** And the king made silver as common in Jerusalem as stone, and he made cedar as plentiful as the sycamore of the Shephe′lah. **28** And Solomon's import of horses was from Egypt and Ku′e, and the king's traders received

g Or *baboons*

---

22. The **fleet of ships of Tarshish** was a merchant fleet of "ocean-going liners." Tarshish is probably the ancient Tartessos, on the Guadalquivir in Spain, a Phoenician settlement. A ship of Tarshish was a ship large and stout enough to venture on what in those days was a long and hazardous voyage.

27. The **sycamore of the Shephelah,** i.e., of the low hills between the Judean highlands and the sea, is of the same genus as the fig, and is known to botanists as *Ficus sycomorus.* The tree is not to be confused with the common sycamore, which is of the same genus as the maple. The wood of the sycamore (spelled variously sycomore and sycamine) is light and porous, much used in Egypt for making mummy cases. The tree was very common in Palestine in ancient times, as is shown by the ancient Greek name for Haifa, which was Sycaminopolis. The wide-spreading branches of the tree afforded plenty of shade, made it greatly esteemed as a wayside tree, and gave a characteristic aspect to the countryside.

28. Most scholars agree with Lenormant and Winckler that מצרים does not here refer to **Egypt,** as usually, but to *Muçri* in north Syria. Similarly, it is generally held

29 And a chariot came up and went out of Egypt for six hundred *shekels* of silver, and a horse for a hundred and fifty: and so for all the kings of the Hittites, and for the kings of Syria, did they bring *them* out by their means.

11 But king Solomon loved many strange women, together with the daughter of Pharaoh, women of the Moabites, Ammonites, Edomites, Zidonians, *and* Hittites;

2 Of the nations *concerning* which the LORD said unto the children of Israel, Ye shall not go in to them, neither shall they come in unto you: *for* surely they will turn

them from Ku'e at a price. 29 A chariot could be imported from Egypt for six hundred shekels of silver, and a horse for a hundred and fifty; and so through the king's traders they were exported to all the kings of the Hittites and the kings of Syria.

11 Now King Solomon loved many foreign women: the daughter of Pharaoh, and Moabite, Ammonite, E'domite, Sido'nian, and Hittite women, 2 from the nations concerning which the LORD had said to the people of Israel, "You shall not enter into marriage with them, neither shall

---

that the difficult word מקוה, **linen yarn,** hides the place name **Kue,** in the plains of Cilicia. This latter is actually the reading of the Vulg. (*de Coa*), and it was found in one variant quoted by Field. This double identification of two place names from the area north of Palestine is supported by Ezek. 27:14, where Togarmah (north Syria and Asia Minor) is given as the name of the area whence the Tyrians imported horses for riding, war horses, and mules. On the other hand, both Deut. 17:16 and Isa. 31:1 say that horses were imported from Egypt. It is possible that Deut. 17:16 is late enough for a mistake to be made in favor of the better-known country, but it is difficult to see how Isa. 31:1 could be wrong. It is therefore better to follow Koenig, who agrees that the second name is **Kue,** but retains Egypt for the first.

3. SOLOMON'S FOREIGN WIVES AND HIS IDOLATRY (11:1-13)

The editor has now told the whole story of Solomon's greatness and splendor. The king who built the temple which was so dear to the Deuteronomic editor fulfilled the Deuteronomic law, was a model king, and was therefore most prosperous. But there was another side to the story of Solomon's reign. The editor has reserved this to the end. Things were far from being as rosy as the preceding chapters suggest. That much can be gathered from this chapter. The editor has so arranged his material as to suggest that all went well at first, and that it was only toward the end of his reign that Solomon failed in his duty as a Deuteronomic king.

11:1. The LXX reads, "a lover of women; and he married many foreign wives." In the original biography of Solomon the statement doubtless appeared without any adverse comments. It may well be that according to the ideas of the time the possession of many wives, especially when some of them were of foreign extraction, was a matter for praise rather than blame. Certainly the marriage with Pharaoh's daughter is regularly represented as being a matter of considerable congratulation.

2. The crime of Solomon's marriages is clearly set forth. It was not so much that he married Pharaoh's daughter, but rather that he married nationals with whom intermarriage was forbidden in Deuteronomic law (Exod. 34:16; Deut. 7:3-4).

---

which the record goes reveals the delight which the recorder takes in the glory that was Solomon's. Later generations found vicarious pride in looking back from their lowered estate to "the good old days" when their Jerusalem was the capital of the world's wealth. But his patriotic zeal did not prevent the Chronicler from exposing the perils inherent in such a regime as Solomon's. The gold begins to tarnish. Solo-

mon's steps of descent are the reverse of Paul's ladder of hope: "Tribulation worketh patience; and patience, experience; and experience, hope" (Rom. 5:3-4). Here we see that power works pride; and pride, arrogance; and arrogance, forgetfulness of God. And then the sensuousness of Solomon leads to sensuality. Here is the sequel to his splendor: **Now King Solomon loved many foreign women.**

away your heart after their gods: Solomon clave unto these in love.

3 And he had seven hundred wives, princesses, and three hundred concubines: and his wives turned away his heart.

4 For it came to pass, when Solomon was old, *that* his wives turned away his heart after other gods: and his heart was not per-

they with you, for surely they will turn away your heart after their gods"; Solomon clung to these in love. 3 He had seven hundred wives, princesses, and three hundred concubines; and his wives turned away his heart. 4 For when Solomon was old his wives turned away his heart after other gods; and

---

3. There is no need to doubt the accuracy of these numbers.

11:4a. Temptations of the Strong.—In ch. 10 Solomon is shown at the peak of his power. That is a point of danger. History is filled with figures who rose on the steppingstones of their virtues to heights of success and then revealed defects that worked their downfall. Power confronts character with subtler temptations than does weakness. Compare with Solomon the case of King Uzziah, of whom it was written: "And his name spread far abroad; for he was marvelously helped, till he was strong. But when he was strong, his heart was lifted up to his destruction" (II Chr. 26:15-16). Here the record is: **For when Solomon was old his wives turned away his heart after other gods.** If the ability of his wives to pervert Solomon's conscience had rested on their physical appeal, he would have been led astray in the younger years of his stronger passions. But now in his age power had gone to his head and heart. His was the weakness hidden in human strength.

Strength is very deceitful. Take the matter of physical health. A wise person is aware that he cannot trust his own feelings as an accurate guide in keeping himself fit. It has been said that those who boast most about their buoyant unbroken health during their first fifty years are quite often the ones who break most quickly after fifty. It quite frequently happens that the bodily organ we think the strongest proves the weakest. In the mental realm strength is even more deceptive. All human knowledge pretends to be more true than it is. Minds are always in danger of being stunted by intellectual pride, which is ignorance of ignorance. Charles F. Kettering, the eminent inventor, has pointed out that progress is due to what he terms "intelligent ignorance." Pioneers of intellectual advance have known enough to know how little they knew. One quality of the meek is that they know their limitations and thus live on the growing edge of life. And in the moral sphere strength is even more dangerously deceitful. How often it happens that a person's character is weakest at the point where he thinks himself strongest. Good traits of character are in personality somewhat as the grain is in wood. It is the grain which gives beauty to lovely wood, but if

you wish to split the wood, just hit it along the grain. Similarly, it is along the grain of his good traits that a man's character is most easily cracked open. Men may feel so sure of their strong points that they leave them unguarded. Or they may become proud of them, and pride makes any good trait bad. Let a man become too proud of his purity, and he becomes priggish and prudish. Let a man become too proud of his thrift, and he is likely to turn penurious and greedy. Let a person pride himself on his strong convictions, and he tends to become dogmatic and intolerant.

Solomon, who "excelled all the kings of the earth in riches and in wisdom" (10:23), had undoubtedly allowed pride to deceive him as to his own strength. It is reported of Francis of Assisi, whose humility of spirit shines across the centuries, that when he was tempted to think too highly of himself because of compliments paid him, he would ask some fellow friar to sit down with him and tell him his faults. That is a service which a good wife renders to a successful man. But Solomon, with all his wives and concubines, presumably had no one of such status and ability that she could correct the king's mounting self-esteem. In fact, the possession of such an enormous household only contributed to his corrupting sense of power, and thus **his wives turned away his heart** from humble submission to Yahweh **after other gods** whom he felt rich enough to patronize as well as placate.

Another temptation which besets the strong is the tendency to abuse their power. Signs of this may be seen in Solomon. The forced labor which he levied (9:15 ff.) and the discrimination made between the children of Israel and the captured foreigners whom he enslaved (9:20-22) reveal that the king was playing fast and loose with his power. Ecclesiastes turns our minds to a sad chapter of human history with his observations, as thoughtfully he ponders "what goes on within this world whenever men have power over their fellows" (Eccl. 8:9 Moffatt). Man has achieved such superb dominion over the earth, the sea, the air, the impersonal things; but when it comes to exercising power

fect with the Lord his God, as *was* the heart of David his father.

5 For Solomon went after Ashtoreth the goddess of the Zidonians, and after Milcom the abomination of the Ammonites.

6 And Solomon did evil in the sight of the Lord, and went not fully after the Lord, as *did* David his father.

his heart was not wholly true to the Lord his God, as was the heart of David his father. **5** For Solomon went after Ash'toreth the goddess of the Sido'nians, and after Milcom the abomination of the Ammonites. **6** So Solomon did what was evil in the sight of the Lord, and did not wholly follow the Lord, as David his father had done.

---

5. The M.T. has **Ashtoreth,** but the correct spelling is "Astarte." She was known as Ishtar in Mesopotamia, but in Syria was the female consort of Baal. She was the goddess of fertility and consequently of sexual love, the parallel to, and also one of the models for, the Greek Aphrodite. She had a great temple in Sidon, which was visited by the second-century A.D. Greek writer Lucian (*The Syrian Goddess* 4). She was often depicted on Sidonian coins as standing on the prow of a galley, leaning forward with right hand outstretched, being thus the original of all figureheads for sailing ships. She was in a special sense **the goddess of the Sidonians.**

The spelling of the M.T. is due to the Masoretes, who substituted the vowels of the word *bôsheth* ("shame") regularly in idolatrous names. In the present verse, at the end,

---

over his fellow men, he has made a sorry job of it.

The abuse of power plays havoc in every sphere of life. In the industrial realm it transforms the comradeship of fellow producers into a struggle for control between management and labor. In governmental affairs the badge of authority often makes petty tyrants out of little people, and the possession of power is perverted into dictatorship. In the sphere of religion one of the dire tragedies of history is that ecclesiastical groups which plead for tolerance when they are in the minority refuse to practice tolerance when they are in the majority. Power is safe only when held in humble hands for the purpose of service. "Ye know that the princes of the Gentiles exercise dominion over them, and they that are great exercise authority upon them. But it shall not be so among you: but whosoever will be great among you, let him be your minister; and whosoever will be chief among you, let him be your servant; even as the Son of man came not to be ministered unto, but to minister" (Matt. 20:25-28). There we have the contrast between the pagan and the Christian use of power. The sons of men want power for the sake of domination; "the Son of man came not to be ministered unto, but to minister." That is one reason why the Christ has outlived the Caesars of the first century and the dictators of the twentieth.

Solomon began by humbly praying for wisdom with which to judge and serve his people. The power which he received deceived him, and he abused it. Power *for* deteriorated into power *over*. That is the beginning of its end.

4b. Not with the Whole Heart.—It would perhaps be unfair to say that Solomon was only

halfhearted in his allegiance to the Lord; but **his heart was not wholly true to the Lord his God, as was the heart of David his father.** And when a person is not wholehearted in any cause, he can hardly be trusted. James Moffatt is reported as having said that the Sixth Beatitude means "Blessed are they who are not double-minded, for they shall be admitted into the intimate presence of God." The Epistle of James indicates a similar understanding of "the pure in heart"—"Purify your hearts, ye double-minded" (Jas. 4:8). The expression "double-minded" suggests instability, unsettledness, even deceitfulness. A person may be double-minded because he lacks integration. He thinks one way today and another way tomorrow, or he is moved one way by one side of his nature and a different way by the other side of his nature. Or a man may be double-minded because he lacks integrity. He thinks one way but speaks another. He has two reasons for what he does: a good reason which he announces, and a real reason which he keeps to himself. But whether he lacks integration or integrity, he is unstable. If we are to be pure in heart we must, as Kierkegaard reminds us, will only one thing, and that the good. And this means willing the good because it is the good, not because we shall get some reward from it or escape the punishment which comes from willing the bad. Solomon's prayer at this stage of his career should have been, "Unite my heart to fear thy name" (Ps. 86:11).

When a person is not wholehearted, there is a looseness of grip. And laxity is usually the first stage of lawlessness. To use Hosea's oft-quoted description of his contemporaries, "They have sown the wind, and they shall reap the whirl-

7 Then did Solomon build a high place for Chemosh, the abomination of Moab, in the hill that *is* before Jerusalem, and for Molech, the abomination of the children of Ammon.

8 And likewise did he for all his strange wives, which burnt incense and sacrificed unto their gods.

9 ¶ And the Lord was angry with Solomon, because his heart was turned from the Lord God of Israel, which had appeared unto him twice,

10 And had commanded him concerning this thing, that he should not go after other gods: but he kept not that which the Lord commanded.

11 Wherefore the Lord said unto Solomon, Forasmuch as this is done of thee, and thou hast not kept my covenant and my statutes, which I have commanded thee, I will surely rend the kingdom from thee, and will give it to thy servant.

7 Then Solomon built a high place for Chemosh the abomination of Moab, and for Molech the abomination of the Ammonites, on the mountain east of Jerusalem. 8 And so he did for all his foreign wives, who burned incense and sacrificed to their gods.

9 And the Lord was angry with Solomon, because his heart had turned away from the Lord, the God of Israel, who had appeared to him twice, 10 and had commanded him concerning this thing, that he should not go after other gods; but he did not keep what the Lord commanded. 11 Therefore the Lord said to Solomon, "Since this has been your mind and you have not kept my covenant and my statutes which I have commanded you, I will surely tear the kingdom from you and will give it to your serv-

the word *shiqqûç*, **abomination,** has actually been substituted for the word "god" (cf. LXX). The name **Milcom** means "king," though the vowels have been altered (cf. vs. 7, where the word *mélekh,* "king," actually is found, though with the vowels of *bôsheth*).

7. Solomon built shrines for the gods of Moab and Ammon on the Mount of Olives, which is to the east of Jerusalem. The M.T. has **before,** i.e., **east,** which is correct.

8. According to the Greek version of Lucian, it was Solomon who burned and slew sacrificial animals to the foreign gods. As elsewhere, the meaning is that Solomon burned whole offerings on the altar and slew animals for the sacred feasts which were a leading feature of all pre-exilic religion in Palestine, whether truly orthodox or tainted with Canaanite rites and interpretations.

9-13. These verses contain the Deuteronomic condemnation of Solomon (cf. also Deut. 17:16-20, which owes a great deal to the misdeeds of this king). The editor makes it appear that all Solomon's sins and troubles belonged to the king's later years. A closer examination of vss. 14-43 shows that the revolts belonged to the earlier part of

wind" (Hos. 8:7). Just as a gentle breeze can be whipped into the destructive rage of a whirlwind, so a little easy, breezy looseness of attitude can develop into gusty passion. In the first stages it may be called tact or agreeableness. The slight compromise of principle may seem quite harmless. But how often the gentle going with the wind of circumstance accelerates the loosening until conscience is "gone with the wind." A British inventor, some time ago, devised a gadget for decreasing automobile accidents. Many of these, he believes, are due to the fatigue of the driver and the resultant relaxing of grip. Hence he designed a buzzer which can be kept quiet only by a firm hand on the wheel. However feasible such an invention may be in the automobile world, it suggests a genuine

value in the moral realm. We need warning signals to tighten our grip on the steering gear of conscience. We need some fixed standards amid our vague ideals.

In the struggle with sin, those who like Solomon try to keep one foot in the godly way and the other outside have a sorry time. A religious experience that is only skin-deep is likely to be full of irritations and pricks, for our nerves are most numerous nearest the surface. When we get under the skin down toward the vital organs, the pain of the wound seems to grow less. Superficial Christians are always bemoaning the burdensome obligations of the church. Their contributions are a continuing source of irritation. But the truly devout man whose religion has become deeply vital never thinks of his

12 Notwithstanding, in thy days I will not do it for David thy father's sake: *but* I will rend it out of the hand of thy son.

13 Howbeit I will not rend away all the kingdom; *but* will give one tribe to thy son for David my servant's sake, and for Jerusalem's sake which I have chosen.

14 ¶ And the LORD stirred up an adversary unto Solomon, Hadad the Edomite: he *was* of the king's seed in Edom.

ant. **12** Yet for the sake of David your father I will not do it in your days, but I will tear it out of the hand of your son. **13** However I will not tear away all the kingdom; but I will give one tribe to your son, for the sake of David my servant and for the sake of Jerusalem which I have chosen."

14 And the LORD raised up an adversary against Solomon, Hadad the E′domite; he

---

the reign. It is almost certain that the building of the apostate shrines also was much earlier than the Deuteronomic editor would allow.

12. The official theory of the O.T. is that sin meets with immediate and sudden doom, so that any lapse of time between the sin and the calamity is due to the forbearance of God. In Ps. 73:18-20 the psalmist accepts this theory, but comforts himself for the untoward flourishing of the wicked with the thought that the doom will be all the more sudden when it comes. God shows forbearance toward the house of David in that, in spite of all Solomon's wickedness, he will not punish the house of David forthwith but will delay the punishment till Solomon is dead.

13. There is always an uncertainty as to whether Benjamin was to be counted among the northern tribes or with Judah. The official numbering is ten for the north and one for the south (cf. vs. 32). Possibly this virtual omission of Benjamin is a reflection of the decimation of that tribe recorded in Judg. 20.

4. Two Revolts (11:14-25)

There were two revolts during the reign of Solomon, for both Hadad of Edom and one of Hadadezer's vassals (cf. II Sam. 10:19) set up independent kingdoms. The author makes it appear that these two revolts, which seriously diminished Solomon's power and resources, took place toward the end of his reign, and thus formed a Deuteronomic judgment on him. It is probable that they belonged to a much earlier time in his reign (see vss. 21, 25).

a) Revolt of Hadad (11:14-22)

Winckler has disentangled with considerable plausibility two interwoven stories in these verses (Burney, *Notes on Hebrew Text of Kings*, pp. 158-60). According to one

---

religious duties as a sacrifice. Henry Drummond once said that he who seeks first the kingdom of God will have some problems, but that he who seeks the kingdom of God second will have nothing but problems.

The record contrasts Solomon's lack of wholehearted loyalty to the Lord with David's perfect devotion (cf. 15:3). David had sinned, as in the memorable case of Uriah. But David's sin of fleshly passion lacked the deteriorating and damning quality inherent in sins of the mind and heart. In the life of the spirit slow changes need more to be watched than sudden shocks. Some sins are a rash, breaking out like measles in a single night. But the seven deadly sins, as traditional theology lists them, suggest slow decay rather than sudden outbreak. Pride, covetousness, lust, anger, envy, gluttony, and sloth are sins which gradually harden the

arteries of the spirit and sap the energies of the will. For this reason Jesus, in line with the record here, is more severe in condemning the sins of the mind and heart than the sins of physical passion and open shame. The latter beget bodily effects and a social disgrace which tend to awaken a spirit of repentance; but the former may be carried so secretly and respectably that there is no sting of the conscience. Consequently, Jesus said to the chief priests and the elders, whose sin-calloused minds were smugly complacent, "The publicans and the harlots go into the kingdom of God before you" (Matt. 21:31).

14-43. *Does God Send Adversaries?*—In this early record Yahweh is pictured as one who in anger vows vengeance. His punishments are prompt and direct. The Lord had said to Solomon, "Since this has been your mind and

15 For it came to pass, when David was in Edom, and Joab the captain of the host was gone up to bury the slain, after he had smitten every male in Edom;

16 (For six months did Joab remain there with all Israel, until he had cut off every male in Edom:)

17 That Hadad fled, he and certain Edomites of his father's servants with him, to go into Egypt; Hadad *being* yet a little child.

18 And they arose out of Midian, and came to Paran: and they took men with them out of Paran, and they came to Egypt, unto Pharaoh king of Egypt; which gave him a house, and appointed him victuals, and gave him land.

19 And Hadad found great favor in the sight of Pharaoh, so that he gave him to wife the sister of his own wife, the sister of Tahpenes the queen.

20 And the sister of Tahpenes bare him Genubath his son, whom Tahpenes weaned

was of the royal house of Edom. 15 For when David was in Edom, and Jo'ab the commander of the army went up to bury the slain, he slew every male in Edom 16 (for Jo'ab and all Israel remained there six months, until he had cut off every male in Edom); 17 but Hadad fled to Egypt, together with certain Edomites of his father's servants, Hadad being yet a little child. 18 They set out from Mid'ian and came to Paran, and took men with them from Paran and came to Egypt, to Pharaoh king of Egypt, who gave him a house, and assigned him an allowance of food, and gave him land. 19 And Hadad found great favor in the sight of Pharaoh, so that he gave him in marriage the sister of his own wife, the sister of Tah'penes the queen. 20 And the

---

story (so Winckler), Hadad was a small boy when David conquered Edom. He was saved from the general massacre and carried off to Egypt, where he was brought up by Pharaoh's wife Tahpenes among the sons of Pharaoh. He returned to Edom after both David and Joab were dead (vs. 25 LXX) and made himself king over Edom. The second story is of a Midianite prince named Adad, who fled to Egypt with some Edomites. He married the sister of Tahpenes and had a son named Genubath, who was brought up in Pharaoh's household. He returned to Midian and set up an independent kingdom there. This second story, as reconstructed by Winckler, is not as convincing as the first, though it may well be true. What does seem to be clear is that Hadad the Edomite revolted quite early in Solomon's reign.

19. The word translated **queen** is גבירה. It refers strictly to the "chief lady" of the harem. Sometimes, therefore, the reference is to the queen mother, and at other times to the queen herself; cf. the important position held by Bathsheba (2:19) and also the special note concerning the removal of Asa's mother from this position (15:13).

---

you have not kept my covenant and my statutes which I have commanded you, I will surely tear the kingdom from you and will give it to your servant" (vs. 11). **And the LORD raised up an adversary against Solomon** (vs. 14; cf. also vs. 23).

Can such passion and promptness be ascribed to God? Our modern minds say no; for we have learned the lesson of Job, that direct connections cannot be traced between goodness and its reward, or between badness and its punishment. As the voice out of the whirlwind revealed to the ancient sufferer, the creator of our vast complex universe does not deal with us after the fashion of an office bookkeeper or a petty police court. His ways are higher than our ways, as the heavens are high above the earth. But

while one should not impute to God our human desire for vengeance or our impatience for direct action, one must not let the primitive ethics of this passage blind us to the stern fact of moral retribution. Evil does defeat itself. The abuse of power begets the loss of power. Our Bible begins with the Genesis story of a gate closing behind those who have sinned their way out of a garden. Some of our moral codes are mere conventions which vary with different countries and different times. Some things which were considered right in the days of Solomon were wrong in the days of Jesus, because "New occasions teach new duties, Time makes ancient good uncouth." [5] But some ethical laws are so basic that they are embedded in the very texture

[5] James Russell Lowell, "The Present Crisis," st. xviii.

in Pharaoh's house: and Genubath was in Pharaoh's household among the sons of Pharaoh.

21 And when Hadad heard in Egypt that David slept with his fathers, and that Joab the captain of the host was dead, Hadad said to Pharaoh, Let me depart, that I may go to mine own country.

22 Then Pharaoh said unto him, But what hast thou lacked with me, that, behold, thou seekest to go to thine own country? And he answered, Nothing: howbeit let me go in any wise.

23 ¶ And God stirred him up *another* adversary, Rezon the son of Eliadah, which fled from his lord Hadadezer king of Zobah:

24 And he gathered men unto him, and became captain over a band, when David slew them *of Zobah:* and they went to Damascus, and dwelt therein, and reigned in Damascus.

sister of Tah'penes bore him Genu'bath his son, whom Tah'penes weaned in Pharaoh's house; and Genu'bath was in Pharaoh's house among the sons of Pharaoh. 21 But when Hadad heard in Egypt that David slept with his fathers and that Jo'ab the commander of the army was dead, Hadad said to Pharaoh, "Let me depart, that I may go to my own country." 22 But Pharaoh said to him, "What have you lacked with me that you are now seeking to go to your own country?" And he said to him, "Only let me go."

23 God also raised up as an adversary to him, Rezon the son of Eli'ada, who had fled from his master Hadade'zer king of Zobah. 24 And he gathered men about him and became leader of a marauding band, after the slaughter by David; and they went to Damascus, and dwelt there, and made him

---

b) REVOLT OF REZON (11:23-25)

23-25. Some have thought that this whole story is due to a confusion between אדם (Edom) and ארם (Aram), two words which are most easily confused in the Hebrew, as indeed they are so confused in vs. 25. But the whole story is much too detailed for this and fits in too well with the story of II Sam. 10. Rezon refused at that time to submit either to his former overlord Hadadezer or to his new overlord David. He was for a time a captain of freebooters, like David, and also like David he took advantage of the difficulties of the true king through invaders. He established himself king, as also did David under similar circumstances, and founded the powerful kingdom of Aram-Damascus (Syria). This kingdom was a grievous thorn in the flesh of the Israelite kings of the ninth and eighth centuries, especially in the time before Ahab's victory (20:23-34) and again after Jehu had adopted an isolationist policy.

---

of human nature. And when we cut through the layers of moral convention which change with time and place, we come to bedrock distinctions on which common universal decency rests.

Solomon had broken his covenant with Yahweh. He had taken the law into his own hands. He had put his own interests first. And the egoist who puts himself first eventually gets in his own way. Jacob, who let no moral concerns stand in the way of his material desires, comes back to meet his brother Esau. In the lonely night watch on the eve of meeting the brother he had wronged, "Jacob was left alone; and there wrestled a man with him until the breaking of the day" (Gen. 32:24). Who was the man? Certainly it was no other human being. We may call this adversary an angel of the Lord, or as Lincoln would say, the "better angel" of Jacob's nature. The truth behind the story is that Jacob had at last come face to face

with the fact that his way was being blocked not by his brother Esau, nor by his father-in-law Laban, but by himself. He had discovered that he was standing in his own way. When a person does stand in his own way, he begins to blame others for being in his way. The spoiled child pouts because he thinks every family regulation is a restriction of his own liberty. The libertine who follows his own impulsive desires looks upon each social decency as a puritanical blue law. The person who takes the road of self-indulgence and self-interest, as followed by Jacob and Solomon, finds himself halted by the exhaustion of his own desires. The prodigal is delighted for a time in the gaiety of the far country, but eventually finds himself surrounded with husks. Francis Thompson may have tried delights of the flesh, but after he had fled from his conscience, "down the nights and down the days," and "under running laughter," he heard the Hound of Heaven pursuing him

25 And he was an adversary to Israel all the days of Solomon, besides the mischief that Hadad *did:* and he abhorred Israel, and reigned over Syria.

26 ¶ And Jeroboam the son of Nebat, an Ephrathite of Zereda, Solomon's servant, whose mother's name *was* Zeruah, a widow woman, even he lifted up *his* hand against the king.

27 And this *was* the cause that he lifted up *his* hand against the king: Solomon built Millo, *and* repaired the breaches of the city of David his father.

king in Damascus. 25 He was an adversary of Israel all the days of Solomon, doing mischief as Hadad did; and he abhorred Israel, and reigned over Syria.

26 Jerobo'am the son of Nebat, an E'phraimite of Zer'edah, a servant of Solomon, whose mother's name was Zeru'ah, a widow, also lifted up his hand against the king. 27 And this was the reason why he lifted up his hand against the king. Solomon built the Millo, and closed up the breach of the city of David his father.

---

5. Jeroboam's Early History (11:26-40)

The author is here giving the prologue to that revolt of the ten northern tribes which robbed the Davidic dynasty of the larger and more prosperous part of its own native territory. He makes it quite plain that this disaster was due to Solomon's neglect of his clear duty as a king after the Deuteronomic pattern. Solomon fostered the worship of other deities, among them the deities of Moab and Ammon, who are particularly to be abhorred in this connection (Deut. 23:3; Neh. 13:1). The insistence upon the worship of the Lord alone is absolute. Nevertheless, God does show his forbearance. Properly, he ought to have punished Solomon forthwith and torn the whole of his kingdom away from him. But God is forbearing and long-suffering. He shows these characteristics here by allowing Solomon to retain the whole kingdom until his death, and then by allowing his son to retain one tribe.

There is a parallel account in the LXX of the whole story of Jeroboam's activities both during Solomon's reign and in connection with the revolt of the Northern Kingdom after Solomon's death. The only difference in the two variant traditions before 12:24 is that in the LXX when the people came to lay their grievances before Rehoboam, Jeroboam was not with them, although he had returned to Israel at the news of Solomon's death. But in the long LXX insertion at 12:24, it is stated that after Solomon had put Jeroboam in charge of the forced labor gangs of the house of Joseph (i.e., of Israel), Jeroboam built Sareira in the hill country of Ephraim, raised a force of three hundred chariots, fortified the city (LXX adds "of David"), and "aspired to the kingdom." This account gives a reason for the statement in the M.T. (11:26) that Jeroboam **lifted up his hand against the king,** i.e., revolted against Solomon.

26. The LXX spelling of **Zeredah,** Jeroboam's birthplace, is Sareira, the scene, according to the LXX, of both of Jeroboam's revolts, one abortive (12:24*b*) and the other successful (12:24*f*). The name of Jeroboam's mother is given in the M.T. as Zeruah, which means "leprous." The name is not found in the LXX, and may well be malicious southern propaganda, invented by southern scribes because of their hatred of the man who broke up the kingdom and set up the idolatrous worship at Bethel. She is called a harlot in the LXX (12:24*b*; cf. John Skinner, *Kings* [New York: Oxford University Press, 1904; "The New-Century Bible"], p. 181).

---

with the words, "All things betray thee, who betrayest Me."

Who are the adversaries the Lord raises up against an egoistic and self-indulgent king? We need not be puzzled to explain the Lord's hand in the insurrections of Hadad and Rezon. Solomon betrayed himself. The straight and narrow way in which he had started his reign had been broadened by compromise. In his

affluence and expansiveness his principles had been adjusted to expediency. He had at last come up against the fact embedded in the story of Balaam, who had started on the road of compromise only to find that "the angel of the Lord stood in the way for an adversary against him" (Num. 22:22). The ass which he rode turned, but Balaam pulled the beast back. Then the angel took his stand in a still narrower

28 And the man Jeroboam *was* a mighty man of valor: and Solomon seeing the young man that he was industrious, he made him ruler over all the charge of the house of Joseph.

29 And it came to pass at that time when Jeroboam went out of Jerusalem, that the prophet Ahijah the Shilonite found him in the way; and he had clad himself with a new garment; and they two *were* alone in the field:

30 And Ahijah caught the new garment that *was* on him, and rent it *in* twelve pieces:

31 And he said to Jeroboam, Take thee ten pieces: for thus saith the LORD, the God of Israel, Behold, I will rend the kingdom out of the hand of Solomon, and will give ten tribes to thee:

28 The man Jerobo'am was very able, and when Solomon saw that the young man was industrious he gave him charge over all the forced labor of the house of Joseph. 29 And at that time, when Jerobo'am went out of Jerusalem, the prophet Ahi'jah the Shi'lonite found him on the road. Now Ahi'jah had clad himself with a new garment; and the two of them were alone in the open country. 30 Then Ahi'jah laid hold of the new garment that was on him, and tore it into twelve pieces. 31 And he said to Jerobo'am, "Take for yourself ten pieces; for thus says the LORD, the God of Israel, 'Behold, I am about to tear the kingdom from the hand of Solomon, and will give you ten

---

29. According to the correct Masoretic reading, Ahijah the Shilonite was the prime mover in the revolt, though he is not mentioned in the LXX until the story is told there (before Jeroboam becomes king, according to the LXX) of the sickness of Jeroboam's son. The revolt had the strong and vigorous support of the descendants of the house of Eli, who had been priests of the ark at Shiloh, and indeed from the earliest days (I Sam. 2:27-28). Later Ahijah the Shilonite became bitterly hostile to Jeroboam, but this was after Jeroboam had made Bethel the chief religious center of the north and a royal sanctuary. Perhaps if Jeroboam had not turned away from the priests of Shiloh and elevated those of Bethel to the royal priesthood the whole story of the north might have been different.

It is necessary to insert the phrase from the LXX, "and he turned him aside from the road," in order to explain how **the two of them were alone in the open country**. The expression **open country** is a sound rendering of the Hebrew שדה, usually translated **field**. Strictly, the word refers to the open country near the town; e.g., "the flower of the field" (Isa. 40:6) is really "the wild flower," the flower that grows of itself in the open country which is not cultivated garden.

31-39. Ahijah's exhortation to Jeroboam is fully Deuteronomic in tone and in phrase. Jeroboam is even promised that if he proves to be a sound Deuteronomic king as David was, his house will stand forever ruling the ten tribes of Israel. Just how this

---

place, and the ass lay down. In the figurative language of Oriental imagery is revealed the truth that when man takes the road of broad and easy compromise he finds it growing narrower and eventually blocked. While we cannot in primitive fashion pick out particular figures and designate them as adversaries sent of God, we can see the truth in Isaiah's interpretation of God's restraining power: "Therefore will I put my hook in thy nose, and my bridle in thy lips, and I will turn thee back by the way by which thou camest" (Isa. 37:29). God does reign in the wrongdoer.

In the mid-twentieth century a new volcano began to form in Mexico, and grew into a mountain two thousand feet high. Its mighty

groaning roar could be heard for miles. From a subsidiary crater near the top a red stream of lava poured like blood from a huge wound. At night the whole mountain was a cone of fire. A Mexican guide turned to two ministers in a party of visitors and said, "You men tell us to be good, but this volcano makes us want to be good." To him the fiery scene was the symbol of divine punishment. While the listeners were not impressed by the volcanic fury as the sign of eternal torment, they were awed into silence by the suggestion of divine power. As they stood watching a force which dwarfed the military might of the warring nations, the words of the psalmist came to mind, "The heathen raged, the kingdoms were moved: he

32 (But he shall have one tribe for my servant David's sake, and for Jerusalem's sake, the city which I have chosen out of all the tribes of Israel:)

33 Because that they have forsaken me, and have worshipped Ashtoreth the goddess of the Zidonians, Chemosh the god of the Moabites, and Milcom the god of the children of Ammon, and have not walked in my ways, to do *that which is* right in mine eyes, and *to keep* my statutes and my judgments, as *did* David his father.

34 Howbeit I will not take the whole kingdom out of his hand: but I will make him prince all the days of his life for David my servant's sake, whom I chose, because he kept my commandments and my statutes:

35 But I will take the kingdom out of his son's hand, and will give it unto thee, *even* ten tribes.

36 And unto his son will I give one tribe, that David my servant may have a light alway before me in Jerusalem, the city which I have chosen me to put my name there.

37 And I will take thee, and thou shalt reign according to all that thy soul desireth, and shalt be king over Israel.

tribes 32 (but he shall have one tribe, for the sake of my servant David and for the sake of Jerusalem, the city which I have chosen out of all the tribes of Israel) , 33 because he[h] has forsaken me, and worshiped Ash'toreth the goddess of the Sido'nians, Chemosh the god of Moab, and Milcom the god of the Ammonites, and has not walked in my ways, doing what is right in my sight and keeping my statutes and my ordinances, as David his father did. 34 Nevertheless I will not take the whole kingdom out of his hand; but I will make him ruler all the days of his life, for the sake of David my servant whom I chose, who kept my commandments and my statutes; 35 but I will take the kingdom out of his son's hand, and will give it to you, ten tribes. 36 Yet to his son I will give one tribe, that David my servant may always have a lamp before me in Jerusalem, the city where I have chosen to put my name. 37 And I will take you, and you shall reign over all that your soul desires, and you shall be

[h] Gk Syr Vg: Heb *they*

could have happened is far from clear, unless the author thought that Jeroboam ought to have reigned over the north, but still to have worshiped at Jerusalem. Possibly he regarded the establishment of the Northern Kingdom, in accordance with the will of God, as the necessary punishment of Solomon's flagrant violation of Deuteronomic standards; at the same time he maintained his Deuteronomic principle of centralized worship at only one sanctuary.

36. The reference to the **lamp** was formerly explained on the analogy of the light which is kept burning continually in poor homes in Palestine, in the belief that when the light is extinguished, so also is the family. The more modern explanation would make this popular custom part of a much wider attitude. The house of David is itself a perpetual light, *nēr tāmîdh,* and the well-being of the nation depends upon the continued life and vigor of the king (cf. 15:4; II Sam. 21:17; II Kings 8:19; W. O. E.

uttered his voice, the earth melted. . . . Be still, and know that I am God" (Ps. 46:6, 10) .

36. *God's Bundle of Life.*—At least four times in this chapter the Lord is interpreted as withholding certain punishments for the sake of his servant David. When God announces to Solomon that his kingdom is to be taken from him because of his transgression, he adds, "For the sake of David your father I will not do it in your days" (vs. 12). And when the Lord promises Jeroboam that he is to have Solomon's kingdom, he holds back the tribe of Judah, **that David my servant may always have a lamp**

before me in Jerusalem (cf. vss. 12, 32, 34; 15:4) .

The persistence of David's power with God recalls the prediction of Abigail in her plea to him, "The soul of my lord shall be bound in the bundle of life with the LORD thy God" (I Sam. 25:29) . Life is always bound in bundles, and growth is ever toward enlarging and enmeshing relationships. The child normally begins its career in the bundle called the family. Then through friendships he begins to enlarge that life, sharing in the joys and sorrows of those linked to him by love. The youth goes to

38 And it shall be, if thou wilt hearken unto all that I command thee, and wilt walk in my ways, and do *that is* right in my sight, to keep my statutes and my commandments, as David my servant did; that I will be with thee, and build thee a sure house, as I built for David, and will give Israel unto thee.

39 And I will for this afflict the seed of David, but not for ever.

40 Solomon sought therefore to kill Jeroboam. And Jeroboam arose, and fled into Egypt, unto Shishak king of Egypt, and was in Egypt until the death of Solomon.

41 ¶ And the rest of the acts of Solomon, and all that he did, and his wisdom, *are* they not written in the book of the acts of Solomon?

42 And the time that Solomon reigned in Jerusalem over all Israel *was* forty years.

43 And Solomon slept with his fathers, and was buried in the city of David his father: and Rehoboam his son reigned in his stead.

12 And Rehoboam went to Shechem: for all Israel were come to Shechem to make him king.

king over Israel. 38 And if you will hearken to all that I command you, and will walk in my ways, and do what is right in my eyes by keeping my statutes and my commandments, as David my servant did, I will be with you, and will build you a sure house, as I built for David, and I will give Israel to you.' " 39 And I will for this afflict the descendants of David, but not for ever.' " 40 Solomon sought therefore to kill Jerobo'am; but Jerobo'am arose, and fled into Egypt, to Shishak king of Egypt, and was in Egypt until the death of Solomon.

41 Now the rest of the acts of Solomon, and all that he did, and his wisdom, are they not written in the book of the acts of Solomon? 42 And the time that Solomon reigned in Jerusalem over all Israel was forty years. 43 And Solomon slept with his fathers, and was buried in the city of David his father; and Rehobo'am his son reigned in his stead.

12 Rehobo'am went to Shechem, for all Israel had come to Shechem to

Oesterley, "Early Hebrew Festival Rituals," in *Myth and Ritual,* ed. S. H. Hooke [London: Oxford University Press, 1933], pp. 142-44).

38. The last phrase of the verse is not in the LXX, neither is vs. 39.

6. DEATH OF SOLOMON (11:41-43)

41-43. The typical Deuteronomic obituary notice for the kings of Judah appears here for the first time.

III. THE TWO KINGDOMS (I Kings 12:1–II Kings 17:41)
A. THE SCHISM (12:1–14:31)
1. JEROBOAM I OF ISRAEL (12:1-33)

The Deuteronomic editor tells the story of the revolt. Having thus begun his account with Jeroboam as the main actor, he continues to tell the whole story of Jeroboam's reign over Israel, the Northern Kingdom. Then having duly recorded the death of Jeroboam, he turns back to give an account of the kings who have succeeded to the throne of Judah, the Southern Kingdom, during that period. This is his usual custom.

school, and the strands in the bundle are increased not only by the fellowship of teachers and other students, but also by comradeship with great minds whose spirits live after them in their books. Then through the church he enters into co-operative comradeship with fellow seekers after righteousness in the whole family of God. From the O.T. concept of being bound in the bundle of life with God, the Christian rises to the concept of membership in the body of Christ. Individuals are not units linked by

social contract. They are cells in a social body. And when the causes for which they live are of God, their lives are preserved in his purposes and programs. "Him that overcometh will I make a pillar in the temple of my God, and he shall go no more out" (Rev. 3:12). David had put his life into the Lord's work. He had served for God's sake. God would go on serving Israel "for David's sake."

12:1-24. Reaping the Whirlwind.—After the extravagance of Versailles came the deluge of

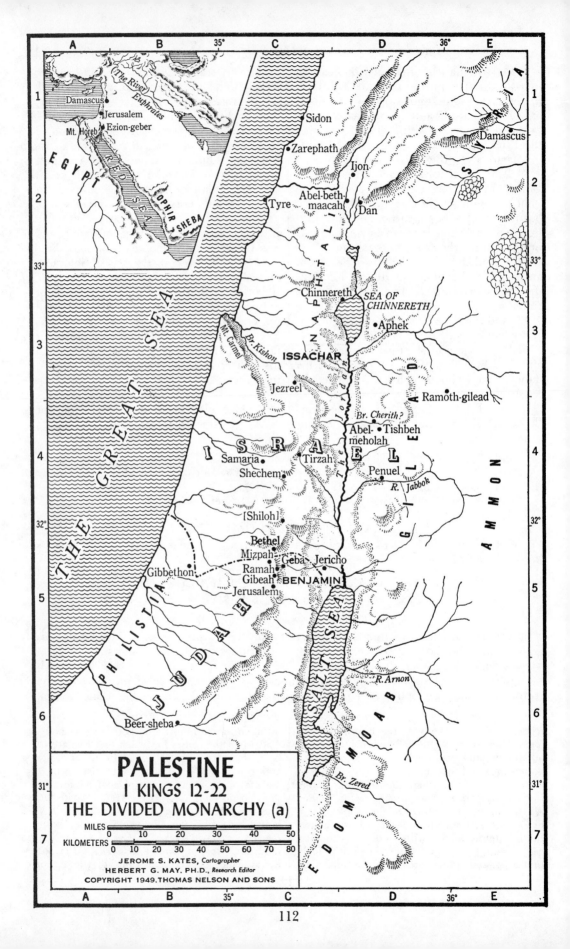

A

B

35°

C

D

36°

E

1

The River Euphrates

Damascus

Jerusalem

Mt. Horeb

Ezion-geber

EGYPT

RED SEA

OPHIR

SHEBA

Sidon

Zarephath

Ijon

Abel-beth-maacah

Damascus

SYRIA

1

Tyre

Dan

2

33°

THE GREAT SEA

Chinnereth

SEA OF CHINNERETH

Aphek

33°

3

Mt. Carmel

Br. Kishon

ISSACHAR

N A P H T A L I

The Jordan

3

Jezreel

Ramoth-gilead

Br. Cherith?

Samaria

I S R A E L

Tirzah

Abel-meholah

Tishbeh

4

Shechem

Penuel

R. Jabbok

G I L E A D

4

32°

[Shiloh]

AMMON

32°

Bethel

Mizpah

Geba

Jericho

Gibbethon

Ramah

Gibeah

BENJAMIN

5

PHILISTIA

Jerusalem

J U D A H

SALT SEA

5

R. Arnon

6

Beer-sheba

M O A B

6

31°

PALESTINE
1 KINGS 12-22
THE DIVIDED MONARCHY (a)

E D O M

Br. Zered

31°

7

MILES

0   10   20   30   40   50

KILOMETERS

0 10 20 30 40 50 60 70 80

JEROME S. KATES, *Cartographer*

HERBERT G. MAY, PH.D., *Research Editor*

COPYRIGHT 1949, THOMAS NELSON AND SONS

7

A

B

35°

C

D

36°

E

2 And it came to pass, when Jeroboam the son of Nebat, who was yet in Egypt, heard *of it,* (for he was fled from the presence of king Solomon, and Jeroboam dwelt in Egypt,)

make him king. **2** And when Jerobo'am the son of Nebat heard of it (for he was still in Egypt, whither he had fled from King Solomon), then Jerobo'am returned from[i]

[i] Gk Vg Compare 2 Chron 10. 2: Heb *dwelt in*

Jeroboam lived through two reigns of southern kings and on into the reign of the third king, Asa.

a) REVOLT OF THE TEN TRIBES (12:1-20)

When Rehoboam came to Shechem to be installed king of Israel the leaders of Israel demanded a change of policy. They refused to submit any longer to the forced labor system by which Solomon had built palaces and temple. When the negotiations broke down, both parties resorted to arms.

There is a long variant (see Skinner, *Kings,* pp. 443-46; also Burney, *Notes on Hebrew Text of Kings,* pp. 163-69) in the LXX after vs. 24, in which it is stated that Jeroboam did not get permission from Pharaoh to leave his court and return to his own country immediately after the death of Solomon. He was thus not present when Rehoboam first went to Shechem (cf. vs. 20 in M.T. and English versions; also part of vs. 2). On the contrary, Pharaoh bribed him to stay in Egypt by giving him Ano, sister of his Queen Tahpenes, as wife, who bore Jeroboam a son, Abijah. Only after this, according to the LXX, was Jeroboam given permission to return. He then gathered the people together and built a fort at his home town Sareira (Zeredah). Then there follows the incident of his son's illness (14:1-18 M.T.), and Ahijah appears for the only time and denounces Jeroboam. The latter then gathers the northern tribes to Shechem, whither Rehoboam also comes. The incident of the torn garment is now told, but the prophet's name is Shemaiah (cf. vs. 22). After Jeroboam is designated king, the story follows the same course as the M.T. (vs. 25).

The LXX account is not nearly as satisfactory as that of the M.T. The reference to the marriage with the sister of Pharaoh's wife looks like a copy of the story of Hadad, including the birth of Genubath. Further, there is no reason for the antagonism of Ahijah, such as is provided in the story of the M.T. (cf. 14:9).

12:1. Rehoboam has to come to Shechem to be installed as king of the north because Shechem was the ancient capital of the north, and there only could any man be anointed king. There was a famous sacred tree at Shechem, venerated from early times, where first Abram worshiped the Lord in the Promised Land (Gen. 12:6). This sacred tree is mentioned time and again in the early histories. Jacob erected an altar there and it was the first "parcel of ground" (so ASV) which he possessed in Canaan (Gen. 33:18-20). There Joseph was buried (Josh. 24:32), and the first attempt at a kingdom was made (Judg. 9:1-5). It was the center of Ephraimite activity all the days of Joshua, just as Hebron was the center of the south.

2. It is evident that Jeroboam did not return from Egypt immediately upon the death of Solomon, so there is a certain amount of truth in the story of the LXX (vs. 24*de*), though whether he was delayed long enough for a son to be begotten and born is open to question (see also vs. 20). It is necessary, therefore, to treat the substance of vs. 2 with reserve, and to delete the name of Jeroboam from vss. 3 and 12. Even according to the general tenor of the M.T., Jeroboam was not present when the first conversations took place at Shechem.

---

revolution. In Israel as in France, the floodgates had been opened by the softening of luxury, the hardness of slave labor, the loosening of moral restraints. Praise for the services of Solomon was now drowned in storms of complaint about his oppression. The revolt against Solomon's luckless son Rehoboam was not motivated by righteous indignation against the godlessness of the rule or by a demand for a return to the true worship. It was a protest against

3 That they sent and called him. And Jeroboam and all the congregation of Israel came, and spake unto Rehoboam, saying,

4 Thy father made our yoke grievous: now therefore make thou the grievous service of thy father, and his heavy yoke which he put upon us, lighter, and we will serve thee.

5 And he said unto them, Depart yet *for* three days, then come again to me. And the people departed.

6 ¶ And king Rehoboam consulted with the old men, that stood before Solomon his father while he yet lived, and said, How do ye advise that I may answer this people?

7 And they spake unto him, saying, If thou wilt be a servant unto this people this day, and wilt serve them, and answer them, and speak good words to them, then they will be thy servants for ever.

8 But he forsook the counsel of the old men, which they had given him, and consulted with the young men that were grown up with him, *and* which stood before him:

9 And he said unto them, What counsel give ye that we may answer this people, who have spoken to me, saying, Make the yoke which thy father did put upon us lighter?

10 And the young men that were grown up with him spake unto him, saying, Thus shalt thou speak unto this people that spake unto thee, saying, Thy father made our yoke

Egypt. 3 And they sent and called him; and Jerobo'am and all the assembly of Israel came and said to Rehobo'am, 4 "Your father made our yoke heavy. Now therefore lighten the hard service of your father and his heavy yoke upon us, and we will serve you." 5 He said to them, "Depart for three days, then come again to me." So the people went away.

6 Then King Rehobo'am took counsel with the old men, who had stood before Solomon his father while he was yet alive, saying, "How do you advise me to answer this people?" 7 And they said to him, "If you will be a servant to this people today and serve them, and speak good words to them when you answer them, then they will be your servants for ever." 8 But he forsook the counsel which the old men gave him, and took counsel with the young men who had grown up with him and stood before him. 9 And he said to them, "What do you advise that we answer this people who have said to me, 'Lighten the yoke that your father put upon us'?" 10 And the young men who had grown up with him said to him, "Thus shall you speak to this people who said to you, 'Your father made our

4. The word **yoke** is not used elsewhere except for the subjugation of a foreign nation. It is more apt here than has been generally recognized, for there was always a radical division between north and south. Most scholars today accept the theory that Joshua brought only the Joseph tribes over Jordan, that Judah came in from the south, and that many of the lesser tribes were never out of Canaan after Jacob came back from Padan-Aram (C. F. Burney, *Israel's Settlement in Canaan* [London: Humphrey Milford, 1918], pp. 34-36; H. H. Rowley, "Israel's Sojourn in Egypt," *Bulletin of the John Rylands Library,* XXII [1938], 266-69). The two groups were never united except in the messianic dreams of the south. Even during David's time there had been two rebellions, the one under Sheba and the other under Absalom, and after Solomon's time the south was subject to the north for long periods (cf. I Kings 22).

10. The M.T. and the Chronicler's parallel (II Chr. 10:10) have "my littleness," and so the LXX and Targ. ("my weakness"). The reference to the **little finger** is due to the Vulg. and Syriac, and is a sound paraphrase. The whole saying is typical of that epigrammatic style which is characteristic of Eastern "wisdom," and can be paralleled often in the Gospels.

heavy taxes and material discomforts. People as well as princes had lost their spirituality. Rebellious people easily seek and find in public circumstances means which they can use to justify their revolt.

Rehoboam was both stupid and arrogant. He

heavy, but make thou *it* lighter unto us; thus shalt thou say unto them, My little *finger* shall be thicker than my father's loins.

11 And now whereas my father did lade you with a heavy yoke, I will add to your yoke: my father hath chastised you with whips, but I will chastise you with scorpions.

12 ¶ So Jeroboam and all the people came to Rehoboam the third day, as the king had appointed, saying, Come to me again the third day.

13 And the king answered the people roughly, and forsook the old men's counsel that they gave him;

14 And spake to them after the counsel of the young men, saying, My father made your yoke heavy, and I will add to your yoke: my father *also* chastised you with whips, but I will chastise you with scorpions.

15 Wherefore the king hearkened not unto the people; for the cause was from the LORD, that he might perform his saying, which the LORD spake by Ahijah the Shilonite unto Jeroboam the son of Nebat.

16 ¶ So when all Israel saw that the king hearkened not unto them, the people answered the king, saying, What portion have we in David? neither *have we* inheritance in the son of Jesse: to your tents, O Israel: now see to thine own house, David. So Israel departed unto their tents.

yoke heavy, but do you lighten it for us'; thus shall you say to them, 'My little finger is thicker than my father's loins.

11 And now, whereas my father laid upon you a heavy yoke, I will add to your yoke. My father chastised you with whips, but I will chastise you with scorpions.' "

12 So Jerobo'am and all the people came to Rehobo'am the third day, as the king said, "Come to me again the third day."

13 And the king answered the people harshly, and forsaking the counsel which the old men had given him, 14 he spoke to them according to the counsel of the young men, saying, "My father made your yoke heavy, but I will add to your yoke; my father chastised you with whips, but I will chastise you with scorpions." 15 So the king did not hearken to the people; for it was a turn of affairs brought about by the LORD that he might fulfil his word, which the LORD spoke by Ahi'jah the Shi'lonite to Jerobo'am the son of Nebat.

16 And when all Israel saw that the king did not hearken to them, the people answered the king,

"What portion have we in David?
We have no inheritance in the son of Jesse.
To your tents, O Israel!
Look now to your own house, David."

---

11. Scorpions: This saying is explained by the Targ. and Syriac as meaning "scourges," probably correctly. The Romans used a scourge made of a long bag of leather filled tightly with sand and studded with spikes, and called this "the scorpion."

15. Rehoboam does not seem to have the slightest understanding of the gravity of the situation. The last man in the world he ought to have sent to quell the disturbance was the one man he did send, Adoram, who had been in charge of the forced labor which caused the trouble. His extraordinary folly is accounted for by the author as a "turn" (so the Hebrew) from the Lord, or as the Targ. puts it, "a fated lot."

16. The reply of the people was in rhythmical form, and is rightly so printed in the RSV. The first line is almost exactly the cry raised by Sheba (II Sam. 20:1) when he led an Israelite revolt against Judah, except that there is a definite negative used there. The phrase **To your tents** does not mean "to arms," but "back home," being an old-fashioned phrase and a survival of the old desert life. The English versions rightly insert **own** in the last line of the reply. The whole point of the people's answer is in the complete divergence between the two groups. The LXX and Targ. read רעה, "to feed as a shepherd," and so "to rule as a king" for ראה, "see," and it may be that this is the correct reading. The Hebrew word *rôʻeh*, "shepherd," is often used as a synonym for "king," "ruler" (cf. Ps. 23:1, where Vulg. has *Dominus regit me*, translated in the Douay Version as "the Lord ruleth me").

17 But *as for* the children of Israel which dwelt in the cities of Judah, Rehoboam reigned over them.

18 Then king Rehoboam sent Adoram, who *was* over the tribute; and all Israel stoned him with stones, that he died. Therefore king Rehoboam made speed to get him up to his chariot, to flee to Jerusalem.

19 So Israel rebelled against the house of David unto this day.

20 And it came to pass, when all Israel heard that Jeroboam was come again, that they sent and called him unto the congregation, and made him king over all Israel: there was none that followed the house of David, but the tribe of Judah only.

21 ¶ And when Rehoboam was come to Jerusalem, he assembled all the house of Judah, with the tribe of Benjamin, a hundred and fourscore thousand chosen men, which were warriors, to fight against the house of Israel, to bring the kingdom again to Rehoboam the son of Solomon.

22 But the word of God came unto Shemaiah the man of God, saying,

23 Speak unto Rehoboam, the son of Solomon, king of Judah, and unto all the house of Judah and Benjamin, and to the remnant of the people, saying,

24 Thus saith the Lord, Ye shall not go up, nor fight against your brethren the children of Israel: return every man to his house; for this thing is from me. They hearkened therefore to the word of the Lord, and returned to depart, according to the word of the Lord.

So Israel departed to their tents. 17 But Rehobo'am reigned over the people of Israel who dwelt in the cities of Judah. 18 Then King Rehobo'am sent Ador'am, who was taskmaster over the forced labor, and all Israel stoned him to death with stones. And King Rehobo'am made haste to mount his chariot, to flee to Jerusalem. 19 So Israel has been in rebellion against the house of David to this day. 20 And when all Israel heard that Jerobo'am had returned, they sent and called him to the assembly and made him king over all Israel. There was none that followed the house of David, but the tribe of Judah only.

21 When Rehobo'am came to Jerusalem, he assembled all the house of Judah, and the tribe of Benjamin, a hundred and eighty thousand chosen warriors, to fight against the house of Israel, to restore the kingdom to Rehobo'am the son of Solomon. 22 But the word of God came to Shemai'ah the man of God: 23 "Say to Rehobo'am the son of Solomon, king of Judah, and to all the house of Judah and Benjamin, and to the rest of the people, 24 'Thus says the Lord, You shall not go up or fight against your kinsmen the people of Israel. Return every man to his home, for this thing is from me.' " So they hearkened to the word of the Lord, and went home again, according to the word of the Lord.

---

17. This verse is not in the LXX, but is based upon II Chr. 11:16, where it is said that a number of pious Israelites emigrated to Judah in order to remain under the rule of the Davidic king, and thus worship the true God in the true way at Jerusalem.

20. Here is the usual discrepancy concerning the number of the tribes who clung to Rehoboam. The LXX avoids the contradiction by adding "and Benjamin" in this verse, thus making the statement here agree with that in vs. 21.

b) Civil War Is Averted (12:21-24)

According to this paragraph, Shemaiah managed to stop civil war between the two groups of tribes. Whether this statement is accurate is to be doubted, since according to 14:30 the two sections never ceased fighting all the time Rehoboam reigned in Judah. Shemaiah's action is probably as fictional as his part in the torn garment incident of the LXX insertion which follows this section.

23. It is best to avoid the word **remnant** (KJV) and to read **rest** (RSV), since the former has a technical sense in the O.T., standing for the faithful and pious nucleus of the people of God. The idea of the remnant occurs first in the name of Isaiah's son Shear-jashub (Isa. 7:3; cf. 10:21-23).

25 ¶ Then Jeroboam built Shechem in mount Ephraim, and dwelt therein; and went out from thence, and built Penuel.

26 And Jeroboam said in his heart, Now shall the kingdom return to the house of David:

27 If this people go up to do sacrifice in the house of the LORD at Jerusalem, then shall the heart of this people turn again unto their lord, *even* unto Rehoboam king of Judah, and they shall kill me, and go again to Rehoboam king of Judah.

28 Whereupon the king took counsel, and made two calves *of* gold, and said unto them, It is too much for you to go up to Jerusalem: behold thy gods, O Israel, which brought thee up out of the land of Egypt.

25 Then Jerobo'am built Shechem in the hill country of E'phraim, and dwelt there; and he went out from there and built Penu'el. 26 And Jerobo'am said in his heart, "Now the kingdom will turn back to the house of David; 27 if this people go up to offer sacrifices in the house of the LORD at Jerusalem, then the heart of this people will turn again to their lord, to Rehobo'am king of Judah, and they will kill me and return to Rehobo'am king of Judah." 28 So the king took counsel, and made two calves of gold. And he said to the people, "You have gone up to Jerusalem long enough. Behold your gods, O Israel, who brought

c) JEROBOAM CONSOLIDATES HIS KINGDOM (12:25-33)

The new king takes precautions against any movement for a return to Judah. He builds and fortifies Shechem and Penuel, then sets up the golden bulls at Bethel and Dan to provide centers for worship other than the shrine which Solomon had built at Jerusalem.

25. Jeroboam makes **Shechem** his capital, thus taking full advantage of the ancient traditions of the place as the center of northern Israelite history. **Penuel** is by the river Jabbok, east of Jordan in the same latitude as Shechem. It dominates the road east from the Jordan Valley, a favorite route for nomad invaders (cf. Judg. 8:8). Penuel was thus built as a forward defense for Shechem.

28-29. Jeroboam sets up the golden bulls at Bethel and Dan. He tells the people that they **have gone up to Jerusalem long enough,** and then follows with the selfsame cry with which the people of old had greeted the golden calf which Aaron made (Exod. 32:4, 8). Here, as in his establishment of Shechem as his capital, Jeroboam was reverting to ancient custom against the innovations of Solomon. W. F. Albright (*From the Stone Age to Christianity* [2nd ed.; Baltimore: Johns Hopkins Press, 1946], p. 203) maintains that these bulls were not representations of Yahweh, but that "the golden calf simply formed the pedestal, on which the invisible Yahweh stood" (cf. the space between the cherubim in Solomon's temple at Jerusalem). It may very well be that the Mosaic religion was strongly "aniconic," and the modern tendency is to give Moses credit for much more advanced ideas than were formerly allowed to be his. The general opinion is that while there was a movement in favor of an imageless worship sponsored by (at any rate) some Levites, yet the Lord was worshiped with images during the time of the judges and during at least part of the time of the kingdoms. The prohibitions against "graven" images (Exod. 20:4 [E, a northern tradition, which incidentally would not exclude the Bethel bull]) and against "molten" images (Exod. 34:17 [J, a southern tradition which would exclude the Bethel bull]) were necessary from the reformers' point of view. It is definitely stated that the people had been making sacrifices to the

took counsel of his courtiers rather than of his Lord. And he took the rash advice of his hotheaded young comrades rather than the more sensible counsel of his seasoned courtiers. By losing his head he lost the larger part of his kingdom. Solomon had sown the wind and Rehoboam reaped the whirlwind.

25-33. *The Gods of Convenience.*—After Jeroboam had taken the ten tribes from Rehoboam and set up the Northern Kingdom, he was worried about the fact that his devout subjects still felt obliged to worship Yahweh at the temple in Jerusalem. Jeroboam feared that if his people were to continue their pilgrimages to Jerusalem

29 And he set the one in Bethel, and the other put he in Dan.

30 And this thing became a sin: for the people went *to worship* before the one, *even* unto Dan.

you up out of the land of Egypt." 29 And he set one in Bethel, and the other he put in Dan. 30 And this thing became a sin, for the people went to the one at Bethel and

---

bronze serpent until Hezekiah destroyed it in his reforming zeal (II Kings 18:4). A good case can be made out for believing that this serpent was the Jebusite fetish image cared for by the original Jerusalem Zadokite priesthood, and that it remained there as the divine symbol even after David had conquered the city (H. H. Rowley, "Zadok and Nehushtan," *Journal of Biblical Literature*, LVIII [1939], 113-41; Adolphe Lods, *Les prophètes d'Israël*, [Paris: La Renaissance du Livre, 1935], p. 130). In the north the divine symbol was the bull. There is a curious phrase in Deut. 33:17, where Joseph is called "the first-born of his bull." Such a passage as Gen. 49:24 suggests that there was a time when the bull was indeed the divine symbol for the Joseph tribes, and this is the most natural explanation of Deut. 33:17. Perhaps this goes back to desert times, but it may be that Jeroboam was reading back the bull image into desert times, just as in the south they read back the serpent into that same period of the wanderings. There are numerous references in the Ras Shamra texts to *Shôr-'ēl* ("the Bull-El"), the same word being used for "bull" as in Deut. 33:17. It is evident that El, the "high god" of Syria, the great creator god, was worshiped in the form of a bull. The setting up of the golden bulls at Bethel and at Dan was fully in accordance with ancient and native Syrian-Canaanite ideas. These images did actually involve a syncretism between the Lord and the gods of Syria (Engnell, *Studies in Divine Kingship*, pp. 136, 154, etc.). This explains why the Deuteronomists regarded the cultus at Bethel with particular horror. It was precisely against this kind of syncretism that all their hatred was directed. Again and again they wrote of the dreadful sin of forgetting the Lord so as to "walk after other gods, and serve them, and worship them" (Deut. 8:19; cf. 6:14; 13:6-7).

Jeroboam's action had not only a religious but also a political aspect. It was necessarily part of his deliberate policy to prevent the people from going up regularly to worship at the Jerusalem shrine. He therefore was compelled politically to do everything he could to encourage them to make their pilgrimages to their own sanctuaries, and in particular to his own royal shrine at Bethel. If he provided good facilities for the proper enjoyment of the harvest meals (cf. I Sam. 1:18 [LXX], Judg. 9:27), local patriotism would doubtless do the rest. He therefore took pains to make the ancient shrine of Bethel worthy in every way to be a royal sanctuary, and the measure of his success can be judged by the vehemence of the threats which Amos uttered against it a century or so later (Amos 3:14; 5:6; 9:1).

30. The RSV is correct here in following Lucian's version.

---

they might come under the influence of Rehoboam, who ruled in that city. He hit upon a plan to obviate this danger. He set up two golden calves and then said to his people, **It is too much for you to go up to Jerusalem: behold thy gods** (vs. 28).

Jeroboam's appeal to convenience seems quite in line with our modern idea of progress. If we were asked how present-day civilization is superior to former modes of living, would not most of us cite our material comforts and conveniences? Our houses are more commodious, hours of work are shorter, labor is being delivered from drudgery. Ours has been called "a sitting civilization." Jeroboam was applying the

principle of comfort and convenience to the realm of religion. And so do we. Our churches are moved to be near our homes. Moreover, we are told that the church would succeed if it gave the people what they want. And the argument sounds plausible. The church is to serve the people. It must therefore reach the people. Religion should be made winsome and attractive. Make the sanctuary as beautiful and comfortable as possible; improve the music; popularize the themes. But how far can this cult of comfort be safely carried in the sphere of religion? There is a certain propriety in the church's studying how to attract people, how to make its message appealing, how to bring to

31 And he made a house of high places, and made priests of the lowest of the people, which were not of the sons of Levi.

32 And Jeroboam ordained a feast in the eighth month, on the fifteenth day of the month, like unto the feast that *is* in Judah, and he offered upon the altar. So did he in Bethel, sacrificing unto the calves that he had made: and he placed in Bethel the priests of the high places which he had made.

33 So he offered upon the altar which he had made in Bethel the fifteenth day of the eighth month, *even* in the month which he

to the other as far as Dan.*j* 31 He also made houses on high places, and appointed priests from among all the people, who were not of the Levites. 32 And Jerobo'am appointed a feast on the fifteenth day of the eighth month like the feast that was in Judah, and he offered sacrifices upon the altar; so he did in Bethel, sacrificing to the calves that he had made. And he placed in Bethel the priests of the high places that he had made. 33 He went up to the altar which he had made in Bethel on the fifteenth day in the eighth month, in the month which he had devised of his own

j Gk: Heb *went to the one as far as Dan*

31. It was legitimate for any devout Israelite to worship the Lord at any of the local shrines. The prohibition of worship at such places belongs to the period following the Deuteronomic reforms. Similarly, it was legitimate for a non-Levite to act as a priest, though as early as the time of the judges there was a popular assumption that a Levite was to be preferred (Judg. 17:5, 10).

32. The feast of Ingathering was celebrated at Bethel in the eighth month of the postexilic calendar, i.e., in Bul, the second month of the pre-exilic calendar. Vs. 33 says that this was an innovation due to Jeroboam's own devising, the author evidently being of the opinion that the first month of the pre-exilic calendar was the proper month everywhere. But Jeroboam was no innovator. On the contrary, he was all for the proper re-establishment of true northern customs against the innovations of the south, and a large part of his success in setting up the Northern Kingdom depended upon this attitude. The feast was held probably a month later in the north than in the south: "The people went to the shrine of their choice at the first full moon after the completion of the harvests of their agricultural year" (see Snaith, *Jewish New Year Festival*, p. 52, where the whole problem of the different dates is discussed). The difference in the climate between the various parts of the country can be judged by the fact that the wheat harvest in Palestine extends from April in the Jordan Valley and in the maritime plain to as late as June in parts of the hill country.

33. Here as elsewhere the pre-exilic meaning of הקטיר is "to sacrifice" and not to burn incense.

aching hearts the healing touch of the Great Physician. But one must remember that the church of the living God must serve the needs of men rather than cater to their desires, must make people be good rather than merely feel good. The cross is not a couch, and the gospel of the crucified Christ cannot be harmonized with physical comfort.

After Jeroboam appeals to his subjects to worship the gods conveniently near at hand, the record adds, **And this thing became a sin** (vs. 30). Why?

To the writer of I Kings the sin lay in the idolatrous worship of golden calves in Dan and Bethel. But transposed into modern thought, the cult of convenience becomes a sin by separating a soul from the one true God. God is a

Father, and we his children keep in communion with him by cultivating the same attitudes which hold children to an earthly parent. If a child is to keep a wholesome relationship with a normal father, he must develop it through obedience, discipline, study, and self-sacrifice. The child's petulant desires of the moment must yield to the parent's longer experience. If the child grows up seeking always his own convenience and pleasure, he becomes spoiled, thus automatically alienating himself from understanding fellowship with the parent. The lad who never learns to put himself out to help or please his father does not learn how to take in what his father can give him. Families who try to run on the principle of personal comfort without sacrificial co-operation are headed for

had devised of his own heart; and ordained a feast unto the children of Israel: and he offered upon the altar, and burnt incense.

13 And, behold, there came a man of God out of Judah by the word of the LORD unto Bethel: and Jeroboam stood by the altar to burn incense.

2 And he cried against the altar in the word of the LORD, and said, O altar, altar, thus saith the LORD; Behold, a child shall

heart; and he ordained a feast for the people of Israel, and went up to the altar to burn incense.

13 And behold, a man of God came out of Judah by the word of the LORD to Bethel. Jerobo'am was standing by the altar to burn incense. 2 And the man cried against the altar by the word of the LORD, and said, "O altar, altar, thus says

---

2. THE MAN OF GOD FROM JUDAH (13:1-34)

The style of the chapter, as Burney points out, is similar to that of the annals of Josiah's time, so that the story as it is told here apparently comes from the hand of the compiler (*ca.* 610 B.C.). Other indications are the specific mention of **Josiah by name** (vs. 2), which is unlikely 330 years before his time, and, especially if this last is held to be an interpolation, the reference (vs. 32) to **the cities of Samaria** (LXX has Samaria only). The town was not built until Omri's time (16:24). Wellhausen suggested that the story owes much to Amos' visit to Bethel (Amos 7:10-16), coupled with the tirade against Bethel in Amos 9:1-9. Budde held that the account is a homiletic story whose sound moral is the sole justification for the telling of it. There is no adequate reason for doubting that this is an ancient tale; the Deuteronomic compiler revived it in order to show that Jeroboam had received full warning and, incidentally, that Judeans should avoid all relations with northerners.

13:1-10. A prophet from Judah appears at Bethel while Jeroboam is actually sacrificing there. He prophesies the destruction of both altar and priests, and gives a sign that his word is true. Jeroboam's arm is paralyzed, the altar is rent, and the ashes are scattered. The man of God relents so far as to permit Jeroboam's arm to be restored, but he follows his divine instructions and firmly refuses all hospitality.

1. The prophet is sent under compulsion of the word of God; this word has the power to get itself spoken, and when it has been spoken, to bring to pass that which has been expressed.

2. The word זבח originally meant "to slaughter," and this rendering is suitable here.

---

the rocks. If we are to take in friendship, love, God, we must put ourselves out. When we try to fashion our religious faith and program to suit ourselves, we separate ourselves from God.

Moreover, the cult of convenience becomes a sin because it stifles our own spiritual growth. When we do only the things we find convenient, when we never put ourselves out to meet and please people, our circles of interest and affection shrink. Henry C. Link, the psychologist, observing this principle in human relations, applied it to the religious realm, and gave the following reasons for going to church:

I go because I would rather lie in bed late on Sunday mornings. . . . I go because I would rather read the Sunday papers. I go because I know it will please my old father, when he learns of it, and my parents-in-law whom I shall undoubtedly see there. I go because I shall meet and have to shake hands with people, many of whom do not interest me in the least; because, if I don't go, my children consider

that they have a good reason for not going to Sunday School; . . . because I may disagree with what the minister has to say. . . . I go because I do not believe in all the doctrines of this church, or any other church. I go, in short, because I hate to go and because I know that it will do me good.[6]

The only way to make room for God in our lives is to put ourselves out. And those who will not be "put out" for him separate themselves from him and stunt their own growth. The ego is like a cell which overasserts itself and causes cancer. The self-centered, self-willed person who wants everything, even his religion, adjusted to suit his own convenience is starting a cancerous growth within his spirit. The gods of comfort lead but to the grave.

13:1-25, 27-34. *This Treasure in Earthen Vessels.*—The O.T. writers were realistic in treating the men of God as well as the kings of men.

[6] *The Return to Religion* (New York: The Macmillan Co., 1936), p. 19. Used by permission.

be born unto the house of David, Josiah by name; and upon thee shall he offer the priests of the high places that burn incense upon thee, and men's bones shall be burnt upon thee.

3 And he gave a sign the same day, saying, This *is* the sign which the Lord hath spoken; Behold, the altar shall be rent, and the ashes that *are* upon it shall be poured out.

4 And it came to pass, when king Jeroboam heard the saying of the man of God, which had cried against the altar in Bethel, that he put forth his hand from the altar, saying, Lay hold on him. And his hand, which he put forth against him, dried up, so that he could not pull it in again to him.

5 The altar also was rent, and the ashes poured out from the altar, according to the sign which the man of God had given by the word of the Lord.

6 And the king answered and said unto the man of God, Entreat now the face of the Lord thy God, and pray for me, that my hand may be restored me again. And the man of God besought the Lord, and the king's hand was restored him again, and became as *it was* before.

7 And the king said unto the man of God, Come home with me, and refresh thyself, and I will give thee a reward.

8 And the man of God said unto the king, If thou wilt give me half thine house, I will not go in with thee, neither will I eat bread nor drink water in this place:

the Lord: 'Behold, a son shall be born to the house of David, Josi'ah by name; and he shall sacrifice upon you the priests of the high places who burn incense upon you, and men's bones shall be burned upon you.' " 3 And he gave a sign the same day, saying, "This is the sign that the Lord has spoken: 'Behold, the altar shall be torn down, and the ashes that are upon it shall be poured out.' " 4 And when the king heard the saying of the man of God, which he cried against the altar at Bethel, Jerobo'am stretched out his hand from the altar, saying, "Lay hold of him." And his hand, which he stretched out against him, dried up, so that he could not draw it back to himself. 5 The altar also was torn down, and the ashes poured out from the altar, according to the sign which the man of God had given by the word of the Lord. 6 And the king said to the man of God, "Entreat now the favor of the Lord your God, and pray for me, that my hand may be restored to me." And the man of God entreated the Lord; and the king's hand was restored to him, and became as it was before. 7 And the king said to the man of God, "Come home with me, and refresh yourself, and I will give you a reward." 8 And the man of God said to the king, "If you give me half your house, I will not go in with you. And I will not eat bread or drink water in this

---

The custom of burning dead men's bones upon an altar had its object in desecrating the sacred site and making it unfit for any sacred purpose.

4. The Hebrews, in complete contradistinction to modern ways of thinking, thought of God himself as being immediately active in all the processes of his world. In this sense a miracle is not a violation of any rule, but rather an outstanding and unusual incident whereby God's active participation in the conduct of his world is particularly evident and designed to point out some religious truth.

6. Entreat now the favor of the Lord is, lit., "make sweet the face of the Lord." The phrase is a strong anthropomorphism describing the process of smoothing away traces of anger from the human face. It is foolish to criticize the use of anthropomorphisms as a matter of principle. The cruder examples are clearly undesirable, but on the other hand, it is impossible for man to speak intelligently of a personal God except in terms borrowed from human experience.

Truly we have the treasure of God in earthen vessels. The unnamed **man of God** who appeared before Jeroboam at Bethel was a messenger of truth, and he demonstrated divine power. If his record had ended with the restoration of the king's hand and his refusal to return by the way he had come to Bethel, he would have left the scriptural stage unsullied.

9 For so was it charged me by the word of the LORD, saying, Eat no bread, nor drink water, nor turn again by the same way that thou camest.

10 So he went another way, and returned not by the way that he came to Bethel.

11 ¶ Now there dwelt an old prophet in Bethel; and his sons came and told him all the works that the man of God had done that day in Bethel: the words which he had spoken unto the king, them they told also to their father.

12 And their father said unto them, What way went he? For his sons had seen what way the man of God went, which came from Judah.

13 And he said unto his sons, Saddle me the ass. So they saddled him the ass: and he rode thereon,

14 And went after the man of God, and found him sitting under an oak: and he said unto him, Art thou the man of God that camest from Judah? And he said, I am.

15 Then he said unto him, Come home with me, and eat bread.

16 And he said, I may not return with thee, nor go in with thee: neither will I eat bread nor drink water with thee in this place:

17 For it was said to me by the word of the LORD, Thou shalt eat no bread nor drink water there, nor turn again to go by the way that thou camest.

18 He said unto him, I am a prophet also as thou art; and an angel spake unto me by the word of the LORD, saying, Bring him back with thee into thine house, that he may eat bread and drink water. But he lied unto him.

place; 9 for so was it commanded me by the word of the LORD, saying, 'You shall neither eat bread, nor drink water, nor return by the way that you came.'" 10 So he went another way, and did not return by the way that he came to Bethel.

11 Now there dwelt an old prophet in Bethel. And his sons[k] came and told him all that the man of God had done that day in Bethel; the words also which he had spoken to the king, they told to their father. 12 And their father said to them, "Which way did he go?" And his sons showed him the way which the man of God who came from Judah had gone. 13 And he said to his sons, "Saddle the ass for me." So they saddled the ass for him and he mounted it. 14 And he went after the man of God, and found him sitting under an oak; and he said to him, "Are you the man of God who came from Judah?" And he said, "I am." 15 Then he said to him, "Come home with me and eat bread." 16 And he said, "I may not return with you, or go in with you; neither will I eat bread nor drink water with you in this place; 17 for it was said to me by the word of the LORD, 'You shall neither eat bread nor drink water there, nor return by the way that you came.'" 18 And he said to him, "I also am a prophet as you are, and an angel spoke to me by the word of the LORD, saying, 'Bring him back with you into your house that he may eat bread

[k] Gk Syr Vg: Heb son

9. The command to eat no bread with any inhabitant of the north country is to be explained by the Eastern idea that two persons who partake of the same food establish between themselves a kind of covenantal relationship.

11-32. The **man of God** from Judah is deceived by a **prophet** from Israel, who says that he has had a command through an angel that the visitor must eat with him. On his way home the man of God is slain by a lion. The prophet thereupon requests that, when he dies, he be buried with the man of God, because his words will surely come true.

18. The idea of the delivery of the divine message by **an angel** is a sign of lateness. Earlier the phrase "the angel of the LORD" was used, but apart from this instance the first occurrences of an angel-messenger are to be found in Ezekiel. We have thus additional evidence that the present story is told in terms which belong to the end of the seventh century B.C. On the other hand, the prophet either was mistaken or else he was lying, and it may be that either he or the compiler hesitated to say directly that it was the word of God, and introduced the angel in order to account for the false message. The pre-

19 So he went back with him, and did eat bread in his house, and drank water.

20 ¶ And it came to pass, as they sat at the table, that the word of the LORD came unto the prophet that brought him back:

21 And he cried unto the man of God that came from Judah, saying, Thus saith the LORD, Forasmuch as thou hast disobeyed the mouth of the LORD, and hast not kept the commandment which the LORD thy God commanded thee,

22 But camest back, and hast eaten bread and drunk water in the place, of the which *the* LORD did say to thee, Eat no bread, and drink no water; thy carcass shall not come unto the sepulchre of thy fathers.

23 ¶ And it came to pass, after he had eaten bread, and after he had drunk, that he saddled for him the ass, *to wit,* for the prophet whom he had brought back.

24 And when he was gone, a lion met him by the way, and slew him: and his carcass was cast in the way, and the ass stood by it, the lion also stood by the carcass.

25 And, behold, men passed by, and saw the carcass cast in the way, and the lion standing by the carcass: and they came and told *it* in the city where the old prophet dwelt.

26 And when the prophet that brought him back from the way heard *thereof,* he said, It *is* the man of God, who was disobedi-

and drink water.' " But he lied to him. 19 So he went back with him, and ate bread in his house, and drank water.

20 And as they sat at the table, the word of the LORD came to the prophet who had brought him back; 21 and he cried to the man of God who came from Judah, "Thus says the LORD, 'Because you have disobeyed the word of the LORD, and have not kept the commandment which the LORD your God commanded you, 22 but have come back, and have eaten bread and drunk water in the place of which he said to you, "Eat no bread, and drink no water"; your body shall not come to the tomb of your fathers.' " 23 And after he had eaten bread and drunk, he saddled the ass for the prophet whom he had brought back. 24 And as he went away a lion met him on the road and killed him. And his body was thrown in the road, and the ass stood beside it; the lion also stood beside the body. 25 And behold, men passed by, and saw the body thrown in the road, and the lion standing by the body. And they came and told it in the city where the old prophet dwelt.

26 And when the prophet who had

---

sumption is that this detail is due to the late compiler, since it is unlikely that the man of God from Judah would be deceived by a message if there had been anything abnormal in it.

22. Not to have burial was a calamity, since it prevented a man from "sleeping with his fathers"—the only consolation which the righteous had after death, according to the ideas of the time.

23. The last phrase is omitted by the LXX. It is the only place in the story where **the man of God who came from Judah** is called a **prophet,** this latter word being elsewhere wholly reserved for the Israelite. Presumably a prophet might be a false prophet, but a man of God is always a man of God.

24. Lions were common in Palestine in the early period, and again after the depopulation of the north which followed the Assyrian conquests (II Kings 17:26) .

But the man of God who resisted a king's invitation yielded to the seduction of a fellow prophet. He was strong enough in his will power but weak in his spiritual perception. He allowed himself to be deceived by his colleague's false assertion that he had received a new commandment from the Lord setting aside the first. He was punished for lack of confidence in his divine commission. Yet the man who deceived

him realized the worth of the erring man of God and asked that his own bones might be buried in the same grave. The whole story has a confused ethic, but human motives are mixed, and even men of God have weak links in their armor.

26. *O Night, What of the Watchman?*—Familiar and timely is the anxious and repeated cry, "Watchman, what of the night?" (Isa. 21:

ent unto the word of the Lord: therefore the Lord hath delivered him unto the lion, which hath torn him, and slain him, according to the word of the Lord, which he spake unto him.

27 And he spake to his sons, saying, Saddle me the ass. And they saddled *him*.

28 And he went and found his carcass cast in the way, and the ass and the lion standing by the carcass: the lion had not eaten the carcass, nor torn the ass.

29 And the prophet took up the carcass of the man of God, and laid it upon the ass, and brought it back: and the old prophet came to the city, to mourn and to bury him.

30 And he laid his carcass in his own grave; and they mourned over him, *saying*, Alas, my brother!

31 And it came to pass, after he had buried him, that he spake to his sons, saying, When I am dead, then bury me in the sepulchre wherein the man of God *is* buried; lay my bones beside his bones:

32 For the saying which he cried by the word of the Lord against the altar in Bethel, and against all the houses of the high places which *are* in the cities of Samaria, shall surely come to pass.

brought him back from the way heard of it, he said, "It is the man of God, who disobeyed the word of the Lord; therefore the Lord has given him to the lion, which has torn him and slain him, according to the word which the Lord spoke to him." 27 And he said to his sons, "Saddle the ass for me." And they saddled it. 28 And he went and found his body thrown in the road, and the ass and the lion standing beside the body. The lion had not eaten the body or torn the ass. 29 And the prophet took up the body of the man of God and laid it upon the ass, and brought it back to the city,[1] to mourn and to bury him. 30 And he laid the body in his own grave; and they mourned over him, saying, "Alas, my brother!" 31 And after he had buried him, he said to his sons, "When I die, bury me in the grave in which the man of God is buried; lay my bones beside his bones. 32 For the saying which he cried by the word of the Lord against the altar in Bethel, and against all the houses of the high places which are in the cities of Samar'ia, shall surely come to pass."

[1] Gk: Heb *he came to the city of the old prophet*

---

11). The world is still living on the defensive, as in the days of Jeroboam. The nights are not filled with the same terrors, but human fears have increased. We are surrounded by very real dangers. Our institutions and ideals are threatened. The faster men and events move the farther ahead is it necessary to look. There are more professional watchmen than ever before—columnists, radio news commentators, government spies. The hurried and worried crowd count heavily on these secular seers, and keep ever asking: "Watchman, what of the night? Will there be war? Will the dawn of peace and justice soon come?"

But what of the watchmen? So much depends on their ability and character. Irresponsible watchmen are worse than none, for they deceive with a false security. Emotional watchmen are a menace, for they excite without cause. Prejudiced watchmen are a peril, for they distort dangers and arouse anxieties in the wrong directions. And worst of all are those professional propagandists who find it more popular and profitable to play upon people's fears and hatreds than upon their sympathy and love. In O.T. times much dependence was put on the divine watchmen. The prophets of God were the seers of the nation. Samuel the prophet

served as guide in choosing Israel's first king, and remained his counselor until Saul lapsed from his high duties. And so on down the list of the great Hebrew prophets. The Christian church played a similar role in the nations of Christendom. Her spokesmen were the watchmen who gave warning of dangers without and within. They served as the nerves of the nations, crying out when human values were imperiled. They have been the keepers of conscience.

In this chapter is the somewhat tangled story of two unnamed prophets. One is called **the man of God.** He came up out of Judah to Bethel, where he boldly confronted King Jeroboam and declared the Lord's condemnation of his apostasy. The king tried to flatter and bribe him, but he resisted the temptation. He announced that he had been commanded of the Lord not to eat bread or drink water in Jeroboam's country, and not to return by the way which he had come to Bethel (vs. 9). All three of these commandments he kept. But a certain "old prophet in Bethel" pursued the departing man of God, overtook him, deceived him with a lying report of having received a more recent command of the Lord, and persuaded him to stop and break bread. As a result of this violation, the man of God was slain by

33 ¶ After this thing Jeroboam returned not from his evil way, but made again of the lowest of the people priests of the high places: whosoever would, he consecrated him, and he became *one* of the priests of the high places.

34 And this thing became sin unto the house of Jeroboam, even to cut *it* off, and to destroy *it* from off the face of the earth.

14 At that time Abijah the son of Jeroboam fell sick.

2 And Jeroboam said to his wife, Arise, I pray thee, and disguise thyself, that thou

---

33 After this thing Jerobo'am did not turn from his evil way, but made priests for the high places again from among all the people; any who would, he consecrated to be priests of the high places. 34 And this thing became sin to the house of Jerobo'am, so as to cut it off and to destroy it from the face of the earth.

14 At that time Abi'jah the son of Jerobo'am fell sick. 2 And Jerobo'am said to his wife, "Arise, and disguise your-

---

33-34. The compiler picks up once more the thread of the main narrative (12:31), repeating part of the last verse and adding a true Deuteronomic moral to the story of the institution of the Bethel altar. The technical term for the consecration of a priest is "to fill the hand"—a phrase used in the same sense in Akkadian. The reference is probably to the first offering made by the priest when he "waved" the prescribed portions in front of the altar according to established rule.

3. DEATH OF JEROBOAM'S SON (14:1-18)

Abijah is ill and likely to die. Jeroboam sends his wife, disguised as an ordinary woman, to the aged and now-blind Ahijah the Shilonite to inquire about the fate of the child. The prophet, blind though he is, recognizes her, tells her even before she asks that the child will die, denounces the king and all his line, prophesies the downfall of the Northern Kingdom. The story ends with the death of the boy.

The original story is to be found in vss. 1-6, 12, 17; the remainder is due to the Deuteronomic compiler who is following his customary habit of pointing out the moral. The LXX parallel is found in the interpolation which follows 12:24, where the incident is recorded as having taken place before Jeroboam becomes king. The M.T. story and its place are preferable.

14:2. Why should the queen so disguise herself? The LXXᴬ, following the M.T., says it was in order that "they should not recognize her," but Josephus understands that

---

a lion. When the prophet who had misled him saw the body he exclaimed, **It is the man of God, who disobeyed the word of the LORD.**

Amid the lights and shadows of this portrayal of two prophets a few points are worthy of notice. First, **the man of God** was faithful to his main and most difficult commission. He had delivered the word of the Lord at great personal risk. Second, he failed in one of the minor commandments. He was undone by his lapse at a point of detail. Having fortified himself for the hard task of denouncing the king, he left himself unguarded against one of his own profession. Perhaps it was the softening reaction which sometimes follows courageous effort. Even the best of men have the "trough" experiences when the crest of the wave has passed. Then, too, he appears to have disobeyed his original command because he innocently believed the other prophet's report of a new revelation from the Lord. But are ignorance

and innocence excusable in a **man of God?** Third, the value of his service was not utterly canceled by his later lapse. The treatment of his body and the tribute to him from the false prophet attest the fact that his courageous stand against Jeroboam's idolatry had not gone for nought. Divine judgment discriminates. There is no cancellation in the moral realm. "Be ye steadfast, unmovable, always abounding in the work of the Lord, forasmuch as ye know that your labor is not in vain in the Lord" (I Cor. 15:58) —even if by some slip you later fall from grace. The good works of the man of God followed him, although he died for his disobedience. But the watchmen of God must be ever on the alert. Unguarded moments often prove the undoing of courageous servants of the Lord.

14:1-31. *The Paths of Glory Lead But to the Grave.*—Jeroboam received his last divine warning for his sins through the illness of his son. In his dire distress the reprobate king turned

be not known to be the wife of Jeroboam; and get thee to Shiloh: behold, there *is* Ahijah the prophet, which told me that *I should be* king over this people.

3 And take with thee ten loaves, and cracknels, and a cruse of honey, and go to him: he shall tell thee what shall become of the child.

4 And Jeroboam's wife did so, and arose, and went to Shiloh, and came to the house of Ahijah. But Ahijah could not see; for his eyes were set by reason of his age.

5 ¶ And the LORD said unto Ahijah, Behold, the wife of Jeroboam cometh to ask a thing of thee for her son; for he *is* sick: thus and thus shalt thou say unto her: for it shall be, when she cometh in, that she shall feign herself *to be* another *woman.*

6 And it was *so,* when Ahijah heard the sound of her feet, as she came in at the door, that he said, Come in, thou wife of Jeroboam; why feignest thou thyself *to be* another? for I *am* sent to thee *with* heavy tidings.

7 Go, tell Jeroboam, Thus saith the LORD God of Israel, Forasmuch as I exalted thee from among the people, and made thee prince over my people Israel,

self, that it be not known that you are the wife of Jerobo'am, and go to Shiloh; behold, Ahi'jah the prophet is there, who said of me that I should be king over this people. 3 Take with you ten loaves, some cakes, and a jar of honey, and go to him; he will tell you what shall happen to the child."

4 Jerobo'am's wife did so; she arose, and went to Shiloh, and came to the house of Ahi'jah. Now Ahi'jah could not see, for his eyes were dim because of his age. 5 And the LORD said to Ahi'jah, "Behold, the wife of Jerobo'am is coming to inquire of you concerning her son; for he is sick. Thus and thus shall you say to her."

When she came, she pretended to be another woman. 6 But when Ahi'jah heard the sound of her feet, as she came in at the door, he said, "Come in, wife of Jerobo'am; why do you pretend to be another? For I am charged with heavy tidings for you. 7 Go, tell Jerobo'am, 'Thus says the LORD, the God of Israel: "Because I exalted you from among the people, and made you

it was solely to disguise herself from the prophet Ahijah (*Antiquities* VIII. 11. 1). This latter explanation is probably correct. Jeroboam had been glad enough of Ahijah's support at the beginning, but evidently he had changed his loyalty after he had become king and had favored the priests of Bethel instead of those of Shiloh, who had been instrumental in raising him to the throne of Israel. Note that the child's name is **Abijah**, a compound name of which one element is a shortened form of the divine name. This is evidence that Jeroboam, in his action of establishing the cult of the calves at Bethel, was not conscious of being an apostate from the worship of the Lord.

3. The word **cracknels** is still in use in England (mainly in the south) to describe small crisp biscuits (cookies), either crescent-shaped or hollow. The word is also used in country districts generally to mean small pieces of pork crisply fried. The Hebrew word is used in Josh. 9:5 of the old dried bread which the Gibeonites used to deceive Joshua. By derivation it has to do with dots, marks, specks, and is used in Ethiopic of worm-eaten wood. A word derived from the same root is used of the speckled sheep in Laban's flock (Gen. 30:32; etc.). The LXXᴬ says that the queen took the crisp biscuits for Ahijah's children. In any case, it was certainly the custom to take a present, however small (I Sam. 9:8), when an oracle was sought from a prophet-seer.

The **cruse** or **jar** was a narrow-necked bottle, so called from the gurgling sound made in pouring out the water: *baqbûq.*

5. She came to the prophet in order to seek an oracle **concerning her son.**

from his hireling priests and false prophets to the man of God, Ahijah. The blind old seer spared no words in denouncing the sins of Jeroboam and predicting the death of his son. He declared the relentless law that sins of the fathers are visited on their offspring. Did Ahijah think that the death of the son would turn the father's heart to God? Sometimes it takes such a

8 And rent the kingdom away from the house of David, and gave it thee: and *yet* thou hast not been as my servant David, who kept my commandments, and who followed me with all his heart, to do *that* only *which was* right in mine eyes;

9 But hast done evil above all that were before thee: for thou hast gone and made thee other gods, and molten images, to provoke me to anger, and hast cast me behind thy back:

10 Therefore, behold, I will bring evil upon the house of Jeroboam, and will cut off from Jeroboam him that pisseth against the wall, *and* him that is shut up and left in Israel, and will take away the remnant of the house of Jeroboam, as a man taketh away dung, till it be all gone.

11 Him that dieth of Jeroboam in the city shall the dogs eat; and him that dieth in the field shall the fowls of the air eat: for the LORD hath spoken *it*.

12 Arise thou therefore, get thee to thine own house: *and* when thy feet enter into the city, the child shall die.

leader over my people Israel, 8 and tore the kingdom away from the house of David and gave it to you; and yet you have not been like my servant David, who kept my commandments, and followed me with all his heart, doing only that which was right in my eyes, 9 but you have done evil above all that were before you and have gone and made for yourself other gods, and molten images, provoking me to anger, and have cast me behind your back; 10 therefore behold, I will bring evil upon the house of Jerobo'am, and will cut off from Jerobo'am every male, both bond and free in Israel, and will utterly consume the house of Jerobo'am, as a man burns up dung until it is all gone. 11 Anyone belonging to Jerobo'am who dies in the city the dogs shall eat; and anyone who dies in the open country the birds of the air shall eat; for the LORD has spoken it." ' 12 Arise therefore, go to your house. When your feet enter the city, the

---

9. **Anger** is an emotion often ascribed to God in the Bible. It stands for his settled attitude toward sin and unrepentant sinners. It is not a sudden, passionate emotion, but a steady reasoned antagonism. Attempts have been made to regard the anger of God as an archaic description of the cause-effect relationship between sin and its consequences, working automatically in the world, and to some extent independently of God (C. H. Dodd, *The Epistle of Paul to the Romans* [London: Hodder & Stoughton, 1932; "The Moffatt New Testament Commentary"], pp. 20-24). But this modern idea, with its tendency toward deism, does not do justice to the biblical idea of the definite and personal opposition to sin which is evident everywhere on the part of God.

The phrase **cast me behind your back** is used of apostasy in Ezek. 23:35; of neglect of God's law in Neh. 9:26; and of the remission of sins in Isa. 38:17. It means "out of sight, out of mind," and in the last case, "out of existence" also—a unique simile for the forgiveness of sins.

10. **Bond and free** represents a phrase whose general sense is clear, but its immediate significance is obscure. The Hebrew phrase is alliterative, so that "fettered and free" (C. F. Keil, *The Book of Kings,* tr. James Martin [2nd ed.; Edinburgh: T. & T. Clark, 1877], p. 211) is an apt rendering. It means "restrained and loosed," and the two categories obviously include all males. Ewald suggested "kept in [by legal defilement] and at large"; Schmidt, "under and over age [i.e., under wardship]"; while the Arabic use of '*azîbh* suggests "married and celibate." The phrase may actually mean "slave and freeman," since Solomon sold men as slaves into Egypt (Deut. 17:16), and there is the definite evidence of Exod. 21:16; II Kings 4:1.

---

calamity to effect a conversion. There is no record that Jeroboam's heart was softened by its breaking.

As for Rehoboam, his ill-starred reign in Judah was five years shorter than Jeroboam's

rule in the Northern Kingdom. His people turned from the true worship to the pagan shrines. His kingdom was invaded by the armies of Egypt, which carried away the richest treasures of Solomon's temple and the royal palace.

13 And all Israel shall mourn for him, and bury him: for he only of Jeroboam shall come to the grave, because in him there is found *some* good thing toward the LORD God of Israel in the house of Jeroboam.

14 Moreover the LORD shall raise him up a king over Israel, who shall cut off the house of Jeroboam that day: but what? even now.

15 For the LORD shall smite Israel, as a reed is shaken in the water, and he shall root up Israel out of this good land, which he gave to their fathers, and shall scatter them beyond the river, because they have made their groves, provoking the LORD to anger.

child shall die. 13 And all Israel shall mourn for him, and bury him; for he only of Jerobo'am shall come to the grave, because in him there is found something pleasing to the LORD, the God of Israel, in the house of Jerobo'am. 14 Moreover the LORD will raise up for himself a king over Israel, who shall cut off the house of Jerobo'am today. And henceforth[m] 15 the LORD will smite Israel, as a reed is shaken in the water, and root up Israel out of this good land which he gave to their fathers, and scatter them beyond the Eu-phra'tes, because they have made their Ashe'rim, provoking the LORD

[m] Heb *obscure*

---

13. Nadab, Jeroboam's son who succeeded him, died a violent death, and that was the end of Jeroboam's dynasty (15:28). The rabbis have a tradition that the action which was found **pleasing to the LORD** occurred when Jeroboam instructed Abijah to prevent the people from going up to worship at the Jerusalem temple, but Abijah tore down the barriers which Jeroboam had set up in order to restrain the people from going up.

15. **The river,** as elsewhere regularly, is **the Euphrates.** This reference to the Assyrian deportations can scarcely have been foreseen in the tenth century; it is a clear indication that the speech of Ahijah the Shilonite is the work of the Deuteronomic compiler.

The **Asherim** were wooden poles commonly set up, either singly or in company with a stone pillar (*maççēbhāh*), at a Canaanite hill shrine beside the altar. There is little justification for the translation **groves,** a reference which is doubtless due to classical associations. An asherah was a wooden pole, stripped of its branches, and it was always associated with a female deity. When the wooden pole was in company with a stone pillar it represented Astarte, the consort of Baal (Jer. 3:9), and this provides the reason for the confusion in Judg. 2:13; 3:7 between "Ashtaroth" and "Asheroth" (ASV). But there is an increasing amount of evidence that there was also a goddess named Asherah. This goddess is mentioned in the Tell el-Amarna tablets (fourteenth century B.C.; the name 'Abad-'Ashrat is found, i.e., "servant of 'Ashrat," on tablet No. 68 in Knudtzon's list [British Museum Bulletin 88-10-13, 58]) and frequently in the Ras Shamra tablets (fifteenth to thirteenth centuries B.C.; J. W. Jack, *The Ras Shamra Tablets* [Edinburgh: T. & T. Clark, 1935], pp. 25, 50; the references are common in the Ras Shamra texts known as I AB and II AB, published by Virolleaud in *Syria,* XII [1931], 193-224; XIII [1932], 113-63; and XV [1934], 226-43). This is the goddess who is associated with the wooden pole when it is not found in company with a stone pillar (e.g., 18:19; II Kings 21:7). She is often styled "Lady Asherah of the Sea" (*rbt 'Ashrt ym;* often in I AB and II AB) —a designation which gives additional point to the title "goddess of the Sidonians" (11:5). On the other hand, there is already confusion in the Tell el-Amarna texts and in the Ras Shamra texts between Astarte, Asherah, and the Babylonian goddess Anath, "the queen of heaven," so that the Israelite confusion was doubtless inherited from the Canaanites whose religion the masses largely adopted. The confusion is not therefore due to a lack of knowledge of the later scribes only (see also René Dussaud, *Les*

Whereas Solomon's shields were of gold, Rehoboam was reduced to shields of bronze. Humiliated and impoverished, the weak and rash son dragged his country through incessant wars until

he slept with his fathers, "unwept, unhonour'd, and unsung."[7]

[7] Sir Walter Scott, *The Lay of the Last Minstrel,* Canto VI, st. i.

16 And he shall give Israel up because of the sins of Jeroboam, who did sin, and who made Israel to sin.

17 ¶ And Jeroboam's wife arose, and departed, and came to Tirzah: *and* when she came to the threshold of the door, the child died;

18 And they buried him; and all Israel mourned for him, according to the word of the LORD, which he spake by the hand of his servant Ahijah the prophet.

19 And the rest of the acts of Jeroboam, how he warred, and how he reigned, behold, they *are* written in the book of the Chronicles of the kings of Israel.

20 And the days which Jeroboam reigned *were* two and twenty years: and he slept with his fathers, and Nadab his son reigned in his stead.

21 ¶ And Rehoboam the son of Solomon reigned in Judah. Rehoboam *was* forty and one years old when he began to reign, and he reigned seventeen years in Jerusalem, the city which the LORD did choose out of all the tribes of Israel, to put his name there. And his mother's name *was* Naamah an Ammonitess.

22 And Judah did evil in the sight of the LORD, and they provoked him to jealousy with their sins which they had committed, above all that their fathers had done.

to anger. 16 And he will give Israel up because of the sins of Jerobo'am, which he sinned and which he made Israel to sin."

17 Then Jerobo'am's wife arose, and departed, and came to Tirzah. And as she came to the threshold of the house, the child died. 18 And all Israel buried him and mourned for him, according to the word of the LORD, which he spoke by his servant Ahi'jah the prophet. 19 Now the rest of the acts of Jerobo'am, how he warred and how he reigned, behold, they are written in the Book of the Chronicles of the kings of Israel. 20 And the time that Jerobo'am reigned was twenty-two years; and he slept with his fathers, and Nadab his son reigned in his stead.

21 Now Rehobo'am the son of Solomon reigned in Judah. Rehobo'am was forty-one years old when he began to reign, and he reigned seventeen years in Jerusalem, the city which the LORD had chosen out of all the tribes of Israel, to put his name there. His mother's name was Na'amah the Ammonitess. 22 And Judah did what was evil in the sight of the LORD, and they provoked him to jealousy with their sins which they committed, more than all that their fathers

---

découvertes de Ras Shamra [Paris: Paul Geuthner, 1937], p. 71; W. F. Albright, *Archaeology and the Religion of Israel* [2nd ed.; Baltimore: Johns Hopkins Press, 1946] pp. 74-79; Engnell, *Studies in Divine Kingship*, p. 115).

17. Tirzah was probably a few miles northeast of Shechem, the modern Nablus, though the site is not certainly identified. It was the royal residence in Jeroboam's time and continued so until the time of Omri, who built Samaria in the seventh year of his reign (16:24). The city was famed for its beauty (Song of S. 6:4).

4. DEATH OF JEROBOAM I (14:19-20)

19-20. The Deuteronomic compiler, having rounded off the story of the sickness and death of Jeroboam's son (vs. 18), now adds his formal obituary notice for the kings of Israel, except that he usually inserts a comparison with Jeroboam son of Nebat himself. Obviously he cannot do that in this particular case.

5. REHOBOAM OF JUDAH (14:21-31)
a) CHARACTERISTICS OF REHOBOAM'S REIGN (14:21-24)

These verses form the Deuteronomic notice for the accession of a new king, giving all the customary formal details (vs. 21). The editor follows with a summary of the king's reign, a story of apostasy and abomination. It is evident that Rehoboam allowed a complete syncretism of the cult of the Lord and the cults of Canaan.

22. The ascription of **jealousy** to God has caused great difficulty. The Hebrew word קנא refers primarily to the color produced in the face by violent emotion; the corresponding Arabic word means "to become intensely red or black with dye." The

23 For they also built them high places, and images, and groves, on every high hill, and under every green tree.

24 And there were also sodomites in the land: *and* they did according to all the abominations of the nations which the Lord cast out before the children of Israel.

had done. 23 For they also built for themselves high places, and pillars, and Ashe′rim on every high hill and under every green tree; 24 and there were also male cult prostitutes in the land. They did according to all the abominations of the nations which the Lord drove out before the people of Israel.

reference is found in Syriac also, but other Semitic languages, including Hebrew, use the word to mean both "zeal for" and "envy against." It is thus similar in usage to the Greek ζῆλος, which can be both the equivalent of φθόνος ("envy") and its exact opposite. The use of the word and idea in reference to God arises from the husband-wife relationship. Just as a husband is zealous for his wife's honor, and jealous of anything that would take her from him, so God is both zealous for Israel and jealously angry at her idolatrous unfaithfulness. The whole picture is anthropomorphic, but no other mode of expression is possible unless we are to divest God of all personal qualities and try to speak of him in terms remote from life itself.

24. There were prostitutes of either sex within the temple in the service of the deity. This custom was common and recognized everywhere in Phoenician cults and in the cults (e.g., that of Aphrodite) which were influenced by them. The custom was a

24. *The Assimilation of Sin.*—The pagan sinners had been killed, but their misdeeds had been preserved by the Israelites. **They did according to all the abominations of the nations which the Lord drove out before the people of Israel.** Such is the tragic aftermath of many a militant crusade against evil. Moral fervor is aroused, and forces are sent forth to remove the wrongdoers. Then the conquerors become infected with the sins of the conquered. The medieval crusaders brought back to Europe germs of sin caught from contact with the Moslem hordes they sought to dislodge. In World War I, millions of youth were slaughtered to make democracy safe from the "Huns." The kaiser was dethroned, but freedom was not established. The aftermath of that war was a diseased society from which sprang a nazism more ruthless than the regime which had been removed. Twenty years later another crusade of passionate reform was whipped up, and more millions were killed in a global conflict called a "war of survival." But what survived World War II? A society so chaotic and diseased that within three years after the victory over nazism, the world was resounding with the cries of alarm over a totalitarianism hailed as the most dangerous yet. So the vicious circle goes on. Like Rehoboam, victors keep on punishing the evildoers and then preserving the evils of their victims.

In this contagion of evil is to be seen the logic behind the apostolic command, "Be not overcome of evil, but overcome evil with good" (Rom. 12:21). We cannot overcome evil with

evil. If our enemy drags us into the gutter to fight him, then he has to that extent at least defeated us. The forces of good must eradicate the evils which poison the minds of sinners. Granted that communism is a pernicious system, its cure lies not in killing the poor victims of its perverted thinking but in removing the poverty, the inequities, the ignorance, the bitterness which breed communists. The abominations practiced by the Canaanite cults were not eradicated by Israel; they were assimilated.

Rehoboam's followers reversed the course of action adopted by the godly man as described in Ps. 1. He too had his residence in the midst of an ungodly and perverse generation. But of him it was said that he "walketh not in the counsel of the ungodly" (Ps. 1:1). Ungodliness may not wear the garb of wickedness. It may observe the social decencies. It simply leaves God out of consideration. Its gods are of this world, as were those of the Canaanite cults. The distinction between godliness and worldliness is not that the former forgoes the enjoyments of this world while the latter revels in them. To enlightened godly persons the world is a joy and a grace; but to them there is something higher, in the name of which they would renounce, if need be, the things of earth. The worldly, on the other hand, are ungodly in the sense that they revere nothing higher than earthly values. Nothing is sufficiently sacred to them that they would sacrifice for it the things they enjoy here and now.

The ungodly are those who, having no sacred spots to safeguard, have taken down the "No

25 ¶ And it came to pass in the fifth year of king Rehoboam, *that* Shishak king of Egypt came up against Jerusalem:

26 And he took away the treasures of the house of the LORD, and the treasures of the king's house; he even took away all: and he took away all the shields of gold which Solomon had made.

27 And king Rehoboam made in their stead brazen shields, and committed *them* unto the hands of the chief of the guard, which kept the door of the king's house.

25 In the fifth year of King Rehobo'am, Shishak king of Egypt came up against Jerusalem; 26 he took away the treasures of the house of the LORD and the treasures of the king's house; he took away everything. He also took away all the shields of gold which Solomon had made; 27 and King Rehobo'am made in their stead shields of bronze, and committed them to the hands of the officers of the guard, who kept the door of

---

feature of Canaanite religion and was common in Mesopotamia from early times. There were three types of sacred prostitutes, two belonging to the temples: the *qadishtu* (the Hebrew word is *qedhēshāh* or, as here, the male *qādhēsh*) and the *ishtaritu*, i.e., a woman connected with the cult of Ishtar. The prophets from Amos to Ezekiel uniformly and vigorously condemned these practices. After the Exile there was no need for condemnation, since the worship was henceforth completely free from sexual ritualism.

b) THE INVASION OF SHESHONK (14:25-28)

Shishak (so M.T.) or Sheshonk (Shoshonq) was the first king of the Twelfth Dynasty. His invasion affected both Israel and Judah, though, judging from the inscriptions on the walls of the temple of Amon at Karnak, Judah suffered the more severely. He is said to have reigned *ca.* 950 B.C., though W. F. Albright (*Archaeology and Religion of Israel*, p. 130) proposes the dates *ca.* 940-920 B.C.

26. Evidently the glory of Solomon's state occasions did not last very long, for in the fifth year of his successor the marvelous golden shields were seized by Pharaoh Sheshonk. The substitute shields of bronze were no longer kept in the forest house of Lebanon but in the guardroom.

Trespass" signs. To walk with them, therefore, is like going with the careless crowd over a lawn without fences and signs, until the lovely green has become a dirty, muddied brown. Living without reverence reduces life to commonness. And he that "walketh . . . in the counsel of the ungodly" finds his sense of duty beginning to weaken. It may be ever so slightly and subtly, just a little lowering here and there of the moral standards, just a little more lenient excusing of shortcomings, just a little more catering to lower natures, just a bit more compromising with the crowd.

The first effect on Judah of their contact with the Canaanites was a loss of reverence. The sanctities of life were lessened. When a people cease to look up to some things as sacred, they start downward. Note the next step of deterioration as depicted by the psalmist, "standeth in the way of sinners" (Ps. 1:1). Consider the case history of a typical young criminal. He began as one of those thousands who grow up in the "counsel of the ungodly," in those homes where God is not considered, where the Lord's Day is not observed, where no sanctities are cultivated.

Growing up with nothing to reverence, nothing to hold to, he drifted with the crowd which hung about the street corners. There he heard the talk of evil and steeped his mind in it. In short, he stood in the way of sinners until his imagination was caught and his conduct conditioned.

The assimilation of evil is the same in principle, whether the victim is caught in the net of the law or immersed in "polite society." There are well-dressed sins which hang around the corners of fashionable society, sins of smugness and pride, of prejudice and bigotry, of self-interest and self-indulgence. If we stand in the way of such sins, if we let our minds dwell on them, if our thoughts return to such sins in our relaxed moments, then we are on the way downward. When we walk in the counsel of the ungodly, we lose our reverence; when we stand in the way of sinners, we lose our virtue. Hetty Sorrel, as George Eliot portrays her in *Adam Bede*, first lost her reverence, then her self-respect, then her purity.

The next step of moral deterioration is to sit "in the seat of the scornful" (Ps. 1:1). When a

28 And it was *so*, when the king went into the house of the LORD, that the guard bare them, and brought them back into the guard chamber.

29 ¶ Now the rest of the acts of Rehoboam, and all that he did, *are* they not written in the book of the Chronicles of the kings of Judah?

30 And there was war between Rehoboam and Jeroboam all *their* days.

31 And Rehoboam slept with his fathers, and was buried with his fathers in the city of David. And his mother's name *was* Naamah an Ammonitess. And Abijam his son reigned in his stead.

15 Now in the eighteenth year of king Jeroboam the son of Nebat reigned Abijam over Judah.

the king's house. 28 And as often as the king went into the house of the LORD, the guard bore them and brought them back to the guardroom.

29 Now the rest of the acts of Rehobo'am, and all that he did, are they not written in the Book of the Chronicles of the Kings of Judah? 30 And there was war between Rehobo'am and Jerobo'am continually. 31 And Rehobo'am slept with his fathers and was buried with his fathers in the city of David. His mother's name was Na'amah the Ammonitess. And Abi'jam his son reigned in his stead.

15 Now in the eighteenth year of King Jerobo'am the son of Nebat, Abi'jam

c) DEATH OF REHOBOAM (14:29-31)

29-31. The formal obituary notice for Rehoboam, according to the regular pattern of the Deuteronomic compiler. The name of the successor is mentioned. The Hebrew text gives the name as **Abijam**, but the versions presuppose "Abijah." Opinion varies as to which spelling is accurate. Many scholars maintain that Abijah is right, but in this case it is difficult to account for the reading Abijam. It may of course be a simple error on the part of some Hebrew scribe, but perhaps it is better to regard the M.T. as being right, with the versions changing the last letter in favor of the better-known name.

B. EARLY WARS BETWEEN ISRAEL AND JUDAH (15:1–16:28)

1. ABIJAM OF JUDAH (15:1-8)

This chapter and the next are the work of the original Deuteronomic compiler of *ca.* 610 B.C., who embodied various extracts from his annalistic sources of the kings of Israel and Judah, and wove them into his general didactic scheme. Vss. 1-3 contain the usual notice with its general estimate of the character of the king in comparison—since he was a king of Judah—with David, the compiler's model king of the days before the good king Josiah. Vss. 7-8 contain the customary obituary notice, with its mention of the successor.

15:1. The name **Abijam** is preferable (cf. Exeg. on 14:29-31).

person has given up trying to be good he begins to make light of goodness. He scorns the old patterns of morality as outmoded and looks upon reformers as narrow souls who do not want others to enjoy the pleasures which they are afraid to take for themselves. Flippantly he says, "Let conscience be your guide," and then wheedles it into a pettifogging attorney for the defense of his desires. And why take conscience seriously, since it is only the echo of social custom? Such is the frosty cynicism which kills the nerves of conscience and faith. From "the counsel of the ungodly" to "the way of sinners" to "the seat of the scornful" is the path toward conformity with the world. The godly man resists this downward drift (cf. Ps. 1); but Reho-

boam's subjects yielded to it until **they did according to all the abominations of the nations which the LORD drove out before the people of Israel.**

15:1-34. *Civil War.*—There are no feuds so bitter as family feuds. Similarities and associations seem to provide places for enmities to fester. The continuing strife between the two Hebrew kingdoms constitutes a sordid story. The Chronicler makes it clear that this tragic hostility was due to godlessness. One god-fearing king redeems this chapter of Hebrew history from unbroken darkness. For forty-one years Asa ruled in Jerusalem doing **what was right in the eyes of the LORD.** He removed idols and restored the votive gifts of true worship. But so

2 Three years reigned he in Jerusalem. And his mother's name *was* Maachah, the daughter of Abishalom.

3 And he walked in all the sins of his father, which he had done before him: and his heart was not perfect with the LORD his God, as the heart of David his father.

4 Nevertheless for David's sake did the LORD his God give him a lamp in Jerusalem, to set up his son after him, and to establish Jerusalem:

5 Because David did *that which was* right in the eyes of the LORD, and turned not aside from any *thing* that he commanded him all the days of his life, save only in the matter of Uriah the Hittite.

6 And there was war between Rehoboam and Jeroboam all the days of his life.

7 Now the rest of the acts of Abijam, and all that he did, *are* they not written in the book of the Chronicles of the kings of Judah? And there was war between Abijam and Jeroboam.

8 And Abijam slept with his fathers; and they buried him in the city of David: and Asa his son reigned in his stead.

began to reign over Judah. **2** He reigned for three years in Jerusalem. His mother's name was Ma′acah the daughter of Abish′alom. **3** And he walked in all the sins which his father did before him; and his heart was not wholly true to the LORD his God, as the heart of David his father. **4** Nevertheless for David's sake the LORD his God gave him a lamp in Jerusalem, setting up his son after him, and establishing Jerusalem; **5** because David did what was right in the eyes of the LORD, and did not turn aside from anything that he commanded him all the days of his life, except in the matter of Uri′ah the Hittite. **6** Now there was war between Rehobo′am and Jerobo′am all the days of his life. **7** The rest of the acts of Abi′jam, and all that he did, are they not written in the Book of the Chronicles of the Kings of Judah? And there was war between Abi′jam and Jerobo′am. **8** And Abi′jam slept with his fathers; and they buried him in the city of David. And Asa his son reigned in his stead.

---

2. The same statement, that the king's mother was **Maacah** the daughter of Absalom (in each case with the same abnormal spelling, **Abishalom**) is made of Asa in vs. 10. Various suggestions have been made to solve the difficulty. It may be that Asa was Abijam's brother and not his son (Wellhausen). Another suggestion is that the mothers of the two kings had in actual fact the same name and that the phrase **the daughter of Abishalom** was wrongly inserted in vs. 10 (Gesenius). Ewald, more probably, proposed that Maacah continued to be head of the harem (her proper title being *gebhirāh*) during the time of her grandson Asa until he took the unusual step of removing her because of her idolatries (vs. 13). This suggestion is all the more probable because Abijam was king for three years at most, and Asa may well have been a minor for some time after he became king. The LXX[B] says that Asa's mother was named Ana (so in vs. 10), but there is no support for this, and it has every indication of being an attempt at correction. Josephus (*Antiquities* VIII. 10. 1) says that Maacah was the granddaughter of Absalom, and that her mother was Tamar (II Sam. 14:27). This is probable since Absalom's daughter must certainly have been older than Rehoboam.

5. The compiler explains why it is that Abijam was permitted to reign in spite of his idolatries. It was because of David's uprightness (11:36). There is a qualification added by some honest scribe who remembered the incident of the wife of Uriah the Hittite, and could not bring himself to let the statement on a perfect David pass without comment. The qualification is not in the LXX.

6. This verse is not in the LXX, and was probably added from 14:30 by some scribe in order to make the record as complete here as it was there.

---

bitter was the enmity between the two Hebrew kingdoms that Asa formed a league with Ben-hadad the Syrian against the Northern Kingdom. David had struggled to unite Israel's tribes into a nation, and now the work of David was un-

done. Solomon had lifted Jerusalem to the pinnacle of unprecedented splendor, and now her glory had departed. To the recorder of the sorry story the reason is clear: Israel was forsaken because she had forsaken God.

9 ¶ And in the twentieth year of Jeroboam king of Israel reigned Asa over Judah.

10 And forty and one years reigned he in Jerusalem. And his mother's name was Maachah, the daughter of Abishalom.

11 And Asa did *that which was* right in the eyes of the LORD, as *did* David his father.

12 And he took away the sodomites out of the land, and removed all the idols that his fathers had made.

13 And also Maachah his mother, even her he removed from *being* queen, because she had made an idol in a grove; and Asa destroyed her idol, and burnt *it* by the brook Kidron.

14 But the high places were not removed: nevertheless Asa's heart was perfect with the LORD all his days.

15 And he brought in the things which his father had dedicated, and the things

9 In the twentieth year of Jerobo'am king of Israel Asa began to reign over Judah, 10 and he reigned forty-one years in Jerusalem. His mother's name was Ma'-acah the daughter of Abish'alom. 11 And Asa did what was right in the eyes of the LORD, as David his father had done. 12 He put away the male cult prostitutes out of the land, and removed all the idols that his fathers had made. 13 He also removed Ma'-acah his mother from being queen mother because she had an abominable image made for Ashe'rah; and Asa cut down her image and burned it at the brook Kidron. 14 But the high places were not taken away. Nevertheless the heart of Asa was wholly true to the LORD all his days. 15 And he brought into the house of the LORD the votive gifts

---

2. ASA OF JUDAH (15:9-24)
a) THE KING'S REFORMS (15:9-15)

The Deuteronomic compiler introduces his account of the reign of Asa with his customary formula. He passes an entirely favorable judgment on the king, in spite of the fact that the latter did not do away with the local shrines according to the perfect pattern of a good king as demanded by the later Deuteronomic reforms. Asa certainly was a great reformer, who did away with the abuses in the cultus of the Jerusalem temple which were due to the assimilation of Canaanite cults that had been permitted in the previous reigns.

12. Cult-prostitutes: See Exeg. on 14:24. The rendering **idols** is inadequate to express the full significance of the Hebrew *gillûlîm*. This word with its proper vowels (M.T. has given it the vowels of *shiqqûṣ;* cf. Exeg. on 11:5) may well have been a proper and respectful term for a god, for the same root is often used in Arabic for the greatness of the dignity of Allah. The Masoretes treated the word as an opprobrious term to mean either "idol-blocks," i.e., logs that can be rolled about or, less likely (though it is the rabbinical exegesis), "balls of dung."

13. Queen mother (RSV) is better than **queen** (KJV) though it should be realized that she was probably his grandmother.

It is uncertain what precisely this **abominable image** (so M.T.) was which Maacah had made. The Hebrew word is found only here and in the parallel II Chr. 15:16. The root means "to tremble," "to shudder," but anything more than this is guesswork. The Vulg. sees a reference to the cult of the phallus, an explanation adopted by some modern scholars. The other versions do not help us. Maacah made the image "to the Asherah" (so the Hebrew). This may mean as an image of the goddess or it may have been something else belonging to the cult of the goddess. The rendering **grove** is due to the LXX ἄλσος, followed by the Vulg. *lucus*.

The king burned the **abominable image** in the Kidron Valley. This is the deep depression to the east of Jerusalem, between the temple heights and the Mount of Olives. It is dry in the summer season and in the winter season also except after heavy rains, though the remains of ancient cave dwellings suggest that in very early times the water supply in the valley was good and regular. From the time of Asa this valley became the regular place where reforming kings destroyed all idolatrous cult objects.

which himself had dedicated, into the house of the Lord, silver, and gold, and vessels.

16 ¶ And there was war between Asa and Baasha king of Israel all their days.

17 And Baasha king of Israel went up against Judah, and built Ramah, that he might not suffer any to go out or come in to Asa king of Judah.

18 Then Asa took all the silver and the gold *that were* left in the treasures of the house of the Lord, and the treasures of the king's house, and delivered them into the hand of his servants: and king Asa sent them to Ben-hadad, the son of Tabrimon, the son of Hezion, king of Syria, that dwelt at Damascus, saying,

19 *There is* a league between me and

of his father and his own votive gifts, silver, and gold, and vessels.

16 And there was war between Asa and Ba'asha king of Israel all their days. **17** Ba'asha king of Israel went up against Judah, and built Ramah, that he might permit no one to go out or come in to Asa king of Judah. **18** Then Asa took all the silver and the gold that were left in the treasures of the house of the Lord and the treasures of the king's house, and gave them into the hands of his servants; and King Asa sent them to Ben-ha'dad the son of Tabrim'-mon, the son of He'zi-on, king of Syria, who dwelt in Damascus, saying, **19** "Let there be

---

b) War Between Asa of Judah and Baasha of Israel (15:16-22)

The war had continued, apparently with little intermission if any, since the days of the secession of the north under Jeroboam. In Asa's time the war had gone so much in favor of the north that the warlike Baasha was able to build a fortress close to Jerusalem itself. Asa then appealed to the Syrian king of Damascus, whom he bribed to attack Baasha and thus relieve the pressure on Judah. In this way Asa rescued his country from a most difficult and awkward predicament.

17. Ramah is only two hours north of Jerusalem, and was evidently the northern limit of the kingdom of Judah at this time. It shows how weak Judah was compared with Israel, since Asa made no attempt himself to hold the town of Ramah, even when Baasha was forced to withdraw. He took the stones with which Baasha had been fortifying Ramah and used them to fortify (probably) Gibeah of Saul, about an hour's journey north of Jerusalem.

18. Some would identify this **Ben-hadad** with the king of the same name in 20:1, but 20:34 is against that. Hadad is the name of "the atmospheric high god" of the Ras Shamra tablets (Engnell, *Studies in Divine Kingship,* pp. 81, 213). He is the Mesopotamian Adad, and was equated with Baal. He "appears to have been adopted at a relatively late date by the Phoenicians" (Dussaud, *Les découvertes de Ras Shamra,* p. 697), and this seems to be reflected in the difficulty of securing the permission of El for the building of a house for Baal (Obermann, *Ugaritic Mythology,* pp. 1-4). The fact that the name Ben-hadad means "son of Hadad" cannot be taken as evidence that the king actually was regarded as the son of the god (Engnell, *op. cit.,* p. 80), since the similar name Benaiah was not the name of any king in Israel. This latter fact supports the statement of S. A. Cook that Ben-hadad "may be a perfectly general name" (J. B. Bury, S. A. Cook, F. E. Adcock, eds., *The Cambridge Ancient History* [New York: The Macmillan Co., 1925], III, 362, n. 3).

The name **Tabrimmon** means "Rimmon is good," and is comparable to the Hebrew Tobiah (as LXX infers). Rimmon is the Assyrian storm god Rammanu, who thus easily becomes equated with Hadad (cf. Zech. 12:11, where the cult is the cult of Tammuz), but it is notoriously difficult to keep the cult of the high storm-god separate from that of the vegetation-god.

Ben-hadad's father, here called **Hezion,** may be the Rezon of 11:23-24, who founded the kingdom of Damascus. There is division of opinion concerning this, but the spelling of the LXX tends to support the identification.

19. If there was indeed a league between the two fathers, then **Let there be a league** cannot be right. This reading arises from the rendering of the LXX. On the other

thee, *and* between my father and thy father: behold, I have sent unto thee a present of silver and gold; come and break thy league with Baasha king of Israel, that he may depart from me.

20 So Ben-hadad hearkened unto king Asa, and sent the captains of the hosts which he had against the cities of Israel, and smote Ijon, and Dan, and Abel-beth-maachah, and all Cinneroth, with all the land of Naphtali.

21 And it came to pass, when Baasha heard *thereof,* that he left off building of Ramah, and dwelt in Tirzah.

22 Then king Asa made a proclamation throughout all Judah; none *was* exempted: and they took away the stones of Ramah, and the timber thereof, wherewith Baasha had builded; and king Asa built with them Geba of Benjamin, and Mizpah.

23 The rest of all the acts of Asa, and all his might, and all that he did, and the cities which he built, *are* they not written in the book of the Chronicles of the kings of Judah? Nevertheless in the time of his old age he was diseased in his feet.

24 And Asa slept with his fathers, and was buried with his fathers in the city of David his father: and Jehoshaphat his son reigned in his stead.

25 ¶ And Nadab the son of Jeroboam began to reign over Israel in the second year of Asa king of Judah, and reigned over Israel two years.

a league between me and you, as between my father and your father: behold, I am sending to you a present of silver and gold; go, break your league with Ba'asha king of Israel, that he may withdraw from me."

20 And Ben-ha'dad hearkened to King Asa, and sent the commanders of his armies against the cities of Israel, and conquered Ijon, Dan, A'bel-beth-ma'acah, and all Chin'neroth, with all the land of Naph'tali.

21 And when Ba'asha heard of it, he stopped building Ramah, and he dwelt in Tirzah.

22 Then King Asa made a proclamation to all Judah, none was exempt, and they carried away the stones of Ramah and its timber, with which Ba'asha had been building; and with them King Asa built Geba of Benjamin and Mizpah. 23 Now the rest of all the acts of Asa, all his might, and all that he did, and the cities which he built, are they not written in the Book of the Chronicles of the Kings of Judah? But in his old age he was diseased in his feet. 24 And Asa slept with his fathers, and was buried with his fathers in the city of David his father; and Jehosh'aphat his son reigned in his stead.

25 Nadab the son of Jerobo'am began to reign over Israel in the second year of Asa king of Judah; and he reigned over Israel

---

hand, if there was already a league in operation between the two kingdoms it is difficult to see why Asa should send such great treasure to the Syrian king. The easiest solution is that there was a lapsed covenant alliance which Asa is seeking to renew. In this case the rendering of the LXX and the RSV has justification, since the syntax of the Hebrew will allow the renderings of both the KJV and the RSV. Asa's sending treasure is, however, really a sending of tribute.

20. The Syrian king raided the whole of the northwestern Israelite territory, including **all Chinneroth,** the fertile plain to the northwest of the Sea of Galilee, now known as el-Ghuwer.

c) Death of Asa (15:23-24)

23-24. The regular obituary notice for a king of Judah. To this there is added a note to the effect that Asa **in his old age . . . was diseased in his feet.** The disease may not actually have been in his feet, since this word is sometimes used as a euphemism for the reproductive organs. If this is the case, the note may mean that Asa ceased to be king before his death, since any man so afflicted would be ineligible to retain any "sacred" office, whether that of priest or of king.

3. Nadab of Israel (15:25-32)

25-32. The account of Nadab's short reign, before he himself was murdered by another usurper, is without significance, except that his destruction of the whole family

26 And he did evil in the sight of the LORD, and walked in the way of his father, and in his sin wherewith he made Israel to sin.

27 ¶ And Baasha the son of Ahijah, of the house of Issachar, conspired against him; and Baasha smote him at Gibbethon, which *belonged* to the Philistines; for Nadab and all Israel laid siege to Gibbethon.

28 Even in the third year of Asa king of Judah did Baasha slay him, and reigned in his stead.

29 And it came to pass, when he reigned, *that* he smote all the house of Jeroboam; he left not to Jeroboam any that breathed, until he had destroyed him, according unto the saying of the LORD, which he spake by his servant Ahijah the Shilonite:

30 Because of the sins of Jeroboam which he sinned, and which he made Israel sin, by his provocation wherewith he provoked the LORD God of Israel to anger.

31 ¶ Now the rest of the acts of Nadab, and all that he did, *are* they not written in the book of the Chronicles of the kings of Israel?

32 And there was war between Asa and Baasha king of Israel all their days.

33 In the third year of Asa king of Judah began Baasha the son of Ahijah to reign over all Israel in Tirzah, twenty and four years.

34 And he did evil in the sight of the LORD, and walked in the way of Jeroboam, and in his sin wherewith he made Israel to sin.

16 Then the word of the LORD came to Jehu the son of Hanani against Baasha, saying,

two years. 26 He did what was evil in the sight of the LORD, and walked in the way of his father, and in his sin which he made Israel to sin.

27 Ba'asha the son of Ahi'jah, of the house of Is'sachar, conspired against him; and Ba'asha struck him down at Gib'bethon, which belonged to the Philistines; for Nadab and all Israel were laying siege to Gib'bethon. 28 So Ba'asha killed him in the third year of Asa king of Judah, and reigned in his stead. 29 And as soon as he was king, he killed all the house of Jerobo'am; he left to the house of Jerobo'am not one that breathed, until he had destroyed it, according to the word of the LORD which he spoke by his servant Ahi'jah the Shi'lonite; 30 it was for the sins of Jerobo'am which he sinned and which he made Israel to sin, and because of the anger to which he provoked the LORD, the God of Israel.

31 Now the rest of the acts of Nadab, and all that he did, are they not written in the Book of the Chronicles of the Kings of Israel? 32 And there was war between Asa and Ba'asha king of Israel all their days.

33 In the third year of Asa king of Judah, Ba'asha the son of Ahi'jah began to reign over all Israel at Tirzah, and reigned twenty-four years. 34 He did what was evil in the sight of the LORD, and walked in the way of Jerobo'am and in his sin which he made Israel to sin.

16 And the word of the LORD came to Jehu the son of Hana'ni against Ba'-

of Jeroboam was in harmony with contemporary ideas. If the whole family was wiped out there was no avenger of blood left, and the murderer was safe. This wholesale slaughter was the regular procedure, and commonly took place on all such occasions (cf. II Kings 10:17).

4. BAASHA OF ISRAEL (15:33–16:7)

These verses contain the customary introduction and the customary obituary notice, together with a short oracle foretelling the speedy doom of Baasha's house.

16:1. Jehu son of Hanani is mentioned by the Chronicler as being responsible for a history which was "inserted into the book of the kings of Israel" (II Chr. 20:34).

16:1. *Messengers of God.*—And the word of the LORD came . . . . This phrase now becomes a frequent expression in the book (cf. 17:8; etc.). Nothing is more certain than that some persons at some moments are carried beyond the usual range of their thought and receive insights which seem to be given them from a higher wisdom. The narrow matter-of-fact work-

2 Forasmuch as I exalted thee out of the dust, and made thee prince over my people Israel; and thou hast walked in the way of Jeroboam, and hast made my people Israel to sin, to provoke me to anger with their sins;

3 Behold, I will take away the posterity of Baasha, and the posterity of his house; and will make thy house like the house of Jeroboam the son of Nebat.

4 Him that dieth of Baasha in the city shall the dogs eat; and him that dieth of his in the fields shall the fowls of the air eat.

5 Now the rest of the acts of Baasha, and what he did, and his might, *are* they not written in the book of the Chronicles of the kings of Israel?

asha, saying, 2 "Since I exalted you out of the dust and made you leader over my people Israel, and you have walked in the way of Jerobo'am, and have made my people Israel to sin, provoking me to anger with their sins, 3 behold, I will utterly sweep away Ba'asha and his house, and I will make your house like the house of Jerobo'am the son of Nebat. 4 Anyone belonging to Ba'asha who dies in the city the dogs shall eat; and anyone of his who dies in the field the birds of the air shall eat."

5 Now the rest of the acts of Ba'asha, and what he did, and his might, are they not written in the Book of the Chronicles

---

According to II Chr. 19:2, he also rebuked Jehoshaphat after the death of Ahab in 852 b.c. This was fully fifty years later, and it is just barely possible that the same man

---

aday experience is suddenly flooded and transformed by the inrush of a vast experience as from another world. Sometimes these flashes and insights come like sudden meteors which leave only a brief trail of fading light; and sometimes they come to persons able by their literary power to preserve them.

Upon examination, these flashes of inspiration are found not to be wholly intrusions from without; they seem to be a spark igniting something within the person. Daniel Webster, telling a friend how he was able to speak for four hours on the meaning of the Constitution of the United States in his famous and inspired "Reply to Senator Hayne," for which he had had no time for specific preparation, said, "It was perfectly easy; I stood up when all of a sudden a smoking thunderbolt came by and I seized it and hurled it at Hayne." [8] Of course that was a figurative and by no means a full explanation. No one else in the Senate that day saw a "smoking thunderbolt." What must have happened was that the occasion released something which had been storing up in Webster's mind through long years of study. Through reading and thought Webster's passion for the Constitution had been charging his mind, and the speech to Hayne was the occasion which released the study of the years. Thus the rational mind becomes a sort of conductor between the oversoul and the unconscious. The person is "carried . . . away in the spirit" (Rev. 17:3). He is in the hands of One "able to do exceeding abundantly above all that we ask or think, according to the power that worketh in us" (Eph. 3:20). He

receives the promise of Christ: "It shall be given you in that same hour what ye shall speak. For it is not ye that speak, but the Spirit of your Father which speaketh in you." (Matt. 10:19-20.)

In studying the nature of mystical insight and divine revelation we need not magnify the mystery of the experience. Imagination at times becomes creative and with a leap of intuition outruns the leaden feet of logic. The poet's insight and the artist's vision are roads to reality, even though they cannot be surveyed with the measuring rod of science. "Poetry," said Shelley, "redeems from decay the visitations of the divinity in man." [9] Moreover, the scientist's flash of discovery bears much resemblance to the intuitive insight of the artist, the poet, and the religious seer. Theories may be verified by elaborate demonstration, but it is creative vision which projects the theories. When asked how he had discovered the law of gravity, Sir Isaac Newton replied: "By thinking about it continuously. . . . I keep the object of my research constantly before me, waiting until the first light begins to dawn, little by little; finally this changes and at last the light is complete." [1] Observation as well as synthesis is sharpened by the subjective element. "It is not true . . . that we observe best when we are entirely devoid of emotion." [2]

In addition to observation, imagination, and intuition, there is a moral set of the soul pre-

[9] Essay, "A Defense of Poetry."

[1] Louis Figuier, *Vies des savants illustres,* Paris, 1870; tr., Barrett H. Clark, *Great Short Biographies of the World* (New York: Robert M. McBride & Co., 1928), p. 713.

[2] Whitehead, *Religion in the Making,* p. 124.

[8] Quoted by Rufus M. Jones, *Pathways to the Reality of God* (New York: The Macmillan Co., 1931), p. 158.

6 So Baasha slept with his fathers, and was buried in Tirzah: and Elah his son reigned in his stead.

7 And also by the hand of the prophet Jehu the son of Hanani came the word of the LORD against Baasha, and against his house, even for all the evil that he did in the sight of the LORD, in provoking him to anger with the work of his hands, in being like the house of Jeroboam; and because he killed him.

8 ¶ In the twenty and sixth year of Asa king of Judah began Elah the son of Baasha to reign over Israel in Tirzah, two years.

9 And his servant Zimri, captain of half *his* chariots, conspired against him, as he was in Tirzah, drinking himself drunk in the house of Arza steward of *his* house in Tirzah.

10 And Zimri went in and smote him, and killed him, in the twenty and seventh year of Asa king of Judah, and reigned in his stead.

11 ¶ And it came to pass, when he began to reign, as soon as he sat on his throne,

of the Kings of Israel? 6 And Ba'asha slept with his fathers, and was buried at Tirzah; and Elah his son reigned in his stead. 7 Moreover the word of the LORD came by the prophet Jehu the son of Hana'ni against Ba'asha and his house, both because of all the evil that he did in the sight of the LORD, provoking him to anger with the work of his hands, in being like the house of Jerobo'am, and also because he destroyed it.

8 In the twenty-sixth year of Asa king of Judah, Elah the son of Ba'asha began to reign over Israel in Tirzah, and reigned two years. 9 But his servant Zimri, commander of half his chariots, conspired against him. When he was at Tirzah, drinking himself drunk in the house of Arza, who was over the household in Tirzah, 10 Zimri came in and struck him down and killed him, in the twenty-seventh year of Asa king of Judah, and reigned in his stead. 11 When he began to reign, as soon as

---

was responsible for both incidents. The statement that Jehu son of Hanani spoke against Baasha is repeated in vs. 7, after the customary closing formula of the 610 B.C. compiler; it is most probably an addition made by the 550 B.C. editor.

5. ELAH OF ISRAEL (16:8-14)

This time the two customary notices are divided by a short account of the rebellion of Zimri, an incident which ended the short-lived dynasty of Baasha.

11. Zimri prevented a blood feud against his house by exterminating all Elah's kinsmen, i.e., every male relation who could act as Elah's *gô'ēl*. The function of the *gô'ēl*

---

requisite to capturing the revelatory experience. As John A. Mackay put it: "There can be no true knowledge of ultimate things, that is to say, of God and man, of duty and destiny, that is not born in a concern and perfected in a commitment." [3] There must be a concern for righteousness and a commitment to righteousness. The seeker must crave to be something, not merely to know something. The will of God must have his vote before he can get its vision. The seer must keep faith with God if he would receive the revelation from God.

When revelatory events occur, their recognition as divine revelation is always "internal history," to use H. Richard Niebuhr's expression.[4] The external or case history of a hospital

[3] *A Preface to Christian Theology* (New York: The Macmillan Co., 1941), p. 45.
[4] Cf. *The Meaning of Revelation* (New York: The Macmillan Co., 1941), ch. ii.

patient as kept by the doctors is very different from the autobiographical experience, or "inner history," of the sick person as he climbs back up the road to health. Yet both are real, and both are history. Case histories cannot be written of those experiences wherein the word of the LORD came to Jehu or Elijah. The exaltation in which Isaiah "saw the Lord sitting upon a throne, high and lifted up" (Isa. 6:1) was an experience which no cameraman could photograph and no anatomist could dissect.

The study of revelation must be approached by way of preparing the mood to receive it. We must look with the seers rather than at them. We cannot show the footprints of revelation, but we can start others on the stairs which lead to the throne of God. The genuine mystical element is probably the greatest single lack in the modern pulpit. Mystical insight must of course be safeguarded by social outlooks. Indi-

that he slew all the house of Baasha: he left him not one that pisseth against a wall, neither of his kinsfolk, nor of his friends.

12 Thus did Zimri destroy all the house of Baasha, according to the word of the LORD, which he spake against Baasha by Jehu the prophet,

13 For all the sins of Baasha, and the sins of Elah his son, by which they sinned, and by which they made Israel to sin, in provoking the LORD God of Israel to anger with their vanities.

he had seated himself on his throne, he killed all the house of Ba'asha; he did not leave him a single male of his kinsmen or his friends. **12** Thus Zimri destroyed all the house of Ba'asha, according to the word of the LORD, which he spoke against Ba'asha by Jehu the prophet, **13** for all the sins of Ba'asha and the sins of Elah his son which they sinned, and which they made Israel to sin, provoking the LORD God of Israel to

---

was that of executor and general vindicator of the deceased. It was his business to see that the deceased got his rights and that his name was perpetuated in Israel. He raised up a posterity to the deceased, if childless, by cohabiting with the widow until a son was born who would then inherit the name and the property of the dead man. It was the further duty of the *gô'ēl*, if the deceased man had been unjustly slain, to avenge his relative's death (Num. 35:19, 21; etc.).

13. The M.T. has **vanities** which the RSV rightly interprets as **idols**. The Hebrew word *hébhel* properly means "vapor," "breath," and it can be used adverbially to mean "to no purpose" (cf. Eccl. 1:2; etc.).

---

vidual confrontation of the Holy Spirit may evaporate without generating any redemptive power. One may experience the apparent symptoms of inspiration without catching a revelation of God. There were false and true prophets in Israel. The two breeds still persist.

12. *Does God Guide?*—The specific and concrete evidence of divine guidance and judgment given in this primitive record arouses skepticism in the modern reader. Repeated reference is made to defeats and destruction which took place **according to the word of the LORD**. Such definitive tracing does not convince, but the question of how and how far God guides will not down.

When we lift our gaze to the long perspective of history it is hard to explain the nexus of events as the push of a "viewless, voiceless Turner of the Wheel," as Thomas Hardy termed the blind purposeless will working through this world.[5] It may be primitive and naïve to see the destruction of **the house of Baasha** as determined by the Lord, but Hebrew history from Baasha to Bethlehem is hardly to be called

> a tale
> Told by an idiot, full of sound and fury,
> Signifying nothing.[6]

When we think back through the aeons of time to the reptiles emerging from the slime; when

[5] *The Dynasts* (New York: The Macmillan Co., 1904), p. 2.

[6] Shakespeare, *Macbeth*, Act V, scene 5.

we think that out of the jungle of beastly gianthood the more intelligent and co-operative animals survived; when our minds try to grasp the stages through which man has worked up from savagery to the arts of speech, music, and painting, to the sciences of telegraphy and television, the only explanation which seems to account for this progress is that behind the universe there is an intelligent purpose, a guiding hand. Can intelligence in man evolve out of an unintelligent creation? Can man's concern for moral values be explained if there is nothing at the heart of the universe that cares?

But granted that the universe viewed in the large gives evidence of divine guidance, can God be counted on as guide in the concrete affairs of individuals and nations? The wisdom writer speaks with assurance, "In all thy ways acknowledge him, and he shall direct thy paths" (Prov. 3:6). The singers of Israel in numerous psalms echo the same confidence. The prophets of Israel claim God's guidance for themselves, and offer it to those who commit the mind and will to him. Hosea puts it very personally when he interprets God as saying, "I drew them with cords of a man, with bands of love" (Hos. 11:4). The cords of a man are not mechanical coercion like the harness of a horse. They are not outside pressure, but inner prescience and intuition. If we could get Hosea's point here, it would help to clear up some misconceptions about divine guidance.

If we are to apprehend God's guiding hand,

14 Now the rest of the acts of Elah, and all that he did, *are* they not written in the book of the Chronicles of the kings of Israel?

15 ¶ In the twenty and seventh year of Asa king of Judah did Zimri reign seven days in Tirzah. And the people *were* encamped against Gibbethon, which *belonged* to the Philistines.

16 And the people *that were* encamped heard say, Zimri hath conspired, and hath also slain the king: wherefore all Israel made Omri, the captain of the host, king over Israel that day in the camp.

17 And Omri went up from Gibbethon, and all Israel with him, and they besieged Tirzah.

anger with their idols. 14 Now the rest of the acts of Elah, and all that he did, are they not written in the Book of the Chronicles of the Kings of Israel?

15 In the twenty-seventh year of Asa king of Judah Zimri reigned seven days in Tirzah. Now the troops were encamped against Gib'bethon, which belonged to the Philistines, 16 and the troops who were encamped heard it said, "Zimri has conspired, and he has killed the king"; therefore all Israel made Omri, the commander of the army, king over Israel that day in the camp. 17 So Omri went up from Gib'bethon, and all Israel with him, and they besieged Tir-

6. Civil War (16:15-22)

15-22. Zimri, who commanded half the chariotry, assassinated Elah while he was feasting, and sought to make himself king, but when the army heard what had happened they supported the claims of their commander, Omri. In the subsequent fighting Omri captured Tirzah, and when Zimri fled into the palace he burned it over his head. This was not the end of the matter, however, for Omri still had to deal with another adversary in his quest for the throne. This man's name was Tibni, but who exactly he was is nowhere stated. It is evident that the civil war was a much more serious and prolonged affair than a cursory reading of the story would suggest. The LXX has an addition at the end of vs. 22 to the effect that "Tibni died and Joram his brother at that time, and Omri reigned instead of Tibni." The civil war seems to have lasted for four years (cf. vss. 16, 23) and, if the LXX is right, Tibni was at one time in a much stronger position than Omri.

we must look for him in the realm of mind and spirit rather than in external physical manifestations. "God is a Spirit: and they that worship him must worship him in spirit and in truth" (John 4:24) . If we are to worship God in spirit, we must expect God to work with us and for us through the spirit. One trouble is that we materially-minded folk look for God's guidance in external, mechanical ways. If there is a washout on the railroad, causing us to miss our appointment, it is not for us to see in that an evidence of God's will that we should not have made the appointment. Or suppose that the train which we had planned to take, but missed, is wrecked with the loss of many lives. Are we to interpret that as God's special providence for us? If so, how shall we explain his attitude toward the unfortunate dead? We must beware lest we confuse coincidence with divine concern, and our personal whims with God's purposes. Nor on the other hand should we make divine guidance a trivial matter. We should begin each day with a prayer for divine illumination and leading, but we should not stop to ask God at

every turn which road to take, which person to speak to, which book to pick up. God leads us "with cords of a man," reason, evidence, and luminous thinking, not by the leading strings of a child.

In addition to the long perspective and the spiritual outlook, we need patience in our apprehension of divine guidance. Devout persons give amazing testimonies to quick answers to prayer. A minister told of needing a thousand dollars for a church enterprise. He prayed for it one evening, and the next morning a check for that amount was in his mail. He believed that was a direct answer to his prayer. It may have been. But when we get to thinking of God working in such quick fashion, we are likely to lose faith when higher help lingers. Too many of us are religious speculators rather than religious investors. We look for the quick returns of religion and are too impatient to be content with long-term investments. Those who gamble on God usually lose their faith, or else deal in counterfeit currency. But devoted souls who put their energies into godly enterprises and sacri-

18 And it came to pass, when Zimri saw that the city was taken, that he went into the palace of the king's house, and burnt the king's house over him with fire, and died,

19 For his sins which he sinned in doing evil in the sight of the LORD, in walking in the way of Jeroboam, and in his sin which he did, to make Israel to sin.

20 Now the rest of the acts of Zimri, and his treason that he wrought, *are* they not written in the book of the Chronicles of the kings of Israel?

21 ¶ Then were the people of Israel divided into two parts: half of the people followed Tibni the son of Ginath, to make him king; and half followed Omri.

22 But the people that followed Omri prevailed against the people that followed Tibni the son of Ginath: so Tibni died, and Omri reigned.

23 ¶ In the thirty and first year of Asa king of Judah began Omri to reign over Israel, twelve years: six years reigned he in Tirzah.

zah. 18 And when Zimri saw that the city was taken, he went into the citadel of the king's house, and burned the king's house over him with fire, and died, 19 because of his sins which he committed, doing evil in the sight of the LORD, walking in the way of Jerobo'am, and for his sin which he committed, making Israel to sin. 20 Now the rest of the acts of Zimri, and the conspiracy which he made, are they not written in the Book of the Chronicles of the Kings of Israel?

21 Then the people of Israel were divided into two parts; half of the people followed Tibni the son of Ginath, to make him king, and half followed Omri. 22 But the people who followed Omri overcame the people who followed Tibni the son of Ginath; so Tibni died, and Omri became king. 23 In the thirty-first year of Asa king of Judah, Omri began to reign over Israel, and reigned for twelve years; six years he

7. OMRI OF ISRAEL (16:23-28)

23-28. Omri must have been a capable, successful, and powerful king, but the southern Deuteronomic writer passes by his reign almost in silence, saying little more than that he built Samaria and reigned wickedly for twelve years. The compiler was interested mainly in religious matters, and in them only in so far as they affected the Deuteronomic principles which were the actual occasion of his writing. Happily we know something of the prowess of Omri from the Moabite stone. According to ll. 4-8, "Omri king of Israel afflicted Moab many days. . . . And Omri had taken possession of the [land ?] of Mĕhēdĕba, and [Israel] dwelt therein during his days and half his son's days, even forty years" (Burney, *Notes on Hebrew Text of Kings*, pp. 371-72). Nothing is mentioned of this subjugation of Moab by Omri in the Bible narrative, though there is a reference to Mesha of Moab's successful revolt (II Kings 3:4). A further tribute to Omri's greatness is found in the annals of the Assyrian King Shalmaneser II, who refers to Jehu as "Ja-u-a . . . the son of Omri" (*ibid.*, p. 375). The Assyrian kings continue to refer to Israel as "the land of the house of Omri" right down to the time when they conquered the country and incorporated it as a province in the Assyrian Empire.

---

ficial service, looking for guidance through spiritual channels, never feel cheated at the end of life. "I know whom I have believed, and am persuaded that he is able to keep that which I have committed unto him against that day" (II Tim. 1:12).

25, 30. The Momentum of Evil.—Omri . . . did more evil than all who were before him. Ahab his son was even worse. Sin rarely stops where the men who start it may expect it to halt. It develops a mounting momentum which gets beyond control.

This truth can be traced in the career of a

single individual or generation. Those who sow the wind often live to reap the whirlwind (Hos. 8:7). When Lot ungenerously chose the Jordan plain for his inheritance, he "pitched his tent toward Sodom" (Gen. 13:12). Lot at first probably had no intention of mingling with the sinners of Sodom. If such a thing had been mentioned to him, he would probably have replied that it was farthest from his thought. But while it was far from intention, it was not far enough from his imagination. His tent was pitched toward the wicked city. That Sodom slope may be gradual, but gravity is at work;

24 And he bought the hill Samaria of Shemer for two talents of silver, and built on the hill, and called the name of the city which he built, after the name of Shemer, owner of the hill, Samaria.

25 ¶ But Omri wrought evil in the eyes of the LORD, and did worse than all that *were* before him.

26 For he walked in all the way of Jeroboam the son of Nebat, and in his sin wherewith he made Israel to sin, to provoke the LORD God of Israel to anger with their vanities.

27 Now the rest of the acts of Omri which he did, and his might that he showed, *are* they not written in the book of the Chronicles of the kings of Israel?

28 So Omri slept with his fathers, and was buried in Samaria: and Ahab his son reigned in his stead.

29 ¶ And in the thirty and eighth year of Asa king of Judah began Ahab the son of Omri to reign over Israel: and Ahab the son of Omri reigned over Israel in Samaria twenty and two years.

30 And Ahab the son of Omri did evil in the sight of the LORD above all that *were* before him.

reigned in Tirzah. **24** He bought the hill of Samar'ia from Shemer for two talents of silver; and he fortified the hill, and called the name of the city which he built, Samar'ia, after the name of Shemer, the owner of the hill.

25 Omri did what was evil in the sight of the LORD, and did more evil than all who were before him. **26** For he walked in all the way of Jerobo'am the son of Nebat, and in the sins which he made Israel to sin, provoking the LORD, the God of Israel, to anger by their idols. **27** Now the rest of the acts of Omri which he did, and the might that he showed, are they not written in the Book of the Chronicles of the Kings of Israel? **28** And Omri slept with his fathers, and was buried in Samar'ia; and Ahab his son reigned in his stead.

29 In the thirty-eighth year of Asa king of Judah, Ahab the son of Omri began to reign over Israel, and Ahab the son of Omri reigned over Israel in Samar'ia twenty-two years. **30** And Ahab the son of Omri did evil in the sight of the LORD more than all that

---

It is evident that they regarded Omri as the founder of the kingdom, and his fame must have been considerable. His building of Samaria showed sound political insight, and it is comparable in wisdom to David's choice of Jerusalem as his capital. The city of Samaria stood on the top of a hill rising some three hundred feet from the surrounding plain, a tremendously strong position for the warfare of those days, and with distinct possibilities for defense even in these. The reference in Mic. 6:16 to "the statutes of Omri" is further testimony to his greatness, since that verse was written some considerable time after Omri's death.

C. AHAB AND ELIJAH (16:29–22:40)

1. AHAB OF ISRAEL (16:29-34)

The formal accession notice is given in vss. 29-30, and the obituary notice is in 22:39-40. We have four other verses in ch. 16 which give additional details of Ahab's

---

and Lot, whose character was revealed by his choice of the low and fertile country, drifted toward further satisfaction of his selfish desires until he found himself caught in the calamities of the corrupt city. When sin has the longer slope of heredity its momentum increases from generation to generation. An evil father furnishes both blood stream and mental environment as channels for sin's cumulative force. Omri does more evil than his predecessors (but see Exeg.), and Ahab, the son who comes after him, outstrips his father's sins.

On the wide social scale sin often has the aspects of a flood. Evil thoughts and practices keep falling like rain back in the hills of men's minds. Tributaries pour their muddy waters into the social mind. The dams of restraint give way. The flood rises with frightening and unbelievable rapidity, engulfing the unsuspecting and sleeping victims. In the kings and people of Israel from Solomon on, the momentum of evil gathers in individual, hereditary, and tribal channels, until in Omri and Ahab it is at the flood.

31 And it came to pass, as if it had been a light thing for him to walk in the sins of Jeroboam the son of Nebat, that he took to wife Jezebel the daughter of Ethbaal king of the Zidonians, and went and served Baal, and worshipped him.

32 And he reared up an altar for Baal in the house of Baal, which he had built in Samaria.

33 And Ahab made a grove; and Ahab did more to provoke the Lord God of Israel to anger than all the kings of Israel that were before him.

34 ¶ In his days did Hiel the Beth-elite build Jericho: he laid the foundation thereof in Abiram his firstborn, and set up the gates thereof in his youngest *son* Segub, according to the word of the Lord, which he spake by Joshua the son of Nun.

were before him. 31 And as if it had been a light thing for him to walk in the sins of Jerobo'am the son of Nebat, he took for wife Jez'ebel the daughter of Ethba'al king of the Sido'nians, and went and served Ba'al, and worshiped him. 32 He erected an altar for Ba'al in the house of Ba'al, which he built in Samar'ia. 33 And Ahab made an Ashe'rah. Ahab did more to provoke the Lord, the God of Israel, to anger than all the kings of Israel who were before him. 34 In his days Hi'el of Bethel built Jericho; he laid its foundation at the cost of Abi'ram his first-born, and set up its gates at the cost of his youngest son Segub, according to the word of the Lord, which he spoke by Joshua the son of Nun.

greater crimes against the true worship of the God of Israel and also make mention of the rebuilding of Jericho, which had been a desolate site for several hundred years. Otherwise, apart from such formal notices as that in II Kings 3:2-3, where the compiler had to mention the accession of a new king, the whole section from I Kings 17:1–II Kings 10:31 is an interpolation from the three or four unnamed sources which have been called "Tales of the North" in the Intro.

31. Ahab's greatest crime in the eyes of the Deuteronomists was that he married **Jezebel** the daughter of Ethbaal, priest-king of Tyre. Whether this marriage was so regarded in the north is open to doubt, since Ps. 45 bears every indication of being a love song in which Ahab and Jezebel appear to be the hero and the heroine (cf. vss. 8, 12-15). Jezebel's father was Ithobal I. According to Josephus (*Against Apion* I. 18. 8), this Ithobal was a priest of Astarte who, at the age of thirty-six, murdered the fratricide Phelles, and then reigned for thirty-two years. Josephus also says that twenty-two years after Ithobal's death, his granddaughter fled from her brother and built Carthage. This is that Dido whom Aeneas is fabled to have met on his journey from Troy to Rome. The zeal of Jezebel for the Tyrian cult may thus be traced to her father's double function and earlier training. This house of Ithobal certainly bred masterful women, for of them three close kinswomen, Jezebel, Athaliah, and Dido, were born to rule.

32. Jezebel's god was Baal-Melkart, tutelary god of Tyre, whose worship was partly assimilated to that of the Baal of the Ras Shamra texts, and who in later years was identified with Hercules (II Macc. 4:19).

34. Hiel of Bethel built Jericho . . . at the cost of . . . his first-born and of his last-born. Thus the ancient curse of Josh. 6:26 accomplished its inevitable fulfillment. Some scholars have thought of this tragedy in terms of a voluntary sacrifice on the part of the father, the spirits of the children being regarded henceforth as guardians of the gate. Others hold that some tragic fate overtook them and that popular opinion recognized a connection with the ancient curse. It is quite possible that we have here an example of the ancient custom of foundation sacrifices, common in widely separated lands. The theory is that the victims were buried beneath the foundations "in order to give strength and stability to the edifice or to guard against enemies" (Frazer, *Folk-lore in the O.T.*, I, 421). Actual examples of such burials have been found at Gezer. Under the foundations of a building there, the excavators found the upper half of the skeleton of an eighteen-year-old boy and two complete skeletons of men (R. A. S. Macalister, *The Excavation of Gezer* [London: J. Murray, 1912], II, 428).

17 And Elijah the Tishbite, *who was* of the inhabitants of Gilead, said unto Ahab, *As* the LORD God of Israel liveth, before whom I stand, there shall not be dew nor rain these years, but according to my word.

2 And the word of the LORD came unto him, saying,

3 Get thee hence, and turn thee eastward, and hide thyself by the brook Cherith, that *is* before Jordan.

17 Now Eli'jah the Tishbite, of Tishbe[n] in Gilead, said to Ahab, "As the LORD the God of Israel lives, before whom I stand, there shall be neither dew nor rain these years, except by my word."

2 And the word of the LORD came to him,

3 "Depart from here and turn eastward, and hide yourself by the brook Cherith,

[n] Gk: Heb *of the settlers*

2. THE FEEDING OF ELIJAH (17:1-24)

Elijah is fed at first by the notoriously voracious ravens, and when the drought has persisted so long that the Wadi Cherith is dried up, he is fed by a poor widow of Phoenicia, herself on the point of starvation when Elijah first searches her out. The chapter concludes with the story of the death and restoration of the widow's son.

17:1. The name **Elijah** means "Yah is El," El being the general Semitic name for the High God. Thus Elijah's own name is the proclamation of his message (see 18:8). It is one of a number of instances in which, perhaps by deliberate intent, the name fits the character or the mission: e.g., Isaiah ("Yah is salvation," cf. Isa. 30:15), Barnabas ("Son of exhortation," Acts 4:36), and even Jesus (Matt. 1:21).

The older scholars follow the M.T., of which the natural interpretation is that Elijah came from **Tishbe** in Naphtali (cf. Tob. 1:2), but that he had settled among the Gileadites east of the Jordan. Modern scholars are unanimous in following the LXX, which reads different vowels (*mittishbê* for *mittôshābhê*), and says that Elijah was a **Tishbite, of Tishbe in Gilead**. It is more than likely that this latter interpretation is right. The word תושב ("sojourner," "settler") is late, the only other case out of a total of fourteen where it is not certainly postexilic being Ps. 39:12, and that reference may be postexilic also.

Josephus says (*Antiquities* VIII. 13. 2) that according to Menander there was a full year's drought in the time of Ethbaal, father of Jezebel, "but when he made supplications there came great thunders."

3. Tradition says that **the brook Cherith** is the Wadi el-Kelt, the traditional Valley of Achor, near which Jericho is situated, but the O.T. makes it plain that it was east of Jordan, one of those rocky defiles through which torrents rush headlong into the Jordan in the time of the rains.

17:1-24. God's Mysterious Moves.—How a modern reporter would describe the events pictured in this chapter, we do not know. When we confront the biblical account of miracles we are impelled to ask just what did happen. Of this we cannot be absolutely sure, because of the changed modes of observing and recording. And when we also ask how the events happened, again we cannot be sure, because our body of scientifically observable data is but an island of charted knowledge surrounded by an ocean of mystery. The larger the island grows, the larger the shoreline of the mysterious. The more we learn, the more we realize how much is beyond our knowing. The eminent physicist, Sir James Jeans, very properly entitled his memorable book *The Mysterious Universe*.

The actual world of the mathematician who wrote *Alice in Wonderland* was as puzzling as the realm described in the little book. Alice was puzzled because the balls and mallets did not stay put in her game. In her wonderland things moved without her moving them. Like the child, we adults have to learn that we are not the only players in the game of living. Things do not always remain as we leave them. Things happen that we do not ask for. There is One also present "able to do exceeding abundantly above all that we ask or think, according to the power that worketh in us" (Eph. 3:20). The living God in his living universe has a range of activity beyond ours, somewhat as the shades of color exceed our reach of vision. Our eyes can catch the colors of the spectrum, and now

4 And it shall be, *that* thou shalt drink of the brook; and I have commanded the ravens to feed thee there.

5 So he went and did according unto the word of the LORD: for he went and dwelt by the brook Cherith, that *is* before Jordan.

6 And the ravens brought him bread and flesh in the morning, and bread and flesh in the evening; and he drank of the brook.

7 And it came to pass after a while, that the brook dried up, because there had been no rain in the land.

8 ¶ And the word of the LORD came unto him, saying,

9 Arise, get thee to Zarephath, which *belongeth* to Zidon, and dwell there: behold, I have commanded a widow woman there to sustain thee.

10 So he arose and went to Zarephath. And when he came to the gate of the city, behold, the widow woman *was* there gathering of sticks: and he called to her, and said, Fetch me, I pray thee, a little water in a vessel, that I may drink.

11 And as she was going to fetch *it,* he called to her, and said, Bring me, I pray thee, a morsel of bread in thine hand.

12 And she said, *As* the LORD thy God liveth, I have not a cake, but a handful of meal in a barrel, and a little oil in a cruse: and, behold, I *am* gathering two sticks, that I may go in and dress it for me and my son, that we may eat it, and die.

that is east of the Jordan. 4 You shall drink from the brook, and I have commanded the ravens to feed you there." 5 So he went and did according to the word of the LORD; he went and dwelt by the brook Cherith that is east of the Jordan. 6 And the ravens brought him bread and meat in the morning, and bread and meat in the evening; and he drank from the brook. 7 And after a while the brook dried up, because there was no rain in the land.

8 Then the word of the LORD came to him, 9 "Arise, go to Zar'ephath, which belongs to Sidon, and dwell there. Behold, I have commanded a widow there to feed you." 10 So he arose and went to Zar'ephath; and when he came to the gate of the city, behold, a widow was there gathering sticks; and he called to her and said, "Bring me a little water in a vessel, that I may drink." 11 And as she was going to bring it, he called to her and said, "Bring me a morsel of bread in your hand." 12 And she said, "As the LORD your God lives, I have nothing baked, only a handful of meal in a jar, and a little oil in a cruse; and now, I am gathering a couple of sticks, that I may go in and prepare it for myself and

4. Attempts to rationalize the story have turned the **ravens** into merchants or into Arabians (both reading *'arābhîm* instead of *'ôrebhîm,* but it is best to leave the story as it is. We have a whole series of wonder stories in these "Tales of the North," and a more-than-human ingenuity is required in order to excise all miraculous elements from them.

9. **Zarephath** is commonly identified with the village of Ṣarafand, some nine miles south of Sidon on the Mediterranean coast.

we have discovered that beyond the red are the infrared and beyond the violet are rays of color called ultraviolet. Who can say what remains to be detected beyond these? As in the days of Elijah, we do not know what wonders are waiting around the corners of the tomorrows.

Yet while

> God moves in a mysterious way
> His wonders to perform,[7]

he is not a whimsical, capricious despot. God does not reverse himself, issuing one order today,

repealing it tomorrow. God's surprises are the surprises not of whim but of plus. Elijah hears the divine call to hide himself by the brook Cherith. The brook dries up. But its drying leads him to new opportunities and resources. Following the Lord's further leading, the prophet is guided from the problem of saving his own life to the privilege of saving a widow's faith and her son's life.

This chapter is a study in the relationship between produce and providence. When Jesus bade his disciples, "Take . . . no thought for the morrow" (Matt. 6:34), he was not counseling them to overlook the morrow, but to look

[7] William Cowper.

13 And Elijah said unto her, Fear not; go *and* do as thou hast said: but make me thereof a little cake first, and bring *it* unto me, and after make for thee and for thy son.

14 For thus saith the LORD God of Israel, The barrel of meal shall not waste, neither shall the cruse of oil fail, until the day *that* the LORD sendeth rain upon the earth.

15 And she went and did according to the saying of Elijah: and she, and he, and her house, did eat *many* days.

16 *And* the barrel of meal wasted not, neither did the cruse of oil fail, according to the word of the LORD, which he spake by Elijah.

17 ¶ And it came to pass after these things, *that* the son of the woman, the mistress of the house, fell sick; and his sickness was so sore, that there was no breath left in him.

18 And she said unto Elijah, What have I to do with thee, O thou man of God? art thou come unto me to call my sin to remembrance, and to slay my son?

19 And he said unto her, Give me thy son. And he took him out of her bosom, and carried him up into a loft, where he abode, and laid him upon his own bed.

20 And he cried unto the LORD, and said, O LORD my God, hast thou also brought evil upon the widow with whom I sojourn, by slaying her son?

my son, that we may eat it, and die." 13 And Eli'jah said to her, "Fear not; go and do as you have said; but first make me a little cake of it and bring it to me, and afterward make for yourself and your son. 14 For thus says the LORD the God of Israel, 'The jar of meal shall not be spent, and the cruse of oil shall not fail, until the day that the LORD sends rain upon the earth.' " 15 And she went and did as Eli'jah said; and she, and he, and her household ate for many days. 16 The jar of meal was not spent, neither did the cruse of oil fail, according to the word of the LORD which he spoke by Eli'jah.

17 After this the son of the woman, the mistress of the house, became ill; and his illness was so severe that there was no breath left in him. 18 And she said to Eli'jah, "What have you against me, O man of God? You have come to me to bring my sin to remembrance, and to cause the death of my son!" 19 And he said to her, "Give me your son." And he took him from her bosom, and carried him up into the upper chamber, where he lodged, and laid him upon his own bed. 20 And he cried to the LORD, "O LORD my God, hast thou brought calamity even upon the widow with whom

---

18. The English versions all paraphrase the Hebrew idiom, which in the O.T. (Judg. 11:12; II Sam. 16:10; 19:22; etc.) and in the N.T. (Matt. 8:29; 27:19; John 2:4) refers to undesired outside interference. It is best therefore to translate, "What have you to do with me?"

The widow thinks that the man of God has brought God so close to her that he has discovered some hidden sin, and that the untimely death of her son is the punishment. Such a primitive idea of God as one who is seeking out unwitting or long-forgotten sins, and being fervent in dealing out strict penalties, is far from dead even today (cf. the frequent question, "What have I done to deserve this?").

19. The **upper chamber** was on the roof, accessible by an outside stairway (Alfred Bertholet, *A History of Hebrew Civilization*, tr. A. K. Dallas [New York: Brentano's, 1926], p. 169).

20. Elijah regards the death of the boy as an act of arbitrary injustice on the part of God. This had happened to the very widow whom God himself had chosen to feed

---

over it to catch the long views of the kingdom ahead. Elijah the Tishbite is being prepared through his contacts with the dribbling brook and the widow's cruse for his larger dealings with kings and entrenched religious cults.

A miracle is an event with which human comprehension has not yet caught up. It is not an interruption of law, but the working of a law which human reason has not yet charted. Difficulty in understanding the precise methods of God's dealing with Elijah should not deter us from standing open-eyed and open-minded be-

21 And he stretched himself upon the child three times, and cried unto the Lord, and said, O Lord my God, I pray thee, let this child's soul come into him again.

22 And the Lord heard the voice of Elijah; and the soul of the child came into him again, and he revived.

23 And Elijah took the child, and brought him down out of the chamber into the house, and delivered him unto his mother: and Elijah said, See, thy son liveth.

24 ¶ And the woman said to Elijah, Now by this I know that thou *art* a man of God, *and* that the word of the Lord in thy mouth *is* truth.

18 And it came to pass *after* many days, that the word of the Lord came to Elijah in the third year, saying, Go, show thyself unto Ahab; and I will send rain upon the earth.

I sojourn, by slaying her son?" 21 Then he stretched himself upon the child three times, and cried to the Lord, "O Lord my God, let this child's soul come into him again." 22 And the Lord hearkened to the voice of Eli'jah; and the soul of the child came into him again, and he revived. 23 And Eli'jah took the child, and brought him down from the upper chamber into the house, and delivered him to his mother; and Eli'jah said, "See, your son lives." 24 And the woman said to Eli'jah, "Now I know that you are a man of God, and that the word of the Lord in your mouth is truth."

18 After many days the word of the Lord came to Eli'jah, in the third year, saying, "Go, show yourself to Ahab;

---

the prophet during the long drought and the subsequent famine and, as if she had not had enough anxiety and privation in the general distress, he has added this extra visitation. It is evident that the ideas concerning the nature and character of God in the ninth century B.C. emphasized his arbitrariness rather than his justice and his mercy. This is a survival of the ancient ideas concerning the denizens of the spirit world, and it behooved all men to be careful since no one knew whether the spirit powers would act for man's weal or woe.

21. The LXX says that Elijah "breathed into the child," but this technique of stretching over the child is mentioned in the other two recorded cases of this type (II Kings 4:34-35; Acts 20:10).

The number **three** shares with the number seven a special magico-religious power (cf. 8:65). It is easy, however, to exaggerate the importance and significance of the number three in primitive ideas. The threefold repetition of an action is not regarded as being effective nearly as often as is generally supposed. Certainly in ancient Hebrew lore the true magic number is seven.

22. The translation **the soul of the child came into him** again is misleading, since it supports the illusion that the word "soul" is used in the Bible for some part of man's nature which is immortal and therefore survives death. Neither the Hebrew *néphesh* nor the N.T. Greek ψυχή refers to an immortal soul of man, even though both words are regularly translated "soul," 460 times in the O.T. and 57 times in the N.T. Usually the best rendering of *néphesh* is "life," in the sense of that ordinary, physical life which ends at death. In the LXX the Greek ψυχή is used in precisely the sense of the Hebrew *néphesh*, and this sense of the word is carried over into the N.T. (N. H. Snaith, "Life after Death," *Interpretation*, I [1947], 309-13).

3. Elijah at Carmel (18:1-46)

The drought is about to end, and Elijah is bidden to appear again before Ahab. The king and his chief steward, Obadiah, are searching the whole country for fodder to keep the chariot horses alive, when suddenly Elijah appears to Obadiah. The narrator interrupts his story to tell of how Obadiah, a faithful adherent of the Lord, has nourished a hundred faithful prophets during the drought and Jezebel's persecution. Obadiah is loath to obey Elijah and to report his presence to Ahab, lest when Ahab comes, Elijah should have disappeared in that strange and miraculous way which men had learned

2 And Elijah went to show himself unto Ahab. And *there was* a sore famine in Samaria.

3 And Ahab called Obadiah, which *was* the governor of *his* house. (Now Obadiah feared the LORD greatly:

4 For it was *so*, when Jezebel cut off the prophets of the LORD, that Obadiah took a hundred prophets, and hid them by fifty in a cave, and fed them with bread and water.)

5 And Ahab said unto Obadiah, Go into the land, unto all fountains of water, and unto all brooks: peradventure we may find grass to save the horses and mules alive, that we lose not all the beasts.

6 So they divided the land between them to pass throughout it: Ahab went one way by himself, and Obadiah went another way by himself.

and I will send rain upon the earth." 2 So Eli'jah went to show himself to Ahab. Now the famine was severe in Samar'ia. 3 And Ahab called Obadi'ah, who was over the household. (Now Obadi'ah revered the LORD greatly; 4 and when Jez'ebel cut off the prophets of the LORD, Obadi'ah took a hundred prophets and hid them by fifties in a cave, and fed them with bread and water.) 5 And Ahab said to Obadi'ah, "Go through the land to all the springs of water and to all the valleys; perhaps we may find grass and save the horses and mules alive, and not lose some of the animals." 6 So they divided the land between them to pass through it; Ahab went in one direction by himself, and Obadi'ah went in another direction by himself.

---

to associate with him. But Elijah swears an oath that he will stay, with the result that Ahab comes. Elijah then bids the king stage a contest on Mount Carmel, in order that all Israel may see who it is that brings the rain, whether the Syrian Baal or the God of Israel. After the failure of the Baal prophets, Elijah calls down fire from heaven. The sacrifice is consumed; Elijah mounts the hill to watch for the coming clouds, and the chapter closes with the deluge of the long-delayed rains; Ahab races across the edge of the Plain of Esdraelon, with Elijah running ahead, lest he be caught in the mud before he reaches the higher ground of the Vale of Jezreel.

18:2. The famine "had a firm hold" on the country. The same word is used of Absalom's head being firmly held by the branches of the tree (II Sam. 18:9).

4. The **prophets of the LORD** were the "sons of the prophets," i.e., the groups of prophets who were attached to the various shrines (II Kings 2:3, 5), or who roamed the countryside (I Sam. 10:5-13; Aubrey R. Johnson, *The Cultic Prophet in Ancient Israel*

---

fore the demonstration of power when a surrendered spirit becomes the instrument of the Infinite.

18:3. Being Good in Bad Places.—Elijah was sent by the Lord to interview King Ahab, of whom it was written that he "did more to provoke the LORD, the God of Israel, to anger than all the kings of Israel who were before him" (16:33). Jezebel, the wife of Ahab, was so conspicuous for her evil-doing that her name has become a synonym for colorful wickedness. She incurred the bitter condemnation of the O.T. writers by her espousal of the priests of Baal. And now Elijah is on his way to beard these royal wrongdoers in their den of idolatry.

Just before Elijah's arrival, Ahab summons the overseer of his household, Obadiah. In describing this official, the record says, **Now Obadiah revered the LORD greatly.** It is a plain little parenthetical statement, but it gives the character of Obadiah a symbolic significance. He was a good man in a bad place. Should a

person who reveres the Lord remain in a pagan court? How can one preserve his reverence and righteousness in such evil surroundings? Can a good man change a bad situation when it is embedded in a system? Obadiah's plight raises many searching questions which are as pertinent today as in the time of Ahab. Even within so-called Christian lands this is still a rather pagan world. Society, as we have it, is the immense and unraveled result of the actions and inactions of an infinite number of people who have wished to be as free from trouble as possible. They therefore have followed the lines of least resistance. These lines have crisscrossed the landscape on which we have to live and have been worn into grooves of convention and compromise. Hence when a person sets out to follow God and his own conscience he has to make his way through a meshwork of systems and traditions.

Just before World War II, the president of an American college said to a graduating class;

7 ¶ And as Obadiah was in the way, behold, Elijah met him: and he knew him, and fell on his face, and said, *Art* thou that my lord Elijah?

8 And he answered him, I *am:* go, tell thy lord, Behold, Elijah *is here.*

9 And he said, What have I sinned, that thou wouldest deliver thy servant into the hand of Ahab, to slay me?

10 *As* the LORD thy God liveth, there is no nation or kingdom, whither my lord hath not sent to seek thee: and when they said, *He is* not *there;* he took an oath of the kingdom and nation, that they found thee not.

11 And now thou sayest, Go, tell thy lord, Behold, Elijah *is here.*

12 And it shall come to pass, *as soon as* I am gone from thee, that the Spirit of the LORD shall carry thee whither I know not;

7 And as Obadi'ah was on the way, behold, Eli'jah met him; and Obadi'ah recognized him, and fell on his face, and said, "Is it you, my lord Eli'jah?" 8 And he answered him, "It is I. Go, tell your lord, 'Behold, Eli'jah is here.'" 9 And he said, "Wherein have I sinned, that you would give your servant into the hand of Ahab, to kill me? 10 As the LORD your God lives, there is no nation or kingdom whither my lord has not sent to seek you; and when they would say, 'He is not here,' he would take an oath of the kingdom or nation, that they had not found you. 11 And now you say, 'Go, tell your lord, "Behold, Eli'jah is here."' 12 And as soon as I have gone from you, the Spirit of the LORD will carry you

---

[Cardiff: University of Wales Press Board, 1944], especially p. 21). Such men have been a common feature of religions from early times, and they are still to be met with in the shamans of Siberia and the dervishes of the Near East.

7. It has been suggested that Obadiah had never seen Elijah before but recognized him only from the memory of popular description. This is unlikely in view of Obadiah's important position at court. Furthermore, his words should be translated, "Is it really you, Elijah?" The form of this question can be sufficiently well explained by Elijah's most mysterious absence during three years and more, and also by his continued disappearance, in spite of the most rigorous search on the part of the king with all the resources at his disposal.

12. It is difficult to be sure whether the word רוח should here be translated by **Spirit** or "wind," since probably the author himself had no thought of making such a distinction. Obadiah means that the mysterious power of God may waft the prophet away and hide him miraculously as had apparently happened during the preceding three years. On account of this belief, Obadiah refuses to carry the message to Ahab until Elijah has

---

"I feel sorry for you as you leave these halls and go out into the world. I feel sorry for you because of what the world will do to you and to your ideals. Too often a man's ideals are in inverse ratio to his distance from college." True indeed! But the temptations which tear at a person's ideals do not begin after graduation from college. Many a student faces at school and college some of the fiercest moral struggles of his life. And the test of being good in bad places comes often before the campus is reached. Not all our homes are wholesome for growing children. Sometimes the character of one or both parents is so bad that the shell of the home has to be broken so that the children can grow up decently. When family attitudes are selfish, when family interests are materialistic, when family loyalties are weakened by distrust and deceit, the home is a hard place in which to

be good. The larger the group, the more difficult it is to permeate it with the principles of personal goodness. In the words of Mandell Creighton:

Christianity beautifies many an individual life and sheds a luster over many a family. Its influence is less conspicuous in the life of business; it pales in the sphere of what is called society and is still dimmer in politics. In the region of international obligations it can scarcely be said to exist.[8]

What can the individual do when he finds himself in a bad place? Sometimes the best thing to do in an evil situation is to leave it. Many of the early Christians did just that. A Christian should get out of a business which is a perpetual rebuke to his conscience. A Christian may have

[8] Quoted by Justin Wroe Nixon, *The Moral Crisis in Christianity* (New York: Harper & Bros., 1931), p. 78.

I KINGS

18:15

and *so* when I come and tell Ahab, and he cannot find thee, he shall slay me: but I thy servant fear the LORD from my youth.

13 Was it not told my lord what I did when Jezebel slew the prophets of the LORD, how I hid a hundred men of the LORD's prophets by fifty in a cave, and fed them with bread and water?

14 And now thou sayest, Go, tell thy lord, Behold, Elijah *is here:* and he shall slay me.

15 And Elijah said, *As* the LORD of hosts liveth, before whom I stand, I will surely show myself unto him to-day.

whither I know not; and so, when I come and tell Ahab and he cannot find you, he will kill me, although I your servant have revered the LORD from my youth. **13** Has it not been told my lord what I did when Jez'ebel killed the prophets of the LORD, how I hid a hundred men of the LORD's prophets by fifties in a cave, and fed them with bread and water? **14** And now you say, 'Go, tell your lord, "Behold, Eli'jah is here"'; and he will kill me." **15** And Eli'jah said, "As the LORD of hosts lives, before whom I stand, I will surely show myself to

---

bound himself by a most solemn oath to stay where he is (vs. 15). It is likely that Obadiah did actually think of Elijah as being carried away by a wind, but he would also think of the wind as being sent especially by God for that purpose.

15. The origin of the full and solemn title LORD of hosts (Yahweh *çebhā'ôth*) is disputed. The most generally accepted explanation is founded on I Sam. 17:45, where the phrase occurs, "The LORD of hosts, the god of the armies of Israel." The reference here is to the actual battalions of the kingdom of Israel, and may be a later insertion, but even if this is the case it is nevertheless a very early explanation of the meaning of the divine title. The phrase LORD of hosts seems largely to belong to the prophets. Smend suggested that it meant originally the armies of heaven, i.e., the elements and the natural forces of the world, with Amos (e.g., 9:5-6) as the pioneer in using it. Another view is that the reference is to armies of angels, the angelic servants of the King of heaven. Actually, the phrase belongs to the ninth century B.C., and it is to be explained on the same lines as the phrase "the chariots of Israel and its horsemen" (II Kings 2:12), an expression especially, and indeed peculiarly, associated with Elijah and his successor Elisha. It is a reference to the armies of God, those angelic beings who obey his commands.

---

to dissociate himself from a social group whose ideals are low and whose practices are degrading. A clean-cut withdrawal has an eloquence of protest which no verbal expostulation can parallel. But as a general rule righteous individuals do not save a situation by merely withdrawing from it. Furthermore, while a man can leave a situation, he cannot so easily leave the whole system in which he is caught. He may pull out of a particular business, but if he is to make a living he cannot easily withdraw from the whole business system. He may feel impelled to leave a political party, but if he is to exercise his duties as a citizen, he must vote in some party, and where is the perfect one? He may conscientiously object to his government's program, as in time of war, but when 90 per cent of a nation's economy is geared to the war effort, even the pacifist can hardly separate himself completely from the system. We are social beings, involved in social systems, and we cannot separate ourselves from all the groups which do things contrary to our consciences. In fact, there can be no effective moral isolation in

God's family. The godly person has to get along with the crowd well enough to help get the crowd along. Jesus prayed for his followers, "Not that thou shouldest take them out of the world, but that thou shouldest keep them from the evil" (John 17:15).

Jesus suggested memorable ways by which his followers might leaven and sweeten bad situations. "Ye are the salt of the earth: but if the salt have lost his savor, wherewith shall it be salted?" (Matt. 5:13.) However evil the place, is the savor of goodness still in us? Can we identify ourselves in fellowship with others and yet keep our judgments independent of theirs? Do we have the courage of our convictions and yet have compassion for those we are trying to convince? Do we have the saltlike quality of bringing out the natural flavor of other personalities? The Master used another figure: "Ye are the light of the world" (Matt. 5:14). And he added that the Christian's light is not to be hid under a bushel but to be set where it can give light to all that are in the house. The godly person must make clear where he stands on

151

16 So Obadiah went to meet Ahab, and told him: and Ahab went to meet Elijah.

17 ¶ And it came to pass, when Ahab saw Elijah, that Ahab said unto him, *Art thou he that troubleth Israel?*

him today." 16 So Obadi′ah went to meet Ahab, and told him; and Ahab went to meet Eli′jah.

17 When Ahab saw Eli′jah, Ahab said to him, "Is it you, you troubler of Israel?"

Associated with this is the fact that in the narratives of Elijah and Elisha the manifestations of the Lord are regularly in fire, e.g., vs. 38, **the fire of the LORD,** which we may assume to be lightning.

16. According to the LXX, Ahab "ran forth" to meet Elijah, a natural and picturesque addition, especially considering that for years so very much had depended upon Ahab's seeing Elijah. It was only according to the spoken word of this prophet that the rains could come (17:1).

17. Ahab sees in Elijah the man who stirs up needless trouble in Israel. The king never really understood what Elijah's object was, and why he did all the things that caused so much difficulty. Two of Ahab's sons had Yahwistic, theophoric names, viz., Ahaziah and Jehoram. It is most unlikely that Ahab would have consented to such a practice unless he had believed himself to be a true worshiper of Yahweh of Israel. In common with most of the people, perhaps in common with all except the prophetic bands (the sons of the prophets), Ahab did not see why he could not combine the worship of the God of Israel with the cult of Baal. Such syncretism is a marked feature

moral principles. He must stand up and show his colors. He can count for righteousness only as he has the courage to stand up and be counted. When his goodness is radiant, it becomes pervasive.

When a good man finds himself in a bad situation, he must not yield to the paralysis of perfectionism. When he is willing to work with imperfect instruments, to use half measures when whole ones are impossible, to do the duty next to him when the ultimate goal is hidden in the haze of distance, he joins his efforts with One "that is able to do exceeding abundantly above all that we ask or think, according to the power that worketh in us" (Eph. 3:20). Moreover, there is a cell principle by which group life can be affected. One thoroughgoing Christian can impart a godly spirit to a family, even though every other member of it may be pagan. A half-dozen devout members, if sufficiently devoted, can change the atmosphere of a church. Group and systems may be more than mere aggregations of atomistic units; they are often organisms possessing a characteristic life of their own. And if a minority, or even a single individual, gets into the blood stream of such a living organism, the results are illimitable.

During World War II a white officer was assigned to take charge of a company of Negro soldiers in training for commissions. Because of his family background, the white commander was so angered by his assignment that he declared, "If any of you get commissions, it will be in spite of me." This so incensed the Negroes that some cried, some cursed, some were for

waylaying the officer. But one quiet member of the company spoke up: "Listen fellows, we are men and soldiers. We are loyal Americans. We are Negroes. Our honor is at stake. We represent the best that our race affords. The eyes of America are upon us. Let's play square soldier for this man, and trust in God." The men heeded his advice. They outdid themselves to obey instructions. As a result 55 per cent, a larger percentage than usual, received commissions. At the close of the training a reception was given by the Negro community to the new officers. The white commander attended, and made a public confession of his change of heart, declaring, "I'm your friend until I die."

Good men in bad places can often do by demonstrations what reformers try and fail to do by agitation.

17. *Divine Troublers.*—Twice elsewhere Elijah is hailed as coming to make trouble (17:18; 21:20). The prophet of God is always a disturber of worldly peace. He comes to give a peace, but "not as the world giveth" (John 14:27). One of the finest tributes ever paid to a modern prophetic preacher was by a layman who said, "He always makes me feel uncomfortable." The prophet is as disturbing to a sinner as heat is to a person who is freezing to death. There comes a stage in the freezing process, so we are told, when it would be more comfortable to sink farther into fatal numbness. With heat there comes pain; but pain is the sign of returning life. At the approach of Jesus a man with an unclean spirit cried, "Let us alone; what have we to do with thee, thou Jesus

18 And he answered, I have not troubled Israel; but thou, and thy father's house, in that ye have forsaken the commandments of the LORD, and thou hast followed Baalim.

19 Now therefore send, *and* gather to me all Israel unto mount Carmel, and the prophets of Baal four hundred and fifty, and the prophets of the groves four hundred, which eat at Jezebel's table.

20 So Ahab sent unto all the children of Israel, and gathered the prophets together unto mount Carmel.

18 And he answered, "I have not troubled Israel; but you have, and your father's house, because you have forsaken the commandments of the LORD and followed the Ba'als. **19** Now therefore send and gather all Israel to me at Mount Carmel, and the four hundred and fifty prophets of Ba'al and the four hundred prophets of Ashe'rah, who eat at Jez'ebel's table."

20 So Ahab sent to all the people of Israel, and gathered the prophets together

---

in all the Ras Shamra texts, and a great deal of evidence in the O.T. shows that the prophets, from Elijah to Jeremiah—in fact, actually in the time of Moses himself and right down to the times of the Maccabees—had to fight hard against it.

18. The Baals are the local fertility gods, worshiped at every village shrine. They are all local manifestations of the great sky-god Baal, who controlled the weather and therefore gave or withheld fertility.

19. Mount Carmel is a ridge which confronts the Mediterranean Sea on the northwest and the Plain of Esdraelon on the southeast. Especially on its southern side it was the most fertile strip of land in the whole country, hence its name "The Carmel," "The Garden Land" (always with the definite article). When Amos (1:2) speaks of the withering of the ridge of Carmel, he means that the last and final disaster which drought can bring has taken place. The actual site of Elijah's exploit is commonly identified with El-Muhraka, i.e., "place of burning," a platform just below the summit on the southern edge, some sixteen hundred feet above sea level, with the brook Kishon (Nahr el-Muqatta') below, and near to it the Tell el-Qassîs ("priest's mound"), the traditional site of the slaughter of the priests of Baal.

---

of Nazareth? art thou come to destroy us?" (Mark 1:24). To him, as to Ahab, the presence of God's representative meant the pain of life coming into lethargy, of light breaking into the darkness loved by evildoers.

The prophet or the Christ disturbs the smugness of complacency. Like those Corinthians who "measuring themselves by themselves, and comparing themselves among themselves, are not wise" (II Cor. 10:12), men seek comfort by settling into moral mediocrity. They develop a clubbable atmosphere of mutual exoneration. Then the appearance of a towering moral personality shames them in their littleness and haunts them with the vision of the "might have been." In the presence of Christlike purity their virtues look like cheap stage jewelry when brought into the sunlight.

Moreover, the prophet often appears as a troubler because he awakens men to added responsibilities. Some years ago a layman said to his minister: "You preachers are making a mistake. We tired businessmen come to church with our problems and burdens, looking for light and lift. And then you of the pulpit leave us with more problems than when we came."

Some sympathy is due his complaint. The church surely ought to comfort the depressed and lighten the loads of the oppressed. But the church is the place where the mind and spirit are stretched in order that they may grow into the fullness of the stature of Christ Jesus our Lord. The church is the body of the Christ who said, "Come unto me, all ye that labor and are heavy laden, and I will give you rest." But read on: "Take my yoke upon you, and learn of me" (Matt. 11:28-29). Christ rests weary men with a yoke, because our deepest need is to be needed, and our souls are not at rest unless they are growing, and souls do not grow toward the fullness of Christ unless they bear "one another's burdens, and so fulfil the law of Christ" (Gal. 6:2).

The purpose of the prophet, as of the Christ, is to cure, not merely to comfort. In its efforts to attract the crowd the pulpit is prone to forget this fact. The strategy of good preaching is to meet people at the level of their desires and lead them up to the level of their needs. Men think they know what they want; they do not always know what they need. Jesus has been likened to a great moral huntsman sweeping

21 And Elijah came unto all the people, and said, How long halt ye between two opinions? if the LORD *be* God, follow him: but if Baal, *then* follow him. And the people answered him not a word.

22 Then said Elijah unto the people, I, *even* I only, remain a prophet of the LORD; but Baal's prophets *are* four hundred and fifty men.

23 Let them therefore give us two bullocks; and let them choose one bullock for themselves, and cut it in pieces, and lay *it* on wood, and put no fire *under:* and I will dress the other bullock, and lay *it* on wood, and put no fire *under:*

24 And call ye on the name of your gods, and I will call on the name of the LORD: and the God that answereth by fire, let him be God. And all the people answered and said, It is well spoken.

at Mount Carmel. 21 And Eli'jah came near to all the people, and said, "How long will you go limping with two different opinions? If the LORD is God, follow him; but if Ba'al, then follow him." And the people did not answer him a word. 22 Then Eli'jah said to the people, "I, even I only, am left a prophet of the LORD; but Ba'al's prophets are four hundred and fifty men. 23 Let two bulls be given to us; and let them choose one bull for themselves, and cut it in pieces and lay it on the wood, but put no fire to it; and I will prepare the other bull and lay it on the wood, and put no fire to it. 24 And you call on the name of your god and I will call on the name of the LORD; and the God who answers by fire, he is God." And all the people answered, "It is

---

21. Both the KJV and the RSV are interpreting. The actual Hebrew word had to do with "clefts," and since it is also used of branches and boughs (Isa. 17:6) we may suppose that in this latter case it means the branching out of the tree, dividing just as legs and limbs divide from the trunk of a human being. Indeed, we do speak of the "limbs" of a tree. There seems to be every justification for Albrecht's claim that the word here means "legs." Elijah's question to all the people is therefore, "How long will you keep hopping [lit., **limping**] from one leg to another?" The emphasis on the need of a choice between Yahweh of Israel and any other god is the contribution of the ninth-century B.C. prophets to the Hebrew religion. They seem to have had no objection to the bull cult of Bethel, but they did maintain that no man could worship any other god if he served the God of Israel. They stood for one God and one God only for Israel— a necessary step if a genuine monotheism was ever to be taught, and perhaps, indeed, a unique characteristic of Yahweh from early times.

23. The test is going to be which god can bring the rain after the long drought. The agreement between the two contending parties is that the god who himself kindles the sacrifice is the God who gives the rain, and therefore is responsible for fertility and life for both land and people. Is it to be Baal, Jezebel's Tyrian god and the rain god of Syria, or is it to be the Lord, the God of Israel, once the God of a desert people (cf. Hos. 2:8)?

---

across the landscape of history, digging men out of the little burrows of complacency and respectability in which they had ensconced themselves.

21. *Dangers of the Middle Road.*—Life flourishes best in the temperate zones. This is true geographically. Our sturdiest races have developed in the zones between the torrid borders of the equator and the frigid circles around the poles. Spiritually, as well as physically, life is healthiest when it avoids certain extremes. Jesus was an illuminating example of sane moderation. He did not join on the one side with the religious radicals of his day, the Essenes and Nazirites, nor on the other side with the con-

servative Pharisees. He practiced self-control but he was not an ascetic. There was none of the narrowness of the fanatic about the Man of Nazareth, who dined with Pharisees and publicans, who chose a Samaritan foreigner as hero for one of his parables, and paid high compliments to Roman centurions.

Nevertheless, true tolerance and genuine moderation have many counterfeits. The middle road between extremes is beset with many pitfalls which have to be avoided if men are not to go, like Ahab's countrymen, limping weakly between two sides. For one thing, they must look to their motives. Are they keeping to the

25 And Elijah said unto the prophets of Baal, Choose you one bullock for yourselves, and dress *it* first; for ye *are* many; and call on the name of your gods, but put no fire *under*.

26 And they took the bullock which was given them, and they dressed *it,* and called on the name of Baal from morning even until noon, saying, O Baal, hear us. But *there was* no voice, nor any that answered. And they leaped upon the altar which was made.

27 And it came to pass at noon, that Elijah mocked them, and said, Cry aloud: for he *is* a god; either he is talking, or he is pursuing, or he is in a journey, *or* peradventure he sleepeth, and must be awaked.

28 And they cried aloud, and cut themselves after their manner with knives and lancets, till the blood gushed out upon them.

29 And it came to pass, when midday was past, and they prophesied until the *time* of the offering of the *evening* sacrifice, that *there was* neither voice, nor any to answer, nor any that regarded.

well spoken." 25 Then Eli'jah said to the prophets of Ba'al, "Choose for yourselves one bull and prepare it first, for you are many; and call on the name of your god, but put no fire to it." 26 And they took the bull which was given them, and they prepared it, and called on the name of Ba'al from morning until noon, saying, "O Ba'al, answer us!" But there was no voice, and no one answered. And they limped about the altar which they had made. 27 And at noon Eli'jah mocked them, saying, "Cry aloud, for he is a god; either he is musing, or he has gone aside, or he is on a journey, or perhaps he is asleep and must be awakened." 28 And they cried aloud, and cut themselves after their custom with swords and lances, until the blood gushed out upon them. 29 And as midday passed, they raved on until the time of the offering of the oblation, but there was no voice; no one answered, no one heeded.

---

26. **Limped** (RSV) is the more accurate rendering (cf. KJV). The reference is to the ritual dance of the priests, who encircled the altar, bending and leaping as they danced around it with innumerable body contortions.

27. The phrase **he has gone aside** may be a corrupt repetition of the previous phrase. Otherwise it is to be regarded as a euphemism. The following phrase, **he is on a journey,** is correctly interpreted by the LXX as "he is engaged on business."

28. The shedding of blood on the part of the worshiper is a custom well established for Syria generally. W. Robertson Smith claimed that the Syriac word *'ethkashshaph* is evidence of the idea's widespread popularity, since the word is used to mean "to make supplication," but means, lit., "to cut oneself" (W. Robertson Smith, *Lectures on the Religion of the Semites* [3rd ed.; New York: The Macmillan Co., 1927], p. 321).

29. According to the KJV the prophets of Baal continued to "prophesy" when midday was past. The RSV has **raved on.** The word used in the Hebrew means "to act as a prophet," but the sense here is that they behaved in an ungoverned manner, having whipped themselves up into a frenzy. This prophetic frenzy or ecstasy was a characteristic feature of early prophecy (I Sam. 18:10; II Kings 9:11; Jer. 29:26). It is Canaanite in

---

middle course in order that they may do justice to both sides, or that they may play safe for themselves? Another danger in taking the middle road is that it will lead to lukewarmness. Too many mistake indifference for tolerance. There is no true tolerance in one who does not care. It is one thing to keep one's head cool enough for impartial judgment; it is another to let one's heart grow cold. Truly warmhearted persons seldom are hotheads. The men who keep the world from stagnation, who strike out

new paths, rouse others to activity, and inaugurate new eras of progress, are men who are full of earnestness. Earnestness conquers where cleverness fails. Furthermore, those who try to be loyal to two differing religious faiths either **go limping** or **halt.** "Every kingdom divided against itself is brought to desolation; and every city or house divided against itself shall not stand" (Matt. 12:25). A mind may entertain a host of different intellectual opinions and scientific theories; but religion involves commit-

30 And Elijah said unto all the people, Come near unto me. And all the people came near unto him. And he repaired the altar of the LORD *that was* broken down.

31 And Elijah took twelve stones, according to the number of the tribes of the sons of Jacob, unto whom the word of the LORD came, saying, Israel shall be thy name:

32 And with the stones he built an altar in the name of the LORD: and he made a trench about the altar, as great as would contain two measures of seed.

30 Then Eli'jah said to all the people, "Come near to me"; and all the people came near to him. And he repaired the altar of the LORD that had been thrown down; 31 Eli'jah took twelve stones, according to the number of the tribes of the sons of Jacob, to whom the word of the LORD came, saying, "Israel shall be your name"; 32 and with the stones he built an altar in the name of the LORD. And he made a trench about the altar, as great as would contain

---

origin (T. H. Robinson, *Prophecy and the Prophets in Ancient Israel* [New York: Charles Scribner's Sons, 1923], p. 34; Harold Knight, *The Hebrew Prophetic Consciousness* [London: Lutterworth Press, 1947], pp. 70-90). The raving dance in which they lashed themselves with whips and gashed themselves with knives was native to Palestine and Asia Minor. It spread into Egypt by the fifth century B.C., and from thence it accompanied the mystery cults throughout the Mediterranean world (W. O. E. Oesterley and T. H. Robinson, *Hebrew Religion, Its Origin and Development* [2nd ed.; New York: The Macmillan Co., 1937], p. 185; Robinson, *Prophecy and Prophets*, pp. 30-37). The dance continued **until the time of the offering of the evening sacrifice.** The word **evening** is not found in the original, and in II Kings 3:20, where the same phrase occurs, it is the morning sacrifice that is intended. The time is not likely the evening twilight ("between the two evenings," Exod. 29:39 ASV mg.), but was probably about three o'clock in the afternoon—the traditional ninth hour of prayer.

30. Apparently there had been a true Yahweh altar on Mount Carmel, probably destroyed by the "reforming" zeal of Jezebel. According to Tacitus (*History* II. 78; also Suetonius, *Lives of the Caesars, Vespasian* V) Vespasian offered sacrifice on Carmel, "the name both of a god and a mountain; but there is neither image nor temple of the god; such are the ancient traditions; we find there only an altar and religious awe."

31. This verse and vs. 32*a* are interpolations by the postexilic Priestly Code editor. In the LXX they are found in the middle of vs. 30.

32. Two seahs (**measures**) of seed amount to about five gallons. This can scarcely have been the cubic capacity of the whole trench. The phrase is used in the Mishnah

---

ment. "Whosoever doth not bear his cross, and come after me, cannot be my disciple" (Luke 14:27). In saying that, Jesus was making no more arbitrary demand than is made by any good physician. A doctor cannot demonstrate his ability to cure a patient until the patient puts himself into the physician's hands and submits to his regimen. Obedience is the way to physical cure and also to spiritual knowledge.

Yahweh and Baal were not guests to be entertained by the Israelites. They were masters to be obeyed and served. "No servant can serve two masters: for either he will hate the one, and love the other; or else he will hold to the one, and despise the other" (Luke 16:13). Elijah was trying to change his hearers from would-be patrons of religion to the only genuinely religious attitude, that of servant. And in religion, as in the state, there must be a seat of sovereignty.

How long would Israel defer decision? To put things off to a more convenient time is one of our deep-seated tendencies. It shows itself in trifles. It has been said that the attics of our houses are filled with our deferred decisions, old, worn-out objects which we cannot quite bring ourselves to discard. And in the serious business of living, who can compute how much folly and failure and sin have resulted from vacillation? The man who is unable to make up his mind is a torment to himself and an object of reproach to others who frequently suffer from his hesitation and fickleness.

The power of decision possesses contagious force. When a person of decisive mind appears in our midst, he disposes men to follow him, as floating objects are drawn into the wake of a speeding vessel. It is men of decision who bring order into a demoralized situation and rally the forces of reconstruction. It was said of William

33 And he put the wood in order, and cut the bullock in pieces, and laid *him* on the wood, and said, Fill four barrels with water, and pour *it* on the burnt sacrifice, and on the wood.

34 And he said, Do *it* the second time. And they did *it* the second time. And he said, Do *it* the third time. And they did *it* the third time.

35 And the water ran round about the altar; and he filled the trench also with water.

36 And it came to pass at *the time of* the offering of the *evening* sacrifice, that Elijah the prophet came near, and said, Lord God of Abraham, Isaac, and of Israel, let it be known this day that thou *art* God in Israel, and *that* I *am* thy servant, and *that* I have done all these things at thy word.

37 Hear me, O Lord, hear me, that this people may know that thou *art* the Lord God, and *that* thou hast turned their heart back again.

two measures of seed. 33 And he put the wood in order, and cut the bull in pieces and laid it on the wood. And he said, "Fill four jars with water, and pour it on the burnt offering, and on the wood." 34 And he said, "Do it a second time"; and they did it a second time. And he said, "Do it a third time"; and they did it a third time. 35 And the water ran round about the altar, and filled the trench also with water.

36 And at the time of the offering of the oblation, Eli'jah the prophet came near and said, "O Lord, God of Abraham, Isaac, and Israel, let it be known this day that thou art God in Israel, and that I am thy servant, and that I have done all these things at thy word. 37 Answer me, O Lord, answer me, that this people may know that thou, O Lord, art God, and that thou hast turned

---

(Shebiith 3:2) as a square measure of a field requiring this quantity of seed. If this is the explanation, then the trench enclosed an area thirty yards square, but this seems to be just as large as the other estimate was small.

33. The pouring of the water was not to make the burning of the sacrifice more difficult, nor was it to preclude any charge of sharp practice. It was the ancient method of procuring rain by sympathetic magic. The operation was repeated thrice to ensure its efficacy. The feature of the incident has occasioned considerable difficulty and has given rise to a legion of rationalizing explanations. The most "efficient" explanation is that they poured naphtha over the sacrifice, since, it is alleged, there was an oil well on or below the ridge of Carmel. The most satisfactory explanation is that the author was telling exactly the truth, and that it was water which was poured out there. The whole incident was a fight between two opposing cults, for Elijah made the giving of the rains the clear central issue. Julian Morgenstern (*Amos Studies* [Cincinnati: Hebrew

---

Pitt that he formed his plans with such promptitude and executed them with such vigor that no one ever spent five minutes with him in conference without leaving a braver man than when he entered. Strength of character is developed by clinching our convictions with decisive action. And our moral foundations are undermined by deferring decisions. How pointedly Jesus or his biographer put this truth at the conclusion of those sayings which we call the Sermon on the Mount. "Whosoever heareth these sayings of mine, and doeth them, I will liken him unto a wise man, which built his house upon a rock: and the rain descended, and the floods came, and the winds blew, and beat upon that house; and it fell not: for it was founded upon a rock. And every one that heareth these sayings of mine, and doeth them

not, shall be likened unto a foolish man, which built his house upon the sand . . . and it fell" (Matt. 7:24-27). To hear the call of duty and do nothing about it; to have our emotions repeatedly stirred and turn away like a theater crowd; to keep on weighing religious opinions and never put them to work—all this disintegrates the rock of character into shifting sand. In view of the dangers of the middle road and deferred decisions, **How long will you go limping with two different opinions?**

37. Ordeal by Fire.—The activity of Elijah on Mount Carmel makes exciting drama. There is a wealth of preaching and teaching value in the sheer courage of the lone prophet pitting himself against the 450 priests of Baal. Such bold faith is bound to win converts even when no miraculous accompaniment seems to authen-

38 Then the fire of the LORD fell, and
consumed the burnt sacrifice, and the wood,
and the stones, and the dust, and licked up
the water that *was* in the trench.

39 And when all the people saw *it*, they
fell on their faces: and they said, The LORD,
he *is* the God; the LORD, he *is* the God.

40 And Elijah said unto them, Take the
prophets of Baal; let not one of them
escape. And they took them: and Elijah
brought them down to the brook Kishon,
and slew them there.

41 ¶ And Elijah said unto Ahab, Get
thee up, eat and drink; for *there is* a sound
of abundance of rain.

42 So Ahab went up to eat and to drink.
And Elijah went up to the top of Carmel;
and he cast himself down upon the earth,
and put his face between his knees,

their hearts back." 38 Then the fire of the
LORD fell, and consumed the burnt offering,
and the wood, and the stones, and the dust,
and licked up the water that was in the
trench. 39 And when all the people saw it,
they fell on their faces; and they said, "The
LORD, he is God; the LORD, he is God."
40 And Eli'jah said to them, "Seize the
prophets of Ba'al; let not one of them
escape." And they seized them; and Eli'jah
brought them down to the brook Kishon,
and killed them there.

41 And Eli'jah said to Ahab, "Go up, eat
and drink; for there is a sound of the rushing of rain." 42 So Ahab went up to eat and
to drink. And Eli'jah went up to the top of
Carmel; and he bowed himself down upon
the earth, and put his face between his

Union College Press, 1941], I, 305-12) produces a considerable amount of evidence on
this point. According to Louis Finkelstein (*The Pharisees* [Philadelphia: Jewish Publication Society of America, 1938], I, 108), the water pouring is an ancient nomadic rite,
and Elijah is here insisting on the efficacy of the old desert ways of the God of Israel
against the Canaanite rites with its bloodletting and all the extravagances in posturing
and frenzy. Certainly he takes care to act and to speak with a calmness and a serenity
which are in marked contrast to the excitement and agitation of the Baal priests, and
the contrast is made all the more clear by the way in which he continues to mock them
while they are frantically performing their rites.

38. The fire of the LORD is a supernatural fire, frequently in the O.T. associated
with the appearance of God. Physically speaking, it may well have been lightning in this
particular case, since the long, hot drought of a semitropical country naturally ends in
thunderstorms of a violence not known in more temperate climates. But to give a physical
explanation of the phenomenon does not do away with the miraculous element in it. The
real point of the incident is that the lightning, if indeed it was actually lightning, came
at that particular time apparently in direct response to Elijah's acted (water pouring)
and spoken prayer. The Hebrew conviction was that whenever the thunder and the
lightning come, they are sent by God, but that there are special occasions such as this
one when he sends them for a particular purpose. The miracle consists in this "coincidence." He sends the lightning when he wills, but there are times fraught with destiny
when he sends it as a specific display of divine grace.

41. Better, "the sound and roar of the downpour." The Hebrew word גשם is used
of the heavy seasonal rains (cf. Ezra 10:9). "In the rainy season the falls are usually

---

ticate it. It was the inexplicable power of such
contagious courage which inspired the ancient
assertion, "One man of you shall chase a thousand" (Josh. 23:10).

It has been said that we never discover the
power of prayer until our prayers look up to
God like wounded animals with great round
eyes of pain. Elijah's prayer on Mount Carmel
was of that type. He was sorely wounded by his
countrymen's indecisive attitude toward the
issue between Yahweh and Baal. For his people

he saw that it was a matter of spiritual life or
death: he was therefore willing to make it a
matter of physical life or death for himself. And
the Lord did not let his prophet down. When
we try to explain the record of the consuming
fire we must take into account the aspects discussed in the Expos. on 17:1-24. The reader
should not be sidetracked into queries as to
whether "the fire of the LORD fell" in the form
of lightning or in some other way. The significant fact is that something happened on

43 And said to his servant, Go up now, look toward the sea. And he went up, and looked, and said, *There is* nothing. And he said, Go again seven times.

44 And it came to pass at the seventh time, that he said, Behold, there ariseth a little cloud out of the sea, like a man's hand. And he said, Go up, say unto Ahab, Prepare *thy chariot,* and get thee down, that the rain stop thee not.

45 And it came to pass in the mean while, that the heaven was black with clouds and wind, and there was a great rain. And Ahab rode, and went to Jezreel.

46 And the hand of the LORD was on Elijah; and he girded up his loins, and ran before Ahab to the entrance of Jezreel.

knees. 43 And he said to his servant, "Go up now, look toward the sea." And he went up and looked, and said, "There is nothing." And he said, "Go again seven times." 44 And at the seventh time he said, "Behold, a little cloud like a man's hand is rising out of the sea." And he said, "Go up, say to Ahab, 'Prepare your chariot and go down, lest the rain stop you.'" 45 And in a little while the heavens grew black with clouds and wind, and there was a great rain. And Ahab rode and went to Jezreel. 46 And the hand of the LORD was on Eli'jah; and he girded up his loins and ran before Ahab to the entrance of Jezreel.

---

heavy, and are accompanied by thunder and lightning, while the wind comes from the W. or S.W." (E. Hull, "Rain," in Hastings, *Dictionary of the Bible,* IV, 195). This is precisely what is happening here. The deluge which follows the burning up of the sacrifice on Mount Carmel is the first downpour of the so-called "former rain," that autumnal rainy season which had been missing for three long years.

43. The seventh look is effective (cf. 8:65). The rain rite and the rain prayer are answered with a thoroughness that satisfies even the most ardent devotee, and should convince the greatest doubter.

46. The hand of the LORD is a regular metaphor for the power of God. The distance from the scene of the sacrifice to the entrance to the Pass of Jezreel is about seventeen miles. This distance Elijah runs in a strength that is not his own, for **the hand of the LORD was on Elijah.** Ahab must hurry to pass through the valley of Esdraelon before it is turned into a quagmire ("black gumbo") as in the days of Sisera and Jael (Judg. 5:21). The race to Jezreel marks the end of Elijah's great demonstration that the Lord is the true God of Israel, he who gives the rain and its consequent fertility, the God to whom alone Israel must look. The victory was apparently short lived, as the next chapter shows. Jezebel was not the woman to take calmly such a feat, nor was she the sort of woman who would let pass the slaughter of the Baal prophets. She threatened vengeance, and Elijah fled. The entire story must be read against the background of the time. The wholesale and ruthless slaughter of the prophets of Baal was considered to be a righteous deed by the oppressed Yahwistic worshipers. The fact that Elijah built up again the altar to the Lord on Carmel is regarded in the story as being meritorious. Such an action was contrary to the principles of the Deuteronomists, who held it against all the kings of Israel and some of the kings of Judah that they permitted altars and shrines elsewhere than at Jerusalem. But in the ninth and eighth centuries such altars were allowed, and the establishment of a true altar to the Lord was to be commended, no matter on what hill it was erected.

Carmel which convinced the spectators that Yahweh was superior to Baal. The event changed the course of Israel's religious history.

This scene of fire and slaughter should be reviewed in the afterglow of Elijah's experiences as described in succeeding chapters. The author is tracing the training and taming of a prophet. The "man of God" who prayed for his answer by fire on Carmel is to learn on Horeb that the Lord is not to be found in the wind and fire. This discovery points in the direction of that wilderness experience centuries later, wherein Jesus of Nazareth resisted the temptation to depend on the spectacularly miraculous to demonstrate divine power. According to the record, the miracle of fire consuming the sacrifice on Carmel converted the early Israelites. The greater miracle is that the sacrifice on Calvary

19 And Ahab told Jezebel all that Elijah had done, and withal how he had slain all the prophets with the sword.

2 Then Jezebel sent a messenger unto Elijah, saying, So let the gods do *to me,* and more also, if I make not thy life as the life of one of them by to-morrow about this time.

3 And when he saw *that,* he arose, and went for his life, and came to Beer-sheba, which *belongeth* to Judah, and left his servant there.

19 Ahab told Jez'ebel all that Eli'jah had done, and how he had slain all the prophets with the sword. 2 Then Jez'ebel sent a messenger to Eli'jah, saying, "So may the gods do to me, and more also, if I do not make your life as the life of one of them by this time tomorrow." 3 Then he was afraid, and he arose and went for his life, and came to Beer-sheba, which belongs to Judah, and left his servant there.

4. ELIJAH AT HOREB (19:1-21)

The reaction sets in and Elijah, threatened by Jezebel, loses his nerve and flees south through the Judahite territory, where he sleeps the sleep of utter exhaustion. He is aroused by an angel and is given supernatural food, in the strength of which he continues his long journey to Horeb, the ancient home of the desert faith. There he hears the voice of God, receives new encouragement, and accepts from God a new policy which he proceeds to put into practice.

19:2-3. Jezebel was apparently not in a position to put Elijah to death in summary fashion, for we may expect her to have acted first and talked afterward if she was in a position to do so. But she did manage to scare Elijah out of the country. (It is best to follow the LXX and Syriac **he was afraid,** a reading which depends on the same consonants but assumes different vowels.) The LXX prefaces Jezebel's message with "As sure as you are Elijah and I am Jezebel." Elijah flees for his life out of Ahab and Jezebel's jurisdiction, and keeps on traveling till he reaches the farthest confines of the settled country. There on the southern boundary of the cultivated land he leaves his servant and continues a day's journey into the southern wilderness.

started a fire in the hearts of men which the centuries cannot put out.

19:3. *The Aftermath of Valor.*—The courage of Elijah in confronting singlehanded the hundreds of Baal priests on Mount Carmel remains an epic undimmed by the difficulty of comprehending the ordeal by fire. How a modern reporter would have described the event, we do not know; but that Elijah routed the priests and aroused the people to their destruction is attested by the results which followed. Jezebel, the patron of the Baal priests, vowed to wreak vengeance on Elijah. **Then he was afraid, and he arose and went for his life.** Just as certain generals like Hannibal and Frederick the Great and Washington were never so dangerous as on the day after a defeat, so some persons are never so vulnerable as on the day after a victory. Elijah's spectacular triumph over the priests had been followed by a reaction. He was passing through that trying time experienced by all idealists when they discover that there are no permanent victories. He was disgusted at the fickleness of the public which had cheered him on Carmel and then turned to follow his foe, Queen Jezebel. It seemed to him that even the

Lord had let him down by leading him into a crisis and then deserting him. Depressed and frightened, he fled into the wilderness.

Courage is the keystone in the arch of character. It gives strength and stability to all our other qualities. If we are not brave, of what avail is our desire for honesty or our concern for justice? And imperative as is the need of valor for overcoming dangers in a crisis, quite as necessary is the quality of fortitude to keep us from being overcome when things run over us. The fleeing Elijah was in need of beliefs to make him brave. One of these was a belief in himself. He needed that resilient courage which enabled young Disraeli to come back confidently after his first speech in Parliament had been jeered down. But it must be something more than mere self-sustained confidence. Elijah needed a God-given belief in himself. "Wait on the LORD: be of good courage, and he shall strengthen thine heart" (Ps. 27:14). Such courage differs in quality from the cocksureness of mere self-reliance. It is more than a success complex built up by repeated triumphs over competitors. The psalmist was counseling a courage rooted in a soil deeper than the subconscious

4 ¶ But he himself went a day's journey into the wilderness, and came and sat down under a juniper tree: and he requested for himself that he might die; and said, It is enough; now, O Lord, take away my life; for I *am* not better than my fathers.

4 But he himself went a day's journey into the wilderness, and came and sat down under a broom tree; and he asked that he might die, saying, "It is enough; now, O Lord, take away my life; for I am no better

---

4. Elijah stops and shelters, exhausted and disillusioned, under a **broom tree.** This bush sometimes grows to a height of as much as ten feet, and is common in the desert wadies of the south. It provides no great amount of shade against the desert sun, but it is the best shade there is. Elijah is utterly at the end of his own courage and his own strength, and dejectedly confesses that in spite of all he has done at Carmel he is no better than his fathers.

---

mind. He was saying that when we wait on the Lord he strengthens our hearts with the feeling that he believes in us, and that begets a belief in ourselves. Elijah had lost faith in himself because he felt the Lord had lost faith in him.

The frightened prophet also needed the belief of others in him. "I, even I only, am left" (vs. 10). Courage has to be sustained by the encouragement of others. It is hard to say how long personal courage could survive in complete isolation of soul. Heroic individuals have put up what we call "lone fights." Athanasius stood so alone against the popular religious trend of his time that the saying arose, "Athanasius against the world." But behind the scenes there must have been a coterie of personal friends whose sympathy sustained the theologian. Gethsemane is the loneliest spot of heroism in all history, for even his own disciples did not keep awake to watch and pray with Jesus; but even there he knew that he had the love of his disciples, wavering as they were. Everyone who has enjoyed the love of another knows how it puts courage and nerve into the soul. To know that there is someone whose heart beats faster when your step is heard on the stair; to know there is one who keeps tryst with you in thought, although absent in person; to know there is one who believes in you when the crowd is howling you down—those are beliefs which make us brave. These Elijah thought he lacked.

4-9. Lifted Out of Our Littleness.—Elijah was in the cave mood. **He came to a cave, and lodged there** (vs. 9). Both his mind and heart had gone into hiding. He was still free from Ahab and Jezebel, but he was a prisoner of himself. He had shut the sunlight out of his mind. He had drawn the shutters of his heart. When doors are slammed against us, we are prone to draw into ourselves and lock our hearts against others. Distrust begets distrust.

In healthy mood, the Hebrews had a dread of being hemmed in. Repeatedly the psalmist sings of the Lord's deliverance as of being led into large places. "He brought me forth also into a large place; he delivered me, because he delighted in me" (Ps. 18:19). "I called upon the Lord in distress: the Lord answered me, and set me in a large place" (Ps. 118:5). Elijah was in need of a larger setting. A mind, like a home, needs proper landscaping. Sometimes this is secured by enlargement of physical outlook. A wise old minister was accustomed throughout a long pastorate to preach one sermon a year on astronomy. When his youthful assistant inquired why the preacher talked about a subject so far removed from the daily walks of life, the pastor replied, "Of course it is no use at all, but it greatly enlarges my idea of God."[1] When a person is shut into the cave mood, he needs a larger mental setting in time as well as in space. However imprisoning the present physical circumstance, the windows of the mind can always be opened to the wisdom of other ages. The physically shut in and the socially shut out can keep company with Plato and Augustine, with Shakespeare and Luther. And the outlook of time can be enlarged into eternity. Whether a dweller in a humble hovel or the hounded victim of disease or persecution, the spirit can catch visions of the Father's house of many mansions (cf. John 14:2).

But mere enlargement of setting does not lift us out of our littleness. Bismarck, while he was the Prussian "Iron Chancellor," expanded his activities to imperial proportions and then, after he was relieved of his command by the young kaiser, retired to his vast estate where he felt himself hemmed in like a prisoner. Bismarck's scale of public operations did not develop in him bigness of soul. John Bunyan, on the other hand, confined in Bedford jail, glimpsed the turrets of the Celestial City.

Elijah needed enlargement of nature as well as of outlook. He had slumped into smallness of soul, where he was victimizing himself by a

[1] Willard L. Sperry, *Yes, But—* (New York: Harper & Bros., 1931), p. 127.

5 And as he lay and slept under a juniper tree, behold, then an angel touched him, and said unto him, Arise *and* eat.

6 And he looked, and, behold, *there was* a cake baked on the coals, and a cruse of water at his head. And he did eat and drink, and laid him down again.

7 And the angel of the LORD came again the second time, and touched him, and said, Arise *and* eat; because the journey *is* too great for thee.

8 And he arose, and did eat and drink, and went in the strength of that meat forty days and forty nights unto Horeb the mount of God.

than my fathers." 5 And he lay down and slept under a broom tree; and behold, an angel touched him, and said to him, "Arise and eat." 6 And he looked, and behold, there was at his head a cake baked on hot stones and a jar of water. And he ate and drank, and lay down again. 7 And the angel of the LORD came again a second time, and touched him, and said, "Arise and eat, else the journey will be too great for you." 8 And he arose, and ate and drank, and went in the strength of that food forty days and forty nights to Horeb the mount of God.

5-7. The thought of angel intermediaries between God and the prophets is not earlier than the Exile. The LXX here has "someone," so that there is every likelihood that the angel is a postexilic interpretation of the original Hebrew. There is a reference to an angel in 13:18, but this particular section is generally held to be a postexilic insertion. The phrase **the angel of the LORD** occurs in vs. 7. This is doubtless the supernatural being of Gen. 16:7, who appears in the earlier histories (J and E) in theophanies as a manifestation of God in human form. The date of the Elijah narratives cannot be far distant from the date of E.

8. Elijah finds his way back to **Horeb the mount of God,** not in his own strength, but in the miraculous strength given to him in the angel's food. Here at Horeb, according to the northern tradition, was the ancient home of the God of Israel, since the name Horeb is peculiar to E and D (Exodus and Deuteronomy). It is the J tradition which has the name Sinai. It is evident that the author of this story knows the E story of Moses at Horeb, there being sufficient similarity in detail between the two accounts to suggest dependence, but at the same time sufficient difference to make that dependence oral rather than literary; cf. the fast of forty days and forty nights (Exod. 34:28) and the "passing across" (M.T. עבר in each case) of God. On the other hand, Moses stood in a cleft of the rock, while Elijah stood in the mouth of a cave; or again, Moses' face is covered by the hand of God, whereas Elijah wraps his face in his mantle. Perhaps even the seven thousand of vs. 18 is in part a reminiscence of the thousands of Exod. 34:7, with whom the Lord keeps faith according to the covenant.

---

vindictive spirit. Fretted by the injustice inflicted upon him, he had lost generosity of judgment and magnanimity of spirit. He was vowing vengeance. Magnanimity is one of the rarest of virtues, for it is much harder to admit merit in others than to achieve it in oneself. Heine, the poet, was only half in jest when, in describing his notion of happiness, he said: "My wishes are a humble dwelling with a thatched roof, a good bed, good food, flowers at my windows, and some fine tall trees before my door. And if the good God wants to make me completely happy he will grant me the joy of seeing six or seven of my enemies hanging from the trees." [2]

Elijah had nursed his depression and vindic-

tiveness into self-pity, one of the mind's most vicious circles. The person who goes around pitying himself bores others with the repeated story of his troubles, and the result is that he is left more and more to himself. Thus he becomes the only audience to which he can pour out his woes, and as these are poured back into himself, they foam up into an ever more bitter and intoxicating drug.

5-18. *Freed from Bitterness.*—Note the steps by which the Lord delivered Elijah from his discouragement. When the despairing prophet had fallen asleep under the broom tree, the divine message to him was, **Arise and eat** (vs. 5). First of all, he was to get up. The body and the will have their part to play in mastering mental depression. God does not spoon-feed minds lying on their backs. Some effort on the

[2] Quoted by Joshua Loth Liebman, *Peace of Mind* (New York: Simon & Schuster, 1946), p. 67.

9 ¶ And he came thither unto a cave, and lodged there; and, behold, the word of the Lord came to him, and he said unto him, What doest thou here, Elijah?

10 And he said, I have been very jealous for the Lord God of hosts: for the children of Israel have forsaken thy covenant, thrown down thine altars, and slain thy prophets with the sword; and I, *even* I only, am left; and they seek my life, to take it away.

11 And he said, Go forth, and stand upon the mount before the Lord. And, behold, the Lord passed by, and a great and strong wind rent the mountains, and brake in pieces the rocks before the Lord; *but* the Lord *was* not in the wind: and after the wind an earthquake; *but* the Lord *was* not in the earthquake:

12 And after the earthquake a fire; *but* the Lord *was* not in the fire: and after the fire a still small voice.

13 And it was *so,* when Elijah heard *it,* that he wrapped his face in his mantle, and went out, and stood in the entering in of the cave. And, behold, *there came* a voice unto him, and said, What doest thou here, Elijah?

9 And there he came to a cave, and lodged there; and behold, the word of the Lord came to him, and he said to him, "What are you doing here, Eli'jah?" 10 He said, "I have been very jealous for the Lord, the God of hosts; for the people of Israel have forsaken thy covenant, thrown down thy altars, and slain thy prophets with the sword; and I, even I only, am left; and they seek my life, to take it away." 11 And he said, "Go forth, and stand upon the mount before the Lord." And behold, the Lord passed by, and a great and strong wind rent the mountains, and broke in pieces the rocks before the Lord, but the Lord was not in the wind; and after the wind an earthquake, but the Lord was not in the earthquake; 12 and after the earthquake a fire, but the Lord was not in the fire; and after the fire a still small voice. 13 And when Eli'jah heard it, he wrapped his face in his mantle and went out and stood at the entrance of the cave. And behold, there came a voice to him, and said,

9. What are you doing here? The construction is similar in part to that in 17:18, where the person addressed is considered to be outside his province, where he had no business to be. Vss. 9a-11a constitute a repetition, though earlier than the LXX, of vss. 13b-14, destroying the dramatic development of the story. The LXX attempts to smooth out the difficulty by inserting "tomorrow," and so also does Josephus (*Antiquities* VIII. 13. 7), perhaps influenced by Exod. 34:2.

12. The traditional rendering is **a still small voice,** but the Hebrew is "a sound of a gentle stillness" (ASV mg.; cf. Job 4:16). The writer thinks of an eerie stillness, so still that it can be heard. The wind, the earthquake, and the fire are the outrunners (cf. II Sam. 15:1) which herald the coming of the king. Such phenomena as these are the regular O.T. accompaniments of a theophany (Exod. 19:16, 18; Ps. 18:7-15).

13. Moses hid his face at the bush because he was afraid to look upon God (Exod. 3:6).

part of the patient is called for. Not yet outmoded by modern psychology is the old maxim, "You never know what you can do till you try." With pleased surprise we all, now and again, complete tasks which we first thought were beyond our powers. Bonaro W. Overstreet would supplement the old sayings with a revised version:

You never try till you know what you can do. The ability and the will to try are not conjured up out of nothing. They are made largely out of past efforts that have brought pleasant rather than painful results. These efforts, many of them, lie so

far back in our infancy and childhood that we have no conscious memory of them. But they are summed up in an attitude that we call self-confidence in life.[3]

This modern version parallels the advice given by Paul to Timothy: "Stir up the gift of God, which is in thee by the putting on of my hands. For God hath not given us the spirit of fear; but of power, and of love, and of a sound mind" (II Tim. 1:6-7). Buried within us are reserves of confidence stored up by past achievements. Elijah, like Timothy, was bidden to **draw upon**

[3] *How to Think About Ourselves* (New York: Harper & Bros., 1948), p. 9.

14 And he said, I have been very jealous for the LORD God of hosts: because the children of Israel have forsaken thy covenant, thrown down thine altars, and slain thy prophets with the sword; and I, *even* I only, am left; and they seek my life, to take it away.

15 And the LORD said unto him, Go, return on thy way to the wilderness of Damascus: and when thou comest, anoint Hazael *to be* king over Syria:

16 And Jehu the son of Nimshi shalt thou anoint *to be* king over Israel: and Elisha the son of Shaphat of Abel-meholah shalt thou anoint *to be* prophet in thy room.

17 And it shall come to pass, *that* him that escapeth the sword of Hazael shall Jehu slay: and him that escapeth from the sword of Jehu shall Elisha slay.

18 Yet I have left *me* seven thousand in Israel, all the knees which have not bowed unto Baal, and every mouth which hath not kissed him.

"What are you doing here, Eli'jah?" 14 He said, "I have been very jealous for the LORD, the God of hosts; for the people of Israel have forsaken thy covenant, thrown down thy altars, and slain thy prophets with the sword; and I, even I only, am left; and they seek my life, to take it away." 15 And the LORD said to him, "Go, return on your way to the wilderness of Damascus; and when you arrive, you shall anoint Haz'ael to be king over Syria; 16 and Jehu the son of Nimshi you shall anoint to be king over Israel; and Eli'sha the son of Shaphat of A'bel-meho'lah you shall anoint to be prophet in your place. 17 And him who escapes from the sword of Haz'ael shall Jehu slay; and him who escapes from the sword of Jehu shall Eli'sha slay. 18 Yet I will leave seven thousand in Israel, all the knees that have not bowed to Ba'al, and every mouth that has not kissed him."

14. The Douay Version here has "zealous," which is more in accordance with the modern usage of the words "jealous" and "zealous" (cf. Exeg. on 14:22).

15. In the sequel it was Elisha who was actually responsible for the anointing of Jehu (II Kings 9:1-6), and also for inciting Hazael to murder his master and to usurp the throne of the Syrian kingdom of Damascus (II Kings 8:7-15). It is therefore assumed, partly because of this, that the Elisha narratives belong to a different cycle of tradition from that of the Elijah stories. The anointing of a prophet is not usual. Apart from Ps. 105:15 (patriarchs as prophets) and Isa. 61:1, only kings are anointed, and priests in the postexilic period only, and then none but the high priest. There is one further exception, that of Cyrus, who is thus divinely commissioned to free the exiles (Isa. 45:1). This last could not have been an actual anointing, so that we have this much evidence that the phrase "anointing" can be used of a special call independently of whether there is any actual ceremony or not.

18. The actual Hebrew refers definitely to the future, so that **I have left me** is wrong. On the other hand, **I will leave** is a paraphrase. It is best to translate, "Yet I will keep a remnant," because the verb which is used is from the same root as *she'ār,* a word which later became the regular and proper term for "the remnant of Israel." The teaching of Isa. 10:20; 11:11-16 is thus anticipated in the Elijah cycle of northern traditions. In spite of all the waywardness and apostasy of the many, there is always a small but solid nucleus of men faithful to Yahweh.

The custom of kissing idols is confirmed in Hos. 13:2; cf. the classical attitude in prayer (Latin, *adoro*), which involved putting the hand to the mouth and moving toward the right. This rite survives in the Moslem custom of kissing the sacred stone

these by bestirring himself. Some physical action, some duty near at hand and within range of present effort, may serve to start the restoration of confidence, even while the fog of despair hides the distant goal.

The Lord's command to get up was followed

by the counsel to look up, **Go forth, and stand upon the mount before the LORD** (vs. 11). A fainting spirit may be revived by a dash of cold water, but mere repetitions of that treatment do not cure anemia. Elijah's mental blood content had to be built up. When Mark Twain

19 ¶ So he departed thence, and found
Elisha the son of Shaphat, who *was* plowing
with twelve yoke *of* oxen before him, and
he with the twelfth: and Elijah passed by
him, and cast his mantle upon him.

20 And he left the oxen, and ran after
Elijah, and said, Let me, I pray thee, kiss
my father and my mother, and *then* I will
follow thee. And he said unto him, Go back
again: for what have I done to thee?

21 And he returned back from him, and
took a yoke of oxen, and slew them, and
boiled their flesh with the instruments of
the oxen, and gave unto the people, and
they did eat. Then he arose, and went after
Elijah, and ministered unto him.

20 And Ben-hadad the king of Syria
gathered all his host together: and
there were thirty and two kings with him,
and horses, and chariots: and he went up
and besieged Samaria, and warred against
it.

19 So he departed from there, and found
Eli'sha the son of Shaphat, who was plowing, with twelve yoke of oxen before him,
and he was with the twelfth. Eli'jah passed
by him and cast his mantle upon him.
20 And he left the oxen, and ran after Eli'-
jah, and said, "Let me kiss my father and
my mother, and then I will follow you."
And he said to him, "Go back again; for
what have I done to you?" 21 And he returned from following him, and took the
yoke of oxen, and slew them, and boiled
their flesh with the yokes of the oxen, and
gave it to the people, and they ate. Then
he arose and went after Eli'jah, and ministered to him.

20 Ben-ha'dad the king of Syria gathered all his army together; thirty-two
kings were with him, and horses and chariots; and he went up and besieged Samar'ia,

(Kaaba) at Mecca and in the Roman practice of kissing the foot of the image of Peter at
Rome.

19. The prophet's **mantle** was made of skin and covered with hair, probably of
goat's skin with the hair turned outward. It was the distinctive clothing of the prophet
(II Kings 1:8; Matt. 3:4; and especially Zech. 13:4). The mantle was the physical means
by which the prophetic power was transferred from Elijah to Elisha (II Kings 2:13-14).
The modern point of view would lead us to suppose that any transference of power by
this means was symbolic, but the storytellers of the time probably accepted the necessity
of some object through which or by means of which the special power could be transferred.

20. The answer of Elijah is difficult, and is most often interpreted to mean "I have
done nothing to you which would prevent a proper leave-taking from your people."
Josephus (*Antiquities* VIII. 13.7) says: "And when he desired leave to salute his parents,
Elijah gave him leave so to do." This, however, is not satisfactory as a translation of
the Hebrew, and we must assume some such translation as "Go [to your parents], and
return [to me], for what have I done to you?" i.e., "You know that I have anointed you
in the name of the Lord, and that he has called you to a special service."

5. AHAB AND THE SYRIANS (20:1-43)

The continuous wars between Syria and Israel have reached the stage when the
Syrian king and his thirty-two vassals have besieged Samaria, Ahab's capital, and
reduced the garrison to the last stage of despair. Ben-hadad, the Syrian king, demands
the complete surrender of the city, and Ahab submits to the harsh terms, but when the
Syrian king adds humiliation to defeat Ahab calls his leading subjects together, and

fell into his moods of cynical doubt it was not
sufficient to say, "Laugh it off." He knew the
power and limitations of humor as few men did.
It was not enough to bid him be brave. He
manifested a high degree of moral and physical
courage. When despair engulfs, it does not
suffice merely to feed the body and flog the will.

The mind must be fed. And that is what the
Lord did for Elijah on the mount. By watching
the storm, the prophet's eyes were opened to his
own weakness and to the divine source of
strength. The wind, the lightning, the earthquake were reminiscent of his own methods
against Ahab and the Baal priests. But the Lord

2 And he sent messengers to Ahab king of Israel into the city, and said unto him, Thus saith Ben-hadad,

3 Thy silver and thy gold *is* mine; thy wives also and thy children, even the goodliest, *are* mine.

4 And the king of Israel answered and said, My lord, O king, according to thy saying, I *am* thine, and all that I have.

5 And the messengers came again, and said, Thus speaketh Ben-hadad, saying, Although I have sent unto thee, saying, Thou shalt deliver me thy silver, and thy gold, and thy wives, and thy children;

6 Yet I will send my servants unto thee to-morrow about this time, and they shall search thine house, and the houses of thy servants; and it shall be, *that* whatsoever is

and fought against it. 2 And he sent messengers into the city of Ahab king of Israel, and said to him, "Thus says Ben-ha'dad: 3 'Your silver and your gold are mine; your fairest wives and children also are mine.'" 4 And the king of Israel answered, "As you say, my lord, O king, I am yours, and all that I have." 5 The messengers came again, and said, "Thus says Ben-ha'dad: 'I sent to you, saying, "Deliver to me your silver and your gold, your wives and your children"; 6 nevertheless I will send my servants to you tomorrow about this time, and they shall search your house and the houses of your

---

they all agree to resist to the end. Guided by a prophet, Ahab makes a desperate sally with the few troops at his disposal and inflicts a crushing defeat on the too confident Syrian king. Ahab is warned that the Syrians will come again, but he wins another victory, and thus frees himself from vassalage to the Syrians, a state of affairs which he seems to have inherited from his father Omri, who had ceded territory to Syria-Damascus and had been forced even to concede trading rights in Samaria itself.

The major difficulty in chs. 20 and 22 is their relation to the circumstances of the Battle of Qarqar (853 B.C.). Opinion differs widely, but the most probable solution is that the battle was fought within a year or so of Ahab's death, and thus between the dates recorded in ch. 20 and those recorded in ch. 22. This makes Ahab, already free from his vassalage, the willing ally of Ben-hadad (Hadad-ezer) at Qarqar when they fought as leaders of the Aramaean league against the Assyrian Shalmaneser III. The Assyrian king claims that he utterly routed his enemies on that occasion, but he does not appear to have continued his advance. Presumably Ahab took advantage of the respite from Assyrian threats which followed the Battle of Qarqar to continue his anti-Syrian policy and to regain what his father had lost, only to meet with his death in the process (W. O. E. Oesterley and T. H. Robinson, *A History of Israel* [Oxford: Clarendon Press, 1932], I, 292-97).

This chapter comes from a source which is favorable in its judgment of Ahab and antagonistic to the Syrians. This is not the attitude of the narrator of chs. 17–19 or of ch. 21. There we find antagonism to Ahab and all his house, while the Syrians are regarded as being something in the nature of a "rod of the LORD's anger" with which he intends to punish Israel for her waywardness and her apostasy. Here Ahab is the savior of his country, generous, wise, and full of courage (cf. 22:35). In particular, his attitude to a beaten foe is in marked contrast to the ruthlessness of the prophetic party who would have every enemy of the Lord mercilessly destroyed.

20:6. Commentators have found a difficulty in realizing that the second demands of Ben-hadad are more fargoing than the first. The difference between the two is that

---

was not in the noisy phenomena. It was after the **still small voice** (vs. 12) that the divine presence became real. The blustering physical forces were superseded by the quiet spiritual resources. The stormy Elijah was learning the gentleness of true gianthood.

A further step was needed to free Elijah's spirit from bitterness. Having gotten up and looked up, he was now bidden to link up. **Go, return on your way to the wilderness of Damascus** (vs. 15). What awaited him there? New work and new friends. He would anoint Hazael

pleasant in thine eyes, they shall put *it* in their hand, and take *it* away.

7 Then the king of Israel called all the elders of the land, and said, Mark, I pray you, and see how this *man* seeketh mischief: for he sent unto me for my wives, and for my children, and for my silver, and for my gold; and I denied him not.

8 And all the elders and all the people said unto him, Hearken not *unto him,* nor consent.

9 Wherefore he said unto the messengers of Ben-hadad, Tell my lord the king, All that thou didst send for to thy servant at the first I will do: but this thing I may not do. And the messengers departed, and brought him word again.

10 And Ben-hadad sent unto him, and said, The gods do so unto me, and more also, if the dust of Samaria shall suffice for handfuls for all the people that follow me.

11 And the king of Israel answered and said, Tell *him,* Let not him that girdeth on *his harness* boast himself as he that putteth it off.

12 And it came to pass, when *Ben-hadad* heard this message, as he *was* drinking, he and the kings in the pavilions, that he said unto his servants, Set *yourselves in array.* And they set *themselves in array* against the city.

13 ¶ And, behold, there came a prophet unto Ahab king of Israel, saying, Thus saith the LORD, Hast thou seen all this great

servants, and lay hands on whatever pleases them,⁰ and take it away.' "

7 Then the king of Israel called all the elders of the land, and said, "Mark, now, and see how this man is seeking trouble; for he sent to me for my wives and my children, and for my silver and my gold, and I did not refuse him." **8** And all the elders and all the people said to him, "Do not heed or consent." **9** So he said to the messengers of Ben-ha′dad, "Tell my lord the king, 'All that you first demanded of your servant I will do; but this thing I cannot do.' " And the messengers departed and brought him word again. **10** Ben-ha′dad sent to him and said, "The gods do so to me, and more also, if the dust of Samar′ia shall suffice for handfuls for all the people who follow me." **11** And the king of Israel answered, "Tell him, 'Let not him that girds on his armor boast himself as he that puts it off.' " **12** When Ben-ha′dad heard this message as he was drinking with the kings in the booths, he said to his men, "Take your positions." And they took their positions against the city.

13 And behold, a prophet came near to Ahab king of Israel and said, "Thus says

⁰ Gk Syr Vg: Heb *you*

---

the first demands involve a complete surrender, but the second a humiliation to the king and his courtiers such as was not originally intended.

11. Ahab's reply actually consisted of three words only, terse and plain: *'al-yithhallēl ḥôgḥēr kimᵉphatteᵃḥ,* one of those witty proverbial sayings in which all men delight, particularly the men of the desert tradition.

13. God is here represented as being favorable to Ahab and willing to aid him, an attitude very different from that portrayed in the Elijah narratives. The phrase **and you shall know that I am the LORD** is rare outside Ezekiel, where it is found about sixty times. Elsewhere it is found only in the Priestly Code and six other times, of which Exod. 10:2 and this verse are the only two early instances.

---

to be king over Syria and Jehu to be king over Israel. He would find seven thousand of the faithful who had not bowed the knee to Baal. And best of all, he would enter into fellowship with Elisha. The prophet who had been wrapped up in himself, cooped in the cave of self-pity, was to find the enlargement that comes from widened interests. He who had been

vainly trying to put comfort and faith into himself was now to put himself into the work of comforting and encouraging others. In those self-forgetting associations Elijah would find his own spirit reinforced by shoulder-to-shoulder contact in service. The prophet whose courage had ebbed during his lonely picket duty in the mountains was returning to the Lord's army.

multitude? behold, I will deliver it into thine hand this day; and thou shalt know that I *am* the LORD.

14 And Ahab said, By whom? And he said, Thus saith the LORD, *Even* by the young men of the princes of the provinces. Then he said, Who shall order the battle? And he answered, Thou.

15 Then he numbered the young men of the princes of the provinces, and they were two hundred and thirty-two: and after them he numbered all the people, *even* all the children of Israel, *being* seven thousand.

16 And they went out at noon. But Ben-hadad *was* drinking himself drunk in the pavilions, he and the kings, the thirty and two kings that helped him.

17 And the young men of the princes of the provinces went out first; and Ben-hadad sent out, and they told him, saying, There are men come out of Samaria.

18 And he said, Whether they be come out for peace, take them alive; or whether they be come out for war, take them alive.

19 So these young men of the princes of the provinces came out of the city, and the army which followed them.

20 And they slew every one his man: and the Syrians fled; and Israel pursued them: and Ben-hadad the king of Syria escaped on a horse with the horsemen.

21 And the king of Israel went out, and smote the horses and chariots, and slew the Syrians with a great slaughter.

22 ¶ And the prophet came to the king of Israel, and said unto him, Go, strengthen thyself, and mark, and see what thou doest: for at the return of the year the king of Syria will come up against thee.

the LORD, Have you seen all this great multitude? Behold, I will give it into your hand this day; and you shall know that I am the LORD." 14 And Ahab said, "By whom?" He said, "Thus says the LORD, By the servants of the governors of the districts." Then he said, "Who shall begin the battle?" He answered, "You." 15 Then he mustered the servants of the governors of the districts, and they were two hundred and thirty-two; and after them he mustered all the people of Israel, seven thousand.

16 And they went out at noon, while Ben-ha'dad was drinking himself drunk in the booths, he and the thirty-two kings who helped him. 17 The servants of the governors of the districts went out first. And Ben-ha'dad sent out scouts, and they reported to him, "Men are coming out from Sa-mar'ia." 18 He said, "If they have come out for peace, take them alive; or if they have come out for war, take them alive."

19 So these went out of the city, the servants of the governors of the districts, and the army which followed them. 20 And each killed his man; the Syrians fled and Israel pursued them, but Ben-ha'dad king of Syria escaped on a horse with horsemen. 21 And the king of Israel went out, and captured[p] the horses and chariots, and killed the Syrians with a great slaughter.

22 Then the prophet came near to the king of Israel, and said to him, "Come, strengthen yourself, and consider well what you have to do; for in the spring the king of Syria will come up against you."

[p] Gk: Heb *smote*

---

14. The word *medhinôth*, **districts,** is found four times in this chapter, rarely elsewhere out of a Persian context. It is an Aramaic word, and became prevalent in the West because Aramaic was the language which the Persians used in their official dealings with their western provinces. They used the word in the sense of **provinces** and its use in this chapter shows that it had a northern origin. In Syriac and in Arabic the word means "city" and is best known in the form *'el-Medina,* the city par excellence of Islam.

17. It is much better to follow the LXX (cf. RSV) as against the M.T. (cf. KJV).

19. The plan of campaign seems to have been to send out a small force only, but composed of desperate fighting men (cf. the modern commandos) who should seem too insignificant in numbers to disturb the feasting Syrians. These men suddenly attacked the unsuspecting Syrians, threw them into confusion, and were quickly reinforced by the seven thousand men whom Ahab had held in reserve. The plan succeeded beyond Ahab's wildest hopes. The Israelites **captured** (so RSV correctly in vs. 21) the chariotry, and used it with devastating effect on the fleeing enemy.

23 And the servants of the king of Syria said unto him, Their gods *are* gods of the hills; therefore they were stronger than we; but let us fight against them in the plain, and surely we shall be stronger than they.

24 And do this thing, Take the kings away, every man out of his place, and put captains in their rooms:

25 And number thee an army, like the army that thou hast lost, horse for horse, and chariot for chariot: and we will fight against them in the plain, *and* surely we shall be stronger than they. And he hearkened unto their voice, and did so.

26 And it came to pass at the return of the year, that Ben-hadad numbered the Syrians, and went up to Aphek, to fight against Israel.

27 And the children of Israel were numbered, and were all present, and went against them: and the children of Israel pitched before them like two little flocks of kids; but the Syrians filled the country.

28 ¶ And there came a man of God, and spake unto the king of Israel, and said, Thus saith the LORD, Because the Syrians have said, The LORD *is* God of the hills, but he *is* not God of the valleys, therefore will I deliver all this great multitude into thine hand, and ye shall know that I *am* the LORD.

29 And they pitched one over against the other seven days. And *so* it was, that in the seventh day the battle was joined: and the children of Israel slew of the Syrians a hundred thousand footmen in one day.

23 And the servants of the king of Syria said to him, "Their gods are gods of the hills, and so they were stronger than we; but let us fight against them in the plain, and surely we shall be stronger than they. 24 And do this: remove the kings, each from his post, and put commanders in their places; 25 and muster an army like the army that you have lost, horse for horse, and chariot for chariot; then we will fight against them in the plain, and surely we shall be stronger than they." And he hearkened to their voice, and did so.

26 In the spring Ben-ha'dad mustered the Syrians, and went up to Aphek, to fight against Israel. 27 And the people of Israel were mustered, and were provisioned, and went against them; the people of Israel encamped before them like two little flocks of goats, but the Syrians filled the country. 28 And a man of God came near and said to the king of Israel, "Thus says the LORD, 'Because the Syrians have said, "The LORD is a god of the hills but he is not a god of the valleys," therefore I will give all this great multitude into your hand, and you shall know that I am the LORD.'" 29 And they encamped opposite one another seven days. Then on the seventh day the battle was joined; and the people of Israel smote of the Syrians a hundred thousand foot sol-

---

23. Here is the crux of the whole story (cf. vs. 28). The Syrians were guilty of belittling the greatness of Israel's God. They said that the Lord was a god of the hills only, not of the plains. The whole story is an account of the punishment of the impious attitude of the Syrians (cf. II Kings 19:20-34).

26. Hostilities were renewed **at the return of the year,** a phrase which is interpreted in the RSV to mean **in the spring.** This interpretation depends upon the Western practice of waging spring campaigns, a practice which seems to have originated with Caesar in the Gallic Wars. It so happens that the two great modern world wars have begun at the close of the harvest rather than at the beginning of spring. In any case, the time when the kings of the Near East went to war was the autumn (Judg. 6:4, 11; II Sam. 17:19; I Sam. 23:1). They had to wait till the harvest was secured. This was for two reasons. In the first place, these lands were too near to starvation ever to risk the loss of a harvest; in the second place, the able-bodied men would not respond to the call until the harvest was gathered (Snaith, *Jewish New Year Festival,* pp. 32-34).

There is a division of opinion as to whether **Aphek** was in the northern part of the Plain of Sharon, eight miles from the sea and fifteen miles northwest of Samaria, or whether it is an unidentified site in the Plain of Esdraelon.

30 But the rest fled to Aphek, into the city; and *there* a wall fell upon twenty and seven thousand of the men *that were* left. And Ben-hadad fled, and came into the city, into an inner chamber.

31 ¶ And his servants said unto him, Behold now, we have heard that the kings of the house of Israel *are* merciful kings: let us, I pray thee, put sackcloth on our loins, and ropes upon our heads, and go out to the king of Israel: peradventure he will save thy life.

32 So they girded sackcloth on their loins, and *put* ropes on their heads, and came to the king of Israel, and said, Thy servant Ben-hadad saith, I pray thee, let me live. And he said, *Is* he yet alive? he *is* my brother.

33 Now the men did diligently observe whether *any thing would come* from him, and did hastily catch *it:* and they said, Thy brother Ben-hadad. Then he said, Go ye, bring him. Then Ben-hadad came forth to him; and he caused him to come up into the chariot.

34 And *Ben-hadad* said unto him, The cities, which my father took from thy father, I will restore; and thou shalt make streets for thee in Damascus, as my father made in

diers in one day. 30 And the rest fled into the city of Aphek; and the wall fell upon twenty-seven thousand men that were left.

Ben-ha′dad also fled, and entered an inner chamber in the city. 31 And his servants said to him, "Behold now, we have heard that the kings of the house of Israel are merciful kings; let us put sackcloth on our loins and ropes upon our heads, and go out to the king of Israel; perhaps he will spare your life." 32 So they girded sackcloth on their loins, and put ropes on their heads, and went to the king of Israel and said, "Your servant Ben-ha′dad says, 'Pray, let me live.' " And he said, "Does he still live? He is my brother." 33 Now the men were watching for an omen, and they quickly took it up from him and said, "Yes, your brother Ben-ha′dad." Then he said, "Go and bring him." Then Ben-ha′dad came forth to him; and he caused him to come up into the chariot. 34 And Ben-ha′dad said to him, "The cities which my father took from your father I will restore; and you may establish bazaars for yourself in Damascus, as my father did in Samar′ia."

---

30. Could a wall fall and destroy **twenty-seven thousand men?** Most commentators take this literally. On the other hand, the destruction of the city wall is often used to describe the capture of the city, so that the verse may actually mean that this large number of men lost their lives when the city was assaulted and taken.

31. The clothing of the Hebrews in the time of the Egyptian bondage consisted of a loincloth made of *saq.* This was a coarsely woven cloth of goat's or camel's hair, almost black in color (Isa. 50:3; Rev. 6:12). The English "sack" is through the Greek derived from the Semitic word, possibly Egyptian in origin. Since it was the garment which the Hebrews wore in slavery, it became the sign of humiliation, slavery, and misery. The significance of the phrase **ropes upon our heads** is unknown, but it was evidently similar in significance to the wearing of the coarse loincloths. Students of English and French history cannot fail to think of the burghers of Calais who came out to Edward III to surrender the city, with ropes around their necks.

33. The messengers were watching for signs, perhaps after the manner of diviners, but perhaps only as men will watch who know that their own fate and that of all their friends depends upon the slightest word. When they heard Ahab use the word **brother,** they made the most of it. The verb חלט is otherwise unknown, but probably is correctly interpreted by the RSV, **took it up,** i.e., they quickly seized on the word.

34. This verse tells us that Omri had been forced to give up territory to the Syrian king and to grant the Syrians trading facilities in Samaria. It does not necessarily mean that Omri was a vassal to the king of Damascus. On the contrary, such was probably not the case since we know that Omri conquered Moab. The probability is that in Omri's time the Damascus king was satisfied with these concessions, and that the situation deteriorated in the earlier part of Ahab's reign. In any case, the tables were

Samaria. Then *said Ahab,* I will send thee away with this covenant. So he made a covenant with him, and sent him away.

35 ¶ And a certain man of the sons of the prophets said unto his neighbor in the word of the LORD, Smite me, I pray thee. And the man refused to smite him.

36 Then said he unto him, Because thou hast not obeyed the voice of the LORD, behold, as soon as thou art departed from me, a lion shall slay thee. And as soon as he was departed from him, a lion found him, and slew him.

37 Then he found another man, and said, Smite me, I pray thee. And the man smote him, so that in smiting he wounded *him.*

38 So the prophet departed, and waited for the king by the way, and disguised himself with ashes upon his face.

39 And as the king passed by, he cried unto the king: and he said, Thy servant went out into the midst of the battle; and, behold, a man turned aside, and brought a man unto me, and said, Keep this man: if by any means he be missing, then shall thy

And Ahab said, "I will let you go on these terms." So he made a covenant with him and let him go.

35 And a certain man of the sons of the prophets said to his fellow at the command of the LORD, "Strike me, I pray." But the man refused to strike him. 36 Then he said to him, "Because you have not obeyed the voice of the LORD, behold, as soon as you have gone from me, a lion shall kill you." And as soon as he had departed from him, a lion met him and killed him. 37 Then he found another man, and said, "Strike me, I pray." And the man struck him, smiting and wounding him. 38 So the prophet departed, and waited for the king by the way, disguising himself with a bandage over his eyes. 39 And as the king passed, he cried to the king and said, "Your servant went out into the midst of the battle; and behold, a soldier turned and brought a man to me, and said, 'Keep this man; if by any means

completely turned by Ahab, and he secured the return of the territory and the same concessions in Damascus for his merchants that Ben-hadad had previously secured in Samaria.

35-43. This section is not from the same source as the rest of the chapter. It is violently antagonistic to that clemency and generosity which is to us such a welcome feature in Ahab's character as portrayed in the previous verses. It reflects the violent ruthlessness of the prophets during this period, when they were at enmity with Ahab because of the syncretism which he encouraged through his alliances with the neighboring peoples. They demanded an isolationist policy and the merciless destruction of all forms, rites, and individuals who were not loyal to the God of Israel. In this particular case the prophet declares to the king that the ancient ban ought to have been enforced whereby the wholesale slaughter of the enemy was demanded (cf. I Sam. 15:3, 21-23; see Snaith, *Distinctive Ideas of O.T.,* pp. 38-41) .

35. The sons of the prophets (a phrase which first occurs here) are members of the prophetic guilds which flourished at that time, and were fanatical in their exclusive devotion to the Lord. This idiomatic Hebrew phrase denotes members of a class, e.g., when Amos says that he is not the son of a prophet, he is not thereby denying that his father was a prophet. He is denying that he was a member of the prophetic guilds which by that time had fallen into disrepute.

36. The insistence upon the absolute obedience to the word of the prophet is to be seen also in ch. 13, which doubtless is from the same origin as these present verses. The similarity extends even to the death by the lion.

37. This acted symbolism is a feature of the technique of the prophets, partly because of its effectiveness as a means of delivering their message, but also because the doing of it in itself was supposed to have "magic" power in actually bringing their acted word to pass.

39. A talent of silver was worth about sixteen hundred dollars.

life be for his life, or else thou shalt pay a talent of silver.

40 And as thy servant was busy here and there, he was gone. And the king of Israel said unto him, So *shall* thy judgment *be;* thyself hast decided *it.*

41 And he hasted, and took the ashes away from his face; and the king of Israel discerned him that he *was* of the prophets.

42 And he said unto him, Thus saith the LORD, Because thou hast let go out of *thy* hand a man whom I appointed to utter destruction, therefore thy life shall go for his life, and thy people for his people.

43 And the king of Israel went to his house heavy and displeased, and came to Samaria.

21 And it came to pass after these things, *that* Naboth the Jezreelite had a vineyard, which *was* in Jezreel, hard by the palace of Ahab king of Samaria.

he be missing, your life shall be for his life, or else you shall pay a talent of silver.'

40 And as your servant was busy here and there, he was gone." The king of Israel said to him, "So shall your judgment be; you yourself have decided it." **41** Then he made haste to take the bandage away from his eyes; and the king of Israel recognized him as one of the prophets. **42** And he said to him, "Thus says the LORD, 'Because you have let go out of your hand the man whom I had devoted to destruction, therefore your life shall go for his life, and your people for his people.'" **43** And the king of Israel went to his house resentful and sullen, and came to Samar′ia.

21 Now Naboth the Jez′reelite had a vineyard in Jezreel, beside the palace

---

42. For **the man whom I had devoted to destruction** the M.T. has "the man of my ḥěrem," i.e., "ban" (cf. 9:21 and Exeg. on vss. 35-43).

6. NABOTH'S VINEYARD (21:1-29)

Ahab wishes to buy Naboth's vineyard which adjoins his palace in Jezreel. Naboth refuses either to sell or to exchange his ancestral plot of land. Ahab goes home vexed and out of temper, lies down with his face to the wall, and refuses to eat. Jezebel finds him thus, discovers the reason, takes action, and has Naboth condemned and executed, all this on the false charge that he had cursed God and the king. Ahab takes possession of the vineyard, but Elijah hears the whole story and threatens Ahab and all his house. The dogs that licked up the dead Naboth's blood will lick up Ahab's blood. To this there is added an even worse fate for Jezebel, and none of Ahab's race will find rest in a grave. Ahab humbles himself before God, and the doom of his house is postponed for a generation.

a) NABOTH'S REFUSAL (21:1-4)

21:1-4. Naboth refuses to part with his vineyard. This vineyard was Naboth's inheritance from his fathers, the hereditary property of his family. It did not therefore

---

20:40. Too Busy for the Main Business.— When Ahab allowed the Syrian King Ben-hadad to escape he committed a sin in the eyes of Israel's prophets. It seemed to undo the results of the sacrifices already made. It left the enemy of Israel still abroad, with more trouble to be expected. The incidents of the escape form an interesting story, and the ruse by which the prophet revealed the Lord's judgment to Ahab is dramatic. Ahab's treatment of his war prisoner and the prophet's interpretation of the Lord's will need not concern us, for the ethics of the primitive time furnish no adequate precedent for our Christian Era. But the explanation of the escape is of perennial significance: As

your servant was busy here and there, he was gone. The prophet interpreted Ahab's failure to his being too busy with other things, his concern to get back the conquered cities, his interest in new trade and profits from Damascus (vs. 34). Too active in his own pursuits, he allowed his divinely-given opportunity to be lost. Thus embedded in the ancient record is a principle which keeps on causing failure.

Like Ahab, we are often too busy to succeed in our main business because excessive activity keeps us from seeing God's priorities. Our minds are sometimes too active for sleep or for orderly thinking. Trains of thought run through our minds, taking on odd and sundry

2 And Ahab spake unto Naboth, saying, Give me thy vineyard, that I may have it for a garden of herbs, because it *is* near unto my house: and I will give thee for it a better vineyard than it; or, if it seem good to thee, I will give thee the worth of it in money.

3 And Naboth said to Ahab, The Lord forbid it me, that I should give the inheritance of my fathers unto thee.

4 And Ahab came into his house heavy and displeased because of the word which Naboth the Jezreelite had spoken to him: for he had said, I will not give thee the inheritance of my fathers. And he laid him down upon his bed, and turned away his face, and would eat no bread.

of Ahab king of Samar'ia. 2 And after this Ahab said to Naboth, "Give me your vineyard, that I may have it for a vegetable garden, because it is near my house; and I will give you a better vineyard for it; or, if it seems good to you, I will give you its value in money." 3 But Naboth said to Ahab, "The Lord forbid that I should give you the inheritance of my fathers." 4 And Ahab went into his house vexed and sullen because of what Naboth the Jez'reelite had said to him; for he had said, "I will not give you the inheritance of my fathers." And he lay down on his bed, and turned away his face, and would eat no food.

---

belong to Naboth, but to his whole family, past and yet to be born. He was perfectly within his rights in refusing to part with the property. Indeed, properly speaking, he could not do otherwise, neither was any other plot of land a suitable exchange. Ahab here found himself in conflict with ancient custom, the rights of the peasant from time immemorial. Ahab himself seems to have realized that there was nothing further he could do about it, but Jezebel with her highhanded action solved his problem. The price they paid for Naboth's vineyard was to make the prophets the champion of the rights of the common man. There were united against them religious zeal and democratic fervor, always a dangerous and usually an effective combination.

---

passengers, but going round and round over the tracks of fixed ideas, getting nowhere. Our bodies add to the restlessness. Physical motion becomes a substitute for sustained thought. Our eagerness to devour new sensations diverts our attention and deteriorates our thinking into "thobbing," to use Henshaw Ward's word.[4] Or the pressure of things to be done drives us toward distraction. The intoxication of activity keeps us going, without reflection as to why we go or whither we go. Like "homeless, drunken mercenaries," we rush hither and yon, selling our labor for that which is not bread.

Our faith in God through Christ should help us to see the divine pattern for our lives. "Seek ye first the kingdom of God, and his righteousness" (Matt. 6:33). When we take time to see the outlines of the life pattern, God's priorities begin to appear in concrete forms. We are enabled to distinguish ends from means. We recognize God as our master and mammon as our servant. We get a singleness of eye which keeps us from darkening and distracting comparisons (Matt. 6:22). We get a singleness of aim which imparts a sense of direction and a sureness of touch.

In Dickens' *Christmas Carol* the miserly Scrooge is confronted by the ghost of his dead

[4] Cf. Ralph W. Sockman, *Men of the Mysteries* (New York: Abingdon Press, 1927), p. 34.

partner, Jacob Marley, who in life had been as stingy as Scrooge. Now from the realm of shadow Marley's ghost tries to save his partner from his own fate. Scrooge seeks to comfort him by saying, "But you were always a good man of business, Jacob." Whereupon Marley's ghost cries: "Business! Mankind was my business. The common welfare was my business; charity, mercy, forbearance, and benevolence, were, all, my business." Too late he had discovered God's priorities.

Activism also allows opportunity to escape by being too busy to keep God's pace. When Ahab impulsively called Ben-hadad into his chariot, he made hasty judgments and rushed from principle to expediency. When we act on the spur of the moment, we are likely to ride recklessly. "He that believeth shall not make haste" (Isa. 28:16). Faith in God does not ignore the urgency of situations, but it avoids the haste that makes waste. "In returning and rest shall ye be saved; in quietness and in confidence shall be your strength" (Isa. 30:15). The prophet was trying to recall his countrymen from their political expedients to the calm of reasoned judgment and divine trust.

Jesus, like the prophets and psalmists before him, sought to help men keep pace with God. He turned to the restless crowds, tiring themselves by their futile strivings, and said: "Come

5 ¶ But Jezebel his wife came to him, and said unto him, Why is thy spirit so sad, that thou eatest no bread?	5 But Jez'ebel his wife came to him, and said to him, "Why is your spirit so vexed that you eat no food?" 6 And he said to her,
6 And he said unto her, Because I spake unto Naboth the Jezreelite, and said unto him, Give me thy vineyard for money; or else, if it please thee, I will give thee *another* vineyard for it: and he answered, I will not give thee my vineyard.	"Because I spoke to Naboth the Jez'reelite, and said to him, 'Give me your vineyard for money; or else, if it please you, I will give you another vineyard for it'; and he answered, 'I will not give you my vineyard.'"
7 And Jezebel his wife said unto him, Dost thou now govern the kingdom of Israel? arise, *and* eat bread, and let thine heart be merry: I will give thee the vineyard of Naboth the Jezreelite.	7 And Jez'ebel his wife said to him, "Do you now govern Israel? Arise, and eat bread, and let your heart be cheerful; I will give you the vineyard of Naboth the Jez'reelite."
8 So she wrote letters in Ahab's name, and sealed *them* with his seal, and sent the letters unto the elders and to the nobles that *were* in his city, dwelling with Naboth.	8 So she wrote letters in Ahab's name and sealed them with his seal, and she sent the letters to the elders and the nobles who dwelt with Naboth in his city. 9 And she wrote in the letters, "Proclaim a fast, and set Naboth on high among the people;
9 And she wrote in the letters, saying, Proclaim a fast, and set Naboth on high among the people:	

b) Jezebel's Plot (21:5-12)

8. The word *ḥôrîm* means "freeborn," "freedman" in other Semitic languages, but in Hebrew it refers to men of somewhat higher station in life, and even means **nobles.** It is properly an Aramaic word, used in the north, and not appearing in the southern literature until the late period, i.e., the time of Nehemiah. It occurs twice in Jeremiah (27:20; 39:6), but neither of these two passages is found in the LXX (S. R. Driver, *An Introduction to the Literature of the Old Testament* [rev. ed.; New York: Charles Scribner's Sons, 1913], p. 553, n.).

9. A fast is called at a time of grave national emergency, caused by a crime which brings the whole of the people into danger from the anger of God. In the O.T. a fast is called at such a time of crisis, either as a sign of contrition or by way of intercession. It was associated with any period fraught with destiny, when a man believed himself to be close to that borderline which divides this world from the other. Thus, in primitive religion the time of death, i.e., the seven days of death, is a time for fasting (I Sam. 31:13), probably on account of the nearness of the spirit world. The fast which Jezebel proclaimed was destined to prepare the people for the alleged approach of the deity, which in turn is due to a serious crime committed against him. God has drawn near, so that a crisis is at hand. Fasting in worship has the same ancient and primitive origin, though here the custom has been re-explained on more developed spiritual lines.

unto me, all ye that labor and are heavy laden, and I will give you rest. Take my yoke upon you, and learn of me. . . . For my yoke is easy, and my burden is light" (Matt. 11:28-30). The young ox must be "broken" to the yoke. At first it is fractious and fuming, rushing ahead, then holding back, wearing itself sore with the yoke. But eventually it learns the timing of the steady, experienced animal with which it is teamed. So Christ's followers were to be his teammates, falling into step with him, and finding thereby a restful pace. And Jesus' own yoke was easy because he was teamed with the Eternal. He was so at one with his heavenly Father that he took things in God's stride. There was urgency in Jesus' program, "I must work the works of him that sent me, while it is day" (John 9:4). But he did not give the impression of being hurried. He had time to talk with little children, to attend festive occasions, to "come apart and rest awhile." He moved calmly, steadily, "with unperturbèd pace" toward his goal. He did not allow regret for joys that were past or anxiety for troubles ahead

10 And set two men, sons of Belial, before him, to bear witness against him, saying, Thou didst blaspheme God and the king. And *then* carry him out, and stone him, that he may die.

11 And the men of his city, *even* the elders and the nobles who were the inhabitants in his city, did as Jezebel had sent unto them, *and* as it *was* written in the letters which she had sent unto them.

12 They proclaimed a fast, and set Naboth on high among the people.

13 And there came in two men, children of Belial, and sat before him: and the men of Belial witnessed against him, *even* against Naboth, in the presence of the people, saying, Naboth did blaspheme God and the king. Then they carried him forth out of the city, and stoned him with stones, that he died.

10 and set two base fellows opposite him, and let them bring a charge against him, saying, 'You have cursed God and the king.' Then take him out, and stone him to death." 11 And the men of his city, the elders and the nobles who dwelt in his city, did as Jez'ebel had sent word to them. As it was written in the letters which she had sent to them, 12 they proclaimed a fast, and set Naboth on high among the people. 13 And the two base fellows came in and sat opposite him; and the base fellows brought a charge against Naboth, in the presence of the people, saying, "Naboth cursed God and the king." So they took him outside the city, and stoned him to death

10. Two witnesses were essential according to ancient law, laid down clearly and specifically by the Deuteronomists (Deut. 17:6; 19:15; Num. 35:30; cf. also Matt. 26:60; Moses and Elijah [Mark 9:5] are the two witnesses to Messiah).

The phrase **sons of Belial** is generally understood to mean "sons of worthlessness" or **base fellows**, "lewd fellows of the baser sort." If this interpretation is correct, the word **Belial** is a compound word made up of *beli* ("not") and *yā'al* ("profit"), i.e., "good-for-nothings." An alternative derivation produces the meaning "ne'er-do-wells," although Burney is of the opinion that such compound words are late, and that we are here dealing with a word which the Masoretes revocalized. He suggests that the word is connected with the root בלע ("to swallow up"), and therefore means "engulfing ruin" (*Notes on Hebrew Text of Kings*, pp. 245-47).

The Hebrew has "blessed," a euphemism which has been deliberately substituted because even to mention the sin of blasphemy is a sin. The English versions have rightly changed the word back again to **cursed**. (The euphemistic usage is found elsewhere in the O.T., e.g., Job 1:5; 2:5, 9; Ps. 10:5.)

c) NABOTH'S DEATH (21:13-16)

13. Here is the crime of which Naboth is accused (cf. Exod. 22:28). It seems strange to us that so much importance should be attached to a spoken curse, for today

to detract from the present. He was "all there" all the time, living each moment to the full. The present moment is never unbearable; it is the fear of what is coming the next minute or the next month which makes for despair. Since we can do only one thing at a time, we should realize that there is only one thing to do at a time.

> So never be troubled about to-morrow;
> to-morrow will take care of itself.
> (Matt. 6:34 Moffatt.)

When a person is not too busy to see God's priorities and to keep God's pace, then he

makes use of God's power. Activity may be the sign of weakness rather than of strength. The pushing, hurrying, aggressive man may be trying to rush his deal through before its weak points are discovered. He may lack reserve because he is short of reserves. On the other hand, he who is sure that he is on the side of the truth is confident of the future. He frets not because of evildoers, knowing that their way will be soon cut off. He commits his way unto the Lord, confident that "he shall bring it to pass" (Ps. 37:1-5). It is understandable why the thirty-seventh psalm was a favorite of Abraham Lincoln, for only such assurance of divine sup-

14 Then they sent to Jezebel, saying, Naboth is stoned, and is dead.

15 ¶ And it came to pass, when Jezebel heard that Naboth was stoned, and was dead, that Jezebel said to Ahab, Arise, take possession of the vineyard of Naboth the Jezreelite, which he refused to give thee for money: for Naboth is not alive, but dead.

16 And it came to pass, when Ahab heard that Naboth was dead, that Ahab rose up to go down to the vineyard of Naboth the Jezreelite, to take possession of it.

17 ¶ And the word of the Lord came to Elijah the Tishbite, saying,

18 Arise, go down to meet Ahab king of Israel, which is in Samaria: behold, he is in the vineyard of Naboth, whither he is gone down to possess it.

19 And thou shalt speak unto him, saying, Thus saith the Lord, Hast thou killed, and also taken possession? And thou shalt speak unto him, saying, Thus saith the Lord, In the place where dogs licked the blood of Naboth shall dogs lick thy blood, even thine.

with stones. 14 Then they sent to Jez'ebel, saying, "Naboth has been stoned; he is dead."

15 As soon as Jez'ebel heard that Naboth had been stoned and was dead, Jez'ebel said to Ahab, "Arise, take possession of the vineyard of Naboth the Jez'reelite, which he refused to give you for money; for Naboth is not alive, but dead." 16 And as soon as Ahab heard that Naboth was dead, Ahab arose to go down to the vineyard of Naboth the Jez'reelite, to take possession of it.

17 Then the word of the Lord came to Eli'jah the Tishbite, saying, 18 "Arise, go down to meet Ahab king of Israel, who is in Samar'ia; behold, he is in the vineyard of Naboth, where he has gone to take possession. 19 And you shall say to him, 'Thus says the Lord, "Have you killed, and also taken possession?"' And you shall say to him, 'Thus says the Lord: "In the place where dogs licked up the blood of Naboth shall dogs lick your own blood."'"

---

a curse is a curse and nothing more. In the ninth century B.C. ancient ideas concerning curses still held. People believed that a curse, like a blessing, had itself active power and therefore itself caused real damage. The speaking of the curse itself did real harm to the one who was cursed, and even a curse against God was supposed in some strange way to have an effectiveness. Everything therefore had to be done to wipe out him who uttered the curse because of the supposed anger of the Deity, who would certainly take action against this man who sought to inflict harm and damage upon God.

15. According to II Kings 9:26, Naboth's sons were also stoned to death. This was necessary in order to prevent the fulfillment of the curse, since they, being his sons, were regarded as being agents in the matter. Further, from Jezebel's point of view this was necessary in order to enable Ahab to become possessor of the vineyard, possession of which reverted to the crown when there was no heir.

16. According to Josephus (*Antiquities* VIII. 13. 8) "Ahab was glad at what had been done, and rose up immediately from the bed whereon he lay," but the LXX says that he "rent his clothes and put on sackcloth."

d) Elijah's Intervention (21:17-29)

17-29. Vss. 20*b*-22, 24 are the work of the earlier Deuteronomic compiler (*ca.* 610 B.C.). The dynasty of Omri is to be wiped out as the dynasty of Jeroboam son of Nebat was

---

port could have sustained him. The man who is timed to God's pace has the strength which comes from knowing that time is on his side. He does not bluster. He does not impatiently and destructively rush in to root out the tares, but waits for the God of the harvest (Matt. 13:24-30).

Fénelon once pointed out to the Duc de

Chevreuse how distracted was his life, and advised him to begin each morning by quietly running over in his mind the chief things he would probably have to do or be asked to do during the coming day. Then when he came to the actual doing of these things, he would succeed in surrounding each act with an air of leisure. It gives poise to take a preview of each

20 And Ahab said to Elijah, Hast thou found me, O mine enemy? And he answered, I have found *thee:* because thou hast sold thyself to work evil in the sight of the LORD.

21 Behold, I will bring evil upon thee, and will take away thy posterity, and will cut off from Ahab him that pisseth against the wall, and him that is shut up and left in Israel,

22 And will make thine house like the house of Jeroboam the son of Nebat, and like the house of Baasha the son of Ahijah, for the provocation wherewith thou hast provoked *me* to anger, and made Israel to sin.

23 And of Jezebel also spake the LORD, saying, The dogs shall eat Jezebel by the wall of Jezreel.

24 Him that dieth of Ahab in the city the dogs shall eat; and him that dieth in the field shall the fowls of the air eat.

25 ¶ But there was none like unto Ahab, which did sell himself to work wickedness in the sight of the LORD, whom Jezebel his wife stirred up.

26 And he did very abominably in following idols, according to all *things* as did the Amorites, whom the LORD cast out before the children of Israel.

27 And it came to pass, when Ahab heard those words, that he rent his clothes, and put sackcloth upon his flesh, and fasted, and lay in sackcloth, and went softly.

20 Ahab said to Eli′jah, "Have you found me, O my enemy?" He answered, "I have found you, because you have sold yourself to do what is evil in the sight of the LORD. **21** Behold, I will bring evil upon you; I will utterly sweep you away, and will cut off from Ahab every male, bond or free, in Israel; **22** and I will make your house like the house of Jerobo′am the son of Nebat, and like the house of Ba′asha the son of Ahi′jah, for the anger to which you have provoked me, and because you have made Israel to sin. **23** And of Jez′ebel the LORD also said, 'The dogs shall eat Jez′ebel within the bounds of Jezreel.' **24** Anyone belonging to Ahab who dies in the city the dogs shall eat; and anyone of his who dies in the open country the birds of the air shall eat."

25 There was none who sold himself to do what was evil in the sight of the LORD like Ahab, whom Jez′ebel his wife incited. **26** He did very abominably in going after idols, as the Amorites had done, whom the LORD cast out before the people of Israel.

27 And when Ahab heard those words, he rent his clothes, and put sackcloth upon his flesh, and fasted and lay in sackcloth,

---

wiped out, and for the same reason: neither line of kings had been faithful to the Deuteronomic ideas. Vss. 25-26 are also Deuteronomic in tone and style, but come from the later Deuteronomic editor (*ca.* 550 B.C.).

Vs. 23 interrupts the sequence. Possibly it is part of the original story of Naboth and his fate, since it is clear that the action of Jezebel was really the action to which the prophet took such grave exception. It is more likely to be part of the original story

---

day's expected events. It also gives power and responsiveness. With a perspective of God's priorities, and an adjustment to God's pace, we are ready for life's "big moments," whether good or bad, and we are not too busy to succeed in our main business.

The record is that when Ahab recognized the prophet and realized the loss he had suffered, he "went to his house resentful and sullen" (vs. 43). Alongside Ahab, consider a father of our own day. Ambitious to succeed, engrossed in his various pursuits, he neglected to cultivate and enjoy the company of his only son. At twenty

the lad was taken. Imagine the father's anguish as he looked up to God and cried, **As your servant was busy here and there, he was gone.**

21:20. Selling One's Soul.—The evil course of Ahab seemed to reach its nadir in his killing of Naboth in order to get possession of a vineyard. His petty greed, his pliability in the hands of the unscrupulous Jezebel, his permission of the trumped-up charge against Naboth, and his complicity in the execution of the innocent man constitute a chapter of unrelieved blackness. When he saw Elijah approaching, the bloodstained Ahab cried, **Have you found me,**

28 And the word of the LORD came to Elijah the Tishbite, saying,

29 Seest thou how Ahab humbleth himself before me? because he humbleth himself before me, I will not bring the evil in his days: *but* in his son's days will I bring the evil upon his house.

22 And they continued three years without war between Syria and Israel.

2 And it came to pass in the third year, that Jehoshaphat the king of Judah came down to the king of Israel.

and went about dejectedly. 28 And the word of the LORD came to Eli'jah the Tishbite, saying, 29 "Have you seen how Ahab has humbled himself before me? Because he has humbled himself before me, I will not bring the evil in his days; but in his son's days I will bring the evil upon his house."

22 For three years Syria and Israel continued without war. 2 But in the third year Jehosh'aphat the king of Judah

---

than an interpolation based on II Kings 9:36, especially since there is evidence both in vss. 27-29 and in the LXX statement in vs. 16 that Ahab clothed himself in sackcloth and ashes, and showed true and real repentance. There is no need at all to assume that the penitence of Ahab was not real.

7. AHAB'S LAST BATTLE (22:1-40)

Apparently part of the territory which Ben-hadad of Syria-Damascus ought to have returned to Ahab after the battle of Aphek (20:34) included Ramoth-gilead. Ahab takes steps to secure the return of this city, important because of its proximity to the eastern caravan route through Gilead. Ahab commands his vassal, Jehoshaphat of Judah, to join him. The Judahite king wishes to consult the prophets over the wisdom of the venture, and they all with one accord prophesy victory. But there is one prophet, Micaiah, whom Ahab has not called, because his oracles are consistently unfavorable to the king. Micaiah is called. He prophesies the death of Ahab and the defeat of Israel. Ahab takes every precaution to prevent the fulfillment of the prophet's words, even to requesting that Jehoshaphat, his vassal, wear his armor. But an archer shoots an arrow without taking particular aim, and Ahab, dressed as a common chariot soldier, is pierced and slain. The dogs of Samaria lick up his blood, and the Deuteronomist adds his customary obituary notice.

In the LXX and Lucian this chapter follows ch. 20, since they have placed ch. 21 after ch. 19. This arrangement is much sounder, since chs. 20 and 22 both tell of Ahab's wars with Ben-hadad of Syria-Damascus.

22:1. The Assyrian menace has passed with the Battle of Qarqar, and Ahab renews his wars against Syria, seeking to repossess all that his father had lost. It appears that Ben-hadad had not fulfilled his promise to give Ramoth-gilead back to Ahab, so Ahab proceeds to take it. Josephus (*Antiquities* VIII. 15. 3) makes the explicit statement that Ben-hadad had taken this city from Omri.

2. Jehoshaphat of Judah comes to Ahab of Israel at the latter's bidding. This involves vassalage on the part of Jehoshaphat. Such a state of affairs is confirmed by

---

O my enemy? To a guilty conscience the prophet of God always looks like an enemy. And Elijah replied, **I have found you, because you have sold yourself to do what is evil in the sight of the LORD.**

Ahab had sold his soul for the price of his neighbor's vineyard. Our minds are arrested by the thought of selling our souls outright as in this case, or as did Faust in the familiar legend, or as George Eliot's Silas Marner sold his soul for his pile of gold, or as did Cardinal Wolsey

for political power. When we contemplate such dramatic cases, we say at once, "What a bad bargain!" The agonized cry of Faust as he contemplates the thought of eternal hell which awaits him, and the mournful soliloquy of Wolsey as he considers the present hell which he has brought on himself, haunt us. Some hold that if we would stress, as our grandfathers did, the dread judgment laid up for such sinners, we could restrain the current trends to evil. But one wonders whether it is the severity

3 And the king of Israel said unto his servants, Know ye that Ramoth in Gilead *is* ours, and we *be* still, *and* take it not out of the hand of the king of Syria?

4 And he said unto Jehoshaphat, Wilt thou go with me to battle to Ramoth-gilead? And Jehoshaphat said to the king of Israel, I *am* as thou *art,* my people as thy people, my horses as thy horses.

5 And Jehoshaphat said unto the king of Israel, Inquire, I pray thee, at the word of the LORD to-day.

6 Then the king of Israel gathered the prophets together, about four hundred men, and said unto them, Shall I go against Ramoth-gilead to battle, or shall I forbear? And they said, Go up; for the Lord shall deliver *it* into the hand of the king.

7 And Jehoshaphat said, *Is there* not here a prophet of the LORD besides, that we might inquire of him?

8 And the king of Israel said unto Jehoshaphat, *There is* yet one man, Micaiah the son of Imlah, by whom we may inquire of the LORD: but I hate him; for he doth not prophesy good concerning me, but evil.

came down to the king of Israel. 3 And the king of Israel said to his servants, "Do you know that Ramoth-gilead belongs to us, and we keep quiet and do not take it out of the hand of the king of Syria?" 4 And he said to Jehosh'aphat, "Will you go with me to battle at Ramoth-gilead?" And Jehosh'aphat said to the king of Israel, "I am as you are, my people as your people, my horses as your horses."

5 And Jehosh'aphat said to the king of Israel, "Inquire first for the word of the LORD." 6 Then the king of Israel gathered the prophets together, about four hundred men, and said to them, "Shall I go to battle against Ramoth-gilead, or shall I forbear?" And they said, "Go up; for the Lord will give it into the hand of the king." 7 But Jehosh'aphat said, "Is there not here another prophet of the LORD of whom we may inquire?" 8 And the king of Israel said to Jehosh'aphat, "There is yet one man by whom we may inquire of the LORD, Micai'ah the son of Imlah; but I hate him, for

---

the part that the Judean king plays in the battle, where the LXX says correctly that Ahab caused Jehoshaphat to array himself in his (Ahab's) robes. This is really clear from the M.T. in vs. 32, where it is evident that the Syrians thought they were attacking Ahab himself, and it was only when Jehoshaphat cried out that they realized their error.

4. The **horses** mentioned here were not riding horses, but chariot horses, since the Hebrew word is סוס, not פרש.

6. The different point of view from that of ch. 18 is plain. Ahab can call upon four hundred prophets of the Lord who are favorable to him and fully loyal. There is but one prophet who takes the attitude which Elijah took, one of antagonism to the house of Ahab, and this prophet is a certain Micaiah ben Imlah.

---

of the punishment or the subtlety of the selling which needs to be watched and emphasized. We can lose possession of our souls without selling them outright.

For instance, we may gradually lose possession of our souls by mortgaging them. We do something shady. Somebody "gets something" on us, as we say, and that gives him a hold over us. It is like a mortgage plastered on our personalities. In the presence of some people we cannot call our souls our own, because we have done things which keep us from being our true selves. Take the case of a teacher. As such, he is dedicated to the imparting of truth. But the school where he teaches is subjected to certain pressure groups which insist that he shall give a desired color to the content of his teaching.

In order to hold his position he gives consideration to pleasing those groups. Thereupon he ceases to be the free agent that Spinoza was when he refused to accept the chair of philosophy at Heidelberg because it might curb his independence of thought. Or consider a minister of the gospel. As a minister, he is ordained to preach the word of God as sincerely as he can know it. But he asks himself, "What good is it to proclaim God's word if I have few to hear it? Am I not the pastor of a congregation, and must I not seek to give my message in such a way that it will win acceptance by my people?" Yet in trying to get his words across, it is so easy to allow his concern for their acceptability to soften the truth! To be a servant of one's parishioners and also a prophet of one's God is

And Jehoshaphat said, Let not the king say so.

9 Then the king of Israel called an officer, and said, Hasten *hither* Micaiah the son of Imlah.

10 And the king of Israel and Jehoshaphat the king of Judah sat each on his throne, having put on their robes, in a void place in the entrance of the gate of Samaria; and all the prophets prophesied before them.

11 And Zedekiah the son of Chenaanah made him horns of iron: and he said, Thus saith the Lord, With these shalt thou push the Syrians, until thou have consumed them.

12 And all the prophets prophesied so, saying, Go up to Ramoth-gilead, and prosper: for the Lord shall deliver *it* into the king's hand.

13 And the messenger that was gone to call Micaiah spake unto him, saying, Behold now, the words of the prophets *declare* good unto the king with one mouth: let thy word,

he never prophesies good concerning me, but evil." And Jehosh'aphat said, "Let not the king say so." 9 Then the king of Israel summoned an officer and said, "Bring quickly Micai'ah the son of Imlah." 10 Now the king of Israel and Jehosh'aphat the king of Judah were sitting on their thrones, arrayed in their robes, at the threshing floor at the entrance of the gate of Samar'ia; and all the prophets were prophesying before them. 11 And Zedeki'ah the son of Chena'anah made for himself horns of iron, and said, "Thus says the Lord, 'With these you shall push the Syrians until they are destroyed.'" 12 And all the prophets prophesied so, and said, "Go up to Ramoth-gilead and triumph; the Lord will give it into the hand of the king."

13 And the messenger who went to summon Micai'ah said to him, "Behold, the words of the prophets with one accord are

---

10. The two kings sit in state, each one in his royal robes, in the entrance of the city gate, the traditional place for judgment from early times (Amos 5:15; Ruth 4:1). The M.T. has **at the threshing floor** (RSV), for which the KJV reads **in a void place,** making the best of the difficulty. Some translators omit the word, for they regard it, perhaps correctly, as an accidental repetition by dittography, בגרן being a "corrected" repetition of בגדם.

11. Here once more we have the "symbolic" actions of the prophets, the very performance of which ensures the future fulfillment of what is portrayed.

---

no easy task, and unless one is very careful he lets the people he serves put a mortgage on his soul.

But this process of selling one's soul is still more subtle. One can lose possession of it merely by keeping quiet. When Job was trying to prove his integrity, he climaxed the evidence of his honesty by saying that he never "kept quiet within doors, afraid of what the crowd would say" (Job 31:34 Moffatt). Sometimes we discover that silence is golden because it pays profits in popularity. Perhaps one is too respectable to run away from a moral fight after it has begun, but he just goes down another street where he will not see it. It was said of a certain diplomat that he knew how to be silent in six languages. We may rationalize our cowardice by calling it diplomacy, or discretion, or tact, for many and subtle are the ways of selling our souls through silence.

Still other aspects involve us in soul selling.

Sinclair Lewis once declared that more good causes had been hindered by the excuse "But I have a wife and children" than by any other single alibi. Most of us are members of families. How can we follow our own clear line of duty without sacrificing the interests of those who lean on us? We are executives of corporations. How can we be loyal to our employees, our stockholders, and the general public? We are citizens of a nation. How can we be loyal to the country that protects us, and yet not sell our souls by participating in governmental programs which seem wrong to us? These are some of the problems we face and the solution is not easy.

Our guiding principle is to have a sovereign loyalty which heads the hierarchy of our other loyalties. Christ insisted that his followers put him and his kingdom first. "He that loveth father or mother more than me is not worthy of me: and he that loveth son or daughter more

I pray thee, be like the word of one of them, and speak *that which is* good.

14 And Micaiah said, *As* the LORD liveth, what the LORD saith unto me, that will I speak.

15 ¶ So he came to the king. And the king said unto him, Micaiah, shall we go against Ramoth-gilead to battle, or shall we forbear? And he answered him, Go, and prosper: for the LORD shall deliver *it* into the hand of the king.

16 And the king said unto him, How many times shall I adjure thee that thou tell me nothing but *that which is* true in the name of the LORD?

17 And he said, I saw all Israel scattered upon the hills, as sheep that have not a shepherd: and the LORD said, These have no master: let them return every man to his house in peace.

18 And the king of Israel said unto Jehoshaphat, Did I not tell thee that he would prophesy no good concerning me, but evil?

19 And he said, Hear thou therefore the word of the LORD: I saw the LORD sitting on

favorable to the king; let your word be like the word of one of them, and speak favorably." 14 But Micai'ah said, "As the LORD lives, what the LORD says to me, that I will speak." 15 And when he had come to the king, the king said to him, "Micai'ah, shall we go to Ramoth-gilead to battle, or shall we forbear?" And he answered him, "Go up and triumph; the LORD will give it into the hand of the king." 16 But the king said to him, "How many times shall I adjure you that you speak to me nothing but the truth in the name of the LORD?" 17 And he said, "I saw all Israel scattered upon the mountains, as sheep that have no shepherd; and the LORD said, 'These have no master; let each return to his home in peace.'" 18 And the king of Israel said to Jehosh'aphat, "Did I not tell you that he would not prophesy good concerning me, but evil?" 19 And Micai'ah said, "Therefore hear the word of the LORD: I saw the LORD sitting

---

14. This is the word of the true prophet, who will speak only the true word of the Lord to him. He is influenced neither by kings nor by majorities. When Micaiah gives a favorable oracle (vs. 15), Ahab is immediately suspicious of it. He knows his man.

17. Micaiah now gives his true oracle, prophesying the doom of Ahab. The oracle is composed in the customary rhythmical and poetical form, being in a 2+2 meter. Micaiah is made to speak this true oracle by the oath with which Ahab adjures him. He can do no other than say exactly what he believes to be the truth.

19. The reference to the angelic host, attendant upon the Lord as he sits on his heavenly throne, as **the host of heaven** is unusual in the books of Kings, where this phrase normally refers to the stars (see II Kings 17:16). We have therefore additional evidence here of the different source from which the material in this chapter has been taken.

---

than me is not worthy of me" (Matt. 10:37). There may be times when our loyalty to Christ seems to work hardship on members of our families. There may come times when the conscientious follower of Christ seems to run counter to what the majority of his countrymen think is good citizenship. But in the long run the person who uses his best intelligence in being loyal to Christ never proves a poor father, a poor husband, or a poor patriot. Those who follow Christ to the end never feel that they have sold their souls.

22:14, 23. *True and False Prophets.*—The charge that religious faith is the manifestation of wishful thinking is refuted by the record of

the true prophets of God, whose pronouncements so frequently ran counter to popular demand. **Micaiah said, "As the LORD lives, what the LORD says to me, that I will speak"** (vs. 14). Micaiah was no sycophant, no private chaplain to the privileged. His sturdy independence stood foursquare to the passing winds. He was not a weather vane, but a guidepost. But Ahab's court did contain its quota of false prophets. **The LORD has put a lying spirit in the mouth of all these your prophets** (vs. 23). The explanation of this **lying spirit** as sent of God represents a stage in the developing conception of monotheism. We no longer read such human deceitfulness into God's purpose. In Ahab's day,

his throne, and all the host of heaven standing by him on his right hand and on his left.

20 And the LORD said, Who shall persuade Ahab, that he may go up and fall at Ramoth-gilead? And one said on this manner, and another said on that manner.

21 And there came forth a spirit, and stood before the LORD, and said, I will persuade him.

22 And the LORD said unto him, Wherewith? And he said, I will go forth, and I will be a lying spirit in the mouth of all his prophets. And he said, Thou shalt persuade *him,* and prevail also: go forth, and do so.

23 Now therefore, behold, the LORD hath put a lying spirit in the mouth of all these thy prophets, and the LORD hath spoken evil concerning thee.

24 But Zedekiah the son of Chenaanah went near, and smote Micaiah on the cheek, and said, Which way went the Spirit of the LORD from me to speak unto thee?

on his throne, and all the host of heaven standing beside him on his right hand and on his left; 20 and the LORD said, 'Who will entice Ahab, that he may go up and fall at Ramoth-gilead?' And one said one thing, and another said another. 21 Then a spirit came forward and stood before the LORD, saying, 'I will entice him.' 22 And the LORD said to him, 'By what means?' And he said, 'I will go forth, and will be a lying spirit in the mouth of all his prophets.' And he said, 'You are to entice him, and you shall succeed; go forth and do so.' 23 Now therefore behold, the LORD has put a lying spirit in the mouth of all these your prophets; the LORD has spoken evil concerning you."

24 Then Zedeki'ah the son of Chena'anah came near and struck Micai'ah on the cheek, and said, "How did the Spirit of the

---

20-24. The problem of the false prophet is one of the most difficult in the O.T. The court prophets were doubtless honest men whose zeal for their country and whose devotion to the successful Ahab made them sure of Ahab's victory. They believed this to be the veritable word of the Lord. Further, even Micaiah, who knew that their message was false, believed that since they were prophets they were actually speaking the word which God had given to them. That is what the prophet does when he speaks. The explanation given, therefore, is that God had deliberately deceived them in order to lure Ahab to his death. It is evidence of various stages in the development of man's ideas about God. The author, equally with Micaiah, believed that all prophecy had a more-than-human origin. If the man himself is in control of his faculties, the word is his and so are the actions. But if a man is not in control of his own faculties, e.g., a prophet in his ecstasy or perhaps a well-known prophet under all circumstances, then either the word of the prophet is the word of the Lord or else it is a message from some spirit alien to God. The prophet Micaiah is enough of a monotheist to reject the idea of any prophetic inspiration in Israel other than that which has been inspired by the God of Israel, so he has to say that the Lord deliberately **put a lying spirit in the mouth of all these your prophets** (vs. 23). By the next century, in the time of Amos, such an answer could scarcely be possible. Yet Jeremiah, in the late seventh century, can talk of God deceiving him when the expected result does not come to pass (Jer. 20:7). Even Paul is not wholly emancipated from this strange way of thinking (II Thess. 2:11-12). The solution of I John 4:1 is that some spirits are not under God's control. The full development in the O.T. is that true prophecy is inspired by "the Spirit of the LORD," *rûaḥ 'adhônāy,* and it is this phrase which foreshadows in the O.T. the Holy Spirit of the

---

as in ours, there are representatives of religion who, like Tito in George Eliot's *Romola,* get "employed everywhere because they are tools with smooth handles."

The world pays high tribute to religion's power by seeking the pulpit's support for almost

every secular cause; but it takes a terrific toll from the church when it lures her preachers as spokesmen for so many secondary and spurious causes. It is one thing to be used of truth; it is quite another to have one's voice and office used to give partisan and passing causes the

25 And Micaiah said, Behold, thou shalt see in that day, when thou shalt go into an inner chamber to hide thyself.

26 And the king of Israel said, Take Micaiah, and carry him back unto Amon the governor of the city, and to Joash the king's son;

27 And say, Thus saith the king, Put this *fellow* in the prison, and feed him with bread of affliction and with water of affliction, until I come in peace.

28 And Micaiah said, If thou return at all in peace, the LORD hath not spoken by me. And he said, Hearken, O people, every one of you.

29 So the king of Israel and Jehoshaphat the king of Judah went up to Ramoth-gilead.

30 And the king of Israel said unto Jehoshaphat, I will disguise myself, and enter into the battle; but put thou on thy robes. And the king of Israel disguised himself, and went into the battle.

31 But the king of Syria commanded his thirty and two captains that had rule over his chariots, saying, Fight neither with small nor great, save only with the king of Israel.

32 And it came to pass, when the captains of the chariots saw Jehoshaphat, that they

LORD go from me to speak to you?" 25 And Micai'ah said, "Behold, you shall see on that day when you go into an inner chamber to hide yourself." 26 And the king of Israel said, "Seize Micai'ah, and take him back to Amon the governor of the city and to Jo'ash the king's son; 27 and say, 'Thus says the king, "Put this fellow in prison, and feed him with scant fare of bread and water, until I come in peace."'" 28 And Micai'ah said, "If you return in peace, the LORD has not spoken by me." And he said, "Hear, all you peoples!"

29 So the king of Israel and Jehosh'aphat the king of Judah went up to Ramoth-gilead. 30 And the king of Israel said to Jehosh'aphat, "I will disguise myself and go into battle, but you wear your robes." And the king of Israel disguised himself and went into battle. 31 Now the king of Syria had commanded the thirty-two captains of his chariots, "Fight with neither small nor great, but only with the king of Israel." 32 And when the captains of the

---

N.T., and ultimately the Third Person of the Trinity of Christian doctrine (N. H. Snaith, "The Spirit of God in Jewish Thought," *The Doctrine of the Holy Spirit* [London: Epworth Press, 1937], pp. 11-21, especially p. 17). The use of the phrase "the Spirit of the LORD" to denote true prophecy may be seen in vs. 24. Zedekiah smites Micaiah on the cheek and demands of him what authority he has to say that he (Micaiah) is right and all the rest of them wrong. The way Zedekiah puts the question is **How did the Spirit of the LORD go from me to speak to you?**

28. The concluding phrase **and he said, "Hear, all you peoples"** is not found in the LXX, but it is a quotation from the opening words of Micah (1:2), inserted on account of a wrong identification of Micaiah ben Imlah with Micah of Moresheth-gath.

31. The command to attack Ahab only is partly a recognition of the skill and prowess of Ahab as soldier and general, but partly also due to the idea that if "the light of Israel" fails, then Israel fails also (cf. II Sam. 21:17). The welfare of the nation is identified with the welfare of the king (see also Exeg. on 11:36).

32. Instead of **turned . . . against him,** it is better to follow the LXX and the parallel II Chr. 18:31, reading "surrounded him." The variation in the Hebrew is small (יסבו for יסרו).

---

semblance of divine truth. There have been few rulers so perverse and few causes so corrupting that they have not found some ecclesiastical supporters to pronounce a blessing upon them. A minister may have sufficient independence to

resist a single royal patron, as Micaiah defied Ahab, and yet sell his soul in the markets of popular patronage. The pulpit is in more danger of bartering away its freedom by catering to the public than by submitting to govern-

said, Surely it *is* the king of Israel. And they turned aside to fight against him: and Jehoshaphat cried out.

33 And it came to pass, when the captains of the chariots perceived that it *was* not the king of Israel, that they turned back from pursuing him.

34 And a *certain* man drew a bow at a venture, and smote the king of Israel between the joints of the harness: wherefore he said unto the driver of his chariot, Turn thine hand, and carry me out of the host; for I am wounded.

35 And the battle increased that day: and the king was stayed up in his chariot against the Syrians, and died at even: and the blood ran out of the wound into the midst of the chariot.

36 And there went a proclamation throughout the host about the going down of the sun, saying, Every man to his city, and every man to his own country.

37 ¶ So the king died, and was brought to Samaria; and they buried the king in Samaria.

38 And *one* washed the chariot in the pool of Samaria; and the dogs licked up his blood; and they washed his armor; according unto the word of the Lord which he spake.

39 Now the rest of the acts of Ahab, and all that he did, and the ivory house which

chariots saw Jehosh'aphat, they said, "It is surely the king of Israel." So they turned to fight against him; and Jehosh'aphat cried out. **33** And when the captains of the chariots saw that it was not the king of Israel, they turned back from pursuing him. **34** But a certain man drew his bow at a venture, and struck the king of Israel between the scale armor and the breastplate; therefore he said to the driver of his chariot, "Turn about, and carry me out of the battle, for I am wounded." **35** And the battle grew hot that day, and the king was propped up in his chariot facing the Syrians, until at evening he died; and the blood of the wound flowed into the bottom of the chariot. **36** And about sunset a cry went through the army, "Every man to his city, and every man to his country!"

37 So the king died, and was brought to Samar'ia; and they buried the king in Samar'ia. **38** And they washed the chariot by the pool of Samar'ia, and the dogs licked up his blood, and the harlots washed themselves in it, according to the word of the Lord which he had spoken. **39** Now the rest of the acts of Ahab, and all that he did, and

---

34. The archer **drew his bow at a venture**, i.e., without aiming it. But it was not by chance that the arrow sped on its way and pierced Ahab apparently in the abdomen. The arrow was guided, so the thought of the time and of the author would say, by that word of God which the prophet Micaiah ben Imlah had spoken. That word was an effective word and, in spite of all that Ahab did, it accomplished its fulfillment.

38. This verse is from the same source as 21:19. The M.T. states quite definitely and clearly that it was at **the pool of Samaria**, where **the harlots washed themselves**. However, the Targ., the Vulg., and the Syriac have taken the Hebrew הזנות (**the harlots**) to be the Aramaic and rabbinical Hebrew word זינא ("armor"). This was probably done for propriety's sake, and this rendering has been followed by the KJV, **and they washed his armor.** There is no doubt of the correctness of the RSV, for the Hebrew verb רחץ is used exclusively of washing flesh, either a part of the human body or the flesh portion of a sacrifice.

39-40. The usual Deuteronomic obituary notice, including the name of the dead king's successor. Ahab was a great builder, and set the fashion of building those ivory

---

mental pressure, real as this latter peril is. When people seem to prefer a religious message which makes them feel good rather than one which makes them be good, it is easy for the preacher

to allow concern for the reception of his message to dull the edge of its thrust.

Ahab was seeking prophets to give him what he wanted. How commonly we hear, "If the

he made, and all the cities that he built, *are* they not written in the book of the Chronicles of the kings of Israel?

40 So Ahab slept with his fathers; and Ahaziah his son reigned in his stead.

41 ¶ And Jehoshaphat the son of Asa began to reign over Judah in the fourth year of Ahab king of Israel.

42 Jehoshaphat *was* thirty and five years old when he began to reign; and he reigned twenty and five years in Jerusalem. And his mother's name *was* Azubah the daughter of Shilhi.

43 And he walked in all the ways of Asa his father; he turned not aside from it, doing *that which was* right in the eyes of the LORD: nevertheless the high places were not taken away; *for* the people offered and burnt incense yet in the high places.

44 And Jehoshaphat made peace with the king of Israel.

45 Now the rest of the acts of Jehoshaphat, and his might that he showed, and how he warred, *are* they not written in the book of the Chronicles of the kings of Judah?

the ivory house which he built, and all the cities that he built, are they not written in the Book of the Chronicles of the Kings of Israel? 40 So Ahab slept with his fathers; and Ahazi'ah his son reigned in his stead.

41 Jehosh'aphat the son of Asa began to reign over Judah in the fourth year of Ahab king of Israel. 42 Jehosh'aphat was thirty-five years old when he began to reign, and he reigned twenty-five years in Jerusalem. His mother's name was Azu'bah the daughter of Shilhi. 43 He walked in all the way of Asa his father; he did not turn aside from it, doing what was right in the sight of the LORD; yet the high places were not taken away, and the people still sacrificed and burned incense on the high places. 44 Jehosh'aphat also made peace with the king of Israel.

45 Now the rest of the acts of Jehosh'aphat, and his might that he showed, and how he warred, are they not written in the Book of the Chronicles of the Kings of

houses which a century later the wealthy magnates of Amos' time favored (Amos 3:15). Additional evidence as to Ahab's prowess in this respect is to be seen in the LXX[A] of Jer. 22:15, where the reading is, "Shalt thou be king because thou dost eagerly strive to excel Ahab?" The preceding verses make it clear that the reference is to building. See also Ps. 45:9, which may well be connected with the marriage of Ahab and Jezebel (cf. the reference to "the daughter of Tyre" in vs. 12).

D. THE ELISHA NARRATIVES (I Kings 22:41–II Kings 8:29)

1. JEHOSHAPHAT OF JUDAH (22:41-50)

The major events of the reign of Jehoshaphat have already been mentioned in the story of Ahab and Ramoth-gilead. This fact was due to the custom of the Deuteronomic editor who deals wholly with the life of one king before he turns back to the reigns of the kings who have meanwhile succeeded in the other kingdom. Most of these verses are from the hand of the editor and contain the usual introductory and obituary notices proper to a king of Judah. Vss. 46-49 are from the annals. From them we learn that Edom was vassal to Jehoshaphat, and that a disastrous attempt was made to open up once more that foreign trade with the East, based at Ezion-geber at the head of the Gulf of Aqabah, which had brought great profit and luxury to Solomon.

church would give me what I want, I would attend its services." Religion, however, cannot be sold on the department store principle that the customer is always right. Ahab got from the false prophets the message which he liked, and it led to the loss of his life. People think they know what they want; they do not always know

what they need. And the minister's prophetic function is to lead men from what they want to what they need.

In 1940 the editors of *Fortune* chided the church's shepherds with following rather than leading their flocks. The result, they said, was a vicious spiral of spiritual disillusionment. And

46 And the remnant of the sodomites, which remained in the days of his father Asa, he took out of the land.

47 *There was* then no king in Edom: a deputy *was* king.

48 Jehoshaphat made ships of Tharshish to go to Ophir for gold: but they went not; for the ships were broken at Ezion-geber.

49 Then said Ahaziah the son of Ahab unto Jehoshaphat, Let my servants go with thy servants in the ships. But Jehoshaphat would not.

50 ¶ And Jehoshaphat slept with his fathers, and was buried with his fathers in the city of David his father: and Jehoram his son reigned in his stead.

51 ¶ Ahaziah the son of Ahab began to reign over Israel in Samaria the seventeenth year of Jehoshaphat king of Judah, and reigned two years over Israel.

52 And he did evil in the sight of the LORD, and walked in the way of his father, and in the way of his mother, and in the way of Jeroboam the son of Nebat, who made Israel to sin:

53 For he served Baal, and worshipped him, and provoked to anger the LORD God of Israel, according to all that his father had done.

Judah? **46** And the remnant of the male cult prostitutes who remained in the days of his father Asa, he exterminated from the land.

47 There was no king in Edom; a deputy was king. **48** Jehosh'aphat made ships of Tarshish to go to Ophir for gold; but they did not go, for the ships were wrecked at E'zion-ge'ber. **49** Then Ahazi'ah the son of Ahab said to Jehosh'aphat, "Let my servants go with your servants in the ships," but Jehosh'aphat was not willing. **50** And Jehosh'aphat slept with his fathers, and was buried with his fathers in the city of David his father; and Jeho'ram his son reigned in his stead.

51 Ahazi'ah the son of Ahab began to reign over Israel in Samar'ia in the seventeenth year of Jehosh'aphat king of Judah, and he reigned two years over Israel. **52** He did what was evil in the sight of the LORD, and walked in the way of his father, and in the way of his mother, and in the way of Jerobo'am the son of Nebat, who made Israel to sin. **53** He served Ba'al and worshiped him, and provoked the LORD, the God of Israel, to anger in every way that his father had done.

47-50. These verses are not found in the LXX MSS, except in Codex A. The reference there, however, is to one ship only. The statement in the M.T. that the deputy was king in Edom, following immediately after the statement that there was no king, is strange though intelligible. It can be taken to mean that there was no native Edomite king reigning, but that Jehoshaphat's deputy reigned in his stead. Bernhard Stade (*The Books of Kings,* tr. R. E. Brünnow and Paul Haupt [Leipzig: J. C. Hinrichs, 1914; "The Sacred Books of the Old Testament"], *ad loc.*) has proposed a reconstruction of vss. 47-48 as follows: "There was no king in Edom, and the deputy of King Jehoshaphat made a ship. . . ."

51-53. The chapter concludes with the formal Deuteronomic introduction of the reign of Ahaziah of Israel. The story of Ahaziah is carried on in an excerpt from the prophetic tales of the north (see II Kings 1:17-18).

---

this was the conclusion: "There is only one way out of the spiral. The way out is the sound of a voice, not our voice, but a voice coming from something not ourselves, in the existence of which we cannot disbelieve. It is the earthly task of the pastors to hear this voice, to cause us to hear it, and to tell us what it says." [5] Micaiah

was dedicated to hear and interpret this divine voice. **What the LORD says to me, that will I speak.** When Micaiah spoke, he received a brutal blow on the cheek and a sentence to prison. But his word would have saved Ahab, as many another life may be saved if the chastening word that comes from God is heard and heeded.

[5] Vol. XXI, p. 27.

II KINGS

TEXT, EXEGESIS, AND EXPOSITION

1 Then Moab rebelled against Israel after the death of Ahab.

2 And Ahaziah fell down through a lattice in his upper chamber that *was* in Samaria, and was sick: and he sent messengers, and said unto them, Go, inquire of Baal-zebub the god of Ekron whether I shall recover of this disease.

1 After the death of Ahab, Moab rebelled against Israel.

2 Now Ahazi'ah fell through the lattice in his upper chamber in Samar'ia, and lay sick; so he sent messengers, telling them, "Go, inquire of Ba'al-ze'bub, the god of Ekron, whether I shall recover from this

2. AHAZIAH OF ISRAEL (II Kings 1:1-18)

1:1. A fuller account of Jehoram's abortive attempt to reconquer Moab is to be found in 3:4-27—a story taken from a source akin to that of I Kings 22:1-37. All these stories portray an interest in the north not shared by the 610 B.C. compiler. According to the Moabite stone (King Mesha's own account of the revolt), Moab revolted from Israelite suzerainty during the time of Omri's son, but Ahaziah's reign was so short that the variation is of no great account.

2-17a. Ahaziah falls through a lattice in the upper chamber of his palace and receives severe injuries. He sends to the shrine at Ekron to inquire whether he will recover. The messengers are met by Elijah, who is full of wrath because the king has sent to this heathen shrine and not to the Lord. Elijah resists capture at the hands of bodies of troops sent to arrest him, and finally goes to the king and foretells his death. This doom is fulfilled, and the chapter concludes with a Deuteronomic obituary notice and a formal note of the name of the successor.

2. The ʿaliyyāh (**upper chamber**) was normally a roof chamber, built over the city gateway (II Sam. 18:33) or on the corner of the house roof (Neh. 3:31), usually with access by a stairway from the street. Josephus is thinking in terms of some such roof chamber (*Antiquities* IX. 2. 1) when he says that Ahaziah fell as he was coming down

---

1:1-6, 16-18. *How Ahaziah Failed.*—Ahaziah was cursed with evil parents. He was reared in a house of cruelty and irreligion. Ahab and Jezebel! How could a son of such a pair do other than come to a bad end? Of course this does not always follow. As we shall see, the Southern Kingdom never had worse rulers than Manasseh and his son Amon. Yet also it never had a better one than good King Josiah, the son of Amon. So today we sometimes see the miracle of a pure and holy life defying all laws of heredity and environment, for the grace of God is not bound and fettered by natural laws. Yet it remains true that generally a child follows in the path of his parents, just as

Ahaziah "walked in the way of his father, and in the way of his mother" (I Kings 22:52). Thus Ruskin has remarked that the history of a nation is written not by its wars, but by its homes. A good home is the surest guarantee of virtue. Houses of luxury, materialism, and indulgence are the breeding places of the evils that threaten civilization. The paramount question is whether we can maintain simplicity of life and high moral standards, or whether we shall be corrupted by the disease that may grow from wealth, by almost unlimited possibilities of pleasure and indulgence which are at our disposal. Thus is destroyed the foundation upon which the whole future organization of society must rest. What is going on in a million homes

For Introduction to II Kings see pp. 3-18.

THE GREAT SEA

SYRIA

Abana
Damascus
R. Pharpar

Ijon

Abel-beth-maacah   Dan

Kedesh

Hazor

BASHAN

M. Lebanon

GALILEE

NAPHTALI

Aphek

MANASSEH

Gath-hepher

Shunem

Megiddo

Jezreel

Ibleam

Ramoth-gilead

M. Carmel

Dothan

Tishbeh

ISRAEL

Samaria   Tirzah

SAMARIA

Baal-shalishah

HILL COUNTRY
OF EPHRAIM

GILEAD

R. Jabbok

AMMON

Gilgal

The Jordan

Bethel

Jericho

Bezer

Ekron   Jerusalem   Gilgal

Beth-shemesh

Nebo

Medeba

Baal-   Jahaz
meon

Libnah

LAND OF THE PHILISTINES

Gath

Zior
(Zair)

Lachish

Ataroth
Kiriathaim
Dibon
Aroer

R. Arnon

SEA OF THE ARABAH
SALT SEA

REUBEN

JUDAH

Beer-sheba

V. of Salt

Kir-hareseth

MOAB

Br. Zered

EDOM

Sela
(Joktheel)

PALESTINE
2 KINGS 1-17
THE DIVIDED MONARCHY (b)

MILES
0   10   20   30   40   50
KILOMETERS
0 10 20 30 40 50 60 70 80

JEROME S. KATES, Cartographer
HERBERT G. MAY, PH.D., Research Editor
COPYRIGHT 1949. THOMAS NELSON AND SONS

MEDIA

ASSYRIA

Gozan

Habor

Hamath
Avva
(Ivvah)

Cuthah

Babylon

Sela

Elath

EGYPT

RED
SEA

3 But the angel of the LORD said to Elijah the Tishbite, Arise, go up to meet the messengers of the king of Samaria, and say unto them, *Is it* not because *there is* not a God in Israel, *that* ye go to inquire of Baal-zebub the god of Ekron?

4 Now therefore thus saith the LORD, Thou shalt not come down from that bed on which thou art gone up, but shalt surely die. And Elijah departed.

sickness." 3 But the angel of the LORD said to Eli'jah the Tishbite, "Arise, go up to meet the messengers of the king of Samar'ia, and say to them, 'Is it because there is no God in Israel that you are going to inquire of Ba'al-ze'bub, the god of Ekron?' 4 Now therefore thus says the LORD, 'You shall not come down from the bed to which you have gone, but you shall surely die.' " So Eli'jah went.

---

from the top of his house. Probably Ahaziah's chamber was more in terms of the "wide and spacious roof chambers" of which Jeremiah (22:14) speaks, with windows cut out. Furthermore, these eastern windows were for letting in the air (not light). Ahaziah fell through the protective latticework of one of these open window spaces in his spacious roof chamber.

He sent messengers to "seek an oracle" or **inquire of Baal-zebub, the god of Ekron.** This was no "obscure local deity," as some commentators have said, but a localized form of the great Baal of Syria, the weather-god, identified with Hadad, and also locally identified with Baal-Melkart, tutelary god of Tyre. He is the Baal of the Ras Shamra tablets. The name **Baal-zebub** means "Lord of flies." It was formerly the custom of commentators to compare him and even to identify him with the Greek god Zeus Apomuios—i.e., Zeus the averter of flies—as a god who possessed the special power of destroying this Eastern pest. Hence the LXX here has μυῖαν θεὸν. It is now certain that the god's true name was Baal-zebul, so that Cheyne's suggestion has proved to be correct. The alteration of the last letter was deliberate on the part of earliest copyists because it was the name of an idol-god. They wished to turn the name into something offensive and ludicrous. The name Baal-zebul has been found in the Ras Shamra tablets in the form *Zbl-b'l.* In one text he is equated with "the rider of the clouds" (III AB, A; cf. Charles Virolleaud, "La révolte de Košer contre Baal," *Syria,* XVI [1935], 29-35), or again he is Aliyan-Baal, the god who controls the springs, wells, and watercourses, and comes to life again from his dwelling (*zebul*) in the earth (I AB, III-IV, 2-3; cf. Virolleaud, "Un poème phénicien de Ras-Shamra," *Syria,* XII [1931], 193-224; also René Dussaud, *Les découvertes de Ras Shamra* [Paris: Paul Geuthner, 1937], pp. 69, 79; W. F. Albright, "The North-Canaanite Epic of 'Al'êyân Ba'al and Môt," *Journal of the Palestine Oriental Society,* XII [1932], 191-92). He is thus the life-god of Syria, and Elijah is protesting against precisely the same syncretism on the part of Ahaziah as he had done in the case of Ahab his father on Mount Carmel. On the former occasion at Carmel it was a choice between Baal-Melkart and the Lord; on this latter occasion it was a choice between Baal-zebul and the Lord (cf. Hos. 2:8). It will be seen that the Greek N.T. is thus correct at Matt. 10:25 and elsewhere in reading *Beelzeboul,* and that some English versions are wrong in assimilating their spelling there to the deliberately erroneous spelling of this verse in II Kings 1:2.

Ekron was one of the five cities of the Philistines (Josh. 13:3). It was about fifteen miles south of the modern Jaffa, and was therefore the most easily accessible of the five to any traveler from Israel.

3. The angel of the LORD is a temporary manifestation of God, and here, as in I Kings 19:5-8, is the medium by which the word of the Lord is given to the prophet.

---

today will determine the kind of world in which we will live tomorrow.

Ahaziah's brief reign was filled from beginning to end with nothing but catastrophe. Weak, faithless, miserable, he caused every-

thing he touched to end in ruin and failure. Once the strong hand of Ahab was removed (vs. 1), there came the quick rebellion of Moab. Then came Ahaziah's own bodily accident (vs. 2). Yet had Ahaziah had faith in the God of

5 ¶ And when the messengers turned back unto him, he said unto them, Why are ye now turned back?

6 And they said unto him, There came a man up to meet us, and said unto us, Go, turn again unto the king that sent you, and say unto him, Thus saith the LORD, *Is it* not because *there is* not a God in Israel, *that* thou sendest to inquire of Baal-zebub the god of Ekron? therefore thou shalt not come down from that bed on which thou art gone up, but shalt surely die.

7 And he said unto them, What manner of man *was he* which came up to meet you, and told you these words?

8 And they answered him, *He was* a hairy man, and girt with a girdle of leather about his loins. And he said, It *is* Elijah the Tishbite.

9 Then the king sent unto him a captain of fifty with his fifty. And he went up to him: and, behold, he sat on the top of a hill. And he spake unto him, Thou man of God, the king hath said, Come down.

10 And Elijah answered and said to the captain of fifty, If I *be* a man of God, then let fire come down from heaven, and consume thee and thy fifty. And there came down fire from heaven, and consumed him and his fifty.

11 Again also he sent unto him another captain of fifty with his fifty. And he answered and said unto him, O man of God, thus hath the king said, Come down quickly.

12 And Elijah answered and said unto them, If I *be* a man of God, let fire come down from heaven, and consume thee and

5 The messengers returned to the king, and he said to them, "Why have you returned?" 6 And they said to him, "There came a man to meet us, and said to us, 'Go back to the king who sent you, and say to him, Thus says the LORD, Is it because there is no God in Israel that you are sending to inquire of Ba'al-ze'bub, the god of Ekron? Therefore you shall not come down from the bed to which you have gone, but shall surely die.' " 7 He said to them, "What kind of man was he who came to meet you and told you these things?" 8 They answered him, "He wore a garment of haircloth, with a girdle of leather about his loins." And he said, "It is Eli'jah the Tishbite."

9 Then the king sent to him a captain of fifty men with his fifty. He went up to Eli'jah, who was sitting on the top of a hill, and said to him, "O man of God, the king says, 'Come down.' " 10 But Eli'jah answered the captain of fifty, "If I am a man of God, let fire come down from heaven and consume you and your fifty." Then fire came down from heaven, and consumed him and his fifty.

11 Again the king sent to him another captain of fifty men with his fifty. And he went up[a] and said to him, "O man of God, this is the king's order, 'Come down quickly!' " 12 But Eli'jah answered them, "If I am a man of God, let fire come down from heaven and consume you and your

[a] Gk Compare verses 9, 13: Heb *answered*

9-14. It is difficult to ascribe this section to the same cycle of stories as the Elijah narratives of I Kings 17–19. The section has closer affinities with the Elisha stories (cf.

Israel he might have surmounted these difficulties. For there are few obstacles in life which faith and courage cannot conquer.

But what did Ahaziah do? He sent messengers **to inquire of Baal-zebub the god of Ekron whether I shall recover of this disease** (vs. 2). For help he looked to pagan gods, instead of to the God of his fathers. And many people today in similar misfortunes do as he did. They do not go to the rich resources of faith contained between the covers of their Bibles, to the unfailing power of real religion. Rather, they inquire of modern Baal-zebubs. They consult

ouijas, astrologists, necromancers, fortunetellers; or they place reliance on a purely secular psychiatry, on theosophy, on various forms of menticulture. But they do not go to the God revealed to us in Scripture, to the strength supplied by Jesus Christ, to the simple faith in the prayer which "availeth much," to the undeniable powers of a true Christian faith to heal disease, to lift one above the levels of depression and despair, and enable one to overcome the evils which beset him.

7-15. The Energies of Elijah.—Once more, and for the last time, Elijah is commissioned to

thy fifty. And the fire of God came down from heaven, and consumed him and his fifty.

13 ¶ And he sent again a captain of the third fifty with his fifty. And the third captain of fifty went up, and came and fell on his knees before Elijah, and besought him, and said unto him, O man of God, I pray thee, let my life, and the life of these fifty thy servants, be precious in thy sight.

14 Behold, there came fire down from heaven, and burnt up the two captains of the former fifties with their fifties: therefore let my life now be precious in thy sight.

15 And the angel of the LORD said unto Elijah, Go down with him: be not afraid of him. And he arose, and went down with him unto the king.

16 And he said unto him, Thus saith the LORD, Forasmuch as thou hast sent messengers to inquire of Baal-zebub the god of Ekron, *is it* not because *there is* no God in Israel to inquire of his word? therefore thou shalt not come down off that bed on which thou art gone up, but shalt surely die.

17 ¶ So he died according to the word of the LORD which Elijah had spoken. And Jehoram reigned in his stead, in the second year of Jehoram the son of Jehoshaphat king of Judah; because he had no son.

fifty." Then the fire of God came down from heaven and consumed him and his fifty.

13 Again the king sent the captain of a third fifty with his fifty. And the third captain of fifty went up, and came and fell on his knees before Eli'jah, and entreated him, "O man of God, I pray you, let my life, and the life of these fifty servants of yours, be precious in your sight. 14 Lo, fire came down from heaven, and consumed the two former captains of fifty men with their fifties; but now let my life be precious in your sight." 15 Then the angel of the LORD said to Eli'jah, "Go down with him; do not be afraid of him." So he arose and went down with him to the king, 16 and said to him, "Thus says the LORD, 'Because you have sent messengers to inquire of Ba'al-ze'bub, the god of Ekron, — is it because there is no God in Israel to inquire of his word? — therefore you shall not come down from the bed to which you have gone, but you shall surely die.' "

17 So he died according to the word of the LORD which Eli'jah had spoken. Jeho'ram, his brother,[b] became king in his stead in the second year of Jeho'ram the son of Jehosh'aphat, king of Judah, because Aha-

[b] Gk Syr: Heb lacks *his brother*

2:23-25), where the moral of reverence for the prophet is instilled in the crudest fashion, at the expense of even ordinary ideas of justice and humanity.

17b-18. These Deuteronomic notices are strange. Vs. 17b normally would follow vs. 18; moreover, it does not agree with the statement of 3:1. There are actually three

do the work of a prophet. He is to confront the messengers of Ahaziah with the indignant question, "Is it because there is no God in Israel that you are going to inquire of Baal-zebub?" (vs. 3). And the same question may well be put by a modern minister of God to many an Ahaziah today. The poor, sick king at Samaria is to be told that he will die because he inquired of Baal-zebub instead of the God of Israel.

The story which follows reveals the undiminished moral energies of Elijah. As he called down the fire on the prophets of Baal, so he called down the fire on the messengers of Ahaziah. Two squads of fifty, we are told, were actually consumed. The third was spared only because its leader begged for mercy. The credibility of such happenings as this will be discussed later (see pp. 215-16). Here we are concerned only with the cruelty of them. It was a barbaric age. There was little sense of the

sanctity of personal life. Deeds of savagery did not offend the moral sense of even the noblest among God's people. They were then, it must be remembered, at the beginnings of their moral education. God took his people in the rough and gradually educated them out of the barbarism of their neighbors. What we find in the Bible is the wonderful story of the slow evolution of moral ideals. The divine seed was sown in corruption, but it was raised in incorruption. Let one compare what he finds in this chapter with what he finds in Rom. 12:19-21 and in Eph. 4:32, and remember that Paul belonged to the same race as Elijah; he discovers then to what high levels of conduct this progressive development led under the tutelage of the Spirit of God as it was finally revealed in Jesus Christ.

The story as it stands, however, has its moral lesson which must not be overlooked. Elijah is

18 Now the rest of the acts of Ahaziah which he did, *are* they not written in the book of the Chronicles of the kings of Israel?

2 And it came to pass, when the LORD would take up Elijah into heaven by a whirlwind, that Elijah went with Elisha from Gilgal.

2 And Elijah said unto Elisha, Tarry here, I pray thee; for the LORD hath sent me to Beth-el. And Elisha said *unto him, As* the LORD liveth, and *as* thy soul liveth, I will not leave thee. So they went down to Beth-el.

zi'ah had no son. 18 Now the rest of the acts of Ahazi'ah which he did, are they not written in the Book of the Chronicles of the Kings of Israel?

2 Now when the LORD was about to take Eli'jah up to heaven by a whirlwind, Eli'jah and Eli'sha were on their way from Gilgal. 2 And Eli'jah said to Eli'sha, "Tarry here, I pray you; for the LORD has sent me as far as Bethel." But Eli'sha said, "As the LORD lives, and as you yourself live, I will not leave you." So they went down to

---

systems of synchronization for the reigns of the kings of Israel and Judah in the M.T., in Lucian, and in the LXX respectively. The system favored by Lucian differs from the LXX twice only, here and in 8:25. In each case Lucian's figure appears in the M.T., in addition to the regular M.T. figure, viz., 8:25 and 9:29; here and 3:1. An editor apparently held that Lucian's figure was right, though only in those instances where Lucian differed from the LXX. (The details are given in parallel columns in C. F. Burney, *Notes on the Hebrew Text of the Books of Kings* [Oxford: Clarendon Press, 1903], pp. xlii-xliii.)

3. ELISHA SUCCEEDS ELIJAH (2:1-18)

Elijah is aware that his work is finished. He therefore bids Elisha come with him as far as Gilgal. Three times, at Gilgal, at Bethel, and at Jericho, Elijah bids Elisha stay behind. Twice the local prophetic guilds ask Elisha if he does not know that the Lord is going that very day to remove his master, as if adding their entreaties to Elijah's orders that Elisha should stay behind. Elisha steadily persists in clinging to his master till the end. They cross the Jordan, miraculously divided for that purpose, and suddenly Elijah is snatched away. Elisha prays for the heirdom of his master's spirit and power, and this is granted him as if accompanying the prophet's mantle. Elisha recrosses the Jordan, again miraculously divided. The local prophets acknowledge him as Elijah's successor. They want to send and find Elijah and persist in their requests till Elisha, for shame, allows them to send. They return from their fruitless errand.

2:1. The idea of **whirlwind** is by no means essential to the Hebrew word. The reference is to the stormwind often associated with the coming of God, either in wrath, or indeed at any time. Only in Ps. 107:25 is the word used of an ordinary tempest (but cf. Isa. 29:6; 40:24; Ezek. 13:11; Zech. 9:14). The translation **whirlwind** is due to the

---

the incarnation of a moral conscience which asserts itself irresistibly against the infidelity of Ahaziah. We are reminded that nothing in all this universe can withstand the truth as this is embodied in the will of God. **A captain of fifty with his fifty!** Such a force might seem sufficient to capture the person of the prophet. But it shrivels into nothingness before the consuming energies of God. The most powerful thing in the world, it has been said, is an idea. And when that idea has behind it and within it the word and will of God, then nothing can withstand it. Thus Catherine of Siena, by the sheer power of that truth of which she was the

living incarnation, bent popes and emperors to her will. A word of Luther, "The just shall live by faith," could undo an ecclesiastical system that had endured for a thousand years. Let anyone today—however much the odds may seem against him, however formidable the opposition which confronts him—speak the truth as God has given him to see and know the truth, and he too will see "the captains with their fifties" disappear before him, consumed by the very breath of God.

2:1-7. *Bible Friendships.*—The story of the assumption of Elijah is told in a style of the loftiest poetry, with an imagination at once

3 And the sons of the prophets that *were* at Beth-el came forth to Elisha, and said unto him, Knowest thou that the LORD will take away thy master from thy head to-day? And he said, Yea, I know *it;* hold ye your peace.

4 And Elijah said unto him, Elisha, tarry here, I pray thee; for the LORD hath sent me to Jericho. And he said, *As* the LORD liveth, and *as* thy soul liveth, I will not leave thee. So they came to Jericho.

5 And the sons of the phophets that *were* at Jericho came to Elisha, and said unto him, Knowest thou that the LORD will take away thy master from thy head to-day? And he answered, Yea, I know *it;* hold ye your peace.

6 And Elijah said unto him, Tarry, I pray thee, here; for the LORD hath sent me to Jordan. And he said, *As* the LORD liveth, and *as* thy soul liveth, I will not leave thee. And they two went on.

7 And fifty men of the sons of the prophets went, and stood to view afar off: and they two stood by Jordan.

8 And Elijah took his mantle, and wrapped *it* together, and smote the waters, and they were divided hither and thither, so that they two went over on dry ground.

Bethel. 3 And the sons of the prophets who were in Bethel came out to Eli'sha, and said to him, "Do you know that today the LORD will take away your master from over you?" And he said, "Yes, I know it; hold your peace."

4 Eli'jah said to him, "Eli'sha, tarry here, I pray you; for the LORD has sent me to Jericho." But he said, "As the LORD lives, and as you yourself live, I will not leave you." So they came to Jericho. 5 The sons of the prophets who were at Jericho drew near to Eli'sha, and said to him, "Do you know that today the LORD will take away your master from over you?" And he answered, "Yes, I know it; hold your peace."

6 Then Eli'jah said to him, "Tarry here, I pray you; for the LORD has sent me to the Jordan." But he said, "As the LORD lives, and as you yourself live, I will not leave you." So the two of them went on. 7 Fifty men of the sons of the prophets also went, and stood at some distance from them, as they both were standing by the Jordan. 8 Then Eli'jah took his mantle, and rolled it up, and struck the water, and the water was parted to the one side and to the other, till the two of them could go over on dry ground.

Vulg. *turbo.* As the itinerary shows, **Gilgal** is not the well-known site between Jericho and the Jordan, but another locality on the high road from Shechem to Bethel, some seven miles north of Bethel.

8. After the fashion of primitive religion, Elijah's hairy **mantle** is endowed with supernatural power. Elisha receives through it the wonder-working power which belonged to his master Elijah (vs. 13); he then smites with it the waters of the Jordan (vs. 14), as if to test whether the power of Elijah is still to be associated with the garment.

exalted and restrained. As literature alone it ranks high among the great chapters of the Bible. And it teaches spiritual lessons of great depth and meaning.

The time had come when the Lord was to remove Elijah from the scene of his tremendous labors. So he left Gilgal, where young prophets were in training, and set out for Bethel. But Elisha, whose name has not been mentioned in the record since his call to be the successor of Elijah (I Kings 19:16-19), refused to leave him. Here we find another illustration of devoted friendship of which the O.T. has already given us conspicuous and beautiful illustrations: of David to Saul, of Jonathan to David, of Ruth to Naomi. This type of devotion lies embedded deep in human character, beneath all outward distinctions of condition or of race, as ele-

mental as religion itself. Is this kind of deathless loyalty rare today? Friendships are all too easily broken; loyalties, when tested, break down; self-interest and prudence win over selfless devotion. Dickens wrote of Dombey that he had not a real friend in the world. One measure of the real worth of a man is the number and the quality of his friendships.

8. *Always a Way Through.*—When Elijah and Elisha came to the Jordan, we read that Elijah **smote the waters, and . . . they two went over on dry ground** (cf. Josh. 3:14-16). Apparently insurmountable obstacles give way before the courage of a real faith. One can march right forward if one is in the path of the will of God. Always there is a thoroughfare into our promised land. Difficulties fairly met will not be too great; duties resolutely undertaken

9 ¶ And it came to pass, when they were gone over, that Elijah said unto Elisha, Ask what I shall do for thee, before I be taken away from thee. And Elisha said, I pray thee, let a double portion of thy spirit be upon me.

10 And he said, Thou hast asked a hard thing: *nevertheless,* if thou see me *when I am* taken from thee, it shall be so unto thee; but if not, it shall not be *so.*

11 And it came to pass, as they still went on, and talked, that, behold, *there appeared* a chariot of fire, and horses of fire, and parted them both asunder; and Elijah went up by a whirlwind into heaven.

9 When they had crossed, Eli'jah said to Eli'sha, "Ask what I shall do for you, before I am taken from you." And Eli'sha said, "I pray you, let me inherit a double share of your spirit." 10 And he said, "You have asked a hard thing; yet, if you see me as I am being taken from you, it shall be so for you; but if you do not see me, it shall not be so." 11 And as they still went on and talked, behold, a chariot of fire and horses of fire separated the two of them. And Eli'jah went up by a whirlwind into

---

9. The **double share** is the **portion** of the heir, the first-born. Elisha desires to succeed to the leadership of the prophetic guilds ("the sons of the prophets"), and so to have the authority and power which belonged to his master. The meaning is not that he should be two thirds as great as Elijah (so Ewald), nor on the other hand that he should be twice as great as Elijah (so Ecclus. 48:13, Vulg.), but that he should be his successor.

The word *rûaḥ* (**spirit**) is not used here of prophetic inspiration so much as in the sense of more-than-human power.

10. "If you have eyes to see the chariotry of the LORD, then your prayer will be answered." It was not every man who could see this heavenly chariotry (6:17). The youth needed to have his eyes opened in order that he might see them. Joash saw the chariotry of the Lord when he visited Elisha on the latter's deathbed (13:14), and he used the same words as those which Elisha used here (vs. 12).

11. The translation of Elijah and his mysterious end have given rise to a whole world of legend. He is the Jewish ancestor of El-Ḥudr, the eternal wanderer of Islamic lore who drank the water of life and never grows old. According to popular beliefs, Elijah is liable at any time to appear suddenly in order to right the wrongs of man. He will return before the day of Messiah (Mal. 4:5). He is the "angel of the covenant," and his chair is a feature to this day at the rite of circumcision. The door is left ajar for his entrance at Passover. The joyous barking of dogs is said to be a sign of his presence (see Eduard König, "Elijah," *The Jewish Encyclopedia* [New York: Funk & Wagnalls, 1903], V, 121-28).

---

will not prove too much for us; temptations boldly challenged will not overcome us. We can smite the Jordan with the mantle of faith and pass over on dry ground.

9. *A Prayer that Is Always Answered.*—When Elisha asked that the spirit of Elijah might rest on him, he was offering the kind of prayer that will always be answered (cf. I Kings 3:5). People who complain that their prayers are not answered are praying for the wrong thing. The best, i.e., the spiritual gifts, can always be ours if we earnestly desire and fervently pray for them (Matt. 7:7-11). Prayer would be given new meaning for us if, when we are told to ask what we will, we should pray that more of God's Holy Spirit may be ours.

10. *Spiritual Eyesight.*—If thou see me when I am taken from thee. Spiritual realities are not discerned by the outward eye, but are perceived only by those who are intent upon and sensitive to them. They are immediately luminous only to those who are tender of heart as well as keen of intellect, who are devout of soul as well as practical in their judgments. If we do not see these realities, it is not because they are not there to be seen, but rather because we have not the eyes with which to see them. The difficulty is not with the thing to be perceived, but with the perceiver.

11-18. *The Fire of the Spirit.*—A chariot of fire, and horses of fire. The truly reverent way is to leave this description of the assumption

12 ¶ And Elisha saw *it,* and he cried, My father, my father, the chariot of Israel, and the horsemen thereof! And he saw him no more: and he took hold of his own clothes, and rent them in two pieces.

13 He took up also the mantle of Elijah that fell from him, and went back, and stood by the bank of Jordan;

14 And he took the mantle of Elijah that fell from him, and smote the waters, and said, Where *is* the LORD God of Elijah? And when he also had smitten the waters, they parted hither and thither: and Elisha went over.

15 And when the sons of the prophets which *were* to view at Jericho saw him, they said, The spirit of Elijah doth rest on Elisha. And they came to meet him, and bowed themselves to the ground before him.

16 ¶ And they said unto him, Behold now, there be with thy servants fifty strong men; let them go, we pray thee, and seek thy master: lest peradventure the Spirit of the LORD hath taken him up, and cast him upon some mountain, or into some valley. And he said, Ye shall not send.

17 And when they urged him till he was ashamed, he said, Send. They sent therefore

heaven. 12 And Eli'sha saw it and he cried, "My father, my father! the chariots of Israel and its horsemen!" And he saw him no more.

Then he took hold of his own clothes and rent them in two pieces. 13 And he took up the mantle of Eli'jah that had fallen from him, and went back and stood on the bank of the Jordan. 14 Then he took the mantle of Eli'jah that had fallen from him, and struck the water, saying, "Where is the LORD, the God of Eli'jah?" And when he had struck the water, the water was parted to the one side and to the other; and Eli'sha went over.

15 Now when the sons of the prophets who were at Jericho saw him over against them, they said, "The spirit of Eli'jah rests on Eli'sha." And they came to meet him, and bowed to the ground before him. 16 And they said to him, "Behold now, there are with your servants fifty strong men; pray, let them go, and seek your master; it may be that the Spirit of the LORD has caught him up and cast him upon some mountain or into some valley." And he said, "You shall not send." 17 But when they urged him till he was ashamed, he

---

12. The rending of garments is the traditional sign of grief. Throwing ashes on the head, lacerating the face and breasts, and shaving the forehead all belong to the general custom of disfigurement, either as a matter of disguise against ghosts or, less likely, as an outward expression of intense sorrow.

14. The phrase **and smote the waters** is repeated verbatim in the M.T., though this is disguised in the translations. The Vulg., Lucian, and the LXX (Complutensian Polyglot 1513-17) have inserted "and they were not divided" after the first occurrence of the phrase. This may be a gloss to account for the repetition, but its effect is to make futile Elisha's first attempt to divide the waters of the Jordan. He has first to say, **Where is the LORD, the God of Elijah?** To this question the word "now" ought to be added, as in the LXX. The mantle of Elijah acts as the carrier of the spirit which Elijah possessed. When Elisha has evoked the deity, the miraculous parting of the waters of the Jordan becomes the first evidence of the transfer of this more-than-human power.

16. This was not the first time that Elijah had mysteriously disappeared (see I Kings 18:9-16).

---

of Elijah in the realm of symbolism, of poetry, of the imagination. Of course the body of Elijah was not found (vss. 16-17). The body of Elijah was not Elijah. No end to Elijah's life could have been more in keeping with the man himself. For Elijah was a whirlwind, and his spirit the incarnation of fire. Everywhere fire accompanies him and illustrates him. This is the final lesson taught by this majestic prophet.

What is it that we most miss in the lives of the conventionally good? Is it not that there is wholly lacking in their moral and religious experience anything which tallies with this word "fire"—what Lowell once called "old Judaea's gift of secret fire"? [1] In no sense can it be said of them that they are on fire for God or truth or righteousness. No character is formed on the

¹ "The Cathedral."

fifty men; and they sought three days, but found him not.

18 And when they came again to him, (for he tarried at Jericho,) he said unto them, Did I not say unto you, Go not?

19 ¶ And the men of the city said unto Elisha, Behold, I pray thee, the situation of this city *is* pleasant, as my lord seeth: but the water *is* naught, and the ground barren.

20 And he said, Bring me a new cruse, and put salt therein. And they brought *it* to him.

21 And he went forth unto the spring of the waters, and cast the salt in there, and said, Thus saith the LORD, I have healed these waters; there shall not be from thence any more death or barren *land*.

22 So the waters were healed unto this day, according to the saying of Elisha which he spake.

said, "Send." They sent therefore fifty men; and for three days they sought him but did not find him. **18** And they came back to him, while he tarried at Jericho, and he said to them, "Did I not say to you, Do not go?"

19 Now the men of the city said to Eli′sha, "Behold, the situation of this city is pleasant, as my lord sees; but the water is bad, and the land is unfruitful." **20** He said, "Bring me a new bowl, and put salt in it." So they brought it to him. **21** Then he went to the spring of water and threw salt in it, and said, "Thus says the LORD, I have made this water wholesome; henceforth neither death nor miscarriage shall come from it." **22** So the water has been wholesome to this day, according to the word which Eli′sha spoke.

---

4. CLEANSING OF THE SPRING AT JERICHO (2:19-22)

This is the first of a series of wonder tales which are associated with the story of Elisha. They are unique in the O.T. They all seek to emphasize the marvelous power of the man of God, or to inculcate respect and reverence for him.

Jericho had a pleasant situation, but the water was bad, and nothing would grow. Elisha cast salt into the spring, and the waters have been sweet and wholesome ever since. It is best not to offer natural explanations for this and other stories of the same type, but rather to leave them alone as wonder stories, belonging to another age than ours.

19. The land is used for "the people" (cf. Lev. 19:29 and often elsewhere). The spring (modern 'Ain es-Sulṭān) has the reputation of causing miscarriages in humans and animals.

The sixteenth-century English **naught** was commonly used for the idea of **bad** (cf. Shakespeare, "The mustard was naught" [*As You Like It*, Act I, scene 2] and Jer. 24:2, "naughty figs").

Bible pattern, or can in the deepest sense be called Christian, which lacks this quality of fire. No man counts for much who does not have passion. We need more Christians today who are "a burning and a shining light" (John 5:35).

19-25. Introducing Elisha.—The character of Elisha cannot measure up to that of his great predecessor. Truly great men appear but seldom on the pages of history. Their followers may carry on their work, but they cannot walk on their heights. Hence we find in the career of Elisha no stupendous scenes, no outstanding achievements, no exhibitions of grandeur of soul. Yet the career of Elisha reminds us that without great capacities, without being heroes, one can do much good in the world.

19-22. The Healing of the Waters.—How simple and homely is the first beneficent deed of Elisha: making pure the water of the springs

near Jericho! The sources of thought and action have become impure in many a modern community. And these have infected our youth. Modern literature is tainted with cynicism. Old standards of rectitude and honor have given way to indulgence and license. The very springs of life have become corrupted so that the fruits of good living have withered and the morals of men have become diseased. Elisha made those waters pure by the infusion of **salt**. Jesus told the disciples that they were to be "the salt of the earth" (Matt. 5:13). Everywhere salt is nature's perpetual foe of decay. And Christian men or women today can perform the same prophetic mission of Elisha for the communities in which they live by opposing their own simple Christian ideas and ideals to each and every corrupting influence with which they come in contact.

23 ¶ And he went up from thence unto Beth-el: and as he was going up by the way, there came forth little children out of the city, and mocked him, and said unto him, Go up, thou bald head; go up, thou bald head.

24 And he turned back, and looked on them, and cursed them in the name of the LORD. And there came forth two she bears out of the wood, and tare forty and two children of them.

25 And he went from thence to mount Carmel, and from thence he returned to Samaria.

3 Now Jehoram the son of Ahab began to reign over Israel in Samaria in the eighteenth year of Jehoshaphat king of Judah, and reigned twelve years.

2 And he wrought evil in the sight of the LORD; but not like his father, and like his mother: for he put away the image of Baal that his father had made.

23 He went up from there to Bethel; and while he was going up on the way, some small boys came out of the city and jeered at him, saying, "Go up, you baldhead! Go up, you baldhead!" 24 And he turned around, and when he saw them, he cursed them in the name of the LORD. And two she-bears came out of the woods and tore forty-two of the boys. 25 From there he went on to Mount Carmel, and thence he returned to Samar'ia.

3 In the eighteenth year of Jehosh'aphat king of Judah, Jeho'ram the son of Ahab became king over Israel in Samar'ia, and he reigned twelve years. 2 He did what was evil in the sight of the LORD, though not like his father and mother, for he put away the pillar of Ba'al which his father

---

5. THE SMALL BOYS AND THE SHE-BEARS (2:23-25)

This story of the small boys who were rude to the prophet has been subjected to various explanations by commentators who have hoped to make it acceptable to proper standards of justice and fairness. It is merely an example of premoral exhortation to respect the prophets as the holy men of God. The story compares most unfavorably with N.T. teaching (Matt. 5:44; Luke 23:34), and indeed will not stand examination from any moral point of view.

23. Baldness was reckoned to be a disgrace in ancient times. The word **baldhead** was a term of reproach among both the Greeks and the Romans (A. Macalister, "Baldness," in James Hastings, ed., *A Dictionary of the Bible* [New York: Charles Scribner's Sons, 1898], I, 234-35).

6. JEHORAM'S MOABITE CAMPAIGN (3:1-27)

3:1-3. These verses contain the formal Deuteronomic introduction to the reign of King Jehoram of Israel, and they come from the 610 B.C. compiler.

2. The M.T. reads, **put away the pillar of Baal,** but the ancient versions read "pillars." It is commonly said that Jehoram's reforms could not have been as thorough as this verse suggests, otherwise Jehu could not have done as he did in 10:18-27. Apparently there was still one pillar (so Lucian, but M.T. has "pillars") in the Baal temple

---

23-25. *The Penalty of Vicious Behavior.*— Here is a story from which the Bible reader shrinks. A careful reading of the text, however, will show us that Elisha did not himself summon the bears. He was not that kind of man. Thus understood, the story, however dreadful, has its sharp significance. The irreverence, lawlessness, hoodlumism of youth are sure to result in moral disaster. The bears that came out of the woods are the symbol of that inevitable retribution which overtakes vicious behavior. The boys of this story are the prototype of thousands of youth today. If they can be taught at home, in school, at church, the lessons of reverence and self-control, they may escape the fate which otherwise will overtake them. Lawless youth may not be torn asunder by bears, but they are rent by passions, devoured by appetite, until their characters and careers and all their hopes for happy, useful living are destroyed.

3:1-3. *Jehoram.*— The brother of Ahaziah, Jehoram, presents us with the type of man who does neither what is all right nor what is all wrong. He was not as wicked as his parents, yet

3 Nevertheless he cleaved unto the sins of Jeroboam the son of Nebat, which made Israel to sin; he departed not therefrom.

4 ¶ And Mesha king of Moab was a sheepmaster, and rendered unto the king of Israel a hundred thousand lambs, and a hundred thousand rams, with the wool.

5 But it came to pass, when Ahab was dead, that the king of Moab rebelled against the king of Israel.

had made. 3 Nevertheless he clung to the sin of Jerobo'am the son of Nebat, which he made Israel to sin; he did not depart from it.

4 Now Mesha king of Moab was a sheep breeder; and he had to deliver annually[c] to the king of Israel a hundred thousand lambs, and the wool of a hundred thousand rams. 5 But when Ahab died, the king of Moab rebelled against the king of Israel.

[c] Tg: Heb lacks annually

---

which Jehu destroyed (10:26). Some hold, however, that this reference is an insertion, but there is no real justification for the suggestion. It is true that in vs. 13 Elisha rebuked Jehoram because of Ahab and Jezebel, but elsewhere the prophet is kindly disposed to the young king. It is therefore more than probable that the young king did actually take steps to reform the cultus, in spite of the fact that his mother Jezebel was still alive and presumably had still some considerable influence. The Deuteronomic verdict is that he did not follow Baal as his parents did. In view of the later story of Jehu's activity, we must assume that the young king was partially successful in his reforming zeal, but that he was not able wholly to extirpate Baal from the land.

4-27. Moab revolts from Israel at the death of Ahab. Ahaziah dies before he can take any action, so his brother Jehoram finds it incumbent upon him to restore the situation. Jehoram commands his vassal Jehoshaphat to join forces with him, and this involves also the king of Edom, vassal of Jehoshaphat. The three kings seek to attack Moab through the Edomite country, but after seven days they are faced with an utter lack of water. The three kings go to seek advice from Elisha, who at first spurns the Israelite king, bidding him go to the prophets of his parents, but he later suggests a stratagem by which Moab is deceived into making a disorderly advance. As a result, the Moabites are driven back in confusion, their country destroyed, their cities taken, until the king of Moab finds himself driven to make a desperate sally with seven hundred swordsmen. The despairing effort fails, so he sacrifices his eldest son, the heir to the throne, on the city wall. This sacrifice is so effective that Israel is driven back in confusion, and Moab retains her independence.

4. Mesha was a *nôqēdh*, i.e., an owner of that breed of sheep which the Arabs call *naqad*. They are small, unprepossessing in appearance ("viler than a *naqad*" is a term of reproach), but giving abundant wool of good quality. Amos was a keeper of such sheep (Amos 1:1).

The M.T. reads "he [Mesha] used to deliver," to which the Targ. inserts **annually** (so RSV). The numbers seem somewhat excessive for an annual tribute, even though Moab was famous as a pastoral country. The LXX therefore infers that it was a single payment paid as an indemnity in the rebellion.

---

he did not abjure calf worship, the sin of Jeroboam. He was like Bunyan's Mr. Facing-both-ways. And so are many men today. They do not descend to the worst sins in society or in business. They are free from the worst excesses of their day. Yet never can they make up their minds to break utterly with everything that is not rooted in conscience and be wholly void of offense toward God and man. They temporize and they compromise. They continue religious habits, but they do not allow their religion to penetrate too far into daily deportment, into

the regulation of the practical affairs of life. It is a poor commentary on a man's life to say that he was not as bad as he might have been. Consider the tragedy of many a man's life that he was not as good as he might have been.

4-10. *The Moabites.*—This chapter is concerned with the conquest of **Moab**, which had revolted when Ahab was dead. What first impresses us is the coalition which undertook this campaign. The allies were **Israel, Judah, Edom.** What a combination of forces was that! Between Israel and Judah there had been nearly a cen-

6 ¶ And king Jehoram went out of Samaria the same time, and numbered all Israel.	6 So King Jeho'ram marched out of Samar'ia at that time and mustered all Israel.

6 ¶ And king Jehoram went out of Samaria the same time, and numbered all Israel.

7 And he went and sent to Jehoshaphat the king of Judah, saying, The king of Moab hath rebelled against me: wilt thou go with me against Moab to battle? And he said, I will go up: I *am* as thou *art,* my people as thy people, *and* my horses as thy horses.

8 And he said, Which way shall we go up? And he answered, The way through the wilderness of Edom.

9 So the king of Israel went, and the king of Judah, and the king of Edom: and they fetched a compass of seven days' journey: and there was no water for the host, and for the cattle that followed them.

10 And the king of Israel said, Alas! that the LORD hath called these three kings together, to deliver them into the hand of Moab!

11 But Jehoshaphat said, *Is there* not here a prophet of the LORD, that we may inquire of the LORD by him? And one of the king of Israel's servants answered and said, Here *is* Elisha the son of Shaphat, which poured water on the hands of Elijah.

6 So King Jeho'ram marched out of Samar'ia at that time and mustered all Israel. 7 And he went and sent word to Jehosh'aphat king of Judah, "The king of Moab has rebelled against me; will you go with me to battle against Moab?" And he said, "I will go; I am as you are, my people as your people, my horses as your horses." 8 Then he said, "By which way shall we march?" Jeho'ram answered, "By the way of the wilderness of Edom."

9 So the king of Israel went with the king of Judah and the king of Edom. And when they had made a circuitous march of seven days, there was no water for the army or for the beasts which followed them. 10 Then the king of Israel said, "Alas! The LORD has called these three kings to give them into the hand of Moab." 11 And Jehosh'aphat said, "Is there no prophet of the LORD here, through whom we may inquire of the LORD?" Then one of the king of Israel's servants answered, "Eli'sha the son of Shaphat is here, who poured water on

8. They decide to attack Moab from the south, marching around the south of the Dead Sea for seven days till they come to the Wadi el-Ḥesā on the southern border of Moab. It is not clear to whom the **he** refers in either sentence, but in view of Jehoram's reply to Elisha in vs. 13, it is more than likely that the march around the south end of the Dead Sea was dictated by an oracle of the Lord.

9. They expected to find water in this border wadi between Edom and Moab, and were astounded when they found none. But Elisha bade them dig pits (vs. 16), with the result that by the next morning the whole valley was flooded. It is still possible to obtain water in this way in this wadi by digging for it. Infiltrations from the mountains of Edom are retained by the underground rocks in the valley (W. Robertson Smith, *The Old Testament in the Jewish Church* [2nd ed.; New York: D. Appleton & Co., 1898], p. 147; cf. the Salinas River of California).

The references here to **the king of Edom** are difficult to reconcile with 8:20; I Kings 22:47. It seems clear that at that time the Edomite king was a vassal to the king of

tury of war, and Edom had been the inveterate foe of both. But before the common threat of Moab they joined forces. That threat removed, however, they immediately fell apart again. Each nation was thinking only in terms of its own interests. None envisaged the possibility of a Hebrew nation reunited in terms of common welfare and destiny. As a consequence, all three of them ultimately went down in ruin.

There is a parable here for the world in which we live. Twice within the memory of living men has this sad story been repeated. For reasons like those in the ancient time, the freedom of the world from the curse of war is in jeopardy. At the root of all our difficulties are national conceit and ingrained selfishness: the refusal to put the welfare of all above the interests of each. Can we learn no better than those three kindred nations in that ancient world? If not, the same fate is in store for us.

11-20. *Jehoram and Elisha.*—How Elisha came to be in the camp of the allies we are not

12 And Jehoshaphat said, The word of the Lord is with him. So the king of Israel and Jehoshaphat and the king of Edom went down to him.

13 And Elisha said unto the king of Israel, What have I to do with thee? get thee to the prophets of thy father, and to the prophets of thy mother. And the king of Israel said unto him, Nay: for the Lord hath called these three kings together, to deliver them into the hand of Moab.

14 And Elisha said, *As* the Lord of hosts liveth, before whom I stand, surely, were it not that I regard the presence of Jehoshaphat the king of Judah, I would not look toward thee, nor see thee.

15 But now bring me a minstrel. And it came to pass, when the minstrel played, that the hand of the Lord came upon him.

16 And he said, Thus saith the Lord, Make this valley full of ditches.

17 For thus saith the Lord, Ye shall not see wind, neither shall ye see rain; yet that valley shall be filled with water, that ye may drink, both ye, and your cattle, and your beasts.

18 And this is *but* a light thing in the sight of the Lord: he will deliver the Moabites also into your hand.

the hands of Eli′jah." 12 And Jehosh′aphat said, "The word of the Lord is with him." So the king of Israel and Jehosh′aphat and the king of Edom went down to him.

13 And Eli′sha said to the king of Israel, "What have I to do with you? Go to the prophets of your father and the prophets of your mother." But the king of Israel said to him, "No; it is the Lord who has called these three kings to give them into the hand of Moab." 14 And Eli′sha said, "As the Lord of hosts lives, whom I serve, were it not that I have regard for Jehosh′aphat the king of Judah, I would neither look at you, nor see you. 15 But now bring me a minstrel." And when the minstrel played, the power of the Lord came upon him. 16 And he said, "Thus says the Lord, 'I will make this dry stream-bed full of pools.' 17 For thus says the Lord, 'You shall not see wind or rain, but that stream-bed shall be filled with water, so that you shall drink, you, your cattle, and your beasts.' 18 This is a light thing in the sight of the Lord; he will also

Judah (cf. 8:22 and the present story), so it is necessary to suppose that the other passages mean that there was no independent king in Edom.

15. The M.T. indicates that this playing on a stringed instrument was customary when Elisha was concerned with the giving of oracles, since it was during the playing that the ecstatic prophetic condition was induced in him. The RSV assumes that the tense of the verb is changed, and that the playing took place only on that particular occasion. The alternative is to conjecture the accidental omission of a sentence which said that a minstrel came and played. Use of music as a means of inducing ecstasy was common not only in Israel but also in Arabia (T. H. Robinson, *Prophecy and the Prophets in Ancient Israel* [New York: Charles Scribner's Sons, 1923], p. 32; W. Robertson Smith, *The Prophets of Israel* [2nd ed.; London: A. & C. Black, 1897], p. 392; see also I Sam. 10:5).

18-19. This oracle tells of the earlier success of the campaign, but not of the later disaster when Israel had to withdraw after the Moabite king had sacrificed his son and

told. The significant thing is that the allies, in spite of their numbers, would have been helpless without the prophet. No water for men or cattle! Elisha would have nothing to do with Jehoram, recreant king that he was. Only for Jehoshaphat's sake did he consent to lend his aid. Jehoram was by far the most powerful of the three kings. Yet he was helpless in the emergency that confronted him. Only divine help of which Elisha was the symbol could save

the allies. Carnal weapons are not enough. Military might can never achieve the final victory for which we wait. The conquest of Moab was not achieved by the legions of Jehoram, but by the Spirit of the Lord. Only the same Spirit can win the victory for us of today. Over against the militarism of our modern world stands the august truth, "Not by might, nor by power, but by my Spirit, saith the Lord of hosts" (Zech. 4:6).

19 And ye shall smite every fenced city, and every choice city, and shall fell every good tree, and stop all wells of water, and mar every good piece of land with stones.

20 And it came to pass in the morning, when the meat offering was offered, that, behold, there came water by the way of Edom, and the country was filled with water.

21 ¶ And when all the Moabites heard that the kings were come up to fight against them, they gathered all that were able to put on armor, and upward, and stood in the border.

22 And they rose up early in the morning, and the sun shone upon the water, and the Moabites saw the water on the other side as red as blood:

give the Moabites into your hand, 19 and you shall conquer every fortified city, and every choice city, and shall fell every good tree, and stop up all springs of water, and ruin every good piece of land with stones." 20 The next morning, about the time of offering the sacrifice, behold, water came from the direction of Edom, till the country was filled with water.

21 When all the Moabites heard that the kings had come up to fight against them, all who were able to put on armor, from the youngest to the oldest, were called out, and were drawn up at the frontier. 22 And when they rose early in the morning, and the sun shone upon the water, the Moabites saw the water opposite them as red as blood.

---

heir. The oracle was true so far as it went. It was thus similar to those Delphic oracles which lured Croesus of Lydia and Pyrrhus of Epirus into a false confidence, though there is no evidence here that Elisha deliberately encouraged the three kings to disaster.

20. The event took place at the time of the offering of the morning sacrifice (see Exeg. on I Kings 18:29, where the reference is to the evening sacrifice). In the second temple the morning sacrifice was offered when the morning sun had lighted the sky as far as Hebron, but before it had actually appeared over the ridge of the Mount of Olives.

22. The redness of the water which deceived the Moabites, who would be stationed on the northern cliffs two thousand feet up, may have been due to seepage through red soil, or to strange reflections in the deep defile in the light of the early dawn. The former explanation is more likely to be correct, since the Hebrew word "Edom" means "red" (cf. Gen. 25:30).

How touching is the detail recorded in vs. 15, **Bring me a minstrel.** Just as the harp of David had calmed the turbulent soul of King Saul, so the playing of this unknown minstrel was to reveal to Elisha the will of God. We think of that nameless man. He had his gift and he used it. How little did he imagine that by its use he would help to win for his people a glorious victory. Yet **when the minstrel played, the power of the LORD came upon** [Elisha]. Every one of us, no matter how humble he may be, can make "undying music in the world." And moral victories are won by it more often than we think.

Music has charms to sooth a savage breast,
To soften rocks, or bend a knotted oak.[2]

To be a minstrel in the troubled world today is to perform a high mission. Thus some cloud may be lifted from another's soul, some light may enter there, some inspiration may be felt,

[2] William Congreve, *The Mourning Bride*, Act I, scene 1.

and the power of the Lord may come to one who sorely needs it.

What follows in the biblical story reads like a miracle. It may, however, have been the sure strategy of one whose mind had been illumined and thus saw what course to take. Trenches were to be dug into which the gathering storm clouds would pour the water needed for man and beast. The gift of God to man comes often in no external or supernatural fashion; comes rather by the clarification of powers of insight and imagination whereby one is enabled to utilize resources that otherwise might remain hidden and unknown. Therein is revealed the function of prayer in the emergencies of life.

21-27. The Defeat of Moab.—The story is pictured in lurid colors. The canvas is splashed with red and crimson. No similar scene is spread before the eye in all O.T. history. The rays of the setting sun, the cobalt red of the soil, these turned the water in the trenches to apparent pools of blood to the eyes of the watching Moabites. This could mean only that the allies had

23 And they said, This *is* blood: the kings are surely slain, and they have smitten one another: now therefore, Moab, to the spoil.

24 And when they came to the camp of Israel, the Israelites rose up and smote the Moabites, so that they fled before them: but they went forward smiting the Moabites, even in *their* country.

25 And they beat down the cities, and on every good piece of land cast every man his stone, and filled it; and they stopped all the wells of water, and felled all the good trees: only in Kir-haraseth left they the stones thereof; howbeit the slingers went about *it*, and smote it.

26 ¶ And when the king of Moab saw that the battle was too sore for him, he took with him seven hundred men that drew swords, to break through *even* unto the king of Edom: but they could not.

27 Then he took his eldest son that should have reigned in his stead, and offered

23 And they said, "This is blood; the kings have surely fought together, and slain one another. Now then, Moab, to the spoil!"

24 But when they came to the camp of Israel, the Israelites rose and attacked the Moabites, till they fled before them; and they went forward, slaughtering the Moabites as they went.*d* 25 And they overthrew the cities, and on every good piece of land every man threw a stone, until it was covered; they stopped every spring of water, and felled all the good trees; till only its stones were left in Kir-har′eseth, and the slingers surrounded and conquered it. 26 When the king of Moab saw that the battle was going against him, he took with him seven hundred swordsmen to break through, opposite the king of Edom; but they could not. 27 Then he took his eldest son who was to reign in his stead, and

d Gk: Heb uncertain

---

23. The Moabites abandoned their almost impregnable position on the mountain and rushed down in disorder to plunder the allied camp. They were met by the waiting armies and driven back with great loss, both in the actual battle itself and in the subsequent rout. The victory of William of Normandy over Harold the Saxon in 1066 was likewise accomplished: the Norman invader tricked the Saxons into thinking that the victory was won, and that all they had to do was to pursue the beaten foe and to drive him back into the sea.

25. This wholesale and deliberate destruction of enemy country is generally pointed out as an instance of the inhumanity of ancient warfare and its wanton damage, whereby men, women, and children are slain indiscriminately. Such comments can still be made, but not by way of contrast with modern warfare.

The RSV is wrong in saying that the slingers **conquered** Kir-haraseth, though this may well be the meaning of the M.T. It is better to keep **smote it** because, although this expression generally means in Hebrew "destroyed," it leaves room for what happened in vs. 26. They assaulted the city until everything was almost lost. Then the king of Moab sacrificed his eldest son on the city wall as a last desperate appeal to the Moabite god Chemosh (vs. 27). This was his final resort after the last attempt to break through the investing armies came to nothing (vs. 26).

27. The **great wrath upon Israel** is the fierce anger of the Moabite god, who was still thought to have effective power in his own territory. It is evident that the tide of battle suddenly and surprisingly turned, and Mesha of Moab was able to extricate himself and his people from an apparently utterly hopeless situation. The early Israelite historian,

---

turned to fighting among themselves, and had stained the water with each other's blood. Thus were the Moabites lured to their ruin. Nowhere in all literature does nature play so large a role as a revelation of the being, the power, and the providence of God as in the Bible. Everything in nature spoke to the Hebrew of God. No wonder, then, if natural phenomena, occurring at the moment of their deepest necessity,

appeared to them as divine and miraculous events designed for their rescue. Here is a preeminent illustration of nature working in behalf of God's people: its ghostly mirage, its awesome spectacle, water turned to blood by rays of sun and color of soil! Never in all Hebrew history was God seen to move in a way more mysterious and incalculable than in the story of the defeat of the Moabites. Who could have foreseen it,

him *for* a burnt offering upon the wall. And there was great indignation against Israel: and they departed from him, and returned to *their own* land.

4 Now there cried a certain woman of the wives of the sons of the prophets unto Elisha, saying, Thy servant my husband is dead; and thou knowest that thy servant did fear the LORD: and the creditor is come to take unto him my two sons to be bondmen.

2 And Elisha said unto her, What shall I do for thee? tell me, what hast thou in the house? And she said, Thine handmaid hath not any thing in the house, save a pot of oil.

3 Then he said, Go, borrow thee vessels abroad of all thy neighbors, *even* empty vessels; borrow not a few.

offered him for a burnt offering upon the wall. And there came great wrath upon Israel; and they withdrew from him and returned to their own land.

4 Now the wife of one of the sons of the prophets cried to Eli'sha, "Your servant my husband is dead; and you know that your servant feared the LORD, but the creditor has come to take my two children to be his slaves." 2 And Eli'sha said to her, "What shall I do for you? Tell me; what have you in the house?" And she said, "Your maidservant has nothing in the house, except a jar of oil." 3 Then he said, "Go outside, borrow vessels of all your neighbors, empty vessels and not too few.

---

from whose early work this narrative has been taken, still thought that while Israel's god was all-powerful in Israel, Moab's god had power in Moab, each god in his own territory (see Exeg. on 5:15). Presumably the sacrifice of Mesha was effective, an angry Chemosh was placated by his people, and he therefore turned and saved them from disaster. This line of reasoning is most likely, since the Moabite stone reads extraordinarily like an early Israelite account. If the names of the god and of the locality were changed, it would be well-nigh impossible to distinguish it from a contemporary Israelite document.

7. STORIES OF ELISHA (4:1–6:23)

This section consists of a group of Elisha stories drawn from a collection of wonder tales concerning him. Each story gives an account of some miraculous deed and thereby demonstrates the extraordinary power and prestige of the prophet. There is nothing to be gained by trying to explain away the miraculous element in these stories. They belong to the same environment as that which often collects around some most unusual personage. The best example of this kind is *The Little Flowers of Saint Francis.*

a) THE VESSELS OF OIL (4:1-7)

The widow of one of the members of the prophetic guilds is threatened with the seizure of her two sons by a creditor who intends to sell them as slaves. She appeals for help to Elisha. He tells her to borrow all the vessels she can and to fill them with the oil she has at hand. Miraculously the oil continues to pour until all the vessels she can borrow are filled. She sells this oil and is able to pay the creditor. The quantity of the oil was limited only by her faith in collecting empty vessels.

4:1. The Targ. identifies the woman as the wife of Obadiah, Ahab's chief steward who saved the hundred prophets (I Kings 18:4), probably on account of the statements

---

or imagined that it could have happened? Thus are we taught that the resources of God for our salvation are beyond all human understanding. Thus do we learn that in moments of danger we too can rely upon his saving power.

4:1-7. *Elisha and the Needy Woman.*—The contrast between Elijah and Elisha is complete. Elijah was a prophet of the wilds, appearing at moments of religious crisis, and then disap-

pearing in the solitudes of the desert. Elisha walked daily among men, interested not only in great events but in the vicissitudes of the personal life, in the needs and sorrows of men in everyday experience. In this respect the ministry of Elisha resembles that of our Lord, who went about doing good. Indeed, ch. 4 reads much like a chapter out of the Gospels (cf. vss. 1-7 with John 2:1-10; vss. 8-36 with Luke 8:49-56;

4 And when thou art come in, thou shalt shut the door upon thee and upon thy sons, and shalt pour out into all those vessels, and thou shalt set aside that which is full.

5 So she went from him, and shut the door upon her and upon her sons, who brought *the vessels* to her; and she poured out.

6 And it came to pass, when the vessels were full, that she said unto her son, Bring me yet a vessel. And he said unto her, *There is* not a vessel more. And the oil stayed.

7 Then she came and told the man of God. And he said, Go, sell the oil, and pay thy debt, and live thou and thy children of the rest.

8 ¶ And it fell on a day, that Elisha passed to Shunem, where *was* a great woman; and she constrained him to eat

4 Then go in, and shut the door upon yourself and your sons, and pour into all these vessels; and when one is full, set it aside."

5 So she went from him and shut the door upon herself and her sons; and as she poured they brought the vessels to her.

6 When the vessels were full, she said to her son, "Bring me another vessel." And he said to her, "There is not another." Then the oil stopped flowing.

7 She came and told the man of God, and he said, "Go, sell the oil and pay your debts, and you and your sons can live on the rest."

8 One day Eli'sha went on to Shunem, where a wealthy woman lived, who urged

---

in each context that he **feared the LORD.** So also Josephus, who adds (*Antiquities* IX. 4. 2) that the money in question was borrowed by Obadiah in order to feed the prophets.

The existence of slavery in Israel is evidenced elsewhere by Exod. 21:7; Lev. 25:39; Neh. 5:5; Isa. 50:1; Jer. 34:8-11. The creditor was not acting contrary to the law in purposing to seize the sons and sell them as slaves in order to recover the debt.

b) THE SON OF THE WOMAN OF SHUNEM (4:8-37)

A wealthy woman of Shunem notices that Elisha often passes that way, and she builds a roof chamber for the convenience of the prophet. Elisha asks his servant what can best be done to recompense his hostess. Learning that her greatest desire is to bear

---

vss. 42-44 with Mark 6:34-44). Elisha was constantly moved with compassion. He used his powers to banish sorrow, to bring hope and cheer into the lives of plain men and women. He was a dispenser of happiness. Thus his is the type of ministry which may be ours. No one of us may be an Elijah, but every one of us may be an Elisha. If possessed by God's Holy Spirit, we may perform deeds of mercy which will seem like miracles in other men's eyes. It is a high calling to move among men and bring courage and happiness into disheartened and bewildered souls. The character and career of Elisha are often disparaged in comparison with the more heroic figure of Elijah. Yet his beneficent life, less spectacular and more humane, is the inspired symbol of a ministry which lies within the reach of us all. Small kindnesses, small courtesies, small considerations, habitually practiced, give a greater charm to the character and often do more good in the world than great accomplishments.

To the casual reader this chapter may seem to present only a series of incredible old wives' tales that have no more moral meaning than a wonderbook of ancient mythology. To the crit-

ical reader it will pose only interesting questions about the origin of these miraculous narratives and the light which they throw on the social life of Israel in that day. The devout reader, however, is not too much concerned with these matters, nor is he at all disturbed by doubt of their literal historicity. Rather he finds in these narratives glimpses of spiritual truth, and these throw light on personal duty and opportunity. Consider this story of the devout woman in financial distress. She applies to Elisha for help, just as many a woman today turns to her minister in times of stress. The quiet, anonymous helpfulness of the church is not the least of the services it is performing in our modern world. But such kindness and consideration to those hard-pressed financially is often rendered by some "man of God," unordained, but having in him a heart of sympathy, some banker, lawyer, financial adviser, who is able to find a way to relieve distress and lift a burden. The story may be ancient, but it is also modern. And in both cases equally a miracle of grace has been performed.

8-37. The Shunammite Woman.—This story is a beautiful one from beginning to end. It is

bread. And *so* it was, *that,* as oft as he passed by, he turned in thither to eat bread.

9 And she said unto her husband, Behold now, I perceive that this *is* a holy man of God, which passeth by us continually.

10 Let us make a little chamber, I pray thee, on the wall; and let us set for him there a bed, and a table, and a stool, and a candlestick: and it shall be, when he cometh to us, that he shall turn in thither.

11 And it fell on a day, that he came thither, and he turned into the chamber, and lay there.

12 And he said to Gehazi his servant, Call this Shunammite. And when he had called her, she stood before him.

13 And he said unto him, Say now unto her, Behold, thou hast been careful for us with all this care; what *is* to be done for thee? wouldest thou be spoken for to the king, or to the captain of the host? And she answered, I dwell among mine own people.

14 And he said, What then *is* to be done for her? And Gehazi answered, Verily she hath no child, and her husband is old.

15 And he said, Call her. And when he had called her, she stood in the door.

16 And he said, About this season, according to the time of life, thou shalt embrace a son. And she said, Nay, my lord, *thou* man of God, do not lie unto thine handmaid.

17 And the woman conceived, and bare a son at that season that Elisha had said unto her, according to the time of life.

him to eat some food. So whenever he passed that way, he would turn in there to eat food. 9 And she said to her husband, "Behold now, I perceive that this is a holy man of God, who is continually passing our way. 10 Let us make a small roof chamber with walls, and put there for him a bed, a table, a chair, and a lamp, so that whenever he comes to us, he can go in there."

11 One day he came there, and he turned into the chamber 12 and rested there. And he said to Geha'zi his servant, "Call this Shu'nammite." When he had called her, she stood before him. 13 And he said to him, "Say now to her, See, you have taken all this trouble for us; what is to be done for you? Would you have a word spoken on your behalf to the king or to the commander of the army?" She answered, "I dwell among my own people." 14 And he said, "What then is to be done for her?" Geha'zi answered, "Well, she has no son, and her husband is old." 15 He said, "Call her." And when he had called her, she stood in the doorway. 16 And he said, "At this season, when the time comes round, you shall embrace a son." And she said, "No, my lord, O man of God; do not lie to your maidservant." 17 But the woman conceived, and she bore a son about that time the following spring, as Eli'sha had said to her.

---

a son, he calls her and announces the fulfillment of her wish. In process of time a boy is born, but one day the growing lad dies of a sunstroke. The widow hurries to the prophet's home on Mount Carmel and Elisha brings the child to life again.

10. The **small roof chamber with walls** is an upper chamber built on the roof with access by an outer stairway, so that the entrance or exit is independent of the house itself.

16. The reading of the KJV is preferable, **About this season, according to the time of life.** The meaning is, "At this season of the year, according to the period of gestation" (cf. Gen. 18:10, 14, where the meaning is that after the usual nine-month period Sarah

---

full of grace and charm. We note that the initial kindness of the woman and her husband was in no expectation of any reward but was the spontaneous expression of hospitable hearts. It was not she who asked anything in return from Elisha. It was he who inquired of his servant Gehazi what he could do for her. There followed the gift of a child and the child's restoration to life after he had died. Poignant is the story of

the woman's grief. We are told that she was a wealthy woman. But grief spares none, high or low. The community of suffering makes the whole world kin. She insisted on going in person to Elisha. She had learned to believe in and trust this man whose power she had begun to know. Perhaps one of the greatest rewards of any "man of God" today is to win the faith and confidence of souls in need.

18 ¶ And when the child was grown, it fell on a day, that he went out to his father to the reapers.

19 And he said unto his father, My head, my head! And he said to a lad, Carry him to his mother.

20 And when he had taken him, and brought him to his mother, he sat on her knees till noon, and *then* died.

21 And she went up, and laid him on the bed of the man of God, and shut *the door* upon him, and went out.

22 And she called unto her husband, and said, Send me, I pray thee, one of the young men, and one of the asses, that I may run to the man of God, and come again.

23 And he said, Wherefore wilt thou go to him to-day? *it is* neither new moon, nor sabbath. And she said, *It shall be* well.

24 Then she saddled an ass, and said to her servant, Drive, and go forward; slack not *thy* riding for me, except I bid thee.

25 So she went and came unto the man of God to mount Carmel. And it came to pass, when the man of God saw her afar off, that he said to Gehazi his servant, Behold, *yonder is* that Shunammite:

26 Run now, I pray thee, to meet her, and say unto her, *Is it* well with thee? *is it* well with thy husband? *is it* well with the child? And she answered, *It is* well.

18 When the child had grown, he went out one day to his father among the reapers. 19 And he said to his father, "Oh, my head, my head!" The father said to his servant, "Carry him to his mother." 20 And when he had lifted him, and brought him to his mother, the child sat on her lap till noon, and then he died. 21 And she went up and laid him on the bed of the man of God, and shut the door upon him, and went out. 22 Then she called to her husband, and said, "Send me one of the servants and one of the asses, that I may quickly go to the man of God, and come back again." 23 And he said, "Why will you go to him today? It is neither new moon nor sabbath." She said, "It will be well." 24 Then she saddled the ass, and she said to her servant, "Urge the beast on; do not slacken the pace for me unless I tell you." 25 So she set out, and came to the man of God at Mount Carmel.

When the man of God saw her coming, he said to Geha'zi his servant, "Look, yonder is the Shu'nammite; 26 run at once to meet her, and say to her, Is it well with you? Is it well with your husband? Is it well with the child?" And she answered, "It is well."

will bear a son). **When the time comes round:** The Hebrew actually reads "according to the living [quickening] time."

23. The distance from Shunem to Carmel is about twenty-five miles. Evidently at that period the sabbath was not observed as in postexilic times. It was probably not known in Israel until the time of the Assyrian domination of the country, with its introduction of many Assyrian customs and ideas such as the observance of the new moon days and of the "seven" days (N. H. Snaith, *The Jewish New Year Festival* [London: Society for Promoting Christian Knowledge, 1947], pp. 117-21).

24. The woman's command to the young man was to follow the beast closely and to keep on beating the ass so that it maintained a good pace all the way to Mount Carmel. The prophet's headquarters were probably at the place where his predecessor Elijah had striven for the Lord against Baal in the time of Jezebel.

Thus is described to us the reciprocal relation of two noble souls. The woman's native sympathy and kindness had caused her to entertain an angel unawares. So, often in human experience a casual gesture of kindness, the simple expression of good will and sympathy, brings in its train rich rewards, unexpected blessings. Elisha, too, might have accepted what was offered him as only what was due to a prophet of God. Not so. What could he do to requite this kindness? At once is revealed the heart of any true "man of God." Inquiry disclosed the woman's secret wants. How often under the external appearance of prosperity and well-being there lies the hidden disappointment! To detect this and to seek to satisfy the hungry soul is one of the finest ministries of any "man of God."

27 And when she came to the man of God to the hill, she caught him by the feet: but Gehazi came near to thrust her away. And the man of God said, Let her alone; for her soul *is* vexed within her: and the Lord hath hid *it* from me, and hath not told me.

28 Then she said, Did I desire a son of my lord? did I not say, Do not deceive me?

29 Then he said to Gehazi, Gird up thy loins, and take my staff in thine hand, and go thy way: if thou meet any man, salute him not; and if any salute thee, answer him not again: and lay my staff upon the face of the child.

30 And the mother of the child said, *As* the Lord liveth, and *as* thy soul liveth, I will not leave thee. And he arose, and followed her.

31 And Gehazi passed on before them, and laid the staff upon the face of the child; but *there was* neither voice, nor hearing. Wherefore he went again to meet him, and told him, saying, The child is not awaked.

32 And when Elisha was come into the house, behold, the child was dead, *and* laid upon his bed.

33 He went in therefore, and shut the door upon them twain, and prayed unto the Lord.

34 And he went up, and lay upon the child, and put his mouth upon his mouth, and his eyes upon his eyes, and his hands upon his hands: and he stretched himself upon the child; and the flesh of the child waxed warm.

27 And when she came to the mountain to the man of God, she caught hold of his feet. And Geha′zi came to thrust her away. But the man of God said, "Let her alone, for she is in bitter distress; and the Lord has hidden it from me, and has not told me."

28 Then she said, "Did I ask my lord for a son? Did I not say, Do not deceive me?"

29 He said to Geha′zi, "Gird up your loins, and take my staff in your hand, and go. If you meet any one, do not salute him; and if any one salutes you, do not reply; and lay my staff upon the face of the child."

30 Then the mother of the child said, "As the Lord lives, and as you yourself live, I will not leave you." So he arose and followed her.

31 Geha′zi went on ahead and laid the staff upon the face of the child, but there was no sound or sign of life. Therefore he returned to meet him, and told him, "The child has not awaked."

32 When Eli′sha came into the house, he saw the child lying dead on his bed. 33 So he went in and shut the door upon the two of them, and prayed to the Lord. 34 Then he went up and lay upon the child, putting his mouth upon his mouth, his eyes upon his eyes, and his hands upon his hands; and as he stretched himself upon him, the flesh

---

29. The command to silence was not in the interests of speed, but to preserve the effectiveness of that power with which the prophet was sending him. Many examples of this necessity of silence are given in books on primitive religion and customs. In Morocco "*baraka* is affected by speaking, especially speaking aloud, whereas there is magic power in silence" (E. A. Westermarck, *Ritual and Belief in Morocco* [London: Macmillan & Co., 1926], I, 253). *Baraka* (the equivalent Hebrew word means "blessing") is the Moroccan equivalent of mana. There are also numerous allusions to the magic power of silence in the various volumes written by Baldwin Spencer and F. J. Gillen on the habits and customs of Australian aborigines. In this particular case the mana carried by the wonder-working staff is not effective, whether it was intended to restore

---

Did Elisha really restore to life the son of the Shunammite woman? If so, this is the only instance of the kind to be found in the O.T. Or is it one of the many legends which attached themselves to the life of Elisha? If so, it loses none of its spiritual significance. For in vs. 34

we are given a graphic description of what it costs to bring the dead to life. Only life can restore life. Only the uttermost giving of self can breathe the breath of life into the otherwise dead. Only the stretching of one's soul upon the soul of one out of which all semblance of life

35 Then he returned, and walked in the house to and fro; and went up, and stretched himself upon him: and the child sneezed seven times, and the child opened his eyes.

36 And he called Gehazi, and said, Call this Shunammite. So he called her. And when she was come in unto him, he said, Take up thy son.

37 Then she went in, and fell at his feet, and bowed herself to the ground, and took up her son, and went out.

38 ¶ And Elisha came again to Gilgal: and *there was* a dearth in the land; and the sons of the prophets *were* sitting before him: and he said unto his servant, Set on the great pot, and seethe pottage for the sons of the prophets.

39 And one went out into the field to gather herbs, and found a wild vine, and gathered thereof wild gourds his lap full, and came and shred *them* into the pot of pottage: for they knew *them* not.

40 So they poured out for the men to eat. And it came to pass, as they were eating of the pottage, that they cried out, and said, O *thou* man of God, *there is* death in the pot. And they could not eat *thereof*.

41 But he said, Then bring meal. And he cast *it* into the pot; and he said, Pour out

of the child became warm. 35 Then he got up again, and walked once to and fro in the house, and went up, and stretched himself upon him; the child sneezed seven times, and the child opened his eyes. 36 Then he summoned Geha'zi and said, "Call this Shu'nammite." So he called her. And when she came to him, he said, "Take up your son." 37 She came and fell at his feet, bowing to the ground; then she took up her son and went out.

38 And Eli'sha came again to Gilgal when there was a famine in the land. And as the sons of the prophets were sitting before him, he said to his servant, "Set on the great pot, and boil pottage for the sons of the prophets." 39 One of them went out into the field to gather herbs, and found a wild vine and gathered from it his lap full of wild gourds, and came and cut them up into the pot of pottage, not knowing what they were. 40 And they poured out for the men to eat. But while they were eating of the pottage, they cried out, "O man of God, there is death in the pot!" And they could not eat it. 41 He said, "Then bring meal." And he threw it into the pot, and said,

---

life or to prevent such further loss of life power as would cause the boy to die. The boy was already dead, and Elisha himself had to restore him by personal contact.

35. The reference to sneezing is not found in the LXX, and is probably an error due to a dittograph. According to the LXX, the prophet stretched himself seven times over the child. This is much more in line with the regular procedure in these matters, especially since the magic number seven is involved in Elisha's own actions.

c) DEATH IN THE POT (4:38-41)

Elisha came to Gilgal in a time of famine. The people gathered together to eat a common meal, but one man unknowingly shredded poisonous gourds into the pot. When this was discovered, presumably because of the taste, they cried out warning, and Elisha, casting some meal into the pot, made the pottage wholesome.

38. There was a seven-year **famine** predicted in 8:1; this may well be that same famine.

39. The plant is called **a wild vine** because of its trailing shoots, and its fruit could easily be mistaken for a gourd cucumber. The plant is usually identified as the colocynth,

---

has vanished can quicken it again. It was by Christ's stretching of himself upon the cross of his infinite sacrifice that he brought to life again men that were dead in their trespasses and sins.

38-44. Two Other Miracles.—The last two stories in the chapter are obscure. The first

records the method of the prophet in making the food of the poor, poisoned by weeds, fit to eat. The second records the feeding of the hungry. Of these and other miracles in the O.T. it may be said in general that they do not stand on the same level as those recorded in the Gospels by so much as those who are reported

for the people, that they may eat. And there was no harm in the pot.

42 ¶ And there came a man from Baal-shalisha, and brought the man of God bread of the firstfruits, twenty loaves of barley, and full ears of corn in the husk thereof. And he said, Give unto the people, that they may eat.

43 And his servitor said, What, should I set this before a hundred men? He said again, Give the people, that they may eat: for thus saith the LORD, They shall eat, and shall leave *thereof*.

44 So he set *it* before them, and they did eat, and left *thereof*, according to the word of the LORD.

5 Now Naaman, captain of the host of the king of Syria, was a great man with his master, and honorable, because by him

"Pour out for the men, that they may eat." And there was no harm in the pot.

42 A man came from Ba'al-shal'ishah, bringing the man of God bread of the first fruits, twenty loaves of barley, and fresh ears of grain in his sack. And Eli'sha said, "Give to the men, that they may eat." **43** But his servant said, "How am I to set this before a hundred men?" So he repeated, "Give them to the men, that they may eat, for thus says the LORD, 'They shall eat and have some left.'" **44** So he set it before them. And they ate, and had some left, according to the word of the LORD.

5 Na'aman, commander of the army of the king of Syria, was a great man with

---

and its fruit is like an orange in shape and size, the pulp of which is a powerful cathartic, and in large quantities is definitely poisonous.

d) THE TWENTY LOAVES (4:42-44)

A man brings twenty loaves and some fresh ears of barley as his first fruits. With this comparatively small quantity of food Elisha feeds a hundred men.

42. The bringing of **first fruits** to the man of God has been thought to be a departure from normal practice. This is not the case, since in old Israel there were prophets at the shrines as well as priests; e.g., Elisha had his main home at the shrine on Mount Carmel (A. R. Johnson, *The Cultic Prophet in Ancient Israel* [Cardiff: University of Wales Press, 1944], p. 26). It was only in postexilic times that the priests had sole rights in the first fruits. The theory involved in the offering of first fruits is that all the produce belongs to the deity, and that he must first receive a token of the harvest, after which the produce is regarded as "common" (*hōl*) and permissible for human use.

The word צִקְלֹן occurs only here, and its meaning is unknown. The rendering **in his sack** is based upon the Vulg., but the Syriac and Targ. have "garment." Possibly the original word, this or another, meant "in his wallet."

e) THE HEALING OF NAAMAN (5:1-19)

Naaman, the Syrian commander in chief, has received every honor that military skill and good fortune can bring, but he is a leper. A little Israelite maid has been captured in a raid and finds herself in the service of Naaman's wife. She tells her mistress of the prophet in Israel. The king of Syria commands the king of Israel to heal Naaman. The peremptory command causes the king of Israel great concern, until he is reminded of Elisha the prophet and his miraculous powers. Elisha bids Naaman bathe seven times in the Jordan. Naaman refuses, but is persuaded by his attendants. The Syrian is healed and returns home with all the gifts which Elisha refuses to take.

5:1. It is remarkable that the victories of Naaman are ascribed to the good favor of the Lord, the God of Israel. The story comes from the Elisha cycle. Since Elisha died

---

to have wrought them do not occupy the altitudes of the personality of Jesus.

5:1-14. *Naaman the Syrian.*—He was . . . a **mighty man of valor, but he was a leper** (see Luke 4:27). To how many men in the world's

history do these words apply. They were mighty in intellect, mighty in capacity, but they were not whole and sound of soul. Hence their great abilities brought no good to the world or even to themselves. Had they been cured of their

the Lord had given deliverance unto Syria: he was also a mighty man of valor, *but he was* a leper.

2 And the Syrians had gone out by companies, and had brought away captive out of the land of Israel a little maid; and she waited on Naaman's wife.

3 And she said unto her mistress, Would God my lord *were* with the prophet that *is* in Samaria! for he would recover him of his leprosy.

4 And *one* went in, and told his lord, saying, Thus and thus said the maid that *is* of the land of Israel.

5 And the king of Syria said, Go to, go, and I will send a letter unto the king of Israel. And he departed, and took with him ten talents of silver, and six thousand *pieces* of gold, and ten changes of raiment.

6 And he brought the letter to the king of Israel, saying, Now when this letter is come unto thee, behold, I have *therewith* sent Naaman my servant to thee, that thou mayest recover him of his leprosy.

his master and in high favor, because by him the Lord had given victory to Syria. He was a mighty man of valor, but he was a leper. 2 Now the Syrians on one of their raids had carried off a little maid from the land of Israel, and she waited on Na′aman's wife. 3 She said to her mistress, "Would that my lord were with the prophet who is in Samar′ia! He would cure him of his leprosy." 4 So Na′aman went in and told his lord, "Thus and so spoke the maiden from the land of Israel." 5 And the king of Syria said, "Go now, and I will send a letter to the king of Israel."

So he went, taking with him ten talents of silver, six thousand shekels of gold, and ten festal garments. 6 And he brought the letter to the king of Israel, which read, "When this letter reaches you, know that I have sent to you Na′aman my servant, that

---

ca. 800 B.C. (cf. 13:14), the date of this story cannot be much earlier than the time of Amos, who could say that the God of Israel brought the Philistines from Crete and the Syrians from Kir (Amos 9:7). We see here, therefore, advancing ideas concerning the power of God side by side with primitive survivals. This need occasion no great surprise since there are many traces of primitive religion still observable in our own times.

5. The present which Naaman brought was large. Apart from the value of the clothing, which may have been considerable, the actual cash amounted to more than $80,000.

6. The tone of the **letter,** and indeed the whole setting of the story, create the impression that at this time Israel was subject to Syria. This impression is confirmed by the later story, according to which the king of Syria was able to send his armies to surround the prophet on the hill at Dothan (6:14). Dothan was scarcely more than ten miles from Samaria, almost due north.

---

leprosy, what names they might have written on the scrolls of time! Or today there may be found proud and forceful men who ride high, achieve wealth and position, and yet are lepers. Some hidden moral defect cancels their real abilities, prevents them from attaining lives of positive influence, from commanding the confidence and respect of their fellow men. Mighty men, but lepers!

And the Syrians . . . had brought away captive out of the land of Israel a little maid. Once more a major role is played by a minor biblical character. How little did she realize, this humble Hebrew girl, what her native piety —her only distinction—was to achieve. She did not hide her faith in God; she used it. And let anyone today, however humble he may be, have

faith in God and declare it to one in physical or moral need and he too may bring like miracles to pass.

So Naaman departed and took much treasure with him. Yet the price which Naaman had to pay to be healed of his leprosy was even greater than that. Money can do much, yet it never yet purchased for a man the healing of his soul nor the peace of his mind. And Naaman had to travel all the way from Syria to Elisha, the man of God, to gain his cure. The gods of Syria were not equal to the task. We have here the touchstone by which we may test the supremacy of Bible religion. It alone is able to purge the soul of man from the leprosy of sin. And only the religion that can do that can claim the final allegiance of the human heart. Other religions

7 And it came to pass, when the king of Israel had read the letter, that he rent his clothes, and said, *Am* I God, to kill and to make alive, that this man doth send unto me to recover a man of his leprosy? Wherefore consider, I pray you, and see how he seeketh a quarrel against me.

8 ¶ And it was *so,* when Elisha the man of God had heard that the king of Israel had rent his clothes, that he sent to the king, saying, Wherefore hast thou rent thy clothes? let him come now to me, and he shall know that there is a prophet in Israel.

9 So Naaman came with his horses and with his chariot, and stood at the door of the house of Elisha.

10 And Elisha sent a messenger unto him, saying, Go and wash in Jordan seven times, and thy flesh shall come again to thee, and thou shalt be clean.

11 But Naaman was wroth, and went away, and said, Behold, I thought, He will surely come out to me, and stand, and call on the name of the LORD his God, and strike his hand over the place, and recover the leper.

you may cure him of his leprosy." 7 And when the king of Israel read the letter, he rent his clothes and said, "Am I God; to kill and to make alive, that this man sends word to me to cure a man of his leprosy? Only consider, and see how he is seeking a quarrel with me."

8 But when Eli'sha the man of God heard that the king of Israel had rent his clothes, he sent to the king, saying, "Why have you rent your clothes? Let him come now to me, that he may know that there is a prophet in Israel." 9 So Na'aman came with his horses and chariots, and halted at the door of Eli'sha's house. 10 And Eli'sha sent a messenger to him, saying, "Go and wash in the Jordan seven times, and your flesh shall be restored, and you shall be clean." 11 But Na'aman was angry, and went away, saying, "Behold, I thought that he would surely come out to me, and stand, and call on the name of the LORD his God, and wave his hand over the place, and cure

---

11. Naaman was aggrieved on two counts: first, that the prophet himself did not come out to heal him in some publicly spectacular way, and second, that he was told to bathe in the river Jordan. "Mostly silent and black in spite of its speed, but now and then breaking into praise and whitening into foam, Jordan scours along, muddy between banks of mud, careless of beauty, careless of life" (George Adam Smith, *Historical Geography of the Holy Land* [25th ed.; London: Hodder & Stoughton, 1931], p. 486) —a sharp contrast to the beauty of the rivers of Damascus. The prophet, however, follows his normal custom of speaking through an intermediary, and insists that Naaman shall

---

contain high and beautiful truths. But from the point of view of freeing the soul from sin there is no such thing as comparative religion. Only the Bible deals finally with that.

Jehoram the king did not know what to do when the message and the gift came from Syria. With all his kingly power, he was powerless. Secular force cannot deal with moral emergency. Only the man of God can assume control. And he tells the Syrian to **go and wash in the Jordan seven times.** Naaman is indignant. His pride is hurt, and he would turn away in disappointed anger. Plenty of people are in the same mood today. Modern prophets are telling them that secular sources of inspiration and illumination will never heal them of their leprosy; that they must wash in the old river Jordan; that they must find their healing in church and sabbath, Bible and prayer. And the modern mind rebels.

There is something too narrow and provincial in this reiterated assertion that a man cannot find health and healing except as he dips into this old Jordan. Are there not splendid waters in our modern world that lie entirely outside this little Judea of religion? The answer is the same today as in the day of Naaman. It is not a question of whether the secular sources of inspiration are not more beautiful than the Jordan. It is a question only of which can heal men of their leprosy.

For the longing to be healed is still the longing of many a man and woman in our modern world. In spite of all that they possess they are really sick at heart, and they know that they are. The friction and the pressure of life always bring with them many impurities which mere appeal to reason cannot remedy, because reason condemns while it cannot cure. The sense of

12 *Are* not Abana and Pharpar, rivers of Damascus, better than all the waters of Israel? may I not wash in them, and be clean? So he turned and went away in a rage.

13 And his servants came near, and spake unto him, and said, My father, *if* the prophet had bid thee *do some* great thing, wouldest thou not have done *it?* how much rather then, when he saith to thee, Wash, and be clean?

14 Then went he down, and dipped himself seven times in Jordan, according to the saying of the man of God: and his flesh came again like unto the flesh of a little child, and he was clean.

15 ¶ And he returned to the man of God, he and all his company, and came, and stood before him: and he said, Behold, now

the leper. 12 Are not Aba'na[e] and Pharpar, the rivers of Damascus, better than all the waters of Israel? Could I not wash in them, and be clean?" So he turned and went away in a rage. 13 But his servants came near and said to him, "My father, if the prophet had commanded you to do some great thing, would you not have done it? How much rather, then, when he says to you, 'Wash, and be clean'?" 14 So he went down and dipped himself seven times in the Jordan, according to the word of the man of God; and his flesh was restored like the flesh of a little child, and he was clean.

15 Then he returned to the man of God, he and all his company, and he came and

[e] Another reading is *Amana*

wash in an Israelite river, since the whole cure is a demonstration **that there is a prophet in Israel** (vs. 8).

12. These two rivers of Damascus are commonly identified with the Nahr Baradā (**Abana**) and the Nahr el-A'waj (**Pharpar**). The name Pharpar is to be recognized in Wadi Barbar, a smaller stream which may at one time have been much larger, and whose waters may have joined those of the Nahr el-A'waj. The effect of Damascus on the desert nomad can scarcely be appreciated by other people. The Arab calls the Oasis of Damascus *Jinnat ed-dinnea* ("the garden of the world"). There is an ancient story that in his youth the prophet Mohammed went to Damascus in a caravan, but when he came to the summit of the southern hills and saw the unexpected view of the oasis with its orchards and its blossoms, he turned away, wrapping his face in his mantle, saying that man may enter but one *jannat* ("garden," "paradise"), and his was above. Mohammed never would enter Damascus.

15. Here again we get an apparently monotheistic statement, side by side with a belief (vs. 17) that this God cannot be worshiped except on Israelite soil. With this latter verse cf. I Sam. 26:19, where David says that being driven off Israelite soil is equivalent to being told to go and worship other gods.

The Hebrew ברכה, usually translated **blessing**, occasionally (Gen. 33:11 and six times in all) means **present** (cf. Prov. 11:25, where "the liberal soul" is a good rendering of what in Hebrew is, lit., "the person of *berākhāh*").

unworthiness remains. And when it comes to this washing of the soul, this cure of life at its center, there is no substitute for the old river Jordan. Culture can do much, but it cannot do this. As simple, contrite-hearted men and women, we must go and wash in this Jordan if we would be clean.

But this demands much of the modern man, just as it did of Naaman. Yet Naaman conquered his pride, stifled his vanity, and, proud soldier that he was, went down and dipped seven times—one dip was not enough—and his **flesh came again like unto the flesh of a little child.** Pride, and only pride, keeps many a modern Naaman from receiving the blessing

which came to the ancient Syrian. If we can but forget our pride, put off our intellectual harness and critical apparatus, and go right down into the stream of the life-giving life of God, then our flesh too will come to us as the flesh of a little child. If each week we bathe our souls in a real sabbath and in worship in the sanctuary, if each day we dip into the Bible and know real moments of consecrating prayer, then the miracle will be wrought for us as truly as it was for Naaman.

15-19. *The House of Rimmon.*—Naaman exhibited after his cure the noble spirit of a noble man. He did not set off at once to Syria but came in reverence to Elisha, confessed his faith

I know that *there is* no God in all the earth, but in Israel: now therefore, I pray thee, take a blessing of thy servant.

16 But he said, *As* the LORD liveth, before whom I stand, I will receive none. And he urged him to take *it;* but he refused.

17 And Naaman said, Shall there not then, I pray thee, be given to thy servant two mules' burden of earth? for thy servant will henceforth offer neither burnt offering nor sacrifice unto other gods, but unto the LORD.

18 In this thing the LORD pardon thy servant, *that* when my master goeth into the house of Rimmon to worship there, and he leaneth on my hand, and I bow myself in the house of Rimmon: when I bow down myself in the house of Rimmon, the LORD pardon thy servant in this thing.

19 And he said unto him, Go in peace. So he departed from him a little way.

stood before him; and he said, "Behold, I know that there is no God in all the earth but in Israel; so accept now a present from your servant." 16 But he said, "As the LORD lives, whom I serve, I will receive none." And he urged him to take it, but he refused. 17 Then Na'aman said, "If not, I pray you, let there be given to your servant two mules' burden of earth; for henceforth your servant will not offer burnt offering or sacrifice to any god but the LORD. 18 In this matter may the LORD pardon your servant: when my master goes into the house of Rimmon to worship there, leaning on my arm, and I bow myself in the house of Rimmon, when I bow myself in the house of Rimmon, the LORD pardon your servant in this matter." 19 He said to him, "Go in peace."

But when Na'aman had gone from him a

---

18. Naaman is referring to the formal state worship of Ramman (**Rimmon**). This name is an epithet of Hadad, the thunder and weather god of Assyria, and actually means "thunderer" (René Dussaud, *Les religions des Hittites et des Hourrites, des Phéniciens et des Syriens* [Paris: Presses Universitaires de France, 1945; "Mana: Introduction à l'histoire des religions"], p. 390) .

---

in the God of Israel, and offered rich payment. The refusal of Elisha to take it is illustrative of the attitude of a true ministry always and everywhere. What a man of God does is done for no other reward than the knowledge that he has been able to save a soul in need. At least this should be said of the ministry: that it shall be above any taint of mercenary motive. Many a man of God cures souls today without receiving or expecting the reward that would be paid to the physician or psychiatrist.

When we read these verses, we instinctively feel a certain sympathy for Naaman. It was a fine, frank thing to tell Elisha of the difficult situation that he foresaw, and to ask the prophet's counsel. We are glad that Elisha trusted him and told him to **go in peace.** How would a purely formal deference to pagan gods involve his new-found loyalty to the God of Israel? Yet the phrase to **bow . . . in the house of Rimmon** (vs. 18) has become a proverbial expression to denote a dangerous and dishonest compromise. The danger was always there that, by bowing in the house of Rimmon, Naaman's new-found faith would be weakened and destroyed. The general principle remains: any deviation from truth and honor, even if circumstance may seem to warrant it, is always dangerous and may even prove fatal. It is often

the beginning of moral disaster. "It is astonishing how soon the whole conscience begins to unravel, if a single stitch drops." [3] True allegiance to God allows of no exceptions. One must serve him with the whole heart or one cannot serve him at all.

In vs. 17 we find a curious request of Naaman before he leaves for Syria. May he not take with him **two mules' burden of earth,** since he is resolved henceforth to offer sacrifice only to the God of Israel? This points to the religious idea of that day that each land had its own god who could be worshiped only there. To leave one land for another was to leave one god for another. Hence, if Naaman was to worship the God of Israel in Syria, he must take some of the soil of Israel with him. To us this appears to be a naïve idea. To those of that day it had definite meaning. The request thus witnesses to the thorough religious sincerity of Naaman, to a conversion whose roots went deep.

The incident has its spiritual meaning and interpretation. Often we leave our native land and go into regions where the God of our fathers is neither worshiped nor honored. We may not have to travel very far. Paganism exists

[3] Charles Buxton, quoted by Mary W. Tileston, *Daily Strength for Daily Needs* (Boston: Little, Brown & Co., 1900), p. 82.

20 ¶ But Gehazi, the servant of Elisha the man of God, said, Behold, my master hath spared Naaman this Syrian, in not receiving at his hands that which he brought: but, *as* the LORD liveth, I will run after him, and take somewhat of him.

21 So Gehazi followed after Naaman. And when Naaman saw *him* running after him, he lighted down from the chariot to meet him, and said, *Is* all well?

22 And he said, All *is* well. My master hath sent me, saying, Behold, even now there be come to me from mount Ephraim two young men of the sons of the prophets: give them, I pray thee, a talent of silver, and two changes of garments.

23 And Naaman said, Be content, take two talents. And he urged him, and bound two talents of silver in two bags, with two changes of garments, and laid *them* upon two of his servants; and they bare *them* before him.

24 And when he came to the tower, he took *them* from their hand, and bestowed *them* in the house: and he let the men go, and they departed.

short distance, 20 Geha'zi, the servant of Eli'sha the man of God, said, "See, my master has spared this Na'aman the Syrian, in not accepting from his hand what he brought. As the LORD lives, I will run after him, and get something from him." 21 So Geha'zi followed Na'aman. And when Na'aman saw some one running after him, he alighted from the chariot to meet him, and said, "Is all well?" 22 And he said, "All is well. My master has sent me to say, 'There have just now come to me from the hill country of E'phraim two young men of the sons of the prophets; pray, give them a talent of silver and two festal garments.'" 23 And Na'aman said, "Be pleased to accept two talents." And he urged him, and tied up two talents of silver in two bags, with two festal garments, and laid them upon two of his servants; and they carried them before Geha'zi. 24 And when he came to the hill, he took them from their hand, and put them in the house; and he sent the men

---

f) GEHAZI THE LEPER (5:20-27)

Elisha has refused any gift from Naaman, but the sight of all the wealth stirs up his servant's greed. Gehazi follows Naaman, tells him that the prophet has changed his mind. Naaman willingly gives him all he asks, and more. When Gehazi returns, he finds the prophet is already aware of what has happened, and is told that the leprosy of Naaman will cling to him and to his family forever.

21. The M.T. reads, lit., "He fell from his chariot," but the Hebrew root נפל is used here of a sudden descent; cf. Amos 3:5, the sudden descent of the bird which sees a lure on the ground (N. H. Snaith, *The Book of Amos* [London: Epworth Press, 1946], II, 58); cf. also Gen. 24:64, Rebekah's sudden descent from her camel when first she saw Isaac. It is best therefore in this present verse to insert "hurriedly."

24. The word 'ôphēl is difficult. It apparently signifies some sort of swelling since it is used in I Sam. 5:6 of a boil or tumor, and there is a similar use in Arabic. But it is also used of a fortification at Jerusalem (southeast spur of the temple mount) and also somewhere in Moab, for the word is found on the Moabite stone (ll. 21-22). The Jerusalem Ophel is comparable to "the great projecting tower" of Neh. 3:27, and the "tower of the flock" of Mic. 4:8. **The hill** is the place where Elisha was living; cf. the

---

near us as well as in distant lands. We must take with us some of the rich, spiritual Palestinian soil, at least two mules' burden, if henceforth, no matter where we are, with whomsoever we may be associated, whatever our environment may be, we are to offer sacrifices not unto other gods but only unto the Lord.

20-27. Gehazi.—It is sad that so noble a chapter should have to record, before it ends, the avarice and deception of this trusted servant

of Elisha. He had never seen such wealth before as Naaman had offered to Elisha. It blinded his eyes and stifled his conscience. Here was easy money for the asking. So he fabricated his story, received from the grateful Naaman twice as much as he asked, returned, and hid his loot. Discovery and penalty swiftly followed. What a chapter is this! It tells of redemption and of retribution. A pagan by an act of faith is cured of his leprosy. An Israelite by an act of dis-

25 But he went in, and stood before his master. And Elisha said unto him, Whence *comest thou,* Gehazi? And he said, Thy servant went no whither.

26 And he said unto him, Went not mine heart *with thee,* when the man turned again from his chariot to meet thee? *Is it* a time to receive money, and to receive garments, and oliveyards, and vineyards, and sheep, and oxen, and menservants, and maidservants?

27 The leprosy therefore of Naaman shall cleave unto thee, and unto thy seed for ever. And he went out from his presence a leper *as white* as snow.

6 And the sons of the prophets said unto Elisha, Behold now, the place where we dwell with thee is too strait for us.

2 Let us go, we pray thee, unto Jordan, and take thence every man a beam, and let us make us a place there, where we may dwell. And he answered, Go ye.

3 And one said, Be content, I pray thee, and go with thy servants. And he answered, I will go.

4 So he went with them. And when they came to Jordan, they cut down wood.

5 But as one was felling a beam, the axe head fell into the water: and he cried, and said, Alas, master! for it was borrowed.

6 And the man of God said, Where fell it? And he showed him the place. And he cut down a stick, and cast *it* in thither; and the iron did swim.

away, and they departed. 25 He went in, and stood before his master, and Eli'sha said to him, "Where have you been, Geha'zi?" And he said, "Your servant went nowhere." 26 But he said to him, "Did I not go with you in spirit when the man turned from his chariot to meet you? Was it a time to accept money and garments, olive orchards and vineyards, sheep and oxen, menservants and maidservants? 27 Therefore the leprosy of Na'aman shall cleave to you, and to your descendants for ever." So he went out from his presence a leper, as white as snow.

6 Now the sons of the prophets said to Eli'sha, "See, the place where we dwell under your charge is too small for us. 2 Let us go to the Jordan and each of us get there a log, and let us make a place for us to dwell there." And he answered. "Go." 3 Then one of them said, "Be pleased to go with your servants." And he answered, "I will go." 4 So he went with them. And when they came to the Jordan, they cut down trees. 5 But as one was felling a log, his axe head fell into the water; and he cried out, "Alas, my master! It was borrowed." 6 Then the man of God said, "Where did it fall?" When he showed him the place, he cut off a stick, and threw it in there, and made

---

hill where Elijah was when the captains with their fifties came to arrest him (1:9) and the hill where Elisha was when the Syrian chariotry came after him (6:17). The LXX and Vulg. think of the evening darkness, evidently translating *'ôphēl* with an *'āleph* instead of an *'ayin.*

g) The Floating Axhead (6:1-7)

6:1-7. The local prophetic guild needs more commodious dwellings, so they go down to the Jordan to fell trees for the building. One of the men loses his axhead in the water and is distressed all the more because it is a borrowed one. Elisha throws a stick on the water, brings the axhead to the surface, and all is well. The story has no particular merit or significance apart from the fact that it emphasizes the supernatural power which the man of God possesses.

---

honor is cursed by it. Thus Gehazi takes his place in Scripture with Aachan, Judas, and Ananias, who sold their souls for gold. And how many successors they have had in all ages since!

6:1-7. *The Axhead.*—This story well illustrates two aspects of O.T. miracles. The first is the triviality and incredibility of some of them, as

in this case. Here the Bible reader may do one of three things. He may accept them literally as they are recorded because they are found in Holy Writ, because with God nothing is impossible, and because they cannot be disproved. Or again, he may explain these miracles as the result of some extraordinary natural phenom-

7 Therefore said he, Take *it* up to thee. And he put out his hand, and took it.

8 ¶ Then the king of Syria warred against Israel, and took counsel with his servants, saying, In such and such a place *shall be* my camp.

9 And the man of God sent unto the king of Israel, saying, Beware that thou pass not such a place; for thither the Syrians are come down.

10 And the king of Israel sent to the place which the man of God told him and warned him of, and saved himself there, not once nor twice.

the iron float. **7** And he said, "Take it up." So he reached out his hand and took it.

8 Once when the king of Syria was warring against Israel, he took counsel with his servants, saying, "At such and such a place shall be my camp." **9** But the man of God sent word to the king of Israel, "Beware that you do not pass this place, for the Syrians are going down there." **10** And the king of Israel sent to the place of which the man of God told him. Thus he used to warn him, so that he saved himself there more than once or twice.

---

h) Capture of the Syrian Army (6:8-23)

The king of Israel again and again avoids falling into ambushes carefully prepared for him by the Syrian king, so much so that the Syrian king suspects a spy in his own court who regularly sends information to the king of Israel concerning the Syrian's military plans. His courtiers deny this and tell the king of the prophet Elisha who, by his miraculous powers, learns the king's innermost secrets. The king sends an army to capture the prophet, who is protected by the heavenly chariotry. "The horses and chariots of Israel" are mentioned again and again in the prophetic stories of the north. The prophet's attendant cannot see these fiery hosts until his eyes are opened. The Syrians are smitten with blindness and are led captive by the prophet into the very center of Samaria. The king of Israel wants to slay them all, but Elisha will have none of this. On the contrary, the army is fed and sent away in peace to its own country. There is no more war between the two countries.

8-9. The last word of vs. 8 presents an unusual form not found elsewhere. It is best to follow the ancient versions and to read "let us make an ambush" instead of **shall be my camp.** Similarly, at the end of vs. 9, read "have concealed themselves" for **are come down,** the Hebrew word being unintelligible.

10. The RSV here provides the sounder translation. It is more intelligible and is preferable in every way.

---

enon in which the Hebrew mind found a sign or symbol of the presence of God in human events. Or he may regard them as legends in which ancient literature abounds. The second aspect of these miracles reveals them as enshrining some moral or religious teaching which is always, everywhere, and eternally true. Thus J. Wilbur Chapman, a truly great evangelist, once based a powerful sermon on this incident. The axhead symbolizes man's essential manhood: his moral rectitude and honor. And a man has lost it. Where did he lose it? **And he showed him the place.** How did he lose it? Why did he lose it? And as little as an ax is good for anything without the axhead, so is a man's life without meaning if conscience, self-respect, and the respect of his fellow men have been lost. How shall it be recovered? He cannot recover it of himself except he is undergirded with the strength of God, the saving power of Jesus Christ. But by divine help the manhood

that has been lost can be restored: **Take it up to thee. And he put out his hand, and took it.** One has but to put out his hand and take the hand of the Lord, and he can recover his axhead and be a man again.

8-17. *Horses and Chariots of Fire.*—Here is a beautiful and spiritually illuminating narrative. A sudden attack by the Syrians had invested Dothan. Elisha's servant—no longer Gehazi—was panic-stricken. But Elisha saw more than the horses and chariots of the Syrians. He beheld the mountains full of horses and chariots of fire, symbol of the enveloping and protecting care of God. Thus he could say, **Fear not: for they that be with us are more than they that be with them,** one of the unforgettable words of Scripture. Then he prayed that the eyes of the young man might be opened, that he might see what the prophet saw, and so have fear replaced by faith in God's pledge of deliverance from danger. Thus we are taught the lesson we need

11 Therefore the heart of the king of Syria was sore troubled for this thing; and he called his servants, and said unto them, Will ye not show me which of us *is* for the king of Israel?

12 And one of his servants said, None, my lord, O king: but Elisha, the prophet that *is* in Israel, telleth the king of Israel the words that thou speakest in thy bedchamber.

13 ¶ And he said, Go and spy where he *is,* that I may send and fetch him. And it was told him, saying, Behold, *he is* in Dothan.

14 Therefore sent he thither horses, and chariots, and a great host: and they came by night, and compassed the city about.

15 And when the servant of the man of God was risen early, and gone forth, behold, a host compassed the city both with horses and chariots. And his servant said unto him, Alas, my master! how shall we do?

16 And he answered, Fear not: for they that *be* with us *are* more than they that *be* with them.

17 And Elisha prayed, and said, Lord, I pray thee, open his eyes, that he may see. And the Lord opened the eyes of the young man; and he saw: and, behold, the moun-

11 And the mind of the king of Syria was greatly troubled because of this thing; and he called his servants and said to them, "Will you not show me who of us is for the king of Israel?" 12 And one of his servants said, "None, my lord, O king; but Eli'sha, the prophet who is in Israel, tells the king of Israel the words that you speak in your bedchamber." 13 And he said, "Go and see where he is, that I may send and seize him." It was told him, "Behold, he is in Dothan." 14 So he sent there horses and chariots and a great army; and they came by night, and surrounded the city.

15 When the servant of the man of God rose early in the morning and went out, behold, an army with horses and chariots was round about the city. And the servant said, "Alas, my master! What shall we do?" 16 He said, "Fear not, for those who are with us are more than those who are with them." 17 Then Eli'sha prayed, and said, "O Lord, I pray thee, open his eyes that he may see." So the Lord opened the eyes of

---

11. The LXX correctly explains the passage with its interpretation, "Who has betrayed me to the king of Israel?"

17. The **horses and chariots of fire** are the heavenly chariotry, a feature of the Elijah-Elisha narratives (cf. 2:11; 13:14).

18. The word translated **blindness** is in the Hebrew a plural of majesty, thus indicating a most intense blindness. The word is of uncertain origin and is used elsewhere

---

most to learn: that in every hour of peril and of apparent defeat the soul that trusts in God is surrounded—if he has but eyes to see it— with divine spiritual agencies equal to any emergency. The trouble with us is not that God's help is not always there, but that we cannot see the **horses and chariots of fire.** "Open our eyes that we may see," must be our deepest prayer. If only we had eyes to see, we should feel ourselves enveloped by the protecting care of God. Martin Luther at a time of difficulty and danger could not sleep. He arose, went to the window, and looked out. Then he saw a marvel. He saw the sky overhead with no visible pillar to hold it up, yet resting serene and still, upheld by the hands of God. So would he too be upheld by him who can thus sustain the skies. A woman who was once in great trouble and mental anxiety lay out of doors and watched the sky. As she saw cloud after

cloud go by, one by one, propelled by an unseen hand, she suddenly realized that her own life was controlled and sustained by the same power, and all fear and foreboding left her. **Horses and chariots of fire** are about us all, if only our eyes are opened to see them. "The angel of the Lord encampeth round about them that fear him, and delivereth them" (Ps. 34:7); "And I will encamp about my house because of the army, . . . for now have I seen with mine eyes" (Zech. 9:8).

> The hosts of God encamp around
> The dwellings of the just;
> Deliverance he affords to all
> Who on his promise trust.[4]

Everywhere and always it is true, **they that be with us are more than they that be with them.**

[4] Nicholas Brady and Nahum Tate, *A New Version of the Psalms of David,* Ps. 34.

tain *was* full of horses and chariots of fire round about Elisha.

18 And when they came down to him, Elisha prayed unto the Lord, and said, Smite this people, I pray thee, with blindness. And he smote them with blindness according to the word of Elisha.

19 ¶ And Elisha said unto them, This *is* not the way, neither *is* this the city: follow me, and I will bring you to the man whom ye seek. But he led them to Samaria.

20 And it came to pass, when they were come into Samaria, that Elisha said, Lord, open the eyes of these *men*, that they may see. And the Lord opened their eyes, and they saw; and, behold, *they were* in the midst of Samaria.

21 And the king of Israel said unto Elisha, when he saw them, My father, shall I smite *them?* shall I smite *them?*

22 And he answered, Thou shalt not smite *them:* wouldest thou smite those whom thou hast taken captive with thy sword and with thy bow? set bread and water before them, that they may eat and drink, and go to their master.

23 And he prepared great provision for them: and when they had eaten and drunk, he sent them away, and they went to their master. So the bands of Syria came no more into the land of Israel.

24 ¶ And it came to pass after this, that Ben-hadad king of Syria gathered all his host, and went up, and besieged Samaria.

the young man, and he saw; and behold, the mountain was full of horses and chariots of fire round about Eli'sha. 18 And when the Syrians came down against him, Eli'sha prayed to the Lord, and said, "Strike this people, I pray thee, with blindness." So he struck them with blindness in accordance with the prayer of Eli'sha. 19 And Eli'sha said to them, "This is not the way, and this is not the city; follow me, and I will bring you to the man whom you seek." And he led them to Samar'ia.

20 As soon as they entered Samar'ia, Eli'sha said, "O Lord, open the eyes of these men, that they may see." So the Lord opened their eyes, and they saw; and lo, they were in the midst of Samar'ia. 21 When the king of Israel saw them he said to Eli'sha, "My father, shall I slay them? Shall I slay them?" 22 He answered, "You shall not slay them. Would you slay those whom you have taken captive with your sword and with your bow? Set bread and water before them, that they may eat and drink and go to their master." 23 So he prepared for them a great feast; and when they had eaten and drunk, he sent them away, and they went to their master. And the Syrians came no more on raids into the land of Israel.

24 Afterward Ben-ha'dad king of Syria mustered his entire army, and went up, and

---

only in Gen. 19:11 of the sudden blindness which miraculously descended upon the men of Sodom. In each case the blindness is ascribed to divine action.

22. Lucian is correct in inserting "not" immediately before **have taken captive**. It was customary to kill all prisoners, since they came under the ban (*ḥērem*) as belonging to a foreign deity; cf. I Kings 20:42, and especially Samuel's ruthless action in hewing Agag in pieces before the Lord (I Sam. 15:33). The command to slaughter every male is to be found in Deut. 20:13. The so-called humanitarianism of Deuteronomy does not extend to non-Hebrews unless they are "sojourners" or household slaves.

j) Siege of Samaria (6:24–7:20)

It is uncertain which king of Israel is to be identified with the king mentioned in this section. Further, the relationship of this story to the remainder of the Elisha narratives

---

18-33. Mercy and Judgment.—The Syrians, smitten with blindness, are decoyed into Samaria and are at the mercy of the Israelites. Elisha, who usually appears as a man of benevolent kindness, decrees that their lives shall be spared. This act in direct opposition to all customs of that age stands out, if authentic, like

an isolated mountain peak, high above the moral level of those days. Thus by centuries was anticipated the precept in Rom. 12:19-21. The hearts of the Syrians were softened only temporarily by this deed of generosity. Evil is not overcome by isolated acts of kindness. Only the continuous warmth of the sun will melt the

25 And there was a great famine in Samaria: and, behold, they besieged it, until an ass's head was *sold* for fourscore *pieces* of silver, and the fourth part of a cab of dove's dung for five *pieces* of silver.

26 And as the king of Israel was passing by upon the wall, there cried a woman unto him, saying, Help, my lord, O king.

27 And he said, If the LORD do not help thee, whence shall I help thee? out of the barnfloor, or out of the winepress?

28 And the king said unto her, What aileth thee? And she answered, This woman said unto me, Give thy son, that we may eat him to-day, and we will eat my son to-morrow.

29 So we boiled my son, and did eat him: and I said unto her on the next day, Give thy son, that we may eat him: and she hath hid her son.

30 ¶ And it came to pass, when the king heard the words of the woman, that he rent his clothes; and he passed by upon the wall,

besieged Samar'ia. 25 And there was a great famine in Samar'ia, as they besieged it, until an ass's head was sold for eighty shekels of silver, and the fourth part of a kab of dove's dung for five shekels of silver. 26 Now as the king of Israel was passing by upon the wall, a woman cried out to him, saying, "Help, my lord, O king!" 27 And he said, "If the LORD will not help you, whence shall I help you? From the threshing floor, or from the wine press?" 28 And the king asked her, "What is your trouble?" She answered, "This woman said to me, 'Give your son, that we may eat him today, and we will eat my son tomorrow.' 29 So we boiled my son, and ate him. And on the next day I said to her, 'Give your son, that we may eat him'; but she has hidden her son." 30 When the king heard the words of the woman he rent his clothes — now he

is disputed. The king of Israel is probably Jehoahaz son of Jehu, the Syrian king is probably Ben-hadad son of that Hazael whom Elisha incited to revolt against his master, and the story is probably from the Elisha cycle, though in many respects it is much closer to the type of story we find in I Kings 20; 22.

(1) THE CITY REDUCED TO STARVATION (6:24-31)

Samaria has been besieged by the Syrians so long that the city is practically reduced to starvation. As the king passes by on the wall, a woman complains to him that she and another woman agreed to eat their two sons, her own son one day and the other's son the next day. When, however, one son has been eaten, the other woman, she who had proposed the arrangement, has hidden her son. Upon hearing this tale of the plight to which the inhabitants have been reduced, the king rends his clothes in sorrow. The people see that beneath his royal robes he is wearing sackcloth. The king blames Elisha for the famine, and swears that he will execute the prophet forthwith.

25. The LXX says "fifty shekels" instead of **eighty**. Even fifty shekels amounts to twenty-eight dollars, a high price to pay for a practically worthless part of an unpalatable animal. There is a reference in Plutarch (*Artaxerxes* XXIV) to sixty drachmas (fifteen shekels) being paid in time of famine for an ass's head. More desperate still is five silver shekels for a pint of **dove's dung**, i.e., rather more than three dollars. Attempts have been made to see here a reference to sour wine or to carob pods, but men eat strange things toward the end of a protracted siege. There is a statement extant to the effect that during a famine in England in 1316 "men ate their own children, dogs, mice, and pigeons' dung" (G. E. Post, "Dove's Dung," in Hastings, *Dictionary of the Bible*, I, 620).

30. The king has been wearing **sackcloth** underneath his robes. The writer rightly shows his admiration both at the action of the king in expressing his sorrow and anxiety

iceberg. The love that never fails must be like the love of him who loved "unto the end." There followed the terrible siege of Samaria. The king held Elisha responsible for this calamity, vowed that Elisha should die, and vehemently renounced his faith in Elisha's God. So men are always wont to hold God responsible for evils of their own making. It is not faith in God that they should lose, but rather faith in themselves.

and the people looked, and, behold, *he had* sackcloth within upon his flesh.

31 Then he said, God do so and more also to me, if the head of Elisha the son of Shaphat shall stand on him this day.

32 But Elisha sat in his house, and the elders sat with him; and *the king* sent a man from before him: but ere the messenger came to him, he said to the elders, See ye how this son of a murderer hath sent to take away mine head? look, when the messenger cometh, shut the door, and hold him fast at the door: *is* not the sound of his master's feet behind him?

33 And while he yet talked with them, behold, the messenger came down unto him: and he said, Behold, this evil *is* of the LORD; what should I wait for the LORD any longer?

7 Then Elisha said, Hear ye the word of the LORD; Thus saith the LORD, To-mor-

was passing by upon the wall — and the people looked, and behold, he had sack-cloth beneath upon his body — **31** and he said, "May God do so to me, and more also, if the head of Eli'sha the son of Shaphat remains on his shoulders today."

32 Eli'sha was sitting in his house, and the elders were sitting with him. Now the king had despatched a man from his presence; but before the messenger arrived Eli'-sha said to the elders, "Do you see how this murderer has sent to take off my head? Look, when the messenger comes, shut the door, and hold the door fast against him. Is not the sound of his master's feet behind him?" **33** And while he was still speaking with them, the king*f* came down to him and said, "This trouble is from the LORD! Why should I wait for the LORD any longer?" **1** But Eli'sha said, "Hear the word of the LORD: thus says the LORD,

f See 7. 2: Heb *messenger*

---

and also at his unostentatious way of performing this act of contrition and humble supplication to God.

31. The king regards Elisha as being responsible for the horrors of the siege. This may be for one of two reasons, and there is no apparent way of deciding between the two. Either Elisha had persuaded the king to hold out, on the expectation of some divine intervention which would remove the Syrian menace perhaps forever even when all seemed lost, or the famine was not due primarily to the siege but to the seven years' drought (8:1), for which Elisha may be regarded as being responsible because he had prophesied it. Vs. 25 favors one alternative; vs. 27, the other.

(2) ELISHA IS NOT EXECUTED (6:32–7:2)

The king sends a messenger, and he himself follows, but Elisha receives supernatural warning of the messenger's approach and of the king's footsteps. Elisha prophesies plenty of food for the morrow and the death of a courtier who is skeptical.

32. There is no need to translate literally **this son of a murderer** since we are dealing with a Hebrew idiom whereby "son of" means that the man belongs to a particular class, e.g., "son of Belial" means "son of worthlessness," i.e., "worthless fellow." Similarly, "son of exhortation" (Acts 4:36) refers to a man peculiarly gifted in encouraging men. Thus the RSV is right with the translation **this murderer.**

33. It is best to read **the king** (RSV) instead of **the messenger** (KJV). This makes the account less confused, the messenger being already there. The change in the text involves the omission of the soundless consonant *'āleph.* The king comes into the prophet's house himself and declares that he can wait no longer for deliverance from the Lord. Elisha replies with an oracle which declares the famine at an end. The courtier who accompanies the king, i.e., the favorite courtier on whom the king rested his arm for support, skeptically mocks at the oracle, and is told that he will see the fulfillment of the oracle but will not himself eat of the plenty.

7:1. The price of the wheat will be $1.50 a bushel; that of the barley, 75¢ a bushel.

7:1-2, 6-7. *The Raising of the Siege.*—How calm and confident was Elisha in the face of the anger of King Jehoram for whom he had pro-

found contempt (6:32). In defiance of all probability he made the extraordinary prediction that by the next day the city would be amply

row about this time *shall* a measure of fine flour *be sold* for a shekel, and two measures of barley for a shekel, in the gate of Samaria.

2 Then a lord on whose hand the king leaned answered the man of God, and said, Behold, *if* the LORD would make windows in heaven, might this thing be? And he said, Behold, thou shalt see *it* with thine eyes, but shalt not eat thereof.

3 ¶ And there were four leprous men at the entering in of the gate: and they said one to another, Why sit we here until we die?

4 If we say, We will enter into the city, then the famine *is* in the city, and we shall die there: and if we sit still here, we die also. Now therefore come, and let us fall unto the host of the Syrians: if they save us alive, we shall live; and if they kill us, we shall but die.

5 And they rose up in the twilight, to go unto the camp of the Syrians: and when they were come to the uttermost part of the camp of Syria, behold, *there was* no man there.

Tomorrow about this time a measure of fine meal shall be sold for a shekel, and two measures of barley for a shekel, at the gate of Samar'ia." 2 Then the captain on whose hand the king leaned said to the man of God, "If the LORD himself should make windows in heaven, could this thing be?" But he said, "You shall see it with your own eyes, but you shall not eat of it."

3 Now there were four men who were lepers at the entrance to the gate; and they said to one another, "Why do we sit here till we die? 4 If we say, 'Let us enter the city,' the famine is in the city, and we shall die there; and if we sit here, we die also. So now come, let us go over to the camp of the Syrians; if they spare our lives we shall live, and if they kill us we shall but die." 5 So they arose at twilight to go to the camp of the Syrians; but when they came to the edge of the camp of the Syrians, be-

---

(3) END OF THE SIEGE (7:3-20)

Four starving lepers that same evening decide to surrender to the enemy, since the worst that the enemy can do is to kill them, and they believe that death is inevitable otherwise. They find the Syrian camp deserted. The explanation offered by the narrator is that the Lord miraculously had caused the Syrians to hear the noise of a great army of chariotry. The Syrians thought that new enemies were upon them and they fled, leaving everything behind them. The lepers eat their full and gather spoil from the empty tents until they remember their fellows within the city. They hurry back with the good news and tell the porter at the gate, who reports it to the king. But the king is wary, thinking that the whole affair is a stratagem to entice the Israelites out of the city. He sends out a small scouting party of chariots, realizing that even if these are lost, the situation is very little worsened. The scouts come back with the story that the Syrians are already beyond the Jordan and the road is everywhere littered with the equipment of an army in flight. This means food enough for all, and in the rush of the starving people the courtier who had mocked Elisha the day before, being this day on guard at the gate, is trampled to death.

---

supplied with food, but that the king's envoy would not live to eat it. There is direct correspondence between the raising of the siege of Samaria by the Syrians under Ben-hadad and the raising of the siege of Jerusalem by the Assyrians under Sennacherib (19:32-36) a century later. In both cases the hosts were mysteriously dispersed. What happened? Sennacherib's army may have been smitten with sudden pestilence. In this case (vs. 6) the Syrians were overtaken by panic (cf. Judg. 7:19-23). In both cases this miraculous deliverance was foreseen

and foretold by the prophets Elisha and Isaiah. How are we to explain this extraordinary prescience? Did some inkling of what was about to happen reach the prophets and form a rational basis for their predictions? Or does all of this lie in the undefinable and unanalyzable region of subconsciousness in which intuitions are born which have such solid assurance in the mind that they are announced with confident conviction? Such psychological phenomena are not rare today. Instances are known when someone, at a time of peril when probability points

6 For the Lord had made the host of the Syrians to hear a noise of chariots, and a noise of horses, *even* the noise of a great host: and they said one to another, Lo, the king of Israel hath hired against us the kings of the Hittites, and the kings of the Egyptians, to come upon us.

7 Wherefore they arose and fled in the twilight, and left their tents, and their horses, and their asses, even the camp as it *was,* and fled for their life.

8 And when these lepers came to the uttermost part of the camp, they went into one tent, and did eat and drink, and carried thence silver, and gold, and raiment, and went and hid *it;* and came again, and entered into another tent, and carried thence *also,* and went and hid *it.*

9 Then they said one to another, We do not well: this day *is* a day of good tidings, and we hold our peace: if we tarry till the morning light, some mischief will come upon us: now therefore come, that we may go and tell the king's household.

hold, there was no one there. 6 For the Lord had made the army of the Syrians hear the sound of chariots, and of horses, the sound of a great army, so that they said to one another, "Behold, the king of Israel has hired against us the kings of the Hittites and the kings of Egypt to come upon us." 7 So they fled away in the twilight and forsook their tents, their horses, and their asses, leaving the camp as it was, and fled for their lives. 8 And when these lepers came to the edge of the camp, they went into a tent, and ate and drank, and they carried off silver and gold and clothing, and went and hid them; then they came back, and entered another tent, and carried off things from it, and went and hid them.

9 Then they said to one another, "We are not doing right. This day is a day of good news; if we are silent and wait until the morning light, punishment will overtake us; now therefore come, let us go and

---

6. A miraculous noise as of countless chariots deceives the Syrians into thinking that they are about to be attacked by their northern neighbors. It is better to read *Muçrîm* for *Miçráyim* (in either case the same consonants, מצרים), i.e., "the kings of *Muçrî*" for **the kings of Egypt.** In the first place, it is not proper or usual to speak of the kings of Egypt in the plural. In the second place, an alliance between the **Hittites** to the north and the Egyptians to the south is wholly unlikely. If we assume the alliance to be between the Hittites and their neighbors in Asia Minor, the *Muçri,* then the whole story becomes more intelligible (for the name "*Muçrî*" see Exeg. on I Kings 10:28).

9. The Hebrew word *'āwôn* is a comprehensive word which includes not only the "iniquity" itself, but also its consequences. Hence the word sometimes refers not to the actual wrong action, but to the consequences of it; cf. Gen. 4:13, where the English rendering is rightly **punishment,** and so also here. The prophets were always insistent that sin could not be separated from its consequences, so much so that the same word can be used for both.

---

straight to disaster, boldly and confidently predicts a deliverance which actually comes to pass. If asked how he knew that, he would answer that he did not know how he knew it. All that he knew was that he knew it. And he did. So these prophets received a divine intuition of which they were so sure that they announced it as positive fact.

3-5, 8-20. The Story of Lepers and Its Sequel.
—The main interest in this narrative lies in the manner of the discovery of the Syrian debacle, and the account of this is one of the most dramatic stories to be found in the O.T. We think of those poor, starving lepers thrust outside the city gates, their plan of desperation to cast themselves on the mercy of the Syrians, their

stupefaction on finding that the enemy had fled, leaving rich food and bounty behind them, and how they voraciously satisfied their hunger. And then comes the great awakening. The starving city must be told of its salvation. So they hurry back with their incredible message. The people rush out, and in fulfillment of Elisha's prophecy the king's envoy loses his life in the crush of the crowds that erupt in wild disorder through the gates.

We do not well: this day is a day of good tidings, and we hold our peace: if we tarry, . . . some mischief will come upon us. In these words we find a profound truth. In no department of life can one receive a great gift and refuse to share it without mischief coming upon

10 So they came and called unto the porter of the city: and they told them, saying, We came to the camp of the Syrians, and, behold, *there was* no man there, neither voice of man, but horses tied, and asses tied, and the tents as they *were*.

11 And he called the porters; and they told *it* to the king's house within.

12 ¶ And the king arose in the night, and said unto his servants, I will now show you what the Syrians have done to us. They know that we *be* hungry; therefore are they gone out of the camp to hide themselves in the field, saying, When they come out of the city, we shall catch them alive, and get into the city.

13 And one of his servants answered and said, Let *some* take, I pray thee, five of the horses that remain, which are left in the city, (behold, they *are* as all the multitude of Israel that are left in it: behold, *I say*, they *are* even as all the multitude of the Israelites that are consumed:) and let us send and see.

14 They took therefore two chariot horses; and the king sent after the host of the Syrians, saying, Go and see.

15 And they went after them unto Jordan: and, lo, all the way *was* full of garments and vessels, which the Syrians had cast away in their haste. And the messengers returned, and told the king.

tell the king's household." 10 So they came and called to the gatekeepers of the city, and told them, "We came to the camp of the Syrians, and behold, there was no one to be seen or heard there, nothing but the horses tied, and the asses tied, and the tents as they were." 11 Then the gatekeepers called out, and it was told within the king's household. 12 And the king rose in the night, and said to his servants, "I will tell you what the Syrians have prepared against us. They know that we are hungry; therefore they have gone out of the camp to hide themselves in the open country, thinking, 'When they come out of the city, we shall take them alive and get into the city.'" 13 And one of his servants said, "Let some men take five of the remaining horses, seeing that those who are left here will fare like the whole multitude of Israel that have already perished; let us send and see." 14 So they took two mounted men, and the king sent them after the army of the Syrians, saying, "Go and see." 15 So they went after them as far as the Jordan; and, lo, all the way was littered with garments and equipment which the Syrians had thrown away in their haste. And the messengers returned, and told the king.

---

13. This verse is difficult, but it can just be translated if the Hebrew *hinnām* ("behold them") is taken to mean "either they . . ." for its first occurrence, and "or they . . ." for its second occurrence. The meaning then is: If we lose the five horses, then they will be lost like all the rest, like those that are already gone, and the rest of us will

---

him. If a man has great wealth and keeps it to himself, he suffers certain moral deterioration. Let a person have benefit of education and use it for personal and selfish ends rather than as an instrument for social serviceableness, and his education becomes a curse, both to himself and to others, rather than a blessing. Thus Matthew Arnold wrote, "The individual is required, under pain of being stunted and enfeebled in his own development if he disobeys, to carry others along with him in his march towards perfection."[5] Anywhere and everywhere the possession of advantage, of the means of happiness, imposes the obligation to share it with those who lack it, else mischief comes upon one.

Thus this is one of the greatest missionary parables to be found in Scripture. For all of us

5 *Culture and Anarchy* (New York: The Macmillan Co., 1898), p. 11.

this is a day of good tidings, the glad tidings of great joy announced by the Christmas angels, which are not for us only but for all people. What would life mean to us if we had no knowledge of Christ or hope for the forgiveness of sin, no knowledge of any life beyond the limits of our present existence? We are living on these riches every day of our lives. And do we hold our peace? Do we forget

> . . . how many thousands still are lying
> Bound in the darksome prison house of sin,
> With none to tell them of the Savior's dying,
> Or of the life he died for them to win?[6]

Are we failing to publish glad tidings? Then mischief will come upon us. If we have received this unspeakable gift, the unsearchable riches

6 Mary A. Thomson, "O Zion, haste, thy mission high fulfilling."

16 And the people went out, and spoiled the tents of the Syrians. So a measure of fine flour was *sold* for a shekel, and two measures of barley for a shekel, according to the word of the LORD.

17 ¶ And the king appointed the lord on whose hand he leaned to have the charge of the gate: and the people trode upon him in the gate, and he died, as the man of God had said, who spake when the king came down to him.

18 And it came to pass as the man of God had spoken to the king, saying, Two measures of barley for a shekel, and a measure of fine flour for a shekel, shall be to-morrow about this time in the gate of Samaria:

19 And that lord answered the man of God, and said, Now, behold, *if* the LORD should make windows in heaven, might such a thing be? And he said, Behold, thou shalt see it with thine eyes, but shalt not eat thereof.

20 And so it fell out unto him: for the people trode upon him in the gate, and he died.

8 Then spake Elisha unto the woman, whose son he had restored to life, saying, Arise, and go thou and thine household, and sojourn wheresoever thou canst so-

---

16 Then the people went out, and plundered the camp of the Syrians. So a measure of fine meal was sold for a shekel, and two measures of barley for a shekel, according to the word of the LORD. 17 Now the king had appointed the captain on whose hand he leaned to have charge of the gate; and the people trod upon him in the gate, so that he died, as the man of God had said when the king came down to him. 18 For when the man of God had said to the king, "Two measures of barley shall be sold for a shekel, and a measure of fine meal for a shekel, about this time tomorrow in the gate of Samar'ia," 19 the captain had answered the man of God, "If the LORD himself should make windows in heaven, could such a thing be?" And he had said, "You shall see it with your own eyes, but you shall not eat of it." 20 And so it happened to him, for the people trod upon him in the gate and he died.

8 Now Eli'sha had said to the woman whose son he had restored to life, "Arise,

---

soon go too; but if all is well, then we will all alike live, both the five and we in the city. There is therefore little to lose and everything to gain by sending out this small scouting party.

k) THE WOMAN OF SHUNEM COMES HOME (8:1-6)

Elisha knows that a seven-year famine is coming, so he tells his hostess at Shunem, the kindly woman who had given him an upper room in which to lodge and whose son

---

of Christ, into our own lives, then it must be upon pain of moral deterioration if we do not have the passion to make this truth prevail. It is thus that world missions prevent what was meant to be our salvation from becoming our condemnation. This is the innermost meaning of the familiar word of Paul, "Woe to me if I do not preach the gospel!" (I Cor. 9:16.)

The same truth holds good in the sphere of our material possessions. We have homes in which to live; millions are homeless. We have food in abundance to eat; millions are hungry, if not starving. We have clothing, warmth, and comfort; millions lack these elementary necessities of life. It is the story of Dives and Lazarus all over again. Can we enjoy our luxuries when we know the misery of others? Do we hold our peace? Then mischief must come upon us. So

Ruskin has written: "Consider whether, even supposing it guiltless, luxury would be desired by any of us, if we saw clearly at our sides the suffering which accompanies it in the world. . . . The cruelest man living could not sit at his feast, unless he sat blindfold." [7] The response of the normal human heart is surely that of the lepers, in gratitude for God's deliverance. It will mean not only the salvation of other lives but the salvation of our own.

8:1-6. Re-enter the Shunammite Woman.— The story contains two lessons of importance to us. In the first place we are reminded of the frequency of famines in the Holy Land. From the early days of Jacob, whose sons came to Egypt (Gen. 41:56–42:1-2), this was the most

[7] John Ruskin, *Unto This Last* (London: George Allen, 1906), pp. 173-74.

journ: for the Lord hath called for a famine; and it shall also come upon the land seven years.

2 And the woman arose, and did after the saying of the man of God: and she went with her household, and sojourned in the land of the Philistines seven years.

3 And it came to pass at the seven years' end, that the woman returned out of the land of the Philistines: and she went forth to cry unto the king for her house and for her land.

4 And the king talked with Gehazi the servant of the man of God, saying, Tell me, I pray thee, all the great things that Elisha hath done.

5 And it came to pass, as he was telling the king how he had restored a dead body to life, that, behold, the woman, whose son he had restored to life, cried to the king for her house and for her land. And Gehazi said, My lord, O king, this *is* the woman, and this *is* her son, whom Elisha restored to life.

and depart with your household, and sojourn wherever you can; for the Lord has called for a famine, and it will come upon the land for seven years." 2 So the woman arose, and did according to the word of the man of God; she went with her household and sojourned in the land of the Philistines seven years. 3 And at the end of the seven years, when the woman returned from the land of the Philistines, she went forth to appeal to the king for her house and her land. 4 Now the king was talking with Geha'zi the servant of the man of God, saying, "Tell me all the great things that Eli'sha has done." 5 And while he was telling the king how Eli'sha had restored the dead to life, behold, the woman whose son he had restored to life appealed to the king for her house and her land. And Geha'zi said, "My lord, O king, here is the woman, and here is her son whom Eli'sha restored

he had restored to life, to migrate for the time being to the Philistine country. This she does. When the seven years are past she comes back and appeals to the king for the return of her house and her property. It so happens that Gehazi is at court, telling the king of Elisha's miraculous deeds, particularly how he has raised the dead to life. So Gehazi turns and points out the woman to the king, who forthwith sends a court official with her to see to it that she gets back her property.

8:2. Isaac had migrated to the land of the Philistines in a time of famine (Gen. 26:1). This trek toward Egypt was evidently the regular movement at such times (Gen. 12:10; 43:2; 46:6).

feared of the scourges that befell the people of God. Palestine was indeed "a dry and thirsty land." If rain was withheld, then famine followed swiftly. It may have been part of the divine education of God's people that lack of material riches would rouse within them the hunger and thirst for the living God. Unable to satisfy the needs of the body, they were driven to find their satisfaction in the plenitude of the mercies of God. One has only to contrast the history of ancient peoples who lived in freedom from want with the history of God's people, who were never free from it, to understand the connection between adversity and character. Today the people who live in hot climates where they do not have to struggle with the elements or with the soil are not those who have produced the world's leaders in any department of life. Those come from lands exposed to the rigors of nature. A visitor to New England, remarking its hard and stony soil, is reported to have asked,

"What can you raise here?" To which the proud reply came, "Here we raise men." Social workers have often observed that the moral diseases which afflict and degrade our social order stem largely from the homes of the idle rich. Famine and faith are closely joined in the Bible. It was a famine which caused the prodigal son to come to himself and resolve to return to his father. We who have never known what famine means, have never known an hour when we did not have enough to eat or when the next meal was not ready, are reminded of the forgotten mercies of God. Here is the justification of the now so often neglected practice of grace before meat. No more powerful means exists for the religious education of children, or for the deepening of the sense of reverence in all who participate in it, than this simple habit of recognizing that every day of our lives the prayer has been answered for us, "Give us this day our daily bread." We are reminded, too, of

6 And when the king asked the woman, she told him. So the king appointed unto her a certain officer, saying, Restore all that *was* hers, and all the fruits of the field since the day that she left the land, even until now.

7 ¶ And Elisha came to Damascus; and Ben-hadad the king of Syria was sick; and it was told him, saying, The man of God is come hither.

8 And the king said unto Hazael, Take a present in thine hand, and go, meet the man of God, and inquire of the LORD by him, saying, Shall I recover of this disease?

to life." 6 And when the king asked the woman, she told him. So the king appointed an official for her, saying, "Restore all that was hers, together with all the produce of the fields from the day that she left the land until now."

7 Now Eli'sha came to Damascus. Ben-ha'dad the king of Syria was sick; and when it was told him, "The man of God has come here," 8 the King said to Haz'ael, "Take a present with you and go to meet the man of God, and inquire of the LORD through him, saying, 'Shall I recover from

---

l) ELISHA AND HAZAEL (8:7-15)

Elisha visits Damascus. Ben-hadad king of Syria is ill and sends Hazael with rich gifts to inquire of the man of God whether he will recover from his sickness. Elisha says that he will, but adds that he will nevertheless die from another cause. The prophet then falls into a half-conscious trance and there comes on his face a look of great horror as he gazes fixedly on Hazael. The prophet weeps and Hazael asks him why. The prophet replies that he weeps because he sees all the sorrow and ruin which Hazael will bring upon Israel when he has become king of Syria. When Hazael returns to Damascus he acts upon the word of the prophet, tells the king he will recover from his sickness, but the next day smothers him with his own pillow. **And Hazael became king in his stead.** The prophet Elisha thus takes the second step toward the fulfillment of the word spoken to his master Elijah on Horeb (cf. I Kings 19:15-16). Elijah had fulfilled one item when he called Elisha from following the plow; here we have the fulfillment of the second item and Hazael is raised up to be an enemy of the house of Ahab from outside the kingdom. Later Jehu is raised up, definitely encouraged by the prophet as was Hazael, to be an enemy from within the kingdom (9:4-10).

8. This rich gift follows the normal practice of taking a present to the seer when he is to be consulted on any matter (cf. I Sam. 9:7; I Kings 14:3). The custom is connected with the principle that no man must appear before God without a gift (Exod. 23:15).

---

those for whom it has not been answered. The simple ritual of passing a mite box after grace and before eating has beauty and significance. Here is the perfect combination of gratitude to God and sympathy for our fellow men.

The other lesson deriving from this incident is taught us by the act of Elisha in remembering this Shunammite woman. We note that this time it was not the woman who appealed to Elisha for help, but Elisha who thought of her. There is here given to us for our inspiration a beautiful illustration of the individualizing of sympathy. Elisha was not so preoccupied with great affairs of public importance that he overlooked the personal welfare of one individual and household. Here lies the weakness of much humanitarianism today. Too often it is abstract, vague, a generalized sentiment of benevolence. It is not focused on a particular individual. But genuine affection can always point to "a certain man," and thus always holds us to

concrete and definite forms of service to individuals. Modern preachers and prophets who find themselves so immersed in practical affairs that they overlook the needs of individuals may well lay to heart the words with which this chapter begins: **Then spake Elisha unto the woman, whose son he had restored to life.**

The conclusion of this story also merits brief mention. The appeal of the woman that her property be restored to her was granted by the king because of Elisha's interest in her. It is a good thing for one to have personal relations with prophets, ancient or modern. Ministers of God have an influence with men in authority. Their word can be depended upon. The people whose cause they espouse can be presumed to be worthy and deserving. Many a time since the days of Elisha the name of a prophet of God has secured justice for those in need.

7-15. Elisha and Ben-hadad.—This passage contains a confused account (see Exeg. for the

9 So Hazael went to meet him, and took a present with him, even of every good thing of Damascus, forty camels' burden, and came and stood before him, and said, Thy son Ben-hadad king of Syria hath sent me to thee, saying, Shall I recover of this disease?

10 And Elisha said unto him, Go, say unto him, Thou mayest certainly recover: howbeit the LORD hath showed me that he shall surely die.

11 And he settled his countenance steadfastly, until he was ashamed: and the man of God wept.

12 And Hazael said, Why weepeth my lord? And he answered, Because I know the evil that thou wilt do unto the children of Israel: their strongholds wilt thou set on fire, and their young men wilt thou slay with the sword, and wilt dash their children, and rip up their women with child.

this sickness?' " 9 So Haz′ael went to meet him, and took a present with him, all kinds of goods of Damascus, forty camel loads. When he came and stood before him, he said, "Your son Ben-ha′dad king of Syria has sent me to you, saying, 'Shall I recover from this sickness?' " 10 And Eli′sha said to him, "Go, say to him, 'You shall certainly recover'; but the LORD has shown me that he shall certainly die." 11 And he fixed his gaze and stared at him, until he was ashamed. And the man of God wept. 12 And Haz′ael said, "Why does my lord weep?" He answered, "Because I know the evil that you will do to the people of Israel; you will set on fire their fortresses, and you will slay their young men with the sword, and dash in pieces their little ones, and rip up their

---

10. Elisha gives the oracle **You shall certainly recover**; he then adds for the hearing of Hazael, but not for him to tell to his master, that Ben-hadad will **certainly die.** Here we get an instance of an oracle which tells the truth but not the whole truth. (A similar case is to be found in 3:18.) The incident is a survival of that natural religion of man whereby he fears the supernatural and regards it as being at least semialien to him. Man must always be careful in his dealings with the other world lest the gods maliciously lure him to his destruction. In this present incident the oracle, true enough in itself, is designed to lure Ben-hadad into a false confidence. Further, the prophet immediately takes steps to ensure that Ben-hadad does die. The famous examples of classical tradition are the "true" oracle which lured Croesus to his doom, and the equally "true" oracle which encouraged Pyrrhus of Epirus to defeat at the hands of Rome. The Delphic Oracle told Croesus that if he crossed the river Halys, his eastern boundary, he would destroy a mighty empire, but it did not tell him that it was his own empire he would destroy. Similarly, the oracle told Pyrrhus that he would conquer the Romans, but when he returned later and complained that the Romans had conquered him, he was told that the oracle should have been read as, "I say that the Romans will conquer you," a translation which can be made of the original Latin, though it is not the obvious one.

11. All the ancient versions found this verse difficult, mostly because of the unique use of the verb which is translated **he fixed his gaze.** The meaning, however, is quite plain. Elisha was suddenly seized with a semitrance. He saw a vision of the horrors of the coming war. This fixed unseeing look of horror lasted so long and was followed by such bitter tears that Hazael inquired the reason. It is better to read, following the Vulg., "His face became fixed with a look of indescribable horror"; then follows the reference to the prophet weeping.

12-15. This is war with its horrors, though now there are alternatives no less terrible. Hazael is far from being horror-stricken at the recital of these terrible doings. On the

---

explanation of the apparent contradiction in vs. 10) of the illness and death of Ben-hadad king of Syria. The chief point of interest relates to the munificent presents sent by the king to Elisha (vss. 8-9). The narrator does not even pause to record that Elisha refused to accept

them. Prophets could not be bought in those days. Neither can they be bought in our day. The dictum "Every man has his price" stops short when we come to men of God. Again we are reminded that there is this inherent dignity and nobility about the profession of the minis-

13 And Hazael said, But what, *is* thy servant a dog, that he should do this great thing? And Elisha answered, The LORD hath showed me that thou *shalt be* king over Syria.

14 So he departed from Elisha, and came to his master; who said to him, What said Elisha to thee? And he answered, He told me *that* thou shouldest surely recover.

15 And it came to pass on the morrow, that he took a thick cloth, and dipped *it* in water, and spread *it* on his face, so that he died: and Hazael reigned in his stead.

16 ¶ And in the fifth year of Joram the son of Ahab king of Israel, Jehoshaphat *being* then king of Judah, Jehoram the son of Jehoshaphat king of Judah began to reign.

17 Thirty and two years old was he when he began to reign; and he reigned eight years in Jerusalem.

18 And he walked in the way of the kings of Israel, as did the house of Ahab; for the daughter of Ahab was his wife: and he did evil in the sight of the LORD.

19 Yet the LORD would not destroy Judah

women with child." 13 And Haz'ael said, "What is your servant, who is but a dog, that he should do this great thing?" Eli'sha answered, "The LORD has shown me that you are to be king over Syria." 14 Then he departed from Eli'sha, and came to his master, who said to him, "What did Eli'sha say to you?" And he answered, "He told me that you would certainly recover." 15 But on the morrow he took the coverlet and dipped it in water and spread it over his face, till he died. And Haz'ael became king in his stead.

16 In the fifth year of Joram the son of Ahab, king of Israel,ᵍ Jeho'ram the son of Jehosh'aphat, king of Judah, began to reign. 17 He was thirty-two years old when he became king, and he reigned eight years in Jerusalem. 18 And he walked in the way of the kings of Israel, as the house of Ahab had done, for the daughter of Ahab was his wife. And he did what was evil in the sight of the LORD. 19 Yet the LORD would not

ᵍ Gk Syr: Heb *Israel, Jehoshaphat being king of Judah*

contrary, he modestly regards himself as being of too low a station in life for the accomplishment of such mighty deeds.

8. JEHORAM OF JUDAH (8:16-24)

Jehoram becomes king of Judah at the death of his father Jehoshaphat. Special mention is made of his wife Athaliah, Ahab's daughter, because of Athaliah's later action in seizing the throne. During this reign Edom and Libnah revolt from the domination of Judah.

16-19. These verses form the Deuteronomist's introduction for the reign of the new king of Judah. The RSV rightly omits the phrase **Jehoshaphat being then king of Judah,** thus following the LXX and Syriac. It is a copyist's error, being an accidental repetition of the last three words of the verse.

18. The new king's wife was Athaliah, a woman of determination and resource, like her Tyrian mother Jezebel and her second cousin, the Carthaginian Dido. It is understandable that there would be no room for the queen mother while Athaliah's husband was king.

19. This verse contains another copyist's error, by which **to his children** (לבניו) was written instead of "before him" (לפניו), i.e., before God (cf. I Kings 11:36).

try: those who enter it may not be influenced by material rewards. Forty camels loaded with presents could not induce a true minister of God to speak what he did not believe to be true, or to serve a cause in which he did not believe. He may not be brilliant or conspicuous. But he must be incorruptible.

16-29. The Southern Kingdom: Jehoram and Ahaziah.—Jehoram's reign was an evil one,

for the daughter of Ahab was his wife (vs. 18). And Ahaziah **did what was evil . . . , for he was son-in-law to the house of Ahab** (vs. 27), and **his mother's name was Athaliah; she was a granddaughter of Omri** (vs. 26). Ahab's wickedness did not end with his life. Wickedness never ends with the life of a wicked man. The infection is transmitted unto coming generations. A great truth could be drawn from the

for David his servant's sake, as he promised him to give him always a light, *and* to his children.

20 ¶ In his days Edom revolted from under the hand of Judah, and made a king over themselves.

21 So Joram went over to Zair, and all the chariots with him: and he rose by night, and smote the Edomites which compassed him about, and the captains of the chariots: and the people fled into their tents.

22 Yet Edom revolted from under the hand of Judah unto this day. Then Libnah revolted at the same time.

23 And the rest of the acts of Joram, and all that he did, *are* they not written in the book of the Chronicles of the kings of Judah?

24 And Joram slept with his fathers, and was buried with his fathers in the city of David: and Ahaziah his son reigned in his stead.

25 ¶ In the twelfth year of Joram the son of Ahab king of Israel did Ahaziah the son of Jehoram king of Judah begin to reign.

26 Two and twenty years old *was* Ahaziah when he began to reign; and he reigned one year in Jerusalem. And his mother's name *was* Athaliah, the daughter of Omri king of Israel.

destroy Judah, for the sake of David his servant, since he promised to give a lamp to him and to his sons for ever.

20 In his days Edom revolted from the rule of Judah, and set up a king of their own. 21 Then Joram passed over to Za'ir with all his chariots, and rose by night, and he and his chariot commanders smote the E'domites who had surrounded him; but his army fled home. 22 So Edom revolted from the rule of Judah to this day. Then Libnah revolted at the same time. 23 Now the rest of the acts of Joram, and all that he did, are they not written in the Book of the Chronicles of the Kings of Judah? 24 So Joram slept with his fathers, and was buried with his fathers in the city of David; and Ahazi'ah his son reigned in his stead.

25 In the twelfth year of Joram the son of Ahab, king of Israel, Ahazi'ah the son of Jeho'ram, king of Judah, began to reign. 26 Ahazi'ah was twenty-two years old when he began to reign, and he reigned one year in Jerusalem. His mother's name was Athali'ah; she was a granddaughter of Omri

---

20-22. This is an extract from the annals of the kings of Judah, but it has been so altered by the compiler as to obscure the fact that in his attempt to resubjugate Edom the king of Judah suffered a military disaster which stopped just short of being complete. He evidently was surrounded by the Edomites and cut his way out with a few chariots only with the utmost difficulty. His punitive expedition was unsuccessful, and Edom secured its independence, to be followed by Libnah, a city to the southwest of Judah, probably in the Philistine country, though the site has not been definitely identified.

23-24. The formal Deuteronomic obituary for a king of Judah, as usual including the name of his successor.

9. AHAZIAH OF JUDAH (8:25-29)

25-29. The Deuteronomic compiler introduces the reign of the new king of Judah. He mentions the fact that Athaliah was the **granddaughter of Omri** (RSV), not **the daughter of Omri** as the M.T. says. Lucian corrects the text to "daughter of Ahab," but this continued reference to Omri is a further tribute to the greatness of Ahab's father, the founder of the dynasty (cf. Exeg. on I Kings 16:23-28). The compiler tells how

---

text "The House of Ahab," tracing the course of evil which, stemming from him, continued to poison the life of both kingdoms for years to come. Note the words, however, in vs. 19. The light flickered low in those days, but it never went out. Darkness enveloped the destinies of Israel and only the providence of God kept that

light alive. The promise holds good for every people, for every soul that God has created. Always a light in the heart of any nation, however degraded; in the soul of any man, however depraved. Always there is the spark of light which awaits only the rightly directed breath of God to be fanned into a flame of life.

27 And he walked in the way of the house of Ahab, and did evil in the sight of the LORD, as *did* the house of Ahab: for he *was* the son-in-law of the house of Ahab.

28 ¶ And he went with Joram the son of Ahab to the war against Hazael king of Syria in Ramoth-gilead; and the Syrians wounded Joram.

29 And king Joram went back to be healed in Jezreel of the wounds which the Syrians had given him at Ramah, when he fought against Hazael king of Syria. And Ahaziah the son of Jehoram king of Judah went down to see Joram the son of Ahab in Jezreel, because he was sick.

9 And Elisha the prophet called one of the children of the prophets, and said unto him, Gird up thy loins, and take this box of oil in thine hand, and go to Ramoth-gilead:

king of Israel. 27 He also walked in the way of the house of Ahab, and did what was evil in the sight of the LORD, as the house of Ahab had done, for he was son-in-law to the house of Ahab.

28 He went with Joram the son of Ahab to make war against Haz'ael king of Syria at Ramoth-gilead, where the Syrians wounded Joram. 29 And King Joram returned to be healed in Jezreel of the wounds which the Syrians had given him at Ramah, when he fought against Haz'ael king of Syria. And Ahazi'ah the son of Je-ho'ram king of Judah went down to see Joram the son of Ahab in Jezreel, because he was sick.

9 Then Eli'sha the prophet called one of the sons of the prophets and said to him, "Gird up your loins, and take this flask of oil in your hand, and go to Ramoth-

Joram and Ahaziah of Judah went to fight against the Syrians, continuing the campaign in which Ahab died, how Joram was wounded, and how Ahaziah went to visit him as he lay sick in his palace at Jezreel. The compiler then has to break off his story because he must tell the story of Jehu's revolt, since this ended in the slaughter of two kings in one day.

E. THE REVOLUTION OF JEHU (9:1–10:28)

These two chapters are taken from the same source as the narratives of I Kings 20; 22. They are thoroughly lively in style and are northern in sympathy and interest. Apart from the Deuteronomic insertions of 9:7-10a and 10:28-31, there is nothing to emphasize the general standpoint of the books of Kings.

1. JEHU IS ANOINTED KING (9:1-13)

Elisha sends one of his disciples to anoint Jehu king of Israel. Jehu is in camp at Ramoth-gilead, fighting against the Syrians. He is anointed secretly within doors, and the young man hurries away, his mission completed. When Jehu's fellow officers hear what has happened they forthwith set up an improvised throne, hail him as king, and the revolution is under way.

9:1. Elisha, leader of **the sons of the prophets** (i.e., of the prophetic guilds), kindles the first spark of the revolution by sending one of his disciples to anoint Jehu secretly, just as Samuel had secretly anointed both Saul and David (I Sam. 10:1; 16:13). These prophets were determined to destroy the dynasty of Omri and they were prepared to go to any length to bring this to pass. Elisha encouraged Hazael to murder his master Ben-hadad in Damascus (8:13), and now he raises up Jehu to be an enemy within Israel itself. These actions apparently saved the Northern Kingdom for some sort of worship

9:1-10. The Fearless Messenger.—This chapter, which records the downfall of the house of Ahab, makes plain the moral retribution that overtakes the workers of iniquity. The dynasty of Omri, Ahab's father, was one of the most powerful in the history of Israel. Ahab himself was a strong monarch who, abetted by Jezebel,

a woman of immense strength of will, had enormously increased the prestige of his people. Yet both were tyrants who flouted the will of God and had no sense of justice, honor, or humanity. Hence Elijah (I Kings 19:15-17) had foretold their doom and had bequeathed to Elisha the fulfillment of this prediction. Elisha

2 And when thou comest thither, look out there Jehu the son of Jehoshaphat the son of Nimshi, and go in, and make him arise up from among his brethren, and carry him to an inner chamber;

3 Then take the box of oil, and pour *it* on his head, and say, Thus saith the LORD, I have anointed thee king over Israel. Then open the door, and flee, and tarry not.

4 ¶ So the young man, *even* the young man the prophet, went to Ramoth-gilead.

5 And when he came, behold, the captains of the host *were* sitting; and he said, I have an errand to thee, O captain. And Jehu said, Unto which of all us? And he said, To thee, O captain.

6 And he arose, and went into the house; and he poured the oil on his head, and said unto him, Thus saith the LORD God of Israel, I have anointed thee king over the people of the LORD, *even* over Israel.

gilead. 2 And when you arrive, look there for Jehu the son of Jehosh'aphat, son of Nimshi; and go in and bid him rise from among his fellows, and lead him to an inner chamber. 3 Then take the flask of oil, and pour it on his head, and say, 'Thus says the LORD, I anoint you king over Israel.' Then open the door and flee; do not tarry."

4 So the young man, the prophet,[h] went to Ramoth-gilead. 5 And when he came, behold, the commanders of the army were in council; and he said, "I have an errand to you, O commander." And Jehu said, "To which of us all?" And he said, "To you, O commander." 6 So he arose, and went into the house; and the young man poured the oil on his head, saying to him, "Thus says the LORD the God of Israel, I anoint you king over the people of the

[h] Gk Syr: Heb *the young man, the young man, the prophet*

of the Lord, but politically they brought the country to its very nadir. It is true that the dynasty of Jehu lasted for a hundred years, but for forty years the kingdom was in continual difficulties with neighboring Damascus-Syria. It was not until Damascus was destroyed by the Assyrian usurper Adadnirari III in 805 B.C. that Israel, under king Jehoash, was able to recover what she had lost. At one time Israel was reduced to fifty horsemen, ten chariots, and ten thousand footmen (13:7). Judah was vassal to Syria (12:18) and Hazael even captured Gath in the Philistine country (12:17). The judgment of a prophet of later date on Jehu's bath of blood is to be found in Hos. 1:4.

2. Jehu is twice called "son of Nimshi" (vs. 20; I Kings 19:16), this being his grandfather's name. In Assyrian inscriptions he is called "son of Omri," a tribute to the power and reputation of the founder of the previous dynasty. The reading of the name of Jehu on the superscription of one of the bas-reliefs on the Black Obelisk of Shalmaneser III (859-824 B.C.) was one of the first achievements in the reading of the Assyrian cuneiform script. This was read by Edward Hincks in 1851. It is the Assyrian record of Jehu paying tribute to the Assyrian king in 841 B.C., and this date is therefore one of the fixed points of Hebrew chronology.

4. The phrase **even the young man the prophet** (KJV) looks like an early gloss, though it may be that the word for **the young man** has been accidentally repeated.

6. The statement that Israel (i.e., the Northern Kingdom) is **the people of the LORD** is definitely a northern statement. The original compiler could scarcely have allowed this to stand, and evidently this story has been taken over without any partisan alterations.

had never forgotten that this was his task, and had awaited the moment which had now come for compassing the destruction of the house of Ahab. He chose a young prophet and ordered him to go and to anoint Jehu as king in Joram's stead. It was a perilous mission. How could the young man know that the captains at the front were ready to revolt; that Jehu was prepared to usurp the throne? Yet he did not hesitate. We find here an illustration of the fearlessness of God's servants which runs all through the

centuries. The O.T. annals are filled with a record of heroism unmatched by any which pagan or secular history can muster. The most irresistible personalities in the world are those filled with a passion for God and the will of God. The absence of such selfless devotion to God and the will of God is the most glaring defect in conventional and contemporary Christian character. What we need to remember is that it is possible to live in simple appreciation of Godlike ideas, to be accounted "interested"

7 And thou shalt smite the house of Ahab thy master, that I may avenge the blood of my servants the prophets, and the blood of all the servants of the LORD, at the hand of Jezebel.

8 For the whole house of Ahab shall perish: and I will cut off from Ahab him that pisseth against the wall, and him that is shut up and left in Israel:

9 And I will make the house of Ahab like the house of Jeroboam the son of Nebat, and like the house of Baasha the son of Ahijah:

10 And the dogs shall eat Jezebel in the portion of Jezreel, and *there shall be* none to bury *her*. And he opened the door, and fled.

11 ¶ Then Jehu came forth to the servants of his lord: and *one* said unto him, *Is* all well? wherefore came this mad *fellow* to thee? And he said unto them, Ye know the man, and his communication.

12 And they said, *It is* false; tell us now. And he said, Thus and thus spake he to me, saying, Thus saith the LORD, I have anointed thee king over Israel.

13 Then they hasted, and took every man his garment, and put *it* under him on the top of the stairs, and blew with trumpets, saying, Jehu is king.

LORD, over Israel. 7 And you shall strike down the house of Ahab your master, that I may avenge on Jez'ebel the blood of my servants the prophets, and the blood of all the servants of the LORD. 8 For the whole house of Ahab shall perish; and I will cut off from Ahab every male, bond or free, in Israel. 9 And I will make the house of Ahab like the house of Jerobo'am the son of Nebat, and like the house of Ba'asha the son of Ahi'jah. 10 And the dogs shall eat Jez'ebel in the territory of Jezreel, and none shall bury her." Then he opened the door, and fled.

11 When Jehu came out to the servants of his master, they said to him, "Is all well? Why did this mad fellow come to you?" And he said to them, "You know the fellow and his talk." 12 And they said, "That is not true; tell us now." And he said, "Thus and so he spoke to me, saying, 'Thus says the LORD, I anoint you king over Israel.'" 13 Then in haste every man of them took his garment, and put it under him on the bare[i] steps, and they blew the trumpet, and proclaimed, "Jehu is king."

[i] The meaning of the Hebrew word is uncertain

7-10a. These verses are an insertion by the Deuteronomic compiler and are based on I Kings 17–19; 21:23. The original story told simply how the young man **opened the door, and fled** (vs. 10*b*) as soon as he had anointed Jehu. This involves the same reticence and silence with which we are familiar in other stories of the delivery of the prophetic message.

8. The phrase **bond or free** is taken from I Kings 21:21 (see Exeg. on I Kings 14:10).

10. The word חלק, **portion**, is from a root meaning "to divide" and refers primarily to the strip of land which each man cultivated in the area of tilled land outside the settlement, whether village or town. This system of strips of land outside the village settlement was extant in England in the Middle Ages.

11. The officers call the young prophet **this mad fellow.** It was partly out of contempt, but with some justification because of the ecstatic, uncontrolled behavior which was common among these earlier prophets (Johnson, *Cultic Prophet in Ancient Israel*, p. 19).

13. The officers make an improvised throne **on the bare steps**, sound the coronation fanfare, and raise the customary cry, **Jehu is king.** The word גרם is difficult, but the Jewish commentator Qimḥi's translation (**bare**) is probably correct.

---

in social ideals, without rising to the conception of the glorious cause of our common humanity which will make us lose sight of ourselves in devotion to it. The real call of the Cross is the highest venture of living in a world which waits to be saved. We need more men in the ranks with the spirit of this young

prophet who hazarded his life in the performance of his mission. The demand today is for the fighting saint. For every sinner as bold as Satan there should be a saint as audacious as the Son of God.

11-37. *The Wages of Sin.*—The narrative of the swift and terrible retribution which overtook

14 So Jehu the son of Jehoshaphat the son of Nimshi conspired against Joram. (Now Joram had kept Ramoth-gilead, he and all Israel, because of Hazael king of Syria.

15 But king Joram was returned to be healed in Jezreel of the wounds which the Syrians had given him, when he fought with Hazael king of Syria.) And Jehu said, If it be your minds, *then* let none go forth *nor* escape out of the city to go to tell *it* in Jezreel.

16 So Jehu rode in a chariot, and went to Jezreel; for Joram lay there. And Ahaziah king of Judah was come down to see Joram.

17 And there stood a watchman on the tower in Jezreel, and he spied the company of Jehu as he came, and said, I see a com-

14 Thus Jehu the son of Jehosh'aphat the son of Nimshi conspired against Joram. (Now Joram with all Israel had been on guard at Ramoth-gilead against Haz'ael king of Syria; 15 but King Joram had returned to be healed in Jezreel of the wounds which the Syrians had given him, when he fought with Haz'ael king of Syria.) So Jehu said, "If this is your mind, then let no one slip out of the city to go and tell the news in Jezreel." 16 Then Jehu mounted his chariot, and went to Jezreel, for Joram lay there. And Ahazi'ah king of Judah had come down to visit Joram.

17 Now the watchman was standing on the tower in Jezreel, and he spied the com-

---

2. ASSASSINATION OF THE TWO KINGS (9:14-29)

Jehu takes immediate action. He prevents any possibility of the news preceding him and sets out in his chariot across the country to Jezreel. It so happened that Ahaziah of Judah was there at the time, visiting his cousin Joram of Israel. With great literary art the narrator now changes the scene and tells of the watcher at the gate seeing the small party racing toward Jezreel. The king sends a messenger to meet them, but Jehu detains the man. The same thing happens to another messenger, and by this time the watchman has recognized Jehu by the furious rate of his driving. Joram and Ahaziah both go out to meet him, each man in his own chariot, apprehensive lest Jehu is bringing bad news from the battlefront. Both are unsuspecting of any hostile intentions, but Jehu's reply to Joram's inquiry leaves no room for doubt. Joram turns to flee, crying out to Ahaziah that treachery is abroad. Jehu shoots Joram dead, has his body cast into the vineyard which once was Naboth's, pursues the fleeing Ahaziah, overtakes him at Ibleam, and shoots him down also. Ahaziah's chariot continues to flee, but by the time the charioteer has reached Megiddo, Ahaziah is dead. His body is taken to Jerusalem and buried there.

14. The reference to Joram's having been **on guard at Ramoth-gilead** is strange, though so far as the actual Hebrew syntax and the sense of the passage are concerned the statement can well stand. It is better, however, to follow the suggestion of Graetz and substitute Jehu for Joram. We now get the statement that Jehu was in charge of the garrison at Ramoth-gilead, holding the place against the Syrians while Joram (Jehoram) was recovering from his wounds in Jezreel. All of this is correct, and the realization of such a situation is essential to the proper understanding of the story.

17. The LXX says that the watchman saw a dust cloud. There is something to be said for such an interpretation since it would account for the long time before the group of chariots was near enough for him to recognize Jehu's style of driving.

Joram, his nephew Ahaziah, the queen mother Jezebel, is told in vivid detail. Jezebel met her awful fate undaunted, an awesome figure to the very last. Commensurate with the wickedness of the house of Ahab was the sordidness of its collapse. There runs—this is the inmost lesson of the whole tragic story—a moral law through the affairs of men. Behind the shifting scene of outward events, the rise and fall of dynasties and of nations, there operates the unvarying principle of righteousness, the righteousness of God. No matter how spectacular the achievements of men may be, however great their ability or genius, let their work be tainted with evil, devoid of justice and humanity, and it will come to the ground at last and so will they. Modern history has furnished us with prodigious examples of the downfall of tyrants

pany. And Joram said, Take a horseman, and send to meet them, and let him say, *Is it* peace?

18 So there went one on horseback to meet him, and said, Thus saith the king, *Is it* peace? And Jehu said, What hast thou to do with peace? turn thee behind me. And the watchman told, saying, The messenger came to them, but he cometh not again.

19 Then he sent out a second on horseback, which came to them, and said, Thus saith the king, *Is it* peace? And Jehu answered, What hast thou to do with peace? turn thee behind me.

20 And the watchman told, saying, He came even unto them, and cometh not again: and the driving *is* like the driving of Jehu the son of Nimshi; for he driveth furiously.

21 And Joram said, Make ready. And his chariot was made ready. And Joram king of Israel and Ahaziah king of Judah went out, each in his chariot, and they went out against Jehu, and met him in the portion of Naboth the Jezreelite.

22 And it came to pass, when Joram saw Jehu, that he said, *Is it* peace, Jehu? And he answered, What peace, so long as the whoredoms of thy mother Jezebel and her witchcrafts *are so* many?

pany of Jehu as he came, and said, "I see a company." And Joram said, "Take a horseman, and send to meet them, and let him say, 'Is it peace?' " 18 So a man on horseback went to meet him, and said, "Thus says the king, 'Is it peace?' " And Jehu said, "What have you to do with peace? Turn round and ride behind me." And the watchman reported, saying, "The messenger reached them, but he is not coming back." 19 Then he sent out a second horseman, who came to them, and said, "Thus the king has said, 'Is it peace?' " And Jehu answered, "What have you to do with peace? Turn round and ride behind me." 20 Again the watchman reported, "He reached them, but he is not coming back. And the driving is like the driving of Jehu the son of Nimshi; for he drives furiously."

21 Joram said, "Make ready." And they made ready his chariot. Then Joram king of Israel and Ahazi'ah king of Judah set out, each in his chariot, and went to meet Jehu, and met him at the property of Naboth the Jezreelite. 22 And when Joram saw Jehu, he said, "Is it peace, Jehu?" He answered, "What peace can there be, so long as the harlotries and the sorceries of your

---

20. The furious driving of Jehu had already become a matter for remark. In our time it is proverbial. The Targ. says that his custom was to drive quietly, while Josephus (*Antiquities* IX. 6. 3) says that he marched slowly and in good order. Possibly these interpretations are due to the fact that it is indeed necessary to allow a fairly long period between the time when the watchman first saw the group coming from the direction of Ramoth-gilead and the time when the two kings went out to meet Jehu. As has been seen, the LXX obtains this necessary period of time by saying that the watchman first saw a dust cloud. The Hebrew, however, clearly says that Jehu was driving "like a madman" (the same root as that used in vs. 11 to describe the young prophet).

22. What peace . . . ? The Hebrew strictly will not allow this rendering which is obtained by the omission of the letter *hē*. The alternative is to alter the vowels as the Targ. has done (*māh hashālôm* for *māh-hashshālôm*) and read, "What 'Is it well?' can there be while . . ." i.e., what is the use of asking such a question when Jezebel is still alive corrupting the country?

Harlotries . . . sorceries: The former is a description of the idolatries of Canaan; its use begins with the J tradition (Num. 14:33) and is common in Hosea, Jeremiah, and

---

whose miserable ends have not been unlike that of the house of Ahab.

The truth that the stability and prosperity of men and of nations depend wholly upon their conformity to the righteousness of God is the uniform teaching of the O.T. These historical books, we must remember, were written

from the prophetic standpoint. They are not mere books of history. They are sermons. And they all teach the same truth: the moral law vindicating in the end the righteousness of God. This was the ultimate basis of the social optimism of the prophets, causing them even in the darkest hour to believe in the final victory of

23 And Joram turned his hands, and fled, and said to Ahaziah, *There is* treachery, O Ahaziah.

24 And Jehu drew a bow with his full strength, and smote Jehoram between his arms, and the arrow went out at his heart, and he sunk down in his chariot.

25 Then said *Jehu* to Bidkar his captain, Take up, *and* cast him in the portion of the field of Naboth the Jezreelite: for remember how that, when I and thou rode together after Ahab his father, the LORD laid this burden upon him;

26 Surely I have seen yesterday the blood of Naboth, and the blood of his sons, saith the LORD; and I will requite thee in this plat, saith the LORD. Now therefore take *and* cast him into the plat *of ground*, according to the word of the LORD.

27 ¶ But when Ahaziah the king of Judah saw *this*, he fled by the way of the garden house. And Jehu followed after him, and said, Smite him also in the chariot. *And they did so* at the going up to Gur, which *is* by Ibleam. And he fled to Megiddo, and died there.

mother Jez'ebel are so many?" **23** Then Joram reined about and fled, saying to Ahazi'ah, "Treachery, O Ahazi'ah!" **24** And Jehu drew his bow with his full strength, and shot Joram between the shoulders, so that the arrow pierced his heart, and he sank in his chariot. **25** Jehu said to Bidkar his aide, "Take him up, and cast him on the plot of ground belonging to Naboth the Jezreelite; for remember, when you and I rode side by side behind Ahab his father, how the LORD uttered this oracle against him: **26** 'As surely as I saw yesterday the blood of Naboth and the blood of his sons — says the LORD — I will requite you on this plot of ground.' Now therefore take him up and cast him on the plot of ground, in accordance with the word of the LORD."

27 When Ahazi'ah the king of Judah saw this, he fled in the direction of Beth-haggan. And Jehu pursued him, and said, "Shoot him also"; and they shot him[j] in the chariot at the ascent of Gur, which is by Ibleam. And he fled to Megid'do, and died

j Syr Vg Compare Gk: Heb lacks *and they shot him*

Ezekiel. Its origin lies partly in the fact that the nature worship of Canaan, with its Baals and Astartes, involved sacred prostitution at the various hill shrines, but mostly on account of the husband-wife simile which had been boldly adopted by Hosea and continued by Ezekiel. This involves the further idea that apostasy on the part of Israel was adultery away from her true husband. The word **sorceries** does not refer to Israel's apostasy so much as to Jezebel's seductive skill in enticing Israel to follow Baal.

27. It is best to leave **Beth-haggan** (lit., **the garden house**) untranslated, taking it to be a place name, and identifying it with En-gannim ("spring of gardens," Josh. 19:21), some seven miles south of Jezreel at the foot of the ridge of Carmel. Jehu and his men thus came within shooting distance of the fleeing Ahaziah just beyond the entrance to

---

right over wrong, truth over falsehood, life over death. Never did they despair, since they knew that nothing could defeat the divine will and purpose. That must be the final foundation of a true optimism today. So only can we have "optimism without frivolity and seriousness without despair." As James Russell Lowell has written:

Though the cause of Evil prosper, yet 'tis Truth alone is strong;
. . . .
Truth forever on the scaffold, Wrong forever on the throne—
Yet that scaffold sways the future, and, behind the dim unknown,
Standeth God within the shadow, keeping watch above his own.[8]

[8] "The Present Crisis."

Jehu's dynasty was the last in the Northern Kingdom. Under his successors Samaria went down in ruins. The career of Jehu reveals him as a bloodthirsty tyrant, a man without conscience or pity. How comes it that Elisha could choose, and that God could use, such a man to accomplish his ends? It is a real problem. Yet it is not a problem which involves the integrity of God or any compromise with the principle of righteousness. Wicked men may perform tasks necessary for the ultimate achievement of righteousness. This does not condone their wickedness or absolve them from its penalties. Blindly and unwittingly they accomplish moral ends. Perhaps no one else could do it. Yet they themselves do not escape final condemnation. So it proved with Jehu.

The problem involved in the career of Jehu

28 And his servants carried him in a chariot to Jerusalem, and buried him in his sepulchre with his fathers in the city of David.

29 And in the eleventh year of Joram the son of Ahab began Ahaziah to reign over Judah.

30 ¶ And when Jehu was come to Jezreel, Jezebel heard *of it;* and she painted her face, and tired her head, and looked out at a window.

31 And as Jehu entered in at the gate, she said, *Had* Zimri peace, who slew his master?

there. 28 His servants carried him in a chariot to Jerusalem, and buried him in his tomb with his fathers in the city of David.

29 In the eleventh year of Joram the son of Ahab, Ahazi'ah began to reign over Judah.

30 When Jehu came to Jezreel, Jez'ebel heard of it; and she painted her eyes, and adorned her head, and looked out of the window. 31 And as Jehu entered the gate, she said, "Is it peace, you Zimri, murderer

the pass of the Plain of Dothan. There Jehu shot him, but Ahaziah's charioteer evidently turned northwest and fled along the road which skirts the northern flank of the Carmel Ridge. He had reached Megiddo, about twelve miles away, when the wounded king died. The charioteer probably continued through the pass of Megiddo and on to Jerusalem. According to the parallel narrative in II Chr. 22:9, Ahaziah managed to reach Samaria and hid there until he was searched out and brought to Jehu, who executed him.

29. This notice is both out of place and contradictory to the notice in 8:25, for there is a discrepancy of one year. Lucian has **in the eleventh year** in both places. The notice belongs to the short account of Ahaziah's reign which is found in Lucian at the end of ch. 10. It is probable, therefore, that 9:30–10:36 is an insertion into an original summary of Ahaziah's reign, still found in Lucian's version, but omitted in the M.T. and the LXX because some of it is now found in ch. 9.

3. END OF JEZEBEL (9:30-37)

Jezebel hears what has happened. Knowing that her death is certain, she takes great pains with her toilette and looks out of her window to greet Jehu mockingly as a second Zimri who murdered his master. At Jehu's word two or three eunuchs throw her out of the window and Jehu tramples her to death with his horses and chariots. Having entered the place to eat and drink, he suddenly remembers that after all Jezebel was a king's daughter and no ordinary wife or concubine to a king. He commands that she receive decent burial, but the dogs of Jezreel have devoured her body. Nothing is left but the skull, the feet, and the palms of her hands. The terrible curse of Elijah has been fulfilled.

Jezebel "set her eyes in antimony" as the Hebrew puts it. She blackened the edges of her eyelids above and below with antimony. This still is a fashion in the East. It makes the eyes appear larger and more brilliant. Her object may have been, as some say, to die bravely, but it is more than likely that she wanted to die in all her beauty; cf. Leonidas and his Spartans at Thermopylae, who followed the custom of combing their hair and beautifying their bodies before battle. They were not effeminate in this, as the Persians thought. Their idea was that a man began the next life, however shadowy that life might be, with a body similar in all respects to his physical body at the time of death, with its blemishes and its amputations, but also with any beauty it possessed (Lucien Lévy-Bruhl, *The "Soul" of the Primitive,* tr. Lilian A. Clare [London: George Allen & Unwin, 1928], pp. 314-15).

31. The translation of the KJV is untenable. The RSV rightly makes the question

may be sketched in broader lines. The wrath of man, it appears, can work to the glory of God. No Ahab or Jehu? No Manasseh or Jehoiakim? Then no Exile with its glories, no

new vision of God through discipline and suffering. No Judas or Caiaphas? No Herod or Pilate? Then no Cross of glory with its revelation of the redemptive love of God. "Who is the wise

32 And he lifted up his face to the window, and said, Who *is* on my side? who? And there looked out to him two *or* three eunuchs.

33 And he said, Throw her down. So they threw her down: and *some* of her blood was sprinkled on the wall, and on the horses: and he trode her under foot.

34 And when he was come in, he did eat and drink, and said, Go, see now this cursed *woman,* and bury her: for she *is* a king's daughter.

35 And they went to bury her: but they found no more of her than the skull, and the feet, and the palms of *her* hands.

36 Wherefore they came again, and told him. And he said, This *is* the word of the LORD, which he spake by his servant Elijah the Tishbite, saying, In the portion of Jezreel shall dogs eat the flesh of Jezebel:

37 And the carcass of Jezebel shall be as dung upon the face of the field in the portion of Jezreel; *so* that they shall not say, This *is* Jezebel.

10 And Ahab had seventy sons in Samaria. And Jehu wrote letters, and sent to Samaria, unto the rulers of Jezreel,

of your master?" 32 And he lifted up his face to the window, and said, "Who is on my side? Who?" Two or three eunuchs looked out at him. 33 He said, "Throw her down." So they threw her down; and some of her blood spattered on the wall and on the horses, and they trampled on her. 34 Then he went in and ate and drank; and he said, "See now to this cursed woman, and bury her; for she is a king's daughter." 35 But when they went to bury her, they found no more of her than the skull and the feet and the palms of her hands. 36 When they came back and told him, he said, "This is the word of the LORD, which he spoke by his servant Eli'jah the Tishbite, 'In the territory of Jezreel the dogs shall eat the flesh of Jez'ebel; 37 and the corpse of Jez'ebel shall be as dung upon the face of the field in the territory of Jezreel, so that no one can say, This is Jez'ebel.' "

10 Now Ahab had seventy sons in Samar'ia. So Jehu wrote letters, and

---

Is it peace? to be a general salutation. Jezebel calls him "Zimri the regicide" and neither gives nor expects mercy.

4. JEHU KING OF ISRAEL (10:1-36)

a) MASSACRE OF THE HOUSE OF AHAB (10:1-14)

Jehu follows the custom of the time and sets out to destroy every male of the royal line which he has supplanted. This is partly to secure the succession to his own family and partly to prevent a blood feud, ensuring that there should be no one to take revenge for the murdered king. Ahab has seventy sons living in Samaria, so Jehu sends a message to their guardians, challenging them to pick their man as king and fight for him. They say to themselves that they can never stand against a man who is so mighty as to kill two kings, so they submit to Jehu and ask for instructions. He commands them to execute all their charges and bring their heads to Jezreel. Jehu bids them leave these heads by the gate overnight, and in the morning says that neither he nor the citizens are responsible, suggesting that this is an act of God who fulfills his word. Jehu then sets out for Samaria and meets Ahaziah of Judah's kinsmen who have gone to greet their northern relatives and are presumably on their way home. Jehu arrests them all and executes them. They too are related to the house of Ahab, since Athaliah, the mother of Ahaziah, was Ahab's daughter.

10:1. Seventy is a frequent number for the sum total of the relatives of a king (Judg. 8:30; 12:14; cf. Bar-Çûr of Ya'di, who also had seventy relatives massacred

---

man, that may understand this? and who is he to whom the mouth of the LORD hath spoken, that he may declare it?" (Jer. 9:12*a*.) Such ultimate mysteries we may well leave to a knowledge that is above and beyond our own.

10:1-14, 16-32. *More on Jehu.*—One reads this chapter with horror and loathing. It is full of unimaginable atrocity and merciless butchery, and it reeks with blood. The whole story is a dreadful nightmare. It is a lurid picture, un-

to the elders, and to them that brought up Ahab's *children,* saying,

2 Now as soon as this letter cometh to you, seeing your master's sons *are* with you, and *there are* with you chariots and horses, a fenced city also, and armor;

3 Look even out the best and meetest of your master's sons, and set *him* on his father's throne, and fight for your master's house.

4 But they were exceedingly afraid, and said, Behold, two kings stood not before him: how then shall we stand?

5 And he that *was* over the house, and he that *was* over the city, the elders also, and the bringers up *of the children,* sent to Jehu, saying, We *are* thy servants, and will do all that thou shalt bid us; we will not make any king: do thou *that which is* good in thine eyes.

6 Then he wrote a letter the second time to them, saying, If ye *be* mine, and *if* ye will hearken unto my voice, take ye the heads of the men your master's sons, and come to me to Jezreel by to-morrow this time. Now the king's sons, *being* seventy persons, *were* with the great men of the city, which brought them up.

7 And it came to pass, when the letter came to them, that they took the king's sons, and slew seventy persons, and put their heads in baskets, and sent him *them* to Jezreel.

sent them to Samar'ia, to the rulers of the city,[k] to the elders, and to the guardians of the sons of Ahab, saying, 2 "Now then, as soon as this letter comes to you, seeing your master's sons are with you, and there are with you chariots and horses, fortified cities also, and weapons, 3 select the best and fittest of your master's sons and set him on his father's throne, and fight for your master's house." 4 But they were exceedingly afraid, and said, "Behold, the two kings could not stand before him; how then can we stand?" 5 So he who was over the palace, and he who was over the city, together with the elders and the guardians, sent to Jehu, saying, "We are your servants, and we will do all that you bid us. We will not make any one king; do whatever is good in your eyes." 6 Then he wrote to them a second letter, saying, "If you are on my side, and if you are ready to obey me, take the heads of your master's sons, and come to me at Jezreel tomorrow at this time." Now the king's sons, seventy persons, were with the great men of the city, who were bringing them up. 7 And when the letter came to them, they took the king's sons, and slew them, seventy persons, and put their heads in baskets, and sent them to him at Jezreel.

[k] Gk Vg: Heb *Jezreel*

(Burney, *Notes on Hebrew Text of Kings,* p. 302). There are traces of this number partaking to some extent of the magic nature of the number seven (Westermarck, *Ritual and Belief in Morocco,* I, 143, II, 263).

The **Jezreel** of the M.T. is difficult. It is better to follow Lucian and the Vulg. and read **the city.** If we read "of the city and to the elders," the error in the Hebrew is much easier than the English translation would suggest.

2-4. Jehu challenges the men to resist him if they dare. Let them pick the best man and fight it out. But the officials submit because Jehu has already killed two kings. Behind this reason for their submission is more than the modern reader readily appreciates. The classical example in the O.T. of this ancient attitude is the case of Gideon's son who is afraid to kill Zebah and Zalmunna, the two kings of Midian (Judg. 8:20-21).

---

equaled in Scripture, of brutality and horror. There is nothing in the whole narrative to indicate that the author of it had the slightest detestation of the horrors that he describes. On the contrary, the inference is that he not only condoned but approved of them (vs. 30). Neither is there anything to show that Elisha recoiled from the terrible sequence of events he had set in motion when he had given Jehu

his mandate to destroy the house of Ahab. Thus we are presented with a dark picture of the state of religion in those ancient days. Yet only a little knowledge of history is needed to show us that even in an era called Christian abominable cruelties have been perpetrated in the name of religion and with the sanction of the church. The religious conscience has freed itself only slowly from its dreadful alliance with cruelty.

8 ¶ And there came a messenger, and told him, saying, They have brought the heads of the king's sons. And he said, Lay ye them in two heaps at the entering in of the gate until the morning.

9 And it came to pass in the morning, that he went out, and stood, and said to all the people, Ye *be* righteous: behold, I conspired against my master, and slew him: but who slew all these?

10 Know now that there shall fall unto the earth nothing of the word of the LORD, which the LORD spake concerning the house of Ahab: for the LORD hath done *that* which he spake by his servant Elijah.

11 So Jehu slew all that remained of the house of Ahab in Jezreel, and all his great men, and his kinsfolk, and his priests, until he left him none remaining.

12 ¶ And he arose and departed, and came to Samaria. *And* as he *was* at the shearing house in the way,

13 Jehu met with the brethren of Ahaziah king of Judah, and said, Who *are* ye? And they answered, We *are* the brethren of Ahaziah; and we go down to salute the

8 When the messenger came and told him, "They have brought the heads of the king's sons," he said, "Lay them in two heaps at the entrance of the gate until the morning."

9 Then in the morning, when he went out, he stood, and said to all the people, "You are innocent. It was I who conspired against my master, and slew him; but who struck down all these? 10 Know then that there shall fall to the earth nothing of the word of the LORD, which the LORD spoke concerning the house of Ahab; for the LORD has done what he said by his servant Eli'jah." 11 So Jehu slew all that remained of the house of Ahab in Jezreel, all his great men, and his familiar friends, and his priests, until he left him none remaining.

12 Then he set out and went to Samar'ia. On the way, when he was at Beth-eked of the Shepherds, 13 Jehu met the kinsmen of Ahazi'ah king of Judah, and he said, "Who are you?" And they answered, "We are the

---

The king was regarded as being a sacred person and therefore as being possessed of special more-than-human power. A man who can slay two kings in one day is thus possessed of a most extraordinary power, and only a fool would lightly take action against him.

9. The people are apprehensive when they see the seventy severed heads at the gates of the city. The city gates marked the site where judgment was dispensed, and the placing of the heads there was naturally interpreted to mean that the city was charged with the murders and involved in the blood guilt for which atonement had to be made. Jehu reassures the people: **You are innocent.** He then proceeds to make out that he had nothing to do with this new massacre either, that it constitutes a divine fulfillment of Elijah's oracle concerning the fate of the house of Ahab. Jehu was not distinguished for his scrupulousness, either here or elsewhere, zealous though he was for the Lord.

11. It is better, instead of reading **all his great men,** to follow Lucian's translation and to read "all his kinsfolk." Jehu was not murdering men indiscriminately. He was eliminating every male related to Ahab and Jezebel, Joram and Ahaziah, who could be "the avenger of blood."

13. The differences in the RSV are important and sound. The Judahite princes were on their way home when Jehu intercepted them. Furthermore, it is correct to read **queen mother,** since the reference is to the men of the king's own generation.

We still witness in time of war the resurgence of unbelievable depravity and cold-blooded inhumanity. Yet the religious conscience today condemns it, loathes it, is arrayed against it, is resolved to overcome it. Thus we can trace slow but sure progress under God in the evolution of morals and religion.

How can we say that God could use such a bloodthirsty tyrant as Jehu for the accomplish-

ment of his ends? The question is sharpened by this catalogue of hideous crime. Is some light thrown on it by vs. 28, **Thus Jehu destroyed Baal?** He possessed the qualities needed: courage, capacity for swift decision, leadership. He could have accomplished his mission without descending to these depths of depravity. The destruction of Baal was a command of God. The method employed was not. Jehu was com-

children of the king and the children of the queen.

14 And he said, Take them alive. And they took them alive, and slew them at the pit of the shearing house, *even* two and forty men; neither left he any of them.

15 ¶ And when he was departed thence, he lighted on Jehonadab the son of Rechab *coming* to meet him: and he saluted him, and said to him, Is thine heart right, as my heart *is* with thy heart? And Jehonadab answered, It is. If it be, give *me* thine hand. And he gave *him* his hand; and he took him up to him into the chariot.

16 And he said, Come with me, and see my zeal for the Lord. So they made him ride in his chariot.

17 And when he came to Samaria, he slew all that remained unto Ahab in Samaria, till he had destroyed him, according to the saying of the Lord, which he spake to Elijah.

kinsmen of Ahazi'ah, and we came down to visit the royal princes and the sons of the queen mother." 14 He said, "Take them alive." And they took them alive, and slew them at the pit of Beth-eked, forty-two persons, and he spared none of them.

15 And when he departed from there, he met Jehon'adab the son of Rechab coming to meet him; and he greeted him, and said to him, "Is your heart true to my heart as mine is to yours?"[l] And Jehon'adab answered, "It is." Jehu said,[m] "If it is, give me your hand." So he gave him his hand. And Jehu took him up with him into the chariot. 16 And he said, "Come with me, and see my zeal for the Lord." So he[n] had him ride in his chariot. 17 And when he came to Samar'ia, he slew all that remained to Ahab in Samar'ia, till he had wiped them out, according to the word of the Lord which he spoke to Eli'jah.

[l] Gk: Heb *Is it right with your heart, as my heart is with your heart?*
[m] Gk: Heb lacks *Jehu said*
[n] Gk Syr Tg: Heb *they*

b) Jehonadab the Rechabite (10:15-17)

Jehu sets out for Samaria and on his way meets Jehonadab, the leader of the Rechabites. He bids him come to see how zealous he is for the Lord, and takes him up into his chariot. Jehu arrives in Samaria and massacres all the residue of the house of Ahab.

15. According to Josephus (*Antiquities* IX. 6. 6), Jehu and Jehonadab were friends of long standing. The Rechabites were of Kenite descent (I Chr. 2:55) and stood firm for the old desert ways. They remained firm and vigorous in this faith in the days of Jeremiah, when they still refused to drink wine, or to possess vineyard, field, or seed (Jer. 35:9). They insisted upon living the old nomad life of their fathers, dwelling in tents and having as little as possible to do with the ways of Canaan. It will be readily seen that they were in wholehearted agreement with all that Jehu did, even to the fierce massacres for which he was responsible. In their vows of abstinence they have a modern parallel in the Wahabis of Saudi Arabia.

missioned to a divine end. The way he executed it was devilish. Actually Jehu did not destroy Baal by these methods. He destroyed Baal worshipers wholesale, but by such means he did not end the cult. Brute force never achieves moral ends. War in our modern world illustrates this truth. No matter how complete the overthrow of the enemy may be, war of itself settles nothing. It raises more problems than it solves. It begets more evils than it destroys. Baal can never be destroyed thus. Only by moral means can a kingdom of righteousness be established on earth. Jehu's kingdom was not established, as the sorry and sordid record shows (vss. 31-33). There was no peace, no prosperity during all this wretched reign. And a century later the

dynasty reared on the rotten foundation of bloodshed and cruelty went down in ruins.

15. The Rechabites.—They were a clan among the Israelites, traced back to Caleb in I Chr. 2:42, 55. Jehonadab was not their founder, but he had acquired such prominence and authority that the Rechabites later regarded him much as the people of Israel regarded Moses. They were devout worshipers of Yahweh, and their clan laws demanded abstinence from wine and made their ancient nomadic habits a matter of religious obligation (Jer. 35:6-7). The purpose of this seems to have been to preserve them from contamination by too close association with the Canaanites, and also to enable them to live a freer and more independent life

| 18 ¶ And Jehu gathered all the people together, and said unto them, Ahab served Baal a little; *but* Jehu shall serve him much. | 18 Then Jehu assembled all the people, and said to them, "Ahab served Ba'al a little; but Jehu will serve him much. 19 Now therefore call to me all the prophets of Ba'al, all his worshipers and all his priests; let none be missing, for I have a great sacrifice to offer to Ba'al; whoever is missing shall not live." But Jehu did it with cunning in order to destroy the worshipers of Ba'al. 20 And Jehu ordered, "Sanctify a solemn assembly for Ba'al." So they proclaimed it. 21 And Jehu sent throughout all Israel; and all the worshipers of Ba'al came, so that there was not a man left who did not come. And they entered the house of Ba'al, and the house of Ba'al was filled from one end to the other. 22 He said to him who was in charge of the wardrobe, "Bring out the vestments for all the worshipers of Ba'al." So he brought out the vestments for them. |

19 Now therefore call unto me all the prophets of Baal, all his servants, and all his priests; let none be wanting: for I have a great sacrifice *to do* to Baal; whosoever shall be wanting, he shall not live. But Jehu did *it* in subtilty, to the intent that he might destroy the worshippers of Baal.

20 And Jehu said, Proclaim a solemn assembly for Baal. And they proclaimed *it*.

21 And Jehu sent through all Israel: and all the worshippers of Baal came, so that there was not a man left that came not. And they came into the house of Baal; and the house of Baal was full from one end to another.

22 And he said unto him that *was* over the vestry, Bring forth vestments for all the worshippers of Baal. And he brought them forth vestments.

c) MASSACRE OF THE BAAL WORSHIPERS (10:18-28)

Jehu pretends great zeal for Baal, and bids every worshiper gather in the temple for a great sacrifice. He makes sure that every Baal worshiper is there, dressed in proper attire. He takes precautions that no true worshiper of the Lord is inside the temple. Then he stations eighty men outside to see that no one escapes and sends in his bodyguard to kill everyone inside the temple. He then demolishes the temple and everything in it.

19-20. It is best to omit **all his worshipers.** The phrase occurs in Lucian's translation after the reference to the **priests,** so it has every appearance of being a gloss which has crept into the text. Further, the worshipers in general are not called until vs. 21, when the prophets and the priests of Baal have made everything ready for them. These prophets and priests are the cult officials of the sanctuary (Johnson, *Cultic Prophets in Ancient Israel,* p. 53).

Jehu uses for **sacrifice** the word זבח which strictly means "slaughter for sacrifice," so it may be that he is continuing his grim humor of vs. 18 and is thinking more of the slaughter than of the sacrifice. Similarly, in vs. 20 the word עצרת, usually translated "common assembly," probably signifies "closing festival" (Deut. 16:8; Lev. 23:36), so that Jehu is actually calling a closing festival for Baal in a double sense.

22. The custom of washing one's clothes (Exod. 19:10) or of putting on a change of clothes (Gen. 35:2) is ancient and widespread, not only in connection with sacred festivals among the Hebrews, whether true worshipers or Baal worshipers, but among

than the settled villager or townsman. This naïve philosophy of life contains a profound truth. There are two elements in human existence which must somehow be reconciled: the instinct for stability and security, and the instinct for freedom, for movement, for escape from limitation and confinement. The solution of this problem lies in two directions. There must be some permanent basis of life, some accepted home of the soul. Without it, freedom becomes aimless wandering, pure eccentricity.

Life lacks coherence, unity. Even the Rechabites stuck to Palestine. This was their spiritual home and they never moved out of it. There is nothing in the Rechabite ideal to justify the reckless experimentation of much modern living. Stability, however, is one thing and immobility is another. Security there must be, but not stagnation. Within some Palestine, some area of settled principles of faith and conduct, every true life must be lived. Yet that life must have within it the spirit of the Rechabite, must live

23 And Jehu went, and Jehonadab the son of Rechab, into the house of Baal, and said unto the worshippers of Baal, Search, and look that there be here with you none of the servants of the LORD, but the worshippers of Baal only.

24 And when they went in to offer sacrifices and burnt offerings, Jehu appointed fourscore men without, and said, If any of the men whom I have brought into your hands escape, *he that letteth him go,* his life *shall be* for the life of him.

25 And it came to pass, as soon as he had made an end of offering the burnt offering, that Jehu said to the guard and to the captains, Go in, *and* slay them; let none come forth. And they smote them with the edge of the sword; and the guard and the captains cast *them* out, and went to the city of the house of Baal.

26 And they brought forth the images out of the house of Baal, and burned them.

27 And they brake down the image of Baal, and brake down the house of Baal, and made it a draught house unto this day.

28 Thus Jehu destroyed Baal out of Israel.

23 Then Jehu went into the house of Ba'al with Jehon'adab the son of Rechab; and he said to the worshipers of Ba'al, "Search, and see that there is no servant of the LORD here among you, but only the worshipers of Ba'al." 24 Then he[o] went in to offer sacrifices and burnt offerings.

Now Jehu had stationed eighty men outside, and said, "The man who allows any of those whom I give into your hands to escape shall forfeit his life." 25 So as soon as he had made an end of offering the burnt offering, Jehu said to the guard and to the officers, "Go in and slay them; let not a man escape." So when they put them to the sword, the guard and the officers cast them out and went into the inner room[p] of the house of Ba'al 26 and they brought out the pillar that was in the house of Ba'al, and burned it. 27 And they demolished the pillar of Ba'al, and demolished the house of Ba'al, and made it a latrine to this day.

28 Thus Jehu wiped out Ba'al from Is-

[o] Gk Compare verse 25: Heb *they*
[p] Cn: Heb *city*

---

the Arabs and elsewhere (W. Robertson Smith, *Lectures on the Religion of the Semites* [3rd ed.; New York: The Macmillan Co., 1927], p. 451). C. M. Doughty describes how the pilgrims to Mecca bathe themselves and put off their ordinary clothes before they enter the sacred city. They put on the *ihram,* the proper regulation clothing for the pilgrim, "and in this guise must every soul enter the sacred precincts" (*Travels in Arabia Deserta* [New York: Random House, 1946], pp. 511 ff., 572). Presumably this ancient custom is the remote origin of the modern "Sunday best."

25. The M.T. reads that the guard and the officers **went to the city of the house of Baal.** This does not make sense, and so it has become the custom to read דביר (**inner room,** "shrine") for עיר. It is now known that the Hebrew text is correct, and that there is a second word of the same form meaning "altar." This undoubtedly is the meaning here.

26. The M.T. has "pillars" (so ASV, ERV), but the singular certainly is intended, for the verse closes with **and burned it.** Since the sacred altar was burned it is generally agreed that the text did not have **the pillar,** which would be of stone, but "the sacred pole" (אשרה) though this is without any support in the ancient versions.

27. The M.T. has **pillar,** which some read **image,** under the impression that the pillar was actually a stone image of the god. Others read מזבח ("altar"), on the plea that there ought to be a reference to the destruction of the altar.

---

in tents, be able to move forward to new ideas, new duties, new outlooks on life. The test of true living is to take counsel not of our timidity but of our courage. The capacity for mental and moral movement is the prerequisite of any strong and achieving character. And it is only so that real stability and ultimate security can be

won. For apparent stability without freedom in thinking and action turns out not to be stable at all. Thus in the political sphere there are these two contending influences at work at the heart of every people. The one holds to the past, entrenching itself in tradition, calling it heresy to depart from the political philosophy of our

29 ¶ Howbeit, *from* the sins of Jeroboam the son of Nebat, who made Israel to sin, Jehu departed not from after them, *to wit,* the golden calves that *were* in Beth-el, and that *were* in Dan.

30 And the LORD said unto Jehu, Because thou hast done well in executing *that which is* right in mine eyes, *and* hast done unto the house of Ahab according to all that *was* in mine heart, thy children of the fourth *generation* shall sit on the throne of Israel.

31 But Jehu took no heed to walk in the law of the LORD God of Israel with all his heart: for he departed not from the sins of Jeroboam, which made Israel to sin.

32 ¶ In those days the LORD began to cut Israel short: and Hazael smote them in all the coasts of Israel;

33 From Jordan eastward, all the land of Gilead, the Gadites, and the Reubenites, and the Manassites, from Aroer, which *is* by the river Arnon, even Gilead and Bashan.

rael. 29 But Jehu did not turn aside from the sins of Jerobo'am the son of Nebat, which he made Israel to sin, the golden calves that were in Bethel, and in Dan. 30 And the LORD said to Jehu, "Because you have done well in carrying out what is right in my eyes, and have done to the house of Ahab according to all that was in my heart, your sons of the fourth generation shall sit on the throne of Israel." 31 But Jehu was not careful to walk in the law of the LORD the God of Israel with all his heart; he did not turn from the sins of Jerobo'am, which he made Israel to sin.

32 In those days the LORD began to cut off parts of Israel. Haz'ael defeated them throughout the territory of Israel: 33 from the Jordan eastward, all the land of Gilead, the Gadites, and the Reubenites, and the Manas'sites, from Aro'er, which is by the valley of the Arnon, that is, Gilead and

d) SUMMARY OF JEHU'S REIGN (10:29-31)

29-31. This is in the normal Deuteronomic style. For all Jehu's zeal for the Lord, the compiler's praise is qualified since the calf worship at Bethel and Dan still continued. Nevertheless, the compiler sees some reward for Jehu's zeal in the fact that four generations of Jehu's line occupied the throne of Israel for an over-all total of a hundred years.

e) ISRAEL'S LOSSES TO SYRIA (10:32-33)

32-33. These two verses are an extract from the Chronicles of the Kings of Israel, telling the sad story of the amount of territory Israel lost to the vigorous and successful Hazael. The weakness of Assyria from *ca.* 840 B.C. left Hazael free to make the most of his opportunities in the west. He took from Israel the whole of the territory east of the Jordan, and this territory was held by Syria until the rise of Adadnirari III, who conquered Damascus in 805 B.C.

fathers, invoking the words but not the spirit of our leaders of a century ago, insisting that we abide within a set of ideas that have become crystallized and unyielding. The other, the Rechabite ideal, holds that new conditions call for new ideas, that an expanding world calls for expanding ideals, that no political philosophy is or can be unalterable, that there are no traditions which may not be changed, and that we must move on and out into a new world at the call of humanity which is the call of God. It is the Rechabite ideal that needs a fresh interpretation in the national mind. Only so can civilization be made secure. And it is just so in personal living. A faith that takes refuge in the past, that refuses to move beyond the fixed traditions and formulas of religion, does not really rest on firm foundations. Besides

attachment to the inward essence of all true religion, fidelity to God, fellowship with Jesus Christ, there must be the Rechabite spirit which always welcomes new ideas and is willing to follow new paths into ever-enlarging conceptions of truth. Only so does faith itself become secure. And in the sphere of material existence the same spirit of independence and freedom is needed. Social security must be established. Yet this ideal is not enough of itself. Because it is the sole ambition of many, there follows inevitably a certain degradation of the higher life of man. If comfort and security are our only ideal, we fall short of our possible moral and spiritual destiny. Such is the lesson taught us by the Rechabites. Only as we learn it shall we dwell secure. Long after Samaria had fallen, the Rechabites went on living in the land.

<table>
<tr><td>

34 Now the rest of the acts of Jehu, and all that he did, and all his might, *are* they not written in the book of the Chronicles of the kings of Israel?

35 And Jehu slept with his fathers: and they buried him in Samaria. And Jehoahaz his son reigned in his stead.

36 And the time that Jehu reigned over Israel in Samaria *was* twenty and eight years.

11 And when Athaliah the mother of Ahaziah saw that her son was dead, she arose and destroyed all the seed royal.

</td><td>

Bashan. 34 Now the rest of the acts of Jehu, and all that he did, and all his might, are they not written in the Book of the Chronicles of the Kings of Israel? 35 So Jehu slept with his fathers, and they buried him in Samar'ia. And Jeho'ahaz his son reigned in his stead. 36 The time that Jehu reigned over Israel in Samar'ia was twenty-eight years.

11 Now when Athali'ah the mother of Ahazi'ah saw that her son was dead, she arose and destroyed all the royal family.

</td></tr>
</table>

f) Conclusion (10:34-36)

Here is the formal Deuteronomic obituary notice for Jehu, together with the name of his successor.

F. From Jehu's Revolution to the Fall of the Northern Kingdom (11:1–17:40)

1. Revolution and Counterrevolution in Judah (11:1-20)

At the death of Ahaziah his mother Athaliah seized the throne of Judah and held it for six years. She massacred all the males of the royal line of Judah except Joash, the infant son of Ahaziah. He was saved by his aunt, the wife of the high priest who was loyal to the Lord. She hid the baby prince in the temple precincts until the seventh year, when Jehoiada, her husband, staged a *coup d'état* on a sabbath at the time when the temple guard was being changed. Athaliah was killed, and the boy king was crowned. The Baal temple was destroyed and the high priest of Baal died a martyr for his faith.

11:1-21. An Unholy Alliance.—The narratives concerning the kings of Israel and of Judah shift from one kingdom to the other (see Exeg.). The historian proceeds in this chapter to describe the consequences of the revolution in the Northern Kingdom on the fortunes of Judah. To make the story complete the reader should consult II Chr. 21. Note also that the J(eh)oram of vss. 2 (son of Ahab, king of Israel) is not to be confused with the Jehoram of II Chr. 21:1, son of Jehoshaphat, king of Judah (cf. 8:16).

Athaliah was a daughter of Ahab and Jezebel (8:18). Doubtless to Jehoshaphat the marriage of his son Jehoram to a daughter of Ahab seemed a master stroke of political wisdom. Thus he could count on Ahab's help in attack upon their common enemies. As the results proved, the marriage brought only disaster upon the Southern Kingdom. Had Jehoshaphat married his son to a true woman who shared his own faith and loyalty to Yahweh the terrible story which this chapter contains would never have been written. One contrasts the folly of Jehoshaphat in marrying his son to a half-Phoenician idolatress with the farsighted wisdom of his progenitor Abraham, who bade his son (Gen. 24:3-4) seek a wife not among the Canaanites

with whom he might have advanced his worldly fortunes but from his own people and kindred. The ruin of Samson was compassed by his marriage with a Philistine woman. The counterpart of the marriage of Jehoram and Athaliah is found over and over again in history and in our modern world. Marriages which have for their purpose only material advantage invariably end in disillusion and disaster. Young men and women in our day can be given no better counsel than to marry one who lives as they live, believes as they believe, shares the same ideals, has the same religious background, is rooted in the same soil. The apostolic injunction, "Do not be mismated with unbelievers" (II Cor. 6:14), has fundamental significance and meaning.

1. Athaliah.—Here was a true daughter of Jezebel. She saw to it that all of her husband's brothers should be murdered so that his authority might go unchallenged (II Chr. 21:4). The worship of Baal was soon made the national religion; the high priest Jehoiada was degraded; all the cruelties, immoralities, and irreligion of the house of Ahab were re-enacted in the Southern Kingdom, which now fell to the lowest level in its history. There followed the miserable

244

2 But Jehosheba, the daughter of king Joram, sister of Ahaziah, took Joash the son of Ahaziah, and stole him from among the king's sons *which were* slain; and they hid him, *even* him and his nurse, in the bedchamber from Athaliah, so that he was not slain.

3 And he was with her hid in the house of the LORD six years. And Athaliah did reign over the land.

2 But Jehosh'eba the daughter of King Joram, sister of Ahazi'ah, took Jo'ash the son of Ahazi'ah, and stole him away from among the king's sons who were about to be slain, and she put*q* him and his nurse in a bedchamber. Thus she*r* hid him from Athali'ah, so that he was not slain; 3 and he remained with her six years, hid in the house of the LORD, while Athali'ah reigned over the land.

q With 2 Chron 22. 11: Heb lacks *and she put*
r Gk Syr Vg Compare 2 Chron 22. 11: Heb *they*

---

a) ATHALIAH SEIZES THE THRONE OF JUDAH (11:1-3)

The queen mother managed to maintain the ways of the house of Ahab for another six years in the kingdom of Judah, but she missed one person in the general massacre of Ahaziah's male kin, and this small boy proved to be the instrument of her final undoing.

11:2. According to II Chr. 22:11, Jehosheba was the wife of Jehoiada, the loyal high priest of the Lord. This fact explains how the boy and his nurse could remain hidden in the temple for six long years. On the night of the slaughter she hid the baby and his nurse **in a bedchamber,** i.e., not in a sleeping apartment but, as is quite clear from Josephus (*Antiquities* IX. 7. 1), in the chamber where the beds (mattresses) and couches were stored.

---

death of Jehoram (II Chr. 21:15, 18-19), and of his son Ahaziah (already narrated in 9:27). These events had no other effect on Athaliah, the wife of the one and the mother of the other, than to beget in her wild dreams whereby she could realize her unbridled ambition to become sole ruler of a kingdom. Hence the events as narrated in this chapter.

Athaliah thus stands out in history as the incarnation of cruelty, a masterful, conscienceless nature, capable of swift resolution, relentless purpose, devoid of any instincts either of natural affection or of common humanity. A sermon might be preached, with her as the supreme example, on the perversion of grand human qualities to ignoble ends. Here was a superb woman who commands admiration for her fearlessness, undaunted courage, immense ability, farseeing intelligence, and contempt of immobility, timidity, weakness and cowardice. These are among the noblest qualities in human nature. Personalities endowed with them rise like mountain peaks above the ruck of our common humanity. What a power for good such qualities could achieve if directed by conscience to moral ends. We are here reminded that a high degree of intelligence and of native ability uncontrolled by morality is far more dangerous to the social order than ignorance and incapacity. If our processes of education result in sharpening the wits of men who use these wits for selfish and unscrupulous ends, it were far better that their wits had not been sharpened

at all. Our most dangerous enemies today are highly trained and capable men who use their intelligence and abilities to circumvent laws enacted for the common welfare. Without moral character at the base, mental discipline becomes a menace, not a blessing. Has one ever asked oneself what place Napoleon might occupy in history had he possessed the moral qualities of George Washington?

Small wonder that the macabre and gripping drama narrated in this chapter appealed to Handel as the theme of one of his oratorios in which the double chorus is used for the first time, and to Racine whose *Athalie* is one of the noblest of his tragedies. He uses the material freely, describes Athaliah as forewarned in a dream, and weakened in advance by nervous apprehension. He even pictures a scene between her and this unknown child whom she interrogates concerning his origin and parentage. This, however, lessens the dramatic effect of the narrative which confronts the queen with a spectacle of which she had no previous intimation.

2-16. *Sic Semper Tyrannis.*—Few more dramatic narratives are to be found in the O.T. than that contained in this chapter: the hiding of the child Joash, reminiscent of that of Moses; the forged plot; the precautions taken by the posting of the guards; the preparation of a festival service announced by the blare of trumpets; the undaunted courage of the queen, who entered the temple and saw young Joash

4 ¶ And the seventh year Jehoiada sent and fetched the rulers over hundreds, with the captains and the guard, and brought them to him into the house of the LORD, and made a covenant with them, and took an oath of them in the house of the LORD, and showed them the king's son.

5 And he commanded them, saying, This *is* the thing that ye shall do; A third part of you that enter in on the sabbath shall even be keepers of the watch of the king's house;

6 And a third part *shall be* at the gate of Sur; and a third part at the gate behind the guard: so shall ye keep the watch of the house, that it be not broken down.

7 And two parts of all you that go forth on the sabbath, even they shall keep the watch of the house of the LORD about the king.

8 And ye shall compass the king round about, every man with his weapons in his hand: and he that cometh within the ranges,

4 But in the seventh year Jehoi'ada sent and brought the captains of the Carites and of the guards, and had them come to him in the house of the LORD; and he made a covenant with them and put them under oath in the house of the LORD, and he showed them the king's son. 5 And he commanded them, "This is the thing that you shall do: one third of you, those who come off duty on the sabbath and guard the king's house 6 (another third being at the gate Sur and a third at the gate behind the guards), shall guard the palace; 7 and the two divisions of you, which come on duty in force on the sabbath and guard the house of the LORD,[s] 8 shall surround the king, each with his weapons in his hand; and whoever approaches the ranks is to be slain. Be with

[s] Heb *the* LORD *to the king*

b) OVERTHROW OF ATHALIAH (11:4-20)

The story is from two sources, the main part being an account of a carefully designed plot on the part of the high priest, supported by the whole of the royal bodyguard. An insertion (vss. 13-18*a*) ascribes to the movement a popular origin with a distinctly religious object. The common people go in a body after the death of Athaliah (vs. 16) and destroy the Baal temple. The second account of the death of Athaliah (vs. 20) belongs to the main story.

4. The Carites were the foreign mercenaries who formed the royal bodyguard (see II Sam. 20:23, where they are identified with the Cherethites [Cretans]). In the parallel account (II Chr. 23:1-21) the Levites take the place of the Carites. This is in accordance with later ideas, for in the postexilic period it was thought to be highly improper that foreigners should be officially employed in the temple service, especially since there is evidence that the foreign guards were also the slaughterers of the sacrificial animals in pre-exilic times (W. Robertson Smith, *O.T. in Jewish Church*, p. 262, n.). The protest first appears in Ezek. 44:7.

5-7. These instructions remain confused even though in the RSV the major part of vs. 6 is regarded as a gloss. The plan seems to have been as follows: One third of the guard was to go off temple duty on the sabbath and watch over the security of the king's palace. But on this occasion they were to stay on duty within the temple itself while the other two thirds were to surround the young King Joash. This procedure enabled Jehoiada to have the whole of the temple guard together at one time, with all of them protecting the king, while at the same time the guard was suddenly withdrawn from the palace itself. This left Athaliah without any military support and provided the maximum safety for the young king. Further, the whole maneuver was performed in such a way that no one would have any idea of any special happening until it was accomplished. The normal procedure was for two thirds of the guard to be on duty at the palace and one third in the temple, except on the sabbath when the positions were reversed. The gloss in vs. 6 may be assumed as describing the positions taken by the sabbath guards on a normal sabbath.

8. The word **ranges** is an old form of the modern word **ranks** (cf. French *rang*).

let him be slain: and be ye with the king as he goeth out and as he cometh in.

9 And the captains over the hundreds did according to all *things* that Jehoiada the priest commanded: and they took every man his men that were to come in on the sabbath, with them that should go out on the sabbath, and came to Jehoiada the priest.

10 And to the captains over hundreds did the priest give king David's spears and shields, that *were* in the temple of the LORD.

11 And the guard stood, every man with his weapons in his hand, round about the king, from the right corner of the temple to the left corner of the temple, *along* by the altar and the temple.

12 And he brought forth the king's son, and put the crown upon him, and *gave him* the testimony; and they made him king, and anointed him; and they clapped their hands, and said, God save the king.

13 ¶ And when Athaliah heard the noise of the guard *and* of the people, she came to the people into the temple of the LORD.

14 And when she looked, behold, the king

the king when he goes out and when he comes in."

9 The captains did according to all that Jehoi'ada the priest commanded, and each brought his men who were to go off duty on the sabbath, with those who were to come on duty on the sabbath, and came to Jehoi'ada the priest. 10 And the priest delivered to the captains the spears and shields that had been King David's, which were in the house of the LORD; 11 and the guards stood, every man with his weapons in his hand, from the south side of the house to the north side of the house, around the altar and the house.[t] 12 Then he brought out the king's son, and put the crown upon him, and gave him the testimony; and they proclaimed him king, and anointed him; and they clapped their hands, and said, "Long live the king!"

13 When Athali'ah heard the noise of the guard and of the people, she went into the house of the LORD to the people; 14 and when she looked, there was the king stand-

[t] Heb *the house to the king*

10. The statement that the priest delivered weapons to the temple guard is extraordinary. Why should they of all people ever be without weapons? John Skinner's explanation is most attractive; he suggests that the verse is a gloss from II Chr. 23:9, where Jehoiada is said to have distributed weapons to the Levites (*Kings* [New York: Oxford University Press, 1904; "The New-Century Bible"], p. 339). If the Chronicler replaced the well-armed mercenaries with unarmed Levites, then he obviously had to arrange for them to be given arms on this special occasion.

11. The king had not yet been brought forward, so the guards can scarcely have been arranged **round about the king**. It is better, therefore, to omit the reference to the king, as in the RSV. On the other hand, it is necessary to make it clear that when the king was indeed brought out the guards were already in such a position as to surround him completely and thus to guard him effectively.

12. The sign of royalty, **the crown**, is placed on the king. The word **testimony** is difficult. It is best to assume the omission of one letter in the Hebrew, and so to read "bracelets" (cf. II Sam. 1:10).

13. Here the interpolated fragment begins, according to which the people, not the bodyguard, are the agents in carrying out the inauguration of the new regime. In the M.T. there has been an attempt to dovetail the two accounts into one and to reconcile them by the insertion of an unusual form of the word which elsewhere means "outrunners," translated **the guard**.

14. The **pillar** by which the king stood can scarcely have been one of the entrance pillars. It was apparently the place where the king stood regularly during worship,

crowned and mitered in royal regalia. She shouted, **Treason, treason,** but her hour had come and her doom was sealed. So in the Southern Kingdom as in the Northern, we gaze upon

the end of the house of Ahab, where it reaches its term in the death of his daughter who incarnated in her nature alike the superb abilities and the utter moral depravity of her parents.

stood by a pillar, as the manner *was,* and the princes and the trumpeters by the king, and all the people of the land rejoiced, and blew with trumpets: and Athaliah rent her clothes, and cried, Treason, treason.

15 But Jehoiada the priest commanded the captains of the hundreds, the officers of the host, and said unto them, Have her forth without the ranges; and him that followeth her kill with the sword. For the priest had said, Let her not be slain in the house of the LORD.

16 And they laid hands on her; and she went by the way by the which the horses came into the king's house: and there was she slain.

17 ¶ And Jehoiada made a covenant between the LORD and the king and the people, that they should be the LORD's people; between the king also and the people.

18 And all the people of the land went into the house of Baal, and brake it down; his altars and his images brake they in pieces thoroughly, and slew Mattan the priest of Baal before the altars. And the priest appointed officers over the house of the LORD.

19 And he took the rulers over hundreds, and the captains, and the guard, and all the people of the land; and they brought down the king from the house of the LORD, and came by the way of the gate of the guard to the king's house. And he sat on the throne of the kings.

20 And all the people of the land rejoiced, and the city was in quiet: and they slew Athaliah with the sword *beside* the king's house.

ing by the pillar, according to the custom, and the captains and the trumpeters beside the king, and all the people of the land rejoicing and blowing trumpets. And Athali'ah rent her clothes, and cried, "Treason! treason!" **15** Then Jehoi'ada the priest commanded the captains who were set over the army, "Bring her out between the ranks; and slay with the sword any one who follows her." For the priest said, "Let her not be slain in the house of the LORD." **16** So they laid hands on her; and she went through the horses' entrance to the king's house, and there she was slain.

17 And Jehoi'ada made a covenant between the LORD and the king and people, that they should be the LORD's people; and also between the king and the people. **18** Then all the people of the land went to the house of Ba'al, and tore it down; his altars and his images they broke in pieces, and they slew Mattan the priest of Ba'al before the altars. And the priest posted watchmen over the house of the LORD. **19** And he took the captains, the Carites, the guards, and all the people of the land; and they brought the king down from the house of the LORD, marching through the gate of the guards to the king's house. And he took his seat on the throne of the kings. **20** So all the people of the land rejoiced; and the city was quiet after Athali'ah had been slain with the sword at the king's house.

---

corresponding to the seats of ecclesiastical dignitaries or to the stalls of the knights of the orders of chivalry in their private chapel. The word used here is עמוד, lit., "station," not מצבה (which refers to idolatrous pillars), and designates the two pillars which stood before the porch.

16. The translation **they laid hands on her** is correct; the translation of the ASV, "they made way for her," has no justification.

18. The full name of the priest was doubtless Mattan-baal ("gift of Baal"), a name frequently found in Phoenician inscriptions, and parallel to the Hebrew Mattaniah ("gift of Yah"), which was the name of the last king of Judah before his name was changed to Zedekiah (24:17). Bad causes have their martyrs equally with good causes.

Was ever more dramatic illustration given of the eternal law, "The soul that sinneth, it shall die" (Ezek. 18:4)? The House of Ahab! It stands like a monolith of warning above the wrecks of time. The figures in the tragedy are grandiose. And commensurate with the magnificence of their conscienceless splendor was the sordidness of their doom.

21 Seven years old *was* Jehoash when he began to reign.

12 In the seventh year of Jehu, Jehoash began to reign; and forty years reigned he in Jerusalem. And his mother's name *was* Zibiah of Beer-sheba.

2 And Jehoash did *that which was* right in the sight of the LORD all his days wherein Jehoiada the priest instructed him.

3 But the high places were not taken away: the people still sacrificed and burnt incense in the high places.

21[u] Jeho'ash was seven years old when he began to reign.

12 In the seventh year of Jehu Jeho'ash began to reign, and he reigned forty years in Jerusalem. His mother's name was Zib'iah of Beer-sheba. 2 And Jeho'ash did what was right in the eyes of the LORD all his days, because Jehoi'ada the priest instructed him. 3 Nevertheless the high places were not taken away; the people continued to sacrifice and burn incense on the high places.

[u] Heb 12. 1

2. JEHOASH OF JUDAH (11:21–12:21)

And so Jehoash becomes king. He is faithful to the Lord, but the local southern shrines remain. The new king had ordered that the priests' perquisites should go to the repair of the temple, but twenty-three years passed and nothing was done. So Jehoash relieved the priests of these perquisites and also of the responsibility of repairing the temple. All this money had to go into a box which stood by the entrance, and this box was handed over at intervals to the builders who bought with it such materials as they needed in their work of renovation. But unfortunately Jehoash, in order to buy off Hazael of Syria, had to empty the temple treasuries and to take all the votive gifts which he and his three predecessors had dedicated to the temple. His reign closed with a conspiracy and his death at the hand of assassins.

a) THE REIGN OF JEHOASH (11:21–12:3)

12:2. The Hebrew says that King Jehoash was faithful to the Lord **all his days, because** of the influence of Jehoiada the priest. This is the interpretation of the RSV, but the KJV follows the ancient versions which say that he was true to the Lord **all his days wherein** he was instructed by Jehoiada. The inference is that the king's conduct deteriorated after the death of Jehoiada, and this is what II Chr. 24:2 says (see details of his conduct in II Chr. 24:17-22).

3. As elsewhere regularly in pre-exilic passages, the Hebrew verb קטר should be translated "sacrifice," not **burn incense.** Read, therefore, "continued to slaughter and to sacrifice," the first word referring to the animals slaughtered for sacred meals, the second to those which were offered up and burned on the altar.

11:21–12:21. ***The Life and Reign of Jehoash.*** —Two divergent accounts are given of the long reign of Joash (or Jehoash), who was crowned when he was seven years old and held the throne for forty years. This chapter records only the effort of the king to rebuild and restore the temple which Athaliah had pillaged, the menacing invasion of Hazael of Syria, who had to be bought off from attacking Jerusalem, and the tragic death of the king at the hands of his servants. In II Chr. 24 we find a different story, which tells of his moral lapse—from which stemmed his downfall—and records the capture of Jerusalem, the wounding of the king in combat, and his subsequent murder. The interpretation of the character and career of Joash depends on which of these two accounts gives us the true picture of the king. Since the account of the history of Israel and Judah which the Chronicler gives is much later than that found in the books of the Kings, and is written from the priestly point of view; since it seems unlikely that Joash, carefully reared as he was, could have been sufficiently corrupted by the princes of Judah to have turned to idolatry, and be guilty of the murder of Zechariah; and since the story of the capture and sack of Jerusalem by Hazael is suspect on historical grounds, we may assume that II Kings gives us the truer description of the life and reign of Joash. He is reckoned among the good kings, together with Amaziah (14:1, 3) and Uzziah (15:1, 3) and Jotham (15:32-34). At the same time, it is possible that in Chronicles there are preserved for us fragments of history not found in the earlier books.

4 ¶ And Jehoash said to the priests, All the money of the dedicated things that is brought into the house of the Lord, *even* the money of every one that passeth *the account*, the money that every man is set at, *and* all the money that cometh into any man's heart to bring into the house of the Lord,

5 Let the priests take *it* to them, every man of his acquaintance: and let them repair the breaches of the house, wheresoever any breach shall be found.

6 But it was *so, that* in the three and twentieth year of king Jehoash the priests had not repaired the breaches of the house.

7 Then king Jehoash called for Jehoiada the priest, and the *other* priests, and said unto them, Why repair ye not the breaches of the house? now therefore receive no *more* money of your acquaintance, but deliver it for the breaches of the house.

4 Jeho'ash said to the priests, "All the money of the holy things which is brought into the house of the Lord, the money for which each man is assessed — the money from the assessment of persons — and the money which a man's heart prompts him to bring into the house of the Lord, 5 let the priests take, each from his acquaintance; and let them repair the house wherever any need of repairs is discovered." 6 But by the twenty-third year of King Jeho'ash the priests had made no repairs on the house. 7 Therefore King Jeho'ash summoned Jehoi'ada the priest and the other priests and said to them, "Why are you not repairing the house? Now therefore take no more money from your acquaintances, but hand it

b) The Repair of the Temple (12:4-16)

The king's first move was to instruct the priests that while they could still accept all the money that was offered in the temple, either by the regular assessment (cf. Lev. 27:2-7, which doubtless is maintaining ancient custom) or by freewill gifts over and above this, yet they were responsible for keeping the temple in repair and they must pay for it out of the money received. The "current money" of the ERV and ASV is an attempt to translate the Hebrew, but it is better to follow the LXX with **the money for which each man is assessed.**

5. The word מכר is not found other than here and again in vs. 7. Its interpretation is doubtful. It means **acquaintance,** and probably refers to the man with whom each priest dealt personally. It is natural to suppose that each priest would have some sort of claim upon the money which he himself received from the worshiper with whom he actually dealt.

7. When at last Jehoash found that the priests were taking the money and not fulfilling their duty in repairing the temple, he directed them to stop taking money themselves. He ordered that all such money should go into a special box in the porch, and he saw to it himself that the repairs were done, his own secretary acting in conjunction with the chief priest (cf. vs. 10).

4-5. Love of the Sanctuary.—The rehabilitation of the temple, in whose precincts Joash had spent the years of his infancy and boyhood, was the new king's first concern. Personal feeling for the temple must have undergirded the religious motive. Consider then the importance of inculcating in the lives of children feelings of affection for the church. No moral influence in the lives of young men or women is more beautiful than the sentiment they often possess for the church in which their childhood has been spent. Let a boy or girl from his earliest years be brought up within the church, have sacred memories that center there, and in later years

these impressions will have their immense effect on character and conduct. Parents who deprive their children of this sacred association, this love of the sanctuary, are failing to endow them with rich spiritual resources. Well may they ponder the relevance of these words, "And he was . . . hid in the house of the Lord six years" (11:3) and "Jehoash . . . said [to the priests], Why repair ye not the breaches of the house?" (12:7).

6-16. Repairing the Temple.—This passage contains suggestive material for church anniversary and dedication occasions. It reminds us that the care and beautifying of the house of

8 And the priests consented to receive no *more* money of the people, neither to repair the breaches of the house.

9 But Jehoiada the priest took a chest, and bored a hole in the lid of it, and set it beside the altar, on the right side as one cometh into the house of the Lord: and the priests that kept the door put therein all the money *that was* brought into the house of the Lord.

10 And it was *so,* when they saw that *there was* much money in the chest, that the king's scribe and the high priest came up, and they put up in bags, and told the money that was found in the house of the Lord.

11 And they gave the money, being told, into the hands of them that did the work, that had the oversight of the house of the Lord: and they laid it out to the carpenters and builders, that wrought upon the house of the Lord,

12 And to masons, and hewers of stone, and to buy timber and hewed stone to repair the breaches of the house of the Lord, and for all that was laid out for the house to repair *it.*

over for the repair of the house." 8 So the priests agreed that they should take no more money from the people, and that they should not repair the house.

9 Then Jehoi'ada the priest took a chest, and bored a hole in the lid of it, and set it beside the altar on the right side as one entered the house of the Lord; and the priests who guarded the threshold put in it all the money that was brought into the house of the Lord. 10 And whenever they saw that there was much money in the chest, the king's secretary and the high priest came up and they counted and tied up in bags the money that was found in the house of the Lord. 11 Then they would give the money that was weighed out into the hands of the workmen who had the oversight of the house of the Lord; and they paid it out to the carpenters and the builders who worked upon the house of the Lord, 12 and to the masons and the stonecutters, as well as to buy timber and quarried stone for making repairs on the house of the Lord, and for any outlay upon the repairs

---

9. The money chest can scarcely have been **beside the altar** since **the priests who guarded the threshold** were responsible for it. It is therefore better to follow the lead of Codex Alexandrinus (LXX^A), which has transliterated the Hebrew word for "pillar," presumably meaning one of the pillars by the porch.

10. There is some doubt whether Jehoiada had anything to do with the counting of the money. In the first place, there is no record of **the high priest** existing in pre-exilic times, though there would certainly be a chief priest. In the second place, the order of the two officials is different in the Syriac. This fact lends color to the suggestion that the mention of the high priest is a postexilic insertion. This is all the more likely since Jehoash had every reason to distrust the whole of the priesthood in the matter of money. Jehoiada must have been a party to the evasion of the king's command whereby at least some of the money which the priests received should be used on repair work. The king probably took the whole matter out of the priests' hands and put in his own nominee to see to it that his intentions and commands were carried out. The suggestion in II Chr. 24:6-14 that there was a break between the king and the priest Jehoiada may well have some foundation, though apparently the fault, to say the least, was not all on the king's side.

God is one of the duties of God's people. Note the following points: The people gave willingly. They often do for such a cause. But the priests did not administer efficiently the money which the people put into their hands. So Joash ordered that the money should no longer be given to the priests, but be put directly into a chest at the temple door and laymen be allowed to administer the funds themselves. Here we have suggested the function of laymen in church affairs. Priests and pastors are often not skilled in finance. It is a mistake to put the burden of raising and administering the funds required for church support on the shoulders of the clergy who have other tasks and duties to perform. Church walls would go up far more rapidly today if it were understood that the church's finances would be cared for by laymen. It is evident from the story in this chapter that one reason why contributions were not sufficient

13 Howbeit there were not made for the house of the LORD bowls of silver, snuffers, basins, trumpets, any vessels of gold, or vessels of silver, of the money *that was* brought into the house of the LORD:

14 But they gave that to the workmen, and repaired therewith the house of the LORD.

15 Moreover they reckoned not with the men, into whose hand they delivered the money to be bestowed on workmen: for they dealt faithfully.

16 The trespass money and sin money was not brought into the house of the LORD: it was the priests'.

17 ¶ Then Hazael king of Syria went up, and fought against Gath, and took it: and Hazael set his face to go up to Jerusalem.

of the house. 13 But there were not made for the house of the LORD basins of silver, snuffers, bowls, trumpets, or any vessels of gold, or of silver, from the money that was brought into the house of the LORD, 14 for that was given to the workmen who were repairing the house of the LORD with it. 15 And they did not ask an accounting from the men into whose hand they delivered the money to pay out to the workmen, for they dealt honestly. 16 The money from the guilt offerings and the money from the sin offerings was not brought into the house of the LORD; it belonged to the priests.

17 At that time Haz′ael king of Syria went up and fought against Gath, and took it. But when Haz′ael set his face to go up

---

13-15. Apparently the gold and silver vessels of the temple had disappeared in the midst of the general neglect. There was not enough money to replace these, for everything had to go to the workmen, of whose honesty special note is made. Perhaps the reason for this emphasis is not unconnected with the lapses of the priesthood.

16. Here the KJV is correct in mentioning **trespass money and sin money**. The renderings **guilt offerings** and **sin offerings** (RSV) are unfortunate, since these offerings proper were a postexilic development. Both words refer to cash payments made by way of compensation for wrong done. In postexilic development the sin offering included an animal (e.g., Lev. 4:3-12) of which the blood and certain sacred parts were brought to the altar, but the rest was definitely and deliberately taken "without the camp," the ritual thus being symbolic of the fact that man's sins no longer remained between him and God. The ritual of the slaying of the animal, etc., was a postexilic addition to the payment of the cash fine (Lev. 5:15), but the cash fine was in force in pre-exilic times. Being the price of sin, it could never be "brought into the house of the LORD," nor could it be used in any way in connection with the repair of the holy buildings. These payments therefore remained the perquisite of the priests.

c) JEHOASH'S REVERSES (12:17-18)

17-18. Hazael of Syria evidently overran the whole of the country as far as the Philistine territory, costing Jehoash all the treasures that had been accumulated since the time of Asa, who had been in similar trouble at the hands of Baasha of Israel a hundred years or so before (I Kings 15:18).

---

was that the people were not sure that money paid directly into the hands of the priests would be properly used. As soon as the new method was tried, the offerings were abundant. The same idea holds good today. Also laymen, if they are wise, will seek to lessen the minister's burden at this point in every possible way. And ministers, if they are wise, will limit their activity in the work of raising funds to the spiritual aspects of these. The reiterated exhortation to an assembled congregation for a "large offering" has a deadening effect on the spirit of worship.

Ministers must never be lax and careless concerning the upkeep of the house of God. The

church building may be neither large nor costly, but it must always be kept clean, neat, and orderly. In this aspect of his duty one can get a clue to the fidelity of a minister to his task. The true minister will not tolerate slovenliness anywhere in his church building. The loving care of God's house is one proof of devotion to God on the part of minister and people alike.

17-21. *The Decline of Joash.*—Whichever account of the reign of Joash is followed, it is clear that it ended in failure and tragedy. In part this was due to the hostility of princes and priests who resented the authority assumed by the king. Then came the invasion of Hazael.

18 And Jehoash king of Judah took all the hallowed things that Jehoshaphat, and Jehoram, and Ahaziah, his fathers, kings of Judah, had dedicated, and his own hallowed things, and all the gold that was found in the treasures of the house of the LORD, and in the king's house, and sent *it* to Hazael king of Syria: and he went away from Jerusalem.

19 ¶ And the rest of the acts of Joash, and all that he did, *are* they not written in the book of the Chronicles of the kings of Judah?

20 And his servants arose, and made a conspiracy, and slew Joash in the house of Millo, which goeth down to Silla.

21 For Jozachar the son of Shimeath, and Jehozabad the son of Shomer, his servants, smote him, and he died; and they buried him with his fathers in the city of David: and Amaziah his son reigned in his stead.

13 In the three and twentieth year of Joash the son of Ahaziah king of Judah, Jehoahaz the son of Jehu began to

against Jerusalem, 18 Jeho'ash king of Judah took all the votive gifts that Jehosh'aphat and Jeho'ram and Ahazi'ah, his fathers, the kings of Judah, had dedicated, and his own votive gifts, and all the gold that was found in the treasuries of the house of the LORD and of the king's house, and sent these to Haz'ael king of Syria. Then Haz'ael went away from Jerusalem.

19 Now the rest of the acts of Jo'ash, and all that he did, are they not written in the Book of the Chronicles of the Kings of Judah? 20 His servants arose and made a conspiracy, and slew Jo'ash in the house of Millo, on the way that goes down to Silla. 21 It was Jo'zacar the son of Shim'eath and Jeho'zabad the son of Shomer, his servants, who struck him down, so that he died. And they buried him with his fathers in the city of David, and Amazi'ah his son reigned in his stead.

13 In the twenty-third year of Jo'ash the son of Ahazi'ah, king of Judah,

d) ASSASSINATION OF JEHOASH (12:19-21)

19-21. The normal Deuteronomic obituary is interrupted by the necessity of saying how the king met his death. According to II Chr. 24:25-26 the assassination was in revenge for his part in the stoning to death of Jehoiada's son Zechariah, who was murdered in the very temple courts themselves. This may well be the cause of Jehoash's death, especially since the king's action in overriding the priests in the matter of repairs to the temple may easily have led to trouble between the king and Jehoiada. This priest has not been the only man to create a king and then to find he could not control the monarch as he had hoped to do.

3. JEHOAHAZ OF ISRAEL (13:1-9)

The story of this reign is one of unrelieved gloom. During the whole of it Israel was under the domination of Syria and was reduced to a state of complete helplessness.

However this turned out, it was a deep humiliation for the kingdom and the king, and it was seized upon by his opponents as proof of his incapacity. Thus we are able to account for his tragic death without assuming that he had sunk into idolatry and personal turpitude. Joash seems to have done well as long as Jehoiada was at his side. He was not strong enough to stand alone. Perhaps he had been kept under the tutelage of Jehoiada too long and had not been taught early enough to stand on his own feet. Children are often mistakenly reared in this way by oversolicitude of parents and teachers. They must learn to stand independently, so that when they move out into life they can maintain themselves against both circumstance

and temptation. That is the test of character; that is the sign as to whether real religion controls their lives. The career of Joash arouses within us the feeling of compassion. His task was too great for him. A man of good intentions, he was carried beyond his depth by the current of events. We think back on the fair-haired youth crowned with Davidic honors, invested with the royal insignia, and then view with pity the inglorious end. If Athaliah had had the virtue of Joash, if Joash had had the strength of Athaliah, how different this history would have been. Neither virtue nor strength is sufficient of itself. Their union alone spells victory.

13:1-9. *Corruption of Israel's Religion.*—We return to the Northern Kingdom which under

reign over Israel in Samaria, *and reigned* seventeen years.

2 And he did *that which was* evil in the sight of the LORD, and followed the sins of Jeroboam the son of Nebat, which made Israel to sin; he departed not therefrom.

3 ¶ And the anger of the LORD was kindled against Israel, and he delivered them into the hand of Hazael king of Syria, and into the hand of Ben-hadad the son of Hazael, all *their* days.

4 And Jehoahaz besought the LORD, and the LORD hearkened unto him: for he saw the oppression of Israel, because the king of Syria oppressed them.

5 (And the LORD gave Israel a saviour, so that they went out from under the hand of the Syrians: and the children of Israel dwelt in their tents, as beforetime.

Jeho'ahaz the son of Jehu began to reign over Israel in Samar'ia, and he reigned seventeen years. 2 He did what was evil in the sight of the LORD, and followed the sins of Jerobo'am the son of Nebat, which he made Israel to sin; he did not depart from them. 3 And the anger of the LORD was kindled against Israel, and he gave them continually into the hand of Haz'ael king of Syria and into the hand of Ben-ha'dad the son of Haz'ael. 4 Then Jeho'ahaz besought the LORD, and the LORD hearkened to him; for he saw the oppression of Israel, how the king of Syria oppressed them. 5 (Therefore the LORD gave Israel a savior, so that they escaped from the hand of the Syrians; and the people of Israel dwelt in their homes

13:1-2. These verses contain the formal Deuteronomic notice introducing the reign of a new king of Israel.

3-7. Israel is reduced to a complete and defenseless vassalage by the vigorous Hazael, suffering equally with the neighboring kingdom of Judah.

3-5. The rendering **all their days**, i.e., all the days of Hazael and his son Ben-hadad, is not strictly accurate. The Hebrew is a little more indefinite. Actually the tide of disaster began to turn in the days of Ben-hadad (vs. 25). This verse bears a striking resemblance to the comments which form the editorial scheme of Judges (cf. Judg. 3:8-9). To the same stratum belong vss. 4-5. They are due to a later editor who was much better disposed toward the Northern Kingdom than either of the two Deuteronomic editors, and it is probable that he had something to do with the final form of vs. 3. The deliverer was Jehoahaz' grandson, Jeroboam II son of Joash.

Jehoahaz, son of Jehu, sank to the lowest levels thus far in its history. The account of his long reign contained in this chapter is evidently fragmentary. It tells us, however, that under his rule religion in Israel was corrupted by the most immoral rites. Not only was the symbolic calf worship of his predecessors continued, but to this Jehoahaz had added the iniquity of reinstating the **Asherah** (vs. 6) in Samaria. This was the pillar of a Phoenician nature goddess which Jezebel had first set up with the apparent approval of Ahab (I Kings 16:33). It stood as a symbol of decadence in the capital city of Israel. We are also told here of Israel's humiliation at the hands of Hazael of Syria. The nation was reduced to the dust (vs. 7). All of this is given in briefest form.

4. *The Prayer of the Unrighteous.*—Thus, we are told at this extremity of his misfortunes, **Jehoahaz besought the LORD, and the LORD hearkened to him.** This is reminiscent of Ps. 107:27-28, "They . . . are at their wits' end. Then they cry unto the LORD. . . ." Here is an

unrighteous man in desperate need which he had brought upon himself. He had forgotten God, forsaken him, betrayed him. But now that he is at his wits' end, he turns to him. This is the only kind of religion many people know. So long as all goes well with them they can manage without religion. But let calamity lay them low, then they turn to God and to prayer. Under the pressure of dire need the soul breaks through the crust of indifference, selfishness, worldliness, and escapes to God for succor. It shows us that there is rarely such a thing as stark atheism. An imagined atheism goes to pieces when a man comes to the depths. When the strong wind arises which lifts up the waves thereof, when the soul melts because of trouble, when it reels to and fro like a drunken man, then the deep instincts within man assert themselves and cry unto the Lord. This is the inevitable prayer of the unrighteous. There is religion in it, but a poor kind of religion. True religion consists in walking with God all the time, not running to him only in an emergency.

6 Nevertheless they departed not from the sins of the house of Jeroboam, who made Israel sin, *but* walked therein: and there remained the grove also in Samaria.)

7 Neither did he leave of the people to Jehoahaz but fifty horsemen, and ten chariots, and ten thousand footmen; for the king of Syria had destroyed them, and had made them like the dust by threshing.

8 ¶ Now the rest of the acts of Jehoahaz, and all that he did, and his might, *are* they not written in the book of the Chronicles of the kings of Israel?

9 And Jehoahaz slept with his fathers; and they buried him in Samaria: and Joash his son reigned in his stead.

10 ¶ In the thirty and seventh year of Joash king of Judah began Jehoash the son

as formerly. 6 Nevertheless they did not depart from the sins of the house of Jerobo'am, which he made Israel to sin, but walked[v] in them; and the Ashe'rah also remained in Samar'ia.) 7 For there was not left to Jeho'ahaz an army of more than fifty horsemen and ten chariots and ten thousand footmen; for the king of Syria had destroyed them and made them like the dust at threshing. 8 Now the rest of the acts of Jeho'ahaz and all that he did, and his might, are they not written in the Book of the Chronicles of the Kings of Israel? 9 So Jeho'ahaz slept with his fathers, and they buried him in Samar'ia; and Jo'ash his son reigned in his stead.

10 In the thirty-seventh year of Jo'ash

[v] Gk Syr Tg Vg: Heb *he walked*

6-7. Vs. 6 is Deuteronomic in style and comment, but the phraseology (**from the sins of the house of Jeroboam**) is sufficiently wide of the stereotyped formula of the Deuteronomic compiler to warrant the assumption that it also is part of the late insertion. Vs. 7 continues the grim story of vs. 3 and tells of an army so sadly reduced as to be well below fighting strength.

8-9. The concluding Deuteronomic formula for the death of a king of Israel.

4. JEHOASH OF ISRAEL (13:10-25)

First we find a formal description of the reign of Jehoash, containing the regular introduction and the regular obituary. This is followed by two stories from the Elisha narratives which presumably were inserted at a later date. On his deathbed Elisha tells the king to shoot with bow and arrows through the window toward Syria. The king is then bidden to strike the ground with his arrows. He strikes three times. At this Elisha is angry and tells him he ought to have struck the ground six or seven times, then he would have conquered Syria. As it is, he will defeat them in battle three times only, according to the number of times he struck the earth with his arrows. The second story concerns the prophet's tomb. A dead man is being buried when there is the warning of a party of raiders. They cast the dead man's body into a handy tomb, which happens to be that of Elisha, and hurry to repel the enemy. When the corpse touches the bones of the prophet, it comes to life again. Next, there is found an extract from the Book of the Kings of Israel, telling of the Syrian wars, how Hazael conquered Israel and how Joash (Jehoash) recovered territory from Hazael's successor.

And the LORD hearkened to him. This surprises us. For seventeen long years Jehoahaz had betrayed God. Yet when the faithless king turned to him, he was ready to hear. Were we ever more vividly reminded of the unwearying love of God? So, if now a man has forgotten God for years and has lived in a fashion that has landed him in disaster, let him not despair. Neither false shame nor a sense of meanness must keep him at such an hour from turning at last to God, from the discovery that God is indeed merciful and gracious, a very present help in time of trouble. How did God deliver

Jehoahaz? Is it possible that the miraculous deliverance of Samaria described in 7:5-7 took place at this time? Or was it the death of Hazael? Or was deliverance to come not in his lifetime, but in that of his son and grandson? We do not know. All that we know is that Israel was given its second chance, misused it, and sank finally into ruin.

10-13. When Deliverance Does Not Deliver.— Here we have a brief chronicle of the reign of Jehoash (his name is contracted to Joash in vss. 12 and 13). It seems incredible that after the Lord's deliverance of Samaria at the petition

of Jehoahaz to reign over Israel in Samaria, *and reigned* sixteen years.

11 And he did *that which was* evil in the sight of the LORD; he departed not from all the sins of Jeroboam the son of Nebat, who made Israel sin: *but* he walked therein.

12 And the rest of the acts of Joash, and all that he did, and his might wherewith he fought against Amaziah king of Judah, *are* they not written in the book of the Chronicles of the kings of Israel?

13 And Joash slept with his fathers; and Jeroboam sat upon his throne: and Joash was buried in Samaria with the kings of Israel.

14 ¶ Now Elisha was fallen sick of his sickness whereof he died. And Joash the king of Israel came down unto him, and wept over his face, and said, O my father,

king of Judah Jeho'ash the son of Jeho'ahaz began to reign over Israel in Samar'ia, and he reigned sixteen years. **11** He also did what was evil in the sight of the LORD; he did not depart from all the sins of Jerobo'am the son of Nebat, which he made Israel to sin, but he walked in them. **12** Now the rest of the acts of Jo'ash, and all that he did, and the might with which he fought against Amazi'ah king of Judah, are they not written in the Book of the Chronicles of the Kings of Israel? **13** So Jo'ash slept with his fathers, and Jerobo'am sat upon his throne; and Jo'ash was buried in Samar'ia with the kings of Israel.

14 Now when Eli'sha had fallen sick with the illness of which he was to die, Jo'ash king of Israel went down to him, and wept

---

a) DEUTERONOMIC SUMMARY (13:10-13)

10. The thirty-seventh year: This date does not agree with the chronology of vss. 1 and 14:1. It ought to be "the thirty-ninth."

13. The phraseology varies considerably from the usual formula, such as that found in 14:15-16, in the middle of the story of the reign of Amaziah of Judah. In addition, Lucian places vss. 12-13 at the end of ch. 13. This is where we would expect the obituary notice to come. The most satisfactory solution of the puzzle is that originally 14:8-14 followed 13:25, but that it was placed subsequently in the history of Amaziah. The story is northern in its sympathies rather than southern, but it does actually fit in much better with the story of Amaziah of Judah. The obituary notice would thus come at the end of what is now 14:8-14, which is where it ought to be. With Lucian the notice was left behind when the transference was made, but a later Hebrew scribe, finding that the notice of the death of King Joash was not where it ought to be (i.e., at the end of ch. 13), wrote an obituary notice roughly in the Deuteronomic style and inserted it here before the Elisha stories (Skinner, *Kings*, p. 349).

b) THE ARROW OF VICTORY (13:14-19)

The scene is Elisha's deathbed, and the king of Israel has come to visit him. The dying prophet seeks to leave a legacy of victory for Israel, but is in part frustrated by the timid action of the king.

14. Jehoash repeats the exact words which Elisha himself spoke when he proclaimed Elijah's departure from this life. The Hebrew means "chariotry," so that **chariots** is preferable to the singular **chariot**.

---

of his father, Jehoash should have continued in his father's evil ways. Thus we are reminded of the sad fact that deliverance from danger is rarely the occasion of permanent personal or social reform. When the crisis is over and the danger past good resolutions are forgotten and men slip back into the old ways. If men simply flee to God in an emergency, instead of walking with him all the time, they have no sure hold on the strength which will carry them through recurring temptations.

14-21. Exit Elisha.—At this point emerges once more and for the last time the figure of Elisha, who had vanished from the pages of Israel's history since the coronation of Jehu. He is now an old man, at least eighty years of age. One more demonstration of his power and the life of the prophet ends. Joash had succeeded Jehoahaz, and was no better than his father. Yet he must have been an able ruler since he thrice defeated the Syrians and recovered much of Israel's lost territory (vs. 25). Elisha was sick

my father! the chariot of Israel, and the horsemen thereof.

15 And Elisha said unto him, Take bow and arrows. And he took unto him bow and arrows.

16 And he said to the king of Israel, Put thine hand upon the bow. And he put his hand *upon it:* and Elisha put his hands upon the king's hands.

17 And he said, Open the window eastward. And he opened *it.* Then Elisha said, Shoot. And he shot. And he said, The arrow of the LORD's deliverance, and the arrow of deliverance from Syria: for thou shalt smite the Syrians in Aphek, till thou have consumed *them.*

18 And he said, Take the arrows. And he took *them.* And he said unto the king of Israel, Smite upon the ground. And he smote thrice, and stayed.

19 And the man of God was wroth with him, and said, Thou shouldest have smitten five or six times; then hadst thou smitten Syria till thou hadst consumed *it:* whereas now thou shalt smite Syria *but* thrice.

before him, crying, "My father, my father! The chariots of Israel and its horsemen!" 15 And Eli'sha said to him, "Take a bow and arrows"; so he took a bow and arrows. 16 Then he said to the king of Israel, "Draw the bow"; and he drew it. And Eli'sha laid his hands upon the king's hands. 17 And he said, "Open the window eastward"; and he opened it. Then Eli'sha said, "Shoot"; and he shot. And he said, "The LORD's arrow of victory, the arrow of victory over Syria! For you shall fight the Syrians in Aphek until you have made an end of them." 18 And he said, "Take the arrows"; and he took them. And he said to the king of Israel, "Strike the ground with them"; and he struck three times, and stopped. 19 Then the man of God was angry with him, and said, "You should have struck five or six times; then you would have struck down Syria until you had made an end of it, but now you will strike down Syria only three times."

16. The drawing of the bow and the shooting of the arrow eastward is in line with those ideas of effective symbolism which are common in popular narratives. This particular incident is similar to Joshua's stretching out his spear toward and against the city of Ai (Josh. 8:18). The drawing of the bow is regarded as actually setting in motion the chariotry of the Lord on its task of delivering Israel from the domination of Syria. Perhaps this is why Elisha tells the king to "make his hand ride" the bow (**draw the bow** and **put thine hand upon** are both paraphrases), the same Hebrew root being used as that which is used for "chariotry," and meaning primarily "mount and ride a chariot."

17. The pointing of the arrow eastward need occasion no difficulty even if the true direction is supposed to be toward Damascus, which is strictly northeast. The direction is eastward because that is precisely where the victory was needed, viz., in that Israelite territory east of Jordan, where Syria had conquered Israelite territory and shorn it away from direct Israelite control. This actually is the direction in which the first Israelite successes against Damascus-Syria did take place (vs. 25).

18-19. The idea of effective symbolism is very plain here. By striking the arrows into the ground three times, the king ensured three victories against Syria. If he had struck more times, he would have ensured more victories. It is customary to see in the king's action the evidence of a vacillating character.

unto death and the king came and wept over him. The prophet was a revered figure. A holy life is always revered. It makes its own impression, and commands universal respect and veneration. Holiness vindicates itself. It is felt to be the highest form of human excellence. One says, "To live like that—whatever else is wrong or right, true or false—this must be right and true." Let anyone, even in the humblest sphere

of life, give this evidence, create this impression of holiness of life, and men in all stations in life, high and low, will pay him homage and weep at his tomb.

And the king said, **O my father, . . . the chariot of Israel, and the horsemen thereof,** the very words which Elisha himself had used at the assumption of Elijah (2:12). Had the words become a tradition in Israel? Did the

20 ¶ And Elisha died, and they buried him. And the bands of the Moabites invaded the land at the coming in of the year.

21 And it came to pass, as they were burying a man, that, behold, they spied a band *of men*; and they cast the man into the sepulchre of Elisha: and when the man was let down, and touched the bones of Elisha, he revived, and stood up on his feet.

22 ¶ But Hazael king of Syria oppressed Israel all the days of Jehoahaz.

20 So Eli'sha died, and they buried him. Now bands of Moabites used to invade the land in the spring of the year. 21 And as a man was being buried, lo, a marauding band was seen and the man was cast into the grave of Eli'sha; and as soon as the man touched the bones of Eli'sha, he revived, and stood on his feet.

22 Now Haz'ael king of Syria oppressed

c) THE LAST MIRACLE OF ELISHA (13:20-21)

The prophet is dead and buried, but his bones still have miraculous power and contain enough mana to bring a dead man to life.

20. The M.T. says that the Moabite raiding parties used to invade the settled lands **at the coming in of the year.** This means in the autumn, at the end of the year, when the harvests were fully gathered. It is an erroneous notion to interpret this Hebrew phrase as meaning **in the spring of the year.** These raids regularly took place after the harvest.

21. Western mentality is misleading here, as in the preceding verse. The Eastern grave is not dug in the ground and filled in with earth, but is hollowed out of a hill and closed with a large stone. The body is wrapped in graveclothes and placed in the grave without coffin. When the Israelites saw the raiders coming they hurriedly rolled back the stone which covered the entrance to the nearest tomb and placed the body inside. It chanced to be Elisha's tomb, and the story is that when the body touched the bones of the prophet, which were lying there on the floor, the dead man was restored to life. The idea that the bones of the dead retain, for a while at least, the supernatural power which the deceased had in his lifetime is common among primitive people. It survives in the veneration which is paid to the bones of the saints, kept by some religious organizations as holy relics.

d) TURNING OF THE TIDE (13:22-25)

This extract from the Chronicles of the Kings of Israel tells how the shooting of the arrows brought its exact fulfillment. King Jehoash defeated the Syrians under Ben-hadad thrice, and no more than thrice.

king mean that, like Elijah, Elisha would mount triumphant over death? The chariots of fire and the horsemen thereof bear every saintly soul into the presence of God.

The final deathbed act of Elisha is involved in some obscurity. The clue to it seems to be found in vs. 19. Had the king struck the ground with his arrow many times more, victory would have been complete. So it often is in life. One shoots but three arrows. But why stop shooting? The hosts of evil are never overcome by momentary, partial, fragmentary effort. That wins the triumph of a day, but not the final conquest of sin. Perseverance, unremitting effort, constant shooting, this is the key to final victory.

The story recounted in vs. 21 is without parallel in Scripture. Nowhere else do we find even a hint of magic power in the bones of the dead. It is a relic of superstitious belief which

somehow crept into the tradition concerning Elisha. But it is at least token of our awareness that in death we have dealings with eternity. To be quickened by contact with the living soul of a holy man, though he were dead, is one thing. For a man to come to life because his dead body touched the bones of a saint is something which finds no warrant elsewhere in what we are taught in the Bible of the ways of God.

22-25. *The Patience of God.*—The passage tells us how the temporary rescue of Israel was achieved. Hazael the Syrian who had oppressed Israel since the reign of Jehoahaz died opportunely and Jehoash recaptured the territory which Hazael had won. One would have looked for only anger and retribution after the repeated apostasy of Jehoash. Instead we read that the Lord had compassion. The patience of God with his recreant children! The O.T. often

23 And the Lord was gracious unto them, and had compassion on them, and had respect unto them, because of his covenant with Abraham, Isaac, and Jacob, and would not destroy them, neither cast he them from his presence as yet.

24 So Hazael king of Syria died; and Ben-hadad his son reigned in his stead.

25 And Jehoash the son of Jehoahaz took again out of the hand of Ben-hadad the son of Hazael the cities, which he had taken out of the hand of Jehoahaz his father by war. Three times did Joash beat him, and recovered the cities of Israel.

14 In the second year of Joash son of Jehoahaz king of Israel reigned Amaziah the son of Joash king of Judah.

Israel all the days of Jeho'ahaz. 23 But the Lord was gracious to them and had compassion on them, and he turned toward them, because of his covenant with Abraham, Isaac, and Jacob, and would not destroy them; nor has he cast them from his presence until now.

24 When Haz'ael king of Syria died, Ben-ha'dad his son became king in his stead. 25 Then Jeho'ash the son of Jeho'ahaz took again from Ben-ha'dad the son of Haz'ael the cities which he had taken from Jeho'ahaz his father in war. Three times Jo'ash defeated him and recovered the cities of Israel.

14 In the second year of Jo'ash the son of Jo'ahaz, king of Israel, Amazi'ah the son of Jo'ash, king of Judah, began to

---

23. This verse seems to be a later interpolation. It is from the same hand as vss. 4-6, and like them it shows a much more favorable attitude to Israel than that shown by either of the two Deuteronomic editors. It dates from after the time when the northern captivity had taken place, since otherwise there would be no mention of their being cast away.

25. The successes of Jehoash in regaining territory lost to the Syrians did indeed follow the death of Hazael, and so took place in the reign of his son Ben-hadad. The main reason for the Israelite success, however, was not the natural weakness of Ben-hadad, though he may easily have been a less formidable antagonist than his father, who had himself carved out a kingdom and an empire. The main reason was the subjection of Damascus by the new Assyrian King Adadnirari III in 805 b.c. This was the year before Jehoash's succession. He made three successful campaigns, and thus the prophecy of Elisha was fulfilled. But the real time of Israelite conquests at the expense of the Syrian kingdom of Damascus took place in the next reign, that of Jeroboam II.

5. Amaziah of Judah (14:1-22)

The new King Amaziah was true to the Lord but did not remove the local shrines. He exercised an unwonted clemency and pardoned the children of his father's murderers. Perhaps that is why he also was murdered. He won a victory over the Edomites and was thereby emboldened to challenge Jehoahaz of Israel. Amaziah would not listen to Jehoahaz' warning that he was asking for trouble, so he was defeated and captured. The Israelite king destroyed a large section of the wall of Jerusalem, took all the treasure he could find, with hostages, and returned home.

a) Deuteronomic Introduction (14:1-4)

These verses constitute the usual introduction for a king of Judah. From the religious point of view Amaziah was as good as any pre-Deuteronomic king could be. The local shrines were still in existence, and there was worship at them all, but there were no serious departures from proper practice.

---

speaks of the mother love of God. A mother never ceases to believe in her child, no matter how wayward he has been or how greatly he may have sinned. In this passage we seem to feel the tender yearning mother love of God. What hope lies here for sinning souls today!

14:1-5. Amaziah's Revenge.—While Joash of Israel was thus restoring the prosperity of the Northern Kingdom by his wise and vigorous rule, Amaziah, who had succeeded his father Jehoash in Judah, was also displaying qualities of real leadership. Evidently the murderers of

2 He was twenty and five years old when he began to reign, and reigned twenty and nine years in Jerusalem. And his mother's name *was* Jehoaddan of Jerusalem.

3 And he did *that which was* right in the sight of the LORD, yet not like David his father: he did according to all things as Joash his father did.

4 Howbeit the high places were not taken away: as yet the people did sacrifice and burnt incense on the high places.

5 ¶ And it came to pass, as soon as the kingdom was confirmed in his hand, that he slew his servants which had slain the king his father.

6 But the children of the murderers he slew not: according unto that which is written in the book of the law of Moses, wherein the LORD commanded, saying, The fathers shall not be put to death for the children, nor the children be put to death for the fathers; but every man shall be put to death for his own sin.

reign. 2 He was twenty-five years old when he began to reign, and he reigned twenty-nine years in Jerusalem. His mother's name was Jeho-ad′din of Jerusalem. 3 And he did what was right in the eyes of the LORD, yet not like David his father; he did in all things as Jo′ash his father had done. 4 But the high places were not removed; the people still sacrificed and burned incense on the high places. 5 And as soon as the royal power was firmly in his hand he killed his servants who had slain the king his father. 6 But he did not put to death the children of the murderers; according to what is written in the book of the law of Moses, where the LORD commanded, "The fathers shall not be put to death for the children, or the children be put to death for the fathers; but every man shall die for his own sin."

14:2. The statement that Amaziah **reigned twenty-nine years** does not agree with the statement that his son Azariah (15:1) became king in the twenty-seventh year of Jeroboam II. If the first statement is right, the second statement ought to say that it was the fifteenth year. The problem of the synchronization of the reigns of the kings of the two kingdoms is most difficult, since there is a discrepancy of at least twenty-one years (possibly as much as twenty-three) between the total number of the years of the kings of Judah and of those of the kings of Israel during the period from the accession of Jehu (841 B.C.) to the fall of Samaria (721 B.C.), the Judah total being the larger. The matter is further complicated by the fact that, according to Assyrian inscriptions, the total number of years of the kings of Israel is already twenty-five years too long. The most satisfactory solution is that given by Oesterley and Robinson, which reduces Jehu from twenty-eight to twenty, and Pekah from twenty to two. For the kings of Judah, Amaziah is reduced from twenty-nine to nine, Uzziah-Azariah from fifty-two to forty-two, with thirteen years of Jotham's sixteen counted in his father's reign as the length of his regency (W. O. E. Oesterley and T. H. Robinson, *History of Israel* [Oxford: Clarendon Press, 1932], I, 454-64).

b) AMAZIAH'S CLEMENCY (14:5-6)

5-6. Amaziah did not execute the children of his father's murderers. These verses are from the annals of the kings of Judah, but the Deuteronomic compiler has supplemented them with a reference to and a quotation from **the book of the law of Moses.**

his father were not strong enough to set aside Amaziah's right to the throne, and as soon as the royal power was firmly in his hands he avenged the death of his father.

6. *An Act of Mercy.*—But the children of the murderers he slew not. Why not? Law and custom did not forbid. The historian quotes a law which only later came into existence (Deut. 24:16) when barbarous practices were somewhat softened. Had Amaziah caused the sons of his father's murderers to be put to death he would but have followed the usual practices of his age. Discretion and policy dictated such a course. We seem here to have illustrated the possibility of the soul of a man suddenly rising above the conventional morality of his time in response to springs of action concealed within him. Often in history and contemporary life this has hap-

7 He slew of Edom in the valley of salt ten thousand, and took Selah by war, and called the name of it Joktheel unto this day.

8 ¶ Then Amaziah sent messengers to Jehoash, the son of Jehoahaz son of Jehu, king of Israel, saying, Come, let us look one another in the face.

7 He killed ten thousand Edomites in the Valley of Salt and took Sela by storm, and called it Jok'the-el, which is its name to this day.

8 Then Amazi'ah sent messengers to Jeho'ash the son of Jeho'ahaz, son of Jehu, king of Israel, saying, "Come, let us look

He has made a substantially accurate quotation from Deut. 24:16, except that he has improved the syntax. The 610 B.C. compiler found in this action of the new king an admirable example of conduct which fitted in with some of the details of that scroll of the law which had been found in the temple in the days when his hero-king Josiah was renovating it. Such an action of clemency is a notable departure from the customs of the old ruthless days when the whole family was wiped out for the sins of the father, e.g., Achan (Josh. 7:24-27) and Naboth (II Kings 9:26). On the other hand, since Amaziah himself was assassinated, perhaps not more than nine years later, it is more than likely that he paid the penalty for his clemency with his life. Probably the men who murdered him were the kinsmen of his father's murderers, whom Amaziah had executed.

c) Amaziah's Victory over Edom (14:7)

7. This extract from the annals of the kings of Judah is necessary because of the story following (vss. 8-14), which tells of the humbling of Amaziah's pride and is probably from the royal annals of Israel. It is generally agreed that the Valley of Salt is the marshy plain to the south of the Dead Sea. Sela (lit., "crag") is usually identified with the rock city of Petra (see Judg. 1:36; Isa. 16:1). There is no reference to this city in the parallel account in II Chr. 25:11-12, where the prisoners are thrown from the top of the crag.

d) Amaziah Challenges Jehoash (14:8-14)

Amaziah is so encouraged by his success over Edom that he seeks to measure his strength against Israel, to whom Judah has been tributary ever since before the days of Ahab. The result is disastrous in the extreme. Amaziah did not manage even to invade Israelite territory. The armies met at Beth-shemesh, some fifteen miles west of Jerusalem, and Amaziah lost everything. The king of Israel even tore down the wall of Jerusalem for some two hundred yards.

pened, and whenever it does it witnesses to the godlike in man and points to higher possibilities of life and conduct. Thus the summons comes to us all to act more nobly, more generously, than common ethics demands of us. It is not to the credit of any man that he lives according to the conventions of his day. True nobility is seen only when he rises above them. Only those whose moral life consists not in conformity to existing standards but in obedience to higher ideals not yet commonly accepted and practiced have helped the world forward to better things.

7. The Edomites.—Always it was Edom (see also II Chr. 25:11-12). Other foes might be vanquished, but Edom never. From Genesis (25:30) to Malachi (1:1-5) there is a continuous record of almost unbroken hostility between Israel and Edom. Yet they were blood brothers. When Jacob defrauded his brother of his birthright, he set in motion an antagonism

which endured right down to the threshold of the Christian Era. The story of Jacob and Esau points a solemn warning to all who are tempted by irritation, by anger, by a sense of injustice, to open a rift in family relationships which may never be healed. To begin with the words "And Esau hated Jacob" (Gen. 27:41), and then to trace the whole story of that enmity through the pages of the O.T., is to have material for a powerful presentation of the danger of family quarrels, from the hour of their inception to their often tragic conclusions.

8-14, 17-20. Pride Goeth Before Destruction.— Amaziah was so flushed with his victory over the Edomites—which, however, was by no means final (II Chr. 28:17)—that he looked about for new worlds to conquer. And his envious eyes fell upon Israel. In the presumption of his pride he challenged Joash to combat, Come, let us look one another in the face. Joash received the first message in unperturbed good humor and,

9 And Jehoash the king of Israel sent to Amaziah king of Judah, saying, The thistle that *was* in Lebanon sent to the cedar that *was* in Lebanon, saying, Give thy daughter to my son to wife: and there passed by a wild beast that *was* in Lebanon, and trode down the thistle.

10 Thou hast indeed smitten Edom, and thine heart hath lifted thee up: glory *of this,* and tarry at home: for why shouldest thou meddle to *thy* hurt, that thou shouldest fall, *even* thou, and Judah with thee?

11 But Amaziah would not hear. Therefore Jehoash king of Israel went up; and he and Amaziah king of Judah looked one another in the face at Beth-shemesh, which *belongeth* to Judah.

12 And Judah was put to the worse before Israel; and they fled every man to their tents.

13 And Jehoash king of Israel took Amaziah king of Judah, the son of Jehoash the son of Ahaziah, at Beth-shemesh, and came to Jerusalem, and brake down the wall of Jerusalem from the gate of Ephraim unto the corner gate, four hundred cubits.

14 And he took all the gold and silver, and all the vessels that were found in the house of the LORD, and in the treasures of the king's house, and hostages, and returned to Samaria.

15 ¶ Now the rest of the acts of Jehoash which he did, and his might, and how he fought with Amaziah king of Judah, *are* they not written in the book of the Chronicles of the kings of Israel?

one another in the face." 9 And Jeho'ash king of Israel sent word to Amazi'ah king of Judah, "A thistle on Lebanon sent to a cedar on Lebanon, saying, 'Give your daughter to my son for a wife'; and a wild beast of Lebanon passed by and trampled down the thistle. 10 You have indeed smitten Edom, and your heart has lifted you up. Be content with your glory, and stay at home; for why should you provoke trouble so that you fall, you and Judah with you?"

11 But Amazi'ah would not listen. So Jeho'ash king of Israel went up, and he and Amazi'ah king of Judah faced one another in battle at Beth-shemesh, which belongs to Judah. 12 And Judah was defeated by Israel, and every man fled to his home. 13 And Jeho'ash king of Israel captured Amazi'ah king of Judah, the son of Jeho'ash, son of Ahazi'ah, at Beth-shemesh, and came to Jerusalem, and broke down the wall of Jerusalem for four hundred cubits, from the E'phraim Gate to the Corner Gate. 14 And he seized all the gold and silver, and all the vessels that were found in the house of the LORD and in the treasuries of the king's house, also hostages, and he returned to Samar'ia.

15 Now the rest of the acts of Jeho'ash which he did, and his might, and how he fought with Amazi'ah king of Judah, are they not written in the Book of the Chron-

---

9. When Amaziah challenged Jehoash the Israelite king told him a parable about **a thistle, a cedar,** and **a wild beast.** This is what happens to little thistles which set themselves up as being equal to cedars. Since the story is a parable and not an allegory there is no need to seek to identify the wild beast.

e) DEATH OF JEHOASH (14:15-16)

This is the formal Deuteronomic notice of the death of a king of Israel. It is out of place here (see Exeg. on 13:10-13).

---

in a little parable reminiscent of Judg. 9:8-15, ironically advised Amaziah to be content with his glory. Yet in his overweening vanity Amaziah persisted in kindling an unprovoked war against the Northern Kingdom, which ended in national and personal disaster. He dragged out several more years of impotent rule until, like his father, he was murdered by conspirators.

How often in the world's history has this

tragic story of unprovoked warfare been repeated, when every dictate of policy and statesmanship would call for co-operation, mutual helpfulness, and brotherhood. The expositor will see in this foolish act of Amaziah as in miniature the picture presented in our modern world of nations, whose welfare and even continued existence depend upon mutual understanding and co-operation, still suspicious of

16 And Jehoash slept with his fathers, and was buried in Samaria with the kings of Israel; and Jeroboam his son reigned in his stead.

17 ¶ And Amaziah the son of Joash king of Judah lived after the death of Jehoash son of Jehoahaz king of Israel fifteen years.

18 And the rest of the acts of Amaziah, *are* they not written in the book of the Chronicles of the kings of Judah?

19 Now they made a conspiracy against him in Jerusalem: and he fled to Lachish; but they sent after him to Lachish, and slew him there.

20 And they brought him on horses: and he was buried at Jerusalem with his fathers in the city of David.

21 ¶ And all the people of Judah took Azariah, which *was* sixteen years old, and made him king instead of his father Amaziah.

22 He built Elath, and restored it to Judah, after that the king slept with his fathers.

icles of the Kings of Israel? 16 And Jeho'ash slept with his fathers, and was buried in Samar'ia with the kings of Israel; and Jerobo'am his son reigned in his stead.

17 Amazi'ah the son of Jo'ash, king of Judah, lived fifteen years after the death of Jeho'ash son of Jeho'ahaz, king of Israel. 18 Now the rest of the deeds of Amazi'ah, are they not written in the Book of the Chronicles of the Kings of Judah? 19 And they made a conspiracy against him in Jerusalem, and he fled to Lachish. But they sent after him to Lachish, and slew him there. 20 And they brought him upon horses; and he was buried in Jerusalem with his fathers in the city of David. 21 And all the people of Judah took Azari'ah, who was sixteen years old, and made him king instead of his father Amazi'ah. 22 He built Elath and restored it to Judah, after the king slept with his fathers.

f) DEATH OF AMAZIAH (14:17-22)

The statement of vs. 17 is a later insertion, possibly made in order to separate the two death notices. It is based on the statements of 13:10 and 14:2. Amaziah probably survived Jehoash by seven years (see Exeg. on vs. 2). The usual obituary notice for a king of Judah has had to be modified in the case of Amaziah because of the unusual circumstances of the king's death. We have therefore (vs. 18) the customary mention of the source in which further details can be found, but to this is added an extract from the source which tells the story of Amaziah's assassination and gives a short summary of the way in which his son was installed as his successor. It appears that when the king heard of the plot he fled toward Egypt but was overtaken at Lachish and there killed. Lachish was the second largest city of Judah, about thirty-five miles southwest of Jerusalem (see Exeg. on 18:13-16).

21. The name of the new king is here given as **Azariah,** but in the parallel account in II Chr. 26:1 the name is Uzziah, and so in the Syriac of Kings. This fact may be accounted for by the accidental omission of one letter, e.g., in Hebrew Azariah is עזריה, Uzziah is עזיה. The different vowels could arise naturally in an attempt of later scribes to vocalize the Hebrew consonants which they found.

22. The position of this verse has occasioned considerable comment. It would naturally appear during the account of the king's reign, not as an isolated piece of

one another, unable to reconcile their differences, compose their quarrels, arrive at broad policies by which the interests of each would be conserved and the welfare of all be achieved. The very same motives which impelled Amaziah to embark so rashly on his ill-fated adventure against Joash are at the heart of the world's disorder today. A selfish and ambitious nationalism is always the foe of world peace. And unless we have learned better ways by the catastrophes which have overtaken our modern world, only the ruin which overtook those two little Jewish kingdoms is in store for us.

21-22. *The Accomplishments of Courage.*—What must have been in the heart of this young boy Azariah when after the murder of his father he was made king! But these verses show us that he was no timid soul, that he did not shrink from danger, that he had in him a resolute heart. **He built Elath and restored it to Judah.**

23 ¶ In the fifteenth year of Amaziah the son of Joash king of Judah, Jeroboam the son of Joash king of Israel began to reign in Samaria, *and reigned* forty and one years.

24 And he did *that which was* evil in the sight of the LORD: he departed not from all the sins of Jeroboam the son of Nebat, who made Israel to sin.

25 He restored the coast of Israel from the entering of Hamath unto the sea of the plain, according to the word of the LORD God of Israel, which he spake by the hand of his servant Jonah, the son of Amittai, the prophet, which *was* of Gath-hepher.

23 In the fifteenth year of Amazi'ah the son of Jo'ash, king of Judah, Jerobo'am the son of Jo'ash, king of Israel, began to reign in Samar'ia, and he reigned forty-one years. 24 And he did what was evil in the sight of the LORD; he did not depart from all the sins of Jerobo'am the son of Nebat, which he made Israel to sin. 25 He restored the border of Israel from the entrance of Hamath as far as the Sea of the Arabah, according to the word of the LORD, the God of Israel, which he spoke by his servant Jonah the son of Amit'tai, the prophet, who

information attached to the formal notice of his accession to the throne. The most probable explanation is that the verse is an addition here from the parallel account in II Chr. 26:2.

Elath is the modern Aqabah, at the head of the northeast arm of the Red Sea. Azariah's capture of the town opened up once more the possibility of overseas trade with the East generally and with Ophir in particular.

6. JEROBOAM II OF ISRAEL (14:23-29)

Jeroboam II was by far the most successful of all the kings of Israel. Profiting by the weakness of his rival, Syria-Damascus, after its subjugation by Adadnirari III in 805 B.C., he extended his kingdom to the farthest northern traditional border of Israel, viz., to **the entrance of Hamath**, the most northerly limit of Solomon's kingdom (I Kings 8:65). **The Sea of the Arabah** is the Dead Sea, the Arabah being that depression which extends from the Jordan Valley to the Red Sea, part of the great rift which appears in East Africa in Lake Tanganyika and the Rift Valley.

25. Jonah the son of Amittai is presumably the prophet under whose name the book of Jonah was later written. Nothing is known of this prophet apart from what is in this verse, **Gath-hepher** being a town in Zebulun (Josh. 19:13). His tomb is shown near Nazareth of Galilee and also as the "mound of repentance" to the east of the site of Nineveh.

Elath was a strategic seaport (I Kings 9:26) in the extreme south of Edom to which it then belonged. To retake it, to rebuild it, demanded foresight and courage. The young ruler thus gave promise of his long and prosperous reign. One can often tell by initial acts what the spirit of a man is. When courage rises with danger, one has an index of the soul. It is true that Elath was finally lost to the Syrians (16:6) but then an irresolute Ahaz was on the throne.

23-29. Prosperity and Righteousness.—Vss. 15-16 of this chapter conclude the record of Joash of Israel, related in the last verses of ch. 13. The solid achievements of his reign were the foundation on which his successor, Jeroboam II, raised Israel to a pitch of material prosperity beyond anything she had hitherto enjoyed. It seems extraordinary that only a few verses in this chapter are devoted to the long and successful career of this exceptionally able

ruler. Israel's territory was enlarged until Jeroboam was lord of a kingdom of Davidic dimensions. He even pushed his conquests two hundred miles north of Samaria. And the result of all this was a long and unwonted peace. Wealth increased. Agriculture and commerce flourished. But religion and morals declined. Luxury, social injustice, immorality, were the order of the day. For a true picture of Israel under Jeroboam one must turn to Amos, the first of the great reformatory prophets. His eye pierced behind the outward splendor and saw in it only the hectic flush on the face of a nation that was morally diseased and bound to perish.

Thus the lesson is held stark and simple before the conscience of men today. Nothing will save from ruin a nation whose policies do not rest on righteousness as between God and man, and man and his fellow men. Outward prosperity and wealth are no sign of the stability

26 For the LORD saw the affliction of Israel, *that it was* very bitter: for *there was* not any shut up, nor any left, nor any helper for Israel.

27 And the LORD said not that he would blot out the name of Israel from under heaven: but he saved them by the hand of Jeroboam the son of Joash.

28 ¶ Now the rest of the acts of Jeroboam, and all that he did, and his might, how he warred, and how he recovered Damascus, and Hamath, *which belonged* to Judah, for Israel, *are* they not written in the book of the Chronicles of the kings of Israel?

29 And Jeroboam slept with his fathers, *even* with the kings of Israel; and Zachariah his son reigned in his stead.

15 In the twenty and seventh year of Jeroboam king of Israel began Azariah son of Amaziah king of Judah to reign.

2 Sixteen years old was he when he began to reign, and he reigned two and fifty years in Jerusalem. And his mother's name *was* Jecholiah of Jerusalem.

3 And he did *that which was* right in the sight of the LORD, according to all that his father Amaziah had done;

was from Gath-he′pher. 26 For the LORD saw that the affliction of Israel was very bitter, for there was none left, bond or free, and there was none to help Israel. 27 But the LORD had not said that he would blot out the name of Israel from under heaven, so he saved them by the hand of Jerobo′am the son of Jo′ash.

28 Now the rest of the acts of Jerobo′am, and all that he did, and his might, how he fought, and how he recovered for Israel Damascus and Hamath, which had belonged to Judah, are they not written in the Book of the Chronicles of the Kings of Israel? 29 And Jerobo′am slept with his fathers, the kings of Israel, and Zechari′ah his son reigned in his stead.

15 In the twenty-seventh year of Jerobo′am king of Israel Azari′ah the son of Amazi′ah, king of Judah, began to reign. 2 He was sixteen years old when he began to reign, and he reigned fifty-two years in Jerusalem. His mother's name was Jecoli′ah of Jerusalem. 3 And he did what was right in the eyes of the LORD, according to all that

---

26-27. This section is an addition by the later editor who was favorable to Israel and was responsible for similar insertions (i.e., 13:23).

28-29. The formal Deuteronomic obituary notice for a king of Israel. The Hebrew has "and Hamath to Judah in Israel," which is unintelligible. The Syriac has "to Israel" for the whole phrase. This makes sense, though some reference to the earlier control of Damascus (if not of Hamath itself) by Judah may well be original. It would scarcely be possible for any writer to speak of the northern boundary of Jeroboam's Israel without thinking of the situation in Solomon's most prosperous days. This may account for the introduction of a reference to Judah. The picture of a sudden and very great prosperity during this reign can be seen in the books of Amos and Hosea, supplemented by such a chapter as Isa. 28.

7. AZARIAH OF JUDAH (15:1-7)

15:1-4. The formal Deuteronomic notice of the accession of a king of Judah. He was a good king, except that he did not conform to the centralizing policy of the compiler.

---

of any nation. A plumb line (Amos 7:7-9) is let down straight into the life of every nation, straight as the laws of righteousness and justice. If that line is not true, then that nation must totter to its fall. What a message is suggested here for any prophet of today! Outward profession in worship and sacrifice of faith in God counts for nothing unless we "let judgment run down as waters, and righteousness as a mighty stream" (Amos 5:24).

Such is the moral lesson drawn from the reign of Jeroboam II of Israel.

15:1-4. *Azariah's Reign.*—This chapter is chiefly concerned with the growing decay of the Northern Kingdom. The first part of it, however (vss. 1-7), and the concluding section (vss. 32-38) deal with the long period of sixty years during which the Southern Kingdom had but two rulers, Azariah and his son Jotham. Azariah appears to have had two names. The Chron-

4 Save that the high places were not removed: the people sacrificed and burnt incense still on the high places.

5 ¶ And the LORD smote the king, so that he was a leper unto the day of his death, and dwelt in a several house. And Jotham the king's son *was* over the house, judging the people of the land.

6 And the rest of the acts of Azariah, and all that he did, *are* they not written in the book of the Chronicles of the kings of Judah?

7 So Azariah slept with his fathers; and they buried him with his fathers in the city of David: and Jotham his son reigned in his stead.

his father Amazi'ah had done. 4 Nevertheless the high places were not taken away; the people still sacrificed and burned incense on the high places. 5 And the LORD smote the king, so that he was a leper to the day of his death, and he dwelt in a separate house. And Jotham the king's son was over the household, governing the people of the land. 6 Now the rest of the acts of Azari'ah, and all that he did, are they not written in the Book of the Chronicles of the Kings of Judah? 7 And Azari'ah slept with his fathers, and they buried him with his fathers in the city of David, and Jotham his son reigned in his stead.

5. Azariah became a **leper,** and from that time took no part in public affairs. According to II Chr. 26:16-21, the leprosy of the king appeared suddenly while he was burning incense in the temple—an unwarranted intrusion upon the sacred duties of the priests. Whether it was such a great sin in Azariah's time as the later priestly writers would have us believe is open to question. This verse is an extract from the royal annals of Judah. It states that King Azariah was not cast out of the city as would have been the case if he had been a common leper, but that he **dwelt in a several house,** the word **several** being good Elizabethan English for **separate.** The verse also states that the king's son and heir, Jotham, acted as regent for the rest of his father's life, probably for thirteen years (see Exeg. on 14:2).

6-7. This customary obituary notice for a king of Judah gives no indication of the new prosperity of the period in which Azariah-Uzziah shared (cf. II Chr. 26:1-15). The year of the king's death was the year of Isaiah's call to be a prophet (Isa. 6:1-6).

icler (II Chr. 26:1) and Isaiah (1:1; 6:1) call him Uzziah and by this name, also found in vs. 32 of this chapter, he seems familiarly to have been known. For a full account of his reign we are referred (vs. 6) to the account in Chronicles (II Chr. 26:2-21) and also to a narrative by Isaiah (II Chr. 26:22) which has not come down to us. The Chronicler records an illustrious reign. Here we are told only that he reigned for no less than fifty-two years, that he was a good king, and that he became a leper. That he did not remove the **high places,** a fact monotonously intoned in these chapters, is nothing against him, since this is a later prophetic commentary on these rulers dating from the time of the Deuteronomic reform when these rural sanctuaries were forbidden.

5. *The Doom of the Arrogant.*—Azariah had taken many a city, but he had not ruled his spirit (II Chr. 26:16-20). His was the spirit of pride and arrogance. Hence he was smitten with leprosy, unable longer to rule as king, allowed to live unmolested in his own house, but dragging out there a miserable existence and buried at last not in a royal sepulcher but in an adjoin-

ing field. What a dramatic plunge was this from the summit of splendor to the horrors of a living death. A victor over his enemies, he was unable to conquer himself. The hardest victory to win in the sphere of morals is that of humility, control, and self-restraint when in the possession of power. Let wealth, continued success, realization of native capacity come to a man and almost inevitably he becomes puffed up. The most dangerous temptation that can come to a man is the possession of power and the knowledge that he possesses it. At the height of his extraordinary career, Dwight L. Moody realized the moral danger that he was in and said that he was praying daily that he might be kept humble. Azariah never offered that prayer. "When he was strong, his heart was lifted up" (II Chr. 26:16). Swinging his censer arrogantly in the face of the priests! And the leprosy starting out at once on his face! The LORD smote [him]. And moral disease, ultimate decay of all that is good in a man, inevitably overtakes one who cannot control his pride and lust for power and walk humbly with his fellow men and with God. Perhaps the greatest victors on the field

8 ¶ In the thirty and eighth year of Azariah king of Judah did Zachariah the son of Jeroboam reign over Israel in Samaria six months.

9 And he did *that which was* evil in the sight of the LORD, as his fathers had done: he departed not from the sins of Jeroboam the son of Nebat, who made Israel to sin.

10 And Shallum the son of Jabesh conspired against him, and smote him before the people, and slew him, and reigned in his stead.

11 And the rest of the acts of Zachariah, behold, they *are* written in the book of the Chronicles of the kings of Israel.

12 This *was* the word of the LORD which he spake unto Jehu, saying, Thy sons shall sit on the throne of Israel unto the fourth *generation*. And so it came to pass.

13 ¶ Shallum the son of Jabesh began to reign in the nine and thirtieth year of Uzziah king of Judah; and he reigned a full month in Samaria.

14 For Menahem the son of Gadi went up from Tirzah, and came to Samaria, and

8 In the thirty-eighth year of Azari'ah king of Judah Zechari'ah the son of Jerobo'am reigned over Israel in Samar'ia six months. 9 And he did what was evil in the sight of the LORD, as his fathers had done. He did not depart from the sins of Jerobo'am the son of Nebat, which he made Israel to sin. 10 Shallum the son of Jabesh conspired against him, and struck him down at Ibleam,[w] and killed him, and reigned in his stead. 11 Now the rest of the deeds of Zechari'ah, behold, they are written in the Book of the Chronicles of the Kings of Israel. 12 (This was the promise of the LORD which he gave to Jehu, "Your sons shall sit upon the throne of Israel to the fourth generation." And so it came to pass.)

13 Shallum the son of Jabesh began to reign in the thirty-ninth year of Uzzi'ah king of Judah, and he reigned one month in Samar'ia. 14 Then Men'ahem the son of Gadi came up from Tirzah and came to

[w] Gk Compare 9. 27: Heb *before the people*

8. ZECHARIAH OF ISRAEL (15:8-12)

8-12. These verses summarize the brief reign of Zechariah. He was the son of Jeroboam and reigned for six months only. There was little indeed which the Deuteronomic compiler could add to his formal notices of accession (vss. 8-9) and of death (vs. 11), except an extract from the royal annals to the effect that the king was murdered by Shallum, as well as a comment (vs. 12) that this murder marked the end of Jehu's dynasty of five kings (as a fulfillment of the prophecy of 10:30). In this year (747 B.C.) there were two kings murdered in Israel, and four kings sat on the throne. This period of anarchy is comparable to that of 69 A.D., when Galba was put to death in the Forum at Rome, and both Otto and Vitellius died, making room for Vespasian. After the death of Jeroboam II the kingdom of Israel lasted for twenty-three years. There were six kings, of whom five seized the throne by murder and violence. The sole exception was Pekahiah, who succeeded his father Menahem in comparatively peaceful circumstances, but he was murdered after two years. As Amos said, the country was like a basket of summer fruit (*qáyiṣ*) which needed to be eaten quickly because it was ripe and doomed to speedy decay: the end (*qēṣ*) was near (Amos 8:2).

9. SHALLUM OF ISRAEL (15:13-15)

13-15. This king maintained his position for one month only, and was in his turn assassinated by Menahem. The paragraph consists of the usual Deuteronomic notices

of time have been not the martyrs to fate, but the masterful and successful who have used their power not for self-glory, but for the welfare of the world in which they live. "Perceiving then that they were about to . . . make him king, Jesus withdrew again" (John 6:15).

8-31. *The Decline and Fall of the Northern Kingdom.*—The story of its final collapse is

reserved for another chapter. But here we are told how rapidly the Northern Kingdom began to disintegrate. Six kings follow in rapid succession. Only two of them died a natural death, and each seems to have been worse than his predecessor. The kingdom was reduced by the Assyrians to a miserable vassalage. Later Tiglath-Pileser III, having disposed of the Syrians,

smote Shallum the son of Jabesh in Samaria, and slew him, and reigned in his stead.

15 And the rest of the acts of Shallum, and his conspiracy which he made, behold, they *are* written in the book of the Chronicles of the kings of Israel.

16 ¶ Then Menahem smote Tiphsah, and all that *were* therein, and the coasts thereof from Tirzah: because they opened not *to him,* therefore he smote *it; and* all the women therein that were with child he ripped up.

17 In the nine and thirtieth year of Azariah king of Judah began Menahem the son of Gadi to reign over Israel, *and reigned* ten years in Samaria.

Samar'ia, and he struck down Shallum the son of Jabesh in Samar'ia and slew him, and reigned in his stead. 15 Now the rest of the deeds of Shallum, and the conspiracy which he made, behold, they are written in the Book of the Chronicles of the Kings of Israel. 16 At that time Men'ahem sacked Tappuah[x] and all who were in it and its territory from Tirzah on; because they did not open it to him, therefore he sacked it, and he ripped up all the women in it who were with child.

17 In the thirty-ninth year of Azari'ah king of Judah Men'ahem the son of Gadi began to reign over Israel, and he reigned

[x] Compare Gk: Heb *Tiphsah*

---

of the king's accession and death, the first followed by a short extract from the royal annals which tells of the murder, the second shorter than usual because of the circumstances (there was no regular succession of the king by his son).

10. Menahem of Israel (15:16-22)

Menahem, having assassinated Shallum in Samaria, proceeded to Tiphsah to eliminate the supporters of Shallum who were holding out there. He conquered it and all in the neighborhood as far as Tirzah who did not surrender to him, treating the cities with the regular brutality of the warfare of the period. Menahem's reign was blighted by the new activity of Assyria under the usurper Tiglath-pileser III, who exacted such heavy tribute that Menahem had to resort to a capital levy.

16. It is possible that the name **Tiphsah** is an erroneous transcription of the little-known place name **Tappuah** (so Lucian), a town on the borders of Ephraim and Manasseh. There is no need, however, to insist upon this alteration; while it is true that the well-known Tiphsah is on the Euphrates, and therefore obviously not the city intended here, there was also another place with the same name about six miles southwest of Shechem.

17-18. These verses form the usual Deuteronomic notice of the king's accession. In this case it had to be preceded by a reference to those events through which Menahem secured the throne. They are followed by an extract from the annals (vss. 19-20) and by the normal editorial obituary.

Tiglath-pileser III seized the Assyrian throne in 745 B.C. and brought to an end a period of weakness. In the first year of his reign he defeated the Armenians who had made great inroads into Assyrian territory during the period which had followed the death of Adadnirari III in 782 B.C. The Armenian King Argistis (780-760 B.C.) had made the most of the opportunities with which weak Assyrian kings had presented him. For seven years Tiglath-pileser sent expeditions south and east and north until he had consolidated his empire. Then in 738 B.C. he began the fourth great Assyrian thrust to the west to reach the Mediterranean. The first had been the successful venture of Tiglath-pileser I, who actually sailed on that western sea toward the end of the twelfth century B.C. The second was that of Shalmaneser III, brought to a halt by Ahab and his allies at Qarqar in 854 B.C. The third was that of Adadnirari III, who had destroyed

---

descended upon it (vs. 29), overran it, and carried off many captives without, however, attempting to take its capital, Samaria. Under Hoshea, puppet ruler, the Northern Kingdom came to its inglorious end.

One has only to turn to the book of Hosea to get an inside view of what was going on in its internal affairs during this period. For Hosea lived and prophesied during the whole of it down to the very brink of final disaster. He

18 And he did *that which was* evil in the sight of the Lord: he departed not all his days from the sins of Jeroboam the son of Nebat, who made Israel to sin.

19 *And* Pul the king of Assyria came against the land: and Menahem gave Pul a thousand talents of silver, that his hand might be with him to confirm the kingdom in his hand.

20 And Menahem exacted the money of Israel, *even* of all the mighty men of wealth, of each man fifty shekels of silver, to give to the king of Assyria. So the king of Assyria turned back, and stayed not there in the land.

21 ¶ And the rest of the acts of Menahem, and all that he did, *are* they not written in the book of the Chronicles of the kings of Israel?

22 And Menahem slept with his fathers; and Pekahiah his son reigned in his stead.

23 ¶ In the fiftieth year of Azariah king of Judah, Pekahiah the son of Menahem began to reign over Israel in Samaria, *and reigned* two years.

ten years in Samar'ia. 18 And he did what was evil in the sight of the Lord; he did not depart all his days from all the sins of Jerobo'am the son of Nebat, which he made Israel to sin. 19 Pul the king of Assyria came against the land; and Men'ahem gave Pul a thousand talents of silver, that he might help him to confirm his hold of the royal power. 20 Men'ahem exacted the money from Israel, that is, from all the wealthy men, fifty shekels of silver from every man, to give to the king of Assyria. So the king of Assyria turned back, and did not stay there in the land. 21 Now the rest of the deeds of Men'ahem, and all that he did, are they not written in the Book of the Chronicles of the Kings of Israel? 22 And Men'ahem slept with his fathers, and Pekahi'ah his son reigned in his stead.

23 In the fiftieth year of Azari'ah king of Judah Pekahi'ah the son of Men'ahem began to reign over Israel in Samar'ia, and

Damascus but apparently had made no further headway. But this disaster to Damascus had made the way easier for the new conqueror, and it had actually sealed the doom of Israel, because now there was no buffer state of any substance to take the shock of the blow. Tiglath-pileser reached the Mediterranean and received homage and tribute from the local kings, among whom were Rezon of Damascus and "Minihummu of Samarinai," who is generally identified as Menahem of Israel, Samaria being his capital city, and Samarina the name by which the Assyrians called that area when they formed it into an Assyrian province some sixteen years later. Menahem paid a tribute of two million gold dollars and was established as a puppet king under the Assyrian overlord. This marks the end of Israel as an independent state. The Hebrew gives the name of the Assyrian king as Pul. He is known by this name in Babylonian inscriptions. It has been suggested that Pul was his own name, and that he took the other as a throne name because of his distinguished predecessor. On the other hand, it was a frequent custom for a king to be known by one name in Assyria and by another in Babylonia. It may well be that this king was actually known in the West by the name which was used in Babylonia.

20. Menahem raised the tribute which he had to pay to the Assyrian king by a capital levy of about thirty-five dollars levied on **all the wealthy men.**

11. Pekahiah of Israel (15:23-26)

The paragraph contains the usual notices, together with an extract from the royal annals of Israel (vs. 25) concerning the king's death.

paints for us a terrible picture of social and political corruption and anarchy. "I gave thee a king in mine anger, and took him away in my wrath" (Hos. 13:11) ; "Ephraim . . . is like a silly dove" (Hos. 7:11) ; "Ephraim is joined to idols" (Hos. 4:17) ; "There is no fidelity, no kindness, and no knowledge of God in the land. Cursing, lying, murder, theft and adultery—they break out, and one crime follows hard upon another" (Hos. 4:1, 2 Amer. Trans) . Worst of all, the very capacity of the people for repentance has been atrophied; only doom awaits

24 And he did *that which was* evil in the sight of the LORD: he departed not from the sins of Jeroboam the son of Nebat, who made Israel to sin.

25 But Pekah the son of Remaliah, a captain of his, conspired against him, and smote him in Samaria, in the palace of the king's house, with Argob and Arieh, and with him fifty men of the Gileadites: and he killed him, and reigned in his room.

26 And the rest of the acts of Pekahiah, and all that he did, behold, they *are* written in the book of the Chronicles of the kings of Israel.

27 ¶ In the two and fiftieth year of Azariah king of Judah, Pekah the son of Remaliah began to reign over Israel in Samaria, *and reigned* twenty years.

28 And he did *that which was* evil in the sight of the LORD: he departed not from the sins of Jeroboam the son of Nebat, who made Israel to sin.

29 In the days of Pekah king of Israel came Tiglath-pileser king of Assyria, and took Ijon, and Abel-beth-maachah, and Janoah, and Kedesh, and Hazor, and Gilead, and Galilee, all the land of Naphtali, and carried them captive to Assyria.

he reigned two years. 24 And he did what was evil in the sight of the LORD; he did not turn away from the sins of Jerobo'am the son of Nebat, which he made Israel to sin. 25 And Pekah the son of Remali'ah, his captain, conspired against him with fifty men of the Gileadites, and slew him in Sa-mar'ia, in the citadel of the king's house;*y* he slew him, and reigned in his stead. 26 Now the rest of the deeds of Pekahi'ah, and all that he did, behold, they are written in the Book of the Chronicles of the Kings of Israel.

27 In the fifty-second year of Azari'ah king of Judah Pekah the son of Remali'ah began to reign over Israel in Samar'ia, and reigned twenty years. 28 And he did what was evil in the sight of the LORD; he did not depart from the sins of Jerobo'am the son of Nebat, which he made Israel to sin.

29 In the days of Pekah king of Israel Tig'lath-pile'ser king of Assyria came and captured I'jon, A'bel-beth-ma'acah, Jano'ah, Kedesh, Hazor, Gilead, and Galilee, all the land of Naph'tali; and he carried the peo-

y Heb adds *Argob and Arieh,* which probably belong to the list of places in verse 29

---

25. The citadel of the king's house was evidently a part of the royal palace which was more than ordinarily secure (cf. I Kings 16:18). The phrase **with Argob and Arieh** is obscure. As the M.T. stands, the reference is to two men who died with Pekahiah at the hands of Pekah and his fifty Gileadite conspirators. But Jerome understood them to be place names, and it has therefore been suggested by Stade that they have come in here by mistake from the list of districts in vs. 29. In this case the names may have been originally Argob, which is a district in Bashan (I Kings 4:13), and Havvoth-jair, an area which is connected with Argob (Deut. 3:14).

12. PEKAH OF ISRAEL (15:27-31)

This paragraph contains the usual editorial notices, together with an extract from the royal annals telling of the great disaster of Pekah's reign, whereby a large part of the kingdom was shorn away and many Israelites carried into captivity by the Assyrian king. The extract also tells of the plot which brought about Pekah's death.

27. The length of Pekah's reign is given as **twenty years** (see Exeg. on 14:2). According to the most satisfactory reconstruction, Pekah's reign is reduced in length to two years.

29. This attack on Israel by Tiglath-pileser followed the Syro-Ephraimite invasion of Judah (16:5-9). It is evident that Pekah was the head of an anti-Assyrian party in Israel who murdered the puppet Pekahiah and forthwith set about revolting against Assyria. Pekah formed an alliance with Rezon of Damascus, who had paid tribute to the Assyrian king three years earlier (738 B.C.) when Menahem also had paid tribute.

---

them. Hosea, who has faith in the unfailing love of God, cannot blind his eyes to the inevitable consequence of deep and ineradicable sin. The problem here presented is one

which the O.T. never solved. Only the Cross points the way to salvation for every lost child of God, however dead he may seem to be in his trespasses and sins.

30 And Hoshea the son of Elah made a conspiracy against Pekah the son of Remaliah, and smote him, and slew him, and reigned in his stead, in the twentieth year of Jotham the son of Uzziah.

31 And the rest of the acts of Pekah, and all that he did, behold, they *are* written in the book of the Chronicles of the kings of Israel.

32 ¶ In the second year of Pekah the son of Remaliah king of Israel began Jotham the son of Uzziah king of Judah to reign.

33 Five and twenty years old was he when he began to reign, and he reigned sixteen years in Jerusalem. And his mother's name *was* Jerusha, the daughter of Zadok.

34 And he did *that which was* right in the sight of the LORD: he did according to all that his father Uzziah had done.

35 ¶ Howbeit the high places were not removed: the people sacrificed and burned incense still in the high places. He built the higher gate of the house of the LORD.

ple captive to Assyria. 30 Then Hoshe'a the son of Elah made a conspiracy against Pekah the son of Remali'ah, and struck him down, and slew him, and reigned in his stead, in the twentieth year of Jotham the son of Uzzi'ah. 31 Now the rest of the acts of Pekah, and all that he did, behold, they are written in the Book of the Chronicles of the Kings of Israel.

32 In the second year of Pekah the son of Remali'ah, king of Israel, Jotham the son of Uzzi'ah, king of Judah, began to reign. 33 He was twenty-five years old when he began to reign, and he reigned sixteen years in Jerusalem. His mother's name was Jeru'sha the daughter of Zadok. 34 And he did what was right in the eyes of the LORD, according to all that his father Uzzi'ah had done. 35 Nevertheless the high places were not removed; the people still sacrificed and burned incense on the high places. He built the upper gate of the house of the LORD.

These two "firebrands" (Isa. 7:4) sought to coerce Ahaz of Judah into a revolt against Assyria, but Ahaz would have none of it and appealed to Assyria for help. This attack was the consequence of Ahaz' appeal, and it reduced Israel to an area of approximately thirty miles by forty miles (734 B.C.). In the following year Pekah himself was murdered by Hoshea. Tiglath-pileser states that he executed Pekah and placed Hoshea on the throne as his nominee. This may or may not be true, but Hoshea certainly started his reign as a pro-Assyrian.

13. JOTHAM OF JUDAH (15:32-38)

The usual Deuteronomic notices of succession and death create some difficulties. The statement that Jotham **reigned sixteen years** (vs. 33) does not agree with that in vs. 30, which says that Hoshea murdered Pekah in Jotham's twentieth year. Also, if Hoshea became king during the time of Jotham, he could not have become king of Judah in Ahaz' twelfth year (17:1). The reconstruction suggested in vs. 27 agrees with a reign of sixteen years, but the statement of vs. 37 cannot be right, since Pekah can scarcely have become king before the sixth year of Ahaz. The history of the last years of the kingdom of Israel was so confused that the Deuteronomic compiler, a hundred years later, was unable to secure any sort of consistency.

35. The upper gate of the house of the LORD which Jotham built is probably "the upper gate of Benjamin" mentioned by Jeremiah (20:2).

32-38. *Jotham's Mistake.*—We return to Judah. Jotham's brief reign appears to have been uneventful. For details we must again turn to the Chronicler (II Chr. 27). Jotham was a builder (vs. 35; II Chr. 27:3-4). But while outer walls and fortresses were going up, the morals of the people were going as steadily down (Isa. 1:4-6). If Jotham had devoted himself not to externals—walls, gates, fortresses— but to the inner reform of his people, he would

have more surely laid the foundations of their prosperity. What a parable for modern times is here! Military bases, defenses, armed forces, will avail us nothing so long as our domestic life is out of order. True security rests on moral and religious foundations. Our main task lies in a thorough reformation of our national life. And evils abound: economic strife, racial antagonisms, decay of family life, the mania for pleasure, luxurious living, secular ideals, ma-

36 ¶ Now the rest of the acts of Jotham, and all that he did, *are* they not written in the book of the Chronicles of the kings of Judah?

37 In those days the LORD began to send against Judah Rezin the king of Syria, and Pekah the son of Remaliah.

38 And Jotham slept with his fathers, and was buried with his fathers in the city of David his father: and Ahaz his son reigned in his stead.

16 In the seventeenth year of Pekah the son of Remaliah, Ahaz the son of Jotham king of Judah began to reign.

2 Twenty years old *was* Ahaz when he began to reign, and reigned sixteen years in Jerusalem, and did not *that which was* right in the sight of the LORD his God, like David his father.

---

36 Now the rest of the acts of Jotham, and all that he did, are they not written in the Book of the Chronicles of the Kings of Judah? 37 In those days the LORD began to send Rezin the king of Syria and Pekah the son of Remali'ah against Judah. 38 Jotham slept with his fathers, and was buried with his fathers in the city of David his father; and Ahaz his son reigned in his stead.

16 In the seventeenth year of Pekah the son of Remali'ah, Ahaz the son of Jotham, king of Judah, began to reign. 2 Ahaz was twenty years old when he began to reign, and he reigned sixteen years in Jerusalem. And he did not do what was right in the eyes of the LORD his God, as his

---

14. AHAZ OF JUDAH (16:1-20)

This king was a great syncretist, and in his time many idolatrous objects and rites were introduced into the Jerusalem temple. He restored the Baal-Astarte cults of Canaan and introduced an altar after a pattern which he had seen at Damascus. He lost control of the Edomite territory and saved himself from Pekah of Israel and Rezin of Damascus only by appealing to Assyria. He stripped all the treasuries bare in order to purchase Tiglath-pileser's help, and made various alterations in the temple edifice and furniture.

a) REIGN OF AHAZ (16:1-4)

Here is the stereotyped Deuteronomic notice of accession, with the compiler's judgment on the religious aspects of the reign. In the opinion of the compiler, Ahaz was thoroughly bad.

16:1. In Tiglath-pileser's inscription the name of this king is given as *Ya'u-ḥazi,* i.e., "Jehoahaz," which was without doubt his full name.

2. If Ahaz was twenty years old when he became king, and if his son Hezekiah was twenty-five at Ahaz' death, then Ahaz was eleven when his first son was born. This is

---

terial interests. Without a just and moral social order there can be no security for any nation. Its inner life must be founded upon the principles of righteousness, sobriety, brotherhood, justice.

16:1-9. Politics and Religion.—While the Northern Kingdom is in the agony of its final dissolution we witness in the kingdom of Judah a state of affairs hardly less tragic. Jotham had died and was succeeded by his son Ahaz. At once the folly of Jotham's policy became apparent. His bulwarks and bastions provided no real security at all. Rather, these were an invitation to attack. No sooner had he completed his forts and turrets than his enemies were in motion (15:37). Ahaz found himself ringed with hostile armies: the Edomites on the east (II Chr. 28:17), the Philistines on the west

(II Chr. 28:18), Israel and the Syrians on the north (vs. 5). The times called for a resolute ruler. Instead, Judah had for her king a timid, irreligious monarch, a tool of politicians and worldly princes, without faith or trust in moral principles or in national honor. The story of this hapless reign, which involved Judah in difficulties from which the nation never again escaped, is told us not only here and in Chronicles but in the early chapters of the book of Isaiah. For at this hour of crisis there appeared on the scene the greatest statesman-prophet of the Hebrew people. One has only to read Isa. 1; 3; 5 to get a vivid picture of the state of affairs within and without the little kingdom.

Ahaz was at his wits' end. He resolved upon a desperate expedient. He would appeal to the

3 But he walked in the way of the kings of Israel, yea, and made his son to pass through the fire, according to the abominations of the heathen, whom the LORD cast out from before the children of Israel.

4 And he sacrificed and burnt incense in the high places, and on the hills, and under every green tree.

5 ¶ Then Rezin king of Syria, and Pekah son of Remaliah king of Israel, came up to Jerusalem to war: and they besieged Ahaz, but could not overcome *him*.

father David had done, 3 but he walked in the way of the kings of Israel. He even burned his son as an offering,[z] according to the abominable practices of the nations whom the LORD drove out before the people of Israel. 4 And he sacrificed and burned incense on the high places, and on the hills, and under every green tree.

5 Then Rezin king of Syria and Pekah the son of Remali'ah, king of Israel, came up to wage war on Jerusalem, and they besieged Ahaz but could not conquer him.

[z] Or *made his son to pass through the fire*

unlikely, though there is evidence that such a fact is possible, especially in the East (cf. C. F. Keil and F. Delitzsch, *The Books of Kings,* tr. James Martin [2nd ed.; Edinburgh: T. & T. Clark, 1877], p. 398). In the LXX and Syriac of II Chr. 28:1, Ahaz' age at accession is given as twenty-five, a figure which eases the problem.

3. In the eyes of the Deuteronomic editors this king was exceeded in wickedness only by his grandson Manasseh. Not only did he walk **in the way of the kings of Israel,** i.e., follow the nature cults of Canaan, but he also reverted to the custom of sacrificing the first-born. The M.T. states that he **made his son to pass through the fire.** Attempts have been made to see in this phrase a reference to a custom whereby the child was passed through the flames in some purification rite, but according to II Chr. 28:3, he actually did burn his son (the plural there is an error), and so here also the correct interpretation is that he **burned his son as an offering.** The sacrifice of the first-born is an ancient rite belonging to heathen religions generally (cf. 17:31; Ezek. 16:21). There are many passages which refer to the first-born as belonging to God (Exod. 13:2; 22:29; 34:19; etc.). The story of the sacrifice of Isaac (Gen. 22:3-14) is the story of the substitution of a ram for the first-born. According to Exod. 13:15, all first-born males are to be sacrificed to God, "but all the first-born of my sons I redeem."

It has been commonly said that Ahaz introduced this custom of the sacrifice of the first-born into the religion of Judah. It is more likely that it was a reversion to ancient Semitic practice, and that it was due to the desperate situation in which the king found himself (cf. 3:27; Jer. 7:18, 31; 44:15-19).

4. The phrase **and under every green tree** is truly Deuteronomic (Deut. 12:2), used in the book of Kings only of Rehoboam (I Kings 14:23), Ahaz (here), and of the northern tribes generally (17:10).

b) SYRO-EPHRAIMITE WAR (16:5-9)

Rezin of Syria-Damascus and Pekah of Israel try to bully Ahaz into joining them in a revolt against their common Assyrian overlord. Ahaz sends for help to Assyria, buying that help with great treasure, and is saved from his two immediate troublers. Damascus is captured, its people exiled, and the king executed. Further details of the war are to be found in Isa. 7 and II Chr. 26. The two kings besieged Jerusalem, but "could not engage

Assyrians who lay north of Syria, and thus compass the destruction of both Syria and the Northern Kingdom. It was a dangerous and short-sighted policy. This alliance with a heathen nation was vigorously opposed by Isaiah (chs. 7–8) who warned Ahaz that if he took this step the Lord would bring upon Judah days such as it had never seen. But Isaiah's counsels fell on

deaf ears. The panic-stricken king and princes sent messengers to Tiglath-pileser III, begging him to come and save them from destruction by Syria and Israel. The Assyrian was only too ready to respond. He descended upon Damascus, took it, and reduced Syria to subjection. What he did to Israel is narrated in ch. 17.

The political philosophy of Ahaz was thus

6 At that time Rezin king of Syria recovered Elath to Syria, and drave the Jews from Elath: and the Syrians came to Elath, and dwelt there unto this day.

7 So Ahaz sent messengers to Tiglathpileser king of Assyria, saying, I *am* thy servant and thy son: come up, and save me out of the hand of the king of Syria, and out of the hand of the king of Israel, which rise up against me.

8 And Ahaz took the silver and gold that was found in the house of the LORD, and in the treasures of the king's house, and sent *it for* a present to the king of Assyria.

9 And the king of Assyria hearkened unto him: for the king of Assyria went up against Damascus, and took it, and carried *the people of* it captive to Kir, and slew Rezin.

6 At that time[a] the king of Edom[b] recovered Elath for Edom,[b] and drove the men of Judah from Elath; and the Edomites came to Elath, where they dwell to this day. 7 So Ahaz sent messengers to Tig'lath-pile'ser king of Assyria, saying, "I am your servant and your son. Come up, and rescue me from the hand of the king of Syria and from the hand of the king of Israel, who are attacking me." 8 Ahaz also took the silver and gold that was found in the house of the LORD and in the treasures of the king's house, and sent a present to the king of Assyria. 9 And the king of Assyria hearkened to him; the king of Assyria marched up against Damascus, and took it, carrying its people captive to Kir, and he killed Rezin.

[a] Heb *At that time Rezin*
[b] Heb *Aram* (Syria)

---

him in battle." He had taken the precaution of securing his water supply (Isa. 7:3), always a problem in the defense of Jerusalem, and was able to hold out till Tiglath-pileser forced "the two tails of these smoking firebrands" to raise the siege. According to II Chr. 28:6-15, Ahaz suffered heavy casualties before he withdrew into Jerusalem, but the Hebrew of vs. 5 scarcely warrants the rendering **could not conquer him.**

6. The RSV is correct in omitting the reference to Rezin, and in reading **Edom** (אדם) for **Syria** (ארם). On the other hand, the M.T. does actually read **Edomites** at the end of the verse, and the KJV is wrong in changing it to **Syrians.** Elath never belonged to Syria, but it did naturally belong to Edom from whom Azariah-Uzziah had taken it not many years before (14:22). Further, it is in the highest degree unlikely that Rezin of Syria would be able to busy himself at this period with faraway Elath when he was concerned mostly with throwing off his allegiance to the Assyrian king.

9. Tiglath-pileser executes Rezin for his general turbulence and virtual rebellion, and deports the inhabitants of Damascus. This did not necessarily involve the whole of the population any more than did the deportation of Israel. It was in accordance with the policy of Assyria, and later of Babylonia. Both empires sought at first to rule through native princes, and when that failed they deported those elements of the population which were most likely to cause trouble and turned the country into a province. The site of **Kir** is unknown; according to Amos 9:7, it was the original home of the Syrians of Damascus.

---

wholly secular, whereas the statecraft of Isaiah was based on faith and religion (Isa. 8:10, 13). Ahaz had no use for anything except power politics. And political expediency, devoid of all moral and religious motives, led his nation down to ruin. The application of all this to our modern world is clear. The interpreter can make good use of it. We have witnessed the appalling results of a purely pagan statecraft. International relations have been determined wholly upon principles of national self-interest. The laws of a personal morality, it has been affirmed, cannot be applied to the relation of one state to another. It has been denied with

vehemence that the state is subject to any ethical principle. There has been no room for God, for the ideals of honor, justice, brotherhood, fair dealing in international relations, for over two centuries of modern history. Ahaz, not Isaiah, has ruled. As a result, the whole world has been convulsed and involved in unimaginable ruin. We are beginning to understand that nothing will avail to save mankind and to restore a semblance of order and sanity in our world order except a repudiation of the Ahaz philosophy and a reintroduction in international relations of the basic ideas of morality and religion as advocated by Isaiah.

10 ¶ And king Ahaz went to Damascus to meet Tiglath-pileser king of Assyria, and saw an altar that *was* at Damascus: and king Ahaz sent to Urijah the priest the fashion of the altar, and the pattern of it, according to all the workmanship thereof.

11 And Urijah the priest built an altar according to all that king Ahaz had sent from Damascus: so Urijah the priest made *it* against king Ahaz came from Damascus.

12 And when the king was come from Damascus, the king saw the altar: and the king approached to the altar, and offered thereon.

13 And he burnt his burnt offering and his meat offering, and poured his drink offering, and sprinkled the blood of his peace offerings, upon the altar.

10 When King Ahaz went to Damascus to meet Tig′lath-pile′ser king of Assyria, he saw the altar that was at Damascus. And King Ahaz sent to Uri′jah the priest a model of the altar, and its pattern, exact in all its details. 11 And Uri′jah the priest built the altar; in accordance with all that King Ahaz had sent from Damascus, so Uri′jah the priest made it, before King Ahaz arrived from Damascus. 12 And when the king came from Damascus, the king viewed the altar. Then the king drew near to the altar, and went up on it, 13 and burned his burnt offering and his cereal offering, and poured his drink offering, and threw the blood of his peace offer-

---

c) AHAZ' VISIT TO DAMASCUS AND ITS RESULTS (16:10-20)

Ahaz goes to Damascus, where Tiglath-pileser is completing his subjugation of the Syrian kingdom, there presumably to do homage to his overlord. While he is in Damascus he sees an altar which takes his fancy. It has been alleged that in copying this altar he was turning away to worship the Syrian gods because they were more successful than his own god of Israel had been. This is indeed the interpretation of II Chr. 28:23; but it rests upon a misunderstanding of Ahaz' action. The gods of Syria had been wholly unsuccessful in preserving their people from disaster. Indeed, they had not been even as successful as the Lord, the God of Israel. Ahaz' action therefore cannot have had such a motive. Two alternatives are open. Either it was an Assyrian altar imported there by Tiglath-pileser at that time, or it was the design of the altar which appealed to Ahaz, and he took plans of it for aesthetic reasons, intending to enrich the ritual of the Jerusalem temple. Urijah the priest was active in the matter. Possibly he was fulfilling the commands of the king and had no real alternative, but it is scarcely likely that Ahaz' motive was wholly wrong, for in that case this priest would never have been one of the two "faithful witnesses" for Isaiah the prophet (Isa. 8:2).

13. There was nothing in pre-exilic belief or practice to prohibit the king from performing personally these sacrificial functions. It was only the postexilic regulations which made Ahaz' action illegal and improper, and the same is true of Uzziah (II Chr. 26:16-20).

The first phrase of this verse is genuinely pre-exilic, since the word translated **burned** is קטר, the root which was used in postexilic literature for burning incense. It meant originally "to cause to smoke" and so "to sacrifice" in pre-exilic writings, as here and generally in the book of Kings. On the other hand, the association in this verse of the

---

10-20. *The New Paganism.*—This chapter ends with one of the most curious stories to be found in these annals. Ahaz, who seems to have been a devotee of aesthetics, had admired the beauties of a pagan altar which he saw in Damascus. So he had a sketch of it made, sent this to Jerusalem with orders to make one like it, and, back in Jerusalem himself, had the ancient altar moved from its place, and offered sacrifice on the new altar. It seems strange that Urijah the priest, well spoken of by Isaiah

(8:2), should not have resisted these innovations of Ahaz, who had become enamored of pagan ideas and wanted to please his Assyrian overlord (vs. 18). Here we have in parable what has been happening in modern life. We too have replaced the ancient altars with those which seem more attractive and pleasing than the old altars of a true sabbath, family prayer, and common worship. We have substituted secular means of culture. As a result our whole social order lacks that solid religious foundation on

14 And he brought also the brazen altar, which *was* before the Lord, from the forefront of the house, from between the altar and the house of the Lord, and put it on the north side of the altar.

15 And king Ahaz commanded Urijah the priest, saying, Upon the great altar burn the morning burnt offering, and the evening meat offering, and the king's burnt sacrifice, and his meat offering, with the burnt offering of all the people of the land, and their meat offering, and their drink offerings; and sprinkle upon it all the blood of the burnt offering, and all the blood of the sacrifice: and the brazen altar shall be for me to inquire *by*.

ings upon the altar. 14 And the bronze altar which was before the Lord he removed from the front of the house, from the place between his altar and the house of the Lord, and put it on the north side of his altar. 15 And King Ahaz commanded Uri'jah the priest, saying, "Upon the great altar burn the morning burnt offering, and the evening cereal offering, and the king's burnt offering, and his cereal offering, with the burnt offering of all the people of the land, and their cereal offering, and their drink offering; and throw upon it all the blood of the burnt offering, and all the blood of the sacrifice; but the bronze altar

meal offering and the drink offering with the whole burnt offering is a postexilic development. Further evidence of later editorial activity is to be seen in alterations at the beginning of vs. 14, since that verse as it stands is untranslatable.

14. The effect of the alteration is to make it appear that Ahaz moved the bronze altar to the north of its original position and put his new altar in its place. If, however, we reconstruct the text in the light of the Syriac, Targ., and LXX, the natural interpretation of the passage is that Ahaz sacrificed his whole burnt offering on the old original altar, as before, and poured out the blood of the slain beasts, which were eaten by the worshipers in the sacred meal, upon this same altar, **which was before the Lord.** He then brought his own altar, the bronze altar which was after the pattern of the altar he had seen in Damascus, and put it at the north side of the original altar. He then issued commands that all the regular sacrifices were to be offered, as before, on the main and original altar, which he left where it was, but that the new bronze altar was for his own use **to inquire by** (vs. 15). The confusion arises because of the assumption that Solomon made a bronze altar when he built the temple. There is no mention of such an altar in I Kings 7, but there is mention of one in I Kings 8:64—a passage which shows many signs of later editing. Scholars generally have found great difficulty in accounting for the omission of any mention of a bronze altar in I Kings 7. The easiest explanation is that there never was one.

15. The list of sacrifices has been worked over more than once. The major part of the verse is probably due to the later compiler, since it shows evident similarities with the proposed ritual of Ezek. 46:1-15. Here we find reference to a regular morning burnt offering, and also (Ezek. 46:4) to a burnt offering of the prince as distinct from the other regular burnt offering. Further the meal (cereal) offering and the drink offering are mentioned in Ezek. 46:14 as accompaniments of the whole burnt offering. The difficulty of the list of offerings which Ahaz commanded lies in the distinction between **the morning burnt offering** and **the evening cereal offering** (מנחה). Such a distinction is made in Jer. 14:12, and may reveal, before the Exile, the existence of the postexilic

which alone it can safely rest and ultimately prosper. Ah, no! The ancient altars must be left in their place. Neither must they be changed or modernized to conform to neopagan ideas. There are no substitutes for the faith that is rooted in God, enshrined for us in Bible and church. Let us set aside the Assyrian altars and see that religion is reborn in the hearts of the people. So shall Judah be secure and rest safely.

Ahaz did not go his pagan way without protest. Urijah may have done what Ahaz told him to do. But Isaiah confronted Ahaz with a message straight from God. Urijah typifies the idea that the church must always take orders from the state; Isaiah, the idea that the church speaks always with a voice of her own. In Isaiah religion asserts itself as an authority above states and kings and secular politics. If we survey

16 Thus did Urijah the priest, according to all that king Ahaz commanded.

17 ¶ And king Ahaz cut off the borders of the bases, and removed the laver from off them; and took down the sea from off the brazen oxen that *were* under it, and put it upon a pavement of stones.

18 And the covert for the sabbath that they had built in the house, and the king's entry without, turned he from the house of the LORD for the king of Assyria.

shall be for me to inquire by." **16** Uri'jah the priest did all this, as King Ahaz commanded.

17 And King Ahaz cut off the frames of the stands, and removed the laver from them, and he took down the sea from off the bronze oxen that were under it, and put it upon a pediment of stone. **18** And the covered way for the sabbath which had been built inside the palace, and the outer entrance for the king he removed from*c* the house of the LORD, because of the king of

c Cn: Heb *turned to*

---

custom of an evening cereal offering as against a whole burnt offering. The general custom of the editors of the book of Kings is to use the term מנחה for both the morning (3:20) and the evening sacrifice (I Kings 18:29, 36). The best solution of the problem of Ahaz' commands is to assume that his original instructions concerned the regular morning and evening sacrifices, but that the whole verse has been edited in order to make it conform to the official ideas of the middle of the sixth century.

Commentators have found difficulty in the interpretation of the phrase **to inquire by,** but the natural explanation is the most likely. Ahaz intended to use his new altar in order to inquire of the Lord, i.e., to seek an oracle. This was by the age-old rite of examining the entrails of the victim which had been slain. In rabbinical Hebrew the root בקר means "to examine closely the sacrificial animals for blemishes," but this is not the original meaning. The corresponding Arabic root means "to cleave," "to slit," from which it may be inferred that there was an early use of the root in the sense of slitting an animal or a bird in order to examine its entrails as a method of inquiring for an oracle from the deity. That this rite was known in old Canaan is instanced by the model of a liver, made of hard-baked red clay covered with vertical and horizontal lines. Found at Gezer, it is an illustration of the ancient method of divination known and practiced in Mesopotamia and also by the Etruscans of ancient central Italy (R. A. S. Macalister, *The Excavation of Gezer* [London: J. Murray, 1912], II, 453-54; also S. A. Cook, *The Religion of Ancient Palestine in the Light of Archaeology* [London: British Academy, 1930], p. 103, and Pl. XXIII, Fig. 2).

17-18. Ahaz robs the temple **because of the king of Assyria.** He had to break up the furniture of the temple in order to pay his tribute to the Assyrian king. Commentators formerly assumed that he hid these treasures so that his Assyrian overlord should not demand them, but it is now generally agreed that they followed Ahaz' other treasures to Assyria.

Vs. 18 is most difficult, chiefly because the word מוסך is unknown. It apparently has something to do with a covering, hence the translation **the covered way for the sabbath.** On the other hand, the LXX has "the foundation [מוסד] of the seat" (reading *shébheth* for *shabbāth*). The best solution seems to be to combine the two readings, and to read מוסך השבת, "the covering of the seat," understanding it to be a reference to a

---

modern political history we discover that the Urijah idea has grown to be a popular dogma. The state is above the church in all secular and political issues, and for the church to resist the state is tantamount to treason. Thus a modern statesman has said, "I resent the interference of the church in affairs of state." In the face of this tendency to absolutize nation and state, it is today the duty of the church to teach

fearlessly that state and nation belong to the sphere of relative and earthly values, whereas the church belongs to the higher sphere of spiritual values and hence cannot be governed in its judgment and attitudes by secular authority. A vigorous challenge to the modern worship of the state is long overdue. We need a few more Isaiahs in our modern world. Thus and thus only will the church assume its rightful dignity

19 ¶ Now the rest of the acts of Ahaz which he did, *are* they not written in the book of the Chronicles of the kings of Judah?

20 And Ahaz slept with his fathers, and was buried with his fathers in the city of David: and Hezekiah his son reigned in his stead.

17 In the twelfth year of Ahaz king of Judah began Hoshea the son of Elah to reign in Samaria over Israel nine years.

2 And he did *that which was* evil in the sight of the LORD, but not as the kings of Israel that were before him.

3 ¶ Against him came up Shalmaneser king of Assyria; and Hoshea became his servant, and gave him presents.

Assyria. 19 Now the rest of the acts of Ahaz which he did, are they not written in the Book of the Chronicles of the Kings of Judah? 20 And Ahaz slept with his fathers, and was buried with his fathers in the city of David; and Hezeki'ah his son reigned in his stead.

17 In the twelfth year of Ahaz king of Judah Hoshe'a the son of Elah began to reign in Samar'ia over Israel, and he reigned nine years. 2 And he did what was evil in the sight of the LORD, yet not as the kings of Israel who were before him. 3 Against him came up Shalmane'ser king of Assyria; and Hoshe'a became his vassal,

---

canopied seat, similar to a choir stall in a cathedral. In this case the LXX is right in assuming that **the house** (KJV) is not **the palace** (RSV), but the house of the Lord, which indeed is the usual meaning of the word. Whatever the reading and the interpretation of the rest of the verse, it seems necessary to read הסר (**removed**) instead of הסב ("surrounded," **turned**), and to read **from** instead of "to" (M.T.).

19-20. The Deuteronomic editor concludes with the formal obituary notice.

15. THE END OF ISRAEL (17:1-40)

a) HOSHEA OF ISRAEL (17:1-6)

This was the last king of the Northern Kingdom. He had to submit to the Assyrian king, but later he rebelled, being enticed by the promises of Egypt. The Assyrian king then imprisoned Hoshea, besieged Samaria, and when the city fell after a three-year siege, deported a large portion of the population.

17:1-2. Here is the usual formal introduction of an Israelite king. The dating is strange, and in accordance with the chronology accepted elsewhere it should be the eighth year of Ahaz. No reason is given for the comparatively favorable judgment which the Deuteronomist passes on this last king of Israel. Perhaps his anti-Assyrian policy is counted to him for righteousness.

3-6. This section is an extract from the royal annals of Israel and is necessarily the last extract. Some have held that vss. 3-4 represent a different stratum from vss. 5-6, and that the first compiler was not aware that Hoshea had been tributary to Assyria from his accession (15:30). He therefore assumed that Shalmaneser made two campaigns against Hoshea, one early in Hoshea's reign (727 B.C.), the other in 724 B.C. The Assyrian records state definitely that there was no campaign in 726 B.C. It is possible to retain the unity of the section by assuming that Hoshea went to pay his tribute and to do homage to the king of Assyria, who had marched west because he had heard rumors that all was not well. He found evidence that Hoshea had been in communication with the Egyptian authorities, imprisoned him, overran the whole country, and laid siege

---

and exert its true influence on human affairs. This does not mean that the modern prophet ceases to be a patriot. At first it may look like a divided loyalty, as if one must choose between loyalty to country and loyalty to God. As a matter of fact, the loyalty is not twain but one. In being loyal to God, Isaiah was far more loyal to his country than was Urijah. So today the

modern prophet who opposes policies of state that contravene the laws of God is far more truly a patriot than he who blindly follows the policies of a state, however flagrantly these may violate the word and will of God.

17:1-23. *Fall of the Northern Kingdom.*— This chapter consists of a long obituary of the Northern Kingdom. Unlike some obituaries,

4 And the king of Assyria found conspiracy in Hoshea: for he had sent messengers to So king of Egypt, and brought no present to the king of Assyria, as *he had done* year by year: therefore the king of Assyria shut him up, and bound him in prison.

5 ¶ Then the king of Assyria came up throughout all the land, and went up to Samaria, and besieged it three years.

6 ¶ In the ninth year of Hoshea the king of Assyria took Samaria, and carried Israel away into Assyria, and placed them in Halah and in Habor *by* the river of Gozan, and in the cities of the Medes.

and paid him tribute. 4 But the king of Assyria found treachery in Hoshe′a; for he had sent messengers to So, king of Egypt, and offered no tribute to the king of Assyria, as he had done year by year; therefore the king of Assyria shut him up, and bound him in prison. 5 Then the king of Assyria invaded all the land and came to Samar′ia, and for three years he besieged it. 6 In the ninth year of Hoshe′a the king of Assyria captured Samar′ia, and he carried the Israelites away to Assyria, and placed them in Halah, and on the Habor, the river of Gozan, and in the cities of the Medes.

---

to Samaria. This solution, proposed by Skinner, is quite satisfactory. In any case, Shalmaneser died before Samaria surrendered, and it was his successor, Sargon, who was responsible for the formation of the country into the province of Samarina, and for the deportation of 27,290 of the inhabitants (according to his own inscription) .

The word מנחה is used here in its original sense of **tribute**. As a sacrificial term it means "tribute offering," and so "sacrifice" in pre-exilic times, and "cereal offering" in the postexilic ritual.

4. The title **So king of Egypt** raises difficulties. Formerly it was the custom to identify this man with one of the first two kings of the Twenty-fifth (Ethiopian) Dynasty, with either Shabaka or Shabataka, but Sargon mentions a certain *Sib′u,* a general of Egypt whom he defeated at Raphia (on the road to Egypt, seventeen miles west of Gaza) in 720 B.C. He mentions also *Pir′u* (Pharaoh) king of Egypt. It is best, therefore, to read *Ṣēwe'* for *Ṣô'* (same consonants—סוא—with different vowels) . Winckler holds that the reference is not to Egypt (*Miçráyim*) at all, but to the north Arabian kingdom of *Muçrî.*

6. The Assyrian king, now Sargon, deports the population to northern Mesopotamia and Media. The year is 721 B.C. In the "Vision of the Man from the Sea," a first-century A.D. writing found in II Esdras 13:39-47, there is a visionary account of the ten tribes taking "this counsel among themselves, that they would leave the multitude of the heathen, and go forth into a further country, where never mankind dwelt, that they might there keep their statutes, which they never kept in their own land." That country is through "the narrow passages of the river Euphrates." The seer says that the Most High will once more dry up these springs when they return, and there is a reminiscence of this in Rev. 16:12. Here are the first stages of those strange beliefs by which many men have identified their own nation with the ten lost tribes.

The site of **Halah** in uncertain. Possibly it is Ḥalaḫḫu, east of Haran in northern Mesopotamia, though the LXX took it to be a river, and in that case it may be the river Balikh, a tributary of the Euphrates, the next river west of the Khābûr. Both these streams run due south, the former joining the Euphrates in the latitude of Aleppo, a hundred miles east of it, and the other, another hundred miles east, but in the latitude of Hamath.

---

however, it makes no effort to gloss over the failures or to exaggerate the virtues of the departed. Here is no eulogy but a dirge. First we have a very brief account of historical events (vss. 1-6) . What the three years' siege of Samaria must have meant to its inhabitants we can learn by referring to 6:24-29, when the city was besieged by the Syrians. Taken at last by Sargon, it was not destroyed, but the better class of its people were carried away captives to a region somewhere north of the Euphrates. Such was the end of the Northern Kingdom. The ten tribes that composed it are never heard of again. Only Judah remained, to maintain a separate existence for another 160 years. Israel fell, unpitied by Judah, smarting under the memories

7 For *so* it was, that the children of Israel had sinned against the Lord their God, which had brought them up out of the land of Egypt, from under the hand of Pharaoh king of Egypt, and had feared other gods,

8 And walked in the statutes of the heathen, whom the Lord cast out from before the children of Israel, and of the kings of Israel, which they had made.

9 And the children of Israel did secretly *those* things that *were* not right against the Lord their God, and they built them high places in all their cities, from the tower of the watchmen to the fenced city.

10 And they set them up images and groves in every high hill, and under every green tree:

11 And there they burnt incense in all the high places, as *did* the heathen whom

7 And this was so, because the people of Israel had sinned against the Lord their God, who had brought them up out of the land of Egypt from under the hand of Pharaoh king of Egypt, and had feared other gods 8 and walked in the customs of the nations whom the Lord drove out before the people of Israel, and in the customs which the kings of Israel had introduced.*d*

9 And the people of Israel did secretly against the Lord their God things that were not right. They built for themselves high places at all their towns, from watch tower to fortified city; 10 they set up for themselves pillars and Ashe'rim on every high hill and under every green tree; 11 and there they burned incense on all the high

d Heb obscure

---

b) A Deuteronomic Homily (17:7-23)

The Deuteronomic compiler makes full use of this golden opportunity to point out the moral of the history and fate of the Northern Kingdom of Israel. The disruption of the kingdom was due to her general waywardness, her neglect of the commands of God, but most of all her breaking away from loyalty to the throne of David and worshiping the golden calf and at a temple other than that of Jerusalem. Some commentators hold that this section is the work of the later editor (*ca.* 550 B.C.) chiefly on account of the references to star worship (vs. 16) and Molech worship (vs. 17), but a writer of the years following Manasseh of Judah would have such things in the very forefront of his mind and would easily add them to his catalogue of northern wickednesses.

7. Strictly speaking the M.T. reads, "And it came to pass, because . . . ," with a long causal clause lasting until the end of vs. 17, a very unlikely Hebrew construction. Lucian reads, "And the anger of the Lord was against Israel, because . . . ," which is much more likely and makes good syntax.

The use of the word "fear" in the sense of worship with awe belongs to the category of the numinous, with its characteristics of awefulness, overpoweringness, and fascination. It arises out of that creature-feeling in the presence of deity which is fundamental to true religion (cf. Rudolf Otto, *The Idea of the Holy,* tr. J. W. Harvey [London: Oxford University Press, 1923], pp. 8-41). When Jacob awoke at Bethel after having seen visions of God, he said, "How dreadful [lit., "to be feared"] is this place!" (Gen. 28:17); see also Job 4:12-15, and the Aramaic Targ. of Jonah 1:5, which reads, "They prayed each to his fear [*daḥlā*']."

8. The concluding phrase makes no sense in the M.T. and is better omitted. The RSV uses considerable freedom with the text.

9. The translation **did secretly** cannot be right since there was nothing at all secret about what they did. The authors of the ancient versions were far from happy about the word, and for the most part have been guessing. It is best to follow Klostermann, and to read ויראפו ("and they devised") for ויחפאו ("and they did secretly"). Possibly the alteration, either deliberate or unconscious, was due to reminiscences of Ezek. 8:7-12.

The modern equivalent to **from watch tower to fortified city** is "from hamlet to city," or "from cottage to palace," or again "from shack to mansion." That the watchtower was typical of the most sparsely populated district can be seen from II Chr. 26:10.

11. Once more the verb קטר means "sacrificed," not **burned incense,** and so in all pre-exilic writings.

the LORD carried away before them; and wrought wicked things to provoke the LORD to anger:

12 For they served idols, whereof the LORD had said unto them, Ye shall not do this thing.

13 Yet the LORD testified against Israel, and against Judah, by all the prophets, *and by* all the seers, saying, Turn ye from your evil ways, and keep my commandments *and* my statutes, according to all the law which I commanded your fathers, and which I sent to you by my servants the prophets.

14 Notwithstanding, they would not hear, but hardened their necks, like to the neck of their fathers, that did not believe in the LORD their God.

15 And they rejected his statutes, and his covenant that he made with their fathers, and his testimonies which he testified against them; and they followed vanity, and became vain, and went after the heathen that *were* round about them, *concerning* whom the LORD had charged them, that they should not do like them.

16 And they left all the commandments of the LORD their God, and made them molten images, *even* two calves, and made a grove, and worshipped all the host of heaven, and served Baal.

17 And they caused their sons and their daughters to pass through the fire, and used divination and enchantments, and sold themselves to do evil in the sight of the LORD, to provoke him to anger.

18 Therefore the LORD was very angry with Israel, and removed them out of his sight: there was none left but the tribe of Judah only.

19 Also Judah kept not the commandments of the LORD their God, but walked in the statutes of Israel which they made.

places, as the nations did whom the LORD carried away before them. And they did wicked things, provoking the LORD to anger, 12 and they served idols, of which the LORD had said to them, "You shall not do this." 13 Yet the LORD warned Israel and Judah by every prophet and every seer, saying, "Turn from your evil ways and keep my commandments and my statutes, in accordance with all the law which I commanded your fathers, and which I sent to you by my servants the prophets." 14 But they would not listen, but were stubborn, as their fathers had been, who did not believe in the LORD their God. 15 They despised his statutes, and his covenant that he made with their fathers, and the warnings which he gave them. They went after false idols, and became false, and they followed the nations that were round about them, concerning whom the LORD had commanded them that they should not do like them. 16 And they forsook all the commandments of the LORD their God, and made for themselves molten images of two calves; and they made an Ashe'rah, and worshiped all the host of heaven, and served Ba'al. 17 And they burned their sons and their daughters as offerings,[e] and used divination and sorcery, and sold themselves to do evil in the sight of the LORD, provoking him to anger. 18 Therefore the LORD was very angry with Israel, and removed them out of his sight; none was left but the tribe of Judah only.

19 Judah also did not keep the commandments of the LORD their God, but walked in the customs which Israel had

[e] Or *made their sons and their daughters pass through the fire*

---

16. It is sometimes doubted whether this Mesopotamian astral worship was known in the Northern Kingdom, because it does not seem to have been introduced into Judah until the time of Manasseh (21:3). But there is evidence for such worship in Israel in Amos 5:26, where "Sakkut" is the Assyrian god Ninurta, whose star was Kewan (Saturn). The two words Sakkut and Kewan have been given the vowels of the Hebrew word *shiqqûç* ("detested thing") because of the idolatrous associations of the words; cf. Exeg. on I Kings 11:5.

18, 21-23. These verses mark the end of the homily which began with vs. 7, but it is renewed, probably by the same author in vs. 21, which actually reads in the Hebrew **For he rent . . .** , and not as in the RSV. The ultimate and crowning wickedness of the Northern Kingdom, according to the Deuteronomic compiler, was the breakaway

20 And the LORD rejected all the seed of Israel, and afflicted them, and delivered them into the hand of spoilers, until he had cast them out of his sight.

21 For he rent Israel from the house of David; and they made Jeroboam the son of Nebat king: and Jeroboam drave Israel from following the LORD, and made them sin a great sin.

22 For the children of Israel walked in all the sins of Jeroboam which he did; they departed not from them;

23 Until the LORD removed Israel out of his sight, as he had said by all his servants the prophets. So was Israel carried away out of their own land to Assyria unto this day.

24 ¶ And the king of Assyria brought *men* from Babylon, and from Cuthah, and from Ava, and from Hamath, and from

introduced. 20 And the LORD rejected all the descendants of Israel, and afflicted them, and gave them into the hand of spoilers, until he had cast them out of his sight.

21 When he had torn Israel from the house of David they made Jerobo'am the son of Nebat king. And Jerobo'am drove Israel from following the LORD and made them commit great sin. 22 The people of Israel walked in all the sins which Jerobo'am did; they did not depart from them, 23 until the LORD removed Israel out of his sight, as he had spoken by all his servants the prophets. So Israel was exiled from their own land to Assyria until this day.

24 And the king of Assyria brought peo-

---

from the Southern Kingdom, involving worship elsewhere than at Jerusalem. And so, having reiterated this charge time and time again, the author concludes his story of the Northern Kingdom with the epilogue of vss. 21-23, making the moral of the whole story plain without any slightest possibility of misunderstanding.

19-20. These two verses form a later comment on vs. 18. They refer to the apostasy of Judah during the last years of the Southern Kingdom, and go on to emphasize the fact that all Israel was rejected by the Lord, and that this included the inhabitants of the northern territory of postexilic times. This passage is a polemic against the descendants of the thenceforth mixed population of the north, later called the Samaritans.

c) ORIGIN OF THE SAMARITANS (17:24-41)

The Assyrian king, having depopulated the northern territory of Palestine, resettled it with populations that had been torn away from their homes in the eastern parts of

---

of injuries inflicted on it by Jehoash (14:9-14) and later under Pekah (16:5). Israel had made wanton war against its blood brothers, close kinship with whom was dictated both by sacred tradition and political wisdom. Isaiah exults at the downfall of Samaria (Isa. 28:1-4).

20-21. The Sin of Schism.—The moral of all this is the subject of the funeral sermon preached by the historian in vss. 7-23. The same sermon may be preached today as a commentary on the catastrophes that have overtaken our modern world. One item in this arraignment of Israel calls for special mention. In addition to its other violations of the word and will of God, Israel had been guilty of the sin of schism. **For he rent Israel from the house of David.** This sin had been Israel's alone. It had broken the bond which united it with the ancient faith which centered in Jerusalem. Therefore to Judah, not to Israel, was to be given the mission of transmitting that faith to the world. Here is a truth which needs fresh emphasis in our day. Many modern men and women have

by this same act of schism cut themselves off from the ancient faith of their fathers, from the sanctuary in which that faith is enshrined. Religion has always incorporated itself in institutional forms, in a church with its order and solidarity, and must always do so if it is to be more than personal sentiment and become a positive force in the world. Only those, therefore, who organically belong to a church do actually become those through whom the religion which is therein enshrined is conserved and perpetuated and brought to bear upon the life of the world. Thus schism from the church means more than mere spiritual loss to the individual. It is essentially an act of disloyalty to that spiritual body, incorporation in which alone enables the individual to transmit to posterity, as did the people of Judah with all their faults, the faith of which Jerusalem for the Jews, and the church for us, is the center and the symbol.

24-28. Lions and Bears.—The subsequent history of the ruined land in the north is sketched

Sepharvaim, and placed *them* in the cities of Samaria instead of the children of Israel: and they possessed Samaria, and dwelt in the cities thereof.

ple from Babylon, Cuthah, Avva, Hamath, and Sepharva'im, and placed them in the cities of Samar'ia instead of the people of Israel; and they took possession of Samar'ia,

---

the empire. But difficulties soon arose, popularly supposed to be due to the ignorance of the new settlers of the way to propitiate the local deity, but actually caused by warfare desolation, which in turn allowed the wild beasts to get the upper hand. The settlers appealed to the Assyrian king, who allowed one of the exiled northern priests to return to Israel in order to instruct the settlers in the proper technique of local worship. The editor says that henceforth the religion of the settlers was syncretistic; they worshiped their own native gods and they worshiped the god of the land. The "cutting edge" of the section is to be seen in vss. 34 and 41. These people in the north, says the writer, still are not true and faithful worshipers of the Lord, and in our days the same attitude must be maintained to them, which our fathers adopted to them in the old days. They are in truth "no better than their fathers."

There are three different strata in this section, vss. 24-28, 29-34a, and 34b-40, with vs. 41 as an editorial conclusion. The first set of verses is drawn from a source which was in general favorable to the northern worship with its calf cult of Bethel (vs. 28). Winckler argued that the colonists mentioned were deported and settled in Israel by Ashurbanipal (668-626 B.C.), and he is supported in this by Ezra 4:10. In Ezra 4:2 the name of Ashurbanipal's predecessor, Esarhaddon (680-669 B.C.), is mentioned. It is evident that there were successive waves of settler-deportees, as one Assyrian king after another followed the traditional Assyrian policy of destroying national patriotism among their defeated subjects by uprooting them from their homes and mixing them thoroughly with other groups also torn away from their roots. Possibly this northern source is the royal annalistic history which has been used for information concerning the northern kings, though it is more likely that this chronicle ceased with the end of the kingdom. In any case, a Deuteronomic editor, perhaps the 610 B.C. compiler, added to this northern account a list of the heathen cults which these foreigners brought with them, and ended by saying that these new inhabitants were no better than their predecessors, but on the whole rather worse. The concluding passage, vss. 34b-40, is of later origin, and denies that the northerners of the interpolator's time were worshipers of the Lord in any proper sense of the term. The section belongs to the period when the differences between the returned exiles of the south and "the inhabitants of the land" (i.e., those who had remained in Palestine) were growing into open antagonism. This division was widening toward the end of the sixth century B.C. (Ezra 4:1-6).

24. Cuthah (in Akkadian, "Kutu") is now a mound and village called Tell Ibrāhîm. It is fifteen miles northeast of Babylon, and before the rise of Babylon it was the leading city of northern Babylonia. The next city mentioned in the Hebrew text is '*Awwā*', which some identify with the Ivvah of 18:34 and 19:13, in which case it is a Syrian city, similar to **Hamath,** on the Orontes, which is also mentioned in these other two chapters. The same applies to **Sepharvaim,** which possibly is the Syrian city of Shabarain, captured by Shalmaneser IV. The reference, however, may be to the two Sippars, the Sippar of the sun-god Shamash and the Sippar of the goddess Anunitum, a double city situated on the Euphrates above Babylon. It is not likely that any Assyrian king settled Syrian exiles in a territory so close to their home as Palestine.

---

in vss. 24-41. Its population, consisting of the dregs of the ten tribes, was augmented by the importation of mongrel peoples from Babylonia. Socially and religiously all was confusion. Helpless, they were set upon by wild beasts, lions, hyenas, bears, jackals, that infested the region. Convinced that the cause of this misfortune was the lack of any one ruling god in the land, they appealed to the king of Assyria to send them a priest of the old Jewish faith to teach the people about the God of the land, the God of Israel, by the fear of whom these beasts could be restrained. So a priest came **and taught them how they should fear the LORD.**

25 And *so* it was at the beginning of their dwelling there, *that* they feared not the LORD: therefore the LORD sent lions among them, which slew *some* of them.

26 Wherefore they spake to the king of Assyria, saying, The nations which thou hast removed, and placed in the cities of Samaria, know not the manner of the God of the land: therefore he hath sent lions among them, and, behold, they slay them, because they know not the manner of the God of the land.

27 Then the king of Assyria commanded, saying, Carry thither one of the priests whom ye brought from thence; and let them go and dwell there, and let him teach them the manner of the God of the land.

28 Then one of the priests whom they had carried away from Samaria came and dwelt in Beth-el, and taught them how they should fear the LORD.

29 Howbeit every nation made gods of their own, and put *them* in the houses of the high places which the Samaritans had made, every nation in their cities wherein they dwelt.

30 And the men of Babylon made Succoth-benoth, and the men of Cuth made

and dwelt in its cities. 25 And at the beginning of their dwelling there, they did not fear the LORD; therefore the LORD sent lions among them, which killed some of them. 26 So the king of Assyria was told, "The nations which you have carried away and placed in the cities of Samar'ia do not know the law of the god of the land; therefore he has sent lions among them, and behold, they are killing them, because they do not know the law of the god of the land." 27 Then the king of Assyria commanded, "Send there one of the priests whom you carried away thence; and let him*f* go and dwell there, and teach them the law of the god of the land." 28 So one of the priests whom they had carried away from Samar'ia came and dwelt in Bethel, and taught them how they should fear the LORD.

29 But every nation still made gods of its own, and put them in the shrines of the high places which the Samaritans had made, every nation in the cities in which they dwelt; 30 the men of Babylon made

f Syr Vg: Heb *them*

For this reason many authorities think that the two Syrian cities, **Avva** and Hamath, have been added here from the lists in chs. 18–19.

25. When the emigrants arrived in the country they found it infested with **lions**, and according to the prevalent ideas of the time they concluded that it was because they did not know the proper way in which the local deity should be conciliated. In Isa. 35:9 the absence of lions and ravenous beasts generally is a sign of the active good will of a god who is favorably disposed to his people.

26. Each land was regarded as having its own deity, and each deity had his own peculiar rites. One of the Bethel priests was brought back and presumably all was well. Evidence for the idea that a deity can be worshiped only on his own territory may be found in 5:17.

29. Here is found for the first time the name **Samaritans**, by which the population of the center and the north was known to the postexilic Jews of Palestine.

30-31. The name **Succoth-benoth** has never been satisfactorily explained. Since the introduction of the cult was due to Mesopotamian settlers, we would expect the names

---

Lions and bears because of the lack of religion in the land! How often has this situation been repeated alike in the life of the individual and the life of society: life attacked by all kinds of alien forces that threaten to tear it to pieces. What is needed in this predicament is the priest who shall teach the fear of the Lord. Many a man who has lived an irreligious life with no thought of God, of sanctuary, of faith, when set upon by lions and bears turns to some

man of God to furnish spiritual means of meeting his emergency. Lions and bears! Are they not let loose today upon a society whose whole security lies in what the priest has to offer? What we most need is that the people shall be taught **the manner of the God of the land** by true spokesmen of God.

29-32. *When Religion Disintegrates.*—Here is described religious anarchy at its worst. **Every nation made gods of their own.** The Baby-

Nergal, and the men of Hamath made Ashima,

31 And the Avites made Nibhaz and Tartak, and the Sepharvites burnt their children in fire to Adrammelech and Anammelech, the gods of Sepharvaim.

32 So they feared the LORD, and made unto themselves of the lowest of them priests of the high places, which sacrificed for them in the houses of the high places.

Suc'coth-be'noth, the men of Cuth made Nergal, the men of Hamath made Ashi'ma, 31 and the Av'vites made Nibhaz and Tartak; and the Sephar'vites burned their children in the fire to Adram'melech and Anam'melech, the gods of Sepharva'im. 32 They also feared the LORD, and appointed from among themselves all sorts of people as priests of the high places, who sacrificed for them in the shrines of the

---

Marduk-Zarbanit or Marduk-Zapanitum. The -benoth (lit., "daughters of") in the M.T. is probably a corruption of the name of the spouse of Marduk, chief god of Babylon, since its consonants are identical with the last three consonants of Zarbanit. The consonants of the first part of the god's name write the word "Sakkut" (the planet Saturn), which is called "the star of justice and right."

Nergal was the god of Kutu. He was the deity of the underworld and in the Mesopotamian astral system was identified with the planet Mars. His special day was the twenty-eighth of the month, the "day of the ravishment of the moon-god," because on this day there was no moon, and Sin, the moon-god, was regarded as having entered the land of the dead. It is on record that when Tiglath-pileser was in Babylonia in 729 B.C. he offered sacrifice to the great gods of Babylonia, of whom Nergal at Kutu was one.

The name Ashima has been found in a compound name, '-s-m–bethel, in the Elephantine papyri. She was apparently worshiped there as the secondary wife of Yahu (Cook, Religion of Ancient Palestine in Light of Archaeology, pp. 149-52). It is probable that the name Ashima should be read in Amos 8:14 for 'ashmath, and then translated "swear by Ashima of Samaria."

The two names Nibhaz and Tartak are wholly unknown, and the words themselves are actually uncertain. Jewish tradition says that one deity was worshiped under the guise of a dog's head, the other under the guise of an ass, but such statements are untrustworthy since the Jews were notoriously abusive when they referred to heathen deities.

The two names Adrammelech and Anammelech should probably be "Adad-melekh" and "Anu-melekh," these two names requiring only the minimum of alteration in the Hebrew consonants, the letter ר for the letter ד. Mélekh means "king," and Adad was one of the ancient gods of Babylonia; he was the god of storm and rain and already by Hammurabi had been hailed as "prince of the heavens and the earth." He was known later in Syria as Hadad, and is so mentioned in the Ras Shamra texts. His ancient home was the unidentified Bit-Karkara. He was identified not with any particular star but with the thunder. The name Adad-melekh means that Adad was worshiped with the rites of the god Melekh. These rites involved the sacrifice of the first-born by burning (Lev. 18:21; Jer. 32:35). Anu was the great sky-god of Babylonia. He too is mentioned by Hammurabi. There were four great nature-gods, Anu of the sky, Enlil of the earth, Ea of the waters, and Nergal of the underworld. The name Anu-melekh means that Anu also was worshiped with a mixed cultus which included the rites proper to Melekh.

32. According to later ideas, it was an offense to appoint any other priests than Levites who claimed descent from Aaron.

---

lonians set up their patron god; the men of Cuth (near Babylon) put up their god Nergal; the men of Hamath (on the river Orontes) chose Ashima, and the Avvites their two gods, while the Sepharvites made human sacrifice to their deities. The very conglomeration of names produces the impression of the wildest moral

and religious disorder. To this degradation had sunk the proud people of the Northern Kingdom, the life of the ten tribes of Israel who had been delivered from Egypt and given possession of the Promised Land. Could we have a more graphic illustration of the truth that "the wages of sin is death"?

33 They feared the Lord, and served their own gods, after the manner of the nations whom they carried away from thence.

34 Unto this day they do after the former manners: they fear not the Lord, neither do they after their statutes, or after their ordinances, or after the law and commandment which the Lord commanded the children of Jacob, whom he named Israel;

35 With whom the Lord had made a covenant, and charged them, saying, Ye shall not fear other gods, nor bow yourselves to them, nor serve them, nor sacrifice to them:

36 But the Lord, who brought you up out of the land of Egypt with great power and a stretched out arm, him shall ye fear, and him shall ye worship, and to him shall ye do sacrifice.

high places. 33 So they feared the Lord but also served their own gods, after the manner of the nations from among whom they had been carried away. 34 To this day they do according to the former manner.

They do not fear the Lord, and they do not follow the statutes or the ordinances or the law or the commandment which the Lord commanded the children of Jacob, whom he named Israel. 35 The Lord made a covenant with them, and commanded them, "You shall not fear other gods or bow yourselves to them or serve them or sacrifice to them; 36 but you shall fear the Lord, who brought you out of the land of Egypt with great power and with an outstretched arm; you shall bow yourselves to

---

34b-40. This section is a collection of Deuteronomic phrases all dovetailed together, claiming that the northerners never obeyed the will of the Lord, either before the fall of the Northern Kingdom or afterward.

---

33. Counterfeit Religion.—Only a mongrel religion existed in the land. Nominally the people worshiped Yahweh, yet each nation made gods of its own. **They feared the Lord, and served their own gods.** How descriptive this is of the kind of religion many people know. They fear the Lord. They count themselves religious people. They observe the outward forms and decencies of religion. But also they serve their own gods: the gods of money, success, pleasure, profit. And this mongrel religion is worth no more today than it was among this degraded people of old. Here lay the root of the contempt felt by the Jews of a later day for the despised Samaritans. Not only was their blood corrupted by intermarriage with these pagan peoples, but their religion was infected with heathenism. Here too lies the root of the contempt which honest people feel for counterfeit religion. One can have greater regard for a man who confesses to no religion at all than for a man who says that he fears the Lord, while in his daily life he serves other gods.

It is a comfort to remember that this is not the final word which the Bible has to utter about these twelve tribes, this family of God whose history began away back in the book of Genesis, whose fortunes we follow down to this terrible and apparently final ruin. One of the most eloquent passages in the Bible is Rev. 7:1-8. There we read the roll call of this family of God. The first time those names were called was in

Gen. 49, when one by one Jacob named his sons and foretold their futures. Thereafter every misfortune which could befall any human family overtook them, including hatred of each other. Finally ten of them disappeared into oblivion. But before the Bible ends, we find them all reunited "when the roll is called up yonder." How unspeakably moving becomes this calling of each separate name: Judah, Reuben, Gad, Asher, and the rest, all present and accounted for. Trial and tribulation, sin and retribution, division and schism all passed, the reunited family are forever together in the home of God. And so, we may believe, is it with our families today, whatever their fortunes may have been:

> For the love of God is broader
> Than the measure of man's mind,
> And the heart of the Eternal
> Is most wonderfully kind.[1]

34-41. Idolatry and Immorality.—The moral is here solemnly drawn from this picture of false religion, of counterfeit religion, of no religion at all. There has been no real "fear of the Lord," no obedience to moral law, no observance of divine commandment. Thus there can be no salvation, no national health and strength. These can come only by keeping the covenant between God and man. Deliverance from foes

[1] Frederick W. Faber, "There's a wideness in God's mercy."

286

37 And the statutes, and the ordinances, and the law, and the commandment, which he wrote for you, ye shall observe to do for evermore; and ye shall not fear other gods.

38 And the covenant that I have made with you ye shall not forget; neither shall ye fear other gods.

39 But the LORD your God ye shall fear; and he shall deliver you out of the hand of all your enemies.

40 Howbeit they did not hearken, but they did after their former manner.

41 So these nations feared the LORD, and served their graven images, both their children, and their children's children: as did their fathers, so do they unto this day.

18 Now it came to pass in the third year of Hoshea son of Elah king of Israel, *that* Hezekiah the son of Ahaz king of Judah began to reign.

him, and to him you shall sacrifice. 37 And the statutes and the ordinances and the law and the commandment which he wrote for you, you shall always be careful to do. You shall not fear other gods, 38 and you shall not forget the covenant that I have made with you. You shall not fear other gods, 39 but you shall fear the LORD your God, and he will deliver you out of the hand of all your enemies." 40 However they would not listen, but they did according to their former manner.

41 So these nations feared the LORD, and also served their graven images; their children likewise, and their children's children —as their fathers did, so they do to this day.

18 In the third year of Hoshe'a son of Elah, king of Israel, Hezeki'ah the son of Ahaz, king of Judah, began to reign.

IV. THE SURVIVING KINGDOM OF JUDAH (18:1–25:30)

A. THE ASSYRIAN PERIOD (18:1–21:26)

1. HEZEKIAH OF JUDAH (18:1–20:21)

This king was a great reformer. He sought to abolish all idolatrous images and objects generally, and he attempted to abolish the local shrines. He joined in a general revolt of the west against Assyria, lost everything except Jerusalem, but was miraculously and unexpectedly saved. He was encouraged and supported by the prophet Isaiah, through whom God announced to him the grant of a further lease of life, but he incurred Isaiah's displeasure and criticism for his favorable reception of an embassy from the Babylonian firebrand, Merodach-baladan.

a) INTRODUCTION (18:1-3)

These verses form the usual stereotyped Deuteronomic notice of succession to the throne. In this case the verdict of the compiler is wholly favorable to the king. Such unqualified praise is found only of Hezekiah and Josiah. Here as elsewhere the synchronization presents difficulties. It is best to assume that Hezekiah became king in

---

both within and without can be won only by that people whose life is governed by a morality that is rooted in real religion. We need the same warning in our day when secularism, greed, immorality, and intolerance threaten the integrity of our national life.

> Judge of the nations, spare us yet,
> Lest we forget—lest we forget! [2]

18:1-3. The Influence of a Mother.—Ahaz and Hezekiah were human opposites: an evil father and a righteous son. Once more we con-

[2] Rudyard Kipling, "Recessional," from *The Five Nations*. Copyright 1903 by Rudyard Kipling, reprinted by permission of Mrs. George Bambridge; Methuen & Co.; The Macmillan Co., Canada; and Doubleday & Co.

front this strange story of heredity. We confront it again in the son of Hezekiah, Manasseh, whose long and evil reign was a curse to his people. How are we to account for this? Does the answer lie in the characters of these kings' mothers, whose names are always mentioned? Hezekiah's mother, we read, was Abi (called Abijah in II Chr. 29:1). She, we are told, was the daughter of Zechariah, who may have been the man of high repute mentioned in Isa. 8:2. If so, we have here a strain of pure blood, a descent from all that was best in the life of the people. Here was young Hezekiah, the son of a renegade father, exposed to all the evils of his day and yet growing up in the fear of the Lord. We think of what Abi did not only for

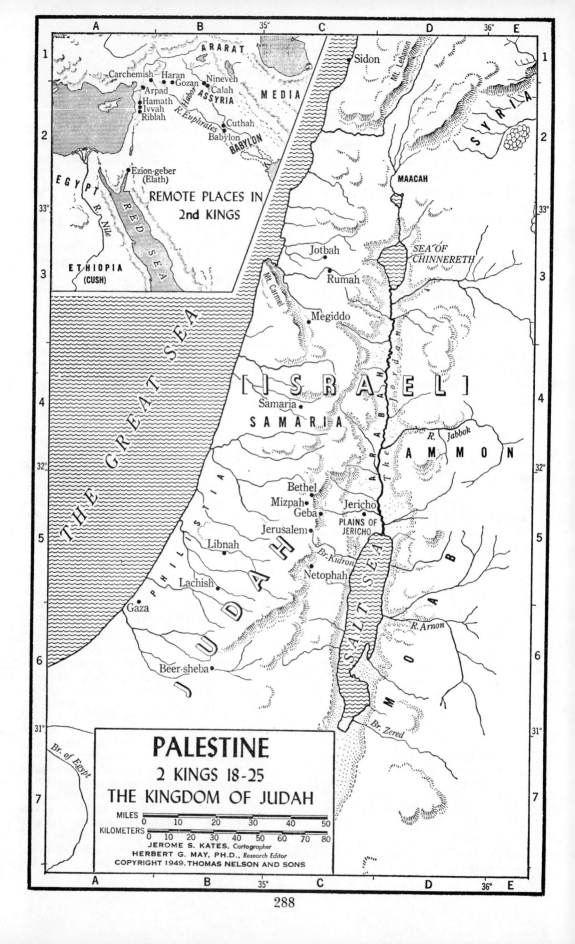

REMOTE PLACES IN 2nd KINGS

A R A R A T

Carchemish Haran Gozan Nineveh MEDIA
Arpad ASSYRIA Calah
Hamath R. Habor R. Tabor
Ivvah
Riblah R. Euphrates Cuthah
Babylon BABYLON

E G Y P T Ezion-geber (Elath)

R. Nile RED SEA

ETHIOPIA (CUSH)

SYRIA

Sidon

Mt. Lebanon

MAACAH

SEA OF CHINNERETH

Jotbah

Rumah

THE GREAT SEA

Mt. Carmel

Megiddo

[I S R A E L]

Samaria

S A M A R I A

The Jordan

A R A B A H

R. Jabbok

A M M O N

P H I L I S T I A

Bethel
Mizpah Geba
Jericho
Jerusalem PLAINS OF JERICHO
Libnah Br. Kidron
Netophah

J U D A H

Lachish

Gaza

Beer-sheba

S A L T   S E A

M O A B

R. Arnon

Br. Zered

Br. of Egypt

PALESTINE
2 KINGS 18-25
THE KINGDOM OF JUDAH

MILES
0   10   20   30   40   50
KILOMETERS
0 10 20 30 40 50 60 70 80

JEROME S. KATES, *Cartographer*
HERBERT G. MAY, PH.D., *Research Editor*
COPYRIGHT 1949, THOMAS NELSON AND SONS

2 Twenty and five years old was he when he began to reign; and he reigned twenty and nine years in Jerusalem. His mother's name also *was* Abi, the daughter of Zachariah.

3 And he did *that which was* right in the sight of the LORD, according to all that David his father did.

4 ¶ He removed the high places, and brake the images, and cut down the groves, and brake in pieces the brazen serpent that Moses had made: for unto those days the children of Israel did burn incense to it: and he called it Nehushtan.

2 He was twenty-five years old when he began to reign, and he reigned twenty-nine years in Jerusalem. His mother's name was Abi the daughter of Zechari'ah. 3 And he did what was right in the eyes of the LORD, according to all that David his father had done. 4 He removed the high places, and broke the pillars, and cut down the Ashe'rah. And he broke in pieces the bronze serpent that Moses had made, for until those days the people of Israel had burned

---

725 B.C., which was Hoshea's eighth year (Oesterley and Robinson, *History of Israel,* I, 459).

18:2. The name **Abi** is a shortened form of Abijah (see II Chr. 29:1).

b) HEZEKIAH'S REFORMS AND SUCCESS IN WAR (18:4-8)

The Deuteronomic compiler summarizes Hezekiah's reforms of the cultus and says that he was the best of all the kings of Judah, whether before his time or after. In vss. 7-8 we find the true Deuteronomic reward of success and prosperity. Hezekiah revolted against his Assyrian overlord, and we are led to assume (vs. 7) that he was successful. We read further that he was successful in wars against the Philistines. The substance of vss. 7-8 is true of the first part of the revolt, but ultimately the revolt was unsuccessful, and Hezekiah was actually in a worse position at the end than he had been at the beginning.

4. According to this verse the reforms of Hezekiah covered exactly the same ground as the reforms of his great-grandson, Josiah, including the centralization of the worship at Jerusalem. Vss. 4-8 are the work of the Deuteronomic compiler of *ca.* 610 B.C., except that vs. 4 shows signs of later authorship. Either the whole of the verse is a later insertion, or it has been remodeled by a later editor, perhaps of postexilic times. The most likely solution is that Hezekiah's reforms involved the destruction of all emblems used in the worship of the Lord which had any pagan association, especially those which were of Assyrian origin. This would involve the destruction of sacred pillars and sacred poles generally, and the suppression of heathen or semiheathen cults wherever they happened to be. In the fullness of his reforming zeal he destroyed even the **bronze serpent,** which was traditionally held to have been made by Moses in the wilderness. There is no information as to the period of his reign during which Hezekiah instituted all these reforms. The most likely date is 705 B.C., which was the year of the general insurrection of the western tributary states against Sennacherib, the new Assyrian king who had come to the throne at the death of Sargon. This rebellion was a bid for national liberty, and the revival of the national religion, with a parallel elimination of extranational

---

her son but for her people in giving such a son to be their king at such a critical hour in their history. What kind of woman was Hezekiah's wife, Hephzibah (21:1), that she should have a son like Manasseh? Thus mothers determine the destinies not only of individuals but of nations. A consecrated motherhood is our deepest social necessity today. Mothers are forgetful of their true mission in life when they imagine that any task or duty is more important than the careful

training of their children in self-control, in high ideals of life and conduct, in knowledge of God, rearing them in homes in which simplicity, honesty, and generosity are practiced, and offering them examples of such living in their own lives.

4-6. Religion and Prosperity.—Ahaz had bequeathed to Hezekiah a kingdom in disorder and peril. But here was a king so righteous in intention and motive that the historian eulo-

5 He trusted in the LORD God of Israel; so that after him was none like him among all the kings of Judah, nor *any* that were before him.

6 For he clave to the LORD, *and* departed not from following him, but kept his commandments, which the LORD commanded Moses.

incense to it: it was called Nehush'tan. 5 He trusted in the LORD the God of Israel; so that there was none like him among all the kings of Judah after him, nor among those who were before him. 6 For he held fast to the LORD; he did not depart from following him, but kept the commandments which

---

rites and customs, invariably coincided with a period of national revival. Similarly, the reforms of King Josiah (621 B.C.) were consequent upon his bid for freedom, for which the death of Ashurbanipal and the breakup of the Assyrian Empire gave opportunity. In cases of such apostate kings as Ahaz and Manasseh, it may well be that their inclination concided with their duty to the overlords of Assyria, but it is nevertheless true that they were compelled to be completely subservient and that this obedience involved religion as well as other aspects of life. Religious reform and national revival went hand in hand. If the reform of Hezekiah was primarily a reaction against Assyrian cults, the reference to the abolition of the local shrines may be due to an editor who read into Hezekiah's time policies which belonged to a later generation.

The **bronze serpent** which Hezekiah destroyed had been an object of worship, since **until those days the people of Israel had** sacrificed (the verb קטר means "to sacrifice" in pre-exilic Hebrew) to it. According to tradition this was actually the serpent which Moses had lifted up in the wilderness (Num. 21:9). It is most probable, however, that the bronze serpent originally had nothing to do with the worship of the Lord God of Israel, but that "it was housed in the shrine kept by Zadok, and that it was the principal sacred object of that shrine until the Ark was brought in to be beside it" (H. H. Rowley, "Zadok and Nehushtan," *Journal of Biblical Literature,* LVIII [1939], 137). Zadok was the original Jebusite priest of Jerusalem, and the bronze serpent was from time immemorial under the special care of that priesthood. The M.T. says that Hezekiah called it **Nehushtan,** "a bronze thing," and the implication is that Hezekiah called it this punning name by way of ridicule, since the Hebrew words for "bronze" (*neḥôsheth*) and "serpent" (*nāḥāsh*) are quite similar. According to some of the ancient versions (Lucian, Syriac, and Targ.), the text read, "And they [i.e., the people] called it. . . ." In this case the name is not to be regarded as an opprobrious word, and possibly it means "bronze god," or "serpent-dragon," or "ancient serpent."

5. This verse seems to have been involved in the revision occasioned by the introduction of vs. 4. The original reading probably was "And there was none like him among all the kings of Judah who were before him." The Deuteronomic editor of Josiah's time would certainly never have agreed that Hezekiah, pious and devout though he was in his reforming zeal, was the equal of Josiah himself.

---

gizes him in words not spoken of any other king of Judah. He began courageously the work of restoring order in his realm. And he began at the bottom. He laid sure foundations. The first task which he undertook was the reformation of religion in the land. More than once in this Exposition attention has been called to the close connection between religion and national prosperity. Irreligion is the ultimate cause of national decay and disaster. Hezekiah understood this and instituted a national religious reformation. And it was thorough. It involved not only the abolition of heathen practices which flourished under Ahaz (16:3, 4) but, and

for the first time, included the destruction of the local altars, **high places.** He destroyed even the brazen serpent, a hoary relic of Israel's wilderness days (Num. 21:9), which seems to have been used for idolatrous purposes. So today, if religion is to reform the life of a nation it must defy old political and economic traditions. Its demands must be uncompromising. Ancient idols of selfish capitalism, economic imperialism, national sovereignty, race supremacy and inequality, must be shattered. Many a brazen serpent revered by our fathers must be smashed. Like Hezekiah, we must go to the roots of national infidelity. Religion must be made a

7 And the LORD was with him; *and* he prospered whithersoever he went forth: and he rebelled against the king of Assyria, and served him not.

8 He smote the Philistines, *even* unto Gaza, and the borders thereof, from the tower of the watchmen to the fenced city.

9 ¶ And it came to pass in the fourth year of king Hezekiah, which *was* the seventh year of Hoshea son of Elah king of Israel, *that* Shalmaneser king of Assyria came up against Samaria, and besieged it.

10 And at the end of three years they took it: *even* in the sixth year of Hezekiah, that *is* the ninth year of Hoshea king of Israel, Samaria was taken.

11 And the king of Assyria did carry away Israel unto Assyria, and put them in Halah and in Habor *by* the river of Gozan, and in the cities of the Medes:

12 Because they obeyed not the voice of the LORD their God, but transgressed his covenant, *and* all that Moses the servant of the LORD commanded, and would not hear *them*, nor do *them*.

the LORD commanded Moses. **7** And the LORD was with him; wherever he went forth, he prospered. He rebelled against the king of Assyria, and would not serve him. **8** He smote the Philistines as far as Gaza and its territory, from watchtower to fortified city.

9 In the fourth year of King Hezeki'ah, which was the seventh year of Hoshe'a son of Elah, king of Israel, Shalmane'ser king of Assyria came up against Samar'ia and besieged it **10** and at the end of three years he took it. In the sixth year of Hezeki'ah, which was the ninth year of Hoshe'a king of Israel, Samar'ia was taken. **11** The king of Assyria carried the Israelites away to Assyria, and put them in Halah, and on the Habor, the river of Gozan, and in the cities of the Medes, **12** because they did not obey the voice of the LORD their God but transgressed his covenant, even all that Moses the servant of the LORD commanded; they neither listened nor obeyed.

---

7. This rebellion of Hezekiah against Assyria was part of the general revolt in which Merodach-baladan of Babylon was involved and all the Syrian and Palestinian kings except Padi king of Ekron. It is more than likely that Merodach-baladan was the chief instigator of the revolt. Padi's subjects revolted against him, wanting to be free from Assyria with the rest, and Hezekiah kept Padi in prison. It was during this period at the beginning of the revolt that Hezekiah undertook his expedition against the Philistines, sweeping everything before him right up to the very walls of Gaza. He thus brought into subjection those few Philistine princelings like Padi of Ekron who had held out against the general revolt. Thus the victories recorded by the Deuteronomic compiler in vs. 8 belong to the period before 701 B.C., the year in which the Assyrian king crushed the revolt. In that year Sennacherib allocated certain territory of Judah to those Philistines who had been faithful to him during the troubled previous four years. The compiler could say that **wherever he went forth** [i.e., to battle], **he prospered** only of the beginnings of the revolt.

c) FALL OF SAMARIA (18:9-12)

9-12. These verses constitute an account of the end of the Northern Kingdom, parallel to that given in 17:5-6. They are from the royal annals of the Southern Kingdom, and conclude (vs. 12) with a comment from the Deuteronomic compiler. Once more there are difficulties over the chronology. In accordance with the solution favored earlier, we should read in vs. 9, "the ninth year of Hoshea," and "the second year of Hezekiah," and in vs. 10, "the twelfth year of Hoshea," and "the fifth year of Hezekiah."

---

real thing in the land. "And the LORD was with him; and he prospered" (vs. 7).

7-37. The Assyrians Come.—When he was strong, **he rebelled against the king of Assyria, and served him not.** This was a dangerous step, for Assyria, having reduced Damascus, had ad-

vanced upon Samaria (vss. 9-10) which fell three years later. Evidently Judah was to come next. Thus Hezekiah faced imminent peril. What to do? To attempt resistance seemed suicidal. To turn to Egypt would be futile (Isa. 30:1-7). It remained only to stand fast and to

13 ¶ Now in the fourteenth year of king Hezekiah did Sennacherib king of Assyria come up against all the fenced cities of Judah, and took them.

13 In the fourteenth year of King Hezeki'ah Sennach'erib king of Assyria came up against all the fortified cities of Judah and

---

d) Sennacherib's Campaign (18:13–19:37)

This narrative, with occasional omissions and insertions, is found also in Isa. 36:1–39:8. It was taken from here and added to the first half of Isaiah in order to provide there the account of additional incidents in the life and work of the prophet. The present text is composed of three separate and independent accounts. These are 18:13-16; 18:17–19:8 (or 9a); 19:9 (or 9b) -35, while vss. 36-37 form the conclusion of the second section, into which the third section has been interpolated.

The first section is an annalistic account of the invasion of Sennacherib which ended in Hezekiah's submission. The second section tells of an attempt of the Assyrians to secure the surrender of Jerusalem by a mixture of threats, promises, and a parade of force. Isaiah strengthens the king's will to resistance, promises that the city will be safe because the Assyrian king will suddenly raise the siege at the receipt of bad news, return home, and there meet with a violent death. The sequel to this is detailed in vss. 36-37. The third section follows the course of the second in general outline, but with marked differences. This time Sennacherib communicates with Hezekiah by letter and there is no parade of force. The substance of the letter is the utter hopelessness of Hezekiah's resistance, on the ground that none of the gods of the rebel states which Sennacherib has been subduing for the four years since his accession have been able to save their people. Neither, says he, can the God of the people of Judah save his people. Hezekiah prays in the temple, and Isaiah intervenes. The Assyrian's letter is an insult to the Lord, the God of Judah. Then follows a taunt song against Assyria (19:21-31) which is from an independent source. The conclusion of the account is that the Lord himself takes action on behalf of Jerusalem and slays the Assyrians that night in their camp to the number of 185,000.

(1) The Annalist's Account (18:13-16)

Hezekiah surrenders to the Assyrian king while the latter has his headquarters at Lachish. The Assyrian king imposes a heavy indemnity, which Hezekiah pays at the cost of clearing both the temple and the royal treasuries and stripping the gold from the door and doorposts of the temple. This account is very close in detail to Sennacherib's own account on the Taylor Cylinder (Burney, *Notes on Hebrew Text of Kings*, pp. 377-79, where a translation of the relevant portion is given). He captured 46 cities of Judah, and took over 200,000 captives, in addition to a huge number of cattle and beasts of every kind. Hezekiah had to pay an indemnity of 800 talents of silver (M.T. says 300) and 30 talents of gold, a total of $2,500,000.

13. The chronology is again at fault. The year was 701 B.C., the twenty-fourth year of Hezekiah's reign. The fourteenth year of his reign was probably the year of his almost fatal sickness (20:1-19).

---

trust in the Lord. This policy was urged by Isaiah (28:16-21) and the few who stood with him. It was natural that Hezekiah should vacillate, beset as he was by such terrific dangers. At first he yielded (vss. 13-14), hoping that Sennacherib could be bought off by giving him treasure. The Assyrian, however, was not appeased and demanded the unconditional surrender of Jerusalem. The story of the parleys between the two occupies the rest of this chapter. The Assyrian envoy made out a strong case

for surrender: resistance was impossible; trust in the Lord their God would not save them. It was an apparently unanswerable argument. And the Judean messengers answered him not a word: for the king's commandment was, . . . Answer him not (vs. 36).

So the issue was joined. Once more it was David confronting Goliath. According to any human calculation, the overwhelming odds were with the Assyrians. What hope indeed had this little community that it could withstand the

14 And Hezekiah king of Judah sent to the king of Assyria to Lachish, saying, I have offended; return from me: that which thou puttest on me will I bear. And the king of Assyria appointed unto Hezekiah king of Judah three hundred talents of silver and thirty talents of gold.

15 And Hezekiah gave *him* all the silver that was found in the house of the LORD, and in the treasures of the king's house.

16 At that time did Hezekiah cut off *the gold from* the doors of the temple of the LORD, and *from* the pillars which Hezekiah king of Judah had overlaid, and gave it to the king of Assyria.

17 ¶ And the king of Assyria sent Tartan and Rabsaris and Rab-shakeh from Lachish to king Hezekiah with a great host against

took them. 14 And Hezeki'ah king of Judah sent to the king of Assyria at Lachish, saying, "I have done wrong; withdraw from me; whatever you impose on me I will bear." And the king of Assyria required of Hezeki'ah king of Judah three hundred talents of silver and thirty talents of gold. 15 And Hezeki'ah gave him all the silver that was found in the house of the LORD, and in the treasuries of the king's house. 16 At that time Hezeki'ah stripped the gold from the doors of the temple of the LORD, and from the doorposts which Hezeki'ah king of Judah had overlaid and gave it to the king of Assyria. 17 And the king of Assyria sent the Tartan, the Rab'saris, and the

---

16. The statement that Hezekiah had overlaid the doors and the doorposts with gold can scarcely be accurate. The name is an error, possibly for Solomon, but more probably for Azariah-Uzziah, since the gold which Solomon had used in the glorification of the temple had gone long since in tribute and indemnities to foreign conquerors.

(2) THE FIRST STORY OF HEZEKIAH'S DELIVERANCE (18:17–19:9a)

The Assyrian king sends his chief officials from Lachish to secure Hezekiah's surrender. They ask for the king, who dispatches his chief officials to meet them. The Assyrian chief minister seeks to show Hezekiah's officials how futile their opposition is. If they are relying upon Pharaoh's promises, they ought to know by this time the worth of such promises. If they are relying upon the Lord, can they reasonably expect assistance from him when Hezekiah has destroyed his shrines and altars? He proposes terms for surrender and ends by saying that the Lord himself has bid him destroy Judah. When the officials ask him to speak in Aramaic so that the people of Jerusalem will not be able to understand, the Assyrian becomes abusive and vulgar, and makes a direct appeal to the common people, promising them peace and quietness in a pleasant land like their own. But they follow the request of their own leaders and make no response. When Hezekiah hears all this, he dresses in sackcloth and sends for Isaiah, who reassures him, tells him that the Lord will stand no impertinence from the Assyrian king. This king will hear bad news from home, will suddenly raise the siege, and when he gets home will die a violent death.

17. In the M.T. **Tartan and Rabsaris and Rab-shakeh** are treated as proper names. Actually they are the titles of Assyrian officials, and the words are rightly so translated in the RSV.

This **conduit of the upper pool, which is on the highway to the Fuller's Field,** is mentioned also in Isa. 7:3 as the place where Isaiah the prophet warned Ahaz of the

---

might of Assyria? There is no verbal or rational answer to that question. Therefore the people held their peace. The answer lies deeper than reason. It lies in moral forces, spiritual resources which are invisible, incalculable according to any outward appearance or measurement. The Assyrians left God out of the reckoning. And that factor turned the balance and was decisive. It is always so. The weakest people, the solitary

individual without apparent means of resistance, yet linked with God, his truth and righteousness, can withstand secular pressure however strong. How often has this issue been joined in history and experience. And always the result has been the same. Babylon and all that it stands for is gone and gone forever. Jerusalem and all it stands for lives and will live forever. Precisely so in individual experience. Here is

Jerusalem: and they went up and came to Jerusalem. And when they were come up, they came and stood by the conduit of the upper pool, which *is* in the highway of the fuller's field.

18 And when they had called to the king, there came out to them Eliakim the son of Hilkiah, which *was* over the household, and Shebna the scribe, and Joah the son of Asaph the recorder.

19 And Rab-shakeh said unto them, Speak ye now to Hezekiah, Thus saith the great king, the king of Assyria, What confidence *is* this wherein thou trustest?

20 Thou sayest, (but *they are but* vain words,) *I have* counsel and strength for the war. Now on whom dost thou trust, that thou rebellest against me?

21 Now, behold, thou trustest upon the staff of this bruised reed, *even* upon Egypt, on which if a man lean, it will go into his hand, and pierce it: so *is* Pharaoh king of Egypt unto all that trust on him.

22 But if ye say unto me, We trust in the LORD our God: *is* not that he, whose high places and whose altars Hezekiah hath

Rab'shakeh with a great army from Lachish to King Hezeki'ah at Jerusalem. And they went up and came to Jerusalem. When they arrived, they came and stood by the conduit of the upper pool, which is on the highway to the Fuller's Field. 18 And when they called for the king, there came out to them Eli'akim the son of Hilki'ah, who was over the household, and Shebnah the secretary, and Jo'ah the son of Asaph, the recorder.

19 And the Rab'shakeh said to them, "Say to Hezeki'ah, 'Thus says the great king, the king of Assyria: On what do you rest this confidence of yours? 20 You think that mere words are counsel and strength for war! On whom do you now rely, that you have rebelled against me? 21 Behold, you are relying now on Egypt, that broken reed of a staff, which will pierce the hand of any man who leans on it. Such is Pharaoh king of Egypt to all who rely on him. 22 But if you say to me, "We rely on the LORD our God," is it not he whose high places and

folly of seeking help from Assyria. The site has not been certainly located, but it was probably a conduit which brought the water supply from the Virgin's Pool, the modern 'Ain Sittī Maryam, to the Pool of Siloam within the city. The water supply was always a problem in the defense of the city, and the Virgin's Pool is the only continuous water supply within easy reach of the city. Hezekiah built an underground conduit in order to make the supply more secure (cf. 20:20).

20-21. The difficulty of vs. 20 may be judged from the differences in the renderings of the KJV and the RSV. The better interpretation is that of the RSV, emphasizing the folly in trusting the words of Egypt as support against Assyria. The willingness to rely upon the promises of Egypt was the fatal error of the statesmen of Judah for generation after generation. The Pharaohs and their successors of the Greek period, the Ptolemies, were always ready to stir up trouble in Palestine for Assyrian, Babylonian, Persian, Greek, whoever happened to be the dominant power in western Asia. They usually promised help but rarely fulfilled their promises, and each time Judah suffered. In this particular instance there is evidence that Pharaoh actually did send an army, which the Assyrians defeated at Eltekeh. It was this defeat, involving the end of his hopes of relief, that forced Hezekiah to surrender to the Assyrians (vs. 14).

22. There is no reason to suppose that Sennacherib and his advisers were unaware of Hezekiah's abolition and destruction of images and shrines during the years of

one born in Judea, with simple faith in God, in moral standards of conduct in which he has been reared. He is confronted by modern Assyrians who mock at all that, bring arguments to bear from secular sources upon these simple and naïve ideals. And they make out a strong case. Jerusalem is apparently at the mercy of

Assyria. What now is the man of Judea to do? Let him keep silent. Argument against the Assyrian rarely carries the day. The real answer to the Assyrian is not in words, but in life. Faith, ideals, standards of righteous conduct, these when incorporated in human character are their own argument and defense. The life

taken away, and hath said to Judah and Jerusalem, Ye shall worship before this altar in Jerusalem?

23 Now therefore, I pray thee, give pledges to my lord the king of Assyria, and I will deliver thee two thousand horses, if thou be able on thy part to set riders upon them.

24 How then wilt thou turn away the face of one captain of the least of my master's servants, and put thy trust on Egypt for chariots and for horsemen?

25 Am I now come up without the LORD against this place to destroy it? The LORD said to me, Go up against this land, and destroy it.

26 Then said Eliakim the son of Hilkiah, and Shebna, and Joah, unto Rab-shakeh, Speak, I pray thee, to thy servants in the Syrian language; for we understand *it:* and talk not with us in the Jews' language in the ears of the people that *are* on the wall.

27 But Rab-shakeh said unto them, Hath my master sent me to thy master, and to thee, to speak these words? *hath he* not *sent*

altars Hezeki'ah has removed, saying to Judah and to Jerusalem, "You shall worship before this altar in Jerusalem"? 23 Come now, make a wager with my master the king of Assyria: I will give you two thousand horses, if you are able on your part to set riders upon them. 24 How then can you repulse a single captain among the least of my master's servants, when you rely on Egypt for chariots and for horsemen? 25 Moreover, is it without the LORD that I have come up against this place to destroy it? The LORD said to me, Go up against this land, and destroy it.' "

26 Then Eli'akim the son of Hilki'ah, and Shebnah, and Jo'ah, said to the Rab'-shakeh, "Pray, speak to your servants in the Aramaic language, for we understand it; do not speak to us in the language of Judah within the hearing of the people who are on the wall." 27 But the Rab'shakeh said to them, "Has my master sent me to speak these words to your master and to you, and

---

independence which followed the revolt of 705 B.C. The suggestion that Hezekiah had gone so far as actually to seek to centralize the worship at Jerusalem is due to the narrator of this prophetic narrative rather than to the Assyrian envoys themselves, but the general argument against his destructive reforms may well have been a contemporary one, and it might easily have been effective.

23. The chief minister tells Hezekiah's officials that they stand no chance whatever against the Assyrian armies. Even if Judah had **two thousand horses,** she could not supply the **riders.**

24. Most authorities omit the word **captain** for reasons of syntax. The Hebrew is certainly made more normal by the omission, but the idea is far from easy to express in Hebrew. The second part of the verse is uncertain. Probably read, "How then can you repulse a single captain among the least of my master's servants? And so you have relied [no wonder you have relied] on Egypt for chariots and horsemen."

25. Cyrus is stated to have said this when he attacked Babylon. Both he and Sennacherib may have honestly believed what they said. That a conqueror or ambitious leader of any kind should believe devoutly that he has a special mission from the Almighty is not a phenomenon exclusive to Assyria and Persia.

26. Aramaic was the language in general use in western Asia in diplomatic and commercial circles. It was not at this period understood by the common people of Judah, though after the Exile it became the common speech of Palestine. The Judahite court officials ask the Assyrian vizier to speak in Aramaic, not in Hebrew, whereupon the

---

of sophistication and experimentalism ends inevitably in disillusionment and often in disaster. But the life that is true to fixed standards of morals and conduct grows year by year in the realization of the solid and permanent

satisfactions of life. If when all seems dark, when teachers perplex and friends mock him, one will still cling obstinately to moral good, his night will become day, and he will know those blessings which come only as the reward of fidelity.

me to the men which sit on the wall, that they may eat their own dung, and drink their own piss with you?

28 Then Rab-shakeh stood and cried with a loud voice in the Jews' language, and spake, saying, Hear the word of the great king, the king of Assyria:

29 Thus saith the king, Let not Hezekiah deceive you: for he shall not be able to deliver you out of his hand:

30 Neither let Hezekiah make you trust in the LORD, saying, The LORD will surely deliver us, and this city shall not be delivered into the hand of the king of Assyria.

31 Hearken not to Hezekiah: for thus saith the king of Assyria, Make *an agreement* with me by a present, and come out to me, and *then* eat ye every man of his own vine, and every one of his fig tree, and drink ye every one the waters of his cistern:

32 Until I come and take you away to a land like your own land, a land of corn and wine, a land of bread and vineyards, a land of oil olive and of honey, that ye may live, and not die: and hearken not unto Hezekiah, when he persuadeth you, saying, The LORD will deliver us.

33 Hath any of the gods of the nations delivered at all his land out of the hand of the king of Assyria?

34 Where *are* the gods of Hamath, and of Arpad? where *are* the gods of Sepharvaim, Hena, and Ivah? have they delivered Samaria out of mine hand?

35 Who *are* they among all the gods of the countries, that have delivered their country out of mine hand, that the LORD should deliver Jerusalem out of mine hand?

36 But the people held their peace, and answered him not a word: for the king's commandment was, saying, Answer him not.

37 Then came Eliakim the son of Hilkiah, which *was* over the household, and Shebna the scribe, and Joah the son of Asaph the recorder, to Hezekiah with *their* clothes rent, and told him the words of Rab-shakeh.

not to the men sitting on the wall, who are doomed with you to eat their own dung and to drink their own urine?"

28 Then the Rab'shakeh stood and called out in a loud voice in the language of Judah: "Hear the word of the great king, the king of Assyria! 29 Thus says the king: 'Do not let Hezeki'ah deceive you, for he will not be able to deliver you out of my hand. 30 Do not let Hezeki'ah make you to rely on the LORD by saying, The LORD will surely deliver us, and this city will not be given into the hand of the king of Assyria.' 31 Do not listen to Hezeki'ah; for thus says the king of Assyria: 'Make your peace with me and come out to me; then every one of you will eat of his own vine, and every one of his own fig tree, and every one of you will drink the water of his own cistern; 32 until I come and take you away to a land like your own land, a land of grain and wine, a land of bread and vineyards, a land of olive trees and honey, that you may live, and not die. And do not listen to Hezeki'ah when he misleads you by saying, The LORD will deliver us. 33 Has any of the gods of the nations ever delivered his land out of the hand of the king of Assyria? 34 Where are the gods of Hamath and Arpad? Where are the gods of Sepharva'im, Hena, and Ivvah? Have they delivered Samar'ia out of my hand? 35 Who among all the gods of the countries have delivered their countries out of my hand, that the LORD should deliver Jerusalem out of my hand?' "

36 But the people were silent and answered him not a word, for the king's command was, "Do not answer him." 37 Then Eli'akim the son of Hilki'ah, who was over the household, and Shebna the secretary, and Jo'ah the son of Asaph, the recorder, came to Hezeki'ah with their clothes rent, and told him the words of the Rab'shakeh.

Assyrian becomes thoroughly offensive, and makes a direct appeal to the common people who are standing on the city wall.

34. These are all Syrian cities which had been reconquered by Sennacherib during his third campaign. **Sepharvaim** here is the Syrian city of Shabarain, originally captured by Shalmaneser IV (cf. Ezek. 47:16). It is best to follow Lucian and the O.L. and to insert "Where are the gods of Samaria?"

19 And it came to pass, when king Hezekiah heard *it*, that he rent his clothes, and covered himself with sackcloth, and went into the house of the LORD.

2 And he sent Eliakim, which *was* over the household, and Shebna the scribe, and the elders of the priests, covered with sackcloth, to Isaiah the prophet the son of Amoz.

3 And they said unto him, Thus saith Hezekiah, This day *is* a day of trouble, and of rebuke, and blasphemy: for the children are come to the birth, and *there is* not strength to bring forth.

19 When King Hezeki'ah heard it, he rent his clothes, and covered himself with sackcloth, and went into the house of the LORD. **2** And he sent Eli'akim, who was over the household, and Shebna the secretary, and the senior priests, covered with sackcloth, to the prophet Isaiah the son of Amoz. **3** They said to him, "Thus says Hezeki'ah, This day is a day of distress, of rebuke, and of disgrace; children have come to the birth, and there is no strength to

---

19:1-7. At last the king and his counselers listen to Isaiah, who has all along been against the alliance with Egypt and all that it implied in rebellion against the Assyrian king (Isa. 30:1-7, 15; 31:1-9). Further, it is Shebna, of all people, who is one of the group which comes to Isaiah (cf. Isa. 22:15-19). Isaiah was fearful lest a rebellion against Assyria should involve the end of the Davidic dynasty and the establishment of a province of Judea. So long as there was a king in Judah, however weak, there was always the chance of a revival, both national and religious, when the power of the conqueror

---

19:1. The Sanctuary.—The people had rent their clothes on hearing the defiant summons to surrender Jerusalem, and when word was brought to King Hezekiah he too tore off his clothes **and covered himself with sackcloth.** For whence could he look for salvation at such a critical hour? See now what Hezekiah did. He tells us all what to do in any time of trouble.

The first thing that Hezekiah did was to go straight **into the house of the LORD.** He took his burden into the sanctuary. And that is what the house of the Lord is for. It is a place of refuge for the harassed soul of man beset with danger from which he sees no escape. How many since the day of Hezekiah have done the same thing, and have found deliverance there! In Ps. 73:16-17 we read of a poor man who was bowed down, bowled over by misfortune and injustice. It was quite too much for him. When he tried to understand it, he became perplexed and bewildered: *until* he "went into the sanctuary of God." Then his burden was lifted; then he came to understand what it all meant; then his vision became clear; then his knowledge of God's encompassing love became strong. There he found rest for his soul, and out of this experience he wrote the psalm which begins and ends in the note of faith and thanksgiving. So it is with men today. So long as all goes well with them they may pass by the sanctuary and give it no place in their lives. But let sorrow come, or danger, let life prove too much for them and failure bring pride to the ground, then they

flee for refuge, just as Hezekiah did, to the house of the Lord. It stands there always, ready to receive them. The church is "the mother of us all" (Gal. 4:26). It is ready to receive its children in every time of need.

2-3. A Man of God.—The next thing that Hezekiah did was to turn to Isaiah. He had at his side a man of God. At such an hour others— politicians, princes, secular advisers—were not what he needed. He needed one who would not give him counsels of expediency, suggest political maneuvering according to the winds that blew. He needed one who would speak with the authority that comes only from fellowship with God and thus with knowledge of the will of God. So he asked Isaiah to help him. And many a man does the same thing today. When critical emergencies occur his deepest need is not for well-meaning, sagacious friends who may suggest ways and means out of his difficulties. His deepest need is for some man of God whose judgment pierces beneath outward circumstance and rests upon the deeper principles of the will and love of God, his power to direct and to save. This man of God may be no ordained priest or prophet. But always he is one who can be trusted to interpret and to utter the hidden counsels of God. Yet he may be a humble parish minister, not gifted perhaps in other ways, but endowed with spiritual wisdom. "It is a good thing," a woman once said, "to have a minister to whom to turn; for one never knows what may happen." To be such a counselor is to play a

4 It may be the LORD thy God will hear all the words of Rab-shakeh, whom the king of Assyria his master hath sent to reproach the living God; and will reprove the words which the LORD thy God hath heard: wherefore lift up *thy* prayer for the remnant that are left.

5 So the servants of king Hezekiah came to Isaiah.

6 ¶ And Isaiah said unto them, Thus shall ye say to your master, Thus saith the LORD, Be not afraid of the words which thou hast heard, with which the servants of the king of Assyria have blasphemed me.

7 Behold, I will send a blast upon him, and he shall hear a rumor, and shall return to his own land; and I will cause him to fall by the sword in his own land.

8 ¶ So Rab-shakeh returned, and found the king of Assyria warring against Libnah: for he had heard that he was departed from Lachish.

9 And when he heard say of Tirhakah

bring them forth. 4 It may be that the LORD your God heard all the words of the Rab'-shakeh, whom his master the king of Assyria has sent to mock the living God, and will rebuke the words which the LORD your God has heard; therefore lift up your prayer for the remnant that is left." 5 When the servants of King Hezeki'ah came to Isaiah, 6 Isaiah said to them, "Say to your master, 'Thus says the LORD: Do not be afraid because of the words that you have heard, with which the servants of the king of Assyria have reviled me. 7 Behold, I will put a spirit in him, so that he shall hear a rumor and return to his own land; and I will cause him to fall by the sword in his own land.' "

8 The Rab'shakeh returned, and found the king of Assyria fighting against Libnah; for he heard that the king had left Lachish. 9 And when the king heard concerning

---

should come to an end. Fortunately Judah was saved on this occasion, though only at the last extremity, and Sennacherib's difficulties elsewhere did not allow him the time to besiege Jerusalem until he actually conquered the city. He was therefore willing to accept Hezekiah's submission and to leave him once more as a subject king. Judah learned her lesson at this time, and she steadfastly refused to join in any other move of the western kinglets against the Assyrian overlord.

7. The rendering **I will send a blast upon him** is not good. It is due to the influence of vs. 35. The meaning is that God will cause the Assyrian king to be driven by a *rûaḥ* (spirit) which he cannot control, so that he will leave Jerusalem inviolate and return to Assyria. It will be a spirit of fear and concern, due to a rumor which he has heard. The word *rûaḥ* is here used in its psychological sense of a dominating impulse which decides a man's actions almost in spite of himself (cf. Exeg. on I Kings 10:5).

9a. The rumor is interpreted to be news of the advance of **Tirhakah king of**

---

great role in the human drama. In many a beleaguered Jerusalem today there stands an Isaiah to whom men and women know they can turn in time of need.

4-7. The Power of Prayer.—Hezekiah, then, through his emissaries told Isaiah how affairs stood. Was it possible that the God of Isaiah, **the LORD thy God,** would hear the taunts of the Assyrians and answer them? Human wisdom did not know how to answer; but would the Lord know what to say? **Wherefore lift up thy prayer.** Here is expressed faith in the intercessory prayer of one whose heart was right toward God. However skeptical one may be about the efficacy of one's own prayers, there remains nethermost in the hearts of most men an inarticulate, unreasoned, but inextinguish-

able faith in the prayers of a man of God. So Tennyson has written in his "Morte d'Arthur":

Pray for my soul. More things are wrought by prayer
Than this world dreams of. Wherefore, let thy voice
Rise like a fountain for me night and day.

. . . .
For so the whole round earth is every way
Bound by gold chains about the feet of God.

Then came to Hezekiah from Isaiah the astounding announcement, **Be not afraid.** The Lord had heard the blasphemies of the Assyrians. He would answer and confound them. Hezekiah had only to stand firm. (For the nature of this prophetic inspiration see Expos. on 7:1-2, 6-7.)

8-13. Cf. Expos. on 18:7-37.

king of Ethiopia, Behold, he is come out to fight against thee; he sent messengers again unto Hezekiah, saying,

10 Thus shall ye speak to Hezekiah king of Judah, saying, Let not thy God in whom thou trustest deceive thee, saying, Jerusalem shall not be delivered into the hand of the king of Assyria.

11 Behold, thou hast heard what the kings of Assyria have done to all lands, by destroying them utterly: and shalt thou be delivered?

12 Have the gods of the nations delivered them which my fathers have destroyed; *as* Gozan, and Haran, and Rezeph, and the children of Eden which *were* in Thelasar?

13 Where *is* the king of Hamath, and the king of Arpad, and the king of the city of Sepharvaim, of Hena, and Ivah?

Tirha'kah king of Ethiopia, "Behold, he has set out to fight against you," he sent messengers again to Hezeki'ah, saying, **10** "Thus shall you speak to Hezeki'ah king of Judah: 'Do not let your God on whom you rely deceive you by promising that Jerusalem will not be given into the hand of the king of Assyria. **11** Behold, you have heard what the kings of Assyria have done to all lands, destroying them utterly. And shall you be delivered? **12** Have the gods of the nations delivered them, the nations which my fathers destroyed, Gozan, Haran, Rezeph, and the people of Eden who were in Tel-assar? **13** Where is the king of Hamath, the king of Arpad, the king of the city of Sepharva'im, the king of Hena, or the king of Ivvah?' "

Ethiopia. This man was first a general of Pharaoh Shabaka, the second pharaoh of the Twenty-fifth (Ethiopian) Dynasty, whom he succeeded in 691 B.C. It is not easy to explain why the rumor of his approach should send Sennacherib posthaste back to Assyria. Further, it is on record that the Assyrian king defeated Pharaoh and his allies at the Battle of Eltekeh in 701 B.C. It is much more likely that the rumor which he heard was that Babylon, whom he had subdued before he marched west in 703 B.C., had once more broken out in rebellion. This did indeed actually take place, and while the revolt was suppressed easily enough, Sennacherib was kept busy fighting in the east for many years (see Oesterley and Robinson, *History of Israel*, I, 397-400, where a full discussion of the historical problems of these narratives is to be found). He undertook an expedition against the Edomites and the Arabs in 691 B.C., but there was no need for him to advance into Palestine again.

(3) DELIVERANCE OF JERUSALEM (19:9b-35)

This is the third of the three accounts. The narrative is best regarded as being wholly independent of what precedes it. The Assyrian king sends a letter to Hezekiah, pointing out how foolish it is for him to expect his God to deliver him since none of the other gods of the nations had been able to save their cities and peoples. Hezekiah takes the letter into the temple and spreads it out for the Lord to read. The message comes to the king through Isaiah, who promises divine aid and speedy relief. That night there is a huge slaughter in the Assyrian camp, and the siege is raised.

12. The name **Gozan** appears as the name of a river in 17:6. **Haran** is the Harran of the Assyrian inscriptions, the Charrae of the Romans, and it was the chief trading city of northwest Mesopotamia. It was situated on the river Balîkh, a tributary of the Euphrates, the next tributary west of the Khâbûr (cf. Exeg. on 17:6), and it was in the same latitude as the Gulf of Issus, the modern Alexandretta. There are many sites named **Rezeph** (*Ra-ṣa-ap-pa*), but this place was on the road from Harran to Palmyra, one day's journey south of the Euphrates. The expression **children of Eden** refers to the Aramaean state known as Bit-'Adinni, north of the Euphrates and in the neighborhood of Harran. The site of **Telassar** is unknown, but it was probably the chief city of this Aramaean state.

13. These names are found also in 18:34, but the **Sepharvaim** of this verse is the Syrian city, not the twin Mesopotamian cities of 17:24. The site of **Hena** is unknown.

14 ¶ And Hezekiah received the letter of the hand of the messengers, and read it: and Hezekiah went up into the house of the LORD, and spread it before the LORD.

15 And Hezekiah prayed before the LORD, and said, O LORD God of Israel, which dwellest *between* the cherubim, thou art the God, *even* thou alone, of all the kingdoms of the earth; thou hast made heaven and earth.

16 LORD, bow down thine ear, and hear: open, LORD, thine eyes, and see: and hear the words of Sennacherib, which hath sent him to reproach the living God.

17 Of a truth, LORD, the kings of Assyria have destroyed the nations and their lands,

18 And have cast their gods into the fire: for they *were* no gods, but the work of men's hands, wood and stone: therefore they have destroyed them.

19 Now therefore, O LORD our God, I beseech thee, save thou us out of his hand, that all the kingdoms of the earth may know that thou *art* the LORD God, *even* thou only.

14 Hezeki'ah received the letter from the hand of the messengers, and read it; and Hezeki'ah went up to the house of the LORD, and spread it before the LORD. 15 And Hezeki'ah prayed before the LORD, and said: "O LORD the God of Israel, who art enthroned above the cherubim, thou art the God, thou alone, of all the kingdoms of the earth; thou hast made heaven and earth. 16 Incline thy ear, O LORD, and hear; open thy eyes, O LORD, and see; and hear the words of Sennach'erib, which he has sent to mock the living God. 17 Of a truth, O LORD, the kings of Assyria have laid waste the nations and their lands, 18 and have cast their gods into the fire; for they were no gods, but the work of men's hands, wood and stone; therefore they were destroyed. 19 So now, O LORD our God, save us, I beseech thee, from his hand, that all the kingdoms of the earth may know that thou, O LORD, art God alone."

14. Hezekiah would actually **spread** the letter out **before the LORD,** unrolling the little scroll so that it could be read. The action would have, according to the ideas of the time, a more than symbolic meaning. He would actually be expecting the Lord to read it.

15. The place between the outstretched wings of the cherubim who were above the oracle was regarded as being the particular place where the presence of the invisible God was localized (cf. I Kings 6:23).

16. The phrase **the living God** is Deuteronomic (Deut. 5:26). It does not emphasize the fact that God is alive—that would be assumed by the Hebrew without any argument—but that he is alive to vindicate his holy Name and to save his people Israel (cf. Josh. 3:10; I Sam. 17:26, 36).

18. The contrast between the Lord and the gods of wood and stone, who are not gods at all, is frequent in Deuteronomy and in Second Isaiah. It belongs to the last days of the Judahite kingdom, and it received great emphasis among the exiles in Babylon because of their idolatrous environment. The faithful were driven for very faith's sake into a firm and rigorous monotheism.

14-19. The Religion of Experience.—When Hezekiah received the pronouncement of Isaiah, he went right back to the house of the Lord and spread it all out before God. Then he offered his own prayer. Any soul so surcharged with grief and gratitude must do just that. Such prayer cannot be suppressed. It wells up from the depths and issues as the inmost utterance of one's being. Note the order of this true prayer. It began in adoration, it went on to supplication, it ended in intercession that all the kingdoms of the earth may know that thou art the LORD God, even thou only.

Thus out of this experience religion had become a real thing to Hezekiah. And many other people have made the same discovery. Religion has been to them a matter of tradition, of custom, but it has not been a personal, vital, inward experience. Then has come danger. They find themselves facing some crisis in life. They pray for deliverance. They make test of God's power and love. However that prayer may be answered, God has become to them a reality. And thereafter religion is for them deeper, vital and real than ever it had been. Thus they know a closer walk with God. Religion such as

20 ¶ Then Isaiah the son of Amoz sent to Hezekiah, saying, Thus saith the LORD God of Israel, *That* which thou hast prayed to me against Sennacherib king of Assyria I have heard.

21 This *is* the word that the LORD hath spoken concerning him; The virgin the daughter of Zion hath despised thee, *and* laughed thee to scorn; the daughter of Jerusalem hath shaken her head at thee.

22 Whom hast thou reproached and blasphemed? and against whom hast thou exalted *thy* voice, and lifted up thine eyes on high? *even* against the Holy *One* of Israel.

23 By thy messengers thou hast reproached the Lord, and hast said, With the multitude of my chariots I am come up to the height of the mountains, to the sides of Lebanon, and will cut down the tall cedar trees thereof, *and* the choice fir trees thereof: and I will enter into the lodgings of his borders, *and into* the forest of his Carmel.

24 I have digged and drunk strange waters, and with the sole of my feet have I dried up all the rivers of besieged places.

20 Then Isaiah the son of Amoz sent to Hezeki'ah, saying, "Thus says the LORD, the God of Israel: Your prayer to me about Sennach'erib king of Assyria I have heard.
21 This is the word that the LORD has spoken concerning him:

"She despises you, she scorns you —
     the virgin daughter of Zion;
she wags her head behind you —
     the daughter of Jerusalem.

22 "Whom have you mocked and reviled?
     Against whom have you raised your voice
and haughtily lifted your eyes?
     Against the Holy One of Israel!
23 By your messengers you have mocked the Lord,
     and you have said, 'With my many chariots
I have gone up the heights of the mountains,
     to the far recesses of Lebanon;
I felled its tallest cedars,
     its choicest cypresses;
I entered its farthest retreat,
     its densest forest.
24 I dug wells
     and drank foreign waters,
and I dried up with the sole of my foot
     all the streams of Egypt.'

21-28. This taunt song against Assyria is in the *qînāh* measure (3+2 meter) which, with its peculiar halting rhythm, is especially suitable for lamentation or satire.

21. The phrase **the virgin daughter of Zion** is common in writings of the period between Hezekiah and Jeremiah, when the continuance of Jerusalem as a city into which a foreign conqueror had never entered was more than once in danger. Zion is still the inviolate, unconquered city (cf. Lam. 1:15).

22. The phrase **the Holy One of Israel** is common in the writings of both First and Second Isaiah. It describes the uniqueness, the separateness, the awesomeness of the God of Israel, especially in respect of his righteous saving power.

23. It is better not to treat the word **Carmel** as a proper name, but actually to translate it (see RSV). The word is composed of the word כרם ("vineyard") with an afformative *lāmedh,* and it means a district of gardenlike fertility. The tract of country which answered most to this description was the Carmel, i.e., the ridge of Carmel, but here the reference seems to be to the most fertile district of **Lebanon.**

24. The M.T. has "and I will dry up," but it is much better to follow the LXX and the Vulg., which read different vowels, and to translate as a past, making the tense "a

---

that is born only out of experience. (Cf. Job 42:5.)

20-37. *The End of Sennacherib.*—The question of the historical character of the events narrated in this chapter must be left to the scholars. Not much of Judea was salvaged after

this invasion. But Jerusalem remained. What actually happened to Sennacherib's hosts we do not know. The account of their destruction may be legendary. What we do find here recorded, however, remains eternally true. Secular forces, however omnipotent they may seem to be, can

25 Hast thou not heard long ago *how* I have done it, *and* of ancient times that I have formed it? now have I brought it to pass, that thou shouldest be to lay waste fenced cities *into* ruinous heaps.

26 Therefore their inhabitants were of small power, they were dismayed and confounded; they were *as* the grass of the field, and *as* the green herb, *as* the grass on the housetops, and *as corn* blasted before it be grown up.

27 But I know thy abode, and thy going out, and thy coming in, and thy rage against me.

28 Because thy rage against me and thy tumult is come up into mine ears, therefore I will put my hook in thy nose, and my bridle in thy lips, and I will turn thee back by the way by which thou camest.

29 And this *shall be* a sign unto thee, Ye shall eat this year such things as grow of themselves, and in the second year that which springeth of the same; and in the third year sow ye, and reap, and plant vineyards, and eat the fruits thereof.

25 "Have you not heard
　　that I determined it long ago?
I planned from days of old
　　what now I bring to pass,
that you should turn fortified cities
　　into heaps of ruins,
26 while their inhabitants, shorn of strength,
　　are dismayed and confounded,
and have become like plants of the field,
　　and like tender grass,
like grass on the housetops;
　　blighted before it is grown?

27 "But I know your sitting down
　　and your going out and coming in,
　　and your raging against me.
28 Because you have raged against me
　　and your arrogance has come into my
　　　　ears,
I will put my hook in your nose
　　and my bit in your mouth,
and I will turn you back on the way
　　by which you came.

29 "And this shall be the sign for you: this year you shall eat what grows of itself, and in the second year what springs of the same; then in the third year sow, and reap, and plant vineyards, and eat their fruit.

perfect of certainty." Actually Sennacherib never invaded Egypt (see Exeg. on vss. 35-36). This adventure was left to his son and successor Esarhaddon (680-669 B.C.), who invaded Egypt in 671 B.C. and seized Memphis. The last word of the verse in the M.T. is **besieged places** (KJV), but the previous word, יארי, is used only of the Nile and its delta streams, so that there is no doubt that we should read מצרים (**Egypt**) for מצור (**besieged places,** "defense"), i.e., **all the streams of Egypt** (RSV).

25. The idea that the heathen conqueror can be the rod of the Lord's anger receives its classical expression in Isa. 10:5-11, where also the punishment of Assyria is prophesied on account of his arrogance and overweening pride (vss. 12-19).

26. The metaphor refers to the grass of the uncultivated land outside the city, here today and gone tomorrow (cf. Isa. 40:7; Matt. 6:30). The **tender grass** or **green herb** is the *deshe'*, the fresh young sweet grass which springs up after the latter rain (i.e., in March). For the **grass on the housetops,** which quickly dies in the summer heat. see Ps. 129:6. The rendering of the RSV involves an adjustment at the end of the verse, and the assumption of some confusion at the end of this verse and the beginning of the next, but it most probably represents the original. The reference to **corn** is due to the rendering of the Vulg.

28. The figure of the **hook** in the **nose** and the **bridle** in the **lips** (i.e., the bit in the mouth) refers to captured wild beasts. There is no evidence that this kind of thing was actually done to prisoners, though no one can say, either then or now, that this or that brutality is impossible.

29-31. The taunt song with its elegiac (*qînāh*) meter is followed by a prophecy wholly in prose. The substance of the passage is that there will be no true harvest until the third year. In the first year what harvest there is will be self-sown, and in the next

30 And the remnant that is escaped of the house of Judah shall yet again take root downward, and bear fruit upward.

31 For out of Jerusalem shall go forth a remnant, and they that escape out of mount Zion: the zeal of the LORD *of hosts* shall do this.

32 Therefore thus saith the LORD concerning the king of Assyria, He shall not come into this city, nor shoot an arrow there, nor come before it with shield, nor cast a bank against it.

33 By the way that he came, by the same shall he return, and shall not come into this city, saith the LORD.

34 For I will defend this city, to save it, for mine own sake, and for my servant David's sake.

35 ¶ And it came to pass that night, that the angel of the LORD went out, and smote in the camp of the Assyrians a hundred fourscore and five thousand: and when they arose early in the morning, behold, they *were* all dead corpses.

30 And the surviving remnant of the house of Judah shall again take root downward, and bear fruit upward; 31 for out of Jerusalem shall go forth a remnant, and out of Mount Zion a band of survivors. The zeal of the LORD will do this.

32 "Therefore thus says the LORD concerning the king of Assyria, He shall not come to this city or shoot an arrow there, or come before it with a shield or cast up a mound against it. 33 By the way that he came, by the same he shall return, and he shall not come into this city, says the LORD. 34 For I will defend this city to save it, for my own sake and for the sake of my servant David."

35 And that night the angel of the LORD went forth, and slew a hundred and eighty-five thousand in the camp of the Assyrians; and when men arose early in the morning,

---

year the harvest will be **what springs of the same,** i.e., what is self-sown from the previous year, the second year of self-sown crops. The Hebrew word so translated is otherwise unknown; according to the medieval scholar Abulwalid, it refers to what grows up from the roots of the previous crop.

30. Here we get that doctrine of the **remnant** which is set forth by Isaiah of Jerusalem (Isa. 10:20-22), though the word used here is "that which is escaped," not the term *she'ār,* which is used by Isaiah.

31. The phrase **the zeal of the LORD** is valuable and noteworthy in that it emphasizes and insists upon God's active interest and deliberate effectiveness in salvation. The deliverance and the renewed life of the people will not be due to any automatic working out of history, or to any natural or economic causes. It will be quite definitely the effective work of an active God.

32-34. This detailed statement bears every appearance of being a contemporary oracle drawn from the biography of Isaiah the prophet. Isaiah was confident that there would be no attack on Jerusalem. This deliverance, miraculous in its unexpectedness, was a vivid demonstration of the soundness of Isaiah's message that Israel's hope and salvation are to be found in the Lord alone (Isa. 30:15; 31:1-5; cf. Ps. 46). It bore good fruit in Isaiah's own day, but bad and bitter fruit a century later when it issued in a false confidence in themselves as the Lord's people and in the city itself as the site of the Lord's temple.

35-37. This wholesale slaughter of the Assyrian army is without any extrabiblical confirmation. It is scarcely to be expected that the Assyrian records would refer to it. There is, however, an Egyptian legend of an overwhelming defeat which Sennacherib suffered at the hands of the Egyptians. According to Herodotus (*History* II. 141), the Assyrian army was routed at Pelusium because their bowstrings and the thongs of their shields had been devoured overnight by an army of field mice. The details of this tradition have little in common with the biblical story except in the matter of the tremendous Assyrian losses, but it is difficult to account for such traditions, although they may have a common basis of fact. It may well be that Sennacherib did suffer a disastrous defeat

36 So Sennacherib king of Assyria departed, and went and returned, and dwelt at Nineveh.

37 And it came to pass, as he was worshipping in the house of Nisroch his god, that Adrammelech and Sharezer his sons smote him with the sword: and they escaped into the land of Armenia. And Esar-haddon his son reigned in his stead.

20 In those days was Hezekiah sick unto death. And the prophet Isaiah the son of Amoz came to him, and said unto him, Thus saith the LORD, Set thine house in order; for thou shalt die, and not live.

behold, these were all dead bodies. 36 Then Sennach'erib king of Assyria departed, and went home, and dwelt at Nin'eveh. 37 And as he was worshiping in the house of Nisroch his god, Adram'melech and Share'zer, his sons, slew him with the sword, and escaped into the land of Ararat. And Esarhad'don his son reigned in his stead.

20 In those days Hezeki'ah became sick and was at the point of death. And Isaiah the prophet the son of Amoz came to him, and said to him, "Thus says the LORD. 'Set your house in order; for you shall die,

---

in an attempted invasion of Egypt, if not in 701 B.C., at least in 691 B.C., when he made a successful campaign against Judah's southern neighbors. For the idea of **the angel of the LORD** as God's active agent in a destructive pestilence see II Sam. 24:16. The migration of rodents at a time of plague is a well-known fact.

Vss. 36-37 form the conclusion of the earlier prophetic narrative which ended at vs. 9a. The assassination of Sennacherib by his son is confirmed from Assyrian sources. There is also a statement quoted by Eusebius to the effect that this king was murdered by his son Adramelus (i.e., the **Adrammelech** of vs. 37), and was succeeded by Nergilus (i.e., Nergal-sharusur, the **Sharezer** of vs. 37; cf. Jer. 39:3, 13), who was executed by Axerdis (i.e., **Esarhaddon**).

36. The site of ancient **Nineveh** is across the river Tigris, on the east bank, opposite the modern Mosul. It had been an important city in the twelfth century B.C., but its rise to greatness as the capital of Assyria was due to Sennacherib. It continued to be the capital of the Assyrian Empire until the collapse of that empire at the death of Ashurbanipal in 626 B.C. It was finally destroyed in 612 B.C. This city came to stand in Hebrew lore as the type of heathendom, the enemy of God, and the last of all the heathen cities on which God could be expected to have mercy (cf. the book of Jonah).

37. The name **Nisroch** is not known, but there was a god named Nusku, a personification of fire. He it was who consumed the burnt offerings and transformed their smoke into an agreeable odor for the gods to smell. He was therefore the messenger of the gods, an intermediary between man and god. At Nippur he was worshiped in company with Ninurta and his spouse. At Ur, he and his wife Sadarnunna were the children of Sin the moon-god and Ningal, and all four were worshiped in Haran, where Ashurbanipal, conqueror and archaeologist, restored the temple of Nusku (Édouard Dhorme, *Les religions de Babylonie et d'Assyrie* [Paris: Presses universitaires de France, 1945; "Mana: Introduction à l'histoire des religions, I"], pp. 59-60, 111-12, etc.).

Ararat is the Assyrian Urartu, i.e., **Armenia**.

e) HEZEKIAH'S ILLNESS (20:1-11)

The king is seized with a fatal illness and is told by the prophet that his death is certain. Hezekiah prays to the Lord for a further lease of life on the grounds of his

---

never withstand the power of moral ideals. In this truth lies the inspiration of this chapter. The reader is reminded of Byron's immortal poem, "The Destruction of Sennacherib."

20:1. Must One Always Tell the Truth?—The dating of the two episodes recorded in this chapter must be left to the scholars (see Exeg.). Neither need the nature of Hezekiah's illness

detain us. All that we know is that he was **sick unto death.** When Isaiah heard of his illness, he came to him at once, for they were friends. Hezekiah was a young man, still in his thirties, and had everything to live for. Probably Hezekiah asked if he would get well. Isaiah answered truthfully that the king must die. This abrupt announcement seems unfeeling and **unwise.**

2 Then he turned his face to the wall, and prayed unto the LORD, saying,

3 I beseech thee, O LORD, remember now how I have walked before thee in truth and with a perfect heart, and have done *that which is* good in thy sight. And Hezekiah wept sore.

4 And it came to pass, afore Isaiah was gone out into the middle court, that the word of the LORD came to him, saying,

you shall not recover.' " 2 Then Hezeki'ah turned his face to the wall, and prayed to the LORD, saying, 3 "Remember now, O LORD, I beseech thee, how I have walked before thee in faithfulness and with a whole heart, and have done what is good in thy sight." And Hezeki'ah wept bitterly.

4 And before Isaiah had gone out of the middle court, the word of the LORD came

---

faithfulness and loyalty to the Lord. The prayer is answered favorably, and Hezekiah is given another fifteen years. Hezekiah asks for a sign that the oracle is true and the shadow goes back ten steps on the sundial of Ahaz.

The date of this incident has given rise to some considerable discussion, since it is closely connected with the date of Merodach-baladan's embassy. If vs. 12 is correct in saying that the apparent and declared reason for the embassy is Hezekiah's remarkable recovery, then it is probable that the date of the illness is 711 B.C. Merodach-baladan established himself as king of Babylonia in 721 B.C. and maintained his position till 710 B.C. He established himself for a few months once more in 702 B.C., but it is not generally thought that he was in a position to send embassies to the west at that time. This argument is precarious, but if we are to count back fifteen years from Hezekiah's death, then the date of his sickness must have been not later than 710 B.C., a time when Merodach-baladan would be seeking allies to help him withstand that onset of Sargon which swept him out of Babylon.

20:1. Set your house in order (lit., "command thy house") : This is the regular phrase for settling one's affairs in the face of death (cf. II Sam. 17:23).

3. The sentiment expressed in this verse is set forth more fully in the opening couplet of Hezekiah's prayer which has been inserted at this point in the parallel narrative in Isa. 38:10. An early death is the reward of the wicked. Added years and a long life are the reward of the righteous. As yet the Hebrew had no hope of any life beyond the grave. When this hope did arise, it was a development of the belief that justice must prevail for the individual in spite of the obvious disparity between good fortune and good deeds in this life. The fact that Hezekiah's prayer was granted became later a signal proof of the efficacy of the prayer of the righteous (cf. II Bar. 63:5).

4. The consonantal Hebrew text says that Isaiah had gone out as far as the middle city (i.e., between the upper and lower city). We know that there were two sections of the city (22:14), but there is no evidence of more than two sections. The Masoretes have corrected the written text with the instruction to read **court**, so that we must understand that Isaiah had gone no farther than **the middle court** (i.e., the courtyard of the palace).

Here we come upon the vexing question if under such circumstances the obligation of telling the truth is still binding. On this point the opinion of an outstanding American physician, Richard C. Cabot, is worth pondering. In an address delivered in 1902 before the Academy of Medicine in New York, he took the position that a lie by a doctor to his patient is never justifiable; that patients exhibit an astonishing power to withstand the full truth and an amazing immunity against its depressing effects; that a lie detected destroys a patient's confidence in the doctor, and that a lie by its poisonous effect on the medium of human intercourse does more

harm than speaking the truth would do. Probably Isaiah did Hezekiah more real good by telling him the truth than by deceiving him with false promises. For this threw the king right back upon God.

2-11. *Prayer and the Sick.*—Hezekiah **turned his face to the wall, and prayed.** Doubtless Isaiah prayed also. And prayer prevailed. The human diagnosis was correct. But this omitted the possibility of a spiritual cure: the immediate contact of the soul with God, the immediate impact of the life of God on soul and body. That prayer is a powerful agency in the healing of the sick is now generally admitted by medical

5 Turn again, and tell Hezekiah the captain of my people, Thus saith the LORD, the God of David thy father, I have heard thy prayer, I have seen thy tears: behold, I will heal thee: on the third day thou shalt go up unto the house of the LORD.

6 And I will add unto thy days fifteen years; and I will deliver thee and this city out of the hand of the king of Assyria; and I will defend this city for mine own sake, and for my servant David's sake.

7 And Isaiah said, Take a lump of figs. And they took and laid *it* on the boil, and he recovered.

8 ¶ And Hezekiah said unto Isaiah, What *shall be* the sign that the LORD will heal me, and that I shall go up into the house of the LORD the third day?

9 And Isaiah said, This sign shalt thou have of the LORD, that the LORD will do the thing that he hath spoken: shall the shadow go forward ten degrees, or go back ten degrees?

to him: 5 "Turn back, and say to Hezeki'ah the prince of my people, Thus says the LORD, the God of David your father: I have heard your prayer, I have seen your tears; behold, I will heal you; on the third day you shall go up to the house of the LORD. 6 And I will add fifteen years to your life. I will deliver you and this city out of the hand of the king of Assyria, and I will defend this city for my own sake and for my servant David's sake." 7 And Isaiah said, "Bring a cake of figs. And let them take and lay it on the boil, that he may recover."

8 And Hezeki'ah said to Isaiah, "What shall be the sign that the LORD will heal me, and that I shall go up to the house of the LORD on the third day?" 9 And Isaiah said, "This is the sign to you from the LORD, that the LORD will do the thing that he has promised: shall the shadow go forward ten

---

5. The phrase **the prince of my people** is not found in the parallel Isa. 38:5. It belongs to that later prophetic type of narrative which was far from being enamored of the kings and hesitated to admit that there could ever be any "king" over Israel apart from the Lord himself (cf. I Sam. 9:16; Ezek. 44:3) .

6. The fifteen added years in addition to the fourteen make a total of twenty-nine years, which agrees with 18:2. The reference to the deliverance from the Assyrian is due to the Deuteronomic compiler rather than to the author of the biography from which the narrative was taken in the first place. The verse contains phrases which are not in the parallel text in Isa. 38, so we must assume that the passage has been worked over by a later writer.

7. A poultice of **figs** was well known in the ancient world as a means of softening and opening hard boils and ulcers.

8-10. There are evidences here of a dislocation of the story, since there is no point in the giving of the sign when Hezekiah had already been cured. In Isa. 38:4-22, the sign comes first (vss. 7-8) and the healing afterward (vs. 21), though even there a request for a sign appears in vs. 22. Apart from this, the order in Isaiah is much to be preferred. Further, in the Isaiah form of the story the sign is given and no alternative is offered. This is also the situation in 20:9, where the Hebrew reads, "The shadow has gone ten steps." Evidently vs. 10, which assumes an alternative, is later and is due to a misunder-

---

science. Thus Alexis Carrel wrote: "I have seen men, after all other therapy had failed, lifted out of disease . . . by the serene effort of prayer. It is the only power in the world that seems to overcome the so-called 'laws of nature.' " [3] But note that Isaiah did not neglect *materia medica*. He applied first aid and laid figs on the diseased spot. A sick man needs two things which should

[3] "Prayer Is Power," *Reader's Digest*, XXXVIII (1941), p. 34; see pp. 33-36.

always go together: prayer and the doctor. Neither should exclude the other. They combine and co-operate in the healing of the sick. Yet Isaiah was careful to remind the king that it was not the figs but the Lord who healed him in answer to his prayer (vs. 5) . Two answered prayers in Hezekiah's life. Could he ever forget that?

When Hezekiah wanted proof that he was to recover, Isaiah suggested a miraculous setting back of the shadow on the sundial of Ahaz.

10 And Hezekiah answered, It is a light thing for the shadow to go down ten degrees: nay, but let the shadow return backward ten degrees.

11 And Isaiah the prophet cried unto the LORD: and he brought the shadow ten degrees backward, by which it had gone down in the dial of Ahaz.

12 ¶ At that time Berodach-baladan, the son of Baladan, king of Babylon, sent letters and a present unto Hezekiah: for he had heard that Hezekiah had been sick.

steps, or go back ten steps?" 10 And Hezeki'ah answered, "It is an easy thing for the shadow to lengthen ten steps; rather let the shadow go back ten steps." 11 And Isaiah the prophet cried to the LORD; and he brought the shadow back ten steps, by which the sung had declined on the dial of Ahaz.

12 At that time Mero'dach-bal'adan the son of Bal'adan, king of Babylon, sent envoys with letters and a present to Hezeki'ah; for he heard that Hezeki'ah had been sick.

g Syr See Is. 38. 8 and Tg: Heb lacks *the sun*

standing of the previous verse, which has indeed in the Hebrew been partly turned into an alternative, since it reads, "Or shall the shadow return?" Apparently the "or" (אם) was inserted in vs. 9 when vs. 10 was added.

11. The use of the word **dial** in the English versions raises the question as to whether there was indeed a properly constructed sundial. The Hebrew has "steps" at the end of the verse, just as there is a reference to steps in all three verses. It is by no means essential that there should have been any dial at all, but only some steps which Ahaz built which served as a rough-and-ready method of measuring the passing of the hours. On the other hand, rough and ready though the reckoning may have been, Ahaz may have built these steps for the very purpose of determining the time of the day, since such determination may have been needed for the proper observance of the cults which he introduced.

f) THE EMBASSY OF MERODACH-BALADAN (20:12-21)

Hezekiah receives this embassy with every mark of delight and shows them all his wealth and resources. Isaiah hears all this, rebukes the king, and prophesies the Babylonian exile. Hezekiah comforts himself with the thought that it will not happen in his lifetime.

The name **Berodach-baladan** is due to an error of transcription in the M.T. since everywhere else the name is spelled correctly. The accidental writing of *bêth* for *mêm* and vice versa is comparatively common, and in the older script was an easy error to make (S. R. Driver, *Notes on the Hebrew Text of the Books of Samuel* [2nd ed.; Oxford: Clarendon Press, 1913], p. lxvii) . Marduk-abal-idinna was king of a little principality in lower Mesopotamia, but always had great ambitions. During the troubles which attended the accession of Sargon in 721 B.C. this princeling seized Babylon and held it till 710 B.C. In that year Sargon, having restored the situation elsewhere, was free to turn to Babylon. Josephus says that the aim of the embassy was to secure Hezekiah as an ally (*Antiquities* X. 2. 2) . That is probably correct. It accounts for the fact that Hezekiah declared his resources, financial and military, to his visitors. The date of the embassy is generally held to be *ca.* 711 B.C., but there are difficulties still not resolved

Thus by outward sign was confirmed the turning back of the disease of the king. Whatever we think of this extraordinary incident, it points to a profound and often forgotten truth that God is not bound by what we call the laws of nature. He is a free moral agent at the heart of the universe, a self-governing and self-determining personality possessing freedom and initiative, not controlled by the universe but in a

real sense controlling and operating it; not limited by its laws except in so far as he chooses to be limited by them; not allowing perpetual variation on the suggestion of occasional moral contingencies, yet always governing according to the principles of his being.

12-21. Hezekiah's Transgression.—It is disquieting to find that Hezekiah, miraculously healed, so soon fell into such error as to merit

13 And Hezekiah hearkened unto them, and showed them all the house of his precious things, the silver, and the gold, and the spices, and the precious ointment, and *all* the house of his armor, and all that was found in his treasures: there was nothing in his house, nor in all his dominion, that Hezekiah showed them not.

14 ¶ Then came Isaiah the prophet unto king Hezekiah, and said unto him, What said these men? and from whence came they unto thee? And Hezekiah said, They are come from a far country, *even* from Babylon.

15 And he said, What have they seen in thine house? And Hezekiah answered, All *the things* that *are* in mine house have they seen: there is nothing among my treasures that I have not showed them.

16 And Isaiah said unto Hezekiah, Hear the word of the LORD.

17 Behold, the days come, that all that *is* in thine house, and that which thy fathers have laid up in store unto this day, shall be carried unto Babylon: nothing shall be left, saith the LORD.

13 And Hezeki'ah welcomed them, and he showed them all his treasure house, the silver, the gold, the spices, the precious oil, his armory, all that was found in his storehouses; there was nothing in his house or in all his realm that Hezeki'ah did not show them. 14 Then Isaiah the prophet came to King Hezeki'ah, and said to him, "What did these men say? And whence did they come to you?" And Hezeki'ah said, "They have come from a far country, from Babylon." 15 He said, "What have they seen in your house?" And Hezeki'ah answered, "They have seen all that is in my house; there is nothing in my storehouses that I did not show them."

16 Then Isaiah said to Hezeki'ah, "Hear the word of the LORD: 17 Behold, the days are coming, when all that is in your house, and that which your fathers have stored up till this day, shall be carried to Babylon;

and from many points of view there is something to be said for the date 702 B.C., following which Hezekiah actually did revolt (see, however, Exeg. on 20:1-11).

13. There is an error in the M.T., which has **And Hezekiah hearkened** [וישמע] **unto them.** The text should read, "And Hezekiah was glad [וישמח] of them" (so LXX, Vulg., Syriac, and the parallel Isa. 39:2, but cf. RSV). Hezekiah showed the messengers **all his treasure house.** This is a better rendering than **all the house of his precious things** (KJV), for the Assyrian phrase *bit nakanti*, which means "treasure house," is a near equivalent of the Hebrew phrase here used.

14. Isaiah, all his prophetic life the friend and counselor of kings, intervenes. He was always against any plots and policies which involved open hostilities with the sovereign power.

17. This prophecy of the captivity in Babylon is generally held to be due to the Deuteronomic editor rather than to the original biographer. Some scholars have thought that it is a reference to the captivity of Manasseh in Babylon (II Chr. 33:11-13). It may well be that Manasseh did find himself in difficulties if he took part in the revolt of *ca.* 647 B.C. of Shamashshumukin against the latter's brother, Ashurbanipal, who

the rebuke of Isaiah. If the incident here recorded occurred after Hezekiah's recovery, it reveals the sad fact often illustrated in human experience that deliverance from danger is in itself rarely the occasion of final resistance to fresh allurements as life unfolds itself. So it appears to have been in the case of Hezekiah. Two prayers answered, and yet forgetting God! Flattered by Babylon's suggestion of an alliance against Assyria, Hezekiah welcomed its ambassadors and proudly exhibited his treasures, concealing nothing. Isaiah's eye pierced beneath the shallow pretense of such an alliance, warned Hezekiah that he was merely exchanging one potential enemy for another, and foretold that the Babylon which the king was courting would be the very power which would ultimately crush Jerusalem. Hezekiah, humbled, comforted himself with the inglorious thought that at least all of this would not happen during his lifetime.

18 And of thy sons that shall issue from thee, which thou shalt beget, shall they take away; and they shall be eunuchs in the palace of the king of Babylon.

19 Then said Hezekiah unto Isaiah, Good *is* the word of the LORD which thou hast spoken. And he said, *Is it* not *good,* if peace and truth be in my days?

20 ¶ And the rest of the acts of Hezekiah, and all his might, and how he made a pool, and a conduit, and brought water into the city, *are* they not written in the book of the Chronicles of the kings of Judah?

21 And Hezekiah slept with his fathers: and Manasseh his son reigned in his stead.

nothing shall be left, says the LORD. 18 And some of your own sons, who are born to you, shall be taken away; and they shall be eunuchs in the palace of the king of Babylon." 19 Then said Hezeki'ah to Isaiah, "The word of the LORD which you have spoken is good." For he thought, "Why not, if there will be peace and security in my days?"

20 The rest of the deeds of Hezeki'ah, and all his might, and how he made the pool and the conduit and brought water into the city, are they not written in the Book of the Chronicles of the Kings of Judah? 21 And Hezeki'ah slept with his fathers; and Manas'seh his son reigned in his stead.

---

had already been king of Assyria for twenty years. There is no evidence, however, that he took any part in this revolt. The whole tradition of Manasseh's imprisonment in Babylon may have arisen from the visit which he paid to Esarhaddon in 667 B.C. to render his tribute and allegiance. Manasseh's name is found in two lists of tributary kings, one in the time of Esarhaddon, the other in the time of Ashurbanipal.

20-21. The Deuteronomic compiler concludes his account of the reign of Hezekiah with his customary obituary notice, here expanded to include a short summary of Hezekiah's good deeds. The expansion has to do partly with his successes in the earlier part of the revolt, and partly with the tunnel which he made, whereby he brought the waters of the Virgin's Spring through the temple mount to the Pool of Siloam (cf. II Chr. 32:30; Ecclus. 48:17). This tunnel has been found, and with it an inscription in the old Hebrew script on the right-hand wall some nineteen feet from the outlet into the Pool of Siloam. The inscription, partly scoured away by running water, tells how the two parties, working from opposite ends, managed to meet in the middle. The length of the tunnel is over 1,700 feet, but the direct line between the two mouths of the tunnel is only 1,090 feet (George Adam Smith, *Jerusalem* [New York: A. C. Armstrong & Son, 1907], I, 92-96; for facsimile, etc., see Driver, *op. cit.,* Pl. II).

Sometimes the life of a good man ends in moral anticlimax. No man's life can be finally assessed until the very last day of it has been lived.

Note vs. 15, **What have they seen in thine house?** The king had shown the pagans all his material wealth. But they had not been shown the altar, the sanctuary, the house and abode of God. They had seen nothing with which they were not perfectly familiar. They were not made aware that the house of Hezekiah differed in any way from their own. He might have shown them something that would have impressed them, awed them, made them feel that the God of Israel possessed a holiness and a strength with which the gods of Babylon were not endowed.

What have they seen in thine house? The question may be asked of many a modern man or woman who believes in Israel's God. Pagans come into the house, strangers to religious ideals. And what do they see? What are they shown? Only silver and gold, material possessions, the outward show of comfort and prosperity? Or do they see something else? Are they made to feel that there is something else, something deeper, sweeter, holier, truer, an atmosphere with which they are not familiar, a suggestion of a spiritual strength and stability wanting in their own homes? A young man once went frequently to a Christian home. He himself made no pretense of possessing religious motives or ideals. But he afterward confessed that what he had seen there had made a better man of him. He had seen something to which he was a stranger. **What have they seen in thine house?** Hezekiah had his chance. And the opportunity he had lost would never come again.

21 Manasseh *was* twelve years old when he began to reign, and reigned fifty and five years in Jerusalem. And his mother's name *was* Hephzi-bah.

2 And he did *that which was* evil in the sight of the LORD, after the abominations of the heathen, whom the LORD cast out before the children of Israel.

3 For he built up again the high places which Hezekiah his father had destroyed; and he reared up altars for Baal, and made a grove, as did Ahab king of Israel; and worshipped all the host of heaven, and served them.

21 Manas'seh was twelve years old when he began to reign, and he reigned fifty-five years in Jerusalem. His mother's name was Heph'zibah. **2** And he did what was evil in the sight of the LORD, according to the abominable practices of the nations whom the LORD drove out before the people of Israel. **3** For he rebuilt the high places which Hezeki'ah his father had destroyed; and he erected altars for Ba'al, and made an Ashe'rah, as Ahab king of Israel had done, and worshiped all the host

2. MANASSEH OF JUDAH (21:1-18)

This king reigned longer than any other king of Judah. His reign coincided with the peak of Assyrian prosperity in the west and he was therefore wholly under Assyrian influence from first to last. Hezekiah's reign had ended under this cloud, though the fact is disguised in the Deuteronomist's account of his reign, but for Manasseh there was no sunshine at all. Manasseh reigned from 696 to 641 B.C., and from 671 B.C. onward, when Esarhaddon invaded Egypt, Assyrian armies were continually marching to and fro along the coastal plain. Egypt did not recover her independence till 652 B.C., during the reign of Ashurbanipal. For all this period the little kingdom of Judah remained at peace, secure while the big warring world passed by, but the peace and security involved complete subservience to the demands of the Assyrian overlord, regular payment of tribute, and the wholesale introduction of foreign religious cults. This last was inevitable to some extent, but Manasseh does not seem to have been averse to these tendencies and probably encouraged them. Only he knows whether he encouraged them because he liked them or because he thought it was the best way to preserve anything at all of his kingdom.

The section contains details of Manasseh's introduction of foreign cults, with two oracles interwoven. The first oracle (vss. 7b-8) is a reiteration of the Deuteronomic commands laid upon David; the second (vss. 11-15) is a Deuteronomic oracle against Manasseh, laying upon him the blame and responsibility for the destruction of temple and kingdom.

21:3. Manasseh reintroduced all the old idolatries and all the cults which his father Hezekiah had abolished with the exception of the serpent worship, which Hezekiah had effectively destroyed by getting rid of the bronze serpent itself. He is the only king of Judah whom the Deuteronomist likens to Ahab of Israel, under whose government the hated Baal-Melkart worship was introduced into the Northern Kingdom. But Manasseh did more than revive the old Canaanite cults. He introduced, doubtless under Assyrian influence and probably under Assyrian pressure, the Assyrian astral cults, and he even built altars for these astral deities of Mesopotamia in the temple itself (vs. 5). This is the period during which the nucleus of the book of Deuteronomy was written, and it is Manasseh's idolatries which are expressly condemned there (Deut. 4:19; 17:3; 18:10-11).

21:1-26. Manasseh the Wicked.—The story of the whole long reign of Manasseh is compressed in this narrative within eighteen verses. As for the brief reign of Amon which followed (vss. 19-26), it was only a miserable and unimportant footnote to Manasseh's career. Amon may be dismissed as a wretched cipher in the annals of Jewish history. Manasseh, however, bulks large. One of the worst of all Judah's kings, he reigned the longest. The boy was only twelve years old when he came to the throne. He was born after Hezekiah's recovery from illness.

4 And he built altars in the house of the Lord, of which the Lord said, In Jerusalem will I put my name.

5 And he built altars for all the host of heaven in the two courts of the house of the Lord.

6 And he made his son pass through the fire, and observed times, and used enchantments, and dealt with familiar spirits and wizards: he wrought much wickedness in the sight of the Lord, to provoke *him* to anger.

of heaven, and served them. 4 And he built altars in the house of the Lord, of which the Lord had said, "In Jerusalem will I put my name." 5 And he built altars for all the host of heaven in the two courts of the house of the Lord. 6 And he burned his son as an offering, and practiced soothsaying and augury, and dealt with mediums and with wizards. He did much evil in the sight

---

5. The whole of this section (vss. 1-6) is the work of the earlier Deuteronomic compiler of 610 b.c. His reference to **the two courts of the house of the Lord** has, however, created some difficulty, since there was but one court in the pre-exilic temple. Either this verse has been adapted by a postexilic writer who knew the second temple or, less likely, the second court is that outer court which included the various royal edifices which Solomon had built.

6. In addition to child sacrifice, Manasseh also revived the ancient practices of **soothsaying** and necromancy. Probably these had never died out, for both are prevalent today in so-called civilized countries, though under more respectable names. It was formerly thought that the reference was to the practice of soothsaying by the observance of the movement of clouds, but this derivation of the root *'ānan* has been abandoned. It is now held that the word refers to the "crooning" of the soothsayer, who made a noise not unlike the cooing of a dove. **Augury** includes every kind of divination, on the basis of any sign (event) on earth or in the heavens which is not caused by human action. The theory is that since it must have been caused by the action of some person, it must have been caused by some supernatural person. The sign-events included the watching of the play of light on a cup of liquid (Gen. 44:5, 15) or the watching of the flight of birds (see Deut. 18:10).

The Hebrew *'ôbh* originally signified "ghost," but it came in practice to mean "medium." Similarly, the word *yidde'ônî* originally meant "knowing one," i.e., the spirit which knew, but in course of time it came to mean "wizard." The intense opposition of the prophets to these practices rested on the fact that they presupposed a belief in a supernatural power other than Yahweh's. They did not doubt that they received signs and instructions from the Lord, but they were quite sure that the other people did not.

One wonders if Hezekiah's moral decline at the end of his life had for its saddest consequence the character of his son. And there was no one strong enough to oppose and restrain him. For Isaiah was dead. The people had doubtless chafed under the heavy hand of reform. Banished were the pleasures associated with heathen rites. Yahweh alone must be worshiped, and he only at Jerusalem. And the religion which he exacted was not the mere offering of sacrifices but rectitude in personal living, justice to one's neighbor, righteousness and morality, precisely the kind of religion which was least easy to render. Princes and politicians were in the saddle, and the nation plunged right back into the old days of idolatry and licentiousness. The priests, too, were eager for it. With the destruction of the **high places** they had lost standing

and revenues. They welcomed the restoration of the old shrines. Altars to Baal were reared in the land. The worship of the stars was an innovation (Jer. 7:18; 19:13; Zeph. 1:5), and human sacrifice and the dark practices of wizardry and enchantments threw an eerie shadow over the whole wild scene. Murders filled the streets with blood. We are told (vss. 10-15) that prophets raised their voices in opposition. Who they were we do not know. Jeremiah had not begun his work. Micah had probably ended his. But conscience was not dead. God had his servants then as always. Even such days could not destroy that inner sense of righteousness and truth which condemned evil and both foresaw and foretold its dreadful consequences.

The first truth which comes out of this tragic

7 And he set a graven image of the grove that he had made in the house, of which the LORD said to David, and to Solomon his son, In this house, and in Jerusalem, which I have chosen out of all the tribes of Israel, will I put my name for ever:

8 Neither will I make the feet of Israel move any more out of the land which I gave their fathers; only if they will observe to do according to all that I have commanded them, and according to all the law that my servant Moses commanded them.

9 But they hearkened not: and Manasseh seduced them to do more evil than did the nations whom the LORD destroyed before the children of Israel.

10 ¶ And the LORD spake by his servants the prophets, saying,

11 Because Manasseh king of Judah hath done these abominations, *and* hath done wickedly above all that the Amorites did, which *were* before him, and hath made Judah also to sin with his idols:

12 Therefore thus saith the LORD God of Israel, Behold, I *am* bringing *such* evil upon Jerusalem and Judah, that whosoever heareth of it, both his ears shall tingle.

of the LORD, provoking him to anger. **7** And the graven image of Ashe'rah that he had made he set in the house of which the LORD said to David and to Solomon his son, "In this house, and in Jerusalem, which I have chosen out of all the tribes of Israel, I will put my name for ever; **8** and I will not cause the feet of Israel to wander any more out of the land which I gave to their fathers, if only they will be careful to do according to all that I have commanded them, and according to all the law that my servant Moses commanded them." **9** But they did not listen, and Manas'seh seduced them to do more evil than the nations had done whom the LORD destroyed before the people of Israel.

10 And the LORD said by his servants the prophets, **11** "Because Manas'seh king of Judah has committed these abominations, and has done things more wicked than all that the Amorites did, who were before him, and has made Judah also to sin with his idols; **12** therefore thus says the LORD, the God of Israel, Behold, I am bringing upon Jerusalem and Judah such evil that the ears of every one who hears of it will

---

7-15. These verses are the work of the later Deuteronomic editor of *ca.* 550 B.C. He lays the blame for the final disaster to Jerusalem and Judah wholly on Manasseh's shoulders. This writer had to account for the fact that Jerusalem was destroyed and the kingdom brought to an end in spite of the good works of King Josiah. According to the Deuteronomic theory, he had to account for the amazing disaster which overtook the best of the Deuteronomic kings, Josiah himself. He does this by laying the blame on Manasseh. It was his opinion that the fifty-five years of idolatry under Manasseh, and the two further years under his son Amon, had created such a dead weight of apostasy and wickedness that not even the zeal of the good King Josiah could avert the doom. All that Josiah could do, that model of what a Deuteronomic king could be, was to avert the final ruin for a time. If Manasseh had observed the Deuteronomic law, the editor held, both in respect of exclusive worship at Jerusalem and in respect of the laws against idolatry and evil-doing generally, then all would have been well.

---

story is that real religion makes its inexorable demands upon men and exacts the inevitable sacrifice of much that the natural man holds dear. The basic reason why Manasseh and princes and people rebelled against the stern religion of the reformation was that it took from them the self-indulgence which the popular religion had so freely gratified, demanded obedience to moral law, abstinence from sins of the flesh, the practice of social justice. Such a conception of worship was too narrow, too restrictive, too prohibitory for them. And it is much the same today. Men have no fault to find

with religion so long as it confers benefits and demands only outward forms of worship. But when they discover that it cuts right into their personal habits, demands an austere morality, affects their ways of doing business, and thus alters the whole aspect of their lives, then they are not enthusiastic about it. The alternative must be pressed home. Either it is a religion like that or no religion at all. Holiness is indeed a formidable word, but we cannot escape it. It means consecration to the highest we know, whatever self-control and self-denial it may involve. It holds us rigidly to certain definite

13 And I will stretch over Jerusalem the line of Samaria, and the plummet of the house of Ahab: and I will wipe Jerusalem as *a man* wipeth a dish, wiping *it,* and turning *it* upside down.

14 And I will forsake the remnant of mine inheritance, and deliver them into the hand of their enemies; and they shall become a prey and a spoil to all their enemies;

15 Because they have done *that which was* evil in my sight, and have provoked me to anger, since the day their fathers came forth out of Egypt, even unto this day.

16 Moreover Manasseh shed innocent blood very much, till he had filled Jerusalem from one end to another; besides his sin wherewith he made Judah to sin, in doing *that which was* evil in the sight of the LORD.

17 ¶ Now the rest of the acts of Manasseh, and all that he did, and his sin that he

tingle. 13 And I will stretch over Jerusalem the measuring line of Samar′ia, and the plummet of the house of Ahab; and I will wipe Jerusalem as one wipes a dish, wiping it and turning it upside down. 14 And I will cast off the remnant of my heritage, and give them into the hand of their enemies, and they shall become a prey and a spoil to all their enemies, 15 because they have done what is evil in my sight and have provoked me to anger, since the day their fathers came out of Egypt, even to this day."

16 Moreover Manas′seh shed very much innocent blood, till he had filled Jerusalem from one end to another, besides the sin which he made Judah to sin so that they did what was evil in the sight of the LORD.

17 Now the rest of the acts of Manas′seh, and all that he did, and the sin that he

---

13. The **line** and the **plummet** obviously stand for judgment (cf. Amos 7:8). Judah and Jerusal⁣ will be judged with exactly the same judgment as Samaria and all the house of Ahab. This meant the end of Jerusalem, just as it had meant the end of Samaria. The figure of the upturned **dish** is vivid and complete.

16-18. The 610 B.C. Deuteronomic editor completes his tale of woe. There is a tradition that Manasseh slew the prophets. Josephus reports (*Antiquities* X. 3. 1) that he slew some every day. A legend also said that he slew the prophet Isaiah by sawing him asunder with a wooden saw. This may well be the case, for Jezebel slew the prophets of the Lord (I Kings 18:13), though generally, however wicked a ruler was, he would stop short of this since prophets, like priests, were reckoned to be sacred persons and therefore enjoyed physical immunity.

17. The normal obituary notice for a king of Judah, with a change in the place of interment. The last kings of Judah, those of them who died in their own land, were buried in private sepulchers of their own (vs. 26; 23:30; 24:6). This was situated close by the temple wall in the royal garden (Ezek. 43:7).

---

ideals of life and conduct. It is a narrow way, but it leads us straight into the only kind of life that is really worth living.

A second truth in this chapter is revealed in the attitude of Manasseh toward Yahweh. It appeared to the king that Yahweh's love of his people, his power and providence, had been discredited by the misfortunes which had befallen them. Faith in God had been shaken by circumstance. And so it is among modern men. So long as all goes well with them, so long as the fabric of their lives remains secure, they have faith in God. But let life break down, hopes fall in ruins all about them, then they "lose their religion," feel that faith in a good and loving God is no longer possible. As a matter of fact, all the material disasters which befell the Jewish people made possible a far

greater destiny than otherwise could have been theirs. They were proof not of the impotence or indifference of God but of his love. So in personal experience the suffering which one endures is never an occasion for loss of faith in God. Rather it is an opportunity for a deeper faith in him who is preparing some better thing than prosperity had given. How often has this truth been illustrated in biography. "Why should I start at the plough of my Lord, that maketh deep furrows on my soul? I know He is no idle husbandman, He purposeth a crop." [4]

17-18. *Character and Desert.*—A final lesson is presented by the glaring contrast between the character of Manasseh and his earthly fortunes.

[4] Samuel Rutherford, quoted in Tileston, *Daily Strength for Daily Needs,* p. 49.

sinned, *are* they not written in the book of the Chronicles of the kings of Judah?

18 And Manasseh slept with his fathers, and was buried in the garden of his own house, in the garden of Uzza: and Amon his son reigned in his stead.

19 ¶ Amon *was* twenty and two years old when he began to reign, and he reigned two years in Jerusalem. And his mother's name *was* Meshullemeth, the daughter of Haruz of Jotbah.

20 And he did *that which was* evil in the sight of the LORD, as his father Manasseh did.

21 And he walked in all the way that his father walked in, and served the idols that his father served, and worshipped them:

22 And he forsook the LORD God of his fathers, and walked not in the way of the LORD.

23 ¶ And the servants of Amon conspired against him, and slew the king in his own house.

24 And the people of the land slew all them that had conspired against king Amon; and the people of the land made Josiah his son king in his stead.

25 Now the rest of the acts of Amon which he did, *are* they not written in the book of the Chronicles of the kings of Judah?

26 And he was buried in his sepulchre in the garden of Uzza: and Josiah his son reigned in his stead.

committed, are they not written in the Book of the Chronicles of the Kings of Judah?

18 And Manas'seh slept with his fathers, and was buried in the garden of his house, in the garden of Uzza; and Amon his son reigned in his stead.

19 Amon was twenty-two years old when he began to reign, and he reigned two years in Jerusalem. His mother's name was Meshul'lemeth the daughter of Haruz of Jotbah. 20 And he did what was evil in the sight of the LORD, as Manas'seh his father had done. 21 He walked in all the way in which his father walked, and served the idols that his father served, and worshiped them; 22 he forsook the LORD, the God of his fathers, and did not walk in the way of the LORD. 23 And the servants of Amon conspired against him, and killed the king in his house. 24 But the people of the land slew all those who had conspired against King Amon, and the people of the land made Josi'ah his son king in his stead. 25 Now the rest of the acts of Amon which he did, are they not written in the Book of the Chronicles of the Kings of Judah? 26 And he was buried in his tomb in the garden of Uzza; and Josi'ah his son reigned in his stead.

3. AMON OF JUDAH (21:19-26)

19-26. This king reigned but two years, and was assassinated at the age of twenty-four. The account of his reign says little more than that he followed in his father's footsteps. The Deuteronomist has added an extract from the royal annals of Judah which gives a few details of his death. It was the courtiers who murdered him, but the people in general avenged his death and made his son Josiah king in his stead.

He was one of the most wicked of Judah's kings. Yet his reign was the longest and one of the least troubled in the annals of either kingdom. Ahab, Jeroboam, Ahaz, these paid with their lives for the evils they had done. But Manasseh, after his long and abominable reign during all of which his kingdom had been at peace, **slept with his fathers, and was buried in the garden of his own house.** This inversion of ethics appeared so unaccountable and irrational to the Chronicler (II Chr. 33:11-16) that he felt that history must be altered in the interest of justice. But there is nothing to corroborate and every-

thing to disprove such an epilogue to the story of Manasseh. It makes sense but it is not history. Here we confront a vivid illustration of the contradiction so often found in human experience. It is one of the most staggering problems presented to faith. The O.T. never solved it. Its dogma that righteousness is rewarded by outward prosperity and wickedness by misfortune is negated by fact. The N.T. gives us the only solution possible to human understanding. We find it stated in Heb. 12:5-11. And, after all, who died the happier man, Manasseh or Jeremiah, Nero or Paul?

22 Josiah *was* eight years old when he began to reign, and he reigned thirty and one years in Jerusalem. And his mother's name *was* Jedidah, the daughter of Adaiah of Boscath.

2 And he did *that which was* right in the sight of the LORD, and walked in all the way of David his father, and turned not aside to the right hand or to the left.

3 ¶ And it came to pass in the eighteenth year of king Josiah, *that* the king sent Shaphan the son of Azaliah, the son of Meshullam, the scribe, to the house of the LORD, saying,

22 Josi'ah was eight years old when he began to reign, and he reigned thirty-one years in Jerusalem. His mother's name was Jedi'dah the daughter of Adai'ah of Bozkath. 2 And he did what was right in the eyes of the LORD, and walked in all the way of David his father, and he did not turn aside to the right hand or to the left.

3 In the eighteenth year of King Josi'ah, the king sent Shaphan the son of Azali'ah, son of Meshul'lam, the secretary, to the

---

B. END OF THE KINGDOM OF JUDAH (22:1–25:30)

1. JOSIAH OF JUDAH (22:1–23:30)

This passage, apart from interpolations, marks the end of the work of the original Deuteronomic compiler of 610 B.C. (23:25a). Josiah was his inspiration and the real burden of his theme throughout, and he measures all the kings, north and south, by this great reformer. He is the king who put into practice the tenets and commands of the lawbook which was found in the temple, and up to 610 B.C. the Lord rewarded him with prosperity and success.

a) INTRODUCTION (22:1-2)

22:1-2. Here is the formal Deuteronomic notice of the accession of a king of Judah. Josiah and his great-grandfather Hezekiah are the only two kings of whom the authors of the book of Kings express unqualified approval.

b) DISCOVERY OF THE BOOK OF THE LAW (22:3-20)

As restoration work was being undertaken at the temple, the priest Hilkiah came forward with a scroll and showed it to the royal scribe, who in turn read it and took it to the king. Josiah rent his clothes in sorrow and alarm when he heard of the dreadful judgment there portrayed for all the idolatry of Judah. He sent his officials to seek an oracle of the Lord, and was told by Huldah the prophetess that the doom was certain but that it would not take place in his time. The oracle of Huldah is composite, and has received additions at the hand of the *ca.* 550 B.C. editor.

The work of repair did not begin until Josiah was in the eighteenth year of his reign (621 B.C.). He would not have been able to do any repairs sufficiently extensive to cause comment before 626 B.C., the year in which Ashurbanipal died, since up to that

---

22:1-2. *Josiah's Reign Begins.*—Great events were impending outside and inside the little kingdom of Judah when young Josiah came to the throne in 638 B.C. From 630-624 occurred the savage invasion of the Scythians (Jer. 4:5-31; 5:15-19; 6:22-30; Zeph. 2:4-5). And during these and the following years came the ominous rise to power of Babylonia. Within the kingdom came once more the voice of articulate prophecy. Jeremiah began his long career in 627 B.C.; Zephaniah's prophecy dates from 628-626; and Nahum wrote in 614-612. None of these events without or within is mentioned by our historian who confines himself to the record of

Josiah's reign. He was one of Judah's noblest kings. How a creature like Amon could have had a son like Josiah presents again the insoluble problem of heredity. Of his mother and her father we know only their names. For eighteen years, or until the king was twenty-six years old, the story of his reign is a blank. For ten years at least the affairs of state must have been in the hands of regents. But then things began to happen.

3-7. *Rebuilding the Temple.*—The temple had fallen into dilapidation during the long and evil reign of Manasseh. Its rebuilding became the new king's first task. He had good

4 Go up to Hilkiah the high priest, that he may sum the silver which is brought into the house of the Lord, which the keepers of the door have gathered of the people:

5 And let them deliver it into the hand of the doers of the work, that have the oversight of the house of the Lord: and let them give it to the doers of the work, which is in the house of the Lord, to repair the breaches of the house,

6 Unto carpenters, and builders, and masons, and to buy timber and hewn stone to repair the house.

7 Howbeit, there was no reckoning made with them of the money that was delivered into their hand, because they dealt faithfully.

house of the Lord, saying, 4 "Go up to Hilki'ah the high priest, that he may reckon the amount of the money which has been brought into the house of the Lord, which the keepers of the threshold have collected from the people; 5 and let it be given into the hand of the workmen who have the oversight of the house of the Lord; and let them give it to the workmen who are at the house of the Lord, repairing the house, 6 that is, to the carpenters, and to the builders, and to the masons, as well as for buying timber and quarried stone to repair the house. 7 But no accounting shall be asked from them for the money which is delivered into their hand, for they deal honestly."

date Josiah was a vassal to the Assyrian king. Further delay was caused by the incursions of hordes of Scythians (Jer. 1:13-15).

4. The title **high priest** is found here, again in vs. 8, and in 23:4. This is properly a postexilic term, the pre-exilic term being "chief priest" and that of the next in precedence "the second priest" (25:18).

The procedure followed in the provision of money to pay for the renovations was that followed by King Jehoash (12:9, 15), even to the practice of not counting the money. Whether the custom of having the box in the porch had fallen into disuse since the time of Jehoash or not, it is impossible to say definitely. It looks as if the boxes had been there all the time but that the money had not gone for repairs. In any case, the box for gifts became a feature in the second temple. In the first century A.D. there were thirteen chests for the reception of charitable gifts. These were then situated around the Court of the Women, where the worshipers congregated. The chests were narrow at the top and wide at the bottom, and were called "trumpets" because of their shape. Nine of the trumpets were for the reception of the various contributions legally due from the worshipers, while the other four were for gifts which were wholly voluntary (Alfred Edersheim, *The Temple, Its Ministry and Services* [New York: Fleming H. Revell Co., 1910], pp. 26-27).

helpers: Shaphan the scribe and Hilkiah the high priest. The people were asked for subscriptions, and the money was so faithfully employed that no accounts were kept (vs. 7; cf. 12:15). The temple was for the Jewish people the symbol, the very incarnation, of religion. Thus in restoring the temple Josiah was seeking to restore the religion that was enshrined within it. We would do well to apply ourselves to a similar task, to the rebuilding of religion into the structure of our society. We have been building everything else, bridges, dams, and highways; we have built temples of finance and industry. But we have neglected the house of God, which has fallen into disrepair. Our civilization from top to bottom has been largely secular. The root trouble with modern society is that religion has

been left out of it. We have left religion out of our business, out of our education, out of our politics. We have not been building religion into the lives of our people or into the life of the nation. The time has come to rebuild the house of God. And this involves fresh loyalty to the church in which religion is always incorporated. For at no time and nowhere has religion existed without incorporating itself in institutional forms. Without a visible church, religion would doubtless remain as a source of private inspiration, but it would not be a continuing and constructive force. Without the church, the Christian religion can achieve nothing as a social dynamic. The church needs to be rebuilt in the loyalties and affections of men if religion is to prosper in the land.

8 ¶ And Hilkiah the high priest said unto Shaphan the scribe, I have found the book of the law in the house of the LORD. And Hilkiah gave the book to Shaphan, and he read it.

9 And Shaphan the scribe came to the king, and brought the king word again, and said, Thy servants have gathered the money that was found in the house, and have delivered it into the hand of them that do the work, that have the oversight of the house of the LORD.

10 And Shaphan the scribe showed the king, saying, Hilkiah the priest hath delivered me a book. And Shaphan read it before the king.

11 And it came to pass, when the king had heard the words of the book of the law, that he rent his clothes.

12 And the king commanded Hilkiah the priest, and Ahikam the son of Shaphan, and Achbor the son of Michaiah, and Shaphan the scribe, and Asahiah a servant of the king's, saying,

13 Go ye, inquire of the LORD for me, and for the people, and for all Judah, concerning the words of this book that is found: for great is the wrath of the LORD that is kindled against us, because our fathers have not hearkened unto the words of this book, to do according unto all that which is written concerning us.

8 And Hilki'ah the high priest said to Shaphan the secretary, "I have found the book of the law in the house of the LORD." And Hilki'ah gave the book to Shaphan, and he read it. 9 And Shaphan the secretary came to the king, and reported to the king, "Your servants have emptied out the money that was found in the house, and have delivered it into the hand of the workmen who have the oversight of the house of the LORD." 10 Then Shaphan the secretary told the king, "Hilki'ah the priest has given me a book." And Shaphan read it before the king.

11 And when the king heard the words of the book of the law, he rent his clothes. 12 And the king commanded Hilki'ah the priest, and Ahi'kam the son of Shaphan, and Achbor the son of Micai'ah, and Shaphan the secretary, and Asai'ah the king's servant, saying, 13 "Go, inquire of the LORD for me, and for the people, and for all Judah, concerning the words of this book that has been found; for great is the wrath of the LORD that is kindled against us, because our fathers have not obeyed the words of this book, to do according to all that is written concerning us."

---

8. The book of the law: It will never be decided whether Hilkiah really found the scroll or whether he knew very well where to look. The general agreement is that the scroll contained the nucleus of the present book of Deuteronomy, probably chs. 12–26 (see Intro. to Deuteronomy, Vol. II, pp. 312-13, 320-23).

12. The king's servant was evidently an official of some considerable standing. This is confirmed by the Tell en-Nasbeh seal, which bears the inscription "To Ya'azanyahu, servant of the king"; it has been suggested that this is actually the army general mentioned in II Kings 25:23; Jer. 40:8 (see facsimile of the impression of this seal in G. Ernest Wright, "Tell en-Nasbeh," *The Biblical Archaeologist,* X [1947], 73, reproduced from the report on the excavations by C. C. McCown).

8-20. *The Rediscovery of the Bible.*—Here is an interesting story. The substance of the book that was found is contained for us in the book of Deuteronomy (see Exeg.). Whether it was purposely hidden there by members of the prophetic party, so that its discovery was in the nature of a pious fraud, or whether Hezekiah's reformers had reduced their principles to writing and concealed this document in the temple for safekeeping, we do not know. But its dis-

covery became the signal of the most thorough reformation of worship that Judah had ever known. The great reformation of Josiah was built solidly upon it.

The rediscovery of the Bible has often marked an epoch in the life of nations and of individuals. For centuries it was a lost book. It existed only in MSS, or, after the advent of printing, only in scarce volumes out of the reach of the common people. Its rediscovery in the days

14 So Hilkiah the priest, and Ahikam, and Achbor, and Shaphan, and Asahiah, went unto Huldah the prophetess, the wife of Shallum the son of Tikvah, the son of Harhas, keeper of the wardrobe; (now she dwelt in Jerusalem in the college;) and they communed with her.

15 ¶ And she said unto them, Thus saith the LORD God of Israel, Tell the man that sent you to me,

16 Thus saith the LORD, Behold, I will bring evil upon this place, and upon the inhabitants thereof, *even* all the words of the book which the king of Judah hath read:

17 Because they have forsaken me, and have burned incense unto other gods, that they might provoke me to anger with all the works of their hands; therefore my wrath shall be kindled against this place, and shall not be quenched.

18 But to the king of Judah which sent you to inquire of the LORD, thus shall ye say to him, Thus saith the LORD God of Israel, *As touching* the words which thou hast heard;

19 Because thine heart was tender, and thou hast humbled thyself before the LORD, when thou heardest what I spake against this place, and against the inhabitants thereof, that they should become a desolation and a curse, and hast rent thy clothes, and wept before me; I also have heard *thee,* saith the LORD.

14 So Hilki'ah the priest, and Ahi'kam, and Achbor, and Shaphan, and Asai'ah went to Huldah the prophetess, the wife of Shallum the son of Tikvah, son of Harhas, keeper of the wardrobe (now she dwelt in Jerusalem in the Second Quarter) ; and they talked with her. 15 And she said to them, "Thus says the LORD, the God of Israel: 'Tell the man who sent you to me, 16 Thus says the LORD, Behold, I will bring evil upon this place and upon its inhabitants, all the words of the book which the king of Judah has read. 17. Because they have forsaken me and have burned incense to other gods, that they might provoke me to anger with all the work of their hands, therefore my wrath will be kindled against this place, and it will not be quenched. 18 But as to the king of Judah, who sent you to inquire of the LORD, thus shall you say to him, Thus says the LORD, the God of Israel: Regarding the words which you have heard, 19 because your heart was penitent, and you humbled yourself before the LORD, when you heard how I spoke against this place, and against its inhabitants, that they should become a desolation and a curse, and you have rent your clothes and wept before me, I also have heard you, says the

14. The king sends to the temple to inquire what should be done, and the word is given by the prophetess Huldah. It has been thought strange that Jeremiah did not give this oracle, but there is no evidence that he was ever attached to the Jerusalem shrine, and it was the cult prophet there who would give the oracle.

15. The tendency of the prophets is to insist that the king is but a man before God, and is therefore no different from any other man. Such a passage as this needs to be remembered in the face of all attempts to show that among the Hebrews the king was regarded as divine.

16-20. The first part of Huldah's speech presupposes a knowledge of the destruction of the temple and of the transportation of the inhabitants of the city into exile. On

of Wycliffe and Luther meant the dawn of a new era in the religious and moral life of Europe and laid the foundation of our modern democracy. As in the life of nations, so in the lives of men. A man has been brought up on the Bible, instructed in it. But in later years he forgets it. He is worshiping gods other than the God of the Bible: material interests, wealth and pleasure, ambition and success. And then some-

day, wearied and disillusioned, he chances on the Bible, buried under an accumulation of secular books and papers. He opens it and begins to read. And then like Josiah, he rends his clothes. The message of psalmist and prophet speaks home to his soul. And the rediscovery of his Bible means a new chapter in that man's life. Or the edifice of a man's life may have collapsed. It lies in ruins all about him. And

20 Behold therefore, I will gather thee unto thy fathers, and thou shalt be gathered into thy grave in peace; and thine eyes shall not see all the evil which I will bring upon this place. And they brought the king word again.

23 And the king sent, and they gathered unto him all the elders of Judah and of Jerusalem.

2 And the king went up into the house of the Lord, and all the men of Judah and all the inhabitants of Jerusalem with him, and the priests, and the prophets, and all the people, both small and great: and he read in their ears all the words of the book of the covenant which was found in the house of the Lord.

3 ¶ And the king stood by a pillar, and made a covenant before the Lord, to walk after the Lord, and to keep his commandments and his testimonies and his statutes with all *their* heart and all *their* soul, to perform the words of this covenant that were written in this book. And all the people stood to the covenant.

Lord. 20 Therefore, behold, I will gather you to your fathers, and you shall be gathered to your grave in peace, and your eyes shall not see all the evil which I will bring upon this place.'" And they brought back word to the king.

23 Then the king sent, and all the elders of Judah and Jerusalem were gathered to him. 2 And the king went up to the house of the Lord, and with him all the men of Judah and all the inhabitants of Jerusalem, and the priests and the prophets, all the people, both small and great; and he read in their hearing all the words of the book of the covenant which had been found in the house of the Lord. 3 And the king stood by the pillar and made a covenant before the Lord, to walk after the Lord and to keep his commandments and his testimonies and his statutes, with all his heart and all his soul, to perform the words of this covenant that were written in this book; and all the people joined in the covenant.

the other hand, vs. 20 was apparently written before Josiah's death. The easiest solution is to suppose that an original oracle of Huldah's has been rewritten by the editor of *ca.* 550 B.C., who took the view that even Josiah's full repentance and adherence to the tenets of the Deuteronomists could only delay and not stave off the inevitable end.

c) Making of the Covenant (23:1-3)

King Josiah gathers all the people together in the temple courts and reads to them the scroll which Hilkiah has found in the temple. The king took up his stand by the pillar and bound himself to the Lord by covenant to observe the demands of the scroll of the law with full consecration of his whole life, and all the people joined themselves with him in this promise. During the ceremony the king stood by the pillar, just as the boy-king Jehoash had done when Jehoiada the chief priest seized the throne for him and proclaimed him king (11:14). It was evidently the regular and proper place for the king to stand when he worshiped in the temple.

23:3. According to the M.T. the people "stood in the covenant." This is the literal translation of the Hebrew, and there is every reason to suppose that here the M.T. is more accurate than the English versions, e.g., KJV, **stood to**, and the RSV, which paraphrases **joined in**. The Hebrew is doubtless descriptive of the actual ceremony

there among the debris lies the Bible. He stumbles upon it and takes it up. And no matter how modern or how self-sufficient he may be, the Bible at a time of failure, of bereavement, brings to him what he can find nowhere else. He discovers in it what no other book, however enlightening, can give him. For the lonely, suffering, sinning soul there is no substitute for the Bible. When it comes to restoring the soul, the law of the Lord is perfect. The re-

discovery of the Bible has meant a turning point in many a man's history.

23:1-28. *The Reforms of Josiah.*—The first part of this long chapter (vss. 1-28) is given up to a detailed description of the drastic reforms of Josiah. He began with the temple (vss. 4-7). Then he went through the whole land from north to south, destroying all idolatrous shrines and abolishing root and branch pagan star worship and all of its trappings (vss. 8-18). The

4 And the king commanded Hilkiah the high priest, and the priests of the second order, and the keepers of the door, to bring forth out of the temple of the LORD all the vessels that were made for Baal, and for the grove, and for all the host of heaven: and he burned them without Jerusalem in the fields of Kidron, and carried the ashes of them unto Beth-el.

4 And the king commanded Hilki'ah, the high priest, and the priests of the second order, and the keepers of the threshold, to bring out of the temple of the LORD all the vessels made for Ba'al, for Ashe'rah, and for all the host of heaven; he burned them outside Jerusalem in the fields of the Kidron,

by which the king and the people bound themselves in the covenant. It is stated by Dictys Cretensis (*De Bello Trojano* I 15) that before the Greeks set out for Troy, the soothsayer Calchas brought a boar into the market place, cut it in two pieces, and placed one piece at the west side of an open space and the other piece at the east side. He then caused every man, with his drawn sword in his hand, to pass between the pieces of the boar and swear enmity against Priam king of Troy. Each man entered into the covenant by passing between the pieces of the animal, thus identifying himself with the life of the animal, and so binding themselves each with the other, into a common brotherhood. It could be said of these Greeks that they "stood in the covenant" in so far as they stood between the pieces of the boar. Pausanias (*Description of Greece* III. 20. 9) says that the suitors of Helen bound themselves to defend her, whoever was her choice of husband, and that they did it by standing on the pieces of a horse which Tyndareus her father had cut up. That some such idea was extant in ancient times among the Hebrews is to be seen in the story of Abraham's covenant (Gen. 15:9-21) where God passed between the pieces of the sacrifices (vs. 17) in the likeness of a flaming torch. The making of a covenant by passing between the pieces of a calf is mentioned in Jer. 34:18, a passage which is contemporary with the making of the covenant in the temple in Josiah's time. We judge therefore that there was some such ceremony at Josiah's dedication of himself and his people to the tasks of reform.

d) REFORM OF THE CULTUS (23:4-15)

Josiah proceeded to sweep away all idolatrous cult objects out of the temple. He burned them in Kidron and disposed of the ashes at Bethel, presumably to ensure the complete desecration of the most offensive of all shrines to a true worshiper of the Lord. He got rid of all idolatrous priests, and brought the genuine priests to Jerusalem, though they were not admitted there as regular sacrificing priests. In general, he began in the temple, continued in Jerusalem, passed over to the Mount of Olives, and thence throughout the country, making a clean sweep everywhere.

4. It is best to read "the second priest" (cf. 25:18, where "the chief priest" and **the keepers of the threshold** are also mentioned).

For **the fields of the Kidron** Lucian has "limekilns of Kidron," which many commentators prefer. The word used in the Hebrew is not used elsewhere in Hebrew prose, and it is very similar to the word for "kilns" (lit., "place of burning"). As a perfect Deuteronomist, he had the refuse carried to Bethel, there to scatter it on the basest altar of all.

crusade was carried even into Samaria (vss. 19-20). Then a great, solemn feast of the Passover was observed (vs. 21). **Like unto him was there no king before him** (vs. 25). Such was the great reform of Josiah.

If one imagines that this ended paganism in Judah, he is mistaken. Reform by suppression only never ends paganism of any kind. Josiah's reform was negative, not positive; destructive,

not constructive. It was carried out with ruthless zeal but not with discretion. It wiped out external evils, it did not create new motives and impulses. It rode roughshod over long-established customs. It did not correct these at their source. Hence nothing was surer than that when the heavy hand that suppressed these customs was removed the old practices would spring to life again. The reformation demanded

5 And he put down the idolatrous priests, whom the kings of Judah had ordained to burn incense in the high places in the cities of Judah, and in the places round about Jerusalem; them also that burned incense unto Baal, to the sun, and to the moon, and to the planets, and to all the host of heaven.

6 And he brought out the grove from the house of the LORD, without Jerusalem, unto the brook Kidron, and burned it at the brook Kidron, and stamped *it* small to powder, and cast the powder thereof upon the graves of the children of the people.

and carried their ashes to Bethel. 5 And he deposed the idolatrous priests whom the kings of Judah had ordained to burn incense in the high places at the cities of Judah and round about Jerusalem; those also who burned incense to Ba'al, to the sun, and the moon, and the constellations, and all the host of the heavens. 6 And he brought out the Ashe'rah from the house of the LORD, outside Jerusalem, to the brook Kidron, and burned it at the brook Kidron, and beat it to dust and cast the dust of it upon the graves of the common people.

---

5. The word used for **the idolatrous priests** whom Josiah "caused to cease" (so M.T.) is *kemārîm*. It is the regular word in Aramaic and Syriac for all priests, whether legitimate or not. The word is also found in Nabataean (North Arabia) and in Punic (Carthage in North Africa), and yet again in an ordinary association in the Elephantine papyri. In the O.T. the word is used rarely, and always for **idolatrous priests** (Hos. 10:5; Zeph. 1:4; and possibly the correct reading in Hos. 4:4). It was formerly thought that the word was connected with the Hebrew root כמר II ("to be black"), on the ground that the priests were supposedly always dressed in black. This is most unlikely, since we do know that the Jerusalem priests were traditionally dressed in white, and it is likely that in this they followed an ancient custom. The word is probably to be connected with the root כמר III ("to lay prostrate"), the priest thus being the man who prostrates himself before God.

Here, as always in passages which are earlier than the Priestly Code, we should read "sacrifice" for **burn incense.**

There has been much discussion concerning the meaning of the Hebrew *mazzālôth*. The word is a loan word from the Assyrian, where it means "a place of standing," and is used of the mansions of the gods, i.e., the territory assigned to them in the skies in the Mesopotamian astral system. In Arabic *'al-manazil* is used of the twenty-eight mansions of the moon. The word in Syriac refers to the signs of the zodiac, while in rabbinical Hebrew the reference is to the twelve signs of the zodiac and also to the planets (so KJV here). The most likely solution is that the word refers to thirty-six stars which governed the year, three being allocated to each month. In the Aries period (i.e., the period when Aries the ram rises in the first month of the year), the regents for the month Sivan were Orion, Canis Major, and Gemini. In the Taurus period (from *ca.* 3000 B.C.), these would be the regents for the month Ayar (S. H. Langdon, *Babylonian Menologies and the Semitic Calendars* [London: British Academy, 1935], pp. 3-10).

6. Wealthy people were buried in caves hollowed out of hillsides, but poor folk were buried in a common graveyard—a large death pit (Jer. 26:23). The contact with the common graves would destroy any holiness which might still cling to the desecrated remains of the idol. Objects could still be regarded at that period as being holy even though they were used in idolatrous cults, and definite desecration was necessary in order to prevent their being regarded as holy.

---

more of the people than they were inwardly prepared to perform. Had Josiah proceeded with greater prudence, removing the most glaring evils in a way to win popular support, and then sought to educate the people out of more innocent practices which they were not ready to abandon, the result might have been different. No reform—and here is a lesson which we

have been slow to learn—can ever be permanent which outruns popular opinion and support. No reform that relies solely on suppression, on negative means, on the heavy hand of the law, can long endure. The solution of no social problem is as simple as that.

Josiah's reforms dealt with externals only. They did not reach the inward spirit. Here we

7 And he brake down the houses of the sodomites, that *were* by the house of the LORD, where the women wove hangings for the grove.

8 And he brought all the priests out of the cities of Judah, and defiled the high places where the priests had burned incense, from Geba to Beer-sheba, and brake down the high places of the gates that *were* in the entering in of the gate of Joshua the governor of the city, which *were* on a man's left hand at the gate of the city.

9 Nevertheless the priests of the high places came not up to the altar of the LORD in Jerusalem, but they did eat of the unleavened bread among their brethren.

10 And he defiled Topheth, which *is* in the valley of the children of Hinnom, that no man might make his son or his daughter to pass through the fire to Molech.

7 And he broke down the houses of the cult prostitutes which were in the house of the LORD, where the women wove hangings for the Ashe'rah. 8 And he brought all the priests out of the cities of Judah, and defiled the high places where the priests had burned incense, from Geba to Beer-sheba; and he broke down the high places of the gates that were at the entrance of the gate of Joshua the governor of the city, which were on one's left at the gate of the city. 9 However, the priests of the high places did not come up to the altar of the LORD in Jerusalem, but they ate unleavened bread among their brethren. 10 And he defiled To'pheth, which is in the valley of the sons of Hinnom, that no one might burn his son or his daughter as an offering to

---

7. The cult prostitutes were males (cf. **sodomites**). This native Palestinian practice was regularly abolished by reforming kings, but found its way back again as soon as the time of the reforms was past (I Kings 14:24; 15:12; 22:46). Prostitutes of both sexes were strictly prohibited in the Deuteronomic Code (Deut. 23:17).

The translation **hangings** depends upon the traditional Jewish interpretation, since the Hebrew has the difficult word "houses." Perhaps further information on the cults of Canaan may clarify the Hebrew meaning. The use of hangings or tents in or around the shrines is confirmed by Amos 5:26 (LXX); Ezek. 16:16, and also the LXX of Amos 2:8, which reads, "And binding their clothes [i.e., those received as pledges] with cords, they have made them curtains near the altar."

8. It is customary and almost certainly correct to read, with Hoffmann, שעירים (*se'îrîm*, "satyrs," "goats") for שערים (*she'ārîm*, **gates**). The reference is then to the "hairy ones," the goat demons who were worshiped in early times (Lev. 17:7; II Chr. 11:15; W. O. E. Oesterley and T. H. Robinson, *Hebrew Religion, Its Origin and Development* [2nd ed.; New York: The Macmillan Co., 1937], pp. 112-13).

9. The Deuteronomic intention (Deut. 18:6-8) was that the dispossessed Levites of the southern local shrines should come up to the central sanctuary at Jerusalem and there be on an equal footing with the Jerusalem priests. They were indeed partly recognized as sacred persons, since **they ate unleavened bread among their brethren,** but they were not admitted as sacrificing priests and so became subordinate officials. In view of the behavior of the priests in the time of Jehoash (12:4-7), and possibly also in the time of Josiah himself (cf. 22:3-7), it is a legitimate assumption that the Jerusalem priests themselves were unwilling to share their perquisites, even though these would be vastly increased by the destruction of the local shrines.

10. It is probable that the word **Topheth** (or Tephath) originally meant "fireplace" and referred to the Valley of Hinnom, where the bodies of child victims were sacrificed

---

are guided by observing the attitude of Jeremiah, the most spiritual of all the prophets, towards this great reform, the greatest effort ever made to bring the life of Israel into conformity to the will of God. At first it won the passionate support of the prophet, who went on a preaching mission in its behalf (Jer. 11:6). Yet as he

watched its results he became increasingly convinced that a truly spiritual religion was not to be won for the people by such external procedure. They could not be legislated into either morality or religion. Conformity to external habits of worship would never make religion a matter of the heart. Though the moral code of

11 And he took away the horses that the kings of Judah had given to the sun, at the entering in of the house of the LORD, by the chamber of Nathan-melech the chamberlain, which *was* in the suburbs, and burned the chariots of the sun with fire.

12 And the altars that *were* on the top of the upper chamber of Ahaz, which the kings of Judah had made, and the altars which Manasseh had made in the two courts of the house of the LORD, did the king beat down, and brake *them* down from thence, and cast the dust of them into the brook Kidron.

13 And the high places that *were* before Jerusalem, which *were* on the right hand of the mount of corruption, which Solomon the king of Israel had builded for Ashtoreth the abomination of the Zidonians, and for Chemosh the abomination of the Moabites, and for Milcom the abomination of the children of Ammon, did the king defile.

Molech. 11 And he removed the horses that the kings of Judah had dedicated to the sun, at the entrance to the house of the LORD, by the chamber of Nathan-melech the chamberlain, which was in the precincts;[h] and he burned the chariots of the sun with fire. 12 And the altars on the roof of the upper chamber of Ahaz, which the kings of Judah had made, and the altars which Manas′seh had made in the two courts of the house of the LORD, he pulled down and broke in pieces,[i] and cast the dust of them into the brook Kidron. 13 And the king defiled the high places that were east of Jerusalem, to the south of the mount of corruption, which Solomon the king of Israel had built for Ash′toreth the abomination of the Sido′nians, and for Chemosh the abomination of Moab, and for Milcom the abomination

[h] The meaning of the Hebrew word is uncertain
[i] Heb *pieces from there*

as burnt offerings. The Masoretes as usual inserted the vowels of the word *bôsheth* ("shameful thing") because of the heathen associations of the word. According to Jerome the site was a green and wooded place watered by the Pools of Siloam. Here as elsewhere (except I Kings 11:7, which is an error for "Milcom," the Ammonite god), the name of the god associated with child sacrifice is given as Molech. This is the Hebrew word *mélekh* ("king") with the vowels of *bôsheth* inserted instead of the proper vowels. The worship of the god Melekh (the heavenly "King") was widespread throughout the Semitic East, and the sacrifice of children was the special and distinctive feature of his cult. It is most probable that the cult observed at Topheth was a syncretism of Yahweh-Melekh.

11. The idea that the sun-god drives across the sky in his chariot is found both in Mesopotamia and in Greece, i.e., both of Shamash and of Helios. Indeed, a solar god can regularly be detected by the fact that he is represented as riding in a winged chariot. This is especially evident in the famous Gaza coin, dating from *ca.* 400 B.C., in which Yahu the God of the Jews, is depicted as a solar Zeus (Cook, *Religion of Ancient Palestine in Light of Archaeology*, pp. 147-48). The "chariot" (so LXX) and its **horses,** which Josiah removed, were situated near the entrance **in the precincts**—some kind of structure which was to the west of the temple itself (I Chr. 26:18). In the Mishnah and in the Targs. the word *parwār* means "suburb" (so KJV) and it is probably to be connected with the Persian *parwār* "kiosk," "summerhouse."

12. The phrase **the upper chamber of Ahaz** is out of construction and appears to be a gloss. The **altars** were on the roof of the temple itself—a natural location for their use in the astral cults which were introduced from Mesopotamia, probably in the time of Ahaz when Assyrian influence became dominant in Judah. It is possible that Ahaz built a roof chamber in connection with them. In this case, the phrase is an intelligent and informed gloss.

13. "The Mount of Olives" (reading *mishḥāh* for *mashḥîth*) had been the site of heathen shrines certainly since the time of Solomon (I Kings 11:7), as the references in

Deuteronomy might exist as a standard, only some deep, inward spiritual principle could make it operative in their lives (Jer. 7:3-16). The people might perform acts of worship as

prescribed, yet go their way as before, living lives of greed and selfishness. True reform, in a word, is the reformation of inward motives, impulses, desires. We must begin there. No out-

14 And he brake in pieces the images, and cut down the groves, and filled their places with the bones of men.

15 ¶ Moreover the altar that *was* at Beth-el, *and* the high place which Jeroboam the son of Nebat, who made Israel to sin, had made, both that altar and the high place he brake down, and burned the high place, *and* stamped *it* small to powder, and burned the grove.

16 And as Josiah turned himself, he spied the sepulchres that *were* there in the mount, and sent, and took the bones out of the sepulchres, and burned *them* upon the altar, and polluted it, according to the word of the LORD which the man of God proclaimed, who proclaimed these words.

17 Then he said, What title *is* that that I see? And the men of the city told him, *It is* the sepulchre of the man of God, which came from Judah, and proclaimed these things that thou hast done against the altar of Beth-el.

18 And he said, Let him alone; let no man move his bones. So they let his bones alone, with the bones of the prophet that came out of Samaria.

19 And all the houses also of the high places that *were* in the cities of Samaria, which the kings of Israel had made to provoke *the* LORD to anger, Josiah took away, and did to them according to all the acts that he had done in Beth-el.

of the Ammonites. 14 And he broke in pieces the pillars, and cut down the Ashe'rim, and filled their places with the bones of men.

15 Moreover the altar at Bethel, the high place erected by Jerobo'am the son of Nebat, who made Israel to sin, that altar with the high place he pulled down and he broke in pieces its stones,^j crushing them to dust; also he burned the Ashe'rah. 16 And as Josi'ah turned, he saw the tombs there on the mount; and he sent and took the bones out of the tombs, and burned them upon the altar, and defiled it, according to the word of the LORD which the man of God proclaimed, who had predicted these things. 17 Then he said, "What is yonder monument that I see?" And the men of the city told him, "It is the tomb of the man of God who came from Judah and predicted these things which you have done against the altar at Bethel." 18 And he said, "Let him be; let no man move his bones." So they let his bones alone, with the bones of the prophet who came out of Samar'ia. 19 And all the shrines also of the high places that were in the cities of Samar'ia, which kings of Israel had made, provoking the LORD to anger, Josi'ah removed; he did to them according to all that he had done at

^j Gk: Heb *he burned the high place*

---

this verse show. The particular site mentioned was at the south end of the ridge, and is commonly identified with the so-called Mount of Offense (Jebel Baṭn 'el-Hawa).

15. The destruction of the shrine and altar at Bethel climaxes the work of cultic purification.

e) JOSIAH AND THE BONES OF THE MAN OF GOD (23:16-20)

16-20. While Josiah is busy making havoc of the altar and shrine at Bethel, he sees the burial caves in the distance and commands that dead men's bones be brought so that he can effectually desecrate the altar and put it out of commission permanently as a holy place. He sees one particular monument and is informed that it marks the grave of the man of God who years ago prophesied the destruction of the altar. So Josiah commands that his bones be left alone, thus fulfilling the ancient prophecy. Josiah continues on to Samaria, destroys all the idolatrous objects there, slaying the priests over their own altars. These verses are a later addition and belong to the same stratum as I Kings 12:32–13:34. The prophet who had protested against Jeroboam's original

---

ward scheme of salvation will avail so long as men themselves remain self-seeking, materially minded, unbrotherly, indulgent. The world for which we wait depends not on outward organizations but upon the revival of a true religion in

the hearts of men. Precisely what we are, the world will become. The reformation of the world depends upon the reformation of the soul. Such are the lessons taught us by the reforms of Josiah.

20 And he slew all the priests of the high places that *were* there upon the altars, and burned men's bones upon them, and returned to Jerusalem.

21 ¶ And the king commanded all the people, saying, Keep the passover unto the LORD your God, as *it is* written in the book of this covenant.

22 Surely there was not holden such a passover from the days of the judges that judged Israel, nor in all the days of the kings of Israel, nor of the kings of Judah;

23 But in the eighteenth year of king Josiah, *wherein* this passover was holden to the LORD in Jerusalem.

24 ¶ Moreover the *workers with* familiar spirits, and the wizards, and the images, and the idols, and all the abominations that were spied in the land of Judah and in Jerusalem, did Josiah put away, that he

Bethel. 20 And he slew all the priests of the high places who were there, upon the altars, and burned the bones of men upon them. Then he returned to Jerusalem.

21 And the king commanded all the people, "Keep the passover to the LORD your God, as it is written in this book of the covenant." 22 For no such passover had been kept since the days of the judges who judged Israel, or during all the days of the kings of Israel or of the kings of Judah; 23 but in the eighteenth year of King Josi'ah this passover was kept to the LORD in Jerusalem.

24 Moreover Josi'ah put away the mediums and the wizards and the teraphim and the idols and all the abominations that were seen in the land of Judah and in

---

infamies has his bones left in peace, a just and fitting reward to the dead for faithfulness to the Deuteronomic ideals.

f) CELEBRATION OF THE PASSOVER (23:21-23)

21-23. The climax of Josiah's reforms was the celebration of the Passover according to the regulations laid down in Deut. 16:1-8. It is stated that there had never been a Passover such as this since the days of the judges. This is undoubtedly true, since the centralizing of all worship at Jerusalem made new regulations necessary. The centralization would not affect the Passover itself, since that was essentially a home festival and not by any means a pilgrimage feast. It was a seasonal apotropaic rite, i.e., a spring festival which had its distant origin in the exorcism and "turning away" of evil spirits (see such regulations as the prohibition of leaving the house, and the removal of every trace of the victim, however slight). The festival came to be associated in Hebrew lore with the redemption of the first-born and with the rescue from Egypt. In the days before Josiah the people could observe the Passover in their own homes on the night of the full moon, and then set out in the morning to celebrate the feast of Mazzoth (Unleavened Bread) at their nearest or favorite shrine. This feast was the barley harvest festival, and like all harvest festivals it was a pilgrimage feast. When the law of the central sanctuary was enforced, different regulations had to be framed so as to make it possible for the people to observe the Passover and still be in Jerusalem for the feast of Mazzoth which followed immediately upon it (Snaith, *Jewish New Year Festival*, pp. 13-25). It was thus essential that the people should have a "home" in Jerusalem, so that they could keep both the home festival, which strictly demanded that they should stay at home, and the pilgrimage feast, which demanded that they should keep it in Jerusalem.

g) CONCLUSION OF THE ORIGINAL BOOK (23:24-25a)

Here is the concluding summary of the Deuteronomic compiler of 610 B.C. Josiah abolished every kind of heathen object and custom in Judah and Jerusalem, and there never was a king like him, who fully and loyally obeyed the law of Moses "with all his heart, and with all his soul, and with all his might" (cf. Deut. 6:5).

24. The **teraphim** were household **images**. They were of various sizes, big enough to be mistaken for a man in a bad light (I Sam. 19:13-16), or small enough to be packed in the saddles of camels (Gen. 31:32, 34). A regular feature of household religion in

might perform the words of the law, which were written in the book that Hilkiah the priest found in the house of the LORD.

25 And like unto him was there no king before him, that turned to the LORD with all his heart, and with all his soul, and with all his might, according to all the law of Moses; neither after him arose there *any* like him.

26 ¶ Notwithstanding, the LORD turned not from the fierceness of his great wrath, wherewith his anger was kindled against Judah, because of all the provocations that Manasseh had provoked him withal.

27 And the LORD said, I will remove Judah also out of my sight, as I have removed Israel, and will cast off this city Jerusalem which I have chosen, and the house of which I said, My name shall be there.

28 Now the rest of the acts of Josiah, and all that he did, *are* they not written in the book of the Chronicles of the kings of Judah?

29 ¶ In his days Pharaoh-nechoh king of Egypt went up against the king of Assyria

Jerusalem, that he might establish the words of the law which were written in the book that Hilki'ah the priest found in the house of the LORD. 25 Before him there was no king like him, who turned to the LORD with all his heart and with all his soul and with all his might, according to all the law of Moses; nor did any like him arise after him.

26 Still the LORD did not turn from the fierceness of his great wrath, by which his anger was kindled against Judah, because of all the provocations with which Manas'seh had provoked him. 27 And the LORD said, "I will remove Judah also out of my sight, as I have removed Israel, and I will cast off this city which I have chosen, Jerusalem, and the house of which I said, My name shall be there."

28 Now the rest of the acts of Josi'ah, and all that he did, are they not written in the Book of the Chronicles of the Kings of Judah? 29 In his days Pharaoh Neco king

---

the early days, they were reckoned to be legitimate even by Hosea (3:4), who regarded the loss of them as a deprivation. They may have been in some way connected with the giving of oracles.

25a. With the phrase **all the law of Moses** the work of the Deuteronomic compiler of 610 B.C. comes to an end. He has told the story of the reforms of Josiah, his hero, the king who more than all that were before him fulfilled the Deuteronomic ideal.

h) DEATH OF JOSIAH (23:25*b*-30)

With the untimely death of Josiah the whole Deuteronomic structure which the first editor had erected fell to the ground. The course of events had falsified it, for if ever a king ought to have lived long and prospered, it was Josiah; yet this monarch died before he was forty years old. But in 561 B.C., forty-seven years later, the exiled king Jehoiachin received favor at the hands of the Babylonian king (25:27-30). This good fortune may have encouraged one writer to believe that in spite of the disaster which had ended Josiah's reign, there was still truth in the tenets of the Deuteronomists. He blamed Manasseh for the disaster, and explained the reduction of Jerusalem and the Exile as a retribution for all the provocations of Manasseh.

28-30. These verses consist of the customary reference which the earlier author made to the source of further information, together with a short and somewhat enigmatic account of Josiah's death and burial. We have the additional information that the people chose Josiah's son, Jehoahaz, as king and installed him in his father's place.

29. Pharaoh Neco II (610-595 B.C.) was the son of Psamtik I, and thus the second Pharaoh of the Twenty-sixth Dynasty. The city of Nineveh had fallen in 612 B.C. (C. J.

**29-37. *In the Wake of Reform.*—First came the tragic death of Josiah at the battle of Megiddo in 608 B.C., when he rashly and foolishly attempted to resist the Egyptians in their

advance against Assyria. An unwise, premature, and impulsive use of the fighting instinct, which fails to choose the proper time and occasion for the risks that it involves, has cost many a man

to the river Euphrates: and king Josiah went against him; and he slew him at Megiddo, when he had seen him.

30 And his servants carried him in a chariot dead from Megiddo, and brought him to Jerusalem, and buried him in his own sepulchre. And the people of the land took Jehoahaz the son of Josiah, and anointed him, and made him king in his father's stead.

of Egypt went up to the king of Assyria to the river Eu-phra'tes. King Josi'ah went to meet him; and Pharaoh Neco slew him at Megid'do, when he saw him. 30 And his servant carried him dead in a chariot from Megid'do, and brought him to Jerusalem, and buried him in his own tomb. And the people of the land took Jeho'ahaz the son of Josi'ah, and anointed him, and made him king in his father's stead.

Gadd, ed., *The Fall of Nineveh* [London: British Museum, 1923], p. 15) to a combined attack of Cyaxares the Mede and Nabopolassar the Babylonian. Neco was marching north and east, either to support the remnants of the Assyrian power, or to carve out an empire for himself. The place at the head of the nations had become vacant with the death of Ashurbanipal in 626 B.C. and the breakup of the Assyrian Empire. Probably Neco was trying to establish the Egyptian power throughout Syria as Thutmose III had done in the fifteenth century B.C. Curiously enough, it was actually at Megiddo that Thutmose III had defeated the Syrian armies and conquered Palestine in 1479 B.C.

The reason for Josiah's advance to Megiddo is unknown, but there is every reason to suppose that Josiah was fighting on his own account in order to extend his own power and authority (cf. II Chr. 35:20-24). He was confident of his own cause; he had already achieved a measure of success, and the Deuteronomic philosophy of history would assure him that he was bound to prosper since he had kept the Deuteronomic law with the utmost devotion and vigor. (According to Herodotus [*History* II. 159], the battle took place at Magdalos by the Egyptian border.) Neco subsequently continued his march eastward to garrison Charchemish on the Euphrates, in company with the Assyrian force, both of them anxious to prevent a Babylonian advance to the north. Neco's army was annihilated there in 605 B.C. by Nebuchadrezzar, son of Nabopolassar, who became king of Babylon in the next year (Jer. 46:2; II Chr. 35:20). This ended the Egyptian bid for power, and the Pharaohs were never again able to interfere in the politics of the Near East until the time of the Ptolemies (after 323 B.C.). The death of Josiah was for Judah a disaster of the first magnitude It was followed by great lamentations (II Chr. 35:25), and the king's memory was greatly treasured for centuries (Ecclus. 49:1-3). His death marked the end of any Judahite hope of independence, and it abruptly interrupted the revival of a purified cultus.

The statement that **Pharaoh-nechoh . . . went up against the king of Assyria** is difficult. Either it means that he went up against whoever happened to be in control in Mesopotamia (cf. Ezra 6:22, where the phrase is used of a Persian) or, more likely, the preposition עַל ("against") should be translated "to," as if it were אֶל. Such a translation suggests that the Egyptian ruler was allying himself with what was left of Assyria.

Mount Megiddo is in Hebrew *har-meghiddô*, and in the Greek *Armagedōn*. It came to be the traditional site of the last great fight against the enemies of God (Rev. 16:16).

30. The people of Judah buried Josiah and installed Jehoahaz as king.

---

his life and freedom many a victory. The death of Josiah sounded the death knell of Judah. To the prophetic party, which had pinned its hopes on this just and good king, his untoward death must have come as a devastating blow to their hopes, must have appeared as a blank mystery in the ways of God. For they could not have foreseen the greater glory which God was preparing for his people through defeat and suffering.

With a few swift strokes the historian dismisses the three months' reign of Jehoahaz, one of Josiah's younger sons. The land was put under tribute, an older half brother of Jehoahaz was made king in his stead, and his name was changed to Jehoiakim. This was the last of the real kings of Judah, a strong but evil-minded man with whom Jeremiah waged one of the most grandiose personal battles in all history. Again we are bewildered by the regularity with

31 ¶ Jehoahaz *was* twenty and three years old when he began to reign; and he reigned three months in Jerusalem. And his mother's name *was* Hamutal, the daughter of Jeremiah of Libnah.

32 And he did *that which was* evil in the sight of the LORD, according to all that his fathers had done.

33 And Pharaoh-nechoh put him in bands at Riblah in the land of Hamath, that he might not reign in Jerusalem; and put the land to a tribute of a hundred talents of silver, and a talent of gold.

34 And Pharaoh-nechoh made Eliakim the son of Josiah king in the room of Josiah his father, and turned his name to Jehoiakim, and took Jehoahaz away: and he came to Egypt, and died there.

35 And Jehoiakim gave the silver and the gold to Pharaoh; but he taxed the land to give the money according to the commandment of Pharaoh: he exacted the silver and the gold of the people of the land, of every one according to his taxation, to give *it* unto Pharaoh-nechoh.

36 ¶ Jehoiakim *was* twenty and five years old when he began to reign; and he reigned eleven years in Jerusalem. And his mother's

31 Jeho'ahaz was twenty-three years old when he began to reign, and he reigned three months in Jerusalem. His mother's name was Hamu'tal the daughter of Jeremiah of Libnah. 32 And he did what was evil in the sight of the LORD, according to all that his fathers had done. 33 And Pharaoh Neco put him in bonds at Riblah in the land of Hamath, that he might not reign in Jerusalem, and laid upon the land a tribute of a hundred talents of silver and a talent of gold. 34 And Pharaoh Neco made Eli'akim the son of Josi'ah king in the place of Josi'ah his father, and changed his name to Jehoi'akim. But he took Jeho'ahaz away; and he came to Egypt, and died there. 35 And Jehoi'akim gave the silver and the gold to Pharaoh, but he taxed the land to give the money according to the command of Pharaoh. He exacted the silver and the gold of the people of the land, from every one according to his assessment, to give it to Pharaoh Neco.

36 Jehoi'akim was twenty-five years old when he began to reign, and he reigned

2. JEHOAHAZ OF JUDAH (23:31-35)

31-35. This king's reign was short. The account consists only of a Deuteronomic condemnation of him (vss. 31-32), together with the statement that he ended his days a prisoner in Egypt. He was not the oldest son of Josiah (cf. vss. 31, 36). Presumably this son supported the nationalistic policy of his father, since Neco almost immediately summoned him to the Egyptian headquarters at Riblah by the Orontes and deposed him in favor of his elder brother, Eliakim, whose name he changed to Jehoiakim. The new king instituted a capital levy in order to pay the tribute which the Egyptian king demanded.

3. JEHOIAKIM OF JUDAH (23:36–24:7)

Jehoiakim reigned for eleven years. During his reign Neco and his army were annihilated at Charchemish on the Euphrates. This event freed Jehoiakim from the Egyptian suzerainty, but his freedom was short lived because when he attempted to resist the Babylonian domination he found himself faced with Nebuchadrezzar and his army. The Judahite king died before the clash of arms and left his son to deal with a desperate situation.

36-37. Here is the normal Deuteronomic notice of the accession of a new king of Judah. If the earlier Deuteronomic compiler of 610 B.C. did indeed complete his work

which an evil king is followed by a good one, and a good one by an evil one. Ahaz and Hezekiah; Hezekiah and Manasseh; Amon and Josiah; Josiah and Jehoiakim. When Jehoahaz and Jehoiakim died in degradation, no tears were shed for them (Jer. 22:10, 18-19). When

Josiah died, there was national lamentation and he was buried in honor. The reward of the righteous man always lies in the honor in which he is held after his death; the fate of the unrighteous lies in the infamy which is forever attached to his name. The best commentary on

name *was* Zebudah, the daughter of Pedaiah of Rumah.

37 And he did *that which was* evil in the sight of the LORD, according to all that his fathers had done.

24 In his days Nebuchadnezzar king of Babylon came up, and Jehoiakim became his servant three years: then he turned and rebelled against him.

2 And the LORD sent against him bands of the Chaldees, and bands of the Syrians, and bands of the Moabites, and bands of the children of Ammon, and sent them against Judah to destroy it, according to the word of the LORD, which he spake by his servants the prophets.

3 Surely at the commandment of the LORD came *this* upon Judah, to remove *them* out of his sight, for the sins of Manasseh, according to all that he did;

eleven years in Jerusalem. His mother's name was Zebi'dah the daughter of Pedai'ah of Rumah. **37** And he did what was evil in the sight of the LORD, according to all that his fathers had done.

24 In his days Nebuchadnez'zar king of Babylon came up, and Jehoi'akim became his servant three years; then he turned and rebelled against him. **2** And the LORD sent against him bands of the Chalde'ans, and bands of the Syrians, and bands of the Moabites, and bands of the Ammonites, and sent them against Judah to destroy it, according to the word of the LORD which he spoke by his servants the prophets. **3** Surely this came upon Judah at the command of the LORD, to remove them out of his sight, for the sins of Manas'seh, accord-

---

before the death of King Josiah, then these verses are the work of the later Deuteronomic editor of *ca.* 550 B.C.

24:1-7. Vs. 1 is the final extract from the royal annals of Judah. Vs. 7 seems to be a fragmentary remnant of a passage which told of the defeat of Pharaoh Neco at Carchemish in 605 B.C. Jehoiakim had evidently become vassal to Nebuchadrezzar when the new king of Babylon overran Syria, either in the year after Carchemish, i.e., 604 B.C. (in which case Jehoiakim's rebellion took place in 601 B.C.) or else in 601 B.C. (in which case the rebellion took place *ca.* 598 B.C.). In the first case we must assume that various robber bands (vs. 2) were acting under Babylonian authority and with Nebuchadrezzar's encouragement in order to keep Jehoiakim busy until Nebuchadrezzar himself was free to deal with the situation. It is more likely that Jehoiakim was free from any outside domination till 601 B.C. Nebuchadrezzar was too busy elsewhere, and the various bands were probably making the most of their opportunities of plunder, consequent upon the collapse of the Egyptian authority in Syria, before Nebuchadrezzar could restore order. For **Syrians** read "Edomites" (אדם for ארם). Lucian adds "and of the Samaritans" (as does LXX in the parallel II Chr. 36:5). The **prophets** mentioned in vs. 2 were Jeremiah and Uriah (Jer. 26:20 ff.).

3. The later Deuteronomist develops his theme that the dead weight of Manasseh's sins brought ruin to Jerusalem in spite of all that Josiah could do.

---

the lives of these kings of Judah is found in the eloquent passage in the apocryphal book of the Wisdom of Solomon (5:1-15), which ought to be more often read in our churches.

24:1-7. Jehoiakim and Jeremiah.—Portentous events now follow in swift succession. In 612 B.C., Nineveh fell with a crash which startled the world (Nah. 2–3). And now Babylon rose to power under her brilliant new King Nebuchadrezzar, defeated the Egyptians at Carchemish (Jer. 46:1-12), and then in the fourth or fifth year of the reign of Jehoiakim swept down upon Palestine. Without a struggle Judah yielded and Jehoiakim became a vassal of Babylon. Jerusalem was spared. But it was a short

respite. After several years, in spite of warnings from Jeremiah (25:9; 36:30-31), Jehoiakim rebelled. Judah was invaded and ravaged and in some skirmish Jehoiakim was slain.

Consider the two contrasted characters and careers of Jehoiakim and Jeremiah, who for a decade faced each other in uncompromising hostility. They were human opposites. The king was worldly, selfish, unscrupulous, wholly irreligious. The prophet was the embodiment of fearless moral courage and of a truly spiritual religion. The one was actuated only by the basest motives; the other was motivated only by complete obedience to the word and will of God. Jehoiakim sought only personal gain;

4 And also for the innocent blood that he shed: for he filled Jerusalem with innocent blood; which the LORD would not pardon.

5 ¶ Now the rest of the acts of Jehoiakim, and all that he did, *are* they not written in the book of the Chronicles of the kings of Judah?

6 So Jehoiakim slept with his fathers: and Jehoiachin his son reigned in his stead.

7 And the king of Egypt came not again any more out of his land: for the king of Babylon had taken from the river of Egypt unto the river Euphrates all that pertained to the king of Egypt.

8 ¶ Jehoiachin *was* eighteen years old when he began to reign, and he reigned in

ing to all that he had done, 4 and also for the innocent blood that he had shed; for he filled Jerusalem with innocent blood, and the LORD would not pardon. 5 Now the rest of the deeds of Jehoi′akim, and all that he did, are they not written in the Book of the Chronicles of the Kings of Judah? 6 So Jehoi′akim slept with his fathers, and Jehoi′achin his son reigned in his stead. 7 And the king of Egypt did not come again out of his land, for the king of Babylon had taken all that belonged to the king of Egypt from the Brook of Egypt to the river Eu-phra′tes.

8 Jehoi′achin was eighteen years old

5-6. The editor adds the customary obituary notice, continuing it in vs. 7 with a note concerning the complete weakness of Egypt after the disaster at Carchemish.

4. JEHOIACHIN OF JUDAH (24:8-17)

This young king inherited an impossible situation, with the Babylonian army besieging the city while he had no resources. He surrendered forthwith and went into exile with all his court. Nebuchadrezzar plundered the temple and carried into captivity all the arms, the craftsmen, and the smiths, everyone who was likely to raise the standard of revolt or could manufacture war material, and left only the lowest stratum of the people.

8-9. Here again is the customary Deuteronomic notice of the accession of a king of Judah. The adverse comment on this king is not in accordance with the judgment of Ezekiel, who seems to regard him favorably (Ezek. 17:22-24).

Jeremiah cared nothing for what became of himself. Such was the contrast. Yet there was a certain identity in their fate. The king came to an unhappy end. But so did the prophet, who never knew the meaning of human happiness. During the whole of this terrible decade he persisted in opposing the policies of Jehoiakim and his parasites, going so far as to predict the conquest of Jerusalem by the Babylonians, thus laying himself open to the charge of treason. It is a mystery that he was allowed to live. As it was, he was flung into a dungeon (Jer. 38:6), and his life ended in sheer tragedy (Jer. 43:1-7). Thus both king and prophet outwardly met much the same fate. Yet in the light of history how different has been their destiny. Jehoiakim's proper epitaph reads, "The name of the wicked shall rot" (Prov. 10:7). The total achievement of Jehoiakim adds up to less than zero. And Jeremiah? His epitaph reads, "Blessed are they which are persecuted for righteousness' sake: for theirs is the kingdom of heaven" (Matt. 5:10). Jeremiah lived in a kingdom of which Jehoiakim knew nothing. For the highest of all joys is that in which one's self is wholly lost in complete devotion to the will of God.

This gives to life its highest unity, consistency, power, peace, and joy. Such was the kingdom in which Jeremiah lived, moved, and had his being. And when he died, he left an immortal bequest to humanity: the concepts of a higher, truer, and more spiritual religion than the world had ever known. Derided in his lifetime, scorned and neglected, Jeremiah both in what he was and in what he did became revered as few were revered who came before or after him. He has his permanent place among this world's immortals. Jehoiakim and Jeremiah! Contemporaries, man and man; living in the same place and under the same circumstances. Did two men standing side by side, by their characters, careers, and destinies ever teach such deep and solemn truths: "The wages of sin is death" (Rom. 6:23); "He that doeth the will of God abideth for ever" (I John 2:17)?

8-9. Jehoiachin.—Came to the throne Jehoiachin. Here is a man to be pitied. He was a favorite of the people (Jer. 22:24), and there must have been something attractive about him, for brief as his reign was—only three months—he was not forgotten (Ezek. 19:8-9), and his Babylonian captors had mercy on him (25:27-

Jerusalem three months. And his mother's name *was* Nehushta, the daughter of Elnathan of Jerusalem.

9 And he did *that which was* evil in the sight of the LORD, according to all that his father had done.

10 ¶ At that time the servants of Nebuchadnezzar king of Babylon came up against Jerusalem, and the city was besieged.

11 And Nebuchadnezzar king of Babylon came against the city, and his servants did besiege it.

12 And Jehoiachin the king of Judah went out to the king of Babylon, he, and his mother, and his servants, and his princes, and his officers: and the king of Babylon took him in the eighth year of his reign.

13 And he carried out thence all the treasures of the house of the LORD, and the treasures of the king's house, and cut in pieces all the vessels of gold which Solomon king of Israel had made in the temple of the LORD, as the LORD had said.

14 And he carried away all Jerusalem, and all the princes, and all the mighty men of valor, *even* ten thousand captives, and all the craftsmen and smiths: none remained, save the poorest sort of the people of the land.

when he became king, and he reigned three months in Jerusalem. His mother's name was Nehush'ta the daughter of Elna'than of Jerusalem. **9** And he did what was evil in the sight of the LORD, according to all that his father had done.

10 At that time the servants of Nebuchadnez'zar king of Babylon came up to Jerusalem, and the city was besieged. **11** And Nebuchadnez'zar king of Babylon came to the city, while his servants were besieging it; **12** and Jehoi'achin the king of Judah gave himself up to the king of Babylon, himself, and his mother, and his servants, and his princes, and his palace officials. The king of Babylon took him prisoner in the eighth year of his reign, **13** and carried off all the treasures of the house of the LORD, and the treasures of the king's house, and cut in pieces all the vessels of gold in the temple of the LORD, which Solomon king of Israel had made, as the LORD had foretold. **14** He carried away all Jerusalem, and all the princes, and all the mighty men of valor, ten thousand captives, and all the craftsmen and the smiths; none remained, except the poorest people of the land.

10-17. Jehoiakim died in time, and it was left for the youthful Jehoiachin to surrender quickly and so to save the city and the temple from destruction.

12. The date of the first captivity is here given as Nebuchadrezzar's **eighth year** (597 B.C.), whereas Jer. 52:28 mentions the "seventh year" (see 25:27).

13-14. These two verses belong to a different stratum of tradition from vss. 15-16. Stade held with some justification that they are more suitable to the deportation of 586 B.C. On the other hand, the figures given, in both vss. 14 and 16, do not agree with

---

30). We are told (vs. 9) that he did evil. But was it he or his mother Nehushta? For it seems likely that she was the real ruler for this brief period (Jer. 13:18). Neither can we forget that her father Elnathan had dragged back Uriah (Jer. 26:22-23) from Egypt to be murdered by Jehoiakim. Evil influences encompassed the young king, only eighteen, who came into such a terrible situation in national affairs. We read of it in Habakkuk, whose prophecy was written a few years earlier. Corruption and irreligion within the kingdom, and the Chaldeans at the gates!

Here, then, we find tragedy of a kind to arouse our deepest compassion: a young man made for better things, who with a different chance in life might have done well, crushed by circumstances over which he had no control,

helpless in the face of events, his hands tied by his elders, having to witness the spectacle of the ruin of his land, and himself to suffer an ignoble fate. Such a career has its counterparts in human experience. There are people today who have no real chance in life, whose deepest impulses, longings, aspirations are never satisfied, who suffer defeat when they merit the opposite. Here lies one of the deepest reasons for feeling that there must be a life beyond this human life of ours, in which the apparent injustice of human event will find its correction, and in which what was denied here will find its completion and fulfillment in the life that is to be.

10-17. *The Great Refusal.*—Catastrophe was not delayed. Nebuchadrezzar soon arrived before Jerusalem. Resistance was useless. **And . . .**

15 And he carried away Jehoiachin to Babylon, and the king's mother, and the king's wives, and his officers, and the mighty of the land, *those* carried he into captivity from Jerusalem to Babylon.

16 And all the men of might, *even* seven thousand, and craftsmen and smiths a thousand, all *that were* strong *and* apt for war, even them the king of Babylon brought captive to Babylon.

17 ¶ And the king of Babylon made Mattaniah his father's brother king in his stead, and changed his name to Zedekiah.

18 Zedekiah *was* twenty and one years old when he began to reign, and he reigned eleven years in Jerusalem. And his mother's name *was* Hamutal, the daughter of Jeremiah of Libnah.

15 And he carried away Jehoi'achin to Babylon; the king's mother, the king's wives, his officials, and the chief men of the land, he took into captivity from Jerusalem to Babylon. 16 And the king of Babylon brought captive to Babylon all the men of valor, seven thousand, and the craftsmen and the smiths, one thousand, all of them strong and fit for war. 17 And the king of Babylon made Mattani'ah, Jehoi'achin's uncle, king in his stead, and changed his name to Zedeki'ah.

18 Zedeki'ah was twenty-one years old when he became king, and he reigned eleven years in Jerusalem. His mother's name was Hamu'tal the daughter of Jere-

---

the very moderate figures of Jer. 52:28-30 (a total of 4,600 for three deportations—including that in 581 B.C. with a total of 745 deportees).

15. This verse agrees with Jer. 27:20, which says that Nebuchadrezzar carried away the king and the nobility but makes no reference to any other groups.

17. Mattaniah (Zedekiah) was full brother to the Jehoahaz who had been carried captive to Egypt by Pharaoh Neco in 608 B.C. He would therefore be supposed to be a safe anti-Egyptian.

5. ZEDEKIAH OF JUDAH (24:18–25:7)

Zedekiah proved unable to resist the pro-Egyptian party, which gained strength mostly because Nebuchadrezzar had unwisely transported the more responsible elements

---

the king . . . went out, . . . he, and his mother. We think of the pair, and the princes and the mighty men of valor! And they were carried away to Babylon. Yet there was something left. There was enough left even then to have preserved the nation from its final fate. Jeremiah was left, devoted heart and soul to the salvation of his people. Alone, he could have saved it. Yet even this last chance was thrown away by unrepentant Judah. Here we are taught the lesson that even in the hour of gravest disaster there remains always the possibility of moral self-recovery. Always there is something left on which character can be rebuilt; and with this rebuilding of character the reconstruction of life. If disaster, deserved or undeserved, can be accepted, if its lessons are learned, if the future is resolutely faced, then salvation is always possible. And this is true alike for the individual and for the state.

24:18–25:21. Conscience and Circumstance.— Here the historian gives us a dry and circumstantial account of the death agonies of the ancient Davidic dynasty. He recounts the terrible results of the rebellion of King Zedekiah. The detail of all of this cannot detain us.

What fastens our attention in this fearful drama is the character of King Zedekiah. Personally he was attractive, likable, and well intentioned. He was treated by Jeremiah with a deference never showed to Jehoiakim. Zedekiah, on his part, revered and honored the prophet, placed great confidence in his character and counsel, and doubtless recognized that to submit to the Babylonians was the wiser course to pursue (Jer. 37:7-9; 38:16-24). His personal convictions coincided with those of the prophet. But he was beset on the other hand by political pressure and popular sentiment that favored rebellion. And this course was further supported by other prophets, notably by Hananiah (Jer. 28:1-3), who declared boldly that within two years the captives in Babylon would return and that the yoke of Babylon would be broken.

Thus we have the tragic picture of a man whose conscience and whose truest friend urged him one way while the whole crowd of politicians and timeserving prophets were hounding him to the opposite course of action. Why has no one dramatized this fearsome episode in literature? Zedekiah, terrorized by the chauvinists, yielded at last, deliberately broke the

19 And he did *that which was* evil in the sight of the LORD, according to all that Jehoiakim had done.

20 For through the anger of the LORD it came to pass in Jerusalem and Judah, until he had cast them out from his presence, that Zedekiah rebelled against the king of Babylon.

25 And it came to pass in the ninth year of his reign, in the tenth month, in the tenth *day* of the month, *that* Nebuchadnezzar king of Babylon came, he, and all his host, against Jerusalem, and pitched against it; and they built forts against it round about.

2 And the city was besieged unto the eleventh year of king Zedekiah.

3 And on the ninth *day* of the *fourth* month the famine prevailed in the city, and there was no bread for the people of the land.

4 ¶ And the city was broken up, and all the men of war *fled* by night by the way of the gate between two walls, which *is* by the king's garden: (now the Chaldees *were*

miah of Libnah. **19** And he did what was evil in the sight of the LORD, according to all that Jehoi′akim had done. **20** For because of the anger of the LORD it came to the point in Jerusalem and Judah that he cast them out from his presence.

And Zedeki′ah rebelled against the king

25 of Babylon. **1** And in the ninth year of his reign, in the tenth month, on the tenth day of the month, Nebuchadnez′zar king of Babylon came with all his army against Jerusalem, and laid siege to it; and they built siegeworks against it round about. **2** So the city was besieged till the eleventh year of King Zedeki′ah. **3** On the ninth day of the fourth month the famine was so severe in the city that there was no food for the people of the land. **4** Then a breach was made in the city; the king with all the men of war fled[k] by night by the way of the gate between the two walls, by

[k] Gk Compare Jer 39. 4; 52. 7: Heb lacks *the king* and *fled*

---

to Babylonia. Apart from the family of Shaphan the scribe, who had been prominent in Josiah's time, the king seems to have had no one left who was capable of supporting the inspired and balanced judgment of the prophet Jeremiah. There is a certain amount of evidence that the accession of Psamtik II to the throne of Egypt in 593 B.C. caused considerable unrest in the western provinces of the Babylonian Empire, but the promised revolt did not take place till Apries (Hophra) secured the Egyptian crown in 588 B.C. Once more the hope of help from the powers of the Nile brought Judah into trouble, and this time it proved to be complete destruction.

25:1. The custom of reckoning the months by number is a postexilic fashion due to Babylonian influence. The siege began about the end of December, on the tenth of the tenth month. By the latter part of June in the next year there was no food left for the civilians.

4. When the city wall was breached, Zedekiah and the surviving fighting men made a sally through the gate which led out from the space between the two ancient Jebusite walls which still existed on the north side of the ancient city. On the other three sides there

---

solemn oath he had made to Nebuchadrezzar, and rebelled. This brought down upon him the scathing condemnation of both Jeremiah and Ezekiel (Ezek. 17:19). Even in those days solemn covenants between nations were held to be more than "a scrap of paper."

How often has this tragedy in the life of Zedekiah been re-enacted in the lives of men, high and low. They are good and well meaning. They know what is right and they want to do it. They are placed in positions which demand stamina, courage, and loyalty to standards of conduct and action in which they themselves believe. They have some friends in whom they

can trust, who urge firmness in standing for what they know is right. Yet in the shifting sphere of politics and business there is the bellowing crowd which tells them that everything will be won in the way of preferment and success by a policy which involves dishonor, the breaking of solemn pledges, parting with conscience and the demands of simple truth and rectitude. The drama was enacted on a high level in the case of Zedekiah. But the issue is the same on any level, high or low. And always the results are the same.

24:20. *The Futility of Rebellion.*—Zedekiah rebelled. And rebellion against the plain and

against the city round about:) and *the king* went the way toward the plain.

5 And the army of the Chaldees pursued after the king, and overtook him in the plains of Jericho: and all his army were scattered from him.

6 So they took the king, and brought him up to the king of Babylon to Riblah; and they gave judgment upon him.

7 And they slew the sons of Zedekiah before his eyes, and put out the eyes of Zedekiah, and bound him with fetters of brass, and carried him to Babylon.

8 ¶ And in the fifth month, on the seventh *day* of the month, which *is* the nineteenth year of king Nebuchadnezzar king of Babylon, came Nebuzar-adan, captain of the guard, a servant of the king of Babylon, unto Jerusalem:

9 And he burnt the house of the LORD, and the king's house, and all the houses of Jerusalem, and every great *man's* house burnt he with fire.

10 And all the army of the Chaldees, that *were with* the captain of the guard, brake down the walls of Jerusalem round about.

the king's garden, though the Chalde'ans were around the city. And they went in the direction of the Arabah. 5 But the army of the Chalde'ans pursued the king, and overtook him in the plains of Jericho; and all his army was scattered from him. 6 Then they captured the king, and brought him up to the king of Babylon at Riblah, who passed sentence upon him. 7 They slew the sons of Zedeki'ah before his eyes, and put out the eyes of Zedeki'ah, and bound him in fetters, and took him to Babylon.

8 In the fifth month, on the seventh day of the month — which was the nineteenth year of King Nebuchadnez'zar, king of Babylon — Nebu'zarad'an, the captain of the bodyguard, a servant of the king of Babylon, came to Jerusalem. 9 And he burned the house of the LORD, and the king's house and all the houses of Jerusalem; every great house he burned down. 10 And all the army of the Chalde'ans, who were with the captain of the guard, broke

were steep ascents, and little other protection was needed, but on the north side extra precautions had been taken. The double walls on the north have been recently discovered (F. Garrow Duncan, "Millo and the City of David," *Zeitschrift für die alttestamentliche Wissenschaft*, XLII [1924], 222-44). To the east the desert country came close up to the city, and this easy access to the desolate lands proved more than once a refuge to the hard-beset defenders of Jerusalem. Many men escaped by this means in the final stages of the resistance against Titus in A.D. 70.

5. Zedekiah followed the same general direction as that by which David had escaped in the first stage of Absalom's revolt, but he was overtaken by the pursuing Babylonians in the Jordan Valley near Jericho.

6. **Riblah** had been the headquarters of Pharaoh Neco also (23:33). It acted as a convenient center for the subjugation of the whole of Syria.

6. Destruction of the Temple and the City (25:8-17)

The Babylonians burned the whole city, temple, palace, and all the houses. They deported the population and left behind only agricultural workers. They took away all the metalwork of the temple, bronze, gold, and silver. The annihilation of the city was complete.

8. According to Jer. 52:29, the destruction took place in Nebuchadrezzar's eighteenth year (587 B.C.), but **the nineteenth** is correct, i.e., 586 B.C. (see Exeg. on 24:12-15).

evident will of God is always folly. However repugnant to the Jewish nationalistic consciousness, nothing was plainer than that it was the will of God that his people must sacrifice pride and accept the humiliation of domination by a foreign power. So urged Jeremiah. They refused. And by their refusal, as a result, final

calamity overtook them. Judah paid dearly for its act of perfidy. And many a nation in our modern world has paid a high price for following a similar course of dishonor. God's judgments are true and righteous altogether.

Zedekiah's rebellion was not only dishonorable; it was also futile. Precisely so in personal

11 Now the rest of the people that were left in the city, and the fugitives that fell away to the king of Babylon, with the remnant of the multitude, did Nebuzar-adan the captain of the guard carry away.

12 But the captain of the guard left of the poor of the land *to be* vinedressers and husbandmen.

13 And the pillars of brass that *were* in the house of the LORD, and the bases, and the brazen sea that *was* in the house of the LORD, did the Chaldees break in pieces, and carried the brass of them to Babylon.

14 And the pots, and the shovels, and the snuffers, and the spoons, and all the vessels of brass wherewith they ministered, took they away.

15 And the firepans, and the bowls, *and* such things as *were* of gold, *in* gold, and of silver, *in* silver, the captain of the guard took away.

16 The two pillars, one sea, and the bases which Solomon had made for the house of the LORD; the brass of all these vessels was without weight.

17 The height of the one pillar *was* eighteen cubits, and the chapiter upon it *was* brass: and the height of the chapiter three cubits; and the wreathed work, and pomegranates upon the chapiter round about, all of brass: and like unto these had the second pillar with wreathed work.

18 ¶ And the captain of the guard took Seraiah the chief priest, and Zephaniah the second priest, and the three keepers of the door:

down the walls around Jerusalem. 11 And the rest of the people who were left in the city and the deserters who had deserted to the king of Babylon, together with the rest of the multitude, Nebu'zarad'an the captain of the guard carried into exile. 12 But the captain of the guard left some of the poorest of the land to be vinedressers and plowmen.

13 And the pillars of bronze that were in the house of the LORD, and the stands and the bronze sea that were in the house of the LORD, the Chalde'ans broke in pieces, and carried the bronze to Babylon. 14 And they took away the pots, and the shovels, and the snuffers, and the dishes for incense and all the vessels of bronze used in the temple service, 15 the firepans also, and the bowls. What was of gold the captain of the guard took away as gold, and what was of silver, as silver. 16 As for the two pillars, the one sea, and the stands, which Solomon had made for the house of the LORD, the bronze of all these vessels was beyond weight. 17 The height of the one pillar was eighteen cubits, and upon it was a capital of bronze; the height of the capital was three cubits; a network and pomegranates, all of bronze, were upon the capital round about. And the second pillar had the like, with the network.

18 And the captain of the guard took Serai'ah the chief priest, and Zephani'ah the second priest, and the three keepers of

---

16-17. There is a fuller description of these bronzes in Jer. 52:20-23. Here the reference to the bronze bulls which supported the bronze sea is omitted. Perhaps this is deliberate and correct, for it has been stated in II Kings 16:17 that Ahaz had removed them to give them to his Assyrian overlord. The Deuteronomic editor of *ca.* 550 B.C. was aware of this, and knew also that other bronzes had disappeared before the final destruction. He therefore omitted the numbers of the pomegranates and reduced the other numbers.

7. EXECUTION OF THE LEADERS (25:18-22)

18-22. These were the men who had been responsible for the revolt. The Babylonians might not be able to stop another revolt, though they intended to do their best, but

---

experience we discover the folly of rebellion against the will of God. Times come in a man's life when he is asked to accept what looks like the undeserved ruin of all his earthly hopes. Pride rebels. He cannot and will not submit. He remains defiant against a fate that is repug-

nant to all his human desires. He resists with all his strength, only to know at last the bitterness of defeat and alienation from the God in whom once he believed. There is but the one way: submission to and acceptance of whatever may seem most intolerable, if this cannot be avoided

19 And out of the city he took an officer that was set over the men of war, and five men of them that were in the king's presence, which were found in the city, and the principal scribe of the host, which mustered the people of the land, and threescore men of the people of the land *that were* found in the city:

20 And Nebuzar-adan captain of the guard took these, and brought them to the king of Babylon to Riblah:

21 And the king of Babylon smote them, and slew them at Riblah in the land of Hamath. So Judah was carried away out of their land.

22 ¶ And *as for* the people that remained in the land of Judah, whom Nebuchadnezzar king of Babylon had left, even over them he made Gedaliah the son of Ahikam, the son of Shaphan, ruler.

23 And when all the captains of the armies, they and their men, heard that the king of Babylon had made Gedaliah governor, there came to Gedaliah to Mizpah, even Ishmael the son of Nethaniah, and Johanan the son of Careah, and Seraiah the son of Tanhumeth the Netophathite, and Jaazaniah the son of a Maachathite, they and their men.

the threshold; 19 and from the city he took an officer who had been in command of the men of war, and five men of the king's council who were found in the city; and the secretary of the commander of the army who mustered the people of the land; and sixty men of the people of the land who were found in the city. 20 And Nebu'zarad'an the captain of the guard took them, and brought them to the king of Babylon at Riblah. 21 And the king of Babylon smote them, and put them to death at Riblah in the land of Hamath. So Judah was taken into exile out of its land.

22 And over the people who remained in the land of Judah, whom Nebuchadnez'zar king of Babylon had left, he appointed Gedali'ah the son of Ahi'kam, son of Shaphan, governor. 23 Now when all the captains of the forces in the open country[l] and their men heard that the king of Babylon had appointed Gedali'ah governor, they came with their men to Gedali'ah at Mizpah, namely, Ishmael the son of Nethani'ah, and Joha'nan the son of Kare'ah, and Serai'ah the son of Tan'humeth the Netoph'athite, and Ja-azani'ah the son of the

[l] With Jer 40. 7: Heb lacks *in the open country*

---

they certainly made sure that these men could not lead a second one. According to Jer. 52:25, there were seven, not five.

8. Gedaliah Governor of Judah (25:23-26)

The editor has reached the last stage in his sad tale. According to Josephus (*Antiquities* X. 9. 1-2), Gedaliah was a man of gentle and generous disposition who won the confidence of the captains of the guerrilla bands. He sought by his kindness and generosity to conciliate them, and he refused to believe in the treachery of Ishmael when Johanan warned him. He himself preferred to be slain rather than to destroy a man who had fled to him for refuge. Such misplaced generosity brought Gedaliah to his death, for Ishmael, encouraged by the king of Ammon, assassinated him and threw everything once more into confusion. Ishmael slew every man he found in Mizpah, both Jews and Babylonians, all the "collaborators" (Jer. 40:1-16).

23. The town of **Mizpah** which was Gedaliah's headquarters was Mizpah of Benjamin, fortified by Asa with the timber and the stones which Baasha had been using in his fortification works at Ramah (I Kings 15:22).

---

and is the plain, even if it remains the mysterious, will of God for us. It is the only pathway to peace and to ultimate victory. Out of the humiliation of earthly hopes often comes the discovery of unsuspected spiritual blessings. "There is only one thing to do," a devout woman once said, "when you have a bitter cup to drink. You must take it in both hands, put

it to your lips, and drink it down to its last dregs. Only so can you absorb it and discover its meaning. So long as you hold it at a distance and refuse to drink it, you will know nothing but bitterness and loss of faith and peace."

25:22-30. Ave Atque Vale.—One more dreadful episode remains for the historian to chronicle. It is narrated in vss. 22-26. The beggarly

24 And Gedaliah sware to them, and to their men, and said unto them, Fear not to be the servants of the Chaldees: dwell in the land, and serve the king of Babylon; and it shall be well with you.

25 But it came to pass in the seventh month, that Ishmael the son of Nethaniah, the son of Elishama, of the seed royal, came, and ten men with him, and smote Gedaliah, that he died, and the Jews and the Chaldees that were with him at Mizpah.

26 And all the people, both small and great, and the captains of the armies, arose, and came to Egypt: for they were afraid of the Chaldees.

27 ¶ And it came to pass in the seven and thirtieth year of the captivity of Jehoiachin king of Judah, in the twelfth month, on the seven and twentieth *day* of the month, *that* Evil-merodach king of Babylon in the year that he began to reign did lift up the head of Jehoiachin king of Judah out of prison;

28 And he spake kindly to him, and set his throne above the throne of the kings that *were* with him in Babylon;

29 And changed his prison garments: and he did eat bread continually before him all the days of his life.

30 And his allowance *was* a continual allowance given him of the king, a daily rate for every day, all the days of his life.

Ma-ac'athite, 24 And Gedali'ah swore to them and their men, saying, "Do not be afraid because of the Chalde'an officials; dwell in the land, and serve the king of Babylon, and it shall be well with you." 25 But in the seventh month, Ishmael the son of Nethani'ah, son of Eli'shama, of the royal family, came with ten men, and attacked and killed Gedali'ah and the Jews and the Chalde'ans who were with him at Mizpah. 26 Then all the people, both small and great, and the captains of the forces arose, and went to Egypt; for they were afraid of the Chalde'ans.

27 And in the thirty-seventh year of the exile of Jehoi'achin king of Judah, in the twelfth month, on the twenty-seventh day of the month, Evil-mero'dach king of Babylon, in the year that he began to reign, graciously freed Jehoi'achin king of Judah from prison; 28 and he spoke kindly to him, and gave him a seat above the seats of the kings who were with him in Babylon. 29 So Jehoi'achin put off his prison garments. And every day of his life he dined regularly at the king's table; 30 and for his allowance, a regular allowance was given him by the king, every day a portion, as long as he lived.

---

9. THE HOPEFUL ENDING (25:27-30)

In the spring of 561 B.C. Jehoiachin, after thirty-seven years of captivity, found himself restored to a position of favor. He was not permitted to return home to Palestine but he did get a measure of preferment. Nebuchadrezzar had died in 562 B.C., and the new king Amel-Marduk (562-560 B.C.) changed his father's policy with respect to the captive king.

27. The phrase **lift up the head** is similarly used in Gen. 40:13 for describing release from actual prison.

29. The custom of eating at the king's table is a high honor (II Sam. 19:33; I Kings 2:7).

30. A number of cuneiform tablets have been recovered from a chamber in the northeast corner of Nebuchadrezzar's southern fort, beneath the ground floor of the

---

remnant of the people, alarmed by the assassination of Gedaliah and in fear of Babylon, fled back to Egypt, carrying the aged prophet Jeremiah with them. Let the Bible reader turn to the book of Exodus, reread the story of the deliverance of God's people from Egypt, then think of this stampede of wretched fugitives back to Egypt, and he will have compassed the whole tragic story of a people whose persistent moral disobedience to the will of God had

brought about this incredible reversal of their fortunes. It did not take forty years for the return through the wilderness to Egypt. Moral retrogression is always swifter than moral advance. And the life of the people goes out in oblivion and obliquity in the very Egypt from which they had once set out on their pilgrim's progress to the Promised Land.

The last word in this book (vss. 27-30) contrasts strangely with what has preceded it. For

palace. Four of these refer to provisions which were supplied to Jehoiachin and his fellow prisoners. They belong to the period 594-569 B.C., so that the last of them is at least eight years earlier than the time of Jehoiachin's good fortune. It is evident therefore that Evil-merodach increased the king's allowance from the meager amount recorded in the tablets (G. R. Driver, "Jehoiakin in Captivity," *Expository Times*, LVI [1945] 317-18) .

The book of Kings ends on a note of hope. It is not the triumphant expectation of the earlier compiler of 610 B.C., the man who conceived the work itself, but it provides a ground of confidence in God's future redemption, the groundwork on which Second Isaiah and Ezekiel built, and out of which there grew the restored community of post-exilic days.

---

it tells of a generous act by one of whom we should least have expected it: the pagan King Evil-merodach. Thus we discover that no human heart but has in it the seeds of kindness and compassion. Our historian wrote during the Exile, and he seems glad to record this touch of mercy which he may have felt to be prophetic of mercies yet to come. And so it proved to be. For in God's own time these exiles, taught by sorrow and disciplined by suffering, were to usher in a new day not only for their own people but for all mankind.

The First and Second Books of

CHRONICLES

Introduction and Exegesis by W. A. L. ELMSLIE
Exposition by W. A. L. ELMSLIE

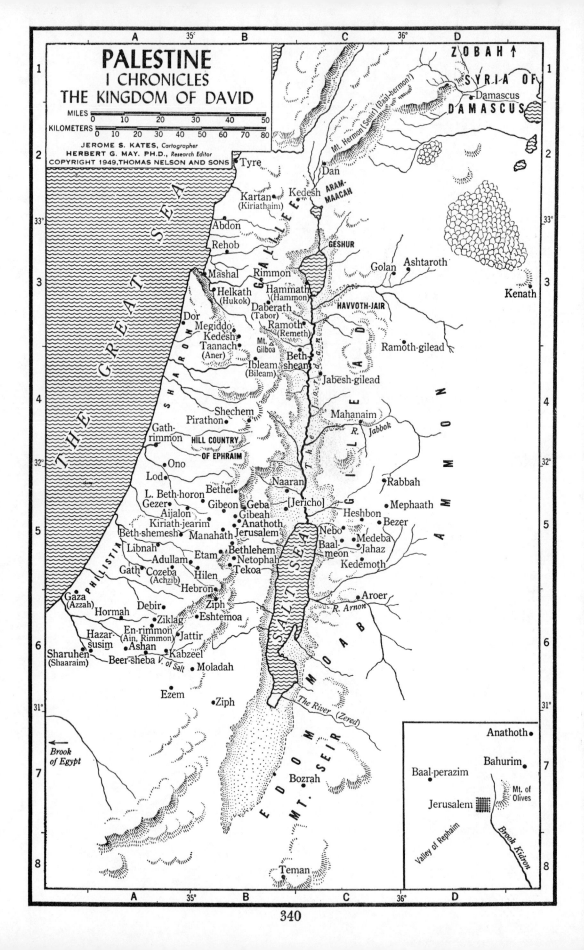

PALESTINE
I CHRONICLES
THE KINGDOM OF DAVID

MILES
0 10 20 30 40 50

KILOMETERS
0 10 20 30 40 50 60 70 80

JEROME S. KATES, *Cartographer*
HERBERT G. MAY, PH.D., *Research Editor*
COPYRIGHT 1949, THOMAS NELSON AND SONS

ZOBAH
SYRIA OF
DAMASCUS
• Damascus

Tyre

Mt. Hermon (Senir) (Baal-hermon?)

Dan

Kartan
(Kiriathaim)

Kedesh

ARAM-
MAACAH

Abdon

Rehob

GESHUR

Golan

Ashtaroth

Kenath

THE GREAT SEA

SHARON

Mashal

Rimmon

GALILEE

Helkath
(Hukok)

Hammath
(Hammon)

HAVVOTH-JAIR

Dor

Megiddo

Daberath
(Tabor)

Ramoth
(Remeth)

Ramoth-gilead

Kedesh

Taanach
(Aner)

Mt.
Gilboa

Ibleam
(Bileam)

Beth-
shean

Jabesh-gilead

Shechem

Pirathon

Mahanaim

R. Jabbok

GILEAD

Gath-
rimmon

HILL COUNTRY
OF EPHRAIM

AMMON

Ono

Naaran

Rabbah

Lod

L. Beth-horon

Bethel

Gezer

Gibeon

Geba

[Jericho]

Mephaath

Aijalon

Gibeah

Heshbon

Bezer

Kiriath-jearim

Anathoth

Nebo

Beth-shemesh

Manahath

Jerusalem

Baal-
meon

Medeba

Jahaz

Libnah

Bethlehem

Etam

Netophah

Kedemoth

PHILISTIA

Gath

Adullam

Cozeba
(Achzib)

Hilen

Tekoa

Hebron

Gaza
(Azzah)

Debir

Ziph

Aroer

R. Arnon

Hormah

Ziklag

Eshtemoa

En-rimmon
(Ain, Rimmon)

Jattir

Hazar-
susim

Ashan

Kabzeel

MOAB

Sharuhen
(Shaaraim)

Beer-sheba

V. of Salt

Moladah

SALT SEA

Ezem

Ziph

The River
(Zered)

Brook
of Egypt

EDOM

Bozrah

MT. SEIR

Teman

Anathoth

Bahurim

Baal-perazim

Mt. of
Olives

Jerusalem

Valley of Rephaim

Brook Kidron

I AND II CHRONICLES

INTRODUCTION

Chronicles is one of the most stimulating books in the Bible, courageous and practical—a splendid achievement. But that high valuation depends on understanding that Chronicles is not what it appears to be. Anyone who supposes that it is a history of Judah, which its author wanted or expected his readers to accept as accurate, is almost certain to consider it for the most part dull and frequently incredible. That impression of its character is widely held, and in consequence these two great books have become virtually deadwood in the Bible. They come alive when the real intentions of the Chronicler and the peculiar method which he used to make his purpose effective are apprehended. Properly understood, Chronicles has a rightful and indeed unique place in the Scriptures. It is the only instance of Hebraic philosophy of history presented on an immense scale. It is theology, powerfully and persuasively inculcating three doctrines: that human life exists under the overruling of an immutable moral order ordained by God; that observance of rightful forms of worship is of paramount importance for the community; and that God's revelation is given not only in past time but in the present— a *living* word of truth. The Chronicler had to urge this philosophy and these doctrines, not by abstract argument, but by a method wholly strange to us although sufficiently clear to his contemporaries. The Chronicler taught by painting a picture of the past, in which sometimes he laid emphasis on the religio-moral causes and consequences of events that actually had happened and sometimes gave a freely imagined delineation of what ought to have happened. Even where he makes use of facts, his aim is to depict "truth of idea." The mode should not be lightly esteemed, unfamiliar though it is. Expositors of the New Testament do not belittle the parables of Jesus on the ground that this and that did not really happen; their penetrating "truth of idea" is thankfully and seriously pondered.

The Chronicler's pictorial method was, of course, dramatic. Drama, except perhaps for the book of Job, is supposed to be unrepresented in Hebrew literature. But Chronicles is essentially a vast and moving drama, ranging from Adam to the destruction of the Judean kingdom. We should see in its first nine chapters a prelude, subtly inviting us to feel that human history from its commencement led up to the radiant morning of David's reign and the noonday splendor of Solomon, culminating in his dedication of the glorious temple for the rightful worship of God. Thereafter the drama unfolds its grim sequel in the succession of those kings of Judah to whom so much had been entrusted, from whom came so seldom good, so often evil. Again and again light shines, only to be swiftly quenched in darkness. (We should ask ourselves, Will evil prevail in human affairs? Will men fatally never learn to see and choose the ways of God?) Toward the end of the drama there are two periods (the reigns of Hezekiah and Josiah) when it seems as if victory may rest with good; but they are transient. At the last, black night descends on the tragedy of Jerusalem: the city is captured and destroyed and its temple burned. Its kings and people had persisted in wickedness until there was no remedy.

This drama could never be acted. It was composed for reading and reflection. But suppose it had been enacted before the eyes of the men of Jerusalem in the time of the Chronicler, long after the sack of Jerusalem, with what thoughts should they have witnessed it? They realized that overwhelming military might had abolished their political independence. They were men in peril of despondency or despair. But they knew that, although seemingly final night had fallen when the Davidic kingdom had been destroyed, light had arisen in darkness.

Their people had rallied on a religion purified and ennobled by the thoughts of God and duty which the prophets had demanded. Jerusalem's temple had been rebuilt; their national consciousness had not ceased. A wonderful, spiritual coherence of Israel was possible, not only among themselves in Palestine, but also among the multitude of their brethren dispersed in many lands. The Chronicler's delineation of the terrible past could therefore stir in them far more than the emotions of pity and terror which great tragic drama creates in the beholder. For them it was a call to the living, a solemn exhortation to faith and hope—that they should trust in the one God of righteousness and remember his precepts to do them. "Believe in the LORD your God, and you will be established; believe his prophets, and you will succeed" (II Chr. 20:20).

I. Characteristics

Unless the purpose and method of the Chronicler are thus realized, a modern reader—especially if he compares Chronicles with Samuel and Kings—is likely to be of the opinion that very little of intellectual and spiritual value would be lost if this strange work had been omitted from the Bible. No doubt he would grant that here and there beautiful verses appear in its long course. Apart from that, Chronicles on a superficial view seems to be for the most part unnecessary, uninteresting, defective in comparison with Samuel and Kings, and in many matters incredible. Consider severally those strictures:

Unnecessary: At least to the extent that fully half of Chronicles copies verbatim, or with some adaptations, parts of Genesis, Samuel, and Kings. What advantage is there in being able to read the same words in two places in the Bible?

Uninteresting: At least in part. Take a glance at the name lists which fill from end to end I Chr. 1–9, and at similar punctilious lists—most of them concerning ancestors of Levites serving the temple in various functions—which recur throughout the book. Presumably these pedigrees interested some Jews dead and buried many centuries ago. But we must ask: "How can they help us to deal with present problems? What value is in them for the spirit of man in the agelong quest for truth and right?"

Defective: Chronicles is lopsided, an exclusive history of Judah which ignores the story of the northern kingdom of Israel, except for a few frowning side glances at times when the doings of certain kings of Israel affected Judah. Not a syllable in Chronicles about Elijah's stand for God and justice! If we want to know fully about the Hebrew monarchies, who would not choose Samuel and Kings? Moreover, even as regards the Judean kingdom, Chronicles strangely omits many of the most memorable and moving narratives told in Samuel and Kings. The acute student, however, will question for two reasons whether this adverse estimate as to deficiency is not too sweeping. He will point out first that Chronicles constantly has modified what it quotes in such a way as to alter the significance of the record. In thus changing the color of things is there justifiable improvement? But the general effect of the changes is that what was vivid and convincing in Samuel and Kings has become stiff and artificial. It is as if the vitality has been taken out of the narratives and, instead, the Chronicler offers us "History in a stained-glass window." For example, in Samuel, David lives before us, an imperfect but very great and attractive personality. In Chronicles, David is an almost perfect saint, his years as monarch concentrated on caring for the sacred ark and its clergy, and on making provision for the future temple. But second, there is in Chronicles a large number of passages—many complete chapters—purporting to give information not recorded in Samuel and Kings. What is their worth? On scrutiny it appears indisputable that they furnish an absolute minimum (if any at all) of reliable new information about the kingdom of Judah. And most of their contents concerns the temple, the organization of its staff, celebrations of religious rites on great occasions. We are bound to ask, "What abiding importance have those matters for us?"

Incredible: Consider the unbelievable features in Chronicles. For one thing, it ascribes to David the institution of elaborate arrangements about the Levites. For overwhelmingly strong reasons, based on other scriptures, what is related is not credible history. Next, the Chronicler exaggerates numbers and amounts out of all possibility; sometimes we are able to contrast his allegations with comparatively reasonable figures in Kings. David and Solomon were rulers of a nascent Palestinian state: the Chronicler declares that between them they amassed for the building and decoration of a small temple treasure of such value that it would suffice to meet the modern world's financial crises. Again, the Chronicler ascribes to certain good Judean kings stupendous armies—to Jehoshaphat 1,160,000 soldiers attending him in Jerusalem. Moreover, the point he drives home is this: that the issues of war turned not upon the vast numbers of soldiers, but upon something radically different. Whenever, he declares, a king of Judah, threatened by foes, sought divine aid and obeyed the guidance of a prophet, victory on a stupendous scale ensued—on occasions without his army needing to strike a blow (II Chr. 20; cf. 13:3-20; 14:9-15). But if the king relied on any other aid save God's, he suffered stupendous defeat, as on the day when Ahaz in a clash with the Israelites lost 120,000 killed, and 200,000 men, women, and children taken captive (II Chr. 28:5-8). This sort of thing was not meant to be read as sober history. The Jews for whom the Chronicler wrote were shrewd men. Moreover, they could, if they chose, compare Chronicles with the plain tale in Samuel and Kings. Obviously the Chronicler expected his readers to look beneath the surface and to perceive a deeper purpose than the attempt to write an accurate account of the past. It was easy for the Chronicler's contemporaries to see what he really meant, however difficult for us.

Our initial difficulty in appreciating the purpose and value of Chronicles is that it is not history in our sense of the word at all. No one at any time can give a completely comprehensive survey of the past, even over a very limited range of events. Any work which aimed simply at that target would turn out to be an imperfect catalogue, dry as dust, useful only as a quarry in which wiser men might dig. Our demand is primarily that a modern historian shall consult the best sources and use them as accurately as possible. If he fails to essay that much his book should be relegated to the scrap heap. But further, as someone has well said, we ask from a historian not a record of history as it has actually happened, but a record of what has mattered, and of what, for that reason, may still be important to us. That is to say, we look to him wisely to select from available knowledge what seem to him the salient, meaningful facts. If it is judged that his selection and handling of facts is palpably prejudiced we call his book tendentious and ask for a fairer, more reliable account. Chronicles does not come up for judgment under any of those descriptions. The Chronicler set out to depict ideas and ideals, and for that end he utilized records of the past, exercising, however, complete freedom to suppress, modify, and inventively add to what he read. The result was that he created a narrative so obviously idealized that his contemporaries could not fail to recognize it for what it was. He held before their minds and consciences a picture: How rightly to live and to worship. All through his work shines his sincerity of conviction that he is portraying the abiding meaning in human life—the reality of God and his righteousness, the continuity of the divine good purpose. In the line and color of his picture the Chronicler hoped to enable men to "see" the ideal; in its sternness and beauty he was persuading them to revere and love its righteousness in order that they and their children after them should translate the abiding ideal into actuality. Then their difficulties would turn into boundless opportunity. Chronicles surpasses all else in the Old Testament in this mode; the stories of the patriarchs in Genesis exemplify it, but in a less exalted degree. In modern literature we have nothing really comparable, the nearest approach being the free treatment of past events found in historical novels or dramas. Shakespeare, for example, drew upon the facts of history to construct his drama of Henry V, but he did so with creative liberty, ascribing to the king a most noble character and the utterance of immortal words. The motion picture added photographic aid to the poet's genius. Who that has seen the result on stage or screen can forget the presented ideal of youthful charm and royal responsibility, of forethought, endurance, courage, and generosity crowned with success? The book of Chronicles asks to be weighed as portrayal of profound principles which enable us rightly to deal with life's vicissitudes and choices. In reading Chronicles do not say, "This cannot possibly have happened as related." That would be a frame of mind which misconceives the intention of the Chronicler, and fails to see the strength of his teaching.

Accordingly, outline realization of the circumstances amid which the Chronicler lived is imperatively necessary. Here are the historical landmarks that would dwell in his own and his fellows' thoughts. (a) In 721 B.C. the kingdom of Israel had come to an end when the Assyrians captured Samaria and removed into captivity some thirty thousand Israelites, replacing them by alien settlers. (b) In 586 ended the kingdom of Judah when the Babylonians sacked Jerusalem, broke down its walls, burned temple and palace, and deported to Babylonia its leading citizens and craftsmen, in number about thirty to fifty thousand persons. (c) In 538, when Cyrus the Persian conquered Babylon, he permitted Jews to go back to Palestine. Some returned to Jerusalem; and among them in all likelihood not a few were sons whose fathers had been members of the Zadokite hierarchy of Solomon's temple. (d) in 520-516 a substitute temple was built; pitiably poor it seemed in comparison with Solomon's; still for the moment hopes ran high. (e) Thereafter for about 150 years nothing in particular happened, until in 384—perhaps not 444, as used to be thought—Nehemiah, coming from Babylonia with authority from its Persian king, rebuilt Jerusalem's walls. (f) Shortly afterward a caravan of some 1,800 Jews led by Ezra (if the event is not exaggerated) returned to Jerusalem from Babylonia, among them being 262 Levites.

II. Purpose

The Chronicler shows absorbing interest in the temple and its staff of priests, Levites, musicians, custodians, and so on. To understand his purpose it is necessary to consider what had been happening to the worship of Yahweh, and its administration, from the fall of the kingdoms down to the Chronicler's period. In conquered Israel the Assyrians in 721 B.C. had prohibited sacrifice to Yahweh at the Hebrew sanctuaries. Many would acquiesce to the fact that Assyrian deities must now be propitiated instead of Yahweh who had "let them down." But obstinate Israelites hated the humiliating religious restriction and began to think seriously about their own God. (Take the Bible away and people will clamor to be allowed to read it.) They reflected that certain prophets had foretold disaster and that it would be just retribution for their social cruelty and for worshiping baals as well as Yahweh. All Israelitish Levites who would not serve Assyrian deities had to seek other employment. Some years after 721 the Assyrians permitted sacrifices to Yahweh, but at one place only in the occupied land, at Bethel. Meantime, many bold Israelites (see Exeg. on II Chr. 30:1–31:27) had accepted an invitation from the Judean King Hezekiah to go to Jerusalem to keep the Passover: they would be impressed by its splendid temple in the still independent kingdom.

When the kingdom of Judah was overthrown in 586 its inhabitants were stunned for a time. But in Judah, as earlier in Israel, the mass of the population—perhaps four out of every five Hebrews—was left in Palestine. The stouthearted did not collapse like weaklings. Hebrews stand up to protracted calamity, a tenacious, resilient people. But what could they do? They carried on with ordinary life and began to take seriously the teachings of the great prophets. They began to believe that the overthrow of their city and kingdom had happened not because the gods of the Babylonians were mightier than Yahweh, but because there really is only one God, the Almighty, whose will is righteousness. The disaster had been, as the prophets had foreseen, his just retribution on their fathers' and their own iniquities (cf. Lam. 2; 4:13). That was an illuminating and re-creative thought. They began to ask how rightly they should treat one another, and how rightly reverence God.

In all probability not very long after 586, and certainly long before 538, worship of Yahweh was resumed at the sacred area in Jerusalem. The ruined temple—its ark and golden vessels gone—was an eyesore; but men could offer sacrifices, prayer, and praise to God at the holy site. By whom was that worship staffed? Thirty-five years before the fall of Jerusalem King Josiah had suppressed the local sanctuaries in Judah as well as any still used in Israel, including that at Bethel. We are told that he wanted to give their Levites the right to serve at Jerusalem; we may guess that the hereditary Zadokites in Solomon's temple did their utmost to make that intention a dead letter: no doubt there were many "country" Levites out of normal employment! When Jerusalem was razed in 586 we may be sure that most of its Zadokite clergy were killed or deported. Although some escaped, the Solomonic hierarchy as an organized body was smashed. Surely the resumed worship during the seventy years was served by a few Zadokites who had escaped and returned, but chiefly by country Levites from Judah and Israel, some of whom would come to reside in Jerusalem. As the city revived, and when in 520 the temple was rebuilt, increase of clergy was needed, for the daily ritual required many ministrants and large augmentation was necessary at the times of the three great religious festivals. Some more "sons of Zadok" may have returned in 538. But many of the clergy in the second temple would be of country Levitical origin, and to the great festivals would come visiting Levites from Judah or Israel who would claim right to officiate—being, so to speak, canons of the cathedral resident only for a portion of the year, serving "by courses," as the Chronicler puts it. Thus in the sixth and fifth centuries there developed a situation offering only too wide scope for clerical jealousies and disputes. One can infer that the permanent staff in Jerusalem began to assert superiority against the "occasional" Levites, especially if they were from Israelitish territory. Against that cruel, narrow-minded, vested-interest attitude the Chronicler set his face. He pleaded that faithful Levites of Israel had full right to serve at Jerusalem. Moreover for the citizens of Jerusalem it was gall and bitterness that Samaria had regained importance as the seat of Persian control. Jerusalem's citizens could be fiercely proud of its ancient prestige, jealous with a great jealousy. Why should Israelites be respected as brethren by the men of Jerusalem, or their Levites be allowed to function in its temple?

Opposed to that horrid, petty antagonism the Chronicler wrote, showing in a picture the goodness of brotherhood and reunion. He urged as the will of God that there should be one Hebrew people. He implored quarrelsome men to forget the ancient enmities, and to see in God-fearing Israelites their brethren. He bade them read that to the coronation of David 400,000 such Israelites had come, and 22,000 Judeans (I Chr. 12:23-38). He related that when two good kings, Hezekiah and Josiah, were reigning in Jerusalem, a huge concourse of Israelites had come to keep Passover, the Hebrew sacrament of deliverance and unity (II Chr. 30; 35). What wise, farsighted teaching that was for the Chronicler's time! Perhaps he had glimpsed an ineffable hope latent in his generous attitude. Did he descry, faintly and afar, that if only bitter men, intent on prestige, eager about so-called principles but blind to the holy purpose of God, did not wreck the hope, there might yet be one people of God throughout the wide world, wherever Jews had taken to heart Jeremiah's inspiration that in any land they could pray to God and be answered, if they would love and serve his righteous will? (Jer. 29:1-14; the Chronicler was aware of Jeremiah's greatness: see II Chr. 36:12.) It is a thought which should stab the sleeping conscience of divided Christendom. In the depressing fifth century, when nothing in particular happened and the walls remained broken down, apathy and worldliness set in. The priests grew slack and slovenly, the people careless about their support and negligent in coming to the great occasions of worship. Against that deadly tendency the Chronicler set himself. He painted "what should be" in a parable of "history"—David's ceaseless care for the sacred ark and the Levites and the future house of God; the splendor of Solomon's temple with its golden vessels, throngs of diligent Levites, countless sacrifices offered by thankful king and people, and magnificence of music; and how, whenever under the good kings this faithfulness had been renewed, there came not only from Judah, but from Israel also, "a multitude keeping festival" (Ps. 42:4). After this fashion the Chronicler idealized the worship of Judah's past kingdom, and in everything was solemnly declaring his fundamental faith concerning life, that out of evil, evil comes, and out of good, good. Again and again he said it, symbolically, with utmost emphasis. He said it with a great confidence upholding him; for he was very sure of the abiding mercy of God. In effect, he told his readers that if they had a million soldiers to protect them, everything would really depend on whether their reliance was in God. If they would trust their lives to the ways of righteousness, would listen to the words of the living God, then no power on earth could defeat their spirit or turn aside their destiny in the high providence of God. Great

teaching for his own period and for many another century since then!

III. Date

The outcome of clerical tension in Jerusalem during the fifth century was that certain Levitical families who could claim descent from Levi through Zadok or, more widely, through Aaron, established themselves as having exclusive sacerdotal rights: they alone were "priests unto God," in contrast to all other Levites (musicians, singers, custodians, porters) whose status was that of "ministers unto their brethren the priests" (see Exeg. on I Chr. 6:1-81). Subsequent to this strict differentiation an orthodox Jew would be careful to refer to "the priests *and* the Levites"; at an earlier stage it was permissible to use the Deuteronomic phrase "the priests, the Levites," and, as the Chronicler does, to allude to Levites (unspecified) as exercising functions later reserved to the Aaronite Zadokites. The superiority of the Aaronite Zadokites was solemnly documented as carrying the authority of Moses by those portions of the Pentateuch which are termed the Priestly Code, and when the whole Pentateuch was promulgated—apparently not earlier than 450 nor later than 350 B.C.—a final settlement had been reached: this, and neither more nor less, was the law of God given by Moses.

Prevailing opinion has been that the Chronicler wrote during the succeeding century, 350-250 B.C. This conclusion would follow if he were the compiler of the books of Nehemiah and Ezra, but the reason assigned for that opinion is not cogent (see Exeg. on II Chr. 36:22-23; a minor argument for a very late date does not now carry weight—see Exeg. on I Chr. 3:19-24). Linguistic features (discussed below) are deemed to imply no earlier period than late in the fourth century. If so, we have to think of the Chronicler as one who lived a long while after the establishment of the system of ritual set forth in the Priestly Code, after the Aaronite Zadokites had attained their supremacy, after the written promulgation of the law immutably given by Moses. It is held, for instance, that the Chronicler's work should be regarded as "a sequel and supplement to the Priestly Code," written as an "endeavor to raise the rank and prestige of the Levites to those of the priests. . . . The Priestly Code . . . became the charter of normative Judaism. The Chronicler is not the great architect of the edifice but a humble restorer and decorator who reverently adds to its usefulness for a subsequent age." [1] But if so,

[1] Robert H. Pfeiffer, *Introduction to the Old Testament* (New York: Harper & Bros., 1941), pp. 785, 797, 786. Cf. also Hermann Vogelstein, *Der Kampf zwischen Priestern*

how incomprehensible and naïve was the Chronicler's mentality! Beyond question he was a devout Jew, in uttermost earnest that all things should be properly and punctiliously performed in the ritual of the temple. How could such a man, living a hundred or at least fifty years after the authoritative, written enactments of the law given by Moses had been in operation, challenge or even speak loosely about its sacrosanct provisions and a cardinal principle in its system? If he did pen such heterodoxy, hoping to induce the entrenched priests to contravene the word of God and admit to their privileges numbers of the inferior clergy, how naïve he was! The optimism of Joshua bidding the sun to stand still in the heavens was by comparison sensible. If, further, he was the author of the entire text of Chronicles as it now stands, how weakly he advanced his astonishing plea! For whenever he alludes to Levites and ritual in a way not incompatible with the earlier Deuteronomic standpoint, but incompatible with the ultimate orthodoxy of the Priestly Code—always there we find qualifying and contradictory phrases and verses to the effect that nevertheless orthodox procedure had been observed on the occasion. There is, however, virtual unanimity that these phrases and verses were not part of the Chronicler's original writing, but are corrective additions inserted into his text at a later date. The motive that would give rise to them is not difficult to perceive (see below, p. 347).

On the other hand, consider whether the Chronicler's original work may be dated in the circumstances of the fifth century; or, say, 450-350 B.C. It would then have been very relevant, and we could credit him with fine qualities and with making a sensible endeavor. The battle for a generous outlook was not yet lost. If he wrote before the Aaronite Zadokites had won complete victory, and before the law as it stands in the Pentateuch had been finally written and declared, then his mode of referring to Levites does not perplex. And his idealizing picture of the past was a moving plea to the Judeans and men of Jerusalem to treat all loyalist Israelites, and not least their Levites, as brethren. This conception of the Chronicler's purpose and period has been powerfully advocated by A. C. Welch,[2] and, in general, it seems that a date in the latter part of the fifth century, or very little later, should be accepted. It gives natural-

und Leviten (Stettin: von Nagel, 1889); and Gerhard von Rad, *Das Geschichtsbild des chronistischen Werkes* (Stuttgart: W. Kohlhammer, 1930; "Beiträge zur Wissenschaft vom Alten und Neuen Testament").

[2] *The Work of the Chronicler* (London: British Academy, 1939). Cf. also his *Post-Exilic Judaism* (Edinburgh: William Blackwood & Sons, 1935), pp. 185-244.

ness to the Chronicler's mind, and the great and complex perplexities which otherwise confront us in the basic characteristics of Chronicles vanish.

A conspicuous problem of style, however, remains to be considered. Chronicles contains many and lengthy quotations from the books of Samuel and Kings. Those books are written in what may be termed "classical" Hebrew, whereas all else in Chronicles—that is, the Chronicler's own composition—differs startlingly in details of vocabulary and syntax from the Hebrew of Samuel and Kings.[3] Obviously the Chronicler, if he had so desired, was learned enough to try to conform his own writing to the "classical" style—much as a modern preacher could shape his sermon in close conformity with strictly biblical English. He made no such attempt whatever. Evidently he wanted his readers to realize without difficulty just when they were reading quotations and when his own idealizing presentation of affairs. The Chronicler's own diction must be that of ordinary contemporary use, and admittedly it is similar to that found in the latest Hebrew writings in the Old Testament.

But even by the middle of the third century B.C. vernacular speech in Jerusalem had, it seems, ceased to be Hebrew and become Aramaic. Moreover, at about 400 B.C. a reference in Neh. 8:8 to a public reading from the Law probably signified that the people understood clearly only when they were given an interpretation in their everyday terms. It may reasonably be asked, How early did ordinary Hebrew diction begin to diverge from the "classical" literary idiom, and how rapid was the process of change? (As soon as thirty years after the issue of the ASV the editors of the RSV found it desirable to alter its remanent archaisms, alike in vocabulary and syntax.) Before summing up, consideration may be given to a suggestion arising from the Chronicler's intense sympathy for loyalist Israelites and their Levites. Was his family home within the bounds of the territory of ancient Israel? Had he or his father before him migrated to Jerusalem and become one of many Levites with Israelitish lineage who served in the second temple, and whose position was being undermined and scorned by the Judean Zadokites? Israelitish Hebrew differed in particulars from the Judean: there is evidence as far back as the compilation of the northern records concerning Elijah and Elisha. In addi-

[3] A long and impressive list of divergencies is given by Edward L. Curtis and Albert A. Madsen, *A Critical and Exegetical Commentary on the Books of Chronicles* (New York: Charles Scribner's Sons, 1910; "International Critical Commentary"), pp. 27-36.

tion to the divergencies from the "classical" mode current in the normal diction of the Jews of Jerusalem in the Chronicler's time, did he also impart to his writing a flavoring of northern variations? That is extremely conjectural.

We know too little about the development of ordinary Hebrew speech to be dogmatic that the Chronicler (being not desirous to disguise his own composition) could not have written as he does during the fifth century, especially toward its close.[4]

IV. Additions

The view of the structure of Chronicles indicated above affords a consistent and reasonable criterion for distinguishing the original writing of the Chronicler from the numerous additions which, as all scholars are agreed, were in course of time introduced into the manuscripts. When the final Law obtained, devout readers were sure to be distressed by passages and verses which conflicted with its provisions, or were ambiguous or perilously vague. In general it would be felt that quite inadequate attention was paid to the primary dignity and rights of the Zadokite-Aaronite priests. What should be done? Let the writing perish? Fortunately its goodness touched good men—its unshakable faith in the reality and providence of God; its stern declaration of moral retribution and reward; its radiant love of the temple and worship; its perception that out of the perishable kingdom had emerged imperishable spiritual strength; its plea that there should be one people of God. Attempts were therefore made to improve it. What seem to be the consequent corrections and amplifications will be pointed out in the Exegesis.

V. Sources

A subordinate and difficult problem is how far, if at all, the Chronicler for his new material availed himself of lost sources, and whether in consequence his work adds anything reliable to what Kings tells about the history of Judah. In Chronicles there is a great parade of alleged sources, among them notably references to lost prophetic writings (e.g., I Chr. 29:29; II Chr. 9:29). But for the most part these references on investigation merge into one general question—whether the Chronicler had before him a large-scale document other than Kings about the history of Judah and Israel (e.g., II Chr. 16:11; 27:7). If he did, it was an edifying

rather than a historically trustworthy work; and he did not quote from it, as he does from Kings, but transmuted into his own style what he wanted to reproduce. Its existence is doubtful; its worth for reliable new information is certainly slender.[5] Nevertheless, it is difficult not to feel that the Chronicler was able to avail himself of some written and oral minor sources of information other than Kings, and to some extent of pre-exilic date, which he used as a basis for numerous details regarding ancestors, places, building operations, and certain events and dates. And indeed, evidence to that effect has grown in recent years: an outstanding instance is II Chr. 16:1-6 (see Exeg.).[6] The most important feature concerns the differences between Kings and Chronicles in respect of the reigns of Hezekiah and Josiah. It is becoming much more likely that what is said in Chronicles about those two kings throws valuable light on efforts made by the Judean kingdom to gain the nationalistic and religious adherence of the northern Hebrews after the fall of Samaria in 721 B.C. As regards postexilic thought and problems, Chronicles as a composite whole is, of course, an invaluable, firsthand source.

VI. Text

The text of Chronicles is in fairly good condition. Where it is faulty, the Septuagint translation does not help; for it was made from a manuscript virtually identical with the present Hebrew text. A Greek translation of II Chr. 35–36, found in I Esdras, differs from the Septuagint of those chapters. It has great interest for study of the relations and characteristics of the Greek versions. Further, we know

---

[4] W. F. Albright did not regard the diction of Chronicles as incompatible with the end of the fifth century, since he has argued that the Chronicler was none other than Ezra ("The Date and Personality of the Chronicler," *Journal of Biblical Literature,* XL [1921], 104-24).

[5] This view is stressed by Curtis and Madsen (*op. cit.,* p. 26), who write, "The unity of style and composition . . . is against this patchwork theory of composition, although its possibility in view of our limited knowledge cannot be denied." As regards the intricate, tenuous subject of sources in Chronicles, reference must be made to studies of specialists, in particular Curtis and Madsen, *op. cit.;* Immanuel Benzinger, *Die Bücher der Chronik* (Leipzig: J. C. B. Mohr, 1901; "Kurzer Hand-Commentar zum Alten Testament"); Rudolf Kittel, *Die Bücher der Chronik* (Göttingen: Vandenhoeck & Ruprecht, 1902; "Handkommentar zum Alten Testament"); J. W. Rothstein and Johannes Hänel, *Kommentar zum ersten Buch der Chronik* (Leipzig: A. Deichert, 1927; "Kommentar zum Alten Testament"); Gerhard von Rad, "Die levitische Predigt in den Büchern der Chronik," *Festschrift Otto Procksch* (Leipzig: A. Deichert, 1934), pp. 113-24, also *Das Geschichtsbild des chronistischen Werkes;* C. C. Torrey, "The Chronicler as Editor and as Independent Narrator," *American Journal of Semitic Languages and Literatures,* XXV (1909), 157-73; 188-217; and Welch, *Work of the Chronicler.*

[6] See W. F. Albright, "A Votive Stele Erected by Ben-Hadad I of Damascus to the God Melcarth," *Bulletin of the American Schools of Oriental Research,* No. 87 (1942), pp. 23-29.

that in the course of manuscript transmission the text in Chronicles was sometimes adjusted to that found in Samuel and Kings; sometimes the reverse process is to be detected.

VII. Place in Canon

The translators of the Septuagint placed Chronicles after Kings, and in consequence that is its position in our Bibles. But it was very nearly excluded from the Jewish scriptures and was set as the last book. An interesting story must lie behind that fact. The immediate purposes for which the Chronicler wrote concerned now-forgotten disputes. The revisers had done their part, and made the book less glaringly out of accord with orthodoxy. Nevertheless, learned Jewish students would not miss the inner inconsistencies; and whereas Samuel and Kings were indispensable, Chronicles was highly debatable. When toward the end of the first century A.D. the rabbis at Jamnia reached decisions as to which writings should be classed as sacred, there must have been anxious discussion about Chronicles. Its virtues prevailed, and it was included. For that we can be thankful. Cleared of the confusing accretions, the Chronicler's own work stands out as a noble creation, wrought by a man who, although he was no poet in words, was poet in soul; a man great in religious convictions and moral integrity, who in this work presented to his contemporaries a moving plea to believe that the issues in life are ruled and overruled by the righteousness of God. His resolute faith and his generous longing that good men should stand together united in spirit in the bond of peace and in holiness of life speak to our needs. One God, one faith, one people—the Chronicler had, in his own way, an ecumenical mind.

VIII. Outline of Contents

IX. Selected Bibliography

CURTIS, EDWARD L., and MADSEN, ALBERT A. *A Critical and Exegetical Commentary on the Books of Chronicles* ("International Critical Commentary") . New York: Charles Scribner's Sons, 1910.

ELMSLIE, W. A. L. *The Books of Chronicles* ("The Cambridge Bible") . Cambridge: Cambridge University Press, 1916.

VON RAD, GERHARD. *Das Geschichtsbild des chronistischen Werkes* ("Beiträge zur Wissenschaft vom Alten und Neuen Testament") . Stuttgart: W. Kohlhammer, 1930.

WELCH, ADAM C. *The Work of the Chronicler.* London: British Academy, 1939.

I CHRONICLES

TEXT, EXEGESIS, AND EXPOSITION

1 Adam, Sheth, Enosh,
2 Kenan, Mahalaleel, Jered,
3 Henoch, Methuselah, Lamech,
4 Noah, Shem, Ham, and Japheth.
5 ¶ The sons of Japheth; Gomer, and Magog, and Madai, and Javan, and Tubal, and Meshech, and Tiras.
6 And the sons of Gomer; Ashchenaz, and Riphath, and Togarmah.

1 Adam, Seth, Enosh; 2 Kenan, Mahal'-alel, Jared; 3 Enoch, Methu'selah, Lamech; 4 Noah, Shem, Ham, and Japheth.
5 The sons of Japheth: Gomer, Magog, Madai, Javan, Tubal, Meshech, and Tiras.
6 The sons of Gomer: Ash'kenaz, Diphath,

I. GENEALOGIES (1:1–9:44)

The Chronicler commenced his idealized history of the kingdom of Judah not with these nine chapters of names, but dramatically with the death of Saul (10:1) as initiating the reign of David. There are cumulative reasons for thinking that these genealogies were not composed or collected by the Chronicler. For one thing, it is sometimes evident that more than one collector was at work; but chiefly they seem in general to emanate from the later period when the final system of the Law was operative, when the Zadokite or Aaronite priests had gained accepted superiority over those Levites who served as musicians, singers, doorkeepers. Accordingly, in this Exeg. the compilers of the name lists in chs. 1–9 will be termed "genealogists."

The genealogists were not pedigree hunters impelled merely by antiquarian curiosity or by pride. Their lists originated in serious and sacred purpose, for they established the rights of the several Levitical families in postexilic Jerusalem to fulfill their various functions; they also supported the claim of other important families in the Jewish community to count themselves truly as children of Abraham, heirs of the divine promise. It meant a great deal to loyal and devout men to read their ancestors' names in an approved list. The genealogical interest was not related only to matters of dignity and of title to emoluments. It rested upon the deep and honorable belief that the elect people had a sacred trust by reason of their knowledge of the one real God, and of the right way to worship him and serve his righteous will. As time passed every scrap of ascertainable genealogical information was gathered, sifted, and eventually co-ordinated to form these (superficially dry-as-dust) nine chapters.

A. THE ANCESTORS OF ALL PEOPLES (1:1-54)

1:1-34. These verses (abbreviated from Gen. 5:3-32; 10:2-29; 25:1-16) name first the antediluvian patriarchs, next the reputed founders of the nations of the world, and so lead up to the first ancestors of the Hebrew people.

1:1. Adam.—The interest of the men who compiled the names in the opening chapters of Chronicles was concentrated on their own people, or rather on certain of the Hebrew tribes, and above all on the Levitical families. Why then did they not begin with Abraham and his sons? The easy and correct reply is to say that they were utilizing the book of Genesis, which has much to relate concerning those who lived before Abraham and were therefore the reputed ancestors of all the peoples of the world. But the question repays closer consideration. Every

349

7 And the sons of Javan; Elishah, and Tarshish, Kittim, and Dodanim.

8 ¶ The sons of Ham; Cush, and Mizraim, Put, and Canaan.

9 And the sons of Cush; Seba, and Havilah, and Sabta, and Raamah, and Sabtecha. And the sons of Raamah; Sheba, and Dedan.

10 And Cush begat Nimrod: he began to be mighty upon the earth.

11 And Mizraim begat Ludim, and Anamim, and Lehabim, and Naphtuhim,

12 And Pathrusim, and Casluhim, (of whom came the Philistines,) and Caphtorim.

13 And Canaan begat Zidon his firstborn, and Heth,

14 The Jebusite also, and the Amorite, and the Girgashite,

15 And the Hivite, and the Arkite, and the Sinite,

16 And the Arvadite, and the Zemarite, and the Hamathite.

17 ¶ The sons of Shem; Elam, and Asshur, and Arphaxad, and Lud, and Aram, and Uz, and Hul, and Gether, and Meshech.

18 And Arphaxad begat Shelah, and Shelah begat Eber.

19 And unto Eber were born two sons: the name of the one *was* Peleg; because in his days the earth was divided: and his brother's name *was* Joktan.

20 And Joktan begat Almodad, and Sheleph, and Hazarmaveth, and Jerah,

21 Hadoram also, and Uzal, and Diklah,

22 And Ebal, and Abimael, and Sheba,

23 And Ophir, and Havilah, and Jobab. All these *were* the sons of Joktan.

and Togar'mah. 7 The sons of Javan: Eli'shah, Tarshish, Kittim, and Ro'danim.

8 The sons of Ham: Cush, Egypt, Put, and Canaan. 9 The sons of Cush: Seba, Hav'ilah, Sabta, Ra'ama, and Sab'teca. The sons of Ra'amah: Sheba and Dedan. 10 Cush was the father of Nimrod; he began to be a mighty one in the earth.

11 Egypt was the father of Ludim, An'amin, Leha'bim, Naph'tuhim, 12 Pathru'sim, Caslu'him (whence came the Philis'tines), and Caph'torim.

13 Canaan was the father of Sidon his first-born, and Heth, 14 and the Jeb'usites, the Amorites, the Gir'gashites, 15 the Hivites, the Arkites, the Sinites, 16 the Ar'vadites, the Zem'arites, and the Ha'mathites.

17 The sons of Shem: Elam, Asshur, Arpach'shad, Lud, Aram, Uz, Hul, Gether, and Meshech. 18 Arpach'shad was the father of Shelah; and Shelah was the father of Eber. 19 To Eber were born two sons: the name of the one was Peleg (for in his days the earth was divided), and the name of his brother Joktan. 20 Joktan was the father of Almo'dad, Sheleph, Hazarma'veth, Jerah, 21 Hador'am, Uzal, Diklah, 22 Ebal, Abim'a-el, Sheba, 23 Ophir, Hav'ilah, and Jobab; all these were the sons of Joktan.

---

nation is guilty of regarding others as a mere circumference around its self-interest; but the Hebrews are often accused of particularly crude nationalism because they esteemed themselves the people preferred by Yahweh, their God, above all other nations. Abundant evidence to that effect can be adduced, and is likely to suffice those whom half a truth will satisfy. It can be urged that even when the Hebrew kingdoms had perished Hebrew-Jewish particularism was intensified in that the Jews, impotent politically, became so proudly conscious of possessing a religion immeasurably superior to the beliefs of polytheistic Gentiles. By way of rebuttal it is not enough to cull a few outstanding, explicit acknowledgments of universalism from the O.T., as if these were the only indications of a

wider outlook. Such passages, in general and in detail, deserve to be emphasized—the prophetic insistence on moral obligation as supernational; recognition that the divine vocation of Israel denoted duty, not favoritism; the parable of Jonah. The point here stressed is that when the Jew worshiped God he believed that he worshiped the Creator and Father of all men, whose "tender mercies are over all his works" (Ps. 145:9). Implicit universalism pervades almost the whole of the great literature of the Jewish period and gives it its timeless quality. The Psalter contains the songs of Zion and her children, but in such wise that Jerusalem seems to be the city of redeemed mankind, and her hymns prove themselves a universal treasure. If the genealogists were to be true to their faith, they

24 ¶ Shem, Arphaxad, Shelah,

25 Eber, Peleg, Reu,

26 Serug, Nahor, Terah,

27 Abram; the same *is* Abraham.

28 The sons of Abraham; Isaac, and Ishmael.

29 ¶ These *are* their generations: The firstborn of Ishmael, Nebaioth; then Kedar, and Adbeel, and Mibsam,

30 Mishma, and Dumah, Massa, Hadad, and Tema,

31 Jetur, Naphish, and Kedemah. These are the sons of Ishmael.

32 ¶ Now the sons of Keturah, Abraham's concubine: she bare Zimran, and Jokshan, and Medan, and Midian, and Ishbak, and Shuah. And the sons of Jokshan; Sheba, and Dedan.

33 And the sons of Midian; Ephah, and Epher, and Henoch, and Abida, and Eldaah. All these *are* the sons of Keturah.

34 And Abraham begat Isaac. The sons of Isaac; Esau and Israel.

35 ¶ The sons of Esau; Eliphaz, Reuel, and Jeush, and Jaalam, and Korah.

36 The sons of Eliphaz; Teman, and Omar, Zephi, and Gatam, Kenaz, and Timna, and Amalek.

37 The sons of Reuel; Nahath, Zerah, Shammah, and Mizzah.

38 And the sons of Seir; Lotan, and Shobal, and Zibeon, and Anah, and Dishon, and Ezar, and Dishan.

39 And the sons of Lotan; Hori, and Homam: and Timna *was* Lotan's sister.

40 The sons of Shobal; Alian, and Manahath, and Ebal, Shephi, and Onam. And the sons of Zibeon; Aiah, and Anah.

41 The sons of Anah; Dishon. And the sons of Dishon; Amram, and Eshban, and Ithran, and Cheran.

42 The sons of Ezer; Bilhan, and Zavan, *and* Jakan. The sons of Dishan; Uz, and Aran.

24 Shem, Arpach'shad, Shelah; 25 Eber, Peleg, Re'u; 26 Serug, Nahor, Terah; 27 Abam, that is, Abraham.

28 The sons of Abraham: Isaac and Ish'mael. 29 These are their genealogies: the first-born of Ish'mael, Neba'ioth; and Kedar, Adbeel, Mibsam, 30 Mishma, Dumah, Massa, Hadad, Tema, 31 Jetur, Naphish, and Ked'emah. These are the sons of Ish'mael. 32 The sons of Ketu'rah, Abraham's concubine: she bore Zimran, Jokshan, Medan, Mid'ian, Ishbak, and Shu'ah. The sons of Joksham: Sheba and Dedan. 33 The sons of Mid'ian: Ephah, Epher, Hanoch, Abida, and Elda'ah. All these were the descendants of Ketu'rah.

34 Abraham was the father of Isaac. The sons of Isaac: Esau and Israel. 35 The sons of Esau: Eli'phaz, Reu'el, Je'ush, Jalam, and Korah. 36 The sons of Eli'phaz: Teman, Omar, Zephi, Gatam, Kenaz, Timna, and Am'alek. 37 The sons of Reu'el: Nahath, Zerah, Shammah, and Mizzah.

38 The sons of Se'ir: Lotan, Shobal, Zib'eon, Anah, Dishon, Ezer, and Dishan. 39 The sons of Lotan: Hori and Homam; and Lotan's sister was Timna. 40 The sons of Shobal: Al'ian, Man'ahath, Ebal, Shephi, and Onam. The sons of Zib'eon: Ai'ah and Anah. 41 The son of Anah: Dishon. The sons of Dishon: Hamran, Eshban, Ithran, and Cheran. 42 The sons of Ezer: Bilhan, Za'avan, and Ja'akan. The sons of Dishon: Uz and Aran.

35-54. These verses trace the descendants of Esau, who forfeited his birthright, and became the ancestor of the desert-dwelling Edomites, whose early chieftains (**dukes,**

had to commence with **Adam, Seth, Enosh,** and proceed to confess the original affinity of Israel with all other races stemming from Adam. We, like them, can lightly affirm that primevally all men were brothers without improving our treatment of other nations. Yet the brotherhood of mankind is a fact which, if it is disregarded, spells calamity. Could God devise other means to bring home to us its significance? Could he show us "a second Adam" in whose life and death we might perceive the obligations which the fact entails?

43 ¶ Now these *are* the kings that reigned in the land of Edom before *any* king reigned over the children of Israel; Bela the son of Beor: and the name of his city *was* Dinhabah.

44 And when Bela was dead, Jobab the son of Zerah of Bozrah reigned in his stead.

45 And when Jobab was dead, Husham of the land of the Temanites reigned in his stead.

46 And when Husham was dead, Hadad the son of Bedad, which smote Midian in the field of Moab, reigned in his stead: and the name of his city *was* Avith.

47 And when Hadad was dead, Samlah of Masrekah reigned in his stead.

48 And when Samlah was dead, Shaul of Rehoboth by the river reigned in his stead.

49 And when Shaul was dead, Baal-hanan the son of Achbor reigned in his stead.

50 And when Baal-hanan was dead, Hadad reigned in his stead: and the name of his city *was* Pai; and his wife's name *was* Mehetabel, the daughter of Matred, the daughter of Mezahab.

51 ¶ Hadad died also. And the dukes of Edom were; duke Timnah, duke Aliah, duke Jetheth,

52 Duke Aholibamah, duke Elah, duke Pinon,

53 Duke Kenaz, duke Teman, duke Mibzar,

54 Duke Magdiel, duke Iram. These *are* the dukes of Edom.

2 These *are* the sons of Israel; Reuben, Simeon, Levi, and Judah, Issachar, and Zebulun,

43 These are the kings who reigned in the land of Edom before any king reigned over the Israelites: Bela the son of Be'or, the name of whose city was Din'habah. 44 When Bela died, Jobab the son of Zerah of Bozrah reigned in his stead. 45 When Jobab died, Husham of the land of the Te'manites reigned in his stead. 46 When Husham died, Hadad the son of Bedad, who defeated Mid'ian in the country of Moab, reigned in his stead; and the name of his city was Avith. 47 When Hadad died, Samlah of Masre'kah reigned in his stead. 48 When Samlah died, Sha'ul of Reho'both on the Eu-phra'tes reigned in his stead. 49 When Sha'ul died, Ba'al-ha'nan, the son of Achbor, reigned in his stead. 50 When Ba'al-ha'nan died, Hadad reigned in his stead; and the name of his city was Pa'i, and his wife's name Mehet'abel the daughter of Matred, the daughter of Me'zahab. 51 And Hadad died.

The chiefs of Edom were: chiefs Timna, Al'iah, Jetheth, 52 Oholiba'mah, Elah, Pinon, 53 Kenaz, Teman, Mibzar, 54 Mag'-di-el, and Iram; these are the chiefs of Edom.

2 These are the sons of Israel: Reuben, Simeon, Levi, Judah, Is'sachar, Zeb'-

vss. 51-54) are named. The archaic English **dukes** (Latin *dux,* "leaders") is sensibly translated **chiefs** by the RSV.

B. Descendants of Judah (2:1-55)

Twelve sons of Jacob are cited, but in the sequel it will appear that the genealogists were absorbingly concerned only with three southern tribes—Judah, Simeon, Benjamin—and with the tribe of Levi.

2:1. *The Sons of Israel.*—The genealogies from this point concern the Hebrew families. Each individual is designated as "the son of . . ." That description has a significance which we do not readily realize, so deeply is our social attitude to others influenced by Greco-Roman civilization which tragically lacked the Hebraic point of view concerning the basis of peaceful relations between men. The individual Hebrew felt that

his very existence was due to his having in his body part of the family's blood: from the totality of his family or kindred he possessed his personal strength and virtue, and to the welfare of its collective life he must contribute his utmost. If he prospered, not only he but also all his family benefited; and no member of his kindred became weak except to the loss of all. Family meant to a Hebrew not a unit household

2 Dan, Joseph, and Benjamin, Naphtali, Gad, and Asher.

3 ¶ The sons of Judah; Er, and Onan, and Shelah: *which* three were born unto him of the daughter of Shua the Canaanitess. And Er, the firstborn of Judah, was evil in the sight of the LORD; and he slew him.

4 And Tamar his daughter-in-law bare him Pharez and Zerah. All the sons of Judah *were* five.

5 The sons of Pharez; Hezron, and Hamul.

6 And the sons of Zerah; Zimri, and Ethan, and Heman, and Calcol, and Dara: five of them in all.

ulun, 2 Dan, Joseph, Benjamin, Naph'tali, Gad, and Asher. 3 The sons of Judah: Er, Onan, and Shelah; these three Bath-shu'a the Canaanitess bore to him. Now Er, Judah's first-born, was wicked in the sight of the LORD, and he slew him. 4 His daughter-in-law Tamar also bore him Perez and Zerah. Judah had five sons in all.

5 The sons of Perez: Hezron and Hamul. 6 The sons of Zerah: Zimri, Ethan, Heman,

---

Three names have special importance: **Ram** (vs. 10) as an ancestor of David, **Caleb** (in vs. 9 **Chelubai** is a variant spelling of Caleb), and **Jerahmeel** (vss. 9, 25, 42). The Calebites and Jerahmeelites were originally not Hebrews but nomadic Edomites who had left the desert and settled in southern Judah about the time of David, and who after the fall of Jerusalem in 586 B.C. moved northward close to Jerusalem, while other Edomites from the desert took their place. In time these Calebite-Jerahmeelite families became an important element—regarded as true Hebrews—in postexilic Jerusalem and its neighborhood (cf. vss. 42-55). Hence the genealogists' keen interest. Modern scholars are even more interested in the incursion and northward shift of these many really Edomitic families (cf. E. L. Curtis and A. A. Madsen, *A Critical and Exegetical Commentary on the Books of Chronicles* [New York: Charles Scribner's Sons, 1910; "International Critical Commentary"], pp. 89-90). For these had their own ancestral ideas and memories, and allowance has to be made for their influence on the distinctively Hebrew "Mosaic" tradition and on the older Canaanitish elements in the O.T. The consequences were certainly not negligible—and may be far-reaching—for study of the biblical narratives; but the possibilities are too subtle and intricate for mention here.

2:6, 21. The fact that no reference is made elsewhere to **the sons of Zerah,** or to the statement that some Hezronites entered Canaan with the Hebrews from Gilead (vs. 21), furnishes one of many indications that the genealogists had some traditions besides those in the canonical books. The rest of the Hezronites entered Judah from the south at a later date.

---

as in our usage, but the whole community—however extensive—of men with whom he could or should have any form of peaceful relations; all those persons were his family or **house,** men of his covenant.

Observe that the Hebrew kingdoms were termed "the house of Judah," "the house of Israel." The point is that every individual was related to all the men of his covenant by no lesser bond of obligation than that of giving utmost brotherly support. Of necessity as well as natural desire, the strong must help the weak, and the weak must help the strong. This principle of social health—the great prophets insisted—the Hebrews knew, and were without excuse if they did not practice it. When that attitude broke down in the later monarchy, hor-

rible cruelty and social chaos calamitously ensued. The climax of Hebrew prophetic hope envisaged a world wherein the nations joyously realized themselves as one family under God, each contributing its gifts in fulfillment of the divine purpose (cf. Isa. 42:5-7; 56:6-7; 60:1-22). For individuals likewise the principle was that no man must be allowed to live unto himself (cf. Rom. 14:7). He who attempts to do so is Cain, the murderer, who cannot be tolerated within the civilized community. The conception of covenantal relationship with all its obligations is fundamental in O.T. religion and morality.

3, 7. *Er and Achar.*—Some men and women single themselves out by their singular infamy, and history is prone to record their memory.

7 And the sons of Carmi; Achar, the troubler of Israel, who transgressed in the thing accursed.

8 And the sons of Ethan; Azariah.

9 The sons also of Hezron, that were born unto him; Jerahmeel, and Ram, and Chelubai.

10 And Ram begat Amminadab; and Amminadab begat Nahshon, prince of the children of Judah;

11 And Nahshon begat Salma, and Salma begat Boaz,

12 And Boaz begat Obed, and Obed begat Jesse.

13 ¶ And Jesse begat his firstborn Eliab, and Abinadab the second, and Shimma the third,

14 Nethaneel the fourth, Raddai the fifth,

15 Ozem the sixth, David the seventh:

16 Whose sisters were Zeruiah, and Abigail. And the sons of Zeruiah; Abishai, and Joab, and Asahel, three.

17 And Abigail bare Amasa: and the father of Amasa was Jether the Ishmaelite.

18 ¶ And Caleb the son of Hezron begat children of Azubah his wife, and of Jerioth: her sons are these; Jesher, and Shobab, and Ardon.

19 And when Azubah was dead, Caleb took unto him Ephrath, which bare him Hur.

20 And Hur begat Uri, and Uri begat Bezaleel.

21 ¶ And afterward Hezron went in to the daughter of Machir the father of Gilead, whom he married when he was threescore years old; and she bare him Segub.

22 And Segub begat Jair, who had three and twenty cities in the land of Gilead.

23 And he took Geshur, and Aram, with the towns of Jair, from them, with Kenath, and the towns thereof, even threescore cities. All these belonged to the sons of Machir the father of Gilead.

Calcol, and Dara, five in all. 7 The sons of Carmi: Achar, the troubler of Israel, who transgressed in the matter of the devoted things; 8 and Ethan's son was Azari'ah.

9 The sons of Hezron, that were born to him: Jerah'meel, Ram, and Chelu'bai. 10 Ram was the father of Ammin'adab, and Ammin'adab was the father of Nahshon, prince of the sons of Judah. 11 Nahshon was the father of Salma, Salma of Bo'az, 12 Bo'az of Obed, Obed of Jesse. 13 Jesse was the father of Eli'ab his first-born, Abin'adab the second, Shim'ea the third, 14 Nethan'el the fourth, Raddai the fifth, 15 Ozem the sixth, David the seventh; 16 and their sisters were Zeru'iah and Ab'igail. The sons of Zeru'iah: Abi'shai, Jo'ab, and As'ahel, three. 17 Ab'igail bore Ama'sa, and the father of Ama'sa was Jether the Ish'maelite.

18 Caleb the son of Hezron had children by his wife Azu'bah, and by Jer'ioth; and these were her sons: Jesher, Shobab, and Ardon. 19 When Azu'bah died, Caleb married Ephrath, who bore him Hur. 20 Hur was the father of Uri, and Uri was the father of Bez'alel.

21 Afterward Hezron went in to the daughter of Machir the father of Gilead, whom he married when he was sixty years old; and she bore him Segub; 22 and Segub was the father of Ja'ir, who had twenty-three cities in the land of Gilead. 23 But Geshur and Aram took from them Havvoth-ja'ir, Kenath and its villages, sixty towns. All these were descendants of Machir, the

---

We ought to be much more mindful of the conspicuously good; or at least be more thankfully conscious of our heritage from the virtuous.

13. Eliab.—The meaning of Eliab is "My god is father." Study of proper names throws light on Hebrew religion, history, and literature to a surprising extent.[1] For example, we know that

[1] See George Buchanan Gray, Studies in Hebrew Proper Names (London: A. & C. Black, 1896).

many names appear in these lists which cannot possibly be of early date but are postexilic. Again, names compounded with "Baal" or "Melech" show the old Canaanitish sense of the gods as masters, owners, kings; whereas those with "El"—such as Eliab—preserve the desert tribesmen's way of thinking of their god in terms of personal relationships. The Hebrews attached great significance to names, for each man was

24 And after that Hezron was dead in Caleb-ephratah, then Abiah Hezron's wife bare him Ashur the father of Tekoa.

25 ¶ And the sons of Jerahmeel the first-born of Hezron were, Ram the firstborn, and Bunah, and Oren, and Ozem, *and* Ahijah.

26 Jerahmeel had also another wife, whose name *was* Atarah; she *was* the mother of Onam.

27 And the sons of Ram the firstborn of Jerahmeel were, Maaz, and Jamin, and Eker.

28 And the sons of Onam were, Shammai, and Jada. And the sons of Shammai; Nadab, and Abishur.

29 And the name of the wife of Abishur *was* Abihail, and she bare him Ahban, and Molid.

30 And the sons of Nadab; Seled, and Appaim: but Seled died without children.

31 And the sons of Appaim; Ishi. And the sons of Ishi; Sheshan. And the children of Sheshan; Ahlai.

32 And the sons of Jada the brother of Shammai; Jether, and Jonathan: and Jether died without children.

33 And the sons of Jonathan; Peleth, and Zaza. These were the sons of Jerahmeel.

34 ¶ Now Sheshan had no sons, but daughters. And Sheshan had a servant, an Egyptian, whose name *was* Jarha.

35 And Sheshan gave his daughter to Jarha his servant to wife; and she bare him Attai.

36 And Attai begat Nathan, and Nathan begat Zabad,

37 And Zabad begat Ephlal, and Ephlal begat Obed,

38 And Obed begat Jehu, and Jehu begat Azariah,

39 And Azariah begat Helez, and Helez begat Eleasah,

father of Gilead. 24 After the death of Hezron, Caleb went in to Eph'rathah,*ᵃ* the wife of Hezron his father, and she bore him Ashhur, the father of Teko'a.

25 The sons of Jerah'meel, the first-born of Hezron: Ram, his first-born, Bunah, Oren, Ozem, and Ahi'jah. 26 Jerah'meel also had another wife, whose name was At'arah; she was the mother of Onam. 27 The sons of Ram, the first-born of Jerah'meel: Ma'az, Jamin, and Eker. 28 The sons of Onam: Sham'mai and Jada. The sons of Sham'mai: Nadab and Abi'shur. 29 The name of Abi'shur's wife was Ab'ihail, and she bore him Ahban and Molid. 30 The sons of Nadab: Seled and Ap'pa-im; and Seled died childless. 31 The sons of Ap'pa-im: Ishi. The sons of Ishi: Sheshan. The sons of Sheshan: Ahlai. 32 The sons of Jada, Sham'mai's brother: Jether and Jonathan; and Jether died childless. 33 The sons of Jonathan: Peleth and Zaza. These were the descendants of Jerah'meel. 34 Now Sheshan had no sons, only daughters; but Sheshan had an Egyptian slave, whose name was Jarha. 35 So Sheshan gave his daughter in marriage to Jarha his slave; and she bore him Attai. 36 Attai was the father of Nathan and Nathan of Zabad. 37 Zabad was the father of Ephlal, and Ephlal of Obed. 38 Obed was the father of Jehu, and Jehu of A'zari'ah. 39 Azari'ah was the father of

ᵃ Gk Vg: Heb *in Caleb Ephrathah*

25-41. Jerahmeelites are not mentioned in pre-exilic O.T. writings. As said above, they became important only after the fall of Jerusalem.

---

deemed realistically to have in him the qualities of his ancestors; hence name in the O.T. is almost equivalent to character. When it is said that God's name is honored, the implication is of reverence paid to God's justice and mercy—to all that is in the divine character. The Hebrews also were prone to extract from names meanings philologically unfounded or dubious, e.g., Jacob, "the trickster" (Gen. 25:26; 27:36).

Many "lessons" could be thus extracted from genealogies, but a modern teacher, when he uses a text as a pretext, should make acknowledgment of the fact. Allegorizing the O.T. is a perniciously dangerous device. Anyone disposed to

40 And Eleasah begat Sisamai, and Sisamai begat Shallum,

41 And Shallum begat Jekamiah, and Jekamiah begat Elishama.

42 ¶ Now the sons of Caleb the brother of Jerahmeel *were,* Mesha his firstborn, which *was* the father of Ziph; and the sons of Mareshah the father of Hebron.

43 And the sons of Hebron; Korah, and Tappuah, and Rekem, and Shema.

44 And Shema begat Raham, the father of Jorkoam: and Rekem begat Shammai.

45 And the son of Shammai *was* Maon: and Maon *was* the father of Beth-zur.

46 And Ephah, Caleb's concubine, bare Haran, and Moza, and Gazez: and Haran begat Gazez.

47 And the sons of Jahdai; Regem, and Jotham, and Gesham, and Pelet, and Ephah, and Shaaph.

48 Maachah, Caleb's concubine, bare Sheber, and Tirhanah.

49 She bare also Shaaph the father of Madmannah, Sheva the father of Machbenah, and the father of Gibea: and the daughter of Caleb *was* Achsa.

50 ¶ These were the sons of Caleb the son of Hur, the firstborn of Ephratah; Shobal the father of Kirjath-jearim,

51 Salma the father of Beth-lehem, Hareph the father of Beth-gader.

52 And Shobal the father of Kirjath-jearim had sons; Haroeh, *and* half of the Manahethites.

53 And the families of Kirjath-jearim; the Ithrites, and the Puhites, and the Shumathites, and the Mishraites; of them came the Zareathites, and the Eshtaulites.

54 The sons of Salma; Beth-lehem, and the Netophathites, Ataroth, the house of Joab, and half of the Manahethites, the Zorites.

55 And the families of the scribes which dwelt at Jabez; the Tirathites, the Shimeathites, *and* Suchathites. These *are* the Kenites that came of Hemath, the father of the house of Rechab.

Helez, and Helez of Ele-a'sah. **40** Ele-a'sah was the father of Sismai, and Sismai of Shallum. **41** Shallum was the father of Jekami'ah, and Jekami'ah of Elish'ama.

42 The sons of Caleb the brother of Jerah'meel: Mare'shah[b] his first-born, who was the father of Ziph. The sons of Mare'shah: Hebron.[c] **43** The sons of Hebron: Korah, Tap'puah, Rekem, and Shema. **44** Shema was the father of Raham, the father of Jor'ke-am; and Rekem was the father of Sham'mai. **45** The son of Sham'mai: Ma'on; and Ma'on was the father of Beth-zur. **46** Ephah also, Caleb's concubine, bore Haran, Moza, and Gazez; and Haran was the father of Gazez. **47** The sons of Jah'dai: Regem, Jotham, Geshan, Pelet, Ephah, and Sha'aph. **48** Ma'acah, Caleb's concubine, bore Sheber and Tir'hanah. **49** She also bore Sha'aph the father of Madman'nah, Sheva the father of Machbe'nah and the father of Gib'e-a; and the daughter of Caleb was Achsah. **50** These were the descendants of Caleb.

The sons[d] of Hur the first-born of Eph'rathah: Shobal the father of Kir'iath-je'arim, **51** Salma, the father of Bethlehem, and Hareph the father of Beth-gader. **52** Shobal the father of Kir'iath-je'arim had other sons: Haro'eh, half of the Menu'hoth. **53** And the families of Kir'iath-je'arim: the Ithrites, the Puthites, the Shu'mathites, and the Mish'ra-ites; from these came the Zo'rathites and the Esh'taolites. **54** The sons of Salma: Bethlehem, the Netoph'athites, At'roth-beth-jo'ab, and half of the Man'aha'thites, the Zorites. **55** The families also of the scribes that dwelt at Jabez: the Ti'rathites, the Shim'e-athites, and the Su'cathites. These are the Ken'ites who came from Hammath, the father of the house of Rechab.

[b] Gk: Heb *Mesha*
[c] Heb *the father of Hebron*
[d] Heb *son*

---

try its slippery paths should consult the article on the subject in *The Encyclopaedia of Religion and Ethics.*[2] The name **Eliab** signified that God is this man's father. What an extraordinary assertion on his parents' part—or his tribe's!

[2] Ed. James Hastings (New York: Charles Scribner's Sons, 1908-27), I, 327-31.

Crudely the desert tribesmen conceived the notion; greedily and grossly the Hebrews of the monarchic period construed the fatherhood of God in terms of an indulgent potentate pampering his royal family. Contrast the exquisite insight of Hosea (11:1-4) as to what fatherhood truly denotes, and the teaching of Christ on the

3 Now these were the sons of David, which were born unto him in Hebron; the firstborn Amnon, of Ahinoam the Jezreelitess: the second, Daniel, of Abigail the Carmelitess:

2 The third, Absalom the son of Maachah the daughter of Talmai king of Geshur: the fourth, Adonijah the son of Haggith:

3 The fifth, Shephatiah of Abital: the sixth, Ithream by Eglah his wife.

4 *These* six were born unto him in Hebron; and there he reigned seven years and six months: and in Jerusalem he reigned thirty and three years.

5 And these were born unto him in Jerusalem; Shimea, and Shobab, and Nathan, and Solomon, four, of Bath-shua the daughter of Ammiel:

6 Ibhar also, and Elishama, and Eliphelet,

7 And Nogah, and Nepheg, and Japhia,

8 And Elishama, and Eliada, and Eliphelet, nine.

9 *These were* all the sons of David, besides the sons of the concubines, and Tamar their sister.

10 ¶ And Solomon's son *was* Rehoboam, Abia his son, Asa his son, Jehoshaphat his son,

11 Joram his son, Ahaziah his son, Joash his son,

12 Amaziah his son, Azariah his son, Jotham his son,

13 Ahaz his son, Hezekiah his son, Manasseh his son,

14 Amon his son, Josiah his son.

15 And the sons of Josiah *were*, the firstborn Johanan, the second Jehoiakim, the third Zedekiah, the fourth Shallum.

16 And the sons of Jehoiakim; Jeconiah his son, Zedekiah his son.

3 These are the sons of David that were born to him in Hebron: the first-born Ammon, by Ahin'o-am the Jez'reelitess; the second Daniel, by Ab'igail the Car'melitess, 2 the third Ab'salom, whose mother was Ma'acah, the daughter of Talmai, king of Geshur; the fourth Adoni'jah, whose mother was Haggith; 3 the fifth Shephati'ah, by Abi'tal; the sixth Ith'ream, by his wife Eglah; 4 six were born to him in Hebron, where he reigned for seven years and six months. And he reigned thirty-three years in Jerusalem. 5 These were born to him in Jerusalem: Shim'e-a, Shobab, Nathan, and Solomon, four by Bath-shu'a, the daughter of Am'mi-el; 6 then Ibhar, Elish'ama, Eliph'elet, 7 Nogah, Nepheg, Japhi'a, 8 Elish'ama, Eli'ada, and Eliph'elet, nine. 9 All these were David's sons, besides the sons of the concubines; and Tamar was their sister.

10 The descendants of Solomon: Rehobo'am, Abi'jah his son, Asa his son, Jehosh'aphat his son, 11 Joram his son, Ahazi'ah his son, Jo'ash his son, 12 Amazi'ah his son, Azari'ah his son, Jotham his son, 13 Ahaz his son, Hezeki'ah his son, Manas'seh his son, 14 Amon his son, Josi'ah his son. 15 The sons of Josi'ah: Joha'nan the first-born, the second Jehoi'akim, the third Zedeki'ah, the fourth Shallum. 16 The descendants of Jehoi'akim: Jeconi'ah his son, Zedeki'ah his

---

C. Descendants of David (3:1-24)

3:1-9. **Bathshua** (vs. 5) is a variant form of Bathsheba. For **Eliada** (vs. 8), see Exeg. on 14:7.

10-18. These verses give the list of the kings of Judah from Solomon to Zechariah. Very surprising is the inclusion of **Johanan** (vs. 15), since the book of Kings does not

---

subject. Jesus said of God, "My Father" and "your Father"; a lifetime is not sufficient to reveal the full meaning of his words.

3:10-18. *The Kings of Judah.*—A few of these Hebrew kings were to be remembered for the good they did; others were to be remembered for their iniquity. We all bear a name; it is a great issue whether the men and women who know us, or come after us, think of good or evil when they recall our name.

17 ¶ And the sons of Jeconiah; Assir, Salathiel his son,

18 Malchiram also, and Pedaiah, and Shenazar, Jecamiah, Hoshama, and Nedabiah.

19 And the sons of Pedaiah *were*, Zerubbabel, and Shimei: and the sons of Zerubbabel; Meshullam, and Hananiah, and Shelomith their sister:

20 And Hashubah, and Ohel, and Berechiah, and Hasadiah, Jushab-hesed, five.

21 And the sons of Hananiah; Pelatiah, and Jesaiah: the sons of Rephaiah, the sons of Arnan, the sons of Obadiah, the sons of Shechaniah.

22 And the sons of Shechaniah; Shemaiah: and the sons of Shemaiah; Hattush, and Igeal, and Bariah, and Neariah, and Shaphat, six.

23 And the sons of Neariah; Elioenai, and Hezekiah, and Azrikam, three.

24 And the sons of Elioenai *were*, Hodaiah, and Eliashib, and Pelaiah, and Akkub, and Johanan, and Dalaiah, and Anani, seven.

4 The sons of Judah; Pharez, Hezron, and Carmi, and Hur, and Shobal.

2 And Reaiah the son of Shobal begat Jahath; and Jahath begat Ahumai, and Lahad. These *are* the families of the Zorathites.

3 And these *were of* the father of Etam; Jezreel, and Ishma, and Idbash: and the name of their sister *was* Hazelelponi:

son; 17 and the sons of Jeconi'ah, the captive: She-al'tiel his son, 18 Malchi'ram, Peda'iah, Shenaz'zar, Jekami'ah, Hosh'ama, and Nedabi'ah; 19 and the sons of Peda'iah: Zerub'babel and Shim'e-i; and the sons of Zerub'babel: Meshul'lam and Hanani'ah, and Shelo'mith was their sister; 20 and Hashu'bah, Ohel, Berechi'ah, Hasadi'ah, and Ju'shab-he'sed, five. 21 The sons of Hanani'ah: Pelati'ah and Jesha'iah, his son[e] Repha'iah, his son[e] Arnan, his son[e] Obadi'ah, his son[e] Shecani'ah. 22 The sons of Shecani'ah: Shemai'ah. And the sons of Shemai'ah: Hattush, Igal, Bari'ah, Neari'ah, and Shaphat, six. 23 The sons of Neari'ah: Eli-o-e'nai, Hizki'ah, and Azri'kam, three. 24 The sons of Eli-o-e'nai: Hod'avi'ah, Eli'ashib, Pela'iah, Akkub, Joha'nan, Dela'iah, and Ana'ni, seven.

4 The sons of Judah: Perez, Hezron, Carmi, Hur, and Shobal. 2 Re-a'iah the son of Shobal was the father of Jahath, and Jahath was the father of Ahu'mai and Lahad. These were the families of the Zo'rathites. 3 These were the sons[f] of Etam: Jezreel, Ishma, and Idbash; and the name

[e] Gk Compare Syr Vg: Heb *sons of*
[f] Gk Compare Vg: Heb *father*

---

mention him, and it appears that he did not reign. **Zedekiah** (vs. 16) was uncle (**son** is a conventional term) of his predecessor Jeconiah, who in II Chr. 36:8 and II Kings 24:6 is called Jehoiachin, and in Jer. 22:24, Coniah.

19-24. These verses give the list of David's descendants after the captivity. The point is that **Zerubbabel,** who was ruler of Jerusalem under the Persians in 520 B.C. (see Hag. 1:1; 2:21), is here recorded to be grandson of the exiled King Jeconiah. In him, therefore, as civil head of the renascent community, the Jews could feel that in some measure "the house of David" had been restored. The names cited thereafter imply for the latest of them a date *ca.* 350 B.C.; while the LXX extends the list to the eleventh generation, *ca.* 250. These facts do not require us to date the Chronicler as late as 350, still less 250 B.C., for there is no solid evidence that the Chronicler wrote these verses. As for the LXX's extension, what more natural than that in the copying of MSS such a list would be kept up-to-date? In vs. 22, omit **And the sons of Shemaiah.**

D. SONS OF JUDAH AND SIMEON (4:1-43)

1. CALEBITES AND OTHERS (4:1-23)

4:1-23. Judah's genealogy has already been given in ch. 2. The present list seems likely to be an older version in view of vs. 9 (a fanciful etymology) and vss. 21-23. Another genealogist later inserted the longer list of ch. 2. In vs. 1 **Carmi** is a textual error for

4 And Penuel the father of Gedor, and Ezer the father of Hushah. These *are* the sons of Hur, the firstborn of Ephratah, the father of Beth-lehem.

5 ¶ And Ashur the father of Tekoa had two wives, Helah and Naarah.

6 And Naarah bare him Ahuzam, and Hepher, and Temeni, and Haahashtari. These *were* the sons of Naarah.

7 And the sons of Helah *were*, Zereth, and Jezoar, and Ethnan.

8 And Coz begat Anub, and Zobebah, and the families of Aharhel the son of Harum.

9 ¶ And Jabez was more honorable than his brethren: and his mother called his name Jabez, saying, Because I bare him with sorrow.

10 And Jabez called on the God of Israel, saying, Oh that thou wouldest bless me indeed, and enlarge my coast, and that thine hand might be with me, and that thou wouldest keep *me* from evil, that it may not grieve me! And God granted him that which he requested.

11 ¶ And Chelub the brother of Shuah begat Mehir, which *was* the father of Eshton.

12 And Eshton begat Beth-rapha, and Paseah, and Tehinnah the father of Ir-nahash. These *are* the men of Rechah.

13 And the sons of Kenaz; Othniel, and Seraiah: and the sons of Othniel; Hathath.

14 And Meonothai begat Ophrah: and Seraiah begat Joab, the father of the valley of Charashim; for they were craftsmen.

of their sister was Hazzelelpo'ni, 4 and Penu'el was the father of Gedor, and Ezer the father of Hushah. These were the sons of Hur, the first-born of Eph'rathah the father of Bethlehem. 5 Ashhur, the father of Teko'a, had two wives, Helah and Na'arah; 6 Na'arah bore him Ahuz'zam, Hepher, Te'meni, and Ha-ahash'tari. These were the sons of Na'arah. 7 The sons of Helah: Zereth, Izhar, and Ethnan. 8 Koz was the father of Anub, Zobe'bah, and the families of Ahar'hel the son of Harum. 9 Jabez was more honorable than his brothers; and his mother called his name Jabez, saying, "Because I bore him in pain." 10 Jabez called on the God of Israel, saying, "Oh that thou wouldst bless me and enlarge my border, and that thy hand might be with me, and that thou wouldst keep me from harm so that it might not hurt me!" And God granted what he asked. 11 Chelub, the brother of Shuhah, was the father of Mehir, who was the father of Eshton. 12 Eshton was the father of Bethra'pha, Pase'ah, and Tehin'nah the father of Irna'hash. These are the men of Recah. 13 The sons of Kenaz: Oth'ni-el and Sera'iah; and the sons of Oth'ni-el: Hathath and Meo'nothai.g 14 Meo'nothai was the father of Ophrah; and Sera'iah was the father of Jo'ab the father of Ge-har'ashim,h so-called

g Gk Vg: Heb lacks *Meonothai*
h That is *Valley of craftsmen*

"Caleb." The mention of skilled craftsmen in vss. 21-23 is a notable feature. As regards the expert **potters**, it has been argued on the basis of some excavated jar handles inscribed with similar names that the men were of Calebite-Jerahmeelite families

---

4:10. *Not a Christian Prayer.*—What Jabez asked from God was earthly prosperity: enlarged territory, success in his ventures, and security against foes. His petition **that thou wouldest keep me from evil** may have little or no ethical meaning. The Hebrew word translated **evil** denoted physical disaster as well as moral iniquity, so that **harm** (RSV) is a more accurate rendering. This wide meaning of the Hebrew word should be borne in mind when reading the O.T.; e.g., "Shall evil befall a city, and the LORD hath not done it?" (Amos 3:6 ERV). Jabez' prayer was crude and selfish. His conscience was not troubled by the thought

that others would suffer if he gained his wishes. But ours should be. Yet how easily and often we also pray amiss. Christian praying is longing to learn and to accept what God would have us be and do; and asking in Christ's name (John 14:13; 15:7) covers only desires that are in accordance with the character of him who prayed in the Garden of Gethsemane, "Father, all things are possible to thee; remove this cup from me; yet not what I will, but what thou wilt" (Mark 14:36). Subject to that understanding and control, it is not asking amiss to pray for natural benefits—health, happiness, security —for ourselves, and how much more for others:

15 And the sons of Caleb the son of Je-phunneh; Iru, Elah, and Naam: and the sons of Elah, even Kenaz.

16 And the sons of Jehaleleel; Ziph, and Ziphah, Tiria, and Asareel.

17 And the sons of Ezra *were,* Jether, and Mered, and Epher, and Jalon: and she bare Miriam, and Shammai, and Ishbah the father of Eshtemoa.

18 And his wife Jehudijah bare Jered the father of Gedor, and Heber the father of Socho, and Jekuthiel the father of Za-noah. And these *are* the sons of Bithiah the daughter of Pharaoh, which Mered took.

19 And the sons of *his* wife Hodiah the sister of Naham, the father of Keilah the Garmite, and Eshtemoa the Maachathite.

20 And the sons of Shimon *were,* Amnon, and Rinnah, Ben-hanan, and Tilon. And the sons of Ishi *were,* Zoheth, and Ben-zo-heth.

21 ¶ The sons of Shelah the son of Judah *were,* Er the father of Lecah, and Laadah the father of Mareshah, and the families of the house of them that wrought fine linen, of the house of Ashbea,

22 And Jokim, and the men of Chozeba, and Joash, and Saraph, who had the do-minion in Moab, and Jashubi-lehem. And *these are* ancient things.

23 These *were* the potters, and those that dwelt among plants and hedges: there they dwelt with the king for his work.

24 ¶ The sons of Simeon *were,* Nemuel, and Jamin, Jarib, Zerah, *and* Shaul:

because they were craftsmen. 15 The sons of Caleb the son of Jephun'neh: Iru, Elah, and Na'am; and the sons of Elah: Kenaz. 16 The sons of Jehal'lelel: Ziph, Ziphah, Tir'i-a, and As'arel. 17 The sons of Ezrah: Jether, Mered, Epher, and Jalon. These are the sons of Bith'i-ah, the daughter of Phar-aoh, whom Mered married;[i] and she con-ceived and bore[j] Miriam, Sham'mai, and Ishbah, the father of Eshtemo'a. 18 And his Jewish wife bore Jered the father of Gedor, Heber the father of Soco, and Jeku'thiel the father of Zano'ah. 19 The sons of the wife of Hodi'ah, the sister of Naham, were the fathers of Kei'lah the Garmite and Esh-temo'a the Ma-ac'athite. 20 The sons of Shimon: Amnon, Rinnah, Ben-ha'nan, and Tilon. The sons of Ishi: Zoheth and Ben-zo'heth. 21 The sons of Shelah the son of Judah: Er the father of Lecah, La'adah the father of Mare'shah, and the families of the house of linen workers at Beth-ashbe'a; 22 and Jokim, and the men of Coze'ba, and Jo'ash, and Saraph, who ruled in Moab and returned to Lehem[k] (now the records[l] are ancient). 23 These were the potters and inhabitants of Neta'im and Gede'rah; they dwelt there with the king for his work.

24 The sons of Simeon: Nem'u-el, Jamin,

[i] The clause: *These are . . . married* is transposed from verse 18
[j] Heb lacks *and bore*
[k] Vg Compare Gk: Heb *and Jashubi-lahem*
[l] Or *matters*

(R. A. S. Macalister, "The Craftsmen's Guild of the Tribe of Judah" and "Occasional Papers on the Modern Inhabitants of Palestine," *Palestine Exploration Fund Quarterly Statement for 1905,* pp. 243-53, 343-56). The conjecture is interesting but not con-vincing.

2. SIMEONITES (4:24-43)

24-43. With these verses cf. Gen. 46:10; Josh. 19:2-8. The two exploits mentioned in vss. 34-43 (not recorded elsewhere) presumably come from an old tradition. In vs. 39

"Give us this day our daily bread." Eventually some of the Hebrews, taught by the great proph-ets, realized how rightly to offer personal and intercessional prayer and practiced it.

But Jabez deserves kinder treatment. His name signified "pain" or "sorrow" and the fact preyed on his imagination, suggesting that he was a man handicapped in life, sure to be un-fortunate. He had the courage to refuse to despond. Face your fears. Put up a fight against

misfortunes and difficulties. Beethoven con-quered deafness and created immortal music to which he could not listen with the hearing of the ear. Jabez had crude ideas about God. But he was wise in thinking that spiritual aid is a reality, available for those who seek it rightly.

23. They Dwelt with the King for His Work. —(See Exeg.) This seemingly plain statement for some reason puzzled or stimulated the Jew-ish interpreters. At any rate the Targ. quaintly

25 Shallum his son, Mibsam his son, Mishma his son.

26 And the sons of Mishma; Hamuel his son, Zacchur his son, Shimei his son.

27 And Shimei had sixteen sons and six daughters; but his brethren had not many children, neither did all their family multiply, like to the children of Judah.

28 And they dwelt at Beer-sheba, and Moladah, and Hazar-shual,

29 And at Bilhah, and at Ezem, and at Tolad,

30 And at Bethuel, and at Hormah, and at Ziklag,

31 And at Beth-marcaboth, and Hazar-susim, and at Beth-birei, and at Shaaraim. These *were* their cities unto the reign of David.

32 And their villages *were*, Etam, and Ain, Rimmon, and Tochen, and Ashan, five cities:

33 And all their villages that *were* round about the same cities, unto Baal. These *were* their habitations, and their genealogy.

34 And Meshobab, and Jamlech, and Joshah the son of Amaziah,

35 And Joel, and Jehu the son of Josibiah, the son of Seraiah, the son of Asiel,

36 And Elioenai and Jaakobah, and Jeshohaiah, and Asaiah, and Adiel, and Jesimiel, and Benaiah,

37 And Ziza the son of Shiphi, the son of Allon, the son of Jedaiah, the son of Shimri, the son of Shemaiah;

38 These mentioned by *their* names *were* princes in their families: and the house of their fathers increased greatly.

39 ¶ And they went to the entrance of Gedor, *even* unto the east side of the valley, to seek pasture for their flocks.

40 And they found fat pasture and good, and the land *was* wide, and quiet, and peaceable; for *they* of Ham had dwelt there of old.

41 And these written by name came in the days of Hezekiah king of Judah, and

Jarib, Zerah, Sha'ul; 25 Shallum was his son, Mibsam his son, Mishma his son. 26 The sons of Mishma: Ham'mu-el his son, Zac'cur his son, Shim'e-i his son. 27 Shim'e-i had sixteen sons and six daughters; but his brothers had not many children, nor did all their family multiply like the men of Judah. 28 They dwelt in Beer-sheba, Mola'dah, Ha'zar-shu'al, 29 Bilhah, Ezem, Tolad, 30 Bethu'el, Hormah, Ziklag, 31 Beth-mar'-caboth, Ha'zar-su'sim, Beth-biri, and Sha-ara'im. These were their cities until David reigned. 32 And their villages were Etam, A'in, Rimmon, Tochen, and Ashan, five cities, 33 along with all their villages which were round about these cities as far as Ba'al. These were their settlements, and they kept a genealogical record.

34 Mesho'bab, Jamlech, Joshah the son of Amazi'ah, 35 Jo'el, Jehu the son of Joshibi'ah, son of Sera'iah, son of As'i-el, 36 Eli-o-e'nai, Ja-ako'bah, Jeshohai'ah, Asa'iah, Ad'i-el, Jesim'i-el, Benai'ah, 37 Ziza the son of Shiphi, son of Allon, son of Jeda'iah, son of Shimri, son of Shemai'ah — 38 these mentioned by name were princes in their families, and their fathers' houses increased greatly. 39 They journeyed to the entrance of Gedor, to the east side of the valley, to seek pasture for their flocks, 40 where they found rich, good pasture, and the land was very broad, quiet, and peaceful; for the former inhabitants there belonged to Ham. 41 These, registered by name, came in the

---

Gedor should perhaps be "Gerar" (LXX), a place on the Philistine border. **Of Ham** (vs. 40) means people of Canaanite ancestry.

---

paraphrased it thus: "They made their dwelling there with the Presence [Shekinah] of the King of the World for the practice of the law." Is that too high an estimate of these **potters** and their skill? Or is it true that whenever men practice their tasks to the best of their ability they draw nigh to the divine Presence, and in their achievements show forth the praise of God?

smote their tents, and the habitations that were found there, and destroyed them utterly unto this day, and dwelt in their rooms: because *there was* pasture there for their flocks.

42 And *some* of them, *even* of the sons of Simeon, five hundred men, went to mount Seir, having for their captains Pelatiah, and Neariah, and Rephaiah, and Uzziel, the sons of Ishi.

43 And they smote the rest of the Amalekites that were escaped, and dwelt there unto this day.

5 Now the sons of Reuben the firstborn of Israel, (for he *was* the firstborn; but, forasmuch as he defiled his father's bed, his birthright was given unto the sons of Joseph the son of Israel: and the genealogy is not to be reckoned after the birthright.

2 For Judah prevailed above his brethren, and of him *came* the chief ruler; but the birthright *was* Joseph's:)

3 The sons, *I say,* of Reuben the firstborn of Israel *were,* Hanoch, and Pallu, Hezron, and Carmi.

4 The sons of Joel; Shemaiah his son, Gog his son, Shimei his son,

5 Micah his son, Reaia his son, Baal his son,

6 Beerah his son, whom Tilgath-pilneser king of Assyria carried away *captive:* he *was* prince of the Reubenites.

7 And his brethren by their families, when the genealogy of their generations was reckoned, *were* the chief, Jeiel, and Zechariah,

8 And Bela the son of Azaz, the son of Shema, the son of Joel, who dwelt in Aroer, even unto Nebo and Baal-meon:

9 And eastward he inhabited unto the entering in of the wilderness from the river Euphrates: because their cattle were multiplied in the land of Gilead.

days of Hezeki'ah, king of Judah, and destroyed their tents and the Me-u'nim who were found there, and exterminated them to this day, and settled in their place, because there was pasture there for their flocks. 42 And some of them, five hundred men of the Simeonites, went to Mount Se'ir, having as their leaders Pelati'ah, Ne-ari'ah, Repha'iah, and Uz'ziel, the sons of Ishi; 43 and they destroyed the remnant of the Amal'ekites that had escaped, and they have dwelt there to this day.

5 The sons of Reuben the first-born of Israel (for he was the first-born; but because he polluted his father's couch, his birthright was given to the sons of Joseph the son of Israel, so that he is not enrolled in the genealogy according to the birthright; 2 though Judah became strong among his brothers and a prince was from him, yet the birthright belonged to Joseph), 3 the sons of Reuben, the first-born of Israel: Hanoch, Pallu, Hezron, and Carmi. 4 The sons of Jo'el: Shemai'ah his son, Gog his son, Shim'e-i his son, 5 Micah his son, Re-a'iah his son, Ba'al his son, 6 Be-er'ah his son, whom Til'gath-pilne'ser king of Assyria carried away into exile; he was a chieftain of the Reubenites. 7 And his kinsmen by their families, when the genealogy of their generations was reckoned: the chief, Je-i'el, and Zechari'ah, 8 and Bela the son of Azaz, son of Shema, son of Jo'el, who dwelt in Aro'er, as far as Nebo and Ba'al-me'on. 9 He also dwelt to the east as far as the entrance of the desert this side of the Eu-phra'tes, because their cattle had multiplied in the land

---

E. Trans-Jordan Tribes (5:1-26)

This list refers to the sons of Reuben, Gad, and Manasseh, who lived on the eastern side of the Jordan.

5:2-22. A prince, i.e., David. The deportation of **Beerah** (vs. 6) is mentioned only here. The phrase **reckoned by genealogies** (vs. 17) is found only in Chronicles, Ezra,

---

5:1-26. *The Point of No Return.*—This chapter concerns the Hebrew tribes dwelling east of the Jordan, in Gilead and Bashan. It has a sting in its tail, for it records (vss. 25, 26) that they

. . . went a whoring after the gods of the people of the land, and were carried away captive by the Assyrians, never to return. They were Hebrews, but they went so far wrong that there

10 And in the days of Saul they made war with the Hagarites, who fell by their hand: and they dwelt in their tents throughout all the east *land* of Gilead.

11 ¶ And the children of Gad dwelt over against them, in the land of Bashan unto Salcah:

12 Joel the chief, and Shapham the next, and Jaanai, and Shaphat in Bashan.

13 And their brethren of the house of their fathers *were,* Michael, and Meshullam, and Sheba, and Jorai, and Jachan, and Zia, and Heber, seven.

14 These *are* the children of Abihail the son of Huri, the son of Jaroah, the son of Gilead, the son of Michael, the son of Jeshishai, the son of Jahdo, the son of Buz;

15 Ahi the son of Abdiel, the son of Guni, chief of the house of their fathers.

16 And they dwelt in Gilead in Bashan, and in her towns, and in all the suburbs of Sharon, upon their borders.

17 All these were reckoned by genealogies in the days of Jotham king of Judah, and in the days of Jeroboam king of Israel.

18 ¶ The sons of Reuben, and the Gadites, and half the tribe of Manasseh, of valiant men, men able to bear buckler and sword, and to shoot with bow, and skilful in war, *were* four and forty thousand seven hundred and threescore, that went out to the war.

19 And they made war with the Hagarites, with Jetur, and Nephish, and Nodab.

20 And they were helped against them, and the Hagarites were delivered into their hand, and all that *were* with them: for they

of Gilead. 10 And in the days of Saul they made war on the Hagrites, who fell by their hand; and they dwelt in their tents throughout all the region east of Gilead.

11 The sons of Gad dwelt over against them in the land of Bashan as far as Sal'-ecah: 12 Jo'el the chief, Shapham the second, Ja'nai, and Shaphat in Bashan. 13 And their kinsmen according to their fathers' houses: Michael, Meshul'lam, Sheba, Jo'rai, Jacan, Zi'a, and Eber, seven. 14 These were the sons of Ab'ihail the son of Huri, son of Jaro'ah, son of Gilead, son of Michael, son of Jeshish'ai, son of Jahdo, son of Buz; 15 Ahi the son of Ab'di-el, son of Guni, was chief in their fathers' houses; 16 and they dwelt in Gilead, in Bashan and in its towns, and in all the pasture lands of Sharon to their limits. 17 All of these were enrolled by genealogies in the days of Jotham king of Judah, and in the days of Jerobo'am king of Israel.

18 The Reubenites, the Gadites, and the half-tribe of Manas'seh had valiant men, who carried shield and sword, and drew the bow, expert in war, forty-four thousand seven hundred and sixty, ready for service. 19 They made war upon the Hagrites, Jetur, Naphish, and Nodab; 20 and when they received help against them, the Hagrites and

---

and Nehemiah, and probably implies a census, taken not for taxation or military ends but for record of families which had kept fully Jewish relationship in the postexilic community.

---

was no recovery, no place for them in the renewal of Jewish life. Chronicles implies that the Judeans and many in Israel did recover because they were willing to learn, acquired finer moral discernment and wiser thoughts as to God and his demands, and so through their faith found strength. Stanley A. Cook has somewhere written that there will be a future for Christianity. But it may not be, as we too lightly assume, in Western civilization. The next stage may be in African and Asian Christianity.

20-22. The God of Battles.—Hapless Hagrites, slaughtered and dispossessed! Hebrews triumphant, because they had obtained the aid of a God mighty in battle (cf. Pss. 24:8; 144:1; but in the Psalter the words are metaphorical). The Chronicler lived many centuries later than this scrap of ancient tradition. Jewish morality and religion had become profound. It would be interesting to ask the Chronicler how he really felt about the ferocity and naïve theology implied in these verses.

Damage beyond calculation has been done to the cause of true religion by the notion that everything said about God in the Bible from cover to cover ought somehow to be jumbled

cried to God in the battle, and he was entreated of them; because they put their trust in him.

21 And they took away their cattle; of their camels fifty thousand, and of sheep two hundred and fifty thousand, and of asses two thousand, and of men a hundred thousand.

22 For there fell down many slain, because the war *was* of God. And they dwelt in their steads until the captivity.

23 ¶ And the children of the half tribe of Manasseh dwelt in the land: they increased from Bashan unto Baal-hermon and Senir, and unto mount Hermon.

24 And these *were* the heads of the house of their fathers, even Epher, and Ishi, and Eliel, and Azriel, and Jeremiah, and Hodaviah, and Jahdiel, mighty men of valor, famous men, *and* heads of the house of their fathers.

25 ¶ And they transgressed against the God of their fathers, and went a whoring after the gods of the people of the land, whom God destroyed before them.

26 And the God of Israel stirred up the spirit of Pul king of Assyria, and the spirit of Tilgath-pilneser king of Assyria, and he carried them away, even the Reubenites, and the Gadites, and the half tribe of Manasseh, and brought them unto Halah, and Habor, and Hara, and to the river Gozan, unto this day.

6 The sons of Levi; Gershon, Kohath, and Merari.

2 And the sons of Kohath; Amram, Izhar, and Hebron, and Uzziel.

all who were with them were given into their hands, for they cried to God in the battle, and he granted their entreaty because they trusted in him. 21 They carried off their livestock: fifty thousand of their camels, two hundred and fifty thousand sheep, two thousand asses, and a hundred thousand men alive. 22 For many fell slain, because the war was of God. And they dwelt in their place until the exile.

23 The members of the half-tribe of Manas'seh dwelt in the land; they were very numerous from Bashan to Ba'al-her'mon, Senir, and Mount Hermon. 24 These were the heads of their fathers' houses: Epher,[m] Ishi, Eli'el, Az'ri-el, Jeremiah, Hodavi'ah, and Jah'di-el, mighty warriors, famous men, heads of their fathers' houses. 25 But they transgressed against the God of their fathers, and played the harlot after the gods of the peoples of the land, whom God had destroyed before them. 26 So the God of Israel stirred up the spirit of Pul king of Assyria and the spirit of Til'gath-pilne'ser king of Assyria, and he carried them away, namely, the Reubenites, the Gadites, and the half-tribe of Manas'seh, and brought them to Halah, Habor, Hara, and the river Gozan, to this day.

6 [n] The sons of Levi: Gershom, Kohath, and Merar'i. 2 The sons of Kohath:

[m] Gk Vg: Heb *and Epher*
[n] Heb Ch 5. 27

---

23. **The half-tribe of Manasseh** means those dwelling east of the Jordan.

F. Sons of Levi (6:1-81)

This long chapter concerning the ministrants of worship raises a subject of prime interest, but also of great obscurity, in relation to Hebrew history and ritual. Comment has already been made regarding it in the Intro. (Succinct and lucid discussion may be found in the article by N. H. Snaith, "The Priesthood and the Temple," in T. W.

---

together in an incongruous amalgam. Follow instead, as key to the permanent value of the Scriptures, the thought that by the patient will of the one eternal God the Hebrews were being brought gradually to discernment of his real nature—were led out of darkness into marvelous light.

What should be felt about the appalling situations that seem so often to confront us in

the modern world? The massacred Hagrites may at least remind us that might may be used to defend right, but never in the interests of greed and cruelty; and that our ultimate purpose must be not less than the welfare of mankind.

6:1-81. *The Sons of Levi.*—These are the men who were responsible for the rightful ordering of Hebrew worship. They based their authority

Manson, ed., *A Companion to the Bible* [Edinburgh: T. & T. Clark, 1943], pp. 418-43. A study of lasting importance is George Buchanan Gray, *Sacrifice in the Old Testament* [Oxford: Clarendon Press, 1925], pp. 179-255.) Levi, like the other "sons of Jacob," was originally a tribe which together with Simeon—at a date in the patriarchal period, long before the time of Moses—attacked the Canaanite town of Shechem, and afterward suffered so great a defeat that the survivors were no longer a coherent group but dispersed families, of whom some wandered here and there in Canaan and others migrated to Egypt and thence returned in the time of Moses (so Gen. 34; 49:5-7). An interesting conjecture is that Levites chanced to become priest-guardians of the Hebrew holy place at Kadesh-barnea before the invasion of Canaan. If so, it would be natural that Levites were chosen to serve the first Hebrew sanctuaries in Canaan, notably at Shiloh where a temple was built. At the time of the Philistine conflicts this shrine was in the charge of Eli (an Aaronite Levite) whose descendant was Abiathar, one of the two principal priests at the end of David's reign. It was, however, legitimate—and long remained so—for any Hebrew to act as a priest in offering sacrifice. But there is irrefutable evidence from the early period of the judges that Levites were especially esteemed and much coveted as the guardians and priests of sanctuaries (Judg. 17–18). Finding employment thus, the Levites—it is agreed—became in time essentially ministers of the cult (Deut. 33:8-11). Yet down to the end of the Judean kingdom in the sixth century b.c., men who were not of Levitical families were employed in ritual duties, as we know to be the case in Solomon's temple (see Ezek. 44:7) where, of course, men claiming descent from Levi through Zadok were dominant and held the important posts. "Levite" resembles a Hebrew verb *lāwāh*, meaning "to attach"; and we can therefore readily understand that non-Levitical men employed in the cult, as attached persons, might in time be credited with Levitical ancestry; Chronicles seems to show two instances, Samuel the Ephraimite (6:28; cf. I Sam. 1:1) and Obed-edom the Gittite (see Exeg. on 13:13; cf. 16:5). Reference has been made in the Intro. to developments after the fall of the two Hebrew kingdoms, which eventually had the result that in the second temple only those men who were deemed to be descended from Zadok, and more widely from Levi through Aaron, were accorded the standing of full priests, while all other Levites discharged subordinate duties and had the standing of ministers "unto their brethren the priests." Ch. 6 is eloquent of that eventual stage: mark the emphasis in vs. 49, But **Aaron and his sons** . . . . Now the original text of the Chronicler has been freely and confusingly subjected to later insertions. It is possible very clearly to screen out those additions and "corrections," if the view set forth in the Intro. is taken, that they were made in the interests of conforming what the Chronicler had written to the final Law, and if the Chronicler himself is regarded as having lived at a somewhat earlier period. The Chronicler belonged to the antecedent period when Levites, other than only the Zadokites, were acting in the priestly duties, later confined to the Zadokites or "sons of Aaron"—as well as in the other functions of the cult. That earlier stage is the attitude found in Deuteronomy, where it is characterized by the phrase "the priests, the Levites"—perhaps also in Malachi, its date being prior to Nehemiah (see J. M. P. Smith, *A Critical and Exegetical Commentary on Haggai, Zechariah, Malachi and Jonah* [New York: Charles Scribner's Sons, 1912; "International Critical Commentary"], p. 38, on Mal. 2:4). It is highly significant that the phrase "the priests, the Levites," is found in 13:13 (LXX); II Chr. 23:18; 30:27 (M.T. and LXXB). It may well be that originally it occurred much more often, for it would give grave offense to men of later times. By inserting in the MS a single Hebrew letter, waw (ו), which means "and," they could indicate the differentiation they expected to read, "the priests and the Levites." It is probable that in not a few places the Chronicler himself wrote simply "the Levites," and the revisers inserted "the priests and." However that may be, if and when the Chronicler wrote "the priests and the Levites," he meant thereby Levites (not merely of Zadokite families) acting as priests by sacrificing, burning incense, sounding the sacred trumpets, together with Levites fulfilling other duties. The revisers would suppose he meant

3 And the children of Amram; Aaron, and Moses, and Miriam. The sons also of Aaron; Nadab and Abihu, Eleazar and Ithamar.

4 ¶ Eleazar begat Phinehas, Phinehas begat Abishua,

5 And Abishua begat Bukki, and Bukki begat Uzzi,

6 And Uzzi begat Zerahiah, and Zerahiah begat Meraioth,

7 Meraioth begat Amariah, and Amariah begat Ahitub,

8 And Ahitub begat Zadok, and Zadok begat Ahimaaz,

9 And Ahimaaz begat Azariah, and Azariah begat Johanan,

10 And Johanan begat Azariah; (he *it is* that executed the priest's office in the temple that Solomon built in Jerusalem:)

11 And Azariah begat Amariah, and Amariah begat Ahitub,

12 And Ahitub begat Zadok, and Zadok begat Shallum,

13 And Shallum begat Hilkiah, and Hilkiah begat Azariah,

14 And Azariah begat Seraiah, and Seraiah begat Jehozadak,

15 And Jehozadak went *into captivity,* when the Lord carried away Judah and Jerusalem by the hand of Nebuchadnezzar.

Amram, Izhar, Hebron, and Uz'ziel. 3 The children of Amram: Aaron, Moses, and Miriam. The sons of Aaron: Nadab, Abi'hu, Elea'zar, and Ith'amar. 4 Elea'zar was the father of Phin'ehas, Phin'ehas of Abishu'a, 5 Abishu'a of Bukki, Bukki of Uzzi, 6 Uzzi of Zerahi'ah, Zerahi'ah of Mera'ioth, 7 Mera'ioth of Amari'ah, Amari'ah of Ahi'tub, 8 Ahi'tub of Zadok, Zadok of Ahim'a-az, 9 Ahim'a-az of Azari'ah, Azari'ah of Joha'nan, 10 and Joha'nan of Azari'ah (it was he who served as priest in the house that Solomon built in Jerusalem). 11 Azari'ah was the father of Amari'ah, Amari'ah of Ahi'tub, 12 Ahi'tub of Zadok, Zadok of Shallum, 13 Shallum of Hilki'ah, Hilki'ah of Azari'ah, 14 Azari'ah of Sera'iah, Sera'iah of Jehoz'adak; 15 and Jehoz'adak went into exile when the Lord sent Judah and Jerusalem into exile by the hand of Nebuchadnez'zar.

"Aaronite priests and subordinate Levites." The importance of this subtle point will be seen in notes on not a few passages.

1. The Aaronite Line (6:1-15)

Transparently it is the final stage, not the Chronicler's view, which appears in this chapter, beginning thus with an impressive list of Aaronic chief priests, through **Zadok** (vs. 8) to **Jehozadak** (vs. 15), taken prisoner to Babylon in 586 b.c.

6:8. Zadok: The list ignores the other chief priest at the end of David's reign—Abiathar (descendant of Eli) who sided with Adonijah against Solomon. However, the Chronicler was not unwilling to mention him (15:11). Other evidence that this list is not by the Chronicler is its curious failure to name two chief priests referred to in Chronicles: Jehoiada (II Chr. 22:11) and Azariah (II Chr. 26:20). Strangely enough, Urijah, named in II Kings 16:11, is mentioned neither here nor elsewhere in Chronicles.

10. The remark about **Azariah** should have been attached to his grandfather of the same name (vs. 9), who was contemporary with Solomon.

to do so on the ground that they were in the line of physical descent from one or other of the three great Levitical families: **Gershom, Kohath, and Merari.** One name in the list prompts reflection—**Zadok** (vs. 8), whom Solomon appointed to be chief priest in Jerusalem when he rejected from his royal service Abiathar, whose forefather had been Eli, priest of

the temple at Shiloh. Recall that eventually the descendants of Zadok arrogated to themselves alone the dominant functions in the second temple. But Zadok's appointment had turned on a king's decision and was a consequence of plots and policy (I Kings 1:1-53; 2:26-28). And all too many of Zadok's "sons" proved themselves to be but priests "after the flesh" in Jerusalem's

16 ¶ The sons of Levi; Gershom, Kohath, and Merari.

17 And these *be* the names of the sons of Gershom; Libni, and Shimei.

18 And the sons of Kohath *were*, Amram, and Izhar, and Hebron, and Uzziel.

19 The sons of Merari; Mahli, and Mushi. And these *are* the families of the Levites according to their fathers.

20 Of Gershom; Libni his son, Jahath his son, Zimmah his son,

21 Joah his son, Iddo his son, Zerah his son, Jeaterai his son.

22 The sons of Kohath; Amminadab his son, Korah his son, Assir his son,

23 Elkanah his son, and Ebiasaph his son, and Assir his son,

24 Tahath his son, Uriel his son, Uzziah his son, and Shaul his son.

25 And the sons of Elkanah; Amasai, and Ahimoth.

26 *As for* Elkanah: the sons of Elkanah; Zophai his son, and Nahath his son,

27 Eliab his son, Jeroham his son, Elkanah his son.

28 And the sons of Samuel; the firstborn Vashni, and Abiah.

29 The sons of Merari; Mahli, Libni his son, Shimei his son, Uzza his son,

30 Shimea his son, Haggiah his son, Asaiah his son.

31 And these *are they* whom David set

16[o] The sons of Levi: Gershom, Kohath,
and Merar'i. 17 And these are the names of
the sons of Gershom: Libni and Shim'e-i.
18 The sons of Kohath: Amram, Izhar, Hebron, and Uz'ziel. 19 The sons of Merar'i:
Mahli and Mushi. These are the families
of the Levites according to their fathers.
20 Of Gershom: Libni his son, Jahath his
son, Zimmah his son, 21 Jo'ah his son, Iddo
his son, Zerah his son, Je-ath'erai his son.
22 The sons of Kohath: Ammin'adab his
son, Korah his son, Assir his son, 23 Elka'-
nah his son, Ebi'asaph his son, Assir his son,
24 Tahath his son, Uri'el his son, Uzzi'ah
his son, and Sha'ul his son. 25 The sons of
Elka'nah: Ama'sai and Ahi'moth, 26 Elka'-
nah his son, Zophai his son, Nahath his son,
27 Eli'ab his son, Jero'ham his son, Elka'nah
his son. 28 The sons of Samuel: Jo'el[p] his
first-born, the second Abi'jah.[q] 29 The sons
of Merar'i: Mahli, Libni his son, Shim'e-i
his son, Uzza his son, 30 Shim'e-a his son,
Haggi'ah his son, and Asa'iah his son.

31 These are the men whom David put

[o] Heb Ch 6. 1
[p] Gk Syr Compare verse 33 and 1 Sam 8. 2: Heb lacks *Joel*
[q] Heb *and Abijah*

2. Other Branches (6:16-30)

The sons of **Gershom** and **Merari** mentioned in the canonical books of the Law were not enough to bridge the generations from Levi to David's time. Accordingly five new names in vss. 39-40, and nine in vss. 44-47, were provided. However, those names are quite certainly not early Hebrew names, but postexilic. Presumably the genealogists, aware that certain Gershonite and Merarite families had long served the second temple, inserted the earliest known forefathers of those families as the missing men so as to provide a pedigree long enough to reach to the time of David.

27. Elkanah his son: Add "Samuel his son," which has accidentally dropped out of the text.

3. The Musical Guilds (6:31-48)

The Levitical descent of the three principal divisions or families serving the music

temple. Jeremiah had sorrowfully to write: "Both prophet and priest are profane; yea, in my house have I found their wickedness, saith the Lord" (23:11). In sixteenth-century Europe if the armies of Protestant princes had altogether prevailed, if the Papacy had ceased, if the apostolic succession had been completely interrupted, what then? Ought not modern priests and presbyters, Catholic and Protestant, to consider spiritually the validity of their claim to descent from Christ, from him who is revered as "very God of very God," and who said, "By this shall all men know that ye are my disciples, if ye have love one to another" (John 13:35)?

31. *Church Music.*—(Cf. Expos. on I Chr. 15:16; II Chr. 5:13-14.) The Chronicler was fa-

over the service of song in the house of the LORD, after that the ark had rest.

32 And they ministered before the dwelling place of the tabernacle of the congregation with singing, until Solomon had built the house of the LORD in Jerusalem: and *then* they waited on their office according to their order.

33 And these *are* they that waited with their children. Of the sons of the Kohathites; Heman a singer, the son of Joel, the son of Shemuel,

34 The son of Elkanah, the son of Jeroham, the son of Eliel, the son of Toah,

35 The son of Zuph, the son of Elkanah, the son of Mahath, the son of Amasai,

36 The son of Elkanah, the son of Joel, the son of Azariah, the son of Zephaniah,

37 The son of Tahath, the son of Assir, the son of Ebiasaph, the son of Korah,

38 The son of Izhar, the son of Kohath, the son of Levi, the son of Israel.

39 And his brother, Asaph, who stood on his right hand, *even* Asaph the son of Berachiah, the son of Shimea,

40 The son of Michael, the son of Baaseiah, the son of Malchiah,

41 The son of Ethni, the son of Zerah, the son of Adaiah,

42 The son of Ethan, the son of Zimmah, the son of Shimei,

43 The son of Jahath, the son of Gershom, the son of Levi.

44 And their brethren the sons of Merari *stood* on the left hand: Ethan the son of Kishi, the son of Abdi, the son of Malluch,

45 The son of Hashabiah, the son of Amaziah, the son of Hilkiah,

46 The son of Amzi, the son of Bani, the son of Shamer,

47 The son of Mahli, the son of Mushi, the son of Merari, the son of Levi.

in charge of the service of song in the house of the LORD, after the ark rested there. 32 They ministered with song before the tabernacle of the tent of meeting, until Solomon had built the house of the LORD in Jerusalem; and they performed their service in due order. 33 These are the men who served and their sons. Of the sons of the Ko'hathites: Heman the singer the son of Jo'el, son of Samuel, 34 son of Elka'nah, son of Jero'ham, son of Eli'el, son of To'ah, 35 son of Zuph, son of Elka'nah, son of Mahath, son of Ama'sai, 36 son of Elka'nah, son of Jo'el, son of Azari'ah, son of Zephani'ah, 37 son of Tahath, son of Assir, son of Ebi'-asaph, son of Korah, 38 son of Izhar, son of Kohath, son of Levi, son of Israel; 39 and his brother Asaph, who stood on his right hand, namely, Asaph the son of Berechi'ah, son of Shim'e-a, 40 son of Michael, son of Ba-ase'iah, son of Malchi'jah, 41 son of Ethni, son of Zerah, son of Ada'iah, 42 son of Ethan, son of Zimmah, son of Shim'e-i, 43 son of Jahath, son of Gershom, son of Levi. 44 On the left hand were their brethren the sons of Merar'i: Ethan the son of Kishi, son of Abdi, son of Malluch, 45 son of Hashabi'ah, son of Amazi'ah, son of Hilki'ah, 46 son of Amzi, son of Bani, son of Shemer, 47 son of Mahli, son of Mushi, son

---

in the second temple: **Korah, Asaph, Ethan.** Korah was originally an Edomite (Calebite) family (see 2:43) .

32. Tabernacle: See Exeg. on 16:37-43. **According to their order** (Hebrew, *mishpāṭ*) signified for the genealogist the duties of their rank in the service of the "Mosaic" tabernacle, not instructions newly issued to them by David.

---

miliar with the provision for the temple music in his own time; it was controlled by guilds of Levites whose ancestors he here names. He believed that even before Solomon, David had taken care to appoint Levites to be in charge of the praises of the Lord. As the centuries passed,

the Levites saw to it that psalms were brought into use which were suitable to accompany the various kinds of sacrifice and appropriate to the sacred festivals and fasts of the year.[3] Moreover,

[3] See John P. Peters, *The Psalms as Liturgies* (New York: The Macmillan Co., 1922).

48 Their brethren also the Levites *were* appointed unto all manner of service of the tabernacle of the house of God.

49 ¶ But Aaron and his sons offered upon the altar of the burnt offering, and on the altar of incense, *and were appointed* for all the work of the *place* most holy, and to make an atonement for Israel, according to all that Moses the servant of God had commanded.

50 And these *are* the sons of Aaron; Eleazar his son, Phinehas his son, Abishua his son,

51 Bukki his son, Uzzi his son, Zerahiah his son,

52 Meraioth his son, Amariah his son, Ahitub his son,

53 Zadok his son, Ahimaaz his son.

54 ¶ Now these *are* their dwelling places throughout their castles in their coasts, of the sons of Aaron, of the families of the Kohathites: for theirs was the lot.

55 And they gave them Hebron in the land of Judah, and the suburbs thereof round about it.

56 But the fields of the city, and the villages thereof, they gave to Caleb the son of Jephunneh.

57 And to the sons of Aaron they gave the cities of Judah, *namely,* Hebron, *the city* of refuge, and Libnah with her suburbs, and Jattir, and Eshtemoa, with their suburbs.

58 And Hilen with her suburbs, Debir with her suburbs,

59 And Ashan with her suburbs, and Beth-shemesh with her suburbs:

of Merar'i, son of Levi; 48 and their brethren the Levites were appointed for all the service of the tabernacle of the house of God.

49 But Aaron and his sons made offerings upon the altar of burnt offering and upon the altar of incense for all the work of the most holy place, and to make atonement for Israel, according to all that Moses the servant of God had commanded. 50 These are the sons of Aaron: Elea'zar his son, Phin'ehas his son, Abishu'a his son, 51 Bukki his son, Uzzi his son, Zerahi'ah his son, 52 Mera'ioth his son, Amari'ah his son, Ahi'tub his son, 53 Zadok his son, Ahim'a-az his son.

54 These are their dwelling places according to their settlements within their borders: to the sons of Aaron of the families of Ko'hathites, for theirs was the lot, 55 to them they gave Hebron in the land of Judah and its surrounding pasture lands, 56 but the fields of the city and its villages they gave to Caleb the son of Jephun'neh. 57 To the sons of Aaron they gave the cities of refuge: Hebron, Libnah with its pasture lands, Jattir, Eshtemo'a with its pasture lands, 58 Hilen with its pasture lands, Debir with its pasture lands, 59 Ashan with its pasture lands, and Beth-shemesh with its

---

4. ADDITIONAL LIST OF AARONITE PRIESTS (6:49-53)

49. The prescriptive rights of the Aaronite priests are emphatically stated: **According to all that Moses the servant of God had commanded.**

5. LEVITICAL CITIES (6:54-81)

These verses reproduce Josh. 21:9-25, 33, 40, save that vs. 54 is new, and the introductory verse in Josh. 21:9 has been utilized here in vs. 65, where, however, its statement is not in keeping with the context.

---

there was no copyright in antiquity. The Levites were free to alter and adapt psalms, discard old and accept new ones. Eventually they did their work well. The Psalter as we have it is truly monotheistic, and may rightly be styled "The Hymnbook of the Second Temple." Are we drastic enough in revising the contents of our hymnbooks? Some hymns which suited the out-

look of a century ago may misrepresent contemporary belief and do harm to impressionable worshipers.

Times of special religious enthusiasm and revival give rise to fresh praising of the Lord, as was seen in the period of the Reformation and the Wesleyan Revival. In Ecclus. 50:16 an account of a religious festival at Jerusalem in

60 And out of the tribe of Benjamin; Geba with her suburbs, and Alemeth with her suburbs, and Anathoth with her suburbs. All their cities throughout their families *were* thirteen cities.

61 And unto the sons of Kohath, *which were* left of the family of that tribe, *were cities given* out of the half tribe, *namely, out of* the half *tribe* of Manasseh, by lot, ten cities.

62 And to the sons of Gershom throughout their families out of the tribe of Issachar, and out of the tribe of Asher, and out of the tribe of Naphtali, and out of the tribe of Manasseh in Bashan, thirteen cities.

63 Unto the sons of Merari *were given* by lot, throughout their families, out of the tribe of Reuben, and out of the tribe of Gad, and out of the tribe of Zebulun, twelve cities.

64 And the children of Israel gave to the Levites *these* cities with their suburbs.

65 And they gave by lot out of the tribe of the children of Judah, and out of the tribe of the children of Simeon, and out of the tribe of the children of Benjamin, these cities, which are called by *their* names.

66 And *the residue* of the families of the sons of Kohath had cities of their coasts out of the tribe of Ephraim.

67 And they gave unto them, *of* the cities of refuge, Shechem in mount Ephraim with her suburbs; *they gave* also Gezer with her suburbs,

68 And Jokmeam with her suburbs, and Beth-horon with her suburbs,

69 And Ajalon with her suburbs, and Gath-rimmon with her suburbs:

70 And out of the half tribe of Manasseh; Aner with her suburbs, and Bileam with her suburbs, for the family of the remnant of the sons of Kohath.

71 Unto the sons of Gershom *were given*, out of the family of the half tribe of Manasseh, Golan in Bashan with her suburbs, and Ashtaroth with her suburbs:

72 And out of the tribe of Issachar; Kedesh with her suburbs, Daberath with her suburbs,

pasture lands; 60 and from the tribe of Benjamin, Geba with its pasture lands, Al'emeth with its pasture lands, and An'athoth with its pasture lands. All their cities throughout their families were thirteen.

61 To the rest of the Ko'hathites were given by lot out of the family of the tribe, out of the half-tribe, the half of Manas'seh, ten cities. 62 To the Gershomites according to their families were allotted thirteen cities out of the tribes of Is'sachar, Asher, Naph'tali, and Manas'seh in Bashan. 63 To the Merar'ites according to their families were allotted twelve cities out of the tribes of Reuben, Gad, and Zeb'ulun. 64 So the people of Israel gave the Levites the cities with their pasture lands. 65 They also gave them by lot out of the tribes of Judah, Simeon, and Benjamin these cities which are mentioned by name.

66 And some of the families of the sons of Kohath had cities of their territory out of the tribe of E'phraim. 67 They were given the cities of refuge: Shechem with its pasture lands in the hill country of E'phraim, Gezer with its pasture lands, 68 Jok'me-am with its pasture lands, Beth-ho'ron with its pasture lands, 69 Ai'jalon with its pasture lands, Gath-rim'mon with its pasture lands, 70 and out of the half-tribe of Manas'seh, Aner with its pasture lands, and Bil'e-am with its pasture lands, for the rest of the families of the Ko'hathites.

71 To the Gershomites were given out of the half-tribe of Manas'seh: Golan in Bashan with its pasture lands and Ash'taroth with its pasture lands; 72 and out of the tribe of Is'sachar: Kedesh with its pasture lands, Dab'erath with its pasture lands,

---

the time of Simon son of Onias, the high priest, glowingly relates: "Then shouted the sons of Aaron, they sounded the trumpets of beaten work, they made a great noise to be heard." The din of the Levitical instruments and the mighty responses of the multitude would perhaps not have satisfied our modern music critics. But to the Hebrews it seemed as if God had come very near: "O thou that inhabitest the praises of Israel" (Ps. 22:3) .

73 And Ramoth with her suburbs, and Anem with her suburbs:

74 And out of the tribe of Asher; Mashal with her suburbs, and Abdon with her suburbs,

75 And Hukok with her suburbs, and Rehob with her suburbs:

76 And out of the tribe of Naphtali; Kedesh in Galilee with her suburbs, and Hammon with her suburbs, and Kirjathaim with her suburbs.

77 Unto the rest of the children of Merari *were given,* out of the tribe of Zebulun, Rimmon with her suburbs, Tabor with her suburbs:

78 And on the other side Jordan by Jericho, on the east side of Jordan, *were given them,* out of the tribe of Reuben, Bezer in the wilderness with her suburbs, and Jahzah with her suburbs,

79 Kedemoth also with her suburbs, and Mephaath with her suburbs:

80 And out of the tribe of Gad; Ramoth in Gilead with her suburbs, and Mahanaim with her suburbs,

81 And Heshbon with her suburbs, and Jazer with her suburbs.

7 Now the sons of Issachar *were,* Tola, and Puah, Jashub, and Shimrom, four.

2 And the sons of Tola; Uzzi, and Rephaiah, and Jeriel, and Jahmai, and Jibsam, and Shemuel, heads of their father's house, *to wit,* of Tola: *they were* valiant men of might in their generations; whose number *was* in the days of David two and twenty thousand and six hundred.

3 And the sons of Uzzi; Izrahiah: and the sons of Izrahiah; Michael, and Obadiah, and Joel, Ishiah, five: all of them chief men.

73 Ramoth with its pasture lands, and Anem with its pasture lands; 74 out of the tribe of Asher: Mashal with its pasture lands, Abdon with its pasture lands, 75 Hukok with its pasture lands, and Rehob with its pasture lands; 76 and out of the tribe of Naph'tali: Kedesh in Galilee with its pasture lands, Ham'mon with its pasture lands, and Kiriatha'im with its pasture lands. 77 To the rest of the Merar'ites were allotted out of the tribe of Zeb'ulun: Rim'mono with its pasture lands, Tabor with its pasture lands, 78 and beyond the Jordan at Jericho, on the east side of the Jordan, out of the tribe of Reuben: Bezer in the steppe with its pasture lands, Jahzah with its pasture lands, 79 Ked'emoth with its pasture lands, and Meph'a-ath with its pasture lands; 80 and out of the tribe of Gad: Ramoth in Gilead with its pasture lands, Mahana'im with its pasture lands, 81 Heshbon with its pasture lands, and Jazer with its pasture lands.

7 The sons[r] of Is'sachar: Tola, Pu'ah, Jashub, and Shimron, four. 2 The sons of Tola: Uzzi, Repha'iah, Je'ri-el, Jah'mai, Ibsam, and Shem'uel, heads of their fathers' houses, namely of Tola, mighty warriors of their generations, their number in the days of David being twenty-two thousand six hundred. 3 The sons of Uzzi: Izrahi'ah. And the sons of Izrahi'ah: Michael, Obadi'ah, Jo'el, and Isshi'ah, five, all of them chief

r Syr Compare Vg: Heb *and to the sons*

G. THE NORTHERN TRIBES (7:1-40)

1. ISSACHAR (7:1-5)

7:1-5. These verses are from an unknown source.

Tunes are perilous to comment on. The zeal of organists and choirs is sometimes rewarded by a responsive congregation. But not always; the unmusical may be coldly indifferent, obstructive, or conventional. How tragic when quarrels arise in consequence! This playing and singing is **in the house of the LORD.**

7:2. Idealizing the Soldier.—The Chronicler skillfully utilized the list of names in order to give an idealistic sketch of the establishment of Yahweh's people in Canaan. His readers would

understand that symbolic, not actual, history is presented. In ch. 6 he has delineated the upbuilding of a devoted hierarchy. Here and in ch. 8 he turns to the civil aspect and by the recurrent phrases **heads of their fathers' houses** and **warriors of their generations,** subtly invites us to reflect that the Canaanites were subdued not because a few adventurous Hebrews became professional soldiers, but because household by household the men of Israel were willing to fight the good fight. The heading "Idealizing

4 And with them, by their generations, after the house of their fathers, *were* bands of soldiers for war, six and thirty thousand *men:* for they had many wives and sons.

5 And their brethren among all the families of Issachar *were* valiant men of might, reckoned in all by their genealogies fourscore and seven thousand.

6 ¶ *The sons* of Benjamin; Bela, and Becher, and Jediael, three.

7 And the sons of Bela; Ezbon, and Uzzi, and Uzziel, and Jerimoth, and Iri, five; heads of the house of *their* fathers, mighty men of valor; and were reckoned by their genealogies twenty and two thousand and thirty and four.

8 And the sons of Becher; Zemira, and Joash, and Eliezer, and Elioenai, and Omri, and Jerimoth, and Abiah, and Anathoth, and Alameth. All these *are* the sons of Becher.

9 And the number of them, after their genealogy by their generations, heads of the house of their fathers, mighty men of valor, *was* twenty thousand and two hundred.

10 The sons also of Jediael; Bilhan: and the sons of Bilhan; Jeush, and Benjamin, and Ehud, and Chenaanah, and Zethan, and Tharshish, and Ahishahar.

11 All these the sons of Jediael, by the heads of their fathers, mighty men of valor,

men; 4 and along with them, by their generations, according to their fathers' houses, were units of the army for war, thirty-six thousand, for they had many wives and sons. 5 Their kinsmen belonging to all the families of Is'sachar were in all eighty-seven thousand mighty warriors, enrolled by genealogy.

6 The sons of Benjamin: Bela, Becher, and Jedi'a-el, three. 7 The sons of Bela: Ezbon, Uzzi, Uz'ziel, Jer'imoth, and Iri, five, heads of fathers' houses, mighty warriors; and their enrollment by genealogies was twenty-two thousand and thirty-four. 8 The sons of Becher: Zemi'rah, Jo'ash, Elie'zer, Eli-o-e'nai, Omri, Jer'emoth, Abi'jah, An'athoth, and Al'emeth. 9 All these were the sons of Becher; and their enrollment by genealogies, according to their generations, as heads of their fathers' houses, mighty warriors, was twenty thousand two hundred. 10 The sons of Jedi'a-el: Bilhan. And the sons of Bilhan: Je'ush, Benjamin, Ehud, Chena'anah, Zethan, Tarshish, and Ahish'-ahar. 11 All these were the sons of Jedi'a-el according to the heads of their fathers'

---

2. BENJAMIN (7:6-12)

6. The sons of Benjamin: The original text undoubtedly was "sons of Zebulun" (the difference is slight in Hebrew). The authentic Benjaminite list is given in 8:1-40.

---

the Soldier" is perhaps less than just to the Chronicler. He is here concerned simply to stress that the whole community willingly shared in the grim ordeal of war. But we should sadly reflect: How many young men died in these battles? How many were maimed? What did the Hebrew women feel when fathers and husbands and sons went to war? Must there always be fighting? Unlike the Western and central Asiatic peoples, the very ancient Chinese civilization did not idealize the soldier. He ranked very low in its grading of society. Suddenly there has taken place a change of opinion in China with incalculable consequences, for China represents a quarter of the world's population. For the nations of the West there is only a hope that the former attitude, during which for two thousand years the man of war was not idealized, may re-emerge in Chinese life.

The Western nations in this awful century

can scarcely be said to idealize war. But they are under the profoundest duty to honor the soldier and to reverence the morale of the fighting services. The morals of the soldier—cut off from normal life and home surroundings, and enduring, it may be, suffering or imminent death—are not perfect. Criticisms may be merited, but not on the lips of the sheltered and the safe.

How about the morale of the Christian army?

> Soldiers of Christ, arise,
> And put your armor on.[4]

11. *Fit to Go Out for War.*—What a memorable, challenging remark this is! It sets a standard: Fit for duty. Apply the test to the community in which we live. Are some thousands of its population careless and undisciplined in

[4] Charles Wesley.

were seventeen thousand and two hundred *soldiers,* fit to go out for war *and* battle.

12 Shuppim also, and Huppim, the children of Ir, *and* Hushim, the sons of Aher.

13 ¶ The sons of Naphtali; Jahziel, and Guni, and Jezer, and Shallum, the sons of Bilhah.

14 ¶ The sons of Manasseh; Ashriel, whom she bare; *(but* his concubine the Aramitess bare Machir the father of Gilead:

15 And Machir took to wife *the sister* of Huppim and Shuppim, whose sister's name *was* Maachah;) and the name of the second *was* Zelophehad: and Zelophehad had daughters.

16 And Maachah the wife of Machir bare a son, and she called his name Peresh; and the name of his brother *was* Sheresh; and his sons *were* Ulam and Rakem.

17 And the sons of Ulam; Bedan. These *were* the sons of Gilead, the son of Machir, the son of Manasseh.

18 And his sister Hammoleketh bare Ishod, and Abiezer, and Mahalah.

19 And the sons of Shemidah were, Ahian, and Shechem, and Likhi, and Aniam.

20 ¶ And the sons of Ephraim; Shuthelah, and Bered his son, and Tahath his son, and Eladah his son, and Tahath his son,

21 ¶ And Zabad his son, and Shuthelah his son, and Ezer, and Elead, whom the men of Gath *that were* born in *that* land slew,

houses, mighty warriors, seventeen thousand and two hundred, ready for service in war. 12 And Shuppim and Huppim were the sons of Ir, Hushim the sons of Aher.

13 The sons of Naph'tali: Jah'zi-el, Guni, Jezer, and Shallum, the offspring of Bilhah. 14 The sons of Manas'seh: As'ri-el, whom his Aramaean concubine bore; she bore Machir the father of Gilead. 15 And Machir took a wife for Huppim and for Shuppim. The name of his sister was Ma'acah. And the name of the second was Zeloph'ehad; and Zeloph'ehad had daughters. 16 And Ma'acah the wife of Machir bore a son, and she called his name Peresh; and the name of his brother was Sheresh; and his sons were Ulam and Rakem. 17 The sons of Ulam: Bedan. These were the sons of Gilead the son of Machir, son of Manas'seh. 18 And his sister Hammo'lecheth bore Ishhod, Abi-e'zer, and Mahlah. 19 The sons of Shemi'da were Ahi'an, Shechem, Likhi, and Ani'am.

20 The sons of E'phraim: Shuthe'lah, and Bered his son, Tahath his son, Ele-a'dah his son, Tahath his son, 21 Zabad his son, Shuthe'lah his son, and Ezer and

This unlucky textual error occurred very early, for some Benjaminite names (e.g., vs. 10) were inserted in the Zebulun genealogy.

12b. The sons of Ir, Hushim the sons of Aher: A textual error; read "the sons of Dan, Hushim his son, [only] one" (cf. LXX; Gen. 46:23).

3. Naphtali and Manasseh (7:13-19)

14. Manasseh, i.e., the part of the tribe living west of Jordan (cf. 5:23-24). In the latter part of the verse read (as LXX and ASV), **whom his Aramaean concubine bore; she bore Machir the father of Gilead,** i.e., Hebrews in Gilead were partly of Aramean (Syrian) blood.

4. Ephraim and Asher (7:20-40)

21-23. An old tradition may underlie this reference to a disastrous attempt by Ephraimites to raid Philistine territory. But it may be mere invention spun out of the fact that **Beriah** resembles the Hebrew for "in disaster."

character, neither willing nor able to do their best in the conflict between right and wrong? Apply it to the Christian congregation. Are its members trained and ready to contend for

Christ? Wiser it is to apply the challenge to oneself; for nothing so swiftly makes one unfit to be a disciple of Jesus as to be censorious of others (cf. Matt. 7:1-5).

because they came down to take away their cattle.

22 And Ephraim their father mourned many days, and his brethren came to comfort him.

23 ¶ And when he went in to his wife, she conceived and bare a son, and he called his name Beriah, because it went evil with his house.

24 (And his daughter *was* Sherah, who built Beth-horon the nether, and the upper, and Uzzen-sherah.)

25 And Rephah *was* his son, also Resheph, and Telah his son, and Tahan his son,

26 Laadan his son, Ammihud his son, Elishama his son,

27 Non his son, Jehoshuah his son.

28 ¶ And their possessions and habitations *were*, Beth-el and the towns thereof, and eastward Naaran, and westward Gezer, with the towns thereof; Shechem also and the towns thereof, unto Gaza and the towns thereof:

29 And by the borders of the children of Manasseh, Beth-shean and her towns, Taanach and her towns, Megiddo and her towns, Dor and her towns. In these dwelt the children of Joseph the son of Israel.

30 ¶ The sons of Asher; Imnah, and Isuah, and Ishuai, and Beriah, and Serah their sister.

31 And the sons of Beriah; Heber, and Malchiel, who *is* the father of Birzavith.

32 And Heber begat Japhlet, and Shomer, and Hotham, and Shua their sister.

33 And the sons of Japhlet; Pasach, and Bimhal, and Ashvath. These *are* the children of Japhlet.

34 And the sons of Shamer; Ahi, and Rohgah, Jehubbah, and Aram.

35 And the sons of his brother Helem; Zophah, and Imna, and Shelesh, and Amal.

36 The sons of Zophah; Suah, and Harnepher, and Shual, and Beri, and Imrah,

37 Bezer, and Hod, and Shamma, and Shilshah, and Ithran, and Beera.

38 And the sons of Jether; Jephunneh, and Pispah, and Ara.

E'le-ad, whom the men of Gath who were born in the land slew, because they came down to raid their cattle. 22 And E'phraim their father mourned many days, and his brothers came to comfort him. 23 And E'phraim went in to his wife, and she conceived and bore a son; and he called his name Beri'ah, because evil had befallen his house. 24 His daughter was She'erah, who built both lower and upper Beth-ho'ron, and Uz'zen-she'erah. 25 Rephah was his son, Resheph his son, Telah his son, Tahan his son, 26 Ladan his son, Ammi'hud his son, Elish'ama his son, 27 Nun his son, Joshua his son. 28 Their possessions and settlements were Bethel and its towns, and eastward Na'aran, and westward Gezer and its towns, Shechem and its towns, and Ayyah and its towns; 29 also along the borders of the Manas'sites, Beth-she'an and its towns, Ta'anach and its towns, Megid'do and its towns, Dor and its towns. In these dwelt the sons of Joseph the son of Israel.

30 The sons of Asher: Imnah, Ishvah, Ishvi, Beri'ah, and their sister Serah. 31 The sons of Beri'ah: Heber and Mal'chi-el, who was the father of Bir'zaith. 32 Heber was the father of Japhlet, Shomer, Hotham, and their sister Shu'a. 33 The sons of Japhlet: Pasach, Bimhal, and Ashvath. These are the sons of Japhlet. 34 The sons of Shemer his brother: Rohgah, Jehub'bah, and Aram. 35 The sons of Heler his brother: Zophah, Imna, Shelesh, and Amal. 36 The sons of Zophah: Su'ah, Har'nepher, Shu'al, Beri, Imrah, 37 Bezer, Hod, Shamma, Shilshah, Ithran, and Be-e'ra. 38 The sons of Jether:

---

24. *His Daughter . . . Built Beth-horon.*—On this a commentator of the last century—let him take shelter in anonymity—remarked, "In verse 24, chapter vii, we actually find a woman doing something." But immediately thereafter he wrote: "What builders women may be! What character they can build in their sons and daughters! What influence they can build round themselves! Women can do a work which men cannot even attempt."

39 And the sons of Ulla; Arah, and Haniel, and Rezia.

40 All these *were* the children of Asher, heads of *their* father's house, choice *and* mighty men of valor, chief of the princes. And the number throughout the genealogy of them that were apt to the war *and* to battle *was* twenty and six thousand men.

8 Now Benjamin begat Bela his firstborn, Ashbel the second, and Aharah the third,

2 Nohah the fourth, and Rapha the fifth.

3 And the sons of Bela were, Addar, and Gera, and Abihud,

4 And Abishua, and Naaman, and Ahoah,

5 And Gera, and Shephuphan, and Huram.

6 And these *are* the sons of Ehud: these are the heads of the fathers of the inhabitants of Geba, and they removed them to Manahath:

7 And Naaman, and Ahiah, and Gera, he removed them, and begat Uzza, and Ahihud.

8 And Shaharaim begat *children* in the country of Moab, after he had sent them away; Hushim and Baara *were* his wives.

9 And he begat of Hodesh his wife, Jobab, and Zibia, and Mesha, and Malcham,

10 And Jeuz, and Shachia, and Mirma. These *were* his sons, heads of the fathers.

11 And of Hushim he begat Abitub and Elpaal.

12 The sons of Elpaal; Eber, and Misham, and Shamed, who built Ono, and Lod, with the towns thereof:

13 Beriah also, and Shema, who *were* heads of the fathers of the inhabitants of Ajalon, who drove away the inhabitants of Gath:

14 And Ahio, Shashak, and Jeremoth,

15 And Zebadiah, and Arad, and Ader,

16 And Michael, and Ispah, and Joha, the sons of Beriah;

Jephun'neh, Pispa, and Ara. **39** The sons of Ulla: Arah, Han'niel, and Rizi'a. **40** All of these were men of Asher, heads of fathers' houses, approved, mighty warriors, chief of the princes. Their number enrolled by genealogies, for service in war, was twenty-six thousand men.

8 Benjamin was the father of Bela his first-born, Ashbel the second, Ahar'ah the third, **2** Nohah the fourth, and Rapha the fifth. **3** And Bela had sons: Addar, Gera, Abi'hud, **4** Abishu'a, Na'aman, Aho'ah, **5** Gera, Shephu'phan, and Huram. **6** These are the sons of Ehud (they were heads of fathers' houses of the inhabitants of Geba, and they were carried into exile to Mana'hath): **7** Na'aman,[s] Ahi'jah, and Gera, that is, Heglam,[t] who was the father of Uzza and Ahi'hud. **8** And Shahara'im had sons in the country of Moab after he had sent away Hushim and Ba'ara his wives. **9** He had sons by Hodesh his wife: Jobab, Zib'i-a, Mesha, Malcam, **10** Je'uz, Sachi'a, and Mirmah. These were his sons, heads of fathers' houses. **11** He also had sons by Hushim: Abi'tub and Elpa'al. **12** The sons of Elpa'al: Eber, Misham, and Shemed, who built Ono and Lod with its towns, **13** and Beri'ah and Shema (they were heads of fathers' houses of the inhabitants of Ai'jalon, who put to flight the inhabitants of Gath); **14** and Ahi'o, Shashak, and Jer'emoth. **15** Zebadi'ah, Arad, Eder, **16** Michael, Ish-

[s] Heb *and Naaman*
[t] Or *he carried them into exile*

H. Sons of Benjamin (8:1-40)

8:1-5. Cf. Gen. 46:21; Num. 26:38.

The twentieth century has seen the rapid extension of women's influence from family life into almost every aspect of communal affairs, not only in the Western world but even, to a lesser degree, in the Islamic countries and China. The transformation may be ascribed to modern freedom of thought breaking down unreasonable conventions, but it is wholly consonant with fundamental implications of Jewish and Christian religion. As Paul put it, "There is neither male nor female; for you are all one in Christ Jesus" (Gal. 3:28).

17 And Zebadiah, and Meshullam, and Hezeki, and Heber,

18 Ishmerai also, and Jezliah, and Jobab, the sons of Elpaal;

19 And Jakim, and Zichri, and Zabdi,

20 And Elienai, and Zilthai, and Eliel,

21 And Adaiah, and Beraiah, and Shimrath, the sons of Shimhi;

22 And Ishpan, and Heber, and Eliel,

23 And Abdon, and Zichri, and Hanan,

24 And Hananiah, and Elam, and Antothijah,

25 And Iphedeiah, and Penuel, the sons of Shashak;

26 And Shamsherai, and Shehariah, and Athaliah,

27 And Jaresiah, and Eliah, and Zichri, the sons of Jeroham.

28 These *were* heads of the fathers, by their generations, chief *men*. These dwelt in Jerusalem.

29 And at Gibeon dwelt the father of Gibeon; whose wife's name *was* Maachah:

30 And his firstborn son Abdon, and Zur, and Kish, and Baal, and Nadab,

31 And Gedor, and Ahio, and Zacher.

32 And Mikloth begat Shimeah. And these also dwelt with their brethren in Jerusalem, over against them.

33 ¶ And Ner begat Kish, and Kish begat Saul, and Saul begat Jonathan, and Malchi-shua, and Abinadab, and Esh-baal.

34 And the son of Jonathan *was* Meribbaal; and Merib-baal begat Micah.

35 And the sons of Micah *were,* Pithon, and Melech, and Tarea, and Ahaz.

36 And Ahaz begat Jehoadah; and Jehoadah begat Alemeth, and Azmaveth, and Zimri; and Zimri begat Moza;

37 And Moza begat Binea: Rapha *was* his son, Eleasah his son, Azel his son.

pah, and Joha were sons of Beri'ah. [17] Zebadi'ah, Meshul'lam, Hizki, Heber, [18] Ish'merai, Izli'ah, and Jobab were the sons of Elpa'al. [19] Jakim, Zichri, Zabdi, [20] Eli-e'nai, Zil'le-thai, Eli'el, [21] Ada'iah, Bera'iah, and Shimrath were the sons of Shim'e-i. [22] Ishpan, Eber, Eli'el, [23] Abdon, Zichri, Hanan, [24] Hanani'ah, Elam, Anthothi'jah, [25] Iphde'iah, and Penu'el were the sons of Shashak. [26] Sham'sherai, Shehari'ah, Athali'ah, [27] Ja-areshi'ah, Eli'jah, and Zichri were the sons of Jero'ham. [28] These were the heads of fathers' houses, according to their generations, chief men. These dwelt in Jerusalem.

29 Je-i'el[u] the father of Gibeon dwelt in Gibeon, and the name of his wife was Ma'acah. [30] His first-born son: Abdon, then Zur, Kish, Ba'al, Nadab, [31] Gedor, Ahi'o, Zecher, [32] and Mikloth (he was the father of Shim'e-ah). Now these also dwelt opposite their kinsmen in Jerusalem, with their kinsmen. [33] Ner was the father of Kish, Kish of Saul, Saul of Jonathan, Mal'chishu'a, Abin'adab, and Eshba'al; [34] and the son of Jonathan was Mer'ib-ba'al; and Mer'ib-ba'al was the father of Micah. [35] The sons of Micah: Pithon, Melech, Tare'a, and Ahaz. [36] Ahaz was the father of Jeho'addah; and Jeho'addah was the father of Al'emeth, Az'maveth, and Zimri; Zimri was the father of Moza. [37] Moza was the father of Bin'e-a; Raphah was his son, Ele-

[u] Compare 9. 35: Heb lacks *Jeiel*

29-38. This list of Saul's ancestors is repeated in 9:35-44, where it becomes the immediate prelude to Chronicles' history of David and of the kings of Judah; for that reason probably it seemed desirable to repeat it there.

33. Eshbaal: The meaning is "Man [worshiper] of baal." In II Sam. 2:8 the name of Saul's son was altered to Ishbosheth, "Man of shame," because that book was read aloud in synagogue services, whereas Chronicles was not. Baal came to denote a god other than Yahweh; in Saul's thought it meant a title of honor, implying that Yahweh was Master (*bá'al*) of Canaan.

The territory anciently occupied by the tribe of Benjamin lay close to Jerusalem on the north. One can understand that after the fall of the kingdom of Israel in 721 B.C. its occupants would turn for support to the surviving capital; likewise, after the fall of Jerusalem in 586 B.C., it would be natural that Hebrews resident in Benjamin would

38 And Azel had six sons, whose names *are* these, Azrikam, Bocheru, and Ishmael, and Sheariah, and Obadiah, and Hanan. All these *were* the sons of Azel.

39 And the sons of Eshek his brother *were,* Ulam his firstborn, Jehush the second, and Eliphelet the third.

40 And the sons of Ulam were mighty men of valor, archers, and had many sons, and sons' sons, a hundred and fifty. All these *are* of the sons of Benjamin.

9 So all Israel were reckoned by genealogies; and, behold, they *were* written in the book of the kings of Israel and Judah, *who* were carried away to Babylon for their transgression.

2 ¶ Now the first inhabitants that *dwelt* in their possessions in their cities *were,* the Israelites, the priests, Levites, and the Nethinim.

3 And in Jerusalem dwelt of the children of Judah, and of the children of Benjamin, and of the children of Ephraim, and Manasseh;

4 Uthai the son of Ammihud, the son of Omri, the son of Imri, the son of Bani, of the children of Pharez the son of Judah.

a'sah his son, Azel his son. 38 Azel had six sons, and these are their names. Azri'kam, Bo'cheru, Ish'mael, She-ari'ah, Obadi'ah, and Hanan. All these were the sons of Azel. 39 The sons of Eshek his brother: Ulam his first-born, Je'ush the second, and Eliph'elet the third. 40 The sons of Ulam were men who were mighty warriors, bowmen, having many sons and grandsons, one hundred and fifty. All these were Benjaminites.

9 So all Israel was enrolled by genealogies; and these are written in the Book of the Kings of Israel. And Judah was taken into exile in Babylon because of their unfaithfulness. 2 Now the first to dwell again in their possessions in their cities were Israel, the priests, the Levites, and the temple servants. 3 And some of the people of Judah, Benjamin, E'phraim, and Manas'seh dwelt in Jerusalem: 4 Uthai the son of Ammi'hud, son of Omri, son of Imri, son of Bani, from the sons of Perez the son of

become closely linked in sympathy and practical interests with the renascent community in Jerusalem. That this did happen is strikingly attested by vs. 28, **These dwelt in Jerusalem,** i.e., Benjaminite families whose forefathers are named in vss. 15-27.

J. JERUSALEM FAMILIES (9:1-16)

9:1. Of Israel: The LXX adds "and Judah." The source cited in this verse was not the canonical book of Kings: see Intro., p. 347.

2a. This list of inhabitants of Jerusalem appears also in Neh. 11:3-19. Vs. 2 is rather less obscure in the parallel Neh. 11:3, where "the chief of the province" is read for **the first inhabitants,** and "the townships of Judah" for the meaningless **in their cities.** The list of course refers to postexilic Jerusalem.

2b-3. Israel here denotes not the long-ago fallen kingdom of Israel, but Jews loyal to postexilic Jerusalem and its worship (cf. II Chr. 30:18; Ps. 80:2). They are said to include men of the areas of **Ephraim, Benjamin,** and **Manasseh,** as well as the Judeans.

9:1. Lessons of the Past.—Hope stirs that the catalogue of ancestors will now end; but the following forty-three verses are packed with names. Only at ch. 10 does the Chronicler begin a readable narrative. His contemporaries were keenly interested in these lists of names. If their families could thus trace back their lineage the fact was warrant for claiming rights and privileges in the Jewish community. The Chronicler's genealogical zeal was not for an unpractical study of antiquity for its own sake: the past was held to have a close bearing on the

present. How far is that attitude sensible or important?

"History is bunk," Henry Ford once said.[5] Yet probably he set himself to acquire thorough knowledge of the history of the internal combustion engine. A nation which ignores or despises past events stands in deadly peril of plunging into errors the consequences of which have been repeatedly made plain in former times. In the sphere of religion the danger is

[5] On the witness stand at Mt. Clemens, Mich., in his libel suit against the *Chicago Tribune,* July, 1919.

5 And of the Shilonites; Asaiah the first-born, and his sons.

6 And of the sons of Zerah; Jeuel, and their brethren, six hundred and ninety.

7 And of the sons of Benjamin; Sallu the son of Meshullam, the son of Hodaviah, the son of Hasenuah,

8 And Ibneiah the son of Jeroham, and Elah the son of Uzzi, the son of Michri, and Meshullam the son of Shephatiah, the son of Reuel, the son of Ibnijah;

9 And their brethren, according to their generations, nine hundred and fifty and six. All these men *were* chief of the fathers in the house of their fathers.

10 ¶ And of the priests; Jedaiah, and Jehoiarib, and Jachin,

11 And Azariah the son of Hilkiah, the son of Meshullam, the son of Zadok, the son of Meraioth, the son of Ahitub, the ruler of the house of God;

12 And Adaiah the son of Jeroham, the son of Pashur, the son of Malchijah, and Maasiai the son of Adiel, the son of Jahzerah, the son of Meshullam, the son of Meshillemith, the son of Immer;

13 And their brethren, heads of the house of their fathers, a thousand and seven hundred and threescore; very able men for the work of the service of the house of God.

Judah. 5 And of the Shi'lonites: Asa'iah the first-born, and his sons. 6 Of the sons of Zerah: Jeu'el and their kinsmen, six hundred and ninety. 7 Of the Benjaminites: Sallu the son of Meshul'lam, son of Hodavi'ah, son of Hassenu'ah, 8 Ibne'iah the son of Jero'ham, Elah the son of Uzzi, son of Michri, and Meshul'lam the son of Shephati'ah, son of Reu'el, son of Ibni'jah; 9 and their kinsmen according to their generations, nine hundred and fifty-six. All these were heads of fathers' houses according to their fathers' houses.

10 Of the priests: Jeda'iah, Jehoi'arib, Jachin, 11 and Azari'ah the son of Hilki'ah, son of Meshul'lam, son of Zadok, son of Mera'ioth, son of Ahi'tub, the chief officer of the house of God; 12 and Ada'iah the son of Jero'ham, son of Pashhur, son of Malchi'jah, and Ma'asai the son of Ad'i-el, son of Jah'zerah, son of Meshul'lam, son of Meshil'lemith, son of Immer; 13 besides their kinsmen, heads of their fathers' houses, one thousand seven hundred and sixty, very able men for the work of the service of the house of God.

---

10. The famous family of the Maccabees traced its descent from **Jehoiarib.**

---

seldom that of ignoring history, but is often that of allowing what our fathers thought and did authoritatively to determine our own outlook. In any extreme form that attitude is a cardinal error, for it is virtual disbelief in the promised guidance of the Holy Spirit, failure to conceive of God as the living God. It induces the devout to seal their minds against the impact of new facts instead of courageously believing that greater knowledge will but enrich understanding of the essential faith. In the nineteenth and early twentieth centuries the attitude of the churches toward the findings of scientific research was for the most part futile, calamitous, and shortsighted. The mistake is now generally realized, but it will take a long time to undo the tragic consequences. Great reverence is due to what wise Christians have believed. Nevertheless, knowledge of the history of Christianity should be our guide but not our chain. The reformers understood and honored the strength and grandeur in medieval theology, but they

were open to try to receive present revelation, and therein were in accord with the deepest conviction of Hebraic prophetic faith and with the Christian doctrine of the Holy Spirit declared in John 16:12-14. With the same great and humble wisdom concerning his own teaching spoke John Robinson in 1612, when he bade the Pilgrim Fathers farewell in these memorable words:

I charge you, before God and His blessed Angels, that you follow me no further than you have seen me follow the Lord Jesus Christ. If God reveal anything to you by any other instrument of His, be as ready to receive it as you were to receive any truth by my ministry, for I am verily persuaded the Lord hath more truth yet to break forth out of His holy word.[6]

13. *Conspicuous Ability.*—We may surmise that not all the priests named were so highly

[6] H. S. Skeats, *A History of the Free Churches of England* (2nd ed.; London: Arthur Miall, 1869), p. 44.

14 And of the Levites; Shemaiah the son of Hasshub, the son of Azrikam, the son of Hashabiah, of the sons of Merari;

15 And Bakbakkar, Heresh, and Galal, and Mattaniah the son of Micah, the son of Zichri, the son of Asaph;

16 And Obadiah the son of Shemaiah, the son of Galal, the son of Jeduthun, and Berechiah the son of Asa, the son of Elkanah, that dwelt in the villages of the Netophathites.

17 And the porters *were*, Shallum, and Akkub, and Talmon, and Ahiman, and their brethren: Shallum *was* the chief;

18 Who hitherto *waited* in the king's gate eastward: they *were* porters in the companies of the children of Levi.

19 And Shallum the son of Kore, the son of Ebiasaph, the son of Korah, and his brethren, of the house of his father, the Korahites, *were* over the work of the service, keepers of the gates of the tabernacle: and their fathers, *being* over the host of the LORD, *were* keepers of the entry.

20 And Phinehas the son of Eleazar was the ruler over them in time past, *and* the LORD *was* with him.

21 *And* Zechariah the son of Meshelemiah *was* porter of the door of the tabernacle of the congregation.

22 All these *which were* chosen to be porters in the gates *were* two hundred and twelve. These were reckoned by their gene-

14 Of the Levites: Shemai'ah the son of Hasshub, son of Azri'kam, son of Hashabi'ah, of the sons of Merar'i; 15 and Bakbak'kar, Heresh, Galal, and Mattani'ah the son of Mica, son of Zichri, son of Asaph; 16 and Obadi'ah the son of Shemai'ah, son of Gal'al, son of Jedu'thun, and Berechi'ah the son of Asa, son of Elka'nah, who dwelt in the villages of the Netoph'athites.

17 The gatekeepers were: Shallum, Akkub, Talmon, Ahi'man, and their kinsmen (Shallum being the chief), 18 stationed hitherto in the king's gate on the east side. These were the gatekeepers of the camp of the Levites. 19 Shallum the son of Ko're, son of Ebi'asaph, son of Korah, and his kinsmen of his fathers' house, the Ko'rahites, were in charge of the work of the service, keepers of the thresholds of the tent, as their fathers had been in charge of the camp of the LORD, keepers of the entrance. 20 And Phin'ehas the son of Elea'zar was the ruler over them in time past; the LORD was with him. 21 Zechari'ah the son of Meshelemi'ah was gatekeeper at the entrance of the tent of meeting. 22 All these, who were chosen as gatekeepers at the thresholds, were two hundred and twelve.

K. DUTIES OF THE TEMPLE STAFF (9:17-34)

17. The porters: Guardians of the gates; preferably rendered gatekeepers.

22. And Samuel: The notion that Samuel assisted David to appoint these men to office may be regarded as an edifying remark, evolved from the statement in I Sam. 3:15 that Samuel as a boy at Shiloh "opened the doors of the house of the LORD."

gifted that it was very easy for them to be proficient. By diligence in learning their tasks and by unfaltering attention to their duties, one and all, however, won the reputation of being **very able men for the work of the service of the house of God.** Were they puffed up by their good qualities? Pride, as Reinhold Niebuhr insists,[7] is the taproot of evil in human nature, and the temptation to it grows stronger and more insidious when we have real merits. In any walk of life it is exceedingly difficult to become a very able personality and yet remain humble in spirit.

[7] *The Nature and Destiny of Man* (New York: Charles Scribner's Sons, 1941), I, 198 ff.

These conspicuous men were priests. If proud they were, then all the more heinous their sin of pride. There is no excuse whatsoever for self-conceit in those (however able) who are engaged in the service of the Lord Jesus Christ, who "being in the form of God, . . . took upon him the form of a servant, . . . and being found in fashion as a man, he humbled himself, and became obedient unto death, even the death of the cross" (Phil. 2:6-8; cf. Mark 10:45; John 13:14) .

17. *Menial Workers.*—The **gatekeepers** or the **porters** were the men charged with custody of the temple and its courts and with many other so-called menial duties. No doubt the priests

alogy in their villages, whom David and Samuel the seer did ordain in their set office.

23 So they and their children *had* the oversight of the gates of the house of the LORD, *namely,* the house of the tabernacle, by wards.

24 In four quarters were the porters, toward the east, west, north, and south.

25 And their brethren, *which were* in their villages, *were* to come after seven days from time to time with them.

26 For these Levites, the four chief porters, were in *their* set office, and were over the chambers and treasuries of the house of God.

27 ¶ And they lodged round about the house of God, because the charge *was* upon them, and the opening thereof every morning *pertained* to them.

28 And *certain* of them had the charge of the ministering vessels, that they should bring them in and out by tale.

29 *Some* of them also *were* appointed to oversee the vessels, and all the instruments of the sanctuary, and the fine flour, and the wine, and the oil, and the frankincense, and the spices.

30 And *some* of the sons of the priests made the ointment of the spices.

31 And Mattithiah, *one* of the Levites, who *was* the firstborn of Shallum the Korahite, had the set office over the things that were made in the pans.

32 And *other* of their brethren, of the sons of the Kohathites, *were* over the showbread, to prepare *it* every sabbath.

33 And these *are* the singers, chief of the

They were enrolled by genealogies in their villages. David and Samuel the seer established them in their office of trust. 23 So they and their sons were in charge of the gates of the house of the LORD, that is, the house of the tent, as guards. 24 The gatekeepers were on the four sides, east, west, north, and south; 25 and their kinsmen who were in their villages were obliged to come in every seven days, from time to time, to be with these; 26 for the four chief gatekeepers, who were Levites, were in charge of the chambers and the treasures of the house of God. 27 And they lodged round about the house of God; for upon them lay the duty of watching, and they had charge of opening it every morning.

28 Some of them had charge of the utensils of service, for they were required to count them when they were brought in and taken out. 29 Others of them were appointed over the furniture, and over all the holy utensils, also over the fine flour, the wine, the oil, the incense, and the spices. 30 Others, of the sons of the priests, prepared the mixing of the spices, 31 and Mattithi'ah, one of the Levites, the first-born of Shallum the Ko'rahite, was in charge of making the flat cakes. 32 Also some of their kinsmen of the Ko'hathites had charge of the showbread, to prepare it every Sabbath.

33 Now these are the singers, the heads of

---

29. Regular use of frankincense (לבונה) is evidence of the late period (see Exeg. on II Chr. 13:11).

33. **And these are . . . :** But no names follow! Perhaps this is the proper conclusion for vss. 14-16, which has been misplaced; or else some names have dropped out of the text at this point.

---

offering the sacrifices, and the Levites rendering the psalms, counted themselves much above these, the very inferior clergy—and let them know it. But, said a psalmist, "I had rather be a doorkeeper in the house of my God, than to dwell in the tents of wickedness" (Ps. 84:10). Lord Keynes and another British peer were once overheard keenly discussing the best way of washing dishes. As they were very able men, no doubt the technique they favored was both efficient and economical. "Whatsoever thy hand

findeth to do, do it with thy might" (Eccl. 9:10). Less secular and more memorable is the verse in George Herbert's "The Elixir."

> Teach me, my God and King,
>   In all things thee to see;
> And what I do in anything,
>   To do it as for thee.

33. *By Night and by Day.*—It is not meant that there was psalmody in the temple during the course of the night. Details of the elaborate

fathers of the Levites, *who remaining* in the chambers *were* free: for they were employed ir. *that* work day and night.

34 These chief fathers of the Levites *were* chief throughout their generations; these dwelt at Jerusalem.

35 ¶ And in Gibeon dwelt the father of Gibeon, Jehiel, whose wife's name *was* Maachah:

36 And his firstborn son Abdon, then Zur, and Kish, and Baal, and Ner, and Nadab,

37 And Gedor, and Ahio, and Zechariah, and Mikloth.

38 And Mikloth begat Shimeam. And they also dwelt with their brethren at Jerusalem, over against their brethren.

39 And Ner begat Kish; and Kish begat Saul; and Saul begat Jonathan, and Malchi-shua, and Abinadab, and Esh-baal.

40 And the son of Jonathan *was* Merib-baal: and Merib-baal begat Micah.

41 And the sons of Micah *were*, Pithon, and Melech, and Tahrea, *and Ahaz*.

42 And Ahaz begat Jarah; and Jarah begat Alemeth, and Azmaveth, and Zimri; and Zimri begat Moza;

43 And Moza begat Binea; and Rephaiah his son, Eleasah his son, Azel his son.

44 And Azel had six sons, whose names *are* these, Azrikam, Bocheru, and Ishmael, and Sheariah, and Obadiah, and Hanan. These *were* the sons of Azel.

10 Now the Philistines fought against Israel; and the men of Israel fled from before the Philistines, and fell down slain in mount Gilboa.

fathers' houses of the Levites, dwelling in the chambers of the temple free from other service, for they were on duty day and night.

34 These were heads of fathers' houses of the Levites, according to their generations, leaders, who lived in Jerusalem.

35 In Gibeon dwelt the father of Gibeon, Je-i'el, and the name of his wife was Ma'acah, 36 and his first-born son Abdon, then Zur, Kish, Ba'al, Ner, Nadab, 37 Gedor, Ahi'o, Zechari'ah, and Mikloth; 38 and Mikloth was the father of Shim'e-am; and these also dwelt opposite their kinsmen in Jerusalem, with their kinsmen. 39 Ner was the father of Kish, Kish of Saul, Saul of Jonathan, Mal'chishu'a, Abin'adab, and Eshba'al; 40 and the son of Jonathan was Mer'ib-ba'al; and Mer'ib-ba'al was the father of Micah. 41 The sons of Micah: Pithon, Melech, Tahr'e-a, and Ahaz;[v] 42 and Ahaz was the father of Jarah, and Jarah of Al'emeth, Az'maveth, and Zimri; and Zimri was the father of Moza. 43 Moza was the father of Bin'e-a; and Repha'iah was his son, Ele-a'sah his son, Azel his son. 44 Azel had six sons and these are their names: Azri'kam, Bo'cheru, Ish'mael, She-ari'ah, Obadi'ah, and Hanan; these were the sons of Azel.

10 Now the Philistines fought against Israel; and the men of Israel fled before the Philistines, and fell slain on Mount

[v] Compare 8. 35: Heb lacks *and Ahaz*

L. ANCESTORS OF SAUL (9:35-44)

See Exeg. on 8:29-38. The list here repeated may have displaced some of the Chronicler's words introductory to his account of Judah's kingdom.

39. Here (and in 8:33) read "begat Abner." **Ner** was Saul's uncle (I Sam. 14:51).

II. THE REIGN OF DAVID (10:1–29:30)

A. THE END OF SAUL (10:1-14)

The Chronicler had in mind a great purpose: to relate how a kingdom, brought into being by the will of God, had in the end been reduced to nought by human perversity.

---

administration in the temple in Herod's time are vividly described in the rabbinical writings called the Mishnah, and in general no doubt similar arrangements obtained in the earlier second temple; vigilant guard was maintained throughout the night hours, and certain priests and Levites slept within the precincts. Just before dawn the altar fires were tended and renewed, and the moment of the appearing of the sun was heralded to the sleeping city. Then the dawn sacrifice of a lamb was prepared and offered, with the singing Levites standing on the

2 And the Philistines followed hard after Saul, and after his sons; and the Philistines slew Jonathan, and Abinadab, and Malchishua, the sons of Saul.

3 And the battle went sore against Saul, and the archers hit him, and he was wounded of the archers.

4 Then said Saul to his armor-bearer, Draw thy sword, and thrust me through therewith; lest these uncircumcised come and abuse me. But his armor-bearer would not; for he was sore afraid. So Saul took a sword, and fell upon it.

5 And when his armor-bearer saw that Saul was dead, he fell likewise on the sword, and died.

6 So Saul died, and his three sons, and all his house died together.

7 And when all the men of Israel that *were* in the valley saw that they fled, and that Saul and his sons were dead, then they forsook their cities, and fled: and the Philistines came and dwelt in them.

8 ¶ And it came to pass on the morrow, when the Philistines came to strip the slain, that they found Saul and his sons fallen in mount Gilboa.

9 And when they had stripped him, they took his head, and his armor, and sent into the land of the Philistines round about, to carry tidings unto their idols, and to the people.

Gilbo'a. 2 And the Philistines overtook Saul and his sons; and the Philistines slew Jonathan and Abin'adab and Mal'chishu'a, the sons of Saul. 3 The battle pressed hard upon Saul, and the archers found him; and he was wounded by the archers. 4 Then Saul said to his armor-bearer, "Draw your sword, and thrust me through with it, lest these uncircumcised come and make sport of me." But his armor-bearer would not; for he feared greatly. Therefore Saul took his own sword, and fell upon it. 5 And when his armor-bearer saw that Saul was dead, he also fell upon his sword, and died. 6 Thus Saul died; he and his three sons and all his house died together. 7 And when all the men of Israel who were in the valley saw that the army[w] had fled and that Saul and his sons were dead, they forsook their cities and fled; and the Philistines came and dwelt in them.

8 On the morrow, when the Philistines came to strip the slain, they found Saul and his sons fallen on Mount Gilbo'a. 9 And they stripped him and took his head and his armor, and sent messengers throughout the land of the Philistines, to carry the good news to their idols and to the people.

[w] Heb *they*

He also wished to show that the high design of God had not been finally frustrated. Out of the fallen kingdom there had come into existence the temple and its worship: a visible sign of faith indestructible. Except for the farewell speech which the Chronicler assigned to David (ch. 29), he was no great artist in words. Nevertheless, steadily and with cumulative effect he pursued his theme with an artist's eye for selecting what mattered and rejecting the irrelevant. He saw that the vivid narratives in Samuel about Saul's life were beside the point, for in Saul the kingdom had made, as it were, a false start. Only Saul's death mattered, because it had been a prelude to David's reign. With that, therefore, he began, quoting I Sam. 31:1-13; skillfully he altered one verse (vs. 6) and added his own reflection (vss. 13-14).

10:1. Now the Philistines fought . . . : Possibly some introductory words by the Chronicler are lost—having been replaced by the genealogical chapters—but not necessarily so. For ancient taste the opening would not seem so abrupt as it does to us.

6. And all his house: His whole family, all his sons (contrast I Sam. 31:6, "all his men," i.e., his soldiers). Yet the Chronicler knew that at least two sons of Saul, Ishbosheth and Mephibosheth, survived Saul's death; for the book of Samuel says much about them, and relates that Ishbosheth (not David) was accepted by the northern and southern tribes, reigning over them as king for two years. He knew that II Sam. 3:1 says, "Now there was long war between the house of Saul and the house of David." He knew that for seven years David was no more than king of the Judeans at Hebron, and became

10 And they put his armor in the house of their gods, and fastened his head in the temple of Dagon.

11 ¶ And when all Jabesh-gilead heard all that the Philistines had done to Saul,

12 They arose, all the valiant men, and took away the body of Saul, and the bodies of his sons, and brought them to Jabesh, and buried their bones under the oak in Jabesh, and fasted seven days.

13 ¶ So Saul died for his transgression which he committed against the LORD, *even* against the word of the LORD, which he kept not, and also for asking *counsel* of *one that had* a familiar spirit, to inquire *of it;*

14 And inquired not of the LORD: therefore he slew him, and turned the kingdom unto David the son of Jesse.

10 And they put his armor in the temple of their gods, and fastened his head in the temple of Dagon. 11 But when all Ja'besh-gil'ead heard all that the Philistines had done to Saul, 12 all the valiant men arose, and took away the body of Saul and the bodies of his sons, and brought them to Jabesh. And they buried their bones under the oak in Jabesh, and fasted seven days.

13 So Saul died for his unfaithfulness; he was unfaithful to the LORD in that he did not keep the command of the LORD, and also consulted a medium, seeking guidance, 14 and did not seek guidance from the LORD. Therefore the LORD slew him, and turned the kingdom over to David the son of Jesse.

---

effectively ruler of all the Hebrews only after he captured Jerusalem (Zion) from the Jebusites. In the same way the Chronicler ignored the narrative which tells how David, late in his reign, was almost overthrown by a rebellion led by his son Absalom. Thus, why did the Chronicler, in face of known facts, deliberately declare that all Saul's family perished when the Battle of Gilboa was fought? Because David as the chosen of the Lord ought at once to have been crowned enthusiastically by all the Hebrews. This verse prepares the way for him to say so. Clearer proof need not be asked to show that the Chronicler was not attempting to write a history to be credited as literal fact, but was obviously setting out to portray an ideal.

13-14. The Chronicler's own comment. Saul perished not in the fortunes of war and because the Philistines were stronger, but because he had defied the injunction of Samuel, the true prophet of God, and sought counsel from the dead.

---

steps leading to the priests' hall, ready to render the psalm when the sacrifice was completed [8] (cf. the hymn attributed to Gregory the Great, "Father, we praise thee, now the night is over").

10:13-14. *A Man Who Failed.*—Notice that the Chronicler chooses to ignore the efforts and successes of Saul's career. He records only his final defeat and death on Mount Gilboa and the action of the valiant men who carried his body to Jabesh. The Chronicler then pronounces verdict. Contrast these verses with the eulogy and lament which David, whom Saul had wronged, composed concerning the fallen king and Jonathan his lovable son (II Sam. 1:17-27).

Does not David's generous tribute exemplify the right attitude in estimating the blend of virtues and faults in a man's character, especially in one who has carried difficult and high responsibility? For long years Saul had striven to rally the quarrelsome Hebrew tribes and prevent their subjugation by the Philistines. Often he

[8] See *The Jewish Encyclopedia* (New York: Funk & Wagnalls, 1906), XII, 81-83.

had fought successfully, and the final battle was lost because the Philistines attacked in great force and were far better armed than the Hebrews. It is true that his unwarranted jealousy of David fatefully weakened his cause. But we should mercifully judge that in Saul's mind there may have been all along a tendency toward derangement. Jealousy gave it actuality: that green-eyed monster from whose insidious influence few are perfectly exempt. Who of us would unreservedly condemn Saul? The Chronicler did so: **Saul died for his transgression which he committed against the LORD.**

The Chronicler was not out to do full justice to the memory of Saul. He was wholeheartedly concerned to insist throughout his account of Judah's history that whenever men flouted what they believed to be the will of God the consequences were not trivial but disastrous. This verse collects the evidence against Saul in that respect, and upon those sad facts alone the harsh verdict results. A deep issue is raised. Does deliberate wrongdoing lead to destruction? "The voice of conscience is the voice of God."

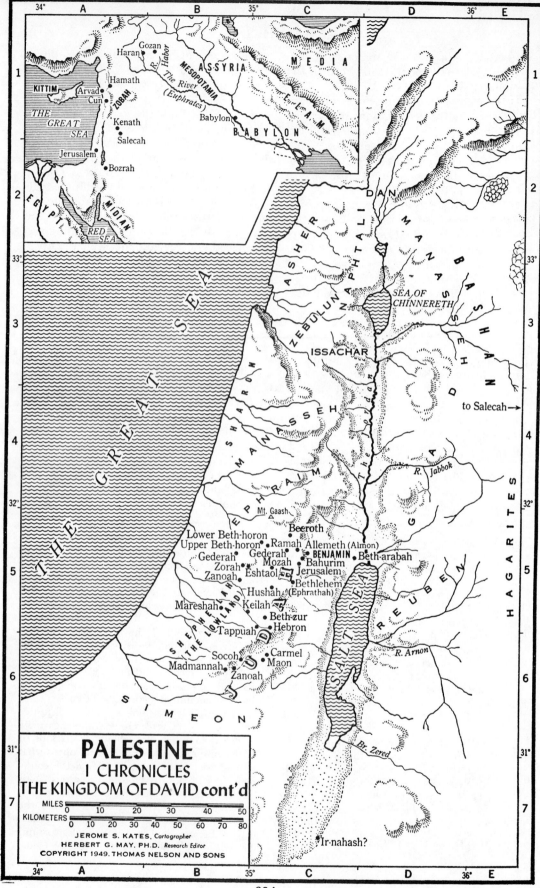

PALESTINE
1 CHRONICLES
THE KINGDOM OF DAVID cont'd

MILES
0   10   20   30   40   50

KILOMETERS
0 10 20 30 40 50 60 70 80

JEROME S. KATES, *Cartographer*
HERBERT G. MAY, PH.D. *Research Editor*
COPYRIGHT 1949, THOMAS NELSON AND SONS

11 Then all Israel gathered themselves to David unto Hebron, saying, Behold, we are thy bone and thy flesh.

2 And moreover in time past, even when Saul was king, thou *wast* he that leddest out and broughtest in Israel: and the LORD thy God said unto thee, Thou shalt feed my people Israel, and thou shalt be ruler over my people Israel.

3 Therefore came all the elders of Israel to the king of Hebron; and David made a covenant with them in Hebron before the LORD; and they anointed David king over Israel, according to the word of the LORD by Samuel.

4 ¶ And David and all Israel went to Jerusalem, which *is* Jebus; where the Jebusites *were,* the inhabitants of the land.

5 And the inhabitants of Jebus said to David, Thou shalt not come hither. Nevertheless David took the castle of Zion, which *is* the city of David.

6 And David said, Whosoever smiteth the Jebusites first shall be chief and captain. So Joab the son of Zeruiah went first up, and was chief.

7 And David dwelt in the castle; therefore they called it the city of David.

11 Then all Israel gathered together to David at Hebron, and said, "Behold, we are your bone and flesh. 2 In times past, even when Saul was king, it was you that led out and brought in Israel; and the LORD your God said to you, 'You shall be shepherd of my people Israel, and you shall be prince over my people Israel.' " 3 So all the elders of Israel came to the king at Hebron; and David made a covenant with them at Hebron before the LORD, and they anointed David king over Israel, according to the word of the LORD by Samuel.

4 And David and all Israel went to Jerusalem, that is Jebus, where the Jeb'usites were, the inhabitants of the land. 5 The inhabitants of Jebus said to David, "You will not come in here." Nevertheless David took the stronghold of Zion, that is, the city of David. 6 David said, "Whoever shall smite the Jeb'usites first shall be chief and commander." And Jo'ab the son of Zeru'iah went up first, so he became chief. 7 And David dwelt in the stronghold; therefore it

B. DAVID'S TRIUMPHS (11:1–12:40)

11:1-3. Instantly, effortlessly, David (says the Chronicler) was acclaimed as king by all the Hebrews. The pretext for this assertion was found in II Sam. 5:1-3, but the whole of II Sam. 1–4 and 5:4-5 had to be ignored.

4-9. The impression is given that David's master stroke in capturing Zion from the Jebusites was an immediate sequel to his coronation, and the text stresses that **all Israel**

Is that truth or delusion concerning human affairs? Horrible deeds have been perpetrated at the dictate of conscience. It is as necessary to educate our moral as our mental sense. We need to let the mind of Christ illumine our conscience and constrain our will.

11:1-3. *Behold the Man!*—Here is a significant fact. A personality appears whose qualities are such that men can take heart again amidst perils that seem overwhelming; and not only so, they can also feel he will bring them more than had ever been hoped. His right to leadership is transparent and is welcomed. In the new enthusiasm former uncertainty and causes of division vanish. It is "a time for greatness."

All Israel was of one mind to make David king. They felt him to be the answer to their common need—"the man born to be king." There are three notable features in these verses.

First, the tribes of the north assert that they, not only the Judeans, are David's kith and kin: **Behold, we are thy bone and thy flesh.** Second, they declare their conviction that David is what he is, and what he will be, through the purpose and power of God. And third, their confidence in his character was not mistaken. David responded to their overture as a true man to his brethren: he **made a covenant with them in Hebron before the LORD.**

National histories afford many parallels for the emergence of a solitary, outstandingly great person. World history shows one supreme instance—Jesus Christ: *Ecce Homo.* Of him it was said, "Behold, the Lamb of God, who takes away the sin of the world!" (John 1:29). All Israel came together to make David king. Jesus said that he would draw all men unto himself. It has not so happened. But it ought to happen. There

8 And he built the city round about, even from Millo round about: and Joab repaired the rest of the city.

9 So David waxed greater and greater: for the LORD of hosts *was* with him.

10 ¶ These also *are* the chief of the mighty men whom David had, who strengthened themselves with him in his kingdom, *and* with all Israel, to make him king, according to the word of the LORD concerning Israel.

11 And this *is* the number of the mighty men whom David had; Jashobeam, a Hachmonite, the chief of the captains: he lifted up his spear against three hundred slain *by him* at one time.

12 And after him *was* Eleazar the son of Dodo, the Ahohite, who *was one* of the three mighties.

13 He was with David at Pas-dammim, and there the Philistines were gathered together to battle, where was a parcel of ground full of barley; and the people fled from before the Philistines.

14 And they set themselves in the midst of *that* parcel, and delivered it, and slew the Philistines; and the LORD saved *them* by a great deliverance.

15 ¶ Now three of the thirty captains went down to the rock of David, into the cave of Adullam; and the host of the Philistines encamped in the valley of Rephaim.

16 And David *was* then in the hold, and the Philistines' garrison *was* then at Bethlehem.

was called the city of David. **8** And he built the city round about from the Millo in complete circuit; and Jo'ab repaired the rest of the city. **9** And David became greater and greater, for the LORD of hosts was with him.

10 Now these are the chiefs of David's mighty men, who gave him strong support in his kingdom, together with all Israel, to make him king, according to the word of the LORD concerning Israel. **11** This is an account of David's mighty men: Jasho'be-am, a Hach'monite, was chief of the three;[x] he wielded his spear against three hundred whom he slew at one time.

12 And next to him among the three mighty men was Elea'zar the son of Dodo, the Aho'hite. **13** He was with David at Pasdam'mim when the Philistines were gathered there for battle. There was a plot of ground full of barley, and the men fled from the Philistines. **14** But hey took his[y] stand in the midst of the plot, and defended it, and slew the Philistines; and the LORD saved them by a great victory.

15 Three of the thirty chief men went down to the rock to David at the cave of Adul'lam, when the army of Philistines was encamped in the valley of Reph'aim. **16** David was then in the stronghold; and the garrison of the Philistines was then at

---

[x] Compare 2 Sam 23. 8: Heb *thirty* or *captains*

[y] Compare 2 Sam 23. 12: Heb *they . . . their*

---

was with him in the enterprise. We see in that emphasis the first indication of the Chronicler's cumulative plea to his contemporaries that the men of Israel ought to be reckoned true Hebrews, brethren of the Judeans (contrast II Sam. 5:6, which alludes merely to "the king and his men") .

10-47. The equivalent passage in II Sam. 23:8-39 suggests correctly that the exploits happened at sundry times during David's life. The Chronicler by placing them together at the outset, implies that all these heroes from all Israel had risked their lives for David even before he became king.

---

need be no delay for the individual to recognize in Christ his king and allow him to dispel the confusion of his mind, heal its divisions, and deliver his soul from peril.

10. *Loyal Helpers.*—In the verses which follow, the Chronicler assembled names, exploits, and numbers of valiant men who served David, as if all of them had been with him in the time of his youth. It is much as if we were to compile

a vast catalogue of those who throughout the centuries had nobly served Christ. Who could read that list understandingly and not be enheartened? To do so should check somber reflections about nominal Christians unworthy of his name. It is a prevalent fault to allow disheartening facts to loom in our thoughts. Paul was wise when he urged us to concentrate attention on whatsoever things are good (Phil. 4:8) .

17 And David longed, and said, Oh that one would give me drink of the water of the well of Beth-lehem, that *is* at the gate!

18 And the three brake through the host of the Philistines, and drew water out of the well of Beth-lehem, that *was* by the gate, and took *it,* and brought *it* to David: but David would not drink *of* it, but poured it out to the LORD,

19 And said, My God forbid it me, that I should do this thing: shall I drink the blood of these men that have put their lives in jeopardy? for with *the jeopardy of* their lives they brought it: therefore he would not drink it. These things did these three mightiest.

20 ¶ And Abishai the brother of Joab, he was chief of the three: for lifting up his spear against three hundred, he slew *them,* and had a name among the three.

21 Of the three, he was more honorable than the two; for he was their captain: howbeit he attained not to the *first* three.

22 Benaiah the son of Jehoiada, the son of a valiant man of Kabzeel, who had done many acts; he slew two lionlike men of Moab: also he went down and slew a lion in a pit in a snowy day.

23 And he slew an Egyptian, a man of *great* stature, five cubits high; and in the Egyptian's hand *was* a spear like a weaver's beam; and he went down to him with a staff, and plucked the spear out of the Egyptian's hand, and slew him with his own spear.

24 These *things* did Benaiah the son of Jehoiada, and had a name among the three mighties.

Bethlehem. 17 And David said longingly, "O that some one would give me water to drink from the well of Bethlehem which is by the gate!" 18 Then the three mighty men broke through the camp of the Philistines, and drew water out of the well of Bethlehem which was by the gate, and took and brought it to David. But David would not drink of it; he poured it out to the LORD, 19 and said, "Far be it from me before my God that I should do this. Shall I drink the lifeblood of these men? For at the risk of their lives they brought it." Therefore he would not drink it. These things did the three mighty men.

20 Now Abi'shai, the brother of Jo'ab, was chief of the thirty.[z] And he wielded his spear against three hundred men and slew them, and won a name beside the three. 21 He was the most renowned[a] of the thirty,[z] and became their commander; but he did not attain to the three.

22 And Benai'ah the son of Jehoi'ada was a valiant man[b] of Kabzeel, a doer of great deeds; he smote two ariels[c] of Moab. He also went down and slew a lion in a pit on a day when snow had fallen. 23 And he slew an Egyptian, a man of great stature, five cubits tall. The Egyptian had in his hand a spear like a weaver's beam; but Benai'ah went down to him with a staff, and snatched the spear out of the Egyptian's hand, and slew him with his own spear. 24 These things did Benai'ah the son of Jehoi'ada, and won a name beside the three

[z] Syr: Heb *three*
[a] Compare 2 Sam 23. 19: Heb *more renowned among the two*
[b] Syr: Heb *the son of a valiant man*
[c] The meaning of the word *ariel* is unknown

17-19. *Grace Before Meals.*—This episode has been an inexhaustible well from which to draw refreshing water. David was not perishing from thirst, but the water available at the stronghold at Adullam was warm with the heat of its rocks, and he longed for the coolness found in Bethlehem's deep well. One may hope that, in consideration for the feelings of the men who risked their lives to evade the Philistine sentinels and fetch it to him, David **poured . . . out** only a token amount of the water and drank most of it. Scholars may point to the widespread custom of offering a libation, pouring out a portion of wine in honor of the gods before drinking the rest. Suffice it to infer that David's

action on the occasion effectively showed that he set the safety of his followers incomparably above his physical desires. Are there comparable testing situations in our lives, when we are in danger of accepting benefits from others without giving due thanks either to them or to God for the self-sacrifice or kindness involved?

22. *The Lion Killer.*—What a quaint verse this is! We could do with a photograph of the **two lionlike men of Moab** whom Benaiah killed. Were their beards so exuberant as to resemble a lion's mane? But as the RSV (**he smote two ariels of Moab**) indicates, the Hebrew is obscure. The original reading may have recorded the comparatively tame fact that Benaiah slew

25 Behold, he was honorable among the thirty, but attained not to the *first* three: and David set him over his guard.

26 ¶ Also the valiant men of the armies *were,* Asahel the brother of Joab, Elhanan the son of Dodo of Beth-lehem,

27 Shammoth the Harorite, Helez the Pelonite,

28 Ira the son of Ikkesh the Tekoite, Abiezer the Antothite,

29 Sibbecai the Hushathite, Ilai the Ahohite,

30 Maharai the Netophathite, Heled the son of Baanah the Netophathite,

31 Ithai the son of Ribai of Gibeah, *that pertained* to the children of Benjamin, Benaiah the Pirathonite,

32 Hurai of the brooks of Gaash, Abiel the Arbathite,

33 Azmaveth the Baharumite, Eliahba the Shaalbonite,

34 The sons of Hashem the Gizonite, Jonathan the son of Shage the Hararite,

35 Ahiam the son of Sacar the Hararite, Eliphal the son of Ur,

36 Hepher the Mecherathite, Ahijah the Pelonite,

37 Hezro the Carmelite, Naarai the son of Ezbai,

38 Joel the brother of Nathan, Mibhar the son of Haggeri,

39 Zelek the Ammonite, Naharai the Berothite, the armor-bearer of Joab the son of Zeruiah,

40 Ira the Ithrite, Gareb the Ithrite,

41 Uriah the Hittite, Zabad the son of Ahlai,

42 Adina the son of Shiza the Reubenite, a captain of the Reubenites, and thirty with him,

43 Hanan the son of Maachah, and Joshaphat the Mithnite,

44 Uzzia the Ashterathite, Shama and Jehiel the sons of Hothan the Aroerite,

45 Jediael the son of Shimri, and Joha his brother, the Tizite,

46 Eliel the Mahavite, and Jeribai and Joshaviah the sons of Elnaam, and Ithmah the Moabite,

mighty men. 25 He was renowned among the thirty, but he did not attain to the three. And David set him over his bodyguard.

26 The mighty men of the armies were As'ahel the brother of Jo'ab, Elha'nan the son of Dodo of Bethlehem, 27 Shammoth of Harod,[d] Helez the Pel'onite, 28 Ira the son of Ikkesh of Teko'a, Abi-e'zer of An'athoth, 29 Sib'becai the Hu'shathite, I'lai the Aho'hite, 30 Ma'harai of Netoph'ah, Heled the son of Ba'anah of Netoph'ah, 31 Ithai the son of Ribai of Gib'e-ah of the Benjaminites, Benai'ah of Pir'athon, 32 Hurai of the brooks of Ga'ash, Abi'el the Ar'bathite, 33 Az'maveth of Baha'rum, Eli'ahba of Sha-al'bon, 34 Hasheme[e] the Gi'zonite, Jonathan the son of Shagee the Har'arite, 35 Ahi'am the son of Sacher the Har'arite, Eli'phal the son of Ur, 36 Hepher the Meche'rathite, Ahi'jah the Pel'onite, 37 Hezro of Carmel, Na'arai the son of Ezbai, 38 Jo'el the brother of Nathan, Mibhar the son of Hagri, 39 Zelek the Ammonite, Na'harai of Be-er'oth, the armor-bearer of Jo'ab the son of Zeru'iah, 40 Ira the Ithrite, Gareb the Ithrite, 41 Uri'ah the Hittite, Zabad the son of Ahlai, 42 Ad'ina the son of Shiza the Reubenite, a leader of the Reubenites, and thirty with him, 43 Hanan the son of Ma'acah, and Josh'aphat the Mithnite, 44 Uzzi'a the Ash'terathite, Shama and Je-i'el the sons of Hotham the Aro'erite, 45 Jedi'a-el the son of Shimri, and Joha his brother, the Tizite, 46 Eli'el the Ma'havite, and Jer'ibai, and Joshavi'ah, the sons of El'na-am, and Ith-

d Compare 2 Sam 23. 25: Heb *the Harorite*
e Compare Gk and 2 Sam 23. 32: Heb *the sons of Hashem*

---

two young lions in their den. On the second part of the verse George Adam Smith comments: "The beast had strayed up from Jordan, and been caught in a snowstorm. Where else [than in Palestine] could lions and snow come together?" [9] An evangelist found in the episode the topics for his three-dimensional sermon: slaying lions—in pits—on snowy days.

[9] *The Historical Geography of the Holy Land* (25th ed.; London: Hodder & Stoughton, 1910), p. 65.

47 Eliel, and Obed, and Jasiel the Mesobaite.

12 Now these *are* they that came to David to Ziklag, while he yet kept himself close because of Saul the son of Kish: and they *were* among the mighty men, helpers of the war.

2 *They were* armed with bows, and could use both the right hand and the left in *hurling* stones and *shooting* arrows out of a bow, *even* of Saul's brethren of Benjamin.

3 The chief *was* Ahiezer, then Joash, the sons of Shemaah the Gibeathite; and Jeziel, and Pelet, the sons of Azmaveth; and Berachah, and Jehu the Antothite,

4 And Ismaiah the Gibeonite, a mighty man among the thirty, and over the thirty; and Jeremiah, and Jahaziel, and Johanan, and Josabad the Gederathite,

5 Eluzai, and Jerimoth, and Bealiah, and Shemariah, and Shephatiah the Haruphite,

6 Elkanah, and Jesiah, and Azareel, and Joezer, and Jashobeam, the Korhites,

7 And Joelah, and Zebadiah, the sons of Jeroham of Gedor.

8 And of the Gadites there separated themselves unto David into the hold to the wilderness men of might, *and* men of war *fit* for the battle, that could handle shield and buckler, whose faces *were like* the faces of lions, and *were* as swift as the roes upon the mountains;

mah the Mo'abite, 47 Eli'el, and Obed, and Ja-asi'el the Mezo'ba-ite.

12 Now these are the men who came to David at Ziklag, while he could not move about freely because of Saul the son of Kish; and they were among the mighty men who helped him in war. 2 They were bowmen, and could shoot arrows and sling stones with either the right or the left hand; they were Benjaminites, Saul's kinsmen. 3 The chief was Ahi-e'zer, then Jo'ash, both sons of Shema'ah of Gib'e-ah; also Je'zi-el and Pelet the sons of Az'maveth; Ber'acah, Jehu of An'athoth, 4 Ishma'iah of Gibeon, a mighty man among the thirty and a leader over the thirty; Jeremiah,*f* Jahazi'el, Joha'nan, Joz'abad of Gede'rah, 5 Elu'zai,*g* Jer'imoth, Beali'ah, Shemari'ah, Shephati'ah the Har'uphite; 6 Elka'nah, Isshi'ah, Az'arel, Jo-e'zer, and Jasho'be-am, the Ko'rahites; 7 and Jo-e'lah and Zebadi'ah, the sons of Jero'ham of Gedor.

8 From the Gadites there went over to David at the stronghold in the wilderness mighty and experienced warriors, expert with shield and spear, whose faces were like the faces of lions, and who were swift as

f Heb verse 5
g Heb verse 6

12:1-40. The colossal assertion of this chapter (without any basis in Samuel) must be regarded mainly as the Chronicler's fertile invention; but some use of popular traditions seems indicated by vss. 2, 8, 15, 17-19, which are not in the Chronicler's colorless style.

2. It is utterly unlikely that more than a few **Benjaminites** joined David, for the tribe as a whole sided with Ishbosheth, Saul's son.

12:1-40. *Unrealized Possibilities.*—This is a lovely chapter, provided its underlying purpose is perceived. At its outset the Chronicler emphasizes the fact that, even when David was no more than a hunted fugitive from Saul, fighting men of surpassing skill and courage came to be with him, some even from Saul's own territory of Benjamin and others from the Israelite regions of Gad and Manasseh. A vast concourse assembled at Hebron—155,000 from the lesser tribes of the north alone, their numbers utterly surpassing the men from Judah. A united people made David king. The Chronicler's contemporaries, who could read the books of Samuel, knew this was not fact. It piles the incredible on the unhistorical. For whom then, for what sort of men, was it written that they might take

to heart its contemporary implications? For self-satisfied men in the Jerusalem of the Chronicler's age, who felt no pity for former Israel but prided themselves that Jerusalem was exclusively the city of God, and they its elite. For men who opposed the view that loyal Israelites should serve in the temple. For cynics who thought the promise of Abraham, that his children should be innumerable as the sand upon the shore of the sea, was sentimental moonshine. The Chronicler was painting a picture of unity so radiant that to see it would be to desire it.

Translate his dream into terms of the unrealized possibilities in Western history. Rancorous cherishing of old wrongs—how prevalent that evil is! But North and South in the United States have seen one such deep wound healed.

9 Ezer the first, Obadiah the second, Eliab the third,

10 Mishmannah the fourth, Jeremiah the fifth,

11 Attai the sixth, Eliel the seventh,

12 Johanan the eighth, Elzabad the ninth,

13 Jeremiah the tenth, Machbanai the eleventh.

14 These *were* of the sons of Gad, captains of the host: one of the least *was* over a hundred, and the greatest over a thousand.

15 These *are* they that went over Jordan in the first month, when it had overflown all his banks; and they put to flight all *them* of the valleys, *both* toward the east, and toward the west.

16 And there came of the children of Benjamin and Judah to the hold unto David.

17 And David went out to meet them, and answered and said unto them, If ye be come peaceably unto me to help me, mine heart shall be knit unto you: but if *ye be come* to betray me to mine enemies, seeing *there is* no wrong in mine hands, the God of our fathers look *thereon,* and rebuke *it.*

18 Then the spirit came upon Amasai, *who was* chief of the captains, *and he said,* Thine *are* we, David, and on thy side, thou son of Jesse: peace, peace *be* unto thee, and peace *be* to thine helpers; for thy God helpeth thee. Then David received them, and made them captains of the band.

gazelles upon the mountains: 9 Ezer the chief, Obadi′ah second, Eli′ab third, 10 Mishman′nah fourth, Jeremiah fifth, 11 Attai sixth, Eli′el seventh, 12 Joha′nan eighth, Elza′bad ninth, 13 Jeremiah tenth, Mach′bannai eleventh. 14 These Gadites were officers of the army, the lesser over a hundred and the greater over a thousand. 15 These are the men who crossed the Jordan in the first month, when it was overflowing all its banks, and put to flight all those in the valleys, to the east and to the west.

16 And some of the men of Benjamin and Judah came to the stronghold to David. 17 David went out to meet them and said to them, "If you have come to me in friendship to help me, my heart will be knit to you; but if to betray me to my adversaries, although there is no wrong in my hands, then may the God of our fathers see and rebuke you." 18 Then the Spirit came upon Ama′sai, chief of the thirty, and he said,

"We are yours, O David;
     and with you, O son of Jesse!
Peace, peace to you,
     and peace to your helpers!
For your God helps you."

Then David received them, and made them officers of his troops.

---

18. This remarkable verse has the rhythmic form of Hebrew poetry: a probable indication of its antiquity.

Imagine a world-wide healing: the nations united peaceably, ancient enmities forgiven. Picture the countless homes from which the shadows of fear and want would pass away. Or turn to Christian history. Suppose there had been no split between Orthodox and Catholic, Catholic and Protestant, because so deeply, so boldly, so generously the followers of Jesus had interpreted his definition of those who are his disciples (John 13:34-35). How vast and vague are these unrealized ideals! But there is one region over which we can exercise some measurable and immediate control—the region of our individual character. There, if we would, we could readily set to work to remedy past wrongs, to forgive, and to rebuild. There has been one Ideal that became fact in this dark world— Jesus of Nazareth.

17. *A Clear Conscience.*—David and his followers who were taking refuge in the cave of Adullam were in great danger. The tribe of Benjamin as a whole supported Saul's son Ishbosheth. If these men from Benjamin approaching the stronghold were hostile and intended to seize him and hand him over to Ishbosheth, it meant that his end had come and he must die in his youth. David had not been a traitor to Saul. Sometimes the Chronicler shoots an arrow straight to the mark. In this moment of mortal peril it was possible for David to say with honesty, there is no wrong in my hands.

18. *A Right Response.*—David had his integrity, and Amasai and the Benjaminites with him were men who knew and admired his spirit. Fire kindled fire. They wished to be his friends, not his foes. So sometimes it happens in life,

19 And there fell *some* of Manasseh to David, when he came with the Philistines against Saul to battle; but they helped them not: for the lords of the Philistines upon advisement sent him away, saying, He will fall to his master Saul to *the jeopardy of* our heads.

20 As he went to Ziklag, there fell to him of Manasseh, Adnah, and Jozabad, and Jediael, and Michael, and Jozabad, and Elihu, and Zilthai, captains of the thousands that *were* of Manasseh.

21 And they helped David against the band *of the rovers:* for they *were* all mighty men of valor, and were captains in the host.

22 For at *that* time day by day there came to David to help him, until *it was* a great host, like the host of God.

23 ¶ And these *are* the numbers of the bands *that were* ready armed to the war, *and* came to David to Hebron, to turn the kingdom of Saul to him, according to the word of the LORD.

24 The children of Judah that bare shield and spear *were* six thousand and eight hundred, ready armed to the war.

25 Of the children of Simeon, mighty men of valor for the war, seven thousand and one hundred.

26 Of the children of Levi four thousand and six hundred.

27 And Jehoiada *was* the leader of the Aaronites, and with him *were* three thousand and seven hundred;

28 And Zadok, a young man mighty of valor, and of his father's house twenty and two captains.

29 And of the children of Benjamin, the kindred of Saul, three thousand: for hitherto the greatest part of them had kept the ward of the house of Saul.

30 And of the children of Ephraim twenty thousand and eight hundred, mighty

19 Some of the men of Manas'seh deserted to David when he came with the Philistines for the battle against Saul. (Yet he did not help them, for the rulers of the Philistines took counsel and sent him away, saying, "At peril to our heads he will desert to his master Saul.") 20 As he went to Ziklag these men of Manas'seh deserted to him: Adnah, Joz'abad, Jedi'a-el, Michael, Joz'abad, Eli'hu, and Zil'lethai, chiefs of thousands in Manas'seh. 21 They helped David against the band of raiders;[h] for they were all mighty men of valor, and were commanders in the army. 22 For from day to day men kept coming to David to help him, until there was a great army, like an army of God.

23 These are the numbers of the divisions of the armed troops, who came to David in Hebron, to turn the kingdom of Saul over to him, according to the word of the LORD. 24 The men of Judah bearing shield and spear were six thousand eight hundred armed troops. 25 Of the Simeonites, mighty men of valor for war, seven thousand one hundred. 26 Of the Levites four thousand six hundred. 27 The prince Jehoi'ada, of the house of Aaron, and with him three thousand seven hundred. 28 Zadok, a young man mighty in valor, and twenty-two commanders from his own father's house. 29 Of the Benjaminites, the kinsmen of Saul, three thousand, of whom the majority had hitherto kept their allegiance to the house of Saul. 30 Of the E'phraimites

[h] Or *as officers of his troops*

---

22. Like the host of God: Superhumanly vast in number; vss. 23-40 supply a fantastic commentary.

23. The deputation (heads of families) that comes to crown David numbers just under 400,000, and all but 22,000 hail from the central and northern tribes. Obviously a symbolic mode of insisting that Israelites had indeed been truly Hebrews. Ponder it, all ye unbrotherly men in Jerusalem—378,000 Israelites did their duty on that great day!

---

when a man can face peril with a good conscience. He may meet the reward he deserves. It is a point of special interest that Amasai's answer, **We are yours, O David,** is cast in the rhythmic form of emotional Hebrew speech. This makes it probable that a really ancient tradition, otherwise unrecorded, is here preserved.

men of valor, famous throughout the house of their fathers.

31 And of the half tribe of Manasseh eighteen thousand, which were expressed by name, to come and make David king.

32 And of the children of Issachar, *which were men* that had understanding of the times, to know what Israel ought to do; the heads of them *were* two hundred; and all their brethren *were* at their commandment.

33 Of Zebulun, such as went forth to battle, expert in war, with all instruments of war, fifty thousand, which could keep rank: *they were* not of double heart.

34 And of Naphtali a thousand captains, and with them with shield and spear thirty and seven thousand.

35 And of the Danites expert in war twenty and eight thousand and six hundred.

36 And of Asher, such as went forth to battle, expert in war, forty thousand.

37 And on the other side of Jordan, of the Reubenites, and the Gadites, and of the half tribe of Manasseh, with all manner of instruments of war for the battle, a hundred and twenty thousand.

38 All these men of war, that could keep rank, came with a perfect heart to Hebron, to make David king over all Israel: and all the rest also of Israel *were* of one heart to make David king.

39 And there they were with David three days, eating and drinking: for their brethren had prepared for them.

40 Moreover they that were nigh them, *even* unto Issachar and Zebulun and Naphtali, brought bread on asses, and on camels, and on mules, and on oxen, *and* meat, meal, cakes of figs, and bunches of raisins, and wine, and oil, and oxen, and sheep abundantly: for *there was* joy in Israel.

13 And David consulted with the captains of thousands and hundreds, *and* with every leader.

twenty thousand eight hundred, mighty men of valor, famous men in their fathers' houses. 31 Of the half-tribe of Manas'seh eighteen thousand, who were expressly named to come and make David king. 32 Of Is'sachar men who had understanding of the times, to know what Israel ought to do, two hundred chiefs, and all their kinsmen under their command. 33 Of Zeb'ulun fifty thousand seasoned troops, equipped for battle with all the weapons of war, to help David[i] with singleness of purpose. 34 Of Naph'tali a thousand commanders with whom were thirty-seven thousand men armed with shield and spear. 35 Of the Danites twenty-eight thousand six hundred men equipped for battle. 36 Of Asher forty thousand seasoned troops ready for battle. 37 Of the Reubenites and Gadites and the half-tribe of Manas'seh from beyond the Jordan, one hundred and twenty thousand men armed with all the weapons of war.

38 All these, men of war, arrayed in battle order, came to Hebron with full intent to make David king over all Israel; likewise all the rest of Israel were of a single mind to make David king. 39 And they were there with David for three days, eating and drinking, for their brethren had made preparation for them. 40 And also their neighbors, from as far as Is'sachar and Zeb'ulun and Naph'tali, came bringing food on asses and on camels and on mules and on oxen, abundant provisions of meal, cakes of figs, clusters of raisins, and wine and oil, oxen and sheep, for there was joy in Israel.

13 David consulted with the commanders of thousands and of hundreds,

[i] Gk: Heb lacks *David*

C. David's Failure to Bring the Ark to Zion (13:1-14)

According to II Sam. 5:6 ff., David (*a*) captured Zion from the Jebusites, then (*b*) proceeded to wage two successful conflicts with the Philistines; (*c*) with aid of materials

---

39. *A Welcome Prepared.*—This verse strikes home to the feelings of any hospitable person for whom the entertaining of a guest has become a problem. The idealistic Chronicler is delightfully practical; for, of course, instead of happiness on the grand occasion there would have been hunger and desperation for the multitudes from Israel come for the coronation, if their Judean brethren had not made generous provision to feed them. On the other hand, it ap-

2 And David said unto all the congregation of Israel, If *it seem* good unto you, and *that it be* of the LORD our God, let us send abroad unto our brethren every where, *that are* left in all the land of Israel, and with them *also* to the priests and Levites *which are* in their cities *and* suburbs, that they may gather themselves unto us:

3 And let us bring again the ark of our God to us: for we inquired not at it in the days of Saul.

4 And all the congregation said that they would do so: for the thing was right in the eyes of all the people.

5 So David gathered all Israel together, from Shihor of Egypt even unto the entering of Hemath, to bring the ark of God from Kirjath-jearim.

6 And David went up, and all Israel, to Baalah, *that is,* to Kirjath-jearim, which *belonged* to Judah, to bring up thence the ark of God the LORD, that dwelleth *between* the cherubim, whose name is called *on it.*

7 And they carried the ark of God in a new cart out of the house of Abinadab: and Uzza and Ahio drave the cart.

with every leader. 2 And David said to all the assembly of Israel, "If it seems good to you, and if it is the will of the LORD our God, let us send abroad to our brethren who remain in all the land of Israel, and with them to the priests and Levites in the cities that have pasture lands, that they may come together to us. 3 Then let us bring again the ark of our God to us; for we neglected it in the days of Saul." 4 All the assembly agreed to do so, for the thing was right in the eyes of all the people.

5 So David assembled all Israel from the Shihor of Egypt to the entrance of Hamath, to bring the ark of God from Kir'iath-je'-arim. 6 And David and all Israel went up to Ba'alah, that is, to Kir'iath-je'arim which belongs to Judah, to bring up from there the ark of God, which is called by the name of the LORD who sits enthroned above the cherubim. 7 And they carried the ark of God upon a new cart, from the house of Abin'adab, and Uzza and Ahi'o[j] were driv-

[j] Or *and his brother*

and craftsmen from the king of Tyre began to build for himself a palace; only thereafter (d) tried to bring the ark to Zion from its humiliating storage at Kiriath-jearim; and (e), in making the attempt, paid no attention to what the Chronicler regarded as being the king's obvious duty, viz., to entrust its transport to the care of the Levites. Conceivably the Chronicler was so shocked by that sequence as to deem it unhistorical. However that may be, his narrative in this and the following chapter effectively reverses the order of events: it declares that after capturing Zion, David's first concern had been for the ark, and that he had at once made a first effort to achieve the perilous task of transporting it to Zion (vss. 1-11).

13:1-5. Introductory verses by the Chronicler, the purpose being to emphasize that David convened **all Israel** to assist him in the task (contrast II Sam. 6:2, "with all the people that were with him"); that all Israel's laity faithfully responded (vs. 5); and that with them came Levites, legitimate ministrants of worship (vs. 2).

2. Very revealing of the Chronicler's postexilic standpoint is the wording of this verse. Mark that **our brethren** are termed men **in all the land of Israel**, and that the remarkable phrase **who remain** appears first in postexilic writings and seems a designation of the Hebrews left in the Israelitish territory after the Assyrian conquest (so Adam C. Welch, *The Work of the Chronicler* [London: British Academy, 1939], pp. 16-17). In vs. 2b read, with RSV, **pasture lands**. In vs. 2c the words **the priests and** may be an instance of the revisers' correction. But further, it is notable that here all MSS of the LXX

pears that those who came from a distance had done their utmost toward self-help.

13:2. Seek Ye First the Kingdom of God.—The ark was deemed to contain two stone tablets on which had been graven the great Commandments and was regarded as the token of

assurance that Yahweh would be with his people. David was determined to set that treasure in the heart of his kingdom. In our world's civilization there is desperate need to establish at its center the Christian faith more wisely and more securely than in the past.

8 And David and all Israel played before God with all *their* might, and with singing, and with harps, and with psalteries, and with timbrels, and with cymbals, and with trumpets.

9 ¶ And when they came unto the threshingfloor of Chidon, Uzza put forth his hand to hold the ark; for the oxen stumbled.

10 And the anger of the LORD was kindled against Uzza, and he smote him, because he put his hand to the ark: and there he died before God.

11 And David was displeased, because the LORD had made a breach upon Uzza: wherefore that place is called Perez-uzza to this day.

12 And David was afraid of God that day, saying, How shall I bring the ark of God *home* to me?

13 So David brought not the ark *home* to himself to the city of David, but carried it aside into the house of Obed-edom the Gittite.

14 And the ark of God remained with the family of Obed-edom in his house three months. And the LORD blessed the house of Obed-edom, and all that he had.

ing the cart. 8 And David and all Israel were making merry before God with all their might, with song and lyres and harps and tambourines and cymbals and trumpets.

9 And when they came to the threshing floor of Chidon, Uzza put out his hand to hold the ark, for the oxen stumbled. 10 And the anger of the LORD was kindled against Uzza; and he smote him because he put forth his hand to the ark; and he died there before God. 11 And David was angry because the LORD had broken forth upon Uzza; and that place is called Pe′rez-uz′za[k] to this day. 12 And David was afraid of God that day; and he said, "How can I bring the ark of God home to me?" 13 So David did not take the ark home into the city of David, but took it aside to the house of O′bed-e′dom the Gittite. 14 And the ark of God remained with the household of O′bed-e′dom in his house three months; and the LORD blessed the household of O′bed-e′dom and all that he had.

[k] That is *The breaking forth upon Uzzah*

---

read the typically Deuteronomic phrase "the priests, the Levites," i.e., that was the reading of the Hebrew MS used in making the LXX translation in the second century A.D.

13. Obed-edom the Gittite: The man derived from the Philistine city of Gath. It disturbed the Chronicler that the king should have placed the sacred ark in the house of one who was not even a pure-blooded Hebrew. Accordingly, in vs. 14 he slightly altered II Sam. 6:11 in order to indicate that the ark was not actually under the Gittite's roof; for the Hebrew of vs. 14 should be translated "by [near] the house of Obed-edom, in its own house." The man's descendants were in the postexilic period engaged in the Levitical service of the temple, and so it comes to pass that in various references to Obed-edom elsewhere in Chronicles, he, as their ancestor, appears respectably transformed into a son of Levi, keeping the doors (15:18, 24; 16:38; 26:4, 8, 15; II Chr. 25:24), or playing a harp in the temple (15:21; 16:5).

---

9. The Death of Uzza.—Here, quoted from the book of Samuel, is an ancient Hebrew story portraying the irascible sanctity of the Deity. It is passing strange to our minds that anyone could have copied such a story without rebuke or alteration of its crude theology. We, however, can see with full understanding that rightful thoughts of God developed slowly in Hebrew history. And realization of that fact answers a thousand "difficulties" which formerly perplexed good men about the authority and value of the Bible. Our primary duty, however, is not condescendingly to despise our forefathers for crudity but ourselves to do better; for to whom

much enlightenment has been entrusted, from them the more is required. Horribly crude ideas of what Christianity believes and teaches still are held by masses of people today. There is plenty of sound teaching to be done in order that the light of Christ may shine with clarity.

12. Reverence.—It is instructive to note the sequence of David's moods in fetching the ark to Zion. First, he regards it as an occasion for solemnity and arranges an impressive ceremonial (vss. 1-7). Then he is jubilant (vs. 8). Then he is—not unreasonably—indignant about the tragic fate of well-intentioned Uzza (vs. 11). Then he becomes afraid.

14

Now Hiram king of Tyre sent messengers to David, and timber of cedars, with masons and carpenters, to build him a house.

2 And David perceived that the LORD had confirmed him king over Israel, for his kingdom was lifted up on high, because of his people Israel.

3 ¶ And David took more wives at Jerusalem: and David begat more sons and daughters.

4 Now these *are* the names of *his* children which he had in Jerusalem; Shammua, and Shobab, Nathan, and Solomon,

5 And Ibhar, and Elishua, and Elpalet,

6 And Nogah, and Nepheg, and Japhia,

7 And Elishama, and Beeliada, and Eliphalet.

8 ¶ And when the Philistines heard that David was anointed king over all Israel, all the Philistines went up to seek David. And David heard *of it,* and went out against them.

9 And the Philistines came and spread themselves in the valley of Rephaim.

10 And David inquired of God, saying, Shall I go up against the Philistines? and wilt thou deliver them into mine hand? And the LORD said unto him, Go up; for I will deliver them into thine hand.

11 So they came up to Baal-perazim; and David smote them there. Then David said, God hath broken in upon mine enemies by mine hand like the breaking forth of waters: therefore they called the name of that place Baal-perazim.

14

And Hiram king of Tyre sent messengers to David, and cedar trees, also masons and carpenters to build a house for him. **2** And David perceived that the LORD had established him king over Israel, and that his kingdom was highly exalted for the sake of his people Israel.

3 And David took more wives in Jerusalem, and David begot more sons and daughters. **4** These are the names of the children whom he had in Jerusalem: Shammu'a, Shobab, Nathan, Solomon, **5** Ibhar, Eli'-shu-a, El'pelet, **6** Nogah, Nepheg, Japhi'a, **7** Elish'ama, Beeli'ada, and Eliph'elet.

8 When the Philistines heard that David had been anointed king over all Israel, all the Philistines went up in search of David; and David heard of it and went out against them. **9** Now the Philistines had come and made a raid in the valley of Reph'aim. **10** And David inquired of God, "Shall I go up against the Philistines? Wilt thou give them into my hand?" And the LORD said to him, "Go up, and I will give them into your hand." **11** And he went up to Ba'al-pera'zim, and David defeated them there; and David said, "God has broken through[l] my enemies by my hand, like a bursting flood." Therefore the name of that place is

---

[l] Heb *paraz*

D. PALACE AND VICTORIES (14:1-17)

14:7. Beeliada: This son of David bears a name compounded with "baal." Perhaps by inadvertence the Chronicler did not alter it to the innocuous "Eliada," found in 3:8.

8. Note the omission of the phrase found in II Sam. 5:17, which clearly points to David's early difficulties, "went down to the hold," i.e., to the cave of Adullam.

Carelessness about the forms of religious practice may indicate triviality about holy things. But equally out of place, and very frequent, is a superficial solemnity. It is a mood which derives from crude ideas of the Deity. There is a world of difference between such solemnity and true reverence. The former we can put on like a garment and plume ourselves that we are properly dressed for Sunday. The spiritual consequence of such an attitude of mind is apt to be only increased self-approval. Our need is an awareness that to God the secrets of our hearts

are open, and consequent consciousness of what truly is sacred in his sight. The famous saying in Prov. 9:10, "The fear of the LORD is the beginning of wisdom," would be better translated, "Reverence for God . . . ." Perhaps we may infer that as a result of poor Uzza's death David began to be really reverent.

14:3. *More Wives.*—David's polygamy is mentioned without censure. In II Chr. 24:3 we are told that the chief priest, Jehoiada, selected two wives for the young king Joash. This of course was consonant with the Eastern assump-

12 And when they had left their gods there, David gave a commandment, and they were burned with fire.

13 And the Philistines yet again spread themselves abroad in the valley.

14 Therefore David inquired again of God; and God said unto him, Go not up after them; turn away from them, and come upon them over against the mulberry trees.

15 And it shall be, when thou shalt hear a sound of going in the tops of the mulberry trees, *that* then thou shalt go out to battle: for God is gone forth before thee to smite the host of the Philistines.

16 David therefore did as God commanded him: and they smote the host of the Philistines from Gibeon even to Gazer.

17 And the fame of David went out into all lands; and the Lord brought the fear of him upon all nations.

15 And *David* made him houses in the city of David, and prepared a place for the ark of God, and pitched for it a tent.

called Ba'al-pera'zim.*m* 12 And they left their gods there, and David gave command, and they were burned.

13 And the Philistines yet again made a raid in the valley. 14 And when David again inquired of God, God said to him, "You shall not go up after them; go around and come upon them opposite the balsam trees. 15 And when you hear the sound of marching in the tops of the balsam trees, then go out to battle; for God has gone out before you to smite the army of the Philistines." 16 And David did as God commanded him, and they smote the Philistine army from Gibeon to Gezer. 17 And the fame of David went out into all lands, and the Lord brought the fear of him upon all nations.

15 David built houses for himself in the city of David; and he prepared a place for the ark of God, and pitched a tent

m That is *Lord of breaking through*

12. The Chronicler completely changes the (to his mind) appalling statement in II Sam. 5:21, "And the Philistines left their idols there, and David and his men carried them away."

E. The Ark in Zion (15:1–16:43)

15:1-3. According to II Sam. 6 David heard that Obed-edom was prospering; he thereupon took courage and made a second attempt to fetch the ark to Zion, and succeeded. The Chronicler transforms the tale in a way that illuminates his principles and methods. David now left nothing undone that he ought to have done (cf. vs. 12). First he made provision to shelter the ark; then by royal proclamation he declared the sole right of the Levites to transport it; finally he **assembled all Israel** to accompany its journey.

tion that increase of children of royal blood was wholly desirable. But the troubles of David's later life (suppressed by the Chronicler) supplied eloquent comment on the disadvantages of royal polygamy, and Solomon's enormously large harem shocked even the Hebrews. Very interesting therefore is the considered criticism of later days expressed in Deut. 17:17, that the king to whom Israel's obedience can be rightly given "shall not multiply wives for himself." Given time, the Jews proved themselves conspicuous in antiquity for the acceptance of monogamy, and for high ideals of marriage and home relationships. Writing about the frightful strain on Jewish family morality when Christian governments and the church enforced on the Jews residence in segregated ghettos, sometimes

setting up brothels in them to add to the ill repute, Israel Abrahams observes:

The purity of the Jewish home-life . . . was even able to resist the terrible squalor and unhealthiness which prevailed in the miserable and infamous Roman ghetto, where at one time as many as 10,000 inhabitants were herded into a space less than a square kilometre. . . . The sufferings of the Jews in that hell upon earth in the papal city were not diminished by the yearly overflowing of the Tiber, which made the Roman ghetto a dismal and plague-stricken swamp.[1]

15:1-2. *A Place for the Ark.*—It is not easy to set "the sacred" in the heart of so-called

[1] *Jewish Life in the Middle Ages* (New York: The Macmillan Co., 1896), p. 68.

2 Then David said, None ought to carry the ark of God but the Levites: for them hath the LORD chosen to carry the ark of God, and to minister unto him for ever.

3 And David gathered all Israel together to Jerusalem, to bring up the ark of the LORD unto his place, which he had prepared for it.

4 And David assembled the children of Aaron, and the Levites:

5 Of the sons of Kohath; Uriel the chief, and his brethren a hundred and twenty:

6 Of the sons of Merari; Asaiah the chief, and his brethren two hundred and twenty:

7 Of the sons of Gershom; Joel the chief, and his brethren a hundred and thirty:

8 Of the sons of Elizaphan; Shemaiah the chief, and his brethren two hundred:

9 Of the sons of Hebron; Eliel the chief, and his brethren fourscore:

10 Of the sons of Uzziel; Amminadab the chief, and his brethren a hundred and twelve.

11 And David called for Zadok and Abiathar the priests, and for the Levites, for Uriel, Asaiah, and Joel, Shemaiah, and Eliel, and Amminadab,

12 And said unto them, Ye *are* the chief of the fathers of the Levites: sanctify yourselves, *both* ye and your brethren, that ye may bring up the ark of the LORD God of Israel unto *the place that* I have prepared for it.

13 For because ye *did it* not at the first, the LORD our God made a breach upon us, for that we sought him not after the due order.

for it. 2 Then David said, "No one but the Levites may carry the ark of God, for the LORD chose them to carry the ark of the LORD and to minister to him for ever." 3 And David assembled all Israel at Jerusalem, to bring up the ark of the LORD to its place, which he had prepared for it. 4 And David gathered together the sons of Aaron and the Levites: 5 of the sons of Kohath, Uri'el the chief, with a hundred and twenty of his brethren; 6 of the sons of Merar'i, Asa'iah the chief, with two hundred and twenty of his brethren; 7 of the sons of Gershom, Jo'el the chief, with a hundred and thirty of his brethren; 8 of the sons of Eliza'phan, Shemai'ah the chief, with two hundred of his brethren; 9 of the sons of Hebron, Eli'el the chief, with eighty of his brethren; 10 of the sons of Uz'ziel, Ammin'adab the chief, with a hundred and twelve of his brethren. 11 Then David summoned the priests Zadok and Abi'athar, and the Levites Uri'el, Asa'iah, Jo'el, Shemai'ah, Eli'el, and Ammin'adab, 12 and said to them, You are the heads of the fathers' houses of the Levites; sanctify yourselves, you and your brethren, so that you may bring up the ark of the LORD, the God of Israel, to the place that I have prepared for it. 13 Because you did not carry it the first time,[n] the LORD our God broke forth upon us, because we did not care for it in the way

[n] The meaning of the Hebrew word is uncertain

2. Note that the Levites are termed ministers unto God, the standpoint of the Chronicler and Deuteronomy. Their position in the final system of the Law is that of ministers to their brethren, the priests.

4-10. From this point appear corrections by revisers trying to bring what the Chronicler wrote about the Levites into conformity with the final Law. Their touches may be seen in vs. 4 (**the sons of Aaron and**; Welch [*op. cit.*, p. 65 n.] points out that LXX[B] has the peculiar reading "the sons of Aaron, the Levites," which may imply that here the original text in Chronicles was "the priests, the Levites"); in vs. 11 (**for Zadok and Abiathar the priests, and**); in vs. 14 (**the priests and**); and probably vs. 15 (as **Moses . . . LORD**). The Levites number 872 men, to whose six leaders (mentioned by name, and in vs. 12 called **the heads of . . . the Levites**) the king's injunction is

"secular life." On his second attempt David succeeded because he had the grace to learn from a failure. He now took thought how rightly to make preparation for the ark's arrival at Zion, and accordingly entrusted its transport to

the proper men for the duty—not laymen but **Levites** (see Exeg.). Our modern mistake is seen in the popular opinion that the maintenance and strengthening of religious belief and practice is the affair of the clergy. Rather it is

14 So the priests and the Levites sanctified themselves to bring up the ark of the LORD God of Israel.

15 And the children of the Levites bare the ark of God upon their shoulders with the staves thereon, as Moses commanded, according to the word of the LORD.

16 And David spake to the chief of the Levites to appoint their brethren *to be the* singers with instruments of music, psalteries and harps and cymbals, sounding, by lifting up the voice with joy.

17 So the Levites appointed Heman the son of Joel; and of his brethren, Asaph the son of Berechiah; and of the sons of Merari their brethren, Ethan the son of Kushaiah;

18 And with them their brethren of the second *degree,* Zechariah, Ben, and Jaaziel, and Shemiramoth, and Jehiel, and Unni, Eliab, and Benaiah, and Maaseiah, and Mattithiah, and Elipheleh, and Mikneiah, and Obed-edom, and Jeiel, the porters.

19 So the singers, Heman, Asaph, and Ethan, *were appointed* to sound with cymbals of brass;

20 And Zechariah, and Aziel, and Shemiramoth, and Jehiel, and Unni, and Eliab, and Maaseiah, and Benaiah, with psalteries on Alamoth;

21 And Mattithiah, and Elipheleh and Mikneiah, and Obed-edom, and Jeiel, and Azaziah, with harps on the Sheminith to excel.

22 And Chenaniah, chief of the Levites, *was* for song: he instructed about the song, because he *was* skilful.

23 And Berechiah and Elkanah *were* doorkeepers for the ark.

that is ordained. 14 So the priests and the Levites sanctified themselves to bring up the ark of the LORD, the God of Israel. 15 And the Levites carried the ark of God upon their shoulders with the poles, as Moses had commanded according to the word of the LORD.

16 David also commanded the chiefs of the Levites to appoint their brethren as the singers who should play loudly on musical instruments, on harps and lyres and cymbals, to raise sounds of joy. 17 So the Levites appointed Heman the son of Jo'el; and of his brethren Asaph the son of Berechi'ah; and of the sons of Merar'i, their brethren, Ethan the son of Kusha'iah; 18 and with them their brethren of the second order, Zechari'ah, Ja-a'ziel, Shemir'amoth, Jehi'el, Unni, Eli'ab, Benai'ah, Ma-ase'iah, Mattithi'ah, Eliph'elehu, and Mikne'iah, and the gatekeepers O'bed-e'dom and Je-i'el. 19 The singers, Heman, Asaph, and Ethan, were to sound bronze cymbals; 20 Zechari'ah, A'zi-el, Shemir'amoth, Jehi'el, Unni, Eli'ab, Ma-ase'iah, and Benai'ah were to play harps according to Al'amoth; 21 but Mattithi'ah, Eliph'elehu, Mikne'iah, O'bed-e'dom, Je-i'el, and Azazi'ah were to lead with lyres according to the Shem'inith. 22 Chenani'ah, leader of the Levites in music, should direct the music, for he understood it. 23 Berechi'ah and Elka'nah

---

addressed, not to Zadok and Abiathar. Zadok was a leading priest at the end of David's reign, but at this time was describable as "a young man mighty in valor" (12:28) .

15. The Priestly Code passages in Numbers do not mention the ark in relation to the transportation of the tabernacle. Num. 4:15 specifically forbids mere Levites to handle the sacred things in the tabernacle until priests had wrapped them up.

17-24. Revisional contributions are present, and in more than one layer. Observe the tangled references to **Obed-edom** and **Jeiel**—now as doorkeepers in vss. 18 and 24 (where **Jehiah=Jeiel**), now as harpists in vs. 21. Perhaps their postexilic descendants rose in status from doorkeepers to musicians.

---

an enterprise that should be regarded by all good men as their bounden duty.

16. *A Joyful Noise.*—Full thought was taken to ensure that the music was worthy of the occasion; and David was fortunate in the choirmaster who directed the music, "for he understood it" (vs. 22) . From many references to temple music and psalmody one gathers that the popular estimate was the more noise the better. Over the choir stalls in a village church in Britain's Cornwall is inscribed this motto: *Amor, non clamor, ascendit in aures Dei;* wise words

24 And Shebaniah, and Jehoshaphat, and Nethaneel, and Amasai, and Zechariah, and Benaiah, and Eliezer, the priests, did blow with the trumpets before the ark of God: and Obed-edom and Jehiah *were* doorkeepers for the ark.

25 ¶ So David, and the elders of Israel, and the captains over thousands, went to bring up the ark of the covenant of the LORD out of the house of Obed-edom with joy.

26 And it came to pass, when God helped the Levites that bare the ark of the covenant of the LORD, that they offered seven bullocks and seven rams.

27 And David *was* clothed with a robe of fine linen, and all the Levites that bare the ark, and the singers, and Chenaniah the master of the song with the singers: David also *had* upon him an ephod of linen.

28 Thus all Israel brought up the ark of the covenant of the LORD with shouting, and with sound of the cornet, and with trumpets, and with cymbals, making a noise with psalteries and harps.

29 ¶ And it came to pass, *as* the ark of the covenant of the LORD came to the city of David, that Michal the daughter of Saul looking out at a window saw king David dancing and playing: and she despised him in her heart.

16 So they brought the ark of God, and set it in the midst of the tent that David had pitched for it: and they offered burnt sacrifices and peace offerings before God.

were to be gatekeepers for the ark. **24** Shebani'ah, Josh'aphat, Nethan'el, Ama'sai, Zechari'ah, Benai'ah, and Elie'zer, the priests, should blow the trumpets before the ark of God. O'bed-e'dom and Jehi'ah also were to be gatekeepers for the ark.

25 So David and the elders of Israel, and the commanders of thousands, went to bring up the ark of the covenant of the LORD from the house of O'bed-e'dom with rejoicing. **26** And because God helped the Levites who were carrying the ark of the covenant of the LORD, they sacrificed seven bulls and seven rams. **27** David was clothed with a robe of fine linen, as also were all the Levites who were carrying the ark, and the singers, and Chenani'ah the leader of the music of the singers; and David wore a linen ephod. **28** So all Israel brought up the ark of the covenant of the LORD with shouting, to the sound of the horn, trumpets, and cymbals, and made loud music on harps and lyres.

29 And as the ark of the covenant of the LORD came to the city of David, Michal the daughter of Saul looked out of the window, and saw King David dancing and making merry; and she despised him in her heart.

16 And they brought in the ark of God, and set it inside the tent which David had pitched for it; and they offered burnt offerings and peace offerings before God.

---

25. The Chronicler's straightforward narrative continues without later corrections from this point to 16:3.

26. They sacrificed: By plain inference the Levites did so. It seems the revisers let the vague phrase pass, feeling that their previous insertions mentioning the presence of priests safeguarded readers.

27. Of the song: The Hebrew means, lit., "of the lifting up," i.e., the carrying of the ark. Someone misunderstood it as "lifting up the voice" and added **with the singers.**

16:1. At Zion in the tent which he had prepared David placed the ark. Later the Chronicler tells how devotedly David longed to build a temple worthy of its permanent reception. At the moment the king could do one thing more, and did it: order Levites to maintain rites of worship there before the ark.

---

for choir and congregation alike. "Love, not loudness, riseth to the ears of God."

27-29. *Enthusiasm and Disdain.*—What could be more vivid, and assuredly historical, than the record of Queen Michal looking down on the procession and despising David because on this day of religious ardor he could deem it fitting to behave as if he were on an equality with the people and the priests? How incredibly imprudent, as well as undignified! He had even

2 And when David had made an end of offering the burnt offerings and the peace offerings, he blessed the people in the name of the LORD.

3 And he dealt to every one of Israel, both man and woman, to every one a loaf of bread, and a good piece of flesh, and a flagon *of wine.*

4 ¶ And he appointed *certain* of the Levites to minister before the ark of the LORD, and to record, and to thank and praise the LORD God of Israel:

5 Asaph the chief, and next to him Zechariah, Jeiel, and Shemiramoth, and Jehiel, and Mattithiah, and Eliab, and Benaiah, and Obed-edom: and Jeiel with psalteries and with harps; but Asaph made a sound with cymbals;

2 And when David had finished offering the burnt offerings and the peace offerings, he blessed the people in the name of the LORD, 3 and distributed to all Israel, both men and women, to each a loaf of bread, a portion of meat,° and a cake of raisins.

4 Moreover he appointed certain of the Levites as ministers before the ark of the LORD, to invoke, to thank, and to praise the LORD, the God of Israel. 5 Asaph was the chief, and second to him were Zechari'ah, Je-i'el, Shemi'ramoth, Jehi'el, Mattithi'ah, Eli'ab, Benai'ah, O'bed-e'dom, and Je-i'el, who were to play harps and lyres; Asaph

° Compare Gk Syr Vg: Heb uncertain

---

4. The revisers did not insert here a correction to the effect that David appointed *priests* to minister (i.e., to offer sacrifice) while the Levites were merely to praise. Probably they inferred that **to invoke, to thank, and to praise** had reference only to musical worship conducted by Levites. But, in fact, **to invoke** (an obscure word) does seem to mean or to cover the function of sacrificing, and the phrase **as ministers** must have implied in the Chronicler's view sacrificial offerings. The revisers, in order to ensure their view of things, ought to have omitted from the text the **and** before **to thank** (see KJV).

5a. Obed-edom and **Jeiel** would seem to have given satisfaction as harpists (15:21).

5b-6. Asaph ... of God: In the final Law, sounding the sacred trumpets was priestly prerogative. These are revisers' words, harmonizing with the previous revisionary insertion (vss. 19-21).

---

put off his regal attire. He was dancing and rejoicing like one of the mob. How barbaric! She, sophisticated daughter of royalty, scorned both him and them.

Religious enthusiasm stands in need of restraint as we well know. But icy disdain for its manifestations has far worse consequences in human life. Michal, at any rate, was wrong; she had no vestige of insight to see that before God all men are equal, and that David was going to establish in Israel a constitutional monarchy, a concept of kingship incomparably finer than the world had ever known.

16:2. *Blessing and Power.*—The king, as the anointed of the Lord, was the mediator of the divine blessing to his people. When kings were no more, the Jewish law entrusted to the priests alone the prerogative of pronouncing a blessing in the rites of worship. The Hebrews counted interchange of blessing—from God to man, from man to God, from individual to individual—to be a realistic necessity. Thus in 29:10, 20 it is related that David, having blessed the congregation in the name of the

Lord, commanded that those who had thus received into their souls the divine strengthening, should in turn "bless the LORD," rendering to God the responsive strength of their human wills. One cannot comprehend this matter clearly without understanding the Hebrew psychological standpoint. So Johannes Pedersen:

> The soul is a whole saturated with power. . . . This vital power, without which no living being can exist, is called by the Israelites bᵉrākhā, blessing. . . . Behind the blessing of the individual stand the fathers; from them he has derived it, and its strength depends on their powers. . . . The blessing connects the souls, and so it must be, because it consists in a communication of the contents of the soul. . . . Great assemblies, cultic or non-cultic, must necessarily conclude with a blessing, so that every one may take away with him the strength of the community.[2]

With due regard for modern psychology, there is wisdom in those beliefs. The man or woman who has not at some time longed for and re-

[2] *Israel, Its Life and Culture, I-II* (London: Oxford University Press, 1926), pp. 182, 194, 200, 203.

6 Benaiah also and Jahaziel the priests with trumpets continually before the ark of the covenant of God.

7 ¶ Then on that day David delivered first *this psalm* to thank the LORD into the hand of Asaph and his brethren.

8 Give thanks unto the LORD, call upon his name, make known his deeds among the people.

9 Sing unto him, sing psalms unto him, talk ye of all his wondrous works.

10 Glory ye in his holy name: let the heart of them rejoice that seek the LORD.

11 Seek the LORD and his strength, seek his face continually.

12 Remember his marvelous works that he hath done, his wonders, and the judgments of his mouth;

13 O ye seed of Israel his servant, ye children of Jacob, his chosen ones.

14 He *is* the LORD our God; his judgments *are* in all the earth.

15 Be ye mindful always of his covenant; the word *which* he commanded to a thousand generations;

16 *Even of the covenant* which he made with Abraham, and of his oath unto Isaac;

17 And hath confirmed the same to Jacob for a law, *and* to Israel *for* an everlasting covenant,

18 Saying, Unto thee will I give the land of Canaan, the lot of your inheritance;

19 When ye were but few, even a few, and strangers in it.

20 And *when* they went from nation to nation, and from *one* kingdom to another people;

8 O give thanks to the LORD, call on his name,
    make known his deeds among the peoples!

9 Sing to him, sing praises to him,
    tell of all his wonderful works!

10 Glory in his holy name;
    let the hearts of those who seek the LORD rejoice!

11 Seek the LORD and his strength,
    seek his presence continually!

12 Remember the wonderful works that he has done,
    the wonders he wrought, the judgments he uttered,

13 O offspring of Abraham his servant,
    sons of Jacob, his chosen ones!

14 He is the LORD our God;
    his judgments are in all the earth.

15 He is mindful of his covenant for ever,
    of the word that he commanded, for a thousand generations,

16 the covenant which he made with Abraham,
    his sworn promise to Isaac,

17 which he confirmed as a statute to Jacob,
    as an everlasting covenant to Israel,

18 saying, "To you I will give the land of Canaan,
    as your portion for an inheritance."

19 When they were few in number,
    and of little account, and sojourners in it,

20 wandering from nation to nation,
    from one kingdom to another people,

7-36. A compilation—drawn from Pss. 105:1-15; 96:1b-13a; 106:1, 47-48—surely not made by the Chronicler (observe that vs. 37 connects smoothly with vs. 6), but by someone who deemed these words would have been appropriate to sing. The compiler

---

ceived the blessing of another has missed one of life's most precious experiences. How much more precious whenever we are able to receive into our soul the strength of the blessing of God!

7-36. *The King's Thanksgiving.*—These verses are quotations drawn together from three of the canonical psalms. It is unlikely (see Exeg.) that they formed part of the Chronicler's original

21 He suffered no man to do them wrong: yea, he reproved kings for their sakes,

22 *Saying,* Touch not mine anointed, and do my prophets no harm.

23 Sing unto the Lord, all the earth; show forth from day to day his salvation.

24 Declare his glory among the heathen; his marvelous works among all nations.

25 For great *is* the Lord, and greatly to be praised: he also *is* to be feared above all gods.

26 For all the gods of the people *are* idols: but the Lord made the heavens.

27 Glory and honor *are* in his presence; strength and gladness *are* in his place.

28 Give unto the Lord, ye kindreds of the people, give unto the Lord glory and strength.

29 Give unto the Lord the glory *due* unto his name: bring an offering, and come before him: worship the Lord in the beauty of holiness.

30 Fear before him, all the earth: the world also shall be stable, that it be not moved.

31 Let the heavens be glad, and let the earth rejoice: and let *men* say among the nations, The Lord reigneth.

32 Let the sea roar, and the fulness thereof: let the fields rejoice, and all that *is* therein.

33 Then shall the trees of the wood sing out at the presence of the Lord, because he cometh to judge the earth.

34 O give thanks unto the Lord; for *he is* good; for his mercy *endureth* for ever.

35 And say ye, Save us, O God of our salvation, and gather us together, and deliver us from the heathen, that we may give thanks to thy holy name, *and* glory in thy praise.

---

21 he allowed no one to oppress them;
　　he rebuked kings on their account,
22 saying, "Touch not my anointed ones,
　　do my prophets no harm!"

23 Sing to the Lord, all the earth!
　　Tell of his salvation from day to day.
24 Declare his glory among the nations,
　　his marvelous works among all the peoples!
25 For great is the Lord, and greatly to be praised,
　　and he is to be held in awe above all gods.
26 For all the gods of the peoples are idols;
　　but the Lord made the heavens.
27 Honor and majesty are before him;
　　strength and joy are in his place.

28 Ascribe to the Lord, O families of the peoples,
　　ascribe to the Lord glory and strength!
29 Ascribe to the Lord the glory due his name;
　　bring an offering, and come before him!
　Worship the Lord in holy array;
30 　tremble before him, all the earth;
　　yea, the world stands firm, never to be moved.
31 Let the heavens be glad, and let the earth rejoice,
　　and let them say among the nations, "The Lord reigns!"
32 Let the sea roar, and all that fills it,
　　let the field exult, and everything in it!
33 Then shall the trees of the wood sing for joy
　　before the Lord, for he comes to judge the earth.
34 O give thanks to the Lord, for he is good;
　　for his steadfast love endures for ever!

35 Say also:
　"Deliver us, O God of our salvation,
　　and gather and save us from among the nations,
　　that we may give thanks to thy holy name,
　　and glory in thy praise.

---

must have lived later than the time (about 200 B.C.) when the Psalter had been divided into five books, for Ps. 106:48 (= vs. 36) is no part of that psalm itself, but a doxology rounding off the fourth book of the Psalms.

36 Blessed *be* the Lord God of Israel for ever and ever. And all the people said, Amen, and praised the Lord.

37 ¶ So he left there before the ark of the covenant of the Lord Asaph and his brethren, to minister before the ark continually, as every day's work required:

38 And Obed-edom with their brethren, threescore and eight; Obed-edom also the son of Jeduthun and Hosah *to be* porters:

39 And Zadok the priest, and his brethren the priests, before the tabernacle of the Lord in the high place that *was* at Gibeon,

40 To offer burnt offerings unto the Lord upon the altar of the burnt offering continually morning and evening, and *to do* according to all that is written in the law of the Lord, which he commanded Israel;

36 Blessed be the Lord, the God of Israel,
    from everlasting to everlasting!"
Then all the people said "Amen!" and praised the Lord.

37 So David left Asaph and his brethren there before the ark of the covenant of the Lord to minister continually before the ark as each day required, 38 and also O'bed-e'dom and his*p* sixty-eight brethren; while O'bed-e'dom, the son of Jedu'thun, and Hosah were to be gatekeepers. 39 And he left Zadok the priest and his brethren the priests before the tabernacle of the Lord in the high place that was at Gibeon, 40 to offer burnt offerings to the Lord upon the altar of burnt offering continually morning and evening, according to all that is written in the law of the Lord which he com-

p Heb *their*

37-43. A key passage as to the present structure of Chronicles. The men who knew the final Law read with growing concern the Chronicler's glowing account of David's transference of the ark and provision of Levites to guard and honor it—duties which, they assumed, must not include offering sacrifices but merely safe custody of the ark and maintenance of musical worship. Accordingly, the Chronicler's words about the Levites' responsibilities were, to say the least, lamentably vague or ambiguous: Why did he not clearly distinguish between priests acting in their appropriate functions and Levites in theirs? And why did he not indicate that David had been punctilious to see that legitimate sacrifices were being offered by qualified priests? In seeking answer the revisers were confronted by a prior perplexity, for on their view of the Mosaic age the tabernacle—containing the ark and sacred vessels, and served by legitimate priests ("sons of Aaron") and by Levites in their respective duties—had journeyed with the tribes in the wilderness. The revisers asked themselves: "When the Hebrews had entered Canaan, what had happened to the sacred tabernacle? Where was it stationed?" Now I Kings 3:4 tells that after Solomon had gained mastery of the throne he went to offer abundant sacrifices at the altar of "the great high place" at Gibeon (six miles northwest of Jerusalem). Some brilliant student of the Chronicler's writing saw in that statement about Solomon a solution of the prior enigma: the ancient, Mosaic tabernacle (he inferred and probably did not in the least realize how historically impossible his notion was) had been placed at Gibeon, and on the altar there Aaronite priests—duly assisted by subordinate musical Levites—were offering legitimate sacrifices. Let that conception be inserted into the text of Chronicles where occasion required, and all would be well: the book would become salutary reading for the pious. Vss. 39-40 are the first instance of these crucial corrections concerning the tabernacle.

38. The middle clause, **Obed-edom . . . Jeduthun,** is probably a gloss, for elsewhere Obed-edom is classed as a singer; **and Hosah** should follow **Obed-edom** at the start of the verse; the required second name is then provided.

---

work. Someone later felt, not unjustly, that at this moment David ought to have raised his musical voice in thanksgiving. The composer chose well. He knew the books of psalms thoroughly, and that is a capacity worth acquiring. R. E. Prothero did a good service when he

compiled from the long centuries of Christian experience records of the use made of the psalms by men and women on great occasions and at solemn moments in their lives.[3] Unfailingly the

[3] *The Psalms in Human Life* (new and enlarged ed.; New York: E. P. Dutton & Co., 1914).

41 And with them Heman and Jeduthun, and the rest that were chosen, who were expressed by name, to give thanks to the LORD, because his mercy *endureth* for ever;

42 And with them Heman and Jeduthun with trumpets and cymbals for those that should make a sound, and with musical instruments of God. And the sons of Jeduthun *were* porters.

43 And all the people departed every man to his house: and David returned to bless his house.

17 Now it came to pass, as David sat in his house, that David said to Nathan the prophet, Lo, I dwell in a house of cedars, but the ark of the covenant of the LORD *remaineth* under curtains.

---

manded Israel. 41 With them were Heman and Jedu'thun, and the rest of those chosen and expressly named to give thanks to the LORD, for his steadfast love endures for ever. 42 Heman and Jedu'thun had trumpets and cymbals for the music and instruments for sacred song. The sons of Jedu'thun were appointed to the gate.

43 Then all the people departed each to his house, and David went home to bless his household.

17 Now when David dwelt in his house, David said to Nathan the prophet, "Behold, I dwell in a house of cedar, but the ark of the covenant of the LORD is under

---

41-42. The muddled reiteration in these verses suggests that late marginal comments were mistakenly brought into the text.

43. This verse contains the Chronicler's own dignified conclusion for the story of the ark's installation at Jerusalem.

F. DAVID'S DESIRE TO BUILD A TEMPLE (17:1-27)

How could conscientious David be content to live in a palace while the ark was sheltered only by the curtains of a tent? His power and resources increased. Surely he must have longed to build a worthy temple. Why did he never do so? The Chronicler found in II Sam. 7 a satisfying answer to that question, and he therefore copied its narrative almost word for word.

17:1. David said to Nathan the prophet: It was wholly congenial to the Chronicler to read that David had consulted a prophet about his desire. In his subsequent account

---

Psalter affords words that not only meet daily needs but also sustain in the testing hour. Heine said that in it is collected "sunrise and sunset, birth and death, promise and fulfillment, the whole drama of humanity."

41. *The Everlasting Mercy.*—(Cf. Pss. 106:1; 107:1.) No wonder that the Jews wove these words like a refrain throughout the texture of their liturgy, that John Masefield found in them the title for a great poem, and that in their certitude countless men and women have been strengthened to feel that their being is within the knowledge and goodness of God. **Mercy,** so we are accustomed to translate the Hebrew word. But our language has no one word adequate to render its rich meanings in Hebrew usage. As between man and man, it denoted relations of integrity and kindness; as between God and men, such **steadfast love,** such unmerited goodness, as can emanate only from the changelessness of divine grace.

43. *Religion in the Home.*—The words of this verse prompt reflection on the fact that Judaism h..s far excelled Christian practice in the skill and fullness whereby religious worship was in-

tegrated into the lives of its people in their homes, and not predominantly concentrated on the services in the synagogues. In the Christian system the impressions made by worship have been, or have become, far too much dependent on what happens in church on Sundays. No one can be other than deeply moved and delighted by the values of religious ritual in the home, if he has ever had the privilege to be present with a Jewish household when father and mother and children alike participate happily and reverently in picturesque and solemn observance of the Passover. For practicing Jews and Christians one day in seven is sacred. But what a contrast between the gloomy, restricted solemnity which that recognition used to take in Puritan circles and the wisdom of Judaism which planned to keep the sabbath holy "by making it a day of delight, cheerfulness, gladness and joy; and many of the regulations . . . such as the lights, the special meals and table-songs, are designed to diffuse this spirit of joy in the Jewish home." [4]

[4] Isidore Epstein, *The Jewish Way of Life* (London: E. Goldston, 1946), p. 181; also pp. 196-209.

2 Then Nathan said unto David, Do all that *is* in thine heart; for God *is* with thee.

3 ¶ And it came to pass the same night, that the word of God came to Nathan, saying,

4 Go and tell David my servant, Thus saith the LORD, Thou shalt not build me a house to dwell in:

5 For I have not dwelt in a house since the day that I brought up Israel unto this day; but have gone from tent to tent, and from *one* tabernacle *to another*.

6 Wheresoever I have walked with all Israel, spake I a word to any of the judges of Israel, whom I commanded to feed my people, saying, Why have ye not built me a house of cedars?

7 Now therefore thus shalt thou say unto my servant David, Thus saith the LORD of hosts, I took thee from the sheepcote, *even* from following the sheep, that thou shouldest be ruler over my people Israel:

8 And I have been with thee whithersoever thou hast walked, and have cut off all thine enemies from before thee, and have made thee a name like the name of the great men that *are* in the earth.

a tent." 2 And Nathan said to David, "Do all that is in your heart, for God is with you."

3 But that same night the word of the LORD came to Nathan, 4 "Go and tell my servant David, 'Thus says the LORD: You shall not build me a house to dwell in. 5 For I have not dwelt in a house since the day I led up Israel to this day, but I have gone from tent to tent and from dwelling to dwelling. 6 In all places where I have moved with all Israel, did I speak a word with any of the judges of Israel, whom I commanded to shepherd my people, saying, "Why have you not built me a house of cedar?" ' 7 Now therefore thus shall you say to my servant David, 'Thus says the LORD of hosts, I took you from the pasture, from following the sheep, that you should be prince over my people Israel; 8 and I have been with you wherever you went, and have cut off all your enemies from before you; and I will make for you a name, like the name of the

of the kings of Judah the Chronicler produced a sequence of otherwise unmentioned prophets who spoke to the monarchs in God's name.

5a. I have not dwelt in a house since the day: Yet I Sam. 3:3 contains memorable record of the ark's having been in the temple of Shiloh, which the Philistines destroyed. Did the writer in II Sam. 7:6 by ignoring that fact wish to suggest—the Chronicler would concur—that no temple other than that in Jerusalem ought ever to have been built?

5b. The Hebrew reads, lit., "but have walked from tent to tent, and in a tabernacle." The concluding words in the phrase make havoc of its sense and quite clearly reveal the revisers' insistence that the Mosaic tabernacle had continued in existence.

6. The judges is the correct text (see II Sam. 7:7 KJV, "the tribes"; but cf. RSV).

17:2-4. *Second Thoughts.*—These verses are of great interest concerning a psychological difference between the many in Hebrew history whom we may rightly call false prophets and the few who, being also gifted with psychic sensitiveness, spoke truth and right as the word of God (cf. Expos. on II Chr. 18:21). Nathan one day in the name of God bids David to build the temple; twenty-four hours later, again claiming divine authority, he commands David not to build. Here is a man positive that he had divine inspiration yet capable of having "second thoughts." What is the reason? Answer should surely be that Nathan was a completely sincere personality, not cocksure about his own inerrancy, not swollen with conceit. God can teach

such men. A remarkable parallel is found in Jeremiah's attitude of mind.

4-11. *The Unfinished Symphony.*—David must understand that he has begun a task so great that it cannot be completed in the span of mortal life. Wonderful as are the achievements he accomplishes, the end is beyond his reaching. Rabbi Tarphon said:

The day is short, and the task is great. . . . It is not for thee to finish the work, nor art thou free to desist therefrom; . . . faithful is the Master of thy work, who will pay thee the reward of thy work, and know that the recompence of the reward of the righteous is for the time to come.[5]

[5] Charles Taylor, *Sayings of the Jewish Fathers* (Cambridge: Cambridge University Press, 1897), pp. 40-41.

9 Also I will ordain a place for my people Israel, and will plant them, and they shall dwell in their place, and shall be moved no more; neither shall the children of wickedness waste them any more, as at the beginning,

10 And since the time that I commanded judges *to be* over my people Israel. Moreover I will subdue all thine enemies. Furthermore I tell thee, that the LORD will build thee a house.

11 ¶ And it shall come to pass, when thy days be expired that thou must go *to be* with thy fathers, that I will raise up thy seed after thee, which shall be of thy sons; and I will establish his kingdom.

12 He shall build me a house, and I will stablish his throne for ever.

13 I will be his father, and he shall be my son: and I will not take my mercy away from him, as I took *it* from *him* that was before thee:

14 But I will settle him in mine house and in my kingdom for ever: and his throne shall be established for evermore.

15 According to all these words, and according to all this vision, so did Nathan speak unto David.

great ones of the earth. 9 And I will appoint a place for my people Israel, and will plant them, that they may dwell in their own place, and be disturbed no more; and violent men shall waste them no more, as formerly, 10 from the time that I appointed judges over my people Israel; and I will subdue all your enemies. Moreover I declare to you that the LORD will build you a house. 11 When your days are fulfilled to go to be with your fathers, I will raise up your offspring after you, one of your own sons, and I will establish his kingdom. 12 He shall build a house for me, and I will establish his throne for ever. 13 I will be his father, and he shall be my son; I will not take my steadfast love from him, as I took it from him who was before you, 14 but I will confirm him in my house and in my kingdom for ever and his throne shall be established for ever.' " 15 In accordance with all these words, and in accordance with all this vision, Nathan spoke to David.

Let no man think that sudden in a minute
　All is accomplished and the work is done;—
Though with thine earliest dawn thou shouldst
　　begin it
　Scarce were it ended in thy setting sun.[6]

13. The Relationship of God to Man.—Personality is the highest category we can conceive, and if we use it concerning God we must employ the terms of human personal relationships and qualities: **I will be his father, and he shall be my son.** In the context of high religious reflection such usage ought not in the least to be regarded as anthropomorphic thinking. To suppose so is stupid. In Hebraism and Judaism the thought that God deals with men as an ideally perfect father with his children was historically fundamental, being inherent even in the nomadic religious and social ideas before the entry into Canaan. It was gravely threatened by the master-slave (or servant) and king-subject ideas to which the Canaanites were accustomed. But the fatherly conception proved radical for the Hebrews, and was sublimely apprehended by the great prophets (cf. Hos. 11:1-4). Isaiah said, "Mine eyes have seen the King, the LORD

of hosts" (6:5); but his whole treatment of the grace of God and the wickedness of the people was inspired and controlled by the father-son relationship (cf. Isa. 1:2). The history of Christian theology has exhibited no end of confusion about this vital matter, to the huge detriment of all concerned, frequently insisting upon interpretations that are consonant only with the authority of kings and the legalism of judges. But the doctrine of the divine fatherhood ought never to have been obscured by other ideas. It was dominant in the mind of Christ and pervaded his teaching ("My father, and your father," John 20:17; see also Matt. 5:45, Luke 15:11-32).

14. The Chief Owner.—In my house and in my kingdom, i.e., in God's house, God's kingdom. The Chronicler altered the text in II Sam. 7:16 where it reads "thine house" and "thy kingdom," meaning David's. This deliberate change indicates the difference between the religious and irreligious view of life's possessions. The godless man says to himself, "This is my house and I will do what I please with it." Jeremiah said to his friend, Baruch, that even our individual life is not our own, but is a trust from God wherewith we may be faithful

[6] Frederic W. H. Myers, *Saint Paul*, st. xv.

16 ¶ And David the king came and sat before the LORD, and said, Who *am* I, O LORD God, and what *is* mine house, that thou hast brought me hitherto?

17 And *yet* this was a small thing in thine eyes, O God; for thou hast *also* spoken of thy servant's house for a great while to come, and hast regarded me according to the estate of a man of high degree, O LORD God.

18 What can David *speak* more to thee for the honor of thy servant? for thou knowest thy servant.

19 O LORD, for thy servant's sake, and according to thine own heart, hast thou done all this greatness, in making known all *these* great things.

20 O LORD, *there is* none like thee, neither *is there any* God besides thee, according to all that we have heard with our ears.

21 And what one nation in the earth *is* like thy people Israel, whom God went to redeem *to be* his own people, to make thee a name of greatness and terribleness, by driving out nations from before thy people, whom thou hast redeemed out of Egypt?

22 For thy people Israel didst thou make thine own people for ever; and thou, LORD, becamest their God.

23 Therefore now, LORD, let the thing that thou hast spoken concerning thy servant and concerning his house be established for ever, and do as thou hast said.

24 Let it even be established, that thy name may be magnified for ever, saying, The LORD of hosts *is* the God of Israel, *even* a God to Israel: and *let* the house of David thy servant *be* established before thee.

25 For thou, O my God, hast told thy servant that thou wilt build him a house: therefore thy servant hath found *in his heart* to pray before thee.

16 Then King David went in and sat
before the LORD, and said, "Who am I,
O LORD God, and what is my house, that
thou hast brought me thus far? 17 And this
was a small thing in thy eyes, O God; thou
hast also spoken of thy servant's house for
a great while to come, and hast shown me
future generations,[q] O LORD God! 18 And
what more can David say to thee for honoring thy servant? For thou knowest thy servant.
19 For thy servant's sake, O LORD, and
according to thy own heart, thou hast
wrought all this greatness, in making known
all these great things. 20 There is none like
thee, O LORD, and there is no God besides
thee, according to all that we have heard
with our ears. 21 What other[r] nation on
earth is like thy people Israel, whom God
went to redeem to be his people, making
for thyself a name for great and terrible
things, in driving out nations before thy
people whom thou didst redeem from
Egypt? 22 And thou didst make thy people
Israel to be thy people for ever; and thou,
O LORD, didst become their God. 23 And
now, O LORD, let the word which thou hast
spoken concerning thy servant and concerning his house be established for ever, and do
as thou hast spoken; 24 and thy name will
be established and magnified for ever, saying, 'The LORD of hosts, the God of Israel,
is Israel's God,' and the house of thy servant
David will be established before thee. 25 For
thou, my God, hast revealed to thy servant
that thou wilt build a house for him; therefore thy servant has found courage to pray

[q] Cn: Heb uncertain
[r] Gk Vg: Heb *one*

to do his will (Jer. 45:5). "The earth is the LORD's, and the fulness thereof," sang the psalmist (24:1), and the final Jewish law magnificently translated the poetry into conscience-searching prose by declaring that the soil belongs to God, and men must cultivate it as his tenants, not in order that the prosperous may build still bigger barns for their own benefit, but in order that there may be plenty for all: other men are our brethren, for each of whom God cares equally. This view has never been popular. Has that anything to do with the fact that despite mankind's unique capacity to make nature productive, dearth and destruction have not been eliminated?

16-27. ***The Doing of God.***—Whoever reads this moving passage will, if he can at all discern reasons for thankfulness in the course of his own life, find in its verses words that speak to his particular experience. Above all, he may so feel about David's saying **Who am I, O LORD God, . . . that thou hast brought me thus far?**

26 And now, LORD, thou art God, and hast promised this goodness unto thy servant:

27 Now therefore let it please thee to bless the house of thy servant, that it may be before thee for ever: for thou blessest, O LORD, and *it shall be* blessed for ever.

18 Now after this it came to pass, that David smote the Philistines, and subdued them, and took Gath and her towns out of the hand of the Philistines.

2 And he smote Moab; and the Moabites became David's servants, *and* brought gifts.

3 ¶ And David smote Hadarezer king of Zobah unto Hamath, as he went to stablish his dominion by the river Euphrates.

4 And David took from him a thousand chariots, and seven thousand horsemen, and twenty thousand footmen: David also houghed all the chariot *horses,* but reserved of them a hundred chariots.

5 And when the Syrians of Damascus came to help Hadarezer king of Zobah, David slew of the Syrians two and twenty thousand men.

6 Then David put *garrisons* in Syria-damascus; and the Syrians became David's servants, *and* brought gifts. Thus the LORD preserved David whithersoever he went.

7 And David took the shields of gold that were on the servants of Hadarezer, and brought them to Jerusalem.

8 Likewise from Tibhath, and from Chun, cities of Hadarezer, brought David very much brass, wherewith Solomon made the brazen sea, and the pillars, and the vessels of brass.

before thee. **26** And now, O LORD, thou art God, and thou hast promised this good thing to thy servant; **27** now therefore may it please thee to bless the house of thy servant, that it may continue for ever before thee; for what thou, O LORD, hast blessed is blessed for ever."

18 After this David defeated the Philistines and subdued them, and he took Gath and its villages out of the hand of the Philistines.

2 And he defeated Moab, and the Mo'abites became servants to David and brought tribute.

3 David also defeated Hadade'zer king of Zobah, toward Hamath, as he went to set up his monument[s] at the river Eu-phra'tes. **4** And David took from him a thousand chariots, seven thousand horsemen, and twenty thousand foot soldiers; and David hamstrung all the chariot horses, but left enough for a hundred chariots. **5** And when the Syrians of Damascus came to help Hadade'zer king of Zobah, David slew twenty-two thousand men of the Syrians. **6** Then David put garrisons[t] in Syria of Damascus; and the Syrians became servants to David, and brought tribute. And the LORD gave victory to David wherever he went. **7** And David took the shields of gold which were carried by the servants of Hadade'zer, and brought them to Jerusalem. **8** And from Tibhath and from Cun, cities of Hadade'-zer, David took very much bronze; with it Solomon made the bronze sea and the pillars and the vessels of bronze.

[s] Heb *hand*
[t] Gk Vg 2 Sam 8. 6 Compare Syr: Heb lacks *garrisons*

G. DAVID'S VICTORIES (18:1–20:8)

In Samuel, David's wars are said to precede Nathan's answer that he must not attempt to build a temple. The Chronicler shows an idealized David, having humbly accepted the divine answer from the lips of the prophet, then proceeding to wage wars: after the kingdom became strengthened and protected, resources could be acquired wherewith to provide preparations for the future temple.

18:1-13. David defeats and despoils Philistines, Moabites, Syrians, Edomites.

(vs. 16) . The similar words of Moses, facing the commencement of his duty, may be recalled: "Who am I, . . . that I should bring forth the children of Israel out of Egypt?" (Exod. 3:11) . In that spirit men should begin, continue, and end their work. Here David, whatever the future has in store, has reached a point where he can look back in humble gratitude. Whatever has been well done, he counts it as accomplished in the providence and by the grace of God. "For we are his workmanship, created in Christ Jesus unto good works, which God hath before ordained that we should walk in them" (Eph. 2:10) .

9 ¶ Now when Tou king of Hamath heard how David had smitten all the host of Hadarezer king of Zobah;

10 He sent Hadoram his son to king David, to inquire of his welfare, and to congratulate him, because he had fought against Hadarezer, and smitten him; (for Hadarezer had war with Tou;) and *with him* all manner of vessels of gold and silver and brass.

11 ¶ Them also king David dedicated unto the LORD, with the silver and the gold that he brought from all *these* nations; from Edom, and from Moab, and from the children of Ammon, and from the Philistines, and from Amalek.

12 Moreover, Abishai the son of Zeruiah slew of the Edomites in the valley of salt eighteen thousand.

13 ¶ And he put garrisons in Edom; and all the Edomites became David's servants. Thus the LORD preserved David whithersoever he went.

14 ¶ So David reigned over all Israel, and executed judgment and justice among all his people.

15 And Joab the son of Zeruiah *was* over the host; and Jehoshaphat the son of Ahilud, recorder;

9 When To'u king of Hamath heard that David had defeated the whole army of Hadade'zer, king of Zobah, 10 he sent his son Hador'am to King David, to greet him, and to congratulate him because he had fought against Hadade'zer and defeated him; for Hadade'zer had often been at war with To'u. And he sent all sorts of articles of gold, of silver, and of bronze; 11 these also King David dedicated to the LORD, together with the silver and gold which he had carried off from all the nations, from Edom, Moab, the Ammonites, the Philistines, and Am'alek.

12 And Abi'shai, the son of Zeru'iah, slew eighteen thousand E'domites in the Valley of Salt. 13 And he put garrisons in Edom; and all the E'domites became David's servants. And the LORD gave victory to David wherever he went.

14 So David reigned over all Israel; and he administered justice and equity to all his people. 15 And Jo'ab the son of Zeru'iah was over the army; and Jehosh'aphat the

12*a.* **Moreover, Abishai the son of Zeruiah:** Almost certainly the original text ran, "And when he [David] returned, he smote Edom." The difference seems extreme but is slight in the Hebrew.

12*b.* **Of the Edomites:** Samuel, obviously by error, has "of the Syrians." Edom (אדם) and Syria (ארם) are so nearly identical that confusion was easy. Indeed, that fact may be the ground for the tradition that David won victories against the powerful Syrians as far as the Euphrates.

14-17. David's high officials. In vs. 16 read, "Abiathar the son of Ahimelech" (cf. 15:11; 24:3). Especially note that David's sons are termed **chief about the king,** whereas the text in Samuel says "were priests." To the Chronicler that was so sacrilegious as to seem certainly unhistorical: he made the arbitrary change.

18:11. *Dedicated Loot.*—To the service of God David dedicated spoils taken from conquered foes. In that breath-taking marvel, the mosque of St. Sophia in Constantinople—originally the metropolitan church of Eastern Christendom—there are looted treasures, including marble columns reputed to be from the temple of Diana at Ephesus. Similarly, in the Christian church of St. Mark in Venice there are looted treasures. Loot is not absent from our museums. But that perhaps is less open to criticism. Is it not good that some artistic treasures from lands which possess abundant evidence of their own past culture should spread knowledge of that culture elsewhere? If the Elgin marbles, now in the British Museum, had been left in Athens they might have perished, for when they were removed few in Greece cared one drachma about their preservation. Perhaps loot in modern times takes on vaster and more sinister forms: the innumerable sales of cherished possessions enforced by poverty, economic squeeze on the colossal scale. But loot in churches does not seem fitting. What should we think about tainted money put to good uses? Regretfully one feels that the Chronicler, still more so the

16 And Zadok the son of Ahitub, and Abimelech the son of Abiathar, *were* the priests; and Shavsha was scribe;

17 And Benaiah the son of Jehoiada *was* over the Cherethites and the Pelethites; and the sons of David *were* chief about the king.

19 Now it came to pass after this, that Nahash the king of the children of Ammon died, and his son reigned in his stead.

2 And David said, I will show kindness unto Hanun the son of Nahash, because his father showed kindness to me. And David sent messengers to comfort him concerning his father. So the servants of David came into the land of the children of Ammon to Hanun, to comfort him.

3 But the princes of the children of Ammon said to Hanun, Thinkest thou that David doth honor thy father, that he hath sent comforters unto thee? are not his servants come unto thee for to search, and to overthrow, and to spy out the land?

4 Wherefore Hanun took David's servants, and shaved them, and cut off their garments in the midst hard by their buttocks, and sent them away.

5 Then there went *certain*, and told David how the men were served; and he sent to meet them: for the men were greatly ashamed. And the king said, Tarry at Jericho until your beards be grown, and *then* return.

6 ¶ And when the children of Ammon saw that they had made themselves odious to David, Hanun and the children of Ammon sent a thousand talents of silver to hire them chariots and horsemen out of Mesopotamia, and out of Syria-maachah, and out of Zobah.

7 So they hired thirty and two thousand chariots, and the king of Maachah and his people; who came and pitched before Med-

son of Ahi'lud was recorder; 16 and Zadok the son of Ahi'tub and Ahim'elech the son of Abi'athar were priests; and Shavsha was secretary; 17 and Benai'ah the son of Jehoi'ada was over the Cher'ethites and the Pel'ethites; and David's sons were the chief officials in the service of the king.

19 Now after this Nahash the king of the Ammonites died, and his son reigned in his stead. 2 And David said, "I will deal loyally with Hanun the son of Nahash, for his father dealt loyally with me." So David sent messengers to console him concerning his father. And David's servants came to Hanun in the land of the Ammonites, to console him. 3 But the princes of the Ammonites said to Hanun, "Do you think, because David has sent comforters to you, that he is honoring your father? Have not his servants come to you to search and to overthrow and to spy out the land?" 4 So Hanun took David's servants, and shaved them, and cut off their garments in the middle, at their hips, and sent them away; and they departed. 5 When David was told concerning the men, he sent to meet them, for the men were greatly ashamed. And the king said, "Remain at Jericho until your beards have grown, and then return."

6 When the Ammonites saw that they had made themselves odious to David, Hanun and the Ammonites sent a thousand talents of silver to hire chariots and horsemen from Mesopota'mia, from Aram-ma'acah, and from Zobah. 7 They hired thirty-two thousand chariots and the king of

---

19:1–20:3. At this point the Chronicler—reluctantly, it may be conjectured—had to omit the fine story in II Sam. 9, concerning David's kindness to Mephibosheth, Saul's grandson and son of Jonathan, David's beloved friend. He could not consistently include

---

actual David, did not realize that loot dedicated to the temple raised a moral problem (see also Expos. on I Chr. 26:27).

19:2-4. *Dark Glasses.*—Does not this miserable episode throw light on a thousand tragic outcomes in international affairs? David's motive, when he sent the courteous message to King

Hanun, was genuine. He sometimes had magnanimity, the power and the will to recall past benefits gratefully. But so poisoned by baseness was the international atmosphere that Hanun's councilors had no difficulty in thinking up a sinister intent on David's part and deciding to return insult for courtesy. So they provoked war

eba. And the children of Ammon gathered themselves together from their cities, and came to battle.

8 And when David heard *of it,* he sent Joab, and all the host of the mighty men.

9 And the children of Ammon came out, and put the battle in array before the gate of the city: and the kings that were come *were* by themselves in the field.

10 Now when Joab saw that the battle was set against him before and behind, he chose out of all the choice of Israel, and put *them* in array against the Syrians.

11 And the rest of the people he delivered unto the hand of Abishai his brother, and they set *themselves* in array against the children of Ammon.

12 And he said, If the Syrians be too strong for me, then thou shalt help me: but if the children of Ammon be too strong for thee, then I will help thee.

13 Be of good courage, and let us behave ourselves valiantly for our people, and for the cities of our God: and let the LORD do *that which is* good in his sight.

14 So Joab and the people that *were* with him drew nigh before the Syrians unto the battle; and they fled before him.

15 And when the children of Ammon saw that the Syrians were fled, they likewise fled before Abishai his brother, and entered into the city. Then Joab came to Jerusalem.

16 ¶ And when the Syrians saw that they were put to the worse before Israel, they sent messengers, and drew forth the Syrians that *were* beyond the river: and Shophach the captain of the host of Hadarezer *went* before them.

17 And it was told David; and he gathered all Israel, and passed over Jordan, and came upon them, and set *the battle* in array against them. So when David had put the battle in array against the Syrians, they fought with him.

Ma'acah with his army, who came and encamped before Med'eba. And the Ammonites were mustered from their cities and came to battle. 8 When David heard of it, he sent Jo'ab and all the army of the mighty men. 9 And the Ammonites came out and drew up in battle array at the entrance of the city, and the kings who had come were by themselves in the open country.

10 When Jo'ab saw that the battle was set against him both in front and in the rear, he chose some of the picked men of Israel, and arrayed them against the Syrians; 11 the rest of his men he put in the charge of Abi'shai his brother, and they were arrayed against the Ammonites. 12 And he said, "If the Syrians are too strong for me, then you shall help me; but if the Ammonites are too strong for you, then I will help you. 13 Be of good courage, and let us play the man for our people, and for the cities of our God; and may the LORD do what seems good to him." 14 So Jo'ab and the people who were with him drew near before the Syrians for battle; and they fled before him. 15 And when the Ammonites saw that the Syrians fled, they likewise fled before Abi'shai, Jo'ab's brother, and entered the city. Then Jo'ab came to Jerusalem.

16 But when the Syrians saw that they had been defeated by Israel, they sent messengers and brought out the Syrians who were beyond the Eu-phra'tes, with Shophach the commander of the army of Hadade'zer at their head. 17 And when it was told David, he gathered all Israel together, and crossed the Jordan, and came to them, and drew up his forces against them. And when David set the battle in array against the

---

it, for he had declared that all the house of Saul perished when the Battle of Gilboa was fought. Therefore he now proceeded, on the basis of II Sam. 10:1-19, to relate David's courtesy to an Ammonite king, and its curious sequel.

---

and incurred defeat. We do not know just when King Nahash, father of Hanun, assisted David, but probably it was when the Ammonites were fighting Saul and David was endangered by Saul's jealousy. Shall we therefore infer that Nahash had been actuated not by kindly desire

to help David, but by intention to do a disservice to Saul? If we do so, we find ourselves imputing bad motives as suspiciously as did Hanun's councilors. Satan, in the sense of the archfiend, is a manufacturer of spectacles—mass-produced dark glasses for us all to wear.

18 But the Syrians fled before Israel; and David slew of the Syrians seven thousand *men which fought in* chariots, and forty thousand footmen, and killed Shophach the captain of the host.

19 And when the servants of Hadarezer saw that they were put to the worse before Israel, they made peace with David, and became his servants: neither would the Syrians help the children of Ammon any more.

20 And it came to pass, that after the year was expired, at the time that kings go out *to battle,* Joab led forth the power of the army, and wasted the country of the children of Ammon, and came and besieged Rabbah. But David tarried at Jerusalem. And Joab smote Rabbah, and destroyed it.

2 And David took the crown of their king from off his head, and found it to weigh a talent of gold, and *there were* precious stones in it; and it was set upon David's head: and he brought also exceeding much spoil out of the city.

3 And he brought out the people that *were* in it, and cut *them* with saws, and with harrows of iron, and with axes. Even so dealt David with all the cities of the children of Ammon. And David and all the people returned to Jerusalem.

4 ¶ And it came to pass after this, that there arose war at Gezer with the Philistines; at which time Sibbechai the Hushathite slew Sippai, *that was* of the children of the giant: and they were subdued.

5 And there was war again with the Philistines; and Elhanan the son of Jair

Syrians, they fought with him. 18 And the Syrians fled before Israel; and David slew of the Syrians the men of seven thousand chariots, and forty thousand foot soldiers, and killed also Shophach the commander of their army. 19 And when the servants of Hadade'zer saw that they had been defeated by Israel, they made peace with David, and became subject to him. So the Syrians were not willing to help the Ammonites any more.

20 In the spring of the year, the time when kings go forth to battle, Jo'ab led out the army, and ravaged the country of the Ammonites, and came and besieged Rabbah. But David remained at Jerusalem. And Jo'ab smote Rabbah, and overthrew it. 2 And David took the crown of their king[u] from his head; he found that it weighed a talent of gold, and in it was a precious stone; and it was placed on David's head. And he brought forth the spoil of the city, a very great amount. 3 And he brought forth the people who were in it, and set them to labor[v] with saws and iron picks and axes;[w] and thus David did to all the cities of the Ammonites. Then David and all the people returned to Jerusalem.

4 And after this there arose war with the Philistines at Gezer; then Sib'becai the Hu'shathite slew Sip'pai, who was one of the descendants of the giants; and the Philistines were subdued. 5 And there was again war

[u] Or *Milcom* See 1 Kings 11. 5
[v] Compare 2 Sam 12. 31: Heb *he sawed*
[w] Compare 2 Sam 12. 31: Heb *saws*

19:18. Divergences between this passage and II Sam. 8:4; 10:18 present insurmountable difficulties (see A. R. S. Kennedy, ed., *The Book of Samuel* [New York: Henry Froude, n.d.; "The New-Century Bible"], p. 240) .

20:4-8. At this point the Chronicler had to omit the section of II Sam. 13:1–21:14 which vividly narrates the revolts of Absalom and Sheba and the vengeance exacted by the Gibeonites on seven surviving sons (or grandsons) of Saul: it was all incompatible with the picture of an idealized David.

5. II Sam. 21:19 reads, "Elhanan . . . the Bethlehemite, slew Goliath," a statement which startlingly conflicts with the famous tale that youthful David slew Goliath (I Sam.

20:5. *Did David Slay Goliath?*—See Exeg., but let not meticulous scholars rob us of "David and Goliath." If necessary, take a hint from the Chronicler, and suppress their vexatious opinion. Rather let us add to the famous tale the following picturesque conjecture: The cave

dwellers, whom the Hebrews, invading Canaan, dislodged with great difficulty from the limestone caverns near Hebron, were exceptionally tall, Stone Age men. Some of the survivors may have found refuge in the Philistines' coastal plain. Therefore a great-grandson of one of

slew Lahmi the brother of Goliath the Gittite, whose spear staff *was* like a weaver's beam.

6 And yet again there was war at Gath, where was a man of *great* stature, whose fingers and toes *were* four and twenty, six *on each hand,* and six *on each foot:* and he also was the son of the giant.

7 But when he defied Israel, Jonathan the son of Shimea David's brother slew him.

8 These were born unto the giant in Gath; and they fell by the hand of David, and by the hand of his servants.

21 And Satan stood up against Israel, and provoked David to number Israel.

2 And David said to Joab and to the rulers of the people, Go, number Israel from

with the Philistines; and Elha'nan the son of Ja'ir slew Lahmi the brother of Goliath the Gittite, the shaft of whose spear was like a weaver's beam. **6** And there was again war at Gath, where there was a man of great stature, who had six fingers on each hand, and six toes on each foot, twenty-four in number; and he also was descended from the giants. **7** And when he taunted Israel, Jonathan the son of Shim'e-a, David's brother, slew him. **8** These were descended from the giants in Gath; and they fell by the hand of David and by the hand of his servants.

21 Satan stood up against Israel, and incited David to number Israel. **2** So David said to Jo'ab and the commanders of

17). Perhaps Elhanan really was the giant killer, the credit being legendarily transferred to David. At any rate, Chronicles circumvented or corrected by saying that Elhanan slew Goliath's brother. **Lahmi** is a mutilated fragment of the word "the Bethlehemite."

H. CENSUS AND PLAGUE (21:1–22:1)

The Chronicler adapted the narrative of II Sam. 24, for although it showed human David presumptuously sinning in taking the census, it related an ideally good sequel. The king heeded the rebuking prophet; he accepted as just chastisement the visitation of plague; he was therefore not only pardoned but he also received from God an inestimable sign of favor. When David was at the threshing floor of Araunah the Jebusite, a vision of an angel of mercy was vouchsafed, and therefore the prophet told him to purchase the ground and to offer thankful sacrifice. In Samuel this story is feebly placed at the very end of the book. When a reader of the book of Samuel turned for sequel to the book of Kings, he read, "Now King David was old and stricken in years." Sensibly and skillfully the Chronicler placed it in the midst of David's career. Moreover, the account in Samuel fails to say that Araunah's threshing floor became the site of the temple! The Chronicler of course seized on that outcome as the really glorious significance of the whole episode. Indeed, he saw in it the pivotal point in the ideal history he was writing.

21:1. Satan stood up against Israel: Satan has not here the later meaning of chief of evil, superhuman beings, opposed to the will of God, but denotes a superhuman being

them may have been brawny Goliath, most useful to the Philistines as their champion in the custom of single combat fighting, wherein the understanding was that the army whose picked representative was slain would on his downfall take to flight. In this instance mighty muscles attached to a stupid brain were no match for young David's skill and courage.

In the course of our earthly pilgrimage there are few who have not sometime to encounter a giant temptation, and then must either slay or be slain. John Bunyan's Christian met such a one when he found himself facing Despair, a far

more deadly opponent than Despondency. What means of defense or attack should anyone in like circumstance seek to possess? "Thou wilt keep him in perfect peace, whose mind is stayed on thee" (Isa. 26:3). "These things I have spoken unto you," said Jesus to his disciples, "that in me ye might have peace. . . . Be of good cheer; I have overcome the world" (John 16:33).

21:1. *Satan or God?*— (See Exeg.) The difference between the statement in II Sam. 24:1, that God incited David to do wrong, and here, **Satan . . . incited David,** is not doctrinal but

Beer-sheba even to Dan; and bring the number of them to me, that I may know *it*.

3 And Joab answered, The LORD make his people a hundred times so many more as they *be:* but, my lord the king, *are* they not all my lord's servants? why then doth my lord require this thing? why will he be a cause of trespass to Israel?

4 Nevertheless the king's word prevailed against Joab. Wherefore Joab departed, and went throughout all Israel, and came to Jerusalem.

5 ¶ And Joab gave the sum of the number of the people unto David. And all *they* of Israel were a thousand thousand and a hundred thousand men that drew sword: and Judah *was* four hundred threescore and ten thousand men that drew sword.

6 But Levi and Benjamin counted he not among them: for the king's word was abominable to Joab.

7 And God was displeased with this thing; therefore he smote Israel.

8 And David said unto God, I have sinned greatly, because I have done this thing: but now, I beseech thee, do away the iniquity of thy servant; for I have done very foolishly.

the army, "Go, number Israel, from Beer-sheba to Dan, and bring me a report, that I may know their number." 3 But Jo'ab said, "May the LORD add to his people a hundred times as many as they are! Are they not, my lord the king, all of them my lord's servants? Why then should my lord require this? Why should he bring guilt upon Israel?" 4 But the king's word prevailed against Jo'ab. So Jo'ab departed and went throughout all Israel, and came back to Jerusalem. 5 And Jo'ab gave the sum of the numbering of the people to David. In all Israel there were one million one hundred thousand men who drew the sword, and in Judah four hundred and seventy thousand who drew the sword. 6 But he did not include Levi and Benjamin in the numbering, for the king's command was abhorrent to Jo'ab.

7 But God was displeased with this thing, and he smote Israel. 8 And David said to God, "I have sinned greatly in that I have done this thing. But now, I pray thee, take away the iniquity of thy servant; for I have

---

(angel, messenger) who furthers the will of God (cf. Job 1:6-12); and particularly Zech. 3:1-2, which indicates that as early as 520 B.C. this mode of expression was well understood as a substitute for the earlier blunt statement that God himself tests ("tempts") men. The parallel text in II Sam. 24:1 reads "He [God] moved David."

6. Not in Samuel. Perhaps a reviser's reservation, since Num. 1:49 exempts Levites from army service. The reason for which **Benjamin** also is exempted defies conjecture.

---

reverential, a matter of expressional sensitiveness. **Satan** is here regarded as an "angelic" agent of God. This does not imply that God was thus mysteriously relieved of ultimate responsibility for the fact that men are confronted by morally testing choices. The metaphysical issue is subject for a volume, not for a brief note. In this chapter the Chronicler was able to relate that David's sinful decision to follow the promptings of power and pride nevertheless resulted in amazingly great good, for David repented, and then God enabled him to see Araunah's (Ornan's) threshing floor as the holy place where the temple should be built.

"O Almighty God, who canst bring good out of evil, and makest even the wrath of men to turn to thy praise. . . ." So begins a beautiful and memorable collect. But it should not be spoken lightly. So startling is its assertion that

it should compel us to reflect. How can evil be overruled for good? How can even God bring good out of evil? This incident declares that David's sin resulted in good, only because penitently he realized that he had done wrong and became willing to accept guidance to do right.

When the Hebrew writers said that God (or Satan) **incited David** in such wise that he sinned, they used a curious idiom of the Hebrew language, and literal translation easily leads to deep misunderstanding on our part. That idiom states a specific decision taken as if it had been the only possibility inherent in the situation and presents the result as if that had been purposed by God. It is not meant that David had no choice when he acted as he did. Two famous examples of this idiom are Isa. 6:9 and Exod. 7:1, 3.

9 ¶ And the LORD spake unto Gad, David's seer, saying,

10 Go and tell David, saying, Thus saith the LORD, I offer thee three *things:* choose thee one of them, that I may do *it* unto thee.

11 So Gad came to David, and said unto him, Thus saith the LORD, Choose thee

12 Either three years' famine; or three months to be destroyed before thy foes, while that the sword of thine enemies overtaketh *thee;* or else three days the sword of the LORD, even the pestilence, in the land, and the angel of the LORD destroying throughout all the coasts of Israel. Now therefore advise thyself what word I shall bring again to him that sent me.

13 And David said unto Gad, I am in a great strait: let me fall now into the hand of the LORD; for very great *are* his mercies: but let me not fall into the hand of man.

14 ¶ So the LORD sent pestilence upon Israel: and there fell of Israel seventy thousand men.

15 And God sent an angel unto Jerusalem to destroy it: and as he was destroying, the LORD beheld, and he repented him of the evil, and said to the angel that destroyed, It is enough, stay now thine hand. And the angel of the LORD stood by the threshingfloor of Ornan the Jebusite.

16 And David lifted up his eyes, and saw the angel of the LORD stand between the earth and the heaven, having a drawn sword in his hand stretched out over Jerusalem. Then David and the elders *of Israel, who were* clothed in sackcloth, fell upon their faces.

done very foolishly." 9 And the LORD spoke to Gad, David's seer, saying, 10 "Go and say to David, 'Thus says the LORD, Three things I offer you; choose one of them, that I may do it to you.' " 11 So Gad came to David and said to him, "Thus says the LORD, 'Take which you will: 12 either three years of famine; or three months of devastation by your foes, while the sword of your enemies overtakes you; or else three days of the sword of the LORD, pestilence upon the land, and the angel of the LORD destroying throughout all the territory of Israel.' Now decide what answer I shall return to him who sent me." 13 Then David said to Gad, "I am in great distress; let me fall into the hand of the LORD, for his mercy is very great; but let me not fall into the hand of man."

14 So the LORD sent a pestilence upon Israel; and there fell seventy thousand men of Israel. 15 And God sent the angel to Jerusalem to destroy it; but when he was about to destroy it, the LORD saw, and he repented of the evil; and he said to the destroying angel, "It is enough; now stay your hand." And the angel of the LORD was standing by the threshing floor of Ornan the Jeb'usite. 16 And David lifted his eyes and saw the angel of the LORD standing between earth and heaven, and in his hand a drawn sword stretched out over Jerusalem. Then David and the elders, clothed in

---

16. Only in Chronicles. The reference to **the angel** in II Sam. 24:15-17 is so awkward in that context that one wonders whether the smoother version in Chronicles was originally the text of Samuel.

9-13. *Into Thy Hands, O Lord.*—Gad the prophet was certain that David's sin of arrogance in taking a census of his subjects must meet with retribution. What form would it take? Gad felt inspired to tell David that God tests him by offering choice between three disasters— **famine,** defeat in battle, or **pestilence.** Plague broke out in the land—on the modern view caused not by an immediate intervention by the Deity, but by insanitary habits or infected vermin. For us the intense religious interest of the narrative is seen in David's moving answer (vs. 13). Gone is his arrogance. Humbly he

asks that the merited disaster may be determined not by human cruelty, but by the justice of God, "whose property is always to have mercy." The story has very deep significance. For one thing, we should note—as David did (vs. 17)—that the sufferings from the plague were endured by innocent men and women in the country: Jerusalem was not affected, David did not contract the disease and die in agony. What then? This solemn reflection—that seldom if ever are the consequences of our wrongdoing confined to ourselves. We do not live in complete isolation from our fellow men. What we are must either

17 And David said unto God, *Is it* not I *that* commanded the people to be numbered? even I it is that have sinned and done evil indeed; but *as for* these sheep, what have they done? let thine hand, I pray thee, O Lord my God, be on me, and on my father's house; but not on thy people, that they should be plagued.

18 ¶ Then the angel of the Lord commanded Gad to say to David, that David should go up, and set up an altar unto the Lord in the threshingfloor of Ornan the Jebusite.

19 And David went up at the saying of Gad, which he spake in the name of the Lord.

20 And Ornan turned back, and saw the angel; and his four sons with him hid themselves. Now Ornan was threshing wheat.

21 And as David came to Ornan, Ornan looked and saw David, and went out of the threshingfloor, and bowed himself to David with *his* face to the ground.

22 Then David said to Ornan, Grant me the place of *this* threshingfloor, that I may build an altar therein unto the Lord: thou shalt grant it me for the full price: that the plague may be stayed from the people.

23 And Ornan said unto David, Take *it* to thee, and let my lord the king do *that which is* good in his eyes: lo, I give *thee* the oxen *also* for burnt offerings, and the threshing instruments for wood, and the wheat for the meat offering; I give it all.

24 And king David said to Ornan, Nay; but I will verily buy it for the full price: for I will not take *that* which *is* thine for the Lord, nor offer burnt offerings without cost.

sackcloth, fell upon their faces. 17 And David said to God, "Was it not I who gave command to number the people? It is I who have sinned and done very wickedly. But these sheep, what have they done? Let thy hand, I pray thee, O Lord my God, be against me and against my father's house; but let not the plague be upon thy people."

18 Then the angel of the Lord commanded Gad to say to David that David should go up and rear an altar to the Lord on the threshing floor of Ornan the Jeb′usite. 19 So David went up at Gad's word, which he had spoken in the name of the Lord. 20 Now Ornan was threshing wheat; he turned and saw the angel, and his four sons who were with him hid themselves. 21 As David came to Ornan, Ornan looked and saw David and went forth from the threshing floor, and did obeisance to David with his face to the ground. 22 And David said to Ornan, "Give me the site of the threshing floor that I may build on it an altar to the Lord — give it to me at its full price — that the plague may be averted from the people." 23 Then Ornan said to David, "Take it; and let my lord the king do what seems good to him; see, I give the oxen for burnt offerings, and the threshing sledges for the wood, and the wheat for a cereal offering. I give it all." 24 But King David said to Ornan, "No, but I will buy it for the full price; I will not take for the Lord what is yours, nor offer burnt

---

20. In Samuel the presence of Araunah only is mentioned. His four sons may be the Chronicler's embellishment—the more witnesses the better.

---

harm or help others. Awareness of that great truth should, if we have any conscience and imagination, restrain us from selfish and wanton impulses.

What is the latent meaning that makes David's answer—**let me fall into the hand of the Lord** —alike so beautiful and so profound, at least for Christian thought? Surely it is seen in our apprehension that the consequences of wrongdoing need not be merely punitive, but can be transformed into good through God's everlasting redemptive mercy, the fullness of which is manifested in the cross of Christ. Who can read the

prayer of David, **let me fall into the hand of the Lord,** and not remember the trust of the sinless One, "Father, into thy hands I commit my spirit" (Luke 23:46).

24. *Bargaining.*—Here is a pleasing and vivid example of Oriental bargaining (for a parallel see the story of Abraham's purchase of the burying place for his wife's body in Gen. 23:1-16). East and West have radically different views about proper procedure in commercial transactions. We aim at no unnecessary expenditure of precious time in effecting a deal. The East considers that there is time to burn.

25 So David gave to Ornan for the place six hundred shekels of gold by weight.

26 And David built there an altar unto the LORD, and offered burnt offerings and peace offerings, and called upon the LORD; and he answered him from heaven by fire upon the altar of burnt offering.

27 And the LORD commanded the angel; and he put up his sword again into the sheath thereof.

28 ¶ At that time when David saw that the LORD had answered him in the threshingfloor of Ornan the Jebusite, then he sacrificed there.

29 For the tabernacle of the LORD, which Moses made in the wilderness, and the altar of the burnt offering, *were* at that season in the high place at Gibeon.

30 But David could not go before it to inquire of God: for he was afraid because of the sword of the angel of the LORD.

22 Then David said, This *is* the house of the LORD God, and this *is* the altar of the burnt offering for Israel.

offerings which cost me nothing." 25 So David paid Ornan six hundred shekels of gold by weight for the site. 26 And David built there an altar to the LORD and presented burnt offerings and peace offerings, and called upon the LORD, and he answered him with fire from heaven upon the altar of burnt offering. 27 Then the LORD commanded the angel; and he put his sword back into its sheath.

28 At that time, when David saw that the LORD had answered him at the threshing floor of Ornan the Jeb′usite, he made his sacrifices there. 29 For the tabernacle of the LORD, which Moses had made in the wilderness, and the altar of burnt offering were at that time in the high place at Gibeon; 30 but David could not go before it to inquire of God, for he was afraid of the sword of the angel of the LORD.

22 Then David said, "Here shall be the house of the LORD God and here the altar of burnt offering for Israel."

---

25. Six hundred shekels of gold: In Samuel, "fifty shekels of silver." But no sum could be too high to pay for such utterly sacred ground. Moreover, according to Gen. 23:15-17, Abraham paid four hundred silver shekels for the cave of Machpelah. No wonder the Chronicler wrote **shekels of gold.**

26b. Here and in 22:1 the Chronicler added to what he read in Samuel an important assertion and inference. When David laid on this altar its first sacrifice, his action was divinely approved by a miracle; whereupon (22:1) there came upon him a revelation: he foreknew that God purposed this place to be the site of the temple, and that on this altar the burnt offerings of the people would be sacrificed.

29-30. The anxious revisers apparently mollified the preceding verse (**he sacrificed there**) by pointing out that the tabernacle and legitimate altar were at Gibeon: David would of course have gone thither to offer this exceptional sacrifice, but for the fact that he was prevented by **the sword of the angel of the Lord!**

Compared with the importance of showing perfect politeness and proffering generosity (of which, however, no gentleman would lower himself by taking advantage), what matter moments or hours or days? Besides, the protracted method is interesting, affords scope for skill, and eventually may reach a decision acceptable to both parties. There is something to be said for and against both methods. At any rate, Westerners lose much of the possible joy of living by being continually in such a hurry. Said an eager Londoner in the complex system of the underground railways, "If we change at this station, we can get a train on the other line which will save two minutes." "And what," said his companion, "shall we do with the two min-

utes?" One way and another, by indolence or by haste, it is only too easy not to make the best use of the fleeting minutes, hours, and days of the years of our life.

And on what basis do we conduct our transactions with God? That is a question which gives food for thought. The Scriptures insist that God gives his gifts freely. In what spirit do we receive them?

22:1-19. Preparation.—This fine chapter prompts various reflections. Certain of them may be grouped together in an initial note. In vs. 1, **This is the house of the LORD**—but not a stone of it was yet laid! The future is seen as realized. Courage of that high order is likely sooner or later to fashion, or cause to be fash-

2 And David commanded to gather together the strangers that *were* in the land of Israel; and he set masons to hew wrought stones to build the house of God.

3 And David prepared iron in abundance for the nails for the doors of the gates, and for the joinings; and brass in abundance without weight;

4 Also cedar trees in abundance: for the Zidonians and they of Tyre brought much cedar wood to David.

5 And David said, Solomon my son *is* young and tender, and the house *that is* to be builded for the LORD *must be* exceeding magnificent, of fame and of glory throughout all countries: I will *therefore* now make preparation for it. So David prepared abundantly before his death.

6 ¶ Then he called for Solomon his son, and charged him to build a house for the LORD God of Israel.

7 And David said to Solomon, My son, as for me, it was in my mind to build a house unto the name of the LORD my God:

2 David commanded to gather together the aliens who were in the land of Israel, and he set stonecutters to prepare dressed stones for building the house of God. 3 David also provided great stores of iron for nails for the doors of the gates and for clamps, as well as bronze in quantities beyond weighing, 4 and cedar timbers without number; for the Sido'nians and Tyrians brought great quantities of cedar to David. 5 For David said, "Solomon my son is young and inexperienced, and the house that is to be built for the LORD must be exceedingly magnificent, of fame and glory throughout all lands; I will therefore make preparation for it." So David provided materials in great quantity before his death.

6 Then he called for Solomon his son, and charged him to build a house for the LORD, the God of Israel. 7 David said to Solomon, "My son, I had it in my heart to build a house to the name of the LORD my

---

J. DAVID'S PREPARATIONS FOR THE TEMPLE (22:2-19)

The passage 22:3–29:30 has no parallel in Samuel. The Chronicler easily thought that David had devotedly sought to prepare for the future building of the temple.

22:5. Magnificent: The form "magnifical" is retained in most editions of KJV. It is sad that this resounding adjective should have grown obsolete.

---

ioned, what it dreams. The great prophets had that quality, penetrating through present darkness, to see the power of a ceaseless divine purpose in the end achieving its aim. Jesus foresaw fulfillment beyond suffering and death. In vs. 3 we are told that David prepared, not only in abundance, but in detail. No other mode of preparation is effective: first, largeness of vision; then meticulous care and toil. It is to be hoped that Solomon—as the Chronicler will charitably but perhaps unhistorically later relate—did not take all the credit to himself when the time came. It is a besetting weakness in human nature to forget indebtedness to predecessors. "Other men labored," said Jesus, "and ye are entered into their labors" (John 4:38). Vs. 5 reminds us that father and son co-operated. It is written that David, conscious of Solomon's immaturity, was also confident of his future strength and believed that he would be free from incessant wars (cf. vs. 9) and would prosper exceedingly, for such was the purpose of God. Yet David did not therefore fold his hands and leave the consummation for Solomon to achieve unaided; instead

he resolved, **I will therefore make preparation for it.** In vs. 13 is expressed a parent's affectionate hope for his son; note that it is taking shape in wise and noble counsel from a father who has won the right to give it.

2. *Manual and Menial.*—The chapter (cf. Expos. on II Chr. 2:17-18) makes a bad start in this verse, with its implication that it was unbecoming for Hebrews to have to bend their backs to hard work, wherefore only strangers (men of Canaanitish families is meant, not resident aliens) should be set to manual labor. In contrast, remember the energy of the Hebrews of Jerusalem and Judah in Nehemiah's time, when with one accord they themselves tackled the tremendous task of rebuilding Jerusalem's broken walls—with the exception of the nobles of Tekoa, who "put not their necks to the work of the Lord" (Neh. 3:5).

7. *It Was in My Heart to Build.*—What of the good projects, the legitimate longings that we know we shall not live to fulfill? Perchance they will not be done by those who come after us, unless we have hoped and planned and prepared for the ends we shall not ourselves attain.

8 But the word of the LORD came to me, saying, Thou hast shed blood abundantly, and hast made great wars: thou shalt not build a house unto my name, because thou hast shed much blood upon the earth in my sight.

9 Behold, a son shall be born to thee, who shall be a man of rest; and I will give him rest from all his enemies round about: for his name shall be Solomon, and I will give peace and quietness unto Israel in his days.

10 He shall build a house for my name; and he shall be my son, and I *will be* his father; and I will establish the throne of his kingdom over Israel for ever.

11 Now, my son, the LORD be with thee; and prosper thou, and build the house of the LORD thy God, as he hath said of thee.

12 Only the LORD give thee wisdom and understanding, and give thee charge concerning Israel, that thou mayest keep the law of the LORD thy God.

13 Then shalt thou prosper, if thou takest heed to fulfil the statutes and judgments which the LORD charged Moses with concerning Israel: be strong, and of good courage; dread not, nor be dismayed.

14 Now, behold, in my trouble I have prepared for the house of the LORD a hundred thousand talents of gold, and a thousand thousand talents of silver; and of brass and iron without weight; for it is in abundance: timber also and stone have I prepared; and thou mayest add thereto.

God. 8 But the word of the LORD came to me, saying, 'You have shed much blood and have waged great wars; you shall not build a house to my name, because you have shed so much blood before me upon the earth. 9 Behold, a son shall be born to you; he shall be a man of peace. I will give him peace from all his enemies round about; for his name shall be Solomon, and I will give peace and quiet to Israel in his days. 10 He shall build a house for my name. He shall be my son, and I will be his father, and I will establish his royal throne in Israel for ever.' 11 Now, my son, the LORD be with you, so that you may succeed in building the house of the LORD your God, as he has spoken concerning you. 12 Only, may the LORD grant you discretion and understanding, that when he gives you charge over Israel you may keep the law of the LORD your God. 13 Then you will prosper if you are careful to observe the statutes and the ordinances which the LORD commanded Moses for Israel. Be strong, and of good courage. Fear not; be not dismayed. 14 With great pains I have provided for the house of the LORD a hundred thousand talents of gold, a million talents of silver, and bronze and iron beyond weighing, for there is so much of it; timber and stone too I have

---

11-12. An interruptive parenthesis which appears to be a pious addition.

14. With great pains: The phrase subtly implies that compared with the wealth which Solomon would possess, David's resources were slender. Now according to I Kings 10:14, Solomon's wealth became so amazing that in one year his revenue was 666 gold talents. At the same rate David in forty years would have accumulated 26,640 talents. The Chronicler picturesquely used a double superlative when he stated that David had set aside toward the temple **a hundred thousand talents of gold,** plus **a million**

---

8. Disqualified.—Note the abysmally lower reason assigned in I Kings 5:3, viz., that David had been too busy fighting to have time to erect the temple. The Chronicler did not regard the wars of David as wrongdoing. Far from it, his victories provided resources for the future temple. All the more remarkable therefore is the sensitiveness of feeling here expressed. The fierce necessities which David's life had to cope with made it incongruous that the structure of the place, where later generations were to wor-

ship the God whose will is righteousness and peace, should be his achieving. Actually David and Solomon would not have seen the point as did the Chronicler, for they thought of God and worship as men did who lived in 1000 B.C., while he was thinking of the temple as men thought of it who lived five hundred years later. That second temple had been built in 520 B.C. by Jews subject to the Persians. No Hebrew king then existed who had shed the blood of other nations; instead, other mighty nations had

15 Moreover, *there are* workmen with thee in abundance, hewers and workers of stone and timber, and all manner of cunning men for every manner of work.

16 Of the gold, the silver, and the brass, and the iron, *there is* no number. Arise *therefore,* and be doing, and the Lord be with thee.

17 ¶ David also commanded all the princes of Israel to help Solomon his son, *saying,*

18 *Is* not the Lord your God with you? and hath he *not* given you rest on every side? for he hath given the inhabitants of the land into mine hand; and the land is subdued before the Lord, and before his people.

19 Now set your heart and your soul to seek the Lord your God; arise therefore, and build ye the sanctuary of the Lord God, to bring the ark of the covenant of the Lord, and the holy vessels of God, into the house that is to be built to the name of the Lord.

23 So when David was old and full of days, he made Solomon his son king over Israel.

provided. To these you must add. 15 You have an abundance of workmen: stonecutters, masons, carpenters, and all kinds of craftsmen without number, skilled in working 16 gold, silver, bronze, and iron. Arise and be doing! The Lord be with you!"

17 David also commanded all the leaders of Israel to help Solomon his son, saying, 18 "Is not the Lord your God with you? And has he not given you peace on every side? For he has delivered the inhabitants of the land into my hand; and the land is subdued before the Lord and his people. 19 Now set your mind and heart to seek the Lord your God. Arise and build the sanctuary of the Lord God, so that the ark of the covenant of the Lord and the holy vessels of God may be brought into a house built for the name of the Lord."

23 When David was old and full of days, he made Solomon his son king over Israel.

---

talents of silver: *credat Judaeus Apella!* (Horace *Satires* I. 5. 100.) Neither the Jewish Chronicler nor his Jewish readers could have imagined that there would ever be anyone so prosaic as to take the golden words literally.

19. Arise and build: Why the urgent imperative? In order to bring into the temple-to-be the ark of the covenant of the Lord. No trace in the Chronicler's text about the matter that bulked in the minds of the revisers—transference of the tabernacle from Gibeon.

K. Duties of the Levites (23:1–26:32)

It is natural to expect that the Chronicler would present David as taking meticulous care to provide that the Levites were organized in accordance with their several duties, and so ready to minister in the coming temple. But whatever he wrote on that theme was scrutinized by the devout in later times, and corrections and additions were probably inserted and gave rise eventually to a highly complicated text. By common consent of scholars these four chapters offer the most disconcertingly intricate critical problems in Chronicles (see Welch, *Work of the Chronicler*, pp. 81-96). This Exeg. takes the view that the Chronicler lived before the rigid distinction between Aaronite priests and the

---

shed abundantly the blood of the Hebrews. No doubt the Chronicler's constant thought of the temple of his time was as the place of prayer for Jewish worship. But one wonders if perchance he had read and pondered the words in Isa. 56:7, "My house shall be called a house of prayer for all peoples" (cf. Mark 11:17).

23:1. Death Draws Near.—Strange it feels when a man knows the hour has come to make

his last arrangements, and that hands other than his will deal with what he thus seeks to set in order. To the utmost of his ability David took pains not to leave that final duty undone. Wrote Horace to his friend,

Alas, . . . not piety nor tears,
Can halt the inexorable passing of the years.[7]

[7] *Odes* II. 14.

2 ¶ And he gathered together all the princes of Israel, with the priests and the Levites.

3 Now the Levites were numbered from the age of thirty years and upward: and their number by their polls, man by man, was thirty and eight thousand.

4 Of which, twenty and four thousand *were* to set forward the work of the house of the Lord; and six thousand *were* officers and judges:

5 Moreover four thousand *were* porters; and four thousand praised the Lord with the instruments which I made, *said David,* to praise *therewith.*

6 And David divided them into courses among the sons of Levi, *namely,* Gershon, Kohath, and Merari.

7 ¶ Of the Gershonites *were* Laadan, and Shimei.

8 The sons of Laadan; the chief *was* Jehiel, and Zetham, and Joel, three.

9 The sons of Shimei; Shelomith, and Haziel, and Haran, three. These *were* the chief of the fathers of Laadan.

10 And the sons of Shimei *were,* Jahath, Zina, and Jeush, and Beriah. These four *were* the sons of Shimei.

11 And Jahath was the chief, and Zizah the second: but Jeush and Beriah had not many sons; therefore they were in one reckoning, according to *their* father's house.

12 ¶ The sons of Kohath; Amram, Izhar, Hebron, and Uzziel, four.

13 The sons of Amram; Aaron, and Moses: and Aaron was separated, that he should sanctify the most holy things, he and his sons for ever, to burn incense before the

2 David assembled all the leaders of Israel and the priests and the Levites. 3 The Levites, thirty years old and upward, were numbered, and the total was thirty-eight thousand men. 4 "Twenty-four thousand of these," David said, "shall have charge of the work in the house of the Lord, six thousand shall be officers and judges, 5 four thousand gatekeepers, and four thousand shall offer praises to the Lord with the instruments which I have made for praise." 6 And David organized them in divisions corresponding to the sons of Levi: Gershom, Kohath, and Merar'i.

7 The sons of Gershom[x] were Ladan and Shim'e-i. 8 The sons of Ladan: Jehi'el the chief, and Zetham, and Jo'el, three. 9 The sons of Shim'e-i: Shelo'moth, Ha'zi-el, and Haran, three. These were the heads of the fathers' houses of Ladan. 10 And the sons of Shim'e-i: Jahath, Zina, and Je'ush, and Beri'ah. These four were the sons of Shim'e-i. 11 Jahath was the chief, and Zizah the second; but Je'ush and Beri'ah had not many sons, therefore they became a father's house in one reckoning.

12 The sons of Kohath: Amram, Izhar, Hebron, and Uz'ziel, four. 13 The sons of Amram: Aaron and Moses. Aaron was set apart to consecrate the most holy things, that he and his sons for ever should burn

[x] Vg Compare Gk Syr: Heb *to the Gershonite*

---

other Levites obtained, and that the chief motive for the revisers' activities in altering and adding to the text he had written was its frequent inconsistency with that distinction.

23:1. It is hinted that long years intervened between this gathering of Levites and David's speech recorded in ch. 22. It is likely that the entire passage was inserted by a reviser, and that his work was in turn subjected in places, e.g., vss. 24-27, 32, to still later amendments.

3. From . . . thirty years: Vs. 27 speaks of Levites taking office at the age of twenty (see Exeg. on vss. 24-27).

6. The strict rendering is: "And David divided them into courses. Concerning the sons of Levi . . . ." Perhaps the first clause concluded vss. 1-5; and what follows, "concerning the sons of Levi . . . ," was the heading for the ensuing name list, which had no original connection with vss. 1-5.

13b. Aaron was set apart: The author stressed the ordinances of the final Law as to the priests.

LORD, to minister unto him, and to bless in his name for ever.

14 Now *concerning* Moses the man of God, his sons were named of the tribe of Levi.

15 The sons of Moses *were*, Gershom, and Eliezer.

16 Of the sons of Gershom, Shebuel *was* the chief.

17 And the sons of Eliezer *were*, Rehabiah the chief. And Eliezer had none other sons; but the sons of Rehabiah were very many.

18 Of the sons of Izhar; Shelomith the chief.

19 Of the sons of Hebron; Jeriah the first, Amariah the second, Jahaziel the third, and Jekameam the fourth.

20 Of the sons of Uzziel; Micah the first, and Jesiah the second.

21 ¶ The sons of Merari; Mahli, and Mushi. The sons of Mahli; Eleazar, and Kish.

22 And Eleazar died, and had no sons, but daughters: and their brethren the sons of Kish took them.

23 The sons of Mushi; Mahli, and Eder, and Jeremoth, three.

24 ¶ These *were* the sons of Levi after the house of their fathers; *even* the chief of the fathers, as they were counted by number of names by their polls, that did the work for the service of the house of the LORD, from the age of twenty years and upward.

incense before the LORD, and minister to him and pronounce blessings in his name for ever. 14 But the sons of Moses the man of God were named among the tribe of Levi. 15 The sons of Moses: Gershom and Elie'zer. 16 The sons of Gershom: Sheb'uel the chief. 17 The sons of Elie'zer: Rehabi'ah the chief; Elie'zer had no other sons, but the sons of Rehabi'ah were very many. 18 The sons of Izhar: Shelo'mith the chief. 19 The sons of Hebron: Jeri'ah the chief, Amari'ah the second, Jahazi'el the third, and Jekame'am the fourth. 20 The sons of Uz'ziel: Micah the chief, and Isshi'ah the second.

21 The sons of Merar'i: Mahli and Mushi. The sons of Mahli: Elea'zar and Kish. 22 Elea'zar died having no sons, but only daughters; their kinsmen, the sons of Kish, married them. 23 The sons of Mushi: Mahli, Eder, and Jer'emoth, three.

24 These were the sons of Levi by their fathers' houses, the heads of fathers' houses as they were registered according to the number of the names of the individuals from twenty years old and upward who were to do the work for the service of the

---

24-27. From twenty years old and upward: Here is a most interesting amendment of the announcement in vs. 3 that the Levites began service at the age of thirty. No specific reason is assigned for the change; in vs. 27 it is merely said that the **twenty years** regulation was made by the last words of David. Obviously in the time of the author of vs. 3 (Chronicler or first reviser) the date line was thirty. At what later period did the change to twenty come to pass? No doubt when the second temple was built in 520 B.C. it required an increase of Levites, but that is too early a date for the composition of Chronicles. It is an attractive conjecture that as and when (perhaps the Nehemiah-Ezra period early in the fourth century B.C.) the Zadokites won their contention for supremacy over the other Levites, numbers of Levites may have refused to acquiesce; and that especially those of Israelite lineage abandoned their claim to serve in Jerusalem and left the city. If so, two consequences might well ensue: on the one hand, a shortage of Levitical man power in Jerusalem necessitating the lowering of the age limit; and on

---

Happier was Paul, who could say to Philemon, "Being such a one as Paul the aged, and now also a prisoner of Jesus Christ" (Philem. 9).

24. *From the Age of Twenty Years.*—Formerly responsibility was not taken up by the Levites

until the age of thirty. Emergency laid the burden on very young shoulders. It always does. Then emergency passes and the seniors resume their sway. Perhaps that is inevitable; but the unrepayable debt they owe to youth's courage,

25 For David said, The LORD God of Israel hath given rest unto his people, that they may dwell in Jerusalem for ever:

26 And also unto the Levites: they shall no *more* carry the tabernacle, nor any vessels of it for the service thereof.

27 For by the last words of David the Levites *were* numbered from twenty years old and above:

28 Because their office *was* to wait on the sons of Aaron for the service of the house of the LORD, in the courts, and in the chambers, and in the purifying of all holy things, and the work of the service of the house of God;

29 Both for the showbread, and for the fine flour for meat offering, and for the unleavened cakes, and for *that which is baked in* the pan, and for that which is fried, and for all manner of measure and size;

30 And to stand every morning to thank and praise the LORD, and likewise at even;

31 And to offer all burnt sacrifices unto the LORD in the sabbaths, in the new moons, and on the set feasts, by number, according to the order commanded unto them, continually before the LORD:

32 And that they should keep the charge of the tabernacle of the congregation, and the charge of the holy *place,* and the charge of the sons of Aaron their brethren, in the service of the house of the LORD.

24 Now *these are* the divisions of the sons of Aaron. The sons of Aaron; Nadab and Abihu, Eleazar and Ithamar.

house of the LORD. 25 For David said, "The LORD, the God of Israel, has given peace to his people; and he dwells in Jerusalem for ever. 26 And so the Levites no longer need to carry the tabernacle or any of the things for its service" — 27 for by the last words of David these were the number of the Levites from twenty years old and upward — 28 "but their duty shall be to assist the sons of Aaron for the service of the house of the LORD, having the care of the courts and the chambers, the cleansing of all that is holy, and any work for the service of the house of God; 29 to assist also with the showbread, the flour for the cereal offering, the wafers of unleavened bread, the baked offering, the offering mixed with oil, and all measures of quantity or size. 30 And they shall stand every morning, thanking and praising the LORD, and likewise at evening, 31 and whenever burnt offerings are offered to the LORD on sabbaths, new moons, and feast days, according to the number required of them, continually before the LORD. 32 Thus they shall keep charge of the tent of meeting and the sanctuary, and shall attend the sons of Aaron, their brethren, for the service of the house of the LORD."

24 The divisions of the sons of Aaron were these. The sons of Aaron: Na-

---

the other hand, the presence in central Canaan, and beyond, of many disgruntled Levites seeking other employment. Such men or their sons would relish the proposal, when it arose, that on Mount Gerizim (not far from Samaria) was a far more venerable holy place than Jerusalem, and that a temple should be built there. When such a temple was built in the fourth century B.C., it most probably did not lack a staff of authentic Levites.

28-32. Clearly a reviser's verses, probably in direct continuation of vss. 24-27. Mark the emphatic declaration that the task of mere Levites was to wait on the Aaronic priests.

24:1-20. To the same revising hand these verses should perhaps be ascribed.

---

energy, and sacrifice ought forever afterward to be remembered by them.

28-32. *Reminder and Reproof.*—This careful catalogue of sacred duties may be an oblique censure of slackness among the postexilic priests. But the unwilling are seldom persuaded to change their tune by being shown a long list of their delinquencies. Different and deeper

treatment is needed: "Create in me a clean heart, O God; and renew a right spirit within me" (Ps. 51:10). We know there were depressing times when the ministers of the second temple were negligent or worse (see the book of Malachi). If we knew more, we might find that the indifference or scorn of the laity had taken the heart out of them.

2 But Nadab and Abihu died before their father, and had no children: therefore Eleazar and Ithamar executed the priest's office.

3 And David distributed them, both Zadok of the sons of Eleazar, and Ahimelech of the sons of Ithamar, according to their offices in their service.

4 And there were more chief men found of the sons of Eleazar than of the sons of Ithamar; and *thus* were they divided. Among the sons of Eleazar *there were* sixteen chief men of the house of *their* fathers, and eight among the sons of Ithamar according to the house of their fathers.

5 Thus were they divided by lot, one sort with another; for the governors of the sanctuary, and governors *of the house* of God, were of the sons of Eleazar, and of the sons of Ithamar.

6 And Shemaiah the son of Nethaneel the scribe, *one* of the Levites, wrote them before the king, and the princes, and Zadok the priest, and Ahimelech the son of Abiathar, and *before* the chief of the fathers of the priests and Levites: one principal household being taken for Eleazar, and *one* taken for Ithamar.

7 Now the first lot came forth to Jehoiarib, the second of Jedaiah,

8 The third to Harim, the fourth to Seorim,

9 The fifth to Machijah, the sixth to Mijamin,

10 The seventh to Hakkoz, the eighth to Abijah,

11 The ninth to Jeshuah, the tenth to Shecaniah,

12 The eleventh to Eliashib, the twelfth to Jakim,

13 The thirteenth to Huppah, the fourteenth to Jeshebeab,

14 The fifteenth to Bilgah, the sixteenth to Immer,

dab, Abi'hu, Elea'zar, and Ith'amar. 2 But Nadab and Abi'hu died before their father, and had no children, so Elea'zar and Ith'amar became the priests. 3 With the help of Zadok of the sons of Elea'zar, and Ahim'elech of the sons of Ith'amar, David organized them according to the appointed duties in their service. 4 Since more chief men were found among the sons of Elea'zar than among the sons of Ith'amar, they organized them under sixteen heads of fathers' houses of the sons of Elea'zar, and eight of the sons of Ith'amar. 5 They organized them by lot, all alike, for there were officers of the sanctuary and officers of God among both the sons of Elea'zar and the sons of Ith'amar. 6 And the scribe Shemai'ah the son of Nethan'el, a Levite, recorded them in the presence of the king, and the princes, and Zadok the priest, and Ahim'elech the son of Abi'athar, and the heads of the fathers' houses of the priests and of the Levites; one father's house being chosen for Elea'zar and one chosen for Ith'amar.

7 The first lot fell to Jehoi'arib, the second to Jeda'iah, 8 the third to Harim, the fourth to Se-o'rim, 9 the fifth to Malchi'jah, the sixth to Mij'amin, 10 the seventh to Hakkoz, the eighth to Abi'jah, 11 the ninth to Jeshua, the tenth to Shecani'ah, 12 the eleventh to Eli'ashib, the twelfth to Jakim, 13 the thirteenth to Huppah, the fourteenth to Jesheb'e-ab, 14 the fifteenth to Bilgah,

---

3. Ahimelech: Read "Abiathar," as also in vs. 6 (see Exeg. on 18:14-17).

5. Echo of an unknown dispute, happily settled by deciding that both parties had rights and should draw lots for the appointments.

24:2. *The Parent Outlived the Children.*— Nadab and Abihu died before their father and had no children. If the father and the two sons loved one another his grief for their early death had an element of poignancy which they would not have suffered had their father lived a natural

length of years and predeceased them. These two died childless. Said a father of his young son killed in battle, "Never again shall I see the wind blowing his hair, or see his marriage and his children." Said David, "O my son Absalom! my son, my son Absalom! would God I had died

15 The seventeenth to Hezir, the eighteenth to Aphses,

16 The nineteenth to Pethahiah, the twentieth to Jehezekel,

17 The one and twentieth to Jachin, the two and twentieth to Gamul,

18 The three and twentieth to Delaiah, the four and twentieth to Maaziah.

19 These *were* the orderings of them in their service to come into the house of the LORD, according to their manner, under Aaron their father, as the LORD God of Israel had commanded him.

20 ¶ And the rest of the sons of Levi *were these:* Of the sons of Amram; Shubael: of the sons of Shubael; Jehdeiah.

21 Concerning Rehabiah: of the sons of Rehabiah, the first *was* Isshiah.

22 Of the Izharites; Shelomoth: of the sons of Shelomoth; Jahath.

23 And the sons *of Hebron;* Jeriah *the first,* Amariah the second, Jahaziel the third, Jekameam the fourth.

24 *Of* the sons of Uzziel; Michah: of the sons of Michah; Shamir.

25 The brother of Michah *was* Isshiah: of the sons of Isshiah; Zechariah.

26 The sons of Merari *were* Mahli and Mushi: the sons of Jaaziah; Beno.

27 ¶ The sons of Merari by Jaaziah; Beno, and Shoham, and Zaccur, and Ibri.

28 Of Mahli *came* Eleazar, who had no sons.

29 Concerning Kish: the son of Kish *was* Jerahmeel.

30 The sons also of Mushi; Mahli, and Eder, and Jerimoth. These *were* the sons of the Levites after the house of their fathers.

31 These likewise cast lots over against their brethren the sons of Aaron in the presence of David the king, and Zadok, and Ahimelech, and the chief of the fathers of the priests and Levites, even the principal fathers over against their younger brethren.

the sixteenth to Immer, 15 the seventeenth to Hezir, the eighteenth to Hap'pizzez, 16 the nineteenth to Pethahi'ah, the twentieth to Jehez'kel, 17 the twenty-first to Jachin, the twenty-second to Gamul, 18 the twenty-third to Dela'iah, the twenty-fourth to Ma-azi'ah. 19 These had as their appointed duty in their service to come into the house of the LORD according to the procedure established for them by Aaron their father, as the LORD God of Israel had commanded him.

20 And of the rest of the sons of Levi: of the sons of Amram, Shu'ba-el; of the sons of Shu'ba-el, Jehde'iah. 21 Of Rehabi'ah: of the sons of Rehabi'ah, Isshi'ah the chief. 22 Of the Iz'harites, Shelo'moth; of the sons of Shelo'moth, Jahath. 23 The sons of Hebron:*y* Jeri'ah the chief,*z* Amari'ah the second, Jahazi'el the third, Jekame'am the fourth. 24 The sons of Uz'ziel, Micah; of the sons of Micah, Shamir. 25 The brother of Micah, Isshi'ah; of the sons of Isshi'ah, Zechari'ah. 26 The sons of Merar'i: Mahli and Mushi. The sons of Ja-azi'ah: Beno. 27 The sons of Merar'i: of Ja-azi'ah, Beno, Shoham, Zaccur, and Ibri. 28 Of Mahli: Elea'zar, who had no sons. 29 Of Kish, the sons of Kish: Jerah'meel. 30 The sons of Mushi: Mahli, Eder, and Jer'imoth. These were the sons of the Levites according to their fathers' houses. 31 These also, the head of each father's house and his younger brother alike, cast lots, just as their brethren the sons of Aaron, in the presence of King David, Zadok, Ahim'elech, and the heads of fathers' houses of the priests and of the Levites.

y See 23. 19: Heb lacks *Hebron*
z See 23. 19: Heb lacks *the chief*

20-31. This list has no integral connection with its context, and how it stands related to the list in 23:6-24 is a puzzle. It looks like a very late addition for it ignores the Gershonites, who may have ceased to function at the time of its compilation.

---

for thee, O Absalom, my son, my son!" (II Sam. 18:33.) If length of life were the same for all and a certainty, so that without fail children would outlive parents, and parents live to see their grandchildren, would that be for the best?

To how great an extent the zest and discipline with which life as it is confronts us would vanish to our detriment! There is contingency. We must live as not knowing what a day may bring forth, and the fact is a summons alike to the

25 Moreover David and the captains of the host separated to the service of the sons of Asaph, and of Heman, and of Jeduthun, who should prophesy with harps, with psalteries, and with cymbals: and the number of the workmen according to their service was:

2 Of the sons of Asaph; Zaccur, and Joseph, and Nethaniah, and Asarelah, the sons of Asaph under the hands of Asaph, which prophesied according to the order of the king.

3 Of Jeduthun: the sons of Jeduthun; Gedaliah, and Zeri, and Jeshaiah, Hashabiah, and Mattithiah, six, under the hands of their father Jeduthun, who prophesied with a harp, to give thanks and to praise the LORD.

4 Of Heman: the sons of Heman; Bukkiah, Mattaniah, Uzziel, Shebuel, and Jerimoth, Hananiah, Hanani, Eliathah, Giddalti, and Romamti-ezer, Joshbekashah, Mallothi, Hothir, *and* Mahazioth:

5 All these *were* the sons of Heman the king's seer in the words of God, to lift up the horn. And God gave to Heman fourteen sons and three daughters.

25 David and the chiefs of the service also set apart for the service certain of the sons of Asaph, and of Heman, and of Jedu'thun, who should prophesy with lyres, with harps, and with cymbals. The list of those who did the work and of their duties was: 2 Of the sons of Asaph: Zaccur, Joseph, Nethani'ah, and Ashare'lah, sons of Asaph, under the direction of Asaph, who prophesied under the direction of the king. 3 Of Jedu'thun, the sons of Jedu'thun: Gedali'ah, Zeri, Jesha'iah, Shim'e-i,[a] Hashabi'ah, and Mattithi'ah, six, under the direction of their father Jedu'thun, who prophesied with the lyre in thanksgiving and praise to the LORD. 4 Of Heman, the sons of Heman: Bukki'ah, Mattani'ah, Uz'ziel, Shebu'el, and Jer'imoth, Hanani'ah, Hana'ni, Eli'athah, Giddal'ti, and Romam'ti-e'zer, Joshbekash'ah, Mallo'thi, Hothir, Maha'zi-oth. 5 All these were the sons of Heman the king's seer, according to the promise of God to exalt him; for God had given Heman fourteen sons and three daughters.

[a] One Ms: Gk: Heb lacks *Shimei*

25:1-31. The chapter taken as a whole may be deemed revisional work, but vss. 1-7 (or a simpler form of them) may be due not merely to the Chronicler himself but to an earlier document which he used. At any rate, it is of the highest interest to note that the heart of the matter concerns not Levites as skilled in music and psalmody, but picked men from the three chief families of musician Levites (**Asaph, Heman,** and **Jeduthun**), whose duty was to produce oracular—prophetic—utterances when in an ecstasy induced by rhythmic music. Only recently have scholars adequately envisaged the fact that these professional prophets were part of the regular staff of the temple. One reflects how

---

young and the old to live aright. In bereavement those who have hold of the Christian faith sorrow not as do those without hope.

25:3. The Forgotten Man.—Six, under the direction of their father. But only five sons are here recorded. The sixth deserved recognition and did not get it. Plenty of instances there are of that sort of thing in life, and those who receive publicity are apt to be forgetful that their brother has been overlooked. The forgotten need to learn to say in their hearts, "The work was done, and thank God I took my part in it." Vs. 17, however, enables us to recover the lost man: he was Shimei. The omission was due to a scribe's error in copying. Those who realize the difficulty of copying perfectly a very ancient Hebrew MS will give the scribe their sympathy. Over the desk of an expert printer who used to deal with Semitic language work in the Cam-

bridge University Press, there hung this motto: "The man who never made a mistake never made anything."

4. Buried Treasure.—Here is one of the oddest facts in the text of the Scriptures. From **Hananiah** onward these names of the sons of Heman are not names of men, but (with thin disguise) words of a poem, a prayer, to this effect: "Be gracious unto me, O God, be gracious unto me. Thou art my God. Thou hast increased and raised up help for him that sat in distress. Do thou make the (prophetic) visions abundant." This fact appears, however, to be remarkable, rather than edifying. Can one extract good counsel from it? Perhaps if we looked with gentler, wiser eyes into the underlying nature and meaning of our lives we might discover, in what we took to be only dull prose, hidden poetry of spiritual significance.

6 All these *were* under the hands of their father for song *in* the house of the LORD, with cymbals, psalteries, and harps, for the service of the house of God, according to the king's order to Asaph, Jeduthun, and Heman.

7 So the number of them, with their brethren that were instructed in the songs of the LORD, *even* all that were cunning, was two hundred fourscore and eight.

8 ¶ And they cast lots, ward against *ward,* as well the small as the great, the teacher as the scholar.

9 Now the first lot came forth for Asaph to Joseph: the second to Gedaliah, who with his brethren and sons *were* twelve:

10 The third to Zaccur, *he,* his sons, and his brethren, *were* twelve:

11 The fourth to Izri, *he,* his sons, and his brethren, *were* twelve:

12 The fifth to Nethaniah, *he,* his sons, and his brethren, *were* twelve:

13 The sixth to Bukkiah, *he,* his sons, and his brethren, *were* twelve:

14 The seventh to Jesharelah, *he,* his sons, and his brethren, *were* twelve:

15 The eighth to Jeshaiah, *he,* his sons, and his brethren, *were* twelve:

16 The ninth to Mattaniah, *he,* his sons, and his brethren, *were* twelve:

17 The tenth to Shimei, *he,* his sons, and his brethren, *were* twelve:

18 The eleventh to Azareel, *he,* his sons, and his brethren, *were* twelve:

19 The twelfth to Hashabiah, *he,* his sons, and his brethren, *were* twelve:

20 The thirteenth to Shubael, *he,* his sons, and his brethren, *were* twelve:

21 The fourteenth to Mattithiah, *he,* his sons, and his brethren, *were* twelve:

22 The fifteenth to Jeremoth, *he,* his sons, and his brethren, *were* twelve:

23 The sixteenth to Hananiah, *he,* his sons, and his brethren, *were* twelve:

24 The seventeenth to Joshbekashah, *he,* his sons, and his brethren, *were* twelve:

6 They were all under the direction of their father in the music in the house of the LORD with cymbals, harps, and lyres for the service of the house of God. Asaph, Jedu'thun, and Heman were under the order of the king. **7** The number of them along with their brethren, who were trained in singing to the LORD, all who were skilful, was two hundred and eighty-eight. **8** And they cast lots for their duties, small and great, teacher and pupil alike.

9 The first lot fell for Asaph to Joseph; the second to Gedali'ah, to him and his brethren and his sons, twelve; **10** the third to Zaccur, his sons and his brethren, twelve; **11** the fourth to Izri, his sons and his brethren, twelve; **12** the fifth to Nethani'ah, his sons and his brethren, twelve; **13** the sixth to Bukki'ah, his sons and his brethren, twelve; **14** the seventh to Jeshare'lah, his sons and his brethren, twelve; **15** the eighth to Jesha'iah, his sons and his brethren, twelve; **16** the ninth to Mattani'ah, his sons and his brethren, twelve; **17** the tenth to Shim'e-i, his sons and his brethren, twelve; **18** the eleventh to Az'arel, his sons and his brethren, twelve; **19** the twelfth to Hashabi'ah, his sons and his brethren, twelve; **20** to the thirteenth, Shu'ba-el, his sons and his brethren, twelve; **21** to the fourteenth, Mattithi'ah, his sons and his brethren, twelve; **22** to the fifteenth, to Jer'emoth, his sons and his brethren, twelve; **23** to the sixteenth, to Hanani'ah, his sons and his brethren, twelve; **24** to the seventeenth, to Joshbekash'ah, his sons and his brethren,

---

radically different were their ways and words from the character and spiritual discernment of the supreme, individual prophets (cf. Jer. 18:18; 23:14-22).

Vs. 6 probably comes from an annotator who missed the point about the duty of prophesying, and was conscious of the three families as musician Levites.

7-8. *Master and Pupil.*—No doubt the beginners stood in full need of instruction in the various instruments and tunes. The teachers had to teach, and the pupils to learn. But it is a pleasing thought that when the time for performance came, the superiority was ignored

25 The eighteenth to Hanani, *he,* his sons, and his brethren, *were* twelve:

26 The nineteenth to Mallothi, *he,* his sons, and his brethren, *were* twelve:

27 The twentieth to Eliathah, *he,* his sons, and his brethren, *were* twelve:

28 The one and twentieth to Hothir, *he,* his sons, and his brethren, *were* twelve:

29 The two and twentieth to Giddalti, *he,* his sons, and his brethren, *were* twelve:

30 The three and twentieth to Mahazioth, *he,* his sons, and his brethren, *were* twelve:

31 The four and twentieth to Romamtiezer, *he,* his sons, and his brethren, *were* twelve.

26 Concerning the divisions of the porters: Of the Korhites *was* Meshelemiah the son of Kore, of the sons of Asaph.

2 And the sons of Meshelemiah *were,* Zechariah the firstborn, Jediael the second, Zebadiah the third, Jathniel the fourth,

3 Elam the fifth, Jehohanan the sixth, Elioenai the seventh.

4 Moreover the sons of Obed-edom *were,* Shemaiah the firstborn, Jehozabad the second, Joah the third, and Sacar the fourth, and Nethaneel the fifth,

5 Ammiel the sixth, Issachar the seventh, Peulthai the eighth: for God blessed him.

6 Also unto Shemaiah his son were sons born, that ruled throughout the house of their father: for they *were* mighty men of valor.

7 The sons of Shemaiah; Othni, and Rephael, and Obed, Elzabad, whose brethren *were* strong men, Elihu, and Semachiah.

8 All these of the sons of Obed-edom: they and their sons and their brethren, able men for strength for the service, *were* threescore and two of Obed-edom.

9 And Meshelemiah had sons and brethren, strong men, eighteen.

10 Also Hosah, of the children of Merari, had sons; Simri the chief, (for *though* he was not the firstborn, yet his father made him the chief;)

11 Hilkiah the second, Tebaliah the third, Zechariah the fourth: all the sons and brethren of Hosah *were* thirteen.

twelve; **25** to the eighteenth, to Hana'ni, his sons and his brethren, twelve; **26** to the nineteenth, to Mallo'thi, his sons and his brethren, twelve; **27** to the twentieth, to Eli'athah, his sons and his brethren, twelve; **28** to the twenty-first, to Hothir, his sons and his brethren, twelve; **29** to the twenty-second, to Giddal'ti, his sons and his brethren, twelve; **30** to the twenty-third, to Maha'zioth, his sons and his brethren, twelve; **31** to the twenty-fourth, to Romam'ti-e'zer, his sons and his brethren, twelve.

26 As for the divisions of the gatekeepers: of the Ko'rahites, Meshelemi'ah the son of Ko're, of the sons of Asaph. **2** And Meshelemi'ah had sons: Zechari'ah the first-born, Jedi'a-el the second, Zebadi'ah the third, Jath'ni-el the fourth, **3** Elam the fifth, Jeho-ha'nan the sixth, El'ieho-e'nai the seventh. **4** And O'bed-e'dom had sons: Shemai'ah the first-born, Jehoz'abad the second, Jo'ah the third, Sacar the fourth, Nethan'el the fifth, **5** Am'mi-el the sixth, Is'sachar the seventh, Pe-ul'lethai the eighth; for God blessed him. **6** Also to his son Shemai'ah were sons born who were rulers in their fathers' houses, for they were men of great ability. **7** The sons of Shemai'ah: Othni, Reph'a-el, Obed, and Elza'bad, whose brethren were able men, Eli'hu and Semachi'ah. **8** All these were of the sons of O'bed-e'dom with their sons and brethren, able men qualified for the service; sixty-two of O'bed-e'dom. **9** And Meshelemi'ah had sons and brethren, able men, eighteen. **10** And Hosah, of the sons of Merar'i, had sons: Shimri the chief (for though he was not the first-born, his father made him chief), **11** Hilki'ah the second, Tebali'ah the third, Zechari'ah the fourth: all the sons and brethren of Hosah were thirteen.

26:1-20. Again probably a reviser's supplementation. The verses present some insoluble puzzles, especially when collated with the genealogists' list of doorkeepers in 9:17-27. Perhaps a main purpose was to assert Levitical descent for certain families whose

12 Among these *were* the divisions of the porters, *even* among the chief men, *having* wards one against another, to minister in the house of the Lord.

13 ¶ And they cast lots, as well the small as the great, according to the house of their fathers, for every gate.

14 And the lot eastward fell to Shelemiah. Then for Zechariah his son, a wise counselor, they cast lots; and his lot came out northward.

15 To Obed-edom southward; and to his sons the house of Asuppim.

16 To Shuppim and Hosah *the lot came forth* westward, with the gate Shallecheth, by the causeway of the going up, ward against ward.

17 Eastward *were* six Levites, northward four a day, southward four a day, and toward Asuppim two *and* two.

18 At Parbar westward, four at the causeway, *and* two at Parbar.

19 These *are* the divisions of the porters among the sons of Kore, and among the sons of Merari.

20 ¶ And of the Levites, Ahijah *was* over the treasures of the house of God, and over the treasures of the dedicated things.

21 *As concerning* the sons of Laadan; the sons of the Gershonite Laadan, chief fathers, *even* of Laadan the Gershonite, *were* Jehieli.

22 The sons of Jehieli; Zetham, and Joel his brother, *which were* over the treasures of the house of the Lord.

23 Of the Amramites, *and* the Izharites, the Hebronites, and the Uzzielites:

24 And Shebuel the son of Gershom, the son of Moses, *was* ruler of the treasures.

25 And his brethren by Eliezer; Rehabiah his son, and Jeshaiah his son, and

12 These divisions of the gatekeepers, corresponding to their chief men, had duties, just as their brethren did, ministering in the house of the Lord; 13 and they cast lots by fathers' houses, small and great alike, for their gates. 14 The lot for the east fell to Shelemi'ah. They cast lots also for his son Zechari'ah, a shrewd counselor, and his lot came out for the north. 15 O'bed-e'dom's came out for the south, and to his sons was allotted the storehouse. 16 For Shuppim and Hosah it came out for the west, at the gate of Shal'lecheth on the road that goes up. Watch corresponded to watch. 17 On the east there were six each day,[b] on the north four each day, on the south four each day, as well as two and two at the storehouse; 18 and for the parbar[c] on the west there were four at the road and two at the parbar. 19 These were the divisions of the gatekeepers among the Ko'rahites and the sons of Merar'i.

20 And of the Levites, Ahi'jah had charge of the treasuries of the house of God and the treasuries of the dedicated gifts. 21 The sons of Ladan, the sons of the Gershonites belonging to Ladan, the heads of the fathers' houses belonging to Ladan the Gershonite: Jehi'eli.[d] 22 The sons of Jehi'eli, Zetham and Jo'el his brother, were in charge of the treasuries of the house of the Lord. 23 Of the Am'ramites, the Iz'harites, the He'bronites, and the Uz'zielites — 24 and Sheb'uel the son of Gershom, son of Moses, was chief officer in charge of the treasuries. 25 His brethren: from Elie'zer were his son Rehabi'ah, and

b Gk: Heb *Levites*
c The meaning of the word *parbar* is unknown
d The Hebrew text of verse 21 is confused

---

lineage had been in question: at any rate, **Obed-edom** (the Gittite of 13:13) appears (vss. 8, 15), and his sons are commended.

14-19. Whoever set down these topographical allusions was writing for men entirely aware of the layout of the second temple. **Parbar** (vs. 18) is unknown.

20-32. The subject matter is baffling, the text exceptionally unreliable. The verses, however, may be scraps of ancient information; note especially vss. 27, 32.

---

and all participated, small and great, teacher and pupil alike. The musical quality of the occasion may not have benefited, but a fine human relationship is implied between young and old, the skilled and the less skilled.

26:14. *Zechariah His Son, a Wise Counselor.* —Concerning him, the best-known preacher in Britain at the end of the nineteenth century, himself a wise counselor, wrote: "Zechariah.... Not a musician, but a wise counsellor; no use

Joram his son, and Zichri his son, and Shelo-mith his son:

26 Which Shelomith and his brethren *were* over all the treasures of the dedicated things, which David the king, and the chief fathers, the captains over thousands and hundreds, and the captains of the host, had dedicated.

27 Out of the spoils won in battles did they dedicate to maintain the house of the LORD.

28 And all that Samuel the seer, and Saul the son of Kish, and Abner the son of Ner, and Joab the son of Zeruiah, had dedicated; *and* whosoever had dedicated *any thing, it was* under the hand of Shelomith, and of his brethren.

29 ¶ Of the Izharites, Chenaniah and his sons *were* for the outward business over Israel, for officers and judges.

30 *And* of the Hebronites, Hashabiah and his brethren, men of valor, a thousand and seven hundred, *were* officers among them of Israel on this side Jordan westward in all the business of the LORD, and in the service of the king.

31 Among the Hebronites *was* Jerijah the chief, *even* among the Hebronites, according to the generations of his fathers. In the fortieth year of the reign of David they were sought for, and there were found among them mighty men of valor at Jazer of Gilead.

32 And his brethren, men of valor, *were* two thousand and seven hundred chief fathers, whom king David made rulers over the Reubenites, the Gadites, and the half tribe of Manasseh, for every matter pertaining to God, and affairs of the king.

27 Now the children of Israel after their number, *to wit*, the chief fathers

his son Jesh'a-iah, and his son Joram, and his son Zichri, and his son Shelo'moth. **26** This Shelo'moth and his brethren were in charge of all the treasuries of the dedicated gifts which David the king, and the heads of the fathers' houses, and the officers of the thousands and the hundreds, and the commanders of the army, had dedicated. **27** From spoil won in battles they dedicated gifts for the maintenance of the house of the LORD. **28** Also all that Samuel the seer, and Saul the son of Kish, and Abner the son of Ner, and Jo'ab the son of Zeru'iah had dedicated — all dedicated gifts were in the care of Shelo'moth[e] and his brethren.

29 Of the Iz'harites, Chenani'ah and his sons were appointed to outside duties for Israel, as officers and judges. **30** Of the He'-bronites, Hashabi'ah and his brethren, one thousand seven hundred men of ability, had the oversight of Israel westward of the Jordan for all the work of the LORD and for the service of the king. **31** Of the He'bron-ites, Jeri'jah was chief of the He'bronites of whatever genealogy or fathers' houses. (In the fortieth year of David's reign search was made and men of great ability among them were found at Jazer in Gilead.) **32** King David appointed him and his breth-ren, two thousand seven hundred men of ability, heads of fathers' houses, to have the oversight of the Reubenites, the Gadites, and the half-tribe of the Manas'sites for everything pertaining to God and for the affairs of the king.

27 This is the list of the people of Israel, the heads of fathers' houses,

 e Heb *Shelomith*

L. MILITARY AND CIVIL ADMINISTRATION (27:1-34)

27:1-22. Probably by the Chronicler in his superlative mood, for we are informed that in the small area of Judah and central Canaan alone the ideal David had no less than 288,000 trained warriors attendant on him, by rotation of 24,000 each month.

---

with firearms, . . . but great in sagacity; nothing with his hands, but an army with his head." [8]

27. *More Loot for God's House.*— (See Expos. on I Chr. 18:11.) The notion was that since

[8] Joseph Parker, *The People's Bible* (New York: Funk & Wagnalls, 1881), IX, 134.

victory had been gained by the help of God, some or all of the plunder should be dedicated to religious use in his honor. This ancient superstitious convention will not do: it was bad theology and must not be condoned. We can extract respectable significance from the verse

and captains of thousands and hundreds, and their officers that served the king in any matter of the courses, which came in and went out month by month throughout all the months of the year, of every course *were* twenty and four thousand.

2 Over the first course for the first month *was* Jashobeam the son of Zabdiel: and in his course *were* twenty and four thousand.

3 Of the children of Perez *was* the chief of all the captains of the host for the first month.

4 And over the course of the second month *was* Dodai an Ahohite, and of his course *was* Mikloth also the ruler: in his course likewise *were* twenty and four thousand.

5 The third captain of the host for the third month *was* Benaiah the son of Jehoiada, a chief priest: and in his course *were* twenty and four thousand.

6 This *is that* Benaiah, *who was* mighty *among* the thirty, and above the thirty: and in his course *was* Ammizabad his son.

7 The fourth *captain* for the fourth month *was* Asahel the brother of Joab, and Zebadiah his son after him: and in his course *were* twenty and four thousand.

8 The fifth captain for the fifth month *was* Shamhuth the Izrahite: and in his course *were* twenty and four thousand.

9 The sixth *captain* for the sixth month *was* Ira the son of Ikkesh the Tekoite: and in his course *were* twenty and four thousand.

10 The seventh *captain* for the seventh month *was* Helez the Pelonite, of the children of Ephraim: and in his course *were* twenty and four thousand.

11 The eighth *captain* for the eighth month *was* Sibbecai the Hushathite, of the Zarhites: and in his course *were* twenty and four thousand.

12 The ninth *captain* for the ninth month *was* Abiezer the Anetothite, of the

the commanders of thousands and hundreds, and their officers who served the king in all matters concerning the divisions that came and went, month after month throughout the year, each division numbering twenty-four thousand:

2 Jasho'beam the son of Zab'di-el was in charge of the first division in the first month; in his division were twenty-four thousand. 3 He was a descendant of Perez, and was chief of all the commanders of the army for the first month. 4 Dodai the Aho'-hite*f* was in charge of the division of the second month; in his division were twenty-four thousand. 5 The third commander, for the third month, was Benai'ah, the son of Jehoi'ada the priest, as chief; in his division were twenty-four thousand. 6 This is the Benai'ah who was a mighty man of the thirty and in command of the thirty; Ammiz'abad his son was in charge of his division.*g* 7 As'ahel the brother of Jo'ab was fourth, for the fourth month, and his son Zebadi'ah after him; in his division were twenty-four thousand. 8 The fifth commander, for the fifth month, was Shamhuth, the Iz'rahite; in his division were twenty-four thousand. 9 Sixth, for the sixth month, was Ira, the son of Ikkesh the Teko'ite; in his division were twenty-four thousand. 10 Seventh, for the seventh month, was Helez the Pel'onite, of the sons of E'phraim; in his division were twenty-four thousand. 11 Eighth, for the eighth month, was Sib'-becai the Hu'shathite, of the Ze'rahites; in his division were twenty-four thousand. 12 Ninth, for the ninth month, was Abi-

f Gk: Heb *Ahohite and his division and Mikloth the chief officer*
g Gk Vg: Heb *was his division*

---

4. The text is faulty: read, perhaps, "Eleazar the son of Dodo the Ahohite."

---

only along metaphorical lines, viz., that it is legitimate and wise to consider that the opponent may not be wholly bad and that perhaps one may usefully learn from him. *Fas est et ab hoste doceri.* For Christian usage that principle of interpretation may be brought into relation to the once-prevalent notion that every-

thing in non-Christian religions is wholly false and foolish. Modern endeavor to perceive and appreciate what is good in other creeds is salutary. It is now becoming apparent that the new Christian communities of the East and of Africa have, or will have, from the heritage of their ancestral beliefs, spiritual treasure in relation

Benjamites: and in his course *were* twenty and four thousand.

13 The tenth *captain* for the tenth month *was* Maharai the Netophathite, of the Zarhites: and in his course *were* twenty and four thousand.

14 The eleventh *captain* for the eleventh month *was* Benaiah the Pirathonite, of the children of Ephraim: and in his course *were* twenty and four thousand.

15 The twelfth *captain* for the twelfth month *was* Heldai the Netophathite, of Othniel: and in his course *were* twenty and four thousand.

16 ¶ Furthermore over the tribes of Israel: the ruler of the Reubenites *was* Eliezer the son of Zichri: of the Simeonites, Shephatiah the son of Maachah:

17 Of the Levites, Hashabiah the son of Kemuel: of the Aaronites, Zadok:

18 Of Judah, Elihu, *one* of the brethren of David: of Issachar, Omri the son of Michael:

19 Of Zebulun, Ishmaiah the son of Obadiah: of Naphtali, Jerimoth the son of Azriel:

20 Of the children of Ephraim, Hoshea the son of Azaziah: of the half tribe of Manasseh, Joel the son of Pedaiah:

21 Of the half *tribe* of Manasseh in Gilead, Iddo the son of Zechariah: of Benjamin, Jaasiel the son of Abner:

22 Of Dan, Azareel the son of Jeroham. These *were* the princes of the tribes of Israel.

23 ¶ But David took not the number of them from twenty years old and under: because the LORD had said he would increase Israel like to the stars of the heavens.

24 Joab the son of Zeruiah began to number, but he finished not, because there fell wrath for it against Israel; neither was the number put in the account of the Chronicles of king David.

e'zer the An'athothite, a Benjaminite; in his division were twenty-four thousand. **13** Tenth, for the tenth month, was Ma'harai the Netoph'athite, of the Ze'rahites; in his division were twenty-four thousand. **14** Eleventh, for the eleventh month, was Benai'ah the Pir'athonite, of the sons of E'phraim; in his division were twenty-four thousand. **15** Twelfth, for the twelfth month, was Heldai the Netoph'athite, of Oth'ni-el; in his division were twenty-four thousand.

16 Over the tribes of Israel, for the Reubenites Elie'zer the son of Zichri was chief officer; for the Simeonites, Shephati'ah the son of Ma'acah; **17** for Levi, Hashabi'ah the son of Kem'uel; for Aaron, Zadok; **18** for Judah, Eli'hu, one of David's brothers; for Is'sachar, Omri the son of Michael; **19** for Zeb'ulun, Ishma'iah the son of Obadi'ah; for Naph'tali, Jer'emoth the son of Az'riel; **20** for the E'phraimites, Hoshe'a the son of Azazi'ah; for the half-tribe of Manas'seh, Jo'el the son of Peda'iah; **21** for the half-tribe of Manas'seh in Gilead, Iddo the son of Zechari'ah; for Benjamin, Ja-a-si'el the son of Abner; **22** for Dan, Az'arel the son of Jero'ham. These were the leaders of the tribes of Israel. **23** David did not number those below twenty years of age, for the LORD had promised to make Israel as many as the stars of heaven. **24** Jo'ab the son of Zeru'iah began to number, but did not finish; yet wrath came upon Israel for this, and the number was not entered in the chronicles of King David.

23-24. Here is a reviser anxious to say that although David sinned in taking a census, he was scrupulous to comply with the priestly regulation (Num. 1:3) which excluded enumeration of males under twenty years old.

---

to Christ that Western Christendom could most usefully acquire—and acquire without robbery. Again, how impoverished those Christians are who are blind to or belittle the wealth of virtue shown by multitudes of nonchurchgoing people.

Sometimes they show an example of faith which some Christians would do well to acquire (cf. Luke 7:9). Again, how much there is to desire and reverence in the rectitude of method and unbiased pursuit of fact shown by scientists.

25 ¶ And over the king's treasures *was* Azmaveth the son of Adiel: and over the storehouses in the fields, in the cities, and in the villages, and in the castles, *was* Jehonathan the son of Uzziah:

26 And over them that did the work of the field for tillage of the ground *was* Ezri the son of Chelub:

27 And over the vineyards *was* Shimei the Ramathite: over the increase of the vineyards for the wine cellars *was* Zabdi the Shiphmite:

28 And over the olive trees and the sycamore trees that *were* in the low plains *was* Baal-hanan the Gederite: and over the cellars of oil *was* Joash:

29 And over the herds that fed in Sharon *was* Shitrai the Sharonite: and over the herds *that were* in the valleys *was* Shaphat the son of Adlai:

30 Over the camels also *was* Obil the Ishmaelite: and over the asses *was* Jehdeiah the Meronothite:

25 Over the king's treasuries was Az′-maveth the son of Ad′i-el; and over the treasuries in the country, in the cities, in the villages and in the towers, was Jonathan the son of Uzzi′ah; 26 and over those who did the work of the field for tilling the soil was Ezri the son of Chelub; 27 and over the vineyards was Shim′e-i the Ra′mathite; and over the produce of the vineyards for the wine cellars was Zabdi the Shiphmite. 28 Over the olive and sycamore trees in the Shephe′lah was Ba′al-ha′nan the Gede′rite; and over the stores of oil was Jo′ash. 29 Over the herds that pastured in Sharon was Shitrai the Shar′onite; over the herds in the valleys was Shaphat the son of Adlai. 30 Over the camels was Obil the Ish′maelite; and over the she-asses was Jehde′iah the Meron′othite. Over the flocks was Jaziz the

25-31. Possibly an old record underlies; but that precisely twelve officials, guarding David's proprietary rights, are named, is suspiciously like the Chronicler.

Appropriations which we may thus make from such sources are not spoliation and can properly be dedicated to the service of the house of God.

27:25-31. *Town and Country.*—The Hebrews did not paint pictures on canvas, or attempt to convey in words elaborate descriptions of natural scenery. But they had the eye of the artist none the less, and were intensely sensitive to nature in its manifold relations to human life. Their swift, pictorial language aided their gifts (cf. Pss. 65:9-13; 104). Living in cities may narrow one's interest in the richness and marvel of nature, until the townsman has eyes and thoughts only for busy streets. When that happens, there is great impoverishment of spirit—perhaps even to an irreligious extent, for "the earth is the Lord's, and the fulness thereof" (Ps. 24:1). "I remember," wrote H. V. Morton, "years ago meeting in the hop-fields of Kent, near Faversham, a slum-bred boy; and he was frightened of the stars! At home, among the street-lamps of Whitechapel, however, he was, I have no doubt, the leader of some Arab gang." [9] An old couple in London were sent to the country for a few days. They went on Friday but returned on Saturday evening to their back-street home. The reason, as Dad explained, was that "the singing of them birds got on Ma's nerves."

The whole Old Testament literature is rich in small fragments of the most delicate observation [of nature] embodied in a sentence, sometimes in a word; but these fragments are strung upon a thread of feeling instead of being set forth by artistic composition and grouping of parts. A typical example is the first chapter of the prophecy of Joel. . . . Each little picture, suggested rather than drawn, is in the most exquisite harmony with the feeling of the prophet. The fig tree stripped of its bark, standing white against the arid landscape; the sackcloth-girt bride wailing for her husband; the night watch of the supplicating priests; the empty and ruinous garners; the perplexed rush of the herds maddened with heat and thirst; or the unconscious supplication in which they raise their heads to heaven with piteous lowing, are indicated with a concrete pregnancy of language which the translator vainly strives to reproduce.[1]

And in these verses in Chronicles, if we pause to perceive it, how vividly the peaceful daily life of the Jewish countryside unfolds.

28-29. *The Final Scene.*—These chapters depict how the ideal David completed his lifework. He must sum up his endeavors in one final

---

[9] *The Call of England* (New York: Robert M. McBride & Co., 1928), p. 16.

[1] W. Robertson Smith, *Lectures and Essays* (London: A. & C. Black, 1912), p. 419. Used by permission.

31 And over the flocks *was* Jaziz the Hagerite. All these *were* the rulers of the substance which *was* king David's.

32 Also Jonathan David's uncle was a counselor, a wise man, and a scribe: and Jehiel the son of Hachmoni *was* with the king's sons:

33 And Ahithophel *was* the king's counselor: and Hushai the Archite *was* the king's companion:

34 And after Ahithophel *was* Jehoiada the son of Benaiah, and Abiathar: and the general of the king's army *was* Joab.

28 And David assembled all the princes of Israel, the princes of the tribes, and the captains of the companies that ministered to the king by course, and the captains over the thousands, and captains over the hundreds, and the stewards over all the substance and possession of the king, and of his sons, with the officers, and with the mighty men, and with all the valiant men, unto Jerusalem.

2 Then David the king stood up upon his feet, and said, Hear me, my brethren, and my people: *As for me,* I *had* in mine heart to build a house of rest for the ark of the covenant of the LORD, and for the footstool of our God, and had made ready for the building:

3 But God said unto me, Thou shalt not build a house for my name, because thou *hast been* a man of war, and hast shed blood.

Hagrite. 31 All these were stewards of King David's property.

32 Jonathan, David's uncle, was a counselor, being a man of understanding and a scribe; he and Jehi'el the son of Hach'moni attended the king's sons. 33 Ahith'ophel was the king's counselor, and Hushai the Archite was the king's friend. 34 Ahith'ophel was succeeded by Jehoi'ada the son of Benai'ah, and Abi'athar. Jo'ab was commander of the king's army.

28 David assembled at Jerusalem all the officials of Israel, the officials of the tribes, the officers of the divisions that served the king, the commanders of thousands, the commanders of hundreds, the stewards of all the property and cattle of the king and his sons, together with the palace officials, the mighty men, and all the seasoned warriors. 2 Then King David rose to his feet and said: "Hear me, my brethren and my people. I had it in my heart to build a house of rest for the ark of the covenant of the LORD, and for the footstool of our God; and I made preparations for building. 3 But God said to me, 'You may not build a house for my name, for you are

---

32-34. Court officials. Read probably, as ASV mg., "Jonathan, David's brother's son" (cf. 20:7).

M. DAVID'S FAREWELL (28:1–29:30)

In conclusion the Chronicler was free to reason what the last words of David should have been—David, obedient to prophets, a king who had done all in his power to provide beforehand for the erection of the temple and the right ordering of the worship there to be offered.

28:1-8. First, David exhorts the nation's leaders.

---

speech to the princes and commanders of the nation, to Solomon his heir, and to the people.

So *ought* a perfect reign to end. Here David dies, leaving his country peaceful, powerful, and contented. . . . He dies believing that his people's true prosperity is in its zeal for the worship of God; and for that end, with the popular approval, he has made marvellous preparation. And lastly he dies, in no vain-glorious spirit, but conscious of the littleness of man and the majesty of God, and in

humble dependence on the continuance of divine Grace.[2]

The much more realistic record in Samuel shows how somber and tragic were the circumstances at the close of David's reign, chiefly as the result of his own faults. But does not the Chronicler's

[2] W. A. L. Elmslie, *The Books of Chronicles* (Cambridge: Cambridge University Press, 1916; "The Cambridge Bible"), p. 158. Its author does not now hold many opinions on Chronicles expressed in that volume.

4 Howbeit the Lord God of Israel chose me before all the house of my father to be king over Israel for ever: for he hath chosen Judah *to be* the ruler; and of the house of Judah, the house of my father; and among the sons of my father he liked me to make *me* king over all Israel:

5 And of all my sons, (for the Lord hath given me many sons,) he hath chosen Solomon my son to sit upon the throne of the kingdom of the Lord over Israel.

6 And he said unto me, Solomon thy son, he shall build my house and my courts: for I have chosen him *to be* my son, and I will be his father.

7 Moreover I will establish his kingdom for ever, if he be constant to do my commandments and my judgments, as at this day.

8 Now therefore, in the sight of all Israel the congregation of the Lord, and in the audience of our God, keep and seek for all the commandments of the Lord your God: that ye may possess this good land, and leave *it* for an inheritance for your children after you for ever.

a warrior and have shed blood.' 4 Yet the Lord God of Israel chose me from all my father's house to be king over Israel for ever; for he chose Judah as leader, and in the house of Judah my father's house, and among my father's sons he took pleasure in me to make me king over all Israel. 5 And of all my sons (for the Lord has given me many sons) he has chosen Solomon my son to sit upon the throne of the kingdom of the Lord over Israel. 6 He said to me, 'It is Solomon your son who shall build my house and my courts, for I have chosen him to be my son, and I will be his father. 7 I will establish his kingdom for ever if he continues resolute in keeping my commandments and my ordinances, as he is today.' 8 Now therefore in the sight of all Israel, the assembly of the Lord, and in the hearing of our God, observe and seek out all the commandments of the Lord your God; that you may possess this good land, and leave it for an inheritance to your children after you for ever.

---

5. Why is Solomon to reign? Not because he is his father's favorite, but because God has providentially so ordained. Contrast this idyllic pronouncement with the horrible facts in I Kings 1:1–2:46 (unmentioned by the Chronicler) concerning the palace intrigues, the murderous violence, through which Solomon secured to himself the throne. Here we are made conscious only of David's profound faith in God and serene trust in a loyal and united people.

---

idealizing suggest a yet deeper truth concerning the essential David, the man who could so wholeheartedly sorrow about his rebel son, the king who in so many ways and through so many years had been faithful to his high responsibility? Despite his faults he had the right to trust:

All I could never be,
All, men ignored in me,
This, I was worth to God, whose wheel the pitcher shaped.[3]

28:8. Vital Religion.—Anyone who has even a slight acquaintance with the history of the Jews throughout the Christian Era cannot fail to be amazed by their racial persistence and their intellectual achievements, not least in the sciences and philosophy.[4] Outwardly their religion may seem to have shown itself in rigid observance of

the precepts of their ancient law. But in fact their theological thought has been a living growth century by century, constructively seeking to relate past truth to developing knowledge. What is the secret of their extraordinary vitality, not only in religion but in other spheres as well? It is indicated in the twofold principle which David is said in this verse to have declared to his people as the condition whereby **you may possess this good land, and leave it for an inheritance to your children after you for ever:** they ought both to **observe and seek out all the commandments of the Lord.** The principle runs far back in Hebrew history to the tradition that Moses had told the tribesmen not only to keep the statutes declared, but also to await and obey the guidance of the living God who would speak his word to future generations by prophets like himself. We see it in the great prophets seeking and finding fresh and fuller truth in relation to the circumstances of their age. When the Hebrew kingdoms perished noth-

---

[3] Browning, "Rabbi Ben Ezra," st. xxv.

[4] See E. R. Bevan and Charles Singer, eds., *The Legacy of Israel* (Oxford: Clarendon Press, 1927).

9 ¶ And thou, Solomon my son, know thou the God of thy father, and serve him with a perfect heart and with a willing mind: for the LORD searcheth all hearts, and understandeth all the imaginations of the thoughts: if thou seek him, he will be found of thee; but if thou forsake him, he will cast thee off for ever.

10 Take heed now; for the LORD hath chosen thee to build a house for the sanctuary: be strong, and do *it.*

11 ¶ Then David gave to Solomon his son the pattern of the porch, and of the houses thereof, and of the treasuries thereof, and of the upper chambers thereof, and of the inner parlors thereof, and of the place of the mercy seat,

12 And the pattern of all that he had by the Spirit, of the courts of the house of the LORD, and of all the chambers round about, of the treasuries of the house of God, and of the treasuries of the dedicated things:

13 Also for the courses of the priests and the Levites, and for all the work of the service of the house of the LORD, and for all the vessels of service in the house of the LORD.

14 *He gave* of gold by weight for *things* of gold, for all instruments of all manner of service; *silver also* for all instruments of silver by weight, for all instruments of every kind of service:

15 Even the weight for the candlesticks of gold, and for their lamps of gold, by weight for every candlestick, and for the lamps thereof: and for the candlesticks of silver by weight, *both* for the candlestick, and *also* for the lamps thereof, according to the use of every candlestick.

9 "And you, Solomon my son, know the God of your father, and serve him with a whole heart and with a willing mind; for the LORD searches all hearts, and understands every plan and thought. If you seek him, he will be found by you; but if you forsake him, he will cast you off for ever. 10 Take heed now, for the LORD has chosen you to build a house for the sanctuary; be strong, and do it."

11 Then David gave Solomon his son the plan of the vestibule of the temple, and of its houses, its treasuries, its upper rooms, and its inner chambers, and of the room for the mercy seat; 12 and the plan of all that he had in mind for the courts of the house of the LORD, all the surrounding chambers, the treasuries of the house of God, and the treasuries for dedicated gifts; 13 for the divisions of the priests and of the Levites, and all the work of the service in the house of the LORD; for all the vessels for the service in the house of the LORD, 14 the weight of gold for all golden vessels for each service, the weight of silver vessels for each service, 15 the weight of the golden lampstands and their lamps, the weight of gold for each lampstand and its lamps, the weight of silver for a lampstand and its lamps, according to the use of each lampstand in the

---

9-20. David exhorts Solomon, his son and heir.

11. Direct revelation to David gave him the architectural plan for the temple—said the Chronicler. Direct revelation to Moses gave the pattern for the tabernacle in the desert, which was the prototype of the temple—said the final Law.

---

ing that really mattered was lost. On the contrary, immense strength was available for the Jews through acceptance of the vitalizing wisdom of the prophetic conception of God. Rightly understood, biblical theology is not static but dynamic belief. So likewise should it be with Christian theology. There is a fossilized form of piety which is satisfied to look at the past, endeavoring merely to keep the known commandments, and dreading or deeming un-

necessary present efforts to seek out what God the Lord will say today. In the long run that attitude of mind is fatal.

9-21. *A Father's Last Charge.*—The aged king next speaks to Solomon concerning the qualities he must have if he is to be sustained in his future duty; then he encourages him (vs. 20) to believe that God will not withhold unfailing aid. In vss. 11-19 he commits to Solomon all that he had so sedulously prepared for the

16 And by weight *he gave* gold for the tables of showbread, for every table; and *likewise* silver for the tables of silver:

17 Also pure gold for the fleshhooks, and the bowls, and the cups: and for the golden basins *he gave gold* by weight for every basin; and *likewise silver* by weight for every basin of silver:

18 And for the altar of incense refined gold by weight; and gold for the pattern of the chariot of the cherubim, that spread out *their wings*, and covered the ark of the covenant of the LORD.

19 All *this, said David*, the LORD made me understand in writing by *his* hand upon me, *even* all the works of this pattern.

20 And David said to Solomon his son, Be strong and of good courage, and do *it:* fear not, nor be dismayed, for the LORD God, *even* my God, *will be* with thee; he will not fail thee, nor forsake thee, until thou hast finished all the work for the service of the house of the LORD.

21 And, behold, the courses of the priests and the Levites, *even they shall be with thee* for all the service of the house of God: and *there shall be* with thee for all manner of workmanship every willing skilful man, for any manner of service: also the princes and all the people *will be* wholly at thy commandment.

29 Furthermore David the king said unto all the congregation, Solomon my son, whom alone God hath chosen, *is yet*

service, 16 the weight of gold for each table for the showbread, the silver for the silver tables, 17 and pure gold for the forks, the basins, and the cups; for the golden bowls and the weight of each; for the silver bowls and the weight of each; 18 for the altar of incense made of refined gold, and its weight; also his plan for the golden chariot of the cherubim that spread their wings and covered the ark of the covenant of the LORD. 19 All this he made clear by the writing from the hand of the LORD concerning it,[h] all the work to be done according to the plan.

20 Then David said to Solomon his son, "Be strong and of good courage, and do it. Fear not, be not dismayed; for the LORD God, even my God, is with you. He will not fail you or forsake you, until all the work for the service of the house of the LORD is finished. 21 And behold the divisions of the priests and the Levites for all the service of the house of God; and with you in all the work will be every willing man who has skill for any kind of service; also the officers and all the people will be wholly at your command."

29 And David the king said to all the assembly, "Solomon my son, whom

[h] Cn: Heb *upon me*

---

19. Reviser's caution, hinting that David in reality had relied not on personal inspiration, but on written authority—the Mosaic legislation.

20. A summarizing sentence at the end of this verse has dropped out of the M.T. and is preserved in the LXX.

21. From the reviser again, dragging in mention of the priests. How his words enfeeble David's peroration!

29:1-21. David's appeal and farewell to the people. The conception and construction

---

future temple—its plan, its furnishings. As the Chronicler envisaged the scene he was enraptured. Here his verses are literature—the gleam of gold and silver, the miracle of craftsman's skill shine in them. For the moment a pedestrian writer has become a poet.

Different thoughts may occur to our mind. Poor David! In time past he had hoped to do all this for Absalom, his best-beloved son. What loving expectation he had had that Absalom would be his heir! But Absalom was dead, leaving behind him a name for reckless courage

and ruthless plotting to overthrow his father. Most bitter of all, David knew that by his own negligence in royal duty he had tempted Absalom to seize the kingship. David had to transfer his hopes. He had to do his best for the second best—for Solomon, child of his guilty passion for Bathsheba. Poor David!

29:1. *The King's Last Will.*—Finally David speaks to his people; and he had won the right to do so. Forbidden in his desire to build the house of the Lord, he had not in chagrin lavished his wealth on building for himself a splen-

young and tender, and the work *is* great: for the palace *is* not for man, but for the LORD God.

2 Now I have prepared with all my might for the house of my God the gold for *things to be made* of gold, and the silver for *things* of silver, and the brass for *things* of brass, the iron for *things* of iron, and wood for *things* of wood; onyx stones, and *stones* to be set, glistering stones, and of divers colors, and all manner of precious stones, and marble stones in abundance.

3 Moreover, because I have set my affection to the house of my God, I have of mine own proper good, of gold and silver, *which* I have given to the house of my God, over and above all that I have prepared for the holy house,

4 *Even* three thousand talents of gold, of the gold of Ophir, and seven thousand talents of refined silver, to overlay the walls of the houses *withal:*

5 The gold for *things* of gold, and the silver for *things* of silver, and for all manner of work *to be made* by the hands of artificers. And who *then* is willing to consecrate his service this day unto the LORD?

6 ¶ Then the chief of the fathers and princes of the tribes of Israel, and the captains of thousands and of hundreds, with the rulers of the king's work, offered willingly,

7 And gave, for the service of the house of God, of gold five thousand talents and ten

alone God has chosen, is young and inexperienced, and the work is great; for the palace will not be for man but for the LORD God. **2** So I have provided for the house of my God, so far as I was able, the gold for the things of gold, the silver for the things of silver, and the bronze for the things of bronze, the iron for the things of iron, and wood for the things of wood, besides great quantities of onyx and stones for setting, antimony, colored stones, all sorts of precious stones, and marble. **3** Moreover, in addition to all that I have provided for the holy house, I have a treasure of my own of gold and silver, and because of my devotion to the house of my God I give it to the house of my God: **4** three thousand talents of gold, of the gold of Ophir, and seven thousand talents of refined silver, for overlaying the walls of the house, **5** and for all the work to be done by craftsmen, gold for the things of gold and silver for the things of silver. Who then will offer willingly, consecrating himself today to the LORD?"

6 Then the heads of fathers' houses made their freewill offerings, as did also the leaders of the tribes, the commanders of thousands and of hundreds, and the officers over the king's work. **7** They gave for the service

---

of the ideal speech is admirable: it culminates in David's confidence in all his subjects, their magnificent response, and his benediction.

1b. For the palace will not be for man but for the LORD God: One must conclude that in some extraordinary way **palace** has been substituted for "house" or "temple," which was in the original text. It is difficult to suppose that at the climax of his speech about the temple-to-be David suddenly interjected a plea to his hearers to be diligent in seeing to it that Solomon's palace would be erected on a divinely worthy scale. The Hebrew word *bîrāh,* rendered **palace,** is known only in postexilic Hebrew; in Neh. 2:10 it occurs in reference to a building overlooking the temple which later became the fortress-tower of Antonia. Perhaps for an obscure reason an owner of a MS chanced to jot down this word in its margin, and later it was inserted in the text (here and in vs. 19) in place of "house" or "temple."

2-5. David invites all to make a freewill offering, and tells them that apart from what he has provided from the national revenue account (22:14), he himself heads the

---

did palace. He was able now to tell the people the magnitude of his personal bequest for the temple; but in doing so he was leading on to the right conclusion. If work is to be done for

God worthily, then something incomparably finer than the great gifts of the wealthy is required, viz., the willing contributions of one and all.

thousand drams, and of silver ten thousand talents, and of brass eighteen thousand talents, and one hundred thousand talents of iron.

8 And they with whom *precious* stones were found gave *them* to the treasure of the house of the LORD, by the hand of Jehiel the Gershonite.

9 Then the people rejoiced, for that they offered willingly, because with perfect heart they offered willingly to the LORD: and David the king also rejoiced with great joy.

10 ¶ Wherefore David blessed the LORD before all the congregation: and David said, Blessed *be* thou, LORD God of Israel our father, for ever and ever.

11 Thine, O LORD, *is* the greatness, and the power, and the glory, and the victory, and the majesty: for all *that is* in the heaven and in the earth *is thine;* thine *is* the kingdom, O LORD, and thou art exalted as head above all.

12 Both riches and honor *come* of thee, and thou reignest over all; and in thine hand *is* power and might; and in thine hand *it is* to make great, and to give strength unto all.

13 Now therefore, our God, we thank thee, and praise thy glorious name.

14 But who *am* I, and what *is* my people, that we should be able to offer so willingly after this sort? for all things *come* of thee, and of thine own have we given thee.

15 For we *are* strangers before thee, and sojourners, as *were* all our fathers: our days on the earth *are* as a shadow, and *there is* none abiding.

of the house of God five thousand talents and ten thousand darics of gold, ten thousand talents of silver, eighteen thousand talents of bronze, and a hundred thousand talents of iron. **8** And whoever had precious stones gave them to the treasury of the house of the LORD, in the care of Jehi'el the Gershonite. **9** Then the people rejoiced because these had given willingly, for with a whole heart they had offered freely to the LORD; David the king also rejoiced greatly.

10 Therefore David blessed the LORD in the presence of all the assembly; and David said: "Blessed art thou, O LORD, the God of Israel our father, for ever and ever. **11** Thine, O LORD, is the greatness, and the power, and the glory, and the victory, and the majesty; for all that is in the heavens and in the earth is thine; thine is the kingdom, O LORD, and thou art exalted as head above all. **12** Both riches and honor come from thee, and thou rulest over all. In thy hand are power and might; and in thy hand it is to make great and to give strength to all. **13** And now we thank thee, our God, and praise thy glorious name.

14 "But who am I, and what is my people, that we should be able thus to offer willingly? For all things come from thee, and of thy own have we given thee. **15** For we are strangers before thee, and sojourners, as all our fathers were; our days on the earth are like a shadow, and there is no

---

subscriptions with his own contribution of approximately $60,000,000. Could one ask for a finer example to be set? Loyally and liberally the people are said to have responded (vss. 6-9).

10-30. Finally the thankful king—his lifework completed at this exalted moment—in noble words (vss. 11-19) pronounces the divine benediction. In turn the people give thanks to God, offer a multitude of sacrifices, and rejoice together **before the LORD on that day with great gladness.** There aesthetically the Chronicler should have ended his

---

10-19. *Te Deum.*—The king could now give thanks to God and bring his speech to its close. If victorious David had been like only too many prosperous persons who call themselves "self-made," how boastful his last words might have been. But David ended by expressing humble and reverent gratitude to the majesty of God.

14. *We Give What We Have Received.*— Mark the reiterated insistence (vss. 11, 12, 16)

on the thought expressed by James: "Every good endowment and every perfect gift is from above, coming down from the Father of lights with whom there is no variation or shadow due to change" (Jas. 1:17). We ought indeed so to conceive of God, even as Christ in his parable thought of the Father as saying, "Son, thou art ever with me, and all that I have is thine" (Luke 15:31). We should feel that not only

16 O Lord our God, all this store that we have prepared to build thee a house for thine holy name *cometh* of thine hand, and *is* all thine own.

17 I know also, my God, that thou triest the heart, and hast pleasure in uprightness. As for me, in the uprightness of mine heart I have willingly offered all these things: and now have I seen with joy thy people, which are present here, to offer willingly unto thee.

18 O Lord God of Abraham, Isaac, and of Israel, our fathers, keep this for ever in the imagination of the thoughts of the heart of thy people, and prepare their heart unto thee:

19 And give unto Solomon my son a perfect heart, to keep thy commandments, thy testimonies, and thy statutes, and to do all *these things,* and to build the palace, *for* the which I have made provision.

20 ¶ And David said to all the congregation, Now bless the Lord your God. And all the congregation blessed the Lord God of their fathers, and bowed down their heads, and worshipped the Lord, and the king.

21 And they sacrificed sacrifices unto the Lord, and offered burnt offerings unto the Lord, on the morrow after that day, *even* a thousand bullocks, a thousand rams, *and* a thousand lambs, with their drink offerings, and sacrifices in abundance for all Israel:

22 And did eat and drink before the Lord on that day with great gladness. And they made Solomon the son of David king the second time, and anointed *him* unto the Lord *to be* the chief governor, and Zadok *to be* priest.

abiding.[i] 16 O Lord our God, all this abundance that we have provided for building thee a house for thy holy name comes from thy hand and is all thy own. 17 I know, my God, that thou triest the heart, and hast pleasure in uprightness; in the uprightness of my heart I have freely offered all these things, and now I have seen thy people, who are present here, offering freely and joyously to thee. 18 O Lord, the God of Abraham, Isaac, and Israel, our fathers, keep for ever such purposes and thoughts in the hearts of thy people, and direct their hearts toward thee. 19 Grant to Solomon my son that with a whole heart he may keep thy commandments, thy testimonies, and thy statutes, performing all, and that he may build the palace for which I have made provision."

20 Then David said to all the assembly, "Bless the Lord your God." And all the assembly blessed the Lord, the God of their fathers, and bowed their heads, and worshiped the Lord, and did obeisance to the king. 21 And they performed sacrifices to the Lord, and on the next day offered burnt offerings to the Lord, a thousand bulls, a thousand rams, and a thousand lambs, with their drink offerings, and sacrifices in abundance for all Israel; 22 and they ate and drank before the Lord on that day with great gladness.

And they made Solomon the son of David king the second time, and they anointed him as prince for the Lord, and Zadok as

[i] Gk Vg: Heb *hope*

picture of the ideal David; and there in all probability he did end—apart from a formal annalistic conclusion which is seen in vs. 28 (note its typical stress on prophetic sources) and in vss. 29-30. Of the intervening vss. 22b-28, vs. 22b may be ascribed to a reviser—note its supercautious **the second time,** as if 23:1 had denoted a first, formal intimation

our material possessions but each good and gracious faculty of mind and heart is God-given, and ought to be dedicated to his service. Thus the apostles felt concerning the new life which had come to them through Christ, "Of his fulness have all we received, and grace for grace" (John 1:16). So Christ felt in his own communion with God, "All mine are thine, and thine are mine" (John 17:10). How searching

are these words of Paul, "You are not your own; you were bought with a price" (I Cor. 6:19, 20).

20. *Amen and Amen.*—David asked for the people's response, and they gave it according to his hope: **And all the congregation blessed the Lord God of their fathers, and bowed down their heads, and worshipped the Lord, and the king.**

23 Then Solomon sat on the throne of the LORD as king instead of David his father, and prospered; and all Israel obeyed him.

24 And all the princes, and the mighty men, and all the sons likewise of king David, submitted themselves unto Solomon the king.

25 And the LORD magnified Solomon exceedingly in the sight of all Israel, and bestowed upon him *such* royal majesty as had not been on any king before him in Israel.

26 ¶ Thus David the son of Jesse reigned over all Israel.

27 And the time that he reigned over Israel *was* forty years; seven years reigned he in Hebron, and thirty and three *years* reigned he in Jerusalem.

28 And he died in a good old age, full of days, riches, and honor: and Solomon his son reigned in his stead.

29 Now the acts of David the king, first and last, behold, they *are* written in the book of Samuel the seer, and in the book of Nathan the prophet, and in the book of Gad the seer,

30 With all his reign and his might, and the times that went over him, and over Israel, and over all the kingdoms of the countries.

priest. 23 Then Solomon sat on the throne of the LORD as king instead of David his father; and he prospered, and all Israel obeyed him. 24 All the leaders and the mighty men, and also all the sons of King David, pledged their allegiance to King Solomon. 25 And the LORD gave Solomon great repute in the sight of all Israel, and bestowed upon him such royal majesty as had not been on any king before him in Israel.

26 Thus David the son of Jesse reigned over all Israel. 27 The time that he reigned over Israel was forty years; he reigned seven years in Hebron, and thirty-three years in Jerusalem. 28 Then he died in a good old age, full of days, riches, and honor; and Solomon his son reigned in his stead. 29 Now the acts of King David, from first to last, are written in the Chronicles of Samuel the seer, and in the Chronicles of Nathan the prophet, and in the Chronicles of Gad the seer, 30 with accounts of all his rule and his might and of the circumstances that came upon him and upon Israel, and upon all the kingdoms of the countries.

---

of Solomon's accession; note also its determination not to leave **Zadok** out of the picture. Vs. 27 cannot conceivably have been penned by the Chronicler; for ever so carefully he had ruled out allusions to David's initial seven-year reign (of sorts) at Hebron preceding David's kingship over all the Hebrews. Someone put it in to correspond with I Kings 2:11. But the remaining four verses are much more interesting; they concern the commencement of Solomon's reign and (in the order of vss. 26, 23-25) may constitute the Chronicler's original introduction to the narrative concerning King Solomon. II Chr. 1:1-6 is another introduction to Solomon's reign supplied by revisers.

II CHRONICLES

TEXT, EXEGESIS, AND EXPOSITION

1 And Solomon the son of David was strengthened in his kingdom, and the LORD his God *was* with him, and magnified him exceedingly.

2 Then Solomon spake unto all Israel, to the captains of thousands and of hundreds, and to the judges, and to every governor in all Israel, the chief of the fathers.

3 So Solomon, and all the congregation with him, went to the high place that *was* at Gibeon; for there was the tabernacle of the congregation of God, which Moses the servant of the LORD had made in the wilderness.

1 Solomon the son of David established himself in his kingdom, and the LORD his God was with him and made him exceedingly great.

2 Solomon spoke to all Israel, to the commanders of thousands and of hundreds, to the judges, and to all the leaders in all Israel, the heads of fathers' houses. 3 And Solomon, and all the assembly with him, went to the high place that was at Gibeon; for the tent of meeting of God, which Moses the servant of the LORD had made in the

---

III. THE REIGN OF SOLOMON (1:1–9:31)

Solomon built and equipped the temple in truly "magnifical" style (cf. I Chr. 22:5 ERV), for his kingdom was strong, his wealth immense. The road was open for the Chronicler to describe an ideal Solomon by ignoring the dark aspects of his reign, which the narrative in Kings relates, and by expatiating on Solomonic glories. To begin, therefore, the Chronicler makes no mention whatever of the material now preserved in I Kings 1–2.

A. SOLOMON'S WISDOM (1:1-17)

1:1-6. A reviser probably substituted these verses for the Chronicler's introductory words concerning Solomon, which he transferred to I Chr. 29:23-26. It was essential from

---

1:1. His Majesty, King Solomon.—Solomon was **strengthened in his kingdom** and was **magnified . . . exceedingly.** But was Solomon truly **great?** If we consider his actions at the commencement of his rule—frankly stated in I Kings 2, but suppressed by the Chronicler—in dealing with real or potential opponents, it is plain that he was a ruthless personality. If we have regard to the continuance of his reign, he made his comparatively small kingdom really powerful. Politically he was adroit in effecting his marriage to an Egyptian princess and in establishing friendly relations with the king of Phoenicia. Militarily he was clever, perceiving the importance of speed in war; the number of Hebrew cavalry and chariots (vs. 14) was vastly

increased, and mobile garrisons were established at strategic places in his realm. Commercially he showed genius. Control of the trade routes from harbors at the Gulf of Aqabah on the Red Sea through Edom and Canaan to the great ports of Phoenicia enabled him to tax the transit of merchandise and to become the equivalent of a multimillionaire. It is true that he became recklessly extravagant, even for his resources; but he cannot be numbered among the many sons of prosperous fathers who have wasted their inheritance in riotous living. Solomon loved grandeur: the riches of his palace and temple, the number of his wives and concubines, were astonishing, even to the eyes of the queen of Sheba (9:1-9). But in the eyes of Jesus the splendor of a single flower surpassed that of

For Introduction to II Chr. see pp. 341-48.

4 But the ark of God had David brought up from Kirjath-jearim to *the place which* David had prepared for it: for he had pitched a tent for it at Jerusalem.

5 Moreover the brazen altar, that Bezaleel the son of Uri, the son of Hur, had made, he put before the tabernacle of the LORD: and Solomon and the congregation sought unto it.

6 And Solomon went up thither to the brazen altar before the LORD, which *was* at the tabernacle of the congregation, and offered a thousand burnt offerings upon it.

7 ¶ In that night did God appear unto Solomon, and said unto him, Ask what I shall give thee.

8 And Solomon said unto God, Thou hast showed great mercy unto David my father, and hast made me to reign in his stead.

9 Now, O LORD God, let thy promise unto David my father be established: for thou hast made me king over a people like the dust of the earth in multitude.

10 Give me now wisdom and knowledge, that I may go out and come in before this people: for who can judge this thy people, *that is so* great?

wilderness, was there. 4 (But David had brought up the ark of God from Kir'iath-je'arim to the place that David had prepared for it, for he had pitched a tent for it in Jerusalem.) 5 Moreover the bronze altar that Bez'alel the son of Uri, son of Hur, had made, was there before the tabernacle of the LORD. And Solomon and the assembly sought the LORD. 6 And Solomon went up there to the bronze altar before the LORD, which was at the tent of meeting, and offered a thousand burnt offerings upon it.

7 In that night God appeared to Solomon, and said to him, "Ask what I shall give you." 8 And Solomon said to God, "Thou hast shown great and steadfast love to David my father, and hast made me king in his stead. 9 O LORD God, let thy promise to David my father be now fulfilled, for thou hast made me king over a people as many as the dust of the earth. 10 Give me now wisdom and knowledge to go out and come in before this people, for who can rule this thy people, that is so great?"

---

the reviser's later standpoint (see Exeg. on I Chr. 16:37-43) to assert that Solomon's first action had been to go to Gibeon—where, as he supposed, the tabernacle was stationed—and to offer there a sacrifice on the **bronze altar** (see also Exeg. on 5:1–7:10).

7-13. Perhaps this story of Solomon's dream was omitted by the Chronicler and inserted by a reviser to conform with I Kings 3:5-15. Note that vs. 14 would link smoothly onto I Chr. 29:23-26, and on the other hand, that the final vs. 13 of the dream-narrative

---

Solomon in all his glory. If we look to the end of Solomon's reign we see a tyrant hated and feared by subjects ready to revolt; and the seeming strength of his kingdom was ready to fall to pieces. David was able to leave to Solomon a considerable fortune. He wanted to bequeath his own virtues to his son. Those Solomon was too weak in character to inherit. He did not become a ruler carrying high responsibility in order to serve his fellow men. Unlike David, he could not see and acknowledge his sins, and be sorry. Dollars do not fully indicate what children may have inherited or failed to inherit from parents.

Unless material things truly sum up all that matters in human life, Solomon was not great. The reason for his power and prosperity was, according to the Chronicler, that **the LORD his God was with him.** It is an oversimple assertion to which in all the circumstances we should

demur. But the Chronicler thought about Solomon from one angle, a consideration which seemed to him paramount: David's son magnificently fulfilled the sacred trust, laid upon him by David, to build the temple.

7-12. *Solomon's Petition.*—In these famous words we read not a verbatim report, but the thoughts of good men in later times setting down what they believed appropriate. Did Solomon in actuality desire and pray to be a good as well as a strong king? We may think it probable that he began well. Unhappily his character deteriorated.

The **wisdom and knowledge** which he is said to have asked from God had in Hebrew usage a wider and deeper significance than intellectual learning; it meant sagacity and prudence in the affairs of life, arising from moral integrity (cf. the Christian conception of true wisdom in Jas. 3:17). Solomon was shrewd (I Kings 3:16-28).

11 And God said to Solomon, Because this was in thine heart, and thou hast not asked riches, wealth, or honor, nor the life of thine enemies, neither yet hast asked long life; but hast asked wisdom and knowledge for thyself, that thou mayest judge my people, over whom I have made thee king:

12 Wisdom and knowledge *is* granted unto thee; and I will give thee riches, and wealth, and honor, such as none of the kings have had that *have been* before thee, neither shall there any after thee have the like.

13 ¶ Then Solomon came *from his journey* to the high place that *was* at Gibeon to Jerusalem, from before the tabernacle of the congregation, and reigned over Israel.

14 And Solomon gathered chariots and horsemen: and he had a thousand and four hundred chariots, and twelve thousand horsemen, which he placed in the chariot cities, and with the king at Jerusalem.

15 And the king made silver and gold at Jerusalem *as plenteous* as stones, and cedar trees made he as the sycamore trees that *are* in the vale for abundance.

16 And Solomon had horses brought out of Egypt, and linen yarn: the king's merchants received the linen yarn at a price.

17 And they fetched up, and brought forth out of Egypt a chariot for six hundred *shekels* of silver, and a horse for a hundred and fifty: and so brought they out *horses* for all the kings of the Hittites, and for the kings of Syria, by their means.

11 God answered Solomon, "Because this was in your heart, and you have not asked possessions, wealth, honor, or the life of those who hate you, and have not even asked long life, but have asked wisdom and knowledge for yourself that you may rule my people over whom I have made you king, 12 wisdom and knowledge are granted to you. I will also give you riches, possessions, and honor, such as none of the kings had who were before you, and none after you shall have the like." 13 So Solomon came from*a* the high place at Gibeon, from before the tent of meeting, to Jerusalem. And he reigned over Israel.

14 Solomon gathered together chariots and horsemen; he had fourteen hundred chariots and twelve thousand horsemen, whom he stationed in the chariot cities and with the king in Jerusalem. 15 And the king made silver and gold as common in Jerusalem as stone, and he made cedar as plentiful as the sycamore of the Shephe'lah. 16 And Solomon's import of horses was from Egypt and Ku'e, and the king's traders received them from Ku'e for a price. 17 They imported a chariot from Egypt for six hundred shekels of silver, and a horse for a hundred and fifty; likewise through them these were exported to all the kings of the Hittites and the kings of Syria.

a Gk Vg: Heb *to*

---

is tame and redundant in view of what had already been asserted regarding Solomon's splendor. Moreover, it would not suit the Chronicler to record that an initial act of the heir of saintly David had been to resort to the high place at Gibeon, and there to sacrifice. If, however, the Chronicler did include it, then the telltale phrase in vs. 13—**from before the tabernacle of the congregation**—is a revisional addition (contrast I Kings 3:15).

It is certain that he took pleasure, and was himself masterly, in the art of uttering sagacious thoughts in pithy, axiomatic words: "He spake three thousand proverbs" (I Kings 4:32). Such was his fame in this respect that when collections were eventually made of Hebrew wise sayings, the books of Proverbs (1:1; 25:1) and Ecclesiastes were ascribed to him; note also the beautiful work in the apocryphal writings called The Wisdom of Solomon (*ca.* 50 B.C. or later). But was Solomon really wise? (See Expos. on vs. 1.)

11-12. God's Response.—Because the king had wisely asked for **wisdom**, therefore wisdom the

more was granted him. What men aim at they are at least much more likely to attain if they are ardent and persistent in their desire (cf. Luke 11:5-13). It is said further that because Solomon prayed for wisdom, God promised him also **riches, possessions, and honor.** What should we make of that? Concerning anxieties for food and clothing, Jesus said, "Seek ye first the kingdom of God, and his righteousness; and all these things shall be added unto you" (Matt. 6:33). Frequently it happens that the virtues inherent in a truly religious spirit conduce to health, happiness, and prosperity; but not invariably so. Jesus put first the will of God,

2 And Solomon determined to build a house for the name of the LORD, and a house for his kingdom.

2 And Solomon told out threescore and ten thousand men to bear burdens, and fourscore thousand to hew in the mountain, and three thousand and six hundred to oversee them.

3 ¶ And Solomon sent to Huram the king of Tyre, saying, As thou didst deal with David my father, and didst send him cedars to build him a house to dwell therein, *even so deal with me.*

4 Behold, I build a house to the name of the LORD my God, to dedicate *it* to him, *and* to burn before him sweet incense, and for the continual showbread, and for the burnt offerings morning and evening, on the sabbaths, and on the new moons, and on the solemn feasts of the LORD our God. This *is an ordinance* for ever to Israel.

5 And the house which I build *is* great: for great *is* our God above all gods.

6 But who is able to build him a house, seeing the heaven and heaven of heavens cannot contain him? who *am* I then, that I should build him a house, save only to burn sacrifice before him?

2 [b] Now Solomon purposed to build a temple for the name of the LORD, and a royal palace for himself. [2c] And Solomon assigned seventy thousand men to bear burdens and eighty thousand to quarry in the hill country, and three thousand six hundred to oversee them. 3 And Solomon sent word to Huram the king of Tyre: "As you dealt with David my father and sent him cedar to build himself a house to dwell in, so deal with me. 4 Behold, I am about to build a house for the name of the LORD my God and dedicate it to him for the burning of incense of sweet spices before him, and for the continual offering of the showbread, and for burnt offerings morning and evening, on the sabbaths and the new moons and the appointed feasts of the LORD our God, as ordained for ever for Israel. 5 The house which I am to build will be great, for our God is greater than all gods. 6 But who is able to build him a house, since heaven, even highest heaven, cannot contain him? Who am I to build a house for him, except

[b] Heb Ch 1. 18
[c] Heb Ch 2. 1

B. BUILDING OF THE TEMPLE (2:1–4:22)

2:4. To dedicate . . . for ever to Israel: This enumeration of the ritual purposes of the temple looks like a heavy-handed addition, and the qualifying clause in vs. 6*b*—**save only to burn sacrifice before him**—transparently so.

---

but he experienced hunger, hardship, disappointments, and an early, excruciating death. His counsel was addressed to "men in the plural." Then how everlastingly true it is; for if communities and nations had the right spirit, and there could be an end of greed, mistrust, and war, well-nigh unimaginable benefit for mankind could be attained in this age of scientific resources. If humanity were to do the will of God as Christ conceived it, welfare would increase "far more abundantly than all that we ask or think" (Eph. 3:20).

2:6. *An Insoluble Problem in Architecture.*— To erect a building commensurate with the glory of God is beyond human contriving; cf. the same acknowledgment in Isa. 66:1-2, but note how far the prophetic insight excels that of Solomon, in that it continues, "For all these things hath mine hand made, and so all these things came to be, saith the LORD: but to this man will I look, even to him that is poor and

of a contrite spirit, and that trembleth at my word" (ERV). Realization that God is transcendent is basic wisdom. "It is the genius and the task of prophetic religion to insist on the organic relation between historic human existence and that which is both the ground and the fulfillment of this existence, the transcendent." [1] Nevertheless, right instinct prompts the utmost endeavor, and when the will to build a magnificent place of worship can command gigantic resources, the results are amazing, even if the potentates giving the order may have had mixed motives touching their own renown. Witness the great mosques in Constantinople, the sublime cathedrals in Europe, wherein majesty and mystery blend. This is apparent even to the artistically sensitive; how much more to the believer. But many a lesser church offers to the soul a marvel of strength and quietude, a spirit-

[1] Reinhold Niebuhr, *An Interpretation of Christian Ethics* (New York: Harper & Bros., 1935), p. 105.

7 Send me now therefore a man cunning to work in gold, and in silver, and in brass, and in iron, and in purple, and crimson, and blue, and that can skill to grave with the cunning men that *are* with me in Judah and in Jerusalem, whom David my father did provide.

8 Send me also cedar trees, fir trees, and algum trees, out of Lebanon: for I know that thy servants can skill to cut timber in Lebanon; and, behold, my servants *shall be* with thy servants,

9 Even to prepare me timber in abundance: for the house which I am about to build *shall be* wonderful great.

10 And, behold, I will give to thy servants, the hewers that cut timber, twenty thousand measures of beaten wheat, and twenty thousand measures of barley, and twenty thousand baths of wine, and twenty thousand baths of oil.

11 ¶ Then Huram the king of Tyre answered in writing, which he sent to Solomon, Because the LORD hath loved his people, he hath made thee king over them.

12 Huram said moreover, Blessed *be* the LORD God of Israel, that made heaven and earth, who hath given to David the king a wise son, endued with prudence and understanding, that might build a house for the LORD, and a house for his kingdom.

as a place to burn incense before him? **7** So now send me a man skilled to work in gold, silver, bronze, and iron, and in purple, crimson, and blue fabrics, trained also in engraving, to be with the skilled workers who are with me in Judah and Jerusalem, whom David my father provided. **8** Send me also cedar, cypress, and algum timber from Lebanon, for I know that your servants know how to cut timber in Lebanon. And my servants will be with your servants, **9** to prepare timber for me in abundance, for the house I am to build will be great and wonderful. **10** I will give for your servants, the hewers who cut timber, twenty thousand cors of crushed wheat, twenty thousand cors of barley, twenty thousand baths of wine, and twenty thousand baths of oil."

11 Then Huram the king of Tyre answered in a letter which he sent to Solomon, "Because the LORD loves his people he has made you king over them." **12** Huram also said, "Blessed be the LORD God of Israel, who made heaven and earth, who has given King David a wise son, endued with discretion and understanding, who will build a temple for the LORD, and a royal palace for himself."

---

ual splendor not contingent on size. The homeliest building is adequate for worship if it is the outcome of sincerity and is cared for diligently. What is despicable is to be eager and lavish about the size, comfort, and adornment of our home, and at the same time be content to let the place of our worship become mean and shabby. The perfect temple is not built with hands; it can be entered anywhere at any time by the honest seeker after God (cf. John 4: 21-23).

7-8. Help From Tyre.—Solomon had cash in abundance for his desired temple, but he lacked architects, craftsmen, and cedars of Lebanon. Therefore he called in the help of the king of Tyre, worshiper of the Phoenician deities, who responded generously to the request. Wherefore in due course Jerusalem's first temple formed a most impressive instance of a great sanctuary patterned after the fashion normal for Semitic places of worship, the one exceptional feature being that in its innermost holy building there was no image of the deity but

only the ancient ark. The alignment conformed with worship appropriate to adoration of the sun; the furnishings were eloquent of "heathen" sacred symbols (cf. II Kings 21:5; 23:11).[2] In short, the impression Solomon's temple was likely to make on Hebrew worshipers was not that their God was the only God and utterly unlike the deities of their neighbors. All this, however, might not have mattered so much if what went on in the temple during the monarchic centuries had been clean rites, very different from the customs of the other Semitic peoples. But the cult practiced in the Solomonic temple was often abominably the reverse of pure.

We are in no danger of building Christian churches in the style and with the adornments of heathen temples. But it is not altogether easy to keep out of our buildings some quite heathenish moods and unchristian ideas of God.

---

[2] See F. J. Hollis, *The Archaeology of Herod's Temple* (London: J. M. Dent & Sons, 1934), pp. 132-39; S. H. Hooke, ed., *Myth and Ritual* (London: Oxford University Press, 1933), pp. 87 ff.

13 And now I have sent a cunning man, endued with understanding, of Huram my father's,

14 The son of a woman of the daughters of Dan, and his father *was* a man of Tyre, skilful to work in gold, and in silver, in brass, in iron, in stone, and in timber, in purple, in blue, and in fine linen, and in crimson; also to grave any manner of graving, and to find out every device which shall be put to him, with thy cunning men, and with the cunning men of my lord David thy father.

15 Now therefore the wheat, and the barley, the oil, and the wine, which my lord hath spoken of, let him send unto his servants:

16 And we will cut wood out of Lebanon, as much as thou shalt need: and we will bring it to thee in floats by sea to Joppa; and thou shalt carry it up to Jerusalem.

17 ¶ And Solomon numbered all the strangers that *were* in the land of Israel, after the numbering wherewith David his father had numbered them; and they were found a hundred and fifty thousand and three thousand and six hundred.

18 And he set threescore and ten thousand of them *to be* bearers of burdens, and fourscore thousand *to be* hewers in the mountain, and three thousand and six hundred overseers to set the people awork.

13 "Now I have sent a skilled man, endued with understanding, Huram-abi, 14 the son of a woman of the daughters of Dan, and his father was a man of Tyre. He is trained to work in gold, silver, bronze, iron, stone, and wood, and in purple, blue, and crimson fabrics and fine linen, and to do all sorts of engraving and execute any design that may be assigned him, with your craftsmen, the craftsmen of my lord, David your father. 15 Now therefore the wheat and barley, oil and wine, of which my lord has spoken, let him send to his servants; 16 and we will cut whatever timber you need from Lebanon, and bring it to you in rafts by sea to Joppa, so that you may take it up to Jerusalem."

17 Then Solomon took a census of all the aliens who were in the land of Israel, after the census of them which David his father had taken; and there were found a hundred and fifty-three thousand six hundred. 18 Seventy thousand of them he assigned to bear burdens, eighty thousand to quarry in the hill country, and three thousand six hundred as overseers to make the people work.

---

17. The laborers were **aliens**, not Hebrew subjects, says the Chronicler, glossing over I Kings 5:13.

---

13. *Craftsmanship.*—The skilled artisan is very nearly squeezed out in our hurried, price-ridden times. We become accustomed to see and to use mass-produced articles. But however well turned out for their purpose, they lack the excellence and interest which the skill and patience of the individual craftsman can impart. In religion there is great loss when the beliefs which we say we hold are accepted in mass-produced form. It makes a world of difference if we apply our own individuality; then beliefs become (so to say) "hand-made," the work of our spirit, our very own (cf. Phil. 2:12-13).

17-18. *Forced Labor.*—Presumably the craftsmen obtained from Huram king of Tyre were very well paid by Solomon, and came willingly to Jerusalem. But the lumbermen whom Huram set to work in the forests of Lebanon, how did they fare? Assuredly Huram exacted from Solo-

mon a price for their labor, but did the money actually pass to them in wages? Vs. 10 notes decorously that Solomon sent a colossal supply of food for their benefit. But significantly the statement is not found in the parallel passage in II Kings. And did the food reach the men? The art of "squeeze" is not a merely modern device.[3] Tyrants like Huram or the kings of ancient Egypt (cf. Exod. 1:11-14) conscripted laborers on bare subsistence or slavery terms.

I Kings 5:13-15 relates that Solomon "raised a levy out of all Israel," to the number of more than 150,000, to toil at his buildings. This the Chronicler interestingly alters by assuring us that no Hebrews were engaged: the 150,000 were aliens in the land, all the aliens whom the king

[3] For a modern example see Henry Longhurst, *You Never Know Till You Get There* (London: J. M. Dent & Sons, 1949), p. 178.

3 Then Solomon began to build the house of the LORD at Jerusalem in mount Moriah, where *the LORD* appeared unto David his father, in the place that David had prepared in the threshingfloor of Ornan the Jebusite.

2 And he began to build in the second *day* of the second month, in the fourth year of his reign.

3 ¶ Now these *are the things wherein* Solomon was instructed for the building of the house of God. The length by cubits after the first measure *was* threescore cubits, and the breadth twenty cubits.

4 And the porch that *was* in the front *of the house,* the length *of it was* according to the breadth of the house, twenty cubits, and the height *was* a hundred and twenty: and he overlaid it within with pure gold.

5 And the greater house he ceiled with fir tree, which he overlaid with fine gold, and set thereon palm trees and chains.

6 And he garnished the house with precious stones for beauty: and the gold *was* gold of Parvaim.

3 Then Solomon began to build the house of the LORD in Jerusalem on Mount Mori'ah, where the LORD had appeared to David his father, at the place that David had appointed, on the threshing floor of Ornan the Jeb'usite. 2 He began to build in the second month of the fourth year of his reign. 3 These are Solomon's measurements[d] for building the house of God: the length, in cubits of the old standard, was sixty cubits, and the breadth twenty cubits. 4 The vestibule in front of the nave of the house was twenty cubits long, equal to the width of the house;[e] and its height was a hundred and twenty cubits. He overlaid it on the inside with pure gold. 5 The nave he lined with cypress, and covered it with fine gold, and made palms and chains on it. 6 He adorned the house with settings of precious stones. The gold was gold of Par-

[d] Syr: Heb *foundations*
[e] 1 Kings 6. 3: Heb uncertain

3:1. Only in this verse is Zion said to be identical with **Mount Moriah** (Gen. 22:2).

4a. A hundred and twenty: Read "twenty." The extra hundred cubits probably is a reader's annotation; he knew that Herod's temple was a hundred cubits in height.

---

could find among his subjects (cf. also 8:7-8). Of course that is not fact; there is the telltale record in 10:4, how immediately after the death of Solomon the people came in fury to Rehoboam, saying, "Lighten the hard service of your father and his heavy yoke upon us, and we will serve you." Why then did the Chronicler believe, or wish to believe, that right-minded Solomon could not have conscripted Hebrews to toil at building the temple? In his generation the men of Jerusalem had to do their own work: they were in no position to conscript aliens. Perhaps the idea derived from eschatological expectations expressed in Hag. 2:6-9 and in Isa. 60. Literally construed, those prophecies that alien nations would restore and adorn Jerusalem seem unworthy. In Isa. 60 the scene is idyllically conceived: God's good purpose has been universally realized; all the peoples of the world know the one true God as their redeemer and come rejoicing to the City of God, where the Jews serve mankind as its priests.[4]

Our peril is to err in two directions. We are prone either to think that somebody else should do the needed work for the church, or else—too

[4] Cf. C. C. Torrey, *The Second Isaiah* (New York: Charles Scribner's Sons, 1928), pp. 111-34.

insistent that nobody can do it properly except ourselves—are afraid and jealous lest others should be asked. There is a happy middle way between the two extremes.

3:3. *The Length and the Breadth.*—Imagination is apt to conceive the temple itself as an immense building, but in fact its ground plan measured only about ninety by thirty feet. What was impressive, however, was the great sacred area surrounding it—the open-air courts of the temple—magnificently located in Jerusalem, as at this day: that, and Solomon's adjoining palace. The seer of Revelation in his vision of the heavenly Jerusalem saw that there was "no temple therein: for the Lord God Almighty and the Lamb are the temple of it" (Rev. 21:22). It is only too easy to allow our minds to equate the church with the faith itself, and then to worship ecclesiasticism more than Christ. The real glory, the spiritual reality, exists in the souls of those who want to serve the Lord and try to comprehend "what is the breadth and length and height and depth [of] the love of Christ which surpasses knowledge" (Eph. 3:18).

4. *Pure Gold.*—In this and the following chapter there is such insistence on the lavish use of **gold** for the adornment of the temple

7 He overlaid also the house, the beams, the posts, and the walls thereof, and the doors thereof, with gold; and graved cherubim on the walls.

8 And he made the most holy house, the length whereof *was* according to the breadth of the house, twenty cubits, and the breadth thereof twenty cubits: and he overlaid it with fine gold, *amounting* to six hundred talents.

9 And the weight of the nails *was* fifty shekels of gold. And he overlaid the upper chambers with gold.

10 And in the most holy house he made two cherubim of image work, and overlaid them with gold.

11 ¶ And the wings of the cherubim *were* twenty cubits long: one wing *of the one cherub was* five cubits, reaching to the wall of the house: and the other wing *was likewise* five cubits, reaching to the wing of the other cherub.

12 And *one* wing of the other cherub *was* five cubits, reaching to the wall of the house: and the other wing *was* five cubits *also*, joining to the wing of the other cherub.

13 The wings of these cherubim spread themselves forth twenty cubits: and they stood on their feet, and their faces *were* inward.

14 ¶ And he made the veil *of* blue, and purple, and crimson, and fine linen, and wrought cherubim thereon.

15 Also he made before the house two pillars of thirty and five cubits high, and the chapter that *was* on the top of each of them *was* five cubits.

va'im. 7 So he lined the house with gold — its beams, its thresholds, its walls, and its doors; and he carved cherubim on the walls.

8 And he made the most holy place; its length, corresponding to the breadth of the house, was twenty cubits, and its breadth was twenty cubits; he overlaid it with six hundred talents of fine gold. 9 The weight of the nails was one shekel[f] to fifty shekels of gold. And he overlaid the upper chambers with gold.

10 In the most holy place he made two cherubim of wood[g] and overlaid[h] them with gold. 11 The wings of the cherubim together extended twenty cubits: one wing of the one, of five cubits, touched the wall of the house, and its other wing, of five cubits, touched the wing of the other cherub; 12 and of this cherub, one wing, of five cubits, touched the wall of the house, and the other wing, also of five cubits, was joined to the wing of the first cherub. 13 The wings of these cherubim extended twenty cubits; the cherubim[i] stood on their feet, facing the nave. 14 And he made the veil of blue and purple and crimson fabrics and fine linen, and worked cherubim on it.

15 In front of the house he made two pillars thirty-five cubits high, with a capital

[f] Compare Gk: Heb lacks *one shekel*
[g] Gk: Heb uncertain
[h] Heb *they overlaid*
[i] Heb *they*

8*b*. Not in Kings. Fifty talents per tribe. As to the impossibly vast value of the gold involved cf. Exeg. on I Chr. 29:2-5.

14. Not in Kings. A reviser's insertion in view of Exod. 26:31 (P).

---

that our mental eyes are dazzled and astonished. The description may serve to remind us of an important fact, viz., the insistence in Hebrew teaching that men must not offer shoddy gifts to God—the first-fruits of the crops must be dedicated, the animals presented as sacrifices must be unblemished, the tithes must be given without deduction (cf. the rebuke in Mal. 1:14; 3:8-10). What do we erect on our profession of belief in God? Agreed that for us the foundation is Christ, and can be no other. But what do we build on that foundation? Ideas that are no better than "wood, hay, stubble" (I Cor. 3:12) or a temple of thoughts throughout expressive

of the very mind of Christ? And wherewith do we adorn the basic structure of our faith? With the very qualities of Christ's spirit? Or with unworthy acts and occasional grudging attention? Who is there that does not need to beware of being mean toward God in many things?

8. *Six Hundred Talents.*—The sum represented fifty talents for each of the twelve tribes; not one of them was omitted. "I beheld, and, lo, a great multitude . . . of all nations, and kindreds, and people, and tongues, stood before the throne" (Rev. 7:9). During the past century the two greatest influences on human thought have been the expansion of the knowl-

16 And he made chains, *as* in the oracle, and put *them* on the heads of the pillars; and made a hundred pomegranates, and put *them* on the chains.

17 And he reared up the pillars before the temple, one on the right hand, and the other on the left; and called the name of that on the right hand Jachin, and the name of that on the left Boaz.

4 Moreover he made an altar of brass, twenty cubits the length thereof, and twenty cubits the breadth thereof, and ten cubits the height thereof.

2 ¶ Also he made a molten sea of ten cubits from brim to brim, round in compass, and five cubits the height thereof; and a line of thirty cubits did compass it round about.

3 And under it *was* the similitude of oxen, which did compass it round about: ten in a cubit, compassing the sea round about. Two rows of oxen *were* cast, when it was cast.

4 It stood upon twelve oxen, three looking toward the north, and three looking toward the west, and three looking toward the south, and three looking toward the east: and the sea *was set* above upon them, and all their hinder parts *were* inward.

5 And the thickness of it *was* a handbreadth, and the brim of it like the work of the brim of a cup, with flowers of lilies; *and* it received and held three thousand baths.

6 ¶ He made also ten lavers, and put five on the right hand, and five on the left, to wash in them: such things as they offered for the burnt offering they washed in them; but the sea *was* for the priests to wash in.

7 And he made ten candlesticks of gold according to their form, and set *them* in the

of five cubits on the top of each. **16** He made chains like a necklace[j] and put them on the tops of the pillars; and he made a hundred pomegranates, and put them on the chains. **17** He set up the pillars in front of the temple, one on the south, the other on the north; that on the south he called Jachin, and that on the north Bo'az.

4 He made an altar of bronze, twenty cubits long, and twenty cubits wide, and ten cubits high. **2** Then he made the molten sea; it was round, ten cubits from brim to brim, and five cubits high, and a line of thirty cubits measured its circumference. **3** Under it were figures of gourds,[k] for thirty[l] cubits, compassing the sea round about; the gourds[k] were in two rows, cast with it when it was cast. **4** It stood upon twelve oxen, three facing north, three facing west, three facing south, and three facing east; the sea was set upon them, and all their hinder parts were inward. **5** Its thickness was a handbreadth; and its brim was made like the brim of a cup, like the flower of a lily; it held over three thousand baths. **6** He also made ten lavers in which to wash, and set five on the south side, and five on the north side. In these they were to rinse off what was used for the burnt offering, and the sea was for the priests to wash in.

7 And he made ten golden lampstands as

j Cn: Heb *in the inner sanctuary*
k 1 Kings 7. 24: Heb *oxen*
l Compare verse 2: Heb *ten*

4:1. The measurements may be those of the altar in the second temple. This **altar of bronze** is (strangely) not mentioned in I Kings 7, but elsewhere in Kings (I Kings 8:64; II Kings 16:14, 15).

6. Not in Kings. Perhaps a gloss to stress the superiority of the priests, inserted by someone insensitive to the inconvenience of **the sea** for such a purpose! The molten sea possibly symbolized divine victory over the waters of chaos at the Creation.

7. The parallel in Kings is suspect as a late addition (cf. Exod. 25:31 ff.; Zech. 4).

---

edge of Jesus Christ, and the spread of communism. Yet the importance of the former fact, even in its merely sociological effects, strangely escaped the notice of the editors of *The Cambridge Modern History,* for in its twelve massive

volumes Christian missions are mentioned only once, and that in a footnote.

4:1-22. *Without! Within?*—The dazzling array of earthly treasure is here summed up. The Solomon of history built for his own glory, and

temple, five on the right hand, and five on the left.

8 He made also ten tables, and placed *them* in the temple, five on the right side, and five on the left. And he made a hundred basins of gold.

9 ¶ Furthermore he made the court of the priests, and the great court, and doors for the court, and overlaid the doors of them with brass.

10 And he set the sea on the right side of the east end, over against the south.

11 And Huram made the pots, and the shovels, and the basins. And Huram finished the work that he was to make for king Solomon for the house of God;

12 *To wit,* the two pillars, and the pommels, and the chapiters *which were* on the top of the two pillars, and the two wreaths to cover the two pommels of the chapiters which *were* on the top of the pillars;

13 And four hundred pomegranates on the two wreaths; two rows of pomegranates on each wreath, to cover the two pommels of the chapiters which *were* upon the pillars.

14 He made also bases, and lavers made he upon the bases;

15 One sea, and twelve oxen under it.

16 The pots also, and the shovels, and the fleshhooks, and all their instruments, did Huram his father make to king Solomon for the house of the LORD, of bright brass.

17 In the plain of Jordan did the king cast them, in the clay ground between Succoth and Zeredathah.

18 Thus Solomon made all these vessels in great abundance: for the weight of the brass could not be found out.

19 ¶ And Solomon made all the vessels that *were for* the house of God, the golden altar also, and the tables whereon the showbread *was set;*

20 Moreover the candlesticks with their lamps, that they should burn after the manner before the oracle, of pure gold;

21 And the flowers, and the lamps, and the tongs, *made he of* gold, *and* that perfect gold;

prescribed, and set them in the temple, five on the south side and five on the north.

8 He also made ten tables, and placed them in the temple, five on the south side and five on the north. And he made a hundred basins of gold. 9 He made the court of the priests, and the great court, and doors for the court, and overlaid their doors with bronze; 10 and he set the sea at the southeast corner of the house.

11 Huram also made the pots, the shovels, and the basins. So Huram finished the work that he did for King Solomon on the house of God: 12 the two pillars, the bowls, and the two capitals on the top of the pillars; and the two networks to cover the two bowls of the capitals that were on the top of the pillars; 13 and the four hundred pomegranates for the two networks, two rows of pomegranates for each network, to cover the two bowls of the capitals that were upon the pillars. 14 He made the stands also, and the lavers upon the stands, 15 and the one sea, and the twelve oxen underneath it. 16 The pots, the shovels, the forks, and all the equipment for these Huram-abi made of burnished bronze for King Solomon for the house of the LORD. 17 In the plain of the Jordan the king cast them, in the clay ground between Succoth and Zer'edah. 18 Solomon made all these things in great quantities, so that the weight of the bronze was not ascertained.

19 So Solomon made all the things that were in the house of God: the golden altar, the tables for the bread of the Presence, 20 the lampstands and their lamps of pure gold to burn before the inner sanctuary, as prescribed; 21 the flowers, the lamps, and

---

9. Solomon's temple had but one sacred court, and beyond it was the large royal area (*'azārāh*) in which stood the palace. This verse suits the layout of the second temple.

18-22. These verses (cf. I Kings 7:48-50, which, however, is suspect as a late addition) awkwardly anticipate the Chronicler's conclusion of the survey (5:1). **The golden altar** (vs. 19) is also puzzling.

22 And the snuffers, and the basins, and the spoons, and the censers, *of* pure gold: and the entry of the house, the inner doors thereof for the most holy *place,* and the doors of the house of the temple, *were of* gold.

5 Thus all the work that Solomon made for the house of the LORD was finished: and Solomon brought in *all* the things that David his father had dedicated; and the silver, and the gold, and all the instruments, put he among the treasures of the house of God.

2 ¶ Then Solomon assembled the elders of Israel, and all the heads of the tribes, the chief of the fathers of the children of Israel, unto Jerusalem, to bring up the ark of the covenant of the LORD out of the city of David, which *is* Zion.

3 Wherefore all the men of Israel assembled themselves unto the king in the feast which *was* in the seventh month.

4 And all the elders of Israel came; and the Levites took up the ark.

5 And they brought up the ark, and the tabernacle of the congregation, and all the holy vessels that *were* in the tabernacle, these did the priests *and* the Levites. bring up.

the tongs, of purest gold; 22 the snuffers, basins, dishes for incense, and firepans, of pure gold; and the sockets[m] of the temple, for the inner doors to the most holy place and for the doors of the nave of the temple were of gold.

5 Thus all the work that Solomon did for the house of the LORD was finished. And Solomon brought in the things which David his father had dedicated, and stored the silver, the gold, and all the vessels in the treasuries of the house of God.

2 Then Solomon assembled the elders of Israel and all the heads of the tribes, the leaders of the fathers' houses of the people of Israel, in Jerusalem, to bring up the ark of the covenant of the LORD out of the city of David, which is Zion. 3 And all the men of Israel assembled before the king at the feast which is in the seventh month. 4 And all the elders of Israel came, and the Levites took up the ark. 5 And they brought up the ark, the tent of meeting, and all the holy vessels that were in the tent; the priests

[m] 1 Kings 7. 50: Heb *the door of the house*

C. CONSECRATION OF THE TEMPLE (5:1–7:10)

Important intricacies are here apparent. The parallel passages in Kings contain some late additions, so we cannot tell exactly what the Chronicler had before him. He probably related, as the grand climax, that Solomon summoned the Levites—priests, musicians, bearers—and that they duly carried the ark into the temple. But such a narrative left the men of later times in a quandary. On their view of the situation Solomon ought also solemnly to have fetched the Mosaic tabernacle from Gibeon, though no one knows what he was to do with it on its arrival at Jerusalem. The legitimate altar at Gibeon he could not shift: they had to say that he made a new altar of brass for the temple, and to declare that it received divine approval by fire from heaven. In the Chronicler's view the rightful altar already existed, being the altar built by David at Araunah's threshing floor, on which the heavenly fire (see I Chr. 21:26; 22:1) had then fallen. Probably the Chronicler's original description is found in 5:1-5a, 6; 6:1-12, 14-42; 7:1, 3-5, and the revisers' additions in 5:5b, 7-14; 6:13; 7:2, 6-10.

5. The tent of meeting: By these words the revisers signified that the tabernacle was brought from Gibeon. **In the tent:** The Chronicler referred to the Davidic "tent of curtains" in Zion.

---

in his pride judged worth by wealth. He might have been wise, but he was foolish toward God. And the splendor of his temple tended only to debase the minds of the priests and people: all glorious without, within it became full of corruption and evil deeds (cf. Jer. 7:1-16). Solomon

never came near understanding what God requires from us, as the great prophets understood the divine will.

5:1. Complete at Last.—The dazzling catalogue has reached conclusion: the temple stands complete. Solomon had given the people a

6 Also king Solomon, and all the congregation of Israel that were assembled unto him before the ark, sacrificed sheep and oxen, which could not be told nor numbered for multitude.

7 And the priests brought in the ark of the covenant of the LORD unto his place, to the oracle of the house, into the most holy place, even under the wings of the cherubim:

8 For the cherubim spread forth their wings over the place of the ark, and the cherubim covered the ark and the staves thereof above.

9 And they drew out the staves of the ark, that the ends of the staves were seen from the ark before the oracle; but they were not seen without. And there it is unto this day.

10 There was nothing in the ark save the two tables which Moses put therein at Horeb, when the LORD made a covenant with the children of Israel, when they came out of Egypt.

11 ¶ And it came to pass, when the priests were come out of the holy place: (for all the priests that were present were sanctified, and did not then wait by course:

and the Levites brought them up. 6 and King Solomon and all the congregation of Israel, who had assembled before him, were before the ark, sacrificing so many sheep and oxen that they could not be counted or numbered. 7 So the priests brought the ark of the covenant of the LORD to its place, in the inner sanctuary of the house, in the most holy place, underneath the wings of the cherubim. 8 For the cherubim spread out their wings over the place of the ark, so that the cherubim made a covering above the ark and its poles. 9 And the poles were so long that the ends of the poles were seen from the holy place before the inner sanctuary; but they could not be seen from outside; and they are there to this day. 10 There was nothing in the ark except the two tables which Moses put there at Horeb, where the LORD made a covenant with the people of Israel, when they came out of Egypt. 11 Now when the priests came out of the holy place (for all the priests who were present had sanctified themselves, without regard to

---

7-14. The revisers hint at the subsequent unimportance of the ark (invisible save for the staves; cf. Exeg. on 35:2-17).

11b-12. This clumsy parenthesis looks like a very late addition to what the revisers had written, made by someone who thought it fitting to say also that the musicians had not trespassed one step farther than was proper.

---

superlative demonstration of religious generosity. It would be treason to ask whether he had really been building ad majorem gloriam Solomonis. Could and should all this treasure have been put to better use? Most of Solomon's subjects were existing in stringent poverty and housed in hovels. The king felt no vestige of concern about social welfare, and it never occurred to him that God does. There are, however, moments when precious things are rightly expended on spiritual purposes (see Matt. 26:6-13).

Men and women are prone to concentrate their energies and resources on the self and the circle of their immediate family, sometimes with set intention, often through lack of sympathetic attention to others. Christ challenged that attitude in the most drastic and searching terms (Matt. 10:37-39; 25:31-46; Luke 6:38).

7. The Real Treasure.—From this point the narrative improves in value. All the splendor of outward things had not made a temple which

was the abode of the Spirit. But now there is solemnly placed in its innermost sanctuary Israel's ancient hallowed ark—felt to be the sign and token of God's being with them; and if the Ten Commandments were inscribed on the stones which Moses put therein, it did indeed contain the essence of Hebrew faith.

Very interesting, but subject of indeterminate discussion, is the history of the ark. The notices of its journeyings from Mount Horeb are exciting (cf. Num. 10:33-36; 14:44; Josh. 3:3-4; 6:6-11; I Sam. 3:3; 4:3-22; II Sam. 6). After it was placed in the temple the record falls silent. Possibly Shishak carried it off (I Kings 14:26), but it may have been in place in Jeremiah's day (Jer. 3:16) and destroyed when the Babylonians sacked Jerusalem in 586 B.C. It is as good as certain that the ark originally contained two stones taken from the Mount of Covenant. It is most unlikely that the Ten Commandments were written on them. After 586 B.C. the Jews, thanks to the great prophets, knew and revered

12 Also the Levites *which were* the singers, all of them of Asaph, of Heman, of Jeduthun, with their sons and their brethren, *being* arrayed in white linen, having cymbals and psalteries and harps, stood at the east end of the altar, and with them a hundred and twenty priests sounding with trumpets:)

13 It came even to pass, as the trumpeters and singers *were* as one, to make one sound to be heard in praising and thanking the LORD; and when they lifted up *their* voice with the trumpets and cymbals and instruments of music, and praised the LORD, *saying*, For *he is* good; for his mercy *endureth* for ever: that *then* the house was filled with a cloud, *even* the house of the LORD;

14 So that the priests could not stand to minister by reason of the cloud: for the glory of the LORD had filled the house of God.

6 Then said Solomon, The LORD hath said that he would dwell in the thick darkness.

their divisions; 12 and all the Levitical singers, Asaph, Heman, and Jedu'thun, their sons and kinsmen, arrayed in fine linen, with cymbals, harps, and lyres, stood east of the altar with a hundred and twenty priests who were trumpeters; 13 and it was the duty of the trumpeters and singers to make themselves heard in unison in praise and thanksgiving to the LORD), and when the song was raised, with trumpets and cymbals and other musical instruments, in praise to the LORD,

"For he is good,
    for his steadfast love endures for ever,"
the house, the house of the LORD, was filled with a cloud, 14 so that the priests could not stand to minister because of the cloud; for the glory of the LORD filled the house of God.

6 Then Solomon said,
"The LORD has said that he would dwell
    in thick darkness.

6:1-42. The Chronicler transcribed Solomon's prayer from I Kings 8:22-50, but gave it a finer conclusion.

1-2. Then Solomon . . . ever: But read, in accordance with the LXX of I Kings 8:12,

Then Solomon said,
    "The LORD has set the sun in the heavens,
        but has said that he would dwell in thick darkness.
    I have built thee an exalted house,
        a place for thee to dwell in for ever."

---

those commandments, and their faith in God was not dependent on the preservation of a wooden box and inscribed stones.

In the sanctuary of Christian belief the treasure is Jesus, and we cannot do without him. Arguments can be advanced for the validity of theism; but in the last resort Jesus is the only indestructible evidence that God is love.

13-14. *Unison.*— (Regarding the music, see Expos. on I Chr. 6:31; 15:16; and for correct translation of the Hebrew text see RSV.) Not until united voices were raised in thankful praise was the mystery of divine acceptance felt and an assurance of God's presence given: **The house . . . was filled with a cloud; . . . for the glory of the LORD filled the house of God.** Apathetic worshipers in church are like a wet blanket of fog, a dismal cloud amidst which the willing long for the clear shining of radiant thankfulness. The unmusical cannot participate in the rendering of hymns with good effect; but there are times of prayer when all can help or

hinder. Worship is easily affected by spiritual "temperature." No religion faces the dark aspects of life so gravely as Christianity. But it has such an answer to give that it should excel all religions in joyousness. The early Christians startled their heathen neighbors in that respect. "As Hermas wrote in his *Shepherd*, The Holy Spirit was a glad spirit. . . . 'It befits Truth to laugh, because she is glad—to play with her rivals, because she is free from fear,' so said Tertullian. . . . And it was Jesus who was the secret of it." [5] "Rejoice in the Lord always: and again I say, Rejoice," urged Paul (Phil. 4:4). A Scottish evangelist rebuked a reticent, gloomy congregation: "If David," said he, "heard you singing the psalms like that, he would take them from you."

6:1-2. *The Hidden God.*— (See Exeg.) Whether the interesting rhythmic utterance was older than Solomon's time and quoted by him

[5] T. R. Glover, *The Jesus of History* (London: Student Christian Movement Press, 1917), p. 214.

2 But I have built a house of habitation for thee, and a place for thy dwelling for ever.

3 And the king turned his face, and blessed the whole congregation of Israel: and all the congregation of Israel stood.

4 And he said, Blessed *be* the LORD God of Israel, who hath with his hands fulfilled *that* which he spake with his mouth to my father David, saying,

5 Since the day that I brought forth my people out of the land of Egypt I chose no city among all the tribes of Israel to build a house in, that my name might be there; neither chose I any man to be a ruler over my people Israel:

6 But I have chosen Jerusalem, that my name might be there; and have chosen David to be over my people Israel.

7 Now it was in the heart of David my father to build a house for the name of the LORD God of Israel.

8 But the LORD said to David my father, Forasmuch as it was in thine heart to build a house for my name, thou didst well in that it was in thine heart:

9 Notwithstanding thou shalt not build the house; but thy son which shall come forth out of thy loins, he shall build the house for my name.

10 The LORD therefore hath performed his word that he hath spoken: for I am risen up in the room of David my father, and am set on the throne of Israel, as the LORD promised, and have built the house for the name of the LORD God of Israel.

11 And in it have I put the ark, wherein *is* the covenant of the LORD, that he made with the children of Israel.

12 ¶ And he stood before the altar of the LORD in the presence of all the congregation of Israel, and spread forth his hands:

2 I have built thee an exalted house,
    a place for thee to dwell in for ever."
3 Then the king faced about, and blessed all the assembly of Israel, while all the assembly of Israel stood. 4 And he said, "Blessed be the LORD, the God of Israel, who with his hand has fulfilled what he promised with his mouth to David my father, saying, 5 'Since the day that I brought my people out of the land of Egypt, I chose no city in all the tribes of Israel in which to build a house, that my name might be there, and I chose no man as prince over my people Israel; 6 but I have chosen Jerusalem that my name may be there and I have chosen David to be over my people Israel.' 7 Now it was in the heart of David my father to build a house for the name of the LORD, the God of Israel. 8 But the LORD said to David my father, 'Whereas it was in your heart to build a house for my name, you did well that it was in your heart; 9 nevertheless you shall not build the house, but your son who shall be born to you shall build the house for my name.' 10 Now the LORD has fulfilled his promise which he made; for I have risen in the place of David my father, and sit on the throne of Israel, as the LORD promised, and I have built the house for the name of the LORD, the God of Israel. 11 And there I have set the ark, in which is the covenant of the LORD which he made with the people of Israel."

12 Then Solomon stood before the altar of the LORD in the presence of all the assembly of Israel, and spread forth his hands.

This rhythmic quatrain is said by the LXX to have come from a collection of ancient Hebrew poems called the "Book of Songs," elsewhere styled the "Book of Jashar" (cf. Josh. 10:13; II Sam. 1:18). Seeing that the initial clause (in Hebrew three words), "The LORD has set his sun in the heavens," was available to the LXX translators, one feels it

---

from the ancient Song of Songs, or was spoken first by him on this solemn occasion and consequently included in the Song of Songs, must be left to conjecture. The contrast between he unendurable brightness of the sun and the impenetrable darkness of the inner sanctuary in

which the ark was deposited is most effective. Jewish religion kept the balance true between divine transcendence and immanence—realization of the infinitude of God himself, and trust that nevertheless he is accessible to man. A Talmudic saying declares: "God is far [for is He

13 For Solomon had made a brazen scaffold, of five cubits long, and five cubits broad, and three cubits high, and had set it in the midst of the court: and upon it he stood, and kneeled down upon his knees before all the congregation of Israel, and spread forth his hands toward heaven,

14 And said, O LORD God of Israel, *there is* no God like thee in the heaven, nor in the earth; which keepest covenant, and *showest* mercy unto thy servants, that walk before thee with all their hearts:

15 Thou which hast kept with thy servant David my father that which thou hast promised him; and spakest with thy mouth, and hast fulfilled *it* with thine hand, as *it is* this day.

16 Now therefore, O LORD God of Israel, keep with thy servant David my father that which thou hast promised him, saying, There shall not fail thee a man in my sight to sit upon the throne of Israel; yet so that thy children take heed to their way to walk in my law, as thou hast walked before me.

17 Now then, O LORD God of Israel, let thy word be verified, which thou hast spoken unto thy servant David.

18 But will God in very deed dwell with men on the earth? Behold, heaven and the heaven of heavens cannot contain thee; how much less this house which I have built!

13 Solomon had made a bronze platform five cubits long, five cubits wide, and three cubits high, and had set it in the court; and he stood upon it. Then he knelt upon his knees in the presence of all the assembly of Israel, and spread forth his hands toward heaven; 14 and said, "O LORD, God of Israel, there is no God like thee, in heaven or on earth, keeping covenant and showing steadfast love to thy servants who walk before thee with all their heart; 15 who hast kept with thy servant David my father what thou didst declare to him; yea, thou didst speak with thy mouth, and with thy hand hast fulfilled it this day. 16 Now therefore, O LORD, God of Israel, keep with thy servant David my father what thou hast promised him, saying, 'There shall never fail you a man before me to sit upon the throne of Israel, if only your sons take heed to their way, to walk in my law as you have walked before me.' 17 Now therefore, O LORD, God of Israel, let thy word be confirmed, which thou hast spoken to thy servant David.

18 "But will God dwell indeed with man on the earth? Behold, heaven and the highest heaven cannot contain thee; how much

must also have been found in the original text of both Kings and Chronicles. What might lead to its eventual deletion? Perhaps a too anxious Jewish scribe, aware that the Solomonic temple had been tainted by sun-cult rites, felt that any allusion whatsoever to the sun was undesirable in Solomon's dedicatory address.

13. The revisers had no cause to alter the noble words of the prayer, yet they took occasion to interject a forehint for their remarks in 7:7. Read **platform**; the Hebrew word is very similar to **scaffold**.

not in the heaven of heavens?], yet He is near. . . . For a man enters a synagogue, and stands behind a pillar, and prays in a whisper, and God hears his prayer, and so it is with all His creatures."[6]

14-42. The King's Prayer.—The Chronicler quotes almost verbatim from I Kings 8:22-50. There are other moving supplications recorded in the O.T., e.g., Exod. 33:12-23; Jer. 15:15-18. None is equal to this in magnitude and sustained quality. The whole utterance has rightfully its place in sublime literature; and that without any intention or striving on the author's

[6] C. G. Montefiore and Herbert Loewe, *A Rabbinic Anthology* (London: Macmillan & Co., 1938), p. 22.

part to produce an artistic achievement. But before attempting to appreciate let us be critical on the literary side. Its invocation (vss. 14-21) is perhaps above criticism: for its length is appropriate to the length of the ensuing prayer, its wording admirable in humility, dignity, and reverence. But thereafter are there not obvious faults in the prayer's construction? The sequence of topics seems somewhat haphazard. Reflections on war have not been brought together under one heading, but are dispersed in vss. 24, 34, 36, with yet another allusion interjected into vs. 28. The reference to experience of captivity is anything but concise. Is there not verbosity in the reiteration of the supplication for pardon for

19 Have respect therefore to the prayer of thy servant, and to his supplication, O LORD my God, to hearken unto the cry and the prayer which thy servant prayeth before thee:

20 That thine eyes may be open upon this house day and night, upon the place whereof thou hast said that thou wouldest put thy name there; to hearken unto the prayer which thy servant prayeth toward this place.

21 Hearken therefore unto the supplications of thy servant, and of thy people Israel, which they shall make toward this place: hear thou from thy dwelling place, *even* from heaven; and when thou hearest, forgive.

22 ¶ If a man sin against his neighbor, and an oath be laid upon him to make him swear, and the oath come before thine altar in this house;

23 Then hear thou from heaven, and do, and judge thy servants, by requiting the wicked, by recompensing his way upon his own head; and by justifying the righteous, by giving him according to his righteousness.

24 ¶ And if thy people Israel be put to the worse before the enemy, because they have sinned against thee; and shall return and confess thy name, and pray and make supplication before thee in this house;

less this house which I have built! **19** Yet have regard to the prayer of thy servant and to his supplication, O LORD my God, hearkening to the cry and to the prayer which thy servant prays before thee; **20** that thy eyes may be open day and night toward this house, the place where thou hast promised to set thy name, that thou mayest hearken to the prayer which thy servant offers toward this place. **21** And hearken thou to the supplications of thy servant and of thy people Israel, when they pray toward this place; yea, hear thou from heaven thy dwelling place; and when thou hearest, forgive.

22 "If a man sins against his neighbor and is made to take an oath, and comes and swears his oath before thy altar in this house, **23** then hear thou from heaven, and act, and judge thy servants, requiting the guilty by bringing his conduct upon his own head, and vindicating the righteous by rewarding him according to his righteousness.

24 "If thy people Israel are defeated before the enemy because they have sinned against thee, when they turn again and acknowledge thy name, and pray and make

---

the penitent—if he turns toward God and this temple, **then hear thou from heaven thy dwelling place, . . . and forgive** (vs. 39). The supplication is finely phrased, but why not have reserved it for the close, or used it at most twice in the course of the prayer? Could not the author have shortened and (so to say) tidied up his writing, and thus have made it suitable for publication?

Not so. These are not faults even of construction, but are signs of authentic praying; the outpouring of a man's soul, touched by the infirmities of his people, striving to cover the whole range of human need, beseeching for erring and suffering men the delivering and restoring mercy of God, who alone **knowest the hearts of the children of men** (vs. 30). Respect and gratitude are due to the man whose words here quoted perhaps gave form to a prayer which countless times has been offered in Christian worship, and finds a lodging in the hearer's conscience: "Almighty God, unto whom all hearts are open, all desires known, and from

whom no secrets are hid; Cleanse the thoughts of our hearts. . . ."

We may now survey the contents of the prayer ascribed to Solomon, remembering that we have before us the thoughts of a Jew who lived after the fall of the Hebrew kingdoms and here prays as Solomon, he feels, should have done.

22-23. Social Sins.—It was wholly appropriate that the first intercession should concern the inner life of the community—the wrongs which men who should be true brethren inflict on one another, injuring all. The suppliant prays that resolute justice may be upheld, the guilty punished, the cause of the innocent vindicated (cf. Deut. 16:20, "That which is altogether just shalt thou follow, that thou mayest live, and inherit the land which the LORD thy God giveth thee").

24, 34, 36. In Time of War.—The intercessor may not personally have known the horrors and anguish of defeat by a pitiless foe—massacre, ruin, slavery—but he had the imagination and heart to comprehend what it does entail for human homes, what miseries it had often brought

25 Then hear thou from the heavens, and forgive the sin of thy people Israel, and bring them again unto the land which thou gavest to them and to their fathers.

26 ¶ When the heaven is shut up, and there is no rain, because they have sinned against thee; *yet* if they pray toward this place, and confess thy name, and turn from their sin, when thou dost afflict them;

27 Then hear thou from heaven, and forgive the sin of thy servants, and of thy people Israel, when thou hast taught them the good way, wherein they should walk; and send rain upon thy land, which thou hast given unto thy people for an inheritance.

supplication to thee in this house; 25 then hear thou from heaven, and forgive the sin of thy people Israel, and bring them again to the land which thou gavest to them and to their fathers.

26 "When heaven is shut up and there is no rain because they have sinned against thee, if they pray toward this place, and acknowledge thy name, and turn from their sin, when thou dost afflict them, 27 then hear thou in heaven, and forgive the sin of thy servants, thy people Israel, when thou dost teach them the good way[n] in which they should walk; and grant rain upon thy land, which thou hast given to thy people as an inheritance.

[n] Gk Syr Vg: Heb *toward the good way*

---

upon his people in times past. He had a quality of soul which the safe and prosperous often lack to their own ruinous impoverishment of spirit (read Jer. 4:5-13, 22-31; Lam. 2; Amos 9:1-4).

Vs. 34, on aggressive warfare, looks like an afterthought, it is so far separated from vs. 24. Perhaps the writer, remembering how often Judean kings had led their young subjects on campaigns for conquest, felt that the matter must be given a place in Solomon's prayer. Jews in his own time were in no position to wage war on others. Nevertheless, to our feelings this is the one blot in the dedicatory intercession. Christian prayers in time of war may rightly supplicate for the men who at their nation's summons are face to face with the perils and horrors of battle, but must include and be inspired by longing that the hearts of all peoples, our own and our foes', will be led into the ways of peace. At a religious meeting in Britain during the appalling crisis in World War I, someone offered a prayer of that nature. He was followed by an indignant and perplexed layman who began, "O Lord, O Lord, we are here tonight to pray for the British Empire."

26-28. *Drought and Famine.*—Anyone who has seen pastures and crops wither into desolation understands the constraint that prayers should be offered for rain. But Jesus called his disciples to hold such a faith in the impartial goodness of God that we shall accept as from his hand the whole dispensation of events—"the changes and chances of this mortal life"—without mistrust that he knows our need. In antiquity Palestine was much more fertile than it now is, and moreover its luxuriance was seen by its inhabitants in contrast with the aridity of the deserts east and south, where the nomads contrived to exist on the near edge of starvation and thirst (cf. Deut. 8:7-9). When pro-

longed drought hit ancient Canaan there was no escape to more fortunate surrounding lands, and from the West came no relief ships carrying cargoes of grain. The cattle perished, the springs dried up, and in the homes of the people men, women, and children thirsted and starved (cf. Amos 4:6-10). In the past century the willingness of Western nations to send famine relief to stricken areas has conspicuously differentiated Christian from non-Christian civilization. In the future perhaps it will be characteristic of modern humanity everywhere, if good will and the sciences can defeat the looming menace of world-wide hunger.

27, 31, 33. *The Purpose of Forgiveness.*—Why should men concern themselves to seek divine forgiveness? Do they hope thus to gain mental assurance that unpleasant consequences will not ensue from their wrongdoing? Is their aim merely to secure the cancellation of one debt in order that they may gaily run again into another debt? Why should God be conceived as so much concerned to forgive? Is it because he finds pleasure in being indulgent, and relishes opportunities to be soft? Heine's witticism, spoken when he was dying—"God will pardon us; it's his business"—was pathetic in its shallowness. The O.T. goes to the root of this deep matter. It relates that Moses was bidden to lead undeserving Israel out of Egypt in order that the people might rightly worship God and learn to keep his commandments. So also in this intercession God is besought to pardon his people, being penitent, in order that he might **teach them the good way** (vs. 27), in order that **they may fear thee and walk in thy ways all the days that they live in the land** (vs. 31); and yet more, **in order that all the peoples of the earth may know thy name and fear thee, as do thy people Israel** (vs. 33).

28 ¶ If there be dearth in the land, if there be pestilence, if there be blasting or mildew, locusts or caterpillars; if their enemies besiege them in the cities of their land; whatsoever sore, or whatsoever sickness *there be:*

29 *Then* what prayer *or* what supplication soever shall be made of any man, or of all thy people Israel, when every one shall know his own sore and his own grief, and shall spread forth his hands in this house:

30 Then hear thou from heaven thy dwelling place, and forgive, and render unto every man according unto all his ways, whose heart thou knowest; (for thou only knowest the hearts of the children of men;)

31 That they may fear thee, to walk in thy ways, so long as they live in the land which thou gavest unto our fathers.

32 ¶ Moreover concerning the stranger, which is not of thy people Israel, but is

28 "If there is famine in the land, if there is pestilence or blight or mildew or locust or caterpillar; if their enemies besiege them in any of their cities; whatever plague, whatever sickness there is; **29** whatever prayer, whatever supplication is made by any man or by all thy people Israel, each knowing his own affliction, and his own sorrow and stretching out his hands toward this house; **30** then hear thou from heaven thy dwelling place, and forgive, and render to each whose heart thou knowest, according to all his ways (for thou, thou only, knowest the hearts of the children of men) ; **31** that they may fear thee and walk in thy ways all the days that they live in the land which thou gavest to our fathers.

32 "Likewise when a foreigner, who is

---

28. In the cities of their land (KJV) : Corrupt text. Read either, **in any of their cities** (so LXX and RSV) , or "by making a breach in their gates."

---

28. *Pestilence and Disease.*—We are at least cushioned against the terrors of disease, and have much reason to hope for recovery from sickness. Medical science and hospital service are at our disposal. In ancient Palestine diseases were as rife, painful, and exhausting as now; but next to nothing was known about sensible remedies. Patients were as likely to recover without as with the treatment given by those who claimed to be physicians (see Expos. on 16:12) . Moreover, the sufferer was oppressed by belief that the calamity had befallen him because he had angered God by some transgression, whether consciously or unconsciously committed by himself or others of his family. Disaster of any sort was deemed to imply the wrath of God (cf. Luke 13:4) . As for plague, wonderfully the bacteriologists have protected modern men against its onset. Formerly it was a horror of horrors—the Black Death in fourteenth-century Europe; the plague in Athens, of which Thucydides wrote an immortal description.[7] When plague ravaged the towns and villages of ancient Palestine with its fierce agony, none knew why it struck this home and that, or how to exclude it from barred doors.

From lightning and tempest; from earthquake, fire, and flood; from plague, pestilence, and famine; from battle and murder, and from sudden death,
Good Lord, deliver us.[8]

[7] *Peloponnesian War* II. 47-52.
[8] Book of Common Prayer, The Litany.

29, 36a. *Individual Need.*—It is helpful in worship when a moment of opportunity is given wherein the individual may prayerfully think of his particular need, **each knowing his own affliction, and his own sorrow.** Manifold beyond enumeration are the strains and stresses which men and women have to bear. This intercessor remembered that. But equally he insists—even as did Jesus (Matt. 6:15) —that the distressed individual must know himself not merely as a person deserving pity but also as one who has wronged others, and should pray to be forgiven, **for there is no man who does not sin.** That profound appraisal of human imperfection, so difficult constantly to accept, became cardinal doctrine in Judaism and Christianity. Will God forgive iniquity? Not unconditionally—there must first be repentance. Solomon's prayer reiterates the solemn teaching. Does God aid men to repent, seeking to persuade our free personalities to perceive and turn away from evil? And to what length does divine mercy go? Judaism insisted, "To the limit of human imagination and beyond" (Gen. 18:22-33) . Christianity answered, "Even to the Cross."

32. *Stranger in a Strange Land.*—A Jewish patriot is praying, his mind seemingly absorbed in thoughts for his own people. But here—it is so unexpected and wonderful—humanely he recalls the strangers in their midst, and asks that they also may receive the same restoring grace of God. Mark that it is through the He-

come from a far country for thy great name's sake, and thy mighty hand, and thy stretched out arm; if they come and pray in this house;

33 Then hear thou from the heavens, *even* from thy dwelling place, and do according to all that the stranger calleth to thee for; that all people of the earth may know thy name, and fear thee, as *doth* thy people Israel, and may know that this house which I have built is called by thy name.

34 If thy people go out to war against their enemies by the way that thou shalt send them, and they pray unto thee toward this city which thou hast chosen, and the house which I have built for thy name;

35 Then hear thou from the heavens their prayer and their supplication, and maintain their cause.

36 If they sin against thee, (for *there is* no man which sinneth not,) and thou be angry with them, and deliver them over before *their* enemies, and they carry them away captives unto a land far off or near;

37 Yet *if* they bethink themselves in the land whither they are carried captive, and turn and pray unto thee in the land of their captivity, saying, We have sinned, we have done amiss, and have dealt wickedly;

38 If they return to thee with all their heart and with all their soul in the land of their captivity, whither they have carried them captives, and pray toward their land, which thou gavest unto their fathers, and *toward* the city which thou hast chosen, and toward the house which I have built for thy name:

not of thy people Israel, comes from a far country for the sake of thy great name, and thy mighty hand, and thy outstretched arm, when he comes and prays toward this house, **33** hear thou from heaven thy dwelling place, and do according to all for which the foreigner calls to thee; in order that all the peoples of the earth may know thy name and fear thee, as do thy people Israel, and that they may know that this house which I have built is called by thy name.

34 "If thy people go out to battle against their enemies, by whatever way thou shalt send them, and they pray to thee toward this city which thou hast chosen and the house which I have built for thy name, **35** then hear thou from heaven their prayer and their supplication, and maintain their cause.

36 "If they sin against thee — for there is no man who does not sin — and thou art angry with them, and dost give them to an enemy, so that they are carried away captive to a land far or near; **37** yet if they lay it to heart in the land to which they have been carried captive, and repent, and make supplication to thee in the land of their captivity, saying, 'We have sinned, and have acted perversely and wickedly'; **38** if they repent with all their mind and with all their heart in the land of their captivity, to which they were carried captive, and pray toward their land, which thou gavest to their fathers, the city which thou hast chosen, and the house which I have built

---

brews' kindly treatment of the **foreigner** that he can dare to hope that eventually the world will be brought to the knowledge of truth and the love of right. This intercession lifts the whole prayer onto the plane of universal, timeless value. Collect from the O.T. or elsewhere in Jewish literature all hostile or contemptuous references to Gentiles that can be found, they weigh not against this verse. Here Jewish religion has risen to perceive that "One touch of nature makes the whole world kin." [1] One cannot credit the actual Solomon in his pride taking compassionate thought about foreign visitors or a handful of aliens settled in his new capital —diplomatic provision for them to worship their own gods, yes (II Kings 23:13), but not tenderhearted concern for their personal feel-

[1] Shakespeare, *Troilus and Cressida*, Act III, scene 3.

ings. What caused the maker of the prayer to have such insight concerning the heart of **the stranger?** He himself may have been among the Jews "captive" in Babylonia, and have been able to return to Jerusalem. We know that from the sixth century onward the Jews of Palestine were very mindful of their brethren dispersed in other lands. But better it is simply to judge that the man from whose soul this great prayer could come had compassion for human beings, had all too rare willingness to realize that the stranger is not exempt from normal anxieties, pains, and sorrows, and that he may be very lonely in a land not his own, heartsick for his former home.

Never was intercession for the stranger in our midst more relevant than in our times. Thousands of refugees may not be altogether

39 Then hear thou from the heavens, *even* from thy dwelling place, their prayer and their supplications, and maintain their cause, and forgive thy people which have sinned against thee.

40 Now, my God, let, I beseech thee, thine eyes be open, and *let* thine ears *be* attent unto the prayer *that is made* in this place.

41 Now therefore arise, O Lord God, into thy resting place, thou, and the ark of thy strength: let thy priests, O Lord God, be clothed with salvation, and let thy saints rejoice in goodness.

42 O Lord God, turn not away the face of thine anointed: remember the mercies of David thy servant.

7 Now when Solomon had made an end of praying, the fire came down from heaven, and consumed the burnt offering and the sacrifices; and the glory of the Lord filled the house.

2 And the priests could not enter into the house of the Lord, because the glory of the Lord had filled the Lord's house.

3 And when all the children of Israel saw how the fire came down, and the glory of the Lord upon the house, they bowed themselves with their faces to the ground upon the pavement, and worshipped, and praised the Lord, *saying*, For *he is* good; for his mercy *endureth* for ever.

for thy name, 39 then hear thou from heaven thy dwelling place their prayer and their supplications, and maintain their cause and forgive thy people who have sinned against thee. 40 Now, O my God, let thy eyes be open and thy ears attentive to a prayer of this place.

41 "And now arise, O Lord God, and go to thy resting place,
thou and the ark of thy might.
Let thy priests, O Lord God, be clothed with salvation,
and let thy saints rejoice in thy goodness.

42 O Lord God, do not turn away the face of thy anointed one!
Remember thy steadfast love for David thy servant."

7 When Solomon had ended his prayer, fire came down from heaven and consumed the burnt offering and the sacrifices, and the glory of the Lord filled the temple. 2 And the priests could not enter the house of the Lord, because the glory of the Lord filled the Lord's house. 3 When all the children of Israel saw the fire come down and the glory of the Lord upon the temple, they bowed down with their faces to the earth on the pavement, and worshiped and gave thanks to the Lord, saying,

"For he is good,
for his steadfast love endures for ever."

40-42. This far finer ending replaces I Kings 8:50-53, and should be credited to the Chronicler.

7:1, 3-5. When the culminating sign of divine approval had been vouchsafed, the king and his people—keeping "the feast of the seventh month" (5:3)—could offer their personal sacrifices.

2, 6-10. These are probably the revisers' insertions, confusing and reiterative: note the allusion (vs. 7) to **the brazen altar** (cf. 4:1); in addition, vss. 8-10 (two weeks plus

---

welcome in the land of refuge, but thousands of them are grateful nonetheless, want to be useful and loyal, and to be received into friendship. Even without intention, the citizens of a country can inflict on such people a sense of isolation in a thousand petty ways; for men tend to be absorbingly interested only in "their own." The wounds may go deep and sore into the alien's spirit. Extend the application. Was there some lonely person—not of the family circle—invited to the Christmas table? Reflect also that "strangers" have been known at times to attend church worship. They can be chill-

ingly observed by the regular congregation, or their presence simply ignored. "I was a stranger," said Jesus, "and you welcomed me" (Matt. 25:35).

40-42. *Finale.*—The last notes of the glorious symphony now are sounded. In I Kings 8:53 the magnificent prayer has a different ending. There the final plea for divine compassion is based on a claim, viz., that Israel is Yahweh's possession because he brought the tribes out of Egypt, the inference being that for that reason he ought to care for his own people. The Chronicler substituted these verses. It is very

4 ¶ Then the king and all the people offered sacrifices before the LORD.

5 And king Solomon offered a sacrifice of twenty and two thousand oxen, and a hundred and twenty thousand sheep. So the king and all the people dedicated the house of God.

6 And the priests waited on their offices: the Levites also with instruments of music of the LORD, which David the king had made to praise the LORD, because his mercy *endureth* for ever, when David praised by their ministry; and the priests sounded trumpets before them, and all Israel stood.

7 Moreover Solomon hallowed the middle of the court that *was* before the house of the LORD: for there he offered burnt offerings, and the fat of the peace offerings, because the brazen altar which Solomon had made was not able to receive the burnt offerings, and the meat offerings, and the fat.

8 ¶ Also at the same time Solomon kept the feast seven days, and all Israel with him, a very great congregation, from the entering in of Hamath unto the river of Egypt.

9 And in the eighth day they made a solemn assembly: for they kept the dedication of the altar seven days, and the feast seven days.

10 And on the three and twentieth day of the seventh month he sent the people away into their tents, glad and merry in heart for the goodness that the LORD had showed unto David, and to Solomon, and to Israel his people.

11 Thus Solomon finished the house of the LORD, and the king's house: and all that

4 Then the king and all the people offered sacrifice before the LORD. **5** King Solomon offered as a sacrifice twenty-two thousand oxen and a hundred and twenty thousand sheep. So the king and all the people dedicated the house of God. **6** The priests stood at their posts; the Levites also, with the instruments for music to the LORD which King David had made for giving thanks to the LORD — for his steadfast love endures for ever — whenever David offered praises by their ministry; opposite them the priests sounded trumpets; and all Israel stood.

7 And Solomon consecrated the middle of the court that was before the house of the LORD; for there he offered the burnt offering and the fat of the peace offerings, because the bronze altar Solomon had made could not hold the burnt offering and the cereal offering and the fat.

8 At that time Solomon held the feast for seven days, and all Israel with him, a very great congregation, from the entrance of Hamath to the Brook of Egypt. **9** And on the eighth day they held a solemn assembly; for they had kept the dedication of the altar seven days and the feast seven days. **10** On the twenty-third day of the seventh month he sent the people away to their homes, joyful and glad of heart for the goodness that the LORD had shown to David and to Solomon and to Israel his people.

11 Thus Solomon finished the house of

---

a day) accord with the final Law, whereas earlier custom was one week only. The text in I Kings 8:65, as LXX and the first words of vs. 66 there show, has been conformed to Chronicles.

D. SOLOMON'S VISION (7:11-22)

The Chronicler may have transcribed from I Kings 9:1-19, but the vision's dismal forebodings are such an anticlimax that one wonders whether it was not added by a gloomy scribe who would not let well enough alone.

---

difficult to improve on a masterpiece, but the Chronicler improved on the version in Kings. Here "the plea rings with greater exultation in the thought of the Temple being the resting-place of Yahweh, the abode of his ark and of his priests, and in remembrance of David or (better) the divine covenant with him."[2] That

appraisal is the just judgment of a biblical scholar. Considered from a literary standpoint, the Chronicler's finale was assuredly a touch of genius.

7:10. Worship and Resolve.—In contrast with I Kings 8:65-66, Chronicles doubles the duration of the religious celebrations (see Exeg.). It is

[2] Edward L. Curtis and Albert A. Madsen, *A Critical and Exegetical Commentary on the Books of Chronicles* (New York: Charles Scribner's Sons, 1910; "International Critical Commentary"), p. 345.

came into Solomon's heart to make in the house of the LORD, and in his own house, he prosperously effected.

12 ¶ And the LORD appeared to Solomon by night, and said unto him, I have heard thy prayer, and have chosen this place to myself for a house of sacrifice.

13 If I shut up heaven that there be no rain, or if I command the locusts to devour the land, or if I send pestilence among my people;

14 If my people, which are called by my name, shall humble themselves, and pray, and seek my face, and turn from their wicked ways; then will I hear from heaven, and will forgive their sin, and will heal their land.

15 Now mine eyes shall be open, and mine ears attent unto the prayer *that is made* in this place.

16 For now have I chosen and sanctified this house, that my name may be there for ever: and mine eyes and mine heart shall be there perpetually.

17 And as for thee, if thou wilt walk before me, as David thy father walked, and do according to all that I have commanded thee, and shalt observe my statutes and my judgments;

18 Then will I stablish the throne of thy kingdom, according as I have covenanted with David thy father, saying, There shall not fail thee a man *to be* ruler in Israel.

19 But if ye turn away, and forsake my statutes and my commandments, which I have set before you, and shall go and serve other gods, and worship them;

20 Then will I pluck them up by the roots out of my land which I have given them; and this house, which I have sanctified for my name, will I cast out of my sight, and will make it *to be* a proverb and a byword among all nations.

the LORD and the king's house; all that Solomon had planned to do in the house of the LORD and in his own house he successfully accomplished. 12 Then the LORD appeared to Solomon in the night and said to him: "I have heard your prayer, and have chosen this place for myself as a house of sacrifice. 13 When I shut up the heavens so that there is no rain, or command the locust to devour the land, or send pestilence among my people, 14 if my people who are called by my name humble themselves, and pray and seek my face, and turn from their wicked ways, then I will hear from heaven, and will forgive their sin and heal their land. 15 Now my eyes will be open and my ears attentive to the prayer that is made in this place. 16 For now I have chosen and consecrated this house that my name may be there for ever; my eyes and my heart will be there for all time. 17 And as for you, if you walk before me, as David your father walked, doing according to all that I have commanded you and keeping my statutes and my ordinances, 18 then I will establish your royal throne, as I covenanted with David your father, saying, 'There shall not fail you a man to rule Israel.'

19 "But if you*o* turn aside and forsake my statutes and my commandments which I have set before you, and go and serve other gods and worship them, 20 then I will pluck you*p* up from the land which I have given you;*p* and this house, which I have consecrated for my name, I will cast out of my sight, and will make it a proverb and a by-

o The word you is plural here
p Heb *them*

13-15. Not in Kings. An old tradition may have been used here by the Chronicler.

---

not said that **on the twenty-third day** the worshipers departed twice as earnestly resolved to conform their conduct to the laws of the Lord. But that issue is the test of the worth of our attendances, long or short, at divine worship.

12-22. *The Stern Mercy of God.*—In this passage the certainty of divine mercy and the certainty of retribution are held together. These words were written by one who if he had not actually witnessed the sack of Jerusalem and the destruction of Solomon's temple by the Babylonians in 586 b.c., could never forget what befell a people who would not take to heart the warnings of the great prophets. Down to that catastrophe the Hebrews as a whole clung to the notion that Yahweh's care for them implied a measure of leniency or indulgence, so that even the light repentance of a day would gain

21 And this house, which is high, shall be an atonishment to every one that passeth by it; so that he shall say, Why hath the LORD done thus unto this land, and unto this house?

22 And it shall be answered, Because they forsook the LORD God of their fathers, which brought them forth out of the land of Egypt, and laid hold on other gods, and worshipped them, and served them: therefore hath he brought all this evil upon them.

8 And it came to pass at the end of twenty years, wherein Solomon had built the house of the LORD, and his own house,

2 That the cities which Huram had restored to Solomon, Solomon built them, and caused the children of Israel to dwell there.

3 And Solomon went to Hamath-zobah, and prevailed against it.

4 And he built Tadmor in the wilderness, and all the store cities, which he built in Hamath.

5 Also he built Beth-horon the upper, and Beth-horon the nether, fenced cities, with walls, gates, and bars;

6 And Baalath, and all the store cities that Solomon had, and all the chariot cities, and the cities of the horsemen, and all that Solomon desired to build in Jerusalem, and in Lebanon, and throughout all the land ·of his dominion.

7 ¶ As for all the people that were left of the Hittites, and the Amorites, and the Per-

word among all peoples. 21 And at this house, which is exalted, everyone passing by will be astonished, and say, 'Why has the LORD done thus to this land and to this house?' 22 Then they will say, 'Because they forsook the LORD the God of their fathers who brought them out of the land of Egypt, and laid hold on other gods, and worshiped them and served them; therefore he has brought all this evil upon them.' "

8 At the end of twenty years, in which Solomon had built the house of the LORD and his own house, 2 Solomon rebuilt the cities which Huram had given to him, and settled the people of Israel in them.

3 And Solomon went to Ha′math-zo′bah, and took it. 4 He built Tadmor in the wilderness and all the store-cities which he built in Hamath. 5 He also built Upper Beth-hor′on and Lower Beth-hor′on, fortified cities with walls, gates, and bars, 6 and Ba′alath, and all the store-cities that Solomon had, and all the cities for his chariots, and the cities for his horsemen, and whatever Solomon desired to build in Jerusalem, in Lebanon, and in all the land of his dominion. 7 All the people who were left of

---

21. **Which is high:** Grammatically, the Hebrew must be translated "which was so high." The text in Kings is corrupt.

E. SOLOMON'S CONSTRUCTIONS AND SACRIFICES (8:1-18)

8:2. What audacity the Chronicler had! He turns upside down what he read in I Kings 9:11-14, where it is said that Solomon sold to the Phoenician king twenty Hebrew towns for 120 gold talents. Perhaps he could not believe that Solomon was ever in need of cash, or could stoop to so ignominious a deal. At any rate, here is nice instance of the freedom the Chronicler exercised to paint his picture of affairs as they should be.

4. Kings reads "Tamar" (in southern Judah) which the Chronicler misread as **Tadmor.** This place in later times was the famous desert town, Palmyra, northeast of

---

renewal of his favor (cf. Hos. 6:1-4). If the prodigal son had returned home unrepentant he could not have been received as the lost son born again. It is always terribly hard to face up to the truth that God's mercy upholds the reality of the moral order.

8:7-9. *Underdogs and Top Dogs.*—Who should be held down in the social scale? Aliens in the land, conquered races, say these verses. Solomon had no hesitations and presumably no scruples about the matter (see Expos. on 2:17-18; I Chr. 22:2). The present world poses com-

izzites, and the Hivites, and the Jebusites, which *were* not of Israel,

8 *But* of their children, who were left after them in the land, whom the children of Israel consumed not, them did Solomon make to pay tribute until this day.

9 But of the children of Israel did Solomon make no servants for his work; but they *were* men of war, and chief of his captains, and captains of his chariots and horsemen.

10 And these *were* the chief of king Solomon's officers, *even* two hundred and fifty, that bare rule over the people.

11 ¶ And Solomon brought up the daughter of Pharaoh out of the city of David unto the house that he had built for her: for he said, My wife shall not dwell in the house of David king of Israel, because *the places are* holy, whereunto the ark of the LORD hath come.

12 ¶ Then Solomon offered burnt offerings unto the LORD on the altar of the LORD, which he had built before the porch,

13 Even after a certain rate every day, offering according to the commandment of Moses, on the sabbaths, and on the new moons, and on the solemn feasts, three times in the year, *even* in the feast of unleavened bread, and in the feast of weeks, and in the feast of tabernacles.

14 ¶ And he appointed, according to the order of David his father, the courses of the priests to their service, and the Levites to their charges, to praise and minister before

the Hittites, the Amorites, the Per'izzites, the Hivites, and the Jeb'usites, who were not of Israel, **8** from their descendants who were left after them in the land, whom the people of Israel had not destroyed — these Solomon made a forced levy and so they are to this day. **9** But of the people of Israel Solomon made no slaves for his work; they were soldiers, and his officers, the commanders of his chariots, and his horsemen. **10** And these were the chief officers of King Solomon, two hundred and fifty, who exercised authority over the people.

11 Solomon brought Pharaoh's daughter up from the city of David to the house which he had built for her, for he said, "My wife shall not live in the house of David king of Israel, for the places to which the ark of the LORD has come are holy."

12 Then Solomon offered up burnt offerings to the LORD upon the altar of the LORD which he had built before the vestibule, **13** as the duty of each day required, offering according to the commandment of Moses for the sabbaths, the new moons, and the three annual feasts — the feast of unleavened bread, the feast of weeks, and the feast of tabernacles. **14** According to the ordinance of David his father, he appointed the divisions of the priests for their service, and the Levites for their offices of praise and

Damascus. It is in the last degree unlikely that Solomon took or fortified (**built**) Tadmor; and the assertion in vs. 3 that he warred against a powerful place in north Syria may be an effort to lead up to this still more extravagant assertion of his power.

12-15. These verses are probably the revisers' work (cf. II Chr. 2:4*b*), inserted to safeguard their belief that the altar of the Lord was not the altar built by David, but a new one; and to cover the full ordinances of the final Law. In I Kings 9:15 the text is unreliable.

parable issues. The problems are grave and difficult. But they ought at least to be regarded as conscience-searching.

11. *Respect for Sacred Things.*—Solomon had contracted a mixed marriage, mixed indeed— Egyptian princess to Hebrew king, worshiper of the many gods of an ancient and mighty realm to worshiper of the one God of an upstart Canaanite kingdom. Solomon, we are here informed, considered that if his foreign queen were to reside within the sacred area in his

capital her presence would pollute its holiness and give offense to Yahweh's jealous pride. The daughter of Pharaoh is likely to have had other and strong views on the subject. Altogether a tense situation is indicated: if she wrote home about it to her father in Egypt, an international complication was in the making. We may, somewhat too readily, take a contemptuous view of Solomon's naïve theology. Realistically we feel that if the queen was a good woman, her presence on the holy ground would have enhanced

the priests, as the duty of every day required: the porters also by their courses at every gate: for so had David the man of God commanded.

15 And they departed not from the commandment of the king unto the priests and Levites concerning any matter, or concerning the treasures.

16 Now all the work of Solomon was prepared unto the day of the foundation of the house of the LORD, and until it was finished. So the house of the LORD was perfected.

17 ¶ Then went Solomon to Ezion-geber, and to Eloth, at the sea side in the land of Edom.

18 And Huram sent him, by the hands of his servants, ships, and servants that had knowledge of the sea; and they went with the servants of Solomon to Ophir, and took thence four hundred and fifty talents of gold, and brought *them* to king Solomon.

9 And when the queen of Sheba heard of the fame of Solomon, she came to prove Solomon with hard questions at Jerusalem, with a very great company, and camels that bare spices, and gold in abundance, and precious stones: and when she was come to Solomon, she communed with him of all that was in her heart.

2 And Solomon told her all her questions: and there was nothing hid from Solomon which he told her not.

ministry before the priests as the duty of each day required, and the gatekeepers in their divisions for the several gates; for so David the man of God had commanded. **15** And they did not turn aside from what the king had commanded the priests and Levites concerning any matter and concerning the treasuries.

16 Thus was accomplished all the work of Solomon from*q* the day the foundation of the house of the LORD was laid until it was finished. So the house of the LORD was completed.

17 Then Solomon went to E'zion-ge'ber and Eloth on the shore of the sea, in the land of Edom. **18** And Huram sent him by his servants ships and servants familiar with the sea, and they went to Ophir together with the servants of Solomon, and fetched from there four hundred and fifty talents of gold and brought it to King Solomon.

9 Now when the queen of Sheba heard of the fame of Solomon she came to Jerusalem to test him with hard questions, having a very great retinue and camels bearing spices and very much gold and precious stones. When she came to Solomon, she told him all that was on her mind. **2** And Solomon answered all her questions; there was nothing hidden from Solomon which he

q Gk Syr Vg: Heb *to*

F. VISIT OF SHEBA'S QUEEN (9:1-31)

This chapter is closely copied from I Kings 10:1-29.

---

its sanctity. The problem was not clear cut for Solomon. He and his subjects, in the manner of ancient belief, carried respect for holy things to absurd and "fear-ful" conclusions. An opposite fault can be committed by modern men: lack of respect for the fact that things can be put to sacred use. "Wherefore whosoever shall eat this bread and drink this cup of the Lord, unworthily, . . ." (I Cor. 11:27) .

9:1. A Royal Visit.—The story of the queen of Sheba visiting Solomon ranks with that of David and Goliath among the best known in the O.T. Even when we take the largest pinch of salt about the size of her **retinue** and the amount of **gold, precious stones,** and finest **spices** that she brought, she still floats romantically and richly in the imagination—like a character in a supplement to *The Arabian Nights.* But real wealth existed behind the theatrical

scene. From remote time the valleys of southern Arabia grew in abundance the trees from which incense was made. The temples in the several civilizations used great quantities of the costly product (cf. Ezek. 27:22) , and the value of its export from South Arabia can be reckoned only in millions of modern money.[3] The traffic in incense was by far the most lucrative in ancient commerce, comparable to the present oil industry. Southern Arabia is some fourteen hundred miles from Jerusalem, and it is not likely that the queen of Sheba came from that distant realm. At this period the Sabean tribes were located much farther north, but probably they exacted lucrative taxes from the incense cara-

[3] For a fascinating description of existing conditions there, including the lofty houses of its powerful families, see Freya Stark, *The Southern Gates of Arabia* (New York: E. P. Dutton & Co., 1936).

3 And when the queen of Sheba had seen the wisdom of Solomon, and the house that he had built,

4 And the meat of his table, and the sitting of his servants, and the attendance of his ministers, and their apparel; his cupbearers also, and their apparel; and his ascent by which he went up into the house of the LORD; there was no more spirit in her.

5 And she said to the king, *It was* a true report which I heard in mine own land of thine acts, and of thy wisdom:

6 Howbeit I believed not their words, until I came, and mine eyes had seen *it:* and, behold, the one half of the greatness of thy wisdom was not told me: *for* thou exceedest the fame that I heard.

7 Happy *are* thy men, and happy *are* these thy servants, which stand continually before thee, and hear thy wisdom.

8 Blessed be the LORD thy God, which delighted in thee to set thee on his throne, *to be* king for the LORD thy God: because thy God loved Israel, to establish them for ever, therefore made he thee king over them, to do judgment and justice.

9 And she gave the king a hundred and twenty talents of gold, and of spices great abundance, and precious stones: neither was there any such spice as the queen of Sheba gave king Solomon.

10 And the servants also of Huram, and the servants of Solomon, which brought gold from Ophir, brought algum trees and precious stones.

11 And the king made *of* the algum trees

could not explain to her. 3 And when the queen of Sheba had seen the wisdom of Solomon, the house that he had built, 4 the food of his table, the seating of his officials, and the attendance of his servants, and their clothing, his cupbearers, and their clothing, and his burnt offerings which he offered at the house of the LORD, there was no more spirit in her.

5 And she said to the king, "The report was true which I heard in my own land of your affairs and of your wisdom, 6 but I did not believe the[r] reports until I came and my own eyes had seen it; and behold, half the greatness of your wisdom was not told me; you surpass the report which I heard. 7 Happy are your wives![s] Happy are these your servants, who continually stand before you and hear your wisdom! 8 Blessed be the LORD your God, who has delighted in you and set you on his throne as king for the LORD your God! Because your God loved Israel and would establish them for ever, he has made you king over them, that you may execute justice and righteousness." 9 Then she gave the king a hundred and twenty talents of gold, and a very great quantity of spices, and precious stones: there were no spices such as those which the queen of Sheba gave to King Solomon.

10 Moreover the servants of Huram and the servants of Solomon, who brought gold from Ophir, brought algum wood and precious stones. 11 And the king made of the algum wood steps[t] for the house of the

[r] Heb *their*
[s] Gk Compare 1 Kings 10. 8: Heb *men*
[t] Gk Vg: The meaning of the Hebrew word is uncertain

---

vans passing through their territory. Astute Solomon was developing traffic by sea to South Arabia from his Red Sea port. Perhaps, then, the anxious Sabeans on the overland route sent to him their queen, furnished with polite and ample gifts, not in order to please her curiosity, but on a commercial mission: to effect, if possible, a *modus vivendi*, a reasonable trade agreement.

6. *Personal Experience.*—Someone hears Christians saying extraordinary things about Jesus. He thinks it strange exaggeration—at any rate, no concern of his. But if he looked into the matter for himself, he would say, **Half the greatness . . . was not told me.**

9-12. *Fair Exchange.*—She gave the king . . . (vs. 9) ; **Solomon gave to the queen . . .** (vs. 12).

When royalties paid visits to foreign courts, or commissioned their representatives to go, it was an invariable custom, both in courtesy and diplomacy, to take and to receive presents. The awkward aspect was that the value of the gifts given and taken was regarded as a measure of the power and prestige of the donors. The Amarna letters of the fourteenth century B.C. furnish amusing evidence—even a letter sent without an accompanying gift "could be almost a diplomatic incident." [4] Royal example had an unhappy consequence in that the convention ran down the entire social scale. A suppliant must offer a gift to his superior when seeking

[4] S. A. Cook, in *The Cambridge Ancient History,* ed. J. B. Bury, S. A. Cook, F. E. Adcock (New York: The Macmillan Co., 1924), II, 297.

terraces to the house of the LORD, and to the king's palace, and harps and psalteries for singers: and there were none such seen before in the land of Judah.

12 And king Solomon gave to the queen of Sheba all her desire, whatsoever she asked, besides *that* which she had brought unto the king. So she turned, and went away to her own land, she and her servants.

13 ¶ Now the weight of gold that came to Solomon in one year was six hundred and threescore and six talents of gold;

14 Besides *that which* chapmen and merchants brought. And all the kings of Arabia and governors of the country brought gold and silver to Solomon.

15 ¶ And king Solomon made two hundred targets *of* beaten gold: six hundred *shekels* of beaten gold went to one target.

16 And three hundred shields *made he of* beaten gold: three hundred *shekels* of gold went to one shield. And the king put them in the house of the forest of Lebanon.

17 Moreover the king made a great throne of ivory, and overlaid it with pure gold.

18 And *there were* six steps to the throne, with a footstool of gold, *which were* fastened to the throne, and stays on each side of the sitting place, and two lions standing by the stays:

19 And twelve lions stood there on the one side and on the other upon the six steps. There was not the like made in any kingdom.

20 ¶ And all the drinking vessels of king Solomon *were of* gold, and all the vessels of the house of the forest of Lebanon *were of* pure gold: none *were of* silver; it was *not* any thing accounted of in the days of Solomon.

LORD and for the king's house, lyres also and harps for the singers; there never was seen the like of them before in the land of Judah.

12 And King Solomon gave to the queen of Sheba all that she desired, whatever she asked besides what she had brought to the king. So she turned and went back to her own land, with her servants.

13 Now the weight of gold that came to Solomon in one year was six hundred and sixty-six talents of gold, 14 besides that which the traders and merchants brought; and all the kings of Arabia and the governors of the land brought gold and silver to Solomon. 15 King Solomon made two hundred large shields of beaten gold; six hundred shekels of beaten gold went into each shield. 16 And he made three hundred shields of beaten gold; three hundred shekels of gold went into each shield; and the king put them in the House of the Forest of Lebanon. 17 The king also made a great ivory throne, and overlaid it with pure gold. 18 The throne had six steps and a footstool of gold, which were attached to the throne, and on each side of the seat were arm rests and two lions standing beside the arm rests, 19 while twelve lions stood there, one on each end of a step on the six steps. The like of it was never made in any kingdom. 20 All King Solomon's drinking vessels were of gold, and all the vessels of the House of the Forest of Lebanon were of pure gold; silver was not considered as anything in the days

---

9:13. About $20,000,000, but a trifle compared with the provision for the temple ascribed to David (I Chr. 22:14).

14. Chapmen: Archaic English for itinerant traders.

---

aid or favor, and a plaintiff likewise when he brought his case to the judge; in degenerate times that meant that the rich man's bribe could be relied on to determine a verdict in his favor.

Nowadays the thoughtful guest may bring some pleasant gift to his host, but happily not with the hope that the hospitality received will be commensurate. There are grudging and

thoughtless persons, only too many of them: some can be summed up in the caustic remark, "All take and no give." Christ said, "Give, and it shall be given unto you" (Luke 6:38); the principle he had in mind was profoundly deeper than calculated material interests.

15. *Shields of Gold.*— (See Expos. on 12:10-11.)

21 For the king's ships went to Tarshish with the servants of Huram: every three years once came the ships of Tarshish bringing gold, and silver, ivory, and apes, and peacocks.

22 And king Solomon passed all the kings of the earth in riches and wisdom.

23 ¶ And all the kings of the earth sought the presence of Solomon, to hear his wisdom, that God had put in his heart.

24 And they brought every man his present, vessels of silver, and vessels of gold, and raiment, harness, and spices, horses, and mules, a rate year by year.

25 ¶ And Solomon had four thousand stalls for horses and chariots, and twelve thousand horsemen; whom he bestowed in the chariot cities, and with the king at Jerusalem.

26 ¶ And he reigned over all the kings from the river even unto the land of the Philistines, and to the border of Egypt.

27 And the king made silver in Jerusalem as stones, and cedar trees made he as the sycamore trees that are in the low plains in abundance.

28 And they brought unto Solomon horses out of Egypt, and out of all lands.

29 ¶ Now the rest of the acts of Solomon, first and last, are they not written in the

of Solomon. 21 For the king's ships went to Tarshish with the servants of Huram; once every three years the ships of Tarshish used to come bringing gold, silver, ivory, apes, and peacocks.

22 Thus King Solomon excelled all the kings of the earth in riches and in wisdom. 23 And all the kings of the earth sought the presence of Solomon to hear his wisdom, which God had put into his mind. 24 Every one of them brought his present, articles of silver and of gold, garments, myrrh, spices, horses, and mules, so much year by year. 25 And Solomon had four thousand stalls for horses and chariots, and twelve thousand horsemen, whom he stationed in the chariot cities and with the king in Jerusalem. 26 And he ruled over all the kings from the Eu-phra'tes to the land of the Philistines, and to the border of Egypt. 27 And the king made silver as common in Jerusalem as stone, and cedar as plentiful as the sycamore of the Shephe'lah. 28 And horses were imported for Solomon from Egypt and from all lands.

29 Now the rest of the acts of Solomon,

---

21. Ships of Tarshish: Tarshish was probably a Phoenician settlement in Spain, and the Chronicler strangely took the phrase literally. But it denoted ocean-going vessels (cf. "Indiamen"), and the cargoes brought back show that the two kings were trading down the Red Sea to India and Africa.

25. Horses and chariots: It is likely that Solomon had at least 1400 horses for his chariots (cf. I Kings 10:26). (The Assyrian Shalmaneser III claimed to have captured 1200 chariots from the King of Syria and 2000 from Ahab of Israel.) That Solomon stationed them in several strategic towns has been interestingly supported by excavations at Megiddo, undertaken by the University of Chicago in 1929, where stabling for 400 horses was found.

26. The river is the Euphrates. That Solomon traded with Mesopotamia we may be sure; that he ruled as far as the Euphrates we may doubt.

29. The rest of the acts: It was all very well for the Chronicler to refer his readers

---

21. Exotic Cargoes.—The king's fleet did not voyage from the Red Sea to Tarshish somewhere in the western Mediterranean via a nonexistent Suez Canal! Ships of Tarshish was a term for ocean-going vessels (see Exeg.). The allusion to a three-year round trip may imply that Solomon's ships went as far as India or East Africa. The authority of William F. Albright is cited for similar rarities named in the

cargo of a Babylonian ship which made a two-year voyage from the Persian Gulf ca. 1830 B.C.[5]

29. God's Interpreters.—There is a typical divergence between this verse and its parallel in I Kings 11:41; whereas Kings cites as source

[5] J. A. Montgomery and H. S. Gehman, *A Critical and Exegetical Commentary on the Books of Kings* (Edinburgh: T. & T. Clark, 1951; "International Critical Commentary"), p. 224.

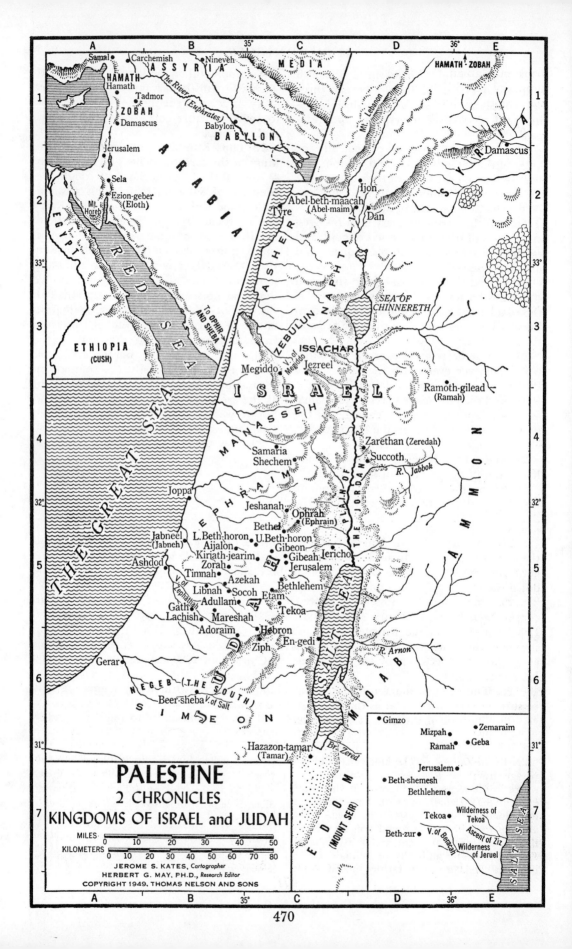

PALESTINE
2 CHRONICLES
KINGDOMS OF ISRAEL and JUDAH

MILES
0 10 20 30 40 50
KILOMETERS
0 10 20 30 40 50 60 70 80

JEROME S. KATES, *Cartographer*
HERBERT G. MAY, PH.D., *Research Editor*
COPYRIGHT 1949, THOMAS NELSON AND SONS

470

book of Nathan the prophet, and in the prophecy of Ahijah the Shilonite, and in the visions of Iddo the seer against Jeroboam the son of Nebat?

30 And Solomon reigned in Jerusalem over all Israel forty years.

31 And Solomon slept with his fathers, and he was buried in the city of David his father: and Rehoboam his son reigned in his stead.

10 And Rehoboam went to Shechem: for to Shechem were all Israel come to make him king.

2 And it came to pass, when Jeroboam the son of Nebat, who *was* in Egypt, whither he had fled from the presence of Solomon the king, heard *it,* that Jeroboam returned out of Egypt.

3 And they sent and called him. So Jeroboam and all Israel came and spake to Rehoboam, saying,

from first to last, are they not written in the history of Nathan the prophet, and in the prophecy of Ahi'jah the Shi'lonite, and in the visions of Iddo the seer concerning Jerobo'am the son of Nebat? 30 Solomon reigned in Jerusalem over all Israel forty years. 31 And Solomon slept with his fathers, and was buried in the city of David his father; and Rehobo'am his son reigned in his stead.

10 Rehobo'am went to Shechem, for all Israel had come to Shechem to make him king. 2 And when Jerobo'am the son of Nebat heard of it (for he was in Egypt, whither he had fled from King Solomon), then Jerobo'am returned from Egypt. 3 And they sent and called him; and Jerobo'am and all Israel came and said to Rehobo'am,

---

to these now lost prophetic sources (see Intro., p. 347). He himself is responsible for omitting much that is written in canonical Kings concerning Solomon—the king's altars to other gods, the troubles of his reign, his immense harem, his increasing and resented tyranny.

IV. The Kings of Judah (10:1–36:23)

The Chronicler proceeds to trace the checkered history of the Davidic kingdom of Judah down to its destruction in 586 b.c. He does so by selecting and adapting from Kings only what furthered his religious intention, and by adding much thereto. The new

---

"the book of the acts of Solomon," the Chronicler names prophets—Nathan, Ahijah, Iddo. Those alleged writings may have been passages in a now lost, didactic account of Judean history, but there is a reason why that is improbable (see Intro., p. 347). The important point is that in this stress on prophets we have the first instance of a method which the Chronicler will deliberately pursue in his survey of the future kings—an insistence that God did not fail to send, as the occasions required, prophets to declare his truth, and that in the reactions of the kings to these interpreters of the divine word the sequel showed God's overruling of men and affairs to establish his righteous will. There are some today who, although not called prophets, are voices of truth and right. Response spells our destiny.

10:1–36:21. The Nation Under God.—In these twenty-seven chapters the Chronicler depicts the kingdom of Judah from the accession of Rehoboam to its fall in 586 b.c. in such a way as to inculcate his fundamental beliefs. The reader is subtly offered "truth of idea," not exact history. Jewish readers were more open

than we to allow pictures rather than polysyllables to speak to their intelligence and conscience.

The fundamental convictions (in our terminology) were these: (a) Human life exists under a moral order which is consequent on God's invariable, righteous will. As surely as the sun rises and sets, goodness produces good, evil produces evil. What excuse is there if we also do not see that the cumulative outcome of individual and national pride, ferocity, greed, and stupidity is calamity? "Are grapes gathered from thorns, or figs from thistles?" (Matt. 7:16.) (b) The maintenance and practice of right religious worship is of paramount importance for the well-being of the community. The Chronicler's elaborations about the Levites and Solomon's temple presented "truth of idea," challenging the men of his time to be scrupulous and zealous concerning the keeping of the law and the service of the second temple. In comparison with Solomon's, that temple was externally a postwar makeshift (see Zech. 4:10). Let none despise it! Out of the destruction of Jerusalem by the Babylonians there had

4 Thy father made our yoke grievous: now therefore ease thou somewhat the grievous servitude of thy father, and his heavy yoke that he put upon us, and we will serve thee.

5 And he said unto them, Come again unto me after three days. And the people departed.

6 ¶ And king Rehoboam took counsel with the old men that had stood before Solomon his father while he yet lived, saying, What counsel give ye *me* to return answer to this people?

7 And they spake unto him, saying, If thou be kind to this people, and please them, and speak good words to them, they will be thy servants for ever.

8 But he forsook the counsel which the old men gave him, and took counsel with the young men that were brought up with him, that stood before him.

9 And he said unto them, What advice give ye that we may return answer to this people, which have spoken to me, saying, Ease somewhat the yoke that thy father did put upon us?

10 And the young men that were brought up with him spake unto him, saying, Thus shalt thou answer the people that spake

---

4 "Your father made our yoke heavy. Now therefore lighten the hard service of your father and his heavy yoke upon us, and we will serve you." 5 He said to them, "Come to me again in three days." So the people went away.

6 Then King Rehobo'am took counsel with the old men, who had stood before Solomon his father while he was yet alive, saying, "How do you advise me to answer this people?" 7 And they said to him, "If you will be kind to this people and please them, and speak good words to them, then they will be your servants for ever." 8 But he forsook the counsel which the old men gave him, and took counsel with the young men who had grown up with him and stood before him. 9 And he said to them, "What do you advise that we answer this people who have said to me, 'Lighten the yoke that your father put upon us'?" 10 And the young men who had grown up with him

---

material is often the product of his own inventive reasoning as to what ought to have happened or been done; and in its contents we perceive most clearly the ruling principles of his faith.

---

emerged the spiritual splendor of faith in the one and only God and knowledge how rightly to live. Similar awareness should be in us concerning the worth of true religion in our civilization. But when the Assyrians destroyed Samaria in 721 B.C. nothing comparable had arisen from its ruins. Therefore it was appropriate to the Chronicler's purpose to ignore the history of the kingdom of Israel, including even the narratives about Elijah and Elisha, which must have stirred his soul. (*c*) But he did not ignore good Israelites, loyal to the true faith. On the contrary, depicting "truth of idea," he exaggerates preposterously their devotion (Levites and laity) to David; he glories in declaring how in vast numbers they responded to the brotherly overtures made to them by Hezekiah and Josiah. Thus he would rebuke contemporaries in Jerusalem who were determined to ostracize or belittle religiously the Hebrew population in Canaan outside their Judean circles. His hope was of one household of faith. What

are our views about Christian inability to transcend ancient dissensions even in face of the rise of the atheistic communist philosophy? (*d*) The Chronicler insists on the constant intervention of inspired prophets, thus urging that God gives not only the heritage of our fathers' insight but also the immediate voices of wise and unflinching servants of truth. Are we willing and swift to perceive and understand their counterpart today?

10:4. *Clogs to Clogs.*—A few decades ago the textile workers in Lancashire wore wooden shoes (clogs) to save expense in shoe leather. There was a saying among them, "Three generations from clogs to clogs": a workman rises from the ranks to become owner of the mill; his son makes a great fortune out of the business; his grandchildren scatter the wealth. David—Solomon—Rehoboam. The shepherd boy became a king; his grandson flung away the heritage.

6-15. *Wise Heads on Old Shoulders.*—Rehoboam had an ultimatum served on him by nine

unto thee, saying, Thy father made our yoke heavy, but make thou *it* somewhat lighter for us; thus shalt thou say unto them, My little *finger* shall be thicker than my father's loins.

11 For whereas my father put a heavy yoke upon you, I will put more to your yoke: my father chastised you with whips, but I *will chastise you* with scorpions.

12 So Jeroboam and all the people came to Rehoboam on the third day, as the king bade, saying, Come again to me on the third day.

13 And the king answered them roughly; and king Rehoboam forsook the counsel of the old men,

14 And answered them after the advice of the young men, saying, My father made your yoke heavy, but I will add thereto: my father chastised you with whips, but I *will chastise you* with scorpions.

15 So the king hearkened not unto the people: for the cause was of God, that the LORD might perform his word, which he spake by the hand of Ahijah the Shilonite to Jeroboam the son of Nebat.

16 ¶ And when all Israel *saw* that the king would not hearken unto them, the people answered the king, saying, What portion have we in David? and *we have* none inheritance in the son of Jesse: every man to your tents, O Israel: *and* now, David, see to thine own house. So all Israel went to their tents.

17 But *as for* the children of Israel that dwelt in the cities of Judah, Rehoboam reigned over them.

said to him, "Thus shall you speak to the people who said to you, 'Your father made our yoke heavy, but do you lighten it for us'; thus shall you say to them, 'My little finger is thicker than my father's loins.

11 And now, whereas my father laid upon you a heavy yoke, I will add to your yoke. My father chastised you with whips, but I will chastise you with scorpions.' "

12 So Jerobo'am and all the people came to Rehobo'am the third day, as the king said, "Come to me again the third day."

13 And the king answered them harshly, and forsaking the counsel of the old men,

14 King Rehobo'am spoke to them according to the counsel of the young men, saying, "My father made your yoke heavy, but I will add to it; my father chastised you with whips, but I will chastise you with scorpions." 15 So the king did not hearken to the people; for it was a turn of affairs brought about by God that the LORD might fulfil his words, which he spoke by Ahi'jah the Shi'lonite to Jerobo'am the son of Nebat.

16 And when all Israel saw that the king did not hearken to them, the people answered the king,

"What portion have we in David?
    We have no inheritance in the son of Jesse.
Each of you to your tents, O Israel!
    Look now to your own house, David."
So all Israel departed to their tents. 17 But Rehobo'am reigned over the people of Israel who dwelt in the cities of Judah.

tenths of his subjects, all except the Judeans: he must accept their stated conditions or there would be an end to their loyalty to his throne. The seniors at his court advised compliance: **If you will be kind to this people and please them, . . . they will be your servants for ever** (vs. 7). It is not always true that "a soft answer turneth away wrath" (Prov. 15:1). Timid yielding to unreasonable and impudent demands will usually be construed as an open opportunity to double the demands. Comparing these verses with I Kings 12:6-7, we find that the Chronicler—if you will be kind—needlessly and feebly modified the wise answer of the old men. According to Kings they counseled, "If you will be a servant to this people today and serve them, . . . then they will be your servants for ever." That advice was based on the realization

that the Israelites' complaint was not only just but radically right: autocratic Solomon had perverted the constitutional, "brotherly" concept of kingship which David had exemplified—the king is to rule as under God that he may serve his fellows. The democratic Greeks admired the mighty Persian Empire except in one respect: "Among the Persians all men are slaves, except one."

Rehoboam's ambition, no doubt, was to equal or surpass the strength of his autocratic father, and, following the cruel opinion of his young advisers, haughtily he told the vexatious complainants that he would rule with a rod of iron. When a vexatious circumstance presents itself, immediate anger is natural enough both in young and old. But second thoughts are likely to be best. Sleep overnight before mailing the

18 Then king Rehoboam sent Hadoram that *was* over the tribute; and the children of Israel stoned him with stones, that he died. But king Rehoboam made speed to get him up to *his* chariot, to flee to Jerusalem.

19 And Israel rebelled against the house of David unto this day.

11 And when Rehoboam was come to Jerusalem, he gathered of the house of Judah and Benjamin a hundred and fourscore thousand chosen *men,* which were warriors, to fight against Israel, that he might bring the kingdom again to Rehoboam.

2 But the word of the LORD came to Shemaiah the man of God, saying,

3 Speak unto Rehoboam the son of Solomon, king of Judah, and to all Israel in Judah and Benjamin, saying,

4 Thus saith the LORD, Ye shall not go up, nor fight against your brethren: return every man to his house; for this thing is done of me. And they obeyed the words of the LORD, and returned from going against Jeroboam.

5 ¶ And Rehoboam dwelt in Jerusalem, and built cities for defense in Judah.

18 Then King Rehobo'am sent Hador'am, who was taskmaster over the forced labor, and the people of Israel stoned him to death with stones. And King Rehobo'am made haste to mount his chariot, to flee to Jerusalem. 19 So Israel has been in rebellion against the house of David to this day.

11 When Rehobo'am came to Jerusalem, he assembled the house of Judah, and Benjamin, a hundred and eighty thousand chosen warriors, to fight against Israel, to restore the kingdom to Rehobo'am. 2 But the word of the LORD came to Shemai'ah the man of God: 3 "Say to Rehobo'am the son of Solomon king of Judah, and to all Israel in Judah and Benjamin, 4 'Thus says the LORD, You shall not go up or fight against your brethren. Return every man to his home, for this thing is from me.' " So they hearkened to the word of the LORD, and returned and did not go against Jerobo'am.

5 Rehobo'am dwelt in Jerusalem, and

A. REIGN OF REHOBOAM (10:1–12:16)

10:19. Mark that I Kings 12:20—"there was none that followed the house of David, but the tribe of Judah only"—is ignored. The Chronicler's purpose would have been impaired if he had frankly admitted the desperate weakness of the Davidic kingdom under Rehoboam. Enough for him to admit Rehoboam's sin of provocation, and to declare that nevertheless Israel's action was a heinous sin of rebellion.

11:1-4. The Chronicler judged that Rehoboam exceeded all bounds when he proposed to attack the apostate brethren, the Israelites. Accordingly, he gladly inserted from I Kings 12:22-24 the tale that a prophet, Shemaiah, forbade, and that the king desisted. Whereupon he expanded the logic of the situation, and—no parallel in Kings— in 11:5-23 indicated Rehoboam's reward for obeying the prophet; but in 12:1-8 (cf. I Kings 14:22, 25-28) he also expatiated on the chastisement which Rehoboam's wicked intention had merited.

---

furious letter. And above all, try carefully to see the other man's point of view, in case you are not entirely in the right.

11:4. By the Will of God.—A notice in 12:15 says that "there were wars between Rehoboam and Jeroboam continually," which should be construed as signifying constant enmity and occasional fighting. Here we are told that Rehoboam wanted to launch an immediate attack on the rebels, but his Judeans would have none of it—because a prophet warned that the disaster of their revolt was in accordance with the

will of God. Disaster the division into two Hebrew kingdoms truly was; the strength of Solomon's realm had vanished like smoke, and the occupant of the throne of David was reduced to being "king of the Castle" in Jerusalem. The prophet was of one mind with the veteran counselors who saw that the attitude of Solomon to his royal duty had been evil, and that the split of the kingdom was evidence of the reality of a moral order in life which is the will of God.

5-10. Lines of Defense.—He built does not imply "built for the first time." Hebron and

6 He built even Beth-lehem, and Etam, and Tekoa,

7 And Beth-zur, and Shoco, and Adullam,

8 And Gath, and Mareshah, and Ziph,

9 And Adoraim, and Lachish, and Azekah,

10 And Zorah, and Ajalon, and Hebron, which *are* in Judah and in Benjamin, fenced cities.

11 And he fortified the strongholds, and put captains in them, and store of victuals, and of oil and wine.

12 And in every several city *he put* shields and spears, and made them exceeding strong, having Judah and Benjamin on his side.

13 ¶ And the priests and the Levites that *were* in all Israel resorted to him out of all their coasts.

14 For the Levites left their suburbs and their possession, and came to Judah and Jerusalem: for Jeroboam and his sons had cast them off from executing the priest's office unto the LORD:

15 And he ordained him priests for the high places, and for the devils, and for the calves which he had made.

he built cities for defense in Judah. 6 He built Bethlehem, Etam, Teko'a, 7 Beth-zur, Soco, Adul'lam, 8 Gath, Mare'shah, Ziph, 9 Adora'im, Lachish, Aze'kah, 10 Zorah, Ai'jalon, and Hebron, fortified cities which are in Judah and in Benjamin. 11 He made the fortresses strong, and put commanders in them, and stores of food, oil, and wine. 12 And he put shields and spears in all the cities, and made them very strong. So he held Judah and Benjamin.

13 And the priests and the Levites that were in all Israel resorted to him from all places where they lived. 14 For the Levites left their common lands and their holdings and came to Judah and Jerusalem, because Jerobo'am and his sons cast them out from serving as priests of the LORD, 15 and he appointed his own priests for the high places, and for the satyrs, and for the calves

6-12. None of the towns were in **Benjamin** (vs. 10); all in **Judah.** Their fortification would assist defense against an Egyptian army. An old tradition may have been utilized here.

12. Having . . . Benjamin on his side: Historically it was not, but in the Chronicler's lifetime the people of that area were closely aligned with the Jerusalem community, and it was fitting to represent Benjamin as not having sided with rebel Israel (see Exeg. on I Chr. 8:1-40).

13-15. The priests and the Levites that were in all Israel: Regarding the reasons for considering the priests and to be a reviser's correction, or for supposing that the original text of the Chronicler was "the priests, the Levites," see Exeg. on I Chr. 6:1-81 and Intro., pp. 345-47. The purport of these verses is to stress that it was only the Israelitish laity who rebelled; the Israelitish Levites on the contrary were so loyal that they suffered persecution from Jeroboam, relinquished their worldly possessions, and

Aijalon were very ancient towns (cf. Num. 13:22; Josh. 14:12; Judg. 1:35). In Hebrew "to build" may denote "to fortify." When the king strengthened the defenses of these places against the possibility of an attacking army coming from Egypt, he knew not that among them **Tekoa** would be famous because of Amos, and **Bethlehem** become the birthplace of One whose kingdom is from everlasting to everlasting.

13-14, 16. *Exaggeration.*—The sanctuaries in the kingdom of Israel were served not exclusively by Levites but also by persons of other lineage. The orthodox compilers of I Kings

(12:31; 13:33) were horrified. It is probable that some, perhaps many, Israelitish Levites decided not to submit to Jeroboam and moved out of his territory to Jerusalem, where its great temple afforded golden hope of employment. The Chronicler inferred that all northern Levites had loyally adhered to the house of David—an exaggeration no doubt, but he may have supposed it a fact. At any rate, he seized the opportunity to emphasize his argument about the existence of faithful Israelites.

15. *Prejudice.*—The Hebrew for **devils or satyrs** means "he-goats," a designation of de-

16 And after them, out of all the tribes of Israel, such as set their hearts to seek the Lord God of Israel came to Jerusalem, to sacrifice unto the Lord God of their fathers.

17 So they strengthened the kingdom of Judah, and made Rehoboam the son of Solomon strong, three years: for three years they walked in the way of David and Solomon.

18 ¶ And Rehoboam took him Mahalath the daughter of Jerimoth the son of David to wife; *and* Abihail the daughter of Eliab the son of Jesse;

19 Which bare him children; Jeush and Shemariah, and Zaham.

20 And after her he took Maachah the daughter of Absalom; which bare him Abijah, and Attai, and Ziza, and Shelomith.

21 And Rehoboam loved Maachah the daughter of Absalom above all his wives and his concubines: (for he took eighteen wives, and threescore concubines; and begat twenty and eight sons, and threescore daughters.)

22 And Rehoboam made Abijah the son of Maachah the chief, *to be* ruler among his brethren: for *he thought* to make him king.

23 And he dealt wisely, and dispersed of all his children throughout all the countries of Judah and Benjamin, unto every fenced city: and he gave them victuals in abundance. And he desired many wives.

12 And it came to pass, when Rehoboam had established the kingdom, and had strengthened himself, he forsook the law of the Lord, and all Israel with him.

2 And it came to pass, *that* in the fifth year of king Rehoboam, Shishak king of

which he had made. 16 And those who had set their hearts to seek the Lord God of Israel came after them from all the tribes of Israel to Jerusalem to sacrifice to the Lord, the God of their fathers. 17 They strengthened the kingdom of Judah, and for three years they made Rehobo'am the son of Solomon secure, for they walked for three years in the way of David and Solomon.

18 Rehobo'am took as wife Ma'halath the daughter of Jer'imoth the son of David, and of Ab'ihail the daughter of Eli'ab the son of Jesse; 19 and she bore him sons, Je'ush, Shemari'ah, and Zaham. 20 After her he took Ma'acah the daughter of Ab'salom, who bore him Abi'jah, Attai, Ziza, and Shelo'mith. 21 Rehobo'am loved Ma'acah the daughter of Ab'salom above all his wives and concubines (he took eighteen wives and sixty concubines, and had twenty-eight sons and sixty daughters) ; 22 and Rehobo'am appointed Abi'jah the son of Ma'acah as chief prince among his brothers, for he intended to make him king. 23 And he dealt wisely, and distributed some of his sons through all the districts of Judah and Benjamin, in all the fortified cities; and he gave them abundant provisions, and procured wives for them.*u*

12 When the rule of Rehobo'am was established and was strong, he forsook the law of the Lord, and all Israel with him. 2 In the fifth year of King Rehobo'am,

u Cn: Heb *sought a multitude of wives*

came to Jerusalem to serve in the Solomonic temple. The assertion was not historic fact; it was the Chronicler's way of urging that Levites of Israelitish families ought to be given full rights to serve—as priests, musicians, or custodians—in the second temple. Note the point that in Israel they are said to have functioned as **priests** (vs. 14) .

18-23. Not in Kings. The details given perhaps imply the use of an old tradition.

12:1. Here and in vs. 6, **Israel** denotes the Judeans as the surviving true "Israel."

2-9. Shishak's plundering of Jerusalem is recorded in I Kings 14:25-28. The Chronicler represented the disaster as merited, not only because Rehoboam had attacked the

monic beings supposed to inhabit waste places. Jeroboam, we may be sure, did not foster devil-worship in his new kingdom. He was anxious to demonstrate his zeal for the worship of Yahweh, and since he could not present a temple rivaling Solomon's he made Bethel and Dan royal sanctuaries and there erected two gold-plated images

in the shape of bulls (**calves**). The monotheist Jews to whom we owe Kings and Chronicles, who scorned idolatry, probably realized that the bulls had been set up in honor of Yahweh. But they made the act a focus of denunciation in respect of the religious practices in the Northern Kingdom which were in fact somewhat more

Egypt came up against Jerusalem, because they had transgressed against the LORD,

3 With twelve hundred chariots, and threescore thousand horsemen: and the people *were* without number that came with him out of Egypt; the Lubim, the Sukkiim, and the Ethiopians.

4 And he took the fenced cities which *pertained* to Judah, and came to Jerusalem.

5 ¶ Then came Shemaiah the prophet to Rehoboam, and *to* the princes of Judah, that were gathered together to Jerusalem because of Shishak, and said unto them, Thus saith the LORD, Ye have forsaken me, and therefore have I also left you in the hand of Shishak.

6 Whereupon the princes of Israel and the king humbled themselves; and they said, The LORD *is* righteous.

7 And when the LORD saw that they humbled themselves, the word of the LORD came to Shemaiah, saying, They have humbled themselves; *therefore* I will not destroy them, but I will grant them some deliverance; and my wrath shall not be poured out upon Jerusalem by the hand of Shishak.

8 Nevertheless they shall be his servants; that they may know my service, and the service of the kingdoms of the countries.

9 So Shishak king of Egypt came up against Jerusalem, and took away the treasures of the house of the LORD, and the treasures of the king's house; he took all: he carried away also the shields of gold which Solomon had made.

10 Instead of which king Rehoboam made shields of brass, and committed *them* to the hands of the chief of the guard, that kept the entrance of the king's house.

11 And when the king entered into the house of the LORD, the guard came and fetched them, and brought them again into the guard chamber.

because they had been unfaithful to the LORD, Shishak king of Egypt came up against Jerusalem 3 with twelve hundred chariots and sixty thousand horsemen. And the people were without number who came with him from Egypt — Libyans, Suk'ki-im, and Ethiopians. 4 And he took the fortified cities of Judah and came as far as Jerusalem. 5 Then Shemai'ah the prophet came to Rehobo'am and to the princes of Judah, who had gathered at Jerusalem because of Shishak, and said to them, "Thus says the LORD, 'You abandoned me, so I have abandoned you to the hand of Shishak.'" 6 Then the princes of Israel and the king humbled themselves and said, "The LORD is righteous." 7 When the LORD saw that they humbled themselves, the word of the LORD came to Shemai'ah: "They have humbled themselves; I will not destroy them, but I will grant them some deliverance, and my wrath shall not be poured out upon Jerusalem by the hand of Shishak. 8 Nevertheless they shall be servants to him, that they may know my service and the service of the kingdoms of the countries."

9 So Shishak king of Egypt came up against Jerusalem; he took away the treasures of the house of the LORD and the treasures of the king's house; he took away everything. He also took away the shields of gold which Solomon had made; 10 and King Rehobo'am made in their stead shields of bronze, and committed them to the hands of the officers of the guard, who kept the door of the king's house. 11 And as often as the king went into the house of the LORD, the guard came and bore them, and brought

Israelites but also (vs. 1) because in his pride **he forsook the law of the LORD.** At the same time the Chronicler emphasized the king's merit in heeding Shemaiah's rebuke

gross and polytheistic than the customs at Judean sanctuaries, though these became vile enough (cf. Jer. 2:20-28). The venom shown by this verse is perhaps pardonable.

12:10-11. Shields of Brass.—Imitation articles in place of the real thing (cf. 9:15)! There is a very human aspect in this incident. How swiftly the bubble of Rehoboam's pride was pricked,

and the glory of Solomon's realm departed. Up came the king of Egypt, and in a twinkling Jerusalem was "off the gold standard." Various reflections are possible. Was anything that mattered really lost? What was the use of gold which set no wheels of trade in motion? The scornful could laugh at the foolish king's pretense, and say about his brass shields, "All that

12 And when he humbled himself, the wrath of the LORD turned from him, that he would not destroy *him* altogether: and also in Judah things went well.

13 ¶ So king Rehoboam strengthened himself in Jerusalem, and reigned: for Rehoboam *was* one and forty years old when he began to reign, and he reigned seventeen years in Jerusalem, the city which the LORD had chosen out of all the tribes of Israel, to put his name there. And his mother's name *was* Naamah an Ammonitess.

14 And he did evil, because he prepared not his heart to seek the LORD.

15 Now the acts of Rehoboam, first and last, *are* they not written in the book of Shemaiah the prophet, and of Iddo the seer concerning genealogies? And *there were* wars between Rehoboam and Jeroboam continually.

16 And Rehoboam slept with his fathers, and was buried in the city of David: and Abijah his son reigned in his stead.

13 Now in the eighteenth year of king Jeroboam began Abijah to reign over Judah.

2 He reigned three years in Jerusalem. His mother's name also *was* Michaiah the daughter of Uriel of Gibeah. And there was war between Abijah and Jeroboam.

3 And Abijah set the battle in array with an army of valiant men of war, *even* four hundred thousand chosen men: Jeroboam

them back to the guardroom. 12 And when he humbled himself the wrath of the LORD turned from him, so as not to make a complete destruction; moreover, conditions were good in Judah.

13 So King Rehobo'am established himself in Jerusalem and reigned. Rehobo'am was forty-one years old when he began to reign, and he reigned seventeen years in Jerusalem, the city which the LORD had chosen out of all the tribes of Israel to put his name there. His mother's name was Na'amah the Ammonitess. 14 And he did evil, for he did not set his heart to seek the LORD.

15 Now the acts of Rehobo'am, from first to last, are they not written in the chronicles of Shemai'ah the prophet and of Iddo the seer?[v] There were continual wars between Rehobo'am and Jerobo'am. 16 And Rehobo'am slept with his fathers, and was buried in the city of David; and Abi'jah his son reigned in his stead.

13 In the eighteenth year of King Jerobo'am Abi'jah began to reign over Judah. 2 He reigned for three years in Jerusalem. His mother's name was Micai'ah the daughter of U'riel of Gib'e-ah.

3 Now there was war between Abi'jah and Jerobo'am. Abi'jah went out to battle having an army of valiant men of war, four

[v] Heb *seer, to enroll oneself*

---

and pointed out that the judgment had been loss of treasure, not total destruction of the kingdom.

15. Concerning genealogies: The text is corrupt.

B. REIGN OF ABIJAH (13:1-22)

13:1-2. Rehoboam having been chastised, it was time that Israel should suffer retribution commensurate with its apostasy and heathenish worship (cf. 11:15). But Rehoboam's son Abijah was not fit to inflict the chastisement, for I Kings 15:1, 2, 6-7 had nothing good to say about him. The Chronicler, however, found a solution for his difficulty when he read in Kings that God for the sake of David's merits allowed Abijah to establish Jerusalem and to be succeeeded by his son, and that fighting with Israel was constant throughout his reign. (In Kings Abijah is called "Abijam.")

3-20. The Battle of Zemaraim has no parallel in Kings. **Zemaraim** was a place on the border between the two kingdoms. Perhaps there was tradition of a fight there won

---

glisters is not gold";[6] but one may also reflect that Rehoboam had the courage to rally from the blow and make the most of such resources as remained to him.

[6] Shakespeare, *The Merchant of Venice,* Act II, scene 7.

13:1-22. *Soft Words and Hard Blows.*—If this chapter is read through to its quaint close, what a dreadful passage it is to encounter in Holy Writ! Abijah's specious plea was backed by the mailed fist. When the Israelites' military

also set the battle in array against him with eight hundred thousand chosen men, *being* mighty men of valor.

4 ¶ And Abijah stood up upon mount Zemaraim, which *is* in mount Ephraim, and said, Hear me, thou Jeroboam, and all Israel;

5 Ought ye not to know that the LORD God of Israel gave the kingdom over Israel to David for ever, *even* to him and to his sons by a covenant of salt?

6 Yet Jeroboam the son of Nebat, the servant of Solomon the son of David, is risen up, and hath rebelled against his lord.

7 And there are gathered unto him vain men, the children of Belial, and have strengthened themselves against Rehoboam the son of Solomon, when Rehoboam was young and tender-hearted, and could not withstand them.

8 And now ye think to withstand the kingdom of the LORD in the hand of the sons of David; and ye *be* a great multitude, and *there are* with you golden calves, which Jeroboam made you for gods.

9 Have ye not cast out the priests of the LORD, the sons of Aaron, and the Levites, and have made you priests after the manner of the nations of *other* lands? so that whosoever cometh to consecrate himself with a young bullock and seven rams, *the same* may be a priest of *them that are* no gods.

10 But as for us, the LORD *is* our God, and we have not forsaken him; and the priests, which minister unto the LORD, *are*

hundred thousand picked men; and Jerobo'am drew up his line of battle against him with eight hundred thousand picked mighty warriors. 4 Then Abi'jah stood up on Mount Zemara'im which is in the hill country of E'phraim, and said, "Hear me, O Jerobo'am and all Israel! 5 Ought you not to know that the LORD God of Israel gave the kingship over Israel for ever to David and his sons by a covenant of salt? 6 Yet Jerobo'am the son of Nebat, a servant of Solomon the son of David, rose up and rebelled against his lord; 7 and certain worthless scoundrels gathered about him and defied Rehobo'am the son of Solomon, when Rehobo'am was young and irresolute and could not withstand them.

8 "And now you think to withstand the kingdom of the LORD in the hand of the sons of David, because you are a great multitude and have with you the golden calves which Jerobo'am made you for gods. 9 Have you not driven out the priests of the LORD, the sons of Aaron, and the Levites, and made priests for yourselves like the peoples of other lands? Whoever comes to conse-

---

by the Judeans. Possibly the victory is the Chronicler's invention. Certainly its colossal scale reveals his symbolic language. Abijah with 400,000 soldiers marched to the frontier, and there in moving terms harangued Jeroboam and the men of Israel, urging them to repent their rebellion; to forgive and forget since Rehoboam had been an impetuous youth misled by bad counselors; to realize now that they were setting themselves against God, who had entrusted his kingdom to the house of David. While the parley went on the Israelites got forces to the rear of the Judeans. Battle was joined, and Israel was defeated with a loss of 500,000 men. The Chronicler must not be blamed for not foreseeing that there might be readers prosaic enough to suppose he meant the tale to be credited as actual fact. He was writing doctrine in parable (cf. 14:9-15; 20:1-30).

9, 10*b*, 11. Clear instance of a late insertion. Of special interest is the reference to the regular burning of **incense** (spices, סמים), with which cf. Exod. 30:7 (P). Incidental

---

maneuver failed, and it is said that 500,000 of their soldiers were slaughtered, the narrator does not seem to turn a hair. But there is no parallel in Kings for the tale. It is of course only the Chronicler's quaint, pictorial way of

arguing that, although Rehoboam had been grievously wrong and the Israelites' revolt in accordance with God's will, nevertheless the fatal schism ought not to have continued; and that since Israel was wrong to persist in aliena-

the sons of Aaron, and the Levites *wait* upon *their* business:

11 And they burn unto the LORD every morning and every evening burnt sacrifices and sweet incense: the showbread also *set they in order* upon the pure table; and the candlestick of gold with the lamps thereof, to burn every evening: for we keep the charge of the LORD our God; but ye have forsaken him.

12 And, behold, God himself *is* with us for *our* captain, and his priests with sounding trumpets to cry alarm against you. O children of Israel, fight ye not against the LORD God of your fathers; for ye shall not prosper.

13 ¶ But Jeroboam caused an ambushment to come about behind them: so they were before Judah, and the ambushment *was* behind them.

14 And when Judah looked back, behold, the battle *was* before and behind: and they cried unto the LORD, and the priests sounded with the trumpets.

15 Then the men of Judah gave a shout: and as the men of Judah shouted, it came to pass, that God smote Jeroboam and all Israel before Abijah and Judah.

16 And the children of Israel fled before Judah: and God delivered them into their hand.

17 And Abijah and his people slew them with a great slaughter: so there fell down slain of Israel five hundred thousand chosen men.

18 Thus the children of Israel were brought under at that time, and the children of Judah prevailed, because they relied upon the LORD God of their fathers.

19 And Abijah pursued after Jeroboam, and took cities from him, Beth-el with the towns thereof, and Jeshanah with the towns thereof, and Ephrain with the towns thereof.

20 Neither did Jeroboam recover strength again in the days of Abijah: and the LORD struck him, and he died.

21 ¶ But Abijah waxed mighty, and married fourteen wives, and begat twenty and two sons, and sixteen daughters.

crate himself with a young bull or seven rams becomes a priest of what are no gods. 10 But as for us, the LORD is our God, and we have not forsaken him. We have priests ministering to the LORD who are sons of Aaron, and Levites for their service. 11 They offer to the LORD every morning and every evening burnt offerings and incense of sweet spices, set out the showbread on the table of pure gold, and care for the golden lampstand that its lamps may burn every evening; for we keep the charge of the LORD our God, but you have forsaken him. 12 Behold, God is with us at our head, and his priests with their battle trumpets to sound the call to battle against you. O sons of Israel, do not fight against the LORD, the God of your fathers; for you cannot succeed."

13 Jerobo'am had sent an ambush around to come on them from behind; thus his troops[w] were in front of Judah, and the ambush was behind them. 14 And when Judah looked, behold, the battle was before and behind them; and they cried to the LORD, and the priests blew the trumpets. 15 Then the men of Judah raised the battle shout. And when the men of Judah shouted, God defeated Jerobo'am and all Israel before Abi'jah and Judah. 16 The men of Israel fled before Judah, and God gave them into their hand. 17 Abi'jah and his people slew them with a great slaughter; so there fell slain of Israel five hundred thousand picked men. 18 Thus the men of Israel were subdued at that time, and the men of Judah prevailed, because they relied upon the LORD, the God of their fathers. 19 And Abi'jah pursued Jerobo'am, and took cities from him, Bethel with its villages and Jesha'nah with its villages and Ephron[x] with its villages. 20 Jerobo'am did not recover his power in the days of Abi'jah; and the LORD smote him, and he died. 21 But Abi'jah grew mighty. And he took fourteen wives, and had twenty-two sons and sixteen

[w] Heb *they*
[x] Another reading is *Ephrain*

allusion, earlier than P passages, would seem to be Ezek. 8:11. Frankincense (לבונה) is first mentioned in Jer. 6:20; its use in the ritual became increasingly important in the postexilic period.

22 And the rest of the acts of Abijah, and his ways, and his sayings, *are* written in the story of the prophet Iddo.

14 So Abijah slept with his fathers, and they buried him in the city of David: and Asa his son reigned in his stead. In his days the land was quiet ten years.

2 And Asa did *that which was* good and right in the eyes of the LORD his God:

3 For he took away the altars of the strange *gods,* and the high places, and brake down the images, and cut down the groves:

4 And commanded Judah to seek the LORD God of their fathers, and to do the law and the commandment.

5 Also he took away out of all the cities of Judah the high places and the images: and the kingdom was quiet before him.

6 ¶ And he built fenced cities in Judah: for the land had rest, and he had no war in those years; because the LORD had given him rest.

7 Therefore he said unto Judah, Let us build these cities, and make about *them* walls and towers, gates and bars, *while* the land *is* yet before us; because we have sought the LORD our God, we have sought *him,* and he hath given us rest on every side. So they built and prospered.

8 And Asa had an army *of men* that bare targets and spears, out of Judah three hundred thousand; and out of Benjamin, that bare shields and drew bows, two hundred and fourscore thousand: all these *were* mighty men of valor.

daughters. 22 The rest of the acts of Abi'jah, his ways and his sayings, are written in the story of the prophet Iddo.

14^y So Abi'jah slept with his fathers, and they buried him in the city of David; and Asa his son reigned in his stead. In his days the land had rest for ten years. 2^z And Asa did what was good and right in the eyes of the LORD his God. 3 He took away the foreign altars and the high places, and broke down the pillars and hewed down the Ashe'rim, 4 and commanded Judah to seek the LORD, the God of their fathers, and to keep the law and the commandment. 5 He also took out of all the cities of Judah the high places and the incense altars. And the kingdom had rest under him. 6 He built fortified cities in Judah, for the land had rest. He had no war in those years, for the LORD gave him peace. 7 And he said to Judah, "Let us build these cities, and surround them with walls and towers, gates and bars; the land is still ours, because we have sought the LORD our God; we have sought him, and he has given us peace on every side." So they built and prospered. 8 And Asa had an army of three hundred thousand from Judah, armed with bucklers and spears, and two hundred and eighty thousand men from Benjamin, that carried shields and drew bows; all these were mighty men of valor.

^{y} Heb Ch 13. 23
^{z} Heb Ch 14. 1

C. REIGN OF ASA (14:1–16:14)

14:3. He took away the foreign altars and the high places: This is the Deuteronomic test of a good king, to which the Chronicler will add his own—obedience to a prophet (15:1-2, 8). But the author of Kings had already credited both Rehoboam and Abijah with sufficient piety to remove the high places. The Chronicler conveniently ignored the inconsistency, and also suppressed the admission in Kings that Asa's fathers had allowed temple prostitutes and idols. I Kings 15:9-24 portrays Asa as a very good king, but tells also that he relied on Syrian help when Baasha of Israel menaced Judah, and that he died of disease in his feet. It was easy for the Chronicler to embroider upon that record.

8. As a very good king, Asa is said to have had 580,000 soldiers. His even more important successor, Jehoshaphat, will be credited with double the number.

---

tion from the house of David, nothing less than condign retribution ought now to have happened; and who was more fitting to inflict the chastisement than Abijah, Rehoboam's worthy successor?

History shows with what tragic facility nations persist in cherishing enmity. In international disputes individuals may feel, not altogether justly, that they can do little to heal the breach. But in the sphere of family life and acquaint-

9 ¶ And there came out against them Zerah the Ethiopian with a host of a thousand thousand, and three hundred chariots; and came unto Mareshah.

10 Then Asa went out against him, and they set the battle in array in the valley of Zephathah at Mareshah.

11 And Asa cried unto the LORD his God, and said, LORD, *it is* nothing with thee to help, whether with many, or with them that have no power: help us, O LORD our God; for we rest on thee, and in thy name we go against this multitude. O LORD, thou *art* our God; let not man prevail against thee.

12 So the LORD smote the Ethiopians before Asa, and before Judah; and the Ethiopians fled.

13 And Asa and the people that *were* with him pursued them unto Gerar: and the Ethiopians were overthrown, that they could not recover themselves; for they were destroyed before the LORD, and before his host; and they carried away very much spoil.

14 And they smote all the cities round about Gerar; for the fear of the LORD came upon them: and they spoiled all the cities; for there was exceeding much spoil in them.

15 They smote also the tents of cattle, and carried away sheep and camels in abundance, and returned to Jerusalem.

9 Zerah the Ethiopian came out against them with an army of a million men and three hundred chariots, and came as far as Mare'shah. 10 And Asa went out to meet him, and they drew up their lines of battle in the valley of Zeph'athah at Mare'shah. 11 And Asa cried to the LORD his God, "O LORD, there is none like thee to help, between the mighty and the weak. Help us, O LORD our God, for we rely on thee, and in thy name we have come against this multitude. O LORD, thou art our God; let not man prevail against thee." 12 So the LORD defeated the Ethiopians before Asa and before Judah, and the Ethiopians fled. 13 Asa and the people that were with him pursued them as far as Gerar, and the Ethiopians fell until none remained alive; for they were broken before the LORD and his army. The men of Judah[a] carried away very much booty. 14 And they smote all the cities round about Gerar, for the fear of the LORD was upon them. They plundered all the cities, for there was much plunder in them. 15 And they smote the tents of those who had cattle,[b] and carried away sheep in abundance and camels. Then they returned to Jerusalem.

[a] Heb *they*
[b] Heb obscure

---

9. Zerah the Ethiopian: Hebrew, "the Cushite," i.e., an Arabian. The KJV—perhaps also the Chronicler—supposed Cush to be Ethiopia and Zerah to be king of Egypt—perhaps Osorkon I or II of the Bubasite dynasty.

9-15. No parallel in Kings. The attack by Zerah's army of a million footmen and three hundred chariots is made the occasion for a marvelous sign of God's satisfaction with Asa. He trusted not in his own army of half a million, but cast all his care upon the Lord (vs. 11).

15. Tents of cattle: Inexplicable, probably a textual error. Perhaps read with the RSV, **tents of those who had cattle.**

---

anceship they can do much, if they choose. "Blessed are the peacemakers: for they shall be called the children of God" (Matt. 5:9).

14:11. *Dauntless Tenacity.*—The quality of this utterance in its confidence and supplication must be measured not as if it were the actual words of King Asa, but as showing the spirit of the Chronicler in relation to his own times and circumstances. All too regularly in warfare victory goes to the big battalions, almost regardless of the merits of the case. One reaction to that fact is a craven materialistic view of life; but another may be dauntless tenacity despite overwhelming peril. If the few do not flinch,

they may sometimes defeat the many. The men and women of the resistance movements in Europe during World War II thought so, and so did the population of Britain in 1940-41, although almost everyone else reckoned total destruction inevitable. The Chronicler had even sterner facts to face. He knew that politically his people had been utterly conquered; the two Hebrew kingdoms had gone down like a pack of cards before the onslaught of the Assyrians and Babylonians. Nevertheless he held that in the ceaseless conflict between right and wrong the things that are right stand ultimately secure in the immutable purpose of God. So in this para-

15 And the Spirit of God came upon Azariah the son of Oded:

2 And he went out to meet Asa, and said unto him, Hear ye me, Asa, and all Judah and Benjamin; The Lord *is* with you, while ye be with him; and if ye seek him, he will be found of you; but if ye forsake him, he will forsake you.

3 Now for a long season Israel *hath been* without the true God, and without a teaching priest, and without law.

4 But when they in their trouble did turn unto the Lord God of Israel, and sought him, he was found of them.

5 And in those times *there was* no peace to him that went out, nor to him that came in, but great vexations *were* upon all the inhabitants of the countries.

6 And nation was destroyed of nation, and city of city: for God did vex them with all adversity.

7 Be ye strong therefore, and let not your hands be weak: for your work shall be rewarded.

8 And when Asa heard these words, and the prophecy of Oded the prophet, he took courage, and put away the abominable idols out of all the land of Judah and Benjamin, and out of the cities which he had taken from mount Ephraim, and renewed the altar of the Lord, that *was* before the porch of the Lord.

15 The spirit of God came upon Azari'ah the son of Oded, 2 and he went out to meet Asa, and said to him, "Hear me, Asa, and all Judah and Benjamin: The Lord is with you, while you are with him. If you seek him, he will be found by you, but if you forsake him, he will forsake you. 3 For a long time Israel was without the true God, and without a teaching priest, and without law; 4 but when in their distress they turned to the Lord, the God of Israel, and sought him, he was found by them. 5 In those times there was no peace to him who went out or to him who came in, for great disturbances afflicted all the inhabitants of the lands. 6 They were broken in pieces, nation against nation and city against city, for God troubled them with every sort of distress. 7 But you, take courage! Do not let your hands be weak, for your work shall be rewarded."

8 When Asa heard these words, the prophecy of Azari'ah the son of Oded,[c] he took courage, and put away the abominable idols from all the land of Judah and Benjamin and from the cities which he had taken in the hill country of E'phraim, and he repaired the altar of the Lord that was in front of the vestibule of the house of the

[c] Compare Syr Vg: Heb *the prophecy, Oded the prophet*

15:1-15. No parallel in Kings. The Chronicler saw an opportunity, perhaps utilizing an old tradition, to introduce two prophets, otherwise unknown, and made Azariah's prophetic intervention lead to exactly what he wanted to impress on his own contemporaries, viz., that as a result of Asa's piety and success Israelites in great numbers came to Jerusalem (vss. 9-15) to celebrate the thanksgiving for the harvest of corn (feast of Weeks).

3-6. A reviser's parenthesis, wrecking the continuity of vss. 2, 7.

8. Renewed the altar: Nowhere previously has it been stated that the altar had been destroyed. **And put away the abominable idols** is out of harmony with the assertion about Asa's reforms (14:2-3).

---

ble he calls us to see, on the one side, Zerah with his 1,000,000 soldiers, on the other, Asa with his 580,000, and to believe that the issue will not turn on numbers: **Help us, O Lord our God, for we rely on thee, and in thy name we have come against this multitude . . . ; let not man prevail against thee.**

15:2, 7, 12, 15. *Reform.*—The little that is said in I Kings 15:9-15 about Asa is good—he "did that which was right in the eyes of the Lord," and "forty and one years reigned he in

Jerusalem." The Chronicler saw in this yet another opportunity to preach his sermon on the theme that, given a chance, there were plenty of good Israelites. So he relates that a prophet was raised up to exhort Asa; that the king obeyed the word of God and strenuously reformed religious conditions in his territory; and that not merely his Judean subjects, but Israelites in abundance (vs. 9) responded to his spirit and came to Jerusalem to keep the harvest festival. Observe two features. First, that

9 And he gathered all Judah and Benjamin, and the strangers with them out of Ephraim and Manasseh, and out of Simeon: for they fell to him out of Israel in abundance, when they saw that the LORD his God *was* with him.

10 So they gathered themselves together at Jerusalem in the third month, in the fifteenth year of the reign of Asa.

11 And they offered unto the LORD the same time, of the spoil *which* they had brought, seven hundred oxen and seven thousand sheep.

12 And they entered into a covenant to seek the LORD God of their fathers with all their heart and with all their soul;

13 That whosoever would not seek the LORD God of Israel should be put to death, whether small or great, whether man or woman.

14 And they sware unto the LORD with a loud voice, and with shouting, and with trumpets, and with cornets.

15 And all Judah rejoiced at the oath: for they had sworn with all their heart, and sought him with their whole desire; and he was found of them: and the LORD gave them rest round about.

16 ¶ And also *concerning* Maachah the mother of Asa the king, he removed her from *being* queen, because she had made an idol in a grove: and Asa cut down her idol, and stamped *it*, and burnt *it* at the brook Kidron.

LORD.[d] 9 And he gathered all Judah and Benjamin, and those from E'phraim, Manas'seh, and Simeon who were sojourning with them, for great numbers had deserted to him from Israel when they saw that the LORD his God was with him. 10 They were gathered at Jerusalem in the third month of the fifteenth year of the reign of Asa. 11 They sacrificed to the LORD on that day, from the spoil which they had brought, seven hundred oxen and seven thousand sheep. 12 And they entered into a covenant to seek the LORD, the God of their fathers, with all their heart and with all their soul; 13 and that whoever would not seek the LORD, the God of Israel, should be put to death, whether young or old, man or woman. 14 They took oath to the LORD with a loud voice, and with shouting, and with trumpets, and with horns. 15 And all Judah rejoiced over the oath; for they had sworn with all their heart, and had sought him with their whole desire, and he was found by them, and the LORD gave them rest round about.

16 Even Ma'acah, his mother, King Asa removed from being queen mother because she had made an abominable image for Ashe'rah. Asa cut down her image, crushed it, and burned it at the brook Kidron.

[d] Heb *the vestibule of the* LORD

16. **An abominable image for Asherah,** i.e., symbolizing the goddess Asherah.

the prophet blended warning with encouragement in addressing king and people, **The LORD is with you, while you are with him** (vs. 2) ; and **Do not let your hands be weak** (vs. 7). God does not do our duty for us, but gives us strength to do our duty. Second, that when the men of Judah together with the faithful out of Israel unitedly and earnestly **entered into a covenant to seek the LORD, the God of their fathers** (vs. 12), it is written that **all Judah rejoiced over the oath** (vs. 15). The Judeans did not look askance at the men from Israel as if at returning prodigals; there was the gladness of brethren united. There have been members of the Christian church who meet wanderers returned to the fold with a dubious glance and a very limp handshake.

13. *Should Be Put to Death.*—The ferocious penalty is matched by passages in Deuteronomy ordering that the Canaanites be slaughtered, and that Hebrews guilty of worshiping gods other than Yahweh be stoned to death (Deut. 7:1-4; 13:6-10) . When Deuteronomy was written the Canaanites as a national entity had long since ceased to exist, but the contamination of their polytheism and gross customs continued as a mental menace to the conception of God and duty which the great prophets had proclaimed and which the makers of Deuteronomy and the Chronicler longed to promote. The seeming mercilessness in this verse is a figurative way of insisting that the community must do all possible to put an end to bad theology and consequent bad morals. There is current in modern society a plenitude of quite primitive theology and a naïve assumption that God and mammon can both be worshiped. Lukewarmness about the

17 But the high places were not taken away out of Israel: nevertheless the heart of Asa was perfect all his days.

18 ¶ And he brought into the house of God the things that his father had dedicated, and that he himself had dedicated, silver, and gold, and vessels.

19 And there was no *more* war unto the five and thirtieth year of the reign of Asa.

16 In the six and thirtieth year of the reign of Asa, Baasha king of Israel came up against Judah, and built Ramah, to the intent that he might let none go out or come in to Asa king of Judah.

2 Then Asa brought out silver and gold out of the treasures of the house of the LORD and of the king's house, and sent to Ben-hadad king of Syria, that dwelt at Damascus, saying,

3 *There is* a league between me and thee, as *there was* between my father and thy father: behold, I have sent thee silver and gold; go, break thy league with Baasha king of Israel, that he may depart from me.

4 And Ben-hadad hearkened unto king Asa, and sent the captains of his armies

---

17 But the high places were not taken out of Israel. Nevertheless the heart of Asa was blameless all his days. 18 And he brought into the house of God the votive gifts of his father and his own votive gifts, silver, and gold, and vessels. 19 And there was no more war until the thirty-fifth year of the reign of Asa.

16 In the thirty-sixth year of the reign of Asa, Ba'asha king of Israel went up against Judah, and built Ramah, that he might permit no one to go out or come in to Asa king of Judah. 2 Then Asa took silver and gold from the treasures of the house of the LORD and the king's house, and sent them to Ben-ha'dad king of Syria, who dwelt in Damascus, saying, 3 "Let there be a league between me and you, as between my father and your father; behold, I am sending to you silver and gold; go, break your league with Ba'asha king of Israel, that he may withdraw from me." 4 And Ben-ha'dad hearkened to King Asa, and

---

17. The statement, transcribed from I Kings 15:14, contradicts what the Chronicler has said in 14:3. Vs. 19 conflicts with vs. 16 in Kings, but this latter divergence is tolerable, since Kings placed the war with Baasha early in Asa's reign, whereas the Chronicler transposed it to the end.

16:1-10. Not in Kings. The Chronicler's assertion that in the thirty-sixth year of his reign Asa was at war with Baasha and successfully obtained aid from Ben-hadad of Damascus conflicts with the chronology given in Kings. But a recently discovered inscription on stone (stele), made by Ben-hadad about 850 B.C., appears decisively to confirm

---

purity and practice of our faith has terrible consequences (cf. Rev. 3:16).

17. *An Inconsistency.*—Here we read that the high places were not taken away by Asa, but in vs. 8 that they were! Strange that the Chronicler should overlook the manifest inconsistency. The reason probably is that this verse was later inserted into the original text. However that may be, we note a factual discrepancy in the Scriptures. What does that sort of thing matter in regard to the true value of the Bible? Nothing at all.

Sin and its consequence, hunger and thirst after righteousness, love, hate and jealousy, heartbreak, grief and tragedy, joy, hope, and the need of God. . . . The strength of the Bible has always been its appeal to this deep and abiding realm of man's basic experiences, for out of that realm the Bible came.[7]

[7] Harry Emerson Fosdick, *The Modern Use of the Bible* (New York: The Macmillan Co., 1925), pp. 56, 59.

In those issues does the Bible yield enlightenment? Were the Hebrews being led into knowledge of the one true God? That is what matters.

16:1-10. *An Impious Alliance Suitably Punished.*—Kings relates nothing to the discredit of Asa, unless failure to take away the high places is to be counted. But it tells that in his old age "he was diseased in his feet" (I Kings 15:23). The Chronicler inferred in that a punishment for some wrongdoing. He then spun partly out of his imagination this story, how Asa, menaced by Baasha king of Israel, persuaded the king of Syria, Ben-hadad, to break his treaty with Baasha and attack Israel. The result of being thus "yoked with an unbeliever" removed the danger to Asa and gained him some useful plunder. But how heinous the king's sin of mistrust in Yahweh! Had not Asa years earlier, by reliance solely on Yahweh, been granted an astounding victory over the invading

against the cities of Israel; and they smote Ijon, and Dan, and Abel-maim, and all the store cities of Naphtali:

5 And it came to pass, when Baasha heard *it,* that he left off building of Ramah, and let his work cease.

6 Then Asa the king took all Judah; and they carried away the stones of Ramah, and the timber thereof, wherewith Baasha was building; and he built therewith Geba and Mizpah.

7 ¶ And at that time Hanani the seer came to Asa king of Judah, and said unto him, Because thou hast relied on the king of Syria, and not relied on the LORD thy God, therefore is the host of the king of Syria escaped out of thine hand.

8 Were not the Ethiopians and the Lubim a huge host, with very many chariots and horsemen? yet, because thou didst rely on the LORD, he delivered them into thine hand.

9 For the eyes of the LORD run to and fro throughout the whole earth, to show himself strong in the behalf of *them* whose heart *is* perfect toward him. Herein thou hast done foolishly: therefore from henceforth thou shalt have wars.

10 Then Asa was wroth with the seer, and put him in a prison house; for *he was* in a rage with him because of this *thing.* And Asa oppressed *some* of the people the same time.

11 ¶ And, behold, the acts of Asa, first and last, lo, they *are* written in the book of the kings of Judah and Israel.

sent the commanders of his armies against the cities of Israel, and they conquered I'jon, Dan, A'bel-ma'im, and all the store-cities of Naph'tali. 5 And when Ba'asha heard of it, he stopped building Ramah, and let his work cease. 6 Then King Asa took all Judah, and they carried away the stones of Ramah and its timber, with which Ba'asha had been building, and with them he built Geba and Mizpah.

7 At that time Hana'ni the seer came to Asa king of Judah, and said to him, "Because you relied on the king of Syria, and did not rely on the LORD your God, the army of the king of Syria has escaped you. 8 Were not the Ethiopians and the Libyans a huge army with exceedingly many chariots and horsemen? Yet because you relied on the LORD, he gave them into your hand. 9 For the eyes of the LORD run to and fro throughout the whole earth, to show his might in behalf of those whose heart is blameless toward him. You have done foolishly in this; for from now on you will have wars." 10 Then Asa was angry with the seer, and put him in the stocks, in prison, for he was in a rage with him because of this. And Asa inflicted cruelties upon some of the people at the same time.

11 The acts of Asa, from first to last, are written in the Book of the Kings of Judah

that it is the figures in Kings which are inaccurate, and allows further chronological inferences to be drawn. The important, wider conclusion follows that the Chronicler was in places utilizing some pre-exilic, annalistic sources which the compilers of Kings neglected or did not possess (cf. W. F. Albright, "A Votive Stele Erected by Ben-Hadad I of Damascus to the God Melcarth," *Bulletin of the American Schools of Oriental Research,* No. 87 [1942], pp. 23-29) .

Asa transgressed by purchasing Syrian assistance against Baasha at the cost of temple treasure—a grievous sin in the eyes of the Chronicler, who proceeded to add that a seer rebuked Asa for his failure to rely on Yahweh and that Asa (who had begun so well) now so far lapsed from grace as to punish the bold prophet.

11-14. It is then told (cf. I Kings 15:23-24) that Asa met his merited end through a disease in his feet, but received high honors at his burial.

Ethiopian host? It is said that **Hanani,** an otherwise unknown seer, administered due reproach and told Asa that if he had relied only on Yahweh he could have beaten both the Israelites and the Syrians as well. Whereupon Asa added

to his iniquity by imprisoning Hanani. Alas! What a falling away from grace was here. The Jewish reader of Chronicles could feel that the disease which came upon once good Asa was fully deserved. The truth we may take to heart

12 And Asa in the thirty and ninth year of his reign was diseased in his feet, until his disease *was* exceeding *great:* yet in his disease he sought not to the LORD, but to the physicians.

13 ¶ And Asa slept with his fathers, and died in the one and fortieth year of his reign.

14 And they buried him in his own sepulchres, which he had made for himself in the city of David, and laid him in the bed which was filled with sweet odors and divers kinds *of spices* prepared by the apothecaries' art: and they made a very great burning for him.

17 And Jehoshaphat his son reigned in his stead, and strengthened himself against Israel.

2 And he placed forces in all the fenced cities of Judah, and set garrisons in the land of Judah, and in the cities of Ephraim, which Asa his father had taken.

3 And the LORD was with Jehoshaphat, because he walked in the first ways of his father David, and sought not unto Baalim;

4 But sought to the LORD God of his father, and walked in his commandments, and not after the doings of Israel.

and Israel. 12 In the thirty-ninth year of his reign Asa was diseased in his feet, and his disease became severe; yet even in his disease he did not seek the LORD, but sought help from physicians. 13 And Asa slept with his fathers, dying in the forty-first year of his reign. 14 They buried him in the tomb which he had hewn out for himself in the city of David. They laid him on a bier which had been filled with various kinds of spices prepared by the perfumer's art; and they made a very great fire in his honor.

17 Jehosh'aphat his son reigned in his stead, and strengthened himself against Israel. 2 He placed forces in all the fortified cities of Judah, and set garrisons in the land of Judah, and in the cities of E'phraim which Asa his father had taken. 3 The LORD was with Jehosh'aphat, because he walked in the earlier ways of his father;*e* he did not seek the Ba'als, 4 but sought the God of his father and walked in his commandments, and not according to the ways

e Another reading is *his father David*

D. REIGN OF JEHOSHAPHAT (17:1–20:37)

Three of the Judean kings are credited in Kings with outstanding virtue and success—Jehoshaphat, Hezekiah, and Josiah. Naturally the Chronicler used and enlarged all that was said to their credit in Kings, but he added a great deal of fresh material. It is a moot question whether the Chronicler derived this new material to a considerable degree, or to some degree, from an extensive lost source, or whether it sprang solely from his creative imagination as to what ideally should have happened. (See the remarks on sources in the Intro. [p. 347] and the Exeg. on 16:1-10; 34:1–35:27.)

It seems that the conjectured large source must have been an edifying work, lacking the comparatively high historical value of canonical Kings. What tells heavily against its existence, and in favor of the Chronicler's own authorship, is that virtually all the

is that if there have been times in our life when wonderfully our faith strengthened us to do right, not one of us but later is in danger of forgetting.

12. Call the Doctor.—On the same principle of sole reliance on God, the Chronicler was shocked because Asa had sought medical aid in his dire suffering: **He sought not to the LORD, but to the physicians.** Certain famous pre-exilic prophets were credited with having possessed astonishing healing powers (see I Kings 17:17-24; II Kings 4:18-37; 20:1-7). The Chronicler's frowning allusion to pre-exilic physicians was probably due to their having employed not only medicinal remedies but also spells and incantations. Interesting is the very different attitude to doctors taken by Ben Sirach, the author of Ecclesiasticus (200 B.C.), who writes, "My son, in thy sickness be not negligent; but pray unto the Lord, and he shall heal thee. Put away wrongdoing, and order thine hands aright, and cleanse thy heart from all manner of sin. . . . Then give place to the physician, for verily the Lord hath created him; and let him not go from thee, for thou hast need of him. There is a time when in their very hands is the issue for good. For they also shall beseech the Lord, that he may prosper them in giving relief and

5 Therefore the Lord stablished the kingdom in his hand; and all Judah brought to Jehoshaphat presents; and he had riches and honor in abundance.

6 And his heart was lifted up in the ways of the Lord: moreover he took away the high places and groves out of Judah.

7 ¶ Also in the third year of his reign he sent to his princes, *even* to Ben-hail, and to Obadiah, and to Zechariah, and to Nethaneel, and to Michaiah, to teach in the cities of Judah.

8 And with them *he sent* Levites, *even* Shemaiah, and Nethaniah, and Zebadiah, and Asahel, and Shemiramoth, and Jehonathan, and Adonijah, and Tobijah, and Tob-adonijah, Levites; and with them Elishama and Jehoram, priests.

9 And they taught in Judah, and *had* the book of the law of the Lord with them, and went about throughout all the cities of Judah, and taught the people.

10 ¶ And the fear of the Lord fell upon all the kingdoms of the lands that *were* round about Judah, so that they made no war against Jehoshaphat.

of Israel. 5 Therefore the Lord established the kingdom in his hand; and all Judah brought tribute to Jehosh'aphat; and he had great riches and honor. 6 His heart was courageous in the ways of the Lord; and furthermore he took the high places and the Ashe'rim out of Judah.

7 In the third year of his reign he sent his princes, Ben-hail, Obadi'ah, Zechari'ah, Nethan'el, and Micai'ah, to teach in the cities of Judah; 8 and with them the Levites, Shemai'ah, Nethani'ah, Zebadi'ah, As'ahel, Shemi'ramoth, Jehon'athan, Adoni'jah, Tobi'jah, and Tobadoni'jah; and with these Levites, the priests Elish'ama and Jeho'ram. 9 And they taught in Judah, having the book of the law of the Lord with them; they went about through all the cities of Judah and taught among the people.

10 And the fear of the Lord fell upon all the kingdoms of the lands that were round about Judah, and they made no war

---

new information is cast in the Chronicler's distinctive style. To Jehoshaphat the Chronicler (not Kings) attributed two important measures—arrangements to teach the people the rightful manner of worshiping Yahweh, and a new judicial system.

17:6. **He took away the high places:** But 20:33 (= I Kings 22:43) states the opposite. For a similar contradiction cf. 14:3 with 15:17 (= I Kings 15:14). Perhaps 15:17 and 20:33 were inserted by an overzealous scribe to conform with the readings in Kings.

7-9. A royal commission to teach the law of Yahweh. There can be little or no doubt that such action was not taken in Jehoshaphat's reign. But in the sixth century, when the second temple had been built, it was wholly natural and necessary that the religious leaders in Jerusalem should make systematic efforts to revive in the people a belief in their God and an understanding of the reformed ritual. They had taken to heart the exhortations, instructions, and encouragement which found expression in Deuteronomy; and it is significant that Deuteronomy, alone in the Pentateuchal codes, insists that diligent instruction must be given the people, and lays on the Levites this

---

in healing for the maintenance of life." (Ecclus. 38:9-14.) Ben Sirach would have done well to leave it there. One does not quite know what he intended to convey by his concluding remark (vs. 15), "He that sinneth before his Maker, let him fall into the hand of the physician." Of the utmost importance are the careful, modern investigations being made regarding the relationship between religious belief and physical health.[8]

[8] Cf. Leslie D. Weatherhead, *Psychology, Religion and Healing* (New York and Nashville: Abingdon-Cokesbury Press, 1951).

17:7-9. *Religious Education.*— (See Exeg.) In this difficult duty and necessity Judaism has excelled. Its system skillfully blends worship in the synagogue and religious customs in the home. Down the centuries the Jews have taken to heart the solemn injunctions in Deut. 6:7-9; 11:18-20, and have stressed that study of the faith should be a lifelong obligation. Christian practice tends to send the child to the church or Sunday school and let religious education end there. It is only too easy to learn to repeat "I believe in . . . ," but to make no sustained effort to apprehend the Creed more deeply.

11 Also *some* of the Philistines brought Jehoshaphat presents, and tribute silver; and the Arabians brought him flocks, seven thousand and seven hundred rams, and seven thousand and seven hundred he goats.

12 ¶ And Jehoshaphat waxed great exceedingly; and he built in Judah castles, and cities of store.

13 And he had much business in the cities of Judah: and the men of war, mighty men of valor, *were* in Jerusalem.

14 And these *are* the numbers of them according to the house of their fathers: Of Judah, the captains of thousands; Adnah the chief, and with him mighty men of valor three hundred thousand.

15 And next to him *was* Jehohanan the captain, and with him two hundred and fourscore thousand.

16 And next him *was* Amasiah the son of Zichri, who willingly offered himself unto the LORD; and with him two hundred thousand mighty men of valor.

17 And of Benjamin; Eliada a mighty man of valor, and with him armed men with bow and shield two hundred thousand.

18 And next him *was* Jehozabad, and with him a hundred and fourscore thousand ready prepared for the war.

19 These waited on the king, besides *those* whom the king put in the fenced cities throughout all Judah.

18 Now Jehoshaphat had riches and honor in abundance, and joined affinity with Ahab.

against Jehosh'aphat. 11 Some of the Philistines brought Jehosh'aphat presents, and silver for tribute; and the Arabs also brought him seven thousand seven hundred rams and seven thousand seven hundred he-goats. 12 And Jehosh'aphat grew steadily greater. He built in Judah fortresses and store-cities, 13 and he had great stores in the cities of Judah. He had soldiers, mighty men of valor, in Jerusalem. 14 This was the muster of them by fathers' houses: Of Judah, the commanders of thousands: Adnah the commander, with three hundred thousand mighty men of valor, 15 and next to him Jeho-ha'nan the commander, with two hundred and eighty thousand, 16 and next to him Amasi'ah the son of Zichri, a volunteer for the service of the LORD, with two hundred thousand mighty men of valor. 17 Of Benjamin: Eli'ada, a mighty man of valor, with two hundred thousand men armed with bow and shield, 18 and next to him Jeho'zabad with a hundred and eighty thousand armed for war. 19 These were in the service of the king, besides those whom the king had placed in the fortified cities throughout all Judah.

18 Now Jehosh'aphat had great riches and honor; and he made a marriage

---

paramount duty (see Deut. 6:6-9; 27:11-26; 31:9-13; cf. Adam C. Welch, *The Work of the Chronicler* [London: British Academy, 1939], pp. 74, 129). Observe the remarkable composition of the commission: five lay nominees of the king, nine Levites, and two priests. Evidently the Chronicler paid scant regard to priests as priests, assigned much responsibility to the laity, but the predominant part to Levites.

14-19. Jehoshaphat's colossal army numbered 1,160,000 soldiers, not including garrison troops in the Judean towns! For similar symbolic exaggerations cf. 11:1; 13:3; 14:8; also I Chr. 12:23 ff.

18:1-34. Here alone a lengthy narrative primarily concerned with the kingdom of Israel is incorporated in Chronicles (see I Kings 22:1-37). The Chronicler needed this

---

All too few persevere in studying the Bible. It is the duty of preachers to expound and commend the doctrines of the faith. But they cannot do justice to the greatness of those themes if most in the congregation have but the sketchiest biblical knowledge; for a teacher must to no small extent adapt his teaching to the comprehension of his hearers. Many preachers feel

driven to all sorts of devices in order to produce merely interesting discourses with a minimum of educative matter. There is a great need that they should feel freer to talk (as it is said) "over the heads of the people," relying on a more general eagerness to apprehend better the substance of the Bible and Christian doctrine. A distinguished British man of letters, who had

2 And after *certain* years he went down to Ahab to Samaria. And Ahab killed sheep and oxen for him in abundance, and for the people that *he had* with him, and persuaded him to go up *with him* to Ramoth-gilead.

3 And Ahab king of Israel said unto Jehoshaphat king of Judah, Wilt thou go with me to Ramoth-gilead? And he answered him, I *am* as thou *art,* and my people as thy people; and *we will be* with thee in the war.

4 ¶ And Jehoshaphat said unto the king of Israel, Inquire, I pray thee, at the word of the LORD to-day.

5 Therefore the king of Israel gathered together of prophets four hundred men, and said unto them, Shall we go to Ramoth-gilead to battle, or shall I forbear? And they said, Go up; for God will deliver *it* into the king's hand.

6 But Jehoshaphat said, *Is there* not here a prophet of the LORD besides, that we might inquire of him?

7 And the king of Israel said unto Jehoshaphat, *There is* yet one man, by whom we may inquire of the LORD: but I hate him; for he never prophesied good unto me, but always evil: the same *is* Micaiah the son of Imla. And Jehoshaphat said, Let not the king say so.

8 And the king of Israel called for one *of his* officers, and said, Fetch quickly Micaiah the son of Imla.

9 And the king of Israel and Jehoshaphat king of Judah sat either of them on his throne, clothed in *their* robes, and they sat

alliance with Ahab. 2 After some years he went down to Ahab in Samar'ia. And Ahab killed an abundance of sheep and oxen for him and for the people who were with him, and induced him to go up against Ramoth-gilead. 3 Ahab king of Israel said to Jehosh'aphat king of Judah, "Will you go with me to Ramoth-gilead?" He answered him, "I am as you are, my people as your people. We will be with you in the war."

4 And Jehosh'aphat said to the king of Israel, "Inquire first for the word of the LORD." 5 Then the king of Israel gathered the prophets together, four hundred men, and said to them, "Shall we go to battle against Ramoth-gilead, or shall I forbear?" And they said, "Go up; for God will give it into the hand of the king." 6 But Jehosh'aphat said, "Is there not here another prophet of the LORD of whom we may inquire?" 7 And the king of Israel said to Jehosh'aphat, "There is yet one man by whom we may inquire of the LORD, Micai'ah the son of Imlah; but I hate him, for he never prophesies good concerning me, but always evil." And Jehosh'aphat said, "Let not the king say so." 8 Then the king of Israel summoned an officer and said, "Bring quickly Micai'ah the son of Imlah." 9 Now the king of Israel and Jehosh'aphat the king of Judah were sitting on their thrones, ar-

veered from caustic agnosticism toward the Christian standpoint, is reported to have said to an archbishop that he had been much impressed by reading an able but brief and inexpensive book on Christianity, priced at less than one dollar. He received this deserved answer, "I am glad to hear that, but, you know, there are books about Christianity which cost more."

18:3. Latent Compulsion.—When Ahab king of Israel politely asked Jehoshaphat if he would join forces with him to attack the Syrians at Ramoth-gilead, the invitation was virtually an "If you please, you must." Omri, Ahab's father, had made the kingdom of Israel powerful, and its strength continued under Ahab. Judah was not quite reduced to the status of a satellite, but its king, Jehoshaphat, sensibly regarded close friendship with Ahab as a better state of affairs than an uneasy peace and occasional fighting between the two Hebrew kingdoms. The ex-

positor who recalls the narratives in Kings about Elijah's adamant antagonism to Ahab's Phoenician queen, Jezebel—fanatically determined that honor and sacrifices should be offered in Israel to her own god, Baal—will perceive that much else was latent in the present situation. For one thing, Jehoshaphat had married his son to Jezebel's daughter, who was as fanatical as her mother—a sinister wedding for Judah, as the future would show (see 21:6; 22:2-3; 23:1-21). The immediate sequel to Jehoshaphat's acceptance of Ahab's request has very great interest. For one thing, it appears that despite Elijah's unflinching opposition to Ahab and Jezebel, Ahab could collect four hundred Israelite prophets who considered themselves inspired in the name of Yahweh to promise victory in the intended campaign.

4-27. Beware of False Prophets.—This intensely interesting passage poses an issue that

in a void place at the entering in of the gate of Samaria; and all the prophets prophesied before them.

10 And Zedekiah the son of Chenaanah had made him horns of iron, and said, Thus saith the LORD, With these thou shalt push Syria until they be consumed.

11 And all the prophets prophesied so, saying, Go up to Ramoth-gilead, and prosper: for the LORD shall deliver *it* into the hand of the king.

12 And the messenger that went to call Micaiah spake to him, saying, Behold, the words of the prophets *declare* good to the king with one assent; let thy word therefore, I pray thee, be like one of theirs, and speak thou good.

13 And Micaiah said, *As* the LORD liveth, even what my God saith, that will I speak.

14 And when he was come to the king, the king said unto him, Micaiah, shall we go to Ramoth-gilead to battle, or shall I forbear? And he said, Go ye up, and prosper, and they shall be delivered into your hand.

15 And the king said to him, How many times shall I adjure thee that thou say nothing but the truth to me in the name of the LORD?

16 Then he said, I did see all Israel scattered upon the mountains, as sheep that have no shepherd: and the LORD said, These have no master; let them return *therefore* every man to his house in peace.

rayed in their robes; and they were sitting at the threshing floor at the entrance of the gate of Samar'ia; and all the prophets were prophesying before them. 10 And Zedeki'ah the son of Chena'anah made for himself horns of iron, and said, "Thus says the LORD, 'With these you shall push the Syrians until they are destroyed.'" 11 And all the prophets prophesied so, and said, "Go up to Ramoth-gilead and triumph; the LORD will give it into the hand of the king."

12 And the messenger who went to summon Micai'ah said to him, "Behold, the words of the prophets with one accord are favorable to the king; let your word be like the word of one of them, and speak favorably." 13 But Micai'ah said, "As the LORD lives, what my God says, that I will speak." 14 And when he had come to the king, the king said to him, "Micai'ah, shall we go to Ramoth-gilead to battle, or shall I forbear?" And he answered, "Go up and triumph; they will be given into your hand." 15 But the king said to him, "How many times shall I adjure you that you speak to me nothing but the truth in the name of the LORD?" 16 And he said, "I saw all Israel scattered upon the mountains, as sheep that have no shepherd; and the LORD said, 'These have no master; let each return to

---

story since it led into what he had subsequently to relate—the dreadful corruption of Judah's dynasty through the marriage of Jehoshaphat's son Jehoram (21:5-6) with Athaliah, the Baal-worshiping daughter of Ahab and Jezebel. He told the story from

---

constantly arises in religious affairs. Two persons, two parties, each sincere, urge divergent views. How should others try to judge which is the right opinion? The problem was peculiarly difficult for the Hebrews who believed that when men spoke as prophets they declared not their own ideas but a message from a supernatural Being, received by them in trance or ecstasy. Here **four hundred** prophets promise victory: that was good enough for Ahab. Mark the Judean king's uneasy instinct that something is being withheld. Reluctantly Ahab summons the prophet Micaiah. He agrees with the four hundred, but with obvious irony. Adjured, he declares that utter defeat is in fact the word which Yahweh has given him to speak. Micaiah himself then accounts for the divergence. He does not question the sincerity of the ecstasy of the

other prophets. But he believes that God, knowing that Ahab is resolved to follow the desires of his own heart, is testing him. If his conscience had been clear he would know that Micaiah spoke truly. We ask, Why did Micaiah's trance-experience show him the coming catastrophe? We can reason that there was in this man a depth of moral sincerity which the others lacked, such that his subconsciousness or superconsciousness saw into the real heart of things and sensed the latent moral evil (cf. the story of Balaam, Num. 23, especially vs. 26). It has been well said that the predictions of the prophets of victory and peace were "the outcome of the imagination working upon the material presented by the desires," whereas "the prophecies of Amos, Hosea, Isaiah, Jeremiah, and others . . . always express the result of profound meditation into

17 And the king of Israel said to Jehosha-phat, Did I not tell thee *that* he would not prophesy good unto me, but evil?

18 Again he said, Therefore hear the word of the LORD; I saw the LORD sitting upon his throne, and all the host of heaven standing on his right hand and *on* his left.

19 And the LORD said, Who shall entice Ahab king of Israel, that he may go up and fall at Ramoth-gilead? And one spake saying after this manner, and another saying after that manner.

20 Then there came out a spirit, and stood before the LORD, and said, I will entice him. And the LORD said unto him, Wherewith?

21 And he said, I will go out, and be a lying spirit in the mouth of all his prophets. And *the LORD* said, Thou shalt entice *him*, and thou shalt also prevail: go out, and do *even* so.

22 Now therefore, behold, the LORD hath put a lying spirit in the mouth of these thy prophets, and the LORD hath spoken evil against thee.

23 Then Zedekiah the son of Chenaanah came near, and smote Micaiah upon the cheek, and said, Which way went the Spirit of the LORD from me to speak unto thee?

24 And Micaiah said, Behold, thou shalt see on that day when thou shalt go into an inner chamber to hide thyself.

25 Then the king of Israel said, Take ye Micaiah, and carry him back to Amon the governor of the city, and to Joash the king's son;

26 And say, Thus saith the king, Put this *fellow* in the prison, and feed him with bread of affliction and with water of affliction, until I return in peace.

27 And Micaiah said, If thou certainly return in peace, *then* hath not the LORD

his home in peace.' " 17 And the king of Israel said to Jehosh'aphat, "Did I not tell you that he would not prophesy good concerning me, but evil?" 18 And Micai'ah said, "Therefore hear the word of the LORD: I saw the LORD sitting on his throne, and all the host of heaven standing on his right hand and on his left; 19 and the LORD said, 'Who will entice Ahab the king of Israel, that he may go up and fall at Ramoth-gilead?' And one said one thing, and another said another. 20 Then a spirit came forward and stood before the LORD, saying, 'I will entice him.' And the LORD said to him, 'By what means?' 21 And he said, 'I will go forth, and will be a lying spirit in the mouth of all his prophets.' And he said, 'You are to entice him, and you shall succeed; go forth and do so.' 22 Now therefore behold, the LORD has put a lying spirit in the mouth of these your prophets; the LORD has spoken evil concerning you."

23 Then Zedeki'ah the son of Chena'-anah came near and struck Micai'ah on the cheek, and said, "Which way did the Spirit of the LORD go from me to speak to you?" 24 And Micai'ah said, "Behold, you shall see on that day when you go into an inner chamber to hide yourself." 25 And the king of Israel said, "Seize Micai'ah, and take him back to Amon the governor of the city and to Jo'ash the king's son; 26 and say, 'Thus says the king, Put this fellow in prison, and feed him with scant fare of bread and water, until I return in peace.' " 27 And Micai'ah said, "If you return in peace, the LORD has

---

the Judean angle, and in Jehoshaphat's worthy attitude toward Micaiah (vss. 6-8) could see an offset to the king's sin in making an alliance with wicked Ahab.

---

the meaning and order of the actual world . . . ; these visions are based upon insight into the moral order." [9]

Hebrew religion in time tried to see some principle by which to judge if a prophet had spoken wrongly. Deuteronomy laid down this rule: If a prophet speaks in Yahweh's name

anything contrary to the fundamental, religious, and moral requirements revealed in the "Mosaic" covenant, he must not be believed (see Deut. 13:1-5; cf. I John 4:1-3).[1] Much more illuminating, however, are the records concerning Jeremiah's wrestling with his perplexity that many prophets of his own time passionately de-

[9] Nathaniel Micklem, *Prophecy and Eschatology* (London: George Allen & Unwin, 1926), p. 44.

[1] Cf. Adam C. Welch, *Deuteronomy, the Framework to the Code* (London: Oxford University Press, 1932), p. 26.

spoken by me. And he said, Hearken, all ye people.

28 So the king of Israel had Jehoshaphat the king of Judah went up to Ramoth-gilead.

29 And the king of Israel said unto Jehoshaphat, I will disguise myself, and will go to the battle; but put thou on thy robes. So the king of Israel disguised himself; and they went to the battle.

30 Now the king of Syria had commanded the captains of the chariots that *were* with him, saying, Fight ye not with small or great, save only with the king of Israel.

31 And it came to pass, when the captains of the chariots saw Jehoshaphat, that they said, It *is* the king of Israel. Therefore they compassed about him to fight: but Jehoshaphat cried out, and the LORD helped him; and God moved them *to depart* from him.

32 For it came to pass, that, when the captains of the chariots perceived that it was not the king of Israel, they turned back again from pursuing him.

33 And a *certain* man drew a bow at a venture, and smote the king of Israel between the joints of the harness: therefore he said to his chariot man, Turn thine hand, that thou mayest carry me out of the host; for I am wounded.

34 And the battle increased that day: howbeit the king of Israel stayed *himself* up in *his* chariot against the Syrians until the even: and about the time of the sun going down he died.

19 And Jehoshaphat the king of Judah returned to his house in peace to Jerusalem.

2 And Jehu the son of Hanani the seer went out to meet him, and said to king Jehoshaphat, Shouldest thou help the un-

not spoken by me." And he said, "Hear, all you peoples!"

28 So the king of Israel and Jehosh'aphat the king of Judah went up to Ramoth-gilead. 29 And the king of Israel said to Jehosh'aphat, "I will disguise myself and go into battle, but you wear your robes." And the king of Israel disguised himself; and they went into battle. 30 Now the king of Syria had commanded the captains of his chariots, "Fight with neither small nor great, but only with the king of Israel." 31 And when the captains of the chariots saw Jehosh'aphat, they said, "It is the king of Israel." So they turned to fight against him; and Jehosh'aphat cried out, and the LORD helped him. God drew them away from him, 32 for when the captains of the chariots saw that it was not the king of Israel, they turned back from pursuing him. 33 But a certain man drew his bow at a venture, and struck the king of Israel between the scale armor and the breastplate; therefore he said to the driver of his chariot, "Turn about, and carry me out of the battle, for I am wounded." 34 And the battle grew hot that day, and the king of Israel propped himself up in his chariot facing the Syrians until evening; then at sunset he died.

19 Jehosh'aphat the king of Judah returned in safety to his house in Jerusalem. 2 But Jehu the son of Hana'ni the seer went out to meet him, and said to King

---

19:1-3. No parallel in Kings. A prophet, Jehu the son of Hanani, rebukes Jehoshaphat on his return to Jerusalem, but he also recognizes his inherent better nature; wherefore the king reverts to pious action and for a time prospers.

---

clared as the word received from Yahweh that all was well, and would be well, with Jerusalem. He saw that they ignored the vices and cruelties rampant in the city, and that their own characters were infected by the evils. That was the criterion by which Jeremiah reached final assurance that those men had not stood, as he had who sought to be pure in heart, in the very

counsel of God and thus had not truly heard his word (cf. Jer. 23) .[2]

19:2. *Inventing a Prophet.*—Conceivably the Chronicler found this mention of **Jehu** . . . the **seer** in a source available to him but not used for Kings. It is much more likely that Jehu is

[2] See John Skinner, *Prophecy and Religion* (Cambridge: Cambridge University Press, 1922), pp. 190-200.

godly, and love them that hate the Lord? therefore *is* wrath upon thee from before the Lord.

3 Nevertheless, there are good things found in thee, in that thou hast taken away the groves out of the land, and hast prepared thine heart to seek God.

4 And Jehoshaphat dwelt at Jerusalem: and he went out again through the people from Beer-sheba to mount Ephraim, and brought them back unto the Lord God of their fathers.

5 ¶ And he set judges in the land throughout all the fenced cities of Judah, city by city,

6 And said to the judges, Take heed what ye do: for ye judge not for man, but for the Lord, who *is* with you in the judgment.

7 Wherefore now let the fear of the Lord be upon you; take heed and do *it:* for *there is* no iniquity with the Lord our God, nor respect of persons, nor taking of gifts.

Jehosh'aphat, "Should you help the wicked and love those who hate the Lord? Because of this, wrath has gone out against you from the Lord. 3 Nevertheless some good is found in you, for you destroyed the Ashe'rahs out of the land, and have set your heart to seek God."

4 Jehosh'aphat dwelt at Jerusalem; and he went out again among the people, from Beer-sheba to the hill country of E'phraim, and brought them back to the Lord, the God of their fathers. 5 He appointed judges in the land in all the fortified cities of Judah, city by city, 6 and said to the judges, "Consider what you do, for you judge not for man but for the Lord; he is with you in giving judgment. 7 Now then, let the fear of the Lord be upon you; take heed what you do, for there is no perversion of justice with the Lord our God, or partiality, or taking bribes."

4-9. Local courts of justice were set up in the provincial towns; in Jerusalem, a court of appeal. No doubt it was so in the postexilic community. There is no solid evidence or probability that Jehoshaphat instituted any such judicial system concerning civil, criminal, and ritual matters. The Chronicler reflected back to the authority of a good king the good institution with which he was cognizant. There was no need, however,

one of the prophets whose presence and words he invented in accordance with his purpose to delineate an ideal history—on such and such an occasion a man of God ought to have appeared to speak truly in rebuke or encouragement.

Inevitably these "Chronicles" prophets are stylized, but their worthiness must not be belittled: Jehu's utterance, by its blending of uncompromising rebuke with insight into the king's measure of virtue, is in the grand manner of the great prophets of truth. Adam C. Welch rightly comments:

In contrast with the tremendous figures of Elijah and Amos and Hosea [the Chronicler's] prophets are colourless and thin, and have become mouthpieces of a recognized message. The historian belonged to a time when prophecy was on its deathbed, as an active force in the life of the nation. . . . But the spirit of the past was not yet dead. . . . A man who could not write the story of his nation without a constant reference to prophecy and its work was alive to its worth.[3]

Moreover, as Welch emphasizes in the context, the vitally important matter is the principle

[3] *The Work of the Chronicler* (London: British Academy, 1939), pp. 49-50.

which the Chronicler sought in this way to affirm. He did not conceive of God merely as the revealer of rules and regulations in past time, but as the living God. How long has reluctance to believe that been the besetting weakness in the history of the Christian church —and is still?

19:2. *Helping the Ungodly.*—Men are fertile in excuses (cf. Luke 14:18-20). Jehoshaphat could argue that friendly relations with Israel greatly advantaged Judah and did not imply that he would countenance in its temple sacrifices in honor of the Phoenician Baal which Jezebel imperiously demanded in Israel. The prophet was forthright, **Should you help the wicked?** It was a memorable saying. For less than affairs of state—for business advantage, social pride, timid impulse—men are tempted to compromise, hoping to touch pitch without being much defiled, and forgetting that wider interests than our own are injured when we attempt to worship God and mammon alike.

6. *The Course of Justice.*—Hebrew religion evolved a sublime conception of the basis of law and the due administration of justice. The foundation of law (right) should not be conceived to be a social contract—the wishes of the

8 ¶ Moreover in Jerusalem did Jehosha-phat set of the Levites, and *of* the priests, and of the chief of the fathers of Israel, for the judgment of the LORD, and for contro-versies, when they returned to Jerusalem.

9 And he charged them, saying, Thus shall ye do in the fear of the LORD, faith-fully, and with a perfect heart.

10 And what cause soever shall come to you of your brethren that dwell in their cities, between blood and blood, between law and commandment, statutes and judg-ments, ye shall even warn them that they trespass not against the LORD, and *so* wrath come upon you, and upon your brethren: this do, and ye shall not trespass.

11 And, behold, Amariah the chief priest *is* over you in all matters of the LORD; and Zebadiah the son of Ishmael, the ruler of the house of Judah, for all the king's mat-ters: also the Levites *shall be* officers before you. Deal courageously, and the LORD shall be with the good.

8 Moreover in Jerualem Jehosh'aphat appointed certain Levites and priests and heads of families of Israel, to give judg-ment for the LORD and to decide disputed cases. They had their seat at Jerusalem. 9 And he charged them: "Thus you shall do in the fear of the LORD, in faithfulness, and with your whole heart: 10 whenever a case comes to you from your brethren who live in their cities, concerning bloodshed, law or commandment, statutes or ordinances, then you shall instruct them, that they may not incur guilt before the LORD and wrath may not come upon you and your brethren. Thus you shall do, and you will not incur guilt. 11 And behold, Amari'ah the chief priest is over you in all matters of the LORD; and Zebadi'ah the son of Ish'mael, the gov-ernor of the house of Judah, in all the king's matters; and the Levites will serve you as officers. Deal courageously, and may the LORD be with the upright!"

---

for him to confer upon it the still more august authority of David. To what king could he more fittingly ascribe its origin than to Jehoshaphat, whose name signifies "Yahweh is judge"?

8a. Mark the composition of the court charged with disputes local to Jerusalem and with appeals. Note also the eminence accorded to **Levites**—they are named first, and they act as its executive officers (vs. 11). For civil trials the lay representative of government presided; for religious ones, the chief priest.

8b. They returned to Jerusalem is a textual error. A slight change in the Hebrew yields the excellent sense, "and for the controversies of the inhabitants of Jerusalem."

10. Concerning bloodshed: I.e., whether the case amounted to manslaughter or murder.

11. Note here and in vss. 6-7 how the solemn demand that the judges shall be incorrupt and fearless corresponds to the like insistence in Deuteronomy which is less precise concerning the institution of the judges—a fact possibly indicating a stage of development rather earlier than Chronicles (see Welch, *op. cit.,* pp. 129-31).

---

governed—or as the principle that might makes right—what the governors find convenient to enforce. Instead, men must support right by an endeavor to attain an absolute standard—the perfection of God's righteousness. Richard Hooker wrote: "of Law there can be no less acknowledged than that her seat is the bosom of God." [4] That was the conception which Jehoshaphat enjoined upon the men whom he is said to have sent out to teach and maintain the ways of true justice in his land: **Ye judge not for man, but for the LORD.** Magnificent words! The administrators of justice must be absolutely incorrupt, the path to justice as cer-tain and easy for the poor as for the rich, for the humble as for the influential. When that ideal has once been stated, ever afterward the

worth of a civilization's culture ought to be measured by its approximation to that standard. And very searching this is for the pride of powerful nations and persons. Are the poor at a disadvantage in our courts? Are our officers of justice, from the greatest to the least, incor-ruptible? Or is it only too true that many litigants have sorrowfully had to conclude that Judge Lynch has a brother named "Fleece"? The practical interpretation of the ideal among the Hebrews improved steadily; the present pas-sage marks an upward stage. Is our standard improving? That is another revealing test of a nation's conscience and capacity. Are we su-pinely tolerant of old abuses, or unable to abolish them? There was a phase in American history when lynch law was in certain places the most practicable defense against crime.

[4] *Ecclesiastical Polity,* Bk. I, sec. 3.

20 It came to pass after this also, *that* the children of Moab, and the children of Ammon, and with them *other* besides the Ammonites, came against Jehoshaphat to battle.

2 Then there came some that told Jehoshaphat, saying, There cometh a great multitude against thee from beyond the sea on this side Syria; and, behold, they *be* in Hazazon-tamar, which *is* En-gedi.

3 And Jehoshaphat feared, and set himself to seek the LORD, and proclaimed a fast throughout all Judah.

4 And Judah gathered themselves together, to ask *help* of the LORD: even out of all the cities of Judah they came to seek the LORD.

5 ¶ And Jehoshaphat stood in the congregation of Judah and Jerusalem, in the house of the LORD, before the new court,

6 And said, O LORD God of our fathers, *art* not thou God in heaven? and rulest *not* thou over all the kingdoms of the heathen? and in thine hand *is there not* power and might, so that none is able to withstand thee?

7 *Art* not thou our God, *who* didst drive out the inhabitants of this land before thy people Israel, and gavest it to the seed of Abraham thy friend for ever?

8 And they dwelt therein, and have built thee a sanctuary therein for thy name, saying,

20 After this the Moabites and Ammonites, and with them some of the Me-u'nites,[f] came against Jehosh'aphat for battle. 2 Some men came and told Jehosh'aphat, "A great multitude is coming against you from Edom,[g] from beyond the sea; and, behold, they are in Haz'azon-ta'mar" (that is, En-ge'di). 3 Then Jehosh'aphat feared, and set himself to seek the LORD, and proclaimed a fast throughout all Judah. 4 And Judah assembled to seek help from the LORD; from all the cities of Judah they came to seek the LORD.

5 And Jehosh'aphat stood in the assembly of Judah and Jerusalem, in the house of the LORD, before the new court, 6 and said, "O LORD, God of our fathers, art thou not God in heaven? Dost thou not rule over all the kingdoms of the nations? In thy hand are power and might, so that none is able to withstand thee. 7 Didst thou not, O our God, drive out the inhabitants of this land before thy people Israel, and give it for ever to the descendants of Abraham thy friend? 8 And they have dwelt in it, and have built thee in it a sanctuary for

f Compare 26. 7: Heb *Ammonites*
g One Ms: Heb *Aram* (Syria)

20:1-30. Overtaken by the **wrath . . . from the LORD** (19:2) which his alliance with Ahab deserved, Jehoshaphat is said to have met his trials in so admirable a spirit that the Chronicler thought it appropriate to add an expository comment.

1-2. For **Ammonites** read **Meunites,** men of the Edomitic desert near Petra; and for **Syria** (ארם) unquestionably read **Edom** (אדם).

5. The new court: Congruous with the second temple but not with Solomon's.

In the West, from the Alleghanies to the Golden Gate, the pioneer settlers resorted to popular justice to get rid of bands of outlaws, and to regulate society during that period when laws were weak or confused, when the laws made in the East did not suit western conditions, and when courts and officials were scarce and distant. . . . However, the lack of regard for law fostered by the conditions described led to a survival of the lynching habit after the necessity for it had passed away.[5]

If the habit still persists, is not the indictment grave? Medieval Jewish justice—in the systems of the *Bêth Dîn*—eventually evolved a way by

[5] Article, "Lynch Law," *Encyclopaedia Britannica* (11th ed.), XVII, 169.

which many disputes could be settled with strict justice, yet on the basis of common sense and appeal to brotherly duty and kindness, a fact worthy of Gentile reflection.

20:1-30. *The Arabian Invasion.*—This tale is the plainest instance of the Chronicler's method of inventively constructing a situation in order to present principles which should govern good men's attitudes to events. He had credited Jehoshaphat with an army of more than a million soldiers (17:14-19). Here he declares that, when the men of the desert were reported to be on the march against Judah, the king did not turn his thoughts to his army but to his God. Then he received guidance from a prophet who called

9 If, *when* evil cometh upon us, *as* the sword, judgment, or pestilence, or famine, we stand before this house, and in thy presence, (for thy name *is* in this house,) and cry unto thee in our affliction, then thou wilt hear and help.

10 And now, behold, the children of Ammon and Moab and mount Seir, whom thou wouldest not let Israel invade, when they came out of the land of Egypt, but they turned from them, and destroyed them not;

11 Behold, *I say, how* they reward us, to come to cast us out of thy possession, which thou hast given us to inherit.

12 O our God, wilt thou not judge them? for we have no might against this great company that cometh against us; neither know we what to do: but our eyes *are* upon thee.

13 And all Judah stood before the LORD, with their little ones, their wives, and their children.

14 ¶ Then upon Jahaziel the son of Zechariah, the son of Benaiah, the son of Jeiel, the son of Mattaniah, a Levite of the sons of Asaph, came the Spirit of the LORD in the midst of the congregation;

15 And he said, Hearken ye, all Judah, and ye inhabitants of Jerusalem, and thou king Jehoshaphat, Thus saith the LORD unto you, Be not afraid nor dismayed by reason of this great multitude; for the battle *is* not yours, but God's.

16 To-morrow go ye down against them: behold, they come up by the cliff of Ziz; and ye shall find them at the end of the brook, before the wilderness of Jeruel.

17 Ye shall not *need* to fight in this *battle:* set yourselves, stand ye *still,* and see the salvation of the LORD with you, O Judah and Jerusalem: fear not, nor be dis-

thy name, saying, 9 'If evil comes upon us, the sword, judgment,[h] or pestilence, or famine, we will stand before this house, and before thee, for thy name is in this house, and cry to thee in our affliction, and thou wilt hear and save.' 10 And now behold, the men of Ammon and Moab and Mount Se'ir, whom thou wouldest not let Israel invade when they came from the land of Egypt, and whom they avoided and did not destroy — 11 behold, they reward us by coming to drive us out of thy possession, which thou hast given us to inherit. 12 O our God, wilt thou not execute judgment upon them? For we are powerless against this great multitude that is coming against us. We do not know what to do, but our eyes are upon thee."

13 Meanwhile all the men of Judah stood before the LORD, with their little ones, their wives, and their children. 14 And the Spirit of the LORD came upon Jahazi'el the son of Zechari'ah, son of Benai'ah, son of Je-i'el, son of Mattani'ah, a Levite of the sons of Asaph, in the midst of the assembly. 15 And he said, "Hearken, all Judah and inhabitants of Jerusalem, and King Jehosh'aphat: Thus says the LORD to you, 'Fear not, and be not dismayed at this great multitude; for the battle is not yours but God's. 16 To-morrow go down against them; behold, they will come up by the ascent of Ziz; you will find them at the end of the valley, east of the wilderness of Jeru'el. 17 You will not need to fight in this battle; take your position, stand still, and see the victory of the LORD on your behalf, O Judah and Jerusalem.' Fear not, and be not dismayed; tomor-

h Or *the sword of judgment*

---

14. It is a **Levite,** inspired to prophesy, who rises to the crisis (cf. I Chr. 25:1-3).

---

the whole people to share their king's reliance. When thereafter king and people set forth to encounter the foe, they went in the strength of the Lord, and not one of the million soldiers needed to strike a blow! Care must be taken not to misunderstand or to underrate the implications of this parable. It was concerned with a choice in life which is ubiquitous and constant. Here, as elsewhere, the Chronicler was striving to teach that if men forget the God of righteousness in their response to life's chal-

lenges all will go amiss, no matter how vast their material resources; whereas whenever in any circumstances, whether of prosperity or peril, they determine their conduct by basic trust in absolute righteousness, then in the deepest sense a marvelous triumph of the human spirit is won. Martin Luther might have found here, as he did in Ps. 46, the inspiration for his famous hymn, "A mighty fortress is our God."

17. *God Is Our Refuge and Strength.*—There are other fine verses in this chapter (e.g., vss.

mayed; to-morrow go out against them: for the Lord *will be* with you.

18 And Jehoshaphat bowed his head with *his* face to the ground: and all Judah and the inhabitants of Jerusalem fell before the Lord, worshipping the Lord.

19 And the Levites, of the children of the Kohathites, and of the children of the Korhites, stood up to praise the Lord God of Israel with a loud voice on high.

20 ¶ And they rose early in the morning, and went forth into the wilderness of Tekoa: and as they went forth, Jehoshaphat stood and said, Hear me, O Judah, and ye inhabitants of Jerusalem; Believe in the Lord your God, so shall ye be established; believe his prophets, so shall ye prosper.

21 And when he had consulted with the people, he appointed singers unto the Lord, and that should praise the beauty of holiness, as they went out before the army, and to say, Praise the Lord; for his mercy *endureth* for ever.

22 ¶ And when they began to sing and to praise, the Lord set ambushments against the children of Ammon, Moab, and mount Seir, which were come against Judah; and they were smitten.

23 For the children of Ammon and Moab stood up against the inhabitants of mount Seir, utterly to slay and destroy *them:* and when they had made an end of the inhabitants of Seir, every one helped to destroy another.

24 And when Judah came toward the watchtower in the wilderness, they looked unto the multitude, and, behold, they *were* dead bodies fallen to the earth, and none escaped.

25 And when Jehoshaphat and his people came to take away the spoil of them, they found among them in abundance both

row go out against them, and the Lord will be with you."

18 Then Jehosh'aphat bowed his head with his face to the ground, and all Judah and the inhabitants of Jerusalem fell down before the Lord, worshiping the Lord. **19** And the Levites, of the Ko'hathites and the Ko'rahites, stood up to praise the Lord, the God of Israel, with a very loud voice.

20 And they rose early in the morning and went out into the wilderness of Teko'a; and as they went out, Jehosh'aphat stood and said, "Hear me, Judah and inhabitants of Jerusalem! Believe in the Lord your God, and you will be established; believe his prophets, and you will succeed." **21** And when he had taken counsel with the people, he appointed those who were to sing to the Lord and praise him in holy array, as they went before the army, and say,

"Give thanks to the Lord,
     for his steadfast love endures for ever."

22 And when they began to sing and praise, the Lord set an ambush against the men of Ammon, Moab, and Mount Se'ir, who had come against Judah, so that they were routed. **23** For the men of Ammon and Moab rose against the inhabitants of Mount Se'ir, destroying them utterly, and when they had made an end of the inhabitants of Se'ir, they all helped to destroy one another.

24 When Judah came to the watchtower of the wilderness, they looked toward the multitude; and behold, they were dead bodies lying on the ground; none had escaped. **25** When Jehosh'aphat and his peo-

---

20. Believe in the Lord your God, so shall ye be established; believe his prophets, so shall ye prosper: Surely the Chronicler had, as the collect puts it, read, marked, learned, and inwardly digested Isaiah's undeviating trust in God (see Isa. 7:9) .

12, 15, 20) , but best of all is this verse. Consider that when it was written other nations had soldiers innumerable, and that Judah was an insignificant part of an outlying province in the vast Persian Empire. **Set yourselves,** said the Chronicler to his people; be resolute, find strength not in soldiers but in your religion and morals. The Persian Empire has crumbled to

dust; its religion is now known only to students of antiquity. Said the Chronicler to the Jews, **Stand ye still, and see the salvation of the Lord with you, O Judah and Jerusalem.** Men and women with that quality keep steady in emergencies, and their soul is invincible.

25. *Dead to Conscience.*—It has somewhere been pungently remarked, "Some people who

riches with the dead bodies, and precious jewels, which they stripped off for themselves, more than they could carry away: and they were three days in gathering of the spoil, it was so much.

26 ¶ And on the fourth day they assembled themselves in the valley of Berachah; for there they blessed the LORD: therefore the name of the same place was called, The valley of Berachah, unto this day.

27 Then they returned, every man of Judah and Jerusalem, and Jehoshaphat in the forefront of them, to go again to Jerusalem with joy; for the LORD had made them to rejoice over their enemies.

28 And they came to Jerusalem with psalteries and harps and trumpets unto the house of the LORD.

29 And the fear of God was on all the kingdoms of *those* countries, when they had heard that the LORD fought against the enemies of Israel.

30 So the realm of Jehoshaphat was quiet: for his God gave him rest round about.

31 ¶ And Jehoshaphat reigned over Judah: *he was* thirty and five years old when he began to reign, and he reigned twenty and five years in Jerusalem. And his mother's name *was* Azubah the daughter of Shilhi.

32 And he walked in the way of Asa his father, and departed not from it, doing *that which was* right in the sight of the LORD.

33 Howbeit the high places were not taken away: for as yet the people had not prepared their hearts unto the God of their fathers.

34 Now the rest of the acts of Jehoshaphat, first and last, behold, they *are* written in the book of Jehu the son of Hanani, who *is* mentioned in the book of the kings of Israel.

35 ¶ And after this did Jehoshaphat king of Judah join himself with Ahaziah king of Israel, who did very wickedly:

36 And he joined himself with him to make ships to go to Tarshish: and they made the ships in Ezion-gaber.

37 Then Eliezer the son of Dodavah of

ple came to take the spoil from them, they found cattle*i* in great numbers, goods, clothing, and precious things, which they took for themselves until they could carry no more. They were three days in taking the spoil, it was so much. 26 On the fourth day they assembled in the Valley of Bera'cah,*j* for there they blessed the LORD; therefore the name of that place has been called the Valley of Bera'cah to this day. 27 Then they returned, every man of Judah and Jerusalem, and Jehosh'aphat at their head, returning to Jerusalem with joy, for the LORD had made them rejoice over their enemies. 28 They came to Jerusalem, with harps and lyres and trumpets, to the house of the LORD. 29 And the fear of God came on all the kingdoms of the countries when they heard that the LORD had fought against the enemies of Israel. 30 So the realm of Jehosh'aphat was quiet, for his God gave him rest round about.

31 Thus Jehosh'aphat reigned over Judah. He was thirty-five years old when he began to reign, and he reigned twenty-five years in Jerusalem. His mother's name was Azu'bah the daughter of Shilhi. 32 He walked in the way of Asa his father and did not turn aside from it; he did what was right in the sight of the LORD. 33 The high places, however, were not taken away; the people had not yet set their hearts upon the God of their fathers.

34 Now the rest of the acts of Jehosh'aphat, from first to last, are written in the chronicles of Jehu the son of Hana'ni, which are recorded in the Book of the Kings of Israel.

35 After this Jehosh'aphat king of Judah joined with Ahazi'ah king of Israel, who did wickedly. 36 He joined him in building ships to go to Tarshish, and they built the ships in E'zion-ge'ber. 37 Then Elie'zer the son of Dodav'ahu of Mare'shah prophesied

i Gk: Heb *among them*
j That is, *Blessing*

35-37. Jehoshaphat, taking a leaf out of Solomon's book, repeats his transgression by joining Ahab's son Ahaziah in a shipping expedition. **To go to Tarshish:** See Exeg. on 9:21.

Mareshah prophesied against Jehoshaphat, saying, Because thou hast joined thyself with Ahaziah, the LORD hath broken thy works. And the ships were broken, that they were not able to go to Tarshish.

21 Now Jehoshaphat slept with his fathers, and was buried with his fathers in the city of David. And Jehoram his son reigned in his stead.

2 And he had brethren the sons of Jehoshaphat, Azariah, and Jehiel, and Zechariah, and Azariah, and Michael, and Shephatiah: all these *were* the sons of Jehoshaphat king of Israel.

3 And their father gave them great gifts of silver, and of gold, and of precious things, with fenced cities in Judah: but the kingdom gave he to Jehoram; because he *was* the firstborn.

4 Now when Jehoram was risen up to the kingdom of his father, he strengthened himself, and slew all his brethren with the sword, and *divers* also of the princes of Israel.

5 ¶ Jehoram *was* thirty and two years old when he began to reign, and he reigned eight years in Jerusalem.

6 And he walked in the way of the kings of Israel, like as did the house of Ahab: for he had the daughter of Ahab to wife: and he wrought *that which was* evil in the eyes of the LORD.

7 Howbeit the LORD would not destroy the house of David, because of the covenant that he had made with David, and as he promised to give a light to him and to his sons for ever.

8 ¶ In his days the Edomites revolted from under the dominion of Judah, and made themselves a king.

9 Then Jehoram went forth with his princes, and all his chariots with him: and he rose up by night, and smote the Edomites which compassed him in, and the captains of the chariots.

10 So the Edomites revolted from under the hand of Judah unto this day. The same time *also* did Libnah revolt from under his

against Jehosh'aphat, saying, "Because you have joined with Ahazi'ah, the LORD will destroy what you have made." And the ships were wrecked and were not able to go to Tarshish.

21 Jehosh'aphat slept with his fathers, and was buried with his fathers in the city of David; and Jeho'ram his son reigned in his stead. 2 He had brothers, the sons of Jehosh'aphat: Azari'ah, Jehi'el, Zechari'ah, Azari'ah, Michael, and Shepha-ti'ah; all these were the sons of Jehosh'aphat king of Judah. 3 Their father gave them great gifts, of silver, gold, and valuable possessions, together with fortified cities in Judah; but he gave the kingdom to Jeho'ram, because he was the first-born. 4 When Jeho'ram had ascended the throne of his father and was established, he slew all his brothers with the sword, and also some of the princes of Judah.[k] 5 Jeho'ram was thirty-two years old when he became king, and he reigned eight years in Jerusalem. 6 And he walked in the way of the kings of Israel, as the house of Ahab had done; for the daughter of Ahab was his wife. And he did what was evil in the sight of the LORD. 7 Yet the LORD would not destroy the house of David, because of the covenant which he had made with David, and since he had promised to give a lamp to him and to his sons for ever.

8 In his days Edom revolted from the rule of Judah, and set up a king of their own. 9 Then Jeho'ram passed over with his commanders and all his chariots, and he rose by night and smote the E'domites who had surrounded him and his chariot commanders. 10 So Edom revolted from the rule of Judah to this day. At that time Libnah also re-

[k] Heb *Israel*

E. REIGNS OF JEHORAM, AHAZIAH, AND ATHALIAH (21:1–23:21)

21:2-4. A fragment of state annals may be the Chronicler's source for the sons' names and the grim event recorded.

10. Libnah, in southern Judah, close to the desert of Edom. From the reign of Jehoshaphat onward (see 20:1-10) the book of Chronicles contains numerous allusions

hand; because he had forsaken the LORD God of his fathers.

11 Moreover he made high places in the mountains of Judah, and caused the inhabitants of Jerusalem to commit fornication, and compelled Judah *thereto*.

12 ¶ And there came a writing to him from Elijah the prophet, saying, Thus saith the LORD God of David thy father, Because thou hast not walked in the ways of Jehoshaphat thy father, nor in the ways of Asa king of Judah,

13 But hast walked in the way of the kings of Israel, and hast made Judah and the inhabitants of Jerusalem to go a whoring, like to the whoredoms of the house of Ahab, and also hast slain thy brethren of thy father's house, *which were* better than thyself:

14 Behold, with a great plague will the LORD smite thy people, and thy children, and thy wives, and all thy goods:

15 And thou *shalt have* great sickness by disease of thy bowels, until thy bowels fall out by reason of the sickness day by day.

16 ¶ Moreover the LORD stirred up against Jehoram the spirit of the Philistines, and of the Arabians, that *were* near the Ethiopians:

17 And they came up into Judah, and brake into it, and carried away all the substance that was found in the king's house, and his sons also, and his wives; so that there was never a son left him, save Jehoahaz, the youngest of his sons.

volted from his rule, because he had forsaken the LORD, the God of his fathers.

11 Moreover he made high places in the hill country of Judah, and let the inhabitants of Jerusalem into unfaithfulness, and made Judah go astray. 12 And a letter came to him from Eli'jah the prophet, saying, "Thus says the LORD, the God of David your father, 'Because you have not walked in the ways of Jehosh'aphat your father, or in the ways of Asa king of Judah, 13 but have walked in the way of the kings of Israel, and have led Judah and the inhabitants of Jerusalem into unfaithfulness, as the house of Ahab led Israel into unfaithfulness, and also you have killed your brothers, of your father's house, who were better than yourself; 14 behold, the LORD will bring a great plague on your people, your children, your wives, and all your possessions, 15 and you yourself will have a severe sickness with a disease of your bowels, until your bowels come out because of the disease, day by day.' "

16 And the LORD stirred up against Jeho'ram the anger of the Philistines and of the Arabs who are near the Ethiopians; 17 and they came up against Judah, and invaded it, and carried away all the possessions they found that belonged to the king's house, and also his sons and his wives, so that no son was left to him except Jeho'ahaz, his youngest son.

(see 25:11-12; 26:6-8; 28:17-18) to fluctuating fighting between Judean kings and Arabians (Edomites), together with Philistines, i.e., inhabitants of the southern coastal plain formerly ruled by the historic Philistines in the time of Saul and David. There may have been some traditional authority for these notices, but it should be remembered that after the fall of Jerusalem pressure from those regions was persistently exerted against the stricken Judeans.

17. This curious verse cannot signify that the Arabians took and plundered Jerusalem. Presumably they carried off royal property from Judah and persons of the royal family who had been with the defeated army.

---

would scruple to rob the dead spend all their time in robbing the living."

21:12-15. Denounced by the Dead.—Elijah, long dead, did not compose this letter to be delivered to a future king of Judah. Why was the Chronicler not content to evoke yet another of his otherwise unknown prophets to reproach Jehoram? Possibly he felt King Jehoram's enormities so flagrant that only the mighty Elijah

would seem adequate to denounce them. A conjecture, however, may be hazarded. Did a deeply wronged citizen inscribe on the walls of Jehoram's palace certain of the flaming words which Elijah had formerly addressed to Ahab and Jezebel? Popular memory of the daring deed may have been transmuted by the Chronicler into **a writing to him from Elijah.** When the ruins of the Maccabean governor's house at

18 ¶ And after all this the LORD smote him in his bowels with an incurable disease.

19 And it came to pass, that in process of time, after the end of two years, his bowels fell out by reason of his sickness: so he died of sore diseases. And his people made no burning for him, like the burning of his fathers.

20 Thirty and two years old was he when he began to reign, and he reigned in Jerusalem eight years, and departed without being desired. Howbeit they buried him in the city of David, but not in the sepulchres of the kings.

22 And the inhabitants of Jerusalem made Ahaziah his youngest son king in his stead: for the band of men that came with the Arabians to the camp had slain all the eldest. So Ahaziah the son of Jehoram king of Judah reigned.

2 Forty and two years old was Ahaziah when he began to reign, and he reigned one year in Jerusalem. His mother's name also was Athaliah the daughter of Omri.

3 He also walked in the ways of the house of Ahab: for his mother was his counselor to do wickedly.

4 Wherefore he did evil in the sight of the LORD like the house of Ahab: for they were his counselors, after the death of his father, to his destruction.

5 ¶ He walked also after their counsel, and went with Jehoram the son of Ahab king of Israel to war against Hazael king of Syria at Ramoth-gilead: and the Syrians smote Joram.

18 And after all this the LORD smote him in his bowels with an incurable disease.

19 In course of time, at the end of two years, his bowels came out because of the disease, and he died in great agony. His people made no fire in his honor, like the fires made for his fathers. 20 He was thirty-two years old when he began to reign, and he reigned eight years in Jerusalem; and he departed with no one's regret. They buried him in the city of David, but not in the tombs of the kings.

22 And the inhabitants of Jerusalem made Ahazi'ah his youngest son king in his stead; for the band of men that came with the Arabs to the camp had slain all the older sons. So Ahazi'ah the son of Jeho'ram king of Judah reigned. 2 Ahazi'ah was forty-two years old when he began to reign, and he reigned one year in Jerusalem. His mother's name was Athali'ah, the granddaughter of Omri. 3 He also walked in the ways of the house of Ahab, for his mother was his counselor in doing wickedly. 4 He did what was evil in the sight of the LORD, as the house of Ahab had done; for after the death of his father they were his counselors, to his undoing. 5 He even followed their counsel, and went with Jeho'ram the son of Ahab king of Israel to make war against Haz'ael king of Syria at Ramoth-gilead.

22:1-9. Ahaziah (son of Jehoram and Athaliah, grandson of Jehoshaphat) was king of Judah for one year only, and on his death Athaliah, the queen mother, seized the throne. Ahab, the king of Israel contemporary with the Judean Jehoshaphat and Jehoram, had married the Baal-worshiping Phoenician princess, Jezebel. They had a daughter and two sons, one of whom, Ahaziah, ruled Israel after Ahab's death for two years only, and was succeeded on the throne by his brother Jehoram. The daughter Athaliah was as strong-minded as her mother; the point is that through her marriage

---

Gezer were excavated, on one of its stones there was found the inscription "Says Pamphras, May fire take Simon's palace!"

20. *Good Riddance.*—II Kings 8:16-24 mentions Jehoram's (Joram's) ill-doings briefly and dismisses him by noting that he "slept with his fathers, and was buried with his fathers in the city of David." The Chronicler judged that much too innocuous a finish for so vile a monarch, and therefore declares that he suffered a

terrible defeat, died in protracted agony, and at burial was shown signal dishonor. One phrase that he used may give us pause: Jehoram *departed with no one's regret.* His people were glad when he died; the world was better without him. How far do we ourselves possess or lack qualities which will make men give thanks that we were born, and mourn for our death?

22:3. *An Evil Heritage.*—It stands written, his mother was his counselor in doing wickedly.

6 And he returned to be healed in Jezreel because of the wounds which were given him at Ramah, when he fought with Hazael king of Syria. And Azariah the son of Jehoram king of Judah went down to see Jehoram the son of Ahab at Jezreel, because he was sick.

7 And the destruction of Ahaziah was of God by coming to Joram: for when he was come, he went out with Jehoram against Jehu the son of Nimshi, whom the LORD had anointed to cut off the house of Ahab.

8 And it came to pass, that, when Jehu was executing judgment upon the house of Ahab, and found the princes of Judah, and the sons of the brethren of Ahaziah, that ministered to Ahaziah, he slew them.

9 And he sought Ahaziah: and they caught him, (for he was hid in Samaria,) and brought him to Jehu: and when they had slain him, they buried him: Because, said they, he is the son of Jehoshaphat, who sought the LORD with all his heart. So the house of Ahaziah had no power to keep still the kingdom.

10 ¶ But when Athaliah the mother of Ahaziah saw that her son was dead, she arose and destroyed all the seed royal of the house of Judah.

11 But Jehoshabeath, the daughter of the king, took Joash the son of Ahaziah, and stole him from among the king's sons that were slain, and put him and his nurse in a bedchamber. So Jehoshabeath, the daughter of king Jehoram, the wife of Jehoiada the priest, (for she was the sister of Ahaziah,) hid him from Athaliah, so that she slew him not.

12 And he was with them hid in the house of God six years: and Athaliah reigned over the land.

And the Syrians wounded Joram, 6 and he returned to be healed in Jezreel of the wounds which he had received at Ramah, when he fought against Haz′ael king of Syria. And Ahazi′ah the son of Jeho′ram king of Judah went down to see Joram the son of Ahab in Jezreel, because he was sick.

7 But it was ordained by God that the downfall of Ahazi′ah should come about through his going to visit Joram. For when he came there he went out with Jeho′ram to meet Jehu the son of Nimshi, whom the LORD had anointed to destroy the house of Ahab. 8 And when Jehu was executing judgment upon the house of Ahab, he met the princes of Judah and the sons of Ahazi′ah's brothers, who attended Ahazi′ah, and he killed them. 9 He searched for Ahazi′ah, and he was captured while hiding in Samar′ia, and he was brought to Jehu and put to death. They buried him, for they said, "He is the grandson of Jehosh′aphat, who sought the LORD with all his heart." And the house of Ahazi′ah had no one able to rule the kingdom.

10 Now when Athali′ah the mother of Ahazi′ah saw that her son was dead, she arose and destroyed all the royal family of the house of Judah. 11 But Jeho-shab′e-ath, the daughter of the king, took Jo′ash the son of Ahazi′ah, and stole him away from among the king's sons who were about to be slain, and she put him and his nurse in a bedchamber. Thus Jeho-shab′e-ath, the daughter of King Jeho′ram and wife of Jehoi′ada the priest, because she was a sister of Ahazi′ah, hid him from Athali′ah, so that she did not slay him; 12 and he remained with them six years, hid in the house of God, while Athali′ah reigned over the land.

to the Judean king named Jehoram, the poison of Jezebel's fanatical zeal for her Phoenician god became venomously active in Jerusalem (vss. 3-4). No wonder that her son, the Judean Ahaziah, was hand-in-glove with his uncle, Jehoram king of Israel (vs. 5). In vs. 2 **granddaughter** is correct. In vs. 9 **Samaria** must denote the territory, not the city itself.

22:10-23:21. Concerning Athaliah's tyranny, and assassination, II Kings 11:1-21 relates that Jehoiada the chief priest gained the aid of army officers for his plot to kill

Frightful epitaph, deservedly inscribed on the memory of Queen Athaliah. Alas for her son Ahaziah, environed by her strong, merciless personality. She had the same disposition as had her imperial mother, Queen Jezebel. Perhaps

it is not masculine prejudice to feel that when a woman is bad she is apt to be venomously bad. History and literature spotlight famous women, not least those in high places whose wickedness entailed great consequences, e.g., Cleopatra,

23 And in the seventh year Jehoiada strengthened himself, and took the captains of hundreds, Azariah the son of Jeroham, and Ishmael the son of Jehohanan, and Azariah the son of Obed, and Maaseiah the son of Adaiah, and Elishaphat the son of Zichri, into covenant with him.

2 And they went about in Judah, and gathered the Levites out of all the cities of Judah, and the chief of the fathers of Israel, and they came to Jerusalem.

3 And all the congregation made a covenant with the king in the house of God. And he said unto them, Behold, the king's son shall reign, as the LORD hath said of the sons of David.

4 This *is* the thing that ye shall do; A third part of you entering on the sabbath, of the priests and of the Levites, *shall be* porters of the doors;

5 And a third part *shall be* at the king's house; and a third part at the gate of the foundation: and all the people *shall be* in the courts of the house of the LORD.

6 But let none come into the house of the LORD, save the priests, and they that minister of the Levites; they shall go in, for they *are* holy: but all the people shall keep the watch of the LORD.

7 And the Levites shall compass the king round about, every man with his weapons in his hand; and whosoever *else* cometh into the house, he shall be put to death: but be ye with the king when he cometh in, and when he goeth out.

8 So the Levites and all Judah did according to all things that Jehoiada the priest had commanded, and took every man his men that were to come in on the sabbath, with them that were to go *out* on the sabbath: for Jehoiada the priest dismissed not the courses.

9 Moreover Jehoiada the priest delivered to the captains of hundreds spears, and bucklers, and shields, that *had been* king David's, which *were* in the house of God.

23 But in the seventh year Jehoi'ada took courage, and entered into a compact with the commanders of hundreds, Azari'ah the son of Jero'ham, Ish'mael the son of Jeho-ha'nan, Azari'ah the son of Obed, Ma-asei'ah, the son of Adai'ah, and Elisha'phat the son of Zichri. 2 And they went about through Judah and gathered the Levites from all the cities of Judah, and the heads of fathers' houses of Israel, and they came to Jerusalem. 3 And all the assembly made a covenant with the king in the house of God. And Jehoi'ada[1] said to them, "Behold, the king's son! Let him reign, as the LORD spoke concerning the sons of David. 4 This is the thing that you shall do: of you priests and Levites who come off duty on the sabbath, one third shall be gatekeepers, 5 and one third shall be at the king's house and one third at the Gate of the Foundation; and all the people shall be in the courts of the house of the LORD. 6 Let no one enter the house of the LORD except the priests and ministering Levites; they may enter, for they are holy, but all the people shall keep the charge of the LORD. 7 The Levites shall surround the king, each with his weapons in his hand; and whoever enters the house shall be slain. Be with the king when he comes in, and when he goes out."

8 The Levites and all Judah did according to all that Jehoi'ada the priest commanded. They each brought his men, who were to go off duty on the sabbath, with those who were to come on duty on the sabbath; for Jehoi'ada the priest did not dismiss the divisions. 9 And Jehoi'ada the priest delivered to the captains the spears and the large and small shields that had been King David's, which were in the house

[1] Heb *he*

Athaliah, and that these laymen (some of them aliens) conspired together within the temple court. But for the Chronicler in later times that connoted sacrilege. Here then the plot is carried out by Levites, and the sanctities are preserved (22:2-6) .

Catherine de Médici, Lady Macbeth. Fortunately life produces women, renowned and unrenowned, whose powers for good are beyond estimation, and whose memory is blessed.

Happy the sons and daughters who receive the influence of such a mother. Some of these children fling away the gift, or are even unconscious of having received it. Alas, sad mothers

10 And he set all the people, every man having his weapon in his hand, from the right side of the temple to the left side of the temple, along by the altar and the temple, by the king round about.

11 Then they brought out the king's son, and put upon him the crown, and *gave him* the testimony, and made him king. And Jehoiada and his sons anointed him, and said, God save the king.

12 ¶ Now when Athaliah heard the noise of the people running and praising the king, she came to the people into the house of the LORD:

13 And she looked, and, behold, the king stood at his pillar at the entering in, and the princes and the trumpets by the king: and all the people of the land rejoiced, and sounded with trumpets, also the singers with instruments of music, and such as taught to sing praise. Then Athaliah rent her clothes, and said, Treason, treason.

14 Then Jehoiada the priest brought out the captains of hundreds that were set over the host, and said unto them, Have her forth of the ranges: and whoso followeth her, let him be slain with the sword. For the priest said, Slay her not in the house of the LORD.

15 So they laid hands on her; and when she was come to the entering of the horse gate by the king's house, they slew her there.

16 ¶ And Jehoiada made a covenant between him, and between all the people, and between the king, that they should be the LORD's people.

17 Then all the people went to the house of Baal, and brake it down, and brake his altars and his images in pieces, and slew Mattan the priest of Baal before the altars.

18 Also Jehoiada appointed the offices of the house of the LORD by the hand of the priests the Levites, whom David had distributed in the house of the LORD, to offer the burnt offerings of the LORD, as *it is* written in the law of Moses, with rejoicing and with singing, *as it was ordained* by David.

of God; 10 and he set all the people as a guard for the king, every man with his weapon in his hand, from the south side of the house to the north side of the house, around the altar and the house. 11 Then he brought out the king's son, and put the crown upon him, and gave him the testimony; and they proclaimed him king, and Jehoi'ada and his sons anointed him, and they said, "Long live the king."

12 When Athali'ah heard the noise of the people running and praising the king, she went into the house of the LORD to the people; 13 and when she looked, there was the king standing by his pillar at the entrance, and the captains and the trumpeters beside the king, and all the people of the land rejoicing and blowing trumpets, and the singers with their musical instruments leading in the celebration. And Athali'ah rent her clothes, and cried, "Treason! Treason!" 14 Then Jehoi'ada the priest brought out the captains who were set over the army, saying to them, "Bring her out between the ranks; any one who follows her is to be slain with the sword." For the priest said, "Do not slay her in the house of the LORD." 15 So they laid hands on her; and she went into the entrance of the horse gate of the king's house, and they slew her there.

16 And Jehoi'ada made a covenant between himself and all the people and the king that they should be the LORD's people. 17 Then all the people went to the house of Ba'al, and tore it down; his altars and his images they broke in pieces, and they slew Mattan the priest of Ba'al before the altars. 18 And Jehoi'ada posted watchmen for the house of the LORD under the direction of the Levitical priests and the Levites whom David had organized to be in charge of the house of the LORD, to offer burnt offerings to the LORD, as it is written in the law of Moses, with rejoicing and with singing, ac-

---

23:11. And gave him the testimony: An ingenius emendation (עדות instead of צעדות, "and the bracelets") possibly restores the correct reading.

18. The priests the Levites: See also 30:27. That the Deuteronomic equation of priests with Levites in general has not everywhere in Chronicles been "corrected" to accord with the standpoint of the final Law ("the priests and the Levites") is most

19 And he set the porters at the gates of the house of the Lord, that none *which was* unclean in any thing should enter in.

20 And he took the captains of hundreds, and the nobles, and the governors of the people, and all the people of the land, and brought down the king from the house of the Lord: and they came through the high gate into the king's house, and set the king upon the throne of the kingdom.

21 And all the people of the land rejoiced: and the city was quiet, after that they had slain Athaliah with the sword.

24 Joash *was* seven years old when he began to reign, and he reigned forty years in Jerusalem. His mother's name also *was* Zibiah of Beer-sheba.

2 And Joash did *that which was* right in the sight of the Lord all the days of Jehoiada the priest.

3 And Jehoiada took for him two wives; and he begat sons and daughters.

4 ¶ And it came to pass after this, *that* Joash was minded to repair the house of the Lord.

5 And he gathered together the priests and the Levites, and said to them, Go out unto the cities of Judah, and gather of all Israel money to repair the house of your God from year to year, and see that ye hasten the matter. Howbeit the Levites hastened *it* not.

6 And the king called for Jehoiada the chief, and said unto him, Why hast thou not required of the Levites to bring in out of Judah and out of Jerusalem the collection, *according to the commandment* of Moses the servant of the Lord, and of the congre-

cording to the order of David. **19** He stationed the gatekeepers at the gates of the house of the Lord so that no one should enter who was in any way unclean. **20** And he took the captains, the nobles, the governors of the people, and all the people of the land; and they brought the king down from the house of the Lord, marching through the upper gate to the king's house. And they set the king upon the royal throne. **21** So all the people of the land rejoiced; and the city was quiet, after Athali'ah had been slain with the sword.

24 Jo'ash was seven years old when he began to reign, and he reigned forty years in Jerusalem; his mother's name was Zib'iah of Beer-sheba. **2** And Jo'ash did what was right in the eyes of the Lord all the days of Jehoi'ada the priest. **3** Jehoi'ada got for him two wives, and he had sons and daughters.

4 After this Jo'ash decided to restore the house of the Lord. **5** And he gathered the priests and the Levites, and said to them, "Go out to the cities of Judah, and gather from all Israel money to repair the house of your God from year to year; and see that you hasten the matter." But the Levites did not hasten it. **6** So the king summoned Jehoi'ada the chief, and said to him, "Why have you not required the Levites to bring in from Judah and Jerusalem the tax levied

---

important evidence that the Chronicler himself used the phrase since it was not unorthodox in his time (see Exeg. on I Chr. 6:1-81).

F. Reign of Joash (24:1-27)

Joash, seven years old, owed his accession to the priest Jehoiada, and his preservation in infancy to Jehoiada's sister (22:11). Joash came to a bad end, but the Chronicler could make the most of his youthful years during which the king was under the good influence of Jehoiada.

24:4-14. The Chronicler could rejoice to credit the young king with making arrangements for the repair and maintenance of the temple, which was in shocking condition

---

of such children! May your reward be great in heaven! In the Lady Chapel of twentieth-century Liverpool Cathedral there are, uniquely, twenty-one windows dedicated to women who were good and great in English history.

24:5. Mercenary Clerics.—Howbeit the Levites hastened it not. The clergy went on a "Go slow strike," dreading lest perhaps the king's collection might lessen their revenues. Shame on them! And there is no reason to suppose

gation of Israel, for the tabernacle of witness?

7 For the sons of Athaliah, that wicked woman, had broken up the house of God; and also all the dedicated things of the house of the LORD did they bestow upon Baalim.

8 And at the king's commandment they made a chest, and set it without at the gate of the house of the LORD.

9 And they made a proclamation through Judah and Jerusalem, to bring in to the LORD the collection *that* Moses the servant of God *laid* upon Israel in the wilderness.

10 And all the princes and all the people rejoiced, and brought in, and cast into the chest, until they had made an end.

11 Now it came to pass, that at what time the chest was brought unto the king's office by the hand of the Levites, and when they saw that *there was* much money, the king's scribe and the high priest's officer came and emptied the chest, and took it, and carried it to his place again. Thus they did day by day, and gathered money in abundance.

12 And the king and Jehoiada gave it to such as did the work of the service of the house of the LORD, and hired masons and carpenters to repair the house of the LORD, and also such as wrought iron and brass to mend the house of the LORD.

13 So the workmen wrought, and the work was perfected by them, and they set the house of God in his state, and strengthened it.

14 And when they had finished *it*, they brought the rest of the money before the king and Jehoiada, whereof were made vessels for the house of the LORD, *even* vessels to minister, and to offer *withal*, and spoons, and vessels of gold and silver. And they

by Moses, the servant of the LORD, on[m] the congregation of Israel for the tent of testimony?" **7** For the sons of Athali'ah, that wicked woman, had broken into the house of God; and had also used all the dedicated things of the house of the LORD for the Ba'als.

8 So the king commanded, and they made a chest, and set it outside the gate of the house of the LORD. **9** And proclamation was made throughout Judah and Jerusalem, to bring in for the LORD the tax that Moses the servant of God laid upon Israel in the wilderness. **10** And all the princes and all the people rejoiced and brought their tax and dropped it into the chest until they had finished. **11** And whenever the chest was brought to the king's officers by the Levites, when they saw that there was much money in it, the king's secretary and the officer of the chief priest would come and empty the chest and take it and return it to its place. Thus they did day after day, and collected money in abundance. **12** And the king and Jehoi'ada gave it to those who had charge of the work of the house of the LORD, and they hired masons and carpenters to restore the house of the LORD, and also workers in iron and bronze to repair the house of the LORD. **13** So those who were engaged in the work labored, and the repairing went forward in their hands, and they restored the house of God to its proper condition and strengthened it. **14** And when they had finished, they brought the rest of the money before the king and Jehoi'ada, and with it were made utensils for the house of the LORD, both for the service and for the burnt offerings, and dishes for incense, and vessels of gold and silver. And they offered burnt

[m] Compare Vg: Heb *and*

---

due to Athaliah and her partisans (sons). He could assign to the Levites charge of the generous contributions for the "fabric fund," which the laity placed in an offertory box. This account subtly differs from II Kings 12:5-16, where seemingly the first intention for effecting repairs was to use part of the clergy's revenues, and the offertory box was resorted to only when the proposal was stultified by clerical opposition. Revisers (in vss. 5, 6, 9, 14a) overlaid what the Chronicler wrote in order to align proceedings with the provisions concerning maintenance of the tabernacle in the desert (see Welch, *op. cit.*, pp. 78-80).

---

that in Solomon's temple the Levites were other than amply supported. Ugly instances of clerical avarice and obstruction of good causes can be gleaned from history. Today the broad fact is

that no learned profession is so cruelly underpaid as a whole. Often it is the minister's family handicapped by financial strain, and his dwelling with worn-out furnishings, which stand

offered burnt offerings in the house of the LORD continually all the days of Jehoiada.

15 ¶ But Jehoiada waxed old, and was full of days when he died; a hundred and thirty years old *was he* when he died.

16 And they buried him in the city of David among the kings, because he had done good in Israel, both toward God, and toward his house.

17 Now after the death of Jehoiada came the princes of Judah, and made obeisance to the king. Then the king hearkened unto them.

18 And they left the house of the LORD God of their fathers, and served groves and idols: and wrath came upon Judah and Jerusalem for this their trespass.

19 Yet he sent prophets to them, to bring them again unto the LORD; and they testified against them: but they would not give ear.

20 And the Spirit of God came upon Zechariah the son of Jehoiada the priest, which stood above the people, and said unto them, Thus saith God, Why transgress ye the commandments of the LORD, that ye cannot prosper? because ye have forsaken the LORD, he hath also forsaken you.

21 And they conspired against him, and stoned him with stones at the commandment of the king in the court of the house of the LORD.

22 Thus Joash the king remembered not the kindness which Jehoiada his father had done to him, but slew his son. And when he died, he said, The LORD look upon *it,* and require *it.*

23 ¶ And it came to pass at the end of the year, *that* the host of Syria came up against him: and they came to Judah and Jerusalem, and destroyed all the princes of the people from among the people, and sent all the spoil of them unto the king of Damascus.

offerings in the house of the LORD continually all the days of Jehoi'ada.

15 But Jehoi'ada grew old and full of days, and died; he was a hundred and thirty years old at his death. 16 And they buried him in the city of David among the kings, because he had done good in Israel, and toward God and his house.

17 Now after the death of Jehoi'ada the princes of Judah came and did obeisance to the king; then the king hearkened to them. 18 And they forsook the house of the LORD, the God of their fathers, and served the Ashe'rim and the idols. And wrath came upon Judah and Jerusalem for this their guilt. 19 Yet he sent prophets among them to bring them back to the LORD; these testified against them, but they would not give heed.

20 Then the Spirit of God took possession of[n] Zechari'ah the son of Jehoi'ada the priest; and he stood above the people, and said to them, "Thus says God, 'Why do you transgress the commandments of the LORD, so that you cannot prosper? Because you have forsaken the LORD, he has forsaken you.' " 21 But they conspired against him, and by command of the king they stoned him with stones in the court of the house of the LORD. 22 Thus Jo'ash the king did not remember the kindness which Jehoi'ada, Zechari'ah's father, had shown him, but killed his son. And when he was dying, he said, "May the LORD see and avenge!"

23 At the end of the year the army of the Syrians came up against Jo'ash. They came to Judah and Jerusalem, and destroyed all the princes of the people from among people, and sent all their spoil to the king

[n] Heb *clothed itself with*

15-26. On the death of Jehoiada a faction which favored Athaliah's unregenerate regime gained the good will of Joash. That may well be true. This development leads up to the dark end of Joash's reign. Threatened by victories of Hazael, the powerful

---

in much more need of repairs than the church; and it is the laity who do not hasten to observe the needs and remedy them.

22. *Black Ingratitude.*—Joash owed the preservation of his life in infancy to the boldness of Jehoiada's wife (22:10-12); owed his succession

to the throne to Jehoiada's courage against Athaliah, and owed how much more in the ensuing years to his support and good counsel. But as soon as his benefactor was dead, he and his nobles undid the reforms that had been made (vss. 17-18), and in the end he slew his

24 For the army of the Syrians came with a small company of men, and the LORD delivered a very great host into their hand, because they had forsaken the LORD God of their fathers. So they executed judgment against Joash.

25 And when they were departed from him, (for they left him in great diseases,) his own servants conspired against him for the blood of the sons of Jehoiada the priest, and slew him on his bed, and he died: and they buried him in the city of David, but they buried him not in the sepulchres of the kings.

26 And these are they that conspired against him; Zabad the son of Shimeath an Ammonitess, and Jehozabad the son of Shimrith a Moabitess.

27 ¶ Now *concerning* his sons, and the greatness of the burdens *laid* upon him, and the repairing of the house of God, behold, they *are* written in the story of the book of the kings. And Amaziah his son reigned in his stead.

25 Amaziah *was* twenty and five years old *when* he began to reign, and he reigned twenty and nine years in Jerusalem. And his mother's name *was* Jehoaddan of Jerusalem.

2 And he did *that which was* right in the sight of the LORD, but not with a perfect heart.

3 ¶ Now it came to pass, when the kingdom was established to him, that he slew his servants that had killed the king his father.

of Damascus. 24 Though the army of the Syrians had come with few men, the LORD delivered into their hand a very great army, because they had forsaken the LORD, the God of their fathers. Thus they executed judgment on Jo'ash.

25 When they had departed from him, leaving him severely wounded, his servants conspired against him because of the blood of the son[o] of Jehoi'ada the priest, and slew him on his bed. So he died; and they buried him in the city of David, but they did not bury him in the tombs of the kings. 26 Those who conspired against him were Zabad the son of Shim'e-ath the Ammonitess, and Jeho'zabad the son of Shimrith the Moabitess. 27 Accounts of his sons, and of the many oracles against him, and of the rebuilding[p] of the house of God are written in the Commentary on the Book of the Kings. And Amazi'ah his son reigned in his stead.

25 Amazi'ah was twenty-five years old when he began to reign, and he reigned twenty-nine years in Jerusalem. His mother's name was Jeho-ad'dan of Jerusalem. 2 And he did what was right in the eyes of the LORD, yet not with a blameless heart. 3 And as soon as the royal power was firmly in his hand he killed his servants

[o] Gk Vg: Heb *sons*
[p] Heb *founding*

---

king of Syria, Joash is said to have purchased immunity by use of temple treasure, and thereafter to have been assassinated by his servants. An old tradition may provide the vivid tale of the murder of the prophet Zechariah (see Luke 11:51).

G. REIGN OF AMAZIAH (25:1-28)

Kings relates that Amaziah, puffed up by a victory over Edom, rashly challenged the king of Israel and was utterly defeated; Jerusalem was taken and part of its wall

---

benefactor's son, Zechariah, who as a prophet denounced his wickedness to his royal face. Now the persons of the prophets were regarded as sacrosanct, since they claimed to be speaking under divine constraint. Angry, defiant kings might go so far as to maltreat them, but when Joash had Zechariah stoned to death, that was appalling sacrilege. The populace must have been horrified; and some even in the palace circles also, for when the opportunity came they

slew Joash in his bed (vs. 25). It is perhaps to the martyrdom of this Zechariah that Christ referred (Matt. 23:35). Ingratitude, we may think to ourselves, so black does not closely concern our character. Are there, however, deeds or frames of mind that might be styled dark, gray, or even white ingratitude?

25:1-28. *Unstable in All His Ways.*—Read through this chapter and it will be apparent that instability (cf. Jas. 4:8) suitably describes

4 But he slew not their children, but *did* as *it is* written in the law in the book of Moses, where the Lord commanded, saying, The fathers shall not die for the children, neither shall the children die for the fathers, but every man shall die for his own sin.

5 ¶ Moreover Amaziah gathered Judah together, and made them captains over thousands, and captains over hundreds, according to the houses of *their* fathers, throughout all Judah and Benjamin: and he numbered them from twenty years old and above, and found them three hundred thousand choice *men, able* to go forth to war, that could handle spear and shield.

6 He hired also a hundred thousand mighty men of valor out of Israel for a hundred talents of silver.

7 But there came a man of God to him, saying, O king, let not the army of Israel go with thee; for the Lord *is* not with Israel, *to wit, with* all the children of Ephraim.

8 But if thou wilt go, do *it,* be strong for the battle: God shall make thee fall before the enemy: for God hath power to help, and to cast down.

9 And Amaziah said to the man of God, But what shall we do for the hundred talents which I have given to the army of Israel? And the man of God answered, The Lord is able to give thee much more than this.

10 Then Amaziah separated them, *to wit,* the army that was come to him out of Ephraim, to go home again: wherefore their anger was greatly kindled against Judah, and they returned home in great anger.

11 ¶ And Amaziah strengthened himself, and led forth his people, and went to the valley of salt, and smote of the children of Seir ten thousand.

who had slain the king his father. 4 But he did not put their children to death, according to what is written in the law, in the book of Moses, where the Lord commanded, "The fathers shall not be put to death for the children, or the children be put to death for the fathers; but every man shall die for his own sin."

5 Then Amazi'ah assembled the men of Judah, and set them by fathers' houses under commanders of thousands and of hundreds for all Judah and Benjamin. He mustered those twenty years old and upward, and found that they were three hundred thousand picked men, fit for war, able to handle spear and shield. 6 He hired also a hundred thousand mighty men of valor from Israel for a hundred talents of silver. 7 But a man of God came to him and said, "O king, do not let the army of Israel go with you, for the Lord is not with Israel, with all these E'phraimites. 8 But if you suppose that in this way you will be strong for war,*q* God will cast you down before the enemy; for God has power to help or to cast down." 9 And Amazi'ah said to the man of God, "But what shall we do about the hundred talents which I have given to the army of Israel?" The man of God answered, "The Lord is able to give you much more than this." 10 Then Amazi'ah discharged the army that had come to him from E'phraim, to go home again. And they became very angry with Judah, and returned home in fierce anger. 11 But Amazi'ah took courage, and led out his people, and went to the Valley of Salt and smote ten thou-

q Gk: Heb *But if you go, act, be strong for the battle*

---

destroyed. Amaziah fled to Lachish, was extradited, and was put to death by his subjects. The Chronicler has woven into that account allusions to two unnamed prophets (vss. 5-10, 14-16). The interesting new material is typical of his method, but may be based on a lost source.

11-12. One hopes that the savage treatment of the **men of Seir,** i.e., the Edomites, is due to some old tradition, not to the Chronicler's own invention.

King Amaziah, at least as Chronicles, amplifying II Kings 14:1-20, portrays his conduct. There is a comical touch in the story. Wanting to attack the Edomites, he hired soldiers from the king of Israel at great expense; warned by a prophet in the usual way that this is sinful, he asked pathetically, How about the money he had spent? Then he deferred to the prophet's injunction and, before setting out on his campaign against Edom, dismissed the Israelite mercenaries—without, however, any payment for their coming, with the not unnatural result

12 And *other* ten thousand *left* alive did the children of Judah carry away captive, and brought them unto the top of the rock, and cast them down from the top of the rock, that they all were broken in pieces.

13 ¶ But the soldiers of the army which Amaziah sent back, that they should not go with him to battle, fell upon the cities of Judah, from Samaria even unto Beth-horon, and smote three thousand of them, and took much spoil.

14 ¶ Now it came to pass, after that Amaziah was come from the slaughter of the Edomites, that he brought the gods of the children of Seir, and set them up *to be* his gods, and bowed down himself before them, and burned incense unto them.

15 Wherefore the anger of the LORD was kindled against Amaziah, and he sent unto him a prophet, which said unto him, Why hast thou sought after the gods of the people, which could not deliver their own people out of thine hand?

16 And it came to pass, as he talked with him, that *the king* said unto him, Art thou made of the king's counsel? forbear; why shouldest thou be smitten? Then the prophet forbare, and said, I know that God hath determined to destroy thee, because thou hast done this, and hast not hearkened unto my counsel.

17 ¶ Then Amaziah king of Judah took advice, and sent to Joash, the son of Jehoahaz, the son of Jehu, king of Israel, saying, Come, let us see one another in the face.

18 And Joash king of Israel sent to Amaziah king of Judah, saying, The thistle that *was* in Lebanon sent to the cedar that *was* in Lebanon, saying, Give thy daughter to my son to wife: and there passed by a wild beast that *was* in Lebanon, and trode down the thistle.

19 Thou sayest, Lo, thou hast smitten the Edomites; and thine heart lifteth thee up to boast: abide now at home; why shouldest thou meddle to *thine* hurt, that thou shouldest fall, *even* thou, and Judah with thee?

sand men of Se'ir. 12 The men of Judah captured another ten thousand alive, and took them to the top of a rock and threw them down from the top of the rock; and they were all dashed to pieces. 13 But the men of the army whom Amazi'ah sent back, without letting go with him to battle, fell upon the cities of Judah, from Samar'ia to Beth-hor'on, and killed three thousand people in them, and took much spoil.

14 After Amazi'ah came from the slaughter of the E'domites, he brought the gods of the men of Se'ir, and set them up as his gods, and worshiped them, making offerings to them. 15 Therefore the LORD was angry with Amazi'ah and sent to him a prophet, who said to him, "Why have you resorted to the gods of a people, which did not deliver their own people from your hand?" 16 But as he was speaking the king said to him, "Have we made you a royal counselor? Stop! Why should you be put to death?" So the prophet stopped, but said, "I know that God has determined to destroy you, because you have done this and have not listened to my counsel."

17 Then Amazi'ah king of Judah took counsel and sent to Jo'ash the son of Jeho'ahaz, son of Jehu, king of Israel, saying, "Come, let us look one another in the face." 18 And Jo'ash the king of Israel sent word to Amazi'ah king of Judah, "A thistle on Lebanon sent to a cedar on Lebanon, saying, 'Give your daughter to my son for a wife'; and a wild beast of Lebanon passed by and trampled down the thistle. 19 You say, 'See, I have smitten Edom,' and your heart has lifted you up in boastfulness. But now stay at home; why should you provoke trouble so that you fall, you and Judah with you?"

---

that they plundered Judean territory on their homeward march. Vss. 14-16 relate another typical instability of purpose; and vss. 17-24 tell that on his return after a victory in Edom the king, angered by the deeds of the unpaid mercenaries, was such an utter fool as to challenge the powerful king of Israel, who promptly defeated and captured him, entered Jerusalem, and broke down part of its northern wall. In the end his subjects rose against Amaziah; he fled to Lachish, was extradited and slain (vs. 27). Altogether this king provides an object lesson

20 But Amaziah would not hear; for it *came* of God, that he might deliver them into the hand *of their enemies,* because they sought after the gods of Edom.

21 So Joash the king of Israel went up; and they saw one another in the face, *both* he and Amaziah king of Judah, at Beth-she-mesh, which *belongeth* to Judah.

22 And Judah was put to the worse before Israel, and they fled every man to his tent.

23 And Joash the king of Israel took Amaziah king of Judah, the son of Joash, the son of Jehoahaz, at Beth-shemesh, and brought him to Jerusalem, and brake down the wall of Jerusalem from the gate of Ephraim to the corner gate, four hundred cubits.

24 And *he took* all the gold and the silver, and all the vessels that were found in the house of God with Obed-edom, and the treasures of the king's house, the hostages also, and returned to Samaria.

25 ¶ And Amaziah the son of Joash king of Judah lived after the death of Joash son of Jehoahaz king of Israel fifteen years.

26 Now the rest of the acts of Amaziah, first and last, behold, *are* they not written in the book of the kings of Judah and Israel?

27 ¶ Now after the time that Amaziah did turn away from following the LORD they made a conspiracy against him in Jerusalem; and he fled to Lachish: but they sent to Lachish after him, and slew him there.

28 And they brought him upon horses, and buried him with his fathers in the city of Judah.

26 Then all the people of Judah took Uzziah, who *was* sixteen years old, and made him king in the room of his father Amaziah.

2 He built Eloth, and restored it to Judah, after that the king slept with his fathers.

3 Sixteen years old *was* Uzziah when he began to reign, and he reigned fifty and two years in Jerusalem. His mother's name also *was* Jecoliah of Jerusalem.

20 But Amazi'ah would not listen; for it was of God, in order that he might give them into the hand of their enemies, because they had sought the gods of Edom. **21** So Jo'ash king of Israel went up; and he and Amazi'ah king of Judah faced one another in battle at Beth-shemesh, which belongs to Judah. **22** And Judah was defeated by Israel, and every man fled to his home. **23** And Jo'ash king of Israel captured Amazi'ah king of Judah, the son of Jo'ash, son of Ahazi'ah, at Beth-she'mesh, and brought him to Jerusalem, and broke down the wall of Jerusalem for four hundred cubits, from the E'phraim Gate to the Corner Gate. **24** And he seized all the gold and silver, and all the vessels that were found in the house of God, and O'bed-e'dom with them; he seized also the treasuries of the king's house, and hostages, and he returned to Samar'ia.

25 Amazi'ah the son of Jo'ash king of Judah lived fifteen years after the death of Jo'ash the son of Jeho'ahaz, king of Israel. **26** Now the rest of the deeds of Amazi'ah, from first to last, are they not written in the Book of the Kings of Judah and Israel? **27** From the time when he turned away from the LORD they made a conspiracy against him in Jerusalem, and he fled to Lachish. But they sent after him to Lachish, and slew him there. **28** And they brought him upon horses; and he was buried with his fathers in the city of David.

26 And all the people of Judah took Uzzi'ah, who was sixteen years old, and made him king instead of his father Amazi'ah. **2** He built Eloth and restored it to Judah, after the king slept with his fathers. **3** Uzzi'ah was sixteen years old when he began to reign, and he reigned fifty-two years in Jerusalem. His mother's

in vacillation. It is always a fault which may lead from small mistakes to ruin.

26:3. *King for Fifty-Two Years.*—Uzziah's prosperous reign ran parallel with the equally long and prosperous rule of Jeroboam II over

Israel. But from the books of Amos, Hosea, and Isaiah vividly we learn that under those monarchs the prosperity of the few was coincident with the miseries of the many and the growth of monstrous social corruption.

4 And he did *that which was* right in the sight of the LORD, according to all that his father Amaziah did.

5 And he sought God in the days of Zechariah, who had understanding in the visions of God: and as long as he sought the LORD, God made him to prosper.

6 And he went forth and warred against the Philistines, and brake down the wall of Gath, and the wall of Jabneh, and the wall of Ashdod, and built cities about Ashdod, and among the Philistines.

7 And God helped him against the Philistines, and against the Arabians that dwelt in Gur-baal, and the Mehunim.

8 And the Ammonites gave gifts to Uzziah: and his name spread abroad *even* to the entering in of Egypt; for he strengthened *himself* exceedingly.

9 Moreover Uzziah built towers in Jerusalem at the corner gate, and at the valley gate, and at the turning *of the wall,* and fortified them.

10 Also he built towers in the desert, and digged many wells: for he had much cattle, both in the low country, and in the plains; husbandmen *also,* and vinedressers in the mountains, and in Carmel: for he loved husbandry.

11 Moreover Uzziah had a host of fighting men, that went out to war by bands, according to the number of their account by the hand of Jeiel the scribe and Maaseiah the ruler, under the hand of Hananiah, *one* of the king's captains.

12 The whole number of the chief of the fathers of the mighty men of valor *were* two thousand and six hundred.

13 And under their hand *was* an army, three hundred thousand and seven thousand and five hundred, that made war with mighty power, to help the king against the enemy.

14 And Uzziah prepared for them throughout all the host shields, and spears, and helmets, and habergeons, and bows, and slings *to cast* stones.

15 And he made in Jerusalem engines, invented by cunning men, to be on the

name was Jecoli'ah of Jerusalem. 4 And he did what was right in the eyes of the LORD, according to all that his father Amazi'ah had done. 5 He set himself to seek God in the days of Zechari'ah, who instructed him in the fear of God; and as long as he sought the LORD, God made him prosper.

6 He went out and made war against the Philistines, and broke down the wall of Gath and the wall of Jabneh and the wall of Ashdod; and he built cities in the territory of Ashdod and elsewhere among the Philistines. 7 God helped him against the Philistines, and against the Arabs that dwelt in Gurba'al, and against the Me-u'nites. 8 The Ammonites paid tribute to Uzzi'ah, and his fame spread even to the border of Egypt, for he became very strong. 9 Moreover Uzzi'ah built towers in Jerusalem at the Corner Gate and at the Valley Gate and at the Angle, and fortified them. 10 And he built towers in the wilderness, and hewed out many cisterns, for he had large herds, both in the Shephe'lah and in the plain, and he had farmers and vinedressers in the hills and in the fertile lands, for he loved the soil. 11 Moreover Uzzi'ah had an army of soldiers, fit for war, in divisions according to the numbers in the muster made by Je-i'el the secretary and Ma-asei'ah the officer, under the direction of Hanani'ah, one of the king's commanders. 12 The whole number of the heads of fathers' houses of mighty men of valor was two thousand six hundred. 13 Under their command was an army of three hundred and seven thousand five hundred, who could make war with mighty power, to help the king against the enemy. 14 And Uzzi'ah prepared for all the army shields, spears, helmets, coats of mail, bows, and stones for slinging. 15 In Jerusalem he made engines, invented by skilful men, to

---

H. REIGNS OF UZZIAH, JOTHAM, AND AHAZ (26:1–28:27)

26:5-15. A turn in the wheel of international circumstance brought forty years of prosperity to Israel under Jeroboam II, and to Judah under Uzziah. The detail in these remarkable verses (no basis in Kings) seems clearly to imply the use of an old document.

towers and upon the bulwarks, to shoot arrows and great stones withal. And his name spread far abroad; for he was marvelously helped, till he was strong.

16 ¶ But when he was strong, his heart was lifted up to *his* destruction: for he transgressed against the Lord his God, and went into the temple of the Lord to burn incense upon the altar of incense.

17 And Azariah the priest went in after him, and with him fourscore priests of the Lord, *that were* valiant men:

18 And they withstood Uzziah the king, and said unto him, *It appertaineth* not unto thee, Uzziah, to burn incense unto the Lord, but to the priests the sons of Aaron, that are consecrated to burn incense: go out of the sanctuary; for thou hast trespassed; neither *shall it be* for thine honor from the Lord God.

19 Then Uzziah was wroth, and *had* a censer in his hand to burn incense: and while he was wroth with the priests, the leprosy even rose up in his forehead before the priests in the house of the Lord, from beside the incense altar.

20 And Azariah the chief priest, and all the priests, looked upon him, and, behold, he *was* leprous in his forehead, and they thrust him out from thence; yea, himself hasted also to go out, because the Lord had smitten him.

21 And Uzziah the king was a leper unto the day of his death, and dwelt in a several house, *being* a leper; for he was cut off from the house of the Lord: and Jotham his son *was* over the king's house, judging the people of the land.

22 ¶ Now the rest of the acts of Uzziah, first and last, did Isaiah the prophet, the son of Amoz, write.

23 So Uzziah slept with his fathers, and they buried him with his fathers in the field of the burial which *belonged* to the kings;

be on the towers and the corners, to shoot arrows and great stones. And his fame spread far, for he was marvelously helped, till he was strong.

16 But when he was strong he grew proud, to his destruction. For he was false to the Lord his God, and entered the temple of the Lord to burn incense on the altar of incense. 17 But Azari'ah the priest went in after him, with eighty priests of the Lord who were men of valor; 18 and they withstood King Uzzi'ah, and said to him, "It is not for you, Uzzi'ah, to burn incense to the Lord, but for the priests the sons of Aaron, who are consecrated to burn incense. Go out of the sanctuary; for you have done wrong, and it will bring you no honor from the Lord God." 19 Then Uzzi'ah was angry. Now he had a censer in his hand to burn incense, and when he became angry with the priests leprosy broke out on his forehead, in the presence of the priests in the house of the Lord, by the altar of incense. 20 And Azari'ah the chief priest, and all the priests, looked at him, and behold, he was leprous in his forehead! And they thrust him out quickly, and he himself hastened to go out, because the Lord had smitten him. 21 And King Uzzi'ah was a leper to the day of his death, and being a leper dwelt in a separate house, for he was excluded from the house of the Lord. And Jotham his son was over the king's household, governing the people of the land.

22 Now the rest of the acts of Uzzi'ah, from first to last, Isaiah the prophet the son of Amoz wrote. 23 And Uzzi'ah slept with his fathers, and they buried him with his fathers in the burial field which belonged

---

16-23. Uzziah died a **leper** (cf. II Kings 15:5). The Chronicler assigned general reason for the king's affliction in vs. 16a. It is probable that the interesting story in vss. 16b-20 is a very late addition; for although the use of **incense**—perhaps not employed until nearly the end of the monarchy—became increasingly prominent in the postexilic period,

---

16. When He Was Strong.—King Uzziah was neither the first nor the last to be spoiled by success. Often the talented man thinks and behaves as if he could ascribe solely to himself all the credit, not only for his native ability but

for the use he has made of his talents. Everyone needs to be on guard against the temptation to ignore the extent to which his prosperity and his virtues may be due not to achievements but to endowment. Self-esteem is always a deadly

for they said, He *is* a leper: and Jotham his son reigned in his stead.

27 Jotham *was* twenty and five years old when he began to reign; and he reigned sixteen years in Jerusalem. His mother's name also *was* Jerushah, the daughter of Zadok.

2 And he did *that which was* right in the sight of the LORD, according to all that his father Uzziah did: howbeit he entered not into the temple of the LORD. And the people did yet corruptly.

3 He built the high gate of the house of the LORD, and on the wall of Ophel he built much.

4 Moreover he built cities in the mountains of Judah, and in the forests he built castles and towers.

5 ¶ He fought also with the king of the Ammonites, and prevailed against them. And the children of Ammon gave him the same year a hundred talents of silver, and ten thousand measures of wheat, and ten thousand of barley. So much did the children of Ammon pay unto him, both the second year, and the third.

6 So Jotham became mighty, because he prepared his ways before the LORD his God.

7 ¶ Now the rest of the acts of Jotham, and all his wars, and his ways, lo, they *are* written in the book of the kings of Israel and Judah.

8 He was five and twenty years old when he began to reign, and reigned sixteen years in Jerusalem.

9 ¶ And Jotham slept with his fathers, and they buried him in the city of David: and Ahaz his son reigned in his stead.

28 Ahaz *was* twenty years old when he began to reign, and he reigned sixteen years in Jerusalem: but he did not *that*

to the kings, for they said, "He is a leper." And Jotham his son reigned in his stead.

27 Jotham was twenty-five years old when he began to reign, and he reigned sixteen years in Jerusalem. His mother's name was Jeru'shah the daughter of Zadok. 2 And he did what was right in the eyes of the LORD according to all that his father Uzzi'ah had done — only he did not invade the temple of the LORD. But the people still followed corrupt practices. 3 He built the upper gate of the house of the LORD, and did much building on the wall of Ophel. 4 Moreover he built cities in the hill country of Judah, and forts and towers on the wooded hills. 5 He fought with the king of the Ammonites and prevailed against them. And the Ammonites gave him that year a hundred talents of silver, and ten thousand cors of wheat and ten thousand of barley. The Ammonites paid him the same amount in the second and the third years. 6 So Jotham became mighty, because he ordered his ways before the LORD his God. 7 Now the rest of the acts of Jotham, and all his wars, and his ways, behold, they are written in the Book of the Kings of Israel and Judah. 8 He was twenty-five years old when he began to reign, and he reigned sixteen years in Jerusalem. 9 And Jotham slept with his fathers, and they buried him in the city of David; and Ahaz his son reigned in his stead.

28 Ahaz was twenty years old when he began to reign, and he reigned six-

---

mention of an **altar** for the purpose (vs. 16) seems to belong only to the latest stage of the P legislation.

27:1-9. Cf. II Kings 15:32-38. Jotham's building operations and the tribute from the Ammonites may have had a basis in an old source. Vs. 2b—**howbeit . . . the LORD**—presumably is from the author of the verses concerning Uzziah's trespass (26:16b-20).

---

menace to character. The fault takes many shapes; e.g., the capable official becomes first efficient, then dictatorial, unable to envisage that even in his case "second thoughts" may be best. Too readily we forget how Paul said that all our gifts are worthless if we lack love—the greatest gift of all (I Cor. 13) ; and, said Paul,

"Let him that thinketh he standeth take heed lest he fall" (I Cor. 10:12) .

27:1. *The Reign of Jotham.*—There is only one good reason why Jotham should be remembered, and that is not due to anything he did himself: during his years on the throne of David, Isaiah was a prophet in Jerusalem.

which was right in the sight of the LORD, like David his father:

2 For he walked in the ways of the kings of Israel, and made also molten images for Baalim.

3 Moreover he burnt incense in the valley of the son of Hinnom, and burnt his children in the fire, after the abominations of the heathen whom the LORD had cast out before the children of Israel.

4 He sacrificed also and burnt incense in the high places, and on the hills, and under every green tree.

5 Wherefore the LORD his God delivered him into the hand of the king of Syria; and they smote him, and carried away a great multitude of them captives, and brought *them* to Damascus. And he was also delivered into the hand of the king of Israel, who smote him with a great slaughter.

6 ¶ For Pekah the son of Remaliah slew in Judah a hundred and twenty thousand in one day, *which were* all valiant men; because they had forsaken the LORD God of their fathers.

7 And Zichri, a mighty man of Ephraim, slew Maaseiah the king's son, and Azrikam the governor of the house, and Elkanah *that was* next to the king.

8 And the children of Israel carried away captive of their brethren two hundred thousand, women, sons, and daughters, and took also away much spoil from them, and brought the spoil to Samaria.

9 But a prophet of the LORD was there, whose name *was* Oded: and he went out before the host that came to Samaria, and said unto them, Behold, because the LORD God of your fathers was wroth with Judah, he hath delivered them into your hand, and ye have slain them in a rage *that* reacheth up unto heaven.

teen years in Jerusalem. And he did not do what was right in the eyes of the LORD, like his father David, 2 but walked in the ways of the kings of Israel. He even made molten images for the Ba'als; 3 and he burned incense in the valley of the son of Hinnom, and burned his sons as an offering, according to the abominable practices of the nations whom the LORD drove out before the people of Israel. 4 And he sacrificed and burned incense on the high places, and on the hills, and under every green tree.

5 Therefore the LORD his God gave him into the hand of the king of Syria, who defeated him and took captive a great number of his people and brought them to Damascus. He was also given into the hand of the king of Israel, who defeated him with great slaughter. 6 For Pekah the son of Remali'ah slew a hundred and twenty thousand in Judah in one day, all of them men of valor, because they had forsaken the LORD, the God of their fathers. 7 And Zichri, a mighty man of E'phraim, slew Ma-asei'ah the king's son and Azri'kam the commander of the palace and Elka'nah the next in authority to the king.

8 The men of Israel took captive two hundred thousand of their kinsfolk, women, sons, and daughters; they also took much spoil from them and brought the spoil to Samar'ia. 9 But a prophet of the LORD was there, whose name was Oded; and he went out to meet the army that came to Samar'ia, and said to them, "Behold, because the LORD, the God of your fathers, was angry with Judah, he gave them into your hand, but you have slain them in a rage which has

---

28:6-15. A comparison between this passage and II Kings 16 illustrates the Chronicler's method. II Kings 16:1-4 gave him warrant for treating Ahaz as a monster of iniquity; but he also read in Kings the story—so vividly recorded in Isa. 7—that Ahaz, when menaced by the kings of Syria and Israel, sought support from the Assyrians, and that the threatened danger from the two kings came to nought. It was contrary to the Chronicler's view of the fitness of things that Ahaz did not suffer as a result of

---

28:8-15. *An Act of Magnanimity.*—Well done, Oded, prophet of the Lord in Samaria! He urged the victorious soldiers of Israel to be magnanimous toward the captive Judeans and let them return to their homes. So finely did he

voice his appeal that it more than succeeded. For his words, we are told, so completely touched the hearts of the captors that instead of a horde of miserable refugees trailing back to Judah, ragged and hungry, there returned a

10 And now ye purpose to keep under the children of Judah and Jerusalem for bondmen and bondwomen unto you: *but are there* not with you, even with you, sins against the LORD your God?

11 Now hear me therefore, and deliver the captives again, which ye have taken captive of your brethren: for the fierce wrath of the LORD *is* upon you.

12 Then certain of the heads of the children of Ephraim, Azariah the son of Johanan, Berechiah the son of Meshillemoth, and Jehizkiah the son of Shallum, and Amasa the son of Hadlai, stood up against them that came from the war,

13 And said unto them, Ye shall not bring in the captives hither: for whereas we have offended against the LORD *already,* ye intend to add *more* to our sins and to our trespass: for our trespass is great, and *there is* fierce wrath against Israel.

14 So the armed men left the captives and the spoil before the princes and all the congregation.

15 And the men which were expressed by name rose up, and took the captives, and with the spoil clothed all that were naked among them, and arrayed them, and shod them, and gave them to eat and to drink, and anointed them, and carried all the feeble of them upon asses, and brought them to Jericho, the city of palm trees, to their brethren: then they returned to Samaria.

16 ¶ At that time did king Ahaz send unto the kings of Assyria to help him.

17 For again the Edomites had come and smitten Judah, and carried away captives.

18 The Philistines also had invaded the cities of the low country, and of the south of Judah, and had taken Beth-shemesh, and

reached up to heaven. 10 And now you intend to subjugate the people of Judah and Jerusalem, male and female, as your slaves. Have you not sins of your own against the LORD your God? 11 Now hear me, and send back the captives from your kinsfolk whom you have taken, for the fierce wrath of the LORD is upon you." 12 Certain chiefs also of the men of E'phraim, Azari'ah the son of Joha'nan, Berechi'ah the son of Meshil'lemoth, Jehizki'ah the son of Shallum, and Ama'sa the son of Hadlai, stood up against those who were coming from the war, 13 and said to them, "You shall not bring the captives in here, for you propose to bring upon us guilt against the LORD in addition to our present sins and guilt. For our guilt is already great, and there is fierce wrath against Israel." 14 So the armed men left the captives and the spoil before the princes and all the assembly. 15 And the men who have been mentioned by name rose and took the captives, and with the spoil they clothed all that were naked among them; they clothed them, gave them sandals, provided them with food and drink, and anointed them; and carrying all the feeble among them on asses, they brought them to their kinsfolk at Jericho, the city of palm trees. Then they returned to Samar'ia.

16 At that time King Ahaz sent to the king[r] of Assyria for help. 17 For the E'domites had again invaded and defeated Judah, and carried away captives. And the Philistines had made raids on the cities in the

[r] Gk Syr Vg Compare 2 Kings 16. 7: Heb *kings*

mistrusting Yahweh and seeking aid from Assyria. Wherefore he ignored the statement in Kings, and instead declared that Ahaz met with double defeat; first at the hands of the Syrians, and second of the Israelites, losing to the latter alone 120,000 killed and 200,000 men, women, and children captured! The second catastrophe, however, had a charming outcome.

16. Having turned the Syrian-Israelite menace upside down, the Chronicler stood in need of further foes to chastise Ahaz for asking aid from Assyria: Philistines and Edomites (see Exeg. on 21:10) duly oblige.

---

multitude of men and women and children who had been fed and cared for, as well as released, and who now could not think of Israelites as pitiless foes but as men who had

shown them kindness (vs. 15). Oded deserved to succeed, for he had said to the victors that they ought to forgive because they themselves needed to be forgiven (vs. 10), and had told

Ajalon, and Gederoth, and Shocho with the villages thereof, and Timnah with the villages thereof, Gimzo also and the villages thereof: and they dwelt there.

19 For the Lord brought Judah low because of Ahaz king of Israel; for he made Judah naked, and transgressed sore against the Lord.

20 And Tilgath-pilneser king of Assyria came unto him, and distressed him, but strengthened him not.

21 For Ahaz took away a portion *out* of the house of the Lord, and *out* of the house of the king, and of the princes, and gave *it* unto the king of Assyria: but he helped him not.

22 ¶ And in the time of his distress did he trespass yet more against the Lord: this *is that* king Ahaz.

23 For he sacrificed unto the gods of Damascus, which smote him: and he said, Because the gods of the kings of Syria help them, *therefore* will I sacrifice to them, that they may help me. But they were the ruin of him, and of all Israel.

24 And Ahaz gathered together the vessels of the house of God, and cut in pieces the vessels of the house of God, and shut up the doors of the house of the Lord, and he made him altars in every corner of Jerusalem.

25 And in every several city of Judah he made high places to burn incense unto other gods, and provoked to anger the Lord God of his fathers.

Shephe'lah and the Negeb of Judah, and had taken Beth-she'mesh, Ai'jalon, Gede'roth, Soco with its villages, Timnah with its villages, and Gimzo with its villages; and they settled there. 19 For the Lord brought Judah low because of Ahaz king of Israel, for he had dealt wantonly in Judah and had been faithless to the Lord. 20 So Til'gath-pilne'ser king of Assyria came against him, and afflicted him instead of strengthening him. 21 For Ahaz took from the house of the Lord and the house of the king and of the princes, and gave tribute to the king of Assyria; but it did not help him.

22 In the time of his distress he became yet more faithless to the Lord — this same King Ahaz. 23 For he sacrificed to the gods of Damascus which had defeated him, and said, "Because the gods of the kings of Syria helped them, I will sacrifice to them that they may help me." But they were the ruin of him, and of all Israel. 24 And Ahaz gathered together the vessels of the house of God and cut in pieces the vessels of the house of God, and he shut up the doors of the house of the Lord; and he made himself altars in every corner of Jerusalem. 25 In every city of Judah he made high places to burn incense to other gods, provoking to anger the Lord, the God of his fathers.

---

24. Shut up the doors of the house of the Lord: As part of the price for Assyrian support Ahaz no doubt had to honor in the temple the great gods of Assyria, but he did not close its doors. It was, however, appropriate for the Chronicler's idealized history to vilify Ahaz thoroughly. Moreover, he thus adroitly prepared for an inspiring sequel in Hezekiah's reign.

---

them that the captives were their brethren (vs. 11). This narrative is not in Kings. The Chronicler devised it. Well done, the Chronicler!

23. *They Were the Ruin of Him.*—The Chronicler was confused (see Exeg.) about the real historical situation, which is clear from II Kings 16:1-20, combined with Isa. 7:1-17. The kings of Syria and Israel were determined to have the Judean army with them in a coalition for defense against the might of the Assyrians which loomed over them. Ahaz refused, sought Assyrian support by paying tribute, later paid honor to their gods in Jerusalem, and **they were the ruin of him.** It was enough for the Chron-

icler to reiterate his standing accusation: failure to rely on God alone. The general application is that when men in difficulties have recourse to what they know to be evil, "the latter end is worse with them than the beginning" (II Pet. 2:20).

24. *Acts of Desperation.*—It is entirely credible that Ahaz was in straits to find treasure enough to provide his bribe to the Assyrians, but from II Kings 16:14-18 the inference to be drawn is not that Ahaz closed the temple area, but that he instituted an altar for sacrifice to Assyria's gods (see Exeg.). That was too outrageous a sacrilege for the Chronicler to believe,

26 ¶ Now the rest of his acts and of all his ways, first and last, behold, they *are* written in the book of the kings of Judah and Israel.

27 And Ahaz slept with his fathers, and they buried him in the city, *even* in Jerusalem: but they brought him not into the sepulchres of the kings of Israel: and Hezekiah his son reigned in his stead.

29 Hezekiah began to reign *when he was* five and twenty years old, and he reigned nine and twenty years in Jerusalem. And his mother's name *was* Abijah, the daughter of Zechariah.

2 And he did *that which was* right in the sight of the LORD, according to all that David his father had done.

---

26 Now the rest of his acts and all his ways, from first to last, behold, they are written in the Book of the Kings of Judah and Israel. 27 And Ahaz slept with his fathers, and they buried him in the city, in Jerusalem, for they did not bring him into the tombs of the kings of Israel. And Hezeki'ah his son reigned in his stead.

29 Hezeki'ah began to reign when he was twenty-five years old, and he reigned twenty-nine years in Jerusalem. His mother's name was Abi'jah the daughter of Zechari'ah. 2 And he did what was right in the eyes of the LORD, according to all that David his father had done.

J. REIGN OF HEZEKIAH (29:1–32:33)

Beyond doubt Hezekiah was a good and enlightened ruler. II Kings 18:3-6 pays unqualified tribute to his virtue: "There was none like him among all the kings of Judah after him, nor among those who were before him." That superlative eulogy seems to leave out of thought David, and the coming Josiah with his decisive reform. It provided full reason for the Chronicler to expatiate in praise of Hezekiah, to depict him indeed as a second "Saint David." It is no surprise to find that in the long section he devoted to Hezekiah more than three chapters (chs. 29–31 and part of ch. 32) present new material. The Chronicler might well ask himself, "What would such a good king, following such a bad king, do in Jerusalem?" It seems that he had an inspiration and he gave a vivid reply. Obviously Hezekiah would rectify the religious abuses of Ahaz's reign. Further, the Chronicler had represented that Ahaz had closed the doors of the

---

and he states that the plundered temple was closed. Churches have been closed for diverse reasons—in periods of persecution, when believers have nobly shown that faith can dispense with buildings; or because the population has departed from a district, as in Central London, with its numerous, ancient parish churches. (Practical sense feels that they should be pulled down, their very valuable sites sold and the proceeds used elsewhere; but sentiment rebels.) When the former members have moved to a distance from a church building, why is it so often that the remaining inhabitants in the district have no use for organized Christianity and that church stands desolate? Where should blame be placed? Does the tragedy arise from too conventional modes of presenting the faith? Or is the fault in the people? The common people heard Jesus gladly (Mark 12:37; cf. Acts 2:41).

29:1–32:33. *Hezekiah's Reign*.—Ahaz died, the ruler who had uncomprehendingly rejected the word of the Lord spoken to him by Isaiah (Isa. 7:3-17) when Jerusalem was menaced by the kings of Syria and Israel, the man whose

"theology" in that crisis impelled him to seek the favor of Yahweh by sacrificing his son as a burnt offering (II Kings 16:3). He was succeeded by Hezekiah, who shares with Josiah (cf. chs. 34–35) chief honors as being the best of the Judean monarchs. During his reign Isaiah was at the height of his prophetic powers. There are satisfying reasons to believe that Hezekiah was zealous for religious reforms, and it is likely that very discreetly he made overtures to loyalist Hebrews in the former kingdom of Israel (from 721 B.C. an Assyrian province) that they should see in Jerusalem a remaining citadel for their trust in Yahweh. Optimists could hope that the house of David might yet again rule over a reunited people of God (see Exeg. on 29:1–32:33).

Ample material was available concerning Hezekiah in II Kings 18–20. It is very interesting to compare the account in Kings with that in Chronicles, and to note how dexterously the Chronicler adapted it to his cardinal purpose, quoting and omitting, abridging and expanding.

29:1-35. *The Purification of the Temple*.—The Chronicler disregarded the dull order of

3 ¶ He in the first year of his reign, in the first month, opened the doors of the house of the LORD, and repaired them.

4 And he brought in the priests and the Levites, and gathered them together into the east street,

5 And said unto them, Hear me, ye Levites; sanctify now yourselves, and sanctify the house of the LORD God of your fathers, and carry forth the filthiness out of the holy *place*.

6 For our fathers have trespassed, and done *that which was* evil in the eyes of the LORD our God, and have forsaken him, and have turned away their faces from the habitation of the LORD, and turned *their* backs.

7 Also they have shut up the doors of the porch, and put out the lamps, and have not burned incense nor offered burnt offerings in the holy *place* unto the God of Israel.

8 Wherefore the wrath of the LORD was upon Judah and Jerusalem, and he hath delivered them to trouble, to astonishment, and to hissing, as ye see with your eyes.

9 For, lo, our fathers have fallen by the sword, and our sons and our daughters and our wives *are* in captivity for this.

3 In the first year of his reign, in the first month, he opened the doors of the house of the LORD, and repaired them. 4 He brought in the priests and the Levites, and assembled them in the square on the east, 5 and said to them, "Hear me, Levites! Now sanctify yourselves, and sanctify the house of the Lord, the God of your fathers, and carry out the filth from the holy place. 6 For our fathers have been unfaithful and have done what was evil in the sight of the LORD our God; they have forsaken him, and have turned away their faces from the habitation of the LORD, and turned their backs. 7 They also shut the doors of the vestibule and put out the lamps, and have not burned incense or offered burnt offerings in the holy place to the God of Israel. 8 Therefore the wrath of the LORD came on Judah and Jerusalem, and he has made them an object of horror, of astonishment, and of hissing, as you see with your own eyes. 9 For lo, our fathers have fallen by the sword and our sons and our daughters and our wives are in captivity

temple (28:24): he could now picture the closed doors being reopened, the temple thoroughly cleansed from its pollution, and thereafter a glorious day of rededication and thanksgiving. Hezekiah's accession is to be dated in 725 or 720—either just before or just after the terrible siege and capture of Samaria which put an end to the kingdom of Israel (see W. O. E. Oesterley and T. H. Robinson, *A History of Israel* [Oxford: Clarendon Press, 1932], I, 460; also John Skinner, *Kings* [Edinburgh: T. C. & E. C. Jack, 1904; "The New-Century Bible"], p. 44).

1. CLEANSING OF THE TEMPLE (29:1-36)

29:3. In the first year of his reign, in the first month: It was logical to infer that the good king would lose not a moment in ordering the good work to begin. How vivid the impression of Hezekiah thus given in comparison with the nebulous account of II Kings 18:1-12 which, after praising him and in a single verse recording that he fought the Philistines, mentions the Assyrian attack on Samaria as happening in his fourth year, and immediately thereafter relates how in his fourteenth year the terrible Assyrian assault on Judah ended in miraculous deliverance. Actually that crisis took place in 701 B.C. toward the very end of Hezekiah's reign.

4-5. The priests and the Levites: In vs. 5 only the Levites are addressed, and the charge laid on them involved their entering the temple sanctuary, a privilege which

events stated in II Kings. He assumed that the good king would put first things first. Ahaz, he had just affirmed, had plundered and closed the temple. Therefore he devised a glowing and elaborate description of its reopening, cleansing, and consecration.

Hezekiah **in the first year of his reign, in the first month, opened the doors of the house of the LORD.** But the reopened temple was in a filthy condition, and its sanctity had been polluted. Next, then, a good king would summon the proper men, **Levites,** to undertake its cleans-

10 Now *it is* in mine heart to make a covenant with the LORD God of Israel, that his fierce wrath may turn away from us.

11 My sons, be not now negligent: for the LORD hath chosen you to stand before him, to serve him, and that ye should minister unto him, and burn incense.

12 ¶ Then the Levites arose, Mahath the son of Amasai, and Joel the son of Azariah, of the sons of the Kohathites: and of the sons of Merari; Kish the son of Abdi, and Azariah the son of Jehalelel: and of the Gershonites; Joah the son of Zimmah, and Eden the son of Joah:

13 And of the sons of Elizaphan; Shimri, and Jeiel: and of the sons of Asaph; Zechariah, and Mattaniah:

14 And of the sons of Heman; Jehiel, and Shimei: and of the sons of Jeduthun; Shemaiah, and Uzziel.

15 And they gathered their brethren, and sanctified themselves, and came, according to the commandment of the king, by the words of the LORD, to cleanse the house of the LORD.

16 And the priests went into the inner part of the house of the LORD, to cleanse *it,* and brought out all the uncleanness that they found in the temple of the LORD into the court of the house of the LORD. And the Levites took *it,* to carry *it* out abroad into the brook Kidron.

17 Now they began on the first *day* of the first month to sanctify, and on the eighth day of the month came they to the porch of the LORD: so they sanctified the house of the LORD in eight days; and in the sixteenth day of the first month they made an end.

18 Then they went in to Hezekiah the king, and said, We have cleansed all the

for this. **10** Now it is in my heart to make a covenant with the LORD, the God of Israel, that his fierce anger may turn away from us. **11** My sons, do not now be negligent, for the LORD has chosen you to stand in his presence, to minister to him, and to be his ministers and burn incense to him."

12 Then the Levites arose, Mahath the son of Ama'sai, and Jo'el the son of Azari'ah, of the sons of the Ko'hathites; and of the sons of Merar'i, Kish the son of Abdi, and Azari'ah the son of Jehal'lelel; and of the Gershonites, Jo'ah the son of Zimmah, and Eden the son of Jo'ah; **13** and of the sons of Eliza'phan, Shimri and Jeu'el; and of the sons of Asaph, Zechari'ah and Mattani'ah; **14** and of the sons of Heman, Jehu'el and Shim'e-i; and of the sons of Jedu'thun, Shemai'ah and Uz'ziel. **15** They gathered their brethren, and sanctified themselves, and went in as the king had commanded, by the words of the LORD, to cleanse the house of the LORD. **16** The priests went into the inner part of the house of the LORD to cleanse it, and they brought out all the uncleanness that they found in the temple of the LORD into the court of the house of the LORD; and the Levites took it and carried it out to the brook Kidron. **17** They began to sanctify on the first day of the first month, and on the eighth day of the month they came to the vestibule of the LORD; then for eight days they sanctified the house of the LORD, and on the sixteenth day of the first month they finished. **18** Then they went in to Hezeki'ah the king and said,

---

the final Law reserved to the Zadokite priests. The conjunction **and** represents a reviser's neat emendation to rule out such a sacrifice.

11. Note the Levites' high standing: they it is who minister to the Lord, not merely to Zadokite priests, and Hezekiah calls them **my sons.**

16. The priests went into: Added by revisers to correct the implication in vs. 15 that Levites other than priests entered the sacred building. Perhaps the phrase **by the words of the LORD** (vs. 15*b*) is also revisional, to avert the idea that the king's order was given solely on his royal authority.

---

ing (vs. 4). And they must be one with him in understanding the sacred nature of their task, conscious of how evil the past had been, how merited the calamity which had befallen the land and its homes (vss. 5-10). Young in years

but old in wisdom, Hezekiah terms the Levites **My sons,** speaking not as a master giving orders (vs. 11). So at last the moment came (vs. 30), when from a temple purified by men of right spirit the sound of instruments and psalms,

house of the LORD, and the altar of burnt offering, with all the vessels thereof, and the showbread table, with all the vessels thereof.

19 Moreover all the vessels, which king Ahaz in his reign did cast away in his transgression, have we prepared and sanctified, and, behold, they *are* before the altar of the LORD.

20 ¶ Then Hezekiah the king rose early, and gathered the rulers of the city, and went up to the house of the LORD.

21 And they brought seven bullocks, and seven rams, and seven lambs, and seven he goats, for a sin offering for the kingdom, and for the sanctuary, and for Judah. And he commanded the priests the sons of Aaron to offer *them* on the altar of the LORD.

22 So they killed the bullocks, and the priests received the blood, and sprinkled *it* on the altar: likewise, when they had killed the rams, they sprinkled the blood upon the altar: they killed also the lambs, and they sprinkled the blood upon the altar.

23 And they brought forth the he goats *for* the sin offering before the king and the congregation; and they laid their hands upon them:

24 And the priests killed them, and they made reconciliation with their blood upon the altar, to make an atonement for all Israel: for the king commanded *that* the burnt offering and the sin offering *should be made* for all Israel.

25 And he set the Levites in the house of the LORD with cymbals, with psalteries, and with harps, according to the commandment of David, and of Gad the king's seer, and Nathan the prophet: for *so was* the commandment of the LORD by his prophets.

26 And the Levites stood with the instruments of David, and the priests with the trumpets.

27 And Hezekiah commanded to offer the burnt offering upon the altar. And when the burnt offering began, the song of

"We have cleansed all the house of the LORD, the altar of burnt offering and all its utensils, and the table for the showbread and all its utensils. 19 All the utensils which King Ahaz discarded in his reign when he was faithless, we have made ready and sanctified; and behold, they are before the altar of the LORD.

20 Then Hezeki'ah the king rose early and gathered the officials of the city, and went up to the house of the LORD. 21 And they brought seven bulls, seven rams, seven lambs, and seven he-goats for a sin offering for the kingdom and for the sanctuary and for Judah. And he commanded the priests the sons of Aaron to offer them on the altar of the LORD. 22 So they killed the bulls, and the priests received the blood and threw it against the altar; and they killed the rams and their blood was thrown against the altar; and they killed the lambs and their blood was thrown against the altar. 23 Then the he-goats for the sin offering were brought to the king and the assembly, and they laid their hands upon them, 24 and the priests killed them and made a sin offering with their blood on the altar, to make atonement for all Israel. For the king commanded that the burnt offering and the sin offering should be made for all Israel.

25 And he stationed the Levites in the house of the LORD with cymbals, harps, and lyres, according to the commandment of David and of Gad the king's seer and of Nathan the prophet; for the commandment was from the LORD through his prophets. 26 The Levites stood with the instruments of David, and the priests with the trumpets. 27 Then Hezeki'ah commanded that the burnt offering be offered on the altar. And

---

21-30. The dedicatory sacrifices are said to have been duplicated. The explanation may be that vss. 25-27 are the Chronicler's statement, to which revisers prefixed vss. 21-24 in order to make the procedure fully consonant with the final Law.

---

the words of David and of Asaph the seer, could rise acceptably to God. We are told that the feelings of the people were roused to enthusiasm, and that they then brought multitudes of sacrifices (vss. 31-33, 35). That is ever

the way: men with souls to conceive better things must toil patiently in hope that general response will in the end be evoked. If they prepare with all diligence, response may be forthcoming, and the rejoicings be really great.

the Lord began *also* with the trumpets, and with the instruments *ordained* by David king of Israel.

28 And all the congregation worshipped, and the singers sang, and the trumpeters sounded: *and* all *this continued* until the burnt offering was finished.

29 And when they had made an end of offering, the king and all that were present with him bowed themselves, and worshipped.

30 Moreover Hezekiah the king and the princes commanded the Levites to sing praise unto the Lord with the words of David, and of Asaph the seer. And they sang praises with gladness, and they bowed their heads and worshipped.

31 Then Hezekiah answered and said, Now ye have consecrated yourselves unto the Lord, come near and bring sacrifices and thank offerings into the house of the Lord. And the congregation brought in sacrifices and thank offerings; and as many as were of a free heart, burnt offerings.

32 And the number of the burnt offerings, which the congregation brought, was threescore and ten bullocks, a hundred rams, *and* two hundred lambs: all these *were* for a burnt offering to the Lord.

33 And the consecrated things *were* six hundred oxen and three thousand sheep.

34 But the priests were too few, so that they could not flay all the burnt offerings: wherefore their brethren the Levites did help them, till the work was ended, and until the *other* priests had sanctified themselves: for the Levites *were* more upright in heart to sanctify themselves than the priests.

35 And also the burnt offerings *were* in abundance, with the fat of the peace offerings, and the drink offerings for *every* burnt offering. So the service of the house of the Lord was set in order.

36 And Hezekiah rejoiced, and all the people, that God had prepared the people: for the thing was *done* suddenly.

when the burnt offering began, the song to the Lord began also, and the trumpets, accompanied by the instruments of David king of Israel. **28** The whole assembly worshiped, and the singers sang, and the trumpeters sounded; all this continued until the burnt offering was finished. **29** When the offering was finished, the king and all who were present with him bowed themselves and worshiped. **30** And Hezeki'ah the king and the princes commanded the Levites to sing praises to the Lord with the words of David and of Asaph the seer. And they sang praises with gladness, and they bowed down and worshiped.

31 Then Hezeki'ah said, "You have now consecrated yourselves to the Lord; come near, bring sacrifices and thank offerings to the house of the Lord." And the assembly brought sacrifices and thank offerings; and all who were of a willing heart brought burnt offerings. **32** The number of the burnt offerings which the assembly brought was seventy bulls, a hundred rams, and two hundred lambs; all these were for a burnt offering to the Lord. **33** And the consecrated offerings were six hundred bulls and three thousand sheep. **34** But the priests were too few and could not flay all the burnt offerings, so until other priests had sanctified themselves their brethren the Levites helped them, until the work was finished — for the Levites were more upright in heart than the priests in sanctifying themselves. **35** Besides the great number of burnt offerings there was the fat of the peace offerings, and there were the libations for the burnt offerings. Thus the service of the house of the Lord was restored. **36** And Hezeki'ah and all the people rejoiced because of what God had done for the people; for the thing came about suddenly.

---

34. A perplexing verse, because normally the lay offerers flayed the carcasses. Also, what lies behind the admission that the priests were slack, whereas the other ministrants

---

Day to day progress often is invisible; when attainment comes, we are startled by its suddenness (vs. 36).

34. *Embarrassing Generosity.*—This verse may be a reviser's addition (see Exeg.). So

abundant were the offerings of the laity that the normal ministrants could not cope with the task. "Generosity may sometimes confuse officialism. If this spirit were to seize the Church, the only man that would feel incommoded by it

30 And Hezekiah sent to all Israel and Judah, and wrote letters also to Ephraim and Manasseh, that they should come to the house of the LORD at Jerusalem, to keep the passover unto the LORD God of Israel.

30 Hezeki'ah sent to all Israel and Judah, and wrote letters also to E'phraim and Manas'seh, that they should come to the house of the LORD at Jerusalem, to keep the passover to the LORD the God of

---

were eager? Perhaps not a few of the leading clergy had been content with the state of affairs in Ahaz's reign, and looked askance on Hezekiah's zeal.

2. The Unprecedented Passover (30:1–31:21)

The Chronicler now credits Hezekiah with a master stroke of human sympathy, which at the same time was astute statesmanship. He relates that Hezekiah sent couriers into the territory of the fallen kingdom of Israel, bearing a letter which invited the subjugated Hebrews to come to Jerusalem and there to keep the Passover and the feast of Unleavened Bread. Presumably his action was taken in the years following soon after the conquest of Samaria in 721, during the period when the Assyrians prohibited the conquered people from worshiping Yahweh, but preceding the date when they allowed the cult of Yahweh to be resumed at Bethel. The Judean king's gesture would be timely and, though risky, adroit. For Assyrian troops could not be everywhere, and Hezekiah's couriers would move circumspectly. In any case the Assyrians, vigilant against signs of revolt, might see no danger if some Hebrews resorted to a religious rite in Jerusalem. Little did they guess how stimulating to nationalist feeling was Passover— the celebration of the deliverance of Hebrews long ago from the tyranny of an Egyptian king. Vss. 10-11 state that many of the Israelites scoffed at the invitation, or—it may be inferred—feared to run the risk, but that many responded and came to Jerusalem. Granting that the Chronicler exaggerates numbers, is this alleged event fiction or fact? The question, as will appear in connection with Josiah's reign, has no small importance concerning the development of Hebrew literature and religious practice. A further matter requires comment. It seems certain that originally the night ritual of Passover was observed by the Hebrews in their homes, after which they resorted to the sanctuaries to keep Mazzoth. But Deuteronomy—a formulation of the Israelites' customs—enjoins that Passover be kept at a sanctuary. It may be therefore that by his time the northern Hebrews had departed from the ancient home method of celebration. If so, for them the unprecedented feature in regard to Hezekiah's proposal would be solely that they should go not to one of their own sanctuaries, but to Jerusalem. Rankling under the Assyrian prohibition to worship Yahweh, not a few may have resolved to hazard the journey. What was unprecedented for the Judeans was that for the first time—or for this once— they were summoned to keep Passover not at home, but at their capital. It is likely enough that, constrained by the king's urgency, they did so. It is true that the Chronicler, following his logic that good Israelites would respond to a good Judean king, was capable of inventing the episode. His logic may chance to have led him to infer an actual event. However, he may have followed a popular tradition or even some written source not utilized in Kings. The historical situation would seem to have afforded Hezekiah an excellent opportunity.

---

would be the treasurer. He would want an increase of assistance." [6]

30:1. A House of Prayer for All People.— Hezekiah could not foresee the universal hope depicted in Isa. 56:7. But he did not confine the rejoicings to the men of Jerusalem, or even to his immediate subjects the Judeans. He wanted

[6] Joseph Parker, *The People's Bible* (New York: Funk & Wagnalls, 1881), X, 72.

all who possibly could to share therein; so he sent an invitation to Israel, as well as to Judah —to the northern Hebrews who were under the heel of the Assyrian conquerors. He took thought to devise means of reaching them (vss. 6-10). Consider the occasion to which he invited them, **to keep the passover.** This was the Hebrews' "Independence Day," release of their forefathers from bondage in Egypt. No other

2 For the king had taken counsel, and his princes, and all the congregation in Jerusalem, to keep the passover in the second month.

3 For they could not keep it at that time, because the priests had not sanctified themselves sufficiently, neither had the people gathered themselves together to Jerusalem.

4 And the thing pleased the king and all the congregation.

5 So they established a decree to make proclamation throughout all Israel, from Beer-sheba even to Dan, that they should come to keep the passover unto the LORD God of Israel at Jerusalem: for they had not done *it* of a long *time in such sort* as it was written.

6 So the posts went with the letters from the king and his princes throughout all Israel and Judah, and according to the commandment of the king, saying, Ye children of Israel, turn again unto the LORD God of Abraham, Isaac, and Israel, and he will return to the remnant of you, that are escaped out of the hand of the kings of Assyria.

7 And be not ye like your fathers, and like your brethren, which trespassed against the LORD God of their fathers, *who* therefore gave them up to desolation, as ye see.

8 Now be ye not stiffnecked, as your fathers *were, but* yield yourselves unto the LORD, and enter into his sanctuary, which he hath sanctified for ever: and serve the LORD your God, that the fierceness of his wrath may turn away from you.

9 For if ye turn again unto the LORD, your brethren and your children *shall find* compassion before them that lead them captive, so that they shall come again into this land: for the LORD your God *is* gracious and merciful, and will not turn away *his* face from you, if ye return unto him.

10 So the posts passed from city to city, through the country of Ephraim and Manasseh, even unto Zebulun: but they laughed them to scorn, and mocked them.

11 Nevertheless, divers of Asher and Manasseh and of Zebulun humbled themselves, and came to Jerusalem.

Israel. 2 For the king and his princes and all the assembly in Jerusalem had taken counsel to keep the passover in the second month — 3 for they could not keep it in its time because the priests had not sanctified themselves in sufficient number, nor had the people assembled in Jerusalem — 4 and the plan seemed right to the king and all the assembly. 5 So they decreed to make a proclamation throughout all Israel, from Beer-sheba to Dan, that the people should come and keep the passover to the LORD the God of Israel, at Jerusalem; for they had not kept it in great numbers as prescribed. 6 So couriers went throughout all Israel and Judah with letters from the king and his princes, as the king had commanded, saying, "O people of Israel, return to the LORD, the God of Abraham, Isaac, and Israel, that he may turn again to the remnant of you who have escaped from the hand of the kings of Assyria. 7 Do not be like your fathers and your brethren, who were faithless to the LORD God of their fathers, so that he made them a desolation, as you see. 8 Do not now be stiff-necked as your fathers were, but yield yourselves to the LORD, and come to his sanctuary, which he has sanctified for ever, and serve the LORD your God, that his fierce anger may turn away from you. 9 For if you return to the LORD, your brethren and your children will find compassion with their captors, and return to this land. For the LORD your God is gracious and merciful, and will not turn away his face from you, if you return to him."

10 So the couriers went from city to city through the country of E'phraim and Manas'seh, and as far as Zeb'ulun; but they laughed them to scorn, and mocked them. 11 Only a few men of Asher, of Manas'seh, and of Zeb'ulun humbled themselves and

---

30:2. **In the second month:** Difficulties in organizing the arrival of the willing Israelites—not the reason adduced (by revisers?) in vs. 3—probably accounted for the postponement from the statutory first month.

12 Also in Judah the hand of God was to give them one heart to do the commandment of the king and of the princes, by the word of the LORD.

13 ¶ And there assembled at Jerusalem much people to keep the feast of unleavened bread in the second month, a very great congregation.

14 And they arose and took away the altars that *were* in Jerusalem, and all the altars for incense took they away, and cast *them* into the brook Kidron.

15 Then they killed the passover on the fourteenth *day* of the second month: and the priests and the Levites were ashamed, and sanctified themselves, and brought in the burnt offerings into the house of the LORD.

16 And they stood in their place after their manner, according to the law of Moses the man of God: the priests sprinkled the blood, *which they received* of the hand of the Levites.

17 For *there were* many in the congregation that were not sanctified: therefore the Levites had the charge of the killing of the passovers for every one *that was* not clean, to sanctify *them* unto the LORD.

18 For a multitude of the people, *even* many of Ephraim and Manasseh, Issachar and Zebulun, had not cleansed themselves, yet did they eat the passover otherwise than it was written. But Hezekiah prayed for them, saying, The good LORD pardon every one

19 *That* prepareth his heart to seek God, the LORD God of his fathers, though *he be* not *cleansed* according to the purification of the sanctuary.

20 And the LORD hearkened to Hezekiah, and healed the people.

21 And the children of Israel that were present at Jerusalem kept the feast of unleavened bread seven days with great glad-

came to Jerusalem. 12 The hand of God was also upon Judah to give them one heart to do what the king and the princes commanded by the word of the LORD.

13 And many people came together in Jerusalem to keep the feast of unleavened bread in the second month, a very great assembly. 14 They set to work and removed the altars that were in Jerusalem, and all the altars for burning incense they took away and threw into the Kidron valley. 15 And they killed the passover lamb on the fourteenth day of the second month. And the priests and the Levites were put to shame, so that they sanctified themselves, and brought burnt offerings into the house of the LORD. 16 They took their accustomed posts according to the law of Moses the man of God; the priests threw the blood which they received from the hand of the Levites. 17 For there were many in the assembly who had not sanctified themselves; therefore the Levites had to kill the passover lamb for every one who was not clean, to make it holy to the LORD. 18 For a multitude of the people, many of them from E'phraim, Manas'seh, Is'sachar, and Zeb'ulun, had not cleansed themselves, yet they ate the passover otherwise than as prescribed. For Hezeki'ah had prayed for them, saying, "The good LORD pardon every one 19 who sets his heart to seek God, the LORD the God of his fathers, even though not according to the sanctuary's rules of cleanness." 20 And the LORD heard Hezeki'ah, and healed the people. 21 And the people of Israel that were present at Jerusalem kept the feast of un-

---

12-27. The text shows confusion: Vss. 12, 15*a*, 17-20 concern Passover; vss. 13-14, 15*b*, 21-27 concern Mazzoth.

---

day of commemoration, save Christmas and Easter, has exercised so mighty and so noble an influence on human hearts. Why? Because the Hebrews ascribed the precious gift of freedom not to their own prowess, but to the high purpose of God in order that they should learn to worship him whose mercy is unfailing.

17-20. Not According to the Rules.—This is a fascinating passage, and it is due to the Chronicler himself. He realized that great numbers who had come from the north could not have complied with the complicated regulations about ceremonial **cleanness**. The fact made strict observance of the ritual rules impossible

ness: and the Levites and the priests praised the Lord day by day, *singing* with loud instruments unto the Lord.

22 And Hezekiah spake comfortably unto all the Levites that taught the good knowledge of the Lord: and they did eat throughout the feast seven days, offering peace offerings, and making confession to the Lord God of their fathers.

23 And the whole assembly took counsel to keep other seven days: and they kept *other* seven days with gladness.

24 For Hezekiah king of Judah did give to the congregation a thousand bullocks and seven thousand sheep; and the princes gave to the congregation a thousand bullocks and ten thousand sheep: and a great number of priests sanctified themselves.

25 And all the congregation of Judah, with the priests and the Levites, and all the congregation that came out of Israel, and the strangers that came out of the land of Israel, and that dwelt in Judah, rejoiced.

26 So there was great joy in Jerusalem: for since the time of Solomon the son of David king of Israel *there was* not the like in Jerusalem.

27 ¶ Then the priests the Levites arose and blessed the people: and their voice was heard, and their prayer came *up* to his holy dwelling place, *even* unto heaven.

31 Now when all this was finished, all Israel that were present went out to the cities of Judah, and brake the images in pieces, and cut down the groves, and threw down the high places and the altars out of all Judah and Benjamin, in Ephraim also and Manasseh, until they had utterly destroyed them all. Then all the children of Israel returned, every man to his possession, into their own cities.

2 ¶ And Hezekiah appointed the courses of the priests and the Levites after their courses, every man according to his service, the priests and Levites for burnt offerings

leavened bread seven days with great gladness; and the Levites and the priests praised the Lord day by day, singing with all their might[s] to the Lord. **22** And Hezeki'ah spoke encouragingly to all the Levites who showed good skill in the service of the Lord. So the people ate the food of the festival for seven days, sacrificing peace offerings and giving thanks to the Lord the God of their fathers.

23 Then the whole assembly agreed together to keep the feast for another seven days; so they kept it for another seven days with gladness. **24** For Hezeki'ah king of Judah gave the assembly a thousand bulls and seven thousand sheep for offerings, and the princes gave the assembly a thousand bulls and ten thousand sheep. And the priests sanctified themselves in great numbers. **25** The whole assembly of Judah, and the priests and the Levites, and the whole assembly that came out of Israel, and the sojourners who came out of the land of Israel, and the sojourners who dwelt in Judah, rejoiced. **26** So there was great joy in Jerusalem, for since the time of Solomon the son of David king of Israel there had been nothing like this in Jerusalem. **27** Then the priests and the Levites arose and blessed the people, and their voice was heard, and their prayer came to his holy habitation in heaven.

31 Now when all this was finished, all Israel who were present went out to the cities of Judah and broke in pieces the pillars and hewed down the Ashe'rim and broke down the high places and the altars throughout all Judah and Benjamin, and in E'phraim and Manas'seh, until they had destroyed them all. Then all the people of Israel returned to their cities, every man to his possession.

2 And Hezeki'ah appointed the divisions of the priests and of the Levites, division by division, each according to his service, the

[s] Compare 1 Chron 13. 8: Heb *with instruments of might*

---

27. The priests the Levites: See 23:18 and Exeg. on I Chr. 6:1-81.

31:1-21. The subject is how to secure adequate maintenance for the clergy—at all times a troublesome problem. The Chronicler here reflects back to Hezekiah's reign

---

on the occasion. He did not think the rules were wrong, but he felt certain that here was a circumstance in which they must be swept aside in order that "the weightier matters of the law" (cf. Matt. 23:23) might be vindicated and

glorified. This was a magnificent decision coming from a king who was a wholehearted ecclesiastic, according to the Chronicler. What a text it offers for today! Translate the matter into the discussions in divided Christendom. What

and for peace offerings, to minister, and to give thanks, and to praise in the gates of the tents of the Lord.

3 *He appointed* also the king's portion of his substance for the burnt offerings, *to wit,* for the morning and evening burnt offerings, and the burnt offerings for the sabbaths, and for the new moons, and for the set feasts, as *it is* written in the law of the Lord.

4 Moreover he commanded the people that dwelt in Jerusalem to give the portion of the priests and the Levites, that they might be encouraged in the law of the Lord.

5 ¶ And as soon as the commandment came abroad, the children of Israel brought in abundance the firstfruits of corn, wine, and oil, and honey, and of all the increase of the field; and the tithe of all *things* brought they in abundantly.

6 And *concerning* the children of Israel and Judah, that dwelt in the cities of Judah, they also brought in the tithe of oxen and sheep, and the tithe of holy things which were consecrated unto the Lord their God, and laid *them* by heaps.

7 In the third month they began to lay the foundation of the heaps, and finished *them* in the seventh month.

8 And when Hezekiah and the princes came and saw the heaps, they blessed the Lord, and his people Israel.

9 Then Hezekiah questioned with the priests and the Levites concerning the heaps.

10 And Azariah the chief priest of the house of Zadok answered him, and said, Since *the people* began to bring the offerings into the house of the Lord, we have had enough to eat, and have left plenty: for the Lord hath blessed his people; and that which is left *is* this great store.

11 ¶ Then Hezekiah commanded to prepare chambers in the house of the Lord; and they prepared *them,*

priests and the Levites, for burnt offerings and peace offerings, to minister in the gates of the camp of the Lord and to give thanks and praise. 3 The contribution of the king from his own possessions was for the burnt offerings: the burnt offerings of morning and evening, and the burnt offerings for the sabbaths, the new moons, and the appointed feasts, as it is written in the law of the Lord. 4 And he commanded the people who lived in Jerusalem to give the portion due to the priests and the Levites, that they might give themselves to the law of the Lord. 5 As soon as the command was spread abroad, the people of Israel gave in abundance the first fruits of grain, wine, oil, honey, and of all the produce of the field; and they brought in abundantly the tithe of everything. 6 And the people of Israel and Judah who lived in the cities of Judah also brought in the tithe of cattle and sheep, and the dedicated things[t] which had been consecrated to the Lord their God, and laid them in heaps. 7 In the third month they began to pile up the heaps, and finished them in the seventh month. 8 When Hezekiah and the princes came and saw the heaps, they blessed the Lord and his people Israel. 9 And Hezeki'ah questioned the priests and the Levites about the heaps. 10 Azari'ah the chief priest, who was of the house of Zadok, answered him, "Since they began to bring the contributions into the house of the Lord we have eaten and had enough and have plenty left; for the Lord has blessed his people, so that we have this great store left."

11 Then Hezeki'ah commanded them to prepare chambers in the house of the Lord;

[t] Heb *the tithe of the dedicated things*

---

what was being done in his own time, or what ought to be done, to obtain fair contributions alike from the Judeans and from the loyalists in the former Israelite localities. But the problem as known in the Chronicler's time had not reached final settlement;

---

a challenge it presents to modern representatives of theology and church order!

31:10. *Superabundance.*—Contributions surpassed even the utmost needed for the main-

tenance of the temple and its ministrants. If anything comparable were to happen today there would be no difficulty in finding how to use the surplus in the furtherance of good causes

12 And brought in the offerings and the tithes and the dedicated *things* faithfully: over which Cononiah the Levite *was* ruler, and Shimei his brother *was* the next.

13 And Jehiel, and Azaziah, and Nahath, and Asahel, and Jerimoth, and Jozabad, and Eliel, and Ismachiah, and Mahath, and Benaiah, *were* overseers under the hand of Cononiah and Shimei his brother, at the commandment of Hezekiah the king, and Azariah the ruler of the house of God.

14 And Kore the son of Imnah the Levite, the porter toward the east, *was* over the freewill offerings of God, to distribute the oblations of the LORD, and the most holy things.

15 And next him *were* Eden, and Miniamin, and Jeshua, and Shemaiah, Amariah, and Shecaniah, in the cities of the priests, in *their* set office, to give to their brethren by courses, as well to the great as to the small:

16 Besides their genealogy of males, from three years old and upward, *even* unto every one that entereth into the house of the LORD, his daily portion for their service in their charges according to their courses;

17 Both to the genealogy of the priests by the house of their fathers, and the Levites from twenty years old and upward, in their charges by their courses;

18 And to the genealogy of all their little ones, their wives, and their sons, and their daughters, through all the congregation: for in their set office they sanctified themselves in holiness:

19 Also of the sons of Aaron the priests, *which were* in the fields of the suburbs of their cities, in every several city, the men that were expressed by name, to give portions to all the males among the priests, and to all that were reckoned by genealogies among the Levites.

20 ¶ And thus did Hezekiah throughout all Judah, and wrought *that which was* good and right and truth before the LORD his God.

and they prepared them. 12 And they faithfully brought in the contributions, the tithes and the dedicated things. The chief officer in charge of them was Conani′ah the Levite, with Shim′e-i his brother as second; 13 while Jehi′el, Azazi′ah, Nahath, As′ahel, Jer′imoth, Jo′zabad, Eli′el, Ismachi′ah, Mahath, and Benai′ah were overseers assisting Conani′ah and Shim′e-i his brother, by the appointment of Hezeki′ah the king and Azari′ah the chief officer of the house of God. 14 And Ko′re the son of Imnah the Levite, keeper of the east gate, was over the freewill offerings to God, to apportion the contribution reserved for the LORD and the most holy offerings. 15 Eden, Mini′amin, Jeshua, Shemai′ah, Amari′ah, and Shecani′ah were faithfully assisting him in the cities of the priests, to distribute the portions to their brethren, old and young alike, by divisions, 16 except those enrolled by genealogy, males from three years old and upwards, all who entered the house of the LORD as the duty of each day required, for their service according to their offices, by their divisions. 17 The enrollment of the priests was according to their fathers' houses; that of the Levites from twenty years old and upwards was according to their offices, by their divisions. 18 The priests were enrolled with all their little children, their wives, their sons, and their daughters, the whole multitude; for they were faithful in keeping themselves holy. 19 And for the sons of Aaron, the priests, who were in the fields of common land belonging to their cities, there were men in the several cities who were designated by name to distribute portions to every male among the priests and to every one among the Levites who was enrolled.

20 Thus Hezeki′ah did throughout all Judah; and he did what was good and right and faithful before the LORD his God.

---

and in vs. 17—where Levites are said to function from the age of twenty (cf. I Chr. 23:24)—the hand of revisers may be recognized.

---

in Christ's name. As it is, churches are often in great straits. Why? Sometimes their members are ungenerous; more often they are generous and nevertheless are ungenerously reproached for not giving more. In Hezekiah's time his goodness and zeal so captivated the hearts of the people that they responded en masse to his appeal, and the treasury was filled.

21 And in every work that he began in
the service of the house of God, and in the
law, and in the commandments, to seek his
God, he did *it* with all his heart, and prospered.

32 After these things, and the establishment thereof, Sennacherib king of
Assyria came, and entered into Judah, and
encamped against the fenced cities, and
thought to win them for himself.

2 And when Hezekiah saw that Sennacherib was come, and that he was purposed to
fight against Jerusalem,

3 He took counsel with his princes and
his mighty men to stop the waters of the
fountains which *were* without the city: and
they did help him.

4 So there was gathered much people together, who stopped all the fountains, and
the brook that ran through the midst of the
land, saying, Why should the kings of Assyria come, and find much water?

5 Also he strengthened himself, and built
up all the wall that was broken, and raised
it up to the towers, and another wall without, and repaired Millo *in* the city of David,
and made darts and shields in abundance.

6 And he set captains of war over the people, and gathered them together to him in
the street of the gate of the city, and spake
comfortably to them, saying,

7 Be strong and courageous, be not afraid
nor dismayed for the king of Assyria, nor
for all the multitude that *is* with him: for
there be more with us than with him.

21 And every work that he undertook in the
service of the house of God and in accordance with the law and the commandments,
seeking his God, he did with all his heart,
and prospered.

32 After these things and these acts of
faithfulness Sennach'erib king of Assyria came and invaded Judah and encamped against the fortified cities, thinking
to win them for himself. 2 And when Hezeki'ah saw that Sennach'erib had come and
intended to fight against Jerusalem, 3 he
planned with his officers and his mighty
men to stop the water of the springs that
were outside the city; and they helped him.
4 A great many people were gathered, and
they stopped all the springs and the brook
that flowed through the land, saying, "Why
should the kings of Assyria come and find
much water?" 5 He set to work resolutely
and built up all the wall that was broken
down, and raised towers upon it,ᵘ and outside it he built another wall; and he
strengthened the Millo in the city of David.
He also made weapons and shields in
abundance. 6 And he set combat commanders over the people, and gathered them together to him in the square at the gate of
the city and spoke encouragingly to them,
saying, 7 "Be strong and of good courage.
Do not be afraid or dismayed before the
king of Assyria and all the horde that is
with him; for there is one greater with us

ᵘ Vg: Heb *and raised upon the towers*

3. The Assyrian Invasion and Hezekiah's Death (32:1-33)

32:1. Thought to win them: According to II Kings 18:13, the Assyrians did capture
the Judean towns; and further, Hezekiah paid tribute, only to find himself duped. The
Chronicler arbitrarily altered the tale because he felt that so good a king ought not to
have been so humiliated.

32:1-8. Piety Unrewarded.—After this manifestation of piety, so genuine and so thorough,
after these things and these acts of faithfulness,
up came the king of Assyria with his overwhelming army. Frequent and daunting are the comparable experiences in life. Heavy labor, we
feel, should be followed by a restful holiday.
After we have battled through a dozen difficulties, surely we should have relief from anxiety
and strain. Kindness should always have a response in gratitude. When we have beaten
down temptations, and have long loved to try
to do the will of God, ought there not to come

a time when we enter into peace on earth? Constantly it does not so happen, and bitter trials
may continue to be our lot. We should learn
that character never can rise above need for
the discipline which changing circumstance ever
presents, and that the true reward of piety is not
in cessation of trials but in increased strength
rightly to encounter them. Not outward but
inward peace is the possession, here and now,
of "the treasure laid up in heaven."

Pious Hezekiah suddenly was faced by deadly
peril: invasion by the merciless Assyrian army,
equipped with terrible siege engines. As for the

8 With him *is* an arm of flesh; but with us *is* the LORD our God to help us, and to fight our battles. And the people rested themselves upon the words of Hezekiah king of Judah.

9 ¶ After this did Sennacherib king of Assyria send his servants to Jerusalem, (but he *himself laid siege* against Lachish, and all his power with him,) unto Hezekiah king of Judah, and unto all Judah that *were* at Jerusalem, saying,

10 Thus saith Sennacherib king of Assyria, Whereon do ye trust, that ye abide in the siege in Jerusalem?

11 Doth not Hezekiah persuade you to give over yourselves to die by famine and by thirst, saying, The LORD our God shall deliver us out of the hand of the king of Assyria?

12 Hath not the same Hezekiah taken away his high places and his altars, and commanded Judah and Jerusalem, saying, Ye shall worship before one altar, and burn incense upon it?

13 Know ye not what I and my fathers have done unto all the people of *other* lands? were the gods of the nations of those lands any ways able to deliver their lands out of mine hand?

14 Who *was there* among all the gods of those nations that my fathers utterly destroyed, that could deliver his people out of mine hand, that your God should be able to deliver you out of mine hand?

15 Now therefore let not Hezekiah deceive you, nor persuade you on this manner, neither yet believe him: for no god of any nation or kingdom was able to deliver his

than with him. 8 With him is an arm of flesh; but with us is the LORD our God, to help us and to fight our battles." And the people took confidence from the words of Hezeki′ah king of Judah.

9 After this Sennach′erib king of Assyria, who was besieging Lachish with all his forces, sent his servants to Jerusalem to Hezeki′ah king of Judah and to all the people of Judah that were in Jerusalem, saying, 10 "Thus says Sennach′erib king of Assyria, 'On what are you relying, that you stand siege in Jerusalem? 11 Is not Hezeki′ah misleading you, that he may give you over to die by famine and by thirst, when he tells you, "The LORD our God will deliver us from the hand of the king of Assyria"? 12 Has not this same Hezeki′ah taken away his high places and his altars and commanded Judah and Jerusalem, "Before one altar you shall worship, and upon it you shall burn your sacrifices"? 13 Do you not know what I and my fathers have done to all the peoples of other lands? Were the gods of the nations of those lands at all able to deliver their lands out of my hand? 14 Who among all the gods of those nations which my fathers utterly destroyed was able to deliver his people from my hand, that your God should be able to deliver you from my hand? 15 Now therefore do not let Hezeki′ah deceive you or mislead you in this fashion, and do not believe him, for no god of any nation or kingdom has been able

---

little towns and villages of Judah, even if no opposition were ventured, there was only a faint hope of being spared from massacre or captivity. Now in II Kings 18:14-16 we are told that Hezekiah's first response to the threat was to try to appease the Assyrians by paying tremendous tribute, and that to obtain the wherewithal he seized the treasures in the temple. Imagine the Chronicler's consternation—that was abject failure to rely on Yahweh; it was Ahaz' sacrilegious sin repeated. To include this information would blacken his portrait of the good king. He met the problem by omitting the damaging verses, and instead related that Hezekiah bravely made all military preparations to resist, and then spoke to his people (vss. 7-8) words that deserve to be immortal: **Do not be afraid**

or dismayed before the king of Assyria and all the horde that is with him; for there is one greater with us than with him. With him is an arm of flesh; but with us is the LORD **our God, to help us and to fight our battles** (cf. II Kings 6:17; Isa. 31:1-3).

What should we think about the Chronicler's refusal to set on record Hezekiah's weakness in the first impact of crisis? Was his decision simply an unpardonable suppression of truth, or was it fairness to a larger truth, viz., the general tenor of the king's character? Men are prone to let a single tragic error devastatingly darken the memory of an upright life. "Judge not, that ye be not judged" (Matt. 7:1).

9-23. *The Great Deliverance.*—From this point the Chronicler could thankfully continue

people out of mine hand, and out of the hand of my fathers: how much less shall your God deliver you out of mine hand?

16 And his servants spake yet *more* against the Lord God, and against his servant Hezekiah.

17 He wrote also letters to rail on the Lord God of Israel, and to speak against him, saying, As the gods of the nations of *other* lands have not delivered their people out of mine hand, so shall not the God of Hezekiah deliver his people out of mine hand.

18 Then they cried with a loud voice, in the Jews' speech, unto the people of Jerusalem that *were* on the wall, to affright them, and to trouble them; that they might take the city.

19 And they spake against the God of Jerusalem, as against the gods of the people of the earth, *which were* the work of the hands of man.

20 And for this *cause* Hezekiah the king, and the prophet Isaiah the son of Amoz, prayed and cried to heaven.

21 ¶ And the Lord sent an angel, which cut off all the mighty men of valor, and the leaders and captains in the camp of the king of Assyria. So he returned with shame of face to his own land. And when he was come into the house of his god, they that came forth of his own bowels slew him there with the sword.

22 Thus the Lord saved Hezekiah and the inhabitants of Jerusalem from the hand of Sennacherib the king of Assyria, and from the hand of all *other*, and guided them on every side.

23 And many brought gifts unto the Lord to Jerusalem, and presents to Hezekiah king of Judah: so that he was magnified in the sight of all nations from thenceforth.

24 ¶ In those days Hezekiah was sick to the death, and prayed unto the Lord: and he spake unto him, and he gave him a sign.

25 But Hezekiah rendered not again according to the benefit *done* unto him; for his heart was lifted up: therefore there was wrath upon him, and upon Judah and Jerusalem.

to deliver his people from my hand or from the hand of my fathers. How much less will your God deliver you out of my hand!' "

16 And his servants said still more against the Lord God and against his servant Hezeki'ah. **17** And he wrote letters to cast contempt on the Lord the God of Israel and to speak against him, saying, "Like the gods of the nations of the lands who have not delivered their people from my hands, so the God of Hezeki'ah will not deliver his people from my hand." **18** And they shouted it with a loud voice in the language of Judah to the people of Jerusalem who were upon the wall, to frighten and terrify them, in order that they might take the city. **19** And they spoke of the God of Jerusalem as they spoke of the gods of the peoples of the earth, which are the work of men's hands.

20 Then Hezeki'ah the king and Isaiah the prophet, the son of Amoz, prayed because of this and cried to heaven. **21** And the Lord sent an angel, who cut off all the mighty warriors and commanders and officers in the camp of the king of Assyria. So he returned with shame of face to his own land. And when he came into the house of his god, some of his own sons struck him down there with the sword. **22** So the Lord saved Hezeki'ah and the inhabitants of Jerusalem from the hand of Sennach'erib king of Assyria and from the hand of all his enemies; and he gave them rest on every side. **23** And many brought gifts to the Lord to Jerusalem and precious things to Hezeki'ah king of Judah, so that he was exalted in the sight of all nations from that time onward.

24 In those days Hezeki'ah became sick and was at the point of death, and he prayed to the Lord; and he answered him and gave him a sign. **25** But Hezeki'ah did not make return according to the benefit done to him, for his heart was proud. Therefore wrath came upon him and Judah and

---

25. The occasion when he showed pride is that referred to in vs. 31 (see II Kings 20:12-19).

26 Notwithstanding, Hezekiah humbled himself for the pride of his heart, *both* he and the inhabitants of Jerusalem, so that the wrath of the LORD came not upon them in the days of Hezekiah.

27 ¶ And Hezekiah had exceeding much riches and honor: and he made himself treasuries for silver, and for gold, and for precious stones, and for spices, and for shields, and for all manner of pleasant jewels;

28 Storehouses also for the increase of corn, and wine, and oil; and stalls for all manner of beasts, and cotes for flocks.

29 Moreover he provided him cities, and possessions of flocks and herds in abundance: for God had given him substance very much.

30 This same Hezekiah also stopped the upper watercourse of Gihon, and brought it straight down to the west side of the city of David. And Hezekiah prospered in all his works.

31 ¶ Howbeit, in *the business of* the ambassadors of the princes of Babylon, who sent unto him to inquire of the wonder that was *done* in the land, God left him, to try him, that he might know all *that was* in his heart.

32 ¶ Now the rest of the acts of Hezekiah, and his goodness, behold, they *are* written in the vision of Isaiah the prophet, the son of Amoz, *and* in the book of the kings of Judah and Israel.

33 And Hezekiah slept with his fathers, and they buried him in the chiefest of the sepulchres of the sons of David: and all Judah and the inhabitants of Jerusalem did him honor at his death. And Manasseh his son reigned in his stead.

33 Manasseh *was* twelve years old when he began to reign, and he reigned fifty and five years in Jerusalem:

Jerusalem. **26** But Hezeki'ah humbled himself for the pride of his heart, both he and the inhabitants of Jerusalem, so that the wrath of the LORD did not come upon them in the days of Hezeki'ah.

27 And Hezeki'ah had very great riches and honor; and he made for himself treasuries for silver, for gold, for precious stones, for spices, for shields, and for all kinds of costly vessels; **28** storehouses also for the yield of grain, wine, and oil; and stalls for all kinds of cattle, and sheepfolds. **29** He likewise provided cities for himself, and flocks and herds in abundance; for God had given him very great possessions. **30** This same Hezeki'ah closed the upper outlet of the waters of Gihon and directed them down to the west side of the city of David. And Hezeki'ah prospered in all his works. **31** And so in the matter of the envoys of the princes of Babylon, who had been sent to him to inquire about the sign that had been done in the land, God left him to himself, in order to try him and to know all that was in his heart.

32 Now the rest of the acts of Hezeki'ah, and his good deeds, behold, they are written in the vision of Isaiah the prophet the son of Amoz, in the Book of the Kings of Judah and Israel. **33** And Hezeki'ah slept with his fathers, and they buried him in the ascent of the tombs of the sons of David; and all Judah and the inhabitants of Jerusalem did him honor at his death. And Manas'seh his son reigned in his stead.

33 Manas'seh was twelve years old when he began to reign, and he

---

K. REIGNS OF MANASSEH AND AMON (33:1-25)

Hezekiah, "a second David," was succeeded by Manasseh, who was tyrant, polytheist,

---

by quoting with some curtailment from II Kings 18:13-37; 19:1-37, the dramatic episode regarding the Assyrian plenipotentiaries at the barred gates of Jerusalem, and the startling retirement of the Assyrian army.

31. God Left Him to Try Him.—God's testing of men continues to the very end; and it is

best so. The Chronicler could be content now to admit that this good king was not quite free from fault (vss. 25, 31), was not quite a perfect saint. But Hezekiah had done very well. *Requiescat in pace.*

33:1-25. After the Best, the Worst.—The sheer perversity of things! Manasseh reigned for fifty-

2 But did *that which was* evil in the sight of the Lord, like unto the abominations of the heathen, whom the Lord had cast out before the children of Israel.

3 ¶ For he built again the high places which Hezekiah his father had broken down, and he reared up altars for Baalim, and made groves, and worshipped all the host of heaven, and served them.

4 Also he built altars in the house of the Lord, whereof the Lord had said, In Jerusalem shall my name be for ever.

5 And he built altars for all the host of heaven in the two courts of the house of the Lord.

6 And he caused his children to pass through the fire in the valley of the son of Hinnom: also he observed times, and used enchantments, and used witchcraft, and dealt with a familiar spirit, and with wizards: he wrought much evil in the sight of the Lord, to provoke him to anger.

7 And he set a carved image, the idol which he had made, in the house of God, of which God had said to David and to Solomon his son, In this house, and in Jerusalem, which I have chosen before all the tribes of Israel, will I put my name for ever:

8 Neither will I any more remove the foot of Israel from out of the land which I have appointed for your fathers; so that they will take heed to do all that I have commanded them, according to the whole law and the statutes and the ordinances by the hand of Moses.

9 So Manasseh made Judah and the inhabitants of Jerusalem to err, *and* to do worse than the heathen, whom the Lord had destroyed before the children of Israel.

reigned fifty-five years in Jerusalem. **2** He did what was evil in the sight of the Lord, according to the abominable practices of the nations whom the Lord drove out before the people of Israel. **3** For he rebuilt the high places which his father Hezeki'ah had broken down, and erected altars to the Ba'als, and made Ashe'rahs, and worshiped all the host of heaven, and served them. **4** And he built altars in the house of the Lord, of which the Lord had said, "In Jerusalem shall my name be for ever." **5** And he built altars for all the host of heaven in the two courts of the house of the Lord. **6** And he burned his sons as an offering in the valley of the son of Hinnom, and practiced soothsaying and augury and sorcery, and dealt with mediums and with wizards. He did much evil in the sight of the Lord, provoking him to anger. **7** And the image of the idol which he had made he set in the house of God, of which God said to David and to Solomon his son, "In this house, and in Jerusalem, which I have chosen out of all the tribes of Israel, I will put my name for ever; **8** and I will no more remove the foot of Israel from the land which I appointed for your fathers, if only they will be careful to do all that I have commanded them, all the law, the statutes, and the ordinances given through Moses." **9** Manas'seh seduced Judah and the inhabitants of Jerusalem, so that they did more evil than the nations whom the Lord destroyed before the people of Israel.

---

and renewer of revolting rites in honor of Yahweh. The compilers of Kings (II Kings 21:11-16; 23:26-27; etc.) regarded the eventual fall of Jerusalem as retribution brought about by Manasseh's sins.

---

five years and was the most evil of all the kings of Judah. Good Hezekiah's lifework was swept away in the twinkling of an eye. The fact that progress often is not conserved is, on the shallow view, a heartbreaking aspect of life, but on deeper reflection, a stimulating challenge. Only the good we have ourselves struggled to attain is truly our own, and every generation must fight its own battle for right or wrong. Vs. 6 sufficiently indicates Manasseh's vileness, but elabo-

ration may be read in II Kings 21:1-16. Consider but one fact: that he revived the frightful rite of sacrificing first-born infants by fire to Yahweh. This and other acts of similar barbarity were perpetrated "religiously" in the ancient world. Justly did the philosophic Roman poet Lucretius exclaim, "So foul the wickedness religion can induce!" [7] It is not so long, as history measures time, since heretics were burned and tor-

[7] *On the Nature of Things* I. 101.

10 And the LORD spake to Manasseh, and to his people: but they would not hearken.

11 ¶ Wherefore the LORD brought upon them the captains of the host of the king of Assyria, which took Manasseh among the thorns, and bound him with fetters, and carried him to Babylon.

12 And when he was in affliction, he besought the LORD his God, and humbled himself greatly before the God of his fathers,

13 And prayed unto him: and he was entreated of him, and heard his supplication, and brought him again to Jerusalem into his kingdom. Then Manasseh knew that the LORD he *was* God.

14 Now after this he built a wall without the city of David, on the west side of Gihon, in the valley, even to the entering in at the fish gate, and compassed about Ophel, and raised it up a very great height, and put captains of war in all the fenced cities of Judah.

15 And he took away the strange gods, and the idol out of the house of the LORD, and all the altars that he had built in the mount of the house of the LORD, and in Jerusalem, and cast *them* out of the city.

16 And he repaired the altar of the LORD, and sacrificed thereon peace offerings and thank offerings, and commanded Judah to serve the LORD God of Israel.

17 Nevertheless the people did sacrifice still in the high places, *yet* unto the LORD their God only.

18 ¶ Now the rest of the acts of Manasseh, and his prayer unto his God, and the words of the seers that spake to him in the

10 The LORD spoke to Manas'seh and to his people, but they gave no heed. 11 Therefore the LORD brought upon them the commanders of the army of the king of Assyria, who took Manas'seh with hooks and bound him with fetters of bronze and brought him to Babylon. 12 And when he was in distress he entreated the favor of the LORD his God and humbled himself greatly before the God of his fathers. 13 He prayed to him, and God received his entreaty and heard his supplication and brought him again to Jerusalem into his kingdom. Then Manas'seh knew that the LORD was God.

14 Afterwards he built an outer wall to the city of David west of Gihon, in the valley, to the entrance by the Fish Gate, and carried it round Ophel, and raised it to a very great height; he also put commanders of the army in all the fortified cities in Judah. 15 And he took away the foreign gods and the idol from the house of the LORD, and all the altars that he had built on the mountain of the house of the LORD and in Jerusalem, and he threw them outside of the city. 16 He also restored the altar of the LORD and offered upon it sacrifices of peace offerings and of thanksgiving; and he commanded Judah to serve the LORD the God of Israel. 17 Nevertheless the people still sacrificed at the high places, but only to the LORD their God.

18 Now the rest of the acts of Manas'seh, and his prayer to his God, and the words of

33:11-13. Kings is silent as to Manasseh's spell in captivity, and his penitence. That he repented in this wise there is no vestige of likelihood; for Josiah had to purge Jerusalem of heathenism. That he was removed to Babylon, but later released, may be fact—if he was suspect in the widespread revolt against Assyria in 648 B.C.

14-17. Not in Kings.

18. The late apocryphal book called The Prayer of Manasses drew its title from this verse, but not its contents.

tured in the cause of Christian orthodoxy; nor has religious persecution vanished from the modern world. "Religion" is a term which constantly requires definition. When Christians urge the need for "a revival of religion" they know with fair accuracy what they intend, but perhaps fail initially to realize that in the thoughts of the irreligious to whom they appeal

religion has denoted a bewildering variety of things true and false, debased and exalted.

10-17. *The Villain Penitent.*—This passage had no warrant in Kings. That Manasseh was for a time compelled to go to Assyria and came back somewhat chastened is not wholly improbable. Record to that effect may have appeared in the hypothetical source named in vs. 18, and

name of the Lord God of Israel, behold, they *are written* in the book of the kings of Israel.

19 His prayer also, and *how God* was entreated of him, and all his sins, and his trespass, and the places wherein he built high places, and set up groves and graven images, before he was humbled: behold, they *are* written among the sayings of the seers.

20 ¶ So Manasseh slept with his fathers, and they buried him in his own house: and Amon his son reigned in his stead.

21 ¶ Amon *was* two and twenty years old when he began to reign, and reigned two years in Jerusalem.

22 But he did *that which was* evil in the sight of the Lord, as did Manasseh his father: for Amon sacrificed unto all the carved images which Manasseh his father had made, and served them;

23 And humbled not himself before the Lord, as Manasseh his father had humbled himself; but Amon trespassed more and more.

24 And his servants conspired against him, and slew him in his own house.

25 ¶ But the people of the land slew all them that had conspired against king Amon; and the people of the land made Josiah his son king in his stead.

34 Josiah *was* eight years old when he began to reign, and he reigned in Jerusalem one and thirty years.

2 And he did *that which was* right in the sight of the Lord, and walked in the ways of David his father, and declined *neither* to the right hand, nor to the left.

the seers who spoke to him in the name of the Lord the God of Israel, behold, they are in the Chronicles of the Kings of Israel. **19** And his prayer, and how God received his entreaty, and all his sin and his faithlessness, and the sites on which he built high places and set up the Ashe'rim and the images, before he humbled himself, behold, they are written in the Chronicles of the Seers.[v] **20** So Manas'seh slept with his fathers, and they buried him in his house; and Amon his son reigned in his stead.

21 Amon was twenty-two years old when he began to reign, and he reigned two years in Jerusalem. **22** He did what was evil in the sight of the Lord, as Manas'seh his father had done. Amon sacrificed to all the images that Manas'seh his father had made, and served them. **23** And he did not humble himself before the Lord, as Manas'seh his father had humbled himself, but this Amon incurred guilt more and more. **24** And his servants conspired against him and killed him in his house. **25** But the people of the land slew all those who had conspired against King Amon; and the people of the land made Josi'ah his son king in his stead.

34 Josi'ah was eight years old when he began to reign, and he reigned thirty-one years in Jerusalem. **2** He did what was right in the eyes of the Lord, and walked in the ways of David his father; and he did not turn aside to the right or to the left.

[v] One Ms Gk: Heb *of Hozai*

21-25. These verses reproduce II Kings 21:19-26, concerning Amon.

---

have been there embroidered in regard to his repentance. That might explain the curious vs. 17, which indicates that, although the local altars in Judah were not abolished, sacrifices were now there offered only to Yahweh and not also to the local spirits, the baals, or to the female deity, Astarte. But against whitewashing stand such verses as Jer. 2:20, 28.

The modern expositor may be inclined to think that if Manasseh's conscience ever was troubled, it would be a case of expediency:

The Devil was sick—the Devil a monk would be;
The Devil was well—the Devil a monk was he.[8]

[8] Rabelais, *Works*, Bk. IV, ch. xxiv.

No more can sensibly be suggested than forlorn hope that conceivably this sinner repented and was not refused the grace of God (vs. 19).

21-25. *Assassinated Amon.*—Amon was like-minded with his father. After two years he was murdered by a party in the palace. But the populace of Jerusalem had had enough of "Manassehism" and of palace plots: they rose and slew Amon's slayers. "This interference in the court by 'the people of the land' is the most democratic action recorded in the history"[9] (but cf. Jer. 26:16-19).

[9] Montgomery and Gehman, *Kings*, p. 521.

3 ¶ For in the eighth year of his reign, while he was yet young, he began to seek after the God of David his father: and in the twelfth year he began to purge Judah and Jerusalem from the high places, and the groves, and the carved images, and the molten images.

4 And they brake down the altars of Baalim in his presence; and the images, that *were* on high above them, he cut down; and the groves, and the carved images, and the molten images, he brake in pieces, and made dust *of them,* and strewed *it* upon the graves of them that had sacrificed unto them.

5 And he burnt the bones of the priests upon their altars, and cleansed Judah and Jerusalem.

6 And *so did he* in the cities of Manasseh, and Ephraim, and Simeon, even unto Naphtali, with their mattocks round about.

7 And when he had broken down the altars and the groves, and had beaten the graven images into powder, and cut down all the idols throughout all the land of Israel, he returned to Jerusalem.

3 For in the eighth year of his reign, while he was yet a boy, he began to seek the God of David his father; and in the twelfth year he began to purge Judah and Jerusalem of the high places, the Ashe′rim, and the graven and the molten images. 4 And they broke down the altars of the Ba′als in his presence; and he hewed down the incense altars which stood above them; and he broke in pieces the Ashe′rim and the graven and the molten images, and he made dust of them and strewed it over the graves of those who had sacrificed to them. 5 He also burned the bones of the priests on their altars, and purged Judah and Jerusalem. 6 And in the cities of Manas′seh, E′phraim, and Simeon, and as far as Naph′tali, in their ruins[w] round about, 7 he broke down the altars, and beat the Ashe′rim and the images into powder, and hewed down all the incense altars throughout all the land of Israel. Then he returned to Jerusalem.

[w] Heb uncertain

L. Reign of Josiah (34:1–35:27)

34:3. In the twelfth year: Josiah would then be twenty years old. An expectable sequence of events is related. The Assyrian Empire was in difficulties, approaching its destruction in 612 B.C., and its hold on central and northern Palestine was probably no more than nominal. Josiah and his counselors could venture on measures to strengthen unity of national feeling among the Hebrews throughout the land. A century earlier—so the Chronicler believed and said—King Hezekiah had brilliantly exploited a comparable but transient opportunity by holding a "Unity Passover" at Jerusalem. Josiah was a decent-minded youth, and there was probably a strong revulsion felt in Jerusalem against the religious polytheism and licentious rites obtaining in Manasseh's reign. What the Chronicler stated is therefore entirely possible: viz., that in the twelfth year of Josiah's reign drastic measures were taken to effect a thorough reform of religious rites, and concurrently to unify the Judean and Israelite Hebrews on the basis of their common worship of Yahweh. Hezekiah's action, so the Chronicler believed, set a precedent, if one was needed. For not only did Josiah cleanse the Augean stables in Jerusalem, but he resolutely destroyed the local sanctuaries both in Judah and in Israelite territory—obviously with the object that the great religious festivals should be observed at Jerusalem and sacrificial worship henceforth confined to its altar. The Chronicler next told that in Josiah's *eighteenth* year (34:8) an impressive document (vs. 14) was

34:3. One Generation to Another.—There is no accounting for the mutations of character from one generation to another: incorrigible Ahaz, followed by teachable Hezekiah; evil-disposed Manasseh and Amon, and then Manasseh's grandson, good King Josiah, who was respected by Huldah (vss. 26-28) and honored by Jeremiah. "He judged the cause of the poor and needy; then it was well with him: was not this to know me? saith the Lord" (Jer. 22:16). In this matter the facts of life, broadly seen, are not depressing. Frequently the child of bad parents becomes disgusted with their ways and learns to meet his own experiences with eyes open and able to discern right from wrong. But it may be added that those who do great good

8 ¶ Now in the eighteenth year of his reign, when he had purged the land, and the house, he sent Shaphan the son of Azaliah, and Maaseiah the governor of the city, and Joah the son of Joahaz the recorder, to repair the house of the LORD his God.

9 And when they came to Hilkiah the high priest, they delivered the money that was brought into the house of God, which the Levites that kept the doors had gathered of the hand of Manasseh and Ephraim, and of all the remnant of Israel, and of all Judah and Benjamin; and they returned to Jerusalem.

10 And they put it in the hand of the workmen that had the oversight of the house of the LORD, and they gave it to the workmen that wrought in the house of the LORD, to repair and amend the house:

11 Even to the artificers and builders gave they it, to buy hewn stone, and timber for couplings, and to floor the houses which the kings of Judah had destroyed.

12 And the men did the work faithfully: and the overseers of them were Jahath and Obadiah, the Levites, of the sons of Merari; and Zechariah and Meshullam, of the sons of the Kohathites, to set it forward; and other of the Levites, all that could skill of instruments of music.

13 Also they were over the bearers of burdens, and were overseers of all that wrought the work in any manner of service: and of the Levites there were scribes, and officers, and porters.

14 ¶ And when they brought out the money that was brought into the house of the LORD, Hilkiah the priest found a book of the law of the LORD given by Moses.

8 Now in the eighteenth year of his reign, when he had purged the land and the house, he sent Shaphan the son of Azali'ah, and Ma-asei'ah the governor of the city, and Jo'ah the son of Jo'ahaz, the recorder, to repair the house of the LORD his God. 9 They came to Hilki'ah the high priest and delivered the money that had been brought in to the house of God, which the Levites, the keepers of the threshold, had collected from Manas'seh and E'phraim and from all the remnant of Israel and from all Judah and Benjamin and from the inhabitants of Jerusalem. 10 They delivered it to the workmen who had the oversight of the house of the LORD; and the workmen who were working in the house of the LORD gave it for repairing and restoring the house. 11 They gave it to the carpenters and the builders to buy quarried stone, and timber for binders and beams for the buildings which the kings of Judah had let go to ruin. 12 And the men did the work faithfully. Over them were set Jahath and Obadi'ah the Levites, of the sons of Merar'i, and Zechari'ah and Meshul'lam, of the sons of the Ko'hathites, to have oversight. The Levites, all who were skilful with instruments of music, 13 were over the burden bearers and directed all who did work in every kind of service; and some of the Levites were scribes, and officials, and gatekeepers.

14 While they were bringing out the money that had been brought into the house of the LORD, Hilki'ah the priest found the book of the law of the LORD given

---

found in the temple; and that thereafter an enthusiastic "Unity Passover" was celebrated in Jerusalem. It might well be that there was strong opposition to the destruction of the local sanctuaries, and that not until six years after the initiation of the reform could the "Unity Passover" be achieved. The Chronicler's order of events, it may be noted, is much more natural than the account in II Kings 22:3-20, where nothing happened until the discovery of the book occurred in Josiah's eighteenth year, and the discovery

---

in life generally began to travel the right way when they were young, as did Josiah **while he was yet a boy.**

14. *Sower and Reaper.*—It is virtually certain that the writing so remarkably discovered in the temple was the book, or the essential part of the book, we know as Deuteronomy (see Exeg.) —teaching belief in the grace of the living God,

showing how his people should worship him and how, as God's people, they should deal with one another. A single reflection is here offered. Think of the men who had gathered together this writing in time past, moved by their faith in the pure purpose of God, hoping that their labor would not be in vain in the Lord; and who died not knowing that it would thus be

15 And Hilkiah answered and said to Shaphan the scribe, I have found the book of the law in the house of the Lord. And Hilkiah delivered the book to Shaphan.

16 And Shaphan carried the book to the king, and brought the king word back again, saying, All that was committed to thy servants, they do *it*.

17 And they have gathered together the money that was found in the house of the Lord, and have delivered it into the hand of the overseers, and to the hand of the workmen.

18 Then Shaphan the scribe told the king, saying, Hilkiah the priest hath given me a book. And Shaphan read it before the king.

19 And it came to pass, when the king had heard the words of the law, that he rent his clothes.

20 And the king commanded Hilkiah, and Ahikam the son of Shaphan, and Abdon the son of Micah, and Shaphan the scribe, and Asaiah a servant of the king's, saying,

21 Go, inquire of the Lord for me, and for them that are left in Israel and in Judah, concerning the words of the book that is found: for great *is* the wrath of the Lord that is poured out upon us, because our fathers have not kept the word of the Lord, to do after all that is written in this book.

22 And Hilkiah, and *they* that the king *had appointed,* went to Huldah the prophetess, the wife of Shallum the son of Tikvath, the son of Hasrah, keeper of the ward-

through Moses. 15 Then Hilki'ah said to Shaphan the secretary, "I have found the book of the law in the house of the Lord"; and Hilki'ah gave the book to Shaphan. 16 Shaphan brought the book to the king, and further reported to the king, "All that was committed to your servants they are doing. 17 They have emptied out the money that was found in the house of the Lord and have delivered it into the hand of the overseers and the workmen." 18 Then Shaphan the secretary told the king, "Hilki'ah the priest has given me a book." And Shaphan read it before the king.

19 When the king heard the words of the law he rent his clothes. 20 And the king commanded Hilki'ah, Ahi'kam the son of Shaphan, Abdon the son of Micah, Shaphan the secretary, and Asai'ah the king's servant, saying, 21 "Go, inquire of the Lord for me and for those who are left in Israel and in Judah, concerning the words of the book that has been found; for great is the wrath of the Lord that is poured out on us, because our fathers have not kept the word of the Lord, to do according to all that is written in this book."

22 So Hilki'ah and those whom the king had sent[x] went to Huldah the prophetess, the wife of Shallum the son of Tokhath, son of Hasrah, keeper of the wardrobe

[x] Syr Vg: Heb lacks *had sent*

---

initiated the reform alike in the capital and in the country, while in the selfsame eighteenth year the "Unity Passover" was triumphantly held! It is arguable that the Chronicler arbitrarily antedated the reform to the twelfth year, on the principle that a good young king should "get going" early. But one asks whether by aid of tradition or written source he happened to know the right order, or else rightly conjectured it. At any rate, it is the compilers of Kings who here presented a stilted, most improbable sequence.

15. **I have found the book of the law:** Unquestionably a remarkable MS concerning rightful worship of Yahweh was found in the temple by workmen carrying out repairs.

---

found in Jerusalem and when the hour came for the dissolution of the Judean kingdom, would serve to hold together their people, to instruct them and enlighten, and by its finest words inspire the faith of countless Jews and Christians. Christ saw in the fact that "one soweth, and another reapeth" no reason for sadness. The sower should rejoice in hope; the reaper should not look upon the golden grain as due to his own merit, but instead rejoice to think that past sowing has come to harvest (John 4:27-38).

22. *Huldah the Prophetess.*—Why did the chief priest not consult the very numerous male prophets in Jerusalem? We would like to know more about Huldah, but never shall. What we

robe; (now she dwelt in Jerusalem in the college;) and they spake to her to that *effect.*

23 ¶ And she answered them, Thus saith the LORD God of Israel, Tell ye the man that sent you to me,

24 Thus saith the LORD, Behold, I will bring evil upon this place, and upon the inhabitants thereof, *even* all the curses that are written in the book which they have read before the king of Judah:

25 Because they have forsaken me, and have burned incense unto other gods, that they might provoke me to anger with all the works of their hands; therefore my wrath shall be poured out upon this place, and shall not be quenched.

26 And as for the king of Judah, who sent you to inquire of the LORD, so shall ye say unto him, Thus saith the LORD God of Israel *concerning* the words which thou hast heard;

27 Because thine heart was tender, and thou didst humble thyself before God, when thou heardest his words against this place, and against the inhabitants thereof, and humbledst thyself before me, and didst rend thy clothes, and weep before me; I have even heard *thee* also, saith the LORD.

28 Behold, I will gather thee to thy fathers, and thou shalt be gathered to thy grave in peace, neither shall thine eyes see all the evil that I will bring upon this place, and upon the inhabitants of the same. So they brought the king word again.

29 ¶ Then the king sent and gathered together all the elders of Judah and Jerusalem.

(now she dwelt in Jerusalem in the Second Quarter) and spoke to her to that effect. 23 And she said to them, "Thus says the LORD, the God of Israel: 'Tell the man who sent you to me, 24 Thus says the LORD, Behold, I will bring evil upon this place and upon its inhabitants, all the curses that are written in the book which was read before the king of Judah. 25 Because they have forsaken me and have burned incense to other gods, that they might provoke me to anger with all the works of their hands, therefore my wrath will be poured out upon this place and will not be quenched. 26 But to the king of Judah, who sent you to inquire of the LORD, thus shall you say to him, Thus says the LORD, the God of Israel: Regarding the words which you have heard, 27 because your heart was penitent and you humbled yourself before God when you heard his words against this place and its inhabitants, and you have humbled yourself before me, and have rent your clothes and wept before me, I also have heard you, says the LORD. 28 Behold, I will gather you to your fathers, and you shall be gathered to your grave in peace, and your eyes shall not see all the evil which I will bring upon this place and its inhabitants.'" And they brought back word to the king.

29 Then the king sent and gathered together all the elders of Judah and Jerusa-

---

And there is no difference between Kings and Chronicles regarding the profound impression which its solemn words made on king and people. It is likely that the writing was an early version of the present book of Deuteronomy—a statement of Israelitish custom made under the influence of prophetic zeal for Yahweh, and somehow deposited in the temple at Jerusalem after the fall of Samaria. But scholars have gone beyond warrant in confidence that it was a version of Deuteronomy which clearly enjoined that sacrifice should be offered to Yahweh at one altar only in all Hebrew territory. All that is known for certain about the contents of the book, and the immediate impression which it made, is that when it was submitted to the prophetess Huldah she somberly declared that there was nothing in it to justify hope that sinful Jerusalem would escape destruction, but that the disaster would not happen in good-intentioned

---

do know is fine—she refused to countenance wishful thinking (vss. 24-25), but she encouraged the young king to believe that his good intentions would not be in vain (vss. 26-28). Little did Josiah and Hilkiah and Huldah

realize that four miles distant from Jerusalem a lad was growing up who, through suffering, would be led to see deeper into the heart of truth than any man who had yet lived—Jeremiah of Anathoth.

30 And the king went up into the house of the LORD, and all the men of Judah, and the inhabitants of Jerusalem, and the priests, and the Levites, and all the people, great and small: and he read in their ears all the words of the book of the covenant that was found in the house of the LORD.

31 And the king stood in his place, and made a covenant before the LORD, to walk after the LORD, and to keep his commandments, and his testimonies, and his statutes, with all his heart, and with all his soul, to perform the words of the covenant which are written in this book.

32 And he caused all that were present in Jerusalem and Benjamin to stand to it. And the inhabitants of Jerusalem did according to the covenant of God, the God of their fathers.

33 And Josiah took away all the abominations out of all the countries that pertained to the children of Israel, and made all that were present in Israel to serve, even to serve the LORD their God. And all his days they departed not from following the LORD, the God of their fathers.

35 Moreover, Josiah kept a passover unto the LORD in Jerusalem: and they killed the passover on the fourteenth day of the first month.

lem. 30 And the king went up to the house of the LORD, with all the men of Judah and the inhabitants of Jerusalem and the priests and the Levites, all the people both great and small; and he read in their hearing all the words of the book of the covenant which had been found in the house of the LORD. 31 And the king stood in his place and made a covenant before the LORD, to walk after the LORD and to keep his commandments and his testimonies and his statutes, with all his heart and all his soul, to perform the words of the covenant that were written in this book. 32 Then he made all who were present in Jerusalem and in Benjamin stand to it. And the inhabitants of Jerusalem did according to the covenant of God, the God of their fathers. 33 And Josi'ah took away all the abominations from all the territory that belonged to the people of Israel, and made all who were in Israel serve the LORD their God. All his days they did not turn away from following the LORD the God of their fathers.

35 Josi'ah kept a passover to the LORD in Jerusalem; and they killed the passover lamb on the fourteenth day of the

Josiah's lifetime (vss. 22-28; see II Kings 22:14-20). Thereafter king and people vowed that they would obey the injunctions of the book and loyally worship Yahweh. At this point Kings states that the whole reform movement was instituted, but Chronicles (34:32-33) that Josiah continued the good work throughout the land which he had begun in his *twelfth* year.

35:1-19. Josiah kept a passover to the LORD in Jerusalem: The Chronicler did not specify exactly when, deliberately refraining at this point (see vss. 18-19) from transcribing II Kings 23:21-23 where the implication is that the great "Unity Passover" was inspired by the finding of the book, and held in that very year. The Chronicler believed Hezekiah to have held just such a Passover a century earlier, when no "book of the law" had been discovered to prompt his action. Welch rightly insists on the great importance of this point for critical study. Other deep-seated differences between what is said of Hezekiah's Passover and Josiah's support the view that the historicity of Hezekiah's Passover should not be dismissed as a fictional reading back to Hezekiah's time of an event which in fact took place only under Josiah. (Cf. Welch, *Work of the Chronicler*, pp. 110, 147: "The fact remains that a responsible writer [the Chronicler], whose book has found its way into the Jewish Canon, had no hesitation in

35:1, 18. *Josiah's Passover.*—Jewish life was enriched because its holidays were so definitely holy days. Western civilization suffers because the celebrations of public leisure have become too deeply sundered from religious consciousness. Popular sentiment loses in that the occasion is apt to be untouched by acknowledgment of man's highest aspirations and hopes. Religion

2 And he set the priests in their charges, and encouraged them to the service of the house of the Lord,

3 And said unto the Levites that taught all Israel, which were holy unto the Lord, Put the holy ark in the house which Solomon the son of David king of Israel did build; *it shall* not *be* a burden upon *your* shoulders: serve now the Lord your God, and his people Israel,

4 And prepare *yourselves* by the houses of your fathers, after your courses, according to the writing of David king of Israel, and according to the writing of Solomon his son:

5 And stand in the holy *place* according to the divisions of the families of the fathers of your brethren the people, and *after* the division of the families of the Levites.

6 So kill the passover, and sanctify yourselves, and prepare your brethren, that *they* may do according to the word of the Lord by the hand of Moses.

7 And Josiah gave to the people, of the flock, lambs and kids, all for the passover offerings, for all that were present, to the number of thirty thousand, and three thousand bullocks: these *were* of the king's substance.

8 And his princes gave willingly unto the people, to the priests, and to the Levites: Hilkiah and Zechariah and Jehiel, rulers of the house of God, gave unto the priests for the passover offerings two thousand and six hundred *small cattle*, and three hundred oxen.

9 Conaniah also, and Shemaiah and Nethaneel, his brethren, and Hashabiah and Jeiel and Jozabad, chief of the Levites, gave unto the Levites for passover offerings five

first month. 2 He appointed the priests to their offices and encouraged them in the service of the house of the Lord. 3 And he said to the Levites who taught all Israel and who were holy to the Lord, "Put the holy ark in the house which Solomon the son of David, king of Israel, built; you need no longer carry it upon your shoulders. Now serve the Lord your God and his people Israel. 4 Prepare yourselves according to your fathers' houses by your divisions, following the directions of David king of Israel and the directions of Solomon his son. 5 And stand in the holy place according to the groupings of the fathers' houses of your brethren the lay people, and let there be for each a part of a father's house of the Levites.[y] 6 And kill the passover, and sanctify yourselves, and prepare for your brethren, to do according to the word of the Lord by Moses.

7 Then Josi'ah contributed to the lay people, as passover offerings for all that were present, lambs and kids from the flock to the number of thirty thousand, and three thousand bulls; these were from the king's possessions. 8 And his princes contributed willingly to the people, to the priests, and to the Levites. Hilki'ah, Zechari'ah, and Jehi'el, the chief officers of the house of God, gave to the priests for the passover offerings two thousand six hundred lambs and kids and three hundred bulls. 9 Conani'ah also, and Shemai'ah and Nethan'el his brothers, and Hashabi'ah and Je-i'el and Jo'zabad, the chiefs of the Levites, gave to the Levites for the passover offerings five

[y] Heb obscure

---

dating the first tentative movement for centralization, and the change of locus for passover in the time of Hezekiah, and that, by doing this, he made it impossible to connect either movement with the discovery of the book of the law.") Deuteronomy exerted a profound influence on the men of the exilic and early postexilic generations; but that is a wider matter.

2-17. No parallel in Kings. Vs. 3*b* (**Put the holy ark . . .**) is probably revisional, for it deprecates the ark's importance (cf. Exeg. on 5:7-14) and intimates that mere Levites, having redeposited the ark, are now to return to their ordinary duties. On the

---

loses in that the worshipers are so few relatively to the total population that the services for the day seem isolated amidst, not indispensable to, the general enjoyment of the welcome freedom from work.

The Chronicler had described a passover held at Jerusalem as the zenith of Hezekiah's reign, with a great concourse of worshipers from both Judah and Israel. But this celebration under Josiah surpassed even that, surpassed all that

thousand *small cattle,* and five hundred oxen.

10 So the service was prepared, and the priests stood in their place, and the Levites in their courses, according to the king's commandment.

11 And they killed the passover, and the priests sprinkled *the blood* from their hands, and the Levites flayed *them.*

12 And they removed the burnt offerings, that they might give according to the divisions of the families of the people, to offer unto the LORD, as *it is* written in the book of Moses. And so *did they* with the oxen.

13 And they roasted the passover with fire according to the ordinance: but the *other* holy *offerings* sod they in pots, and in caldrons, and in pans, and divided *them* speedily among all the people.

14 And afterward they made ready for themselves, and for the priests: because the priests the sons of Aaron *were busied* in offering of burnt offerings and the fat until night; therefore the Levites prepared for themselves, and for the priests the sons of Aaron.

15 And the singers the sons of Asaph *were* in their place, according to the commandment of David, and Asaph, and Heman, and Jeduthun the king's seer; and the porters *waited* at every gate; they might not depart from their service; for their brethren the Levites prepared for them.

16 So all the service of the LORD was prepared the same day, to keep the passover, and to offer burnt offerings upon the altar of the LORD, according to the commandment of king Josiah.

17 And the children of Israel that were present kept the passover at that time, and the feast of unleavened bread seven days.

thousand lambs and kids and five hundred bulls.

10 When the service had been prepared for, the priests stood in their place, and the Levites in their divisions according to the king's command. **11** And they killed the passover lamb, and the priests sprinkled the blood which they received from them while the Levites flayed the victims. **12** And they set aside the burnt offerings that they might distribute them according to the groupings of the fathers' houses of the lay people, to offer to the LORD, as it is written in the book of Moses. And so they did with the bulls. **13** And they roasted the passover lamb with fire according to the ordinance; and they boiled the holy offerings in pots, in caldrons, and in pans, and carried them quickly to all the lay people. **14** And afterward they prepared for themselves and for the priests, because the priests the sons of Aaron were busied in offering the burnt offerings and the fat parts until night; so the Levites prepared for themselves and for the priests the sons of Aaron. **15** The singers, the sons of Asaph, were in their place according to the command of David, and Asaph, and Heman, and Jedu'thun the king's seer; and the gatekeepers were at each gate; they did not need to depart from their service, for their brethren the Levites prepared for them. **16** So all the service of the LORD was prepared that day, to keep the passover and to offer burnt offerings on the altar of the LORD, according to the command of King Josi'ah. **17** And the people of Israel who were present kept the passover at that time, and the feast of unleavened bread seven

other hand, vss. 2-3a (**And . . . to the LORD**), 4 (the **and** should be omitted as the revisers' linking word), and 5 are by the Chronicler, who gives the Levites the status later reserved to the Zadokites: they are said to be **holy to the LORD**, and to **stand in the holy place.** As for vss. 6-17, the Chronicler's mention that large cattle as well as lambs were permissible victims (so only in Deut. 16:2), and that the flesh was boiled, accords with Deuteronomy, but not with the final Law (cf. Deut. 16:7 with Exod. 12:9 in the RSV). It appears, however, that the revisers were content to obscure the matter by

former years had known. The multitude of families who participated were of the utmost diversity of mind. Many were devout, many were by no means so; but we may suppose there

were very few who did not in some degree benefit spiritually because this great holiday was conceived by the whole community as essentially a holy day.

18 And there was no passover like to that kept in Israel from the days of Samuel the prophet; neither did all the kings of Israel keep such a passover as Josiah kept, and the priests, and the Levites, and all Judah and Israel that were present, and the inhabitants of Jerusalem.

19 In the eighteenth year of the reign of Josiah was this passover kept.

20 ¶ After all this, when Josiah had prepared the temple, Necho king of Egypt came up to fight against Carchemish by Euphrates: and Josiah went out against him.

21 But he sent ambassadors to him, saying, What have I to do with thee, thou king of Judah? *I come* not against thee this day, but against the house wherewith I have war: for God commanded me to make haste: forbear thee from *meddling with* God, who *is* with me, that he destroy thee not.

22 Nevertheless Josiah would not turn his face from him, but disguised himself, that he might fight with him, and hearkened not unto the words of Necho from the mouth of God, and came to fight in the valley of Megiddo.

23 And the archers shot at king Josiah; and the king said to his servants, Have me away; for I am sore wounded.

24 His servants therefore took him out of that chariot, and put him in the second chariot that he had; and they brought him to Jerusalem, and he died, and was buried in *one of* the sepulchres of his fathers. And all Judah and Jerusalem mourned for Josiah.

25 ¶ And Jeremiah lamented for Josiah: and all the singing men and the singing women spake of Josiah in their lamentations to this day, and made them an ordinance in Israel: and, behold, they *are* written in the lamentations.

26 Now the rest of the acts of Josiah, and his goodness, according to *that which was* written in the law of the LORD,

days. 18 No passover like it had been kept in Israel since the days of Samuel the prophet; none of the kings of Israel had kept such a passover as was kept by Josi'ah, and the priests and the Levites, and all Judah and Israel who were present, and the inhabitants of Jerusalem. 19 In the eighteenth year of the reign of Josi'ah this passover was kept.

20 After all this, when Josi'ah had prepared the temple, Neco king of Egypt went up to fight at Car'chemish on the Eu-phra'tes and Josi'ah went out against him. 21 But he sent envoys to him, saying, "What have we to do with each other, king of Judah? I am not coming against you this day, but against the house with which I am at war; and God has commanded me to make haste. Cease opposing God, who is with me, lest he destroy you." 22 Nevertheless Josi'ah would not turn away from him, but disguised himself in order to fight with him. He did not listen to the words of Neco from the mouth of God, but joined battle in the plain of Megid'do. 23 And the archers shot King Josi'ah; and the king said to his servants, "Take me away, for I am badly wounded." 24 So his servants took him out of the chariot and carried him in his second chariot and brought him to Jerusalem. And he died, and was buried in the tombs of his fathers. All Judah and Jerusalem mourned for Josi'ah. 25 Jeremiah also uttered a lament for Josi'ah; and all the singing men and singing women have spoken of Josi'ah in their laments to this day. They made these an ordinance in Israel; behold, they are written in the Laments. 26 Now the rest of the acts of Josi'ah, and his good deeds according to what is written in the law of

introducing the confusing remarks about burnt offerings, and the quite mysterious reference to holy offerings found in vss. 12-13.

18-19. Here are the verses found in II Kings 23:22-23, for which the Chronicler (see Exeg. on vss. 1-19) substituted the dateless phrase **such a passover as Josiah kept.** These verses were probably inserted here by an annotator who perhaps failed to realize that the Chronicler's long and glowing description of the keeping of this Passover more than compensated for the omission of II Kings 23:22. What is significant is that neither the annotator nor the Chronicler thought it worth while to transcribe II Kings 23:21,

27 And his deeds, first and last, behold, they *are* written in the book of the kings of Israel and Judah.

36 Then the people of the land took Jehoahaz the son of Josiah, and made him king in his father's stead in Jerusalem.

2 Jehoahaz *was* twenty and three years old when he began to reign, and he reigned three months in Jerusalem.

3 And the king of Egypt put him down at Jerusalem, and condemned the land in a hundred talents of silver and a talent of gold.

4 And the king of Egypt made Eliakim his brother king over Judah and Jerusalem, and turned his name to Jehoiakim. And Necho took Jehoahaz his brother, and carried him to Egypt.

5 ¶ Jehoiakim *was* twenty and five years old when he began to reign, and he reigned eleven years in Jerusalem: and he did *that which was* evil in the sight of the LORD his God.

6 Against him came up Nebuchadnezzar king of Babylon, and bound him in fetters, to carry him to Babylon.

7 Nebuchadnezzar also carried of the vessels of the house of the LORD to Babylon, and put them in his temple at Babylon.

8 Now the rest of the acts of Jehoiakim, and his abominations which he did, and that which was found in him, behold, they *are* written in the book of the kings of Israel and Judah: and Jehoiachin his son reigned in his stead.

the LORD, 27 and his acts, first and last, behold, they are written in the Book of the Kings of Israel and Judah.

36 The people of the land took Jeho'-ahaz the son of Josi'ah and made him king in his father's stead in Jerusalem. 2 Jeho'ahaz was twenty-three years old when he began to reign; and he reigned three months in Jerusalem. 3 Then the king of Egypt deposed him in Jerusalem and laid upon the land a tribute of a hundred talents of silver and a talent of gold. 4 And the king of Egypt made Eli'akim his brother king over Judah and Jerusalem, and changed his name to Jehoi'akim; but Neco took Jeho'ahaz his brother and carried him to Egypt.

5 Jehoi'akim was twenty-five years old when he began to reign, and he reigned eleven years in Jerusalem. He did what was evil in the sight of the LORD his God. 6 Against him came up Nebuchadnez'zar king of Babylon, and bound him in fetters to take him to Babylon. 7 Nebuchadnez'zar also carried part of the vessels of the house of the LORD to Babylon and put them in his palace in Babylon. 8 Now the rest of the acts of Jehoi'akim, and the abominations which he did, and what was found against him, behold, they are written in the Book of the Kings of Israel and Judah; and Jehoi'achin his son reigned in his stead.

---

which says, "Keep the passover, . . . as it is written in this book of the covenant." Evidently they did not attach importance to the general phrase as denoting a specific order to come to Jerusalem for the purpose, instead of—as hitherto—observing the rite in the homes.

M. LAST KINGS OF JUDAH (36:1-23)

36:1-11. This section reproduces with some freedom II Kings 23:26–24:6; but vss. 12-20 give the Chronicler's own indictment of Zedekiah, final king of Judah, who would not obey even Jeremiah, and of the unteachable people who mocked the prophets sent by God, until at last **there was no remedy** (vs. 16) .

36:1-23. The End.—Rapidly in this chapter the Chronicler mentions the kings of Jerusalem during its final twenty years of independence. Incidentally, his brevity is less than fair to the last of them, Zedekiah (vs. 12). The pitiful details mattered not; he hastens on to enforce the supreme reason for the tragedy. If the

utterances of Jeremiah were sufficiently known to him, he must have agreed with the great prophet's interpretation of the decline and fall of the throne of David: Jeremiah's sad realization of the incorrigible nature of the religious blindness and moral perversity of the rulers and the people; his insight that the coming capture

9 ¶ Jehoiachin *was* eight years old when he began to reign, and he reigned three months and ten days in Jerusalem: and he did *that which was* evil in the sight of the LORD.

10 And when the year was expired, king Nebuchadnezzar sent, and brought him to Babylon, with the goodly vessels of the house of the LORD, and made Zedekiah his brother king over Judah and Jerusalem.

11 ¶ Zedekiah *was* one and twenty years old when he began to reign, and reigned eleven years in Jerusalem.

12 And he did *that which was* evil in the sight of the LORD his God, *and* humbled not himself before Jeremiah the prophet *speaking* from the mouth of the LORD.

13 And he also rebelled against king Nebuchadnezzar, who had made him swear by God: but he stiffened his neck, and hardened his heart from turning unto the LORD God of Israel.

14 ¶ Moreover all the chief of the priests, and the people, transgressed very much after all the abominations of the heathen; and polluted the house of the LORD which he had hallowed in Jerusalem.

15 And the LORD God of their fathers sent to them by his messengers, rising up betimes, and sending; because he had compassion on his people, and on his dwelling place:

16 But they mocked the messengers of God, and despised his words, and misused his prophets, until the wrath of the LORD arose against his people, till *there was* no remedy.

17 Therefore he brought upon them the king of the Chaldees, who slew their young men with the sword in the house of their sanctuary, and had no compassion upon young man or maiden, old man, or him that stooped for age: he gave *them* all into his hand.

9 Jehoi'achin was eight years old when he began to reign, and he reigned three months and ten days in Jerusalem. He did what was evil in the sight of the LORD. 10 In the spring of the year King Nebuchadnez'zar sent and brought him to Babylon, with the precious vessels of the house of the LORD, and made his brother Zedeki'ah king over Judah and Jerusalem.

11 Zedeki'ah was twenty-one years old when he began to reign, and he reigned eleven years in Jerusalem. 12 He did what was evil in the sight of the LORD his God. He did not humble himself before Jeremiah the prophet, who spoke from the mouth of the LORD. 13 He also rebelled against King Nebuchadnez'zar, who had made him swear by God; he stiffened his neck and hardened his heart against turning to the LORD, the God of Israel. 14 All the leading priests and the people likewise were exceedingly unfaithful, following all the abominations of the nations; and they polluted the house of the LORD which he had hallowed in Jerusalem.

15 The LORD, the God of their fathers, sent persistently to them by his messengers, because he had compassion on his people and on his dwelling place; 16 but they kept mocking the messengers of God, despising his words, and scoffing at his prophets, till the wrath of the LORD rose against his people, till there was no remedy.

17 Therefore he brought up against them the king of the Chalde'ans, who slew their young men with the sword in the house of their sanctuary, and had no compassion on young man or virgin, old man or aged; he gave them all into his hand.

---

9. Read probably "eighteen." Jehoiachin was king for three months only. Note therefore how conventional is the adverse verdict pronounced upon him.

---

of Jerusalem and destruction of its temple could work for good in the wisdom and purpose of God by enabling the survivors to cease to trust in outward things and to find their strength in the eternal truths of the spirit. But the Chronicler was impressively seeking to teach the same wisdom in his own way. The drama of his narrative, from Adam to Zedekiah, taught that the kingdom of Judah had come to an end because its kings and people persisted in rejecting the prophet-messengers of the living God—**till there was no remedy.**

18 And all the vessels of the house of God, great and small, and the treasures of the house of the LORD, and the treasures of the king, and of his princes; all *these* he brought to Babylon.

19 And they burnt the house of God, and brake down the wall of Jerusalem, and burnt all the palaces thereof with fire, and destroyed all the goodly vessels thereof.

20 And them that had escaped from the sword carried he away to Babylon; where they were servants to him and his sons until the reign of the kingdom of Persia:

21 To fulfil the word of the LORD by the mouth of Jeremiah, until the land had enjoyed her sabbaths: *for* as long as she lay desolate she kept sabbath, to fulfil threescore and ten years.

22 ¶ Now in the first year of Cyrus king of Persia, that the word of the LORD *spoken* by the mouth of Jeremiah might be accomplished, the LORD stirred up the spirit of Cyrus king of Persia, that he made a proclamation throughout all his kingdom, and *put it* also in writing, saying,

18 And all the vessels of the house of God, great and small, and the treasures of the house of the LORD, and the treasures of the king and of his princes, all these he brought to Babylon. 19 And they burned the house of God, and broke down the wall of Jerusalem, and burned all its palaces with fire, and destroyed all its precious vessels. 20 He took into exile in Babylon those who had escaped from the sword, and they became servants to him and to his sons until the establishment of the kingdom of Persia, 21 to fulfil the word of the LORD by the mouth of Jeremiah, until the land had enjoyed its sabbaths. All the days that it lay desolate it kept sabbath, to fulfil seventy years.

22 Now in the first year of Cyrus king of Persia, that the word of the LORD by the mouth of Jeremiah might be accomplished, the LORD stirred up the spirit of Cyrus king of Persia so that he made a proclamation throughout all his kingdom and also put it

21. **Her sabbaths:** The final Law enjoined, idealistically, that every seventh year the soil should rest uncultivated. Ten such occasions would therefore total **threescore and ten years.** The verse is a late addition to imply that legitimate worship of Yahweh was in abeyance from the fall of Jerusalem in 586 B.C. until in 538 loyal, uncontaminated Hebrew priests and laymen returned to Jerusalem from captivity in Babylon, and in 518-516 the second temple was built and dedicated.

22-23. These verses occur as Ezra 1:1-3*a*. But it does not follow that they must have been the conclusion of the Chronicler's book and that he was therefore the compiler of Ezra and Nehemiah. The contrary inference may be drawn: "Men do not take the trouble to stitch together two documents, unless they have been originally separate" (Adam C. Welch, *Post-exilic Judaism* [Edinburgh: William Blackwood & Sons, 1935],

This last chapter reads like the tolling of a funeral bell. But Chronicles was not mere delineation of a tragedy, if one recollects when and for whom it was written. This drama spoke to Jews of his time in solemn warning, but also as a command to do their duty and as an exhortation to hope. It warned them that they should "hate evil and love good"; then they would be entitled to believe that God would be with them (cf. Amos 5:14-15). It warned them to perceive that suddenly or insidiously wickedness brings ruin as its sequel. Let them honor and follow after truth and righteousness. The picture of the fallen state was so drawn that they could perceive why the disaster had happened—even as we should understand the con-

vulsions in our past history and learn how to build civilization on strong foundations.

The continuance of the kingdom had been always conditioned on the obedience of the kings to the word of prophecy which had brought the kingdom into existence. The condition was so absolute in its character that when the last king, ignoring the lessons of the past [vss. 12, 15-16], despised the message of the prophet, his kingdom fell. . . . But it had not fallen until it had created that house of God, through which the divine purpose with Israel was continued in force.[1]

Therefore let them take heart and hope, who knew that light had arisen out of darkness; who

[1] Welch, *Work of the Chronicler*, pp. 48, 158.

23 Thus saith Cyrus king of Persia, All the kingdoms of the earth hath the LORD God of heaven given me; and he hath charged me to build him a house in Jerusalem, which *is* in Judah. Who *is there* among you of all his people? The LORD his God *be* with him, and let him go up.

in writing: 23 "Thus says Cyrus king of Persia, 'The LORD, the God of heaven, has given me all the kingdoms of the earth, and he has charged me to build him a house at Jerusalem, which is in Judah. Whoever is among you of all his people, may the LORD his God be with him. Let him go up.' "

---

p. 186). The probability is that, when Chronicles was relegated to the position of the very last of the Hagiographa, these verses were added to the MSS of Chronicles in order that the Hebrew Bible should conclude on a note of hope.

---

knew that wondrously God had had compassion on his stricken people to give them a continuance and a hope, that through them his will for mankind might be fulfilled. The Chronicler wrote for men who had seen their house of God built for a second time. He was urging them to believe that their future depended on whether they would comprehend that the temple's structure was no more than visible sign of invisible grace. If they could rise to the moral demands made by a true conception of the living God, then the divine glory would fill the second temple because righteousness filled their lives. Chronicles can be an inspiring work for us if we relate its essential heroism and its spiritual insight to the circumstances of our own age.

The Book of

EZRA

and

The Book of

NEHEMIAH

Introduction and Exegesis by RAYMOND A. BOWMAN
Exposition by CHARLES W. GILKEY

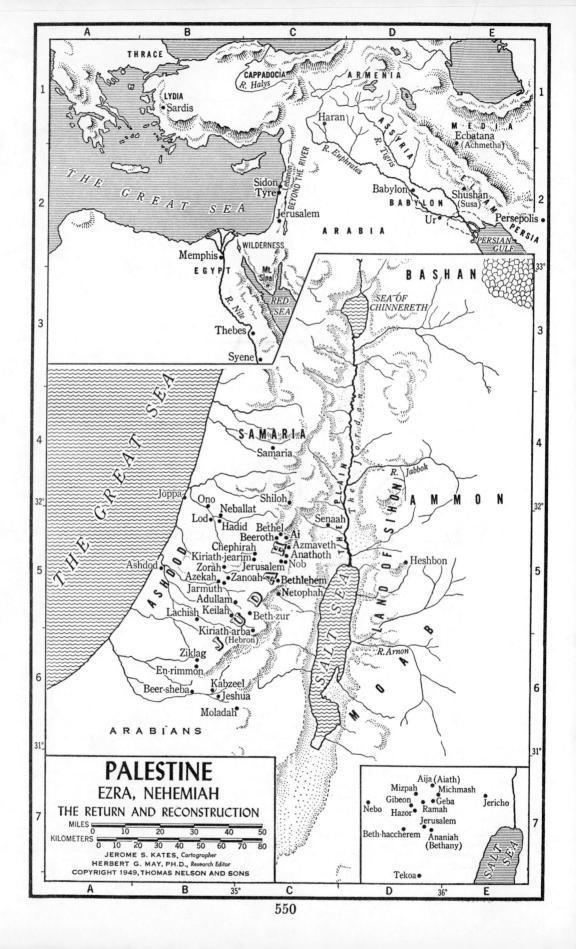

THRACE

CAPPADOCIA
R. Halys

LYDIA
Sardis

ARMENIA

ASSYRIA

R. Tigris

MEDIA

Ecbatana
(Achmetha)

Haran

R. Euphrates

THE GREAT SEA

BEYOND THE RIVER

Sidon
Tyre
Lebanon

Babylon
BABYLON

ELAM

Shushan
(Susa)

PERSIA

Persepolis

Jerusalem

ARABIA

Ur

PERSIAN
GULF

WILDERNESS

Memphis

EGYPT

Mt.
Sinai

RED
SEA

BASHAN

33°

SEA OF
CHINNERETH

R. Nile

Thebes

SALT SEA

Syene

THE GREAT SEA

SAMARIA

Samaria

The Jordan

The Plain

R. Jabbok

AMMON

32°

Joppa

Ono

Shiloh

Lod

Neballat

Senaah

Hadid
Bethel
Beeroth
Chephirah
Kiriath-jearim
Zorah
Azekah
Jarmuth
Adullam
Lachish
Keilah
Kiriath-arba
(Hebron)
Ziklag

Ai
Azmaveth
Anathoth
Jerusalem
Nob
Zanoah
Bethlehem
Netophah

Heshbon

ASHDOD

Ashdod

JUDAH

Beth-zur

LAND OF SIHON

MOAB

R. Arnon

En-rimmon

Kabzeel
Beer-sheba
Jeshua

Moladah

ARABIANS

31°

PALESTINE
EZRA, NEHEMIAH
THE RETURN AND RECONSTRUCTION

MILES 0   10   20   30   40   50
KILOMETERS 0 10 20 30 40 50 60 70 80

JEROME S. KATES, *Cartographer*
HERBERT G. MAY, PH.D., *Research Editor*
COPYRIGHT 1949, THOMAS NELSON AND SONS

Aija (Aiath)
Mizpah   Michmash
Gibeon
Nebo   Hazor   Geba
Ramah   Jericho
Jerusalem
Beth-haccherem   Ananiah
(Bethany)

SALT
SEA

Tekoa

EZRA AND NEHEMIAH

INTRODUCTION

The books known as Ezra and Nehemiah are named not for the author but for the principal personalities encountered in each. It is apparent from the versions that in antiquity all that is now included in these books was known under the title of Ezra. Indeed, in addition to the canonical books there were two other writings that bore the name Ezra (Esdras) : a recension of the canonical work, now known as the Greek Ezra, and an apocalypse in the Apocrypha with the same title.[1] There exists, therefore, the following ambiguity in the use of the name Ezra in the Greek and Latin versions:

I Esdras in the LXX = Greek Ezra (cf. p. 561)
I Esdras in Old Latin MSS = Greek Ezra (I Esdras)
I Esdras in later Latin MSS
  (post-Vulgate)   = canonical Ezra-Nehemiah as one book

II Esdras in the LXX (major MSS)   = canonical Ezra-Nehemiah as one book (chs. 1–10 = Ezra; chs. 11–23 = Nehemiah)

II Esdras in LXX[L][2] = Greek Ezra (I Esdras)
II Esdras in later Latin MSS = chs. 1–2 of the Ezra Apocalypse

III Esdras in the Vulgate = Greek Ezra (I Esdras)
IV Esdras in later Latin MSS   = chs. 3–14 of the Ezra Apocalypse

V Esdras in later Latin MSS = chs. 15–16 of the Ezra Apocalypse

[1] See article, "The Literature and Religion of the Apocrypha," Vol. I, pp. 397-98.
[2] LXXL, as elsewhere in Exeg., signifies not a single MS but the Lucianic recension.

It was Jerome (Prologus Galeatus) who first used the name "Nehemiah" for the second part of II Esdras.

I. Unity and Relationships

English Bibles treat Ezra and Nehemiah as separate books, but such practice has not always prevailed. Division into two books is first mentioned by Origen (A.D. 185-253), with the implication that such usage is Hebrew practice. But in accordance with the Talmudic tradition,[3] the oldest Hebrew codices treat Ezra-Nehemiah as a single book,[4] and the division into two books is not found in the Hebrew Bible until the Bomberg edition of 1525. Evidence for the original unity of the books in the Hebrew Bible is also seen in the fact that, though now separated, the Masoretic statistics and comments, usually found after each book of the Bible, are missing after Ezra 10:44, but are found for the entire work after Neh. 13:31. Furthermore, the Masoretic indication of the middle of the book is found only at Neh. 3:32, which is not the middle of Nehemiah but of the combined work.

The recognition of the two books, now established Christian practice, is first found in the Vulgate, and Jerome is the first to use the title Nehemiah. Not all Christian churches, however, recognized the separate books, for both Eusebius[5] and Melito of Sardis[6] knew but "Ezra," and the oldest Christian indices of Old Testament books recognized but a single work.

[3] Baba Bathra 15a.
[4] Cf. G. B. de Rossi, Variae lectiones Veteris Testamenti (Parma: Ex regio typographeo, 1784-88), IV, 157.
[5] Church History IV. 26. 14.
[6] See article, "The Canon of the Old Testament," Vol. I, p. 40.

Although the Septuagint later separated Ezra-Nehemiah into two books, doubtless under Christian influence and the example of the Vulgate, it originally recognized but one book. Codex Vaticanus (LXX[B]) proceeds without interruption from Ezra to Nehemiah and designates all as II Esdras (Esdras[β1]). The Greek Ezra recension (I Esdras; cf. below) treats the books as a unit, showing no sign of a break between them or a knowledge of their separate existence. It has been assumed, however, from the silence about Ezra in Ecclus. 44:1–49:13 and II Macc. 2:13, which mention only Nehemiah, that the story of Nehemiah may have circulated separately.[7]

The evidence is overwhelming that Ezra and Nehemiah, now separated, were once regarded as a literary unit and should now be so considered from the standpoint of authorship, purpose, and teaching. Under such circumstances it is easy to understand how some of the Ezra narrative has intruded into the book of Nehemiah.

But the original literary unit was even greater than Ezra-Nehemiah. It is a striking fact that II Chr. 36:23 concludes abruptly in the middle of Cyrus' edict and that II Chr. 36:22-23 is repeated in Ezra 1:1-3a, finishing the fragmentary ending of the Chronicles. The "Greek Ezra," another recension from the Hebrew text, includes even more of Chronicles, through II Chr. 35–36. Such duplication seems a deliberate device to indicate an original connection between Ezra-Nehemiah and the books of Chronicles. The conclusion that Ezra-Nehemiah was originally part of Chronicles is further supported by the fact that the same late Hebrew language, the same distinctive literary peculiarities that mark the style of the Chronicler, are found throughout Ezra-Nehemiah. The same presuppositions, interests, points of view, and theological and ecclesiastical conceptions so dominate all these writings that it is apparent that Chronicles-Ezra-Nehemiah was originally a literary unit, the product of one school of thought, if not of a single mind, that can be called "the Chronicler."

II. Canon

In the English Bible Ezra and Nehemiah follow the Chronicles as they did originally. The English order follows the Hellenistic (Alexandrian) treatment of the books, which abolished the Jewish distinction between "the Prophets" and "the Writings." In the tripartite division of the Hebrew Bible (Law, Prophets, and Writings) Ezra and Nehemiah, along with

Chronicles, are classified not among the "prophetic" books (as Samuel and Kings are), but among "the Writings" (like Psalms, Job, and Ecclesiastes). Such location is a witness to their relatively late composition, when the other divisions of the Hebrew Bible were regarded as closed canonically.

Modern printed Hebrew Bibles follow the German Hebrew manuscripts, which place Nehemiah between Daniel and Chronicles. The Babylonian Jewish practice placed Ezra and Chronicles after Esther, concluding the section of "the Writings,"[8] while Palestinian manuscripts began "the Writings" section with Chronicles and concluded it with the single work Ezra, placed after Esther and Daniel.

Old Latin Bibles differed greatly in the placement of Ezra-Nehemiah. Cassiodorus[9] placed them between Judith and the books of Maccabees, while Augustine[10] put them between the Maccabees and the Psalms. They are omitted entirely in a list from the last half of the fourth century A.D. found by Theodor Mommsen[11] at Cheltenham.

Doubtless mere chance accounts for the omission of any reference to Ezra or Nehemiah in the New Testament, but there is a definite repudiation of Chronicles-Ezra-Nehemiah in the canon of the Syrian Christians. Chronicles was originally omitted from the Syrian translation of the Bible. When a Jewish Targum of the book[12] was adopted in its stead, Aphraates quoted from it, but Ephraim omitted any commentary on the book and it was not generally accepted. There is no Targum for Ezra-Nehemiah. Theodore of Mopsuestia omitted Ezra-Nehemiah as well as Chronicles, Esther, and Job in his conception of the canon. The Nestorian canon and that adopted by several Monophysite groups omit all of Chronicles-Ezra-Nehemiah.

III. Author

Ezra and Nehemiah unquestionably have been formed and transmitted by the anonymous person known as the Chronicler, the author of the books of Chronicles.[13] Only what can be learned of him from his work is known. Since he is greatly concerned with the temple and its cultus, it is assumed that he was a minister in the temple, quite possibly a Levite; and because he shows a special interest in the musicians, which were one of the minor orders of temple servants, it has been conjectured that the

---

[7] Cf. Theodor Nöldeke, "Bemerkungen zum hebräischen Ben Sirā," Zeitschrift für die alttestamentliche Wissenschaft, XX (1900), 89.

[8] Cf. Babylonian Talmud: Baba Bathra 14b.

[9] De institutione divinarum literarum XIV.

[10] On Christian Doctrine II. 8. 13.

[11] "Zur lateinischen Stichometrie," Hermes, XXI (1886), 142 ff.; cf. Adolf Harnack's review in Theologische Litteraturzeitung, XI (1886), 175.

[12] Cf. article, "Text and Ancient Versions of the Old Testament," Vol. I, p. 57.

[13] See Intro. to Chronicles, pp. 341-42.

Chronicler was probably one of the singers of the guild of Asaph.[14]

The peculiar interests and points of view of the author of the books of Chronicles, which are best learned from his work in Chronicles, where there is a control in the canonical sources that he used, also are constantly in evidence in Ezra-Nehemiah. His striking literary style [15] is also much in evidence in Ezra-Nehemiah, indicating that his literary activity also extended there.

The view that Ezra was the author of Chronicles-Ezra-Nehemiah, presented in the Talmud (Baba Bathra 15a), is also held by the rabbis, the church fathers, and most of the older commentators.[16] Even today William F. Albright has argued that the Chronicler was Ezra.[17]

IV. Date

From the nature of his work the Chronicler has left but few clues in the form of historical allusions from which to date Chronicles-Ezra-Nehemiah. In I Chr. 3:15-24 a genealogy purporting to list the descendants of David appears to extend six generations beyond Zerubbabel (ca. 520 B.C.). Counting thirty years to a generation,[18] the last generation mentioned, which was presumably the Chronicler's own, must be dated no earlier than ca. 350 B.C. Support for such a date is claimed in the list of high priests in Neh. 12:10 ff., which includes Jaddua, whom Josephus claims (cf. Neh. 13:28) was high priest at the time of Alexander the Great (ca. 332 B.C.). Principally on such basis the majority of scholars now date the work of the Chronicler 350-250 B.C.[19] Resorting to more subjective criteria for dating, such as style, vocabulary, and polemics, some urge the still later date of 300-250 B.C.[20] or even as late as some time after

Ben Sirach (ca. 180 B.C.).[21] By thus assuming that the Chronicler was writing more than a century after the events he records, it is easy to understand why his statements can be challenged as unhistorical.

However, there has been a reaction to such a late date for the Chronicler. It is argued that in the crucial passage, I Chr. 3:21, a later hand has corrupted the text, and that originally there were but four generations after Zerubbabel.[22] If with Rudolf Kittel the generation is computed at twenty instead of thirty years,[23] six generations would extend to 400 B.C., and four would be 440 B.C. for the period of the Chronicler. But it is now widely believed that I Chr. 1–9 was originally not part of the Chronicler's work.[24] This view eliminates I Chr. 3 as evidence for the Chronicler's date. Furthermore, the other passage, Neh. 12:10 ff., has also been regarded as a secondary addition to the text.[25] With the elimination of these supposed historical allusions and the interpretation of the supporting evidence adduced from linguistic and polemic bases in other ways, the only remaining evidence for date is the time of the last datable event in the books—the mission of Ezra.

Those who insist that Ezra arrived in Palestine during the interval between Nehemiah's administrations (cf. Ezra 7:8) argue for a date soon after 432 B.C.[26] and no earlier than 433 B.C., the end of Nehemiah's first administration.[27] Since the Chronicler faultily places Ezra before Nehemiah (see below), it is suggested that several generations must have elapsed for the

Making and Meaning (Nashville: Cokesbury Press, 1937), p. 77; Pfeiffer, *Intro. to O.T.*, pp. 811-12.

[21] Adolphe Lods, *The Prophets and the Rise of Judaism* (tr. S. H. Hooke; New York: E. P. Dutton & Co., 1937), p. 299.

[22] Cf. Curtis and Madsen, *op. cit.*, pp. 6, 102; J. W. Rothstein and Johannes Hänel, *Kommentar zum ersten Buch der Chronik* (Leipzig: A. Deichert, 1927; "Kommentar zum Alten Testament"), pp. 43, 46-47; Aage Bentzen, *Introduction to the Old Testament* (Copenhagen: G. E. C. Gad, 1948-49), II, 215; Wilhelm Rudolph, *Esra und Nehemia* (Tübingen: J. C. B. Mohr, 1949; "Handbuch zum Alten Testament"), p. xxiv.

[23] *Die Bücher der Chronik* (Göttingen: Vandenhoeck & Ruprecht, 1902; "Handkommentar zum Alten Testament"), p. 26.

[24] Cf. Adam C. Welch, *Post-Exilic Judaism* (Edinburgh: William Blackwood & Sons, 1935), pp. 185-86; *The Work of the Chronicler* (London: British Academy, 1939), pp. 1, 12, n. 1; Christopher R. North, *The Old Testament Interpretation of History* (London: Epworth Press, 1946), p. 116; Martin Noth, *Überlieferungsgeschichtliche Studien I* (Halle: M. Niemeyer, 1943), p. 120, n. 1; Rudolph, *loc. cit.*

[25] Noth, *loc. cit.*; Rudolph, *loc. cit.*; Howard Crosby, *The Book of Nehemiah* (New York: Armstrong & Co., 1877; "Lange's Commentary"), p. 2.

[26] Rothstein and Hänel, *op. cit.*, p. lxix.

[27] Artur Weiser, *Einleitung in das alte Testament* (2d ed.; Göttingen: Vandenhoeck & Ruprecht, 1949), p. 237.

[14] Cf. R. H. Pfeiffer, *Introduction to the Old Testament* (New York: Harper & Bros., 1941), p. 797; C. C. Torrey, *Ezra Studies* (Chicago: University of Chicago Press, 1910), p. 211.

[15] Cf. S. R. Driver, *An Introduction to the Literature of the Old Testament* (new ed.; New York: Charles Scribner's Sons, 1913), pp. 535-40; Francis Brown, "Chronicles, I and II," in James Hastings, ed., *Dictionary of the Bible* (New York: Charles Scribner's Sons, 1898), I, 389-97; Edward L. Curtis and Albert A. Madsen, *A Critical and Exegetical Commentary on the Books of Chronicles* (New York: Charles Scribner's Sons, 1910; "International Critical Commentary"), pp. 27-36.

[16] Otto Zöckler, *The Books of the Chronicles* (tr. J. G. Murphy; New York: Armstrong & Co., 1877; "Lange's Commentary"), pp. 8-11.

[17] "The Date and Personality of the Chronicler," *Journal of Biblical Literature*, XL (1921), 104-24; cf. "A Brief History of Judah from the Days of Josiah to Alexander the Great," *The Biblical Archaeologist*, IX (1946), 15.

[18] E.g., Curtis and Madsen, *op. cit.*, p. 5.

[19] E.g., W. O. E. Oesterley and T. H. Robinson, *An Introduction to the Books of the Old Testament* (London: Society for Promoting Christian Knowledge, 1934), pp. 111-12; Driver, *op. cit.*, p. 518.

[20] E.g., H. Wheeler Robinson, *The Old Testament: Its*

Chronicler to have won uncomplaining acceptance of his proposed order, and the date must be about 400 B.C., with perhaps the latitude of a decade more. Rudolph warns that not much more time can be allowed since the secondary insertions in I Chr. 3:15 ff. and Neh. 3:10 ff. reach only to about 400 B.C. when reckoned as above,[28] and the lists in Neh. 12:1-9, 12-26 must be dated before the death of Darius II (405 B.C.) and thus were probably incorporated not long afterward.[29] Albright, who identifies the Chronicler with Ezra, now ascribes Ezra's activity to 427 B.C., during the reign of Artaxerxes I (cf. Ezra 7:8), and thus dates the "Chronicler" about 400 B.C., just as Martin Noth did in his earlier work.[30]

Such dating, which is possible only by emending Ezra 7:8, is weak in that it rests on the assumption that Ezra's activity fell within the reign of Artaxerxes I, which is less likely than that he arrived during the time of Artaxerxes II (cf. Ezra 7:8). In the latter case the Chronicler's work could be no earlier than 397 B.C., but with a similar allowance to that mentioned above of time elapsed between the activity of Ezra and the work of the Chronicler, the date of the Chronicler would be no earlier than about 365-350 B.C.

V. Sources

The question of sources is closely related to that of date. An eyewitness may stand on his own account (e.g., Nehemiah), but one removed a century or more from the events he records needs reliable sources of information if his credibility is to be maintained. The great controversy over Ezra-Nehemiah is centered in this issue. Those who posit a very late date for the Chronicler find it easy to be critical of his narrative and suspicious of his results. They insist that the few sources he employed were preserved almost literally (e.g., Nehemiah), but most of his work is thought to be his own composition, the product of his fertile imagination and therefore unhistorical. He is regarded as a person of great imagination, inventive skill, and firm convictions, who wrote his work as fiction, forging speeches and documents as needed, and even deliberately distorting known facts to support his peculiar theses. "It is evident," so Torrey claims, "that the Chronicler became an editor more from necessity than from choice. By taste and gift he was a novelist. He would doubtless have preferred to give freer rein to his imagination in composing the story of the Jews and their antecedents. But he was now

writing not to interest, but with an apologetic purpose."[31] Such scholars believe that he had almost no sources for the events he portrays, and the sources that he mentions by name (Neh. 7:5; 12:23) are regarded with suspicion as part of his "imaginary library."[32] Wherever the Chronicler's strikingly peculiar literary style or his favorite concepts are manifest it is assumed that the work is the Chronicler's own invention and hence unhistorical.

Others tend to assign to the Chronicler a date almost contemporary with the events he records, in which case the sources are less important. Nevertheless they insist that he used many sources in the framing of his narrative. While they agree that he could reproduce his sources literally, without much of his tampering so long as the material did not conflict with his own ideas,[33] and that in his editorial activity he created passages to join his sources and give a consecutive narrative, such scholars minimize the creative activity of the Chronicler. Where the Chronicler's characteristics are impressed on the material, it is recognized that he may have created those passages concerned with his favorite themes and interests, but it is also believed that lying behind the Chronicler's façade there may be credible sources that he has employed, working over them thoroughly and leaving on them the evidence of his activity. Therefore such scholars give greater historical weight to the Chronicler's narrative and attempt, wherever possible, to probe behind his text to the sources he seems to employ.[34]

The major difference between the two schools of interpretation thus concerns primarily that material in which the Chronicler's style and ideas are clearly apparent. It can exist because even after extensive study of the Chronicler's activity in the books of Chronicles, where the canonical texts of Samuel and Kings, etc., are indisputably his sources,[35] the results of such analysis are not decisive. It is apparent that the Chronicler could and did copy, revise, and compose even where he was obviously using a canonical source. The editorial technique of the Chronicler, demonstrable in the books of Chronicles, must be that employed in Ezra-Nehemiah with whatever sources he used, even though his work cannot be checked against the originals, as in Chronicles.

Even a casual reader will be impressed by the

---

[28] Rothstein-Hänel, op. cit., pp. lxvii-lxviii.

[29] Rudolph, loc. cit.

[30] Die Gesetze im Pentateuch (Halle: M. Niemeyer, 1940), p. 67, n. 2.

[31] Ezra Studies, pp. 250-51.

[32] Ibid., p. 141, n. 5.

[33] Rudolph, op. cit., p. xxiii.

[34] Cf. L. S. Batten, A Critical and Exegetical Commentary on the Books of Ezra and Nehemiah (New York: Charles Scribner's Sons, 1913; "International Critical Commentary"), p. 24.

[35] Cf. Zöckler, Books of Chronicles, pp. 25-27; Torrey, Ezra Studies, pp. 208-51.

evidences of the Chronicler's use of sources in Ezra-Nehemiah. The narrative does not always run smoothly and continuously. Gaps occur where no actual sources were available, e.g., during the reign of Cambyses and during the interval between the time of Ezra and the coming of Nehemiah, as the Chronicler understood the chronology.[36] Often there are abrupt transitions between passages. A narrative is begun and is stopped abruptly when it is realized that a letter to be employed would duplicate the story (cf. Ezra 5:3-5). Twice there is a shift in language from Hebrew to Aramaic as the source appears in the Aramaic language (Ezra 4:8–6:18; 7:12-26), and there is a perplexing shift from the use of the third-person pronoun to the first (cf. Ezra 8:15–9:15; Neh. 1:1–7:7; 12:31; 13:6 ff.) which appears to be of greater significance than a slip on the part of the author.

Further evidence for sources may be seen in the fact that the Chronicler did not always understand the significance of his sources and therefore ignorantly misused them. A list is used twice in different contexts (Neh. 11:3-24; cf. I Chr. 9:1-44), and a source indicating antagonism toward the building of the city wall is treated as opposition to the rebuilding of the temple (Ezra 4:11 ff.).

A. Claimed Sources.—Twice in Ezra-Nehemiah the Chronicler actually mentions records, "the book of the genealogy" (Neh. 7:5) and "the book of the Chronicles," which is not his canonical work but presumably a temple chronicle containing historical data as well as lists (cf. Neh. 12:23). These supposed records are not considered seriously by some[37] but are regarded as being on the same plane as the many otherwise unknown sources mentioned in the books of Chronicles. Driver, however, agrees with Wellhausen's conjecture that the "Book of Chronicles" may be one of the "older sources, accessible to the compiler."[38]

B. Earlier Canonical Sources.—The Chronicler's knowledge of earlier canonical books of the Bible and his use of them is demonstrated in his books of Chronicles but is less readily observed in Ezra-Nehemiah where no earlier canonical records existed for so much of the narrative. The historical references to Haggai and Zechariah in Ezra 5:1-2 were doubtless part of the Aramaic source, but the allusion to Hag. 2:1-4 in Ezra 3:12-13 seems to come from the Chronicler's hand. The scriptural dependence in Neh. 1:5, 7-8 may be due to him also, but the more extensive prayers (Ezra 9:5 ff.; Neh. 9:6 ff.), which also show extensive familiarity with scripture, may have come from elsewhere.

C. Nehemiah's Memoirs.—Although the extent of Nehemiah's narrative is debated, no one challenges the authenticity of the memoir concerning him that the Chronicler has incorporated in his work. Without making allowance for minor touches by the Chronicler, the general limits of the memoir of Nehemiah seem to be Neh. 1:1–7:73a; 11:1-2; 12:27-43; 13:4-31.

The following are some of the variations from the description given above of the extent of the Nehemiah story as found among scholars: In ch. 1 Batten omits vss. 5-11a.[39] In ch. 2 he regards only vss. 1-7 as genuine,[40] while Torrey holds vss. 1-6, 9b-20 as Nehemiah's.[41] Ch. 3 is regarded by Torrey as the Chronicler's work[42] and it is clearly intrusive in Nehemiah's memoirs, but Batten denies that the Chronicler composed it,[43] and Rudolph suggests that Nehemiah himself incorporated it into his narrative.[44] In ch. 7, while all regard vss. 1-5 as authentic, Rudolph includes the list in vss. 6-73a as one Nehemiah himself included in the record.[45] In ch. 11 usually only vss. 1-2 are regarded as Nehemiah's, but Rudolph would also include vss. 20, 25a,[46] while Carl Steuernagel holds that the kernel of vss. 3-24 are also Nehemiah's.[47] The passage 12:27-43 is regarded as authentic,[48] but Steuernagel would limit the genuine material to vss. 31-32, 37-40,[49] and Rudolph indicates as Nehemiah's vss. 27aα, 30, 31-32, 37-40, 43.[50] The lists of names (vss. 33-36, 41-42) are doubtless supplements to the text. Some reject ch. 13 as the Chronicler's work,[51] but those who find anything genuine in the chapter find it in vss. 4-31. Batten, however, begins the authentic material with vs. 6.[52]

Nehemiah's memoirs, written not very long after 432 B.C. (cf. Neh. 5:14) and preserved by the Chronicler literally, with relatively little interpolation or reworking,[53] are one of the most accurate historical sources in the Old Testament, the only undisputed source for Jewish history between 520-175 B.C. The memoirs appear to be a memorial inscription, a type

[36] Cf. Rudolph, *loc. cit.*
[37] Torrey, *Ezra Studies*, p. 141, n. 5.
[38] Driver, *Intro. to the Literature of the O.T.*, p. 551.

[39] *Op. cit.*, pp. 188-89.
[40] *Ibid.*, pp. 15, 197.
[41] *The Composition and Historical Value of Ezra-Nehemiah* (Giessen: J. Ricker, 1895; "Beihefte zur Zeitschrift für die alttestamentliche Wissenschaft"), p. 50.
[42] *Ibid.*, pp. 37-38.
[43] *Op. cit.*, p. 207.
[44] *Op. cit.*, p. 211.
[45] *Ibid.*
[46] *Ibid.*, pp. 187-88.
[47] *Lehrbuch der Einleitung in das Alte Testament* (Tübingen: J. C. B. Mohr, 1912), pp. 423, 426.
[48] Otto Eissfeldt, *Einleitung in das Alte Testament* (Tübingen: J. C. B. Mohr, 1934), pp. 588-89.
[49] *Op. cit.*, p. 426.
[50] *Op. cit.*, p. 198.
[51] Torrey, *Composition*, pp. 42-50.
[52] *Op. cit.*, pp. 289-90.
[53] Rudolph, *op. cit.*, pp. 211-12.

familiar in the ancient Near East.[54] By placing his memoirs before God in the temple Nehemiah doubtless sought to stir the memory of the Lord regarding his good works and thereby to be assured of the "name" that he as a eunuch (cf. Neh. 2:1) could not obtain through his posterity (cf. Isa. 56:3-5).[55] It was probably there in the temple archives that the Chronicler found Nehemiah's text.

D. Ezra's Report.—Since Ezra's narrative, like Nehemiah's, is written partly in the first person (Ezra 7:27-28; 8:1-34; cf. 9:1-15) it has the appearance of being autobiographical and is often assumed to be so. But lexical and syntactical analysis of the material indicates no real linguistic difference between the "I" portions of the story and those written in the third person, and it is asserted that therefore no "primitive" Ezra story can be dissociated from the rest of the Chronicler's work in which it is supposedly set.[56] It is usually assumed that the language of the whole is the Chronicler's since it seems uniformly to agree with his literary style, and those who regard the Chronicler's work with suspicion deny historicity to the Ezra narrative; some even deny the existence of Ezra himself (cf. p. 565).[57] Such scholars regard the use of the first-person pronoun as a literary device to gain greater vividness in the narrative. As such it would have its parallels in Enoch, Tobit, the Aḥiqar papyrus, and other works from the Near East.[58] The shift from first to third person in the narrative is believed to depend upon the extent to which the author imaginatively enters into his narrative.

More recently there have been challenges to the former use of linguistic statistics to relate the whole composition to the Chronicler. The attack attempts to show that the Chronicler's language is merely that of late Hebrew. A com-

parison of the linguistic usage in the Ezra memoirs with that of the Chronicler as seen elsewhere may show that when those linguistic phenomena which have their parallels elsewhere in late Hebrew are excluded, there remains but one element (the expression "there should be no . . ." in Ezra 9:14) that the Ezra source and the Chronicler have in common.[59] It is assumed that "Ezra himself is the composer of the Ezra narrative" but that the Chronicler has here and there worked it over, leaving his trace which is so distinctive that his work can easily be distinguished from the original.[60] In the Ezra memoirs the passages in the first person are claimed to be "clearly extracts from some record which Ezra kept of his work; and they appear to be *verbatim* extracts" while those in the third person "may well offer the gist of extracts from the same source."[61] Some hold that in addition to the first-person narrative the Chronicler, who shaped the Ezra story, had at his disposal a revised and amplified edition of Ezra's memoirs.[62] It has been conjectured that the Ezra narrative was written by a contemporary of Ezra who was still alive in 430-420 B.C., and that except for Ezra 7:1-26; 8:14 the Ezra materials are a unified whole, a valuable source of information.[63]

Judged by the narrative itself, rather than on purely linguistic grounds, the Ezra story includes Ezra 7:11–10:44; Neh. 7:73*b*–9:5. For the original sequence of events see pp. 560-61.

There is more scholarly variation in estimating the extent of the Ezra narrative than in that of Nehemiah.[64] Although Torrey also defines the Ezra story, he nevertheless regards it all as unhistorical fiction. The following differences occur: Ezra 7 is accepted in its entirety by some,[65] although Lods believed that 7:1-10 is by a redactor who used Ezra's memoirs and amplified them.[66] Others, however, limit the original material to vss. 1-10, 27-28[67] or more usually

[54] Cf. Sigmund Mowinckel, *Stadtholderen Nehemia* (Kristiania: 1916), pp. 89-159; "Die vorderasiatischen königs-und fürsteninschriften," in Hans Schmidt, ed., ΕΥΧΑΡΙΣΤΗΡΙΟΝ (Göttingen: Vandenhoeck & Ruprecht, 1923), p. 278; N. H. Snaith, "The Historical Books," in H. H. Rowley, ed., *The Old Testament and Modern Study* (Oxford: Clarendon Press, 1951), pp. 112-13.

[55] Rudolf Kittel, *Geschichte des Volkes Israel* (2nd ed.; Stuttgart: W. Kohlhammer, 1929), III, 610; Eissfeldt, *op. cit.*, p. 589; Gustav Hölscher, *Die Bücher Ezra und Nehemia* (4th ed., E. Kautzsch and A. Bertholet; Tübingen: J. C. B. Mohr, 1923), p. 497; Rudolph, *op. cit.*, p. 212; Bentzen, *Intro. to O.T.*, I, 247.

[56] Cf. Arvid S. Kapelrud, *The Question of Authorship in the Ezra-Narrative* (Oslo: J. Dybwad, 1944), pp. 95-96.

[57] Maurice Vernes, *Précis d'histoire juive* (Paris: Hachette, 1889), pp. 572 ff.; Torrey, *Composition*, pp. 51-65; *Ezra Studies*, pp. 238-48; Hölscher, *Esra und Nehemia*, pp. 491 ff.; Alfred Loisy, *La religion d'Israël* (3rd ed.; Paris: Emile Nourry, 1933), pp. 228-29; Pfeiffer, *Intro. to O.T.*, pp. 816-30.

[58] Cf. Torrey, *Ezra Studies*, pp. 244-46; Sigmund Mowinckel, *Ezra den Skriftlaerde* (Kristiania: 1916), pp. 49-61; Kapelrud, *op. cit.*, p. 95.

[59] Cf. Rudolph, *op. cit.*, pp. 163-65; cf. Kittel, *Geschichte des Volkes Israel*, III, 543-44.

[60] Cf. Rudolph, *op. cit.*, p. 165.

[61] Oesterley and Robinson, *Intro. to Books of O.T.*, p. 125.

[62] W. W. Baudissin, *Einleitung in die Bücher des Alten Testamentes* (Leipzig: S. Hirzel, 1901), p. 289; Kittel, *Geschichte des Volkes Israel*, III, pp. 542-44; cf. Pfeiffer, *Intro. to O.T.*, p. 832, n. 11.

[63] Frieder Ahlemann, "Zur Esra-Quelle," *Zeitschrift für die alttestamentliche Wissenschaft*, LIX (1942-43), 77-98.

[64] Cf. Pfeiffer, *Intro. to O.T.*, pp. 830-31.

[65] Julius A. Bewer, *The Literature of the Old Testament* (rev. ed.; New York: Columbia University Press, 1933), p. 282; Friedrich Bleek, *Einleitung in das Alte Testament* (4th ed.; Berlin: Georg Reimer, 1878), p. 282; H. H. Schaeder, *Esra der Schreiber* (Tübingen: J. C. B. Mohr, 1930; "Beiträge zur historischen Theologie"), p. 9.

[66] *Histoire de la littérature hébraïque et juive* (Paris: Payot, 1950), p. 548.

[67] Torrey, *Ezra Studies*, p. 157.

to vss. 11-28 [68] or vss. 12-28.[69] Still others would limit the Ezra narrative to vss. 27-28.[70] Most authorities regard all of Ezra 8 as part of the Ezra memoirs, but some would conclude the original material at vs. 34 [71] and Batten limits it to vss. 15-19, 21-25, 28-29, 31-32, with vs. 36 dubious.[72] The tendency is to attribute all of Ezra 9 to the Ezra memoirs, but Eissfeldt is suspicious of the prayer and regards only vss. 1-5 as fundamentally genuine.[73] Batten holds that in ch. 9, vss. 1-11a, 13-15 are part of the Ezra story.[74] Ezra 10 is regarded by almost all as part of the Ezra narrative, but Cornill suggests that the memoirs "suddenly break off at ix.15 . . . due to the interposition of a strange hand: the events of the next thirteen years were clearly of too dismal a character to make it desirable to perpetuate the memory of them." [75] Some regard Ezra 10 as indirectly genuine, based on the original memoirs.[76]

Part of the Ezra memoirs have intruded into the book of Nehemiah (cf. pp. 560-61) . Schaeder considers Neh. 7:6-73 to be part of the Ezra memoirs.[77] Torrey considers only vss. 70-73 part of the Ezra story,[78] but the majority of scholars consider only vs. 73b as authentic.[79] All of Neh. 8 is usually attributed to the Ezra memoirs, but some regard it as derived indirectly through a document based on the original narrative.[80] Oesterley and Robinson, however, recognize as authentic Ezra narrative only

8:12-18.[81] Most scholars consider all of Neh. 9 as part of Ezra's memoirs, but Cornill, regarding vs. 5 as rewritten, limits the authentic portion to vss. 6-38.[82] Most probably, however, only Neh. 9:1-5 belongs to the Ezra story.[83] Many scholars consider Neh. 10 also a part of the Ezra story,[84] either received directly or indirectly as an expansion of the original Ezra memoirs.[85] Oesterley and Robinson consider Neh. 10 "in the main" part of the Ezra memoirs.[86] But it is much more likely that the narrative there is related to the Nehemiah records.[87]

E. Aramaic Source.—The Aramaic material in Ezra is so concentrated (Ezra 4:7–6:18; 7:12-26) that at least Ezra 4:7–6:18 was probably part of a single source. Aside from a few small sections (Ezra 5:1-5; 6:14-18) and some connecting links (Ezra 4:23-24; 6:1-2) , the Aramaic material purports to be correspondence between the foes of the Jews and the Persian court (Ezra 4:7-22; 5:6-17; 6:3-12) and the royal firman given to Ezra (Ezra 7:12-26) . Thus all are purported to be official documents, written as might be expected in Aramaic, one of the important languages of the Persian empire.[88] The narrative sections in Aramaic, written by the compiler, show native skill and indicate that he was not a mere copyist.[89]

It has been argued unsuccessfully that Ezra 1–2 has been translated to Hebrew from an Aramaic original,[90] just as Ezra 4:6-7 probably has been, and that Ezra 5:1–6:15 has been converted from Hebrew to Aramaic.[91] But the block of Aramaic (Ezra 4:7–6:18) is considered as a unit that came to the hand of the Chronicler, who compiled Ezra-Nehemiah. It has been explained as the product of a Jew, working with the friendly Persian official Mithredath to transmit to the court a historical document referring

[68] Eissfeldt, *op. cit.*, p. 585.

[69] C. C. Cornill, *Introduction to the Canonical Books of the Old Testament* (tr. G. H. Box; London: Williams & Norgate, 1907), p. 244; Driver, *Intro. to the Literature of the O.T.*, p. 550; Ernst Sellin, *Einleitung in das Alte Testament*, ed. Leonhard Rost (8th ed.; Heidelberg: Quelle & Meyer, 1950), p. 178.

[70] Batten, *op. cit.*, pp. 16, 316; Baudissin, *op. cit.*, p. 288, n. 5; Alfred Bertholet, *Die Bücher Esra und Nehemia* (Tübingen: J. C. B. Mohr, 1902; "Kurzer Hand-Commentar zum Alten Testament"), pp. xiv, 34-35; Kittel, *Geschichte des Volkes Israel*, III, 567; Carl Siegfried, *Esra, Nehemia, und Esther* (Göttingen: Vandenhoeck & Ruprecht, 1901; "Handkommentar zum Alten Testament"), pp. 9, 55.

[71] Bertholet, *op. cit.*, pp. xiv, 38; W. H. Kosters, "Ezra-Nehemiah," in T. K. Cheyne and J. Sutherland Black, eds., *Encyclopaedia Biblica* (New York: The Macmillan Co., 1901), Vol. II, col. 1479; Oesterley and Robinson, *op. cit.*, p. 125.

[72] *Op. cit.*, pp. 16, 320-30.

[73] *Op. cit.*, p. 586.

[74] *Op. cit.*, p. 16, 330 ff.

[75] *Op. cit.*, p. 245.

[76] Bertholet, *op. cit.*, pp. xiv, 42; Kosters, in Cheyne and Black, *Encyclopaedia Biblica*, Vol. II, col. 1479; Siegfried, *op. cit.*, p. 9; Steuernagel, *Lehrbuch der Einleitung in A.T.*, p. 421; cf. Batten, *op. cit.*, p. 17.

[77] *Esra der Schreiber*, p. 15.

[78] *Ezra Studies*, p. 267.

[79] Oesterley and Robinson, *loc. cit.*; Rudolph, *op. cit.*, pp. 26-27, 141-42; Steuernagel, *op. cit.*, p. 424; *et al.*

[80] Cornill, *op. cit.*, p. 249; Steuernagel, *op. cit.*, pp. 424-25.

[81] *Loc. cit.*

[82] *Op. cit.*, p. 248.

[83] Cf. Exeg., *ad loc.*; Rudolph, *op. cit.*, pp. 155-56.

[84] Torrey, *Ezra Studies*, pp. 272-73, 282-84.

[85] Baudissin, *op. cit.*, pp. 292, 297; Bleek, *op. cit.*, p. 281; Cornill, *op. cit.*, pp. 245-46, 248-49; Driver, *op. cit.*, pp. 550-51; Siegfried, *op. cit.*, pp. 5-6; Steuernagel, *loc. cit.*

[86] *Loc. cit.*

[87] Cf. Exeg. *ad loc.*; Lods, *Histoire de la littérature hébraïque*, p. 551; Rudolph, *op. cit.*, pp. 172-81.

[88] Cf. Raymond A. Bowman, "Aramaeans, Aramaic, and the Bible," *Journal of Near Eastern Studies*, VII (1948), 76-84.

[89] Cf. Oesterley and Robinson, *op. cit.*, p. 126.

[90] Albin Van Hoonacker, "Zorobabel et le second temple," *Le Muséon*, X (1891), 72-96, 232-60, 379-97, 489-515, 634-44.

[91] W. M. L. De Wette, *Lehrbuch der historischen-kritischen Einleitung in die kanonischen und apokryphischen Bücher des Alten Testamentes* (ed. Eberhard Schrader; Berlin: Georg Reimer, 1860), p. 387; W. H. Kosters, *Die Wiederherstellung Israels in der persischen Periode* (Heidelberg: J. Hörning, 1895), p. 62, n. 1; Torrey, *Composition*, p. 13.

to the persecution of the Jews and showing that the Persian court had always resulted in supporting them. The purpose of the document was to gain royal support against the enemies of the Jews (cf. Exeg. on Ezra 4:7-16).[92] This interpretation, which is also intended to explain that the disordered Persian chronology of the Aramaic material was due to the carelessness of the original compiler rather than to late Jewish ignorance of Persian chronology, sounds attractive, but it has weaknesses and is unlikely.[93] The incorrect chronological order must be explained otherwise (cf. Exeg. on Ezra 4:4b–6:22).

Torrey once (1910) regarded the several documents as separate sources received by the Chronicler, whose hand he saw only in Ezra 6:9-10, 15-18,[94] although formerly (1896) he had recognized the Chronicler's touch also in Ezra 4:9-10, 24.[95] Later, however, he followed Nöldeke in treating the Aramaic material as the work of the Chronicler.[96] The historical validity of the Aramaic documents in Ezra is still hotly debated. H. H. Graetz, who declared them all forgeries,[97] has been followed by many others.[98] Pfeiffer claims that each of the Aramaic documents must be judged separately, and concludes that the Persian documents in Ezra are spurious. "They were written by the author of the narratives in which they are contained."[99]

Since the discovery of the Aramaic papyri of the Persian period it has been common practice to conclude, as some Aramaic specialists have done, that the style of the Aramaic in Ezra approximates that of the papyri of the fifth century B.C.[100] Torrey, to the contrary, assigns all biblical Aramaic to the second and third centuries B.C., where it would support his date for the Chronicler's authorship.[101] Later exhaustive comparative studies indicate that the Aramaic in Ezra is doubtless later than that of the papyri, but there is still some confusion as to just how late it is. Walter Baumgartner dates the Aramaic of Ezra perhaps a few decades or at most a century earlier than the Aramaic of Daniel, which he assigns to the second or third centuries B.C.,[102] while H. H. Rowley suggests that "the Aramaic sections of Ezra may have been written in the fourth or third centuries B.C."[103]

The severe judgment against the historicity of the Aramaic parts of Ezra is based largely on the Jewishness of some of them, but there are other explanations for such a characteristic (e.g., Ezra 7:11-12). There is an increasing recognition of the genuine elements in the Aramaic documents in Ezra. Kosters, who rejected most of the Aramaic material as unhistorical, nevertheless recognized some of it as genuine,[104] and the historian Eduard Meyer defended the authenticity of all of the Persian documents in Ezra, except for the Cyrus edict.[105] Now even that (Ezra 1:2-4) has its defenders.[106] Pfeiffer says of Ezra 4:6-24: "The fact that the Chronicler misunderstood these texts and placed them in the wrong context proves that he could hardly have been their author [and] the fact that these are the only Aramaic documents in which the enemies of the Jews triumph and the Persian king opposes Jewish aspirations, could be adduced in favor of their authenticity."[107]

The Aramaic documents of Ezra have by no means yet been proved a forgery. Increasingly it is found that their substance is in agreement with what is revealed by our growing knowledge of the Persian period (see Exeg.).[108]

F. Lists.—As in the book of Chronicles, the editor here shows a distinct liking for lists and seems to supply them whenever possible. Almost anywhere else such lists would be taken at face value and presumed to be authentic, but here as part of the Chronicler's work they are usually regarded with suspicion and considered to be the product of his imagination. Since one at least is falsely connected (Ezra 7:1-5), all are on trial, and in each case it is a question as to what extent the Chronicler invented them or used authentic material. The lists remain a challenge to be proved or disproved, and it is

[92] Schaeder, *Esra der Schreiber*, p. vi; *Iranische Beitrage I* (Halle: M. Niemeyer, 1930), pp. 14-27; cf. A. T. Olmstead, *History of the Persian Empire* (Chicago: University of Chicago Press, 1948), p. 314.

[93] Cf. Eissfeldt, *op. cit.*, pp. 594-95.

[94] *Ezra Studies*, p. 158.

[95] Torrey, *Composition*, pp. 7-9.

[96] "Medes and Persians," *Journal of the American Oriental Society*, LVI (1946), 13-14.

[97] *Geschichte der Juden* (Leipzig: O. Leiner, 1911), Bd. II, Heft 2, pp. 87n, 100n, 128n.

[98] Julius Wellhausen, "Die Rückkehr der Juden aus dem babylonischen Exil," *Nachrichten von der königliche Gesellschaft der Wissenschaften zu Göttingen* (1895), pp. 169, 175-76; Theodor Nöldeke, *Die semitischen Sprachen* (2nd ed.; Leipzig: C. H. Tauchnitz, 1899), p. 35, n. 1; Torrey, *Composition*, pp. 51-65; *Ezra Studies*, pp. 142-57; "Medes and Persians," pp. 13-14; Laurence E. Browne, *Early Judaism* (Cambridge: Cambridge University Press, 1920), pp. 36-39, 44-45.

[99] *Intro. to O.T.*, p. 824.

[100] A. H. Sayce and A. E. Cowley, *Aramaic Papyri Discovered at Assuan* (London: A. Moring, 1906), p. 20; Eduard Sachau, *Aramäische Papyrus und Ostraka* (Leipzig: J. C. Hinrichs, 1911), p. xxvi; A. E. Cowley, *Aramaic Papyri of the Fifth Century B.C.* (Oxford: Clarendon Press, 1923), p. xv; Batten, *op. cit.*, p. 22; Bentzen, *Intro. to O.T.*, II, 200.

[101] *Ezra Studies*, p. 161.

[102] "Das Aramäische im Buche Daniel," *Zeitschrift für die alttestamentliche Wissenschaft*, XLV (1927), 118, 122.

[103] *The Aramaic of the Old Testament* (London: Oxford University Press, 1929), p. 156.

[104] *Wiederherstellung Israels*, pp. 24-25, 54-63.

[105] *Die Entstehung des Judenthums* (Halle: M. Niemeyer, 1896), pp. 8-71.

[106] Cf. Olmstead, *op. cit.*, pp. 57, 305.

[107] *Intro. to O.T.*, p. 829.

[108] Cf. Lods, *Histoire de la littérature hébraïque*, pp. 540-43.

impossible to do either in every case with convincing finality. The use of the phrase "mentioned by name" (Ezra 8:20) would indicate that the author had a list available, which for some reason he refrained from using, while the lack of a list in Ezra 10:16 where one would be expected indicates that none was available. Such practices should lend more confidence than is usually given to the lists supplied throughout Ezra-Nehemiah.

Various kinds of lists are presented in Ezra-Nehemiah. Many are lists of names, sometimes grouped as genealogies (cf. Ezra 7:1-5) or more commonly by professions. There are a great many lists of temple ministrants, each designated by class. A few such lists identify leaders who participate in civic projects (Neh. 3:1-32; 12:35-36, 41). Sometimes the word "number" (Neh. 7:7) in a list of considerable size suggests a census, either of members of a caravan (cf. Ezra 2:2b-20; 8:1-14) or of settlers in the land (Ezra 2:21-35). At least one list is geographical (Neh. 11:25-35). In a few cases there are inventories of animals (Ezra 2:66-67) or of gifts to the temple (Ezra 2:69; Neh. 7:70-72). That in Ezra 1:9-11 has been regarded as the translation of an official document, originally in Aramaic, which was attached to Sheshbazzar's orders.[109] It suggests another, of the time of Ezra, the purpose and use of which can be seen in Ezra 8:25-27, 30, 34.

Whence came such lists, if they are genuine? Such independent lists are not unknown in the Persian period. They are found among the Aramaic papyri [110] and a clay label bearing the single Aramaic word "priests," found at Persepolis, seems to indicate its use as a label for a list or series of lists of names of priests to which it was attached. At least one such list has been found among the Elamite tablets from the "treasury" at Persepolis.[111] Since most of the lists used in Ezra-Nehemiah relate to the temple, its history, administration, and cultic affairs, the suggestion has been plausibly made that an important source of information used by the Chronicler was the temple archives, which might be available to him as a temple ministrant.[112]

It is entirely probable that the temple at Jerusalem had a library—like that found associated with the temple of Baal at Ugarit—or at least an archival room where important documents were preserved. This seems indicated by the reference to a Levite official who was over the external business of the temple (Neh. 11:16), and by the use of written records in Ezra 8:34. Josephus, too, who lived while the temple stood and is therefore a good witness to the temple practice of his time, implies a depository for documents when he declares that Nehemiah's orders were presented before God and when he insists that Hezekiah placed the letters of the Assyrian general "within the temple" (cf. Neh. 2:9). It was apparently there that the Chronicler also obtained Nehemiah's memorial. The "book of the chronicles" in which the Levites were registered (Neh. 12:23) was probably a journal of the temple for the postexilic period (cf. Neh. 12:23).[113] It is obvious from Ezra 2:62 that at least the temple ministrants were registered by genealogy, and it is probable that not only the family leaders but the ordinary citizens were likewise registered by families (cf. Ezra 10:25-41). Such official records would be increasingly important, especially as later Judaism tended to stress ethnic purity, although it need not indicate that such lists arose only after the practice of exclusivism began.

The use of the same list in two different contexts (Neh. 11:3 ff.; cf. I Chr. 9:2-3) indicates that one must carefully distinguish between the source and the use to which it is put. Even that which is obviously now in error (Ezra 7:1-5) is faulty only in the interpretation that is made of the list. It is also imperative, in assessing the value of the lists, to distinguish between the lists supplied by the Chronicler referring to events long past and such lists as Nehemiah may have included in his own memoirs (cf. Neh. 3), since the latter were almost contemporary with the events and therefore more probably accurate.

G. Tradition.—More nebulous but equally real as sources are the traditions current during the time of the Chronicler. It is perhaps too much to see the force of tradition in "the choice of words, tone of the language and stylistic effects" of the present text, but undoubtedly oral tradition shaped the Ezra narrative, particularly in governing the order in which available sources would be employed, the identification of lists, and in some measure at least also in the philosophy and theology that color the narrative. It is probable too that such tradition has spoken where there were gaps in the available sources, so that the substance of the Chronicler's additional narrative reflects not so much his individual whims or fancies as the tradition of his time. It has been conjectured also that "the additions and elaborations" suspected in Nehemiah's narrative, too, may be due to current

[109] Kurt Galling, "Der Tempelschatz nach Berichten und Urkunden im Buche Esra," *Zeitschrift des deutschen Palastina-vereins,* LX (1937), 177-83; cf. Schaeder, *Esra der Schreiber,* pp. 28-29.

[110] Cowley, *op. cit.,* Nos. 12, 19, 22, 23, 51, 52, 53, 74.

[111] George G. Cameron, *Persepolis Treasury Tablets* (Chicago: University of Chicago Press, 1948), p. 25.

[112] Cf. Eissfeldt, *op. cit.,* p. 592; Bentzen, *op. cit.,* I, 245; Rudolph, *Esra und Nehemia,* pp. xxiii-xxiv, 173-74.

[113] Cf. *ibid.,* pp. 193-94.

tradition, and that even the historical inaccuracies and deficiencies in knowledge, formerly attributed to the Chronicler, may be due actually to the traditions put at the editor's disposal.[114]

It is impossible to trace such tradition, but there is evidence for its persistence and its development into rather grotesque forms in the Hellenistic period (cf. II Macc. 1:18-22, 31-36; 2:13). Strong evidence for the force of tradition and the Chronicler's response to it is found in the persistence of a tradition about Sheshbazzar in the time of Cyrus, even when that ran counter to another tradition stressing the importance of Zerubbabel (cf. Exeg. on Ezra 2:1-67; 5:16). Too strong to be ignored, the tradition was preserved by the Chronicler and kept in its proper historical setting in the Aramaic document (cf. Ezra 5:14-16).

VI. Order

The present chaotic order of the Ezra-Nehemiah narrative, which intermixes the story of Ezra with that of Nehemiah, is not that originally produced by the Chronicler. It has been suggested that the Nehemiah memoirs, which may have circulated separately (cf. p. 552), were not originally used by the Chronicler, who produced the Ezra story. S. Granild argues that the Nehemiah material, together with all of the Aramaic, was inserted by a late editor who wanted to credit Nehemiah rather than Ezra with the founding of Judaism.[115] Albright has conjectured that the Chronicler later simply added Nehemiah's memoirs at the conclusion of his own work.[116] There is no question but what Nehemiah's memoirs were originally a separate document but it is evident that the Chronicler has made an effort to incorporate them in the plan of his total work.

Rudolph has stressed the symmetrical structure of the Chronicler's original story of how, through the providence of God and the sympathetic co-operation of the Persian court, the Hebrew community and its temple, destroyed because of the sin of the people, were restored under the leadership of three men: Zerubbabel (Ezra 1:1–6:22); Ezra (Ezra 7:1–8:36; Neh. 7:73b–8:18; Ezra 9:1–10:44; Neh. 9:1–10:40); and Nehemiah (Neh. 1:1–7:73a; 11:1–13:31). Symmetrically, each of the three episodes began with an act of grace as the Persian ruler permitted or commissioned a Jewish leader to lead his fellow Jews to Palestine from exile. In each instance those who returned promptly and vigorously began the special task of reconstruction to which they had been dedicated: rebuilding the temple (Zerubbabel); reinstituting the law (Ezra); and the fortification of the city and re-establishment of the cult in the light of that law (Nehemiah). In each case the task, despite opposition, was continued to a successful conclusion, which was then celebrated as a great festival. The result was a rejuvenated community loyal to God and his law.[117] In the light of such symmetry it is likely that for the Chronicler the story of Nehemiah ended with the ceremony of the dedication of the wall and the exclusion of all foreigners from the community (Neh. 12:27–13:3), and that Neh. 13:4-31 was an appendix to his work, communicated, perhaps reluctantly, because it concerned cultic matters.[118]

In the first episode it was doubtless the Chronicler who disrupted the order of his Aramaic source and thereby caused confusion in chronology by shifting Ezra 4:6-23 from its proper place after 5:1–6:15 so that his narrative would move smoothly, directly from the completion of the temple (6:15) to the story of its ceremony of dedication (6:16-22). He was obviously more concerned with the temple, central in the episode, than with the accurate chronology.

It has been conjectured that the work of Ezra failed[119] and that the original conclusion of the Ezra narrative, which supposedly ended as a confession of failure to solve the problem of mixed marriages, has since been displaced by the Chronicler by a substitution of the positive story of the popular acceptance of the law, which supposedly was first associated with Nehemiah's activity.[120] Such speculation, however, is without foundation and there is no real evidence for Ezra's failure.[121]

The present order, which puts part of the Ezra narrative (Neh. 7:73b–8:18) in the book of Nehemiah, is due to an editor later than the Chronicler.[122] It was apparently he too who put the name of Nehemiah in Neh. 8:9 and the reference to Ezra in Neh. 12:36 which falsely suggest that they were contemporaries in Jeru-

---

[114] Cf. Kapelrud, *Question of Authorship in the Ezra-Narrative*, p. 96.

[115] *Ezrabogens literaere Genesis undersøgt med Henblik paa et efterkronistik Indgreb* (1949) cited by Snaith in Rowley, *O.T. and Modern Study*, p. 113; cf. Bentzen, *op. cit.*, II, 210.

[116] "Date and Personality of the Chronicler," p. 123.

[117] Cf. Rudolph, *op. cit.*, pp. xxii-xxiii.

[118] *Ibid.*, p. xxiii.

[119] Cf. J. S. Wright, *The Date of Ezra's Coming to Jerusalem* (London: Tyndale Press, 1947), pp. 25-26; Joseph Fischer, *Die chronologischen Fragen in den Büchern Esra und Nehemia* (Freiburg i. B.: Herder, 1903; "Biblische Studien"), pp. 73-74; H. M. Wiener, "The Relative Dates of Ezra and Nehemiah," *Journal of the Palestine Oriental Society*, VII (1927), 157.

[120] Cf. Rudolph, *op. cit.*, p. xxiv.

[121] Cf. H. H. Rowley, *The Servant of the Lord and Other Essays on the Old Testament* (London: Lutterworth Press, 1952), pp. 141-42.

[122] Torrey, *Ezra Studies*, p. 258; Rudolph, *op. cit.*, p. 144.

salem. That such confusion is relatively late is seen in the fact that in I Esdras and Josephus, Ezra precedes Nehemiah in Jerusalem and Nehemiah is not mentioned in I Esdras (cf. p. 561). It was perhaps this late editor, or another like him, who placed Neh. 10 at the conclusion of the Ezra story (cf. Exeg. on Neh. 9:38–10:39), incorporated Neh. 9:5b-37, and added the supplement in 11:22-23, which reflects substantially later times.

VII. I Esdras (Greek Ezra) and Josephus

Evidence of a different and doubtless earlier sequence of the Ezra-Nehemiah materials is found in I Esdras (the Greek Ezra), which is believed to reflect a better text of the Hebrew Bible than that now found in the Masoretic Text.[123] The most significant differences between I Esdras and the Masoretic Text are:

1. I Esdras begins with two full chapters of duplication of II Chronicles (35:1–36:21) instead of just a few verses (Ezra 1:1-3a=II Chr. 36:22-23).

2. The Artaxerxes correspondence regarding the building of the wall (Ezra 4:7-24) is found after the narrative of the return with Sheshbazzar (Ezra 1:3b-11). It was perhaps the reference to "the Jews that have come up from you to us" in I Esdras 2:18 (=Ezra 4:12), appearing after the reference to the return under Zerubbabel (I Esdras 2:1-15), that was responsible for the transfer of the section (Ezra 4:7-24) in I Esdras 2:16-30.

3. After the story in Ezra 4:17-24 there is a long interpolation (I Esdras 3:1–5:6) of unique material regarding three guardsmen in the court of Darius. It is a pagan story, possibly Persian in origin,[124] written originally in the Aramaic language,[125] but adapted to Jewish use to explain how Zerubbabel won permission to go from exile to Jerusalem.

4. The omission of Neh. 1:1–7:73a leaves I Esdras without a reference to Nehemiah. Silence regarding Nehemiah may be due to the fact that I Esdras is but a fragment from which the Nehemiah portion is missing. The text is incomplete, concluding abruptly after the first few words of Neh. 8:13a. The most striking and significant fact is that in I Esdras, Neh. 7:73 follows Ezra 10 and is followed by Neh. 8:1 ff., just as the Masoretic Text is now conjectured to have been originally. Thus the Ezra material,

now transferred to Nehemiah in the Masoretic Text, is here still attached to the book of Ezra.

When I Esdras concludes, Josephus, who used I Esdras rather than the Septuagint or Masoretic Text as his source for the period of Ezra-Nehemiah, proceeds to tell the story of Nehemiah in a form somewhat different from that in the present Masoretic Text and Septuagint. It is conjectured that he then uses an independent Greek narrative as his source,[126] but it is possible that he merely continues his work of presenting the story as originally completed in I Esdras.

In his work it is noted that Josephus gives "the substance of the first six chapters [of Nehemiah], making brief but plain allusion to 7:4; 11:1; 12:27, and 13:10 f. Of chapters 9 and 10 he makes no use." [127] It is significant that in one sentence (*Antiquities* XI. 5. 8) he refers in its first part to 7:4 and the latter part to 11:1, suggesting that in Josephus' Greek source Neh. 7 was followed immediately by Neh. 11—as originally was the case [128] (cf. Neh. 7:73a; 11:1-2).

Josephus did not reproduce his source literally but dealt with it freely, omitting tedious parts at will (cf. Ezra 2:1-67) and "correcting" his text as it pleased him. He corrects the impossible order of the Persian kings in I Esdras, which actually reverses the historical sequence, and he puts them in their proper relationship. Thus the "Artaxerxes" of Ezra 4:7-24 becomes "Cambyses" in Josephus [129] and, although he still has Ezra precede Nehemiah, both men are located in the reign of Xerxes instead of Artaxerxes (Ezra 7:1–10:44; Neh. 7:73–8:13a).[130] While such chronology is superior to that which he displays elsewhere (cf. Exeg. on Neh. 13:28), the solution proposed for the disruption of the proper sequence of Persian kings given above (cf. p. 560) is preferable.

VIII. The Priority of Nehemiah

Affixing the book of Nehemiah to that of Ezra, whether by the Chronicler or by a later editor (cf. p. 560), created a chronological problem regarding the order of appearance of Ezra and Nehemiah in Jerusalem. It is natural to assume that the one mentioned first was the first to arrive, and this traditional order has many defenders.[131] The problem is complicated by the

---

[123] Bernhard Walde, *Die Esdrasbücher der Septuaginta* (Freiburg i. B.: Herder, 1913), pp. 92-96; cf. R. H. Pfeiffer, *History of New Testament Times* (New York: Harper & Bros., 1949), p. 241.

[124] *Ibid.*, pp. 251-54.

[125] Torrey, *Ezra Studies*, pp. 23-25, 50-56; Edmund Bayer, *Das dritte Buch Esdras* (Freiburg i. B.: Herder, 1911; "Biblische Studien"), pp. 123-35; Walde, *op. cit.*, pp. 119-20.

[126] Pfeiffer, *History of N.T. Times*, p. 245.

[127] C. C. Torrey, *The Apocryphal Literature* (New Haven: Yale University Press, 1945), p. 46.

[128] *Ibid.*, p. 47.

[129] *Antiquities* XI. 2. 1.

[130] *Ibid.*, XI. 5. 1; cf. XI. 5. 6.

[131] Cf. Eissfeldt, *Einleitung in das A.T.*, p. 597; B. D. Eerdmans, *The Religion of Israel* (Leiden: Universitaire Pers Leiden, 1947), pp. 233-41; J. S. Wright, *op. cit.*; Olmstead, *History of the Persian Empire*, pp. 304-7; *et al.*

dating of the arrivals of both ambiguously to the time of "Artaxerxes," and the present text treats them as contemporaries (Neh. 8:9; 12:36), which is highly improbable (cf. p. 562).

In solution of the chronological problem it was proposed in 1889 that Nehemiah was active under Artaxerxes I (464-423 B.C.) while Ezra, if historical, came to Jerusalem under Artaxerxes II (404-358 B.C.). This thesis, propounded, expanded, and defended for years by Albin Van Hoonacker, until it has become associated with his name, has always been under attack but has nevertheless gained many adherents.[132] The principal considerations that have made this view persuasive are: [133]

1. It is unlikely that the same king would send to Palestine two men with official support and authority at the same time. The powers granted Ezra and Nehemiah were so similar that it is improbable that they could have exercised them simultaneously. Nor was there a division of labor whereby Nehemiah left religious matters to Ezra the priest, for he was himself concerned with regulating the priests (Neh. 7:64 ff.; 10:32 ff.), the tithes and temple treasures (Neh. 13:10-11), and the sabbath (Neh. 13:15 ff.).

2. Ezra and Nehemiah ignore each other in a way that would be surprising if they were contemporaries. Ezra is not mentioned until Neh. 8, and then only in a passage originally not part of the Nehemiah story. In all his reforms Nehemiah nowhere gives the slightest indication that he is enforcing the law introduced by Ezra and accepted by the people. Nor does either mention the other who, like himself, had an official royal commission. "Wherever their names are found together one is a mere passenger, whose name can be dropped without the slightest consequence to the narrative" [134] (cf. Neh. 8:9; 12:36).

3. Nehemiah would scarcely have designated the inhabitants of Jerusalem as those who had escaped exile (Neh. 1:2-3) if shortly before a great caravan had arrived there from Babylonia with Ezra.

4. In preparation for a census Nehemiah is concerned with the list of those who had returned with Zerubbabel some time before (Neh. 7:1-73), but he is silent regarding those who returned with Ezra (Ezra 8:1-14).

5. Nehemiah found Jerusalem almost uninhabited and subsequently took steps to repopulate it (cf. Neh. 7:4; 11:1-2), whereas Ezra lived and worked in a busy city (Ezra 9:4; 10:1).

6. In Ezra 8:29; 10:5 the priests, Levites, and heads of families were dwelling in Jerusalem,

while according to Neh. 11:1 ff., Nehemiah had sent them to the capital.

7. Nehemiah found the defenses of Jerusalem destroyed (Neh. 1:3; 2:13, 17; cf. 3:1-32; 4:6), but Ezra thanks God for the "wall" in Jerusalem (cf. Ezra 9:9).

8. No members of the families that returned with Ezra (Ezra 8:1-20) can be identified with certainty in the list of those who built the wall of Jerusalem with Nehemiah. Hashabiah (Neh. 3:17; Ezra 8:19, 24) and Meshullam (Neh. 3:4, 30; [6:18]; Ezra 8:16) are too common to identify, and it is obvious that the Davidic Hattush son of Shechaniah (Ezra 8:21) is not Hattush son of Hashabneiah (Neh. 3:10).

9. Whereas Nehemiah was a contemporary of the high priest Eliashib (cf. Neh. 3:1, 20-21; 13:4, 7, 28), Ezra lived during the period of the high priest Jehohanan, the grandson of Eliashib (Ezra 10:6; cf. Neh. 12:10-11, 22). Jehohanan is attested by the Aramaic papyri as high priest in Jerusalem in 407 B.C., under Darius II.[135] This most important evidence indicates that Ezra was active under Artaxerxes II, at least a generation after Nehemiah.

10. The papyrus mentioning the high priest Jehohanan, contemporary of Ezra (cf. paragraph 9 above), also indicates that the power of Samaria then was in the hands of the sons of Sanballat, who was apparently an old man,[136] rather than in his own, since he personally had been the active opponent of Nehemiah (Neh. 2:10; 4:1-2; 6:1-2).

11. Nehemiah appointed a commission of temple treasurers (Neh. 11:16; 13:13) and when Ezra arrived he found a similar one (Ezra 8:33). The priest Jozabad, whom Nehemiah appointed over the outside business of the temple (Neh. 11:16), may not be the one of that name functioning in that role in the time of Ezra (Ezra 8:34), but the interval between is proper for him to have been the grandson (cf. Eliashib and Jehohanan in paragraph 9 above). Grandsons often bore the names of their grandfathers.

12. Meremoth the son of Uriah was of the family of Koz, which could not authenticate its priestly status in the time of Zerubbabel (Ezra 2:61-62). He appears as a builder of the wall without priestly title in the time of Nehemiah (Neh. 3:4, 21), assuming a double portion, apparently in youthful enthusiasm. His family doubtless regained its priestly status during Nehemiah's administration, for at Ezra's arrival he is a priest, perhaps an aged man, who received the treasure from Ezra.[137]

13. The rigorous reforms instituted by Nehe-

132 Cf. Rowley, Servant of the Lord, pp. 131 ff.
133 Cf. Batten, Ezra and Nehemiah, pp. 28-30.
134 Rowley, Servant of the Lord, p. 156.

135 Cowley, Aramaic Papyri, No. 30, l. 18.
136 Ibid., l. 29.
137 Cf. Rowley, Servant of the Lord, pp. 158-59.

miah would hardly be necessary if Ezra had won popular acceptance of the law and its implied loyal support of the cultus. Those who maintain the traditional order must posit a failure for Ezra's efforts or an apostasy by the people shortly after they accepted the law.

14. The matter of tithes and the consequent flight of the Levites (Neh. 13:10-11) would be surprising so soon after the popular acceptance of the law. It appears that Nehemiah was not merely restoring conditions temporarily upset but was correcting a situation of long neglect and abuse.

15. While the matter of mixed marriages could have been a recurring problem, the situation faced by Nehemiah was one of some years' standing, since he found children speaking in their foreign mothers' tongues (Neh. 13:23-24), a situation unlikely if Ezra's reforms occurred shortly before. Moreover, there is a greater psychological motive for Nehemiah's reform in that a member of the high priest's family had married into the family of Nehemiah's enemy (Neh. 13:28). It is also likely that Nehemiah's violent approach to the problem would not be as effective and give as enduring results as that of Ezra's, which depended upon voluntary co-operation and an appeal to the law.

Not all of the foregoing considerations are of equal weight in determining the priority of Nehemiah, but their cumulative effect is strong, arguing that it is most probable that Nehemiah preceded Ezra in Palestine. Rebuttals to this view are strictly defensive and are often devious and ingenious rather than persuasive.[138] In the course of debate over this chronological problem, alternate solutions are proposed by those who admit the priority of Nehemiah but believe that Ezra too served under Artaxerxes I. It is suggested that the Chronicler has just reversed the dates of Ezra and Nehemiah, that Nehemiah came in the seventh year (458/457 B.C.) and Ezra in the twentieth year (445/444 B.C.) of Artaxerxes I.[139] Some emend the Masoretic Text to gain a later date for Ezra. It was suggested that the numeral twenty has been lost from the text, and that the date of Ezra's arrival should be the twenty-seventh year (438-437 B.C.),[140] but this would place Ezra in the midst of Nehemiah's administration (445-433 B.C.). Others conjecture that Ezra's mission came after Nehemiah's first administration and before his second one (cf. Ezra 7:7-8), after 432 B.C.[141] In support of the latter view it is argued

that representatives of the priestly groups Phinehas and Ithamar, which came with Ezra (Ezra 8:2), are lacking in the population list during Nehemiah's first administration (Neh. 11:10 ff.), but that the family of Daniel the son of Ithamar is present during Nehemiah's second administration (Neh. 10:6). Still others consider that the numeral thirty has been lost and that Ezra's arrival was during the thirty-seventh year of Artaxerxes I (428/427 B.C.).[142] As an alternative, Markwart proposes the fortieth year of Artaxerxes I (425/424 B.C.), but that is textually more difficult.

More radical solutions have been proposed. Hugo Winckler substitutes the name Darius for that of Artaxerxes, and thus dates Ezra during the seventh year of Darius,[143] while others cut the Gordian knot by denying the historicity of Ezra entirely.

All such proposals are purely conjectural, without the support of the Hebrew text or the versions. The chronological problem seems best solved by assigning Ezra to the period of Artaxerxes II, as suggested long ago.

IX. Historicity

Whatever is attributed to Nehemiah is regarded as "admittedly genuine beyond the shadow of a doubt,"[144] but a great gulf is fixed between scholars regarding the historicity of the events of the Ezra narrative and in the Chronicler's work in general.

For those who, on the basis of a theory of literal inspiration of scripture, accept Ezra-Nehemiah at its face value as historical, there is no problem of chronology or historicity, since the biblical narrative is regarded as the truth with which the present puzzling chronology is someday expected to be seen in agreement. Those at the other extreme, who hold that the Chronicler writes unhistorical fiction instead of history, forging speeches and documents and expounding his fictional "history" as he imagined it occurred, likewise have no chronological or historical problems. They reject all of the Chronicler's views out of hand as unhistorical, and regard it impossible to know the actual historical truth of the Persian period in Palestine since Neh. 1:1–7:73a "is the only unimpeachable source for Jewish history between Haggai and Zechariah in 520-516 and I Maccabees for the period 175-135."[145] For them the historical problem is transmuted into the

[138] Cf. the arguments pro and con in Rowley, *Servant of the Lord*, pp. 131-59.
[139] Sidney Jellicoe, "Nehemiah-Ezra: A Reconstruction," *Expository Times*, LIX (1947-48), 54.
[140] Wellhausen, "Die Rückkehr der Juden," p. 186.
[141] Cf. Rudolph, *Esra und Nehemia*, pp. xxiv, 70-71.

[142] Josef Markwart, *Fundamente israelitischer und jüdischer Geschichte* (Göttingen: Dieterich, 1896), p. 36; Julius Bewer, *Der Text des Buches Ezra* (Göttingen: Vandenhoeck & Ruprecht, 1922), p. 68.
[143] *Altorientalische Forschungen*, Reihe 2, Bd. II, p. 242.
[144] Pfeiffer, *Intro. to O.T.*, p. 829.
[145] *Ibid.*

psychological one of determining what has led the Chronicler to distort and jumble historical data as he is reputed to have done. Between these extremes are the many who recognize the errors and inaccuracies in the Chronicler's narrative but also acknowledge that there is more or less historical material in his work. For them problems of chronology and historical validity are vital but troublesome considerations. They agree with the dictum: "We are in the direct need of information as to the history of the Jews in the Persian period, and every scrap of material that promises help ought to be treasured and put to use. But no extremity of need can outweigh the obligation to follow the evidence." [146]

Adequate criteria for distinguishing the true from the false in the Chronicler's work are greatly needed. Those who deny historical validity to the Chronicler's narrative do so because they mistrust him as one who uses more imagination than objective sources. This attitude has arisen as a result of a study of the Chronicler's technique in the books of Chronicles, where canonical biblical books that he used as sources are still available as a check. The reputation he earned there is transferred to Ezra-Nehemiah where, however, canonical and even uncanonical data which could serve as a check on his practices are largely lacking.

But other scholars, carefully working over the same material, have obtained widely conflicting results. The questions that divide scholars here are whether the Chronicler's function was that of an editor, compiling and arranging his sources, adding bits where necessary to produce a smooth narrative and on occasion even reworking his sources to make them conform to his own conceptions, or whether he was predominantly an author, using few sources and those verbatim with little addition by himself but, on the other hand, writing from his own imagination great stretches of material, including official documents which he forges and supposed "sources" which he names (cf. Neh. 7:5; 12:23). The latter view, supported by Torrey after much research,[147] has resulted in the radical view that the Chronicler's work is unhistorical fiction, while the former, held by Batten among many others, has led to his statement, "I find myself among the number who must still take the Ezra story seriously." [148]

Linguistic study of the Chronicler's work has been extensive. Comparative studies in the books of Chronicles have resulted in the compilation of long lists of the lexical, syntactical,

and conceptual peculiarities of the Chronicler.[149] It is said, "There is no writer, in all the Old Testament, whose peculiarities of language and style are so strongly marked, or who can so easily and certainly be recognized, as the Chronicler."[150] Hence the principal criterion for historicity employed by Torrey and his followers in Ezra-Nehemiah is a linguistic one. Wherever in the text of Ezra-Nehemiah such "telltale signs of the Chronicler" are recognized, the passage is presumed to be the Chronicler's composition and it is automatically regarded as unhistorical. Even though the Chronicler may explain that a source is being used by him, it is assumed that none existed.

Although literary criticism is a valid technique, it must be used with discretion and not regarded as the sole criterion for determining historical validity. The medium is easily subject to abuse. A single telltale mark of what is called the Chronicler's style does not allow the critic to judge an entire passage. Such a practice would imply that the Chronicler had a monopoly on his usage. Although Torrey has scored the assumption of "a generation or more ago" that the Chronicler's style was merely late postexilic Hebrew prose,[151] there is now an increasing tendency to defend that proposition. Driver suggested that "Ezra's style approaches slightly more than Nehemiah's does to that of the compiler," [152] and Kapelrud claims that "the choice of words, tone of the language and stylistic effects [of the Ezra narrative] are now those that were natural in [the Chronicler's] circles."[153] Geissler's studies have produced a long list of words and phrases in common between Ezra and the Hexateuch,[154] and Rudolph, after careful study, concludes that there is but a single linguistic phenomenon shared by Ezra and the Chronicler that is not also encountered elsewhere in Hebrew.[155] Admittedly the Chronicler has favorite expressions, but it is dangerous to assume that no one else could use them and that they form a sure clue to the Chronicler's authorship of any passage.

As valuable as linguistic evidence is as a technique for indicating source and relationship, it is not the sole criterion but must be

---

[146] Torrey, Ezra Studies, p. 157.
[147] Composition, pp. 51-52, 57, 60; Ezra Studies, pp. 238-48.
[148] Ezra and Nehemiah, pp. 17-18.

[149] See Intro. to Chronicles, pp. 342-44; cf. Driver, Intro. to the Literature of the O.T., pp. 535-40; Torrey, Composition, pp. 16-20, 22-25; Johannes Geissler, Die litterarischen Beziehungen der Esramemoiren (Chemnitz: J. C. F. Pickenhahn, 1899), pp. 5-12.
[150] Torrey, Ezra Studies, p. 240; cf. S. R. Driver, "Chronicles, Books of," in Cheyne and Black, Encyclopaedia Biblica, Vol. I, col. 772.
[151] Loc. cit.
[152] Op. cit., p. 553.
[153] Question of Authorship in the Ezra-Narrative, p. 96.
[154] Op. cit., pp. 12-21; but cf. Torrey, Ezra Studies, p. 241, n. 45.
[155] Op. cit., pp. 163-65.

used along with every other test. S. A. Cook properly warns that "historical criticism cannot start from the untrustworthiness of Chronicles, and minimize the extent of the 'chronicler' in [Ezra-Nehemiah] or exaggerate it . . . , or assume that all other records are necessarily superior." [156] It is strange that the Chronicler's statements to be credible must be authenticated by another witness, while material in the books of Samuel and Kings, under similar circumstances, is at once accepted as true. All of our rapidly growing knowledge of the history and culture of the Near East must be brought to bear on the interpretation of the Ezra-Nehemiah narrative. While our knowledge of events in Palestine during the Persian period is still unfortunately incomplete, enough has been accomplished to permit Albright to state, "We are justified in rejecting [Torrey's] position completely, without any concessions—except that Torrey's searching criticism of the sources and their interpretation have been of immense heuristic value." [157]

In Ezra-Nehemiah the test of plausibility, whether the event fits the total picture as known from all other evidence, is important. If there is agreement with known facts, then even though there is linguistic evidence of the Chronicler's hand, the data may still be valid. In the light of the Chronicler's imposition of his style upon everything he touched, a broader scale of judgment than simply true and false must be used. While searching for the truth we must be satisfied at times, at least temporarily, with the classifications "possible" and "probable." Attitude also is important, for incredulity is not the only virtue of a historian, and experience shows that a negative attitude breeds negative results, whereas critical readiness to believe, when not simple credulity, opens the door to constructive knowledge and often to the ultimate solution of historical problems.

One of the fruits of the radical criticism of Ezra-Nehemiah is the denial of the existence of an Ezra narrative, which is then described as "spurious Memoirs of Ezra patterned after Nehemiah's" [158] and even the denial of the existence of the person Ezra. It is stressed that Ezra "appears relatively late in tradition, but continues to grow in reputation. He is absent from both Ben Sira xlix. 12 seq. and 2 Macc. i. seq., and here [Nehemiah] is particularly prominent." [159] Torrey refers to "the Chronicler's 'creation of the character' of Ezra," and claims that "Ezra" himself is the personification of the Chronicler's interests, completely identi-

cal with the Nehemiah of Neh. 13 and (mutatis mutandis) with each of the long list of ecclesiastical heroes and reformers created by the Chronicler. [160] Pfeiffer, who usually agrees with Torrey, is somewhat reluctant here, but ultimately also denies the historicity of the Ezra narrative as he remarks: "Ezra need not be a purely fictitious character. He may well have been a devout Jew living in Jerusalem in the days of Nehemiah, whose name was remembered in later generations. The Chronicler . . . apparently selected Ezra for the role of founder of the guild of the scribes and concocted his fictitious biography." He also claims: "His [Ezra's] 'Memoirs' lack the genuine historicity of those of Nehemiah and his life is far more legendary." [161]

Such a negative conception has not found wide acceptance. Many prefer to say, "The probability is that Ezra was indeed a real person, who came to Jerusalem and did substantially what the Chronicler says he did." [162] Albright is willing to admit that the Chronicler wrote the Ezra narratives, but he identifies that author with Ezra himself. [163] Such a concept is quite extreme, however, and is not held widely.

It is usual to regard Ezra as the embodiment of the later particularistic and legalistic Judaism, but it is clear that he was also its fountainhead. Cowley has declared:

It was Ezra who made modern Judaism, by instituting (or re-instituting) the ceremonial law and formulating regulations for the national festivals. The books of Ezra and Nehemiah show this as clearly as the early literature shows the lack of them. . . . The importance of the new revelation [law] is that in it we see the birth of modern Judaism, which could never have developed by natural process from pre-exilic Judaism. The subsequent development of it down to the present day is easily traced. . . . All this is the natural growth of the system born under Ezra: it could not have grown out of a religious system such as that of the colonists of Elephantine. [164]

The story of Ezra-Nehemiah for the most part rings true. It makes good sense when understood from the standpoint of what is known otherwise of the history of the Jews during the exilic and postexilic periods (cf. Robinson, "The History of Israel," Vol. I, pp. 284-88) and of the history and culture of the world in which

[156] "First Esdras," in R. H. Charles, ed., The Apocrypha and Pseudepigrapha of the Old Testament (Oxford: Clarendon Press, 1913), I, 5, n. 1.

[157] W. F. Albright, From the Stone Age to Christianity (2nd ed.; Baltimore: Johns Hopkins Press, 1946), p. 247.

[158] Pfeiffer, Intro. to O.T., p. 838.

[159] Cook, "First Esdras," in Charles, Apocrypha and Pseudepigrapha, I, 17.

[160] Ezra Studies, pp. 247-48.

[161] Intro. to O.T., pp. 833, 819; cf. Gustav Hölscher, Geschichte der israelitischen und jüdischen Religion (Giessen: Alfred Töpelmann, 1922), p. 140.

[162] Snaith in Rowley, O.T. and Modern Study, p. 113.

[163] "Date and Personality of the Chronicler," pp. 104-24; cf. also The Archeology of Palestine and the Bible (New York: Fleming H. Revell, 1932), pp. 218, n. 97.

[164] Aramaic Papyri, p. 62, xxviii.

the Jews then lived (cf. Albright, "The Old Testament World," Vol. I, pp. 268-71).

X. Theological Significance

Since Ezra-Nehemiah is part of the Chronicler's work (cf. Intro., p. 552), the work shares the general purpose of the books of Chronicles (cf. Intro. to Chronicles, pp. 344-45). The Chronicler rewrote and supplemented the hisorical books which were already canonical. He intended chiefly to include in the national history an account of the origin and development of the Jerusalem temple and its cultus. Because those books concluded with the negative narration of the destruction of Jerusalem (II Kings 25:1-30), its temple, and cultus, the Ezra-Nehemiah portion of the narrative, without a counterpart in the canonical works, was especially significant for the Chronicler: In a positive way, it describes the rebuilding of Jerusalem, its defenses and its temple, and the reinstitution of the temple administration and religious practices. It concludes with a message dear to the Chronicler, that the Jews of the postexilic period became a united, self-conscious people, avoiding all foreign contamination and maintaining a fierce loyalty to the law of their God.

However, each of the major sources employed by the Chronicler had its own purpose. The now-fragmentary Aramaic source seems to have preserved a factual account of the reconstruction of Jerusalem in the face of unbelievable opposition by the neighbors of the Jews. Although Nehemiah's work, too, is basically factual, the key to its purpose is to be found in its frequent petition to God to "remember" what Nehemiah had done for Jerusalem and the cause of religion there. His work was designed presumably to be preserved as a memorial before God in the temple in order that the perpetuation there of the good deeds of Nehemiah the eunuch might gain for him salvation, the preservation of his name and reputation, which would otherwise have been lost and forgotten since he could leave no posterity (cf. Neh. 13:14). Ezra's account has been described as a report to his king regarding the faithful discharge of the commission with which he was sent to Palestine.[165] Obviously the writer aimed particularly at describing the means employed by Ezra in getting the Jewish people to accept God's law as binding on their actions, making them a community ideally subservient to his will, and at showing how, in consequence of such law, or an expansion of it, the community purged itself of every foreign element that might seduce the people religiously, as they had been led astray in the dark days just past. Such particularistic emphases strongly marked later Judaism.

[165] Cf. Rudolph, op. cit., p. xxvii.

With a more recent development of universalistic thought and of impatience with legal restrictions, especially in religion, the work of Ezra-Nehemiah has been greatly neglected, regarded as negative in character, and considered significant only for its possible factual content. Properly understood, however, the value of the work goes far beyond its historical import. Rarely in the Bible is there expressed such a sense of intimate relationship with God and consciousness of his providence as is found in Nehemiah's frequent observations that the "hand of God" guided and defended him in his holy work (cf. Neh. 2:8, 18). Always Nehemiah was confident that the almost impossible task of reviving the desolate Jewish community could not be accomplished without the guidance and support of God. Thus his work is no mere human boast of achievement but an account of faithful stewardship to his Lord.

The work of Ezra, too, although often scorned today because of its particularism and legalism, likewise has enduring significance when seen in proper perspective. It is true that the emotional intensity, prophetic boldness, and beautiful language of the major prophets are not encountered in the work of Ezra, but it is a fact that in a great measure Ezra made a practical application of the prophetic ideal and realistically implemented the prophetic message. The great prophets had declaimed against the menace of Canaanite and other foreign religious influences and had declared that continued acceptance of such seducing forces would lead to divine displeasure, exile, and destruction. Ezra admitted the truth of the prophetic contention and, recognizing that all intimate foreign contacts inherently presented an insidious possibility of contamination of the cult, he urged that such "cancerous growths" should be removed, surgically if necessary, in order that a sound Jewish cult might survive, avoiding a repetition of divine displeasure and of the destruction which had come, as the prophets had warned, because of the ready acceptance of foreign influences, particularly in religion. Judaism lost much of cultural benefit, to be sure, by the rigid rejection of all foreign influences, but the cost was counted worth while when the purity of its religion and the identity of its people were maintained. The real test of the value of the policy of exclusion came with the onset of the Hellenistic Age (cf. Robinson, "The History of Israel," Vol. I, pp. 288-90). As might be expected, some Jews accepted Hellenism and reveled in their new freedom but it was such conservative and exclusivistic groups as the Hasidim that preserved Judaism and led the way toward Christianity.

Since Paul, Christians have looked with contempt upon the legalistic development of Judaism and have rejected the "burden" of the Law as a means of salvation. But such a view often distorts the truth. Even Paul had to combat in the church the antinomian tendencies that his words and attitudes on the subject had released. Although not all Jewish laws need be binding upon Christians, nevertheless there were Christian laws or principles by which religious conduct must be guided, and Paul himself was often most explicit about these. There are few men with adequate religious sensitivity and discernment to understand and appreciate and make effective the law that God writes in every human heart. Historically, the result of human attempts to make that law explicit has been confusion, contradiction, and crossed purposes. Nevertheless, most men require an objective guide of conduct. Such abstractions as "holiness" and "righteousness" must be spelled out in concrete expression. The average man wants these explanations to be adequate but in minimal terms. He asks, *"How far* can I go and still be righteous?"* or *"What* must I do to be saved?" Jewish law met the issue by supplying a specific code of conduct, recognized as the will of God. Strict adherence to it constituted righteousness. Therein lay both its positive force and its corrupting influence.

XI. Outline of Contents

EZRA

I. Sheshbazzar's return (1:1–2:70)
  A. Preliminary (1:1-4)
    1. Introduction (1:1)
    2. Edict of Cyrus (1:2-4)
  B. Preparation for the return (1:5-11)
    1. Chiefs of fathers (1:5)
    2. Support of neighbors (1:6)
    3. Cyrus' return of temple vessels (1:7-11)
  C. Returning Israelites (2:1-70)
    1. Superscription (2:1-2a)
    2. The principal list (2:2b-67)
      a) Laymen (2:2b-35)
        (1) By family (2:2b-20)
        (2) By city (2:21-35)
      b) Temple ministrants (2:36-58)
        (1) Priests (2:36-39)
        (2) Levites (2:40)
        (3) Singers (2:41)
        (4) Porters (2:42)
        (5) Temple servants (2:43-54)
        (6) Descendants of Solomon's servants (2:55-58)
      c) Uncertified clans (2:59-63)
      d) Summaries (2:64-67)
        (1) Congregation (2:64)
        (2) Private property (2:65-67)
    3. Temple donations (2:68-70)
II. Building the temple under Darius (3:1–6:22)
  A. Reconstruction of the altar and re-establishment of sacrifices (3:1-6)
    1. Erection of the altar (3:1-3a)
    2. Institution of program of offerings (3:3b-6)
  B. Work on the temple (3:7–6:22)
    1. Work begins (3:7-13)
      a) Supplies and labor (3:7-9)
      b) Subfoundation laid and dedicated (3:10-11)
      c) Popular reaction to the building (3:12-13)
    2. The Samaritan conflict (4:1–6:22)
      a) Offer of assistance (4:1-2)
      b) Rejection of assistance (4:3)
      c) Plots and frustrations (4:4-5)
      d) Reigns of Xerxes and Artaxerxes (4:6-24)
        (1) Complaints made to Xerxes and Artaxerxes (4:6-16)
        (2) Letters of Artaxerxes to Rehum and Shimshai (4:17-22)
        (3) Work stopped at Jerusalem (4:23-24)
      e) Reign of Darius (5:1–6:22)
        (1) The temple building is begun (5:1-2)
        (2) Official investigation of the building of the temple (5:3-5)
        (3) Report of Tattenai to Darius (5:6-17)
        (4) Answer of Darius (6:1-12)
        (5) Completion of the temple (6:13-18)
        (6) The feasts of Passover and Unleavened Bread (6:19-22)
III. Ezra's return (7:1–8:36)
  A. Introduction of Ezra (7:1-10)
    1. Genealogy of Ezra (7:1-5)
    2. Summary of Ezra's career (7:6-10)
  B. Ezra's commission (7:11-26)
    1. Introduction (7:11-12)
    2. Permission to return (7:13-14)
    3. Gifts for the temple (7:15-19)
    4. Additional funds (7:20-24)
    5. Ezra and the law (7:25-26)
    6. Ezra's poem of praise (7:27-28)
  C. Those returning with Ezra (8:1-14)
  D. Acquisition of temple servants (8:15-20)
  E. Final preparation before departure (8:21-23)
  F. Delegation to transport treasure (8:24-30)
  G. Departure and arrival (8:31-36)
IV. Mixed marriages 9:1–10:44)
  A. Report of mixed marriages (9:1-2)
  B. Ezra's reaction to the mixed marriages (9:3-15)
    1. Ezra's mourning (9:3-5)
    2. Ezra's prayer (9:6-15)
  C. Public reaction to Ezra's distress (10:1-6)
  D. Public assembly (10:7-15)
  E. Action of the Jerusalem commission (10:16-19)
  F. List of those who married foreign women (10:20-44)

NEHEMIAH

I. Nehemiah hears news of Jerusalem (1:1-11a)
  A. The news (1:1-4)
  B. Nehemiah's prayer (1:5-11a)
II. Nehemiah's petition is granted (1:11b–2:8)

XII. Selected Bibliography

ALBRIGHT, W. F. "The Date and Personality of the Chronicler," *Journal of Biblical Literature*, XL (1921), 104-24.

BATTEN, L. W. *A Critical and Exegetical Commentary on the Books of Ezra and Nehemiah* ("International Critical Commentary"). New York: Charles Scribner's Sons, 1913.

BROWNE, LAURENCE E. *Early Judaism.* Cambridge: Cambridge University Press, 1920.

ROWLEY, H. H. *The Servant of the Lord and Other Essays on the Old Testament.* London: Lutterworth Press, 1952. Pp. 131-59.

RUDOLPH, WILHELM. *Esra und Nehemia* ("Handbuch zum Alten Testament"). Tübingen: J. C. B. Mohr, 1949.

SIMONS, J. J. *Jerusalem in the Old Testament.* Leiden: E. J. Brill, 1952.

TORREY, C. C. *The Composition and Historical Value of Ezra-Nehemiah* ("Beihefte zur Zeitschrift für die alttestamentliche Wissenschaft"). Giessen: J. Ricker, 1895.

——. *Ezra Studies.* Chicago: University of Chicago Press, 1910.

EZRA

TEXT, EXEGESIS, AND EXPOSITION

The Book of Ezra.—In Thornton Wilder's novel *The Ides of March,* set in the last days of Julius Caesar, the author explains that he has deliberately displaced one historical event by seventeen years, and that he has for his own purposes kept several of his historical characters alive long after the actual dates of their deaths. But he points out that "historical reconstruction is not among the primary aims of this work," and calls it rather "a fantasia on certain events and persons of the last days of the Roman republic." [1]

Likewise, in his well-known long poem *John Brown's Body,* [2] Stephen Vincent Benét has incorporated into his account of Brown's attack on Harper's Ferry, and of his later trial and execution, the actual words which Brown uttered in explanation and defense. Benét then portrays, through characters and events of his own creation, the powerful influence of John Brown's words and deeds upon the course of the Civil War and the history of the American people.

Both these twentieth-century procedures illuminate the present-day relevance of the book of Ezra. Benét and Wilder have written in an age when the standards and methods of responsible historical scholarship have become widely established, and about periods of history for which the written sources of our knowledge are abundant. Ezra, on the other hand, as the Intro. and Exeg. show, was written some generations—perhaps even a century or two—after the events with which it deals, about one of the most obscure periods in Hebrew history, on the basis of written sources that were scanty and ambiguous, by an author whose knowledge on

[1] New York: Harper & Bros., 1948, p. vii.
[2] New York: Doubleday, Doran & Co., 1928.

many historical questions was confused and inaccurate. Its author had little if any comprehension of what we now mean by historical scholarship; but like Wilder, who does know a great deal about it, his primary aim in any case was not that of historical reconstruction. He was chiefly interested in the maintenance and enrichment of the temple ritual and its development after the rebuilding of the temple, which he undertook to recount; and he was equally concerned in the elaboration and enforcement of the early Jewish religion of the law, which was developing so fast in his own time.

Seeing the danger to later Judaism in any relaxation of these developing ceremonies and traditions—especially through intermarriage with the surrounding peoples, whose religious practices were much less strict than his own—he used his scanty sources and limited knowledge of earlier times to write what a modern scholar has called "idealized history." He carried back the origins of the ceremonial observances and legalistic conformities by which in his own day he set such store, into an earlier period when our fuller sources show that these practices had not yet developed. By the great influence of his book, and especially of its hero Ezra, upon the course of later Judaism, he gave both direction and powerful impetus to the elaboration of the ceremonialism, the legalism, and the exclusive "particularism" which thus became characteristic of later Judaism.

It cannot be too strongly emphasized that in all this there was no conscious falsification on the author's part. Like his successors of whom the N.T. speaks, he fully believed that he was doing both God and God's chosen people a great service. The course of later history seems to us Christians to show that God's purposes

1 Now in the first year of Cyrus king of Persia, that the word of the Lord by the mouth of Jeremiah might be fulfilled, the Lord stirred up the spirit of Cyrus king of Persia, that he made a proclamation throughout all his kingdom, and *put it* also in writing, saying,

1 In the first year of Cyrus king of Persia, that the word of the Lord by the mouth of Jeremiah might be accomplished, the Lord stirred up the spirit of Cyrus king of Persia so that he made a proclamation throughout all his kingdom and also put it in writing:

I. Sheshbazzar's Return (1:1–2:70)

A. Preliminary (1:1-4)

1. Introduction (1:1=II Chr. 36:22; I Esdras 2:1-2)

Ezra 1:1-3*a* reproduces II Chr. 36:22-23 almost exactly. The final sentence, incomplete in II Chronicles, is finished in Ezra, where Cyrus' decree is given in full. Duplication is even more extensive in I Esdras 1:1-58 where two full chapters of II Chronicles (35:1–36:23) are repeated. This is usually regarded as evidence of the original unity of Chronicles-Ezra-Nehemiah (cf. Intro., p. 552). With the present division of the books the passage forms both an optimistic conclusion to II Chronicles and a fitting introduction to the Ezra-Nehemiah story of reconstruction.

The **first year** was not Cyrus' first regnal year (559 b.c.) but his first as king of Babylon (538 b.c.), when the Jews had their first major contact with him (cf. 5:13). **King of Persia** was Cyrus' title as early as the Nabonidus Chronicle (col. 2, 1. 15) where it describes him before the capture of Babylon (Sidney Smith, tr., *Babylonian Historical Texts* [London: Methuen & Co., 1924], pp. 112, 116). Since more inclusive titles were used within three weeks after the capture of Babylon, **king of Persia** is usually regarded as anachronistic, an evidence of the Chronicler's authorship. It has been defended, however, as representing the title popular in the West (R. D. Wilson, "Titles of the Persian Kings," *Festschrift Eduard Sachau* [Berlin: Georg Reimer, 1915], pp. 179-207; E. J. Bickerman, "The Edict of Cyrus in Ezra 1," *Journal of Biblical Literature*, LXV [1946], 254-56).

The expression **stirred up the spirit,** used especially in late Hebrew, describes divine motivation, often indicating God's control over Gentiles (cf. I Chr. 5:26; II Chr. 21:16-17; 36:22; Jer. 51:11; Hag. 1:14). Second Isaiah regarded Cyrus as divinely commissioned (Isa. 44:28; 45:1-5, 13) and Cyrus himself, in the Cyrus Cylinder (11. 13-15) recognizes divine call and assistance (of the foreign God Marduk) in his conquest of Babylon (for texts of the Cyrus Cylinder see F. H. Weissbach, ed., *Die Keilinschriften der Achämeniden* [Leipzig: J. C. Hinrichs, 1911], pp. 2-9; Robert William Rogers, ed., *Cuneiform Parallels to the Old Testament* [2nd ed.; New York: Abingdon Press, 1926], pp. 380-84; G. A. Barton, *Archaeology and the Bible* [7th ed.; Philadelphia: American Sunday School Union, 1937], pp. 484-85; A. L. Oppenheim in J. B. Pritchard, ed., *Ancient Near Eastern Texts* [Princeton: Princeton University Press, 1950], p. 315).

Jeremiah prophesied a return to Palestine after the period of exile (Jer. 29:10; 25:12). The Chronicler has already cited the prophecy in its negative aspect, the duration of exile (II Chr. 36:21), and now refers to the positive implication, the promise of restoration. Because of divine incitement Cyrus **made a proclamation.** The Hebrew text has, lit., "he made a voice pass through," which means "he sent a herald through." Ernst Herzfeld (*Zoroaster and His World* [Princeton: Princeton University Press, 1947], I, 172,

were moving toward other ends, and were being fulfilled by other means than those on which he laid such stress. We read and interpret his book in the light of the fuller revelation of God's character and purposes which has been given to us in Jesus Christ, and through Christ's servant Paul. Inevitably we often find that the

chief ethical and spiritual values of the book of Ezra for our own time lie at points other than those which its author was most concerned to emphasize.

1:1-4. The Hand of God in History.—Alike for Ezra in his memoirs, and for the Chronicler in this later revision of them, the tolerant reli-

2 Thus saith Cyrus king of Persia, The LORD God of heaven hath given me all the kingdoms of the earth; and he hath charged me to build him a house at Jerusalem, which *is* in Judah.

2 "Thus says Cyrus king of Persia: The LORD, the God of heaven, has given me all the kingdoms of the earth, and he has charged me to build him a house at Jerusa-

---

n. 9) finds essentially a translation of this expression in the Persian word for "herald" in Dan. 3:4 (כרוז), which he derives from Persian *kāra*, "pass through," and *vāč*, "voice." Such heralds are mentioned often in Greek sources (Herodotus *History* III. 62; VII. 119; Xenophon *Anabasis* II. 1. 7; etc.) and are implied in the "commandment" and "decree" in Esth. 1:19-20, 22; 3:14; 8:13. After the **proclamation** the herald left a **writing** confirming the message (cf. II Kings 19:9-14). **Writing** here is a technical term used in Hebrew almost always for formal inscriptions (Bickerman, *op. cit.*, pp. 272-73). It is perhaps this writing, with some editing, that is given in ch. 6.

2. EDICT OF CYRUS (1:2-4=6:3-5; II Chr. 36:22-23; I Esdras 2:3-7)

Cyrus' edict appears in both 1:2-4 (in Hebrew) and in 6:3-5 (in Aramaic), in somewhat different forms. Those who feel impelled to choose between the accounts usually favor the Aramaic text. Bickerman, however (*ibid.*, pp. 249-53), insists that no choice is necessary since the Hebrew text may represent the oral proclamation of the herald, while the Aramaic text may be the official written decree.

L. W. Batten rightly claims, "In the Heb. edict . . . there is no note of improbability, save in the matter of Baby. contributors" (*A Critical and Exegetical Commentary on the Books of Ezra and Nehemiah* [New York: Charles Scribner's Sons, 1913; "International Critical Commentary"], p. 61). Phrases in the decree frequently suggest Persian bureaucratic style as known from extrabiblical sources and reflect concepts found in Cyrus' other inscriptions. These have been regarded by some as deliberate imitations of Persian style to give a semblance of authenticity to a decree forged entirely by the Chronicler (C. C. Torrey, *Ezra Studies* [Chicago: University of Chicago Press, 1910], p. 152). Probably, however, they are traces of a genuine source used by the Chronicler. Like the record in II Kings 18:17-25, 27-35; 19:10-13, the proclamation is not preserved verbatim but transmits the essence of the herald's words, including some of the official terminology.

2. Thus says Cyrus resembles the prophetic declaration "Thus saith the LORD," but it doubtless represents the official Persian formula of royal inscriptions. It appears in all versions of the Behistun inscription (Weissbach, *op. cit.*, pp. 8-75; A. E. Cowley, ed., *Aramaic Papyri of the Fifth Century B.C.* [Oxford: Clarendon Press, 1923], pp. 251-71, col. 1, ll. 7, 12; col. 2, ll. 16, 17, 22; col. 3, l. 37; col. 4, ll. 50, 59), the Gadatas inscription (tr. C. J. Ogden in G. W. Botsford and E. G. Sihler, *Hellenic Civilization* [New York: Columbia University Press, 1915], p. 162), and in trilingual inscriptions from Susa (V. Scheil, *Inscriptions des Achéménides à Suse* [Paris: E. Leroux, 1929], Nos. 3, 7, 9, 10, 14, 16 C, 16 E, 18, 20, 21, 23, 25, 26, 28, 29). Since the formula always concludes with "the king," the additional **of Persia** is due to the Chronicler (cf. vs. 1). The assertion **God . . . has given me all the kingdoms of the earth** has its counterpart in an inscription of Cyrus from Ur which claims, "The great Gods have delivered all the lands into my hand" (C. J. Gadd and Léon Legrain, *Ur Excavations Texts: Royal Inscriptions* [London and Philadelphia: British Museum & the Museum of the University of Pennsylvania, 1928], p. 58, No. 194), and the Cyrus Cylinder (l. 12) which states, "to sovereignty over the whole world he [Marduk] appointed him [Cyrus]." This view

---

gious policy of Cyrus toward the gods and shrines of his subject peoples is here interpreted as a fulfillment of Jeremiah's unspecified prophecies, and as a direct result of the working of God on the mind of the king. This religious view of human history, which anticipates the later doctrine of the divine providence, becomes for us, in our anxiety about the course and outcome of history, the most relevant aspect of this opening chapter. Little as Ezra and the Chron-

3 Who *is there* among you of all his
people? his God be with him, and let him
go up to Jerusalem, which *is* in Judah, and
build the house of the LORD God of Israel,
(he *is* the God,) which *is* in Jerusalem.

4 And whosoever remaineth in any place
where he sojourneth, let the men of his
place help him with silver, and with gold,
and with goods, and with beasts, besides the
freewill offering for the house of God that
is in Jerusalem.

lem, which is in Judah. 3 Whoever is among
you of all his people, may his God be with
him, and let him go up to Jerusalem, which
is in Judah, and rebuild the house of the
LORD, the God of Israel — he is the God
who is in Jerusalem; 4 and let each survivor,
in whatever place he sojourns, be assisted
by the men of his place with silver and gold,
with goods and with beasts, besides freewill
offerings for the house of God which is in
Jerusalem."

---

of Cyrus' divine mission is shared by Second Isaiah (44:28; 45:1-3, 13). **God of heaven**
was not employed by Hebrews in pre-exilic times, presumably because it was used by
the Aramaeans for Hadad and by the Canaanites for Baal. It is used in the postexilic
period in the Jewish Aramaic papyri (Cowley, *op. cit.*, No. 30, ll. 2, 15, 27-28; No. 31,
ll. 26-27; No. 32, ll. 3-4; No. 38, ll. 3, 5) and by Nehemiah (1:4-5; 2:4, 20). Since Ormazd,
the Persian god, was a celestial god, portrayed with a winged sun disk in the heavens
and acknowledged as creator of heaven and earth, the epithet may have been adopted
by the Persians for their god and then popularized as one inoffensive and acceptable to
most of the subject peoples. Cyrus was receptive toward the gods of his subjects. He
"worshiped" Marduk of Babylon (Cyrus Cylinder, ll. 23, 35) and repatriated the gods
exiled to Babylon by Nabonidus along with their worshipers (*ibid.,* ll. 32, 35). To the
restored gods he gave "habitations for all time" (*ibid.,* l. 32), "habitations giving joy
to their hearts" (*ibid.,* l. 34).

3. His God be with him: "Let his God go with him." The Jewish God is permitted
to return home with his adherents, just as the Babylonian gods were. Since there was
no image to transport to Jerusalem, the concept is Persian rather than Jewish. The
Nabonidus Chronicle (col. 3, ll. 21-22) states that after the fall of Babylon (Oct. 13,
539 B.C.) "from Kislimu [November-December] to Addaru [February-March] they returned
the gods of Akkad, whom Nabonidus had brought up to Babylon, to their cities" (Sidney
Smith, *Babylonian Historical Texts*, pp. 113-14, 118). Apparently the Jewish return
was part of that movement. Cyrus claims that during the conquest of Babylon Marduk
went with him, "going by his side as friend and companion" (Cyrus Cylinder, l. 15).
Since heraldic proclamations are known from other sources to begin with a question
(Xenophon *Cyropaedia* V. 8. 1; Herodotus *History* VII. 134; cf. Judg. 7:3), it is preferable
to translate **who is there among you** instead of **whoever is among you,** thus obtaining
a smoother reading. The M.T. permits either. **All,** omitted in I Esdras 2:5, is unnecessary,
reflecting the Chronicler's idea that northern Israelites who had been in pre-exilic
Jerusalem (I Chr. 9:3; II Chr. 11:16; 30:11, 21; 31:6) were also to return.

4. Each survivor presumes those "that had escaped from the sword" (II Chr. 36:20),
those returning to Judah; but more probable is the interpretation "everyone remaining
behind" (cf. I Chr. 13:2; Num. 11:26), those who refused to go to Judah. Some interpret
men of his place to include Gentiles as well as Jews, and thus see the hand of the
Chronicler laboring under the influence of the story of the exodus from Egypt (Exod.
11:2; 12:35). But the reference is rather to Jews who followed Jeremiah's advice and
developed such strong roots in Babylonia, acquiring wealth and position (Jer. 29:4-10),

---

icler knew about events that had taken place a
century before Ezra, and possibly 250 years before the Chronicler, and free as they both felt
to fill in and even to reset the picture, they
shared deeply the conviction of the greater
Hebrew prophets that human history is finally

in the hands of God. Holding this theocentric
faith, they here represent Cyrus' tolerant policy
toward the religions of all his subject peoples
as involving (vs. 3) an explicit recognition of
the God of Israel as the source and support (vs.
2) of his own kingly authority.

5 ¶ Then rose up the chief of the fathers of Judah and Benjamin, and the priests, and the Levites, with all *them* whose spirit God had raised, to go up to build the house of the LORD which *is* in Jerusalem.

6 And all they that *were* about them strengthened their hands with vessels of silver, with gold, with goods, and with beasts, and with precious things, besides all *that* was willingly offered.

5 Then rose up the heads of the fathers' houses of Judah and Benjamin, and the priests and the Levites, every one whose spirit God had stirred to go up to rebuild the house of the LORD which is in Jerusalem; 6 and all who were about them aided them with vessels of silver, with gold, with goods, with beasts, and with costly wares,

---

that they decided to remain. These were expected to assist those who wished to return. **Help him:** Lit., "support him." The verb may also mean "supply him" (cf. I Kings 9:11). Such supplies were to enable the emigrants to make the long journey.

B. PREPARATION FOR THE RETURN (1:5-11)

1. CHIEFS OF FATHERS (1:5=I Esdras 2:8)

5. The Chronicler portrays immediate response to the permissive edict. **Chief of the fathers** abbreviates **the heads of the fathers' houses** (cf. Exod. 6:14; I Chr. 5:24), "clan chieftains" according to I Esdras 2:8. **Judah and Benjamin** were regarded by the Chronicler as constituting the postexilic community, presumably because they alone had remained loyal to the house of David (4:1; II Chr. 11:12; I Chr. 12:16; Neh. 11:4) and were the elements of the pre-exilic kingdom last taken into captivity. **The priests and the Levites** were the religious personnel needed for the temple. **Levites** were priests of a lower order, treated as servants of the regular priests (Num. 3:9-10).

With all them seems to imply another class of emigrants, but the Hebrew text should be translated "namely," indicating those already mentioned, since all who returned were **stirred** by God (vs. 1). **Rose up . . . to,** idiomatic for "began at once to . . . ," means "Then they began at once to go up to build . . . ." **To go up,** rather than simply "to go," indicates Palestinian usage where the height of Jerusalem above other sites necessitates ascent to the capital.

2. SUPPORT OF NEIGHBORS (1:6=I Esdras 2:9)

6. The influence of vs. 4 is apparent here, but the Chronicler amplifies or alters some of the expressions. "Those remaining" (vs. 4) becomes **all who were about them,** which could refer to Gentile neighbors as well as Jews. **Strengthened their hands:** An idiom meaning **aided them** is used for the "supply him" of vs. 4. Instead of **with vessels** (בכלי), I Esdras 2:9 reads a graphically similar Hebrew text as "in all things" (בכל). The latter is preferable since **vessels** may be due to vs. 7. In addition to things listed in vs. 4, mention is made of **costly wares** (cf. Gen. 24:53; II Chr. 21:3; 32:23), possibly under the influence by the exodus story (Exod. 3:22; 11:2; 12:35). The Hebrew words rendered **besides** are a unique combination without that meaning elsewhere. Part of the Hebrew expression itself (על) may mean "in addition to" (cf. Gen. 28:9; 31:50). The remainder of the Hebrew text (לבד) should be translated "in abundance" (לרב), correcting a scribal error of a graphically similar text (cf. I Esdras 2:9 and Syriac).

5-11. *A Heritage Becomes a Task.*—In the light of the pathetic picture of the situation and morale of the returned exiles in Jerusalem given in Hag. 1, and of the difficulty the prophet plainly encountered in arousing the people to rebuild their temple, which he explicitly says (Hag. 2:3) was in such depressing contrast to "its former glory," these verses seem to throw a rosy glow of magnifying patriotism and piety over the actual scale of the rebuilding of Jerusalem, as not only Haggai but the archaeological evidences indicate it. This picture of an emigration of leading citizens from Babylon to Jerusalem to rebuild the temple, bringing with them not only large gifts freely offered, but **five thousand four hundred and sixty-nine . . . vessels of gold and of silver** from Solomon's temple, now restored to them by Cyrus for this **purpose,**

7 ¶ Also Cyrus the king brought forth the vessels of the house of the LORD, which Nebuchadnezzar had brought forth out of Jerusalem, and had put them in the house of his gods;

8 Even those did Cyrus king of Persia bring forth by the hand of Mithredath the treasurer, and numbered them unto Shesh-bazzar, the prince of Judah.

9 And this is the number of them: thirty chargers of gold, a thousand chargers of silver, nine and twenty knives,

besides all that was freely offered. 7 Cyrus the king also brought out the vessels of the house of the LORD which Nebuchadnez'zar had carried away from Jerusalem and placed in the house of his gods. 8 Cyrus king of Persia brought these out in charge of Mith'redath the treasurer, who counted them out to Shesh-baz'zar the prince of Judah. 9 And this was the number of them: a thousand[a] basins of gold, a thousand ba-

^a 1 Esdras 2. 13. Heb thirty

3. CYRUS' RETURN OF TEMPLE VESSELS (1:7-11=I Esdras 2:10-12)

7-8. The Hebrew text stresses the royal contribution, the returning of precious vessels taken by the Babylonians (Jer. 52:18-20; II Kings 25:14-15), by placing **the king** before **Cyrus**. The **vessels** were dedicated as a trophy of war (cf. I Sam. 5:2; 31:9-10; II Chr. 5:1) in the temple Esagila, **the house of his gods** in Babylon, by **Nebuchadnezzar** (605-562 B.C.) who destroyed Jerusalem in 586 B.C. **Mithredath** is a Persian name (Mithradata) and the title **treasurer** is also a Persian word which was adopted by the Akkadian, Aramaic, and Hebrew languages.

Shesh-bazzar is a corruption of Babylonian Shamash-ab-uṣur (so M.T. and LXX) or Sin-ab-uṣur (I Esdras and Josephus). The Lucianic recension of I Esdras suggests Shamash-apal-uṣur, but lack of support of the reading by the O.L. (Sasabalassar) suggests that it is a late revised spelling. Like Zerubbabel (cf. 2:2), he bears a Babylonian name but is the prime secular Jewish leader. His title (נשיא) often means **prince,** but may be simply "chief" or "leader" (Gen. 17:20; 25:16). Some identify him with Shenazzar (I Chr. 3:18), the son of Jehoiakim and uncle of Zerubbabel (I Chr. 3:19). If so, the title **prince** would be appropriate. The Chronicler wrongly identifies **Shesh-bazzar** with Zerubbabel. Here I Esdras 2:11 calls him "governor" (προστάτης), anticipating the title applied elsewhere (5:14).

9-11. **Vessels** is too limited since the Hebrew term could include implements of various kinds as well. The **bowls** (vs. 10) are Babylonian kaparu, food bowls. **Chargers,** "platters" (ASV), or **basins** represent a Hebrew word (אגרטל) of uncertain origin and meaning. It appears non-Semitic, possibly Aryan, but proposed identification with Greek "basket" (κάρταλλος) or "wine mixing bowl" (κρατήρ) is precarious. The LXX renders "wine cooler" (ψυκτῆρες) and I Esdras (2:9) here has "libation vessel" (σπονδεῖα). **Censers,** too, represents an obscure word rendered elsewhere as **knives** (so Vulg.; Syriac; Talmud) and "changes of garments" (LXX). I Esdras employs the same word **(censers)** used by the LXX in II Kings 25:14 for the Hebrew word "hand" (כף), which may indicate the hand-shaped "censers" of ivory and steatite found at Megiddo (Herbert G. May, *Material Remains of the Megiddo Cult* [Chicago: University of Chicago Press, 1935], pp. 18-19, Pl. XVII). Julius A. Bewer would omit the word (מחלפים) entirely, regarding it as a corrupt repetition of the preceding word "two thousand" (*Der Text des Buches Ezra* [Göttingen: Vandenhoeck & Ruprecht, 1922], p. 16). Kurt Galling revocalizes the Hebrew word to translate "substitute fittings," which appears inappropriate ("Der Tempelschatz nach Berichten und Urkunden im Buche Esra," *Zeitschrift*

sounds in the sober light of Haggai very much like "idealized history." But Americans, who have not always looked back through the cool clear light of critical scholarship at Pilgrim ancestors as they landed on Plymouth Rock, or at the "founding fathers" as they wrote the

Constitution, or at the pioneers as they moved out in their covered wagons to the "winning of the West," can surely understand something of this Jewish pride and gratitude that magnified as through a powerful reading lens not only the major achievements of their forefathers but

10 Thirty basins of gold, silver basins of a second *sort* four hundred and ten, *and* other vessels a thousand.

11 All the vessels of gold and of silver *were* five thousand and four hundred. All *these* did Sheshbazzar bring up with *them of* the captivity that were brought up from Babylon unto Jerusalem.

2 Now these *are* the children of the province that went up out of the captivity, of those which had been carried away, whom Nebuchadnezzar the king of

sins of silver, twenty-nine censers, **10** thirty bowls of gold, two thousand[b] four hundred and ten bowls of silver, and a thousand other vessels; **11** all the vessels of gold and of silver were five thousand four hundred and sixty-nine.[c] All these did Shesh-baz'zar bring up, when the exiles were brought up from Babylonia to Jerusalem.

2 Now these were the people of the province who came up out of the cap-

[b] 1 Esdras 2. 13. Heb *of a second sort*
[c] 1 Esdras 2. 14. Heb *five thousand four hundred*

---

des deutschen Palästina-vereins, LX [1937], 180-81). Wilhelm Rudolph (*Esra und Nehemia* [Tübingen: J. C. B. Mohr, 1949; "Handbuch zum Alten Testament"], p. 5) treats it as a marginal comment, "to be corrected," which has been accidentally taken into the text. **Of a second sort** (vs. 10), which separates an item from its total, is also difficult. The Hebrew word means either "double" (LXXMSS; Syriac; Ethiopic) or **second sort**, neither of which suits the context. Since I Esdras has a larger number than the M.T. in this verse, the Hebrew word (חלפים) has been regarded as a corruption of **two thousand** (אלפים).

The figures are in hopeless confusion. Totals vary in the versions, and except for I Esdras the grand total does not agree with that obtained by adding the given items. The grand total 5,400 of the M.T. is 2,901 more than the figure arrived at by addition. Figures given in the KJV and ASV are those of the M.T. and LXX, while those of the RSV follow I Esdras.

Explanations of the discrepancies differ considerably. Rudolph (*ibid.*) makes few emendations of the M.T. and explains the differences between items and total by the assumption that the grand total includes items accidentally lost from the M.T. Bewer (*loc. cit.*) prefers emendation, reading "two thousand" for **censers** (vs. 9) and another **two thousand** for **a second sort** (vs. 10). He contends that the original total was 5,499, that obtained by adding his emended figures. He assumes that from that figure the number "ninety-nine" was lost from the Hebrew text to leave the round number 5,400 in the M.T. and LXX.

A list of articles taken from the Jerusalem temple is given in II Kings 25:14 ff. but without enumeration. The figures in vss. 9-11 are fantastically large, apparently exaggerated according to the Chronicler's well-recognized custom.

C. Returning Israelites (2:1-70)

In 1:11 the Chronicler presumes the substance of ch. 2, which he introduces from Neh. 7:6-73, where the list is designated as "those who came up at the beginning" (Neh. 7:5). He assumes that it describes those returning with Sheshbazzar, although that name is not mentioned therein. Such identification is possible only because the Chronicler wrongly identifies Sheshbazzar with Zerubbabel. Since traditionally each headed a return to Jerusalem (vs. 2; 1:11*b*), and each began to build the temple (3:8; 5:2), it is perhaps inevitable that there should be confusion, even though a later document used

---

even the details of their adventurous journeyings through what were doubtless "days of small things." God had been at work in their national history, as in that of the United States, through the courage and faith of little-known men "whose hearts God had touched" (I Sam. 10:26) with the energy and patience to overcome great

odds, and to finish what began as a precarious undertaking.

2:1-67. *The Role of Inconspicuous Individuals.*
—This religious view of history in retrospect illuminates also the longer range significance of the extensive lists and numbers of family and regional groups that make up so large and, for

Babylon had carried away unto Babylon, and came again unto Jerusalem and Judah, every one unto his city;	tivity of those exiles whom Nebuchadnez'-zar the king of Babylon had carried captive to Babylonia; they returned to Jerusalem and Judah, each to his own town. 2 They came with Zerub'babel, Jeshua, Nehemi'ah,
2 Which came with Zerubbabel: Jeshua, Nehemiah, Seraiah, Reelaiah, Mordecai,	

by the Chronicler (5:2, 14, 16) makes it evident that historically Sheshbazzar under Cyrus must be differentiated from Zerubbabel, who was active under Darius I.

Zerubbabel and Jeshua in vs. 2 suggest that the list originally described a return at the time of Darius I, but it is probable that the list does not all come from the same period, for differing formulas in the list of laymen (vss. 2b-35) indicate that it has been supplemented by data drawn from other sources. In I Esdras 5:7-46 it purports to list those returning with Zerubbabel. The list was so highly regarded by the Chronicler that its clan names and their sequence are employed whenever a tabulation of postexilic Judeans is required. Its influence is found in the list of those sealing the covenant (Neh. 10:14-27), in the list of those who had taken foreign wives (10:18-44), and elsewhere. Josephus knew the list but purposely omitted it lest it interrupt his narrative (*Antiquities* XI. 3. 10).

1. Superscription (2:1-2a=Neh. 7:7; I Esdras 5:8)

2:1. These in the superscription signifies not only those in vs. 2 but all in the list. **The province** was technically the Judean subdivision of the fifth Persian satrapy. The point of view of the list is Palestinian and postexilic. The Chronicler ignores Jews who remained in Judea and the temporary fugitives who returned to the land early, and regards as true Israel the people of Judah and Benjamin who returned from exile. Names in the list indicate that some at least of the clan founders were descendants of those exiled and had not themselves seen pre-exilic Judea. **Each to his own town** (cf. vs. 70) unrealistically ignores the fact that many pre-exilic sites were not subsequently reoccupied. The rabbis claimed, "Many cities which were conquered by the Israelites who came up from Egypt were not reconquered by those who came up from Babylon" (Isidore Epstein, ed., *The Babylonian Talmud: Seder Ḳodashim* [London: Soncino Press, 1948]; Ḥullin I, 7a), and archaeology confirms this view. Destroyed Jerusalem could not house all of its pre-exilic inhabitants (cf. Neh. 2:17; 7:4). Doubtless the immigrants sought to settle at pre-exilic ancestral homes wherever possible, but many obviously had to start anew elsewhere.

2a. A simple list of people, given without genealogy perhaps because they were well-known personages, precedes the principal list. The record is ambiguous since it could be, as in the KJV, a list of those who returned with Zerubbabel or (with ASV, RSV, and the American Jewish Translation) an account of leaders of diverse periods, of whom Zerubbabel was but one, who led Jews back to Judea. They were "guides" (προηγούμενοι) according to I Esdras 5:8, and Josephus (*loc. cit.*) calls them "rulers" who were "distinguished from the multitude." According to Rudolph (*op. cit.*, p. 19, n. 4), R. Fruin has suggested that they were a series of governors of the province of Judea (cf. "Is Esra een Historisch Persoon?" *Nieuw Theologisch Tijdschrift*, XVIII [1929], 132 ff.). If so, several, like **Zerubbabel** and **Jeshua**, may have been contemporaries, for the list is much too long. Sheshbazzar, of course, would be omitted by virtue of identification with **Zerubbabel**. If "Azariah" (Neh. 7:7), the name of which Ezra is an

us of today, so tedious a part of ch. 2. As the Exeg. shows, these long lists were made up not only from different sources but from different categories—some genealogical, others geographical. The Chronicler was greatly interested in such lists of the men of other days, and made	them do duty for various purposes. They are reminders to every subsequent generation that its own history and civilization have been forgotten or perhaps confused. Who knows today the names of more than a very few of the American pioneers who first settled the thirteen

Bilshan, Mizpar, Bigvai, Rehum, Baanah. The number of the men of the people of Israel:

3 The children of Parosh, two thousand a hundred seventy and two.

4 The children of Shephatiah, three hundred seventy and two.

5 The children of Arah, seven hundred seventy and five.

Serai'ah, Re-el-ai'ah, Mor'decai, Bilshan, Mispar, Big'vai, Rehum, and Ba'anah.

The number of the men of the people of Israel: 3 the sons of Parosh, two thousand one hundred and seventy-two. 4 The sons of Shephati'ah, three hundred and seventy-two. 5 The sons of Arah, seven hundred and

---

abbreviation, is read instead of **Seraiah,** the order of **Nehemiah** and "Azariah" may be significant. In addition to **Zerubbabel,** a Persian **Bigvai** is mentioned as governor of Judea under Darius II (Cowley, *Aramaic Papyri,* No. 30, l. 1; Josephus, too, mentions a vice-regent of the same name in Palestine [*Antiquities* XI. 7), and a **Rehum** figures prominently as a Palestinian official contemporary with Nehemiah (cf. 4:8-9, 17, 23). Such a theory, obviously incapable of proof, would explain the preponderance of foreign names, since more than half are non-Jewish and distinctly postexilic in type. **Bigvai** is Persian and in addition to **Zerubbabel** ("Seed of Babylon"), **Mordecai** (an abbreviation of a name with the god element *Marduk*) and **Bilshan** (probably the popular abbreviation Bel-shunu) are Babylonian names.

2. The Principal List (2:2*b*-67)

The principal list presents the number of each clan that returned, followed by a list of their servants and beasts, concluding with a listing of donations to the temple (vss. 68-69). The list, divided by headings into different categories, begins, contrary to the Chronicler's preference, with a list of laymen rather than priests and Levites. Introductory formulas show that the original lay list (vss. 3-20), wherein the clans are identified by ancestors who founded them, has been supplemented several times (vss. 21-28, 29-35) from sources which identify those returning by geographical names.

Although described as a "book of genealogy" (Neh. 7:5), a stress on number rather than name has led some to regard the list as an official Persian census of the Jewish community (Robert H. Pfeiffer, *Introduction to the Old Testament* [New York: Harper & Bros., 1941], pp. 822, 836; G. Hölscher, *Die Bücher Esra und Nehemia* [4th ed., E. Kautzsch and A. Bertholet; Tübingen: J. C. B. Mohr, 1923], II, 503-4). This concept seems to be supported by the use of geographical rather than personal names, but numbers are just as important in a tally of immigrants, and vss. 65-67, inexplainable as part of a census, are appropriate to an account of a return (cf. Rudolph, *op. cit.,* pp. 15-16).

Where personal names are found they are not all of the same order. In addition to the usual Hebrew sentence names (e.g., vs. 4, **Shephatiah,** "The Lord Judges") there are partial names, used in abbreviation (e.g., vs. 9, **Zaccai** for such a name as Zechariah, "The Lord Has Remembered"), animal names (e.g., vs. 3, **Parosh,** "Flea"; vs. 5, **Arah,** "Ox"), and nicknames (e.g., vs. 19, **Hashum,** "Broad Nose"). Interesting is **Pahath-moab** (vs. 6), which is not a personal name but the title "Governor of Moab." The foreign names **Elam** (vss. 7, 31), **Bigvai** (vs. 14), and **Ater** (vs. 16) reflect the Exile.

Since the lists all name rather remote ancestors, the words **sons of** should here be understood as "descendants of."

a) Laymen (2:2*b*-35=Neh. 7:7*b*-38; I Esdras 5:7-23)

(1) By Family (2:2*b*-20)

5. Arah ("Ox") has parallels in Babylonia and among Arabs, but only the Chronicler uses it in the Bible. He names a pre-exilic descendant of Asher, a "chief of princes" who was a "head" of a "father's house" (I Chr. 7:39-40). Of widely differing totals in the versions, the original figure appears to have been either 652 (as in the M.T. of Neh. 7:10

6 The children of Pahath-moab, of the children of Jeshua *and* Joab, two thousand eight hundred and twelve.

7 The children of Elam, a thousand two hundred fifty and four.

8 The children of Zattu, nine hundred forty and five.

9 The children of Zaccai, seven hundred and threescore.

10 The children of Bani, six hundred forty and two.

11 The children of Bebai, six hundred twenty and three.

12 The children of Azgad, a thousand two hundred twenty and two.

13 The children of Adonikam, six hundred sixty and six.

14 The children of Bigvai, two thousand fifty and six.

seventy-five. 6 The sons of Pa′hath-mo′ab, namely the sons of Jeshua and Jo′ab, two thousand eight hundred and twelve. 7 The sons of Elam, one thousand two hundred and fifty-four. 8 The sons of Zattu, nine hundred and forty-five. 9 The sons of Zac′-cai, seven hundred and sixty. 10 The sons of Bani, six hundred and forty-two. 11 The sons of Be′bai, six hundred and twenty-three. 12 The sons of Azgad, one thousand two hundred and twenty-two. 13 The sons of Adoni′kam, six hundred and sixty-six. 14 The sons of Big′vai, two thousand and

---

and I Esdras 5:10 in the Lucianic recension) or 752 (with the LXXBא of Neh. 7:10 and the Lucianic Greek text there).

6. Pahath-moab ("Governor of Moab") designates an early Hebrew person who ruled Moab. Under David (II Sam. 8:2) and Solomon, Judeans dominated Moab. The Chronicler suggests that Judeans ruled Moab (Neh. 3:11) and lists a Judean Saraph ("Serpent") as ruler of Moab (I Chr. 4:22). The clan was subdivided into those of **Jeshua and Joab** (cf. 8:9; Neh. 3:19).

7. Elam is used by the Chronicler to designate a Benjaminite (I Chr. 8:24). The name probably has connection with the country east of the Tigris (Gen. 10:22) later ruled by Cyrus, a place to which exiled Israelites were sent (Isa. 11:11).

10. Bani (בני) appears as "Binnui" (בנוי) in Neh. 7:15 and as "Bunni" (בני) in Neh. 10:15. Since two names are found in the list in both Ezra 10:29, 34 and Neh. 10:13-15, it is probable that the original list contained two very similar names, representing different clans, and that identical spelling in the C.T. caused the loss of one here. Read for 642 the 648 of Neh. 7:15 and I Esdras 5:13.

12. Azgad ("Gad Is Strong") like Gaddiel ("Gad Is God") in Num. 13:10 contains the name of the god Gad, "Fortune" (cf. Gen. 30:11; Isa. 65:11). For the **one thousand two hundred and twenty-two** of Ezra read 2,222 with the Lucianic recension of Ezra and Nehemiah (cf. Neh. 7:12). The text in Ezra is easily explained by the loss of a letter which makes two thousand (אלפם) read **one thousand** (אלף). The loss was easy before **two hundred** (מאתים), which begins with the same letter that was lost.

13. Adonikam ("My Lord Has Arisen") has the element Adoni- ("My Lord") found in the early names Adoniram (I Kings 4:6) and Adonijah (I Kings 1:8; II Sam. 3:4), where it substitutes for the name of God. Read 667 with Neh. 7:18 and I Esdras 5:14 for the **six hundred and sixty-six** of Ezra.

14. Bigvai (cf. vs. 2), a Persian name, could be a clan name no earlier than the time of the Exile. Greek texts and Josephus (*Antiquities* XI. 7) show that the first

---

colonies or those who crossed the continent by covered wagon? It was such nameless men who became the first Christian missionaries to the Gentiles (Acts 11:20), and thereby changed the course of Western history. Lists of names like these may be inaccurate or ambiguous, and are

certainly tedious reading in public worship or private devotion today; but they remind us of humanity's unpayable debt to nameless men and women who have made posterity their heavy debtors by the courage and persistence that were the historical price of our human heritage.

15 The children of Adin, four hundred fifty and four.

16 The children of Ater of Hezekiah, ninety and eight.

17 The children of Bezai, three hundred twenty and three.

18 The children of Jorah, a hundred and twelve.

19 The children of Hashum, two hundred twenty and three.

20 The children of Gibbar, ninety and five.

21 The children of Beth-lehem, a hundred twenty and three.

fifty-six. 15 The sons of Adin, four hundred and fifty-four. 16 The sons of Ater, namely of Hezeki′ah, ninety-eight. 17 The sons of Be′zai, three hundred and twenty-three. 18 The sons of Jorah, one hundred and twelve. 19 The sons of Hashum, two hundred and twenty-three. 20 The sons of Gibbar, ninety-five. 21 The sons of Bethlehem,

---

syllable is Persian *baga-* ("God"). Aramaic papyri spell **Bigvai** (בגוי) as בגוהי, the name of a Persian governor of Judea (Cowley, *op. cit.*, No. 30, 1. 1; No. 32, 1. 1; cf. p. 109).

16. Ater as Hebrew could be either "Cripple" or "Lefty," but is probably the very common abbreviated name Etir, found often in business documents of the Neo-Babylonian and Persian periods. The spelling of the name is the same as that of the element Etir in the names in Aramaic endorsements on cuneiform tablets (Louis Delaporte, *Épigraphes araméens* [Paris: Paul Geuthner, 1912], p. 52, No. 38; p. 57, No. 53). For **of Hezekiah** read "namely of Hezekiah," since the Babylonian name, given in the Exile, had displaced the old clan name **Hezekiah**.

Here I Esdras 5:15 adds four names not in the list in the Hebrew text. The first two are corruptions of Ezra 2:31 (Bewer, *Der Text des Buches Ezra*, pp. 21-22) but from Neh. 10:18-19 it is clear that the other two (υἱοὶ Ἀζούρου, 432, υἱοὶ Ἀννίας [for αυδιας], 101) represent the Azzur of Neh. 10:17, and a corruption of Hodijah of Neh. 10:18 (KJV), now lost from the Hebrew lists. Bewer arbitrarily assumes that the 101 of I Esdras 5:15 was originally 110 in order to obtain a larger grand total.

17-19. I Esdras 5:16 supports the order of verses in Neh. 7:22-24 (cf. Neh. 10:18-19), where the substance of vs. 19 here appears before that of vs. 17. **Bezai** abbreviates Bezalel (10:30; cf. Exod. 31:2; 35:30). **Jorah** ("Autumn Rain"; cf. Deut. 11:14; Jer. 5:24; Hos. 6:3), unique in Ezra, is "Hariph" in Neh. 7:24; 10:19 and originally in I Esdras 5:16. Since Arabic *harîf* means either "freshly gathered fruit" or "autumn rain," it has been argued that **Jorah** and Hariph may be equivalents (Martin Noth, *Die israelitischen Personennamen im Rahmen der Gemeinsemitischen Namengebung* [Stuttgart: W. Kohlhammer, 1928; "Beiträge zur Wissenschaft vom Alten und Neuen Testament"], pp. 228, 244; cf. Rudolph, *op. cit.*, p. 8).

20. Gibbar appears in Neh. 7:25 as the place name "Gibeon," perhaps because of proximity to the names that follow, but Gibeon, northwest of Jerusalem, should not appear before vs. 25 in a list which works northward. The LXX^A vocalizes Gaber which is probably the abbreviated Babylonian name Gabria (for Ilu-gabri) found in cuneiform tablets of the Persian period.

(2) By City (2:21-35)

21-28. (Cf. Neh. 7:26-32; I Esdras 5:17-21.) With vss. 21-28 the introductory formula changes from "the sons of" to **the men of,** and the listing is by geographical home rather than by ancestor. The significance of the shift is not clear. It may indicate later supplementation from another source, but some have thought that it indicated a different type of citizen. K. F. Keil suggested that the previous clans were all of Jerusalem, in contrast to those listed geographically (*Chronik, Esra, Nehemia und Esther* [Leipzig: Dörffling & Franke, 1870; "Biblischer Commentar über das Alte Testament"], pp. 415-17), but the figures given are much too large. Others have suggested that those in vss. 3-20

22 The men of Netophah, fifty and six.

23 The men of Anathoth, a hundred twenty and eight.

24 The children of Azmaveth, forty and two.

25 The children of Kirjath-arim, Chephirah, and Beeroth, seven hundred and forty and three.

26 The children of Ramah and Gaba, six hundred twenty and one.

one hundred and twenty-three. 22 The men of Neto'phah, fifty-six. 23 The men of An'athoth, one hundred and twenty-eight. 24 The sons of Az'maveth, forty-two. 25 The sons of Kir'iathar'im, Chephi'rah, and Be-er'oth, seven hundred and forty-three. 26 The sons of Ramah and Geba, six hun-

---

were landed property holders, the freemen, the "people of the land," in contrast to those without property, "the poor of the land" (II Kings 25:12; Jer. 40:7), who were not listed by clan (Eduard Meyer, *Die Entstehung des Judenthums* [Halle: M. Niemeyer, 1896], pp. 152 ff.; Rudolf Kittel, *Geschichte des Volkes Israel* [2nd ed.; Stuttgart: W. Kohlhammer, 1929], III, 359-61; Rudolph, *op. cit.*, p. 20).

It is uncertain whether the places mentioned represent pre-exilic ancestral homes to which the immigrants returned or centers at which returning Jews actually settled. From vss. 1, 70 it is clear that the Chronicler thought that all Jews could return to their pre-exilic homes. It is significant that there is no reference to towns of the Negeb, far in the south, which Jeremiah (13:19) claims were plundered in 598 B.C. and cut off from Judah so that no prisoners were taken from that region in 586 B.C. (Albrecht Alt, "Judas Gaue unter Josia," *Palästinajahrbuch*, XXI [1925], 108). The towns listed begin with the southernmost, in the vicinity of Bethlehem, and proceed northward through familiar sites that appear largely to have escaped the destruction which made the rest of Judea quite a desolate region during the Exile.

21-22. For **The sons of Bethlehem** read "the men of Bethlehem," with vss. 22 ff.; Neh. 7:26. **Bethlehem** is modern Beit Laḥm, about five miles south of Jerusalem. **Netophah** is probably Khirbet Bedd Fâlûḥ, about three miles south of Bethlehem, near the road to Tekoa, the home of Amos (Alt, "Das Institut im Jahre 1931," *Palästinajahrbuch*, XXVIII [1932], 9 ff.; Konrad Kob, "Netopha," *ibid.*, pp. 47-54).

23. Anathoth, home of some of David's men (II Sam. 23:27), of Abiathar (I Kings 2:26), and of Jeremiah (1:1; 32:6-15), is Râs el-Kharrûbeh near 'Anāta, about three miles northeast of Jerusalem.

24. Read "men of" as in Neh. 7:28 and I Esdras 5:18 instead of **sons of.** For **Azmaveth** read "Beth-azmaveth," as in Neh. 7:28 and I EsdrasAB 5:18. It is modern Hizmeh, about five miles north-northeast of Jerusalem. The name is Canaanite, preserving the divine name Mot now found in the Ugaritic texts.

25. As in vs. 24, read "men of" with Neh. 7:29 and I Esdras 5:19. **Kiriatharim** ("Village of Cities") is obviously an error for "Kiriath-jearim" ("Village of the Woods") as Neh. 7:29 and the LXX show (cf. Josh. 9:17; 15:9; etc.). It is probably Tell el-Azhar, about nine miles from Jerusalem toward Lydda, nearly six miles southwest of Gibeon. **Chephirah** is Nhirbet el Kefîreh, five miles west of Gibeon, commanding its approaches from the west, about two miles north of Kiriath-jearim. **Be-eroth,** which presumably guarded Gibeon from the north, is not yet exactly identified but Eusebius locates it "under the hill of Gabaon" (Erich Klostermann, *Das Onomasticon der biblische Ortsnamen* [Leipzig: J. C. Hinrichs, 1904]; cf. Peter Thomsen, "Palästina nach dem Onomasticon des Eusebius," *Zeitschrift des deutschen Palästina-vereins*, XXVI [1903], 97-188).

26. Read "men of" with Neh. 7:30 and I EsdrasAB 5:20. **Geba** is modern Jeba', a Benjaminite town commanding the pass at Michmas, east of **Ramah**, which as modern Er-Râm is five miles north of Jerusalem, opposite Bethel. **Ramah** was a frontier outpost of Benjamin, lying between the ancient kingdoms of Israel and Judah (I Kings 15:17, 22).

27 The men of Michmas, a hundred twenty and two.

28 The men of Beth-el and Ai, two hundred twenty and three.

29 The children of Nebo, fifty and two.

30 The children of Magbish, a hundred fifty and six.

31 The children of the other Elam, a thousand two hundred fifty and four.

32 The children of Harim, three hundred and twenty.

33 The children of Lod, Hadid, and Ono, seven hundred twenty and five.

dred and twenty-one. 27 The men of Michmas, one hundred and twenty-two. 28 The men of Bethel and Ai, two hundred and twenty-three. 29 The sons of Nebo, fifty-two. 30 The sons of Magbish, one hundred and fifty-six. 31 The sons of the other Elam, one thousand two hundred and fifty-four. 32 The sons of Harim, three hundred and twenty. 33 The sons of Lod, Hadid, and

---

27. Michmas, modern Mukhmâs (cf. I Sam. 14:5), lies northeast of Geba, on the road from Jericho to Ai.

28. Bethel and **Ai** cross the border of Judah-Benjamin into former Ephraimite territory. Alt ("Judas Gaue unter Josia," pp. 108-9) has argued that it was Josiah's policy of expansion that added the marginal district to Judah in pre-exilic times. **Bethel,** modern Beitîn, lies on the road to Shechem (Nablus), about twelve miles north of Jerusalem. **Ai** ("The Ruin") was et-Tell near Dēr Dīwân, on a rocky terraced mound almost two miles east of **Bethel.** Excavation shows the site deserted from about 2200 B.C., except for a few houses about 1000 B.C. Although it is improbable that the place was resettled in any serious fashion during the postexilic period, Rudolph would identify it with Aiath (Isa. 10:28) and Aija (Neh. 11:31).

29-35. (Cf. Neh. 7:33-38; I Esdras 5:21-24.) From "men of" the formula changes to "sons of," as in vss. 3-20, indicating another source. Since the names from vs. 33 are indisputably geographical, it must be true of the whole list that "sons of" must mean "inhabitants of" (cf. Joel 3:6).

29. Most MSS of I Esdras 5:21 support Ezra in reading "sons of" rather than "men of." Nebai (Neh. 10:19) and Nob (Neh. 11:32; cf. Isa. 10:32) suggest a reading Nub or Nob for **Nebo** here (Meyer, *op. cit.,* pp. 145, 149). It has nothing to do with Mount Nebo (Deut. 32:49) or Nebo of Trans-Jordan (Num. 32:3) but is probably Beit Nûbā, north of Aijalon (Yâlō).

30. Magbish is omitted in Neh. 7:33-34, but appears as "Magpiash" in Neh. 10:20. Its location is uncertain but the name signifying "made massive" or "heaped up" suggests a place. Etymological difficulty prevents acceptance of C. R. Conder's identification with Khirbet Maḥbiyeh, about four miles northwest of Nebo (Nûbā) (*Map of Western Palestine* [London: Ordnance Survey Office, 1880], Sheet XXI, sec. JV; cf. F. M. Abel, *Géographie de la Palestine* [Paris: J. Gabalda, 1938], II, 398, *s.v. Nébo*).

31. Other Elam contrasts with the Elam of vs. 7. Conder (*loc. cit.*) identifies this place with Beit ʿĀlam, about three and a half miles south of Khirbet Maḥbiyeh and somewhat west-southwest of Nûbā. The total is the same as that in vs. 7, but Rudolph (*op. cit.,* p. 9) rightly insists that such a coincidence does not justify the omission of vs. 31. The larger figure of 2,254 in the LXX of Ezra and Nehemiah, which apparently derives from an alternate Hebrew text, is preferable.

32. Conder (*loc. cit.*) identified **Harim** with Khirbet Hôrân, about one mile northwest of Khirbet Maḥbiyeh (cf. vs. 30).

33. Lod, modern Ludd or Lydda, lies in the Plain of Sharon, about eleven miles southeast of Jaffa. **Hadid,** modern el-Hadîtheh, about three and one-quarter miles northeast of **Lod** (Alt, "Das Institut im Jahr 1927," *Palästinajahrbuch, XXIV* [1928], 71-72). **Ono,** modern Kefr ʿAnā, lay northwest of **Lod,** almost due east of Jaffa.

These cities, far from Jerusalem, may have been added to Judah under Josiah in pre-exilic times (Alt, "Judas Gaue unter Josia," pp. 110-11), but in postexilic times they

34 The children of Jericho, three hundred forty and five.

35 The children of Senaah, three thousand and six hundred and thirty.

36 ¶ The priests: the children of Jedaiah, of the house of Jeshua, nine hundred seventy and three.

37 The children of Immer, a thousand fifty and two.

38 The children of Pashur, a thousand two hundred forty and seven.

39 The children of Harim, a thousand and seventeen.

Ono, seven hundred and twenty-five. 34 The sons of Jericho, three hundred and forty-five. 35 The sons of Sena'ah, three thousand six hundred and thirty.

36 The priests: the sons of Jedai'ah, of the house of Jeshua, nine hundred and seventy-three. 37 The sons of Immer, one thousand and fifty-two. 38 The sons of Pashhur, one thousand two hundred and forty-seven. 39 The sons of Harim, one thousand and seventeen.

---

appear to have been in a neutral zone between the provinces of Ashdod and Samaria (Neh. 6:2; Alt, "Judas Nachbarn zur Zeit Nehemias," *Palästinajahrbuch*, XXVII [1931], 72, n. 5). Rudolph (*op. cit.*, pp. 20-21) holds that this verse cannot refer to the time of Cyrus or Darius and must be a supplement from a later period.

34. Jericho lies at the ruins of Tell es-Sultân, about a mile and a half northwest of modern Jericho, at the eastern foot of the Judean hills. Formerly under control of the Northern Kingdom (cf. I Kings 16:34; II Kings 2:4 ff.), Jericho by late pre-exilic times came under the authority of Judah presumably during the reign of Josiah (Alt, "Judas Gaue unter Josia," p. 109), and it appears to be Judean in the time of Nehemiah (cf. Neh. 3:2).

35. Senaah was probably classical Magdalsenna ("Tower of Sena'a"), controlling the route from the Jordan Valley to Baal Hazor. Abel (*op. cit.*, II, 455) identifies it with the ruin Sheikh Tarûni near Khirbet el 'Auja el Fôqa, about eight miles northeast of Jericho.

b) TEMPLE MINISTRANTS (2:36-58=Neh. 7:39-60; I Esdras 5:24-35)

After the laymen, the list includes those who ministered in the temple, presented by classes and assigned to clans according to ancestors as in vss. 3-20.

(1) PRIESTS (2:36-39)

36-39. Very early the tribe of Levi became official priests; in the Deuteronomic Code the priests are called "the sons of Levi." In David's court his priest Abiathar (I Sam. 22:20; 23:6) served with Zadok (II Sam. 15:27, 36), who was not of the ancient priesthood and possibly not of Levitical lineage. With the banishment of Abiathar (I Kings 1:25, 42 ff.) his post was given to Zadok (I Kings 1:32 ff.), who dominated the Jerusalem temple priesthood. In the Ezekiel Code the priests are called "sons of Zadok." In the Holiness Code (Lev. 17–26) the priests are called "the sons of Aaron" (Lev. 21:1), a restriction perhaps due to the non-Zadokite priests whose legitimacy was denied by the Zadokite group. Thus in Neh. 10:38 the priests are "the sons of Aaron." But later tradition furnished a priestly genealogy for Zadok, appropriate to his eminent position, as a descendant of the eldest son of Aaron (I Chr. 24:3).

Only four clans of priests are listed in Ezra 2 but the number of individuals is proportionally very large (4,289), approximately one tenth of those returning. During the Exile the priests more than others must eagerly have awaited the opportunity to return to rebuild the temple and participate in its cultus. Each of the clans appears related to members of the priestly courses in David's temple, as recognized by the Chronicler. A **Jedaiah** (vs. 36) was the head of the second course of priests in David's temple (I Chr. 24:7). **Jedaiah** is identified as being **of the house of Jeshua**, presumably Jeshua the high priest (vs. 2). Such identification of **the house of Jeshua**, as of the clan of **Jedaiah**, must be a later insertion, made after the return of Jeshua and his

40 ¶ The Levites: the children of Jeshua and Kadmiel, of the children of Hodaviah, seventy and four.

41 ¶ The singers: the children of Asaph, a hundred twenty and eight.

42 ¶ The children of the porters: the children of Shallum, the children of Ater,

40 The Levites: the sons of Jeshua and Kad'mi-el, of the sons of Hodavi'ah, seventy-four. 41 The singers: the sons of Asaph, one hundred and twenty-eight. 42 The sons of the gatekeepers: the sons of Shallum, the sons of Ater, the sons of Talmon, the sons

---

establishment as high priest (Kittel, *Geschichte des Volkes Israel*, III, 396-97). Since **Jeshua,** but not **Jedaiah,** occurs in 10:18 ff., it appears that the Chronicler equated the names.

Immer (vs. 37) was in the sixteenth course of priests in David's temple (I Chr. 24:14). **Harim** (vs. 39) was a priest in the third course (I Chr. 24:8). **Pashhur** (vs. 38), who bears an Egyptian name like some other Levites, should belong to the early period. Since a priest **Pashhur,** the descendant of Malchijah, is mentioned in Neh. 11:12 (cf. I Chr. 9:12), it is possible that he is of the same clan, and that the distinguished remote ancestor Malchijah was the member of the fifth course of priests in David's organization (I Chr. 24:9).

(2) LEVITES (2:40)

40. All Levites were originally regarded as priests, equal to the Zadokites (Deut. 18:6-8), but after the Deuteronomic reform in actual practice they were degraded to become the hereditary servants of the acting priests (Num. 3:9-10), compelled to contribute part of their tithe to the priests (Num. 18:21-29; Neh. 10:38). They acted as butchers of sacrifices, doorkeepers, singers (I Chr. 15:22), scribes, teachers (II Chr. 35:3; Neh. 8:7, 9), and even temple beggars (II Chr. 24:5 ff.). Such secularization greatly depleted the numbers willing to serve in the temple after 586 B.C., for many apparently entered secular employment. Thus very few (seventy-four) Levites are mentioned here, and Ezra found it difficult to get any Levites to return (8:18 ff.). If Neh. 3:17 ff. seems to imply any great number of Levites in Jerusalem, it was perhaps because many could have been recruited from those who had remained in secular service in Judea (Meyer, *op. cit.,* pp. 176 ff.; Kittel, *op. cit.,* III, 394, 404 ff.; Rudolph, *op. cit.,* p. 22).

For **Jeshua and Kadmiel** read "Jeshua, namely of Kadmiel" with Neh. 7:43, for **Jeshua** was the great ancestor and the others named are but subdivisions of the clan. Instead of **sons of** (בני) I Esdras 5:26 has the name "Bannas," but other Greek texts suggest either "Bani" (בני) or "Bunni" (בני), as in vs. 10. Levites with both names occur in Neh. 9:4-5. The word **of** before **the sons of** must be omitted as due to dittography.

(3) SINGERS (2:41)

41. The singers, called "The holy singers" in I Esdras 5:27, were a single clan, the descendants of **Asaph,** one of three Levites whom David set over the song in the temple (I Chr. 15:16; cf. I Chr. 6:31-32, 39). Since only men served in the temple, the singers of vs. 65 were a different and secular group. Under Nehemiah they lived near Jerusalem (Neh. 12:29) and received regular support (Neh. 11:22 ff.) but when neglected, they, like the Levites, turned to secular work in the fields (Neh. 13:10).

(4) PORTERS (2:42)

42. The gatekeepers of the temple are not mentioned in extant pre-exilic literature, although Samuel apparently kept the door of a shrine (I Sam. 3:15). Postexilic gatekeepers did more than tend the door (I Chr. 9:17-32). They are sometimes regarded as Levites (I Chr. 9:26; II Chr. 8:14; 23:4; etc.; Neh. 12:25; 13:22) but sometimes are differentiated as here (II Chr. 35:15).

Shallum, Talmon, and **Akkub** appear in I Chr. 9:17 with **Shallum** as chief. A **Shallum** occurs as ancestor of a gatekeeper in the time of Jeremiah (Jer. 35:4). **Talmon**

the children of Talmon, the children of Akkub, the children of Hatita, the children of Shobai, *in* all a hundred thirty and nine.

43 ¶ The Nethinim: the children of Ziha, the children of Hasupha, the children of Tabbaoth,

44 The children of Keros, the children of Siaha, the children of Padon,

45 The children of Lebanah, the children of Hagabah, the children of Akkub,

46 The children of Hagab, the children of Shalmai, the children of Hanan,

47 The children of Giddel, the children of Gahar, the children of Reaiah,

48 The children of Rezin, the children of Nekoda, the children of Gazzam,

49 The children of Uzza, the children of Paseah, the children of Besai,

50 The children of Asnah, the children of Mehunim, the children of Nephusim,

of Akkub, the sons of Hati'ta, and the sons of Sho'bai, in all one hundred and thirty-nine.

43 The temple servants:[d] the sons of Ziha, the sons of Hasu'pha, the sons of Tabba'-oth, 44 the sons of Keros, the sons of Si'aha, the sons of Padon, 45 the sons of Leba'nah, the sons of Hag'abah, the sons of Akkub, 46 the sons of Hagab, the sons of Sham-lai, the sons of Hanan, 47 the sons of Giddel, the sons of Gahar, the sons of Re-ai'ah, 48 the sons of Rezin, the sons of Neko'da, the sons of Gazzam, 49 the sons of Uzza, the sons of Pase'ah, the sons of Besai, 50 the sons of Asnah, the sons of Me-u'nim, the sons of

[d] Heb *nethinim*

---

is a postexilic Aramaic form of Solomon, abbreviated as "Telem" in 10:24. **Akkub** and **Ater** (or Etir; cf. Exeg. on vs. 16) are found as abbreviated Neo-Babylonian names.

(5) Temple Servants (2:43-54)

The **Nethinim** are literally those "given" or "dedicated" as **temple servants**. The Chronicler reports that David and the princes dedicated them for the service of the Levites (8:20). Some were Hebrews (I Sam. 1:11, 24-28) but more frequently they were foreigners, captives of war, who became temple slaves (Num. 31:30, 47) and "hewers of wood and drawers of water" in the cult (Josh. 9:27). Such **temple servants** are strongly parallel to the Babylonian *shirkûtu* (R. P. Dougherty, *The Shirkûtu of Babylonian Deities* [New Haven: Yale University Press, 1923]). They dwelt in the "house of the Nethinim" (Neh. 3:31; cf. Babylonian *Bît Shirki*), supervised by overseers (Neh. 11:21; cf. *Râb Shirki*). When they married outside of their class, their offspring too were reckoned as temple servants (cf. Mishnah: Kiddushin III. 12; Yebamoth II. 4).

The names of the **temple servants** are significantly largely foreign. Two names are national rather than personal. **Meunim** (vs. 50) were the Arabs at Ma'an (I Chr. 4:39-41; II Chr. 26:7) and the **Nephisim** (vs. 50) are the Naphish Ishmaelites (Gen. 25:15; I Chr. 1:31; 5:19). **Ziha** (vs. 43) and **Asnah** (vs. 50) are Egyptian; **Barkos** (vs. 53) is Edomite; **Rezin** (vs. 48) is probably Aramaean (cf. Isa. 7:1 ff.); and **Sisera** (vs. 53) is non-Semitic (cf. Judg. 4:1–5:31). Many names are such informal nicknames as might be given to servants. **Hasupha** ("Quick," vs. 43), **Gahar** ("Humble," vs. 47), and **Neziah** ("Faithful," vs. 54) express approval, while **Lebanah** ("White," vs. 45); **Giddel** (for "Gadhol," "Big," vs. 47), **Nekoda** ("Spotted" or "Freckled," vs. 48), **Paseah** ("Lame," vs. 49) **Hakupha** ("Stooped," vs. 51), and **Harsha** ("Deaf" or "Dumb," vs. 52) indicate physical condition. **Hatipha** ("Snatched," vs. 54) and **Mehida** (for "Mehira," "Bought," vs. 52) indicate how the servants were acquired.

45-46. After **Akkub** I Esdras 5:30 and the LXX of Neh. 7:48 have additional names "Outa" and "Ketab" (cf. "Ketar" in LXX of Neh. 7:48), which are probably corruptions of names now lost in Hebrew lists. Read "Shalmai" for **Shamlai,** with Neh. 7:48 and Hebrew *Qerê* in 2:46.

47. Vocalization in I Esdras[A] 5:30 (Καθουα) suggests reading for **Giddel** the "Gadhol" (גדול) found often in the Aramaic papyri.

51 The children of Bakbuk, the children of Hakupha, the children of Harhur,

52 The children of Bazluth, the children of Mehida, the children of Harsha,

53 The children of Barkos, the children of Sisera, the children of Thamah,

54 The children of Neziah, the children of Hatipha.

55 ¶ The children of Solomon's servants: the children of Sotai, the children of Sophereth, the children of Peruda,

56 The children of Jaalah, the children of Darkon, the children of Giddel,

57 The children of Shephatiah, the children of Hattil, the children of Pochereth of Zebaim, the children of Ami.

58 All the Nethinim, and the children of Solomon's servants, *were* three hundred ninety and two.

59 And these *were* they which went up from Tel-melah, Tel-harsa, Cherub, Addan, *and* Immer: but they could not show their father's house, and their seed, whether they *were* of Israel:

60 The children of Delaiah, the children of Tobiah, the children of Nekoda, six hundred fifty and two.

Nephi'sim, 51 the sons of Bakbuk, the sons of Haku'pha, the sons of Harhur, 52 the sons of Bazluth, the sons of Mehi'da, the sons of Harsha, 53 the sons of Barkos, the sons of Sis'era, the sons of Temah, 54 the sons of Nezi'ah, and the sons of Hati'pha.

55 The sons of Solomon's servants: the sons of So'tai, the sons of Hasso'phereth, the sons of Peru'da, 56 the sons of Ja'alah, the sons of Darkon, the sons of Giddel, 57 the sons of Shephati'ah, the sons of Hattil, the sons of Po'chereth-hazzeba'im, and the sons of Ami.

58 All the temple servants[d] and the sons of Solomon's servants were three hundred and ninety-two.

59 The following were those who came up from Tel-me'lah, Tel-har'sha, Cherub, Addan, and Immer, though they could not prove their fathers' houses or their descent, whether they belonged to Israel: 60 the sons of Del-ai'ah, the sons of Tobi'ah, and the sons of Neko'da, six hundred and fifty-two.

[d] Heb *nethinim*

---

(6) DESCENDANTS OF SOLOMON'S SERVANTS (2:55-58)

55-58. A subdivision of the **temple servants** are **the sons of Solomon's servants,** who are included among the temple servants in Neh. 10:28 and in the total in vs. 58. Nothing certain is known of their history or function. They may be Canaanite prisoners of war, possibly Gibeonites (Josh. 9:27; I Kings 9:20-21; I Chr. 8:7-9; Rudolph, *op. cit.*, p. 23), who became state slaves (Isaac Mendelsohn, "State Slavery in Ancient Palestine," *Bulletin of the American Schools of Oriental Research*, No. 85 [1942], pp. 16-17). Like the **temple servants,** their names are informal and descriptive: **Peruda** (or "Perida" in Neh. 7:57) is "Lonely" or "Solitary" (vs. 55); **Hattil,** "The Babbler" (vs. 57); and **Darkon,** "Rough" (vs. 56). **Giddel** (vs. 56) should be "Gadhol," as in vs. 47. **Hassophereth** (vs. 55) means "The Teacher" and **Pochereth-hazzebaim** is "The Gazelle Hunter" (vs. 57; cf. Rudolph, *op. cit.*, p. 14). Although a relatively large number of names of the temple servants are given, the group itself was quite small—**three hundred and ninety-two**—averaging about eight per family.

c) UNCERTIFIED CLANS (2:59-63=Neh. 7:61-65; I Esdras 5:36-40)

The Mishnah declares that Ezra did not rest until Babylonia was "sieved like fine meal" (Kiddushin IV. 1. 69*b*, 71*b*; Yalkut II. 106-7), and that Ezra himself had his own line certified before he left Babylonia (Baba Bathra 15*a*). Pure-blooded Jews were called "fine meal" and the others were designated "mixed dough" (Hugo Graetz, "Illegitime Mischehen in Judäa," *Monatsschrift für Geschichte und Wissenschaft des Judenthums,* XXVIII [1879], 481-508). It is usually assumed that such racial consciousness and striving for purity did not exist until the reforms of Ezra (9:1–10:44) and Nehemiah (13:23-30), but the great list implies the keeping of strict genealogical records during the Exile. There may have been little such concern in Palestine, but there was evidently such interest abroad, especially among such conservative folk, as contributed to the Return.

61 ¶ And of the children of the priests: the children of Habaiah, the children of Koz, the children of Barzillai; which took a wife of the daughters of Barzillai the Gileadite, and was called after their name:

62 These sought their register *among* those that were reckoned by genealogy, but they were not found: therefore were they, as polluted, put from the priesthood.

63 And the Tirshatha said unto them, that they should not eat of the most holy things, till there stood up a priest with Urim and with Thummim.

61 Also, of the sons of the priests: the sons of Habai′ah, the sons of Hakkoz, and the sons of Barzil′lai (who had taken a wife from the daughters of Barzil′lai the Gileadite, and was called by their name) . 62 These sought their registration among those enrolled in the genealogies, but they were not found there, and so they were excluded from the priesthood as unclean; 63 the governor told them that they were not to partake of the most holy food, until there should be a priest to consult Urim and Thummim.

The six clans, three lay and three priestly, who remained uncertified were appended to the great list. These may have derived from proselytes or may have lacked proper credentials. **Their seed** (vs. 59) means **their descent.** They came from five Babylonian places not yet identified. Since the element Tel- means a ruined mound of an earlier habitation (Josh. 8:28; Deut. 13:16; Jer. 49:2) at least two places were Jewish resettlements.

61. Omit the introductory **the sons of** with Neh. 7:63 and I Esdras 5:38. **Habaiah** is unique but its variant "Hobiah" may be related to the abbreviation "Hubbah" in I Chr. 7:34 (*Qerê,* Vulg.) . **Hakkoz** ("The Thorn") also appears without the article as Koz (I Chr. 4:8; Neh. 3:4, 21). It is argued from Neh. 3:4, 21 that the clan was later reinstated. Possible relationship to the ancient nonpriestly **Barzillai** (II Sam. 17:27; 19:32-37; I Kings 2:7) doubtless brought into question the status of the priestly clan of **Barzillai.**

62. Their registration is, lit., "their writing," which is described as **those that were reckoned by genealogy.** This "writing" is a priestly list like the list of Levites in Neh. 12:22-23 and the much later list of priests mentioned by Josephus (*Against Apion* I. 7) . It is preferable to read, "They sought in their writing," as in the Syriac. It is better to read, with Neh. 7:64, "They were not found," since the subject is the clan, not the writing in which the other priests (cf. vss. 39-42) were listed.

Uncertified laymen could doubtless remain in the community, possibly with some restrictions, until lineage could be established. But the priests posed a greater problem because of their prerogatives and the possibility of contaminating the cultus. To avoid defilement of holy things by uncertified priests those challenged were "desecrated from the priesthood." "Desecrated," a term in late Hebrew usage, is preferable to **polluted.**

63. The order restricting the uncertified priests was given by the **Tirshatha,** the Jewish authority in charge. **Tirshatha** is not the title **governor** but an Iranian epithet "The One to Be Feared," which could signify "His Excellency." Its use in Neh. 8:9; 10:1 for Nehemiah as governor is responsible for the intrusion of Nehemiah into I Esdras 5:40 alongside the epithet transliterated as "Attharias." The Syriac text of I Esdras has Nehemiah alone, but the Peshitta declares that "the heads of Israel" gave the order.

According to the M.T., the uncertified priests were forbidden to share in **the most holy food,** special portions reserved for male descendants of Aaron (Lev. 2:3; 7:31-33) , but I Esdras 5:40 excluded them from "all holy things," the ordinary priestly food (Lev. 7:3-6; 10:14; 22:10, 13*b*) . This is interpreted in the RSV as **they were excluded from the priesthood** (vs. 62). The exclusion was not intended to be permanent, but only until a divine decision could be made through the sacred lot, the **Urim and Thummim** (cf. I Sam. 14:41) . Rabbinical tradition lists the sacred lot as among things lacking in the postexilic temple (Tosephta Sota XIII. 2; Yalkut II. 150. 568; Yoma 21*b*) , and despite Josephus (*Antiquities* III. 8. 9) , there is no evidence for sacred lot in the postexilic temple. The rabbis regarded the statement in vs. 63 as meaning "until the dead

64 ¶ The whole congregation together *was* forty and two thousand three hundred *and* threescore,

65 Besides their servants and their maids, of whom *there were* seven thousand three hundred thirty and seven: and *there were* among them two hundred singing men and singing women.

66 Their horses *were* seven hundred thirty and six; their mules, two hundred forty and five;

67 Their camels, four hundred thirty and five; *their* asses, six thousand seven hundred and twenty.

68 ¶ And *some* of the chief of the fathers,

64 The whole assembly together was forty-two thousand three hundred and sixty, 65 besides their menservants and maidservants, of whom there were seven thousand three hundred and thirty-seven; and they had two hundred male and female singers. 66 Their horses were seven hundred and thirty-six, their mules were two hundred and forty-five, 67 their camels were four hundred and thirty-five, and their asses were six thousand seven hundred and twenty.

68 Some of the heads of families, when

---

are resurrected" or "until Elijah comes" (Tosephta Sota XIII. 1; Sota 48*b*; Ketuboth 24*b*; Shebuoth 16*a*; Jerusalem Kiddushim IV. 1; Tosaphoth Yoma 21*b*).

A priest would be appropriate in pre-exilic times when any Levite could use the lot (Deut. 33:8), but it was later restricted to the high priest (Exod. 28:30; Lev. 8:8; Num. 27:21; cf. "a priest" in Neh. 7:65). The "high priest" is specified in the Peshitta, Vulg., and I Esdras^ALN. If the high priest is meant, it would indicate that none was yet recognized in the community and the date of the document must be before 520 B.C.

d) SUMMARIES (2:64-67=Neh. 7:66-69; I Esdras 5:41-43)

(1) CONGREGATION (2:64)

64. Together indicates that all of the lists were used in the total. As in 1:9-11, the figures do not agree in all versions and there is a discrepancy between the given grand total and that obtained by addition. By emendation (vss. 12, 16, 31) Bewer (*Der Text des Buches Ezra*, p. 33) derives a sum 32,360, ten thousand less than that in vs. 64. Rudolph (*op. cit.*, p. 25) assumes that the difference is due to the inclusion of women in the given total, as in vs. 65. By adding "from twelve years old," I Esdras 5:41 excludes children, since adulthood was reckoned from that age (cf. Luke 2:42).

(2) PRIVATE PROPERTY (2:65-67)

65-67. It has been argued that the great list ended with the total in vs. 64, and that what follows has been added by the Chronicler (Hölscher, *Esra und Nehemia*, II, 504), but the arguments are not persuasive (cf. Rudolph, *op. cit.*, pp. 7, 9-10). **Besides** indicates that what follows was not counted in the **assembly.** The **servants** or "slaves" were private property, as were the **singers,** whose secular role is seen by the inclusion of women who were not employed in the temple. Such **singers,** to be differentiated from those in vs. 41, entertained the wealthy and served as minstrels (II Sam. 19:35; II Chr. 35:25; Eccl. 2:8).

The animals (vss. 66-67) were needed for the caravan. **Mules** were sometimes used to carry burdens (II Kings 5:17; cf. Judith 2:17; 15:11) but were generally prized for riding (II Sam. 13:29; 18:9), while **asses** were used as pack animals (II Sam. 16:1), and I Esdras 5:43 here calls them "beasts of burden" (ὑποζύγια). Read **their asses** with seven MSS, the LXX, Vulg., and Ethiopic versions and the other nouns in the verses.

3. TEMPLE DONATIONS (2:68-70=Neh. 7:70-73; I Esdras 5:44-46)

68-70. Vss. 68-69 have been regarded as dislocated, originally following either 1:11 (Hölscher, *loc. cit.*) or 8:36 (C. C. Torrey, *The Composition and Historical Value of*

68-70. *Building Campaigns in Every Generation.*—However inaccurate may be the total figures given for the temple building fund in

vs. 69, there is one touch of agelong human nature in vs. 68 which every minister or layman who has ever shared in a church building cam-

when they came to the house of the LORD which *is* at Jerusalem, offered freely for the house of God to set it up in his place:

69 They gave after their ability unto the treasure of the work threescore and one thousand drams of gold, and five thousand pounds of silver, and one hundred priests' garments.

70 So the priests, and the Levites, and *some* of the people, and the singers, and the porters, and the Nethinim, dwelt in their cities, and all Israel in their cities.

3 And when the seventh month was come, and the children of Israel *were* in the cities, the people gathered themselves together as one man to Jerusalem.

they came to the house of the LORD which is in Jerusalem, made freewill offerings for the house of God, to erect it on its site;

69 according to their ability they gave to the treasury of the work sixty-one thousand darics of gold, five thousand minas of silver, and one hundred priests' garments.

70 The priests, the Levites, and some of the people lived in Jerusalem and its vicinity;*e* and the singers, the gatekeepers, and the temple servants lived in their towns, and all Israel in their towns.

3 When the seventh month came, and the sons of Israel were in the towns, the people gathered as one man to Jerusalem.

e 1 Esdras 5. 46. Heb lacks *lived in Jerusalem and its vicinity*

Ezra-Nehemiah [Giessen: J. Ricker, 1896; "Beihefte zur Zeitschrift für die alttestamentliche Wissenschaft"], pp. 30-34; *Ezra Studies,* pp. 256, 267). But in the first instance the reason for the disruption of context by the long list is left unexplained, while in the latter one must overlook the fact that Ezra's gifts were already delivered in 8:33 ff. It is better to see the passage as original in the list (cf. Rudolph, *op. cit.,* p. 10).

II. BUILDING THE TEMPLE UNDER DARIUS (3:1–6:22)

A. RECONSTRUCTION OF THE ALTAR AND RE-ESTABLISHMENT OF SACRIFICES (3:1-6)

Throughout this narrative concerned with the cultus the Chronicler's interests and literary habits are observable. What, if any, sources were at his disposal cannot now be determined. It is probable that some sound tradition lay behind the story of the reconstruction of an early altar before the temple was rebuilt. It could exist without the temple and was greatly needed for the rehabilitation of the cult. David had an altar in Jerusalem before the construction of the temple (II Sam. 24:25) and sacrifices continued to be made there even after the temple was destroyed (Jer. 41:5; Hag. 2:14). Less plausible is the Chronicler's inference that the depleted and distressed community at once instituted a sacrificial system on the grand scale that the Chronicler himself knew.

1. ERECTION OF THE ALTAR (3:1-3a=I Esdras 5:47-50a)

3:1. Comparison of vs. 1 with I Esdras 5:47 and Neh. 7:73*b* shows that the material formed the conclusion of the document incorporated in Ezra 2:2-70. In Nehemiah it introduces the narrative of the reading of the law in the reign of Artaxerxes but here, as in I Esdras, it leads to the erection of an altar prior to the building of the temple in a much earlier period. Such differences in context have compelled some modification in content.

The **seventh month** would fit the context in Nehemiah, where the next previous date is the sixth month, when the walls were completed (Neh. 6:15; 7:1). But since the **seventh month** was a festal period when there would be great need for an altar, the

---

paign will recognize at once. Idealize his history as the Chronicler may well have done, he is nevertheless frank enough to admit that some of the heads of families **made freewill offerings for the house of God . . . according to their ability,** but he also implies that some others gave only sparingly and under pressure, and

that some did not give at all. So has it been with church building funds from that day to this.

3:1-13. Youth and Age in Changing Times.— An even more authentic touch of human nature, under the stress of one of the most poignant of human experiences, quickens into life for us

2 Then stood up Jeshua the son of Joza-dak, and his brethren the priests, and Zerub-babel the son of Shealtiel, and his brethren, and builded the altar of the God of Israel, to offer burnt offerings thereon, as *it is* written in the law of Moses the man of God.

3 And they set the altar upon his bases; for fear *was* upon them because of the people of those countries: and they offered

2 Then arose Jeshua the son of Jo'zadak, with his fellow priests, and Zerub'babel the son of She-al'ti-el with his kinsmen, and they built the altar of the God of Israel, to offer burnt offerings upon it, as it is written in the law of Moses the man of God. 3 They set the altar in its place, for fear was upon them because of the peoples of the lands,

---

time would also be appropriate for the Ezra narrative. Nevertheless, the taboos prevailing at the beginning of the **seventh month** (cf. vs. 6) raise some question as to the validity of the date for the Ezra narrative. The numerical reckoning of the **seventh month,** which was Ethanim in the pre-exilic Canaanite calendar (I Kings 8:2) and Tishri in the postexilic Babylonian one, reflects the postexilic change in calendar, when the Babylonian names (cf. 6:15; Neh. 1:1; 2:1; 6:15) had not yet come into general use (cf. Hag. 1:1, 15; etc.).

The year date is difficult to determine since there was none in the original document. The Chronicler apparently considered it to be during the first year of Cyrus (1:1) but Rudolph (*op. cit.,* p. 29) contends that six months would be too short for the return and settlement, and suggests possibly the second or even third year of Cyrus as the actual date. Since Babylon fell in 539 b.c. and the gods were returned during the rest of that year (1:3), the actual interval of preparation and return may have been longer than six months. But it is obvious that the Chronicler identified Sheshbazzar with Zerubbabel and thinks of the days of Darius I as in I Esdras (cf. I Esdras 5:2, 6).

The assembly, according to Ezra, was held in **Jerusalem,** but Nehemiah, which reflects a much later date, located it in the plaza before "the Water Gate" (cf. Neh. 8:1) in restored Jerusalem, while I Esdras 5:47, influenced by I Esdras 9:38, placed it in the plaza before the temple porch. The latter would be appropriate only if it is understood as being before the temple ruins, since in I Esdras, as in Ezra, the temple is not yet rebuilt.

2. Jeshua and **Zerubbabel** (2:2) indicate the time of Darius rather than that of Cyrus (cf. Hag. 1:1–2:23 and Zech. 1:1–8:23). Elsewhere **Zerubbabel,** as secular ruler, is mentioned first (vs. 8; 2:2; 4:3; 5:2; Neh. 12:1) but **Jeshua** precedes him here where matters of cult are involved. Surprisingly, Jeshua's title "high priest" is here omitted (cf. Neh. 12:10 ff.; Hag. 1:1, 14; 2:2). **His brethren** used of **Jeshua** means **his fellow priests;** used of **Zerubbabel,** it signifies not princely brothers but fellow laymen.

The **altar** was hastily constructed in less than a day (vs. 6) of field stones in accord-ance with the earliest prescriptions for altars in **the law of Moses** (Exod. 20:25; cf. Deut. 27:6). It was described by Hecateus of Abdera (cf. Josephus *Against Apion* I. 22) and lasted down to Maccabean times (I Macc. 4:47, 54). **Man of God** is applied not only to Moses (cf. Deut. 33:1; Josh. 14:6; I Chr. 23:14; II Chr. 30:16) but also to Samuel (I Sam. 9:6), Elijah (I Kings 17:18), and Elisha (II Kings 4:7) as a prophetic title. It is used also of David (Neh. 12:24, 36) and of Timothy (I Tim. 6:11; II Tim. 3:17).

3a. The **bases** of the altar signify "foundation" rather than "site," since the altar was erected on a platform or pavement (cf. Ezek. 43:13-14, 17). But Josephus, influenced by the Greek text, paraphrases, "He then built the altar on the same place it formerly had been built" (Josephus *Antiquities* XI. 4. 1).

---

the confused palimpsest of obscure history that has come down as ch. 3. Whatever may have been the chronological and ceremonial confu-sion that have been so carefully disentangled by the Exeg., every subsequent older generation knows only too well the nostalgia for "the days

that are no more" [3] that still throbs with such moving pathos within this brief account. The tears of older folk who could remember the size and splendor of Solomon's former temple were mingled with the shouts of happy young people

[3] Tennyson, *The Princess,* Part IV.

burnt offerings thereon unto the LORD, *even* burnt offerings morning and evening.

4 They kept also the feast of tabernacles, as *it is* written, and *offered* the daily burnt offerings by number, according to the custom, as the duty of every day required;

5 And afterward *offered* the continual burnt offering, both of the new moons, and of all the set feasts of the LORD that were consecrated, and of every one that willingly offered a freewill offering unto the LORD.

and they offered burnt offerings upon it to the LORD, burnt offerings morning and evening. 4 And they kept the feast of booths, as it is written, and offered the daily burnt offerings by number according to the ordinance, as each day required, 5 and after that the continual burnt offerings, the offerings at the new moon and at all the appointed feasts of the LORD, and the offerings of every one who made a freewill offering to the

---

A difficult and confused Hebrew text lies behind the translation **for fear was upon them because of the peoples of the lands.** It is best explained as an intrusive comment which may once have explained some such word as "adversaries" in 4:1. Rudolph (*op. cit.*, p. 28) regards the gloss as relevant, indicating that the motive for restoring the cultus was to assure the help of God against their enemies. The **people of those countries** were the non-Jews sent in to repopulate the land (4:9-10) but the Chronicler would also include those Jews who had remained in the land and married Gentile women (cf. 6:21).

2. INSTITUTION OF PROGRAM OF OFFERINGS (3:3*b*-6=I Esdras 5:50*b*-53)

3*b*-4. Burnt offerings in the earliest postexilic period would probably have followed the simple prescriptions of the Deuteronomic Code (Deut. 12:5-7, 13-14, 27), but the Chronicler doubtless regarded them as following the priestly practices of his own day (Num. 28:1-8; cf. Exod. 29:38-42). The sacrifices were prescribed **as each day required** (cf. Neh. 11:23). This is specified as being either according to **custom** (cf. I Sam. 27:11; Gen. 40:13) or according to the **ordinance** (Lev. 5:10; 9:16; Neh. 8:18), since the Hebrew word used (*mishpāṭ*) can mean either. The latter is perhaps intended (cf. Neh. 8:18) since the complete expression is frequently found in later legislation regarding the **feast of booths** (cf. Num. 29:18, 21, 24, 27, 30, 33).

The **feast of tabernacles** or **booths**, originally a Canaanite agricultural festival (Judg. 9:27), named for the temporary shelters of branches (cf. Neh. 8:15) erected in the fields for the harvest laborers (cf. Isa. 1:8; 4:6; Jonah 4:5) is the oldest festival in the Hebrew cultic calendar. Frequently called simply "the feast" or "the feast of the Lord," it is the only one mentioned in the historical literature (Judg. 9:27; I Sam. 1:1 ff.; I Kings 12:32). Originally a joyous harvest celebration at the close of the year (Exod. 34:22; 23:16; Deut. 16:13-16), in the later Priestly Code it lost its joyful character, and beginning on the fifteenth day of the seventh month (Lev. 23:33-36, 39-43; Num. 29:12-40) it lasted eight days.

5-6. The Chronicler's hand is most apparent here where he assumes that from its completion the altar was as busy with offerings as it was later in his own day. The offerings are listed as in the priestly legislation (Num. 28-29). The **continual burnt offering** was that repeated with regularity **morning and evening** (vs. 3). The pre-exilic burnt offering was made each morning and a meal offering was made each evening (I Kings 18:29-30; II Kings 16:15), but later priestly legislation called for two burnt offerings, morning and evening, each accompanied by a subordinate meal offering (Num. 28:3-8). The latter, which prevailed in the Chronicler's day (cf. I Chr. 16:40; II Chr.

---

who knew nothing beyond or before the comparative drabness and smallness of the new. The old men who had seen the first house, wept with a loud voice when they saw the foundation of this house being laid, though many shouted aloud for joy; so that the people could

not distinguish the sound of the joyful shout from the sound of the people's weeping (vss. 12-13).

That same strange mingling of the diverse emotions of age and youth over the same situation can still be heard by sensitive ears at

6 From the first day of the seventh month began they to offer burnt offerings unto the LORD. But the foundation of the temple of the LORD was not *yet* laid.

7 They gave money also unto the masons, and to the carpenters; and meat, and drink,

LORD. 6 From the first day of the seventh month they began to offer burnt offerings to the LORD. But the foundation of the temple of the LORD was not yet laid. 7 So they gave money to the masons and the carpenters, and food, drink, and oil to the

---

13:11; 31:3) is here clumsily transported back to the simple ritual of the early postexilic period. Such a burnt offering is later called simply the "continual" (Dan. 11:31).

With the **new moon** a new month began and it was the sign of a period of danger and taboo, when labor had to cease and sacrifices had to be made. Important sacrifices were held by clans (I Sam. 20:6) and in court (I Sam. 20:5) at that time. Pre-exilic prophets condemned **new moon** celebrations (Isa. 1:14; Hos. 2:11) apparently because of association with Canaanite rites. Although there is abundant evidence for observance of **new moons** in the early cultus, there is no pre-exilic legislation regarding it. Later legislation is found in Num. 28:11-15. The **new moon,** superseded by the sabbath, continued down into late times (Judith 8:6; Col. 2:16). Reference to the sabbath, frequently associated with the continual sacrifices (Num. 28:9 ff.; II Chr. 2:4; 8:13; Neh. 10:33) and **new moons** (Amos 8:5), is missing here in Ezra but is found in I Esdras 5:52, where it may be original.

The **set feasts** were **the appointed feasts** recurring yearly at fixed times (cf. Gen. 1:14). Those meant here are doubtless those of the later priestly calendar (Lev. 23:1-44), the Passover, the feast of Weeks, New Year, the day of Atonement, and the feast of Booths. **A freewill offering** was a sacrifice made usually in thanksgiving and was not mandatory by law or because of a vow (cf. 1:4; Deut. 12:17; Lev. 22:17 ff.; Num. 15:1 ff.). No such offerings are mentioned in I Esdras 5:53 but instead sacrifices due to vows, presumably those made for the safe journey from Babylonia. These are linked to the following verse: "And all they that made any vow to God began to offer sacrifices to God from the new moon of the seventh month." Some have preferred this version (Gustav Jahn, *Die Bücher Esra [A und B] und Nehemja* [Leiden: E. J. Brill, 1909], p. 30), and Batten (*Ezra and Nehemiah,* p. 111) has regarded the Hebrew of Ezra as ungrammatical, since the reference to freewill offerings dangles awkwardly, but as Bewer insists (*Der Text des Buches Ezra,* p. 40), the reference goes back to **they offered burnt offerings** in vs. 3*b*. The M.T., grammatically correct, seems distinctly preferable. The Chronicler may have thought of the offerings brought from Babylonia to the temple (1:4).

The **first day of the seventh month** was a most holy time during which later legislation decreed that no servile work was to be done (Lev. 23:23-25; Num. 29:1). If such prohibition also existed earlier, it would be extremely unlikely that the labor here described took place on that day. **But the foundation of the temple of the LORD was not yet laid** interprets a Hebrew text which is, lit., "But the temple of the LORD was not restored." Thus there need be no direct reference to a **foundation.**

B. WORK ON THE TEMPLE (3:7–6:22)

1. WORK BEGINS (3:7-13)

The conclusion of vs. 6 leads to preparation for the rebuilding of the temple. It is evident that the narrative here has been influenced by the Chronicler's account of the building of Solomon's temple (II Chr. 2; cf. I Kings 5). Such literary dependence need not indicate unhistorical character since the process of building a temple at Jerusalem would necessarily involve the same problems and procedures in every age (cf. Rudolph, *op. cit.,* p. 31).

a) SUPPLIES AND LABOR (3:7-9=I Esdras 5:54-58)

7. Coined **money** was known in the Persian period but was not common until later. Precious metals were still weighed out. Solomon's "hire" was paid in commodities (I Kings

and oil, unto them of Zidon, and to them of Tyre, to bring cedar trees from Lebanon to the sea of Joppa, according to the grant that they had of Cyrus king of Persia.

8 ¶ Now in the second year of their coming unto the house of God at Jerusalem, in the second month, began Zerubbabel the son of Shealtiel, and Jeshua the son of Jozadak, and the remnant of their brethren

Sido'nians and the Tyrians to bring cedar trees from Lebanon to the sea, to Joppa, according to the grant which they had from Cyrus king of Persia.

8 Now in the second year of their coming to the house of God at Jerusalem, in the second month, Zerub'babel the son of She-al'ti-el and Jeshua the son of Jo'zadak made a beginning, together with the rest of their

---

5:6, 11), and references here to **food, drink, and oil** indicate that such was still the basic medium of payment. The **masons** were miners who quarried the stone (cf. I Kings 5:15; Isa. 5:2; 22:16). **Carpenters** were "engravers" who worked in many mediums. Batten (*op. cit.,* p. 119) plausibly suggests that they dressed and carved the temple stones, but the term also described wood carvers and those who chased metals.

Zidon and **Tyre** were famous in antiquity for their trade (Ezek. 27), especially for **cedar trees from Lebanon** brought from the mountains nearby. Because the cedars furnished the long, massive, tough beams essential for the construction of such large structures as palaces and temples, the forests of Lebanon supplied all the kingdoms of the Near East. As Solomon (I Kings 5:6-10) and Nehemiah (Neh. 2:8) needed cedars for their building, so new cedars would be necessary for rebuilding the burned temple (II Kings 25:8-9). No royal grant of timber is mentioned in the Cyrus edict (Ezra 1:2-4; 6:3-5), and the parallel passage in I Esdras 4:48, which refers to such a grant but assigns the act to Darius, is probably based on Ezra 3:7, with some influence possibly from Neh. 2:8. Josephus here (*Antiquities* XI. 4. 1), influenced by I Esdras, describes a shipment of logs in the days of Darius, which he claims was ordered by Cyrus.

8. From 4:24; 5:16 it would appear that **the second year** refers to the first attempts at reconstruction of the temple in the reign of Cyrus. But in blundering fashion the Chronicler introduces **Zerubbabel** and **Jeshua** of the time of Darius I (521-485 B.C.). For him Zerubbabel was Sheshbazzar. Both I Esdras and Josephus place the events during the reign of Darius I. Work on the temple began on the twenty-fourth day of the sixth month of the second year of Darius (Sept. 21, 520 B.C.) according to Hag. 1:15. Although the Chronicler finds it impossible to do so, historically an abortive attempt at rebuilding by Sheshbazzar in the time of Cyrus must be kept separate from the successful one by Zerubbabel during the reign of Darius. Influence of the Chronicler's narrative of the building of Solomon's temple (II Chr. 3:2) may be seen in the statement that work began in the **second month** (Iyyar, i.e., May). But it is plausible that the work should have started then, when the rainy season had ended and the harvest was gathered (Kittel, *Geschichte des Volkes Israel,* III, 428-29; Rudolph, *loc. cit.*). **Began** dangles incompletely in the Hebrew text, without specifying the action begun. **Made a beginning** does not reflect the awkwardness of the original. The Chronicler's sentence might well be completed, as in I Esdras 5:57, by supplying "And they laid the foundation of the house of God."

The subject of **began** is extremely long and complex. It suggests that in Hag. 1:12, 14, but there Haggai is silent regarding the priests and Levites in whom the Chronicler is much interested. To Haggai, who never mentions Babylonian Jews, the **remnant** means

---

almost any wedding. It is even more evident through periods of rapid and far-reaching change in the life of a community, a nation, or a generation. It recurs likewise in the experience of almost every church, especially in changing city or suburban or rural neighborhoods, when a strategic site has to be given up, or a

beloved building torn down, or a traditional program radically modified. The older members weep nostalgic tears as they look back to the way things were when they were young; but their eventual successors, with no such memories of "the good old days," look forward in hope and faith, and are in a mood to celebrate.

the priests and the Levites, and all they that were come out of the captivity unto Jerusalem; and appointed the Levites, from twenty years old and upward, to set forward the work of the house of the LORD.

9 Then stood Jeshua *with* his sons and his brethren, Kadmiel and his sons, the sons of Judah, together, to set forward the workmen in the house of God: the sons of Henadad, *with* their sons and their brethren the Levites.

10 And when the builders laid the foundation of the temple of the LORD, they set the priests in their apparel with trumpets, and the Levites the sons of Asaph with cymbals, to praise the LORD, after the ordinance of David king of Israel.

11 And they sang together by course in praising and giving thanks unto the LORD; because *he is* good, for his mercy *endureth* for ever toward Israel. And all the people

brethren, the priests and the Levites and all who had come to Jerusalem from the captivity. They appointed the Levites, from twenty years old and upward, to have the oversight of the work of the house of the LORD. **9** And Jeshua with his sons and his kinsmen, and Kad'mi-el and his sons, the sons of Judah, together took the oversight of the workmen in the house of God, along with the sons of Hen'adad and the Levites, their sons and kinsmen.

10 And when the builders laid the foundation of the temple of the LORD, the priests in their vestments came forward with trumpets, and the Levites, the sons of Asaph, with cymbals, to praise the LORD, according to the directions of David king of Israel; **11** and they sang responsively, praising and giving thanks to the LORD,

"For he is good,
for his steadfast love endures for ever toward Israel."

---

those who had not been exiled, while the Chronicler applies the term to the returned exiles alone. The **Levites** (cf. 2:40) were assigned **to have the oversight of the work** (cf. Neh. 11:16). The Hebrew word used means "to be pre-eminent," and used by the Chronicler it has the sense "to oversee" or "to superintend." The **twenty years** minimum age for Levites contrasts with the twenty-five (Num. 8:24) and thirty (Num. 4:3) years of the priestly legislation. Harmonizers have suggested that the difference was due to the scarcity of Levites at the time when many were needed, or that the younger men would be needed for the work of heavy transport. It is questionable whether the Levites were used to any great extent for actual manual labor (cf. vs. 9). More likely the difference in age reflects the practice of the Chronicler's own time (cf. I Chr. 23:24-27; II Chr. 31:17), before changing social and economic conditions compelled a change in age.

9. The names must be emended as in the RSV, in accordance with the Greek texts, to include "Binnui" (בנוי), whose name has been translated as **his sons** (בניו), and "Hodaviah" (הודויה or הודוה, "Hodevah," in Neh. 7:43), which has been corrupted to the graphically similar **Judah** (יהודה). But a **Judah** does appear elsewhere as the head of a family of Levites (Neh. 12:8). **Henadad** does not appear in 2:40, but is mentioned in Neh. 3:18, 24; 10:9, and may have been introduced here secondarily from Nehemiah. It is separated from the other names by text in the M.T. but is joined with them in I Esdras 5:58. Meyer (*Entstehung des Judenthums,* p. 177) believed the name to be missing in 2:40 because the family had not gone into captivity but had remained in Palestine. **Stood . . . together** means were mutually responsible. **To set forward** (cf. vs. 8) is properly rendered in I Esdras by "to serve as taskmasters" (ἐργοδιῶκται). While some MSS read "the doers of the work" instead of **the workmen,** it is better to read with the M.T. "the doing of the work." Here "work" is the task of rebuilding (cf. Hag. 1:14) and must not be restricted simply to "worship" as Meyer inclines to suggest (*ibid.,* p. 195).

b) SUBFOUNDATION LAID AND DEDICATED (3:10-11=I Esdras 5:59-62)

10-11. The celebration occurred before the temple was completed (4:1-3) but there is no specific reference to a **foundation** in the verse (cf. vs. 6). For **they set** read with thirteen MSS, the LXX, and I Esdras, "they stood," which the RSV interprets

shouted with a great shout, when they praised the Lord, because the foundation of the house of the Lord was laid.

12 But many of the priests and Levites and chief of the fathers, *who were* ancient men, that had seen the first house, when the foundation of this house was laid before their eyes, wept with a loud voice; and many shouted aloud for joy:

13 So that the people could not discern the noise of the shout of joy from the noise of the weeping of the people: for the people shouted with a loud shout, and the noise was heard afar off.

And all the people shouted with a great shout, when they praised the Lord, because the foundation of the house of the Lord was laid. **12** But many of the priests and Levites and heads of fathers' houses, old men who had seen the first house, wept with a loud voice when they saw the foundation of this house being laid, though many shouted aloud for joy; **13** so that the people could not distinguish the sound of the joyful shout from the sound of the people's weeping, for the people shouted with a great shout, and the sound was heard afar.

came forward. The Hebrew "dressed" is interpreted as **in their apparel** and in I Esdras "clad in vestments" (ἐστολισμένοι). Josephus expands this to "adorned with their customary garments." It is possible that a word, perhaps "in fine linen" (בוץ), has dropped from the text. The **trumpets** were the long tubelike clarions with flaring bell such as are portrayed among the plunder of the temple on the Arch of Titus at Rome. They were the priests' instruments (cf. Num. 10:8), used on ceremonial occasions (cf. I Chr. 16:6). The Levites played **cymbals** (cf. II Sam. 6:5; I Chr. 15:19). The Levitical musicians were the **sons of Asaph** (2:41). David was the one who ordered the Levites to be musicians, according to the Chronicler (II Chr. 29:25-26). The Hebrew "they answered" is properly interpreted as **they sang responsively.** Josephus and I Esdras 5:61 indicate that hymns were sung; the line of song quoted here (found also in Pss. 106:1; 136:1; cf. Jer. 33:10 ff.), was a favorite of the Chronicler (cf. I Chr. 16:34; II Chr. 5:13; 7:3). **Toward Israel** was added early by someone who did not recognize the quotation.

c) Popular Reaction to the Building (3:12-13=I Esdras 5:63-65)

12-13. Popular reaction to the temple must be understood in the light of Hag. 2:1-4, in which the prophet encourages the people who were disappointed with the appearance of the structure. Any **old men** who had seen the first temple would have been greatly in the minority in the crowd in 520 B.C., since that temple had been destroyed sixty-six years before.

Part of vs. 12 is in Hebrew quite rough and grammatically impossible, reading, lit., ". . . the old man who had seen the first house in its establishment, this the house, with their eyes. . . ." The expression "this the house" may be a correct gloss to the pronoun "its" (Rudolph, *op. cit.,* p. 30); or the pronoun זה, "this," may be a fragment of an original verb נבזה, "despised," in a parenthetical comment explaining the weeping on such an occasion: ". . . at the time of its rebuilding the house was despised in their eyes" (Arnold B. Ehrlich, *Randglossen zur hebräischen Bibel* [Leipzig: J. C. Hinrichs, 1914], VII, 163; Bewer, *op. cit.,* pp. 45-46). This conforms to the sense of Hag. 2:3. According to I Esdras 5:65, "The people did not hear the trumpets because of the weeping of the people," a view reflected by the Peshitta. But the Chronicler believed that the complaints of the weepers were concealed by the loud shouts of the others who outnumbered them. Josephus explains: "But the people in general were content with their present condition, and because they were allowed to build themselves a temple they desired no more, and neither considered nor remembered nor tormented themselves at all with the comparison of that one and the former temple, as though this were below their expectations" (*Antiquities* XI. 4. 2).

The intrusion of several words in vs. 13 obscures the meaning. Of three occurrences of **the people** only the last seems original. The first instance is lacking in the Vulg. and the second, which may be a dittograph, is missing in the LXX. Ehrlich's emendations

4 Now when the adversaries of Judah and Benjamin heard that the children of the captivity builded the temple unto the LORD God of Israel;

4 Now when the adversaries of Judah and Benjamin heard that the returned exiles were building a temple to the LORD, the

---

further improve the text, reading **discern** as singular and inserting the preposition "of" before the first occurrence of **sound**. As emended, vs. 13 should read: "And there was not a discerning of the sound of the shout of joy from the sound of weeping, for the people were shouting a great shout."

2. THE SAMARITAN CONFLICT (4:1–6:22)

In ch. 4 the Chronicler explains why the temple, begun during Cyrus' reign (539-530 B.C.), was not finished until the time of Darius I (521-486 B.C.). Ignoring economic reasons (Hag. 1:9) and Jewish reluctance to undertake the task (Hag. 1:2), he suggests that the delay was due to persecution by the neighbors of the Jews, whose offer of co-operation was rejected (4:1-5). He illustrates such persecution by offering excerpts from an Aramaic source (cf. Intro., p. 557) which showed that in all periods, through correspondence with the Persian court, the enemies of the Jews tried to stop the reconstruction of Jerusalem and succeeded temporarily (4:6-24).

Through his usual confusion of Zerubbabel with Sheshbazzar, the Chronicler transports events of the time of Darius I back to that of Cyrus. Thus he is enabled to expound his views that the returned exiles began work on the temple at once, and that from the beginning the Jews rejected the contamination of associating with foreigners, no matter what religion they professed. While the actual date of the first open break between the returned Jews and their neighbors cannot yet be determined, tension between them must have increased from the very start on economic and political as well as religious grounds. As J. W. Rothstein's correct interpretation of Hag. 2:14b shows, already by the time of Haggai "the people of the land" were regarded as "unclean" (*Juden und Samaritaner* [Leipzig: J. C. Hinrichs, 1908; "Beiträge zur Wissenschaft vom Alten Testament"], pp. 31-41).

a) OFFER OF ASSISTANCE (4:1-2=I Esdras 5:66-69)

4:1. The **adversaries**, now identified in vss. 2, 9-10, may once have been explained here rightly by the migrant gloss "the peoples of the lands," now in 3:3. They appear to be the folk of mixed blood inhabiting the province of Samaria, where the Hebrews of the Northern Kingdom had dwelt. Although tradition associates **Benjamin** with the northern tribes at their secession (I Kings 11:32, 36; 12:17, 20; Hos. 5:8), ultimately it was linked with Judah (cf. Jer. 33:12-13), where it is regularly associated in postexilic sources (cf. 2:20-34; I Chr. 7–8; 9:7-9; 12:2-7; Neh. 11:7 ff.). **The LORD** represents the proper name of the Jewish God which was probably pronounced "Yahweh."

4:1-24. Sectarianism and Racialism.—Whatever the chronological confusions, and the variety of sources both Hebrew and Aramaic that have been interwoven into this puzzling chapter, as these have been so strangely mingled by the Chronicler and so patiently disentangled by present-day scholarship, there is one aspect of this chapter which modern eyes, in the light of subsequent history, must note with sadness of heart. The offer of co-operation by the Samaritans, with its reminder of a common heritage in faith and worship—**Let us build with you; for we worship your God as you do** (vs. 2b)— is curtly rebuffed by the exclusiveness character-

istic of sectarianism in every age, and of racialism in every land: **You have nothing to do with us in building a house to our God** (vs. 3). This refusal of the returned exiles in Jerusalem to allow their Samaritan coreligionists any share in the worship of the rebuilt temple, a refusal which according to Josephus actually dated from the end of the Persian period, is here projected back by the Chronicler to this first attempt to rebuild the temple—in the face of his own admission in II Chr. 34:9 that money had earlier been sent from Samaria for the repair of the temple under Josiah. The Chronicler is of course in entire sympathy with the stress of

2 Then they came to Zerubbabel, and to the chief of the fathers, and said unto them, Let us build with you: for we seek your God, as ye *do;* and we do sacrifice unto him since the days of Esar-haddon king of Assur, which brought us up hither.

3 But Zerubbabel, and Jeshua, and the rest of the chief of the fathers of Israel, said unto them, Ye have nothing to do with us

God of Israel, 2 they approached Zerub'babel and the heads of fathers' houses and said to them, "Let us build with you; for we worship your God as you do, and we have been sacrificing to him ever since the days of E'sar-had'don king of Assyria who brought us here." 3 But Zerub'babel, Jeshua, and the rest of the heads of fathers' houses in Israel said to them, "You have

---

2. As I Esdras 5:68 shows (cf. Ezra 4:3), "and to Jeshua," now lost from the M.T., should be added after **Zerubbabel. We seek your God** (cf. 6:21) reflects the tradition in II Kings 17:25-28, 32 (cf. Josephus *Antiquities* IX. 9. 3). According to II Chr. 34:9, money was sent from Samaria for the temple in the time of King Josiah. Later the sons of the governor of Samaria (cf. Neh. 2:9-10) bore the good Jewish names Delaiah and Shelemiah; the Jews in Egypt, when their temple was destroyed, appealed to the Samaritans for aid in 408 B.C. (Cowley, *Aramaic Papyri,* pp. 108-24); and the relative of a Jewish high priest married the daughter of the governor of Samaria (Neh. 13:28). They accepted the Jewish Pentateuch as their sacred scripture. Thus, essentially Jewish in religion, the Samaritans felt they had a common interest with the Jews in their cult and made an apparently sincere offer of co-operation. Josephus claims that they were permitted to worship at the temple after its completion (*Antiquities* XI. 4. 3; XVIII. 2. 2).

Some have seen a political motive in the Samaritan offer. The Samaritans under the Assyrians and Neo-Babylonians had prestige as the ruling group in the province until the Persian rule began. Jewish newcomers from the East, who had the consent and support of the Persian court and could thus form a new and powerful upper class in the region, were menacing the established position of the Samaritans. By joining the new Jewish group in their venture the Samaritans may have sought identification with them and thus a salvaging of something of their political position (Rudolph, *op. cit.,* pp. 33-34).

Reference to Assyrian King **Esar-haddon** (680-669 B.C.) shows that the adversaries were not those settled in Samaria after its conquest by Sargon in 721 B.C. (II Kings 17:24 ff.) but a group exiled there later. Esar-haddon's annals indicate that the Syrian coast was subdued and organized as an Assyrian province from which Syrians were exiled and to which Eastern folk were sent for settlement in 677-676 B.C. (D. D. Luckenbill, *Ancient Records of Assyria and Babylonia* [Chicago: University of Chicago Press, 1926-27], II, 211-12, sec. 527; A. T. Olmstead, *History of Assyria* [New York: Charles Scribner's Sons, 1923], pp. 374-75). The neighboring province of Samaria may then have received the Easterners mentioned in vs. 2. It has also been suggested that the settlement was made in connection with the fall of Tyre and Esar-haddon's Egyptian campaign of 671 B.C. (Rudolph, *op. cit.,* p. 33).

b) REJECTION OF ASSISTANCE (4:3=I Esdras 5:70-71)

3. The Jewish rejection was, lit., "It is not for you and for us," which is properly interpreted as **You have nothing to do with us** or, in the Amer. Trans., "You have nothing in common with us." **We ourselves together** signifies the Jews banded together against

---

both Ezra and Nehemiah on racial purity as a prerequisite for any sharing in the worship of the God of their fathers. But as Julius A. Bewer[4] points out in his discussion of the book of Ruth, the "broader sympathies" and "larger-hearted

[4] *The Literature of the Old Testament and Its Historical Development* (rev. ed.; New York: Columbia University Press, 1933), pp. 282, 284.

view" so memorably set forth in that exquisite little idyl did not prevail against the "nativists, led by Nehemiah and Ezra."

In the light of the tragic story of anti-Semitism down the centuries, of its cruel climax in mid-twentieth century Germany, and of its ominous echoes in other countries, one can only speculate as to how different the course of history

to build a house unto our God; but we ourselves together will build unto the LORD God of Israel, as king Cyrus the king of Persia hath commanded us.

4 Then the people of the land weakened the hands of the people of Judah, and troubled them in building,

5 And hired counselors against them, to frustrate their purpose, all the days of Cyrus king of Persia, even until the reign of Darius king of Persia.

nothing to do with us in building a house to our God; but we alone will build to the LORD, the God of Israel, as King Cyrus the king of Persia has commanded us."

4 Then the people of the land discouraged the people of Judah, and made them afraid to build, 5 and hired counselors against them to frustrate their purpose, all the days of Cyrus king of Persia, even until the reign of Darius king of Persia.

---

the Samaritans. **We alone** follows the Vulg. and I Esdras, but such a meaning for the M.T. is not otherwise supported in Hebrew.

Cyrus . . . commanded us appeals to the royal edict (1:2-3; 5:13, 15; 6:1-4) to exclude Samaritans, taking advantage of a technicality to exclude undesirables. The Chronicler believed that none but returned Jewish exiles built the temple. Jewish reluctance to co-operate may have been due historically to the fact that the Samaritans were not pure monotheists but had merely added the Jewish God, as the god of the land, to their regular pantheon (II Kings 17:29-34a; cf. *ibid.*) .

c) PLOTS AND FRUSTRATIONS (4:4-5=I Esdras 7:72-73)

From an Aramaic document at his disposal (cf. Intro., pp. 557-58) the Chronicler presented evidence of the scheming antipathy of the adversaries who sought royal support in preventing Jewish reconstruction. Only part of the material refers to the temple, and that from the time of Darius (5:1–6:15) . None was available from the periods of Cyrus and Cambyses to explain the stoppage to which the Chronicler's verse (4:24) would intend the opposition to refer. Apparently because the Chronicler desired to lead directly from the completion of the temple (5:15) to reinstitution of cultic services as a preliminary to the story of Ezra (7:1–10:44) , he shifted the later material of 4:6-23, which would have interrupted his narrative, from after 5:1–6:18 to its present location. He was more concerned with the religious history than with accurate chronology. Evidently for him the data from the reigns of Xerxes and Artaxerxes amply illustrated the type of opposition which he believed also marked the period prior to Darius. With the shift the statement in 4:6 was translated from Aramaic to Hebrew and the reference to the letter in vs. 7 was but partially so translated.

4. Weakened the hands (cf. Neh. 6:9), lit., "relaxing the hands," an old Hebrew idiom (cf. II Sam. 4:1; Isa. 13:7; Jer. 6:24; 50:43; etc.), means to cause someone to lose heart and be discouraged to the point of inefficiency and even of inability to work. It is now found in a Hebrew ostracon from Lachish, referring to a prophet accused of lowering the morale of the country in a critical moment (Harry Torczyner, *et al., The Lachish Letters* [London: Oxford University Press, 1938], pp. 104-5, 117, No. VI, l. 6) .

The **hired counselors** could have been Jewish traitors (cf. Neh. 6:12-13) or, since the term is used of royal advisers (7.28) , bribed Persian officials. The accusations are general, presumably because specific data were lacking for the early Persian period. The Chronicler records a persistent tradition of the beginning of the temple by Sheshbazzar during the reign of Cyrus, but he could supply no details. It was common knowl-

---

might have been had the wider horizons and sympathies of the books of Ruth and Jonah prevailed instead of the relentless racialism of Ezra, had these proffered seeds of co-operation in work and worship instead of the dragon's teeth of racial prejudice and arrogance been

sown in Palestine 2,400 years ago. The Chronicler is at least explicit in his summary of the bitter harvest: **Then the people of the land discouraged the people of Judah, and made them afraid to build, and hired counselors against them to frustrate their purpose. . . .**

6 And in the reign of Ahasuerus, in the beginning of his reign, wrote they *unto him* an accusation against the inhabitants of Judah and Jerusalem.

7 ¶ And in the days of Artaxerxes wrote Bishlam, Mithredath, Tabeel, and the rest of their companions, unto Artaxerxes king of Persia; and the writing of the letter *was* written in the Syrian tongue, and interpreted in the Syrian tongue.

6 And in the reign of Ahasu-e′rus, in the beginning of his reign, they wrote an accusation against the inhabitants of Judah and Jerusalem.

7 And in the days of Ar-ta-xerx′es, Bishlam and Mith′redath and Tab′e-el and the rest of their associates wrote to Ar-ta-xerx′es king of Persia; the letter was written in

edge, from the work of Haggai and Zechariah, that the temple was actually constructed by Zerubbabel and Jeshua in the time of Darius. The Chronicler harmonizes his traditions in part by identifying the leaders of the two periods and in part by the contradictory hypothesis of a compulsory work stoppage between the reigns.

d) REIGNS OF XERXES AND ARTAXERXES (4:6-24)

(1) COMPLAINTS MADE TO XERXES AND ARTAXERXES (4:6-16=I Esdras 2:16-24)

6. As indicated above, **Ahasuerus** here is anachronistic if it refers to Xerxes. Both I Esdras and Josephus omit this verse. **Ahasuerus** (cf. Esth. 10:1; Dan. 9:1) is a corrupt form of a Persian name. It has been called a corruption of Cyaxares, confused with the name Xerxes. This has been taken as evidence that the Chronicler shared the later Jewish concept of Persian chronology which, faulty and unhistorical, recognized Cyaxares (II), a fictitious Median king reputed to be the son of "Darius the Mede" (Dan. 5:31) and the successor of Cyrus (C. C. Torrey, "Medes and Persians," *Journal of the American Oriental Society,* LXVI [1946], 3, 6-9). This ingenious interpretation would explain the unusual order of kings in vss. 6 ff. but it is not persuasive. More likely is the usual identification with Xerxes (486-465 B.C.). In explaining the unhistorical sequence of kings, Xerxes and Artaxerxes have been regarded as being used as typical Persian names (Alfred Bertholet, *Die Bücher Esra und Nehemia* [Tübingen: J. C. B. Mohr, 1902; "Kurzer Hand-Commentar zum Alten Testament"], p. 13). We probably have here a genuine reference to King Xerxes which has been drawn from its proper chronological position in the original Aramaic document (see *ibid.* and Rudolph, *op. cit.,* pp. 35, 37, 41).

The **accusation** is not explicit. Presumably the Chronicler (or the author of the Aramaic source) did not regard it as being as important or as relevant as those letters given in full. Lack of detailed knowledge of events in Palestine during the time of Xerxes makes it impossible to recover the substance of the letter or its occasion. **The beginning of his reign** means Xerxes' accession year, when he ascended the throne (December, 486 B.C.) to fill out the last year of his predecessor before beginning his own first year on April 6, 485 B.C. A papyrus describes such a year as "the beginning of the reign, when . . . the king sat upon his throne" (Cowley, *op. cit.,* p. 16, No. 6, ll. 1-2).

7. Like vs. 6, the letters to **Artaxerxes** I (464-423 B.C.) are out of chronological order. The two Artaxerxes letters are combined in I Esdras 2:16 by listing together all the senders. Josephus (*Antiquities* XI. 2. 1) corrects the chronology of both the M.T. and I Esdras by making Cambyses (530-522 B.C.) the recipient of the letter. He prefaces the document with a statement that during the reign of Cyrus the satraps were bribed to oppose Jewish reconstruction without the knowledge of Cyrus, who was preoccupied with

Then the work on the house of God which is in Jerusalem stopped. (Vss. 4-5a, 24.) In these sensitive matters, not least, the children on both sides reap what their fathers have sown; and the history not only of the Jewish people, but of our Western civilization as well, might have

been different had the outlook of the books of Ruth and Jonah prevailed over that of Ezra.

And yet, just as we are on the point of such speculation about what the course of history might have been and was not, a realistic question arises to give us pause. In the pathetically

8 Rehum the chancellor and Shimshai the scribe wrote a letter against Jerusalem to Artaxerxes the king in this sort:

Aramaic and translated./ 8 Rehum the commander and Shim'shai the scribe wrote a letter against Jerusalem to Ar-ta-xerx'es the

/ Heb adds *in Aramaic*, indicating that 4. 8-6. 18 is in Aramaic. Another interpretation is *The letter was written in the Aramaic script and set forth in the Aramaic language*

war elsewhere. Thus he does what the Chronicler leads one to expect by his vs. 24. But he does so only by mentioning the reconstruction of the temple which he already found in I Esdras 2:18, 20, although it is not in any of the Artaxerxes correspondence in the M.T. which should postdate the completion of the temple (but cf. 6:14).

The senders of the first letter (vs. 7) were the Persian **Mithredath** (Old Persian *Mithradata;* cf. 1:8) and the Aramaean **Tabe-el** (like Hebrew Tobiah), about whom nothing more definite is known. It has been conjectured that **Tabe-el** was a Jew, sympathetic toward rebuilding Jerusalem, who wrote the Aramaic document (cf. Intro., pp. 557-58) to **Mithredath** (cf. LXXᴮ) for transmission to the king (H. H. Schaeder, *Iranische Beiträge I* [Halle: M. Niemeyer, 1930], pp. 16-17). The M.T., however, only permits both men to share in sending the letter. Despite I Esdras 2:16, **Bishlam** is not a proper name but the Aramaic for "in peace." It could be part of a salutation in a letter (cf. vs. 17; 5:7), but the verse is not an introduction in form, and the word order would be unusual for a salutation. Rudolph (*op. cit.,* p. 34) therefore suggests reading בירושלם, "against Jerusalem," for בשלם, **Bishlam.**

Although vs. 7 is in Hebrew, its original Aramaic is still evident in the spelling of **unto** and in the use of loan words for **companions** (vss. 9, 17, 23; 5:3, 6; 6:6, 13) and **letter** (vss. 18, 23; 5:5). **Writing,** too, is an Aramaic word, a gloss to explain the Persian loan word for **letter. Written** could refer to the use of square **script** or to the use of **the Aramaic language. In the Syrian tongue** is, lit., **in Aramaic** the language which was the lingua franca of the Persian Empire (R. A. Bowman, "Aramaeans, Aramaic, and the Bible," *Journal of Near Eastern Studies,* VII [1948], 65-90). The last occurrence of **in the Syrian tongue,** not found in the LXX, is probably an addition, inserted as in Dan. 2:4 to indicate transition to the Aramaic language which follows (4:8–6:18).

8-16. The second Artaxerxes letter is given in full. Within vss. 8-11a are several introductions to the letter, each differing in the identification of the senders. Vss. 9-10, which interrupt the narrative, are an interpolated explanatory comment identifying the **companions** of the senders (cf. Torrey, *Ezra Studies,* p. 178). Schaeder (*Iranische Beiträge I,* p. 22) assumes that the long list of vss. 9-10 originally followed vs. 11b, but that the Chronicler first omitted them and later put them back in the margin whence they migrated to the present position after vs. 8, where they are relevant. As the letter actually begins in vs. 11b, the senders are now grouped anonymously under a general title. Josephus makes Cambyses the recipient of the letter (cf. vs. 7) instead of Artaxerxes.

Each section of the complex (vss. 8-11a) concludes with a peculiar expression, lit., **and thus** (vs. 8) or **and now** (vss. 10, 11), usually incorrectly translated **in this sort, as follows,** or "at such a time" (vs. 11). Such an expression regularly in the Aramaic papyri marks the division between the salutation and the body of the letter (Cowley, *op. cit.,* No. 17, 1. 2; No. 21, 1. 3; No. 26, 1. 1; No. 37, 1. 2; etc.).

8. Rehum ("Merciful") abbreviates such an Akkadian name as ᵐ*Rahim-ili* or ᵐ*Rahim-sharri.* His title was "Holder of a (royal) decree," the Aramaic equivalent of

weak and difficult situation of these returning exiles, amid the racial, cultural, and spiritual mixtures and dilutions that surrounded them, would their great heritage of prophetic and ethical religion have been preserved for posterity without the hard protective shell of the rigid racialism that speaks out so positively, not only in vs. 3b, **We alone will build to the LORD, the God of Israel,** but likewise throughout both Ezra and Nehemiah? Would Judaism, the law and the prophets alike, have survived amid the rising flood of Hellenistic syncretism through

9 Then *wrote* Rehum the chancellor, and Shimshai the scribe, and the rest of their companions; the Dinaites, the Apharsathchites, the Tarpelites, the Apharsites, the Archevites, the Babylonians, the Susanchites, the Dehavites, *and* the Elamites,

10 And the rest of the nations whom the great and noble Asnapper brought over, and set in the cities of Samaria, and the rest *that are* on this side the river, and at such a time.

king as follows — 9 then wrote Rehum the commander, Shim'shai the scribe, and the rest of their associates, the judges, the governors, the officials, the Persians, the men of Erech, the Babylonians, the men of Susa, that is, the Elamites, 10 and the rest of the nations whom the great and noble Osnap'par deported and settled in the cities of Samar'ia and in the rest of the province

---

Persian *farmānkara*. He was not a military leader but a bureaucrat representing the king (Herzfeld, *Zoroaster and His World*, I, 171; the Persian equivalent, *prmnkr*, is found in Cowley, *op. cit.*, No. 26, ll. 4, 8). The title was borrowed from Assyria, where it was held by officials of high rank, sometimes even by the chief priest (E. G. Klauber, *Politisch-Religiöse Texte aus der Sargonidenzeit* [Leipzig: E. Pfeiffer, 1913], pp. xxiv-xxv; cf. No. 137, reverse, l. 2; No. 103, reverse ll. 9-10; No. 111, reverse l. 4; No. 116, reverse l. 3). Klauber calls the official the "reporter," the meaning found also in I Esdras 2:17, 25 and in Josephus, who interprets the title "the recorder of all things that happen" (*Antiquities* XI. 2. 1). Such royal investigators were sent out yearly to the Persian satrapies to investigate and report conditions (Xenophon *Cyropaedia* VIII. 6. 16). Neither **chancellor** nor **commander** adequately renders the title or function.

Shimshai is found frequently in Akkadian records as *mShamshai*, an abbreviation of a name including the name of the Babylonian sun-god Shamash. Since a common **scribe** would not be mentioned in the salutation, **Shimshai** must be an official. Rudolph (*op. cit.*, p. 42) identifies him as Rehum's secretary. He probably was such a royal appointee as the scribe attached to officials during the Persian period to spy upon them and report directly to the king (Herodotus *History* III. 128; cf. George Rawlinson, *The History of Herodotus* [New York: D. Appleton & Co., 1859], II, 426, n. 9). Thus both men were required to investigate suspicious acts such as the fortification of Jerusalem. **Letter** here represents an Akkadian word (*egirtu*) borrowed by both the Aramaic and the Hebrew languages.

9-10. The list of names is a commentary on the "adversaries" (vs. 1), "the people of the land" (vs. 4). Although the M.T. treats all the names as gentilics, and some are definitely geographic, many are official titles.

The **Dinaites** are the **judges** (Persian *dâtabhar*), found often in the Aramaic papyri (Cowley, *op. cit.*, No. 6, l. 6; No. 8, l. 24; No. 27, l. 9; No. 80, l. 8; No. 82, l. 1). The Lucianic recensions of the LXX and of I Esdras 2:17 translate as **judges,** and Josephus calls them "the judges of the council" (*Antiquities* XI. 2. 1). Herodotus (*History* III. 31) claims that their authority derived from the king, and a papyrus links them with "observers" and "police" as part of the spy network of the province (Cowley, *op. cit.*, No. 27, ll. 8-9).

The **Apharsathchites** were not **governors** but "envoys" (Persian *frēstaka* or *fraistaka;* Rudolph, *op. cit.*, p. 36, cites Wilhelm Eilers, *Iranische Beamtennamen in der keilschriftliche Überlieferung* [Leipzig: F. A. Brockhaus, 1940], pp. 39, n. 1, 100; cf. Herzfeld,

---

the centuries between the O.T. and the N.T., except within that shell of legalism and exclusivism which Ezra himself did so much to create and to harden? The same kind of question, in terms not so much racial as cultural and theological, has faced the younger Christian

churches in India and China. And if Judaism had not survived as a distinctive culture and faith, would there have arisen any Jesus of Nazareth four hundred years after Ezra, or any Christian church universal under Paul? Who of us is wise enough to answer these highly

11 ¶ This *is* the copy of the letter that they sent unto him, *even* unto Artaxerxes the king; Thy servants the men on this side the river, and at such a time.

12 Be it known unto the king, that the Jews which came up from thee to us are

Beyond the River, 11 and now this is a copy of the letter that they sent — "To Ar-ta-xerx'es the king: Your servants, the men of the province Beyond the River, send greeting. 12 And now be it known to the king that the Jews who came up from you to us

---

Zoroaster and His World, I, 171). I Esdras 6:7, translating the "Apharsachites" of Ezra 5:6; 6:6, has "governors." None of the many explanations of the **Tarpelites** is convincing but its position suggests some kind of **officials.** The **Apharsites** are usually rendered as **Persians** (so also Rudolph, *loc. cit.*) but Herzfeld relates them to a possible Neo-Babylonian official, the *amiprasakanu,* whose identity is yet undetermined (Herzfeld, *Zoroaster and His World,* I, 171). Since the *-ka* sign is damaged in the text, the name is probable but not certain. Harry Torczyner ("Aryans and non-Aryan Persians in the Bible," *Bulletin of the Jewish Palestine Exploration Society,* XIV [1947-48], pp. 1, 6) regards the **Archevites** (ארכויא) as representing the Aryans, the "free-born" Persians (αριακοι) and the **Tarpelites** (reading טפליא and comparing שרביט for שביט) as "affiliated" or "dependent" Persians, the Babylonians and Shushanites that follow in the list. But this hypothesis depends on reading "Persians" for titles otherwise identifiable (**Apharsites** and **Apharsathchites**) and if the affiliated Persians are those listed, **Tarpelites** should appear just before the ethnic names.

Archevites are doubtless the **men of Erech** (Gen. 10:10), of the ancient city Uruk (modern Warka) in southern Babylonia. Since the other names are those of cities, the **Babylonians** apparently are those of the city of Babylon. **Susanchites** were men of the city of Shushan or **Susa** (Neh. 1:1; Dan. 8:2; Esth. 1:2, 5; 3:15), the capital of ancient Elam. **Dehavites** must be revocalized with two MSS and LXXB and translated **that is** linking the **Susanchites** with the **Elamites,** which was doubtless originally an explanatory gloss to the less familiar **Susanchites.** The **Elamites** were a non-Semitic folk who dwelt in the great plain of the lower Tigris, along the northern shore of the Persian Gulf, and in the mountains enclosing the plain to the north and east. They frequently joined the Babylonians against the Assyrians (George G. Cameron, *History of Early Iran* [Chicago: University of Chicago Press, 1936], pp. 4-5).

Asnapper is certainly a corruption of Ashurbanipal, the last Assyrian king (669-633 B.C.), since only he captured Shushan (Susa) from which the captives (vs. 9) were brought (H. Gelzer, "Die Colonie des Osnappar," *Zeitschrift für aegyptische Sprache,* XIII [1875], 81-82; Cameron, *History of Early Iran,* pp. 198-207). **Deported and settled** indicates that the Hebrew exile was not unique but a regular political technique used by the Assyrians with rebels. In exile people would be too busy adjusting to a new environment to be a threat to Assyria. Read the plural, **cities of Samaria,** with the LXX and Vulg. (cf. II Kings 17:24-26).

11. After the long list, a brief reference to the letter is needed to resume the subject. The salutation here greatly resembles that in the Aramaic papyri when a superior is addressed (Cowley, *op. cit.,* No. 30, l. 1; cf. No. 17, l. 1).

12. Be it known to the king is appropriate for the report of royal informants and may have been a standard formula for introducing such reports (cf. vs. 13; 5:8). Such

---

speculative questions, much less to presume to correct the actual course of history? All that we can fairly say is that Ezra and Nehemiah did then prevail over the authors of Ruth and Jonah, but that Jesus and Paul were later, "in God's own good time," raised up out of that very heritage. This also "is the Lord's doing;

it is marvelous in our eyes" (Ps. 118:23). And in this reminder from the actual course of history there is agelong encouragement for all who to this day have to live and work in a world where sectarianism and racialism are still powerful, sowing their dragon's teeth as of old.

come unto Jerusalem, building the rebellious and the bad city, and have set up the walls *thereof,* and joined the foundations.

have gone to Jerusalem. They are rebuilding that rebellious and wicked city; they are finishing the walls and repairing the foun-

---

a report would normally reach the king indirectly through a scribe who would read it to him. Some Assyrian reports addressed to the king contain personal notes to the scribal intermediaries. One begins: "To king Sargon himself, my lord, may this come . . . . Speak as follows to the king, my lord . . ." (Leroy Waterman, *Royal Correspondence of the Assyrian Empire* [Ann Arbor: University of Michigan Press, 1930], Part II, p. 217, No. 1027). Another appends the note: "Whoever you are O scribe who reads this, do not conceal it from the king your lord. Speak kindness before the king. May Bel (and) Nabû command kindness for you before the king" (*ibid.,* Part II, p. 371, No. 1250). The very formula may be reflected in the appended note: "Now I have written to the king my lord. May the king my lord know" (*ibid.,* Part I, pp. 120-21, No. 177; Part II, p. 29, No. 753).

Came up from you, lit., "came up from with you," need not imply a return from Ezra's group, for the expression may be merely geographical, meaning "from the East," where the king was. Since Nehemiah arrived at Jerusalem and built the walls before Ezra came (cf. Intro., pp. 561-62), the reference could not be to Ezra and his group. Rudolph (*op. cit.,* pp. 44-45) dates this incident shortly before 445 B.C., possibly in 448 B.C., while the satrap Megabyzos was in revolt against Artaxerxes. **Rebellious and wicked** describe Jerusalem from the standpoint of overlords who had to send expeditions to crush rebels in the western provinces (II Kings 18:7-11, 13-20; 24:1-2; 25:1-6, 25-26).

The correspondence here is not concerned with the temple, as in I Esdras 2:18, 20, but with the city walls. The temple was finished by the time of Artaxerxes (but cf. 6:14). The Chronicler in placing the letter here merely illustrates the hostility of the adversaries. Torrey ("Medes and Persians," p. 2) contends that the Chronicler understood that the adversaries were playing a trick; by a lying accusation regarding the city wall the enemies succeeded in stopping all construction, including the temple, which was their real goal. But there is no temple mentioned in Ezra and its presence in I Esdras is easily explained as due to a misunderstanding of "palace" in Ezra 4:14 as "temple" since the same Hebrew word is used for both (Rudolph, *op. cit.,* p. 43, n. 1).

Since the walls are still incomplete in vs. 13, "have finished the walls" (ASV) or **have set up the walls** is surely wrong. One can read **are finishing,** but it is preferable to follow Rudolph's emendation (*ibid.,* p. 38), which suggests that the verb "they have begun" (ושריו) has been lost by haplography after the very similar "the walls" (שוריא), and that the verb following should be read "to finish," thus, "they have begun to finish the walls."

The long debated **foundations,** which represents a hitherto enigmatic Aramaic word ('*ushshayyā*'), is now explained plausibly as a distinctly Mesopotamian architectural term (Sumerian *USH;* Akkadian *ushshu*) referring to a subfoundation double the thickness of the planned walls into which the walls were laid (Sidney Smith, "Foundations: Ezra iv, 12; v, 16; vi, 3," in I. Epstein, E. Levine, and C. Roth, eds., *Essays in Honor of the Very Reverend Dr. J. H. Hertz* [London: E. Goldston, 1944], pp. 385-96). The *ushshu* is mentioned in an Akkadian building inscription by Artaxerxes (Ernst Herzfeld, *Altpersische Inschriften* [Berlin: Dietrich Reimer, 1938], p. 45, No. 22, l. 5; R. G. Kent, "Old Persian Texts," *Journal of Near Eastern Studies,* IV [1945], 228). Perhaps such a structure is what Darius describes in his record of the building of his palace at Susa when he says, "Downward the earth was dug, until I reached rock in the earth. When the excavation had been made, rubble was packed down, some 40 cubits in depth, another (part) 20 cubits in depth. On that rubble the palace was constructed." (R. G. Kent, *Old Persian* [New Haven: American Oriental Society, 1950], pp. 142-44, Darius Susa F., ll. 22-27, sec. 3*e;* cf. George G. Cameron, *Persepolis Treasury Tablets* [Chicago: University

13 Be it known now unto the king, that, if this city be builded, and the walls set up *again, then* will they not pay toll, tribute, and custom, and *so* thou shalt endamage the revenue of the kings.

14 Now because we have maintenance from *the king's* palace, and it was not meet for us to see the king's dishonor, therefore have we sent and certified the king;

15 That search may be made in the book of the records of thy fathers: so shalt thou find in the book of the records, and know that this city *is* a rebellious city, and hurt-

dations. **13** Now be it known to the king that, if this city is rebuilt and the walls finished, they will not pay tribute, custom, or toll, and the royal revenue will be impaired. **14** Now because we eat the salt of the palace and it is not fitting for us to witness the king's dishonor, therefore we send and inform the king, **15** in order that search may be made in the book of the records of your fathers. You will find in the book of the

---

of Chicago Press, 1945], p. 17, n. 112.) Since architectural problems differed in stony Jerusalem from those in muddy Mesopotamian plains, the easterners who wrote the letter apparently applied the term they knew to some similar process employed by the Jews. With such a meaning for **foundations** the verb is best translated "being dug out" with the American Jewish Translation, supported by the Peshitta. Obviously the work was not very far along and the officials believed that prompt action would prevent the fortification of Jerusalem.

13. Tribute is an Akkadian loan word (*mandatu*) meaning a more or less voluntary gift made to an overlord (cf. Neh. 5:4 KJV). Usually closely linked with it is the *biltu,* the assessed tribute imposed by the overlord. That is apparently related to the second term in the series (Aramaic בלו) which is attested as "his tax" (בלוה) in an Aramaic ostracon from Egypt (Mark Lidzbarski, *Ephemeris für semitische Epigraphik* [Giessen: A. Töpelmann, 1908], II, 238-39). The third term, usually translated **custom** or **toll** because of its similarity to the Hebrew verb "go" (הלך), is still another Akkadian word (*ilku*) meaning *corvée,* taskwork, or feudal service owed the overlord, or its cash equivalent. It occurs (as הלך) in the Aramaic notes in the margins of cuneiform tablets concerned with the *ilku* (Delaporte, *Épigraphes araméens,* p. 67, No. 73; p. 70, No. 78; pp. 70-71, No. 79).

Revenue is but an incorrect guess based on context. The difficult word is probably a Persian adverb meaning "in the end" (as in the ASV) or "finally" (Persian *apatam-am;* Schaeder, *Iranische Beiträge* I, p. 74). The warning **thou shalt endamage** would hardly be addressed to a king by his subjects. Better sense is given by a simple emendation (reading מלכי מהנזק for מלכים תהנזק), "My king will be damaged" (Kittel, *Geschichte des Volkes Israel,* III, 601, n. 1; Rudolph, *op. cit.,* p. 39).

14. Since **we eat** incorrectly translates the verb "we have salted" (*melaḥnā'*), it is preferable to revocalize the word as the noun "our salt" (*milḥanā'*), reading, "Our salt is the salt of the palace" (Eberhard Nestle, *Marginalien und Materialien* [Tübingen: J. J. Heckenhauer, 1893], pp. 30 ff.; cf. Rudolph, *op. cit.,* p. 40). The reference is to a salt covenant (cf. Lev. 2:13; Num. 18:19; II Chr. 13:5) whereby contracting parties pledge to help and defend one another. Modern Arabs say "There is salt between us" and modern Persians describe a disloyal person as "untrue to salt" (H. C. Trumbull, *The Covenant of Salt* [New York: Charles Scribner's Sons, 1899]; W. R. Smith, *Lectures on the Religion of the Semites* [3rd ed.; New York: The Macmillan Co., 1927], p. 270; Adela M. Goodrich-Freer, *Arabs in Tent and Town* [London: Seeley, Service & Co., 1924], pp. 115-18). **Not fitting** represents the Persian *ariyaka,* "worthy of an Aryan" (Isidor Scheftelowitz, *Arisches im Alten Testament* [Berlin: S. Calvary & Co., 1901], I, 79). **Dishonor** is, lit., "nakedness" (cf. Gen. 9:22-23).

15. The book of the records is actually, as in I Esdras, the LXX[L], and Vulg., "books of memoranda," records kept by the Persian bureaucrats and their predecessors (cf.

ful unto kings and provinces, and that they have moved sedition within the same of old time: for which cause was this city destroyed.

16 We certify the king that, if this city be builded *again,* and the walls thereof set up, by this means thou shalt have no portion on this side the river.

17 ¶ *Then* sent the king an answer unto Rehum the chancellor, and *to* Shimshai the scribe, and *to* the rest of their companions that dwell in Samaria, and *unto* the rest beyond the river, Peace, and at such a time.

18 The letter which ye sent unto us hath been plainly read before me.

19 And I commanded, and search hath been made, and it is found that this city of old time hath made insurrection against kings, and *that* rebellion and sedition have been made therein.

20 There have been mighty kings also over Jerusalem, which have ruled over all *countries* beyond the river; and toll, tribute, and custom, was paid unto them.

records and learn that this city is a rebellious city, hurtful to kings and provinces, and that sedition was stirred up in it from of old. That was why this city was laid waste. **16** We make known to the king that, if this city is rebuilt and its walls finished, you will then have no possession in the province Beyond the River."

17 The king sent an answer: "To Rehum the commander and Shim'shai the scribe and the rest of their associates who live in Samar'ia and in the rest of the province Beyond the River, greeting. And now **18** the letter which you sent to us has been plainly read before me. **19** And I made a decree, and search has been made, and it has been found that this city from of old has risen against kings, and that rebellion and sedition have been made in it. **20** And mighty kings have been over Jerusalem, who ruled over the whole province Beyond the River, to whom tribute, custom, and toll were paid.

N. Schneider, "Die Urkundenbehälter von Ur III und ihre archivalische Systematik," *Orientalia,* N.S.IX [1940], 7; Cameron, *Persepolis Treasury Tablets,* pp. 9 ff., 20-23). **Your fathers** is not "your ancestors" but "your predecessors," the Babylonian kings. The Persians regarded themselves as the legitimate successors of the Neo-Babylonians, for the writers here have in mind the earlier revolts leading to the destruction of Jerusalem. Nothing certain is known of Palestinian revolts under the early Persian kings. But the incidents of Zech. 6:9-15 and the sudden disappearance of Zerubbabel suggest that the Jews may have proved rebellious during the reign of Darius (A. T. Olmstead, *History of the Persian Empire* [Chicago: University of Chicago Press, 1948], pp. 138-39).

(2) LETTER OF ARTAXERXES TO REHUM AND SHIMSHAI (4:17-22=I Esdras 2:25-29)

17. Instead of Artaxerxes I (cf. vs. 8), Josephus has Cambyses, whom he describes as "naturally bad." **Answer** represents a Persian word (*paitigāma*) which in modern Persian (*paigam*) means "message" (Scheftelowitz, *op. cit.,* I, 51). The abrupt **To Rehum** is characteristic of address to an inferior also in the Aramaic papyri (Cowley, *op. cit.,* No. 26, l. 1). **Peace** or "well-being" suggests the χαίρειν of Greek letters (cf. Acts 15:23; 23:26; Jas. 1:1) but it is also found alone in the papyri (*ibid.,* Nos. 39, 42, etc.), where it may be an abbreviation of the lengthy salutation, "The welfare of . . . may the god seek abundantly at all times" (*ibid.,* No. 30, ll. 1-2; No. 17, ll. 1-2; No. 21, l. 2, etc.).

18. Plainly read is rather "translated," since it is a technical term referring to extempore translation by a scribe, in the presence of the king, of material written in a foreign language into Persian, which the king could understand. Its Hebrew equivalent is in vs. 7. In Neh. 8:8 the term is used for translation from Hebrew to Aramaic (cf. Schaeder, *Iranische Beiträge I,* pp. 1-14). Since all versions, including the LXX, are confused by the term, its use here argues against fabrication of the letter in the late period and for the originality of the document containing it.

19-20. Search has been made implies search in the Babylonian files. Like the Assyrians, they must have kept full reports on political events in all areas of their

21 Give ye now commandment to cause these men to cease, and that this city be not builded, until *another* commandment shall be given from me.

22 Take heed now that ye fail not to do this: why should damage grow to the hurt of the kings?

23 ¶ Now when the copy of king Artaxerxes' letter *was* read before Rehum, and Shimshai the scribe, and their companions, they went up in haste to Jerusalem unto the Jews, and made them to cease by force and power.

24 Then ceased the work of the house of God which *is* at Jerusalem. So it ceased unto the second year of the reign of Darius king of Persia.

21 Therefore make a decree that these men be made to cease, and that this city be not rebuilt, until a decree is made by me.

22 And take care not to be slack in this matter; why should damage grow to the hurt of the king?"

23 Then, when the copy of King Ar-ta-xerx'es' letter was read before Rehum and Shim'shai the scribe and their associates, they went in haste to the Jews at Jerusalem and by force and power made them cease.

24 Then the work on the house of God which is in Jerusalem stopped; and it ceased until the second year of the reign of Darius king of Persia.

---

empire (cf. vs. 15; Waterman, *Royal Correspondence,* Part IV, pp. 23-24). **Ruled over all . . . beyond the river** is an unhistorical exaggeration since **Jerusalem** never approximated rule over all Palestine and Syria. The verse looks like an expression of Jewish nationalistic pride and as such may be a Jewish expansion of a more moderate statement. But Batten (*Ezra and Nehemiah,* pp. 178-79) suggests that the threat of a strong Judean king, such as is found in the cuneiform record of Hezekiah's strong resistance to Sennacherib (Luckenbill, *Ancient Records of Assyria and Babylonia,* II, 119-21, sec. 240) may have been sufficient to move a suspicious Persian ruler to such action.

21-22. Since only the king had the prerogative to do so (cf. 6:12), **make a decree** shows the men to be his representatives. **Until a decree is made by me,** lacking in I Esdras, may be a later addition, anticipating the granting of permission in Neh. 2:4-6. "The throne" would properly interpret **the kings** of the M.T.

(3) Work Stopped at Jerusalem (4:23-24=I Esdras 2:30)

23-24. Rehum's title (vss. 8, 9, 17) has been lost here as one MS, the LXX[L], and the Peshitta show. **By force and power** is, lit., "by arm and force." "Arm" is often a symbol of strength (Ezek. 31:17; Prov. 31:17; Dan. 11:15, 31). **Power** or "force" (חיל) is used for "army" in the Aramaic papyri. In I Esdras the text is interpreted, "with horsemen and a multitude in battle array," and Josephus does likewise. Rudolph (*op. cit.,* p. 44) plausibly suggests that whatever had been built in Jerusalem was then destroyed, leaving the desolation which caused Nehemiah's grief (Neh. 1:3). Vs. 24 is probably due to the Chronicler, who disturbed the original order of the Aramaic document (cf. Intro., p. 559) and then had to revert to the situation in vs. 5 in order to resume his narrative in ch. 5. The expression **king of Persia,** which he uses elsewhere (vss. 5, 7; 1:1-2, 8; 3:7; 7:1) supports this view. The word **then** which introduces the verse and relates it to the chronological sequence that precedes (Darius, vss. 2-3; Xerxes, vs. 6; and Artaxerxes, vss. 7-22), suggests that the Chronicler may have confused Darius I (522-486 b.c.) with Darius II (423-404 b.c.), which would be too late for the completion of the temple. Schaeder regards **then** as a reference to events in the days of Cyrus which he believes were originally in the Aramaic document but were omitted because the Chronicler had already dealt with them (1:1–4:4). Schaeder (*Iranische Beiträge* I, p. 23) suggests that **then** was copied unthinkingly, thus making a false chronology. This hypothesis cannot be proved. Rudolph (*op. cit.,* pp. 39-40) believes that the Chronicler who wrote the verse in Hebrew wrote "Thus" (כזאת) in Hebrew, which was corrupted to **then** when it was translated into Aramaic (אדין > באדין > בדין > כדן > כזאת).

5 Then the prophets, Haggai the prophet, and Zechariah the son of Iddo, prophesied unto the Jews that *were* in Judah and Jerusalem in the name of the God of Israel, *even* unto them.

2 Then rose up Zerubbabel the son of Shealtiel, and Jeshua the son of Jozadak, and began to build the house of God which *is* at Jerusalem: and with them *were* the prophets of God helping them.

5 Now the prophets, Hag'gai and Zecha-ri'ah the son of Iddo, prophesied to the Jews who were in Judah and Jerusalem, in the name of the God of Israel who was over them. 2 Then Zerub'babel the son of She-al'ti-el and Jeshua the son of Jo'zadak arose and began to rebuild the house of God which is in Jerusalem; and with them were the prophets of God, helping them.

e) REIGN OF DARIUS (5:1–6:22)

The story of the temple, interrupted at 4:5, is resumed in 5:1–6:18, part of the Aramaic document already encountered in 4:6-23. As the sequence of kings shows, 5:1–6:18 must have preceded 4:6-23 originally.

After brief reference to resumption of work on the temple under the stimulus of Haggai and Zechariah (5:1-2) the writer describes an official investigation of the Jewish activity in Jerusalem (5:3-5) and incorporates verbatim the official report to the king (5:6-17), which explains the situation the officials found (5:8) and gives a statement of the Jewish defense (5:11-16). The officials called for a check of Jewish claims and requested further instructions (5:17).

(1) THE TEMPLE BUILDING IS BEGUN (5:1-2=I Esdras 6:1-2)

5:1-2. In Darius' second year (520 B.C.), after Haggai's first prophecy (Aug. 29, 520 B.C.; cf. Hag. 1:1), the work on the temple was resumed (Sept. 21, 520 B.C.; cf. Hag. 1:15). The date in Hag. 1:1 was doubtless the source of both that in Ezra 4:24b and I Esdras 6:1. The name **Haggai** is found frequently in the postexilic periods in the cuneiform records of Babylonia as well as in the Aramaic papyri. The paternity of **Haggai** is never given, but he is always called "the prophet" (Hag. 1:1, 12; 2:1, 10; cf. Ezra 6:14). The RSV wrongly follows I Esdras here in omitting the title. **Zechariah** ("God Has Remembered"), on the basis of Zech. 1:1, should be the "descendant" of **Iddo** the prophet rather than his **son** or "grandson." In cuneiform records of the period the third name in a paternal record usually refers to a distinguished ancestor whose name is proudly perpetuated. According to the Chronicler (II Chr. 13:22) "Iddo the prophet" was a person of distinction in the time of King Abijah (913-911/910 B.C.). Such abbreviation of genealogy is found elsewhere in the cases of Ezra (7:1; cf. I Chr. 6:14-15), Laban (Gen. 29:5; cf. Gen. 24:24), and Jehu (I Kings 19:16; II Kings 9:20; cf. II Kings 9:2, 14).

The God of Israel is found elsewhere several times, particularly in the Aramaic material (6:14; 7:15; I Chr. 5:26), but the Chronicler usually has "The LORD, the God of Israel" (cf. I Chr. 15:12, 14; 16:4, 36; etc.), which I Esdras and the LXXA have here. **Even unto them:** The last word in vs. 1 dangles awkwardly, disconnected and meaningless. Its alternate translation, **who was over them**, makes good sense, although the ambiguous pronoun could mean either the Jews or the prophets.

For **Zerubbabel** and **Jeshua** see Exeg. on 2:2; 3:2. **Began to build** need not mean ignorance of the work of Sheshbazzar since he is mentioned in vs. 16. The Aramaic word here translated **began**, like later Greek ἤρξατο (ἤρξαντο), is often redundantly prefixed to a verb in narration without temporal significance (Gustaf Dalman, *The*

5:1–6:22. Prophetic Persistence Through Obstructions.—Resuming his story of the rebuilding of the temple that had been interrupted in 4:6, the Chronicler avails himself of further Aramaic source material bearing on the political legitimacy of the undertaking, as having the written sanction of a Persian king and his officials. In so doing he gives incidental recognition (5:1-2) to the actual movers in the whole enterprise, the prophets **Haggai and Zechariah**. The respective roles of the prophet and the layman in every constructive achievement, then

3 ¶ At the same time came to them Tat-nai, governor on this side the river, and Shethar-boznai, and their companions, and said thus unto them, Who hath commanded you to build this house, and to make up this wall?

3 At the same time Tat'tenai the governor of the province Beyond the River and She'thar-boz'enai and their associates came to them and spoke to them thus, "Who gave you a decree to build this house and to

---

Words of Jesus, tr. D. M. Kay [Edinburgh: T. & T. Clark, 1909], pp. 26-28; Torrey, *Ezra Studies,* p. 51, note d, p. 189). But since apparently little evidence remained of the former work, which seems limited to substructure (vs. 16), Zerubbabel actually began again with a new substructure (3:10-11). **Rebuild** is more accurate. While **helping** could mean manual labor, it is probable that the prophetic "help" means moral support and encouragement (cf. 6:14). The same verb is used in the Aramaic version of the Behistun inscription in the sense of "support" in Darius' claim " (the God) Ahuramazda helped me" in battle (Cowley, *op. cit.,* pp. 251-59, ll. 2, 5, 13, 19, 28). Josephus, too, interpreted it as moral support, claiming that the prophets "urged them to take courage and not to be apprehensive of any untoward action by the Persians" (*Antiquities* XI. 4. 5).

(2) OFFICIAL INVESTIGATION OF THE BUILDING OF THE TEMPLE (5:3-5= I Esdras 6:3-6)

The narrative of the investigation by officials of the Persian court was begun and the line of questioning was indicated, but when the writer realized that the story would be duplicated in the letter to follow (vss. 3-4; cf. vss. 9-10), he stopped abruptly and appended the letter itself (Rudolph, *op. cit.,* p. 51).

3. The date intended by **at the same time** cannot be determined closely, but the narrative suggests that it was soon after building was begun, when enough had been done to attract attention to the project. External walls had been raised (vs. 8) and work was progressing rapidly. Since the beginning of Darius' reign was marked by revolts throughout the empire, alert officials reported the seeds of sedition wherever they began to sprout. The tone of the letter suggests a routine visit by unbiased officials (vs. 17), but the Chronicler (4:5) and Josephus regard it as part of a deliberate campaign of harassment of the Jews, perpetrated by the Samaritans through persuasion or bribery of local officials. Josephus (*Antiquities* XI. 4. 4) departs from biblical tradition to reflect the natural concern of the official who inquired "who it was that had given them permission to build the temple in such a way that it was more like a fortress than a sanctuary."

Since Zerubbabel is not mentioned specifically in vss. 5, 9, and **the elders** are mentioned, some have dated the visit after the sudden disappearance of Zerubbabel. While it is true that he may have been included in the list of elders, silence regarding him in this situation is surprising, and may possibly be evidence for the date of this episode. A. T. Olmstead linked Zerubbabel's disappearance with a Jewish revolt timed to coincide with that of Nebuchadrezzar III and with Darius' Egyptian campaign ("Darius and His Behistun Inscription," *American Journal of Semitic Languages and Literatures,* LV [1938], 410-12; cf. the same author's *History of the Persian Empire,* pp. 138-40). But it has been shown that the revolts were past, and for Zerubbabel's disappearance one must "presuppose a comparatively peaceful situation in the Persian Empire," perhaps "immediately after the Jews resumed work on the temple, i.e., somewhere in the latter part of Darius' second year of reign" (519 B.C.; Arno Poebel, "The Duration of the Reign

---

and now, are shrewdly suggested in 5:2: the laymen **rose up**—and there was no enduring accomplishment until they did; but **with them were the prophets of God helping them.** There is likewise specific mention (vss. 14, 16) of the apparently abortive early attempt at rebuilding

under Cyrus, made by Sheshbazzar (1:8, 11), whom later tradition, as the Exeg. points out, either slurred over, or confused with Zerubbabel, or sought to erase altogether. Into most of the major accomplishments of history go such premature attempts and failures. Their final

4 Then said we unto them after this manner, What are the names of the men that make this building?

finish this structure?" 4 They^g also asked them this, "What are the names of the men

^g Gk Syr: Aramaic We

---

of Smerdis, the Magian, and the Reigns of Nebuchadnezzar III and Nebuchadnezzar IV," *American Journal of Semitic Languages and Literatures*, LVI [1939], 145). Rudolph (*loc. cit.*), because he believes that the inner walls were erected and the temple almost completed, dates the incident to 517 B.C., closer to 515 B.C. when the temple was finished (6:15) than to its beginning in 520 B.C. But this hypothesis rests heavily upon a faulty interpretation of a word (אשרנא in vs. 3 below) which he translates as "paneled."

Tattenai, formerly identified with **Ushtannu** (Hystanes), the satrap over Babylonia and Trans-Euphratia (Bruno Meissner, "תתני," *Zeitschrift für die alttestamentliche Wissenschaft*, XVII [1897], 191-92), was apparently his subordinate. He is almost certainly mentioned in a business document of the time of Darius I as "the governor [NAM=*pakhat*] of Trans-Euphratia" (A. T. Olmstead, "Tattenai, Governor of 'Across the River,'" *Journal of Near Eastern Studies*, III [1944], 46). The title **governor** is thus quite elastic, sometimes indicating the great satrap, sometimes, as here, his subordinate, ruling but part of the satrapy, and at times even a more limited subordinate (Hag. 1:1) whose authority was confined to Judea, a part of Trans-Euphratia (cf. Abel, *Géographie de la Palestine*, II, 115, n. 3). Albrecht Alt would interpret the latter as simply "commissioner," insisting that the official had but temporary authority to complete a limited and specific task to which he was appointed ("Die Rolle Samarias bei der Entstehung des Judentums," *Festschrift Otto Procksch* [Leipzig: J. C. Hinrichs, 1934], pp. 23-24).

Shethar-bozenai need not be emended to Shatibarzana (cf. Rudolph, *op. cit.*, p. 46; cf. Cowley, *op. cit.*, pp. 11-12, No. 5, 1. 16) since it would form a good Persian name (Shathrabujyāna; "Delivering the Kingdom"), which may also be found in the papyri (Raymond A. Bowman, "An Aramaic Journal Page," *The American Journal of Semitic Languages and Literatures*, LVIII [1941], 305, 312; col. C, 1. 4). The second element of the name is found alone as an epithet in the Aramaic incantations (J. A. Montgomery, *Aramaic Incantation Texts from Nippur* [Philadelphia: University Museum, 1913], No. 40, ll. 17-18, cf. pp. 252-54). Like Shimshai (4:8), this official was probably a royal scribe. **Their companions** are identified as "the investigators" (vs. 6).

This wall is proved an incorrect translation by the several occurrences of the Aramaic word it represents (*'ushsharnâ*) in the papyri (Cowley, *op. cit.*, No. 26, ll. 5, 9, 21; No. 27, 1. 18; No. 30, 1. 11). There the term refers to materials required to repair a boat, to objects stolen from a temple, and to some material from a temple which could be burned. It has been recognized that the word "must be taken in a wide sense" (*ibid.*, p. 102). It has been well translated as "material" or "equipment" by Harry Torczyner who, however, finally wrongly identifies the word here in Ezra with the building itself ("Anmerkungen zu den Papyrusurkunden von Elephantine," *Orientalische Literaturzeitung*, XV [1912], 399). The Greek χορηγία, used by the LXX here and in vs. 9, seems appropriate for it can mean "supplies" (for war) or "apparatus" (for a banquet or for the stage). In Ezra it could refer either to prepared stones, beams, or other materials awaiting the builders, or to equipment or furnishings for the completed temple.

4. "We told them" of the ASV, appropriate in the letter that follows (vss. 7-17), is out of place in a narrative in the third person. **They also asked** is better but inexact, since the verb of the M.T. is **said.** Render with the LXX, Ethiopic, Peshitta versions and one

---

achievement is made possible by a creative combination of the initiative of men with the ripeness of the times and the conditions, under what 5:5 calls **the eye of their God**—a symbol of "providential watchfulness" (Exeg.). Such co-operation between different callings, and

between different generations, is energized by the religious faith that can continue to say alike of unfinished tasks from the past and of new beginnings for the future, **We are the servants of the God of heaven and earth** (5:11).

In chs. 5–6 the Chronicler is plainly concerned

5 But the eye of their God was upon the elders of the Jews, that they could not cause them to cease, till the matter came to Darius: and then they returned answer by letter concerning this *matter*.

6 ¶ The copy of the letter that Tatnai, governor on this side the river, and Shethar-boznai, and his companions the Apharsachites, which *were* on this side the river, sent unto Darius the king:

7 They sent a letter unto him, wherein was written thus; Unto Darius the king, all peace.

who are building this building?" 5 But the eye of their God was upon the elders of the Jews, and they did not stop them till a report should reach Darius and then answer be returned by letter concerning it.

6 The copy of the letter which Tat'tenai the governor of the province Beyond the River and She'thar-boz'enai and his associates the governors who were in the province Beyond the River sent to Darius the king; 7 they sent him a report, in which was written as follows: "To Darius the king, all

---

MS, "they said to them as follows." It is lacking in I Esdras and may be an addition from vs. 9 (so Meyer, *Entstehung des Judenthums*, p. 26; Hermann Guthe and L. W. Batten, *The Books of Ezra and Nehemiah* [Leipzig: J. C. Hinrichs, 1901; "The Sacred Books of the Old Testament"], p. 34; Rudolph, *op. cit.*, pp. 46-47). **What are the names?** Lit., "Who are they, the names?" an idiom found also in Judg. 13:17. The names, which may have included Zerubbabel and Jeshua, are nowhere preserved. After answering the first question (vs. 3), the names may have been forgotten as unimportant. More likely they were sent in a separate list. In I Esdras 6:12 it is said that the Jews were required to furnish such a list "in writing."

5. **The eye of their God** symbolized providential watchfulness (Pss. 33:18-19; 34:15-16). **The matter**, elsewhere translated "the decree" (6:14) is here **a report**, in the sense customary in Akkadian (cf. 4:8; Dan. 6:2). **The report** is the letter that follows (vss. 7-17). **The answer** (cf. 4:18, 23) is found in 6:6-12. **By letter** is implied by the narrative but has no counterpart in Aramaic.

(3) REPORT OF TATTENAI TO DARIUS (5:6-17=I Esdras 6:7-22)

6. **Copy** (cf. 4:11, 23) and **letter** (cf. 4:8, 11). are loan words from the Persian and Akkadian respectively. **Apharsachites** are not the governors (RSV); the latter renders "the rulers" (οἱ ἡγεμόνες) of I Esdras 6:7. Nor is the term a transcription of Greek ἔπαρχος, **governor** (Torrey, *Ezra Studies*, p. 174; contra W. F. Albright, "The Date and Personality of the Chronicler," *Journal of Biblical Literature*, XL [1921], 114). The LXX and Vulg. treat it incorrectly as a proper name. Herzfeld (*Zoroaster and His World*, I, 171) identified the **Apharsachites** with the "Apharsites" of 4:9. Eilers most plausibly identifies them with the Persian *frasaka*, "investigator," which is also implied by the "watcher" (*nawaṭir*) of the Ethiopic version (cf. Rudolph, *op. cit.*, p. 50).

7. **A letter** (cf. 4:17) is preferable to **a report** since it represents the Persian word used in 4:17. The **all** of **all peace** is unique in Aramaic epistolary salutation, but the word is attested by I Esdras 6:8 where, however, as "all things" it is transferred to the next sentence. The word translated **all** is really an adverb (J. A. Montgomery, "Adverbial *kúlla* in Biblical Aramaic and Hebrew," *Journal of the American Oriental Society*, XLIII [1923], 391-95). The expression resembles superficially the "Heartiest greetings" (πλεῖστα χαίρειν) or "Many greetings" (πολλα χαίρειν) sometimes found in Greek letters of Hellenistic Egypt. But it is probably a token abbreviation of a longer Aramaic greeting

---

to make full use of all Aramaic sources at his disposal, showing the political approval given by various Persian kings to the rebuilding of the temple. In ch. 6 he cites a memorandum of Cyrus to his officials, and another of instruction by Darius I (under whom the temple was

completed in 515 B.C.), promising both official sanction and financial support in the great task, in accordance with Persian policy in these matters. Either because he found the name of Artaxerxes interpolated in his texts, or because he himself was confused as to the Persian king

8 Be it known unto the king, that we went into the province of Judea, to the house of the great God, which is builded with great stones, and timber is laid in the walls, and this work goeth fast on, and prospereth in their hands.

9 Then asked we those elders, *and* said unto them thus, Who commanded you to build this house, and to make up these walls?

peace. **8** Be it known to the king that we went to the province of Judah, to the house of the great God. It is being built with huge stones, and timber is laid in the walls; this work goes on diligently and prospers in their hands. **9** Then we asked those elders and spoke to them thus, 'Who gave you a decree to build this house and to finish this

---

(cf. 4:17; 7:12) such as "The welfare (שלם) of ——— may the Gods altogether (כלא) seek abundantly at all times" (Cowley, *op. cit.,* p. 140, No. 41, l. 1). Since "and now," which usually marks the end of the salutation (cf. 4:12, 13, 17), is missing here, Bewer (*Der Text des Buches Ezra,* p. 58) regards the **all** as an early corruption of that expression.

8. For **be it known** see Exeg. on 4:12. **The province of Judea,** a subdivision of the satrapy of "Babylon and Trans-Euphratia," may represent such an administrative division as that over which Assyria formerly had appointed a "district ruler" (*ᵃmbêl-pakhati;* cf. Abel, *op. cit.,* II, 115).

I Esdras 6:8 has additional material, at least part of which apparently has been lost from the M.T. since some of the data is presupposed later (e.g., "those elders" in vs. 9). Therefore, after **the province of Judea,** read, "We found in the city of Jerusalem the elders of the Jews building . . . ," which must be genuine (cf. Guthe and Batten, *op. cit.,* p. 35; Bewer, *loc. cit.;* Rudolph, *loc. cit.*). The object of "building" is **the house.** Thus what is translated **to** is actually an Aramaic indicator of the object. **The great God** has long been regarded as strange for a Persian official and therefore evidence of Jewish composition. But as I Esdras 6:9 shows, **great** here modifies not **God** but **the house of . . . God.** Thus we read, "We went to the province of Judea [and we found, in the city of Jerusalem, the elders of the Jews building] the great house of God."

As the Greek versions show, **great stones** is certainly wrong. The LXX has "choice" for **great,** while I Esdras 6:9 has the double translation "polished and costly" (cf. I Kings 7:9-11) with no indication of size. The usual explanation, deriving **great** from "round," is forced and impossible (Batten, *Ezra and Nehemiah,* p. 140). The word (גלל) is now found in Aramaic also on a series of mortars and pestles of gray-green chert from Persepolis (E. F. Schmidt, *The Treasury of Persepolis* [Chicago: University of Chicago Press, 1939], pp. 61-62 and Fig. 41) which bear in part the inscription "[So and so] made this mortar of *gll*" (עבד הון זנה זי גלל). It is encountered also in a Mandaic incantation text, where Cyrus H. Gordon translates it as "unsplit stone" (גלאלא) ("Aramaic and Mandaic Magical Bowls," *Archiv Orientalni,* IX [1937], pp. 96-97 and Pl. XII, Bowl M, l. 20). Although its etymology remains uncertain, the context suggests some kind of stone or "stone" in general. The Semitic **stones** here and in 6:4 may then be an explanatory gloss to the foreign word.

Timber is laid in the walls (cf. 6:4) is too ambiguous for identifying the type of construction. Timber with brick is found even in early times in Egypt, Babylonia, and Greece, but stone and timber, a weak combination, is more rare. Cretan houses of

---

under whom the task was finished, he ascribes the latter document to Artaxerxes. Complicated as are these textual and chronological problems, they suggest the difficulties against which the returning exiles labored, and the importance to them of official support against the opposition of their neighbors and the paucity of their own resources, thus confirming the picture of poverty

and apathy given in the books of Haggai and Zechariah. More important than official support in overcoming these obstacles was the indomitable Hebrew faith reflected in 6:12, 22. The God whom they served would **overthrow** their enemies, provide new allies, and give them strength of hand and joy of heart for **the work of the house of God, the God of Israel.**

10 We asked their names also, to certify thee, that we might write the names of the men that *were* the chief of them.

11 And thus they returned us answer, saying, We are the servants of the God of heaven and earth, and build the house that was builded these many years ago, which a great king of Israel builded and set up.

12 But after that our fathers had provoked the God of heaven unto wrath, he gave them into the hand of Nebuchadnezzar the king of Babylon, the Chaldean, who destroyed this house, and carried the people away into Babylon.

13 But in the first year of Cyrus the king of Babylon, *the same* king Cyrus made a decree to build this house of God.

structure?' 10 We also asked them their names, for your information, that we might write down the names of the men at their head. 11 And this was their reply to us: 'We are the servants of the God of heaven and earth, and we are rebuilding the house that was built many years ago, which a great king of Israel built and finished. 12 But because our fathers had angered the God of heaven, he gave them into the hand of Nebuchadnez'zar king of Babylon, the Chalde'an, who destroyed this house and carried away the people to Babylonia. 13 However in the first year of Cyrus king of Babylon, Cyrus the king made a decree that this

---

masonry had great wooden beams tying in the stone both horizontally and vertically (J. D. S. Pendlebury, *The Archaeology of Crete* [London: Methuen & Co., 1939], pp. 98, 132, 188; and Pls. XXI, 1; XXIX; XXX, 1). But this is not the usual conception of the Jewish temple and is improbable. Stone and wood were used together in the walls of the temple court (cf. I Kings 6:36; 7:12) but scarcely in the walls of the temple itself. Rudolph, thinking of his interpretation in vs. 3, regards the wood as paneling for the inner walls (cf. I Kings 6:15), but this, too, is improbable. The reference is probably to the fixing of cedar beams into and across the walls to support the roof (cf. I Kings 6:9). **Goeth fast on** or **goes on diligently** interprets a Persian word (Old Persian *usprna*) which Schaeder identifies (in a personal communication to Rudolph, *loc. cit.*) as "completely." Read here, "And that work is being done thoroughly" (cf. 6:8, 12-13; 7:17, 21, 26).

11-17. This long Jewish answer to the first question of the officials (vss. 3, 9), a long-range historical review, was a favorite device of Jewish writers (cf. Neh. 9:6-37). A more direct answer could have been given, but this type of answer is certainly more effective. Because of its apologetic tone and because its course of history is that stressed by the Chronicler, many conclude that the Chronicler has worked it over or may have even written it himself. But since the explanation is a Jewish defense, such as might be expected under the circumstances, there seems no good reason to challenge its validity as an actual scribal record of the Jewish answer.

11. Answer, here used of oral response, is the same Persian word elsewhere used of a "letter" (4:17; 5:7). The **great king,** of course, was Solomon (I Kings 5:1–7:51).

12. Angered or **provoked . . . unto wrath** implies very violent anger, for the verb, meaning "to tremble violently," is also used of the movement of earthquake. When the people ignored or rejected an agreement made between their fathers and God (cf. Jer. 7:17-20; 11:1-12), it was believed that God need no longer defend Israel but could become their vengeful enemy (II Chr. 36:14-16). **Gave them** expresses the belief that God could and did use foreign people as instruments for the punishment of Israel (cf. 1:2; Judg. 2:13-15; 4:1-2; 6:1; etc.). Nebuchadrezzar II (604-562 B.C.) besieged and destroyed Jerusalem in 586 B.C. and carried off many Jews to Babylon (Jer. 39:1-18; II Kings 24:1–25:30). **Chaldean** indicates the tribal groups from which Nebuchadrezzar descended; not of the line of old Babylonian kings but of a nomadic tribe that settled at the headwaters of the Persian Gulf about the tenth century B.C. and became the Neo-Babylonian rulers after the decline and fall of Assyria.

13. With this verse the narrative reaches the point at which 1:1 begins. If the Chronicler were author, we should expect a reference to the return from Babylon, one

14 And the vessels also of gold and silver of the house of God, which Nebuchadnezzar took out of the temple that *was* in Jerusalem, and brought them into the temple of Babylon, those did Cyrus the king take out of the temple of Babylon, and they were delivered unto *one,* whose name *was* Sheshbazzar, whom he had made governor;

15 And said unto him, take these vessels, go, carry them into the temple that *is* in Jerusalem, and let the house of God be builded in his place.

16 Then came the same Sheshbazzar, *and* laid the foundation of the house of God

house of God should be rebuilt. 14 And the gold and silver vessels of the house of God, which Nebuchadnez'zar had taken out of the temple that was in Jerusalem and brought into the temple of Babylon, these Cyrus the king took out of the temple of Babylon, and they were delivered to one whose name was Shesh-baz'zar, whom he had made governor; 15 and he said to him, "Take these vessels, go and put them in the temple which is in Jerusalem, and let the house of God be rebuilt on its site." 16 Then this Shesh-baz'zar came and laid the founda-

---

of his favorite themes. **King of Babylon** (cf. 1:1) is corrected to "k̄ing of Persia" in the Peshitta, but it is justified in I Esdras by the explanation "the first year that Cyrus reigned over the country of Babylon." For the **decree** cf. 1:2-4; 6:3-5.

14. For **vessels** see 1:7-11; 6:5; II Kings 25:13-17. The **temple of Babylon,** "his own temple" in I Esdras 6:18, was Esagila, of which Nebuchadrezzar calls himself "patron." Herodotus (*History* I, 181-83) describes some of the glories of that temple (cf. G. R. Tabouis, *Nebuchadnezzar* [New York: McGraw Hill Book Co., 1931], pp. 29 ff.; Vincent Scheil and M. Dieulafoy, *Esagil ou le Temple de Bêl-Marduk à Babylone* [Paris: Imprimerie Nationale, 1913]. **Whose name was Sheshbazzar** (cf. 1:8) is, lit., Sheshbazzar, his name." The expression "his name" is good Persian and must not be omitted with the Greek versions, H. L. Strack (*Grammatik des biblisch Aramäischen* [4th ed.; Leipzig: J. C. Hinrichs, 1905], p. 3*, note s), and Bewer (*op. cit.,* p. 60) as an accidental anticipation of the **whom he had made,** which has the same consonantal structure (שמה). "His name" also occurs in the Aramaic copy of the Behistun Inscription after proper names where the Old Persian text has *nāma,* and also in several other papyri (Cowley, *op. cit.,* Nos. 28, 33, 66:1, and the Ahiqar Papyrus; cf. Dan. 2:26; 4:8, 19; Antoine Meillet, *Grammaire du Vieux-Perse,* ed. E. Benveniste [Paris: É. Champion, 1931], p. 179; E. L. Johnson, *Historical Grammar of the Ancient Persian Language* [New York: American Book Co., 1917], p. 234, sec. 596). In 1:8 **Sheshbazzar** was simply "prince of Judah." His title, here translated **governor,** is an ambiguous one (cf. Exeg. on vs. 3). Like Zerubbabel (Hag. 1:1) and Nehemiah (Neh. 5:14), he would be ranked below Tattenai (Ezra 5:3). Possibly the title here was equivalent to the later Greek ethnarch. Others posit for him more limited authority, temporary assignment to a specific task (cf. vs. 3) and some render "deputy" (cf. Kurt Galling, *Syrien in der Politik der Achaemeniden* [Leipzig: J. C. Hinrichs, 1937; "Der Alte Orient"], p. 32; Rudolph, *op cit.,* pp. 62, 64).

15. The usual interpretation has a contradiction between the two parts of the verse, the first half presumes a standing temple while the second permits the building of one. Batten (*op. cit.,* pp. 137-38) omits reference to **the temple,** and implies storage in Jerusalem in some temporary place. The word translated **temple** here and in vs. 14 may also be translated "palace" (cf. 4:3; Dan. 4:29; 5:5; 6:18). Bewer (*loc. cit.*) therefore avoids the contradiction by translating "palace," implying the governor's palace. Rudolph (*op. cit.,* p. 52) objects, but his solution through an explicatory conjunction ("it, namely the House of God, shall be built") is implausible and unsatisfactory. It is probable that **the temple** here anticipates the building of such a structure. The same word, **place** or **site,** is used in an Aramaic papyrus for the site of the former Jewish temple in Egypt on which a new one was to be built (Cowley, *op. cit.,* No. 32, l. 8).

16. Laid the foundation involves Sheshbazzar in an act elsewhere assigned to Zerubbabel (4:12). Here men of the time of Zerubbabel refer to Sheshbazzar as someone who lived some time before. Tradition of the return and attempt at reconstruction under

which *is* in Jerusalem: and since that time even until now hath it been in building, and *yet* it is not finished.

17 Now therefore, if *it seem* good to the king, let there be search made in the king's treasure house, which *is* there at Babylon, whether it be *so,* that a decree was made of Cyrus the king to build this house of God at Jerusalem, and let the king send his pleasure to us concerning this matter.

6 Then Darius the king made a decree, and search was made in the house of the rolls, where the treasures were laid up in Babylon.

tions of the house of God which is in Jerusalem; and from that time until now it has been in building, and it is not yet finished.'

17 Therefore, if it seem good to the king, let search be made in the royal archives there in Babylon, to see whether a decree was issued by Cyrus the king for the rebuilding of this house of God in Jerusalem. And let the king send us his pleasure in this matter."

6 Then Darius the king made a decree, and search was made in Babylonia, in the house of the archives where the docu-

---

Sheshbazzar persisted and could not be ignored, even though, for sentimental as well as historical reasons, Zerubbabel was associated with the building of the second temple. The persistent memory of an earlier attempt at building embarrassed later generations who could not explain the failure of so holy a mission, and it confused historians of later times who tried to record the history of the temple. Sheshbazzar's acts were first slurred over, then deliberately identified with those of Zerubbabel. Deliberate attempts were made in ancient times to erase Sheshbazzar from Jewish history, and such efforts have continued down to our own day. But it is likely that a relatively small but enthusiastic group returned in the time of Cyrus and also that an attempt at building the temple was made. Conditions were even more unfavorable then than in the time of Haggai, and the crude beginning was abortive. About eighteen years later traces of the effort were no longer discernible and a new beginning had to be made.

For **foundation** see Exeg. on 4:12. Not **laid** but "gave" is the verb used here (cf. 4:12). Guthe and Batten (*op. cit.,* p. 63) see Persian influence here, since Old Persian *dâ* means both "give" and "make," and in trilingual inscriptions Babylonian "give" (*nadânu*) has the same significance, presumably under Persian influence. Such use of "give" is also found in the Aramaic papyri (Cowley, *op. cit.,* No. 81, l. 111; Ahiqar, l. 170).

17. With vs. 16 the Jewish account is finished. The transition to the officials' own request is marked by **Now, therefore** or **Therefore**—literally the same "and now" which elsewhere separated the salutation from the body of the letter (4:8, 10, 11). **If it seem good** is a characteristic deferential statement used in correspondence of the Persian period when subordinates ventured to make suggestions or petitions to their superiors. Similar usage is found in the papyri (Cowley, *op. cit.,* No. 27, ll. 19, 21, 22; No. 30, l. 23a; No. 31, l. 22. The **treasure house** is, lit., "the house of the treasures." **The royal archives** reflects the translation of I Esdras 6:21. No archival rooms have yet been found at Babylon, but they must have been similar to those excavated at the treasury at Persepolis. There documents were deposited in several rooms adjacent to the Court of Reception. Nearly eight hundred clay tablets were found in a tablet room, while in the papyrus and parchment room nearby only a few bits of charred cloth and some clay labels (*bullae*) bearing the seals of Darius and Xerxes bore witness to the very hot fire that had destroyed the flammable contents of the room at the burning of Persepolis (Schmidt, *Treasury of Persepolis,* pp. 33-37, Fig. 11). **Babylon** would be a natural place to look for early records of Cyrus. It was there that Hormuzd Rassam found the famous and valuable Cyrus Cylinder now in the British Museum (cf. O. E. Hagen, "Keilschrifturkunden zur Geschichte des Königs Cyrus," *Beiträge zur Assyriologie,* II [1891-93], 205).

(4) ANSWER OF DARIUS (6:1-12=I Esdras 6:23-34)

The requested search for Cyrus' edict (5:17) is first described (vss. 1-2) and its substance is quoted (vss. 3-5) before Darius' own instructions to his officers are given.

2 And there was found at Achmetha, in the palace that *is* in the province of the Medes, a roll, and therein *was* a record thus written:

3 In the first year of Cyrus the king, *the same* Cyrus the king made a decree *concerning* the house of God at Jerusalem, Let

ments were stored. 2 And in Ecbat′ana, the capital which is in the province of Media, a scroll was found on which this was written: "A record. 3 In the first year of Cyrus the

---

His orders grant the Jews permission to build the temple without molestation and provide for its support when it is finally completed (vss. 6-12). As a result of the king's assistance the temple was finished (vss. 14-15) and dedicated (vss. 16-18). The Chronicler then appended a description of the Passover and the feast of Unleavened Bread, which fell due shortly after the dedication of the building (vss. 19-22).

6:1-2. Then means when the report (5:7-17) was received at the Persian court. Instead of **made a decree** one expects an informal "gave an order" here, but the Persian king used only the decree in his administration. **House of the rolls** is, lit., "house of letters" or "house of documents." Josephus and I Esdras interpret it as **archives.** Since such rooms for documents were found in association with the treasury at Persepolis (cf. 5:17) it is not necessary to transpose the text to read "the storeroom where the documents were stored" (Julius Wellhausen, "Die Rückkehr der Juden aus dem babylonischen Exil," *Nachrichten von der königliche Gesellschaft der Wissenschaft zu Göttingen* [1895], p. 176; Torrey, *Ezra Studies,* p. 192; Rudolph, *op. cit.,* p. 54), and we can retain with the M.T., **where the treasures were laid up.** Although search may have been made **in Babylon,** as had been suggested (5:17), the edict was actually found at **Ecbatana** (modern Hamadân), the former capital of Media which, because of its elevation and pleasant climate, became the summer resort of the Persian kings. Cyrus spent two summer months in **Ecbatana,** three spring months in Susa, and the rest of the year at Babylon (Xenophon *Cyropaedia* VIII. 6. 22; Strabo *Geography* XI. 13. 1). Shortly after his accession Cyrus retired to Ecbatana (539-538 B.C.), leaving the government at Babylon first to his general Gobryas and later to Crown Prince Cambyses (cf. Nabonidus Chronicle, col. III, ll. 24 ff. in Sidney Smith, *Babylonian Historical Texts,* p. 118; Olmstead, *History of the Persian Empire,* p. 57). Read neither **palace** nor **capital** to designate **Ecbatana** but translate "fortress" (Akkadian *birtu*) as descriptive of a fortified city. Such usage is regular in the Aramaic papyri of the Persian period; in the Behistun Inscription the word is used to translate Old Persian "stronghold" (*didā;* Cowley, *op. cit.,* Behistun Inscription, ll. 77-78). Ecbatana was a great fortress, as classical and other writers testify (Herodotus *History* I. 98; Judith 1:2-4; cf. Zend-Avesta, the second fargard of the Vendidad Jemshid). Since the record was probably a single sheet of parchment or papyrus (Bowman, "Aramaeans, Aramaic, and the Bible," p. 77), **a roll** is preferable to **a scroll,** which suggests something more formal and elaborate.

3-5. (Cf. 5:13-15.) Both 5:13-15 and 6:3-5 deal with the same situation; the former as narrative, the latter as prescription. Strong resemblances have led some to regard 6:3-5 as a corruption of 5:13-15, so that 6:3-5 might be emended on the basis of 5:13-15. Thus 6:4 has been excised because it was not in the other passage, and the text of 5:15b has been substituted for 6:5b by some (cf. Batten, *op. cit.,* pp. 143-44). But 5:15b seems to be superfluous, and 6:5b is quite appropriate in its present context (cf. Bewer, *op. cit.,* p. 62, n. 1). Since Aramaic tends toward stereotyped forms of expression, in the same situation some identical vocabulary and word order might be expected. Furthermore, **the first year of Cyrus** (cf. 1:1) and **Cyrus the king . . . made a decree** quote Tattenai's letter (5:13), just as an Aramaic memorandum later reflects passages in the official letter to which it responds (Cowley, *op. cit.,* cf. No. 32 with No. 30). Bickerman contends that 6:3-5 represents a written document in contrast to the oral heraldic proclamation in 1:1-4 (cf. 1:1). Plausible is the suggestion that 6:3-5 is not a formal decree but the abstraction of relevant portions of a more extensive document which may have been

the house be builded, the place where they offered sacrifices, and let the foundations thereof be strongly laid; the height thereof threescore cubits, *and* the breadth thereof threescore cubits;

4 *With* three rows of great stones, and a row of new timber: and let the expenses be given out of the king's house:

king, Cyrus the king issued a decree: Concerning the house of God at Jerusalem, let the house be rebuilt, the place where sacrifices are offered and burnt offerings are brought; its height shall be sixty cubits and its breadth sixty cubits, 4 with three courses of great stones and one course of timber; let the cost be paid from the royal treasury.

---

concerned with permission for rebuilding the temples of other gods also (Galling, *op. cit.*, p. 31; Cyrus Cylinder, ll. 30-36; Sidney Smith, *op. cit.*, p. 91, col. 6, l. 18). It has been supposed that the builders in the time of Darius had either the edict or an abstract of it, apparently as part of the temple archives (Rudolph, *op. cit.*, p. 53). **Record** (vs. 2), lit., "memorandum," favors the idea of abstraction of data from a more extensive document. A similar memorandum in the Aramaic papyri deals with official permission to rebuild the Jewish temple in Egypt (Cowley, *op. cit.*, pp. 122-24, No. 32), and the same word "memorandum" is found frequently on the reverse of the papyri bearing the Behistun Inscription (*ibid.*, No. 61, ll. 1, 10; No. 63, ll. 10, 12, 14; No. 68, l. 2).

3. Several MSS and the versions show the translation "the house of God which is in Jerusalem" (cf. vs. 12; 4:24; 5:2, 16); cf. the statement in the papyri, "the temple of Yahu the God which is in the fortress Yeb" (*ibid.*, No. 30, l. 6). Such a reference to the temple here appears to be a superscription, possibly to distinguish the Jerusalem grant from others which may have been in the same document. The designation **the place where sacrifices are offered** suggests the official Persian description of the Jewish temple in Egypt as "the house of the sacrificial altar" (*ibid.*, No. 32, ll. 3-4).

Because the verb means not **laid** but **brought,** there have been many attempts to emend the word translated **foundations** (*ushshu* as in 4:12). It has been altered to "his fire offerings" (Paul Haupt in Guthe and Batten, *op. cit.*, p. 36) or **burnt offerings** (Torrey, *Ezra Studies*, p. 192). In the present context, however, not **offerings** but some transition to the following building instructions is expected. The architectural term **foundations,** as "substructure," suits the present context and needs no emendation. As "let them carry," the verb might refer to carrying the fill for the substructure. If "carry" could have the sense of "bear" or "support," as in English, **foundations** could be the subject, connected with the dimensions of the building: "And its substructures shall support its height," etc. Unfortunately since such use is not attested, the problem remains unsolved.

A dimension is lacking in the specifications. Data about Solomon's temple, the pattern here, shows that due to the many references to **cubits,** a scribe has omitted some Hebrew text, including the height of the building, which is thirty cubits in I Kings 6:2. The **sixty** now attached to **its height** is the missing measure of length (cf. I Kings 6:2; II Chr. 3:3; see Rudolph, *op. cit.*, pp. 54-55). The **breadth** measure has been assimilated to the previous **sixty** and should be "twenty" as the Peshitta shows (cf. I Kings 6:2; II Chr. 3:3; Ezek. 41:2). Since the **cubit** varied in length, the size of the building cannot be determined. The Jewish **cubit** was about 17.6 inches but Ezek. 41:8 mentions a "great cubit," apparently the royal cubit, described as "a cubit and a handbreadth" (about 20.57 inches at Jerusalem), which must have been used for such a building.

4. **Courses** is now attested as an Akkadian word (*nadbak*) in a tablet of the time of Nebuchadrezzar, in which a foreman of bricklayers specifies the number of bricks in each **course** in the construction of a palace wall (H. F. Lutz, *Neo-Babylonian Administration Documents from Erech* [Berkeley: University of California Press, 1927], p. 74, No. 82, ll. 3, 11). As in 5:8, **great stones** is incorrect. Instead of **new timber,** read with the LXX^{AB} and two MSS **one course of timber** (cf. I Kings 6:36; 7:12). The specifications are for the walls of the temple court and must not refer to the temple walls, which apparently had no binding timbers (cf. 5:8).

5 And also let the golden and silver vessels of the house of God, which Nebuchadnezzar took forth out of the temple which *is* at Jerusalem, and brought unto Babylon, be restored, and brought again unto the temple which *is* at Jerusalem, *every one* to his place, and place *them* in the house of God.

6 Now *therefore*, Tatnai, governor beyond the river, Shethar-boznai, and your companions the Apharsachites, which *are* beyond the river, be ye far from thence:

7 Let the work of this house of God alone; let the governor of the Jews and the elders of the Jews build this house of God in his place.

5 And also let the gold and silver vessels of the house of God, which Nebuchadnez'zar took out of the temple that is in Jerusalem and brought to Babylon, be restored and brought back to the temple which is in Jerusalem, each to its place; you shall put them in the house of God."

6 "Now therefore, Tat'tenai, governor of the province Beyond the River, She'thar-boz'enai, and your associates the governors who are in the province Beyond the River, keep away; 7 let the work on this house of God alone; let the gevernor of the Jews and the elders of the Jews rebuild this house

---

5. It was expected that the temple vessels taken by the Babylonians would be restored to Jerusalem (cf. Jer. 27:21-22), and postexilic Jews believed that one of the first acts of Cyrus after his capture of Babylonia was their return (cf. 1:7-11; 5:14-15). Since the subject is the **vessels**, the words **and also let . . . be . . . brought**, lit., "and let it go," are awkward. But it is unnecessary to make the verb plural to agree with the subject from which it is so far separated (Ehrlich, *Randglossen zur hebräischen Bibel*, VII, 168; contra Eduard König, *Historisch-comparative Syntax der hebräischen Sprache* [Leipzig: J. C. Hinrichs, 1897], sec. 348*t*; cf. Rudolph, *op. cit.*, p. 56). It may be translated according to its sense as "and let it [all] come . . ." (Torrey, *Ezra Studies*, p. 193). **Every one to his place**, impossible here, is perhaps an intrusion under the influence of "upon its place" in 5:15. **And place them** includes an object not in the M.T. which has "you shall lay down." The best sense is obtained by emending the text to read, "And let it all be caused to be deposited . . ." (*ibid.*). Such emendation is favored by the fact that the verb is translated passively in the versions and the result (ויינחת) has some graphic similarity to the present text (ותחת).

6-12. With **now** in vs. 6 attention shifts abruptly to Darius' answer to the officials (cf. 5:6) who had asked for instructions (5:17). Such a sharp transition, without formal epistolary introduction, suggests that a portion of the text is missing between vs. 5 and vs. 6. **Now**, here as elsewhere (cf. 4:8, 10; 5:17), seems to mark a transition, a shift from reference to Cyrus' edict to Darius' own order based on the edict. But the connection between vs. 2 and vs. 3 is too close and smooth to conjecture that the salutation and part of the letter ever stood there. Josephus, too, felt the need for some introduction here, and he supplied a covering letter for the Cyrus edict, but there is nothing in the M.T. or in I Esdras to support his informal, rather Hellenistic note (*Antiquities* XI. 4. 7). It is proposed to introduce something like "Thereupon Darius wrote to Tattenai . . ." (cf. Rudolph, *op. cit.*, p. 48), but there is no present means for recovering the text which was lost so early that none of the versions preserve a trace of it.

6. With **now** Darius begins to explain "his pleasure" (5:17) about the Jewish temple. Since his throne was still somewhat uncertain at the beginning of his reign, he found it expedient to confirm Cyrus' edict and thereby to gain the good will of the Jews who could form for him a buffer against Egypt (Olmstead, *History of the Persian Empire*, pp. 140-41). In the Gadatas inscription, too, in his "policy towards the gods" Darius is motivated by the concern of his "forefathers towards the god . . ." (Botsford and Sihler, *Hellenic Civilization*, p. 162).

7. This verse is better translated, "Let the governor of the Jews and the elders of the Jews alone for the work of that house of God; and let them build that house of God upon its site" (cf. Vulg.; Torrey, *Ezra Studies*, p. 193, note n). **The governor**, a gloss

8 Moreover I make a decree what ye shall do to the elders of these Jews for the building of this house of God: that of the king's goods, *even* of the tribute beyond the river, forthwith expenses be given unto these men, that they be not hindered.

9 And that which they have need of, both young bullocks, and rams, and lambs, for the burnt offerings of the God of heaven, wheat, salt, wine, and oil, according to the

of God on its site. **8** Moreover I make a decree regarding what you shall do for these elders of the Jews for the rebuilding of this house of God; the cost is to be paid to these men in full and without delay from the royal revenue, the tribute of the province from Beyond the River. **9** And whatever is needed — young bulls, rams, or sheep for

---

for agreement with 5:3, is responsible for the further expansion to "Zerubbabel, the servant of the Lord" in I Esdras 6:27. As might be expected of a distant king, the Aramaic text has "that house of God" instead of **this.**

8. In the ambiguous text here, **do to the elders** could mean, as in I Esdras 6:27-28, "work along with the elders," but such help would have been refused (cf. 4:2-3). **Do for these elders** is less likely than "do about those elders." As in vs. 7 the pronouns indicate remote objects, "those elders," "that house," and "those men." Vs. 8*b* is introduced by an explicative conjunction, "namely."

Reaffirming Cyrus' edict (6:4), Darius orders the **expenses** of building withheld from **the royal revenue**—lit., from **the king's goods**—collected by his agents in Trans-Euphratia. Since it represents a Persian word for "thoroughly" (cf. 5:8), **in full** is better than **forthwith. That they be not hindered,** presumably referring to the workmen, reflects the LXX and Peshitta, but the M.T. has "that it may not be made to stop," which refers to payments for the work. "Without stopping" is therefore more accurate than **without delay.**

The verse has been ridiculed as unauthentic because Hag. 2:3; Zech. 4:7-10 reflect no use of such funds (Jahn, *Esra [A und B] und Nehemja,* p. 54; Hölscher, *Esra und Nehemia,* II, 514), but it would be difficult to collect the grant from hostile officials far from the court even if it were made (cf. Batten, *Ezra and Nehemiah,* p. 146; Rudolph, *op. cit.,* pp. 56-57). Furthermore, since the work was not stopped by the officers (cf. 5:8), it is probable that before any grant could be collected the plans and construction would be too far advanced to admit any major changes.

9-10. Part of the expenses of the cult, too, were to be paid by the king. On the assumption that a Persian king would not be likely to make such concessions and would be uninterested in such details of Jewish cult, these verses have been regarded as unhistorical forgeries. But the Persepolis treasury texts show just such royal concern for detail (cf. Cameron, *Persepolis Treasury Tablets,* pp. 12-13). Such interest is known to have extended to the cult of subject peoples. Cyrus was concerned with Babylonian gods and temples (cf. 1:2-3). Cambyses was personally concerned about Egyptian temples and the distribution of supplies for their sacrifices (cf. Olmstead, *History of the Persian Empire,* p. 91; Wilhelm Spiegelberg, ed., *Die sogennante demotische Chronik* [Leipzig: J. C. Hinrichs, 1914], pp. 32-33). He showed special concern for the Jewish temple in Egypt (Cowley, *Aramaic Papyri,* p. 113, No. 30, ll. 13-14). Darius I also supported a foreign god favored by his predecessors and reproved an official for taxing a religious community and for making them cultivate unhallowed ground (cf. Botsford and Sihler, *op. cit.,* p. 162). Darius II later sent to Egypt detailed orders for the keeping of the Jewish festival of Unleavened Bread (and Passover?) and, in granting permission to rebuild the Jewish temple in Egypt, the types of sacrifice permitted were specified (Cowley, *op. cit.,* No. 21 and No. 32).

It may be deduced from vs. 10 that not all sacrifices but only the daily burnt offerings and their supplements which were connected with prayers for the royal house were supplied (Bertholet, *Esra und Nehemia,* p. 27; Rudolph, *op. cit.,* pp. 58-59). Cyrus, too, expected daily intercession with the Babylonian gods he had re-established (Cyrus

appointment of the priests which *are* at Jerusalem, let it be given them day by day without fail:

10 That they may offer sacrifices of sweet savors unto the God of heaven, and pray for the life of the king, and of his sons.

11 Also I have made a decree, that whosoever shall alter this word, let timber be pulled down from his house, and being set up, let him be hanged thereon; and let his house be made a dunghill for this.

burnt offerings to the God of heaven, wheat, salt, wine, or oil, as the priests at Jerusalem require — let that be given to them day by day without fail, **10** that they may offer pleasing sacrifices to the God of heaven, and pray for the life of the king and his sons. **11** Also I make a decree that if anyone alters this edict, a beam shall be pulled out of his house, and he shall be impaled upon it, and his house shall be made a

---

Cylinder, ll. 34-36). Later Jews in Egypt similarly offered to pray and sacrifice on behalf of a Persian official who might help with the restoration of their temple (Cowley, *op. cit.,* p. 114, No. 30, ll. 25-28).

Thus the substance of vss. 9-10 is historically probable, but they can also be challenged on other grounds. The accuracy of terminology and the knowledge of Jewish practices there demonstrated may be explained as due to the influence of a Jewish secretary, like the later Ezra, as advisor to the royal court (Rudolph, *op. cit.,* pp. 57-58). But the verses are just such an expansion as the Chronicler might make in the interest of the cultus and there are definite indications of the Chronicler's literary style. The sacrifices are listed in an order favored by the Chronicler (I Chr. 29:21; II Chr. 29:21, 32; Ezra 6:17; 7:22; 8:35) and the expression **day by day** is such as he favors (I Chr. 12:22; 16:23; II Chr. 8:13; 24:11; 30:21). The verses are best explained as an expansion by the Chronicler (cf. Torrey, *Composition,* p. 10; *Ezra Studies,* p. 158).

Wheat was offered as fine flour, either alone (Lev. 5:11-13), mixed as dough (Lev. 2:1-3), or as cakes (Lev. 2:4 ff.). Josephus here specifies "fine flour." **Salt** (cf. 7:22) was offered with all oblations (Lev. 2:13; Mark 9:49), and meal offerings are particularly specified as needing **salt** seasoning (Lev. 2:13). **Wine** was presented as a libation with every public burnt offering (Exod. 29:40-41; Lev. 23:13, 18, 37; Num. 15:24; etc.). It was poured from a chalice to the base of the altar (Ecclus. 50:15; cf. Josephus *Antiquities* III. 9. 4). Olive **oil** figured prominently in the meal offering. **Sweet savors,** as the odor of sacrifice, here means the regular **pleasing sacrifices** (cf. Exod. 29:18, 25; Lev. 1:9, 13, 17; etc.).

11-12. Severe penalties were prescribed for those who violated the royal decree. Neither **hanged** nor "fastened" (ASV) reflects the violence of the act. The M.T. has, lit., "let a timber be pulled away from his house and, when erected, let him be struck upon it." The victim was **impaled** on the sharpened timber. It was thrust into the body either just below the ribs or between the legs (cf. W. D. Birch and T. G. Pinches, *The Bronze Ornaments of the Palace Gates of Balawat* [London: Society of Biblical Archaeology, 1902], pp. 2b, 4b, 10a; Pls. B2, D4, J3). The Assyrians used impalement to punish only the most abhorrent crimes (Olmstead, *History of Assyria,* pp. 87, 112, 308, 551; Bruno Meissner, *Babylonien und Assyrien* [Heidelberg: C. Winter, 1920], I, 112), and Herodotus (*History* III. 159) calls it a Persian practice also. The **house** of the offender was pulled down (cf. Dan. 2:5; 3:29) and the ruin was made into a **dunghill** or public privy (II Kings 10:27; J. A. Montgomery, *A Critical and Exegetical Commentary on the Book of Daniel* [New York: Charles Scribner's Sons, 1927; "International Critical Commentary"], pp. 148-49).

Warnings of punishment for violation of royal decree are not unusual. Unlike the Daniel passages, vs. 12 promises additional punishment for future kings or people who would change the decree favoring the temple. The KJV wrongly makes **alter** (vs. 12) refer to the temple, but the implied object of the verb, as vs. 11a shows, is the **edict.** As usual in such threats, God is expected to defend the decree and the temple, since he would be vitally concerned and would survive the king himself.

12 And the God that hath caused his name to dwell there destroy all kings and people, that shall put to their hand to alter *and* to destroy this house of God which *is* at Jerusalem. I Darius have made a decree; let it be done with speed.

13 ¶ Then Tatnai, governor on this side the river, Shethar-boznai, and their companions, according to that which Darius the king had sent, so they did speedily.

14 And the elders of the Jews builded, and they prospered through the prophesying of Haggai the prophet and Zechariah the son of Iddo. And they builded, and finished *it,* according to the commandment of the God of Israel, and according to the commandment of Cyrus, and Darius, and Artaxerxes king of Persia.

15 And this house was finished on the third day of the month Adar, which was in the sixth year of the reign of Darius the king.

dunghill. 12 May the God who has caused his name to dwell there overthrow any king or people that shall put forth a hand to alter this, or to destroy this house of God which is in Jerusalem. I Darius make a decree; let it be done with all diligence."

13 Then, according to the word sent by Darius the king, Tat'tenai, the governor of the province Beyond the River, She'thar-boz'enai, and their associates did with all diligence what Darius the king had ordered. 14 And the elders of the Jews · built and prospered, through the prophesying of Haggai the prophet and Zechari'ah the son of Iddo. They finished their building by command of the God of Israel and by decree of Cyrus and Darius and Ar-ta-xerx'es king of Persia; 15 and this house was finished on the third day of the month of Adar, in the sixth year of the reign of Darius the king.

The God who has caused his name to dwell there is a distinctly Hebraic expression, common in Deuteronomic literature (cf. Deut. 12:11; 14:23; 16:2, 6, 11; 26:2; etc.). Its Jewishness has been explained as due to Jewish advice in the drafting of the document in the Persian chancellory (Bertholet, *op. cit.,* pp. 27-28; Rudolph, *op. cit.,* p. 58). The **name** of God, representing his revealed character and attributes, is sometimes equivalent to the person of God (Pss. 5:11; 7:17; 20:1), and in the late Jewish period it becomes a substitute for "God" (Lev. 24:11-16). The Persian word translated **done with speed** or **done with all diligence** is better rendered as "done thoroughly" (cf. 5:8; 6:8).

(5) COMPLETION OF THE TEMPLE (6:13-18=I Esdras 7:1-9)

Darius' officials (5:3) promptly followed his orders. With "they decided to act accordingly," Josephus implies reluctance, in keeping with his idea of bribed officials (cf. 4:7), but it does not represent the M.T. In vs. 13 as in vs. 12, read "thoroughly" instead of **speedily.**

14. The narrative in vs. 14 reflects the situation in 5:1-2. The same Aramaic word is used for both the **command** of God and the **decree** of the Persian kings. The **commandment** of God may rest ultimately on II Sam. 7:12-13; I Kings 5:4-5, but more directly upon Ezra 1:2. The **decree of Cyrus** is in 1:2-3; 6:3-5; that of **Darius** is in 6:7-8. Since the temple was finished under Darius I (vs. 15), the reference to **Artaxerxes** (464-423 B.C.) must be an addition made by someone who thought of the king's aid to Ezra (7:12-27) and Nehemiah (Neh. 2:5-8), and especially of the king's intention (Ezra 7:27). But a tradition persisted that there was some rebuilding of the temple in the time of **Artaxerxes** (cf. S. A. Cook, "I Esdras" in R. H. Charles, ed., *The Apocrypha and Pseudepigrapha of the Old Testament* [Oxford: Clarendon Press, 1913], p. 13).

15. About four and a half years after it was started (Sept. 21, 520 B.C.; cf. Hag. 1:14-15) the temple was finished. **Adar** (February-March) was the last Babylonian month. The **third day** (Mar. 12, 515 B.C.) of the M.T. is less likely than the "twenty-third day" of I Esdras 7:5 (Apr. 1, 515 B.C.), since the "twenty" is easier lost than gained in the text. Furthermore, the **third day** was a sabbath, when no work could be done, while the "twenty-third day" was a Friday (F. X. Kugler, *Von Moses bis Paulus* [Münster in Westfalen: Aschendorff, 1922], p. 215). It is unnecessary to substitute "they continued"

16 ¶ And the children of Israel, the priests, and the Levites, and the rest of the children of the captivity, kept the dedication of this house of God with joy,

17 And offered at the dedication of this house of God a hundred bullocks, two hundred rams, four hundred lambs; and for a sin offering for all Israel, twelve he goats, according to the number of the tribes of Israel.

18 And they set the priests in their divisions, and the Levites in their courses, for the service of God, which is at Jerusalem; as it is written in the book of Moses.

19 And the children of the captivity kept the passover upon the fourteenth day of the first month.

16 And the people of Israel, the priests and the Levites, and the rest of the returned exiles, celebrated the dedication of this house of God with joy. 17 They offered at the dedication of this house of God one hundred bulls, two hundred rams, four hundred lambs, and as a sin offering for all Israel twelve he-goats, according to the number of the tribes of Israel. 18 And they set the priests in their divisions and the Levites in their courses, for the service of God at Jerusalem, as it is written in the book of Moses.

19 On the fourteenth day of the first month the returned exiles kept the passover.

---

for **was finished** (so Batten, *op. cit.*, p. 149) since the verb is Akkadian and usage in that language permits a translation "completed" when used of finishing a temple (Carl Bezold, *Babylonisch-Assyrisches Glossar* [Heidelberg: C. Winter, 1926], p. 59, col. 2, *s.v. aṣû*, III₁), as also in later Targumic Aramaic (Marcus Jastrow, *A Dictionary of the Targumim* [New York: G. P. Putnam's Sons, 1903], II, 1567, *s.v.* שׁישׁי). Because of its precise date and because he feels that vs. 14 closes an episode, Torrey (*Ezra Studies*, p. 158) regards vs. 15 as a new section (6:15-18) by the Chronicler, but that would leave unexplained the transition from Aramaic to Hebrew at vss. 18-19.

16-18. The ceremony of dedication at the completion of the temple is reminiscent of that of the time of Solomon (I Kings 8). Such celebration is historically probable and the report may rest on the temple archives. Such stress on priestly activity is widely regarded as evidence of the Chronicler's authorship, but in several instances the evidence points away from him. The tripartite concept of the restored community (vs. 16) suggests the Chronicler's view but **all Israel** and the sacrifice of **twelve he-goats** (cf. 8:35), representing **the tribes of Israel** (vs. 17), indicate that there is a more inclusive view operative in the narrative. The sacrifices, too, are relatively modest when compared with those at the earlier dedication (I Kings 8:5), especially according to the Chronicler's account (II Chr. 7:5). In Lev. 4:13-21 the **sin offering** calls for a bullock rather than a he-goat.

With renewal of sacrifices the temple staff was inducted (vs. 18), and I Esdras 7:9 adds that doorkeepers were stationed at every gate (cf. I Esdras 1:16). Organization of the clergy into **divisions** and **courses** is traced to **the book of Moses** (cf. 3:2), but Pentateuchal law contains no such provisions. The reference, however, may be simply to priestly dedication (Exod. 29:1-46; Lev. 8:1-36) and the appointment of Levites (Num. 3:5-9; 8:5-22). It has been recognized that if the Chronicler were the author, one should expect reference to Davidic authority for clerical organization, since that was his understanding of its origin (cf. 3:10; 8:20; I Chr. 23:1–26:32; Neh. 12:24, 45; cf. Rudolph, *op. cit.*, p. 61). For **the service of God** read with the Peshitta and the LXXL "the service of the house of God," since "house" has been lost from the M.T.

(6) THE FEASTS OF PASSOVER AND UNLEAVENED BREAD (6:19-22=I Esdras 7:10-15)

The Aramaic section is concluded with vs. 18, and the Hebrew language, dropped at 4:6, is resumed. As most authorities agree, the author is the Chronicler. But it has been suggested that he has only adapted one of his sources, fitting it to its present context and modifying it to suit his own ideas (Batten, *Ezra and Nehemiah*, pp. 151-52).

19. The **passover**, originally a pastoral festival, finally was regarded as celebrating

20 For the priests and the Levites were purified together, all of them *were* pure, and killed the passover for all the children of the captivity, and for their brethren the priests, and for themselves.

21 And the children of Israel, which were come again out of captivity, and all such as had separated themselves unto them from the filthiness of the heathen of the land, to seek the LORD God of Israel, did eat,

22 And kept the feast of unleavened bread seven days with joy: for the LORD had

20 For the priests and the Levites had purified themselves together; all of them were clean. So they killed the passover lamb for all the returned exiles, for their fellow priests, and for themselves; 21 it was eaten by the people of Israel who had returned from exile, and also by every one who had joined them and separated himself from the pollutions of the peoples of the land to worship the LORD, the God of Israel. 22 And they kept the feast of unleavened bread seven days with joy; for the LORD had made

---

Israel's deliverance from Egyptian bondage (Exod. 12:1-30). It is not mentioned in the earliest Hebrew legislation but is prominent in the later codes and is described at length by the Chronicler (II Chr. 35:1-19). The **fourteenth day of the first month**, i.e., Nisan (cf. Exod. 12:2-3, 6), in 515 B.C. was April 21, shortly after the completion of the temple. Torrey (*Composition*, p. 10) holds the Chronicler responsible for the chronology which neatly makes the Passover occur right after the dedication. The expression **the children of the captivity**, excluding non-exiled Jews, presents the Chronicler's conception of the restored community, but it is slightly expanded in vs. 21. The "children of Israel" found here in I Esdras 7:10, however, is not original but is derived from I Esdras 7:6 (=Ezra 6:16).

20. The pro-Levite bias of the Chronicler (II Chr. 29:34) is seen in his insistence that **the Levites** killed the sacrifice for the priests (II Chr. 35:3-6, 10-11, 14). Vs. 20*b* shows that only the Levites **were purified**. A later writer who missed them added **the priests. Purified themselves together**, lit., "purified themselves as one," is properly translated as "purified themselves to a man" by the Amer. Trans. **Pure** or **clean** is a technical term meaning "ceremonially clean." This signifies freedom from such contamination as would prevent the ritual act from being efficacious. Such purification was done with water (cf. Exod. 29:4; Num. 8:7), just as Babylonian priests purified themselves with river water before entering the sanctuary (Johannes Pedersen, *Israel, Its Life and Culture, II-III* [London: Oxford University Press, 1940], pp. 747-48).

21. The community of vs. 19 was augmented by **every one who had joined them**, by proselytes drawn from Gentiles and half-caste Jews who had intermarried with the Gentiles (cf. 9:1-2, 12, 14; Neh. 13:23-24). According to Jewish legislation, all "clean" Jews were expected to share the Passover under penalty of ostracism (Num. 9:13); circumcised foreigners could participate on the same basis as the Jews (Num. 9:14); but all uncircumcised were forbidden to partake (Exod. 12:43-45, 48-49).

Filthiness or **pollutions** means "ceremonial uncleanness," just the opposite of the ceremonial purity of vs. 20. In I Esdras 7:13 it is interpreted as "the abominations" or "the detestable things" (βδέλυγμα; cf. Luke 16:15; Matt. 24:15; etc.), the influences of foreign culture, particularly in religion (cf. 9:1, 11; Neh. 13:23-24, 26). The tragedy of Babylonian captivity was attributed to such foreign contamination (9:13-14), and later Jewish exclusiveness and the strong aversion to mixtures are deeply rooted in this antipathy to non-Jewish influence. **To seek** (cf. 4:2) is distinctly the Chronicler's own term. Although it has been interpreted as **to worship**, the word may have been weakened to merely "revere" (S. R. Driver, *Introduction to the Literature of the Old Testament* [9th ed.; New York: Charles Scribner's Sons, 1913], p. 536, No. 7). The implied object of **did eat** is the Passover, which is made explicit in the LXX.

22. The **feast of unleavened bread**, originally a Canaanite harvest festival (Exod. 34:18-26 [J]; 23:14-16 [E], followed on the day after the Passover, the fifteenth day (cf. Lev. 23:6), and continued for **seven days. Turned the heart** means "changed the mind" (or "the will" or "the purpose"). **King of Assyria** is anachronistic in the Persian period.

made them joyful, and turned the heart of the king of Assyria unto them, to strengthen their hands in the work of the house of God, the God of Israel.

7 Now after these things, in the reign of Artaxerxes king of Persia, Ezra the son of Seraiah, the son of Azariah, the son of Hilkiah,

2 The son of Shallum, the son of Zadok, the son of Ahitub,

them joyful, and had turned the heart of the king of Assyria to them, so that he aided them in the work of the house of God, the God of Israel.

7 Now after this, in the reign of Ar-ta-xerx'es king of Persia, Ezra the son of Serai'ah, son of Azari'ah, son of Hilki'ah, 2 son of Shallum, son of Zadok, son of Ahi'-

Jewish scholars assume a Persian king and Josephus so translates it (*Antiquities* XI. 4. 8). **Assyria** may be loose usage or even a scribal error for "Syria" (cf. Hölscher, *Esra und Nehemia*, II, 516). The unidentified **king** is most probably Artaxerxes, whose harshly unfavorable decision (4:21-22) is about to be changed in the following narrative (7:1-28), which the Chronicler here anticipates. Artaxerxes is recalled as a supporter of the work of both Ezra and Nehemiah and as beautifier of the house of the Lord (7:27). As the versions show, **the work of the house of God, the God of Israel** is awkward in the M.T. Expected is either "the house of the God of Israel" (as in the LXX) or "the house of the Lord, the God of Israel" (as in the Vulg., I Esdras, and Peshitta).

III. Ezra's Return (7:1–8:36)
A. Introduction of Ezra (7:1-10=I Esdras 8:1-8)
1. Genealogy of Ezra (7:1-5)

7:1-5. The general chronological note, **after these things** (cf. II Chr. 32:1; Esth. 2:1; 3:1), covers an interval of 117 years, between the completion of the temple (6:15) and the journey of Ezra to Judah (7:7).

Ezra ("Help") abbreviates such a full name as Azariah (cf. 2:2). The genealogy supplied (vss. 1:5) is an unhistorical reflection of the conviction of the Chronicler's age that so important a person as Ezra must have had a significant ancestry. As priest (cf. vss. 11-12, 21), he was not only a descendant of Aaron (vs. 5), like all Jewish priests returned from Babylonia (8:2), but he was also related to the house of the high priest. Such relationship was suggested perhaps by the name of Ezra's father, **Seraiah** (vs. 1), which was the same as that of the high priest slain at the fall of Jerusalem, about 188 years before Ezra's arrival in Palestine (cf. II Kings 25:18-21). Since about five generations separated Ezra from the high priest **Seraiah**, Ezra could not have been his son. If the link with the family of the house of the high priest is intended, the genealogy should have been carried down to a high priest closer to Ezra. The missing generations have been explained by supposing that from the time of **Seraiah** onward the family of Ezra was not directly in the line of the high priest but collateral to it (Ernst Bertheau, *Die Bücher Esra, Nechemia und Ester*, ed. Victor Ryssel [2nd ed.; Leipzig: S. Hirzel, 1887; "Kurzgefasstes exegetisches Handbuch zum Alten Testament"], p. 88; Keil, *Chronik, Esra, Nehemia und Esther*, p. 457).

7:1-26. Ezra: The "Ready Scribe."—At last we meet the hero whose name the whole book bears; but at first only through an introduction in the third person, evidently written long afterward by some author (either the Chronicler or some intermediate redactor), whose major interests are at any rate those of the Chronicler. His emphasis is still, as in chs. 5–6, on the political approval and financial support given by different Persian kings to the rebuilding of the temple; but even more now (cf. vss. 6-10 with vss. 25-26) on the special qualifications of Ezra to teach and enforce the law of Moses in the full authoritative sense which it had acquired in the Jerusalem community by the time of the Chronicler—as **statutes and ordinances** laid down by God himself, under penalties that included not only **imprisonment** and **banishment**, but even **death** (vs. 26).

3 The son of Amariah, the son of Azariah, the son of Meraioth,
4 The son of Zerahiah, the son of Uzzi,
the son of Bukki,
5 The son of Abishua, the son of Phinehas, the son of Eleazar, the son of Aaron the
chief priest:
6 This Ezra went up from Babylon; and
he *was* a ready scribe in the law of Moses,
which the LORD God of Israel had given:
and the king granted him all his request,
according to the hand of the LORD his God
upon him.

tub, 3 son of Amari'ah, son of Azari'ah, son
of Merai'oth, 4 son of Zerahi'ah, son of Uzzi,
son of Bukki, 5 son of Abi'shu-a, son of
Phin'ehas, son of Elea'zar, son of Aaron the
chief priest — 6 this Ezra went up from
Babylonia. He was a scribe skilled in the
law of Moses which the LORD the God of
Israel had given; and the king granted him
all that he asked, for the hand of the LORD
his God was upon him.

The genealogy is based on data in I Chr. 6:3-15, 50-53 (cf. Neh. 11:11), but comparison shows the list in Ezra to be textually defective (cf. Rudolf Kittel, *Die Bücher
der Chronik* [Göttingen, Vandenhoeck & Ruprecht, 1902; "Handkommentar zum Alten
Testament"], pp. 39-42). Assuming three generations to a century, the present list would
reach back only about 567 years, not to Aaron but to about the time of Saul (*ca.* 1150
B.C.). In addition to the generations missing between the fall of Jerusalem and Ezra,
the present list lacks the generations named in I Chr. 6:8b-12a, which were lost apparently
accidentally, due to the similarity of names. A scribe's eyes passed from one **Amariah** (cf.
I Chr. 6:7) to another (cf. I Chr. 6:11), omitting the seven intervening names. The
genealogy does, however, share the glaring error of I Chr. 6:12 in identifying **Zadok**
as the son of **Ahitub** (cf. 7:2). If I Sam. 2:22-36 has any real value, **Zadok** cannot be
identified as the son of **Ahitub**, Abiathar's grandfather (cf. William R. Arnold, *Ephod
and Ark* [Cambridge: Harvard University Press, 1917], pp. 14-15). This faulty genealogy
is secondary to the Ezra narrative and does not represent Ezra's true ancestry, which
must have been originally simply "Ezra the son of Seraiah."

2. SUMMARY OF EZRA'S CAREER (7:6-10)

6. This Ezra, repeating the subject of vs. 1 after the long genealogical insertion,
identifies the person of the genealogy with the principal character in the narrative that
follows. The M.T. permits **from Babylon,** but **from Babylonia** is more likely since, in
late Jewish use the term but rarely refers to the city. **Scribe** (cf. 4:8) can mean an official
secretary of the court (cf. II Sam. 8:17; II Kings 18:18, 37; 19:2; Esth. 3:12; 8:9). It is
argued that Ezra, like the later Jewish exilarch (*rēsh gālûthā'*), was a high court official
who advised the king in all matters concerning the Jewish people (cf. Neh. 11:24; H. H.
Schaeder, *Esra der Schreiber* [Tübingen: J. C. B. Mohr, 1930; "Beiträge zur historischen
Theologie"], pp. 46-49; cf. Rudolph, *op. cit.,* p. 73). The word translated **ready** (*māhîr*)
is used of scribes in Egypt in the sense of "experienced" or "skillful" (W. M. Müller,
Asien und Europa [Leipzig: W. Engelmann, 1893], p. 173) and elsewhere during the
Persian period and before. An Aramaic papyrus calls Ahiqar, an Assyrian scribe, "a wise
and skillful [מהר] scribe" (Cowley, *Aramaic Papyri,* p. 212, l. 1; cf. pp. 220, 226). It is
the Chronicler who transformed Ezra the royal official to the later distinctly Jewish
Bible scribe, the specialist in scripture, more familiar in his own day (cf. I Chr. 2:55;
Neh. 12:26; Ecclus. 38:24–39:11; Matt. 2:4).

It is said of Ezra that the king **granted him all his request,** but the Ezra story begins
abruptly and there is preserved no account of Ezra's session with the king, such as is
found in the story of Nehemiah (cf. 2:1-8). The nature of **his request** can be learned
only from the edict of the king (vss. 13-26). It would appear that as an official in the
Persian court Ezra persuaded the king that it would be to the advantage of the empire
to establish Jewish law as normative in Palestine. Apparently convinced that peace and

7 And there went up *some* of the children of Israel, and of the priests, and the Levites, and the singers, and the porters, and the Nethinim, unto Jerusalem, in the seventh year of Artaxerxes the king.

8 And he came to Jerusalem in the fifth month, which *was* in the seventh year of the king.

7 And there went up also to Jerusalem, in the seventh year of Ar-ta-xerx′es the king, some of the people of Israel, and some of the priests and Levites, the singers and gate-keepers, and the temple servants. 8 And he came to Jerusalem in the fifth month, which

---

security would be fostered by such a measure, and that the re-establishment of the Jewish cult at Jerusalem would result in greater loyalty of his subjects and the support of the powerful Jewish God for the royal house, Artaxerxes **granted him all that he asked.** The **hand of the LORD** (vs. 28; 8:22, 31; cf. 7:9; 8:18; Neh. 2:8, 18) indicates the favor of God. **According to the hand** implies success in proportion to God's support, but the sense is improved by following the LXX in reading, **for the hand of the LORD . . . was upon him.**

7-8. Because in vs. 7 attention is turned suddenly but briefly from Ezra to returning exiles, the verse has been regarded as an addition to the text (Josef Markwart, *Fundamente israelitische und jüdische Geschichte* [Göttingen: Dieterich, 1896], p. 34; Sigmund Mowinckel, *Ezra den Skriftlaerde* [Kristiania: 1916], p. 2; Hölscher, *op. cit.*, II, 518). But a simple emendation from **and there went up** (ויעלו) to "he sent up" (ויעל) would refocus the attention on Ezra and eliminate the chief motive for omitting the verse (Rudolph, *op. cit.*, p. 67). The classes of people mentioned are those found in Ezra 2:1-70, but Hölscher argues that the treatment of **the singers and gate-keepers** as distinct from **the Levites** (2:41; 3:10) is contrary to the Chronicler's point of view, and is thus evidence for the secondary character of the verse. It is true that the **singers and gate-keepers** are not named among the returning Jews in 8:15 ff., but they are here a later addition derived from the Levites in 8:18-19, probably under the influence of 7:24, and possibly also with 2:41-42 in mind (*ibid.*, p. 72). Vs. 8, which almost duplicates vs. 7*b*, has also been regarded as an addition (Martin Noth, *Überlieferungsgeschichtliche Studien I* [Halle: M. Niemeyer, 1943], p. 125), but the verse does advance the thought, reverting to Ezra from his companions and specifying **the fifth month** (July-August) as part of the date.

One of the most perplexing and controversial problems of Ezra-Nehemiah is that of the date of Ezra's arrival in Jerusalem. Traditionally **Artaxerxes** is identified with Artaxerxes I (464-424 B.C.), whose **seventh year** was 458 B.C. Since Ezra followed Nehemiah to Palestine (cf. Intro., pp. 561-62) and was not his contemporary, the **Artaxerxes** must have been Artaxerxes II (404-359 B.C.), whose **seventh year** was 398 B.C. (H. H. Rowley, *The Servant of the Lord and Other Essays on the Old Testament* [London: Lutterworth Press, 1952], pp. 131-59). It is always possible that Ezra may have come to Jerusalem some time during the reign of Artaxerxes I, after the end of the first administration of Nehemiah in 432 B.C. (Neh. 5:14), but any satisfactory date in this period is highly conjectural, without textual support. Some have arbitrarily assigned Ezra's arrival to the thirty-second year of Artaxerxes I (433/432 B.C.), when Nehemiah left (W. H. Kosters, *Die Wiederherstellung Israels in der persischen Periode* [tr. A. Basedow; Heidelberg: J. Hörning, 1895], pp. 95 ff., 116; Bertholet, *Esra und Nehemia*, pp. 30-31; R. H. Kennett, *Old Testament Essays* [Cambridge: Cambridge University Press, 1928], p. 85; formerly also W. F. Albright, *The Archaeology of Palestine and the Bible* [New York: Fleming H. Revell Co., 1932], p. 219). Others have sought textual support for a date in the "thirty-seventh year" of Artaxerxes I (428 B.C.) by assuming the loss of "thirty" (שלשים) from the text due to similarity to the beginning of the spelling of seven (שבע) in vss. 7-8 (Markwart, *op. cit.*, p. 36; Bewer, *Der Text des Buches Ezra*, p. 68; W. F. Albright, *From the Stone Age to Christianity* (2nd ed.; Baltimore: Johns Hopkins Press,

9 For upon the first *day* of the first month began he to go up from Babylon, and on the first *day* of the fifth month came he to Jerusalem, according to the good hand of his God upon him.

10 For Ezra had prepared his heart to seek the law of the LORD, and to do *it,* and to teach in Israel statutes and judgments.

11 ¶ Now this *is* the copy of the letter that the king Artaxerxes gave unto Ezra the

was in the seventh year of the king; 9 for on the first day of the first month he began[h] to go up from Babylonia, and on the first day of the fifth month he came to Jerusalem, for the good hand of his God was upon him.

10 For Ezra had set his heart to study the law of the LORD, and to do it, and to teach his statutes and ordinances in Israel.

11 This is a copy of the letter which King

[h] Vg See Syr: Heb *that was the foundation of the going up*

1946), p. 366; Rudolph, *op. cit.,* pp. 71, 168). The date cannot be determined accurately but it must have been at least after the first administration of Nehemiah.

9. Chronological data already given in vss. 7-8 is recapitulated here. Such information, lacking in the present Ezra narrative, must have been drawn by the Chronicler from the now missing beginning of Ezra's own report. **He began to go up** attempts to make sense of a corrupt Hebrew text, **that was the foundation of the going up.** For **the foundation** (*yeṣudh*) read the verb "was decided upon" (*yiṣṣadh;* cf. Esth. 1:8). Earlier, perhaps, **the first month** was followed by an explanatory gloss "that is [the month] Nisan," of which נסן, "Nisan," was lost because of some similarity to the verb יסד, "was decided upon" (cf. Ehrlich, *Randglossen zur hebräischen Bibel,* VII, 171; Rudolph, *op. cit.,* p. 67). Thus we translate, "For upon the first of the month (that is Nisan) the going up was decided upon." Such emendation avoids a conflict with 8:31, according to which the departure occurred on the twelfth day (Apr. 16, 398 B.C.) instead of the **first day** (Apr. 5, 398 B.C.). There need be no contradiction in any case since there was some delay (8:15-30) before the actual departure.

10. This verse comments on vs. 6, explaining the reason for Ezra's success through divine support and portraying him as the ideal Jewish scribe dedicated to the threefold task of seeking the law, obeying it, and propagating it. **Set his heart** means "set his mind" (cf. 1:1). The **law of the LORD** is "the law of Moses" (vs. 6). **To seek the law** means **to study** it, to determine its implications for daily life. Such study ultimately produced the oral law and the Talmud. But study was not enough, for it was obedience to the law that led to a virtuous life. Thus Judaism stresses activity rather than belief as the avenue to salvation. Such emphasis is found insistently in the older Hebrew legislation. Scribal legalism was not merely individual but also social. The learned had a missionary task to perform. **Statutes and ordinances** are terms found in earlier legislation (cf. Exod. 15:25; Josh. 24:25; I Sam. 30:25), especially in Deuteronomy where they are synonyms (Deut. 4:1, 5, 8, 14; 5:1; 11:32; 12:1; 26:16). **Statutes** originally meant something "inscribed" and a related word in Arabic means "to be right" or "to be obligatory." **Ordinances,** lit., **judgments,** signify legal decisions based on an earlier inscribed code.

B. EZRA'S COMMISSION (7:11-26=I Esdras 8:8-24)

1. INTRODUCTION (7:11-12)

An editorial verse in Hebrew (vs. 11) introduces a long document (vss. 12-26) which, like all official correspondence in the book, is written in the Aramaic language (cf. 4:8-22; 5:6–6:12). Purportedly a royal decree, it contains Ezra's commission, a statement of his authority, and a list of powers at his disposal to assure the success of his mission. The phraseology of the decree is very surprising for a Persian ruler, since it shows intimate acquaintance with Jewish terminology (cf. vss. 13, 15) and with cultic distinctions and practices prevailing in the later Jewish temple (cf. vs. 24). Such Jewishness has led to a charge that the document was forged (cf. Torrey, *Ezra Studies,* pp. 157-58; Pfeiffer, *Intro. to O.T.,* p. 826), or at least that an original document has been edited, supplemented, or even rewritten by a Jew (Driver, *Intro. to Literature*

priest, the scribe, *even* a scribe of the words of the commandments of the LORD, and of his statutes to Israel.

12 Artaxerxes, king of kings, unto Ezra the priest, a scribe of the law of the God of heaven, perfect *peace*, and at such a time.

Ar-ta-xerx'es gave to Ezra the priest, the scribe, learned in matters of the commandments of the LORD and his statutes for Israel: 12 "Ar-ta-xerx'es, king of kings, to Ezra the priest, the scribe of the law of the

---

of O.T., p. 550). A plausible explanation is presented by those who regard Ezra as an official in the Persian court, the adviser to the king for Jewish affairs (cf. vs. 6). As such, Ezra himself could have written the document or dictated its terms to be endorsed by the king and issued as an official decree (Meyer, *Entstehung des Judenthums*, pp. 64 ff.; Kittel, *Geschichte des Volkes Israel*, III, 583; Schaeder, *Esra der Schreiber*, pp. 9, 42, 55; Rudolph, *op. cit.*, pp. 73, 76).

11. Copy (cf. 4:11; 5:6) implies a written source behind the Aramaic text. **Artaxerxes** (cf. vss. 7-8) is the king according to the M.T. and I Esdras, but Josephus, aware of chronological difficulty in conflict with dates in Nehemiah, and believing that Ezra has preceded Nehemiah, has substituted "Xerxes" (485-465 B.C.), the predecessor of Artaxerxes I, as the one who gave Ezra his commission. Vs. 11*b* obviously is a later gloss on **the scribe,** based on the substance of vs. 10.

12. The title **king of kings,** used here in the superscription, was frequently employed by the Persian rulers (cf. Dan. 2:37), as by the Babylonians before them (Ezek. 26:7). Ezra is identified as **priest,** but, as in the Aramaic papyri (Cowley, *op. cit.*, No. 30, ll. 1, 18; No. 38, ll. 1, 12), the word used is Hebrew (*kôhēn*) rather than Aramaic (*kumrā*). Thus it would appear that the Hebrew term had been adopted in official use (cf. Schaeder, *Esra der Schreiber*, p. 43). Apparently on the basis of the genealogy of vss. 1-5, Ezra is identified as the "chief priest" in I Esdras 9:40 and Josephus (*Antiquities* XI. 5. 1), but that is incorrect. Schaeder (*Esra der Schreiber*, pp. 46-48) has also insisted that the second title of Ezra, **scribe of the law,** was in the Persian period an official one, a trace of which is found in the later name of the secretariat for law (*dādh dawirih*). Here the term used for **law** is Persian (*dât*) rather than Hebrew (*tôrāh;* cf. 3:2). The concept was always important in Persian thought. Nor did the Persians distinguish sharply between sacred and secular law. In the Avesta, the Persian holy book, as also in later Pahlavi literature, there is no distinction between moral and legal crimes, between ecclesiastical and civil jurisprudence, for the priestly code of the Avesta, the Vendidad, is a medley of all sorts of ritual, moral, civil, and even hygienic laws (James Darmesteter, *The Zend-Avesta;* Part I, "The Vendidad" [Oxford: Clarendon Press, 1880; "The Sacred Books of the East"], pp. lxx-lxxi, lxxxii, lxxxiv).

Under such circumstances Ezra might be expected to be successful in gaining royal support in his attempt to introduce sacred **law** into the Judean province. He was directed to set up authorities in a secular manner (vs. 25), and his law was to be regarded as equivalent to the law of the king (vs. 26). Royal support was doubtless forthcoming on the assumption that the land could be made secure and peaceful for Persia through the instrumentality of Jewish law (cf. Rudolph, *op. cit.*, p. 76). Identification of the **law** as that of the **God of heaven** (cf. 5:11; 6:9) has led Schaeder (*Esra der Schreiber*, pp. 48-49) to insist that Ezra was secretary for Jewish affairs in the Persian court.

The verse literally concludes "finished, and now." The words **and now** are the normal conclusion of the salutation of a letter (cf. 4:10), but "finished" (cf. 5:16) is a corruption which has no counterpart in the versions and is therefore omitted entirely in the RSV. Part of the corrupt word (גמר) is probably a distorted fragment of the word "peace" (שלם) and its remainder (יר) is a likely distorted duplication of the letters which follow (וכ; Bewer, *op. cit.*, p. 69). The presence of "peace" in the Peshitta and I Esdras 8:9 seems to support the addition of the word "peace" in emending the text.

13 I make a decree, that all they of the people of Israel, and *of* his priests and Levites, in my realm, which are minded of their own free will to go up to Jerusalem, go with thee.

14 Forasmuch as thou art sent of the king, and of his seven counselors, to inquire concerning Judah and Jerusalem, according to the law of thy God which *is* in thine hand;

15 And to carry the silver and gold, which the king and his counselors have freely offered unto the God of Israel, whose habitation *is* in Jerusalem,

16 And all the silver and gold that thou canst find in all the province of Babylon,

God of heaven. And now **13** I make a decree that any one of the people of Israel or their priests or Levites in my kingdom, who freely offers to go to Jerusalem, may go with you. **14** For you are sent by the king and his seven counselors to make inquiries about Judah and Jerusalem according to the law of your God, which is in your hand, **15** and also to convey the silver and gold which the king and his counselors have freely offered to the God of Israel, whose dwelling is in Jerusalem, **16** with all the silver and gold which you shall find in the whole province of

2. Permission to Return (7:13-14)

13. This verse is strongly Jewish in terminology. **Any one . . . who freely offers** represents an expression unusual in Aramaic but common in later Hebrew, especially in the work of the Chronicler (I Chr. 29:5, 6, 9, 14, 17; II Chr. 17:16; cf. Ezra 1:6; 2:68; Neh. 11:2) . Such usage, the distinction between **priests** and **Levites** (cf. 2:36, 40) , and the use of **people of Israel** to designate secular persons in contrast to the clergy, where the Persians would say "Jews" (cf. 4:12, 23; 5:1, 5; 6:7-8, 14) , all suggest Jewish rather than Persian composition. Since those wanting to go to Judah were to go **with** Ezra, his commission included leading a caravan to Jerusalem.

14. The Persian king ruled absolutely, without a regularly established council. But he occasionally called in judges, political or military experts, or even just the "noblest Persians" as advisers (Herodotus *History* III. 31; VII. 8; VIII. 67) . In Esth. 1:14 the counselors are described as "the seven princes of Persia and Media, who saw the king's face, and sat first in the kingdom." The basis for the number **seven** cannot yet be determined, but as late as the revolt of Cyrus the Younger (403-401 B.C.) the council consisted of seven of the most distinguished Persians of his staff (Xenophon *Anabasis* I. 6. 4-5) . **To make inquiries** means "to investigate," as in 4:15, 19; 5:17; 6:1. Thus Ezra was to investigate the degree to which Jewish law was being effectively obeyed in Judah.

Your God indicates that there was no ambiguity regarding the nature of the **law.** It was distinctly Jewish and not confused with Persian legislation. **In your hand** identifies the law as that favored and promoted by Ezra. The nature of this **law,** much debated, is not yet certainly identified. It was a code already known to the people (vs. 25; Neh. 8:1) , but the law brought by Ezra from Babylonia cannot be identified with any special code of the Bible. It was probably a form of the Deuteronomic Code, with which there had been considerable concern during the Exile, but it was a form of that code that had been somewhat modified in the direction of the Priestly Code developed during the Exile (cf. Neh. 8:1-2) .

3. Gifts for the Temple (7:15-19)

15-16. With (vs. 16) indicates that two distinct groups of donors are mentioned in vs. 16, since vs. 16*a* is not qualified by vs. 16*b*, which certainly refers to Jews. The phrases **all the silver and gold** and **in the whole province** suggest a large group of donors. Some have seen here the influence of 1:4, and possibly the story of the Exodus (Exod. 10:25; 12:35-36; cf. Torrey, *Ezra Studies,* p. 158) . As an alternative it has been proposed that Ezra was privileged to levy a tax on Jewish property in Babylonia for

with the freewill offering of the people, and of the priests, offering willingly for the house of their God which *is* in Jerusalem:

17 That thou mayest buy speedily with this money bullocks, rams, lambs, with their meat offerings and their drink offerings, and offer them upon the altar of the house of your God which *is* in Jerusalem.

18 And whatsoever shall seem good to thee, and to thy brethren, to do with the rest of the silver and the gold, that do after the will of your God.

19 The vessels also that are given thee for the service of the house of thy God, *those* deliver thou before the God of Jerusalem.

20 And whatsoever more shall be needful for the house of thy God, which thou shalt have occasion to bestow, bestow *it* out of the king's treasure house.

Babylonia, and with the freewill offerings of the people and the priests, vowed willingly for the house of their God which is in Jerusalem. **17** With this money, then, you shall with all diligence buy bulls, rams, and lambs, with their cereal offerings and their drink offerings, and you shall offer them upon the altar of the house of your God which is in Jerusalem. **18** Whatever seems good to you and your brethren to do with the rest of the silver and gold, you may do, according to the will of your God. **19** The vessels that have been given you for the service of the house of your God, you shall deliver before the God of Jerusalem. **20** And whatever else is required for the house of your God, which you have occasion to provide, you may provide it out of the king's treasury.

---

the funds, but there is no evidence for such action (Carl Siegfried, *Esra, Nehemia und Esther* [Göttingen: Vandenhoeck & Ruprecht, 1901; "Handkommentar zum Alten Testament"], p. 52). The non-Jewish donors were probably "his lords'" (cf. 8:25). Delivery of the gifts is mentioned in 8:24-26, 33-34.

17-18. Knowledge of Hebrew terminology and custom is evident in these verses. Not only the proper sacrifices are mentioned, but also the **cereal offerings** and **drink offerings** that regularly accompanied them (cf. Num. 15:1-10). But the usage is not that preferred by the Chronicler for designating the sacrificial animals. **Speedily** should be rendered "faithfully" (cf. 5:8; 6:8, 12, 13). Since it is assumed (vs. 18) that the collected funds will be more than enough for the sacrifices, the surplus is to be disposed of under Ezra's direction, but only for such cult purposes as will please the Jewish God. **Will of . . . God** represents a word meaning "pleasure" or "desire," found only here and in late Hebrew. **Your brethren** means Ezra's fellow priests.

19. **Vessels** should be "utensils" in a wider sense than pots and jars, as the LXX (σκεύη) shows (cf. 1:10-11). Although I Esdras 8:17 seems to interpret them as temple vessels that had been plundered (1:7-11; 5:14; 6:5), this is but an assumption. They may have been dedicated by their donors to the **service** of the temple. The abrupt **God of Jerusalem** would be unique in the Aramaic documents. Since the LXX and Vulg. have "in Jerusalem," it is probable that the Peshitta is right in reading "the God who is in Jerusalem" (cf. 1:3). But it is possible also that the original text was "the God of Israel, who is in Jerusalem" (cf. vs. 15).

4. Additional Funds (7:20-24)

20-24. If additional funds are needed for the temple beyond the donations, such requirements are to be met by a grant of funds from **the king's treasury** (cf. 5:17; 6:1). **You may provide it** seems addressed to Ezra, who was not in position to draw on royal funds. Therefore there is incorporated in Ezra's orders a special section (vss. 21-24) which is addressed to **the treasurers** who are to pay the funds (cf. 1:8). These officials are to take orders from **Ezra** (cf. vs. 12), but in a businesslike way practical limits are put on his possible demands (vs. 22). Again **speedily** is "faithfully" or "exactly" (cf. 5:8).

The Chronicler's tendency to exaggerate statistics concerning the temple (cf. I Chr. 29:7) has led those who regard him as the author here to be suspicious of the royal grants (Jahn, *Esra [A und B] und Nehemja*, p. 63). The list of gifts and prerogatives

21 And I, *even* I Artaxerxes the king, do make a decree to all the treasurers which *are* beyond the river, that whatsoever Ezra the priest, the scribe of the law of the God of heaven, shall require of you, it be done speedily,

22 Unto a hundred talents of silver, and to a hundred measures of wheat, and to a hundred baths of wine, and to a hundred baths of oil, and salt without prescribing *how much.*

23 Whatsoever is commanded by the God of heaven, let it be diligently done for the house of the God of heaven: for why should there be wrath against the realm of the king and his sons?

24 Also we certify you, that, touching any of the priests and Levites, singers, porters, Nethinim, or ministers of this house of God, it shall not be lawful to impose toll, tribute, or custom, upon them.

21 "And I, Ar-ta-xerx'es the king, make a decree to all the treasurers in the province Beyond the River: Whatever Ezra the priest, the scribe of the law of the God of heaven, requires of you, be it done with all diligence, 22 up to a hundred talents of silver, a hundred measures of wheat, a hundred baths of wine, a hundred baths of oil, and salt without prescribing how much. 23 Whatever is commanded by the God of heaven, let it be done in full for the house of the God of heaven, lest his wrath be against the realm of the king and his sons. 24 We also notify you that it shall not be lawful to impose tribute, custom, or toll upon any one of the priests, the Levites, the singers, the doorkeepers, the temple servants, or other servants of this house of God.

---

has been called "not quite incredible" (Torrey, *Ezra Studies,* p. 206, note u), but Meyer did not think the sums mentioned excessive (*Entstehung des Judenthums,* pp. 68-69). Egyptian records reveal both Persian interest in the sacrificial cultus of their subjects and Persian generosity in supporting it (Speigelberg, *Die sogennante demotische Chronik,* pp. 32-33; cf. Olmstead, *History of the Persian Empire,* p. 91).

Since no uniform standard of weight was recognized in the ancient Near East, even for weights bearing the same name, the actual measure of Persian generosity cannot be determined. **Talents** weighed about sixty-five pounds each. **Measures** represents the *kōr,* which held about eleven and two-thirds bushels of grain (however, see Vol. I, p. 155). **Baths** held about nine gallons apiece. **Oil** translates a word meaning "anointing," apparently an abbreviation of the Hebrew expression "the oil of anointing" (cf. Exod. 25:6; 29:7; etc.). The same word is used in 6:9 and in the Aramaic papyri, but one would not expect a Persian official to use it without Jewish prompting or instruction. There would not be a very heavy demand for **salt** (cf. 6:9), and no limit was set for its expenditure.

23. The motive for royal support of the temple was to win the favor of the Jews and their God and to prevent their antipathy against the royal family and the Persian Empire. Practical considerations doubtless prevailed. Artaxerxes II long hoped to emulate his predecessors as conquerors of Egypt. The weak Egyptian kings of the Twenty-eighth and Twenty-ninth Dynasties (525-332 B.C.) seemed to hold promise of Persian victory, and a friendly Palestine on the flank and rear would be a military necessity for success.

24. All temple attendants (cf. 2:36, 40-43) were to be exempt from **tribute, custom, or toll,** by which is meant taxes and forced labor (cf. 4:13). The clergy were often granted special privileges and exemptions (J. A. Wilson in Pritchard, *Ancient Near Eastern Texts,* p. 212). The Gadatas inscription reflects just such favors by Darius and his predecessors (Botsford and Sihler, *Hellenic Civilization,* p. 162), and Josephus (*Antiquities* XII. 3. 3) claims that Antiochus the Great later granted such exemption from taxation. The list of attendants certainly shows Jewish influence in its compilation. Since **singers** represents a word (*zammar*) signifying either "singer" or "player," the term "musicians" presents the same ambiguity as the Aramaic word. **Ministers** or **servants**

25 And thou, Ezra, after the wisdom of thy God, that *is* in thine hand, set magistrates and judges, which may judge all the people that *are* beyond the river, all such as know the laws of thy God; and teach ye them that know *them* not.

26 And whosoever will not do the law of thy God, and the law of the king, let judgment be executed speedily upon him, whether *it be* unto death, or to banishment, or to confiscation of goods, or to imprisonment.

25 "And you, Ezra, according to the wisdom of your God which is in your hand, appoint magistrates and judges who may judge all the people in the province Beyond the River, all such as know the laws of your God; and those who do not know them, you shall teach. 26 Whoever will not obey the law of your God and the law of the king, let judgment be strictly executed upon him, whether for death or for banishment or for confiscation of his goods or for imprisonment."

is related to the term "service" in vs. 19. It is properly rendered as "menials," since it presumably refers to "the sons of Solomon's servants" of 2:55.

5. Ezra and the Law (7:25-26)

25-26. With **you, Ezra** the letter again turns to Ezra himself. **The wisdom of your God** means "the law of your God" (cf. vs. 14). The equation of **wisdom** and **law**, found frequently in late Hebrew, anticipates the usage in Ben Sirach (Ecclus. 15:1; 19:20; 21:11; 24:23-29; 34:8). This too is evidence for Jewish composition. A secular organization was to be set up for judging in accordance with the law of Ezra. **Magistrates** and **judges** are synonymous terms. Only the latter (*dayyān*) is used in the Aramaic papyri of the Persian period (cf. 4:9). The former is Hebrew (cf. 10:14) and is not used elsewhere in Aramaic. Instead, the LXXABL have "scribes and judges," which presupposes an original "secretaries and judges." Such "scribes" were secular officers, like the "notaries of the provinces" mentioned in the Aramaic papyri (Cowley, *Aramaic Papyri*, p. 53, No. 17, ll. 1, 6).

All the people seems to mean all Jews and Gentiles of Syria and Palestine (Torrey, *Ezra Studies*, p. 206, notes u, v), but **such as know the laws of your God** limits the authority to Jews alone, wherever they were found in **the province Beyond the River** (cf. Batten, *Ezra and Nehemiah*, pp. 313-14; Meyer, *op. cit.*, p. 67). The injunction to **teach** the law to those ignorant of it doubtless refers to those Jews who had abandoned Judaism and to the more remote Jewish groups who had not kept abreast of the development of Jewish law. Official control over all Jews in the West, even outside of Palestine, is well illustrated by the instructions sent to Egypt about the observance of the feast of Unleavened Bread in 419 B.C. (Cowley, *op. cit.*, pp. 60-62).

26. Royal approval made Jewish law **the law of the king,** and willful disobedience to it was to be punished with the same severity used against other law breakers. **Speedily** is better rendered **strictly** here (cf. 5:8). The punishments, arranged with decreasing severity, gave Ezra power which he appears to have been reluctant to use. Ezra's friends threaten **confiscation** and **banishment** (cf. 10:8), but there is no evidence of the execution of that threat. The rendering **banishment** assumes that the problematical word שרשו represents a Semitic root (שרש), which can mean "uproot" (Ps. 52:5 [Hebrew 52:7]); from this an abstract noun **banishment** can be produced. Such etymology is rejected by Batten (*op. cit.*, p. 316), who nevertheless regards the conjectured meaning as most probable. But somewhere in a truly Persian list should be found "beating," the most common Persian form of punishment. The LXXAB, indeed, renders the M.T. as "chastisement" (παιδείαν; cf. Heb. 12:5, 7-11; Prov. 15:5; and often in the LXX). If this is the correct interpretation of the word, it may be non-Semitic, possibly an abbreviation of "the scourge," "whip," or "thong" (*sraoshô-careman*), one of the two implements for beating mentioned in the later Persian law book (Vendidad IV, 17-21; V, 43-44; etc.; cf. Darmesteter, *The Zend-Avesta,* p. xcvi, n. 3).

27 ¶ Blessed *be* the LORD God of our fathers, which hath put *such a thing* as this in the king's heart, to beautify the house of the LORD which *is* in Jerusalem:

28 And hath extended mercy unto me before the king, and his counselors, and before all the king's mighty princes. And I was strengthened as the hand of the LORD my God *was* upon me, and I gathered together out of Israel chief men to go up with me.

27 Blessed be the LORD, the God of our fathers, who put such a thing as this into the heart of the king, to beautify the house of the LORD which is in Jerusalem, 28 and who extended to me his steadfast love before the king and his counselors, and before all the king's mighty officers. I took courage, for the hand of the LORD my God was upon me, and I gathered leading men from Israel to go up with me.

6. EZRA'S POEM OF PRAISE (7:27-28)

27-28. The Aramaic edict is followed by a doxology in Hebrew (vss. 27-28). With these verses begins the Ezra document (cf. Intro., pp. 556-57) which, with some exceptions, is written in the first person. Ezra supposedly is the speaker throughout. The beginning of the Ezra document, now lost (Batten, *op. cit.,* p. 316), must have given some account of Ezra's audience before the king and his counselors (vss. 14, 28), which resulted in his winning the right to go to Judea to establish Jewish law there. Some of the data of the original document must have been used by the Chronicler for his editorial introduction (vss. 1-26), but the beginning of the Ezra document was omitted, apparently because its substance was greatly duplicated in the Artaxerxes letter (vss. 12-26).

In I Esdras 8:25 (LXXA) vs. 27 is introduced by the note, "Then said Esdras the scribe . . . ," but this is obviously a late editorial note identifying the speaker of the "I" section, for it is missing in I EsdrasBL. **Such a thing as this,** lit., "like this," refers not to the preceding document but to the whole idea of Ezra's return and all it implied. Thus I Esdras has "these things." Those things most in the writer's mind are then specified. **In the king's heart** means "in the king's mind" (cf. 6:22). A similar view is found in I Sam. 21:12; Job 22:22, as well as in the Ahiqar papyri (Cowley, *op. cit.,* p. 225, l. 163). **Beautify** represents a word much used under the influence of the book of Isaiah (cf. 10:15; 44:23; 49:3; 55:5; 60:7, 9, 13, 21; 61:3; cf. Exod. 8:9 [Hebrew 8:5]; Judg. 7:2; Ps. 149:4; Arvid S. Kapelrud, *The Question of Authorship in the Ezra-Narrative* [Oslo: J. Dybwad, 1944], p. 43). Although much support of the temple is attributed to Artaxerxes, there is no evidence that he was responsible for such building or decoration of the temple as is implied in 6:14.

Extended means "offered," as in I Chr. 21:10. The idiom means "to let one find mercy" (cf. Gen. 39:21). **Steadfast love** (*ḥeṣedh*) is often used by the Chronicler and by the later psalmists, but it is not found in the Jewish papyri. There, however, in a similar context, the word "mercy" (*raḥmîn*), as also used in Neh. 1:11 (cf. Neh. 9:19, 27-28, 31), is found. For **counselors** see vs. 14. **I was strengthened** means "I strengthened myself," in the sense of **I took courage** (cf. II Chr. 15:8). For **hand of the LORD** see 7:6. **Gathered** implies a process of selection. Later Jewish tradition insisted that Ezra himself selected those who were to return, that, as Rabbi Eleazar said, "Ezra did not go up from Babylon until he made it like pure sifted flour . . . " by sifting those of pure lineage ("fine

27-28. *Ezra's Doxology.*—Not only "Ezra's memoirs" in the first person, but an authentic note of firsthand religion appears at last in this hymn of praise. It is **the God of our fathers** who has moved the Persian king's heart and strengthened Ezra's hand for this great undertaking; it is his guiding **hand** that has called forth and led this little company across the desert. The Chronicler in his later time looks back on that journey as Leonard Bacon in 1833 looked back on the founding of New Haven, two hundred years earlier, and on the landing of the Pilgrims at Plymouth in 1620:

O God, beneath thy guiding hand
Our exiled fathers crossed the sea.

In that American hymn, as in this Jewish doxology, patriotism and religion meet and blend in a paean of praise and thanksgiving.

8 These *are* now the chief of their fathers, and *this is* the genealogy of them that went up with me from Babylon, in the reign of Artaxerxes the king.

2 Of the sons of Phinehas; Gershom: of the sons of Ithamar; Daniel: of the sons of David; Hattush.

3 Of the sons of Shechaniah, of the sons of Pharosh; Zechariah: and with him were reckoned by genealogy of the males a hundred and fifty.

8 These are the heads of their fathers' houses, and this is the genealogy of those who went up with me from Babylonia, in the reign of Ar-ta-xerx'es the king: 2 Of the sons of Phin'ehas, Gershom. Of the sons of Ith'amar, Daniel. Of the sons of David, Hattush, 3 of the sons of Shecani'ah. Of the sons of Parosh, Zechari'ah, with whom were

---

unmixed meal") from the intermarried peoples ("mixed dough"; Babylonian Talmud, Kiddushin 69b, 71b, cf. Jerusalem Talmud, Kiddushin IV, 1; cf. Haggada, Yalkut II, 1067).

C. THOSE RETURNING WITH EZRA (8:1-14=I Esdras 8:28-40)

8:1-14. In accordance with the royal edict (7:13), Ezra planned to lead back those Jews who desired to go to Judea. Josephus (*Antiquities* XI. 5. 2) adds a comment that a copy of the royal correspondence was sent by Ezra to his kinsmen in Media (cf. II Kings 17:6) and that "many of them, taking along their possessions also, came to Babylon out of longing to return to Jerusalem. But the Israelite nation as a whole remained in the country." As usual, he omits the extended lists of returnees given in the Bible, lest it interrupt the flow of his narrative.

The authenticity of the list has been challenged by those who regard it as an invention, based on 2:1-70 and interrupting the connection between 7:28 and 8:15 (cf. Hölscher, *Esra und Nehemia*, II, 493, 519-20). But the originality of the list has been vigorously defended (cf. Rudolph, *Esra und Nehemia*, p. 79). The expression "chief men" of 7:28 is related to the **chief of their fathers** in vs. 1, and vs. 15 fits well as the resumption of narrative when the author has interpolated a relevant list (cf. Noth, *Überlieferungsgeschlichtliche Studien* I, p. 125).

It is incorrect to regard the genealogy as "an extract of those in Ezr 2 and Neh 7" (Kapelrud, *op. cit.*, p. 45), for there are important differences. Unlike that in 2:1-70, this genealogy first lists the priests (vs. 2), with no heading to identify them. Only the ancestral names indicate the priestly connection. Those listed are not Zadokites (cf. 2:36) but descendants of Aaron who became prominent in Babylonia between the time of Zerubbabel and Ezra and were not yet recognized as dominant in Palestine as late as the time of Ezra (10:18 ff.; cf. Kittel, *Geschichte des Volkes Israel*, III, 402-7). The descendants of the two Aaronitic families are later most important, according to the Priestly Code (cf. Num. 3:1 ff.; 25:6-15). It has been conjectured that the priests are here listed first in deference to Ezra the priest (7:11-12), and that the family of **Phinehas** precedes because that was the one to which Ezra belonged (7:5; cf. Rudolph, *op. cit.*, p. 79). But **Ithamar** was the youngest son of Aaron (Exod. 6:23) and might therefore be listed second. In Neh. 10:6 **Daniel** appears among the priests sealing the covenant. Since Ezra later selected a dozen priests who came up with him (vs. 24), the two men mentioned must have been family heads, as among the laymen.

Hattush was an individual, a prince of the line of David through Solomon and Zerubbabel. The words **of the sons of Shecaniah** (vs. 3) refer to **Hattush** and indicate

---

8:1-20. *The Caravan on Its Way.*—Again the narrative in the first person is interrupted by the insertion of another of the genealogical lists of which the Chronicler was so fond; but at last in vs. 15 the caravan begins to "get organized" for

its long journey. Then Ezra discovers (vss. 15-20) that he has with him for the proper service of the temple neither Levites nor their helpers the Nethinim, an interesting hint that there were plenty of plausible reasons why the ma-

4 Of the sons of Pahath-moab; Elihoenai the son of Zerahiah, and with him two hundred males.

5 Of the sons of Shechaniah; the son of Jahaziel, and with him three hundred males.

6 Of the sons also of Adin; Ebed the son of Jonathan, and with him fifty males.

7 And of the sons of Elam; Jeshaiah the son of Athaliah, and with him seventy males.

8 And of the sons of Shephatiah; Zebadiah the son of Michael, and with him fourscore males.

registered one hundred and fifty men. 4 Of the sons of Pa'hath-mo'ab, Eli-e-ho-e'nai the son of Zerahi'ah, and with him two hundred men. 5 Of the sons of Zattu,[i] Shecani'ah the son of Jahazi'el, and with him three hundred men. 6 Of the sons of Adin, Ebed the son of Jonathan, and with him fifty men. 7 Of the sons of Elam, Jeshai'ah the son of Athali'ah, and with him seventy men. 8 Of the sons of Shephati'ah, Zebadi'ah the son of Michael, and with him eighty men.

[i] Gk 1 Esdras 8. 32. Heb lacks *of Zattu*

that he was the grandson (cf. 5:1) of Shecaniah (I Chr. 3:22). According to J. W. Rothstein and Johannes Hänel (*Kommentar zum ersten Buch der Chronik* [Leipzig: A. Deichert, 1927; "Kommentar zum Alten Testament"], p. 43), "and the sons of Shemaiah" is to be omitted in I Chr. 3:22, which would make **Hattush** the son of Shecaniah as here and I Esdras 8:29.

It is largely the list of lay families (vss. 3-14) that causes the genealogy to be regarded with suspicion, since many of the family names found in 2:3 ff. (=Neh. 7:8 ff.) are encountered here. Although the names of remote ancestors are identical, there is some difference in order. All the names found in vss. 3-14 are encountered among the first thirteen names in ch. 2, but only a dozen families are found here in ch. 8. "Arah" and "Zaccai" are surprisingly missing, and no names beyond 2:15 are found. Although it is not mentioned specifically, the number twelve is presumably selected to represent the twelve Hebrew tribes, for the symbolism occurs elsewhere in the Ezra narrative (cf. vss. 24, 35). Although **Jeshaiah** and **Athaliah** (vs. 7) are Benjaminite (cf. Neh. 11:7; I Chr. 8:26), it is impossible to assign the families mentioned to the twelve original Hebrew tribes.

The formula here calls for listing the ancestral name, the family leader who returned with Ezra, identified by his father's name, together with the sum of the males of that family who returned at that time. Where the formula is incomplete (vss. 5, 10) the need for restoration of text is apparent, and in the one instance of departure from the formula (vs. 13) the change is significant. Thus the name of the father of **Zechariah** (vs. 3) no longer survives. In vs. 4 **Pahath-moab** (2:6) apparently has come to indicate the family of Jeshua alone (2:6) since "Joab" appears independently later in the list (vs. 9). Missing in vs. 5 is the name of the remote ancestor, but it can be restored as "Zattu" (2:8) on the basis of the "Zathoes" of the LXX. Similarly, in vs. 10 the LXX ("Boani") and I Esdras[AB] ("Banias") indicate that the missing ancestral name was "Bani" (cf. 2:10). **Ebed** ("Servant of . . .") in vs. 6 (cf. Judg. 9:26) could be an abbreviation of such a name as "Abdiel," but the Greek texts suggest an original "Obed" (Ruth 4:17, 21; I Chr. 2:12; Matt. 1:5), which abbreviates **Obadiah** (cf. vs. 9). The name **Jeshaiah** (vs. 7) is identical with the name "Isaiah." The feminine name **Shelomith** (vs. 10; cf. Lev. 24:11) should be vocalized "Shelomoth" (cf. I Chr. 23:9; 24:22; 26:25-28), as the Greek versions show. **Hakkatan** ("The Little One") in vs. 12 may be an epithet meaning either "small" or "young" (cf. Judg. 3:9 and "James the less" in Mark 15:40).

jority of the exiles preferred to remain in the relative comfort and security of Babylon, rather than to risk so long and dangerous a journey to what proved to be so precarious a livelihood. But with the help of **a man of discretion** and

by **the good hand of our God upon us** (vs. 18), this ceremonial lack was supplied. As so often in the undertakings that make history, both human wisdom and divine guidance and blessing "had a hand" in the outcome.

9 Of the sons of Joab; Obadiah the son of Jehiel, and with him two hundred and eighteen males.

10 And of the sons of Shelomith; the son of Josiphiah, and with him a hundred and threescore males.

11 And of the sons of Bebai; Zechariah the son of Bebai, and with him twenty and eight males.

12 And of the sons of Azgad; Johanan the son of Hakkatan, and with him a hundred and ten males.

13 And of the last sons of Adonikam, whose names *are* these, Eliphelet, Jeiel, and Shemaiah, and with them threescore males.

14 Of the sons also of Bigvai; Uthai, and Zabbud, and with them seventy males.

15 ¶ And I gathered them together to the river that runneth to Ahava; and there

9 Of the sons of Jo'ab, Obadi'ah the son of Jehi'el, and with him two hundred and eighteen men. 10 Of the sons of Bani,ʲ Shelo'mith the son of Josiphi'ah, and with him a hundred and sixty men. 11 Of the sons of Be'bai, Zechari'ah, the son of Be'bai, and with him twenty-eight men. 12 Of the sons of Azgad, Joha'nan the son of Hak'katan, and with him a hundred and ten men. 13 Of the sons of Adoni'kam, those who came later, their names being Eliph'elet, Jeu'el, and Shemai'ah, and with them sixty men. 14 Of the sons of Big'vai, Uthai and Zakkur, and with them seventy men.

15 I gathered them to the river that runs

ʲ Gk 1 Esdras 8. 36. Heb lacks *Bani*

In vs. 13 the formula is broken and three names are given without reference to paternity. The word translated **last** is obscure in the context. It is unnecessary to omit the word as a dittograph (cf. Ehrlich, *Randglossen zur herbräischen Bibel*, VII, 174; Bewer, *Der Text des Buches Ezra*, p. 74; Hölscher, *op. cit.*, II, 520). **Who came later** is nonsense in the light of the **went up with me** in vs. 1. The LXX^AB and I Esdras, which have "the last ones," show the way to the proper interpretation. The three individuals comprise the last of the family of **Adonikam** (2:13) that remained in Babylonia. The three men were apparently of equal rank.

Of the family of **Bigvai** (2:14), **Uthai** appears to have been the son of **Zabbud** (or **Zakkur**), as the reading in I Esdras shows (cf. Bewer, *loc. cit.*). The Greek versions show that in agreement with the single name the correct reading of the M.T. is "with him" rather than **with them**. After the corruption of the text to read two names, the text was altered to **with them** in agreement, and that "correction" is found in the Vulg., Peshitta, and about ninety MSS. **Zabbud** represents the written tradition of the M.T., but Hebrew oral tradition, supported by the Vulg. and the LXX^L has **Zakkur**. The names are easily confused in writing and it is impossible to determine which was original.

D. Acquisition of Temple Servants (8:15-20=I Esdras 8:41-49)

15. As with every large caravan about to get under way, an open space away from the big city was used as an assembly point where the people could be organized and the equipment prepared for the expedition (cf. Jer. 41:17). Here the emigrees **abode . . . in tents** during the necessary period. Ezra's camp was located on a stream flowing toward **Ahava,** a place not yet certainly identified. Instead of **river,** translate "stream" or "canal" (cf. Ezek. 1:1; 3:15). Identification which would place **Ahava** on the Euphrates must be wrong since that river would not be described as in vs. 15. Many attempts at identification have been made, but the most probable links it with modern Mečin, the classical Maschana or Scenae, on the canal now called Ad-Dugejl (Alois Musil, *The Middle Euphrates* [New York: Czech Academy of Sciences and Arts, 1927], Appendix XX, pp. 360-63). The classical name, which means "tented settlement," suits well the description of **Ahava.** The place is located on the transport route along the right bank of the Tigris River at the point where it branches into two caravan routes, one leading northwest, the other going westward across central Mesopotamia.

Some have seen the prototype of the **three days** in the Nehemiah memoirs (Neh.

abode we in tents three days: and I viewed the people, and the priests, and found there none of the sons of Levi.

16 Then sent I for Eliezer, for Ariel, for Shemaiah, and for Elnathan, and for Jarib, and for Elnathan, and for Nathan, and for Zechariah, and for Meshullam, chief men; also for Joiarib, and for Elnathan, men of understanding.

to Aha'va, and there we encamped three days. As I reviewed the people and the priests, I found there none of the sons of Levi. 16 Then I sent for Elie'zer, Ar'i-el, Shemai'ah, Elna'than, Jarib, Elna'than, Nathan, Zechari'ah, and Meshul'lam, leading men, and for Joi'arib and Elna'than, who

---

2:11; Kapelrud, *op. cit.*, p. 46), but three days is only a reasonable time to delay for organization (cf. vs. 32 for disbanding the caravan). It was apparently on the third day that the absence of the Levites was discovered, but it was not until the twelfth day that the lack was remedied and the caravan was ready to depart (vs. 31).

Perhaps in ancient times, as today in mass migrations, the chieftains rode together in advance of the caravan, followed by the various households together with their stock. At each encampment the families erected tents in a place selected by the family leader so that a halted caravan was actually a series of family camps (Charles M. Doughty, *Travels in Arabia Deserta* [New York: Random House, 1946], pp. 257, 161-62; cf. C. P. Grant, *The Syrian Desert* [New York: The Macmillan Co., 1938], p. 226). Stress on family groups explains the family structure of the genealogy. Thus, too, the absence of Levites was detected when Ezra **reviewed the people and the priests.**

The Levites apparently refused to leave their security and position in Babylonia for the insecurity of menial duties in the Jerusalem temple (cf. Neh. 13:10). Later Jews, embarrassed by such reluctance, rationalized the Levites' behavior by explaining that since Abraham had once dwelt in Babylonia, and the Babylonian language was similar to Hebrew, the Levites and other Jews felt at home there (Tosephta Baba Kama VII, 3; Pesaḥim 87*b*). Some insisted that Levites were in the caravan (cf. 7:7), but that they were old men who had made themselves unfit for temple service by biting off their fingers (cf. Lev. 21:16-24) rather than play their instruments at Nebuchadrezzar's orders (Yalkut II, 884; Midrash Tehillim, 137). But Ezra found no Levites and had to recruit some.

16. A group of men were appointed to represent Ezra in the gathering of the Levites. They are called **leading men,** but aside from **Zechariah** (vss. 3, 11) and **Shemaiah** (vs. 13), who bear very common names, none is listed among the family leaders in the genealogy (vss. 3-14). Nor can it be determined just how many members the delegation had. The M.T., LXX, and Vulg. list eleven; I Esdras[AB] has ten; while I Esdras[L] has only seven. Several names seem to be duplicated. **Elnathan** appears thrice and the abbreviation **Nathan** once, while **Jarib** and **Joiarib** are variants of the same name. One **Elnathan** may be a corruption of another name for which six MSS have "Jonathan." **Joiarib** and **Elnathan,** now separated from the others at the end of the verse, obviously duplicate the earlier **Jarib** and **Elnathan,** as I Esdras[L] shows. Their omission restores to the noun "chieftains" (lit., "heads") its adjectival modifier "intelligent," so that all men listed, not just the last two, are characterized as "intelligent leaders," as in I Esdras 8:44.

Grammatical ambiguity makes possible the translations "I sent to Eliezer" as well as **I sent for Eliezer,** as though the men were located somewhere apart from Ezra in Babylonia. But Ezra sent them to Iddo (vs. 17). No preposition is given in the Vulg. and the Lucianic Greek texts, apparently because it was recognized as the sign of the object, as in Aramaic (E. F. Kautzsch, *Gesenius' Hebrew Grammar*, tr. A. E. Cowley [2nd English ed.; Oxford: Clarendon Press, 1910], sec. 143*e*; cf. Driver, *Intro. to Literature of O.T.*, p. 538, No. 39; Torrey, *Ezra Studies*, p. 265; Bewer, *op. cit.*, p. 75), and the translation should be "I sent Eliezer."

17 And I sent them with commandment unto Iddo the chief at the place Casiphia, and I told them what they should say unto Iddo, *and* to his brethren the Nethinim, at the place Casiphia, that they should bring unto us ministers for the house of our God.

18 And by the good hand of our God upon us they brought us a man of understanding, of the sons of Mahli, the son of Levi, the son of Israel; and Sherebiah, with his sons and his brethren, eighteen;

were men of insight, 17 and sent them to Iddo, the leading man at the place Casiphi'a, telling them what to say to Iddo and his brethren the temple servants[k] at the place Casiphi'a, namely, to send us ministers for the house of our God. 18 And by the good hand of our God upon us, they brought us a man of discretion, of the sons of Mahli the son of Levi, son of Israel, namely Sherebi'ah with his sons and kins-

[k] Heb *nethinim*

---

17. I sent them with commandment reflects the conflate reading of the M.T., but only one of the ideas, either "send" or "command," should be translated. Hebrew oral tradition and the Peshitta call for "I commanded them," as in the American Jewish Translation. This is understood as meaning "directing them [to]" or "I dispatched them" (cf. Exod. 6:13; Jer. 27:4). Hebrew written tradition, the LXX[AB], and Arabic versions call for a translation **I sent them.** The **Iddo** (אדו) to whom the delegation was sent must not be confused with the Iddo (עדו) of I Kings 4:14; Zech. 1:7; II Chr. 12:15, which is spelled differently. The name abbreviates one containing the element "Lord" (*'ādhôn*), such as Adonijah. It may be found in Neo-Babylonian texts as *mid-du-u-a* (Oluf Krückmann, *Neubabylonische Rechts- und Verwaltungs-texte* [Leipzig: J. C. Hinrichs, 1933], No. 9, l. 38). Like the leaders who accompanied Ezra (8:1, 16), **Iddo** is a "head" or **leading man** of the Jews.

Iddo was found at **the place Casiphia** which also is not yet identified but must have been near **Ahava.** Because 9:8 uses **place** for the holy place in Jerusalem, it has been suggested that **Casiphia** was a sanctuary, a Babylonian Jewish "temple" parallel to the Jewish temples in Egypt (Laurence E. Browne, "A Jewish Sanctuary in Babylonia," *Journal of Theological Studies*, XVII [1916], 400-401; cf. the same author's *Early Judaism* [Cambridge: Cambridge University Press, 1920], p. 53). It has also been conjectured that **Casiphia** was a training school for Levites (Bertheau, *Esra, Nechemia und Ester,* p. 104). But it is more probable that **Casiphia** was a city or village with a large Jewish colony. **Place** is used of a city in Hebrew when its name is already known (cf. II Kings 18:25), but the word may be used here as a determinative, an aid in reading as in Akkadian (cf. Gen. 12:6; Jer. 19:13; cf. W. E. Staples, "The Reading of Hebrew," *American Journal of Semitic Languages and Literatures*, LVIII [1941], 139-45). It has been suggested that the name **Casiphia** has been distorted to Ctesiphon, the city lying just across the river from Seleucia (Hugo Winckler, "Kasiphja-Ktesiphon," *Altorientalische Forschungen* [Leipzig: E. Pfeiffer, 1901], Reihe 2, Bd. III, pp. 509-30). Such identification cannot be regarded as certain, but the site would be suitable if the antiquity of Ctesiphon could be demonstrated archaeologically.

The senseless combination "his brother the Nethinim" in the M.T. has been corrected to **his brethren the Nethinim.** It is better to read with the versions, "Iddo and his brethren." But **Iddo** was probably a Levite rather than one of the Nethinim and **brethren** here merely indicates mutual interest and professional relationship, as elsewhere (cf. 3:2). As I Esdras shows, originally the text had "and the Nethinim," but the conjunction was lost accidentally since it was identical with the last letter of **his brethren.** Thus we should read, "Iddo and his brethren and the Nethinim." **Ministers** is, lit., "servants," but as a cultic title it could be applied even to priests (cf. Exod. 28:35; 30:20); here it indicates menial servants, the lowly assistants of the priests.

18-20. Josephus summarizes these verses but, as usual, in the interest of the narrative he supplies no names. **The good hand** is as in 7:6. As I Esdras[AB] shows, the **man of discretion** was **Sherebiah,** who plays an important role in the Ezra story (8:18, 24; Neh. 8:7; 9:4-5; 10:12; 12:8, 24). Thus **and** before his name should be regarded as explicative

19 And Hashabiah, and with him Jeshaiah of the sons of Merari, his brethren and their sons, twenty;

20 Also of the Nethinim, whom David and the princes had appointed for the service of the Levites, two hundred and twenty Nethinim: all of them were expressed by name.

21 ¶ Then I proclaimed a fast there, at the river of Ahava, that we might afflict our-

men, eighteen; 19 also Hashabi'ah and with him Jeshai'ah of the sons of Merar'i, with his kinsmen and their sons, twenty; 20 besides two hundred and twenty of the temple servants, whom David and his officials had set apart to attend the Levites. These were all mentioned by name.

21 Then I proclaimed a fast there, at the

(cf. 6:8), translated **namely. Sherebiah** is traced to Jacob (**Israel**) through **Levi** (cf. Exod. 6:19; Num. 3:20). All of the Levites mentioned were of the line of **Merari** the son of **Levi** (cf. I Chr. 6:47), the family which traditionally served the tent of meeting (Num. 4:29-33, 42-45) and helped to bear the tabernacle (Num. 10:17). **Hashabiah** is listed with **Jeshaiah** (vs. 7) as being of the sons of **Merari** (I Chr. 6:44-45). The antecedent of **his brethren** is Sherebiah of vs. 18, but **their sons** refers to the families of **Hashabiah** and **Jesaiah.**

Only thirty-eight Levites were assembled, but the number of servants was swelled by the relatively large number of **Nethinim** (cf. 2:43) who were induced to go to Jerusalem. Because the **Nethinim** are not mentioned in vs. 15, the reference to them has been regarded as an addition to the text. But 7:7 lists them as among those who returned with Ezra, and it is probable that with so few Levites returning, some special inducements may have been offered to bring servants of any order to the temple. The unusual form of the relative pronoun in vs. 20 suggests that the clause, **whom David and the princes,** etc., may have been added to the text. Since the Chronicler uses the relative particle several times (I Chr. 5:20; 27:27), this may be the work of his hand. There was no need to comment on the origin of the Nethinim here, and it is only here that there is preserved the tradition that **David and the princes** were responsible for instituting the **Nethinim.** The Chronicler elsewhere declares that the temple cultus derived from the time of David, but the **Nethinim** do not come into prominence until the postexilic period.

Mentioned by name is associated with lists of names elsewhere in the work of the Chronicler (I Chr. 12:31; 16:41; II Chr. 28:15; 31:19) and in Num. 1:17. It indicates that a full list was available and could have been given but was omitted because too many names were involved.

E. Final Preparation Before Departure (8:21-23 = I Esdras 8:50-53)

Ezra assumed leadership at once, and as leader combined his secular and religious functions in seeking the protection of God for his caravan. He had assured the king that God would protect his own and therefore did not request a bodyguard (vs. 22), but he was aware of the robbers who would try to loot his caravan (vs. 31) to get the rich and valuable treasure he carried (vss. 25-28). Through fasting and prayer he sought divine protection (vss. 21-23), and the temple treasure was placed in the charge of God's holy priests (vss. 24-30). The move was successful, for although the caravan was attacked they finished the journey safely (cf. vss. 23, 31).

21-23. The self-inflicted hunger pains of a **fast** were calculated to influence God to pity the fasting petitioner (cf. II Sam. 12:16 ff.; Isa. 58:3) and thus gain a favorable

---

21-36. *Prayer and Fasting.*—Here some sense of historical reality and religious urgency breaks through the genealogical and ceremonial framework within which the Chronicler is so concerned to set his story; and we begin to feel something of the firsthand authenticity that is

so marked in Nehemiah's memoirs. Ezra proclaims a period of fasting and prayer, because he is ashamed to ask the king for a military guard after he has so explicitly put his reliance on **the hand of our God** (vs. 22) for guidance and protection.

selves before our God, to seek of him a right way for us, and for our little ones, and for all our substance.

22 For I was ashamed to require of the king a band of soldiers and horsemen to help us against the enemy in the way: because we had spoken unto the king, saying, The hand of our God *is* upon all them for good that seek him; but his power and his wrath *is* against all them that forsake him.

23 So we fasted and besought our God for this: and he was entreated of us.

24 ¶ Then I separated twelve of the chief of the priests, Sherebiah, Hashabiah, and ten of their brethren with them,

river Aha′va, that we might humble ourselves before our God, to seek from him a straight way for ourselves, our children, and all our goods. 22 For I was ashamed to ask the king for a band of soldiers and horsemen to protect us against the enemy on our way; since we had told the king, "The hand of our God is for good upon all that seek him, and the power of his wrath is against all that forsake him." 23 So we fasted and besought our God for this, and he listened to our entreaty.

24 Then I set apart twelve of the leading priests: Sherebi′ah, Hashabi′ah, and ten of

---

answer to prayer. The **right way** means a **straight** or "even" way (cf. Isa. 26:7; Jer. 31:9). In I EsdrasAB 8:50 it is interpreted as a "favorable journey" (εὐοδίαν). The Amer. Trans. renders it "a safe journey." Because of danger of ambush by local raiders who would plunder the caravan while passing through lonely desert wastes en route to the west, during the Persian period the government in control sometimes on request furnished a military escort (cf. Neh. 2:9), just as the Turks supplied janizaries during the early part of the Ottoman period (cf. Grant, *op. cit.,* pp. 128, 137-39) and the French did in Syria in modern times. The rendering **band of soldiers,** lit., "a force" (cf. 4:23), represents a word used in the Jewish papyri for the detachment of soldiers posted at Assuan, and also in the Behistun papyri for the Assyrian and Persian armies. **To help us,** like the M.T., implies a readiness of the Jews themselves to fight, but **to protect us,** which is based on the Greek versions, stresses absolute dependence upon the armed escort. The great concern was felt for the children and possessions. The word translated **little ones** (vs. 21) is found frequently in early Hebrew but is relatively rare in the late period (cf. Isa. 9:6; Esth. 3:13; 8:11; II Chr. 20:13; 31:18). The Greek versions translate it as **our children. Substance** (Hebrew *rekhûsh;* cf. 1:4, 6) can mean "livestock," as in I Esdras 8:50, but here the broader interpretation of the term, accumulated **goods,** is preferable since Ezra sought safe arrival not only of his beasts but of the treasure (vss. 25-28) being delivered.

In Ezra's refusal to ask for a bodyguard some have seen a rebuke to Nehemiah for lack of faith and a lauding of Ezra as superior (cf. Kapelrud, *Question of Authorship in the Ezra-Narrative,* pp. 52-53). It is thus supposed that the Ezra narrative here is dependent upon Nehemiah and is thus historically improbable. It may, however, be merely the expected contrast between the realistic and practical administrator Nehemiah and the religious idealist Ezra.

F. DELEGATION TO TRANSPORT TREASURE (8:24-30=I Esdras 8:54-60)

Lacking an armed bodyguard, Ezra sought some way to protect the treasure entrusted by the Persian court for delivery to the temple in Jerusalem. As material set apart for divine use, the vessels and the metals were **holy unto the LORD** (vs. 28). Both men, as priests and Levites (cf. Lev. 21:6; II Chr. 23:6), and temple paraphernalia (cf.

To Americans, vss. 21-23 may well seem the most momentous in the entire book in their far-reaching historical consequences. William Bradford's *History of Plymouth Plantation* tells us that this was the text of John Robinson's last sermon at Leyden, before he sent his little

band of Pilgrims forth in 1620 to face the perils of the North Atlantic in autumn, and the rigors of "a stern and rock-bound coast"[5] through that first terrible winter at Plymouth,

[5] Felicia Dorothea Hemans, "The Landing of the Pilgrim Fathers."

25 And weighed unto them the silver, and the gold, and the vessels, *even* the offering of the house of our God, which the king, and his counselors, and his lords, and all Israel *there* present, had offered:

26 I even weighed unto their hand six hundred and fifty talents of silver, and silver vessels a hundred talents, *and* of gold a hundred talents;

their kinsmen with them. 25 And I weighed out to them the silver and the gold and the vessels, the offering for the house of our God which the king and his counselors and his lords and all Israel there present had offered; 26 I weighed out into their hand six hundred and fifty talents of silver, and silver vessels worth a hundred talents, and

Josh. 6:19; Zech. 14:20-21) were consecrated and were then no longer subject to common use but were henceforth surrounded by taboos and restrictions placed on all of God's property. Only holy men should handle holy things. The knowledge that the valuables belonged neither to Ezra nor the people but to their God would serve to make the holy men guarding the wealth unquestionably honest and especially vigilant until their responsibilities should be discharged in Jerusalem. Implied also is the fact that God would in a special way protect what was his own.

24. Set apart means selected for the special task. **Twelve** was a popular number among the Hebrews, but it is here not a symbol for the twelve tribes since all of the clerics were of the same tribe. No laymen were permitted to handle holy things. In addition to the dozen priests there were as many Levites selected (cf. vs. 30). Since **Sherebiah** and **Hashabiah** were not priests (cf. 8:2) but leaders of Ezra's newly acquired Levites (cf. vss. 18-19), it is necessary to read with I Esdras the conjunction "and" before each name. It has been suggested that something like "and the Levites" has been omitted after **priests** (Torrey, *Ezra Studies*, p. 266). Josephus (*Antiquities* XI. 5. 2) identifies the group as "treasurers who were of priestly descent." **Their brethren** means the Levites.

25. Of the treasure the **silver** and **gold** constituted the **freewill offering** (vs. 28) collected in Babylonia for the temple (cf. 7:15 ff.). In addition to the **king** and **counselors** (vs. 25) mentioned in 7:15, the M.T. adds a third group, **his lords**, which appear as "leaders" in the LXX and "grandees" or "noblemen" in I Esdras. Josephus here omits the third group as in 7:15. Unworked precious metal, presumably in bars or ingots, is listed by weight alone, but the manufactured articles are listed by number and appraised value. As elsewhere, **vessels** may better be translated "implements" (cf. 1:7). In listing the treasure the most common and abundant metal is listed first, then gold, and finally the rare and valuable objects.

26. The figures here given, much too large to be historically probable, are doubtless the Chronicler's contribution, for he becomes overly enthusiastic in his statistics where the temple is concerned (cf. II Chr. 7:5), even where his figures can be checked against an earlier source (II Sam. 24:24; I Chr. 21:25).

The **hundred talents** assigned to the silver vessels does not represent the M.T., which has, lit., "a hundred silver vessels worth talents." It has been proposed to read the **talents** as dual, "two talents," rather than as plural (Bewer, *Der Text des Buches Ezra*, p. 77; cf. Rudolph, *Esra und Nehemia*, p. 82). But such a modest sum seems inappropriate in the light of the other figures. It is more probable that the actual figure, which should follow **talents**, has been lost from the text (cf. Meyer, *Entstehung des Judenthums*, p. 69; Torrey, *Ezra Studies*, p. 266). Since a **talent** weighed about sixty-five

during which half the company of the "Mayflower" perished. Thus the "idealized history" of the Chronicler kindled some at least of the spiritual dynamic that sustained a longer and riskier journey than Ezra's, and through the "Mayflower Compact" signed in Provincetown Harbor became a creative part of the social and religious heritage of American democracy. The congregation at Leyden, like the caravan at the river Ahava, proclaimed a "day of solleme humiliation . . . powering out prairs to ye Lord with great fervencie, mixed with abundance of tears." Robinson's sermon on this text took most of the day "very profitably," and his

27 Also twenty basins of gold, of a thousand drams; and two vessels of fine copper, precious as gold.

28 And I said unto them, Ye *are* holy unto the LORD; the vessels *are* holy also; and the silver and the gold *are* a freewill offering unto the LORD God of your fathers.

29 Watch ye, and keep *them,* until ye weigh *them* before the chief of the priests and the Levites, and chief of the fathers of Israel, at Jerusalem, in the chambers of the house of the LORD.

30 So took the priests and the Levites the weight of the silver, and the gold, and the vessels, to bring *them* to Jerusalem unto the house of our God.

a hundred talents of gold, 27 twenty bowls of gold worth a thousand darics, and two vessels of fine bright bronze as precious as gold. 28 And I said to them, "You are holy to the LORD, and the vessels are holy; and the silver and the gold are a freewill offering to the LORD, the God of your fathers. 29 Guard them and keep them until you weigh them before the chief priests and the Levites and the heads of fathers' houses in Israel at Jerusalem, within the chambers of the house of the LORD." 30 So the priests and the Levites took over the weight of the silver and the gold and the vessels, to bring them to Jerusalem, to the house of our God.

---

pounds (cf. 7:22), the silver gift would come to more than twenty-one tons, while the **hundred talents** of gold would come to about three and a quarter tons, worth considerably more than the silver. The ratio of silver to gold in the Persian period is as yet unknown, but in the Chaldean age, just before the Persian conquest, the ratio of silver to gold varied between ten and thirteen to one (W. H. Dubberstein, "Comparative Prices in Later Babylonia," *American Journal of Semitic Languages and Literatures,* LVI [1939], 23).

27. The **bowls** are of the same type as those in 1:10. The term rendered **drams** or **darics** is spelled as in I Chr. 29:7 (*'adharkōnîm*) rather than as in Ezra 2:69 (cf. Neh. 7:70-72). However, the confusion in the LXX^ABL suggests that the spelling of the M.T. was once that in 2:69, for the error there, "the road" (τὴν ὁδόν), points to a confusion of the Hebrew "road" (דרך) with the beginning letters of **darics** ([מנים] דרכ).

The list of treasure concludes with the unique vessels of special type and great value. They are described as being as **precious as gold,** but Josephus calls them "more precious than gold," which would account for their being last in a list that is apparently in an ascending scale. Since the same word is used in Hebrew for both **copper** and **bronze,** the nature of the material is uncertain and it has even been suggested that it was "a rare amalgam" (George Rawlinson, *Ezra and Nehemiah* [New York: Anson D. F. Randolph & Co., 1891], p. 23). The description given here seems to favor copper as a metal of beauty that could be highly polished. The KJV omits the modifier found in the M.T., which in the RSV is translated **bright,** apparently because the LXX has

---

departing flock never forgot what he said to them:

I charge you before God and his blessed Angels to follow me no further than I follow Christ, . . . and if God shall reveal anything to you by any other Instrument of his, be as ready to receive it as ever you were to receive any truth by my ministry. [Two days later they left Leyden], that goodly and pleasant citie, which had been their resting place near 12 years; but they knew they were pilgrimes, and looked not much on those things, but lift[ed] up their eyes to ye heavens, their dearest cuntrie, and quieted their spirits.[6]

[6] George F. Willison, *Saints and Strangers* (New York: Reynal and Hitchcock, 1945), pp. 119-20.

So Ezra's faith and courage for his journey across the Arabian Desert quickened the Pilgrims' faith and courage that dared both the Atlantic and the winter wilderness two thousand years later, passing over thus into the spiritual heritage of the western continent to mold the history of the New World. In view of the historical results of the journeys of both these little companies, the religiously minded among their children's children have had reason aplenty to join in the grateful acknowledgment of their "founding fathers": **The hand of our God was upon us, and he delivered us from the hand of the enemy and from ambushes by the way** (vs. 31*b*).

31 ¶ Then we departed from the river of Ahava on the twelfth *day* of the first month, to go unto Jerusalem: and the hand of our God was upon us, and he delivered us from the hand of the enemy, and of such as lay in wait by the way.

32 And we came to Jerusalem, and abode there three days.

31 Then we departed from the river Aha'va on the twelfth day of the first month, to go to Jerusalem; the hand of our God was upon us, and he delivered us from the hand of the enemy and from ambushes by the way. 32 We came to Jerusalem, and

---

"glittering" and I Esdras has "glittering like gold." In the Amer. Trans. it is interpreted as "burnished." But the M.T. has "reddened" (cf. Arabic *ṣahiba*, "be red") and the term appears to be a translation of the Akkadian "red-gleaming copper" (*sipparu ruššu*).

G. Departure and Arrival (8:31-36=I Esdras 8:61-64)

The first stage of the journey to Jerusalem began on the first of the first month (7:9) in the seventh year of Artaxerxes (7:7-8). But Josephus, basing his narrative on I Esdras 8:6 (=Ezra 7:8), wrongly places the movement during the seventh year of Xerxes (479 b.c.), which is too early. The delay at Ahava (cf. 8:15 ff.) took some time, but after the temple servants were gotten and the caravan organized, the departure was made on the twelfth day of the first month (Apr. 16, 398 b.c.).

31. **We departed** translates a word used among nomads meaning "pull up stakes" and then "depart," a word rare in late Hebrew (Job 4:21; 19:10) as might be expected, but it is appropriate here for the departure of a tented community (cf. 8:15). Josephus declares that the group "set out from the Euphrates" but that is much less likely than from the Tigris. The route along the Euphrates would be difficult and dangerous during early spring (Rawlinson, *Ezra and Nehemiah*, pp. 32-35). Musil (*Middle Euphrates*, p. 361) says: "There was no corn ripe as yet in early April on the Euphrates, and the Jews would therefore have found neither food for themselves nor pasture for their animals. Moreover, the chiefs of the different settlements along the Euphrates, always more or less independent, would undoubtedly have troubled them with their demands. The chiefs from the surrounding country would not have hesitated to fall upon a body of strangers not protected by Persian soldiery and who, as they knew or at least imagined, had plenty of money and supplies." The alternate route, longer but safer, through more inhabited territory "led first along the right bank of the Tigris northward nearly as far as Mosul of today; then it turned west along the foot of the northern mountain range and went through the region between the desert and the settled country as far as the Euphrates, which it reached at the ford of Thapsacus in the neighborhood of the present Bâlis ruins" (*ibid.*).

Ezra's journey took four months, culminating at Jerusalem on the first day of the fifth month (7:9), July 31, 398 b.c., including necessary delays and the journey from Syria southward to Jerusalem. Strabo (*Geography* XVI. 1. 8, 26-27) describes the same route as traveled by merchants of his day, and indicates that it took twenty-five days from the ford of the Euphrates (at Anthemusia) to Scenae (=Ahava) on camel back (Musil, *op. cit.*, pp. 361-62). Ezra's large group with its livestock could scarcely match the speed of small merchant caravans.

32. Upon arrival at **Jerusalem** there were **three days** of encampment, apparently for rest and orderly demobilization of the caravan. Immigrants would have to be settled and the inevitable conflicts between the newcomers and the people in the land would have to be adjusted. Because in Neh. 2:11 a similar interval followed Nehemiah's arrival, vs. 32 here has been regarded as a borrowing from that passage by the Chronicler (cf. Siegfried, *Esra, Nehemia und Esther*, p. 60; Kapelrud, *op. cit.*, p. 57), but there is nothing implausible in the narrative here. In fact, such a period would be even more necessary with Ezra's caravan than with Nehemiah's smaller company.

33 ¶ Now on the fourth day was the silver and the gold and the vessels weighed in the house of our God by the hand of Meremoth the son of Uriah the priest; and with him *was* Eleazar the son of Phinehas; and with them *was* Jozabad the son of Jeshua, and Noadiah the son of Binnui, Levites;

34 By number *and* by weight of every one: and all the weight was written at that time.

35 *Also* the children of those that had been carried away, which were come out of the captivity, offered burnt offerings unto the God of Israel, twelve bullocks for all Israel, ninety and six rams, seventy and seven lambs, twelve he goats *for* a sin offering: all *this was* a burnt offering unto the LORD.

there we remained three days. 33 On the fourth day, within the house of our God, the silver and the gold and the vessels were weighed into the hands of Mer'emoth the priest, son of Uri'ah, and with him was Elea'zar the son of Phin'ehas, and with them were the Levites, Jo'zabad the son of Jeshua and No-adi'ah the son of Bin'nui. 34 The whole was counted and weighed, and the weight of everything was recorded.

35 At that time those who had come from captivity, the returned exiles, offered burnt offerings to the God of Israel, twelve bulls for all Israel, ninety-six rams, seventy-seven lambs, and as a sin offering twelve he-goats; all this was⁀ a burnt offering to

---

33-34. On the **fourth day,** after the caravan had disbanded, Ezra turned to the less pressing but important duty of delivering the temple treasure. It was presumably turned in at "the chambers," the storerooms or treasuries of the temple (cf. vs. 29; Neh. 10:37-39). Since the M.T. says that the things were "weighed out upon the hands" of the treasurers, it is better to read **weighed into the hands of . . .** rather than "under the direction of . . ." (Torrey, *Ezra Studies,* p. 267). **By the hand of** is certainly too ambiguous, since it is clear from the M.T. that **Meremoth** was the recipient of the treasure, not the one bringing it. In businesslike fashion the goods were checked **by number and by weight** against the inventory at Jerusalem. Such concern about accounting has led to the conclusion that the Ezra document is no mere memoir or edifying treatise but an actual report back to the king and court regarding the progress of the tasks to which Ezra was entrusted (cf. Rudolph, *op. cit.,* pp. 83-84). Because "the same peculiar construction and the same words" are used in I Chr. 28:14-18, it has been suggested that the Chronicler has written this passage (Torrey, *loc. cit.*), but both passages are concerned with tabulation, and the agreement is not as verbally exact as the theory implies. The **priest, Meremoth,** is mentioned as having come up from Babylonia at an earlier day (cf. 2:61). Since he was of the family of Koz, who could not authenticate their right to priestly office (2:61-62), and since he is mentioned without priestly title as a builder of the wall in the days of Nehemiah (Neh. 3:4, 21), the presence of the title **priest** here is significant. It has been conjectured that Meremoth's double share of work on the wall (Neh. 3:4, 21) gained his priestly investiture (cf. Aage Bentzen, "Priesterschaft und Laien in der jüdischen Gemeinde des fünften Jahrhunderts," *Archiv für Orientforschung,* VI [1931], 285). Such evidence would indicate the priority of Nehemiah's arrival and activity in Jerusalem (cf. Rowley, *Servant of the Lord,* pp. 158-59). **Eleazar** may be the priest accused of marrying a foreign wife in 10:18. **Jozabad** and **Noadiah** were Levitical assistants to the priests. A **Jozabad** was one of the chief Levites who had oversight of the outside business of the temple in the days of Nehemiah (Neh. 11:16), a role in which he appears to be functioning here. A Levite of the same name married a foreign woman (10:23). **Noadiah** appears only here, but he is of the important family of **Binnui** which, like that of **Jeshua,** is listed as having come up from Babylonia with Zerubbabel (Neh. 12:8).

35-36. Appended to the Ezra narrative are these verses in which the Chronicler's hand is apparent both in interest and style. But the content need not be regarded as unhistorical, at least in its broad outlines, although the Chronicler may have heightened

36 ¶ And they delivered the king's commissions unto the king's lieutenants, and to the governors on this side the river: and they furthered the people, and the house of God.

the LORD. 36 They also delivered the king's commissions to the king's satraps and to the governors of the province Beyond the River; and they aided the people and the house of God.

some of the details. The verses complete the episode by disposing of elements presumably neglected in the Ezra document: the presenting of the sacrifices at the temple (7:17) and the delivery of royal instructions (cf. 7:21) to the secular officials of the western provinces. Both matters lie within the peculiar interests of the Chronicler, for they concern the history and fortunes of the temple.

At that time (vs. 34 KJV) is an example of faulty verse division, since it should introduce vs. 35, as in the RSV, which here follows the LXX^AB. Josephus (*Antiquities* XI. 5. 2) indicates that the sacrifices were made "when he [Ezra] had given these [treasures] over to the priests." The nature of the **offerings** is not clear. He explains them not as special gifts but as regular "whole burnt offerings customarily made." But the verse here stresses that it was the returning Jews, not those already in the land, who made the sacrifices. This would suggest that they may have been, like the thanksgiving (*tôdhāh*) sacrifices (Lev. 7:11-12; 22:29-30) or "joyous sacrifices" (*šalmê simḥâh*) of the later period, thanksgiving for a safe journey. In I Esdras 8:66 the sacrifice is called a "peace offering" (σωτηρίον), the word regularly used in the LXX to translate the Hebrew *shélem*. But only a portion of the peace offerings and thank offerings was burned; the rest was eaten by the worshiper and his friends. The only public peace offerings were the two lambs at Pentecost (cf. Lev. 23:19). Public sacrifices, as a rule, were either **burnt offerings** (*'ôlāh*) or the **sin offering** (*ḥaṭṭā'th*). Therefore Josephus declares the sacrifices were "as an atonement for sins," and thus agrees with the M.T., which mentions a **sin offering**. The term **sin offering** may apply only to the **twelve he-goats** (cf. 6:17; Lev. 7:1-38).

The figures in this verse indicate the author's belief that the restored community represented all the twelve tribes of Israel (cf. vss. 1-14, 24), since all sacrifices are twelve or multiples of it. Obviously the **seventy-seven** lambs is corrupt and should be "seventy-two," as is rendered in I Esdras^AL and Josephus. The figures here presented suggest those of the tribal sacrifices at the dedication of the early altar according to Num. 7:12-88, but the number of **rams** is extraordinarily large, for in Num. 7:87-88 the number of rams and lambs is identical.

36. For **commissions** the M.T. has, lit., "the laws" (Persian *data;* cf. 7:12), but the meaning is clearly weakened to mean "instructions" or "orders." The **commissions** here mentioned are usually identified as those incorporated in the king's letter (7:21-24), but the latter are addressed to the "treasurers" whereas the officers here mentioned as the **king's lieutenants** are his **satraps** (Persian *khshathrapāvan*) and **governors** (Babylonian *paḥatu;* cf. 5:3, 6, 14; 6:6, 7, 13). The **satraps** were the vice-regents of satrapies, and as such, among the highest officials in the kingdom. **Governors** was a Semitic title which in the Persian period was ambiguous and could be applied to any official, including the satrap himself (cf. 5:3). Here, as in Daniel (3:2-3, 27; 6:7) and Esther (3:12; 8:9), the Persian and Babylonian titles are found side by side. It is sometimes assumed that **governors** is an explanatory gloss to **satraps** (Batten, *Ezra and Nehemiah*, p. 330) or vice versa (Bertholet, *Esra und Nehemia*, p. 38), and Guthe has suggested that the conjunction might be explicative, "namely" (cf. 6:8; 8:18).

They furthered or **they aided** reflects a verb meaning "to lift" or "to carry," which is extended to mean "they gave support to," as in the Amer. Trans. (cf. 1:4; I Kings 9:11; Esth. 9:3). In the M.T. the subject could be Ezra and his companions, the **they** of vs. 36*a*, but Josephus (*Antiquities* XI. 5. 2) clarifies the subject as the officials who received the royal orders, for he says: "Being compelled to carry out his [Artaxerxes'] commands they [the officials] honored the Jewish nation and assisted it in all necessary ways."

9 Now when these things were done, the princes came to me, saying, The people of Israel, and the priests, and the Levites, have not separated themselves from the people of the lands, *doing* according to their abominations, *even* of the Canaanites, the Hittites, the Perizzites, the Jebusites, the Ammonites, the Moabites, the Egyptians, and the Amorites.

9 After these things had been done, the officials approached me and said, "The people of Israel and the priests and the Levites have not separated themselves from the peoples of the lands with their abominations, from the Canaanites, the Hittites, the Per'izzites, the Jeb'usites, the Ammonites, the Moabites, the Egyptians, and the Amo-

The transition from 8:36 to 9:1 is decidedly too abrupt to be original. The necessary sequel to ch. 8 is Neh. 7:70-73, which is quite out of place in the story of Nehemiah. The entire passage Neh. 7:70–8:18 belongs between Ezra 8 and Ezra 9 (Torrey, *Ezra Studies*, p. 256). Rudolph (*op. cit.*, p. 85; cf. pp. 14-15) would move from 8:36 to Neh. 7:72*b*.

IV. MIXED MARRIAGES (9:1–10:44)
A. REPORT OF MIXED MARRIAGES (9:1-2=I Esdras 8:68-70)

9:1. After these things had been done suggests that the crisis of chs. 9–10 occurred during the fifth month, shortly after Ezra's arrival at Jerusalem (cf. 7:8-9), but Josephus claims it was "some time afterwards," and 10:6-9 indicates a date in the ninth month (Dec. 14, 398 B.C.), almost five months after Ezra's arrival. The events of the seventh month (Neh. 7:70–8:18) had thus intervened, and **these things** must refer to the acceptance of the law and the celebration of the feast of Tabernacles (Neh. 8:1-18), a part of the Ezra story that has been transported to the book of Nehemiah. The proper order of the Ezra narrative would have Neh. 7:70–8:18 between Ezra 8 and 9 (cf. Torrey, *Ezra Studies*, pp. 255-60).

Since it is unlikely that Ezra would have remained so long ignorant of the situation concerning mixed marriages, or would have made no attempt to combat that trend, the account of earlier, futile attempts by Ezra to solve the problem may have been editorially suppressed by the Chronicler as being unworthy behavior by the community he recognized as ideal (cf. 4:1; 5:1). But it is possible also that Ezra himself had omitted from his official report the previous failures in favor of the detailed account of the more successful measures which is preserved (cf. Rudolph, *op. cit.*, pp. 85, 87).

The term **princes** (*sārîm*, vs. 2) is used by Nehemiah for district leaders (Neh. 3:9; 12:31-32). **Peoples of the lands** (cf. 3:3) are those found in Judea by those who returned from the Exile. The long list of people which follows is intended as a commentary on **peoples of the lands.** But the list is a worthless and unhistorical addition to the text, since it includes people who had long since disappeared from the scene, exterminated or assimilated by the Canaanites and Hebrews. **Canaanites, Hittites, Perizzites, Jebusites, Egyptians,** and **Amorites** were no threat to the Jews in the time of Ezra. For **Amorites** I Esdras 8:69 has "Edomites," which would be historically suitable since the Edomites pushed into southern Judea during the Exile and formed part of the population when Ezra arrived (cf. Neh. 2:19). **Ammonites,** too, were still active in Palestine (cf. Neh. 4:3, 7; 13:7-8), as were the **Moabites** (cf. Isa. 25:10-11; Ps. 83:6; Neh. 13:1). **Ammonites and Moabites** may appear because of Deut. 23:3-4 (cf. Neh. 13:1), and the list may well have been derived by the Chronicler from the injunction against foreign contacts in Deut. 7 (especially vss. 1, 3-4).

9:1-15. Family Complications.—Hard as some of us find it to sympathize with Ezra's acute concern and ruthless attitude toward mixed marriages, as that attitude appears in chs. 9–10, there is one aspect of his prayer of public con-fession that has touched our own consciences to the quick. Under the influence of the greater Hebrew prophets and of the Christian "social gospel," we have felt it a part of our responsibility as Christian ministers to declare and

2 For they have taken of their daughters for themselves, and for their sons: so that the holy seed have mingled themselves with the people of *those* lands: yea, the hand of the princes and rulers hath been chief in this trespass.

3 And when I heard this thing, I rent my garment and my mantle, and plucked off the hair of my head and of my beard, and sat down astonished.

rites. 2 For they have taken some of their daughters to be wives for themselves and for their sons; so that the holy race has mixed itself with the peoples of the lands. And in this faithlessness the hand of the officials and chief men has been foremost."

3 When I heard this, I rent my garments and my mantle, and pulled hair from my

---

2. The negative statement of vs. 1 becomes positive accusation here. **They** refers to the Jewish men. **Holy race** is, lit., **holy seed** (cf. Isa. 6:13), the "seed of Abraham" (II Chr. 20:7), the "holy people" (Deut. 7:6). Believing that God abhorred mixtures (cf. Lev. 19:19), the Jews were rebuked for mingling with their non-Jewish neighbors. Jewish leaders rather than the average Jews were guilty of the practice of foreign marriages. **Rulers** represents a Babylonian title for a variety of appointed **officials,** from governors to simple deputies, and in the Persian period even for superintendents or foremen (cf. Ezek. 23:6, 12, 23; Jer. 51:23, 57; Isa. 41:25). Its degradation in the post-exilic period is apparent in its listing between the nobles and the people (Neh. 4:14). Here they are probably only local deputies or minor leaders. The **princes** or **officials** (cf. vs. 1) should probably be identified with the "nobles," for in Neh. 4:14, in a listing similar to that found here, the officials linked with the "deputies" are called "nobles" (*ḥôrîm*) instead of **princes** (*sārîm*), as here. The two titles are usually regarded as identical (Meyer, *Entstehung des Judenthums,* p. 132) and it has been proposed to omit the former title since the **princes** in vs. 1 are the informers (cf. Hölscher, *Esra und Nehemia,* II, 522) and the LXXAB has but one title. But the two groups need not be identical, for the **princes** of vs. 1 may be those who returned with Ezra, while those in vs. 2 may represent those long resident in Judah (Rudolph, *op. cit.,* p. 86).

The Hebrew word translated **trespass** suggests perfidy and is best rendered **faithlessness.** The LXX has "breach of covenant" (ἀσυνθεσία). The word, characteristic of late Hebrew, is often used by the Chronicler (cf. I Chr. 9:1; 10:13; II Chr. 28:19; 29:19; 33:19; 36:14).

B. Ezra's Reaction to the Mixed Marriages (9:3-15)

1. Ezra's Mourning (9:3-5=I Esdras 8:71-73; cf. Neh. 13:23-28)

Sensitive Ezra was severely shaken by the news that there were Jews who were married to foreigners, since he knew that the entire community was endangered by their misbehavior. Unlike Nehemiah (13:25), Ezra's action was turned against himself. So different are the reactions in the same situation that it has been regarded as evidence of a basic difference in personality, which makes it highly improbable that Nehemiah can be "simply Ezra (i.e., the Chronicler) under another name," as Torrey (*Ezra Studies,* p. 248) has declared (cf. Batten, *op. cit.,* p. 46).

3. **Rent my garment** expresses very violent action, originally the tearing off of all clothing to the point of nakedness (cf. Mic. 1:8; Isa. 20:2-4), although the practice was severely modified later (Morris Jastrow, tr., "The Tearing of Garments as a Symbol of Mourning," *Journal of the American Oriental Society,* XXI [1900] 23-39; "Baring of

---

confess the sins of our own day and generation; but we have not always been equally ready to recognize our individual and group responsibility as sharers in these social sins. We do well to note that Ezra himself had no slightest share in the sins of his people which he so movingly

confesses in vss. 3-15; and yet, like a true shepherd of souls, he identifies himself with his wandering and wayward flock before the judgment seat of God. From beginning to end, the words **we, us,** and **our** appear in his prayer of confession: **O my God, I am ashamed and**

4 Then were assembled unto me every one that trembled at the words of the God of Israel, because of the transgression of those that had been carried away; and I sat astonished until the evening sacrifice.

4 Then all who trembled at the words of the God of Israel, because of the faithlessness of the returned exiles, gathered round me while I sat appalled until the evening sacrifice.

the Arm and Shoulder as a Sign of Mourning," *Zeitschrift für die alttestamentliche Wissenschaft,* XXII [1902], 117-20). The attention that Ezra attracted indicates that he did more than minor damage to his clothing. The M.T. has simply **my garment,** using a general word for clothing, which the LXX and Syriac wrongly understood as the plural, **my garments.** Undergarment must be meant here, since an outer garment, a **mantle,** was also worn. The description of the **mantle** (Exod. 28:31-35) suggests that it was fashioned like a Greek chiton with a neck-hole in the midst of the cloth and highly embroidered or otherwise decorated. Mantles were worn by kings and men of high station (Immanuel Benzinger, *Hebräische Archäologie* [Freiburg i. B.: J. C. B. Mohr, 1894], p. 100). In I Esdras 8:71 the word is rendered as "holy garment," presumably influenced by the use of the term mantle as part of the high priest's vestments (Exod. 28:31-32).

Pulled hair is preferable to **plucked off the hair,** since the M.T. indicates that but part of the hair was pulled. Such plucking was the counterpart of the more formal cutting or shaving of hair as a sign of mourning (Amos 8:10; Jer. 16:6; Ezek. 7:18; Job 1:20), a practice forbidden by Hebrew law (Lev. 19:27; 21:5; Deut. 14:1; Ezek. 44:20).

Overcome by emotion, Ezra fell to the ground. **Appalled** merely suggests the emotion of terror and awe involved in the Hebrew word. "Horror-stricken" is preferable, since the word is used in Hebrew to describe objects that cause horror and abhorrence (cf. Dan. 9:27). The expression of sorrow was genuine, but Ezra seems to have made use of the occasion deliberately to gather a crowd and set the stage emotionally for his message. Josephus (*Antiquities* XI. 5. 3) interprets Ezra's experience by saying: "He reasoned that if he commanded them to put away their wives and children born to them he would not be listened to [so] he remained lying on the ground." Ezra has been called a "master of psychology" (Kittel, *Geschichte des Volkes Israel,* III, 595), and such seems to be the case since he renounced the use of force, despite his great authority (cf. 7:25-26), and used such subtle means to influence men to do what he desired of their own volition (cf. Rudolph, *op. cit.,* p. 170).

4. The plight of Ezra, lying torn and disheveled in the street before the temple (cf. 10:1), stunned by the shock of the terrible news, would naturally attract a crowd of pious Jews, particularly if he was recognized as the prominent religious leader who but recently had led the community to an acceptance of the law (cf. Neh. 9–10). Doubtless it was the spectacle of silent Ezra himself rather than a full knowledge of the situation behind his shock and grief that gathered and held the people. Hence **because of the faithlessness,** etc., in vs. 4 is awkward in its present place. Its inappropriateness is sensed by I Esdras, where it is freely translated as "while I mourned for the iniquity," while Josephus (*loc. cit.*) states that Ezra acted thus "because the chief men among the people were guilty of the charge." The difficult words fit better at the conclusion of vs. 3 (Ehrlich, *Randglossen zur hebräischen Bibel,* VII, 177; Bewer, *Der Text des Buches Ezra,* pp. 80-81). **The words of the God of Israel** need not refer to an exact passage of scripture

blush to lift my face to thee, my God, for our iniquities have risen higher than our heads, and our guilt has mounted up to the heavens. From the days of our fathers to this day we have been in great guilt. . . . Behold, we are before thee in our guilt, for none can stand before thee be-

cause of this. (Vss. 6-7, 15.) The first person plural in his prayers was possibly part of the secret of the radical reforms Ezra was apparently able to bring about during his own lifetime, and of the far-reaching influence which he certainly exerted over successive generations.

5 ¶ And at the evening sacrifice I arose up from my heaviness; and having rent my garment and my mantle, I fell upon my knees, and spread out my hands unto the LORD my God,

6 And said, O my God, I am ashamed and blush to lift up my face to thee, my

5 And at the evening sacrifice I rose from my fasting, with my garments and my mantle rent, and fell upon my knees and spread out my hands to the LORD my God, 6 saying:

"O my God, I am ashamed and blush to

---

banning foreign marriages; the phrase suggests, rather, scripture in general, and identifies the crowd as those who had accepted the law which Ezra introduced. All versions show that the original text was "the word of the God of Israel," i.e., the law.

5. Ezra remained the center of attention until the time of **the evening sacrifice** (cf. 3:3), which the Peshitta explains as "the ninth hour," 3 P.M. (cf. Acts 3:1). It was an appropriate time for Ezra to cease his self-abasement and to begin to pray, for in later Judaism that time was recognized as one of the three periods prescribed for prayer (cf. Benzinger, *op. cit.,* pp. 462-64). **I arose** need not imply that Ezra stood before kneeling (cf. Batten, *op. cit.,* p. 332); he merely shifted from abject prostration to a kneeling posture. There was no prescribed attitude of prayer in ancient times. One might stand (cf. I Sam. 1:26), sit (cf. I Chr. 17:16), or kneel (I Kings 8:54; II Chr. 6:13). Prostration preceded and may have followed prayer in standing or kneeling position (Benzinger, *op. cit.,* p. 464). **Hands** were either lifted (Pss. 28:2; 134:2; cf. Neh. 8:6) or, as here, were **spread out** (Exod. 9:29; Isa. 1:15; I Kings 8:22). It has been suggested that the hands were oriented toward the altar at first, but toward heaven in the later period (Wilhelm Nowack, *Lehrbuch der hebräischen Archäologie* [Freiburg i. B.: J. C. B. Mohr, 1894], I, 122, Figs. 6-7; II, 260). Palms were turned upward in the gesture familiar from the *orans* figure in Christian catacomb art (Walter Lowrie, *Monuments of the Early Church* [New York: The Macmillan Co., 1923], pp. 201-4). **Heaviness** translates a Hebrew word later rendered as **fasting**, since that was the primary expression of self-abasement in later Judaism (cf. 8:21). Thus I Esdras 8:73 has "fasting" (νηστείας), but though Ezra of necessity had gone without food, nothing had previously been mentioned about fasting. The LXX quite adequately translates as "humiliation" (ταπείνωσις) since the word refers to the distressed state described in vs. 3. The Amer. Trans. properly renders it as "self-abasement." The present M.T. and LXX suggest that Ezra further tore his clothes before the prayer, and it is conjectured that it was for that purpose that he **arose** (Batten, *loc. cit.*), but such action is inappropriate just before prayer and it is better to emend the text to read, "with my garments and my mantle torn" (Ehrlich, *op. cit.,* VII, 177; Bewer, *op. cit.,* p. 81), a rendering supported by I Esdras 8:73 and reflected in the RSV.

2. EZRA'S PRAYER (9:6-15=I Esdras 8:74-90)

Since ancient authors often put into the mouths of their characters speeches consistent with their personalities and appropriate to the occasion, it is difficult to determine how much of the prayer may be authentic and how much invention. It has been regarded as "thoroughly characteristic" of the Chronicler's work (Torrey, *Ezra Studies,* p. 270, note n) and it is claimed that "from the beginning to the end we have characteristic Chronicle terminology" (Kapelrud, *Question of Authorship in the Ezra-Narrative,* p. 70). But the prayer has been defended as genuine, "a verbal extract from Ezra's memoirs" (Siegfried, *op. cit.,* p. 61; Bertholet, *Esra und Nehemia,* p. xiv). Rudolph (*op. cit.,* pp. 90-91) even conjectures that Ezra, while lying on the ground, planned what he would say and later could therefore record quite literally what was said. Although literary characteristics associated with the Chronicler must be admitted, the prayer does not have an artificial or secondary nature, but is psychologically as well as historically appropriate. It is relevant to the occasion and necessary for the development of the situation (cf. Batten, *op. cit.,* pp. 336-37).

God: for our iniquities are increased over *our* head, and our trespass is grown up unto the heavens.

7 Since the days of our fathers *have* we *been* in a great trespass unto this day; and for our iniquities have we, our kings, *and* our priests, been delivered into the hand of the kings of the lands, to the sword, to captivity, and to a spoil, and to confusion of face, as *it is* this day.

8 And now for a little space grace hath been *showed* from the LORD our God, to leave us a remnant to escape, and to give us a nail in his holy place, that our God may lighten our eyes, and give us a little reviving in our bondage.

lift my face to thee, my God, for our iniquities have risen higher than our heads, and our guilt has mounted up to the heavens. **7** From the days of our fathers to this day we have been in great guilt; and for our iniquities we, our kings, and our priests have been given into the hand of the kings of the lands, to the sword, to captivity, to plundering, and to utter shame, as at this day. **8** But now for a brief moment favor has been shown by the LORD our God, to leave us a remnant, and to give us a secure hold[l] within his holy place, that our God may brighten our eyes and grant us a little

[l] Heb *nail* or *tent-pin*

Reviewing the recently passed period of humiliation and suffering of the Hebrews due to the sins of the fathers (vss. 7, 13), Ezra notes the current short interval of success, when by the grace of God Persian support had been obtained for the return of a remnant and the reconstruction of Jerusalem (vss. 8-9). He then confesses that his Jewish contemporaries by intermarrying with foreigners were offending against God's law (vss. 10-12). For the offense Ezra anticipates the utter destruction of all Jews, since there were no mitigating circumstances to warrant expectation of mercy from the divine Judge (vss. 14-15). The prayer ends suddenly on a note of fear and apprehension which gives it strength. Through the prayer Ezra deliberately sought to move his audience not by assurance of divine forgiveness but by the motive of fear that the Jerusalem community, still in the uncertain throes of reconstruction, would again return to disgrace, bondage, and justified divine destruction.

6. The prayer begins in a personal vein (vs. 6a) but soon shifts (vs. 6b) to group expression as Ezra reaches out to his audience. With **I am ashamed**, innocent Ezra associates himself with the guilty. **Lift my face** indicates the attitude of prayer but also refers to the former state of humility and fear. **Guilt** (cf. vss. 7, 13, 15) translates a Hebrew word often used by the Chronicler (I Chr. 21:3; II Chr. 24:18; 28:10, 13; 33:23; cf. Driver, *Intro. to Literature of O.T.*, p. 536, No. 19).

7. In general terms Ezra reviews Hebrew history in the light of the Deuteronomic philosophy of history, which accounts for the disasters of Israel as punishment for sin (cf. Judg. 2:11-23). The **sword** (cf. II Kings 25:6-7, 20-21); **captivity** (II Kings 17:5-6; 24:14-16; 25:6-7); **plundering** (II Kings 24:13; 25:13-17), a word used only in late Hebrew (cf. Esth. 9:10, 15-16; Dan. 11:24, 33); and **confusion of face**, which the LXXAB renders more exactly as "shame of face," meaning **utter shame** or "humiliation" (cf. Jer. 7:19; Ps. 44:15; Lam. 2:15-16; etc.)—all symbolize the divine punishments. By the expression **kings of the lands** Ezra was certainly suggesting Assyria (II Kings 17:5-6) and especially Babylonia (II Kings 24:14-15; 25:6-7), who brought Israel to ruin and degradation. He expresses no resentment against the nations for their acts against Israel, since he considered all of it, and even more, as justly deserved for Israel's sin (vs. 13).

8. And now (cf. vss. 10, 12) marks a rapid transition in thought from the pre-exilic and exilic past of vs. 7 to the near-past and postexilic times. **A brief moment** refers to the interval between 538 B.C. (cf. Ezra 1:1) and the time of Ezra, which was marked not by God's vindictive anger but by his **favor**, even though it was undeserved (cf. vs. 13). The favor was shown first by God's failure to blot out offending Israel entirely and by his leaving **a remnant** or nucleus for a new start. Such a concept of a remnant is found in the most optimistic passages in the prophetic books (cf. Amos 5:15; Isa. 4:3;

9 For we *were* bondmen; yet our God hath not forsaken us in our bondage, but hath extended mercy unto us in the sight of the kings of Persia, to give us a reviving, to set up the house of our God, and to repair the desolations thereof, and to give us a wall in Judah and in Jerusalem.

reviving in our bondage. 9 For we are bondmen; yet our God has not forsaken us in our bondage, but has extended to us his steadfast love before the kings of Persia, to grant us some reviving to set up the house of our God, to repair its ruins, and to give us protection*m* in Judea and Jerusalem.

m Heb *a wall*

6:13; 10:22; Jer. 24:8; etc.) where the idea of **escape** is stressed. Sometimes the remnant was thought to be the Jews who escaped exile, but to Ezra, like the Chronicler, the remnant meant the exiles who later returned to Judea. Another evidence of favor was the **nail** or **tent-pin** the Jews had in God's **holy place**, Judea and Jerusalem. The figure is that of a tent peg driven in to give **a secure hold.** The reference is to the security of the re-established Jewish community. The nomadic figure would be natural for one who had but a few months before traveled far, living in a tent (cf. 8:15), and would be appreciated by others who had made a similar journey. A third token of favor was the brightening of the eyes, the restoration of the spirit and life of the people (cf. I Sam. 14:29; Pss. 13:3; 19:8; Prov. 29:13). A fourth sign of favor was the **little reviving** the Jews had enjoyed in their restored community. The rare Hebrew word used (*miḥyâh*) means "preservation of life" (cf. Gen. 45:5; II Chr. 14:13). Because a reference to **bondage** seemed difficult here during the Persian period, it was proposed to revocalize the Hebrew text of **in our bondage** (*be'abhduthēnû*) to read "by means of our works" (*ba'abhōdhāthēnû;* Ehrlich, *op. cit.,* VII, 177-78). But vs. 9 seizes and presumably expands the concepts of **bondage** and **little reviving** of vs. 8, as though it were a commentary on them.

9. As an admission of subjection to Persia (cf. Neh. 9:36-37), it is preferable to read **we are bondmen** rather than **we were bondmen,** referring to earlier times, for even under the Persians Judea was not free. Favor **before the kings of Persia** resulted in the revival of Jewish life, re-establishment of the temple, the repair of the city ruins, and the building of the city wall.

The **wall in Judah and in Jerusalem** has caused much debate. The word used for **wall** (*gādhēr*) is rare in late Hebrew and then is used only of an actual low wall or fence about vineyards (Isa. 5:5; Ps. 80:12), bordering a road (Num. 22:24; cf. Eccl. 10:8), or in the temple court (Ezek. 42:7). It is debatable whether the term is used of the city wall in Mic. 7:11 (Heinrich Kaupel, "Die Bedeutung von גדר in Esr 9, 9," *Biblische Zeitschrift,* XXII [1934], 89-92; "Zu גדר en Esr. 9, 9," *Biblica,* XVI [1935], 213-14; Andrés Fernández, "La Voz גדר en Esd. 9, 9," and "Esdr. 9, 9 y un Texto de Josefo," *Biblica,* XVI [1935], 82-84; XVIII [1937], 207-8). Since Ezra is listing actual accomplishments—progress toward recovery—the wall must be an actual one (cf. Mowinckel, *Ezra den Skriftlaerde,* p. 71; W. O. E. Oesterley and T. H. Robinson, *A History of Israel* [Oxford: Clarendon Press, 1932], II, 117; Kapelrud, *op. cit.,* pp. 66-67; Rowley, *Servant of the Lord,* pp. 140-43). The reference may be to a defensive city wall, but one cannot argue for the priority of Nehemiah in Jerusalem from this fact, for, as some have recognized, the poignancy of Nehemiah's grief over the ruined walls of Jerusalem can best be explained by news of a recent destruction of the city walls (cf. 4:23) rather than that long before, in 586 B.C. (J. S. Wright, *The Date of Ezra's Coming to Jerusalem* [London: Tyndale Press, 1947], pp. 7, 18-19). The earliest attempts to rebuild Jerusalem must have involved the building of some sort of defensive rampart, even before the coming of Nehemiah. The location of the wall **in Judea and Jerusalem** is awkward and somewhat tautological but by no means impossible. It is unnecessary to omit either of the terms, as has been proposed (Batten, *op. cit.,* p. 334). Nor is it necessary, therefore, to regard the expression as figurative rather than literal (cf. Rudolph, *op. cit.,* p. 88) and to translate **protection** instead of **wall,** even though a similar word (*gédher*) is used

10 And now, O our God, what shall we say after this? for we have forsaken thy commandments,

11 Which thou hast commanded by thy servants the prophets, saying, The land, unto which ye go to possess it, is an unclean land with the filthiness of the people of the lands, with their abominations, which have filled it from one end to another with their uncleanness.

12 Now therefore give not your daughters unto their sons, neither take their daughters unto your sons, nor seek their peace or their wealth for ever: that ye may be strong, and eat the good of the land, and leave it for an inheritance to your children for ever.

13 And after all that is come upon us for

10 "And now, O our God, what shall we say after this? For we have forsaken thy commandments, 11 which thou didst command by thy servants the prophets, saying, 'The land which you are entering, to take possession of it, is a land unclean with the pollutions of the peoples of the lands, with their abominations which have filled it from end to end with their uncleanness. 12 Therefore give not your daughters to their sons, neither take their daughters for your sons, and never seek their peace or prosperity, that you may be strong, and eat the good of the land, and leave it for an inheritance to your children for ever.' 13 And after all

in a figurative sense by the later rabbis when they refer to "a fence [gédher] around the law," i.e., a protection for the biblical precepts when restrictions were imposed to curb violations of biblical law (Julius H. Greenstone, "Gezerah," *Jewish Encyclopedia* [New York: Funk & Wagnalls Co., 1906], V, 648b).

10-12. Again with **and now** (cf. vs. 8) attention suddenly shifts to the terrible contemporary situation. Vss. 11-12 present the scriptural basis for Ezra's marriage reforms. As elements in a prayer they are not precise citations of scripture such as might be expected of one whose prime mission was to teach and establish the law. But the data are presented as prophetic teaching rather than law, and the writer seems unaware of the sharp distinction between law and prophecy which is characteristic of later Judaism. The usage reflects a fluid stage in the formulation of legislation, when the sources are regarded as prophetic (cf. Bertholet, *op. cit.,* p. 41). Only in Malachi (2:11-16), however, does prophetic teaching involve this problem of foreign marriage. The verses are a medley of scriptural bits quoted sometimes in slightly modified form from Deuteronomy (cf. 7:1, 3, 12; 23:6) and loosely joined by biblical allusions which, in one instance at least (vs. 11; cf. Lev. 18:24-30), represent a free adaptation of other biblical texts. The writer, well versed in scripture, seems not bound to be exact, and can therefore freely adapt biblical ideas to make his own case clear and impressive. The Chronicler's hand is evident throughout and Torrey, who finds similar treatment of scripture in II Chr. 36:21, claims: "The Chronicler quotes as he writes—carelessly and irresponsibly" (*Ezra Studies,* p. 271, note s).

To possess it is a characteristic Deuteronomic expression (cf. Deut. 7:1). The words **unclean** and **filthiness** or **pollutions** are characteristic of priestly writings in Ezekiel and Leviticus, where they have specific ritualistic connotation. Canaan was regarded not as **unclean** but as desirable when the Hebrews entered (cf. Deut. 8:7 ff.; Num. 13:27-28). Involved here, as in Lev. 18:24-30, is the idea that the good land can be defiled by contagion (cf. 8:28) of **unclean** foreigners and their practices. **Give not your daughters,** etc., is adapted from Deut. 7:3. But Ezra mentions no Jewish women married to foreigners. **Nor seek their peace** loosely quotes Deut. 23:6 but extends the prohibitions against Ammonites and Moabites to all foreigners. **Their . . . prosperity** is, lit., "their good things." On **peace** and **prosperity,** cf. Jer. 33:9; Lam. 3:17. **That you may be strong** is a fragment of Deut. 11:8. The expression, **eat the good of the land**—i.e., its best produce (Gen. 45:18, 20) —seems to be drawn from Isa. 1:19.

13-14. These verses form a single sentence interrupted abruptly by a parenthetical comment (vs. 13b). Such incomplete expression is characteristic of the Chronicler's style

our evil deeds, and for our great trespass, seeing that thou our God hast punished us less than our iniquities *deserve,* and hast given us *such* deliverance as this;

14 Should we again break thy commandments, and join in affinity with the people of these abominations? wouldest not thou be angry with us till thou hadst consumed *us,* so that *there should be* no remnant nor escaping?

15 O Lord God of Israel, thou *art* righteous; for we remain yet escaped, as *it is* this day: behold, we *are* before thee in our trespasses; for we cannot stand before thee because of this.

10 Now when Ezra had prayed, and when he had confessed, weeping and casting himself down before the house of God, there assembled unto him out of Israel

that has come upon us for our evil deeds and for our great guilt, seeing that thou, our God, hast punished us less than our iniquities deserved and hast given us such a remnant as this, **14** shall we break thy commandments again and intermarry with the peoples who practice these abominations? Wouldst thou not be angry with us till thou wouldst consume us, so that there should be no remnant, nor any to escape? **15** O Lord the God of Israel, thou art just, for we are left a remnant that has escaped, as at this day. Behold, we are before thee in our guilt, for none can stand before thee because of this."

10 While Ezra prayed and made confession, weeping and casting himself

(Driver, *op. cit.,* p. 537, No. 27). **All that has come** presents syntax found often in his work (cf. vs. 17; 8:25) and probably not elsewhere (Kautzsch, *Gesenius' Hebrew Grammar,* sec. 138*i-k*). The reference is to the Exile and the accompanying degradation (cf. vs. 7). The comment in vs. 13*b* in English interprets an awkward Hebrew text, ". . . has held back downwards more than our sins [deserve]" or ". . . has held back downwards some of our sins." For "has held back" (חשכת) nine Hebrew MSS and the Peshitta have the graphically similar "hast reckoned" (חשבת), which may be original. Although the punishment of Israel was heavy (vs. 7), it would have been even greater if they had received retribution proportionate to the offense. God's grace lightened the punishment and saved a remnant as a nucleus for rebuilding (vs. 8). **Deliverance** (vs. 13) is closer than **remnant** to the original Hebrew word "escape" (cf. vs. 8). Josephus comments: "For though they had done things deserving of death, it was in keeping with the kindness of God to exempt even such sinners from punishment" (*Antiquities* XI. 5. 3).

15. In a dramatically effective emotional passage Ezra draws his audience with him in humility before the bar of the divine Judge without a defense. All confess their **guilt**. **Stand before** probably has the judicial meaning of "to win vindication." **Righteous** or **just** used of God is a confession that God has a just case against Israel (cf. II Chr. 12:6). Mercy is hoped for but no merciful second chance is expected. For two-time offenders full and complete punishment is expected, possibly with additional severity to compensate for the mercy formerly granted but abused. The tense emotional scene is psychologically contrived to induce just such action as is described in ch. 10.

C. Public Reaction to Ezra's Distress (10:1-6=I Esdras 8:91–9:2)

The narrative of ch. 9 continues without interruption through ch. 10, but with a shift after the prayer (9:6-15) from the first person (7:27–9:15) to the third person (cf. 7:1-26). The shift has been explained by the hypothesis that the Chronicler here used a revised and amplified edition of the Ezra narrative and was thus responsible for recasting

10:1-44. *Effectual Repentance.*—The final chapter raises another question for the Christian message that goes well beneath all the issues concerning the historicity of this last unhappy scene, about which scholars differ widely; and likewise beyond the question of the rights and

wrongs of Ezra's harsh policy in breaking up mixed marriages regardless of the rights of the wives and children involved, as we in our later day see and feel them. The strength of Ezra's own conviction, and the moving sincerity of his prayer of confession on behalf of his people, for

a very great congregation of men and women and children: for the people wept very sore.

2 And Shechaniah the son of Jehiel, *one* of the sons of Elam, answered and said unto Ezra, We have trespassed against our God, and have taken strange wives of the people of the land: yet now there is hope in Israel concerning this thing.

3 Now therefore let us make a covenant with our God to put away all the wives, and such as are born of them, according to the counsel of my lord, and of those that tremble at the commandment of our God; and let it be done according to the law.

down before the house of God, a very great assembly of men, women, and children, gathered to him out of Israel; for the people wept bitterly. 2 And Shecani'ah the son of Jehi'el, of the sons of Elam, addressed Ezra: "We have broken faith with our God and have married foreign women from the peoples of the lands, but even now there is hope for Israel in spite of this. 3 Therefore let us make a covenant with our God to put away all these wives and their children, according to the counsel of my lord and of those who tremble at the commandment of our God; and let it be done according to the law.

---

it. But the existence of such a document, called "both elusive and imaginary," cannot be otherwise demonstrated (Pfeiffer, *Intro. to O.T.*, p. 832, n. 11). The difference in person has sometimes been explained as a reflection of the mood of the Chronicler who, when the third person was used, "did not happen to identify himself, in imagination, with his hero" (Torrey, *Ezra Studies*, p. 272, note w; cf. p. 245).

10:1. Hebrew MSS support both translations, **when Ezra had prayed** and **while Ezra prayed,** but the latter is preferable since it was the action and prayer that attracted the crowd. Such use of temporal clauses at the beginning of a sentence has been recognized as a stylistic characteristic of the Chronicler (Driver, *op. cit.*, p. 538, No. 37; cf. E. L. Curtis and Albert A. Madsen, *A Critical and Exegetical Commentary on the Books of Chronicles* [New York: Charles Scribner's Sons, 1910; "International Critical Commentary"], p. 35). **Casting himself down** might imply further prostration during prayer (cf. Neh. 8:6) but it probably means simply "fallen to his knees" (cf. 9:5). Ezra prayed **before the house of God** (cf. 4:24; 5:8; etc.), a place favored for prayer (Isa. 56:7; cf. Luke 18:10; Acts 3:1). **Confession** refers to the admission of guilt in the prayer (9:7, 13, 15). Unlike some prophets (cf. Jer. 31:29-34; Ezek. 18:1-9), Ezra stressed the older concept of group responsibility wherein one sinner contaminated his whole group, making even the innocent subject to penalty (cf. Josh. 7:24 ff.). The concept was fortified by the fact that captivity, exile, and return were regarded as group experiences, shared by guilty and innocent alike. Ezra attracted spectators from among the pious who had come to pray (cf. 9:4). The informal group is better called "crowd" or "multitude," as in I Esdras, even though it is described by a Hebrew term (*qāhāl*) later used for the formal **assembly** or **congregation.** Since **out of Israel** is used in an ethnic rather than geographical sense, it means "of the people of Israel."

2-4. Spokesman for the bystanders was a descendant of **Elam** (cf. 2:7, 31), **Shecaniah,** whose name resembles the *mši-kin-iliᵖˡ* of a cuneiform document of the time of Darius (A. T. Clay, *Business Documents of Murashû Sons of Nippur Dated in the Reign of Darius II* [Philadelphia: University of Pennsylvania, 1904], No. 110, I. 3). Since he was probably the son of one who had married a foreign woman (cf. vs. 26), the problem was a vital one for him. Like Ezra, he placed himself among the guilty by using the words **we have,** but there is no evidence that he was an actual offender. Josephus

---

sins of which he himself was not guilty, made such a deep impression—not only on leaders like Shecaniah (vs. 2), but on many of the people (vs. 12)—that in spite of division and opposition in some quarters (vs. 15), the laborious task of investigation and decision, by what we

would nowadays call a commission, was carried out through a period of three months.

We are mercifully spared any account of the heartaches and cruelties which any such thoroughgoing policy must have involved; and we would be interested to know how generally the

4 Arise; for *this* matter *belongeth* unto thee: we also *will be* with thee: be of good courage, and do *it*.

5 Then arose Ezra, and made the chief priests, the Levites, and all Israel, to swear that they should do according to this word. And they sware.

4 Arise, for it is your task, and we are with you; be strong and do it." 5 Then Ezra arose and made the leading priests and Levites and all Israel take oath that they would do as had been said. So they took the oath.

---

calls him "the head [*prōtos*] of the people of Jerusalem," but there is no evidence that he had official position.

More optimistic than Ezra, Shecaniah announced **even now there is hope for Israel.** On the basis of Arabic usage one might suggest the reading **in spite of this** for the M.T., **concerning this thing** (cf. 8:23; 9:15; Torrey, *Ezra Studies*, p. 272). The proposal for mending the broken relationship with God called for undoing as far as possible the "wrong" that had been done, and for trusting in the grace of God for forgiveness for what could not be undone. The remedy is harsh, ignoring human anguish and reflecting the low estimate of women and children as chattels to be disposed of at will, disregarding their desire and ignoring their human rights. It is in full agreement with the historically ruthless attitude of the Hebrews toward non-Hebraic inhabitants of Palestine (cf. Josh. 9:24-27; 11:20, 22-23; I Sam. 27:9, 11; II Sam. 8:2; 11:1; etc.). **Put away,** however, means not annihilation since it is, lit., "eject" or "send forth," implying brutal exclusion from the Jewish community of loved ones, many of whom were partially of Hebrew blood. The expression **these wives** or "such wives" (*ibid.*) interprets the M.T., which has "all women," without further qualification. But the original text must have been "all our wives," as in I Esdras^AB, since such an error is easy in written Hebrew (Rudolph, *Esra und Nehemia*, p. 92).

The reform was to constitute a renewal of the **covenant** between the people and their God, the contractual obligation whereby God was to guarantee the prosperity and protection of Israel in exchange for their recognition of him as the only God and their unquestioned obedience to his will. By **the law** is meant that which Ezra had recently introduced in Judea (cf. Neh. 8), but the present Pentateuchal legislation has no prohibition against foreign marriages in general (cf. 9:11-12). Because the matter was regarded as an infraction of the law, it was recognized as **the task** of Ezra, the proponent of the law (cf. 7:6, 11, 14, 25-26; Neh. 8:1-18).

5-6. With public support proposed for a campaign against foreign marriage, Ezra's plan to induce reform was a success and he was able to abandon his humble state. At once he required an **oath** of the leaders who surrounded him, to the effect that they would support the proposed reform. The oath was a religious act creating mutual confidence because it was a sincere and solemn promise before God (cf. Judg. 11:10), who participated in the action, watching over the agreement. The oath makers were not the comprehensive group indicated by **the chief priests,** etc., which reflects the Chronicler's idea of the whole community, but the leaders of those groups as they were present in the crowd.

The fasting and prayer took place before the temple (cf. vs. 1), which is described as "the court [αὐλῆς] of the temple" in I Esdras 9:2. Withdrawing, Ezra went to a

---

letter of the law was still being carried out when the Chronicler wrote this account. But we are vividly reminded of the power of strong conviction to multiply itself when it is genuinely held even by a comparative few, and of the power of such conviction to mold the future of a nation's thought and life. **We have broken faith with our God . . . , but even now there is hope for**

Israel in spite of this. Therefore let us make a covenant with our God. . . . Arise, for it is your task, and we are with you; be strong and do it. (Vss. 2-4.)

On that soul-searching note the book abruptly closes. But all later Judaism brings its cumulative evidence of the tenacious influence of such contagious repentance and resolve.

6 ¶ Then Ezra rose up from before the house of God, and went into the chamber of Johanan the son of Eliashib: and *when* he came thither, he did eat no bread, nor drink water: for he mourned because of the transgression of them that had been carried away.

7 And they made proclamation throughout Judah and Jerusalem unto all the children of the captivity, that they should gather themselves together unto Jerusalem;

6 Then Ezra withdrew from before the house of God, and went to the chamber of Jehoha'nan the son of Eli'ashib, where he spent the night,[n] neither eating bread nor drinking water; for he was mourning over the faithlessness of the exiles. 7 And a proclamation was made throughout Judah and Jerusalem to all the returned exiles that

[n] 1 Esdras 9. 2. Heb *where he went*

---

chamber (cf. 8:29), which I Esdras 9:1 and Josephus interpret as the priests' quarters (παστοφόριον). Such rooms, connected with the sanctuary, were sometimes used as storerooms (cf. Neh. 13:4 ff.), which led to the translation "treasury" in the LXX. Jeremiah's prophecy was read before an assembly in such a room (Jer. 36:10).

The **chamber** belonged to **Jehohanan the son of Eliashib**, whose identity, much debated, is important for the problem of the chronological sequence of Ezra and Nehemiah (cf. Intro., p. 562). Although **Jehohanan** is a common name in the postexilic period, it appears in Ezra-Nehemiah twice with the same paternity, evidently for the same person. **Eliashib** was high priest in the time of Nehemiah (3:1) and **Jehohanan** is high priest in the time of Darius II (*ca.* 408 B.C.; Cowley, *Aramaic Papyri,* p. 114, No. 30, l. 18). Since **Jehohanan** was grandson or descendant of **Eliashib**, rather than his son (Neh. 12:10-11, 22; cf. Ezra 5:1), several generations separated the two high priesthoods. Since Nehemiah was a contemporary of **Eliashib** (Neh. 3:1; 13:4) and **Jehohanan** is here a contemporary of Ezra, the sequence Nehemiah-Ezra is demonstrated (A. Van Hoonacker, "La succession chronologique Néhémie-Esdras," *Revue Biblique* XXXII [1923], 481-94; XXXIII [1924], 33-64). But it has been denied that **Jehohanan** in 10:6, who does not bear the title of high priest, has anything to do with the high priesthood (Wellhausen, "Die Rückkehr der Juden aus dem babylonischen Exil," p. 168). It is also proposed that **Jehohanan** may have been a son of the high priest **Eliashib** and a brother of Joiada (cf. Neh. 12:10-11, 22), not in the line of succession and therefore not the later high priest of the name but only a simple priest with quarters at the sanctuary (Wright, *Date of Ezra's Coming to Jerusalem,* p. 20). But lack of title is not significant since, unlike Neh. 3:1, the high priest is never given a title in the Ezra story (3:2, 8, 9; 4:3; 5:2). Inasmuch as there is no further description of **Jehohanan**, some well-known person must be meant (cf. Bernhard Stade, *Geschichte des Volkes Israel* [Berlin: G. Grote, 1888], II, 153, n. 1). A semiofficial person like Ezra would scarcely be entertained by an unknown or subordinate official within the sanctuary; his host must therefore have been the high priest (Albright, "Date and Personality of the Chronicler," p. 121). The verb וילך, **and when he came**, is a simple scribal corruption of וילן, **where he spent the night**, as I Esdras 9:2, the Peshitta, and the LXX[L] show. There Ezra continued the fast begun that day (9:5).

D. PUBLIC ASSEMBLY (10:7-15=I Esdras 9:3-15)

7-8. Actual reform began with a great public assembly summoned by the secular authority in Jerusalem, the leaders and elders (vs. 8). The M.T. can be read either **they made proclamation**, with an indefinite subject, or **a proclamation was made.** The **proclamation** presupposes a courier (cf. 1:1) to spread the summons through **Judah and Jerusalem.** The **order** issued, which the LXX translates "decree" (βουλή), is the same word used in "the counsel of my lord" in vs. 3. Promptness and full participation were ensured by a severe penalty imposed on laggards and those who ignored the summons. The penalties were within Ezra's power to impose (cf. 7:26), but he delegated his powers as an administrator, as elsewhere (cf. 8:24-29; Neh. 8:4, 7-8). As part of the

8 And that whosoever would not come within three days, according to the counsel of the princes and the elders, all his substance should be forfeited, and himself separated from the congregation of those that had been carried away.

9 ¶ Then all the men of Judah and Benjamin gathered themselves together unto Jerusalem within three days. It *was* the ninth month, on the twentieth *day* of the month; and all the people sat in the street of the house of God, trembling because of *this* matter, and for the great rain.

10 And Ezra the priest stood up, and said unto them, Ye have transgressed, and have taken strange wives, to increase the trespass of Israel.

11 Now therefore make confession unto the LORD God of your fathers, and do his pleasure: and separate yourselves from the

they should assemble at Jerusalem, 8 and that if any one did not come within three days, by order of the officials and the elders all his property should be forfeited, and he himself banned from the congregation of the exiles.

9 Then all the men of Judah and Benjamin assembled at Jerusalem within the three days; it was the ninth month, on the twentieth day of the month. And all the people sat in the open square before the house of God, trembling because of this matter and because of the heavy rain. 10 And Ezra the priest stood up and said to them, "You have trespassed and married foreign women, and so increased the guilt of Israel. 11 Now then make confession to the LORD the God of your fathers, and do

---

Persian Empire, subject to control and close observation (4:11 ff.; 5:6-17), not even a Jewish executive council could act in the proposed highhanded manner without such consent of the government as Ezra had won (7:26). **Property** of the guilty was to be confiscated, but the term used originally meant that it was to be devoted to God and condemned to human use (cf. Josh. 6:17-21). Both I Esdras 9:4 and Josephus interpret it here as "seized for the use of the temple."

The guilty were to be **banned**, ostracized from the society of true Israel. The Hebrew word translated **congregation** (*qāhāl*; cf. vs. 1) here means the politico-ethnic group of Jews. Only **exiles** were believed to constitute this group, but the Peshitta properly interprets it as "the people of Israel." In vs. 9, as in 1:5; 4:1, **Judah and Benjamin** indicate the extent of the restored community. The northern boundary of Judah was traced south of Jerusalem (Josh. 15:8; 18:16), which was counted as Benjaminite (Judg. 1:21), as in the Talmud later, where it is claimed that the major part of the temple was in Benjamin with the great altar of sacrifice on Judean soil (Sanhedrin 54; Yoma 12). Although the sympathies of Benjamin were largely with the seceding tribes at the division of the kingdom (cf. II Sam. 20:1-2; I Kings 12:20), the Chronicler, as well as the priestly writer later, regarded **Judah and Benjamin** as the two tribes loyal to the house of David (I Kings 12:12=II Chr. 11:1).

9. The assembly was held at the end of three days (vs. 8), on the twentieth day of the ninth month (Kislev), presumably in the year of Ezra's arrival (7:8), which would be December 18, 397 B.C. The month usually marks the beginning of **the great rain** of Palestine, when the **heavy rain** (cf. I Kings 18:41; Ezek. 13:11) saturates the earth and fills the cisterns. It was, as I Esdras 9:6 interprets, "the onset of winter storms," for the rains, often icy cold, reached the peak of intensity during December and January, and snow could fall and the temperature could drop below freezing. The crowd, temporarily gathered into the city and unhoused, were **trembling** in the open, apparently in the plaza where the law was read (Neh. 8:1, 3, 16). The Hebrew word (*reḥôbh*) denotes breadth of space and is used sometimes parallel to "outside" (Jer. 5:1). It is often used of a place near a gate (cf. II Chr. 32:6; Job 29:7) where assemblies were held (II Chr. 29:4) and proclamations and speeches were made (Prov. 1:20; Esth. 6:9, 11).

10-11. Ezra first accused the anxious but uncomfortable people of contracting foreign marriages, and with "and now" (cf 5:17) he turned abruptly to outline things to be done to avert disaster. After **confession** there must be a positive pleasing of God shown

people of the land, and from the strange wives.

12 Then all the congregation answered and said with a loud voice, As thou hast said, so must we do.

13 But the people *are* many, and *it is* a time of much rain, and we are not able to stand without, neither *is this* a work of one day or two: for we are many that have transgressed in this thing.

14 Let now our rulers of all the congregation stand, and let all them which have taken strange wives in our cities come at appointed times, and with them the elders of every city, and the judges thereof, until the fierce wrath of our God for this matter be turned from us.

his will; separate yourselves from the peoples of the land and from the foreign wives." 12 Then all the assembly answered with a loud voice, "It is so; we must do as you have said. 13 But the people are many, and it is a time of heavy rain; we cannot stand in the open. Nor is this a work for one day or for two; for we have greatly transgressed in this matter. 14 Let our officials stand for the whole assembly; let all in our cities who have taken foreign wives come at appointed times, and with them the elders and judges of every city, till the fierce wrath of our God over this matter be averted from

---

by the avoidance of contamination by foreign marriages. **Do his pleasure** approximates the M.T., while **do his will** reflects the interpretation of I Esdras, which pointedly stresses obedience to the law. With **separate yourselves** Ezra endorses the remedy proposed by Shecaniah (vs. 3). Since the Jews were in the majority, the exclusion of the others is implied (cf. vs. 19; Neh. 13:30).

12-15. The people readily accepted Ezra's proposals, but there were differences of opinion regarding practical procedure (vs. 13). The **loud voice** (vs. 12) is stressed to indicate the earnestness and like-mindedness of the group. There was but little opposition (cf. vs. 15). But the people argued that the number of cases needing investigation, the size of the unhoused crowd, and the severity of the weather prevented an immediate solution. **The people** were not the foreigners to be excluded, since they would be called "foreign women" (cf. vss. 2, 11), so the motive was not consideration for the victims but concern for the shivering crowd. **We cannot stand** (vs. 13) is idiomatic for "we cannot remain" (Torrey, *Ezra Studies,* p. 273). **In the open** translates the M.T. literally.

It was determined (vs. 14) to establish a Jerusalem commission to hear the cases of those accused after the assembly dispersed. The cases were to be forwarded to Jerusalem for trial from the villages and cities where preliminary hearings and investigations were held. Local officials at **appointed times** (vs. 14) accompanied the accused to Jerusalem, presumably as complaining witnesses and observers. The author reflects the Chronicler's view of local judgeships (cf. II Chr. 19:5-7), and it was one of Ezra's functions to appoint judges (cf. 7:25). Reference to local as well as higher courts in the Persian judicial system (Cowley, *op. cit.,* pp. 50-51, No. 16 [435 b.c.]) makes it likely that there could have been such organization in the time of Ezra.

Although the M.T. may be understood as **until the fierce wrath . . . be turned** (vs. 14), it is preferable to regard it as purposive with the LXX, "to turn away the fierce wrath." The former would indicate that the reform would not be stopped short of its goal, even though the community were to feel that it had done enough to be safe from God's wrath. For the M.T. "until this matter," the versions show that the reading should be **over this matter,** for על, **over,** has been changed to the similar עד, **until,** perhaps under the influence of **until the fierce wrath.**

It has been suggested that Neh. 9:1-2, now out of place, should follow Ezra 10:14 to introduce popular mourning and confession on the twenty-fourth day of the ninth month (Dec. 20, 398 b.c.), an ancient annual fast day for the winter solstice (Julian Morgenstern, "The Chanukkah Festival and the Calendar of Ancient Israel," *Hebrew Union College Annual,* XX [1947], 19-22). But under such circumstances the actual separation of the mixed families (Neh. 9:2) would occur before the completion of the

15 ¶ Only Jonathan the son of Asahel and Jahaziah the son of Tikvah were employed about this *matter:* and Meshullam and Shabbethai the Levite helped them.

16 And the children of the captivity did so. And Ezra the priest, *with* certain chief of the fathers, after the house of their fathers, and all of them by *their* names, were separated, and sat down in the first day of the tenth month to examine the matter.

17 And they made an end with all the men that had taken strange wives by the first day of the first month.

us." 15 Only Jonathan the son of As'ahel and Jahzei'ah the son of Tikvah opposed this, and Meshul'lam and Shab'bethai the Levite supported them.

16 Then the returned exiles did so. Ezra the priest selected men,[o] heads of fathers' houses, according to their fathers' houses, each of them designated by name. On the first day of the tenth month they sat down to examine the matter; 17 and by the first day of the first month they had come to the end of all the men who had married foreign women.

[o] 1 Esdras 9. 16. Syr: Heb *and there were selected Ezra,* etc.

---

preparation to do so (Ezra 10:16 ff.; cf. Rudolph, *Esra und Nehemia,* p. 155). It is preferable to regard Neh. 9 as a continuation of Ezra 10 (cf. Torrey, *Composition,* p. 32; *Ezra Studies,* pp. 254, 274, note p; Rudolph, *op. cit.,* p. 154).

Vs. 15 parenthetically indicates opposition to the reform procedure. Although **all the assembly** agreed with Ezra (vs. 12), several men opposed the ruthless proposal. Such opposition should be expected (cf. Neh. 13:25, 28), but admission of it runs counter to the Chronicler's view (cf. vss. 12-13). Although such detail lends verisimilitude to the story, it has been regarded by some as a realistic touch created by the Chronicler (cf. instances of such a practice in I Chr. 21:6; II Chr. 28:12; 30:10-11, 18; Neh. 7:61-65; etc.; Torrey, *Ezra Studies,* p. 273, note h). The interpretation **were employed** (cf. I Esdras 9:14) rests upon a faulty text of the LXX. The M.T. has simply "stood," but the word should be read with the following preposition "against," to mean **opposed.** The restrictive **only,** introducing the verse, indicates but light opposition. **Meshullam** (cf. 8:16) is a name found in late cuneiform documents and was also popular among Jews of the Persian period (K. L. Tallqvist, *Neubabylonisches Namenbuch* [Helsingfors: 1905], pp. 113, 114; Cowley, *op. cit.,* p. 298). **Shabbethai** is a Babylonian-type name also found frequently in cuneiform sources and the papyri (Samuel Daiches, "Einige nach babylonischem Muster gebildete hebräische Namen," *Orientalische Literaturzeitung,* XI [1908], 278). **Shabbethai** is called a **Levite** (cf. 2:40), but several Hebrew MSS, the LXX[L], and I Esdras[L] have "the Levites," including **Meshullam** also in the group.

Them of **supported them** is ambiguous. By reading "but Meshullam" for **and Meshullam** the Levites are regarded as loyal to Ezra and the majority, but it is possible that **them** refers to the dissident faction (Morgenstern, *op. cit.,* p. 25).

E. ACTION OF THE JERUSALEM COMMISSION (10:16-19=I Esdras 9:15-20)

16. Did so now refers to the substance of vs. 14, the appearance of the guilty at the Jerusalem court. The present Hebrew text is corrupt and difficult to interpret. It seems to describe the constitution of the Jerusalem court. To read **Ezra the priest selected men,** the passive verb of the M.T. must be revocalized and made singular. The LXX[L], I Esdras 9:16, and the Peshitta have "Ezra the priest selected for himself." The "for himself" (לו) has been combined with the verb **selected** to produce the clumsy plural verb "they selected."

If **did so** refers to the action of Neh. 9:1-2, the keeping of a festival and the actual separation from foreigners, and not to the organization of the Jerusalem court, the reference to **Ezra** must be excised and the passive plural verb must be retained with "certain men" as its subject: "certain men were selected." Thus, "And certain men, family heads, . . . separated themselves" (Morgenstern, *loc. cit.*).

The men **selected** were chosen by ancestral line. Such lines are clearly discernible in the organization of the lists given in Ezra (cf. vss. 25 ff.; 2:3 ff.) and Nehemiah. The

18 ¶ And among the sons of the priests there were found that had taken strange wives: *namely,* of the sons of Jeshua the son of Jozadak, and his brethren; Maaseiah, and Eliezer, and Jarib, and Gedaliah.

19 And they gave their hands that they would put away their wives; and *being* guilty, *they offered* a ram of the flock for their trespass.

20 And of the sons of Immer; Hanani, and Zebadiah.

18 Of the sons of the priests who had married foreign women were found Maasei'ah, Elie'zer, Jarib, and Gedali'ah, of the sons of Jeshua the son of Jo'zadak and his brethren. 19 They pledged themselves to put away their wives, and their guilt offering was a ram of the flock for their guilt. 20 Of the sons of Immer: Hana'ni and Zebadi'ah.

---

number is uncertain but the Peshitta independently inserts the figure "twenty." That number may represent a rounding of the number of secular families in 2:3-20 since, if Joab (2:6; 8:9) is regarded as a separate family, there are nineteen primary secular families in the list. **By name** may be a vestige of the formula "expressed by names" (cf. 8:20) favored by the Chronicler (cf. I Chr. 4:38, 41; 12:31; 16:41; etc.; cf. Num. 1:17; Driver, *Intro. to Literature of O.T.,* p. 536, No. 12). Lack of a list here indicates that none was available for the Chronicler, who liked lists and would have inserted it in full. That none is composed here by him is important in estimating the validity of lists he does present. It has been suggested however that **by name** might mean "with names," indicating that the men described were "persons of reputation" (cf. Gen. 6:4; Morgenstern, *loc. cit.*).

It is proposed to place Neh. 10:28-30 [Hebrew 10:29-31] between vs. 16*a* and vs. 16*b* (*ibid.,* pp. 23-28), since that description of the action of separation from the foreigners and the taking of an oath would be more appropriate here than in its present location.

The date of the first session of the Jerusalem commission was December 26, 398 B.C., about thirteen days after the great assembly (cf. vs. 9). By the **first day of the first month** the work was finished at Jerusalem—April 23, 397 B.C., assuming the intercalation of an extra month in Palestine as in the Babylonian calendar in 397 B.C., which extended the period of examination somewhat (R. A. Parker and W. H. Dubberstein, *Babylonian Chronology 626 B.C.–A.D. 45* [Chicago: University of Chicago Press, 1942], p. 32). Since **they made an end** refers not to the punishment of the guilty but to the conclusion of the processing of those investigated, it is preferable to read **they had come to the end of.**

18-19. Foreign marriages constituted a **trespass** (vs. 19), an unintentional breach of faith which could be rectified. The term "ignorance," (ἄγνοια) is used for it in I Esdras 9:20. One guilty of **trespass** must first right the wrong done and then make peace with God through a **guilt offering.** It is preferable to read **their guilt offering** (אשמם) for the impossible **guilty** (אשמים) of the M.T. (Abraham Kuenen, *Gesammelte Abhandlungen zur biblischen Wissenschaft,* tr. Karl Budde [Leipzig: J. C. B. Mohr, 1894], p. 245; cf. Rudolph, *op. cit.,* p. 96). **A ram of the flock** (cf. 7:17) suggests the law of Lev. 5:15, but I Esdras 9:20, the Vulg., and the Peshitta have "rams" here.

The location of vs. 19*b* prevents misunderstanding that each offender made a sacrifice. Only guilty relatives of the high priest (3:2; 2:36; Hag. 1:12) were expected to offer rams. As in the later law regarding the sin offering (Lev. 4:3, 13-14, 22-23, 27-28, 32), the higher the office and the more responsibility, the greater the penalty exacted for transgression. Listed first and separately (vs. 18) are the guilty of the family of the high priest, who might be expected to set an example for the entire people. These **gave their hands** during the oath, just as Zedekiah took the hand of Nebuchadrezzar in pledging allegiance (Pedersen, *Israel, Its Life and Culture,* I-II, p. 304).

F. List of Those Who Married Foreign Women (10:20-44=I Esdras 9:21-36)

20-23. Although guilty members of the high priest's family are singled out for special attention (vs. 18), guilty persons were found in all four priestly families (cf.

21 And of the sons of Harim; Maaseiah, and Elijah, and Shemaiah, and Jehiel, and Uzziah.

22 And of the sons of Pashur; Elioenai, Maaseiah, Ishmael, Nethaneel, Jozabad, and Elasah.

23 Also of the Levites; Jozabad, and Shimei, and Kelaiah, (the same is Kelita,) Pethahiah, Judah, and Eliezer.

24 Of the singers also; Eliashib: and of the porters; Shallum, and Telem, and Uri.

25 Moreover of Israel: of the sons of Parosh; Ramiah, and Jeziah, and Malchiah, and Miamin, and Eleazar, and Malchijah, and Benaiah.

26 And of the sons of Elam; Mattaniah, Zechariah, and Jehiel, and Abdi, and Jeremoth, and Eliah.

27 And of the sons of Zattu; Elioenai, Eliashib, Mattaniah, and Jeremoth, and Zabad, and Aziza.

28 Of the sons also of Bebai; Jehohanan, Hananiah, Zabbai, and Athlai.

29 And of the sons of Bani; Meshullam, Malluch, and Adaiah, Jashub, and Sheal, and Ramoth.

21 Of the sons of Harim: Ma-asei'ah, Eli'jah, Shemai'ah, Jehi'el, and Uzzi'ah. 22 Of the sons of Pashhur: Eli-o-e'nai, Ma-asei'ah, Ish'mael, Nethan'el, Jo'zabad, and Ela'sah.

23 Of the Levites: Jo'zabad, Shi'me-i, Kelai'ah (that is, Keli'ta), Petha-hi'ah, Judah, and Elie'zer. 24 Of the singers: Eli'ashib. Of the gatekeepers: Shallum, Telem, and Uri.

25 And of Israel: of the sons of Parosh: Rami'ah, Izzi'ah, Malchi'jah, Mi'jamin, Elea'zar, Hashabi'ah,[p] and Benai'ah. 26 Of the sons of Elam: Mattani'ah, Zechari'ah, Jehi'el, Abdi, Jer'emoth, and Eli'jah. 27 Of the sons of Zattu: Eli-o-e'nai, Eli'ashib, Mattani'ah, Jer'emoth, Zabad, and Azi'za. 28 Of the sons of Be'bai were Jeho-ha'nan, Hanani'ah, Zab'bai, and Ath'lai. 29 Of the sons of Bani were Meshul'lam, Malluch, Adai'ah,

[p] 1 Esdras 9. 26. Gk: Heb Malchijah

2:36-39), described as his [i.e., Jeshua's; cf. vs. 18] brethren (cf. 3:2). Following the priests (vss. 18, 20-22), the guilty Levites, who are always associated with the priests (cf. 2:40), are listed (vs. 23). Kelaiah (vs. 23) is identified as Kelita (cf. Neh. 8:7; 10:10) by a gloss older than I Esdras. It has been suggested that the identification may be a parenthetical comment by the Chronicler himself (Bewer, Der Text des Buches Ezra, p. 89). But one singer (2:41) was involved (vs. 24), and there is no reference to guilty Nethinim or children of Solomon's servants (2:43-57), the lowest orders of temple servants, since they were already largely foreigners and outside the law.

25-33. Following the list of temple servants is the much larger list of guilty belonging to the secular families of Israel (cf. 2:2-35). Malchijah (vs. 25) is named twice, but the LXX[NA] and I Esdras[AB] show that the second is an error for Hashabiah. Mijamin (cf. Neh. 10:7; 12:5) is a contraction of Miniamin (Neh. 12:17, 41), found in Neo-Babylonian and Persian cuneiform documents (Clay, Business Documents of Murashû Sons of Nippur, No. 104, l. 2; No. 205, l. 14). The Peshitta has "Benjamin" here, and it is conjectured that the names should be equated (Noth, Personennamen, p. 60, n. 2; Rudolph, op. cit., p. 98). Abdi (vs. 26) abbreviates "Abadiah" (cf. I Esdras[AB]).

Zabad (vs. 27) is for such a name as Zabadiah (cf. 8:8), for which Zabbai (vs. 28; cf. Neh. 3:20) may also be an abbreviation. Names with the element Zabad-, which are found in Babylonian tablets and the papyri, occur with great frequency in the Chronicler's lists and are represented in the N.T. by Zebedee (Matt. 4:21; Mark 1:19; John 21:2; Luke 5:10; Noth, Personennamen, p. 47). Since Bani (vs. 29; cf. 2:10) is read in vs. 34, another name must have been originally here or there. The LXX[BN] suggests "Binnui" (cf. Neh. 7:15), but that also is found in vs. 38 and must be excluded. Graphically similar "Bigvai" (2:14) has been proposed here (Rudolph, op. cit., p. 99). A Meshullam (vs. 29) was among those opposing Ezra's reform (cf. vs. 15). For the unique Sheal (vs. 29) the Peshitta has "Shaul" (Saul), which is better (Jahn, Esra [A und B] und Nehemja, p. 85), but the unusual conjunction before the name may be the corruption

30 And of the sons of Pahath-moab; Adna, and Chelal, Benaiah, Maaseiah, Mattaniah, Bezaleel, and Binnui, and Manasseh.

31 And *of* the sons of Harim; Eliezer, Ishijah, Malchiah, Shemaiah, Shimeon,

32 Benjamin, Malluch, *and* Shemariah.

33 Of the sons of Hashum; Mattenai, Mattathah, Zabad, Eliphelet, Jeremai, Manasseh, *and* Shimei.

34 Of the sons of Bani; Maadai, Amram, and Uel,

35 Benaiah, Bedeiah, Chelluh,

36 Vaniah, Meremoth, Eliashib,

37 Mattaniah, Mattenai, and Jaasau,

38 And Bani, and Binnui, Shimei,

39 And Shelemiah, and Nathan, and Adaiah,

40 Machnadebai, Shashai, Sharai,

Jashub, She'al, and Jer'emoth, 30 Of the
sons of Pa'hath-mo'ab: Adna, Chelal, Be-
nai'ah, Ma-asei'ah, Mattani'ah, Bez'alel,
Bin'nui, and Manas'seh. 31 Of the sons of
Harim: Elie'zer, Isshi'jah, Malchi'jah,
Shemai'ah, Shim'e-on, 32 Benjamin, Mal-
luch, and Shemari'ah. 33 Of the sons of
Hashum: Matte'nai, Mat'tattah, Zabad,
Eliph'elet, Jer'emai, Manas'seh, and
Shim'e-i. 34 Of the sons of Bani: Ma-ada'i,
Amram, Uel, 35 Benai'ah, Bedei'ah, Chel'-
uhi, 36 Vani'ah, Mer'emoth, Eli'ashib,
37 Mattani'ah, Matte'nai, Ja'asu. 38 Of the
sons of Bin'nui:[q] Shim'e-i, 39 Shelemi'ah,
Nathan, Adai'ah, 40 Machnad'ebai, Shashai,

[q] Gk: Heb *Bani, Binnui*

---

of a letter, and I Esdras^{AB}, as well as Oriental MSS, suggests the name Yishal (Bewer, *op. cit.*, p. 91; Rudolph, *loc. cit.*).

Bezalel (vs. 30) is a late type of name (cf. I Chr. 2:20; II Chr. 1:5) from a Babylonian prototype (*^{m}Ina-ṣil-^{d}Nabû;* Tallqvist, *op. cit.*, p. 78; Noth, *Personennamen*, pp. 32, 152). **Manasseh** (vs. 30), like **Joseph** (vs. 42), **Judah** (vs. 23), **Shimeon** (vs. 31), and **Benjamin** (vs. 32), indicates a revival of the use of patriarchal names in postexilic times. For "and the sons of" (vs. 31) many Hebrew MSS and the versions indicate the use of the usual formula **and of the sons of** (KJV).

34-43. These verses are the most corrupt in the list. The twenty-seven names assigned to **Bani** (vss. 34-42) appear excessive since the next largest total is eight (vss. 30-31). Obviously several clans are combined in the total, but it is impossible to sort out the names and identify them by family in every case. The unique **Uel** (vs. 34) is corrupt and should be read "Joel" (cf. Neh. 11:9), as I Esdras^{ABL}, the LXX^{BL}, and the Peshitta show. **Cheluhi** (vs. 35) is corrupt, but it cannot be "Koliahu" or "Jecoliahu" (cf. Bewer, *op. cit.*, p. 92) since the divine name element is otherwise not -iahu in Ezra-Nehemiah (cf. Rudolph, *loc. cit.*). **Vaniah** (vs. 36), which appears to be a Persian name (*Vānya*, "Worthy of Love"), is found also in the Aramaic papyri and ostraca (Cowley, *Aramaic Papyri*, p. 68, No. 22, l. 40; *Corpus Inscriptionum Semiticarum* [Paris: E. Reipublicae Typographeo, 1889], Part II, Vol. I, No. 154, l. 3), but the Peshitta and I Esdras indicate a corrupt text. It is suggested that the versions have the name Jonas (Bewer, *loc. cit.*), but since that does not occur as a family name, it is thought that it might be a corruption for Jorah (cf. 2:18), and that at this point (vs. 36) a new family name is perhaps introduced (Rudolph, *loc. cit.*). For **and Bani** (ובני) in vs. 38 read here the graphically similar **And of the sons of** (ומבני) of the formula (cf. vs. 29), with the LXX^{AB} (cf. LXX^{L} and I Esdras^{L}), and the corrupt Peshitta text.

Machnadebai (vs. 40) seems to contain the element nadbi-, as in Nadbi-el (Lidzbarski, *Ephemeris*, III, 279; cf. Nedabiah in I Chr. 3:18), and in such names as the Moabite Kammusu-nadbi found in a cuneiform document (Luckenbill, *Ancient Records of Assyria and Babylonia*, II, 119, sec. 239). But no god Mach- is known and the Hebrew name may be corrupt. The LXX^{B} with Machad-Nabou suggests the name Nabû or Nebo (2:29), but that family is mentioned in vs. 43. The reading "And of the sons of Ezora" is found in I Esdras^{AB} but that name is otherwise unknown and may represent such a graphically similar name as Azzur (Guthe and Batten, *Ezra and Nehemiah*, p. 43), or more probably Zaccai (זכי; cf. 2:9), which closely resembles the final letters of the element -nadebai (דבי; Bewer, *op. cit.*, p. 93). **Shashai** (vs. 40), found also in the

41 Azareel, and Shelemiah, Shemariah,
42 Shallum, Amariah, *and* Joseph.
43 Of the sons of Nebo; Jeiel, Mattithiah, Zabad, Zebina, Jadau, and Joel, Benaiah.
44 All these had taken strange wives:
and *some* of them had wives by whom they
had children.

Sha'rai, 41 Az'arel, Shelemi'ah, Shemari'ah,
42 Shallum, Amari'ah, and Joseph. 43 Of the
sons of Nebo: Je-i'el, Mattithi'ah, Zabad,
Zebi'na, Jaddai, Jo'el, and Benai'ah. 44 All
these had married foreign women, and they
put them away with their children.[r]

[r] 1 Esdras 9. 36. Heb obscure

---

papyri (Cowley, *op. cit.*, p. 154, No. 49, l. 1), abbreviates a name with the element
mentioning the god Shamash (cf. Sheshbazzar in 1:8). **Zabad** (vs. 43; cf. vss. 27, 33) is
Zaccur in one Hebrew MS and the Peshitta. **Zebina** (vs. 43) is found frequently in
Neo-Babylonian documents. Its meaning ("Bought") has been believed to apply to
orphan or abandoned children (Noth, *Personennamen,* pp. 231-32), but it can as well
signify "Bought from God by means of sacrifices or prayers" (E. R. Bevan, *The House of
Seleucus* [London: Edward Arnold, 1902], II, 305-6).

44. This verse is obviously corrupt since it is ungrammatical and vs. 44*b* is senseless.
All these refers to the guilty men (vss. 18-43). For the Hebrew **taken as married** see 9:2.
And some of them had wives, stating the obvious, reflects the awkward Hebrew text,
"And there were of them wives." But I Esdras reads, "And they sent them away with
children," which supplies the desired conclusion to the reform program (cf. vss. 3, 11)
and forms the basis for most emendations and the translation in the RSV. In the writing
of the postexilic period, as seen in the Jewish Aramaic papyri, an original text, וישלחום,
"And they sent them," could easily be corrupted to the ויש מהום, "And there were of
them . . . ," of the M.T. (Bewer, *loc. cit.*). The verb וישימו, **and they put,** which makes
nonsense of vs. 44*b*, is but a dittograph of ו נשים, **women, and . . . .** The original text
was, "All these had taken foreign women but they sent them away, women and children."

Corruption of the verse led some to conclude that Ezra's reform failed (cf. Pfeiffer,
Intro. to O.T., p. 815). But if the guilt offering (vss. 18-19) is historical the reform was
successful, for such offering could be made only when the wrong had been righted.
Moreover, the Chronicler certainly desired to leave the impression that the exclusive
Judaism of Ezra was victorious and the restored community had been purged of all
foreign influences. The whole story has anticipated and prepared for a successful purge.
As Torrey points out (*Ezra Studies*, pp. 278-79), "The immediate sequel in Neh. 9 f.
asserts again that they did separate themselves completely, not only from the heathen
wives and their children (10:29-31), but also from all the other foreigners (9:2, cf.
especially Ezr. 9:1, 10:11)." Josephus shared this view in saying, "So then, having
rectified the wrong doing of the forementioned men in marrying, Ezra purified the
practice relating to this matter so that it remained fixed for the future" (*Antiquities*
XI. 5. 4). The Ezra narrative continues in Neh. 9:1-5, which describes the confession
required by Ezra (vs. 11), and relates the actual separation of the mixed families.

NEHEMIAH

TEXT, EXEGESIS, AND EXPOSITION

1 The words of Nehemiah the son of Hachaliah. And it came to pass in the month Chisleu, in the twentieth year, as I was in Shushan the palace,	1 The words of Nehemi′ah the son of Hacali′ah. Now it happened in the month of Chislev, in the twentieth year, as I was in Susa

I. NEHEMIAH HEARS NEWS OF JERUSALEM (1:1-11)

Nehemiah was read in Greek as a separate book as late as the time of Ben Sirach (*ca.* 180 B.C.) and when II Macc. 2:13 was written (Ecclus. 49:13; Theodor Nöldeke, "Bemerkungen zum hebräischen Ben Sīrā," *Zeitschrift für die alttestamentliche Wissenschaft,* XX [1900], 89). Nehemiah is not mentioned in I Esdras, but Josephus uses the memoirs in a form somewhat different from that in the M.T. and the LXX. He may have used an independent Greek narrative as his source when the Ezra story terminated in the MS of I Esdras that he used (Robert H. Pfeiffer, *History of New Testament Times* [New York: Harper & Bros., 1949, p. 245]).

A. THE NEWS (1:1-4)

1:1. The title of the book is doubtless introduced by the Chronicler or a later editor who incorporated Nehemiah's text into the present literary complex of Ezra-Nehemiah. It is missing in the LXX[L]. The phrase **The words of** usually introduces prophetic books (cf. Amos 1:1; Jer. 1:1) but the Hebrew text can also be read as "the acts of," which would be more appropriate for Nehemiah's factual, historical account. The word translated **words** is used as the Hebrew title of the books called Chronicles.

Nehemiah ("The Lord has comforted"), sometimes abbreviated Nahum (cf. 7:7; Nah. 1:1), Naham (I Chr. 4:19), or Nahamani (7:7). The name is found in old Hebrew letters on a pre-exilic Israelite scarab (C. Clermont-Ganneau, "Sceaux et cachets," *Journal Asiatique;* Ser. 8, Vol. I [1883], p. 156, No. 42). It is found only in postexilic material in the Bible and is not found in the Aramaic papyri. Many attempts

1:1-3. Words That Began as Deeds.—The words of Nehemiah, as Robert H. Pfeiffer points out,[1] are "from the literary point of view . . . something new. They are the earliest autobiography extant written by a man who was not a king, with the exception of the grave inscriptions of Egyptian nomarchs in the Middle Kingdom."

Here then we have the personal reminiscences of a leader in a national, cultural, and religious crisis, who emerged not by birth and only secondarily by official appointment, but rather by what Arnold J. Toynbee has called "challenge and response," in the midst of the crisis

For Introduction to Nehemiah see pp. 551-69.
[1] *Introduction to the Old Testament* (New York: Harper & Bros., 1941), p. 837.

itself. In that sense Nehemiah's memoirs, as O.T. scholars frequently call them, have become even more than our chief firsthand source for an obscure period in Hebrew history twenty-four hundred years ago; they have also become what Homer called "winged words," borne far down on the winds of history to us of today; words both revelatory and prophetic of something characteristic in what we mean by "the democratic way of life." For here we can trace the voluntary assumption of responsibility and initiative in the midst of a social crisis by an individual whom God called and equipped for leadership, and whom men thereupon recognized and followed. As centuries afterward Lincoln, "The Rail Splitter," without benefit of birth, breeding, or education, emerged from the

2 That Hanani, one of my brethren, came, he and *certain* men of Judah; and I asked them concerning the Jews that had escaped, which were left of the captivity, and concerning Jerusalem.	the capital, 2 that Hana'ni, one of my brethren, came with certain men out of Judah; and I asked them concerning the Jews that survived, who had escaped exile, and con-

have been made to explain the name **Hacaliah** (cf. 10:1), but none is persuasive and it remains one of the most difficult to interpret (George Buchanan Gray, *Hebrew Proper Names* [London: A. & C. Black, 1896], p. 221; Martin Noth, *Die israelitischen Personennamen im Rahmen der Gemeinsemitischen Namengebung* [Stuttgart: W. Kohlhammer, 1928; "Beiträge zur Wissenschaft vom Alten und Neuen Testament"], p. 32, n. 3).

Postexilic Jewish events, like later Babylonian and Persian business documents, are dated exactly by month, year, and usually also by the day (cf. Hag. 1:1, 15; 2:1, 10; Zech. 1:1, 7; 7:1). **Chislev** is the ninth Babylonian month (*Kislimu* or *Kisliwu*), a type of reckoning adopted by the Jews in postexilic times. The **twentieth year** was clearly that during the reign of Artaxerxes (2:1), presumably Artaxerxes I (*Longimanus*, 464-423 B.C.). The date of vs. 1 is thus sometime between December 5 and January 3, 445-444 B.C. But since the later event of 2:1 is dated in the first month, that in vs. 1 is obviously wrong and must be earlier. The date has been regarded as an interpolation, possibly derived from 5:14 (cf. L. W. Batten, *A Critical and Exegetical Commentary on the Books of Ezra and Nehemiah* [New York: Charles Scribner's Sons, 1913; "International Critical Commentary"], p. 182), but the error must be for the "nineteenth year" (Dec. 17 to Jan. 14). Josephus (*Antiquities* XI. 5. 6) wrongly places both Ezra and Nehemiah in the reign of Xerxes, reserving the reign of Artaxerxes for the story of Esther (*ibid.* XI. 6. 1-13).

Shushan or **Susa** (cf. Ezra 4:9), capital of Elam, was the winter residence of the Persian kings (Xenophon *Cyropaedia* VIII. 6. 22). For **the palace** or **the capital** after the name, read "the fortress" (cf. Ezra 6:2).

2. Hanani abbreviates Hananiah (cf. 3:8, 30). **Brethren** is as elastic in Hebrew as in English. It may mean simply a fellow Jew (Exod. 2:11; Deut. 15:12), an intimate friend (II Sam. 1:26; I Kings 9:13; 20:32-33), a kinsman with some degree of actual relationship, or a blood brother. From 7:2 it seems likely that he was a genuine brother.

---

obscurity of the American wilderness to save his country in a crisis, so Nehemiah, the layman, emerged from the indignities of an exiled people, to save his nation, its culture, and its religion in a perilous time.

We do well to note that this historic achievement was first a bold and creative deed—and only afterward became a written narrative. For that reason the marginal rendering of the ASV, "The history of Nehemiah," or as the Exeg. suggests, the "acts of Nehemiah," tells us more about the total event in its historical and spiritual significance than words alone can ever tell. This sequence of historic deeds, afterward recounted in "winged words" that in turn quicken new and fruitful deeds, is characteristic because often repeated in our Jewish-Christian religious heritage—a heritage deeply rooted in the soil of history itself. So "saints, apostles, prophets, martyrs" speak to us still across the centuries—as Nehemiah speaks— even more by their example than by their utterance. So above all speaks still to Christian faith "the Word . . . made flesh" who "dwelt

among us, . . . full of grace and truth" (John 1:14). All Christian theologies of the Incarnation bear witness to this primacy of the historic fact and the creative deed which preceded the written or even the spoken word; and our latest N.T. scholarship emphasizes this same order and sequence in the earliest history of the Christian gospel itself. Only in the mind and purpose of God does the "Word" come first: in our human experience and history Goethe's famous line tells the oft-repeated story, "In the beginning was the deed."

This same sequence—deeds first, then words— reveals to us the core of Nehemiah's character, and the secret of his influence and success. As Pfeiffer puts it:

Nehemiah was essentially a man of action. Deeply concerned over the plight of the pitiful Jewish community in Jerusalem, through his indomitable energy, self-denial, and shrewd unmasking of hostile plots, he brought new life to it. . . . He revived the dying Jewish community in Palestine and endowed it with deathless vigor.[2]

[2] *Ibid.*

3 And they said unto me, The remnant that are left of the captivity there in the province *are* in great affliction and reproach: the wall of Jerusalem also *is* broken down, and the gates thereof are burned with fire.

cerning Jerusalem. 3 And they said to me, "The survivors there in the province who escaped exile are in great trouble and shame; the wall of Jerusalem is broken down, and its gates are destroyed by fire."

He does not appear in Josephus' version (*Antiquities* XI. 5. 6), which describes Nehemiah as walking before the city walls where he overheard Hebrew spoken by travelers. **Hanani and his companions** have been regarded as a special embassy sent to ask their fellow Jew in a prominent position to intercede with the king on behalf of his fellow Jews in Jerusalem (A. T. Olmstead, *History of the Persian Empire* [Chicago: University of Chicago Press, 1948], pp. 313-14). But **I asked** indicates that Nehemiah took the initiative in questioning the men, and there is no evidence of a petition presented to Nehemiah. **Who had escaped** and **which were left** show concern for Jews who survived the catastrophe of 586 B.C., possibly those Judeans who fled for safety when the enemy approached (II Kings 25:22-26; Jer. 40:11-12). The viewpoint is distinctly Palestinian, in contrast to that of the Chronicler who viewed the survivors as those who returned from exile to found the restored postexilic community (cf. Ezra 2:1).

3. The **province** is Judea, a subdivision of the satrapy (cf. Ezra 2:1; 4:15; 7:16). **Great affliction** and **great trouble** translate the Hebrew "great evil." Josephus (*loc. cit.*) expands the narrative: "The surrounding nations were inflicting many injuries on the Jews, overrunning the country and plundering it by day and doing mischief by night, so that many had been carried off as captives from the country and from Jerusalem itself; and every day the roads were found full of corpses." The opponents are clear from 2:10, 19 (cf. Ezra 4:6-23). For **reproach** or **shame** see 2:19; 4:1-4; Ezra 9:7.

The **wall of Jerusalem** is described as "pulled down" or "demolished" in 586 B.C. (II Kings 25:10; Jer. 39:8; cf. Lam. 2:8-9) but the term here is simply "breached" (cf. 4:3; II Kings 14:13; II Chr. 25:23). The huge wooden **gates** such as barred access to ancient cities (cf. Jer. 17:27; 51:58) were **burned with fire.** Late Assyrian sculpture shows attacks made on city gates, using battering rams and fire (Bruno Meissner, *Babylonien und Assyrien* [Heidelberg: C. Winter, 1920], I, 110 and Pl. 64; C. J. Gadd, *Assyrian Sculptures* [London: British Museum, 1934], p. 41), practices which were widely

---

It is plain from these memoirs that in a real sense Nehemiah created his own crisis by the way in which he grappled responsibly with a situation the seriousness of which others either did not recognize or were content to evade. His creative deeds, that is to say, sprang out of his vivid imagination, his sensitive conscience, and his courageous loyalty, all active in a situation which his fellows were content to regard as none of their affair. These characteristic qualities begin to appear in the first sentence of his memoirs (vs. 2). Nehemiah was "well fixed" personally, with an important post in the royal palace at Susa. He could easily have let the situation in faraway Jerusalem take care of itself: just as every citizen who learns of a sore spot in his own neighborhood, or every nation in our own shrunken world that hears rumblings from a crisis on the other side of the earth, can easily ignore it, in the complacent hope that "everything will turn out all right."

The process by which Nehemiah developed

into the leader and savior of his people, already under way in this first sentence of his narrative, involved the initiative and co-operation of others besides himself. The significant part played in it by his kinsman Hanani—so often repeated in the life history of leaders who themselves are guided into their high calling by other hands that history barely remembers, or more often forgets—was a role that doubtless seemed outwardly insignificant but was inwardly indispensable. As L. W. Batten describes it:

Hanani apparently had not been in Judah himself, but he had heard tidings from a company of returning pilgrims, and had brought them to the cup-bearer, because of his high position and commanding influence, as well as his known interest in the welfare of Jerusalem. The visit was scarcely accidental, and so Hanani deserves credit for starting the important mission of Nehemiah.[3]

[3] *A Critical and Exegetical Commentary on the Books of Ezra and Nehemiah* (New York: Charles Scribner's Sons, 1913; "International Critical Commentary"), p. 183.

4 ¶ And it came to pass, when I heard | 4 When I heard these words I sat down
these words, that I sat down and wept, and |

---

imitated. Modern Jewish behavior at the so-called Wailing Wall in Jerusalem (*Kauthal ma'arbê*; Karl Baedeker, *Palestine and Syria* [5th ed.; New York: Charles Scribner's Sons, 1912], pp. 65-66) shows that tragedies long past may be mourned, but the poignancy of Nehemiah's grief suggests that it was a rather fresh catastrophe that shocked him. The obscurity of the history of Palestine during the Persian period makes it difficult to determine the date and circumstance of such a destruction. Since a great revolt swept the West at the accession of Xerxes (*ca.* 486-485 B.C.) it is possible that the trouble at Jerusalem occurred then (S. A. Cook, "The Fall and Rise of Judah," in J. B. Bury, S. A. Cook, F. E. Adcock, eds., *The Cambridge Ancient History* [New York: The Macmillan Co., 1925], III, 418; "Israel Before the Prophets," *ibid.,* III, 488). But it is more probable that the destruction occurred during the time of Artaxerxes himself (cf. Ezra 4:11-23; Olmstead, *History of the Persian Empire,* pp. 313-14).

4. **These words** can also be "these things" (cf. vs. 1). **For days** usually means "for some time" (cf. Gen. 40:4; I Kings 17:15; etc.). The interval of mourning between **Chislev** (1:1) and **Nisan** (2:1) would be three or four months, but Josephus asserts that Nehemiah appeared before the king almost at once. For **fasted, and prayed** see Ezra 9:5; for **God of heaven** see 2:4, 20; Ezra 1:2.

Hanani reminds us therefore that many of us in every generation exert our greatest influence through other people more highly gifted or strategically placed than ourselves, the switch of whose life history at some critical moment we are in a position to throw toward some main track that leads them to usefulness greater than we ourselves can ever match, or may ever even know about afterward. In the pages of scripture we think at once of what Eli did for Samuel, Andrew for Peter, Philip for Nathanael—and John the Baptist for Jesus himself. There were incalculable results from a brief visit in 1886 to the Cornell University campus by J. K. Studd, a famous Cambridge cricketer and Christian leader. In one address, followed by a personal interview, he turned the thinking of an ambitious sophomore named John R. Mott toward Christian service as a lifework, and so vicariously influenced tens of thousands of students on hundreds of college campuses the world around, through ten succeeding student generations.[4] We remember likewise Abraham Lincoln's stepmother, and thank God for all the mothers and aunts and grandmothers, the neighbors and family friends, not least the teachers in Sunday schools and public schools, whose greatest work is done through the children they mold for later usefulness and leadership.

So like a sword the son shall roam
    On nobler missions sent;
And as the smith remained at home
    So sits the while at home the mother well content.[5]

[4] B. J. Mathews, *John R. Mott—World Citizen* (New York: Harper & Bros., 1934), pp. 34-35.
[5] Robert Louis Stevenson, "It is not yours, O mother, to complain," st. viii.

The conditions in Jerusalem reported by Hanani's friends in vs. 3, which, as Batten points out, seem to "require a recent calamity," are such as in twentieth-century postwar periods could be reported from all the war-devastated countries of Europe, and likewise from those parts of the Near and the Far East, where civil or guerrilla warfare prevailed. Nehemiah could have ignored or forgotten these reports, but he had imagination enough to see what they meant, and sense of loyalty and responsibility enough to regard them as his own concern. In spite of his own high and affluent position, he felt the "great trouble and shame" of the handful of his fellow countrymen in Jerusalem as if they were his own. The sufferings and wrongs of minority groups, and of the underprivileged or oppressed in every age and scene of human history, have had to wait for their redemption until some individual or group, frequently like Nehemiah in a position of privilege or influence, has felt them as if they had befallen themselves, and taken the responsibility of their amelioration. One thinks at once of the part played in the development of British democracy in the early nineteenth century by Richard Cobden and John Bright, and by the "liberal Tories," on whose strategic and forward-looking role G. M. Trevelyan lays such stress in his *British History in the Nineteenth Century.*[6] Nehemiah is a shining example of such social awareness and personal self-dedication.

4-11a. Prayers—Corporate and Personal.— Nehemiah's concern for his fellow countrymen in Jerusalem, and his grief over the low estate of the ancient capital of his people, drove him

[6] London: Longmans Green & Co., 1922, pp. 196-97.

mourned *certain* days, and fasted, and prayed before the God of heaven,

5 And said, I beseech thee, O Lord God of heaven, the great and terrible God, that

and wept, and mourned for days; and I continued fasting and praying before the God of heaven. 5 And I said, "O Lord God of heaven, the great and terrible God who

---

B. Nehemiah's Prayer (1:5-11*a*)

Josephus (*Antiquities* XI. 5. 6) states: "Then Nehemiah burst into tears out of pity for the misfortune of his countrymen and, looking up to heaven, said, 'How long, O Lord, wilt thou look away while our nation suffers these things, having thus become the prey and spoil of all?' " This prayer may be an abstract or a brief paraphrase of what Josephus found in his source, but it is appropriate to the occasion and has something of the businesslike directness and simplicity of Nehemiah's language as it is known elsewhere. In sharp contrast the biblical prayer is a rambling, indirect effusion of stilted Deuteronomic phrases having little or no bearing on the situation that evoked the prayer. Although even C. C. Torrey has regarded the prayer as authentic (*The Composition and Historical Value of Ezra-Nehemiah* [Giessen: J. Ricker, 1895; "Beihefte zur Zeitschrift für die alttestamentliche Wissenschaft"], p. 36) and it has been defended as genuine (Wilhelm Rudolph, *Esra und Nehemia* [Tübingen: J. C. B. Mohr, 1949; "Handbuch zum Alten Testament"], p. 105), its integrity has not been unchallenged (H. G. Mitchell, "The Wall of Jerusalem According to the Book of Nehemiah," *Journal of Biblical Literature,* XXII [1903], 87; Batten, *op. cit.,* p. 188; so also Sigmund Mowinckel, *Ezra den Skriftlaerde* [Kristiania: 1916]; Gustav Hölscher, *Die Bücher Ezra und Nehemia* [4th ed., E. Kautzsch and A. Bertholet; Tübingen: J. C. B. Mohr, 1923], *et al.*). It is strongly liturgical and might well be classified as a "folk lament" (Hermann Gunkel and Joachim Begrich, *Einleitung in die Psalmen* [Göttingen: Vandenhoeck & Ruprecht, 1933; "Göttinger Handbuch zum Alten Testament"], pp. 121 ff.). It has been suggested that the Chronicler "took this prayer [1:5-11a] from the Temple Liturgy and put it into the mouth of Nehemiah" (W. O. E. Oesterley, "Ezra-Nehemiah," in A. S. Peake, ed., *A Commentary on the Bible* [New York: Thomas Nelson & Sons, n.d.], p. 330). But it closely resembles the work of the Chronicler himself, who weaves together Deuteronomic phrases as prayers (cf. Ezra 9:6-15; Batten, *loc. cit.*).

Since **this man** (vs. 11*a*) is senseless in its context, and the parenthetical comment that follows indicates that it refers to Artaxerxes, who has not yet been mentioned, it is probable that the prayer is misplaced, drawn from 2:4, where a definite prayer is mentioned (*ibid.,* pp. 188, 192). That prayer must have been brief, silent, and almost instantaneous. "At this time" (vs. 6) and **this day** (vs. 11) would be pertinent but **day and night** (vs. 6) could be a later gloss to adapt it to a context in which Nehemiah

---

into a prolonged period of what our ancestors, as well as his, called "fasting and prayer." The fact that a similar prayer of national confession in Ezra 9:6-15 is set in a similar frame of personal humiliation and strong emotion suggests that the hand of the Chronicler may well have cast or recast both the substance and the setting of these prayers into patterns of his own. We are told that both Ezra and Nehemiah, with an emotional intensity which is characteristically Oriental and Semitic, but is conspicuously not an Anglo-Saxon trait, wept bitter tears, and that Ezra rent his clothes in a penitence before the God of his fathers that was both personal and national. The prayers that follow at length, here in vss. 5-11, and in Ezra 9:6-15, bear marked resemblances to a similar and even longer prayer

in Dan. 9:4-19. All three of these prayers make large use of Deuteronomic phrases and ideas: there are four marginal references to Deuteronomy in Nehemiah's prayer, one in Ezra's, five in Daniel's. Apparently the book of Deuteronomy became for later Judaism a kind of literary and spiritual quarry, from which were brought forth not only words and phrases for written prayers, but religious insights and attitudes proper before altars of private devotion; somewhat as phrases from George Washington's well-known prayer for his country have reappeared in liturgies for public and private worship.

Whatever the critical problems and the literary relationships which scholarship may uncover within and among those four O.T. books, they

keepeth covenant and mercy for them that love him and observe his commandments:

6 Let thine ear now be attentive, and thine eyes open, that thou mayest hear the prayer of thy servant, which I pray before thee now, day and night, for the children of Israel thy servants, and confess the sins of the children of Israel, which we have sinned against thee: both I and my father's house have sinned.

keeps covenant and steadfast love with those who love him and keep his commandments;

6 let thy ear be attentive, and thy eyes open, to hear the prayer of thy servant which I now pray before thee day and night for the people of Israel thy servants, confessing the sins of the people of Israel, which we have sinned against thee. Yea, I and my father's

---

mourned for **certain days** (vs. 4). Similarly "thy servant" (vs. 10) is expected but **and to the prayer of thy servants who delight to fear thy name** (vs. 11) must be a gloss making a personal prayer a communal one. Batten (*ibid.,* p. 189) claims that "if [Nehemiah] recorded his prayer at all, it has been so elaborately worked over that the original cannot be recovered." But it is tempting to conjecture that the original prayer, appropriate after 2:4, might have been, "I beseech thee, O LORD, God of Heaven [vs. 5], that thou mayest hear the prayer of thy servant which I pray before thee now for the children of Israel, thy servants [vs. 6]. Give success, I pray thee, to thy servant now and grant him compassion in the sight of this man." Such a prayer, transferred to its present context, appears to have displaced an earlier prayer, the substance of which may be preserved by Josephus.

5. This verse differs but slightly from Dan. 9:4. A habit of stereotyped prayer may account for the presence of the personal name of God, translated LORD (cf. Ezra 1:2), found only here in Nehemiah, and for **the children of Israel** (vs. 6), also not used elsewhere by Nehemiah. **Great and terrible** are attributes of God. **Terrible** means "awe-inspiring" (cf. Joel 2:31; Mal. 4:5). Despite fearsome powers, God is faithful to his **covenant** (cf. Ezra 10:3). **Mercy** or **steadfast love** is not to be regarded in a sentimental sense alone, for it always implies faithful compliance with the accepted terms of the covenant contract (cf. Nelson Glueck, *Das Wort ḥesed im alttestamentlichen Sprachgebrauche* [Giessen: Alfred Töpelmann, 1927]). It is "the feeling of fellowship between the Israelites themselves and between them and their God" (Johannes Pedersen, *Israel, Its Life and Culture III-IV* [London: Oxford University Press, 1940], p. 541). **Steadfast love,** like the covenant, is limited to those in the agreement who love God and express that love by obedience to his **commandments.**

6. Because "hearken" has nothing to do with **eyes,** reference to open eyes has been called a later addition based on II Chr. 6:40 (Rudolph, *op. cit.,* p. 104), but the expression is found elsewhere (II Chr. 7:15; Isa. 37:17). For **ear** the LXX[L], Vulg., and Peshitta have "ears," as in II Chr. 6:40; Ps. 130:2, but the expression here is exactly as found in Isa. 37:17. God is implored to hear the plea and observe the pitiable plight so that both sight and sound might move him to respond. **Thy servant** is a humble formula of

---

represent in any case a deep and sound religious insight, from which the Christian minister may profit both in the conduct of public worship and in the practice of private devotion. Personal religion has some of its deepest roots not only in its family and national heritage (vss. 6, 10), but in its ancestral and contemporary social experiences of collective temptation and failure (vss. 6-7), leading to a religious confession of social sin before the God of the generations. Not only are the sins of the fathers visited on their children, but the repentance of the children is indispensable if there is to be redemp-

tion for either generation. Our most urgent interracial and international problems are bedeviled by our inherited racial prejudices; and our economic difficulties both at home and abroad are complicated by habitual attitudes of isolation, irresponsibility, and "every man for himself." Only if we repent individually and collectively of our fathers' sins as well as of our own can either they or we be forgiven—or our children saved in their day and generation.

It is deeply significant that Nehemiah, like Ezra (9:6-7, 15), identifies himself in his prayer with the wrongdoing of his fellows and his

7 We have dealt very corruptly against thee, and have not kept the commandments, nor the statutes, nor the judgments, which thou commandedst thy servant Moses.

8 Remember, I beseech thee, the word that thou commandedst thy servant Moses, saying, *If* ye transgress, I will scatter you abroad among the nations:

9 But *if* ye turn unto me, and keep my commandments, and do them; though there were of you cast out unto the uttermost part of the heaven, *yet* will I gather them from thence, and will bring them unto the place that I have chosen to set my name there.

house have sinned. **7** We have acted very corruptly against thee, and have not kept the commandments, the statutes, and the ordinances which thou didst command thy servant Moses. **8** Remember the word which thou didst command thy servant Moses, saying, 'If you are unfaithful, I will scatter you among the peoples; **9** but if you return to me and keep my commandments and do them, though your dispersed be under the farthest skies, I will gather them thence and bring them to the place which I have chosen, to make my name dwell there.'

polite address toward equals or superiors (cf. Gen. 18:3; I Sam. 20:7-8; etc.), used also in Assyrian letters. **Now**, lit., "today" (vs. 11), seems original while **day and night** seems a later addition (cf. above). Since **night** and not "evening" is used, the reference is not to the three periods appointed for prayer (Dan. 6:10; Ps. 55:17). Confession of guilt plays a large part (vss. 6-7) before the actual petition, as in Ezra's prayer (Ezra 9:5-15). **Thy servants** are the Jews (cf. 1:11; 2:20), for Nehemiah frequently used **servant** and calls the Jews "this people" (5:19), which may lie behind the "our nation" in the prayer in Josephus. The LXX[L], Peshitta, and Vulg. have "they have sinned" which, with **the children of Israel,** may be an earlier reading, but this has been changed (M.T. and LXX[AB]) to **we have sinned,** whereby Nehemiah, like Ezra (9:6), includes himself among the sinners. **I and my father's house** has been called an addition (Gustav Jahn, *Die Bücher Esra [A und B] und Nehemja* [Leiden: E. J. Brill, 1909], p. 91), but Batten (*op. cit.*, p. 186), who thinks it genuine, infers Davidic descent for Nehemiah from it, since "the sin of his house is separated from that of the people generally" (cf. 2:3, 5).

7-8. Didst command . . . saying should preface a direct scriptural quotation, but the words cited (vss. 8-10) are no more than an assemblage of Deuteronomic phrases largely reminiscent of Deut. 30:1-5. "Trespass" or **transgress** is a favorite term of the Chronicler (cf. Ezra 10:2, 10). The substance of the passage is found in Deut. 4:27; 28:64, but a closer parallel is found in Lev. 26:14-15, 33. **Commandments . . . statutes . . . ordinances** are terms characteristic of Deuteronomy (cf. 5:31; 6:1; cf. also Ezra 7:11). **Moses,** who gives the commandments (Deut. 28:13-15), is frequently called the **servant** of God (cf. Neh. 9:14).

9. The idea of return to God, found in the prophets (cf. Jer. 4:1; 24:7), is a prominent theme of Deuteronomic writers (cf. I Kings 8:47-48=R[D]). Only with a real change of heart can the result of repentance be manifested in loyal obedience to the commandments. Such obedience consists in keeping the covenant, the only guarantee of life and prosperity (Deut. 28:1-2). The awkward **though there were of you cast out**

fathers, even though he himself has had neither part nor lot in it. **Yea, I and my father's house have sinned** (vs. 6b). On this identification of himself and his family with the national wrongdoing rests no small part of the leverage Nehemiah was able to bring to bear for national repentance and reform. In every generation there are plenty of people ready to confess the sins of other races and social groups than their own; and there are likewise always some who are equally ready to confess the sins of their

own group or nation—while explicitly disclaiming all personal responsibility therefor. But it is those who, like Nehemiah and Ezra, are ready to say, "From the days of our fathers to this day we have been in great guilt" (Ezra 9:7), who have been able to move their less sensitive fellows toward collective repentance and conversion.

Conversely, when Nehemiah confessed so humbly the national sins of his fathers and of his own generation, and renewed his own faith

10 Now these *are* thy servants and thy people, whom thou hast redeemed by thy great power, and by thy strong hand.

11 O Lord, I beseech thee, let now thine ear be attentive to the prayer of thy servant, and to the prayer of thy servants, who desire to fear thy name: and prosper, I pray thee,

10 They are thy servants and thy people, whom thou hast redeemed by thy great power and by thy strong hand. 11 O Lord, let thy ear be attentive to the prayer of thy servant, and to the prayer of thy servants who delight to fear thy name; and give

---

is improved by reading **though your dispersed be,** for the Hebrew participle as a substantive means someone who is "banished" or "thrust away." For **your dispersed** the LXX has "your scattering," using a word (*diaspora*) which became a technical term for all Jews outside of Palestine. **Under the farthest skies** interprets the Hebrew "unto the ends of the heavens." There is no implication of human habitation in the skies, for the reference is to the farthest horizon, where earth and sky meet. For **gather them** read with the LXX[L], Vulg., and Peshitta, "gather you" to agree with **if you return.**

The place which I have chosen is not found outside of Deuteronomy in the Pentateuch (Deut. 12:5, 11, 14; 16:6, 11; etc.). The place is the site of the temple in Jerusalem, which is described as "chosen" by later Deuteronomic editors (cf. I Kings 8:16, 44, 48; 11:13, 32; etc.). For **my name** and the expression **set my name** see Ezra 6:12.

10-11a. Words attributed to Nehemiah are resumed in vs. 10, after the conclusion of the "quotation" in vs. 9. Vs. 10 is apparently a paraphrase of Deut. 9:29. Reference is to exiled Jews, but Nehemiah's own interest is not in exiles, neither at home nor abroad, but in the people of Jerusalem who survived the disaster of 586 B.C. (cf. vss. 2-3). For "thou didst bring out" of Deut. 9:29, vs. 10 uses **thou hast redeemed,** which is more appropriate in the historical context in Nehemiah. Such a concept of redemption is prominent in Deuteronomic thought (Deut. 7:8; 9:26; 13:5; 15:15; 21:8; 24:18), as is also the use of **strong hand** (Deut. 3:24; 4:34; 5:15;. etc.).

The petition begun in vss. 5-6 is resumed in vs. 11 with almost the same words of vs. 6, but with no reference to open eyes. **The prayer of thy servants** might be a recognition by Nehemiah of the constant prayer of Jews who, like himself, sought God's aid for the welfare of their people. But following **the prayer of thy servant,** which appears original (cf. above), it seems to be an addition to the text, presumably to give it liturgical value. The paradoxical **delight to fear** combines two aspects of Jewish religion (cf. Ps.

---

in and dependence on the God of his fathers, who had revealed himself in their history as a nation, he began to get clear light on his own duty in the contemporary situation. Kneeling individually before that social altar, he found there new awareness both of the judgment and of the mercy of God in his people's history (vss. 8-9), and new confidence in God's redeeming purposes and power (vs. 10). There too he found guidance and reinforcement in the crisis of his own personal obligation and opportunity to serve and save his people (vs. 11). This final petition, as Pfeiffer points out, doubtless has more of Nehemiah's own authentic words and spirit, and fewer signs of the Chronicler's later editorial hand, than any other part of this prayer.

For all ministers of religion who are so often asked to offer prayer on public occasions, and quite as often to counsel their parishioners in the practice of private and family devotion, there are both illumination and guidance in the

apparent relation between the authentic core of Nehemiah's brief prayer for personal help before his critical interview with the king (vs. 11) and the longer and much more liturgical prayer of collective compassion and intercession **for the people of Israel thy servants** (vs. 6), into which the Chronicler has expanded Nehemiah's brief petition. As the Exeg. points out, Josephus reports a prayer of a single sentence before the interview: "How long, O Lord, wilt thou look away while our nation suffers these things, having thus become the prey and spoil of all?" [7] Even more relevant to the actual situation is the cry for personal help in vs. 11: **Give success to thy servant today, and grant him mercy in the sight of this man.**

Either of these instances of what our contemporary phrase has called "ejaculatory prayer"—even if in a sudden crisis it is no more than "O Lord, help me now," or the even briefer outcry "O God!"—is the quick upreach

[7] *Antiquities* XI. 5. 6.

thy servant this day, and grant him mercy in the sight of this man. For I was the king's cupbearer.	success to thy servant today, and grant him mercy in the sight of this man." Now I was cupbearer to the king.

112:1) : **delight,** which implies eagerness or zealousness to act because one is pleased to do so (cf. Pss. 1:2; 40:8; 112:1; cf. Rom. 7:22) , and **fear,** connoting awe and reverence before a mighty power. The biblical concept of fear of God is complex, ranging from elemental terror to the more refined emotion implied here (H. A. Brongers, "La crainte du Seigneur," in *Oudtestamentische Studiën,* ed. P. A. H. De Boer [Leiden: E. J. Brill, 1948], V, 151-73) . **My name** (vs. 9) signifies God himself, evidence that the Jews' unwillingness to pronounce the personal name of God had already begun to show itself (cf. Lev. 24:11) .

The actual petition, appropriate in the context of 2:1-4, begins with **give success. Mercy:** a plural form signifying compassionate feelings (cf. Rom. 12:1; Phil. 2:1; Heb. 10:28) . Under similar circumstances a Jewish writer in Egypt used almost the same expression to wish that a Persian official might find favor before the royal court (A. E. Cowley, ed., *Aramaic Papyri of the Fifth Century B.C.* [Oxford: Clarendon Press, 1923], No. 30, 1. 2) . **This man,** awkward and meaningless as it stands, would be intelligible in a prayer in the context of 2:4. The **man** is certainly "the king" of 2:5, previously identified as Artaxerxes (2:1) .

II. Nehemiah's Petition Is Granted (1:11b–2:8)

Nehemiah's story resumes with **now** in 1:11b (cf. 1:1b) but faulty verse division puts the first sentence in ch. 1 where it appears as a parenthetic comment on 1:11a. As the Peshitta shows, it is actually the beginning of the narrative in ch. 2.

11b. As royal **cupbearer** (cf. Gen. 40:2) Nehemiah illustrates the success of ambitious Jews of the Diaspora against whom few avenues of advancement were closed. The office, one of the oldest and highest court positions in Babylonia (Alfred Jeremias, *Das Alte Testament im Lichte des Alten Orients* [2nd ed.; Leipzig: J. C. Hinrichs, 1906], p. 54; Heinrich Zimmern, "Über Bäcker und Mundschenk im Altsemitischen," *Zeitschrift der deutschen morgenländischen Gesellschaft,* LIII [1899], 115-19) , remained "an honor of no small account in Persia" (Herodotus *History* III. 34) . The **cupbearer** served partly

---

of the hand of man toward God for support and guidance which gives reality and urgency to all prayer, whether short or long. Such brief and instant prayer is the elementary school in which we all begin to learn the practice of communion with God.

But when on some public or solemn occasion the minister has to lead the "great congregation" (not yet delivered from what John Bright's noble invocation calls "coldness of heart and wanderings of mind") "unto the throne of grace"—the very phrase in Heb. 4:16 is a vivid symbol of the paradoxical combination of authoritative judgment and undeserved support in our human experience of God, which H. H. Farmer has finely called "absolute demand and final succour"—then the minister in that priestly function does well, like the Chronicler, to stir complacent consciences with reminders of what God always has demanded from his people, and to widen their narrow horizons out toward the perspectives of the God who is "our dwelling place in all generations," in whose sight "a

thousand years . . . are but as yesterday when it is past" (Ps. 90:1, 4). And the priestly instinct of the Chronicler is likewise a sound one, which on such ceremonial occasions sent not only his thought but his very phrases back to the scriptures of their fathers, as a reminder and bequest from the spiritual heritage and the reawakened insights of their race and nation. It was some such combination of sense for the nation's religious heritage, with his own personal prophetic insight, that made Phillips Brooks's prayer at the Harvard memorial service in 1865—at which James Russell Lowell read his well-known "Commemoration Ode"—one of the abiding memories of that historic occasion for all who were present, even though the actual words of the memorable prayer were never accessible afterward.[8]

1:11b–2:8. The Critical Moment.—Protestant theology from Luther onward has emphasized the spiritual significance of vocation; and

[8] A. V. G. Allen, *Life and Letters of Phillips Brooks* (New York: E. P. Dutton, 1900), I, 548-54.

2 And it came to pass in the month Nisan, in the twentieth year of Artaxerxes the king, *that* wine *was* before him: and I took up the wine, and gave *it* unto the king. Now I had not been *beforetime* sad in his presence.

2 In the month of Nisan, in the twentieth year of King Ar-ta-xerx'es, when wine was before him, I took up the wine and gave it to the king. Now I had not been sad

---

as taster of the king's wine and partly as guardian of the royal apartment (cf. Xenophon *Cyropaedia* I. 3. 8-9. 11). Presumably each royal residence had its own **cupbearer.** Persian reliefs show the importance of the office by placing the **cupbearer** in attendance upon the king before the bearer of the royal weapons and just behind the crown prince (E. F. Schmidt, *The Treasury of Persepolis* [Chicago: University of Chicago Press, 1939], pp. 23-24, 26-27, Fig. 14). Beardlessness of the **cupbearer,** portrayed with his napkins and fly-whisk, indicates that at least from the time of Xerxes such intimate servants were eunuchs in Persia, as they were elsewhere (cf. Gen. 40:7; Josephus *Antiquities* XVI. 8. 1). Thus Nehemiah, too, who also served the queen (vs. 6), was a eunuch (Peter Browe, *Zur Geschichte der Entmannung* [Breslau: Müller & Seiffert, 1936], pp. 37 ff.; Olmstead, *History of the Persian Empire*, p. 314). Emasculation should have excluded him from the Jewish community (Deut. 23:1), but in postexilic times there was a tendency to include such persons. Ps. 127 has been regarded as directed against Nehemiah, and Isa. 56:3 has been considered a reply to that attack (Alfred Bertholet, *Die Bücher Esra und Nehemia* [Tübingen: J. C. B. Mohr, 1902; "Kurzer Hand-Commentar zum Alten Testament"], p. 48).

2:1. Artaxerxes is Artaxerxes I, Longimanus (464-423 B.C.). Arguments for the identification with Artaxerxes II, Mnemon (404-358 B.C.), are not persuasive (H. H. Rowley, *The Servant of the Lord and Other Essays on the Old Testament* [London: Lutterworth Press, 1952], pp. 137 ff., 150 ff.). The **twentieth year** is probably 445 B.C. The first month, **Nisan** (Apr. 13-May 11), marked the end of the rainy season, when luxuriantly sprouting foliage made conditions most pleasant at Susa (cf. 1:1; George Rawlinson, *Biblical Topography* [New York: James Pott & Co., 1887], pp. 64-65; *Ezra and Nehemiah* [New York: A. D. F. Randolph & Co., 1891], pp. 76-77). For three or four months (cf. 1:4), during the season of heavy rains (December-March), Nehemiah had brooded at Susa while the king was absent, presumably at his winter palace in Babylon.

For **before him** read with the LXX "before me," which can mean "under my supervision" (Num. 8:22; I Sam. 3:1). The **wine** was prepared by others, but Nehemiah **gave it to the king.** Sad here translates the Hebrew "bad." By stressing the pleasing appearance of Herod's cupbearer and other intimate servants, Josephus (*Antiquities* XVI. 8. 1) indicates that a prime qualification for intimate royal servants was a good personal appearance. Here he interprets the Hebrew "bad" as unwashed and unkept. But vs. 2 requires "sad of face," and it is better to read thus with the LXX[L] and the Vulg.

Robert L. Calhoun in *God and the Common Life* [9] has given our own generation a noble interpretation of this characteristic Protestant conviction that all "callings," first received from and then consecrated to God, are thereby rendered sacred. The very word "calling" carries some of these deep religious overtones that are implicit in its Latin-derived synonym "vocation." In the brief transitional sentence with which ch. 1 closes—**Now I was cupbearer to the king**—introducing in ch. 2 Nehemiah's own vivid memories of the critical moment (*kairos*,

as Tillich would call it) which opened the way for his great enterprise, the prophet gives us a glimpse of a similar conviction about his own daily work. His office as cupbearer brought him his responsibility and gave him his opportunity. Missionaries to the Far East point out that the Chinese word for "crisis" has been built up out of two shorter words meaning "danger" and "opportunity." Both these elements were plainly present in this crisis of Nehemiah's own life and of his people's future.

It was the genuineness of Nehemiah's concern for his fellow countrymen, and for the low estate

[9] New York: Charles Scribner's Sons, 1935.

2 Wherefore the king said unto me, Why *is* thy countenance sad, seeing thou *art* not sick? this *is* nothing *else* but sorrow of heart. Then I was very sore afraid,

3 And said unto the king, Let the king live for ever: why should not my countenance be sad, when the city, the place of my fathers' sepulchres, *lieth* waste, and the gates thereof are consumed with fire?

4 Then the king said unto me, For what dost thou make request? So I prayed to the God of heaven.

in his presence. 2 And the king said to me, "Why is your face sad, seeing you are not sick? This is nothing else but sadness of the heart." Then I was very much afraid. 3 I said to the king, "Let the king live for ever! Why should not my face be sad, when the city, the place of my fathers' sepulchres, lies waste, and its gates have been destroyed by fire?" 4 Then the king said to me, "For what do you make request?" So I prayed to the

---

2. The intimate relationship between king and cupbearer is understandable in the light of the isolation imposed on the Persian ruler by court etiquette (cf. George Rawlinson, *The Seven Great Monarchies of the Ancient Eastern World* [New York: J. B. Alden, 1885], II, 351; *Ezra and Nehemiah*, p. 86). Josephus (*op. cit.* XI. 5. 6) sets the scene "after dinner, when the king . . . was relaxed and in a more pleasant mood than usual." In asking **Why is your face sad?** (cf. Gen. 40:7) the wise king recognized that, lacking physical distress, Nehemiah's trouble was mental. **Sadness of the heart** is "pain [lupe] of heart" in the LXX[L]. Since **heart** signifies "mind" (cf. Ezra 6:22; 7:10), that expression would be identical with the Greek "pain of mind" used to describe "grief." Doubtless Nehemiah was afraid of punishment or dismissal, which might be expected for disturbing the king by his unpleasant appearance.

3. The response begins with a characteristic deferential salutation for Oriental kings (cf. I Kings 1:31; Dan. 2:4; 3:9; etc.) and builds on the king's own deduction (vs. 2). With what has been called "the eunuch's subtlety" (Olmstead, *History of the Persian Empire*, p. 314), Nehemiah in his request nowhere mentions by name Jerusalem or its fortifications, for Artaxerxes had stopped building there until further orders (Ezra 4:21-22). Nehemiah required just such countermanding orders. Jerusalem he described as **the place of my fathers' sepulchres.** Since all Orientals were concerned about ancestral tombs, and the king was preparing his own burial chamber among the royal Persian tombs at Naqsh-i-Rustam, Nehemiah may have won sympathy through such choice of words. He lightly mentions the ruined **gates** (cf. 1:3) but he is silent about the walls over which there had been controversy (Ezra 4:21-22).

4. The abrupt **For what do you make request?** gave Nehemiah the favorable opportunity he sought. His hasty prayer before answering is lost, but traces of it may be seen in 1:5-11*a*, especially in the words "in the sight of this man" (1:11*a*).

---

of the capital city of his fathers, that gave him his chance in this sudden crisis to intercede with the king on behalf of both. Neither habitual disconsolateness nor calculated "play acting" would have opened to him the long road toward the shaping of Jewish history so effectively as did his own quick-thinking sincerity. Social concern about the evils of our own time that gets no farther than a constant depression of spirit beneath the burden of anxiety about them, or no farther than putting on an occasional dramatic scene out of their poignancy, is liable now as then to miss its chance to change the very situation which it deplores. Every such crisis of responsibility and opportunity, as Nehemiah himself realized, is pregnant with

danger to all concerned—in a democracy as well as under a despotism. **Then I was very much afraid** (vs. 3*a*).

When his great moment came, Nehemiah was prepared to put his case before the king vividly, tactfully, and briefly. He had thought so much and so clearly about it previously in private, that (like Lincoln at Gettysburg) he could now condense the situation, as he had slowly come to see it, into a memorable summary touched with personal and contagious emotion. **The city, the place of my fathers' sepulchres, lies waste.** That was not the first nor yet the last time that old social evils have finally been lifted or removed by the leverage of a genuine personal

5 And I said unto the king, If it please the king, and if thy servant have found favor in thy sight, that thou wouldest send me unto Judah, unto the city of my fathers' sepulchres, that I may build it.

6 And the king said unto me, (the queen also sitting by him,) For how long shall thy journey be? and when wilt thou return? So it pleased the king to send me; and I set him a time.

God of heaven. 5 And I said to the king, "If it pleases the king, and if your servant has found favor in your sight, that you send me to Judah, to the city of my fathers' sepulchres, that I may rebuild it." 6 And the king said to me (the queen sitting beside him), "How long will you be gone, and when will you return?" So it pleased the king to send me; and I set him a time.

5. After the prayer Nehemiah began humbly with his request, prefacing it with the deferential **if it please the king** (Ezra 5:17) and **if your servant has found favor in your sight.** The latter expression seems related to an old Hebrew formula (cf. Gen. 34:18; 41:37; 45:16; cf. Esth. 5:14). With **send me unto Judah** Nehemiah avoids reference to notorious Jerusalem (Ezra 4:12, 15), which was ruined and largely depopulated (cf. 11:1-2).

6. The king's answer is interrupted unexpectedly by the words **the queen sitting beside him.** In later rabbinical usage the word here translated **queen** almost never has the polite sense of "wife" but usually implies promiscuity. The LXX renders it "concubine" (*pallakē*). But biblical usage strongly contrasts the word to those used for inferior harem women (cf. Ps. 45:9; Dan. 5:2-3, 23; cf. J. A. Montgomery, *A Critical and Exegetical Commentary on the Book of Daniel* [New York: Charles Scribner's Sons, 1927; "International Critical Commentary"], p. 251), and the Talmud (Rosh Hashanah 4a) usually uses it for **queen.** Here, as in Ps. 45:9 and in Daniel, the Vulg. translates **queen.** As queen she could be only Damaspia, the one legitimate queen of Artaxerxes I (cf. Ctesias *Persian Fragments,* sec. 44; Ernst Herzfeld, *Zoroaster and His World* [Princeton: Princeton University Press, 1947], I, 165-69). Since palace wives never appeared in public (Plutarch *Symposium* I. 1; Macrobius *Saturnalia* VII; Aelian, *Variae historiae* XII. 1), the scene is an intimate one. Reference to the queen is appropriate, since feminine influences and resulting harem intrigues were strong during Artaxerxes' reign (W. W. Tarn, "Persia, from Xerxes to Alexander," in *Cambridge Ancient History,* VI, 2-3; Olmstead, *History of the Persian Empire,* pp. 312, 344). According to the LXXABL and the Vulg., the queen spoke sympathetically to Nehemiah and she may have used her influence to aid him (P. H. Hunter, *After the Exile* [London: Oliphant, Anderson, & Ferrier, 1890], I, 294; Rawlinson, *Ezra and Nehemiah,* p. 89; Rudolf Kittel, *Geschichte des Volkes Israel* [2nd ed.; Stuttgart: W. Kohlhammer, 1929], III, 616). It is even conjectured that the queen sat by the king as the result of a previous arrangement with Nehemiah (Olmstead, *History of the Persian Empire,* p. 315).

Nehemiah could scarcely answer the question **How long?** since he did not know the magnitude of his task. The Hebrew text may be translated more appropriately, "When is your going?" (Batten, *op. cit.,* p. 193). For **I set him a time** the Peshitta has more plausibly, "he gave me a time," which may be original (Hugo Winckler, *Altoriental-*

concern, vigorously applied at just the right, the "providential," moment.

Across almost twenty-four hundred years we can still feel in this vivid recital the mounting tensions of this fateful interview, and we are carried thereby past the hand of the Chronicler who edited it generations afterward, and are brought closer to the mind and heart of Nehemiah himself, who participated in it and soon thereafter put his own account in writing. The king's question, **For what do you make request?**

stirred him to "ejaculatory prayer"—a cry to God for guidance and help—before he made reply: So I **prayed to the God of heaven. And I said to the king.** Prayer to God for the right word and spirit at this critical moment followed upon the thorough preparation of his own mind for all eventualities which the whole account reflects. God could and would give the right word more quickly and surely to a man who had already done some hard thinking, doubtless then also with a similar prayer **for**

7 Moreover I said unto the king, If it please the king, let letters be given me to the governors beyond the river, that they may convey me over till I come into Judah; 8 And a letter unto Asaph the keeper of the king's forest, that he may give me timber to make beams for the gates of the palace which *appertained* to the house, and for the wall of the city, and for the house that I shall enter into. And the king granted me, according to the good hand of my God upon me.

7 And I said to the king, "If it pleases the king, let letters be given me to the governors of the province Beyond the River, that they may let me pass through until I come to Judah; 8 and a letter to Asaph, the keeper of the king's forest, that he may give me timber to make beams for the gates of the fortress of the temple, and for the wall of the city, and for the house which I shall occupy." And the king granted me what I asked, for the good hand of my God was upon me.

---

ische Forschungen [Leipzig: E. Pfeiffer, 1901], Reihe 2, Bd. III, p. 473, n. 3; Herbert Gotthard, *Der Text des Buches Nehemia* [Riga: Ernst Plates, 1932-38], p. 63; Batten, *op. cit.*, p. 194). The period of absence was actually at least twelve years (5:14), but Nehemiah must have asked for much less than that and had his leave renewed from time to time.

7-8. These verses, dealing with further requests, have sometimes been rejected as the work of the Chronicler (Torrey, *Composition*, p. 36) or considered to be so edited that "one can pick out but little of the original" (Batten, *loc. cit.*). The verses are usually regarded as genuine, with some traces of editorial revision (cf. Robert H. Pfeiffer, *Introduction to the Old Testament* [New York: Harper & Bros., 1941], p. 835). Much is missing in Nehemiah's commission, however, for there is no reference to his escort (2:9) or to his appointment as governor of Judea (5:14). The journey could not be made without documents identifying him as a servant of the king and granting him proper authority. Ezra also had required such letters (Ezra 7:21; 8:36), including a passport (Persian *parvānak* or *fravartak*) to guarantee safe conduct to Judea (cf. Herzfeld, *Zoroaster and His World*, I, 229-30). The **governors** (cf. Ezra 8:36) were the underlings of the satrap of the land **Beyond the River** (cf. Ezra 4:10) who could refuse passage through their districts. Also needed was an order (*farmān*) for materials necessary for the reconstruction. Huge timbers were scarce in the Near East except in the Lebanon district (Ezra 3:7; 6:4). From Assyrian times the Lebanons were a royal preserve and the area is here (vs. 8) called a "park" (Persian *pairidaēza*), a term usually used for the enclosed pleasure gardens surrounding the residences of Persian kings and satraps (cf. Song of S. 4:13; Eccl. 2:5; Xenophon *Anabasis* I. 2. 9; II. 4. 16).

The great distance between the Lebanons and Jerusalem and the use of the Hebrew name **Asaph** (cf. Ezra 2:41) have led to attempts at discovering for the royal preserve a Palestinian location in the sycamore woods of the Shephelah (I Chr. 27:28; K. F. Keil, *Chronik, Esra, Nehemia und Esther* [Leipzig: Dörffling & Franke, 1870; "Biblischer Commentar über das Alte Testament"], p. 507) or the gardens of Solomon at 'Etam (Tell 'Eitun), about seven miles from Jerusalem (Frants Buhl, *Geographie des alten Palästina*

---

guidance and help. In this profoundly religious sense "God helps those who help themselves" and realize their need of further aid humbly and hopefully enough to ask for God's help. Most ministers finally learn, as much through their failures as by their successes, that God still gives to careful preparation for every kind of speaking—so long as the preacher himself does not turn his words into an idol or a dogma— the fulfillment which Jesus promised, "It shall be given you in that same hour what ye shall speak" (Matt. 10:19).

So there begins to take shape, in Nehemiah's reply to the king's question, that "great work" from which, in the best-known sentence of these memoirs (6:3), he later refused to come down. At this earliest stage of its inception we can already see that it included for him, as indispensable factors in its performance: (*a*) his own initiative and continuing responsibility, strikingly focused in his request to the king that you **send me to Judah;** (*b*) the king's understanding and support for his mission; and (*c*) God's continuous guidance and blessing upon its

9 ¶ Then I came to the governors beyond the river, and gave them the king's letters. Now the king had sent captains of the army and horsemen with me.

9 Then I came to the governors of the province Beyond the River, and gave them the king's letters. Now the king had sent with me officers of the army and horsemen.

[Freiburg i. B.: J. C. B. Mohr, 1896], pp. 90-92) . But the distance from Lebanon was always regarded as negligible when the quality of its timber was considered (I Kings 5:6-10; Ezra 3:7) . Moreover, Nehemiah would scarcely know the name of a minor official in Palestine, but as an intimate palace official he might know the name of the Syrian official who furnished timbers for the royal builders at Susa from "a mountain named Lebanon" (V. Scheil, *Inscriptions des Achéménides à Suse* [Paris: E. Leroux, 1929], pp. 3 ff., 16 ff.; R. G. Kent, "The Record of Darius's Palace at Susa," *Journal of the American Oriental Society,* LIII [1933], 1-23; Olmstead, *History of the Persian Empire,* p. 168) . The name **Asaph,** moreover, need not be Hebrew but could abbreviate Phoenician Milki-ashapa (D. D. Luckenbill, *Ancient Records of Assyria and Babylonia* [Chicago: University of Chicago Press, 1926-27], Vol. II, p. 266, sec. 690; p. 340, sec. 876; cf. feminine *Asept* in *Corpus Inscriptionum Semiticarum* [Paris: E. Reipublicae Typographeo, 1889], Part II, Vol. I, No. 119) or some Persian name with the common element aspa-, such as Aspis (Cornelius Nepos *Lives of Eminent Commanders* XIV. 4. 1 ff.; Ferdinand Justi, *Iranisches Namenbuch* [Marburg: N. G. Elwert, 1895], p. 46) .

Timber could be "trees." For **palace** read **fortress** (cf. Ezra 6:2) . The **fortress of the temple,** defending the north approach to the temple, included the Tower of Hananel (3:1) and possibly also the Tower of the Hundred (3:1; 12:39; J. J. Simons, *Jerusalem in the Old Testament* [Leiden: E. J. Brill, 1952], p. 429, n. 2) . Timbers were needed **for the wall of the city** (I Kings 7:11-12; Ezra 5:8; 6:4) . **Which I shall occupy** interprets a literal **that I shall enter into,** the latter perhaps indicating a repaired house rather than a new one. Since he did not use the abode of a former governor (cf. 5:15) , he may not yet have been governor. Nor did he divert labor or supplies from his main project, the city fortification, to provide for his own comfort. For **according to the good hand** see Ezra 7:6; 8:18, 22.

III. Nehemiah, Governor of Judea (2:9-20)

A. Arrival in Trans-Euphratia (2:9-11)

9. The Chronicler's hand has been seen in vss. 9-10 but with insufficient reason (Torrey, *loc. cit.;* Batten, *loc. cit.*) . **Officers of the army** accompanied Nehemiah, but since the Peshitta and the LXX[L] have a single officer with the **horsemen,** the plural form has been regarded as due to a tendency to increase the glory of Nehemiah (Gotthard, *op. cit.,* p. 66) . The **governors** (cf. Ezra 5:3, 6) were apparently the deputies of the satrap of Trans-Euphratia who controlled the areas through which Nehemiah had to pass. Josephus indicates that Nehemiah picked up Jewish emigrees in Babylon who followed

---

progress. Without these factors the "great work" could hardly come to completion.

It is evident that in vss. 6-8 the text is confused and may not be intact (see Exeg.) . But in spite of such gaps, and of possible later revisions, certain characteristics of Nehemiah still shine through the account as we have it. He knew that the time element in the situation was not only urgent but short, and he accepted a definitely limited liability for his own personal participation (vs. 6) . He had looked ahead in anticipation to the middle distance, the region where the plans of so many of us, like our focus of forethought, turn fuzzy; he

made careful provision for that middle journey (vs. 7) , even though he could not see ahead all the way to the end of the road. And he took the happy outcome of this initial interview with the king as additional assurance for his faith that **the good hand of my God . . . upon me** would guide and support him to the end (vs. 8) . So every "hero of faith" has to continue to "walk by faith, not by sight" (II Cor. 5:7) , alike through success and failure, life and death.

9-11. *There Are Many Adversaries.*—It is an indication that we have in our present account a firm warp of Nehemiah's actual experience, as well as a woof interwoven by the Chronicler's

10 When Sanballat the Horonite, and Tobiah the servant, the Ammonite, heard *of it,* it grieved them exceedingly that there was come a man to seek the welfare of the children of Israel.	10 But when Sanbal'lat the Hor'onite and Tobi'ah the servant, the Ammonite, heard this, it displeased them greatly that someone had come to seek the welfare of the children of Israel.

him to Jerusalem. The letters (vs. 7) were given to the governors, but Josephus asserts that Nehemiah "showed the letters to God" just as he elsewhere (*Antiquities* X. 1. 4) insists that Hezekiah placed the letters of the Assyrian general (II Kings 19:14) "within the temple."

10. **Displeased them greatly** and **grieved them exceedingly** both interpret the literal Hebrew text, "And it was bad for them a great badness." **Welfare** (Hebrew "good") is interpreted as "prosperity" in the Vulg. **Sanballat** bears the Babylonian name *md Sin-uballit* (K. L. Tallqvist, *Neubabylonisches Namenbuch* [Helsingfors: 1905], p. 276, No. 168). Men of Babylon, Cutha, and other Babylonian cities were settled in North Israel (II Kings 17:24, 29-31). **Sanballat** is associated with Samaria (4:2) and Josephus (*Antiquities* IX. 14. 3) regularly calls the Samaritans "Cutheans." The Hebrew names of his sons (Delaiah and Shelemiah; Cowley, *Aramaic Papyri*, No. 30, l. 29; cf. Neh. 6:10; 7:62 and 3:30; 13:13), like the Samaritan attempt to worship with the Jews (Ezra 4:1-2), are doubtless due to Jewish missionary activity in Samaria (II Kings 17:26-28). **The Horonite** is perhaps an epithet linking **Sanballat** with Beth-horon of Ephraim (modern Beit 'Ur et-Taḥta and Beit 'Ur el-Fōqā), commanding the most difficult passages of the ancient road from Jerusalem to Lydda and the seacoast (F. M. Abel, *Géographie de la Palestine* [Paris: J. Gabalda, 1938], II, 93, 220; W. M. Thomson, *The Land and the Book* [London: Thomas Nelson & Sons, 1880], pp. 533, 670). Its site was strategic for keeping in touch with Jewish affairs without neglecting Samaria where he was "governor." It is straining credulity too far to assume that another Sanballat lived under similar circumstances in the time of Alexander the Great (Isaac Spak, *Der Bericht des Joesphus über Alexander den Grossen* [Königsberg: Hartung, 1911]; C. C. Torrey, "Sanballat 'The Horonite,'" *Journal of Biblical Literature*, XLVII [1928], 384, 386). Too many coincidences are essential to such a view (Cowley, *op. cit.*, p. 110; Ralph Marcus, tr., *Josephus* [Cambridge: Harvard University Press, 1927; "Loeb Classical Library"], IV, 498-511).

Tobiah is the Hebrew equivalent of Tabe-el (Ezra 4:7). **The Ammonite** indicates residence in Trans-Jordan, just north of ancient Moab. The family of Tobiah was prominent in Ammon down to Hellenistic times (C. C. Edgar, "Selected Papyri from the Archives of Zenon," *Annales du Service des Antiquités*, XVIII [1918], 164-66; 231-32; Hugo Gressmann, *Die ammonitischen Tobiaden* [Berlin: W. de Gruyter, 1921], pp. 663-71; H. Willrich, "Zur Geschichte der Tobiaden," *Archiv für Papyrusforschung*, VII [1924], 61-64). The homestead of the Tobiah family was found at 'Araq el-Emir, about a dozen miles east of the Jordan and about ten miles northwest of ancient Heshbon, Moab (Josephus *Antiquities* XII. 4. 11; H. C. Butler, *Ancient Architecture in Syria* [Leyden: E. J. Brill, 1907], I, 1-25; Carl Watzinger, *Denkmäler Palästinas* [Leipzig: J. C. Hinrichs, 1935], Vol. II, Pl. XXII). The name Tobiah found carved there may be dated as early as the time of the **Tobiah** who was contemporary with Nehemiah (B. Maisler, בית טוביה ("The House of Tobias"), *Tarbiz*, XII [1941], 109-23; Marcus, *op. cit.*, VII, 117, note *c*). The puzzling epithet **the servant** does not indicate subservience to Sanballat (as proposed by Rudolph, *Esra und Nehemia*, p. 109) but rather to the Persian king, apparently as the highest Persian official over Ammon (Albrecht Alt,

idealizing hand, that in spite of the letters and soldiers the king had given him, enemies of his cause appeared even before he reached Jerusalem. Their names and residences are explicitly given. There is a distinct hint of what we moderns should be tempted to call anti-Semitism in the attitude of these non-Jewish neighbors (cf. vs. 20c) as it is stated in vs. 10.

11 So I came to Jerusalem, and was there three days.

12 ¶ And I arose in the night, I and some few men with me; neither told I *any* man what my God had put in my heart to do at Jerusalem: neither *was there any* beast with me, save the beast that I rode upon.

11 So I came to Jerusalem and was there three days. 12 Then I arose in the night, I and a few men with me; and I told no one what my God had put into my heart to do for Jerusalem. There was no beast with me

---

"Judas Nachbarn zur Zeit Nehemias, *Palästinajahrbuch*, XXVII [1931], 70) . Gashmu the Arabian (cf. vs. 19) may have borne the same title. He has been regarded as a "governor" of Trans-Jordan (Ernst Sellin, *Geschichte des israelitisch-jüdischen Volkes* [Leipzig: Quelle & Meyer, 1932], II, 152) , as a deputy of a higher "governor" or satrap. Such officials functioned like the later ethnarchs of whom Origen (*Epistle to Africanus* XIV) claims that the ethnarch of Palestine in his day was "differing in nothing from a king." Nebuchadrezzar's vassals were called his "servants" (II Kings 24:1, 10-11) and Darius, in the Behistun inscription, calls his officials "subject" (Persian *bandaka*) , which becomes "servant" (*gallâ*) in the Babylonian version and "servant" or "slave" (עילם misspelled for עלים) in the Aramaic version (Cowley, *op. cit.*, pp. 253, 259, restoration in Aramaic Behistun inscription, Col. III, l. 38) . The name "Castle of the Servant" (Qaṣr il-'Abd) , now applied to the fortress 'Araq el-Emir, might possibly preserve the earlier title **servant** and not derive from the legend of the black slave and the emir's daughter, as recorded by C. R. Conder (*Heth and Moab* [3rd ed.; London: Macmillan & Co., 1892], p. 363) .

The arrival of Nehemiah with royal support disturbed the foes of the Jews because it meant a delimitation of the powers they may have previously exercised, possibly as nonresident governors supervising Judea. Upon arrival, Nehemiah rested for **three days** (cf. Ezra 8:32) .

B. Inspection of the City Wall (2:12-15)

After three days Nehemiah secretly set out to assess the damage to the city wall and the magnitude of the task of reconstruction. Upon his arrival he probably approached from the north and noted the state of the walls there. He appears to have resided in the southwestern part of the city, where he could have examined the western wall for three days. Thus he set forth with a small group secretly, moving counterclockwise, to examine the southern and eastern walls.

12. Inspection **in the night** could be done only in bright moonlight (cf. Rudolph, *op. cit.*, p. 110; cf. vs. 15) . **I told no one** refers to the Jews who had not yet been told of Nehemiah's identity or purpose. For **at Jerusalem** the M.T. has, lit., "to Jerusalem" (as in LXXᴸ) or **for Jerusalem**. The **few men** were his servants since they were unmounted. The Peshitta explains that they "had come with" Nehemiah but there is nothing to indicate that Hanani (cf. 1:2) was in the group (Batten, *op. cit.*, p. 199) . The Hebrew for **beast** merely means a domestic animal (cf. Gen. 1:24-25) , without defining its kind. A single mounted rider accompanied by servants on foot would draw less attention than a mounted party.

11-16. First Count the Cost.—Whatever may have been Nehemiah's own thinking in advance, however careful his formulation of a program for his mission, he took time enough after his arrival in Jerusalem to look around for himself; and he supplemented what others had told him about the actual situation by firsthand investigations of his own. The story of his secret midnight inspection of the ruined walls is one of the most vivid accounts of personal experience in the O.T., and its sharpness of detail, as he recalls what befell him and the animal he rode, persuades us that we have here what his own observant eye saw through the darkness, rather than any "tendentious" generalities and inventions of the Chronicler. Nehemiah was canny enough not to tell even the leaders of his own party what he had in mind until he had looked over the ground carefully himself, just as he had been canny enough in his interview with

13 And I went out by night by the gate of the valley, even before the dragon well, and to the dung port, and viewed the walls of Jerusalem, which were broken down, and the gates thereof were consumed with fire.

but the beast on which I rode. 13 I went out by night by the Valley Gate to the Jackal's Well and to the Dung Gate, and I inspected the walls of Jerusalem which were broken down and its gates which had been de-

---

13. The **Valley Gate,** important in the fortification of Jerusalem (cf. II Chr. 26:9), has been located by scholars on various sides of the city (cf. Simons, *op. cit.,* pp. 124-25). Since **the Valley** (Hebrew *gai*) invariably means the Valley of Hinnom (Wadi er-Rabâbeh), to the south of Jerusalem, the **Valley Gate** was certainly in the south wall, opening toward that valley. But the exact location in the south wall is uncertain since there is a dispute as to whether the southwestern hill of Jerusalem was occupied so early. As a result of the latest excavation on the hill, it is concluded that "while the pottery would go to show that the western hill was inhabited at least towards the end of the Monarchy, it has still to be established that it was fortified then, for no well-dated masonry of that period has yet come to light" (C. N. Johns, "The Citadel, Jerusalem," *The Quarterly of the Department of Antiquities in Palestine,* XIV [1950], 152). The fact that the earliest fortification found there is early Hellenistic (*ibid.,* pp. 127 ff.; 150 ff.) has supported the view of those who insist that in the time of Nehemiah the city was confined to the southeastern hill (J. Germer-Durand, *Topographie de l'ancienne Jérusalem* [Jerusalem: Hôtellerie de Notre-Dame de France, 1925]; Albrecht Alt, "Das Taltor von Jerusalem," *Palästinajahrbuch,* XXIV [1928], 74-98; Kurt Galling, "Jerusalem," *Biblisches Reallexikon* [Tübingen: J. C. B. Mohr, 1937; "Handbuch zum Alten Testament"], pp. 297-309; W. F. Albright, "Excavations at Jerusalem," *Jewish Quarterly Review,* XXI [1930-31], 167; "Recent Works on the Topography and Archaeology of Jerusalem," *ibid.,* XXII [1931-32], 414-16). The discovery of a strong early wall on the western side of the southeast hill has further strengthened the one-hill hypothesis (J. W. Crowfoot and G. M. Fitzgerald, *Excavations in the Tyropoeon Valley, Jerusalem, 1927* [London: Palestine Exploration Fund, 1927]). But the archaeological evidence, contrary though it appears, need not yet be regarded as conclusive since but little excavation has been done on the southwestern hill and the wall on the western rim of the southeastern hill may be merely evidence of persistent circumvallation of the royal compound on Ophel (Simons, *op. cit.,* p. 126). Moreover, scriptural allusions and other considerations make it probable that the southwestern hill was walled in the late pre-exilic times (*ibid.,* pp. 226-81). As Simons has indicated, "Not only the number of gates to be placed along the circumference of the city, but more especially the problem of the site of the Valley Gate is an insuperable obstacle to the one-hill-theory, every form of which so far devised is forced to detach it from the Hinnom Valley, to which its name inseparably unites it" (*ibid.,* p. 281).

The **Valley Gate** is perhaps best located in the south wall, close to the southwest corner, in the same relative position as the later gate found by F. J. Bliss (*Excavations at Jerusalem* [London: Committee of the Palestine Exploration Fund, 1898], pp. 16 ff., Pl. II, pp. 342-44; Simons, *op. cit.,* pp. 279-80; Mitchell, "Wall of Jerusalem," p. 112). According to 3:13 the so-called **Dung Gate** lay about one thousand cubits (about fifteen hundred feet) from the **Valley Gate.** At a little greater distance to the east from the Bliss Gate (about nineteen hundred feet), at the terminus of the southern wall and exactly at the mouth of the central (Tyropoeon) valley and on its western slope, a massive gate has been found (Bliss, *op. cit.,* pp. 88 ff., Pl. X; Simons, *op. cit.,* pp. 123-24, 162; Mitchell, *op. cit.,* p. 114). The ancient **Dung Gate,** if in a similar position, thus lay on the road down the Tyropoeon Valley on which the modern **Dung Gate** (*Bāb el-Mughâribeh*) opens. The Bliss wall, to be sure, is later than the time of Nehemiah, but it has been claimed that "besides the hypothesis of a wall earlier than that of Bliss on a slightly more restricted line, there is also the possibility that the wall of Bliss itself replaced a much earlier one along the same course" (Simons, *op. cit.,* p. 272). Thus the position

14 Then I went on to the gate of the fountain, and to the king's pool: but *there was* no place for the beast *that was* under me to pass.

stroyed by fire. 14 Then I went on to the Fountain Gate and to the King's Pool; but there was no place for the beast that was

---

of the Zion Gate (Bāb en-Nebi Dāūd) appears to be "a successor to the Gate of the Essenes and the Valley Gate on a more restricted course of the city-wall" (*ibid.*, p. 280, n. 1). The **Dung Gate** is more accurately the "Refuse Gate," since **Dung** translates a word equated with "dust" in poetic parallelism (cf. Ps. 113:7; I Sam. 2:8), and the gate is doubtless identical with the "Gate of the Potsherds" of Jer. 19:2a.

Mentioned between the **Valley Gate** and the **Dung Gate** is the **dragon well**, which is found nowhere else in the Bible. It may be a popular name for a well elsewhere designated differently. It is better to read with the M.T., LXX^L, and Vulg., **dragon** (*tannîn;* cf. Gen. 1:20-21; Ps. 74:13; Ezek. 29:3; 32:2) rather than **Jackal's** (*tannîm;* Mic. 1:8; Lam. 4:3) since the mythical monster in ancient as in modern times was believed to lie within rivers, pools, or springs, especially when the waters tasted medicinal (cf. Ezek. 32:2) or were intermittent in their flow (cf. Strabo *Geography* XVI. 2. 7; Josephus *Jewish Wars* V. 3. 2; W. Robertson Smith, *Lectures on the Religion of the Semites* [3rd ed.; New York: The Macmillan Co., 1927], pp. 168-69, 171-72; Edward Robinson, *Biblical Researches in Palestine, Mount Sinai and Arabia Petraea* [New York: J. Leavitt, 1841], I, 507). The well was probably En-rogel, lying deep in the valley, at the juncture of the Kidron and Hinnom valleys, where the "Serpent's Stone" (I Kings 1:9) was also located. It is also called the "Well of Nehemiah" because of the tradition that he retrieved from it the sacred fire of the temple that had been concealed within it during the Exile (II Macc. 1:19-22; *ibid.*, I, 491, n. 1). Since Nehemiah followed the wall and did not descend to the valley floor, the translation **to the . . . Well** is wrong. The complex Hebrew preposition "to the front of" indicates that he passed the wall at a point opposite the well. The LXX^L translates "opposite" (*kata prosōpon*); the Vulg. and Peshitta read "before."

14. The **Fountain Gate**, lit., "the Gate of the Spring," led to a spring much used by the city. Opinion is divided as to whether it was the Gihon Spring or En-rogel (cf. vs. 13) but the latter seems most likely. The gate is probably to be identified with the ancient gate found before the stairs of the City of David (cf. 3:15), discovered at the southeastern corner of the city (Raymond Weill, *La cité de David* [Paris: Paul Geuthner, 1920], pp. 120, 123; Hugues Vincent, "Notes and Queries," *Palestine Exploration Fund Quarterly Statement for 1926*, pp. 160-62; Simons, *op. cit.*, pp. 121-24, 449). The **King's Pool** has been sought both within the city wall (Alt, "Das Taltor von Jerusalem," pp. 92 ff.) and in the Kidron Valley outside of it (Galling, *Biblisches Reallexikon*, p. 305). Its name has caused it to be sought in the valley southeast of the city near the king's garden (3:15), as a basin fed by a canal from the Gihon Spring (Simons, *op. cit.*, pp. 192-93). Many have identified it with the "Lower Pool" or "Pool of Shiloah" (cf. 3:15; Birket el Ḥamra), lying within the city wall just before the **Fountain Gate** at the end of the central valley (Gustav Dalman, "Die Wasserversorgung des ältesten Jerusalem," *Palästinajahrbuch*, XIV [1918], 65 ff.; J. Fischer, "Die Quellen und Teiche des Biblischen Jerusalem," *Das Heilige Land*, LXXVII [1933], 97; Weill, *op. cit.*, p. 94). But the **King's Pool** lay beyond the **Fountain Gate**, which is mentioned before it. A rock-cut basin in front of the Gihon Spring (the Spring of the Stairs, 'Ain Umm ed-Deraj, the Fountain of the Virgin) would meet the requirements (Edward Robinson, *op. cit.*, Vol. II, p. 311, n. 5, p. 499; Hugues Vincent, "La cité de David," *Revue Biblique*, XXX [1921], 567-69).

---

the king not to stress the connection of his plans with the city of Jerusalem, about which the king had evidently received unfriendly information.

Here again is the combination of careful planning with religious vision and faith which was so steadily characteristic of this man of action.

15 Then went I up in the night by the brook, and viewed the wall, and turned back, and entered by the gate of the valley, and so returned.

16 And the rulers knew not whither I went, or what I did; neither had I as yet told it to the Jews, nor to the priests, nor to the nobles, nor to the rulers, nor to the rest that did the work.

17 ¶ Then said I unto them, Ye see the distress that we are in, how Jerusalem lieth waste, and the gates thereof are burned with fire: come, and let us build up the wall of Jerusalem, that we be no more a reproach.

under me to pass. 15 Then I went up in the night by the valley and inspected the wall; and I turned back and entered by the Valley Gate, and so returned. 16 And the officials did not know where I had gone or what I was doing; and I had not yet told the Jews, the priests, the nobles, the officials, and the rest that were to do the work.

17 Then I said to them, "You see the trouble we are in, how Jerusalem lies in ruins with its gates burned. Come, let us build the wall of Jerusalem, that we may no

15. Beyond the **King's Pool** the walls approached the precipitous side of the Kidron Valley, the deep ravine running east of the city (I Macc. 12:37). **By the brook** is meant the torrent bed of the Kidron stream which gives the valley its name. Since the valley floor rises gradually north of the Virgin's Spring, **went up** correctly describes northward progress. It is debatable whether Nehemiah continued around the city (Ernst Bertheau, *Die Bücher Esra, Nechemia und Ester*, ed. Victor Ryssel [2nd ed.; Leipzig: S. Hirzel, 1887; "Kurzgefasstes exegetisches Handbuch zum Alten Testament"], p. 148; Hölscher, *Ezra und Nehemia*, p. 528; Simons, *op. cit.*, p. 444; and with some doubts Bernhard Stade, *Geschichte des Volkes Israel* [Berlin: G. Grote, 1888], II, 166) or turned back the way he came (Bertholet, *Esra und Nehemia*, p. 52; Alt, "Das Taltor von Jerusalem," p. 91; Rudolph, *Esra und Nehemia*, p. 112). Practical experience has shown that he could not profitably continue to inspect the walls from the valley even on a moonlight night (Selah Merrill, *Ancient Jerusalem* [New York: Fleming H. Revell, 1908], pp. 341-42).

C. Nehemiah's Announcement to the Leaders (2:16-18)

Josephus (*Antiquities* XI. 5. 7) omits the secret inspection of the walls and claims that on his arrival Nehemiah gathered "all of the people" to Jerusalem and addressed them "in the middle of the temple court." The Bible indicates that he did not inform the Jewish leaders regarding his authority and plans until after his inspection of the walls.

16. The **rulers** (cf. Ezra 9:2) were the local **officials,** probably non-Jewish deputies in the city. **The Jews** is an inclusive term, covering the specified classes of leaders. **Nobles** means "freemen" and the LXX^{אAB} uses here the word (*tois entimois*) employed by Xenophon to designate Persian nobles. With the **nobles** Nehemiah usually links the **rulers,** the politicians and bureaucrats who governed the people directly (cf. Ezra 9:2).

Generally the leaders are balanced against "the rest of the people" (4:14, 19) but here is found "the rest of the doing of the work" or preferably, with other Hebrew MSS and the Peshitta, "the rest of those doing the work." **That were to do the work** is interpretative, anticipating work on the wall (5:16), limiting the group unreasonably. The reference is probably to the administrative personnel, those in charge of the business (Esth. 3:9; 9:3; I Chr. 29:6; Heinrich Kaupel, "Der Sinn von המלאכה עשה in Neh. 2, 16," *Biblica*, XXI [1940], 40-44; Rudolph, *op. cit.*, p. 110). Nehemiah got in touch with the people through the aristocrats and government officials.

17. Josephus indicates that the distress of Jerusalem was due to the ill will of its neighbors, whereas the M.T. finds it due to physical damages to the fortifications of the city (cf. 1:3).

17-19a. Let Us Rise Up and Build.—With such thorough preparation in advance, Nehemiah's summons to co-operative action brought forth immediate and energetic response on the part of his previously disheartened fellow countrymen. He knew them well enough to

18 Then I told them of the hand of my God which was good upon me; as also the king's words that he had spoken unto me. And they said, Let us rise up and build. So they strengthened their hands for *this* good *work.*

19 But when Sanballat the Horonite, and Tobiah the servant, the Ammonite, and Geshem the Arabian, heard *it,* they laughed us to scorn, and despised us, and said, What *is* this thing that ye do? will ye rebel against the king?

longer suffer disgrace." 18 And I told them of the hand of my God which had been upon me for good, and also of the words which the king had spoken to me. And they said, "Let us rise up and build." So they strengthened their hands for the good work.

19 But when Sanbal'lat the Hor'onite and Tobi'ah the servant, the Ammonite, and Geshem the Arab heard of it, they derided us and despised us and said, "What is this thing that you are doing? Are you rebelling

---

18. Characteristic terminology of Nehemiah is seen in **the hand** (vs. 8; 1:10), indicating divine guidance; **my God** (vss. 8, 12; 5:19; 6:14; etc.) ; and **upon me for good** (vs. 8; cf. Ezra 9:12). **The king's words** refer to the entire scene of vss. 4-8. For **Let us rise up and build** the M.T. has "We will arise and build," which is more resolute. The expression **strengthened their hands** (cf. 6:9; Ezra 4:4) seems parallel to the Akkadian *kunnu qātē* ("to make hands fast") which, when used with an infinitive (cf. Ezra 6:22), means "to prepare to do something" (cf. Carl Bezold, *Babylonisch-Assyrisches Glossar* [Heidelberg: C. Winter, 1926], p. 135, col. 1, *s.v. kânu,* III, 1). Here the Peshitta has "to do good"; Josephus concludes, "And the Jews prepared for the work."

D. Conflict with Neighboring Officials (2:19-20)

19. In addition to **Sanballat** and **Tobiah** (vs. 10) as an enemy of the Jews is **Geshem the Arabian** (also called "Gashmu" in 6:6). Arabic names suggest Gushamu (Julius Euting, *Sinaitische Inschriften* [Berlin: Georg Reimer, 1891], pp. 10-11; Theodor Nöldeke, "Wellhausen's Reste arabischen Heidenthumes," *Zeitschrift der deutschen morgenländischen Gesellschaft,* XLI [1887], 715, n. 1). An official mentioned in first place in the date formula of a Lihyanite Arabian inscription found at Hegra (cf. F. V. Winnett, *A Study of the Lihyanite and Thamudic Inscriptions* [Toronto: University of Toronto Press, 1937], pp. 14, 16, 50-51) has been identified with the **Geshem** of vs. 19 (H. Grimme, "Beziehungen zwischen dem Staate der Lihjān und dem Achämenidenreiche," *Orientalische Literaturzeitung,* XLIV [1941], 343; Olmstead, *History of the Persian Empire,* p. 295; Rudolph, *op. cit.,* pp. 112-13). The *'Abd* which follows the name may be another example of the title "the servant" (cf. vs. 10), designating him as the highest Persian official of the Arabian district (Alt, "Judas Nachbarn zur Zeit Nehemias," pp. 73 ff.). **The Arabian** is an administrative rather than ethnic term, indicating the province of Arabia which, during the Persian period, incorporated the earlier land of Edom, to the south of Judah, about which Nehemiah is strangely silent (Abel, *Géographie,* II, 122-23). Edomites have been regarded as "Arabs" in the later period (Gustav Hölscher, *Palästina in der persischen und hellenistischen Zeit* [Berlin: Weidmann, 1903], pp. 19 ff.). During the Exilic period Edom was an aggressive neighbor (Mal. 1:2-5; Obad. 1-21; Lam. 4:1-22; I Esdras 4:48-56; S. A. Cook, "First Esdras," in R. H. Charles, ed., *The Apocrypha and Pseudepigrapha* [Oxford: Clarendon Press, 1913], I, 13; "The Inauguration of Judaism," in *Cambridge Ancient History,* VI, 176-88; R. H.

---

include in his call to action a reference to the support of the king, and above all to **the hand of my God which had been upon me for good;** their response echoes like an antiphonal trumpet, **Let us rise up and build.** His courage and faith quickened them into resolution and confidence.

19b-20. Derision and Threat.—As so often in crises, with the progress of the enterprise came stiffening of the opposition. Now it is charges of political rebellion and treason that Nehemiah and his followers have to face, as well as the ridicule that a "despised minority" often finds even harder to meet than misrepresenta-

20 Then answered I them, and said unto them, The God of heaven, he will prosper us; therefore we his servants will arise and build: but ye have no portion, nor right, nor memorial, in Jerusalem.

3 Then Eliashib the high priest rose up with his brethren the priests, and they builded the sheep gate; they sanctified it,

against the king?" 20 Then I replied to them, "The God of heaven will make us prosper, and we his servants will arise and build; but you have no portion or right or memorial in Jerusalem."

3 Then Eli'ashib the high priest rose up with his brethren the priests and they

---

Kennett, "The Date of Deuteronomy," *The Journal of Theological Studies,* VII [1906], 487). Nabataean pressure pushed Edomites into Judea, where they took over former Jewish settlements. The Persian palace at Lachish (Tell ed-Duweir) may have been the administrative center of the Arabian territory (Abel, *op. cit.,* II, 123; J. L. Starkey, "Tell Duweir," *Palestine Exploration Fund Quarterly Statement for 1933,* p. 193, Plates III-IV; "Fourth Season at Tell Duweir," *ibid.,* 1936, p. 188, Plates VII, IX).

20. The God of Heaven will make us prosper indicates Nehemiah's sense of mission (cf. vss. 8*b*, 18*a*) with divine as well as royal support. **And we his servants,** supported by the Vulg., is less exact than **therefore we his servants,** which links the servanthood (1:10) more directly with the divine support which promises success. **We . . . will arise** usually initiates an action which is then more fully specified (cf. Ezra 1:5). **But** draws a sharp contrast between the industrious Jews and their watching opponents. **Portion,** "part" or "share," indicates possession of property. **Right** has the technical sense of "just claim" (H. E. Ryle, *The Books of Ezra and Nehemiah* [Cambridge: Cambridge University Press, 1893; "Cambridge Bible"], p. 171; Carl Siegfried, *Esra, Nehemia und Esther* [Göttingen: Vandenhoeck & Ruprecht, 1901; "Handkommentar zum Alten Testament"], p. 79; Bertholet, *loc. cit.*), or even "authority" (Batten, *Ezra and Nehemiah,* p. 204), referring to legal right of possession or even the assumption of authority such as the neighbors claimed before Nehemiah's arrival. **Memorial** is, lit., "remembrance." There was not to remain, even in the memory of man, a shred of evidence that the opponents ever had any connection with the Jewish territory.

IV. Building the Wall of Jerusalem (3:1–4:23)

Ch. 3 is clearly intrusive in the Nehemiah document, interrupting the narrative which is then resumed in ch. 4. Its literary style, unlike Nehemiah's, has been likened to that of the Chronicler, and some (e.g., Torrey, *Composition,* p. 37) have regarded him as the editor who introduced the list. But evidence of such authorship is by no means clear, and the chapter is not a worthless fiction by the Chronicler, as is sometimes assumed. It preserves important topographic data, including local landmarks, of the Jerusalem of Nehemiah's day, and mentions important persons and settlements which were active in the reconstruction of the city. Despite its information, however, the actual extent of the city and the exact location of the walls, gates, and other phenomena cannot be determined with certainty (cf. 2:13). Nor is it always possible to discover whether the gates mentioned were in the city wall or somewhere within the city (cf. vss. 28-30).

A complete circuit of the city wall is described, in counterclockwise fashion, from the Sheep Gate to the Sheep Gate. Nevertheless, because of a shift in formula and

---

tion. But Nehemiah met this opposition (more confidently doubtless than his supporters would have done) with an assurance born of his own ultimate religious faith: **The God of heaven will make us prosper, and we his servants will arise and build.** And even if we of today, acutely sensitized to interracial and intercultural frictions, find it hard to sympathize with the

narrow and sharply exclusive particularism with which his confession of religious faith concludes, we can at least see that this attitude was no small factor in his success at that time, whatever seeds of trouble it planted for his successors to this day.

3:1-32. *A Record of Co-operative Accomplishment.*—As the Exeg. points out, this lengthy

and set up the doors of it; even unto the tower of Meah they sanctified it, unto the tower of Hananeel.

built the Sheep Gate. They consecrated it and set its doors; they consecrated it as far as the Tower of the Hundred, as far as the

---

emphasis (cf. vs. 13) the unity of the chapter has been questioned. The first part describes the course of the wall by listing in succession the workmen assigned to its repair, while the latter part generally describes the assignments on the wall by reference to nearby landmarks. But the apparent shift in formulas may be a literary device to relieve the monotony in a long list (cf. Millar Burrows, "Nehemiah 3:1-32 as a Source for the Topography of Ancient Jerusalem," *Annual of the American Schools of Oriental Research,* XIV [1933-34], 116-21), and the increasing reference to landmarks may indicate merely that the northern and western parts of the city were residential while the older eastern part of the city, where such public features as the water works, the royal compound, and the temple area were located, abounded in familiar and significant landmarks.

A. WORKERS ON THE WALL (3:1-32)

1. THE NORTH WALL (3:1-5)

3:1. Eliashib the high priest (cf. 12:10-11) is important as a contemporary of Nehemiah, in demonstrating the chronological priority of Nehemiah (cf. Ezra 10:6; Intro., p. 562). Close to the temple area the **priests** are expected. The circuit of the walls begins (vs. 1) and ends (vs. 32) with the **Sheep Gate,** located close to the northeastern corner of the city. There was the market (vss. 31-32) where animals could be bought for sacrifices (cf. John 5:2). Between the **Sheep Gate** and the **Fish Gate** (vs. 3) lay the "fortress of the temple" (cf. 2:8) guarding the relatively weak northern approach to the city (cf. 2:8; 7:2). Part of the fortress was the **Tower of the Hundred.** Some follow the Vulg. in considering the **hundred** as a dimension in cubits (Gustaf Dalman, *Jerusalem und sein Gelände* [Gütersloh: C. Bertelsmann, 1930], p. 115), but it probably has military significance as the headquarters of the centurion in charge of his hundred. Officers over hundreds are found in the early period (cf. II Sam. 18:1; II Kings 11:4), in the Persian period (Cowley, *Aramaic Papyri,* No. 2, l. 11; No. 3, l. 11; No. 22, ll. 19-20), and into Roman times (Matt. 8:5; Mark 15:39; Luke 7:2; Acts 27:43). The **Tower of Hananel** (cf. 12:39; Jer. 31:38; Zech. 14:10) apparently stood near the northwest corner of the temple area, at the most northerly point of the city, "where the Mishneh Wall [Zeph. 1:10] crossed the crest of the ridge which was later called Bezetha" (Simons, *Jerusalem in the O.T.,* p. 343). The fortress was later the site of the Maccabean Baris (Josephus *Antiquities* XV. 11. 4; *Jewish War* I. 3. 3), and the Herodian Antonia (Josephus *Antiquities* XVIII. 4. 3; *Jewish War* I. 401), at the northwestern corner of the present Haram area (Mitchell, "Wall of Jerusalem," p. 144). Josephus (*Jewish War* V. 5. 8) indicates that Herod's fortress also had a tower at each of its ends.

Built (cf. vss. 2, 13-15), used almost always of work on the gates, implies considerable construction. Since it is only in the north wall that both the walls and gates are **built,** it is apparent that the greatest damage was suffered at that vulnerable place. Elsewhere the word "repaired" is used. The **priests** there **sanctified** the restored wall. Because such action is not described elsewhere until the general consecration (12:27 ff.), it is proposed to read קרוהו, "they timbered it" (cf. vss. 3, 6) for קדשׁוהו, **sanctified it** (Torrey, *Composition,* p. 38; Siegfried, *loc. cit.;* Bertholet, *op. cit.,* p. 53; similarly, Arnold B. Ehrlich, *Randglossen zur hebräischen Bibel* [Leipzig: J. C. Hinrichs, 1914], VII, 188, who reads קרשׁוהו). But the conjecture is textually unsupported and such action by the **priests** in the temple area is understandable (cf. I Kings 8:64).

---

chapter interrupts Nehemiah's own vivid memoirs with a colorless memorandum of assignments and co-operating groups in the rebuilding of the walls, written in a style which is "unlike Nehemiah's" and recorded after the completion and dedication of the work. This record may have been incorporated by the Chronicler as one of the various available lists of names and

2 And next unto him builded the men of Jericho. And next to them builded Zaccur the son of Imri.

3 But the fish gate did the sons of Hassenaah build, who *also* laid the beams thereof, and set up the doors thereof, the locks thereof, and the bars thereof.

4 And next unto them repaired Meremoth the son of Urijah, the son of Koz. And next unto them repaired Meshullam the son of Berechiah, the son of Meshezabeel. And next unto them repaired Zadok the son of Baana.

Tower of Hanan'el. 2 And next to him the men of Jericho built. And next to them[a] Zaccur the son of Imri built.

3 And the sons of Hassena'ah built the Fish Gate; they laid its beams and set its doors, its bolts, and its bars. 4 And next to them Mer'emoth the son of Uri'ah, son of Hakkoz repaired. And next to them Meshul'lam the son of Berechi'ah, son of Meshez'abel repaired. And next to them

[a] Heb *him*

2. The phrase **next unto him** (vss. 8, 10, 12, 17, 19) or **next to them** (vss. 4-5, 7, 9-10) introduces the workmen on the walls in proper succession. Next, lit., "at hand," like Akkadian "to hand" (*ana idi*), means "at the side of" or "beside" (cf. Num. 13:29; Exod. 2:5), but its use in a series is only in late Hebrew (Num. 34:3; Judg. 11:26; Job 1:14; II Chr. 17:15-16, 18; 31:15). **Unto him** refers to Eliashib (vs. 1) but because of **the priests** (vs. 1) the LXX has **them**. Such disagreement in number is frequent in the list (cf. vss. 12, 23, 29, 4, 5, 10) as attention shifts from the leader to his workmen. **Men of Jericho:** Cf. Ezra 2:34. **Zaccur:** Cf. Ezra 8:14. **Imri** abbreviates Amariah (10:3; 11:4; Ezra 7:3), as the LXX and Vulg. show.

3. For **Hassenaah** the Vulg., Peshitta, and most Greek texts have Senaah (cf. Ezra 2:35). Since he was a remote ancestor, as usual in this list, read "descendants of" for **sons of.** The **Fish Gate** (12:39; Zeph. 1:10) was the port of entry for fish from the seacoast. The exact location depends upon the extent of the city (cf. 2:13). Those who confine it to the southeastern hill locate it, as the Corner Gate (Jer. 31:38) where the wall bends southward, at the western city wall (Kurt Galling, "Archäologischer Jahresbericht," *Zeitschrift des deutschen Palästina-vereins*, LIV [1931], pp. 87-88). More likely, since the Phoenicians controlled the fish trade (13:16), it was located like the modern Damascus Gate (Bāb el-'Amūd) in the north wall, where the central (Tyropoeon) valley entered the city (Simons, *op. cit.*, p. 291, n. 3). Thus it was identical with the "Middle Gate" (Jer. 39:1-3) in the middle of the north wall (Mitchell, *loc. cit.*). **Laid the beams** describes the timbering of the gate frames. **Set up the doors,** which was a later operation (cf. 6:1), indicates the relatively late date of the list. **Bolts** were the metal strips fixed to the gates into which the **bars** (I Kings 4:13; Isa. 45:2) were placed.

4. The family of the priest **Meremoth** had been deprived of its status (cf. Ezra 2:59-61), but he later received the things brought to the temple by Ezra (Ezra 8:33). Thus he had apparently achieved his priestly status in the interim. His double assignment on the wall (cf. vs. 21) has been regarded as the means by which his priestly rights were regained (Aage Bentzen, "Priesterschaft und Laien in der jüdischen gemeinde des fünften Jahrhunderts," *Archiv für Orientforschung*, VI [1930-31], 285), but it is unlikely that the status could be obtained so easily. **Meshullam** (cf. vs. 30; Ezra 8:16) was the father-in-law of Tobiah the Ammonite (cf. 6:18). **Meshezabel,** his ancestor, bears the Babylonian name *mMushezib-dilu*. **Zadok** abbreviates Zedekiah or Jehozadek. **Baana** was his remote ancestor (cf. Ezra 2:2). Instead of "built" (cf. vs. 3) the action is here **repaired,**

family connections so dear to his editorial heart; but it seems to "preserve authentic data," and as Pfeiffer also notes, it "is an invaluable source for the topography of ancient Jerusalem."[1]

Unfamiliar as its long lists of names and

[1] *Intro. to O.T.*, p. 835.

places must sound in our restless modern ears, this chapter remains a literary symbol of the careful division of labor and of the efficient co-operation of many individuals and groups that combined to make possible the rapid completion of this "great work." As in all large

5 And next unto them the Tekoites repaired; but their nobles put not their necks to the work of their Lord.

6 Moreover the old gate repaired Jehoiada the son of Paseah, and Meshullam the son of Besodeiah; they laid the beams thereof, and set up the doors thereof, and the locks thereof, and the bars thereof.

Zadok the son of Ba'ana repaired. 5 And next to them the Teko'ites repaired; but their nobles did not put their necks to the work of their Lord.[b]

6 And Joi'ada the son of Pase'ah and Meshul'lam the son of Besodei'ah repaired the Old Gate; they laid its beams and set

[b] Or lords

---

lit., "made strong," which, as the LXX[L] and Peshitta show, means "strengthened," "restored," or "fortified."

5. The **Tekoites** were from Tekoa (Amos 1:1), modern Tequ', about eleven miles south of Jerusalem or five miles south of Bethlehem. Use of a different word here for **nobles** (אדיר) from that employed by Nehemiah (חרים) may indicate an author other than Nehemiah. **Put their necks to** is an agricultural figure of an ox plunging its neck into the yoke to move a heavy load (cf. Jer. 27:11-12), indicating voluntary co-operative effort in the task. Instead of "yoke" the M.T. has **the work of.** For "their lords" of the M.T., which could refer to Nehemiah and his foremen (Siegfried, *op. cit.*, p. 80; Bertholet, *loc. cit.*), the Complutensian Polyglot text has "their lord," which could mean Nehemiah (cf. Ezra 10:3; Jer. 27:11-12; Gotthard, *Text des Nehemia,* p. 78; Rudolph, *Esra und Nehemia,* p. 116). The Vulg. with "their Lord" and the LXX[L] with "the Lord" refer to God but since "Lord" as surrogate for God is found elsewhere only with the pronoun "our" (Ehrlich, *op. cit.*, p. 189), the M.T. plural is preferable, referring to those supervising the work (cf. vs. 27). The **nobles** spurned subservience and menial labor.

2. THE WEST WALL (3:6-12)

6. The **Old Gate,** as translated by the Vulg. and Peshitta, is grammatically impossible. The M.T. is, lit., "the Gate of the Old," to which some such substantive as "city," "wall," or "pool" must be appended. But nouns cannot be applied at will (Rudolph, *loc. cit.*) and it is unlikely that the substantive would be lost in two widely separated places (here and 12:39; Simons, *op. cit.*, p. 276). Greek texts transliterate it as a proper name which has been identified with the "Jeshanah" of II Chr. 13:19 and the Isana of Josephus (*Antiquities* VIII. 11. 3; XIV. 15. 12), the modern Burj el-Isâneh on the Nablus Road, about twenty miles north of Jerusalem (W. F. Albright, "New Identifications of Ancient Towns," *Bulletin of the American Schools of Oriental Research,* No. 9 [1923], pp. 7-8; Abel, *Géographie,* II, 364; Galling, *Biblisches Reallexikon,* p. 304). Thus, like the Damascus Road, the gate is named for the major place toward which its road led and has been identified with the "Gate of Ephraim" (8:16; 12:39; cf. II Kings 14:13), which is missing in ch. 3 (Hugues Vincent, "Les murs de Jérusalem d'après Néhémie," *Revue Biblique,* XIII [1904], 66-67; Dalman, *Jerusalem,* p. 236; Otto Procksch, "Das Jerusalem Jesajas," *Palästinajahrbuch,* XXVI [1930], 28; E. J. Fischer, "Die Mauern und Tore des biblischen Jerusalem," *Theologische Quartalschrift,* CXIII [1932], 225). But because the "Jeshanah Gate" precedes the Ephraim Gate by at least one section of wall, it has been regarded as a separate gate and some propose to emend the name to המשנה, "the Mishneh," instead of הישנה, "the Jeshanah" (cf. Vincent, "Les murs de Jérusalem," pp. 62, 67; Simons, *op. cit.*, p. 306), and to locate it, opening northward, at the head of what Josephus calls "the southern portion" of the Mishneh Wall, the north-south wall which formed part of the western boundary of the city (Simons, *op. cit.*, pp. 305-6, 443, Fig.

---

human enterprises to this day, there are plain hints of disaffection here and there. The aristocrats of Tekoa (Amos' home town) seem to have fallen down badly: **Their nobles did not put their necks to the work of their Lord** (vs.

5b). Nevertheless one senses through this roster of workers, so carefully catalogued by name, a pride of residence (cf. vs. 2a), a pride of heritage (cf. vs. 2b), and toward the end a pride of calling (vss. 31-32). Nehemiah evidently knew

7 And next unto them repaired Melatiah the Gibeonite, and Jadon the Meronothite, the men of Gibeon, and of Mizpah, unto the throne of the governor on this side the river.

8 Next unto him repaired Uzziel the son of Harhaiah, of the goldsmiths. Next unto him also repaired Hananiah the son of *one*

its doors, its bolts, and its bars. 7 And next to them repaired Melati'ah the Gibeonite and Jadon the Mero'nothite, the men of Gibeon and of Mizpah, who were under the jurisdiction of the governor of the province Beyond the River. 8 Next to them Uz'ziel the son of Harhai'ah, goldsmiths, repaired.

---

56). **Joiada** was a "descendant" of **Paseah** (Ezra 2:49) and **Besodeiah** has a name of Babylonian type similar to that of Bezalel (Ezra 10:30).

7. Gibeon is a mound beside modern Ej-Jîb, about six miles northwest of Jerusalem (W. F. Albright, "Recent Works on the Topography and Archaeology of Jerusalem," *Jewish Quarterly Review XXII* [1931-32], 415-16; Dalman, *Jerusalem*, pp. 218 ff.). Meronoth (I Chr. 27:30) is identified with Beit Unia, about three miles north-northwest of **Gibeon** (Abel, *op. cit.*, II, Map VII). Tell en-Naṣbeh, about eight miles north of Jerusalem, meets all topographic requirements for **Mizpah** (cf. James Muilenburg, "Survey of the Literature on Tell en-Naṣbeh," in C. C. McCown, ed., *Tell en-Naṣbeh, Archaeological and Historical Results* [Berkeley and New Haven: Palestine Institute of the Pacific School of Religion and The American Schools of Oriental Research, 1947], pp. 13-49; Abel, *op. cit.*, II, 335). **Unto the throne** suggests a terminus for an assignment, but another Hebrew word is used for **unto** with other termini (cf. vss. 1, 8, 13, 15). Because the M.T. can mean "at the chair," it is suggested that the seat of the governor in Jerusalem was here (Laurence E. Browne, *Early Judaism* [Cambridge: Cambridge University Press, 1920], p. 148; Burrows, "Source for Topography of Ancient Jerusalem," p. 137), and its location has been conjectured to be in the "Middle Tower" built against the exterior of the wall lying under the Russian Hospice, east of the Church of the Holy Sepulchre (C. Schick, "Der Lauf der zweiten Mauer Jerusalems," *Zeitschrift des deutschen Palästina-vereins*, VIII [1885], 267; "Nehemiah's Mauerbau in Jerusalem," *ibid.*, XIV [1891], 47; cf. Simons, *op. cit.*, p. 321). But that tower had defensive function and it is unlikely that the governor resided in depopulated Jerusalem. **The throne** has been regarded as the "judgment seat" of the Persian officer, parallel to the Roman procurator's praetorium (Hölscher, *Esra und Nehemia*, p. 531, note *a*), but since **Mizpah** was the Judean administrative center after 586 B.C. (cf. II Kings 25:23; Jer. 40:5-10), and the Persian administrator may have held court there (cf. G. A. Smith, *Jerusalem* [London: Hodder & Stoughton, 1907-8], II, 354), "the seat of the governor," etc., is appositive to **Mizpah,** and instead of **unto** "namely" is required (cf. Ezra 1:5, 11; Jer. 1:18; II Kings 12:6). The RSV is purely interpretative.

8. The unique **Harhaiah** is difficult as an ancestral name. It is proposed to read instead either "the associates of the . . ." (חברי ה; cf. Job 41:6) or "the guild of the . . ." (חבר ה; Rudolph, *loc. cit.;* Ehrlich, *loc. cit.*). **Goldsmiths,** lit., "smelters" or "refiners," are jewelers as in vs. 31. As the Vulg. and LXX^L indicate, the **perfumers** were the mixers of ointments.

The M.T. seems to indicate that in addition to repairing their wall, the men of vs. 8 **abandoned Jerusalem as far as the Broad Wall,** by which is understood the altering of the line of the old wall to exclude part of the former city (cf. Batten, *op. cit.*, p. 211; Burrows, "Source for Topography of Ancient Jerusalem," p. 123; Gotthard,

---

how to enlist diverse loyalties in a common enterprise, a major qualification for leadership.

Of course such endless lists of names, with their oft-recurring verbal formulas, quickly become for modern readers monotonous and tire-

somely repetitious, until we remember that so would any similar catalogue of the colonists who settled our own Atlantic seaboard, of the pioneers who shared in the "winning of the West," of the missionaries who carried the Christian

of the apothecaries, and they fortified Jerusalem unto the broad wall.

9 And next unto them repaired Rephaiah the son of Hur, the ruler of the half
part of Jerusalem.

Next to him Hanani'ah, one of the perfumers, repaired; and they restored[c] Jerusalem
as far as the Broad Wall. **9** Next to them
Rephai'ah the son of Hur, ruler of half the

[c] Or *abandoned*

---

op. cit., p. 82). The puzzling **abandoned,** which occurs again in 4:2, has led to a search
for some meaning more relevant to the idea of reconstruction found in this chapter.
It has been proposed to read instead of יעזב, **abandoned,** either יעזר, "enclosed" (cf.
עזרה, "enclosure," in Ezek. 43:14; Ehrlich, *loc. cit.*), or יאזר, "girdled" (Siegfried, *op. cit.,*
p. 81), but by appeal to the Arabic meaning of the word (South Arabic עדב), and to
Akkadian (*ezêbu*), a meaning "completed" is obtained (J. H. Mordtmann, "Neue
himjarische Inschriften," *Zeitschrift der deutschen Morgenländischen Gesellschaft,*
XXXIX [1885], 230; Burrows, "Source for Topography of Ancient Jerusalem," p. 123,
n. 9). Such conjecture is responsible for the interpretative **fortified** and **restored,** but
the verb indicates some action apparently not applicable in the other assignments, and
no convincing solution is at hand.

A **Broad Wall** is difficult to locate. Its identification with a broad wall at the eastern
rim of the Pool of Hezekiah (Schick, "Der Lauf der zweiten Mauer," p. 270) has been
regarded as impossible (Merrill, *Ancient Jerusalem,* p. 359). It has been recognized as
a fragment of earlier wall abutting the western city wall or part of the latter wall itself
(Millar Burrows, "The Topography of Nehemiah 12:31-43," *Journal of Biblical Literature,*
LIV [1935], 36-37), possibly part of the west wall which Galling ("Archäologischer
Jahresbericht," p. 87; cf. Pl. VI) conjectures curved southeastward across the Tyropoeon
Valley. Others have conjectured a place in the north wall where Joash destroyed about
four hundred cubits of ancient wall (II Kings 14:13) which Hezekiah later restored,
presumably with a much "broader" wall (Dalman, *Jerusalem,* p. 236). But instead of
Broad Wall, the Vulg. and LXXABא render the M.T. as "The Wall of the Square" (cf.
Ezra 10:9), a reading requiring but the slight emendation in Hebrew from רחבה, "broad,"
to רחוב, "square" (cf. George St. Clair, "Nehemiah's South Wall, and the Locality of the
Royal Sepulchres," *Palestine Exploration Fund Quarterly Statement for 1889,* p. 99;
cf. Mitchell, "Wall of Jerusalem," p. 132, n. 35). This "Wall of the Square" may be
identified with the western section of the north wall of the city, lying between the
Ephraim Gate, at the western wall of the Mishneh, and the Corner Gate, a wall which
formed the southern margin of the "square" just outside the Gate of Ephraim (cf. 8:16;
Simons, *op. cit.,* pp. 277, 300, 443, Fig. 56).

9. Hur, an Akkadian name (*ḫûru,* "child"; Noth, *Personennamen,* p. 221), persisted
through the Persian period (Cowley, *Aramaic Papyri,* No. 23, l. 3; No. 38, ll. 4, 6, 8) and
into Hellenistic times (Tallqvist, *Neubabylonisches Namenbuch,* p. 68; cf. J. N.
Strassmaier, "Arsaciden-Inschriften," *Zeitschrift für Assyriologie und verwandte Gebiete,*
III [1888], 149, No. 10, l. 25; cf. p. 136, l. 25). **Ruler of half the district** has led to some
broad conclusions regarding the political organization of Jerusalem and Judea, since
ancient cities were sometimes divided into administrative areas and the Assyrian title
"chief of the districts" (*rab pilkâni;* Leroy Waterman, *Royal Correspondence of the
Assyrian Empire* [Ann Arbor: University of Michigan Press, 1930], Pt. I, pp. 358-59,
No. 512) could possibly be the equivalent of **ruler of . . . the district** (*sar . . . pélekh*).
But it is improbable that either depopulated Jerusalem or such small places as Keilah
(vss. 17-18) would be under divided control. The Hebrew *pélekh* could refer to a

---

gospel to the Far East, or, centuries ago, to our
own Anglo-Saxon ancestors. All great social enterprises are carried on the shoulders of a multitude of laborers whose names have been forgotten or survive only in colorless lists like

these. Monotonous they inevitably are for the
reading of their successors who inherit what
they made possible; but it was their co-operative
labor and sacrifice that under God changed the
course of human history.

10 And next unto them repaired Jedaiah the son of Harumaph, even over against his house. And next unto him repaired Hattush the son of Hashabniah.

11 Malchijah the son of Harim, and Hashub the son of Pahath-moab, repaired the other piece, and the tower of the furnaces.

12 And next unto him repaired Shallum the son of Halohesh, the ruler of the half part of Jesusalem, he and his daughters.

district of[d] Jerusalem, repaired. 10 Next to them Jedai'ah the son of Haru'maph repaired opposite his house; and next to him Hattush the son of Hashabnei'ah repaired.

11 Malchi'jah the son of Harim and Hasshub the son of Pa'hath-mo'ab repaired another section and the Tower of the Ovens.

12 Next to him Shallum the son of Hallo'hesh, ruler of half the district of[d] Jerusalem, repaired, he and his daughters.

[d] Or foreman of half the portion assigned to

district, but it certainly here refers to much less. The cognate Assyrian term (*pilku*), in a text dealing with the building of a wall and gate, is used repeatedly for "assigned portion" (*ibid.*, pp. 340-43, No. 486), usage which is applicable here where in each case two assignments are mentioned. **Ruler** then means simply the **foreman** or "overseer" (cf. Gen. 39:21, 23; 47:6; Exod. 1:11; etc.) responsible for "half of the assignment" of the town.

10. Harumaph ("Flat nose") is a nickname (Noth, *Personennamen*, p. 227; cf. Lev. 21:18). **Hattush:** Cf. Ezra 8:2. Unique **Hashabneiah** is difficult but "Hashabniah" is found in 9:5 (where the Peshitta has "Hashabiah"; cf. Ezra 8:19) and "Hashabnah" is found in 10:25. These families (vs. 10) have been regarded as non-Jewish (Eduard Meyer, *Die Entstehung des Judenthums* [Halle: M. Niemeyer, 1896], p. 147). Here, as in vss. 23, 28-29, each man was assigned to a small portion of wall opposite his own house.

11. Malchijah the son of Harim here and in Ezra 10:31 has been used as evidence for the chronological priority of Ezra (J. S. Wright, *The Date of Ezra's Coming to Jerusalem* [London: Tyndale Press, 1947], p. 21), but such a conclusion is unnecessary. **Malchijah** is a common name and he is the "descendant" of **Harim** (Ezra 2:39), for whom many "sons" are listed (cf. 7:35, 42). Since the grandfather's name is often given, the **Malchijah** of Ezra 10:31 may have been a grandson of the person named here (Rowley, *Servant of the Lord*, pp. 157-58). **Hasshub**, abbreviating "Hashabiah" (cf. vs. 17), is a descendant of **Pahath-moab** (cf. Ezra 2:6). Some men, like some cities, had two assignments (with vs. 4 cf. vs. 21; with vs. 5 cf. vs. 27; with vs. 18 [LXX] cf. vs. 24). "Second section" implies a previous assignment. Lack of such earlier assignment here (cf. also vss. 19-20, 30) is regarded as evidence for the incompleteness of the list and a serious omission is conjectured before this verse (Bertholet, *Ezra und Nehemia*, p. 54; Hölscher, *Esra und Nehemia*, p. 529; Batten, *op. cit.*, p. 213).

Tower of the Ovens is preferable to **tower of the furnaces** since the Hebrew word (*tannûr*) refers to bakers' ovens rather than to kilns or to smelteries (cf. Mitchell, *op. cit.*, 130, n. 30; Merrill, *op. cit.*, p. 364; Wilhelm Nowack, *Lehrbuch der hebräischen Archäologie* [Freiburg i. B.: J. C. B. Mohr, 1894], I, 146 ff.). It appears to have been located at the northwest corner of the city as part of the fortification of the Corner Gate (Jer. 31:38; II Kings 14:13) which Uzziah fortified (II Chr. 26:9). Strategically the tower protected the corner, "near the narrow neck of land linking the N.W. Hill to the S.W. Hill" (Simons, *op. cit.*, pp. 234, 304). The assignment seems to include a section of the wall and the tower but some see the tower as a terminus (Hölscher, *Esra und Nehemia*, p. 531). An alternate proposal is to read את, "at" (cf. I Kings 9:26; II Kings 9:27), and translate "a second assignment . . . at the Gate of the Ovens" (Rudolph, *op. cit.*, p. 117).

12. Hallohesh ("The Whisperer") is a professional title used for "snake charmer" (Ps. 58:5; Eccl. 10:11). It is not found in Ezra 2. **Shallum** was a foreman (cf. vs. 9). **His daughters** is an unusual and unexpected note since it is assumed that women would do a large share of the labor in each section. A proposed emendation to "its daughters," referring to Jerusalem and its dependent hamlets (cf. 11:25-31; Num. 21:25; 32:42; Josh. 15:45, 47; etc.) is attractive but is not supported by the M.T. or the versions.

13 The valley gate repaired Hanun, and the inhabitants of Zanoah; they built it, and set up the doors thereof, the locks thereof, and the bars thereof, and a thousand cubits on the wall unto the dung gate.

14 But the dung gate repaired Malchiah the son of Rechab, the ruler of part of Beth-haccerem; he built it, and set up the doors thereof, the locks thereof, and the bars thereof.

15 But the gate of the fountain repaired Shallun the son of Col-hozeh, the ruler of part of Mizpah; he built it, and covered it, and set up the doors thereof, the locks

13 Hanun and the inhabitants of Zano'ah repaired the Valley Gate; they rebuilt it and set its doors, its bolts, and its bars, and repaired a thousand cubits of the wall, as far as the Dung Gate.

14 Malchi'jah the son of Rechab, ruler of the district of[d] Beth-hac'che'rem, repaired the Dung Gate; he rebuilt it and set its doors, its bolts, and its bars.

15 And Shallum the son of Colho'zeh, ruler of the district of[d] Mizpah, repaired the Fountain Gate; he rebuilt it and cov-

[d] Or *foreman of half the portion assigned to*

---

3. THE SOUTH WALL (3:13-14)

13. Hanun abbreviates Hananiah or Hananiel. **Zanoah** (Khirbet Zānû‘) in the Judean foothills, about twelve and a half miles west of Bethlehem (Albrecht Alt, "Die Ausflüge: Sanoah," *Palästinajahrbuch*, XXIV [1928], 27-28; Abel, *Géographie*, II, 90, 489; W. F. Albright, "Topographical Researches in Judea," *Bulletin of the American Schools of Oriental Research*, No. 18 [1925], p. 11), is associated with Jarmuth and Adullam (cf. 11:30). For the **Valley Gate** and **Dung Gate** see Exeg. on 2:13. Because of the extraordinary distance between the **Valley Gate** and the **Dung Gate,** the **thousand cubits** that separated them is specified. Because the distance is considerably above the average, the text has been regarded as corrupt, and it is claimed that "all calculations based upon the distance stated are therefore unreliable" (Burrows, "Source for Topography of Ancient Jerusalem," p. 131). But since some assignments were as small as half the length of a house (vss. 20-21) the sections were by no means the same and an "average" section is hypothetical. The men of **Zanoah** may have been numerous and the southern wall may not have needed extensive repairs. Although the listing of some workmen on the southern wall may have been lost from the present M.T., the distance mentioned, as "a rounded underestimation," is approximately right (cf. 2:13; Simons, *op. cit.*, pp. 280, 439). Like the **Dung Gate** and the **Fountain Gate** (2:14) in the south of the city, the **Valley Gate** is described as both **repaired** and **rebuilt,** the former apparently referring to the masonry and the latter to the woodwork which had been burned (cf. 1:3).

14. Rechab may be the remote ancestor of the Rechabites (cf. II Kings 10:15, 23; Jer. 35:1-19). **Beth-haccherem** ("The House of the Vineyard"), a fertile place with a lofty peak nearby from which fire signals could be sent (Jer. 6:1), was probably modern 'Ain Karîm ("Spring of Vineyards"), about four miles west of Jerusalem, at the foot of the ridge Jebel 'Ali, upon which was found a huge cairn (Rujm et Târûd), well suited to the purpose of a beacon (C. R. Conder, "Lieutenant Conder's Reports," *Palestine Exploration Fund Quarterly Statement for 1881*, pp. 271-72; Abel, *op. cit.*, II, 295). For **ruler of the district** see Exeg. on vs. 9. "Laid the beams," found elsewhere (vss. 3, 6), is omitted here but is reflected in the LXX.

4. THE EAST WALL (3:15-31)

15. For the unique **Shallun** read **Shallum** (cf. Ezra 2:42) with five Hebrew MSS and the Vulg. and Peshitta versions. **Col-hozeh** was an ancestor rather than the father (cf. 11:5). The name ("All-Seeing") is a title (cf. vs. 12) indicating that **Shallum** descended from a prominent seer. Since **Mizpah** (cf. vs. 7) had two assignments (vss. 15, 19) the word "half" has been lost from the title (cf. vs. 9). For "laid the beams" (vss. 3, 6) the text here has **covered it,** a change which, together with the use of Aramaic rather than Hebrew spelling, has been regarded by some as evidence for composite structure of the chapter (but cf. above).

thereof, and the bars thereof, and the wall of the pool of Siloah by the king's garden, and unto the stairs that go down from the city of David.

16 After him repaired Nehemiah the son of Azbuk, the ruler of the half part of Beth-zur, unto *the place* over against the sepul-

ered it and set its doors, its bolts, and its bars; and he built the wall of the Pool of Shelah of the king's garden, as far as the stairs that go down from the City of David.

16 After him Nehemi'ah the son of Azbuk, ruler of half the district of[d] Beth-zur, re-

[d] Or *foreman of half the portion assigned to*

The **Fountain Gate** (cf. 2:14) was both **rebuilt** and **repaired** (cf. vs. 13). At the **Fountain Gate** the counterclockwise progress ceases momentarily to describe an important defensive architectural complex lying behind the city wall between the Dung Gate and the **Fountain Gate** and connected with the latter. Within that gate a rock-cut staircase descended from the **City of David** to the **Fountain Gate** where, "long before Zedekiah [II Kings 25:4] the exit from the city *via* the 'stairs of the City of David' and the Fountain Gate led through a 15 metres long corridor enclosed between two strong walls" (Simons, *op. cit.*, p. 127; cf. Figs. 10, 56).

The **Wall of the Pool of Shelah** was doubtless one of the two strong walls forming the corridor behind the city wall. The inner wall, crossing the Tyropoeon Valley and joining the eastern and western hills of the city, formed the barrage of the **Pool of Shelah,** the Lower Pool (Birket el Ḥamra; *ibid.*, p. 109). The spelling **Shelah** may be an attempt to avoid identification with the Pool of Siloam, as is done by the Vulg. and some modern scholars (G. Ernest Wright and Floyd V. Filson, *The Westminster Historical Atlas to the Bible* [Philadelphia: Westminster Press, 1945], p. 98). The original name was apparently Shiloah (cf. Isa. 8:6), as some Hebrew MSS and most scholars agree. **The Wall** could have been the inner wall, the barrage of the reservoir itself, but the outer wall, the city wall about which the list is otherwise silent, could have taken the name of the **Pool** that it protected (Simons, *op. cit.*, pp. 108-9, 121-22, n. 2). As part of the corridor, the **Wall** did not go by the **king's garden** nor was it of that **garden,** but it ran "toward" the **garden,** which lay below the city, at the southern end of the Kidron Valley (*ibid.*, pp. 10, 193, 231, n. 7, 455) where the Dragon Well (2:13) sometimes overflowed from its mouth, watering the plain where gardens once extended southward from Siloam along the Kidron Valley (cf. Edward Robinson, *Biblical Researches,* I, 491-92; Josephus *Jewish War* V. 2. 2). The waters of the Gihon Spring may also have come by canal to the **garden** area into "the King's Pool" (cf. 2:14; Simons, *op. cit.*, pp. 10, 193).

The **City of David,** site of pre-Hebrew Jerusalem (II Sam. 5:6-9), lay high on the southeastern hill where it was limited to the "Stronghold of Zion," described as "the area around and including the large tower in the northeast part of the fortifications of Jebusite Jerusalem and the gate identified by the excavators as the water-gate, the two features which overlook and guard the approaches to the Spring of Gîhôn, the only source of water supply in the Jerusalem of the period" (S. Yeivin, "The Sepulchers of the Kings of the House of David," *Journal of Near Eastern Studies,* VII [1948], 40-41, 43). **Stairs** descended about 165 feet in several rock-cut stages to the lower levels of the hill at the south of the city (*ibid.*, p. 44).

16. Azbuk ("Buq Is Mighty") is a pagan name in form like Azgad (Ezra 2:12), Azmaweth (II Sam. 23:31), and Uzziah (Jahn, *Esra [A und B] und Nehemja*, p. 101; Rudolph, *op. cit.*, p. 118). **Beth-zur** (Khirbet et-Ṭubeiqah) lies about a half mile northwest of modern Burj es-Sur, about four miles north of Hebron (Abel, *op. cit.*, II, 283). It was destroyed by Nebuchadrezzar and resettled in the Persian period, when it shows a complete cultural change with strong influence of Greek culture (O. R. Sellers, *The Citadel of Beth-Zur* [Philadelphia: Westminster Press, 1933], pp. 10, 41, 43, 70).

Three landmarks near the city wall define the terminus of Nehemiah's assignment. The **sepulchres of David** (Acts 2:29) lay north of the Fountain Gate and near the east wall. Roman period quarrying has left the area mutilated with empty, demolished graves. The most likely location for the royal cemetery is within the great curve of Hezekiah's

chres of David, and to the pool that was made, and unto the house of the mighty.

17 After him repaired the Levites, Rehum the son of Bani. Next unto him repaired Hashabiah, the ruler of the half part of Keilah, in his part.

18 After him repaired their brethren, Bavai the son of Henadad, the ruler of the half part of Keilah.

19 And next to him repaired Ezer the son of Jeshua, the ruler of Mizpah, another piece over against the going up to the armory at the turning *of the wall*.

paired to a point opposite the sepulchres of David, to the artificial pool, and to the house of the mighty men. **17** After him the Levites repaired: Rehum the son of Bani; next to him Hashabi'ah, ruler of half the district of[d] Kei'lah, repaired for his district. **18** After him their brethren repaired: Bav'vai the son of Hen'adad, ruler of half the district of[d] Kei'lah; **19** next to him Ezer the son of Jeshua, ruler of Mizpah, repaired another section opposite the ascent to the

[d] Or *foreman of half the portion assigned to*

---

tunnel, where several ancient imposing rock-cut tombs have been found (Weill, *La cité de David*, pp. 103-4, 157-83, 190-92, Pls. V, XVIII, XIX; Gustaf Dalman, "Zion, die Burg Jerusalems," *Palästinajahrbuch*, XI [1915], 75 ff., Pl. 5; *Jerusalem*, p. 135; Simons, *op. cit.*, pp. 205, 208, 213, 216-20). The **pool that was made**, an **artificial pool**, lay nearby but its location is uncertain. Water was usually conducted from the springs outside the city to constructions within the city for defensive purposes, but it has been conjectured that this pool may have been outside the walls, in the Kidron Valley (Rudolph, *op. cit.*, p. 119). Also nearby but not yet identifiable was the **house of the mighty men**, the house of the warriors, the name of which suggests David's "heroes" (II Sam. 10:7; 16:6; 23:8; I Kings 1:10). It was presumably the barracks for the royal bodyguard.

17. Since **Levites** (cf. Ezra 2:40) are next in line (vss. 17-21), **Bani** is not the layman of Ezra 2:10. **Hashabiah** (Ezra 8:19), who bears a popular Levite name (cf. Neh. 10:11; I Chr. 27:17), was an administrator (vs. 9) in charge of part (cf. vs. 18) of the assignment of **Keilah** (Khirbet Qîlā), a place about eight miles northwest of Hebron, near the Philistine border. This verse has led to the hypothesis that **Keilah** was settled by Levites in the Persian period (Meyer, *Entstehung des Judenthums*, p. 178). Since **Hashabiah** was a "foreman" rather than a **ruler** (cf. vs. 9), it need no longer be denied that he was a Levite (Batten, *Ezra and Nehemiah*, p. 217). Read **his part** rather than **for his district** since the preceding preposition is neither **in** nor **for** but the indicator of the object (cf. 9:32; 11:2; Ezra 8:16).

18. Their brethren (vss. 18-21) were also Levites. Several Hebrew MSS, the Peshitta, and corrupt Greek texts show that the **Bavvai** of the M.T. should be **Binnui** (cf. Ezra 2:10), as in vs. 24 (cf. 10:9; Gotthard, *Text des Nehemia*, p. 90). **Henadad** ("Favor of Adad") is not necessarily pre-exilic (Batten, *loc. cit.*) but, like Mordecai (*Mardukaia*), is postexilic, for it is of a Neo-babylonian type *mhinni-ilâni* (Tallqvist, *Neubabylonisches Namenbuch*, pp. 68, 316 *s.v* חנן; cf. Hanniel in Num. 34:23) and the divine name Adad is common also in that period (*ibid.*, pp. 1-3, 22-26).

19. Corrupt text, confusing syntax, technical terms, and uncertainty concerning topography make this verse extremely difficult. Ancients were as baffled as moderns by it, and the versions are almost useless in restoring the text. The apparent stylistic change may rest on scribal error (Batten, *loc. cit.*) or it may indicate deliberate variation to avoid monotonous repetition of the same formula (Burrows, "Source for Topography of Ancient Jerusalem," p. 119). **Ezer**, abbreviated like Ezra (Ezra 7:1), was presumably a descendant of the Levite **Jeshua** (Ezra 2:40). Like Shallum (vs. 15), he was a "foreman" rather than a **ruler** (cf. vs. 9). Since **Mizpah** had two assignments (vss. 15, 19) the text must be emended as in vs. 15 (cf. Meyer, *op. cit.*, p. 167).

The meaning of the word translated **ascent** is yet uncertain. It could be "upper chamber" (עליה) as in vss. 31-32, or "above," in the sense of "northward" with the rising ground (Mitchell, "Wall of Jerusalem," p. 155). Topographically, however, **ascent** seems most promising, and this sense is required by the Vulg. and Peshitta versions.

20 After him Baruch the son of Zabbai earnestly repaired the other piece, from the turning *of the wall* unto the door of the house of Eliashib the high priest.

21 After him repaired Meremoth the son of Urijah the son of Koz another piece, from the door of the house of Eliashib even to the end of the house of Eliashib.

22 And after him repaired the priests, the men of the plain.

---

armory at the Angle. 20 After him Baruch the son of Zab'bai repaired another section from the Angle to the door of the house of Eli'ashib the high priest. 21 After him Mer'-emoth the son of Uri'ah, son of Hakkoz repaired another section from the door of the house of Eli'ashib to the end of the house of Eli'ashib. 22 After him the priests,

---

To derive such sense the M.T. must be revocalized (from *'alōth* to *'ōlōth;* cf. Ezek. 40:26), but it is usually emended to מעלת, "stairs," as in vs. 15 (see 12:37; Ezra 7:9; cf. Gotthard, *op. cit.,* p. 91).

Armory represents a Hebrew word which elsewhere can mean "equipment" or "weapons" (Ezek. 39:9; Isa. 22:8; I Kings 10:25; II Kings 10:2). Since the word alone can scarcely mean **armory,** it is usually emended to "the house of weapons," with that meaning. But the Hebrew root from which it derives normally means "to bring into close contact" and "to kiss," a concept implied in the LXX, "where it meets," where there is no reference to an **armory.**

Even more difficult is the final word, usually translated **turning,** with the assumption that the wall changed direction (cf. Burrows, "Source for Topography of Ancient Jerusalem," p. 139). But there is no evidence for any sharp change in the direction of the wall until the vicinity of the Horse Gate (vs. 28), where a different term, **corner** (*pinnāh*), is used to describe it (vs. 31; Jer. 31:38; Simons, *op. cit.,* p. 120). As an architectural term it signifies a buttress (cf. Ezek. 46:21-22) or, on a smaller scale, the corner post of an altar (Ezek. 41:22), which is reflected in the "corner buttress" of the Amer. Trans. The LXX and Vulg. both suggest **Angle** assumed to mean "a corner formed by the city-wall and a wall perpendicularly abutting on it from inside the city" (*ibid.,* n. 1). Other Semitic languages suggest the meaning "cut off," and the cognate Arabic noun means "something cut off" or "something ending abruptly." Since the term in the M.T. stands in apposition to the preceding word, usually translated **armory,** they must have the same significance. Thus the present M.T. could mean "from opposite the ascent of the contact, the barrier." As such the terminus would be something **opposite** the wall and close to it. Apparently only one such structure existed (*ibid.,* p. 119; cf. II Chr. 26:9) but the mention of eight assignments (vss. 19-25) suggests that it was of considerable length. No topographical evidence exists for identifying the "contact," but the present M.T. suggests a natural or artificial barrier within the city, arising at some distance from the wall (vs. 19), proceeding toward the city wall to make contact with it (vs. 24), and moving away again (vs. 25).

20. **Baruch** ("Blessed") abbreviates such a name as Berechiah (vs. 4) or Barachel (cf. Job 32:2, 6). In twenty-three Hebrew MSS, the Vulg., and the Peshitta, **Zabbai** (cf. Ezra 10:28) is "Zaccai" (cf. Ezra 2:9). **Earnestly:** Lit., "he burned," but forced and unparalleled in this sense in Hebrew since the verb (ההרה), usually used of anger, interrupts a familiar formula. It is lacking in seven Hebrew MSS, the LXXᴬᴮℵ, and the Ethiopic and Arabic versions and is apparently a corrupt and incorrect repetition of the similar **after him** (אחריו) which precedes it and is rightly omitted in the RSV. **Another section** (cf. vss. 19, 21, 24, 27, 30) is unexpected since **Baruch** is mentioned only here. His terminus was the "doorway" of the house of the high priest **Eliashib** (cf. vs. 1).

21. **Meremoth** (cf. vs. 4) had but a short "second assignment," to the **end** of Eliashib's house.

22. Because the Hebrew word translated **plain** (*kikkār*) usually means the Jordan Valley (cf. Gen. 13:10-12; 19:17, 25; Deut. 34:3), the Peshitta has **the men of the plain,** and the Vulg. has "men of the plains of the Jordan." But the priests dwelt in the

23 After him repaired Benjamin and Hashub over against their house. After him repaired Azariah the son of Maaseiah the son of Ananiah by his house.

24 After him repaired Binnui the son of Henadad another piece, from the house of Azariah unto the turning *of the wall,* even unto the corner.

25 Palal the son of Uzai, over against the turning *of the wall,* and the tower which lieth out from the king's high house, that *was* by the court of the prison. After him Pedaiah the son of Parosh.

the men of the Plain, repaired. 23 After them Benjamin and Hasshub repaired opposite their house. After them Azari'ah the son of Ma-asei'ah, son of Anani'ah repaired beside his own house. 24 After him Bin'nui the son of Hen'adad repaired another section, from the house of Azari'ah to the Angle 25 and to the corner. Palal the son of Uzai repaired opposite the Angle and the tower projecting from the upper house of the king at the court of the guard. After

---

suburbs of Jerusalem (cf. Jer. 1:1; Luke 1:39 ff.) , scarcely as far from the temple as the Jordan Valley. The term may refer to the district about Jerusalem (cf. 12:28) and means here "the men of the vicinity."

Lack of reference to a landmark has led to the conjecture that the verse is either incomplete or a later interpolation, possibly by the Chronicler (cf. Gotthard, *op. cit.,* p. 93) or that it is now misplaced (Batten, *op. cit.,* p. 218) . But exact specification, lacking elsewhere (cf. vss. 2, 4-5, 9-10, 12, 17-18) , need not be insisted upon here (Rudolph, *op. cit.,* p. 120) . Nor need the use of **after him** in vs. 23, following **the priests,** be evidence for the intrusion of the verse, for such disagreement is not unusual (cf. vs. 2) and has no textual significance (*ibid.,* p. 114) .

23. Benjamin (cf. Ezra 10:32) and **Hasshub** (cf. vs. 11) lived together. **Ananiah,** only here in the Bible, is common in the Jewish Aramaic papyri, both in its full form and in its abbreviation ʿ*Anani* (Cowley, *Aramaic Papyri,* No. 6, l. 20; No. 8, l. 32; No. 30, ll. 18-19) .

24. Henadad: Cf. vs. 18. Because **the turning** is so far from the last reference to it (vs. 19) , another is presumed here (Batten, *loc. cit.*) , but it is presumably the same one which here joins the wall, for "to the barrier" indicates a terminus at the wall. **Corner** implies a sharp turn (cf. vss. 31-32; Job 1:19; I Kings 7:34) . But if the corner of the Horse Gate (Jer. 31:40) was not in the city wall (cf. vs. 28) , no **corner** is expected until the juncture with the north wall of the city. The **corner** here has been regarded as an intrusion (cf. Mitchell, *op. cit.,* p. 157; Simons, *op. cit.,* p. 456) , but as **even unto the corner** the reference may not be to the city wall but to the **corner** of the "barrier," which here touches the wall and again turns away (cf. vs. 19) . Nothing is gained by the radical expedient of transporting **and to the corner** to the beginning of vs. 25 as in the RSV (cf. Burrows, "Source for Topography of Ancient Jerusalem," pp. 125-26) .

25. Lack of an introductory "after him" and of a verb indicates textual damage here. **Repaired** must be supplied. **Palal** abbreviates Pelaliah (cf. 11:12) and the unique **Uzai** may be a short form of Azaniah (10:9; Noth, *Personennamen,* p. 185) , but the form Uzain (אוזין) should be expected. **Opposite** indicates that "the barrier" (vs. 19) has again moved away from the wall. Nearby a **tower** projected from the **house of the king,** which is called the **upper house** to distinguish it, the "Solomonic" palace, from the older "House of David," on the southern part of the hill (cf. E. J. Fischer, "Die Mauern und Tore des Jerusalem," p. 260; Burrows, "Source for Topography of Ancient Jerusalem," p. 130; Simons, *op. cit.,* p. 130) . Some, denying that there were two palaces (Batten, *op. cit.,* pp. 218, 223-24; Gotthard, *op. cit.,* p. 94; Rudolph, *op. cit.,* p. 120) , translate **high** instead of **upper,** thinking of a **high house,** with the Vulg., or of higher and lower towers, with the LXX. **Which lieth out** suggests a free-standing tower, discon-nected from the palace. But the M.T. has, lit., "the one going out" or **projecting.** The tower is most probably the very large tower with a projection of 22½ feet found by Warren at his Ophel Wall where it came into line with the present Haram Wall (Charles W.

26 Moreover the Nethinim dwelt in Ophel, unto *the place* over against the water gate toward the east, and the tower that lieth out.

27 After them the Tekoites repaired another piece, over against the great tower that lieth out, even unto the wall of Ophel.

28 From above the horse gate repaired the priests, every one over against his house.

him Pedai'ah the son of Parosh 26 and the temple servants living[e] on Ophel repaired to a point opposite the Water Gate on the east and the projecting tower. 27 After him the Teko'ites repaired another section opposite the great projecting tower as far as the wall of Ophel.

28 Above the Horse Gate the priests repaired, each one opposite his own house.

[e] Cn: Heb *were living*

Wilson and Charles Warren, *The Recovery of Jerusalem* [New York: D. Appleton & Co., 1871], pp. 228-29; Mitchell, *loc. cit.;* Simons, *op. cit.,* pp. 118-19, 142, 456). Since three assignments are described with relation to the **tower** (vss. 25, 26, 27), which was only twenty-six feet wide, one must agree that the text here is "hopelessly out of order" and that the **tower** must have followed the Water Gate, as in vs. 26 (cf. *ibid.,* p. 456; cf. p. 123, n. 1). The **court of the guard** was the enclosure in the house of the king in which Jeremiah was shut up (Jer. 32:2). The name **Pedaiah** ("The Lord Has Ransomed"; cf. Neh. 8:4; 11:7; 13:13) is also found in the papyri (Cowley, *op. cit.,* No. 43, 1. 12).

26. The reference to **the temple servants** (the **Nethinim;** cf. Ezra 2:43), co-workers with Pedaiah, has been called "a parenthetic expression which has strayed from its original place" (Batten, *op. cit.,* p. 219), and it is thought to be a gloss to **Ophel** in vs. 27, borrowed ultimately from 11:21 (Gotthard, *op. cit.,* pp. 95-96; Rudolph, *loc. cit.*). But an emendation of the M.T. היו ישבים, "were living," to היושבים, "those living," preserves the double subject (Burrows, "Source for Topography of Ancient Jerusalem," p. 125).

Ophel ("swelling"; cf. Deut. 28:27; I Sam. 5:6, 9, 12; 6:4) is an eminence or bulge, a mound or hill, that was fortified (cf. II Kings 5:24 and the Moabite stone, 1. 22). At Jerusalem later popular usage applied the term to the whole southeastern hill (II Chr. 33:14), but it was earlier confined to the Kidron side of the hill, near the angle of the present Haram, where the first bulge of the temple hill proper overhangs the Kidron Valley, above the City of David (cf. Simons, *op. cit.,* pp. 64-67). The **Water Gate** gave access to the Gihon Spring outside the city wall (cf. Bertholet, *Esra und Nehemia,* p. 55; Simons, *op. cit.,* p. 121) but there is yet no evidence for such a gate in the eastern wall (*ibid.,* pp. 122-23). **Opposite** suggests that the gate was near the city wall but not in it. It has been regarded as a door in the eastern part of the palace (Bertholet, *loc. cit.;* Rudolph, *op. cit.,* p. 119), but the unusual **on the east** may signify a gate east of the city wall. Such an ancient gate, found by Parker (Hugues Vincent, *Jérusalem sous terre* [London: H. Cox, 1911], p. 29, col. 2 and Pl. VI), lying a few yards below the brink of the hill exactly above the Gihon Spring, may have been "an element in the communication between the city and the shaft leading to the Spring of the Steps" (cf. Simons, *op. cit.,* pp. 83, 165). According to the Mishnah a **Water Gate** was located as the most easterly one in the later south wall of the temple court (Shekalim 6:3; Sukkah 4:9; Middoth 1:4; 2:6). Possibly the words **on the east** are used to distinguish the gate from one within the city. Some, however, ignore the **opposite** and locate the **Water Gate** in the city wall (cf. Burrows, "Source for Topography of Ancient Jerusalem," p. 127; Simons, *op. cit.,* p. 452). A great open place lay before the **Water Gate** (cf. 8:1, 3, 16).

27. The **wall of Ophel,** the terminus of the second **section** of the **Tekoites** (cf. vs. 5), might have been part of the city wall (*ibid.,* p. 456), but lack of reference to the rebuilding of it suggests a landmark rather than a part of the external fortification with which Nehemiah was most concerned. It could be Warren's "Ophel Wall" (cf. vs. 25; *ibid.,* n. 1) or some other internal wall that joined the city wall somewhere just below the southeast corner of the present Haram.

28. The **Horse Gate** has been recognized as a city gate close to the palace, used as a private gate to the royal quarters (*ibid.,* p. 339), but it is probably the same as

29 After them repaired Zadok the son of Immer over against his house. After him repaired also Shemaiah the son of Shechaniah, the keeper of the east gate.

30 After him repaired Hananiah the son of Shelemiah, and Hanun the sixth son of Zalaph, another piece. After him repaired Meshullam the son of Berechiah over against his chamber.

31 After him repaired Malchiah the goldsmith's son unto the place of the Nethinim, and of the merchants, over against the gate Miphkad, and to the going up of the corner.

29 After them Zadok the son of Immer repaired opposite his own house. After him Shemai′ah the son of Shecani′ah, the keeper of the East Gate, repaired. 30 After him Hanani′ah the son of Shelemi′ah and Hanun the sixth son of Zalaph repaired another section. After him Meshul′lam the son of Berechi′ah repaired opposite his chamber. 31 After him Malchi′jah, one of the goldsmiths, repaired as far as the house of the temple servants and of the merchants, opposite the Muster Gate,ᶠ and to the upper

ᶠ Or Hammiphkad Gate

---

the "horses' entrance to the king's house" (II Kings 11:16) leading from the southeastern part of the temple compound to the royal stable, which was presumably such a subterranean structure as "the stables of Solomon," on which the southern end of the present platform of the Haram area rests (Mitchell, op. cit., p. 160; Simons, op. cit., pp. 347 ff.). If the gate were thus in a relatively deep location (cf. Bertholet, op. cit., p. 56), the use of **above** to describe the terminus on the city wall towering over it would be intelligible. Such an area, adjacent to the temple compound, was naturally a quarter for the priests.

29. Zadok (cf. vs. 4) was a "descendant" of **Immer** (Ezra 2:37) the priest, and **Shemaiah** (Ezra 8:13) the "descendant" of **Shechaniah** (cf. 12:3) may also have been a priest, but since the gatekeepers were Levites (cf. Ezra 2:42; Ezek. 44:11) and the names are common, he may have been a Levite (cf. Ezra 2:40). Some identify the **East Gate** with the Water Gate of vs. 26 (cf. Burrows, "Source for Topography of Ancient Jerusalem," pp. 120-21), but it more probably was in the wall of the temple court where Ezekiel's plans called for an **East Gate** reserved for the prince, opened only on holy days (Ezek. 46:1 ff.). The Mishnah also mentions but one gate on the East "on which was portrayed the Palace of Shushan," a gate through which the high priest who burned the red heifer and his party went out to the Mount of Olives (Middoth 1:3-4). This gate might have been the predecessor of the present "Golden Gate" (Bāb ed-Dâhirîyeh) in the eastern wall of the Haram area (cf. Simons, op. cit., p. 340).

30. Hananiah (cf. Ezra 10:28) of vs. 8 and **Hanun** of vs. 13, neither of whom were given paternal names earlier, collaborated in this second assignment. For **Shelemiah** the LXXᴮᴺ have "Telemiah," suggesting the "Telem" of Ezra 10:24 and the "Talmon" of 7:45; 11:19; 12:25 (cf. Gotthard, op. cit., p. 97). **Zalaph** means "Caper Bush." **Sixth son** is without parallel in genealogical lists. It is due to a very early textual corruption of possibly a marginal note correcting Telemiah to **Shelemiah** (ibid.), or of some such place of origin as "the Shemeshite" (of 'Ain Shemesh; cf. Josh. 15:7; 18:17; Jahn, Esra [A und B] und Nehemja, p. 103) or, since **Hanun** is associated with Zanoah (vs. 13), as a corrupt fragment of an earlier "inhabitants of Zanoah" (Bertheau, Esra, Nechemia und Ester, p. 175; Bertholet, loc. cit.). **Meshullam**, with two assignments (cf. vs. 4), was the father-in-law of Tobiah the Ammonite (cf. 6:18). Instead of "his house" (cf. vss. 23, 28-29) the M.T. has **his chamber** (cf. Ezra 8:29; 10:6). This could have been a dwelling (Ezra 10:6) or a storeroom (Ezra 8:29) and the Vulg. and LXX here render "his treasury" (cf. Neh. 10:38-39; John 8:20). Could this be the **chamber** later used by Tobiah (cf. 13:4-7, 7-9)?

31. A Masoretic note at vs. 31, "half the book," indicates the belief that Ezra-Nehemiah formed a single work. Since **son** in the M.T. can mean guild membership (cf. vs. 8), **Malchijah** (cf. Ezra 10:25) was not **the goldsmith's son** but **one of the goldsmiths.** The terminus of his assignment was a **house** in which the **Nethinim** (cf. Ezra 2:43) and **merchants** (cf. vs. 32) were associated. Its nature is uncertain but its location in a

32 And between the going up of the corner unto the sheep gate repaired the goldsmiths and the merchants.

4 But it came to pass, that when Sanballat heard that we builded the wall, he was wroth, and took great indignation, and mocked the Jews.

chamber of the corner. 32 And between the upper chamber of the corner and the Sheep Gate the goldsmiths and the merchants repaired.

4 g Now when Sanbal'lat heard that we were building the wall, he was angry and greatly enraged, and he ridiculed the

g Ch 3. 33 in Heb

---

shop area indicates that it was not a residence (cf. vs. 26; 11:21) but a place of employment.

The significance of the word rendered **Muster** is uncertain since it could mean also "visit," "attend," or "appoint." It has been regarded as a gate between "the less sacred part of the enclosure, where the traders did business, [and] the sanctuary proper" (Mitchell, *op. cit.*, p. 161). It is also considered to be a gate leading to "the appointed place" (*miphqād*) belonging to the temple, outside of the sacred area (cf. Ezek. 43:21; Rudolph, *op. cit.*, pp. 120-21). Some, calling it the "Inspection Gate," locate it near the northern end of the east wall of the city and identify it with the Benjamin Gate (cf. Jer. 37:12-13; Dalman, *Jerusalem*, p. 140; Simons, *op. cit.*, pp. 340-42). If **opposite** refers to the gate rather than to the house of the Nethinim and merchants, the gate would be a landmark, not part of the city wall. The later temple court had but one gate in its eastern wall (Middoth 1:4). Another point of reference, according to the M.T. and Vulg., was **an upper chamber** (עלית; cf. Judg. 3:23-25; I Kings 17:19, 23), apparently a protecting watchtower at the northeast corner of the city (cf. Bertholet, *loc. cit.;* Simons, *op. cit.,* pp. 342, 452). The LXX and Peshitta render the word less plausibly as **the going up** (עלת; cf. vs. 19).

5. REMAINDER OF THE NORTH WALL (3:32)

32. The circuit of the defenses is completed with the restoration of the section of wall from the **upper chamber** (vs. 31) to the **Sheep Gate** (cf. vs. 1). This was repaired by **the goldsmiths and the merchants** whose business lay in that area. Then, as today, the **goldsmiths** were bankers (cf. Mark 11:15; Matt. 21:12). Together with **the merchants** they "sold and bought in the temple" (Mark 11:15). Presumably such tradesmen, in the vicinity of the **Sheep Gate,** dealt in sacrificial animals (cf. John 2:14) and other materials for use in the temple.

B. REACTION OF THE JUDEANS' NEIGHBORS (4:1-3=Hebrew 3:33-35)

Nehemiah's narrative, interrupted at 2:20 by the intrusion of ch. 3, is resumed in ch. 4. Since 4:1-6 presumes some progress in restoration beyond the situation in ch. 2, the effect of the insertion of ch. 3 is somewhat to indicate a lapse of time. But such progress as is assumed is not enough to ensure final success (cf. vs. 6), and certainly not the completeness suggested by 3:3, 6.

4:1-2. Here **when** signifies "after" rather than "at the time that." **Sanballat** (cf. 2:10) acted promptly when reports indicated that work had begun. **We were building** is

---

4:1-6. Increasing Tensions.—Various as are the interpretations that have been offered, and the textual emendations that have been proposed for the better understanding of this chapter (see Exeg.) the events of the middle of the twentieth century have provided a revealing social and psychological commentary on the tensions in which Nehemiah's project speedily became involved. The problems and

attitudes which confronted early Zionism in Palestine twenty-four centuries ago have emerged again in the similar but more violent conflict between the Jews who have returned to their ancient homeland to re-establish Israel there and the long-time Arab inhabitants of that same land. Thus can history repeat itself centuries afterward—on an enlarging scale and with more complicated results.

2 And he spake before his brethren and the army of Samaria, and said, What do these feeble Jews? will they fortify themselves? will they sacrifice? will they make an end in a day? will they revive the stones out of the heaps of the rubbish which are burned?

Jews. 2 And he said in the presence of his brethren and of the army of Samar'ia, "What are these feeble Jews doing? Will they restore things? Will they sacrifice? Will they finish up in a day? Will they revive the stones out of the heaps of rubbish, and

---

preferable to **we builded,** since the work was still far from complete. The corrupt text of vs. 2 has perplexed both ancient and modern translators. So divergent are their results that the versions help but little in recovering a convincing text. Confusion increases when the questions in the verse are regarded as mocking in character (cf. vs. 1), since those of **Sanballat** are best understood as a serious assessment of the situation. Tobiah introduced the note of ridicule. **Brethren** indicates allies (cf. Amos 1:9) as well as fellow Samaritans, since Tobiah was a member of the group (cf. vs. 3). The Hebrew "force" (*ḥáyil*), often rendered **army** (cf. Ezra 4:23), is not translated adequately by the "multitude" (*frequentia*) of the Vulg. The term has been assumed to mean the upper-class Samaritans, the political, economic, and military leaders (Albrecht Alt, "Die Rolle Samarias bei der Entstehung des Judenthums," *Festschrift Otto Procksch* [Leipzig: J. C. Hinrichs, 1934], pp. 12-13), but that would call for some differentiation from **brethren** that is not readily apparent. As governor of Samaria (cf. 2:10) **Sanballat** had troops and Nehemiah clearly expected armed intervention at Jerusalem (vss. 13 ff.). **Brethren** reflects civil leaders and **the army** indicates the military officers at the conference over the Jewish problem. To object to **army** because a fight would have been the result (Batten, *Ezra and Nehemiah,* p. 226) is to assume that the council was held within sight of Jerusalem, but the M.T. has no such setting. **These feeble Jews** might seem to indicate such a locale, but that rendition of the LXX^L does not agree with the M.T., the Vulg., and the Peshitta which have simply "the feeble Jews." The council may have met in Samaria.

Since Sanballat was informed both directly (2:19-20) and by rumor (vs. 1) of the Jewish plans, the question concerns motive (cf. 2:19; 6:6-7), and the translation is best as "What are the feeble Jews about to do?" (Hölscher, *Esra und Nehemia,* p. 474, note g). **Fortify** translates the difficult word which is usually rendered "abandon" (cf. 3:8) but cannot mean that here. **Things** is purely interpretative, for the M.T. has "for themselves." **Will they sacrifice?** may be but a faulty repetition of **Will they restore** (cf. Ehrlich, *Randglossen,* p. 191), but it is probably the serious question "Will they [only] sacrifice?" which implies that royal protection was previously confined to the religious cult, but raising the city defenses might indicate an interest in rebellion (cf. 3:19; 6:6-7) which would go beyond the permitted sacrificing. **Will they make an end in a day?** follows the Vulg., but the question is about the building itself, not the speed of the work. It is possible that the text is corrupt and should read, "Will they continue their building to the end?" (*ibid.;* Rudolph, *op. cit.,* p. 122). **Revive** sometimes means restoring to life (e.g., I Sam. 2:6; Deut. 32:39; Hos. 6:2), but it is also used of restoring a city (I Chr. 11:8), as in Phoenician (Zellig S. Harris, *A Grammar of the Phoenician Language* [New Haven: American Oriental Society, 1936], p. 100; Julian Obermann, *Discoveries at Karatepe* [Baltimore: American Oriental Society, 1948], pp. 15, 38). **Burned ones at that** renders a trailing circumstantial clause, "and they are burned."

Part of the tension that Nehemiah faced seems to have arisen from genuine anxiety and fear on the part of his Samaritan neighbors. The Exeg. agrees with Batten that "Sanballat seems to have been seriously alarmed at Nehemiah's activity." Tobiah, on the other hand, was disposed to ridicule the Jewish effort: **If a fox goes up on it he will break down their stone wall!** (Vs. 3*b*.) This combination of angry suspicion and bitter mockery stirred the volatile personality of Nehemiah to an outburst of imprecatory prayer against the enemies of his

3 Now Tobiah the Ammonite *was* by him, and he said, Even that which they build, if a fox go up, he shall even break down their stone wall.

4 Hear, O our God; for we are despised: and turn their reproach upon their own head, and give them for a prey in the land of captivity:

5 And cover not their iniquity, and let not their sin be blotted out from before thee: for they have provoked *thee* to anger before the builders.

burned ones at that?" 3 Tobi′ah the Ammonite was by him, and he said, "Yes, what they are building — if a fox goes up on it he will break down their stone wall!"

4 Hear, O our God, for we are despised; turn back their taunt upon their own heads, and give them up to be plundered in a land where they are captives. 5 Do not cover their guilt, and let not their sin be blotted out from thy sight; for they have provoked thee to anger before the builders.

---

3. Tobiah (cf. 2:10), reacting to Sanballat's seriousness, mocks the Jewish efforts. For **fox** (read by all the versions) it is possible to translate "jackal" (*shû'al;* cf. Judg. 15:4; Ezek. 13:4; Lam. 5:18; Ps. 63:10; Batten, *op. cit.,* p. 225). **Break down,** used elsewhere of breaching a wall (cf. II Kings 14:13), here means to "dig through."

C. Nehemiah's Imprecation (4:4-5 = Hebrew 3:36-37)

Although the imprecation has been regarded as the Chronicler's (C. C. Torrey, *Ezra Studies* [Chicago: University of Chicago Press, 1910], p. 226), its brevity suggests Nehemiah's work (cf. 1:11) rather than the Chronicler's wordy compositions (cf. 1:5-11; 9:6-38; Ezra 9:6-15). Its violence, too, bespeaks the volatile personality of Nehemiah (cf. 13:25).

4. The salutation is such as is found in Pss. 54:1-2; 64:1; Dan. 9:17. **Our god** reflects Nehemiah's style (cf. 5:9). The idea of being **despised** was one of the inducements that brought Nehemiah to Judea (1:3). He sought to reverse the situation so that the enemies would suffer Israel's fate. Instead of **give them up to be plundered** the Vulg. and LXX translate as though the "plunder" of the M.T. (*bizzāh*) were the "scorn" (*buzzāh*) mentioned just before.

5. In lines borrowed from Jer. 18:23*b*, God is urged not to forgive the sins of the enemies of the Jews. Nehardean tradition would make the text conform more closely to that of Jeremiah by omitting the initial **and** which links vs. 5 closely to what precedes (Bertheau, *Esra, Nechemia und Esther,* p. 226; Gotthard, *Text des Nehemia,* pp. 108-9). **Cover** (כסה), meaning "to hide," used of God's gracious concealing of sin (Pss. 32:1; 85:2), replaces the more familiar verb (כפר) with the same meaning used in the Jeremiah passage. **Blotted out** means "to wipe out," and its cognate in Arabic means "efface," "erase," "obliterate." **Iniquity** or **guilt** (עוֹן) means not perversity but error, "deviation from the right path," as its Arabic cognate shows (Paul Lagarde, *Mittheilungen von Paul de Lagarde* [Göttingen: Dieterich, 1884], I, 236-37). **Their sin** likewise means error or going wrong in the sense of "missing the mark." As error rather than perversity the sin in Jer. 18:23*b* would seem to indicate common human frailty, but the writer here,

---

people (vss. 4-5). The violence of his imprecation grates harshly on modern ears; but it must be remembered that such vehemence against enemies appears more than once in the psalms (cf. Pss. 79:4-12; 123:3-4; 137:7-9). So likewise does the confident readiness to identify the feelings of patriotic Zionists with the purposes of God (cf. Ps. 69:19, 27-28). The prior religious question, whether the ethical and spiritual conditions, long since laid down by the major prophets for the successful reoccupation of their Promised Land, under the judgment and with

the blessing of their God, had as yet been met by the Jewish people themselves—that crucial question is here not even raised, much less faced with searching of heart and conscience. And the deeper religious problem of the right of mortal man to identify his immediate projects with the purposes of God, and then to pray for divine vengeance on those who oppose them (as Paul later faced that problem so searchingly in Rom. 12:19), is even more completely bypassed. It is not only Jesus' parable of the Pharisee and the publican that raises these

6 So built we the wall; and all the wall was joined together unto the half thereof: for the people had a mind to work.

7 ¶ But it came to pass, *that* when Sanballat, and Tobiah, and the Arabians, and the Ammonites, and the Ashdodites, heard that the walls of Jerusalem were made up, *and* that the breaches began to be stopped, then they were very wroth,

6 So we built the wall; and all the wall was joined together to half its height. For the people had a mind to work.

7[h] But when Sanbal'lat and Tobi'ah and the Arabs and the Ammonites and the Ash'dodites heard that the repairing of the walls of Jerusalem was going forward and that the breaches were beginning to be closed,

[h] Ch 4. 1 in Heb

---

sensing the fact that the quotation does not exactly fit his specific case, appends the central reason for need of punishment, a reason indicating not simple "error" but deliberate, malicious, perverse conduct. The present awkward Hebrew text does not clearly state the reason, and the versions are of little help in recovering it. The M.T. has, lit., "for they provoked to anger before the builders." **They have provoked thee** reflects the Arabic version (cf. Deut. 31:29), but while the verb is used of Hebrew action, some argue that it was not used of a similar action by heathen people (Browne, *Early Judaism,* p. 97). Omitting the **before,** the Vulg. has "they mocked the builders" (cf. 2:19; 4:1). The Peshitta, if an obvious doublet is omitted ("the building") has "because they were furious against the builders," and this may be original.

D. Further Progress in Construction of the Wall (4:6=Hebrew 3:38)

6. Nehemiah reported that the work progressed despite opposition. If **all the wall** is retained, then **unto the half thereof** must indicate **its height,** but the versions do not all have such a text. The **all** is omitted by the Peshitta and it has been argued that walls to be repaired (3:4) must have stood, at least in part, more than half their height when the work began. Then the reference would be to their circumference rather than their height (Gotthard, *op. cit.,* p. 109; Hölscher, *Esra und Nehemia,* p. 532, note *c;* Rudolph, *op. cit.,* p. 123). But the height would be necessary for the stopping of the breaches (4:1; Batten, *op. cit.,* p. 228). However, neither height nor circumference alone may have been thought of, and the writer may have had in mind just half of the complete task of construction. The statement that the people **had a mind to work** is surprising in the light of the morale reflected in vs. 10. Since the Peshitta has "all" (כל) instead of "heart" (לב=**mind;** cf. Ezra 6:22; 7:10), the text may have been, "it was half finished and all the people were working" (cf. Gotthard, *loc. cit.*).

E. Conspiracy Against Jerusalem (4:7-12=Hebrew 4:1-6)

7. When Jewish success was apparent in the fortification of Jerusalem, their neighbors on all sides were aroused. The **Arabians** were on the south, holding lands formerly belonging to Edom (cf. 2:19). After **Tobiah,** the Arabic version lists "Gashmu the Arabian," as in 2:19. The **Ashdodites** were named for one of the five principal Philistine cities (Josh. 11:22), Ashdod (modern Esdûd), about three miles from the sea and about midway between Joppa and Gaza. It was the chief city of an Assyrian province (A. T.

---

deeper questions so inescapably for the Christian conscience today: they were squarely faced centuries before Christ by the greatest of the Hebrew prophets themselves (cf. Jer. 31:27-34; Amos 2:4-5; 5:14-27), as they were faced at a crisis in American history by Abraham Lincoln in his Second Inaugural Address.

We are on firmer religious ground in vs. 6, when Nehemiah (or the Chronicler) ceases to be so dogmatically certain about the purposes of the Almighty and so sure of the impossibility

of God's forgiving Israel's enemies, and returns rather to the prosecution of his own immediate and God-given task. **So we built the wall. . . . For the people had a mind to work.** It is always man's part to do that which will not be done by other than human hands in the sustaining faith that God in his own time and way will "establish . . . the work of our hands upon us" (cf. Ps. 90:17 with Phil. 2:12*b*-13).

7-14. *Without Were Fightings, Within Were Fears.*—When suspicion and ridicule did not

8 And conspired all of them together to come *and* to fight against Jerusalem, and to hinder it.

9 Nevertheless we made our prayer unto our God, and set a watch against them day and night, because of them.

10 And Judah said, The strength of the bearers of burdens is decayed, and *there is* much rubbish; so that we are not able to build the wall.

they were very angry; 8 and they all plotted together to come and fight against Jerusalem and to cause confusion in it. 9 And we prayed to our God, and set a guard as a protection against them day and night.

10 But Judah said, "The strength of the burden-bearers is failing, and there is much rubbish; we are not able to work on the

---

Olmstead, *History of Assyria* [New York: Charles Scribner's Sons, 1923], p. 309) and the name may have survived to designate that district in the Persian period when the Persians adopted the administrative areas of the Assyrian provincial system (Albrecht Alt, "Nachwort über die territorialgeschichtliche Bedeutung von Sanheribs Eingriff in Palästina," *Palästinajahrbuch*, XXV [1929], 84; "Judas Nachbarn zur Zeit Nehemias," p. 72, n. 1). Thus the **Ashdodites** were the western neighbors of Judea. Omitted by Josephus, the Arabic version, and the LXXAB, the word **Ashdodites** is usually regarded as a later addition, under the influence of 13:23 ff. But the M.T. is supported by the Peshitta and the Vulg., and some Greek MSS have a corrupted name resembling the later Greek name of Ashdod, "Azotus" (cf. Acts 8:40). The province survived into the later Persian period (cf. 13:23-24) and Ashdod was sacked in the Hellenistic period (I Macc. 5:68; 10:84).

Were made up or **going forward** interprets a M.T. that uses for the progress on the wall the figure of the healing of a wound (cf. Jer. 8:22; 30:17; 33:6) which is rendered by the Vulg., "the wounds of the wall were closed" (cf. II Chr. 24:13). After vs. 6, **began to be stopped** is difficult unless "half of it" represents the height of wall (cf. Batten, *loc. cit.*). But **began** may be a redundant, nontemporal use of the word (cf. Ezra 5:2). Since 6:1 indicates that **breaches** still existed then, **began** here means simply that the work of filling the breaches was just starting.

8. It is unnecessary after vs. 1 ff. and 2:19 ff. to say that the enemies **plotted together** or **conspired**. The "assembled" of the Vulg. and the LXX is due to the **to fight** which follows immediately. **To cause confusion** is closer to the M.T. than the interpretative **to hinder**. **Confusion** renders a Hebrew noun elsewhere found as "error" (Isa. 32:6), quite similar in meaning to "iniquity" (cf. vs. 5). It is probable that the meaning here is to be explained by the cognate Arabic word in the sense of "din of battle," from a verb meaning "to make war" or "to make an uproar" (cf. Ehrlich, *loc. cit.*). **It** and **in it** represent the Hebrew "for him," which, because cities are feminine gender (cf. 2:17), is sometimes emended to "for her." More probably it (לו) is a scribal error for "for us" (לנו) or "for me" (לי), as in the LXXL, which is even more characteristic of Nehemiah's style (Batten, *loc. cit.*; Rudolph, *op. cit.*, p. 124).

9. For עליהם, **against them**, the Peshitta reads עלינו, "over us," but the original may have been עליה, "over her," referring to Jerusalem, for the Vulg., apparently influenced by vs. 13, has "we set watchmen upon the wall." For **because of them** the M.T. has, lit., "from their face," which can mean **as a protection against them** (cf. Gen. 7:7; Jer. 35:11).

10. Tension in the narrative is heightened by the realistic revelation of weakness in the Jewish camp. Surprising after 4:6, it reflects just the situation expected as the difficult work progressed. Since the context is military here, such reference to labor has led to the charge that the verse is intrusive (Batten, *op. cit.*, p. 229; Rudolph, *loc. cit.*). It is recognized as a fragment of a lament of the **burden-bearers** and its metric structure (*Qînāh* meter) and internal rhyme (*sabbāl* and *nûkhal*) support the conjecture. The meter requires that **and Judah said** be part of the poem, not an introduction to it (Hölscher, *Esra und Nehemia*, p. 532; Kittel, *Geschichte des Volkes Israel*, III, 633). **Judah** means not the ancient tribe but the entire postexilic community. **Decayed and**

11 And our adversaries said, They shall not know, neither see, till we come in the midst among them, and slay them, and cause the work to cease.

12 And it came to pass, that when the Jews which dwelt by them came, they said unto us ten times, From all places whence ye shall return unto us *they will be upon you.*

13 ¶ Therefore set I in the lower places behind the wall, *and* on the higher places, I even set the people after their families with their swords, their spears, and their bows.

wall." 11 And our enemies said, "They will not know or see till we come into the midst of them and kill them and stop the work." 12 When the Jews who lived by them came they said to us ten times, "From all the places where they live[i] they will come up against us."[j] 13 So in the lowest parts of the space behind the wall, in open places, I stationed the people according to their families, with their swords, their spears, and

[i] Cn: Heb *you return*
[j] Compare Gk Syr: Heb uncertain

---

failing, used here of failing strength (cf. Ps. 31:10), renders a Hebrew word meaning "to stagger," elsewhere used of tottering from weakness due to fasting (cf. Ps. 31:10). The LXX has, more dramatically, "shattered."

11. The opening words may have been suggested by those of vs. 10, as attention shifts suddenly from Judah to its enemies. **Our adversaries,** lit., "our besiegers," is rendered **our enemies** by the Peshitta.

12. The Hebrew text is incomplete and its last part is so corrupt as to make nonsense. Again the versions differ widely as they make the best of a corrupt text. The first part of the verse is clear and the general context of the message can be calculated from Nehemiah's reaction (vss. 13 ff.). An attack, threatened in vs. 11, is confirmed in vs. 12 by rumors of it reported from all sides.

Reports came in from the outlying Jews who **lived by them,** i.e., by the enemies of Jerusalem. The words **came** and **ten times** suggest that the Jews of outlying towns (cf. 3:5, 7, 13-14, 16-17) periodically went home and later returned with news of their districts, or that increasing tension drew a certain number of outlying Jews to Jerusalem for safety. **Ten times** is a general round·number (cf. Gen. 31:7, 41; Lev. 26:26; Num. 14:22; I Sam. 1:8; Job 19:3).

Because מכל-המקמות, **from all the places,** is difficult to connect in the M.T., it is proposed to read instead כל-המזמות, "all the plans," and חשבו, "they planned," for תשובו, **ye shall return,** translating "all the plots that they devised against us" (cf. Ehrlich, *op. cit.,* p. 192; Rudolph, *loc. cit.*), but the versions do not support that ingenious emendation. The incomplete M.T., lit., "from all the places where," is filled out by **they live** in the Peshitta, and the LXXABℵ suggests that the verb ויעלו, "they will come up," has been lost from the M.T., possibly because of its similarity to עלינו, **against us.** The verse is best translated by the Amer. Trans. which has, "When the Jews came who dwelt beside them, they said to us ten times, 'From all the places where they dwell they will come up against us.'"

F. Jewish Defensive Measures (4:13-23=Hebrew 4:7-17)

13. The object of the first **set I,** lost in textual transmission, was probably "builders" or "workmen." **In the lower places** does not reproduce the M.T., which has "from" rather than **in. Lowest parts,** as "the places below," could refer to places at the base of the wall outside the city where building stones were being prepared. **Higher places**

---

stop the enterprise, mockery passed over into the threat of aggressive attack. This was the more dangerous because complaints over the hard labor and difficult conditions of the work were already weakening the morale of the Jews them-

selves (cf. vs. 10). To this outward and inward crisis Nehemiah applied his own characteristic combination of confidence in God (vss. 9, 14) with preparedness for all eventualities (vss. 9b, 13). The situation was one that exposed

14 And I looked, and rose up, and said unto the nobles, and to the rulers, and to the rest of the people, Be not ye afraid of them: remember the Lord, *which is* great and terrible, and fight for your brethren, your sons, and your daughters, your wives, and your houses.

15 And it came to pass, when our enemies heard that it was known unto us, and God had brought their counsel to nought, that we returned all of us to the wall, every one unto his work.

16 And it came to pass from that time forth, *that* the half of my servants wrought in the work, and the other half of them held both the spears, the shields, and the bows, and the habergeons; and the rulers *were* behind all the house of Judah.

their bows. 14 And I looked, and arose, and said to the nobles and to the officials and to the rest of the people, "Do not be afraid of them. Remember the Lord, who is great and terrible, and fight for your brethren, your sons, your daughters, your wives, and your homes."

15 When our enemies heard that it was known to us and that God had frustrated their plan, we all returned to the wall, each to his work. 16 From that day on, half of my servants worked on construction, and half held the spears, shields, bows, and coats of mail; and the leaders stood behind all the

---

translates a word elsewhere meaning "bare," in reference to a smooth, cleared rock surface (Ezek. 24:7-8; 26:4, 14). The LXX^L has **open places,** perhaps "cleared places." The word seems intended to determine more exactly the preceding general statement, **behind the wall** (Hermann Guthe and L. W. Batten, *The Books of Ezra and Nehemiah* [Leipzig: J. C. Hinrichs, 1901; "The Sacred Books of the Old Testament"], p. 47). It indicates cleared working areas within the walls to which the workmen were transferred so that work could be continued with safety. **Families** indicate the larger social groups, such as the clan. Lacking a professional Jewish army, weapons were in the hands of all the workmen.

14. The awkward **and I looked** is improved by the introduction of the object to read "I saw their fear" (Bertholet, *Esra und Nehemia,* p. 59; Gotthard, *op. cit.,* p. 120) or "I saw that they were afraid" (Rudolph, *op. cit.,* p. 126). Josephus (*Antiquities* XI. 5. 8). declares "the Jews were so alarmed that they nearly gave up building," and vs. 15 indicates that work stopped and the workmen left their posts on the wall. Again three groups are distinguished (cf. 2:16) as Nehemiah urges the Jews to share his trust in God (cf. vs. 20: 2:18). The words **great and terrible** again characterize God (cf. 1:5; Deut. 7:21; 10:17).

15. Their counsel is **their plan** or "their purpose" (cf. Ezra 4:5). No violence is implied, but Josephus (*ibid.*) claims that "they killed many of the Jews."

16. From that time forth means from the setting of the guard, when the Jews were persuaded to return to work. **Servants,** lit., "youths," were Nehemiah's own men who could be appointed to work on the walls (cf. 5:16) or to guard duty (cf. 13:19). Such "youths" were not slaves, for they had funds of their own (5:10), but were military retainers (Gen. 14:24; I Sam. 25:5 ff.; II Sam. 2:14 ff.; I Kings 20:14 ff.). They have been called part of Nehemiah's bodyguard (Batten, *op. cit.,* p. 231) and their equipment suggests the short **spears,** wicker **shields,** long **bows** and iron-scaled armor of the Persian soldier (cf. Olmstead, *History of the Persian Empire,* p. 239). Lacking is "the short sword slung from a girdle on the right hip," but since the list begins with **and** it is possible that the "swords" were originally listed also (cf. Bertholet, *op. cit.,* p. 60). **Coats of mail**

---

scattered workers to hostile surprise, rumors of which had been cunningly spread abroad. The psychology on both sides of the "cold war" between Russia and the Western democracies after World War II will help us to understand

better the seriousness and the complexity of Nehemiah's problem at this crisis.

15-23. *Both . . . and.*—At this critical point the practical-minded Nehemiah introduced a new division of labor that produced surprising

17 They which builded on the wall, and they that bare burdens, with those that laded, *every one* with one of his hands wrought in the work, and with the other *hand* held a weapon.

18 For the builders, every one had his sword girded by his side, and *so* builded. And he that sounded the trumpet *was* by me.

19 ¶ And I said unto the nobles, and to the rulers, and to the rest of the people, The work *is* great and large, and we are separated upon the wall, one far from another.

house of Judah, 17 who were building on the wall. Those who carried burdens were laden in such a way that each with one hand labored on the work and with the other held his weapon. 18 And each of the builders had his sword girded at his side while he built. The man who sounded the trumpet was beside me. 19 And I said to the nobles and to the officials and to the rest of the people, "The work is great and widely spread, and we are separated on the wall,

---

is preferable to the archaic **habergeons,** which indicated mail covering of the neck and breast, for Herodotus (*History* IX. 22) and Pausanius (*Description of Greece* I. 27. 1) mention golden-scaled armor worn by the Persian Masistius and fragments of iron and bronze scale armor were found at Persepolis, as well as some gold-covered iron scales (Schmidt, *Treasury of Persepolis,* pp. 44-46, Figs. 27 *b, c, d, e*).

Behind all the house is enigmatic unless it means that **the servants** stood guard over workers. The present M.T. indicates that **the rulers** stood back, apparently out of danger, but that seems unlikely. To render "supported" for **behind** is to employ modern idiom. A clear context demands the elision of the troublesome **rulers** (Rudolph, *loc. cit.*) even though the word is used by Nehemiah (12:32) and is here well attested by the versions (Kittel, *op. cit.,* III, 633; Gotthard, *op. cit.,* p. 124). It could easily be a dittograph (השרים) of the preceding **coats of mail** (השרינים; Hölscher, *Esra und Nehemia,* p. 533). **House of Judah** means "Judeans" (Zeph. 2:7; Zech. 8:13, 15, 19; 10:3, 6; 12:4; Jer. 3:18). As the LXX and Vulg. show, **who were building on the wall** of vs. 17 should follow **house of Judah** in explanation. Both the burden-bearers and masons (vss. 17-18) were included in this group.

17. Perhaps because the soldiers were few the builders also were armed for defense. **With those that laded** suggests a second class of laborers, a view supported by the Vulg. and Peshitta. But the M.T. has a plural participle of uncertain meaning. **Laded** presumes a faulty spelling in the M.T. (עמס for עמש). The LXX[L] translation "armed" (*enoploi*) suggests that the difficult word, עמשים, may be an error for חמשים, "were armed" (Siegfried, *Esra, Nehemia und Esther,* p. 88; Gotthard, *op. cit.,* pp. 125-26; Rudolph, *loc. cit.*). **Weapon** here suggests something thrown, and the LXX[ABℵ] renders it thus (*bolida*). Burden-bearers, who carried smaller stones or baskets of debris on their heads or shoulders, would usually have one hand free for the missile.

18. As the Peshitta indicates, the **builders** here were stonemasons, in contrast to the laborers of vs. 17. Since they needed both hands for work, their weapon had to be **girded** where it would be available but out of the way. The **sword** was perhaps a short one (cf. Judg. 3:16), such as Persian soldiers used (cf. vs. 16).

18*b*-20. Because the work on the walls was **widely spread** and there were relatively few defenders at any point, a system of alarms had to be instituted. A horn was to summon the workmen in time of attack. The **trumpet** (*shôphār*) was a curved horn of a

---

results. It is difficult to tell from the ambiguous account and the frequently obscure text, which is all we now have to go on, whether vss. 17-18 are a typically Oriental symbolism (defensive weapon in one hand, constructive tool in the other) for the fact that both guarding and

building went forward together within the well-organized group, or whether vs. 16, with its picture of half the company at work and half on guard, is an original account which the Chronicler later combined with the other picture in vss. 17-18, characteristically not noticing,

20 In what place *therefore* ye hear the sound of the trumpet, resort ye thither unto us: our God shall fight for us.

21 So we labored in the work: and half of them held the spears from the rising of the morning till the stars appeared.

22 Likewise at the same time said I unto the people, Let every one with his servant lodge within Jerusalem, that in the night they may be a guard to us, and labor on the day.

23 So neither I, nor my brethren, nor my servants, nor the men of the guard which

far from one another. 20 In the place where you hear the sound of the trumpet, rally to us there. Our God will fight for us."

21 So we labored at the work, and half of them held the spears from the break of dawn till the stars came out. 22 I also said to the people at that time, "Let every man and his servant pass the night within Jerusalem, that they may be a guard for us by night and may labor by day." 23 So neither I nor my brethren nor my servants nor the

---

cow or ram. **By me** of the M.T. and Vulg. (vs. 18*b*) suggests that a single trumpeter accompanied Nehemiah, who expected to be at the point of attack where the alarm would be sounded. But that would give the foe the advantage, and good generalship would call for a number of trumpeters at strategic points to spread the alarm. The LXX and Peshitta, reading "next to him," referring to the builder, suggest a system of alarms, and Josephus (*loc. cit.*) claimed that Nehemiah "stationed trumpeters at intervals of five hundred feet, with the command to give the signal to the people if the enemy appeared." Nehemiah concludes his instruction with the comforting promise that the Jews would not face the enemy alone but with the support of God, in whose cause they labored.

21. The words **half of them held the spears** obviously intrude from vs. 16, presumably because **labored at the work** is found in both verses.

22. Most Judeans lived in the outlying towns (cf. 3:2, 5, 7, 14-17) with relatively few people in the city (7:4; 11:1-3). The new security of the city made it advisable for those in the vicinity to come within its completed walls in time of danger. It is sometimes assumed that the order (vs. 22) was directed to workmen in Jerusalem who were from out of town and had gone back and forth to their homes to gain recruits for the night watch, to prevent shirkers from being absent without leave, and to avoid possible contacts between Jewish traitors and the enemy (Rudolph, *op. cit.*, p. 127). But the order was perhaps general, part of the means for defending the city.

His servant translates a word used in vs. 16 for military personnel, but it is unlikely that each Jew had a military retainer. Some have proposed to emend the text to read "like my servants," with reference to Nehemiah's men (vs. 16; *ibid.*). Others prefer emending to "his followers" (cf. Gen. 14:24; I Sam. 25:5 ff.). These critics limit the term to the officials of outlying towns and their followers, but that the word ever meant "fellow citizens" is unlikely. The word here most probably is collective, used for household servants of the people about to move to Jerusalem.

The verse should conclude with a balanced expression with nouns of the same force. Some Hebrew MSS have "for a guard" and "for work," but the M.T. **labor** is not exactly parallel to the preceding word **guard**. It would be preferable to read "a working force," but such usage is not attested elsewhere (cf. Batten, *op. cit.*, p. 234).

23. Josephus (*loc. cit.*) summarizes this verse by saying of Nehemiah: "He himself made the rounds of the city by night, never tiring either through work or lack of food and sleep, neither of which he took for pleasure but as a necessity." But the verse

---

or more probably not caring, about the resulting obscurities. In any case, Nehemiah's gift for executive leadership knew how to enlist both workers and leaders in the forefront of the common task; how to guard against daytime

surprises by their enemies at weak or isolated points (vss. 9, 18*b*-20); and how to protect his men against surprise or deceit at night, when the suburban workers had returned to their homes (vs. 22). Such foresightedness and effi-

followed me, none of us put off our clothes, *saving that* every one put them off for washing.

5 And there was a great cry of the people and of their wives against their brethren the Jews.

men of the guard who followed me, none of us took off our clothes; each kept his weapon in his hand.*k*

5 Now there arose a great outcry of the people and of their wives against their

k Cn: Heb *each his weapon the water*

---

indicates that his associates were also under pressure, ready to work or fight as needed. Since **brethren,** usually "fellow Jews," is more restricted in 5:14, it could refer here to close kinsmen (cf. 7:2). **Servants** were retainers of Nehemiah (cf. vs. 16). **Men of the guard** could mean the Persian bodyguard (2:9; cf. Bertholet, *loc. cit.*), but it also could refer in general to any who guarded the workmen (cf. vss. 13, 21). It is unlikely that **who followed me** indicates "who supported me" (cf. vs. 16). With "who escorted me" the Amer. Trans. identifies the guardsmen (2:9) but this is invalid if the reference is to armed Jews. The clause is perhaps a mistaken gloss under the influence of **behind all the house of Judah** (vs. 16; cf. Rudolph, *loc cit.*). It contributes nothing but confusion and should be omitted.

The conclusion of the M.T., "every man his missile the water," is nonsense. It is disputed both in ancient and modern times whether the word rendered **his weapon** (שלחו) should be the noun "his missile" (cf. vs. 17) or the verb "stripped himself" (שלחו). The Vulg. interprets, "Every man stripped himself when he was to be washed" (cf. KJV, **every one put them off for washing**). But the verb is not used of "undressing," even though the rendition "let down" appears in an entirely different context in Jer. 38:6. Furthermore, the reference to remaining clothed (vs. 23*a*) is adequate. One expects, then, a reference to having weapons ready constantly for an emergency. But if **his weapon** is correct, **the water** (המים) must be wrong. It could be emended to **in his hand** (בידו; Torrey, *Composition,* p. 39, n. 1; Guthe and Batten, *Ezra and Nehemiah,* p. 68), as in II Chr. 23:10, or to "lay at his right hand" (הימינו; cf. II Sam. 14:19; Keil, *Chronik, Esra, Nehemia und Esther,* p. 536; Rudolph, *op. cit.,* pp. 126-27).

V. Economic Problems (5:1-19)

A. Internal Jewish Problems (5:1-13)

Again the story is unexpectedly interrupted by extraneous material, purely socioeconomic problems not directly connected with the building of the wall. The interpolation may again be a device to indicate a lapse of time (cf. 4:1), but it is possible that the insertion was made to illustrate further hindrance to the reconstruction due this time to internal conflict.

Since the wall was completed in the short interval of fifty-two days (6:15), it is unlikely that the economic situation was due to the draining of farm labor to construction work in the city (cf. Rudolph, *op. cit.,* p. 128). The situation presumed in the chapter was certainly the result of a long drought (cf. vs. 3), possibly the disaster that depleted the temple stores and drove the Levites to seek a livelihood in the country (cf. 13:5, 10-12). The substance and tone of the chapter suggest the circumstances of ch. 13 and the date in vs. 14 indicates that the narrative was written toward the end of Nehemiah's administration, long after the walls were completed.

---

ciency of organization put heavy burdens on the endurance and loyalty of each and every worker from the break of dawn till the stars came out (vs. 21), and then forbade them (including their leader himself who shared their exposure to attack) to rest at night without their clothes on their backs and their weapons at hand. Such was the complete and patient co-operation that made possible the accomplishment of the "great work" (6:15).

5:1-13. *A Man's Foes . . . They of His Own Household.*—Nehemiah's account of his problems with the enemies of his people suddenly shifts to an acute difficulty within his own group, one which has a curiously contemporary sound. Then, and ever since, great undertakings

2 For there were that said, We, our sons, and our daughters, *are* many: therefore we take up corn *for them*, that we may eat, and live.

Jewish brethren. 2 For there were those who said, "With our sons and our daughters, we are many; let us get grain, that we

---

1. IMPOVERISHED JEWS FORCED INTO SLAVERY (5:1-5)

Small Jewish landowners were reluctant to relinquish their inherited property (cf. I Kings 21:1-16), for from the land they both earned their living and paid their taxes and the property was capital that could be mortgaged for funds to prevent acute distress. But in real-estate loans the creditor took over the property, and the produce of the fields was applied toward the interest on the loan (F. R. Steele, *Nuzi Real Estate Transactions* [New Haven: American Oriental Society, 1943], pp. 44-49; Olmstead, *History of the Persian Empire*, p. 299). Every loan, however small, required collateral as a pledge— even so little as a cloak (Exod. 22:26; Deut. 24:13). Those without property who needed considerable sums to redeem their property or for living expenses were sometimes driven to the extremity of selling the services of their daughters (Exod. 21:7), sons (II Kings 4:1), or themselves (Lev. 25:39) as collateral. Sometimes the poor were sold into virtual slavery for as little as a pair of shoes (Amos 2:6; 8:6).

As early as the Covenant Code (Exod. 21:2-3) humanitarian considerations provided that Hebrew bondsmen were to be released every seventh year, the year of jubilee, and such provisions were found in the later codes (Deut. 15:12), but in the Priestly Code the interval between jubilees was increased to fifty years (Lev. 25:10). With Ezekiel real estate, too, was then to be restored to its original owners (Ezek. 46:17) and the Priestly Code made similar provisions, at least concerning lands outside of Jerusalem (Lev. 25:10, 13, 23, 28, 31; cf. 27:20-24; Num. 36:4). But reality worked against such idealistic legislation, and it is doubtful whether the jubilee ordinances were ever observed. In the one recorded instance of observance (Jer. 34:14-17) the bondsmen were re-enslaved almost at once, and later generations circumvented the laws of jubilee by means of the *prosbol* invented by Rabbi Hillel.

5:1. The complaint of the poor regarding their lot was chronic in the ancient Near East, but the **great outcry** against the wealthy **Jewish brethren,** who stood to profit from loans, was an unusual and concerted protest against prevailing practices which could not be ignored.

2-3. The M.T. of vs. 2 seems to complain that large families required much food and this has been interpreted to mean that "the population had increased faster than the means of support" (Batten, *op. cit.*, p. 238). But Hebrews never complained about large families, and the real grievance is about the gradual loss of property and subsequent enslavement. It is better to read instead of רבים, **many,** the graphically similar ערבים, "pledging," making the construction agree with **we are mortgaging** in vs. 3 (Siegfried, *Esra, Nehemia und Esther*, p. 89; Gotthard, *Text des Nehemia*, p. 131; Rudolph, *loc. cit.*). It is highly probable that vs. 2 is but an early corruption of vs. 3, for the verses begin alike and are almost identical in Hebrew word order. **Our daughters** (בנתינו, vs. 2) is a corruption of **our houses** (בתינו, vs. 3). Then **our fields, our vineyards** of vs. 3, which would have been unintelligible before **our daughters,** was replaced by **our sons,** perhaps under the influence of vs. 5. As indicated above, **many** (vs. 2) corrupts **mortgaging** in

---

have been beset and often betrayed inside their own camp by familiar weaknesses within human nature itself. In every generation gifted leaders like Nehemiah, facing crises in front and on each flank, have had to turn their attention and energies from the battle to deal with the readiness of some of their own followers to exploit the crisis for personal or partisan profit,

even though they risk thereby the common and far greater cause.

Nehemiah's forthright account of the economic situation among his fellow Jews is no sociological study in such exploitation. It is vibrant with his own quick sympathy for those who were having to pay too much for their food, or to see their families rise still hungry from the

3 *Some* also there were that said, We have mortgaged our lands, vineyards, and houses, that we might buy corn, because of the dearth.

4 There were also that said, We have borrowed money for the king's tribute, *and that upon* our lands and vineyards.

5 Yet now our flesh *is* as the flesh of our brethren, our children as their children: and, lo, we bring into bondage our sons

may eat and keep alive." 3 There were also those who said, "We are mortgaging our fields, our vineyards, and our houses to get grain because of the famine." 4 And there were those who said, "We have borrowed money for the king's tax upon our fields and our vineyards. 5 Now our flesh is as the flesh of our brethren, our children are as their children; yet we are forcing our sons

---

vs. 3. It is better to read ונקחה, "And we have taken" (Ehrlich, *Randglossen*, p. 194), for the M.T. **let us get.** In the present context of vs. 2 the concluding **that we may eat, and live** is logical. In the Vulg. "for their price" (בערך) in vs. 2 seems a corruption of the similar **because of the dearth** (ברעב) of vs. 3. Greek texts refer to eating in vs. 3, and the Peshitta in vs. 3 adds "and live" after **because of the dearth.** Needless repetition and anticipation of material is avoided and no essential substance is lost if vs. 2 is regarded as a corrupt duplicate of vs. 3. For **we are mortgaging** the Peshitta interprets, "we are selling." Instead of "we have taken," it is possible to render **that we might buy,** since the Hebrew verb later has that sense (Marcus Jastrow, *A Dictionary of the Targumim* [New York: G. P. Putnam's Sons, 1903], II, 717), which is also attested by the Akkadian cognate (*laqû*; Bezold, *Babylonisch-Assyrisches Glossar,* p. 161, col. 2). To interpret the Hebrew word for **dearth** to mean the farmer's need for grain when he has used up his own produce (Batten, *op. cit.,* pp. 238-39) is an unjustified softening of the meaning, for the word, meaning "be hungry," elsewhere signifies not mere "need" but actual **famine** (Rudolph, *op. cit.,* p. 129). Frequent famines were encountered in the relatively infertile mountain regions, strongly dependent upon rain (cf. Gen. 42:5; I Kings 18:1-2; II Kings 6:25 ff.).

4. The **king's tribute** was an additional tax to that of vs. 15, assessed for the needs of the kingdom (cf. Ezra 6:8; 7:20). The fifth satrapy, including Cyprus, Syria, and Palestine, was assessed 350 talents (Herodotus *History* III. 91). Little ever returned to the satrapy, and the king's tendency to insist on payment in metal drained the empire of gold and silver and drove the landowners into the hands of local loan sharks everywhere in the empire (Olmstead, *History of the Persian Empire,* pp. 298-99). It is unnecessary to omit **our lands and vineyards,** which is appended awkwardly in the M.T., under the assumption that the property has already changed hands (Guthe and Batten, *op. cit.,* pp. 47-48; Siegfried, *loc. cit.;* Bertholet, *Esra und Nehemia,* p. 61), for the pledging and borrowing was a constant process and not all lands were yet held as pledge. The versions all boldly attempt to retain the words, and the LXXᴬᴮℵ adds "and our houses." The preposition "upon" is introduced in the LXXᴸ, as though the properties were collateral for a loan, and this may be original (Jahn, *Esra [A und B] und Nehemia,* p. 110; Gotthard, *op. cit.,* p. 132; Rudolph, *op. cit.,* p. 128).

5. Although the Peshitta begins this verse with the formula used to begin vss. 3, 4, the **yet now** of the M.T. in the conclusion of the protests is intended to show the most extreme results of the economic policy, since each protest was increasingly more severe. **Our flesh** and **our children** do not declare that the poor are as good as the rich, but emphasize the fact of racial unity between the oppressors and their victims. This is made explicit in the LXXᴸ, which adds after **our sons** the words "for we are one flesh."

---

table because they could not afford to buy more food; for those likewise who had mortgaged their property to buy food when it was scarce, or had sold their children into slavery to pay their taxes. Even warmer was his indignation

at his fellow Jews who had taken advantage of hard times and short supplies to enrich themselves at the cost of their own Jewish brethren. **I was very angry** (vs. 6).

Twenty-four centuries have passed between

and our daughters to be servants, and *some of our daughters are brought into bondage already:* neither *is it* in our power *to redeem them;* for other men have our lands and vineyards.

6 ¶ And I was very angry when I heard their cry and these words.

7 Then I consulted with myself, and I rebuked the nobles, and the rulers, and said unto them, Ye exact usury, every one of his brother. And I set a great assembly against them.

and our daughters to be slaves, and some of our daughters have already been enslaved; but it is not in our power to help it, for other men have our fields and our vineyards."

6 I was very angry when I heard their outcry and these words. 7 I took counsel with myself, and I brought charges against the nobles and the officials. I said to them, "You are exacting interest, each from his brother." And I held a great assembly

---

Flesh is used in our sense of "blood." Not a foreign tyrant but a racial brother was responsible for the abuses and the distress. If parents had to make a shocking confession, at least there lay behind it the implication that their fellow Jews were actually responsible for the situation.

Brought into bondage (כבש) means "to press," then "to tread," and finally, "to oppress," but the addition of **to be slaves** after it indicates that enslavement is not involved in the verb itself. After specific reference to enslavement of both sexes, the charge is repeated with reference to **some of our daughters.** Some omit the repetitious material (Jahn, *loc. cit.*), but if it is retained obviously the verb must have a different meaning. In Esth. 7:8 that verb definitely has sexual significance, for the LXX there has, "Wilt thou even force the woman in my house?" Here the verb "press" or "tread" is a euphemism for rape (cf. C. D. Buck, *A Dictionary of Selected Synonyms in the Principal Indo-European Languages* [Chicago: University of Chicago Press, 1949], p. 279). The LXX[L] here has "some of our daughters have been taken by force," but this has been explained as arising through dittography (cf. Gotthard, *loc. cit.*).

Stripped of their capital, the complainants were helpless, unable to do more than pay the interest on their debt. **Neither is it in our power** is incomplete and, as does the M.T., needs something like **to redeem,** as in the Vulg., or **to help it.** The M.T. has, lit., "And there is not the power of our hands" (cf. Deut. 28:32). To **our fields and our vineyards** the Peshitta adds "and our possessions." For לאחרים, "belongs to others" (M.T.), the LXX has לחרים, "belongs to the nobles," which some regard as original (Jahn, *loc. cit.;* Gotthard, *op. cit.*, p. 133), but that reading, although it gives the proper interpretation, seems to be wholly conjectural and the M.T. is preferable (Ehrlich, *loc. cit.;* Rudolph, *op. cit.*, p. 128).

2. NEHEMIAH'S PROTEST AND SOLUTION (5:6-13)

6. Nehemiah became violently angry when his moral sense was aroused (13:8, 21, 25). **Their outcry** is the complaint of vss. 2-5. **These words** may mean "these things." Instead of **I was very angry,** which renders the Hebrew idiom (cf. 4:1; 4:7), the Peshitta and the LXX[AB][א] have "and I was much grieved." This probably is due to the beginning of vs. 7, but the M.T., supported by the Vulg., seems original, for it fits well the temper of "and I contended" in vs. 7.

7. Consulted with myself is translated by the LXX as "my heart took counsel within me," and the Vulg. has "my heart thought with myself." Thus the "heart" in the M.T. indicates "mind" (cf. Ezra 6:22; 7:27). The Amer. Trans. interprets the M.T. properly

---

this very human story of long ago and the "chiselers," "scroungers," war profiteers, and black market operators and customers of our own experience. Most communities, especially the smaller ones, still find it hard to forgive or

forget the leaders of organized religion who "devour widows' houses, and . . . make long prayers" (Mark 12:40) —though not always "for a pretense." And every generation may have its share of politicians who in a time of

8 And I said unto them, We, after our ability, have redeemed our brethren the Jews, which were sold unto the heathen; and will ye even sell your brethren? or shall they be sold unto us? Then held they their peace, and found nothing *to answer.*

9 Also I said, It *is* not good that ye do: ought ye not to walk in the fear of our God

against them, 8 and said to them, "We, as far as we are able, have bought back our Jewish brethren who have been sold to the nations; but you even sell your brethren that they may be sold to us!" They were silent, and could not find a word to say.

9 So I said, "The thing that you are doing

---

with "after thinking it over," but such translations are possible only by adopting the Aramaic or Akkadian meaning of the verb "to counsel" (cf. Dan. 4:27). Hebrew usage demands a translation "my heart was king over me" (Batten, *op. cit.,* p. 240). Those who believe that Nehemiah acted impulsively, motivated by emotion, emend the text to "my heart was turned within my body" (cf. Hos. 11:8; Ehrlich, *op. cit.,* pp. 194-95) or "my heart trembled" (Jahn, *op. cit.,* p. 111), and the Peshitta has "my heart was broken within me." The M.T. is preferable.

As usual, Nehemiah dealt with the officials before going directly to the people (cf. 2:16). **I rebuked** and **I brought charges against** represent the M.T., "I contended with." The complaint seems not against **exacting interest** or against **usury,** which was illegal (cf. Deut. 23:20), but against the demand for important capital as a pledge. The verb involved (נשה) always means "to loan on pledge" (Rudolph, *op. cit.,* p. 130) so the complaint is properly rendered by the American Jewish Translation as "Ye lend upon pledge" (cf. Deut. 24:10). Unsuccessful with the nobles themselves, Nehemiah appealed to the people directly through a popular **assembly** (cf. vs. 13).

8. Jews enslaved by Jews were to be released in the year of jubilee (Lev. 25:10, 13, 39-41) but those enslaved by **the heathen** or **the nations** had to be redeemed (cf. Lev. 25:47-49). Nehemiah here indicates that such ransoms were being paid to redeem fellow Jews. The M.T. "acquired" is interpreted as **bought back** or **redeemed.** Some consider the practice limited to Jews brought home from Persia (Bernhard Stade, *Biblische Theologie des Alten Testaments* [Tübingen: J. C. B. Mohr, 1905], I, 323), but others think only of Jews in Gentile hands in and about Judea (cf. Batten, *op. cit.,* p. 241). The program of purchase was limited only by "the sufficiency among us," which means, as the Vulg. shows, **as far as we are able.** The LXX[AB]ℵ has "of our free will," which some regard as better than the M.T. (Gotthard, *op. cit.,* p. 135; Batten, *loc. cit.*). An ambiguous M.T. is rendered by the Vulg. and the LXX as those **who have been sold,** but the American Jewish Translation, "that sold themselves," is preferable, indicating such sales as in vss. 2, 5.

The leaders were berated for driving fellow Jews to desperation with their demand for pledges. As in the Vulg. and the LXX, the Amer. Trans. presents the statement to the leaders as a rhetorical question, implying that the greedy Jews were responsible for Jewish enslavement. The practice was economically as well as morally wrong since it compelled the spending of the limited Jewish capital for the ransom. For the M.T. **shall they be sold unto us** it is proposed to read ונכרו לנו, "so that we should purchase" (Rudolph, *loc. cit.;* cf. Vulg. "for us to redeem them").

9. Fear was to be the basis for reform. The nobles stood in relation to God as their subservient underlings did to them (cf. Ps. 123:2), trembling lest they displease (Ps. 119:120). Since God is "terrible" (cf. 1:5; 4:14) it is difficult to see how **fear** could be separated from "dread" (cf. Batten, *op. cit.,* p. 242). Jewish devotion moved between

---

national and world crisis can see nothing farther away or more important than winning the next election, by fair means or foul.

Nehemiah's method of dealing with these perennial human problems was characteristically

forthright. He was not satisfied to "view with alarm" in a political or commencement address before an audience in which the offenders were scantily represented, or even to write vigorous letters to the newspapers. He went straight to

because of the reproach of the heathen our enemies?

10 I likewise, *and* my brethren, and my servants, might exact of them money and corn: I pray you, let us leave off this usury.

11 Restore, I pray you, to them, even this day, their lands, their vineyards, their oliveyards, and their houses, also the hundredth *part* of the money, and of the corn, the wine, and the oil, that ye exact of them.

is not good. Ought you not to walk in the fear of our God to prevent the taunts of the nations our enemies? **10** Moreover I and my brethren and my servants are lending them money and grain. Let us leave off this interest. **11** Return to them this very day their fields, their vineyards, their olive orchards, and their houses, and the hundredth of money, grain, wine, and oil which you have

---

the poles of fear and love. The loving God sometimes chastised his children (Prov. 3:11-12), but the respectful and obedient experienced God's love. The **fear** of God was thus synonymous with righteousness (cf. Job 1:1, 8) and inseparable from it (Ps. 111:10; Prov. 1:7; cf. Pedersen, *Israel, Its Life and Culture III-IV*, pp. 623-27). The righteous found freedom from fear in his relationship with God because the fear of God consumed all other fears (cf. Ps. 27:1).

Failure to fear God meant divine reprisals, both personal punishment and national degradation. **Taunts** suggests the return of destruction and disgrace (cf. 1:3). The M.T. now identifies **the nations** as **enemies,** a common concept in later Judaism; but here some would reserve the first term, **nations,** for the Gentiles who bought Jews as slaves (cf. vs. 8) and the second, **enemies,** for Nehemiah's foes, and would omit one of the terms (cf. Batten, *op. cit.,* p. 248). But the omission of **the nations** here by the LXXABℵ is no more than an easy error in copying, and the LXX^L with the other versions has both terms.

10. Nehemiah and his companions also made loans to the needy. **Brethren** may mean actual kinsmen (cf. 4:23). The Peshitta has "my sons" but reads **my brethren** for **my servants,** which follows in the M.T. **Servants** (cf. 4:16) is again misunderstood by the LXX, which has "my acquaintance." With **Let us leave off,** Nehemiah and his people associate themselves with those who are guilty of the now-condemned practice of taking pledges. To avoid this conclusion, to which both the M.T. and the Vulg. point, it is proposed to emend the text to read, "And we have remitted this interest" (*ibid.,* pp. 242-43), but there is no textual support for such translation. Others hold that Nehemiah not only condemned holding a pledge and charging interest but also favored the remission of the principal loan itself as an extension of the practice planned for the year of jubilee (cf. Deut. 15:1-11), a view expressed also by the Vulg., "Let us forgive the debt that is owing to us" (Bertholet, *op. cit.,* p. 62). Because of its similarity in content to vs. 11, and possibly because of the uncertainty of the Hebrew word translated **interest** or **usury** (cf. vs. 7), the versions differ widely at the end of the verse. The M.T. must mean "Let us leave off, I pray, this taking on pledge."

11. Among the items to be restored by the wealthy, in addition to those listed in vs. 3, are added **olive orchards,** which are constantly mentioned in the Deuteronomic legislation underlying Nehemiah's proposals (cf. Deut. 6:11), and **wine** and **oil,** which do not appear in the complaints (vss. 2-5) but were likely commodities to be pledged. The **oil** is fresh oil of the new crop (*yishār*) and the **wine** is "new wine" (*tîrôsh*). Thus creditors were not to substitute old stock that they would like to move in exchange for the fresh crop that was pledged.

Hundredth part is difficult to interpret since a return of 1 per cent would have no

---

his offending brethren, not only in private but in public (vs. 7). He used appeals not only to their better nature (vs. 9a) but also to their patriotic pride (vs. 9b). He was not satisfied with their promises to emend their ways, but

put them on public oath (vs. 12). And he even went so far as an imprecatory prayer that to our modern ears sounds very much like a curse upon those who did not keep their promise (vs. 13). According to his own account of the

12 Then said they, We will restore *them,* and will require nothing of them; so will we do as thou sayest. Then I called the priests, and took an oath of them, that they should do according to this promise.

13 Also I shook my lap, and said, So God shake out every man from his house, and from his labor, that performeth not this promise, even thus be he shaken out, and emptied. And all the congregation said, Amen, and praised the LORD. And the people did according to this promise.

14 ¶ Moreover from the time that I was appointed to be their governor in the land

been exacting of them." 12 Then they said, "We will restore these and require nothing from them. We will do as you say." And I called the priests, and took an oath of them to do as they had promised. 13 I also shook out my lap and said, "So may God shake out every man from his house and from his labor who does not perform this promise. So may he be shaken out and emptied." And all the assembly said "Amen" and praised the LORD. And the people did as they had promised.

14 Moreover from the time that I was

---

appreciable effect on the economic situation (cf. Batten, *op. cit.,* p. 243). Even 1 per cent per month or 12 per cent per year (cf. Bertholet, *loc. cit.*) would be suspiciously low interest for the Persian period when elsewhere 20 per cent and often more was charged (Olmstead, *History of the Persian Empire,* pp. 77, 84-85). Instead of the מאת, **hundredth part,** emend to read משאת, "the loan on pledge of" (cf. Deut. 24:10; Bertholet, *loc. cit.;* Gotthard, *op. cit.,* p. 139; Rudolph, *loc. cit.*), which is graphically very similar.

12-13. In the presence of the great assembly (vss. 7, 13) the reluctant nobles accepted Nehemiah's proposal. Unwilling that their important concession should rest upon a simple promise which might later be broken, Nehemiah at once required **an oath. The priests** administered the most solemn oaths as representatives of God (cf. Num. 5:21 ff.). Such oaths were frequently followed by a statement of penalties against one who breaks the oath. Perjury was a crime abhorrent to God, whose name was thereby taken in vain (Ps. 15:4; Ezek. 17:13, 16, 18-19). Perjurers were to be deprived of home and livelihood (cf. Ezra 7:26; 10:8). Since the wealthy were not "laboring" men, it is preferable to translate "fruit of labor" or "acquired property" (Hag. 1:11; Ps. 109:11) instead of **labor.**

Like the prophets, Nehemiah dramatized the penalties before the people by a symbolic act. The perjurer was to be shaken loose from his things and thus be in an "empty" state. The word translated **my lap** (*ḥōçen*), not clearly understood by the versions, means a "sash" or "girdle" (Neo-Babylonian *ḥusannu*), from a root meaning "to hold" or "to carry" (*ḥaṣânu;* Arthur Ungnad, "Lexikalisches," *Zeitschrift für Assyriologie und verwandte Gebiete,* XXXI [1917-18], 258-61; cf. Erich Ebeling, *Keilschrifttexte aus Assur religiösen Inhalts* [Leipzig: J. C. Hinrichs, 1919, 1922], Vol. XXVIII, No. 66, 1. 8; Vol. XXXIV, No. 298, 1. 27; W. F. Albright, "Notes on Assyrian Lexicography and Etymology," *Revue d'Assyriologie et d'Archéologie Orientale,* XVI [1919], 183). It was thus used for carrying things (cf. II Sam. 20:8 and the LXX of Deut. 23:13 [14]). By shaking his sash violently he spilled out the contents, then waved the sash as he shouted "empty." **Amen** means "certainly" or "assuredly." Since only the nobles made a pledge, **the people** who **did as they had promised** must have been the wealthy nobles.

B. PRINCIPLES OF NEHEMIAH'S ADMINISTRATION (5:14-19)

In contrast to the selfishness of the moneylenders, Nehemiah as an administrator was generous. The material here considered was not included in Nehemiah's remarks to

---

matter, these direct and vigorous methods worked—as well they might in what we should call so small a group, and on so small a scale.

14-19. *Beyond the Line of Duty.*—Nehemiah was himself in position to take so strong a line

because of his own scrupulous practice in such matters. Unlike political leaders who defend themselves or their followers whose ethics are under public scrutiny by protesting that they have done "nothing illegal," Nehemiah had

of Judah, from the twentieth year even unto the two and thirtieth year of Artaxerxes the king, *that is*, twelve years, I and my brethren have not eaten the bread of the governor.

15 But the former governors that *had been* before me were chargeable unto the people, and had taken of them bread and wine, besides forty shekels of silver; yea, even their servants bare rule over the people: but so did not I, because of the fear of God.

appointed to be their governor in the land of Judah, from the twentieth year to the thirty-second year of Ar-ta-xerx'es the king, twelve years, neither I nor my brethren ate the food allowance of the governor. 15 The former governors who were before me laid heavy burdens upon the people, and took from them food and wine, besides forty shekels of silver. Even their servants lorded it over the people. But I did not do so, because

---

the moneylenders for if, as seems likely, the date **twelve years** (vs. 14) is genuine, the passage could not have been earlier than the end of his administration (433/432 B.C.).

14-15. Subject peoples had to support the local Persian bureaucracy (vs. 15) in addition to tax and tribute (Ezra 4:13). During the **twelve years** of his administration Nehemiah refused to make such local assessments, which would have meant an additional burden on the Jewish economy. He paid the expenses of his administration himself.

Only here does Nehemiah refer to his appointment. He was not a "satrap" (Batten, *op. cit.*, p. 245) but a minor official, perhaps more the rank of the later Greek ethnarch (cf. Ezra 5:14). **Governor** is an ambiguous term, but the satraps themselves sometimes gave their title to their subordinates (George Rawlinson, *The History of Herodotus* [New York: D. Appleton & Co., 1859], II, 462). Nothing certain is known about the **former governors** (cf. Ezra 2:2), but probably some at least were Jewish (Julius Wellhausen, *Israelitische und Jüdische Geschichte* [Berlin: G. Reimer, 1894], p. 150; Meyer, *Entstehung des Judenthums*, p. 88, n. 1). Ezra's silence regarding them has been regarded as evidence for the arrival of Nehemiah before Ezra (Albin Van Hoonacker, "Néhémie et Esdras," *Le Muséon*, IX [1890], 160-61).

Bread of the governor was **the food allowance** (cf. Mal. 1:7-8), since **bread** (vs. 15) means **food** in general. But the **forty shekels of silver** were not **besides** the food, for the word in the M.T., אחר, "after," is never used in the sense of "in addition" in Hebrew (cf. Rudolph, *op. cit.*, p. 132). English versions usually ignore the preposition ב before the word **bread** in the M.T. and the versions, but the American Jewish Translation rightly translates "for bread" (cf. E. F. Kautzsch, ed., *Gesenius' Hebrew Grammar*, tr. A. E. Cowley [2nd English ed.; Oxford: Clarendon Press, 1910], sec. 119*p*; Eduard König, *Historisch-comparative Syntax der hebräischen Sprache* [Leipzig: J. C. Hinrichs, 1897], sec. 332*o*; Rudolph, *loc. cit.*). Thus the silver was the amount collected by the governor for food. The Vulg., which has "every day" (*quotidie*), suggests an original Hebrew text "for one day" (ליום אחד), of which the words "for day" (ליום) have been lost before the graphically similar word **bread** (לחם) and the "one" (אחד), also read by the Ethiopic version, has been altered to the quite similar "after" (אחר) of the present text. The original text was thus, "and they took from them for bread for one day forty shekels of silver." **And wine** is an intrusion due to its presence in vs. 18 (cf. Rudolph, *loc. cit.*).

Were chargeable unto interprets the M.T., "they made heavy upon the people." Since the LXX^L includes the word "collar" (*kloion*), it is assumed that עיל, "yoke,"

---

shown a fine sense of personal responsibility by maintaining a large official household at his own expense, in view of the general destitution, instead of demanding for them **the food allowance of the governor**. And if his final appeal to God, **Remember for my good . . . all that I have done for this people** (vs. 19), strikes on

our modern ears as a bit like trying to drive a religious bargain with a God before whose righteous judgments "all have sinned and fall short" (Rom. 3:23), we Christians must remember that both he and the Chronicler, who preserved his memoirs for us, were alike living not under grace but under "the law."

16 Yea, also I continued in the work of this wall, neither bought we any land: and all my servants *were* gathered thither unto the work.

17 Moreover *there were* at my table a hundred and fifty of the Jews and rulers, besides those that came unto us from among the heathen that *are* about us.

cause of the fear of God. 16 I also held to the work on this wall, and acquired no land; and all my servants were gathered there for the work. 17 Moreover there were at my table a hundred and fifty men, Jews and officials, besides those who came to us from the nations which were about us.

---

has dropped from the M.T. in error before the similar על, **upon. Laid heavy burdens upon** presumes such emendation (cf. Isa. 47:6; I Kings 12:10, 14).

The verb rendered **bare rule over** or **lorded it over,** related to the word "sultan," means in late Hebrew "to domineer" or "to be master." The youthful subordinates of the **former governors** did not share the rule but rather were insolent and haughty toward the Jews (Batten, *loc cit.*). Nehemiah protests his innocence of such exploitation (cf. Paul in I Cor. 9:12; II Cor. 11:9). He did not use his full power because he was a God-fearing man (vs. 9).

16. This seems an intrusion into the statement of the expenses of the governor's table (vss. 14-18) but it is a side comment introduced because of the reference to presumptuous servants in vs. 15*b*. Here Nehemiah offers positive assertion that he and his staff were not like his predecessors. Both he (cf. 4:18, 21, 23) and his servants (4:16, 23) worked on the wall. Since they had no special assignments (ch. 3) the **servants** apparently worked where needed, while Nehemiah moved about (4:18, 20) as supervisor. His activity is described as "strengthening" the wall (cf. 3:4). Because the verb "be strong" has many meanings, the versions have such divergent renditions as "I did not treat them harshly" (LXXAB*ℵ*), "I was of good courage" (Peshitta), and "I prevailed" (LXXL).

This wall (M.T. and Peshitta) suggests Palestinian authorship, but the Vulg. and the LXX have "the wall." Reference to the purchase of land in connection with the building of the wall led to the suggestion that the material is out of place and should be with vss. 1-5 since Nehemiah refused to take advantage of the needy as the wealthy had done to acquire property cheaply (*ibid.*, p. 246). It has been suggested that in the building of the wall property owners had a particular responsibility and that Nehemiah, without property, was doing more than was required. But it is clear in ch. 3 that all workmen were not property owners in Jerusalem. It is also suggested that during Nehemiah's administration there was a general redistribution of land (Wilhelm Bolle, *Das israelitische Bodenrecht* [Berlin: Dissertation, 1940], pp. 86 ff.), but this is unlikely, for Nehemiah would have given the details of such an important reform. **Bought we** involves the "servants" in Nehemiah's action and this interpretation is defensible (cf. Rudolph, *loc. cit*), but at least five Hebrew MSS and all the ancient versions indicate that the M.T. should be emended to **I . . . acquired.**

17. Resuming the subject of vss. 14-15, Nehemiah describes the size of his household and the expense of feeding it. Just as Solomon supported his court (I Kings 4:22-23), it was perhaps the Persian custom for administrators to feed their own staff and retainers (cf. Meyer, *op. cit.*, pp. 132-33). Satraps collected more than the royal assessment of tribute to support their establishments (Rawlinson, *History of Herodotus,* II, 462) and lesser officials were likewise responsible (cf. vs. 14). **Jews and rulers** implies two groups, but since the **officials** were Jews (cf. 2:16; 4:14, 19; Ezra 9:2), it is best, with the Peshitta, to make the terms identical and read, "the Jews, namely the officials." Such **officials** resided in Jerusalem (cf. 11:1). The second group, which fluctuated so much in size that no exact number could be given, were apparently visiting officials and their retinue, part of the steady flow of supervisors necessary for the functioning of the extended bureaucracy of the empire. These came to Judea **from the nations** round about. It is unnecessary to identify this group as Jewish refugees newly arrived who were cared

18 Now *that* which was prepared *for me* daily *was* one ox *and* six choice sheep; also fowls were prepared for me, and once in ten days store of all sorts of wine: yet for all this required not I the bread of the governor, because the bondage was heavy upon this people.

19 Think upon me, my God, for good, *according* to all that I have done for this people.

18 Now that which was prepared for one day was one ox and six choice sheep; fowls likewise were prepared for me, and every ten days skins of wine in abundance; yet with all this I did not demand the food allowance of the governor, because the servitude was heavy upon this people. 19 Remember for my good, O my God, all that I have done for this people.

---

for until they could be established in the community (Batten, *loc. cit.*). Such persons would perhaps be considered part of the former group of Jews.

Like Solomon (I Kings 4:22 ff.), Nehemiah lists the food necessary for a single day. The quantity has been estimated to be sufficient for four or five hundred people if, as seems probable, other foods supplemented those listed (*ibid.*, pp. 246-47). For **sheep** the Vulg. has "rams," and through confusion of similar Hebrew words, the LXX^{AB}, Ethiopic, and Peshitta versions have "goats" (צפירים; cf. Ezra 8:35) for **fowls** (צפרים). Solomon lists fowl (I Kings 4:23), and birds were regular items in the diet of the Persian period (cf. Olmstead, *History of the Persian Empire*, p. 183). In addition to doves, geese, and such clean (cf. Deut. 14:11) wild birds as partridge (I Sam. 26:20), quail (Exod. 16:13; Num. 11:31), and the sparrow (cf. Matt. 10:29; Luke 12:6), chickens were eaten. A cock appears on a seal as early as *ca.* 600 B.C. (W. F. Albright and P. E. Dumont, "A Parallel Between Indic and Babylonian Sacrificial Ritual," *Journal of the American Oriental Society*, LIV [1934], 109, n. 7) and chickens are common from the Persian period onward (Olmstead, *History of the Persian Empire*, pp. 349-50).

Wine was supplied but the awkward M.T. cannot tell the quantity. **Every ten days** or **once in ten days** translates a Hebrew text "in the interval of ten days" (cf. Ludwig Köhler, "Hebräische Vokabeln III," *Zeitschrift für die alttestamentliche Wissenschaft*, LVIII [1941], p. 229). Jahn (*Esra [A und B] und Nehemja*, p. 113) emends the text to "and of wine ten baths every day," but the quantity (almost eighty gallons) seems excessive and the required emendation is too severe. Assuming the loss of כלי, "vessels," before כל, "all," which it resembles, the text would be "vessels of all kinds of wine" (cf. Rudolph, *loc. cit.*). Two Hebrew MSS which have "a skin [נבל] of wine" suggest that instead of בכל, **of all sorts**, the original may have been **skins of** [נבלי] **wine in abundance**. The M.T. needs such a verb as "I gave," supplied in the Vulg., but it is reasonable to suppose that the verb was originally understood to be **prepared**.

Bondage, used of taskwork in Egypt (Exod. 1:14; 2:23), has more implication of slavery than the context here requires. It would be suitable for the arduous task of working on the wall (cf. Gotthard, *Text des Nehemia*, p. 144), but since the reference in vs. 18 is to "service" required to pay taxes during difficult economic times, "service" or **servitude** is sufficiently strong.

19. Nehemiah's declaration of virtue is not a self-righteous boast (cf. Luke 18:11-14) but an expression in harmony with the ancient Egyptian proverb, "A man's virtue is his monument; forgotten is the man of evil repute" (cf. James H. Breasted, *The Dawn of Conscience* [New York: Charles Scribner's Sons, 1933], p. 160). It parallels similar statements, such as that of Ameni of Beni Hasan, *et al.*, in both Egypt and Babylonia (*ibid.*, pp. 213-14; cf. Kittel, *Geschichte des Volkes Israel*, III, 650). Here, as elsewhere (13:14, 22, 31), with an eye to the future, Nehemiah pleads that he may be remembered for his virtuous acts, just as did the Egyptian Uzahor who said, "O thou gods of Sais! Think of all the good that the Chief Physician Uzahor-empiris has done!" (Cf. H. K. Brugsch, *A History of Egypt Under the Pharaohs*, tr. Philip Smith [London: John Murray, 1881], II, 306; cf. Bertholet, *Esra und Nehemia*, p. 63.)

6 Now it came to pass, when Sanballat, and Tobiah, and Geshem the Arabian, and the rest of our enemies, heard that I had builded the wall, and *that* there was no breach left therein; (though at that time I had not set up the doors upon the gates;)

2 That Sanballat and Geshem sent unto me, saying, Come, let us meet together in *some one of* the villages in the plain of Ono. But they thought to do me mischief.

6 Now when it was reported to Sanbal'lat and Tobi'ah and to Geshem the Arab and to the rest of our enemies that I had built the wall and that there was no breach left in it (although up to that time I had not set up the doors in the gates), 2 Sanbal'lat and Geshem sent to me, saying, "Come and let us meet together in one of the villages in the plain of Ono." But they in-

---

VI. Continuation of Work on the Wall (6:1-19)

A. Psychological Attacks on Nehemiah (6:1-14)

1. Plot to Trap Nehemiah Away from Home (6:1-4)

6:1. This chapter resumes the narrative of the building of the wall (ch. 4). Again the interpolation of the digressive material in ch. 5 may serve as a literary device to indicate a lapse of time (cf. ch. 3) during which the work progressed, for in 6:1 there is no longer a **breach** in it and the gate openings have been completed (cf. 2:13). But a parenthetic note states that the **doors,** the wooden leaves to replace those burned (cf. 1:3; 2:17), had not been set in their sockets. This comment has been termed a gloss (Hölscher, *Esra und Nehemia,* p. 536; Gotthard, *op. cit.,* p. 146), but its substance is essential for understanding Nehemiah's excuse (cf. vs. 3b) after claiming that the wall was finished (vs. 1) and the later (vs. 15) announcement of the completion of the wall.

The success of the Jews **was reported** to their **enemies.**

Tobiah has been regarded as added in vs. 1 because he is missing in vs. 2, and there is no preposition before his name in vs. 1 (Hölscher, *loc. cit.;* Rudolph, *op. cit.,* p. 134); but the preposition is found in twenty-three Hebrew MSS as well as in the Peshitta and the LXX[L] (Gotthard, *op. cit.,* p. 145), and the absence in vs. 2 may be explained otherwise. **Sanballat and Tobiah** are usually mentioned together (cf. 2:10, 19). **The rest of our enemies** doubtless included the Ashdodites (cf. 4:7).

2. By messenger Sanballat and Geshem (2:19) sought to trap Nehemiah away from home. The Vulg. interprets the M.T. to declare that the meeting was in order to frame a treaty, but this merely reflects the influence of "let us take counsel together" (vs. 7; cf. Gotthard, *op. cit.,* p. 146). Such apparently harmless meetings were a common deceitful means for eliminating enemies (cf. Jer. 41:1-3; I Macc. 12:39-53; 16:11-24). **To do me harm** shows Nehemiah's suspicion and explains his reluctance to go. Some think "Tobiah" has been lost accidentally in this verse, but it is possible that he dissociated himself from the action because he disapproved of the personal violence anticipated (cf. Batten, *op. cit.,* p. 249). **Ono** (cf. Ezra 2:33) lay in the Wadi Muṣâra, in the Sharon Plain, almost nineteen miles from Jerusalem. It was possibly selected for the meeting because the area had long been a neutral district directly under Persia and not part of the provinces of Philistia, Judea, or Samaria, perhaps even from late Assyrian times (Alt, "Judas Nachbarn zur Zeit Nehemias," pp. 72-73, n. 5; Gustav Beyer, "Die Stadtgebiete

---

6:1-9. *An Ancient War of Nerves.*—What had been in ch. 4 merely mockery and threats on the part of the enemies of Nehemiah's undertaking pass over now into subtler forms of what we call "a war of nerves." No small part of the present-day relevance of these memoirs comes from their plain indication of the way in which Nehemiah met and overcame these even more searching tests of his courage, patience, and faith.

The first attempt of his persistent and unscrupulous enemies was their apparently innocent proposal of a private conference in a village at some distance, which Nehemiah viewed as a trap to do him bodily harm. He met it with a combination of personal fearlessness and social responsibility that reveals a real leader at his best. **I am doing a great work and I cannot come down. Why should the work stop while I leave it and come down to you?**

3 And I sent messengers unto them, saying, I *am* doing a great work, so that I cannot come down: why should the work cease, whilst I leave it, and come down to you?

4 Yet they sent unto me four times after this sort; and I answered them after the same manner.

5 Then sent Sanballat his servant unto me in like manner the fifth time with an open letter in his hand;

tended to do me harm. 3 And I sent messengers to them, saying, "I am doing a great work and I cannot come down. Why should the work stop while I leave it and come down to you?" 4 And they sent to me four times in this way and I answered them in the same manner. 5 In the same way Sanbal'lat for the fifth time sent his servant to

---

von Diospolis und Nikopolis," *Zeitschrift des deutschen Palästina-vereins,* LVI [1933], 236-38).

3-4. Nehemiah dealt subtly (cf. 2:3) with his foes, concealing his suspicions and fears, gaining time with each exchange of messages, but never committing himself to a definite appointment. His constant excuse was that his **great work** would not permit his absence from Jerusalem. **Why,** inappropriate in Nehemiah's letter, is not found in the versions. The LXX, Vulg., Ethiopic, and Peshitta all render "lest," which is a possible translation of the Hebrew word למה (Ezra 4:22; 7:23; cf. Gen. 27:45; Ehrlich, *Randglossen,* p. 196; Rudolph, *loc. cit.*). Although the M.T. expresses a definite refusal to meet, the LXX merely defers decision on an indefinite basis, "As soon as I shall have finished it, I will come down to you." This presupposes no other Hebrew text but translates רפה, **leave,** in the sense "leave off," "be finished" (cf. *ibid.*). **In this way** indicates that the letters were all substantially the same (cf. II Sam. 15:6), urging a meeting, but they doubtless became more urgent and stronger as time went on.

2. Charge of Sedition (6:5-9)

With the fifth letter Sanballat put greater pressure upon Nehemiah by charging that the work was preliminary to rebellion and that Nehemiah intended to proclaim his kingship. The real pressure came with the threat that the king would be informed (vs. 7). The letter in Ezra 4:8-16, addressed to Artaxerxes, if not one written before Nehemiah's arrival (cf. Neh. 1:3), could be just such a letter instigated by the Samaritans (cf. Ezra 4:10).

5-6. The Ethiopic version interprets **open letter** as meaning "not sealed." Some explain that an unsealed letter would be an insult (Thomson, *Land and Book,* p. 132; cf. Gotthard, *op. cit.,* p. 148), but one would scarcely insult a person being enticed to a meeting (Batten, *op. cit.,* p. 252). It could have been an unsealed papyrus sheet, but even more probably it was an ostracon, a letter on a pottery fragment which could be neither folded nor sealed. Such are known from the time of Jeremiah (Harry Torczyner, *et al., The Lachish Letters* [London: Oxford University Press, 1938]; G. R. Driver, *Semitic Writing from Pictograph to Alphabet* [London: British Academy, 1948], Pl. 53, No. 3) and even earlier (Raymond A. Bowman, "Arameans, Aramaic, and the Bible," *Journal of Near Eastern Studies,* VII [1948], G. R. Driver, *op. cit.,* Pl. 55, No. 1).

(Vs. 3.) How often through the centuries since has that trumpetlike reaffirmation of the significance and urgency of a present responsibility heartened the resolution of other leaders in later crises, and lifted the spirits of their followers with its contagious confidence! No wonder this stirring sentence has echoed down the generations as probably the most oft-quoted text from Nehemiah, and his most characteristic spiritual bequest to posterity. Nor is it simply

a text for church leaders who in every generation must "rebuild the walls of Zion" and "strengthen her gates." It has its own message to all of us modern folk who have to live and do our daily work within reach of the telephone, the postman, and the doorbell. From the early morning hours when we try to keep a few moments clear in our closet for private devotion, or together before the family altar, to the end of the day when we try to drop to sleep

6 Wherein *was* written, It is reported among the heathen, and Gashmu saith *it, that* thou and the Jews think to rebel: for which cause thou buildest the wall, that thou mayest be their king, according to these words.

7 And thou hast also appointed prophets to preach of thee at Jerusalem, saying, *There is* a king in Judah: and now shall it be reported to the king according to these words. Come now therefore, and let us take counsel together.

me with an open letter in his hand. 6 In it was written, "It is reported among the nations, and Geshem[l] also says it, that you and the Jews intend to rebel; that is why you are building the wall; and you wish to become their king, according to this report. 7 And you have also set up prophets to proclaim concerning you in Jerusalem, 'There is a king in Judah.' And now it will be reported to the king according to these words. So now come, and let us take counsel

[l] Heb *Gashmu*

As the LXX and Peshitta show, vs. 6 is to be tied closely to what precedes by restoring in the M.T. the "and" that has been lost through haplography at the beginning of the verse. **According to these words** is a senseless, disturbing intrusion from vs. 7. If **nations** has its derogatory connotation, **heathen,** it is Nehemiah's rather than Sanballat's term, for the latter would have used the word "peoples," as in Ezra 4:10. The letter is possibly but a summary of the original (cf. Siegfried, *Esra, Nehemia und Esther,* p. 94). **It is reported** (cf. I Cor. 5:1), lit., "it is heard" (cf. Deut. 4:32), indicates that the letter passes on gossip among the neighbors of Judea regarding Jewish motives. **Gashmu,** mentioned parenthetically, is the **Geshem** of vs. 1; 2:19.

Most serious, if the charge reached the king, was the accusation that Nehemiah had set himself up as king, for the Persian rulers dealt harshly with usurpers, as the Behistun Inscription shows. The Hebrew behind **thou mayest be their king** is "thou art being a king for them," but the Vulg. renders freely, "thou hast a mind to set thyself king over them," which is a possible translation of the M.T. (Gotthard, *op. cit.,* p. 149). The LXX and Ethiopic versions likewise express purpose with **you wish to become their king.**

7. **Prophets,** long connected with kingship in Israel, selected such usurpers as Jeroboam (I Kings 11:29-31) and Jehu (II Kings 9:1 ff.), stirring rebellion against the existing king (cf. Jer. 28:1-4, 11). The Jews had a reputation as a rebellious people (cf. Ezra 4:12, 15). There may have been some foundation to the rumor, for the success of Nehemiah in refortifying Jerusalem, rallying the Jews, and defeating their adversaries may have induced some enthusiastic prophets to consider that the messianic age had come and that Nehemiah would be king (cf. Bertholet, *op. cit.,* p. 64; Batten, *op. cit.,* p. 253; Rudolph Smend, "Über die Genesis des Judenthums," *Zeitschrift für die alttestamentliche Wissenschaft,* II [1882], 147), just as Haggai (2:21-23) and Zechariah (3:8; 4:6-10; 6:10-15) favored Zerubbabel. But it is inconceivable that Nehemiah started the rumors or favored the idea.

without taking too much anxious thought for the morrow, some peremptory ring of interruption or distraction or plausible appeal keeps bidding for our limited supply of time, attention, energy. How slowly, and through how many mistakes in perspective or decisiveness, do we learn to say to all the enemies of our major responsibilities, **I am doing a great work and I cannot come down.**

After this stratagem and reply had been repeated four times, the next device of Nehemiah's enemies was an open letter, charging his people with planning rebellion, and him with personal ambition to be king—all this to be reported promptly to the Persian king. Their plausible proposal then was for a conference to consider what to do about these current reports. This misrepresentation Nehemiah met with a flat denial and the countercharge that the reports themselves were a deliberate "plant." His shrewd insight into the motives behind all this— to weaken the morale of his people, and to arouse fear in his own heart—led him, so the English texts would suggest, into a moving prayer to God for strength of hands and heart in the face of such unscrupulous opposition:

8 Then I sent unto him, saying, There are no such things done as thou sayest, but thou feignest them out of thine own heart.

9 For they all made us afraid, saying, Their hands shall be weakened from the work, that it be not done. Now therefore, O God, strengthen my hands.

together." 8 Then I sent to him, saying, "No such things as you say have been done, for you are inventing them out of your own mind." 9 For they all wanted to frighten us, thinking, "Their hands will drop from the work, and it will not be done." But now, O God, strengthen thou my hands.

---

8. Bluntly and directly Nehemiah denies the rumors and charges his foes with fabricating them. **Thou feignest them** and **you are inventing them** are milder and less exact renderings than the LXX, "You are falsifying them." Here again **heart** renders the M.T. literally, but its significance is psychologically **mind.**

9. This has been regarded as but a fragment of the original text (Ehrlich, *Randglossen,* pp. 197-98) or as "an interpolation by the Chronicler or a modification of some comment of Nehemiah" (Batten, *op. cit.,* p. 254). But it is Nehemiah's statement concluding the episode, interpreting and evaluating it. It progresses beyond the preceding narrative. **They all** includes all of those conspiring with Sanballat (cf. vs. 1). The Jews had been fearful earlier, when strong force threatened an almost defenseless people (cf. 4:8, 11-12, 14), but the threat to accuse them of sedition was even more terrifying because they stood to lose everything in an act of retaliation. **Their hands shall be weakened** idiomatically signifies demoralization (cf. II Sam. 4:1; Isa. 13:7; Jer. 6:24; 50:43; Ezek. 7:17; Zeph. 3:16; and Torczyner, *Lachish Letters,* No. VI, ll. 5-6). With the following **from the work** it constitutes a pregnant construction in the sense "so that they cease working" (Siegfried, *op. cit.,* p. 95; cf. Kautzsch, *Gesenius' Hebrew Grammar,* sec. 119*y*). But the Vulg., with "our hands would cease," thinks of a literal meaning, "to let the hands hang lax."

The M.T. exhorts **strengthen my hands,** to which **O God** is added in the English translations without textual authority, interpreting the words as a hasty prayer. But the versions have no prayer here and it is unlikely that one was intended. Without the "my God" of 5:19, or some sort of introduction, the M.T. begins too abruptly (cf. Bertholet, *loc. cit.;* Ehrlich, *Randglossen,* p. 197). It is too late at the time of writing for such a prayer to be effective (Rudolph, *loc. cit.*) and the terminology, when used elsewhere, always refers to human rather than divine support (Ehrlich, *loc. cit.*). The expression makes most sense as Nehemiah's evaluation of the entire episode. Since he had won additional support by his conduct it is better to translate with the Vulg., "I strengthened my hands all the more."

But now, O God, strengthen thou my hands (vs. 9*b*; yet see Exeg.).

Though Nehemiah had never heard of the "isms" that baffle and tax the patience of later generations, or of the propaganda techniques on a world-wide scale that modern newspaper and radio publicity have made possible, he confronted tactics which required wisdom and patience, as these also are required now. Amid all the equivocations and slipperiness around him, Nehemiah steadied himself, and found a new and greatly needed supply of patience in the dependability and integrity of God. Here is a resource in both private and public prayer of which in our own time we have special need, as it becomes daily more evident that ahead of us lie at the best long years of difficult dealing

with similar disingenuousness and unscrupulousness, alike on the part of political and social groups at home and of powerful nations and other types of mind abroad. Anglo-Saxons especially, with a heritage of forthrightness and fortitude in conflict, and then of good sportsmanship afterward, and the assumption that if only representatives of both sides can "get together" around a conference table they can surely work out some agreed solution, simply are not used to and have little patience with psychological and social problems of this kind. We shall have to develop new resources, not only in our politics and diplomacy but in our personal and social religion as well, if we are to meet the tests and run the long gantlets of the years ahead.

| 10 Afterward I came unto the house of Shemaiah the son of Delaiah the son of Mehetabeel, who *was* shut up; and he said, Let us meet together in the house of God, within the temple, and let us shut the doors of the temple: for they will come to slay thee; yea, in the night will they come to slay thee. | 10 Now when I went into the house of Shemai'ah the son of Delai'ah, son of Mehet'abel, who was shut up, he said, "Let us meet together in the house of God, within the temple, and let us close the doors of the temple; for they are coming to kill you, at |

---

3. ATTEMPT AT BETRAYAL THROUGH FALSE FRIENDS (6:10-14)

A more subtle attempt to betray Nehemiah and turn his people against him was now made by Tobiah and Sanballat (vs. 12). They hired a prominent Jew, who pretended to be a protecting friend, to damage Nehemiah's reputation.

10. Shemaiah (cf. Ezra 8:13, 16) the son of **Delaiah** (cf. Ezra 2:60) was a descendant of **Mehetabel,** whose name otherwise is known only as that of an Edomite princess (Gen. 36:39; I Chr. 1:50). Sometimes he has been regarded as a prophet, principally because meter was discovered in his pronouncement. The metrical material, however, is not a prophetic oracle but the simple disclosure of a plot. Since **Shemaiah** apparently had access to the temple area, and there is no reproof from Nehemiah to the suggestion that they should meet within it, we may conjecture that he was a priest, possibly one of those who were particularly friendly with Tobiah (cf. vss. 12, 18-19; 13:7-9).

The enigmatic **who was shut up** (cf. Jer. 36:5) has led to much speculation. Those who consider **Shemaiah** a prophet think here of ecstatic seizure (cf. Isa. 8:11; Ezek. 3:14; Kittel, *Geschichte des Volkes Israel,* III, 630, n. 2). Others suggest cultic impurity (cf. I Kings 14:10; Jer. 36:5; Bertholet, *op. cit.,* pp. 64-65), but Nehemiah would have avoided contact with him, and the very thought of a defiled one entering the temple would be abhorrent. Some suggest that the reference is to a prophet's symbolic action (cf. Isa. 20:1 ff.; I Kings 22:11 ff.; etc.)—self-enclosure to emphasize the message that Nehemiah must be shut up to save his life (*ibid.*). None of these explanations is persuasive; nor does the similar expression in Jer. 36:5 help. In both instances the "shutting up" could be voluntary withdrawal because life was endangered. **Shemaiah** may have been, or pretended to be, a hunted man like Nehemiah. It is best, however, to translate, "who was confined at home," as in the Amer. Trans., and admit our ignorance of its meaning. The Vulg. interprets by context "in secret."

Shemaiah's initial proposal, that Nehemiah should seek refuge in the temple area, was legitimate, for Israelites had the right of asylum in the holy place (Exod. 21:13; I Kings 1:50-53; 2:28-34), but that did not involve entering the temple building since the altar of asylum was outside (I Kings 8:64; II Kings 16:14). It was the suggestion that they enter the building itself and shut the doors for greater safety that shocked Nehemiah. The only entrance to the building was closed by cypress doors (I Kings 6:33-34). It is unnecessary to insist that Shemaiah urged Nehemiah to hide in the holy of holies (*debhîr;* cf. Batten, *op. cit.,* p. 256; Gotthard, *op. cit.,* p. 152; Ehrlich, *op. cit.,* p. 199) for Shemaiah mentioned only the *hêkhāl,* a term used for the temple itself but more specifically for the large, principal room just before the holy of holies.

10-14. Hired Prophets.—Then came the subtlest stratagem of all, one that may well give pause to all servants of organized religion, because it reveals the temptations and perversions to which religious men and spiritual leaders in every generation are themselves personally exposed. Even Jesus himself, as the story of the temptation in the wilderness plainly shows, had to meet and overcome plausible arguments for his personal satisfaction and prestige that appealed to his assured conviction of a commission from God, and were buttressed by quotations from scripture—for the devil's own purposes!

Now Nehemiah's enemies hired two religious prophets (one of them a woman?), who are specifically named in the story, besides others who are referred to as a group (vs. 14b), to

11 And I said, Should such a man as I flee? and who *is there,* that, *being* as I *am,* would go into the temple to save his life? I will not go in.

12 And, lo, I perceived that God had not sent him; but that he pronounced this prophecy against me: for Tobiah and Sanballat had hired him.

13 Therefore *was* he hired, that I should be afraid, and do so, and sin, and *that* they might have *matter* for an evil report, that they might reproach me.

14 My God, think thou upon Tobiah and Sanballat according to these their works,

night they are coming to kill you." 11 But I said, "Should such a man as I flee? And what man such as I could go into the temple and live?[m] I will not go in." 12 And I understood, and saw that God had not sent him, but he had pronounced the prophecy against me because Tobi'ah and Sanbal'lat had hired him. 13 For this purpose he was hired, that I should be afraid and act in this way and sin, and so they could give me an evil name, in order to taunt me. 14 Remember Tobi'ah and Sanbal'lat, O my God, according to these things that they did, and

[m] Or *would go into the temple to save his life*

11. Although sometimes frightened (cf. vs. 9; 2:2), Nehemiah was a courageous man. His fear of violating the temple was greater than his fear of personal attack. **Such a man as I** here means one "holding the highest position in the state, and so carrying great responsibilities" (Batten, *op. cit.,* pp. 256-57). A second reason for refusal to enter is indicated by **being as I am.** Since the temple building was for priests alone, and intruders were subject to death (cf. Num. 18:7), the expression might mean that Nehemiah had no priestly status that would permit his entry. But since he was a eunuch (cf. 1:11*b*) the words would have even greater significance, since such blemished men would profane the sanctuary (cf. Lev. 21:17-20, 23; Deut. 23:1).

12-13. Briefly Nehemiah commented on the real basis of his refusal. An unusual placement of the negative in Hebrew produces "a not-God sent him," a text stronger than **God had not sent him,** contrasting divine and human commissions. Not divine inspiration but money motivated Shemaiah. The plot appears to be the subtle work of **Tobiah,** whose name is appropriately listed first. Because of this and the singular word **hired,** it is suggested that mention of **Sanballat** is intrusive (Hölscher, *Esra und Nehemia,* p. 537). If the name is retained, the M.T. must be emended with the versions to read "they hired him." Also with the LXX[BN], Ethiopic, and Peshitta versions **against me** should be added, but the Peshitta, "to kill me," is perhaps due to vs. 10.

For this purpose he was hired should be omitted as a dittograph (cf. Guthe and Batten, *Ezra and Nehemiah,* p. 48); **and sin** also is an editorial addition, perhaps by the Chronicler who regarded lay intrusion into the temple as a grievous sin (cf. II Chr. 26:16, 18; Rudolph, *op. cit.,* p. 138). **Evil name** means "a bad reputation." Religious laxity in a cult-conscious community would undermine the governor's authority and destroy his leadership.

14. The episode concludes with a general imprecation against Nehemiah's enemies (cf. 4:4-5; 13:29). Although the Vulg. has "remember me," the simple **remember** is preferable. As Nehemiah pleaded with God to remember his good deeds, presumably for reward (cf. 5:19), so he now asks that the deeds of his enemies be remembered for punishment. Again **Tobiah** is listed first and **Sanballat** may be added (Hölscher, *loc. cit.;*

appeal to his rightful concern for his personal safety by advising him to take refuge in the temple, under cover of darkness, from threats against his own life, with a view then to charging him with cowardice and sacrilege. But Nehemiah saw through this attempt to prostitute religion to the service of private schemes and ulterior ends; and with a courage which

echoes like a trumpet down the centuries, he made his stouthearted reply. **Should such a man as I flee? and who is there, that, being as I am, would go into the temple to save his life? I will not go in.** (Vs. 11.)

Whatever his private suspicions or fears may have been, Nehemiah gave no ear to them; but as so often when under pressure, betook

and on the prophetess Noadiah, and the rest of the prophets, that would have put me in fear.

15 ¶ So the wall was finished in the twenty and fifth *day* of *the month* Elul, in fifty and two days.

also the prophetess No-adi'ah and the rest of the prophets who wanted to make me afraid.

15 So the wall was finished on the twenty-fifth day of the month Elul, in fifty-two

---

Rudolph, *op. cit.,* p. 136), for the M.T. and the LXX have simply "his deeds." The tendency to augment the list of enemies is seen in the Arabic and Peshitta versions, which add to the M.T., "and their companions." **Their works** and **these things that they did** represent emendations based on the LXX, Peshitta, and Vulg. after the list of names had been expanded.

The imprecation passes from **Tobiah** to **the prophets** who aided him against Nehemiah. **The rest** means not all of the prophets but just those who were antagonistic. Some Greek texts (LXXB‍א; Codex 55) and the Ethiopic version have "priests" instead of **prophets. Noadiah** (Ezra 8:33), called a **prophetess,** is given special attention. Although prophetesses functioned in Judah (cf. II Kings 22:14), they were rare. All versions except the LXXᴸ have "prophet" here. The suggestion that **Noadiah** was the one who warned Nehemiah that Shemaiah was a false prophet (cf. vs. 12; Batten, *op. cit.,* p. 258) is unlikely. Nothing is known of any incident involving **Noadiah,** but it has been argued that fragmentary traces of some such episode survive (cf. vs. 10) in the present Nehemiah narrative (Ehrlich, *op. cit.,* pp. 198-99).

B. Completion of the Wall (6:15-16)

15-16. Nehemiah attained his goal by completion of the wall after **fifty-two days.** Work began on August 11, 445 b.c., and was completed on October 2, within six months of his obtaining leave from the king. Josephus (*Antiquities* XI. 5. 8), who places the work during the reign of Xerxes (cf. Ezra 4:6), presents quite different figures. He claims that the work took two years and four months (about 850 days) and was completed during the ninth month (Kislev; cf. Neh. 1:1; Dec. 11-Jan. 10) of the twenty-eighth year of Xerxes (478-477 b.c.). Some have conjectured that Josephus had another text of Nehemiah (cf. Marcus, *Josephus,* VI, 391, note *f*), but the difference is perhaps due to copyist errors in a faulty Greek text (J. A. Bewer, "Josephus' Account of Nehemiah," *Journal of Biblical Literature,* XLIII [1924], 224-26). The shortness of the time has led to a challenge of the integrity of the verse. It is argued that Nehemiah could scarcely have been in Jerusalem much more than two months, and that "the whole verse looks like the work of the Chronicler" (Batten, *op. cit.,* p. 259), a view even more radical than that of Torrey (*Ezra Studies,* p. 227), who claims: "It appears that Nehemiah's own personal memoir ended either with 6:15 or with 6:19." The shortness of time, however, may merely indicate that most of the task was the repair of already standing walls (cf. Hölscher, *loc. cit.*). Furthermore, the work was pressed to its conclusion in a sustained drive, even at great sacrifice of personal comfort (cf. 4:6, 21, 23). The project is comparable to the building of the wall of Athens under the urging of Themistocles (Herodotus *History* VIII. 71).

The enemy reaction to the completion of the walls has been regarded as "hopeless as it stands" (Batten, *loc. cit.*). The **enemies** were Sanballat and his colleagues, while

---

himself to prayer. And even if his prayer sounds to us directed rather more toward vengeance on his enemies and on these hired prophets than toward courage for himself or God's guidance and blessing for his "great work," we can plainly see that not the least of its answers

came in the reinforcement of the stouthearted-ness and shrewd insight of which he already possessed so much.

15-19. *Victory at Last.*—Beneath the reserve of what sounds to us like understatement we can sense both the gratitude and the pride of

16 And it came to pass, that when all our enemies heard *thereof,* and all the heathen that *were* about us saw *these things,* they were much cast down in their own eyes: for they perceived that this work was wrought of our God.

17 ¶ Moreover in those days the nobles of Judah sent many letters unto Tobiah, and *the letters* of Tobiah came unto them.

18 For *there were* many in Judah sworn unto him, because he *was* the son-in-law of Shechaniah the son of Arah; and his son

days. 16 And when all our enemies heard of it, all the nations round about us were afraid[n] and fell greatly in their own esteem; for they perceived that this work had been accomplished with the help of our God. 17 Moreover in those days the nobles of Judah sent many letters to Tobi'ah, and Tobi'ah's letters came to them. 18 For many in Judah were bound by oath to him, because he was the son-in-law of Shecani'ah

[n] Another reading is *saw*

---

the nations round about were the close neighbors of the Jews. Although several Hebrew MSS by their spelling (וייראו) remove the ambiguity of the text (ויראו) to read were afraid, it seems probable that the RSV mg. reading they saw is correct, for the passage reflects the chagrin and frustration of the foe at their inability to stop the building. The enemies heard the reports of the completion of the work but the immediate neighbors saw the task completed.

The apodosis is ambiguous. The M.T., unique in the O.T., has, lit., "Then they fell much in their eyes." This is usually taken to mean "they fell in their own estimation" and so is rendered in their own eyes or in their own esteem. But "they" might refer to the enemy, and their to the nations, indicating a loss of prestige for Sanballat and his allies among the neighbors of the Jews, who witnessed the completion of the fortification despite the plots and blustering of the foes of the Jews.

Because "fall" is not used elsewhere in the figurative sense of "to decrease [in esteem]," it has been proposed to emend the M.T., ויפלו, to read ויפלא, "and it was marvelous" (August Klostermann, *Geschichte des Volkes Israel* [Munich: C. H. Beck, 1896], p. 219; Ehrlich, *op. cit.,* p. 200; Jahn, *Esra* [*A und B*] *und Nehemja,* p. 116; Siegfried, *Esra, Nehemia und Esther,* pp. 96-97; Rudolph, *op. cit.,* p. 137). Thus "fear" is eliminated and a better connection with the last part of the verse is obtained, "It was very marvelous in their eyes and they knew" (cf. Ps. 118:23). The marvel was accomplished not by human effort alone but by the assistance of God. The verse is an apt and fitting conclusion to the story of the building of the wall. Josephus (*loc. cit.*) concludes his story of Nehemiah: "He was a man of kind and just nature and most anxious to serve his countrymen, and he left the walls of Jerusalem as his eternal monument."

C. Jewish Correspondence with Tobiah (6:17-19)

17-19. After the completion of the walls one expects their dedication, which does not appear until 12:27 ff. Instead, there follows a statement concerning Tobiah's connections with Judeans who served as his propagandists and spies. As part of the plots against Nehemiah to hinder the building the material is anticlimactic, and the expression in those days seems to indicate that period of conflict. If intended to introduce the story of Tobiah's activity in Jerusalem (13:4-8), the verses are much too early. Torrey

---

the leader whose foresight, organizing gift, and personal courage had been sustained and blessed by God all the difficult way through to the accomplishment of his great undertaking on behalf of his people: So the wall was finished on the twenty-fifth day of the month Elul, in fifty-two days. And it is a very human (even if obviously less-than-Christian) touch in his

vivid memoirs that led him to exult in the discomfiture of his enemies and the exaltation of his own people above the nations round about, at least as much as sincerely to give God the glory (vs. 16).

It must come as a comfort to many Christian ministers who have to work with and through very human folk in their own churches, and

Johanan had taken the daughter of Me-shullam the son of Berechiah.

19 Also they reported his good deeds before me, and uttered my words to him. *And* Tobiah sent letters to put me in fear.

the son of Arah: and his son Jehoha'nan had taken the daughter of Meshul'lam the son of Berechi'ah as his wife. **19** Also they spoke of his good deeds in my presence, and reported my words to him. And Tobi'ah sent letters to make me afraid.

---

first (1896) assigned the verses to Nehemiah (*Composition*, p. 50), but later (1910) was convinced that they were the Chronicler's (*Ezra Studies*, pp. 226, 248, n. 51). Usually the verses are regarded as genuine (cf. Batten, *op. cit.*, p. 15; Pfeiffer, *Intro. to O.T.*, p. 837), possibly a supplement added by Nehemiah himself (Rudolph, *op. cit.*, p. 139).

Tobiah (cf. 2:10) married the daughter of **Shechaniah** (cf. 3:29), a noble of the family of **Arah** (cf. Ezra 2:5), and contrived to have his son **Jehohanan** marry the daughter of **Meshullam the son of Berechiah,** who repaired two sections of wall (cf. 3:4, 30). Hebrew usage requires that "to wife" **(as his wife)** be added to the M.T., **had taken,** and the LXX, Ethiopic, and Arabic versions do so. Through such contacts Tobiah had many friends among the Jewish **nobles** who were **bound by oath to him.** The Hebrew "lords of an oath" translates the Akkadian term meaning "a sworn ally" (*bêl adê*; Bezold, *Babylonisch-Assyrisches Glossar*, p. 83, col. 1). The Peshitta explains that there could be no enmity between parties under oath (II Sam. 21:7).

The text of vs. 17 is awkwardly un-Hebraic and obviously corrupt and the versions have great difficulty with it. It is best explained as a nominative absolute construction (cf. Hebrew of Gen. 34:8): "As for many of the nobles of Judah, their letters were passing to Tobiah." This translation assumes that the first letter of the word translated "multiplied" (מרבים) is a dittograph of the last letter of the preceding word "those" (ההם). Without the extra letter the word is **many** (רבים). The preposition "of" (מ) has been lost before **nobles** (חרי) through haplography (Ehrlich, *loc. cit.*; Rudolph, *op. cit.*, p. 137).

Good deeds is interpretative of the M.T., which has "his good things." Ten Hebrew MSS, instead of "his good things" (טובותיו), spell out the word in such fashion (טבותיו) that it can be vocalized as "his rumors," with reference to the Aramaic word for "rumor" (טבה), and such emendation has been proposed (Abraham Geiger, *Urschrift und uebersetzungen des Bibel* [Breslau: J. Hainauer, 1857], p. 44; Immanuel Löw, "Miscellen; No. 3, טבותיו. Neh. 6:19," *Zeitschrift für die alttestamentliche Wissenschaft*, XXXIII [1913], 154-55). Both the Peshitta and Arabic versions understand the word as "favorable reports."

My words (vs. 19) could mean "my business" (cf. I Sam. 21:8) or "my acts" (II Chr. 13:22; 35:27; I Kings 11:41). The nobles were informers who kept Tobiah in touch with Nehemiah's activities in Jerusalem. **Letters** also came directly, presumably to Nehemiah himself. Such information is introduced abruptly in the M.T., but the versions all show that the conjunction **and** added in the English versions is justified. It has been lost in the M.T. through haplography, due to the last letter of the preceding word (לו).

---

equally with and in spite of very human attitudes and limitations within their own all-too-human hearts, that Nehemiah likewise found the iron of religious faith so constantly mixed with the clay of racial and national pride and of family and party relationships in the ore (to borrow William R. Inge's fine figure) of all our human experience. Even in this hour of his triumphant achievement, intrigues and faction-

alism continued to plague and divide his followers; and he had still to be on his guard against disloyalties within his own camp, as well as against bitter enemies outside. What a very human story it all is—but by the grace of God what a gallant and victorious leader he became! Hence the example and the value of his achievement to all those who in every generation "rebuild the walls of Jerusalem."

7 Now it came to pass, when the wall was built, and I had set up the doors, and the porters and the singers and the Levites were appointed,

2 That I gave my brother Hanani, and Hananiah the ruler of the palace, charge over Jerusalem: for he *was* a faithful man, and feared God above many.

7 Now when the wall had been built and I had set up the doors, and the gate-keepers, the singers, and the Levites had been appointed, 2 I gave my brother Hana'ni and Hanani'ah the governor of the castle charge over Jerusalem, for he was a more faithful and God-fearing man than

---

VII. Reorganization of Jerusalem (7:1-73a)
A. Appointment and Instruction of Watchmen (7:1-3)

The events of 7:1-3 would have occurred shortly after the completion of the walls and should have been expected after 6:16, which might have followed 7:3; but since 6:17 ff. is of an extraneous nature, the former order is preferable.

7:1. The reference to the setting up of the **doors** is parallel to **was built,** as a second note of time. Not yet in place in 6:1, the doors were certainly in position in 6:16. **Gatekeepers** were appointed when the city fortifications were completed. Since **the singers and the Levites** tended not the city gates but the temple gates (cf. vss. 43-45), the words are intrusive here from vss. 43 ff. (cf. Rudolph, *op. cit.,* p. 138). **The singers and the Levites** is unusual in reversing the order in which they are normally mentioned (cf. Gotthard, *Text des Nehemia,* p. 160). The Vulg. has "I appointed," which Gotthard favors, but since such minor officials were perhaps appointed by a subordinate it is better to read **were appointed.** The Chronicler is held responsible for the intrusive **the singers and the Levites** (Rudolf Smend, *Die Listen der Bücher Esra und Nehemia* [Basel: Schultze, 1881], p. 26; Gotthard, *op. cit.,* p. 160), and Torrey (*Ezra Studies,* p. 227), who holds that Nehemiah's record ended at 6:15 or 6:19, insists that vs. 1*b* "could have been written by no one else" but the Chronicler, who believed that all such services were a cultic feature from the beginning and were restored by Nehemiah when the walls were completed (*Composition,* pp. 41 ff.).

2. In preparation for his return to Susa at the conclusion of his work, Nehemiah was concerned to appoint someone to be in charge of the city in his absence. Some assume that two men were appointed (*ibid.,* p. 42; Rudolph, *op. cit.,* p. 140), but it is improbable that two officials bearing the same name would rule Jerusalem simultaneously (Gotthard, *loc. cit.*). **Hanani** and **Hananiah** are identical names, the former an abbreviation of the latter. Obviously **and** joining the names is explicative (cf. Ezra 6:8; 8:18; see Kautzsch, *Gesenius' Hebrew Grammar,* sec. 154a, n. 1*b*): "My brother Hanani, that is Hananiah." He is perhaps the "brother" of 1:2. Because the second element of the title (*bîrāh*) is used of the temple complex (I Chr. 29:1, 19), and the Vulg. translates it "house," Torrey (*loc. cit.*) sees in the title the "ruler of the temple" (*prostatēs tou hierou*) of II Macc. 3:4 (cf. Josephus *Antiquities* XX. 6. 2), and "the ruler of the house of God" of I Chr. 9:11; II Chr. 31:13 (cf. Emil Schürer, *A History of the Jewish People in the Time of Jesus Christ,* tr. S. Taylor and P. Christie [Edinburgh: T. & T. Clark, 1885], Div. II, Vol. I, p. 267). The LXX[L] renders it as "citadel" (*bareōs*), and the Peshitta uses the word found in Ezra 6:2. It has been assumed that "the fortress" mentioned was connected with the temple (cf. 2:8; I Macc. 11:20-24; Batten, *op. cit.,* pp. 262-63), but the term could be used of Jerusalem itself as a fortified place (cf. 1:1; Ezra 6:2; Esth. 1:2, 5; etc.). The title is then parallel to "commander of the city" (Judg. 9:30; I Kings 22:26; II Kings 23:8) and "the one over the city" or "the general of the

---

7:1-4. *Keeping on Guard.*—In the face of these complications it is small wonder that Nehemiah kept the charge of the city in the hands of men whom he could trust (vs. 2), or that he used the new walls and gates to protect the

city alike against surprise and treachery. There is a vivid glimpse of the odds against which he had carried out his "great work," and likewise of the scanty support and small resources at his disposal, in what may be the final phrases

3 And I said unto them, Let not the gates of Jerusalem be opened until the sun be hot; and while they stand by, let them shut the doors, and bar *them:* and appoint watches of the inhabitants of Jerusalem, every one in his watch, and every one *to be* over against his house.

many. 3 And I said to them, "Let not the gates of Jerusalem be opened until the sun is hot; and while they are still standing guard[o] let them shut and bar the doors. Appoint guards from among the inhabitants of Jerusalem, each to his station and each

[o] Heb obscure

city," later found at Alexandria and elsewhere (Pierre Jouquet, *Macedonian Imperialism and the Hellenization of the East* [tr. M. B. Dobie; New York: Alfred A. Knopf, 1928], p. 89). The title presumably indicates his post after appointment. Possibly it was he who appointed the gatetenders and supervised the guarding of the city.

3. Because an attack of the city under cover of darkness was still anticipated, emergency regulations were instituted. Oral tradition (*Qerê*) and the versions (cf. also 5:9) indicate that Nehemiah gave the orders, but it seems probable that Hananiah did, as the Hebrew written tradition (*Kethîbh*) has it.

The **gates** were open during daylight hours but the Hebrew text is obscure in setting the time of opening. It suggests that they remained closed after sunrise until the sun was rather high in the sky. Closing must have been before dusk, but no definite time can be ascertained from the present M.T. Its "until [or "while"] they are standing" is meaningless. **And while they stand by** reflects the Vulg., "and while they were yet standing by." **They** (הם) is ambiguous. It cannot refer to Hanani and Hananiah (cf. above), but there is no other antecedent. It has been considered a corruption of "the people" (העם; Ehrlich, *op. cit.*, p. 202), but the closing would scarcely be determined by the sleeping habits of the citizens (cf. Rudolph, *op. cit.*, p. 138). A similar view is obtained by regarding "standing" as opposite to "lying down," giving the meaning "while the people are still up and about" (cf. the *Kethîbh* of Ps. 134:1; Ehrlich, *loc. cit.*), but it is doubtful whether the verb עמד, "stand," can support such a meaning. Others interpret **they** to mean the "guards" (cf. vs. 1), leading to "while they were watching" in the LXX and **while they are still standing guard,** but this has been challenged as "much too obvious" and its use of "stand" is regarded as unparalleled (Rudolph, *loc. cit*). Other interpretations require emendation of the Hebrew text. On the basis of the Peshitta, "while the day is standing," it has been rendered "while it [the sun] stands" in the sky before sunset (Gotthard, *op. cit.*, p. 42; Batten, *op. cit.*, p. 265). More extensive change lies behind the conjecture "while it [the sun] is yet over the sea" with the meaning "before it sinks into the sea" (Rudolph, *loc. cit.*). This emendation employs some consonants of the M.T. but presumes corruptions which, while possible, seem improbable.

When closed for the night the gates were to be made fast, since the M.T. means not merely "closed" but "made fast" or "barred." By relating the Hebrew root אחז to the word חידה, "riddle," which is derived from the Aramaic cognate (אחד) of the Hebrew root אחז, the verb has been explained as "locked up" (*ibid.*).

In addition to the gatekeepers (vs. 1) other **watches** were posted, presumably at the wall. **Opposite his own house** (cf. 3:10, 23, 28-29) seems to indicate that guards mounted the wall opposite their houses. Rudolph (*ibid.*), thinking of a partitive construction, suggests that part of the guards were at fixed posts and part patrolled before the individual houses. But while the expression is used distributively, there is no evidence for

of his own memoirs: **The city was wide and large, but the people within it were few and no houses had been built.**

How many Christian ministers and missionaries in every generation have had to occupy new territory for the church against similar odds, and with like pioneering resourcefulness! But Nehemiah's faith and courage had long

since looked far into the future, and had built not for the present actualities of the situation, which were small enough, but for the unrealized possibilities which he foresaw through the eyes of his faith and hope in God. In that sense he was not only a "man of action": he was also a "hero of faith," one who might well have been included in the honor roll of Heb. 11.

4 Now the city *was* large and great: but the people *were* few therein, and the houses *were* not builded.

5 ¶ And my God put into mine heart to gather together the nobles, and the rulers, and the people, that they might be reckoned by genealogy. And I found a register of the genealogy of them which came up at the first, and found written therein,

opposite his own house." 4 The city was wide and large, but the people within it were few and no houses had been built.

5 Then God put it into my mind to assemble the nobles and the officials and the people to be enrolled by genealogy. And I found the book of the genealogy of those who came up at the first, and I found written in it:

---

the partitive construction in Hebrew, and it is certainly not mandatory in Isa. 3:5, which is cited in support. Torrey (*Composition*, pp. 41-42), thinking of the guards in I Chr. 26:12-19 and the later police of Jerusalem (cf. Schürer, *op. cit.*, Div. II, Vol. I, pp. 264-68), thinks that just such an organization is proposed here by the Chronicler. But no elaborate or permanent organization need be implied, for what is involved is a setting up of a temporary group to function during the emergency, until the city should have a larger population.

B. The Populating of Jerusalem (7:4-73a)

4. Jerusalem was ruined and relatively uninhabited, with little for the new fortification to protect. Nehemiah, like Alexander and his successors who established cities, had the problem of populating it (cf. Jouquet, *op. cit.*, pp. 88, 367 ff.). **Wide and large** translates a M.T. "wide of hands and large." The word "hands" so troubled translators that it is omitted in the LXX, Ethiopic, Peshitta, and Vulg. and some propose to omit it here (Gotthard, *loc. cit.*), but the idiom appears elsewhere (Gen. 34:21; Judg. 18:10; Isa. 22:18; 33:21; Ps. 104:25; I Chr. 4:40). Its origin doubtless lies in the gesture of spreading the arms in order to convey the idea of "stretching widely to the right and left." **Large** here presumably indicates great length.

No houses had been built directly contradicts vs. 3 and other passages in which "his house" means a building within the city (cf. 3:10, 23, 28-29). Some interpret "house" figuratively as "family" (cf. Gen. 18:19; Deut. 25:9; etc.), referring to the fact that during the Exile many families were extinguished, never to be restored (cf. Paul Haupt, "Batim lo benuyim," *Johns Hopkins University Circulars*, XIII [1894], 108; cf. Guthe and Batten, *Ezra and Nehemiah*, p. 49; Siegfried, *Esra, Nehemia und Esther*, p. 98; Rudolph, *op. cit.*, p. 140). It could mean literally that no new buildings had yet been erected within the city. Josephus (*Antiquities* XI. 5. 8) understood the words literally, claiming that Nehemiah "prepared houses for them at his own expense" and Ben Sirach too (Ecclus. 49:13), in addition to praising Nehemiah for his work on the walls, adds that he "raised up our homes again."

Josephus seems to link vs. 4 with 11:1 ff., and it has been suggested that his Greek source had ch. 11 immediately after vs. 4 (Torrey, *Ezra Studies*, pp. 32-33; cf. Jahn, *Esra [A und B] und Nehemja*, p. 118). But the genealogy (vss. 5-73a) could have been in his source, for Josephus was inclined toward omitting long genealogies lest they encumber his narrative (cf. *Antiquities* XI. 3. 10; cf. Exeg. on Ezra 2:1).

5. Preliminary to the redistribution of the population Nehemiah planned to make, he undertook an assembly of the people for a census (I Chr. 9:22; Luke 2:1-4), which he regarded as an act of divine inspiration (cf. 2:12, 16). With **my God** the M.T. has the informal and personal style of Nehemiah (cf. 2:8, 12, 18; 5:19; 6:14; etc.) but the

---

5-73. *The Role of Inconspicuous Individuals.* — (See Expos. on 3:1-32; Ezra 2:1-67.) Even the uncritical reader of our English versions can sense the change of style and mood that marks the insertion into Nehemiah's terse and vivid memoirs, by the Chronicler's later editorial

hand, of another of the endless genealogical lists of names by families, of which the Chronicler himself was so fond. The insertion here is another version of Ezra 2, different in minor details, but plainly based on the same or a variant source.

6 These *are* the children of the province, that went up out of the captivity, of those that had been carried away, whom Nebuchadnezzar the king of Babylon had carried away, and came again to Jerusalem and to Judah, every one unto his city;

7 Who came with Zerubbabel, Jeshua, Nehemiah, Azariah, Raamiah, Nahamani, Mordecai, Bilshan, Mispereth, Bigvai, Nehum, Baanah. The number, *I say,* of the men of the people of Israel *was this;*

8 The children of Parosh, two thousand a hundred seventy and two.

9 The children of Shephatiah, three hundred seventy and two.

10 The children of Arah, six hundred fifty and two.

11 The children of Pahath-moab, of the children of Jeshua and Joab, two thousand and eight hundred *and* eighteen.

12 The children of Elam, a thousand two hundred fifty and four.

6 These were the people of the province who came up out of the captivity of those exiles whom Nebuchadnez'zar the king of Babylon had carried into exile; they returned to Jerusalem and Judah, each to his town. 7 They came with Zerub'babel, Jeshua, Nehemi'ah, Azari'ah, Ra-ami'ah, Naham'ani, Mor'decai, Bilshan, Mis'pereth, Big'vai, Nehum, Ba'anah.

The number of the men of the people of Israel: 8 the sons of Parosh, two thousand a hundred and seventy-two. 9 The sons of Shephati'ah, three hundred and seventy-two. 10 The sons of Arah, six hundred and fifty-two. 11 The sons of Pa'hath-mo'ab, namely the sons of Jeshua and Jo'ab, two thousand eight hundred and eighteen. 12 The sons of Elam, a thousand two hun-

---

versions all have simply **God**, which has been regarded as original (Gotthard, *loc. cit.*). **My mind** rather than **mine heart** properly interprets Hebrew psychology (cf. Ezra 6:22; 7:27). The intent implied by **to gather together** or **to assemble** is possible through a slight change of vowels in the M.T. which can now be read only "and I assembled." The purpose of the assembly is lost in the LXX, which has "I gathered into companies." The Vulg. "to muster them" indicates a census, and the Peshitta adds "according to their families" (cf. Luke 2:2-4).

During the census, which involved written records (cf. vs. 64; Ezra 2:62), a genealogical list was found which was purported to list Jews who had returned from Babylonia (vss. 6-73*a*; Ezra 2:1-67). There is considerable controversy over the authorship of the list. It has been regarded by some as the Chronicler's work (Torrey, *Ezra Studies,* p. 227; Jahn, *op. cit.,* p. 119; Guthe and Batten, *loc. cit.*), but others argue for its authenticity (cf. Bertholet, *Esra und Nehemia,* p. 67; Rudolph, *op. cit.,* p. 141). The whole list is certainly not as early as the time of Cyrus, where the Chronicler puts it (Ezra 1:1), and the present context indicates a time prior to the arrival of Nehemiah; but some want to date the passage as late as *ca.* 400 B.C., shortly after the time of Nehemiah (Hölscher, *Esra und Nehemia,* p. 502; Pfeiffer, *Intro. to O.T.,* pp. 822, 836).

The connection between **the book of the genealogy** and **of those who came up at the first** is decidedly awkward. The second element is supplemental: "the book of genealogy, those coming up," etc. The Peshitta lacks "those coming up at the first," which is usually regarded as a gloss by the Chronicler (Siegfried, *loc. cit.;* Guthe and Batten, *loc. cit.;* Josef Markwart, *Fundamente israelitische und jüdische Geschichte* [Göttingen: Dieterich, 1896], p. 35; Hermann Guthe, *Geschichte des Volkes Israel* [Freiburg i. B: J. C. B. Mohr, 1899], p. 259). The principal argument for the deletion (cf. Gotthard, *loc. cit.;* Bertholet, *op. cit.,* p. 68), however, is not syntactical roughness or omission from the Peshitta, but the belief that **the first** refers to the time of Cyrus, when the list does not exactly reflect conditions of that period. But the words can mean "previously" (cf. II Sam. 7:10; 20:18; Jer. 7:12; Isa. 52:4), which is suitable here since the list seems to refer to various returns to Palestine from the time of Cyrus (cf. Ezra 1:1) down to 515 B.C. (cf. Rudolph, *op. cit.,* pp. 15-17).

6-73*a*. For detailed notes on the great list see Ezra 2:1-67 which is almost identical.

13 The children of Zattu, eight hundred forty and five.

14 The children of Zaccai, seven hundred and threescore.

15 The children of Binnui, six hundred forty and eight.

16 The children of Bebai, six hundred twenty and eight.

17 The children of Azgad, two thousand three hundred twenty and two.

18 The children of Adonikam, six hundred threescore and seven.

19 The children of Bigvai, two thousand threescore and seven.

20 The children of Adin, six hundred fifty and five.

21 The children of Ater of Hezekiah, ninety and eight.

22 The children of Hashum, three hundred twenty and eight.

23 The children of Bezai, three hundred twenty and four.

24 The children of Hariph, a hundred and twelve.

25 The children of Gibeon, ninety and five.

26 The men of Beth-lehem and Netophah, a hundred fourscore and eight.

27 The men of Anathoth, a hundred twenty and eight.

28 The men of Beth-azmaveth, forty and two.

29 The men of Kirjath-jearim, Chephirah, and Beeroth, seven hundred forty and three.

30 The men of Ramah and Gaba, six hundred twenty and one.

31 The men of Michmas, a hundred and twenty and two.

32 The men of Beth-el and Ai, a hundred twenty and three.

33 The men of the other Nebo, fifty and two.

34 The children of the other Elam, a thousand two hundred fifty and four.

35 The children of Harim, three hundred and twenty.

36 The children of Jericho, three hundred forty and five.

37 The children of Lod, Hadid, and Ono, seven hundred twenty and one.

38 The children of Senaah, three thousand nine hundred and thirty.

dred and fifty-four. 13 The sons of Zattu, eight hundred and forty-five. 14 The sons of Zac'cai, seven hundred and sixty. 15 The sons of Bin'nui, six hundred and forty-eight. 16 The sons of Be'bai, six hundred and twenty-eight. 17 The sons of Azgad, two thousand three hundred and twenty-two. 18 The sons of Adoni'kam, six hundred and sixty-seven. 19 The sons of Big'vai, two thousand and sixty-seven. 20 The sons of Adin, six hundred and fifty-five. 21 The sons of Ater, namely of Hezeki'ah, ninety-eight. 22 The sons of Hashum, three hundred and twenty-eight. 23 The sons of Be'zai, three hundred and twenty-four. 24 The sons of Hariph, a hundred and twelve. 25 The sons of Gibeon, ninety-five. 26 The men of Bethlehem and Neto'phah, a hundred and eighty-eight. 27 The men of An'athoth, a hundred and twenty-eight. 28 The men of Beth-az'maveth, forty-two. 29 The men of Kir'iath-je'arim, Chephi'rah, and Be-er'oth, seven hundred and forty-three. 30 The men of Ramah and Geba, six hundred and twenty-one. 31 The men of Michmas, a hundred and twenty-two. 32 The men of Bethel and Ai, a hundred and twenty-three. 33 The men of the other Nebo, fifty-two. 34 The sons of the other Elam, a thousand two hundred and fifty-four. 35 The sons of Harim, three hundred and twenty. 36 The sons of Jericho, three hundred and forty-five. 37 The sons of Lod, Hadid, and Ono, seven hundred and twenty-one. 38 The sons of Sena'ah, three thousand nine hundred and thirty.

39 ¶ The priests: the children of Jedaiah, of the house of Jeshua, nine hundred seventy and three.

40 The children of Immer, a thousand fifty and two.

41 The children of Pashur, a thousand two hundred forty and seven.

42 The children of Harim, a thousand and seventeen.

43 ¶ The Levites: the children of Jeshua, of Kadmiel, *and* of the children of Hodevah, seventy and four.

44 ¶ The singers: the children of Asaph, a hundred forty and eight.

45 ¶ The porters: the children of Shallum, the children of Ater, the children of Talmon, the children of Akkub, the children of Hatita, the children of Shobai, a hundred thirty and eight.

46 ¶ The Nethinim: the children of Ziha, the children of Hashupha, the children of Tabbaoth,

47 The children of Keros, the children of Sia, the children of Padon,

48 The children of Lebana, the children of Hagaba, the children of Shalmai,

49 The children of Hanan, the children of Giddel, the children of Gahar,

50 The children of Reaiah, the children of Rezin, the children of Nekoda,

51 The children of Gazzam, the children of Uzza, the children of Phaseah,

52 The children of Besai, the children of Meunim, the children of Nephishesim,

53 The children of Bakbuk, the children of Hakupha, the children of Harhur,

54 The children of Bazlith, the children of Mehida, the children of Harsha,

55 The children of Barkos, the children of Sisera, the children of Tamah,

56 The children of Neziah, the children of Hatipha.

57 ¶ The children of Solomon's servants: the children of Sotai, the children of Sophereth, the children of Perida,

58 The children of Jaala, the children of Darkon, the children of Giddel,

59 The children of Shephatiah, the children of Hattil, the children of Pochereth of Zebaim, the children of Amon.

60 All the Nethinim, and the children of Solomon's servants, *were* three hundred ninety and two.

39 The priests: the sons of Jedai'ah, namely the house of Jeshua, nine hundred and seventy-three. **40** The sons of Immer, a thousand and fifty-two. **41** The sons of Pashhur, a thousand two hundred and forty-seven. **42** The sons of Harim, a thousand and seventeen.

43 The Levites: the sons of Jeshua, namely of Kad'mi-el of the sons of Ho'-devah, seventy-four. **44** The singers: the sons of Asaph, a hundred and forty-eight. **45** The gatekeepers: the sons of Shallum, the sons of Ater, the sons of Talmon, the sons of Akkub, the sons of Hati'ta, the sons of Sho'bai, a hundred and thirty-eight.

46 The temple servants:*p* the sons of Ziha, the sons of Hasu'pha, the sons of Tabba'oth, **47** the sons of Keros, the sons of Si'a, the sons of Padon, **48** the sons of Leba'na, the sons of Hag'aba, the sons of Shalmai, **49** the sons of Hanan, the sons of Giddel, the sons of Gahar, **50** the sons of Re-ai'ah, the sons of Rezin, the sons of Neko'da, **51** the sons of Gazzam, the sons of Uzza, the sons of Pase'ah, **52** the sons of Besai, the sons of Me-u'nim, the sons of Nephush'esim, **53** the sons of Bakbuk, the sons of Haku'pha, the sons of Harhur, **54** the sons of Bazlith, the sons of Mehi'da, the sons of Harsha, **55** the sons of Barkos, the sons of Sis'era, the sons of Temah, **56** the sons of Nezi'ah, the sons of Hati'pha.

57 The sons of Solomon's servants: the sons of So'tai, the sons of So'phereth, the sons of Peri'da, **58** the sons of Ja'ala, the sons of Darkon, the sons of Giddel, **59** the sons of Shephati'ah, the sons of Hattil, the sons of Po'chereth-hazzeba'im, the sons of Amon.

60 All the temple servants and the sons of Solomon's servants were three hundred and ninety-two.

p Heb *nethinim*

61 And these *were* they which went up *also* from Tel-melah, Tel-haresha, Cherub, Addon, and Immer: but they could not show their father's house, nor their seed, whether they *were* of Israel.

62 The children of Delaiah, the children of Tobiah, the children of Nekoda, six hundred forty and two.

63 ¶ And of the priests: the children of Habaiah, the children of Koz, the children of Barzillai, which took *one* of the daughters of Barzillai the Gileadite to wife, and was called after their name.

64 These sought their register *among* those that were reckoned by genealogy, but it was not found: therefore were they, as polluted, put from the priesthood.

65 And the Tirshatha said unto them, that they should not eat of the most holy things, till there stood *up* a priest with Urim and Thummim.

66 ¶ The whole congregation together *was* forty and two thousand three hundred and threescore,

67 Besides their manservants and their maidservants, of whom *there were* seven thousand three hundred thirty and seven: and they had two hundred forty and five singing men and singing women.

68 Their horses, seven hundred thirty and six: their mules, two hundred forty and five:

69 *Their* camels, four hundred thirty and five: six thousand seven hundred and twenty asses.

70 ¶ And some of the chief of the fathers gave unto the work. The Tirshatha gave to the treasure a thousand drams of gold, fifty basins, five hundred and thirty priests' garments.

71 And *some* of the chief of the fathers gave to the treasure of the work twenty thousand drams of gold, and two thousand and two hundred pounds of silver.

72 And *that* which the rest of the people gave *was* twenty thousand drams of gold, and two thousand pounds of silver, and threescore and seven priests' garments.

73 So the priests, and the Levites, and the porters, and the singers, and *some* of the

61 The following were those who came up from Tel-me'lah, Tel-har'sha, Cherub, Addon, and Immer, but they could not prove their fathers' houses nor their descent, whether they belonged to Israel: **62** the sons of Delai'ah, the sons of Tobi'ah, the sons of Neko'da, six hundred and forty-two. **63** Also, of the priests: the sons of Hobai'ah, the sons of Hakkoz, the sons of Barzil'lai (who had taken a wife of the daughters of Barzil'lai the Gileadite and was called by their name). **64** These sought their registration among those enrolled in the genealogies, but it was not found there, so they were excluded from the priesthood as unclean; **65** the governor told them that they were not to partake of the most holy food, until a priest with Urim and Thummim should arise.

66 The whole assembly together was forty-two thousand three hundred and sixty, **67** besides their menservants and maidservants, of whom there were seven thousand three hundred and thirty-seven; and they had two hundred and forty-five singers, male and female. **68** Their horses were seven hundred and thirty-six, their mules two hundred and forty-five,[q] **69** their camels four hundred and thirty-five, and their asses six thousand seven hundred and twenty.

70 Now some of the heads of fathers' house gave to the work. The governor gave to the treasury a thousand darics of gold, fifty basins, five hundred and thirty priests' garments. **71** And some of the heads of fathers' houses gave into the treasury of the work twenty thousand darics of gold and two thousand two hundred minas of silver. **72** And what the rest of the people gave was twenty thousand darics of gold, two thousand minas of silver, and sixty-seven priests' garments.

73 So the priests, the Levites, the gatekeepers, the singers, some of the people, the

[q] Ezra 2. 66 and the margins of some Hebrew Mss Heb lack *their horses . . . forty-five*

73a. The versions differ in their distribution of this text between ch. 7 and ch. 8. Like the M.T., the Peshitta concludes ch. 7 with vs. 73, but the LXX, Vulg., and I Esdras use vs. 73*b* as an introduction to ch. 8, a distribution supported by some Hebrew MSS

| people, and the Nethinim, and all Israel, dwelt in their cities; and when the seventh month came, the children of Israel *were* in their cities. | temple servants, and all Israel, lived in their towns.
 And when the seventh month had come, the children of Israel were in their towns. |

which have a space between vs. 73a and vs. 73b and by the fact that in Ezra 3:1 this portion of the long dittograph (see below) introduces a new narrative. The Amer. Trans., the American Jewish Translation, and the RSV attach vs. 73b to the beginning of ch. 8.

The difficulty of the passage apparently arises from the fact that vs. 73 is the result of the conflation of two originally quite similar sentences (cf. *ibid.*, pp. 14-15). One, which formed the proper conclusion to the list of ch. 7, originally resembled the text of Ezra 2:70, where the text is better preserved. The other, which originally formed the conclusion of Ezra 8, following Ezra 8:36, must have been quite similar, referring also to a return of exiles and employing similar categories. Some statement about the distribution of the people in Ezra's caravan has long been sought (Kittel, *Geschichte des Volkes Israel*, III, 588-89; H. H. Schaeder, *Esra der Schreiber* [Tübingen: J. C. B. Mohr, 1930; "Beiträge zur historichen Theologie"], pp. 22-23; Rudolph. *loc. cit.*). It has been suggested that Ezra 8:36 should be followed by such a concluding statement as, "And the priests and Levites and some of the people dwelt in Jerusalem and the rest of the people were in the cities of Judea" (Rudolph, *op. cit.*, p. 15), after which the narrative would continue with Neh. 7:73b (*ibid.*, p. 85; cf. pp. 14-15). The "in Jerusalem" of the above conjecture is not found in the M.T. but it is in I Esdras 5:46.

The consolidation of the similar sentences produced some inconsistencies. The **singers** and **porters**, appropriate in the great list (vss. 44-45), must have been absent from the conclusion of Ezra 8, since those categories were not included in his caravan (cf. Ezra 8:15-20). Furthermore, it is contradictory to read both **some of the people** and **all Israel** in the same verse. **All Israel** would be inappropriate for the relatively small group accompanying Ezra, but would be suitable in a list describing a number of people settled in Judea. **Some of the people** could indicate the distribution of Ezra's caravan, but it would really fit the situation better after Nehemiah had repopulated Jerusalem (cf. 11:3, 20).

VIII. READING THE LAW (7:73b–8:18)

With this chapter, suddenly Ezra, not Nehemiah, is the principal figure and it is doubtful whether Nehemiah plays any role (cf. vs. 9). Obviously it is part of the Ezra narrative and should be linked in sequence with Ezra 8 (cf. Torrey, *Composition*, p. 34; "The Ezra Story in Its Original Sequence," *American Journal of Semitic Languages and Literatures*, XXV [1909], 279 ff.; *Ezra Studies*, pp. 255-58, 265-78; Winckler, *Altorientalische Forschungen*, Reihe 2, Bd. III, p. 472; Rudolph, *op. cit.*, p. 142). The present disorder of text has been explained as a disruption of the Chronicler's final work, occurring perhaps near the end of the third century B.C. when a copyist, who regarded Neh. 7:70-73 as a simple variant of Ezra 2:68-70, having copied Ezra 8:36, transferred the section which he considered the true sequel of Neh. 7 to the book of Nehemiah. It was then necessary to transpose Neh. 9:1–10:39 from Ezra also to follow the reading of the law in Neh. 8 (Torrey, *Ezra Studies*, p. 258). Less mechanically it can be explained that the late editor, with a bias against foreigners, placed the mixed marriage reform as Ezra's first act and reserved the popular acceptance of the law until the city was organized and secure enough to guarantee the continuance of the postexilic community devoted to the law (cf. Rudolph, *op. cit.*, p. 144).

Because constructions and vocabulary toward which the Chronicler is partial are unquestionably found in the chapter, there is considerable difference of opinion regarding the historicity of the events that it relates. Pfeiffer (*Intro. to O.T.*, pp. 832, 827-28), noting that Neh. 8–10, or parts of it, are generally attributed to Ezra's memoirs, admits

8 And all the people gathered themselves together as one man into the street that *was* before the water gate; and they spake unto Ezra the scribe to bring the book of the law of Moses, which the Lord had commanded to Israel.

8 And all the people gathered as one man into the square before the Water Gate; and they told Ezra the scribe to bring the book of the law of Moses which the

---

that "we gain the impression that the Chronicler himself is writing freely or at least restating in his own words the contents of a source," and that while "we cannot exclude the possibility that the Chronicler utilized a book on Ezra," he insists that "the historicity of any part of Neh. 8–10, when critically examined, must remain as doubtful as the chronology." Schaeder (*Esra der Schreiber*, p. 8) contends that the chapter is from Ezra's memoirs and Mowinckel (*Ezra den Skriftlaerde*, cited by Pfeiffer, *op. cit.*, p. 831) insists that it was written by an eyewitness to the events. Others see in the chapter just fiction, "merely an imaginary repetition of Josiah's promulgation of the Deuteronomic Code in 621" (*ibid.*, p. 828; cf. Bertholet, *op. cit.*, p. 70; Martin Kegel, *Die Kultusreformation des Esra* [Gütersloh: C. Bertelsmann, 1921], pp. 54, 183; Hölscher, *Esra und Nehemia*, p. 543). But the parallels assumed are exaggerated and unjustified (cf. Rudolph, *op. cit.*, p. 151, n. 2), and the assembly instigated by the people must have been just such a popular movement as Ezra had been planning and preparing for from the moment of his arrival in Jerusalem.

A. Assembly to Hear the Law (7:73b–8:2)

7:73b–8:2. The **seventh month** raises a chronological problem. The last reference to Ezra was some eighteen years earlier (Apr. 23, 397 B.C.; Ezra 10:17). If Ezra preceded Nehemiah to Jerusalem the silence of Nehemiah regarding him would be most surprising. To explain the silence it is claimed that after a brief ministry Ezra left the country not to return until the time of Neh. 8 (cf. Andreas Fernández, "Epoca de la Actividad de Esdras," *Biblica*, II [1921], 431 ff.; Joseph Fischer, *Die Chronologischen Fragen in den Büchern Esra und Nehemia* [Freiburg i. B.: Herder, 1903; "Biblische Studien"], pp. 74, 90), or that after a preliminary failure Ezra went into temporary retirement (C. T. Wood, "Nehemiah-Ezra," *Expository Times*, LIX [1947-48], 53-54) but neither explanation is plausible. Inasmuch as the chapter belongs after Ezra 8, as indicated above, the **seventh month** would fall in 398 B.C., the year of Ezra's arrival at Jerusalem (Ezra 7:9), since Ezra, whose prime mission was to introduce the law (Ezra 7:14, 25-26), would probably begin his task as soon as he arrived. In I Esdras 9:37 ff., where the assembly follows the narrative in Ezra 10, the **seventh month** would fall in Ezra's second year, about six months after the events of Ezra 10:17 (397 B.C.; Bertholet, *op. cit.*, p. 68; Markwart, *Fundamente Geschichte*, p. 36), but that is less likely since the reference in I Esdras 9:37 (=Neh. 7:73a) to a settlement of the people is more suitable after Ezra 8:31-32, which mentions people to be settled. The **first day of the seventh month**, New Year's Day, was particularly holy (cf. Ezra 3:6). The assembly has been regarded as a celebration of the New Year (cf. Hölscher, *Esra und Nehemia*, pp. 542 ff.), but the short duration of the meeting and the apparent lack of preparation for it mark the event as something extraordinary (Rudolph, *op. cit.*, p. 149). The assembly began on September 28, 398 B.C. (cf. Ezra 7:8).

The **Water Gate** cannot yet be located with certainty (cf. 3:26). Josephus and I Esdras, under the influence of Ezra 10 and possibly of the later **Water Gate** of the

---

8:1-18. *Repentance a Road to the Joy of Forgiveness.*—There is general agreement among O.T. scholars that this chapter was originally part of the Ezra story, following Ezra 8 (as it does in the earliest Greek translation

which we know as I Esdras). There is likewise a widespread belief that the events it narrates, like the expedition of Ezra as a whole, took place after Nehemiah's first visit to Jerusalem in 445 B.C. to rebuild its walls—possibly during

2 And Ezra the priest brought the law before the congregation both of men and women, and all that could hear with understanding, upon the first day of the seventh month.

LORD had given to Israel. 2 And Ezra the priest brought the law before the assembly, both men and women and all who could hear with understanding, on the first day

---

temple, locate the meeting in the temple area. If the **Water Gate** were in the city fortifications rather than the temple area, it would mark the assembly as a unique and extemporaneous civic movement rather than as a religious festival (cf. *ibid.,* p. 145). Instead of **street** read "the broad place" or "plaza" (cf. Ezra 10:9).

All the people (vs. 1) included **both men and women,** a situation unusual enough for comment since **women** ordinarily had little share in religious meetings. **All that could hear with understanding** (vs. 2) doubtless included the "sons and daughters" (cf. 10:28) who had shown ability to understand the law (Joseph Klausner, *Jesus of Nazareth* [tr. Herbert Danby; New York: The Macmillan Co., 1926], pp. 237-38). As in Ezra 2:64 (cf. Ezra 10:8, 12, 14), the assembly is described technically as a formal **congregation,** but the Vulg. and I Esdras have "multitude," and the Peshitta has simply "before the people."

Scribe (cf. Ezra 7:6) is an appropriate title for Ezra as one concerned with the law (Ezra 7:10, 21) but, as elsewhere, he is also called **the priest** (cf. Ezra 7:11). The Peshitta and I Esdras use the double title as in Ezra 7:11-12, 21. The people called for the **law of Moses** [cf. Ezra 3:2] **commanded** by God (Ezra 7:23).

Attempts to identify the law read by Ezra are numerous, varied, and inconclusive (cf. Rudolph, *op. cit.,* p. 169). The editor certainly regarded it as the whole Pentateuch, a view shared by some modern scholars (cf. Julius Wellhausen, *Prolegomena zur Geschichte Israels* [5th ed.; Berlin: Georg Reimer, 1905], pp. 407-8; August Dillmann, *Die Bücher Numeri, Deuteronomium und Josua* [2nd ed.; Leipzig: S. Hirzel, 1886], pp. 672 ff.; Schaeder, *Esra der Schreiber,* p. 69; Sellin, *Geschichte,* II, 140 ff.), but none of the citations made from it (vss. 14-15; Ezra 9:11-12) agrees with the Pentateuch, and the day of Atonement (Lev. 16) does not appear in Neh. 8. Usually it is thought to be a specific code, and some attempts are made to identify it by the elapsed time of the reading (cf. J. M. Powis Smith, *The Origin and History of Hebrew Law* [Chicago: University of Chicago Press, 1931], pp. 118-19; Browne, *Early Judaism,* p. 188; Bertholet, *op. cit.,* p. 69). But due to the variable element of interpretation, which took some time (cf. vs. 8), such identifications can be but tentative and uncertain. Possibly instead of reading a full code in sequence a series of judiciously selected passages were read to arouse popular repentance and create a will to adopt the law as binding (Kegel, *op. cit.,* pp. 135 ff.; 173 ff.; Rudolph, *op. cit.,* p. 145). The law was presumably the law "in his hand" which Ezra brought from Babylonia (Ezra 7:14, 25 ff.). As such it has been identified with the Holiness Code or Ezekiel's plan of restoration "both of which had been written in Babylonia a century before" (Pfeiffer, *loc. cit.*). Thus usually the law of Ezra is identified with the Priestly Code or some work of which that was a part (cf. Batten, *op. cit.,* p. 373; Harlan Creelman, *An Introduction to the Old Testament* [New York: The Macmillan Co., 1917], p. 244), but J. M. P. Smith (*op. cit.,* p. 119), who is inclined toward that view, recognizes that "the Code as introduced by Ezra was in an earlier form than that in which we now have the Priestly Code." Torrey (*Ezra Studies,* p. 262, n. 14) claims that "the laws quoted and accepted in the story do not belong, as a rule,

---

or shortly after his second visit in 433. The Chronicler, as usual little concerned with historical accuracy, and ready to use any existing sources for his present purposes, is very much concerned to emphasize and dignify the religion

of the law, as under Ezra's influence it had developed in his own time. He now makes use of this other material to dramatize its importance, and to ascribe to the earlier days of Nehemiah and Ezra the origin of the feast of

3 And he read therein before the street that *was* before the water gate from the morning until midday, before the men and the women, and those that could understand; and the ears of all the people *were attentive* unto the book of the law.

4 And Ezra the scribe stood upon a pulpit of wood, which they had made for the

of the seventh month. 3 And he read from it facing the square before the Water Gate from early morning until midday, in the presence of the men and the women and those who could understand; and the ears of all the people were attentive to the book of the law. 4 And Ezra the scribe stood on a

---

to the priestly legislation." What appears to be priestly material is regarded by some as the Chronicler's own contribution based on later usage (*ibid.,* pp. 187-88, 192-94).

The strongly Deuteronomic tone of Ezra-Nehemiah has led to the conjecture that Ezra's law was the Deuteronomic Code (cf. *ibid.,* pp. 186-88). The objection of Smith (*loc. cit.*) to such identification because Deuteronomy was pre-exilic and Ezra's law was new is scarcely valid since the code need not have been one drawn up by Ezra or edited by him. In fact, there would be special merit in one that would be binding because of its antiquity (cf. vs. 9). Ezra 7:25a and Neh. 8:1 seem to forbid the assumption of a new law. Ezra could have brought the Deuteronomic legislation from Babylonia for that code, which had a profound effect upon the development of exilic thought, was being supplemented and edited down to about 400 b.c., close to the time of Ezra (cf. Pfeiffer, *Intro. to O.T.,* pp. 182, 187). Rather than a full code, some think of an assemblage of pre-exilic laws with some new passages in addition (Martin Noth, *Die Gesetze im Pentateuch* [Halle: M. Niemeyer, 1940], p. 62; cf. p. 1, n. 2; *Überlieferungsgeschichtliche Studien I* [Halle: M. Niemeyer, 1943], p. 100; Gerhard von Rad, *Das Geschichtsbild des chronistischen Werkes* [Stuttgart: W. Kohlhammer, 1930], pp. 38 ff.; Rudolph, *op. cit.,* p. 169).

B. The Reading of the Law (8:3-8)

8:3. Because the scroll is not opened until vs. 5, some argue that vs. 3 should be omitted (cf. Hölscher, *Esra und Nehemia,* p. 543), but possibly after a mere statement of the fact of the reading (vs. 3), the author felt the need of describing the procedure in detail (vss. 4 ff.) because the unusual event was significant for future practice (cf. Bertholet, *loc. cit.*). The M.T. and versions here read **and he read** but **and they read** (vs. 8) indicates that Ezra's companions participated in the reading. Since the reading session was long (cf. vs. 3), Ezra would need relief. Reading began at daylight—"from the light," which I Esdras interprets as "from dawn," and the LXX as "from the hour of the sun's giving light."

4-8. Close parallels have been recognized between this detailed description of the reading of the law and the Chronicler's account of Josiah's presentation of the Deuteronomic Code (cf. above) and there are some broad parallels with the assembly in the time of Solomon described in II Chr. 5-7 (Torrey, "Ezra Story in Its Original Sequence," pp. 287 ff.; *Composition,* p. 59). Both meetings were during the seventh month (vs. 2; cf. II Chr. 5:2-3); the leader mounted a platform (vs. 4; cf. II Chr. 6:13), the people stood at the blessing (vss. 5-6; II Chr. 6:3) and dispersed to keep the feast with joy after the ceremony (vs. 12; II Chr. 7:8-9). The Chronicler could have used a book of Ezra as his model (cf. Pfeiffer, *Intro. to O.T.,* p. 832), but it is usually assumed that the Chronicler's narrative served as a model here. It has been suggested that the scene reflects the synagogue at the time of the Chronicler, but it has also been suggested that Neh. 8 formed the prototype of the service of the later synagogue (Ismar Elbogen, *Der jüdische Gottesdienst* [Leipzig: G. Fock, 1913], p. 157). What the Chronicler missed in the Ezra source here, he perhaps supplied from the synagogue service of his own day (cf. vs. 7; Rudolph, *op. cit.,* p. 149).

4. Ezra **stood** on a wooden structure which placed him **above all the people** (vs. 5), so that he could be seen by the great crowd. The word *mighdāl* is elsewhere rendered

purpose; and beside him stood Mattithiah, and Shema, and Anaiah, and Urijah, and Hilkiah, and Maaseiah, on his right hand; and on his left hand, Pedaiah, and Mishael, and Malchiah, and Hashum, and Hashbadana, Zechariah, *and* Meshullam.

5 And Ezra opened the book in the sight of all the people; (for he was above all the people;) and when he opened it, all the people stood up:

wooden pulpit which they had made for the purpose; and beside him stood Mattithi'ah, Shema, Anai'ah, Uri'ah, Hilki'ah, and Ma-asei'ah on his right hand; and Pedai'ah, Mish'a-el, Malchi'jah, Hashum, Hash-bad'-danah, Zechari'ah, and Meshul'lam on his left hand. 5 And Ezra opened the book in the sight of all the people, for he was above all the people; and when he opened it all

---

"tower," except in 9:4, where the same object is described. Although its use suggests the tall pulpit (*mimbar*) of the Arab mosque, it was considerably larger, for at least a dozen men sat with Ezra upon it. Doubtless it was wooden scaffolding made **for the purpose.** The LXXABℵ omits **for the purpose,** but because the same consonants (לדבר) can be read "for speaking," the LXXL, Peshitta, Arabic, and Vulg. versions read thus, and the LXXL adds "to the people."

The importance of the meeting was shown by the presence of important men who shared the platform with Ezra. There is no evidence to support the frequent assumption that the men were priests or Levites. In fact, the lack of titles and the presence of such rare names as **Anaiah** (cf. 10:22) and **Hashum** (cf. 7:22) indicate that they were laymen (cf. *ibid.*, p. 147). Since it was "the people" who called for the law (vs. 1), laymen are not unexpected. Presumably there was the same number of men on each side of Ezra, but there is a question whether the number was seven, so favored by the Jews (so Guthe and Batten, *Ezra and Nehemiah,* p. 50; Bertheau, *Esra, Nechemia und Ester,* p. 272), or six, which might very well symbolize, if not represent, the twelve tribes (cf. Ezra 8:35; so Bertholet, *loc. cit.;* Torrey, *Ezra Studies,* p. 268, note *c*). The M.T. and versions agree in naming the six men at Ezra's right, but there are confusion and difficulty with those to the left. **Meshullam,** omitted in I Esdras 9:44, may be the superfluous name in the M.T. since it (משלם) may be the result of a corruption (as משמל) of "on the left hand" (משמאלו), which it resembles (cf. *ibid.,* note *b*).

The names have been regarded as worthless (Meyer, *Entstehung des Judenthums,* p. 179, n. 4) and, lacking evidence of paternity, they cannot with certainty be identified with similar names in other lists. As the LXX and Vulg. show, the full name of **Shema** was Shemaiah (cf. Ezra 8:13). Most of the names occur elsewhere. **Zechariah** may be the Zaccur of 10:12 and the anomalous **Hashbaddannah,** which is certainly corrupt, suggests the Hashabnah of 10:25 (cf. Hashabniah of 3:10; 9:5).

5-6. The book was not a codex but a scroll. The process of opening was actually one of unrolling (cf. Isa. 34:4). The people, seated on the ground in Oriental fashion, showed their respect for the law when they **stood up.** The verb "stand" (עמד) often means to "rise" (cf. Job 29:8; Ezek. 2:1; Dan. 10:11; 12:13; Esth. 8:4), and while not inappropriate, it is unnecessary to translate "stood still," indicating intent listening (cf. Ehrlich, *Randglossen,* p. 202). The standing may have been a spontaneous act, but it appears that there may have been some liturgical procedure already accepted for the reading of scripture (Bertholet, *loc. cit.*). The blessing (vs. 6) might have been an extended prayer (cf. Dan. 2:19*b* ff.) or the words of a song (e.g., I Chr. 16:8 ff.; Bertheau, *op. cit.,* p. 273). The Chronicler might have been expected to insert a long prayer on this occasion (cf. I Chr. 29:10 ff.; Ezra 9:6 ff.) but it may have been somewhat

---

Tabernacles or Booths, which had come to be widely celebrated in his own later time.

But along with these evident interests of the genealogist and the ceremonialist go certain insights into vital religion of every age. According to the Chronicler's deep conviction, the first result of the fuller understanding of the law as the revealed will of God for his people (as the Priestly Code now set it forth) was a sudden sense of judgment and of guilt before

6 And Ezra blessed the Lord, the great God. And all the people answered, Amen, Amen, with lifting up their hands: and they bowed their heads, and worshipped the Lord with *their* faces to the ground.

7 Also Jeshua, and Bani, and Sherebiah, Jamin, Akkub, Shabbethai, Hodijah, Maaseiah, Kelita, Azariah, Jozabad, Hanan, Pelaiah, and the Levites, caused the people to understand the law: and the people *stood* in their place.

the people stood. 6 And Ezra blessed the Lord, the great God; and all the people answered, "Amen, Amen," lifting up their hands; and they bowed their heads and worshiped the Lord with their faces to the ground. 7 Also Jeshua, Bani, Sherebi′ah, Jamin, Akkub, Shab′bethai, Hodi′ah, Maasei′ah, Keli′ta, Azari′ah, Jo′zabad, Hanan, Pelai′ah, the Levites,[r] helped the people to understand the law, while the people remained in their places.

r 1 Esdras 9. 48 Vg: Heb *and the Levites*

shorter (Rudolph, *loc. cit.*). Benedictions are usual even today before reading scripture, and various formulas for that purpose are given in the Talmud (Berakoth 11b). The epithet **the great god,** rather unusual in Hebrew (cf. 9:32; Deut. 10:17; Jer. 32:18; Ezra 5:8), is found in the Jewish papyri (Cowley, *Aramaic Papyri*, No. 72, l. 15). It suggests the Neo-Babylonian use of that title (*ilu rabû*; Sidney Smith, *Babylonian Historical Texts* [London: Methuen & Co., 1924], Pl. I obverse, l. 3) and the similar "great Lord" (*bêlu rabû*), used of the god Marduk in the Cyrus Chronicle.

The repetition of **Amen** (cf. 5:13) expresses great emphasis (cf. John 1:51; 3:3; 5:19; etc.). Public prayer was concluded with an amen in the time of the Chronicler (cf. I Chr. 16:36), and Paul expected it "at the giving of thanks" (I Cor. 14:16). The popular utterance was accompanied by such a **lifting up** of hands as Ezra had done during prayer (cf. Ezra 9:5), and as Ezra had cast himself down (Ezra 10:1) the people **bowed** and "fell down before the Lord." **Bowed,** which always precedes the verb **worshiped** (I Chr. 29:20; II Chr. 29:30; cf. Bertheau, *loc. cit.*), means "bending over" in the first stages of prostration. Thus **bowed their heads** is less accurate than "bowed," and the Peshitta interprets it as "they knelt," which suggests Ezra's humble posture in Ezra 9:5. Since it is obvious that the final state of prostration, **with their faces to the ground** (cf. Ezra 10:1) would not be held during the entire meeting, there is no explicit reference to rising from it.

7-8. Reading the law (vs. 8) should follow directly after the preparatory acts of vss. 4-6, but reference to the interpretation of the law, which normally would follow the reading, is made to precede it. If vs. 7 is genuine, with a reference to interpretation, it is obviously out of place. Some regard it as the Chronicler's work, possibly added to give to the Levites the greater prominence in the role of interpreters which they enjoyed in the Chronicler's day (Guthe and Batten, *op. cit.*, p. 18; Rudolph, *op. cit.*, pp. 147, 149; Gerhard von Rad, *Deuteronomium-Studien* [Göttingen: Vandenhoeck & Ruprecht, 1947], pp. 8 ff.). Others consider the reference to the Levites as genuine, although the list of names may be supplementary (cf. Bertholet, *loc. cit.*). Priestly law enjoined the descendants of Aaron to teach the law (Lev. 10:11), and the Levites in vs. 9 are described as teaching it. "The Levites . . . taught the people" (vs. 9) has been regarded as a title of habitual office (Albin van Hoonacker, *Le sacerdoce lévitique* [London: Williams & Norgate, 1899], p. 50 ff.), and Johannes Nikel (*Die Wiederherstellung des jüdischen Gemeinwesens nach dem babylonischen Exil* [Freiburg i. B.: Herder, 1900; "Biblische Studien"], pp. 22, 171, 226), who translated it as "teachers," believed that such professional teachers instructed the people in the law, whereas the "scribes" expounded and supplemented it. The versions, however, have no reference in vs. 7 to Levitical

God on the part of all the people. But the Chronicler puts upon the lips of Nehemiah as governor, and of Ezra as priest, his own profound conviction that this fuller understanding of the will of God was in a deeper sense a

reason for joy and gratitude to God who had made it possible (vs. 10c).

It is significant that the whole stress of this chapter is on the understanding of the law as the will of God for his people—as if that were

8 So they read in the book in the law of God distinctly, and gave the sense, and caused *them* to understand the reading.

mained in their places. **8** And they read from the book, from the law of God, clearly;[s] and they gave the sense, so that the people understood the reading.

[s] Or *with interpretation*

---

instruction but present the Levites in the role of marshals. The Peshitta claims that they "were attending to [מְשַׁמְּשִׁין] the people" while the Vulg. more explicitly states, "The Levites made silence among the people in order to hear the law." In vss. 11 and 9:4-5 some of the Levites are marshals for the crowd, directing them in liturgical performance. Hölscher (*Ezra und Nehemia*, p. 546, note *h*) suggests that the Levites taught the people in groups or classes as in a church school. Such an interpretation would suit the last statement of the verse if that is to be rendered **the people stood in their place,** possibly as a result of the activity of the Levites. The verb "stand" can mean "stand still" (cf. Ehrlich, *loc. cit.*; Rudolph, *op. cit.*, p. 146; cf. Job 30:20), but the M.T. lacks the verb which gives such an interpretation, although it is present in the Vulg. and Peshitta. If the M.T. is to be understood in agreement with the Peshitta and Vulg., the verse would not be out of order, for it was necessary to quiet the crowd before the reading.

None of the thirteen men named (vs. 7) is listed among the laymen seated with Ezra (vs. 4), but the majority can be identified with Levites elsewhere. Seven are among those in ch. 10 and four of them are also found directing the people in 9:4-5. For **Shabbethai** and **Jozabad** see 11:16; Ezra 8:33; 10:23. Since most of them are identifiable as **Levites,** it may be assumed that all were, and it is preferable to read "namely the Levites" for **and the Levites** or to omit **and** as in I Esdras 9:48, the Vulg., and the RSV. Inclusion of **Akkub** (cf. Ezra 2:42) the gatekeeper (7:45; 11:19; 12:25), if he is the same person, may indicate the Chronicler's hand here, for while the gatekeepers are carefully distinguished from the Levites in 7:45 ff. (=Ezra 2:42 ff.), the Chronicler regarded them as Levites (cf. I Chr. 23:5).

They read now means the Levites of vs. 7, but if vs. 7 is interpolated the readers would be Ezra and his companions (vs. 4). **Distinctly** represents the technical term used in Ezra 4:18, meaning "translated at sight." It is wrong to think here of translation into Hebrew from Babylonian laws (Cowley, *op. cit.*, p. xxvi, n. 1), for the original Hebrew text was doubtless translated aloud as Aramaic, the common speech of postexilic Palestine (Bowman, "Arameans, Aramaic, and the Bible," pp. 81-82). The rabbis regarded this verse as the earliest reference to the Targ. They said, " 'And they read'— that is the text; 'explained,' that is the Targums" (Megillah 18*b*; Jerusalem Megillah I, 9; IV, 1; Genesis Rabbah, 36, 8; Jalkut II, 61, 1071). The Babylonian Talmud asserts, "Originally the Law was given to Israel in Hebrew writing and the holy language. It was again given to them in the days of Ezra in the Assyrian [i.e., Aramaic] writing and the Aramaic language" (Babylonian Talmud: Sanhedrin 21*b*; Nedarim 37*b*; cf. Megillah 3*a*; Jerusalem Megillah 74*d*). **Distinctly** should thus be interpreted "translating at sight and giving understanding." Since the concluding words of the verse refer to the result of reading in the prescribed manner, it is better to render **so that** rather than **and.**

---

all they needed (vss. 2-3, 8-9, 12-13). It was reserved for their descendant Paul centuries later, through his own early experience of life under the law, and then through the forgiving and redeeming grace of God revealed to him on the Damascus road and in the life and death and resurrection of Jesus Christ, to discover that legalistic religion by its very nature puts burdens on the consciences and wills of sensitive-souled men which they are not able

to carry, burdens from which only the forgiving love and power of God as revealed through Christ could admit Paul and his fellow Christians to **the joy of the LORD** (cf. Rom. 6:7-23). In this deeper sense the good news of the N.T. gives a profounder meaning and fulfillment to vs. 10 than the "understanding of the law" (on which the Chronicler laid such stress), by its very nature and in view of human nature as we all know it within ourselves, could ever do.

9 ¶ And Nehemiah, which *is* the Tirshatha, and Ezra the priest the scribe, and the Levites that taught the people, said unto all the people, This day *is* holy unto the LORD your God; mourn not, nor weep. For all the people wept, when they heard the words of the law.

10 Then he said unto them, Go your way, eat the fat, and drink the sweet, and send portions unto them for whom nothing is prepared: for *this* day *is* holy unto our

9 And Nehemi′ah, who was the governor, and Ezra the priest and scribe, and the Levites who taught the people said to all the people, "This day is holy to the LORD your God; do not mourn or weep." For all the people wept when they heard the words of the law. 10 Then he said to them, "Go your way, eat the fat and drink sweet wine and send portions to him for whom nothing

C. Injunction to Celebrate with Joy (8:9-12)

The weeping after the reading of the law is usually explained as due to repentance for past sins and fear of punishment to come (cf. Josephus *Antiquities* XI. 5. 5). Browne (*Early Judaism,* p. 188) conjectured that the reading for the first day covered Deut. 1–15, "which contained enough commandments and threats to cause all the weeping of the people." An entirely new law would scarcely have had this effect. It must have been regarded as the ancient, binding law of Moses which had been neglected in Palestine during the exilic and postexilic periods. Later Jewish teachers taught that Ezra re-established the law in Palestine when the law was forgotten (Midrash: Sukkah 20*a*; Sifre on Deut. 48, p. 84*b*; Tanaim, p. 43), and he was later often placed on a par with Moses because of it (Tosefta Sanhedrin IV, 7; Jerusalem Megillah I, 9; Talmud: Sanhedrin, 21*b*). Another interpretation of the weeping denies that it was due to a reaction to the law and finds in it evidence of an old Canaanite festival which began with rites of mourning for dead Tammuz. In combating this popular celebration the Deuteronomic revision of the feast of Booths stressed rejoicing rather than cultic weeping (Julian Morgenstern, "Supplementary Studies in the Calendars of Ancient Israel," *Hebrew Union College Annual* X [1935], 54, n. 82). The teaching here is then understood to be an affirmation of the joyous character of the feast of Booths about to be described. Since the festival is unnamed and its announcement found some Jews unprepared for it (vs. 10), the feast was probably not an ancient, well-established one. It has been regarded as a special festival instituted without precedent to celebrate the recovery of the law (cf. Ryle, *Ezra and Nehemiah,* p. 244). Such unique festivals are found elsewhere (cf. Esth. 9:16 ff.; I Macc. 4:59; II Macc. 10:6-8; 15:36; John 10:22). The attitude of joy and thanksgiving at the reception of the law reflects the spirit of Deuteronomy (cf. Deut. 12:12; 14:26; 16:11 ff.).

9. The M.T. includes **Nehemiah** in the gathering, but he plays no significant part. The omission of him in I Esdras 9:49 is not important since that version, which ignores him otherwise, would naturally omit him here. As **Ezra** and **Nehemiah** were not contemporaries (cf. Intro., p. 562), the name of **Nehemiah** must be an addition, possibly inserted by the editor who transposed chs. 8–9 to its present position, which thus made the men contemporary (cf. Rudolph, *op. cit.,* p. 148). The epithet **Tirshatha** (cf. Ezra 2:63), interpreted by some as **the governor,** is not applied elsewhere (5:14, 18; 12:26) to **Nehemiah,** who is always called "governor" (*peḥah;* cf. Ezra 5:3; 8:36). Some regard the epithet as genuine and the name **Nehemiah** as a gloss (Guthe and Batten, *op. cit.,* p. 50; Torrey, *Ezra Studies,* p. 269, note *e*; Gotthard, *Text des Nehemia,* p. 43; van Hoonacker, *Le sacerdoce lévitique,* p. 50 and note). But **which is the Tirshatha** appears also to be a gloss, possibly from 10:1, which may have been added when **Nehemiah** was inserted, or even later as a gloss on a gloss (cf. Siegfried, *Esra, Nehemia und Esther,* p. 102; Smend, *Die Listen,* p. 18; Nikel, *op. cit.,* p. 200, n. 1; Stade, *Geschichte des Volkes Israel,* II, 177, n. 1; Rudolph, *loc. cit.*).

10. The day is called **holy unto our Lord,** but the basis for its holiness is not explained. Nor do the people appear to be aware of the significance of the first day of the

Lord: neither be ye sorry; for the joy of the Lord is your strength.

11 So the Levites stilled all the people, saying, Hold your peace, for the day *is* holy; neither be ye grieved.

12 And all the people went their way to eat, and to drink, and to send portions, and to make great mirth, because they had understood the words that were declared unto them.

13 ¶ And on the second day were gathered together the chief of the fathers of all the people, the priests, and the Levites, unto Ezra the scribe, even to understand the words of the law.

is prepared; for this day is holy to our Lord; and do not be grieved, for the joy of the Lord is your strength." 11 So the Levites stilled all the people, saying, "Be quiet, for this day is holy; do not be grieved."

12 And all the people went their way to eat and drink and to send portions and to make great rejoicing, because they had understood the words that were declared to them.

13 On the second day the heads of fathers' houses of all the people, with the priests and the Levites, came together to Ezra the scribe in order to study the words

---

seventh month. Although it became New Year's Day in postexilic times (cf. Ezra 3:1), and later the feast of Trumpets (Lev. 23:23-25; Num. 29:1-6), there is no more expectation of a feast here than in Ezra 3:1. Batten (*op. cit.,* p. 357) claims that "the observance of the day as described does not conform to the law," and he sees in the absence of all reference to trumpets or to a "holy convocation," an indication that Ezra was ignorant of the Priestly Code that some suppose he introduced into Palestine.

The fat, a plural term, means such "fat pieces" as the Oriental regarded as the daintiest morsels, rich food in contrast to ordinary fare. **The sweet,** also plural in Hebrew, could mean **sweet wine** (cf. LXX; Amos 9:13), but it meant as well any supersweet nectarlike drink served at special celebrations. The Vulg. interprets it as wine sweetened with honey (*mulsum*). **Portions** were gifts of food (cf. 13:10; I Sam. 1:4; Esth. 9:19, 22) which have been compared to the gifts given by Arabs to their guests (*lawiyya;* Julius Wellhausen, *Reste arabischen Heidentums* [Berlin: Georg Reimer, 1887], p. 114) and are evidence of generous hospitality connected with festal offerings (cf. I Sam. 9:13; II Sam. 6:19; 15:11; etc.). The LXX and I Esdras wrongly consider that the **portions** were for the poor "that have nothing" (Batten, *op. cit.,* p. 358), for they were sent to others as well (cf. Esth. 9:22). The M.T. behind **to him for whom nothing is prepared** presents unusual Hebrew syntax favored by the Chronicler and in prose found almost exclusively in Chronicles-Ezra-Nehemiah (cf. Arvid S. Kapelrud, *The Question of Authorship in the Ezra-Narrative* [Oslo: J. Dybwad, 1944], p. 86; Kautzsch, *Gesenius' Hebrew Grammar,* sec. 152v; König, *Historisch-comparative Syntax,* sec. 380f). Its sense is properly rendered by the Peshitta, "to whoever has not prepared for himself." Emphasis is on brotherly assistance to help kinsmen, caught unprepared by the short notice, to celebrate the feast.

11. Because it is largely repetitive, this verse is regarded by some as an unnecessary addition by the Chronicler (cf. Rudolph, *op. cit.,* p. 149). But it is not mere repetition for it supplements the preceding statement, "describing more particularly the method by which the people were quieted" (Batten, *loc. cit.;* cf. vs. 3 supplemented by vss. 4-8). Again (cf. vs. 7) the Levites are portrayed as marshals, keeping the crowd in order and passing instructions on to them.

D. Celebration of the Feast of Booths (8:13-18)

13. A smaller group, secular and ecclesiastical leaders who needed to know the law to enforce it, met **on the second day. Heads of fathers' houses** is used in the Ezra story (8:1) but never in Nehemiah's work. **Unto Ezra** has been called an interpolation (Albin van Hoonacker, *Nouvelles études sur la restauration juive après l'exil de Babylone* [Paris: Ernest Leroux, 1896], p. 239; cf. Batten, *op. cit.,* p. 360), but probably means simply that Ezra presided (Siegfried, *op. cit.,* p. 103). The LXX, Vulg., and Peshitta omit **even** before **to understand** or **to study** and are rightly followed by the RSV.

14 And they found written in the law which the LORD had commanded by Moses, that the children of Israel should dwell in booths in the feast of the seventh month:

15 And that they should publish and proclaim in all their cities, and in Jerusalem, saying, Go forth unto the mount, and fetch olive branches, and pine branches, and myrtle branches, and palm branches, and branches of thick trees, to make booths, as *it is* written.

16 ¶ So the people went forth, and brought *them,* and made themselves booths, every one upon the roof of his house, and in their courts, and in the courts of the house

of the law. 14 And they found it written in the law that the LORD had commanded by Moses that the people of Israel should dwell in booths during the feast of the seventh month, 15 and that they should publish and proclaim in all their towns and in Jerusalem, "Go out to the hills and bring branches of olive, wild olive, myrtle, palm, and other leafy trees to make booths, as it is written." 16 So the people went out and brought them and made booths for themselves, each on his roof, and in their courts and in the

---

14. The Pentateuch nowhere presents **written** instructions for keeping the feast of Booths as described in this section. Closest parallels are in the Holiness Code (Lev. 23:39-43), but there are striking differences. There the festival begins on the fifteenth day (Lev. 23:39), while here it is the third, and the reference to the Exodus, prominent in the Holiness Code (Lev. 23:43), is unmentioned here. It has been argued that Neh. 8 reflects the original date in the Holiness Code (Lev. 23:33-43) before that was altered in harmony with the later priestly legislation (Morgenstern, "Studies in Calendars," pp. 53, 56, 69). The implication that the harvest was still in progress points to a date in Neh. 8 at the beginning of the seventh month rather than at its middle (*ibid.*, pp. 61-62, n. 97). For **booths** and **the feast** see Exeg. on Ezra 3:4.

15. Nowhere is it **written in the law** (vs. 14) that the leaders are to **publish and proclaim** the feast. **Unto the mount** suggests that one mountain could supply all the branches named. **The hills** reflects the idea that not a single mountain but the hill country of Judah is meant. The writer may have had in mind the wooded area west of Jerusalem, in the mountains west of 'Ain Kārim (cf. Gustaf Dalman, *Arbeit und Sitte in Palästina* [Gütersloh: C. Bertelsmanns, 1928], I, 77).

As in Lev. 23:40, boughs were to be used during the festival, but the lists have only the **palms** and **thick trees** in common. The **olive** appears in Nehemiah, but there is no reference to the willows of Lev. 23:40. The **myrtle** (עלי הדס) graphically resembles somewhat the spelling of the "goodly trees" (עץ הדר) of Leviticus. The latter suggests the *ligni pulcherrimi* of the Vulg. for "the oil tree" of the M.T., which the Peshitta interprets as "nut trees" and the LXX as "cypress." This tree has been identified with the **wild olive** (oleaster; cf. Isa. 41:19), but since the **wild olive** has few if any berries, and those without oil (Thomson, *Land and Book,* p. 53; Dalman, *op. cit.,* I, 68), the identification is incorrect for "oil tree." Early Jewish commentators (Saadiah, Aruch, Kimḥi on Isa. 41:19) agree with the LXX that the "oil tree" was the resiniferous cypress or **pine.** Luther called it the balsam. **Leafy trees** were perhaps dense foliage which could easily form a crude shelter. Although Jewish tradition calls such trees "myrtle" (J. H. Hertz, ed., *The Pentateuch and Haftorahs: Leviticus* [London: Oxford University Press, 1932], p. 256), which is here mentioned specifically, the Peshitta has "willow" (Lev. 23:40). **Palm** branches, too, would be useful for building, but though **palm** is mentioned a number of times (cf. Judg. 4:5; Joel 1:12), it was as rare in Palestine in ancient as in modern times (Dalman, *op. cit.,* I, 64 ff.), and was not commonly in the highlands. There is not now in scripture any **written** legislation concerning the building of the booths.

16-17. The festal celebration is regarded as unique in Hebrew history. By regarding **son of Nun** (Josh. 1:1) as an interpolation, some identify **Jeshua** with the high priest contemporary with Zerubbabel instead of with Joshua the leader during the conquest

of God, and in the street of the water gate, and in the street of the gate of Ephraim.

17 And all the congregation of them that were come again out of the captivity made booths, and sat under the booths: for since the days of Jeshua the son of Nun unto that day had not the children of Israel done so. And there was very great gladness.

courts of the house of God, and in the square at the Water Gate and in the square at the Gate of E'phraim. 17 And all the assembly of those who had returned from the captivity made booths and dwelt in the booths; for from the days of Jeshua the son of Nun to that day the people of Israel had not done so. And there was very great re-

---

of Canaan (J. D. Michaelis, *Übersetzung des Alten Testament mit Anmerkung für Ungelehrte* [Göttingen: Wittwe Vandenhoeck, 1783], XII, 66; Klostermann, *Geschichte des Volkes Israel,* p. 247; Siegfried, *op. cit.,* p. 104), and a single Hebrew MS supports such emendation. The name **Jeshua** is spelled Joshua elsewhere. It is the same as that used for the high priest (Ezra 2:2) and others (cf. 3:19; 7:11, 43; 8:7; 9:4-5; Ezra 2:6, 36, 40; 3:9; 8:33). The spelling alone, however, is insufficient evidence for emendation, and no historical facts warrant departure from the M.T. If it were the high priest, the paternity "son of Jozadak" (cf. Ezra 3:2, 8; 5:2) would be expected (Bertholet, *Esra und Nehemia,* p. 72).

There is considerable dispute as to the basis for regarding the festival described here as unique in Hebrew history. Some consider that the institution was entirely new (cf. Batten, *op. cit.,* p. 362), but the feast was certainly an old one (cf. Ezra 3:4) which the Chronicler mentions elsewhere (II Chr. 8:13). Others find the novelty in the dwelling in booths (Bertheau, *Esra, Nechemia und Ester,* p. 279; Kegel, *Kultusreformation des Esra,* p. 190), but that practice too was ancient, and the feast is already called the feast of Booths in Deut. 16:13, 16. Ryle (*Ezra and Nehemiah,* p. 248), stressing **done so** (vs. 17), sees the new element in the strictness of the observance. More probably the uniqueness lay in the complete centralization of the feast in Jerusalem, so that not only was the festal sacrifice made in Jerusalem (cf. Deut. 16) but the booths were confined to Jerusalem also (Kittel, *Geschichte des Volkes Israel,* III, 593-94; Sellin, *Geschichte,* II, 139; Rudolph, *op. cit.,* p. 153).

Such centralization explains the distribution of the booths within the city (vs. 16). Because of congestion in the ruined city, the **booths** were set up in every available place. Some were erected on the flat roofs of the houses, where huts of summer boughs were sometimes erected by the poor when they had no cool upper chamber (cf. Nowack, *Lehrbuch,* I, 140-41; Gottlieb Schumacher, *Across the Jordan* [London: Richard Bentley & Son, 1886], p. 89). Although the Canaanites used their roof tops for places of sacrifice (cf. II Kings 23:12; Jer. 19:13; 32:29; Zeph. 1:5), it is unnecessary to regard the booths of vs. 16 as "a certain counter-weight for Yahwe," as a concession to the Jews who were still inclined toward the ancient Canaanite practice (cf. Kapelrud, *op. cit.,* pp. 89-90); this would not account for the other booths. The **courts** of the houses, where booths were set up, were paved areas, often planted with trees and containing a well (II Sam. 17:18), which lay before the houses, separated from the street by a high wall. Booths were also erected in the temple courts. **House of God** (cf. Ezra 1:3) for the temple (cf. Ps. 135:2) is one of the Chronicler's preferred expressions (cf. Ezra 1:3-5, 7; 2:68; etc., *ibid.,* p. 90). Other **booths,** presumably for those from outside Jerusalem, were erected in the "broad place" (cf. Ezra 10:9) of the **Water Gate** (cf. 3:26) and the **Gate of Ephraim.** The **Gate of Ephraim** (cf. 12:39) was so named because its road led northward to Ephraim. It is located about four hundred cubits (about twelve hundred feet) from the Corner Gate (cf. 3:11; Jer. 31:38), according to II Kings 14:13. From 12:39 one may assume that it lay between the Wall of the Square (3:8) and the Mishneh Gate (3:6) and is probably identical with the "first gate" of Zech. 14:10 (Simons, *Jerusalem in O.T.,* p. 278). The gate was located approximately in the middle of the first north wall, where the principal east-west and north-south roads now cross, between the citadel and the Haram-es-sherif (C. Schick, "Der Lauf der zweiten Mauer," pp. 279 ff.; cf. Simons,

18 Also day by day, from the first day unto the last day, he read in the book of the law of God. And they kept the feast seven days; and on the eighth day *was* a solemn assembly, according unto the manner.

18 And day by day, from the first day to the last day, he read from the book of the law of God. They kept the feast seven days; and on the eighth day there was a solemn assembly, according to the ordinance.

op. cit., p. 234). The **square** where the booths were erected was doubtless the square north of the city wall, the "square" of the Wall of the Square (3:8), the "place" of the "first gate" (Zech. 14:10; *ibid.*, p. 278, n. 1).

All the assembly (cf. Ezra 10:1) is here identified as returned exiles, ignoring those who had not been exiled. Such a view is usually associated with the Chronicler (Ezra 9:8). Some have claimed that the attitude "is a result of theoretical deliberation on the basis of Ezra 1–6, and has nothing to do with reality" (Kapelrud, *loc. cit.*); but it is possible that the returned exiles were so numerous as to give their name to the entire community (Bertholet, *loc. cit.*).

18. The expression **day by day**, favored by the Chronicler (S. R. Driver, *Introduction to the Literature of the Old Testament* [new ed.; New York: Charles Scribner's Sons, 1931], p. 505), occurs only in Chronicles and Ezra-Nehemiah (I Chr. 12:22; II Chr. 8:13; 24:11; 30:21; Ezra 3:4; 6:9). An **eighth day** celebration (vs. 18) is not mentioned in earlier legislation where the feast of Booths is but **seven days** long (Deut. 16:13; Ezek. 45:25; Lev. 23:34, 36*a*, 39*a*). The reference to such a day in the Holiness Code (Lev. 23:39) has been regarded as a later priestly interpolation (*ibid.*, p. 55; J. M. P. Smith, *Origin and History of Hebrew Law*, p. 86; cf. Morgenstern, "Studies in Calendars," p. 53), for it is found in the Priestly Code (Lev. 23:36; Num. 29:35) where, however, it was celebrated on the twenty-second day of the seventh month. Usually the **eighth day** is ascribed to the Chronicler, who also supplied it in II Chr. 7:8-10 (cf. I Kings 8:66; Browne, *Early Judaism*, p. 188). It is possible, however, that the custom of an **eighth day** was already in practice in the time of Ezra, who adopted it without reference to earlier legislation (Morgenstern, "Studies in Calendars," pp. 56-57, 64).

Legislation in Deut. 31:10-11 requires that the **law** should be read "at the end of seven years, at the exact moment of the sabbatical year, at the feast of Tabernacles," which has been interpreted as meaning at the end of every seven-year period (Carl Steuernagel, *Übersetzung und Erklärung der Bücher Deuteronomium und Josua* [Göttingen: Vandenhoeck & Ruprecht, 1923; "Handkommentar zum Alten Testament"], p. 111). Morgenstern, who believes that Ezra read the law in 458-457 B.C., has determined that the year was such a sabbatical year, and that Ezra was acting in conformity with the legislation of Deut. 31:10-11 ("Studies in Calendars," pp. 70-71, n. 107). It is unlikely that such a date for Ezra can be maintained (cf. Ezra 7:7-8). More probably the daily reading of the law during the feast was one of its unique features (cf. vs. 17), since it is not elsewhere prescribed in Jewish legislation. Later, when a festal day was established to mark the completion of the annual cycle of the reading of the Pentateuch, this celebration (Simhath Torah: "The Joy of the Law") was placed in the calendar on the **eighth day** of the festival, at the close of the celebration of the feast of Booths—celebrated on the twenty-second day of the seventh month (*ibid.*, pp. 9-10).

According to the ordinance (vs. 18) corresponds to **as it is written** (vs. 15), but no commands are preserved for the observance of the **eighth day** service on the tenth day of the seventh month. Priestly law calls for its observance on the twenty-second day of that month (Lev. 23:36; Num. 29:35-38).

With the successful completion of his mission, the story of Ezra is concluded (cf. Hölscher, *Esra und Nehemia*, p. 544). Josephus (*Antiquities* XI. 5. 5) observes: "And it was his fate, after being honored by the people, to die an old man and be buried with great magnificence in Jerusalem." With the increasing importance of the law in Judaism, the stature of Ezra increased in the minds of his people, and later traditions

9 Now in the twenty and fourth day of this month the children of Israel were assembled with fasting, and with sack-clothes, and earth upon them.

9 Now on the twenty-fourth day of this month the people of Israel were assembled with fasting and in sackcloth, and with

---

abound concerning his life, his devotion to the law and its propagation, his founding of synagogues, and his death and burial (cf. M. Munk, *Esra ha sofer* [Frankfurt: Israelit & Hermon, 1933]).

IX. MIXED MARRIAGE REFORM (9:1-5a)

The expression **this month** now links ch. 9 with ch. 8, but it is out of place, for the transition from joyous celebration (ch. 8) to deep mourning (ch. 9) is hardly understandable. The idea that the mood of 8:9 returned after the brief festival (e.g., Bertholet, *loc. cit.*) is psychologically improbable (Jahn, *Esra [A und B] und Nehemja,* pp. 128-29). Vs. 2 shows that the sorrow was due not to the reading of the law but to mixed marriages. Some scholars transpose ch. 8 to follow chs. 9–10 (W. H. Kosters, *Die Wiederherstellung Israels in der persischen Periode* [tr. A. Basedow; Heidelberg: J. Hörning, 1895], pp. 64 ff.), but it is more likely that ch. 9 should be related to Ezra 10, which is also concerned with mixed marriage. Others insert Neh. 9:1-2 between vs. 14 and vs. 15 of Ezra 10 (Julian Morgenstern, "The Chanukkah Festival and the Calendar of Ancient Israel," *Hebrew Union College Annual,* XX [1947], 22), or between vs. 15 and vs. 16 of that chapter (Frieder Ahlemann, *Die Esra-Quelle; ein literarkritische Untersuchung* [Greifswald: Dissertation, 1941] cited by Rudolph, *op. cit.,* p. xxxi; Ahlemann, "Zur Esra-Quelle," *Zeitschrift für die alttestamentliche Wissenschaft,* LIX [1942-43], 78, 85, 88 ff.), but such proposals place the actual separation of the mixed families (9:2) before the preparation to do so (Ezra 10:16 ff.; cf. Rudolph, *op. cit.,* p. 155). It is better to have ch. 9 follow Ezra 10:44 (Torrey, *Composition,* p. 32; *Ezra Studies,* pp. 254, 274, note *p*; Rudolph, *op. cit.,* p. 154) as a second stage of the marriage reform, after Ezra's most extreme measures had been carried out.

Some regarded vss. 4-5a as the work of the Chronicler, who missed the Levites in vss. 1-2 and introduced them on the basis of late Levitical custom (Siegfried, *Esra, Nehemia und Esther,* pp. 105-6; Rudolph, *op. cit.,* p. 156; *et al.*). But lacking knowledge of the place of Levites in services at the time of Ezra, it seems arbitrary to conclude that the practice in vss. 4-5a was foreign to his age and therefore reflects later times. Reading the law (vs. 3), however, intrudes into a context otherwise concerned with fasting, weeping, and penitence. It is possibly a post-Chronicler supplement inserted by the editor who disrupted the order of the Ezra narrative, or by a later person who felt it necessary to have the reading of the law here as in previous assemblies (e.g., 8:2-8, 18). Vs. 3 shows strong influence of 8:7b-8a (cf. *ibid.,* p. 155).

9:1. This month is the first (Nisan) of 397 B.C. (cf. Ezra 10:17) and its **twenty-fourth day** was May 16. For **fasting** see Ezra 8:21. **Sackcloth** (*saq*) was a coarse hairy cloth worn as a sign of mourning (H. F. Lutz, *Textiles and Costumes Among the Peoples of the Ancient Near East* [Leipzig: J. C. Hinrichs, 1923], pp. 25, 176-77). Originally worn as a loincloth (Gen. 37:34; I Kings 20:31) bound with a rope directly against the skin without the benefit of soft undergarments (I Kings 21:27; II Kings 6:30; Jer. 48:37; Job 16:15), the later garment may have been somewhat more extensive. **Earth** appears in the Peshitta as "ashes." Such material has been identified as dust taken originally from the grave and ashes from articles burned with the body (II Chr. 16:14; 21:19;

9:1-37. Collective Confession and Intercession. —The setting of this entire chapter is that of a general assembly of the people, planned with liturgical care (vss. 4-5), for the further reading of the law (vs. 3a), and then for a public service of worship and confession (vs. 3b). In this solemn setting Ezra the priest offers a lengthy prayer (vss. 6-37) of national confession, beginning with a doxology of praise (vs. 6). The history of God's covenant dealings with his

2 And the seed of Israel separated themselves from all strangers, and stood and confessed their sins, and the iniquities of their fathers.

3 And they stood up in their place, and read in the book of the law of the LORD their God *one* fourth part of the day; and *another* fourth part they confessed, and worshipped the LORD their God.

4 ¶ Then stood up upon the stairs, of the Levites, Jeshua, and Bani, Kadmiel, Shebaniah, Bunni, Sherebiah, Bani, *and* Chenani, and cried with a loud voice unto the LORD their God.

earth upon their heads. 2 And the Israelites separated themselves from all foreigners, and stood and confessed their sins and the iniquities of their fathers. 3 And they stood up in their place and read from the book of the law of the LORD their God for a fourth of the day; for another fourth of it they made confession and worshiped the LORD their God. 4 Upon the stairs of the Levites stood Jeshua, Bani, Kad'mi-el, Shebani'ah, Bunni, Sherebi'ah, Bani, and Chena'ni; and they cried with a loud voice to the LORD

W. Robertson Smith, *Religion of the Semites*, pp. 413-14; cf. Johannes Geissler, *Die literarischen Beziehungen der Esramemorien, insbesondere zur Chronik und den hexateuchischen Quellenschriften* [Chemnitz: J. C. F. Pickenhahn & Sohn, 1899], p. 13) . **Their heads,** in the LXX[L] but lacking in the M.T., correctly indicates the practice among ancient Orientals (cf. I Sam. 4:12; II Sam. 1:2; 15:32; Job 2:12), as well as among the ancient Greeks, who dusted their heads as a sign of deep distress (T. H. Seymour, *Life in the Homeric Age* [New York: The Macmillan Co., 1907], p. 476) .

2. If ch. 9 is a sequel to ch. 8, **separated themselves** means nothing, but it is intelligible as the final formal proclamation of divorce if Ezra 9–10 is antecedent (Browne, *op. cit.,* p. 191) . The contrast here is between **the seed of Israel,** the "holy seed" (Ezra 9:2) , and the **strangers,** who, as early as the time of Haggai (cf. Ezra 4:1) , were excluded from the Judean community. The **foreigners** are clearly the non-Israelite "people of the land" (Ezra 9:1) . The confession of sin is not only personal but collective (cf. 1:6*b*) , covering all sins during Israel's history. **Sins** and **iniquities** (cf. 4:5) appear as synonyms, indicating cultic failure to obey God's law rather than personal moral defects.

3. Someone stood while the law was read (cf. 8:5) , but the pronoun **they** is ambiguous; it apparently refers to the **seed of Israel** (vs. 2) , but it was probably intended to designate "the Levites" of vs. 4, those who were to read (cf. F. W. Schultz, *Esra, Nehemia und Esther* [Leipzig: Velhagen & Klasing, 1876], p. 172) . The verb too is ambiguous, since it would mean "to take places" (cf. 8:7) or "to rise" from a kneeling position. For **in their place** see 8:7*b*.

According to 8:3, the reading lasted half a day, but here, where the half day is divided between reading and confession, the reading time is less. A quarter day is assumed to be three hours. The LXX indicates that the confession was directed "to the Lord." It is suggested that the act was not private confession but public participation in the hearing of the penitential psalm (vss. 5*b*-37; Bertheau, *op. cit.,* p. 281) , but that psalm is entirely unrelated to this episode. For **worshiped** the M.T. has, lit., "prostrated themselves," which is understood to mean that the confession was made while lying prostrate (Siegfried, *op. cit.,* p. 105) .

4-5*a*. Here again (cf. 8:7, 11) the Levites appear as marshals, leading the crowd and directing the service. Each list (vss. 4, 5*a*) in the M.T. has eight Levites, but the totals differ in the versions and the passage has been called textually hopeless (Bertholet, *loc. cit.*) . It is conjectured that the original figure was the round number seven (cf. 8:7;

---

chosen people Israel is then reviewed at great length and in detail, with the steady refrain of God's mercy (vss. 17*b*, 20, 31) and justice (vs. 33) , in spite of the presumption (vs. 16) and disobedience (vss. 17, 26, 30-31, 34) of Israel.

(On such public liturgical prayers see Expos. on 1:4-11; Ezra 9:1-15.) The occasion of this elaborate service and lengthy prayer is plainly intimated in vs. 2; the issue is that of mixed marriages, as in Ezra 9–10. The details of setting

5 Then the Levites, Jeshua, and Kad-miel, Bani, Hashabniah, Sherebiah, Hodijah, Shebaniah, *and* Pethahiah, said, Stand up *and* bless the LORD your God for ever and ever: and blessed be thy glorious name, which is exalted above all blessing and praise.

their God. 5 Then the Levites, Jeshua, Kad'mi-el, Bani, Hashabnei'ah, Sherebi'ah, Hodi'ah, Shebani'ah, and Pethahi'ah, said, "Stand up and bless the LORD your God from everlasting to everlasting. Blessed be thy glorious name which is exalted above all blessing and praise."

Guthe and Batten, *Ezra and Nehemiah*, p. 51), or that the sum of the two lists was originally eleven, six in vs. 4 and five in vs. 5, which, with Ezra himself, would make the number twelve, the traditional number of Hebrew tribes, a number favored by the Chronicler (Torrey, *Ezra Studies*, p. 280).

Usually the lists are regarded as originally identical, as in the Peshitta, and variants are explained away as textual corruptions. But such duplication appears senseless, and there must originally have been some basis of differentiation not now ascertainable. It is conjectured that the first group (vs. 4) began the ceremony with an invocation, and the second (vs. 5) then called the group to participate in the prayer (*ibid.*). But five of the eight Levites have identical names. **Jeshua, Bani,** and **Kadmiel,** usually first when listed (cf. 8:7; 10:9), here also head the lists. **Shebaniah** and **Sherebiah** appear in their usual order in vs. 5 but are reversed in vs. 4. For **Shebaniah** some Hebrew MSS and the LXX^AL have Shechaniah (cf. Ezra 8:3), which is favored by some (*ibid.*, p. 279; Rudolph, *op. cit.*, p. 152) but is found in only a few MSS of Neh. 10, to which the names here listed seem to be related. The other names are found elsewhere for Levites: **Chenani** (vs. 4) abbreviates Chenaniah (I Chr. 15:22); **Hashabneiah** is an error for Hashabiah (cf. 10:11; 12:24). For **Hodiah,** cf. 8:7; 10:13. **Pethahiah** (cf. Ezra 10:23), missing in 10:9 ff., is probably the Pelaiah of 8:7; 10:10 (*ibid.*).

Stairs is used only here in the sense of a platform if it is intended to represent the structure of 8:4, but "the stair of the Levites" seems to refer to a well-known cult apparatus used by the Levites on such occasions. The **loud voice** led to the suggestion that the Levites, responsible for working with groups out of doors, cultivated high, loud, far-carrying voices (Batten, *Ezra and Nehemiah*, p. 364).

X. PENITENTIAL PSALM (9:5b-37)

This section presents not prose narrative but a long penitential psalm. The LXX links the psalm with the narrative by introducing in vs. 6, **and Ezra said,** which is widely accepted as a "probable" emendation. But the psalm begins with a doxology (vs. 5b) and the words **and Ezra said** would be an obvious intrusion. There is no clear evidence of strophic structure in the entire psalm, but Rudolph (*op. cit.*, p. 157) observes that if dubious vs. 22 is omitted, Neh. 9:9 ff. shows symmetrical structure with a preliminary section in three strophes (16+8+8=32 lines); a central seven-line strophe (vss. 24-25); and a final section of four strophes (8+8+8+8=32 lines).

The date and authorship of the original psalm have been much debated but with widely varying results. It has been called "a litany written for the worship of Northern Israel on the occasion of a day of fasting, confession, and prayer," soon after 722 B.C. (Adam C. Welch, "The Source of Nehemiah IX," *Zeitschrift für die alttestamentliche Wissenschaft*, XLVII [1929], 130-37; *Post-Exilic Judaism* [Edinburgh: William Blackwood & Sons, 1935], pp. 42-43), but such a view is as extreme as that which assigns it to the

---

and date are not quite the same as that of the similar assembly reported in Ezra 10:9-12, but the purpose is the same—bluntly stated in vs. 38. The worship is to lead up to a signed and sealed written declaration by their political and religious leaders of their purpose with regard

to mixed marriages. The account is set in the third person with Ezra as officiating priest, assisted by Levites who are named (vss. 4-5). The prayer itself, cast in Deuteronomic phrase and forms of thought, presumably by the Chronicler whose philosophy of Jewish history it

6 Thou, *even* thou, *art* LORD alone; thou hast made heaven, the heaven of heavens, with all their host, the earth, and all *things*

6 And Ezra said:[t] "Thou art the LORD, thou alone; thou hast made heaven, the heaven of heavens, with all their host, the

[t] Gk: Heb lacks *and Ezra said*

Greek period (Batten, *op. cit.*, p. 365). Although some argue that the diction of vss. 6-37, like that of Ezra 9:6-15, shows less relationship to that of the Chronicler than to the narrative parts of Ezra's memoirs (Geissler, *op. cit.*, p. 12), that conclusion is challenged by Torrey, who argues that "the literary qualities of the narrative in Ezr. 8–10 and Neh. 8–10 are exactly those of the independent narrative in I and II Chron. . . . Both the subject matter and the manner of treating it are the Chronicler's own" (*Ezra Studies*, p. 246; cf. Rudolph, *op. cit.*, pp. 155-56). He declares that the psalm is a "tissue of quotation," characteristic of the Chronicler's work elsewhere (e.g., Ezra 9). But definite signs of the Chronicler's style are few and the quotations are here treated differently from those in Ezra 9 (cf. Batten, *loc. cit.*)

The attitude toward foreign overlords (vss. 8 ff.), which might be construed as treasonable, has been argued to preclude Ezra's authorship (Rudolph, *op. cit.*, pp. 156-57; Batten, *loc. cit.*); but just such ideas were expressed by Jews in the Achaemenid period (cf. vs. 8). Evidence that the writer was also familiar with the work of the priestly redactor of the Pentateuch (vss. 7-8) has been offered in arguing for a late post-Ezra date for the psalm (cf. Rudolph, *op. cit.*, p. 163). But it is also suggested that such priestly evidence is possibly a late gloss in vss. 7-8, and that its excision leaves the psalm with a distinctly Deuteronomic flavor, closely resembling Pss. 78; 106 and the framework of the book of Judges (Morgenstern, "Chanukkah Festival," pp. 19-20, n. 33). Absence of reference to the sin of foreign marriage in the psalm suggests that it belongs to a period before Ezra and Nehemiah, as part of the liturgy of the early synagogue (*ibid.*, p. 21, n. 34). It appears to be an independent composition incorporated by the Chronicler or a later editor because it seemed appropriate to the occasion.

The psalm is well organized, moving steadily to its climax. It begins with an invocation to praise God (vs. 5*b*), the all-powerful Creator (vs. 6), who elected Abraham and brought him to Canaan, which he promised to give to him and his descendants (vss. 7-8). Despite great obstacles to the keeping of the promise, such as Egyptian domination (vss. 9-15) and the apostasy of Israel itself (vss. 16-23), the promise was kept by the successful conquest of Canaan (vss. 24-25). But the Israelites did not keep their part of the covenant and were disloyal and stubbornly resisted the will of their God, who therefore punished them (vss. 26-31) by temporarily withdrawing Canaan from their control and making Israel a subject people. The author regarded the foreign domination of his day as being due to punishment for ancestral sins. He confesses such sin, admits the righteousness of God, and then, throwing himself and his generation on the mercy of the gracious God, ever ready to forgive, begs for the withdrawal of the punishment (vss. 32-37) and, with his plaintive, urgent cry, **We are in great distress,** seeks pity and salvation by God, as the Deuteronomic writers had always taught was possible.

A. Doxology (9:5*b*)

5*b*. The psalm is introduced by a doxology similar to those in Pss. 41:13; 106:48 (cf. Gunkel and Begrich, *Einleitung in die Psalmen*, pp. 34, 40; cf. Torrey, *Ezra Studies*, pp. 280-81). **Name** is used in substitution for God (cf. 1:9, 11). The phrase **above all blessing and praise** indicates that God is so transcendent that any blessing and praise would be inadequate.

B. God the Unique and Powerful Creator (9:6)

6. Vss. 6-11 have been adopted in the Jewish liturgy as part of the daily morning prayer (J. H. Hertz, tr., *The Authorized Daily Prayer Book* [New York: Bloch Publishing Co., 1948], pp. 98-101). After the doxology (vs. 5*b*), God is adored in vs. 6 as the unique

that *are* therein, the seas, and all that *is* therein, and thou preservest them all; and the host of heaven worshippeth thee.

7 Thou *art* the Lord the God, who didst choose Abram, and broughtest him forth out of Ur of the Chaldees, and gavest him the name of Abraham;

earth and all that is on it, the seas and all that is in them; and thou preservest all of them; and the host of heaven worships thee.

7 Thou art the Lord, the God who didst choose Abram and bring him forth out of Ur of the Chaldees and give him the name

creator and preserver of all. **And Ezra said** could only be intrusive in such a context, as indicated above. The uniqueness of the Lord paraphrases Deut. 6:4, and Deuteronomic thought is reflected throughout the verse as well as through the entire poem. Although a different Hebrew verb is used for "created," the references to creation are based on Gen. 1:1, 6-8; 2:1. The combination of **heaven** and **the heaven of heavens** may derive from Deut. 10:14. **Heaven of heavens,** indicating belief in a plurality of heavens (cf. Deut. 10:14; I Kings 8:27; Pss. 68:33; 148:4; II Enoch 8:1–9:1; 10:1-6; 21:6-22; cf. Eph. 4:10; II Cor. 12:2-4), means "the highest heaven" (cf. Deut. 10:14; I Enoch 60:1; 71:5). A **host** is a well-ordered army (cf. Isa. 40:26; 45:12), but the **host** of heaven is a group created by God (Gen. 2:1) and described as standing, in attendance like courtiers, on each side of God's throne (see I Kings 22:19). They are described as the sun, moon, and stars (Deut. 4:19; Isa. 40:26), sometimes personified (cf. Judg. 5:20; Job 38:7; Ps. 148:3) and brought under God's subjection (cf. Isa. 24:21). The verb **thou preservest**, lit., "enlivenest," implies both "bringing into existence" and "preserving" (cf. I Sam. 2:6; Deut. 32:39; Ezek. 13:18-19).

C. Election of the Hebrews and the Covenant (9:7-8)

7-8. With vs. 7 begins a retrospective examination of Israel's history such as is characteristic of later Jewish writing strongly influenced by the Deuteronomic philosophy of history (cf. Pss. 78; 105; 106). In it the poet shows the faithfulness of God to his chosen people despite their faithlessness. Although the Exodus is usually stressed as prime evidence of God's favor, and it has been argued that all pre-Sinaitic covenants are secondary (cf. Kurt Galling, *Die Erwählungstraditionen Israels* [Giessen: A. Topelmann, 1928], p. 54), it is recalled that in that event God's act was but the consequence of his oaths to the patriarchs (Deut. 7:8). Like the E writer, our poet counts Hebrew history from the call of Abraham and God's covenant with him, the basis of God's promises to Israel.

Although the writer depends largely upon sources that are Deuteronomic or earlier, there is unmistakable evidence of familiarity with the work of the later priestly redactor in the reference to the change of the name of **Abram** (cf. Gen. 17:5) and the migration from **Ur of the Chaldees** (Gen. 11:31). Such evidence has argued for a late date for the psalm, and those who would date it early must explain its presence. The proposal to regard vss. 7-8 as additions to the text (Welch, "Source of Nehemiah IX," p. 132) is extreme since these verses contain the all-important promise. It is preferable to regard only the troublesome priestly element as the redactor's gloss and thus to omit **Abram and bring him forth out of Ur of the Chaldees and give him the name** (cf. Julian Morgenstern, "Chanukkah Festival," p. 20, n. 33). Although **Abram** and **Abraham** are but variant spellings of the same Amorite name (*Abi-ram;* cf. Num. 16:1; J. A. Montgomery, *Arabia and the Bible* [Philadelphia: University of Pennsylvania Press,

strongly reflects, is the longest in Ezra-Nehemiah, and even longer than the similar prayer ascribed to Daniel (Dan. 9:3-19). It oscillates between the goodness and patience of God (vss. 28*b*-31), and the stubbornness and blindness of Israel down its long history (vss. 26-30). **Thou hast dealt faithfully and we have acted wickedly**

(vs. 33). **Behold, we are slaves . . . and we are in great distress** (vss. 36-37). Suffering follows disobedience as its divine penalty—so simple is the prayer's doctrine of evil, on which Job has not yet thrown his more discerning light, still less the suffering servant of the Lord in Isa. 40–55.

8 And foundest his heart faithful before thee, and madest a covenant with him to give the land of the Canaanites, the Hittites, the Amorites, and the Perizzites, and the Jebusites, and the Girgashites, to give *it, I say,* to his seed, and hast performed thy words; for thou *art* righteous:

9 And didst see the affliction of our fathers in Egypt, and heardest their cry by the Red sea;

10 And showedst signs and wonders upon Pharaoh, and on all his servants, and on all the people of his land: for thou knewest that they dealt proudly against them. So didst thou get thee a name, as *it is* this day.

Abraham; 8 and thou didst find his heart faithful before thee, and didst make with him the covenant to give to his descendants the land of the Canaanite, the Hittite, the Amorite, the Per'izzite, the Jeb'usite, and the Gir'gashite; and thou hast fulfilled thy promise, for thou art righteous.

9 "And thou didst see the affliction of our fathers in Egypt and hear their cry at the Red Sea, 10 and didst perform signs and wonders against Pharaoh and all his servants and all the people of his land, for thou knewest that they acted insolently against our fathers; and thou didst get thee a name,

---

1934], pp. 167-68), it is probable that the name was here originally **Abraham,** as in Deut. 1:8; 6:10; 9:5. Abraham's selection appears arbitrary, but it was found that **his heart** ("mind," Ezra 6:22) was **faithful.** The Hebrew word rendered **faithful** means "firm," "steady," "reliable." The LXX translates it **faithful** as in Gal. 3:9. Of God's promises to Abraham (Gen. 12:1-4, 7) the poet stresses "unto thy seed will I give this land." For **to give the land** the versions have "to give him the land," which may be original (Gotthard, *Nehemia,* p. 43).

The list of peoples (vs. 8), superficially in agreement with Gen. 15:18-21 (J), is closer to Exod. 3:17 (RD), which adds the "Hivites." But the LXXL, Peshitta, and Arabic versions add the Hivites before the **Jebusites** in Neh. 9:8 and some would so emend the M.T. (*ibid.*). Hivites were found in central Palestine, chiefly at Gibeon (Josh. 9:7) and Shechem (Gen. 34:2) and were made subject to taskwork after the time of Solomon (I Kings 9:20 ff.). To the five peoples of Ezra 9:1 the M.T. here adds the **Girgashites,** who are apparently identical with the Qaraqisha of Hittite records (Abel, *Géographie,* I, 325; cf. W. F. Albright, reviewing F. M. Abel's *Géographie de la Palestine, Journal of the Palestine Oriental Society,* XV [1935], 189). They appear to have lived in Trans-Jordan, for they joined Jericho against Israel (Josh. 24:11). The LXX of the parallel text (Exod. 3:17) also lists the **Girgashites.**

D. EGYPTIAN SOJOURN AND EXODUS (9:9-11)

From the promise to Abraham the writer's mind leaped to the Egyptian sojourn, the first great threat to fulfillment of the promise. By his power, revealed through signs and wonders, God broke the bonds that held his people and frustrated the pursuers who would pull Israel back to Egypt.

9-10. Vs. 9 paraphrases Exod. 3:7 (J), changing "afflictions of my people," referring to Egyptian persecution (Exod. 1:8-16), to **affliction of our fathers. Their cry,** which in Exod. 3:7 refers to the reaction to the taskmasters, here occurs **at the Red Sea,** apparently influenced by the thought of Exod. 14:10. As usual the "Sea of Reeds" of the M.T. is called **the Red Sea** in the Vulg. and LXX. The words **signs and wonders** show the influence of Deut. 6:22. The chronological sequence in vs. 10 should make **signs and wonders** follow the Exodus, if not signify the Exodus itself. But in Deut. 6:22 they included the plagues (Exod. 7–12), which the words **and on all the people of his land** show is true here also. The phrase "all his household" of Deut. 6:22 is here rendered **all his servants,** which the Peshitta interprets as "all his army."

One motive for God's intervention was that the Egyptians **acted insolently** against Israel, here expressed in the actual words used by Jethro in Exod. 18:11 (J). **Against them** (M.T.) is interpreted as **against our fathers** but without textual authority. Another motive, popular in later times, was to increase God's reputation (**name;** cf.

11 And thou didst divide the sea before them, so that they went through the midst of the sea on the dry land; and their persecutors thou threwest into the deeps, as a stone into the mighty waters.

12 Moreover thou leddest them in the day by a cloudy pillar; and in the night by a pillar of fire, to give them light in the way wherein they should go.

13 Thou camest down also upon mount Sinai, and spakest with them from heaven, and gavest them right judgments, and true laws, good statutes and commandments:

14 And madest known unto them thy holy sabbath, and commandedst them precepts, statutes, and laws, by the hand of Moses thy servant:

as it is to this day. 11 And thou didst divide the sea before them, so that they went through the midst of the sea on dry land; and thou didst cast their pursuers into the depths, as a stone into mighty waters. 12 By a pillar of cloud thou didst lead them in the day, and by a pillar of fire in the night to light for them the way in which they should go. 13 Thou didst come down upon Mount Sinai, and speak with them from heaven and give them right ordinances and true laws, good statutes and commandments, 14 and thou didst make known to them thy holy sabbath and command them commandments and statutes and a law by Moses thy

---

Exod. 9:16; Isa. 63:12, 14). In associating the **signs and wonders** with the **name,** the writer shows dependence upon Jer. 32:20.

11. The crossing of the Red Sea closely paraphrases Exod. 14:21-22, with some recollection of words of the Song of Moses (Exod. 15:5, 10). For "they sank" (Exod. 15:5, 10) the poet has **thou didst cast,** under the influence of Exod. 14:27. **Into the mighty waters,** found in Exod. 15:10 but with a different adjective, here is influenced by Isa. 43:16, which uses the words of Neh. 9:11. **Persecutors** for the **pursuers** of the M.T., LXX, and Peshitta shows the influence of the Vulg.

E. The Wilderness Wandering (9:12-21)

12-21. After frustrating the enemy (vss. 9-11), to keep his promise of delivering Canaan to Israel God had to save his people from such natural terrors of the wilderness as loss of direction, famine, death by thirst, and finally from the results of Israel's own rebellion and apostasy.

1. Salvation from Natural Dangers (9:12-15)

12. Moreover, or "furthermore," omitted by the RSV, links vs. 12 with what precedes. God guided Israel through the wilderness (cf. Exod. 13:21-22 [J]). The J writer thought of God as being "in a pillar" but "in" can also mean **by** instrumentally. **To give them light** (cf. Exod. 13:21) could refer only to the **pillar of fire,** but the Vulg., "that they might see," could refer to both pillars. By changing the number of the pronoun, Deut. 1:33 is expertly adjusted to **in the way wherein they should go.**

13-14. Inevitably the giving of the law at Sinai (Exod. 19:18, 20 [J]; 20:22b [R]; Deut. 4:36a) would be mentioned in the story of the wilderness, since it was part of the plot of the psalm that Israel later disobeyed those laws. Despite its importance, the writer who places the matter of the law almost parenthetically between references to salvation from natural terrors (vss. 12, 15) is much more moderate in his treatment of the subject than might be expected of the Chronicler under the circumstances.

The imagery is drawn from the J account (Exod. 19:18c, 20), but **from heaven** (cf. Exod. 20:22b [R]) indicates that the writer shares the concept of revelation from heaven rather than the earlier view that God spoke "face to face" with Moses (Deut. 5:4; 34:10). For **judgments** see 1:7; for **statutes** and **commandments** see Ezra 7:11. Only the **sabbath** law is given special attention. Although there was some early concern about the sabbath (Amos 8:5), it becomes a principal concern in the postexilic period (13:15-21; Jer. 17:19-27; Mark 2:23-28; Luke 13:10-17).

15 And gavest them bread from heaven for their hunger, and broughtest forth water for them out of the rock for their thirst, and promisedst them that they should go in to possess the land which thou hadst sworn to give them.

16 But they and our fathers dealt proudly, and hardened their necks, and hearkened not to thy commandments,

17 And refused to obey, neither were mindful of thy wonders that thou didst among them; but hardened their necks, and in their rebellion appointed a captain to return to their bondage: but thou *art* a God ready to pardon, gracious and merciful, slow to anger, and of great kindness, and forsookest them not.

servant. 15 Thou didst give them bread from heaven for their hunger and bring forth water for them from the rock for their thirst, and thou didst tell them to go in to possess the land which thou hadst sworn to give them.

16 "But they and our fathers acted presumptuously and stiffened their neck and did not obey thy commandments; 17 they refused to obey, and were not mindful of the wonders which thou didst perform among them; but they stiffened their neck and appointed a leader to return to their bondage in Egypt. But thou art a God ready to forgive, gracious and merciful, slow to anger and abounding in steadfast love, and

15. Rescue from hunger and thirst is indicated by passing reference to the miracles of the **bread from heaven** (cf. Exod. 16:3-27 [J]) and the **water . . . from the rock** (cf. Exod. 17:6 [J]; Num. 20:7-13 [R]), which are mentioned again in vs. 20. The section concludes with a reference to the treasured promise of God. **To go in to possess the land** is a Deuteronomic expression (cf. Deut. 9:5). **Which thou hadst sworn** interprets a Hebrew text, "which thou hast lifted up thy hand," referring to the gesture of making an oath (cf. Exod. 6:8; Ezek. 20:28, 42; 47:14; Ps. 106:26). God swore to give Canaan to Israel (Gen. 26:3; Exod. 33:1; Num. 14:23) and the poet is ever eager to affirm it.

2. ISRAEL'S REBELLION AND APOSTASY (9:16-18)

Not only the wilderness but also the deliberate acts of Israel could have frustrated God's plan to fulfill his promise. But God resolved to keep his promise despite all the difficulties Israel put in the way of its fulfillment.

16. If **and** is retained in **they and our fathers, they** would refer to Moses' contemporaries and **our fathers** to the poet's more immediate ancestors. Since both probably refer to the same people, ancestors in general, **and** should be rendered "namely," as explicative (cf. 7:2; Ezra 6:8; Siegfried, *op. cit.*, p. 108; Bertholet, *Esra und Nehemia*, p. 73; Rudolph, *Esra und Nehemia*, p. 158). **Dealt proudly** is the same as the expression used in vs. 10 of the hated Egyptians (cf. Deut. 1:43; 17:13). **Stiffened their neck,** a figure borrowed from the driving of oxen who resist guidance, indicates stubbornness (cf. Deut. 10:16; Jer. 7:26; 17:23; 19:15).

17-18. Easy forgetfulness of God's wonders performed for Israel (Exod. 3:20) was regarded as evidence of disbelief in the power of God (Num. 14:11). Seven Hebrew MSS, the LXX, and Ethiopic versions show that במרים, **in their rebellion,** is an easy error for במצרים, **in Egypt,** as in Num. 14:4. **Appointed a leader** makes a mere proposal in Num. 14:4 into a historical fact for which there is no evidence elsewhere. The crowning sin of the wilderness was the rejection of the Lord for the **molten calf** (Exod. 32:1-8) and the identification of that **calf** with the rescuer and protector of Israel. The LXX and Peshitta assimilated the M.T. text here to that of Exodus by substituting "these are the gods" (Exod. 32:4, 8) for **this is thy God,** and the Peshitta adds the vocative "O Israel." For such perfidy Israel deserved to be punished and abandoned by its God but, despite the hindrances and provocations, God continued to help Israel, to fulfill his promise. The concept of **a God ready to forgive** is found elsewhere (cf. Exod. 34:6-7; Amos 7:2; Ps. 130:4; etc.). The exact expression is in Dan. 9:9, from where it is supposed to have been borrowed (Siegfried, *loc. cit.*), but more probably Neh. 9:18 may depend on Num. 14:19-20 (J) and Daniel may borrow from here.

18 Yea, when they had made them a molten calf, and said, This *is* thy God that brought thee up out of Egypt, and had wrought great provocations;

19 Yet thou in thy manifold mercies forsookest them not in the wilderness: the pillar of the cloud departed not from them by day, to lead them in the way; neither the pillar of fire by night, to show them light, and the way wherein they should go.

20 Thou gavest also thy good Spirit to instruct them, and withheldest not thy manna from their mouth, and gavest them water for their thirst.

21 Yea, forty years didst thou sustain them in the wilderness, *so that* they lacked nothing; their clothes waxed not old, and their feet swelled not.

22 Moreover thou gavest them kingdoms and nations, and didst divide them into corners: so they possessed the land of Sihon, and the land of the king of Heshbon, and the land of Og king of Bashan.

didst not forsake them. 18 Even when they had made for themselves a molten calf and said, 'This is your God who brought you up out of Egypt,' and had committed great blasphemies, 19 thou in thy great mercies didst not forsake them in the wilderness; the pillar of cloud which led them in the way did not depart from them by day, nor the pillar of fire by night which lighted for them the way by which they should go. 20 Thou gavest thy good Spirit to instruct them, and didst not withhold thy manna from their mouth, and gavest them water for their thirst. 21 Forty years didst thou sustain them in the wilderness, and they lacked nothing; their clothes did not wear out and their feet did not swell. 22 And thou didst give them kingdoms and peoples, and didst allot to them every corner; so they took possession of the land of Sihon king of Heshbon and the land of Og king

3. God's Protection in the Wilderness (9:19-21)

19. Due to his forgiving nature and his determination to fulfill his promise to Abraham, God did not forsake Israel (cf. Ezra 9:9) in the wilderness. For the pillars see Exeg. on vs. 12.

20-21. In vs. 20 the poet apparently plays on the words "withheld" (*māna'*) and **manna** (cf. vs. 15). But the gifts of God were not all material. Possibly with the ideas of vss. 13-14 in mind, the poet declares that God gave his **good Spirit to instruct them** (cf. Num. 11:17, 25). The LXXᴸ renders **good spirit** (cf. Ps. 143:10) as "the Holy Spirit." The Pentateuch does not mention the gift of the Holy Spirit, but the idea "is in harmony with the later conception [Isa. 63:11]" (Batten, *Ezra and Nehemiah*, p. 368).

Vs. 21 is a "free quotation" of passages in Deut. 8:4, 9 (*ibid.*), mentioning the material needs of Israel supplied by God during forty years in the wilderness. For **didst thou sustain them** (vs. 21) the Vulg. has properly, "thou didst feed them," since the Hebrew verb means "to supply with food" (Gen. 50:21), an idea not found in Deut. 8:4. The Deuteronomist was also concerned about the supply of clothing during the wandering. Our poet takes over his statement, **their clothes did not wear out.** Later Jewish teachers, concerned about children outgrowing their clothes, taught that the clothes of their children grew with their bodies, "like the shell of a snail" (cf. Rashi on Deut. 8:4; Justin *Dialogue with Trypho* 131). Deut. 8:4 also refers to the problem of sore feet. Since the Hebrew verb is later used of the "swelling" of dough, **swell** is appropriate, but the versions differ in interpretation. The Vulg. has "their feet were not worn" (*attriti*), apparently assimilation to the statement about the clothes, and the Peshitta and LXX have "were not split open."

F. Conquest of Canaan (9:22-25)

The climax of the poet's story is the delivery of Canaan to Israel by God, in fulfillment of his promise to Abraham.

22. This verse, which anticipates the conquest in vs. 24, appears to be intrusive, since vs. 23 belongs with vs. 21, and vs. 22 disrupts the strophic structure of vss. 9-37 (cf. Rudolph, *op. cit.*, pp. 157, 160). Israel's first successes were against the **kingdoms and**

23 Their children also multipliedst thou as the stars of heaven, and broughtest them into the land, concerning which thou hadst promised to their fathers, that they should go in to possess it.

24 So the children went in and possessed the land, and thou subduedst before them the inhabitants of the land, the Canaanites, and gavest them into their hands, with their kings, and the people of the land, that they might do with them as they would.

25 And they took strong cities, and a fat land, and possessed houses full of all goods, wells digged, vineyards, and oliveyards, and fruit trees in abundance: so they did eat, and were filled, and became fat, and delighted themselves in thy great goodness.

of Bashan. 23 Thou didst multiply their descendants as the stars of heaven, and thou didst bring them into the land which thou hadst told their fathers to enter and possess. 24 So the descendants went in and possessed the land, and thou didst subdue before them the inhabitants of the land, the Canaanites, and didst give them into their hands, with their kings and the peoples of the land, that they might do with them as they would. 25 And they captured fortified cities and a rich land, and took possession of houses full of all good things, cisterns hewn out, vineyards, olive orchards and fruit trees in abundance; so they ate, and were filled and became fat, and delighted themselves in thy great goodness.

---

peoples of Trans-Jordan (Num. 21:21-35). The defeat of the Amorites **Sihon** and **Og** was long remembered as a great providential event in Hebrew history (Pss. 135:11; 136:19-20). **Heshbon** (Tell Heṣbân), capital of Sihon's kingdom, lay east of the Jordan, between the Arnon and Jabbok rivers (Num. 21:24; Deut. 1:4; 2:26-27; John Garstang, *The Foundations of Bible History: Joshua-Judges* [London: Constable & Co., 1931], p. 384). **Bashan** was the broad fertile land in Trans-Jordan lying southward from Mount Hermon as far as the land of Gilead. It was famous for its oaks (Isa. 2:13; Zech. 11:2; Ezek. 27:6) and its cattle (Amos 4:1; Ps. 22:12).

Into corners translates a Hebrew text, "according to a corner," which is difficult to interpret. Ancient translators were as confused as moderns. The usual interpretation **every corner** or "to its utmost extent" (Francis Brown, S. R. Driver, C. A. Briggs, eds., *A Hebrew and English Lexicon of the Old Testament* [Boston: Houghton Mifflin Co., 1928], p. 802) is forced and unsuitable. Since the word also means "side," "edge," "border," and is used for the points of the compass (cf. Ezek. 47:17-20; Josh. 15:5; 18:12, 14-15, 20), it is proposed to read the plural form (*lappĕ'ôth*) and translate it as "boundaries" (cf. Ehrlich, *Randglossen*, VII, 206; Rudolph, *op. cit.*, p. 160) or as "according to designated boundaries" (Bertholet, *op. cit.*, p. 74; Guthe and Batten, *Ezra and Nehemiah*, p. 51).

23-24. Didst multiply their descendants affirms further fulfillment of the promise to Abraham (Gen. 15:5; 22:17; 26:4; Deut. 1:10). **The children** were Joshua's Israelite contemporaries. **Thou didst subdue** clearly indicates that the conquest was not the work of Israel but God's deed, in fulfillment of his promise. The use of the verb **subdue** (כנע; cf. Deut. 9:3 RSV; Judg. 4:23) suggests a play on the word **Canaanites** (כנענים) in the same verse (cf. "manna" in vs. 20; Ehrlich, *loc. cit.*; Siegfried, *op. cit.*, p. 109; Bertholet, *loc. cit.*; Rudolph, *op. cit.*, p. 109). **Subdue** indicates that the writer did not share the view that the Canaanites were exterminated (cf. Josh. 1–12) but the LXX here interprets as "thou didst destroy."

25. Since the Israelites were to do with the Canaanites as they pleased (vs. 24), a general description of the conquest is given in vs. 25. Most of the expressions are taken from Deuteronomy (cf. Deut. 6:10-11; 8:7-9; etc.). The Deuteronomist favors **fortified cities** (cf. Deut. 3:5). **Fat land** means a fertile, **rich land** (cf. vs. 35; Num. 13:20). Beginning with **houses full of,** the rest of the verse largely abbreviates Deut. 6:11. For **hewn out** the Vulg. has "made by others," obviously assimilating Deut. 6:11, "which thou diggest not." **Fruit trees** are not mentioned in Deut. 6:11, but to cut down **fruit trees** during a siege of a city is forbidden (Deut. 20:19-20).

26 Nevertheless they were disobedient, and rebelled against thee, and cast thy law behind their backs, and slew thy prophets which testified against them to turn them to thee, and they wrought great provocations.

27 Therefore thou deliveredst them into the hand of their enemies, who vexed them: and in the time of their trouble, when they cried unto thee, thou heardest *them* from heaven; and according to thy manifold

26 "Nevertheless they were disobedient and rebelled against thee and cast thy law behind their back and killed thy prophets, who had warned them in order to turn them back to thee, and they committed great blasphemies. 27 Therefore thou didst give them into the hand of their enemies, who made them suffer; and in the time of their suffering they cried to thee and thou didst hear them from heaven; and according to

Amid great plenty the long half-starved Israelites ate and were satisfied, and the poet lauds the **great goodness** of God who gave such plenitude. The verb rendered **delighted themselves** or "lived bountifully" appears only here but seems related to a word for "luxury" or "dainty" (II Sam. 1:24; Jer. 51:34). In Syriac the verb has the sense of "to revel" or "to live licentiously," and it may have been chosen here to indicate the apostasy that accompanied the prosperity. The expression **became fat** has the same force, since in Deuteronomy "becoming fat" is derogatory, associated with apostasy (cf. Deut. 32:15).

G. SIN AND PUNISHMENT IN CANAAN (9:26-31)

After keeping his promise to deliver Canaan to Israel, God expected the Israelites to keep their part of the covenant, obeying his commandments. But well fed and at ease, Israel felt no need of God for sustenance and guidance. They concentrated on the luxuries he provided and ignored his demands. They rebelled and provoked him greatly, rejected his law (vs. 26), ignored his commands (vss. 29-30), resisted co-operation (vs. 29), and acted insolently (vs. 26). Despite such behavior, God was gracious, merciful (vs. 31), and patient (vs. 30). Repeatedly he warned his people (vss. 26, 29-30) to turn to him (vs. 26) and his law (vs. 29). His Spirit (vs. 30; cf. vs. 20) warned through the prophets (vs. 30), but Israel killed the prophets (vs. 26) and ignored God. To reach his people and hold them God had to use other means. Here the poet adopts the Deuteronomic view of Hebrew history as a series of cycles of oppression, salvation, freedom, and apostasy which led to still more oppression (cf. Judg. 2:11 ff.).

In times of apostasy God withdrew his protection from his disobedient people, abandoning them to hostile neighbors (vss. 27, 30) who oppressed and dominated Israel (vss. 27-28). In distress Israel cried pitifully to God (vs. 27), who heard them from heaven and each time answered by giving a savior (vs. 27) to rescue them from their tormentors and restore them in loyalty to their God. He never forsook his people (vss. 30-31) or let them lose their racial identity completely. But Israelite loyalty was short-lived. After an interval of rest and ease (vs. 28) the cycle was renewed with rebellious disobedience and the rejection of God and his law.

26. The violence of Israel's rejection of God is indicated by the statement that they **cast [God's] law behind their back.** Earlier the expression referred to the casting of God himself (cf. I Kings 14:9; Ezek. 23:35). Since **law** was something of a surrogate for God himself (cf. vs. 26 with vs. 29) the expressions may be identical. Death of the prophets indicates the kingdom period, from which some murder stories are known (I Kings 18:4, 13; 19:10, 14; Jer. 2:30, 34; 26:20 ff.). Such crimes were most grievous since the prophets were regarded as channels for the Spirit of God (vs. 30; cf. Jer. 26:15). **Testified against,** a favorite Deuteronomic expression, means "to bear witness." The figure is drawn from the courts, and the prophets and God (cf. vs. 29) are regarded as accusers of guilty people. The new **provocations,** which implies contemptuous or blasphemous acts, translates the same Hebrew word used in the molten calf episode (vs. 18).

27. The word for **enemies** differs from that in vs. 28 and the translation "into the hand of the tormentors and they tormented them, and in the time of their torment" indicates a possible play on the word "torment" (cf. vss. 20, 24; Batten, *op. cit.*, p. 369).

mercies thou gavest them saviours, who saved them out of the hand of their enemies.

28 But after they had rest, they did evil again before thee: therefore leftest thou them in the hand of their enemies, so that they had the dominion over them: yet when they returned, and cried unto thee, thou heardest *them* from heaven; and many times didst thou deliver them according to thy mercies;

29 And testifiedst against them, that thou mightest bring them again unto thy law: yet they dealt proudly, and hearkened not unto thy commandments, but sinned against thy judgments, (which if a man do, he shall live in them;) and withdrew the shoulder, and hardened their neck, and would not hear.

30 Yet many years didst thou forbear them, and testifiedst against them by thy Spirit in thy prophets: yet would they not give ear: therefore gavest thou them into the hand of the people of the lands.

31 Nevertheless for thy great mercies' sake thou didst not utterly consume them,

thy great mercies thou didst give them saviors who saved them from the hand of their enemies. **28** But after they had rest they did evil again before thee, and thou didst abandon them to the hand of their enemies, so that they had dominion over them; yet when they turned and cried to thee thou didst hear from heaven, and many times thou didst deliver them according to thy mercies. **29** And thou didst warn them in order to turn them back to thy law. Yet they acted presumptuously and did not obey thy commandments, but sinned against thy ordinances, by the observance of which a man shall live, and turned a stubborn shoulder and stiffened their neck and would not obey. **30** Many years thou didst bear with them, and didst warn them by thy Spirit through thy prophets; yet they would not give ear. Therefore thou didst give them into the hand of the peoples of the lands. **31** Nevertheless in thy great mercies thou didst not make an end of them or for-

---

From heaven: Cf. vs. 13. **Saviors who saved them** may be another word play. In Judg. 2:16 "judges" is used instead of **saviors**, but the latter is used in II Kings 13:5 as here. The **manifold mercies** of God were responsible for salvation.

28. Had rest refers to the period of peace and freedom after God's protection was restored (cf. Judg. 2:19). **Many times** indicates the frequency of the cycle of apostasy, oppression, and salvation. The difficulty of the Hebrew text, which has been called "unhebraic" (Ehrlich, *loc. cit.*) and "impossible on any just principles of Hebrew syntax" (Batten, *loc. cit.*), is glossed over by translators. Rudolph (*op. cit.*, p. 164), however, argues that the adjective **many** appears in an unusual position by analogy to the syntax of numerals (cf. Jer. 16:16; I Chr. 28:5).

29. Israel's sins are specified in vs. 29. The parenthetic comment associated with the **commandments** and **ordinances** quotes from memory Lev. 18:5 (cf. Ezek. 20:11). Probably a later addition to the text, it is best interpreted as **by the observance of which a man shall live.** On the basis of Lev. 18:5 the later rabbis taught that aside from public idolatry, murder, and adultery, all commandments are in abeyance whenever life is endangered (Hertz, *Pentateuch and Haftorahs: Leviticus,* p. 175). Israel is here portrayed again as a stubborn ox (cf. vs. 16). The imagery is apparently derived from Zech. 7:11 (Hos. 4:16). **Withdrew the shoulder** is, lit., "gave a withdrawing shoulder," describing an ox refusing to accept the yoke. For **stiffened their neck** see Exeg. on vs. 16.

30. For **many years** see Exeg. on **many times** in vs. 28. **Thou didst bear with them** should probably be emended as in the American Jewish Translation to "didst extend mercy unto them," in agreement with such passages as Pss. 36:10; 109:12; Jer. 31:3 (Gotthard, *Nehemia,* p. 44; Batten, *op. cit.,* p. 370; Bertholet, *op. cit.,* p. 75; Rudolph, *op. cit.,* p. 166). **By thy Spirit through thy prophets** seems to reflect Zech. 7:12 (cf. II Pet. 1:21). The **prophets** are the organs through which the divine agent, the Spirit, takes effect.

31. Despite Israel's guilt, God **did not make an end of them.** Because God was **gracious and merciful,** Israel still existed as a people (cf. Jer. 5:18; 30:11).

nor forsake them; for thou *art* a gracious and merciful God.

32 Now therefore, our God, the great, the mighty. and the terrible God, who keepest covenant and mercy, let not all the trouble seem little before thee, that hath come upon us, on our kings, on our princes, and on our priests, and on our prophets, and on our fathers, and on all thy people, since the time of the kings of Assyria unto this day.

33 Howbeit thou *art* just in all that is brought upon us; for thou hast done right, but we have done wickedly:

34 Neither have our kings, our princes, our priests, nor our fathers, kept thy law, nor hearkened unto thy commandments and thy testimonies, wherewith thou didst testify against them.

sake them; for thou art a gracious and merciful God.

32 "Now therefore, our God, the great and mighty and terrible God, who keepest covenant and steadfast love, let not all the hardship seem little to thee that has come upon us, upon our kings, our princes, our priests, our prophets, our fathers, and all thy people, since the time of the kings of Assyria until this day. **33** Yet thou hast been just in all that has come upon us, for thou hast dealt faithfully and we have acted wickedly; **34** our kings, our princes, our priests, and our fathers have not kept thy law or heeded thy commandments and thy warnings which thou didst give them.

H. Plea for Mercy and Salvation (9:32-37)

With **now** (vs. 32) the writer turns from remote history to more recent times, especially his own day. In the sin—repentance—redemption cycle to which the poet subscribed he finds himself and his fellows in the period of foreign domination. From his anguish the psalmist cries as his ancestors had done many times before, with the expectation that, as always before, God would pity his people and provide a savior.

32. The chain of divine epithets here is strongly reminiscent of 1:5 (cf. Deut. 10:17). **Trouble** or **hardship** means "weariness" and is used of Israel's distress in Egypt (Num. 20:14) and in the wilderness (Exod. 18:8). The word has been regarded as almost technical, like "the Exile," consisting of all the defeats, humiliations, and persecutions suffered at foreign hands with God's consent. **Us** includes Israelites in all periods who suffered hardships, down to the writer's own day. Since **all thy people** are mentioned, **our fathers** may come from vs. 34 (Rudolph, *op. cit.*, p. 168). Such **hardship** is thought to have begun in Assyrian times (cf. Ezra 9:7; Siegfried, *op. cit.*, p. 111), but there were many complaints earlier, as in the book of Judges. For **kings of Assyria** the Vulg. and Peshitta have "the king of Assyria," which may have meant Sennacherib (701 B.C.; cf. Rudolph, *op. cit.*, p. 161); but it is preferable to read **kings** with the M.T. and regard the expression in a general sense of "from the time that foreign kings began to rule over Israel" (Bertheau, *op. cit.*, p. 290).

33-35. The writer here declares that despite Israel's hardships, God has not acted unjustly. The verses have been regarded as "the expanded counterpart" of Ezra 9:9, 13, 15 (Torrey, *Ezra Studies*, p. 275, note *w*). Because the two passages are concerned with a similar situation and are both influenced by Deuteronomic reasoning, it is to be expected that the ideas will sometimes be similar, but there is scarcely enough verbal similarity to show actual dependence. For the justice of God (cf. vs. 8*b*; Ezra 9:15) see Deut. 32:4. **In all that has come** (cf. M.T. of Ezra 9:13): The preposition can be rendered "about" or "concerning." The expression **hast done right**, lit., "hast done truth" or "hast exemplified the truth" (Amer. Trans.), is rendered **hast dealt faithfully** due to the LXX, "made faith." The contrasting expression, **have done wickedly**, exhibits the usage of late Hebrew (cf. Dan. 9:5; 12:10).

34. The people listed are the former lawless generations. Prophets, mentioned in vs. 32, are here omitted because they were obedient instruments of God (cf. vss. 26, 30). For the testimony of God see vs. 30. **Commandments** and **testimonies** are grouped in Deut. 6:17; II Kings 23:3. **Testimonies** or **warnings** is a term favored in Deuteronomy (cf. 4:45; 6:17, 20; etc.).

35 For they have not served thee in their kingdom, and in thy great goodness that thou gavest them, and in the large and fat land which thou gavest before them, neither turned they from their wicked works.

36 Behold, we *are* servants this day, and *for* the land that thou gavest unto our fathers to eat the fruit thereof and the good thereof, behold, we *are* servants in it:

37 And it yieldeth much increase unto the kings whom thou hast set over us because of our sins: also they have dominion over our bodies, and over our cattle, at their pleasure, and we *are* in great distress.

35 They did not serve thee in their kingdom, and in thy great goodness which thou gavest them, and in the large and rich land which thou didst set before them; and they did not turn from their wicked works. 36 Behold, we are slaves this day; in the land that thou gavest to our fathers to enjoy its fruit and its good gifts, behold, we are slaves. 37 And its rich yield goes to the kings whom thou hast set over us because of our sins; they have power also over our bodies and over our cattle at their pleasure, and we are in great distress."

35. **They** contrasts with **we** in vs. 36. In the contrast between the failure of the ancestors to serve God (vs. 35) and the consequent servitude to foreigners (vs. 36) the writer may be playing on the word "service" (cf. vss. 20, 23-24; cf. Ehrlich, *loc. cit.*; Rudolph, *op. cit.*, p. 162). **Their kingdom** refers to the independent pre-exilic Hebrew monarchy. "Thy kingdom," found in two Hebrew MSS, the LXX, and Peshitta versions, is assimilated to **thy great goodness**, which follows. **Great goodness** is the abundance of material blessings (cf. Jer. 31:12, 14). The preposition **in** is textually well attested but is awkward and meaningless as usually translated. It is better read "in exchange for" (Kautzsch, *Gesenius' Hebrew Grammar*, sec. 119*p*), since the preposition is elsewhere so used with the verb "serve" (cf. Gen. 29:18, 20; Hos. 12:12). For **gavest before them** or **set before them** it is preferable to read with the Peshitta and Arabic versions "gave to them" (Gotthard, *loc. cit.*).

36-37. The play on the verb "serve" in **we are servants** (cf. Ezra 9:9) is lost by rendering the noun as **slaves**. The masters are the **kings** of vs. 37. Because the Persian period was regarded as a relief from Babylonian bondage (cf. Ezra 1:3), it has been thought that the miseries of the Greek period are reflected here (cf. Batten, *op. cit.*, p. 371). But though life was not too severe under Persia, there was always a desire for independence (cf. Hag. 2:6-8; Zech. 3:8-10; 6:10-12). The overlords were presumably Persian kings whom God **set over** the Jews (Ezra 5:12) because of their sins.

Foreign domination rankled, but the primary and immediate concern of the author was the economic loss in Palestine as goods were passed over to foreign lords. **Eat the fruit thereof** (cf. vs. 25) and **enjoy . . . its good** suggest Jer. 2:7 (cf. Isa. 1:19). The Persian kings, who continued the Assyro-Babylonian assessments of tribute in the provinces (Esth. 10:1), are accused of draining off the best produce of the land, and their excessive demands often created economic disaster (cf. 5:2-4).

They have power also over our bodies refers to forced labor, either as taskwork (cf. Ezra 4:13) or military conscription (A. H. Sayce, *An Introduction to the Books of Ezra, Nehemiah, and Esther* [3rd ed.; London: Religious Tract Society, 1889], p. 60; Bertholet, *loc. cit.*; Bertheau, *op. cit.*, p. 291). **Cattle** were taken for draft purposes in war and, since the word is also used for riding animals (cf. 2:12, 14), perhaps also for the cavalry.

The psalm has often been regarded as fragmentary, mangled in its conclusion. Some expect a supplication for the restoration of Israel (Guthe and Batten, *Ezra and Nehemiah*, p. 51; Kosters, *Wiederherstellung Israels*, p. 67; Siegfried, *op. cit.*, p. 112) and Rudolph (*loc. cit.*) expects some promise to rectify the former neglect of the law, but he explains its lack by the hypothesis that ch. 10 was considered to satisfy such a need. However, the poem seems complete, ending forcibly (cf. Ezra 9:15) with the anguished cry, **we are in great distress,** an appeal for the pity of the merciful God (vs. 32) who had proved himself ever ready to help his people who called on him in their distress (cf. vs. 27). Anything more would weaken the effectiveness of the conclusion.

38 And because of all this we make a sure *covenant*, and write *it*; and our princes, Levites, *and* priests, seal *unto it*.

38ᵘ Because of all this we make a firm covenant and write it, and our princes, our Levites, and our priests set their seal to it.

ᵘ Ch 10. 1 in Heb

XI. PLEDGE OF REFORM (9:38–10:39)

It has been conjectured that this section is the report of an agreement made before Cyrus' edict in 538 B.C. between Palestinian Jews who survived the captivity of 586 B.C. and fellow Israelites who remained behind after the disaster of 722 B.C. It is suggested that the religious agreement was effected to preserve the national Israelite identity in the time of crisis (Adam C. Welch, "The Share of N. Israel in the Restoration of the Temple Worship," *Zeitschrift für die alttestamentliche Wissenschaft*, XLVIII [1930], 179-87). This hypothesis is not demonstrable. The late religious concepts reflected in the chapter make it extremely improbable. Many regard it rather as part of the Ezra story in some way associated with the reading of the law (ch. 8) and the psalm in ch. 9. As such ch. 10 is usually regarded as the Chronicler's work, an attempt to show that although Ezra's efforts may have failed (cf. Rudolph, *op. cit.*, p. 173), his work with the law had a successful conclusion (Torrey, *Composition*, p. 34; *Ezra Studies*, p. 246).

More probably the chapter has nothing to do with the Ezra narrative (Winckler, *Altorientalische Forschungen*, Reihe 2, Bd. III, 472; cf. Bertholet, *op. cit.*, pp. 75-76; Rudolph, *loc. cit.*), but its principal section (9:38; 10:28-39) shows a definite relationship with ch. 13. Stylistic relationships with ch. 13, which have been posited (Bertholet, *op. cit.*, p. 76), are held not demonstrable (cf. Hölscher, *Esra und Nehemia*, pp. 545-46; Rudolph, *loc. cit.*; Torrey, *Ezra Studies*, p. 246; see Exeg. on 9:5b-37). Nevertheless, there is such undeniable agreement in subject matter between the two passages that it seems likely that apart from the list of names (vss. 1-27), ch. 10 is best explained as a summary of the items included in the oath which Nehemiah required during his second administration (cf. 13:25). As such the material is now dislocated and belongs after ch. 13 (cf. Winckler, *op. cit.*, Reihe 2, Bd. III, p. 483; Batten, *op. cit.*, p. 373; Rudolph, *loc. cit.*).

Such unity as ch. 10 now has is due to the editor who placed it here as a conclusion to the Ezra story, for the chapter contains diverse elements drawn from sources having nothing to do with Ezra. The long list of names (vss. 1-27) intrudes into the material (9:38; 10:28-39) which outlines the principal laws to which the pledge was given. If the Chronicler were the author and the list of names referred to those approving Ezra's law, the name of Ezra rather than Nehemiah would have headed the list (cf. Rudolph, *loc. cit.*). But the rest of ch. 10 is also composite. Two hands are "fairly clearly marked," with vss. 33, 37b-39a as a later addition (Browne, vss. 33, 37-39a; cf. his *Early Judaism*, p. 192; Rudolph, *op. cit.*, p. 178). Many have regarded the Chronicler as the author of the chapter (cf. Torrey, *Composition*, pp. 21, 27-28), but the view is by no means unanimous. Though the Chronicler might be regarded as editor, it has been argued that he was using a genuine source, apparently drawn from the temple archives (Rudolph, *op. cit.*, pp. 173-74; Otto Eissfeldt, *Einleitung in das alte Testament* [Tübingen: J. C. B. Mohr, 1934], p. 592). More extreme is the view that the author was a layman of the time of Nehemiah's second administration, "one of the participants [in] the measures taken by the people to perpetuate Nehemiah's reforms" (Batten, *op. cit.*, pp. 372-73).

A. INTRODUCTION (9:38=Hebrew 10:1)

The LXX, Peshitta, and Vulg. all treat 9:38 as the conclusion of ch. 9, but the M.T. regards it as the beginning of ch. 10. It is actually an editorial insert to connect the two chapters. As a conclusion to ch. 9 it is a weak anticlimax, destroying the effectiveness of 9:37, but its substance is now necessary as background for 10:1. Some think 9:38 too abrupt for transition to 10:1, and insist that a more full account of the framing of the document mentioned in 10:1 has been lost (Kosters, *op. cit.*, p. 65; Meyer, *Entstehung des Judenthums*, p. 135; Siegfried, *loc. cit.*). Others regard that hypothesis as unnecessary,

10 Now those that sealed *were*, Nehemiah, the Tirshatha, the son of Hachaliah, and Zidkijah,

10[v] Those who set their seal are Nehemi′ah the governor, the son of Hacaliah,

[v] Ch 10. 2 in Heb

and Torrey (*Ezra Studies*, pp. 275-76, note *w*), who regards the Chronicler as author, considers the transition as "smoothness itself" when compared with the Chronicler's links found elsewhere (e.g., 12:27; I Chr. 28:19; Ezra 2:68; 7:27).

9:38. Since ch. 9 offers no good basis for a covenant, the antecedent of the enigmatic **because of all this** is ambiguous. If the Hebrew preposition "in" here signifies **because,** the antecedent is the reading of the law and its consequences (Ezra 9 ff.), of which Neh. 9 is but a minor, intrusive element (cf. *ibid.*, p. 276 and note *x*; Bertholet, *op. cit.*, p. 75). But the preposition can mean "in spite of" (cf. Isa. 5:25; 9:12, 17, 21; 10:4; Ps. 78:32), thus signifying "despite all this distressing situation" (i.e., 9:35-37), which is reflected in the rendering "And yet for all this" (ASV and American Jewish Translation; cf. Ehrlich, *Randglossen*, VII, 207). The latter rendition puts the Jews in the fine light of taking the initiative in the reconciliation with God.

Instead of the word for **covenant** (9:8; Ezra 10:3), the M.T. here uses one which is related to the word "firm" and is found elsewhere only in 11:23. The noun, here rendered "faith" by the LXX, perhaps means "a firm, trustworthy agreement," and the entire expression is a late variation of the earlier "cut a covenant" (Ludwig Köhler, ed., *Lexicon in Veteris Testamenti Libros* [Leiden: E. J. Brill, 1950], p. 62). Nothing in the M.T. justifies **seal** or **set their seal to it,** which is added for smooth reading. The word used, "the one sealed," means a "sealed document." Seals were used in antiquity to ensure privacy and protect business documents and as substitutes for signatures, but neither use seems pertinent here. It was not necessary to conceal or protect the public document and it is probable that, as in the Jewish papyri of the period, no seals accompanied the Jewish signatures. The expression "sealed document" which may once have signified a business document with appended witnesses' names, sealed externally for security (cf. Jer. 32:11, 14), seems later to mean simply a signed document, a development indicated by later Jewish use of *ḥittûm* for "signature" and Aramaic *ḥathôm* for "signer" or "witness" (Jastrow, *Dictionary of Targumim, s.v.* חיתום and חתומא). The document is not given verbatim but in an abstracted form. "For what purpose the record was made we are not informed" (Batten, *op. cit.*, p. 374), but it is obvious from ch. 13 that the document was a pledge to support some laws that needed special confirmation during or after Nehemiah's second administration.

B. SIGNERS OF THE DOCUMENT (10:1-27=Hebrew 10:2-28)

The hand of the Chronicler is seen in the list because the eighty-four signatures form a multiple of twelve, a device which has been regarded as favored by the Chronicler (Torrey, *Ezra Studies*, p. 284). But it is probable that the number is not significant since some names seem to have been lost from the list (cf. vss. 14-27; Rudolph, *op. cit.*, p. 174).

In 9:38 the listing was said to be "princes," "Levites," and "priests," but the actual list (10:1-27), from a different source, names two secular leaders followed by the priests, Levites, and princes (cf. Ezra 8:1 ff.; 10:18 ff.). **Levites** are before the priests in II Chr. 19:8; 30:21, but the order princes, Levites, and priests is unique.

10:1-39. The Law and the Testimony.—The declaration thus solemnly signed and sealed by the leaders of the people, beginning with Nehemiah as governor, priests, Levites, and princes pledges them by **a curse and an oath** (vs. 29) to renounce mixed marriages, not to buy or sell on the sabbath, and to contribute regularly to the support of the temple ritual (vs. 39*b*). Ceremonial religion is henceforth to have full trial and complete obedience, so far as documents and pledges can guarantee them on behalf of frail and forgetful human nature.

2 Seraiah, Azariah, Jeremiah,
3 Pashur, Amariah, Malchijah,
4 Hattush, Shebaniah, Malluch,
5 Harim, Meremoth, Obadiah,
6 Daniel, Ginnethon, Baruch,
7 Meshullam, Abijah, Mijamin,
8 Maaziah, Bilgai, Shemaiah: these *were*
the priests.

li'ah, Zedeki'ah, 2 Serai'ah, Azari'ah, Jeremiah, 3 Pashhur, Amari'ah, Malchi'jah, 4 Hattush, Shebani'ah, Malluch, 5 Harim, Mer'emoth, Obadi'ah, 6 Daniel, Gin'nethon, Baruch, 7 Meshul'lam, Abi'jah, Mi'jamin, 8 Ma-azi'ah, Bil'gai, Shemai'ah; these

---

1. Civil Authorities (10:1)

10:1. The introductory phrase in the M.T., "and over those being sealed," is difficult. "Seal unto it" or "at the sealing" (cf. Batten, *loc. cit.*) cannot derive from the M.T., nor can the passive M.T. produce **those that sealed** or **those who set their seal.** The plural form of the M.T. has been emended to "the sealed document" (Siegfried, *loc. cit.*) as parallel to 9:38, but that is regarded as "a violent measure" (Rudolph, *op. cit.*, p. 172). The plural noun clearly refers to those named in the list, as both the LXX and Vulg. show. Some propose to emend the present M.T., חתומים, to חותמים, "the ones sealing" (Torrey, *Ezra Studies,* p. 282), but it is possible simply to revocalize the present C.T., החתומים, to read *haḥathômîm,* "the signers," or *haḥittûmîm,* "the signatures" (cf. 9:38 above). The Hebrew preposition before "the signers," already present in the LXX and the M.T. due to the influence of 9:38, is difficult. It must either be omitted, as in the Vulg., or be displaced by "these" (אלה), as in the Peshitta and Arabic versions.

Hecaliah and **Zedekiah** are the secular authorities in Judea (cf. 7:7; Ezra 2:2). **Nehemiah** is identified as the **governor** by his father's name, **Hacaliah** (cf. 1:1), and by the title **Tirshatha** (cf. 7:65, 70; Ezra 2:63). The title is inserted awkwardly before the father's name. The presence of Nehemiah rather than Ezra is significant (cf. above). Torrey (*Ezra Studies,* p. 284) claims that Ezra "was regarded as above the necessity of taking this oath, which had in it something of the nature of a confession of evil-doing (cf. 9:1 ff., 10:29 f. . . .)," but it would be natural for Nehemiah, as governor and viceroy, to head the list.

The ancestry and office of **Zedekiah** are unknown, but his presence in the list shows that he was a prominent person. He has been regarded as possibly an official secretary (Rudolph, *op. cit.,* p. 174), and it is proposed to identify him with the Zadok of 13:13, whose name abbreviates **Zedekiah,** who is conjectured to be the one who drew up the document (Rawlinson, *Ezra and Nehemiah,* p. 48). Others, with greater likelihood, regard **Zedekiah** as a local leader, perhaps chief of a council of elders (Meyer, *op. cit.,* p. 136; Siegfried, *loc. cit.;* cf. 11:8), in contrast to Nehemiah the viceroy. It is unlikely that he is an unhistorical creation of the Chronicler (cf. Torrey, *Ezra Studies,* p. 283), for a forger would have used a better-known name (cf. Rudolph, *loc. cit.*).

2. Priests (10:2-8=Hebrew 10:3-9)

2-8. The list of priests is closely related to that in 12:1-6 of the time of Zerubbabel, and that in 12:10-21 from the time of the father of the high priest Eliashib. Comparison of the lists, which are almost identical in order, indicates that what seem unique names in each list are usually only abbreviations or scribal errors (see Exeg. on 12:1-6, 10-21).

The names are not those of individual contemporaries of Nehemiah but of eponymous ancestors (cf. 12:12-18), and they apparently are to be understood as indicating individuals of the later day, the actual signers, who were representative of the earlier families. From the list it has been concluded "that the priestly families in Palestine had been newly arranged and that now there was actually a striving for the order in I Chr. 24, wherein all are traced to Aaron and his sons" (Kittel, *Geschichte des Volkes Israel,* III, 406; cf. Rudolph, *op. cit.,* p. 175).

9 And the Levites: both Jeshua the son of Azaniah, Binnui of the sons of Henadad, Kadmiel;

10 And their brethren, Shebaniah, Hodijah, Kelita, Pelaiah, Hanan,

11 Micha, Rehob, Hashabiah,

12 Zaccur, Sherebiah, Shebaniah,

13 Hodijah, Bani, Beninu.

14 The chief of the people; Parosh, Pahath-moab, Elam, Zatthu, Bani,

15 Bunni, Azgad, Bebai,

16 Adonijah, Bigvai, Adin,

17 Ater, Hizkijah, Azzur,

18 Hodijah, Hashum, Bezai,

19 Hariph, Anathoth, Nebai,

are the priests. 9 And the Levites: Jeshua the son of Azani'ah, Bin'nui of the sons of Hen'adad, Kad'mi-el; 10 and their brethren, Shebani'ah, Hodi'ah, Keli'ta, Pelai'ah, Hanan, 11 Mica, Rehob, Hashabi'ah, 12 Zaccur, Sherebi'ah, Shebani'ah, 13 Hodi'ah, Bani, Beni'nu. 14 The chiefs of the people: Parosh, Pa'hath-mo'ab, Elam, Zattu, Bani, 15 Bunni, Azgad, Be'bai, 16 Adoni'jah, Big'vai, Adin, 17 Ater, Hezeki'ah, Azzur, 18 Hodi'ah, Hashum, Be'zai, 19 Hariph, An'-

3. Levites (10:9-13)

9-13. Three prominent Levites are mentioned, followed by a larger group of **their brethren.** However remote, there was a blood tie between all Levites, but it is difficult to determine here whether **brethren** means blood ties or priestly office (cf. Batten, *op. cit.,* p. 375). **Jeshua** is identified as **the son of Azaniah** (vs. 9), presumably to differentiate him from Jeshua the contemporary of Zerubbabel. The versions, Neh. 12:8, and some twenty-nine Hebrew MSS show that the conjunction before **Jeshua** in the M.T. should be elided. Again there is confusion here between **Binnui** (3:24; Ezra 8:33) and Bani (8:7; 9:4, 5), but it is preferable to read **Binnui** (cf. 12:8). For **sons of Henadad** (3:18, 24; Ezra 3:9) and for **Kadmiel** see Ezra 2:40; 3:9; etc.

Most of the names are found elsewhere in the lists of Levites (8:7; 9:4-5; Ezra 8:18-19, 33). Duplications cause some uncertainty. Repetition of **Shebaniah** and **Hodiah** (vs. 10; cf. vss. 12-13) in the same order looks like a doublet, but **Shebaniah** (vss. 10, 12) might be an error for Shechaniah in either passage and the latter is supported by some Hebrew MSS and the Peshitta (cf. 9:5). **Shebaniah** has better textual support and is associated with Levites while, except in twenty Hebrew MSS in 9:4, Shechaniah has no Levitical connections. **Beninu** (vs. 13) has been called "unintelligible" (Rudolph, *op. cit.,* p. 172) and is found nowhere else in Hebrew. The proposal to read "Chenani" (cf. 9:4) instead (*ibid.*) is unsupported by MSS or versions, and it is preferable to read "Binnui" (3:24; 12:8; Ezra 8:33). **Micha** (vs. 11), which abbreviates Michael ("Who Is Like God") or Michaiah ("Who Is Like the Lord"), is the name of a Levite in 11:17. **Rehob** (vs. 11) is not a Levite elsewhere.

As with the priests, ancestral rather than personal names are listed, doubtless indicating either families or family representatives. Those listed are apparently not only descendants of exiles (cf. Ezra 2:40) but also of those who had remained in the land. It is suggested that the Levites in postexilic times were largely not organized into families. Hence some personal names should be expected in the list, and **Kelita** (vs. 10; Ezra 10:23) has been proposed as such a name (Meyer, *op. cit.,* p. 179; Rudolph, *op. cit.,* p. 175).

4. Laymen (10:14-27)

14-27. The label **chiefs of the people** is unusual since "the chief of the fathers" is preferred in Ezra-Nehemiah (Ezra 1:5; 4:2, 3; 8:1; 10:16; Neh. 7:70; 8:13; 12:12, 22-23). Part of the list (vss. 14-19) shows relationship to the great list in Ezra 2 and Neh. 7 but it is apparently not directly dependent upon either list. It is perhaps derived from a prototype of the great list. Like Ezra 2:30, the list includes **Magpiash** (vs. 20), which Neh. 7 omits, and like Neh. 7:24 and I Esdras 5:16, it includes the **Hariph** (vs. 19) lacking in Ezra 2. The order **Hashum, Bezai** (vs. 18) is as in 7:22-23 in contrast to

20 Magpiash, Meshullam, Hezir,
21 Meshezabeel, Zadok, Jaddua,
22 Pelatiah, Hanan, Anaiah,
23 Hoshea, Hananiah, Hashub,
24 Hallohesh, Pileha, Shobek,
25 Rehum, Hashabnah, Maaseiah,
26 And Ahijah, Hanan, Anan,
27 Malluch, Harim, Baanah.

28 ¶ And the rest of the people, the priests, the Levites, the porters, the singers, the Nethinim, and all they that had separated themselves from the people of the lands unto the law of God, their wives, their sons, and their daughters, every one having knowledge, and having understanding;

athoth, Ne'bai, 20 Mag'piash, Meshul'lam, Hezir, 21 Meshez'abel, Zadok, Jud'du-a, 22 Pelati'ah, Hanan, Anai'ah, 23 Hoshe'a, Hanani'ah, Hasshub, 24 Hallo'hesh, Pi'lha, Shobek, 25 Rehum, Hashab'nah, Ma-asei'ah, 26 Ahi'ah, Hanan, Anan, 27 Malluch, Ha-rim, Ba'anah.

28 The rest of the people, the priests, the Levites, the gatekeepers, the singers, the temple servants, and all who have separated themselves from the peoples of the lands to the law of God, their wives, their sons, their daughters, all who have knowl-

---

Ezra 2:17-19. In several respects it differs from either of the other lists: both **Bani** and **Bunni** are found in vss. 14-15, and in vss. 17-18 are included **Azzur** and **Hodiah**, missing from the other lists, but **Azzur** is found in I Esdras 5:15; and in vs. 15 the order **Assad, Bebai** is opposite to that in 7:16-17; Ezra 2:11-12.

Furthermore, there is here in ch. 10 no reference to the families of Shephatiah, Arah, and Zaccai (Ezra 2:4-5, 9). It is suggested that the editor omitted them because they were not in Ezra 10:25 ff. (Hölscher, *Esra und Nehemia*, p. 545), but others then should also be missing. It is unlikely that the families refused to subscribe to the pledge (Bertheau, *Esra, Nechemia und Ester*, p. 300), nor is it likely that they died out after the time of Zerubbabel. The names have probably been accidentally lost from the list (Meyer, *op. cit.*, p. 154) in which case the original number of names would be larger than eighty-four and the thesis that used the multiple of twelve as a clue to the Chronicler's authorship would fail (cf. Exeg. on vs. 1).

Almost all the place names of the great list (7:25 ff.; Ezra 2:20 ff.) are omitted, but the inclusion of **Anathoth** (vs. 19) indicates that the names were available (cf. 7:27; Ezra 2:23). **Anathoth** has been regarded as a slip by the "forger" of the document (Hölscher, *loc. cit.*), but it is here a personal name (cf. I Chr. 7:8), perhaps indicating that people of **Anathoth** who established a new family elsewhere bore the name of their former home (Meyer, *op. cit.*, p. 156; Rudolph, *loc. cit.*).

Beginning with **Meshullam** (vs. 20) the great "standard" list is supplemented by a series of personal names (vss. 20-27) which have been regarded as those of the political leaders of the places mentioned in the great list (Ezra 2:20 ff.; Bertheau, *loc. cit.*; Meyer, *loc. cit.*) or the names of the builders in ch. 3 (Hölscher, *loc. cit*). Rudolph (*loc. cit.*) has shown that the names here do not closely follow the order of names in ch. 3, as Hölscher has charged. Even though some of the names might be identical with those in ch. 3, it is clear that the standard list is augmented by new families, some of which may have split off from the older houses.

C. ABSTRACT OF SIGNED DOCUMENT (10:28-39=Hebrew 10:29-40)

1. MIXED MARRIAGES (10:28-30)

28. Since vss. 1-27 are interpolated, vs. 28 originally followed 9:38. In the original document, then, the signers were not named and the list was supplied by the editor who thought it relevant. **The rest of the people** refers to those who did not sign the document. Only this is original and the remainder of the verse is an elaboration by the Chronicler, showing his special interest in cult personnel (*ibid.*, p. 174). It is claimed that "this verse, which betrays the Chronicler's authorship with almost every phrase, fairly represents the whole chapter. From this point on to the end, we can recognize everywhere his peculiar style and diction, and his own special hobbies" (Torrey, *Ezra Studies*, p. 276,

29 They clave to their brethren, their nobles, and entered into a curse, and into an oath, to walk in God's law, which was given by Moses the servant of God, and to observe and do all the commandments of the LORD our Lord, and his judgments and his statutes;

edge and understanding, 29 join with their brethren, their nobles, and enter into a curse and an oath to walk in God's law which was given by Moses the servant of God, and to observe and do all the commandments of the LORD our Lord and his

---

note *c*). Although most scholars see frequent evidence of the Chronicler's hand here, it is by no means certain that he is the author. The document may have been an authentic source which he adapted to his purpose (cf. Rudolph, *op. cit.,* p. 173).

The priests, the Levites, etc., are parallel to **the rest of the people,** but the Chronicler is not responsible for all the classes listed. Since the **gatekeepers, singers,** and **Nethinim** are here, as in Ezra 2:41 ff., listed separately, while the Chronicler includes them all in the one category of Levites (cf. I Chr. 15:22-23; 23:3 ff.), the names following **the Levites** must be a post-Chronicler addition. Perhaps a trace of the junction is to be seen in the "and" before the **gatekeepers** in some Hebrew MSS. For **separated themselves** see Ezra 6:21; for **peoples of the lands** see Ezra 3:3.

As in 8:2-3, women and children were involved in the pledge. Younger children are excluded by the phrase **all who have knowledge and understanding** (cf. 8:2). The conjunction linking **knowledge and understanding** is found in the LXX and Peshitta but not in the M.T. The Vulg. has simply "all that could understand," and some have regarded the word **understanding** as a gloss to **having knowledge** (Ehrlich, *Randglossen,* VII, 207; Paul Haupt in Guthe and Batten, *Ezra and Nehemiah,* p. 70), but **and** could be rendered "namely," as an explicative (cf. 9:16). Rudolph, rejecting all emendation, reads the M.T. as "everyone who understands to have insight," comparing "knowing how to play" in I Sam. 16:16 (*op. cit.,* p. 174; cf. König, *Historisch-comparative Syntax,* sec. 410*e*; but cf. Kautzsch, *Gesenius' Hebrew Grammar,* sec. 120*b*).

29. For **their nobles,** in apposition to **their brethren** (cf. 3:5), the noun used is that found in 3:5 rather than that favored by Nehemiah (cf. 2:16; 4:14; 5:7; 6:17; 7:5), and is therefore regarded as originating from another source, conjectured to be the temple archives (Rudolph, *op. cit.,* p. 173). **Entered into a curse** (cf. Ezek. 17:13): accepted the threat of dire consequences if a person proved unfaithful to his oath. Such penalties were normally written out (cf. Deut. 29:20-21) and may originally have been specified in the document. The word used for **curse** (*'ālāh*) had the implication of a poisonous, disintegrating effect (cf. Pedersen, *Israel, Its Life and Culture I-II,* p. 437). The **oath** was a promise (cf. Lev. 5:4) or a vow (cf. Num. 30:3, 11, 14; Josh. 9:20). **To walk in God's law** is reminiscent of the Deuteronomic "to walk in his ways" (cf. Deut. 8:6; 11:22; 26:17; 30:16; etc.). Deuteronomic phraseology is also seen in **to observe and do all the commandments** (Deut. 28:15; cf. Deut. 15:5; etc.) and in **the LORD our Lord** (Deut. 1:6, 19, 20, 25; etc., lit., "Yahweh, our Lord"; cf. Ezra 1:1). **Which was given by Moses** means "which the Lord had commanded by Moses" (cf. 8:14). For **servant of God** see 1:8; 9:14.

The actual text of the document (cf. 9:38) is gone. What remains are "the specific forms of an agreement," as though the provisions of the document were abstracted. Each of the items of agreement is introduced by a conjunction that is usually rendered **and,** but, because it is explanatory (cf. Ezra 8:18), is better translated "to wit" (Torrey, *Ezra Studies,* p. 276). The editor doubtless thought of the law involved as that brought by Ezra, but since the material here is related to events at the time of Nehemiah's second administration (cf. 13:10), the identification of the law rests on the chronological sequence of Ezra and Nehemiah (cf. Ezra 7:7-8). It is said of this chapter (see above, Exeg. on 9:38–10:39), "Two hands are fairly clearly marked, verses 34, 38-40*a* (E. V. 33, 37-39*a*) being additions. The later hand is undoubtedly the Chronicler. The earlier hand might quite well be the actual covenant." (Browne, *Early Judaism,* p. 192.) The

30 And that we would not give our daughters unto the people of the land, nor take their daughters for our sons:

31 And *if* the people of the land bring ware or any victuals on the sabbath day to sell, *that* we would not buy it of them on the sabbath, or on the holy day: and *that* we would leave the seventh year, and the exaction of every debt.

32 Also we made ordinances for us, to charge ourselves yearly with the third part

ordinances and his statutes. 30 We will not give our daughters to the peoples of the land or take their daughters for our sons;

31 and if the peoples of the land bring in wares or any grain on the sabbath day to sell, we will not buy from them on the sabbath or on a holy day; and we will forego the crops of the seventh year and the exaction of every debt.

32 We also lay upon ourselves the obli-

---

earlier stratum reflects Deuteronomic legislation, while the later shows the ideas and practices of the late priestly laws.

30. Foreign marriages were forbidden by the reform of Nehemiah (13:23-27) as well as that of Ezra (9:1–10:44). These contacts violated early Hebrew legislation (Exod. 34:16; Deut. 7:3). **Peoples of the land** (cf. Ezra 9:2, 11) included those of Ashdod, Ammon, and Moab.

2. Sabbath Observance (10:31)

31. Another area of Nehemiah's reforms was **sabbath** observance (13:15 ff.). Foreigners brought their wares to the city on the sabbath (13:16), tempting the Jews to trade and violate the day (13:15, 17). The Jews here pledge to ignore the tradesmen and keep the sabbath and the **holy day.** The latter may mean fast days (cf. Exod. 12:16; Num. 28:18, 26; 29:1, 7, 12, 35) as well as the new moon festivals which were usually linked with the sabbath (Amos 8:5; II Kings 4:23). **Wares** is explained by the words following, since the conjunction should be rendered not **or** but "especially" or "namely" (cf. Ezra 6:8). **Grain** (*shébher*) means threshed grain rather than **victuals** (cf. Gen. 42:1-2, 19, 26; Amos 8:5).

The sabbatical year (cf. 5:1) is naturally thought of in connection with the **sabbath.** The pledge **we would leave the seventh year** is exceedingly compressed and doubtless textually corrupt. Collocation of **leave** and **seventh year** clearly indicates that the subject is the law requiring the farmer to leave his field fallow during the **seventh** [sabbatical] **year** (Exod. 23:11; cf. Lev. 25:2-7). The word *tebhû'ath*, "product" (cf. Exod. 23:10; Lev. 25:3), which has been omitted accidentally, should be restored to read **the crops of the seventh year** (cf. Torrey, *Ezra Studies*, p. 276, note *d*). Frequently a shortage of grain is reported as due to the keeping of the law of the sabbatical year (cf. I Macc. 6:49, 53; Josephus *Antiquities* XIII. 8. 1; XIV. 16. 2), and the statement of Tacitus (*History* V. 4) and Caesar's remission of tribute during a sabbatical year both attest the observance of the law (Josephus *Antiquities* XIV. 10. 6).

The abrupt phrase **the exaction of every debt** is an afterthought appended to the pledge of sabbatical year observance. It pledges to forego the collection of debts during the sabbatical year (cf. 5:1; Deut. 15:1-4). Connection here with 5:7, 10 is apparent in the use for **exaction** of a Hebrew word meaning "a loan made on pledge" in 5:7, 10. The M.T. has "the loan of every hand." A creditor in Deut. 15:2 is called "the lord of the loan of his hand," which means "'the loan which his own hand has given,' and which, therefore, it has a right to call in" (S. R. Driver, *A Critical and Exegetical Commentary on Deuteronomy* [New York: Charles Scribner's Sons, 1895; "International Critical Commentary"], p. 175). Thus here "hand" means that hand which holds a document proving debt.

3. Temple Tax (10:32-33)

32-33. The temple tax pledge is consonant with Nehemiah's great concern during his second administration regarding the support of the temple (cf. 13:10-14). In postexilic

of a shekel for the service of the house of our God;

33 For the showbread, and for the continual meat offering, and for the continual burnt offering, of the sabbaths, of the new moons, for the set feasts, and for the holy

gation to charge ourselves yearly with the third part of a shekel for the service of the house of our God: 33 for the showbread, the continual cereal offering, the continual burnt offering, the sabbaths, the new moons,

---

times, without the financial support of the monarchy, the temple was dependent directly upon the community. This does not contradict Ezra 6:4; 7:20 ff., which point to Persian aid, for that royal support was in the form of limited amounts of material which ultimately had to be replenished (cf. Bertheau, *op. cit.*, pp. 304-5; Rudolph, *op. cit.*, p. 178).

Ezekiel planned temple dues payable to the prince who would then be responsible for the expenses of public worship (Ezek. 45:13 ff.), but this was never put into effect. It was apparently Nehemiah in his concern for temple support who established an assessment of one-third shekel payable yearly as a head tax for this purpose. Later the tax is one-half shekel yearly (cf. Matt. 17:24, 27), and the Chronicler assumed that this amount was first fixed by Moses (II Chr. 24:6, 9), since the priests believed that in Moses' day a special assessment of one-half shekel was imposed on all males twenty years old and above for the work of the tabernacle (cf. Exod. 30:11 ff.; 38:25 ff.).

The discrepancy between the one-third shekel (vs. 32) and the half shekel (Exod. 30:11-12) has been perplexing. It is possible that an earlier tax was raised when it was found insufficient, but it is more probable that the tax was constant and the variant figures are based on different standards of weight. Persian coinage consisted of one-third, one-fourth, one-sixth, and one-twelfth shekels (cf. Olmstead, *History of the Persian Empire,* p. 188), and the one-third shekel was introduced into Palestine during the Persian period (cf. Immanuel Benzinger, *Hebräische Archäologie* [Leipzig: J. C. B. Mohr, 1894], pp. 193-94). Based on the Babylonian standard, this Persian system was current as far as Persian Lydia in the west. One-third shekel of that standard weighed about 112.2 grams troy weight. The later half shekel was apparently based on the standard of the Phoenician tradesmen, which became that used for coinage in Persian Syria and presumably for early Hebrew coins (cf. G. F. Hill, "Shekel," in T. K. Cheyne and J. Sutherland Black, eds., *Encyclopaedia Biblica* [New York: The Macmillan Co., 1903], Vol. IV, col. 4446). Such a Phoenician standard half shekel also weighed about 112.2 grams troy weight and was thus the equivalent of the earlier one-third shekel. Thus vs. 32 indicates a source earlier than the Chronicler and at variance with the practice of his day.

Ordinances (cf. Ezra 7:10) is preferable to **obligation** or "charge" since the noun is plural. The word is usually rendered "commandments," referring to God's commands found in a code of law. Assessment is specified as **for the service** of the temple, reflecting the Chronicler's manner of indicating the cult (cf. Ezra 8:20).

33. The appended list (vs. 33) of items covered by the temple tax is a later addition, possibly by the Chronicler. It reflects conformity to the later priestly legislation rather than to Deuteronomy. **Showbread** is mentioned early (I Sam. 21:6; I Kings 7:48) as sacred bread, a dozen unleavened cakes each of one-fifth ephah of fine flour, placed in two piles on a table in the shrine or temple. Originally, as in Babylonia (Heinrich Zimmern, *Beiträge zur Kenntniss der babylonischen Religion* [Leipzig: J. C. Hinrichs, 1901], pp. 94-95), it was intended as food for the God. After a week the cakes were replaced and the old ones eaten by the priests within the sanctuary (cf. Exod. 25:23 ff.; Lev. 24:5-9). The Chronicler calls it "the bread of piling" (I Chr. 28:16) or "bread of arrangement" (I Chr. 9:32; 23:29; etc.), and **showbread** is used only in the Priestly Code (Exod. 25:23 ff.; 35:13; 39:36; Lev. 24:5 ff.).

For the **continual** offerings see Ezra 3:2-5; 7:17. **Sabbath** offerings were supplementary sacrifices made on the sabbath (cf. Num. 28:9-10). For **new moons** and **set**

things, and for the sin offerings to make an atonement for Israel, and *for* all the work of the house of our God.

34 And we cast the lots among the priests, the Levites, and the people, for the wood offering, to bring *it* into the house of our God, after the houses of our fathers, at

the appointed feasts, the holy things, and the sin offerings to make atonement for Israel, and for all the work of the house of our God. 34 We have likewise cast lots, the priests, the Levites, and the people, for the wood offering, to bring it into the house of

---

feasts see Ezra 3:5. **Holy things** must be public sacrifices purchased with temple funds. They are usually regarded as those mentioned in II Chr. 29:33; 35:13. The **sin offering** (cf. Ezra 8:35) is not prominent in legislation until the time of Ezekiel (40:39; 42:13; 43:9-25; etc.) and the Priestly Code (Lev. 4:1 ff.). For **atonement** see 8:18 (cf. I Chr. 6:49; II Chr. 29:24; Lev. 4:13-21; 16:21-28). Because another Hebrew word is used here for **work,** not that in vs. 32, which means cultic functions, it is argued that **all the work** means not all other unspecified cultic functions but work of construction and repair in the temple (cf. II Kings 12:5 ff.; 22:3 ff.; Bertholet, *Esra und Nehemia,* p. 79; Rudolph, *op. cit.,* p. 179).

4. Wood Offering (10:34)

34. The **wood offering** was another item with which Nehemiah had been concerned (13:31). Since a fire had to burn perpetually on the great altar (Lev. 6:12; cf. Josephus *Jewish War* II. 17. 6), an adequate supply of trees and brush for fires (cf. Josh. 9:21-22; I Kings 17:10; Jer. 7:18; etc.) was essential for the sacrificial system (cf. Gen. 22:3; Lev. 1:7; I Kings 18:23). Hewers of wood are mentioned in references to subject peoples in the early period (cf. Josh. 9:21, 23, 27), but nowhere until the time of Nehemiah (13:31) is there any provision for systematically supplying wood. Hence, **as it is written** is perplexing and has been regarded as evidence of the Chronicler's irresponsibility (Torrey, *Ezra Studies,* p. 277, note g). But it is not clear whether the statement refers to Lev. 6:12 alone or to the entire matter of the wood offering. If the latter is intended, we must assume that some such prescription as that covered in vs. 33 was once in the law but is no longer preserved (cf. Bertholet, *loc. cit.;* Browne, *op. cit.,* p. 193; cf. Julius Wellhausen, "Die Rückkehr der Juden aus dem babylonischen Exil," *Nachrichten von der königliche Gesellschaft der Wissenschaft zu Göttingen* [1895], p. 174, n. 1; cf. Rudolph, *op. cit.,* p. 180).

The term **fathers' houses** (cf. Ezra 2:59) means family groups. It has been argued that **the priests** would not have gathered wood (Batten, *Ezra and Nehemiah,* pp. 377-78), but though the list of classes may have been additional, the text must reflect ancient usage, for the Talmud mentions "the wood-offerings of the priests" (Henry Malter, ed., *The Treatise Ta'anit of the Babylonian Talmud* [Philadelphia: Jewish Publication Society of America, 1928], p. 215). The versions and several Hebrew MSS indicate that "and" has been lost before **the Levites** in the M.T. The rotation of the task was determined by casting **lots,** the Urim and Thummim (cf. Ezra 2:63), manipulated by the priests (cf. Judg. 18:14-21; Deut. 33:3, 8, 10; Raymond A. Bowman, "Yahweh the Speaker," *Journal of Near Eastern Studies,* III [1944], 7-8). Since **the lots** apparently could answer only a simple question with "Yes" or "No," the process was tedious and prolonged where many people were involved (cf. I Sam. 10:19-24). While **year by year** indicates yearly assignment, **at times appointed** (cf. Ezra 10:14) refers to intervals within the year. According to the Mishnah, the wood supply was replenished nine times each year (Malter, *op. cit.,* pp. 200-201), and Josephus (*Jewish War* II. 17. 6) mentions a festival of wood carrying.

It is unnecessary to charge that vs. 34 interrupts a list of sacrifices (vss. 33, 35) and is therefore out of place (Batten, *op. cit.,* p. 378) for, if vs. 33 is recognized as the interpolation, there is no list of sacrifices in which to intrude, and vs. 32, concerned with a money gift to the temple, is followed in vs. 34 by a gift of material. Vs. 35, also dealing with commodities, follows naturally.

times appointed year by year, to burn upon the altar of the LORD our God, as *it is* written in the law:

35 And to bring the firstfruits of our ground, and the firstfruits of all fruit of all trees, year by year, unto the house of the LORD:

36 Also the firstborn of our sons, and of our cattle, as *it is* written in the law, and the firstlings of our herds and of our flocks, to bring to the house of our God, unto the priests that minister in the house of our God:

our God, according to our fathers' houses, at times appointed, year by year, to burn upon the altar of the LORD our God, as it is written in the law. 35 We obligate ourselves to bring the first fruits of our ground and the first fruits of all fruit of every tree, year by year, to the house of the LORD; 36 also to bring to the house of our God, to the priests who minister in the house of our God, the first born of our sons and of our cattle, as it is written in the law, and the firstlings of our herds and of our flocks;

5. First Fruits (10:35-36)

35-36. The first fruits (*bikkûrîm;* Lev. 23:17, 20 [J]; Exod. 34:22, 26 [E]) were an important part of Nehemiah's reform (13:31) because they formed the basis for Levite support (cf. 13:10-12). Semitic nomads sacrificed the first-born of cattle and flocks (cf. S. A. Cook, "Sacred Tribute in Arabia," in W. Robertson Smith, *Religion of the Semites,* pp. 458-65), and the sacrifice of **first fruits** was part of the Canaanite cultus adopted by the Hebrews (René Dussaud, *Les origines cananéennes du sacrifice israélite* [Paris: E. Leroux, 1921], pp. 163-73; Georges Contenau, *La civilisation phénicienne* [Paris: Payot, 1928], pp. 137-40). Like the first mowings of the field paid to the king (Amos 7:1), the **first fruits** were a charge on the produce of the land, paid as tribute to the Deity as "landlord." Nothing of the new crop could be eaten until the divine proprietor received his due (Lev. 23:14). It was probably believed that the whole nature of the yield of a commodity was inherent in the first of the produce, that the **first fruits** represent the whole, and that "the entire power and blessedness of the harvest are concentrated in them" (cf. Pedersen, *Israel, Its Life and Culture III-IV,* p. 301).

The double use of **all** in the KJV reflects the cumbersome M.T. and Vulg. but the LXXABℵ omits the first **all,** as in vs. 37, and the Peshitta and many Hebrew MSS omit the second one. **First born** of stock and men were also to be offered according to the law (Exod. 13:2). **First born** males were sacrificed on the eighth day (Exod. 22:30; Deut. 15:19-20). Human sacrifice perhaps developed subsequent to animal sacrifices and by analogy to them (W. O. E. Oesterley and T. H. Robinson, *Hebrew Religion, Its Origin and Development* [2nd ed.; New York: The Macmillan Co., 1937], p. 182; Pedersen, *op. cit.,* p. 318 and note on p. 697) and was apparently taken over by the Hebrews in imitation of the Canaanites. It is argued that the Phoenicians abandoned human sacrifice between the eighth and sixth centuries B.C. but that Hebrew religion sanctioned such sacrifices prior to 621 B.C. (Otto Eissfeldt, *Molk als Opferbegriff im punischen und hebräischen und das Ende des Gottes Moloch* [Halle: M. Niemeyer, 1935], pp. 48-55; *Ras Schamra und Sanchunjaton* [Halle: M. Niemeyer, 1939], pp. 69-71) ; however, the latter statement has been vigorously repudiated (W. F. Albright, *Archaeology and the Religion of Israel* [2nd ed.; Baltimore: Johns Hopkins Press, 1946], pp. 163-64; cf. Pedersen, *loc. cit.*). Vs. 36 is silent about the redemption of human first born (Exod. 13:13; 34:20; Num. 18:15; cf. Luke 2:22-24), which was doubtless presumed in the pledge. **Cattle** in a general sense means "beasts" (cf. 2:12, 14), usually domestic but sometimes wild animals (Mic. 5:8; Deut. 28:26; Isa. 18:6). Pure animals were sacrificed and unclean ones were slain or redeemed (Exod. 13:13; 34:20; Num. 18:15-16).

As it is written refers not only to the practices mentioned but also to those assumed. The reference to the law has been regarded as out of place, perhaps drawn from vs. 34 (cf. Batten, *loc. cit.*), since **the firstlings,** etc., which follows, is best seen as explanatory to **cattle.** But the explanatory matter also may be a secondary gloss (*ibid.;* Rudolph, *op. cit.,* p. 178; *et al.*).

37 And *that* we should bring the first-fruits of our dough, and our offerings, and the fruit of all manner of trees, of wine and of oil, unto the priests, to the chambers of | 37 and to bring the first of our coarse meal, and our contributions, the fruit of every

---

6. Voluntary Contributions and Tithes (10:37a)

37a. The first (*rē'shîth*) literally translates a word meaning either chronologically "first" or, in a qualitative sense, "prime." The term is used ambiguously in Deuteronomy, sometimes equal to the "first fruits" (*bikkûrîm*) of vs. 35, and sometimes in the wider sense of "contribution," parallel in use to the word rendered **contributions** (*terûmāh*) here and in vs. 39 (cf. G. B. Gray, *A Critical and Exegetical Commentary on Numbers* [New York: Charles Scribner's Sons, 1903; "International Critical Commentary"], pp. 227-29). In the former sense it refers to raw produce brought to the temple (vs. 36; cf. Num. 18:13) and presented with ceremony (cf. Deut. 26:2-10), while in the latter sense it is rather a prepared gift brought to the priest (vs. 37; cf. Deut. 18:4) at his call, given apparently with little or no ceremony. Furthermore, the nature of **the first** as a simple contribution, rather than **first fruit** offering, is seen in the fact that some of the gifts do not fall into the seven categories specified for the **first fruits** (wheat, barley, wine, figs, pomegranates, olives, and honey; cf. Deut. 8:8; Mishnah, Bikkurim 1:3; 3:9).

Among the donations for the support of the clergy was a substance identified as **coarse meal** (*'arêsāh*), apparently related to an Akkadian word (*arsânu*) for "grain grits" (cf. Bezold, *Babylonisch-Assyrisches Glossar*, p. 69, col. 1), in Syriac "hulled barley" (Paul Lagarde, "Kleinigkeiten," *Nachrichten von der königliche Gesellschaft der Wissenschaft Göttingen* [1889], pp. 301 ff.), and in New Hebrew "barley meal" (Jacob Levy, *Neuhebräisches und chaldäisches Wörterbuch* [Leipzig: F. A. Brockhaus, 1883], III, 702, *s.v.* עָרְסָ). But the term is used in the Talmud and is known in Armenia as a prepared porridge or paste of barley meal or wheat, related to the Arabic *keshk* (Persian *kashk*; Babylonian Talmud, Nedarim 41b; cf. A. R. S. Kennedy, "Food," in Cheyne and Black, *Encyclopaedia Biblica*, Vol. II, col. 1539; Lagarde, "Kleinegkeiten," pp. 301-2; Dalman, *Arbeit und Sitte*, III, 271). Since the substance could be made into a "cake" (Num. 15:20-21), it is probable that the gift to the priests was **dough** in its first mixed stage (cf. Mishnah, Hallah 1:9; Tosefta Hallurin; Targum Jerusalem 1; cf. Dalman, *op. cit.*, IV, 52). In the LXX of Num. 15:20-21 the text uses the same word "dough" (φύραμα) found in Rom. 11:16. Furthermore, since there is no prescription of first fruits of fruit trees in the Torah (cf. Pedersen, *op. cit.*, p. 302), the reference here to **the fruit of every tree** must be to a special voluntary gift. References here to **wine** and **oil** (5:11) are also to gifts additional to "first fruits."

Since the word rendered **our contributions** is but a parallel and later term to that translated **the first**, the former (cf. vs. 39) must be omitted, as in the LXX^ABℵ. Some conjecture that it has been inserted from Ezek. 44:30 (Meyer, *Entstehung des Judenthums*, pp. 212 ff.; Rudolph, *loc. cit.*). The word **tithes**, related to the word "ten," seems based on the secular practice whereby a king claimed the prime part of his subjects' produce. In Egypt the common assessment was 10 per cent (cf. G. C. C. Maspero, *The Struggle of the Nations* [tr. M. L. McClure; New York: D. Appleton & Co., 1897], p. 312), also in Babylonia (Otto Eissfeldt, "Zum Zehnten bei den Babyloniern," in Wilhelm Frankenberg, ed., *Abhandlungen zur semitischen religionskunde und sprachwissenschaft, Wolf Wilhelm grafen von Baudissin* [Giessen: A. Töpelmann, 1918], pp. 163-74), and among the Hebrews (I Sam. 8:15, 17). The divine assessment is known at least as early as the eighth century B.C. (Amos 4:4; cf. Gen. 14:20; 28:22), but legislation for it is not found until the Deuteronomic Code, when it apparently was already an ancient custom in Israel (Deut. 14:22-29; cf. J. M. Powis Smith, "The Deuteronomic Tithe," *American Journal of Theology*, XVIII [1914], 119-26; cf. S. R. Driver, *Deuteronomy*, pp. 166-73). As in Deut. 14:22-29, the tithes here are of **our ground**, levied on crops alone (cf. Num. 18:21-24). The Mishnah declares: "Everything that is eaten and is watched over and grows out

the house of our God; and the tithes of our ground unto the Levites, that the same Levites might have the tithes in all the cities of our tillage.

38 And the priest the son of Aaron shall be with the Levites, when the Levites take tithes: and the Levites shall bring up the tithe of the tithes unto the house of our God, to the chambers, into the treasure house.

39 For the children of Israel and the children of Levi shall bring the offering of the corn, of the new wine, and the oil, unto the

tree, the wine and the oil, to the priests, to the chambers of the house of our God; and to bring to the Levites the tithes from our ground, for it is the Levites who collect the tithes in all our rural towns. **38** And the priest, the son of Aaron, shall be with the Levites when the Levites receive the tithes; and the Levites shall bring up the tithe of the tithes to the house of our God, to the chambers, to the storehouse. **39** For the people of Israel and the sons of Levi shall bring the contribution of grain, wine, and

---

of the ground is subject to tithe" (Maaseroth 1:1). The most scrupulous tithing was done by Pharisees, who were even concerned about "mint and anise and cummin" (Matt. 23:23; cf. Luke 11:42).

The **tithes** originally belonged to the farmer (Deut. 14:22 ff.), who, when they were eaten, was to share them with the Levites and the needy (Deut. 12:12, 19; 14:27; 16:11, 14; 26:12). The statement that **the tithes** are to be brought **to the Levites** indicates a later development of the law. As the need of the cult developed, it was believed that God ceded his tithe to the priests (Num. 18:11 ff. [P]) and it was given to the Levites (Num. 18:21-24).

7. Chronicler's Supplement (10:37b-39a)

These verses, which reflect the cultic ideas and practices of the later period, are usually regarded as supplemental, added by the Chronicler to make the material conform to the practices of his own day.

37b-38. A later conception of the **tithes** is reflected in the priestly collection of them. When the Levites were given the **tithes,** they had to turn over a portion, **the tithe of the tithes,** to the priests (Num. 18:25-32). As a tax due to the clergy, the **tithe** was not always collectible (cf. 13:10-13) and later provision was made for the Levites to go after it. The presence of a **priest** with the Levite collector may be to ensure a proper share for the priests (Batten, *op. cit.*, p. 379). **Son of Aaron** indicates the sharp cleavage between the Levite and the true priest in the Priestly Code, wherein the Levites are the priests' servants (cf. Ezra 2:40-42). By the Christian period the priests themselves collected the tithe (cf. Josephus *Antiquities* XX. 8. 8; XX. 9. 2). In the definite character of **the priest** is seen an attempt by the writer to indicate the practice of his day (Torrey, *Ezra Studies,* p. 277, note i). Jewish scholars, recognizing the discrepancy between Deuteronomic legislation and the usage of their day, reasoned that Ezra deprived the Levites of their tithe because of their reluctance to return to Palestine (cf. Ezra 8:15; Talmud: Kethuboth 26a; Yebamoth 86ab; Hullin, 131b; cf. Munk, *Esra ha sofer,* p. 26).

Since **cities** would scarcely produce agricultural material for tithes, it is proposed to interpret the M.T. as "hamlets" or **towns** (cf. Batten, *loc. cit.*), as in the Peshitta. The final word of vs. 37, lit., "our work," is rendered as **our tillage,** and interpreted as "dependent on our agriculture" (Amer. Trans.). Since the tithe was collectible also in Jerusalem, the interpretation **rural towns** is inadequate (Rudolph, *loc. cit.*). "Our work" can have cultic meaning (cf. vs. 32; Ezra 8:20), and "the cities of our work" can mean "the cities of our cultus," signifying "wherever the Hebrew law of the tithe was operative" (cf. Siegfried, *Esra, Nehemia und Esther,* p. 116; Rudolph, *loc. cit.*).

39a. This verse, beginning with **for,** is a supplementary explanation of the preceding and may be an even later addition to the M.T. (Jahn, *Esra [A und B] und Nehemja,* pp. 145-46). **The people** are to bring the "first fruits" (vss. 35-37; cf. II Chr. 31:5-7), while **the Levites** gather the tithes (vs. 38, cf. 13:12). But here **the Levites,** who in vs. 38

chambers, where *are* the vessels of the sanc- | oil to the chambers, where are the vessels
tuary, and the priests that minister, and the | of the sanctuary, and the priests that minis-
porters, and the singers: and we will not | ter, and the gatekeepers and the singers.
forsake the house of our God. | We will not neglect the house of our God.

11 And the rulers of the people dwelt at Jerusalem: the rest of the people also cast lots, to bring one of ten to dwell in | 11 Now the leaders of the people lived in Jerusalem; and the rest of the

---

collect the tithes, are also to gather the **contribution** (cf. vs. 37) as well, an expansion of clerical rights. **Contribution** (*terûmāh*), incorrectly often called "heave offering," implies no rite of elevation, but rather indicates what is *"lifted off* a larger mass, or separated from it, for sacred purposes." The word is used usually of "contributions" and only exceptionally of sacrifices (S. R. Driver, *Deuteronomy*, p. 142). These voluntary gifts were of materials of a wider range than those of the first fruits. Such was the gift of gold and silver presented at the temple (Ezra 8:25), and in later times it included such items as cucumbers, melons, onions, etc. (Mishnah: Terumoth 2:5-6; 3:1; 9:6). No fixed amount of contributions was established by law. A generous gift was between one thirtieth to one fortieth of the crop; the average expected was about one fiftieth of the produce and only one sixtieth was expected of the parsimonious (Terumoth 4:3).

The **chambers** (cf. Ezra 8:29) held not only the produce gathered but also **the vessels of the sanctuary** (cf. Ezra 1:9; 7:19). The **vessels** need not be limited to storage jars (cf. 13:9) since the term is more inclusive (cf. Ezra 1:6).

In listing the order of the clergy residing in the **chambers** (cf. Ezra 10:6), the M.T. omits the Levites but the Peshitta mentions them, and the term "ministers" in the LXX and Vulg. implies them (cf. Num. 3:5 ff.). The present M.T. must now be read **the priests that minister,** interpreted as those who must reside in the temple during their course of duty. But the LXX, Vulg., and Peshitta indicate that the M.T. has omitted the conjunction "and" before "the ministers," which apparently refers to the Levites. **The porters, and the singers** (Ezra 2:42) dwelt in the chambers, but the Nethinim (Ezra 2:43) lived in Ophel (3:26). **The singers** too lived outside the temple (12:29), apparently when not on duty.

8. Pledge to Support the Temple (10:39*b*)

39*b*. We will not neglect is, lit., **we will not forsake.** The conjunction is like that preceding each pledge in the original document (cf. vss. 29, 31, 32, 34, 35, etc.). By omitting it and emending the verb to read "They will not neglect," the passage has been made part of the supplemented material (Jahn, *op. cit.*, p. 146), but the M.T. and versions are firmly against such emendation. The text has been regarded as concluding a construction begun in vs. 31, summing up the preceding details to form a proper conclusion to the Ezra story. But the statement seems more natural and appropriate as a reaction to Nehemiah's question in 13:11 (cf. Meyer, *op. cit.*, p. 213).

XII. Distribution of Peoples (11:1-36)

This chapter begins abruptly, showing relationship with ch. 10 neither chronologically nor in substance. Since chs. 8–10 are out of order (cf. Exeg. on 7:73*b*), the connection suggested by the conjunction **now** or **and** is usually considered to be with 7:73*a*. After a few verses relating the repopulation of Jerusalem (vss. 1-2), the chapter

---

11:1-36. *A Census by Families of Jerusalem and Its Environs.*—Here follows another genealogical list, arranged this time by places of residence in and around Jerusalem. **One out of ten** (vs. 1) lived within the new city walls: they were chosen by lot, or by their function as priests, Levites, and temple servants in the maintenance of the elaborate temple ritual. The other nine tenths dwelt in the villages outside the walls, the names of which (though not of their inhabitants) are listed with meticulous care.

Jerusalem the holy city, and nine parts *to* *dwell* in *other* cities.	people cast lots to bring one out of ten to live in Jerusalem the holy city, while nine

consists of two diverse lists, purporting to give the population of rebuilt Jerusalem (vss. 3-24) and the other cities and towns of Judea (vss. 25-36).

A. Repopulation of Jerusalem (11:1-2)

Since vss. 1-2 belong after 7:73a, there are some who insist that they are part of an earlier document from the time of Zerubbabel, indicating the distribution of Judeans during the period following the first return in the time of Cyrus (*ibid.*, p. 99, n. 2; Heinrich Ewald, *The History of Israel* [tr. J. E. Carpenter; London: Longmans, Green & Co., 1874], V, 159, n. 2; Stade, *Geschichte des Volkes Israel*, II, 98, n. 1). Inasmuch as it is probable that ch. 7 was part of Nehemiah's memoirs (cf. Rudolph, *op. cit.*, pp. 11-15, 141), the verses may properly represent the distribution of population in Nehemiah's own day. They are but a fragmentary introduction to the lists that follow, but they appear to be an authentic reflection of another of Nehemiah's social reforms. They belong in the general context of 7:4 ff., but the actual connection is conjectural. The fragmentary character of vss. 1-2 and their present association suggest that although they may have been part of Nehemiah's document, they are not in their original form but are a later editor's application of them (cf. Bertholet, *Esra und Nehemia*, p. 81). It has been proposed that at the beginning a sentence now lost explained that the census list (7:6-73a) suggested to Nehemiah how the city should be populated and that 11:1 ff. indicated that solution (Rudolph, *op. cit.*, p. 181). It is possible, however, that there was originally a more extensive passage between the list in ch. 7 and vss. 1-2. It is conjectured that as a result of the meeting (7:5) the leaders volunteered to go to Jerusalem, but that even then the population there was insufficient, and that at a second meeting it was decided to follow the plan reflected in vss. 1-2 (cf. Bertheau, *Esra, Nechemia und Ester*, p. 311).

Such violent population shifting as is here presumed has many parallels in antiquity, for great transportations of people were made in late Assyrian times (cf. Ezra 2:1; 5:12), and in the Achaemenid period and later people were forcibly transplanted to populate the cities that were being founded (Diodorus of Sicily XVII. 83. 7; XVIII. 4. 4; Herodotus *History* VII. 156; Pausanius *Description of Greece* VIII. 27. 3-5). Thus, when depopulated Jerusalem (7:4) had been fortified and was ready for its people, it was only natural that efforts should be made to restore authority there and increase its population for its defense and to augment its prestige.

11:1. The original Hebrew title "princes" (ASV) was gradually weakened to **rulers** or **leaders** (cf. Ezra 10:14), and the Peshitta here interprets as "elders." These were the "nobles" (6:17), doubtless the "heads of families" or "chiefs of the people" (cf. vs. 3; 7:70; Ezra 2:68), in contrast to the Jewish masses. The leaders were actually in Jerusalem during Nehemiah's administration (cf. 6:17) and later, in the time of Ezra (cf. Ezra 8:29). The leaders alone were insufficient to guarantee its defense and dignify its status as religious and civil center. Problems of reconstruction that remained within the city, even after the walls were completed (7:4), made it difficult to induce Judeans to leave the countryside to accept the obvious hardships and difficulties of the city. Compulsion was exerted through the casting of **lots** (cf. 10:34), since that was recognized as the voice of God. **One out of ten** seems to indicate an individual basis of selection, which would disrupt family groups. But it is probable that selection was made on a family basis. The goal seems to have been a Jerusalem containing one tenth of the community (cf. Smend, *Die Listen*, p. 23). Since **nine parts** renders a M.T. that is, lit., "nine handfuls," which may have had its origin in distribution of commodities by handfuls (cf. Bertheau, *op. cit.*, p. 312), the expression may indicate family or clan groups as the basis of selection.

The **nine tenths** not drafted remained in their places in the country. The M.T., **"in the cities,"** is usually interpreted as **in other cities** or **in the other towns,** indicating

2 And the people blessed all the men, that willingly offered themselves to dwell at Jerusalem.

3 ¶ Now these *are* the chief of the province that dwelt in Jerusalem: but in the cities of Judah dwelt every one in his pos-

tenths remained in the other towns. 2 And the people blessed all the men who willingly offered to live in Jerusalem.

3 These are the chiefs of the province who lived in Jerusalem; but in the towns

---

a contrast between Jerusalem and smaller places (vss. 25-29). For **cities** the Peshitta interprets "villages" or "hamlets."

Holy city, previously used by Second Isaiah (48:2; 52:1), is used here as it frequently is later (cf. Dan. 9:24; Tob. 13:9; Matt. 4:5; 27:53; etc.). The title is preserved in the modern Arabic name for Jerusalem, "The Holy" (El-Quds). From the "holy of holies" of the temple, the place par excellence where God met man, it was believed that God's holiness spread to the whole temple, the whole temple mount, the whole city of which that mount was a part, and finally to the whole land, of which Jerusalem was the capital.

Before the long process of lot (cf. 10:34) was completed, some volunteered to move to Jerusalem. They have been regarded as additional to the ten per cent selected (Batten, *op. cit.,* p. 267), but the reaction of the people indicates that the volunteers diminished the number to be chosen and therefore were to be applauded for their sacrifice. It is argued that the Hebrew text demands that "the leaders," not **the people,** should be the subject of **blessed,** and the translation should be, "And they, namely the leaders of the community, thanked the people who were called; not all, but only such as those who volunteered" (cf. Ehrlich, *Randglossen,* VII, 209). Although three Hebrew MSS support such an interpretation, the usual one is grammatically defensible and is preferable (cf. Rudolph, *op. cit.,* p. 182; Kautzsch, *Gesenius' Hebrew Grammar,* secs. 117n, 145b,c).

Characteristically, Nehemiah stresses the joyful aspects of the situation and sublimates the trials, hostility, and difficulties. Later writers credit Nehemiah not only with the fortification of the city but also with the building of houses for the people brought to the city (Ecclus. 49:13; Josephus *Antiquities* XI. 5. 8).

B. Leaders Dwelling in Jerusalem (11:3-24)

Reference to the settlement of Jerusalem (vss. 1-2) suggests the relevance of the list of leaders who dwelt at Jerusalem (vss. 3-24), which indubitably is related in some fashion to the list in I Chr. 9:2-34. Although it has been suggested that the list was a pre-exilic one incorporated by Nehemiah (F. X. Kugler, *Von Moses bis Paulus* [Münster in Westfalen: Aschendorff, 1922], pp. 289-90, 300), it is improbable that such a list would have survived the Exile, and it is likely that the document was not part of the Nehemiah record but a supplement added by the Chronicler who believed it relevant.

The exact relationship to the material in I Chr. 9 has been long disputed. Some, noting that the Chronicler was concerned about the distribution of peoples, believed that he would be expected to show interest in the settlement of Jerusalem (cf. Meyer, *op. cit.,* p. 186), and frequently argue that both passages are his unhistorical invention (Torrey, *Composition,* pp. 42-43, 50; Pfeiffer, *Intro. to O.T.,* p. 830; Meyer, *op. cit.,* pp. 189 ff.; Hölscher, *Esra und Nehemia,* p. 551; cf. Edward L. Curtis and Albert A. Madsen, *A Critical and Exegetical Commentary on the Books of Chronicles* [New York: Charles Scribner's Sons, 1910; "International Critical Commentary"], p. 168). But others contend that I Chr. 9 is an interpolated document, not the work of the Chronicler (Immanuel Benzinger, *Die Bücher der Chronik* [Tübingen: J. C. B. Mohr, 1901; "Kurzer Hand-commentar zum Alten Testament"], p. 35; Noth, *Überlieferungsgeschichtlichestudien,* p. 122; J. W. Rothstein and Johannes Hänel, *Kommentar zum ersten Buch der Chronik* [Leipzig: A. Deichert, 1927; "Kommentar zum Alten Testament"], pp. 180-89; Rudolph, *op. cit.,* p. 183). It is probably a postexilic list (Smend, *Die Listen,* p. 7), which is conjectured to be excerpted from the temple archives (cf. Rudolph, *loc. cit.*). The

session in their cities, *to wit*, Israel, the priests, and the Levites, and the Nethinim, and the children of Solomon's servants.

4 And at Jerusalem dwelt *certain* of the children of Judah, and of the children of Benjamin. Of the children of Judah; Athaiah the son of Uzziah, the son of Zechariah, the son of Amariah, the son of Shephatiah, the son of Mahalaleel, of the children of Perez;

of Judah every one lived on his property in their towns: Israel, the priests, the Levites, the temple servants, and the descendants of Solomon's servants. 4 And in Jerusalem lived certain of the sons of Judah and of the sons of Benjamin. Of the sons of Judah: Athai'ah the son of Uzzi'ah, son of Zechari'ah, son of Amari'ah, son of Shephati'ah, son of Mahal'alel, of the sons of

---

original list, some claim, now exists in two different recensions as the Chronicler has adapted it to differing contexts (cf. Bertholet, *op. cit.*, p. 82). In I Chr. 9 the list is assigned to the time of the first return from Exile (cf. Neh. 7:5), while here it is by implication from the time of Nehemiah, after the city has been repopulated.

1. Judean Laymen (11:3-6)

3. Since vss. 25-36, dealing with towns instead of individuals, is a separate supplement with its own title (vss. 20, 25), the reference to the **towns of Judah** is irrelevant, but the LXX, Peshitta, and Vulg. include it as part of the title, doubtless considering the chapter as a whole. The M.T. connects **in the cities of Judah** with **every one lived,** but the LXX[L], Peshitta, and presumably the Vulg. show that the M.T. should be emended to "and everyone dwelt" (cf. Gotthard, *Nehemia,* p. 44). **The province** is Judea (cf. 1:3; 7:6; Ezra 2:1). The **chiefs** are **the leaders** of vs. 1. Since **his property** is awkward with **in their cities,** which follows, it is better to read "in their possessions," as in I Chr. 9:2. Such a concept of return to ancestral properties is largely unrealistic (cf. Ezra 2:1). Jahn (*Esra [A und B] und Nehemja,* p. 147) prefers "the sons of Israel" instead of **Israel,** but the latter agrees with I Chr. 9:2. **The descendants of Solomon's servants** (cf. Ezra 2:55), not in I Chr. 9:2, is probably from 7:57 (cf. Rothstein and Hänel, *op. cit.,* p. 185; Rudolph, *op. cit.,* p. 182). Batten expects also "the porters" and "the judges" (*sic* for "singers") mentioned in 11:19, 22-23, but these are absent in I Chr. 9:2.

Because the text of the list is incomplete and the figures may indicate not the total population but merely householders (cf. *ibid.,* p. 186), it is impossible to use the statistics for computing the population of Jerusalem or for judging between the relative proportions of the classes within the city.

4a. As in I Chr. 9:3 and elsewhere (Ezra 1:5; 4:1; 10:9), **Judah** and **Benjamin** constitute the lay population of Judea. Some regard **Benjamin** with suspicion, believing it had no status in postexilic times, but there was such tribal consciousness as late as Roman times (cf. Rom. 11:1; Phil. 3:5; Kittel, *Geschichte des Volkes Israel,* III, 642). After the reference to **Benjamin,** many MSS reserve an unusual space, possibly in recognition of the reference to "Ephraim and Manasseh," added in I Chr. 9:3. Because they are ignored in the rest of the chapter, the names are regarded by some with suspicion, as an addition to fit the list to a different context (cf. Curtis and Madsen, *op. cit.,* p. 170). But they may have been original in the list, since the Chronicler thought that members of these tribes were adherents to Judah (cf. II Chr. 28:7; 30:11, 18; 34:9). It is suggested that they are omitted here because they would represent the Samaritans, rejected and hated in the time of Nehemiah (cf. 4:2-3; Ezra 4:1-2; Rudolph, *op. cit.,* p. 184). There is other evidence of omission in the verse, for although a member of "the sons of Zerah" is mentioned in vs. 24 and in I Chr. 9:6, that family is not represented here. Similarly, of the four families mentioned in I Chr. 9:8, only one, **the children of Benjamin,** is listed (vs. 7).

4b. Athaiah, abbreviated "Uthai" (cf. Ezra 8:14) in I Chr. 9:4, descends from **Perez,** a son of Judah and Tamar (Gen. 38:29). A descendant of Zerah, the twin of **Perez,** is mentioned in vs. 24, but his family has been dropped accidentally from the list. For

5 And Maaseiah the son of Baruch, the son of Col-hozeh, the son of Hazaiah, the son of Adaiah, the son of Joiarib, the son of Zechariah, the son of Shiloni.

6 All the sons of Perez that dwelt at Jerusalem *were* four hundred threescore and eight valiant men.

7 And these *are* the sons of Benjamin; Sallu the son of Meshullam, the son of Joed, the son of Pedaiah, the son of Kolaiah, the son of Maaseiah, the son of Ithiel, the son of Jesaiah.

8 And after him Gabbai, Sallai, nine hundred twenty and eight.

Perez; 5 and Ma-asei'ah the son of Baruch, son of Col-ho'zeh, son of Hazai'ah, son of Adai'ah, son of Joi'arib, son of Zechari'ah, son of the Shilo'nite. 6 All the sons of Perez who lived in Jerusalem were four hundred and sixty-eight valiant men.

7 And these are the sons of Benjamin: Sallu the son of Meshul'lam, son of Jo'ed, son of Pedai'ah, son of Kolai'ah, son of Ma-asei'ah, son of I'thi-el, son of Jeshai'ah. 8 And after him Gabba'i, Sal'lai, nine hun-

---

Zechariah (cf. Ezra 5:1) I Chr. 9:4 has Ammihud. For **Amariah** I Chr. 9:4 has its abbreviation "Imri," and also a corrupt doublet in the form "Omri." Since "Zaccur" abbreviates **Zechariah**, "Zaccur the son of Imri" (cf. 3:2) seems relevant here and the present list must thus be several generations later than the time of Nehemiah. **Shephatiah** was an ancestral leader in the time of Ezra (cf. 7:9; Ezra 2:4; 8:8), but I Chr. 9:4 omits **Shephatiah, the son of Mahalalel** and has instead "the son of Bani." The total of the descendants of **Perez** (vs. 6), not found in I Chr. 9, is out of place and should precede vs. 5.

5. **Maaseiah** (cf. Ezra 10:18), corrupted as "Asaiah" in I Chr. 9:5, is descended from "Shelah," third son of Judah, by the Canaanite Shuah (Gen. 38:2-5), but only the Peshitta properly identifies Shelah. **Shiloni** of the M.T. and I Chr. 9:5 is the gentilic **the Shilonite**, "the man from Shiloh," which would be inappropriate since Shiloh lay not in Judah but in Ephraim, north of Bethel (cf. Judg. 21:19). **Zechariah** is one of the "Shelanites" of Num. 26:20 and the word השלני, **the Shilonite**, must be revocalized as "the Shelanite." **Baruch** (ברוך, cf. 3:20) is corrupted to "first born" (בכור) in I Chr. 9:5, where the text is then deliberately abbreviated to "and his sons." **Colhozeh:** Cf. 3:15. **Adaiah:** Cf. Ezra 10:29, 39. **Joiarib:** Cf. Ezra 8:16. **Hazaiah** ("The Lord Has Seen") is found only here.

6. While I Chr. 9:6 omits the total of the sons of Perez, it does give a greater total (690), which may represent all the Judeans in Jerusalem.

2. BENJAMINITE LAYMEN (11:7-9)

7. Cf. I Chr. 9:7. The only Benjaminite chieftain listed is **Sallu,** a descendant of **Jeshaiah,** whose relationship to Benjamin is uncertain. No **Sallu** is found among the Benjaminites in Gen. 46:21 or in the Chronicler's catalogue of grandsons and great-grandsons (I Chr. 7:6-12). **Meshullam:** Cf. Ezra 8:16. **Pedaiah:** Cf. 3:25. **Maaseiah:** Cf. vs. 5; Ezra 10:18. **Jeshaiah:** Cf. Ezra 8:7. **Joed** ("The Lord Is Witness") and **Ithiel** ("God Is with Me") are found only here but the latter is abbreviated as "Ithai" (I Chr. 11:31) and "Ittai" (II Sam. 23:29). **Kolaiah,** known from pre-exilic times (Jer. 29:21), is found in I Esdras and the LXX of Ezra 10:23, where the M.T. has "Kelaiah."

8. Cf. I Chr. 9:9a. The Hebrew text is corrupt and unintelligible. The words "his brothers" in the LXX[L] show that ואחריו, **and after him,** should be emended to ואחיו, "and his brothers." The intrusive letter ר has apparently migrated from the following word, now the senseless גבי, **Gabbai,** which must have been originally גברי, "the men of" (cf. Guthe and Batten, *Ezra and Nehemiah*, p. 53). What follows should be חיל, "strength," to form the common expression גברי חיל, "mighty men of valor," as found, also with the numeral, in vs. 14. The name סלי, **Sallai,** could easily have been corrupted from חיל, "strength," under the influence of "Sallu" in vs. 7 (cf. Rudolph, *op. cit.*, p. 183). The emended text would thus parallel that in vs. 14a. The total of Benjaminites for the

9 And Joel the son of Zichri *was* their overseer: and Judah the son of Senuah *was* second over the city.

10 Of the priests: Jedaiah the son of Joiarib, Jachin.

dred and twenty-eight. 9 Jo'el the son of Zichri was their overseer; and Judah the son of Hassen'u-ah was second over the city.

---

single family is 928, but in I Chr. 9:9, where three additional families are included, the total is only 956.

9. Concluding the data on the laymen is a supplementary note without parallel in I Chr. 9, which indicates that two special officers were "over them." "Them" by position might seem to refer to Benjamin alone, but **over the city** indicates broader responsibility. Since the other classes of citizens also had officials (cf. vss. 14*b*, 21-22), it is probable that these were selected by the several groups to represent their own interests in some sort of cabinet or council that worked with the governor in the administration of the city. The title of the chief representative (*pāqîdh*) is the equivalent of *amelpaqudu*, known from cuneiform sources from late Assyrian times down at least into the Persian period. The Assyrian title has been rendered as "the prefect," but "mayor" would serve as well (Sidney Smith, *Babylonian Historical Texts*, pp. 14-15, rev. 1. 16). Thus in the seventh year of Artaxerxes a *mBel-ittannu* was the *paqudu* official of the city of Nippur (C. E. Keiser, *Letters and Contracts from Erech* [New Haven: Yale University Press, 1918], No. 169, 1. 14). The Hebrew word, meaning "appointed," is reflected in the Vulg. (*praepositus*). The LXX, supported by such passages as II Kings 25:19, interprets it as **overseer** (Greek *episkopos*). The lay representative was **Joel the son of Zichri** (cf. Ezra 10:43), whose name abbreviates "Zechariah." His assistant was **Judah** (cf. Ezra 3:9) the descendant of **Hassenuah** (cf. 3:3; Ezra 2:35). In I Chr. 9:7 **Hassenuah** is the remote ancestor of the Benjaminite Sallu. His title is **second** (*mishneh*), "second in charge." It is unnecessary to limit his authority to "the second city," the *mishneh* quarter of Jerusalem (cf. 3:6; Simons, *Jerusalem in the O.T.*, p. 291, n. 2) since this title too has its parallel in cuneiform sources, where as *amelShanû* it is used from Assyrian to Hellenistic times for the "second officer," "assistant," or "substitute."

3. Priests (11:10-14)

Of the four priestly families in Ezra 2:36-39 (=Neh. 7:39-42) only that of Harim is not represented here. It is unlikely that the family had been secularized and therefore not required to go to Jerusalem (cf. Kittel, *op. cit.*, III, 399), since it is well attested in postexilic times (cf. 10:5; Ezra 10:31). The omission is perhaps due to loss of text, as in the case of the laymen (cf. vs. 4). The silence regarding the Aaronite priests who returned with Ezra has been seen as evidence that the list was prepared before Ezra's return (Rudolph, *op. cit.*, p. 185).

10-11. In I Chr. 9:10 the first three names of vs. 10 are given in sequence without evidence of genealogical relationship. The names before **Seraiah**, the last pre-exilic high priest (cf. Ezra 7:1), are part of the genealogy of the family of the high priest, as in the LXX[L]. The chief **Jedaiah** is "of the house of Jeshua," the high priest contemporary with Zerubbabel (7:39; cf. Ezra 2:36). **Joiarib** and **Jachin** have been regarded as intrusive from I Chr. 24:7, 17 (cf. Hölscher, *Esra und Nehemia*, p. 553). Because the Hasmonean clan was of the **Joiarib** family (I Macc. 2:1), it is argued that the name was interpolated as late as the second century B.C., no earlier than the time of Jonathan the Maccabee (161-143 B.C.; *ibid.*, p. 499). The Peshitta omits **Jachin**.

Joiarib (cf. Ezra 8:16) may have been substituted for an earlier "Joiakim" the son of Jeshua (cf. 12:10; Rudolph, *op. cit.*, p. 184). This is graphically possible and is supported by the statement that Jedaiah was of the house of Jeshua (7:39; cf. Ezra 2:36). **Jachin** (יכין) then may be a corruption of "son of" (בר). Thus **Jedaiah** the son of "Joiakim" was a brother of Eliashib, the contemporary of Nehemiah (3:1). If this reconstruction is correct, the genealogy is again defective, lacking the names Jeshua

11 Seraiah the son of Hilkiah, the son of Meshullam, the son of Zadok, the son of Meraioth, the son of Ahitub, *was* the ruler of the house of God.

12 And their brethren that did the work of the house *were* eight hundred twenty and two: and Adaiah the son of Jeroham, the son of Pelaliah, the son of Amzi, the son of Zechariah, the son of Pashur, the son of Malchiah,

13 And his brethren, chief of the fathers, two hundred forty and two: and Amashai the son of Azareel, the son of Ahasai, the son of Meshillemoth, the son of Immer,

10 Of the priests: Jedai'ah the son of Joi'arib, Jachin, 11 Serai'ah the son of Hilki'ah, son of Meshul'lam, son of Zadok, son of Merai'oth, son of Ahi'tub, ruler of the house of God, 12 and their brethren who did the work of the house, eight hundred and twenty-two; and Adai'ah the son of Jero'ham, son of Pelali'ah, son of Amzi, son of Zechari'ah, son of Pashhur, son of Malchi'jah, 13 and his brethren, heads of fathers' houses, two hundred and forty-two; and Amash'sai, the son of Az'arel, son of Ah'zai, son of Meshil'lemoth, son of Im-

and Jozadak (12:10; cf. Ezra 2:36). It is that of the high priest, with but a few differences. Seraiah's father was not **Hilkiah** (vs. 11) but "Azariah" (cf. Ezra 7:1; I Chr. 6:14); but in I Chr. 9:11 **Seraiah** is not mentioned and "Azariah" is the son of **Hilkiah**. Furthermore, **Meraioth** (cf. Ezra 7:3-4; I Chr. 6:6-7), here as in I Chr. 9:11, is intruded as the son of **Ahitub**, who elsewhere appears as the great-grandson of **Meraioth** (Ezra 7:2-3). **Meshullam** (cf. Ezra 8:16) is abbreviated "Shallum" in Ezra 7:2; I Chr. 6:13.

Ruler (נגיד), lit., "the one in front" or "the conspicuous one," was a title sometimes borne by kings but later given to such minor officers as the attendant of the temple treasurer (I Chr. 26:24). Frequently applied to the high priest (Jer. 20:1; I Chr. 9:11; II Chr. 31:13; Dan. 11:22), it was not his alone, for there were several priests with the same title. It has been compared with the later title (*prostatēs*) applied to the high priest in his civil capacity (cf. Ecclus. 45:24; Josephus *Antiquities* XII. 4. 2; Hugo Graetz, "Beiträge zur Sach- und Worterklärung des Buches Daniel," *Monatsschrift für Geschichte und Wissenschaft des Judenthums*, XX [1871], 395-400), or with that given to Simon Maccabee as the high priest, general, and leader (*hēgoumenos*) of the Jews (I Macc. 12:42; cf. Montgomery, *Daniel*, p. 379). A more modern parallel is the Arabic *imām*, a title applied to both temporal and spiritual leaders, but especially to the latter (A. A. Bevan, *A Short Commentary on the Book of Daniel* [Cambridge: Cambridge University Press, 1892], p. 156, n. 1).

12-13*a*. Adaiah (cf. Ezra 10:29) led the family of **Pashhur** (7:41; cf. Ezra 2:38) and his genealogy is traced to **Malchijah** the father of **Pashhur**. **Jeroham** ("May He Be Compassionate"), which abbreviates such a name as "Jerahmeel" ("God Has Mercy"), is favored by the Chronicler (I Chr. 8:27; 9:8; 12:7; 27:22; II Chr. 23:1). **Pelaliah** ("The Lord Has Intervened") is found only here, and **Amzi**, abbreviating "Amaziah" ("The Lord Has Been Mighty"), appears only here as priest. In I Chr. 9:12 the genealogy is incomplete, lacking **Pelaliah, Amzi,** and **Zechariah.** Since **heads of fathers' houses** applies to **Adaiah** alone, the plural form is incorrect. Furthermore, since it is a lay title it is surprising as applied to priests (Batten, *Ezra and Nehemiah*, p. 270; Bertholet, *Esra und Nehemia*, p. 83), and is perhaps introduced from I Chr. 9:13, displacing some other designation not now recoverable (cf. Keil, *Chronik, Esra, Nehemia und Esther*, p. 573; Rudolph, *loc. cit.*).

13*b*. Cf. I Chr. 9:12. **Amashsai** (עמשסי), the name of the leader of the family of **Immer** (cf. Ezra 2:37), is an un-Hebraic monstrosity, produced by combining two variant spellings, עמסי (cf. LXX and Peshitta) and עמשי. The name abbreviates "Amasiah" ("The Lord Has Carried"; cf. II Chr. 17:16; Noth, *Personennamen*, p. 178). The name "Maasai" in I Chr. 9:12, which looks like an abbreviation of "Maaseiah" (cf. Ezra 10:18), is merely due to the incorrect transposition of the first two letters of "Amasai." **Azarel** (cf. Ezra 10:41) is Adiel ("My Witness Is God") in I Chr. 9:12. **Ahzai** is omitted in the LXX, and in I Chr. 9:12 appears as "Jahzerah," which may

14 And their brethren, mighty men of valor, a hundred twenty and eight: and their overseer *was* Zabdiel, the son of *one of* the great men.

15 Also of the Levites: Shemaiah the son of Hashub, the son of Azrikam, the son of Hashabiah, the son of Bunni;

mer, 14 and their brethren, mighty men of valor, a hundred and twenty-eight; their overseer was Zab'diel the son of Haggedo'-lim.

15 And of the Levites: Shemai'ah the son of Hasshub, son of Azri'kam, son of

---

be a corruption of "Jahzeiah" (cf. Ezra 10:15). **Meshillemoth,** perhaps to be vocalized *Meshallēmôth (ibid.,* p. 250, No. 913), abbreviates such a name as Meshelemiah (I Chr. 9:21). The name is a postexilic imitation of such Akkadian names as *Mushallim-Shamash,* etc. *(ibid.,* p. 145). The "Meshullam" in I Chr. 9:12 is apparently a doublet.

14a. Since the reference here is to the leader alone, not his ancestors, **their brethren** must be emended to "his kinsmen," as in the LXX. **Mighty men of valor,** scarcely a priestly title (cf. Exeg. on vs. 8), was perhaps inserted in the original list through carelessness, for it is found also in I Chr. 9:13, where it has been interpreted as "very able men."

Here, as in vss. 12-13, a total is given for each priestly family, following the genealogy of its leader; but these are lacking in I Chr. 9:10-13, where a single total is given for the whole priestly class. Figures in Neh. 11:12-14 total 1,192 but that in I Chr. 9:13 is 1,760.

In a note without parallel in I Chr. 9, **Zabdiel** ("Gift of God") is listed as the **overseer** (cf. vs. 9) of the priests, as Joel was for laymen. The distinction between ruler (vs. 11) and **overseer** (vs. 14) is not clear but, since there was a tendency to differentiate between the sacred and the secular functions of the clergy (vs. 16), the ruler may have governed internal, sacred affairs, while the **overseer** controlled the more secular aspects of the priestly community.

Haggedolim, meaning **the great men,** is ridiculous as a personal name. Possibly the word is a corruption of a personal name of similar appearance, such as "Giddel" (Ezra 2:47), but the prefixed article would still be difficult. Since "high priest" in Hebrew is "great priest" (cf. 3:1), the original text may have been "the son of the high priest" (Rudolph, *loc. cit.*). But **the great men** may have been thought of here as the succession of high priests in the sense of the house of the high priest. The genealogy of **Zabdiel** is not given but he may have been a collateral descendant of the high priest.

4. Levites (11:15-18)

Despite the divergences, the lists of Levites (here and in I Chr. 9:14-16) must originally have been identical. Some LXX MSS (ABℵ) reduce the bulk of the M.T. by half, and it is suggested that the Greek texts show "how these genealogical records have grown even in late times" (Batten, *op. cit.,* p. 271). But little genealogical data is actually missing in the LXX, for the omissions are chiefly of parenthetic remarks and notices of official standing (cf. vss. 16, 17, 19, 20, 21). The major Greek lack is the ancestry of **Shammua** (vss. 17-18a), which was lost through carelessness and carried with it the essential introduction to the numeral in vs. 18. The missing Greek text is restored in the LXXᴸ and by the corrector of the LXXℵ.

Of the four Levite leaders in I Chr. 9, three are found here and the fourth, Berechiah (I Chr. 9:16), is omitted apparently because that group dwelt not in Jerusalem but "in the villages of the Netophathites."

15. Shemaiah (cf. Ezra 8:13) was the descendant of Merari (I Chr. 9:14), the youngest son of Levi (Gen. 46:11; Exod. 6:16) and the eponymous ancestor of the largest Levite clan (cf. Num. 4:36, 40, 44). Merari (I Chr. 9:14) is preferable to **Bunni** (cf. 9:4; Bertheau, *Esra, Nechemia und Ester,* p. 320). The father of **Hasshub** (cf. 3:11) was **Azrikam** ("My Help Has Arisen"; cf. Noth, *Personennamen,* pp. 129-30, 176). **Hashabiah** (cf. Ezra 8:19) is among the sons of Merari in I Chr. 6:45 (cf. Ezra 8:19).

16 And Shabbethai and Jozabad, of the chief of the Levites, *had* the oversight of the outward business of the house of God.

17 And Mattaniah the son of Micha, the son of Zabdi, the son of Asaph, was the principal to begin the thanksgiving in prayer: and Bakbukiah the second among his brethren, and Abda the son of Shammua, the son of Galal, the son of Jeduthun.

Hashabi'ah, son of Bunni; 16 and Shab'-
bethai and Jo'zabad, of the chiefs of the
Levites, who were over the outside work
of the house of God; 17 and Mattani'ah the
son of Mica, son of Zabdi, son of Asaph,
who was the leader to begin the thanksgiving in prayer, and Bakbuki'ah, the second among his brethren; and Abda the son
of Sham'mua, son of Galal, son of Jedu'-

---

16. In this portion of the list the parenthetic material, found usually at the end of each group (cf. vss. 9, 14), is interspersed between the various families. **Shabbethai** (cf. Ezra 10:15) and **Jozabad** (cf. Ezra 8:33), prominent in the time of Ezra (Neh. 8:7), apparently belong to the family of vs. 15. Their presence in the list is regarded as positive evidence for dating the list in the time of Nehemiah (Rudolph, *op. cit.,* p. 185). **Outside work is** explained as the performance of menial secular tasks (Batten, *loc. cit.*) but **outside** probably means merely in contradistinction to the cultic activities of the priests, "perhaps the maintenance of temple buildings, protecting the income and public traffic, principally" (Rudolph, *op. cit.,* p. 186). The Levite **Jozabad** received the treasure brought to the temple by Ezra (8:33). The LXX$^{AB\aleph}$ omits this note of office.

17. Mattaniah (cf. Ezra 10:26), the second Levite leader, was the descendant of **Asaph,** the psalmist and musician (cf. Ezra 2:41). **Zabdi** (זבדי), which abbreviates "Zabdiel" (vs. 14), appears here in the LXX^{L} and in I Chr. 9:15 as the similar name "Zichri" (זכרי; cf. vs. 9) and some prefer that reading (Guthe and Batten, *Ezra and Nehemiah,* p. 53; Gotthard, *Nehemia,* p. 45). The title of **Mattaniah,** lit., "head of the beginning; thanksgiving for the prayer," is senselessly corrupt. In 12:8 he is described as "in charge of the songs of thanksgiving." The LXX^{L} and Vulg. indicate that instead of התחלה, "the beginning," the text should have the quite similar התהלה, "the praise." Moreover, what is rendered **the thanksgiving** is not a noun but the verb "let him praise." The title should therefore be, lit., "The leader of the song of praise, 'Let him praise,' of the prayer." Thus "Mattaniah was the leader of the Thank-Hymn who, like his ancestor Asaph [I Chr. 16:7] had to lead the prayer *'hodu leYahweh'* " (Rudolph, *loc. cit.*). **Bakbukiah,** whose name is the full form of "Bakbuk" (Ezra 2:51), was apparently of the same family as **Mattaniah.** His title **second** (cf. vs. 9) signifies that he assisted **Mattaniah.**

Abda (cf. I Kings 4:6) headed the third Levite family. The name may be an abbreviation of the form "Obadiah" (cf. Ezra 8:9), which appears here in the LXX^{L} and in I Chr. 9:16. But **Abda** is found as a name frequently in the late Assyrian and Neo-Babylonian business documents. **Shammua** (Num. 13:4; II Sam. 5:14) abbreviates such a name as "Shemaiah," which appears here in the LXX^{L} and in I Chr. 9:16 and is favored by some (cf. Gotthard, *op. cit.,* p. 44). A similar name, *Sa-mu-u-a,* is found in the cuneiform documents of the times of Nebuchadrezzar (J. N. Strassmaier, *Inschriften von Nabuchodonosor, König von Babylon* [Leipzig: E. Pfeiffer, 1889], No. 310, l. 2) and of Artaxerxes (H. C. Hilprecht and A. T. Clay, *Business Documents of Murashû Sons of Nippur Dated in the Reign of Artaxerxes I* [Philadelphia: University of Pennsylvania, 1898], No. 15, l. 20). His father **Galal,** whose name may be identical with that abbreviated "Gilalai" in 12:36, has a name also found in Achaemenid business documents (R. C. Thompson, *Cuneiform Texts from Babylonian Tablets in the British Museum* [London: The Trustees, 1906], Part XXII, Pl. XXXII, No. 174, l. 29; J. B. Nies and C. E. Keiser, *Historical, Religious and Economic Texts and Antiquities* [New Haven: Yale University Press, 1920], No. 111, ll. 3, 6; Arthur Ungnad, *Neubabylonische Kontrakte und Sonstige Urkunden* [Leipzig: 1907], No. 164, l. 22). **Jeduthun,** like **Asaph,** belonged to the Levite singers, but he has been regarded as "a shadowy figure: originally a musical tonality or mode . . . transformed into a person and . . . identified with Ethan (cf. I Chr. 15:17, 19) as the eponym of one of the three guilds of

18 All the Levites in the holy city *were* two hundred fourscore and four.

19 Moreover the porters, Akkub, Talmon, and their brethren that kept the gates, *were* a hundred seventy and two.

20 ¶ And the residue of Israel, of the priests, *and* the Levites, *were* in all the cities of Judah, every one in his inheritance.

21 But the Nethinim dwelt in Ophel: and Ziha and Gispa *were* over the Nethinim.

22 The overseer also of the Levites at Jerusalem *was* Uzzi the son of Bani, the son of Hashabiah, the son of Mattaniah, the son of Micha. Of the sons of Asaph, the singers *were* over the business of the house of God.

thun. 18 All the Levites in the holy city were two hundred and eighty-four.

19 The gatekeepers, Akkub, Talmon and their brethren, who kept watch at the gates, were a hundred and seventy-two. 20 And the rest of Israel, and of the priests and the Levites, were in all the towns of Judah, every one in his inheritance. 21 But the temple servants lived on Ophel; and Ziha and Gishpa were over the temple servants.

22 The overseer of the Levites in Jerusalem was Uzzi the son of Bani, son of Hashabi'ah, son of Mattani'ah, son of Mica, of the sons of Asaph, the singers, over the

---

singers (I Chr. 16:41; 25:1-6; II Chr. 5:12; 29:13-15; 35:15; Pfeiffer, *Intro. to O.T.*, p. 800). Several of these Levites appear in 12:25, not as musicians but as gatekeepers, just as the sons of **Jeduthun** appear as porters in I Chr. 16:42.

18. Since the figures given show more than four times as many priests as Levites, their servants, the data are regarded as evidence for the shortage of Levites in Jerusalem (cf. Ezra 8:15 ff.) and the readiness with which they abandoned the temple service (cf. 13:10; Batten, *loc cit.*); but the incompleteness of the list makes all such judgments precarious (cf. vs. 3).

5. Supplements (11:19-24)

19. As in I Chr. 9, the listing of Levite leaders is followed immediately by that of the gatekeepers, but the passage here presents but little of the abundant data regarding the **gatekeepers** found in Chronicles. In the separate listing of the **gatekeepers,** with their own total, has been seen evidence that the list was not created by the Chronicler, who grouped both the singers and gatekeepers with the Levites (Rudolph, *op. cit.*, p. 185); but Torrey (*Composition*, pp. 22-23) regards such an argument as invalid.

Of the six **gatekeepers** in Ezra 2:42, only **Akkub** and **Talmon** are here listed. Presumably, unless there is a simple omission in the list, the families of Shallum and Ahiman dwelt outside Jerusalem. Since the list here is that of individuals (cf. vs. 3a) rather than ancestors, if this portion is genuine, the leaders of both families by coincidence must have borne the names of their ancestors. The total (172) is less than that in I Chr. 9:22 (212), but there the families of Shallum and Ahiman are also named.

20. This verse, practically a repetition of vs. 3b, is not found in the major Greek MSS but is supplied in the LXX[L]. It seems to have been connected originally with vs. 25 as an introduction to the list of towns (vss. 25-36). The verses intervening between vs. 20 and vs. 25 are supplementary. **In his inheritance** (cf. vs. 3) may imply that exiles returned to their ancestral property which, in at least some cases, was unrealistic (cf. vs. 3).

21. The conclusion of vs. 20 suggested the **Nethinim** (cf. Ezra 2:43), who also dwelt in a special place (cf. 3:26) and are usually listed after the Levites. For **Ophel** see 3:26. Although the title "overseer" is not used, **Ziha** (cf. Ezra 2:43) and **Gishpa** are declared leaders of the **Nethinim. Gishpa,** found only here, is probably a corruption of "Hasupha" (Ezra 2:43; Batten, *op. cit.*, p. 272). The **Nethinim** are not mentioned in I Chr. 9 nor in the LXX[ABℵ] and the Peshitta omits reference to their leaders. The verse is clearly supplemental.

22-23. Also additional are vss. 22-23, inserted by someone who missed a reference to an **overseer** (vs. 9) of the Levites, as such leaders were named for other groups (cf. vss. 9, 14, 21). Since the **overseer** here is **Uzzi** (cf. "Uzziah," Ezra 10:21), the great

23 For *it was* the king's commandment concerning them, that a certain portion should be for the singers, due for every day.

24 And Pethahiah the son of Meshezabeel, of the children of Zerah the son of Judah, *was* at the king's hand in all matters concerning the people.

25 And for the villages, with their fields, *some* of the children of Judah dwelt at Kirjath-arba, and *in* the villages thereof, and at

---

work of the house of God. 23 For there was a command from the king concerning them, and a settled provision for the singers, as every day required. 24 And Pethahi'ah the son of Meshez'abel, of the sons of Zerah the son of Judah, was at the king's hand in all matters concerning the people.

25 And as for the villages, with their fields, some of the people of Judah lived in

---

grandson of **Mattaniah the son of Mica** (vs. 17), the supplement must reflect a substantially later time (Rudolph, *op. cit.*, p. 187). **The business** of the temple suggests its secular affairs, but the literal translation **work** does not imply that. The Vulg. interprets it as "the ministry," which closely approximates the meaning of the word in some contexts (cf. vs. 12; 10:33). **Over** is also a doubtful translation for a Hebrew word meaning "before," and the LXX and Peshitta which render it literally make nonsense. Probably the word (נגד) is related to the word for "guide" or "leader" in vs. 11, and the phrase should be "for the guidance of the work." The Levites and **singers** did the **work** (13:10) and the Levites guided the service of worship (cf. 8:7, 9-11; 9:4-5).

A command from the king is usually considered a reference to David who, according to the Chronicler, instituted the temple ritual (cf. 12:24; I Chr. 25). But since the Persian kings were interested in the local cults (cf. Ezra 6:9-10), the expression could refer to the Persian ruler (Olmstead, *History of the Persian Empire*, p. 91; Rudolph, *loc. cit.*). The word rendered **portion** or **settled provision** ("sure covenant" in 9:38) refers to a synonym in 12:47. The Vulg. (*ordo*) and some minor Greek MSS (A. E. Brooke, N. McLean, and H. St. John Thackeray, *The Old Testament in Greek* [Cambridge: Cambridge University Press, 1935], Vol. II, Part IV, p. 656), which have "arrangement," interpret it to imply royal regulation of the cult through specific orders for the daily work of the singers.

24. Perhaps the reference to the king in vs. 23 is responsible for the supplement here, which scarcely belongs in a list of residents of Jerusalem since **at the king's hand** implies residence abroad, at the Persian court. **Pethahiah** (cf. Ezra 10:23) son of **Meshezabel** (cf. 3:4) was apparently the ambassador who mediated between the Judean and the Persian court. He was a Judean, seemingly of the nobility, a descendant of **Zerah**, the twin of "Perez" (cf. vs. 4; Gen. 38:30; Num. 26:20). Omission of the family of **Zerah** in the list of Judeans (vss. 4-6) may be accidental but, since this verse is supplemental, the family may not yet have returned to Judea when that list was compiled.

C. Towns Settled Outside of Jerusalem (11:25-36)

25-36. After the list of residents of Jerusalem, the editor completes the picture by appending a list of towns outside of Jerusalem settled by the Jews (vss. 25-35). The settlements, relatively few, are quite scattered in four areas: the south (the Negeb); the hill country (Shephelah); the mountains just north and west of Jerusalem; and a small group far to the west in the coastal plain. There is a surprising silence regarding many places mentioned elsewhere in Ezra-Nehemiah: Tekoah (3:5); Beth-haccherem (3:14); Beth-zur (3:16); Keilah (3:17); Bethlehem and Netophah (7:26); Kiriath-jearim (7:29); Gibeon, Mizpah, and Meronoth (3:7); Chephirah and Beeroth (7:29); Jericho (7:36); and Gilgah (12:29 KJV).

The scattered character of the settlements leads many to consider the list as artificial and unhistorical. From Ezra 9 ff. some assume that the settlements were clustered around Jerusalem, arguing that it would be suicide for the tiny community to overextend itself as described in vss. 25-36 (Julius Wellhausen, *Israelitische und jüdische Geschichte* [3rd ed.; Berlin: Georg Reimer, 1897], p. 160). Hence the list is

Dibon, and *in* the villages thereof, and at Jekabzeel, and *in* the villages thereof,	Kir'iath-ar'ba and its villages, and in Dibon and its villages, and in Jekab'zeel and its

usually regarded as the work of the Chronicler, reflecting his motives, wording, and style (Torrey, *Composition*, pp. 42-43; Meyer, *Entstehung des Judenthums*, p. 186; Bertholet, *Esra und Nehemia*, p. 84; Siegfried, *Esra, Nehemia und Esther*, p. 120), and some conclude that in it "there is nothing . . . that may be used confidently for the history of Nehemiah's time" (Pfeiffer, *Intro. to O.T.*, p. 830).

Others, while rejecting the list for the time of Nehemiah, consider it a genuine list of historical value for either pre-exilic or Maccabean times. The criterion is the number of settlements in the south, which was strongly populated in pre-exilic times, overrun by Edomites during the Exile and early postexilic times, and not regained for the Jews until 164 B.C., when the Edomites were defeated and Hebron was recovered (I Macc. 5:65). Thus it is possible for the list to reflect the extent of Judah before the Exile (Stade, *Geschichte des Volkes Israel*, II, 111; Kugler, *Von Moses bis Paulus*, pp. 299-300; Rudolf Smend, *Lehrbuch der alttestamentlichen Religionsgeschichte* [Leipzig: J. C. B. Mohr, 1893], p. 340, n. 1), possibly during the time of Josiah (640-608 B.C.; Albrecht Alt, "Judas Gaue unter Josia," *Palästinajahrbuch*, XXI [1925], pp. 110 ff.), when the coastal plain was acquired by Judah, and Bethel too was taken over (II Kings 23:15). The use of archaic **Kiriath-arba** (vs. 25) for Hebron is better explained also by an earlier date. As a Maccabean product, which is much less likely, it would have to be "a very late insertion" into the book of Nehemiah (Rudolph, *op. cit.*, p. 190).

The list has been more recently defended as a genuine post-exilic document, not from the time of Nehemiah but earlier, before there was any extensive return. The omission of towns mentioned in chs. 3 and 7 has been explained by the fact that "this part of the province was virtually uninhabited when the exiles began to return after 538 B.C.E." (W. F. Albright, "The Biblical Period," in Louis Finkelstein, ed., *The Jews, Their History, Culture, and Religion* [New York: Harper & Bros., 1949], I, 52-53), for the Chaldean invasion left Jewish settlers only in the Negeb and in the district north of Jerusalem, which at the time of the fall of the city (586 B.C.) was under the control of the Babylonian governor of Samaria (W. F. Albright, *From the Stone Age to Christianity* [2nd ed.; Baltimore: Johns Hopkins Press, 1946], p. 247; cf. Rudolph, *op. cit.*, p. 189). The far-flung settlements in the list have also been regarded (Abel, *Géographie*, II, 121) not as returned Exile settlements, but as those of people who did not go into captivity, "the people of the land, rebellious against the new community and living in good relationship with the foreigners residing in Judea [i.e., in Edomite-Arabic and Ashdod districts]." Such a situation is reflected in 13:23-24. Adduced also is the close relationship between the Judean clans (Perez, Shelah) and the semi-Edomite Zerah (cf. vs. 24), for Jeduthun (vs. 17) was of Edomite ancestry since Ethan belonged to the Edomite clan of Zerah (I Kings 4:31) and was not recognized until the Zerah clan became Judean (Gen. 38:30; Num. 26:20; Josh. 7:1, 18, 24; cf. Cook, "First Esdras," in Charles, *Apocrypha and Pseudepigrapha*, I, 12).

1. Judean Settlements (11:25-30)

25a. Originally vs. 25a must have joined vs. 20 to form the title. **And for, and as for** do not translate the Hebrew, which is, lit., "and to" (אל) but it is preferable to read "and these are," since an easy scribal error could account for the loss of the letter which made the original אלה, "these," read אל, "to," before the Hebrew article (ה) of the next word (cf. Gotthard, *Nehemia*, p. 45). The Hebrew term חצר, translated **villages,** means "enclosure," and **their fields** refers to surrounding farm and pasture lands. **Villages** is criticized because some places mentioned were large cities, but "cities" would be equally wrong since most of them were relatively small, especially in the postexilic period. A compromise term such as "settlement" would be preferable.

26 And at Jeshua, and at Moladah, and at Beth-phelet,

27 And at Hazar-shual, and at Beer-sheba, and *in* the villages thereof,

28 And at Ziklag, and at Mekonah, and in the villages thereof,

villages, 26 and in Jeshua and in Mol'adah and Beth-pelet, 27 in Ha'zar-shu'al, in Beer-sheba and its villages, 28 in Ziklag,

---

25b. The cities of Judah listed begin in the south with Hebron and proceed southward roughly in clockwise fashion back toward Hebron. **Kiriath-arba** is perhaps properly identified with Hebron in Judg. 1:10 but Hölscher (*Esra und Nehemia,* p. 652) is not persuaded that the equation is correct. Hebron (El-Khalî) is at the crossroads of the southern highlands, about nineteen miles south and somewhat west of Jerusalem. The ancient site is identified with the Deir el Arba'în, crowning the ridge El Rumeidah overlooking Hebron from the southeast (Garstang, *Foundations of Bible History: Joshua-Judges,* pp. 170, 209-10, 383-84). **Its villages,** lit., "her daughters," refers to tiny settlements dependent upon and perhaps founded by a larger, neighboring mother city. **Dibon,** not to be confused with Dibon of Moab (Num. 21:30), is perhaps the Dimonah of Josh. 15:22 (Paul Haupt, "Über den Halbvokal *u* im Assyrischen," *Zeitschrift für Assyriologie und verwandte Gebiete,* II [1887], 268, n. 2; Gotthard, *loc. cit.*; Bertholet, *op. cit.,* p. 83; Rudolph, *op. cit.,* p. 187), located at El Qebâb east of Tell el-Milḥ (Abel, *op. cit.,* II, 89). The M.T. **Jekabzeel,** unsupported by the versions, is difficult. Many Hebrew MSS agree with the Peshitta, Vulg., and the LXX^L in reading "Kabzeel" (cf. Josh. 15:21a; II Sam. 23:20), usually located at Khirbet Ḥôra, northwest of Khirbet Sa'wi (cf. **Jeshua,** vs. 26) and northeast of Beer-sheba (*ibid*).

26. Jeshua, only here, has been regarded as the postexilic name of "Shema" of Josh. 15:26 (W. F. Albright, "Egypt and the Early History of the Negeb," *Journal of the Palestine Oriental Society.* IV [1924], 152), identified with Khirbet Sa'wi, about four miles north-northwest of El Meshash (cf. vs. 27) and about three miles northwest of Tell el-Milḥ (C. R. Conder and H. H. Kitchener, *The Survey of Western Palestine: Judea* [London: Palestine Exploration Fund, 1883], III, 409-10). **Moladah,** near the southern border of Judah (Josh. 15:26), has been identified by Abel (*op. cit.,* II, 391-92) with Tell el-Milḥ, a deserted site about ten miles southwest of Arad (cf. Wright and Filson, *Westminster Atlas,* p. 110), but Albright ("Egypt and the Early History of the Negeb," pp. 152-54) objects and identifies it with Roman Malatha at Khirbet Quṣeifeh, about four miles from Arad. **Beth-pelet** (Josh. 15:27c), once identified with Tell el Fâr'ah, has been located at Tell el-Milḥ by Albright, "because the order of towns within their groups in this passage of Nehemiah is remarkably exact" (*ibid.,* p. 153; "Progress in Palestinian Archaeology During the Year 1928," *Bulletin of the American Schools of Oriental Research,* No. 33 [1929], p. 7). But Abel (*op. cit.,* II, 89) identifies it with Khirbet el-Meshash (cf. vs. 27).

27. Hazar-shual ("Enclosure of the Jackal") is located by Albright ("Egypt and the Early History of the Negeb," pp. 153-54) at Khirbet el-Meshash, about three and one-half miles west of el-Milḥ, but Abel (*op. cit.,* II, 51, 89) places it at Khirbet Waṭan, east of **Beer-sheba** and west of Horma. **Beer-sheba,** usually identified with the modern site (Bir es-seba') about twenty-eight miles southwest of Hebron (Abel, *op. cit.,* II, 89; Alois Musil, *Arabia Petraea* [Vienna: Alfred Hölder, 1907-8], II, 165-69; Albrecht Alt, "Beiträge zur historischen Geographie und Topographie des Negeb," *Journal of the Palestine Oriental Society,* XV [1935], 320 ff.; cf. Walther Zimmerli, *Geschichte und Tradition von Beerseba im Alten Testament* [Giessen: A. Töpelmann, 1932]), may anciently have been at Tell es-Seba', about four miles east of the modern city (so Abel, *op. cit.,* I, 307; but cf. II, 89, where he identifies it with Horma; Wright and Filson, *op. cit.,* p. 108).

28. Ziklag (Tell el-Khuweilfeh) lay about ten miles east of Tell esh-Sherî'a (Alt, "Geographie und Topographie des Negeb," pp. 317-22). **Meconah** nearby is not yet

29 And at En-rimmon, and at Zareah, and at Jarmuth,

30 Zanoah, Adullam, and *in* their villages, at Lachish, and the fields thereof, at Azekah, and *in* the villages thereof. And they dwelt from Beer-sheba unto the valley of Hinnom.

31 The children also of Benjamin from Geba *dwelt* at Michmash, and Aija, and Bethel, and *in* their villages,

in Meco'nah and its villages, 29 in En-rim'-mon, in Zorah, in Jarmuth, 30 Zano'ah, Adullam, and their villages, Lachish and its fields, and Aze'kah and its villages. So they encamped from Beer-sheba to the valley of Hinnom. 31 The people of Benjamin also lived from Geba onward, at Michmash,

---

certainly identified. Albright ("Egypt and the Early History of the Negeb," pp. 160-61) made a "rather precarious" suggestion to emend to "Meronah" and identify it with Khirbet Marrân, and Batten (*op. cit.,* p. 273) would emend to "Madmannah" (Josh. 15:31), which has been identified with Umm Deimneh in the hills south of 'Anâb (Albright, *loc. cit.;* "Researches of the School in Western Judea," *Bulletin of the American Schools of Oriental Research,* No. 15 [1924], p. 6).

29a. En-rimmon ("Spring of the Pomegranates"; Josh. 15:32; 19:7), probably the Rimmon of Zech. 14:10, is Khirbet Umm et-Ramāmîm, about nine miles northeast of Beer-sheba (Abel, *op. cit.,* II, 52).

Beginning with **Zorah** the list proceeds southward, roughly clockwise. All the Judean towns were between Beer-sheba—always the southern extremity of Jewish Palestine (cf. I Sam. 3:20; I Kings 4:25; etc.)—and the Valley of Hinnom (cf. 2:13), which was the northern boundary of Judah (cf. Josh. 15:8).

29b. Zorah (Josh. 15:33), modern Ṣar'ah, lay about twenty-two miles west of Jerusalem (Abel, *op. cit.,* II, 85; Wright and Filson, *op. cit.,* p. 112, Rudolph, *op. cit.,* p. 188). Garstang (*op. cit.,* pp. 335, 404) finds it at Ṣur'ah, crowning a ridge overlooking the Valley of Sorek (Wadi es-Ṣur'ah; Judg. 16:4), about fifteen miles west of Jerusalem (cf. W. F. Albright, "From Jerusalem to Gaza and Back," *Bulletin of the American Schools of Oriental Research,* No. 17 [1925], pp. 4-5). **Jarmuth** (Khirbet Yarmûk; cf. Josh. 15:35), near the Valley of Elah (Wadi es-Sanṭ), overlooks Tell Zakarîyeh (cf. vs. 30) and the coastal plain (Abel, *op. cit.,* II, 90; Garstang, *op. cit.,* p. 386; Rudolph, *loc. cit.*).

30. Zanoah (Josh. 15:34; Khirbet Zānû' or Zānûḥ) lay one mile northeast of Jarmuth (vs. 29) and almost two miles south of Beth-shemesh ('Ain Shems; Albright, "To Engedi and Masada," p. 11; Abel, *op. cit.,* II, 90, 489; Wright and Filson, *loc. cit.;* Rudolph, *loc. cit.*). **Adullam** (Josh. 15:35; Khirbet 'Id-el-mā) lay about nine and one-half miles northeast of Beit Jibrîn in the Valley of Elah "on the most direct route from Jerusalem to Lachish" (Abel, *op. cit.,* II, 85, 90, 239; Garstang, *op. cit.,* p. 176; Albright, "Researches of the School in Western Judea," pp. 3-4). **Lachish** (Josh. 15:39) lay at Tell ed-Duweir, a few miles southwest of Beit Jibrîn and near modern el-Qubeibeh (cf. G. L. Harding, *Guide to Lachish: Tell ed-Duweir* [Jerusalem: Commercial Press, 1943], pp. 11, 15-16). Some, however, still prefer to identify Lachish with Tell el-Haṣi, west of Tell ed-Duweir, as was formerly done (Anton Jirku, "Lag das alte Lakiš auf dem Tell ed-Duweir" *Zeitschrift für die alttestamentliche Wissenschaft,* LVII [1939], 152-53; Rudolph, *loc. cit.*), even though the excavator of Tell el-Haṣi was not certain of its identification (C. M. Watson, *Fifty Years' Work in the Holy Land* [London: Palestine Exploration Fund, 1915], p. 106). **Azekah** (Josh. 15:35; Tell es-Zakarîyeh) lay not far west of Jarmuth (cf. vs. 29b; Garstang, *op. cit.,* p. 360).

2. BENJAMINITE SETTLEMENTS (11:31-36)

The settlements in Benjamin were located in part in the mountains north and northwest of Jerusalem and in part as a small cluster in the far west in the coastal

32 *And* at Anathoth, Nob, Ananiah,	Ai'ja, Bethel and its villages, 32 An'athoth,
33 Hazor, Ramah, Gittaim,	Nob, Anani'ah, 33 Hazor, Ramah, Git'taim,
34 Hadid, Zeboim, Neballat,	34 Hadid, Zebo'im, Nebal'lat. 35 Lod, and
35 Lod, and Ono, the valley of craftsmen.	Ono, the valley of craftsmen. 36 And cer-
36 And of the Levites *were* divisions *in* Judah, *and* in Benjamin.	tain divisions of the Levites in Judah were joined to Benjamin.

plain (cf. 7:37; Ezra 2:33). The mountain settlements north and northwest of Jerusalem, in old Benjaminite territory, began with **Geba** (vs. 31) and moved in an irregular circuit counterclockwise, bending northeast to **Michmash**, northwest to **Aija**, westward to **Bethel**, far southeast to **Anathoth**, southwest to **Nob**, southeast to **Ananiah**, northwest to **Hazor**, and northward to **Ramah**, which lay almost directly west of the starting point Geba.

31. Read, "And some of the sons of Benjamin," parallel to vs. 25, for **from** or "some of" which belongs there is wrongly placed before **Geba** (Gotthard, *op. cit.*, p. 31; Batten, *Ezra and Nehemiah*, p. 274; Guthe and Batten, *Ezra and Nehemiah*, p. 53; Rudolph, *loc. cit.*); **Geba:** cf. "Gaba," Ezra 2:26; **Michmash:** cf. Ezra 2:27; **Aija** is but the Aramaic equivalent of Ai (Ezra 2:28); **Bethel:** cf. Ezra 2:28.

32. Anathoth: cf. Ezra 2:23 (Neh. 7:27); **Nob** is the "Nebo" of Ezra 2:29 (Neh. 7:33; cf. Batten, *loc. cit.*). **Ananiah** is best identified with the Bethany of the N.T. (el-'Azarîyeh; Albright, "New Identifications of Ancient Towns," pp. 9-10; Abel, *op. cit.*, II, 243).

33ab. Hazor is found only here in reference to Benjamin. Since Khirbet Hazzûr, formerly identified with it (*ibid.*, II, 345; Wright and Filson, *op. cit.*, p. 109; Rudolph, *op. cit.*, p. 189), has proved to be a late site, Roman and later, Alt ("Die Ausflüge: Hazor," *Palästinajahrbuch*, XXIV [1928], 12-13; cf. W. F. Albright, "The Jordan Valley in the Bronze Age," *Annual of the American Schools of Oriental Research*, VI [1924-25], 21) conjectures its earlier site to be on a mountain west of Khirbet Hazzûr, perhaps on El burdsch or Nebi Samwil, and Albright locates it provisionally at El-Mughâr just southeast of Khirbet Hazzûr. For **Ramah** see Ezra 2:26. Because of the difficulty of identifying some sites, it is impossible to observe any regular plan of listing the coastal sites.

33c-35. With **Gittaim** (cf. II Sam. 4:3) the Benjaminite list leaps to the coastal plain. **Gittaim** has been located at the ruined group called Khirbet el-Kelch and Nebi-Zakaria, lying northwest of Berfîlia (Crusaders' Porphilia) and southeast of **Hadid** (cf. Ezra 2:33.; Albrecht Alt, "Gittaim," *Palästinajahrbuch*, XXXV [1939], 100-4). Albright (reviewing Abel's *Géographie de la Palestine, Journal of Biblical Literature*, LVIII [1939], 179) identifies it with the *Qdtm* of Shishak's list (No. 25) and places it between Beth-horon of Ephraim and Ajalon of Dan. For **Hadid** (el-Haditheh), **Lod** (Lydda), and **Ono** (Kefr 'Anā) see Ezra 2:33. **Zeboim,** possibly the *alu* Ṣabuma of the Amarna letters (J. A. Knudtzon, *Die El-Amarna-Tafeln* [Leipzig: J. C. Hinrichs, 1915], II, 1328-29, No. 274, l. 16), could be Khirbet Sabieh, north of Lydda (Abel, *op. cit.*, II, 28, 452). **Neballat,** probably Beit Nabala, northeast of Lydda (Siegfried, *Esra, Nehemia und Esther*, p. 120; Abel, *op. cit.*, II, 397; Wright and Filson, *op. cit.*, p. 111; Rudolph, *loc. cit.*), may have been named for a Nabu-uballit who was "presumably a powerful Assyrian Governor of Samaria at the beginning of the 7th century B.C." (W. F. Albright, "Excavations and Results at Tell el-Fûl (Gibeah of Saul)," *Annual of the American Schools of Oriental Research*, IV [1922-23], 106, n. 15; "The Date and Personality of the Chronicler," *Journal of Biblical Literature*, XL [1921], 111, n. 17).

The **valley of craftsmen** (cf. I Chr. 4:14) possibly lay in the richly wooded region about **Lod** or **Ono** (Rudolph, *loc. cit.*). Perhaps it is to be identified with the Sarafand el-Kharab, in a valley formed by a tributary of the Nahr Rûbîn (Abel, *op. cit.*, II, 405). The Ethiopic and Peshitta versions attest an **and** before the last name which has been lost because it was a single letter identical with the last letter of the name **Ono** (Gotthard, *op. cit.*, p. 45; Guthe and Batten, *loc. cit.; et al.*).

12 Now these *are* the priests and the Levites that went up with Zerubbabel the son of Shealtiel, and Jeshua: Seraiah, Jeremiah, Ezra,

2 Amariah, Malluch, Hattush,

12 These are the priests and the Levites who came up with Zerub'babel the son of She-al'ti-el, and Jeshua: Serai'ah, Jeremiah, Ezra, 2 Amari'ah, Malluch, Hattush,

XIII. CLERICAL GENEALOGIES (12:1-26)

Chapter 12 is a composite work recording clerical genealogies of the postexilic period (vss. 1-26), an account of the dedication of the city walls (vss. 27-43), and finally a statement from the Chronicler's viewpoint regarding the ideal status of the cultus in the postexilic period (vss. 44-47). The genealogies list the individuals or representatives of priests and Levites in various periods, from the return under Darius II to the time of the high priest Jaddua.

A. PRIESTS (12:1-7)

The first list purports to be the priests who returned with Zerubbabel. As such, it should parallel 7:39-42, but instead of the four families of ch. 7, there are twenty-two here. It is argued that the author had no information regarding priests of the time of the high priest Joshua (Hölscher, *Esra und Nehemia*, p. 553), and it has been thought unlikely that all families were developing independent lines for the future in the time of Joshua (Rudolph, *op. cit.*, p. 191). Others, however, contend that after their arrival in Palestine there may have been a subdivision of families with one group retaining the old family name while the others assumed the names of their contemporary family leaders (cf. Bertholet, *Esra und Nehemia*, p. 84; Abraham Kuenen, *Gesammelte Abhandlungen zur biblischen Wissenschaft* [tr. Karl Budde; Leipzig: J. C. B. Mohr, 1894], p. 379). There seems to have been some concern about re-establishing the status of the nine priestly families that had lost their privileges (7:61-65). Some prefer to see in the list a record not of the time of Zerubbabel but of Joiakim (cf. vss. 12-21).

With several additions and omissions, but with the names otherwise in the identical order, the same list of priests is found in 10:2-8, which presumably comes from a time after Nehemiah. The unusual "and" in the midst of the list, before Joiarib (vs. 19), marks all that follows as of secondary origin (Meyer, *Entstehung des Judenthums*, p. 173). Since the Maccabees were descended from Joiarib (I Macc. 2:1), who appears as a correction of the name Joiakim (cf. 11:10), the addition may be as late as Maccabean times (Hölscher, *op. cit.*, p. 553; Rudolph, *loc. cit.*).

12:1. Since the title "the Levites" is in vs. 8, it is possible that only **the priests** was original in vs. 1 (cf. Batten, *op. cit.*, p. 275). However, if the full title were used here, it could be that after the lengthy matter of the priests was finished the need for another title was felt in vs. 8. In the LXXL **Jeshua** is identified as high priest through the insertion of his genealogy (Ezra 3:2). **Ezra** (cf. vs. 13) abbreviates Azariah (cf. Ezra 7:1) as in 10:2.

2. Amariah: Cf. Ezra 7:3. The LXX, Vulg., and Peshitta versions support the reading **Malluch**, which abbreviates Malchiah (cf. Ezra 10:25). **Hattush** (cf. Ezra 8:2) is omitted in 12:14 and in all major Greek MSS, but its presence in 10:4 points to an accidental loss in vs. 14 (cf. Rudolph, *op. cit.*, p. 190). Since the family of Passhur existed in the community (cf. 10:3; 11:12*b*), its absence in vss. 1*b*-7, 12-21 apparently indicates loss of text here (*ibid.*).

12:1-30. *A Census of Priests, Levites, and Singers.*—By the use of various categories and classifications the Chronicler may well have made full use of all the lists of names and families that had come down to him, from the earliest returning exiles under Zerubbabel (cf. Ezra 2:1-2). At a time when mixed marriages were under the ban, especially for the priests and Levites, such genealogies were obviously important.

3 Shechaniah, Rehum, Meremoth,
4 Iddo, Ginnetho, Abijah,
5 Miamin, Maadiah, Bilgah,
6 Shemaiah, and Joiarib, Jedaiah,
7 Sallu, Amok, Hilkiah, Jedaiah. These *were* the chief of the priests and of their brethren in the days of Jeshua.

3 Shecani'ah, Rehum, Mer'emoth, 4 Iddo, Gin'nethoi, Abi'jah, 5 Mi'jamin, Ma-adi'ah, Bilgah, 6 Shemai'ah, Joi'arib, Jedai'ah, 7 Sallu, Amok, Hilki'ah, Jedai'ah. These were the chiefs of the priests and of their brethren in the days of Jeshua.

3. **Shechaniah** (cf. Ezra 8:3) is Shebaniah in three Hebrew MSS and the Vulg. here and in the lists in 10:4; 12:14, but the M.T. here is supported by the LXX$^{\aleph L}$ in 12:14 and by the LXX and Peshitta versions here. By the transposition of letters the name חרם ("Harim"; 7:42; 10:5; 12:15; Ezra 2:32) has been corrupted to רחם (**Rehum**; cf. Ezra 2:2). As the Vulg. and Peshitta versions show, **Meremoth** (cf. 10:5; Ezra 8:33) is preferable to Meraioth (cf. Ezra 7:3).

4. Because **Iddo** (Ezra 5:1) appears in the written tradition (*Kethîbh*) of 12:16 as "Adaiah" (cf. Ezra 10:29) and that is found here in the LXX^L, it is conjectured that the name here should be Obadiah (cf. Ezra 8:9; Gotthard, *loc. cit.*), but in 12:16 the oral tradition (*Qerê*) also had **Iddo. Ginnethoi** is a corruption of "Ginnethon" (cf. 10:6). The correct name is given in about thirty-four Hebrew MSS and the Vulg., and in 10:6; 12:16.

5. **Mijamin** (cf. Ezra 10:25) contracts the "Miniamin" of vss. 17, 41 (cf. II Chr. 31:15), which appears in Babylonian records as *mmi-in-ia-a-me-en* (A. T. Clay, *Business Documents of Murashû Sons of Nippur Dated in the Reign of Darius II* [Philadelphia: University of Pennsylvania, 1904], No. 81, ll. 12, 23; No. 84, ll. 13, 21; etc.), and *mmi-in-ia-mi-i-ni* (Hilprecht and Clay, *Business Documents of Murashû Sons of Nippur in Reign of Artaxerxes I*, No. 14, l. 11). **Maadiah** is the Moadiah of 12:17. "Maaziah" (cf. I Chr. 24:18) is found for it here in the LXX^L and in the M.T. of 10:8, and that familiar priestly name (cf. 10:8; I Chr. 24:18) is favored here by some (Gotthard, *loc. cit.;* Bertholet, *loc. cit.; et al.*).

6. In the parallel list (10:2-8) the names after **Shemaiah** (cf. Ezra 8:13, 16) are omitted. With **and Joiarib** begins a new section, apparently added later. Since **Joiarib** appears to "correct" an original "Joiakim" (cf. 11:10) and **Joiarib** was a Maccabean ancestor (I Macc. 2:1), the addition may be Maccabean (Hölscher, *op. cit.*, p. 553; Rudolph, *op. cit.*, p. 191).

7. As the LXX^L and Vulg. show, **Sallu** (cf. 11:7) is preferable to the Sallai of vs. 20. **Amok** ("Deep") is perhaps a metaphorical "Inscrutable" or "Wise." The name appears among Babylonian names as *mE-muq* (A. T. Clay, *Babylonian Business Transactions of the First Millennium B.C.* [New York: Private Printing, 1912], Vol. I, No. 32, l. 14). Since the element appears in such names as *me-muq^{d}bêl* (Georges Contenau, *Contrâts néobabyloniens* [Paris: P. Geuthner, 1927], Vol. I, No. 2, l. 2) and *me-muq^{d}Adad* (L. W. King, *Babylonian Boundary Stones in the British Museum* [London: British Museum, 1912], Pl. XXII, col. 2, l. 12), the full name was perhaps "Amoqiah" or "Amoqel." Because **Jedaiah** (cf. Ezra 2:36) occurs twice (cf. vs. 6), it was conjectured that in one instance another name must be displaced by it. The LXX^L suggests "Hodaviah" (cf. Ezra 2:40), otherwise unknown as a priestly name (Bertholet, *op. cit.*, p. 85), and others suggest for **Jedaiah** (ידעיה) the name "Adaiah" (עדיה; Guthe and Batten, *loc. cit.;* Bertheau, *Esra, Nechemia und Ester*, p. 327), believed to be represented by the Ethiopic version (Gotthard, *loc. cit.*). But Rudolph (*op. cit.*, p. 190) disapproves of such substitution and argues that a common name could be repeated.

The antecedent of **their brethren** is not clear. If it refers to the chiefs, then **priests** and brothers are identical and the conjunction is needless (cf. *ibid*). The words **and of their brethren** could have been copied mechanically and needlessly from 11:12-14 (*ibid.*; Batten, *op. cit.*, p. 276). Since the Levites are normally so designated, it should refer to them. Possibly vs. 7*b* should follow vs. 9, where **their brethren** would refer to

8 Moreover the Levites: Jeshua, Binnui, Kadmiel, Sherebiah, Judah, *and* Mattaniah, *which was* over the thanksgiving, he and his brethren.

9 Also Bakbukiah and Unni, their brethren, *were* over against them in the watches.

10 ¶ And Jeshua begat Joiakim, Joiakim

8 And the Levites: Jeshua, Bin'nui, Kad'mi-el, Sherebi'ah, Judah, and Mattani'ah, who with his brethren was in charge of the songs of thanksgiving. 9 And Bakbuki'ah and Unni their brethren stood opposite them in the service. 10 And Jeshua was the

---

the Levites listed in vss. 8-9, forming a good connection between vs. 10 and the previous pericope (cf. Rudolph, *loc. cit.*) .

B. Levites (12:8-9)

As usual **the Levites** follow the priests. The list is regarded as highly artificial, expanding a nucleus of three ancestral names (7:43-44; Ezra 2:40) by adding those of contemporaries of Nehemiah and Ezra (*ibid.*) . The identity and order of the Levites is essentially that of other lists (7:43; 8:7; 9:4-5; 10:9; 12:24-25) .

8-9. As always, except for 12:24, **Jeshua** (Ezra 2:2; 3:2) the son of Azaniah (cf. 10:9) heads the list of Levites. As in 10:9, **Binnui** the son of Henadad is listed second. The usual confusion between **Binnui** and Bani (cf. 7:15; Ezra 2:10) is found here, for the name appears as "Bani" in the other lists (cf. 8:7; 9:4-5; and possibly 12:24) . In 7:43 **Kadmiel** (cf. Ezra 2:40) is listed second, but he is third elsewhere, except in 8:7, where the name is omitted.

Sherebiah (cf. Ezra 8:18) , not found in 7:43, appears to have been not of the time of Zerubbabel but from the time of Nehemiah (10:13) and Ezra (Ezra 8:18, 24; Neh. 8:7; 9:4-5) . The name is regularly in later lists, but not always fourth. Some deny that **Judah** (cf. Ezra 3:9) was a Levite name (*ibid.*) and it is possible that **Judah** (יהודה) is a corruption of Hodiah (הודיה) , as in 8:7; 9:5; 10:10, 13 (Bertheau, *loc. cit.;* Siegfried, *Esra, Nehemia und Esther,* p. 120; Gotthard, *loc. cit.; et al.*) or Hodaviah (הודויה; cf. Ezra 2:40; Neh. 7:43; Rudolph, *loc. cit.*) . But **Judah** is also in Ezra 3:9; 10:23 and the Vulg. and Peshitta here support the M.T.

Mattaniah and his brethren led the singing of the thanksgiving hymn (11:17) . The Vulg., "they and their brethren," indicates that all Levites were responsible. Rudolph (*ibid.*) thinks of an antiphonal choir of many men. **Bakbukiah** (cf. 11:17) and **Unni** (I Chr. 15:18, 20) are associated in some activity contrasting with that of the Levites. They are with the gatekeepers in vs. 25. Some read instead of **Unni** a verb "and they used to answer" (Bertheau, *op. cit.,* p. 328; Bertholet, *loc. cit.;* Guthe and Batten, *loc. cit.*) or "and they answered" (Edouard Reuss, *Chronique ecclésiastique de Jérusalem* [Paris: Sandoz & Fischbacher, 1878], p. 254, n. 2) , and omit **and Bakbukiah** as a gloss from 11:17. But since the name is attested in the LXX[L], the emendation to a verb is impossible (Rudolph, *loc. cit.*) . Some change **Unni** to 'Abdî for Obadiah (vs. 25) and Abda (11:17) wherever **Unni** is found in this list (van Hoonacker, *Nouvelles études sur la restauration,* p. 253) . The word is the common abbreviation either of Anaiah (cf. 8:4) or of Ananiah (3:23) ; cf. Rudolph, *loc. cit.*) . In I Chr. 15:18, 20, it refers to a Levite in the time of David.

Stood opposite them may refer to antiphonal singing or to the changes of orders for different occasions (cf. Batten, *loc. cit.*) The verse concludes with "according to functions," meaning "according to the Levitical divisions for service." It is interpreted as "according to their offices" (ASV) , **in the service,** or "in the execution of their official duties" (Amer. Trans.) .

C. Postexilic High Priests (12:10-11)

In I Chr. 6:1-14 the list of high priests concludes with Jehozadak, who went into captivity. Here the list, without a title, begins with **Jeshua** (cf. Ezra 2:2) , the first

also begat Eliashib, and Eliashib begat Joiada,

11 And Joiada begat Jonathan, and Jonathan begat Jaddua.

12 And in the days of Joiakim were priests, the chief of the fathers: of Seraiah, Meraiah; of Jeremiah, Hananiah;

father of Joi'akim, Joi'akim the father of Eli'ashib, Eli'ashib the father of Joi'ada, 11 Joi'ada the father of Jonathan, and Jonathan the father of Jad'du-a.

12 And in the days of Joi'akim were priests, heads of fathers' houses: of Serai'ah,

---

postexilic high priest, contemporary with Zerubbabel (Hag. 1:1; Zech. 3:1 ff.), and concludes with **Jaddua,** who was probably contemporary with the editor.

10. Jeshua: Cf. Ezra 2:2. **Joiakim** was high priest during the period covered by vss. 12-21, 25-26. The interval between **Jeshua** (*ca.* 520 B.C.) and **Eliashib** (*ca.* 445 B.C.) has been regarded as too great for **Joiakim** alone. It is sometimes assumed that at least one name is lost from the list (Hölscher, *op. cit.,* p. 553; Kittel, *Geschichte des Volkes Israel,* III, 649), but possibly **Joiakim** had an unusually long period in office (Rudolph, *op. cit.,* p. 192). **Joiada** (3:6) was the son of **Eliashib,** but in 13:28 the title "high priest" could refer to either **Joiada** or **Eliashib.** It is claimed that Josephus (*Antiquities* XI. 7. 1) regarded Eliashib's successor as "Judah" (Rudolph, *loc. cit.*) but the best text of Josephus has *Jōdas,* a corruption of the **Joiada** of the M.T. (cf. Marcus, *Josephus,* VI, 456-57, 456, note *d*).

11. Jonathan is an error for "Johanan" (cf. vss. 22-23). Mowinckel suggested that **Jonathan** may have been a link between "Johanan" and **Jaddua,** but this is not confirmed by vs. 22, and Josephus (*loc. cit.*) recognizes *Jōannēs* (=Johanan) as the successor of *Jōdas* (=Joiada). It is argued that in vs. 23 "Johanan the son of Eliashib" (cf. Ezra 10:6) means that Johanan was a brother rather than a son of **Joiada** (Rudolph, *loc. cit.;* Hölscher, *loc. cit.*), but the text means "Johanan the descendant of Eliashib" (cf. Ezra 5:1). Johanan can be dated through his contact with the Jews of Egypt who sent him a letter in 410 B.C. (Cowley, *Aramaic Papyri,* No. 30, l. 18; No. 31, l. 17). Josephus (*loc. cit.*) furthermore declares that Johanan killed his brother for plotting with Bagoas, Artaxerxes' general, to displace him in the high priesthood. Bagoas is probably the governor (cf. "Bigvai," Ezra 2:2) named in the same Aramaic papyrus that mentions Johanan during the reign of Darius II (423-404 B.C.; Cowley, *op. cit.,* No. 30, l. 1; No. 32, l. 1). Possibly he may have continued to serve under Artaxerxes II (404-358 B.C). Since Johanan was contemporary with Ezra (Ezra 10:6), the Artaxerxes of the Ezra story is Artaxerxes II, called Mnemon, and Ezra was preceded by Nehemiah, who was a contemporary of Eliashib (cf. 3:1, 20-21; 13:4, 7), the grandfather of Johanan (cf. Rowley, *Servant of the Lord,* pp. 134-45). **Jaddua** is linked with Alexander the Great (332 B.C.) by Josephus (*Antiquities* XI. 8. 2; cf. 13:28). While Josephus' story of such a relationship may be largely legendary, it may nevertheless preserve the valid evidence that **Jaddua,** as an old man, lived to the time of Alexander (Marcus, *op. cit.,* VI, 525-32).

D. Priests Under Joiakim (12:12-21)

This list, purporting to name priests of the time of Joiakim the father of Eliashib (cf. vs. 10), is actually a double one naming both the remote ancestor and the contemporary representative of that family.

12. The versions suggest a different title, "And in the days of Joiakim, his brothers the priests and the heads of the fathers' houses were . . . ." For היו כהנים, **were priests,** the versions suggest the graphically similar אחיו כהנים, "his brethren, priests" (Gotthard, *loc. cit.*). The LXX and Peshitta indicate that the reading should be "the priests," and the LXX and Vulg. show that "and" belongs before **heads of fathers' houses. Of Seraiah** is, lit., "belonging to [the family of] Seraiah." In the Peshitta "belonging to" is omitted and the double list is rendered as a tabulation, "Seraiah: Meraiah," etc. **Seraiah:** Cf. vs. 1; 10:2; Ezra 2:2). **Meraiah,** like Meraioth (11:11), may be an abbreviation of a fuller name, but it could be of a later Aramaic type including the element "Lord" (*mar*),

13 Of Ezra, Meshullam; of Amariah, Jehohanan;

14 Of Melicu, Jonathan; of Shebaniah, Joseph;

15 Of Harim, Adna; of Meraioth, Helkai;

16 Of Iddo, Zechariah; of Ginnethon, Meshullam;

17 Of Abijah, Zichri; of Miniamin, of Moadiah, Piltai;

18 Of Bilgah, Shammua; of Shemaiah, Jehonathan;

19 And of Joiarib, Mattenai; of Jedaiah, Uzzi:

20 Of Sallai, Kallai; of Amok, Eber;

21 Of Hilkiah, Hashabiah; of Jedaiah, Nethaneel.

Merai'ah; of Jeremiah, Hanani'ah; 13 of Ezra, Meshul'lam; of Amari'ah, Jeho-ha'-nan; 14 of Mal'luchi, Jonathan; of Shebani'ah, Joseph; 15 of Harim, Adna; of Merai'oth, Hel'kai; 16 of Iddo, Zechari'ah; of Gin'-nethon, Meshul'lam; 17 of Abi'jah, Zichri; of Mini'amin, of Moadi'ah, Pil'tai; 18 of Bilgah, Sham'mu-a; of Shemai'ah, Jehon'-athan; 19 of Joi'arib, Matte'nai; of Jedai'ah, Uzzi; 20 of Sal'lai, Kal'lai; of Amok, Eber; 21 of Hilki'ah, Hashabi'ah; of Jedai'ah, Nethan'el.

like the names Marachad (מראחד) or Marbaraki (מרברך; *Corpus Inscriptionum Semiticarum*, Part II, Vol. I, Nos. 79, 85), meaning "My Lord is Yah," parallel in meaning to "Adonijah." **Jeremiah:** Cf. 10:2; 12:1. **Hananiah:** Cf. 3:30; Ezra 10:28.

13-16. For **Ezra** the Peshitta has "Azariah," as in 10:2. **Meshullam:** Cf. Ezra 8:16. **Amariah:** Cf. vs. 2; 10:3; Ezra 7:3. The Peshitta contracts **Jehohanan** (cf. Ezra 10:28) to "Johanan" (cf. Ezra 8:12). **Malluchi** is "Malluch" (cf. vs. 2), to which the first letter of the name Jonathan has been attached as a dittograph (Rudolph, *loc. cit.*). **Jonathan:** Cf. Ezra 8:6; 10:15. **Shebaniah** (cf. 10:4), also read by the Vulg., should be "Shechaniah," as in vs. 3, as about seventeen Hebrew MSS, the LXX[L], and Peshitta show. **Joseph:** Cf. Ezra 10:42. **Harim:** Cf. 10:5; "Rehum" in 12:3. **Adna:** Cf. Ezra 10:30. The LXX[L] and Peshitta show that **Meraioth** (cf. Ezra 7:3) should be "Meremoth," as in vs. 3; 10:5. **Helkai** abbreviates "Hilkiah" (cf. 8:4). The LXX[L] and Vulg. support the written tradition of the M.T., "Adaiah" (cf. Ezra 10:29), but it is preferable to read **Iddo** with the oral tradition, the Peshitta, and vs. 4. **Zechariah** (cf. Ezra 5:1) might be the prophet (*ibid.*, p. 193), but it is unnecessary to assume that Zechariah's father bore the name of his ancestor, for "son" may mean "descendant" (Ezra 5:1). **Ginnethon** (cf. 10:6) is preferable to "Ginnethoi" (vs. 4). **Meshullam:** Cf. Ezra 8:16.

17-18. **Abijah:** Cf. vs. 4; 10:7. **Zichri:** Cf. 11:9. **Miniamin** is the full form of "Mijamin" (vs. 5; 10:7) read by two Hebrew MSS here. The name of his descendant is lost. **Moadiah,** only here, is "Maadiah" in vs. 5, and "Mazziah" in 10:8. The former, supported here by five Hebrew MSS and the LXX, seems preferable. **Piltai,** which is also found in the Aramaic papyri (Cowley, *op. cit.*, No. 40, l. 1), abbreviates "Phaltiel" ("God Has Rescued"; II Sam. 3:15), which also appears as Phalti (I Sam. 25:44), or "Pelatiah" ("The Lord Has Rescued"; Ezek. 11:1, 13). **Bilgah** (cf. vs. 5) is preferable to "Bilgai" (10:8). **Shammua:** Cf. 11:17. **Shemaiah:** Cf. vs. 6; 10:8. **Jehonathan** (cf. Ezra 10:28) appears in the versions as "Jonathan."

19-21. As in vs. 6, the remainder of the list, omitted in 10:2-8, is introduced by **and** in the M.T. For **Joiarib** (vs. 6) the Peshitta has "Joiada" (vs. 10). **Mattenai:** Cf. Ezra 10:33, 37. **Jedaiah:** Cf. vs. 6. **Uzzi:** Cf. 11:22; Ezra 7:4. For **Sallai** (vs. 20) read "Sallu" with vs. 7 and the LXX[L]. **Kallai,** only here, abbreviates a full name that can no longer be fully ascertained but may be "Kelaiah" (cf. 10:10; Ezra 10:23). **Amok:** Cf. vs. 7. For **Eber** (Gen. 10:21; I Chr. 5:13; 8:12, 22), supported by "Heber" in the Vulg., it is proposed to read "Ebed" (cf. Ezra 8:6), as in the Peshitta, LXX, and several Hebrew MSS. **Hilkiah:** Cf. vs. 7; also "Helkai," vs. 15. **Hashabiah:** Cf. Ezra 8:19, 24. **Jedaiah** (cf. vs. 7) is rendered "Hoduiah" by the LXX[L], and it is proposed to read here "Adaiah" (עדיה) as in vs. 7 (Gotthard, *loc. cit.*) but that is unnecessary. **Nethanel:** Cf. Ezra 10:22.

22 ¶ The Levites in the days of Eliashib, Joiada, and Johanan, and Jaddua, *were* recorded chief of the fathers: also the priests, to the reign of Darius the Persian.

23 The sons of Levi, the chief of the fathers, *were* written in the book of the

22 As for the Levites, in the days of Eli'-ashib, Joi'ada, Joha'nan, and Jad'du-a, there were recorded the heads of fathers' houses; also the priests until the reign of Darius the Persian. 23 The sons of Levi,

---

E. Source of the Genealogical Lists (12:22-23)

After the priests (vss. 12-21), a list of the Levites of the same period is expected but that is not given until vss. 24-25, separated from the former list by an interpolated passage concerning the registration of genealogies.

22. The words, **the Levites,** out of place here, were apparently part of the original heading of the list in vss. 24-25. But they have also been conjectured to be a marginal gloss to **the sons of Levi** in vs. 23 that has migrated to vs. 22 (Rudolph, *op. cit.,* p. 194). The primary concern in this verse, which appears to be a supplement to the preceding list, is the priestly families. Although the M.T. has the indefinite **chief of the fathers,** the definite form **the heads of fathers' houses** is regarded as essential and is supported by several Hebrew MSS and the Peshitta (cf. Guthe and Batten, *Ezra and Nehemiah,* p. 54; Gotthard, *loc. cit.*). It is necessary if the conjunction **also** is retained before **the priests.** Then two groups would be involved, as in the double list in vss. 12-21. Thus **the heads of fathers' houses** would be a clerical rather than lay designation, as in 11:13. But some, appealing to a single MS, omit **also** to make a single group, "the heads of the families of the priests" (Winckler, *Altorientalische Forschungen,* Reihe 2, Bd. II, p. 221; Rudolph, *loc. cit.*). Then the article is unnecessary before **fathers' houses** since **the priests** makes the whole expression definite (Kautzsch, *Gesenius' Hebrew Grammar,* sec. 127a,d; cf. Isa. 10:12; 21:17).

Although the Vulg. and LXX read "in the reign of Darius," neither "in" nor **until** properly renders the Hebrew preposition עַל, which is usually "upon," or in late Hebrew, under Aramaic influence, **to.** Since sixteen Hebrew MSS have עַד, until, instead of עַל, "upon," it is usual to read the former and regard the latter as a scribal error (Bertheau, *Esra, Nechemia und Ester,* pp. 330-31; Guthe and Batten, *loc. cit.;* Gotthard, *loc. cit.*). More probable is the suggestion that the skipping eyes of a copyist moved from עַל, "upon," in the expression **in the book of the Chronicles** (vs. 23) to a later similar preposition, thus dropping the whole phrase (Rudolph, *loc. cit.*). Vs. 22 should thus be read: "In the days of Eliashib, Joiada, and Johanan. and Jaddua, the chiefs of the fathers and the priests were written in the book of Chronicles during the reign of Darius the Persian."

Because **the Persian** suggests that the Persian period was past, and because Josephus associated **Jaddua** with Alexander the Great (cf. vs. 11), **Darius** is usually identified with Darius III, "Codomanus" (336-332 B.C.; cf. Siegfried, *Esra, Nehemia und Esther,* p. 121; Bertholet, *Esra und Nehemia,* p. 85; Kittel, *Geschichte des Volkes Israel,* III, 674; Pfeiffer, *Intro. to O.T.,* p. 819; *et al.*). But since **the Persian** could be written even earlier, during the Persian period (cf. Ezra 1:1; cf. R. D. Wilson, "Titles of the Persian Kings," *Festschrift Eduard Sachau* [Berlin: Georg Reimer, 1915], p. 193), as Herodotus does (*History* II. 110, 158), **Darius** could as well be Darius II, "Ochus" (423-404 B.C.). **The days of Eliashib,** etc., must all fall within the reign of **Darius the Persian.** It is conceivable that **Eliashib** could have continued under Darius II from the reign of Artaxerxes I, and **Johanan** was deposed in favor of **Jaddua** toward the end of the reign of Darius II (cf. vs. 23). But if **Darius** is Darius II, only the very beginning of Jaddua's high priesthood could be involved. It is argued that **Jaddua** is missing in vs. 23 because, although he is listed among the high priests, the list of Levites had not yet been recorded (Rudolph, *loc. cit.*). But **Jaddua** is difficult in vs. 22 and it seems to be a later addition to the list, which already was terminated by **and Johanan.**

23. In contrast to vs. 22, this verse is concerned with the Levites alone, and while it too is an interpolation it now furnishes a preface to the list of Levites which follows.

Chronicles, even until the days of Johanan the son of Eliashib.

24 And the chief of the Levites: Hashabiah, Sherebiah, and Jeshua the son of Kadmiel, with their brethren over against them, to praise *and* to give thanks, according to the commandment of David the man of God, ward over against ward.

heads of fathers' houses, were written in the Book of the Chronicles until the days of Joha'nan the son of Eli'ashib. 24 And the chiefs of the Levites: Hashabi'ah, Sherebi'ah, and Jeshua the son of Kad'mi-el, with their brethren over against them, to praise and to give thanks, according to the commandment of David the man of God, watch

---

The book of the Chronicles, bearing the actual title of the canonical books of Chronicles, was not that work but another source. Torrey regards it as part of the Chronicler's "imaginary library" and does not consider it seriously. He contends, "There is not the least internal evidence that he had a written source before him in compiling these lists" (*Ezra Studies,* p. 141, n. 5). But not all take such a negative attitude. Wellhausen considered it as one of the Chronicler's postexilic sources (cf. Friedrich Bleek, *Einleitung in das Alte Testament* [4th ed.; Berlin: Georg Reimer, 1878], p. 268; Stade, *Geschichte des Volkes Israel,* II, 153, n. 1), and Meyer (*Entstehung des Judenthums,* p. 104) regarded it as the Chronicler's sole source for the postexilic period. Some think that it differs from the "book of the genealogy" (7:5) in the fact that it contained historical data as well as lists of clerical personnel (cf. Batten, *Ezra and Nehemiah,* p. 277; Bertholet, *loc. cit.*), and thus may have been the official temple chronicle for the postexilic period (cf. Rudolph, *op. cit.,* pp. 193-94). **Until the days of Johanan the son of Eliashib** means roughly, as in vs. 22, to the end of the reign of Darius II. Since Bagoas set aside **Johanan** for the murder of his brother (cf. vs. 11), the high priest must have been deposed sometime between 408 B.C., when he was still in office according to the papyri (Cowley, *op. cit.,* No. 30, l. 18) and 405 B.C., when Darius II died (cf. Rudolph, *op. cit.,* p. 193).

F. Levites Under Joiakim (12:24-26)

This list, expected in vs. 22, should consist of names from the time of Joiakim and it is usually so regarded (*ibid.,* p. 194), but Siegfried (*op. cit.,* p. 122) believes that it is extended to cover the period of Johanan also, and wonders at the omission of Jaddua (cf. vs. 22).

24. The names given are not of individual leaders but are common Levite names, apparently representing the individuals. Since **Jeshua** usually heads the lists of Levites (cf. vs. 8), the name **Hashabiah** (cf. Ezra 8:19) in first place, followed by **Sherebiah** (cf. 8:7; 9:4; 10:12), is surprising. These men must not be confused with men of those names who accompanied Ezra (8:18-19), since they could not also have been in the time of Joiakim. **Jeshua** only here is called **the son of Kadmiel,** but this is erroneous, as the Peshitta and LXX show, for **Kadmiel** usually appears independently (cf. 7:43; 9:4-5; 10:9; Ezra 2:40). Comparison of lists indicates that the word **son of** (בן) is actually another name, either "Bani" (בני; cf. 8:7; 9:4) or "Binnui" (בנוי; cf. vs. 8; 10:9). The latter is preferable and is supported by the erroneous "his sons" (בניו) of the LXX[L], which differs from "Binnui" (בנוי) only in the transposition of two letters (Bertholet, *loc. cit.;* Guthe and Batten, *loc. cit.;* Rudolph, *loc. cit.*). **With their brethren** implies other Levites, but it is difficult to see, in conformity with the title, how they too could be family heads. The LXX[L] has "his brothers," referring to **Kadmiel.**

One of the Levite duties involved the singing of **praise** and **thanks** (cf. vs. 8; 11:17). This occurred principally in connection with giving burnt offerings (I Chr. 23:30). It is clear from the versions and Ezra 3:11 (cf. I Chr. 16:4; 23:30) that the text should be **and to give thanks.** As in vs. 9, the position of the singers is described, and in the characteristic terminology of the Chronicler (I Chr. 25:8; 26:16) the organization of the Levites is described as "watch next to watch" (ASV) or **watch corresponding to watch** (cf. vs. 9). The watches were perhaps the courses by which the Levites were organized,

25 Mattaniah, and Bakbukiah, Obadiah, Meshullam, Talmon, Akkub, *were* porters keeping the ward at the thresholds of the gates.

26 These *were* in the days of Joiakim the son of Jeshua, the son of Jozadak, and in the days of Nehemiah the governor, and of Ezra the priest, the scribe.

corresponding to watch. 25 Mattani'ah, Bakbuki'ah, Obadi'ah, Meshul'lam, Talmon, and Akkub were gatekeepers standing guard at the storehouses of the gates. 26 These were in the days of Joi'akim the son of Jeshua son of Jo'zadak, and in the days of Nehemi'ah the governor and of Ezra the priest the scribe.

---

although the words might mean the arrangements of positions for antiphonal singing (Batten, *loc. cit.*). The Chronicler attributes Levitical organization to the **commandment of David** (cf. I Chr. 25; II Chr. 8:14). The title **man of God,** applied elsewhere to Moses (cf. Ezra 3:2), is given to **David,** as in II Chr. 8:14. The Peshitta has "prophet of the Lord," usage interpreted as indicating that David's "authority in the regulation of the temple service was not royal but prophetic" (*ibid.*).

25. The LXXBAℵ omits the six names here given, which are understood to be **gatekeepers,** but at least **Mattaniah** (vs. 8) and **Bakbukiah** (vs. 9) are associated with singers in vss. 8-9; 11:17. **Obadiah** (cf. Ezra 8:9) is the full name of "Abda" (11:17) who, as a descendant of Jeduthun, could also have been a musician. But he could have been a gatekeeper, for it was the family of Obed-Edom who guarded the house of the stores (I Chr. 26:15). Some propose to insert המשוררים, "the singers," after **Obadiah** (Jahn, *Esra [A und B] und Nehemja,* p. 162); it is possible that the word was lost due to graphic similarity to the name משלם, **Meshullam,** or may be concealed in that name itself (Rudolph, *loc. cit.*), for, although Shallum is associated with gatekeepers (I Chr. 9:17; Ezra 2:42) and the name abbreviates **Meshullam,** this **Meshullam** does not appear to be related to the Shallum of I Chr. 9:17, who may have been contemporary with the Chronicler (cf. I Chr. 9:18a; *ibid.,* p. 195). The Peshitta here has "Shallum," which is favored by some (Gotthard, *loc. cit.*).

"Shallum," **Talman,** and **Akkub** are family names (cf. 2:42), not those of individuals, which vs. 24 leads one to expect. It is conjectured that a copyist erroneously put the names, familiar to him, in the text (Guthe and Batten, *op. cit.,* p. 71; van Hoonacker, *Le sacerdoce lévitique,* pp. 64 ff.). The list expresses the Chronicler's view that the doorkeepers and singers are Levites, but a somewhat later list treats the gatekeepers as a separate class (11:19).

For "watching gates" of the M.T. some read "were the ones watching in the gates" (cf. 11:19), but usually the words are inverted to read **were gatekeepers standing guard,** which prevents "keeping" from being separated from its object "watch" (Keil, *Chronik, Esra, Nehemia und Esther,* p. 583; Guthe and Batten, *op. cit.,* p. 54; Bertholet, *op. cit.,* pp. 85-86; Rudolph, *op. cit.,* p. 195). **Thresholds of the gates** presumes a reading **thresholds** (*sippê*) for the difficult Hebrew '*asuppê,* as in the Peshitta, Targ., and I Chr. 26:15. A "keeper of the threshold" was an important temple official (cf. Jer. 35:4), possibly a priest (II Kings 12:9) but more probably a Levite (cf. II Chr. 34:9; Jahn, *loc. cit.;* Batten, *op. cit.,* p. 278). But it is clear from I Chr. 26:15, 17, which mentions Levites posted over the South Gate and the "House of '*Asuppim,*" that the Hebrew word is not **threshold** but **storehouses,** to be identified with the Akkadian *bît a-su-up-pu* used in that sense frequently in cuneiform documents of the Neo-Babylonian and Persian periods (Bezold, *Babylonisch-Assyrisches Glossar,* p. 52, col. 2).

26. Vss. 24-25 have a subscript, by the final editor who transmitted the lists, which assigns the preceding list to the time of **Joiakim.** Vs. 26b contains a synchronism intended to connect the preceding genealogies with the narrative that follows. In the present disordered text of Ezra-Nehemiah, such synchronism is understandable, for if Nehemiah was contemporary with Eliashib the son of Joiakim and therefore possibly with Joiakim too, then Ezra, who was believed contemporary with Nehemiah, would likewise have been in the time of Joiakim. But the synchronism is historically invalid since Nehemiah

27 ¶ And at the dedication of the wall of Jerusalem they sought the Levites out of all their places, to bring them to Jerusalem, to keep the dedication with gladness, both with thanksgivings, and with singing, *with* cymbals, psalteries, and with harps.	27 And at the dedication of the wall of Jerusalem they sought the Levites in all their places, to bring them to Jerusalem to celebrate the dedication with gladness, with thanksgivings and with singing, with cymbals, psalteries, and with harps.

may not have been in Judea under Joiakim the father of the Eliashib who was his contemporary (3:1, 20), and Ezra came to Palestine later than Nehemiah, under Artaxerxes II (cf. vs. 11).

XIV. DEDICATION OF THE WALLS OF JERUSALEM (12:27-43)

Through dedication secular products are made holy and placed under divine protection. The ancient Hebrews did not confine such dedication to distinctly religious edifices, for apparently even private houses were so dedicated (cf. Deut. 20:5; O. S. Rankin, *The Origins of the Festival of Hanukkah* [Edinburgh: T. & T. Clark, 1930], pp. 30-31). Such rites were thus apparently recognized as the final act of building, just as the sacrifice of first fruits was the final essential act of the agricultural operation. Thus it is natural to suppose that when the walls of the "holy city" (cf. 11:1) were rebuilt, they would be dedicated to ward off possible catastrophe and put them under the protection of God. Since such dedication would be a practical as well as a religious concern, it is strange to learn that "there is nothing in this story of the dedication of the walls that deserves to be taken seriously. The necessity of such a ceremony would of course be keenly felt by the Chronicler; it is not so likely it would have occurred to Nehemiah" (Torrey, *Composition*, pp. 43-44).

Because the narrative is in the first person, it is usually assumed to have been originally part of Nehemiah's record, but others consider the entire passage (12:27–13:13) as the work of the Chronicler, with "nothing whatever to indicate a written source." The Nehemiah of this section has been called simply "Ezra [i.e., the Chronicler] under another name," attempts to isolate even a nucleus of what might be genuine narrative have been ridiculed as "a curious specimen of literary criticism," and it is assumed that "there is no use for analysis here anywhere." All is the work of the Chronicler, false and fanciful (Torrey, *Ezra Studies*, pp. 248-49). Use of the first person subject is rejected as a criterion for assigning material to Nehemiah since "there is no linguistic or stylistic difference between the sections written in the first person and the others [usually attributed to the Chronicler]" (Kapelrud, *Question of Authorship in the Ezra-Narrative*, p. 95; cf. Mowinckel, *Ezra den Skriftlaerde*, pp. 49-61).

The hand of the Chronicler is recognized throughout the narrative, even by those rejecting the extreme view of Torrey, but it is regarded as an editorial rather than a creative hand, thoroughly working over a plausible and probable basic source, attributable to Nehemiah (cf. Batten, *op. cit.*, p. 279). In attempts at recovering the original narrative the use of the first person pronoun is still regarded as a promising clue. Thus Ryssel (*Die Heilige Schrift des Alten Testaments*, ed. Emil Kautzsch [Leipzig: J. C. B. Mohr, 1894], p. 934) suggested that Nehemiah wrote vss. 31-32, 37-40 and the Chronicler vss. 27-30, 33-36, 41-43. Bertholet (*op. cit.*, p. 86) attributes vss. 27-29, 31-32, 37-40 to Nehemiah and vss. 33-36, 41-43 to the Chronicler. Rudolph (*loc. cit.*) in general agrees with Bertholet, but except for the first three words of vs. 27, which he believes to be Nehemiah's, he assigns vss. 27-29 to the Chronicler. It is impossible here to recover with certainty any true text of Nehemiah and the problem is complicated by the fact that, no matter what authorship, the description of the ritual of dedication would have to employ such cultic terminology as the Chronicler was disposed to use. Although the actual words of Nehemiah may be lost, the narrative preserves something of the order of events in the ceremony of dedication: the assembling of the Levites and musicians (vss. 27-29); purification rites (vs. 30); ritual circumambulation (vss. 31-39); and sacrificial celebration (vss. 40-43).

A. Assembling the Levites and Musicians (12:27-29)

These verses are usually attributed to the Chronicler, who is especially interested in the Levites and musicians, but Bertholet (*loc. cit.*) assigns them to the Nehemiah narrative. For a service stressing songs of thanksgiving (vs. 27) and instrumental music (vss. 27, 36), it would be necessary to bring to Jerusalem the Levite musicians who lived outside of the city (cf. vs. 29).

27. The celebration was a "dedication" (Hanukkah) service, like that of the rededication of the temple in Maccabean times (I Macc. 4:52-59) which is still celebrated (Rankin, *op. cit.*). The words **And at the dedication of the wall of Jerusalem** have been regarded as Nehemiah's (Rudolph, *op. cit.*, p. 198), but it is likely that he would have assumed the name of the city (Batten, *loc. cit.*). **At the dedication** scarcely dates the event which has been claimed to have occurred three months (Bertholet, *op. cit.*, p. 87) or even a dozen years (Rawlinson, *Ezra and Nehemiah*, p. 158) after the completion of the walls. More probably the walls were dedicated shortly after they were finished on October 2, 445 B.C. (cf. 6:15; Rudolph, *op. cit.*, p. 195, n. 2).

Gladness can modify either **dedication** or **thanksgivings.** Many follow the LXX[L] in reading **with gladness,** but others retain the M.T. and render "to keep the dedication and the joyous festival" (cf. 8:12; *ibid.*, p. 196). As the versions show, "and" before **with thanksgivings** in the M.T. should be deleted (*ibid.*; Gotthard, *loc. cit.*). Since **singing** is implied in the **thanksgivings,** the word *shîr* means "music," and the names of the instruments refer to it (e.g., "music of cymbals," etc.). It is then unnecessary to insert **with** before the instruments, as in Ezra 3:10 (*ibid.*; Siegfried, *Esra, Nehemia und Esther*, p. 122). The instruments are mentioned in the service of dedication (cf. I Macc. 4:54; I Chr. 15:16; 16:5; etc.). **Cymbals:** Cf. Ezra 3:10. The following two instruments usually associated were used at feasts (Isa. 5:12) and religious services (Pss. 33:2; 43:4), always on joyous occasions (Gen. 31:27; Isa. 24:8) and never for mourning (cf. Ps. 137:2; Job 30:31). Both were stringed but little is known of their exact type.

That rendered **psalteries** (*nébhel*) was known to the Greeks as a Phoenician instrument, especially from Sidon (Athenaeus *Deipnosophistae* IV. 175; cf. Eusebius *Preparation for the Gospel* I. 10. 27). Although the earlier model had but ten strings (Ps. 33:2), that of Josephus' day had twelve, played with the fingers (*Antiquities* VII. 12. 3; Ovid *The Art of Love* III. 327). As such, it was a type of **harp.** Church Fathers (Augustine, Eusebius, Hilary) indicate that it had a resonant chamber above, covering the ends of the strings, and Jerome, who also mentions the resonance chamber, describes it as having the shape of a delta. Like the portable Assyrian harps of similar type (cf. S. R. Driver, *The Books of Joel and Amos* [2nd ed.; Cambridge: Cambridge University Press, 1915; "Cambridge Bible"], p. 235), the *nébhel* could be played while walking (cf. I Sam. 10:5; II Sam. 6:5).

To judge from the greater number of references to it (forty-four times to twenty-seven), the second portable stringed instrument, the instrument of David (I Sam. 16; 23), was more popular than the **harp.** Used often for secular purposes, it was apparently the favorite instrument of the harlot (Isa. 23:16). The same Church Fathers describe the *kinnôr* as having a drum-shaped sound chamber below, with its belly turned downward. Such description, together with the constant Greek translation of the Hebrew word as *kithara*, suggests that the instrument was a **lyre.** Like the lyre, its strings were struck with a plectrum (Josephus *Antiquities* VII. 12. 3). Jewish coins show the *kinnôr* with three, five, or six strings (cf. Benzinger, *Hebräische Archäologie*, p. 273, Figs. 128-30), and in the Talmud it is said to have seven strings (Samuel Krauss, *Talmudische Archäologie* [Leipzig: G. Fock, 1910-1912], III, 85), but Josephus (Marcus, *Josephus*, V, 523, note *c*) declares it had ten, a number apparently derived from Pss. 33:2; 144:9, taking *nébhel* there in apposition to *kinnôr*. It is assumed that the musicians were Levites, many of whom dwelt outside the city in Judah and Benjamin (cf. 11:3, 20, 36). **In all their places** refers to their scattered abodes mentioned in vss. 28-29.

28 And the sons of the singers gathered themselves together, both out of the plain country round about Jerusalem, and from the villages of Netophathi;

29 Also from the house of Gilgal, and out of the fields of Geba and Azmaveth: for the singers had builded them villages round about Jerusalem.

30 And the priests and the Levites purified themselves, and purified the people, and the gates, and the wall.

31 Then I brought up the princes of Judah upon the wall, and appointed two

bals, harps, and lyres. 28 And the sons of the singers gathered together from the circuit round Jerusalem and from the villages of the Netoph'athites; 29 also from Beth-gilgal and from the region of Geba and Az'maveth; for the singers had built for themselves villages around Jerusalem. 30 And the priests and the Levites purified themselves; and they purified the people and the gates and the wall.

31 Then I brought up the princes of

28-29. In 3:22 the plain country is "the vicinity" of Jerusalem, but since round about here would then be unnecessary, and the place is contrasted with the villages around Jerusalem (vs. 29), the plain country perhaps means "the plains of the Jordan" (Amer. Trans.), as elsewhere (Gen. 13:10-11; 19:17, 25). This is supported if the Beth-gilgal is the Gilgal of Josh. 15:7. Geba (11:31; Ezra 2:26) and Azmaveth (Ezra 2:24) lay north of Jerusalem, while Netophah (Ezra 2:22) was about fifteen miles southwest of the city. By the villages of the Netophathites (I Chr. 9:16) is meant the "daughter" settlements (cf. 11:25) about Netophah.

B. Purification (12:30)

30. An indispensable part of the ritual was the preliminary purification of the structures and of participants in the ceremony. Those who had been occupied with secular affairs were regarded as ritually unclean and unfit to participate in the ceremony. Priests were always purified before ceremonies (cf. Ezra 6:20), and laymen too had to be "pure" before joining in cultic ritual (cf. I Sam. 21:5). The mode of purification may have been fasting (Rudolph, op. cit., p. 199), but it is probable that sacrifice also was involved and perhaps sprinkling with blood (cf. Exod. 12:22; Lev. 14:4-7) or with holy water (Num. 19:9, 17-18, 21). Although the phraseology is the Chronicler's, the verse in substance reflects a probable historical situation and may well have been part of Nehemiah's narrative (cf. ibid., p. 197).

C. Circumambulation (12:31-42)

Part of the ritual of dedication was a procession about the walls of Jerusalem. The formal organization of the parading groups and the dual direction of their movement indicate that the purpose of the procession was not mere inspection or simple progress to a destination, but an actual ritual act, such as is found elsewhere. Thus the site of the cathedral of Armagh was consecrated by a sunwise procession led around it by St. Patrick, and Scattery Island was hallowed by St. Senan through a similar procession; and the Roman Catholic Church still employs circumambulation in the consecration of

31-40. Nehemiah in Action Once More.— Here at long last the modern reader rejoices to find himself, after so much colorless third-person narrative from the later times and different concerns of the Chronicler, once more back in the midst of the vivid firsthand brevities of Nehemiah's own memoirs, perhaps from his notes for the double procession in celebration of the completion of the city walls. He is as careful as the Chronicler himself to be sure that his ecclesiastical officials have the proper priestly

antecedents; his notes for the routes are as specific as were those of his first tour of inspection by night around the walls of Jerusalem (cf. 2:12-16) or the report on the assignment of sections of the wall and the gates to various groups for the rebuilding (cf. ch. 3). Nehemiah was a master of organization, whether of a co-operative enterprise or a complicated celebration. Such a ceremony of recognition and dedication should never be regarded as a means whereby the "secular" is made "holy." (Cf. Exeg. on 13:9.)

great *companies of them that gave* thanks, *whereof one* went on the right hand upon the wall toward the dung gate:

32 And after them went Hoshaiah, and half of the princes of Judah,

33 And Azariah, Ezra, and Meshullam,

34 Judah, and Benjamin, and Shemaiah, and Jeremiah,

Judah upon the wall, and appointed two great companies which gave thanks and went in procession. One went to the right upon the wall to the Dung Gate; **32** and after them went Hoshai′ah and half of the princes of Judah, **33** and Azari′ah, Ezra, Meshul′lam, **34** Judah, Benjamin, She-

---

churches (Goblet d' Alviella, "Circumambulation," in James Hastings, ed., *Encyclopaedia of Religion and Ethics* [New York: Charles Scribner's Sons, 1911], III, 657).

Each of the two groups involved moved in a different direction, covering approximately half of the circumference of the wall. The groups appear to have been identical in form, symmetrically arranged. In each a choir (vss. 31, 38*a*) was followed by a high secular official leading half of the lay leaders (vss. 32, 38*b*; cf. vs. 40), followed by a group of seven priests (vss. 33-34, 41) and they by eight Levites (vss. 35-36*a*, 42). The symmetrical structure is disturbed by a later intrusion of Ezra the scribe into the first group (vs. 36).

1. THE ASSEMBLY (12:31*a*)

31*a*. The place of assembly was in the southwest corner of the city, near the Valley Gate (cf. 2:13), which is not mentioned in the procession (cf. Bertholet, *loc. cit.*). That was apparently a center of activity in the time of Nehemiah (cf. 2:11, 13). Because of the preposition used (מעלה ל), some suggest that the starting point was higher than the city wall, but it need not mean "above" the wall and can mean **upon** it (Gen. 1:7; I Sam. 17:39; Jonah 4:6) or even "beside" it (cf. II Chr. 26:19; Rudolph, *op. cit.*, p. 196; Brown, Driver, Briggs, *Lexicon*, p. 759, *s.v.* על IV*e*). The **princes** were the community leaders (cf. 11:1; Ezra 9:1). **Brought up** could mean brought to Jerusalem (cf. Ezra 1:3), but since the rulers resided there (11:1) it means **brought up** to the top of the broad city wall to join the priests and Levites who apparently had purified the structures (vs. 30). The width of the wall is unspecified but adequate for a procession. Even at rustic Gibeah the wall was eight to ten feet thick and fourteen feet at Gezer. An Egyptian wall at Tell el Far'ah was twenty-two feet thick, and at Jericho houses could be built upon the wall (Josh. 2:15). The procession moved **upon the wall.**

Nehemiah first divided the group into two equal sections, each of which was to go in an opposite direction until they met in the temple area, in the northeastern part of the city, to conclude the services. For **I . . . appointed** the LXX has "they appointed," presuming that the **princes,** or possibly the "priests," gave the orders. **Companies** renders a word elsewhere translated "thanksgiving" (*tôdhāh;* cf. vs. 27), but it here means a praise-singing choir (cf. Jer. 30:19), and the Vulg. has "two great choirs."

2. THE COUNTERCLOCKWISE COMPANY (12:31*b*-37)

31*b*. **Went in procession** interprets a unique and corrupt Hebrew word (תהלוכות). The arbitrary "and they went" of the LXX*L*, Peshitta, and Vulg. is clearly wrong, for vs. 38 indicates that but one choir is involved. Better than the emendation "the one going" (Smend, *Die Listen,* p. 11, n. 13) or "and the one choir goes" (Kautzsch, *Heilige Schrift des A.T.,* p. 934), is "and the one went" (והאחת הלכת), which is easily corrupted to the present M.T. (Kosters, *Wiederherstellung Israels,* p. 50; Batten, *op. cit.,* p. 281; Rudolph, *loc. cit.*). The first group moved **to the right,** following Nehemiah's former route (cf. 2:13-15).

32-34. After progress to the **Dung Gate** (vs. 31; cf. 2:13), the procession is interrupted by a list of the members of the first company. After the choir came **Hoshaiah** ("The Lord Has Saved"), a leader of half of the laymen, who is otherwise unknown. Since he

35 And *certain* of the priests' sons with trumpets; *namely,* Zechariah the son of Jonathan, the son of Shemaiah, the son of Mattaniah, the son of Michaiah, the son of Zaccur, the son of Asaph:

36 And his brethren, Shemaiah, and Azarael, Milalai, Gilalai, Maai, Nethaneel, and Judah, Hanani, with the musical instruments of David the man of God, and Ezra the scribe before them.

mai'ah, and Jeremiah, **35** and certain of the priests' sons with trumpets: Zechari'ah the son of Jonathan, son of Shemai'ah, son of Mattani'ah, son of Micai'ah, son of Zaccur, son of Asaph; **36** and his kinsmen, Shemai'ah, Az'arel, Mil'alai, Gil'alai, Ma'ai, Nethan'el, Judah, and Hana'ni, with the musical instruments of David the man of God; and Ezra the scribe went before them.

holds a prominent position, corresponding to Nehemiah in the other group (vss. 38*b*, 40), he was doubtless, like the Zedekiah of 10:1, a person of considerable importance.

The names, presumably interpolated by the Chronicler, could refer in vs. 33 to either the **princes** or the priests. It is probable that, as in vs. 41, the priests followed the laymen, and except for **Judah** and **Benjamin** all the names are found elsewhere for priests. It is clear from vs. 41 that there were seven priests in each group. **Azariah** (cf. Ezra 7:1) is **Ezra** (cf. 8:9; Ezra 7:1), not the eminent scribe and priest but another of the same name (cf. vss. 1, 13). **Meshullam:** Cf. Ezra 8:16. **Shemaiah:** Cf. 10:8. **Jeremiah:** Cf. vs. 1. **Judah** and **Benjamin,** regarded as impossible names for priests, are considered by some as evidence for the worthlessness of the list (Bertholet, *loc. cit.*). But **Benjamin** is perhaps a corruption of "Miniamin" (cf. vss. 5, 17), which the LXX[L] has here, a change that could easily occur in the presence of **Judah** (Rudolph, *op. cit.,* p. 197). Although **Judah** appears as a Levite (vs. 36), the name is nowhere used of a priest.

35. The **priests' sons** are not an additional group but some of the priests just named, for **son** may be used in an occupational sense (cf. 3:31), and it is the **priests** who use the **trumpets** in vs. 41. They were not the Levites, for the **trumpets** were the priests' instruments (cf. Ezra 3:10). The conjunction should be omitted before **the priests' sons,** as in the Arabic version, and inserted before the name of **Zechariah,** which introduces the list of Levites, as in the Ethiopic version (Gotthard, *Nehemia,* p. 46; Rudolph, *loc. cit.;* Guthe and Batten, *Ezra and Nehemiah,* p. 54; *et al.*).

Zechariah (cf. Ezra 8:3), leader of the Levites, is traced to his ancestor **Asaph** (cf. Ezra 2:41). According to the genealogy, **Zechariah** lived several generations after the Mattaniah of 11:17 and I Chr. 9:15, which would be possible if 11:17 referred to the first return—the view of the editor of I Chr. 9 but not of the Chronicler (Rudolph, *op. cit.,* pp. 185, 197). But the words **son of Micaiah, son of Zaccur** may have been an addition to identify **Mattaniah** with the one in 11:17. For **Micaiah** the Peshitta and Arabic versions have "Micah" (cf. 11:17; I Chr. 9:15). Some prefer "Zichri" for **Zaccur** as in I Chr. 9:15 (Guthe and Batten, *loc. cit.*). For **Jonathan** the LXX[B×] has "Johanan."

36. Shemaiah: Cf. Ezra 8:13. **Azarel** (cf. Ezra 10:41) is "Azriel" in the LXX[L] but "Uzziel" in the LXX[AB×] (cf. I Chr. 25:4, 18). **Milalai** could abbreviate "Millaliah" ("The Lord Has Spoken"), but it is probably a corrupt dittograph of **Gilalai** and should be omitted, as in the LXX and Arabic versions (cf. Gotthard, *loc. cit.;* Rudolph, *op. cit.,* p. 197). Such omission leaves a company of eight Levites, as in vs. 42. **Gilalai,** like "Galal" (11:17) may abbreviate a name "Tortoise" (Noth, *Personennamen,* p. 230 and n. 12). **Maai,** also found as "Mei," so sharply abbreviates a full name that the original cannot be recovered. **Nethanel** (cf. Ezra 10:22) is a Levite name in II Chr. 35:9. **Hanani** (cf. 1:2; Ezra 10:20) is the name of a musician in David's service (I Chr. 25:4, 25).

Musical instruments, "instruments of song," indicate those used in accompanying singing, in contrast to the priests' clarions (vs. 35; Ezra 3:10). They are associated with king **David** (cf. Amos 6:5), again called **the man of God** (cf. vs. 24). Ezra the scribe (cf. Ezra 7:6, 11; etc.) intrudes into the narrative, since he and Nehemiah were not contemporary (Meyer, *Entstehung des Judenthums,* p. 200; Siegfried, *Esra, Nehemia und Esther,* p. 123; Browne, *Early Judaism,* p. 178; *et al.*). Inasmuch as the Chronicler knew

37 And at the fountain gate, which was over against them, they went up by the stairs of the city of David, at the going up of the wall, above the house of David, even unto the water gate eastward.

38 And the other *company of them that gave* thanks went over against *them,* and I after them, and the half of the people upon the wall, from beyond the tower of the furnaces even unto the broad wall;

37 At the Fountain Gate they went up straight before them by the stairs of the city of David, at the ascent of the wall, above the house of David, to the Water Gate on the east.

38 The other company of those who gave thanks went to the left, and I followed them with half of the people, upon the wall, above the Tower of the Furnaces, to the

---

of no incident in which they were contemporary, the addition, which now destroys the symmetry of the companies, is later than the time of the Chronicler. **Before them** ambiguously can refer to either the Levites, the priests, the laymen, or the whole company. The editor who made the insertion doubtless meant that **Ezra** led the whole group, but there is no equivalent leader in the second company.

37. The route of the first company, begun in vs. 31, is now resumed. The verse begins quite abruptly, apparently damaged by the intrusion of vss. 33-36, so that at least a verb to introduce the verse has been lost. Such a loss could easily occur if ויעלו, "and they ascended" (Gotthard, *loc. cit.*), or ויעברו, "and they passed over" (Rudolph, *loc. cit.*), had been before על, at. With a verb the preposition על could be either "toward" (2:7; 4:6; 6:17) or "unto" (Gen. 49:13; Josh. 2:7; 18:13; etc.), but it is preferable to read, "and they went over to the Fountain Gate" (cf. 2:14; 3:15).

Which was over against them, lit., "and opposite them," is associated in the M.T. with what precedes, according to the verse accent, and some prefer such a translation even though unable to identify what was opposite (Gotthard, *loc. cit.*). But it is equally possible to translate **straight before them** (cf. Josh. 6:5; Amos 4:3; Jer. 31:39) for **over against them.** Then, disregarding the Hebrew verse accent, the sentence begins, [And] **straight before them** (cf. Rudolph, *loc. cit.*). **Went up** might suggest that somewhere the first group descended from the wall, crossed the **city of David** (cf. 3:15), and did not again ascend until in the vicinity of David's palace (cf. Siegfried, *loc. cit.;* Ryle, *Ezra and Nehemia,* p. 302; Rudolph, *op. cit.,* pp. 197, 199). More probably there was no descent but the company on the wall **went up** with its natural ascent (Batten, *op. cit.,* p. 282).

Fountain Gate: Cf. 2:14; 3:15. **The stairs** and **the city of David:** Cf. 3:15. It is argued that **the house of David** was not the palace of Solomon (3:25) but David's own palace (II Sam. 5:11) in the city of David. It has been suggested that the old building still survived (Hermann Guthe, "Ausgrabungen bei Jerusalem," *Zeitschrift des deutsches Palästina-vereins,* V [1882], 332), but, though the actual building may have been destroyed, its site may have been shown in later times (Bertholet, *op. cit.,* p. 88). Ignorance of specific topography prevents a certain translation of the Hebrew preposition rendered **above.** That interpretation is possible (cf. Exod. 28:27; Jer. 35:4), but the word may also mean "near" the palace (cf. II Chr. 26:19) or "by" the palace (cf. vs. 38). **Ascent of the wall** may mean "where the wall ascends," since the ascending wall may have been higher than the palace site (*ibid.,* p. 87), but the word במעלה, **at the ascent,** may be vocalized as "on the stairs" (cf. Ezra 7:9), possibly referring to the stairway of 3:19. To the **east** again describes **the Water Gate** (3:26), apparently differentiating it from another gate to the west.

3. The Clockwise Company (12:38-42)

38. The starting point of the second **company** (cf. vs. 31) was apparently also in the vicinity of the Valley Gate. The M.T. indicates that they moved "to the fore," which is rendered **over against them** and interpreted as "to the opposite side" in the Vulg. (cf. Guthe and Batten, *loc. cit.*). But למואל, "to the fore," is obviously a scribal error for

39 And from above the gate of Ephraim, and above the old gate, and above the fish gate, and the tower of Hananeel, and the tower of Meah, even unto the sheep gate: and they stood still in the prison gate.

40 So stood the two *companies of them that gave* thanks in the house of God, and I, and the half of the rulers with me:

Broad Wall, 39 and above the Gate of E'phraim, and by the Old Gate, and by the Fish Gate and the Tower of Hanan'el and the Tower of the Hundred, to the Sheep Gate; and they came to a halt at the Gate of the Guard. 40 So both companies of those who gave thanks stood in the house of God, and I and half of the officials with me;

לשמואל, **to the left,** correlative to "to the right" in vs. 31. The pronoun **I** refers to Nehemiah, who, like Hoshaiah (vs. 32), led half of the lay leaders. If **the people** is retained, it must mean the secular leaders, since half of the secular group (vs. 32) is involved. Some, however, emend the M.T. to read "the rulers," as in vs. 40 (Ehrlich, *Randglossen,* VII, 210), but others hold that "princes" has been lost and should be restored to read, as in vs. 32, "half of the princes" (Guthe and Batten, *loc. cit.*) The **Tower of the Furnaces:** Cf. 3:11. **The Broad Wall:** Cf. 3:8.

39. Gate of Ephraim: Cf. 8:16. **Old Gate:** Cf. 3:6. **Fish Gate:** Cf. 3:3. **Tower of Hananel** and **Tower of the Hundred:** Cf. 3:1. **Sheep Gate:** Cf. 3:1, 32. The **Gate of the Guard** or **prison gate** is related to the court of the guard (3:25), and should not be confused with the Muster Gate (3:31; cf. Simons, *Jerusalem in the O.T.,* p. 340). Since in the itinerary of the first company there is no parallel to **came to a halt,** some argue that the final clause in vs. 39 is an addition (cf. Stade, *Geschichte des Volkes Israel,* II, 175; Jahn, *Esra [A und B] und Nehemja,* p. 165; Guthe and Batten, *loc. cit.;* Simons, *loc. cit.*). It is lacking in the LXXᴬᴮ but is restored in the LXXᴸ. A halt at the **Gate of the Guard** would not leave the company standing **in the house of God** (vs. 40), for, although it has been suggested that the **prison** may have been at the place of Bêra-Antonia, north of the temple area (Hermann Hupfeld, "Die topographische Streitfrage über Jerusalem," *Zeitschrift der deutschen morgenlandischen Gesellschaft,* XV [1861], 231; Bertheau, *Esra, Nechemia und Ester,* p. 341), it is usually located south of the temple compound (3:25). A location south of the temple raises topographic problems, for the itinerary would presume a crossing through the temple compound, which is not mentioned, or that the second company crossed the Kidron Valley to the Mount of Olives to approach the city again from the south, entering with the first company (Schultz, *Esra, Nehemia und Esther,* p. 121). The latter alternative is unlikely, for such an extended movement would have been described. It is preferable to regard the reference to the **halt** at the **prison gate** as a later addition, and to consider the second group as entering the temple area at the **Sheep Gate.** The wall east of the temple area was not traversed, apparently because that section, close to the temple, had already been dedicated by the priests who rebuilt it (cf. 3:1).

40. In the house of God means "at the house of God" (Amer. Trans.) since the groups stood in the temple court, possibly in the open plaza east of the temple (Bertheau, *op. cit.,* p. 342; Siegfried, *op. cit.,* p. 124), not in the building itself. The reference to Nehemiah and **the officials** in vs. 40*b* is, as it stands, a second subject to vs. 40*a*, but it is usually assumed that originally something more was told about Nehemiah and the

---

40-47. In Rosy Retrospect.—Here once again the Chronicler's familiar editorial hand appears, concentrating on the liturgy and choral assignments for the service of thanksgiving, and eager to impress on his contemporaries his very questionable assumption that the support of the elaborate temple ritual, as it was in his own day, had been continuous ever since the earliest returning groups of exiles under Zerubbabel and

Nehemiah. Here within ten verses we can sense the different perspectives and valuations of the ceremonialist who idealized history as he looked back upon it through the eyes of his own special interest; and on the other hand, of the man of action who made history against heavy odds in a day of small things. But both Nehemiah and the Chronicler plainly agreed upon one point, and both contributed greatly to it (vs. 43*b*).

41 And the priests; Eliakim, Maaseiah, Miniamin, Michaiah, Elioenai, Zechariah, *and* Hananiah, with trumpets;

42 And Maaseiah, and Shemaiah, and Eleazar, and Uzzi, and Jehohanan, and Malchijah, and Elam, and Ezer. And the singers sang loud, with Jezrahiah *their* overseer.

43 Also that day they offered great sacrifices, and rejoiced: for God had made them rejoice with great joy: the wives also and the children rejoiced: so that the joy of Jerusalem was heard even afar off.

41 and the priests Eli'akim, Ma-asei'ah, Mini'amin, Micai'ah, Eli-o-e'nai, Zechari'ah, and Hanani'ah, with trumpets; 42 and Ma-asei'ah, Shemai'ah, Elea'zar, Uzzi, Jeho-ha'-nan, Malchi'jah, Elam, and Ezer. And the singers sang with Jezrahi'ah as their leader. 43 And they offered great sacrifices that day and rejoiced, for God had made them rejoice with great joy; the women and children also rejoiced. And the joy of Jerusalem was heard afar off.

---

officials and that the text has been lost with the intrusion of the list of names that follows (Guthe and Batten, *op. cit.*, p. 55; Batten, *op. cit.*, p. 283). The present text has Nehemiah's party as observers (Siegfried, *loc. cit.*) but nothing is said of Hoshaiah and the other officials (cf. vs. 32). It is suggested that all of the secular leaders had gathered in the **Gate of the Guard** (vs. 39) to watch the ceremony (Rudolph, *op. cit.*, p. 198).

41-42. Inserted into the narrative, apparently by the Chronicler, is another list representing the clergy in the second company. The list is intrusive and inappropriate here, after reference to the joining of the two groups, and would fit better after vs. 38*a* (Batten, *loc. cit.*). Those listed in vs. 41 are the priests, parallel to those in vss. 33-35*a*, while those in vs. 42*a* are the Levites, parallel to those in vss. 35*b*-36*a*.

Eliakim ("God Will Establish") is only here in Ezra-Nehemiah. **Maaseiah:** Cf. 8:47; Ezra 10:18, 21, 22. **Miniamin:** Cf. 12:17. **Michaiah:** Cf. 12:35. **Elioenai:** Cf. Ezra 10:22. **Zechariah:** Cf. 11:12; 12:16, 35; Ezra 5:1; 8:4. **Hananiah:** Cf. 3:8; 12:12; Ezra 10:28. Like the priests' sons of vs. 35, these priests had **trumpets.** In the list of Levites in vs. 42 the use of **and** before each name (KJV) shows that it is of different origin. It is suggested that the names in the list are each representative of a division of Levites rather than of individuals (Bertheau, *loc. cit.*). Although the office of the men is not indicated, they too, like those in vs. 36, were probably musicians. **Maaseiah:** Cf. vs. 41. **Shemaiah:** Cf. 11:15. **Eleazar:** Cf. Ezra 7:5; 8:33. **Uzzi:** Cf. 11:22. **Jehohanan** (cf. Ezra 10:28) is a musician only here. **Malchijah:** Cf. 8:4; Ezra 10:25. **Elam** (cf. Ezra 2:7) is otherwise a secular name. **Ezer:** Cf. 3:19.

Jezrahiah ("The Lord Shines Forth") was the **leader** (cf. 11:9) of the Levites, just as Zechariah led in the first company (vs. 35). Since the LXXABℵ omits reference to him, the name has been called "a bald interpolation by the Chronicler" (Batten, *loc. cit.*). Instead of **their leader,** the M.T. has "the leader." The mention of music when the two companies met in the temple court has been regarded as authentic but Rudolph (*op. cit.*, p. 199) regards the music of vs. 42 as the Chronicler's contribution.

D. Sacrifice and Celebration (12:43)

43. This verse is the climax of the dedication (vss. 27-42). Although something of this nature must have been included in Nehemiah's account, the present text is from the Chronicler, whose interests are readily apparent (cf. Ezra 3:13; 6:22; II Chr. 20:27). **That day** is the day of dedication (cf. vs. 27). The **great sacrifices** were slaughter offerings followed by an offering meal of celebration, which united the Judean community. **Women and children** joined in the celebration (cf. 8:2-3). So great is the stress on **joy** that it is found in five separate references in the Hebrew text. The LXX, Ethiopic, and Peshitta versions have "joy in Jerusalem" instead of **joy of Jerusalem.** The noise of celebration **was heard afar off** (cf. Ezra 3:13).

44 ¶ And at that time were some appointed over the chambers for the treasures, for the offerings, for the firstfruits, and for the tithes, to gather into them out of the fields of the cities the portions of the law for the priests and Levites: for Judah rejoiced for the priests and for the Levites that waited.

44 On that day men were appointed over the chambers for the stores, the contributions, the first fruits, and the tithes, to gather into them the portions required by the law for the priests and for the Levites according to the fields of the towns; for Judah rejoiced over the priests and the

XV. THE IDEAL COMMUNITY (12:44–13:3)

Form and content both indicate that this section is from someone especially interested in the regulation of the cult, and the prominence of singers and gatekeepers suggests that it was the Chronicler. Here the author portrays an ideal community with respect to the cultus, which might serve as a model for his own day (cf. Kosters, *Wiederherstellung Israels,* p. 94). Thus the Chronicler asserts that the cultic relationships at the time of Ezra and Nehemiah were exemplary, comparing favorably with those of the days of Hezekiah (II Chr. 31:4 ff.; cf. Rudolph, *op. cit.,* p. 201). Reference to **Zerubbabel** (vs. 47) indicates that the author thought the ideal situation for the cult was normal for the postexilic period, even prior to Ezra and Nehemiah.

It is likely that this section was placed here to prepare the reader for the portrayal of faults and negligence in cult matters detailed in ch. 13 (*ibid.*). The author thereby suggests that the behavior as recorded in ch. 13 was not normal but a temporary lapse from the ideal circumstances portrayed in vss. 44-47. These verses seem to depend upon 13:9, 11, 13 (cf. Meyer, *Entstehung des Judenthums,* p. 97, n. 2), but Batten (*loc. cit.*) suggests relationship with 10:28-39.

44. On that day (cf. vs. 43): The phrase may be indeterminate, meaning simply "afterward" or "later" (P. A. Munch, *The Expression Bajjōm Hahū* [Oslo: J. Dybwad, 1936], p. 8). **Chambers** were temple cells (3:30) where the stores were kept (cf. 10:38-39; Ezra 8:29). **For the treasures** means **for the stores** (cf. I Chr. 26:20, 26). The **offerings,** often called "heave offerings," were the **contributions** of 10:39; Ezra 8:25. **First fruits** (cf. 10:37) and **tithes** (10:37-38) were significant parts of clerical support fixed by law (cf. 13:5). Since reference to **the law** is omitted in the LXXABℵ and Ethiopic versions, it is proposed to delete it from the text (cf. Gotthard, *Nehemia,* p. 46). The Vulg., instead of תורה, **law,** has the graphically similar תודה, "thanksgiving," which is accepted by the Amer. Trans., and agrees in substance with the conclusion of the verse.

The word לשדי, **according to the fields,** appears as לשרי, "for the chiefs," in several Hebrew MSS and the versions—a reading which could be expected after similar references to priests and Levites (cf. 9:38). Such interpretation is preferred by those who believed that "general officers were delegated to make collections for the whole country instead of intrusting the task to the local officials" (Batten, *op. cit.,* p. 284). But such a reading is usually rejected as complete nonsense (Rudolph, *op. cit.,* p. 200). Those favoring **according to the fields** believe that collections were made in a predetermined geographical sequence (e.g., Bertholet, *Esra und Nehemia,* p. 89; Siegfried, *op. cit.,* p. 125). This view is also highly impractical and unlikely (Batten, *loc. cit.*). The best solution is suggested by the LXXᴸ, which has **out of the fields** (Gotthard, *loc. cit.*). Evidently the original preposition מן, "from," has been displaced by ל, "for" or "according to," which occurs with greater frequence before nouns in this verse.

The fields were the arable lands around the cities. Storehouses were filled because the people were pleased with the clergy. Therefore read **rejoiced over the priests** rather than **rejoiced for the priests.** The expression seems to reflect such a construction as "to rejoice over" (cf. I Chr. 29:9). **That waited,** lit., "those standing," describing the action of the clerics, is usually regarded as an elliptical expression signifying "standing before the Lord" (cf. Deut. 10:8; II Chr. 29:11; Siegfried, *loc. cit.;* Rudolph, *loc. cit.*) or "standing before God" (Gotthard, *loc. cit.*) in priestly service. A similar result is obtained

45 And both the singers and the porters kept the ward of their God, and the ward of the purification, according to the commandment of David, *and* of Solomon his son.

46 For in the days of David and Asaph of old *there were* chief of the singers, and songs of praise and thanksgiving unto God.

47 And all Israel in the days of Zerubbabel, and in the days of Nehemiah, gave the portions of the singers and the porters, every day his portion: and they sanctified *holy things* unto the Levites; and the Levites sanctified *them* unto the children of Aaron.

Levites who ministered. 45 And they performed the service of their God and the service of purification, as did the singers and the gatekeepers, according to the command of David and his son Solomon. 46 For in the days of David and Asaph of old there was a chief of the singers, and there were songs of praise and thanksgiving to God. 47 And all Israel in the days of Zerub'babel and in the days of Nehemi'ah gave the daily portions for the singers and the gatekeepers; and they set apart that which was for the Levites; and the Levites set apart that which was for the sons of Aaron.

---

by emending the M.T. from העמדים, "those standing," to the graphically very similar העבדים, "those serving" (Ehrlich, *Randglossen*, VII, 210). **Who ministered** satisfactorily interprets the meaning.

45. The expression **kept the ward** or "kept the charge," lit., "watched the watch," is generally used of cultic service (cf. Num. 3:10) but almost always of the work of the Levites (Benzinger, *Hebräische Archäologie*, p. 407, n. 1; Siegfried, *loc. cit.*); **performed the service** interprets it properly. In keeping with his interest, the Chronicler mentions especially the **service of purification**, which was particularly the Levite's task (cf. I Chr. 23:27 ff.). Since it was a priestly function, the reference to **the singers and the gatekeepers** is probably a clumsy interpolation by one stressing that what is said of the Levites was valid also for the **singers** and **gatekeepers**, who were also Levites. As usual, the Chronicler attributes regulation of the temple service to **David** (I Chr. 23:1–26:32) and **Solomon** (II Chr. 8:14). About twenty-six Hebrew MSS and the versions place **and** before **Solomon**.

46. Reference to **David** and the singers in vs. 45 suggests this "historical" note, which concerns the institution of the singers, a special interest of the Chronicler. **Of old** (מקדם), rendered "from the beginning" in the Vulg. and "originally" in the LXX, is a superfluous and awkward intrusion if meant to be parallel to **in the days of David,** and some would omit the words from the M.T. (Gotthard, *loc. cit.*). Others regard them as a corruption of the Hebrew text and read instead מקדם, of old, מפקדים, "were appointed," rendering, "For in the days of David and Asaph the chiefs of the singers were appointed" (cf. I Chr. 16:7; 25:1 ff.; cf. Bertholet, *loc. cit.*). While such emendation clears the first part of the verse, its end must be construed in the sense **and there were songs of praise and thanksgiving.**

Association of **David** and **Asaph** has been criticized, and it is proposed to read "Solomon" for **Asaph,** as in vs. 45. But they are associated also in II Chr. 29:30; 35:15. Since one Hebrew MS, the LXX, Peshitta, Ethiopic, and Arabic versions omit **and** before **Asaph,** it probably should be dropped from the M.T. (Gotthard, *loc. cit.;* Guthe and Batten, *Ezra and Nehemiah*, p. 55). Rudolph (*loc. cit.*) emends מקדם, of old, to פקדם, "their leaders," and further drastically alters the text to read, "For in the days of David, Asaph was the chief of the singers and their leader in the songs of praise and thanksgiving songs unto God."

47. Here the Chronicler returns to the delineation of the ideal cult in the time of **Nehemiah.** By linking **Nehemiah** with **Zerubbabel,** as though the latter's immediate successor, he stresses the continuity of the ideal cultic community throughout the postexilic period. For **every day his portion** see 11:23. The subject of **sanctified** or "hallowed" is presumably **all Israel** (cf. 10:37). The verb means **set apart,** in the sense of presentation to God at the temple so that thereafter all profane use was forbidden (cf. Lev. 27:9). To illustrate the proper relationship between members of the clergy the

13 On that day they read in the book of Moses in the audience of the people; and therein was found written, that the Ammonite and the Moabite should not come into the congregation of God for ever;

2 Because they met not the children of Israel with bread and with water, but hired Balaam against them, that he should curse them: howbeit our God turned the curse into a blessing.

13 On that day they read from the book of Moses in the hearing of the people; and in it was found written that no Ammonite or Moabite should ever enter the assembly of God; 2 for they did not meet the children of Israel with bread and water, but hired Balaam against them to curse them — yet our God turned the curse into

---

author indicates that the Levites gave part of their tithe to the priests (cf. 10:38). **Sons of Aaron** are priests in contrast to the Levites (cf. 10:38).

13:1-3. Since 13:4 ff. concerns Nehemiah (see Exeg., *ad loc.*), vss. 1-3 might be expected to be part of his work, but the lack of reference to him in vss. 1-3, and the fact that the shift from third person to first begins in vs. 4, preclude any connection with Nehemiah's memoirs. These verses have been linked with Ezra's fight against mixed marriages (Ezra 9:1–10:44; Markwart, *Fundamente Geschichte*, p. 36; Geissler, *Literarischen Beziehungen*, p. 45), and it has been suggested that the verses belong in Ezra 10, between vs. 9, the assembling at Jerusalem, and vs. 10, the beginning of Ezra's condemnation of the guilty (W. Robertson Smith, *The Old Testament in the Jewish Church* [2nd ed.; New York: D. Appleton, 1892], p. 427, n. 2). But since the results of Ezra's activity are given in Ezra 9:2, there is no place for vs. 3 in the Ezra narrative (Rudolph, *op. cit.*, p. 202; cf. Mitchell, "Wall of Jerusalem," p. 97). Some see in the passage a somewhat abbreviated account of Deut. 23:3-5 (Batten, *op. cit.*, p. 287; Noth, *Überlieferungsgeschichtliche Studien*, I, p. 131). But vss. 1-3 are the Chronicler's work, a continuation of 12:44-47 with the same motive, to indicate that cultic laws were rigidly observed in the postexilic period, and that the incidents about to be detailed were unusual, temporary departures from the norm, condemned by the community (Jahn, *Esra [A und B] und Nehemja*, p. 167; Rudolph, *loc. cit.*).

1. **On that day** is indefinite (12:44). **They read** supposes an assembly like that in ch. 8, which Rudolph (*ibid.*, pp. 71, 143) insists occurred during the interval between Nehemiah's two administrations. But it is argued that Ezra's assembly must have been later, for the situation of vs. 3 could scarcely have occurred after Ezra's exclusion of foreigners (Batten, *op. cit.*, p. 288). As the work of the Chronicler, however, no historical setting is needed, apart from the Chronicler's assumption that the passage in Deut. 23:3-5 was read at some public assembly. The **book of Moses** is the Pentateuch (8:1). The citation of Deut. 23:3-5 has the inexactitude of a quotation from memory. The **Ammonite** (Ezra 9:1) was the people led by Tobiah, Nehemiah's enemy (vss. 4-8; 2:10). The **Moabite** was the people adjacent to Ammon, to the south. The incident of vs. 2 occurred during the Exodus (Num. 20:14–23:20; cf. Deut. 23:3-5) but in neither Num. 20:14–23:20 nor in Deut. 2:19 ff. is there a reference to Ammonite antagonism to justify linking Ammon with Moab, the real offender, in the condemnation in Deut. 23:3-5 and here. But it is probable that there was an ancient tradition linking Ammon with Moab against Israel during the Exodus (cf. Num. 22:5; Rudolph, *op. cit.*, p. 203, and reference cited there).

2. **Balaam** was brought from abroad by Moab to curse Israel (Num. 22:5; Deut. 23:4). Since it is less likely that he came from Mesopotamia (Deut. 23:4) than from

---

13:1-3. *Strict Racialism.*—It is easier for us to be tolerant of the Chronicler's liturgical meticulousness than of his rigid racialism, having seen what horrors racial pride and prejudice, whether positively in Nazi Germany or negatively in

anti-Semitism throughout the world, can let loose on all mankind. For the Chronicler, the Ammonites and the Moabites of his own day must go on paying forever (vs. 1) for the attitudes of their fathers toward the Hebrews when

3 Now it came to pass, when they had heard the law, that they separated from Israel all the mixed multitude.

4 ¶ And before this, Eliashib the priest, having the oversight of the chamber of the house of our God, *was* allied unto Tobiah:

a blessing. 3 When the people heard the law, they separated from Israel all those of foreign descent.

4 Now before this, Eli'ashib the priest, who was appointed over the chambers of the house of our God, and who was con-

---

"the river of the land of the children of Ammon," as the Peshitta, Vulg., and Samaritan versions of Num. 22:5 declare (Gray, *Numbers*, pp. 315, 325-26), the present antipathy against Ammon is better understood. For the efficacy of a **curse** (Num. 22:6) see Exeg. on vs. 25; 10:29. Use of the singular verb **hired**, referring to Balak, instead of "they hired," referring to Moab and Ammon, as in Deut. 23:4 and here in the LXX, Vulg., and Peshitta versions, indicates that the Chronicler had the narrative of Numbers in mind. **Our God** was the agent who turned the curse and thereby not only negatively averted the catastrophe of an effective malediction but positively **turned the curse into a blessing** to advance the fortune of Israel.

3. The **law** reflects Deut. 23:3, which excludes Moabites and Ammonites from "the assembly of the Lord." The abbreviated form here is even stronger, for reference to "the tenth generation" is omitted and the exclusion was extended to **all those of foreign descent**. The word rendered **mixed multitude,** "alien mixture" (American Jewish Translation), or **those of foreign descent** means "mixture" and is well attested as such in Syriac, Targumic Aramaic, and Neo-Hebrew. Its root means "to enter," in the sense of "intrusion," for the noun here used elsewhere indicates "a heterogeneous body attached to a people," used of those associated not only with Israel (Exod. 12:38 [E]) but also with Egyptians (Jer. 25:20) and with Chaldeans (Jer. 50:37; Brown, Driver, Briggs, *Lexicon,* p. 786, *s.v.* ערב I) .

The extent of the "separation" from the community is much debated, due to the ambiguous nature of the word "assembly" (*qāhāl*) in Deut. 23:3, for it can be used in a general sense, even of Gentiles (Ezra 2:64; cf. Gen. 35:11), and of Israel it may be used of the entire community (8:2, 17; Ezra 10:8) or, more narrowly, in the sense of the cultic services of the group (cf. 5:13; II Chr. 20:5; 30:25). Hence some interpret "separation" as banishment from the community (cf. Ezra 10:15-44; Rawlinson, *Ezra and Nehemiah,* p. 154), while others think merely of exclusion from the privileges of the temple and the cult ceremonies.

XVI. Nehemiah's Reforms (13:4-31)

Some (e.g., Torrey, *Ezra Studies,* p. 227) consider that the work of Nehemiah was concluded with the completion of the city walls. Whether or not he considered his work finished, Nehemiah had to return to the Persian court at the appointed time (cf. 2:6), possibly after some extension of his original leave. After twelve years (445-433 B.C.) as governor of Judea (2:1; 5:14), in the thirty-second year of Artaxerxes I (433-432 B.C.), Nehemiah returned to the Persian king. But according to vs. 6, he sought permission to return to Jerusalem and this chapter largely purports to be further episodes in Nehemiah's activity in Palestine, presumably during a second administration. Some

---

the latter first entered Canaan, without ever being able to discharge the account. It seems not to have occurred to the Chronicler's racial exclusiveness that the God who, as he himself points out, could and did turn Balaam's hired curses upon Israel into ultimate blessing, might be concerned to turn Israel's own unforgiving bitterness toward its neighbors into something a little more neighborly, and more conducive to the peace and prosperity not only of Palestine

then, but of the Near East and of the whole world in a later century. But these are perspectives easier for the centuries than for the years and the generations to see, easier for other countries and peoples to understand than for those whose racial memories and emotions are most involved.

4-31. Nehemiah as Reforming Zealot.—It is Nehemiah himself, with the frank forthrightness of his vivid memoirs, who makes it plain

contend that, like the later visit of Arsames, an official of Egypt, "to the king" (Cowley, *Aramaic Papyri,* No. 30, ll. 4-5, 30), Nehemiah's trip to Persia was but temporary and routine and that he retained his governorship meanwhile (Rudolph, *op. cit.,* p. 203). Probably, however, he left Jerusalem with finality and was later induced to seek further leave for another visit to Jerusalem when he learned of difficulties there. Vs. 6 presupposes that originally his narrative gave some information detailing what had caused his return to Judea, and it has been suggested that vss. 1-5 reflect the situation that brought him back (cf. Batten, *op. cit.,* pp. 46-47), but this seems unlikely (cf. vss. 1-3).

The date of his arrival in Jerusalem for the second time cannot be determined with certainty. From vss. 4-9 it appears that there was a considerable lapse of time since his leaving and that his return did not accord with any set time but was a surprise to the leaders. **After some time,** lit., "the end of days," which dates the beginning of the second administration, is ambiguous and indefinite (cf. vs. 6). Rudolph (*op. cit.,* pp. 65-71, 203), who holds that Ezra's activity occurred during the absence of Nehemiah, suggests that since the journey would take about six months (cf. Ezra 8:31 ff.) and the work of Ezra took about a year, Nehemiah's return was *ca.* 430 B.C. But if Ezra followed Nehemiah and was not active under Artaxerxes II, such computation is impossible.

Torrey argues that there was no return by Nehemiah and that ch. 13 is unhistorical, the Chronicler's fiction. Although he recognizes that vss. 15-27 show less evidence of the Chronicler's style, he contends that the evidence of the Chronicler's authorship of 11:1–13:31 is conclusive. He insists that "there is *nothing in the text* to justify the assumption that an older narrative was worked over, or that any paragraph or verse came from another source than the [Chronicler's] active brain" (*Composition,* pp. 44, 48-49). He holds that in 12:27–13:31 Nehemiah "is simply Ezra (i.e., the Chronicler) under another name" (*Ezra Studies,* p. 248). His extreme conception of ch. 13 has not prevailed among scholars. Although there is general agreement that vss. 1-3 are the Chronicler's work, there is a strong tendency to regard the remainder as basically Nehemiah's document. While the style and linguistic peculiarities of the Chronicler as editor are recognized here and there in the chapter, it is usually concluded that the striking "vividness and concreteness of the narrative" and other characteristics, which are "entirely in the manner of Nehemiah," lead one to believe that "the kernel" of vss. 4-31 is "part of Nehemiah's Memoirs (though retouched by the Chronicler)" (Pfeiffer, *Intro. to O.T.,* p. 837).

Obviously the Chronicler as editor has given but a small part of Nehemiah's narrative of his second administration. Nothing is said of what induced Nehemiah to return and that which is given is very incomplete.

A. Expulsion of Tobiah (13:4-9)

Despite Torrey's argument (*Composition,* pp. 44-45, 48-49), the narrative of Nehemiah's expulsion of Tobiah probably derives from Nehemiah's narrative rather than from the hand of the Chronicler, who wrote vss. 1-3. Here the first person pronoun is resumed in the narrative.

As long as Nehemiah was at Jerusalem, his foe Tobiah (2:10) merely corresponded freely with friends within the city (6:17-19), but when Nehemiah left for Persia Tobiah used his influence to obtain quarters within the protection of the temple precincts, where he might stay when in Jerusalem, or at least where he might deposit some property for safekeeping. With the apparently unexpected return of Nehemiah an awkward situation was uncovered, since Ammonites were excluded by law from the Jewish community (cf. vs. 3; Deut. 23:3).

Jesus' cleansing of the temple (Matt. 21:12-13; Mark 11:15-16; Luke 19:45-46; John 2:13-22), sometimes compared with this incident, is but a superficial parallel. A closer one exists in Egypt, in the time of Cambyses, when a protest was made that foreigners had settled in the temple of Neith. At the king's orders the huts of the foreigners were torn down, their goods cast out, and the foreigners were kept out of the temple compound (Brugsch, *History of Egypt*, II, 304-6; Olmstead, *History of the Persian Empire*, p. 91; Bertholet, *Esra und Nehemia*, p. 91).

4. **Before this** does not mean "and formerly" (Rudolph, *loc. cit.*) and is not a reference to the past in general, as in vs. 5 (Batten, *op. cit.*, p. 289), but refers to some specific incident, perhaps to something in Nehemiah's narrative that has now been lost by the Chronicler's omission. It could have been some reference to Nehemiah's trip to Persia and his return (Bertheau, *Esra, Nechemia und Ester*, p. 346; Siegfried, *Esra, Nehemia und Esther*, p. 126). But Torrey (*Composition*, p. 44) insists that the acceptance of this view "is to shut the eyes to what is obvious, and moreover, to get into trouble at once." He regards the words as the Chronicler's attempt at making a smooth connection between vss. 1-3 and the narrative which follows (cf. Bertholet, *op. cit.*, p. 90; Rudolph, *loc. cit.*).

Although **Eliashib the priest** is usually identified with the high priest (3:1, 20-21; 12:10, 22; cf. Bertheau, *loc. cit.*; Batten, *op. cit.*, p. 288; Jahn, *op. cit.*, p. 168; *et al.*), the identification has been denied by some (Levi Herzfeld, *Geschichte des Volkes Jisrael* [Leipzig: Carl Wilfferodt, 1863] I, 146), and others argue that Eliashib had been deposed from the high priesthood, reduced to the status of simple priest (Winckler, *Altorientalische Forschungen*, Reihe 2, Bd. II, pp. 235-36), or that he had not yet become high priest (Jahn, *loc. cit.*). It would be unusual for the high priest to do the limited work of superintending temple cells, a task more appropriate for a minor official. Furthermore, it would be strange for one who favored Nehemiah and helped in his work to turn suddenly to support his foes.

The word indicating that **Eliashib** was **connected with Tobiah** means "near of kin" in Ruth 2:20, but is literally just "near to." It is usually understood to signify close relationship (Brown, Driver, Briggs, *op. cit.*, p. 898, *s.v.* קרב I, *c*; Wilhelm Gesenius and F. H. W. Buhl, *Hebräisches und aramäisches Handwörterbuch über das Alte Testament* [Leipzig: F. C. W. Vogel, 1921], *s.v.* קרוב; Ryle, *Ezra and Nehemia*, p. 309; Siegfried, *loc. cit.*; *et al.*) but the degree of relationship cannot be determined. In 6:18 Tobiah's relationships by marriage are recalled, but nothing is said of Eliashib, who would certainly have been mentioned if it were possible to connect him with the family of the high priest. Some argue that since Tobiah was related by marriage to Sanballat (13:28), it is not likely that he was also so related to the high priest (cf. Batten, *loc. cit.*). **Connected with** is therefore thought to signify merely close friendship, such as can be indicated by the ambiguous **was allied unto**. However, political marriages with those high in authority were common (cf. vs. 26). Josephus so characterizes the relationship of the relative of the high priest with Sanballat (cf. vs. 28). Such a relationship could have had the intended result of affecting the high priest's attitude toward Nehemiah.

Was appointed over is, lit., "was given with respect to." The classical form requires על, **over**, instead of the M.T. ב, "with respect to" (cf. Gen. 41:41). Since some priests occupied temple cells (cf. Ezra 10:6), the LXX has here "Eliashib the priest dwelt [*oikōn*] in the treasury." Both the LXX and Vulg. render the Hebrew as "the treasury," but **the chamber** is familiar from Ezra 8:29; 10:6; etc. Usually the word לשכת is revocalized from **the chamber of** to **the chambers of** (cf. Ewald, *History of Israel*, V. 160, n. 1).

---

that strict conformity to the rigid legalism of the religion of the law, as Ezra proclaimed it and as the Chronicler eulogized it, was by no means as complete in reoccupied Jerusalem as the latter's account implies. And it is a very human man of action who stands forth clearer than ever in this concluding section of his own memoirs. It is evident that he returned to Jerusalem as governor for a second visit, twelve years after his first leave of absence from the Persian court. Apparently he found the eco-

nomic situation in and around Jerusalem one of scarcity and difficulty, in which the earlier pledges of regular tithes for the support of the costly temple ritual had not all been fully kept up. The Exeg. makes the illuminating suggestion that not only ch. 13 avowedly, but possibly ch. 5 as well, may come from or be based upon Nehemiah's own written account of this second visit, in a time of economic scarcity leading to ceremonial laxity.

In any case Nehemiah found certain abuses

5 And he had prepared for him a great chamber, where aforetime they laid the meat offerings, the frankincense, and the vessels, and the tithes of the corn, the new wine, and the oil, which was commanded *to be given* to the Levites, and the singers, and the porters; and the offerings of the priests.

nected with Tobi'ah, 5 prepared for Tobi'ah a large chamber where they had previously put the cereal offering, the frankincense, the vessels, and the tithes of grain, wine, and oil, which were given by commandment to the Levites, singers, and gatekeepers, and

5. Because of its great concern for cultic matters, this verse is usually regarded as being much edited by the Chronicler (cf. Jahn, *loc. cit.*). It is loosely joined with vs. 4 by a verb introducing the apodosis to the names standing absolutely there (cf. II Kings 25:22; cf. Kautzsch, *Gesenius' Hebrew Grammar*, sec. 111*h*; Bertholet, *op. cit.*, p. 90; Rudolph, *op. cit.*, p. 204). Since the verb of the M.T. would usually signify "and he made," the Peshitta has "he built a great building for himself there." Some have thought of actual construction, the combining of several cells into a single large room by removing internal walls (Siegfried, *loc. cit.*; Bertholet, *loc. cit.*), but more plausible is the translation **prepared** in the sense of "provided" (Gesenius and Buhl, *Handwörterbuch, s.v.* עשה I, 1, e-f; cf. Rudolph, *loc. cit.*). For the ambiguous M.T. לה the LXXB× and Vulg. incorrectly read "for himself," when the proper interpretation is "for him," **for Tobiah**. It had been hallowed by the storage of ingredients for temple offerings and the contributions for the support of the clergy (II Chr. 31:11 ff.). Since regular arrangements are indicated (cf. 12:47), it is better to read "they were in the habit of putting" for **they laid** or **they had . . . put** (cf. Siegfried, *loc. cit.*).

The items mentioned are ingredients rather than the offerings themselves. **Meat offerings:** Better, **cereal offering** (cf. 10:33; Ezra 9:4-5). **Frankincense** was incense made by crushing the resin of plants (*Boswellia carteri* and *Frereana*) from Hadhramauth and Somaliland (cf. Immanuel Löw, *Die Flora der Juden* [Leipzig: R. Löwit, 1928], I, 312-14). It was put upon the flour offering (Lev. 2:15), or as part of a mixture (Exod. 30:34-38) was burned on the altar of incense (Exod. 30:1-10) or in censers (Lev. 10:1; Num. 16:17-18). Prophets rejected the use of incense as useless and idolatrous (Jer. 6:20; 48:35; cf. Lev. 10:1; II Chr. 34:25). No altar of incense is mentioned in the oldest account of the temple (I Kings 6:1–8:66) or in Ezekiel. The earliest biblical reference to **frankincense** is in Jer. 6:20, but it is found regularly in the postexilic cultus.

The **vessels** were probably not the temple treasures (Ezra 1:7; 8:25-28, 30, 33) but ordinary equipment for the service (Siegfried, *op. cit.*, pp. 126-27)—not only containers but also paraphernalia of all kinds (cf. 10:39; Ezra 1:7, 10-11). For **the tithes** see Exeg. on 10:37-39. Since **commandment** (מצות) means "legal obligation" only with difficulty, and that concept is usually expressed by *mishpāṭ* in Hebrew (cf. Deut. 18:3; Ezra 3:4; 7:10), the Vulg. has instead "portions" (מניות), which is easily obtained from the M.T. with but slight emendation (Batten, *op. cit.*, pp. 288-89; Gotthard, *Text des Nehemia*, p. 46; Rudolph, *loc. cit.; et al.*). The words after **oil** have been regarded as the Chronicler's interpretation (cf. Jahn, *loc. cit.*; Noth, *Überlieferungsgeschichtliche Studien I*, p. 150, *et al.*).

The literal rendering, **offering of the priests**, is here misleading since that involved was given **for the priests**. Such offering (*terûmāh*; 10:37, 39; 12:44; Ezra 8:25) was not limited to the "tithe of the tithes" of the Levites (10:37 ff.; Bertholet, *op. cit.*, p. 91; Siegfried, *op. cit.*, p. 127) but included the **contributions** to the priests as well (cf.

being practiced or condoned in the temple ritual and support, among them special privileges provided in the temple itself for his old enemy Tobiah. Nehemiah himself is very frank about his way of dealing with this situation.

I was very angry, and I threw all the household furniture of Tobiah out of the chamber (vs. 8). He was equally strict and firm in enforcing the payment of the tithes that had been promised for the support of the temple services

6 But in all this *time* was not I at Jerusalem: for in the two and thirtieth year of Artaxerxes king of Babylon came I unto the king, and after certain days obtained I leave of the king:

7 And I came to Jerusalem, and understood of the evil that Eliashib did for Tobiah, in preparing him a chamber in the courts of the house of God.

the contributions for the priests. 6 While this was taking place I was not in Jerusalem, for in the thirty-second year of Ar-ta-xerx'es king of Babylon I went to the king. And after some time I asked leave of the king 7 and came to Jerusalem, and I then discovered the evil that Eli'ashib had done for Tobi'ah, preparing for him a chamber

---

Ezra 8:25). The material, not mentioned again in vs. 9, is apparently an amplification by a later hand to bring the story up to date (Batten, *op. cit.*, p. 289). Since the editor did not include the **singers** and **gatekeepers** among the Levites, Rudolph (*op. cit.*, pp. 204-5) insists that he was not the Chronicler.

6. Interrupting the narrative, this verse is obviously an addition strategically placed after the description of the circumstances and before Nehemiah's reaction to them, to excuse Nehemiah from blame for the situation over which he had no control. He should not be held accountable for the deterioration of the cult during his absence. The excuse parallels that in the Aramaic papyri releasing the absent Arsames from blame for the persecution of the Egyptian Jews (Cowley, *Aramaic Papyri*, No. 30, 11. 4, 30; No. 31, ll. 4, 29).

Since Nehemiah usually has simply "the king" (cf. 2:1; 5:14) the **king of Babylon** (cf. Ezra 6:22) is regarded as evidence of an editorial hand (Mowinckel, *Ezra den Skriftlaerde*, pp. 59 ff.; Hölscher, *Esra und Nehemia*, p. 559, note *b*; Kittel, *Geschichte des Volkes Israel*, III, 648-69; Sellin, *Geschichte*, II, 158; Jahn, *op. cit.*, pp. 168-69; Noth, *loc. cit.*; Batten, *loc. cit.*). But the title is historically accurate and defensible, for the Persian king was also **king of Babylon.** Rudolph (*op. cit.*, p. 203), who declares "There is not the least basis for ascribing the exculpating remark to an editor," assumes here that the name and title were added to Nehemiah's remark by the later editor of the chapter.

For the literal **in all this time,** render **while this was taking place,** referring to the events of vss. 4-5. Artaxerxes' **thirty-second year** (433-432 B.C.) marked the end of Nehemiah's twelve years of administration (5:14). Unless he was still governor after his departure, it is inconsistent to declare that in the same year he was in Jerusalem, finishing his twelfth year (5:14), and in Persia asking permission to return to Jerusalem (vs. 6). His original leave must have been short, much less than twelve years (Jahn, *op. cit.*, p. 169; Pfeiffer, *Intro. to O.T.*, p. 835; Browne, *Early Judaism*, p. 157), but perhaps extended as required. Torrey (*Composition*, p. 45) considers that the date of vs. 6 is derived from 5:14, but others hold the reverse to be true (Jahn, *loc. cit.*; Pfeiffer, *loc. cit.*). The **thirty-second year** is usually regarded as the time of Nehemiah's second visit to Jerusalem but Rudolph computes the date of his return as 430 B.C. (cf. above).

7. Beginning abruptly, without explaining what induced the return or describing incidents involved in that return (cf. 2:1-11), this verse follows naturally from vs. 6 but does not join smoothly to vs. 5, which it partially repeats. **Discovered** is less accurate than **understood** or "observed" in rendering the Hebrew *bin,* which means not so much "to see" as "to understand fully all the implications of a situation."

The evil, a superfluous addition (Jahn, *loc. cit.*; Rudolph, *op. cit.*, p. 204), was the pollution of the temple cells (vs. 5) by Tobiah, who was forbidden by law to be there because he was an Ammonite (cf. vs. 1). Reference to the house of Tobiah in vs. 8

(vss. 10-14), and in requiring conformity by non-Jews with the strict requirements of the law concerning sabbath observance (vss. 15-22). But his zeal as a crusading reformer is most

clearly shown in his own account of his treatment of his fellow Jews who had married foreign wives, and whose children did not always speak the language of the Jews (vs. 24). **I con-**

8 And it grieved me sore: therefore I cast forth all the household stuff of Tobiah out of the chamber.

9 Then I commanded, and they cleansed the chambers: and thither brought I again the vessels of the house of God, with the meat offering and the frankincense.

in the courts of the house of God. 8 And I was very angry, and I threw all the household furniture of Tobi'ah out of the chamber. 9 Then I gave orders and they cleansed the chambers; and I brought back thither the vessels of the house of God, with the cereal offering and the frankincense.

leads some to see in **preparing** (cf. vs. 5) a setting up of an apartment in the temple area where Tobiah could stay when in Jerusalem (Siegfried, *loc. cit.;* Bertheau, *Esra, Nechemia und Ester,* p. 348; *et al.*). But others think only of a place for storage of Tobiah's property. It is unlikely that any building was involved (cf. vs. 5). **Chamber** is spelled as in 3:30; 12:44 (נשכה) rather than as in vss. 4-5; 10:37; Ezra 8:29 (לשכה). The temple chambers apparently opened upon one of the broad spaces which surrounded **the house of God** (cf. 6:10; 8:16; Ezra 1:4).

8. Usually for **it grieved me** (2:10), here, lit., "it was evil to me," the Hebrew has "it appeared evil in my eyes" (cf. Gen. 21:11-12). While **I was very angry** is in keeping with Nehemiah's volatile personality (cf. vs. 25), the idea would be expressed otherwise in Hebrew (cf. 5:6). But anger is expressed in the violence of Nehemiah's action, for the verb **threw . . . out** is also used of slinging stones. **Household furniture** is, lit., "the utensils of the house." Some insist that general household goods are meant (cf. vs. 7), while others believe that it was just the equipment used in the celebration of the offering meal (Bertholet, *loc. cit.;* Rudolph, *loc. cit.*). The latter, however, implies for the Ammonite Tobias a greater participation in the Jewish cultus than seems probable. He may have taken advantage of the holy character of the site to store some of his property in the chamber and thereby gained the added protection that the temple afforded. Jahn (*loc. cit.*) omits the "house of Tobiah" everywhere as an interpolation, and suggests that it was Eliashib himself who appropriated the chamber and misused it.

9. The word **commanded** indicates the extent of Nehemiah's authority during his second administration, and the fact that the priests did as ordered, without protest or complaint, indicates their subservience. The Chronicler would scarcely have presented matters thus.

The cleansing was a ritual act to decontaminate the space polluted by Tobiah and to restore it to its holy condition (cf. II Chr. 29:15-16, 18; 34:3, 5, 8). Hebrew practice involved washing and scouring (cf. Lev. 6:27-28); sprinkling blood in a symbolical manner (cf. Ezek. 45:18-19), and sacrificing (Lev. 15:1-33). Purification of a Babylonian temple involved sprinkling with water, beating drums, the use of censer and torch, the smearing of the doors with cedar resin, the slaughtering of a ram, and the recitation of exorcisms (cf. A. Sachs, "Temple Program for the New Year's Festival at Babylon," in J. B. Pritchard, ed., *Ancient Near Eastern Texts Relating to the Old Testament* [Princeton: Princeton University Press, 1950], p. 333, ll. 335-70; cf. Pedersen, *Israel, Its Life and Culture III-IV*, pp. 747-48). As in Babylonia, where not only the temple but the whole vicinity was contaminated and had to be purified, **the chambers** nearby also were cleansed (cf. Rudoph, *loc. cit.*). However, because the singular noun is used everywhere else, **chambers** is incorrectly emended to "the chamber" here, as in the LXX[L], Peshitta, and the Arabic versions.

After the purge, the temple implements and stores (cf. vs. 5) were replaced. **Cereal**

tended with them and cursed them and beat some of them and pulled out their hair (vs. 25a).

We recognize at once in such impetuous physical and spiritual violence the sincere but pitiless Puritan reformer in every generation,

race, and religion. We can see likewise that these characteristics—what Pfeiffer calls "his rabid intolerance, his despotic methods and overbearing tactlessness" [2]— were the defects of Nehemiah's best qualities: his passionate zeal

[2] *Intro. to O.T.*, p. 837.

10 ¶ And I perceived that the portions
of the Levites had not been given *them:* for
the Levites and the singers, that did the
work, were fled every one to his field.

10 I also found out that the portions of
the Levites had not been given to them; so
that the Levites and the singers, who did

---

offering and **frankincense** have been regarded as insertions from vs. 5 (Jahn, *loc. cit.*),
but possibly the lack here of specification of the gifts may be evidence of abbreviation of
the account (Rudolph, *loc. cit.*).

B. Restoration of Levitical Support (13:10-14)

Tobiah acquired a temple chamber presumably because the storeroom, which
customarily held material for the support of the clergy, was either empty or seriously
depleted. The incident with Tobiah (vss. 7-9) was thus indirectly responsible for the
discovery of two major failures of the cult: failure of the people to pay their tithes and,
as a direct result, the desertion of the temple by the Levites. Such problems gave additional
challenge to Nehemiah, whose previous administration was concerned largely with secular
matters. The centrality of the cultic concern of the chapter has naturally led some to
believe that the Chronicler has composed all of it, but the whole tenor suggests the
practical interests and the vigorous and efficient methods of Nehemiah as encountered
elsewhere in his memoirs. Some touches by the Chronicler, expected in any material
dealing with the cult, are clearly observable here (cf. vss. 10, 13).

10. I perceived, representing a different verb (ידע) from that in vs. 7, means to learn
by inquiry (cf. Siegfried, *loc. cit.*). Through investigation Nehemiah **found out** that the
temple stores were exhausted because **the portions [for] the Levites had not been given**
(10:37-39). In **the portions** (cf. II Chr. 31:4), Torrey (*loc. cit.*) sees the influence of the
Chronicler, since the plural form is found elsewhere in the Bible only in 12:44, 47.

Although priests had other sources of support (Num. 18:8 ff.), the Levites were
entirely dependent upon tithes for their living (vs. 12). Like Malachi (3:10), Nehemiah
expected the people to bring in their tithes to the temple storehouse. It is presumed
that the Levites regularly collected their **portions** from the time of Zerubbabel (cf.
12:47), but despite the supposed organization for collecting the tithes (cf. 12:44) it is
evident that there was considerable laxity during the Persian period in the presentation
of gifts to the temple (cf. Mal. 3:8 ff.).

With the cessation of their support, the Levites stopped doing their tasks and **fled**,
leaving the temple "forsaken" (vs. 11). **Each to his field** indicates a return to the farm
areas from which Nehemiah had brought them (12:28-29), where they might till their
own fields or hire themselves to others to earn sustenance. Deut. 18:1-2 indicates that
Levites could not own property. **His field** indicates that the Levitical cities of the Priestly
Code (Num. 35; Josh. 21) were priestly postulates without historical validity (cf. Jahn,
op. cit., pp. 169-70; Rudolph, *op. cit.*, p. 205, n. 2). The **Levites** are to be understood
in the narrowest sense for, except by the Chronicler (cf. I Chr. 23:3-5), the **singers** and
"gatekeepers" are regarded as distinct groups (7:44-45; Ezra 2:41-42). **The singers** here
is a gloss introduced apparently because they are described as living outside the city (cf.
12:28-29). The gatekeepers, usually associated with them, are not mentioned.

---

and his contagious power to turn high resolutions into action.

What is almost as difficult for Christian eyes
and hearts to accept as Nehemiah's "last word"
is the prayer three times offered in this chapter (literally the seven final words of the book
that bears his name down the generations):
Remember me, O my God, for good! (vs. 31*b*).
The merits which, in the *quid pro quo* letter

and spirit of all legalistic religion, he pleads
before the final judgment of God, are not his
incalculable services to the city, the nation, and
the religion of his passionate loyalty, as one of
the great men of action and faith in their long
history. Rather he pleads his uncompromising
insistence as governor on "the letter of the law."
The Christian inevitably reads these vivid memoirs in the revealing light of one of the pro-

11 Then contended I with the rulers, and said, Why is the house of God forsaken? And I gathered them together, and set them in their place.

12 Then brought all Judah the tithe of the corn and the new wine and the oil unto the treasuries.

13 And I made treasurers over the treasuries, Shelemiah the priest, and Zadok the scribe, and of the Levites, Pedaiah: and next to them *was* Hanan the son of Zaccur, the son of Mattaniah: for they were counted faithful, and their office *was* to distribute unto their brethren.

the work, had fled each to his field. 11 So I remonstrated with the officials and said, "Why is the house of God forsaken?" And I gathered them together and set them in their stations. 12 Then all Judah brought the tithe of the grain, wine, and oil into the storehouses. 13 And I appointed as treasurers over the storehouses Shelemi′ah the priest, Zadok the scribe, and Pedai′ah of the Levites, and as their assistant Hanan the son of Zaccur, son of Mattani′ah, for they were counted faithful; and their duty was to

11. As usual, Nehemiah complained to **the rulers** whom he held responsible for negligence in the administration of the law (cf. 5:7). As so often in Ezra-Nehemiah, the temple is called the **house of God** (cf. 6:10; 8:16; 11:16, 22; 12:40; etc.). Nehemiah's concern over temple affairs has been regarded as evidence of the Chronicler's authorship here (cf. vs. 9), but it is as possible to claim that "Nehemiah was the last layman to interfere effectively with the priestly constitution, by virtue of the powers invested in him by the Persian crown" (W. F. Albright, *The Archaeology of Palestine and the Bible* [New York: Fleming H. Revell, 1932], p. 175). As before (12:27 ff.), Nehemiah **gathered . . . together** the dispersed clergy and re-established them in their **stations** in the temple, even before there was public support. It was apparently presumed that it was the Levite's obligation to serve, just as it was the layman's to contribute (cf. Rudolph, *loc. cit.*).

12. With the temple again in operation, the laymen resumed paying their tithe (vs. 5) for the support of the clergy. Only vegetable tithe is mentioned (vs. 5) and nothing is said of a tithe of livestock (cf. II Chr. 31:6). **The treasuries** were the temple cells or storerooms (vs. 5; 10:37-38). Evidence for Nehemiah's fiscal reforms has been adduced from some Early Iron III seal impressions on jar handles from Judea bearing the Aramaic name "Judah," written as in Ezra 5:1, 8; 7:14 (Albright, *Archaeology of Palestine*, pp. 173-74; "Notes on Early Hebrew and Aramaic Epigraphy," *Journal of the Palestine Oriental Society*, VI [1926], 93-102).

13. "The *style* of this verse marks it sufficiently as belonging to [the Chronicler], even without 'the Levites' and the usual enumeration of temple officials" (Torrey, *Composition*, p. 46). Although the Chronicler's hand is apparent, there is nothing improbable about Nehemiah's establishment of such an organization. According to the Chronicler, the neglect of the tithe occurred despite the fact that officials had been appointed to superintend the tithe (cf. 12:44). Nehemiah here makes specific appointments for the same task.

I made treasurers, based upon a very doubtful Hebrew word, derives its meaning by assuming that the verb is denominative from the noun "treasure" (cf. König, *Historisch-comparative Syntax,* sec. 338v; Kautzsch, *Gesenius' Hebrew Grammar,* sec. 53g,n; Bertheau, *op. cit.,* p. 349). Instead of the M.T. אוצרה, rendered **I made treasurers,** about

foundest of the parables of Jesus: the story of the Pharisee and the publican in the temple (Luke 18:9-14). By the light of the teaching and most of all by the life and death and resurrection of Jesus, the N.T. writers had been led to a quite different conception of the status of man in the presence of God. It is put with beautiful simplicity in Tit. 3:4-5: "When the

goodness and loving kindness of God our Savior appeared, he saved us, not because of deeds done by us in righteousness, but in virtue of his own mercy." Before that "everlasting mercy" Nehemiah's very human limitations as they appear in this chapter and his historic achievements and the rare personal qualities that made them possible, will not escape recognition.

14 Remember me, O my God, concerning this, and wipe not out my good deeds that I have done for the house of my God, and for the offices thereof.

15 ¶ In those days saw I in Judah *some* treading winepresses on the sabbath, and bringing in sheaves, and lading asses; as also wine, grapes, and figs, and all *manner of* burdens, which they brought into Jerusalem on the sabbath day: and I testified *against them* in the day wherein they sold victuals.

distribute to their brethren. 14 Remember me, O my God, concerning this, and wipe not out my good deeds that I have done for the house of my God and for his service.

15 In those days I saw in Judah men treading wine presses on the sabbath, and bringing in heaps of grain and loading them on asses; and also wine, grapes, figs, and all kinds of burdens, which they brought into Jerusalem on the sabbath day; and I warned them on the day when they

---

twenty Hebrew MSS spell the word as אצרה, which could be an easy error for אצוה, I appointed, especially when it is similar to אוצרות, treasuries, which follows (cf. Rudolph, *op. cit.,* p. 206). Thus it is preferable to emend the M.T. to read with the LXX^אL and Peshitta versions, I appointed or "I commanded." The men appointed were not over the rooms but over the distribution of the produce (cf. Acts 6:1-3), the portions of the Levites (cf. vs. 10). Because not all temple employees could be trusted with the gifts to the temple (cf. II Kings 12:4 ff.), faithfulness was a desirable trait in the appointment. By faithful is meant "reliable" or "trustworthy" (cf. 7:2; I Cor. 4:2).

Because the names are not unusual, and paternity is not indicated, it is impossible to identify the appointees with others of the same name elsewhere. Since Zadok is the scribe (cf. Ezra 7:6), he was probably a professional "secretary" (Schaeder, *Esra der Schreiber,* p. 41; Bertholet, *loc. cit.;* Siegfried, *op. cit.,* p. 128; *et al.*), possibly one of a group of Levites (cf. II Chr. 34:13). The Levite Pedaiah can scarcely be identical with Pedaiah in 3:25. Despite his full genealogy, Hanan cannot be identified with certainty. It is conjectured that he was a Levite, a descendant of Mattaniah, leader of the musicians (cf. 11:17, 22; 12:8), and hence represented the singers (Bertheau, *op. cit.,* pp. 349-50). Next to them, lit., "at their hand" (cf. 3:4), which is interpreted by the words as their assistant, is rendered "and with them" by the Peshitta, thus indicating no subordination.

14. Characteristically the narrative is interrupted by a direct appeal to God (cf. 4:4-5; 5:19; 6:14; 13:22, 29, 31). Remember me is written with reference to the divine record book wherein God as a scribe was believed to keep records (Exod. 32:32-33), recording the good deeds of the righteous for credit in the final judgment (cf. Mal. 3:16; Isa. 66:6; Dan. 7:10). Such credits were not final but for just cause could be expunged from the record. The good deeds here are specified as what Nehemiah had done for the house of my God, the re-establishment of the cult through the renewal of support for the Levites. And for his service, lacking in the LXX, has been regarded as the Chronicler's gloss to the text (Batten, *Ezra and Nehemiah,* p. 293), but both the Vulg. and Peshitta include it. Since the suffix is ambiguous in the M.T., the text can be rendered either and for his service, with reference to God, or "its services" (Amer. Trans.), concerning the temple. Since the noun is plural, the latter is preferable.

C. Sabbath Reforms (13:15-22)

Like Amos (8:5), Jeremiah (17:21-27), and Ezekiel (20:13; 22:8; 23:38), Nehemiah found people impatient with the delay caused by the required sabbath observance (cf. 9:14; 10:31).

15. In those days (cf. 12:44) may signify merely the beginning of a new episode. On a journey or series of journeys during his second administration, Nehemiah noticed farmers working during the sabbath. Since several different crops seem to be involved, Nehemiah's observations apparently extended over a period of months before he acted. Treading grapes with bare feet, their clothes stained by splashing juice (Isa. 63:2-3), people of all ages shouted and sang (Isa. 16:10; Jer. 48:33; Dalman, *Arbeit und Sitte,* IV,

16 There dwelt men of Tyre also therein, which brought fish, and all manner of ware, and sold on the sabbath unto the children of Judah, and in Jerusalem.

sold food. **16** Men of Tyre also, who lived in the city, brought in fish and all kinds of wares and sold them on the sabbath to the

---

369-71, Figs. 97-98). **Wine presses** were rectangular, oval, or circular floors hewn from the rock. Some had a receptacle for clearing and gathering the juice, or a duct that led the juice to a lower basin for clearing before it was put in jars (Jer. 48:11) or skins (Job 32:19; *ibid.*, IV, 356-63, Figs. 95-96, 99-111; J. G. Duncan, *Digging Up Biblical History* [New York: The Macmillan Co., 1931], II, 34, and plates facing pp. 29, 36). Since grapes for wine were harvested during the seventh month (Tishri=September-October; Jubilees 7:1; Dalman, *op. cit.*, IV, 339-40), and the grain was harvested earlier, during the second or third months (Iyyar or Sivan=April-May or May-June; *ibid.*, III, 1-6), the word rendered **sheaves,** lit., **heaps,** must be the product in another form. It is unlikely that it was straw (Ryle, *Ezra and Nehemiah,* p. 314) and quite probable that the **heaps of grain** were sacked, threshed grain of the harvest (J. G. Wetzstein, "Die syrische Dreschtafel," *Zeitschrift für Ethnologie* V [1873], 279, n. 2). The **loading** of the grain **on asses** has been regarded as supplementary, a description of part of the harvest process, the **bringing in** of the grain (cf. Deut. 26:2). But it could also describe the bringing of such produce to the market at Jerusalem (Rudolph, *op. cit.*, p. 205).

And also introduces other produce put **on asses** for marketing. The lack of "and" before **grapes** has suggested the reading "wine of grapes" (Batten, *op. cit.*, p. 298), but it is probable that during the grape harvest the grapes would be fresh, although some suggest that both the **figs** and **grapes** were dried (Siegfried, *op. cit.*, p. 129; cf. Dalman, *op. cit.*, IV, 349-54). Elsewhere, however, another word (*simmûqîm*) is used for grapes dried as raisins (I Sam. 25:18).

I warned, lit., "I bore witness," is the verb used of the prophets in 9:26. The necessary object, now lacking in the M.T. but supplied as **them** or **against them,** is apparently concealed in the corrupt text rendered **in the day** (ביום). One Hebrew MS and the Peshitta, Arabic, and Ethiopic versions have **against them,** which was probably original (Gotthard, *Text des Nehemia*, p. 46; Rudolph, *op. cit.*, p. 206). Instead of the M.T., "their selling" **(when they sold),** the LXX^ABℵ has the noun "their sale" (Siegfried, *loc. cit.*), and some, following the LXX^L and other Greek and Ethiopic MSS, emend to "when they were selling" (במכרם; Bertholet, *op. cit.*, p. 92; Jahn, *Esra [A und B] und Nehemja,* p. 171; Batten, *loc. cit.*). But since the Peshitta has "that they should not sell," it seems preferable to emend the M.T. by prefixing the preposition *min* of negative consequence (cf. Ezra 2:62; Kautzsch, *Gesenius' Hebrew Grammar,* sec. 119*x,y*), which could easily be omitted by a scribe, to read "that they should not sell" (ממכר; Ehrlich, *Randglossen*, p. 211 under vs. 16; Guthe and Batten, *Ezra and Nehemiah*, p. 55; Rudolph, *loc. cit.*). No word corresponding to **food** or **victuals** is found in the M.T. or the LXX, Vulg., or Ethiopic versions and it should be omitted (Jahn, *loc. cit.;* Gotthard, *loc. cit.;* Siegfried, *loc. cit.; et al.*). The original text thus must have been, "I bore witness against them that they should not sell." In this context "bear witness" signifies "warn."

16. Because the **men of Tyre** (cf. Ezra 3:7) are lacking in the LXX^BA, Peshitta, and Arabic versions, and are not mentioned again in the narrative, some would omit them here (Gotthard, *loc. cit.;* Siegfried, *loc. cit.;* Batten, *op. cit.*, p. 295). Hölscher emends הצרים, "the Tyrians," to הצדים, "the fishermen" (*Esra und Nehemia,* p. 560; Winckler, *Altorientalische Forschungen,* Reihe 2, Bd. III, pp. 486-87), but it is unlikely that fishermen lived so far inland, and the word as emended cannot mean "fish merchants" (Rudolph, *op. cit.*, p. 207). **The people of Judah,** if genuine, indicates foreigners, and there is no good reason for rejecting Tyrians here, for they were the outstanding tradesmen of the ancient world (Ezek. 27) and these may have been agents of the great mercantile houses of Phoenicia (*ibid.*). They were doubtless but visitors to Jerusalem, for the

NEHEMIAH

17 Then I contended with the nobles of Judah, and said unto them, What evil thing *is* this that ye do, and profane the sabbath day?

18 Did not your fathers thus, and did not our God bring all this evil upon us, and upon this city? yet ye bring more wrath upon Israel by profaning the sabbath.

19 And it came to pass, that when the gates of Jerusalem began to be dark before the sabbath, I commanded that the gates should be shut, and charged that they should not be opened till after the sabbath: and *some* of my servants set I at the gates, *that* there should no burden be brought in on the sabbath day.

17 Then I remonstrated with the nobles of Judah and said to them, "What is this evil thing which you are doing, profaning the sabbath day? 18 Did not your fathers act in this way, and did not our God bring all this evil on us and on this city? Yet you bring more wrath upon Israel by profaning the sabbath."

19 When it began to be dark at the gates of Jerusalem before the sabbath, I commanded that the doors should be shut and gave orders that they should not be opened until after the sabbath. And I set some of my servants over the gates, that no burden might be brought in on the sabbath day.

---

verb ישב, **lived,** can also mean merely "to abide," apparently for the duration of the market period (Bertheau, *op. cit.,* p. 351).

17. As usual (cf. vs. 11; 5:7), Nehemiah first protested to the secular officials. The LXX^BA^א indicates that the original reading was "the sons of Judah." The **nobles** (cf. 11:1) may have been a later addition (Jahn, *loc. cit.;* Batten, *op. cit.,* pp. 296, 298-99). For **contended** cf. vs. 11. The sabbath infractions were regarded as an **evil thing** (cf. Josh. 22:16). **Profaning the sabbath day,** a late expression with priestly overtones, is found elsewhere only in Exod. 31:14 (P); Isa. 56:2, 6; and in Ezekiel.

18. Batten (*ibid.,* p. 296) claims that this verse "is couched in the hackneyed terms of which [Nehemiah] is free," and that in many ways it suggests Ezra 9:14; 10:10, 14. He therefore regards it as the work of the Chronicler, a "conventional prophetic utterance" replacing Nehemiah's own originally more forceful utterance. Rudolph (*loc. cit.*), however, insists that it is Nehemiah's own, attesting his excellent knowledge of the prophets (Jer. 17:19-27; Ezek. 20:12 ff.; cf. Bertheau, *loc. cit.*).

All this evil comprehensively includes the sufferings of the Jews in the recent generations, including the destruction of Jerusalem, the Exile, and the trials of the postexilic period of reconstruction. The **evil** was brought by God when his people deserved it (cf. 9:26-27; Ezra 5:12; 9:13), and, as in Jer. 17:21 ff., the **fathers** of the earlier generations were held responsible for the disaster and distress. **Thus** implies that it was just such profanation of the sabbath as Nehemiah condemned that brought on the destruction and Exile. Jahn (*op. cit.,* p. 172) holds that the Chronicler believed national misfortune was due to sabbath infractions. Historically, however, it was general disobedience and unfaithfulness that were stressed in the pre-exilic period as being responsible for the disasters. **And upon this city** is a clumsy, superfluous addition (Jahn, *loc. cit.;* Rudolph, *loc. cit.*). **You bring more wrath** is, lit., "you causing to add wrath" (cf. Ezra 10:10).

19. When the **gates** were completed, Nehemiah ordered them closed at night (7:3), but with peace came laxity and the heavy doors were not shut. Now Nehemiah asserts his political authority to close the gates during the sabbath. **When it began to be dark** presumes the development of a Hebrew verb from a root related to the Arabic "be black," which resulted in the noun "shadow." But the versions make no reference to darkness or evening. The Vulg. has "when the gates . . . were at rest," and the LXX^L^ could mean the same (cf. *ibid.*). It is suggested that the M.T. צללו is corrupted from an original חדלו, "they ceased" (Jahn, *loc. cit.*), but it is preferable to see here the Babylonian *ṣalālu,* in the sense of "to rest," "be idle," "be not in use" (Bezold, *Babylonisch-Assyrisches Glossar,* p. 237, col. 1). A parallel Babylonian text has "Idle lies [*ṣa-lil*] the ferry; idle is the quay; all the sailors are idle" (K. L. Tallqvist, *Die assyrische Besch-*

813

20 So the merchants and sellers of all kind of ware lodged without Jerusalem once or twice.

21 Then I testified against them, and said unto them, Why lodge ye about the wall? if ye do *so* again, I will lay hands on you. From that time forth came they no *more* on the sabbath.

22 And I commanded the Levites, that they should cleanse themselves, and *that* they should come *and* keep the gates, to

20 Then the merchants and sellers of all kinds of wares lodged outside Jerusalem once or twice. 21 But I warned them and said to them, "Why do you lodge before the wall? If you do so again I will lay hands on you." From that time on they did not come on the sabbath. 22 And I commanded the Levites that they should purify themselves and come and guard the gates, to keep the

---

wörungsserie Maqlû [London: Harrison & Sons, 1894], pp. 92-93, ll. 8-9). **Gates** here refers to the centers of social and business activity adjacent to the gates. At sundown on Friday evening the usual bustling activity ceased and the gates were to be closed. **I commanded** indicates the governor's authority (cf. vs. 9; Ezra 2:63). Since another word (דלתות) is used, meaning "door leaves," it is better to render **doors** rather than **gates**. **Till after the sabbath** means until after sundown on Saturday. Nehemiah posted some of his private servants (cf. 4:16, 23; 6:10, 16) to see that his orders were obeyed. This was temporary police duty until a permanent service was established (cf. Torrey, *Composition*, pp. 46-47). Since none could enter closed gates, such posting of guards has been regarded as a superfluous precaution (Winckler, *op. cit.*, Reihe 2, Bd. III, p. 487), but the guards were doubtless intended to guarantee that no one reopened the gates or smuggled in merchandise during the sabbath (Keil, *Chronik, Esra, Nehemia und Esther*, p. 595; Bertheau, *op. cit.*, pp. 351-52; Rudolph, *loc. cit.*; Batten, *op. cit.*, p. 297).

20-21. Instead of returning home, those who brought produce to Jerusalem on the sabbath and found the gates closed settled down outside the walls to wait out the sabbath. **Lodged** need not mean "spent the night" but can be simply "encamped" (*ibid.*, p. 299). As a result, the market was moved outside the walls and merchants waited for buyers who would smuggle their goods into the city (Browne, *Early Judaism*, p. 158). The camping did not violate the law, but the spirit of the law was violated by an impatient wishing for the sabbath to pass quickly. This irritated Nehemiah as it had angered Amos (8:5-6). The LXX, which interprets with "and they all lodged and engaged in business outside of Jerusalem," gives a clue to the more severe measures of Nehemiah, after the merchants had acted thus **once or twice**, a matter of several weeks.

Warned them: Cf. vs. 15. **If you do so again** (cf. I Kings 18:34) is, lit., "if you repeat" (Amer. Trans.). The expression "stretch forth the hand" is elsewhere used of giving charity (cf. Prov. 31:20), but the Hebrew text, "against you," indicates violence (cf. vs. 25). The interpretation "I shall arrest you" (Amer. Trans.) is less likely than **I will lay hands on you** (cf. vs. 25), for instead of the M.T., "a hand," the LXX, Ethiopic, and Arabic versions have "my hand."

22a. The verse is widely recognized as an addition by the Chronicler who did not want the Levites ignored (Jahn, *loc. cit.*; Batten, *op. cit.*, pp. 297-98). But it is unlikely that the Chronicler would assign to secular tasks the Levites who otherwise work only in the temple (cf. Rudolph, *op. cit.*, p. 208).

According to 7:1-2, the Levites were put in charge of the city gates as they already were of the temple gates. It is possible that Nehemiah's servants functioned beside the Levites or other gatekeepers who were not trusted to follow Nehemiah's orders. It is probable, however, that **the Levites** ultimately released the "servants" for their normal duties by returning to posts that they had abandoned (cf. vs. 10). The functions of the Levites at the gates cannot be determined exactly. Some regard them as supplementing the regular gatekeepers (Keil, *op. cit.*, p. 596). Responsible for this view is the former translation, "that they should come in to the watches," which has been considered both linguistically impossible and factually improbable (Rudolph, *op. cit.*, p. 207). The verb

sanctify the sabbath day. Remember me, O my God, *concerning* this also, and spare me according to the greatness of thy mercy.

23 ¶ In those days also saw I Jews *that* had married wives of Ashdod, of Ammon, *and* of Moab:

24 And their children spake half in the speech of Ashdod, and could not speak in the Jews' language, but according to the language of each people.

sabbath day holy. Remember this also in my favor, O my God, and spare me according to the greatness of thy steadfast love.

23 In those days also I saw the Jews who had married women of Ashdod, Ammon, and Moab; **24** and half of their children spoke the language of Ashdod, and they could not speak the language of Judah, but

---

"guarding" (שמרים) is parallel to **come** (lit., "coming," באים) and the text can be interpreted, "that they should come and take their places as watchers" (*ibid.*, p. 206). The Levites, as replacements for the "servants," perform divine service in the city gates in the protection of the sabbath (Rawlinson, *Ezra and Nehemiah,* p. 153; Rudolph, *op. cit.,* p. 208).

A religious aspect is definitely found in connection with the Levites' work at the gates, for they are expected to **purify themselves.** Such a demand for lustration has been regarded as surprising. It is held that only those Levites are involved who were secular gatekeepers on Friday, and had therefore to be purified before joining in the cultic ceremonies of the sabbath, or that the Levites visited the gates to proclaim to the regular gatekeepers the arrival of the sabbath, possibly to pronounce a formula or perform a cultic rite in the gate to usher in the sabbath. It seems probable, however, that even guarding the gates of the holy city during the sabbath was divine service enough to require proper purification before it was undertaken (Rudolph, *loc. cit.*).

22b. The pericope closes with the usual plea for remembrance (cf. vs. 14). **Spare me** suggests a similar use of the verb in Joel 2:17 (cf. Akkadian *ḫâsu*). Salvation here depends not on Nehemiah's deeds (cf. vs. 14) but on God's, on his **steadfast love.**

D. Mixed Marriage Reforms (13:23-29)

23. In those days may be a general reference of time (cf. vs. 15), but the words have been linked with the foregoing as a secondary result of Nehemiah's tours of observation in Judea (cf. Siegfried, *Esra, Nehemia und Esther,* p. 131). **The Jews** are specifically those who married foreign women. **Had married** is, lit., "had made to dwell" (cf. Ezra 10:2). The mixed couples seem to have been found principally on the margins of Judea in the vicinity of the people mentioned. **Ashdod:** Cf. 4:7. **Ammon** (cf. vs. 1; 2:10; Ezra 9:1) and **Moab** (cf. vs. 1; Ezra 9:1) have been regarded as additions to the text by the writer of vss. 1-3, possibly on the basis of Deut. 23:3-5 (Batten, *op. cit.,* p. 299; Browne, *op. cit.,* p. 159; Hölscher, *Esra und Nehemia,* p. 561; *et al.*), but **each people** (vs. 24), if genuine, indicates that more than **Ashdod** (cf. 4:7) is involved (Rudolph, *loc. cit.*). Curiously, the Samaritans (cf. vs. 28) are not mentioned here.

24. Reference to the linguistic ability of the children indicates that the mixed marriages were not a recent threat but a problem of long standing. Those who place Ezra before Nehemiah must admit either that the children were born before Ezra's reforms or that Ezra's work failed and that the couples again came together, ignoring the popular acceptance of the law banning such marriages (*ibid.*). **Half** of the **children** used a foreign tongue and did not understand Jewish speech. On the basis of the Arabic version some assume that **half** refers to a mixed language, a patois or gibberish, half Jewish and half foreign (Rawlinson, *Ezra and Nehemiah,* p. 144; Rudolph, *op. cit.,* pp. 208-9, n. 1), but this view, denied by the reference to inability to use Jewish speech, is now usually repudiated. Since no trace of **the language of Ashdod** of that time survives, its exact nature cannot be determined. Some insist that the ancient Philistine language was still spoken (H. H. Schaeder, *Iranische Beiträge I* [Halle: M. Niemeyer, 1930], p. 29; G. R. Driver, "The Modern Study of the Hebrew Language," in A. S. Peake, ed., *The*

25 And I contended with them, and cursed them, and smote certain of them, and plucked off their hair, and made them swear by God, *saying,* Ye shall not give your daughters unto their sons, nor take their daughters unto your sons, or for yourselves.

the language of each people. 25 And I contended with them and cursed them and beat some of them and pulled out their hair; and I made them take oath in the name of God, saying, "You shall not give your daughters to their sons, or take their daughters for your sons or for yourselves.

People and the Book [Oxford: Clarendon Press, 1925], p. 74). Because **Ashdod** and its environs had long been an Assyrian province (cf. 4:7), some would emend the M.T. אשדודית, "Ashdodite," to the graphically similar אשורית, "Assyrian" (Winckler, *op. cit.,* Reihe 2, Bd. III, p. 488; Jahn, *loc. cit.*). Since the Ashdodites accepted the Semitic god Dagon (cf. Judg. 16:23) and other Semitic elements, some regard it likely that by the time of Nehemiah the tongue of **Ashdod** may have been Semitic, either a corrupt form of Hebrew (Bertheau, *op. cit.,* p. 354; Siegfried, *loc. cit.;* Kautzsch, *Gesenius' Hebrew Grammar,* sec. 2w) or, more probably, Nabataean, the Aramaic-Arabic dialect that prevailed in southern Palestine at that time (cf. 2:19; cf. A. Neubauer, "On Some Newly-Discovered Temanite and Nabataean Inscriptions," *Studia Biblica* [Oxford: Clarendon Press, 1885], p. 230; Otto Eissfeldt, *Philister und Phönizier* [Leipzig: J. C. Hinrichs, 1936; "Der Alte Orient"], pp. 33, 36-37; Batten, *op. cit.,* pp. 299-300).

Not all children spoke "Ashdodite," for they would likely use their mothers' speech and therefore **the language of each people.** Often the words **according to the language of each people** have been regarded as a clumsy addition intended to define what precedes. But Ehrlich (*Randglossen,* p. 212) emends the M.T. to "the language of their people," and regards it as epexegetical to "Jewish." The word rendered **the language of Judah** or **the Jews' language** is, lit., "Jewish," an expression found in the Bible elsewhere only in II Kings 18:26, 28; Isa. 36:11, 13; II Chr. 32:18. It is used here of the language in which the Hebrew portions of Ezra, Nehemiah, Malachi, and some other postexilic Hebrew works were written (cf. Batten, *loc. cit.;* Bertheau, *op. cit.,* p. 355). Josephus extended the term to include "Aramaic," which was also widely used by the Jews in postexilic times (Kautzsch, *Gesenius' Hebrew Grammar,* sec. 2c; cf. G. A. Smith, *Jerusalem,* II, 165, n. 5).

25. There is considerable contrast between Ezra's reaction and that of Nehemiah to the same problem of mixed marriages. Ezra turned his disappointment and fury upon himself (Ezra 9:3), while Nehemiah reacted violently against the offenders (cf. Batten, *op. cit.,* p. 46). **Contended with:** Cf. vss. 11, 17. Since the Hebrew verb rendered **cursed** means "to be slight" or "to be trifling," and its Akkadian equivalent means "to despise" or "to dishonor," it seems best to translate, "I treated them with contempt" or "I vilified them."

Those who consider violence unworthy of Nehemiah object to the statement that he **beat** some offenders, claiming either that he only permitted others to do so (Rawlinson, *Ezra and Nehemiah,* p. 153, n. 2) or that the words are a later addition by a fanatical Jew (Jahn, *op. cit.,* p. 173), much as the Peshitta expanded it to "I killed some of them and buried them." The Peshitta קמרת, "I buried," is due to a transposition of letters of אמרטם, **I . . . pulled out their hair.** Ezra pulled out his own hair (Ezra 9:3). Usually the beard was **plucked** (Isa. 50:6), for loss of the beard was a disgrace (cf. II Sam. 10:4). To claim that all hair was pulled out (Batten, *op. cit.,* p. 300) is extreme, for it is unlikely that Ezra was made bald (Ezra 9:3) and in Arabic and Neo-Hebrew the verb means simply "to pluck hair."

Since the first person is not used in vs. 25b, and vss. 26-29 seem to some not to be an oath, it is proposed to read, "I adjured them" rather than **made them swear** (cf. Bertheau, *loc. cit.;* Rudolph, *op. cit.,* p. 208). It is possible, however, that the trace of just such an oath is to be found in 10:28 ff. Although it is specified that Hebrew daughters are not to be given to foreign men (cf. Deut. 7:3), Nehemiah actually found the reverse. **Or for**

26 Did not Solomon king of Israel sin by these things? yet among many nations was there no king like him, who was beloved of his God, and God made him king over all Israel: nevertheless even him did outlandish women cause to sin.

27 Shall we then hearken unto you to do all this great evil, to transgress against our God in marrying strange wives?

28 And *one* of the sons of Joiada, the son of Eliashib the high priest, *was* son-in-law to Sanballat the Horonite: therefore I chased him from me.

26 Did not Solomon king of Israel sin on account of such women? Among the many nations there was no king like him, and he was beloved by his God, and God made him king over all Israel; nevertheless foreign women made even him to sin. 27 Shall we then listen to you and do all this great evil and act treacherously against our God by marrying foreign women?"

28 And one of the sons of Jehoi′ada, the son of Eli′ashib the high priest, was the son-in-law of Sanbal′lat the Hor′onite;

---

yourselves has been called a scribal addition because the words, not in the LXX, destroy the parallelism (Jahn, *loc. cit.*, p. 173). But since Nehemiah dealt with actual offenders, that statement has also been called "the most appropriate part of the oath" (Batten, *op. cit.*, p. 301).

26. It is argued that even **Solomon** could not contract foreign marriages without sinning. **These things** are the multiple foreign marriages, presumably largely diplomatic, political marriages, and their consequences (cf. I Kings 11:1-8). **No king like him:** Cf. I Kings 3:12. **Beloved by his God** was suggested by II Sam. 12:24b-25, for Jedidiah is "Beloved of the Lord." **Cause to sin** is rendered in the LXX by "turned aside," under the influence of I Kings 11:3-4.

Although Nehemiah may have regarded Solomon as a "horrible example" (Bertholet, *Esra und Nehemia*, p. 93; Rudolph, *op. cit.*, p. 209), vss. 26-27 lack the directness of his approach, and the references to the fathers and their sins suggest that the verses may be a homily or midrash by the Chronicler indicating that he shared the Deuteronomic view that censured Solomon (cf. I Kings 1:9-13). But in reproducing the passages in Kings the Chronicler is silent regarding the foreign marriages (I Kings 3:1; 11:1-8), and it is strange that he should expound the subject here.

27. The first verb may be rendered either as a rhetorical question, **Shall we then listen to you?** as in Ezra 9:14, with a negative answer expected, or "Shall we obey?" The LXX, introducing the expected negative, has "so we will not listen to you," which Batten prefers, with "listen to" understood as "tolerate." The Vulg. and Arabic, also introducing a negative, have "shall we also be disobedient?"

The passage is connected with vs. 26, for a contrast is drawn between mighty, God-favored Solomon, who nevertheless could not escape sinning, and Nehemiah's weak contemporaries, who believed that they could contract such foreign unions with impunity. The passage has been translated, "Is it then heard concerning you that you yourselves do exactly the same great evil?" (Rudolph, *op. cit.*, p. 208.) **Great,** absent in the LXX, has been omitted by Jahn as an "unnecessary heightening" of the idea. **Transgress:** Cf. 1:8; Ezra 9:2; 10:2, 10. The nature of the **evil** is reflected in the rendering "to break faith" (Amer. Trans.), which follows the Peshitta, and in the LXX, "to break covenant" (Ezra 9:2). **By marrying** is a gloss inserted in imitation of Ezra 10:2, 10.

28. Only one important case of mixed marriage is detailed by Nehemiah, apparently because it involved a relative of his enemy **Sanballat** (cf. 2:10; 4:1, 3; 6:1) and a member of a high priestly family. The culprit was **one of the sons of Jehoiada** (cf. 12:10-11, 22; II Kings 1:4; etc.) who was a son of **Eliashib** (3:1). Since **high priest** could indicate either person, it cannot be determined whether **Eliashib** was still alive and functioning (Bertheau, *op. cit.*, p. 356) or merely part of the genealogy. The offender could not be Jonathan, the successor of **Jehoiada.** Josephus, who apparently records the same marriage (*Antiquities* XI. 7. 2), gives the identity as Manasseh the brother of Jaddua, the successor of Jonathan (cf. 12:11), and he calls Sanballat's daughter "Nikaso," which may be a

Hellenized form of a Semitic name, possibly the Aramaic "Nikesa" ("Sacrifice" [?]; Marcus, *op. cit.*, VI, 461, note *e*). He declares that Sanballat arranged the match for political reasons. But Josephus dates the event about a century later than the time of Nehemiah, in the reign of Darius III (335-330 B.C.) and Alexander the Great (*ca.* 332 B.C.). Aside from the faulty chronology there is nothing implausible in his narrative.

Confronted by such similar narratives with such a wide chronological divergence, scholars differ greatly in their interpretation of the relationships between them. Some hold that they are separate, unrelated incidents with but fortuitous similarities (H. Petermann, "Samaria," in J. J. Herzog, ed., *Realencyklopädie für protestantische Theologie und Kirche* [Leipzig: J. C. Hinrichs, 1860], XIII, 366-67; Spak, *Der Bericht des Josephus über Alexander den Grossen*). Yet it is rightly objected that "the view that there were two Sanballats, each governor of Samaria and each with a daughter who married a brother of a High Priest at Jerusalem, is a solution too desperate to be entertained" (Cowley, *Aramaic Papyri*, p. 110). Others favor the biblical narrative, and regard that in Josephus as an unhistorical midrash on Nehemiah (J. A. Montgomery, *The Samaritans, the Earliest Jewish Sect* [Philadelphia: J. C. Winston Co., 1907], pp. 67-68, n. 47; Browne, *op. cit.*, pp. 206-7). Still others prefer Josephus' account and regard the narrative in Nehemiah as the work of the Chronicler writing in the Hellenistic period. Torrey (*Ezra Studies*, p. 235, n. 35; p. 249, n. 52; p. 331; *Composition*, p. 48) argues that Nehemiah's narrative is dependent upon that of Josephus, showing how the Chronicler believed that Nehemiah would have dealt with such a case as that of Manasseh. He insists that if the Chronicler's narrative were earlier, Josephus would not have omitted reference to Nehemiah or the name of the high priest (*Ezra Studies*, pp. 330-31).

Many accept Josephus' data but reject his chronology, regarding him as being "absolutely irresponsible in Persian history and chronology" (Montgomery, *Samaritans*, p. 68; cf. C. C. Torrey, "Medes and Persians," *Journal of the American Oriental Society*, LXVI [1946], 1-15; Munk, *Ezra ha sofer*, pp. 67 ff.). It is claimed that late Jewish writers frequently permitted the period of Alexander to follow that of Nehemiah (cf. Karl Budde, *Der Kanon des Alten Testaments* [Giessen: J. Ricker, 1900], pp. 22-23, 32; Markwart, *Fundamente Geschichte*, p. 67; Siegfried, *Esra, Nehemia und Esther*, p. 132), and it is suggested that Josephus too telescopes Jewish history. His claim that Sanballat was sent to Samaria by Darius (*Antiquities* XI. 7. 2) might be correct if Darius II was meant, but he confuses him with Darius III (338-331 B.C.), possibly because of the reference to Alexander the Great, and calls him "Darius, the last king," thus putting events nearly one hundred years too late (Cowley, *loc. cit.*). He may also have confused the quite similar names of the high priests **Jehoiada** and "Jaddua" (Herzfeld, *Geschichte des volkes Jisrael*, I, 146).

Discrepancies in the narratives of Nehemiah and Josephus are best explained as the preserving of two versions of the same incident. Adolf Buchler ("La relation de Josèphe concernant Alexandre le Grand," *Revue des Études Juives*, XXXVI [1898], 1-26; cf. also Montgomery, *Samaritans*, pp. 68-69) considers the Manasses-Sanballat story in Josephus to be of Samaritan origin. The Jaddua-Alexander portion of Josephus' narrative he regards as of Jewish origin.

Instead of **the Horonite** (cf. 2:10), Josephus calls Sanballat a "Cuthean" (cf. II Kings 17:24, 30), a person of the ancient city of Kutu, about twenty miles northeast of Babylon. By **I chased him** is meant banishment from Jerusalem (cf. Ezra 7:26). **From me**, lit., "from upon me," indicates that Nehemiah was no longer responsible for the banished offender.

The Bible tells nothing more about the banished priest, but Josephus (*Antiquities* XI. 8. 2) understood the incident as the occasion for the final break with the Samaritans and the establishment of the Samaritan cult. He records that Manasseh refused to divorce his Samaritan wife and appealed to Sanballat, who made him the Samaritan high priest at Mount Gerizim, where the Samaritan temple was erected. Then to Manasseh's side came many Jewish priests and laymen who also refused to divorce their foreign wives.

29 Remember them, O my God, because they have defiled the priesthood, and the covenant of the priesthood, and of the Levites.

30 Thus cleansed I them from all strangers, and appointed the wards of the priests and the Levites, every one in his business;

31 And for the wood offering, at times appointed, and for the firstfruits. Remember me, O my God, for good.

therefore I chased him from me. 29 Remember them, O my God, because they have defiled the priesthood and the covenant of the priesthood and the Levites.

30 Thus I cleansed them from everything foreign, and I established the duties of the priests and Levites, each in his work; 31 and I provided for the wood offering, at appointed times, and for the first fruits. Remember me, O my God, for good.

29. Again Nehemiah asks God to **remember** (cf. vss. 14, 22; 1:8) but instead of a pious plea the request is an imprecation, as in 6:14. **Them** seems to refer to priests, but since only one offender is mentioned, the plural suffix is thought to refer to the priests as a group (Bertheau, *loc. cit.*). Others see in it a reference to the schismatic Samaritan cult which, according to Josephus, included many other Jewish priests (Siegfried, *loc. cit.*). But the Bible does not mention that group.

Defiled (cf. Ezra 2:62) follows the Vulg. in verbalizing the plural noun "defilings" of the M.T. The Peshitta and the LXX have a singular noun. The LXX has "concerning rights of inheritance of the priesthood." Because the Hebrew root (גאל) can either mean "defile" (Isa. 59:3; Zeph. 3:1) or describe a close kinsman (*gō'ēl*; cf. Lev. 25:25; Ruth 2:20), it is thought that the text means "they have sought kinship with the priesthood," a charge leveled against the house of Sanballat (Batten, *op. cit.*, p. 302; cf. Jahn, *Esra [A und B] und Nehemja*, p. 176). The **covenant** was apparently that in Mal. 2:4-9 (cf. Deut. 33:9), a covenant with all Levites, including the priests. It is thus a Deuteronomic rather than priestly concept of the priesthood, for the latter considers the priests as "sons of Zadok" (Ezek. 44:15) or "sons of Aaron" (Lev. 8:1-36; 21:1). One Hebrew MS, the LXX[L], Peshitta, Ethiopic, and Arabic versions indicate that the M.T. should be emended from **the priesthood** to "the priests."

E. RECAPITULATION (13:30-31)

It is suggested that Nehemiah's narrative closed with a series of short declarations, referring to the preceding detailed accounts (Bertheau, *op. cit.*, p. 357). Thus vs. 30 may summarize the incidents of the chapter (with vs. 30a cf. vss. 23-29 and possibly vss. 4-9; with vs. 30b cf. vss. 10-13; Rudolph, *op. cit.*, p. 210). But since Nehemiah always concludes a section with a plea (vs. 29), vs. 30a cannot continue vss. 23-28 and, without connection, it must be a gloss to vss. 23-28 (Hölscher, *Esra und Nehemia*, p. 561, note c; Rudolph, *loc. cit.*; Batten, *loc. cit.*; Jahn, *loc. cit.*). Torrey (*Composition*, p. 48) sees the Chronicler's hand in almost every word in the verse, and its priestly content is more in the interest of the Chronicler than of Nehemiah. **Cleansed:** Cf. 12:30; Ezra 6:20. **Them** possibly refers to the entire restored community (Bertheau, *loc. cit.*), but in the light of the foregoing narrative, it could mean the priests and Levites (Van Hoonacker, "Néhémie et Esdras," p. 346; Bertholet, *Esra und Nehemia*, pp. 93-94). For **all strangers**, which follows the Vulg. and Peshitta, the M.T. has **everything foreign**, which is supported by the LXX.

Establishment of **the duties** of the clergy in part reflects the restoration of the Levites (vss. 10-13). Instead of **in his work**, which follows the Vulg. and Peshitta, some prefer the LXX[BL], "according to his work" (Guthe and Batten, *Ezra and Nehemiah*, p. 55; Bertholet, *loc. cit.*; Jahn, *loc. cit.*).

31. **First fruits** has no counterpart in ch. 13, but arrangements for their collection are presumed to be Nehemiah's work (10:35-38), as was the **wood offering** (10:34). Torrey (*loc. cit.*) remarks that the "noticeable expression" **at appointed times** is found elsewhere only in 10:34; Ezra 10:14, which he regards as the Chronicler's work. The conclusion of the book, the characteristic plea for remembrance (cf. vss. 14, 22; 5:19) here suggests 5:19 with its abrupt concluding words **for good** (cf. Ezra 8:22).

The Book of

ESTHER

Introduction and Exegesis by BERNHARD W. ANDERSON
Exposition by ARTHUR C. LICHTENBERGER

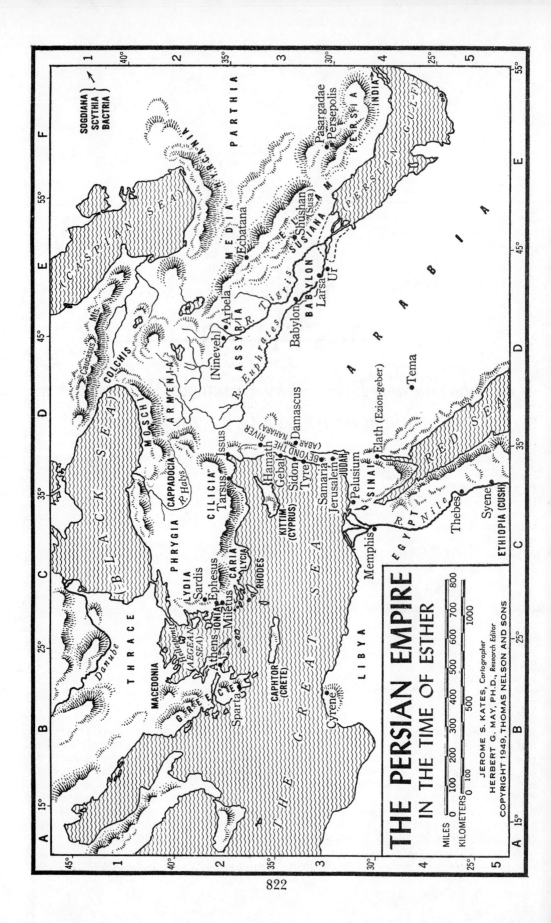

THE PERSIAN EMPIRE
IN THE TIME OF ESTHER

MILES
0 100 200 300 400 500 600 700 800
KILOMETERS
0 100 200 300 400 500 1000

JEROME S. KATES, Cartographer
HERBERT G. MAY, PH.D., Research Editor
COPYRIGHT 1949, THOMAS NELSON AND SONS

ESTHER

INTRODUCTION

Esther is unique among the books of the Old Testament. Not only is it set apart by being the only book which may be called a festal writing in the strict sense, but it contains no explicit religious or ethical teachings. In fact, superficially it seems to be indifferent to the theology and institutions of Judaism. And yet it is an extremely important book for understanding the ethos of Judaism. Last of the five festal scrolls (Megilloth) of the Hebrew Bible in point of arrangement and sequence of reading in the synagogue, it is actually first in the hearts of the Jewish people, among whom it is known universally as *the* Scroll (Megillah).

I. The Story

Purporting to be a chapter from the history of the Dispersion, the story of Esther relates intrigues of Persian court life at Susa which had far-reaching repercussions throughout the empire of Xerxes. On the deposition of Queen Vashti, Esther—not known to be a Jewess and kin of Mordecai—was chosen from all of the beautiful maidens of the empire to become the new queen. In her favored position she used her charms upon the king—though not without personal risk—to frustrate the plot of the grand vizier Haman, who out of hatred for Mordecai had determined to exterminate all Jews of the empire on a single day, the thirteenth of Adar. On account of her intervention, as well as of a series of singular coincidences, the king ordered the execution of Haman on the very gallows prepared for Mordecai, and elevated the Jew to the rank of grand vizier. In this capacity Mordecai sent out a new royal edict which counteracted Haman's previous though irrevocable decree, and allowed the Jews to slaughter their enemies on the very day Haman had determined by "lot" for their destruction. The day after the carnage (fourteenth of Adar) the Jews of the provinces celebrated triumphantly. The Susa Jews, however, did not celebrate until the next day (fifteenth of Adar), since Esther had asked for an additional day of slaughtering in the capital. To commemorate Jewish deliverance, the feast of Purim ("lots") was instituted as an annual two-day festival on the authority of letters sent out by Mordecai and Esther.

II. Additions

The Septuagint contains several major additions and various minor deviations from the Hebrew version of the story, making the standard Greek text slightly over one hundred verses longer than the Hebrew text. Moreover, even when the Septuagint parallels the Masoretic Text closely, there seems to be a striking literary independence even to the modification of important details of the plot. These facts raise the question as to whether the Hebrew story is an abbreviated version of an original story preserved more accurately in the Greek, or whether the standard Septuagint is a free translation or paraphrase of the story now found in the Hebrew Bible. The latter view seems to represent the prevailing opinion of scholars.[1] According to this view, the deviations and additions of the Septuagint were made in the interests of rectifying the religious shortcomings of the story and enlivening the terse original with rhetorical language and fanciful embellishment. The fact that most of these additions were found in the Septuagint at an early period—perhaps in the

[1] See, however, C. C. Torrey, "The Older Book of Esther," *Harvard Theological Review,* XXX (1937), 1-40.

late second century B.C. when the Septuagint "letter of Purim" allegedly was brought into Egypt,[2] and certainly in the first century A.D. when it was followed largely by Josephus [3]— indicates the great popularity which the expanded story enjoyed at an early date. Similar extravagant embellishments are found in the Talmud, the First and Second Targums (Aramaic paraphrases), and the numerous Midrashim (homiletical stories) based on Esther.

The major Septuagint additions are now included in the Apocrypha, although confusingly severed from their proper contexts by the influence of the Vulgate. In making his Latin translation, Jerome faithfully reproduced the Hebrew, but not wishing to ignore the Septuagint, he appended the additions with explanatory notes to indicate their proper place in the narrative. These chapters (10:4–16:24 Vulg.) were declared canonical by several church councils, from that of Carthage (397) to that of Trent (1546). Luther, however, transferred these seven chapters from the canonical books to the Apocrypha, where they now appear as "The Additions to the Book of Esther."

III. Unity

Most scholars agree that the Hebrew text is singularly well preserved, with the exception of a few corrupt or difficult passages (see Exeg. on 1:22; 2:19; 7:4). In regard to the integrity of the book, however, there is no such consensus. Since 1783, when J. D. Michaelis called attention to peculiarities of the passage 9:20–10:3, many critics have pronounced this concluding section spurious, either wholly or in part. The arguments adduced are twofold: (a) linguistic and stylistic differences which allegedly are peculiar to this section; and (b) inconsistencies and contradictions—specifically (i) the distinction between country and city Jews is ignored (9:19), with the result that both days of Purim are made binding on all Jews, and (ii) the details of the recapitulation in 9:24-25 are said to be out of harmony with the earlier narrative. The presence of the passage is variously explained: either it was drawn from an earlier Purim source and put at the conclusion of the book by the author of Esther, or it was added subsequently by a later editor who sought to justify the different Purim custom of his day.

Although this theory seemingly has won the favor of a majority of scholars, the arguments which sustain it are indecisive. A careful literary analysis will reveal that the author's characteristic style is found throughout the book, socalled differences in the latter section resulting naturally from a change of subject matter.[4] The second argument, concerning the dates of the observance of Purim, rests on a misunderstanding of the real purpose of the book of Esther and the relation between the situation in 9:19 and the festal arrangement of 9:20-32 (see below). On closer consideration other alleged inconsistencies disappear, as will be shown in the Exegesis.

Admittedly, the emphasis upon Purim is confined to 9:20-32; yet it is anticipated by the earlier incident of casting a *pûr* or "lot" (3:7). But even the latter passage has been attacked on the grounds that it awkwardly severs the context and gives a secondary etymology of Purim which Josephus supposedly did not find in the Greek version of the story. However, not only is the etymology probably correct (see below), but the incident of casting lots is so organically related to the narrative as a whole that it cannot be removed without the most drastic textual surgery. It is introduced at the natural point in the development of the plot, and no more awkwardly than the episode described in 2:19-23, which is likewise indispensable in the plot. Clearly 3:7 demands the retention of the concluding section, where the feast is named explicitly for the first time and regulated in accordance with the events of the story. Thus the structure of the book, in which the end is anticipated at the beginning, reveals its unity. The Septuagint, which contains practically all of 9:20–10:3, gives some support to this conclusion.

IV. Purpose

The governing purpose of the book is to explain and justify the celebration of a festival for which there is no basis in the Law, by appealing to "history" to furnish the reason for its origin and institution. Esther is a festal legend which attempts both to explain the origin of Purim and to authorize its continued celebration. Even those who regard the concluding section as a later addition usually agree on this point.

If the book is a unity the purpose was not merely to justify but also to regulate the annual observance of Purim. Outside the book the earliest reference to Purim apparently is found in II Macc. 15:36, where the day after "Nicanor's Day" (thirteenth of Adar) is called the "Day of Mordecai" (fourteenth of Adar). If this refers to Purim, it seems to indicate that one day only was observed among the Jews to whom II Maccabees was addressed. Likewise, in Esther there is a parenthetical passage (9:19) which implies that at the time of the author

---

[2] See the colophon at end of LXX.
[3] *Antiquities* XI. 6.
[4] See especially Hans Striedl, "Untersuchung zur Syntax und Stilistik des hebräischen Buches Esther," *Zeitschrift für die alttestamentliche Wissenschaft*, LV (1937), 73-108.

Purim was observed only on the fourteenth of Adar by rural Jews. The author's purpose was to reconcile divergent customs in the celebration of the festival and to legalize "these two days" (9:27) on the Jewish calendar. Accordingly, he provided an explanation of the origin of the custom of keeping two different days—an explanation which gave equal prestige to both the provincial date and the Susa date; and further, he recorded how, after the first spontaneous and unordered celebration on the two different dates, letters were sent out by Mordecai and Esther on the basis of which the Jews "confirmed" and "accepted as a tradition" the unification of Jewish custom throughout the empire.

Eventually this calendar regulation came to be more than a paper law. According to the witness of Josephus (*ca.* A.D. 90), both days of Purim were observed by Jews.[5] By the time of the Mishnah (*ca.* A.D. 200) the two days were definitely legalized in the Jewish calendar, although Talmudic scholars engaged in lengthy discussions as to the precise difference between a walled city and an unwalled village (cf. 9:19). This tradition has been preserved throughout the centuries. Today the celebration of Purim is largely if not exclusively confined to the fourteenth of Adar (February-March) among the great majority of Jews. However, in Jerusalem, which is clearly a walled city, both days of Purim are observed, and in eastern Europe even "Shushan Purim" is something of a holiday, especially for the children. Despite this variation in custom, both days are regarded, at least in a traditional sense, as official dates in the Jewish calendar.

V. The Festival of Purim

Little if anything can be said confidently about the ultimate origin and character of Purim. Scholars have variously attempted to explain it as a Babylonian New Year feast or a Persian celebration in honor of the dead,[6] which was appropriated by the Jews of the Dispersion just as ancient Canaanite agricultural festivals were adopted by the Hebrews and nationalized. The shortcoming of these theories is indicated by the theory of R. H. Pfeiffer, who maintains that the author invented both the festival and its name. The success of this "brilliant hoax," says R. H. Pfeiffer, was due to the fact that the publication of Esther was carefully timed to express and reinforce the patriotic emotions of the Maccabean period.[7]

It remains probable that the feast of Purim ultimately was of non-Jewish origin. The very fact that the author felt it necessary in 3:7 and 9:24 to explain the word *pûr* ("lot") by what he considered its Hebrew equivalent suggests that the word, and therefore the festival it describes, are of foreign origin. This is confirmed by cuneiform evidence. W. F. Albright states [8] that beginning as early as the nineteenth century B.C. the word *puru'um* (later *pûru*) appears in Assyrian texts of different periods in the sense of "lot," "die," followed by a verb meaning "to throw," "to cause to fall."

It seems likely, then, that Jews of the Dispersion came to observe a non-Jewish festival, just as many modern Jews have observed Christmas as a secular holiday. However, in the Jewish tradition the festival was nationalized by being made a memorial of deliverance from enemies and a channel through which Jewish patriotic fervor could be expressed. Eventually Purim was popularized in Palestine, although certain passages in the Talmud (Megillah 7a; Y. Megillah I) suggest that at first Palestinian Jews were opposed to observing it.

From the first the Jewish festival was convivial and "secular" in character. As described in 9:19, 22, the feast was and still is a time of feasting and drinking. Besides the giving of dainties to one another and charity to the poor, other customs were added in the course of time, such as the reading of the scroll of Esther in the synagogue, the fast of the thirteenth of Adar, masquerading, hanging Haman in effigy, noisemaking with rattlers, Purim plays, and so forth.[9] Purim has never been known as a religious holy day. Indeed, its popularity may be accounted for in part by the fact that it is the only worldly holiday in the Jewish calendar for the expression of the lighthearted side of life.

VI. Historicity

Superficially, the book of Esther appears to be sober history. As though it were a continuation of the historical books, it begins with the conventional formula "and it came to pass" (ויהי), and ends, after the manner of the books of Kings and Chronicles, by appealing to a source in which the reader may verify the facts (10:2).

---

[5] *Antiquities* XI. 6. 13.

[6] See Julius Lewy, "The Feast of the 14th Day of Adar," *Hebrew Union College Annual*, XIV (1939), 127-51.

[7] *Introduction to the Old Testament* (New York: Harper & Bros., 1941), pp. 745-46.

[8] In private correspondence. Further discussion of this matter is found in: Albright, "Some Recent Archaeological Publications," *Bulletin of the American Schools of Oriental Research*, No. 67 (Oct., 1937), p. 37; Julius Lewy, "Old Assyrian *puru'um* and *pûrum*," *Revue Hittite et Asianique*, V (1939), 117-24; E. F. Weidner, "Die assyrischen Eponymen," *Archiv für Orientforschung*, XIII (1941), 308b.

[9] See article, "Purim" in *The Jewish Encyclopedia* (New York: Funk & Wagnalls, 1906), X, 274-79. A very readable discussion is given by Hayyim Schauss, *The Jewish Festivals* (Cincinnati: Union of American Hebrew Congregations, 1938), pp. 237-71.

The impression of historicity is strengthened further by a profusion of precise dates and Persian names, and many accurate allusions to Persian customs and court life. Because of these pretensions to veracity, as well as the great popularity of Purim, Jewish authorities hesitantly declared the book canonical. Since then its historicity has been accepted by all ancient and many modern Jews and Christians.

Several difficulties arise if the book is regarded as a literal chapter of Jewish history during the reign of Xerxes I (485-465 B.C.). According to the Greek historian Herodotus, who lived in the period mentioned in the book of Esther, Xerxes' queen was neither Vashti nor Esther, but a Persian general's daughter named Amestris. It is phonetically impossible to identify this name with that of Esther despite the apparent similarity. Moreover, as yet we have no extrabiblical evidence of a general Jewish persecution during Xerxes' reign. Strangely, there is not a single explicit reference to the most memorable event in Xerxes' reign—his unsuccessful invasion of Greece, which according to the chronology of Esther would have taken place in approximately the four-year interval between the deposition of Vashti and the coronation of Esther. The book, however, implies that the king spent this time in Susa seeking a queen!

Some scholars have attempted to overcome these difficulties by arguing, on the basis of the Septuagint, that the events took place during the reign of Artaxerxes II (404-358 B.C.), whose queen's name, Stateira, is alleged to be roughly the same as Hebrew Vashti.[10] According to this view, the book describes a threatened persecution of Jews which was occasioned by their traitorous opposition to the imperial cult of the goddess Anahita. Their deliverance from danger, it is claimed, was the occasion for the institution of Purim—a memorial to the triumph of Jewish monotheism. Aside from the questionable accuracy of the Septuagint reading, "Artaxerxes," this theory obviously labors under the further difficulty that the book nowhere intimates that the proposed Jewish massacre was to be a religious persecution.

At the other extreme, many scholars have explained the story as a faded myth which was attached to the festival of Purim or its prototype. In its pure form the myth supposedly described the rivalry between the chief gods of Elam and Babylon, the triumph of the latter signalizing the political ascendancy of Babylonia over its hostile neighbor. The name Mordecai is said to be derived from Marduk, the chief god of the Babylonian pantheon; Esther allegedly is the equivalent of Ishtar, the chief Babylonian goddess who likewise carried the title "bride" (cf. 2:7, "Hadassah"). As in the parallel case of Mordecai and Esther, Marduk and Ishtar were cousins in Babylonian mythology. Arrayed against these deities were the gods of Elam, the capital of which, Susa, is the scene of the story. Haman is identified with Humman, the chief Elamite god; and Vashti suggests the name of an Elamite goddess. According to this view, Jews of the Dispersion became familiar with the festival celebrating the triumph of the Babylonian pantheon, and in the course of time emptied the mythology of its pagan, polytheistic content.

Other scholars, denying both the historical and mythological interpretation, maintain that the book is fiction, pure and simple. That a wealthy and impressionable king should depose his Persian wife and choose an unknown Jewess out of a bevy of beautiful maidens, that he should first issue a decree for a Jewish massacre on a day fixed eleven months away and subsequently issue a contradictory edict allowing Jews to butcher his own subjects at will, that the cunning of a woman should bring about the downfall of an Amalekite grand vizier and the elevation of a Jew to a position next in rank to the king—these features, it is argued, are designed to tickle Jewish fancy, but hardly to accord with the facts of real life. Like Judith, which likewise gives an air of historicity with its profusion of dates and names, Esther is said to belong in a class of pseudohistorical romances, of which there are many examples in the literature of late Judaism.

All these views must be evaluated in the light of the revolutionary announcement of an undated cuneiform text in which there is reference to a certain Mordecai (Mardukâ), who was a high official at the court of Susa during the reign of Xerxes I, and even before the third year of his reign (cf. 11:3 LXX), probably under Darius I.[11] Ungnad asserts that this text from Barsippa is our first and only extrabiblical reference to the Mordecai of the Esther story. If this is true, the discovery definitely administers a *coup de grâce* to any mythological interpretation of the book. Plainly the author intends the names Mordecai and Esther (even if they are theophorous) to refer to human, not divine, beings; and his story concerns the historical vicissitudes of a people, not an Olympic battle of the gods.

[10] Jacob Hoschander, *The Book of Esther in the Light of History* (Philadelphia: Dropsie College for Hebrew and Cognate Learning, 1923); followed by A. T. Olmstead, *History of Palestine and Syria to the Macedonian Conquest* (New York: Charles Scribner's Sons, 1931), pp. 612-14.

[11] A. Ungnad, "Keilinschriftliche Beiträge zum Buch Esra und Ester," *Zeitschrift für die alttestamentliche Wissenschaft*, LVIII (1940-41), 240-44; also in the same journal, LIX (1942-43), 219.

The question remains, however, as to whether Esther is pure fiction or whether it contains some historical elements. Patently the book is filled with chronological inaccuracies, exaggerations, strange coincidences, inconsistencies, and other fanciful details which make the story "too good to be true." Moreover, the portrait of the weak, sensual, and capricious king is a traditional distortion of the Xerxes known to modern historians.[12] Thus Hoschander's treatment of the book [13] as an accurate historical account, even to the smallest detail, is obviously farfetched, for this scholar ignores the literary features which make the story artificial at so many points. However, Ungnad's observations serve timely warning against any dogmatic judgment that the book is only "a tissue of improbabilities and impossibilities." [14] Though embellished with the author's imagination and literary genius, the story may well preserve genuine reminiscences of Xerxes' court, and may rest upon the historical fact of a deliverance from persecution experienced by Jews of the Dispersion. In this case, Esther should be classed as a "historical novel," a novel—like those of Scott—in which a nucleus of historical truth has been embellished imaginatively. Historians and archaeologists have already confirmed the fact that the author possessed an amazingly accurate knowledge of Persian palaces and manners. Further light on this dark period of Jewish history may reveal that the author's claim for the historicity of his story is not totally erroneous.

VII. Date

The question of date must be considered in terms of two types of evidence.

A. External Evidence.—Not a single pre-Christian writer refers specifically to Esther, and it is not quoted once in the New Testament. The first evidence for the existence of the book is the Septuagint version. Josephus quotes freely from the Septuagint Esther, and implicitly includes Esther among twenty-two books long held sacred.[15] Clearly the Septuagint Esther is pre-Christian, but the exact date of this translation (second century B.C.?) is a moot question. More decisive, perhaps, is the negative witness of the Wisdom of Ben Sirach (ca. 180 B.C.), which many scholars use to establish the earliest possible date of the Hebrew story. Ben Sirach's failure to mention Mordecai or Esther in his "Hymn of the Fathers" (Ecclus. 44–49) seems to

imply that the book was not in existence, or at least not yet known in Palestine in the early second century B.C. However, an argument from silence is notably precarious, especially in view of the fact that the great name of Ezra is also lacking in Ben Sirach's list.

B. Internal Evidence.—There is not a single statement in the book which gives unambiguous witness as to date. The glorious reign of Xerxes is spoken of in the past tense in such a way as to suggest the lapse of a long period of time (1:1, 13-14; 4:11; 8:8; 10:2). That the author lived considerably later than the time of which he wrote is indicated by his vague knowledge of the chronology of the Persian period (see Exeg. on 2:6). Moreover, the description of the Jews as a people "scattered abroad and dispersed" (3:8) indicates that the Dispersion is a long-accomplished fact. This evidence suggests that the book—on the most conservative view—was written sometime late in the Persian period (538-333 B.C.). Whether this date is pushed down farther into the Hellenistic period, early or Maccabean, depends upon other considerations with respect to content. The spirit of the book points to a time when intense bitterness and hatred for Gentiles were engendered by an aggressive threat to Jewish life and culture.

These considerations have produced two schools of thought. A great many scholars, following the lead of Spinoza, believe that the historical background of the book is the intense patriotism of the Maccabean revolution which had been precipitated by Antiochus Epiphanes' attempt to superimpose Hellenistic culture upon Palestine (168-165 B.C.). Haman may be none other than Antiochus IV in disguise, whose policy it was, like Haman's (cf. 3:8), to eliminate all unassimilable elements in his domain (I Macc. 1:41-50). Haman's edict of destruction (3:12-15) may be a veiled allusion to Antiochus' determination to exterminate the Jews and repopulate their land with Hellenists (I Macc. 3:34-36). Moreover, the description of the Jews in 3:8 suggests the Dispersion of the Greek period (cf. Matt. 23:15), and the references to mass conversions to Judaism (8:17; 9:27) call to mind the coercive proselytizing of the Greek period when the Jews reversed Antiochus' policy of removing the marks of circumcision. Accordingly, many scholars date the book sometime after the deliverance from Antiochus' persecutions under the leadership of Judas Maccabaeus (165 B.C.)—more precisely ca. 125 B.C., i.e., during the decadent era of John Hyrcanus, when the religious passion of the first stirring decades of the revolution had weakened into a more worldly attitude.[16]

---

[12] See A. T. Olmstead, *History of the Persian Empire* (Chicago: University of Chicago Press, 1948), ch. xvii.

[13] *Op. cit.*

[14] Theodor Nöldeke, Article, "Esther," in T. K. Cheyné and J. Sutherland Black, eds., *Encyclopaedia Biblica* (New York: The Macmillan Co., 1901), Vol. II, cols. 1400-7.

[15] *Against Apion* I. 8.

[16] For a persuasive presentation of this position see Pfeiffer, *Intro. to O.T.*, pp. 740-42.

Tempting as this hypothesis is, there are certain facts which make it impossible to exclude dogmatically the possibility of an earlier date. In the story the Jews fight not for their religion (as in Daniel) but for their lives; in no passage is Jerusalem or any of Palestine alluded to even implicitly; and the narrative indicates that Jewish hope lies not in patriotic exclusivism, but in winning the foreign administration to favor the Jews. These facts resist any easy dating in the Maccabean period. Thus a number of important scholars (e.g., Streane, Gunkel, Eissfeldt) argue plausibly that the book was written at the very last of the Persian period (fourth century B.C.) and that it reflects the historical situation of the Jewish dispersion. Evidence for this is found in the Persian loan words scattered throughout the book, and the author's uncanny knowledge of Persian royal palaces and customs. Ben Sirach's apparent ignorance of Esther is accounted for by the supposition that both the book and the festival of Purim originated in the eastern Dispersion, and did not become familiar to Palestinian Jews until the Maccabean period, when they were adopted as appropriate vehicles for the expression of an awakened patriotism.

Until we know more about Jewish history in the eastern Dispersion from the fourth to the second centuries B.C., this question must remain unsettled.

VIII. Authorship

On account of a misunderstanding of 9:20, 32, a number of ancient and modern commentators have supposed that Mordecai was the author of Esther. Actually the author is completely unknown. If a Maccabean dating is followed, he may have been a Palestinian Jew who resided in or near Jerusalem and who acquired his acquaintance with Persian customs and architecture through archaeological learning or extensive traveling in the East. On the basis of a Persian dating he was probably a Persian Jew who lived in Susa or thereabouts shortly before the final overthrow of the empire.

IX. Sociological Significance

"Typical in many regards of the perennial fate of the Jews, and recalled even more vividly by their daily experience than by the annual reading of the Megillah at Purim," [17] the book of Esther is the symbol of a sanguinary history of persecution. Haman is the prototype of a succession of leaders who have sought to blot out the memory of the Jew from the earth, and his edict of destruction, counteracted in the story but too often a dreadful fact in real life, has found expression in repeated pogroms of

[17] "Esther," *Jewish Encyclopedia*, V, 233-34.

which the so-called civilized twentieth century displays the most horrible examples.

The issues dramatized in Esther are of pressing relevance today. Being an expression of the life of the Jewish people, the book provides the basis for a realistic discussion of anti-Semitism. Haman's accusation was made on the basis of the unassimilable characteristics of the Jews (3:8) —rooted no doubt in their religion and maintained by a tenacious devotion to the ties of blood and kin. To be sure, Esther and Mordecai rose to power through the violation of the Jewish prohibition against marriage with uncircumcised Gentiles, a thing which troubled the Septuagint and later Jewish commentators. This, however, is merely a necessity of the plot, and must not be construed as advocating cultural assimilation.[18] The author intends to show that their action, though governed by expediency, was taken in the interests of preserving the cultural and racial integrity of the widely dispersed Jewish people (cf. 10:3). It is this characteristic devotion to blood and culture which so often has led to the accusation that the Jews are in some sense "a nation within a nation." One of the most significant features of modern Jewish life is the repudiation, even on the part of liberal Jews, of a policy of total assimilation, and the appearance of a heightened group consciousness. As in Esther, so also in the case of contemporary Jews, this ethnocentricism (symbolized by "Zionism") is rooted in their cultural-religious background and is reinforced by the hostility of which they have been the unfortunate victims.

The book provides at least one explanation of the existence of anti-Semitism. Contrary to the Septuagint, the Hebrew text does not suggest that there had been a long-standing hatred between Jew and Gentile, "hostile always and now" (13:7 LXX). Haman's speech in ch. 3 gives no inkling of a general hostility to the Jews. Rather, at the beginning of the book the Jews have only one "hater" in Haman, who, because of enmity to a single Jew, whips up anti-Semitism by calling attention to peculiar customs and appealing to popular desire for plunder. In ch. 9, however, the situation is different: there is a universal Jewish hatred, and the Jews, fully prepared and poised for attack, are ready to take vengeance on their "enemies" (cf. 8:13). Thus the book seems to claim that anti-Semitism did not arise out of a perennial conflict between Jew and Gentile (cf. Mordecai's dream in LXX), but was created by

[18] Contrary to A. E. Morris, "The Purpose of the Book of Esther," *Expository Times*, XLII (1930-31), 124-28, who believes that the author's purpose was to break down Jewish exclusiveness by advocating a policy of compromise and intermarriage.

Haman's measures so effectively that it could not be quenched even though Haman was executed and was succeeded by a pro-Jewish administration. Admittedly anti-Semitism is occasioned by the fact of unassimilable differences, but invariably it has been awakened by those who would exploit those differences in the interests of their ambitions for power, or by those who fashion a Jewish stereotype (cf. Shylock, Fagin) out of their antipathy for a single obnoxious Jew.

Also, the book describes in most realistic terms the natural reaction to unjust oppression. It is futile to try to justify the story of Esther by arguing that the original prototype contained no vindictive elements (so Torrey), for the Hebrew book of Esther is a fact. Equally futile is the attempt to tone down the element of revenge by making Jewish action purely defensive (see Exeg. on 8:13). Even if the book were only fiction, as many scholars contend, the situation would not be altered substantially, for Christian ethics makes no fine distinction between the imagination of the heart and the overt act of vindictive slaughter. The book is "down to earth," in that it vividly describes the natural vindictiveness generated under persecution (cf. also III Maccabees). The story can be matched with many tales inspired by the hatred which seethed under Nazi oppression.

The rabbis hesitated to admit to the canon a book which might be interpreted as showing contempt for Gentiles. However, the popularity of Esther increased in proportion to the persecution suffered, until in the course of time it became, as it still is, the book most beloved and well known by the Jews. Its immense popularity invited many extravagant embellishments of the story (see the fanciful additions in the two Targums), and much artistic skill was devoted to the production of beautifully adorned texts and cases. As the story was read in the synagogue at the close of the thirteenth of Adar, it became customary for the congregation to participate in the dramatic events by repeating after the reader the passages describing the victory of Jews over their enemies, while at the mention of Haman's name, the people—particularly children—hissed, shook their fists, stamped, and went through various actions indicating that Haman's name should be blotted out. These and other evidences of the popular prestige of the book of Esther must be evaluated in the light of the history of a persecuted people for whom the annual dramatization of Haman's downfall has been a refuge and a hope.

X. Religious Significance

Because only a minimum recognition is given to religion (4:16), and the name of God is not mentioned once explicitly, Esther is an anomaly among the books of the Old Testament. This fact, together with its vindictive spirit and the institution of a festival for which there is no provision in the Law, made it one of the several books whose canonization was opposed by leading rabbis. Even after it was admitted to the Jewish canon (probably at the Council of Jamnia, A.D. 90), the discussion about its inspiration seems to have continued (cf. Talmud, Megillah 7a). In Christian circles, likewise, there was a period of uncertainty as to its canonical status, although its recognition as a part of the Christian Bible was finally secured in A.D. 397 by the action of the Council of Carthage.

The reason for the author's apparent indifference to Judaism, which clearly is not accidental but deliberate, is a debatable matter. Some scholars argue that the author, coarse and worldly in spirit, had a rather cynical attitude toward religion when it claimed to be anything more than conventional forms. Trusting primarily in political intrigue and the power of the sword rather than in divine intervention, he deliberately went out of his way to avoid any religious reference, and even treated the sacred institutions and prohibitions of the Law with bold sarcasm. The author, says Pfeiffer, "appears to have made no demands on God and to have expected that God would make none of him." [19]

However, to say that God and Judaism have no place in the book is an extreme judgment. Since the book is a festal legend for Purim, it does not articulate one man's faith but professes to express the mentality of the whole Jewish people. And the Jewish people, even at the height of their worldly power in the Maccabean period, were always a profoundly religious people. In view of this fact it is strange that the author deliberately goes out of his way to avoid the mention of prayer or God even when the context demands it, as, for instance, in 4:14 where "place" is commonly regarded as a substitute for "God." He seems almost to be afraid of using even the formal and conventional religious terminology. The reason is probably to be found in the heathen origin and "secular" character of the Purim festival at which Esther was read. From the earliest days Purim was a time of noisy merrymaking, even to the point of the excess recommended in the Talmud, "Drink wine until you are no longer able to distinguish between 'Blessed be Mordecai' and 'Cursed be Haman'" (Megillah 7b). Says an old proverb, "On Purim anything is allowed," even to the transgression of priestly law. It seems plausible that because of the danger of blasphemy in connection with a festival

[19] Intro. to O.T., p. 743.

when considerable license was allowed, the author deliberately avoided religious references which in any way would lead to the profaning of the sanctities of Judaism. If this is true, he was actually governed not by a sarcastic religious indifference but by profound reverence.

In any case, the Jews have always found in the story the expression of real religious sentiment. Every development of the plot, though seemingly the result of pure coincidence, has been regarded as the expression of divine guidance and deliverance, as the Septuagint and the Targums interpret. To the Jew the book teaches the indestructibility of Israel, "the eternal miracle of Jewish survival." In spirit it is not alien to the interpretation of the "election of Israel," which found expression extravagantly in the late patriotic and apocalyptic writings of Judaism. Indeed, the Septuagint interpretation of Mordecai's dream (10:4-13) brings out the religious conviction on which the book rests: two lots were cast, one for the chosen nation, the other for the wicked nations who sought to destroy it; but God intervened to save his inheritance, "the nation of the upright." So the story is implicitly religious to the Jew, even though it is couched in nonreligious language and deals with natural rather than supernatural circumstances. As S. Goldman states, it proclaims the faith of the psalmist, "Behold, he that keepeth Israel shall neither slumber nor sleep" (Ps. 121:4).

Nevertheless, it cannot be denied that as we pass to Esther from other books of the Old Testament, "we fall as if from heaven to earth," as Heinrich Ewald once put it.[20] Amos and Hosea do not speak here, for there is no note of divine judgment against the rebellious house of Israel. The suffering servant of Second Isaiah is not here, for there is no suggestion that Israel's sufferings will bring the nations to see the salvation of God. One looks in vain for any trace of the spirit of the classical prophets who had refused to identify the purpose of God with the national interests of Israel.

Indeed, it may be said that because of the immense popularity of the book among Jews and the vehement disapproval which a discerning Christianity has manifested, Esther may be regarded as a clue to the fundamental cleavage between historic Judaism and prophetic Christianity, a cleavage which is sharply drawn in the pages of the New Testament, even though the book is not quoted once. The famous medieval Jewish philosopher, Maimonides (d. 1204), asserted that when all the rest of the Old Testament canon passed away in the days of the coming of the Messiah, Esther and the Law would remain. The rabbis of the Talmud sometimes put Esther not merely on par with but above the Law and the Prophets, reasoning perhaps that if the Jews as a people were to disappear, the Law and the prophetic commentary upon it would vanish likewise. These high claims bear witness to the inextricable connection between Judaism and the Jewish people. Luther, on the other hand, said in his *Table Talk:* "I am so hostile to the book [II Maccabees] and to Esther that I wish they did not exist at all; for they Judaize too much and have much heathen perverseness."[21] The fact is that in so far as Esther links the community of Israel, and implicitly the purpose of God, with race and culture, it is at radical variance with New Testament Christianity where the distinctions of class, race, and culture are obliterated in the "New Israel," and where the purpose of God is not identified with any ethnic group or cultural expression (cf. Col. 3:11).

In one sense the inclusion of Esther in the canon was an accident, resulting chiefly from the popularity of Purim; but from another point of view its canonicity is defensible. Modern objections to Esther are too often based on a purely moralistic evaluation. Weighed in the balance of modern social ideals, the book is found sadly wanting. But if this standard is used, many passages in the Law, the Prophets, and the Writings also must be declared "noncanonical." The Bible, however, does not claim in the first instance to be a book of lessons designed to make men morally better. Rather, its literature is the interpretative record of the history of a people who under God wrestled with the question of the meaning and destiny of their communal life. Esther is the literary deposit of this community in one of its perilous hours of history. To be sure, its understanding of the basis of community and its implicit interpretation of its history do not reflect the prophetic view which was accepted as normative by Christianity. Yet it is in line with much of the literature of Judaism in which the prophetic view was either weakened or distorted and, in a sense, carries the premises of Judaism to their logical conclusion.

Moreover, from the perspective of the New Testament this book has an indispensable place in the record of the providential working of God in Israel's history. Postexilic Judaism did not go the way of II Isaiah; instead, it followed Ezekiel and Ezra into an increasing provincialism and self-consciousness. But the tragic realities of history in this period were such that, humanly speaking, this was inevitable. In a time of foreign domination and aggressive cul-

---

[20] *The History of Israel* (London: Longmans, Green & Co., 1869), I, 197.

[21] No. 3391a. *Tischreden* (Weimar: Herman Böhlaus, 1914), III, 302.

tural influence the only course of action seemed to be a narrowing of loyalty if the vitality of Israel's tradition was to be preserved. The alternative would have been not merely the loss of a sense of peoplehood but the weakening of Israel's faith during a period of cultural syncretism. Particularistic Judaism attempted to say with Elijah, "I have been very jealous for the Lord God of hosts" (I Kings 19:10). Thus the book of Esther is a symbol of the deepening tragedy of Israel's communal existence which in the fullness of time was illumined only by the Cross. It would be false to find specific christological references in Esther; but, since Judaism cradled Christianity, the Christian church justifiably may find in the tragic history of postexilic Israel evidence of the providential design of God who, as the psalmist said, can make even the wrath of man to praise him.[22]

By itself, however, Esther stands as witness to the fact that men in their pride either make nationalism their religion in complete indifference to God, or presumptuously identify their partial purposes with God's purpose ("God and uranium were on our side!"). Since the presuppositions of the book have been superseded in Christian civilization in theory, but so rarely in fact, the words of Jesus are an appropriate commentary on any negative judgment against Esther or the Jewish estimate of the book: "He that is without sin, . . . let him first cast a stone" (John 8:7).

XI. Literary Value

After a thorough literary analysis, Striedl has come to the conclusion, to which one may readily assent, that the author was one of the skillful literary artists of his time, and that Esther deserves to be reckoned among the masterpieces of literature.[23] Although the style lacks the crispness and rhythmic elegance of the narratives of the classical period of Hebrew prose, the story moves along smoothly, keeping the reader in suspense as each new complexity of the plot is introduced, until the denouement is reached in a powerfully dramatic moment in Esther's second banquet (ch. 7). In keeping with Hebrew literary art, the characters are never described by adjectives; rather, their portrait is formed in the mind of the reader by concrete action. The author knows how to make actions speak more effectively than words (witness 7:9 [7:10 RSV], where the king's dramatic sentence of death is scarcely more than a gesture in the direction of the gallows).

The characters, which are clearly drawn, are really types rather than unique individuals. The king is the typical impulsive and impressionable Oriental despot; Haman is the typical "enemy of the Jews," drunk with pride and power; Esther is the beautiful but artful woman (cf. Judith) who knows how to use her charms bewitchingly; and Mordecai is the shrewd leader of the Jews who knows how to seize the opportune moment. Unlike Shakespeare, the author is not concerned with either the feelings or the psychological motivation of his characters. Thus the reader is left to wonder why Vashti refused to come at the king's summons, why Mordecai refused to bow to Haman, or why the king left the banquet hall when the full meaning of the plot dawned upon him. Usually these are necessities of the plot, carefully timed to produce the proper stage effect. The author is not too concerned over inconsistencies, or the seemingly awkward introduction of episodes which are indispensable (3:8; 2:19-23). The action moves inexorably and dramatically toward the realization of his purpose: the justification of the two-day Purim festival.

Various literary techniques are employed in order to achieve the greatest vividness and power of expression. The most subtle and ingenious of these is the construction of the plot upon the ancient blood feud between Amalek and Israel, which "Haman, the Agagite" and "Mordecai, the Jew" inherit (see Exeg. on 3:1). Moreover, the author is a master in the use of contrast and dramatic irony. Probably there is no finer example of irony than chs. 6–7, the account of Haman's humiliation and fall. Indeed, the writer delights to show how the tables were turned completely. The once-proud and ambitious Haman falls into his own trap and is reduced to a position of begging for his life at the queen's feet. Likewise the "unlucky thirteenth" turns out to be unlucky for the opponent of the Jews and, in terror, "many from the peoples of the country declared themselves Jews," i.e., proselytes. There is humor in Esther, but it is the kind which is appreciated only by the victor.

Several literary themes, familiar in folk literature in general, are woven together against the background of a possibly historical persecution of the Jews in the Persian period. The main literary motif—a woman whose beauty captures the heart of the enemy and thereby saves her people from destruction—is found also in other Jewish folk stories (especially Judith). Moreover, Jewish fancy delighted in the story of a Jew who, as courtier of the king, won favor for his people (cf. the story about Zerubbabel in the court of Darius I related in

---

[22] See further Bernhard W. Anderson, "The Place of the Book of Esther in the Christian Bible," *Journal of Religion*, XXX (1950), 32-43.

[23] "Untersuchung zur Syntax und Stilistik des hebräischen Buches Esther," pp. 107-8.

I Esdras). Furthermore, the theme of a ruler who at first planned to destroy the Jews, but later became their best friend, appears also in III Maccabees and is repeated in Josephus' *Against Apion* in a version which describes the king's paramour interceding for the Jews. And finally, it has long been recognized that the "gathering of the maidens" is reminiscent of a theme from the *Arabian Nights,* according to which the king takes a different girl each night until eventually Scheherazade finds favor in his eyes.

Quite apart from one's conclusions as to critical or religious questions involved, undoubtedly this book is a work of considerable literary value. Its dramatic possibilities are indicated in such a play as Racine's *Esther.*

XII. Outline of Contents

XIII. Selected Bibliography

DAVIES, T. W., ed. *Ezra, Nehemiah and Esther* ("New-Century Bible"). New York: Oxford University Press, 1909.

GOLDMAN, SOLOMON. "Esther" in *The Five Megilloth,* ed. A. Cohen. Hindhead, Surrey: Soncino Press, 1946.

GUNKEL, HERMANN. *Esther.* Tübingen: J. C. B. Mohr, 1916.

OLMSTEAD, A. T. *History of the Persian Empire.* Chicago: University of Chicago Press, 1948. Pp. 107-288.

PATON, L. B. *A Critical and Exegetical Commentary on the Book of Esther* ("International Critical Commentary"). New York: Charles Scribner's Sons, 1908.

PFEIFFER, R. H. *Introduction to the Old Testament.* New York: Harper & Bros., 1941. Pp. 732-42.

STREANE, A. W. *Esther* ("Cambridge Bible"). Cambridge: Cambridge University Press, 1907.

ESTHER

TEXT, EXEGESIS, AND EXPOSITION

It has been said frequently that Esther is a remarkable book but that it has no religious significance. Some interpreters have judged it even more harshly, saying with Heinrich Ewald that "its story . . . knows nothing of high and pure truths." [1] If that is so, then there is little reason to expound the book; the Christian preacher or teacher might better turn his attention to other parts of the Bible, as Luther did. He did not hesitate to say that he wished the

[1] *The History of Israel* (London: Longmans, Green & Co., 1869), I, 197.

book did not exist. But Esther is in the O.T. canon, and we find when we accept it for what it is that its presence in the Bible is neither puzzling nor embarrassing. We do not need to pass over it hurriedly or apologize for it. If Esther is important for an understanding of the ethos of Judaism (see Intro., p. 823), then it is important for an understanding of the community of the new Israel.

The Book of Esther and Purim.—To begin with, one who interprets Esther should be familiar with the festival of Purim, its significance

ESTHER

In the LXX (11:2-12:6) the story opens with Mordecai's genealogy, a description of a dream which he had in the second year of "Artaxerxes," and an account of his being made a member of the royal court because of his discovery of a plot against the king's life.

and its history. A full account of it is given in *The Jewish Encyclopedia*,[2] in the *Universal Jewish Encyclopedia*,[3] and in *The Jewish Festivals* by Hayyim Schauss.[4]

Purim is a celebration of deliverance. In contrast to Hanukkah, another festival of deliverance in which the achievement of religious liberty is celebrated and the preservation of Israel remembered, Purim commemorates the preservation of the Jewish people. The book of Esther provides the story: a colony of Jewish people living in Persia is threatened with destruction, but the massacre is averted. The story of Esther is a symbol, as Purim is a symbol, of the deliverance of the Jews. The nation, the people, are spared. This is not an isolated event, but is typical of Israel's history; as the people have been persecuted time and again, so they have often been delivered. Whatever the origin of Purim, and here there can be only conjecture, the festival has one clear meaning: it is a constant reminder year after year that though persecution may come to the Jews, deliverance is certain.

As has been pointed out in the Intro. (p. 825), there is nothing solemn about the Purim observance. From the earliest times it has been a joyous festival, with much eating and drinking, plays by mummers, masquerades, and revelry. An essential part of the celebration, however, is the reading of the book of Esther,[5] for that is the classic account of the triumph of the Jewish people over those who would destroy them; it is a distillation of intense nationalism, the will of the Jews to survive as a distinct people. That is why some rabbis have taught that though all the prophetic books may be forgotten Esther will always be remembered, Purim will always be observed.

Purim, then, is the symbolic name for deliverance, and it was inevitable that many lesser Purims should be patterned after the original festival to celebrate in the same way occasions when families or communities had been spared suffering or persecution. Many such special

Purims are described in the *Jewish Encylopedia*.[6] This is the story of one of the best-known local observances: the governor of Egypt in 1524 arrested and imprisoned twelve Jewish citizens of Cairo, with the intention of forcing them to pay him a large sum of money. One of the twelve was the chief rabbi, David ibn Abi Zimra. The governor intended also to kill every Jew in the city. But on the day scheduled for the massacre he was stabbed by one of his subordinates and the Jews were delivered. In commemoration of this, the "Purim of Cairo" is celebrated each year.

Special Purims are observed not only by communities but by families. Schauss[7] tells of such a festival observed by the family of Rabbi Abraham Danzig. On a certain day in 1804 there was an explosion of gunpowder in Vilna. Many houses were demolished and thirty-one people killed. But although Rabbi Danzig's house was destroyed and he and all his family were seriously injured, they survived. This deliverance, the rabbi ordered, was to be remembered each year with a fast and a Purim feast at which prayers and psalms were chanted.

In all these observances—the Purim observed annually by all Jews, the special community and family Purims—the meaning of the story of Esther becomes quite evident.

The Book of Esther has always been for Jews an allegory depicting the Jewish life and Jewish lot among the nations. It is a book in which not just one period is depicted, but all periods; it is a book that remains forever new because Jewish enemies will not allow it to grow old. It is a book that breathes of love for Jews, of the tie that unites the Jews, the Jew of the masses to the one who has attained kingly honors.[8]

This is what the writer of Esther had to say, this is what it means to the people whose life it depicts. We cannot answer the question "What does it mean to Christians?" without understanding this; we cannot answer the question "What value does it have for Christians?" without appreciating what it means to Jews. Its essential meaning has been put concisely in one phrase, "The indestructibility of Israel." When Esther was written, the indestructibility of Israel was a religious idea; Israel would be preserved because this was God's plan. This is not explicitly stated in Esther; there is no mention

[2] New York: Funk & Wagnalls, 1906, X, 274-79.

[3] Isaac Landman, ed. (New York: The Universal Jewish Encyclopedia, Inc., 1942), IX, 36-42.

[4] Cincinnati: Union American Hebrew Congregations, 1938.

[5] All are required to read Esther on Purim, women as well as men. Children are prepared for the reading as they become old enough. The book can be read privately or in the synagogue; the requirement can be fulfilled by hearing the book read.

[6] Vol. X, pp. 280-83.

[7] *Op. cit.*, p. 256.

[8] *Ibid.*, p. 254.

1 Now it came to pass in the days of Ahasuerus, (this *is* Ahasuerus which reigned from India even unto Ethiopia, *over* a hundred and seven and twenty provinces,)

1 In the days of Ahasu-e′rus, the Ahasu-e′rus who reigned from India to Ethiopia over one hundred and twenty-seven prov-

---

I. Affairs in the Court of Susa (1:1–2:23)
A. The Wealth and Glory of Ahasuerus (1:1-9)

1:1. Ahasuerus: It is clear from a study of Persian monuments that the Hebrew *'Aḥashwērôsh* (cf. Ezra 4:6) is an attempt to represent the Persian *Khshayârsha*, from

---

there of God's purpose, but it seems to be implicit throughout. "The divinest element in the book is perhaps to be found in the profound sense of the indestructibility of Israel, and the duty of an Israelite to maintain the cause of his people at whatever risk. . . . It was this probably that caused its final inclusion in the O.T. canon." [9]

Whether the book is fact or fiction is not crucial to our understanding of the story's significance (cf. Intro., pp. 825-27). The parable of the sower conveys a truth about the call of God's kingdom which does not depend upon the historical existence of the sower described. When Jesus told this story he may have had a particular farmer in mind, he may have been describing a sower he knew, or he may have been picturing the process of sowing. It does not matter; that is not essential to the story. The truth which the parable tells is illuminated by the description of a familiar sight: "Listen! A sower went out to sow" (Mark 4:3). We read Esther as we read the parables. Jews have been persecuted, there has been a Haman; Jews have been delivered, there have been a Mordecai and an Esther—if not with these names then with other names—men who foment anti-Semitism, Jews whose loyalty to Israel is without limit.

If Esther is a "historical novel" with a large element of imagination, that imagination nevertheless has to do with a particular people as illustrated in a particular time. Concerned with the one central truth, "the indestructibility of Israel," its historical reference has been indicated in the Intro. and here. The temptation of many preachers has been to allegorize the story into farfetched and unnatural references. So great a preacher as Jonathan Edwards, troubled perhaps by the lack of explicit religious teaching in the book, proceeded to supply it. "It appears to me very probable, that this book of Esther is an history that is a shadow of gospel things and times. . . . The great feast that Ahasuerus made, is the gospel feast. . . .

Vashti, the queen, is the church, or God's people." [1] Upon Vashti's refusal to appear before the king, Ahasuerus repudiates her, "So we find the rejection of the Jews and calling of the Gentiles compared to God's repudiating his ancient church, and taking another better than she. . . . Mordecai is the gospel ministry." [2] But Edwards read into the book, and so took out of it, meanings which were never originally there. It is true that the chief figures of the book, Ahasuerus, Vashti, Haman, Mordecai, and Esther may be taken as types (Vashti disappears from the story after ch. 1), but certainly as types to be found in Jewish history and not to be identified with persons and events of the gospel story.

Because Esther is written as a continuous story and, as the Intro. has pointed out (see p. 825), does not include sentences which carry in themselves a specific religious content, it is hardly possible in the Expos. to follow the regular pattern of *The Interpreter's Bible,* which is to list homiletic suggestions under particular texts. It would seem more useful to treat the book in relation to the several characters which make up its drama, and to think of those qualities of good and evil which these characters reveal. Consequently, the Expos. follows this method, and the verse references are those in which the name of each character first appears. It is necessary, however, that the whole story should first be read and held in mind in order that as the characters are considered they shall be seen in the light of the relationships which show their motivations and their meanings. The last two suggested topics, "Nationalism" and "Christianity and Judaism," cover the book as a whole.

1:1. Ahasuerus.—Although Ahasuerus is used not very successfully to set the historical scene, he is also a type: a ruler antagonistic to the Jews, who is won over and becomes their friend and protector. At first Ahasuerus gives the order "to destroy, to kill, and to cause to perish, all Jews" (3:13). Later he countermands

---

[9] Charles Gore, H. L. Goudge, Alfred Guillaume, eds., *A New Commentary on Holy Scripture* (New York: The Macmillan Co., 1928), p. 305.

[1] *Notes on the Bible,* in *Works* (New York: G. & C. & H. Carvill, 1830), IX, 328.
[2] *Ibid.*

2 *That* in those days, when the king Ahasuerus sat on the throne of his kingdom, which *was* in Shushan the palace,

3 In the third year of his reign, he made a feast unto all his princes and his servants; the power of Persia and Media, the nobles and princes of the provinces, *being* before him:

inces, 2 in those days when King Ahasu-e′rus sat on his royal throne in Susa the capital, 3 in the third year of his reign he gave a banquet for all his princes and servants, the army chiefs[a] of Persia and Media and the nobles and governors of the provinces

[a] Heb *the army*

---

which was derived the Greek name Xerxes. Unquestionably this refers to Xerxes I (485-465 B.C.), who inherited from his father, Darius I, a world empire extending **from India to Ethiopia.** In one of his inscriptions discovered at Persepolis (quoted in Jack Finegan, *Light from the Ancient Past* [Princeton: Princeton University Press, 1946], pp. 199-200), Xerxes proclaims himself as "the great king, the king of kings, the king of the land of many tribes, the king on this wide, far-stretching earth," and lists the nations over which he ruled, including "the Indus land" and "the Cushites" (Ethiopians). This is the king who is conspicuous in history for his gigantic but abortive campaign against Greece, immortalized by Herodotus (*History* VII-IX).

One hundred and twenty-seven provinces: The Persian Empire was divided into satrapies (twenty, according to Herodotus *ibid.* III. 89), which apparently were subdivided into provinces administered by governors (cf. 3:12).

2. When King Ahasuerus sat: The Hebrew כשבת occasions some difficulty because the verb has the force of a preterit, and does not express duration. Some scholars, connecting the phrase with the words **in the third year of his reign** (vs. 3), find here an allusion to the postponement of the king's accession until he could establish himself securely against all rivals. So the Talmud (Megillah 11*b*) interprets: "when he was established." Others, calling attention to the fact that the Medo-Persian Empire had several capitals in which the king held court in rotation, interpret: "when he took up residence in Susa." Elsewhere, however, the author gives no indication that the king held court in any city other than Susa, even though the events of the book cover a period of several years. The difficulty is partially relieved by the consideration that the temporal phrase in vs. 3*a* is intended to date the banquet, not necessarily the beginning of the king's reign in Susa.

Susa, capital of ancient Elam, was rebuilt as a royal citadel by Darius I and used as a residence until Persepolis became the main capital. Xerxes likewise had his main residence at Persepolis, although apparently he spent his winters in Susa (see especially A. T. Olmstead, *History of the Persian Empire* [Chicago: University of Chicago Press, 1948], chs. xii-xiii, xx).

3-4. There is no reason to suppose that this lavish **banquet** (lit., "a drinking") was either Xerxes' coronation feast held **in the third year of his reign** (see on vs. 2) or an assembly of satraps to make arrangements for the attack on Greece (Herodotus *op. cit.* VII. 8). This is the author's exaggerated way of emphasizing Xerxes' glory and wealth. The sheer extravagance of Persian wine banquets, at which as many as fifteen thousand guests are said to have been entertained at once, made a deep impression upon the imagination of ancient writers (cf. Olmstead, *op. cit.*, pp. 182-83).

The power of Persia and Media, i.e, the army. There is no textual support for the reading **army chiefs** (RSV). Judith 1:16 likewise speaks of a king feasting his entire

---

this order, the Jews that were in every city were "to stand for their life, to destroy, to slay, and to cause to perish, all the power of the people and province that would assault them, both little ones and women, and to take the spoil of them for a prey" (8:11). Not only were the Jews allowed to defend themselves, they "should

be ready against that day to avenge themselves on their enemies" (8:13). Ahasuerus, then, is the potential enemy and destroyer of the Jews, who becomes their benefactor. This is his role in the book. Therefore all moralizing about his character is without point. He has been described as "a mere puppet worked by those

4 When he showed the riches of his glorious kingdom and the honor of his excellent majesty many days, *even* a hundred and fourscore days.

5 And when these days were expired, the king made a feast unto all the people that were present in Shushan the palace, both unto great and small, seven days, in the court of the garden of the king's palace;

6 *Where were* white, green, and blue *hangings,* fastened with cords of fine linen and purple to silver rings and pillars of marble: the beds *were of* gold and silver, upon a pavement of red, and blue, and white, and black marble.

7 And they gave *them* drink in vessels of gold, (the vessels being diverse one from another,) and royal wine in abundance, according to the state of the king.

8 And the drinking *was* according to the law; none did compel: for so the king had appointed to all the officers of his house, that they should do according to every man's pleasure.

9 Also Vashti the queen made a feast for the women *in* the royal house which *belonged* to king Ahasuerus.

being before him, 4 while he showed the riches of his royal glory and the splendor and pomp of his majesty for many days, a hundred and eighty days. 5 And when these days were completed, the king gave for all the people present in Susa the capital, both great and small, a banquet lasting for seven days, in the court of the garden of the king's palace. 6 There were white cotton curtains and blue hangings caught up with cords of fine linen and purple to silver rings[b] and marble pillars, and also couches of gold and silver on a mosaic pavement of porphyry, marble, mother-of-pearl and precious stones. 7 Drinks were served in golden goblets, goblets of different kinds, and the royal wine was lavished according to the bounty of the king. 8 And drinking was according to the law, no one was compelled; for the king had given orders to all the officials of his palace to do as every man desired. 9 Queen Vashti also gave a banquet for the women in the palace which belonged to King Ahasu-e'rus.

[b] Or *rods*

army for 120 days. Perhaps the reference is to the king's elite bodyguard, the famous Ten Thousand Immortals (*ibid.* VII. 83), which included detachments of Persians and Medes. The latter peoples, coming from the same racial stock, jointly established the Medo-Persian Empire, but since the time of Cyrus (549 B.C.) the Persians held the hegemony. This may explain the mention of Persia first in this passage.

5-7. At the close of the six-month banquet for the army and dignitaries, a seven-day banquet was given for all the male citizens (cf. vs. 9) who had gathered at the citadel. Further evidences are given of the dazzling wealth of Xerxes, including the costly marble pillars and mosaic pavement, remains of which archaeologists have found (cf. Olmstead, *op. cit.,* pp. 170-71).

8. **Drinking was according to the law:** If אין אנס means **none did compel,** we must suppose that the usual rule of Persian carousals, according to which drinking was enforced or perhaps directed by a toastmaster, was in this case suspended. Perhaps, however, the meaning is that, with wine flowing freely, no one restricted the amount consumed (cf. LXX). In other words, the drinks were "on the house."

9. Simultaneously Queen Vashti gave a seven-day feast for women only. Since Persian custom did not demand that men and women eat separately (cf. 5:6; 7:1), it is possible that the narrator had in mind the necessity of dividing the guests because

who successively gain his ear . . . ; helplessly weak."[3] Yet Haman did not gain his ear and persuade him to send out the order for the massacre because Ahasuerus was "a mere puppet,"

[3] A. W. Streane, *The Book of Esther* (Cambridge: Cambridge University Press, 1907; "Cambridge Bible"), p. xxi.

but because of the necessities of the plot. Again, the king did not change his mind and tell the Jews to defend themselves because he was "helplessly weak," but because that action is part of the story. Esther is to save her people threatened with annihilation by the king, and Ahasuerus is that king. He granted Haman's

10 ¶ On the seventh day, when the heart of the king was merry with wine, he commanded Mehuman, Biztha, Harbona, Bigtha, and Abagtha, Zethar, and Carcas, the seven chamberlains that served in the presence of Ahasuerus the king,

11 To bring Vashti the queen before the king with the crown royal, to show the people and the princes her beauty: for she *was* fair to look on.

12 But the queen Vashti refused to come at the king's commandment by *his* chamberlains: therefore was the king very wroth, and his anger burned in him.

13 ¶ Then the king said to the wise men, which knew the times, (for so *was* the king's manner toward all that knew law and judgment:

14 And the next unto him *was* Carshena, Shethar, Admatha, Tarshish, Meres, Marsena, *and* Memucan, the seven princes of Persia and Media, which saw the king's face, *and* which sat the first in the kingdom,)

15 What shall we do unto the queen Vashti according to law, because she hath not performed the commandment of the king Ahasuerus by the chamberlains?

10 On the seventh day, when the heart of the king was merry with wine, he commanded Mehu'man, Biztha, Harbo'na, Bigtha and Abag'tha, Zethar and Carkas, the seven eunuchs who served King Ahasue'rus as chamberlains, 11 to bring Queen Vashti before the king with her royal crown, in order to show the peoples and the princes her beauty; for she was fair to behold. 12 But Queen Vashti refused to come at the king's command conveyed by the eunuchs. At this the king was enraged, and his anger burned within him.

13 Then the king said to the wise men who knew the times — for this was the king's procedure toward all who were versed in law and judgment, 14 the men next to him being Carshe'na, Shethar, Adma'tha, Tarshish, Meres, Marse'na, and Memu'can, the seven princes of Persia and Media, who saw the king's face, and sat first in the kingdom — : 15 "According to the law, what is to be done to Queen Vashti, because she has not performed the command of King Ahasu-

---

of the great number. Xerxes' queen, however, was not Vashti, but an imperious and superstitious woman named Amestris (Herodotus *op. cit.* VII. 61; IX. 108-112; see Intro., p. 826).

B. Dethronement of Vashti (1:10-22)

10-12. Why did Vashti refuse to come before the inebriated king so that he might display his greatest wealth, his beautiful queen? Jewish commentators early puzzled over this question, and with typical rabbinical ingenuity deduced from the text that the king had commanded her to appear at his banquet naked, i.e., with only the **royal crown on her head** (so II Targum). Actually the author does not reveal the psychological motivation for her refusal. Vashti's insolence is a literary excuse for her deposition and the subsequent elevation of Esther.

13-15. "The learned men who knew the laws" is an improvement over **wise men, which knew the times** (i.e., astrologers; cf. I Chr. 12:32), and demands only a slight textual change (הדתים instead of העתים). Although this change is not supported by the ancient versions, it seems justified by the parallel reference **all who were versed in law and judgment.** These jurists are described as **the seven princes of Persia and Media—** doubtless the famous Council of Seven (*ibid.* III. 31. 84; Ezra 7:14). As the highest ranking men in the kingdom, they **saw the king's face,** i.e., had access to him at all times except when he was in the harem. The names here and in vs. 10 are Persian.

---

request to slaughter the Jews, he was won over by Esther and reversed his order, so that it was his own Persian subjects who were killed, not the Jews. This is not a description of a vacillating man, this is the statement of one theme of

the book: a man of political power bent on destroying the Jews becomes their champion.

This is not to say, however, that Ahasuerus is simply a robotlike figure used by the author to express a theme of the story. He is a type, but a

16 And Memucan answered before the king and the princes, Vashti the queen hath not done wrong to the king only, but also to all the princes, and to all the people that *are* in all the provinces of the king Ahasuerus.

17 For *this* deed of the queen shall come abroad unto all women, so that they shall despise their husbands in their eyes, when it shall be reported, The king Ahasuerus commanded Vashti the queen to be brought in before him, but she came not.

18 *Likewise* shall the ladies of Persia and Media say this day unto all the king's princes, which have heard of the deed of the queen. Thus *shall there arise* too much contempt and wrath.

19 If it please the king, let there go a royal commandment from him, and let it be written among the laws of the Persians and the Medes, that it be not altered, That Vashti come no more before king Ahasuerus; and let the king give her royal estate unto another that is better than she.

20 And when the king's decree, which he shall make, shall be published throughout all his empire, (for it is great,) all the wives shall give to their husbands honor, both to great and small.

21 And the saying pleased the king and the princes; and the king did according to the word of Memucan:

e'rus conveyed by the eunuchs?" 16 Then Memu'can said in presence of the king and the princes, "Not only to the king has Queen Vashti done wrong, but also to all the princes and all the peoples who are in all the provinces of King Ahasu-e'rus. 17 For this deed of the queen will be made known to all women, causing them to look with contempt upon their husbands, since they will say, 'King Ahasu-e'rus commanded Queen Vashti to be brought before him, and she did not come.' 18 This very day the ladies of Persia and Media who have heard of the queen's behavior will be telling it to all the king's princes, and there will be contempt and wrath in plenty. 19 If it please the king, let a royal order go forth from him, and let it be written among the laws of the Persians and the Medes so that it may not be altered, that Vashti is to come no more before King Ahasu-e'rus; and let the king give her royal position to another who is better than she. 20 So when the decree made by the king is proclaimed throughout all his kingdom, vast as it is, all women will give honor to their husbands, high and low." 21 This advice pleased the king and the princes, and the king did as Memu'can

---

16-18. As in the similar case of Cambyses (*ibid.* III. 31), the seven were quick to suggest a legal sanction for the king's intention. Vashti's punishment, they point out, is demanded not merely by the king's personal grudge, but by public policy. If other wives of lesser rank follow the example of the defiant queen, the empire will be thrown into anarchy.

19-20. It is proposed that the king act decisively by making the decree concerning Vashti irrevocable, despite any later change of mood (cf. 3:1). Here in a whimsical vein the author introduces the theme of the unalterable character of Persian law (cf. Dan 6:8, 12, 15) in preparation for the crucial passage 8:8.

21-22. To every province in its own script: An exaggeration which emphasizes the thoroughness with which the king dealt with domestic insubordination throughout his empire. Persian kings used Aramaic for royal decrees, and regularly employed three official languages in their inscriptions, viz., Elamite, Akkadian, and Persian (e.g., Darius' famous inscription on Mount Behistun).

---

plausible type, a living person. This is true certainly of all the people who pass before us in this story. Vashti's refusal to come before the king at his call is a requirement of the plot and the author tells us no more than this. "But the queen Vashti refused to come at the king's

commandment" (1:12). We may not therefore read into the story more than is there; we may not moralize about the character of Ahasuerus and Vashti. But although the author of Esther does not actually tell us that Ahasuerus thought of his queen as someone to be manipulated and

22 For he sent letters into all the king's provinces, into every province according to the writing thereof, and to every people after their language, that every man should bear rule in his own house, and that *it* should be published according to the language of every people.

2 After these things, when the wrath of king Ahasuerus was appeased, he remembered Vashti, and what she had done, and what was decreed against her.

2 Then said the king's servants that ministered unto him, Let there be fair young virgins sought for the king:

3 And let the king appoint officers in all the provinces of his kingdom, that they may gather together all the fair young virgins unto Shushan the palace, to the house of the women, unto the custody of Hege the king's chamberlain, keeper of the women; and let their things for purification be given *them:*

4 And let the maiden which pleaseth the king be queen instead of Vashti. And the thing pleased the king; and he did so.

proposed; 22 he sent letters to all the royal provinces, to every province in its own script and to every people in its own language, that every man be lord in his own house and speak according to the language of his people.

2 After these things, when the anger of King Ahasu-e'rus had abated, he remembered Vashti and what she had done and what had been decreed against her. 2 Then the king's servants who attended him said, "Let beautiful young virgins be sought out for the king. 3 And let the king appoint officers in all the provinces of his kingdom to gather all the beautiful young virgins to the harem in Susa the capital, under custody of Hegai the king's eunuch who is in charge of the women; let their ointments be given them. 4 And let the maiden who pleases the king be queen instead of Vashti." This pleased the king, and he did so.

Speak according to the language of his people: A difficult phrase. Ancient Jewish commentators took it to mean that in the case of a mixed marriage the husband should compel his wife to speak his tongue. Paul Haupt has suggested that the phrase has the idiomatic meaning of speaking clearly in the mother tongue, i.e., "talk plain English to her," as we would say. The clause was omitted by the LXX—evidently an early witness to the obscurity of the Hebrew original. In any case, the notion that a king would take thorough measures to ensure that **every man be lord in his own house** is obviously a fanciful feature.

C. The Search for a New Queen (2:1-4)

2:1. Remembered Vashti: The author subtly suggests that the king desired to reinstate Vashti now that he was in a calmer mood, but was helpless because he had issued an irrevocable decree. The LXX says she was "no longer" remembered, which destroys the point. Since Vashti has been introduced only to show how her place was taken by Esther, the author feels no need of telling the reader what happened to her.

2-4. Here the author ignores the Persian custom which stipulated that the king could marry only a Persian (according to the Avesta and Herodotus *op. cit.* III. 84). The theme of a king choosing a queen out of the most beautiful maidens of his kingdom appears in folk literature all over the world.

---

exhibited (1:11), surely that is how the king, and therefore other men of that day, thought of their wives. Again, whatever Vashti's motives for refusing to obey the king, such a course was possible in actual life as well as in fiction.

The events of this story therefore present us with a comparison and a contrast with our own day. We do not from our point in history pass judgments on people like Ahasuerus and Vashti. We say rather: this is what people thought and

did some two thousand years ago. When we do that, it is profitable for us to look also at ourselves. Do we manipulate people? Do we use them for our own pleasure and advantage? The answer can be found only in an examination of our twentieth-century ways. For the very subtlety of our contemporary devices for "handling" people can convince us that without doubt we do believe in the dignity of persons and the equality of men and women. But do we?

5 ¶ *Now* in Shushan the palace there was a certain Jew, whose name *was* Mordecai, the son of Jair, the son of Shimei, the son of Kish, a Benjamite;

6 Who had been carried away from Jerusalem with the captivity which had been carried away with Jeconiah king of Judah, whom Nebuchadnezzar the king of Babylon had carried away.

5 Now there was a Jew in Susa the capital whose name was Mor'decai, the son of Ja'ir, son of Shim'e-i, son of Kish, a Benjaminite,

6 who had been carried away from Jerusalem among the captives carried away with Jeconi'ah king of Judah, whom Nebuchad-nez'zar king of Babylon had carried away.

D. MORDECAI AND ESTHER (2:5-7)

5. The son of Jair: Probably not Mordecai's immediate ancestors, as some scholars hold, but his remote ancestors (so Josephus, Targ., and Midrash), following the Jewish practice of omitting intermediate links in a genealogy. Both **Shimei** and **Kish** are well-known members of the tribe of Benjamin, the former appearing as the enemy of David (II Sam. 16:5-13; I Kings 2:8, 36-46) and the latter being the famous father of Saul (I Sam. 9:1; 14:51). Mordecai is not a direct descendant of Saul (in which case Saul would certainly be mentioned), but comes from another line stemming from Kish.

6. Who had been carried away: A reference to the deportation of 597 B.C. Thus by implication Mordecai is described as a leader of the Jews, for it was only the cream of the population which Nebuchadrezzar carried away with Jehoiachin (II Kings 24:14-17). This statement, however, presents a chronological problem. If Mordecai was no more than a lad in 597, he would have been well over one hundred years of age at the time of Xerxes' accession (485), and Esther must have been about seventy when she captivated the king with her virgin charms. Some commentators attempt to evade the difficulty either by assuming that the relative pronoun **who** refers to Kish (who would then be the father of Mordecai, not of Saul), or that **carried away** means only that he had sprung from an exiled family, i.e., that he lived in captivity because of the Exile. Both interpretations violate the natural meaning of the Hebrew. Probably the author, being

---

2:5. *Mordecai.*—Mordecai is the friend at court. **Now in Shushan the palace there was a certain Jew, whose name was Mordecai** (2:5). It was his influence which brought Esther to the attention of the king, and he was the ultimate cause, therefore, of the delivery of his people. Purim at one time was called also "Mordecai's Day." There is a story like the Mordecai story in I Esdras 3-4. Darius the king gave a feast for all the princes of Media and Persia. After the guests had departed, the king went to his bedchamber and slept, but he was restless and soon awoke. Then three young men of his bodyguard wrote, each of them, a sentence. The first wrote, "Wine is the strongest." The second wrote, "The king is strongest." The third wrote, "Women are strongest." When the king read the sentences in the morning, he called the young men, and each in turn declared and defended what he had written. Zerubbabel, who had written "Women are strongest," pleased the king most by his argument, and Darius promised him whatever he should ask. Zerubbabel wanted but one thing: permission to rebuild the temple in Jerusalem, and this the king granted at once—permission and much assist-

ance. Zerubbabel in this story replaces Nehemiah, who had gained permission from King Artaxerxes I to build a wall around Jerusalem. But the very multiplication of stories about the accomplishments of Jews who were in the favor of foreign rulers indicates that this was a favorite theme.

If Mordecai is presented as an unselfish man who was motivated only by devotion to his people, he ceases to be a real person. Human motives are rarely unmixed. It should be remembered that the book ends not with praise for Esther, but with an account of Mordecai's greatness. "And all the acts of his power and of his might, and the declaration of the greatness of Mordecai, whereunto the king advanced him, are they not written in the book of the chronicles of the kings of Media and Persia? For Mordecai the Jew was next unto king Ahasuerus, and great among the Jews, and accepted of the multitude of his brethren, seeking the wealth of his people, and speaking peace to all his seed" (10:2-3). It is not necessary to think that such an outcome was uppermost in Mordecai's mind when he sent Esther to the king. If the thought occurred to him, why is it neces-

7 And he brought up Hadassah, that *is*, Esther, his uncle's daughter: for she had neither father nor mother, and the maid *was* fair and beautiful; whom Mordecai, when her father and mother were dead, took for his own daughter.	7 He had brought up Hadas'sah, that is Esther, the daughter of his uncle, for she had neither father nor mother; the maiden was beautiful and lovely, and when her father and her mother died, Mor'decai

ignorant of the chronology of the period, assumed that Nebuchadrezzar's reign was followed immediately by that of Xerxes. A similar telescoping of history is found in other writings of Judaism (cf. Ezra 4:6; Dan. 1:21; 5:30; 6:1; Tob. 14:15; *et passim*). According to Ezra 2:2 and Neh. 7:7 a certain Mordecai was among the exiles who had been carried away by Nebuchadrezzar. Perhaps the author intended to identify the two (so Targ.). Mordecai is a non-Hebraic name such as would have been given to a Jew of the Dispersion, though its original theophorous meaning probably had been forgotten (see Intro., p. 826).

7. Hadassah: Perhaps a Hebrew maiden name ("Myrtle") which was superseded by the royal name, **Esther**, at her coronation. Some scholars, however, attempt to connect Hadassah with an Assyrian word meaning "bride." **Esther** is variously derived from the Persian *stara* ("star") or from the name of the Babylonian goddess Ishtar.

The daughter of his uncle: I.e., Mordecai's cousin—not his niece, as is often claimed (see Vulg.). The blood kinship and filial relationship between Mordecai and Esther are important in the story.

sary to suppose that this was the ultimate reason for his actions?

Mordecai is a patriot, devoted to his people. Many a patriot since his day has been rewarded for his wisdom and his zeal. To say after the event that his behavior was carefully calculated, a result of his desire for the reward, is to indulge in the sin of detraction. Mordecai's appeal to Esther (4:13-14) is the honest plea of a man who was one with his people. He was not thinking of himself but of his countrymen when he "rent his clothes, and put on sackcloth with ashes, and went out into the midst of the city, and cried with a loud and a bitter cry" (4:1). May we not believe that his cry was addressed to God? The author does not say so, but it is difficult to believe that a Jew could do all this, could cry out for deliverance, and think only of what man could do. The people were God's people, and Mordecai the patriot was God's man.

There is no explanation given of Mordecai's refusal to prostrate himself before Haman. The king had given the command that all should bow down and reverence Haman, and when Mordecai refused and was questioned about his refusal, he would not listen (3:2-4). If Haman and Mordecai typify the feud between Amalekite and Israelite (see Exeg. on 3:1-6), we may find the explanation there. But we meet in this incident, as elsewhere in the book, a difficulty. How much did Mordecai's behavior contribute to Haman's attitude? The separatism of Mordecai and the Jewish community was given by Haman as the reason for his intended persecution. But without such separatism the Jews would not have survived as a people in exile. So the very element, "the indestructibility of Israel," which is the central theme of Esther, while it preserves the Jews in persecution, seems by the manner in which it is lived out to be a factor in the rise of persecution. This is not to say that an excuse for anti-Semitism is to be found in such separatism. It is rather to state the fact that a people which is separatist and unassimilable, whatever its motive for remaining apart, presents a sociological problem. The tension created may in a democratic society be lessened, but the tension remains; in a totalitarian state the tension cannot be tolerated, and the separatist group is liquidated.

7. Esther.—The central figure of the book, of course, is Esther. She is beautiful and courageous, she is cunning and resourceful. We are not told what Esther thought of the plan to make her queen in place of Vashti; it appears that she went to the king's house voluntarily (2:8), but the implication is that this was the first step and a necessary one in Mordecai's plans. At any rate, if the plot is going to develop as it does, Esther must be queen. So Mordecai is the knowing one who makes the necessary arrangements. Esther may have been reluctant to become the bride of a Gentile, but once she accepted her mission she played her part heroically.

Upon Esther depended the deliverance of her people. There is no threat to the Jews when

8 ¶ So it came to pass, when the king's commandment and his decree was heard, and when many maidens were gathered together unto Shushan the palace, to the custody of Hegai, that Esther was brought also unto the king's house, to the custody of Hegai, keeper of the women.

9 And the maiden pleased him, and she obtained kindness of him; and he speedily gave her her things for purification, with such things as belonged to her, and seven maidens, *which were* meet to be given her, out of the king's house: and he preferred her and her maids unto the best *place* of the house of the women.

10 Esther had not showed her people nor her kindred: for Mordecai had charged her that she should not show *it*.

adopted her as his own daughter. 8 So when the king's order and his edict were proclaimed, and when many maidens were gathered in Susa the capital in custody of Hegai, Esther also was taken into the king's palace and put in custody of Hegai who had charge of the women. 9 And the maiden pleased him and won his favor; and he quickly provided her with her ointments and her portion of food, and with seven chosen maids from the king's palace, and advanced her and her maids to the best place in the harem. 10 Esther had not made known her people or kindred, for Mor'decai had charged her not to make it known.

E. Esther Chosen Queen (2:8-18)

8. Was taken: By implication, voluntarily. I Targum reads into this the meaning "taken forcibly," and II Targum explains that Mordecai hid Esther when the king's officers searched the land. Likewise, the LXX (14:3-19) introduces a prayer by Esther in which she vows that she married an uncircumcised Gentile only under compulsion. The obvious meaning of the Hebrew verb was offensive to the stricter elements of Judaism.

9. Like Daniel (Dan. 1:5), Esther is provided with delicacies (lit., **her portion**). According to additions in the LXX and II Targum, she refuses them. But the Hebrew story does not give the slightest evidence that Esther remained faithful to the dietary laws of Judaism, as did Daniel and his friends and Judith.

10. Here there is nothing of the martyr spirit of Daniel or the strict devotion of Judith, both of whom displayed their Judaism at all costs. The author seems to commend Esther's cleverness in hiding her Jewish identity, knowing that as a Jewess she would have little if any chance of becoming queen of Persia. It is useless to ask how such secrecy could have been maintained, for this is one of the requirements of the plot.

Mordecai [emphatic position] **had charged her:** Cf. 2:20. Why did Mordecai give this counsel, which clearly involved disobedience of the laws of Judaism, at a time when the Jewish people were not yet threatened? Jewish commentators have had trouble with this passage, as is indicated by this interpretation of a Midrash: "He thought to himself: How is it possible that this righteous maiden should be married to a non-Israelite?

Esther becomes queen. Haman has not yet been promoted, Mordecai has not offended him, there is no indication that the king will order the slaughter of the Jews in his provinces. But nevertheless, all this "is to come." The book does not tell us that Esther is providentially queen, but every pious Jew would know that this was an act of God: Esther was the instrument by which this community of Israel would be delivered.

Esther accepts her role and gives herself to it. She has no foreknowledge of what will be required of her, but she meets each demand as it comes. The first thing she has to do is to make herself pleasing to the king. On Mor-

decai's instructions she makes known neither "her people nor her kindred" (2:10). When she goes into the king's presence she wants to be as he would desire her, and so she takes the advice of the chamberlain Hegai (2:15). Not only because of her beauty, but because of her shrewdness, Esther becomes queen.

When Haman's plot to exterminate the Jews develops and becomes known, Esther faces the most difficult assignment of her mission. It is quite natural, and not due to weakness of character, that she should at first try to avoid her responsibility. When Mordecai sends Hathach to Esther (4:8), asking her to intercede with the king, she sends back word that she

11 And Mordecai walked every day before the court of the women's house, to know how Esther did, and what should become of her.

12 ¶ Now when every maid's turn was come to go in to king Ahasuerus, after that she had been twelve months, according to the manner of the women, (for so were the days of their purifications accomplished, to wit, six months with oil of myrrh, and six months with sweet odors, and with other things for the purifying of the women,)

13 Then thus came every maiden unto the king; whatsoever she desired was given her to go with her out of the house of the women unto the king's house.

14 In the evening she went, and on the morrow she returned into the second house of the women, to the custody of Shaashgaz, the king's chamberlain, which kept the concubines: she came in unto the king no more, except the king delighted in her, and that she were called by name.

11 And every day Mor'decai walked in front of the court of the harem, to learn how Esther was and how she fared.

12 Now when the turn came for each maiden to go in to King Ahasu-e'rus, after being twelve months under the regulations for the women, since this was the regular period of their beautifying, six months with oil of myrrh and six months with spices and ointments for women — 13 when the maiden went in to the king in this way she was given whatever she desired to take with her from the harem to the king's palace. 14 In the evening she went, and in the morning she came back to the second harem in custody of Sha-ash'gaz the king's eunuch who was in charge of the concubines; she did not go in to the king again, unless the king delighted in her and she was summoned by name.

It must be because some great calamity is going to befall Israel who will be delivered through her." (Quoted by S. Goldman, "Esther" in *The Five Megilloth*, ed. A. Cohen [Hindhead, Surrey: Soncino Press, 1946], p. 204.)

It is only in the context of the drama as a whole, in which Esther's elevation became the only hope for an imperiled people, that one could claim that the end justified the means. If the story is true to life at this stage in the development, it would not be farfetched to suspect that Mordecai's shrewdness was motivated by his ambition for political advancement in the court at Susa, to realize which he was willing to use his cousin. Some commentators, however, stress the beautiful spirit of filial devotion which Esther manifested.

11. Only the eunuchs could enter the harem (vs. 3; 1:10; 4:5; etc.), but Mordecai could find out about Esther through them. It seems strange that Mordecai, who was known to be a Jew, could show such solicitude for Esther without Persian officials suspecting her Jewish extraction.

14. The second harem: After the marriage was consummated, the girl, with the status of a concubine, returned to another division of the harem where she remained a virtual widow unless the king happened to have a fancy for her (cf. the *Arabian Nights*,

---

cannot do this because it would mean death for her. "Whosoever, whether man or woman, shall come unto the king into the inner court, who is not called, there is one law of his to put him to death" (4:11). Esther's reluctance to go to the king without his bidding may seem unheroic and selfish, but it is the reaction which almost anyone would have at first in a similar situation. Esther's behavior is the "heroism of the unheroic," and is therefore the more appealing. She loved her people, but she was afraid to face death and looked for a way out. Then she realized on second thought that for

this she was queen: she must take the risk of death. The second thought, it is true, came from Mordecai; it was his urging which induced Esther to go to the king (4:13-14). But our second thoughts are often prompted in us by others, by circumstances, by pressures from outside. Do they not often come from our waiting upon God? "Among mortals second thoughts are the wisest." [4] The important point here is not that it was through Mordecai's urging that Esther went to the king, but that Esther was able to see her duty and respond to it. "So will

[4] Euripides *Hippolytus*. 436.

15 ¶ Now when the turn of Esther, the daughter of Abihail the uncle of Mordecai, who had taken her for his daughter, was come to go in unto the king, she required nothing but what Hegai the king's chamberlain, the keeper of the women, appointed. And Esther obtained favor in the sight of all them that looked upon her.

16 So Esther was taken unto king Ahasuerus into his house royal in the tenth month, which is the month Tebeth, in the seventh year of his reign.

17 And the king loved Esther above all the women, and she obtained grace and favor in his sight more than all the virgins; so that he set the royal crown upon her head, and made her queen instead of Vashti.

18 Then the king made a great feast unto all his princes and his servants, even Esther's feast; and he made a release to the provinces, and gave gifts, according to the state of the king.

15 When the turn came for Esther the daughter of Ab'ihail the uncle of Mor'decai, who had adopted her as his own daughter, to go in to the king, she asked for nothing except what Hegai the king's eunuch, who had charge of the women, advised. Now Esther found favor in the eyes of all who saw her. 16 And when Esther was taken to King Ahasu-e'rus into his royal palace in the tenth month, which is the month of Tebeth, in the seventh year of his reign, 17 the king loved Esther more than all the women, and she found grace and favor in his sight more than all the virgins, so that he set the royal crown on her head and made her queen instead of Vashti. 18 Then the king gave a great banquet to all his princes and servants; it was Esther's banquet. He also granted a remission of taxes[c] to the provinces, and gave gifts with royal liberality.

[c] Or a holiday

where Shehriyar had a new wife each evening, but did not allow her to come to him a second time).

15. She asked for nothing: Not because of her modesty necessarily, or because of her indifference to being chosen queen, but because her unexcelled beauty made extra make-up superfluous. Esther shrewdly trusted the judgment of Hegai, who knew the royal taste.

16. Seventh year, i.e., four years after the deposition of Vashti (cf. 1:3). Why was the king without a queen for this long period of time? Those who defend the historicity of the book claim that during most of the interval (Xerxes' sixth and seventh years) the king was occupied with the Greek campaign. If Xerxes started home from his ignominious defeat in 479 B.C. he could have reached Susa in time to marry Esther in his seventh year, but this would not have left much time for many virgins to have had their turn before Esther. Apparently the author implies that this entire period was necessary for the abating of the king's wrath, the issuing of the royal edict, the gathering of the virgins in the harem, Esther's year of beauty treatment, and the extensive testing of other virgins before Esther was chosen.

18. A release (lit., "a causing to rest"): This amnesty has been variously interpreted as a **remission of taxes** (I Targum, RSV), a release from work, i.e., **a holiday** (Syriac,

I go in unto the king, which is not according to the law: and if I perish, I perish" (4:16).

Is this an act of faith in God, resignation to his will? When Jacob sent his sons the second time into Egypt, not knowing whether they would return again, he said, "If I be bereaved of my children, I am bereaved" (Gen. 43:14). But Jacob makes explicit reference to God. He says, "God Almighty give you mercy before the man" (Gen. 43:14). There is no doubt that Jacob's trust is in God; the outcome of his sons' journey into Egypt is in God's hands. The omission of any reference to God at this point and

elsewhere in the book of Esther seems deliberate (see Intro., pp. 829-30). The interpolation here in the LXX of a prayer by Mordecai and a prayer by Esther brings into the story that which every devout Jew would expect to find there. And it is unlikely that a Jew at the time when Esther was written would have said, "If I perish, I perish," without thinking of God.

In this connection Esther's words in answer to Mordecai should also be taken into consideration: "Go, gather together all the Jews that are present in Shushan, and fast ye for me" (4:16). A modern Western man who went on a hunger

19 And when the virgins were gathered together the second time, then Mordecai sat in the king's gate.	19 When the virgins were gathered together the second time, Mor'decai was sitting at the king's gate. 20 Now Esther had
20 Esther had not *yet* showed her kindred nor her people, as Mordecai had charged her: for Esther did the commandment of Mordecai, like as when she was brought up with him.	not made known her kindred or her people, as Mor'decai had charged her; for Esther obeyed Mor'decai just as when she was

Vulg., Amer. Trans., RSV mg.), a release of prisoners (cf. I Macc. 10:33; Matt. 27:15), or a release from military service, i.e., a furlough (cf. Eccl. 8:8; Herodotus *op. cit.* III. 67). As in the case of the royal birthday (*ibid.* IX. 110), the king distributed gifts to the Persians on the occasion of Esther's coronation banquet.

F. Attempt on the King's Life (2:19-23)

This passage interrupts the flow of the narrative in order to introduce an episode which later plays an important part in the plot. The LXX awkwardly repeats the incident at the beginning of the apocryphal book (12:1-6), and makes it the explanation of Mordecai's political prominence in Susa and Haman's hatred of him.

19. When the virgins were gathered together the second time: It is strange that there should have been a second gathering of virgins when vss. 16-17 imply that the levy of maidens had already accomplished its purpose. The text at this point is completely unintelligible. The LXX omits the troublesome words—perhaps an evidence of the early obscurity of the Hebrew.

Mordecai sat: The KJV takes this to be the apodosis of the previous temporal clause of vs. 19a. Actually, as a number of commentators point out, the words seem to be a second temporal clause, in which case they should be translated, **Mordecai was sitting at the king's gate** (RSV). If this is true, the clause should be followed by a dash to indicate that all of vs. 20 is a parenthesis (so the American Jewish Translation).

20. This parenthetical verse explains why Mordecai was still occupying a subordinate position at the king's gate, despite Esther's elevation, viz., Esther had not been allowed to disclose her Jewish identity and her kinship with Mordecai (cf. 8:1, where the

strike as a form of protest against the government might do so with no thought of God, and his act would carry no religious implications. But our world is not Esther's; then, fasting in time of stress or penitence meant fasting and prayer. Esther not only asks all the Jews in the city to fast, she and her attendants will fast also (4:16). To what purpose? Not to make herself more attractive to the king! Fasting for three days would have quite the opposite effect. This must mean that Esther recognized her need for God's help. This is her preparation for her perilous task: all her people in the city and those about her would join her in a Godward act. What she had to do, she could not do in her own strength.

As with the other figures in the book, there is one central point in the characterization of Esther: here is a woman who gives herself, her beauty, her shrewdness for the sake of her people; she will risk death for them. As the story is told, Esther emerges as a real person; therefore her motives are mixed, but in the end

she accomplishes the work given her to do. It is beside the point, then, to examine every detail of her life and to moralize about her behavior. This is usually unprofitable anyway. We lift a person out of his time and then judge him by his acts as they appear in the light of our standards; our estimate of him would be different if we used as our criteria the standards of his day and the practice of ours.

It is easy to condemn Esther and Mordecai for their thirst for vengeance; their slaughter of the Persians went far beyond necessary measures of defense. There is no doubt of that. There is in the book a spirit of revenge. But it is not necessary for us either to attempt to explain away that spirit, to say it is not there, or to defend it, any more than it is necessary for us to condemn the actions of Esther. We do not approve of what she did to the inhabitants of Shushan or praise her for it. But the story of retaliation which is told in the closing chapters of the book is the story of what happens or may happen when the tension between

21 ¶ In those days, while Mordecai sat in the king's gate, two of the king's chamberlains, Bigthan and Teresh, of those which kept the door, were wroth, and sought to lay hand on the king Ahasuerus.

22 And the thing was known to Mordecai, who told *it* unto Esther the queen; and Esther certified the king *thereof* in Mordecai's name.

23 And when inquisition was made of the matter, it was found out; therefore they were both hanged on a tree: and it was written in the book of the chronicles before the king.

brought up by him. 21 And in those days, as Mor'decai was sitting at the king's gate, Bigthan and Teresh, two of the king's eunuchs, who guarded the threshold, became angry and sought to lay hands on King Ahasu-e'rus. 22 And this came to the knowledge of Mor'decai, and he told it to Queen Esther, and Esther told the king in the name of Mor'decai. 23 When the affair was investigated and found to be so, the men were both hanged on the gallows. And it was recorded in the Book of the Chronicles in the presence of the king.

disclosure of this information changed Mordecai's position). The notion that Mordecai was an "idler" at the king's gate (Paton) is less probable than the view that he had some official capacity, along with other courtiers (3:2-3), in the king's service (so also LXX 12:5). According to a cuneiform text translated by A. Ungnad (see Intro., p. 826), a certain Mordecai was among the Persian dignitaries who received payment of money, evidently for official service at Susa.

21. The expression **in those days** refers to vs. 19, in continuation of the sentence interrupted by the long parenthesis.

Who guarded the threshhold: A reference to the bodyguards who protected the king's private apartment (cf. *ibid.* III. 77, 118) and thus had easy access to the king. As a matter of fact, Xerxes was finally assassinated in such a court conspiracy. If the story presupposes that Mordecai was already in the king's service, his overhearing the plot becomes more credible.

22. In the name of Mordecai, but without disclosing that he was related to her (cf. 8:1).

23. Before the king, i.e., **in the presence of the king,** and therefore at his direction.

The Book of the Chronicles: Lit., "the book of the acts of the days," i.e., the royal chronicles (cf. Ezra 4:15). Herodotus records (*ibid.* VIII. 90) how Xerxes ordered his scribes to write in a diary the names of his captains who performed worthy exploits, in order that they might be rewarded and enrolled among "the king's benefactors" (cf. *ibid.* VIII. 85). In the Hebrew story there is no other reason for the king's inadvertent failure to reward one who had saved his life than the requirement of the plot. The incident proves decisive in the sequel (6:1-11).

two racial groups is strained to the breaking point. The book of Esther is not, after all, fiction. The particular events related there may never have taken place; Esther, Mordecai, Haman may be creations of the author, but the story he tells is all too true. The numbers of those slain are greatly exaggerated, but the pattern is familiar. The writer was describing, perhaps better than he knew, how racial and cultural antagonisms arise, how they are fed, how they break out into violence. This was not the author's intended story. He wrote it as a simple tale of persecution that is averted and turned against the persecutor. But for us there is much more to it than that: so long as racial antagonisms exist, this book will shed light on their nature and origin.

In its original purpose, however, Esther is the story of the Jews protecting themselves against their persecutors. It is the story of a people who are delivered. Is God their deliverer? If the book may be taken as a symbol of the struggle of the Jews throughout history, then, although God is not mentioned in the book, God no doubt is their savior. Mordecai and Esther are his instruments. The community of Jews is saved. This is the message of the book. Nothing is said or implied as to Israel's mission; it is the story of the preservation of the people as a nation which is told in Esther and celebrated in the feast of Purim. Esther is above all others the book of Jewish nationalism; Purim is the great national day. It is significant that Esther's Hebrew name, Hadassah (2:7), is

3 After these things did king Ahasuerus promote Haman the son of Hammedatha the Agagite, and advanced him, and set his seat above all the princes that *were* with him.

2 And all the king's servants, that *were* in the king's gate, bowed, and reverenced Haman: for the king had so commanded concerning him. But Mordecai bowed not, nor did *him* reverence.

3 After these things King Ahasu-e′rus promoted Haman the son of Hammeda′tha the Ag′agite, and advanced him and set his seat above all the princes who were with him. 2 And all the king's servants who were at the king's gate bowed down and did obeisance to Haman; for the king had so commanded concerning him. But Mor′decai did not bow down or do obeisance.

II. The Feud Between the House of Amalek and the House of Benjamin (3:1–9:19)

A. The Feud Between Haman and Mordecai (3:1-6)

3:1. Agagite: Josephus (*Antiquities* XI. 6. 5) interpreted this to mean "Amalekite," implying that Haman was a descendant of the Amalekite king of Saul's time—the only Agag mentioned in the O.T. (I Sam. 15:8). This interpretation, found also in the Talmud and the Targ., is adopted by many modern Jewish and Christian scholars. Thus the author constructs his plot upon a traditional blood feud—the most ancient and bitter in Israel's history—which is inherited by Mordecai, a descendant of an ancient Benjaminite line (2:5), and Haman, of the seed of King Agag. This fierce feud, which began when the Israelites were attacked by the Amalekites in the wilderness, is recalled by two ancient passages embedded in the book of Exodus (17:14, 16), the burden of which is that the Lord declares eternal war against Amalek until his memory is blotted out. Baalam's oracle (*ca.* 1000 B.C.) promises that Israel's king shall be "higher than Agag" (Num. 24:7), and Amalek is emphatically cursed in the Law (Deut. 25:17-19). According to the narrative of I Sam. 15, Saul received from Samuel the divine commission to fulfill the curse against the Amalekites, but because in his leniency with Agag he was not willing utterly to destroy them, his kingdom was taken from him and Samuel himself had to hew "Agag in pieces before the Lord" (I Sam. 15:33). From this perspective the book of Esther may be regarded as the inexorable working out of the divine curse against Amalek, remnants of which persisted even after their alleged total destruction in the days of Hezekiah (I Chr. 4:43). This explains why Haman is regarded as "the enemy of the Jews" (vs. 10). The LXX reading "Macedonian" for "Agagite" in 9:24 (cf. also 16:10 LXX) merely brings out the same idea to readers for whom the Greek power, ever since the infamous tyranny of Antiochus Epiphanes, was a symbol of hostility to the Jews. In the present verse the LXX "Bougaean" (Βουγαῖον, cf. 9:10; 12:6 LXX) is obscure. If it is not corrupt (Vulg. follows M.T. here and in 9:24), it is possibly another synonym of reproach.

Set his seat above all the princes: He was made grand vizier, a position second only to that of the king (cf. 10:3; Gen. 41:39-45).

2-4. The reason for Mordecai's insolence is given in vs. 4: **He had told them that he was a Jew.** But why should the fact of being a Jew make it impossible to participate in

the name of the women's Zionist organization of the United States. Originally called the Daughters of Zion, Hadassah is the largest Jewish women's organization in the United States and in the world. Hadassah—Esther—is a symbol of the loyalty and devotion every Jew owes to his people.

3:1. Haman.—Haman is in our terminology an anti-Semite. He is promoted by Ahasuerus to the position of grand vizier (3:1), and he is

deeply offended when Mordecai "bowed not, nor did him reverence" (3:2). This may be symbolic of the feud between the Israelites and the Amalekites (see Exeg. on 3:1-6), but Haman by extension has become the Jew-hater, a universal figure. It is not a personal feud between Haman and Mordecai that is related in Esther and remembered on Purim; anti-Semitism is not the hatred of one Gentile for one Jew. To Haman, Mordecai is typical of all

3 Then the king's servants, which *were* in the king's gate, said unto Mordecai, Why transgressest thou the king's commandment?

4 Now it came to pass, when they spake daily unto him, and he hearkened not unto them, that they told Haman, to see whether Mordecai's matters would stand: for he had told them that he *was* a Jew.

5 And when Haman saw that Mordecai bowed not, nor did him reverence, then was Haman full of wrath.

6 And he thought scorn to lay hands on Mordecai alone; for they had showed him the people of Mordecai: wherefore Haman sought to destroy all the Jews that *were* throughout the whole kingdom of Ahasuerus, *even* the people of Mordecai.

3 Then the king's servants who were at the king's gate said to Mor'decai, "Why do you transgress the king's command?" 4 And when they spoke to him day after day and he would not listen to them, they told Haman, in order to see whether Mor'decai's words would avail; for he had told them that he was a Jew. 5 And when Haman saw that Mor'decai did not bow down or do obeisance to him, Haman was filled with fury. 6 But he disdained to lay hands on Mor'decai alone. So, as they had made known to him the people of Mor'decai, Haman sought to destroy all the Jews, the people of Mor'decai, throughout the whole kingdom of Ahasu-e'rus.

the Persian court ceremony, when prostration before superiors was a universal custom in the ancient Orient (cf. I Sam. 24:8; II Sam. 14:4; I Kings 1:16; *et passim*)? According to an old interpretation, Haman claimed divine honors for himself (so 13:14 LXX; I Targum gratuitously adds that he wore an idol on his clothing). But this can hardly be the intended meaning, since Mordecai later could not have become grand vizier without giving Xerxes the honors he refused Haman, and on other points he displayed no religious scruples when adherence to the principles of Judaism was inexpedient. Observing that the king had given orders of a special kind to enforce prostration before Haman, some scholars have concluded that Haman was of low origin—an upstart before whom those of the established aristocracy were loath to bow. This likewise reads meaning into the text. Actually, a traditional antipathy flares up between "Mordecai the Jew" and "Haman the Agagite" when each knows who the other is, and thus provides the literary reason for Haman's plot to liquidate the Jews. II Targum suggests in connection with vs. 3 that no self-respecting Benjaminite could bow before the seed of the ancient enemy of the Jews.

5-6. The reason for Haman's self-restraint is given in the words **for they had showed him the people of Mordecai** (RSV obscures this connection by its sentence division). As a hereditary enemy of the Jews, Haman's vengeance falls not merely upon one man but upon the entire community of which he is a part. His vengeance is postponed not because of his tolerance or the desire to maintain the dignity of his office but because literary considerations of the plot demand it.

Jewish people; he is different, he does not conform. This is the way all Jews are: "And Haman said unto King Ahasuerus, There is a certain people scattered abroad and dispersed among the people in all the provinces of thy kingdom; and their laws are diverse from all people; neither keep they the king's laws" (3:8).

Minority groups are always subject to suspicion. In the early years of the twentieth century many Protestants living in the Middle West believed that every time a boy was born into a Roman Catholic family a rifle was stored in the basement of the local church for his use against the Protestants when the time should come. It was widely believed in China that

Christians took children to their orphanages and hospitals and there made medicine out of their eyes. Examples of such suspicions are numerous. Wherever a minority group is sufficiently different from the people around it, it is suspect. Then if there is an individual or a group who make these rumors articulate, multiply them, spread them, persecution follows. This was Haman's method: "If it please the king, let it be written that they may be destroyed" (3:9).

Anti-Semitism is a modern term. It appeared first apparently in Germany about 1875, and was used in a pamphlet written by the founder of an anti-Semitic league, Wilhelm Marr. It is

7 ¶ In the first month, that *is,* the month Nisan, in the twelfth year of king Ahasuerus, they cast Pur, that *is,* the lot, before Haman from day to day, and from month to month, *to* the twelfth *month,* that *is,* the month Adar.

8 ¶ And Haman said unto king Ahasuerus, There is a certain people scattered abroad and dispersed among the people in all the provinces of thy kingdom; and their laws *are* diverse from all people; neither keep they the king's laws: therefore it *is* not for the king's profit to suffer them.

7 In the first month, which is the month of Nisan, in the twelfth year of King Ahasu-e'rus, they cast Pur, that is the lot, before Haman day after day; and they cast it month after month till the twelfth month, which is the month of Adar. 8 Then Haman said to King Ahasu-e'rus, "There is a certain people scattered abroad and dispersed among the peoples in all the provinces of your kingdom; their laws are different from those of every other people, and they do not keep the king's laws, so that it is not

---

B. Haman's Plot (3:7-15)

7. Pur: This non-Hebraic word is explained by the Hebrew גורל, **lot.** The correctness of the Hebrew synonym is now attested by a number of Assyrian texts in which *pūru* has the meaning of **lot,** "die," and is employed in connection with a verb, "to throw," "to cause to fall" (see Intro., p. 825). In the Hebrew story Haman resorts to the lot in order to ascertain the propitious day for his proposed pogrom. This passage anticipates the conclusion of the book which describes the institution of Purim (i.e., "lots"). On the question of the genuineness of the verse see Intro., p. 824.

From day to day: Does this mean that the lot was cast each day successively, and that the process went on for some eleven months? Probably not, in view of the fact that in vs. 12 the scribes draft the edict in the thirteenth of the first month, evidently a short time after the casting of lots in the same month. Either the priests who manipulated the lot tried all of the days in a single act of divination, or first they tried the days, until the thirteenth was determined, and then the months until the twelfth was appointed. Perhaps Haman is described as carrying on the divination in the first month of Nisan (March-April) because, according to Babylonian religion, the gods came together at the New Year to seal the fate of men for the coming year; therefore any oracle obtained in that month would be peculiarly effective (so Gunkel).

"Till the lot fell on the thirteenth day of": These words which are lacking in the M.T. (but cf. vs. 13; 8:12; 9:1), should perhaps be restored according to the LXX. The omission was due to the fact that a scribe inadvertently passed over a whole clause (haplography).

8. Scattered abroad and dispersed: A clear reference to the Dispersion which began with the Exile and reached its peak in the Greek and Roman periods.

Their laws are different: An allusion to the barrier of the law, which even in the Dispersion protected the Jew from cultural and racial assimilation. While Jews admit that this part of Haman's charge is true, they rightly argue that it does not necessarily make them unloyal subjects (see Jer. 29:7). Significantly, Haman does not mention Mordecai's disobedience of a royal decree (vss. 2-3), for Mordecai is only a single example of a general Jewish disloyalty to the king. So his antipathy for Mordecai finds expression in a political pogrom directed against all "traitorous" Jews, ostensibly in the interests of public welfare (on the sociological implications of this passage see Intro., pp. 828-29).

---

only in the twentieth century that the demonic power of anti-Semitism has been fully understood and used with complete logic as a political tool. But persecutions of the Jews antedate Christianity, and hostility to them is an ancient phenomenon. Some scholars believe that Esther is a concealed description of anti-Jewish movements in the period of Antiochus Epiphanes, others that the book is a fictionalized account of the fortunes of the Jews in Palestine under Demetrius, a Syrian king, nephew of Antiochus Epiphanes. However that may be, Haman belongs to no one age or nation. He may be a man without power who peddles stories and spreads

9 If it please the king, let it be written that they may be destroyed: and I will pay ten thousand talents of silver to the hands of those that have the charge of the business, to bring *it* into the king's treasuries.

10 And the king took his ring from his hand, and gave it unto Haman the son of Hammedatha the Agagite, the Jews' enemy.

11 And the king said unto Haman, The silver *is* given to thee, the people also, to do with them as it seemeth good to thee.

12 Then were the king's scribes called on the thirteenth day of the first month, and there was written according to all that Haman had commanded unto the king's lieutenants, and to the governors that *were* over

for the king's profit to tolerate them. 9 If it please the king, let it be decreed that they be destroyed, and I will pay ten thousand talents of silver into the hands of those who have charge of the king's business, that they may put it into the king's treasuries." 10 So the king took his signet ring from his hand and gave it to Haman the Ag'agite, the son of Hammeda'tha, the enemy of the Jews. 11 And the king said to Haman, "The money is given to you, the people also, to do with them as it seems good to you."

12 Then the king's secretaries were summoned on the thirteenth day of the first month, and an edict, according to all that

---

9. Ten thousand talents of silver: Undoubtedly the narrator intends to suggest that the "estate of Haman" (8:1) was worth this fantastic figure (about $18,000,000)—not that Haman hoped to reap that much money for the royal treasury by confiscating the property of prosperous Jews, for vs. 13 implies that those who were to carry out the massacre would get the plunder. Although individuals did amass great fortunes during the Persian period, this figure—estimated at easily two thirds of the annual revenue of the Persian Empire—is obviously an exaggeration.

10. The giving of **his signet ring** (cf. Gen. 41:42) in modern terms would be the same as granting permission to affix the royal signature to official documents. Thus the "enemy of the Jews" was given unlimited power and, as events later showed, the king remained blissfully ignorant about the "certain people" (vs. 8) condemned to destruction by his own edict.

11. The money is given to you: Does the author intend to say that the king refused this handsome bribe as a grandiose gesture of his immense royal wealth (cf. Herodotus *History* VII. 27-29, where Xerxes turns down a fabulous private fortune)? Or is this an example of Oriental court politeness, which implies that the king really expected that it would "seem good" to Haman to pay the money (cf. the bargaining described in Gen. 23:7-18)? The latter interpretation probably represents the intention of the author, for according to 4:7 Mordecai's information indicates that acceptance of the bribe was part of the deal (cf. also 7:4, "For we are sold").

The people: Significantly, the Jews were not mentioned by name in the interview between Haman and the king (cf. vs. 8, "a certain people"). In view of the king's subsequent honoring of Mordecai the Jew (ch. 6), it would seem as if the author suggests that the careless and indifferent king was kept in the dark as to the people consigned to destruction. If so, this caricature of Xerxes as an impressionable monarch who, on the slenderest evidence presented by his crafty vizier, lightheartedly allowed the liquidation of one of the (unnamed) peoples of his empire, serves to exaggerate the fact of the unjust and wanton treatment of the Jews. The Xerxes of the book of Esther is a weakling who is completely dominated by his eunuchs and court officials. This is not the "historical" Xerxes (see Intro., p. 827).

---

rumors about the Jews. He may be a man possessing little but a burning hatred of Jewish people, gathering about that fire of enmity those who will persecute and destroy. He may be a man of position who knows what a weapon anti-Semitism is and uses it for his own gain.

But whoever he may be, his fate will be the fate of Haman. This is what the story of Esther tells about Haman, the enemy of the Jews, the fate which he had prepared for Mordecai is his. "So they hanged Haman on the gallows that he had prepared for Mordecai" (7:10). This is the

every province, and to the rulers of every people of every province according to the writing thereof, and *to* every people after their language; in the name of king Ahasuerus was it written, and sealed with the king's ring.

13 And the letters were sent by posts into all the king's provinces, to destroy, to kill, and to cause to perish, all Jews, both young and old, little children and women, in one day, *even* upon the thirteenth *day* of the twelfth month, which *is* the month Adar, and *to take* the spoil of them for a prey.

14 The copy of the writing for a commandment to be given in every province was published unto all people, that they should be ready against that day.

15 The posts went out, being hastened by the king's commandment, and the decree was given in Shushan the palace. And the king and Haman sat down to drink; but the city Shushan was perplexed.

Haman commanded, was written to the king's satraps and to the governors over all the provinces and to the princes of all the peoples, to every province in its own script and every people in its own language; it was written in the name of King Ahasu-e'rus and sealed with the king's ring. **13** Letters were sent by couriers to all the king's provinces, to destroy, to slay, and to annihilate all Jews, young and old, women and children, in one day, the thirteenth day of the twelfth month, which is the month of Adar, and to plunder their goods. **14** A copy of the document was to be issued as a decree in every province by proclamation to all the peoples to be ready for that day. **15** The couriers went in haste by order of the king, and the decree was issued in Susa the capital. And the king and Haman sat down to drink; but the city of Susa was perplexed.

---

13. Couriers (lit., "runners"): An allusion to the famous Persian postal system first introduced by Cyrus (*ibid.*, V. 14; VIII. 98; Xenophon *Cyropaedia* VIII. 6. 17-18). It was similar to the pony express of American history. **To destroy, to slay, and to annihilate:** While there is no extrabiblical evidence of the wholesale slaughter of Jews during Xerxes' reign, Haman's decree has literally been put into effect many times, from the persecutions of Antiochus IV to the Nazi ovens at Buchenwald. **To plunder their goods:** An inducement to the people to engage in indiscriminate slaughter of men, women, and children.

(After vs. 13 the LXX [13:1-7] interpolates an imaginary copy of "Artaxerxes'" anti-Jewish decree.)

14. The massacre did not begin at once, but was set for a day exactly eleven months from the issuing of the edict. The postponement is a literary device, conveniently based on Haman's casting lots. The author needs to allow a sufficient interval for the frustration of Haman's plot and the turning of the tables (cf. 9:1). There is no thought of allowing time for the Jews to escape (where could they flee from the vast Persian Empire?) or increasing Jewish suffering through prolonging the suspense.

15. The king and Haman sat down to drink: An effective piece of literary contrast (cf. III Macc. 5:3). It is an example of a Nero fiddling while Rome burns.

The city of Susa was perplexed: I.e., thrown into consternation over the ominous developments which had taken place in the citadel. Far from being animated by any anti-Semitism, the peace-loving citizens of Susa, though predominantly Gentile, mirrored Jewish feelings of dismay over such an outrageous and arbitrary edict (cf. 8:15).

---

fate of every Haman, he is "Hoist with his own petard."[5]

Nationalism.—The intense nationalism of the book of Esther cannot be explained away, but it can be understood. The particularism of the Jews in the exilic and postexilic periods was the form in which the content of Hebrew

religion was preserved. We can imagine what might have happened if the Jews had been assimilated into the culture of Babylon, and we know with what determination they remained Jews; in the Exile they could maintain their distinctiveness only by a strict separatism. It was literally impossible for them to tolerate anything non-Jewish and remain Jews. "If I forget

[5] Shakespeare, *Hamlet*, Act III, scene 4.

4 When Mordecai perceived all that was done, Mordecai rent his clothes, and put on sackcloth with ashes, and went out into the midst of the city, and cried with a loud and a bitter cry;

2 And came even before the king's gate: for none *might* enter into the king's gate clothed with sackcloth.

3 And in every province, whithersoever the king's commandment and his decree came, *there was* great mourning among the Jews, and fasting, and weeping, and wailing; and many lay in sackcloth and ashes.

4 When Mor'decai learned all that had been done, Mor'decai rent his clothes and put on sackcloth and ashes, and went out into the midst of the city, wailing with a loud and bitter cry; 2 he went up to the entrance of the king's gate, for no one might enter the king's gate clothed with sackcloth. 3 And in every province, wherever the king's command and his decree came, there was great mourning among the Jews, with fasting and weeping and lamenting, and most of them lay in sackcloth and ashes.

C. Mordecai's Plans (4:1-17)

4:1. Rent his clothes: The ancestral custom of mourning included tearing the garment, putting on haircloth (Hebrew, *saq*), covering the head with **ashes** or dust, fasting and **wailing.** In these rites (cf. vs. 16) the author comes as close to the practical religion of Judaism as he does anywhere. In Judith 4:9-12 the rites are employed to implore God's intervention on behalf of the Jews. This thought may be in the background of the author's mind here, although Mordecai's actions are motivated also by his attempt to arouse the curiosity of Esther in the palace.

2. Mordecai could go only as far as the open square of the city which was in front of the king's gate (vs. 6), because he was in a state of mourning and therefore ceremonially unclean.

---

thee, O Jerusalem, let my right hand forget her cunning. If I do not remember thee, let my tongue cleave to the roof of my mouth; if I prefer not Jerusalem above my chief joy" (Ps. 137:5-6). The people learned how to "sing the Lord's song in a strange land" (Ps. 137:4). They were not contaminated by the paganism of their environment. When, after the Exile, they returned to Jerusalem, they were no less exclusive.

They had been compelled to magnify their particularisms if Babylon was not to absorb them, and they had done this with such notable success that then, as now, they maintained their unconquerable distinctness. Moreover, the new community on Zion was able to maintain itself only by vehement exclusiveness, so that in the end the survival of Israel would hardly have been possible without fierce nationalism, uncompromising racial prejudice, and bigoted devotion to religious peculiarities.[6]

It was this spirit which preserved for us the religion of Israel. And although in Esther we have only the nationalism, the means by which the faith was kept intact, we value the book for its characterization of a people determined to preserve their heritage at whatever cost.

However, it is this very thing in the book,

"the fiery heart of Jewish nationalism," which presents the chief difficulty for the Christian expositor. Julian Morgenstern has described the effect of separatism on the mission of the Jews and its formative influence on Christianity:

This feeling of peoplehood, this consciousness of uniqueness and separateness in the world, narrowed, but at the same time deepened, the application of the principle of universalism in Judaism. It held Judaism back from a world-wide proselytizing program of absolute universalism, and thus actually called Christianity into being, as its daughter-religion, and gave to it its mission to become the proselytizing religion of the western world, transcending all differences of peoplehood and nationhood.[7]

This, it appears, was the divine mission of the Jews. But what of the persistence and continuance of Jewish nationalism? The separatism which was so necessary for the Jews in the Exile and in the postexilic period has persisted; they resist assimilation today. This resistance is met frequently with hostility, and the hostility strengthens the resistance. Since Esther is regarded by Jewish scholars as presenting "the war that Jews must carry on from time to time,

[6] Harry Emerson Fosdick, *A Guide to Understanding the Bible* (New York: Harper & Bros., 1938), p. 33.

[7] In an address given at The Hebrew Union College, 1943, published by the College in pamphlet form under the title, *Nation, People, Religion—What Are We?*

4 ¶ So Esther's maids and her chamberlains came and told *it* her. Then was the queen exceedingly grieved; and she sent raiment to clothe Mordecai, and to take away his sackcloth from him: but he received *it* not.

5 Then called Esther for Hatach, *one* of the king's chamberlains, whom he had appointed to attend upon her, and gave him a commandment to Mordecai, to know what it *was,* and why it *was.*

6 So Hatach went forth to Mordecai unto the street of the city, which *was* before the king's gate.

7 And Mordecai told him of all that had happened unto him, and of the sum of the money that Haman had promised to pay to the king's treasuries for the Jews, to destroy them.

8 Also he gave him the copy of the writing of the decree that was given at Shushan to destroy them, to show *it* unto Esther, and to declare *it* unto her, and to charge her that she should go in unto the king, to make supplication unto him, and to make request before him for her people.

9 And Hatach came and told Esther the words of Mordecai.

10 ¶ Again Esther spake unto Hatach, and gave him commandment unto Mordecai;

4 When Esther's maids and her enunchs came and told her, the queen was deeply distressed; she sent garments to clothe Mor'decai, so that he might take off his sackcloth, but he would not accept them. **5** Then Esther called for Hathach, one of the king's eunuchs, who had been appointed to attend her, and ordered him to go to Mor'decai to learn what this was and why it was. **6** Hathach went out to Mor'decai in the open square of the city in front of the king's gate, **7** and Mor'decai told him all that had happened to him, and the exact sum of money that Haman had promised to pay into the king's treasuries for the destruction of the Jews. **8** Mor'decai also gave him a copy of the written decree issued in Susa for their destruction, that he might show it to Esther and explain it to her and charge her to go to the king to make supplication to him and entreat him for her people. **9** And Hathach went and told Esther what Mor'decai had said. **10** Then Esther spoke to Hathach and gave him a message for Mor'-

---

4. Sent garments: So Mordecai could resume his accustomed place in the city gate (cf. vs. 2). According to Talmudic Judaism, one should not make a public show of his personal bereavement and thus inflict his sufferings upon others. Mordecai's refusal to accept the clothing was an evidence to Esther that his actions were caused not by a personal sorrow, but by an unusually dire public calamity.

7. The exact sum of money: A reference to Haman's bribe. This allusion loses its point if 3:11 does not imply that the king intended to accept the money. Of course it might be assumed that Mordecai was misinformed; however, since it is repeatedly implied that he had access to an inside source of information, the most natural interpretation is that acceptance of the blood money was part of the transaction.

---

against the enemies that seek to destroy them,"[8] the book does provide "the basis for a realistic discussion of anti-Semitism" (see Intro., p. 828). Both Jew and Christian can combat anti-Semitism most effectively when they understand its historical elements.

It is true that the form which anti-Semitism takes "has practically nothing to do with the Jews at all," the charges made against them have "*absolutely no foundation of fact whatever in any action of any Jew or group of Jews now*

[8] Schauss, *Jewish Festivals*, p. 240.

or in the past."[9] The charges that Jews control the press and government, hold financial power in many countries, and are leagued together in a plot to take over the world, are the creation of those who would destroy the Jews. Anti-Semitism is a manifestation of demonic power, and its most violent and destructive outbreak has come in the twentieth century of the Christian Era in a country which had known the Christian message for a thousand years!

[9] James Parkes, "The Jewish Question To-day," *Christian News Letter*, Supplement to No. 102, Oct. 8, 1941,

11 All the king's servants, and the people of the king's provinces, do know, that whosoever, whether man or woman, shall come unto the king into the inner court, who is not called, *there is* one law of his to put *him* to death, except such to whom the king shall hold out the golden sceptre, that he may live: but I have not been called to come in unto the king these thirty days.

12 And they told to Mordecai Esther's words.

13 Then Mordecai commanded to answer Esther, Think not with thyself that thou shalt escape in the king's house, more than all the Jews.

14 For if thou altogether holdest thy peace at this time, *then* shall there enlargement and deliverance arise to the Jews from another place; but thou and thy father's house shall be destroyed: and who knoweth

decai, saying, **11** "All the king's servants and the people of the king's provinces know that if any man or woman goes to the king inside the inner court without being called, there is but one law; all alike are to be put to death, except the one to whom the king holds out the golden scepter that he may live. And I have not been called to come in to the king these thirty days." **12** And they told Mor'decai what Esther had said. **13** Then Mor'decai told them to return answer to Esther, "Think not that in the king's palace you will escape any more than all the other Jews. **14** For if you keep silence at such a time as this, relief and deliverance will rise for the Jews from another quarter, but you and your father's

---

11. It is true that Persian kings were surrounded by ceremonial customs which protected them from unnecessary annoyance or attempted assassination; but according to Herodotus and Xenophon any subject could ask for an interview and, if his credentials were proper, be summoned. Was the queen ignorant of this aspect of Persian court etiquette? Undoubtedly the author here introduces a fanciful feature by which he intends to magnify the later heroism of Esther. A Jewish scholar observes with realistic candor that initially Esther was more concerned about her own safety than about the welfare of her people (Jacob Hoschander, *The Book of Esther in the Light of History* [Philadelphia: Dropsie College for Hebrew and Cognate Learning, 1923], p. 192).

These thirty days: Perhaps this implies that Esther had lost favor with the moody king, thus making a request to be announced out of the question, or an uninvited appearance extremely hazardous.

13. Mordecai rebukes Esther's thought of personal safety by appealing to her enlightened self-interest in these terms: "You have nothing to lose, but perhaps everything to gain." Going to the king may involve the risk of death, but keeping silent will mean certain death for all Jews, the queen and her family included.

14. From another place: The meaning of this phrase is one of the most debated issues in the study of Esther. According to the oldest view, represented by Lucian's LXX, Josephus, and the Targs., **place** (מקום) is a substitute for the name of God, following the practice in late Judaism of avoiding direct mention of the sacred Name (cf. "mercy" in I Macc. 16:3 or "heaven" in the Matthaean phrase, "the kingdom of heaven"). While many modern scholars accept this interpretation, others believe that the reference is to political help which will come **from another quarter,** i.e., abroad (e.g., from Rome in the Maccabean period; cf. I Macc. 8:17; 12:1). The issue hinges upon one's view as to the reason for the author's deliberate avoidance of religious terminology in passages where the context seemingly demands it (see Intro., p. 829). However, even though the latter view is adopted, it by no means precludes the possibility that the author had in mind some providential working through a human agency.

You and your father's house will perish: According to the traditional view, this would be divine judgment upon Esther for the neglect of her opportunity and responsibility.

Who knows whether you have not come . . . : Having formulated his initial argument in terms of Esther's best interests, Mordecai here suggests that she has a higher vocation. This is only a "perhaps," but the possibility is reticently suggested that

whether thou art come to the kingdom for *such* a time as this?

15 ¶ Then Esther bade *them* return Mordecai *this answer,*

16 Go, gather together all the Jews that are present in Shushan, and fast ye for me, and neither eat nor drink three days, night or day: I also and my maidens will fast likewise; and so will I go in unto the king, which *is* not according to the law: and if I perish, I perish.

17 So Mordecai went his way, and did according to all that Esther had commanded him.

5 Now it came to pass on the third day, that Esther put on *her* royal *apparel,* and stood in the inner court of the king's house, over against the king's house: and

house will perish. And who knows whether you have not come to the kingdom for such a time as this?" **15** Then Esther told them to reply to Mor'decai, **16** "Go, gather all the Jews to be found in Susa, and hold a fast on my behalf, and neither eat nor drink for three days, night or day. I and my maids will also fast as you do. Then I will go to the king, though it is against the law; and if I perish, I perish." **17** Mor'decai then went away and did everything as Esther had ordered him.

5 On the third day Esther put on her royal robes and stood in the inner court

---

Providence has exalted Esther **to the kingdom** (better with the American Jewish Translation, "to royal estate") in order that she might be the savior of her people in a critical time.

16. Fast on my behalf: Since fasting was usually accompanied by prayer (II Sam. 12:16; Dan. 9:3; Jonah 3:5-9, *et passim*), these words seem to carry the force of intercessory prayer, i.e., "pray for me." This is another instance in which the author studiously avoids religious terminology even when the context demands it.

I and my maids will also fast: Here Esther proposes to engage in a purely religious act, for she needs not only moral but spiritual support in her dangerous enterprise. Her religious act, which in this instance is not a mere sign of mourning, seems to suggest that she has understood Mordecai's words in vs. 14 to have a religious meaning.

If I perish, I perish: This climactic utterance has been variously estimated. According to the Jewish commentator Solomon Goldman, it is "a simple, but sublime and courageous statement of resignation to God's will" ("Esther," p. 218). On the other hand, L. B. Paton describes it as "a despairing expression of resignation to the inevitable," and adds: "No religious enthusiasm lights up Esther's resolve. She goes, as one would submit to an operation, because there is a chance of escaping death in that way." (*A Critical and Exegetical Commentary on the Book of Esther* [New York: Charles Scribner's Sons, 1908; "International Critical Commentary"], p. 226.) Both views oversimplify the case by failing to consider the ambiguous mixture of self-consideration and altruistic devotion to her people which finally motivated Esther to risk her life.

(Here the LXX interpolates a prayer by Mordecai [13:8-18] and a prayer by Esther [14:1-19].)

D. ESTHER'S AUDIENCE (5:1-8)

5:1. Stood in the inner court: Since the author is concerned with plot rather than character, he does not pause to describe Esther's emotions in this situation. The LXX,

---

Quite apart from organized and directed anti-Semitic movements, there remains the question of Jewish nationalism and its consequences. Does the creation of the state of Israel make the Christian apologetic for the Jew more difficult? Will it in time make Jewish citizens of other states hyphenates? There is the possi-

bility that Israel may become a thoroughly secular Jewish state. What then would become of the spiritual mission of the Jews?

When the Christian considers such issues as these, he faces a responsibility which is most serious, for here is disclosed "the fundamental cleavage between historic Judaism and pro-

the king sat upon his royal throne in the royal house, over against the gate of the house.

2 And it was so, when the king saw Esther the queen standing in the court, *that* she obtained favor in his sight: and the king held out to Esther the golden sceptre that *was* in his hand. So Esther drew near, and touched the top of the sceptre.

3 Then said the king unto her, What wilt thou, queen Esther? and what *is* thy request? it shall be even given thee to the half of the kingdom.

4 And Esther answered, If *it seem* good unto the king, let the king and Haman come this day unto the banquet that I have prepared for him.

5 Then the king said, Cause Haman to make haste, that he may do as Esther hath said. So the king and Haman came to the banquet that Esther had prepared.

6 ¶ And the king said unto Esther at the banquet of wine, What *is* thy petition? and it shall be granted thee: and what *is* thy request? even to the half of the kingdom it shall be performed.

7 Then answered Esther, and said, My petition and my request *is;*

8 If I have found favor in the sight of the king, and if it please the king to grant my petition, and to perform my request, let the king and Haman come to the banquet that I shall prepare for them, and I will do to-morrow as the king hath said.

of the king's palace, opposite the king's hall. The king was sitting on his royal throne inside the palace opposite the entrance to the palace; 2 and when the king saw Queen Esther standing in the court, she found favor in his sight and he held out to Esther the golden scepter that was in his hand. Then Esther approached and touched the top of the scepter. 3 And the king said to her, "What is it, Queen Esther? What is your request? It shall be given you, even to the half of my kingdom." 4 And Esther said, "If it please the king, let the king and Haman come this day to a dinner that I have prepared for the king." 5 Then said the king, "Bring Haman quickly, that we may do as Esther desires." So the king and Haman came to the dinner that Esther had prepared. 6 And as they were drinking wine, the king said to Esther, "What is your petition? It shall be granted you. And what is your request? Even to the half of my kingdom, it shall be fulfilled." 7 But Esther said, "My petition and my request is: 8 If I have found favor in the sight of the king, and if it please the king to grant my petition and fulfil my request, let the king and Haman come tomorrow[d] to the dinner which I will prepare for them, and tomorrow I will do as the king has said."

[d] Gk: Heb lacks *tomorrow*

---

however, expands vss. 1-2 at length, vividly describing Esther's feelings and appearance as she went before the king.

King's hall: The multipillared apadana or audience chamber, like the one archaeologists have discovered at Persepolis (see Olmstead's description of Xerxes' apadana, and the king giving audience in the chamber: *History of Persian Empire*, pp. 280-83) .

2. The king found Esther's beauty irresistible, just as Holofernes was bewitched by Judith's charms. The versions (LXX, O.L., Lucian) interpret that it was God who changed the attitude of the king.

4-8. Why does Esther postpone, not merely once but twice, taking advantage of the king's benevolent mood? The rabbis were troubled over this in view of the fact that Esther was gambling with the lives of many Jews who were depending upon her. Again literary considerations have dictated the postponement. This not only builds up a situation of suspense, but allows an interval of time during which important developments take place.

---

phetic Christianity" (see Intro., p. 830) . That cleavage cannot be ignored or denied, and yet out of that cleavage has come, often from Christian communities, violent anti-Jewish out-

breaks. So the Christian senses the full weight of his responsibility, and always as the servant of God, "who hath reconciled us to himself by Jesus Christ, and hath given to us the ministry

9 ¶ Then went Haman forth that day joyful and with a glad heart: but when Haman saw Mordecai in the king's gate, that he stood not up, nor moved for him, he was full of indignation against Mordecai.

10 Nevertheless Haman refrained himself: and when he came home, he sent and called for his friends, and Zeresh his wife.

11 And Haman told them of the glory of his riches, and the multitude of his children, and all *the things* wherein the king had promoted him, and how he had advanced him above the princes and servants of the king.

12 Haman said moreover, Yea, Esther the queen did let no man come in with the king unto the banquet that she had prepared but myself; and to-morrow am I invited unto her also with the king.

13 Yet all this availeth me nothing, so long as I see Mordecai the Jew sitting at the king's gate.

14 ¶ Then said Zeresh his wife and all his friends unto him, Let a gallows be made of fifty cubits high, and to-morrow speak thou unto the king that Mordecai may be hanged thereon: then go thou in merrily with the king unto the banquet. And the thing pleased Haman; and he caused the gallows to be made.

9 And Haman went out that day joyful and glad of heart. But when Haman saw Mor'decai in the king's gate, that he neither rose nor trembled before him, he was filled with wrath against Mor'decai. 10 Nevertheless Haman restrained himself, and went home; and he sent and fetched his friends and his wife Zeresh. 11 And Haman recounted to them the splendor of his riches, the number of his sons, all the promotions with which the king had honored him, and how he had advanced him above the princes and the servants of the king. 12 And Haman added, "Even Queen Esther let no one come with the king to the banquet she prepared but myself. And tomorrow also I am invited by her together with the king. 13 Yet all this does me no good, so long as I see Mor'decai the Jew sitting at the king's gate." 14 Then his wife Zeresh and all his friends said to him, "Let a gallows fifty cubits high be made, and in the morning tell the king to have Mor'decai hanged upon it; then go merrily with the king to the dinner." This counsel pleased Haman, and he had the gallows made.

E. Pride Goes Before the Fall (5:9-14)

9. Esther invited Haman to the wine banquets to inflate his pride, and thus to heighten the contrast between his rise and his fall. Mordecai, still unobsequious before his ancient enemy, had evidently heard from inside sources that Esther was favorably received by the king, for he had removed his sackcloth (cf. 4:2) and was sitting in his accustomed place **in the king's gate.**

11-12. **The splendor of his riches** included a large family of sons, which was regarded as an evidence of honor to either a Persian or a Jew. The author introduces this scene of Haman's boasting in order to accentuate the later scene of his humiliation.

14. **Fifty cubits high,** i.e., eighty-three feet. The exorbitant height of the **gallows** (lit., "tree") should not be taken too seriously. The author suggests that the one who has dared offend the vanity of the grand vizier must be executed in a spectacular manner as a warning to all.

He had the gallows made, so confident was he that the king, who had already granted the total massacre of the Jews, would approve this also. Here the author has

---

of reconciliation; to wit, that God was in Christ, reconciling the world unto himself" (II Cor. 5:18-19). Ultimately, then, the Jewish problem is a religious problem.[1]

[1] For an illuminating discussion of this see Alan Richardson, *Christian Apologetics* (New York: Harper & Bros., 1947), pp. 139-44.

Christianity and Judaism.—The issues presented by the book of Esther center for the Christian in the relation of Judaism to Christianity. The Christian position is this: The historic mission of Judaism has been carried out, and its fulfillment is found in the Christian church. Do the Jewish people still have the

6 On that night could not the king sleep, and he commanded to bring the book of records of the chronicles; and they were read before the king.

2 And it was found written, that Mordecai had told of Bigthana and Teresh, two of the king's chamberlains, the keepers of the door, who sought to lay hand on the king Ahasuerus.

3 And the king said, What honor and dignity hath been done to Mordecai for this? Then said the king's servants that ministered unto him, There is nothing done for him.

4 ¶ And the king said, Who *is* in the court? Now Haman was come into the outward court of the king's house, to speak unto the king to hang Mordecai on the gallows that he had prepared for him.

5 And the king's servants said unto him, Behold, Haman standeth in the court. And the king said, Let him come in.

6 So Haman came in. And the king said unto him, What shall be done unto the man whom the king delighteth to honor? Now Haman thought in his heart, To whom would the king delight to do honor more than to myself?

6 On that night the king could not sleep; and he gave orders to bring the book of memorable deeds, the chronicles, and they were read before the king. 2 And it was found written how Mor'decai had told about Bigthana and Teresh, two of the king's eunuchs, who guarded the threshold, and who had sought to lay hands upon King Ahasu-e'rus. 3 And the king said, "What honor or dignity has been bestowed on Mor'decai for this?" The king's servants who attended him said, "Nothing has been done for him." 4 And the king said, "Who is in the court?" Now Haman had just entered the outer court of the king's palace to speak to the king about having Mor'decai hanged on the gallows that he had prepared for him. 5 So the king's servants told him, "Haman is there, standing in the court." And the king said, "Let him come in." 6 So Haman came in, and the king said to him, "What shall be done to the man whom the king delights to honor?" And Haman said to himself, "Whom would the king delight

cleverly created a situation of suspense. Haman still has the confidence of the king, and the king does not know Mordecai's relation to Esther. Esther has postponed making her request to the zero hour, with the result that the fate of Mordecai and the Jews hangs in the balance.

F. An Unrewarded Service (6:1-5)

These verses describe a series of striking coincidences which are decisive in the development of the plot. Admittedly fact is sometimes stranger than fiction, but the perfect timing of these events makes this part of the story too good to be true. Jewish commentators have found here not the working of chance, but God's intervention to save Israel.

6:1. The king could not sleep: Since this is necessary in the plot, it is useless to speculate on the cause. The sleeplessness of kings, of course, is a favorite theme of literature (cf. Dan. 6:18; I Esdras 3:3; Shakespeare, *King Henry IV*, Part 2, Act III, scene 1). The versions (LXX, O.L., Lucian) and Targs. add that it was God who took away his sleep.

Book of records of the chronicles: I.e., the royal annals mentioned in 2:23.

Were read: Lit., "they were being read," i.e., the scribes kept on reading far into the night, with the hope that the reading would have a soporific effect upon the king.

4. A fine touch of irony! In view of vs. 1, Haman must have arrived extremely early in the morning. Thus by a concrete action detail the author describes Haman's eagerness which proved to be his undoing.

G. Haman's Humiliation (6:6-14)

It is important to notice that the king is not at all suspicious of Haman at this point (see 7:5-10, where his eyes are first opened). Therefore it is wrong to construe

7 And Haman answered the king, For the man whom the king delighteth to honor, 8 Let the royal apparel be brought which the king *useth* to wear, and the horse that the king rideth upon, and the crown royal which is set upon his head: 9 And let this apparel and horse be delivered to the hand of one of the king's most noble princes, that they may array the man *withal* whom the king delighteth to honor, and bring him on horseback through the street of the city, and proclaim before him, Thus shall it be done to the man whom the king delighteth to honor. 10 Then the king said to Haman, Make haste, *and* take the apparel and the horse, as thou hast said, and do even so to Mordecai the Jew, that sitteth at the king's gate: let nothing fail of all that thou hast spoken. 11 Then took Haman the apparel and the horse, and arrayed Mordecai, and brought him on horseback through the street of the city, and proclaimed before him, Thus shall it be done unto the man whom the king delighteth to honor.

to honor more than me?" 7 And Haman said to the king, "For the man whom the king delights to honor, 8 let royal robes be brought, which the king has worn, and the horse which the king has ridden, and on whose head a royal crown is set; 9 and let the robes and the horse be handed over to one of the king's most noble princes; let him*e* array the man whom the king delights to honor, and let him*e* conduct the man on horseback through the open square of the city, proclaiming before him: 'Thus shall it be done to the man whom the king delights to honor.' " 10 Then the king said to Haman, "Make haste, take the robes and the horse, as you have said, and do so to Mor'decai the Jew who sits at the king's gate. Leave out nothing that you have mentioned." 11 So Haman took the robes and the horse, and he arrayed Mor'decai and made him ride through the open square of the city, proclaiming, "Thus shall it be done to the man whom the king delights to honor."

e Heb *them*

---

the following verses to mean that the king tries to draw Haman into a trap and impose upon him the first installment in his punishment. The passage is an excellent example of irony. In the same moment that Haman had intended to ask the king for vengeance, he is forced to honor his enemy, although the unsuspecting king remains ignorant of the fact that he deals a crushing blow to the pride of his grand vizier.

6. Mordecai's name is unmentioned because it is part of the author's literary scheme to have the conceited villain pronounce judgment upon himself with his own mouth. "It is a fine stroke of literary art by which Haman himself is made to decide what honours shall be paid to the man whom he has decided to hang" (Paton, *op. cit.*, p. 247).

8. "The king's benefactor"—to use Herodotus' phrase (*History* VIII. 85)—is to be decorated with the highest marks of distinction in characteristically Oriental fashion (cf. Gen. 41:38-44).

On whose head: I.e., the horse's head. The reading **his head** (KJV) is unnecessary, since Assyrian reliefs picture horses wearing tall crownlike head ornaments.

10-11. Why did the king single out a Jew for these special honors when an anti-Jewish edict had already been sent out in his name? We must not suppose that the king had discarded Haman's sanguinary scheme as soon as he recalled Mordecai's meritorious act, for this would fail to explain the king's surprise on hearing Esther's request (7:7). Rather, it seems that the king, totally oblivious to what was going on under his very eyes, did not connect Mordecai the Jew with the unnamed people of 3:8 (cf. 3:11), even as he did not connect Mordecai with Esther at this stage. According to this interpretation, there is no inconsistency in the story.

"appointed mission of calling the attention of the rest of the world to the truth that God exists and has a purpose in history"? [2] This was the calling and the privilege of the Hebrews;

[2] *Ibid.*, pp. 142-43.

it may be that it is still their mission. But the Christian sees that mission as part of a process; it is a preparation for the gospel.

Two points then are clear. First, Christian teaching and preaching must be biblical, its

12 ¶ And Mordecai came again to the king's gate. But Haman hasted to his house mourning, and having his head covered.

13 And Haman told Zeresh his wife and all his friends every *thing* that had befallen him. Then said his wise men and Zeresh his wife unto him, If Mordecai *be* of the seed of the Jews, before whom thou hast begun to fall, thou shalt not prevail against him, but shalt surely fall before him.

14 And while they *were* yet talking with him, came the king's chamberlains, and hasted to bring Haman unto the banquet that Esther had prepared.

7 So the king and Haman came to banquet with Esther the queen.

2 And the king said again unto Esther on the second day at the banquet of wine, What *is* thy petition, queen Esther? and it shall be granted thee: and what *is* thy request? and it shall be performed, *even* to the half of the kingdom.

12 Then Mor'decai returned to the king's gate. But Haman hurried to his house, mourning and with his head covered. 13 And Haman told his wife Zeresh and all his friends everything that had befallen him. Then his wise men and his wife Zeresh said to him, "If Mor'decai, before whom you have begun to fall, is of the Jewish people, you will not prevail against him but will surely fall before him."

14 While they were yet talking with him, the king's eunuchs arrived and brought Haman in haste to the banquet that Esther had prepared.

7 So the king and Haman went in to feast with Queen Esther. 2 And on the second day, as they were drinking wine, the king again said to Esther, "What is your petition, Queen Esther? It shall be granted you. And what is your request? Even to the half of

---

12. Although he had been recognized as "the king's benefactor," Mordecai's position had not changed in the court. Thus he **returned to the king's gate.** Only the later disclosure of his relation to Esther brought about his elevation to a higher rank (cf. 8:1).

His head covered: A sign of despair and wretchedness (cf. II Sam. 15:30; Jer. 14:3-4). With the exception of this faint suggestion, the author does not develop the emotional reactions of Haman or Mordecai (as does LXX), because as usual his interest centers in plot rather than character.

13. This scene, which contrasts Haman's despairing mood with the boasting spirit displayed at the previous family gathering (5:10-14), is introduced for the purpose of allowing Haman's closest friends to predict his downfall. One of the author's favorite literary techniques is that of repeating a situation in order to bring in some further feature of the plot (cf. 2:19[?]; 5:9; 6:2; 7:1 ff.; 8:3 ff.; 9:12-13).

Wise men: The **friends** mentioned in this verse and in 5:10, 14. Goldman suggestively points out that this time the friends are called wise men with deliberate irony: they are wise after the event. Previously they had incited him to take vengeance upon the Jew. "Now, conveniently forgetting that Haman's humiliation was largely the fault of their suggestion, they heap coals on his head and, perhaps deriving some malicious satisfaction from his miserable predicament, warn him that this is the beginning of [the] end." ("Esther," p. 226.) With real wisdom his friends and wife see that this is no mere temporary reversal, for Haman has already **begun to fall** even though he still has the king's favor and an anti-Jewish edict is in effect. Probably the author implies that they have in mind the realization that Haman's doom is foreordained because of the ancient curse against Amalek which still possesses deadly power (see Exeg. on 3:1). An Agagite has no chance against a Benjaminite. Jewish writers delighted to place upon the lips of a

---

source found in both the O.T. and the N.T. Much contemporary Christian preaching touches only lightly on the preparation, on the heritage of the religion of Moses and the prophets. In a survey of 1,845 sermons published between 1914 and 1942, only 55 by Christian ministers

were found to have made any basic or illustrative use of the eighth-century prophets.[3] This is indicative of a tendency in Christian preaching to use only the N.T. The N.T. is a new cove-

[3] G. Ernest Wright, *The Challenge of Israel's Faith* (Chicago: University of Chicago Press, 1944), p. 100.

3 Then Esther the queen answered and said, If I have found favor in thy sight, O king, and if it please the king, let my life be given me at my petition, and my people at my request:

4 For we are sold, I and my people, to be destroyed, to be slain, and to perish. But if we had been sold for bondmen and bondwomen, I had held my tongue, although the enemy could not countervail the king's damage.

5 ¶ Then the king Ahasuerus answered and said unto Esther the queen, Who is he, and where is he, that durst presume in his heart to do so?

6 And Esther said, The adversary and enemy *is* this wicked Haman. Then Haman was afraid before the king and the queen.

my kingdom, it shall be fulfilled." **3** Then Queen Esther answered, "If I have found favor in your sight, O king, and if it please the king, let my life be given me at my petition, and my people at my request. **4** For we are sold, I and my people, to be destroyed, to be slain, and to be annihilated. If we had been sold merely as slaves, men and women, I would have held my peace; for our affliction is not to be compared with the loss to the king." **5** Then King Ahasu-e'rus said to Queen Esther, "Who is he, and where is he, that would presume to do this?" **6** And Esther said, "A foe and enemy! This wicked Haman!" Then Haman was in ter-

---

heathen such confessions of the inevitable triumph of the chosen people (Judith 5:20-21; III Macc. 3:8-10; 5:31; etc.).

H. HAMAN'S DOWNFALL (7:1-10)

7:3. According to Goldman (*ibid.,* p. 227), the words of Esther's request "have a specially poignant appeal to the Jew who is conscious of the interdependence of the fate of the individual Jew and the fate of the Jewish people," and are included in two of the most beautiful liturgies of the Jewish penitential prayers.

4. We are sold: The verb "sell" (מכר), which in the book of Judges is used in the general sense of "deliver up to enemies," seems in this case to allude to Haman's bribe (see Exeg. on 3:11; 4:7).

Our affliction . . . loss to the king: Here Esther is contrasting the hypothetical situation of the enslavement of the Jews with the actual situation of their imminent destruction. However, the M.T. is very obscure, and a variety of translations and interpretations have been proposed. Perhaps the meaning is represented by the following paraphrase: Esther would have kept silent were it merely a case of Haman having "sold" the Jews into slavery, since in their loyalty to Xerxes they would have considered the king's gain derived from the success of his plot to be more important than their humiliation; but since it is a case of their being "sold" into total destruction (vs. 4*a*), Esther feels it her duty to intervene, even though this means that the king might suffer considerable financial loss. The RSV fails to take into consideration that vs. 4*b*β actually is governed by the hypothetical clause, **if we had been sold merely as slaves,** of vs. 4*b*α. Therefore translate: "Since [in that case] the affliction *were* not to be compared . . . (cf. Amer. Trans. "would not have been"). The words **loss to the king** evidently refer to the loss of the ten thousand talents (3:9) which the royal treasury would suffer if Haman's plot were frustrated.

While this seems to be the best interpretation, some translators (cf. KJV) believe that צר should not be translated **affliction,** "calamity," but **enemy,** "adversary" (i.e., Haman; cf. איש צר in vs. 6). So the American Jewish Translation reads, "For the adversary is not worthy that the king be endamaged."

5. The king's question does not indicate that he has forgotten his previous grant to Haman, or that he is dull because of being intoxicated with wine (Hoschander). Rather, it shows that the king fails to see any connection between Esther and the unnamed people whose destruction he had allowed (3:13). The king is naïvely unaware of the plot which has developed in his own court and which he has abetted by his own actions.

7 ¶ And the king arising from the banquet of wine in his wrath *went* into the palace garden: and Haman stood up to make request for his life to Esther the queen; for he saw that there was evil determined against him by the king.

8 Then the king returned out of the palace garden into the place of the banquet of wine; and Haman was fallen upon the bed whereon Esther *was*. Then said the king, Will he force the queen also before me in the house? As the word went out of the king's mouth, they covered Haman's face.

ror before the king and the queen. 7 And the king rose from the feast in wrath and went into the palace garden; but Haman stayed to beg his life from Queen Esther, for he saw that evil was determined against him by the king. 8 And the king returned from the palace garden to the place where they were drinking wine, as Haman was falling on the couch where Esther was; and the king said, "Will he even assault the queen in my presence, in my own house?" As the words left the mouth of the king,

---

7. The author introduces the king's dramatic exit for two reasons: (*a*) to suggest by an action the impact of Esther's words upon him, as he suddenly realized how his own vizier had duped him in a plot which threatened his queen; and (*b*) to allow time for the introduction of an incident which proved to be all that was necessary to incite the angry king to decisive action. Notice that in the dialogue of the preceding verses Esther had not revealed her Jewish identity, but had based her request on her position as queen. So in the present situation it is enough for the king to know that the lives of his queen and her people have been threatened.

8. Haman was falling on the couch: In the posture of a supplicant, he was doubtless "seizing the feet" (cf. 8:3; II Kings 4:27; Matt. 28:9) of the queen who was on the couch where she had been reclining in the customary Persian manner during the banquet. In this ludicrous episode the reader sees all three characters as they really are: Haman, actually an arrogant bully who turns into a whining coward when trapped; the king, capricious and impressionable, and weak despite his show of power; and Esther, victorious through the exercise of her feminine charms, but callous and indifferent as the once-proud heathen asks for mercy. Though Esther could have spoken a word in explanation of Haman's action, or even insisted that he be allowed to speak in self-defense, she looked on in cold silence.

They covered Haman's face: This is usually explained as a mark of capital punishment, corresponding to the ancient Greek and Roman practice of covering the face of a criminal before he was led away to execution. However, there is no evidence that this was a Persian custom. C. C. Torrey argues that the original read, "and Haman's face was covered" (which in Hebrew would be represented by חפוי instead of חפו—so Syriac; cf. I Targum), in which case it was Haman who covered his face as a sign of wretchedness and despair, as in 6:12. Some claim on the basis of the LXX that the text should be changed slightly to read, "his face became flushed" (חפרו), i.e., with dismay and shame.

---

nant, but while it is a fulfillment of the O.T., it does not cancel it out. And it is impossible to understand the N.T. without an understanding of the O.T.

The Old Testament, we find, is of vital significance for our understanding of the mind and thought of Jesus. We perceive that, while we may be hampered by a limited acquaintance with the New Psychology, we are entirely disqualified for the investigation if we do not know the Law, the Prophets, and the Psalms.[4]

[4] Vincent Taylor, *Jesus and His Sacrifice* (London: Macmillan & Co., 1937), p. 4.

But it is also true that the O.T. is incomplete without the N.T. This is the basic Christian conviction: Christ is Lord, he is Lord of all men. He has "broken down the middle wall of partition" (Eph. 2:14). "There is neither Jew nor Greek, there is neither bond nor free, there is neither male nor female; for ye are all one in Christ Jesus" (Gal. 3:28). Christianity is a missionary religion, Judaism is not. This is the distinction between them in operational terms. The gospel is to be proclaimed, then, to Jews as well as to other non-Christians. There is, of course, always the danger that we shall preach

9 And Harbonah, one of the chamberlains, said before the king, Behold also the gallows fifty cubits high, which Haman had made for Mordecai, who had spoken good for the king, standeth in the house of Haman. Then the king said, Hang him thereon.

10 So they hanged Haman on the gallows that he had prepared for Mordecai. Then was the king's wrath pacified.

8 On that day did the king Ahasuerus give the house of Haman the Jews' enemy unto Esther the queen. And Mordecai came before the king; for Esther had told what he *was* unto her.

they covered Haman's face. 9 Then said Harbo′na, one of the eunuchs in attendance on the king, "Moreover, the gallows which Haman has prepared for Mor′decai, whose word saved the king, is standing in Haman's house, fifty cubits high." 10 And the king said, "Hang him on that." So they hanged Haman on the gallows which he had prepared for Mor′decai. Then the anger of the king abated.

8 On that day King Ahasu-e′rus gave to Queen Esther the house of Haman, the enemy of the Jews. And Mor′decai came before the king, for Esther had told what

9. **Moreover, the gallows . . . is standing:** The word בַּם (**Moreover**) has the force of an additional accusation. Harbonah adds further insult to injury by suggesting that Haman had attempted to do away with one of "the king's benefactors" to whom Xerxes was indebted for his life. Knowing that the king had already determined evil against Haman (vs. 7), the eunuch's remark is carefully timed to suggest to the impressionable king a method by which the villain's punishment might be carried out with appropriate poetic justice.

10. The author is a master of irony. Unwittingly Haman had been digging his own grave (cf. Prov. 26:27). As Goldman observes, this is truly "measure for measure." The punishment meted out here is a foreshadowing of the measure-for-measure vengeance which the triumphant Jews were to inflict later upon their enemies.

J. Mordecai's Advancement (8:1-2)

8:1. The house of Haman: His estate (cf. 7:9). The state had the power to confiscate the property of condemned criminals.

Mordecai came before the king: He was raised to the rank of the small group of officials who had the right to "see the king's face" (1:14) without the necessity of awaiting ceremonial summons.

What he was to her: Previously Mordecai had risen on his own merits to the rank of royal benefactor, but immediately had retired to his former position in the king's

ourselves and not Christ Jesus, that we shall think ourselves superior, racially superior. Anti-Semitic propaganda has come often from the Christian church. It is an evil found even within the church.

Anti-Semitism antedates Christianity and it is not suggested that it is a purely Christian phenomenon, but it is aided by false Christian teaching and it results in the appalling situation present in several countries where Christian churches are reluctant, or frankly refuse, to receive a Jewish convert. It is plain that where racial and physical conditions of church membership override the conversion of heart and will, the Christian religion has ceased to exist except in a vain form.[5]

[5] Statement of the International Missionary Council's Committee on the Christian Approach to the Jews, quoted in Conrad Hoffmann, Jr., *The Jews Today* (New York: Friendship Press, 1941), p. 51.

The Christian missionary motive and the problem involved in the Christian approach to the Jew are stated thus by A. E. Garvie:

God has no favourites individual or national; but His love impartially embraces all and He wills that all be saved. Even liberal Jews are opposed to Christian missions to the Jews, and among orthodox as well as liberal Jews alike the missionary motive for their own faith is lacking. As I was engaged in friendly talk on this matter with a Jewish scholar and saint I put the argument for missions thus: "If I possess a treasure I value above all, and if I know that others have as great need of it as I have, can you blame me if I want to share it?" He gave a sincere assent; that meant a permanent change of attitude in him as at a later meeting he confessed. This is the primary missionary motive.[6]

[6] "The Jewish Problem," *International Review of Missions*, XXX (1941), 220-21.

2 And the king took off his ring, which he had taken from Haman, and gave it unto Mordecai. And Esther set Mordecai over the house of Haman.

3 ¶ And Esther spake yet again before the king, and fell down at his feet, and besought him with tears to put away the mischief of Haman the Agagite, and his device that he had devised against the Jews.

4 Then the king held out the golden sceptre toward Esther. So Esther arose, and stood before the king,

5 And said, If it please the king, and if I have found favor in his sight, and the thing *seem* right before the king, and I *be* pleasing in his eyes, let it be written to reverse the letters devised by Haman the son of Hammedatha the Agagite, which he wrote to destroy the Jews which *are* in all the king's provinces:

6 For how can I endure to see the evil that shall come unto my people? or how can I endure to see the destruction of my kindred?

7 ¶ Then the king Ahasuerus said unto Esther the queen and to Mordecai the Jew, Behold, I have given Esther the house of Haman, and him they have hanged upon the gallows, because he laid his hand upon the Jews.

he was to her; 2 and the king took off his signet ring, which he had taken from Haman, and gave it to Mor'decai. And Esther set Mor'decai over the house of Haman.

3 Then Esther spoke again to the king; she fell at his feet and besought him with tears to avert the evil design of Haman the Ag'agite and the plot which he had devised against the Jews. 4 And the king held out the golden scepter to Esther, 5 and Esther rose and stood before the king. And she said, "If it please the king, and if I have found favor in his sight, and if the thing seem right before the king, and I be pleasing in his eyes, let an order be written to revoke the letters devised by Haman the Ag'agite, the son of Hammeda'tha, which he wrote to destroy the Jews who are in all the provinces of the king. 6 For how can I endure to see the calamity that is coming to my people? Or how can I endure to see the destruction of my kindred?" 7 Then King Ahasu-e'rus said to Queen Esther and to Mor'decai the Jew, "Behold, I have given Esther the house of Haman, and they have hanged him on the gallows, because he

gate (6:12). However, his position was altered because the queen, some time after the events described in ch. 7, had disclosed to the king her Jewish identity and the fact that Mordecai was her cousin and foster father.

2. By delegating to him the administration of this valuable property (cf. 3:9; 5:11), Esther endowed her foster father with the prestige befitting a grand vizier. Here Mordecai is described as possessing everything that once belonged to "the enemy of the Jews": his wealth, his title, his authority. Indeed, the tables have been turned!

K. Esther's Petition (8:3-8)

4. Again the author resorts to his favorite literary device of repeating a previous scene (see Exeg. on 6:13), viz., Esther's audience with the king (5:1-4), in order to deal with the fate of the Jews in the empire. Usually commentators assume that in this case Esther took her life in hand a second time by going to the king unsummoned, but in view of the fact that the **scepter** was extended after her impassioned plea in behalf of her people, this can hardly be the meaning intended. Moreover, Mordecai at this time had constant access to the king, and the cousins surely could have arranged a summons without Esther's having to resort to unnecessary personal risk. Probably the extension of the scepter was merely an indication that the king, moved to sympathy because of her emotional plea, desired her to rise from the posture of a supplicant and continue her speech. It is unnecessary to assume that the author limits the king's use of the scepter to one function, viz., granting immunity from the stringent Persian law (cf. 4:11; 5:2).

7. **Said to Queen Esther and to Mordecai:** Although Mordecai is not mentioned in the above verses, we may assume that he was in the throne room too. To be sure, some

8 Write ye also for the Jews, as it liketh you, in the king's name, and seal *it* with the king's ring: for the writing which is written in the king's name, and sealed with the king's ring, may no man reverse.

9 Then were the king's scribes called at that time in the third month, that *is*, the month Sivan, on the three and twentieth *day* thereof; and it was written according to all that Mordecai commanded unto the Jews, and to the lieutenants, and the deputies and rulers of the provinces which *are* from India unto Ethiopia, a hundred twenty and seven provinces, unto every province according to the writing thereof, and unto every people after their language, and to the Jews according to their writing, and according to their language.

10 And he wrote in the king Ahasuerus' name, and sealed *it* with the king's ring, and sent letters by posts on horseback, *and* riders on mules, camels, *and* young dromedaries:

11 Wherein the king granted the Jews which *were* in every city to gather themselves together, and to stand for their life, to destroy, to slay, and to cause to perish, all the power of the people and province that would assault them, *both* little ones and women, and *to take* the spoil of them for a prey,

would lay hands on the Jews. 8 And you may write as you please with regard to the Jews, in the name of the king, and seal it with the king's ring; for an edict written in the name of the king and sealed with the king's ring cannot be revoked."

9 The king's secretaries were summoned at that time, in the third month, which is the month of Sivan, on the twenty-third day; and an edict was written according to all that Mor'decai commanded concerning the Jews to the satraps and the governors and the princes of the provinces from India to Ethiopia, a hundred and twenty-seven provinces, to every province in its own script and to every people in its own language, and also to the Jews in their script and their language. 10 The writing was in the name of King Ahasu-e′rus and sealed with the king's ring, and letters were sent by mounted couriers riding on swift horses that were used in the king's service, bred from the royal stud. 11 By these the king allowed the Jews who were in every city to gather and defend their lives, to destroy, to slay, and to annihilate any armed force of any people or province that might attack them, with their children and women, and

---

versions (LXX, O.L., Syriac) omit the phrase **and to Mordecai the Jew,** but the plurals in vs. 8 make it unwise to change the text at this point. In his speech the king does not imply that he has done all that can be reasonably expected and that Esther should be satisfied, but merely emphasizes that his past actions show his predisposition in favor of the Jews.

8. The king rejects Esther's appeal that the letters be annulled (vs. 5) because the story presupposes that Persian law is unalterable (cf. 1:19) once it is sealed with the king's signet. However, within the limits of Persian law he permits the previous decree to be neutralized in effect. There is no extrabiblical evidence that Persian decrees were irretractable. Undoubtedly this is a fictitious detail (cf. Dan. 6:8, 12, 15) which is introduced to justify the subsequent day of massacre (cf. 9:1-10).

L. A NEW DECREE (8:9-14)

10. This time the couriers (3:13, 15) went out in unusual haste because they were furnished with superior horses from the royal stables. The KJV misunderstands the difficult words in the M.T.

11. **Defend their lives** (RSV), lit., **stand for their life** (KJV): Valiant efforts have been made, especially by those who have an apologetic interest in Esther, to show that this verse means only that the Jews were given the right of self-defense. It is argued that whereas the previous decree had implied that the Jews must submit quietly to massacre (3:13), this decree gave only the right of organized resistance which any people would claim. Probably the author does intend to say that the Gentiles would make the first move, since they had the authorization of a prior irrevocable edict.

12 Upon one day in all the provinces of king Ahasuerus, *namely,* upon the thirteenth *day* of the twelfth month, which *is* the month Adar.

13 The copy of the writing for a commandment to be given in every province *was* published unto all people, and that the Jews should be ready against that day to avenge themselves on their enemies.

14 *So* the posts that rode upon mules *and* camels went out, being hastened and pressed on by the king's commandment. And the decree was given at Shushan the palace.

15 ¶ And Mordecai went out from the presence of the king in royal apparel of blue and white, and with a great crown of gold, and with a garment of fine linen and purple: and the city of Shushan rejoiced and was glad.

16 The Jews had light, and gladness, and joy, and honor.

17 And in every province, and in every city, whithersoever the king's commandment and his decree came, the Jews had joy and gladness, a feast and a good day. And many of the people of the land became

to plunder their goods, 12 upon one day throughout all the provinces of King Ahasu-e'rus, on the thirteenth day of the twelfth month, which is the month of Adar. 13 A copy of what was written was to be issued as a decree in every province, and by proclamation to all peoples, and the Jews were to be ready on that day to avenge themselves upon their enemies. 14 So the couriers, mounted on their swift horses that were used in the king's service, rode out in haste, urged by the king's command; and the decree was issued in Susa the capital.

15 Then Mor'decai went out from the presence of the king in royal robes of blue and white, with a great golden crown and a mantle of fine linen and purple, while the city of Susa shouted and rejoiced. 16 The Jews had light and gladness and joy and honor. 17 And in every province and in every city, wherever the king's command and his edict came, there was gladness and joy among the Jews, a feast and a holiday. And many from the peoples of the country

---

However, the language of the decree indicates that the Jews were to take vengeance (cf. vs. 13) on their enemies not only by slaying **any armed force of any people or province that might attack them,** but also by slaughtering defenseless **children and women** and plundering their property. The phrase **with their children and women** clearly does not refer to enemy action against Jewish women and children, even though the English translation might suggest it. According to Hebrew grammar, these words are also objects of the infinitives **to destroy, to slay, and to annihilate,** and thus refer to legalized Jewish action. This is truly measure-for-measure retaliation, patterned after the sanguinary terms of Haman's original decree, and recalling the ancient ban (*ḥĕrem*) vowed against all "Amalekites" (cf. I Sam. 15:3). Indeed, the language used is strikingly similar to that of Haman's decree, indicating that the terms of the original anti-Jewish edict were to be put into reverse application. Of course it is fantastic that a Persian king would allow a Jewish minority to take the law in its hands and massacre his subjects at will.

(After vs. 12, the LXX interpolates twenty-four verses [16:1-24] purporting to be a copy of the new decree of "Artaxerxes.")

M. POPULAR REACTION (8:15-17)

15. The city of Susa shouted and rejoiced: This is a description of the ovation which greeted the new grand vizier as he went forth from the palace, pompously robed in the royal colors. In contrast to the perplexity which was the popular reaction to Haman's first act in office (3:15), Mordecai's statesmanship—evidenced in the pro-Jewish edict—was hailed enthusiastically. Here the author projects his own sentiments into the predominantly Gentile city.

16. The Jews had light: A symbol of well-being (cf. Job 22:28; 30:26; Ps. 97:11).

17. Many . . . became Jews, i.e., proselytes (cf. 9:27). So much had Jewish prestige risen since the execution of Haman that it actually was dangerous not to bear the mark of circumcision!

Jews; for the fear of the Jews fell upon them.

9 Now in the twelfth month, that *is*, the month Adar, on the thirteenth day of the same, when the king's commandment and his decree drew near to be put in execution, in the day that the enemies of the Jews hoped to have power over them; (though it was turned to the contrary, that the Jews had rule over them that hated them,)

2 The Jews gathered themselves together in their cities throughout all the provinces of the king Ahasuerus, to lay hand on such as sought their hurt: and no man could withstand them; for the fear of them fell upon all people.

3 And all the rulers of the provinces, and the lieutenants, and the deputies, and officers of the king, helped the Jews; because the fear of Mordecai fell upon them.

4 For Mordecai *was* great in the king's house, and his fame went out throughout all the provinces: for this man Mordecai waxed greater and greater.

5 Thus the Jews smote all their enemies with the stroke of the sword, and slaughter,

declared themselves Jews, for the fear of the Jews had fallen upon them.

9 Now in the twelfth month, which is the month of Adar, on the thirteenth day of the same, when the king's command and edict were about to be executed, on the very day when the enemies of the Jews hoped to get the mastery over them, but which had been changed to a day when the Jews should get the mastery over their foes, 2 the Jews gathered in their cities throughout all the provinces of King Ahasu-e′rus to lay hands on such as sought their hurt. And no one could make a stand against them, for the fear of them had fallen upon all peoples. 3 All the princes of the provinces and the satraps and the governors and the royal officials also helped the Jews, for the fear of Mor′decai had fallen upon them. 4 For Mor′decai was great in the king's house, and his fame spread throughout all the provinces; for the man Mor′decai grew more and more powerful. 5 So the Jews smote all their enemies with the sword,

---

N. The Day of Vengeance (9:1-10)

9:1. The enemies of the Jews: Throughout this chapter it is assumed that there is a universal hatred of the Jews (vss. 2, 5, 16; cf. 8:11-13). No mention of this overt anti-Semitism had been made by Haman in his report to the king, in which he described "a certain people" as being eccentric, disobedient, and undesirable citizens (3:8). At that point the Jews had only one "hater"; here they have many "haters." Evidently it is the author's intention to show that Haman's policy had created anti-Semitism among peace-loving citizens by calling attention to differences and appealing to popular greed for plunder. Hence the mere execution of a "Hitler" could not eradicate a prejudice which in the intervening months had poisoned the bloodstream of the entire empire. The picture given here is that of two hostile, fully prepared parties poised and ready to fly at each other's throats, each claiming the authority of a royal edict.

Was turned to the contrary: The key verb in the story (cf. vs. 22). Just as the tables had been turned on Haman, so the thirteenth of Adar ironically proved to be the "unlucky thirteenth" for the Jews' enemies. In this sentence there is again a careful avoidance of reference to God.

2. No one could make a stand against them: Some commentators, following the Vulg., interpret the Hebrew to mean that when the time came the heathen, paralyzed with fear, did not make an attack and yet were destroyed despite their nonresistance. However, the context indicates (e.g., **such as sought their hurt**) that the author intends to say that the enemies were the aggressors who hoped to rule over the Jews (cf. vs. 1). But they could not withstand the superior power and morale of the Jews, and were found in the position of feebly supporting an obviously lost cause (cf. vs. 3; 8:17).

5. Did as they pleased to those who hated them: The Jews took the law into their own hands with the co-operation of officials throughout the empire (cf. vs. 3). Although from a technical standpoint the Jews did not engage in unprovoked aggression, their

and destruction, and did what they would unto those that hated them.

6 And in Shushan the palace the Jews slew and destroyed five hundred men.

7 And Parshandatha, and Dalphon, and Aspatha,

8 And Poratha, and Adalia, and Aridatha,

9 And Parmashta, and Arisai, and Aridai, and Vajezatha,

10 The ten sons of Haman the son of Hammedatha, the enemy of the Jews, slew they; but on the spoil laid they not their hand.

11 On that day the number of those that were slain in Shushan the palace was brought before the king.

12 ¶ And the king said unto Esther the queen, The Jews have slain and destroyed five hundred men in Shushan the palace, and the ten sons of Haman; what have they done in the rest of the king's provinces? now what is thy petition? and it shall be granted thee: or what is thy request further? and it shall be done.

13 Then said Esther, If it please the king, let it be granted to the Jews which are in Shushan to do to-morrow also according unto this day's decree, and let Haman's ten sons be hanged upon the gallows.

14 And the king commanded it so to be done: and the decree was given at Shushan; and they hanged Haman's ten sons.

slaughtering, and destroying them, and did as they pleased to those who hated them. 6 In Susa the capital itself the Jews slew and destroyed five hundred men, 7 and also slew Par-shan-da'tha and Dalphon and Aspa'tha 8 and Pora'tha and Ada'lia and Arida'tha 9 and Parmash'ta and Ar'isai and Ar'idai and Vaiza'tha, 10 the ten sons of Haman the son of Hammeda'tha, the enemy of the Jews; but they laid no hand on the plunder.

11 That very day the number of those slain in Susa the capital was reported to the king. 12 And the king said to Queen Esther, "In Susa the capital the Jews have slain five hundred men and also the ten sons of Haman. What then have they done in the rest of the king's provinces! Now what is your petition? It shall be granted you. And what further is your request? It shall be fulfilled." 13 And Esther said, "If it please the king, let the Jews who are in Susa be allowed tomorrow also to do according to this day's edict. And let the ten sons of Haman be hanged on the gallows." 14 So the king commanded this to be done; a decree was issued in Susa, and the ten sons

action was hardly confined to mere self-defense. Gentile losses were heavy (cf. vs. 16), but not a single Jewish casualty is mentioned. Evidently the Gentile rout turned into a veritable massacre, for the king had allowed the Jews to act in the same measure as their enemies would have done. This is a case of "do unto others as they would have done unto you."

10. The ten sons of Haman: So was the last remnant of Amalek blotted out. Although there is no previous mention of the sons' having participated in Haman's conspiracy, they too were hereditary enemies of the Jews and thus shared in their father's guilt.

They laid no hand on the plunder in spite of the permission given in 8:11. This recurring statement (cf. vss. 15-16) is strange. Some conjecture that it means that the self-respecting Jews were not motivated by mercenary considerations (cf. Gen. 14:22-24). Is it possible that here as elsewhere the author has in mind the narrative of I Sam. 15 (especially vs. 19), where divine judgment fell upon Saul and his army because they laid hand on the spoil after conquering the Amalekites?

O. "Shushan Purim" (9:11-15)

13. Those who argue that the Jews were not governed by a spirit of revenge have difficulty in defending Esther's request for a second day of slaughter, even though the Jews had already won an overwhelming victory, and her further desire that the dead bodies of Haman's sons be impaled as an additional act of disgrace and revenge upon

15 For the Jews that *were* in Shushan gathered themselves together on the fourteenth day also of the month Adar, and slew three hundred men at Shushan; but on the prey they laid not their hand.

16 But the other Jews that *were* in the king's provinces gathered themselves together, and stood for their lives, and had rest from their enemies, and slew of their foes seventy and five thousand, but they laid not their hands on the prey,

17 On the thirteenth day of the month Adar; and on the fourteenth day of the same rested they, and made it a day of feasting and gladness.

18 But the Jews that *were* at Shushan assembled together on the thirteenth *day* thereof, and on the fourteenth thereof; and on the fifteenth *day* of the same they rested, and made it a day of feasting and gladness.

19 Therefore the Jews of the villages, that dwelt in the unwalled towns, made the fourteenth day of the month Adar *a day of* gladness and feasting, and a good day, and of sending portions one to another.

of Haman were hanged. 15 The Jews who were in Susa gathered also on the fourteenth day of the month of Adar and they slew three hundred men in Susa; but they laid no hands on the plunder.

16 Now the other Jews who were in the king's provinces also gathered to defend their lives, and got relief from their enemies, and slew seventy-five thousand of those who hated them; but they laid no hands on the plunder. 17 This was on the thirteenth day of the month of Adar, and on the fourteenth day they rested and made that a day of feasting and gladness. 18 But the Jews who were in Susa gathered on the thirteenth day and on the fourteenth, and rested on the fifteenth day, making that a day of feasting and gladness. 19 Therefore the Jews of the villages, who live in the open towns, hold the fourteenth day of the month of Adar as a day for gladness and feasting and holiday-making, and a day on which they send choice portions to one another.

---

the house of Agag (cf. I Sam. 31:10). Some argue that this action was necessary to prevent further anti-Jewish outbreaks. But of course all war atrocities are "necessary" in that they are intended to have a deterrent effect upon the enemy. Obviously these acts go far beyond mere self-defense. However, the real motive for the repetition of the massacre is literary. This is the author's technique of introducing and explaining certain historical developments which help to justify the celebration of the feast of Purim on two days (see Exeg. below).

P. ORIGIN OF THE TWO DIFFERENT DAYS OF PURIM (9:16-19)

This section is not a continuation of the preceding narrative, but a summary of the events which have already been described. Vss. 16-17 supplement the description of events in the provinces (vss. 2-5); vs. 18 recapitulates the account of events in the city of Susa (vss. 14-15).

16. Seventy-five thousand: The LXX reduces the casualty list to 15,000, but the M.T. is supported by Josephus, Vulg., Syriac, and Targs. The massacre of 75,000 Gentiles is comparable to the report of I Macc. 11:47 that the Jews "did as they pleased" (cf. Esth. 9:5) and slew 100,000 in a single day.

19. The author explains why provincial Jews observed the fourteenth of Adar, in contrast to others who kept the Susa date ("Shushan Purim," as it is known in the Jewish calendar today). This is probably a case of inventing history in order to account for divergent customs (see Exeg. on vs. 13). According to the context, the distinction is made between Jews of the provinces and Jews of the capital of Susa. However, the verse introduces a new distinction, viz., **Jews of the villages, who live in the open towns** and (implicitly) those living in walled cities. Thus some LXX codices expand the Susa class to include all city dwellers by the addition, "But those who dwell in the cities keep also the fifteenth of Adar as a joyous and good day by sending dainties to their neighbors." In the course of time the implication of vs. 19 gave rise to elaborate Talmudic discussion as to the difference between an (unwalled) hamlet and a walled city. The

20 ¶ And Mordecai wrote these things, and sent letters unto all the Jews that *were* in all the provinces of the king Ahasuerus, *both* nigh and far,

21 To establish *this* among them, that they should keep the fourteenth day of the month Adar, and the fifteenth day of the same, yearly,

22 As the days wherein the Jews rested from their enemies, and the month which was turned unto them from sorrow to joy, and from mourning into a good day: that they should make them days of feasting and joy, and of sending portions one to another, and gifts to the poor.

23 And the Jews undertook to do as they had begun, and as Mordecai had written unto them;

24 Because Haman the son of Hammedatha, the Agagite, the enemy of all the Jews, had devised against the Jews to destroy them, and had cast Pur, that *is*, the lot, to consume them, and to destroy them;

20 And Mor'decai recorded these things, and sent letters to all the Jews who were in all the provinces of King Ahasu-e'rus, both near and far, 21 enjoining them that they should keep the fourteenth day of the month Adar and also the fifteenth day of the same, year by year, 22 as the days on which the Jews got relief from their enemies, and as the month that had been turned for them from sorrow into gladness and from mourning into a holiday; that they should make them days of feasting and gladness, days for sending choice portions to one another and gifts to the poor.

23 So the Jews undertook to do as they had begun, and as Mor'decai had written to them. 24 For Haman the Ag'agite, the son of Hammeda'tha, the enemy of all the Jews, had plotted against the Jews to destroy them, and had cast Pur, that is the lot, to

---

rabbis concluded that cities which had been walled since the days of Joshua were under obligation to observe "Shushan Purim." Vs. 19 is of the nature of a parenthesis, and without it the connection between vss. 18 and 20 is excellent.

III. REGULATIONS FOR THE ANNUAL OBSERVANCE OF PURIM (9:20–10:3)

A. MORDECAI LEGALIZES BOTH PURIM DATES (9:20-28)

Up to this point the author has been concerned with explaining the "historical" origin of the custom of observing Purim on different dates. In the following passage he shows that Mordecai's action, shortly after the first spontaneous celebration on the different dates in the provinces and Susa respectively, legalized both days in the Jewish calendar. The author goes out of his way to show that this arrangement, for which there is no basis in the Torah, was legalized by (*a*) Mordecai's festal letter, (*b*) the Jews' acceptance of Purim as a "tradition" (vss. 23, 27), and (*c*) the letter of confirmation sent out jointly by Esther and Mordecai.

20. The words **these things** refer to the substance of what has gone before in the Esther narrative, but should not be construed to mean that Mordecai was the author of the foregoing material (Rashi). Mordecai's festal letter contained not only the authorization of an annual two-day festival, but also some account of the plot which was the background of the deliverance to be commemorated (cf. vss. 24-25).

22. **Gifts to the poor:** This feature did not accompany the original spontaneous celebration of Purim, according to vs. 19, but was made mandatory by Mordecai's festal letter. Says Goldman, "It is a characteristically Jewish addition; a thought for the needy has to accompany every occasion of rejoicing" ("Esther," p. 239).

23. This verse sums up the situation. **To do as they had begun** refers to the original spontaneous celebration of Jewish triumph on the two dates; **as Mordecai had written to them** refers to his authorization that (*a*) the festival be celebrated annually, and (*b*) that the Susa date and the provincial date should both be recognized as official festal days.

24. Probably this and vs. 25 should be understood as a direct continuation of vs. 23, giving an epitome of the Purim legend which Mordecai included in his festal letter (cf. **these things** of vs. 20). The LXX rightly understands the introductory particle כִּי (**for,**

25 But when *Esther* came before the king, he commanded by letters that his wicked device, which he devised against the Jews, should return upon his own head, and that he and his sons should be hanged on the gallows.

26 Wherefore they called these days Purim after the name of Pur. Therefore for all the words of this letter, and *of that* which they had seen concerning this matter, and which had come unto them,

crush and destroy them; 25 but when Esther came before the king, he gave orders in writing that his wicked plot which he had devised against the Jews should come upon his own head, and that he and his sons should be hanged on the gallows. 26 Therefore they called these days Purim, after the term Pur. And therefore, because of all that was written in this letter, and of what they had faced in this matter, and of what had

---

because) as an indication that the substance of Mordecai's letter follows, and therefore renders "how that" (πῶς).

To crush . . . them: The Hebrew verb (*hummām*) seems to be a word play on Haman.

25. When Esther came before the king: This is one of the most troublesome clauses in the book. The difficulty arises out of the uncertainty as to the subject of the clause. Since the subject is feminine in the Hebrew (lit., "she came"), many translators (Vulg., Syriac, Targ., KJV, American Jewish Translation, and RSV) find in the feminine subject a reference to **Esther.** It would be fitting to introduce the heroine into the recapitulation of the plot, but since Esther is not mentioned in the context (she is last mentioned in 9:13) this translation is unnatural. Some modern translators (ERV, ASV, Amer. Trans.) treat the feminine as a neuter "it" or "this," i.e., the matter of Haman's conspiracy which came before the king at Esther's second banquet. This interpretation has the approval of many scholars. However, it rests upon a translation which is questionable ("This is hardly Hebrew," says the eminent Semitist, C. C. Torrey). Possibly the LXX, which offers still a third interpretation, might give a clue to the solution of the problem. In view of the facts that Haman is the subject in vs. 24 and that vs. 25 likewise deals with the king's judgment upon him, it is not surprising that the LXX reads, "when he [Haman] came before the king" (בבאו instead of בבאה; see C. C. Torrey's defense of this translation on the basis of his theory of an Aramaic original, "The Older Book of Esther," *Harvard Theological Review,* III, 37-38). In any case, it is unnecessary to bring Esther into this verse. Since the plot is radically abbreviated in this two-verse résumé, and since the author is making only one point, viz., that Haman's intention to destroy the Jews recoiled "on his own head," the failure to mention Esther is neither inconsistency nor evidence of the literary independence of this section. If vss. 24-25 had come from the hand of a later editor, he would not have been content with such brevity and the neglect of both Esther and Mordecai.

He gave orders in writing: An attempted translation of a peculiar word sequence in the M.T. (אמר עם־הספר). The king never did command in writing that Haman be hanged (cf. 7:9), although according to 9:14, he did in the case of Haman's sons. Of course, in a general sense the king gave written command through Mordecai that Haman's plot should return on his head posthumously in the promulgation of the edict of 8:8-13. But the words make such strange Hebrew that in all probability the text must be regarded as corrupt at this point. Interestingly, the LXX reads, "saying to hang Mordecai" (cf. 6:4), and thus alludes to the fact that Haman began to fall when he went before the king to ask for Mordecai's life.

He and his sons: Haman and his sons were not hanged at the same time. The seeming inaccuracy results from telescoping the account of Haman's plot into the brief compass of two verses.

26. They called these days Purim: This is the first explicit reference to the festival of Purim (a Hebrew plural form built on the loan word **Pur;** cf. 3:7; 9:24). The explanation and authorization of these two days (cf. vs. 27) has been the governing

27 The Jews ordained, and took upon them, and upon their seed, and upon all such as joined themselves unto them, so as it should not fail, that they would keep these two days according to their writing, and according to their *appointed* time every year;

28 And *that* these days *should be* remembered and kept throughout every generation, every family, every province, and every city; and *that* these days of Purim should not fail from among the Jews, nor the memorial of them perish from their seed.

29 Then Esther the queen, the daughter of Abihail, and Mordecai the Jew, wrote with all authority, to confirm this second letter of Purim.

30 And he sent the letters unto all the Jews, to the hundred twenty and seven provinces of the kingdom of Ahasuerus, *with* words of peace and truth,

befallen them, 27 the Jews ordained and took it upon themselves and their descendants and all who joined them, that without fail they would keep these two days according to what was written and at the time appointed every year, 28 that these days should be remembered and kept throughout every generation, in every family, province, and city, and that these days of Purim should never fall into disuse among the Jews, nor should the commemoration of these days cease among their descendants.

29 Then Queen Esther, the daughter of Ab'ihail, and Mor'decai the Jew gave full written authority, confirming this second letter about Purim. 30 Letters were sent to all the Jews, to the hundred and twenty-seven provinces of the kingdom of Ahasu-

---

purpose of the book from the outset. **This letter:** Mordecai's festal letter mentioned in vs. 23.

27. All who joined them: A reference to proselytes (cf. 8:17). **Without fail** (the same words as in 1:19), i.e., without any possibility of alteration or abrogation. Says a Midrash: "Even if all the Festivals should be annulled, Purim will never be annulled." Throughout this section (vss. 26-28) the author displays an almost legal style in order to stress the fact that a two-day festival, for which there is no basis in the Torah and which originated among patriots rather than priests, is as legally binding upon Jews as the irrevocable laws of the Medes and Persians.

B. Esther Adds Her Authorization (9:29-32)

In this section the Hebrew text is not beyond suspicion. The question arises as to whether this new letter was sent out by Esther alone or by Esther and Mordecai jointly. In vs. 29 Esther and Mordecai are coauthors, but in vs. 30 the verb is masculine singular. Some critics omit all references to Mordecai and change the verb in vs. 30 to the feminine. But it is best to follow the M.T. (so LXX in vs. 30) in regarding this as a joint letter. There is no suggestion that this second letter was necessitated by the fact that the Jews had taken objection to the festal observance commanded by Mordecai in his previous letter. The twofold issuing of letters seems to be a further attempt to lend legal sanction to the observance of the two days of Purim.

29. This second letter about Purim: To what does **second** refer? Usually it is taken to refer to the joint letter which is described in vss. 29-31. But it would seem strange for Esther and Mordecai to write to confirm their own letter, and furthermore it is stated explicitly in vs. 31 that the purpose of the joint letter was to give additional confirmation to Mordecai's previous festal letter. Since the word "second" is lacking in the LXX, the O.L., and the Syriac, it is possibly a gloss introduced by a scribe who thought that the reference was to "this second letter which follows." If so, the phrase אגרת הפורים הזאת refers to "this letter" (האגרת הזאת) mentioned in vs. 26. Torrey, however, argues (*ibid.*, pp. 31-33) that the second letter of Purim is the present book of Esther, and that the first letter was the Aramaic prototype.

31 To confirm these days of Purim in their times *appointed,* according as Mordecai the Jew and Esther the queen had enjoined them, and as they had decreed for themselves and for their seed, the matters of the fastings and their cry.

32 And the decree of Esther confirmed these matters of Purim; and it was written in the book.

10 And the king Ahasuerus laid a tribute upon the land, and *upon* the isles of the sea.

2 And all the acts of his power and of his might, and the declaration of the greatness of Mordecai, whereunto the king advanced him, *are* they not written in the book of the chronicles of the kings of Media and Persia?

e'rus, in words of peace and truth, 31 that these days of Purim should be observed at their appointed seasons, as Mor'decai the Jew and Queen Esther enjoined upon the Jews, and as they had laid down for themselves and for their descendants, with regard to their fasts and their lamenting. 32 The command of Queen Esther fixed these practices of Purim, and it was recorded in writing.

10 King Ahasu-e'rus laid tribute on the land and on the coastlands of the sea. 2 And all the acts of his power and might, and the full account of the high honor of Mor'decai, to which the king advanced him, are they not written in the Book of the Chronicles of the kings of Media and Persia?

---

31. **Mordecai . . . enjoined:** Does this refer to the content of the joint letter, or to the previous letter of Mordecai and the consequent action of the Jews (9:20-23)? The context seems to demand the latter interpretation. In this case the words **and Queen Esther** must be regarded as a gloss (so Gunkel, Haupt, Paton, *et al.*) since the previous letter was sent out by Mordecai alone.

With regard to their fasts and their lamenting: Many commentators believe on the basis of this phrase that the purpose of the joint letter was to introduce fasting as an essential part of the festival, and that this verse thus gave a legal precedent for the custom, which developed probably about the ninth century A.D., of observing the thirteenth of Adar as "Esther's Fast" (cf. 4:16). Probably, however, this is merely a reference to Mordecai's previous command (vs. 22) that the Jews annually observe the memorial of their sorrow and mourning (Torrey)—a command which they had already subscribed to as a result of his first letter (cf. vs. 27). The joint letter introduced nothing new: it was written for the sole purpose of ratifying the previous "letter of Purim" by linking Esther's prestige with that of Mordecai.

32. **In writing:** The word הספר does not refer to the book of Esther, as earlier commentators believed, or to another Purim source used by the author of Esther. It is precisely the same word which is used for "letters" in vs. 30.

C. The Greatness of Mordecai (10:1-3)

10:1. The author ends, as he began, with a description of Xerxes' imperial wealth and power, which in this instance had been augmented by making Mordecai grand vizier and by following his statesmanlike policy. The object of Xerxes' tribute, then, is purely literary. It is needless to suppose that the king had to resort to additional taxation in order to compensate for the loss of Haman's bribe or to recover from his unsuccessful wars with Greece. Indeed, the author shows no knowledge of the empire-shaking events which took place in the **coastlands** of the Mediterranean during Xerxes' reign.

2. This prosaic statement, which is modeled after the recurring formulas of the books of Kings and Chronicles (e.g., I Kings 11:41; II Chr. 25:26), is very important, for it purports to validate the authenticity of the previous story by referring the reader to the archives in which the facts may be confirmed. Probably the archives were no more available than another text which an ancient author assured his readers could be found

3 For Mordecai the Jew *was* next unto king Ahasuerus, and great among the Jews, and accepted of the multitude of his brethren, seeking the wealth of his people, and speaking peace to all his seed.

3 For Mor'decai the Jew was next in rank to King Ahasu-e'rus, and he was great among the Jews and popular with the multitude of his brethren, for he sought the welfare of his people and spoke peace to all his people.

in the original, inscribed in gold, on a great pillar in the Indian Ocean (cited by E. J. Bickerman, "The Colophon of the Greek Book of Esther," *Journal of Biblical Literature,* LXIII [1944], 352-53). Some scholars suppose that **the Book of the Chronicles of the kings of Media and Persia** refers to a Jewish book, in circulation at that time, which described the history and experiences of Jews during the Persian regime. However, the author doubtless alludes to the official Persian annals mentioned previously in 2:23 and 6:1, where the same phraseology is employed.

(After 10:3, the LXX has an addition of eleven verses [10:4–11:1], which gives the interpretation of Mordecai's dream, concluding with a colophon which witnesses to the date and authenticity of the LXX "letter of Purim.")

The Book of

JOB

Introduction and Exegesis by SAMUEL TERRIEN
Exposition by PAUL SCHERER

JOB

INTRODUCTION

The book of Job is one of the most celebrated writings of the whole Bible and also one of the least known. Everyone who speaks of "the patience of Job" (Jas. 5:11) shows thereby that he has but a vague acquaintance with the poem (3:1–42:6), or probably none at all. More thoroughly informed laymen and even biblical students who praise the book as a literary masterpiece, sometimes in immoderate terms,[1] often apologize for its failure to solve the problem of innocent suffering. Yet was the poet's purpose to discover the secret of that mystery? Was it even to

> assert eternal Providence,
> And justify the ways of God to men?[2]

In order to answer these questions—and some others pertaining to the understanding of the book—the critic must ask, How and when was the document written? How was it preserved for the contemporary reader? What was the purpose of its publication? What is its place within the total environment of Scripture? What is its relevance for the modern Christian?

I. Title and Place in the Canon

Like Joshua, Ruth, Ezra, Nehemiah, Daniel, and Esther, the book of Job bears as its title the

[1] "Magnificent and sublime as no other book of Scripture" (Luther); "Single and unparalleled in the sacred volume" (Lowth); "The greatest poem of ancient and modern times" (Tennyson); "A noble Book; all men's Book! . . . There is nothing written, I think, in the Bible or out of it, of equal literary merit" (Carlyle).

[2] Milton, *Paradise Lost*, Bk. I, ll. 25-26.

name of the hero, אִיּוֹב, *'iyyôbh*, a dissyllabic word which has been "Hellenisticized" into Ἰώβ (see German *Hiob*) and Latinized into *Job*, a monosyllabic word which has passed into the English language.

In the Hebrew manuscripts the book is found among the Hagiographa or Holy Writings,[3] usually after Psalms and Proverbs. In the Septuagint manuscripts, as well as in the Greek and Latin lists of biblical books, its place varies greatly, but Western tradition, under the influence of the Vulgate, lists Job at the head of the poetic books.

II. Subject and Literary Form

According to popular opinion, the book of Job is the story of a man's trials and restoration. But in point of fact, it is for the most part a collection of poems dealing with the meaning of life and religion. The book falls naturally into five parts: (*a*) a prologue in prose (1:1–2:13) introducing the hero and his sudden misfortunes, as well as three friends who come to comfort him; (*b*) a poetic discussion (3:1–31:40) which goes back and forth between these

[3] These were not considered part of canonical Scripture until the end of the first century A.D. (cf. article "The Canon of the Old Testament," Vol. I, p. 43). It is probably on account of this fact that the book of Job appears to have been practically unknown by Jesus and the early Christians (cf. I Cor. 3:19, the only passage of the N.T. which seems to be a quotation from the book [5:13 LXX]). Parallels of thought or terminology have been observed in about eighteen other passages of the N.T.

friends and the hero; (c) a poetic rebuke and advice offered by a fourth friend hitherto unmentioned and thereafter ignored (32:1–37:24); (d) a series of poetic challenges and questions addressed by Yahweh to Job, and the latter's repentance (38:1–42:6); (e) an epilogue in prose (42:7-17) which records the hero's rehabilitation and return to happiness.

The literary form of the book is not homogeneous. The prologue and the epilogue suggest the genre of patriarchal traditions, with its stylized patterns, its profound psychology under the cover of naïveté, and its folkloric use of hyperbole. The poetic parts, on the contrary, which constitute the bulk of the book (3:1–42:6), belong to the wisdom type of literature, with two significant differences: unlike Proverbs, Ecclesiastes, and other books of their kind, the Joban poems deal with a single theme and represent discourses which are meant to be spoken by various characters. The word "dialogue" does not strictly apply to them, however, because the respective length of each piece precludes the conversational "give-and-take," the exchanges, interruptions, and other rhetorical devices which characterize, for instance, the Dialogues of Plato.[4] For the same and other reasons one should consider the book not as a drama composed for theatrical production,[5] but as a lyrical meditation with a dramatis personae, in some respects similar to the Song of Songs.[6]

The subject as well as the literary form seems

to be original with the poet of Job. However, he may have been influenced by sages of the ancient Near East and by international folklore.

III. Oriental Background

The Old Testament is no longer studied in a cultural vacuum.[7] Archaeological discoveries of the last hundred years have shown eloquently the debt which Israel owed to the religions and literatures of her neighbors.[8] It is therefore imperative to ask whether foreign influences have had any effect at all as regards the origin and development of the book of Job. The question is the more legitimate since the wisdom literature of the Old Testament in general, and the book of Job in particular, display an international—or at least a nonspecifically Hebraic—spirit or outlook.[9]

A. Edomitic Wisdom.—Since the action and the characters of the book are located in Edom (see Exeg. on 1:1; 2:11), it is quite possible that Israel received the story from the Edomites, those seminomads who lived southeast of the Dead Sea and enjoyed a reputation for wisdom.[10] It is also possible that the use of the

[4] See Carl Fries, Das philosophische Gespräch von Hiob bis Plato (Tübingen: J. C. B. Mohr, 1904); Oskar Holtzmann, "Das Ende des jüdischen Staatswesens und die Entstehung des Christenthums," in Bernhard Stade, Geschichte des Volkes Israel (Berlin: G. Grote, 1888), II, 331.
[5] See H. M. Kallen, The Book of Job as a Greek Tragedy (New York: Moffat, Yard & Co., 1918), and C. G. Montefiore's critical discussion of this book in The Harvard Theological Review, XII (1919), 219-24; see also a comparison between Job and Sophocles' Oedipus at Colonus by Robert Lowth, Lectures on the Sacred Poetry of the Hebrews, tr. G. Gregory (Boston: J. Leavitt, 1829), pp. 273-81.
[6] "All general classifications fail to do justice to the overflowing abundance of its forms, moods, and thoughts: it is not exclusively lyric (W. W. Baudissin, P. Volz), nor epic (J. F. Genung, The Epic of the Inner Life. Boston, 1891), nor dramatic (B. Szold, Das Buch Hiob, p. xvii. Baltimore, 1886; J. Ley, Neue Jahrb. f. Philos. und Pädagogik, Vol. 154, pp. 126 f.), nor didactic or reflective (most of the critics), unless the poem is cut down to fit a particular category (as F. Baumgärtel and E. G. Kraeling are inclined to do). Even the more comprehensive characterizations, such as that of Friedr. Delitzsch (Das Buch Hiob, p. 15. Leipzig, 1902), 'a poem with dramatic movement and essentially didactic tendency,' or better still that of J. G. von Herder (Vom Geist der Ebräischen Poesie, Vol. I, p. 148), 'an epopee of mankind, a theodicy of God,' fail to do justice to the scope of the work." (Robert H. Pfeiffer, Introduction to the Old Testament [New York: Harper & Bros., 1941], p. 684. Used by permission.)

[7] See article "The Old Testament World," Vol. I, pp. 233-71. "Much light has been cast on the Old Testament by a comparison with other literatures, especially Babylonian, Assyrian, and Egyptian, and much more light will come from this study" (Julius A. Bewer, The Literature of the Old Testament [Rev. ed.; New York: Columbia University Press, 1933], p. 438).
[8] See Alfred Jeremias, Das Alte Testament im Lichte des alten Orients (4th ed.; Leipzig: J. C. Hinrichs, 1930); Anton Jirku, Altorientalischer Kommentar zum Alten Testament (Leipzig: A. Deichert, 1923); Charles F. Jean, Le milieu biblique avant Jésus-Christ (Paris: Paul Geuthner, 1922-36); Hugo Gressmann, ed., Altorientalische Texte zum Alten Testament (2nd ed.; Berlin: Walter de Gruyter, 1926); T. E. Peet, A Comparative Study of the Literatures of Egypt, Palestine and Mesopotamia (London: Oxford University Press, 1931); George A. Barton, Archaeology and the Bible (Philadelphia: American Sunday-School Union, 1937); James B. Pritchard, ed., Ancient Near Eastern Texts Relating to the Old Testament (Princeton: Princeton University Press, 1950).
[9] See article "The Wisdom Literature," Vol. I, p. 212; A. Causse, "L'origine étrangère et la tendance humaniste de la sagesse juive," Actes du Congrès International d'Histoire des Religions (Paris: Champion, 1925), II, 45-54; Hugo Gressmann, Israels Spruchweisheit im Zusammenhang der Weltliteratur (Berlin: Karl Curtius, 1926); W. O. E. Oesterley, The Wisdom of Egypt and the Old Testament (New York: The Macmillan Co., 1927); Paul Humbert, Recherches sur les sources égyptiennes de la littérature sapientiale d'Israël (Neuchâtel: Secrétariat de l'Université, 1929); Walter Baumgartner, Israelitische und altorientalische Weisheit (Tübingen: J. C. B. Mohr, 1933); Johannes Fichtner, Die altorientalische Weisheit in ihrer israelitisch-jüdischen Ausprägung (Giessen: A. Töpelmann, 1933); J. Coert Rylaarsdam, Revelation in Jewish Wisdom Literature (Chicago: University of Chicago Press, 1946).
[10] See I Kings 4:30-31; Jer. 49:7; Baruch 3:22-23; cf. Robert H. Pfeiffer, "Edomitic Wisdom," Zeitschrift für die alttestamentliche Wissenschaft, XLIV (1926), 13-25.

JOB

divine name Eloah, which is common in the poetic discussion and extremely rare elsewhere in the Bible, indicates a familiarity with Teman in Edom.[11] Quite remarkably the name Eloah is also used by Agur (see Prov. 30:5), an Arabian sage, whose language may have been Edomitic.[12] These observations, however, are not sufficiently weighty for the modern historian to conjecture that "the author of the book was an Edomite."[13]

B. International Folklore.—The theme of the righteous man who suffers ignominy because he is being tested by rival deities or divine beings (see 1:6-12; 2:1-7a) probably belongs to the international folklore of the ancient East. The story of Hariscandra, for instance, appears in India under many different forms [14] and rests upon very ancient traditions.[15] According to one variant of the tale,[16] the gods and goddesses were assembled with the seven Menus in the heaven of Indra. The question was asked whether a single human prince could be found who would be without stain or blemish. Most of the members of the divine assembly were of the opinion that there was none, but Vasishta insisted that a certain Atschandira (Hariscandra) was perfect. Shiva Rutren ("the destroyer") offered to prove the contrary if the prince were delivered into his power. Vasishta accepted the challenge, and it was agreed that, depending upon the issue of the wager, one would yield to the other all merits acquired in a long series of penance. Shiva Rutren thereupon submitted Atschandira to all sorts of trials, deprived him of his wealth, kingdom, wife, and only son, but the prince persisted in his virtue. The gods rewarded him with munificence and returned to him his previous estate. Shiva Rutren gave his own merits to Vasishta, who passed them on to the hero.

Another form of the wager between heavenly beings—this time the archangels Gabriel and Michael—is found among the Suahelis.[17] Thus it appears that the motif is common to several cultural groups. The biblical story, with its wager between Yahweh and "the Satan," has undeniably a polytheistic flavor, and may have been partly inspired from a folkloric theme. But one essential difference far outweighs the similarity. The biblical writer ignores the value of merits among heavenly beings, and even denies it among mortals. His sole purpose is precisely to show that Job serves God for nought.

C. Egyptian Pessimism.—Much more pertinent are the parallels which have been discovered between Job and the Egyptian literature.[18] The literary form which introduces and concludes a poetic dialogue with a prose narrative is most unusual for Israel but quite common in Egypt. For instance, The Complaints of the Eloquent Peasant [19] is composed of nine discourses in a semipoetic form which are framed in a prologue and an epilogue in prose. Likewise, The Prophecy of Nefer-Rohu [20] is prefaced and concluded by a narrative. There is little doubt that the poet of Job was acquainted with Egypt, perhaps even with the Egyptian language (see 3:14; 9:26; 21:32; 28:1 ff.; 29:18; 31:4, 6; 38:14, 17, 33, 36; 39:13 ff.; 40:15 ff.; 41:7 ff.). More decisive still is the comparison in form and content which has often been made between the poetic discussion of Job and the Egyptian Dialogue of the Man Weary of Life with His Soul.[21] The beginning of the composition is lost, but it may be assumed from the poem itself that the Egyptian hero, like Job, fell sick and consequently endured all kinds of ill treatment: his friends and even his brothers departed from him, the good deeds which he had accomplished in the past were forgotten, and his neighbors robbed him. In his extremity he decided to die; but his soul, conceived as an independent being, vehemently opposed his de-

---

[11] See Hab. 3:3; cf. Paul Dhorme, *Le livre de Job* (Paris: J. Gabalda, 1926; "Études bibliques"), p. lxxxix, n. 7.

[12] See Eliezer ben Yehudah, "The Edomite Language," *Journal of the Palestine Oriental Society*, I (1921), 113-15.

[13] See Pfeiffer, *Intro. to O.T.*, p. 683; cf. p. 684.

[14] Jeremias, *Das A. T. im Lichte des alten Orients*, pp. 628-31; Paul Volz, *Hiob und Weisheit* (2nd ed.; Göttingen: Vandenhoeck & Ruprecht, 1921; "Die Schriften des Alten Testaments"), pp. 8-9; Paul Bertie, *Le poème de Job* (Paris: Rieder, 1929), p. 54; Emil G. Kraeling, *The Book of the Ways of God* (New York: Charles Scribner's Sons, 1939), pp. 187-88.

[15] F. E. Pargiter, *The Mārkandeya Purāna Translated with Notes* (Calcutta: The Asiatic Society, 1904; "Bibliotheca Indica"), p. xx.

[16] Cf. Adolphe Lods, *Histoire de la littérature hébraïque et juive* (Paris: Payot, 1950), pp. 691-92.

[17] Volz, *op. cit.*, p. 9.

[18] See especially Humbert, *op. cit.*, pp. 75-106.

[19] This work has been preserved in MSS of the Middle Kingdom (twentieth–eighteenth centuries B.C.); see translations and commentaries by Friedrich Vogelsang, *Kommentar zu den Klagen des Bauern* (Leipzig: J. C. Hinrichs, 1913; "Untersuchungen zur Geschichte und Altertumskunde Aegyptens"); A. H. Gardiner, "The Eloquent Peasant," *Journal of Egyptian Archaeology*, IX (1923), 5-25; Adolf Erman, *The Literature of the Ancient Egyptians* (London: Methuen & Co., 1927), pp. 116-31; John A. Wilson, in Pritchard, *op. cit.*, pp. 407-10.

[20] A text of the Middle Kingdom, preserved in MSS of the Eighteenth Dynasty. See translations by A. H. Gardiner, "New Literary Works from Ancient Egypt," *Journal of Egyptian Archaeology*, I (1914), 100-6; Erman, *op. cit.*, pp. 110-15; Wilson, in Pritchard, *op. cit.*, pp. 444-46.

[21] Text in a palimpsest of the Middle Kingdom; see translations by Erman, *op. cit.*, pp. 86-92; Hermann Ranke, "Das Gedicht vom Lebensmüden," in Gressmann, *Altorientalische Texte*, pp. 25-28; Peet, *op. cit.*, pp. 112 ff.; Alexander Scharff, *Der Bericht über das Streitgespräch eines Lebensmüden mit seiner Seele* (Munich: Bayerischen Akademie der Wissenschaften, 1937; "Sitzungsberichte der philosophisch-historische Klasse"); R. Weill, in *Bulletin de l'Institut Français d'Archéologie Orientale*, XLV (1946), 89-154; Wilson, in Pritchard, *op. cit.*, pp. 405-7.

termination. Like Job, the Egyptian hero breathes out his lament:

> To whom can I speak today?
> (One's) fellows are evil;
> The friends of today do not love.
> To whom can I speak today?
> Hearts are rapacious:
> Every man seizes his fellow's goods. . . .
> Goodness is rejected everywhere. . . .
> There are no righteous;
> The land is left to those who do wrong. . . .
> To whom can I speak today?
> I am laden with wretchedness
> For lack of an intimate (friend) .[22]

Apparently convinced by his soul that death is not desirable, the life-weary man returns to the consideration of the earthly situation, but the spectacle of human society throws him back to his previous resolve to commit suicide. Death is for him

> (Like) the recovery of a sick man, . . .
> Like the odor of myrrh,
> Like sitting under an awning on a breezy day, . . .
> Like the odor of lotus blossoms,
> Like sitting on the bank of drunkenness, . . .
> Like the return of men to their houses from an
> expedition, . . .
> Like the clearing of the sky, . . .
> Like the longing of a man to see his house (again),
> After he has spent many years in captivity.[23]

Unlike the Semites in general or the Hebrews in particular, Job was at times attracted by the prospect of death (see 3:13-22; cf. 10:18, 19; 14:13; 17:13, 14), and this attitude suggests a distinctly Egyptian point of view.[24] However, there is no direct literary influence from Egypt upon the biblical poem. For the Egyptians, the fact of apparently undeserved suffering presented a problem, to be sure; but their belief in retributive justice was safeguarded by their hope in a moral judgment after death. For the Hebrews, death presented a harassing question because they were unable, until the late postexilic period, to postpone righteous retribution to a life beyond the grave.[25]

It is probable that the Joban poet was acquainted with some manifestations of Egyptian pessimism,[26] but it must be noted that he dealt

with human life in a totally different mood, for his outlook was conditioned by an extraordinarily urgent faith in one God, creator and ruler of the universe. His anxiety was therefore derived more from his theology than from his observation of human misery. Moreover, as will be seen below,[27] his purpose was not to discuss philosophically the inequities of existence.

D. Babylonian Skepticism.—For years many critics have turned to the Akkadian literature in an effort to discover possible sources of the book of Job. Over against a multitude of texts which uphold the idea that prosperity, good health, and long life are the product of virtue— and conversely, sickness, poverty, affliction, and premature death are punishment for sins, overt or concealed, sometimes unknown even to those who perpetrate them—a few documents reveal a skeptical trend of bold independence. One of these is known as The Poem of the Righteous Sufferer, often called the Babylonian Job.[28] In its present form the document appears to be a psalm of thanksgiving. The hero has been healed of a mysterious disease, and he now praises the god who delivered him. There is no trace of a dialogue with visiting friends,[29] but in the course of a long monologue several ideas parallel with those of Job may be recognized. At first the sufferer describes his condition:

> . . . I am like a deaf man.
> Although I was powerful, I am become a slave. . . .
> By day, sighing, by night, weeping;
> Monthly lament; sorrow each year.
>
> .   .   .   .
> If I look around me, [there is] evil, evil!
> Oppression has increased upon me, I do not see my
> right.[30]

---

[22] John A. Wilson, tr., "A Dispute over Suicide," in J. B. Pritchard, ed., *Ancient Near Eastern Texts Relating to the Old Testament* (Princeton: Princeton University Press, 1950), pp. 406-7. Used by permission.

[23] *Ibid.*, p. 407.

[24] Humbert (*op. cit.*, p. 76) remarks that the Egyptian sufferer, like Job (3:1) begins his lament with the unusual expression, "I opened my mouth (to speak) to my soul, and I answered to what it said."

[25] See Job 14:7-15; cf. 19:24-25.

[26] See also Job's protest of innocence (31:1-40), which strikingly recalls The Negative Confession in The Book of the Dead, ch. cxxv (see *The Papyrus of Ani*, ed. E. A.

Wallis Budge [New York: G. P. Putnam's Sons, 1913], II, 576-96).

[27] Pp. 897 ff.

[28] See transcriptions, translations, and/or commentaries in: Heinrich Zimmern, "Babylonische Hymnen und Gebete," *Der alte Orient*, VII, 3 (1906), 28 ff.; Morris Jastrow, "A Babylonian Parallel to the Story of Job," *Journal of Biblical Literature*, XXV (1906), 135-91; S. H. Langdon, *Babylonian Wisdom* (London: Luzac & Co., 1921), pp. 35-66; Paul Dhorme, *Choix de textes religieux assyro-babyloniens* (Paris: J. Gabalda, 1907), pp. 372-79; François Martin, "Le Juste Souffrant Babylonien," *Journal Asiatique*, XVI (1910), 75-143; Simon Landersdorfer, *Eine Babylonische Quelle für das Buch Job?* (Freiburg i. B.: Herder, 1911: "Biblische Studien"), pp. 14-28; Erich Ebeling, "Die Geschichte eines Leidenden und seine Erlösung," in Gressmann, *Altorientalische Texte*, pp. 273-81; Robert William Rogers, ed., *Cuneiform Parallels to the Old Testament* (2nd ed.; New York: Abingdon Press, 1926), pp. 164-69; Robert H. Pfeiffer, "I Will Praise the Lord of Wisdom," in Pritchard, *op. cit.*, pp. 434-37.

[29] There is, however, the mention of some fellow (or fellows) who apparently spoke to the sufferer as Job's "comforters" did. "The fury of the companions has destroyed me" (Tablet I, obverse, l. 14); "in the assembly, he has cursed me" (*ibid.*, l. 18); "at the mention of my prosperity, his mouth is a cavern" (*ibid.*, l. 19).

[30] Tablet I, ll. 11, 13, 20-21; Tablet II, ll. 2-3.

The supplications made to the god and goddess have received no answer:

I have cried to the god, but he did not show his face.
I have invoked my goddess, but she did not lift up her head.[31]

Ritual practices have proved ineffective, and the hero is led to formulate his pessimism over life in general:

What perverse events in the world!
I look behind: distress pursues.[32]

He refuses to interpret his afflictions as a punishment for sin or ritual failure:

As if I had not set aside the libation for the god,
And had not, at meal-time, remembered my goddess,
Had not bowed my face, and had not [made] adoration.[33]

He recalls at length his past deeds of piety:

Whereas I, myself, thought only of prayer and supplication,
Supplication was my practice, sacrifice my rule.
The day of the worship of the god was the joy of my heart,
The day of the procession of the goddess was for me gain and riches. . . .
I taught my country to guard the names of the god,
I instructed my people to honor the names of the goddess,
The praise of the king I made like to that of the god,
The fear of the palace I taught to the people,
Truly I knew that such things are pleasant to the god![34]

Eventually the lamenter realizes that he did not know what was agreeable to the deity, and implies that his deeds of devotion were useless:

What seems good to oneself is worthless before the god,
And what is rejected by one's heart finds favor with the god.
Who will comprehend the will of the gods in the midst of the heavens?
The counsel of the god is full of obscurity; who will know it?[35]
How will mortals learn the way of the god?[36]

The reason for man's ignorance is apparently his mortal condition:

He who was alive in the evening is dead the next morning.

In a moment he is cast into grief; suddenly he is crushed down.
In an instant he sings and plays; in a twinkling of the eye he wails like a mourner.[37]

The constant prospect of death without warning may explain man's frailty and fickleness, his enslavement to the emotional insecurity of his condition:

Like day and night their will-power changes.
If they are hungry, they look like corpses;
Are they satiated? they rival their god!
In prosperity they talk of ascending to Heaven;
Are they in distress? they speak of descending to Irkalla.[38]

The text of the lines which follow has deteriorated, but the sufferer apparently returns to his lament and describes realistically his physical condition.[39] The priests and incantators have failed to discover his "state of sickness," and worse still, the deities seem to be indifferent. Death is expected at any moment; the grave is open; the dying man's treasures are being divided among his survivors; the professional mourners begin their dirges; the hero's enemies rejoice. Suddenly hope springs up in the midst of distress.[40] The mercy of Marduk is proclaimed, rituals of purification are performed. The hero is healed, and the poem ends with a hymn of praise.[41]

Thus the Babylonian poet, like Job, protests his innocence, describes his piety, charges the deity with indifference, thereby implying a doubt as to divine justice, confesses the general ignorance of man concerning the ways of the godhead, and is filled with deep pessimism concerning human destiny. However, while Job insists on his ethical righteousness, the Babylonian sufferer mentions only his ritual deeds. Since the Akkadian poem was well known before the Babylonian exile,[42] it is possible that the biblical poet was acquainted with it, but no trace of literary dependence can be demonstrated. In any case, the originality of the Joban master cannot successfully be impugned.

Another cuneiform text has largely escaped the attention of the exegetes of Job, although its similarities to the biblical book are most

[31] Ibid., ll. 4-5.
[32] Ibid., ll. 10-11.
[33] Ibid., ll. 12-14.
[34] Ibid., ll. 23-26, 29-33.
[35] The word i-ha-ak-kim is derived from a root cognate of the Hebrew ḥākham, "to be wise."
[36] Ibid., ll. 34-38; cf. Job 9:1-12; 15:8; etc.
[37] Ibid., ll. 39-41.
[38] I.e., "the land of the dead"; ibid., ll. 42-46.
[39] Mention is made of "cleaved bones" and "bowels": cf. 30:17, 27a. At night the "pursuer" does not give the hero any respite: cf. 7:13; 9:18.
[40] Ibid., ll. 52-53.
[41] Tablets II, reverse, III and IV.
[42] Several copies of it were made during the seventh century B.C., and the existence of a philological commentary explaining the archaisms of its language points to its relatively wide circulation. The exact date of its composition is uncertain, but it is considerably older than Job.

striking. It is an Acrostic Dialogue on Theodicy [43] in which a sufferer discusses with his friend the problem of divine justice and the meaning of life. The poem consists of twenty-seven stanzas of eleven lines each, and the initial syllables within each stanza are identical. If they are read vertically, they form a sentence of twenty-seven syllabic signs, meaning "I, [Sha]-ag-gi-il-ki[-i-na-am]-ub-bi-ib,[44] the incantator, worship the god and the king." Thus the poet may have been aware of the boldness of his position, and may have tried to convince his readers of his orthodoxy; or else he may have passed through a skeptical phase, and at last overcome his doubts. Each of the interlocutors speaks alternatively, the sufferer in sts. i, iii, v, etc., and his friend in sts. ii, iv, vi, etc.

The hero asks for a learned companion who would listen to his complaint, for he wants to expose "the grief of his heart" and to receive "consolation." The friend sympathizes:

Dreadful, my friend, is the grief of which thou speakest.
To the beloved of thy heart thou exposest an evil:
Thy proud mind thou hast caused to resemble that of a fool;
Thy bright face thou hast darkened.[45]

But is not the fate of man in general a sad one?

(Men) are begotten, and immediately they walk on the path of death.
"The river *Khubur* thou wilt cross," so (runs) the old saying! [46]

And he implies that prosperity is the lot of the righteous:

Look at all men together, the people of the community (?),
The wealthy one, they praise him and . . . .
He who sees the face of the god is the owner of a threshold demon,
He who fears the goddess anxiously, abundance is heaped up (on him).[47]

To this evocation of the traditional doctrine of individual retribution, the sufferer replies sarcastically:

A well, my friend, such is thy heart which collects all the . . . .
Splendor (?), the mass of the sea which goes (to) thy knowledge (?).
. . . I shall ask thee; understand my speech,
Listen for a while, and hear my words:
Prosperity has ceased, neediness . . . ,
My happiness has passed, . . . has come,
My strength has weakened, . . . has disappeared,
Want and despair have darkened. . . .[48]

The answer of the comforter is poorly preserved, but he recommends prayer to the god, who "will grant pardon." [49] The sufferer replies that he has already practiced all the possible deeds of piety. The friend retorts, like the comforters of Job, by appealing to the observation of nature, "the palm-tree," "the blameless wild-ass," "the star" which becomes dark. Early death is a punishment for sin:

Has the lion committed a crime? The trap for him remains open!
The treasurer, the wealthy one, who has amassed power (?),
In the fire, before his fate comes, Malik will burn him! [50]

And the friend appealingly concludes: "The way which these have traveled dost thou desire to go?" [51] Like Eliphaz, the Babylonian comforter exhorts the sufferer to find reconciliation with his god: "The accomplishment of the god's pleasure seek thou for ever!" [52] The skeptic's reply is touched with irony, and may be likened to that of Job upon a similar occasion:

A north wind is thy answer, a beautiful breeze for men!
Noble and precious is thy . . . advice!
Let me submit [a reply] to thee! [53]

Experience, he avows, contradicts the orthodox theory of a relationship between affliction and crime:

They go the walk of happiness, those who do not seek the god!
They become poor and embittered, those who piously pray to the god[dess]!
. . . In the earliest bud [54] I sought the will of the god,

[43] See translations in: François Martin, *Textes religieux assyriens et babyloniens* (Paris: E. Bouillon, 1903), II, 164 ff.; Erich Ebeling, "Ein babylonischer Kohelet," *Berliner Beiträge zur Keilschriftkunde*, I (1922), 1 ff.; Paul Dhorme, "Ecclésiaste ou Job?" *Revue Biblique*, XXXII (1923), 1-27; Ebeling, "Klage eines Weisen über die Ungerechtigkeit der Welt," in Gressmann, *Altorientalische Texte*, pp. 287-91; also "Bruchstücke von Kommentaren zum 'Babylonischen Kohelet,'" *Aus fünf jahrtausenden morgenländischer Kultur; Festschrift Max freiherrn von Oppenheim* (Berlin: E. F. Weidner, 1933), pp. 27-34; B. Landsberger, "Die babylonische Theodizee," *Zeitschrift für Assyriologie und verwandte Gebiete*, XLIII (1936), 32-76; Robert H. Pfeiffer, "A Dialogue About Human Misery," in Pritchard, *op. cit.*, pp. 438-40.
[44] "O Shagil, declare the righteous pure!"
[45] Ll. 12-15; cf. Job 4:3-5.
[46] Ll. 16-17.
[47] Ll. 18-19, 21-22.
[48] Ll. 23-30.
[49] L. 44.
[50] Ll. 62-64. "Malik" is probably the god Nergal.
[51] L. 65.
[52] L. 66; cf. Job 22:15-16, 23 ff.
[53] Ll. 67-69; cf. Job 12:2 ff.
[54] I.e., "since my childhood."

With prostration and prayer I contemplated the goddess!
A feudal-burden (?) which gives no profit, I draw the yoke (?)!
The god allows me, instead of wealth, poverty!
Even the weak rises against me, the fool affronts me in the face (?)
They have taken away my . . . and I am debased.[55]

Thereupon the interlocutor, like the friends of Job, attacks more directly:

Truly, thou art possessor of intelligence! Thou hast concealed (?) unclean deeds!
Justice and truth thou hast rejected! The command of the god thou hast scorned. . . .[56]

The discussion continues back and forth, and no progress appears to be made until the last preserved stanza, when the sufferer, like Job, humbly implores the understanding of his friend:

Be merciful, my friend! Hear my complaint!
Come to my help, see my torment, and know!
A slave (?) wise and humble I am! . . .
Help and protection, not for one instant, have I experienced! [57]

He alludes to the humiliations which await him on the streets of his city, and in desperation turns to the deities, hostile as these may be:

Help might he give me, the god who rejected me!
Mercy might she grant me, the goddess who . . . .
The Shepherd, the Sun, might rise, like a god, he might . . . .[58]

The next stanza is entirely broken, and the end of the document is unknown. The last expression of hope, dim as it is, suggests that the lamenter, like Job,[59] expected an ultimate vindication.

The fact of similarity in form, theme, and ideas between the Acrostic Dialogue and the biblical poem cannot be denied, and the date of the Akkadian text [60] allows the hypothesis of an influence upon Job.

Another document, A Pessimistic Dialogue Between Master and Servant,[61] needs to be

quoted in part, for although its mood is quite different from either that of the Acrostic Dialogue on Theodicy or that of Job it illustrates the religious skepticism and utter hopelessness which prevailed in some circles of Mesopotamia. The master summons his slave, expresses a desire, and receives the acquiescence of the slave who then praises the course of action contemplated. The master immediately changes his mind, and the slave in truly "servile" manner applies the same earnest spirit in defending with complete cynicism a course opposite to that previously outlined. Social ambition, pleasures of banqueting, traveling and escapism, building houses, political plotting, forgiving of enemies, love of women, banking, and all aspects of human existence are in turn extolled and condemned. Here is a strophe which deals with the futility of religion.

—O slave, hearken unto me!
　—Yes, my lord, yes!
—Hasten, order me water for my hands!
Give it to me, and I will make sacrifice unto my god!
　—Do it, my lord, do it!
　The man who makes sacrifice unto his god,
　Glad is his heart,
　Loan upon loan he makes!
—Nay, O slave, a sacrifice unto my god
I will not make!
　—Do it not, my lord, do it not!
　Wouldst thou teach the god
　To walk after thee like a dog?
　He might require a ritual;
　He might say, Do not inquire [an oracle];
　Or he might demand something else from thee.[62]

Concerning the vanity of benefaction, the slave declares:

Ascend to the ruins of the cities of old,
Behold the skulls of earlier and latter [men]:
Who is now an evil doer? Who is now a benefactor? [63]

As the master finally asks, "Now then what is good?" the slave replies:

　To break my neck and thy neck,
　To fall into the river is good.
　Who is tall enough to climb to heaven?
　Who is broad enough to grasp the earth?

But the master retorts:

　—Nay, O slave, I will slay thee,
　And cause thee to go before me.

Thereupon the cynic has the last word:

—Would my lord live three days after me? [64]

H. Pfeiffer, "A Pessimistic Dialogue Between Master and Servant," in Pritchard, *op cit.*, pp. 437-38.
[62] St. viii (ll. 61-68).
[63] St. x (ll. 82-83).
[64] St. xi (ll. 84-91).

---

[55] Ll. 70-77; like Job, the Babylonian sufferer has to endure the scorn of his fellow men (cf. Job 30:9 ff.).
[56] Ll. 78-79.
[57] Ll. 287-90; cf. Job 19:21.
[58] Ll. 295-97.
[59] See 31:35 ff.; it may be interesting to note that the points of contact which may be found between the Akkadian and the biblical poem concern Job and Eliphaz rather than Bildad and Zophar.
[60] Dhorme (*Le livre de Job*, p. 27) and Landsberger ("Babylonische Theodizee," pp. 35-36) believe that the present MS is a copy of an older document which was probably anterior to the ninth century B.C.
[61] See translations by Ebeling, "Ein pessimistisches Zwiegespräch zwischen einem Herrn und seinem Knecht," in Gressmann, *Altorientalische Texte*, pp. 284-87; Robert

This document in its present state probably dates from the ninth century B.C.

Thus, the dialogue form appears to have been widely used by Mesopotamian wise men, and the biblical poet probably found among the writings of oriental wisdom his model for the exterior structure of his theological meditation and perhaps for some of his ideas.

IV. Composition and Date

Considerable discussion has been given to the way in which the book of Job, with its diverse parts of prose and poetry, came into being and received its final form. Was it written by a single poet, or by a school of wise men, editors, annotators, and copyists? An answer to this question is important for students who wish to place the book of its *Sitz im Leben* ("situation in life"), to learn the date, locale, and purpose of its composition, and thus to obtain some clues to the correct interpretation of its meaning.

Ever since the rise of modern criticism, especially with the study of the Hexateuchal or synoptic sources and the analysis of the prophetic sermons, biblical exegetes have suspected that the various prose and poetic parts of Job did not originate from the same hand.[65] The literary problems raised by Job, however, differ quite markedly from those of the Hexateuch or of the Gospels, for the prologue, epilogue, and poetic discourses are related to a single theme in such a way that none could have existed independently. If the book in its present form were proved to be a compilation, it would be a priori not an artificial collection of hitherto isolated and autonomous units, but an organic whole which grew through a process of internal development by the grafting of additions to a *Grundschrift*. The question must therefore be asked: Is the book a compendium, and if so, what is the fundamental document? In an attempt to discover the answer, the critic must analyze each section separately.

A. Prologue and Epilogue.—The prologue (1:1–2:13) and epilogue (42:7-17) appear to form a literary piece of homogeneous character, for each needs the other if the story is to make any sense at all.[66] To be sure, the account of

Job's restoration may have been expanded by a later hand,[67] under the audience's craving for concrete details of the hero's renewed happiness, but some account of his rehabilitation (42:7-11) was necessary even in the earliest form of the narrative.

Some scholars have cast doubt on the originality of the scenes at the heavenly court (1:6-12; 2:1-7a). They argue that one may easily remove the passages from the context without disrupting the smoothness of the action or obscuring its intelligibility.[68] According to this conjecture, the original narrative implied only that Yahweh himself had stricken the hero (cf. 42:11b), but a later editor refused to admit that God could be the direct author of evil and so introduced the figure of "the Satan" in order to clear the Deity of any immoral responsibility (see a somewhat similar process in II Sam. 24:1; I Chr. 21:1). If such an excision were made, however, the story would lose its *raison d'être*. The point of the whole prose narrative is that Job is not guilty of any offense, and this fact must be unambiguously stated: hence the presence of the scenes at the heavenly court. Moreover, the motif of a wager between Yahweh and a member of the divine assembly has a popular, picturesque, even humorous flavor which suggests a polytheistic background (see p. 879), and is quite incompatible with the monotheistic spirit and the reverent tone of biblical editors generally.

Most critics accept the unity of the prose story, but they are sharply divided on the question of its literary relationship to the poetic discussion.[69] A first group of scholars maintain that the poet himself wrote the prose story as it now exists in the prologue and epilogue, although he may have been inspired by some ancient oral

---

[Philadelphia: Jewish Publication Society of America, 1938], I, 235) doubt the early date of the latter; see also Shalom Spiegel, "Noah, Danel, and Job" in *Louis Ginzberg Jubilee Volume* (New York: American Academy for Jewish Research, 1945), pp. 323-36.

[67] See Exeg. on 42:12-17; cf. Moses Buttenwieser, *The Book of Job* (New York: The Macmillan Co., 1922), pp. 67-69; cf. also L. W. Batten, "The Epilogue to the Book of Job," *Anglican Theological Review*, XV (1933), 125-28; Albrecht Alt, "Zur Vorgeschichte des Buches Hiob," *Zeitschrift für die alttestamentliche Wissenschaft*, LV (1937), 265-68.

[68] See Eduard König, *Einleitung in das Alte Testament* (Bonn: Eduard Weber, 1893), p. 415; Morris Jastrow, Jr., *The Book of Job* (Philadelphia: J. B. Lippincott Co., 1920), pp. 52 ff.; Finkelstein, *op. cit.*, I, 235; Johannes Lindblom, *La composition du livre de Job* (Lund: C. W. K. Gleerup, 1945), pp. 22 ff.; Pfeiffer, *Intro. to O.T.*, p. 669. It may be admitted that the connection of 1:13 with 1:5 is more natural than with 1:12, but a different text is needed in 2:7b in order to make it follow 1:22.

[69] For the history of the various theories proposed up to the twentieth century, see Karl Kautzsch, *Das sogenannte Volksbuch von Hiob* (Tübingen: J. C. B. Mohr, 1900), pp. 3 ff.

---

[65] For the history of literary criticism on Job see Otto Eissfeldt, *Einleitung in das Alte Testament* (Tübingen: J. C. B. Mohr, 1934), pp. 506 ff.; Adolphe Lods, "Recherches récentes sur le livre de Job," *Revue d'Histoire et de Philosophie Religieuses*, XIV (1934), 501-19; Pfeiffer, *Intro. to O.T.*, pp. 667-78.

[66] Nevertheless, some critics consider the prologue and epilogue as two separate pieces; Eduard König (*Das Buch Hiob* [Gütersloh: C. Bertelsmann, 1929], pp. 3-9) rejects the originality of the former, but Kember Fullerton ("The Original Conclusion to the Book of Job," *Zeitschrift für die alttestamentliche Wissenschaft*, XLII [1924], 116-36) and Louis Finkelstein (*The Pharisees*

traditions, possibly of Edomite origin.[70] A second group of critics believe that the prose narrative was added to the poem by some late redactor.[71] A third group of exegetes consider the prologue and epilogue as an ancient *Volksbuch* or folk tale which existed in a written form long before the time of the poet who used it as a framework in order to introduce his theological meditation in dialogue form.[72] A

[70] *Ibid.*, pp. 45-88; article "Job" in T. K. Cheyne and J. Sutherland Black, eds., *Encyclopaedia Biblica* (New York: The Macmillan Co., 1901), II, col. 2469; Johannes Meinhold, *Einführung in das Alte Testament* (Genf: Veranlassung der Kriegsgefangenenhilfe, n.d.), pp. 277-79; Carl Steuernagel, *Lehrbuch der Einleitung in das Alte Testament* (Tübingen: J. C. B. Mohr, 1912), p. 694; Dhorme, *Le livre de Job*, pp. lvii ff.; J. E. McFadyen, *An Introduction to the Old Testament* (2nd ed.; New York: A. C. Armstrong & Son, 1906), pp. 274-77; Eissfeldt, *op. cit.*, pp. 512-13; Gustav Hölscher, *Das Buch Hiob* (Rev. ed.; Tübingen: J. C. B. Mohr, 1952; "Handbuch zum Alten Testament"), pp. 1-5. Buttenwieser (*op. cit.*, pp. 24-26) belongs to this class of critics as far as his view of the prologue is concerned.

[71] This hypothesis was already proposed by Richard Simon in 1685 and defended by Schultens in 1737, Hasse in 1789, de Wette in 1807, J. Louis Bridel in 1818, Knobel in 1842. S. Lee, in 1837, believed that the dialogue had been recorded from oral tradition by Moses, who then added the prologue and epilogue as necessary background to the understanding of the poetic discussion. In recent times the conjecture of the anteriority of the poetic discussion over the prologue and epilogue has been given new attention: see Robert H. Pfeiffer, *Le problème du livre de Job* (Genève: Albert Kundig, 1915) and *Intro. to O.T.*, pp. 669-70; Kraeling (with serious qualifications), *Book of the Ways of God*, pp. 179-93; B. D. Eerdmans, *Studies in Job* (Leiden: Burgersdijk & Niermans, 1939), pp. 17-20; W. B. Stevenson, *The Poem of Job* (London: British Academy, 1947), pp. 73 ff.

[72] Julius Wellhausen (in a review of August Dillmann, *Das Buch Hiob*), *Jahrbücher für deutsche Theologie*, XVI (1871), pp. 555-58; Karl Budde, *Beiträge zur Kritik des Buches Hiob* (Bonn: A. Marcus, 1876), pp. 29-62, and *Das Buch Hiob* (2nd ed.; Göttingen: Vandenhoeck & Ruprecht, 1913; "Handkommentar zum Alten Testament"), pp. xiii-xxxix; Maurice Vernes, "Bulletin critique de la religion juive," *Revue de l'Histoire des Religions*, I (1880), 232-33; T. K. Cheyne, *Job and Solomon* (London: Kegan Paul, Trench & Co., 1887), pp. 66-70; Gustav Bickell, *Das Buch Job* (Wien: Carl Gerold's Sohn, 1894), pp. 7-8; Bernhard Duhm, *Das Buch Hiob* (Freiburg i. B.: J. C. B. Mohr, 1897; "Kurzer Hand-Commentar zum Alten Testament"), pp. vii-xiii; Ludwig Laue, *Die Composition des Buches Hiob* (Halle: J. Krause, 1896), pp. 1-7, 118-43; D. B. Macdonald, "The Original Form of the Legend of Job," *Journal of Biblical Literature*, XIV (1895), 63-71, and "Some External Evidence on the Original Form of the Legend of Job," *American Journal of Semitic Languages and Literatures*, XIV (1898), 137-64; Lucien Gautier, *Introduction à l'Ancien Testament* (2nd ed.; Paris: Librairie Fischbacher, 1914), II, 98-99; Volz, *Hiob und Weisheit*, p. 16; Adolphe Lods, "Recherches récentes," pp. 508-13, and *Histoire de la littérature hébraïque*, pp. 673 ff.; Lindblom, *op. cit.*, pp. 30 ff.; W. O. E. Oesterley and T. H. Robinson, *An Introduction to the Books of the Old Testament* (New York: The Macmillan Co., 1934), pp. 171-74; also, accepting this view provisionally and with qualifications, S. R. Driver and G. B. Gray, *A Critical and Exegetical Commentary on the Book of Job* (New York: Charles Scribner's Sons, 1921; "International Critical Commentary"), I, xxxiv ff.

great many variations to these three theories have also been proposed, and it may safely be maintained that almost all possible solutions have been examined, a fact which should make the literary problem one of the most vexing questions in biblical criticism.

(1) Some of the evidences of discrepancy between the prose narrative and the poem are not conclusive:

(*a*) In the prologue and epilogue, as well as in the prose verses introducing the poetic discourses of the Lord and the response of Job (39:1; 40:1, 3, 6; 42:1), the narrator uses the name of Yahweh for designating the Deity. There is nothing surprising in this fact, since he is writing obviously as a Hebrew author for a Hebrew circle of hearers and readers. In the poetic discussion, the hero and his three friends always speak of God—as foreigners should—by using nonnational designations such as El, Eloah, Shaddai, Elohim, but never Yahweh.[73] In the prologue, on the contrary, Job utters three times the sacred name (1:21). To many commentators this peculiarity reveals the existence of two different authors: the prose narrator, unlike the poet, was not moved by any theological scruple, or else he was careless of local color, or else again he lived at a very early time when the name Yahweh was not considered to be the exclusive property of the covenant people; but the poet, on his part, knew very well that Job and his friends—foreigners, and Edomites at that—could not utter the sacred tetragrammaton. This argument, however, may lose its importance if one conjectures that the only formula of blessing known to the writer was a Yahwistic one and observes that, even in the prologue, "the Satan," Job's wife, and Job himself—outside of the formula of blessing (1:21) — use the non-Hebraic name Elohim (1:5, 9; 2:9, 10).

(*b*) In the prologue and epilogue Job appears to be a nomad, for he is the owner of considerably large herds and flocks (1:3) spread over a vast area (1:13-17); whereas in the poetic discussion the hero, although a possessor of ewes (31:20, 31), is a tiller of the soil (31:8, 12, 24, 34, 38-40) and is respected by the elders of a city (29:7) where he appears to dwell (19:15). Thus, it is suggested, the point of view of the narrator is not the same as that of the poet.

According to Artur Weiser, the poet is the creator of the narrative, although he adapted it for his own purposes: *Einleitung in das Alte Testament* (2nd ed.; Göttingen: Vandenhoeck & Ruprecht, 1949), p. 214, and *Das Buch Hiob* (Göttingen: Vandenhoeck & Ruprecht, 1951), p. 7.

[73] One verse of the poetic discussion (12:9) appears at first sight to constitute an exception, but most critics agree on other grounds in considering this text as a part of some editorial addition (see Exeg., *ad loc.*).

This second argument, however, like the first, loses its strength when one observes that even in the prologue and epilogue Job (42:11) and his sons (1:4) live in houses, while in the poem he happens to refer to his tent (31:31)! In all probability the hero is pictured quite consistently throughout the book as a seminomad of Edom, living in a walled city during the winter season and migrating with his herds during the long months of spring, summer, and autumn.[74]

(c) In the prologue and epilogue Job has lost all his children (1:19), but in the poem, according to some commentators, he still has sons (19:17). However, the expression "sons of my womb" means most probably "uterine brothers" (see Exeg., ad loc.); moreover, in the poem itself Bildad alludes to the death of the hero's sons (8:4). This third argument, therefore, seems devoid of weight.

(d) In the prologue the suffering of Job is explained as the result of a trial (1:6-12; 2:1-7a), but in the poem not a single allusion is made to this explanation, even in a hypothetical way. Is it conceivable that the poet, if he were also responsible for the prologue, would fail to introduce some reference to the testing? But this matter also is open to question. For neither Job nor his friends know the story of the wager between Yahweh and "the Satan"; so the poet, utterly respectful of the human limitations of his characters, could not bring such a theme into their minds without committing a gross error in psychology. Thus the impact of the fourth argument is considerably weakened, or at any rate made inconclusive.

(2) There are nonetheless other considerations which strongly suggest a composite authorship:

(a) In the prologue and epilogue sacrifices— specifically burnt offerings—play an important part in the hero's piety and in that of the three friends, as they did in all ancient Semitic religions (1:5; 42:8-9). It is obvious that the narrator unqualifiedly approves sacrificial worship, even when it is performed by foreigners. In the poem, on the contrary, sacrifices are conspicuously absent. To be sure, this is an argument e silentio, but it cannot be dismissed easily, for it would be strange indeed, if the poet were also the writer of the narrative, that neither the friends in their admonitions nor the hero in his defense should mention this elementary mode of approach to the Deity.

(b) In the prologue and epilogue Job is innocent of all possible crimes, explicit and implicit, personal and domestic, ethical and

religious. He has the complete approval of God, not only before and during his trial (1:8; 2:3), but also afterward (42:7b, 8c, 10). The narrator presents his hero as the supreme model of faith (1:21, 22; 2:10). The poet, on the contrary, daringly portrays a blasphemer, a doubter, a frenzied rebel, a proud giant, a challenger of God, who in the end must cast himself down in utter humiliation and repent in dust and ashes (42:6).

(c) In the epilogue the narrator's judgment is extremely and unexpectedly severe upon the friends (42:7-10), whereas in the discussion the poet displays toward them an attitude of objective fairness, and certainly does not place in their mouths any statement which justifies the divine wrath of the epilogue.

(d) More striking still is the fact that the atmosphere of the prologue and epilogue is that of a legendary idyl. Job is "the greatest of all the Orientals" (1:3b) and his wealth (1:3a; 42:12) as well as his old age and patriarchal death (42:16, 17), even the status of his daughters (1:4; 42:15b) and their beauty (42:15a) are truly fabulous. Furthermore, the dramatic description of the disasters, with the repeated motif, "And I alone have escaped to tell thee. While he was yet speaking . . ." (1:15b-16a, 16c-17a, 17c-18a), suggests a stylized element, a typical trait of the ancient folk tales. On the contrary, every aspect of the discussion is true to life in the raw, realistically told and realistically appraised. The impression of two literary hands —indeed, two literary worlds—imposes itself upon the reader. The prose narrative suggests to our imagination the haunting strains of a nursery tale, with its villain and its happy ending, whereas the poetic discussion has the ring of grim history.

(e) In the prologue and epilogue the narrator shows exceptionally polished craftsmanship and psychological penetration. He succeeds in creating sympathy for his hero while he as author remains the observer. On the contrary, in the discussion between Job and the friends, the poet is the hero, and yet is also able to portray the friends or to spell out "the voice from the whirlwind" with the creative imagination of an extraordinarily versatile and sensitive thinker. The narrator is a literary master; but the poet is greater still, for when he lends his words to Job even the casual student cannot but sense the voice of introspective authenticity. Both the narrator and the poet are consummate artists, but the former writes about somebody else while the latter writes about himself. The narrator is heir to centuries of storytelling at night before the campfire, and his literary personality was probably not that of an individual

---

[74] Alois Musil has even located an Edomite locality called Chirbet el 'Is, which may be the ancient Uz (Arabia Petraea [Vienna: Alfred Hölder, 1908], II, 337 and 339, note d).

but rather that of a sociological entity—the folk creativity of the ages. The poet on the contrary is a man who has suffered the pangs and throes which he transmutes into verse. When he ascribes to Job laments, soliloquies, prayers, vituperations, protests, invectives, and sheer shouts of pain, the blood of his own heart is spilled before our very eyes, and his agony is laid so starkly bare that we almost avert our gaze. The narrator moves us, but the poet probes us. The former evokes, but the latter embarrasses; the former thrills, but the latter compels with the grip of existential communication.

In view of the above discussion we shall maintain that the prose narrative and the poem originated from two different men, and the first theory (see p. 884) is hereby rejected. But a question remains: Did the poem exist independently of the prose story (second theory), or did the poet borrow the narrative and adapt it as a framework for his poetic discussion (third theory)? An incontrovertible demonstration of either view appears to be impossible on the basis of the present evidence. However, the following points may be entered on the record.

(a) It is not probable that the poet began his work *in medias res* with the sentence, "And Job opened his mouth and cursed his day" (3:1). The so-called parallels from the book of Ruth or the Gospel of Mark [75] are not relevant, for the action in these writings does not presuppose any previous information, whereas the soliloquy of Job is unintelligible without a preface. It requires a plot, a situation, a story. Of course the poet may have assumed that everybody knew that story, just as the prophet Ezekiel alluded to Job together with Daniel and Noah (Ezek. 14:14, 20) without taking time to be specific about them. But if that was the case, the Joban narrative must have existed already in such a fixed form—albeit oral—that the poet took it for granted as common literary property. Then the question whether it was the poet or one of his admirers and disciples who committed the narrative to manuscript form is of secondary and almost immaterial importance.

(b) A linguistic comparison of the prose narrative with the poetic discussion reveals an astounding number of affinities [76] between these two sections of the book:

(i) The word תם, "perfect" (outside of Job only in Gen. 25:27; Ps. 64:5; Prov. 29:10): 1:1; cf. 8:20; 9:20-22.

(ii) The word תמה, "perfection" (outside of Job only in Prov. 11:3): 1:3, 9; cf. 27:5; 31:16.

(iii) The adverb חנם, "for nought": 1:9; 2:3; cf. 9:17; 22:6.

(iv) The expression ואולם, "and yet" (only nine times outside of Job): 1:11; cf. 11:5; 12:7; 13:4; 14:8. Likewise, אולם, "yet": 2:5; cf. 5:8; 13:3.

(v) The verb נגע, "to strike," constructed with the preposition ב: 1:11, 19; cf. 5:19; 19:21.

(vi) The expression על-פני or אל-פני, "to the face of": 1:11; 2:5; cf. 6:28; 13:15; 21:31.

(vii) The use of both genders in the same sentence for the masculine or feminine noun רוח, "wind," "spirit": 1:19; cf. 4:15.

(viii) The expression, יצא מבטן, "to come out of the womb": 1:21; cf. 3:11; 38:29.

(ix) The verb חזק in the Hiphil with the preposition ב, "to hold fast": 2:3, 9; cf. 8:15, 20; 27:6.

(x) The verb בלע in the Piel, "to destroy," "to ruin": 2:3; cf. 8:18; 10:8.

(xi) The noun רעים, "friends": 2:11; 42:7; cf. 19:21.

(xii) The noun כאב, "grief," "sorrow": 2:13; cf. 16:6.

(xiii) The noun ידעים, "acquaintances": 42: 11; cf. 19:13.

(xiv) The expression ראשית, . . . אחרית, "beginning" and "latter end": 42:12; cf. 8:7.

No decisive argument should be drawn from the fact of these affinities, however, because an equally great number of dissimilarities between the vocabulary and grammar of the narrative and those of the poem can easily be noted. E.g., the prologue favors the expression שים לב על, "to consider" (1:8), whereas the poem prefers שית לב אל (7:17); the prologue understands the idiomatic expression מעשה ידים as "the work which man's hands undertake" (1:10) whereas the poem takes it to mean "the completed work of God's hands" (14:15). Moreover, while the poem presents the most peculiar language of the Old Testament, being filled with words of Aramaic, Arabic, Akkadian, and even Egyptian origin, the narrative is written in pure, classical Hebrew,[77] in spite of the presence of one word (קבל in the Piel, "to receive"; 2:10) which has cognates in Arabic and Aramaic but is not necessarily a sign of decadence. The linguistic affinities between the narrative and the poem probably suggest that the poet was intimately acquainted with the prose story and has erected his poetic monument upon its foundation.

(c) The date of the prose narrative cannot be ascertained with scientific rigor, for objective criteria offer conflicting evidence. Many

---

[75] "Now it came to pass in the days when the judges ruled . . ." (Ruth 1:1); "As it is written in the prophets . . ." (Mark 1:2).

[76] Cf. Kautzsch, *Das sogenannte Volksbuch von Hiob*, pp. 24 ff., 40 ff.; Dhorme, *Le livre de Job*, pp. lxv ff.

[77] "The prose narrative is written in a clean and elegant Hebrew while the tongue of the poem is permeated with Aramaisms" (Friedrich Delitzsch, *Das Buch Hiob* [Leipzig: J. C. Hinrichs, 1902], p. 13, n. 1). See p. 72.

critics propose the end of the sixth century B.C., because the name "Satan" appears with the definite article (השטן) exactly as in the book of Zechariah (3:1 ff.). Several considerations render this date improbable, if not impossible:

(i) The scenes at the heavenly court have nothing in common with those of the high priest's trial in Zechariah; on the contrary they are closely akin to the ninth-century vision of Micaiah ben Imlah (I Kings 22:19-23; cf. Exeg. on Job 1:6-8).

(ii) The language and style of the prose story are similar to those of the patriarchal traditions which were gathered by the Yahwist in the tenth or ninth century and to the ninth- or eighth-century narratives now preserved in the books of Samuel and Kings. See among many others the expression איש היה, "there was a man" (1:1; cf. II Sam. 12:1); ויהי היום "and there was a day" (1:13; 2:1; cf. I Sam. 1:4; 14:1).

(iii) A story which presents an Edomite sheik as a hero of faith, uniquely approved by Yahweh, can hardly have been written or orally adapted in Hebrew during the sixth century or later, at a time when the attitude of the Judaeans—and afterward the Jews—against the Edomites was one of hostility bordering on fanatic hatred (see Pss. 83:4-6; 137:7; Isa. 34:5-6; Jer. 49:7-22; Lam. 4:21; Ezek. 25:12-14; 35:2; Obad. 10-14). The mere fact of the Edomitic origin of Job almost requires the conclusion that the story was "Hebraicized" long before the end of the seventh century B.C.[78]

Thus the date of the narrative must be at least pre-exilic, and perhaps as early as the ninth or eighth century B.C.

On account of all these considerations, one is inclined to propose that the poet—who did not live before the sixth century B.C. (see below) — borrowed for a preface a tale which had existed in a fixed literary form, oral or written, for several generations. The consequence of this view is important: the theological message of the poet is free from the implications of the tale, such as divine pride in a man's integrity or the idea of a God who allows human suffering for the purpose of winning a heavenly wager; and more particularly, it does not make the poet responsible for the fabulous ending with its double portion of sheep, camels, oxen, and she-asses.

B. Poetic Discussion.—The dialogue between Job and his three friends seems to be a homogeneous composition. Critics, however, have questioned the authenticity of some sections of the third cycle (chs. 24–27) and the hymn on wisdom (ch. 28).

The third cycle differs from the first two because in it (a) Job appears at times to defend the point of view of his friends (24:18-24; 26:5-14; 27:13-23); (b) the discourse of Bildad is unusually short (25:1-6); and (c) the expected discourse of Zophar is absent. In order to account for these peculiarities commentators have proposed many different rearrangements or excisions.[79] In all probability a late editor has attempted to tone down Job's heretical statements by attributing to him sections which were lifted out of the third discourse of Bildad (26:5-14) and of Zophar (24:18-24; 27:13-23), and by censoring Job's reply to Zophar. Any restoration of the original text remains conjectural, but the following is the most simple and probable:

> Eliphaz: 22:1-30
> Job: 23:1–24:17, 25
> Bildad: 25:1-6; 26:5-14
> Job: 26:1-4; 27:1-12
> Zophar: 24:18-24; 27:13-23
> Job: [?]

Thus restored, each discourse yields excellent sense, fits the positions of the respective speakers, and presents satisfactory sequences of ideas. For instance, the third discourse of Bildad deals with the heavenly beings (25:2-3), man (25:4-6), and the shades in the underworld (27:5-6). Likewise, Job's invective (26:2-4) leads normally to his protest (27:2 ff.), and Zophar's description of the wicked (24:18-24) is naturally followed by a picture of the fate awaiting the oppressors' offspring (27:14 ff.), with a pivotal line between the two developments (27:13; see Exeg., ad loc.).

The hymn on wisdom (ch. 28) raises a problem of its own. Since it undoubtedly interrupts Job's soliloquy and contains a concept of wisdom which is neither that of Job nor that of his friends (see Exeg., ad loc.), many critics regard it as an editorial addition.[80] Yet the language and style show close affinities with those of the discourses of Yahweh (see Exeg., ad loc.). The hymn may therefore be a product of the same poetic hand and may have been preserved at this place by a member of the Joban school.

The date of the poem can be determined with some degree of accuracy as that of the

---

[78] Such details as the mention of the Chaldeans as nomads (1:17), or the use of the "kesitah" (42:11), a piece of uncoined money of the patriarchal period (cf. Exeg., ad loc.), do not necessarily indicate an early date but may reflect the writer's "archaeological" intent.

[79] See detailed lists in A. Regnier, "La distribution des chapitres 25-28 du livre de Job," *Revue Biblique*, XXXIII (1924), 186-200; Pfeiffer, *Intro. to O.T.*, pp. 671-72; cf. G. A. Barton, "The Composition of Job 24–30," *Journal of Biblical Literature*, XXX (1911), 66-77.

[80] Driver and Gray, *op. cit.*, I, xxxviii; Eissfeldt, *Einleitung in das A.T.*, p. 508; Lods, *Histoire de la littérature hébraïque*, p. 680; Pfeiffer, *Intro. to O.T.*, p. 672; et al.

first part of the sixth century B.C. A *terminus a quo* is provided by the facts that Job's soliloquy (3:3-26) has been inspired by one of the confessions of Jeremiah (20:14-18), and that the Joban meditation upon the prosperity of the wicked (21:7 ff.) is an elaboration of that same prophet's anxious query (Jer. 12:1-3).

There is ample evidence, for example, to prove that Job's soliloquy is a literary amplification of Jeremiah's cry of distress: [81]

(*a*) Jeremiah's tone and form are spontaneous, harsh, and violent; those of Job are solemn and sophisticated: his emotion is recollected in serene creativity.

(*b*) The relative particle אשר, "in which," is twice used by the prophet (Jer. 20:14*ab*) and omitted by the poet (Job 3:3): an addition by the former would be pointless, but an omission by the latter indicates poetic flair.

(*c*) The Pual perfect ילדתי, "I was brought forth" (Jer. 20:14*a*), suggests colloquial abruptness, but the Niphal imperfect אולד, "I was born," implies reflection on time (cf. Greek aorist).

(*d*) To the curse of the day of birth (Jer. 20:14) the poet adds a malediction of the conception night (Job 3:3*b*).

(*e*) For the man announcing the news (Jer. 20:15) the poet substitutes the personification of night (Job 3:3*b*).

(*f*) The prophet's awkward mention of בן זכר, "a male son" (Jer. 20:15), becomes גבר, "a he-man" (Job 3:3*b*), although the child is only conceived.

(*g*) The poet develops the curses with mythological allusions (Job 3:4-10) and then returns to the prophet's anxious "Why?" (Jer. 20:18) which he amplifies in a threefold way (Job 3:11, 12, 16).

On the matter of a *terminus ad quem*, scholars are widely divided,[82] but a careful comparison between the Joban poem and Second Isaiah definitely indicates the anteriority of the former over the latter. As Pfeiffer has shown,[83] there are between the two books numerous parallels of thought and even points of verbal contact. For instance, one may note in both pieces the use of rare words, like רק, "spittle" (7:19; 30:10; cf. Isa. 50:6); עכביש, "spider" (8:14; cf. Isa. 59:5); חוג, "vault" (22:14; cf. Isa. 40:22); צאצאים, "offspring" (5:25; 21:8; 27:14; cf. Isa. 44:3; 48:19). Significantly, many of these common expressions or idioms occur in theological contexts, where both poets depict the transcendence of God or the ephemerality and finiteness of man:

(*a*) God is "mighty in strength" (9:4*a*; cf. Isa. 40:26). "Who can hinder him?" (11:10*b*; cf. Isa. 43:13.) "Who will say to him, 'What doest thou?'" (9:12*b*; cf. Isa. 45:9*b*.) God "alone stretched out the heavens" (9:8*a*; cf. Isa. 44:24*d*). "By his understanding [תבונה; cf. Isa. 40:28*e*] he smote Rahab" (26:12*b*; cf. Isa. 51:9*e*) and "he stirred up the sea" (26:12*a*; cf. Isa. 51:15). "Will any teach God knowledge?" (21:22*a*; cf. Isa. 40:14*c*.) Divine thoughts are beyond man's reach (11:7; cf. Isa. 40:28*e*; cf. also Job 5:9; etc.). God is truly *Deus Absconditus* (9:11; 23:8-9; cf. Isa. 45:15). In none of these passages, examined in their respective contexts, is it possible to maintain that Job is dependent upon Second Isaiah. If he had been, he could not have afforded to omit the motif of creation by fiat which is one of the trade-marks of the prophet, or to ignore for example the word ברא, "to create" (Isa. 42:5; etc.).

(*b*) Man is "made" by God's "hands" out of "clay" (10:8-9; cf. Isa. 45:9); he is "fashioned . . . in the womb" (31:15; cf. Isa. 44:24*b*); he receives his "breath" from his maker (12:10; cf. Isa. 42:5*d*). Yet his life "withers" like a flower or like grass (14:1-2; cf. Isa. 40:27*c*). God "frustrates" (מפר) "the devices of the crafty" (5:12*a*) and "the omens of the liars" (Isa. 44:25*a*); he "makes fools" (יהולל) of judges (12:17*b*) and diviners (Isa. 44:25*b*); he is the absolute master of "the nations" (12:23; cf. Isa. 40:15, 17). Man's life is comparable to a "military service" (7:1*a*; 14:14*b*; cf. Isa. 40:2), "a worm" or "a maggot" (25:6; cf. Isa. 41:14 [LXX]), "a moth-eaten garment" (13:28*b*; cf. Isa. 51:8*a*). His "way is hid" (3:23*a*; cf. Isa. 40:27*c*).

(*c*) More particularly, it will be observed that the figure of the servant in Second Isaiah is described in a way which is strongly reminiscent of Job and shows that Job is not the borrower. Several words and expressions are identical in both poems, but Job uses them in concrete, personal clauses, with a preference for active verbal forms which claim chronological priority over "stative," fresco-like propositions, couched in passive participial forms, and characteristic of the servant songs. Job declares, "The hand of God has struck me" (19:21*b*), but Second Isaiah says that the servant was "stricken of God" (Isa. 53:4*c*). One complains that "men . . . smote [him] upon the cheek" (16:10*b*),

---

[81] Cf. Budde, *Hiob*, ad loc.; Duhm, *Hiob*, ad loc.; Dhorme, *Le livre de Job*, pp. cxxvi ff.; *et al.*

[82] See Driver and Gray, *op. cit.*, I, lxv ff.; Pfeiffer, *Intro. to O.T.*, pp. 675-78; *et al.*

[83] In "The Dual Origin of Hebrew Monotheism," *Journal of Biblical Literature*, XLVI (1927), 193-206; see also T. K. Cheyne, *The Prophecies of Isaiah* (New York: Thomas Whittaker, 1888), II, 259-68, and *Job and Solomon*, p. 84; August Dillmann, *Hiob* (4th ed.; Leipzig: S. Hirzel, 1891), pp. xxxiii-xxxiv. The many points of contact between the poet and the Psalms and parts of Proverbs (cf. especially Job's parody of Ps. 8 in 7:17-18) cannot help to determine the date of Job since those psalms and proverbs which influenced the poet are themselves of highly uncertain date.

but the other states that the servant was "smitten" (Isa. 53:4d). One says, "My kinsfolk have failed" (חדלו; 19:14a) while the other writes that the servant was "rejected of men" (חדל אישים; Isa. 53:3a). One exclaims, "Even young children despise me" (מאסו בי; 19:18a), while of the servant the other merely says, "He was despised" (נבזה; Isa. 53:3a). One asks, "Is there wrong on my tongue?" (6:30a), or protests, "Although there is no violence [חמס] in my hands" (16:17a), and the other echoes in two consecutive lines, "Although he had done no violence [חמס], and there was no deceit in his mouth" (Isa. 53:9cd; cf. Job 31:5b). If the poet of Job had known Second Isaiah and borrowed these expressions from the servant songs, why should he have scattered them in widely different contexts? Finally, the Joban poet has tried again and again to explain the cause of human suffering. He has investigated all possible theories. But he has never heard of the theme of vicarious suffering. He does not allude to it; he does not polemize against it; he ignores it completely. All the above considerations converge toward the same conclusion: he does not know Second Isaiah.

The poet of Job may thus be pictured as a man who lived probably between 580 and 540 B.C. He was acquainted with the international circle of the wise; had traveled widely in Arabia, Mesopotamia, Egypt, and of course the Fertile Crescent; forged for himself an elegant poetic idiom,[84] and was deeply impressed, not only by his personal experience of sorrow, but also by the profound social and political disturbances of the ancient Near East at the beginning of the Neo-Babylonian empire.[85] His outlook was thoroughly Hebraic, although he was completely detached from love of promised land, covenant law, temple, or Davidic royal family.[86]

C. Discourses of Elihu.—The genuineness of Elihu's speeches (32:1–37:24) has been questioned for a long time;[87] and although some serious defense of their authenticity has been mustered,[88] most contemporary critics regard

them as the addition of an early reader or scribe who intended to correct the hero's statements, chasten the friends for their failure to silence Job (see 32:11-16), and perhaps in a veiled way improve upon the discourses of Yahweh (see 36:2 ff., 37:1 ff.). The main arguments may be summed up as follows:

(a) The character of the speaker is not mentioned outside of chs. 32–37, a fact especially significant in the epilogue where Yahweh pronounces his verdict upon the three friends (42:7 ff.).

(b) The introduction of Elihu is couched in a ponderous, redundant, and obviously scribal style (32:1-6).

(c) The challenge of Job at the end of his fiery oath of clearance (31:35-37) calls not for any Elihu, but for an immediate answer of the voice from the whirlwind (38:1 ff.)

(d) Elihu quotes Job verbatim (cf. 33:8-11 with 13:24, 27; 34:5-9 with 27:3; 35:3 with 7:20; etc.) and addresses him by name (32:12; 33:1, 31; 34:5, 7, 35, 36; 35:16; 37:14), whereas the poet never elsewhere used this method in the poetic discussion. The manner of Elihu gives the impression of academic and even scholastic argumentation. The author of these speeches seems to have studied the poem in a manuscript form.

(e) The language strangely reveals Aramaic influence (see, among others, the Aramaic רעע, "to break" [34:24], for the Hebrew רצץ; the Aramaic מעבד, "deed" [34:25], for the Hebrew מעשה; the wholly Aramaic sentence, כתר-לי זעיר ואחוך, "Bear with me a little, and I will show you" [36:2a]; the Aramaic פעל, "to do" [36:3], for the Hebrew עשה; the Aramaic למכביר, "in abundance" [36:31], for the Hebrew לרב; probably also the Aramaic words על-עולה, "tempest" [36:33]; הוא, "to fall" [37:6]; מפלאות, "wondrous works" [37:16]; בהיר, "bright" [37:21]), the use of late Hebrew terms or expressions (e.g., the first person pronoun אנכי rather than אני, except in 33:31 [which quotes 31:3a] and in 33:9b [for the sake of parallelism], and several words or verbal forms which are not found in the poetic discussion (e.g., דע, "knowledge" [32:6, 10, 17; 36:3; 37:16], instead of דעת [cf. 13:2; etc.]; יחל in the Hiphil, "to wait for" [32:11, 16], instead of the Piel [cf. 6:11; etc.]; צדק in the Piel, "to justify" [33:32], instead of the Hiphil [cf. 27:5]; אנשי, "the men of . . ." [34:8, 10, 34, 36], instead of מתי [cf. 11:11; 19:19; etc.]; the unusual חף

[84] See pp. 892-93.

[85] See article "The Old Testament World," Vol. I, pp. 267-68. The poet had heard of or witnessed mass deportations and ruthless oppression (cf. 12:17-19); he may have also observed, like the aged Jeremiah (44:15-19), the attractiveness of moon worship (Job 31:26-28).

[86] See p. 898.

[87] M. H. Stuhlmann (1804), W. De Wette (1817), J. C. Eichhorn (1824), *et al.* up to the present time; cf. W. A. Irwin, "The Elihu Speeches in the Criticism of the Book of Job," *Journal of Religion*, XVII (1937), 37-47.

[88] E. F. Rosenmüller (1824), F. W. Umbreit (1832), J. G. Stickel (1842); more thoroughly, Karl Budde, *Beiträge zur Kritik des Buches Hiob*, pp. 65-80; C. H. Cornill, *Introduction to the Canonical Books of the Old Testament*, tr. G. H. Box (London: Williams & Norgate, 1907), pp. 425-31; Gerrit Wildeboer, *Die Literatur des Alten Testaments* (Göttingen: Vandenhoeck & Ruprecht,

1895); Wenzel Posselt, *Der Verfasser der Eliu-reden* (Freiburg i. B.: Herder, 1909; "Biblische Studien"); Martin Thilo, *Das Buch Hiob* (Bonn: A. Marcus & E. Webers, 1925), pp. 135-38. Paul Szczygiel, *Das Buch Hiob* (Bonn: Peter Hanstein, 1931; "Die Heilige Schrift des Alten Testaments"), p. 22; Louis Dennefeld, "Les discours d'Élihou," *Revue Biblique*, XLVIII (1939), 163-80.

"pure" [33:9], instead of the common בר [cf. 11:4]; etc.).[89]

It would be an error to underestimate the value and sometimes the beauty and even the brilliance of this later contribution. Although the author of Elihu is distinctly a lesser poet than the master who penned the poetic discussion, he offers significant views on the educational purpose of suffering (36:7*b*-11) ; he insists on the love of God (37:13*b*, provided the text is correctly preserved) ; more especially, he presents the startling idea of the angel mediator (33:23-25), and develops explicitly the poet's implicit grasp of the mystery of salvation by faith (33:26-28; cf. Exeg. *ad loc.*) .

D. Discourses of Yahweh.—A number of critics reject the discourses of Yahweh (38:1–42:6) in part or *in toto*.[90] These scholars argue that nothing in these chapters applies directly to Job or to the discussion of innocent suffering, which is supposedly the theme of the dialogue. They point out also that the three friends and Job himself have already acknowledged the omnipotence of the divine ruler of the universe, and that the purpose of the insertion is to demonstrate Job's folly and to show his unconditional submission to the Almighty. A clumsy editor thought that Job's rebelliousness required explicit condemnation and undertook a major grafting without realizing that the intrusion of the hero's repentance (42:1-6) contradicted Yahweh's verdict of approval in the epilogue (42:7-10) .

The vast majority of critics, however, while admitting that some developments may well represent later amplifications or interpolations,[91] recognize that these chapters on the whole constitute an indispensable part—indeed, the crowning element—of the original poem.[92] The arguments may be summarized as follows:

(*a*) It is not correct to assert that the discourses of Yahweh condemn purely and simply the attitude of Job and thereby nullify what the poet has accomplished in the dialogue. While it is true that the poet himself is his own hero and paints in Job his own experience of the depths of despair and of the heights of rebellion, he does not imply anywhere in the dialogue that he endorses the innocence of that hero. Nor is it correct to maintain that the author of Yahweh's speeches either condemns the hero's ethical behavior or proclaims the dogma of individual retribution. In effect, the dialogue portrays a man who speaks without knowledge, and the purpose of the divine discourses is to reveal to him this truth. The speeches of Yahweh do not contradict the purpose of the dialogue: they introduce a new dimension by raising the issue at stake from the finite level of man to the infinite level of God.[93]

(*b*) It is hardly conceivable that a man of the poet's magnitude would leave his work in suspense with Job's protest of innocence. The hero has most solemnly called for God's intervention (31:35-37) . To be sure, he has asked for it only for the purpose of obtaining his own vindication (9:2, 3, 14-16, 17, 20, 29-31; 10:6, 7; 13:15-21) : he craved to meet God, but on his own terms since he planned to greet him as a prince welcomes an equal (31:37) ! On the contrary, when Yahweh speaks out of the whirlwind, not a word of vindication is uttered, and the noble sheik prostrates himself in the dust (42:6) . The difference of attitudes between Job's demanding the divine intervention and his receiving it may suggest a logical contradiction, but certainly not a rhetorical, psychological, or theological discrepancy. To reject the genuineness of 38:1–42:6 on the basis of ideological analysis betrays incomprehension of the poet's purpose and religion.

(*c*) From the points of view of language and style, the discourses of Yahweh reveal the closest affinities with the dialogue and represent at least the same degree of virtuosity and brilliance. Who would seriously believe that a postexilic scribe could imitate and at times surpass the poetic genius who brought forth the dialogue?

In conclusion, let it be recognized that the book of Job, like most other writings of the Bible, does not have a strictly individual authorship. The ancient Edomitic folk tale of the suffering servant of God captured the imagination and the inspiration of a poet who asked,

[89] Cf. statistics of prepositions and other grammatical characteristics in Driver and Gray, *Job*, I, xlii ff.; also Dhorme, *Le livre de Job*, pp. lxxxi ff.

[90] Vernes, "Bulletin critique de la religion juive," p. 232; G. L. Studer, *Das Buch Hiob* (Bremen: M. Heinsius, 1881), pp. 137-44; Cheyne, *Job and Solomon*, pp. 66-70; A. van Hoonacker, "Une question touchant la composition du livre de Job," *Revue Biblique*, XII (1903), 161-89; Volz, *Hiob und Weisheit*, pp. 84-87; Bertie, *Le poème de Job*, pp. 48-54; Johannes Hempel, *Die althebräische Literatur* (Potsdam: Akademische Verlagsgesellschaft Athenaion, 1930), p. 179; Friedrich Baumgärtel, *Der Hiobdialog* (Stuttgart: W. Kohlhammer, 1933), p. 1; Kraeling, *Book of the Ways of God*, pp. 143-63; W. A. Irwin, "Job and Prometheus," *Journal of Religion*, XXX (1950), 94; see also article "The Wisdom Literature," Vol. I, pp. 216-17. Other scholars accept the originality of a few lines; e.g., Eissfeldt (*Einleitung in das A.T.*, p. 514) admits the authenticity of 40:6-14; 42:1-6.

[91] E.g., the poem on the ostrich (39:13-18) and parts of the development on Leviathan (41:12-34); see Exeg. *ad loc.*

[92] Cf. Dhorme, *Le livre de Job*, pp. lxxi ff.; Lods, "Recherches récentes," p. 515; *Histoire de la littérature hébraïque*, pp. 677 ff.; Pfeiffer, *Intro. to O.T.*, pp. 674-75;

Weiser, *Einleitung in das A.T.*, p. 215, and *Hiob*, pp. 20-21.

[93] See p. 902.

"Who is God? What does God require of man? What is the meaning of human life?" His answer has been fairly well preserved, in spite of a few excisions and editorial corrections (especially in chs. 24–27).

V. Language and Poetic Structure

A. Original Tongue.—In view of the Edomitic character of the story, several students have conjectured not only that the poet was an Edomite [94] but also that he wrote in Arabic, of which the present book is a Hebrew translation.[95] None of the arguments which have been advanced in favor of this linguistic hypothesis is valid,[96] and the mere idea that a Jewish poet would have translated an Arabic poem—necessarily during the early part of the postexilic period and before the insertion of the discourses of Elihu [97]—is rather fanciful.

The weight of present evidence seems to indicate that the poem of Job (dialogue and discourses of Yahweh) was written in Hebrew, though undoubtedly the poet—like any true genius of the art of verse—has forged for himself a notably original tongue. The Joban master imitated but seldom. If he had a model, he did not copy but adapted and re-created according to his own mold.[98] His vocabulary is extraordinarily rich and includes a large number of words or expressions which are found nowhere else in the Hebrew Bible.[99] Many of these have been explained with the help of the Arabic (e.g., the feminine forms נהרה, "light" [3:4b]; עננה, "cloud" [3:5b]; חילה, "pain" [6:10b]; the hapax legomena כידור, "attack" [15:24b]; הכר, "to mistreat" [19:3b]; etc.), Aramaic (נתע, "to break" [4:10b]; סד, "stocks" [13:27a]; etc.), Akkadian (e.g., מזיח, "belt" [12:21b]; אבה, "reed" [9:26a]; etc.), and even Egyptian (e.g., the two words טחות, "ibis," and שכוי, "rooster" [38:36ab]; perhaps a few others). In addition, several Aramaic words are used for the

sake of poetic parallelism whenever synonyms of Hebrew words are lacking (cf. the Hebrew עד, "witness," and the Aramaic שהד [16:19ab]; the Hebrew פרא, "wild ass," and the Aramaic ערוד [39:5ab]; the Hebrew עצם, "bones," and the Aramaic גרם [40:18a and b]), and a few Aramaic terms are systematically preferred to their Hebrew equivalents (e.g., the Hebrew מלים, "words," is used ten times and the Aramaic מלין, thirteen times; but cf. the Aramaic כפן, "famine" [5:22a]; כפים, "rock" [30:6b]). However, while the Aramaic influence is indisputable, it is neither exclusive nor overwhelming—as in the discourses of Elihu—and should not be exploited in any way as an argument for the postexilic date of the poem. The lexicographic wealth, moreover, does not preclude the conclusion that the language is genuinely Hebrew, for the vocabulary, morphological inflections, and syntactic connections are on the whole closely akin to those of the other poetic books of the Hebrew Bible.

B. Style.—The literary mastery of the poet is unsurpassed in the Old Testament, and his stylistic versatility, vigor, conciseness, and elegance are probably superior to those of any other Hebrew poet. Like the best wise men, he was able to fashion his thought and sharpen it into gnomic terseness (as in 6:14), to clinch an argument with a proverbial quotation (as in 6:6), to pack a rhetorical question with double entendre (as in 22:2), and to titillate the hearer's wit and imagination with enigmatic aphorisms (as in 17:5).

He could develop at length an abstract theme with a wealth of concrete illustrations (as in 21:7-13), evoke a scene with the touch of the storyteller (as in 4:12-16), and embroider in a dozen different ways on hackneyed motifs for which he entertained nothing but dislike (as in 5:2 ff.). He was didactic in the best manner, but he had also a dramatic flair for suspense. For instance, he withheld until the end of the soliloquy (3:23) the mention of God, although it was expected at the outset of the curse (3:3). He was ignorant of the art of the swift dialogue, but he cultivated the highly original method of "delayed reaction," by which Job or a friend answers the argument not of the immediately preceding, but of the penultimate speaker (as in 9:2 ff., which replies to 4:17 ff.). He also displayed a subtle sense of rhetoric by inserting at strategic positions a pivotal sentence which at once could bind up a development and usher in another (as in 4:21). He made the hero indulge in blasphemous statements as "shock warnings" (as in 13:13-14); he could toy with a theme, abandon it, and then reintroduce it with deeper intensity (as in 14:7, 14); he was careful to place emotional climaxes not at the end but

---

[94] J. G. von Herder, *The Spirit of Hebrew Poetry*, tr. James Marsh (Burlington: E. Smith, 1833), I, 103-11; Voltaire, article "Job" in *Dictionnaire philosophique* (Paris: P. Didot l'Aîné, 1816), IX, 229; cf. Pfeiffer, *Intro. to O.T.*, pp. 678-83. Ernest Renan suggested that the poem was an echo of the wisdom of Teman (*Le livre de Job* [3rd ed.; Paris: Michel Lévy Frères, 1865], p. xxvii).

[95] F. H. Foster, "Is the Book of Job a Translation from an Arabic Original?" *American Journal of Semitic Languages and Literatures* XLIX (1932-33), 21-45.

[96] Not even that which is drawn from the expression "thy fear" (Job 4:6; etc.), meaning "thy fear of God" and corresponding exactly to the well-known Arabic idiom (Koran 2:193; etc.). Such a so-called "Arabism" (cf. Foster, *op. cit.*, p. 32), as well as many others, only shows that the poet was acquainted with Arabic ways and possibly with an Arabic dialect.

[97] See pp. 890-91.

[98] See p. 889 and also n. 83.

[99] Delitzsch, *Hiob*, pp. 125 ff.; Dhorme, *Le livre de Job*, pp. cxl ff.

before the completion of a discourse, thus making room for a calming decrescendo (as in 16:22, following vs. 18).

He was equally at home in the genre of the lament (as in 3:3 ff.) or in that of the doxology (as in 9:4 ff.). He was able to transmute a soliloquy into a colloquy; and to make a meditation explode with emotional pressure into a prayer (as in chs. 6–7). He was well versed in the art of forensic eloquence (as in 31:1 ff.), but he could also restrain his powers of oratory and impose silence upon his volubility (as in 42:6). He ran the whole gamut of tones: he could be coarse (as in 15:2) or vehement (as in 16:18), gruesome (as in 17:14) or humorous (as in 17:16), tender (as in 14:13 ff.) or passionate (as in 19:13-19). He used all the shades of irony, from earthly sarcasm (as in 12:2) to heavenly persiflage (as in 38:3 ff.).

His versatility of style was coupled and enhanced with an exquisite sense of the beauty of nature which furnished him at will with ready imagery. The theme of the failure of friendship, for example, led him to picture the swollen streams, overflowing with snow water in springtime, soon to vanish in torrid wastes (6:15 ff.). Thus he could summon, for the sake of heightening the effect or of coloring the debate, all sorts of visions and vignettes: the thunderstorms and the desert hurricanes (21:18; 27:21; etc.), the flash floods in mountain valleys (14:19), the hunger of the lioness and her whelps (4:10-11; cf. the five synonyms for "lion"), the soaring of vultures (5:7) or the swooping of eagles (9:26), the shock of heavy grain at the threshing floor (5:26), the sands innumerable along the surf (6:3), the wild ass grazing against the distant sky (6:5), the papyrus growing in the marsh and the reed blooming in the canal (8:11), the constellations moving in the night, not only the Bear and Orion or the Pleiades, but even the Southern Cross (9:9), and the morning stars singing together (38:7).

In lending words to his hero, he suggested the conflicts of moods (as in 7:21); in ascribing utterances to the friends, he was fair toward ideas which he rejected; in daring to make audible "the voice from the whirlwind," he could transcend the human lack of perspective and borrow for a while the eternal glance. As a dramatic poet, he was the Shakespeare of the Old Testament; as a theological poet, he was brother of the Hebrew prophets.

C. Metrical Forms.—Although many treatises have been written on the subject,[100] the study

of Hebraic prosody is a science which is still in its infancy. Thanks mostly to the discovery of the Ugaritic texts,[101] exegetes have learned to exercise extreme caution before correcting the text in order to make it conform to the rhythm, for the simple reason that they now refuse to state a priori what that rhythm should be, and they reject the Procrustean uniformity which has been for too long imposed upon the Hebrew meter.[102]

The poetic form of Job is as versatile as its style. The colon, which constitutes the essential element of the line, is made up of a clause or sentence containing two, three, or perhaps (but in any case infrequently) four beats or accented syllables. The line itself is formed generally with two cola (bicolon or couplet), occasionally three (tricolon or triad),[103] thus creating a wide variety of combinations such as 2+2, 2+3, 3+2, 3+3, 2+2+2, possibly also 3+4, 4+4, 4+3. These meters are intimately linked with the ideas, which may from colon to colon be repeated (synonymous parallelism), developed by contrast (antithetic parallelism), amplified (synthetic parallelism) or qualified (restrictive parallelism). The Joban poet is astoundingly at ease in most of these forms, and he uses them with striking effects. The most common form, however, is that of synonymous parallelism in 3+3. A few examples of other rhythms follow. They should be read in their respective contexts.

(a) Synonymous parallelism in 2+2:

> haḥēqer 'elôah timçā'
> 'im 'adh-takhlith shadday timçā' (11:7)

> Canst thou find out the depth of God?
> Canst thou discover the limit of the Almighty?

Müller (1896, etc.), Condamin (1899, etc.), Sievers (1901), Schlögl (1912), Gray (1913), Zorrel (1914), König (1914, etc.), Podechard (1918, etc.). On the meter of Job see especially Paul Vetter, *Die Metrik des Buches Hiob* (Freiburg i. B.: Herder, 1897; "Biblische Studien"); Joseph Hontheim, *Das Buch Hiob als strophisches Kunstwerk nachgewiesen* (Freiburg i. B.: Herder, 1904; "Biblische Studien"); Driver and Gray, *Job*, I, lxxvii-lxxviii; Dhorme, *Le livre de Job*, pp. cxlv ff.; Edward J. Kissane, *The Book of Job* (Dublin: Browne & Nolan, 1939), pp. l-lx; Stevenson, *Poem of Job*, pp. 56-59.

[101] Cf. article "The Old Testament World," Vol. I, pp. 259 ff.

[102] Still visible in G. Hölscher, *Das Buch Hiob*, rev. ed. (1952).

[103] The Ugaritic texts have helped Hebraists to understand that a poetic section with a predominating two-cola rhythm may suddenly include a line of three cola (as in 17:1, 11) for the sake of emphasis, aesthetic variation, or strophic structure (see p. 895); cf. C. L. Feinberg, "The Poetic Structure of the Book of Job and the Ugaritic Literature," *Bibliotheca Sacra*, CIII (1946), 283-92.

[100] Cf. the pioneering works of Lowth (1753) and Herder (1782-83); see article "History of the Interpretation of the Bible, III. Modern Period," Vol. I, pp. 131-32; also the monographs of Le Hir (1873), Bickell (1882, etc.), Budde (1882, etc.), Ley (1886), Zenner (1896),

(b) Synonymous parallelism in 3+2 (so-called *Qinâh* rhythm) :

*yehedhephuhû mē'ôr 'el-hôsheq
wûmittēbhēl yenidduhû* (18:18)

They thrust him from light into darkness,
And drive him out of the world.

(c) Restrictive parallelism in 2+3:

*hale'ēl yiṣkon-gábher
ki-yiṣkōn 'ālêmō maskîl* (22:2)

Can a he-man be profitable to God?
(Even) a wise-man profits (only) himself!

(d) Synthetic parallelism in 2+2+2:

*rûḥi ḥubbālāh
yāmay niz'ākhû
qebhārîm lî* (17:1)

My spirit is deranged,
(Yea,) my days are extinct,
The graveyard is mine.

(e) Antithetic parallelism in 4+4:

*yô'bhadh yôm 'iwwáledh bó
wehallâyelāh 'āmar hōrāh ghábher* (3:3)

Perish the day wherein I was born,
And the night which said, A he-man is conceived!

The Joban poem, like all the other Semitic poems, was originally chanted, and the fluctuations of rhythms—no doubt also the tonal melodies—punctuated and inflected the meaning of the sentences in a unique espousal of thought to sound,[104] which tended to induce within the hearer's threshold-consciousness a receptivity proper to psycho-aesthetic comprehension. In its original tongue the poem surely cast a spell upon its audience, in a magnetism comparable with that of the monotony—with subtle departures—of the desert wind drumming on the sand dunes.

D. Strophic Patterns.—Scholars generally have been slow to admit the existence of strophes in Hebrew poetry, perhaps because some proposals of strophic analysis were artificially systematic; because the existence of tricola within sections of bicola was not recognized; and because Greek, rather than Semitic, forms of articulation were imposed upon the poetic texts.[105] Valuable work has been done on the strophic structure of Job,

but this particular study is still in the embryonic stage.[106] It is not possible here to discuss the many different arrangements which have been proposed; let it be noted only that the Joban poet appears to manifest in this particular area of craftsmanship a singular mastery. One example will suffice.

The long first discourse of Eliphaz (4:2–5:27) presents a model of strophic composition.[107] The first part (4:2-11) falls in two sections (vss. 2-6, 7-11), each of which divides itself into two strophes of *three* and *two* lines (couplets or bicola) respectively.

The second part (4:12-21) has an identical pattern in reverse. Each of the two sections (4:12-16 and 17-21) divides itself in two strophes of *two* and *three* lines respectively (instead of *three* and *two*), and the usual couplets or bicola make room twice for triads or tricola (vss. 16, 19), obviously for the sake of special emphasis on the ideas expressed.

The third part (5:1-7), anticipated by the pivotal verse which precedes (4:21), is made up of a single strophe which conveys in seven couplets the central message of the discourse and is crowned with the capital verse (5:7).

The fourth part (5:8-27) falls into two sections, an appeal (5:8-17) and a promise (5:18-27), each made up of three strophes of three couplets and followed by a concluding couplet beginning with the word "Behold!" (vss. 17, 27).

It will be observed that this strophic arrangement respects in every way the Masoretic Text. To be sure, not all the poems of the book readily present such a striking pattern; but those in chs. 3, 6–7, 12–14, 19, 28, and others, display similar structures and indicate that the artistry of the poet was not confined to language, style, and meter, but included an architectural plan of eloquent design. The poet did not often develop a theme at random; he did not allow his imagination to carry his mind away without the reins of a chosen motif. He worked within the pattern which would best express his thinking. Like many psalmists (cf. Pss. 29; 42–43; 46; etc.) and prophets, especially Amos, Isaiah, Jeremiah, and Second Isaiah, he was an authentic poet, linking truth with beauty.

[104] As Hebrew poetry generally, the Joban verse is also characterized by consonantal and vocalic assonances; cf. especially Stevenson, *op. cit.*, pp. 60-61, 98-100.

[105] F. B. Köster, "Die Strophen, oder der Parallelismus der Verse der hebräischen Poesie," *Theologische Studien und Kritiken*, IV (1831), 40-114; cf. also the monographs of scholars mentioned above (p. 893, n. 100).

[106] Bickell, *Hiob;* Hontheim, *Hiob;* Max Löhr, "Beobachtungen zur Strophik im Buche Hiob," in Wilhelm Frankenberg, ed., *Abhandlungen zur semitischen religionskunde und sprachwissenschaft, Wolf Wilhelm grafen von Baudissin* (Giessen: A. Töpelmann, 1918), pp. 303-21; cf. Dhorme, *Le livre de Job*, p. cxlix; Kissane, *op. cit.*, pp. lvi-lx; also W. A. Irwin, "Poetic Structure in the Dialogue of Job," *Journal of Near Eastern Studies*, V (1946), 26-39.

[107] Albert Condamin, *Poèmes de la Bible* (Paris: G. Beauchesne et ses fils, 1933), pp. 196-98.

a) The Dogma of Divine Justice (4:2-11)

    (1) Confidence in Integrity (4:2-6)

(*a*) 2. If one assay to commune with thee, wilt thou be grieved?
      But from speaking, who can refrain?
    3. Behold, thou hast instructed many,
      And the weak hands, thou hast strengthened.
    4. Thy words have upholden him who was stumbling,
      And made firm the feeble knees.

(*b*) 5. But now, it is come upon thee and thou art impatient;
      It toucheth thee, and thou art dismayed.
    6. Is not thy fear of God thy confidence,
      And the integrity of thy ways, thy hope?

    (2) Harvest of Trouble (4:7-11)

(*a*) 7. Remember, I pray thee, whoever perished being innocent?
      Or where were the upright cut off?
    8. As I have seen it, they that plow iniquity,
      And sow trouble, reap the same.
    9. By the breath of God they perish,
      And by the blast of his anger are they consumed.

(*b*) 10. The roaring of the lion, and the voice of the fierce lion,
      And the teeth of the young lions, are broken.
    11. The old lion perisheth for lack of prey,
      And the whelps of the lioness are scattered abroad.

b) The Mystery of Suffering (4:12-21)

    (1) Vision in the Night (4:12-16)

(*a*) 12. A word was brought to me stealthily,
      And mine ear received a whisper thereof,
    13. In thoughts from the visions of the night,
      When deep sleep falleth over men.

(*b*) 14. Dread came upon me, and trembling,
      Which made all my bones to shake;
    15. A breath of air swept over my face,
      And the hair of my flesh bristled up;
    16. Someone was standing still, of undiscernible aspect;
      A form was before mine eyes;
      There was silence. Then, I heard a voice:

    (2) The Human Situation (4:17-21)

(*a*) 17. "Can mortal man be righteous before God?
      Can a strong man be pure before his Maker?
    18. "Behold! in his own servants God putteth no trust,
      And his messengers he chargeth with folly!

(*b*) 19. "How much more them that dwell in houses of clay,
      And whose foundation is in the dust!
      They are crushed like a moth.
    20. "Betwixt morn and even they are beaten small;
      Without any regarding it, forever they perish.
    21. "Is not their pre-eminence departed from them?
      They die, and not of wisdom!"

c) The Fruit of Obstinacy (5:1-7)

    1. Call now: is there any one who can answer thee?
      To which of the holy ones wouldst thou turn?
    2. For surely the wrath of God will slay the fool,
      And his jealousy will bring the silly one to death.
    3. Yea, I have seen the fool taking root;
      But suddenly his abode became rotten.

4. His sons are far from safety;
   They are crushed at the gate, and none shall deliver them.
5. His harvest the hungry will eat up,
   Or God will take it away by drought [?],
   And the thirsty will pant after his milk [?].
6. For affliction cometh not from the dust,
   Neither doth trouble spring out of the ground:
7. It is man who begetteth trouble,
   As surely as the sparks fly upward.

d) The Duty of Man on Earth (5:8-27)
(1) The Appeal (5:8-17)

(*a*) 8. As for me, I would seek unto God,
   And unto God would I commit my cause;
9. He doeth great things and unsearchable,
   Marvellous things without number:
10. He giveth rain upon the face of the earth,
   And sendeth water upon the face of the fields.

(*b*) 11. He setteth the lowly on high,
   And they that mourn are exalted to safety.
12. He frustrateth the devices of the crafty,
   So that their hands cannot perform their enterprise.
13. He taketh the wise in their own craftiness,
   And the counsel of the froward is carried headlong.

(*c*) 14. They meet with darkness in the daytime,
   And grope in the noonday as in the night.
15. But he saveth from the sword the guileless,
   And the poor from the hand of the mighty.
16. Thus hope cometh to the destitute,
   And iniquity stoppeth her mouth.

(*d*) 17. *Behold!* Happy is the man whom God correcteth!
   Therefore, despise not thou the chastening of the Almighty!

(2) The Promise (5:18-27)

(*a*) 18. For he maketh sore, but he bindeth up;
   He woundeth, but his hands heal.
19. From six troubles he shall deliver thee;
   Yea, in seven there shall no evil touch thee.
20. In famine he shall redeem thee from death,
   And in war from the power of the sword.

(*b*) 21. Thou shalt be hid from the scourge of the tongue,
   Neither shalt thou be afraid of destruction when it cometh.
22. At destruction and dearth thou shalt laugh,
   Neither shalt thou be afraid of the beasts of the earth.
23. For thou shalt be in league with the stones of the field,
   And the wild beasts shall be at peace with thee.

(*c*) 24. Thou shalt know that thy tent is in peace,
   And thou shalt inspect thy fold, and miss nothing.
25. Thou shalt know also that thy seed shall be great,
   And thine offspring as the grass of the earth.
26. Thou shalt come to thy grave in full vigor,
   As a shock of grain cometh up in its season.

(*d*) 27. *Behold!* This we have searched out; it is true!
   Hear it, and know thou it for thy good!

VI. Text and Versions

It is to be expected that an ancient writing composed in highly original poetry and presenting many unusual words and grammatical constructions, several repetitions of motifs in various garbs, a style which cultivates subtleties of expression bordering sometimes on the esoteric, and more especially a theological outlook which could never become popular, would suffer at the hand of pedestrian editors and copyists. To say that the Hebrew text of Job is not well preserved is therefore an understatement. Yet the fact that it was preserved at all deserves recognition. Lower critics have done considerable research on the Joban text,[108] although it must be added that some of them have wrought more damage even than censorious editors and careless scribes have done in the early years of transmission.[109]

Scrutiny of the Masoretic Text and comparison with the ancient versions, especially that of the Septuagint,[110] have revealed a number of graphic errors, particularly omissions of letters, words, and lines, as well as some transpositions.[111] However, the critic should be slow to tamper with the text without due warrant. Modern discoveries, especially in the field of comparative linguistics, have proved more than once that a strange form or supposedly "faulty spellings" had been rightly preserved by the Masoretes. Moreover, the testimony of the versions, especially that of the Septuagint, is not always helpful, for the Alexandrine and other translators often paraphrased and sometimes deliberately corrected the wording and the ideas of the original in order to elucidate an obscure passage or even to impose a theological bias.[112]

Among the versions other than those depend-

---

[108] Inaugurated by the pioneering work of Louis and Jean Cappel in the seventeenth century and C. F. Houbigant in the eighteenth, the textual criticism of Job has attracted in modern times the attention of many students, among whom may be mentioned Merx (1871), Beer (1896, etc.; cf. the critical apparatus prepared in 1906 and 1932 for Rudolf Kittel's *Biblia Hebraica* [1937]), Ehrlich (1908, etc.), Houtsma (1925), G. R. Driver (1936, etc.), and all the standard exegetes (see "Selected Bibliography," p. 905).

[109] E.g., Bickell (in the second edition of his work, 1894), Torczyner (1920; 1941), Ball (1922), Richter (1927), and Stevenson (1951).

[110] See article "Text and Versions of the Old Testament," Vol. I, pp. 53-54, 58-59.

[111] For a detailed list see Dhorme, *Le livre de Job*, pp. cliv ff.; cf. also Driver and Gray, *Job*, I, lxxi ff.

[112] E.g., in the famous text of 13:15, the Masoretes apparently preserved in the *Qᵉrê* a tradition which objected to the idea of Job's despair (see Exeg. *ad loc.*), but the Greek translators went further and rejected also the idea that God might slay Job, thus reading:

If the ruler masters me, even when he has become first,
Verily I shall speak and bring to the proof before him.

See Henry S. Gehman, "The Theological Approach of the Greek Translator of Job 1-15," *Journal of Biblical Literature*, LXVIII (1949), 235; other illustrations in pp. 231-40; cf. J. Ziegler, "Der textkritische Wert der Septuaginta des Buches Hiob," *Miscellanea Biblica*, II (1934), 277-96; Gillis Gerleman, *Studies in the Septuagint: I. Book of Job* (Lund: C. W. K. Gleerup, 1946); Donald H. Gard, *The Exegetical Method of the Greek Translation of the Book of Job* (Philadelphia: Society of Biblical Literature and Exegesis, 1953; "Journal of Biblical Literature, Monograph Series").

---

ing on the Septuagint (Jerome's Recension, Syro-hexaplar, Coptic-Sahidic, Coptic-Bohairic, and Septuagintian Arabic), some are quite useful for the restoration or the explanation of the text; that is, the translations of Aquila, Symmachus, and Theodotion, the Targum, and the Peshitta. The Vulgate has literary beauty but it shows undue obedience to the Septuagint and Symmachus, and so is not of primary importance for the textual reconstruction of Job.

VII. Theological Significance

It is often maintained that the book of Job was written in order to answer the question, "Why do the righteous suffer?" But actually the ancient tale as well as the poem utilizes the problem of undeserved suffering for the pursuit of a broader and higher purpose. Important and even crucial as the enigma of unrequited pain may have been for the Hebrews, and especially for those Judeans of the sixth century B.C. under whose feet a world had crumbled, a much more fundamental issue was at stake—namely, what is the meaning of faith? This is in the strict sense of the word a theological matter, for it involves no less than man's knowledge of God.

At the critical end of an era the scattered men of Judah and Jerusalem either gave way to despair or at best found refuge in quietism, musing:

It is good to hope and silently to wait
For the deliverance of the Lord (Lam. 3:26);

and a few generations later in similar straits even some Greeks confessed, "Not to meditate, herein lies the good life." [113] But the poet of Job resolutely faced the dark riddle of existence, looked beyond the wisdom of men, and sought the wisdom of God.

For the onset of his argument he borrowed an acute case history which showed in extreme terms the shock of adversity upon integrity. Such a setting allowed him to scrutinize man's situation at its worst—demonic depth or sickness unto death—and to repudiate the comforts which theism traditionally afforded. Traveling into the theological unknown, he was led unwittingly to imply the necessity of a Christ, learned the sufficiency of grace, and was brought to the threshold of pure religion.

A. Adversity Against Integrity.—Many scholars deny that the book of Job deals with a problem of theology properly speaking. They say that it is the protest of a "humanist" against the tyranny of stultified orthodoxy, the revolt of individual conscience against organized religion, the claim of man against ecclesiasticism.

[113] Sophocles *Ajax* 554.

It is true that the question of selfless piety upon which the folk tale is articulated (cf. 1:9) is never developed explicitly within the poem, which on the contrary concerns itself again and again with the dogma of retributive justice. The purpose of the poet, however, must be sought in the total context of the book, which ends not with the hero's protest of innocence but with the theophany and its subsequent effect upon Job. The poet's use of the tale and his handling of the discussion between the hero and the friends must therefore be viewed in the light of the poem's denouement—the immediate revelation of God and the hero's response to the divine intervention. With a keen sense of drama and a profound knowledge of psychology, the poet withholds until the climax of his work the secret of his intention, which is to show the divinity of God, the humanity of man, and the specific nature of the relation between a God who is truly God and a man who is truly man—namely, one of grace alone apprehended by faith.

Now to separate this particular object of study from its vast context—spatial and temporal—in human life is not an easy task. The poet wished to concentrate his powers of vision upon man as man, man disentangled from the environment of society, history, and cosmos. He selected therefore an appropriate setting for his investigation. At the same time, since he was not an academic theologian trained in the methods of conceptual thinking, he followed the only course open to him: he exhibited a concrete sample of humanity. As a true poet, he could not deal with abstractions. His material had to be the very stuff of life, delineated sharply and compellingly in an existential situation. The story of the man from Uz fulfilled these requirements. It furnished him opportunity to look at a representative of the human species unencumbered with national or religious peculiarities. The figure of Job, Edomitic as it may have been in its origin, transcended time and space. By lending words to him, the poet could present *homo sapiens,* or rather, plainly and merely, *homo vivens,* isolated from racial, cultural, political, and especially ritual characteristics. Moreover, he could not use an average man, leading an average life, moderately good and bad, reasonably happy and unhappy. For his microscopic scrutiny he needed not an average example of manhood, endowed with ordinary gifts and encountering an ordinary fate, but a hero, a model of the most uncommon integrity swept by the most extraordinary kind of adversity. And since "All actual heroes are essential men," [114] his scalpel did not lay bare

[114] Elizabeth Barrett Browning, *Aurora Leigh,* Bk. V, l. 151.

the soul of an Edomite sheik only, but the core of essential man.

Job, then, is pictured with the poet's endorsement as "perfect and upright, and one that feared God, and eschewed evil" (1:1). His integrity means that his personality is "integrated" within himself and within its environment (see Exeg., *ad loc.*). His relationships are of the "right" kind, toward himself, his family, his God. This co-ordination of "right" relations creates in him a legitimate sense of "righteousness," [115] which translates and demonstrates itself by "peace" (shālôm), a healthy (shālēm) wholeness, wealth, and—the crown of prosperity—a happy progeny.[116] His sense of responsibility for the welfare of his home is such that he even anticipates the possibility, not of criminal deeds, but of inward sins among his sons; and he performs atonement for them (1:5). His piety matches his morality.

Misfortune strikes in heroic proportions,[117] and with an incredible magnanimity the hero accepts his fate as the expression of the divine will (1:20-22; 2:10). Adversity meets integrity head on, and integrity is not defeated.

It is at this very point that the poet intervenes. Lifting the hero from a world of legend, he brings him to the level of psychological reality and portrays the "disintegration" of this fabulous integrity. The perfect man who had blessed the divine name is now a man who, still conscious of his integrity, has no alternative in the face of injustice but to curse his own life (3:3 ff.).

B. Sickness unto Death.—Much more than mortal illness is here described. The patient suffers not only from bereft love, destitution, bodily pain, and social isolation; he is estranged from God and knows enough of God to evaluate his loss. If he could only dismiss that God from his world, he would dissolve his burden in the woe of his initial soliloquy (3:3 ff.). For many beside him have said,

> Not to be born is the most
> To be desired; but having seen the light,
> The next best is to go whence one came
> As soon as may be.[118]

But he is different from ancient and modern pagans because he clings to his belief in a just

[115] See Johannes Pedersen, *Israel, Its Life and Culture,* I-II (London: Oxford University Press, 1926), pp. 316 ff., 363 ff.

[116] Notice the unusual status of the daughters among their brothers (1:4b; cf. 1:18; 42:15).

[117] The scenes at the heavenly court (1:6-12; 2:1-7a) have been preserved by the poet because they confirm the hero's integrity (1:8; 2:3) and at the same time raise the question of his selfishness (1:9; 2:4-5). They should not be construed as a reflection of the poet upon the nature of the Deity.

[118] Sophocles *Oedipus at Colonus* 1225.

and omnipotent Deity. Were he to yield to unbelief, his problem would immediately cease to exist. His physical and moral grappling with undeserved evil would remain, but his spiritual torture would end. Thus the path of his agony is not comparable to a continuous descent into hell; it is an incessantly up-and-down movement, a conflict between denial and affirmation, doubt and certainty, revolt and acceptance, "a struggle against God and a hope in him, a flight from before God and a longing to encounter him." [119] Even this belief, this hope, and this longing are in a profound sense misguided; for Job believes not in God, but in his own conception of God. He aspires to meet God, but on his own terms, in order to have his integrity vindicated. To be sure, his statements concerning the power of the Creator, Provider, and Ruler of nature and man are theologically correct (see 9:5-10, 18; 14:4, 20; 17:4; 21:22; 23:3, 8-9, 13; 30:21-23; 31:13-15; etc.), but his attitude toward God is not that of a creature acknowledging creatureliness. It is rather that of a man who (a) uses his sense of innocence as a claim upon the Deity's will, and (b) when unable to reconcile his righteousness with his fate challenges the Deity's justice and stands erect as the judge of his creator.

(a) While Job admits that, as a human being, he is not pure in comparison with God (14:1-6), and even confesses that he may have committed some misdeeds in the time of his youth (13:26), he also knows that his sufferings are out of all proportion to the pettiness of his failures. He therefore shouts that God attacks him "without cause" (9:17). The omniscient Ruler must know that his victim is not guilty (10:7), so until the end Job will hold fast to his righteousness (27:6) and carry it as a trophy, a crown of glory and a badge of honor (31:36). He concludes the poetic discussion with an eloquent rehearsal of his virtuous deeds (30:1 ff.) in a way which demonstrates the fact that he has never abandoned his belief in the dogma of retribution.

(b) Job does not doubt for an instant that God is directly responsible for his plight. It is in God that he seeks the reason for his suffering. "The friends declare that Job is a sinner. Job declares that God is arbitrary, unjust, immoral. The root of the matter is not in him but in God." [120] He constantly implies and often explicitly states that the Deity behaves with him as a capricious tyrant (9:18-19), a corrupt judge (9:20-29), a wild beast which has torn his flesh (16:7, 9), a ruthless warrior (6:4, 9; 16:12-14; 19:8-12) who takes him for a target (7:17-21) and will soon deliver the death blow (13:15).

Physical pain and theological anxiety combined are slowly leading him to magnify his own person. He fancies himself to be playing the part of God's mythical enemy, the cosmic antagonist (7:12) against whom the Creator, like a general in the field, must hurl wave upon wave of fresh hosts (10:17; 16:13-14; 19:12).

With a strange contradiction which reveals the utmost confusion of his mind, he condemns the justice of God and yet expects to receive from him a verdict of acquittal (23:3-7). He desperately seeks the presence of a God who forever eludes his pursuit (23:8-10), but at the same time is terrified by a presence which overwhelms him more completely than the thick darkness of his impending death (23:11-17). But he is determined to maintain his stand at all costs, and his last word is one of unrelieved defiance. "Neither to change, nor falter, nor repent," [121] is the vain glory of a Titan who hopes to meet God as a prince welcomes an equal (31:37), and to take advantage of a divine encounter for the ultimate assertion of the self. There is no place for divine grace in his quest. "Rather than seek help he would prefer to be himself—with all the tortures of hell, if so it must be." [122] He asks for recognition of his worth, but not for mercy; and there lies the root of his "sickness unto death."

C. The Mixed Comforts of Theism.—The discourses of the friends provide an eloquent example of blundering with truth. Eliphaz, Bildad, and Zophar, each in his own way, exalt the greatness, the wisdom, the power, and the justice of God (4:17 ff.; 5:9 ff.; 8:3, 20; 11:7-9; 22:2 ff.; etc.). They are right when, in order to extol divine glory, they point out the "great gulf" which separates God from man, and even from his heavenly servants (4:17-21; 15:15; 25:4-6); but they are wrong when, for the sake of safeguarding the absolute freedom of God, they declare that it is no "pleasure to the Almighty if [man is] righteous" (22:2-3). They are right when they discern that Job's sin lies in his proud refusal to accept the limitations of his manhood:

Art thou the first man that was born?
  Or wast thou made before the hills?
Hast thou listened in the secret council of God?
    (15:7-8a) ;

but they are wrong when they attempt to explain the misfortune of this haughty well-doer as an exact penalty for the sins of his sons (8:4) or for his own ethical crimes (11:14; 15:15; 18:21; 22:5 ff.). They are right when they advise

---

[119] Weiser, *Hiob*, p. 12.
[120] Bewer, *Literature of O.T.*, pp. 321-22.

[121] Shelley, *Prometheus Unbound*, Act IV.
[122] Søren Kierkegaard, *The Sickness unto Death*, tr. Walter Lowrie (Princeton: Princeton University Press, 1941), p. 114.

him to seek God with humble trust and to make supplication unto the Almighty (5:8; 8:5; 11:13; 22:21-22), and they strike a note of delicate and profound beauty when they describe the joy of communing with God (22:25-26); but they are wrong when they uphold mechanically the dogma of retribution as an impersonal law which always finds its verification in historical experience (5:17-27; 8:6-22; 11:15-20; 15:17-35; 18:5-21; 27:13-23). By doing so, they unwittingly fall into Job's fundamental error, because they hold to a merely moralistic view of salvation. They believe that it is man who, by his own will and power, is the author of his fate and the master of his destiny (11:14 ff.; 22:21).

In the friends' conception of the relationship between God and man, as in that of Job, there is no room for the category of divine grace, just as there is no place for man's pure love of God. Like "the Satan" of the folk tale, they do not actually believe that man serves God for nought. Worse, they do not understand the mercy of God. Religion for them is a bargain, humility the best policy, and morality the coin which purchases peace. On the surface they profess a magnificent creed and their theism appears at first sight to be free from flaw. But their belief is not faith. Their orthodoxy, learned in the schools and scrupulously maintained from the tradition of old, is a devious attempt to maintain the sense of their own honor. It is not God they defend, but rather their own security. Indeed, it is their pride which they uphold when they condemn Job, and it is their sin which they reveal when they pay tribute to divine sovereignty. They arrogate to themselves the right to speak ex cathedra, and like other self-appointed vicars of God (15:11) they soon eschew the elementary virtue of human kindness (6:14; see Exeg., ad loc.; cf. 12:5). The presumption of these ethically honest men is comparable to that of the morally evil men who "have brought God into their own hands" (12:6). Their theism has become a subtle form of idolatry.

When orthodoxy becomes a source of theological sin, however, it fulfills a paradoxical function: it sharpens the quest of the heretic into a frantic search for light; and it transforms him, wrong as he may be in the midst of his rebelliousness, into a herald of truths hitherto concealed or unborn.[123] Thus the injustice of the friends not only accentuates the torture of

[123] It is not correct to assert—with many commentators—that the purpose of the poet is to defend the dignity of man. The poet knows that man "is but a driven leaf in autumn, a thing of nought, petty, ephemeral and infinitely to be pitied" (James Strahan, *The Book of Job* [Edinburgh: T. & T. Clark, 1913], p. 11). But he does uphold the right of individual man to oppose the tradition of the past or the dictum of the majority.

Job but also quickens his power of vision: the lamenting hero becomes a prophet.

D. The Necessity of a Christ.—Comfortless solitude among men leads at times to a solitude with God, but Job is alone even before God. Yet a luminous thread runs through the drab canvas. Any one of the details taken separately may be of little significance, but viewed together they reveal the authenticity of the poet's inspiration as well as the height of his literary genius.

Job prodded by the cruelty of his friends, who not unlike the sneering thief cry, "Save thyself!" answers only in his *hubris,* "I do not need salvation, but demand only the vindication of my honor." Such is the impasse, the dead end, the bottom of the pit, wherein he lies. And slowly, almost imperceptibly, his self-sufficiency breaks down. He knows that he cannot throw a bridge which might give him access to the good will of God, but the paradox of his faith prevents him from believing that God will abandon him forever. Above the darkness a light glimmers.

First, there is the strange irony of a hope which is thwarted as soon as entertained:

Why shouldest thou not pardon my transgression
    and take away my iniquity?
For now I shall lie in the earth;
    thou wilt seek me, but I shall be no more (7:21).

Picture the bold image: God is groping in the darkness which precedes dawn for the creature who is lost (see Exeg., ad loc.), but it is too late. Self-pity? Perhaps. But at the same time there is the thought of a God who cares. The idea of divine love may be at this juncture an idle fancy; yet it enters the mind of the hero as a seed is buried in the ground.

Second, there is the remarkable awareness of man's impotence with regard to his own salvation. If Job cleanses himself and washes his hands in snow water and lye (9:30), the outraged Giant will throw him into the ditch (9:31). No path to God can man beat out for himself. "Man cannot be his own *pontifex.*"[124] Ceremonies are of no avail. The rituals of all religions and the deeds of all moralisms are vain. Against the absolute will of God every human attempt at clearance miscarries. Job knows that techniques for self-purification result only in worse helplessness. God is God, and forever above man (9:32). But if there were only a daysman, a mediator, who would place his hands upon the shoulders of God and of man, and bring God and man face to face (9:33)! For a Semite, a prince of monotheism, this is a stupendous thought. If only the awful

[124] Weiser, *Hiob*, p. 75.

gap between Creator and creature could be bridged! If only the abyss between God transcendent and man impure could be spanned! If only some being, at once God and man, could effect reconciliation and beget peace! Of course the text is no witness to the Christian mystery of the Incarnation, but it prophetically proclaims, through some *via negativa*, the necessity of a Christ.

Third, Job toys with the prospect of an afterlife. Taking up the sure surmise of a God who will not let him go (7:21), he is allured by the fancy of resurrection:

Oh, that thou wouldest hide me in Sheol,
.　.　.　.　.　.　.　.　.　.　.　.
　　that thou wouldest appoint for me a set time,
　　　and then, remember me (14:13)!

Again the image of a loving God haunts his distraught spirit. As elsewhere in the Old Testament (cf. Pss. 16:8-11; 73:23-26), the thought of a life after the grave originates in man's desire for the continuation or the inception of an intimate dialogue with God himself:

If a man die, shall he live again?
　All the days of my service I would wait,
　till my release should come.
Thou wouldest call, and I would answer thee;
　thou wouldest long for the work of thy hands
　　(14:14-15).

This hope, however, is withdrawn as soon as expressed, for the Hebraic mind, perhaps in reaction against the fantastic emphasis of Egyptian culture upon rituals designed for ensuring immortal bliss, lived for a thousand years in the affirmation of the finality of the grave (cf. Ps. 88:10-12; etc.).

Fourth, the theme of the daysman reappears in a new form as the sufferer suddenly discerns beyond the miseries of the present the face of a heavenly witness. His blood will be shed unto death (16:18), but his last breath will not mean the closing of his case:

Even now, behold, my witness is in heaven,
　and he that vouches for me is on high.
.　.　.　.　.　.　.　.　.　.　.　.
And he will maintain the right of man with God
　like that of a man with his neighbor (16:19, 21).

To be sure, the interpretation of this passage is uncertain (see Exeg., *ad loc.*). It seems, however, that this heavenly figure is different from God and will fulfill Job's ultimate desire, not the restoration of worldly happiness, but the vindication of human honor. This too the hero will have to surrender.

Fifth and last, therefore, in the climactic passage of the redeemer, the motifs of the daysman

and of the witness, combined with the hope of a resurrection, seize the hero's imagination and grip him with the intensity of unshakable conviction. This time, however, he no longer seeks acquittal:

For I know that my Redeemer liveth;
　and at last he shall stand upon the earth;
And after my skin hath been thus destroyed,
　then, within my flesh shall I see God,
Whom I shall see for myself;
　and mine eyes shall behold, and not another.
My heart is consumed within me (19:25-27).

His fellow creatures have utterly failed the hero (19:13-19) and the hope of a distant rehabilitation by generations to come offers no comfort (19:23-24), but there is now for Job a *gō'ēl* (see Exeg., *ad loc.*) who will live beyond Job's death and will usher him into the holy presence. The hero himself, within his flesh, and not as a stranger, will contemplate with his own eyes the fullness of the Divine. Not a word is now hinted about God's recognition of his innocence. He expects now neither reward nor clearance. The vision of God is enough. The agelong repugnance to lift the veil of death is broken, but only for the sake of communing with the Deity. This is not a belief in the natural immortality of the soul, nor is it the hope that man is able by his own power to find access to God: Job now surrenders all claim and trusts solely in the power of a heavenly high priest to present him before the holy of holies.[125]

The flash, however, is momentary. Although the hero seems ready to understand the sufficiency of grace, he relapses into his former self,[126] below heavens which remain closed, upon an earth where God is absent (21:2 ff.; 23:3 ff.; especially 24:12); and his final protest of innocence shows that his arrogance has not abated. He will not capitulate unless the heavens open and the voice is heard from the whirlwind. This is not man's doing; it is the initiative of God.

---

[125] It is clearly incorrect to maintain—as a number of exegetes do—that the thought of Job remains stagnant throughout the poetic discussion; cf. W. A. Irwin, "An Examination of the Progress of Thought in the Dialogue of Job," *Journal of Religion*, XIII (1933), 150-64.

[126] Inasmuch as the third cycle bears traces of editorial deletions and alterations (see p. 888), and in view of the poet's rhetorical, dramatic, psychological, and theological mastery, one may entertain the conjecture that in the original form of the work the passage on the redeemer (19:25-27) did not constitute the climax of the hero's thinking. The absence of a reply to Zophar may be due to the "curtailment of erstwhile sceptical material" (Kraeling, *Book of the Ways of God*, p. 100; cf. p. 199), perhaps also to an editorial censure of another and even bolder expression of Job's faith in an intercessor between God and himself. It should be observed that Elihu (33:23 ff.) pursues the same theme and draws its soteriological consequences (see Exeg., *ad loc.*).

E. The Sufficiency of Grace.—"Let the Almighty answer me!" (31:35.) Such is the final challenge of Job and of natural man. But the divine answer is always different from human expectations. From the whirlwind Yahweh does not answer questions: he asks them (38:3 ff.). Because the Lord does not explain the mysteries of the universe, solve philosophically the problem of evil, or publicly declare the righteousness of his servant, many scholars have expressed their disappointment. Some have even gone so far as to condemn the divine irony as a display of refined cruelty, if not of devilish scorn. This is not apparently the way Job himself felt (42:5).

By boldly lending human words to the transcendent Deity, the poet succeeds in the most delicate task: the hero becomes aware of the divinity of God, and at the same time senses that a God who is truly God, creator and ruler of the cosmos, consents to incline himself toward the creature of his hands and grants him the vision of divine glory. Job is raised from prison into the wind-swept pageant of the universe. He leaves the enclosure of his aching self and discovers a world. Will he condemn God that he may be justified (40:8)? He learns in awe and wonder that God stands beyond and above the traditions, the ideals, and the wisdom of men.[127] He who had expected to "come forth as gold" (23:10) bows in adoration and repentance (42:1-6). In the presence of the most holy God all pain is stilled, for grace is sufficient (see Exeg., *ad loc.*). Job becomes aware of his sinfulness at the very instant of his reconciliation. He is saved at the moment of his surrender. He receives all when he surrenders all. God's judgment is none other than the blossoming of his mercy. The shattered giant no longer attempts "To grasp this sorry Scheme of Things entire,"[128] for he now understands that the will of his Sovereign is to make him a witness of the holiness and care displayed by "the faithful Creator":

I have heard of thee by the hearing of the ear;
but now mine eye seeth thee (42:5).

Thus, one cannot say that the book of Job "is an exhortation to emulate God's unconquerable will."[129] On the contrary, one is led to conclude that the book is an appeal to yield by faith to the grace of God. It is also from the vantage point of *sola gratia* that the epilogue in prose and its account of Job's worldly restoration should be appreciated and enjoyed. Whatever its literary origin, the conclusion is now part of the book in its canonical form; and in its present context—coming immediately after the hero's repentance—the story of the hero's rehabilitation appears in the light not of his righteousness, but of the grace which is freely and divinely granted him.

F. The Poetry of Pure Religion.—The theological significance of the book of Job quite clearly by-passes the problems of undeserved suffering and of theodicy. That the mystery of human pain and of divine justice is discussed by Job and his three friends, none will deny. But the poet did not write his book for this purpose. Instead of standing still before the problem, he goes forward through it; and he proposes not a speculative answer (he has not asked the question), but a way of consecrated living. Of him one may say, as of the poet of Ps. 73:

In his fellowship with God he has found that nothing matters in comparison with that fellowship. . . . The man who has found fellowship with God is rich though he possesses nothing. That is the real solution—not an answer to the riddle, but the attainment of a state of mind in which there is no desire to ask it.[130]

The poet stands with the prophets and the psalmists at the core of Hebraic faith, and like some of them he goes beyond the limits of the Old Testament; for above the peculiarities of race, ritual, and law, he knows and shows that the chief and highest end of man is to glorify God and fully to enjoy him forever. Indeed, the poet of Job conveys the poetry of pure religion because he understands, almost as well as Paul,[131] that righteousness is not the work of man but the gift of God. The book of Job is not at the fringe of the Old Testament literature. Like the prophecy of Second Isaiah, it asks the most profound question of Hebraism and it leads directly to the New Testament.

VIII. Outline of Contents

I. Prologue in prose (1:1–2:13)
  A. Presentation of the hero (1:1-5)
    1. Job's country, name, and character (1:1)
    2. Job's family, wealth, and fame (1:2-3)
    3. An illustration of Job's piety (1:4-5)

---

[127] "It is as though he were saying, in the mood of certain trends of modern theology, that the righteousness of God is distinct in kind from human morality, so that only an ignorant presumption will demand that God be just according to our standards" (Irwin, "Job and Prometheus," p. 107). This admission is the more remarkable in that its author disparages the speeches of Yahweh.

[128] *The Rubáiyát of Omar Khayyám*, st. xcix.

[129] Ralph Marcus, "Job and God," *The Review of Religion*, XIV (1949), 29.

[130] William Temple, *Nature, Man and God* (London: Macmillan & Co., 1934), p. 43.

[131] Cf. Rom. 11:33-35 not only with Isa. 40:13-14 and Jer. 23:18 but also with Job 11:7-8; 15:8; 36:22-23. Cf. also Rom. 11:35 with Job 35:7; 41:11. See R. P. C. Hanson, "St. Paul's Quotations of the Book of Job," *Theology*, LIII (1950), 250-53.

IX. Selected Bibliography

DHORME, PAUL. *Le livre de Job* ("Études bibliques"). Paris: J. Gabalda, 1926.

DRIVER, S. R., and GRAY, G. B. *A Critical and Exegetical Commentary on the Book of Job* ("International Critical Commentary"). New York: Charles Scribner's Sons, 1921.

HÖLSCHER, GUSTAV. *Das Buch Hiob* ("Handbuch zum Alten Testament"). Rev. ed. Tübingen: J. C. B. Mohr, 1952.

KISSANE, EDWARD J. *The Book of Job.* Dublin: Browne & Nolan, 1939.

KÖNIG, EDUARD. *Das Buch Hiob.* Gütersloh: C. Bertelsmann, 1929.

KRAELING, EMIL G. *The Book of the Ways of God.* New York: Charles Scribner's Sons, 1939.

PEAKE, A. S. *Job* ("The Century Bible"). London: T. C. & E. C. Jack, 1904.

STRAHAN, JAMES. *The Book of Job.* Edinburgh: T. & T. Clark, 1913.

STEVENSON, W. B. *The Poem of Job.* London: British Academy, 1947.

————. *Critical Notes on the Hebrew Text of The Poem of Job.* Aberdeen: Aberdeen University Press, 1951.

WATSON, ROBERT ADDISON. *The Book of Job* ("The Expositor's Bible"). New York: A. C. Armstrong & Son, 1899.

WEISER, ARTUR. *Das Buch Hiob.* Göttingen: Vandenhoeck & Ruprecht, 1951.

JOB

TEXT, EXEGESIS, AND EXPOSITION

The Book of Job.—This is one of the most sublime books of Scripture. To many it seems at first glance one of the most bewildering. Certainly it is one of the most often quoted—or misquoted!—and perhaps one of the least often read. For the casual reader it has comparatively little to offer; and that little is at times hardly more than the distorted remnant of an idea, torn away from the context, and interpreted without any too careful regard for the original intent. Those who do actually sit down to it rarely seem prepared, for one reason or

By special arrangments with Abingdon Press the author used the substance of his Exposition of Job as his James A. Gray lectures delivered at Duke University in 1951 prior to the publication of this volume of *The Interpreter's Bible.*

Pp. 905-7 include the expositor's introduction. Text and Exegesis begin on p. 908. Editors.

another, to come to their task with an open mind. To approach it as if it were an object lesson in patience under trial is to go utterly wrong at the start. If there is any single key word to some measurably adequate understanding of the whole, that word is not "patience" but "impatience." To assume that its aim is to furnish some kind of philosophical clue to the enigma of innocent suffering is to miss the author's purpose entirely. The Hebrew mind was not primarily a philosophical mind; primarily it was a religious mind. Even when it asked philosophical questions, it gave religious answers. No merely speculative solution of any one of the knotty problems here raised is either given or arrived at. More than that, the half dozen suggestions which are thrown down in the hurly-burly of the argument are for the most part introduced in order to be refuted. Some would see it as a drama, strikingly reminiscent in many ways of Greek tragedy. They would think of the friends as serving the function of the chorus, and of the Almighty, like some *deus ex machina,* as providing the denouement. Yet it must be said that there is little or no action anywhere save in Job's own mind, and there is certainly little if any plot.[1] Those who would have it a theodicy, an attempt to "justify the ways of God to men," are embarrassed by the fact that nowhere does the author seem particularly interested in making out a very convincing case; nor is God himself allowed to do so. From beginning to end the point is by no means what man thinks of God; rather is the point everywhere and by all means what God thinks of man. Here is no character study, nor is it in any proper sense a discussion—after the manner of the wisdom schools of the ancient East. There is nothing about it that can be called objective or dispassionate. More than that, the thread of the controversy seems bent on getting lost, only to appear again, while the over-all pattern itself, so much of it as can readily be discerned, seems in no particular haste to emerge.

Is there nothing left for us then but to deal with this book as if it were no more than one of the masterpieces of the world's great literature? To that at least it can lay undisputed claim. J. A. Froude, somewhat extravagantly perhaps, would set it "far above all the poetry of the world." Carlyle wrote of it with even less restraint:

I call [it], apart from all theories about it, one of the grandest things ever written with pen. . . . It is our first . . . statement of . . . man's destiny and God's ways with him here in this earth . . . ; grand

[1] Morris Jastrow, Jr., *The Book of Job* (Philadelphia: J. B. Lippincott Co., 1920), pp. 174-81.

in its sincerity, in its simplicity; in its epic melody, and repose of reconcilement . . . Sublime sorrow, sublime reconciliation; oldest choral melody as of the heart of mankind—so soft, and great; as the summer midnight, as the world with its seas and stars! There is nothing written, I think, in the Bible or out of it, of equal literary merit.[2]

In despair of ever arriving at any very clear-cut conclusion as to what it all means, shall it be read and reread simply for the sheer enjoyment of its lyrics and elegies, its monologues and rhapsodies? Surely that would be to surrender without a struggle, to acknowledge defeat before ever the battle is joined.

Whoever will devote to it serious effort must begin with the critical problems raised by the text itself. As the Intro. points out, the work in its present form gives conclusive evidence of composite authorship. Suffice it to say that we have before us to begin with a prose folk tale, here possibly for the first time committed to writing. No matter what its provenance, pagan (Edomitish?) or Israelitish, it was widespread; no matter what its basis in fact, and there is a truth far more profound than any mere chronicle of events can record, it had become the stock in trade of those who would inculcate (or deride?) humble and unquestioning submission to the dispensations of an inscrutable Providence. To take that tale as it now stands, in chs. 1–2 and in 42:7-17, is to come at once upon the origin of the proverb about "the patience of Job" (Jas. 5:11), and no doubt at the very outset to catch an inkling of the author's purpose. As of some Horatio Alger novel, packed with sweetish virtues, or better still, as of some old-fashioned Sunday-school lesson, with its inevitable moral tag,[3] this genuine realist among the Jewish people, this Shakespeare of the O.T., is saying in effect: "That time-worn story just isn't so, as you have heard it all your life: the rich and upright Arab sheik, and the almost unbelievable misfortunes that overtook him—how he quietly bowed his head before them, and 'sinned not, nor charged God foolishly,' and how 'the Lord blessed the latter end of Job more than his beginning.' There is nothing wrong with the first part of it, or with the last part either; but let me tell you what actually happened in between!" His new and profounder version of "what actually happened in between"—new because nobody in the O.T. had ever before seriously challenged the doctrine of God's evenhanded justice—begins with Job's lament in ch. 3, and continues through the three cycles of debate, in each of

[2] *On Heroes, Hero Worship, and the Heroic in History,* "The Hero as Prophet." An impressive list of such "appreciations" is given in James Strahan, *The Book of Job* (2nd ed.; Edinburgh: T. & T. Clark, 1914), pp. 28-29.

[3] Jastrow, *op. cit.,* pp. 26 ff.

which the friends address Job in turn, one by one to be answered, formally if not directly, by Job himself. Whereupon, after the intrusion of Elihu's speech, and with the entrance on the scene of Yahweh in very person, the resolution of the "tragedy" is complete (see Intro. for further details).

Obviously some such general and preliminary blueprint is necessary as a minimum before even an attempt can be made to understand or expound the meaning of the whole or of any of its parts. But structure is not the only consideration to which the would-be student of the book must give himself if he would dig at all below its surface. He must familiarize himself also with the historical situation out of which the poem sprang. All of the great classics, Dante's *Divine Comedy*, Milton's *Paradise Lost*, Goethe's *Faust*, speak in the name of the ages. So does Job. But that speaks best to the ages which best speaks to its own age. Of what it speaks is one thing; to what it speaks is of scarcely less importance. Lift it out of its moment in the march of the years, and its voice grows relatively muffled and indistinct. Eternity finds its only sharp focus in the transient. The temporal is the timeless on its way through the calendar. It is the perennial mysteries of human existence that thrust themselves to the top in the tragic lot of this ancient Titan of the East, who is represented as having dragged out the weary length of his days while Abraham sought a city whose builder and maker is God, and Isaac digged again the wells of his father, and Jacob served for Rachel in Paddan-aram in the house of Bethuel. Into that distant past the author projects those ultimate questions about God and sin and suffering, about life and death and justice, which had begun to disturb his own generation as few others had ever been disturbed (see Expos. on 15:20).

Israel was standing at the crossroads (read again carefully Intro., pp. 897-902), and it was no longer possible for either the nation or the individual to hold fast the balanced simplicities of the traditional faith in that holy will which with an equal hand, according to the oracles of the prophets, weighed out to man for his rebellion terrible and sure disaster, for his obedience peace and power and measureless bounty. With his poignant sense of humanity's burdensome lot, its grief and pain and unexplained misery, the author of Job would scrutinize the whole wide area of human experience for whatever sign of God's justice might be there; and he finds few enough. The facts were not so clear and unequivocal as the pious liturgy of the faithful would seem to make them, the mumbled phrases of men who would con patience by heart and preach it to all the neighbors by rote. Life

was not like that. And he said it with such "madness in the brain" as comes of being "wroth with one we love." [4]

For madness indeed it is, not doubt. Doubt is no name for the wild tumult in Job's heart. In whatever age we come upon it, the word doubt is "modern" as the mood is "modern." Here is the bitter challenge of a man whose faith will not be denied and cannot be dismissed: the somber and stately defiance of an outraged devotion, at its feet the edge of an abyss unillumined, the stiff upper lip of hell; across its face, intermittently, like bats flying, the impenetrable shadows of what all too often in the darkest chambers of the mind seems an evil, cosmic tyranny. There is nothing paltry about it because there is nothing paltry about Job. Though the idea of tragedy is not congenial to Scripture, his are at least the dimensions of the tragic hero. Such a figure cannot be knocked together out of the flotsam and jetsam of life in the streets. He stands up to the full height of his stature, an epic grandeur among the ruins, stark in a stark world: a world not yet bedeviled with things, still asking great questions; a brave world, where the souls of men, baffled by the endless riddles of being, were betaking themselves from the rude shelter of all the old, habitual answers into the storm and stress of a new freedom. Out of the moral and intellectual flux of the times, under "the acids of modernity," in the hard laboratory of events, a universal cult of "wisdom" had begun to make its influence felt in the shaping of both sage and saint (see Intro., p. 878). Another order was emerging. A strange wine was being poured into the ancient wineskins. The conventionalized faith of the prophets was giving ground before another faith that was yet the same. Within its vaster reach was a nation sorely tried, spelling out syllable by syllable the clue to its destiny; in closer perspective was a solitary life, its "horn in the dust," its eyes red with weeping, but ready at last,

> like the catholic man who hath mightily won God out of knowledge and good out of infinite pain,

ready at last to whisper,

> As the marsh-hen secretly builds on the watery sod,
> Behold I will build me a nest on the greatness of God:
> I will fly in the greatness of God as the marsh-hen flies
> In the freedom that fills all the space 'twixt the marsh and the skies.[5]

It is with this "folk tale at the crossroads" that our study begins (for a summary interpretation of the whole see Expos. on 38:1; 42:5).

[4] Coleridge, "Christabel," Part II.
[5] Sidney Lanier, "The Marshes of Glynn," sts. vi, vii.

1 There was a man in the land of Uz, whose name *was* Job; and that man was perfect and upright, and one that feared God, and eschewed evil.

1 There was a man in the land of Uz, whose name was Job; and that man was blameless and upright, one who feared God,

---

I. PROLOGUE IN PROSE (1:1–2:13)

The purpose of the prologue is to present the hero and protagonists of the poem. Composed in a crisp and serene style, after the manner of the patriarchal narratives, the story moves swiftly without psychological transitions. It is a drama in two parallel acts, preceded by a prelude and followed by a postlude. The drama itself offers an introduction to the poetic discussion.

A. PRESENTATION OF THE HERO (1:1–5)

1. JOB'S COUNTRY, NAME, AND CHARACTER (1:1)

1:1. The land of Uz has been variously located, either in the Hauran (Trachonitis), at the northeast of Palestine, on account of various remains associated with Job in Christian and Moslem traditions, or (as is more probable) around the territory of Edom, at the southeast of Palestine, as indicated by biblical allusions (Jer. 25:19 ff.; Lam. 4:21) and by the homes of the hero's friends (2:11).

The name **Job** (*'iyyôbh*) has been related to the Hebrew verb *'āyabh*, "to be hostile," "to treat as enemy," and it might mean "object of enmity and persecution." It has also been connected with the Arabic stem *'wb*, "to come back," "to be penitent," and thus its meaning might be "one who is converted." Indeed, the epithet *'awwābh*, "repentant," is attributed by the Koran (38:16, 44) to both David and Job. In all probability *'iyyôbh* was the proper name of a well-known figure of the ancient past, associated with such righteous men as Daniel and Noah (see Ezek. 14:14, 20). A certain *A-ia-ab* (*Ayab*)

1:1. Once Upon a Time.—As children invariably ask of their parents, so many a maturer mind has wanted to know at the very outset whether or not this is "a true story." Luther was sure that the Job of history, whoever he was, did not speak as the Job of the Bible is said to have spoken. What has come down through the years is the tradition of his patience, not the violence of his revolt. Back of it all perhaps (see Exeg.) was the experience of some great Oriental emir. G. K. Chesterton once remarked that legend is the only "true" history, true in the deepest of all senses. Certainly there is much in the daily exchange of human life which is far likelier to be preserved by frequent telling, particularly if it enshrines a truth that transcends the truth of fact, than ever it is to get itself set down on some written page. Under the figure of one whose pious resignation had long since become a proverb, as his hapless friends are now, the author propounds the enigma of Israel's election and her woe (cf. Isa. 42:1-4, 19-20, 22, 24-25; 53; also Expos. on 3:20). Yet he does it in such terms that his hero cannot possibly be regarded as nothing more than the personification of God's chosen people (see Expos. on 13:15). It was precisely now, since the days of Jeremiah and Ezekiel, that the relevance of the divine justice to the varying fortunes of every living soul had begun to occupy the foreground of Jewish thought (cf. Jer. 31:29-30; Ezek. 18). "Evenhanded," said the fathers. "None but the impious would question it," said the friends. "Nonsense, I tell you," cried Job. "Look around!" And he stood up alone to do his battle, against a wide, unanswering sky. Not for a moment will he truckle, let Omnipotence do what it will. He cannot prevail, but not an inch will he yield. The delirium of another world seems to be shut up inside him. When God took a handful of clay and hid in it the very torment of eternity, he got him a turmoil out of it. And why not? But the birds of heaven and the beasts of the field looked on with wondering eyes; for this strange creature had its heart among the stars, and its head was only a little lower than the angels! **There was a man.** To obscure that, or lose sight of it in a figure of speech, is to miss the innermost circle of the poet's concern (see Expos. on 4:12-21, 19-21; 6:1-7:21; 9:14-19; 13:15; 15:20).

1. Does Faith Matter?—The picture given us of Job is of a man sound in body and mind, honest and forthright in all his ways (see Exeg.). This is really the first of the three profound unities presented in the opening verse. With them

was mentioned in the fourteenth century B.C. in one of the Tell el-Amarna tablets (EA, No. 256; see translation in J. B. Pritchard, ed., *Ancient Near Eastern Texts Relating to the Old Testament* [Princeton: Princeton University Press, 1950], p. 486) as prince of Ashtartu in Bashan (see W. F. Albright, "Two Little Understood Amarna Letters from the Middle Jordan Valley," *Bulletin of the American Schools of Oriental Research*, No. 89 [Feb., 1943], pp. 7-15).

The character of Job is indicated by a pair of twofold expressions, **perfect and upright, and one that feared God, and eschewed evil.** Like Noah (Gen. 6:9), Abraham (Gen. 17:1), and Jacob (Gen. 25:27), Job was **perfect** (*tām*). Yahweh himself attributed this quality to him (vs. 8; 2:3), and even the hero's wife recognized his "integrity" (*tummāh*, 2:9). Likewise, in the poetic discussion Job never doubted that he was *tām* (9:20, 21, 22) or *tāmîm* (12:4), or that he possessed *tummāh* (27:5; 31:6). The Hebrew idea of perfection referred to physical and mental health, soundness, completeness, entirety, "roundness." A perfect man was comparable to a "finished product." Job was not only well rounded, self-possessed, and balanced, he was also well adapted to his social environment, **upright** (*yāshār*), by practicing straightforwardness and justice in his dealings with his fellow men. Integrity and uprightness are complementary ideas (see Pss. 25:21; 37:37; Prov. 29:10). The narrator proves to be a master of psychology. He shows that Job had a "well-integrated personality" (to use the modern expression), as evidenced by a sense of social integrity. But he goes farther than modern psychologists when he indicates in another double expression the secret spring of that mental equilibrium: Job **feared God, and eschewed evil.** Psychological unity and social adaptability depend upon religion and morality. Furthermore, religion is always accompanied by morality (Prov. 3:7; 14:16), and morality is the direct expression of religion (Ps. 15:1 ff.). It is the fear of God which gives man the power to avoid evil (Prov. 16:6). The language and theology of the Oriental sages is here apparent. Note the use of the word Elohim **(God)** rather than the national name, Yahweh, for Job is represented as a foreigner, an Arab, one of "the sons of the East" (vs. 3).

---

the Hebrew never even thought of tampering. But *we* have, and with singularly unfortunate results! (*a*) Man in himself, and man in community **(perfect and upright):** The religious, social, political, and economic heresies of the twentieth century have sprung largely out of the antithesis that has been set up between the two. Religion has been defined as "the flight of the alone to the Alone," or "what the individual does with his own solitariness." So all around the circle the doctrine of "rugged individualism" puts in its appearance, to strive every step of the way with a totalitarianism that succeeds in correcting its vagaries very much as death corrects disease. (*b*) Man as man **(perfect and upright),** and man under God **(one who feared God, and turned away from evil):** For four hundred years and more, ever since the dawn of modern history in the Renaissance, and on through the Enlightenment, man has struggled to know himself as man—it is almost impossible to assess the gains that have come by way of that struggle— only to have such catastrophes overtake him at last as would seem once and for all to underscore the fact that he cannot even know himself as man unless he knows himself under God. "Where there is no God, there is no man." Wit-

ness Lidice and Buchenwald. Nothing, says Berdyaev, is so truly terrible as humanity when there ceases to be anything above it.[6] (*c*) Religion as reverence **(one who feared God)** and religion as singleness of heart **(turned away from evil):** A civilization which undertakes to discount the one and live on "the ethical capital" of the other is a civilization doomed to moral bankruptcy. Sooner or later, possessed of demons, it rushes headlong down a steep place into the sea. The Sermon on the Mount, dissociated from the "theology" implicit in it, is as ethics altogether visionary and unrealistic. Paul in his letters, while consistently intent on moralizing religion, never makes the mistake which since his day has shaken the world to its foundations: the failure to religionize what morals had been left over to it from "the age of faith." We have to do here with a man, among men and under God, not sinless (7:21; 13:26; 14:16-17) but whole—*integer vitae, scelerisque purus.* (See Expos. on 25:2-6; 29:2-20.) And we are not permitted to cavil about it, or explain what follows by supposing that maybe it was not so. The seal is heaven's own (vs. 8). The verdict is God's.

[6] *Freedom and the Spirit*, tr. O. F. Clarke (New York: Charles Scribner's Sons, 1935), pp. 196 ff.

2 And there were born unto him seven sons and three daughters.

3 His substance also was seven thousand sheep, and three thousand camels, and five hundred yoke of oxen, and five hundred she asses, and a very great household; so that this man was the greatest of all the men of the east.

4 And his sons went and feasted *in their* houses, every one his day; and sent and

and turned away from evil. 2 There were born to him seven sons and three daughters. 3 He had seven thousand sheep, three thousand camels, five hundred yoke of oxen, and five hundred she-asses, and very many servants; so that this man was the greatest of all the people of the east. 4 His sons used to go and hold a feast in the house of each on his

---

2. Job's Family, Wealth, and Fame (1:2-3)

2-3. The use of the consecutive imperfect tense, **and there were born unto him,** provides a swift link between the description of Job's character and that of his posterity. Divine approval of man is demonstrated by man's fecundity and estate. Total health leads to wealth. Sons are the inheritance of Yahweh, and the fruit of the womb is a reward (Pss. 127:3; 128:3). Thus the narrator subtly suggests to well-informed and expectant listeners that Job might not continue to fear God and live righteously were it not for the enjoyment of an extraordinarily full compensation.

The number of children and cattle (seven and three, seven and three, five and five) reveals the artistic, frescolike nature of the story.

3. An Illustration of Job's Piety (1:4-5)

4-5. The sons of this Edomitic prince were apparently unmarried, yet each one kept his own house in a regal manner (II Sam. 13:7; 14:28 ff.). So unusual was the

---

2-3. *Greatness: Inner and Outer.*—The relation between piety and prosperity is one of the major motifs in the vast symphony of the poem with its varied movements. That there is actually such a relation in the unspoiled harmonies of the divine order is an assumption the poet himself would never deny. (See Expos. on 29:2-20.) By the very fact that he allows the epilogue to stand as it is (see Expos. on 42:10), he reverts to a faith in what Robert Louis Stevenson once called the ultimate decency of things; and for that faith the seers of the O.T. must be given due credit (see Expos. on 5:23). To link man's inner greatness to the outward form was to see life as a sacrament; and to link them in the teeth of all seeming contradiction was to respond in high and uncalculating devotion to the self-revealing but never self-seeking goodness of God. How could they ever be unlinked, and why, and what to do when that happened? These are the questions which the author poses, and to them he makes his own reply (see Expos. on 42:5). It is hardly necessary to point the hazard which associates itself with every system of ethics that "defines and enforces moral obligation by its relation to happiness or personal well-being."[7] The history of all religions points it, not less the Hebrew and the Christian (see Expos. on vss. 6-12). The cult of a quasi-psychi-

[7] *Webster's New International Dictionary*, s.v., "Eudaemonism."

atric evangel points it. When religion is made the highway to mental health or the bulwark of democracy, morality all too easily becomes prudential, the Beatitudes platitudes, and the Golden Rule no more than a maxim culled from *Poor Richard's Almanac.* The "good" man who is *not* "happy" sets the dilemma (cf. Luke 21:12-19; etc.). To the Greeks foolishness, to the Jews a stumblingblock (I Cor. 1:23). With the resolution of it in Job cf. Robert Louis Stevenson's "If This Were Faith" (see Expos. on 3:20-21):

God, if this were enough,
That I see things bare to the buff
And up to the buttocks in mire;
That I ask nor hope nor hire,
Nut in the husk,
Nor dawn beyond the dusk,
Nor life beyond death:
God, if this were faith?

.   .   .   .

To go on for ever and fail and go on again,

.   .   .   .

With the half of a broken hope for a pillow at night
That somehow the right is the right
And the smooth shall bloom from the rough:
Lord, if that were enough?

4-5. *Sin's Disguise.*—**It may be that my sons have sinned, and cursed God in their hearts.** Job was anxious lest all inadvertently they be enticed away (see Expos. on vss. 20-22) by the very ceaseless round of their pleasures, and so grow forgetful of him who is the giver of every

called for their three sisters to eat and to drink with them.

5 And it was so, when the days of *their* feasting were gone about, that Job sent and sanctified them, and rose up early in the morning, and offered burnt offerings *according* to the number of them all: for Job said, It may be that my sons have sinned, and cursed God in their hearts. Thus did Job continually.

6 ¶ Now there was a day when the sons

day; and they would send and invite their three sisters to eat and drink with them.

5 And when the days of the feast had run their course, Job would send and sanctify them, and he would rise early in the morning and offer burnt offerings according to the number of them all; for Job said, "It may be that my sons have sinned, and cursed God in their hearts." Thus Job did continually.

6 Now there was a day when the sons of

---

brotherly harmony that they regularly gathered for family banquets to which they invited even their sisters—an exceptional custom, as it would seem, in the ancient Near East. So keen was the father's religious concern for his children that he offered on their behalf a series of burnt offerings in order to atone for their possible crimes of secret misbehavior. The narrator thus indicates that Job's conception of man's duty to God was of the most scrupulous kind. At the same time the hero's understanding of true worship was not confined to a superficial recognition of the divine demands upon man, nor was it satisfied with outward acts of devotion. Above and beyond the formal performance of a ritual or the correct enunciation of a theological creed, Job's religion penetrated to psychological attitudes and inner dispositions. He cared not only for the outward religiosity of his sons, but also for what they thought of God **in their hearts.**

The description of Job's character reflects the moralistic optimism of the wise men and proposes an idealized picture of human nature. To be sure, Job is not represented as being endowed with the attributes of divine perfection. He was neither blameless nor sinless. In the poetic discussion he acknowledged that even the angels were not pure in comparison with the purity of God (13:26; 14:16; etc.), and he confessed the possibility of having committed sin (7:20-21; 13:23[?], 26; 14:17; etc.); but he was not conscious of sinfulness before God. Here is the "something" lacking. Job, as a man, had nothing of which to repent. He did not ask for the mercy of God; he felt no need of it. He was in some measure ancestor of the Pharisee, with his faults and virtues (Luke 18:9-14).

B. FIRST ACT OF THE DRAMA (1:6-22)

1. THE HEAVENLY COURT (1:6-12)

a) YAHWEH COMMENDS JOB (1:6-8)

6-8. The sons of God were conceived as divine beings who shared in the nature of the Deity (cf. 2:1; 38:7; Gen. 6:2; Pss. 29:1; 82:1, 6; 89:6; Dan. 3:25), and they "presented

---

good and perfect gift (Jas. 1:14-17; cf. Deut. 8:7-14, 17-18). Humanity's besetting sin is not avowed godlessness but idolatry, whether barefaced or implicit (Rom. 1:21, 25), what has been called "a loving out of [away from] God." Against even the chance of it, against the chance of it even **in their hearts,** Job with unremitting regularity would set, in purification and atonement, what reverent safeguards he could.

But there is more than one gate into the citadel of Mansoul; and evil provides itself with more than one disguise. Prosperity carries its threat, and adversity its peril. There came a day when the sin Job feared for others stalked him: when, not under sunny skies but under a frowning Providence, his heart became a desolate place, and with his lips he cried out against God.

So manifold is the temptation that assails us! Nor is it any the less destructive because it leaps on us unrecognized and unexpected. Psychoanalysis is replete with instances: The condemnation of pride in others which is itself a revelation of pride; the contempt for self that wears the mask of contempt for neighbor. In Hawthorne's *Scarlet Letter* both Hester Prynne's lover and her husband furnish tragic examples. Read Rom. 2:1, 3, 17-24. His it is who stands to take heed lest he fall (I Cor. 10:12). The prodigal of all prodigals was the prodigal who never left home (Luke 15:25-32). "Watch ye therefore, and pray always" (Luke 21:36; see Expos. on 31:24-28).

6. Behind the Scenes.—Here and in 2:1 we are given access for a moment to the secret

of God came to present themselves before the LORD, and Satan came also among them.

7 And the LORD said unto Satan, Whence comest thou? Then Satan answered the LORD, and said, From going to and fro in the earth, and from walking up and down in it.

8 And the LORD said unto Satan, Hast thou considered my servant Job, that *there is* none like him in the earth, a perfect and an upright man, one that feareth God, and escheweth evil?

God came to present themselves before the LORD, and Satan[a] also came among them. 7 The LORD said to Satan, "Whence have you come?" Satan answered the LORD, "From going to and fro on the earth, and from walking up and down on it." 8 And the LORD said to Satan, "Have you considered my servant Job, that there is none like him on the earth, a blameless and upright man, who fears God and turns away

[a] Heb *the adversary*

---

themselves before Yahweh," their father and ruler, at regular intervals (see I Kings 22:19; Zech. 6:5) in a manner reminiscent of the royal courts in the ancient East. Before Yahweh "came also the Satan." Nothing is told about him, except by implication that he was not one of the sons of God, but **among them.** The use of the definite article (as in Zech. 3:1, 2) shows that the word **Satan** was not then a proper name (as in I Chr. 21:1) but designated a special function, presumably that of instigator of evil upon the earth, or at least of accuser and prosecutor; hence Moffatt's translation, "the Adversary" (cf. RSV mg.). In Arabic the verb *shatana* means "to be remote," especially from truth or God. The scene is closely similar to that of the vision described by the prophet Micaiah ben Imlah (I Kings 22:19-23). There, however, the "being which stood before Yahweh" in order to "entice Ahab" was merely a "spirit" which apparently did not specialize in evil-doing, and which consequently had not the professional title of *"the* Satan." Similarly, the "angel of Yahweh placed himself in the way of *a* satan against" Balaam (Num. 22:22).

This adversary is pictured as a shady character, yet Yahweh seemed to tolerate and perhaps even to enjoy his presence. Just as a king would inquire of one of his most corrupt and attractive minions, Yahweh asked, "Where dost thou come from, thou rogue?" And the fellow retorted impudently, without answering the question, "Oh, just from roving

---

counsels of the Most High, and so provided, as often in Greek tragedy, with information that the hero lacks. The result is a certain heightening of the dramatic tension, a silhouetting of both Job and his friends against the faraway landscape of eternity. In his engravings Blake makes frequent use of the same device. Paul does all his thinking in that perspective (Rom. 9–11). Earth's struggle in the footlights; heaven's secret in the shadows. We are to understand from the very beginning that Job is not being punished. He is not even being disciplined. He is being tried. And that not because God himself intends the trial; God permits it. Not as testing, but confidently and proudly as vindication. Evil is not ascendant in the universe. Back of its mystery is another mystery greater still: a love that "beareth all things, believeth all things, hopeth all things, endureth all things" (I Cor. 13:7). What but that is the meaning of the Cross? (See Expos. on 33:14; 36:8-25; 38:1; 42:5.) In George Eliot's phrase, there are "deal-in's wi' us."

6-12. Will a Man Serve God for Nought?— Without in the least desiring to squeeze a

sophisticated theology out of an ingenuous and untutored narrative, it may yet be remarked:

(*a*) The trials of Job are Satan's idea (cf. vs. 9; 2:5; Matt. 13:27-28*a*; Expos. on 16:11). This is not a rational view. It is a religious view. Elizabeth Barrett Browning has it in those lines of hers:

> You who keep account
> Of crisis and transition in this life,
> Set down the first time Nature says plain "no"
> To some "yes" in you, and walks over you
> In gorgeous sweeps of scorn. We all begin
> By singing with the birds, and running fast
> With June days, hand in hand: but once, for all,
> The birds must sing against us, and the sun
> Strike down upon us like a friend's sword caught
> By an enemy to slay us, while we read
> The dear name on the blade which bites at us!—
> That's bitter and convincing: after that,
> We seldom doubt that something in the large
> Smooth order of creation . . . has gone wrong.[8]

(*b*) God on his part undertakes, as one might look with a patient smile on a jaundiced lad, to point out that surely matters on earth are

[8] *Aurora Leigh*, Bk. II, ll. 750-63.

9 Then Satan answered the Lord, and said, Doth Job fear God for nought?

10 Hast not thou made a hedge about him, and about his house, and about all that he hath on every side? thou hast blessed the work of his hands, and his substance is increased in the land.

11 But put forth thine hand now, and touch all that he hath, and he will curse thee to thy face.

from evil?" 9 Then Satan answered the Lord, "Does Job fear God for nought? 10 Hast thou not put a hedge about him and his house and all that he has, on every side? Thou hast blessed the work of his hands, and his possessions have increased in the land. 11 But put forth thy hand now, and touch all that he has, and he will curse

---

in the earth and roaming about it." The Deity challenged the villain, "Hast thou observed my servant Job?" No one should at this juncture remark, "Why invite trouble? Let sleeping dogs lie!" For the narrator was not a theologian. He was not concerned with a description of divine attributes. He was not even conscious of the theological implications which might follow God's endorsement of Job's virtues. He merely retold a popular tale, probably of early origin (see Intro., pp. 887-88), because he wanted to introduce his poem with the skeptical question of "the Satan."

b) The Doubt and Plan of the Satan (1:9-12)

9-12. The adversary had to concede that "there was none like Job in the earth," but he seemed to know more than Yahweh about human nature. He implied that the Deity was naïve. **Doth Job fear God for nought?** Here is the starting point of the discussion, the nerve of the drama, the basic verse of the whole book. Here is a valid criticism of historical religions. Is not Job pious, as any other man, in exchange for his privileges? Does not every devotee understand piety as part of a bargain? It pays to be religious. "The Satan" probed to the hidden pride of clericalism—by which "holy men" yield the central shrine to the devil. The astounding fact is that the concept of disinterested religion was keenly sensed by the narrator and the hearers of this folk tale. The disturbing question was not primarily that of undeserved suffering, but that of genuine

---

not so bad as Satan would have everybody think, and gently reminds him of Job as a case in point. Recall 1:1, and notice the addition to it here.

(c) The disasters which follow are nevertheless attributed by Job as well as by the friends to God himself. There was no ultimate dualism in the Hebrew mind. There was no knowledge of "secondary causes," which for us seem to postpone the perplexity at least until we can turn the page; no nice distinctions between "absolute will" and "contingent will." There was no theory of chance either. To walk under a ladder and at that precise moment have a paint bucket fall on one's head was not bad luck. When creeds disappear charms take their place. As faith vanishes superstition runs wild. The universe, in "the strange world of the Bible," belonged to God, and it belonged to him from top to bottom. It was instinct with him. Nature and history were the manifestations of his sovereignty. The hosts of heaven were "ministers of his, that do his pleasure." Through them he executed mercy and judgment. All "powers" and all "mights" were his messengers. Whatever

man's response might make of the message, whether good or bad, they went on their appointed rounds to the ends of the earth, "hearkening unto the voice of his word" (see Expos. on 3:23; 4:8; 6:4).

So are the roles assigned and the stage set. Whereupon, with a promptness that reveals if not the author's primary intent then one at least of his major concerns, the problem which has already been subtly suggested (vss. 2-3) is raised into bold relief. **And the Lord said unto Satan, Whence comest thou? Then Satan answered the Lord, and said,** with his hands in his pockets, his tongue in his cheek, and a shrug of his shoulders, "From all over." He seems to have had no particular province allotted to him, as some of the others had. His is a roving commission. He is a kind of ambassador at large. There is not yet about him any of the full-blown malevolence of the figure that writhes and flashes its way through the drawings of Blake.[9] This is

[9] *Illustrations of the Book of Job*, invented and engraved by William Blake; interpreted by S. Foster Damon, *The Doctrine of Job* (New York: United Book Guild, 1950).

12 And the Lord said unto Satan, Behold, all that he hath is in thy power; only upon himself put not forth thine hand. So Satan went forth from the presence of the Lord.

thee to thy face." 12 And the Lord said to Satan, "Behold, all that he has is in your power; only upon himself do not put forth your hand." So Satan went forth from the presence of the Lord.

piety and authentic devotion. They did not ask, with Habakkuk and the psalmists, "Why do the righteous suffer?" but rather, "Is there on earth a man faithful to God for the sake of God?" In spite of the traditional statements to the contrary, the primary and essential question of the book of Job is not theodicy but true worship. The enigma of suffering is not the central concern of the poet: it is merely the instrument of his argument.

Yahweh confidently accepted the challenge, for "the Satan" received permission to put Job on trial by striking his estate and his posterity. Again it is necessary to remark that the narrator was not conscious of theological problems raised by such a development, and that any comment on divine cruelty is out of place.

not Milton's fallen angel, Lucifer, son of the morning; nothing nearly so magnificent as that captain of heaven's rebellious legions, standing there in *Paradise Lost,* stripped of all his honors:

> As when the sun new-ris'n
> Looks through the horizontal misty air,
> Shorn of his beams, or from behind the moon,
> In dim eclipse, disastrous twilight sheds
> O'er half the nations, and with fear of change
> Perplexes monarchs.[1]

The Satan of Job is a kind of devil in the making, already more enamored of his faultfinding than is quite decent. He can fairly be seen kicking up the star dust and looking around with a smirk, as if the cynicism he harbors in his heart were a sweet morsel on his tongue. He does not think too highly of God's government; much less has man been able to pull the wool over his eyes. He is the "nobody's child" of the universe,[2] who has seen it all and likes none of it. It is the mention of Job that sets him off. **None like him** —I dare say! But who does not know why? Does he **fear God for nought? Hast not thou made a hedge about him?** (Cf. 3:23.)

Almost inevitably that question arises every time the claims of Christianity are presented. "Do You Want Abundant Life?" "How to Tap the Springs of Power." And of course the only correct answer is that nobody serves God for nought. Nobody can. Jesus was very explicit on that point. (Luke 18:28-30. Cf. Mark 10:28-30, with the significant variant. In Matt. 19:27-30 the promise is followed by the parable of the laborers in the vineyard, which carries its own moral in that connection. In all three instances we are already standing within the shadow of the Cross. In Mark and Matthew there is in addi-

tion the pathos of that brief story about the sons of Zebedee.) Some wish it might be otherwise. H. G. Wells used to insist that the prospect of heaven, with its pearly gates and golden streets, was altogether too much of an enticement to righteousness. He preferred to be good—for nothing. And no man can be, in a world that is God's world. There is always something. Virtue is its own reward, but not its only reward. There is a harvest to the sower. Friendship has its benefits. So does piety. God makes something of the pious—at cost. He that is in Christ is a new creation. But the man who fixes his eye on the new creation is not in Christ! The trouble is that the only truth Satan knows—and it is a truth—carries back of it a cynical lie. To that lie, here in the book of Job, the lie is given (see Expos. on vss. 20-22; 2:1-6, 7-10; 17:9; 27:2-6; 31:2-4). This is part at least of the author's meaning. And there is no delay in getting at it. **Put forth thine hand now,** and see what happens. I give you my oath, **he will curse thee to thy face.** Not *my* hand, answers the Lord, *thy* hand. **All that he hath** is there. Only touch not his person. And swiftly, eagerly, Satan is gone, to bide his time (see Expos. on vss. 2-3, 13). How near he comes to winning his wager, the sequel will disclose. And how far short—by what breadth, and length, and depth, and height! He is not pitted against Job. He is pitted against God!

12. Why Does God Permit Evil?— (See Expos. on vs. 6.) To the author of Job this was not a problem for the mind to tease; it was a problem for the soul to wrestle with. The "wisdom" of this book, and indeed of all Jewish literature, has to do with life and not with logic. It has to do with the sweeping passions of the human heart, with the stalwart qualities of the human will, and not alone with the calculating processes of the human mind, which incidentally may well belong more to the mind itself than to what-

---

[1] Bk. I, ll. 594-99.

[2] James McKechnie, *Job, Moral Hero, Religious Egoist, and Mystic* (Greenock: James McKelvie & Sons, 1926), p. 23; (New York: George H. Doran Co., 1927), p. 26.

13 ¶ And there was a day when his sons and his daughters *were* eating and drinking wine in their eldest brother's house:

14 And there came a messenger unto Job, and said, The oxen were plowing, and the asses feeding beside them:

15 And the Sabeans fell *upon them,* and took them away; yea, they have slain the servants with the edge of the sword; and I only am escaped alone to tell thee.

16 While he was yet speaking, there came also another, and said, The fire of God is fallen from heaven, and hath burned up the sheep, and the servants, and consumed them; and I only am escaped alone to tell thee.

13 Now there was a day when his sons and daughters were eating and drinking wine in their eldest brother's house; 14 and there came a messenger to Job, and said, "The oxen were plowing and the asses feeding beside them; 15 and the Sabe'ans fell upon them and took them, and slew the servants with the edge of the sword; and I alone have escaped to tell you." 16 While he was yet speaking, there came another, and said, "The fire of God fell from heaven and burned up the sheep and the servants, and consumed them; and I alone have es-

2. First Visitation of Evil (1:13-22)

a) Four Messengers of Woe (1:13-19)

13-19. The action immediately shifts back to the world of men as the news of four disasters reaches Job in quick succession. The **oxen** and the **asses** were carried away and their attending servants slain in a typical raid by some Arabs (vss. 13-15); the **sheep** and their shepherds were struck in a sudden desert storm (vs. 16); the **camels** were stolen and their drivers slain by bands of Aramaean nomads (vs. 17); and in a climactic stroke the **sons** and the **daughters** of the hero perished in a hurricane (vss. 18-19). The symmetrical and stylized character of the scene is evident. Each bearer of bad news escaped alone, for the seemingly single purpose of telling the tale, and was still speaking when

ever it is in the universe that is ultimately "real"! Bertrand Russell has said that even the so-called laws of nature are of necessity little more than human conventions. Reason has its proper work to do, and within its sphere can bear true witness. But it is not sovereign. Nor does it have the last word (see Expos. on 36:8-25). The philosopher may suggest that evil is contingent upon whatever freedom of moral choice is requisite to moral stature. He may think of it as implicit in all moral achievement. But somebody before long will call for the previous question: If God did indeed fashion the world so, why did he not fashion it otherwise? And to that any man's self-born answer is as good as any other's. What the problem needs is a change of venue, which is precisely what the Bible gives it: not why is evil permitted, but how is evil overcome? The book of Job hints at the one, but cries out its assurance of the other. Beyond this world, and in it too—God! "Whom I shall see for myself, and mine eyes shall behold, and not another" (19:27). It is in life's arena that the battle is joined and the victory won. There all our tentative little theodicies, our little arguments on God's behalf (13:4, 7-8), break down. Such efforts may be pious enough in their intent to defend the Almighty against the assaults of

reason. To the modern religious person they may seem quite obviously necessary if religious faith is to justify itself in the eyes of the intelligentsia. But to the seer and the poet they are—what other word is there for it?—wicked. In Thornton Wilder's novel *The Bridge of San Luis Rey* [3] half a dozen people meet their death in the collapse of that bridge, are plunged into the dark abyss of Nature and of God without any warning; so senseless a thing, so utterly casual, that a young priest sets about tracing through those lives one after the other to see what pattern there might be beyond all appearance of meaninglessness and grinning chance. In the end he succeeds in establishing the fact that for every one of them death came promptly at the right moment of all moments; whereupon he himself is burned as a heretic for attempting to justify the ways of God! And that too makes sense! "Verily," cries the prophet Isaiah, "thou art a God that hidest thyself" (45:15). To proceed on any other hypothesis is to climb the last pinnacle of pride and evil presumption. Read Browning's "Mihrab Shah."

13. *There Was a Day.*—"There was a man" (vs. 1), and "there was a day"—in heaven (vs. 6). Then a day on earth, and another day in

[3] New York: A. & C. Boni, 1928.

17 While he was yet speaking, there came also another, and said, The Chaldeans made out three bands, and fell upon the camels, and have carried them away, yea, and slain the servants with the edge of the sword; and I only am escaped alone to tell thee.

18 While he was yet speaking, there came also another, and said, Thy sons and thy daughters *were* eating and drinking wine in their eldest brother's house:

19 And, behold, there came a great wind from the wilderness, and smote the four corners of the house, and it fell upon the young men, and they are dead; and I only am escaped alone to tell thee.

20 Then Job arose, and rent his mantle, and shaved his head, and fell down upon the ground, and worshipped,

caped to tell you." **17** While he was yet speaking, there came another, and said, "The Chalde'ans formed three companies, and made a raid upon the camels and took them, and slew the servants with the edge of the sword; and I alone have escaped to tell you." **18** While he was yet speaking, there came another, and said, "Your sons and daughters were eating and drinking wine in their eldest brother's house; **19** and behold, a great wind came across the wilderness, and struck the four corners of the house, and it fell upon the young people, and they are dead; and I alone have escaped to tell you."

20 Then Job arose, and rent his robe, and shaved his head, and fell upon the

---

the next messenger arrived. The first and third blows were due to human evil, while the second and fourth resulted from natural phenomena. Here is another indication of the sophisticated aspect of the narrative. By concentrating in one instant four different calamities, gathered from four corners of life's horizon, the narrator produces a sense of supernatural awe in the minds of his hearers. Modern readers' attention, like theirs, is focused with anguish and pity upon a rich man made poor, a sheik stripped of his heirs, and a godly worshiper smitten with inexplicable adversity.

b) The Resignation and Faith of Job (1:20-21)

20-21. Now that his life was rent and sunlight had vanished from his day, the hero silently rose and performed the traditional ritual of grief. Then, after his prostration was consummated, he avowed in a couplet, now most famous, his resignation and his faith (vs. 21). Resignation, because he was born destitute and destitute he will return to the

---

heaven (2:1). So back and forth, like a metronome, ticks the clock of destiny. Suddenly the blow falls. First the human stroke, then—or so it would seem—the divine; only to have man strike again, then heaven (vss. 15-18). A sledge hammer is rising and crashing to its target, with vast muscles behind it, each blow heavier than the last, hardly a breath between. And all on a day. Not just any day would do. That day of holy remembrance, when the round of their feasting was gone about, and they were ready to meet again in their eldest brother's house; that day when "early in the morning" (vs. 5) Job had sent for his sons and daughters and offered burnt offerings for them. "Blessed is he whose transgression is forgiven, whose sin is covered. Blessed is the man unto whom the Lord imputeth not iniquity" (Ps. 32:1-2). To get up from your knees like that, and brush the dust from them, and walk right out—into what? It was on Sunday, December 7, 1941, that the bombs fell on Pearl Harbor. You pray, and a child dies. You receive the Lord's Supper, and go

home to get a telegram from the War Office. What sort of world is this? Surely the only final sense there is in it is the sense that God makes. And he is under no compulsion to make our kind of sense. The only security there is in it is his kind of security. You can sit in the nook and chimneyside of his favor, cleansed of all your sin; and there lose your fortune and lose your health—without ever losing the favor, or missing by so much as a hairbreadth the best he has in store for you. If Job had known that, if the Hebrew people had known it, life might have been spared many a Calvary—and been the poorer for it!

20-22. *The Hand of the Giver.*— (Cf. Expos. on 2:7-10; 29:1-25.) To Satan's lie the lie is given. Job maintains his piety. There in that desolation of grief, hemmed in below by "man's inhumanity to man," above by the silent and inscrutable sky, the uncomplaining victim— rending his mantle and shaving his head, as they were wont to do who had plunged into the dark loneliness of some bleak disaster—lifts his

21 And said, Naked came I out of my mother's womb, and naked shall I return thither: the LORD gave, and the LORD hath taken away; blessed be the name of the LORD.

22 In all this Job sinned not, nor charged God foolishly.

ground, and worshiped. 21 And he said, "Naked I came from my mother's womb, and naked shall I return; the LORD gave, and the LORD has taken away; blessed be the name of the LORD."

22 In all this Job did not sin or charge God with wrong.

---

womb of the earth his mother (Gen. 3:19; Ps. 139:13, 15; Ecclus. 40:1) ; faith, because Yahweh owns all and his name shall always be blessed (cf. I Sam. 3:18; Eccl. 5:15) .

The benediction of the name of Yahweh placed on the lips of an Arab prince is unexpected and disconcerting. Elsewhere in the prologue Job spoke of Elohim (vs. 5; 2:10) , and so did the Satan (vs. 9) , the messenger (vs. 16) , Job's wife (2:9) and Yahweh himself (vs. 8; 2:3) .

Duhm's conjecture that the text originally had the word Elohim, which was then accidentally transformed into Yahweh by an absent-minded scribe, is attractive yet gratuitous. But another hypothesis may help to explain the anomaly: the narrator may have introduced a thoroughly Hebraic benediction, for that was the only one known to his listeners—a poetic strophe of a liturgical character. Indeed, one may say that the blessing of the name would not have been possible to the Hebrew mind unless it were the name of Yahweh (Ps. 113:2). Even today in northwestern Arabia, according to Emil G. Kraeling, the survivors of a dead person intone a liturgical formula, "His lord gave him, his lord has taken him away" (*The Book of the Ways of God* [New York: Charles Scribner's Sons, 1939], p. 184) .

The first act of the drama draws to a close (vs. 22) with an indication of Job's refusal to "ascribe to God any folly." The word *tiphlāh*, "tastelessness," applies to moral capriciousness and ill behavior. Job did not accuse the Deity of immoral caprice and misrule.

---

eyes and worships God in the waste. The hand that has added without desert may subtract without reproach. Let Swinburne have his bitter fling at the God who "gives a star and takes a sun away" [4] (see Expos. on 10:1-22) .

For whatever reason (see Exeg. for one of the likeliest conjectures) , the Israelitish name for God is used at this dramatic moment in the prologue, not to occur again, with two exceptions that are perhaps to be accounted for as accidental (12:9; 28:28), until the Lord himself appears (38:1) ; but from that point on increasingly, and consistently in the epilogue. It can hardly be without artistic significance, as the work now stands, that here at the beginning and at the end the mood of reverence so long associated with that name prevails, a reverence so profound that the devout Jew would not even allow his lips to frame the word. Through the cycles of debate, which are kept doubling on their tracks with ever more caustic reiteration, as well as in passages elsewhere that are not intended to reflect the covenant relation, the God to whom reference is made is the God of nature and of all the nations and races of men, a strange, remote, and mighty God, of whom so

little is known, dwelling somewhere outside the intimacies he had established with his people, a God about whom the Arab sheik and his friends converse almost as if they had been orphaned of his presence, a vast and shadowy God, far from the affairs of men. From the warmth and love of one who had made himself known, we are to move farther and farther into the realm where only whispers are heard; until we come back at last to that dear name, and the majesty that kindles again its flame on the hearth of a life restored.

Observe too the double meaning of the word "to bless." It could be a benediction, or it could be a curse. It could be an open door to friendship, or it could be a door slammed in a man's face. The context alone is decisive. It stands in vss. 5 and 11; and in 2:5, 9 (see Exeg. on 2:9-10) . In each instance the word may be a euphemism, as if the very thought of cursing God were intolerable, and the divine name itself, so to speak, had drawn the venom of the curse and by some celestial alchemy had made of it a blessing. A. B. Davidson and H. C. O. Lanchester,[5] however, cite a "similar secondary

[4] *Atalanta in Calydon.*

[5] *The Book of Job* (Cambridge: Cambridge University Press, 1918; "The Cambridge Bible"), p. 6.

2 Again there was a day when the sons of God came to present themselves before the LORD, and Satan came also among them to present himself before the LORD.

2 And the LORD said unto Satan, From whence comest thou? And Satan answered the LORD, and said, From going to and fro in the earth, and from walking up and down in it.

3 And the LORD said unto Satan, Hast thou considered my servant Job, that *there is* none like him in the earth, a perfect and an upright man, one that feareth God, and escheweth evil? and still he holdeth fast his integrity, although thou movedst me against him, to destroy him without cause.

2 Again there was a day when the sons of God came to present themselves before the LORD, and Satan also came among them to present himself before the LORD. 2 And the LORD said to Satan, "Whence have you come?" Satan answered the LORD, "From going to and fro on the earth, and from walking up and down on it." 3 And the LORD said to Satan, "Have you considered my servant Job, that there is none like him on the earth, a blameless and upright man, who fears God and turns away from evil? He still holds fast his integrity, although you moved me against him, to destroy him

---

C. SECOND ACT OF THE DRAMA (2:1-10)

1. THE HEAVENLY COURT (2:1-6)

a) NEW PRAISE OF JOB BY YAHWEH (2:1-3)

2:1-3. The second dialogue—again artistically stylized—between Yahweh and "the Satan" is strictly parallel to the first one. But Yahweh now testifies that his servant has maintained his integrity, and he accuses the adversary of having tormented the hero without cause.

---

use" in the Latin *valere,* which could be for greeting, or for taking leave—permanently. So may one in English speak poetically of "the Blessed Damozel," and a moment later, peering down for a collar button under the lowest-swung article of furniture in the room, mutter imprecations, in colloquial if not vulgar prose, on "the blessed thing"! **Blessed be the name of the LORD.** In any case, what distance is there between that humility and the rebellious defiance which is soon to leap in the face of heaven? To bless, to curse—it is a kind of contrapuntal minor theme, weaving its way in and out of a melody that stands trembling now on the brink of crashing, shuddering discords. The turning of a hand: shall it be El Shaddai, the Almighty, curse him!—or Yahweh, Adonai, blessed be his holy name forever!

In all this Job did not sin. Be prepared for what follows; but at this point, to say no more, the answer to Satan's question comes up roundly from the earth: "Yes! By the eternal LORD of Sinai and the wilderness, of Canaan and the Exile, a man *will* serve God for nought!" There is nothing any more in Job's hands that could possibly account for his piety. His forehead is in the dust. Yet on his lips there is a prayer, and in his heart no sign of a thought that God had dealt unjustly with him; no slightest murmur against what the Hebrew called "foolishness" in heaven's high place, no whispered

charge that on the throne of the universe was wrong, not right, standing there among the shadows, keeping watch above its own (7:12-20). "God, it isn't fair! This should never have happened to me! I don't deserve it!" None of that, not now. Only a man, God's servant, none like him in the earth; and God still proud of him in heaven, still justified in that pride. The first bout with Satan is over—the liar, and the father of lies. In Job's victory God has won.

There is a faith that stands: stands in the peace of remembered good, in the confidence that back of all life's riddles there is meaning, that over all its evil there is God. In the memoirs of Dr. John Brown occurs this passage:

> We were all three awakened by a cry of pain—sharp, insufferable, as if one were stung. . . . We found my father standing before us, erect, his hands clenched in his black hair, his eyes full of misery and amazement, his face white as that of the dead. He frightened us. He saw this, or else his intense will had mastered his agony, for, taking his hands from his head, he said, slowly and gently, "Let us give thanks," and turned to a little sofa in the room; there lay our mother, dead.[6]

2:1-6. *The Final Cynicism.*—The curtain has been lowered only to rise again, this time on a second assembly in heaven, almost identical

[6] "My Father's Memoir," *Spare Hours* (Boston: Ticknor & Fields, 1862), pp. 130-31.

4 And Satan answered the Lord, and said, Skin for skin, yea, all that a man hath will he give for his life.

5 But put forth thine hand now, and touch his bone and his flesh, and he will curse thee to thy face.

6 And the Lord said unto Satan, Behold, he *is* in thine hand; but save his life.

7 ¶ So went Satan forth from the presence of the Lord, and smote Job with sore

without cause." 4 Then Satan answered the Lord, "Skin for skin! All that a man has he will give for his life. 5 But put forth thy hand now, and touch his bone and his flesh, and he will curse thee to thy face." 6 And the Lord said to Satan, "Behold, he is in your power; only spare his life."

7 So Satan went forth from the presence

---

b) New Doubt and Plan of the Satan (2:4-6)

4-6. Skin for skin, or "a hide for a hide," is probably a popular expression familiar to bartering traders and reflects the view that religion too is a bargaining method for obaining happiness. The precise meaning of the proverb is now obscure, but its general application is made clear by the context. "The Satan" was not convinced after the first trial that Job was selflessly devoted to the Deity he worshiped. Property, even posterity, are less precious than physical existence and well-being. According to such a line of reasoning, Job merely executed a strategic retreat and by continuing lip devotion to his God hoped to salvage the only property he still owned—his health. To prove the fallacy of that argument, Yahweh was willing to have the hero put to torture.

2. Second Visitation of Evil (2:7-10)

a) The Disease (2:7-8)

7-8. Job was smitten upon his whole body by an "evil inflammation" (*shehin rā'*). The word for leprosy is not used here, although it was well known to O.T. writers (see

---

with the first. The throne of God is there, and before it the Adversary. One day Job will think of God himself in that role, so near to winning did Satan come. Once more the question, **Whence comest thou?** And once more the answer, nonchalant and unpersuaded, "From all over." Never mind the piety and the patience he has seen, there is still that tongue in his cheek, and the shrug on his shoulders. Tauntingly, as if torn between pain and anger,[7] God throws in the teeth of his perennial cynic, his angel of the sneer, the very words he had used that other day in kindness. **Hast thou considered my servant Job? . . . Still he holdeth fast his integrity.** So that thou **movedst me against him** without reason, goading me to let thee swallow him up for nothing. He was met with the most satanic suggestion Satan has to make: **All that a man hath will he give for his life.** It is a churlish sort of proverb, spoken with what is perhaps the familiarity of an old and licensed retainer who will not have his master imposed on: Let nobody fool you. His possessions are gone, and his children are gone, but with him that barely scratches the surface. Where he is concerned, what counts, apparently, is that he himself is still safe enough.

Not only will Satan report no good—he will

leave that to others more naïve: he will abandon the kind of cynicism that anybody could trot out, and go in for something wholly sophisticated and mature. Here on his lips now is humanity's shout of derision for the image of God in the human soul. "Everybody has his price." Only those could ever be guilty of it who are so obsessed with self that they have begun to mistake their own blindness for sight. There is enough wrong in the world to give it birth, as with all the lies that cradle themselves by the side of truth; but beyond the wrong there is enough right to keep even the man who yields from yielding his own consent. Beyond the wrong, and out of its reach, is an integrity which cannot be bought or had, with threat or bribe. Beyond the wrong, saints and martyrs, how many of them unsung! Beyond, a God who is willing to risk it with anybody! "Behold, not my hand, but thine. I will leave him there, though not his life. That I require of thee, no more." Still that immemorial pride, staking now its love, its confidence, its honor, its hope, laying away in store only death itself, lest there be no foothold left on earth for the soul's triumph. Job will not reckon that a kindness. He will call it the very last of all cruelties. To him it will be doom to live and not die.

7-10. Shall We Receive Good and Not Evil?— So are we rushed at once into the maelstrom of

---

[7] In Blake's illustrations (V and VI), the ineffable sorrow on the face of the Lord is set over against Satan's sadistic glee.

boils from the sole of his foot unto his crown.

8 And he took him a potsherd to scrape himself withal; and he sat down among the ashes.

of the LORD, and afflicted Job with loathsome sores from the sole of his foot to the crown of his head. **8** And he took a potsherd with which to scrape himself, and sat among

---

Lev. 13:9-11; Deut. 24:8; II Kings 5:3) , but the *shehin* was a symptom of one of the worst forms of leprosy (Lev. 13:18-23) ; the same word was used for describing the effects of one of the Egyptian plagues (Exod. 9:9-11) as well as the illness of Hezekiah (II Kings 20:7; Isa. 38:21) . The *shehin rā'* is listed in the curses of Deuteronomy (28:35) as appearing upon the skin, like Job's ailment, "from the sole of the foot to the top of the skull." In the same passage the disease is called "Egyptian" (Deut. 28:27) . Since the ancient writers considered elephantiasis as specifically Egyptian (Pliny *Natural History* XXVI. 5; Lucretius *Of the Nature of Things* VI. 1104-5) , early commentators on Job identified his disease with leprosy. There is no valid reason, however, for maintaining the traditional view. Modern exegetes have conjectured a number of identifications with various dermatic ailments (see S. R. Driver and G. B. Gray, *A Critical and Exegetical Commentary on the Book of Job* [New York: Charles Scribner's Sons, 1921; "International Critical Commentary"], I, 23-24) . A case might be made for a skin disorder known as *pemphigus foliaceus* which, unlike Hansen's disease, appears suddenly and reaches almost at once an acute stage. It is particularly common among young adults endowed with vigorous vitality (cf. 3:13; etc.; Job describes himself fourteen times as a גבר, "strong man") , and it is characterized by bulbous inflammation (cf. 30:30) which produces intense itching (cf. vs. 8) . Atrophic changes appear on the skin of the face (cf. 2:12) and generalized blistering produces an offensive, musty odor. The patient becomes extremely emaciated (cf. 19:20) and suffers from cyclical evening rises of temperature followed by periods of apparent improvement. These are terminated by relapses which reveal constant deterioration, until death eventually comes, sometimes after twenty years (see Rupert Hallam, M.D., "Pemphigus Foliaceus," in *The British Encyclopaedia of Medical Practice* [London: Butterworth & Co., 1938], IX, 490-92) . In spite of several allusions to Job's pathological state which may be found in the poetic discussion (see 7:5; 16:13, 15; 19:17; 30:17, 30) , no diagnosis can be assured.

Scraping himself with a potsherd, Job left his house for a heap of dung ashes—the *mazbala,* which exists to this day outside Arabian towns—and there he sat, amid rubbish, rotting carcasses, playing urchins, homeless beggars, village idiots, and howling dogs. The respected prince was now an outcast, awaiting death, tormented by pain, and rent by mental anguish.

---

mystery and disaster. This time there is no lull before the storm. No sooner is permission given than Satan hurries forth from the divine presence to smite with putrefying sores (see Exeg.) , from head to foot, the man he had already stripped and bereaved. Hell lets loose its bolts, but all within the providence of heaven: for nothing can befall a man outside that circle. The evil is not to be thought of as deliberately willed of God. Explicit in the prologue, and implicit throughout, is the realization that the problem of God's providence may not be so simply resolved. The exercise of it lies rather in the fact that even the wiles of Satan are no more than an instrument in his hands. There was a purpose beyond Satan's purpose, whatever that other purpose was (see Expos. on 36:8-25; 42:5) , and to this purpose Satan's purpose and

man's response alike could do nothing but contribute. Otherwise the permission given Satan would itself have been satanic.

Writes James McKechnie:

It is not enough to say that [Satan] loses in spite of his gains—that does not express the full irony of his position—for, indeed, he loses by and through his gains. He makes Job a rebel, and in rebellion Job lays grip on a deeper loyalty. He provokes him into complaints against God, yet these complaints mark not a renunciation of, but agonising struggles after God. He makes him a heretic, a passionate repudiator of the faith of his people, yet even while the old faith is being destroyed, a new and nobler faith is taking root in his heart. Satan is thus, in most unforeseeable fashion, duped by his own activities. Yet if, after our facile manner, we sum up the results of Job's Ordeal by saying that good comes out of evil, let us beware in what sense we use the

9 ¶ Then said his wife unto him, Dost thou still retain thine integrity? curse God, and die.

10 But he said unto her, Thou speakest as one of the foolish women speaketh. What? shall we receive good at the hand of God, and shall we not receive evil? In all this did not Job sin with his lips.

the ashes. 9 Then his wife said to him, "Do you still hold fast your integrity? Curse God, and die."

10 But he said to her, "You speak as one of the foolish women would speak. Shall we receive good at the hand of God, and shall we not receive evil?" In all this Job did not sin with his lips.

---

b) THE RESIGNATION AND FAITH OF JOB (2:9-10)

9-10. One may wonder why Job's wife had mysteriously survived the tragic blows of ch. 1. Chrysostom and others maintained that the narrator meant thereby to increase the sufferer's torture to a climactic degree: In the light of subsequent events it becomes clear that Job would have found relief in becoming a widower. The woman's question and advice may be interpreted in two ways: (a) "Do you still pretend to be a perfect man? Do you not see that such a fantastic succession of calamities proves beyond doubt that you are a sinner? Bid God farewell and die!" Or (b) "Do you still ridiculously believe that your perfection is recognized by a righteous God? Let blasphemy bring its certain and immediate consequence. Curse God and die." The idea is in line with that expressed in Isa. 8:21-22.

The second interpretation seems preferable, for the verb *bērēkh,* "to bless," had already been used euphemistically by the Satan in the sense of "to curse" (vs. 5; 1:11). In other words, the desperate and bewildered woman, still confident in her husband's integrity, unable to hope for his healing, and profoundly sympathizing with his plight, found her only recourse in the idea of euthanasia, and prescribed for her husband a theological method of committing suicide. Death by a curse was better than a slowly dying life. Such a piece of advice seems to have been inspired by love and common sense. Yet one may understand why Augustine called Job's wife "the adjutant of the devil," a spiritual sister of the woman in the story of the garden (Gen. 3:1 ff.), for she tempted the hero to forsake his Creator.

Job did not fall into this temptation. He recognized in her seemingly reasonable proposal the sign of frenzy. Faith offered to him a reason higher than human reason. He saw only folly in the apparent reasonableness of the scheme, and said, "You speak as one of the *nebhālôth."* The masculine singular form of the same word (*nābhāl*) designates the fool who "said in his heart, There is no God" (Ps. 14:1). The insanity of human wisdom is opposed to the sanity of faith. Job was outspoken, but he remained courteous: he did not accuse his wife of being a fool but only of using fools' language. He understood that she too was suffering in agony. His final expression of trust in God took the form of a rhetorical question, in a loving attempt to win her over to his own

---

words. Never by way of natural and necessary sequence does good come out of evil. It is as a glad surprise, a miracle and triumph of grace, that it comes. Satan accomplishes nothing for God, though God may accomplish much through Satan.[8]

Hell makes its moves on the checkered squares of human existence; but all its moves are on heaven's own chessboard. The Adversary himself has an Adversary (see Expos. on 9:20-24; 19:6; 29:1-25; 34:14; 36:5-15). There are no feints, no sham battles lost or won. There is a

profound sense in which by Job's testing God is tested. He will fail if Job fails. If Job now stands, he will stand.[9] It is his handiwork that is cast into the fire and furnace of life's peril and sorrow—there on the refuse heap beyond the town, where the scavenger dogs of the East prowl among the ashes. There the issue will be drawn—and settled. And there the last prop of Job's thus far stalwart soul is struck from beneath him. Blake represents Job's wife as the faithful attendant upon all her husband's misery. We may perhaps be permitted to assume

⁸ *Job, Moral Hero, Religious Egoist, and Mystic* (Greenock: James McKelvie & Sons, 1926), pp. 26-27; (New York: George H. Doran Co., 1927), pp. 30-31. Used by permission.

⁹ Cf. Robert Frost, *A Masque of Reason* (New York: H. Holt & Co., 1945). The treatment is essentially anthropocentric and yet suggestive.

11 ¶ Now when Job's three friends heard of all this evil that was come upon him, they came every one from his own place; Eliphaz the Temanite, and Bildad the Shuhite, and Zophar the Naamathite: for they had made an appointment together to come to mourn with him, and to comfort him.

11 Now when Job's three friends heard of all this evil that had come upon him, they came each from his own place, Eli'phaz the Te'manite, Bildad the Shuhite, and Zophar the Na'amathite. They made an appointment together to come to condole with

submission to the divine will and assurance in God's righteousness of purpose and omnipotence. He spoke on her behalf as well as on his own, and perhaps in the name of all men who suffer. By using the first person plural pronoun he became the type of mankind crucified. His humility was as perfect as his faith because his theological belief was true to the strictest form of Hebraic monism. In most horrible torment he remembered the grace which had been granted him, and the memory of that grace was sufficient. God's apparent evil could not make him forget God's good. In spite of traditional interpretations to the contrary, his attitude contains nothing of the stoic. He did not resign himself to an impersonal fate but trusted the Almighty. His submission had nothing to do with the honor of man: it was due to his sense of the glory of God. Such a faith reveals not Hellenistic stoicism but Hebraic theocentrism. The argument of the Satan was defeated; **Job did not sin with his lips.** There is no implication, as the rabbis suggested, that he sinned in his heart (Baba Bathra 16*a*).

D. Presentation of the Hero's Friends (2:11-13)
1. Names and Countries of the Friends (2:11)

11. After a certain lapse of time, perhaps weeks or even months, during which, it may be presumed, Job's health deteriorated, three of his friends heard of his misfortunes.

Eliphaz was a resident of Teman, in Edom (Gen. 36:4, 11; Jer. 49:7; Obad. 9; Ezek. 25:13; Amos 1:12)—a country famous for its wisdom (cf. Robert H. Pfeiffer, "Edomitic Wisdom," *Zeitschrift für die alttestamentliche Wissenschaft*, XLIV [1926], 13-25). His name may have meant "God crushes." **Bildad** belonged to the tribe of Shuah, probably associated with Aramaean nomads who migrated somewhere in the southeast

that the gentle remonstrance in vs. 10 won her back to her fealty; but at this moment she fails him. Whether out of the unutterable depths of her compassion or because, whatever her husband might do, she could herself no longer bear a life with every visible token of God's favor and presence gone from it (cf. 1:9-11), she cries out against the whole impossible horror (see Exeg., and recall vss. 3, 5). On this tremendous ground, which only heroes can take, Job meets her: "The good is none of ours. It is not even our due. It comes from God. Shall we not then acknowledge his sovereign hand when the shadows fall and evil is our lot? [See Expos. on 1:20-22.] All our light is no more than a borrowed ray; and the dark no other than a mantle which God spreads over us. Shall we then be godly in the day, and in the night godless?" So it is before a man's self gets in the way and he begins to brood. For Job there is still the vision of God, high and lifted up; and no matter how far he wanders from it in the course of the argument, driven like a wind-tossed ship under a leaden sky, he will return to it, and

find there the peace which passes understanding, and hear again the words that are hardly lawful for a man to utter. Around the splendor of that same throne and majesty the persecuted church of Christ was rallied, centuries on centuries later, with "the removing of those things that are shaken, . . . that those things which cannot be shaken may remain" (Heb. 12:27). What did it matter if they were despised and rejected of men? "Ye are a chosen generation, a royal priesthood, a holy nation, . . . that ye should show forth the praises of him who hath called you out of darkness into his marvelous light" (I Pet. 2:9). What if evil did seem rampant in the world? "Alleluia: for the Lord God omnipotent reigneth" (Rev. 19:6). The flag has been run up full mast. **In all this did Job not sin with his lips** (cf. vs. 5; 1:11, 20-22). God is justified, Satan vanquished. But around those sunny heights now the clouds gather.

11-13. *Job's Comforters.*—It is a mistake to deal harshly with these men. They have become a proverb; but not all proverbs are fair, because not all the people who fashion proverbs are fair.

| 12 And when they lifted up their eyes afar off, and knew him not, they lifted up their voice, and wept; and they rent every one his mantle, and sprinkled dust upon their heads toward heaven. | him and comfort him. 12 And when they saw him from afar, they did not recognize him; and they raised their voices and wept; and they rent their robes and sprinkled dust upon their heads toward heaven. |

of Palestine (Gen. 25:2, 6). His name may be derived from the Aramaic, "Beloved of the Lord." **Zophar** (a name with an uncertain meaning, perhaps "twittering bird" or "sharp nail" or "goatlike jumper") lived in Na'amah, perhaps Djebel-el-Na'ameh, in northwestern Arabia.

2. MOURNING OF THE FRIENDS (2:12)

12. The narrator tells how the three friends met at an appointed place, apparently in order to plan together a common strategy of pastoral ministration. This feature is another indication of the artistic character of the story. **They lifted up their eyes afar off,** as well they would, since Job was sitting on the prominent top of the *mazbala* outside the town. So terrible were the ravages of the disease that **they did not recognize him.** Thereupon they performed the approved ritual of mourning for the dead (II Sam. 12:16; Lam. 2:10).

Neither was Job. What he says of his friends will appear. But what he says is never to be taken with too great literalness. He is a man distraught, who yet gives many a sign that in his heart of hearts he yearns toward them (19:21). They had been grieved to hear of his calamities, they had fixed their rendezvous and come to him, and they meant him the best they knew. That they failed in their mission should never have fastened on them the stigma they have borne through the years. The only thing that can be said of them justly is that they were poorly equipped for their ministry of consolation. They were "too white"; and "the flower of life is red." They lacked most where the need was greatest. The world perishes not of dark but of cold. The soul in its deep distress seeks not light but warmth, not counsel but understanding. If they had ever suffered any themselves, it might have been different.[10] As it was, they came with a theory to meet a person, were of one mind and one will; but the heart is the place of meeting. They undertook their task with certain premises —as who does not: all sufficiently true to give rise to the problem of the book, and lend it even now a peculiar poignancy; and all sufficiently false to stir anybody's affliction into rebellion (cf. Expos. on 32:6). God punishes the evil and rewards the good, so ran their logic. His mercy is toward them that fear him; and his wrath upon the disobedient, that they may forsake their wicked ways and live. The man whom catastrophe overtakes, that man has sinned. Let him repent and his deliverance is sure. If he will not, the very stars in their

courses will fight against him. That was the Hebrew faith, straight out of Deuteronomy and the prophets; and it was their faith. There was certainly nothing contagious about it, to bring a soul, for all the loneliness of its anguish, to cry out "Immanuel, God with us!" Quite the contrary. But they could not themselves afford to become involved with anyone who would break with it, as Job had broken with it. For it had been his faith too, until he saw that never again for him could it cover the facts. He was one of those facts. He had done nothing commensurate with this disaster. There was no answer that way. But what other way was there, and what other answer? The friends twisted and squirmed and guessed and supposed and hurled it back at him over and over again. It was by their traditional piety that Job was goaded into a passionate fury, while round by round their vehemence turned into venom. Less and less did they concern themselves about the sufferer; more and more it was "the principle of the thing" that mattered. They were not intentionally cruel. Theirs was the cruelty of those who "for conscience toward God" would see to it that you "endure grief and suffer wrongfully" (I Pet. 2:19). And it distorted everything they said. It made abysmal folly of their wisdom (cf. Expos. on 4:1–5:27; 6:14).

Through Blake's drawings there runs the suggestion that the debate which staggers back and forth through the body of the poem is little more in reality than the conversation that went on in Job's own mind, between himself the accuser and himself the accused (see Expos. on 19:25). No doubt it is altogether too fanciful, yet almost irresistible, to think of Eliphaz the seer as the word of the prophets of Israel, knock-

---

[10] See Thornton Wilder, *The Angel That Troubled the Waters* (New York: Coward-McCann, 1928); cf. Expos. on 5:8.

| 13 So they sat down with him upon the ground seven days and seven nights, and none spake a word unto him: for they saw that *his* grief was very great. | 13 And they sat with him on the ground seven days and seven nights, and no one spoke a word to him, for they saw that his suffering was very great. |

3. Silence of Job and the Friends (2:13)

13. The friends had intended "to condole with [Job] and comfort him" (vs. 11), but **seven days and seven nights** of silence were more eloquent than words. He himself remained mute with woe. He did not try to take his life, perhaps because he had reached a state of complete despair. "When a man attempts suicide, it means he cares about something. He cares whether he's alive or dead. . . . But real despair means there is no hope, no door, no escape. . . . We never do try to commit suicide in that circle of hell, which is the lowest of all. It is as if we were already dead, rotting, yet still suffering." (William Seabrook, *Asylum* [New York: Harcourt, Brace & Co., 1935], p. 195.) On the other hand, it may be that Job, like most ancient Semites, did not consider at all the idea of bringing death upon himself; and that he kept silence because a remnant of faith prevented him, not from despair, but from a desperate act. He faced death but he did not hasten its coming, like another of whom it was later said,

> The parching thirst of death
> Is on Thee, and Thou triest
>
> The slumb'rous potion bland, and wilt not drink:
> Not sullen, nor in scorn, like haughty man
>   With suicidal hand
>   Putting his solace by.
>   (John Keble, *The Christian Year*, "Tuesday Before Easter.")

The narrative is now brought to a solemn pause, and dramatic pathos is created in the mind of the listeners with a minimum of devices. The last notes of the overture have been played, leaving the audience in suspense. The poetic opus may now begin.

ing at the door of Job's misery. And Bildad the wise as the incarnation of all the wisdom of the Jewish people, treading on the heels of the prophets. And Zophar, the man whose very presence would seem to say continually, "Know ye not the way of the Lord, how straight it is? Then walk ye in it!"—what if Zophar were the very thundering of the law in Job's own heart? Here then would be the three categories of the sacred writings, Law, and Prophets, and Wisdom. Together they stood up in Job's memory to condemn him. Of how much of his violence might not that be the secret! Never is the spirit so bitter as when an inner voice keeps whispering "Yes" to the accusations that are brought against us. With these, one by one, Job held his colloquy. He could not yield himself to their indictment, and they kept indicting him. It was his controversy with all he knew of religion; and so very little of what he knew met his case. It was the controversy of the Jewish people with all they knew of God; and so little, so very little of what they knew answered to their need. They were being driven, as was Job, to wider horizons and broader views and deeper insights.

There was a devout and faithful woman whose extraordinarily gifted son had been killed in World War II. She said it was past her understanding. It seemed to make no sense if one stipulated a good God. And she said that nothing in her religion seemed to help her. Nor anything that religious people said to her. They just aggravated her grief and her bewilderment. "They tell me that I must take it patiently and see it through; that there will be some kind of dawn if I wait for it. But they can't show me any that seems worth waiting for. They say I can be thankful he died a hero, and not a profligate, as some men die. But he died, didn't he? They want me to believe I'll be a stronger woman for it, and kinder, and truer. Did he then have to give up his life to make a stronger woman of me? Wasn't there some other way? Then they remind me that I'm not the only one who has suffered such bereavement, I must think of the thousands like myself. If I should think of them, I'd go mad. And if I found any solace in thinking of them, I should be a monster" (see Expos. on 7:1-6). And so for hours she talked, veering around at last to her son's life-

3 After this opened Job his mouth, and cursed his day.

2 And Job spake, and said,

3 Let the day perish wherein I was born, and the night *in which* it was said, There is a man child conceived.

4 Let that day be darkness; let not God regard it from above, neither let the light shine upon it.

3 After this Job opened his mouth and cursed the day of his birth. 2 And Job said:

3 "Let the day perish wherein I was born, and the night which said, 'A man-child is conceived.'

4 Let that day be darkness! May God above not seek it, nor light shine upon it.

II. The Poetic Discussion (3:1–31:40)

A. Lament of Job (3:1-26)

After weeks and perhaps months of solitude (see 7:3) and seven days and nights of friendly presence without words, Job himself broke the silence. Far from the height of submissive faith in which he had last spoken (2:10), he apparently fell into an abyss of hopelessness. Not quite total, however, for in absolute despondency man cares for nothing and speaks not. Job broke into a curse, not against God, but against his own existence, and he expressed three wishes: (a) that he had never been born (vss. 2-10); (b) that he had died at birth (vss. 11-19); and (c) that he might die now (vss. 20-26). Ignoring both his friends and his God, he let his soliloquy rise as a rhythmic cry of wounded animality.

1. The Curse (3:1-10)

3:1-10. Job . . . cursed his day, viz., the day in which he was born (vss. 1-2). Days and nights, according to ancient beliefs (see Ps. 19:3), were endowed with a kind of

long compassion for the Negro, away there in the deep South where he came from. And suddenly her eyes shone with a strange light. "Maybe," she said, "I ought to go back and carry on where he left off." It was as near as she came to smiling. Softly the door closed behind her as she left. There was no answer that day; but there was a stirring, and a kind of peace that was like the brush of an angel's wing.

So they sat down with him upon the ground. With every manifestation of grief, as those who mourn the dead, stricken as he was stricken, all the verdure of his life no more than dust, they waited for him to speak, not daring themselves to begin. And it was like rain to the parched ground of Job's lonely soul. The flood gates of his sorrow swung wide open (see Matt. 27:36 for purposes of contrast and comparison).

3:1-26. *Job's Lament.*— (Cf. Jer. 20:14-18; Expos. on 6:2-7, 4, 6, 8-13.) In the release that so often comes when a sufferer finds himself as he thinks among those who will assuredly understand, and not take amiss anything he says, Job lets loose the pent-up torrent of his anguish. In verses of somber beauty, breaking out at once into imprecation solemn and sustained (vss. 3-10; on vss. 4, 6 see Expos. on 10:19-22), then dying away, with a change of mood quite characteristic of the poem, into a kind of wistful tranquillity (vss. 11-19), only to surge again

like the tide (vss. 20-26), he pours out his lament. It is the beating of a pulse behind a tired and aching forehead, the writhing of a human soul under incredible torture of mind and body. If only the night had never conceived him, or the day when he first saw the light had never dawned! (Cf. Milton's "Lycidas," l. 26, "the opening eye-lids of the morn.") Surely, with all the possibilities, something else could have happened to him—not this. He could have died before he was born. He could have died at birth, or after. Why not? It would have made no difference when. Why was he ever taken up and owned, or fed with milk at his mother's breast? He might have lain down and been at peace with the great dead—or the not so great. What of it? Where high and low were alike: kings and princes, the wicked and the weary, every one of them at rest now, the prisoner and the slave. Life had no business going on as it was: not when men, multitudes of them, longed for death as frantically as he longed for it, he whose way was hid, not knowing how to go, or which turn to take, or what to do but to cry out and tremble with pain.

1. *The Anatomy of Despair.*—In 1621 Robert Burton published what was intended to be a medical treatise under the title *The Anatomy of Melancholy.* There he explored with a great wealth of learning not only the cause and cure

5 Let darkness and the shadow of death stain it; let a cloud dwell upon it; let the blackness of the day terrify it.

6 As for that night, let darkness seize upon it; let it not be joined unto the days of the year; let it not come into the number of the months.

7 Lo, let that night be solitary; let no joyful voice come therein.

8 Let them curse it that curse the day, who are ready to raise up their mourning.

9 Let the stars of the twilight thereof be dark; let it look for light, but have none; neither let it see the dawning of the day:

10 Because it shut not up the doors of my mother's womb, nor hid sorrow from mine eyes.

---

5 Let gloom and deep darkness claim it.
  Let clouds dwell upon it;
  let the blackness of the day terrify it.

6 That night — let thick darkness seize it!
  let it not rejoice among the days of the year,
  let it not come into the number of the months.

7 Yea, let that night be barren;
  let no joyful cry be heard[b] in it.

8 Let those curse it who curse the day,
  who are skilled to rouse up Leviathan.

9 Let the stars of its dawn be dark;
  let it hope for light, but have none,
  nor see the eyelids of the morning;

10 because it did not shut the doors of my mother's womb,
  nor hide trouble from my eyes.

[b] Heb come

---

autonomous existence. If only the day of Job's birth—nay, the night of his conception—had never come to pass, if **Leviathan** had been stirred up (vs. 8), then chaos would have overcome the created order and Job would not have received life. The pain he now endures never would have excruciated him. Leviathan is a sea monster which in ancient Semitic mythology belonged to the world of chaos that the creator God had to subdue in order to establish a livable earth. In Isa. 27:1 Leviathan is an enemy of God, while in Ps. 104:26 he has become a mere plaything of Yahweh. Job 41:1 ff. and Ps. 74:14 use the term in order to convey the feeling of elemental fear produced by the crocodile. Like *tannîn* (7:12) and Rahab (9:13; 26:12), Leviathan has become a personification of cosmic antagonism to God. To stir and wake them is to bring the world back to primeval chaos. The sufferer wished that the earth had come to an end before he had been conceived.

---

of melancholy, but the nature of it, and its relation to love, to religion, and indeed to all of human life. There is no doubt that its springs lie deep in man's heart. His literature celebrates it endlessly, at times romanticizes it. To live is to suffer from a disease that only death can cure. It is to set out on an uneasy pilgrimage. It is to be the butt of a cosmic jest, or a cosmic blunder; the unsuspecting victim of a lie, a cheat—bubble, dance, dream, shadow, what word you please. Any good encyclopedia of familiar quotations will provide stanza and verse. From momentary whim to poetic mood to settled tedium and dejection, man's finitude, coupled with the manifold frustrations of his existence, has left its mark on him—to say nothing of the sin that clouds his sky and blots out his sun.

But there is something other than melancholy here. There are premonitions of despair. The problem is theological to the core. At first no mention is made of God: partly because of a lingering reverence, but partly too because God is becoming a stranger. It is that which little by

little will prove the most terrible thing of all. The anchor is beginning to drag in the storm. The lines that have held Job fast to eternity are giving way. And it makes of life an answerless riddle and a curse. It turns light into darkness, wipes out the good, and spreads over the past, the present, and the future the shadow of evil (see Exeg. on vss. 20-26). That shadow will not lift until the old relationship can somehow be restored.

It is certainly worth noting too that to the Hebrew—and so by transfer here to Job—life was essentially good, and death evil (see Exeg. on vss. 11-19; 6:8-13). Only in such a context can there be any despair that is profoundly religious in character. This is by no means the *Weltschmerz* of the poet, or the despondency of the suicide; obviously it is anything but the impassive acquiescence of the Stoic or the Buddhist. This is the unrestrained cry of an outraged faith, the torment of a spirit no longer at home in a world where at least some measure of being at home is possible.

11 Why died I not from the womb? *why* did I *not* give up the ghost when I came out of the belly?

12 Why did the knees prevent me? or why the breasts that I should suck?

13 For now should I have lain still and been quiet, I should have slept: then had I been at rest,

14 With kings and counselors of the earth, which built desolate places for themselves;

15 Or with princes that had gold, who filled their houses with silver:

16 Or as a hidden untimely birth I had not been; as infants *which* never saw light.

17 There the wicked cease *from* troubling; and there the weary be at rest.

18 *There* the prisoners rest together; they hear not the voice of the oppressor.

19 The small and great are there; and the servant *is* free from his master.

11 "Why did I not die at birth,
   come forth from the womb and expire?

12 Why did the knees receive me?
   Or why the breasts, that I should suck?

13 For then I should have lain down and
      been quiet;
   I should have slept; then I should have
      been at rest,

14 with kings and counselors of the earth
   who rebuilt ruins for themselves,

15 or with princes who had gold,
   who filled their houses with silver.

16 Or why was I not as a hidden untimely
      birth,
   as infants that never see the light?

17 There the wicked cease from troubling,
   and there the weary are at rest.

18 There the prisoners are at ease together;
   they hear not the voice of the task-
      master.

19 The small and the great are there,
   and the slave is free from his master.

2. The Query (3:11-19)

11-19. The aggressiveness of the lamenter soon subsided into an inquiring mood as the curse of the first strophe became an anxious question and awakened Job to pained curiosity: **Why died I not from the womb?** This inquiry was not immediately pursued, however, for the idea of death began to engage his morbid fancy. While Hebrew thought considered death as evil, Job looked upon it, with some Egyptian and Babylonian pessimists (see Intro., pp. 879-80), as a state of tranquillity and sleep (vs. 13) in which he might have enjoyed rest in the company of the former princes of the earth (vss. 14-15). He contemplated for an instant even the state of nonexistence, such as that of infants dead *in utero* (vs. 16). There is no reason to maintain (with Duhm *et al.*) that this verse is now out of place and should be reinserted after vs. 11. To be sure, a copyist's error is always possible, but it may also be that the poet used here the stylistic device of the afterthought. Job, having apparently completed the first theme (vss. 3-10), started

11. Why Not?—**Why died I not from the womb?** To Job anything would have been better —if anybody had cared to manage it so: death at birth, death in infancy, best of all, death before birth; but if none of these, then death now! With everything there was to choose from, why should very worst turn out to be very fact? Why not this, or that, or some other thing? Almost everybody whose lot it is to suffer finds himself on the verge of asking that question sooner or later. It keeps repeating itself like a recurring decimal. Sometimes men ask it of the wide and lambent air, as Job asked it. Sometimes they ask it about God, not bold enough to face him straight (cf. 10:18). Always they ask it out of an ignorance that would petulantly offer itself as wisdom. One often wonders if the choice had really been ours what we would have done with it, had we too been troubled with omniscience,

as God is. His choices must not be so simply made, or painless for him. To trust that wisdom which is beyond our own, reckoning on the power that in all things works for good with those who answer his love with theirs—what might that not make of life, the life of which so many say they can make nothing at all? The facts are yet facts, even after we have given up wondering about them; and not one of them so trivial or so tragic but that men and women by unnamed thousands have taken its like in their hands and fashioned a splendor of it.

17. There the Wicked Cease From Troubling. —(Cf. 15:20; Isa. 57:20-21.) Both the oppressor and his victim find in Sheol "surcease of sorrow." The text is frequently misconstrued. The reference is not to the repose of the blessed, delivered at last from the hand of the tormentor. Moral distinctions had not yet been carried over

20 Wherefore is light given to him that is in misery, and life unto the bitter *in* soul;	20 "Why is light given to him that is in misery, and life to the bitter in soul,

to develop the second (vss. 11-15), and in the midst of its unfolding introduced a parenthetical hypothesis which logically belonged to the first (vs. 16). He then proceeded to bring the second theme to completion (vss. 17-19).

The contemplation of the quietude of the dead suggested another vision, that of their harmlessness (vs. 17) and social equality (vss. 18-19). This image in turn introduced a third development.

3. THE CRY (3:20-26)

20-26. Job's desire for a quick death was not expressed in the subjective mood of modern romanticists. Once again he spoke in bitter question and in the name of any

into the life beyond. It was the wicked themselves who in that shadowy place were no longer troubled. So completely was the world we know identified with God's world, and the time we know—we talk sometimes of killing it!—caught up into his time, that no other world, no aftertime, seemed able to hold out any promise or carry any threat which the years did not already carry. So full and rich was life, so immediate God's Word, so urgent the necessity for instant obedience, so present and real in each day's experience, and in the movements of history, God's judgment and God's mercy! Strange to think of how much more than with us. man's being here mattered—more, not less—and that in spite of the veil which was to be done away in Christ (II Cor. 3:14; see Expos. on 14:1-6).

20. Why?—It is out of Job's wrestling with these ultimate mysteries of providence, without ever allowing them, by some mystery of grace, finally to alienate him from the divine Protagonist, that the flashing insights come (14:14; 16:19; 17:3; 19:25-27), and the resolution of all mystery in the mystery of a presence (42:5). Certain it is that much of man's knowledge both of God and of the world has been mediated to him through just such struggle (see Expos. on 10:1-7, 8-12). Supremely true was it that the religion of Israel was inseparable from the suffering of Israel as a nation (yet see Expos. on 1:1). In a letter one young scholar of the O.T. writes:

It is obvious in the servant passages that the meaning of Israel's loss of selfhood is being explored, with an effort not so much to find a solution as to indicate a redemptive line of reaction and to make God's dealing with the chosen people intelligible at this point. . . . Israel [is] seeking to understand her vocation, and her relation to God: whether the covenant will hold or not. [If the same is true in Job] then the Vindicator passage (19:25-27) can have all sorts of meaning, possibly messianic. The feeling which keeps haunting me is that the book

is certainly not a theological discussion of the problem of suffering, or merely a satire on the orthodox doctrine of retribution, or a story for its own sake. But primarily it seems on a par with Isa. 52–53 in its summing up of all that disturbed the exilic and postexilic community in its understanding of God's dealing with them. The cataclysmic element, the stubborn and unimaginative reactions, the search and longing for some revelation from God of his purpose in it all, and the final conclusion (so similar to Isa. 40:12 ff., and indeed all of Second Isaiah), which emphasizes the sovereignty of God—all this makes me feel that Job and Second Isaiah belong together as the two great witnesses to the surviving awareness of community and of Israel as still related to Yahweh, if she will but find out how. It seems to be a kind of glorious rebuke to those who would seek an allegorical interpretation at every point in history ("This bit of destruction means that God is angry with us"; or "We have prospered, now he has forgiven"), with the answer in terms of a vast depiction of the nature of God. And that's all they need to know; it turns their attention toward vocation, rather than to justification of past tribulations.[10]

But not only does the revelation come through the conflict; it comes in its fullness only when the conflict itself gives place to high commitment (cf. 42:10). Both **misery** and bitterness of soul have been known to yield light and life; but not for the man who tarries in either of them. The implication in Job's question is that if the purpose of God had not been hidden from him—and that it was, is one of the major points of the prologue—he could have borne his affliction with greater fortitude. It is hard to say. Even if we knew the end God has in mind, most of us would prefer some other means. The "Why?" may not die on a man's lips with the granting of an answer; if it dies anywhere, it will die in his hands.

20-21. Through Dark Glasses.—(Cf. 7:1-6; 29:1-25.) Under the figure of men frantically

[10] Grace Edwards, formerly Assistant Professor of Philosophy and Religion, Hollins College, Virginia. Used by permission.

21 Which long for death, but it *cometh* not; and dig for it more than for hid treasures;	21 who long for death, but it comes not, and dig for it more than for hid treasures;
22 Which rejoice exceedingly, *and* are glad, when they can find the grave?	22 who rejoice exceedingly, and are glad, when they find the grave?

man who **is in misery** (vs. 20), **whose way is hid, and whom God** [Eloah] **hath hedged in** (vs. 23). At last the Deity was remembered, but only as the author of evil. Still, even a fleeting reference to an absent and hostile God represented a step forward, away from the depth of the seven days and nights of dumbness. With consummate skill and profound knowledge of the human spirit, the poet moves his hero toward theological argument. The champion had not yet attacked the Deity, but he was ready to begin the fight. He had challenged the validity of the gift of **life to the bitter in soul** (vs. 20). He had questioned the reasons for living against one's longing for death (vs. 21). He had implicitly doubted the purposes of the creator of life by explicitly accusing him of making a strong man (*gébher*) intellectually blind and impotent (vs. 23). By another skillful transition the poet makes Job turn back to himself to suggest a comparison between his fate and that of a wild and powerful animal **hedged in** with no chance of escape.

The energy he managed to muster for his roarings (vs. 24) has now been spent. The opening curse has given way to the shocked amazement of an apprentice philosopher, which in turn subsides into a childish wailing of tortured flesh (vss. 25-26). Then Job lapses again into silence.

According to some commentators, the last verses do not constitute a complaint against physical pain but reveal the mental anguish which seized Job at the anticipation of the friends' rebuke. In favor of this interpretation one may point out (*a*) the abstract and general character of the fear mentioned in vs. 25, and (*b*) the use of the word *róghez* in vs. 26, which does not mean **trouble** but "raging," "wrath," "rumbling of thunder," and may admirably apply to the theological frenzy that Job may suspect he has inspired in his learned and pious listeners. Against this it must be said that vs. 24 introduces the

digging for hidden treasure, Job represents what to him seems, among the multitudes of mankind, the all too widespread longing for death. Freud and his disciples have made much of the so-called "death wish," life's own deep shudder at life, the desire that being has for not-being; but when every due allowance has been made, it is the unhealthy and jaundiced that see, as a result of their own misery and bitterness of soul, any appreciable number **who rejoice exceedingly, and are glad, when they can find the grave.** Many a weary traveler lies down with no protest on his lips, and nothing but welcome in his eyes; but the broader one's acquaintance with human sorrows the greater one's awareness of the almost incredible tenacity with which life clings to living. Ecclesiastes set down his dolorous conclusion, "Wherefore I praised the dead which are already dead, more than the living which are yet alive. Yea, better . . . than both they [is he] which hath not yet been, who hath not seen the evil work that is done under the sun" (4:2-3). But Ecclesiastes himself must have got a good deal of satisfaction out of writing a book about it. And no doubt

he wanted to finish his book before anything untoward happened to him. More than that, however, and nearer the purpose, courage is too often born under circumstances, and cradled in conditions, that would seem to make dying a boon. Robert Louis Stevenson sent back home from his sickbed such valorous bits so light-heartedly that one reviewer, not knowing him, hazarded the opinion that their author had never felt even a twinge of rheumatism (see Expos. on 1:2-3; 11:7; 30:1, 9, 16, 24). To be sure, facile optimism belongs as little to this world as morbid pessimism; but it gets around more, is much better liked, and fool though it is because facile, stands often closer to the facts. If what a man sees is monstrous, hate not love, ugliness not beauty, gloom not gladness, the chances are that he is staring as in a mirror at his own image. It is not just the life around him, it is the life within, that calls for a cleansing, healing touch. In Dickens' *Christmas Carol* Christmas had not changed; Scrooge had, and more than once! Read Gen. 1 and catch that insistent refrain, "and God saw that it was good." When Satan looked, he saw not that, but

23 *Why is light given* to a man whose way is hid, and whom God hath hedged in?

24 For my sighing cometh before I eat, and my roarings are poured out like the waters.

23 Why is light given to a man whose way is hid,
    whom God has hedged in?
24 For my sighing comes as[c] my bread,
    and my groanings are poured out like water.

[c] Heb *before*

---

everything else. He but rubbed the itch of his opinion and made himself scabs (Shakespeare, *Coriolanus*, Act I, scene 1).

23. A Man Whose Way Is Hid.—Here is at once the tragedy and the romance of human existence. It was more than pain, it was the bewilderment through which Job was passing, the first vague premonitions of estrangement from God (see Expos. on vs. 1; cf. 1:20-22), that threw him off center, driving him in upon himself, narrowing his horizons, shutting off the view, until even God's goodness in the days that were gone seemed like calculated malevolence (10:10-17). His way was hid because he was already traveling in the wrong direction. There was nothing ahead but a dead end. To get out he would have to reverse his steps. There is little use in saying that he should not have allowed any such thing to happen (4:4-5). Man as he ought to be, would not (see Exeg. on vss. 20-26); man as he is, does. He suffers from many a disease of the eye that no oculist can treat: pride, lust, and prejudice (Matt. 6:22-23). "None so blind," writes Matthew Henry, "as those that will not see."

But who sees, and who is blind (see Expos. on 5:14)? From even the keenest eye the future is veiled, and how much of the present and the past! We talk of justice. Who knows what it is? Do wars even approximate it? What is justice for the South Side, for Harlem, for the East End, for the neighbor next door? So is man's way hidden in clouds and thick darkness. Wrote John Henry Newman:

> I do not ask to see
> The distant scene—one step enough for me.[1]

What step? "Lead thou me on!" "O Lord, be not far from me" (Ps. 35:22). "Thy word is a lamp unto my feet, and a light unto my path" (Ps. 119:105). Only the unimaginative and the unadventurous would have it otherwise (see Expos. on 4:7; 5:14).

> So, let him wait God's instant men call years;
> Meantime hold hard by truth and his great soul,
> Do out the duty! Through such souls alone
> God stooping shows sufficient of his light
> For us i' the dark to rise by.[2]

[1] "Lead, kindly Light."
[2] Browning, *The Ring and the Book*, "Pompilia." Cf. Expos. on Luke 21:19.

Job was sure that once he had been able to see clearly. In 12:3; 13:2 he boasts his knowledge of God; in 42:1-6 he calls that knowledge little more than ignorance (see also Expos. on 1:4-5). The way, when it seemed clearest, was hidden; when it seemed utterly hidden, it was growing clear! Once more the memory of all God's goodness in the past will flood his mind (ch. 29). It will seem to him then like "sorrow's crown of sorrow," until, rid of too much self, he sees it again in the presence of God, and knows it for a pledge.

23. Whom God Hath Hedged In.— (Cf. 1:10.) The barrier which God had fashioned to keep the danger out (?) proved to be Job's most vulnerable point (Luke 18:24); the wall which God now seems to have built in order to keep the misery in (?) proves to be the gate "which leadeth unto life" (Matt. 7:14). Is heaven's dealing with us bane or blessing? Are the Ten Commandments safeguard or imprisonment? Are they perhaps both? And who determines which they are (see Expos. on 2:1-6)? Or transforms the one into the other—and how (see Expos. on 1:6-12, paragraph [c])? Read any Thanksgiving Proclamation. The wealth of mine and field and factory—God's good angels, or bad?

It is in this passage for the first time that Job directly attributes his calamity to God. He does not say that it is unjust, not yet; he does say that God has done it, and that it has made sixes and sevens out of everything. The shafts he has been hurling at the universe find their mark at last. And there seems less of evasion, there seems more of the strong man's (*gébher*, vs. 23) honesty about it (see Expos. on John 18:11). One can almost see by this time not the surreptitious glances—they no doubt have been in evidence from the beginning—but the horrified gestures of the friends. They will not be able long to hold their peace.

24. The Impatience of Job.—Job's cries of wretchedness are now his food and drink; a fear is no sooner feared than it becomes fact (not as in KJV; cf. 29:18), in very waves of trembling, like the seizures of an epileptic, or the chill that shakes the body in fever (yet see Exeg.). From that as its source is shortly to break a welter of magnificent imagery, poignant yearning, repetitive debate, charge and counter-

25 For the thing which I greatly feared is come upon me, and that which I was afraid of is come unto me. 26 I was not in safety, neither had I rest, neither was I quiet; yet trouble came.	25 For the thing that I fear comes upon me, and what I dread befalls me. 26 I am not at ease, nor am I quiet; I have no rest; but trouble comes."

subject of physical pain, and that almost every discourse of Job in the poetic discussion ends, in traditionally Oriental fashion, with a lament over his bodily ailments.

Job has said nothing of his past; he has forgotten the blessings of his youth and early manhood. He has said nothing of his present; the consciousness of his innocence remains beyond the range of his pain. He has expressed no hope for deliverance: death is his only future, and it tarries.

The soliloquy stands at the beginning of the round of disputations. It is a poem of rarely equaled magnitude, for its style has not aged, its themes find echo in the mind of every man who has been crushed, and the unraveling of its threefold plan, with its curse, query, and cry, is true to the pattern of smitten life.

The Job of the prologue is a hero of legend; the Job of the soliloquy is still alive. One is man as he should be; the other is merely man of our flesh and age.

charge, fond memory, eager anticipation, abysmal despair, blasphemy: waves that come roaring in out of the deep against some mountainous, rock-bound shore, hurling their crests high into the air, then slithering back by half a hundred tortuous ways to gather their fury for another onslaught. There will be heard now the tumult that in the words of Reinhold Niebuhr "begins with a mystery which is felt to be instinct with meaning, and ends with a meaning which is felt to be instinct with mystery." [3]

We may not talk any longer of patience. There is yet no outright defiance, but there is implied rebellion. Is this the man who laid his forehead in the dust, submissive before God, and said, "The LORD gave, and the LORD hath taken away; blessed be the name of the LORD"? Is this the man who asked of his wife, "Shall we receive good at the hand of God, and shall we not receive evil?" The answer obviously is "No." It is not the same man: unless indeed, as the poet more than once seems to wish we would assume, his protracted sufferings have almost unhinged his mind. It is Job the titan who will soon begin in his madness to take issue with the Almighty.

It is sometimes said that suffering cleanses the soul and purifies the spirit and ennobles the life. Only bear it with fortitude and patience. Somerset Maugham dipped his pen in venom to say that it crushes the soul and breaks the spirit and degrades the life. Be that as it may, there is surely a kind of hypocrisy that makes a virtue of necessity, and in the midst of anguish puts on the mask of piety and resignation. It is that in

his friends against which Job will rail and cry out.[4] It were better almost, were it not, to defy heaven than to assume a counterfeit humility, or achieve patience and quietness of spirit by refusing to wrestle with the ghastly contradictions which life and experience seem to throw up in the face of God's goodness? The Bible itself attaches no such meaning to the word patience. "That we," writes Paul, "through patience and comfort of the Scriptures might have hope" (Rom. 15:4). The very word itself in Greek is a twisting and a turning; a holding on, like Jacob to the angel, "I will not let thee go, except thou bless me" (Gen. 32:26). The book of Job is not an object lesson in our kind of patience; it is an object lesson in that kind of patience. A patience too proud to cover its hurt, too honest to make light of it, too brave to deal in platitudes, too truthful to call black white, too decent to whine, and too stanch to quit. It is an object lesson in the kind of patience of which Miguel de Unamuno, the Spanish philosopher, must have been thinking when he wrote, "May God deny you peace, but give you glory!" [5] In that imprecation—or should we say in that prayer?—the epic of Job unfolds itself. God no doubt was still in his heaven, but all was not right with the world. Definitely not right.

[4] Cf. John Stuart Mill, *An Examination of Sir William Hamilton's Philosophy* (London: Longmans, Green, Reader & Dyer, 1867), p. 124: "I will call no being good, who is not what I mean when I apply that epithet to my fellow-creatures; and if such a being can sentence me to hell for not so calling him, to hell I will go."

[5] *The Tragic Sense of Life* (London: Macmillan & Co., 1921), p. 330.

[3] Cf. *Discerning the Signs of the Times* (New York: Charles Scribner's Sons, 1946), pp. 152-73.

4 Then Eliphaz the Temanite answered and said,

2 *If* we assay to commune with thee, wilt thou be grieved? but who can withhold himself from speaking?

4 Then Eli′phaz the Te′manite answered:

2 "If one ventures a word with you, will you be offended? Yet who can keep from speaking?

B. First Cycle of Discussion (4:1–14:22)

1. First Discourse of Eliphaz (4:1–5:27)

There is no reason to believe that the friends came to Job with hostile intentions. They traveled from afar in order to comfort him (2:11). Their initial silence probably was due to respect and compassion as well as bewilderment (2:13). When Job had shown in his lament that he could not accept his fate with fortitude, the friends felt compelled to speak. Friendship is a favorite theme in Oriental and Hebrew wisdom literatures; and the ancient sages liked to say that friends should reprove as well as sympathize (Prov. 27:6, 17; etc.). Eliphaz spoke first, presumably because he was the oldest and most learned of the three. (For the strophic structure see Intro., pp. 894-96.)

a) Dogma of Divine Justice (4:1-11)

(1) Confidence in Integrity (4:1-6)

4:2. If one ventures a word: Tactful and cautious, Eliphaz does not intend deliberately to start an academic discussion. He knows that even a considerate reproof will

---

4:1–14:22. The First Cycle.—The argument of the friends in the first cycle of the debate presents one of humanity's false approaches to the problem of innocent human suffering. In a word, it sets forth Browning's thesis, though not with Browning's discernment:

> God's in his heaven—
> All's right with the world! [6]

There is nothing wrong with the intent. Eliphaz, Bildad, and Zophar have it in mind to turn the sufferer from thought of self to thought of God. Beside it our quasi-religious, quasi-psychiatric attempts to deal with anguish of body or anguish of soul seem rather pitiful, almost in themselves a profanity. In all such efforts to rid the self of self, the self is centered upon the self and its ailments; with the result, frequently enough, that even the gospel becomes involved in the failure of a technique. One often wonders what would have happened to Paul, with his thorn in the flesh, if somebody from a pulpit had talked to him about relaxing, about getting free of his inferiority complex, about saying to himself after each meal, and three times on going to bed, "Every day in every way I'm getting better and better." Can there be any question that if the preacher had made any easy identification of that with the Christian faith the world would have lost its greatest apostle?

But the friends were wrong nevertheless. They were wrong because the point they fastened on was already becoming a sore point

[6] "Pippa Passes," Pt. I.

with Job. People may restrain themselves from recommending to you patience under affliction; but if they are pious people, they will hardly resist the temptation to refer you to God's ordering of his universe. It is no soulless place, they will tell you. It is inhabited by a holy God, high and lifted up. Surely you can trust him. And that sounds all right. It is simply inept at times, and peculiarly inept. The man who is suffering does not always feel like that about the universe and the God who inhabits it. Your words may be true, and yet not speak to his condition. It is precisely this that happens (see Expos. on 5:9-16).

4:1–5:27. The Word of the Seer.—Eliphaz begins considerately, and proceeds with notable gentleness and courtesy; notable in view of the provocation which Job's lament must undoubtedly have occasioned not only to the settled pattern of his faith, but also to the reverend and ancient piety of his spirit. That singularly happy metathesis attributed to W. A. Spooner, once warden of New College, Oxford, "The tearful chidings of the gospel," might well serve to strike off the tenor and content of Eliphaz' first speech. What few tears—if any—there are in his voice, however, are not for the sufferer; they are for the unseemliness of that impassioned outburst. Entirely apart from the question of Job's innocence or guilt, he deprecates the violent reaction which has outraged his sense of the fitness of things, and to his way of thinking has already given more than sufficient indication of a bearing far less than "perfect" and "upright." Extraordinary as the whole performance is, there

hurt the sufferer's feelings. He suspects that he should remain silent, but he cannot stand any longer the vagaries of a smitten man. According to other interpretations, he apologizes for having remained silent too long.

is in it no healing for a mind distraught, because there is no understanding of what it is in that mind that has gone wrong. Without any realization of what Job has endured, Eliphaz cannot endure what Job has said (see Expos. on 2:11-13; 3:1). "A strange sight this," so we might put the gist of it, "that the comforter of many is now comfortless! You should be finding your strength in the sense of your own integrity. People like you do not finally perish. Remember that. Only the wicked, who make a profession of their wickedness. Let them cry out and complain. Nobody on earth has any right to do such a thing. Nobody on earth or in heaven either. Who is righteous when you come down to it? Who is pure? Is not God's dealing with us then forever just? If I were you, I should turn to him, whose goodness is everlasting, whose retribution never fails. He will deliver you, nothing is so sure; and with tender mercy establish your ways in peace."

There is much that is lofty and impressive about it all, much that from a literary point of view is rarely if ever surpassed anywhere in the book. But there is also a certain uncalculated aloofness about it, which is all too thoroughly calculated to leave Job's misery a cold misery and kindle his anger: a kind of unintentional remoteness, as if the speaker, not consciously, but without meaning to do it—which is worse—conceived of the matter in hand as a fit subject for careful diagnosis and therapeutic counsel. Something is not as it should be when the moment you open your mouth you either apologize for not opening it sooner (see Exeg. on vs. 2), or say, "I've got to talk to you about all this. It won't be pleasant, but I must do it." And then go on to remind one who is in the depths of despair that of old he himself was the source of strength to others; why in the world is he unable to bear up under misfortune when it comes near him? Eliphaz does not yet doubt Job's essential piety; but he is secretly convinced that some undisclosed fault must lie behind such suffering, particularly because of the mood in which the sufferer has responded to it. He regards the situation in the abstract, impersonally, in accordance with his own systematized theological presuppositions; and that ruins everything. He speaks of Job's integrity as if that should be a solace; and to Job it is the very core of the problem. He tries to persuade Job that when all is said and done, everybody has sinned and "come short of the glory of God" (Rom. 3:23). Why should anyone then be offended at

the suggestion that some kind of sin is inseparably bound up with calamity?

And to Job, while there was nothing the matter with that as theory, there was a great deal the matter with it as fact. No doubt every man who shared man's common lot could say, "He hath not dealt with us after our sins; nor rewarded us according to our iniquities" (Ps. 103:10). But if a saint had said it while he was being hurried to the lions—if Jesus had said it on the cross—it might have carried another meaning, sardonic and ghastly. Whereupon Eliphaz went on to recommend a different course. In view of God's greatness and power (5:9-11), the impatience and resentment of the ungodly (5:2) can be nothing but the precursor of doom; in view of God's beneficence (5:17-27), "If I were in your shoes" (16:4-5)—may heaven deliver us from all such!—"I should turn to God for my refuge." And to Job God's power will seem terrible, because God's beneficence seems a thing of the past. Curiously enough, very much as Satan's plans miscarry (see Expos. on 2:7-10), so does Eliphaz' comfort. It becomes an irritant. Instead of a soothing poultice, it turns out to be a mustard plaster. It is a comment from the side lines, with a bit of good advice thrown in. The kind of thing Carlyle once said Emerson did quite too often: like someone safely up on the beach throwing a cheery word or two to poor souls wrestling in the great dark deeps, with the huge billows knocking the breath out of them. What Job needs is the compassion of a human heart. What he gets is a series of absolutely "true" and absolutely beautiful religious clichés and moral platitudes.

It should perhaps be remarked as the debate begins that no great progress is made anywhere in the argument. For the most part it swings around in circles, with some shift of center from heaven to earth to Job himself. And when Job answers, what he says seems often to have little relevance to what has gone immediately before: much more at times to what was said before that. He is a man dazed, trying to find his bearings; while little by little it dawns on him that these friends are not friends at all, never mind their sincerity: they are adversaries, treading softly at first, then as he persists in refusing to admit his guilt of any great transgression, growing more and more outspoken. And somehow he is unable to take it all in at once. The horror of it keeps piling up. While one is speaking, something another has said suddenly stabs his mind awake. Nothing could be more faithful, line upon line,

3 Behold, thou hast instructed many, and thou hast strengthened the weak hands.

4 Thy words have upholden him that was falling, and thou hast strengthened the feeble knees.

5 But now it is come upon thee, and thou faintest; it toucheth thee, and thou art troubled.

| 3 Behold, you have instructed many,
and you have strengthened the weak hands.
4 Your words have upheld him who was stumbling,
and you have made firm the feeble knees.
5 But now it has come to you, and you are impatient;
it touches you, and you are dismayed.

3-5. Job had given lessons to others in the past. He had encouraged them when they were in distress. But **now, it has come** (the feminine subject is not expressed: an Oriental way of alluding to misfortune), and like anybody else, he is **impatient** and **dismayed.**

than the portrait which the author paints of a soul in torment.

4:3-4. Physicians of a Mind Diseased.—Aeschylus says that "words are the physicians of a mind diseased." And indeed they may be. Eliphaz pays sincere and grateful tribute to one who in the past, with mild reproof and kindly sympathy and unfailing encouragement, had **strengthened** and **upheld** and **made firm** many a life dejected and spiritless, halting along under burdens too heavy for anybody to carry. What Job had said to others must have been very much what Eliphaz is now saying to him (see Exeg., outline of chs. 4–5); but with a world of difference.

Certainly it will never do to underrate the ministry of words. Only the petulant would ever say with Brabantio

But words are words; I never yet did hear
That the bruis'd heart was pierced through the ear.[7]

Too many bruised hearts have been (see Expos. on 19:2). It were even better perhaps to be deprived of sight than to be bereft of hearing; for speech is a kind of sacrament that keeps life bound in the fellowship of life. Significantly, to the Hebrew, words both good and evil were deeds in the doing. The Greek better understood our contrast between word and deed; yet his very word for "poem" was derived from the word "to do" (cf. Jas. 1:23).

Sticks and stones may break my bones,
But words can harm me never.

Nothing much sillier ever took such firm hold of the popular fancy. For Jesus judgment waited upon the vain and "idle" word (Matt. 12:36), and eternity upon his own (see Expos. on Luke 21:33). Words that strengthen and uphold and make firm must be spoken not with the lips only, but with the mind and the heart: the mind to keep them from "folly" (5:2-3; cf. Jas. 3:13-

[7] Shakespeare, *Othello*, Act I, scene 3.

17), and the heart to keep them from being like the words of Eliphaz,

Faultily faultless, icily regular, splendidly null,
Dead perfection, no more.[8]

Blake (Illustration V) has Job doling out his charity with the left (material) hand, symbol of the fact that true sympathy is absent. Such a suggestion seems quite gratuitous, though no doubt there will be a new dimension in everything he says and does when the story of his own suffering is over. Meanwhile we are not permitted to cavil about the warmth of his spirit. "Did not I weep for him that was in trouble? was not my soul grieved for the poor?" (30:25.) And with the words that he spoke went deeds to match them. "I was eyes to the blind, and feet was I to the lame" (29:15). "If I have withheld the poor from their desire, . . . or have eaten my morsel . . . alone . . . ; then let mine arm fall from my shoulder blade, and mine arm be broken from the bone. . . . The stranger did not lodge in the street: but I opened my doors to the traveler." (31:16, 17, 22, 32.) Human life needs nothing so sorely, nor is any service a man can render so well within every man's daily reach. It is a very sign of the cross, and a seal of all true greatness (Matt. 20:26-28).

5. *When Trouble Draws Near.*—Something of tact has gone out of Eliphaz' speech. He intends to be kind. What he says is not said with a grin or a raised eyebrow, "Why on earth can't you take your own medicine?" He seems genuinely troubled by this physician who cannot heal himself, who at the first touch (!) of misfortune goes to pieces. But the observation, even if altogether accurate, cannot be regarded as particularly soothing. It may be that reproof is at times in order (see Exeg.); but "the manner of giving is worth more than the gift." To reprove does not often mean "to rub in."

[8] Tennyson, "Maud," Part I, Sec. 2. See Expos. on 6:24-27.

6 *Is* not *this* thy fear, thy confidence, thy hope, and the uprightness of thy ways?

7 Remember, I pray thee, who *ever* perished, being innocent? or where were the righteous cut off?

6 Is not your fear of God your confidence, and the integrity of your ways your hope?

7 "Think now, who that was innocent ever perished?
Or where were the upright cut off?

---

6. Is not . . . thy fear [of God] **thy confidence?** The word **fear** used without object refers to faith and piety (cf. 15:4; 22:4). "Let your religion reassure you" (Moffatt). The friend does not doubt at this stage the **integrity** (*tōm*) of Job. On the contrary, he finds in it a ground for **hope** (*tiqwāh,* "tense but hopeful expectation").

(2) THE HARVEST OF TROUBLE (4:7-11)

7. To be sure, the origin of affliction is sometimes an enigma, but the fact remains, **who ever perished, being innocent?** Eliphaz appeals to Job's knowledge and experience,

---

Nevertheless there is that here which is profitable for learning. Says Alexander Pope, "I never knew any man in my life who could not bear another's misfortunes perfectly like a Christian." [9] But such vicarious courage may not always spring merely from lack of sympathy. It may well be because "another's misfortunes" never quite cloud our vision, while we are all too often blinded by our own. What we see of sorrow and perplexity in other lives we can see if we will in truer perspective than we are able when tears are in our eyes and tumult in our mind. Why else does "talking it over with a friend" serve so frequently to clarify the issues?

For all that, however, the peril is real and twofold: (*a*) that we shall never in any deep sense, deliberately and with imagination, attempt to make another man's burden our burden, or to enter into his condition and feel as he feels, think as he thinks (Ezek. 3:15; see Expos. on Job 5:8). It is very easy to become doctrinaire in matters of morality, race segregation, religious prejudice, national prerogative, without ever making the slightest effort to understand as if they were our own the loves and hates, the hopes and fears, the ambitions and frustrations with which we have to deal in other lives as in our own. And (*b*) that when **it is come upon us,** we shall discover ourselves to be possessed of knowledge uninformed with power. That not only can happen, it does happen; and it happens with a regularity that should stagger even the most confident. Eliphaz lectures Job on patience, and as his counsel meets with shorter shrift than he is sure it deserves, first lets his own patience slip a notch, then loses it outright. "To will is present with me; but how to perform that which is good I find not" (Rom. 7:18). If there had been any genuine compassion in the heart of Eliphaz, reminiscent of that

[9] *Thoughts on Various Subjects.*

which is in the heart of God, who "knoweth our frame," and "remembereth that we are dust" (Ps. 103:14), he might himself, as a steward of the mysteries, have entered in and **strengthened failing hands** and **made firm the feeble knees** (see Expos. on vs. 7).

6. *Religion that Reassures.*—In the O.T. "the fear of the LORD" is that dread which steals into the human soul—Eliphaz describes it in vss. 12-16—with the realization of God's awful holiness, and is the mainspring of "faith and piety" (Exeg.). It is a fear that troubles man's conscience and humbles his pride; for before God no mortal can stand, nor any angel. It is a fear that commands his allegiance and brings the whole of his life into the unity of a willing and reverent obedience. It is not the fear that love casts out (I John 4:18). Rather is it the fear that casts out all other fears (Matt. 10:28), and by the coming of Christ, in his life, his death, his resurrection, is "made perfect in love."

What is there about that to reassure a life which like Job's has fallen away into the dark night of despair? It is the majesty and "otherness" of God that terrify him. It is the purity and holiness of God that his own experience seems to call into question. The **integrity** of his **ways** is precisely what he *has* relied on; and it has offered no stay to calamity. Why all at once should it become the "ground for tense but hopeful expectation" (Exeg.)? The prime purpose of the poem is to portray the shifting of that "ground" from man to God. "Hope in God: for I shall yet praise him, who is the health of my countenance, and my God" (Ps. 43:5). Not man's faith, but God's faithfulness. Not man's piety, but God's love. Who did anything about mediating that to Job? (Cf. II Sam. 9:1, 3.)

7. *Mistaking the Case.*—Not only does Eliphaz consistently fail to understand what the trouble

8 Even as I have seen, they that plow iniquity, and sow wickedness, reap the same.	8 As I have seen, those who plow iniquity and sow trouble reap the same.

Remember, I pray thee. Surely Job still accepts the traditional doctrine of a material, individual, and this-worldly retribution. This is the reason why Eliphaz is shocked by Job's half-blasphemous lament. Since the **upright** are never **cut off** prematurely, Job should not yield to despair. If such is the undertone of this verse, then Eliphaz, while well intentioned, misunderstood Job, who is not afraid of dying but rather longs for death.

8. The progression of thought is smooth. Vs. 7 suggests that the sufferer is innocent, but vs. 8 shows a decided change of tone. **Those who . . . sow trouble reap the same.**

was (see Exeg.); he gives the distinct impression, as McKechnie aptly points out,[1] of not understanding that there is anything to understand. He has lived a long time, and he has pondered much; he has read many opinions, and sought diligently: and he knows the answers (5:27). He does not know Job. Instead of interesting him, Job horrifies him. He judges "human nature without taking human nature into account." He reasons in a vacuum. The answers he has arrived at are no longer theory: "theories preserve an attitude of questioning humility to the facts of life." They are dogma, and dogma that has lost contact with reality. "Something of chaos seems to cling round . . . reality." Eliphaz' answers were tidy, and so not true answers. They were "flouted by the mystery [they] professed to explain." And they were answers to the wrong questions (see Expos. on vs. 5).

It was not death that Job feared, it was life. To be **cut off** at a stroke did not seem to him any more, as it still seemed to the friends, a signal judgment: it would have seemed a signal mercy. It was not so much the pain gnawing at his body that troubled him; it was the perplexity eating its way into his mind: not the calamity, but the fact that in a world of God he could make no sense of it. Eliphaz could, without turning his hand. So could the others. Job's premise was wrong: it was as simple as that. Why try to explain a fact when you could rub the fact out, and so have nothing to explain? **Who ever perished, being innocent?** "Who ever, being innocent as I am innocent, and suffering as I suffer, would not long to perish?" **Where were the upright cut off?** "Why not, in God's name, when they are wretched?" Every arrow is beside the mark (see Expos. on vs. 6). Every word is salt in a wound. It is the ceaseless dilemma of multitudes of pious and well-meaning people. Little wonder that most of the effective counsel given by friend or loved one, by pastor or psychiatrist, is neither admonition nor exhortation. The best word for it is contagion.

The issue for "a man whose way is hid" (3:23) cannot be provided by the recovery of

[1] *Job, Moral Hero,* pp. 38, 46, 47.

lost ideas or the acceptance of rejected standards: it appears in some place of meeting, where heart lies bare to heart, heart of man to heart of man, or heart of man to heart of God. There and there alone can the sufferer talk out his grief; there and only there can it be resolved—proximately and partially in that dimension of love which is temporal and human; wholly and ultimately in that other dimension of love which is divine and eternal.

8-11. The Evolution of the Self-Righteous.—(Cf. 5:3-4, 6-8.) "I have observed," says Eliphaz. He has already made one observation that utterly missed the point, attempting to buttress it with an appeal to Job's better judgment—not better than his, but better than that expressed in ch. 3. "Remember, I pray thee" (vs. 7). The upshot of it was that when calamity overtakes the righteous, there is nothing final about it. Now he opines, on what is to him the unimpeachable authority of his own long acquaintance with life, devoting four verses of choice rhetoric to it, that when calamity overtakes those who are habitually and deliberately wicked they are completely and devastatingly done for. The Exeg. conceives him as musing darkly on the problem of suffering in its relation to innocence and guilt—though it must be added that the guilt takes up more of his time. The implications, one may be quite sure, were not lost on Job. And it is all done with such scrupulous objectivity, such superior (see Expos. on 4:1–5:27) and almost studied remoteness, as to suggest the kind of complacency, secure and undisturbed, which is always the first step in the evolution of the self-righteous. Only God knows how troubled such complacency ought to be, and how insecure it is (42:7-8). Certainly his own "fear of God" is Eliphaz' "confidence"; the "integrity" of his ways is the hope of his soul. From that point on, through growing suspicion to final and outright accusation (22:5; cf. Expos. on 6:28-30), the movement is slow but steady. So did the Pharisees begin, continue, and end (Luke 18:9; 11:15-16; John 8:48). Over against it, in the N.T. Jesus set the parable of the Pharisee and the publican (Luke 18:9-14), and

Does Eliphaz mean to comfort Job by contrasting him with **those who plow iniquity,** or on the contrary does he suggest that in all cases, including Job's, misfortune is the harvest of evil sowing? The word **trouble,** '*āmāl,* has already been used by Job in 3:10, but Eliphaz is not necessarily alluding to that verse, for the word **trouble** and its parallel **iniquity** are familiar expressions of his (cf. 5:6; 15:35). In all probability he does not know at this stage whether Job is innocent or guilty, and he merely muses darkly on both possibilities. However, the poet skillfully anticipates the general pessimism of the next strophe (vs. 17). While the fate of the innocent is considered only in a brief rhetorical question (vs. 7), that of the wicked is described at some length (vss. 8-11).

---

his inimitable story of the good Samaritan (Luke 10:25-37): the one to humble a man toward God, the other to gird him toward his neighbor.

8. They that Plow Iniquity.—These are the people "whose sinning is, so to speak, a business which they practice as the farmer ploughs and sows his field, and whose harvest is unfailing." [2] The doctrine of divine retribution, as Eliphaz propounds it, is in itself a sound doctrine. It means that we live in an orderly and righteous universe (Matt. 7:2), where men do not gather "grapes of thorns, or figs of thistles" (Matt. 7:16); not because of some "natural law" that grinds out results as a printing press grinds out newspapers, but by reason of that law which is the will of God. There is in very truth an "even-handed justice," not only in heaven but on earth, that

Commends the ingredients of our poison'd chalice
To our own lips. [3]

But it is a justice which calls for greater discrimination in the reading of it than any of the friends could show. (a) They were right on two counts. First in their insistence that

God's good time
. . . does not always fall on Saturday
When the world looks for wages. [4]

Life does not seem very promptly partial to the righteous. Quite the contrary (Matt. 10:16-39). Else what value in their righteousness? Nor does it seem very promptly prejudiced against the wicked (Matt. 5:45). So much the friends knew (yet see Expos. on 20:2*b*); though about "the iniquities of the fathers" which are visited upon the children, which they put forward again and again (5:4; 8:13-19; 20:10) as their protest against a too simple and individual and immediate view of divine retribution, Job himself has something to say by way of protest (21:19). They were right, second, in their insistence on the fact that God's justice in being retributive is at the same time intended as redemptive (8:21; 11:14-19; *passim;* cf. Heb. 3:2). (b) But

they were wrong on two counts. They were wrong not only in arguing from a doctrine to a particular case, always a disastrous procedure, but also in their inclination to read history as if it could be neatly interpreted in the light of their doctrine—as Job shows, to his own satisfaction at least, in ch. 21. All the "wise" men who tag events—as people did the Lisbon earthquake, and labeled the tag "the righteous judgment of God," bringing down on themselves the still more righteous if vitriolic wrath of Voltaire; or as others wrote down their liberation from German prison camps to "the lovingkindness of the Most High"—all such "wise" men would be wiser if they understood that life is somewhat more complicated than they think. Hamlet says bluntly, "There is nothing either good or bad, but thinking makes it so." [5] To the Hebrew, as we have seen, the angels themselves, God's messengers, were good or bad in accordance with the human response made to their message (see Expos. on 1:6-12, p. 913; 3:23). Every Sunday devout Christians praise God for his bounty. Can bounty itself be judgment, and ruin mercy?

They that plow iniquity [in 5:6 the word is translated "affliction"] **reap the same.** In what divers ways Eliphaz never dreamed! He would hardly have included himself among the plowers of iniquity and the sowers of trouble; yet already he was standing in the face of God's wrath (42:7-8). Writes Seneca: "The greatest chastisement that a man may receive who hath outraged another, is to have done the outrage; and there is no man who is so rudely punished as he that is subject to the whip of his own repentance." [6] But how many are?

Though the mills of God grind slowly,
Yet they grind exceeding small. [7]

That may be. Still, "how unsearchable are his judgments, and his ways past finding out!" (Rom. 11:33.) The apostle was much more careful in his stating of the law of the harvest (Gal. 6:7-8).

[5] Act II, scene 2.
[6] *Minor Dialogues* V. 26.
[7] Longfellow, "Poetic Aphorisms: Retribution." From the *Sinngedichte* of Friedrich von Logau.

[2] Davidson and Lanchester, *Job,* p. 35.
[3] Shakespeare, *Macbeth,* Act I, scene 7.
[4] Browning, "Prince Hohenstiel-Schwangau."

9 By the blast of God they perish, and by the breath of his nostrils are they consumed.

10 The roaring of the lion, and the voice of the fierce lion, and the teeth of the young lions, are broken.

11 The old lion perisheth for lack of prey, and the stout lion's whelps are scattered abroad.

12 Now a thing was secretly brought to me, and mine ear received a little thereof.

9 By the breath of God they perish,
   and by the blast of his anger they are
      consumed.

10 The roar of the lion, the voice of the
      fierce lion,
   the teeth of the young lions, are broken.

11 The strong lion perishes for lack of prey,
   and the whelps of the lioness are scattered.

12 "Now a word was brought to me stealthily,
   my ear received the whisper of it.

---

9. Premature death is the result of God's wrath, an idea expressed almost in the same words in Ps. 90:7.

10-11. There is no reason to dismiss these verses as revealing the hand of an inferior poet. It is possible that **the roaring of the lion** (vs. 10*a*) is a subtle reference to Job's "my roarings" (3:24*b*): if Job roars like a lion, let him remember that this animal symbolizes the evildoer (cf. Pss. 17:12; 34:10; etc.), and worse still, that **the whelps of the lioness are scattered** (vs. 11*b*). Is this a veiled allusion to the fate of Job's children? Perhaps not an insinuation consciously made. But the poet is possibly anticipating here the pointed remark of 5:4, and especially Bildad's crushing meanness (8:4).

b) THE MYSTERY OF SUFFERING (4:12-21)

(1) VISION IN THE NIGHT (4:12-16)

This famous description of dread in the dark constitutes a wise man's literary attempt to indicate the suprahuman origin of his knowledge. The style and the ideas are quite different from those of the prophets' accounts of their own visions.

9-11. *The Breath of God.*—In two dramatic figures Eliphaz dashes off the fate of the wicked. "The breath of God"—as a wind, favoring or ill, blows upon a ship—came upon Saul and worked a mighty deliverance (I Sam. 11:6); it departed from him, giving way to an "evil spirit from the Lord" that troubled him (I Sam. 16:14). It clothed itself with Gideon and went out to deliver Israel (Judg. 6:34); it stirred up strife "between Abimelech and the men of Shechem" (Judg. 9:23), that God might render to all of them their due. It blows, and there are those who travel with it. It keeps blowing, and men try to battle their way against it. Here it is the burning, devastating sirocco, sweeping up from the arid deserts of the south, leaving behind it a scorched earth. In the second figure the "dens of iniquity" are laid waste. As has been frequently pointed out, there are five different words for **lion** in these verses; four hundred such words in Arabic, and no doubt ample opportunity to use all of them. Could we chart the contours of our culture by means of the words for which we have the greatest number of synonyms? One finds, for instance, far more synonyms for the ability to give pain than for

the ability to give pleasure. The list for "possessions" and its kindred runs to whole pages. That under "disapprove" is twice as long as that under "approve." "Flattery" and "detraction" are of about equal length. Upon the **fierce lion** as he roars over his prey, upon the **young lions** and the **strong lion**, upon the **lioness** and her **whelps** the stroke falls (cf. 5:3-5). Nature in all her aspects, terrible and benign, was the agent of God's awful sovereignty. As for man and his destiny, what mattered was the way his face was set. "All things work together for good to them that love God" (Rom. 8:28). But the workers of iniquity, he "shall cut them off in their own wickedness." (See Ps. 94:23, where Job's problem is the nation's problem.)

12-21. *Why Do the Righteous Suffer?*—Eliphaz knows. The riddle that puzzles Job is no riddle at all. "There is none righteous, no, not one" (Rom. 3:10). It is knowledge that has come to him by revelation. In the time when men sleep, when the hustle and bustle of life are stilled, he has fallen into a trance and sees clearly with the inward eye what is beyond the realm of sight. While he is meditating on it all, troubled and mystified, a dread experience is vouchsafed him.

13 In thoughts from the visions of the night, when deep sleep falleth on men,	**13** Amid thoughts from visions of the night, when deep sleep falls on men,
14 Fear came upon me, and trembling, which made all my bones to shake.	**14** dread came upon me, and trembling, which made all my bones shake.
15 Then a spirit passed before my face; the hair of my flesh stood up:	**15** A spirit glided past my face; the hair of my flesh stood up.
16 It stood still, but I could not discern the form thereof: an image *was* before mine eyes, *there was* silence, and I heard a voice, *saying,*	**16** It stood still, but I could not discern its appearance. A form was before my eyes; there was silence, then I heard a voice:
17 Shall mortal man be more just than God? shall a man be more pure than his Maker?	**17** 'Can mortal man be righteous before[d] God? can a man be pure before[d] his Maker?

[d] Or *more than*

15. Not a spirit but "a wind." The word *rûaḥ*, normally used in the feminine, may be translated either way, but when used in the masculine, as here, it always refers to a breath of air (cf. 41:16; Exod. 10:13; Eccl. 1:6; 3:19). Moreover, in the O.T., a *rûaḥ* is never a ghost or a disembodied spirit. Samuel's shade is called *'elōhîm*, "a god" (I Sam. 28:13).

16. Someone **stood** (the subject is unexpressed), whose appearance was unrecognizable, although Eliphaz could see a *temûnāh*, **a form**, or "a figure." **There was silence**, and then he **heard a voice** (cf. the "voice of silence" in I Kings 19:12; the poet of Job may have been acquainted with the story of Elijah's theophany on Mount Horeb).

(2) The Human Situation (4:17-21)

17. The M.T. could be rendered "more just than God," but the truth revealed to Eliphaz would then be trivial and obvious. The preposition *min*, usually translated "from" or **more than,** sometimes means "in comparison with," "on the part of," "from the point of view of," or "before," especially when it is constructed with the verb *ṣādhēq,*

Apparently he is wide awake when it happens. Suddenly he trembles, and the hair of his flesh stands up. As he tells of it, it seems to be happening all over again, so vivid is the memory of it. A breath passes before his face, and behold, there is a presence, as if someone were in the room unseen; vague, specterlike, he cannot make it out. He strains his eyes, but sees nothing, only a dim form, yet not a form, intangible, filling the heart with awe of the unknown. Then a faint, thin voice, with a hush all around. And this, from beginning to end, in order to declare the surpassing purity of God, whose holiness sullies even the angels, to say nothing of man with his frail mortality.

We are tempted to wonder if a vision was necessary to convey it. For all the exquisite artistry, perhaps the more so because of it, there would seem to be a certain laboring of the commonplace, so that what we have is much ado about comparatively little, a heavenly visitant delivering himself of a pious platitude beautifully wrought and thoroughly inept. God's whisper in the ear turns out to be a sort of banality that solves Job's problem by dismissing it. If Eliphaz is saying anything by appropriating the celestial announcement as his own, he is saying (a) that whatever happens to men in general, we may be sure they deserve it; while to make the point doubly impressive, he is willing to assume (b) such an exalted view of God as to dwarf humanity's stature to the level of insignificance (see Expos. on 9:2-10). What are people anyhow, by and large, but denizens of a day, their houses clods of earth, their **foundation . . . in the dust,** the span of their life from dawn to dark, **crushed** as easily as one would crush a **moth**—and who cares? All their boasted mastery, which so often makes rebels of them (see Exeg.), gone like a flame that has

> lighted fools
> The way to dusty death.[8]

Of course such an "explanation" of suffering renders explanation unnecessary by abolishing not only the ground but the importance of the question. And Job resents it. You cannot undercut the whole thing from the bottom up: the

[8] Shakespeare, *Macbeth*, Act V, scene 5.

18 Behold, he put no trust in his servants; and his angels he charged with folly:

19 How much less *in* them that dwell in houses of clay, whose foundation *is* in the dust, *which* are crushed before the moth?

18 Even in his servants he puts no trust, and his angels he charges with error;

19 how much more those who dwell in houses of clay, whose foundation is in the dust, who are crushed before the moth.

"to be just" (cf. 32:2; Gen. 38:26; Num. 32:22; Jer. 51:5; see also Ps. 139:12 [Hebrew]). The verse may then be rendered:

> Can a mortal be just before God?
> Can even a strong man be pure before his maker?

The ancient versions support this interpretation: ἐναντίον τοῦ κυρίου (LXX), *Dei comparatione* (Vulg.). Of course Job has not compared himself with God, but he has spoken as if he had forgotten the distinction which separates "mortal man" (*'enôsh*) from the transcendent Godhead (*'elôah*), or even a "strong man" (*gébher*) from his creator. The verb *çādhēq*, which sometimes in the poem means "to be in the right," "to have a just cause" (9:15, 20; 13:18; 33:12; 34:5; cf. Gen. 38:26), whence "to be justified in one's plea" (Job 11:2; 40:8), should be rendered, "to be righteous in life and character," in the light of its parallel *ṭāhēr*, "to be clean and pure" (usually referring to ritual purity, but sometimes to ethical cleanness, as in Prov. 20:9). According to human standards, Job may be considered blameless, but in comparison with God's holiness, or from the standpoint of divine glory, no mortal can make the claim of innocence. This is an idea of theological sinfulness which transcends ethics.

18-20. Even **angels** are charged with *toholāh*, **folly** (a *hapax legomenon*): a fortiori, men **whose foundation is in the dust** (cf. Gen. 2:7; 3:19). The poet does not intend in vs. 18 to discredit the angels; he merely wishes to exalt the perfection of God. Thus the rising sun outshines the brightness of planets and constellations. The frailty of men's nature explains their mortality, which is described in a threefold way: they are **crushed** [like] **a moth** (vs. 19c; "like" rather than **before**: cf. 3:24; I Sam. 1:16; also LXX and

---

righteous do suffer (6:5, 28-30). And you cannot just snub it all from the top down. God cares, if nobody else does (cf. vs. 20b with 6:4; 7:12, 17, 20). At least he cares enough to take a man for his target (see Exeg. on vss. 18-20; Expos. on 1:1). It would not be likely meanwhile to escape Job's attention that Eliphaz was sufficiently impressed with the sense of his own significance the while he was denying to others a like dignity. He had the air of one who was condescending to illumine the unillumined. Mankind was sinful. It was an unfortunate fact, but he had it straight out of heaven. He was not himself very noticeably involved in it, but there it was. If this indeed is what the author intended to convey, then Eliphaz was not the first, and he will not be the last, of whom it might be said, as Phaedrus said, among others:

> The mountain groaned in pangs of birth:
> Great expectation filled the earth;
> And lo! a mouse was born! [9]

"Nothing so resembles a swelling as a hollow."

[9] *Fables* IV. 22. 1.

19-21. *The Poverty of Man's Estate.*— (*a*) His body is clay, its foundation no more than dust. (*b*) His life is frail, like the moth's. Death comes to him all too easily (vs. 19c). It comes to him all too soon (vs. 20a). He may be here today, but tomorrow he is gone. It comes to him all too inconspicuously (vs. 20b), causing no great stir anywhere on earth, perhaps not even in heaven. (*c*) His excellence, everything that marks him off from the brute creation, is snatched from him, and he dies, far from that wisdom which is his goal. It is a somber view of human existence; but it suits Eliphaz' book to be somber. That it is in reality Eliphaz' view—a "slant," not a divinely bestowed insight; the two are often confused—is made manifest enough by its very onesidedness (see Exeg. on vss. 18-20). The Bible knows man quite differently. It knows him, even on what we would call his physical aspect, as a paradox of dust and divinity; on what we would call his moral aspect —though there is no such artificial cleavage in the earlier writings of the O.T.—it knows him as potentially both angel and devil. So Pascal. To lose sight of the devil is to leave the divine

20 They are destroyed from morning to evening: they perish for ever without any regarding *it*.

21 Doth not their excellency *which is* in them go away? they die, even without wisdom.

20 Between morning and evening they are destroyed;
they perish for ever without any regarding it.

21 If their tent-cord is plucked up within them,
do they not die, and that without wisdom?'

Vulg.) ; they last less than a day (vs. 20*a*) ; and when **they perish for ever,** no one pays attention or cares (vs. 20*b*). The expression **without any regarding it,** if it is correctly rendered by these words, reveals the gulf which separates the God of Eliphaz from that of the Hebrews in general and of Job in particular (cf. 22:3). It illustrates the process by which a truth (such as divine transcendence or human finiteness) is twisted into an error by the complete one-sidedness with which it is viewed and formulated. A God who does not care for a dying man is a majestic but un-Hebraic figure. Some critics believe, however, that instead of the M.T. מבלי משים, the LXX has read מבלי מ[ו]שיע, "without any one delivering," or "for want of a savior" (Merx, Graetz, Ginsburg, Dhorme, *et al.*). Other scholars conjecture the reading מבלי משיב, "without any one restoring [to life]" (Ehrlich, Kissane, *et al.*), an expression which suggests an idea familiar to the poet (cf. 7:10; 10:21; 14:10-12). The Vulg. reads *et quia nullus intelligit,* and this is possibly close enough to the meaning of the original: nobody among mortal men pays attention to his own impending death (Ewald) or takes much notice of another's. "One knows well from experience that men deceive themselves and run to ruin when they imagine . . . that they will always remain on this earth" (Calvin).

21. Excellency: There are in the Hebrew Bible two different words *yéther* which are written exactly alike. One means "lute-string" or "bow-string," the other "what remains," "advantage," "abundance," "wealth," "excellence," "pre-eminence." Most modern scholars read **tent-cord,** although this meaning is not attested elsewhere in biblical Hebrew. Others correct יתרם into יתדם (Olshausen, Hitzig, Siegfried, *et al.*) and read "their tent-peg," a word which fits the verb "is pulled out" (cf. Isa. 33:20). However,

---

judgment out of account and become the fool who no longer believes in God (Ps. 14:1). To lose sight of the angel is to leave the divine grace out of account and become the cynic who cannot believe even in man. Writes James Strahan:

It is evidently one of the main purposes of the poet to assert the moral rights of personality. He realises two things with equal sureness—the meanness and the dignity of man. Job knows that he is but a driven leaf, a thing of nought, petty, ephemeral, infinitely to be pitied. But he knows also that he is a moral being; and, as he cannot deny his primal certainties, he vindicates his rights against wanton infringements not only at the hands of man, but also at the hands of a despotic God.[1]

20b. The God of Eliphaz.— (Cf. Exeg. on vss. 18-20; Expos. on 5:9-16; 6:14; 12:13-19.) One might perhaps speak with equal fitness of "the God of the orthodox." Not that one would either decry or attempt to discredit orthodoxy. "Right doctrine," however, is not necessarily

[1] *The Book of Job* (2nd ed.; Edinburgh: T. & T. Clark, 1914), p. 11. Used by permission. See Expos. on 1:1.

the doctrine which is in line with ancient tradition. God has always new truths to reveal. He will not contradict himself in the revelation. That revelation is self-consistent when properly understood. For this reason "the rule of faith" has its uses. But its purpose is to illumine, not to obscure by shutting out the new light which is forever shining from God's Word, whereby he supplements and corrects man's fragmentary knowledge. Eliphaz' God was majestic (vss. 9-10) but remote, dealing justly (vss. 12-16), infinitely pure (vss. 17-18), showing mercy (vss. 17-26), but never for a moment involved in his world. Man's "righteousness" was no gain to him (cf. also Elihu, 35:5-8), and man's sin no hurt. In that much at least he would have agreed with Job (7:20*a*). There are traces all through the poem of this remoteness, a reflection no doubt of what was happening just then to Israel's faith (see Expos. on 18:2-4). But the poet himself would not have it so. Neither would Job. He had his moods of alienation: but never was it an alienation in space, so to speak; it was an alienation of the heart from one with whom he had

5 Call now, if there be any that will answer thee; and to which of the saints
wilt thou turn?

5 "Call now; is there any one who will
answer you?
To which of the holy ones will you
turn?

---

if this textual correction is accepted, the image of the tent is abruptly superimposed upon that of the house of clay (vs. 19a) without adding any significant idea to a pericope already overloaded with a threefold description of death (vss. 19c, 20ab). Moreover, there is no support for this correction in the ancient versions. The LXX read an entirely different text (perhaps borrowed from Isa. 40:24b), but a variant of the LXX (Complutensian, Cod. 248; see Paul Dhorme, *Le livre de Job* [Paris: J. Gabalda, 1926; "Études bibliques"], *ad loc.*) agrees with the Vulg., Syriac, and perhaps Targ., in reading the other word *yéther,* which means "excellence," "abundance" (cf. Gen. 49:3; Prov. 17:7; Ps. 17:14). Eliphaz uses this word in a similar context (22:20). The poetic parallelism suggests that the word **wisdom** in vs. 21b calls for an abstract term in vs. 21a. If *yéther* is translated "pre-eminence," the strophe is climaxed in a powerful and original way. "Is not their pre-eminence pulled away from them?" The preposition ב, used in Job after a verb expressing separation, means "from" (cf. 20:20). After the verb מות, "to die," the preposition ב indicates the cause of death (i.e., "to die of thirst" [Judg. 15:18], "to die by the sword" or "to die by famine" [Jer. 11:22]). The verse may thus be translated,

> Is not their pre-eminence departed from them?
> They die, and not of wisdom.

A sense of excellence does not enable men to perceive or to reach the goal of human existence, but merely gives them the vanity of self-satisfaction; the awareness of their "pre-eminence" (over nature and the animals) tends to make them self-sufficient, if not rebellious against the warnings of God. Their claim to perfection, perhaps tinged by arrogance, is taken away from them, and thus they die, but certainly not from superabundance of wisdom!

c) FRUIT OF OBSTINACY (5:1-7)

Eliphaz now applies his general understanding of the human situation to the case at hand. The sequence of his thought is tightly interwoven throughout the poetic development. He has noticed that Job had never surrendered, in the presence of the friends, in a prayer of commitment. A pious man would have bowed in trust in God (4:2-6). He may be, underneath his surface of integrity, one of the plowers of iniquity (4:7-11). In the end all men, and even angels, are impure before the Most High (4:12-16, 17-21). If Job refuses to commit himself to God (vss. 1-5) does it mean that he intends to use the intercession of mediators? That in itself would constitute an act of lese majesty.

5:1. According to a method of development which is familiar to the poet, Eliphaz, who has just mentioned the angels (4:18), is suddenly wondering whether Job's failure to

---

been on terms of intimacy (29:4b). From it hate might spring—or valiant love; mere orthodoxy, correct dogma and no more, could not. The God of Eliphaz was in Eliphaz' image. The God of Job will "in the fullness of time" reveal himself as the God and Father of our Lord Jesus Christ. Again the balance is to be preserved (as in Expos. on vss. 12-21; 9:2-10): between man's need for a God nearer than hands and feet, and man's need for a transcendent and mighty God, ruler of heaven and earth. "God was from the beginning transcendent in that He was different from man, but He was by no

means transcendent in that He was remote from man."[2]

5:1-5. Which of the Holy Ones?— (Cf. Ps. 73, especially vs. 25.) In Scripture, mediation between God and man takes place as the result of God's initiative toward man—as through Moses, the prophets, and Christ—and then as the result of man's response Godward—as through priesthood. The sense of separation always lurks in the background, whether it is the separation due to the divine transcendence (difference, not

[2] N. H. Snaith, *The Distinctive Ideas of the Old Testament* (Philadelphia: Westminster Press, 1946), p. 58.

2 For wrath killeth the foolish man, and envy slayeth the silly one.
 	
3 I have seen the foolish taking root: but suddenly I cursed his habitation.
 	
4 His children are far from safety, and they are crushed in the gate, neither *is there* any to deliver *them*.
 	
5 Whose harvest the hungry eateth up, and taketh it even out of the thorns, and the robber swalloweth up their substance.
	2 Surely vexation kills the fool,
	    and jealousy slays the simple.
	3 I have seen the fool taking root,
	    but suddenly I cursed his dwelling.
	4 His sons are far from safety,
	    they are crushed in the gate,
	    and there is no one to deliver them.
	5 His harvest the hungry eat,
	    and he takes it even out of thorns;*e*
	    and the thirsty*f* pant after his*g* wealth.

e Heb obscure
f Aquila Symmachus Syr Vg: Heb *snare*
g Heb *their*

---

pray to God does not indicate a recourse to intermediaries like the heavenly beings. He ironically asks then, **Which of the holy ones** would be a representative of man and would approach God on man's behalf? **The holy ones** are probably angels, as in 15:15 (cf. Zech. 14:5; Dan. 8:13). At this early stage the poet may purposely have placed in the mouth of the friend a suggestion which will haunt the tormented mind of Job and which will gain concreteness as the dialogue progresses.

> Call now; is there any one (besides God) who can answer thee?
> And (anyway) to which of the holy ones wouldst thou turn?

The idea of intercessory angels may well constitute the first sign of a trend of thought which will lead to the vision of the "mediator" (9:33), the "heavenly witness" (16:19), and the "Redeemer" (19:25).

2. Surely vexation kills the fool: The transition appears to be abrupt, and several commentators have consequently thought that the original text has suffered some disorder. It is possible that vs. 1 was originally placed between vs. 7 and vs. 8, which would leave vs. 2 following easily 4:21 (in addition, 4:21a is placed by the same critics between 5:5b and 5:5c). If the present M.T. is accepted as original, however, one may surmise quite naturally that the poet is weaving an elliptic pattern of reasoning. If Job really did think of begging for the intercession of the angels (vs. 1), this shows how deeply mistaken he was about God's intention toward him. Surely a man who judges God is a **fool,** and his theological resentment a crime whose fatal issue is certain. In Moffatt's free translation, "'Tis death for a fool to flame out against God." Indeed, men do not die from a surplus of wisdom (an echo of 4:21).

3-5. To be sure, the fool may sometimes appear to take root, **but suddenly his dwelling** is "consumed" (LXX), and his sons will suffer after him in solidarity with his guilt. The text of vs. 5bc seems to be corrupt beyond the possibility of interpretation.

---

remoteness), or the separation due to man's sin. For the Protestant Christian both of these have in Christ been resolved. One may well inquire just how far the idea of mediation through church or priest or saint is still to be associated, as Eliphaz suggests here, with man's feeling of alienation, and that in spite of the Christian gospel, conceivably even with his impatience (**vexation;** see 6:2; the word is just another irritant) and indignation (**jealousy**). At any rate the thought of such mediation would seem to take root in Job's mind (see Exeg.). What Eliphaz is sure will result in God's swift judgment (vs. 2) becomes the occasion of the most penetrating insights.

To enforce his warning in vs. 1 and the maxim he draws from it in vs. 2 Eliphaz sketches in the fate of **the fool.** No matter how much he seems to prosper for the moment, the curse is fast (**suddenly**) on his heels, for every man to see it and call it by its name. His house is brought low, his children oppressed, his fields overrun, his fences broken through (vs. 5b?); his wealth no more than bait for the covetous (vs. 5c?), to make some stranger's mouth water. Eliphaz had seen it with his own eyes (vs. 3) and understood it thoroughly. For such ignorance, not only of Job but of God—it is his ignorance parading as knowledge, not Job's ignorance parading as violence, that comes

6 Although affliction cometh not forth of the dust, neither doth trouble spring out of the ground;

7 Yet man is born unto trouble, as the sparks fly upward.

8 I would seek unto God, and unto God would I commit my cause:

6 For affliction does not come from the dust,
　　nor does trouble sprout from the ground;

7 but man is born to trouble
　　as the sparks fly upward.

8 "As for me, I would seek God,
　　and to God would I commit my cause;

6-7. With vs. 6, Eliphaz apparently continues to make objective statements. In fact, it is hard to escape the impression that he formulates opinions concerning life without thinking of the situation which confronts Job. He does not admit that physical evil is independent of man's behavior. Everyone knows that **affliction** does not sprout from the ground ('*adhāmāh*): "it is man ['*ādhām*] who begets sorrow" as surely as **the sparks fly upward.** The verb יולד is pointed *yûlladh* by the Masoretes, and therefore should be translated **is born.** However, the presence of a *mater lectionis* suggests (in spite of Judg. 18:29) a form other than Pual. The LXX reading (γεννᾶται) and the sequence of thought from vs. 6 to vs. 7 make the pointing *yôlidh* in the Hiphil most probable: "Man brings trouble on himself" (Moffatt). Some commentators follow the ancient versions in understanding the expression "sons of the flame" to mean "vultures" or "eagles" rather than **sparks.** With such a rendering the idea of man's responsibility for his suffering is further stressed: it is by his own will and power that man brings an evil fate upon himself, just as mighty birds fly high by sheer exertion of their muscles.

d) The Duty of Man on Earth (5:8-27)

(1) The Appeal (5:8-17)

Vs. 8 may constitute another veiled allusion to Job's readiness to address a power other than the Godhead. One may even ask whether his original lament (ch. 3) did not

---

sharply into focus—he will himself need a mediator (42:8). So completely does the real differ from the actual.

6-7. Affliction Cometh Not Forth of the Dust. —This verse appeared as a banner headline in the Paris press the day Hitler marched in. It is one of the profound truths to which Eliphaz not infrequently gives utterance. Unfortunately, as is always the case with him, he sets it in a context that distorts his wisdom into folly (see Expos. on 2:11-13). He is the classical embodiment of all the men since the beginning of time who have said the right thing in the wrong place.

He means that **affliction** never just happens (cf. 4:8). Man by his sinfulness brings trouble on himself. And it all goes on as naturally and inevitably **as the sparks fly upward.** Which of course is quite true. One must remember, however, that there is no suggestion of any automatism in the process. It is God himself who is active in judgment. The wages of sin are not doled out by the nature of things. Nor altogether on the basis of an individualist ethic (4:17). There may even be here some intimation that suffering is so bound up with the

divine order that neither the "wicked" nor the "righteous" can hope to be immune.[3] In any case, it belongs to humanity's primeval lot (Gen. 3:16-19; see Expos. on 36:8-25), and in Job is represented by the friends as largely punitive, with certain probationary, disciplinary, and redemptive overtones; though like death, it had its entrance not by way of God's original purpose, being itself foreign to his nature, but by way of sin, which is man's warping and twisting of that purpose.

Certain it is that no view, whether secular or religious, of the role that suffering plays in human life makes any sense at all unless due account is taken of the relationship it obviously bears to what the Bible calls sin. Every Utopia men have imagined without the one has had to omit the other from the *res gestae*. The problem lies not in the fact but in the distribution. It is with this that the psalmists wrestle. Most of their conclusions will appear in Job as matter for rebuttal (cf. Pss. 37; 39; 49; etc.).

8. If I Were You.—But that is precisely what is not and can never be (see Expos. on 2:11-13).

[3] See W. B. Stevenson, *The Poem of Job* (London: British Academy, 1947), p. 38.

9 Which doeth great things and unsearchable; marvelous things without number:

10 Who giveth rain upon the earth, and
sendeth waters upon the fields:

11 To set up on high those that be low;
that those which mourn may be exalted to
safety.

9 who does great things and unsearchable,
marvelous things without number:
10 he gives rain upon the earth
and sends waters upon the fields;
11 he sets on high those who are lowly,
and those who mourn are lifted to
safety.

---

contain some such unguarded vagary, even an intention of a polytheistic nature, which
would fully justify Eliphaz' polemics against the intercession of the "holy ones." On
the other hand, there may be in this verse only an invitation to pray in an attitude of
humility and trust which Job has notably lacked. It will be seen that so far the friend's
tact and delicacy have prevented him from making any formal accusation of sinfulness,
and that his advice on prayer has not explicitly included a request that Job should make
a confession of sin.

Vss. 9-11 form a doxology which justifies the idea of an appeal to the Godhead by
describing both his power and his justice. Vs. 9, which is almost identical with 9:10, may
be an interpolation at this place.

It need hardly be said that the easiest thing in
the world, and the one utterly impossible thing,
is to see what is right for someone else (see
Expos. on 4:5). There are of course traditions
and standards which may not be flouted; but
when one person undertakes to prescribe for
another he is always at the point of assuming a
superiority which he does not possess, a knowledge which he does not have, and an assurance
of what he himself would do in similar circumstances to which he has not even the shadow of
a claim. In view of the fact, says Eliphaz, that
everybody manufactures his own misery, **I would
seek unto God** if I were you, if my soul were in
your soul's stead (see Expos. on 16:4), that he
might raise me up (vs. 11). He would never
have dared such presumption, amounting almost to effrontery, in the days of Job's prosperity. You may hand over one of your truisms,
brocaded with rhetoric, to one who is down
and out, though it would be a peculiarly grace-
less thing to do; you would never think of dealing with him in such fashion when he is up and
in. More than that, the man who slaps a homemade poultice on a cancer may be a courteous
fool, even a well-intentioned fool, but nevertheless a fool. Eliphaz was guilty on both counts,
and never dreamed he was guilty. He was doing
the best he knew. He is a warning, not an object
for derision. He is to be pitied, not despised.

It is among the ironies of life that men like
Eliphaz are the first to offer themselves as soul-
physicians to the afflicted. They have cartloads of
wholesome advice to bestow, and who but the
afflicted are their lawful dumping ground? It is
always permissible to take liberties with misery.
Advice may be the frankest form of friendship; but

when pressed on the unfortunate it may be the most
offensive form of patronage. It is offered on the
assumption that a man, just because he is unfortunate, must be on a lower moral or intellectual plane
than his prosperous adviser. . . . Job was no longer
great, therefore he need no longer be counted enlightened. . . . How these men took advantage of
their position! How they dinned rudimentary counsel into the ears of the man at whose feet they had
once been willing to sit! [4]

9-16. My Soul Doth Magnify the Lord.— (Cf.
Luke 1:46-55.) To turn a man's thought of self
to thought of God is an altogether praiseworthy
attempt (see Expos. on 4:1–14:22) ; but when a
man's thought of God has already become confused the strategy is not apt to prove effective.
The more Job dwells on the theme which the
friends keep urging, the less God seems like the
God he had once known. Everything was going
very well with them; why should they not
"magnify the Lord"? But saying so never makes
it so. Job will assent to every word as theology;
but not to a single sentence as either competent
or final.

But the author sets up no men of straw. He
expends much of his skill on just such passages
as this, from vs. 9 to the end of the chapter.
Eliphaz particularly, among other things, is an
orator. Here he extols in ordered and stately
rhythm the majesty of God and his beneficence
(see Expos. on 4:20b), his justice and his mercy,
applying it all at last to Job, in an idyllic picture
of the sufferer's restoration. Only—not one item

[4] James McKechnie, *Job, Moral Hero, Religious Egoist,
and Mystic* (Greenock: James McKelvie & Sons, 1926),
pp. 34-35; (New York: George H. Doran Co., 1927), pp.
38-40. Used by permission.

12 He disappointeth the devices of the crafty, so that their hands cannot perform *their* enterprise.

13 He taketh the wise in their own craftiness: and the counsel of the froward is carried headlong.

14 They meet with darkness in the daytime, and grope in the noonday as in the night.

15 But he saveth the poor from the sword, from their mouth, and from the hand of the mighty.

16 So the poor hath hope, and iniquity stoppeth her mouth.

12 He frustrates the devices of the crafty,
    so that their hands achieve no success.
13 He takes the wise in their own craftiness;
    and the schemes of the wily are brought
      to a quick end.
14 They meet with darkness in the daytime,
    and grope at noonday as in the night.
15 But he saves the fatherless from their
    mouth,[h]
    the needy from the hand of the mighty.
16 So the poor have hope,
    and injustice shuts her mouth.

[h] Cn: Heb uncertain

12-14. Eliphaz is a wise man and a great admirer of wisdom, but this does not prevent his knowing that its efficiency depends ultimately not on the work of man, but on the will of God. He is not a moralistic humanist. He knows that some wise men are **crafty** ('*ārûm*, a word used of the snake in Gen. 3:1), and that **success** (*tûshiyyāh*) is ultimately the result of inward disposition. Vs. 13*a* is the only part of Job quoted in the N.T. (I Cor. 3:19).

---

of it fits. Every bit of it had been true in those "dear, dead days" that were gone; every bit of it would again be true in "the giant mass of things to come" (42:10-17). It was the present that was Job's prison house. "As it was in the beginning, . . . and ever shall be"—but *is not now!* At the moment Job had his own way of looking at the past (10:13), and he had his own way of looking at the rosy future which his counselors held out to him (17:11). There are times when praise may not be comely for the upright. "Ye ought rather to . . . comfort him, lest perhaps such a one should be swallowed up with overmuch sorrow" (II Cor. 2:7).

12-16. God's Great Reversals.—The **crafty**, the **wise**, and the **wily** find themselves frustrated, fall into the pit which they themselves have dug, and are foiled by having their plans come to nothing. It is iniquity that is struck dumb (vs. 16), while the **lowly** are set up on high . . . and those who mourn are lifted up to safety, and the poor have hope. We are forever dwelling on the mystery of life's inequities. Why not dwell at times on the mystery of life's reversals? It is a favorite subject in the N.T. (Matt. 10:39; 18:3; 20:16, 27; Luke 12:18, 20; 14:11). Meditating on the greatest of all reversals, that which took place between the Crucifixion and the Resurrection, Paul discovers in it the clue to God's plan of redemption (I Cor. 1:23-29), and to many another mysterious providence along the way of his own life (II Cor. 12:10). There was a notable meeting of eight great industrialists and business tycoons in Chicago during the era of prosperity when Calvin Coolidge was president

of the United States. They controlled more wealth among them than was available to the national government from taxation. Eight years later seven of the eight had either died in poverty, been imprisoned, or committed suicide. Without arguing as Eliphaz would have argued, we may at least stop long enough to inquire who are the weak and who are the strong, and who are the likelier to prove themselves quite the contrary—by the grace or the judgment of God.

14. Groping at Noonday.—(Cf. Isa. 59:10; Deut. 28:29.) In vivid metaphor Eliphaz sets forth the fate of those who "take counsel together, against the LORD" (Ps. 2:1-5). Their blindness is the kind of judicial blindness which "smote the men that were at the door" of Lot's house in Sodom (Gen. 19:11). It smote the heart of Pharaoh (Exod. 8:15, 19; 9:12). It smote the host of the king of Syria at the word of Elisha the prophet (II Kings 6:18). It smote the politicians and "wise men" of Isaiah's day. At the very moment when their policies seemed likeliest to prevail, the prophet had for them just this one devastating footnote, "Yet he also is wise" (Isa. 31:2; see Expos. on 3:23). In such fashion does God's light become darkness. Read again Paul's terrible indictment of the Gentile world in Rom. 1:18-32, with its downward plunge from revelation (vs. 19) to self-sufficiency (vss. 21-22) to idolatry (vs. 23) to degeneracy (vss. 24-27) to the collapse of society (vss. 28-31) and the deliberate encouragement of vice (vs. 32). Ps. 1 graphically describes the entrance upon such a course: walking, standing,

17 Behold, happy *is* the man whom God correcteth: therefore despise not thou the chastening of the Almighty:

18 For he maketh sore, and bindeth up: he woundeth, and his hands make whole.

17 "Behold, happy is the man whom God reproves;
    therefore despise not the chastening of the Almighty.

18 For he wounds, but he binds up;
    he smites, but his hands heal.

---

17. Although Eliphaz hinted several times at all sufferers' guilt (vs. 2-3, 7, 12-13), he did not wish to dwell on this dark aspect of his yet unformulated diagnosis. He preferred to extol the purifying aspect of suffering, and so quoted a beatitude on the benefit of *mûṣār* (**chastening,** "correction"). The word **happy** is probably derived from a root meaning "to go forth," "to reach for a distant goal," "to walk briskly forward," and does not correspond to a static blessedness but connotes an idea of constant development or ongoing process. Misfortune is thus used as a warning and as a method of improving the self.

(2) THE PROMISE (5:18-27)

18-27. If God **wounds** and **smites,** he also **binds up** and heals. One who does not despise the Almighty's lesson (vs. 17*b*) will escape all evil (vss. 19-22).

---

sitting; then goes on to portray, in terms very much like these that Eliphaz employs, the contrast between the righteous and the ungodly. It is a contrast, as we have seen, which cannot be wrought out with such exactness; neither can it be dismissed. The office of the psychiatrist is filled with people who have tried.

17. *Happy Is the Man Whom God Correcteth.* —(For vs. 17*a* see Ps. 94:12; for vs. 17*b*, Prov. 3:11. In Heb. 12:5-13 is a brief homily on the subject.) Strahan[5] objects that none of the three friends—only Elihu—regards suffering as discipline; they regard it at most as probation. The sufferer is under trial. If he proves tractable, all will yet be well with him; if not, he will perish (4:7-11). In any case, the word **happy** (see Exeg.) serves to indicate the kind of issue which Eliphaz envisions for Job: but only on condition that he receives God's **chastening** in a humble and contrite spirit; not shrug it off, as he has been doing, while violently protesting the fact of it. In all times of persecution men have found great comfort in the thought that "whom the Lord loveth he chasteneth." Their very suffering has seemed to them, especially under the Christian dispensation, a signal mark of sonship. Not that God ever willingly afflicts any of his children; but chiefly no doubt because in an evil world it is the good that has to pay the price of its goodness, as Christ paid; and because out of that dark, all through the years, such light has shone as "never was, on sea or land."

One word of caution, however, needs to be uttered against all such bright hopes as these which Eliphaz and the others hold out (see

Expos. on 6:2-7; 8:7; 23:13): in reality they constitute an avoidance of the issue. P. T. Forsyth writes of the method in general:

1. The first effort of a philosophic theodicy is to ease the jar. . . . The assault on the beneficent scheme of the world is admitted, but it is less than it seems, especially less than it seems to the victims. . . .

But . . . personality has a sense of shock and damage to it from evil too severe and deep to be met by pooh-pooh treatment from the morbidly robust. . . . The reaction . . . against such consolations goes so far that it tends to bound into the extreme of pessimism, or a denial of any possible mitigation. . . .

2. So recourse is had to the second method, which is not to soften the collision by a buffer but to avert it by a shunt. . . . Banes are boons, indirect or inchoate. . . . Evil is but good in the making. . . .

This view . . . like the other . . . is resented by the moral personality. . . . The right sense of the blessed whole would be an anodyne submerging our contributory pain. . . . But this cosmic elevation is not every man's affair, and pain and guilt are. And, in the failure of such a nepenthe, the mind falls again to pessimism . . . and again comes to hope but in a dissolution of reason, and a Nirvana in chaos.[6]

18. *Piety or Policy?*—The stress of Eliphaz' first speech is largely on man's duty toward God. Notice in the outline provided by the Exeg. the number of strophes devoted to it specifically. Now the theme is repentance; but it is repentance with an end in view. It is a turning to God as just about the only way there is of getting out of trouble, out of any number of

[5] *Job*, p. 68.
[6] *The Justification of God* (London: Independent Press, 1948), pp. 140-42. Used by permission.

947

19 He shall deliver thee in six troubles: yea, in seven there shall no evil touch thee.	19 He will deliver you from six troubles; in seven there shall no evil touch you.
20 In famine he shall redeem thee from death: and in war from the power of the sword.	20 In famine he will redeem you from death, and in war from the power of the sword.
21 Thou shalt be hid from the scourge of the tongue: neither shalt thou be afraid of destruction when it cometh.	21 You shall be hid from the scourge of the tongue, and shall not fear destruction when it comes.
22 At destruction and famine thou shalt laugh: neither shalt thou be afraid of the beasts of the earth.	22 At destruction and famine you shall laugh, and shall not fear the beasts of the earth.
23 For thou shalt be in league with the stones of the field: and the beasts of the field shall be at peace with thee.	23 For you shall be in league with the stones of the field, and the beasts of the field shall be at peace with you.

Prosperity (vss. 23-24), posterity (vs. 25), and long life (vs. 26) will follow Job's appeal to God. The conclusion of the discourse (vs. 27) reveals on the part of the speaker a certain impatience and perhaps a tinge of superiority. He will not allow any questioning of his own view of existence, for it has come by long probing and investigation: **Lo, this we have searched out** [by digging]; **it is true.** Experience, moreover, is

---

troubles (vs. 19). Is the author setting down his own mordant criticism of Israel's popular faith? God **wounds;** but even so, if the wound is ever to be bound up, who is there besides God that can do it? He **smites,** but who else is there that can **make whole?** If Job will admit that he is under judgment (whether justly or unjustly it is not his to inquire, God is not likely to be wroth because of his "integrity") ; if he will submit himself, as any Oriental would and should do before a high and mighty potentate (Strahan), then he is really not to be commiserated at all, but rather congratulated. He is in line for something the very thought of which is the note that sets off a lyrical outburst, prompts Eliphaz to deliver himself of nine lovely couplets (vss. 18-26), one after the other, with the greatest of ease, only to have Job take no stock in any of his facile conceits. First there is deliverance from all danger, from famine and war and "the scourge of the tongue," from robbers and devastation and drought and wild beasts (so Edward J. Kissane[7]) ; after that, assurance of prosperity, of peace both in tent and fold, of offspring beyond numbering, and of vigorous, "ripe old age" (vss. 24-26). All of it is the symphonic re-entrance of that discordant motif which was Satan's first cynicism in the court of heaven (1:9; see Expos. on 1:6-12; 8:7). None of it can bring a human soul within hailing distance of anything that could possibly be

mentioned in the same breath with repentance. That comes of meeting God face to face. It is not induced by threat of penalty or hope of reward. As honesty turns dishonest, so piety turns impious, when policy comes down stage (cf. Matt. 10:39; 16:24).

23. *In League with the Stones of the Field.*—There was a sermon preached in London during World War II which promised to all men and women of faith that no bomb would come nigh their dwelling (cf. Ps. 91). For all that, the psalmist was no fool; neither was the prophet (Isa. 11:6-9). Paul speaks of "the earnest expectation of the creature"; indeed of "the whole creation" as groaning and travailing "in pain together until now, . . . waiting for the adoption, to wit, the redemption of our body" (Rom. 8:19, 22-23). Without trying to make prose of poetry, it is perhaps worth noting that the biblical view of life and nature is sacramental throughout, a view cherished by the Eastern Church in its traditions and practices far more than by the West. "The prophet . . . views nature within the orbit of the situation vis-à-vis God in which he stands, and is led to see all creation as sharing the history of rebellion-and-return."[8] There is a wholeness, a vast unity, about God's order, moral and physical, which is not always to be apprehended, but will nevertheless suffer no final contradiction or infringement. We would no doubt have other "explana-

[7] *The Book of Job* (Dublin: Browne & Nolan, 1939), p. 31.

[8] Paul S. Minear, *Eyes of Faith* (Philadelphia: Westminster Press, 1946), pp. 60-61.

24 And thou shalt know that thy tabernacle *shall be* in peace; and thou shalt visit thy habitation, and shalt not sin.	24 You shall know that your tent is safe, and you shall inspect your fold and miss nothing.
25 Thou shalt know also that thy seed *shall be* great, and thine offspring as the grass of the earth.	25 You shall know also that your descendants shall be many, and your offspring as the grass of the earth.
26 Thou shalt come to *thy* grave in a full age, like as a shock of corn cometh in in his season.	26 You shall come to your grave in ripe old age, as a shock of grain comes up to the threshing floor in its season.
27 Lo this, we have searched it, so it *is;* hear it, and know thou *it* for thy good.	27 Lo, this we have searched out; it is true. Hear, and know it for your good."ⁱ
6 But Job answered and said, 2 Oh that my grief were thoroughly weighed, and my calamity laid in the balances together!	6 Then Job answered: 2 "O that my vexation were weighed, and all my calamity laid in the balances!

ⁱ Heb *for yourself*

---

strengthened by tradition: "We have heard it" (LXX; a rendering which the Hebrew letters of the C.T. make possible). "But thou [observe the abrupt contrast between "we" and "thou"] learn it for thyself!" This final imperative is intended to leave the sufferer with a sharp sense of inferiority, and justifies in the mind of the poet the rebellious character of Job's reply (chs. 6–7).

2. JOB'S REPLY TO ELIPHAZ (6:1–7:21)

The reply of Job to the first discourse of Eliphaz is composed of nine strophes grouped together in three rhetorical parts: a soliloquy (6:2-20), an invective (6:21–7:7), and a prayer (7:8-21).

---

tions" to offer of the relationship that can be traced easily enough between war and famine, between human greed and the cattle that choke to death in dust bowls, between man's thoughtless pillage of earth's resources and the floods that sweep away his property; but the relationship is there, and "explanations" are not invariably profound, nor do they invariably explain (cf. Expos. on 1:2-3). Recall the words of Lennox, just before the discovery of Duncan's murder:

The night has been unruly: where we lay,
Our chimneys were blown down; and, as they say,
Lamentings heard i' the air; strange screams of death;
And prophesying, with accents terrible,
Of dire combustion and confus'd events,
New hatch'd to the woeful time.⁹

27. Learn It for Thyself.—(See Exeg.) Eliphaz and his companions have not only heard all this, they have gone to a good deal of trouble inquiring about it, digging into it, thinking it through. They are willing to stand by it now.

⁹ *Macbeth,* Act II, scene 3.

They will set their seal to it that **it is true.** If Job knows what is good for him he will take their word for it. If not, he will have to come to it the hard way. And with that Eliphaz dismisses the subject (see Expos. on vs. 8; 4:8-11).

It is almost inconceivable that a man should fold his arms and conclude what he is prepared to call "the consolations of God" (15:11) with a bolt like that. It shifts the center of gravity from person to precept, from pain to panacea, and the whole weight of responsibility from the shoulders of Eliphaz to the shoulders of Job; the while moving down from such Olympian heights as to suggest instead of the intimacies of friendship the condescensions of an impossible omniscience.

6:1–7:21. Job's Reply to Eliphaz.—The book of Job is an "epic of the inner life." Luther in one passage compares the sufferer with Vergil's Aeneas, type of the eternal hero, led through all waters and seas, through all hostelries, until he becomes a capable and skillful warrior. There is simply no such thing in Job. The poem is thoroughly Oriental, its speeches hung like pearls on so tenuous a string of narrative as almost to shimmer, each in its own right, in midair. Instead of journeys, there are kaleidoscopic moods of the soul (cf. Expos. on 2:11-13). Instead of new scenes, there are visions and images, hopes and fears, memories, all the shifting phantoms of the mind. Instead of new faces, there are faces that are old and familiar: the face of God and the faces of men; but shadows sweep over them, as clouds sweep over the sky—the divine lovingkindness hiding itself away behind implacable enmity, or so it seems; human friendliness darkening over with suspicion, to blaze out at last in livid flashes of resentment and horror. The German poet Herder was eager to imagine that the author himself had endured the calamities and wrestled his way through the misery of which he writes. In "noble words" he addresses that great unknown:

Wast thou thyself the narrator of thy sufferings and thy triumph, of thy victorious and yet conquered wisdom, thou the fortunate Unfortunate, the tortured and rewarded? If so, thou didst give vent a second time to the lamentations of thy heart and didst spread abroad thy victory over the ages and across continents. Out of thy ashes there has gone forth in this book a Phoenix, a rejuvenated palmtree whose roots drink water. Ever since thou didst die in thy nest in accordance with thy wish, its incense has been wafted about, has refreshed much faintness of heart and will continue to do so until the end of time.[1]

Whether or not we draw any such conclusions must be a matter largely left to the individual fancy. There is nothing in the book—beyond a persistent sense of the author's own involvement in the tragedy of his hero—which would tend to support them, as there is nothing in *Macbeth* which would identify the Scottish chief with Shakespeare himself, nothing in *Hamlet* to make the Bard of Avon a Danish prince. Jonathan Swift once wrote of introducing Aristotle to his commentators: in the course of the ensuing conversation the ancient philosopher fell out with all of them, and the experiment ended in name-calling. All that can be said with any assurance is that Job portrays the struggle which goes on in human life against a too easy resolution of its central problem. And its central problem is not suffering but God. In a time when religion was self-seeking and when the people who needed it most—people who were aware in their own flesh of the slings and arrows of the Almighty—were thought of as cut off from the divine favor, in such a time this book would assert, against all the conclusions drawn from an oversimplified view of the relationship between

God and man, that pain and loss need not separate anybody from the Maker and Upholder of the universe. More than that, it would assert the continuing dignity and worth of the sufferer himself (see Expos. on 1:1). It was not only the nation that mattered; it was the individual life that mattered. That life, precious as it was, could never be caught in the toils of a depersonalized fate; it was held in the hands of God. The complexities of the situation were all there, and its manifold dimensions; the sweep of it, the mountains and valleys, the brooks and thickets; but God was there too, and a man could serve him in the very abyss, among the ruins of mind and body and estate.

In chs. 6–7 we enter again the unlit depths of Job's despair, the twistings and writhings of his lonely passion: unlit except for the fitful gleams that seem to make the gloom all the more impenetrable. He cannot be known apart from them. His spirit cannot be measured except as it swings down into these chasmed fears on its way through the storm toward the sunshine of that place where at last he stands naked and in awe before God, the place of peace. The road he has to travel can be laid down by inches on a straight line; but not with light years on the line of his soul's vast epic.

Oh, that my calamity were weighed in some balance, with the crying out of my heart over against it! Then you would see how just is my complaint. I am not making much ado about nothing, some mountain out of a molehill. I know that my words have been rash. But this my affliction—and never think it is just the pain of my body, the whole weight of my distress—is heavier than the sand of the seas. And it comes from God. The arrows of the Almighty are within me; it is their poison that my spirit drinketh up.

Goethe, writing of the Lisbon earthquake, which took place on November 1, 1755, when he was just six years old, and in which the toll of the dead reached sixty thousand, records the impression it made on him.

Perhaps the demon of terror did not at any time so quickly and powerfully spread his tremors over the earth. The boy who repeatedly became aware of this was not a little disturbed. God the Creator of heaven and earth, whom Luther's explanation of the first article of the creed presented as so wise and merciful, had by no means shown himself fatherly in consigning the righteous to destruction along with the wicked. In vain the young mind sought to stabilize itself over against these impressions, which was the more impossible since the wise men and scribes could not agree as to how a phenomenon of this kind was to be regarded.[2]

---

[1] Quoted by Emil G. Kraeling, *The Book of the Ways of God* (New York: Charles Scribner's Sons, 1939), p. 231. See Expos. on 19:23-24.

[2] *Ibid.*, p. 249.

3 For now it would be heavier than the sand of the sea: therefore my words are swallowed up.	**3** For then it would be heavier than the sand of the sea; therefore my words have been rash.

a) Soliloquy (6:1-20)

(1) The Weight of Anguish (6:1-7)

Vss. 2-3 may be given two different interpretations. One may consider that **my grief** (vs. 2*a*) and **my calamity** (vs. 2*b*) are to be weighed separately: either one of them would then be found **heavier than the sand of the sea** (vs. 3*a*). That is a sufficient explanation and defense of Job's lament (vs. 3*b*). Alternately, one may insist on the importance of the word **together** (vs. 2*b*) and understand that **my grief**, or rather, **my vexation**, "my impatient irritation," should be estimated, criticized, and perhaps condemned, only if it is compared in the same scales with **my calamity** (read with *Qerê*, *hawwāthî*, "my fall," "gulf," "chasm," "abyss," "hell"). Since the latter is intolerable and of unheard of proportions, Eliphaz should recognize the reason for which **my words have been** "wild" (vs. 3*b*).

We seem to have no great difficulty with the thought that a ship laden with instruments of death may make its way safely through the hurricane, while another, with its cargo of missionaries, may founder on some hidden reef. Ours is a world where there is "chance" and yet not-chance (see Expos. on 1:12). Job lived in a world where all wretchedness and misery were from God direct, though for the reader the alien figure of Satan broods over the darkness to keep it from being too simply God's darkness. The beleaguering army of perplexing thoughts and fears was the very army of the Almighty, organized into cohorts of evil. That was the burden which his soul could not carry. He was not just the plaything either of circumstance or of natural law in the autonomous world of which science likes to think. He was a man hungry for that goodness of God which he had known; and it was a hunger accursed because denied now of its food.

Doth the wild ass bray when he hath grass? or loweth the ox over his fodder? Life to me now is tasteless, like the white of an egg (?) on my lips. I loathe it. Oh, that God would let loose his hand and cut me off! Is my strength the strength of stones, or my flesh brass? You ought to show me kindness—even the impious man needs that. And you are like a brook run dry. The caravan of all my years turns aside into the desert to perish. I have not asked you to give me anything. I want none of your substance. That might have been too great a strain on your friendship. Teach me, and I shall hold my peace. Look at me. Would I lie to your face? I tell you, my cause is just! (See Expos. on 7:1-21.)

2-7. The Spirit of Heaviness.—A man does not always mean everything he says when he lets himself say everything he thinks he means. Job's passionate lament in ch. 3 should never

have been countered by Eliphaz' dispassionate logic in chs. 4-5 (see Expos. on 5:17). Almost as if talking to himself, Job the comfortless now begins to brood over the chasm that has already yawned between him and his would-be comforters (see Exeg. on vs. 30). Eliphaz has not weighed the utterance against the provocation. To cry out in anguish was as natural as for a **wild ass to bray** when it has no **grass,** or for an **ox to low** in its empty stall. Sheer animal need was enough to account for it. And Job is no animal. He is a man desolate, bereaved, stricken; not in body alone, but in mind. The arrows that have stuck fast in his flesh are **the arrows of the Almighty.** Their poison is the **poison** that his **spirit drinks.** The **terrors** that beset him are God's terrors. What wonder that his **words have been rash!** What wonder that life on his lips is tasteless! How is it possible for anybody to have an **appetite** for living when living makes him sick, like **food that is loathsome,** so that he wants to spew it out of his mouth (see Exeg. on vss. 4, 5-7)? Result had followed cause. It was the cure that Job sought—and found at last, though sadly enough with no human help (cf. 38:1 and 40:3-5; 40:6; 42:1-6; cf. Luke 4:18-21 with Isa. 61:1-3). There is "beauty for ashes." There is "oil of joy for mourning." There is "the garment of praise for the spirit of heaviness." There is more for the Christian, far more even than

> That blessed mood,
> In which the burthen of the mystery,
> In which the heavy and the weary weight
> Of all this unintelligible world,
> Is lightened.[3]

[3] Wordsworth, "Lines Composed a Few Miles Above Tintern Abbey."

4 For the arrows of the Almighty *are* within me, the poison whereof drinketh up my spirit: the terrors of God do set themselves in array against me.

5 Doth the wild ass bray when he hath grass? or loweth the ox over his fodder?

6 Can that which is unsavory be eaten

4 For the arrows of the Almighty are in me;
  my spirit drinks their poison;
    the terrors of God are arrayed against
    me.

5 Does the wild ass bray when he has grass,
  or the ox low over his fodder?

6 Can that which is tasteless be eaten without salt,

---

4. Moreover, the excess of suffering, which of course comes from the **Almighty,** has acted as a poison in the hero's **spirit:** God himself, compared here to a brutal warrior or hunter who is not scrupulous about his choice of weapons, has brought about Job's mental and religious undoing.

5-7. Eliphaz has severely judged the hero's language, but has he reflected upon the cause of the sufferer's rashness? Would Job have cried out in anguish had he been

---

4. *The Arrows of the Almighty.*—It would have been of some comfort to Job had he been able to think as we think, of a universe where it is of God's own ordaining, lest men lose their souls, that the good should "chance it" with the bad, earthquake and flood, famine, and pestilence, and sudden death, the righteous with the wicked. Ecclesiastes sees in it token of the divine indifference, if nothing worse (Eccl. 9:2; 11:3). Jesus sees in it token of the divine forbearance (Matt. 5:45). It might conceivably have been of some comfort to Job if he had been able to think that God had had nothing to do with what had happened to him; though when all is said and done, there could scarcely be a more desolate view. A man whose wife had gone down with the "Titanic" said to a friend, "I don't believe for a moment that God had anything to do with it." Said his friend, with sad and unearthly insight, "Don't you wish you could believe that he had?" It might have been of some comfort to Job if he had been able to think of his calamity as allowed of God, though not sent; allowed for reasons beyond our reasons. So the prologue suggests. But as in so much of the Greek drama, such knowledge, while provided for those of us now who look on, was denied the sufferer himself. It might have been of some comfort to him had he been able to think of his pain as punishment. That he bitterly resents. For *every* ounce of truth in it there is likely to be a pound of falsehood. "Pastor," sobbed a woman, "our family doctor has just told my sister that she has cancer. Mother died of it two years ago. You know that. What have we done? Tell me. Something is the matter. We have been faithful to the church. You know that too—you must know it. What have we done that God should deal with us like this? It is more than I can bear." No other comment is necessary than that such people have to quit believing in a God like that (Lam. 3:33).

Job had already quit. Not so his friends. To him there was more. And he was right. There is. He was wrong only in this: that he could not yet read the text of life's multitude of sorrows in the context of a love that for all its hiddenness was love still. It was in such a context that George Matheson read his blindness, and the broken troth of a woman who could not face with him the threat of those dark years.

> O Love that wilt not let me go,
> .   .   .   .   .   .
> I give thee back the life I owe,
> That in thine ocean depths its flow
>   May richer, fuller be.

And the "borrowed ray," and the cross that lifted up his head. To tug at **the arrows of the Almighty** is one thing. To enter some little way into what Studdert-Kennedy called "the sorrows of God" is another. Job had not come far enough along for that. His friends, with their angry God, were in his way. They were in Calvary's way. It was there that God shot his last arrow.

6. *Dead Sea Fruit.*—Life to Job was

> Like to the apples on the Dead Sea's shore,
> All ashes to the taste.[4]

When he drew a line under the days and added them all up, that is what he got. So with Hamlet:

> O, that this too too solid flesh would melt,
> Thaw and resolve itself into a dew!
> Or that the Everlasting had not fix'd
> His canon 'gainst self-slaughter! O God! O God!
> How weary, stale, flat, and unprofitable,
> Seem to me all the uses of this world![5]

Job recovered. Hamlet died of it. Everybody has to make up his mind sooner or later what to do

[4] Byron, *Childe Harold's Pilgrimage,* Canto III, st. xxxiv.
[5] Act I, scene 2.

without salt? or is there *any* taste in the white of an egg?

7 The things *that* my soul refused to touch *are* as my sorrowful meat.

or is there any taste in the slime of the purslane?*j*

7 My appetite refuses to touch them;
they are as food that is loathsome to me.*k*

j The meaning of the Hebrew word is uncertain
k Heb obscure

---

prosperous and satisfied? Is not his resentment as natural as animal hunger (vs. 5)? Likewise, does not man feel instinctive repugnance before insipid food or **the slime of the purslane** (vs. 6)? In other words, man needs not only food like the animals but also a decent and attractive food. Man wants not only life but also a worth-while existence: otherwise he rejects it and protests the compulsion to live (vs. 7). The proverbial allusions of these verses may well have a secondary and additional meaning (Duhm, *et al.*): "Do you really think," Job indirectly asks Eliphaz, "that I can accept your tasteless consolations and your repugnant advice?" According to this exegesis, Job is no longer on the defensive, as in vs. 5, but challenges the right of a prosperous friend to comfort him by reprimand (vss. 6-7).

---

about it, because it is not exactly an unknown mood to anybody who has lived a while.

Life has a way of becoming unpalatable. Sometimes whole generations seem to lose heart. They adopt some naïve view of history and affirm the doctrine of inevitable progress. Then one morning they see how their ideals, their beliefs, their hopes, and even their rebellions have turned out. The word "disillusion" was born into the common vocabulary of every day and grew up full size in the first quarter of the twentieth century. At about that time Will Durant was addressing an open letter to a few of his "famous contemporaries." What is the meaning of life? he asked them. Thought seems to have destroyed itself. Knowledge has brought disillusion. Truth has not made us free. Why did we hurry so to find it? It has taken from us every reason for existence except the moment's pleasure and tomorrow's trivial hope.[6] Walter Lippmann took up the chorus, telling us of brilliant atheists who had all at once become very nervous; of women who had emancipated themselves from the tyranny of their homes, and with the intermittent but expensive help of the psychoanalyst were enduring liberty at last as interior decorators; of young men who were world weary at twenty-two, and crowds enfranchised by the blood of heroes who could not be persuaded to take an interest in their own destiny.[7] In that world Nazism sprang up like a weed. Hitler knew that men and women who were fed to the gills with the whole sorry mess were ready to take a chance on anything.

[6] "An Anthology of Doubt," in Thomas S. Kepler, ed., *Contemporary Religious Thought* (New York and Nashville: Abingdon-Cokesbury Press, 1941), pp. 89-90.

[7] *A Preface to Morals* (New York: The Macmillan Co., 1929), p. 6.

And Stalin knew it too. So all unconsciously do men allow the subtle process of the years to rob them of the very stuff out of which they might otherwise have built a hopeful view of mankind's strange pilgrimage on this earth (Eph. 2:12). The most imperious of all their necessities, God and the human soul, fellowship and love, mercy and truth, slip over into the margin; while wealth and comfort, achievement and mastery, learning and pleasure, everything that belongs in the margin, they undertake to write down in the text. The result is sure enough, and much too swift for comfort. It is never long before the life that has no meaning beyond its own narrow horizons begins to grow emptier and emptier. With no interest left but self-interest, there is soon no interest left. With Job it was disaster (see Expos. on 3:1-26); with others, routine, a listless boredom that plods down the hours watching the clock; with others still, just sin. They start out with a smacking of the lips; they wind up with nausea in a third-rate hell, where everybody seems to be elaborately and intolerably dull.

And what is the answer? When the zest goes out of life? When the only flag a man has is flying perpetually at half-mast, as if somebody were dead? Whoever will spell that "somebody" with a capital *S* will have the secret in his hand. It was not just the majesty and mystery of life that dawned on Job at the last. What he stammered out was the only thing that could have taken him bodily and lifted him out of himself and his pain: "I have heard of thee by the hearing of the ear; but now mine eye seeth thee" (42:5). Life had found its center again. It has been said that true happiness consists in having someone to love, something to do, and something to hope for. Paul had his own way of say-

8 Oh that I might have my request; and that God would grant *me* the thing that I long for!

9 Even that it would please God to destroy me; that he would let loose his hand, and cut me off!

10 Then should I yet have comfort; yea, I would harden myself in sorrow: let him not spare; for I have not concealed the words of the Holy One.

11 What *is* my strength, that I should hope? and what *is* mine end, that I should prolong my life?

12 *Is* my strength the strength of stones? or *is* my flesh of brass?

13 *Is* not my help in me? and is wisdom driven quite from me?

8 "O that I might have my request,
    and that God would grant my desire;
9 that it would please God to crush me,
    that he would let loose his hand and
    cut me off!
10 This would be my consolation;
    I would even exult[l] in pain unsparing;
    for I have not denied the words of the
    Holy One.
11 What is my strength, that I should wait?
    And what is my end, that I should be
    patient?
12 Is my strength the strength of stones,
    or is my flesh bronze?
13 In truth I have no help in me,
    and any resource is driven from me.

[l] The meaning of the Hebrew word is uncertain

(2) The Boon of Death (6:8-13)

8-13. The sufferer will therefore reassert the desire to die which he expressed in his initial lament (ch. 3). Death at the hand of an unloving God (Eloah) is preferable to a continuation of existence under conditions of misery. Job picks up the thread of vs. 4 and hopes that a brutal Deity (again Eloah) will soon **crush** him (vs. 9). He feels that disintegration of his spirit has gone so far that, if his agony lasts a little longer, he might reject the commandments of a holy God (vs. 10c). An immediate death would be a means of overcoming the temptation of blasphemy and therefore a comfort (vs. 10a). He would **even exult in pain unsparing** (vs. 10b), for **then,** he would not have **denied the words of the Holy One** (vs. 10c). As it is, he has no moral or physical strength left within him (vss. 11-13), and **any resource** that he might find in his wisdom is **driven** away by Eliphaz' clumsy and supercilious recommendations.

ing it (Col. 1:12-13, 10, 11). God had willed and done so great a thing for him and for all human life that no matter what happened he was left there in front of it with a doxology trembling on his lips every time he turned a corner and looked up. Even the rough going carried with it a kind of relish. He said one day that God had made his life "a constant pageant of triumph" (II Cor. 2:14 Moffatt); then began to pass the whole parade in review: "Of the Jews five times received I forty stripes save one. Thrice was I beaten with rods, once was I stoned, thrice I suffered shipwreck, a night and a day I have been in the deep." But read on, and listen to the bands playing; after that the steady tramping of feet (II Cor. 11:24-27). It is a great mistake to suppose that when life goes stale what a man lacks is nothing but something to do, and that anything will do. He can go all to pieces right in the middle of his fuss and bother, with half a dozen irons in the fire. Paul's motion was creative motion. And beyond it, in a world instinct with God's love, a promise, "My grace is sufficient for you" (II Cor. 12:9). Just a level cupful it must have seemed at the

time, no more. Enough, that was all. Except that when the promise was made good, all back and forth around the rim of that Mediterranean world, it seemed to Paul like a rushing torrent: "The grace of our Lord flooded my life" (I Tim. 1:14 Moffatt).

8-13. At the Bottom of the Cup.—There may be those who find it strange that no thought of suicide, man's final thrust not only at self but at the world and God (Judg. 9:54; I Sam. 31:4; II Sam. 17:23—the only three suicides in the O.T., men mortally wounded, or expecting to be slain), ever seems to have entered Job's mind. The Hebrew's verdict on life was that it was good. Death was no boon. Sheol was a place of shadows, where being could hardly be called being, cut off as it was from God (yet see Pss. 16:10; 49:15; 86:13; 139:8). No man who was not beside himself could long for it (cf. Expos. on 3:1). Job's own yearning appears at times no more than a cry caught halfway between life and death, hardly knowing in what direction to turn. It would have been quite impossible for him to adopt our romantic if not sentimental view, taking to flowers and soft music, as if

14 To him that is afflicted pity *should be showed* from his friend; but he forsaketh the fear of the Almighty.

14 "He who withholds[m] kindness from a friend
  forsakes the fear of the Almighty.

[m] Syr Vg Compare Tg: Heb obscure

---

(3) THE FAILURE OF FRIENDSHIP (6:14-20)

14. A *crux interpretum*. All ancient and modern versions reveal attempts to make the best of an obscure and probably corrupt text.

(*a*) Many translators have understood the first word *maṣ* as derived from the verb מסס, "to melt," "to dissolve," "to faint," "to grow fearful or desperate." Hence the literal rendering:

> To the man in despair kindness (is due) from his friend,
> And he [the man in despair] forsaketh the fear of the Almighty.

What is the sequence of thought between the two lines?

(i) On the basis of similar uses of the copulative *waw,* "and," it is possible to translate (with Dillmann, Budde, ERV, ASV, Amer. Trans., *et al.*) :

> A friend should show kindness to a man in despair,
> Even [to a man who] is about to forsake the fear of the Almighty.

This idea is boldly modern and probably unique in the O.T., but the poet of Job is unique and modern in many respects. He is not afraid of placing blasphemous statements on the lips of his hero. This translation presents the advantage of respecting the Hebrew

---

death were anything but an alien, like sin, its full brother. Death was terrible (Deut. 30:15, 19; Ps. 55:4-5), and he knew it. To lie about that would have been to lie about life. Yet so terrible was life, so fraught with weakness of body (vss. 12-13) and peril of soul (vs. 10*c*, cf. Exeg.) that even death was better, that last abyss of **pain unsparing.** The expositor might do well to trace the relation between the modern man's concept of life and his concept of death. All through history to blunder on either count is to be deceived on the other. Settembrini, in Thomas Mann's novel *The Magic Mountain,*[8] is sure that in the cemeteries of the future, each with its own "Hall of Life," there will be no awe of death. Every remnant of such superstition will have disappeared. Poetry and song, glow of light, beauty of stone and canvas will see to that. With one accord they will lift their unanimous voice, and for every grief-stricken mother or father, husband, wife, son, daughter, brother, sister, "sorrow shall be turned into joy" (John 16:20-22). The Christian faith affirms life by refusing to deny death. "To live is Christ." Only when that is so can the sentence be completed, "to die is gain" (Phil. 1:21).

14. Sounding Brass.—There was something missing in what Eliphaz had said. In I Cor. 13 Paul takes that "lost chord" and makes a hymn of it. You do not add to life the love of which he is speaking and so augment the grace of liv-

[8] New York: Alfred A. Knopf, 1944, p. 458.

ing: you subtract it and life blows up. Lack of it does not make the world poorer; lack of it makes the world impossible. Without it you turn into a meaningless clamor the tongues of men and of angels. You cancel prophecy and miracle, generosity and martyrdom. You upset the whole basket of human virtues and reduce everything to nothing. Conceivably Eliphaz may have signed all his letters, "With kindest regard and every good wish, Sincerely yours." He may have made a habit of chanting in every ear and sundry his favorite motto, "Keep Smiling." He may have been full to the scuppers of what he believed to be forgiveness. He may even have gone so far as to get his face slapped, without doing anything about it except to turn the other cheek. He may never have cherished a grudge. He may have prayed God morning and evening to make everybody happy, friend and foe alike. All of it would have been a substitute, and there is none.

Apparently Eliphaz knew nothing of the spontaneity of God's love (Deut. 7:7-8). The only aspect of it with which he was familiar was that which seemed conditional on man's behavior (cf. Deut. 7:9-13); and it begat in him its sorry counterpart (see Expos. on 4:20*b*). It is precisely the love of God that manifests itself in his justice. It is the justice of God that carries, as the only cutting edge it has, God's love. That love is concerned about men, whatever they are, good men and bad men, not for

text and of fitting admirably with the context preceding and following, for it points back to the sufferer's fear of religious denial (vs. 10c), and it also anticipates his indictment of the friends' lack of understanding (vss. 15 ff.). Job has received no real sympathy from Eliphaz. His expectation of comfort has been thwarted, and he now senses that his faith is about to founder on the rocks of his sorrow.

(ii) On the basis of syntactic parallels one may alternatively suggest (with ASV mg., Moffatt, et al.):

A friend should show kindness to a man in despair,
Or else [this man] will forsake the fear of the Almighty.

In this case Job would threaten his friends with the theological consequences of his loneliness and of their blundering ministrations. He makes them responsible in advance for his blasphemy. In view of the fear expressed in vs. 10c, this is the most likely interpretation.

(b) Other students point out that none of the ancient versions seems to have followed one and the same Hebrew text. In vs. 14a, the Syriac and the Vulg. (perhaps also Targ.), instead of למס have read either המנע, המש, or המאס ("the withholder," "the remover," "the refuser"), and appear to have omitted the copulative waw at the beginning of vs. 14b. Hence the translation (Graetz, Beer, Duhm, Driver, et al.):

[Whoever] withholds kindness from a friend
forsakes the fear of the Almighty.

If such is the meaning, then Job is sharply indicting Eliphaz for a grave lack of friendship: pastoral failure is the equivalent of religious apostasy. Faith is betrayed whenever love is absent from a neighbor in need. It is not Job who is in danger of abandoning his religion, but the prosperous theologian who condemns blindly and mercilessly the rashness of the sufferer. Such an idea is just as revolutionary as that suggested by the first translations. It is equally unique in the O.T. and it constitutes in effect a foreshadowing of Jesus' teaching as revealed by the parable of the good Samaritan. Scholars who reject the first interpretations on the ground of their modernity might likewise refuse to accept the second.

---

its own sake, but for theirs. It asks Cain, "Where is thy brother Abel?" But it asks Abel too, "Where is thy brother Cain?" It asks those who are up and in about those who are down and out. But Eliphaz had heard no whisper of it. And Job heard none in him. The love that is at the heart of the universe is a stern and splendid thing, deep and tragic. C. S. Lewis calls it the intolerable compliment which God has paid us. We are something, he goes on, that God is making, and he will not be satisfied with anything less than he wants us to be.

Over a sketch made idly to amuse a child, an artist may not take much trouble. . . . But over the great picture of his life—the work which he loves . . .—he will take endless trouble—and would, doubtless, thereby give endless trouble to the picture if it were sentient. One can imagine a sentient picture, after being rubbed and scraped and re-commenced for the tenth time, wishing that it were only a thumb-nail sketch whose making was over in a minute.[1]

[1] The Problem of Pain (New York: The Macmillan Co., 1944), pp. 30-31.

There is a passion for torn and bleeding life which has to root itself at the foot of a cross if it roots itself anywhere. Hosea understood. Eliphaz had heard no whisper of it. So Job heard none in him. George Buttrick tells of a knock which sounded on the door of a poor little house in Japan. A voice answered it, "Don't come in. I have a contagious disease." Said the man who knocked, "I have something far more contagious than that: the love of God in Christ Jesus." As he entered, there on the bed lay Kagawa.

14. The Test of True Piety.— (See Exeg. for possible interpretations.) However we read the passage, the point is clear enough: there is nothing that can remit the debt of kindness that man owes to man under God, and friend to friend. The piety that wears on its face no such authentic seal is counterfeit piety: and the counterfeit imperils all genuine currency. It is often the only encouragement that impiety needs. Austere virtue sits in the pew. Is that why profanity walks the street? Prodigals leave home

15 My brethren have dealt deceitfully as a brook, *and* as the stream of brooks they pass away;	15 My brethren are treacherous as a torrent-bed, as freshets that pass away,
16 Which are blackish by reason of the ice, *and* wherein the snow is hid:	16 which are dark with ice, and where the snow hides itself.
17 What time they wax warm, they vanish: when it is hot, they are consumed out of their place.	17 In time of heat they disappear; when it is hot, they vanish from their place.
18 The paths of their way are turned aside; they go to nothing, and perish.	18 The caravans turn aside from their course; they go up into the waste, and perish.

(c) Other renderings have been proposed on the basis of various textual conjectures:

(i) By postulating from the Arabic *lamasa* a Hebrew verb למס (which respects fully the C.T.), one may read:

> He has requested kindness from his friend
> And he (now) abandons the fear of the Almighty.

Vs. 14 would then constitute a scribal reflection inserted in the margin.

(ii) By considering מרעהו as a noun without prepositional prefix (see Gen. 26:26; II Sam. 3:8), and by reading מאס for למס, one may also suggest the rendering (with Dhorme):

> His friend has despised kindness
> And he [i.e., Job] has abandoned the fear of the Almighty.

The verse would again be a marginal annotation.

(iii) By translating חסד not "kindness," but "reproach," "shameful thing" (see Lev. 20:17; Prov. 14:34; cf. Prov. 25:10), a few authorities have proposed:

> If reproach comes from his friend to the desperate man,
> He may forsake the fear of the Almighty.

(iv) By correcting חסד into חסר, one might translate (with Kissane):

> When his friend faileth him who is in despair,
> He forsakes the fear of the Almighty.

Notice that these two last renderings yield a meaning which is not distant from that of the first translations mentioned above.

15-20. The rest of the strophe contains several details which are of doubtful interpretation, but the general sense is clear. Job accuses his **brethren** of failing him precisely

because elder brothers stay there. There are "stale saints" and "attractive sinners"; and there are times when the relationship between them is nothing less—and nothing more—than cause and effect (cf. Luke 6:27-36; John 15:12-13; I John 3:14; 4:20-21). The church that is not somewhere in the slums, the church of the unconcerned, whether in peace or in war, Dives' church, would do well to tear down its steeple and quit pretending to point a finger at the sky (cf. Ps. 123:3-4 for the plea of a man who has come to the limit of his endurance).

18. Caravans that Turn Aside.—Such grim righteousness as Eliphaz had shown was like dashing a cup of cool water from the lips of one who was dying of thirst. To Job friendship of that sort was a dried-up brook, not a trickle left across the hot sands. You came staggering up from the distant horizon with a parched throat and swollen tongue; then you turned back into the desert to die. There is no more accurate description anywhere of the part played by some people. There were scribes and Pharisees like that, for instance, in the time of our Lord: fancy applying to them for friendliness and counsel. A Carpenter from Nazareth stood there before them, with love in his eyes and the whole world on his heart, yearning to make of life

| 19 The troops of Tema looked, the companies of Sheba waited for them. | 19 The caravans of Tema look,
    the travelers of Sheba hope. |
| 20 They were confounded because they had hoped; they came thither, and were ashamed. | 20 They are disappointed because they were confident;
    they come thither and are confounded. |

when he needs them. The images of a deceitful **brook** and of thirsty **caravans** lost in the **waste** (*tōhû;* cf. Gen. 1:2) arouse haunting pathos. Friendship has failed him. He remains alone in his misery.

---

what God had always intended it to be: and had his yearning hurled back in his teeth. "Samaritan! Devil! Who do you think you are?" while they looked around for a few handy stones (John 8). There had been no refreshment in them either for Matthew, or for Mary of Magdala, or for Peter, or Zacchaeus. That in part was why Matthew was still Matthew when Jesus found him, and Zacchaeus still Zacchaeus. These religious folk who were good, but with no understanding, righteous but without tenderness—you made your way into their company wanting far more than you dared to ask, as people always do; and you might as well have kept to yourself, or better, out there on the burning sands: no tiniest bit of moisture in them to slake the blazing thirst of a man's soul.

Surely every life is a kind of caravan, carrying its hopes and fears somewhere, many a long mile; hardly knowing where, perhaps, quite lost now and then, looking about today and tomorrow, always anxiously, for anything that may help it to keep going, put heart into it, make it feel that holding on is worth while, across an all too trackless waste. And surely there is some human pilgrimage that turns aside from its distant quest and sets in toward us: feet that come running up, and stop for a moment eagerly; other feet that trudge along slowly, and wait without enthusiasm—the sound of them after a while dying away in the distance, all of them somehow steadier, or a little more weary, for having skirted yonder the edge of our life.

Sympathy is one of the things they come seeking of us. And we are living in a world where just now of all times we can least afford to be without it. Not the cheap kind, which is nothing but diluted sentiment: the kind that costs something, that makes its way deliberately into the center of another man's condition, and instead of lording it about there with criticism and advice bows its head. We can get along with considerably less rubber-gloved diagnosis and ten-foot charity and transatlantic indignation. Wrongs are not righted with distant chatter, or the tips of the fingers. No use opening the grill and looking sad when somebody lays down

his burden on your step: the question then is, How much can you carry and how far can you go? We like to talk about how complicated, how very complicated, everything is. That gives us a comfortable sense of being unable to do anything about it. Congress must act. Mass meetings must be held. Resolutions must be adopted. And where is there anyone who is laying hold with great, strong hands on the life that falters yonder at his door, pressing it for even a moment, like God, to his heart?

Good cheer is another of the things they come seeking of us. We need a surplus of that for sharing. They used to say of Phillips Brooks that the sun seemed to break through the clouds every time he set his foot on the streaming pavements of Boston and raised his umbrella. There are enough people who go about helping along the twilight and doing it theologically. A sick world is not likely to improve if we all keep jerking up the shades in the morning and saying, "Well, I see it's worse today." Perhaps a sign should be posted for a while on the poor patient's door: "No Visitors." There is nothing to be had of grinning or of slapping every third person on the back. There is much in being the kind of soul who has deep and hidden resource. Read again the three "good cheers" of Jesus (Matt. 9:2; 14:27; John 16:33). The apostles go marching through the Acts singing their songs and waving their hands to us. They had something to be gloomy about; but no man can lay his life alongside of Stephen's or Peter's or Paul's and not have his pulses quickened. There was a triumph on which they drew in the midst of disaster; not a chirp and twitter practiced for the occasion; but a note resonant, like the diapason of an organ, leaving all the life around it quivering and glad.

Faith is still another thing men come seeking of us. Do we find it such difficult business holding on to our own that there is hardly enough for us, let alone a margin for anybody else? In one painting of the Crucifixion the hands of God may be seen, through the darkness that shrouds the Cross, supporting the two pierced hands of Jesus, and beyond, the face of God, fuller still of agony than the face of the Crucified,

21 For now ye are nothing; ye see *my* casting down, and are afraid.
 	
22 Did I say, Bring unto me? or, Give a reward for me of your substance?
 	
23 Or, Deliver me from the enemy's hand? or, Redeem me from the hand of the mighty?
 	
24 Teach me, and I will hold my tongue: and cause me to understand wherein I have erred.
 	
25 How forcible are right words! but what doth your arguing reprove?
	21 Such you have now become to me;[n]
	    you see my calamity, and are afraid.
	22 Have I said, 'Make me a gift'?
	    Or, 'From your wealth offer a bribe for me'?
	23 Or, 'Deliver me from the adversary's hand'?
	    Or, 'Ransom me from the hand of oppressors'?
	
	24 "Teach me, and I will be silent;
	    make me understand how I have erred.
	25 How forceful are honest words!
	    But what does reproof from you reprove?
	
	[n] Cn Compare Gk Syr: Heb obscure

b) INVECTIVE (6:21–7:7)

(1) "SHOW ME MY ERROR!" (6:21-27)

Job's tone rises from weary melancholy to abrupt bitterness. The mood of soliloquy turns suddenly into the passion of invective.

21*a*. "Thus, you are now as if you did not exist": Lit., "You are . . . , no!" The text may be corrupt. More probably, the syntactic incoherence may indicate emotional upset and outburst.

21*b*. "You see (my) terror, and you are afraid!" Pastoral counseling is sometimes vitiated from the start when the spectacle of sorrow freezes into fright the would-be comforter.

22-23. In his destitution Job expected not material help, but true sympathy and intelligent understanding.

24-27. A convincing argument from Eliphaz might at least have reduced Job to silence, but the friend's insinuations have not been concrete or compelling. Job would be ready to give up the discussion if he only knew in what way he has **erred**: the verb *shāghāh* usually means "to reel in drunkenness" (Isa. 28:7; Prov. 20:1), and may refer to a ritual error of ignorance (Lev. 4:13; etc.) or to an act of moral turpitude (I Sam. 26:21; Prov. 5:23). But Job does not confess here any ethical crime (cf. 19:4). He probably thinks of the rashness of the language he has used in his initial lament (an

with the thorns on its brow. Facing the facts is gallant work. But what facts? And did you find God in any of them? Were there no hands back of them, and no face? It is not realism just to grit your teeth and clench your fists and run out and get in the dirt. Nobody will swing along more bravely for it. Or less bravely for the man who lifted up his clear eyes on Calvary and said even in that desperate place, seeing as he saw, "It is finished. Father, into thy hands I commend my spirit" (John 19:30; Luke 23:46).

21-27. When Friendship Misses the Mark.— There is a spurious brand of friendship that on occasion fades away into the background as if it were not (see Exeg. on vs. 21*a*). At other times it proves cowardly (see Exeg. on vs. 21*b*; there may possibly be here a hint that the friends are afraid to take Job's part lest they compromise

their own standing before the Almighty). Always it withholds *itself*, that cheapest but rarest of gifts (vss. 22-23); the gift which is no strain on any man's generosity or courage, yet is the spring of both in others. And always it is lacking in insight (vss. 25*b*-26). In any case, it is bane instead of boon. It both hurts and gets hurt (see Exeg. on vs. 27; Expos. on vss. 14, 18).

24-27. *The Force of Honest Words.*— (Cf. Expos. on 4:4; Ps. 120.) Job would not have Eliphaz "by indirections find directions out." He wants a straight hewing to the line: When a man is desperate, do you mistake what he says for wind? Will you "charm ache with air, and agony with words"? You think I have been reeling and staggering back and forth like a drunken man. Deal plainly with me. Show me what I have done, and I shall hold my peace.

26 Do ye imagine to reprove words, and the speeches of one that is desperate, *which are* as wind?

27 Yea, ye overwhelm the fatherless, and ye dig *a pit* for your friend.

28 Now therefore be content, look upon me; for *it is* evident unto you if I lie.

29 Return, I pray you, let it not be iniquity; yea, return again, my righteousness *is* in it.

26 Do you think that you can reprove words,
when the speech of a despairing man is wind?

27 You would even cast lots over the fatherless,
and bargain over your friend.

28 "But now, be pleased to look at me;
for I will not lie to your face.

29 Turn, I pray, let no wrong be done.
Turn now, my vindication is at stake.

---

interpretation confirmed by vs. 26*b*). Passing now from defense to attack, he insinuates that Eliphaz has been dishonest. **How forceful** [would be] **honest words!** But what do arguments prove, coming from you? (Vs. 25.) His mental agony leads him to use an unjustified hyperbole (vs. 27). As so often happens in a quarrel, Job, being hurt, tries to hurt in his turn. **You would even . . . bargain over your friend.** As the next verse may imply, Eliphaz, upon hearing this, gives sign of an abrupt leave-taking.

(2) "Is There Any Wrong on My Tongue?" (6:28-30)

It is now the turn of the sufferer to give advice. His anger has subsided. "Come back, please! let no wrong be done" (vs. 29*a*). The certainty of his innocence has never left him. Perhaps the friends again made as if to leave (Renan). Thus he repeats more insistently, and without the precative particle, "Come back! My righteousness is still in it," i.e., "in the plea that I make," or "in this matter" (Dhorme rightly points out the neutral use of this expression in Gen. 24:14). On the other hand, the meaning of the imperative may well be: "Convert yourselves!" lit., "Change your course," **let no wrong be done!** It is the friends who need conversion, not Job (see vs. 14). By assuming a double metathesis some read, "Recognize my right in this affair" (*La Sainte Bible* [Paris: Société Biblique de Paris, 1947], III, 222).

That would be a kindness. Anything else is cruel. It's like casting **lots over the fatherless.** It's like selling out a friend.

There are not a few who will come up to you, take you by the lapel and say, "Now I'm going to be honest with you." And nine times out of ten what comes out is something nasty. There has to be self-forgetful love behind the honesty to make it honest; and behind the self-forgetful love a conscience, not one that tells its neighbor when he goes wrong, but one that first of all has learned to stay at home and keep house. The force of honest words is not so much in them as behind them (I Cor. 13:4-7). "Faithful are the wounds of a friend; but the kisses of an enemy are deceitful" (Prov. 27:6; see also Ps. 141:5; Matt. 7:1-5). "There are two elements," writes Emerson, "that go to the composition of friendship. . . . One is Truth. . . . The other . . . is Tenderness." [2]

28-30. *Beyond Misunderstanding.*—(See Exeg.) For one who will follow the progress of the dialogue, character by character, from beginning to end, there could scarcely be a more

[2] Essay on "Friendship."

forceful illustration of what happens when no heed is taken of Jesus' word, "Judge not, that ye be not judged" (Matt. 7:1-5; Luke 6:37-45). There is a suggestive and inevitable parallel between (*a*) the movement through the speeches of the friends—from well-intended criticism, veiled and considerate, to downright accusation, dogmatism meanwhile stiffening into *rigor mortis,* and sensitiveness turning into personal resentment; and (*b*) the movement through the speeches of Job—from what is hardly more than the cry of an animal in pain, to the blasphemies of one who more and more sees himself deserted not only by man but by God as well, in a world where nothing but death makes sense any longer. The whole situation has its origin in the presumption against which Jesus uttered his warning. The issue of it is mutual abuse (see Expos. on 4:5, 7, 8-11). But that time has not yet come. Here, in an appeal filled with pathos, and reminiscent of that solemn moment in our courts when the clerk is about to call for the verdict—"Members of the jury, look upon the prisoner. Prisoner, look upon the jury"—Job entreats his comforters: "Don't turn away from

30 Is there iniquity in my tongue? cannot my taste discern perverse things?

7 *Is there* not an appointed time to man upon earth? *are not* his days also like the days of a hireling?

30 Is there any wrong on my tongue? Cannot my taste discern calamity?

7 "Has not man a hard service upon earth, and are not his days like the days of a hireling?

---

30. Is there any wrong on my tongue? The word **wrong** is the same as that in vs. 29*a* and means "perversion," "wickedness." Job insists not only on his uprightness, but also on the soundness of his discernment. "Am I too blunted to be sure of that?" (Moffatt.) **Cannot my taste discern** *hawwôth* (vs. 30*b*)? This word is used in the plural of majesty and refers to a chasm or abyss (cf. the singular use of the same word in vs. 2). The psalmists generally apply it to an evil wrought by their enemies (Pss. 38:12; 52:4; 55:11; etc.). Thus by a single word Job lets his friends know that he is quite aware of their inward dispositions toward him. But he may allude to the abyss of blasphemy on the edge of which he now perilously hangs. The word may even suggest his fear of the annihilation which he had previously desired, and which he now both seeks and loathes, in common with all suffering humanity. This idea, if present in the poet's mind at this place, would in turn admirably introduce the poem which follows.

(3) "LIFE IS WITHOUT HOPE" (7:1-6)

7:1-6. Job suffers because human life in general is a **hard service.** He is subjected to the condition of mortal man (אֱנוֹשׁ), who leads the existence of a soldier or mercenary (vss. 1-3). Physical pain makes nights and days appear to be endless (vss. 4-5). Job

---

me. You do me wrong. I am telling you the truth. I am innocent. Not a fact have I twisted with my tongue. I know the difference between white and black. Give me credit for that." Indeed, one of the most difficult things in the world is to give another credit, to assume the best and not the worst (I Cor. 13:7 Moffatt). In his *Small Catechism*, Luther, writing of "false witness," contrasts it with speaking well of our neighbor, and putting "the most charitable construction on all his actions." [3] There is risk in it, of course: risk of the give and take of harm. But it is love's risk. Ultimately it is God's risk. The only help there is for anybody lies on the other side of it (see Expos. on 16:21). Better, it may be, than mistaken judgment is mistaken kindness. Better than either is that flame which only God can light on the world's hearth to cleanse them both.

7:1-21. *A Medley of Pathos and Complaint, Appeal and Remonstrance.*—Innocent as he has professed himself to be (6:28-30), yet wretched as who could know better than he, Job with utter pathos looks out for a moment upon the world—and upon the life from which so many wish to be free, wish to be paid off like a hireling, wish to find some rest in the shadow. Days are like months, and the months are all nothing; yet swifter are they than a weaver's shuttle. He hardly knows how life seems. In the nights there is no relief. There ought to be pity

for him somewhere up in heaven—with only the grave to look forward to, and that

> undiscover'd country from whose bourn
> No traveller returns.[4]

I will be quiet no longer. I will speak out my mind and not hold back. Am I a sea, O God, that you set a watch over me, a dragon that has to be crushed before any of your creation can be? Sleeping, you afflict me with dreams. Waking, I choke. Let me die. I am not worth the pains you are taking to torment my soul. What if I have sinned? Forgive me, and have done. Or one day you shall seek me and I shall not be.

The wistfulness is the pathetic wistfulness of a child, looking up through its tears at the father who has chastised it, whimpering out of the love that tugs at its heart, as children do, "You'll be sorry sometime. You'll be sorry when I'm dead." There are those who call the book of Job a gloomy book. If it were the story of life in its natural condition, that would be gloomy, with gloom impenetrable; but it is the story of a life that is lost, away from its home and its Father's house, in a far country. For such a life there is always the possibility of return. So has the doctrine of man's fall been called a pessimistic doctrine. Rather is it that if man as he is were not fallen man, there would be no gleam of light at all. For fallen man there

[3] Explanation to the Eighth Commandment.

[4] Shakespeare, *Hamlet*, Act III, scene 1.

2 As a servant earnestly desireth the shadow, and as a hireling looketh for *the reward of* his work;	² Like a slave who longs for the shadow, and like a hireling who looks for his wages,
3 So am I made to possess months of vanity, and wearisome nights are appointed to me.	³ so I am allotted months of emptiness, and nights of misery are apportioned to me.
4 When I lie down, I say, When shall I arise, and the night be gone? and I am full of tossings to and fro unto the dawning of the day.	⁴ When I lie down I say, 'When shall I arise?' But the night is long, and I am full of tossing till the dawn.
5 My flesh is clothed with worms and clods of dust; my skin is broken, and become loathsome.	⁵ My flesh is clothed with worms and dirt; my skin hardens, then breaks out afresh.

should logically renew his plea for death (see 6:9), but instead of wishing to die he clings to the drear and awful lot that is left to him and he complains, **My days are swifter than a weaver's shuttle** (vs. 6a). Such an inconsistency is true to the experience of men everywhere. They call for death, but if they face it they generally ask for a reprieve,

> For who would lose,
> Though full of pain, this intellectual being,
> Those thoughts that wander through eternity,
> To perish rather, swallow'd up and lost
> In the wide womb of uncreated night?
> (Milton, *Paradise Lost*, Bk. II, ll. 146-50.)

On the other hand, there may be no psychological contradiction in Job's desire both to die and to remain alive, but only a poetic ellipsis: "If life could be passed without constant

is a true estate. For Job in his blackest mood there is a future in the hands that even now are weaving it; and the pattern is God's.

1-6. Life's a Pain, and but a Span.—(Cf. Expos. on 3:1, 20-21.) What began in 3:19, reverently enough, as a lament induced by his own life's misery, proceeded as an indictment of life's misery in general (3:20-22), and then to direct accusation of God as the only responsible author of it all (3:23). Job now turns from his effort at self-justification in the eyes of his friends (6:28-30) to what he is ready to assert is God's allotment of time all too brief and labor all too constant and unremitting, not only to mankind, but to Job himself par excellence, part and parcel as he is of the weariness and the woe which he sees all about him. A soldier, trudging out the forced marches of a hard campaign; a slave who draws his breath in great gulps and longs for evening to come; worse still, a man brought in off the streets and set his day's backbreaking toil, with nothing at the end but being paid off and let go (yet see Exeg.): what else is there in the world? (See Expos. on 6:6.) He might, indeed—some sunnier morning before his universe went wrong, and the God of it—have answered his own question; he might have thrown in on the other side of the scale everything that belonged there.

But not now. So greedy is the evil that strikes the eye, or fills the mind, or assaults the body, to swallow up the good that lies in the memory or stands around waiting for a welcome.

> The angels keep their ancient places;—
> Turn but a stone and start a wing!
> 'Tis ye, 'tis your estrangèd faces,
> That miss the many-splendoured thing.[5]

In Job's unique case—of that he was persuaded—what solace in any event could there be in the contemplation of such widespread wretchedness (see Expos. on 2:11-13)?

> That loss is common would not make
> My own less bitter, rather more;
> Too common! Never morning wore
> To evening, but some heart did break.[6]

What on earth was there to live for? With days as long as empty months, and no **shadow** of the evening to bring him a little respite; nothing but **tossings to and fro** from dusk to dawn. Would God it were day! And every day, Would God it were night! (Deut. 28:67.) His flesh worm-eaten, hardening into scabs, then break-

[5] Francis Thompson, "The Kingdom of God," from *Collected Works*, ed. Wilfred Meynell (Westminster, Md.: Newman Press, 1947). Used by permission.
[6] Tennyson, *In Memoriam*, Part VI, st. ii.

6 My days are swifter than a weaver's shuttle, and are spent without hope.

7 O remember that my life *is* wind: mine eye shall no more see good.

8 The eye of him that hath seen me shall see me no *more:* thine eyes *are* upon me, and I *am* not.

6 My days are swifter than a weaver's shuttle,
   and come to their end without hope.

7 "Remember that my life is a breath;
   my eye will never again see good.

8 The eye of him who sees me will behold me no more;
   while thy eyes are upon me, I shall be gone.

---

pain, its brevity [would be] an evil, since none would willingly exchange its warm glow and thrilling interest for the cold and colourless monotony of Sheol" (A. S. Peake, *Job* [Edinburgh: T. C. & E. C. Jack, 1904; "The Century Bible"], p. 101). As it is, man's existence is too short precisely because it is **without hope** beyond the grave (vs. 6*b*).

c) Prayer (7:7-21)

(1) Appeal (7:7-11)

7-8. At last Job breaks into prayer. Not a sharp remonstrance, but a plaintive request. **Remember that my life is a breath** (vs. 7*a*). Job appeals to God's pity. He believes that the seemingly aggressive or impassive Deity may be moved to compassion by the spectacle of man's despair. Even at this early stage of the discussion Job's prayer presupposes a faith in the kindness of God. Only, when God will at last seek him out, it will be too late. "Thine eyes shall be upon me, but I shall be no more" (vs. 8*b*). Thus, at the precise moment when Job states that life is without hope (vs. 6*b*), he also believes that there is a God who will wish to find him after death, but in vain.

---

ing out again into festering sores; and no hope of anything better, none at all, either here or hereafter (see Exeg.). But Job did not have the last word. God had it (cf. Expos. on 30:1, 9, 16, 24).

6. Swifter than a Weaver's Shuttle.— (Cf. 4:19-21; 9:25-26.) The brevity of life was no uncommon theme with the psalmists (Pss. 78:39; 103:16; 144:4). That brevity could never have been regarded as an evil had not life itself been held as a dear possession, with God as its source (see Expos. on 3:1; 6:8-13), his law its charter (Ps. 34:12-14), his providences in judgment and mercy its sanction (Pss. 27:1; 63:3). Job's charge against heaven is that for him existence is both evil and brief—brief in fact if not in seeming. But never is his being here discounted as a matter of little worth. Any good concordance (*s.v.* "now") will provide evidence enough and to spare of (*a*) how dominant throughout the O.T. was the sense of the value and significance of life; (*b*) how urgent its swift and moving finger (Ps. 90:12; contrast the fatalism of Omar Khayyám, *The Rubáiyát,* st. lxxi); (*c*) how sure its foothold in the infinite (concordance, *s.v.* "establish"; Ps. 90:17; see Expos. on 14:1-6).

7-10. Appeal for God's Compassionate Intervention.—From beginning to end Job complains less of God's injustice as the author of his calamities than of God's injustice in failing to intervene as the vindicator of his "righteousness." That there is no such intervention is the very seedbed of the bitterest of all his complaints (10:9-13). He will not bide God's time; he will have God wait upon his.

Says Abraham Lincoln in Stephen Vincent Benét's *John Brown's Body:*

I am a patient man, and I can wait
Like an old gunflint buried in the ground
While the slow years pile up like moldering leaves
Above me, underneath the rake of Time.

. . . .

That is my only virtue as I see it.

Then his thought goes back to his childhood and on to the death of Ann Rutledge, which had left his world so empty, and he remarks that despite what "the smarter people" say:

I can't be smart the way that they are smart.
I've known that since I was an ugly child.
It teaches you—to be an ugly child.
It teaches you—to lose a thing you love.[7]

Far from being a thing of no possible import in this universe, Job regards his very frailty and

[7] From *Selected Works of Stephen Vincent Benét* published by Rinehart & Co., Inc. Copyright, 1927, 1928, by Stephen Vincent Benét. Used by permission.

9 *As* the cloud is consumed and vanisheth away; so he that goeth down to the grave shall come up no *more.*

10 He shall return no more to his house, neither shall his place know him any more.

11 Therefore I will not refrain my mouth; I will speak in the anguish of my spirit; I will complain in the bitterness of my soul.

12 *Am* I a sea, or a whale, that thou settest a watch over me?

9 As the cloud fades and vanishes,
　　so he who goes down to Sheol does not
　　come up;
10 he returns no more to his house,
　　nor does his place know him any more.

11 "Therefore I will not restrain my mouth;
　　I will speak in the anguish of my spirit;
　　I will complain in the bitterness of my
　　soul.
12 Am I the sea, or a sea monster,
　　that thou settest a guard over me?

9-11. There is no resurrection (vss. 9-10). **Therefore I will not restrain my mouth.** The thought of the finality of death prompts him to ignore all moderation of language, even with God: the almost tender mood in which the prayer began is now turning into bitter expostulation. Almost every other blasphemous statement in the discourses of Job is thus announced by the hero's warning.

(2) Defiance (7:12-16)

12. Am I the sea, or a sea monster? The sea is the primeval ocean which the Creator has to keep within bounds in order to maintain security and peace in the inhabited world (Ps. 89:9 ff.; etc.). It is mentioned in parallelism with Rahab (26:12; Ps. 74:13) or Tehom (28:14; 38:16), and here with *tannin,* **a sea monster,** a poisonous snake (see Exod. 7:9 ff.; Deut. 32:33; Ps. 91:13) which lives in the sea or in the subterranean abysses (Gen. 1:21; Pss. 74:13; 148:7; Isa. 27:1). The name *tannin* may be linguistically connected with those of Leviathan (see 3:8) and *neḥûshtān,* the serpent of brass. Job's query reveals a touch of satirical humor which is not without grandeur at this time of his spiritual extremity. A tortured man is here in effect saying to God, "Art thou afraid of me? Am I so important and powerful a hero that I risk endangering the whole universe?" The poet is a thoroughly Hebraic theologian, but his language is deeply marked by reminiscences of the ancient myths of creation. **That thou settest a watch over me**

---

wretchedness as a kind of compulsion weighing on the heart of God. **O remember that my life is wind**—a breath of air which stirs for a moment in the treetops, and ripples swiftly across some field of grain; with never a chance of any happy issue, either in this world or in the next (vs. 7*b*). But more: beyond a mere capacity and willingness to respond, he attributes to God a lovingkindness which is already moving out on its immemorial quest, making through all human history, as we know now, its journey toward a Cross (see Exeg. on vss. 7-8, 21*b*; the RSV, mistakenly it would seem, interprets the appeal in vss. 7-10 as if it were addressed to the friends).

11. *Under the Circumstances.*—Victim as he is of life's brevity and death's dominion, Job half reluctantly, half defiantly, gives the Almighty notice that he is girding himself to the challenge. Caught in the grip of relentless facts, themselves almost transcended in the aching wistfulness of his attempt to state them, the prospect of breaking through his bondage into mastery, with all the travail of a rebirth even now begun,

hardly seems to occur to him. At the top of his mind—Why not risk it? nothing worse can happen (13:15)—is the helpless rage of the vanquished, a man trapped and done for by his divine antagonist. He will therefore hurl his taunts at heaven and shake his fist. In the depths of his soul is the whispered answer of a love that cannot die to the Love that will never quit its search and go back home. Job as yet is unable to see himself anywhere but *under* the circumstances. And God sets no man there.

12-16. *The God Who Takes Advantage.*—In our finiteness we both yearn toward the infinite and resent it. There are tides in our being, like the systole and diastole of God's own heartbeat; now broadly welcomed, away up some spreading estuary, lifting the world's traffic to the sea; thrown back now from every cliff and headland, as if for all our frailty we ourselves were saying, "Hitherto shalt thou come, but no further: and here shall thy proud waves be stayed" (38:11). And indeed to refuse God's incessant offer of himself is to make one's self God. With

13 When I say, My bed shall comfort me, my couch shall ease my complaint;

14 Then thou scarest me with dreams, and terrifiest me through visions:

15 So that my soul chooseth strangling, *and* death rather than my life.

16 I loathe *it;* I would not live alway: let me alone; for my days *are* vanity.

17 What *is* man, that thou shouldest magnify him? and that thou shouldest set thine heart upon him?

13 When I say, 'My bed will comfort me,
   my couch will ease my complaint,'

14 then thou dost scare me with dreams
   and terrify me with visions,

15 so that I would choose strangling
   and death rather than my bones.

16 I loathe my life; I would not live for ever.
   Let me alone, for my days are a breath.

17 What is man, that thou dost make so
   much of him,
   and that thou dost set thy mind upon
   him,

---

alludes to the Akkadian poem in which Marduk, having overcome the dragon, "drew a bolt and posted a watch, and charged them not to suffer her waters to come forth" (*Enûma eliš* IV. 138-40; see Pritchard, *Ancient Near Eastern Texts,* p. 67).

13-14. Thou scarest me: The patient is now discerning God's deliberate hostility as it is displayed both in his own physical suffering and in his mental vagaries. Nightmares and insomnia entail a psychological disintegration which is ascribed to divine enmity.

15. My soul chooseth strangling: Again Job expresses the wish to die, but probably not by his own hands. "Death rather than my pains": Reiske and most modern scholars emend the Hebrew מֵעַצְמוֹתָי, **rather than my bones,** into מֵעַצְבוֹתָי.

16. The first word in the Hebrew is difficult. The verb מאס generally means "to despise," "to reject," "to spurn," but it is used here intransitively. If an unexpressed direct object is supplied, like "death" (vs. 15) or **life,** then the sequence of thought between vs. 16aα and vs. 16aβ is rather perplexing. The word מאס is probably the result of a scribal corruption (it does not appear in the LXX), and the original verb probably belonged to the preceding line (vs. 15*b*), which is now too short (see Jerome's recension and the Syro-Hexaplaric version). In the present M.T. the verb מאס may be associated with its cognate מסס, and the meaning may then be "I am pining away" or "I waste away" (ASV mg.; cf. Vulg., *desperavi*). Thus Job, once more having asked for death, once more reflects on the brevity of life and begs for a moment of respite: **Let me alone—** before I die!

(3) Bewilderment (7:17-21)

17-18. What is man, that thou shouldest magnify him? Most commentators agree in recognizing in this strophe a parody of Ps. 8 (provided, of course, that the latter

---

sardonic humor Job wants to know if the Almighty sees anything in him like that vast swelling of primeval waters, that chaos which had to be overcome before Creation could have its way. What else does God see in every one of us? He sees in us a life of his own devising able to resist not his might—that never really comes under consideration—but his love. It is not of our human weakness that he sets himself to take advantage: it is of our human strength, his own free gift, that he must set himself to make what advantage he can. The bonds that hold us fast (vs. 12*b*) are not by his decree, but by our consent. The plagues (vss. 13-15) are for those who are on his other side, away in an alien land (Exod. 11:7). **Let me alone;** and God would not. There is no respite. **For my days are vanity;** they would have been if he had had his way—a

wraith of cloud under a burning sun, if heaven had loosed its hold. He was sure that God was against him. Who then could be for him? Even so, intuition kept making its demands (9:33; 17:3) and would not be denied. History will one day put another question on human lips (Rom. 8:31-32). A man may think he hears

> Down the fair-chambered corridor of years,
> The quiet shutting, one by one, of doors.[8]

But there is a hand that opens them too; and Job will catch sight of it.

17-18. *Parodies of the Faith.*—There are times when a man's sense of his own insignificance, astronomically, geologically, and biologically sends through him a sort of cosmic chill, with

[8] Hermann Hagedorn, "Doors." Used by permission.

| 18 And *that* thou shouldest visit him every morning, *and* try him every moment? | 18 dost visit him every morning, and test him every moment? |
| 19 How long wilt thou not depart from | 19 How long wilt thou not look away from me, |

poem antedates Job). While the psalmist wonders that the Creator of the starry skies would confer upon man dominion over nature, the tormented Arab wonders, not without irony, why such a great God makes him the center of divine attention. He asks why the Lord of the universe should **visit** puny man **every morning, and test him every moment.** Here again the language is similar to that of Ps. 8 (vs. 4*b*), although the verb פקד in the psalm means "to visit with favor," whereas it is rightly translated in Job "to inspect critically," or "to visit with punishment." Another psalmist deals with the same theme with an almost identical intent and, like Job, links the idea of life's brevity (7:16) with that of God's exaggeration of the importance of man's sinfulness:

> What is man that thou takest knowledge of him?
> Or the son of man that thou shouldest think of him?
> Man is like a silent breath;
> His days are a shadow that passeth away (Ps. 144:3-4).

19. Till I swallow my spittle: Probably an Arabic proverbial expression. In 9:18, Job requests time to catch his breath.

results in modern life that scarcely need to be elaborated (cf. vss. 20*a*; 21:15; 22:12-14; Expos. on 9:14-19; 25:6; 38:1—40:5). At other times it but underscores his bewildered awareness of that in him which by God's grace and condescension is warrant enough for all the tumult he has caused in the history of salvation (Ps. 8). Pascal has said it for us:

Man is only a reed, the feeblest in nature; yet he is a thinking reed. It is not necessary for the Universe to take up arms in order to crush him. A vapor, a drop of water is enough to destroy him. Yet were the Universe to crush him, he would still be more noble than that which has destroyed him, because he knows that he dies, he knows that the Universe has the upper hand. The Universe knows nothing about any of it.[9]

In bitter mood Job parodies the psalmist's faith, deliberately and resentfully twisting the words out of their context of wonder and awe to make them serve his turn of satirical reproach (cf. **magnify** with "thou hast made him a little lower than the angels"; **set thine heart upon him,** i.e., regard him with such fixed and hostile attention, with "that thou art mindful of him"; **dost visit him every morning** with "that thou visitest him"). The story is told of a soldier in World War I, his heart filled with thought of home and loved ones, fatally wounded just an hour before the armistice, looking up at the chaplain and gasping out brokenly with his last

breath, as the roar of the guns suddenly ceased, "Isn't this just like God!" Worse, however, than the bitter travesties which find their way to such lips are those that rarely if ever get put into words, though unnumbered thousands there are who live by them. "The state is my shepherd; I shall not want." "Our privilege, which is of heaven, hallowed be thy name. Thy kingdom come. Thy will be done." "I believe in my own right arm, wherewithal to shape my world, and in the success that comes of it." Always the parody has its origin in the heart's idolatry: in Job's case not materialism or self-complacency, as Blake would make out, but a traditional God, who had been fashioned by the tradition itself far too closely in man's image. Let some heavy hammer of adversity shatter that idol, or any other, and faith turns into irony. Let the irony run its course, and what was a sneer becomes cold and calculating evil: gibes climb into crucifixions. Calvary was the place where God did his utmost to bring about a reversal, and to set Job's final *Te Deum* (40:4*b*; 42:6) in every man's heart.

19. *Let Me Alone.*— (Cf. Expos. on vss. 12-16; Luke 5:8.) In Francis Thompson's "The Hound of Heaven" the drama of this same deep human resentment is wrought out.

Act I. The Flight of the Soul:

> I fled Him, down the nights and down the days;
> I fled Him, down the arches of the years;
> I fled Him, down the labyrinthine ways
> Of my own mind. . . .

[9] *Thoughts,* "The Greatness and Littleness of Man."

me, nor let me alone till I swallow down my spittle?

20 I have sinned; what shall I do unto thee, O thou preserver of men? why hast thou set me as a mark against thee, so that I am a burden to myself?

nor let me alone till I swallow my spittle?

20 If I sin, what do I do to thee, thou watcher of men?
Why hast thou made me thy mark?
Why have I become a burden to thee?

---

20. If I sin, what do I do to thee, thou watcher of men? Job does not acknowledge any crime, but he becomes concerned with the possibility of his sinfulness. He had already rejected any suggestion of his "error" (6:24). Now for the first time he uses the technical term אטה, "to be a sinner," and he wonders whether he has committed any sin which might explain the depth of his misery. But no, even if he had sinned, he should not be punished in such a singular fashion. How can a human action concern the divine glory? With incomparable skill and penetration the poet reveals how acutely aware he is both of the nature of sin and of the character of God. By implication he indicates on the one hand that Job at this early stage still considers sin as moral failure rather than as offense or a revolt against God; and on the other hand, that essential sinfulness lies in refusing to recognize that man's behavior is the constant concern of God. Job calls for a Deity who would be impassive and insensitive to human conduct. That implied wish constitutes his real blasphemy. Should not the God of the universe be far beyond any reach of man's capacity to hurt him? The hero portrays himself as if he were a theologian intent upon the seemingly noble task of purging his conception of the Deity from any stain of anthropopathy. But such a god is an idol, the product of the mind of man.

Act II. The Unhurrying Chase:

Still with unhurrying chase,
And unperturbèd pace,
Deliberate speed, majestic instancy,
Came on the following Feet,
And a Voice above their beat—
"Naught shelters thee, who wilt not shelter Me."

Act III. The Child's Mistake:

All which I took from thee I did but take,
Not for thy harms,
But just that thou might'st seek it in My arms.
All which thy child's mistake
Fancies as lost, I have stored for thee at home.[2]

20a. The Watcher of Men.—H. G. Wells has told of the great eye painted on the wall of a Sunday-school room just above the platform, with the inscription that ran beneath it, "Thou God seest me" (Gen. 16:13); and of how the memory of it day after day rankled in his mind when he was a boy. When he had his hand in the cracker box, it was no comfort. So it is that what God does in mercy (cf. Ps. 121:4-5) is mistaken for what he does in judgment. To the rebellious heart, as to the guilty conscience, the **watcher** (or **preserver**) becomes the spy (cf. 1:10; 3:23b; 34:21-28), and "so much the better" gives way to "so much the worse."

[2] From *Collected Works*, ed. Wilfred Meynell (Westminster, Md.: Newman Press, 1947). Used by permission.

Go, bitter Christ, grim Christ! haul if Thou wilt
Thy bloody cross to Thine own bleak Calvary!

.   .   .   .

I am battered and broken and weary and out of heart,
I will not hear of talk of heroic things,

.   .   .   .

Men were not meant to walk as priests and kings.

Thou liest, Christ, Thou liest; take it hence,
That mirror of strange glories; I am I:
What wouldst Thou make of me? O cruel pretence,
Drive me not mad so with the mockery
Of that most lovely, unattainable lie!

O King, O Captain, wasted, wan with scourging,
Strong beyond speech, and wonderful with woe,
Whither, relentless wilt Thou still be urging
Thy maimed and halt that have not strength to go? . . .
Peace, peace, I follow. Why must we love Thee so?[3]

20a, 21a. Can a Man Hurt God?—Job misapprehends not only the true nature of sin, but also the true nature of God (see Exeg.). On both counts he falls far below the level of the O.T. Sin is more than transgression, or deviation, or defilement, ritual or moral. It is a breaking of the covenant relation, a rebellion against God that "injures the community" and distorts the

[3] Anonymous. See George Stewart, ed., *Redemption: An Anthology of the Cross* (New York: George H. Doran Co., 1927), p. 307.

21 And why dost thou not pardon my transgression, and take away mine iniquity? for now shall I sleep in the dust; and thou shalt seek me in the morning, but I *shall* not *be*.

21 Why dost thou not pardon my transgression
and take away my iniquity?
For now I shall lie in the earth;
thou wilt seek me, but I shall not be."

Why have I become a burden to thee? The reading **to myself** (KJV) is that of the M.T., which in turn represents one of the eighteen corrections of the scribes (cf. Vol. I, p. 51). The LXX has preserved the original with its rendering ἐπὶ σοί. Jewish scribes of the early Christian Era, influenced as they were by philosophical beliefs in divine impassibility, could not accept the idea that man may be **a burden** upon God, although such a bold statement should not be surprising in this context.

21a. Why dost thou not pardon my transgression? Is not forgiveness the essential attribute of God? *Dieu me pardonnera, c'est son métier,* exclaimed Voltaire. "God will forgive me, it's his job." A further display of the hero's incomprehension of the theological dimension of sinfulness.

21b. The titan's boldness is now spent. The idea of forgiveness has crossed the threshold of his consciousness and leads him back to the motif of vs. 8. He once more considers God not as the suspected marksman, but as the compassionate seeker of the creature. **Thou wilt seek me:** The verb שחר, coined from a noun meaning "dawn" or "deep darkness before dawn," is used of wild asses eagerly seeking their food (24:5) or of man longing for God (Hos. 5:15; Isa. 26:9; Pss. 63:1; 78:34; Prov. 7:15; cf. Prov. 1:28;

---

life. It *is* that distortion (Ps. 51:4; Jer. 17:9).[4] To speak therefore of sin as if it might conceivably be of little or no account to God (cf. 21:15; 22:12-14) —**what do I do to thee?**—is to counterfeit truth, to disclaim responsibility, and to dissemble very near the center of the religious consciousness. To speak of God as if conceivably he might not care one way or the other—so some of the sages, but never any of the prophets—is to destroy the center itself. Man is precisely God's only "stumbling block" **(mark)**—surely he strikes himself against nothing else—and **burden** (see Exeg.).

I've worked it over till my brain is numb.
. . . I've tried—
You know it—tried to catch live fire
And pawed cold ashes. Every spark has died.
It won't come right! I'd drop the thing entire,
Only—I can't! I love my job.

You, who ride the thunder,
Do you know what it is to dream and drudge and throb?
I wonder.
Did it come at you with a rush, your dream, your plan?
If so, I know how you began,

[4] See Kenneth Grayston, "Sin," in Alan Richardson, ed., *A Theological Word Book of the Bible* (New York: The Macmillan Co., 1951), pp. 226-28; cf. the doctrine of sins, venial and mortal, in the Roman Catholic tradition with Jas. 2:10.

Yes, with rapt face and sparkling eyes,
Swinging the hot globe out between the skies,

.   .   .   .

And then—
Men!
I see it now.
O God, forgive my pettish row!
I see your job. While ages crawl
Your lips take laboring lines, your eyes a sadder light.
For man, the fire and flower and center of it all—
Man won't come right!
After your patient centuries,
Fresh starts, recastings, tired Gethsemanes
And tense Golgothas, he, your central theme,
Is just a jangling echo of your dream.
Grand as the rest may be, he ruins it.
Why don't you quit?
Crumple it all and dream again! But no;
Flaw after flaw, you work it out, revise, refine—
Bondage, brutality, and war, and woe,
The sot, the fool, the tyrant and the mob—
Dear God, how you must love your job!
Help me, as I love mine.[5]

To say to such a God, **Why dost thou not pardon my transgression?**—forgive me and have done with it—was blasphemy against the human soul and the Love that one day would die for it.

21c. Half Love Is Half Hate.—(See Expos. on vss. 7-10.) The mind of Job is a battlefield.

[5] Badger Clark, "The Job." Used by permission. See Expos. on 40:6–42:6.

8:17; even 13:24). Thus the hero is once more reaching for the hope already expressed in vs. 8b. Through a swift—and quickly spent—reversal of mood which is quite characteristic of human psychology, he obtains in a flash the vision of a loving God. The transition from vs. 21ab to vs. 21c is quite clear. Why should not God forgive the man who is a sinner, especially—Job assumes—if that man is not a sinner? Of course, some day God will once more move eagerly toward his servant. "He will long to renew the old communion" (Peake, *Job*, p. 106). It is possible, however, that the poet did not intend to convey this idea at all. Inasmuch as the Piel of the verb שחר was well known in the sense of "to look diligently and eagerly," one can understand how the traditional interpretation arose. The poet may have even used another verb שחר meaning "to blacken" (rabbinical Hebrew Hiphil, Aramaic Pael). If this were the case, Job would merely describe, in utter dejection, the deathly prospect which is before him:

> For now I am going to lie down in the dust
> And thou shalt darken my face, and I shall not be.

It would be strange, however, that the poet would have used this uncommon verb here while using the other and better known one in Job 24:5, and would thus have run the risk of being misunderstood. The traditional interpretation, therefore, is probably correct. Thus the sufferer is expressing the certainty that God will in the end go about in the gloom of Sheol, groping in the obscurity, looking diligently for his human friend, in an earnest gesture of salvation—but it will be too late: "I shall be no more." The ebb and flow of the sufferer's moods are faithfully and subtly recorded. Receding from the aggressiveness of a persecuted animal, Job rediscovers for a short while the security of being loved as a son, but even this fleeting certainty is cut short by the ultimate bitterness: Death will be final, and God's belated move will be in vain. Thus the poet twists man's desperate clinging to the belief in God's love into a grim joke upon the Deity's frustration.

Every image that lifts above the horizon is raked with crossfire.

Between him and the God of wrath, who hates him, as his afflictions prove, there rises a vision of the God of grace, who surely still loves him, as blessed memories and a good conscience assure him; and at once the sufferer's loud and bitter cries soften to notes of pleading remonstrance. Since God must, as he assumes, sooner or later forgive the sins which have offended Him (whatever they may be), and come back to renew the old fellowship, he pathetically asks why not now, ere it be too late? [6]

God does indeed speak:

Poor human heart,
I know the ecstasy of all thy pain,
The anguish of thy joy.
The smile thou wearest
Cannot hide from Me
The traces of thy tears,
Or fill the deep hollows of remembered grief.
Thou bearest thyself so bravely:
I wish thou wert less assured!
Then might this orphaned pity in My breast
Find solace for itself
In the coverless pleading of thine eyes—
And tend thy hurt,
And tending be at peace!

[6] James Strahan, *The Book of Job* (2nd ed.; Edinburgh: T. & T. Clark, 1914), p. 86.

But Man answers:

I heed Thee not.
I was not fashioned for Thy care,
To lean on Thee and hope
And wait Thy slow compassion
To overtake my lot.
Speak when Thou art spoken to!
I keep my silence,
Let Thy mercy bide with Thee:
I care not for it!
My eyes are clear—
Save for this one last shadow
That steals across my sun;
And the chill wind that shudders down the valleys!
God! I cannot go! Art Thou near enough to hear? [7]

Sterile indifference is the one mood that is absent. Job is a house divided (Matt. 12:25). The psychologist would talk of split personality, the physicist of unstable equilibrium. The condition cannot long persist without getting better or worse. The best that can be said of it is that it is fraught with possibilities. Fecundity, not sterility, is the word now. The man who comes out of it will be anything but neutral (cf. Mark 9:40, tolerance of others, with Matt. 12:30, intolerance as regards the self). He will

[7] Paul Scherer, "Dialogue." Authorship acknowledged by request. Editors.

8 Then answered Bildad the Shuhite, and said,

2 How long wilt thou speak these *things?* and *how long shall* the words of thy mouth *be like* a strong wind?

8 Then Bildad the Shuhite answered:

2 "How long will you say these things, and the words of your mouth be a great wind?

---

3. First Discourse of Bildad (8:1-22)

a) Divine Justice (8:1-7)

8:2-4. Bildad's position is basically the same as that of Eliphaz, but his attack is different. He begins abruptly, as if out of anger. He cannot endure the irreverence with which Job has spoken (ch. 7) of "the ways of God with men." He is probably a nervous, impulsive, extremely convinced believer, whose religious feelings have been painfully hurt. That may be the reason why he starts without the traditional considerations of courtesy. "How long wilt thou discourse like that?" (Vs. 2*a*.) For him Job's eloquence is comparable to a "stormy wind" (vs. 2*b*) since it is directed against the cardinal dogma of divine righteousness. **Doth God pervert . . . justice** (vs. 3*a*)? In Bildad's mind a rhetorical question is sufficient to dispose of the mystery of apparent injustice upon

---

tend to be all love (creative) or all hate (destructive).

8:1-22. A Word from the Wise.—How long will you go on talking such violent nonsense? It is Bildad's turn, and he makes no attempt to conceal his impatience. His is the mood of one who would say

> I am Sir Oracle,
> And when I ope my lips, let no dog bark! [8]

What! **God pervert justice?** The **Almighty?** Who could ever conceive of such a thing? Take your own case for example. Without any further beating about the bush, the suspicion which has been lying dormant in the mind of each of the friends begins to break out into words: Your **children** have been cut off. Surely that was the result of their sin. While the very fact that you yourself have been spared is indication enough that if you will repent, and so become **pure and upright,** God will bestir himself for you, and establish you far more firmly than of old. That would be fair enough, would it not? Then in mellower strain: Our fathers' fathers have taught us, in those days when men lived long and were wise, that the godless are rooted out—like the tender green reeds, they used to say, that wilt and perish when the waters recede, before anybody lays a hand on them. The **confidence** of the wicked, so runs the ancient proverb, is no more than **a spider's web.** They **trust** in their wealth, and lo, they are gone. They lay hold on the stones and wither. Their place knows them no more. They die, with none of their offshoots surviving, and others come after them. It is as if they had not been. So just is God. He will not then destroy you in your integrity. But neither shall any evil stand before his face. You

shall rejoice with us, and with others like us who are your friends. It is rather your enemies, and all such ungodly folk, that shall go down into the dust.

Bildad feels certain that Job, judging from some of the things he has said (6:29; 7:3, 11 ff.), is making the most fatuous of all possible mistakes: he is denying to God the moral discernment which he claims for himself (6:30). Eliphaz, on the basis of knowledge immediate and revealed, had wanted him to see himself as God saw him; Bildad, on the basis of knowledge which had been handed down from generation to generation, wanted him to give God credit for seeing with some clarity. If Job could tell white from black, so could the Almighty. He was not likely to be confused as between the sheep and the goats. What had happened was proof enough. The only difference between Job and his children was that his sin had not yet proved fatal. He still had a chance. Never mind the man's suffering. Never mind his repeated avowals of innocence. Never mind any of the accusations he had brought against his three friends. All of that was beside the point. Dismiss it. What was not beside the point was this: that God unfailingly does away, not with the righteous, but with the godless. You could look it up in the books and see. Every fine old maxim of the past, every sonorous tradition of the fathers, put it beyond question. Let Job take it to heart (vss. 20-22). Already he had had a taste of it. One can hardly keep from noting the parallels with his experience in vss. 14-19 (cf. vs. 14*a* with 4:6*b*). How could he possibly be right and everybody else be wrong?

1-7. Recipe for Revolt.—How long . . . ? So does Cicero begin his orations against Catiline, "How long wilt thou continue to abuse our

---

[8] Shakespeare, *The Merchant of Venice,* Act I, scene 1.

3 Doth God pervert judgment? or doth the Almighty pervert justice?

4 If thy children have sinned against him, and he have cast them away for their transgression;

3 Does God pervert justice?
Or does the Almighty pervert the right?

4 If your children have sinned against him, he has delivered them into the power of their transgression.

---

earth. His anger prompts him to be cruel. While Eliphaz had true sympathy for Job and had not intended insult, Bildad, on the contrary, posing as God's champion (or thinking himself to be—as his name suggests—"God's darling") sharpens his dagger to wound Job precisely where he knew he would hurt the most: at the heart of a father whose children are dead. "Thy sons were sinners, and that is the reason for their sudden and premature death. God hath delivered them into the power of their transgression." This remarkable formula may imply that death is not so much a penalty which is inflicted after the judge of all men has considered the merits of the case: The omnipotent ruler of the universe, conceived in strictly monistic terms, allows death to follow sin in a quasi-impersonal process, as an immediate and inherent result of man's crime; or rather, **transgression** is boldly personified (cf. Gen. 4:7)—it possesses within itself the **power** (Hebrew, "hand") of destruction.

---

patience?" But it was a "patient," not a criminal, whom Bildad was treating with impatience. Nothing but revolt can come of it. Accuse the sick, and let the sickness go. If somebody violates your principles, or offends your faith, or hurts your feelings, never deal with the cause; it is so much easier to deal with the person. Tell him he talks too much, what he says makes no sense. Show your resentment. Fasten on the wild words he has spoken. Undoubtedly the misfortunes he has suffered are an excellent illustration of the inevitable results. Explain him to himself. Make it clear to him how stupid he is. And be sure you hold fast to your theories at this point. No matter about the facts. Hold out to him glib promises, if only he will change his way of looking at things and adopt yours. Labor, the Negro, communism: the world has any number of "patients" on its hands. Treat them with impatience. There is no surer means of getting on—with the revolution!

3. *Dismissing a Mystery.*—Not infrequently is the attempt made to dismiss a mystery with a rhetorical question (see Exeg.). Here the mystery is the mystery of innocent suffering. No "explanation" of it is possible. Explanations are therefore not called for. Every suggestion that can be offered is bound to oversimplify the problem in one way or another. In John 9 the Jews asked Jesus about the man born blind, "Did this man sin, or his parents?" And Jesus would have none of it. They tried again in Luke 13, this time about the Galileans, "whose blood Pilate had mingled with their sacrifices." And Jesus would have none of it. Only that sharp word, "Except ye repent, ye shall all likewise perish." The perplexity will not be resolved anywhere but on the field of action (see Expos.

on 1:12). Bildad's strategy is particularly futile. He tries to get around the difficulty when nobody is looking. He will execute a flanking movement. Laugh it out of court. Use exclamation points. Scare people away from it. The emphasis in both lines of vs. 3 is first on the subject and then on the verb. There may well have been subtle innuendoes in the very tone of Bildad's voice. Inflection often takes the place of argument, and carries a sharper sting in its tail. *"You* perhaps; not *God!"*

The trouble is that when you meet trouble with a truism you make trouble. To say that whatever apparent discrepancies there are in the divine ordering of the universe will be set right in good time (vss. 5-7) may qualify you, strangely enough, as either a wise man or a fool: a wise man for believing it (cf. 42:12-17), a fool for saying it. Far better to acknowledge the mystery—which remains mystery for all your pains. Better still to have traveled that way yourself in faith and fortitude (John 20:27; see Expos. on 36:18-25). Something may happen then. Not otherwise. Meanwhile, no short cuts! No fool's gold that can pave nothing but a fool's paradise. One might wish, for instance, that hate would be born only of blindness, that love would come with sight. Poets have said so—and in saying so have got no more than the soles of their feet wet in the facts. Ignorance is not the only "maker of hell"; nor do "sympathy, charity, kindness" [9] always come of knowledge. They come of love, which has its cradle neither in blindness nor in sight, but elsewhere—in the very heart of the mystery.

4. *The Mills of God.*—One would not impugn the moral order; but must we be forever exalting

[9] See William Watson, "England to Ireland," st. ii.

5 If thou wouldest seek unto God betimes, and make thy supplication to the Almighty;

6 If thou *wert* pure and upright; surely now he would awake for thee, and make the habitation of thy righteousness prosperous.

7 Though thy beginning was small, yet thy latter end should greatly increase.

5 If you will seek God
　　and make supplication to the Almighty,
6 if you are pure and upright,
　　surely then he will rouse himself for you
　　and reward you with a rightful habitation.
7 And though your beginning was small,
　　your latter days will be very great.

To be sure, Bildad may conversely have meant, by accusing the dead sons, to excuse the father still alive, and his words would then have been inspired by a pastoral intent. If that is the case, "God's darling" is the type of the fumbling counselor.

5-6. If you will seek God and make supplication to the Almighty: Lit., "implore grace" (Hithpael). If Job becomes **pure and upright,** God will do his part and "bring peace, health, and prosperity [שׁלום] to the home of [Job's] righteousness" (vs. 6c). Such a conditional restoration reveals a strange conception of "grace": Bildad's words presuppose between God and man a moralistic relation in which man achieves his own righteousness and remains the author of his salvation.

7. "Thy former state will appear insignificant compared to thy future greatness." As Dhorme points out, **beginning** (ראשׁית) and **end** (אחרית) refer respectively to a man's former and latter conditions (cf. 42:12, where the same words are used; see also the LXX rendering of this verse, τὰ μὲν πρῶτά σου . . . τὰ δὲ ἔσχατα σου; cf. Matt. 12:45; Luke 11:26; II Pet. 2:20).

---

it above measure? There is something almost automatic about the operation of divine justice as Bildad conceives of it here (see Exeg.; so also Eliphaz in 4:8; 15:31, 35; Bildad again in 18:7-8; Zophar in 20:12-16). The tendency to speak of God as if he were shadowy and distant is no doubt a reflection of what is happening to Israel's faith: his providence is little by little depersonalized, his judgments are an item in "the nature of the case," *ex necessitate rei.*

> Though the mills of God grind slowly,
> Yet they grind exceeding small;
> Though with patience he stands waiting,
> With exactness grinds he all.[1]

The mills of God were by way of fact; the presence of God by way of courtesy. In a world where even the so-called "laws of nature" have been written down as a kind of "convention," and that by no less a luminary than Bertrand Russell, may it not be that "the moral order" is another plum we pull out of the Christmas pie by putting in a thumb? G. K. Chesterton once remarked that the sun rises every morning because God says, "Get up!" Deism believed in a Person, but got rid of him. He became an absentee landlord. Christianity confronts him. What else is there to do at last with a Person, a troublesome Person, who keeps saying "I" and "thou" in daily encounter? Bildad's words are filled with very considerate if's (vss. 4-6); and

all of them raise in Job's mind very considerable but's—which no circumlocution will ever circumvent, least of all this dodging behind a process (9:17-18, 24c, 31a; 13:24-27).

7. All Will Come Right.—Each insists on it: Eliphaz, with all the ornaments of rhetoric (5:17-26); Bildad, in the present passage, with something more of prose than of poetry; Zophar, with much more detailed reference than either of the others to Job's immediate condition (11: 15-19). After the first cycle they give it up unanimously as an unlikely prospect. Of course the disconcerting response in all such circumstances is "How do you know?" And Job in effect makes it (14:7-12). These men must not, however, be reckoned meanwhile as sheer optimists. There is more here than the mood which flourishes best, as another has put it, in the lunatic asylum; more than what Voltaire once called "the madness of maintaining that everything is right when it is wrong." [2] They at least base their forecasts on Job's fundamental integrity and God's elemental justice (vss. 20-22). What they say misses the mark nonetheless, not because there is no truth in it—their prophecies are fulfilled to the letter—but chiefly because future relief is never a very potent remedy for present grief. Add to that two footnotes, and the indictment will be complete: (a) They all alike take it for granted that Job is hurt more in body and estate than in mind. Satan too was

---

[1] Longfellow, "Retribution."

[2] *Candide,* ch. xix.

8 For inquire, I pray thee, of the former age, and prepare thyself to the search of their fathers:	8 "For inquire, I pray you, of bygone ages, and consider what the fathers have found;

8 For inquire, I pray thee, of the former age, and prepare thyself to the search of their fathers:

9 (For we *are but of* yesterday, and know nothing, because our days upon earth *are* a shadow:)

10 Shall not they teach thee, *and* tell thee, and utter words out of their heart?

11 Can the rush grow up without mire? can the flag grow without water?

12 Whilst it *is* yet in his greenness, *and* not cut down, it withereth before any *other* herb.

13 So *are* the paths of all that forget God; and the hypocrite's hope shall perish:

8 "For inquire, I pray you, of bygone ages,
 and consider what the fathers have found;
9 for we are but of yesterday, and know nothing,
 for our days on earth are a shadow.
10 Will they not teach you, and tell you,
 and utter words out of their understanding?

11 "Can papyrus grow where there is no marsh?
 Can reeds flourish where there is no water?
12 While yet in flower and not cut down,
 they wither before any other plant.
13 Such are the paths of all who forget God;
 the hope of the godless man shall perish.

---

b) TESTIMONY OF THE PAST (8:8-19)

8-10. The tradition of the ancient sages (vs. 8) is needed by man whose life is too short to afford adequate experience (vs. 9). Bildad is more of a didactic dogmatician than Eliphaz. The latter had appealed to his own brand of revelation: "A ghost in the night came and told me" (4:12 ff.). He probably fancied that he was in some way like the prophets of old. Bildad, on the contrary, is a mere teacher of religion. He knows the creed and that is enough. The source of his enlightenment is not a personal contact with a present God, but scholarly learning and archaeological hoarding. He is a "paleo-orthodox" type of theologian appealing to the past without realizing that the present requires the rethinking of formulas which are no longer adequate.

11-13. The wisdom of the former sages as preserved in proverbs (vss. 11-12) shows that **all who forget God** wither before others (vs. 13a). The *ḥānēph* (vs. 13b),

---

certain that these would prove his vulnerable points (1:11; 2:5). They were not at all. His vulnerable point was a relationship which he thought had been destroyed. (*b*) They all alike misconceive the nature of man, the grace of God, and the proximate cause of true repentance (see Exeg.; Expos. on 5:18).

8-10. *The Tyranny of Tradition.*—Inquire, I pray thee, of the former age. The habit of romanticizing the past is well-nigh universal. To Bildad the age of the patriarchs, when men lived long and grew wise, was the golden age. It is interesting enough to take casual note of the fact that the setting of the poem is itself, from beginning to end, a patriarchal setting (cf. 1:5; 42:16). Whether or not by inadvertence, the author represents Bildad as belonging to the very time which he so highly esteems, yet given over to the praise of a time gone by—a not uncommon state of affairs. Such people always discount the present, which a moment's thought might tell them is "the heir of all the ages" and therefore in a better position than any of its forebears to profit by inheritance. So does tradi-

tion lay its "dead hand" on the living. Instead of serving from its place of vantage as a lookout, it takes over the helm. The thrill of it is lost in quotation marks. Proverbs turn into burial grounds. To recapture the life that gave rise to it is to break the bonds of its tyranny and live again: to seek as others before us sought (vs. 8*b*), rather than simply to con their wisdom by rote (cf. the use too often made of the Apostles' Creed as a test of orthodoxy; at most it is the soul's avowal of trust in response to an ultimate Beckoning, at least it is a kind of "invitation to pilgrimage") until we too can speak as they spoke, uttering words out of our heart (vs. 10*b*).

11-19. *The End of Those Who Forget God.*—(Cf. Expos. on 5:12-16, 14.) Eliphaz speaks of them as frustrated, trapped, blind men groping at noonday; Bildad, in the manner of the *International Encyclopedia of Prose and Poetical Quotations*, records the brilliant metaphors of the past. The godless are a reed, a spider, a plant, their trust betrayed (cf. vs. 15 with Amos 5:19), no trace of them left on the earth. There is enough fact in it (Ps. 37) to make it

14 Whose hope shall be cut off, and whose trust *shall be* a spider's web.

15 He shall lean upon his house, but it shall not stand: he shall hold it fast, but it shall not endure.

16 He *is* green before the sun, and his branch shooteth forth in his garden.

17 His roots are wrapped about the heap, *and* seeth the place of stones.

18 If he destroy him from his place, then it shall deny him, *saying,* I have not seen thee.

19 Behold, this *is* the joy of his way, and out of the earth shall others grow.

---

14 His confidence breaks in sunder,
   and his trust is a spider's web.[o]

15 He leans against his house, but it does not stand;
   he lays hold of it, but it does not endure.

16 He thrives before the sun,
   and his shoots spread over his garden.

17 His roots twine about the stone-heap;
   he lives among the rocks.[p]

18 If he is destroyed from his place,
   then it will deny him, saying, 'I have never seen you.'

19 Behold, this is the joy of his way;
   and out of the earth others will spring.

[o] Heb *house*
[p] Gk Vg: Heb uncertain

---

originally "a profane person" (Jer. 3:1; Ps. 106:38), is a renegade and disbeliever who betrays (or forswears) his holy mission (cf. Isa. 10:6).

14-19. Bildad admits that strange situations appear to contradict the dogma of God's righteousness. Ultimately, however, the evildoer will receive his retribution. His confidence is without solid basis (vss. 14-15) and his security superficial (vss. 16-18). **Behold, this is the joy of his way.** Such an exclamation should be interpreted ironically, unless the M.T. is corrupt. Instead of משוש, **joy,** the LXX probably read משאת or מסוס (Beer, *et al.*) since they translated καταστροφή. Dhorme conjectures that the spelling משוש may easily be a variant for מסוס, which in turn could derive from a verbal stem סוס, meaning "to decay." Thus the poet would continue here the image of the plant, and vs. 19 might be translated as follows:

Behold, here he is, rotten on his way,
And from the soil another will sprout

(i.e., out of the renegade's own decay). Forceful language, and a fitting climax to the strophe.

---

stranger than fiction, and enough fiction in it (ch. 21) to make all of it too tenuous for any rating with empirical fact. As proof of God's justice it is of doubtful value; as witness to life's often ambiguous, yet always persistent disavowal of the evil, it is as valid today as ever it was. Around that disavowal a whole body of the world's great literature has grown up. The Bible, with its belief in God's decisive intervention (apocalypse) and its doctrine of the last things (eschatology), is not the only book which is aware of some ultimate meaning in the ups and downs of human life and civilization: a meaning decipherable only to the eyes of faith. To leave God out of it all, and so to reduce the whole thing to gibberish, is one of the prerogatives of moral freedom; to be rid of him by leaving him out is not. Arthur James Balfour tried his hand at it one night, and wailed on to his heart's content.

[Man's] very existence is an accident, his story a brief and transitory episode in the life of one of the meanest of the planets, . . . with conscience enough to feel that it is vile, and intelligence enough to know that it is insignificant . . . : blood and tears, . . . wild revolt, . . . stupid acquiescence, [going] down into the pit, [where] all his thoughts will perish. . . . Matter will know itself no longer. . . . Death itself, and love stronger than death, will be as though they had never been. Nor will anything that *is* be better or be worse for all that the labour, genius, devotion, and suffering of man have striven through countless generations to effect.[3]

Job never even thought to make the attempt. Meaning kept forever intruding itself, intolerably. Life's tragic inequities grinned at all the glib talk about a just God. Let him rather then have his say about a God who was unjust

[3] *The Foundations of Belief* (New York: Longmans, Green & Co., 1895), pp. 30-31.

20 Behold, God will not cast away a perfect man, neither will he help the evildoers:

21 Till he fill thy mouth with laughing, and thy lips with rejoicing.

22 They that hate thee shall be clothed with shame; and the dwelling place of the wicked shall come to nought.

9 Then Job answered and said,
2 I know *it is* so of a truth: but how should man be just with God?

---

20 "Behold, God will not reject a blameless man,
  nor take the hand of evildoers.
21 He will yet fill your mouth with laughter,
  and your lips with shouting.
22 Those who hate you will be clothed with shame,
  and the tent of the wicked will be no more."

9 Then Job answered:
2 "Truly I know that it is so:
  But how can a man be just before God?

---

c) THE DIVINE WELCOME TO THE INNOCENT (8:20-22)

20-22. God will not reject a blameless man: Job still has time to change his attitude. Like Eliphaz, Bildad still hopes that Job is essentially a man of integrity (see William A. Irwin, "An Examination of the Progress of Thought in the Dialogue of Job," *Journal of Religion*, XIII [1933], 151; "The First Speech of Bildad," *Zeitschrift für die alttestamentliche Wissenschaft*, LI [1933], 205-16). It seems as if, toward the end of his speech, Bildad regrets the violence of his exordium or outburst. His peroration is thus warmer, more friendly than one might have expected. While Eliphaz was long-winded and not quite convincing in his description of Job's future restoration (see 5:23-27), Bildad is surprisingly concise and concrete. God will yet **fill thy mouth with laughing, and thy lips with rejoicing.** Those who now **hate** Job **will be clothed with shame.** Once more the poet deserves high praise. His characters are not wooden types. They live. They are men. We recognize ourselves in their portraiture.

4. JOB'S REPLY TO BILDAD (9:1–10:22)

As pointed out in the Intro. (pp. 892-93), the poet appears to follow a method of discussion which might be called "delayed reaction." Job answers not the immediately preceding speaker, but the penultimate one. The first part of his present discourse (9:2-31) is a discussion of the thesis of Eliphaz; the second part (9:32–10:22) is a meditation on the character of God which again turns into a prayer.

a) MAN'S GUILT BEFORE GOD (9:1-31)
(1) REASON FOR MAN'S GUILT (9:1-7)

9:2-7. As if he had had time to meditate on the first speech of Eliphaz, Job quotes the latter's cardinal statement with seeming approval:

(9:30-31; 10:13). If there were nothing that could gather up that dreadful contradiction into a reality beyond, a reality that could affirm the justice without a simple denial of the injustice, there could be for him no renewal of faith. It was a problem that had to be lived out, not thought out. Always it must wait for "the final account God gives of Himself." [4] There is no theodicy apart from theophany. God's justification is his self-revelation. "The supreme theodicy is atonement."

20-22. *Just You Wait!*— (See Expos. on vs. 7.) There is more to do, always more to do, than just to wait. Waiting in Scripture has content.

[4] Forsyth, *Justification of God*, p. 36.

It is not a form of idleness (see concordance *s.v.* "wait"). For all three friends the interval was to be marked by repentance (vs. 5; cf. 5:8; 11:13-19). If Job had allowed them to persuade him, he would thereby have uttered the final blasphemy against God (2:3) and his own soul (13:15); for what they urged upon him would have been a denial of the one and a betrayal of the other. His waiting was quest, and it came into its own.

9:1–10:22. *Job's Reply to Bildad.*— For a moment Job seems scarcely to have heard Bildad at all. He has been brooding over something Eliphaz said. But one thing will lead to another, and he will catch up soon enough. The sequence

Truly I know that it is so:
But how can a man be just before God?

The RSV presupposes that this verse is addressed to Bildad, and perhaps the first phrase is thus intended, but the words of the second are almost identical with those of the ghostly visitor in Eliphaz' vision (4:17). However, Job's assent to the dogma is rooted not in a severe judgment of man's propensity to wreck his own destiny by the perpetration

of thought becomes clear when we understand what his mind, embittered by his pain and bewildered by his wretchedness, has been doing. It can fairly be seen twisting and pulling at the stuff that has been given it to work with, as he thinks out loud about Eliphaz' revelation, with its swelling and sententious maxim, "Can mortal man be righteous before God?" (4:17.) In chs. 6–7 he has attempted to justify his complaint on the ground of (a) the acuteness of his misery; and as if his cup were not already full, (b) the spurious comfort of his friends; to say nothing of what meant most, (c) the gratuitous suffering with which the Almighty has afflicted him. In chs. 9–10 he comes to both the explanations that have been offered. Throwing logic to the winds, out of his passion he frames his own solution: no man can be just before God for the very simple reason that God will not permit it. There may be nothing at all wrong with the man. There must therefore be something wrong with God, Bildad notwithstanding. He does "pervert judgment" (8:3). "If . . . not he, who then is it?" (9:24c.) The premise is the premise of all human helplessness: man stands accused before God because God wants it that way, and has power enough to see to it. Job realizes that for one reason or another a trial of sorts is on foot, and he is at the bar, whether as defendant (9:3) or plaintiff (9:16) makes no difference. Something is being held against him—his misfortunes make that self-evident—and he has no way of knowing what it is. The one thing quite plain to him is that he is bound to lose the case. One might well compare Franz Kafka's novel, *The Trial.*[5] There the hero "K"—scarcely an impenetrable veil for the concealment of Kafka himself—is shadowed, arrested, accused, arraigned, tried, and executed without ever finding out really what it is all about. The whole movement of Job's mind comes very near lending itself to the interpretation which Kafka would have us put on K's mind: as an allegory of human existence, a study in the psychology of guilt, a transcript from the records of almost any psychiatrist.

How could anybody make good his case against God? You talk of angels (4:18); I say anybody: poor run-of-the-mill humanity, men wise and mighty (9:4) even the gods themselves

[5] London: Secker & Warburg, 1947.

(9:13; see Exeg. on 9:8-13). That Power yonder can do as he likes. The world is his from tip to toe. He can make it or break it, he can adorn it or ravish it (9:12), and who will say him nay? What is there to do but to give up (9:15)? He will not listen to anybody. Here am I with my sores. He would strike me dumb. I could only mumble out who knows what. But I will not be browbeaten by him. Come what may, I tell you he makes no distinction between the good and the evil. Where to draw the line indeed! He laughs when the innocent suffer. He not only puts up with wickedness, he arranges for it. With my life fast ebbing out of me, he keeps pronouncing his verdict on me, no matter what I do. He keeps saying that I am guilty. If he were only a man! If only somebody who knows us both could step in between us! But there is no such thing. I am alone (9:35b; see Exeg.), and sick of my life anyway (10:1). God, why do you do it? Of what possible good is it? What pleasure, or profit, or seemliness? Or is it all simply inhuman? There is no conceivable reason for it. You know very well I am not guilty. Was all your kindness to me just a cover for the malice in your heart from the beginning? Did you plan it like this at the start? For pity's sake, have done with it, and let me go to my grave.

2-10. God the All-terrible.—Job is quite willing to recognize and affirm the truth of much that has been said (see Exeg.); but **it is so** because of God's omnipotence, not because of any sense he might have of fair play (8:3).[6]

[6] Cf. the speech of Ahab in Herman Melville, *Moby Dick,* ch. cxix: "Oh! thou clear spirit of clear fire, whom on these seas I as Persian once did worship, till in the sacramental act so burned by thee, that to this hour I bear the scar; I now know thee, thou clear spirit, and I now know that thy right worship is defiance. To neither love nor reverence wilt thou be kind; and e'en for hate thou canst but kill; and all are killed. No fearless fool now fronts thee. I own thy speechless, placeless power; but to the last gasp of my earthquake life will dispute its unconditional, unintegral mastery in me. In the midst of the personified impersonal, a personality stands here. Though but a point at best; whencesoe'er I came; wheresoe'er I go; yet while I earthly live, the queenly personality lives in me, and feels her royal rights. But war is pain, and hate is woe. Come in thy lowest form of love, and I will kneel and kiss thee; but at thy highest, come as mere supernal power; and though thou launchest navies of full-freighted worlds, there's that in here that still remains indifferent. Oh, thou clear spirit, of thy fire thou madest me, and like a true child of fire, I breathe it back to thee."

3 If he will contend with him, he cannot answer him one of a thousand.

4 *He is* wise in heart, and mighty in strength: who hath hardened *himself* against him, and hath prospered?

3 If one wished to contend with him,
  one could not answer him once in a thousand times.

4 He is wise in heart, and mighty in strength
  — who has hardened himself against him, and succeeded? —

---

of evil, but solely in his recognition of God's arbitrary omnipotence. In a contest of strength with the Deity, mortal man would be silenced at once (vs. 3). Even among the best of human beings, the **wise in heart, and mighty in strength: who hath hardened himself against him, and** has remained whole? Against the versions one may perhaps consider the words **wise in heart, and mighty in strength** not as attributes of God, but

---

Nobody has ever been able to stiffen his neck like an ox restive under the yoke, plant his feet in the ground, and hold out against the God who rips **the mountains** wide open with his fire and hardly even knows it (so A. S. Peake;[7] Kissane takes it of the victims[8]). Who could possibly answer the questions he would ask (cf. 38:3; 40:4, 7; 42:2-6)? Even one question in a thousand? He **shakes the earth** to its very foundations (38:4-7), blots out the sun with storm cloud and eclipse, shuts up the stars in their secret place (Isa. 40:26), stretches **out the heavens** like a tent (Isa. 40:22), tramples down **the waves of the sea** (38:8; Ps. 104:2-9), frames the constellations against the blue of the evening sky, and away there (in?) the far-off **chambers of the south.** So with all the **marvelous things without number** (5:9). What are they but the glitter and dash of God the All-terrible? Let anybody try having it out with him (see Expos. on 16:11).

Such power without love is intolerable (see Expos. on 4:12-21; 20b; 23:13). Job would lift Lord Acton's aphorism to the *n*th degree: "Power corrupts; absolute power corrupts absolutely." Set that down on the level of the divine, and might not only makes right; right is transformed into might. Retain in the mind the thought of omnipotence, while you let slip from the heart all knowledge of the love that informs it, and you have a world with nothing but unlimited caprice at the center. Nowadays we have made available for ourselves, in order to lessen the strain somewhat, certain substitutes for God: natural law, social and economic forces, the Third Reich, or the fourth or the fifth—we can still count!—Americanism, "There will always be an England," any one of a dozen hard necessities, whether of blood or soil. No maneuvers of that kind were open to Job (see Expos. on 6:1–7:21; 6:4). There were left for him only irony

and bitterness and resentment and fear—when love was gone (cf. I John 4:14-19). But there is something more to be said.

Love without power is impotent (see Expos. on vs. 24). It is not permitted that we open Paul's Epistle to the Romans and begin reading at ch. 8. We may not exult in denatured love, or water down the judgment and the might in order to satisfy a taste for concentrated solutions of goodness and mercy. Men of old used to turn loose all the music in their souls on

Come hither, ye faithful, triumphantly sing;
Come see in the manger the angels' dread King!

But "dread King" proved altogether too robust. The lines had to be made safe for boys and girls:

O come, all ye faithful, joyfully triumphant,
O come ye, O come ye to Bethlehem!

It was marked "irregular" because nobody could scan it, and even to untrained ears it sounded like three wooden legs and a half. But it got rid of that word "dread." No one, not even the youngest, need be frightened anymore. They used to sing, those men of old, another hymn that set out bravely enough: "God the All-terrible! King, who ordainest." Somewhat later it was made to read, "God the Omnipotent . . . ," trimming it down a little. That, however, was still too strong for delicate constitutions; so a good many hymnals omitted a stanza and began with "God the All-merciful." Then somebody noticed that even this went on to speak of how man had forsaken the ways of the Eternal and slighted his word. Whereupon that too was dropped. Quite a number of versions now had nothing at all about "man hath defied thee" or "the fire of thy chastening": just

God the All-righteous One! When we obey thee,
Earth shall to freedom and truth be restored.

Three fifths of the original had been lost in the interests of sweetness and light. When suddenly

---

[7] *Job* (Edinburgh: T. C. & E. C. Jack, 1905; "The Century Bible"), p. 112.
[8] *Job*, p. 53.

5 Which removeth the mountains, and they know not; which overturneth them in his anger;	5 he who removes mountains, and they know it not, when he overturns them in his anger;
6 Which shaketh the earth out of her place, and the pillars thereof tremble;	6 who shakes the earth out of its place, and its pillars tremble;
7 Which commandeth the sun, and it riseth not; and sealeth up the stars;	7 who commands the sun, and it does not rise; who seals up the stars;
8 Which alone spreadeth out the heavens, and treadeth upon the waves of the sea;	8 who alone stretched out the heavens, and trampled the waves of the sea;*q*
	q Or *trampled the back of the sea dragon*

as characteristics of men who dare to oppose the Deity. The sequence of thought would then be quite clear from vs. 2 to vs. 4. How could man, a weakling (אנוש), be **just with God?** Even the wisest and mightiest man cannot safely oppose him. The traditional rendering, nevertheless, is probably right, for there is no example of qualifying adjectives preceding the interrogative pronoun מי. Vs. 4a may therefore constitute the anticipation of the doxology which is unfolded in vss. 5 ff.

(2) THE AMORALITY OF OMNIPOTENCE (9:8-13)

8-12. The doxology continues in the second strophe and is cut short as Job applies its significance to his own case: if God so completely transcends the created cosmos, no

God entered the pulpit, and preached in his own way by deeds. And his sermons were long and taxing, and they spoiled the dinner. So P. T. Forsyth put it toward the end of World War I:

Clearly God's problem with the world is much more serious than we dreamed. We are having a revelation of the awful and desperate nature of evil. The task which the Cross has to meet is something much greater than a pacific, domestic, fraternal type of religion allows us to face. Disaster should end dainty and dreamy religion, and give some rest to the winsome Christ and the wooing note. . . . It is a much wickeder world than our good nature had come to imagine, or our prompt piety to fathom. We see more of the world Christ saw. . . . And it must cast us back on resources in that Saviour which the mental levity of comfortable religion, lying back for a warm bath in its pew, was coming to stigmatise as gratuitous theology. The salvation of the world is a much greater agony and victory than any but the very *élite* of the Church's faith had seen, and it calls for more than a Cross merely kind and sacrificial, or a Gospel but blithe and wise.[9]

We have to realize, however, the limitations which God himself has set on his power, that men might rise to their full stature, unencumbered by an obtrusive and self-asserting omnipotence. He does not sign his sunsets as Turner did, or blazon his name across the tempest or the earthquake in letters monstrous high. Whatever other purpose the speeches of the Almighty have (see Expos. on 38:1–42:6), they are not intended to cow Job into submis-

[9] *The Justification of God* (London: Independent Press, 1948), pp. 28-29. Used by permission.

sion. He does not deliberately do precisely what Job implores him not to do (see Expos. on 30-35). It is of the very essence of majesty that on occasion it is able to lay majesty aside. Fascinating stories have been told about Harun al-Rashid, caliph of Bagdad, under whom the Eastern caliphate, at about the turn of the ninth century, reached its greatest height. Yet he is best known to us from the tales of *The Arabian Nights*, where in humble disguise he goes out at evening time from his palace to move unknown among his people, if by any chance he might right their wrongs or steady their hearts. So is true majesty best revealed when best hidden. There is much in this queer world that God cannot do without contradicting himself and the whole wide universe. Quarrels cannot be stopped until men are ready to stop them. People cannot be made good until they want to be made good. The wickedness of evil lives cannot be kept from spilling over and hurting the innocent, or airplanes from dropping bombs on children, or shells from bursting and killing somebody we love. God got into all of it on Calvary, just so that he could go on being God forever without asking or needing anybody's permission or forgiveness. His glory is not so much in a "devouring fire on the top of the mount" (Exod. 24:17) as in the compassion that made its way down a steep hill toward a city, and wept (Luke 19:41; cf. I Cor. 1:18-29). There are citadels in the human soul where power cannot come; only weakness can get in.

8-13. The Wholly Other.—It can readily be conceded that the "liberal" theology which in

9 Which maketh Arcturus, Orion, and Pleiades, and the chambers of the south;

10 Which doeth great things past finding out; yea, and wonders without number.

11 Lo, he goeth by me, and I see *him* not: he passeth on also, but I perceive him not.

12 Behold, he taketh away, who can hinder him? who will say unto him, What doest thou?

13 *If* God will not withdraw his anger, the proud helpers do stoop under him.

9 who made the Bear and Orion,
    the Plei'ades and the chambers of the
    south;
10 who does great things beyond under-
    standing,
    and marvelous things without number.
11 Lo, he passes by me, and I see him not;
    he moves on, but I do not perceive him.
12 Behold, he snatches away; who can hin-
    der him?
    Who will say to him, 'What doest
    thou'?

13 "God will not turn back his anger;
    beneath him bowed the helpers of
    Rahab.

---

wonder then that **I do not perceive him** (vs. 11). Are human standards of morality applicable to a being of absolute power? If **he snatches away; who can hinder him** (vs. 12a)? The verb חתף, "to prey upon," is a *hapax legomenon,* but its stem refers elsewhere to human violence (Prov. 23:28; etc.). God is implicitly compared to a thief or a kidnaper whom no man can resist, or even criticize and censure. **Who will say unto him, What doest thou?**

13. According to the usual translations, this verse does not clearly follow the idea of the preceding line. Since the word Eloah is placed in an emphatic position, and sometimes designates not God but "a god" (see 12:6; II Kings 17:31; II Chr. 32:15; Dan. 11:37), it may be understood as an excellent parallel to **the helpers of Rahab** in vs. 13b. Thus vs. 13a might be read, "Even a god could not turn back his wrath" (Kissane). Incidentally, such a translation supports the conjectural rendering of vs. 4a mentioned above. Job's process of thinking may follow a slow gradation: naturally mortal man (vs. 2) cannot be just with God; the wise and mighty cannot defy him unscathed (vs. 4); even a god is powerless before him (vs. 13). Kissane rightfully notes that if this translation is correct, Job makes a further allusion to the discourse of Eliphaz (4:18; 5:1 ff.), who had stated that men, even angels, are impure before God. Job replies that men, heroes, and even gods are powerless before God.

---

the last half of the nineteenth century and the first quarter of the twentieth seemed primarily intent on making a gentleman out of God, a Christian gentleman, a Protestant Christian gentleman, sadly needed the corrective of a theology that was intent on making God "the Wholly Other." It can just as readily be conceded that this "Wholly Other" often tends to become too wholly other. The line from man to God is not one unbroken line. We may not argue from the human to the divine, whether we have in mind philosophical concepts, emotional states, or ethical standards (Isa. 55:8-9). But unless somewhere there is a common denominator between man and God, the result of God's own creative or revelatory act, then "the fruit of the Spirit" (Gal. 5:22-23) is Dead Sea fruit "upon this bank and shoal of time." God's judgments are still unsearchable, and "his ways past finding out" (Rom. 11:33); but they may

not ultimately offend that image of himself in human life which is his own handiwork. Otherwise his wonders would become "wonders" indeed (10:16).

With this Power, across the unbridged gulf, Job knows he has to do. It is not a dogma, not a theory, not an abstraction, not just there, out of all relation to man and his needs, but there *in* that relation, inseparable *from* that relation: invisible, incomprehensible, indomitable, with none even to criticize what goes on. How can anybody do anything about the brush of a wing he cannot see, or the uncanny sound of a footfall in an empty house? The divine snatcher-away—as in Job's own case—will not stop long enough to be questioned or called to account. Even chaos itself is but the footstool of his might (7:12; 26:12). He does not will a thing because it is good; it is "good" because he wills it. His is an amoral freedom, subject to no

14 How much less shall I answer him, *and* choose out my words *to reason* with him?

15 Whom, though I were righteous, *yet* would I not answer, *but* I would make supplication to my judge.

16 If I had called, and he had answered me; *yet* would I not believe that he had hearkened unto my voice.

17 For he breaketh me with a tempest, and multiplieth my wounds without cause.

14 How then can I answer him,
    choosing my words with him?
15 Though I am innocent, I cannot answer
    him;
    I must appeal for mercy to my accuser.*r*
16 If I summoned him and he answered me,
    I would not believe that he was listen-
    ing to my voice.
17 For he crushes me with a tempest,
    and multiplies my wounds without
    cause;

r Or *for my right*

The helpers of Rahab (vs. 13*b*), like Leviathan (see 3:8) and *tannîn* (see 7:12), are monsters of the sea (26:12) which are tamed by the creator God. In the Akkadian poem of creation (*Enûma eliš* IV. 107; see Pritchard, *Ancient Near Eastern Texts*, p. 67), the gods who fight Marduk are called "the helpers" of Tiamat.

(3) Futility of Contending with God (9:14-19)

14-19. If even the primeval forces of chaos bowed beneath him (vs. 13*b*), how much less can Job answer him (vs. 14*a*)? The image is now that of a lawsuit in which Job fancies himself to be either a hopeless defendant (vss. 14-15) or a plaintiff powerless to compel a hearing (vs. 16). That Job still holds fast to his integrity is obvious from the expression **I am innocent** (אצדק), or rather, "I am in the right" or "I am righteous" (vs. 15*a*). Indeed, Job may be answering Bildad's advice to make supplication to the Almighty and to have recourse to God's grace (התחנן, 8:5); Job, being falsely accused, concedes that his only chance is to **appeal for mercy** (התחנן, identical verb) to his **accuser** (vs. 15*b*); but apparently the Arabian nobleman rejects such an attitude of contemptible humiliation and demands instead the vindication due his honor. Thus Job understands better than Bildad the implications of the biblical reality of grace (חן), but at this stage of the drama he rejects it completely. His relation to God is placed on a footing of equality—equality in right if not in might. Human pride leads to unfaith: "If I sum-

---

restraint, whether of others or of self; a liberty which is license, and license full-blown is immorality (vss. 22-24). In some such fashion, were the gulf between man and God still unbridged by word or deed, would the vast Presence toward whom humanity's heart seems always to have yearned, even if only in a weird sort of challenge (23:3, 8-9), become the hateful Unseen, before which all humanity's ways would be helpless.

14-19. The Bill of Rights.—(See Expos. on 1:1.) What standing can a man have in such a trial as that which in vs. 3 Job for the first time dimly envisions? For one driven into a corner and taken into custody by omnipotence, there could be no careful choosing of **words.** Innocence could do no more than stammer like guilt, and beg for mercy (cf. 8:5; see Exeg.). If a summons could be served on the Almighty, it would be to no purpose. Were he to answer, he would still turn a deaf ear to every complaint. The proof of it is in Job's own body, crushed and wounded for a trifle, and kept that way (vs.

18, RSV; with KJV cf. 7:19; 14:6) as evidence of his "guilt," his mind filled with **bitterness.** For **strength,** there he stands ready, this God (vs. 19*a*; cf. vss. 8-13). Who will enter the lists with him? As for **justice,** who can get a hearing? (Cf. vss. 14-18.)

Against the utter helplessness and hopelessness of that situation Job revolts. He has no rights because he has no standing in court. The conclusion, on the premises, is unavoidable—and much too grievous to be taken lying down. Man's pride will sooner justify itself in blasphemy than surrender itself to sheer wanton, arbitrary power. And properly so. There is something else in God besides wayward, contrary, captious might, and something other. Job is on the way to it; but the abyss yawns at his feet. He is the protagonist of all mankind, and the facts are very much as he sees them, though at deeper levels than he dreams. Man may assert his rights against man—if there is nothing better for him to do—and so hammer out for his society some kind of approximate

18 He will not suffer me to take my breath, but filleth me with bitterness.

19 If *I speak* of strength, lo, *he is* strong: and if of judgment, who shall set me a time *to plead?*

20 If I justify myself, mine own mouth shall condemn me: *if I say,* I *am* perfect, it shall also prove me perverse.

21 *Though* I *were* perfect, *yet* would I not know my soul: I would despise my life.

---

18 he will not let me get my breath,
but fills me with bitterness.

19 If it is a contest of strength, behold him!
If it is a matter of justice, who can summon him?[s]

20 Though I am innocent, my own mouth
would condemn me;
though I am blameless, he would prove
me perverse.

21 I am blameless; I regard not myself;
I loathe my life.

[s] Compare Gk: Heb *me.* The text of the verse is uncertain

---

moned him and he answered me, I do not believe [אָמִין לֹא; cf. Isa. 7:9] that he would listen to my voice" (vs. 16). At any rate, this hope is idle fancy, for in the present reality **he crushes me with a tempest** (vs. 17*a*). The Targ. and Syriac read the same consonants as those of the M.T. (בשׂערה) with a slightly different vocalization, *besaʿarāh* instead of *bisʿārāh,* "with a hair," i.e., "for a trifle" (Ehrlich, *et al.*); this meaning would provide an excellent parallel to **without cause** (vs. 17*b*). However, the reading "storm" or **tempest** is not excluded, inasmuch as the verb שׁוּף is used not only for the "crushing" of the head of the serpent's seed and the "bruising" of the heel of the woman's posterity (Gen. 3:15), but also for the "overwhelming" of man by darkness (Ps. 139:11).

Job knows that in a contest of strength God is stronger, and that in a judicial suit none **can summon him** (vs. 19).

(4) THE MOCKING LAUGHTER OF GOD (9:20-24)

20-24. The sense of injustice brings the sufferer to issue the most vehement protest of innocence. Although in the presence of the almighty Tyrant he might be so overcome by fear that his **own mouth would condemn** him (vs. 20*a*), he knows that he is **perfect** (תם, vs. 20*b*). The repetition of the ejaculation, "I am perfect" (vs. 21*a*), reveals the passion which now animates the hero. The violence of his feeling of self-righteousness, no doubt heightened by physical pain and mental agony, prompts him to deny any preoccupation with self-preservation. "I do not care about my *néphesh!*" (Vs. 21*b*.) "I despise

---

justice. He may assert them against nature, and out of her rough granite hew for himself a kind of progress. His struggles are chapters in the history of civilizations. Always he wins, and always he loses: his victories almost incredible, every one of them ambiguous, none of them final. But against God? What "right" has being to assert against the ground of being? What "right" has the mind to assert against the life that animates it? Yet where there is no right against, there may be claim upon. And this Job vaguely but increasingly senses (7:8*b*; 10:9-12; 14:15; 19:25 ff.; etc.). It is God who has himself fashioned humanity's "rights," and honors them (Deut. 7:7-8; Isa. 46:4). What Job saw was (*a*) that man was a good deal more than nothing in the sight of God—the fact and being of God were the very source and substance of his integrity—and (*b*) that he had of himself no inherent "rights" which he could assert against the Almighty. What Job could not yet see was the divine love that not only gives man his

standing, but undertakes to make it good against man's own betrayal of it. Calvary was God's mark, his seal and signature, on the bill of rights which he drew up at Creation. And more: it was the vindication at cost of that holiness in him which is the only hope humanity has, and of that power which alone can give his love "eternal and righteous effect."

20-24. *He That Sitteth in the Heavens.*—In the twisted agony of Job's mind is mirrored a distorted world. He sees himself, for all his innocence, driven to confess his guilt. All despotisms know how to bring that about. Though **blameless,** God would **prove** him **perverse.** What matter then if he should live or die? Life he despises. Let God strike him dead. He will risk it, and say what he thinks. There is no line drawn on earth between good men and evil (4:7; 8:20): they all perish alike (Eccl. 9:2). In flood and pestilence, in war and famine, there is only laughter in heaven, as the righteous go down with the wicked (vs. 23). "On

22 This *is* one *thing*, therefore I said *it*, He destroyeth the perfect and the wicked.	22 It is all one; therefore I say,
	he destroys both the blameless and the wicked.
23 If the scourge slay suddenly, he will laugh at the trial of the innocent.	23 When disaster brings sudden death,
	he mocks at the calamity[t] of the innocent.
24 The earth is given into the hand of the wicked: he covereth the faces of the judges thereof; if not, where, *and* who *is* he?	24 The earth is given into the hand of the wicked;
	he covers the faces of its judges —
	if it is not he, who then is it?

[t] The meaning of the Hebrew word is uncertain

my life!" (Vs. 21c.) Such declarations constitute the usual build-up for the utterance of a blasphemy (cf. 7:11 ff.; 13:13 ff.; etc.). "Therefore I say: Both the perfect and the wicked he exterminates" (vs. 22). This is a direct reply to the creed enunciated by Eliphaz (4:7) and Bildad (8:20). Not only is God devoid of a sense of justice, but he lacks even any human decency, any humane sense of pity. **He mocks at the calamity of the innocent** (vs. 23). He is responsible also for social injustice and political oppression (vs. 24b). Perhaps anticipating polemics on the extreme monism of his theology, Job adds defiantly, **If it is not he, who then is it?** (vs. 24c).

earth as it is in heaven"? God turns the whole place over to the oppressor, and justice is blind. He sees to that. Who else?

Living and dying may indeed be matters of indifference; but for other reasons (Phil. 1:21-24): in part at least, because of that same strange laughter in heaven (Phil. 1:12-20); but it is laughter at the wicked, not at the innocent (Ps. 2:4; Prov. 1:26; Jer. 48:27, 39; Gal. 6:7). God mocks only man's mockery (Mark 10:34). The sound of man's mockery was heard at the Crucifixion; the Resurrection is the echo of God's. It is he who laughs best—and last.

There is a judgment which is not visitation but irony. Its tarrying works upon us more than its coming. . . . It broods evasive, provoking, potent. If God do not yet intervene on earth He sits in heaven —sits and laughs. And His smile is inscrutable, and elusive, only not cruel: the smile of endless power and patience, very still, and very secure, and deeply, dimly kind. . . . The heavens are not so simple as they seem, nor is God so mocked as He consents to appear, and to appear for long. He gives our desire, and it shrivels our soul. Of our pleasant vices He is making instruments to scourge us. . . . Satan's last chagrin is his contribution to God's kingdom. [See Expos. 2:7-10.] This is the irony of history—when the very success of an idea creates the conditions that belie it, smother it, and replace it. Catholicism becomes the Papacy. The care for truth turns to the Inquisition. . . . A revival movement becomes a too, too prosperous and egoistic Church. Freedom as soon as it is secured becomes tyranny. . . . Misfortune need not be judgment, nor need defeat; but victory may be. And defeat may be victory. . . .
In Christ's moral, historic, final Cross alone do we learn to interpret the irony of history as the irony of Providence, the tender, portentous smile

of a victorious, patient God. If His words are acts, so is that slow smile. . . . It is a smile more immeasurable than ocean's [sic] and more deep; it is an irony gentler and more patient than the bending skies, the irony of a long love and the play of its sure mastery; it is the smile of the holy in its silent omnipotence of mercy.[1]

24. *If Not He, Who Then?*—To Job's defiant question many answers have been given (see Expos. on 1:6-12; 6:12; 10:13-17). Some have written down much of humanity's anguish, both of mind and body, to the account of a universe sublimely (!) indifferent to all things human. Others have found man himself the chief culprit —back of him, it may be, a devil (as in the prologue). In any case, the ultimate responsibility is God's. There is no other answer when you add omniscience to omnipotence. But what if, instead of shirking the responsibility he should assume it, binding by it not just his creation but himself, in a purpose transcending every purpose which the human mind can attribute to him (see Expos. on 10:8-12; 24:2-12). Marc Connelly, author of *The Green Pastures,* dissatisfied with the cheap and smart agnosticism of his generation, felt that he simply had to say something about the basic dignity of faith: no matter if he had anything to eat or not; no matter if what he had to say could find a producer or not. The play actually did lie on the shelf for nearly seven months—that stately tale of a God perplexed; a God who over and over again ran into this human willfulness of ours, to be beaten back in the patriarchs, stoned in the prophets, and crucified in his Christ. The

[1] *Ibid.,* pp. 204-7.

25 Now my days are swifter than a post: they flee away, they see no good.	25 "My days are swifter than a runner; they flee away, they see no good.
26 They are passed away as the swift ships: as the eagle *that* hasteth to the prey.	26 They go by like skiffs of reed, like an eagle swooping on the prey.
27 If I say, I will forget my complaint, I will leave off my heaviness, and comfort *myself;*	27 If I say, 'I will forget my complaint, I will put off my sad countenance, and be of good cheer,'
28 I am afraid of all my sorrows, I know that thou wilt not hold me innocent.	28 I become afraid of all my suffering, for I know thou wilt not hold me innocent.
29 *If* I be wicked, why then labor I in vain?	29 I shall be condemned; why then do I labor in vain?
30 If I wash myself with snow water, and make my hands never so clean;	30 If I wash myself with snow, and cleanse my hands with lye,

---

(5) "Thou Wilt Not Hold Me Innocent" (9:25-29)

25-29. Again the poet reveals himself as a profound master of psychology. Job has just made a heretical pronouncement at the risk of his life, and he immediately afterwards complains of the brevity of his days. Having spoken of life with contempt, he soon reveals his fear of death in three images of appealing beauty: the runner (vs. 25), the ships (vs. 26a), and the eagle (vs. 26b). When his brave resolutions to **be of good cheer** (vs. 27) are broken by the excesses of his pain, he turns to God in a prayer of melancholy (vs. 28), which again leads to a philosophical query, **Why then do I labor in vain?** (vs. 29).

b) Intentions of God Toward Man (9:30–10:22)
(1) Need of a Mediator (9:30-35)

30-35. This strophe provides a second landmark in Job's spiritual journey (cf. 7:21d). Although he has recently said that God blindly destroys both perfect and wicked men

---

pastures were not green at all. They were desolate, barren wastes, until a man shouldered a Cross and by Paul's "patience and long-suffering with joyfulness" (Col. 1:11) put his own downfall to rout, drubbed his own drubbing, and made the desert blossom like a rose!

There was never such a fateful experiment as when God trusted man with freedom. But our Christian faith is that He well knew what He was about. He did not do that as a mere adventure, not without knowing that He had the power to remedy any abuse of it that might occur, and to do this by a new creation more mighty, marvellous, and mysterious than the first. . . . If the first creation drew on His might, the second taxed His all-might. . . . To redeem creation is a more creative act than it was to create it. It is the last thing omnipotence could do.[2]

25-29. *Why Labor in Vain?*—Job's efforts to vindicate himself are futile. His days glide swiftly by. In one of Jerome Kern's songs, "Ol' Man River," the Negro laborer on a levee along the Mississippi is "tired o' livin' " and "scared o' dyin' " (cf. Hamlet's soliloquy, Act III, scene 1). So is Job torn. He longs for God and fears

him. He hates life and loves it. Every time he decides to brighten up a bit and **forget** all about his trouble, there is something to remind him of it, some twinge of pain to tell him that God still has it in for him (see Expos. on 10:1-7, 13-17). "He hath a spite against me, that I know." [3] What then was the use of it all?

There are thousands who make of his despondent mood their only comment on life itself. Stark across the years of their striving stands the specter: their wages are earned only to be put "into a bag with holes" (Hag. 1:6). But there is no hole in the middle of our going round and round, our hurrying to and fro; no hole through which are poured at last our human loves and human hopes, our human defeats and human victories. God is there. Even Job's labor was by no means in vain (read I Cor. 15:2, 10, 14, 58).

9:30–10:22. *Who Hath Known the Mind of the Lord?*—Whatever man can know of the mind of God—and on that quest Job is now beginning to embark—must be known by revelation, not by speculation. The facts from which Job argues are summarized in 9:30-31. They seem to him by this time well enough estab-

[2] *Ibid.*, p. 123.

[3] Browning, "Caliban upon Setebos."

| 31 Yet shalt thou plunge me in the ditch, and mine own clothes shall abhor me. | 31 yet thou wilt plunge me into a pit, and my own clothes will abhor me. |
| 32 For *he is* not a man, as I *am, that* I should answer him, *and* we should come together in judgment. | 32 For he is not a man, as I am, that I might answer him, that we should come to trial together. |

(vs. 22), he dimly realizes that he is persecuted by God because he is considered guilty (vs. 28). Now in an aside he proclaims the inability of man to save himself against the will of God (vss. 30-31). The text, of course, must not be pressed excessively, but one may recognize here a man in need of salvation by grace. While the penitent theologian of the *sola gratia* implores God, "Wash me, and I shall be whiter than snow" (Ps. 51:7), Job exclaims, **If I wash myself with snow, . . . yet thou wilt plunge me into a pit.** Like the psalmist, Job realizes that he cannot wash himself, but unlike the psalmist, he does not give up the idea of self-purification and yield to the divine bounty, crying, "Have mercy upon me!"

A thought of stupendous dimensions, however, invades the consciousness of this Semitic monotheist. He admits that God is infinitely transcendent. He perceives that the absolute remoteness of God makes intimacy with man—nay, even colloquy—impossible. There is no common ground between them. There is no meeting place between heaven and earth. God and man may not **come together in judgment,** since **he is not a man, as I am** (vs. 32). The thought of God becoming man, of God made flesh, does not possess the poet's mind, but it enters there for a fleeting instant. The noble Arabian prince is not a prophet of the Christian mystery of the Incarnation, nor is he able to glance at the "shocking" spectacle of a God Incarnate. Yet the poet is desperately trying to bridge the awful gap which separates Creator from creature, to fill the abyss which keeps impure man apart from the holy God. Toying with the idea of a human God for a short while, Job rejects it almost as soon as it is conceived. But for a moment he dwells on the new perspective thereby opened at the edge of his despair. He cannot altogether abandon this impossible thought. Obstinately he clings to his foolish fancy and goes groping in the

lished. The difficulty is canvassed in 9:32-35: God is not man, but he acts like a man (10:1-7) and worse (10:8-12). There is but one explanation: if God is omnipotent, he is not good. The other possibility, that if God is good he is not omnipotent, could hardly have occurred to Job. Beyond question, the Almighty is predisposed to evil, with malice aforethought (10:13-17), and never will let up even for a moment (10:18-22).

Is this not always the risk that speculation runs? Out of its understanding of events it would read its understanding of God. Let any man try that method on any other and see where it leads him. Life will not be read—save as a ghastly and answerless riddle—without regard to its beginning and its end (Rev. 1:8, 11). Posit faith, then read events: Israel's history becomes God's history, and the history of man's salvation; Bethlehem and Calvary, the trouble he went to, and the price he paid. Events are words; but they do not always say what we think they say. The interpretation comes of faith—or of unfaith.

30-35. The Foolishness of the Gospel.—In these verses we peer "through a glass, darkly" (I Cor. 13:12), catching but the dim forms of

things unknown. First a kind of nightmare (vss. 30-31), which often enough is a disguise that the naked truth tries to wear. There is a difference between Job's **if I wash** and the "wash me" of the psalmist (Ps. 51:7). How much nearer the realities of human experience it would have been had Job exchanged his subjects in the condition and the conclusion of his sentence! There is no psychologist but would be inclined to ask him, on the basis of such a statement as his, "Why do you hate—yourself?" Second, there is a kind of folly, with fact behind it (vs. 33; cf. Expos. on 19:25; see Exeg.; set the fact against the folly in Luke 24:11). Perhaps the lines that Keats wrote "On First Looking into Chapman's Homer" might almost serve as a footnote.

Then felt I like some watcher of the skies
When a new planet swims into his ken;
Or like stout Cortez when with eagle eyes
He stared at the Pacific—and all his men
Looked at each other with a wild surmise—
Silent, upon a peak in Darien.

The very foolishness which Job rejects even while he clings to it is the foolishness of the

33 Neither is there any daysman betwixt us, *that* might lay his hand upon us both.

34 Let him take his rod away from me, and let not his fear terrify me:

35 *Then* would I speak, and not fear him; but *it is* not so with me.

33 There is no[u] umpire between us,
     who might lay his hand upon us both.

34 Let him take his rod away from me,
     and let not dread of him terrify me.

35 Then I would speak without fear of him,
     for I am not so in myself.

[u] Another reading is *Would that there were*

---

darkness of his theological thinking, spurred on by his passionate search for a way to bring God and man face to face. **Would that there were** (reading אל as *lu'* instead of *lô'* with several Hebrew MSS, LXX, and Syriac) a third party, a neutral observer, an arbitrator, a middle man, a mediator, yes, a **daysman** or **umpire between us** (vs. 33*a*)! The word מוכיח applies to a person who decides, judges, and convinces, sometimes corrects and rebukes. The astounding significance of its use in this verse lies in the fact that it refers here to some hypothetical being who would be different from God and man, and **who might lay his hand upon us both** (vs. 33*b*). Since God is not a man, and a human God remains an impossibility in terms, let there be someone else who might understand the respective standpoints of both God and man, who might terminate their mutual estrangement, make them intelligible to one another, reconcile their differences, and resolve their reciprocal antagonism into the unity of peace.

To be sure, the image of the **umpire** still suggests primarily a juridical settlement, as if man, on equal terms with God, had rights of his own to safeguard. But the overtone of the figure goes beyond the realm of justice. A conciliator who places his hands over the shoulders of two enemies is more than a judge who imposes a verdict. He not only mediates justice, he also fosters harmony and inspires love. In the words of James Strahan (*The Book of Job* [Edinburgh: T. & T. Clark, 1913], p. 102): "The man who uses such language is ostensibly pleading for justice; but deeper down he is seeking reconciliation, he is thirsting for love. Job is no conscious prophet, but his instinctive cry for a God in human form, and for a daysman between God and man, is an unconscious prophecy of incarnation and atonement. His faith is creative, his heart's intuitions are precursors of revelation."

Vs. 34, according to most translators, begins a new sentence, with God as the unexpressed subject: **Let him take his rod away from me.** It is syntactically more natural, however, to consider the **umpire** of vs. 33 as the third person masculine singular agent of

---

gospel (I Cor. 1:21-29). Finally, there is the nonsense with which he dismisses the subject, "It is not so" (Exeg.; the more usual interpretation of vs. 35*c* would make of it another assertion that the sufferer's conscience is clear and his spirit in itself unafraid; cf. Heb. 4:15-16); and the negation of all hope that comes of it, "I am alone."

T. Z. Koo has told in his lectures of his first experience of an air raid in the days when the Japanese sent their planes in wave after wave over China. Said he: We had to go out into the fields because we had no dugouts in the city. Everybody took his rug and waited. Soon the final warning sounded, and we knew that in ten minutes the planes would arrive. In that short ten minutes I lived through the experiences of a lifetime. A feeling of utter helplessness swept over me. The usual things with which we surround our lives suddenly lost their significance. Most of us had been thinking that if we had

money in the bank we would be fairly secure; but as I sat on that rug waiting, I realized that no amount of money, not even of American dollars, could be of any help to me. I used to pride myself on the fact that I was a university man; but what could a Ph.D. do for me as I sat on that rug waiting for those planes? One after another all these things fell away, until I saw that out there under the sky in the fields I was before my Maker just as I was, stripped of everything, nothing more in life to fall back on. And my lips began to whisper, "Yea, though I walk in the shadow of death, I will fear no evil; for thou art with me." That was no doctrine then. It was no precept in a code of ethics. It was not a beautiful phrase in a poem. It meant that I was not alone, that I had found something in life which even war could not wipe out! (Cf. I Pet. 4:19.)

33. *Is Life a Game Without an Umpire?*—See Expos. on 7:7-10, 21; 14:15; 17:3; 19:25-27.

10 My soul is weary of my life; I will leave my complaint upon myself; I will speak in the bitterness of my soul.

10 "I loathe my life; I will give free utterance to my com· plaint; I will speak in the bitterness of my soul.

the verb in vs. 34 (Dhorme). The mediator would not only bring God and man together but also remove God's rod from the sufferer's back so that the latter might no longer speak under duress (vs. 35a).

Job ceases abruptly from indulging in this daydream. "For it is not so. I am [alone] with myself." (Vs. 35b.) Such is possibly the meaning of this difficult phrase. In other words, "I am left to my own resources." This would provide an admirably concise transition between the lofty flight of the preceding verses and the relapse which follows.

(2) HUMAN BEHAVIOR OF GOD (10:1-7)

Confronting the misery of his existence (vs. 1), Job goes back to God himself and begs not to be condemned without knowing first what charges are brought against him

10:1-22. The Nature of God.—Chs. 9–10 tell the story of how near Satan came to winning his wager (2:5). They mark the nadir of all Job's moods of resentment and despair. In the second cycle of speeches the fury of the storm has spent itself. The center of it seems to pass somewhere between the two chapters with which we are presently concerned. In 10:2 Job begins again to address the God who in ch. 9 appears as the nameless personification of cosmic terror, and gives proof, if not direct then indirect, of a violence somewhat abated. He is occupied now not so much with the argument of his friends or with his own misery and wretchedness, but with the nature of God; and it is precisely in this area that the resolution of his problem will take place, is in a sense already taking place.[4] Under the sound of his words is a heartbeat. Bewildered and weary (vs. 1), he stands up again to the fray; but the old yearning is on him more urgently than before toward the God he has lost. Not the God who acts like some human monster in a torture chamber (vs. 7), but the God about

[4] See E. L. Allen, *The Self and Its Hazards* (New York: The Philosophical Library, 1951), pp. 39-40: "If conscience finds the course of things unjust, whence did conscience arise? For conscience is part of the world it condemns. Strange world, indeed, to make provision thus for an adverse judgment to be passed upon itself! This protest also must be from God. So man realizes with awe what is happening. Like Job, he is appealing from God as men have misunderstood him to God as in his heart of hearts he knows him to be. So that, in the last analysis, his opposition to God is the work of God in him. God wants men to challenge him and bring all things under the judgment of conscience, even if in so doing they pit themselves against him. For he knows that even their rebellion is a form of service which he can accept with joy, since what he desires is the homage of free spirits, of persons who have it in them to rebel against him but who instead surrender themselves to him in utter trust and loyalty. Such surrender is only possible to those who have first dared to call God himself to account." (Used by permission.)

whose very coming (ch. 38) there will be something reminiscent of Hosea's God, with that "Galilean accent" of his, "I am God, and not man. How shall I give thee up?" (Hos. 11:9, 8). Not some mad craftsman (vss. 9-12) who is ready to **turn about and destroy** the work of his own hands, but the God "who provideth for the raven his food," and causeth "it to rain on a land where no man is" (38:41, 26). Not some watcher (7:20) and hunter of men (vs. 16), but the God who "hath begotten the drops of dew," hath gendered "the hoary frost of heaven," who knoweth "the time when . . . the hinds do calve," and sendeth out "the wild ass free" (38:28, 29; 39:1, 5). Job asks his questions (vss. 3-5), but the answers are already struggling up through his heart into his mind (16:19). He makes his appeal like a child aghast, holding its breath (vss. 8-12); only to surrender with a sigh (vs. 20) to the mystery of evil (vss. 13-17), where for him there can be no dwelling place.

That mystery is still with us (see Expos. on 1:12; 16:11). It taunted Swinburne until his lines dripped with bitterness:

None hath beheld him, none
Seen above other gods and shapes of things,
Swift without feet and flying without wings,
Intolerable, not clad with death or life,
    Insatiable, not known of night or day,
The lord of love and loathing and of strife
    Who gives a star and takes a sun away.[5]

It is a mystery that at its deepest never gets itself adequately expressed. But over against it waits still the mystery of good. Why Truth should go on living in a world like this, when it is so very inconvenient and so painful and costs so much! Why you can drive great nails through its hands and feet, and can never, never

[5] *Atalanta in Calydon.*

2 I will say unto God, Do not condemn me; show me wherefore thou contendest with me.

3 *Is it* good unto thee that thou shouldest oppress, that thou shouldest despise the work of thine hands, and shine upon the counsel of the wicked?

4 Hast thou eyes of flesh? or seest thou as man seeth?

---

2 I will say to God, Do not condemn me; let me know why thou dost contend against me.

3 Does it seem good to thee to oppress, to despise the work of thy hands and favor the designs of the wicked?

4 Hast thou eyes of flesh? Dost thou see as man sees?

(vs. 2). **Does it seem good to thee . . . to despise the work of thy hands?** (Vs. *3ab*.) Is there a streak of sadism in the temperament of this creative artist? "Dost thou derive pleasure [lit., "radiance"] from the designs of the wicked?" (Vs. *3c*.) This last question is considered by many commentators as a gloss, for it introduces an idea apparently alien to the context. But the mind of the poet must not be placed in a strait jacket. The persecution of the righteous leads normally by association to the thought of the success of the wicked.

10:4-7. Hast thou eyes of flesh? or seest thou as man seeth? Job's grim mockery appears like a twisted afterthought of his recent wish for the advent of a human God. Having rejected the idea of an incarnation, he seems to reflect on the Deity's strange behavior toward him and to conclude, "Yes, this God acts as a man, in man's inhumanity

---

hammer it down! Thrust a spear into its side, and get nowhere at all! Why loyalty should go on living in such a faithless world, and sacrifice, and a thousand shining things men give their lives for! Is that not mystery too? Except that now, as in Correggio's "Holy Night," all the light there is at the end of every adventure Godward, shining through the clouds into the thick darkness, comes from Christ (see Expos. on vss. 1-7).

1-7. Let Me Know Why.—Job can never abide any of his moods long. In 7:20 he suggested what Pliny the Elder once set down in so many words: "It is ridiculous to suppose that the great head of things, whatever it be, pays any regard to human affairs."[6] There is none of that here. Rather are three entirely different ideas turned up in quick succession and discarded: God takes some kind of pleasure in the wickedness and destruction that are going on (vs. 3); God shares himself in "man's inhumanity to man" (vs. 4); God is just like any other tyrant who knows very well that the victim is innocent, but gloats over the fact that he cannot escape, and tries to wring a confession out of him. (Vss. 5-7. See Exeg.; also Expos. on vss. 13-17. Does Elihu quote from this speech in 33:10? And are the shadows of Eliphaz, Bildad, and Zophar back of vss. 2-7? Is God as they are?)

But none of it would do. The only way for Job to get out was to get in, deeper and deeper. It was not a dilemma for the mind. It was a pilgrimage for the soul. And there was no

escape from it (see Expos. on 19:25). Certainly no escape by the simple device of canceling God out of the picture entirely. Nowadays we may find it possible to fool ourselves, scientifically and philosophically, into believing that all reality must somehow be commensurate with human reason and subject to the tests of human logic. Some things no doubt do lie outside the reach of our general propositions; they seem a bit beyond nature as we know it, will not readily submit themselves to the laboratory method. Macneile Dixon in *The Human Situation*[7] lists quite a number of them, e.g., that "blazing mass," that "incandescent whirlpool" of matter, which we are told set to, one Wednesday at 8 A.M., and dizzily turned out an empire, and a statue by Praxiteles, and Beethoven's *Fifth Symphony*. Or space, as it has now been "photographed with the mathematical 'lenses' of a 'cosmic camera'": no longer one thing at all—unless there have been some changes since! —but "two identical sheets joined by many new bridges." Never mind, though. What we do not understand today we shall no doubt be able to decipher tomorrow; and without having recourse to the supernatural. You will not likely catch us trying to smuggle anything "occult" past the customs. God is not an indispensable factor in our equations. For Job there could be no equation without him. The failure of every other hypothesis was driving him to one which seemed for the time being altogether final (vss. 13-17). But it was not, and could not be.

Perhaps we need life's riddles if we are to

---

[6] *Natural History* II. 5. 20.

[7] London: Edward Arnold & Co., 1937, pp. 299-300, 169.

5 *Are* thy days as the days of man? *are* thy years as man's days,

6 That thou inquirest after mine iniquity, and searchest after my sin?

7 Thou knowest that I am not wicked; and *there is* none that can deliver out of thine hand.

8 Thine hands have made me and fashioned me together round about; yet thou dost destroy me.

---

5 Are thy days as the days of man,
　　or thy years as man's years,

6 that thou dost seek out my iniquity
　　and search for my sin,

7 although thou knowest that I am not
　　guilty,
　　and there is none to deliver out of thy
　　hand?

8 Thy hands fashioned and made me;
　　and now thou dost turn about and de-
　　stroy me.*v*

v Cn Compare Gk Syr: Heb *made me together round about and thou dost destroy me*

---

to man." A slightly different meaning is proposed by the majority of commentators: God does not distinguish between justice and injustice, for his discernment is imperfect, like that of man. The first exegesis, however, is preferable, for it is confirmed by vss. 5 ff.

Are thy days as the days of man [אנוש, a "weakling"]? or even **thy years as man's years** [גבר, a "strong man," a "hero"]? The idea is not that God hastens to torture Job because time is short for him as well as for mortal beings, but rather that his behavior under the circumstances is similar to that of a human animal—an unscrupulous detective, a brutal policeman who must hasten to take vengeance while he has a chance, before his victim dies or can be rescued—**Thou knowest that I am not guilty** (vs. 7*a*; cf. 9:28). Why then dost thou try by torture to extract from me a confession of guilt? **There is none to deliver out of thy hand** (lit., "there is no deliverer"). This remark is perhaps a faint echo of the lingering hope for a mediator which had been expressed in the preceding strophe (9:33).

(3) THE ARTIST AND HIS HANDIWORK (10:8-12)

The thought of the artist's cruelty for the work of his hand (see vs. 3) emerges once more, but this time it is purified of its derisiveness and conveys a sentiment of desperate

---

hold on at all to any sense of God's greatness, and not just waste our time pottering about with a Deity who is indeed very like other men, the grocer at the corner, or the neighbor across the street (see Expos. on 3:20), throwing open the windows of heaven in the morning, doing the day's chores, and pulling down the shades at night. Remember the black curtain that fell on "Nebo's lonely mountain" when Moses died there (Deut. 34:1-6), looking out over a land of promise he would never enter. In some far-off way it was like the curtain that fell on Calvary, with something of the same sublime pathos, the sadness of inexplicable defeat. Yet strangely enough it serves only to make us conscious of how awful a thing the soul of man is. Life is not futile, life is nobler for it: less trivial because of the victory that was not won and the trumpets that were not blown. Riddles without an answer are in part the hope we too have of being found of God. The dark must fall before the stars can show themselves, flaming this way and that, countless jewels set against the soft cushions of the night.

Job lowers himself away into the mystery. It is as if a ship were leaving her cradle, gliding first into the backwaters of a sullen bay. Arthur Porritt in *The Best I Remember* speaks of the

drear, everlasting moment [of her launching] when the props have been knocked from under the hull and a soft whistle announces . . . that the ship is free. . . . The silence is so heavy that literally one hears the breathing of one's neighbours. . . . A second passes, two, three, perhaps four; and still the great ship . . . stands poised and motionless. Then the yard hands raise a cheer. Quick to detect the first faint movement, their eager eyes have observed what to others is an imperceptible stirring of the dead weight. Two seconds more and . . . the mighty hull begins to glide with ever accelerating speed down the greased ways till like a rushing wind she speeds down the slips. Her bows cleave the waters amid a roar of cheering.[8]

8-12. Why Hast Thou Made Me Thus?—(Cf. Rom. 9:20; Isa. 45:9.) Implicit in Job's words from first to last, the ground of all his complaining, the premise of every taunt, is his faith in God as creator, even as father. Between that faith and what seems to be his lot in the world

[8] New York: George H. Doran Co., 1923, p. 166.

9 Remember, I beseech thee, that thou hast made me as the clay; and wilt thou bring me into dust again?

10 Hast thou not poured me out as milk, and curdled me like cheese?

11 Thou hast clothed me with skin and flesh, and hast fenced me with bones and sinews.

12 Thou hast granted me life and favor, and thy visitation hath preserved my spirit.

9 Remember that thou hast made me of clay;w

and wilt thou turn me to dust again?

10 Didst thou not pour me out like milk and curdle me like cheese?

11 Thou didst clothe me with skin and flesh, and knit me together with bones and sinews.

12 Thou hast granted me life and steadfast love;

and thy care has preserved my spirit.

w Gk: Heb *like clay*

---

abandon, with the undertone of helpless reproach, as that of a rejected child to his unnatural parent—worse still, of the horror of a son about to be murdered by his own father (vs. 8). As in Ps. 139:14 ff., Job describes with the images which were appropriate in his time the mystery of embryonic growth, but he insists less on the wonder of this process than on the painstaking love and delicate skill displayed by his maker (vss. 9-12). His rebuke is the more piercing, for it hints at frustrated sonship, and so teaches by implication the doctrine of the fatherhood of God. Instead of defending his own right to live, the son of this inhuman father appeals to whatever feeling of tenderness or of creative pride may remain in the heart of his progenitor: **Remember, I pray . . .** (vs. 9).

12. Thy care has preserved my spirit: Rather, "my breath" (רוּחִי).

---

he can make no adjustment that will satisfy mind and heart and soul (see Expos. on 3:20). The friends of course were sure that he should never have allowed any such question on his lips (vss. 8-9). But it is an honest question, a universal, human question. By asking it and not being able to answer it, except on the basis of suppositions (vs. 13) that neither human reason nor human experience (vs. 12) can readily abide, many a man has found the barred shutters of his life loosened and swung open, as if by an unseen hand, on vast horizons (see Expos. on 19:25; 21:19). So Tennyson:

> Thou wilt not leave us in the dust:
> Thou madest man, he knows not why,
> He thinks he was not made to die;
> And thou hast made him; thou art just.[9]

If the universe is like a mad witch, fashioning with infinite care the most intricate patterns of lace, only to tear them to bits at the last, and with an idiotic grin scatter them over her dust heap, then no

> choir invisible
> Of those immortal dead who live again
> In minds made better by their presence[1]

can rid it of its witless incongruity (cf. 21:19).

What troubles Job, however, is not annihilation (vss. 21-22) but the manifest unreason of

[9] *In Memoriam,* Prologue, st. iii.
[1] George Eliot, "O May I Join the Choir Invisible."

his present state. His appeal is to "a faithful creator" (I Pet. 4:19) who has already by the very act of creation involved himself (see Expos. on 34:14). **Remember, I beseech thee, that thou hast made me.** In both Joshua and Judges is written the story of Caleb (Josh. 15:16-19; Judg. 1:12-15). He promised his daughter one day, in an expansive mood, to any warrior who would subdue a certain portion of the land of Canaan. His nephew—or some relative of his at any rate —went out and took it. Caleb gave the daughter as he had promised. But they were young people, and had nothing with which to begin their life together; so Caleb, musing no doubt on what it is in the world that keeps dragging a man in deeper and deeper, gave them a field. But in the field there was no water; and his daughter came to him saying, "Thou hast given me a south land; give me also springs of water." So Caleb, with perhaps a gesture of desperate and unpromised bounty, gave her both the upper and the nether springs. He had begun it, and in decency he had to see it through. Some such claim would Job lay on God's continuing favor. And it is this claim to which God finally responds (cf. Jer. 18:4, "And the vessel . . . was marred . . . ; so he made it again another vessel"). There is more than purpose in God's dealing; there is the purpose of a God who is always himself: not full of whims and dispositions, not angry and tender by fits and starts, always what we have now seen him to be in Christ. On Calvary words had stopped counting;

13 And these *things* hast thou hid in thine heart: I know that this *is* with thee.

14 If I sin, then thou markest me, and thou wilt not acquit me from mine iniquity.

15 If I be wicked, woe unto me; and *if* I be righteous, *yet* will I not lift up my head. *I am* full of confusion; therefore see thou mine affliction;

16 For it increaseth. Thou huntest me as a fierce lion: and again thou showest thyself marvelous upon me.

13 Yet these things thou didst hide in thy heart;
   I know that this was thy purpose.
14 If I sin, thou dost mark me,
   and dost not acquit me of my iniquity.
15 If I am wicked, woe to me!
   If I am righteous, I cannot lift up my head,
 for I am filled with disgrace
   and look upon my affliction.
16 And if I lift myself up,ˣ thou dost hunt me like a lion,
   and again work wonders against me,

ˣ Syr: Heb *he lifts himself up*

(4) The Unscrupulous Hunter (10:13-17)

13. With the KJV, one should consider the demonstrative pronouns as referring to what follows. The conjunction is one of antithesis: **Yet these things thou didst hide in thy heart.**

14-15. If I sin, . . . if I am wicked, . . . if I am righteous: As the third expression shows, Job is not making any admission of culpability. He merely states that whatever his conduct, his fate would remain the same. The translation "drunk with affliction" (vs. 15*b*) is probably correct, reading with Geiger *et al.* רוה for the *hapax legomenon* ראה, and thus obtaining an excellent parallel to **filled with disgrace.**

16-17. The first word, ויגאה, "and he rises up," is disconcerting. One may perhaps read with the Syriac the first person, ואגאה, **and if I lift myself up.** Dhorme's emendation into ויגע is phonetically possible and fits the context: "And (when I am) exhausted like

only deeds mattered (cf. Isa. 46:4, "I have made, and . . . I will carry").

13-17. The Dread Perhaps.— (See Expos. on 23:3.) Carlyle once called the religion of Burns "at best . . . an anxious wish; like that of Rabelais, 'a great Perhaps.' "[2] His reference was to Rabelais's deathbed metaphor, *"Je m'en vais chercher un grand Peut-être."* To Job, by the process of elimination, the trend of the argument at the moment seems altogether inescapable. His is a faith that in the agony of its desolation can only twist into nightmarish shapes, writhing in every nerve and muscle against the background of what looks to him like an evil, cosmic tyranny, coming to rest now in one of the rigid, misbegotten distortions of a Caliban's brain:

His spirits hear me,
And yet I needs must curse. But they'll nor pinch,
Fright me with urchin-shows, pitch me i' the mire,
Nor lead me, like a firebrand, in the dark
Out of my way, unless he bid 'em; but
For every trifle are they set upon me:
Sometimes like apes, that mow and chatter at me
And after, bite me; then like hedgehogs, which
Lie tumbling in my barefoot way and mount
Their pricks at my footfall; sometime am I

[2] Essay on "Burns."

All wound with adders who with cloven tongues
Do hiss me into madness.[3]

There is no "perhaps" about it: **I know that this was thy purpose.** By God's goodness he has been tricked into believing in the goodness of God. And all the while the only end in view was the consummation of "his misery by giving him that remembrance of happier things which is a sorrow's crown of sorrow. . . . Human doubt reaches its *ne plus ultra* in the terrible conclusion that behind a smiling providence God hides a frowning face. . . . This was the last of life for which the first was planned." So writes Strahan, and continues:

The poet evidently intended such a theory to be the *reductio ad absurdum* of the traditional doctrine of retribution. It is bound up with a theology —even now not quite extinct—which makes one exclaim, "Your God is my devil!" There is a very famous passage in Calvin's *Institutes* (iii. 23. 7): "The decree, I admit, is dreadful (Decretum quidem horribile, fateor); and yet it is impossible to deny that God foreknew what the end of man was to be before He made him, and foreknew, because He had so ordained by His decree."[4]

[3] *The Tempest*, Act II, scene 2.
[4] *The Book of Job* (2nd ed.; Edinburgh: T. & T. Clark, 1914), pp. 106-7. Used by permission.

17 Thou renewest thy witnesses against me, and increasest thine indignation upon me; changes and war *are* against me.

18 Wherefore then hast thou brought me forth out of the womb? Oh that I had given up the ghost, and no eye had seen me!

19 I should have been as though I had not been; I should have been carried from the womb to the grave.

20 *Are* not my days few? cease *then, and* let me alone, that I may take comfort a little,

21 Before I go *whence* I shall not return, *even* to the land of darkness and the shadow of death;

---

17 thou dost renew thy witnesses against me,
   and increase thy vexation toward me;
   thou dost bring fresh hosts against me.*y*

18 "Why didst thou bring me forth from the womb?
   Would that I had died before any eye had seen me,

19 and were as though I had not been,
   carried from the womb to the grave.

20 Are not the days of my life few?*z*
   Let me alone, that I may find a little comfort*a*

21 before I go whence I shall not return,
   to the land of gloom and deep darkness,

y Cn Compare Gk: Heb *changes and a host are with me*
z Cn Compare Gk Syr: Heb *Are not my days few? Let him cease*
a Heb *brighten up*

---

a (pursued) lion, thou huntest me." The comparison, however, applies to the hunted, not to the hunter, and the idea is in line with the general opinion that Job has of himself. His capacity for resistance is such that the hunter, in order to subdue him, must rally all his forces. **Thou renewest thy** [attacks] **against me,** and **fresh hosts** must be brought into the fight. The word עֵדֶיךָ, **thy witnesses,** is reintroducing a juridical image. It may, however, derive from the stem עדה, "to advance in an aggressive mood" (cf. 28:8).

(5) Respite Before Death (10:18-22)

18-22. Inasmuch as death did not put an end to this ludicrous life before it began (vss. 18-19; cf. 3:11 ff.), let there be a truce now for the few days which remain (vs. 20) before the voyage to **the land** of no return (vss. 21-22). The pathos in the thought of

---

Temporarily, for Job, it is the only solution that makes sense, and morbidly he clings to it, explores it, proves it. If he commits some trivial **sin** (vs. 14; cf. Expos. on 7:20*a*), God looks around for it, peers under everything (cf. vs. 6), holds it against him. If he is deliberately **wicked** (cf. vs. 7), for him the bell tolls. If **righteous,** he dare not lift up [his] head, but must go about **filled with disgrace,** and drunk with **affliction.** What else can all that mean? When for an instant he does lift himself, to steal a furtive glance around, like a weary lion, God renews his "wonderful works" (5:9; 9:10; 12:7-25), calls up other witnesses, increases his wrath, throws in fresh troops!

But the answer will not come by elimination. Or by any "philosophic theodicy" (cf. Expos. on 5:17). It comes by other means. (See Expos. on 19:25; 23:13, 15.)

O world, thou choosest not the better part!
It is not wisdom to be only wise,
And on the inward vision close the eyes,
But it is wisdom to believe the heart.
Columbus found a world, and had no chart,
Save one that faith deciphered in the skies;

To trust the soul's invincible surmise
Was all his science and his only art.[5]

18-22. Let Me Brighten Up a Little Before I Go.—(Cf. Ps. 39:13.) Throughout the poem there are themes that enter and re-enter, as in a symphony. This is one of them, a motif in minor key (cf. 3:11 ff.; 6:8 ff.; 14:13; 16:22; etc.). Why did you not repent of your evil purpose before ever I was born? **The days of my life** (reading **of my life** [RSV] for **cease then** [KJV]) are few enough. Go somewhere else (see Expos. on 7:19), that I may brighten up a little (9:27) before I leave for "the land of no return," [6] where there is darkness like the shadow of death (vs. 21), where the night is as chaos (**without any order** [KJV], i.e., with no moon or stars to light it), and so the day (cf. 3:4, 6; Job would

[5] George Santayana, "The Better Part," from *Poems.* Used by permission of Charles Scribner's Sons and Constable & Co., publishers.
[6] A phrase used to describe the underworld in the Babylonian poem, "The Descent of Ishtar"; so Kissane, p. 61. In Hamlet's soliloquy (Act III, scene 1), it is
   The undiscover'd country, from whose bourn
   No traveller returns.

22 A land of darkness, as darkness *itself;* *and* of the shadow of death, without any order, and *where* the light *is* as darkness.

11 Then answered Zophar the Naamathite, and said,

2 Should not the multitude of words be answered? and should a man full of talk be justified?

3 Should thy lies make men hold their peace? and when thou mockest, shall no man make thee ashamed?

22 the land of gloom[b] and chaos,
    where light is as darkness."

11 Then Zophar the Na'amathite answered:

2 "Should a multitude of words go unanswered,
    and a man full of talk be vindicated?

3 Should your babble silence men,
    and when you mock, shall no one shame you?

[b] Heb *gloom as darkness, deep darkness*

---

eternal death is accentuated by a rhythm that has been slowed down to a monotonous beat by the accumulation of synonyms for **darkness**.

5. First Discourse of Zophar (11:1-20)

a) Job's Iniquity (11:1-6)

11:2-6b. Zophar, like Eliphaz and Bildad, defends the dogma of divine justice, but his temper is even more immoderate than that of his immediate predecessor. He believes that Job is less a misguided heretic than **a man full of talk** (lit., "a man of lips," vs. 2), and he dismisses the sufferer's passionately sincere apologia as mere **babble** (vs. 3), which nevertheless deserves a rebuke. How can Job say, **My doctrine is pure, and I am**

---

relegate to very Sheol itself the night of his conception and the day of his birth). But the darkest hour is that before the dawn. Job's world will yet be "changed like clay under the seal, and . . . dyed like a garment" (38:14).

11:1-20. The Word of the Zealot.—Zophar is a man of the way called not only Straight but Narrow. He has listened attentively to all that has been said. He has heard Job hinting and then stating outright that God is lacking in moral discernment (6:30; 9:22-24). Eliphaz had done the best he could: Job should at least try to see himself as God saw him. Bildad had taken a hand: all the hoary traditions of the past gave witness to God's clear-eyed justice, and what had happened to Job himself was evidence enough that he would neither "cast away a perfect man" (Job had not yet perished utterly) nor "help the evildoers" (8:20). The implication was clear: something simply had to be wrong with Job, even if Job had no awareness of it. It was Job's reply in chs. 9–10 that left Zophar no choice, or so he thought. The sufferer had now to be dealt with, and roundly.

How you do talk! Do you expect us to pay no attention to it, and have no word to say? You claim that right is on your side, and want God to speak out. Would to heaven he might! He would tell you with sufficient clarity what all this is about. It is about you. God is tracking you down because you are guilty. Say you are not conscious of any wrongdoing. Does that

mean there has been none? Do you know the mind of God? Will you never learn "how unsearchable are his judgments, and his ways past finding out"? How stupid can a man be? Come to your senses. **Set your heart right,** and turn to him. **Let not wickedness dwell in your tents.** Never say there is no hope but in the grave (6:8-10a; 10:18-22; cf. vs. 15 with 10:15). There is. **You will forget your misery . . . as waters that have passed. Only the eyes of the wicked will fail. Their hope** is in tragic fact what you fancy yours to be: nothing is left for them but **to breathe their last.**

2-6. Knowing What Cannot Be Known.— There is a strange, interesting, and highly suggestive contradiction in what Zophar is at such pains to point out. The assumption that lies back of it, and is of course theologically quite sound, is that ultimately God is unknowable (see Expos. on vs. 7). If we understood him, we would do well to doubt him. The trouble is that Zophar understands him without doubting him. For a man to quote Rom. 11:34, and then not pursue it to its proper issue in mystery (cf. Expos. on 8:3) and awe, is to climb the very pinnacle of presumption, which is pride. It is to profess the undefinable by defining it. Zophar knows what cannot be known, and in the light of his knowledge Job's passionate assertions of innocence (9:20-21; 10:7a) seem no more than **talk,** the mere **babble** of some "stupid" fellow (vs. 12) who has about as much chance to "get

4 For thou hast said, My doctrine *is* pure, and I am clean in thine eyes.	4 For you say, 'My doctrine is pure, and I am clean in God's eyes.'
5 But oh that God would speak, and open his lips against thee;	5 But oh, that God would speak, and open his lips to you,
6 And that he would show thee the secrets of wisdom, that *they are* double to that which is! Know therefore that God exacteth of thee *less* than thine iniquity *deserveth.*	6 and that he would tell you the secrets of wisdom! For he is manifold in understanding.*c* Know then that God exacts of you less than your guilt deserves.

c Heb obscure

---

clean in thine eyes (vs. 4), when he does not know the secrets of wisdom (vss. 5-6a), or rather, its "secret potency" or "potent mysteries" (תעלמות; LXX, δύναμιν)? They are "like stupendous marvels" [in vs. 6b read כפלאים for M.T., כפלים], incomprehensible to human reason.

6c. "Know then that God is pursuing thee [read ישחלך for the obscure ישה לך] on account of thy guilt." At last the charge has been made explicitly. Eliphaz dropped cautious innuendos. Bildad spoke of the sins of the sons. Now that Job has reiterated emphatically that he is perfect, Zophar feels that he may proceed to a direct attack. The poet slowly increases the tension by withholding a specific accusation until the speech of the third friend.

Although Zophar is even more devoid of sympathy than Bildad, and certainly lacks entirely the courteous approach of Eliphaz, his intellectual powers are not to be denied. He may be the "most rasping disputant of the three" (Peake, *Job,* p. 125), but it must

---

understanding" as "a wild ass's colt" has of being "born a man." What God would say if God would speak is no secret to anybody whose very agnosticism has become dogmatic. Such people first preen their feathers; then they look down the nose (see Expos. on 5:8); then they point the finger (see Expos. on 4:8-11). Until at last they are almost bound to essay the role of the prophet (vss. 13-19), unveiling the things that shall be, with many a fair inducement to those who think as they do (see Expos. on 8:7), and much ominous shaking of the head over those who do not (vs. 20; cf. Expos. on 8:11-19). A swelling is of all things else most like a hollow. "Why should the spirit of mortal be proud?" [7] It never is, except when it has seen nothing in heaven above or in earth beneath to humble it. The self that is filled with self is the self that is emptier than any self can be and remain a self (see Expos. on vs. 5).

5. *Man's Word and God's.*—It is never very difficult to confuse the two. There is a God who fashions men, and there are gods that men fashion. Who cannot put words in the mouth of a god that he brings in his hand (12:6; cf. Expos. on 4:20b)? It is a kind of pious ventriloquism in which human life has always been terrifyingly adept. *Deus vult!* And thousands marched out on the First Crusade. "Immanuel! God with us!" And we head north or south, as

[7] William Knox, "Mortality," st. i.

we like, east or west, or perhaps a little on the bias. *Dieu et mon droit* is emblazoned on the British royal arms; but how easily in our minds the order reverses itself—or worse: given time, "my right" can learn how to identify itself with God; more time, and identification can no longer be distinguished from elimination.

Said Cromwell to Samuel Rutherford, a Scottish divine whom he found quite troublesome, "Have you ever considered the possibility that you may be mistaken?" (*a*) To Eliphaz a word had come in the watches of the night. (*b*) Bildad had found it in the past, embalmed in all the sayings of the wise. (*c*) Zophar's insight is relatively keener; only—the relative has for him become the absolute. His doxy is orthodoxy—as whose is not? But the first hazard is neither the where nor the how nor the what: the first hazard is the self—and the last. "Except a man be born again" was Christ's way of putting it (John 3:3). "He that is of God heareth God's words" (John 8:47). There is a touch that cleanses: and the deaf hear, and the blind see, and the lame walk (cf. Matt. 11:2-6). The word that comes then in the stillness (*a*) may well be God's Word. It can stride up now to meet us (*b*) out of the years, from prophet and apostle. It is able at last to speak to us (*c*) in the age-long testimony of the Christian church, in the creeds that have been hammered out on the anvil of Christian experience, in the sacraments

7 Canst thou by searching find out God? canst thou find out the Almighty unto perfection?

8 *It is* as high as heaven; what canst thou do? deeper than hell; what canst thou know?

9 The measure thereof *is* longer than the earth, and broader than the sea.

10 If he cut off, and shut up, or gather together, then who can hinder him?

11 For he knoweth vain men: he seeth wickedness also; will he not then consider *it?*

12 For vain man would be wise, though man be born *like* a wild ass's colt.

7 "Can you find out the deep things of God?
    Can you find out the limit of the Almighty?

8 It is higher than heaven[d] — what can you do?
    Deeper than Sheol — what can you know?

9 Its measure is longer than the earth,
    and broader than the sea.

10 If he passes through, and imprisons,
    and calls to judgment, who can hinder him?

11 For he knows worthless men;
    when he sees iniquity, will he not consider it?

12 But a stupid man will get understanding,
    when a wild ass's colt is born a man.

[d] Heb *The heights of heaven*

---

be admitted at the same time that he is in a way a profound theologian. While Eliphaz appealed to a specific revelation, like a wise man playing the prophet, while Bildad pompously rehearsed the tradition of the ancients, Zophar grasps the significance of a reverent type of agnosticism: God is greater than human thoughts and he escapes man's precise formulations. Zophar is not therefore the rationalistic dogmatist, as some critics assert. Yet he is wrong in the very midst of his rightness, for if Job has not received **the secrets of wisdom,** how can Zophar claim to possess them? How does he know that Job's fate is the result of **guilt?**

b) God's Infinity (11:7-12)

7-12. Once again Zophar states a valid truth and clothes it, incidentally, in incomparably beautiful poetry. **Can you find out the deep things of God** (vs. 7a)? The word חקר refers to the object of searching, which is here the essence and true nature of God (cf.

---

that have ministered the grace of God to Christian faith. But it is a Word never to be possessed; it is a Word to possess us: normative, but not in its highest function; in its highest function creative, moving beyond judgment into love (see Expos. on 6:28-30). "This is my commandment, That ye love one another, as I have loved you" (John 15:12).

7. The Inscrutable God.—Canst thou by searching find out God? (Cf. Expos. on vss. 2-6; 9:30–10:22; 23:3.) It is a rhetorical question, but a question that we need to answer in all soberness, and with sober intent to abide by the answer that we know very well has to be given it. We do not arrive at God by adding one to two and the sum to infinity. Job cast up the total of his wretchedness and said God was like that (10:13). Somerset Maugham, in his autobiographical novel, *Of Human Bondage,*[8] has a lad who argues from a clubfoot to God. Turn

[8] New York: George H. Doran Co., 1915.

the argument around, argue as Robert Louis Stevenson argued, from God to the tuberculosis that racked him with its cough, and the result may well be a hero (see Expos. on 3:20-21). The friends cast up the total of Job's wretchedness too, as much of it as they could understand, and kept setting down under it insistently Job's guilt and God's justice. In every case the addition was wrong (cf. Expos. on 12:2-6).

It is precisely this direction which thought seems so inevitably to take that Kierkegaard attacked in Hegel with all the weapons of scorn and ridicule. Comparing the two, Richard Kroner comments:

Hegel speaks as if there were no distance between man . . . and God not to be overcome by thought. About the realm of pure thought as it unfolds in the succession of categories Hegel writes: "This realm is the Truth as it is without any veil, in and for itself." And he goes on to add words which always have seemed to be utterly blasphemous to

13 If thou prepare thine heart, and stretch out thine hands toward him;

14 If iniquity *be* in thine hand, put it far away, and let not wickedness dwell in thy tabernacles.

15 For then shalt thou lift up thy face without spot; yea, thou shalt be steadfast, and shalt not fear:

16 Because thou shalt forget *thy* misery, *and* remember *it* as waters *that* pass away:

---

13 "If you set your heart aright,
   you will stretch out your hands toward him.

14 If iniquity is in your hand, put it far away,
   and let not wickedness dwell in your tents.

15 Surely then you will lift up your face without blemish;
   you will be secure, and will not fear.

16 You will forget your misery;
   you will remember it as waters that have passed away.

28:16; Ecclus. 42:19). Job has questioned the motives of the Deity's attitude toward him, and he has thereby presumptuously inquired into the very character of the Godhead. **Can you find out the limit of the Almighty?** (Vs. 7*b*.) The word תכלית derives from the root כלה, "to be complete and perfect," and thus means either "the end," **the limit** (26:10; 28:3), or "perfection" (Ps. 139:22). Indeed, Job is right when he realizes that no one **can hinder** God (vs. 10; cf. 9:11-12), but he is wrong when he assumes that God does not distinguish between righteous and **worthless men** (vs. 11; cf. 9:22). The proverb about a **stupid man** (vs. 12) applies to him squarely. As in the preceding strophe, Zophar spoils a correct principle by his gratuitous application of it, or rather by his failure to apply it to himself.

c) FRUITS OF CONVERSION (11:13-20)

13-20. In spite of his forthright bluntness (vs. 6), Zophar does not give Job up as a hopeless reprobate. He therefore concludes with the customary appeal to repent, pray,

---

every believer: "One may therefore express it thus that this content shows forth God as he is in his eternal essence before the Creation of Nature and of a Finite Spirit" (*Logic*, vol. I, p. 60). He who does not feel the religious impossibility of such a statement, cannot be persuaded to do so. . . . Hegel never realizes that such a relation [between knowledge and object] which might be possible in any other case is certainly not possible in the case of man's relation to God, if God is understood in the light of the Bible. . . . "Christianity [says Kierkegaard, *Concluding Unscientific Postscript to the Philosophical Fragments*, tr. David F. Swenson; Princeton: Princeton University Press, 1944; p. 339] is not a doctrine but an existential communication"—that is: it is not a theology, but a living religion, and its truth cannot be severed from the living faith of those who profess and practice that religion.[9]

Between man and God there is no distance; there is a gulf: and a gulf cannot be crossed by a series of small jumps. The profoundest religious question that can be asked is the question that all human history puts to God: "Canst thou by searching find out man?" Calvary is the focal point of that search. God is known in Christ, who indeed says, "Seek, and ye shall find." But

find what? What but the God who prompted the seeking by his finding? "I should never have sought thee hadst thou not already found me." (See Luke 15:3-7.) The terms of that parable are not interchangeable. It is the shepherd who seeks. "That ye, being rooted and grounded in love, may be able to comprehend with all saints what is the breadth [vs. 9*b*], and length [vs. 9*a*], and depth [vs. 8*b*], and height [vs. 8*a*]; and to know the love of Christ, which passeth knowledge, that ye might be filled with all the fulness of God" (Eph. 3:17-19).

16. *As Waters that Pass Away.*— (Cf. Expos. on 5:17, 18, 23; 8:7, 20-22.) "Someday you will look back on this and smile to think that you were so troubled." What cold comfort it is, even if it should be true, when the warmth of a friend's heart is the only thing under the sun that can mediate the warmth of God's! Besides, it is not always true. It happened to be true in this instance (42:12-17). But it did not turn out so because of anything the friends recommended (see Expos. on 17:12). Not even truth is a substitute for love; and this "truth" is too often a falsehood. A man may be repentant, and still find himself in the very middle of trouble. Repentance may actually land him there. Forever

---

[9] "Kierkegaard or Hegel?" *Revue Internationale de Philosophie*, No. 19 (1952), pp. 7-8.

17 And *thine* age shall be clearer than the noonday; thou shalt shine forth, thou shalt be as the morning.

18 And thou shalt be secure, because there is hope; yea, thou shalt dig *about thee, and* thou shalt take thy rest in safety.

19 Also thou shalt lie down, and none shall make *thee* afraid; yea, many shall make suit unto thee.

20 But the eyes of the wicked shall fail, and they shall not escape, and their hope *shall be as* the giving up of the ghost.

17 And your life will be brighter than the noonday;
its darkness will be like the morning.

18 And you will have confidence, because there is hope;
you will be protected*e* and take your rest in safety.

19 You will lie down, and none will make you afraid;
many will entreat your favor.

20 But the eyes of the wicked will fail;
all way of escape will be lost to them,
and their hope is to breathe their last."

e Or *you will look around*

and amend. A willful decision and a prayer of supplication (vs. 13ʃ, followed by moral purification (vs. 14), will bring back security without fear (vs. 15). The present misery will be forgotten (vs. 16) and life again will be worth living (vss. 17-19). This bright prospect, however, is topped by a stern, final warning: there is no way of escape for the wicked.

A brilliant performance, no doubt dictated by genuine conviction, but based upon the familiar moralism of the wise men who believed in salvation by works.

lengthening over the world broods the shadow of a cross; and of One who, needing no repentance, died with nails through his hands and feet. "Because he hath set his love upon me, therefore will I deliver him" (Ps. 91:14). Jesus "bearing his cross went forth" (John 19:17). "I will set him on high, because he hath known my name" (Ps. 91:14). "And sitting down they watched him there" (Matt. 27:36). One grows suspicious of the happy ending—unless one knows what a happy ending really is.

18. *Because There Is Hope.*—Zophar was quite right. There is. If Job had not thought of himself as being "without God in the world" (Eph. 2:12), an alien now to the love he had once known (10:9-12), taught by everything in his religion—against which he rebelled, to the saving of his own soul—that his misery was the very symbol and token of that alienation, he too would have known the meaning of hope; but it would not have been Zophar's meaning. Even with things as they were, he clung to it desperately, with his finger tips (14:13-15; 16:19; etc.). Roget's *Thesaurus* gives as synonyms for "hope" "Utopia," "fool's paradise," "castle in Spain." Cynicism like that is surely no accident. It comes of patterned hopes: and life all too frequently smashes the patterns. The way to keep from being disillusioned is to have no illusions. Trace the word "hope" through Scripture. See it blossom in the psalms, when there were no signs of it in the times. The noun does not appear in the Gospels. What need is there, with Christ in every passing moment of the day?

In its full biblical-Christian sense [it] is hardly found before we reach the Epistles, and this is not surprising, since Christian hope is grounded on the Resurrection of Christ: "Blessed be the God and Father of our Lord Jesus Christ who . . . begat us again unto a living hope by the resurrection of Jesus Christ from the dead" (I Pet. 1:3). . . . The NT conception of hope has nothing at all to do with any this-worldly prospects; it is as far removed as possible from any notion of an earthly Utopia or any secular optimism. [See Expos. on 8:7.] It is through and through eschatological, always bearing reference to the return of the Lord Jesus at the end of the age.[1]

It is born in despair, not in bright ideas and happy hunches. Job was infinitely nearer the N.T. than any of his friends. His hope, what was left of it, was not a patterned hope; theirs was. His hope had to do not with the things the friends set first (17:13-16); it had to do in very truth with "the last things" (19:25-27*b*; cf. Expos. on 12:13-19). In *The Age of Anxiety*, W. H. Auden has Rosetta, a Jewess, say to all "conventional, hearty and bumptious Christians [that they] cannot know what real desperate faith means, as we anxious Jews have to know it. You have a nice 'household god' that brings you luck, and a 'Harpist's Haven for hearty climbers' to look forward to in the next life."[2]

[1] Alan Richardson, "Hope," *A Theological Word Book of the Bible.* Copyright 1951 by The Macmillan Co. and used with their permission.

[2] New York: Random House, 1947, p. 124. Paraphrase by Amos N. Wilder, *Modern Poetry and the Christian Tradition* (New York: Charles Scribner's Sons, 1952), p. 220.

12 And Job answered and said,
2 No doubt but ye *are* the people,
and wisdom shall die with you.

3 But I have understanding as well as
you; I *am* not inferior to you: yea, who
knoweth not such things as these?

12 Then Job answered:
2 "No doubt you are the people,
and wisdom will die with you.
3 But I have understanding as well as you;
I am not inferior to you.
Who does not know such things as
these?

---

6. JOB'S REPLY TO ZOPHAR (12:1–14:22)

This discourse concludes the first cycle of discussion. Its traditional division into three chapters fits quite accurately its organic plan: (*a*) an empirical critique of providence (12:1-25); (*b*) an indictment of the friends' ministrations leading to a new attack upon God (13:1-27); (*c*) a prayerful meditation on the tragedy of life (13:28–14:22).

a) AN EMPIRICAL CRITIQUE OF PROVIDENCE (12:1-25)

(1) THE SPECTACLE OF THE WORLD (12:1-6)

Against the dogma of retribution Job has only one answer: his own experience and the observation of injustice which remains unpunished.

12:2-3. No doubt you are the people: The ancient versions support the M.T., and corrections of modern scholars are conjectural. The traditionally accepted interpretation (see KJV and RSV) is uncertain but possible. Job sarcastically magnifies the opinions of his three comforters as representing the general consensus of mankind. He thereby emphasizes his position as a lonely dissenter, giving affront to the approved beliefs of the human race, or at least of the international school of wisdom (see vs. 2*b*). He probably feels the pride and the bitter satisfaction of the nonconformist who stands alone against the world. Zophar has in effect appealed to a knowledge of God's secret wisdom (see 11:6), and Job raises unwittingly the question of epistemological criterion. His adversaries claim to own a monopoly on knowledge: **wisdom will die with** them (vs. 2*b*). But he himself has **understanding as well as** they (vs. 3*a*). The choice of the word לבב ("heart" is the seat of intellectual and volitive processes) suggests that Job has been deeply wounded by Zophar's use of the proverb on the colt of the wild ass (see 11:12). He is not "a stupid man [unable to] get understanding." His mental as well as

---

12:2–14:22. Job's Reply to Zophar.—No doubt you know everything that can be known. The **wisdom** you have been talking so much about **will die with you.** Let me tell you this: I understand as much about the Almighty as you do. I understand that if you call on him, he will treat you as he has treated me (see Exeg.). I understand that the man who succeeds has no time for the man who has failed. Down with him a little farther! I understand that **peace** is for robbers, and security for idolaters, and for **those who provoke God. The beasts of the field, the fowls of the air, the fish of the sea**—they will **tell you how God rules in the affairs of earth.** It has to be God. Who else is there? **Wisdom is with the aged.** I do not care for the taste of it (vs. 11). Your God of wisdom **and might tears down and shuts . . . in,** makes **fools** out of **judges** and slaves out of **kings.** Grant his power, but quit talking of his justice. How is that for understanding (13:1-2)? I want to say it to God; you want to **whitewash** him **with lies.** It would be wisdom to hold your tongue. Lest he break

out against you for trying to defend him with falsehood and deceit. Come what may, I challenge him. There is no hope for me in anything else (see Exeg. on 13:16). Who will say that I am guilty? Give me a fair trial, O God. Show me my **iniquities. Hide** not thy face from me. What am I but **a driven leaf?** And thou rememberest the sins of my youth, holdest my feet in prison. I am but mortal, **of few days, and full of trouble** (13:28–14:1). Why dost thou stare at me so? I am unclean, as all men are. **Look away from** me for a moment. I shall die soon enough, and **not awake. Hide me in Sheol . . . until thy wrath be past.** O God, keep me in mind! I will not let thee go. If only a man could **live again!** Hast thou no **desire** to the work of thy hands? Instead, thou dost **number my steps,** dost mark every move I make; thou dost hoard my iniquity in a bag. Have it thy way! Death be thy victory! And forgetfulness of all but the dread ache of it.

12:2-6. The Dissent of Common Sense.—Traditional piety and orthodox theology have done their best. Job now turns on his friends, an-

| 4 I am *as* one mocked of his neighbor, who calleth upon God, and he answereth him: the just upright *man is* laughed to scorn. | 4 I am a laughingstock to my friends; I, who called upon God and he answered me, a just and blameless man, am a laughingstock. |

his moral capacities are not inferior to those of his interlocutors (vs. 3b may be out of place here: see 13:2b), but his sources of information are different. They are not the esoteric privilege of an elite, but the common man's property: **Who does not know such things as these?** (vs. 3c).

4-6. These verses are omitted by Siegfried, Duhm, *et al.* It is argued that the idea expressed therein interrupts the thread of vs. 3, which is precisely picked up in vs. 7. It is also noted that the LXX offers at this point a widely different reading, and even omits vs. 4ab. Any hypothesis of a gloss, however, must be viewed in the light of the poet's conception of rhetoric and his shrewd sensitivity to the swift transformation of psychological moods.

It is far from obvious that vss. 4-6 interrupt the sequence presented by vss. 3 and 7. What are "these things" which everyone knows (vs. 3c)? First, "he is [read with Syriac יהיה for the M.T. אהיה] a laughingstock to his neighbor, (the man) who called upon God and God afflicted him" (vs. 4ab). The traditional rendering, **who calleth upon God, and he answereth him,** is grammatically exact but fails to identify the subject and the object of the second clause of the line. The general and proximate context shows, against RSV's conjecture, that God has not yet answered the petitioner. Kissane understands that the **just and blameless man** is one who prays unto God and obeys him, one who is kindly responsive and obedient to the divine will (see I Kings 12:7; Hos. 2:15). In other words, the two verbs depend upon the same subject. Job would then describe himself in the terms of the prologue, as "perfect and upright, one who feared God, and turned away from evil" (1:1). Nevertheless, as the traditional translators have seen, the change of construction in vs. 4b from the participle קרא, "one who calls," to the consecutive imperfect, ויענהו, **and he answereth him,** most probably indicates a change of subject. An attractive possibility is to consider ויענהו as the consecutive imperfect Hiphil of ענה III (see Akkadian *enû*, "to do violence to") which is well attested in biblical Hebrew (see I Kings 8:35, and many uses of this verb in the Piel). Vs. 4b would then read, "One who called upon God, but he [God] afflicted him." The hero is **a laughingstock to [his] friends,** precisely because his prayers are futile and his affliction invalidates his claim to uprightness. Here lies the scandal of Job's situation, the irreducible antinomy which confronts his inquiring mind. His piety and his behavior have not produced any fruit. The dogma of retribution is disproved by his own fate.

swering them all together by entering the plain and simple demurrer of what he believes to be common sense. Devout folk and even theologians do sometimes get too far away from the hard realities of existence, and by their very remoteness are betrayed into talking nonsense—about answers to prayer, God's judgment of the wicked, his tender care of all the righteous; the way of love, the value of sacrifice, the "happy issue" out of all our afflictions (see Expos. on 13:8; 19:21). One good look at the world should suffice. One good look at the Cross should have kept us from being so startled by that one good look at the world. Job's summary of things as they are is of course embittered by the **wisdom** which his friends have claimed as their prerogative. Zophar must have been sorry that he ever used the word. Job twists it and turns it over in his mouth, smacks his lips, and makes a wry face. What he says is no truer than what the others have said; but if allowance is made for the bitterness, one may contend that at least it outlines the case for the prosecution (see Expos. on 3:20-21; 7:1-6; 16:10; 18:21; 21:1-34). However pious the theory there can be no adjustment of the facts to fit it. Cynically Job counts them off on his fingers: **blameless** people who are a **laughingstock;** poor unfortunates for whom the fortunate need have no pity (see Exeg.)—if their foot slips, give them another push, they deserve it; and there all the while, on the other side, the people who "help themselves"—gen-

5 He that is ready to slip with *his* feet *is as* a lamp despised in the thought of him that is at ease.

6 The tabernacles of robbers prosper, and they that provoke God are secure; into whose hand God bringeth *abundantly*.

7 But ask now the beasts, and they shall teach thee; and the fowls of the air, and they shall tell thee:

5 In the thought of one who is at ease there
     is contempt for misfortune;
   it is ready for those whose feet slip.
6 The tents of robbers are at peace,
     and those who provoke God are secure,
   who bring their god in their hand.*f*

7 "But ask the beasts, and they will teach
     you;
   the birds of the air, and they will tell
     you;

f Hebrew uncertain

Another possibility may be considered: without correcting the C.T. but by altering slightly the Masoretic pointing, Hölscher reads *weya'anēhû* instead of *wayya'anēhû.* The clause might then mean, "One who called upon God so that God might answer him." Job would imply that his prayers remain unanswered.

5. Here is the second of these **things** (vs. 3) which are obvious to common sense. A happy man's motto is "Contempt for disaster" (vs. 5*a*). The text is difficult, but if one admits that it is well preserved, its meaning is possibly this: **One who is at ease**—i.e., "secure and serene"—can afford to despise **misfortune** and to minimize its significance. More probably Job is observing that a privileged man normally entertains a contemptuous attitude for men affected by calamity—a thought which would admirably prepare that of the parallel clause in vs. 5*a*, a blow **for those whose feet slip.** According to this translation, the word נכון is not taken as a Niphal of the verb כון (see RSV), but as a derivative of נכה, "to strike." In other words, the popular attitude is summed up in the advice, "Push a stumbling man to the gutter and help him to fall!" This is the practice of the jungle, where strong and healthy animals develop unusual cruelty toward their wounded or ailing mates. Job knows that in primitive society the weak man shows by his very weakness his inadequacy to fulfill his place in the tribal or the civic frame, and that furthermore his ruined life shows that the Deity has abandoned him. It is therefore both socially and religiously correct to attack him. One should side with the majority group and with God by spurning the destitute. Thus the poet indirectly inveighs against a vicious type of morality—vicious even though varnished by a perverted theology.

6. The third of these **things** (vs. 3) that anyone can observe is that **the tents of robbers are at peace, and those who provoke God are secure.** This is the counterpart of the preceding two observations, and it clinches the argument against the dogma of retribution. Vs. 6*c* adds a striking note: those **who bring their god in their hand,** or with Moffatt those "who make a god of their own power" (cf. Vergil's words, *dextra mihi deus* [*Aeneid* X. 773]; Hab. 1:11). If the text is well preserved (ancient versions differ widely from the Hebrew), this phrase refers to the man who thinks he can "bring God in his hand." True idolaters are those who do not submit themselves to the will of God, whatever it may be, but attempt to use God for their own aims and to manipulate religion for selfish gain.

(2) A MONISTIC VIEW OF THE UNIVERSE (12:7-12)

7-12. The whole passage may be spurious for the following reasons: (*a*) It begins with the conjunction and adverb ואולם, "but indeed," "rather," a strong adversative

---

erously. They are the ones God helps (cf. ch. 21). It is a strange world, and will not be reduced to simple formulas. Job knows better than Zophar how hard it is to understand God (see Expos. on 10:1-7; 11:7). The only fact there

is that can make the other facts stand down is the faith which God can fashion in the human heart. What answer to any fact but a Person?

7-25. *What Great Things God Hath Done!*—
The Exeg. summarizes the difficulties to be en-

8 Or speak to the earth, and it shall teach thee; and the fishes of the sea shall declare unto thee.

9 Who knoweth not in all these that the hand of the Lord hath wrought this?

10 In whose hand is the soul of every living thing, and the breath of all mankind.

11 Doth not the ear try words? and the mouth taste his meat?

12 With the ancient is wisdom; and in length of days understanding.

8 or the plants of the earth,[g] and they will teach you;
　　and the fish of the sea will declare to you.

9 Who among all these does not know
　　that the hand of the Lord has done this?

10 In his hand is the life of every living thing
　　and the breath of all mankind.

11 Does not the ear try words
　　as the palate tastes food?

12 Wisdom is with the aged,
　　and understanding in length of days.

[g] Or speak to the earth

which does not fit the context; (b) it is addressed to a single person, not to the friends in the plural (and thus might have been originally directed to Job himself either by one of his friends—in which case it has been accidentally displaced—or else by a scandalized scribe who made a marginal comment); (c) it contains the sacred tetragrammaton יהוה (vs. 9b), a fact which violates the consistent practice of the poet throughout the discourses of Job and his friends, since they are supposed to be Arabs rather than members of the covenanted people; (d) it includes in vs. 9b an exact quotation from Isa. 41:20, and this suggests a scribal rather than an original hand, especially since the pronoun **this** does not refer to any identifiable noun in the present context; (e) the thought that **wisdom is with the aged, and understanding in length of days** (vs. 12) is surprising in the mouth of Job (unless it is a sarcastic statement which then needs to be introduced by such an expression as "Yes, indeed . . ."), but normal under the pen of a conventionally-minded annotator; (f) vs. 12 conflicts so sharply with the statement of the context which follows (vs. 13) that many exegetes are compelled to suppose that Job is here quoting the friends, and therefore they supply some syntactic link in order to make the sequence of ideas intelligible: i.e., "Wisdom, you argue, lies with aged men. . . . Nay, . . ." (Moffatt; see Robert Gordis, "Quotations as a Literary Usage in Biblical, Oriental and Rabbinic Literature," *Hebrew Union College Annual*, XXII [1949], 209-10).

To be sure, the monistic view of the universe which is expounded in vs. 10 agrees with Job's thesis:

**In his hand is the life of every living thing
and the breath of all mankind** (cf. 9:22-24).

This verse, however, may constitute a remnant of Job's original exposition on God's indiscriminate and therefore unjust government of men's affairs.

countered in vss. 7-12. The verses may well be spurious. If not, Job is here marshaling against Zophar the weight of all creation's knowledge, viz., that God cannot be let off so easily: he is responsible for every bit of it, good and bad. The prophets say so (vs. 9; cf. 9:24). See now what the bad is like. Nobody with any sense can swallow the kind of **wisdom** the friends have been doling out. Might, yes; understanding, yes (vs. 13); but what great things has God done with them? The record is set down in vss. 14-25 (vs. 22 is perhaps a gloss). It is the kind of

record that Oscar Wilde once set down. He was sure there was enough misery in one narrow London lane to disprove the notion that God is love. In later years when calamity after its kind overtook him, he seemed equally sure that love of some sort is the only possible explanation of the extraordinary amount of suffering there is in the world. The story of human existence can be read both ways. Possibly vss. 17-25 reflect the sad disillusion of the Exile. If so, it would be an interesting comment on the ambiguities of history to list the profound changes wrought in

13 With him *is* wisdom and strength, he hath counsel and understanding.	13 "With God[h] are wisdom and might; he has counsel and understanding.
14 Behold, he breaketh down, and it cannot be built again: he shutteth up a man, and there can be no opening.	14 If he tears down, none can rebuild; if he shuts a man in, none can open.
15 Behold, he withholdeth the waters, and they dry up: also he sendeth them out, and they overturn the earth.	15 If he withholds the waters, they dry up; if he sends them out, they overwhelm the land.
16 With him *is* strength and wisdom: the deceived and the deceiver *are* his.	16 With him are strength and wisdom; the deceived and the deceiver are his.
17 He leadeth counselors away spoiled, and maketh the judges fools.	17 He leads counselors away stripped, and judges he makes fools.
18 He looseth the bond of kings, and girdeth their loins with a girdle.	18 He looses the bonds of kings, and binds a waistcloth on their loins.
19 He leadeth princes away spoiled, and overthroweth the mighty.	19 He leads priests away stripped, and overthrows the mighty.
20 He removeth away the speech of the trusty, and taketh away the understanding of the aged.	20 He deprives of speech those who are trusted, and takes away the discernment of the elders.
21 He poureth contempt upon princes, and weakeneth the strength of the mighty.	21 He pours contempt on princes, and looses the belt of the strong.
22 He discovereth deep things out of darkness, and bringeth out to light the shadow of death.	22 He uncovers the deeps out of darkness, and brings deep darkness to light.
23 He increaseth the nations, and destroyeth them: he enlargeth the nations, and straiteneth them *again*.	23 He makes nations great, and he destroys them: he enlarges nations, and leads them away.
24 He taketh away the heart of the chief of the people of the earth, and causeth them to wander in a wilderness *where there is* no way.	24 He takes away understanding from the chiefs of the people of the earth, and makes them wander in a pathless waste.
25 They grope in the dark without light, and he maketh them to stagger like a drunken man.	25 They grope in the dark without light; and he makes them stagger like a drunken man.
	[h] Heb *him*

(3) An Indiscriminate Ruler of Men (12:13-25)

13-25. The world reveals the absoluteness of the power of God, but not his justice. He is the sole author of all events (vss. 13-21). Even the **deeps** of the cosmos (see 10:21; 11:8) and the utter **darkness** of Sheol are within his grasp (vs. 22) —a thought which is most unusual for the Hebrew mind, according to which Sheol lies beyond the borders of God's jurisdiction (Ps. 6:5; etc.; contrast the exceptional passages: 26:6; Amos 9:2; Ps. 139:8, 11; Prov. 15:11). Not only the fate of individuals but also the rise and fall of nations depend upon his almighty fiat (vss. 23-25). It cannot be denied that there is an austere grandeur in this completely theocentric philosophy of existence. But Job does not submit without protest to the iron rule. The whole passage is to be considered as a prelude to the aggressive thrust of the lines which follow.

the Hebrew-Christian tradition by those years of suffering (cf. Expos. on 7:19 [Act III]; 11:18). Must we not say that God's redeeming purpose, and his power to effect it, are conditioned, relatively though not absolutely, by man's freedom? The Cross itself is the measure both of his weak-ness and his might (see I Cor. 1:25; cf. Expos. on 9:2-10, 14-19). It is not God's power that we should take for granted. We can stand in the way of it. What we may and should take for granted is his bitter intent to our good, whatever the cost. A leper came one day to Jesus,

13 Lo, mine eye hath seen all *this,* mine ear hath heard and understood it.

2 What ye know, *the same* do I know also: I *am* not inferior unto you.

3 Surely I would speak to the Almighty, and I desire to reason with God.

4 But ye *are* forgers of lies, ye *are* all physicians of no value.

5 Oh that ye would altogether hold your peace! and it should be your wisdom.

6 Hear now my reasoning, and hearken to the pleadings of my lips.

7 Will ye speak wickedly for God? and talk deceitfully for him?

8 Will ye accept his person? will ye contend for God?

9 Is it good that he should search you out? or as one man mocketh another, do ye *so* mock him?

13 "Lo, my eye has seen all this, my ear has heard and understood it.

2 What you know, I also know; I am not inferior to you.

3 But I would speak to the Almighty, and I desire to argue my case with God.

4 As for you, you whitewash with lies; worthless physicians are you all.

5 Oh that you would keep silent, and it would be your wisdom!

6 Hear now my reasoning, and listen to the pleadings of my lips.

7 Will you speak falsely for God, and speak deceitfully for him?

8 Will you show partiality toward him, will you plead the case for God?

9 Will it be well with you when he searches you out? Or can you deceive him, as one deceives a man?

---

b) DEFIANCE OF FRIENDSHIP AND GODHEAD (13:1-27)

(1) THE INCOMPETENT HEALERS (13:1-12)

13:3. The expression ואולם אני, "but as for me," is identical with that which opens Eliphaz' advice in 5:8 and may indicate on the part of Job a sarcastic intent. The friend had said, "As for me, I would seek God." Job replies, "But as for me, I would speak to the Almighty." Before he will directly **argue . . . with God,** Job denounces the futility or rather the viciousness of the friends' endeavors. They are "plasterers of lies" (vs. 4) because they **speak falsely for God** (vs. 7) and defend him with **proverbs of ashes** (vs.

---

and kneeling down to him said, "If thou wilt, thou canst make me clean" (Mark 1:40). In a very real sense we are given there the pagan view of God. The Christian on his knees will rather bow his head and whisper, "If thou canst, my mulishness being what it is, thou wilt make me clean."

13:1-12. Check and Countercheck.—Job's "magnificent inconsistency" (Exeg.) provides both a check on his own jaundiced account of God's dealing—one can hardly help feeling that he is dimly aware of it, despite all his bravado and arrogance—and a countercheck on the friends' bootless if not indeed downright reprobate attempt to take God's part by brandishing around half a dozen "old saws." If Job's mind is in danger of becoming godless, his heart is not: for all that and all that, there is a God who will have no truck with lies, not even when you tell them in his behalf. One thing we still have to be: honest. Never for God's sake try to make black seem white. That kind of trickery fools nobody; least of all him. The **rebuke** may fall where you least expect it. Maybe you are in greater danger than I am, he says to his friends. And they were (42:7). It is the "soul's invincible

surmise" [3] that is to be trusted. Nothing else. And Job seems always to be within hailing distance of that. God is not away somewhere, remote and indifferent. There is still a knocking at the door. The sound of it is quite audible in many of the lines that follow: he will not suffer **a godless man** to **come before him**—he is that just (vs. 16), and Job will profit by it; it is not God that would be vindicated in such a trial, but Job himself—so much justice remains with the Unjust. Note also the misgivings that have begun to shake the foundations of his boasted innocence (vss. 23, 26). No wonder that what starts out to be blasphemy turns into appeal (vss. 20-25) before it settles down again into brooding (vss. 26-27); and no wonder that despair for a moment gives way to hope (vs. 16) before the shadow falls once more, darker than ever (14:1-12), with nothing but the light of fitful fires that blaze (14:14-15) and die down (14:18-22). A life is at its wit's end when the self contradicts the self, and God's "Yes" grapples with man's "No." It is the moment of death and birth.

8. Pleading God's Cause.— (Cf. II Sam. 6:6-7). These attorneys for the defense (see Expos. on

[3] George Santayana, "The Better Part."

10 He will surely reprove you, if ye do secretly accept persons.

11 Shall not his excellency make you afraid? and his dread fall upon you?

12 Your remembrances *are* like unto ashes, your bodies to bodies of clay.

13 Hold your peace, let me alone, that I may speak, and let come on me what *will.*

14 Wherefore do I take my flesh in my teeth, and put my life in mine hand?

---

10 He will surely rebuke you
    if in secret you show partiality.
11 Will not his majesty terrify you,
    and the dread of him fall upon you?
12 Your maxims are proverbs of ashes,
    your defences are defences of clay.

13 "Let me have silence, and I will speak,
    and let come on me what may.
14 I will take^i my flesh in my teeth,
    and put my life in my hand.

^{i} Gk: Heb *Why should I take?*

---

12). Having just expounded the indiscriminate character of God's rule over the universe of men, Job is now certain, with a magnificent inconsistency, that the same God **will surely rebuke** these self-appointed defenders (vs. 10). Thus the blasphemer says that God is unjust toward him, but he still believes in God's retributive justice toward his friends!

(2) A God Who Murders (13:13-19)

As is his wont, Job prefaces a daring thought (vs. 15) with a solemn call to attention (vs. 13) and a forewarning of his boldness (vs. 14). The RSV is correct in following the Greek and in omitting at the beginning of vs. 14 the words עַל־מָה, why, which appear to be a dittography of the immediately preceding עלי מה at the end of vs. 13.

14. I will take my flesh in my teeth is paralleled by the clause **and put my life in my hand.** Job will speak, notwithstanding the most severe risks involved (cf. 9:35–10:1). The image of vs. 14b is comparable with that of Judg. 12:3 (cf. I Sam. 19:5; 28:21; Ps. 119:109). The expression of vs. 14a, on the contrary, is not found elsewhere in the O.T.

---

vss. 1-12) were working up their brief out of manifest falsehood—manifest at least to Job. They stood in peril of their own "just" God. So do all men who discount the hazards of faith and misrepresent the claims of the Christian gospel in their altogether laudable effort to win for it a hearing. "Try God," wrote Mary Pickford. "Why not aspirin?" answered Halford Luccock. All *quid pro quo* religion—"You do this and God will do that"—is an attempt to do the Almighty the kind of favor (vs. 8a; the emphasis falls on **God** in vss. 7-8) which he is apt very promptly to repudiate (Mic. 6:8). **Partiality** is preference shown out of relation to any ground that would warrant it (see Expos. on 12:2-6). It is the essence of hypocrisy. It will genuflect before the altar and cheat its neighbor. It will cross itself and shut up "the bowels of its compassion." God will not be beholden to fraud and deceit. Ultimately of course he needs no defense at all that we can offer; nor any persuading by fair words, either on our behalf or his (see Expos. on 22:12-20). A drowning man is not saved by some argument that aims to set forth the advantages of learning how to swim.

12. *Proverbs of Ashes.*—What made them so? There was truth in them; but it was not the kind of truth that heals. It was the kind that embodies the results of experience. It was the kind that could forewarn. It was not the kind that can give peace to a tortured soul. All the capsuled wisdom of the ages cannot do that. It is a startling fact that most of our secular maxims are prudential: "Honesty is the best policy." "Pride goeth before a fall." "A penny saved is a penny earned." "A stitch in time saves nine." Whatever human life thinks worth embalming is likely to prove either a way to get out of difficulty or a way to keep from getting in (see Expos. on 2:11-13; 5:18). The "wisdom" of the Bible is an almost totally different thing. Always it is theological at its core, whether "speculative" in character, as often in Job and Ecclesiastes, or "practical," as in Proverbs. But even so, particularly in the form of quotation *post eventum,* it can scarcely "minister to a mind diseased." Love, and love alone, knows the healing art (see Expos. on 19:21). All other **defences** may have been bulwarks once; to Job they were **clay** now.

13-19. *The Hope Born of Despair.*—(See Exeg. above, also on 16:12-17; cf. Expos. on 12:7-25; 11:18; 19:25.) Fightings without and

15 Though he slay me, yet will I trust in him: but I will maintain mine own ways before him.

15 Behold, he will slay me; I have no hope; yet I will defend my ways to his face.

It may refer to a proverbial trope similar to that quoted by Moses Buttenwieser (*The Book of Job* [New York: The Macmillan Co., 1922], p. 196), "Salim escaped with his life between his jaws" (i.e., "his life was leaving him"). It may also allude to a man who places between his teeth or his hands his most treasured property—in this case, his life—as a challenge to his enemies, and thus implies the taunt, "Come and take it, if you dare!"

15. The RSV differs sharply from the KJV. The sublime expression of selfless faith, **Yet will I trust in him** (KJV), is translated not from the M.T., but from the marginal note of the Masoretes. Both the text (*Kethîbh*) and the marginal correction (*Qerê*) sound alike when read aloud, but the former is spelled לא איחל, *lō' 'ayaḥēl*, the latter לו איחל, *lô 'ayaḥēl*. The famous English rendering of this verse introduces in the text a syntactic link, **yet,** which is neither in the consonantal MSS nor in the marginal correction, but which makes the meaning apparently intended by the Masoretes more intelligible to the readers of the translations. The question of the original text is most difficult.

On the one hand, the M.T. לא, "not," is perhaps the result of an accidental corruption, for the marginal correction לו, "to him," is supported by several versions which are anterior to the time when the M.T. was fixed (LXXA, Syriac, Targ., Vulg.). The only certain fact is that the KJV is an impossibility, for even if the marginal reading לו were adopted as authentic, the natural sense of the verse would be either (*a*) "I shall wait for him," i.e., "to strike me," and I shall be in a state of defiant expectation; or (*b*) "I shall wait for it," i.e., "death," and I shall be adamant in my claim unto the end.

Against these various renderings, and consequently against the authenticity of the marginal reading לו, one must argue that the verb יחל, as it is used elsewhere in biblical Hebrew with the preposition ל, suggests the sense of "waiting" not for evil but for good (see 30:26). Yet one cannot translate in the direction of the KJV, "I shall wait for him (with confidence)," because such a statement could not be followed immediately by the restrictive word אך, "only," "but," "nevertheless," in vs. 15*b*. If, then, one accepts the M.T. as authentic, the translation is **I have no hope** (RSV).

The conjecture of an accidental corruption, through metathesis, of the verb איחל from an original אחיל is attractive. Job expects to be killed by God, and he adds, "I do not tremble" (Graetz, Ehrlich, *et al.*). However, such a hypothesis cannot be clearly proved.

Another translation is possible and even probable. The first word of vs. 15, הן, is usually understood as an interjection meaning, "Behold!" In many cases, however (see

---

fears within: there is no escape from them by means of educational processes or psychological techniques or planned economies. Man has learned how to alleviate a good many of the pains of living; if he had the will to apply what he knows, he could make human existence almost incredibly more tolerable than it is. What he does not readily learn is that he is himself his own insoluble problem. Job is beginning to show some signs of what the lawyers call a change of venue. He is beginning to contend not so much with God as with himself. His confidence in his own unaided innocence, in his ability to save himself by himself, is being shaken: the issue is going to turn, far more surely than he had thought, on the kind of God who

beyond all injustice is just. Blake [4] precisely at this point represents Job as lifting his eyes to God, away from the accusing figures of his friends, only to see that the "God of Justice" all of them had been commending to him was in reality Eliphaz' God, with a cloven hoof (see Expos. on 4:20*b*). There are the first faint indications now of a straining toward God's "proper work," which is mercy. That can happen only when the hard protective shell of humanity's misplaced reliance on itself is broken.

15. *An Inspired Mistake?*— (See Exeg.) To how many has this "sublime mistranslation" brought courage and peace! (Cf. 19:25.) It cannot be held to convey the original meaning of

[4] Illustrations X, XI.

16 He also *shall be* my salvation: for a hypocrite shall not come before him.

16 This will be my salvation, that a godless man shall not come before him.

Exod. 4:1; Lev. 25:20; etc.), and especially in Job (see 4:18; 12:14, 15; etc.), it introduces a conditional clause and corresponds to the Aramaic conjunction "if." Granted that such is its meaning in this passage, vs. 15a becomes intimately connected with vs. 15b (which otherwise follows without a strict sequence of thought) and the meaning of the C.T. becomes:

> If he slays me, I have no hope!
> Nevertheless, I will defend my behavior in his very presence!

All indications point to an imminent death, and Job agrees with his friends that if the Almighty God, in whose existence he believes, intends to exterminate him, there is not for him any prospect of salvation upon this earth. But he will not be silenced by the threat or the fear of death. His courage—one might even say his arrogance—is intensified by the certainty of his innocence. He will speak at all costs. He has nothing to lose. Indeed, he has everything to gain because, if God murders him, Job will at least meet his divine enemy who has heretofore refused to answer his cry.

16. The prospect of meeting God at last, face to face, even if it means death, brings a new thought to Job's frenzied mind. At the precise moment of his extremity, just when he considers the loss of his life to be inevitable, and therefore gives up any hope for the vindication of his righteousness, Job sees a faint glimmer in the recesses of his gloom. A new hope emerges from his very despair: "Even this [read with LXX היא instead of the M.T. הוא] might become for me (the cause of my) salvation, for no godless man ever dares to face him" (lit., "ever comes to his face").

This is one of the most profound statements of the poem and its import would be considerably lessened, if not altogether eclipsed, were one to accept the traditional English rendering of vs. 15aβ, **yet will I trust in him**. Indeed, it can hardly be maintained that the honest abandonment of this sublime mistranslation impoverishes the Bible in general or the poem of Job in particular.

In effect, the correct rendering **I have no hope** is rhetorically, psychologically, and theologically far more pregnant with meaning than the statement of "faith at all cost," when it is viewed in the light of the whole context, especially of the unexpected and dramatic lifting of tension in vs. 16. Job has announced in vs. 13 that he was going to risk his life by uttering a blasphemy. Surely it would be rhetorically grotesque were such a spiritual earthquake to peter out into an expression of submissive faith. On the contrary, one can appreciate the degree of awe with which Job himself must have said, "If he murders me, I have no hope." Likewise, there is an incomparable upsurge of diction as Job passes from the statement of his despair in vs. 15 to the sudden renewal of his hope

---

the poet; but out of the confusion and uncertainty of the text it leans its way instinctively toward the selfless devotion in which alone Job's questions can find their answer. That answer can never be written out: it has to be lived out in faith—between persons. "Father, into thy hands I commend my spirit" (Luke 23:46).

In either of the translations preferred by the Exeg. stress should be laid on the heightening of that sense of human worth and dignity which is so marked a characteristic of the poem as a whole (see Expos. on 1:1). There are times when Job seems almost to feel that he is dwarfed

against the background of God's ineffable majesty and power (cf. vs. 25; 14:3; etc.). Here indeed is one of his perils: he might well have come to think that in the magnificence and vastness of this universe—for he understands God's greatness better than the friends—he amounted to nothing at all. Yet he never gives way to it (see Expos. on 9:14-19; 17:9). On the contrary, he insists that not even God himself can be suffered to maneuver or coerce a man's conscience. Eliphaz, Bildad, Zophar—each has maintained that if only Job would give up that pretension to innocence, God would deal merci-

17 Hear diligently my speech, and my declaration with your ears.	17 Listen carefully to my words, and let my declaration be in your ears.
18 Behold now, I have ordered *my* cause; I know that I shall be justified.	18 Behold, I have prepared my case; I know that I shall be vindicated.
19 Who *is* he *that* will plead with me? for now, if I hold my tongue, I shall give up the ghost.	19 Who is there that will contend with me? For then I would be silent and die.

in vs. 16. Psychologically, the poet reveals once again his sharp and penetrating knowledge of human moods. Job is man himself, buffeted without, fractured within. But he must reach the extremity of anguish before he can be found by the new truth which shall make him free. Theologically at last Job takes his place among all men of honor and achievement who need to lose all hope in their own merit in order to grasp the basic fact of man's inability to save himself. At this stage the hero is still a long way from discovering either the theological dimensions of his sinfulness or the all-inclusiveness of God's mercy. Nevertheless, the conviction of his innocence will soon be shaken (see vss. 23 ff.). While he still tries to vindicate himself (vs. 15b), he no longer dares to say at this juncture that he is "righteous and perfect." He begins to turn, at the very depth of his hopelessness, to a thought which creates a new hope—that no *hānēph,* i.e., no profane, irreligious man, no apostate (see 8:13) would ever wish or be rash enough to dare meeting God face to face. If Job had not said in vs. 15a that he had no hope, he would not have been able to comprehend that a real bond still existed between the Almighty and himself. Thus his theological perception is growing in profundity: while God, for no apparent reason, may murder man, and therefore may be judged as amoral, he is at the same time so much God that only a certain type of man may approach him. In a sense, therefore, the poet anticipates the evangelical saying, "Blessed are the pure of heart: for they shall see God" (Matt. 5:8).

17-19. Listen carefully: Rather, "Keep on listening," "hear again and again," a prophetic expression (see Isa. 6:9; 55:2) which is used in a context of antagonism and anticipates a negative reaction.

I know that I shall be vindicated (vs. 18b) sums up the stage of spiritual development which Job has reached at the end of the first cycle of discussion. Although he no longer asserts his innocence, he is certain that his righteousness will be proclaimed at the time of his trial (contrast with 19:25a, "I know that my Redeemer liveth").

The challenge of vs. 19a is parallel to the question of the servant of Yahweh in

fully with him; and Job has more than half believed them. But he will not be bribed or threatened into doing it. Not even to secure God's favor will he be false to himself.

Pascal says:
"Were the Universe to crush him, man would still be more noble than that which has slain him, because he knows that he dies, and that the Universe has the better of him. The Universe knows nothing of this." While the modern writer admires intelligent man facing an unintelligent Universe, which has the power to crush him, the ancient poet is awed at the thought of man as a moral being confronting the Maker and Ruler of an immoral Universe, who may have the will to annihilate him. The one reveals the majesty of mind opposing matter, the other the still greater majesty of conscience opposing omnipotent tyranny.[5]

[5] James Strahan, *The Book of Job* (2nd ed.; Edinburgh: T. & T. Clark, 1914), pp. 126-27. Used by permission.

"I will take my life in my teeth, and defend my ways to his face." There is a dignity about that, and a grandeur. It broke into life afresh at the Reformation, the kind of integrity and stature that will challenge any hand to strike it down, even God's hand. "Though devils all the world should fill. . . ."[6] Recall old Andrew Melville, clutching at the robes of Scotland's peevish monarch as he ranted up and down the room prating of his divine right as king: "There are two kings and two kingdoms in Scotland: there is King James the head of this commonwealth, and there is Christ Jesus the King of the church, whose subject James the Sixth is, and of whose kingdom he is not a king, nor a lord, nor a head, but a member."[7]

[6] Martin Luther, "A mighty fortress is our God."
[7] Thomas McCrie, *Life of Andrew Melville* (Edinburgh: William Blackwood, 1824), I, 391-92.

20 Only do not two *things* unto me; then will I not hide myself from thee.	20 Only grant two things to me, then I will not hide myself from thy face:
21 Withdraw thine hand far from me: and let not thy dread make me afraid.	21 withdraw thy hand far from me, and let not dread of thee terrify me.
22 Then call thou, and I will answer: or let me speak, and answer thou me.	22 Then call, and I will answer; or let me speak, and do thou reply to me.
23 How many *are* mine iniquities and sins? make me to know my transgression and my sin.	23 How many are my iniquities and my sins? Make me know my transgression and my sin.

Isa. 50:8, "Who will contend with me?" The difference is great, however, between the two passages; for in the latter the challenger is assured of God's help and protection, while in the former Job is left alone, still contending against God. Since the transition between vs. 19*a* and vs. 19*b* is elliptical, and the word עתה (vs. 19*b*) may mean either **now,** "soon," or **then,** the whole verse is susceptible of at least two interpretations: (*a*) According to most commentators, Job is certain of his case and therefore asks, "Who is he that will risk contending with me? (If there should be such a man, and if he should succeed in proving me wrong), then [עתה] I would be silent and die." (*b*) More probably the verse indicates that Job's cocksureness is beginning to weaken as doubts enter his mind precisely at the instant of his claim, **I know that I shall be justified** (vs. 18*b*). In order to dispel this tantalizing uncertainty, let a challenge be issued, "Who is [he] that will plead against me? (He should do it right early), for then [עתה] I shall be silent and expire."

Job is asking for a speedy court action in view of the imminent prospect of his death. He has already said, "Presently, I shall lie in the earth" (7:21). It is God, not man, with whom he implicitly wants to plead. This interpretation is confirmed by the prayer of the next lines, for which vs. 19*a* constitutes a subtle transition.

(3) Summons to God (13:20-27)

20-27. As on two earlier occasions (7:12 ff.; 10:2 ff.), Job is led by the intensity of his religious emotion to turn abruptly from a discourse on God to a direct appeal. There cannot be a fair trial if the defendant is abused by torture. As in 9:34, he makes a preliminary request (vss. 20-21); then he accepts in advance the type of judicial procedure which will be agreeable to his divine opponent: he is ready to plead either as defendant or as complainant (vs. 22). Since God remains silent, Job proceeds with the latter course: he will attack.

But his long-asserted consciousness of innocence has at last been shattered: "How many iniquities and sins have I?" (vs. 23*a*). The sufferer is searching his conscience as well as asking God. He has no clear conviction of guilt, but his friends have suggested in diverse manners that his sins are the direct cause of his plight. Is he utterly blind about himself? He begs for clear understanding: "Reveal unto me my transgression and my sin" (vs. 23*b*). As again the prayer remains unanswered, the crouching giant, now at the point of yielding, recovers enough self-assurance to consider another explanation of his

20-21. Only Two Things.—There can be no bargaining with God. Job says, "If only thou wilt ease my pain and remove from my heart the terror of thy presence, **I will not hide myself from thy face**" (cf. 9:34-35). Observe that these are the **two things** which God does not do (38:1–42:6). The change that takes place (40:4-5; 42:2-6) takes place in spite of it. The suffering has not yet passed, but there is no resentment any more. The terror is vaster than even Job had dreamed, but there is no groveling before it. God moves in his own mysterious ways, not by our charts and compass, to a better good than ours.

20-27. Questions that God Turns Around.—Already in vs. 19*a* Job has entertained the shadow of a thought that disturbs him (see Exeg.). Now, one after the other, he puts four

24 Wherefore hidest thou thy face, and holdest me for thine enemy?

25 Wilt thou break a leaf driven to and fro? and wilt thou pursue the dry stubble?

26 For thou writest bitter things against me, and makest me to possess the iniquities of my youth.

27 Thou puttest my feet also in the stocks, and lookest narrowly unto all my paths; thou settest a print upon the heels of my feet.

28 And he, as a rotten thing, consumeth, as a garment that is moth-eaten.

24 Why dost thou hide thy face,
    and count me as thy enemy?

25 Wilt thou frighten a driven leaf
    and pursue dry chaff?

26 For thou writest bitter things against me,
    and makest me inherit the iniquities of
    my youth.

27 Thou puttest my feet in the stocks,
    and watchest all my paths;
    thou settest a bound to the soles of my
    feet.

28 Man^j wastes away like a rotten thing,
    like a garment that is moth-eaten.

^{j} Heb *He*

misery: If I am not a criminal, then, **Why dost thou hide thy face, and count me as thy enemy?** (vs. 24). The word for **enemy** (אויב) is probably a cognate of the name Job (איוב). The hero is stunned by the seeming hostility of the master of men. For this deeply consecrated believer all calamities—loss of wealth, children, health, friendship, and honor—are less excruciating than spiritual loneliness and the sense of abandonment by God. He could well ask with another, "My God, my God, why hast thou forsaken me?" (Ps. 22:1). God hides his face when he is angry (Ps. 27:9; Isa. 54:8) or indifferent (Ps. 30:7), and his enmity is the more baffling since it follows so abruptly a long-enjoyed communion and favor.

Failing to find an answer to the second question, Job asks a third (vs. 25): He has now become a shadow of his former self. Is **a driven leaf** or **dry chaff** worth divine pursuit, or dangerous enough to warrant divine persecution? (See 7:12, 20.) A fourth idea strikes his distraught mind. Is then his calamity due to the **iniquities of** [his] **youth** (vs. 26b; cf. Ps. 25:7)? He is desperately trying to "justify the ways of God to men" (Milton, *Paradise Lost*, Bk. I, l. 26). Since no sin of his manhood can explain his ill fate, is it conceivable that God should now make him bear the guilt of errors committed in his early youth? Notice that the word נעורים suggests "shy, early adolescence" rather than "exuberant, lustful, vigorous, and mature youth" (which would have been expressed by the word עלומים), and thus considerably minimizes the gravity of a "guilt" which could not be described as even "the sowing of wild oats." The mystery of his present suffering thus remains almost entire. However irresponsible his behavior may have been when he was a youngster, surely the stringency of the penalty (vs. 27) remains out of all proportion to the vagaries of his early adolescence.

c) Fate of Mortal Man (13:28–14:22)

The third discourse of Job, and with it the first cycle of discussion, is brought to a close with a poem on human destiny which divides itself into four strophes: the first strophe paints the picture of man's mortality (13:28–14:6); the second deals with the finality of man's death (14:7-12); the third wildly imagines an afterlife (14:13-17); the fourth falls back upon the theme of man's irrevocable fate of annihilation (14:18-22).

(1) Picture of Man's Mortality (13:28–14:6)

Most exegetes recognize that 13:28 either is out of place or represents a marginal notation. The verse begins with **And he,** which obviously refers to **man,** although this

questions which are in reality questions his own conscience is putting to him: Guiltless, you say (vs. 23)? Abandoned are you (vs. 24)? Of no moment to God (vs. 25)? The victim of some long-forgotten ill that flesh is heir to (vs. 26)?

To ask is to be forced to answer, every man for himself. "Art thou he that should come?" "Is it lawful to pay tribute to Caesar?" "When shall these things be?" "Art thou a king then?" Every one of them hurtling up toward heaven—and

14 Man *that is* born of a woman *is* of few days, and full of trouble.

2 He cometh forth like a flower, and is cut down: he fleeth also as a shadow, and continueth not.

3 And dost thou open thine eyes upon such a one, and bringest me into judgment with thee?

4 Who can bring a clean *thing* out of an unclean? not one.

14 "Man that is born of a woman
is of few days, and full of trouble.

2 He comes forth like a flower, and withers;
he flees like a shadow, and continues not.

3 And dost thou open thy eyes upon such a one
and bring him[k] into judgment with thee?

4 Who can bring a clean thing out of an unclean?
There is not one.

[k] Gk Syr Vg: Heb *me*

word does not appear before the next line (14:1). According to several commentators its original place may have been after 14:6b, where the sequence of thought is rhetorically striking and the tenses of the verbs are in agreement (ירצה, "he will enjoy," in 14:6b and יבלה, "he will waste away," in 13:28). The reading of 14:6 and 13:28 together would then be as follows:

> Look away from him, and desist,
> that he may enjoy, like a hireling, his day (14:6).

> [But he] wastes away like a rotten thing,
> like a garment that is moth-eaten (13:28).

Other critics prefer to preserve the present order undisturbed, pointing out that the emphatic use of the pronoun והוא at the beginning of 13:28a may easily stand for an original feminine (in English, neuter) והיא, meaning: "And it is like a rotten [tree which] wastes away." This comparison would then echo the image of the "driven leaf" in 13:25, and thus could stay at its present place. Yet the location of the line after 14:6 might just as well be defended on the ground that it prepares for the image of the tree in 14:7 ff.

14:1-3. Man . . . born of a woman: As in 7:1 ff., Job speaks for the whole of mankind ('*ādhām*), but the present train of his thought bears more heavily on life's brevity than on life's misery. In any case, man's insignificance does not justify God's sharp scrutiny (vs. 3; cf. 7:17-19). The shift of person from **such a one** (vs. 3a) to **me** (vs. 3b) shows once more that Job cannot dwell on the general without soon falling back on the particular. However, the LXX, Vulg., and Syriac read ואתו, **and . . . him** (RSV), rather than the M.T. ואתי, **and . . . me** (KJV).

4. Who can bring a clean thing out of an unclean? not one: Several exegetes consider this verse as a marginal note for three reasons: (*a*) it is an unusually short line; (*b*) it is missing in one Hebrew MS; (*c*) it introduces a note of sinfulness in a passage concerned

echoing to the earth again. "What think ye?" "How readest thou?"

14:1-6. The Brevity of Life.—(Cf. Expos. on 7:1-6, 6.) Job makes the point that life is both short and troubled. It is **like a flower, . . . a shadow:** the familiar similes of how many generations! Its end is decreed, its bounds are set (vs. 5). Surely, being short, it should be happy; but it is not. The only pleasure a man can possibly have in it is the pleasure **a hireling** gets out of his drudgery. Eliphaz has said (5:7) that **trouble** is somehow a part of man's primeval inheritance: he is both born to it and respon-

sible for it. Job is interested here merely in stating the fact (see Expos. on 6:8-13). And in arguing from it that God should not add to its burden, but should show a little compassion, **look away** for pity's sake (7:19; 10:20), not hold people to such strict account; especially since everybody is **unclean** anyway—Job no more than the others—and nobody important enough (7:20a, 21a; 13:24-25) for God to stare at him so intently (see Browning's "Instans Tyrannus" and Blake's Illustration XI, the God of the cloven hoof). On the same premises it could have been argued (*a*) that the only sense **to be**

5 Seeing his days *are* determined, the number of his months *are* with thee, thou hast appointed his bounds that he cannot pass;

6 Turn from him, that he may rest, till he shall accomplish, as a hireling, his day.

7 For there is hope of a tree, if it be cut down, that it will sprout again, and that the tender branch thereof will not cease.

5 Since his days are determined,
   and the number of his months is with thee,
   and thou hast appointed his bounds that he cannot pass,
6 look away from him, and desist,[l]
   that he may enjoy, like a hireling, his day.

7 "For there is hope for a tree,
   if it be cut down, that it will sprout again,
   and that its shoots will not cease.

[l] Cn: Heb *that he may desist*

only with life's transitoriness. These are precarious arguments: (*a*) the Hebrew meter is not inflexible and often adapts itself to the abruptness of a poetic idea; (*b*) one MS may have an accidental omission; (*c*) in the same chapter Job is indeed concerned with his "sin," "transgression," and "guilt" (vss. 16-17). In addition, the idea of mankind's uncleanness may have been brought to the poet's mind by the formula of vs. 1, **man . . . born of a woman,** since the thought it represents is akin to that of Ps. 51:5 (cf. Ps. 14:3). Job, like Eliphaz (4:17), acknowledges the universality of man's impurity and thus makes an implicit plea for God's understanding: his own case is not different from that of his fellow human beings. No more than the text of Ps. 51:5 does this line refer to any ritual impurity involved in the act of conception itself (against the paraphrasing of Vulg., *de immundo conceptum semine*); it merely points out the corporate solidarity of the human race and the deep connection of its sinful nature with universal death.

(2) FINALITY OF MAN'S DEATH (14:7-12)

7-12. Religious rites and beliefs in the ancient Near East cultivated the hope of a resurrection after the grave. Job polemizes bluntly against these attractive illusions: **Man**

made out of trouble lies in the victory that can be won over it; and (*b*) that the brevity of life may conceivably underscore the urgency both of duty and love. W. Cosby Bell records the legend of Jubal: how in the days before death came, life seemed to be shallowing out. It "had neither gravity nor greatness." Tomorrow would do as well as today. Endless opportunity, endless boredom. Then suddenly there was an empty place by the fire. A footstep that had grown familiar would never be heard again. There might be no tomorrow—only today, and its infinitely dear and precious hours (see Expos. on 3:17).

Human relationships took on a new depth and tenderness in the knowledge that not forever would they run on unbroken; and one day a man risked his life to save his friend from the leap of a beast, and that was the birthday of heroism in the world. So did death breathe into life the spirit from which came all things fine and great.[8]

[8] *If a Man Die* (New York: Charles Scribner's Sons, 1934), pp. 65-66.

7-12. When a Man Dies He Is Dead.—"If you are dead, then you *are* dead." In *The Church's Witness to God's Design,*[9] prepared under the auspices of the World Council of Churches, this was listed by Emil Brunner as one of the axioms of modern man. He has an idea that he knows what kind of world he lives in. Death seems to him on the face of it fairly conclusive. Aldous Huxley said that he and his friends, in the years of their untrammeled youth, preferred it that way. Job of course is not speaking with any of the scientific or philosophical presuppositions of the twentieth century: the poet is having him speak out of the context of the Hebrew religion. This is precisely the popular Hebrew notion of the so-called "life" after death: it goes on as being, but it amounts to no more than a dreary sort of not-being (see Exeg. on 12:13-25; Expos. on 3:17). Even though the whole face of nature is changed, the dead will be forever the same (vss. 11-12; so Kissane).

What has to be said for Job in this connection is that he seems to understand how incongruous

[9] New York: Harper & Bros., 1948, p. 84.

8 Though the root thereof wax old in the earth, and the stock thereof die in the ground;

9 *Yet* through the scent of water it will bud, and bring forth boughs like a plant.

10 But man dieth, and wasteth away: yea, man giveth up the ghost, and where *is* he?

11 *As* the waters fail from the sea, and the flood decayeth and drieth up;

12 So man lieth down, and riseth not: till the heavens *be* no more, they shall not awake, nor be raised out of their sleep.

13 Oh that thou wouldest hide me in the grave, that thou wouldest keep me secret,

8 Though its root grow old in the earth,
  and its stump die in the ground,
9 yet at the scent of water it will bud
  and put forth branches like a young plant.
10 But man dies, and is laid low;
  man breathes his last, and where is he?
11 As waters fail from a lake,
  and a river wastes away and dries up,
12 So man lies down and rises not again;
  till the heavens are no more he will not awake,
  or be roused out of his sleep.
13 Oh that thou wouldest hide me in Sheol,
  that thou wouldest conceal me until thy wrath be past,

---

lies down and rises not again (vs. 12*a*). In vss. 11 and 12*b* (cf. Isa. 19:5) the poet may be thinking of Egyptian ideas about the afterlife, and thus contemplating for an anxious moment the possibility of a new existence after death. The determination with which he rejects this hope betrays the fascination that such beliefs exercise on his mind. He rejects them, but he cannot help dwelling upon them a little longer in the lines following.

(3) VISION OF AN AFTERLIFE (14:13-17)

Doubt arises immediately after the specific denial. Not as a result of intellectual speculation, but as the fruit of religious groping in prayer: **Oh that thou wouldest . . . remember me!** (vs. 13). Once again Job has risen from the level of meditation to that of warm and intimate dialogue. This call from person to person enables him to restate his wildly imaginative hope in the form of a question, **If a man die, shall he live again?**

---

such an issue is (see Expos. on vss. 13-15), not only because man is "the work" of God's "hands" (vs. 15; see Expos. on 10:8-12), but because God is the kind of God Job still deeply thinks he is (see Exeg. on vss. 13-17). Moreover, there is no surrender of human dignity in any event (see Expos. on 13:15). It has been said that the pessimism of the author of Job is profounder than that of any other of the writers of Israel, profounder even than that of Ecclesiastes: for in Job both to the poet and the hero life seems "incurably evil, unbearably sad, atrociously tragic." Certainly Job understands the wretchedness of it; yet he knows its grandeur too, and that must not be forgotten. Thomas Huxley bitterly resented the suggestion that this life, without any belief in a life to come, would inevitably sink to the level of the bestial. Job would have resented it too. Let be what will be, he will hold his ground (13:14-15; 17:9). The reason for it, however, is that for him God is still in the picture and cannot be got out. Has even the self-professed atheist that much of the image of God in him still?

13-15. What If . . . ?—Kissane thinks that for the sake of a more logical order vss. 13-17 should precede vss. 7-12, not follow them;[1] but "logical order" is hardly a prime requisite in the mind of a man distraught. In their present context these verses record Job's sudden and instinctive (?) revulsion from the impenetrable gloom into which his mood of a moment before had settled; such a prospect as that would not come near making man meaningless, it would come near making God meaningless (see Expos. on vss. 7-12; 10:8-12, 13-17). Job seems to be halfway *out* of the prevailing view with regard to death—a God like God could not allow his handiwork to slither away into nothingness like that, out of all relation to him and the love he bore it (vs. 15; cf. 10:3); yet still halfway *in* (vss. 7-12), without even the poor this-worldly solace a Hebrew would have found in the thought of his posterity (vss. 21-22; cf. Eccl. 9:5-6). It is this movement from one to the other that in the O.T. records God's steady self-revealing invasion of human life, until Job's "What if?" becomes the "What then" of Rom. 8:31.

13. Until Thy Wrath Be Past.—(See Ps. 103; especially vs. 9.) There is still a whisper in

[1] *Job*, pp. 82-83.

until thy wrath be past, that thou wouldest appoint me a set time, and remember me!

14 If a man die, shall he live *again?* all the days of my appointed time will I wait, till my change come.

15 Thou shalt call, and I will answer thee: thou wilt have a desire to the work of thine hands.

that thou wouldest appoint me a set time, and remember me!

14 If a man die, shall he live again?
All the days of my service I would wait,
till my release should come.

15 Thou wouldest call, and I would answer thee;
thou wouldest long for the work of thy hands.

(vs. 14*a*). Philosophical skepticism usually undermines in a negative way the acceptance of a positive dogma. Job's doubt, on the contrary, spurred by a prayer which will not let God go, undermines a negative certainty to prepare for an affirmative faith. The question of vs. 14*a* is not asked by a thinker observing the human situation but by a lover preimagining his partner's attitude: **Thou wouldest hide me, . . . conceal me, . . . appoint me a set time** ["make a date with me"], **. . . remember me** [vs. 13], **call, . . . long for** [lit., "become pale with the passion of desire," or "faint from delayed or thwarted expectation"; cf. Ps. 84:2].

This is not merely the hope of an afterlife. It is the certainty of the unbrokenness, beyond physical death, of a communion which unites God and man on earth (cf. Ps. 73:24-26[?]). If Job knew that at the end of his **service** (vs. 14*b*) God would **call** (vs. 15)

Job's heart. Is it God's whisper? Is there still somewhere in this mysterious universe a love that will not let us go; that in a compassion on the other side of wrath will hide a man away, keep him in secret for a while, bring to an end too at some appointed time his sojourn there in Sheol (cf. vs. 5)? O God, **remember me!** With all the stored-up yearning of his soul he reaches out his hands for what his mind has forbidden him. Is the wish father to the thought, or is God father to the wish? "All the days of my service I would wait." Said an officer in World War I: "I have seen a captain send one of his men to certain death; and I have seen that man salute and turn on his heel to obey. Shall I not do as much, whatever God bids me suffer, wherever he bids me go?"

14. The Doubt that Unsettles Doubt.— (See Exeg. on vss. 13-17, and Expos., pp. 905-7.) Strahan[2] quotes from Browning's "Bishop Blougram's Apology,"

Just when we are safest, there's a sunset touch,
A fancy from a flower-bell, some one's death,
A chorus-ending from Euripides,—
And that's enough for fifty hopes and fears
As old and new at once as nature's self,
To rap and knock and enter in our soul,

and adds that here it is not "a fancy from a flower-bell" but "a fancy from an old tree-stem, as good as dead, and yet, at the scent of water, shooting up again in green felicity." Perhaps it were better for us to doubt our doubts than to doubt our faith. Are we as ready to give a

² *Job*, pp. 133-34.

reason for the faith that is in us as we are to give a reason for the doubt that tries to undermine it? And how closely do we scrutinize the "reasons"? There is much in the world to unsettle the doctrinaire, wherever he throws in his lot, with the "Yes" or with the "No" (read Wordsworth's "Intimations of Immortality"; see Expos. on 10:8-12, 13-17). What of birth, which must be to the infant very much as death is to us? What of the Resurrection, and the gospel that sprang out of it full-grown, as Minerva sprang from the head of Jove? What of the church which that gospel fashioned? Is all of it meaningless? Or is there still a whisper of God in the ear? Whisper or shout? (See Expos. on vss. 1-6, 13; 19:25.)

14*b*. The Sufferings of This Present Time.— Job says that if he could believe what he yearns to believe, he could go through with anything— both here and hereafter (on "waiting" see Expos. on 8:20-22). To what extent in actual fact does the faith we profess in the life that shall be change the aspect of the life that now is? In Eugene O'Neill's play *Lazarus Laughed*,[3] the brother of Mary and Martha comes back to the world with a strangely inverted sense of values. Maybe the "great" things are small, and the "small" great. Maybe we ourselves are greater than we thought.

15. The God Beyond God.—In Blake's engravings, all through the prologue the figure of God appears right foot forward, symbol of spirit and good. In Illustration XI, as has been noted (see Expos. on 13:13-19), the left foot is a

³ New York: Horace Liveright, 1927.

16 For now thou numberest my steps:
dost thou not watch over my sin?

17 My transgression *is* sealed up in a bag,
and thou sewest up mine iniquity.

16 For then thou wouldest number my steps,
thou wouldest not keep watch over my
sin;

17 my transgression would be sealed up in a
bag,
and thou wouldest cover over my
iniquity.

---

then, not unlike Jacob serving for Rachel, he would gladly endure his present "forced labor" and would **answer** the divine invitation. The question of life eternal is not asked here or elsewhere in the Bible on philosophical or ethical grounds; it is raised by the love of man for God, and the response of man to God's **desire** or longing for **the work of [his] hands.**

16. This verse is translated in two conflicting ways: (*a*) The KJV, followed by the ERV, ASV, Amer. Trans., and many exegetes, considers that the initial words כי עתה, "but now," establish a brutal contrast between lyrical fantasy and present realities. Vs. 16*a* is thus rendered, **For now thou numberest my steps:** A pejorative expression, suggesting the sharp watchfulness of a spy (cf. 7:20*b*; 31:4, 37; 34:21). Vs. 16*b*, however, reads, lit., "Thou dost not watch over my sin," which for the sake of consistency is either interpreted as an interrogative sentence (KJV) or corrected into an affirmative clause (by deletion of the negative לא). The difficulty may not have been sensed by the translators of the LXX, for they read, "Thou dost not overlook any of my sins," presumably presupposing such a verb as תערב instead of M.T. תשמר. (*b*) The RSV and several modern exegetes consider that vs. 16 continues the picture of intimate harmony with God delineated in vss. 13-15, and thus interpret the initial words of vs. 16*a*, כי עתה, as referring to the future, **For then.** In this way the rendering of vs. 16*b* would be quite satisfactory: **Thou wouldest not keep watch over my sin,** but vs. 16*a* would have to be understood in a good sense: **For then thou wouldest number my steps** (with loving care), an interpretation which is not supported by other usages of the same idiom (see above). A possible way out of the difficulty would be to follow the reading of the Syriac (which introduces the negative לא in vs. 16*a*) and to translate, "Then thou wouldest *not* number my steps." On the other hand, if the present M.T. is correct one might follow Dhorme's suggestion and suppose that vs. 16*a* refers to the present, while vs. 16*b* returns to the contemplation of God's future favor: "Whereas *now* thou numberest my steps (then) thou wouldest not watch over my sin." However, vs. 17 most probably indicates that Job's turn of thought has already fallen back on the dark present, and consequently the first interpretation of vs. 16 (see above) seems definitely preferable.

17. This verse at first sight presents the same ambiguity as vs. 16, and many critics hold that its meaning depends on the latter's interpretation. An opposite reasoning is just as tenable. Some translators and commentators (see KJV) believe that the sealing of a transgression in a bag (vs. 17*a*) refers to the maintenance of its memory for the purpose of eventual indictment. Others (see RSV) find in the same expression the assurance that Job's transgression will be hidden from God's sight and thus eventually forgotten. Likewise, in vs. 17*b*, some interpreters (see KJV) hold that the verb טפל means

---

cloven hoof: "The God of Justice is only Satan, masquerading as an angel of light." [4] In Illustration XIII God answers Job out of the whirlwind, right foot forward once more. The artist-poet has caught the kaleidoscopic changes wrought in the mind of Job by the conflict between longing and resentment going on in his soul (see Expos. on 7:21*c*; 10:8-12, 13-17; see

[4] Damon, *Doctrine of Job, ad loc.*

also 7:7-10, 21; 9:33; 17:3; 19:25-27). Job for a moment envisions the day when "the God of grace" will call him back again to life and to the restoration of that fellowship which "the God of wrath" has broken off. The eternal gospel casts its Shadow before (John 1:17; Rom. 8:1; yet see Exeg. on 16:18-22; Expos. on 16:19).

16. The Watcher of Men.—Cf. Exeg. on vs. 17; Expos. on 7:20*a*; 16:13; etc.

18 And surely the mountain falling cometh to nought, and the rock is removed out of his place.	**18** "But the mountain falls and crumbles away, 　　and the rock is removed from its place;
19 The waters wear the stones: thou washest away the things which grow *out* of the dust of the earth; and thou destroyest the hope of man.	**19** the waters wear away the stones; 　　the torrents wash away the soil of the earth; 　　so thou destroyest the hope of man.

"to glue over," "to smear," "to plaster," and therefore describes figuratively the process by which Job's guilt is carefully preserved and remembered. Other exegetes (see RSV) find in it an allusion to its "covering," not for the sake of its preservation, but on the contrary for its concealment and eventual disappearance.

Three considerations seem to have been overlooked. (*a*) The sealing of a transgression in a bag (vs. 17*a*) can hardly be done for the purpose of hiding and forgetting. The צרור is a purse or pouch used for storing and safekeeping (Gen. 42:35; Prov. 7:20). Even when figuratively used, the word is never connected with the idea of eventual loss, but reveals on the contrary the anxious desire to preserve (I Sam. 25:29; especially Song of S. 1:13). (*b*) Likewise, the verb טפל (vs. 17*b*) does not mean to **cover** in the sense of "passing over," "overlooking," or "forgiving," but is used with an evil intent in Job (13:4) as well as elsewhere (Ps. 119:69). (*c*) If Job were still thinking in vs. 17 of his future happiness in an afterlife, and explicitly believing in God's act of forgiveness, he would thereby acknowledge implicitly the validity of his friends' accusations; in other words, he would admit the reality of his guilt; he would recognize that his future life of communion with God would be possible only if God overlooked his transgression and covered up his sinfulness; in brief, he would plead guilty. Such an attitude is shown in neither the specific nor the general context of the dialogue: to the end (ch. 31) Job protests his innocence. For these reasons vs. 17 (and consequently vs. 16) should be understood as referring to the present tragic reality.

After having indulged for a few fleeting moments in the luxury of imagining an afterlife born of divine tenderness (vss. 13-15), the miserable creature is thrown back into his—our—world. Life is such that God appears to watch every step, ready to pounce upon man at the first intimation of sin. "Sealed in a purse is my transgression, and thou hast glued over my guilt." There is no divine intention of pardon. Furthermore, Job acknowledges his guilt as little here as in 13:23. He attempts only to explain the hostility displayed by God against him.

(4) MAN'S IRREVOCABLE ANNIHILATION (14:18-22)

18-19. These verses are absent in the Coptic Sahidic version; they are marked with asterisks in Jerome's recension and in the Syro-hexaplaric version; the present text of the

---

18-22. *In Gorgeous Sweeps of Scorn.*—See Expos. on 1:6-12; cf. Prospero's speech in *The Tempest:*

> The cloud-capp'd towers, the gorgeous palaces,
> The solemn temples, the great globe itself,
> Yea, all which it inherit, shall dissolve
> And, like this insubstantial pageant faded,
> Leave not a rack behind. We are such stuff
> As dreams are made on, and our little life
> Is rounded with a sleep.[5]

As the slow process of time eats away at a granite cliff, so God prevails in the end (vs. 20). As **waters wear away the stones,** and **torrents wash**

away the soil, so God brings over the face of human life the vacant stare of death (vs. 20). If our being here is so important, why are we snuffed out so ruthlessly? If love and beauty are so precious, why does the whole created universe act as if they were the merest accident? It will take more than a flower or two of speech to cover that (see Expos. on vs. 13; 6:18-13). See vs. 20, **he passeth;** still a common enough euphemism for death. Says Strahan, "If Revelation consents to retain the word 'passeth,' she does so only on the condition that she shall be allowed to give it an entirely new content"; then quotes I John 3:14.[6]

[5] Act IV, scene 1.

[6] *Job*, p. 136.

20 Thou prevailest for ever against him, and he passeth: thou changest his countenance, and sendest him away.

21 His sons come to honor, and he knoweth *it* not; and they are brought low, but he perceiveth *it* not of them.

22 But his flesh upon him shall have pain, and his soul within him shall mourn.

20 Thou prevailest for ever against him, and he passes;
thou changest his countenance, and sendest him away.

21 His sons come to honor, and he does not know it;
they are brought low, and he perceives it not.

22 He feels only the pain of his own body,
and he mourns only for himself."

15 Then answered Eliphaz the Temanite, and said,

15 Then Eli'phaz the Te'manite answered:

LXX has been supplied from Theod.; the initial word ואולם, "but on the contrary," indicates some disturbance of the original text. In spite of these difficulties, the general idea is clear: as the seemingly most endurable elements of nature—mountains, rocks, and soil—disintegrate under the various phenomena of erosion, so man's hope is destroyed little by little, drop by drop.

20-22. A dead man is unaware of the fate of his descendants (see 21:21). He may retain some kind of psychological consciousness (cf. in contrast Eccl. 9:5-6), but his preoccupation is confined to his own fate: "Only upon himself does his flesh ache and his soul mourn" (vs. 22). The use of the two words **flesh** and **soul** does not indicate a dualistic anthropology, for they are placed in poetic parallelism. The flesh in the grave is devoured by worms, or at least disintegrates, and thus "suffers" in the natural process of decay (vs. 20*b*). The soul, also in the grave, retains the sense of its identity, but is busily engaged in the intoning of an eternal dirge.

At the end of the first cycle of discussion Job has fallen into a slough of despond perhaps deeper than the pessimism of his initial lament. There he looked at death as a state of rest, perhaps of serenity (3:13 ff.); here he grimly faces an endless continuation of dull pain. There he was "half in love with easeful Death"; here he stands alone before "the grisly terror."

C. Second Cycle of Discussion (15:1–21:34)

1. Second Discourse of Eliphaz (15:1-35)

The friends have heretofore displayed a total lack of comprehension; yet they have honestly thought that Job was not beyond man's comfort and God's salvation. The proud way in which the sufferer reacted to their pastoral suggestions has steadily deepened the gulf that from the start had alienated him from them. The tone of the dialogue has now sharpened to such an extent that Eliphaz, who had at first observed the rules of Oriental civility with almost exquisite gentleness (4:2) now drops all circumlocutions of courtesy.

15:1–21:34. The Second Cycle.—In the first round of the conversation which goes on between Job and his three friends it becomes clear how chock-full his would-be comforters are of wise and helpful comments culled from experience, tradition, and the current theology—none of which fits Job's case. They try to bring him what solace they can, albeit with something of the condescension which too often turns the milk of human kindness sour (12:5), by sharing with him many a choice bit of wisdom. And the only result is that they irritate him. The poultice proves to be a mustard plaster. For the simple reason that all of them lack that quiet understanding and deep sympathy which would suffer with the sufferer, silently perhaps; for silence can be a balm when there are no words to utter. What they lack is love; what they have in irksome abundance is a collection of explanations that fail to explain, and exhortations based on them that can therefore incite to nothing but resentment. They try to take his mind off himself and direct it to God; which would have been all right if at the moment he had happened to

2 Should a wise man utter vain knowledge, and fill his belly with the east wind?

3 Should he reason with unprofitable
talk? or with speeches wherewith he can do
no good?

2 "Should a wise man answer with windy
knowledge,
    and fill himself with the east wind?
3 Should he argue in unprofitable talk,
    or in words with which he can do no
    good?

a) A Threefold Indictment (15:2-16)

(1) Job's Self-Incrimination (15:2-6)

15:2-6. The attack is abrupt. There are no conciliating preliminaries. Job had
claimed that he possessed a wisdom of his own (12:3; 13:2), but **should a wise man
utter vain knowledge, and fill his belly with the east wind** (vs. 2)? A "science of wind"
(vs. 2*a*) is without substance, foundation, or purpose (cf. 8:2). Not only is Job's thesis
without consistency and even empty, but it has within itself the germ of destruction
and may be compared to **the east wind** (vs. 2*b*), a hot breath of death which dries up
vegetation and suffocates man and beast. It brings only pain and sterility. Job's reasonings
are not only profitless (vs. 3), they are ruinous. "Thou even disruptest piety" (vs. 4*a*;
cf. Moffatt, "You undermine religion"). Lit., "Thou breakest fear." The verb means
"to violate" (the covenant) or "to make ineffectual" (a counsel or a vow). **Fear** in
gnomic Hebrew designates the pious forms of religion. Job is thus accused of exercising
pernicious influence, presumably upon his friends themselves, who perhaps cannot
help being impressed by his heroic courage and even bewildered and baffled by the
mystery of his fate. The parallel line confirms this interpretation: He is **hindering**

like God. They talk of holiness and justice and
omniscience. But by this time Job has been so
put upon by their insistent if somewhat veiled
assumption of his guilt that he breaks out in
rebellion against the kind of God who would
deal with a man as they keep saying their God
does. So the friends grow increasingly disagree-
able. Job does too. They see nothing else for it
now but that he is the very kind of wicked
person they have been talking about. They
quit making their glib promises of restoration
(see Expos. on 17:12). He has despised the
consolation of God; let him hearken to the
terrors of the Almighty. His conscience has to
be prodded wide awake. Head in the air then,
feet on the ground: the wicked, with God at his
back, must be compelled to behold the wicked's
fate. So in the three cycles do the areas of discussion converge to a point, like vertical cross
sections of an inverted cone, from God to man
to the sufferer himself.

Job does not at first seem to realize the enormity of what is going on. From the very start he
has been lagging a step or two behind, unable
to cope promptly with the hints and innuendoes that he has no desire to hear and refuses
to entertain. As the drift of the argument sets
in toward him more unrelentingly than ever
and with even greater ruthlessness, he sees
himself lonelier than he thought it possible for
a human soul to be: no pity in heaven, and
none on earth. His tortured mind comes back to

it over and over again, pacing up and down,
hardly hearing what anybody says, like a wild
beast in a cage, just looking through the bars
at the desolation that has somehow been
wrought in his world. Until all at once it dawns
on him that everybody has been mouthing the
same old nonsense, building the same old house
of cards: "The Lord knoweth the way of the
righteous: but the way of the ungodly shall
perish" (Ps. 1:6). And with one sweep of his
arm (ch. 21) he scatters it to the winds. Anybody can look around and see for himself what
ridiculous sophistry it is.

15:1-35. *The Speech of Eliphaz.*—Bildad was
right (8:2). If you are a **wise man**, why do you
talk like a windbag? There is no profit in it,
it does no good. You are impious and upsetting
(see Exeg. on vs. 4). You talk as you do because
you are what you are (vs. 5*a*). Then you put a
front on it (vs. 5*b*). You have condemned yourself out of **your own mouth.** Who in the world
do you think you are? Older than anybody?
Wiser than everybody? In what we have said
God has tried to deal **gently with you**—and
your eyes flash. Good heavens—even they are
not good!—nobody on earth (vs. 14) can make
such claims as you have made. **Much less** one
who gulps down **iniquity like water!** Listen.
Experience and tradition alike—before all these
foreigners got in and corrupted it (vs. 19)—
teach what you have had the effrontery to deny
(cf. vss. 20-35 with 9:22-24; 12:6; etc.): that the

4 Yea, thou castest off fear, and restrain-
est prayer before God.

5 For thy mouth uttereth thine iniquity,
and thou choosest the tongue of the crafty.

6 Thine own mouth condemneth thee,
and not I: yea, thine own lips testify against
thee.

7 *Art* thou the first man *that* was born? or
wast thou made before the hills?

4 But you are doing away with the fear of
God,
  and hindering meditation before God,
5 For your iniquity teaches your mouth,
  and you choose the tongue of the crafty.
6 Your own mouth condemns you, and not
  I;
  your own lips testify against you.

7 "Are you the first man that was born?
  Or were you brought forth before the
  hills?

---

meditation before God (vs. 4b). Eliphaz acknowledges, and not obliquely, that his apparent composure hides some deep disturbance. But not for long; he has sensed the attractiveness of heresy, and reacts the more swiftly to this beguilement which threatens his orthodoxy. Like any inquisitor, he thrusts in the sword of accusation: **Your iniquity teaches your mouth** (vs. 5a). Job reveals his own guilt (עָוֹן) by his words. He has chosen **the tongue of the crafty** (vs. 5b), a word used for describing the snake in the story of universal man's temptation to set himself as a judge of the Deity's purpose by casting doubts upon the Deity's motives (Gen. 3:1). Eliphaz may have intended the allusion. Now Job has offered, in his own defense, ground for incrimination, and Eliphaz spares himself the task and burden of pronouncing a verdict: **Thine own mouth condemneth thee, and not I** (vs. 6a). The echo may be heard across the centuries: "What further need have we of witnesses?" (Matt. 26:65).

(2) Job's Self-Delusion (15:7-11)

7a. Since Job has conceded that "in old age is wisdom" (12:12), he must be very old indeed, for he claims monopoly of knowledge (cf. vs. 10). Irony leads Eliphaz to indulge in hyperbole: **Art thou the first man that was born?** (vs. 7a). This question does not necessarily refer to the myth of the primeval man brought forth into existence before the creation of the world, for it may be rendered, "Wert thou born the first of mankind ['ādhām]?" In this case the allusion is to the biblical account of the garden, just as "the crafty" in vs. 5b may have referred to the snake (see Exeg. on vss. 2-6).

7b. This verse is almost identical with Prov. 8:25b, in which the personified figure of wisdom sings, "Before the hills was I brought forth." Inasmuch as this line is the

---

wicked are doomed. They are afraid even when they are well to do. Like you, they are filled with foreboding because they have defied the Almighty (vss. 25-26) and oppressed the poor (vss. 27-28). They will have their **recompense.** Did you ever see a withered vine? A dead tree? Childless homes? Dwelling places gutted by fire (vs. 34b)? And do you know what it means? It means **paid in full** (vs. 32).

4. *Doing Away with Religion.*—All those who do not think as convention does are likely enough to incur the charge. One great revolutionary after another—pioneers in science, economics, sociology, and religion—has been accused of it (see Exeg. on 18:21; Expos. on 23:2). Some of them have been put to death. Jesus of Nazareth was. God moves ahead with great seven-league boots; and we in bedroom slippers. It is "a dreadful thing" to fall into the clutches

of a closed mind. Such a mind is not merely "closed for repairs": it is closed! Pride had closed the mind of Eliphaz, and Job had wounded it (cf. vss. 2-3, 10). Tradition had closed Bildad's. Using his brains without his heart had slammed the door of Zophar's, and locked it. After that, no matter how right other men are—e.g., Job—they are wrong morally (vs. 5a), deliberately (vs. 5b), and obviously (vs. 6). Everything they say spells "guilty." The only thing anyone has to do is to listen (see Exeg. on vs. 6a; Expos. on vss. 7-16).

7-16. *The None Too Gentle Art of Disparagement.*—Eliphaz is still confident of his privileged position. When you are where he was you cannot avoid stooping if you are to have any dealing at all with somebody who is where Job was. Well, the least said the soonest mended. Yet there is evidence that the aged seer has

8 Hast thou heard the secret of God? and dost thou restrain wisdom to thyself?

9 What knowest thou, that we know not? *what* understandest thou, which *is* not in us?

10 With us *are* both the grayheaded and very aged men, much elder than thy father.

11 *Are* the consolations of God small with thee? is there any secret thing with thee?

8 Have you listened in the council of God?
And do you limit wisdom to yourself?

9 What do you know that we do not know?
What do you understand that is not clear to us?

10 Both the grayhaired and the aged are among us,
older than your father.

11 Are the consolations of God too small for you,
or the word that deals gently with you?

---

counterpart of its preceding (Prov. 8:25*a*) and belongs to a homogeneous poem (Prov. 8:22-31), the probability is that the poet of Job borrowed it from the gnomic literature. Does Job think himself to be a demigod, a suprahuman being, a hypostasis of the Godhead, a mythological hero, or even the prototype of humankind? Or did he derive knowledge from listening in the [secret] **council of God** (vs. 8*a*)? Is Job a prophet to whom is revealed the divine secret (סוד; cf. Amos 3:7), or a sage who violates professional etiquette by keeping for himself an esoteric kind of wisdom (vs. 8*b*)? In what way is he, a mere youngster (vs. 10), better informed (vs. 9*a*) or more perceptive (vs. 9*b*) than his friends? All three of them have spoken hopefully about God's method of educating man (5:17-27; 8:5-8; 11:13-20), but Job has spurned their **gently** spoken words; he has belittled even **the consolations of God** himself (vs. 11).

---

been losing some of his composure (see Exeg. on vss. 2-6). What Job has been saying has succeeded in getting under his skin in more ways than one. Job has not been showing any of them proper respect—after they had come all that way to commiserate with him. And he has been delivering himself of certain sentiments that were calculated to annoy any truly pious man: they came too near the uneasy facts to be comfortable. Said a woman the first time she ever heard of Darwin's theory: "My dear! Descended from apes? How perfectly awful! Let us hope that it is not true. And if it is, let us pray that it may not become widely known." All this sparring might very well turn out to be quite awkward. The gloves had to come off now, or things would get worse. The ground had begun to feel shaky enough. Who wants to lose an argument? (Cf. Expos. on 4:8-11.)

So—the "none too gentle art." Begin with an unexamined assumption: (*a*) that with age is the secret of wisdom, and (*b*) that some people who claim to be God's confidants are anything but . . . ; you know who is. Then inquire into the other man's credentials, comparing them with your own. Tell him he has scarcely reached the years of maturity (vss. 7, 10). Ask him if he has a private listening post, and has overheard the counsels of the Almighty (vs. 8). If that is why he limits wisdom to himself—and will not permit you to have all of it. Never breathe a word of what *you* are doing; tell him *he* is doing it. Put it to him: Do you think you know any-

thing **that we do not know?** Some of us are **older than your father.** And we have been offering you the very **consolations of God,** straight from the source (see Expos. on vs. 11). Next, explain your opponent to himself (see Expos. on 22:12-20). Say he must indeed be out of his mind; at any rate what he is spouting out of his mouth is presumptuous and **abominable** (vss. 14-16). And quote what you have said before, while you are about it (4:17-19). Nothing could distress him more. You may wind it all up after that by telling him what he has to look forward to if he keeps on (vss. 17-35).

To such as Eliphaz it is the self that matters, all pretensions to the contrary: the self and what it sees as it looks out on the world. Of all things else, people matter least. And that, being against God and against man, is the destroyer of self! "Inasmuch as ye have done it unto one of the least of these my brethren, ye have done it unto me" (Matt. 25:40).

11. The Consolations of God.—Eliphaz preens himself on having merely hinted that Job was guilty of wrongdoing, and on having held out to him steadily the assurance that his suffering was a blessing in disguise and that everything would come right in the end (5:17-27). So with Bildad and Zophar, though not so considerately. But Job was not interested in either the approach or the prospect: he was interested in having somebody understand how it was with him. Analysis, warning, the promise of a happy issue one of these days—none of it was consolation.

12 Why doth thine heart carry thee away? and what do thy eyes wink at,

13 That thou turnest thy spirit against God, and lettest *such* words go out of thy mouth?

14 What *is* man, that he should be clean? and *he which is* born of a woman, that he should be righteous?

15 Behold, he putteth no trust in his saints; yea, the heavens are not clean in his sight.

16 How much more abominable and filthy *is* man, which drinketh iniquity like water?

17 I will show thee, hear me; and that *which* I have seen I will declare;

18 Which wise men have told from their fathers, and have not hid *it*:

19 Unto whom alone the earth was given, and no stranger passed among them.

20 The wicked man travaileth with pain all *his* days, and the number of years is hidden to the oppressor.

---

12 Why does your heart carry you away, and why do your eyes flash,

13 that you turn your spirit against God, and let such words go out of your mouth?

14 What is man, that he can be clean? Or he that is born of a woman, that he can be righteous?

15 Behold, God puts no trust in his holy ones, and the heavens are not clean in his sight;

16 how much less one who is abominable and corrupt, a man who drinks iniquity like water!

17 "I will show you, hear me; and what I have seen I will declare

18 (what wise men have told, and their fathers have not hidden,

19 to whom alone the land was given, and no stranger passed among them).

20 The wicked man writhes in pain all his days, through all the years that are laid up for the ruthless.

---

(3) Job's Self-Assertion (15:12-16)

12-16. It is not merely a human agency of pastoral ministration that the sufferer has opposed: **Thou turnest thy spirit against God** (vs. 13*a*). The word *rûaḥ,* "breath," "wind," **spirit,** may sometimes mean "wrath," "animosity" (θυμός, *animus;* cf. Judg. 8:3; 9:23; Prov. 16:32). His passionate boasting of innocence is the very proof of his spiritual rebellion. Eliphaz reiterates his own thesis of human depravity in more brutal terms than heretofore: man is **abominable** (lit., "disgusting"; cf. the cognate in 9:31) and **corrupt** (cf. Pss. 14:3; 53:3); he **drinks** "injustice" (עולה; cf. 5:16; 11:14) **like water,** i.e., with uncontrollable avidity. He "thirsts after sin, and finds delight in it" (Strahan, *Job,* p. 143).

b) The Evil Man's Destiny (15:17-35)

The sage now lets his eloquence run unbridled. He knows whereof he speaks, for he has learned it both from personal revelation (**what I have seen** [in a vision? the verb *ḥāzāh* is used of prophetic gazing; cf. *ḥōzeh,* "a seer"]) and a tradition of the **wise men** which is unadulterated by foreign influences (vs. 19). The evil man **writhes in pain all his days** (vs. 20*a*), or if he lives **in prosperity** (vs. 21*b*), **the destroyer will** [suddenly] **come upon him** in the midst of his illusory "peace" (an obvious allusion to Job's prosperity in the prologue).

To call it so was to do away with religion in dead earnest (vs. 4). And that is exactly what it almost accomplished. When God consoles he enters into a man's solitude as a companion and a bearer of burdens (Gal. 6:2).

17-35. *The Fate of the Wicked.*—A vivid picture, quite without any hint of the sorrow that

is in the heart of God—there was no sorrow in the heart of the God that Eliphaz was sure he served (see Expos. on 22:2-5, 12-20). Here is what the seer of visions has seen (4:8; 5:3), here is what he has learned from the fathers of long ago when the faith was pure (vs. 19). Much of it he undoubtedly still believes, with

21 A dreadful sound *is* in his ears: in prosperity the destroyer shall come upon him.

22 He believeth not that he shall return out of darkness, and he is waited for of the sword.

23 He wandereth abroad for bread, *saying*, Where *is it?* he knoweth that the day of darkness is ready at his hand.

24 Trouble and anguish shall make him afraid; they shall prevail against him, as a king ready to the battle.

25 For he stretcheth out his hand against God, and strengtheneth himself against the Almighty.

26 He runneth upon him, *even on his* neck, upon the thick bosses of his bucklers:

27 Because he covereth his face with his fatness, and maketh collops of fat on *his* flanks.

28 And he dwelleth in desolate cities, *and* in houses which no man inhabiteth, which are ready to become heaps.

29 He shall not be rich, neither shall his substance continue, neither shall he prolong the perfection thereof upon the earth.

---

21 Terrifying sounds are in his ears;
   in prosperity the destroyer will come
      upon him.
22 He does not believe that he will return
      out of darkness,
   and he is destined for the sword.
23 He wanders abroad for bread, saying,
      'Where is it?'
   He knows that a day of darkness is
      ready at his hand;
24 distress and anguish terrify him;
   they prevail against him, like a king
      prepared for battle.
25 Because he has stretched forth his hand
      against God,
   and bids defiance to the Almighty,
26 running stubbornly against him
   with a thick-bossed shield;
27 because he has covered his face with his
      fat,
   and gathered fat upon his loins,
28 and has lived in desolate cities,
   in houses which no man should in-
      habit,
   which were destined to become heaps
      of ruins;
29 he will not be rich, and his wealth will
      not endure,
   nor will he strike root in the earth;[m]

[m] Vg: Heb obscure

---

22. He does not believe that he will return out of darkness: This verse does not refer to Job's recent denial of resurrection (14:7 ff.), for it should be translated, "He does not expect [cf. 9:16; 39:12] to escape [cf. 33:30; Ps. 35:17] misfortune" (cf. vss. 23, 30; 19:8).

25-27. The evil man will receive his punishment because his crimes have primarily not an ethical but a theological origin. He is God's adversary. "He plays the hero against the Almighty" (vs. 25*b*).

28-29. By implication Eliphaz accuses Job of having also practiced social and economic oppression.

---

a belief which his very misgivings have rendered violent; the rest of it he hopes is true. In any case, he pulls out all the stops. Job has said:

> The tents of robbers are at peace,
>   and those who provoke God are secure (12:6).

Rather is it for this very reason (vs. 25) they suffer out their allotted time (vs. 20)—and Eliphaz must have looked straightly at Job as he said it. They "hear things" (vs. 21; 22:10). In the very midst of prosperity dread premonitions of destruction at the hands of God (vs. 22*b*), visions of their dead bodies picked at by vul-

tures (vs. 23*a* Kissane), disturb their fancied peace. They have grown rich (vs. 27) exploiting the poor (vs. 28 Kissane; cf. 20:19; 22:5-7); their stubborn defiance (vs. 25) will have no dwelling place left, not even a tent in the desert (vs. 29*b* Kissane). Like withered trees blasted by the wind and the heat, evil shall come upon them by evil begotten (vs. 31; cf. 4:8). This shall be their **recompense** in the midst of the years (vs. 32*a*; 22:16*a*), promise without fulfillment, flower without fruit (vs. 33; cf. 20:18). None shall come after them (cf. 1:18-19): only "the fire of God . . . fallen from heaven" (cf. 1:16), and the "affliction" that

30 He shall not depart out of darkness; the flame shall dry up his branches, and by the breath of his mouth shall he go away.

31 Let not him that is deceived trust in vanity: for vanity shall be his recompense.

32 It shall be accomplished before his time, and his branch shall not be green.

33 He shall shake off his unripe grape as the vine, and shall cast off his flower as the olive.

34 For the congregation of hypocrites *shall be* desolate, and fire shall consume the tabernacles of bribery.

35 They conceive mischief, and bring forth vanity, and their belly prepareth deceit.

16 Then Job answered and said,
2 I have heard many such things: miserable comforters *are* ye all.

3 Shall vain words have an end? or what emboldeneth thee that thou answerest?

---

30 he will not escape from darkness;
the flame will dry up his shoots,
and his blossom[n] will be swept away[o]
by the wind.

31 Let him not trust in emptiness, deceiving himself;
for emptiness will be his recompense.

32 It will be paid in full before his time,
and his branch will not be green.

33 He will shake off his unripe grape, like the vine,
and cast off his blossom, like the olive tree.

34 For the company of the godless is barren,
and fire consumes the tents of bribery.

35 They conceive mischief and bring forth evil
and their heart prepares deceit."

16 Then Job answered:
2 "I have heard many such things;
miserable comforters are you all.

3 Shall windy words have an end?
Or what provokes you that you answer?

[n] Gk: Heb *mouth*
[o] Cn: Heb *will depart*

30-35. Premature death (vss. 31-33) and lack of posterity (vs. 34) are the penalty of the **godless.** The dogma of retribution, delayed but certain, is upheld to the end.

2. Second Reply of Job to Eliphaz (16:1–17:16)

a) The Sorrow-Making "Comforters" (16:1-6)

16:2-6. Since Eliphaz has confused divine truth with the beliefs of his own class and has identified his soothing words with "the comforts of God," Job retorts at once that his friends are **comforters** who inspire only "weariness and sorrow" (vs. 2). He could speak so if only he could exchange his pain for their ease (vss. 3-5). Whether he

---

"cometh not forth of the dust" (vs. 35a; cf. 5:6a). Out of their own **belly** (vs. 2b) the lie (vs. 35b; Ps. 7:14) that dashes the cup from their lips.

It is all strangely reminiscent of the day when Tertullian pictured himself leaning over the battlements of heaven, rubbing his hands together and chortling with satisfaction over the torments of the damned (cf. 22:19). Job is there now—in the flames; and none to "dip the tip of his finger in water" and cool his tongue (Luke 16:24). There was another day when one who saw the multitudes had compassion on them.

16:1–17:16. The Answer of Job.—Windbag yourself! Why keep on at me? If you were in my place, and I in yours, I should not find it difficult to be the kind of word-mouthing comforters you are. With me it is all the same: the

pain is no less whether I speak or hold my peace. Then let me speak. That strange God of yours has tormented me and made men sure of my guilt (vs. 8), so that they take off after me, panting along at my heels like wild beasts (cf. 9:12), making me the butt of all their insults (vs. 10). It is thou, God. Thou didst seize me by the throat (vs. 12), wound me with thine arrows (vs. 13). Thou dost storm at me with thy hosts of evil (vs. 14; cf. 10:17). All my gladness and my honor have gone from me (vs. 15). Yet, Eliphaz, I am not what you want me to believe (see Exeg. on vss. 12-17; cf. vs. 17a with 15:34; vs. 17b with 15:4). Let my death cry out to heaven for justice (vs. 18). Surely someone there will answer for me. God, I beseech thee (vs. 20b), uphold my cause somewhere, somehow! I am on the brink of the grave (16:22–17:1), with nothing but mocking on every side

4 I also could speak as ye *do:* if your soul were in my soul's stead, I could heap up words against you, and shake mine head at you.

5 *But* I would strengthen you with my mouth, and the moving of my lips should assuage *your grief.*

6 Though I speak, my grief is not assuaged: and *though* I forbear, what am I eased?

7 But now he hath made me weary: thou hast made desolate all my company.

8 And thou hast filled me with wrinkles, *which* is a witness *against me:* and my leanness rising up in me beareth witness to my face.

9 He teareth *me* in his wrath, who hateth me: he gnasheth upon me with his teeth; mine enemy sharpeneth his eyes upon me.

---

4 I also could speak as you do,
  if you were in my place;
  I could join words together against you,
    and shake my head at you.

5 I could strengthen you with my mouth,
    and the solace of my lips would assuage
    your pain.

6 "If I speak, my pain is not assuaged,
    and if I forbear, how much of it leaves
    me?

7 Surely now God has worn me out;
    he has*ᵖ* made desolate all my company.

8 And he has*ᵖ* shriveled me up,
    which is a witness against me;
  and my leanness has risen up against me,
    it testifies to my face.

9 He has torn me in his wrath, and hated
    me;
  he has gnashed his teeth at me;
    my adversary sharpens his eyes against
    me.

ᵖ Heb *thou hast*

---

continues the discussion or keeps silent, his pain remains (vs. 6): he will therefore speak bluntly.

b) The Relentless Hostility of God (16:7-11)

7-11. Nothing can explain the origin of his misery except the hostility of God, who is compared (**he** or **thou** in vss. 7-8) to a beast of prey which "tears" (טרף), and to an **adversary** who detests, pursues relentlessly, and "persecutes" (the verb שטם is probably akin to שטן, a cognate of the word "Satan"). One might almost conjecture that the poet wished subtly to suggest that Job, although ignorant, of course, of "the Satan's" part played in the prologue, is on the verge of discovering the cause of his dismay (vs. 9). This impression is strengthened by vs. 11a, "God has delivered me into the hands [cf. use of the verb הסגיר in 11:10] of a knave" [עויל, lit., "irresponsible boy"; cf. plural עוילים

(vs. 2). Strike hands with me thyself (vs. 3). Who else will? These friends of mine in their blindness? Let them not triumph over me (vs. 4; yet see Exeg.). Sycophants, calling me to account—may they be blind fathers of the blind (vs. 5; lit., "suffer misfortune")—helping to turn my life into a byword (like the life of the Jewish exiles). It is enough to stagger a saint and stir his wrath against the world's injustice (vs. 8). But it will not swerve him from his course—or me either. Come back, my friends (see Exeg.). You can only prove yourselves wrong (vs. 10) and the hopes you have held out to me false. I am filled with wretchedness and brokenhearted (vs. 11). You want me to think this is the dawn (cf. 5:17; 8:20; etc.), and I know it is night (vs. 12). I am already blood-kin to the grave (vs. 14). What hope is there in that

—except to take Death for my bride, and go down with her into the dust (vs. 16)?

4. If You Were in My Place.—Eliphaz knows what he would do if he were in Job's place (see Expos. on 5:8), and Job has not forgotten it. If the roles were actually reversed, he is sure he could make a better go of it than any of them. Kissane does not feel the irony of that, and takes all the rest of the passage (vss. 5-6) in sober earnest. But the mood of Job is bitter. That they show him no sympathy is bad enough; that they will not even play fair (13:7) is worse. They have turned religion into a hollow and meaningless thing on both counts. They would have done him more good if they had been less "pious." They might even have been more compassionate. So he gives back with interest what is sent. If only he could change places with one

| 10 They have gaped upon me with their mouth; they have smitten me upon the cheek reproachfully; they have gathered themselves together against me. | 10 Men have gaped at me with their mouth, they have struck me insolently upon the cheek, they mass themselves together against me. |
| 11 God hath delivered me to the ungodly, and turned me over into the hands of the wicked. | 11 God gives me up to the ungodly, and casts me into the hands of the wicked. |

in 19:18; 21:11; perhaps a cognate of עֹלָה, "injustice," wrong," used in 6:29; etc.). Social ostracism quite naturally follows (vss. 10, 11*b*).

of them, it would be so easy for him to do as they had done: stringing **words together,** shaking his head, and saying fiddledeedee—a fig for your piety!—girding them all around with chatter, soothing their pain with platitudes (vss. 4*b*-5). "The consolations of God" indeed!

"If I were you" is usually the preface to a bit of unsolicited advice; "if you were I," preface to the implicit or explicit claim that very few have ever been so put upon or bewildered. "If you were in my place," what would you do? Not that it will necessarily make any difference. "If I were in your place," I could give you a few pointers on how to behave. Always that dream of turning the tables and coming out on top.

There have been men indeed who have done it—and suffered in the place of other men. God did it. A distraught father whose twenty-one-year-old son had been killed in an accident ran into a minister's study, took him by the lapels of the coat, shook him and asked, "Where was your God when my son was killed?" Quietly and promptly the answer came, "Just where he was when his own Son was killed."

10. *The Lot of the Outcast.*—It must be remembered throughout that Job is afflicted far more in mind than in body, which is precisely what adds such poignancy to human suffering. Both the spiritual dimensions of human existence are involved in it: his relationship to God and his relationship to his fellow men. These belong to the very substance of religion and life. When anything goes wrong with either, something goes dreadfully wrong with the integrity of the self. Witness the disintegration of selfhood in the modern world, and the manufactured substitutes for both God and community which are responsible in such large measure for the demonism of totalitarian regimes.

In the course of the second cycle Job's sense of alienation from God (note the feeling of distance implicit in the pronoun "he," vss. 7-8) is aggravated by the growing realization of the gulf that has yawned between himself and his fellow men. The very foundations of his being

seem about to crumble. Again and again he reverts to the sheer human loneliness moving in upon him like some intolerable weight (see Expos. on 15:1–21:34; cf. vss. 20-21; 17:2, 6; 19:13-19). So it was all too often in the O.T., under the Deuteronomic Code: calamity argued unrighteousness (vss. 7-8). At the very moment when a man became most acutely conscious of his need he was taught to regard himself as the object of God's wrath. What then could the "pious" do in such a situation but take God's part, whatever the cost (see Expos. on 12:2-6; 13:8, 12), and keep themselves from any too close and contaminating association with the victim? To be "a friend of publicans and sinners" was for centuries to prove one of the gravest of risks.

One need hardly comment—cannot without fear and trembling—on our own treatment of the "outcast." It is Christendom's badge of infamy, worn in many a land with the specious sanctions of what goes by the name of religion. Did not God himself decree these differences of race and status? "The poor always ye have with you" (John 12:8). Is it not our bounden duty to be the enemy of the enemies of our faith? But ours is a faith in one whose word it was "I say unto you, Love your enemies" (Matt. 5:44). There is a fellowship of his Son which God has fashioned to the intent that men should come to their full stature in love of him and one another. What place in it has a story that originated during the last years of World War II? The graduating class in a high school was assigned as the subject for a composition, "What just punishment should be meted out to Adolf Hitler?" A Negro girl won the prize by developing the thesis that he should be put into a black skin and set down in the midst of a white community. "Whoso shall offend one of these little ones . . . , it were better for him that a millstone were hanged about his neck, and that he were drowned in the depth of the sea" (Matt. 18:6).

11. *An Enemy Hath Done This.*—Cf. Exeg. on vss. 7-11, 12-17; see Expos. on 1:6-12; 9:2-10;

12 I was at ease, but he hath broken me asunder: he hath also taken *me* by my neck, and shaken me to pieces, and set me up for his mark.

13 His archers compass me round about, he cleaveth my reins asunder, and doth not spare; he poureth out my gall upon the ground.

14 He breaketh me with breach upon breach; he runneth upon me like a giant.

15 I have sewed sackcloth upon my skin, and defiled my horn in the dust.

12 I was at ease, and he broke me asunder;
    he seized me by the neck and dashed
      me to pieces;
  He set me up as his target,
13   his archers surround me.
  He slashes open my kidneys, and does
      not spare;
    he pours out my gall on the ground.
14 He breaks me with breach upon breach;
    he runs upon me like a warrior.
15 I have sewed sackcloth upon my skin,
    and have laid my strength in the dust

c) "My Prayer Is Pure" (16:12-17)

12-17. Job felt acutely the sting in Eliphaz' oblique references to the sudden rupture of his "peace" (15:21) and the extinction of his progeny (15:33-34). He refers to these two disasters respectively in vss. 12a and 15b, which may constitute a further allusion to the events of the prologue. He has emptied the cup of bitterness and tasted the uttermost forms of humiliation. Then at the point of utter dejection the hero lifts his head, gathers up his pride, and renews his fight.

> Although there is no violence in my hands,
>   and my prayer is pure (vs. 17).

The double proposition has often been compared with that of Isa. 53:9b, "Although he had done no violence, neither was any deceit in his mouth." Job's innocence is directly linked to the integrity of his religion. Such a certainty remains as his last possession. He clings to it with the passion of a dying man. All is not lost so long as it endures.

10:1-22, 13-17.) Human experience comes to know the evil in the universe as more than a quality of things done or planned; as a power. Paul's word for it is lordship, dominion (see Expos. on 12:13-19). The threat to modern life is not superstition: at least one of the threats lies in not taking evil seriously enough. One need not be overdogmatic about either the existence or the nonexistence of a personal devil. Consult William Temple, *Nature, Man and God;* [7] C. S. Lewis, *Screwtape Letters;* [8] Denis de Rougemont, *The Devil's Share.* If "myth" he is, the myth says a great deal that it is better to bear in mind. Writes de Rougemont: "The Devil . . . says to us, like Ulysses to the Cyclops, 'My name is *Nobody.* There is nobody. Whom should you be afraid of? Are you going to tremble before the non-existent?' " [9] And so he vanishes in his success and his triumph is his incognito. Two of his questions in Scripture, the only two that he raises in person, are enough to make anybody tremble: "Hath God said, . . . ?" (Gen. 3:1) and "Doth Job fear God for nought?" (1:9).

[7] London: Macmillan & Co., 1934, p. 503.
[8] New York: The Macmillan Co., 1943.
[9] Tr. Haakon Chevalier (New York: Pantheon Books, 1944), p. 17.

13. God's Target.— (See Expos. on 6:4; 7:20a, 23:2.) There had been a time when Job was sure that God's very special favor rested on him. It was no very far cry from that to the time when he was equally sure that he was the very special object of God's implacable hostility. In both cases the self was at the center, which is life's fundamental and persistent "distortion." Many of our so-called religious problems have their origin just there: "answered" and "unanswered" prayer—who shall say which is what? "Why does God allow this to happen to me?" The whole doctrine of "election" can become thoroughly self-centered. What else was wrong with the conviction the Jews had of being the chosen people? It may well be that we are chosen not for shelter through time and eternity, but for peril in time, and only the God who is love can know about eternity. The old mountaineer revivalist was nearer right than most. "Election?" he asked. "That is one of the easiest of doctrines to understand. God has one vote, and that is always for you. The devil has one vote, and that is always against you. And you have one vote. That vote decides the election." How many of the muddles in which we find ourselves are due to the fact that we think we are in the middle! To learn that we are not is a

16 My face is foul with weeping, and on my eyelids *is* the shadow of death;	16 My face is red with weeping, and on my eyelids is deep darkness;
17 Not for *any* injustice in mine hands: also my prayer *is* pure.	17 although there is no violence in my hands, and my prayer is pure.
18 O earth, cover not thou my blood, and let my cry have no place.	18 "O earth, cover not my blood, and let my cry find no resting place.

This sudden recovery paves the way for both the outburst and the sublimity of the following strophe. "There is no hope more creative than that of the despairing [man]" (Miguel de Unamuno, *The Agony of Christianity*, tr. Pierre Loving [New York: Payson & Clarke, 1928], p. 37).

d) "MY WITNESS IS IN HEAVEN" (16:18-22)

18-22. The poet's technique once more proves itself true to the profoundest psychology. Job's sense of a new light is always subsequent to his fall into utter darkness. His picture of God the murderer, together with the awareness of his own innocence, combine to induce a state of such frenzy that he cries out:

> O earth, cover not my blood,
> and let my cry find no resting place (vs. 18).

There is more here than the double use of personification. The blood spilled on the soil by malfeasance calls for vengeance (Gen. 4:10-11), and continues to do so as long as it is not covered with dust (Ezek. 24:7). Job summons the personified earth to come to his aid (cf. Isa. 26:21*b*); his cry, delivered from his own murdered self, will continue to rise without **resting place** and will pursue his murderer. For how long? There comes the sublime and unexpected certitude:

> Even now, behold, my witness is in heaven,
> and he that vouches for me is on high (vs. 19).

tough lesson, and God sometimes has to use sinewy means to teach it. Frederick Norwood used to tell of a pious young preacher in Australia. During a prolonged drought he called on a ranchman who had never been known for his piety, and whose ranch was fairly burning up under the blistering sun. "Would you wish me to pray with you for rain?" the young preacher inquired after a while. "Come over here," said the ranchman, "and listen." They went over to the side of the house, and there heard the sound of sheep dying of thirst: "Ugh! Ugh!"—like a man coughing. "Can you pray like that?" the ranchman wanted to know. "And if you can, will the God who does not answer their prayer answer yours?" "Behold, I send you forth as lambs among wolves. Carry neither purse, nor scrip, nor shoes" (Luke 10:3-4). "Can ye drink of the cup that I drink of?" (Mark 10:38; cf. ch. 13; see John 16:2).

16. The Shadow of Death.—According to Strahan, weeping and dimness of sight were among the symptoms of Job's disease. He sees in them the approaching **shadow of death**. Upon

whose **eyelids** does it not rest (see Expos. on 6:8-13; 14:1-6)? Job's only hope lies in his innocence (vs. 17), and in God's ultimate recognition of it. Is there a hint in this verse (cf. Isa. 53:9) that at least the sufferings of the children of Israel, if not indeed Job's, were regarded by the author as in some sense vicarious? Aside from that, note that when the transfer of the center is made from the self to God, hope changes its grip from the innocence which is Job's to the divine favor which is God's. Already in Job's mind that transfer is understood as essential (13:16). It is brought on toward completion for "the man in Christ" (see Expos. on 13:13-19; 17:3).

19. The Witness in Heaven.—(See Exeg.; also Expos. on 7:21*c*; 9:30-35; 13:15; 19:25.) Kissane conceives of Job's "cry" as the **witness**, the advocate with God, pleading that the just man may hold to his way (17:9).[1] Certainly, however, the notion that in heaven there is one who will vouch for him (an angel?) fascinates Job's mind. May his blood be not covered (Gen.

[1] *Job*, p. 102.

19 Also now, behold, my witness *is* in heaven, and my record *is* on high. 20 My friends scorn me: *but* mine eye poureth out *tears* unto God.	19 Even now, behold, my witness is in heaven, and he that vouches for me is on high. 20 My friends scorn me; my eye pours out tears to God,

Who is this heavenly witness of the shocking, wholly unjustifiable murder of Job which is about to be committed by God himself? Commentators generally do not hesitate to identify this mysterious figure with that same God who controls Job's fate, and they develop the thesis of a paradoxical contradiction in Job's conception of the Deity. They represent him as appealing from God to God, from the God of wrath to the God of grace. Such an exegesis ignores three facts: (*a*) For Job, God is already a witness and an accuser (vs. 8), a prosecutor and an adversary (vss. 12-14). How could a witness for the prosecution be sufficiently transformed to become at once, **even now,** before the crime is committed, a defense witness and the initiator (perhaps the executor) of the victim's avenging? (*b*) The **witness** of vs. 19 is the same figure who in vs. 21 will **maintain the right of a man with God** and who is *ipso facto* differentiated from that God. (*c*) The **witness** of vs. 19 is also to be identified with the "avenger" of 19:25 (note how the idea of the blood redeemer was introduced in the present passage by the apostrophe to the earth in vs. 18 and was suddenly aborted through a return of the poet's attention to the idea of witness). Now since the "avenger" of 19:25 is differentiated from God (see Exeg., *ad loc.*), it follows that the witness in this text is not God but someone else.

It seems therefore quite clear that Job has by now abandoned the idea of winning God's favor. He had once entertained the hope that some intermediary being could be found who would bring God toward him. But the mediator of 9:33*a* was a creation of desperate fancy, rejected almost as soon as conceived. The poet is now reattacking the divine unknown from a new angle: man may perish when an omnipotent monster fells him; yet there must be a nemesis for that kind of God. Thus, without any hope of salvation on this earth or of resurrection in the hereafter (cf. vs. 22), Job is satisfied to know that his innocence will be proclaimed **in heaven,** since someone **vouches for [him] on high.** The question should not be asked, "Why does not this witness, even now, intervene in Job's favor, while there is yet time?" The poet is not intent upon describing the nature of God, nor is he even concerned with the quest for theodicy; he is engaged in the task of portraying a miserable human being, buffeted and cornered, who battles no longer for his life but for his name and honor. Nevertheless, in so doing he is beginning to lift the veil from the mystery of the Godhead. He does not indicate whether the **witness** is a divine being, a "son of Elohim" (cf. 1:6), a "servant" or "messenger" (cf. 4:18), or again a "holy one" (cf. 15:15). By presenting the figure of the witness and by respecting the anonymity of that figure, he reopens the theme of the mediator (9:33), prepares the motif of the redeemer (19:25), and thus lays the basis for Christian meditation (see Sigmund Mowinckel, "Hiobs gō'ēl und Zeuge im Himmel," in Karl Budde, ed., *Karl Marti zum siebzigsten Geburtstage gewidmet* . . . [Giessen: A. Töpelmann, 1925], pp. 207-12).

4:10) until there shall appear in the lists one who will defend him against both God and man! Note Tennyson's "Despair":

Ah, yet—I have had some glimmer, at times, in my gloomiest woe,
Of a God behind all—after all—the great God, for aught that I know;
But the God of Love and of Hell together—they cannot be thought,
If there be such a God, may the Great God curse him and bring him to nought! [2]

[2] St. xix.

At any rate, "the idea of mediation is essential to the biblical understanding of the relations between God and man," [3] whether the movement is thought of as from God to man (in the case of the prophet) or as from man to God (in the case of the priest). See Expos. on 5:1; Heb. 8:6; *et passim*. If Job is to hold fast any vestige of his old religion there has to be something that can correspond to it. The phoenix of a new faith is rising out of the ashes.

[3] F. J. Taylor, "Mediator," in Richardson, ed., *Theological Word Book of the Bible*, p. 141.

21 Oh that one might plead for a man with God, as a man *pleadeth* for his neighbor!

22 When a few years are come, then I shall go the way *whence* I shall not return.

21 that he would maintain the right of a man with God,
like*q* that of a man with his neighbor.

22 For when a few years have come
I shall go the way whence I shall not return.

q Syr Vg Tg: Heb *and*

Vs. 20 appears to be a parenthesis which interrupts the sequence of thought. It may represent a momentary aside, reflecting the response of the interlocutors. To the outburst of vss. 18-19, the audience most likely reacts with expressions of mockery. Job is fully conscious of this reaction, and he therefore interrupts the course of his thinking to say, **My friends** [may very well] **scorn me** [for entertaining the idea of a heavenly witness; and I myself have no weapon, except the tears of bitterness which I shed before impending injustice. Thus] **my eye pours out tears to God** (vs. 20). He then continues, picking up the thread of vs. 19, "But let him"—my witness—**maintain the right of man with God, like that of a man with his neighbor** (vs. 21). There is no doubt that the poet is here referring again to the strange figure of vs. 19, someone who must necessarily be different from both God and man alike in order to plead with God on the behalf of man. At the same time, by the skillful use of the verb יוכח, "let him argue the right," he resummons the elusive person of the מוכיח, the "mediator," of 9:33 (notice the cognation of the two words). This time, however, the "mediating" third party will not intervene on the behalf of a doomed man, but will merely act upon the memory of a man who is unjustly brought to death.

It would be unexpected and unnatural to find that, after having spoken of his end as imminent, Job adds in vs. 22, **When a few years are come, then I shall go the way whence I shall not return.** Thus several commentators accept a conjectural emendation of the text and read, instead of שנות מספר, **a few years,** either (*a*) מספר שנות, "the number of [my] years" (has come to an end); or (*b*) נשות מספר, "the women of mourning" (are coming). These proposals are not satisfactory. At any rate, it would be anomalous if in vs. 22 death were envisaged as a somewhat distant event, when in the following strophe (17:1) the same prospect is faced as an imminent reality.

21. As a Man Pleadeth for His Neighbor.—(Cf. Gen. 18:23-33; Exod. 32:11-14, 31-32; John 17.) In Hebrew the **man** of vs. 21*a* is the "hero," the "Titan," like Job (cf. Exeg. on 21:7-13); the **man** of vs. 21*b* is a "son of earth." Job thinks of himself as a prince (31:37) in his relation to God, and as a mortal with his fellow mortals: in both cases there is a **right** to be maintained, and he would have God himself to do it. There is nevertheless an almost irresistible suggestion in the mistranslation of the KJV. Interestingly enough, Kissane, from a slightly different point of view, supports it: Job's cry "is pleading for him before God as one man might plead for another before a human judge."⁴ If instead of the endless recriminations there were such pleading! (See Expos. on vs. 19; 6:28-30.)

Observe that over and over again Job still turns to God in prayer; and recall Browning's lines from "Instans Tyrannus":

I struck him, he grovelled of course—
For, what was his force?
I pinned him to earth with my weight
And persistence of hate:

. . . .

Round his creep-hole, with never a break,
Ran my fires for his sake;
Over-head, did my thunder combine
With my underground mine:
Till I looked from my labor content
To enjoy the event.

When sudden . . . how think ye, the end?
Did I say "without friend"?
Say rather, from marge to blue marge
The whole sky grew his targe
With the sun's self for visible boss,
While an Arm ran across
Which the earth heaved beneath like a breast
Where the wretch was safe prest!
Do you see? Just my vengeance complete,
The man sprang to his feet,
Stood erect, caught at God's skirts, and prayed!
—So, *I* was afraid!

⁴ *Loc. cit.*

17 My breath is corrupt, my days are extinct, the graves *are ready* for me.

2 *Are there* not mockers with me? and doth not mine eye continue in their provocation?

3 Lay down now, put me in a surety with thee; who *is* he *that* will strike hands with me?

17 My spirit is broken, my days are extinct,
　　the grave is ready for me.
2 Surely there are mockers about me,
　　and my eye dwells on their provocation.

3 "Lay down a pledge for me with thyself;
　　who is there that will give surety for me?

---

e) HELD WITHOUT BAIL (17:1-5)

17:1. This verse is in a different meter from that of the context. It is composed of three short stichs, as if the rhythm itself suggested the state of breathless agony in which the dying man labors:

> My breath is labored,
> My days are extinct,
> The graveyard is mine.

Vs. 1*a* is usually translated, **My spirit is broken.** The word *rûaḥ* means either "breath" or "spirit" in the sense of vital principle (cf. 10:12; 12:10); but the rendering of *ḥubbālāh* as **broken** is strained. This word is usually derived from חבל II, and thus may refer to a broken yoke. Its Arabic cognate may mean "corrupt," "unsound," and if this sense could be found in Hebrew usage the phrase would indicate that Job is becoming aware of his mental undoing: "My spirit is deranged." More probably, however, the word may be derived from חבל I, meaning "to bind," "to twist," hence, in the Piel voice, "to writhe in travail" (cf. Song of S. 8:5), and in the Pual, "to be halted," under the pangs of agony. This interpretation fits the immediate context: Job recognizes in his panting breath one of the prodromes of his death.

2. Witnessing the signs of Job's impending end, his friends refuse more than ever to consider his claim to innocence, and they persist in their attitude of **provocation.**

3-4. The hero, however, does not yield any ground and renews the fight directly with God himself in a prayer of defiance: **Lay down a pledge for me with thyself** (reading with Syriac, *'erbhōnî* instead of *'orbhēnî*). Since God is acting as if he too considers Job as a criminal, let him accept a guarantee until Job's innocence is established. But who is willing to take such a risk? **Who is there that will give surety for me?** Lit., **that will strike hands with me** (KJV), i.e., that will give me now the assurance that he will appear before God on my behalf (cf. Prov. 6:1; 11:15; 17:18; 22:26) and provide bail until a trial may be arranged. No one will take such a risk, and Job is left alone in the midst of his friends, for God has **closed their minds to understanding** (vs. 4*a*). Divine enmity is responsible not only for Job's plight but also for his friends' misunderstanding.

17:3. The God Who Goes Bail.— (See Expos. on 14:15; 16:16, 19.) **Lay down a pledge for me with thyself.** No one else will do it, no one else can. Job is compelled to fall back on the same "impossible possibility" which keeps occurring to him: the God who is himself the judge must himself go bail, and when the case comes up, somewhere on the other side of death, see to it that all the wrongs are set right. Only in that way, by God's own gracious act, can the old relationship which has so mysteriously been broken off ever be restored, or better still, yield to another which shall be deeper and richer.

It is not that Job ever expects to be "justified" by reason of his "works"; he pleads for a justification that shall have its source in the very being of God. So it is in the N.T., becoming there the very mainspring of the Christian ethic. To Paul the whole of mankind is, in Job's figure of speech, out on bail, to be brought back into fellowship with God by faith and faith alone (Rom. 3:20-26; 11:32; etc.): "Behold therefore the goodness and severity of God" (Rom. 11:22). There is no question of tempering the divine justice with mercy: unless indeed one understands what tempering really means.

4 For thou hast hid their heart from understanding: therefore shalt thou not exalt *them*.

5 He that speaketh flattery to *his* friends, even the eyes of his children shall fail.

---

4 Since thou hast closed their minds to understanding,

therefore thou wilt not let them triumph.

5 He who informs against his friends to get a share of their property, the eyes of his children will fail.

---

4. Therefore thou wilt not let them triumph: This translation is based on a correction of *terōmēm* ("thou shalt exalt") into either *terōmemēm* or *terīmēm* (which provides the necessary direct object in the form of the pronominal suffix **them**). The sequence of thought, however, remains obscure. Dhorme, followed by Hölscher, corrects תרומם into תרום ידם, and translates the clause, "No hand has been raised [in my favor]." The sense thus obtained fits the context, but the emendation is highly conjectural. One might respect the C.T. תרומם, vocalize *terōmām* (Polal; cf. Ps. 66:17), and render the clause, "Therefore, thou shalt not be exalted." (The Polel is used with God; cf. Ps. 30:1: "I shall exalt thee, Yahweh!") According to this interpretation, Job concludes his aggressive prayer by making another blasphemous statement: Since God has left Job destitute, surely he cannot expect praise from his victim! The Masoretes naturally would have preserved a reading more conducive to reverence, although it represented a *non sequitur:* "Therefore thou shalt not exalt," while the LXX merely omitted the difficult phrase. If the interpretation here proposed is correct, the prayer ends abruptly with a shocking invective. Tortured by his divine enemy and accused by his uncomprehending friends, the lonely titan scoffs at ingratiating softness. He has given up the hope of winning God by begging. He stands on his ground, bloody but unbowed. At the threshold of the grave he throws a taunting threat at the Godhead and almost viciously shouts: "Therefore thou shalt not be exalted!" It must be acknowledged, however, that this interpretation also is conjectural. The meaning of vs. 4*b* probably depends on the context following, and two possibilities remain: (*a*) If vs. 5 refers to Job's friends, then it is likely that vs. 4*b* alludes to them also, since this clause comes after vs. 4*a*, in which the allusion to the same men can hardly be denied. Thus the reading *terīmēm* (Hiphil of *rûm* with pronominal suffix of the third person plural) may be tentatively proposed as doing least violence to the M.T. Job's chain of thought would then be, "Therefore thou shouldest not let them triumph [by dispatching me to the grave]. It is true that they are unable to discern my innocence since thou hast thickened their minds [vs. 3]. But that is not a reason for offering them a vindication by the spectacle of my death. Thou shouldest now prove to them the outrageous error of their position by restoring me from death." (*b*) If, however, vs. 5 does not refer to the friends, then it is at least possible that Job has concluded his aggressive prayer in the mood of defiance described above.

5. This verse unfortunately is also obscure. Assuming that the text is not hopelessly corrupt, commentators have proposed five widely divergent interpretations:

(*a*) **He that speaketh flattery to his friends, even the eyes of his children shall fail.** The KJV obtains this meaning by considering the noun *ḥēleq* as derived from חלק II, "to be smooth," "slippery" (cf. Prov. 7:21), and by construing it as the direct object of the verb יגיד, "he reveals," "informs," "proclaims" (thus ignoring the prepositions). Even if this rendering were supported by syntactic usage, it is hard to see how the idea thus obtained would fit the context.

It does not mean to tamper with, nor does it mean to water down. It means "to bring to a proper degree of hardness and toughness." The mercy of God is what gives his justice its cutting edge. Else why the psalmist's word, "But there is forgiveness with thee, that thou mayest

be feared" (Ps. 130:4)? It is not the majesty of God or his wrath that works awe in the soul; it is his lovingkindness and tender mercy.

Rufus M. Jones, the great Quaker, has told of how that was brought home to him in his youth. His mother and father went out one hot

(b) The RSV (cf. ERV, ASV, Amer. Trans., etc.) understands the verb יגיד in the sense of "he denounces" (cf. Lev. 5:1; Josh. 2:14; Prov. 29:24; Jer. 20:10), and takes the word *ḥēleq* as derived from חלק I, "to divide."

> **He who informs against his friends to get a share of their property,**
> **the eyes of his children will fail.**

Such a translation is grammatically sound, and may support the view that the verse is a popular proverb quoted by Job. But in what way is the maxim applicable to the situation? How could Job suggest that his friends are greedy for his estate when the whole poetic discussion (let alone the prose prologue) shows that he is completely destitute? In addition, how could Job warn his friends with threats directed to their children when he himself (in 21:19) repudiates the doctrine according to which the sons receive retribution for the sins of their fathers?

(c) "He that denounceth his friends for the sake of flattering, even the eyes of his children shall fail." According to this rendering (American Jewish Translation), which combines elements of both (a) and (b) and skillfully avoids the grammatical difficulties raised by either one, Job states that the friends' hostility is motivated by their abject submission to God's capricious and immoral omnipotence, and they merely denounce Job in order to pay court to a divine tyrant. This interpretation, however, faces the same objection as that mentioned above (in connection with the threat of a punishment inflicted upon the children for the cruelty of the fathers), and it also contradicts the statement of vs. 4a, for it assumes that the friends are perfectly clear about Job's situation and inwardly know that he is innocent.

(d) "Somebody invites his friends to share [his goods] while the eyes of his own children are failing [from want]." Such a translation, which is accepted with minor variations by a great many commentators (Hitzig, Budde, Peake, Dhorme, et al.; cf. Vulg.), also suggests that Job quotes a gnomic saying: How can his friends teach him anything significant, offer him a share of their wisdom, while their own households are devoid of it? Physician, heal thyself! This rendering is grammatically possible, for the verb יגיד, usually followed by a preposition introducing a personal object, may be constructed in directly transitive fashion (II Kings 7:9; Ezek. 43:10; cf. especially Job 26:4; 31:37). However, the meaning "to invite" is not supported by parallel uses (as noted by Driver and Gray), and the construction of this verb with *leḥēleq*, "for a share," or *leḥalleq* (pointing לחלק as Piel infinitive), "in order to share," remains highly hypothetical.

(e) Kissane follows the translation mentioned immediately above, but he holds that this verse introduces vs. 6 and refers to the Deity:

> As one inviteth friends to partake,
> While the eyes of his children languish. . . .

Accordingly, Job likens God to some heartless and senseless man who bids his friends to a feast while allowing his own children to starve; and this comparison means that "God permits the wicked to prosper while the just suffer calamity" (Kissane, *The Book of Job* [Dublin: Browne & Nolan, 1939], p. 104). Such an exegesis is ingenious and attractive, for it would fit the present stage of Job's hostility toward God and even widen the cleavage between them, while implying a sarcasm and stressing a pathetic paradox. Yes,

---

summer day and gave him strict charge in their absence to weed the turnip patch. He said he had never quite understood the meaning of the biblical phrase, "from everlasting to everlasting," until that afternoon he looked down those long rows. Just then two of his friends came by with bait and fishing tackle. They pro-

posed that he go with them for a while, promising to help him once they got back. Such a bargain was scarcely to be despised by a boy of fourteen, so off they went. But no fisherman has ever yet marked the passing of time. When he trudged up the path to his front door late that afternoon, his mother was waiting for him. He

6 He hath made me also a byword of the people; and aforetime I was as a tabret.	6 "He has made me a byword of the peoples,
	and I am one before whom men spit.
7 Mine eye also is dim by reason of sorrow, and all my members *are* as a shadow.	7 My eye has grown dim from grief,
	and all my members are like a shadow.
8 Upright *men* shall be astonished at this, and the innocent shall stir up himself against the hypocrite.	8 Upright men are appalled at this,
	and the innocent stirs himself up against the godless.
9 The righteous also shall hold on his way, and he that hath clean hands shall be stronger and stronger.	9 Yet the righteous holds to his way,
	and he that has clean hands grows stronger and stronger.

Job's interlocutors are the *friends* of God, he admits, and their good fortune proves it! But he, Job, is a *child* of God! He was once standing closer to him than they are now, yet he is abandoned by his inhuman father. The validity of this interpretation cannot, however, be demonstrated. In view of the unsatisfactory or conjectural character of all proposed translations, the critic should provisionally accept the fact that the M.T. does not represent the original wording of the verse. In all probability the poet did not allude to "friends" in vs. 5*a* (for Theod. and Symm. both read the word רעים not as *rē'im,* "friends," as the M.T. does, but as *rā'im,* "evil things"). In addition, the LXX (which omits vs. 5*a*) may have read in vs. 5*b* a text quite different from that of the Masoretes, for it renders, "and my eyes pined away for my sons." If this reading had any support, vs. 5*b* would constitute an appropriate climax for the whole passage. Job would realize that no one around him will offer a surety on his behalf (vs. 3). Some would have done it gladly, his own sons. But they are gone.

f) A Byword in the World (17:6-10)

6-7. So extraordinary is Job's fate that he has become a **byword** in the world (vs. 6*a*; cf. Ps. 69:11) and an object of abhorrence and curse (vs. 6*b*). His **grief** has dimmed his **eye . . . and all** his "thoughts" (reading with Syriac ויצרי as *wîçāray*) **are like a shadow** (vs. 7).

8-10. These verses seem to interrupt the development, and some interpreters (Duhm, Peake, *et al.*) have attempted to solve the difficulty by transposing this passage into the second speech of Bildad (after 18:3). If the original order has been preserved in the present text, however, one may clarify the meaning by translating the verbs in the future tense. Job, aware that he will have proverbial significance for generations to come, knows that **upright men shall be astonished at this** (vs. 8*a*), and **the innocent** will find comfort in his example: he will **stir up himself against the hypocrite** (*ḥānēph;* cf. 8:13). Men like Job who are truly **righteous** and have **clean hands** will not by calamity or calumny be shaken out of their conviction of innocence. He himself will **hold on his way,**

---

was sure he knew what was in store, and he had no word to offer in extenuation. He knew he deserved it. Silently she led him to his room; whereupon he was doubly sure. It always happened there.

But a miracle happened instead. Mother put me in a chair, kneeled down, put her hands on me and told God all about me. She interpreted her dream of what my life was to be. She portrayed the boy and the man of her hopes. She told God what she had always expected me to be. And then how I disappointed her hope. "O God," she said, "take this boy of mine and make him the boy and man he is divinely designed to be." Then she bent over

and kissed me and went out and left me alone in the silence with God.[5]

It is the human heart that somehow has to be broken before anything else can happen (Rom. 2:4).

9. With Head Bloody but Unbowed.—"Let God be true, but every man a liar." So Paul (Rom. 3:4). Job comes very near reversing it. Even if God is the kind of God Job is more than half afraid he is (10:13), the **righteous** man can still **hold on his way;** and more, be

5 Louis Finkelstein, ed., *American Spiritual Autobiographies* (New York: Harper & Bros., 1948), pp. 122-23.

10 But as for you all, do ye return, and come now: for I cannot find *one* wise *man* among you.

11 My days are past, my purposes are broken off, *even* the thoughts of my heart.

12 They change the night into day: the light *is* short because of darkness.

10 But you, come on again, all of you,
　　and I shall not find a wise man among
　　you.

11 My days are past, my plans are broken off,
　　the desires of my heart.

12 They make night into day;
　　'The light,' they say, 'is near to the
　　darkness.'[r]

[r] Heb obscure

he will persist in the assertion of his integrity and even be **stronger and stronger** in maintaining his righteousness. This interpretation is confirmed by the dramatic injunction which follows (vs. 10). Horrified by Job's insuperable pride (this could not be the case if vss. 8-9 constituted a tame acceptance of orthodoxy or were not in their original position), Eliphaz and his companions make as if to go, leaving their interlocutor to his mad obstinacy. Job is therefore moved to entreat them to stay (as he has already done in a similar situation; cf. 6:29). "But all of you, will you turn back? Come back, please!" (Vs. 10*a*.) Note the alliteration in *we'ullām kullām*, "but indeed, all of them," instead of *kullekhem*, "all of you" (a reading which nevertheless appears in five MSS). Why should the sufferer call back his friends? He has no hope of convincing them. He knows that he will **not find a wise man among** them, yet such is the isolation of misunderstood misery that it clings to the shreds of time-honored friendships. True wisdom, so Job implies, is not to be discovered among its professionals. Perhaps we have here an anticipation of the thought expressed in ch. 28.

g) Communing with Worms (17:11-16)

11-12. Having had his bitter say, the hero now relapses, as is his wont at the end of his speeches (cf. 3:24-26; 7:21; 10:20-22; 14:18-22), into a quiet wailing over the approach of death. The Hebrew of vs. 11 presents several difficulties which are overlooked by the traditional translators. The punctuation of the M.T. favors the rendering, "My days are spent; my projects are broken, [even] the desires of my heart." However, while the first verb, "to pass over," may be used intransitively in the sense of "to pass by," it is

stronger and stronger (see Expos. on 13:15; 23:10; etc.). F. W. Robertson, when assailed by doubt, was accustomed to budget what light he had, and rehearse in his mind against all the odds those things still most certainly true: that courage is better than impurity, that honor is better than dishonor, that truth is better than falsehood, and love better than hate. Said he:

In that fearful loneliness of spirit . . . I know not but one way in which a man may come forth from his agony scathless; it is by holding fast to those things which are certain still—grand, simple landmarks of morality. In the darkest hour through which a human soul can pass, whatever else is doubtful, this at least is certain. If there be no God, and no future state, yet even then it is better to be generous than selfish, better to be chaste than licentious, better to be true than false, better to be brave than to be a coward. . . . Thrice blessed is he who,—when all is drear and cheerless within and without . . . —has obstinately clung to moral good. Thrice blessed, because *his* night shall pass into clear, bright day.[8]

[8] Stopford A. Brooke, *The Life and Letters of Frederick W. Robertson* (Boston: Ticknor & Fields, 1865), I, 108-9.

A profounder question, however, asserts itself: Why are courage, and hope, and purity, and honor, and truth, and love better than their opposites? (Cf. Expos. on 14:7-12.) Can these things be cut free of God, like flowers from the stem? (See Expos. on 1:1, "Does Faith Matter?") It is for this reason, as Strahan points out,[7] that vss. 8-10*a* have to some scholars seemed more appropriate in the mouth of Bildad (after 18:3), where they would mean that no matter how unjust Job is to his friends, they will stick to their course. If we take the verses in their present context, one may understand something of the pride which God seems to have in Job (cf. 1:8; 2:3; Expos. on 1:20-22; cf. also Matt. 7:21).

12. False Hopes.—(See Exeg.; Expos. on 11:16, 18; 13:13-19.) It has already been noted that in the first cycle each of the friends holds out to Job the prospect of ultimate restoration on condition of his repentance (cf. Expos. on 5:18, 23; etc.). In the second cycle they have given up the illusions they once cherished: Job

[7] *Job*, p. 159.

13 If I wait, the grave *is* mine house: I have made my bed in the darkness.	¹³ If I look for Sheol as my house, if I spread my couch in darkness,
14 I have said to corruption, Thou *art* my father: to the worm, *Thou art* my mother, and my sister.	¹⁴ if I say to the pit, 'You are my father,' and to the worm, 'My mother,' or 'My sister,'
15 And where *is* now my hope? as for my hope, who shall see it?	¹⁵ where then is my hope? Who will see my hope?
16 They shall go down to the bars of the pit, when *our* rest together *is* in the dust.	¹⁶ Will it go down to the bars of Sheol? Shall we descend together into the dust?"

unlikely that the word *zimmāh* could designate Job's "plans" or "projects," for everywhere else in biblical Hebrew (including 31:11), it refers to "evil devices" and especially to various acts of sexual immorality (cf. Lev. 18:17; 20:14; Judg. 20:6; Jer. 13:27; etc.). Furthermore, the position of the phrase **the desires of my heart**, its lack of connecting word or prefix, and the abrupt shortness of the meter (two nouns in construct relation are not sufficient here to form a colon) render the usual translations highly suspect. In addition, the LXX (ἐν βρόμῳ) considers *zimmōthay* not as the first subject of the second verb, but as the qualitative object of the first verb, and takes it to mean "uproar," "groaning" (apparently from the Aramaic root זמם). Finally, the *hapax legomenon* *mōrāshê lebhābhî*, which is usually translated **the desires of my heart** (through the hypothetical derivation of the word *mōrashîm* from ארש; Akkadian, *erêsu*), can hardly fit in this case the concrete and physical meaning of the verb *nitteqû*, "are torn apart" (cf. τὰ ἄρθρα τῆς καρδίας in the LXX). One may therefore turn to an Aramaism (see the Syriac *maršo;* cf. "the walls of my heart" in Jer. 4:19), and the whole verse may then be translated, in full respect of meter, grammar, and lexicography:

> My days are overfilled with my groanings:
> The ligaments[?] of my heart are torn apart.

Job, aware of his physiological condition, is once more expressing the conviction that he cannot hope to regain his health.

Vs. 12 offers no difficulty of translation, but its meaning is quite obscure. **They change the night into day.** Who are **they?** Dhorme and others connect this clause with the last words of vs. 11 (thereby admitting the difficulty mentioned in connection therewith) and read, "The desires of my heart change the night into day" (vss. 11*b*, 12*a*); i.e., they produce insomnia (cf. 7:3-4, 13-15). However, in addition to the fact that vs. 11 forms a poetic whole (see above), there is an obvious parallel between **night** and **day** in vs. 12*a* and **light** and **darkness** in vs. 12*b*. For this reason the whole line is generally understood as referring to the friends of Job. They pretend—he exclaims in a despondent aside— that his night will soon be day (vs. 12*a*) and that "light is nearer than the presence of darkness" (vs. 12*b*; perhaps a delayed allusion, according to the poet's technique, to Zophar's speech in 11:17), but Job knows better than to delude himself.

13-16. His only hope is that **Sheol** will be his home. Observe the similar imagery in Ps. 139:8, where a cognate of the word *yeçûʻay*, **my couch**, is used. Some details of translation are uncertain (e.g., the conjunction **if** in vs. 13*a* should not be repeated in vss. 13*b*, 14; cf. RSV), but the general meaning is clear. The friends have told Job to repent and to shake off his despair, and he retorts in the face of the inescapable imminence

is definitely not planning to repent. Confident, therefore, that God has given him up to a reprobate mind, they no longer dangle any bribe in front of his eyes: it is now only the threat of retribution they would have him envisage (see Expos. on 15:1–21:34). But the mind of	Job still lingers behind. The friends are always blithely ahead of his anguished soul. Deliverance out of all his trouble! The very idea of it! There will be no such thing. "It is darkest just before the dawn." Is there no other ground more sure than that, on which a man's hope may

18 Then answered Bildad the Shuhite, and said,

2 How long *will it be ere* ye make an end of words? mark, and afterward we will speak.

18 Then Bildad the Shuhite answered: 2 "How long will you hunt for words? Consider, and then we will speak.

---

of death that any hope would be a delusion. Another touch of dark humor is here: "My hope and I," the lamenter remarks, as if he were speaking of a bride, **shall we descend together into the dust?** (vs. 16b).

3. SECOND DISCOURSE OF BILDAD (18:1-21)

While Job is blazing a trail in a hitherto unexplored jungle and is moving thus toward a goal which still eludes him, the friends have already arrived at a conclusion. Arrived? They do not seem to have traveled one inch in any direction. By the words which he places in the mouths of his characters, the poet reveals a profound and intimate knowledge of religious men everywhere. Some, like Job, may be branded as heretics by a stable and therefore static majority; but their daring, in spite of its inherent danger and occasional folly, is constructive and prophetic in the true sense of the word. Others, like the friends, are pious and learned transmitters of well-tried formulas, who persist in perpetrating error in the face of some unquestionable truth. Thus, Bildad, speaking from the treasure of tradition, does not see that a "universal" law always admits of exceptions.

a) DISTURBING THE NATURAL ORDER (18:1-4)

18:2. The M.T. in this verse has plural verbs, and accordingly Bildad is addressing not Job but several auditors at once: either the other two friends or some hypothetical bystanders. Such a procedure, however, constitutes a departure from the pattern of the poetic discussion in which a friend always addresses Job and never his own colleagues, even less an unnamed and silent audience. Furthermore, the end of the strophe (vs. 4) is spoken directly to Job in the second person singular. Many scholars therefore follow the reading of the LXX, which has the singular in vs. 2 as well as in vs. 4. Nevertheless, while the plural תבינו in vs. 2b may easily be explained by dittograph (. . . תבינ[ו] ואחר), it is hard to imagine how a singular תשים could have produced the plural תשימון in vs. 2a. If the M.T. is correct, we have to admit that Bildad begins his discourse, not unlike Elihu (32:3), by rebuking his own friends. **How long will you hunt for words?** The RSV offers an attractive but not demonstrable rendering by relating the strange word to the Arabic *qanaça,* "to hunt," and by conjecturing for it the meaning of "snare" or "trap." If Bildad is speaking in the plural (M.T.) to his colleagues, then he is chiding them for not attacking Job's position more directly and forcefully. He continues in vs. 2b

---

stand? That the issue, for example, if not the best as he sees it, will yet be the best as God knows it?

18:1-21. The Speech of Bildad.—The two of you should quit dealing with this man so gently. Come out with it. (See Exeg. It may be better to assume that Bildad addresses Job at once: How long are you going to keep this up? Shall we have to listen to you forever?) **Stupid cattle you** call us, you who are the only beast in the picture. God is not tearing at you, neither are we (16:9-10); you are tearing **yourself in your** anger. Do you think you can substitute your own ideas for God's, and turn the whole universe topsy-turvy so that you can get away with

it? Not in a million years! In spite of all you say, **the wicked** man is doomed. The very stars in their courses fight against him. He is harassed **on every side.** Calamity yearns for him. Deadly plague marches him off toward death. Root and branch he is gone and forgotten, the horror of mankind (vs. 18, lit., "they shall drive"), with none to come after him, an abomination the world around (vs. 20). Your lot is no more than the common lot of the man **who knows not** God.

2-4. The Moral Order.—The speeches of the friends in the second cycle, Eliphaz in considerable measure, Bildad and Zophar in a manner still more pronounced, veer off from God, who

3 Wherefore are we counted as beasts, *and* reputed vile in your sight?

4 He teareth himself in his anger: shall the earth be forsaken for thee? and shall the rock be removed out of his place?

---

3 Why are we counted as cattle? Why are we stupid in your sight?

4 You who tear yourself in your anger, shall the earth be forsaken for you, or the rock be removed out of its place?

---

by bidding them to **consider** thoroughly the case which is before them, and he concludes, **then we will speak**. If, on the contrary, Bildad is speaking in the singular (LXX) to Job, he is derisively asking him to put an end to his rhetoric. Instead of looking for new forms of eloquence, Job should **consider** the situation, **and then we will speak** together, one with the other (in this case the verb נדבר should be vocalized as a Niphal rather than as a Piel). Other critics suggest that the word קנצי is connected with the Akkadian *qinçu*, "fetter," and they translate vs. 2a, "How long will you put restraint on words?" With this rendering, again, Bildad might address his colleagues, urging them not to tone down their rebuke of Job but rather to denounce his crime mercilessly. Or Bildad might be saying to the rebellious heretic, "How long wilt thou attempt to silence us?" Although this latter meaning would fit the context following (vss. 3-4), the exegete must confess that there is no objective clue to a correct translation, and thus no satisfactory interpretation.

3-4. Bildad now defends the knowledge and wisdom of his friends and of himself. Job had said in his reply to Zophar, "But ask the beasts, and they will teach you" (12:7), thereby inferring that even the lower creatures, such as the hippopotamus, have more intelligence than the professionals of learning and reflection. Bildad apparently felt the sting of the insult, for he now retorts, "Why should we pass for a beast, and be obtuse in thy sight?" (vs. 3). The M.T. has נטמינו, "we are defiled" or **reputed vile**, but it is better to read with three MSS נטמנו (*neṭammōnú*), from the verb טמם, "to stop up" (cf. the LXX, "we are become dumb"). The thought of **stupid** animals suggested to Bildad a new invective. It is Job who is a beast, but of course not a silent one: "O thou who tearest thyself in thine anger . . ." (vs. 4a). There is no need to conjecture that one line is missing here. Job has just accused God of tearing him apart (16:9). Bildad suggests that it is Job who stupidly, in a brutish fashion, is hurting himself. More than this, would Job fain be like the blind giant shaking the pillars of Dagon's temple out of their base and engulfing the crowd of his enemies within his own death (Judg. 16:30)? By the reiteration of his blasphemies would Job risk the catastrophe of an aroused divine wrath not only upon himself but also upon his community? Has he not lost all perspective in the complex of a monstrous egotism which prompts him to disregard the safety of others for the sake of his own vindication? Does the welfare of one man count more than the fate of the people? In brief, **shall the earth be forsaken for you** (vs. 4b)? In the next line, however, Bildad's thought seems to swerve in another direction: **or shall the rock be**

---

in the preceding chapters had been the constant focus of their argument, toward the constitution of the universe, the way things are (cf. Expos. on 19:6). To see that movement against the background of Israel's history is to see the first steps taken within the Hebrew-Christian tradition which were bound sooner or later to result in the depersonalizing of God and human existence. The tendency toward abstraction, the movement away from person in the direction of idea, is evident in the very names used for the Deity (cf. Expos. on 4:20b). It is now underscored by the shift from a justice personally administered to a justice arrived at in the nature of life itself—life human (vs. 18) and subhuman

(vs. 10, *et passim*; cf. Judg. 5:20; Expos. on 8:4). Of course God is back of it all in theory; but he *is* "back of it." So it is that when the old prophetic faith, where God's immediate act was his direct word, seems in some excess of calamity to be no longer so naïvely tenable, recourse is had to more empirical sanctions. This encroachment of "philosophy" on religion in the years following the Exile, as in eighteenth-century Deism, is often enough reflected in the modern pulpit. The form the sermon takes is all too frequently somewhat as follows: (*a*) We stand at a fork in the road: on the left an antithesis, God or man; on the right, a synthesis, God and man. (*b*) We dare not choose "God or man";

5 Yea, the light of the wicked shall be put out, and the spark of his fire shall not shine.

6 The light shall be dark in his tabernacle, and his candle shall be put out with him.

7 The steps of his strength shall be straitened, and his own counsel shall cast him down.

---

5 "Yea, the light of the wicked is put out,
　　and the flame of his fire does not shine.
6 The light is dark in his tent,
　　and his lamp above him is put out.
7 His strong steps are shortened
　　and his own schemes throw him down.

---

removed out of its place? (vs. 4c). He may remember here Job's own allusion to the universal law of decay in the realm of nature ("and the rock is removed from its place," 14:18b), while satirically asking, "Do you believe that your little self is so important as to warrant a change in the order of the universe?"

Another interpretation is possible for both lines (vs. 4bc). Instead of directing the questions to Job himself, Bildad may be attempting to interpret his opponent's attitude, saying in effect, "According to your opinion, Job, does your own fate demonstrate that the earth *is* now forsaken by its creator? Has the rock been removed from its place?" In other words, Job is accused of practical atheism. Since the law of retribution is not verified in his own case, he probably concludes—so Bildad insidiously presumes—that God has left the earth, that the world of man has become a moral void, and that an insane confusion presides over the destiny alike of nature and mankind. This interpretation presents the advantage of introducing smoothly the second part of Bildad's discourse, which describes "the lot of him that knoweth not God" (18:21b).

b) Fate of the Ungodly Man (18:5-21)

After the thrust of his direct attack has been spent, Bildad seemingly turns to the didactic mode and paints with dexterity and gusto the picture of the *reshā'im,* "evil men" (vs. 5). In fact, he pursues with remarkable skill his fixed intent, which is the undermining of Job's self-assurance. As the various details of the portrait of the wicked unfold, the sufferer cannot help recognizing there himself, with the inescapable disclosure that such a man is really godless.

(1) Quenching His Light (18:5-7)

5-7. Bildad admits that **the wicked** may for a while enjoy what appears to be happiness. This theme is familiar to him (8:11-19). But he maintains that soon comes a time when their **lamp . . . is put out** (vss. 5:6). Notice that he speaks from the point of view of a nomad accustomed to living in a **tent** (vs. 6a). The flame of the campfire (vs. 5), as well as the light of the lamp (vs. 6), are symbols of prosperity, warmth, good cheer, and even luxury. "I will banish from them the voice of mirth and the voice of gladness, the voice of the bridegroom and the voice of the bride, the grinding of the millstones and the light of the lamp" (Jer. 25:10). As a result of the ensuing darkness, the evil man is compelled to walk slowly and cautiously, and **his strong steps are shortened** (vs. 7a).

---

that way we run headlong into the moral order. Something, apparently, like the law of gravity. (c) We must choose "God and man," the only choice with a promise. Whereupon the whole matter may be laid down with the benediction— all of it safely out of sight of either the O.T. or the N.T. Both Testaments understand that "God and man" plunges us at once into the profoundest of all dilemmas: "we must" and we cannot! The O.T. begins with that; the N.T. resolves it.

Yet of course there is truth in what Bildad

says. To keep the partial truth in relation to the truth that makes it whole is the task that interpretation sets us—and life itself (see Exeg. on vss. 1-21; Expos. on vss. 5-21).

5-21. Hoist with His Own Petard.—It is a striking and lurid picture that Bildad draws, with much gilding of the lily. When there is little to say that has not already been said, take it all up in your hands again—he reverts freely to the speech which he first delivered himself (e.g., at vs. 14 to 8:15; at vs. 16 to 8:11-14, 16-17)—and decorate it with the air of a man who

8 For he is cast into a net by his own feet, and he walketh upon a snare.	8 For he is cast into a net by his own feet, and he walks on a pitfall.
9 The gin shall take *him* by the heel, *and* the robber shall prevail against him.	9 A trap seizes him by the heel, a snare lays hold of him.
10 The snare *is* laid for him in the ground, and a trap for him in the way.	10 A rope is hid from him in the ground, a trap for him in the path.
11 Terrors shall make him afraid on every side, and shall drive him to his feet.	11 Terrors frighten him on every side, and chase him at his heels.

Better, "the steps of his vigor," or "his lusty steps" (Kissane), since the word אוֹן means more than **strength,** "force," or "power," but designates "manly vigor" (Gen. 49:3; Hos. 12:3). Perhaps Bildad is subtly alluding to the horror which was felt among the ancient Semites whenever a family's name was in danger of extinction (cf. vs. 19). **His own schemes throw him down** (vs. 7b), or better, "make him stumble" (reading with LXX תכשילהו instead of תשליכהו). The hidden purpose of the evil man will sooner or later cause him to make a false move or take a wrong step. In darkness he will no longer be able to find the right direction. Worse, the evil character of his intentions will lead him to his ruin.

(2) Laying Snares About Him (18:8-11)

8-11. Such a man has a bad conscience: if he stumbles, it is because he feels surrounded by traps. More than this, he walks toward his own fall, **he is cast into a net by his own feet** (vs. 8). It is probably dangerous for the interpreter to seek a specific meaning

is uttering great and momentous judgments. The similes trip each on the other's heels, all of them meaning much the same thing. Only the emphasis is changed. Now it is not so much God who deals out the retribution: a kind of necessity inherent in the world itself has taken charge, surrogate of the Almighty (see Expos. on vss. 2-4). For **the wicked** the **fire** at the door of his tent has died down (vs. 5), the **light** that hangs above his head is gone out (vs. 6; cf. 21:7). No longer is his stride vigorous and sure: it is his heart within (vs. 7b) that makes his feet to stumble (vs. 8). Everything is a **snare** and a **trap** (cf. Ps. 9:16), a **pitfall** and a noose. He cannot stay where he is (vs. 11a), he cannot go anywhere else (vs. 11b). Catastrophe gapes for him like a hungry monster, ruin holds out its arms waiting for him to stumble (vs. 12; cf. 12:5-6). So indeed the world seems to a man hag-ridden by his conscience (see Exeg. on vss. 8-11). Innuendo gives place now to images less remote (cf. Expos. on 22:12-20). One may almost observe the accompanying gesture, and trace back each successive item to the prologue. **Disease** (leprosy?) eats into his flesh. He is rooted out of his dwelling, where he thought himself secure (8:15), and bundled off toward death. One is reminded of W. Somerset Maugham's story in *Sheppey.* Death says in Act III:

There was a merchant in Bagdad who sent his servant to market to buy provisions and in a little while the servant came back, white and trembling,

and said, Master, just now when I was in the market-place I was jostled by a woman in the crowd and when I turned I saw it was death that jostled me. She looked at me and made a threatening gesture; now, lend me your horse, and I will ride away from this city and avoid my fate. I will go to Samarra and there death will not find me. The merchant lent him his horse, and the servant mounted it, and he dug his spurs in its flanks and as fast as the horse could gallop he went. Then the merchant went down to the market-place and he saw me standing in the crowd and he came to me and said, Why did you make a threatening gesture to my servant when you saw him this morning? That was not a threatening gesture, I said, it was only a start of surprise. I was astonished to see him in Bagdad, for I had an appointment with him to-night in Samarra.[8]

Strangers, goes on Bildad, dwell where he dwelt; his house is accursed. His life withers away (see Exeg. on vss. 16-18), his name is no more abroad (vs. 17b; "field" for **street**). Even his fellows will have nothing to do with him (cf. 17:6; the theme will be further elaborated by Zophar in ch. 20). His family is cut off. Wherever men are, they are **appalled** at the sight (see Exeg. on vs. 20). So secure (12:6) are the **ungodly;** so permanent their lot (cf. 8:13, 19)!

11. Conscience Does Make Cowards of Us All. —Richard III, Macbeth, and Hamlet all bear witness to it. Whatever the origin of that voice within, whether from the ways of our mother

8 Used by permission of the author and William Heinemann, Ltd., publishers.

12 His strength shall be hunger-bitten, and destruction *shall be* ready at his side.

13 It shall devour the strength of his skin: *even* the firstborn of death shall devour his strength.

14 His confidence shall be rooted out of his tabernacle, and it shall bring him to the king of terrors.

15 It shall dwell in his tabernacle, because *it is* none of his: brimstone shall be scattered upon his habitation.

16 His roots shall be dried up beneath, and above shall his branch be cut off.

17 His remembrance shall perish from the earth, and he shall have no name in the street.

18 He shall be driven from light into darkness, and chased out of the world.

---

12 His strength is hunger-bitten,
  and calamity is ready for his stumbling.

13 By disease his skin is consumed,*
  the first-born of death consumes his limbs.

14 He is torn from the tent in which he trusted,
  and is brought to the king of terrors.

15 In his tent dwells that which is none of his;
  brimstone is scattered upon his habitation.

16 His roots dry up beneath,
  and his branches wither above.

17 His memory perishes from the earth,
  and he has no name in the street.

18 He is thrust from light into darkness,
  and driven out of the world.

* Cn: Heb *it consumes the limbs of his skin*

---

for every one of the synonymous terms here employed: **net** and "lattice work" (vs. 8), **gin** and **snare** (vs. 9), **rope** and **trap** (vs. 10). Briefly, the enumeration is summed up in the statement that "from every direction terrors surround him" if he remains stationary, so that he is paralyzed with fright (vs. 11*a*), "and they pursue him close in his tracks" as soon as he resumes his journey (vs. 11*b*). Standing or moving, the evil man is overwhelmed by fear, and his outward happiness is thwarted by his inward disintegration.

(3) MARCHING HIM TO THE KING OF TERRORS (18:12-15)

12-13. Rather than **His strength is hunger-bitten,** the text of vs. 12*a* means, lit., "His calamity is hungry [for him]" (cf. *La Sainte Bible*), or with a slight correction, "Ruin is ravenous for him" (Moffatt), which provides an excellent parallelism to "and distress stands ready at his side" in vs. 12*b*. **By disease his skin is consumed** (reading with RSV בדוי for בדי in vs. 13*a*) and **the first-born of death,** i.e., the plague or a similar epidemic visitation, **consumes his limbs** (vs. 13*b*).

14-15. As a result of this mortal sickness, "he is torn out of his tent, the refuge of his confidence," and "she [female personification of the plague?] shall march him to the king of terrors" (vs. 14). Another will occupy his dwelling after it has been disinfected with sulphur (vs. 15).

(4) ERADICATING HIS MEMORY (18:16-18)

16-18. The image of the tree is familiar to Bildad since he has already used it in his first discourse (8:16-19). Job had regretted the fact that man, unlike a tree when it is cut off, has no capacity for rebirth after death (14:7-9). Thereupon Eliphaz had retorted that indeed, as far as the evil man was concerned, his shoots would be consumed and his blossoms blown away (15:30). Now Bildad stresses once again the truth of his colleague's pronouncement. The **roots** of the evil man **dry up beneath,** and as a consequence of his

---

earth or the will of our father God—the two may not be so neatly divorced as many have seemed to wish—it is here, and it is troublesome, and it has to be dealt with. In the dealing there comes a time when its function is no longer pedagogical but punitive. Modern psychology has spent much time exploring the dark recesses of what it chooses to call "the feeling of guilt"

(see Kafka's novel, *The Trial*; cf. Expos. on 9:1–10:22; see also Kenneth Fearing, "Confession Overheard in a Subway" [9]). Is it not true (except for psychotic guilt) that when one *feels* guilty the chances are that one *has been* guilty; and that what one needs to be rid of is not so

[9] *The Afternoon of a Pawn-Broker and Other Poems* (New York: Harcourt, Brace & Co., 1943), pp. 19-21.

19 He shall neither have son nor nephew among his people, nor any remaining in his dwellings.	19 He has no offspring or descendant among his people, and no survivor where he used to live.
20 They that come after *him* shall be astonished at his day, as they that went before were affrighted.	20 They of the west are appalled at his day, and horror seizes them of the east.
21 Surely such *are* the dwellings of the wicked, and this *is* the place *of him that* knoweth not God.	21 Surely such are the dwellings of the ungodly, such is the place of him who knows not God."

inward desiccation, **his branches wither above** (vs. 16). While the righteous are held in everlasting remembrance (cf. Ps. 112:6), even the name of the wicked man is forgotten (vs. 17). In a word, he shall be **driven out of the world** (vs. 18*b*). The use of the word תבל, **world**, shows how complete will be his departure, or rather, his annihilation.

(5) A FRIGHTFUL WONDER FOR WEST AND EAST (18:19-21)

19. The evil man, Bildad concludes, is deprived of the most elemental hope: he shall have neither נין nor נכד (notice the alliterative sounds), neither **offspring** nor **descendant** (cf. Gen. 21:23; Isa. 14:22). **No survivor** shall remain in the places of his sojourn: thus in finality his name shall utterly vanish from the face of the earth.

20. Before such a spectacle the whole of mankind is shocked: "The Westerners are appalled at his fate and the Easterners are seized with a shudder." The ancient versions rendered אחרנים and קדמנים as "the last" and "the first," i.e., the future and the past generations. But one may ask whether the former or the latter could be witnesses of the evil man's end as described by Bildad. The dead might in some way hear of it in Sheol, but how could the men of the future be **astonished** if even his memory has been wiped out? Modern commentators generally, following Schultens, understand the verse as referring to both parts of civilized mankind, the Occidentals and the Orientals; cf. similar expressions in "the western sea" (Deut. 11:24; etc.), i.e., "the Mediterranean," and "the eastern sea" (Ezek. 47:18; etc.), i.e., "the Dead Sea." Thus in a paradoxical sense and in an indirect way Bildad is actually paying tribute to the exceptional stature of Job. At the beginning of his discourse he had been trying subtly to inject the idea that after all the sufferer is not the champion of suffering humanity or the unique target of God Almighty, but on the contrary a quite ordinary man belonging to the rank and file of humanity (cf. vs. 4). But now Bildad is offering oblique homage to Job's stature. Such a fantastic fate must be explained by a fantastic crime. The speaker is now ready to make his final condemnation.

21. The evil man is the unrighteous man, **the ungodly**, one who deviates from the right course (עול, probably the same word as in 16:11); the cause of his ill behavior is the fact that he **knows not God** (cf. "all those who forget God" in 8:13*a*). Bildad is a deeply sincere religionist who happens to be right theoretically about the organic relation of religion and ethics. Indeed, in the face of Job's hostile judgments on the intentions of

---

much the feeling as the guilt? In the "pedagogical" stage, to be a coward is often the better part of valor; in the "punitive" stage, it is the Augean stables of the self that need cleansing.

21. *The Truth that Is Half a Lie.*—The exposition of every speech of the friends must reckon with the truth that is no better than half a lie. There are of course distortions aplenty in the mind of Job; but they are the reflexes of truth, so to speak, the involuntary reactions of a truth that has not lost its courage, and is indeed itself a very passion (see Exeg.). With Eliphaz,

Bildad, and Zophar the case is different: their sincerity is no more in question than Job's; their point of departure is. They proceed from systems to persons; and persons come first in God's world (see Expos. on 2:11-13). The result is that their half lies come too near for comfort to being sneak lies, told consciously or unconsciously in order to buttress a "safe" truth. What they say about the inside of life is always truer than what they say about the outside; but even that is not unfailingly true. There are wicked men whose conscience seems no longer

19 Then Job answered and said,
2 How long will ye vex my soul, and break me in pieces with words?

19 Then Job answered:
2 "How long will you torment me, and break me in pieces with words?

God, one can understand Bildad's severity and even sympathize with the violence of his indignation. But for Bildad to infer that Job is one **who knows not God** constitutes the ultimate error. Job's personal acquaintance with God cannot be denied. Indeed, it is because the sufferer has been on intimate terms of trust, dependence, and hope with his Creator that he cannot help addressing him in arrogant and rebellious tones. Job's open hostility is the sign of his familiarity with the divine. He speaks to the Most High with the boldness of a son and the daring of a saint. This peculiarity of religious psychology has not escaped the attention of the poet, who at the same time creates in Bildad's character a model both of honor and of blindness.

4. Job's Reply to Bildad (19:1-29)

The sensitive mind of Job has not missed the insinuations of Bildad's peroration. He is now fully aware of his friends' total lack of comprehension (vss. 2-6), and this awareness intensifies the sense of his isolation: cornered by God (vss. 7-12) and ostracized by man (vss. 13-22), he is brought to such a paroxysm of misery that in the rebound of despair he dreams once more of a heavenly witness (16:19). Nay, he rises to heights beyond its comforting light, breaks the limits of his present condition (vss. 22-24), transcends the inevitable prospect of imminent death, and seizes in triumph upon the certainty of his ultimate vision of God (vss. 25-29).

a) The Unrighteousness of God (19:1-6)

19:2-3. Under Bildad's provocation Job smarts with anger and impatience. At the prosperous and pompous man's vilifying hints he is outraged and retorts without the

---

to trouble them at all. They either do not know or do not care. Certainly no such lurid descriptions as are given here can pass for realism. The moral aspects of God's rule have to be taken with a greater seriousness than any of which they are capable. Warning placards are not set up along the way that leads to death— not in any such profusion as this (see Expos. on 4:8); nor are any such obvious and vulgar inducements held out to the righteous (see Expos. on 1:6-12). The first step in any attempt to interpret the facts is to gather all of them. And who can? Prescription number one: humility. Even the Omniscience that has no need of knowing has shown itself quite capable of that! The second step is to face them. Prescription number two: honesty. Ultimately, however, it is not the interpretation that matters so much as the faith of one kind or another which is bound to do the interpreting. Prescription number three: "The fear of the Lord," which "is wisdom" (28:28; see Expos. on 21:5-6; 23:2).

19:1-29. The Answer of Job.—How long? you say. I say it too. How long will you go on driving at me, over and over again, wearing me down? Have you no shame? If I can be said to have done any wrong at all, even the slightest, it is over and done with (vs. 4, see Exeg.; or "I should certainly know about it myself"; perhaps,

"It has worked you no harm," or "It is none of your business," as in 7:20). You want to puff yourselves up by taking me down (vs. 5). Well, I fling it back in your teeth (**know then**): you ask if the Almighty perverts justice (8:3b; see Exeg.). I am not afraid to answer, Yes, he does. God, and God alone, has twisted the truth about me all out of shape and sprung his trap on me (cf. 18:8). What else can you make of his silence, while I keep crying, "Help! Help!" (vs. 7)? Every time I try to move he stops me short, and whenever I try to see he cuts off my view (vs. 8). He has **stripped** me naked of all I had, my wealth, my standing, my honor (vs. 9). **I am gone,** like the rubble of a ruined house; the hope that grew in my heart has been rooted out as if it had been a tree. All his doing (vss. 9-10). His wrath beleaguers my little tent like an army throwing up its ramparts for the assault (vss. 11-12). Far and near, from fringe to center, he has made me **a stranger** (vss. 13-15). My very servants, who at the barest motion of my hand or eye used to run my errands, refuse to listen now when I beg them (vs. 16). I am loathsome even to my wife. Children make fun of me, and you men whom **I** loved shrink from me in horror (vss. 17-19). Look at me. I am nothing but skin and bones. I have lost everything (vs. 20). For God's sake (see Expos. on

3 These ten times have ye reproached me: ye are not ashamed *that* ye make yourselves strange to me.

4 And be it indeed *that* I have erred, mine error remaineth with myself.

3 These ten times you have cast reproach upon me;
   are you not ashamed to wrong me?

4 And even if it be true that I have erred,
   my error remains with myself.

---

forms of courtesy. His words hide a bitterness hitherto unspoken at the outset of his replies. As Bildad has done twice previously (cf. 8:2; 18:2), he begins with **How long . . . ?** This may be a conscious or an unconscious attempt to mock the friend by imitation. **How long will you torment me?** or, better, "How long will you harrow my soul?" (Moffatt). The LXX reads תגיעון, "Will you weary . . . ?" instead of תוגיון (M.T.), "Will you afflict . . . ?" The verb יגה (M.T.) has a powerful impact; its Arabic cognate refers to physical violence (*wajay, castravit; wajiya,* "to be abraded" [used of the foot]); it is commonly found on the tongue of the persecuted Judeans during the sixth century B.C. (Lam. 1:4, 5, 12; 3:32, 33; cf. Isa. 51:23). A term of similar force appears in the next line, "And how long will you crush me with words?" (vs. 2*b*; cf. 22:9; Lam. 3:34; Isa. 53:5). Moral torture is similar to physical torment and no less hurtful. Perhaps the friends by their attacks are attempting to bring Job to "contrition" (cf. the image of "crushing" in the root of the Hebrew word "contrite": Isa. 57:15), but they succeed only in increasing his sufferings. **These ten times,** i.e., often, repeatedly (cf. Gen. 31:7; Num. 14:22), they have attempted "to bring him to complete humiliation" (vs. 3*a*). Are they not "ashamed of mistreating" him (vs. 3*b*)? The Hebrew word is uncertain; it has been variously translated by **make yourselves strange to me** (KJV), **wrong me** (RSV), etc. Ewald, followed by many modern commentators, has suggested that the Hebrew הכר is related to the Arabic *hakara,* "to oppress," "to torment," "to torture." The meaning of the word should be strong enough to match those which precede.

4. **And be it indeed that I have erred** [*shāghîthî,* cf. 6:24; 12:16], **mine error** [*meshûghāthî*] **remaineth with myself:** As in 7:20, Job is not making a confession of culpability. He is merely offering a conjecture for the sake of the discussion. Vs. 4*b* is susceptible of several interpretations. (*a*) "If I had erred (which I have not), my error would dwell with me and remain in my memory. I would remember it, but I do not;

---

vs. 21) have pity on me. He has none (vs. 21). Why do you keep stalking me as he does (cf. 10:16), tearing my good name to shreds (vs. 22)? If only I could plead my case before generations yet to come (vss. 23-24)! No, not that. Of what use would it be? Now at this very moment **I know that my Redeemer lives.** I shall die, he will not. When they bury me, he will **stand . . . at the last on my grave** (vs. 25). Though my body is destroyed—mind you this—**in my flesh shall I see God,** even I, see him **for myself, I, and not another.** How can I possibly wait for it (vss. 26-27)? Mutter as much as you like, "Now we have him cornered. Close in. The whole trouble is with him" (vs. 28). I warn you. Beware of God's vengeance. There is still some justice left (vs. 29)!

2. *Words that Crush.*— (See Expos. on 4:4; 6:24-27.) Contrition is what they were aiming at; attrition is what they accomplished. Words can do untold damage when they issue from pride (see Expos. on 6:28-30), from lack of true understanding and sympathy (see Expos. on 6:14, 18), from fear (see Expos. on 6:21-27),

from presumption (see Expos. on 6:28-30). With their "correct" attitude toward a man so manifestly under God's judgment, the friends enhanced their own sense of importance, and by refusing to align themselves with the sufferer they fortified themselves against a like disaster. What a psychologist would no doubt call "the defense mechanism" was in full swing. Significantly enough, the very word "mechanism," by making the process seem automatic, provides abundant reason for attributing none of the blame to ourselves. "Out of the abundance of the heart the mouth speaketh" (Matt. 12:34).

4. *Only for a Night?*— (See Exeg.; any one of the four or five possible readings could prove suggestive.) For Job to assume that if he had done any evil he should certainly have been conscious of it is to say the least about as insecure a position as one could possibly take. So too with the idea that what happened a long time ago cannot possibly matter any longer; or that our "lapses" hurt nobody (cf. Expos. on 7:20*a*-21*a*), are our business, at the most are only "temporary aberrations." In the drama it

therefore, I have never violated the commandments of the Almighty, I have not made even a mistake." This exegesis is unlikely, since the word שׁגה and its derivatives appear to refer to an act of offense by ignorance, inadvertence, or default, e.g., in a state of intoxication and irresponsibility caused by drunkenness or the passion of love (Lev. 4:14; Num. 15:22; Ezek. 45:20; etc.); thus, Job might be accused of having been unconscious of his crime, a charge that he definitely denies.

(*b*) A second interpretation would be most attractive were it not based upon a wholly conjectural though slight emendation of the text. Following the suggestion of Richter, one might propose to read, instead of אמנם, "in truth" (M.T.), אם נער, "if as an adolescent" (I have erred; cf. 13:26; Ps. 25:7), and then to consider the subsequent clause as a question, "Should my error remain forever with me?" Not only is the proposed correction unsupported by the MSS or the ancient versions, but also the translation "remain forever" is hardly possible, since the verb לין literally means "to sojourn for a night."

(*c*) A third interpretation might follow the lines already sketched in 7:20. Even if Job has lapsed into moral failure, surely he has hurt no one, neither God nor men. His **error** should not therefore bring upon him a punishment which is out of all proportion to a hypothetical peccadillo. This interpretation is possible, for although Job elsewhere (especially in ch. 31) shows that he is uncommonly scrupulous in matters of ethics and religious observance, he might conceivably maintain that a private and secret failure has no social consequences as long as it has not caused offense to another human being; and that in any case it should not affect the equanimity of God.

(*d*) The context following (vs. 5), nevertheless, suggests the possibility of a third meaning for vs. 4. Even if Job has committed a *meshûghâh*, this **error** or "mistake" (as opposed to a sin of intention) would be his own business and should not concern his friends. Some commentators believe that this thought is unlikely to have arisen in the mind of Job, who—as Eliphaz had appropriately remarked (4:3)—was always in the past eager to exercise his pastoral responsibilities toward others, and begged his would-be comforters to teach him what "errors" he had committed (6:24). But it will be observed that actually his relations with his "friends" have deteriorated so far that the ordinary canons of "friendship" no longer apply. This verse seems therefore to open up the theme of social isolation, which will be the object of a pathetically eloquent and even gripping description in the course of the next few lines.

(*e*) Following the LXX, which gave to the verb לין (vs. 4*b*) its literal meaning, one should probably render the verse as follows:

> If in truth I had erred,
> My error would have remained with me only for a night.

In other words, it would have been an aberration without any lasting effect. It would not offer a satisfactory explanation of Job's present misery. This exegesis is strengthened by the fact that the Greek translators include at this point two lines which are not found in the Hebrew text:

> I have spoken words which should not have been spoken,
> My sayings were in error, and they were not fitting.

This may very well represent the original, now accidentally dropped from the M.T. If this passage is authentic, then Job admits that he has made some utterances which were

---

is not the hero's own consciousness of innocence that is decisive: it is God's verdict that counts (1:8; 2:3), and the fact that Job cannot be bribed into what for him would be sheer dishonesty (13:15). The friends may indeed seem to take sin more seriously than he takes it; but their very seriousness is morbid. About Job there is something of Luther's *pecca fortiter*. While it is possible for people to be "picayunish" about their own sins, nobody may make light of sin itself. Item by item, sin is precisely what all the interpretations would have Job saying it is

5 If indeed ye will magnify *yourselves* against me, and plead against me my reproach; 6 Know now that God hath overthrown me, and hath compassed me with his net.	5 If indeed you magnify yourselves against me, and make my humiliation an argument against me, 6 know then that God has put me in the wrong, and closed his net about me.

out of order (perhaps an allusion to the curse on his day in ch. 3), but such an admission is comparable to the jettisoning of ballast which enables an aeronaut to climb to a higher level and to reach thereby a stronger and more secure position. The confession of an error in words, temporarily entertained, carries a denial of any graver guilt which would have permanently stained the record of the sufferer and would have been, according to the friends' thesis, the cause of his torments. Far from pleading guilty, Job turns to the offensive, and in the next lines delivers the thus-far mightiest blow of his encounter with the three antagonists.

5-6. If indeed you magnify yourselves against me: Rather, "on my account" (vs. 5*a*). The sufferer understands that his "friends" reveal by the cruelty of their attitude an attempt to justify themselves as well as their ideas. Their rabidity is a sign of their insecurity. They reaffirm their self-esteem as they "try to prove [his] infamy" (vs. 5*b*). Bildad rhetorically asked in his first speech, "Does God pervert justice?" (8:3*a*). Job answers now in the affirmative.

> Know ye then that it is Eloah who hath perverted my right,
> And hath compassed me with his net (vs. 6).

The rendering of '*iwwethānî* is not easy, for the verb עות, used in the Piel, means "to falsify," "to bend," "to subvert," "to make crooked," and is here linked directly with the personal pronoun "me" instead of with a concrete object like "scales" (as in Amos 8:5) or an abstract substantive like "justice" (as in 8:3). In any event, the general meaning is clear, for Job is plainly and bluntly stating that God, the author of his plight, has willfully distorted the truth concerning him. It is a grave charge. Once more one of the devices of the dialogue technique used by the poet appears in full light. It seems that the hero has slowly and silently meditated upon the statement made by Bildad in the first speech. To the question "Doth the Almighty pervert righteousness?" (8:3*b*) Job did not immediately make open reply. But now, cornered like a hunted animal, he dares to utter the blasphemy: "I tell you, it is God who has falsified my case." James Strahan observes (*Job*, p. 171) that "Job stops short of saying that God needs to be forgiven,

not, or vice versa: it is not a "temporary aberration"; it is everybody's business, for "no man sinneth unto himself"; it does hurt; it matters, for years and ages it matters, whether a man is conscious of it or unconscious. By as much as Job is wrong, so much the more right is he than any of the others. What he is really rebelling against is the doctrine of a meticulous retributive justice; he insists simply that no such explanation fits his case. A God like that would be an evil God. There is a profundity in the very contradictions that are waging their war inside his soul.

6. Calling God to Account.—Blasphemy it is, no less (1:11; 2:5). But nothing that Satan did is responsible for it (see Expos. on 1:6-12; 2:7-10). It is the blasphemy of a new faith in the agony of its encounter with the old (see Expos. on 7:21*c*; 10:13-17; 13:13-19). We are in the presence of a mind outraged by an antiquated idea of God and his dealing with human life; more important still, we are in the presence of a man whose heart will not follow where his mind has been driven. It is his picture of God that he hates, and that is perhaps the most deeply religious act of his life. When the heart denies what the mind affirms, the issue lies with the heart, where God is listening at the door.

Be it said to his credit, Job does not for an instant desert the ground on which he means to stage his controversy (see Expos. on 10:1-22). It is not the moral order that concerns him (cf. Expos. on 18:2-4); God concerns him (see Expos. on 21:5-6; 23:2). Even when he cries out

7 Behold, I cry out of wrong, but I am not heard: I cry aloud, but *there is* no judgment.

8 He hath fenced up my way that I cannot pass, and he hath set darkness in my paths.

9 He hath stripped me of my glory, and taken the crown *from* my head.

10 He hath destroyed me on every side, and I am gone: and mine hope hath he removed like a tree.

7 Behold, I cry out. 'Violence!' but I am
    not answered;
  I call aloud, but there is no justice.

8 He has walled up my way, so that I cannot pass,
  and he has set darkness upon my paths.

9 He has stripped from me my glory,
  and taken the crown from my head.

10 He breaks me down on every side, and I
  am gone,
  and my hope has he pulled up like a
  tree.

---

or of offering, with Omar Khayyám, to share with Him the responsibility, 'Man's forgiveness give, and take.' " Of course such an idea is entirely foreign to the poem. Nevertheless, Job's statement is exceptionally intrepid and borders on titanic usurpation of divine powers. By asserting that Eloah has distorted his right (cf. Rom. 3:5), he judges the Deity's conduct, motivation, and nature. He, the finite dwarf, the son of clay, the ephemeral moth, has lost the sense of his dependence upon God. Job denounces and rebukes his Creator. Man condemns God.

b) The Enmity of God (19:7-12)

In the second strophe Job rises to the stature of the noble damned by substantiating the charges he has just made against the nature of the divinity. However, he does not continue explicitly to accuse the Lord of the universe of acting unjustly. He concentrates on the task of offering evidence that God is not indifferent but hostile and malicious.

7-8. "If I cry 'Violence!' I do not receive any answer" (vs. 7a). The word הן, as in Aramaic, means not **behold** but "if" (cf. 4:18; 11:11; 12:14; 13:15; etc.). The thought and the expressions are closely related to those of Hab. 1:2; Jer. 20:8. **I call aloud** [cf. vs. 7b; again Hab. 1:2], **but there is no justice** [cf. Lam. 3:8]. The silence of God could not be interpreted as a sign of his indifference. He has maliciously blocked all the exits (vs. 8a) and in addition has blinded his prisoner (vs. 8b).

9-12. The dealings of the Deity with his servant are graphically described. It is not readily apparent whether the words **glory** and **crown** (vs. 9) refer to the princely station which Job enjoyed in the midst of his community or suggest a spiritual quality which he prized more deeply than social distinction and political influence, viz., a state of proud dignity vis-à-vis God as well as men. Probably both categories are included here, as one could not easily then separate them. Once more the poet may be alluding to the

---

to his friends for pity (vs. 21), it is of God he is thinking (see Expos.). He is obsessed with God. He is God-possessed. Ultimately his blasphemy will prove to be nothing but the mask which faith can sometimes be tortured into assuming.

7. The Silences of God.—There are many times in life when a shut door seems to be the only valid symbol of reality. Knock on it ever so hard: whoever lives there—if anybody does—apparently pays no attention. A minister once had printed at the bottom of the paper he used for his correspondence the words "Prayer Changes Things"; but they failed to prevent his using that paper in order to write a friend how impossible it was for him and his wife to

agree. There are things which prayer does not change. The one thing it can change is life itself. And that "answer" is not often the answer we want; nor are we always willing to wait for it. Job cried "Help! Help!" and nothing happened. Or did it? When God is silent it is not to be taken for granted that he is doing nothing. Even his silences, when they are not judicial (Luke 23:9) or an indication that matters have already got beyond speech (Mark 15:5), are creative. In the story of the Canaanitish woman (Matt. 15:21-28) it is recorded that Jesus "answered her not a word." Was it because of something in her? She had no right to call him "Son of David." It sounds almost like a pagan charm on her lips. Was it because of something in God?

11 He hath also kindled his wrath against me, and he counteth me unto him as *one of his enemies*.	11 He has kindled his wrath against me, and counts me as his adversary.

12 His troops come together, and raise up their way against me, and encamp round about my tabernacle.	12 His troops come on together;
	    they have cast up siegeworks[t] against me,
	    and encamp round about my tent.

13 He hath put my brethren far from me, and mine acquaintance are verily estranged from me.	13 "He has put my brethren far from me, and my acquaintances are wholly estranged from me.

[t] Heb *their way*

psalm which describes the majesty that God has bestowed on man in the universe: "Thou . . . hast *crowned* him with *glory* and magnificence" (Ps. 8:5; cf. Job 7:17). In contrast with his former status, the sufferer feels not only **stripped** (vs. 9a) but also marked for the final onslaught. According to the blunt colloquialism, "he is a goner" (cf. "I am gone," vs. 10a) and even his **hope** either of restoration before death or of resurrection afterward has been **pulled up like a tree** (vs. 10b). Such a treatment only demonstrates divine **wrath** (vs. 11a) and hostility: [God] **counteth me unto him as one of his enemies** (vs. 11b). This figure of speech is given poetic development. God is compared to a commander in the field, and Job to an isolated point of resistance. God's **troops come on together** (vs. 12a). Everything which has happened to the sufferer, the loss of his property, posterity, health, social standing, religious righteousness, and now his friendships, represents in military language the concerted effort of assailants getting ready to compel a fortress to surrender. The trials he has endured and now endures more sharply than ever are assaults directed against his own defense in the conviction of his integrity. **They have cast up siegeworks against me** (vs. 12b), preparing for the final attack. They **encamp round about my tent** (vs. 12c), they are lying in wait for the propitious moment. My surrender is only a question of time. How long shall I be able to hold out?

c) The Hostility of Men (19:13-19)

13-19. God's enmity is the root of Job's torture, made the more bitter by the fact that the community of the tortured man recognizes it and glibly upholds what appears to be God's side.

It is God who has spurred and wrought his enemy's social seclusion. Through a relentless and gradual tightening of the circles which close upon the hero to ensure thereby his utter loneliness, the strophe moves to its climax of desolation and horror. As in some *symphonie fantastique*, one can hear below and behind the musical phrasing, sustained by strings and winds, the haunting, growing, inevitably faster and faster rhythm of the percussion instruments. Here is more than a mere enumeration of terms or a sociological catalogue. Here is the poetic expression of an isolation which prepares

One may not oversimplify the "problems" which he has to face (see Expos. on 3:11). What will happen if he does as we say? (Cf. Luke 17:18; is Luke 11:24-26 a warning to the dumb man who was healed in vs. 14 of that chapter?) Love is acting when it seems most idle. Leslie Weatherhead tells of going one day to a hospital with a member of his congregation whose three-year-old child had to undergo an operation. The father waited, holding the lad in his arms, until the doctors came; then loosened the fingers that clung so tightly to his lapel, one by one, shut

his ears to the child's crying because his heart was open to the child's need, and even in the midst of the sobbing, "Daddy, don't let them take me. Please don't!" handed his son over to the physicians (see Expos. on vss. 23-24, 25).

13-19. *Job's Desperate Loneliness.*— (See Expos. on 16:10.) These verses, with their constantly narrowing circle of reference, plumb the depths of human loneliness. The sympathy of man might have mediated the compassion of God (II Cor. 1:4). To be explicitly denied the one and implicitly deprived of the other is to

14 My kinsfolk have failed, and my familiar friends have forgotten me.

15 They that dwell in mine house, and my maids, count me for a stranger: I am an alien in their sight.

16 I called my servant, and he gave *me* no answer; I entreated him with my mouth.

17 My breath is strange to my wife, though I entreated for the children's *sake* of mine own body.

18 Yea, young children despised me; I arose, and they spake against me.

19 All my inward friends abhorred me: and they whom I loved are turned against me.

---

14 My kinsfolk and my close friends have
    failed me;
15   the guests in my house have forgotten
     me;
   my maidservants count me as a stranger;
     I have become an alien in their eyes.
16 I call to my servant, but he gives me no
     answer;
   I must beseech him with my mouth.
17 I am repulsive to my wife,
     loathsome to the sons of my own
     mother.
18 Even young children despise me;
     when I rise they talk against me.
19 All my intimate friends abhor me,
     and those whom I loved have turned
     against me.

---

psychologically for the birth of hope told in the subsequent strophe (vss. 23-29). Observe the monotonous and yet progressive accumulation of words: **My brethren,** the men of my covenant (vs. 13*a*; not brothers in the strict sense: cf. vs. 17*b*), **my acquaintances** (vs. 13*b*), **my kinsfolk and my close friends** (vs. 14), **the guests in my house, my maids** (vs. 15), **my** personal **servant** (vs. 16), **my wife** (vs. 17*a*) and even my own blood brothers, **the sons of my own mother** (lit., "the sons of my [mother's] womb," vs. 17*b*), "little urchins" (vs. 18), and finally, as the worst of all forms of ostracism, the rejection wrought by **my intimate friends, . . . those whom I loved,** presumably Eliphaz, Bildad, and Zophar (vs. 19). The word **I loved** is reserved for the end of the list. Its strategic position makes all the previously mentioned degrees of relationship fade into comparative unimportance. "In this lyric of blighted affections the hardest word to utter—'I loved'—is reserved to the last. The natural reward of a love so tender and true is a responsive love that overflows, instead of drying up, when the lover became a sufferer. The Book of Job was written [partly] against a theology which bred suspicion, soured the milk of human kindness, alienated bosom friends, and covered with infamy those who should have been crowned with honour and glory." (Strahan, *ibid.,* pp. 173-74.)

As may be expected, critics do not agree upon the correct translation of these verses. It is commonly held, for example, that **my brethren** (vs. 13*a*) must be taken literally to mean Job's actual brothers rather than metaphorically the members of his "fraternal" consanguinity. Likewise, some scholars maintain that the expression "the sons of my womb" (in vs. 17*b*), instead of referring to "the offspring of my mother," i.e., "my uterine brothers" (Hitzig, Budde, *et al.*), signifies the sufferer's own sons (Dhorme, Moffatt, *La Sainte Bible, et al.*). It may indeed be argued that the word בטן, "womb," may in a popular way be used of a man's generative powers (cf. Deut. 28:53; Mic. 6:7 ["the fruit of my womb"]; Pss. 127:3; 132:11); and this passage, thus interpreted, is used as a weapon by those who claim that the poet is not the author of the folk tale (in which the sons of Job have all died; cf. 1:18-21) and even that he was not aware of it.

---

have the very stuff and content, the very mold and matrix, of personal existence destroyed. It is not for nothing that solitary confinement is regarded as one of the most terrible of punishments. Herbert H. Farmer in *The Servant of the Word,*[1] calls attention to the fact that the deaf so often seem to suffer more from loss of hearing than the blind from loss of sight, and

[1] New York: Charles Scribner's Sons, 1942, pp. 44-45.

suggests that the reason may well lie in the "sacramental" character of speech and its function in serving the interests of community. Certain it is that modern man, so vulnerable at the point of his faith in God, and finding himself so frequently isolated from his fellows by the very individualism with which he has sought to compensate for his dwindling stature in a world given over to science, to the mass, and to the

20 My bone cleaveth to my skin and to my flesh, and I am escaped with the skin of my teeth.

20 My bones cleave to my skin and to my flesh,
and I have escaped by the skin of my teeth.

Other critics (Wetzstein, W. Robertson Smith, Nestle, *et al.*) suggest that the word בטן needs to be explained here through the Arabic *baṭn*, "clan," and that consequently Job is referring to his clansmen. Against these views the following facts provide a weighty objection: (*a*) Job has already spoken of the "womb" in referring to his mother (cf. 3:10) ; (*b*) the poet is well aware of the fact that the hero's sons are dead (cf. 8:4; 29:5) ; (*c*) the **brethren** in vs. 13*a* are parallel with the **acquaintances** in vs. 13*b* (even Moffatt, strangely enough, renders "my children" in vs. 17*b* and yet realizes rightly that "my brothers" in vs. 13*a* are actually "my clansmen") ; (*d*) there is, as indicated above, a sharp climactic rise in the listing of the members of Job's community, and it is natural that his "brothers" should be mentioned after his wife among the closest of his social relations.

d) Final Plea to Men (19:20-24)

In his extremity and wretchedness Job makes a final attempt to regain his friends' comprehension or, in failing to reach that end, tries to vindicate himself among the future generations of mankind. Vs. 19 in the preceding strophe is a hinge for the transition which leads in this strophe to the most passionate appeal yet made to man in the dialogue, either to contemporaries (vss. 21-22) or to posterity (vss. 23-24). Before this final plea to men is uttered, however, the sufferer needs to state clearly and finally the horror of his physical condition (vs. 20).

20. Although the general meaning of this verse is obvious, both lines present a great deal of uncertainty and they have challenged the ingenuity of interpreters. Some of them observe that **skin** may cleave to **bones** but not vice versa, **bones** to **skin.** Others admit that **bones** may cleave either to **skin** or **flesh,** but deny that they may do so to both **skin** and **flesh** at once. The LXX offers evidence of a different text from the present M.T. when it translates:

Under my skin my flesh is corrupted;
My bones are held in [my?] teeth.

On the basis of the Greek translation of vs. 20*a*, one may correct דבקה into רקבה (the M.T. would then be the result of a tittle growth and metathesis) and read, "My bones are rotten within my skin and flesh."

Vs. 20*b* has become a proverbial saying, **I have escaped by the skin of my teeth;** it has therefore received a great deal of exegetical scrutiny, but no certain interpretation seems to be possible. Most critics conclude that the M.T. is corrupt and they emend it in many different ways, which may be summed up as follows:

(*a*) Since the LXX does not read בעורי in vs. 20*b*, one may omit this word (Bickell [2nd ed.], Duhm, Moffatt, *et al.*) , and also correct ואתמלטה into ויתמלטו, thus rendering, "and my teeth are falling out" (cf. the use of the same verb with a similar meaning in 41:11 [Hebrew]) .

(*b*) One may consider the verb מלט as a parallel of מרט, "to shave," "to polish," or "to gnaw," and thus consider (with Beer, Hölscher, *et al.*) that Job refers to the hairless skin of his jaws, or rather, of his cheeks (the loss of beard was of course the acme of disgrace in some parts of the ancient Near East) .

---

machine, is in constant peril of sinking to subhuman levels and becoming less than a person. It is this that totalitarianism succeeds only in aggravating. Through chs. 16–17 Job's mind lashes out at his loneliness like a caged beast. In ch. 19 it almost crushes him. There has to be

an exit somewhere. The door at vs. 21 is slammed in his face. The door at vss. 23-24 seems to swing slowly shut on its hinges. The break-through comes in vss. 25-27.

20. *The Skin of Our Teeth.*—The title of a play by Thornton Wilder: he sets down in

21 Have pity upon me, have pity upon me, O ye my friends; for the hand of God hath touched me.

21 Have pity on me, have pity on me, O you my friends,
for the hand of God has touched me!

(c) As a variation of the above procedure, one may follow the LXX, and transfer the word עצמי, **my bones,** from the first to the second line, and omit the word בעור, "in the skin of" from the latter (Dhorme), and thus read, "I am so lean that I can gnaw my bones with my teeth."

(d) By vocalizing שני as *shēnî*, "a second time," instead of *shinnāy*, **my teeth,** one may render, "I have escaped a second time [only] with my skin" (Hoffmann).

(e) By correcting בעור שני into בעורי בשני, some translate, "I have escaped with my skin [a synonym of flesh] in my teeth" (Lods, *et al.*).

(f) By correcting more boldly בעור שני into בשרי בשני, one may render, "I have escaped with my flesh in my teeth" (a direct parallel in 13:14; Bickell [1st ed.], Budde, Driver and Gray, J. M. P. Smith, *et al.*).

(g) By correcting still more boldly, one may read vs. 20b as ועצמי התמלטה בשנים, "And my bones protrude in sharp points" (Kissane).

The extraordinary variety of these corrections (and of others which might easily be added to this list) reveals the wholly hypothetical nature of the attempt. Several scholars therefore assume that the Hebrew text has been correctly preserved and that the traditional translation, **I have escaped by the skin of my teeth,** represents an idiomatic expression, the precise meaning of which may only be guessed. (a) Some critics (i.e., Schultens, Rosenmüller, Morris Jastrow) maintain that the "skin of the teeth" designates the "gums"; thus Job is saying that he has lost all his teeth. (b) Others (Renan and Buttenwieser) observe that since teeth have no skin, Job is merely stating the hopeless prospect which faces him, saying, "I have not escaped at all; I am utterly lost." (c) Taking the expression **skin of my teeth** in the physical sense, one might argue in an entirely different direction. Although the teeth of an adult are not covered by skin, the teeth of infants are protected against lactate acids by a cutaneous tissue called Nasmyth's membrane, which wears out after the weaning process. If this fact had been known to the learned poet (who reveals throughout the book an astoundingly wide and accurate acquaintance with natural phenomena), one could suggest the following interpretation: **The skin of** [his] **teeth** is for Job the symbol of his childhood innocence. Although conscious of the extremely advanced stage of his pathological condition (vs. 20a), he adds in vs. 20b, "Let me escape [אתמלטה, it will be noted, is in the cohortative] with my integrity intact!" (d) Following the Vulg., one may argue that **the skin of my teeth** is an unusual way of saying "my lips." Job would thus declare, "And only my lips are left around my teeth." This statement in turn might mean, "Nothing is at my disposal except the possibility of speech" (Norbert Peters). (e) Job's enigmatic saying should be compared with that of 13:14a, "I will take my flesh in my teeth," which refers to the deadly risks taken by the sufferer in his blasphemy. Here Job refers to his bare survival; he is at the very brim of the great void, with a foot in the tomb. So far he has escaped the final fall, but now almost nothing, **the skin of** [his] **teeth,** keeps him on the brink of the bottomless precipice. He barely survives; he is more dead than alive. "He has escaped with the loss of everything" (Peake, *Job,* pp. 189-90; cf. Weiser). This is the traditional and most probable interpretation.

21-22. Having described in moving terms his dereliction (vss. 12-19) and reiterated in a swift comment that his physical dejection has reached the final stage (vs. 20), the

---

dramatic form the hairbreadth escapes humanity has had through the ages, historic and prehistoric; and the jeopardy in which it now stands.

21. For God's Sake.— (Cf. 6:14, KJV and RSV; see Expos. on 6:14, 18, 21-27, 28-30.) Job implores his friends for pity, and (to motivate it) assigns the very consideration which prompts them to reject his appeal. They will give him no quarter whom God gives none. They dare not. Besides, to have done so would have necessitated

22 Why do ye persecute me as God, and are not satisfied with my flesh?	22 Why do you, like God, pursue me? Why are you not satisfied with my flesh?

sufferer changes his tone as his defiance subsides. Under stress of agony the pride and anger which have prompted many of his invectives abate at last. He had previously refused, against the explicit advice he had received (8:5), to implore the grace, mercy, or pity of God (9:15). He has however come to implore—in vain—the pity of his own slave (19:16); and now in the depth of his distress he beseeches these three friends, who are still willing to remain with him, to speak and to listen to him: he begs, **Have pity upon me, have pity upon me, O ye my friends** (vs. 21a). This sudden break in the pride of the lone eagle offers another evidence of the profound incisiveness with which the poet probes into the recesses of human nature. Job is completely misunderstood by his friends, and he claims that they are entirely wrong in the judgment which they pass upon his case and are even cruel in the way they treat him. Nevertheless he craves their approval. He cannot endure their contempt. He forswears defiance and throws himself on their mercy. He cannot yet bring himself to pray for the grace or the pity of God (cf. Ps. 123:3), because it is precisely **the hand of God** which **hath touched** him (vs. 21b; cf. the use of the same verb in the confession of the suffering servant in Isa. 53:4). This is the reason for which he appeals to the pity of his friends. Yet this appeal is "all the more hopeless that the reason he urges is the very reason why the friends will not respond. How should God's sycophants succour him whom God has smitten?" (Peake, op. cit., p. 190.) As will be seen in the following strophe (vss. 25-29), Job is reaching the supreme moment of his theological adventure, as described in the poetic discussion, at least in the form in which it has been preserved. But he cannot poetically, emotionally, and spiritually, enter the land of discovery until all other possibilities have been exhausted. The friends are unable to help him, for they know as well as he does that his misery is wrought by the divine will. Nevertheless, their friendship should at least restrain them from outward aggressiveness. Thus Job asks, **Why do ye persecute me as God?** (vs. 22a). Men are apt to become as monsters just at the moment when they believe themselves to be divine. One of the friends has already linked his own consolations with those of God (15:11). Men easily delude themselves into believing that they are Godlike whenever they presume to speak in the name of God. In one sentence Job castigates all religious inquisitors who justify their inhumanity to man by the illusory claim of being divinely appointed to their task. "Yea, the time cometh, that whosoever killeth you will think that he doeth God service" (John 16:2). Are not Job's interlocutors tired of making false accusations? "To

an almost total revamping of their theology (see Expos. on 2:11-13); and that they either would not or could not face. Had it been otherwise, in the company of his friends Job might well have been led back into the companionship of the Almighty (see Expos. on vss. 6, 13-19). The three representatives of the orthodox Hebrew faith were zealous for God; but their zeal was without knowledge. They tried to justify the ways of God (see Expos. on 13:8) by discounting the hazards faith has to run (see Expos. on 12:2-6). The truest service they could have rendered God would have been to channel something of his compassion (cf. I John 2:11; 3:17).

22a. God, Men, and Monsters.—Eliphaz, Bildad, and Zophar were so sure they were spokesmen for the Almighty (15:11) that the ethical was on the point of disappearing in the theological, right living was about to find a substitute in right thinking, simple human kindness in sterile human virtue (see Exeg. on vss. 21-22). Austerity had taken the place of forbearance; magnanimity had given way to punctiliousness. There is a morbid satisfaction to be had in the process, a kind of exhilaration. Decry the human in order to exalt the divine. Depreciate self "to the glory of God the Father." "Oh, to be nothing, nothing! A broken vessel for the Master's use!" So may men turn into beasts, and God into a devil. There have been saints "hell-bent for heaven." God became man in order that man, in his effort to be God, may not become a monster (see Expos. on 23:2).

22b. Tearing a Good Name to Shreds.—To devour the flesh was to slander. The friends are

23 Oh that my words were now written! oh that they were printed in a book!

24 That they were graven with an iron pen and lead in the rock for ever!

23 "Oh that my words were written! Oh that they were inscribed in a book!

24 Oh that with an iron pen and lead they were graven in the rock for ever!

eat the flesh of someone" is an Aramaic and Arabic idiom for "slandering" (Dan. 3:8; cf. Job 31:31).

23-24. Having recognized the futility of appealing to the pity of his friends, Job tries a different method. The present and the imminent future stand before him like a closed door. But the distant future remains an obscure possibility. If nobody vindicates him now, he will appeal to the verdict of posterity. **Oh that my words were written!** (Vs. 23a.) Like the psalmist (Ps. 102:19), the sufferer acquires for an instant the perspective of history; he trusts that if his words are preserved for the generations to come his honor will at last be proclaimed. If his story **were inscribed in a book**, i.e., "on a scroll of parchment" (vs. 23b), like a document in the official archives of some neighboring kingdoms, then an eventual reader, endowed with the wider outlook of a new era, would understand and declare his innocence to the world. But papyrus or parchment is too fragile and ephemeral a substance, because a long time would be required for the human race to overcome prejudices of this kind. **Oh that with an iron pen and lead [my words] were graven in the rock for ever!** (Vs. 24.) Some commentators observe that there is no progression from vs. 23 to vs. 24 because the verb חקק means "to engrave," and thus the noun ספר, "scroll," should be understood as a Hebrew equivalent of the Akkadian *siparru*, "brass," "bronze" (cf. Judg. 5:14; Isa. 30:8[?]). This brilliant suggestion has found support in the discovery—near the Dead Sea—of two scrolls of copper inscribed with Hebrew characters (cf. William L. Reed, "Report of the Director of the School in Jerusalem," *Bulletin of the American Schools of Oriental Research,* No. 128 [Dec., 1952], p. 6).

In any event, the tormented sufferer is overcoming the limitations of the present time. He imagines his own case being inscribed on the side of a cliff with a hard metal stylus (manufactured with an alloy of **iron** and **lead** [cf. Ezek. 22:20]; the poet has perhaps seen such inscriptions left by great conquerors in Phoenicia or Egypt). Even this literary fancy, however, fails to satisfy his desire. He realizes that an eventual vindication in the distant future would be of no significance. More than a wish for recognition by posterity is needed. The fetters of his isolation, not only from men but also from God, must be broken now. Thus, pushed to the extreme limit of agony, he rejects the dream of a human verdict of acquittal in the centuries to come and enters the yet unexplored world of personal certainty: he looks for a defense and a vindication now and in the afterlife (vs. 25 ff.).

represented as not being content with their calumny, their false representations in the matter of Job's once widely reputed piety: with no more than the shreds of his good name in their mouths they must yet hound him to death like God.

To give a dog a bad name has become a proverb. To give a man a bad name is to destroy one of his most precious possessions (see Expos. on Luke 19:2). And it can be done so readily: with a word, sometimes by the lifting of an eyebrow. Besides, the very doing of it ministers to one's own self-esteem. There is more in a name than we think. The Hebrews knew that better than we. The "name" one has often enough

determines the scope and opportunity one is given (see Rev. 3:12).

23-24. Strange Fulfillments.—Job has indeed been permitted to plead his cause at the bar of how many generations then unborn! (Cf. Expos. on 6:1–7:21.) A great British statesman of years gone by, whenever his policies met with defeat in Parliament, would bow to the will of the majority, and fingering the flower in the lapel of his coat appeal to the arbitrament of the future. To be in the dangerous van of one's own time is to wear the emblem of a pioneer in the time to come. Job longed for justification with man and reconciliation with God. The sincerest desires of his heart were granted; but in God's way, not his.

25 For I know *that* my Redeemer liveth, and *that* he shall stand at the latter *day* upon the earth:	25 For I know that my Redeemer[u] lives, and at last he will stand upon the earth;[v]

[u] Or *Vindicator*
[v] Or *dust*

e) "I Know that My Redeemer Liveth" (19:25-29)

25-27. The appeal to friends has failed (vss. 21-22). The entreaty to future generations is fanciful and in any case wholly inadequate (vss. 23-24). Thus the final plea to men makes room for the most momentous expression of faith which may be found in the poem and perhaps in the entire Hebrew Bible. **For I know . . .** (vs. 25a): Better, "But as for me, I know," since the pronoun is emphatically used and the conjunctive letter *waw* does not imply a link of logical sequence with the preceding verses, but on the contrary suggests an adversative sense. Earthly wishes are brought to vanity, *but* there is a knowledge to which Job now clings, **My Redeemer liveth.**

The word *gō'ēl* represents (*a*) the man, usually next of kin, who is the avenger of the blood, i.e., of the blood which has been shed by murder (II Sam. 14:11); (*b*) the man, also next of kin, who has the right to buy or "redeem" the estate of a dead person or to raise up a posterity for him (Deut. 25:5-10; Ruth 2:20; 3:9; 4:4 ff., cf. Lev. 25:25; Num. 5:8); (*c*) by extension, the defender of the oppressed (Prov. 23:10-11), and especially therefore the defender par excellence, i.e., God. The verb *gā'al* or the participial noun *gō'ēl* is used for the Deity when (i) Israel is delivered from the Egyptian bondage (Exod. 6:6; 15:13; Ps. 74:2; etc.) and from the Exile (Isa. 41:14; 43:1; etc.); (ii) individuals are saved from oppression (Ps. 119:154; Prov. 23:11; Jer. 50:34), evil (Gen. 48:16), or death (Pss. 69:18; 72:14; 103:4; Lam. 3:58; Hos. 13:14). Which one of these meanings is intended by the poet of Job at this point?

It is generally agreed that the *gō'ēl* in vs. 25 cannot be a human being since the hero's sons are dead and his relatives have deserted him. Thus commentators usually maintain that Job, through an upsurge of passionate will to be vindicated, suddenly breaks through the wall of his isolation, passes from the stage of vain wish (vss. 23-24) into that of positive conviction, and declares his unshakable knowledge that God himself will be the vindicator of his innocence, the defender of his good name, and the restorer of his honor. It is pointed out that (*a*) the word *ḥay*, "alive," "living," is a common designation of the Deity (Josh. 3:10; Hos. 1:10 [Hebrew 2:1]; etc.) and is used also in the formula of the oath (Judg. 8:19; etc.; cf. Job 27:2); (*b*) the word *'aḥarôn*, **last,** clearly describes the *gō'ēl* (cf. Isa. 48:12; especially 44:6, "Thus saith Yahweh, the King of

25. Victory Through Defeat.—From his friends to the future, and back from the future to God. Read Ps. 130. Defeat is many a time necessary before victory is possible. There is in man a hard and outer shell that has to be broken. In the phrase "ultimate reliance" the word "ultimate" is not without meaning: every other reliance may have to be proved illusory; not in spite of defeat, by means of it. Certainly in the Christian gospel tragedy and triumph are inseparably related, death and life. To be obsessed with the tragedy and lose sight of the triumph is to become a pessimist whose worst fears are likely to be realized; to be obsessed with the triumph and lose sight of the tragedy is to become an optimist whose fondest hopes are little more than the paradise that fools live in. The world is not a place for whistling jaunty tunes; whistling may well be a sign of nervousness. It is not a place where every story has to end as we like. Since Jesus of Nazareth lived in it and died in it, it is a place where more clearly than ever before we can see how closely the tragedy and the triumph are interwrought.

With thy living fire of judgment
  Purge this realm of bitter things;
Solace all its wide dominion
  With the healing of thy wings.[2]

The fire and the solace, the purge and the healing, belong together now.

25. My Redeemer Liveth.—The sense in which Job uses these words must not be con-

[2] Henry Scott Holland, "Judge eternal, throned in splendor." From *The English Hymnal*, by permission of the Oxford University Press.

Israel and his *gô'ēl*, Yahweh of hosts, I am first and I am last ['*aḥarôn*] . . ."); (*c*) the verb *yāqûm*, **he shall stand** (vs. 25*b*), or rather, "he shall rise up" (cf. 16:8), is the *terminus technicus* for the theophanies (Artur Weiser, *Das Buch Hiob* [Göttingen: Vandenhoeck & Ruprecht, 1951], *ad loc.*; cf. many parallels, e.g., "For the oppression of the poor, for the sighing of the needy, now will I arise . . ." [Ps. 12:6]); (*d*) the expression *'al-'āphār*, **upon the dust** (vs. 25*b*), is identical with that found in 41:33 (cf. 5:6; 8:19; 14:8): it indicates that God will come down from heaven and appear within the frame of history to take up the defense of his hero. According to this interpretation, Job recaptures his faith in "the living God" at the very moment when he gives up the illusion of defending himself. The poet reveals in the inner structure of the poem that he knows in its very essence the worship of the covenanted people. As Yahweh will appear at the eschatological time ("the last") to save Israel in her extremity, so also will God appear to Job; and it will be his judgment, not that of men, which will constitute the final act of the drama (see *ibid.*).

Against this prevailing interpretation it may be argued that (*a*) the *gô'ēl* cannot be God, for Job has heretofore consistently thought of the Deity as an implacably hostile being, and (much more important) continues to do so in the remaining part of the poetic discussion (cf. 27:2); (*b*) it is hard, if not impossible, to believe that Job, who has just declared that God persecutes him (vs. 22), at once would completely reverse his position and declare that God is his eternal vindicator (vs. 25); (*c*) those who hold the above interpretation assume that Job is, here as well as in 16:19, opposing God to God and appealing from God the enemy to God the defender; but it has been seen (cf. Exeg. on 16:18-22) that the witness in heaven is to be distinguished from God, and that therefore the identification of the *gô'ēl* with God cannot find any support from the text of 16:19 ff.; (*d*) the words "living," **last, shall stand,** and **upon the earth** may well apply to the mysterious being whom Job conceived for a moment as a "mediator" (9:33), and later recalled to his psychological consciousness not merely as the object of a fleeting fancy but as the heavenly person "who vouches for [him] on high and will maintain the right of man with God" (16:19, 21). Now that irrepressible confidence once more enraptures him, and at this climactic moment he shouts, "But I know that my defender lives! He will survive my unjust death, and over the dust of my grave [cf. the use of the word *'āphār* in 7:21; 17:16; 20:11; 21:26; also 10:9; 34:15; Ps. 104:29] he will stand at the last instant. Through his intermediation, by his activity, he will summon God and me together, and bring me before the face of God!" Such an interpretation offers more than possibility, for it has two specific advantages over the others: (*a*) it enables the exegete to understand why at this point in the poetic discussion Job remains as far as ever from renewing his communion with a God who now seems more distant from him than before (cf. 23:3 ff.); (*b*) it overcomes the otherwise insurmountable difficulty raised by the fact that in the end of the poem, in spite of the weighty opinion of several critics to the contrary, God does not reveal himself as the *gô'ēl* of Job but rather as the transcendent and holy Deity who, far from upholding the honor and integrity of the sufferer, casts him down into utter self-abhorrence and repentance (42:2-6). In this connection it is important to note that if this exegesis is correct, Job has indeed begun to abandon the hope of defending or justifying himself, but nevertheless remains adamant in the conviction of his innocence. His pride stands, exactly as it shows itself to the end of the poetic discussion (31:40).

---

fused with the sense in which the Christian uses them (see Exeg.). To "redeem" from the wrong done one's honor is far other than to redeem from sin and guilt. Job's sudden vision of one who even now stands between him and God—one who **lives,** and is not, as he is, to be accounted already dead—and stands there to vindicate him before the tribunal of God and

man alike, is neither arrived at rationally nor grasped at frantically, a mere straw and trick of the fancy. Call it intuition, which to the man of faith is that something within set there to instruct and to lead. Call it "the soul's invincible surmise" (see Expos. on 9:30-35; 10:1-7, 8-12, 13-17), but know that there is more of response in it than of mere divination.

A liturgical formula from the Ugaritic literature presents a verbal parallel to vs. 25*a* which may be either purely accidental or extremely important and significant, especially in the light of the above discussion. The worshiper declares in the course of a liturgical celebration of a seasonal festival,

wid' khy aliyn b'l
kit zbl b'l arṣ

And I know that the powerful baal liveth,
Existent is the prince, Lord of the earth!

(Cyrus H. Gordon, *Ugaritic Handbook* [Roma: Pontificium Institutum Biblicum, 1947], p. 138; cf. Charles Virolleaud, I AB [iii:8-9], in "Un poème phénicien de Ras-Shamra," *Syria*, XII [1931], 212-13; Pritchard, *Ancient Near Eastern Texts*, p. 140.) This formula is repeated in the sequence of the Ugaritic text (I AB, iii:3-4, 8-9, 20-21), and appears to be a ritual rubric used in celebrating the festival of the dying and rising god. Its emphasis upon the life of the deity is thus an intrinsic part of the ceremonial. On the contrary, Job's insistence upon the "living" character of his redeemer, in terms almost identical with those of the proto-Phoenician poem, is rather unexpected in its present context. Why has he not merely said, "I know that I have a redeemer"? Why has he chosen to contrast the "living" quality of his *gŏ'ēl* with the fact of his own dying? Again, let it be made clear that it is not possible to demonstrate the play of the polytheistic influence of some ancient Semitic cult upon the Joban poet. Yet one can reasonably conjecture that the hero, forsaken of all men and separated from God, may have pinned his hope upon the existence of a heavenly being who would survive his own untimely death and bring about the miracle of a divine-human confrontation. "The parallel may merely be accidental. But it is equally possible that archaic religious terminology about a god who had been dead but was now alive (and therefore able to act decisively) comes to the surface in this formulation. The prolonged absence of divine help may well have led the poet to think of the situation that existed in the pagan world when a god had departed for the land of the dead, while the joyous moment of his restoration to life and the resumption of his accustomed helpful rôle is recaptured in the assertion that 'he lives.' If so the time-honoured interpretation which took 19:25 as a reference to the resurrection of Christ had in it a grain of truth." (Emil G. Kraeling, *The Book of the Ways of God* [London: Society for Promoting Christian Knowledge; New York: Charles Scribner's Sons, 1939], p. 89. Used by permission.)

In any case, and although Job is in no way alluding to a Messiah, the passage foreshadows an obstinacy of faith which transcends the limitations of the original poem. Christian interpreters—as well as the innumerable hearers of Handel's oratorio, *The Messiah*—have a right to find in this passage a prefiguration of the Christian experience of salvation.

Vs. 26*a* is in a state of textual corruption which defies the resources of exegesis. The Hebrew of the M.T. is syntactically incoherent. The words mean, lit., "And after" (preposition introducing a noun, or conjunction governing a verb) or "afterwards" (adverb), "my skin" (masculine noun), "they have stricken off" (Piel of נקף I; cf. Niphal in Isa. 10:34 and the Akkadian *nakpu*, "to mutilate") or "they surrounded" (hypothetical Piel of נקף II; cf. Qal in Isa. 21:1 and Hiphil in Job 1:5; 19:6; Ps. 22:17;

It has been said above (see Expos. on vs. 7) that love is acting when it seems most idle. Job's salvation from the very beginning lay in the fact that in the mercy of God there is always a better self at work within the self. That better self never quite let go. It was never altogether quiescent. It never gave up. It would not quit. That was God, if Job had only known it. There was a man, who, though one of the bitterest of souls, continually railing at Providence, was yet one of the stanchest. At sixty-seven he was able to secure employment, as he had been at sixty-three and at sixty-five. He worked thoroughly, was honest, and loving, and beyond reproach. But God got no credit for any of it. It was his doing. God was doing nothing. Job's fortunes

26 And *though* after my skin *worms* destroy this *body,* yet in my flesh shall I see God:

26 and after my skin has been thus destroyed,
then without[w] my flesh I shall see God,[x]

[w] Or *from*
[x] The meaning of this verse is uncertain

---

etc.), "this" (feminine pronoun). The ancient versions differ widely from the present M.T. and also among themselves; e.g., the LXX translates vs. 26a as a sequence of vs. 25 and reads,

> For I know that he who is about to release me is eternal; (25a)
> Upon earth may he raise up my skin (25b)
> Which exhausteth [or "goeth through"] this . . . (26a).

The Greek translators have therefore omitted ואחר at the beginning of vs. 26a, considered עורי, "my skin" (Hebrew, vs. 26a), as the object of the verb יקים (vs. 25b) which they read as a Hiphil instead of the M.T. יקום, and read נקפו־זאת as *nôqēph-zôth* instead of *niqqephû-zôth*. Furthermore, instead of עורי, "my skin," LXXA has μου τὸ σῶμα, "my body" (which may be an interpretation of "my skin") while other Greek MSS have σπέρμα, "posterity," a word which may have been original rather than either δέρμα or σῶμα (cf. the Arabic version of the LXX, ed. W. W. Baudissin, *Translationis antiquae arabicae libri Iobi* [Leipzig: Doerffling & Franke, 1870]). On the basis of this reading one may suggest that the original Hebrew text had זרעי instead of עורי. Thus Job would have said in effect, "Although I have no longer any descendants, I know that my redeemer will survive me."

The Vulg. has detached the clause of vs. 25b from that of vs. 25a and reads vss. 25-26a as follows:

> *Scio enim quod Redemptor meus vivit,* (25a)
> *Et in novissimo die de terra surrecturus sum;* (25b)
> *Et rursum circumdabor pelle mea . . .* (26a).

Thus the Latin translator read the word יקום, "he shall rise" (vs. 25b), as אקום, "I shall rise"; the words ואחר עורי, "and after my skin," as ועוד [ב?]עורי, "and again with my skin"; the difficult נקפו־זאת probably as נקפתי (*niqqaphti;* a hypothetical Niphal of נקף II).

Vs. 26a has also been translated, "and after my skin will have swollen, this shall be . . ." (Targ.) and "these things surround and my skin and my flesh" (Syriac). The uncertainties of the text are revealed in the KJV which renders, **And though after my skin worms destroy this body,** and offers a marginal substitute, construing עורי, **my skin,** as the construct infinitive of the verb עור, "to awake," thus proposing to read, "And after I shall awake, though this body be destroyed. . . ." The RSV, following the ERV, corrects נקפו־זאת into נקף כזאת and reads, **And after my skin has been thus destroyed. . . .** All textual emendations suggested by modern critics (and their number is high) represent skillful but wholly conjectural proposals. It is better to leave the clause of vs. 26a untranslated, allowing for the possibility that the idea expressed therein referred to violence and perhaps destruction.

The Hebrew of vs. 26b appears at first sight to be clear and well preserved, but its meaning is ambiguous, and the evidence from the ancient versions suggests the probability

---

were laid waste; but there was One who stood guard in his soul. Was it not a whisper from this Other that even the dead might live again (see Expos. on 14:14)? Was it not a whisper from this Other that one day Job would see for himself of the travail of his soul and be satisfied (Isa. 53:11; the ideal Israel?)? Plato gave his grounds for believing that this world is not the only world; Job could give none, except that injustice could not possibly triumph: the Greek by way of reason, the Oriental by way of agony. It was Job's very weakness that led him to this display of strength, the weakness of his seeing faith as it gave way before the intensity of his

of textual corruption here also. It reads, lit., "And from my flesh I shall see God." The preposition מִן, however, may mean either "from within" or "from without." Hence the conflicting translations, **in my flesh** (KJV) and **without my flesh** (RSV). Although the LXX has rendered, "For from the Lord all this was accomplished for me," thus reading perhaps וּמִשַּׁדִּי for וּמִבְּשָׂרִי and אֱלֹהַּ for אֱלוֹהַּ, there is no valid reason for challenging the accuracy of the present M.T., since vs. 27 obviously indicates that Job expected to see God. Two questions remain: (a) Will this experience take place before his death or afterward? (b) If the answer to the preceding question is "afterward," in what mode of existence will Job face the Deity—as a disincarnated spirit, or in a form of being which is described pictorially as *in carne?*

On the one hand, it will be observed that the preposition מִן assumes a privative meaning not only with verbs of motion and separation (as is ordinarily the case), but also in spatially neutral contexts such as Num. 15:24; Judg. 5:11; Prov. 1:33; 20:3; Jer. 48:45 (other passages such as Job 11:15; 21:9; 28:4 which are often adduced in support of this meaning in 19:26 are not relevant parallels). On the other hand, there is no doubt that when used with a verb expressing vision or perception, the same preposition מִן refers to the point of vantage, the locale from which or through which the function of sight operates. Thus "Yahweh looketh from [מִן] heaven, . . . from [מִן] the place of his habitation" (Ps. 33:13-14) or "My beloved looketh forth through [מִן] the windows, . . . through [מִן] the lattice" (Song of S. 2:9). It is therefore evident that 19:26*b* should be translated with the KJV, **in my flesh shall I see God.** This exegesis is confirmed (a) negatively by the fact that the idea of a bodiless mode of human existence is totally foreign to the Semitic mentality (as proved by the growth and development of the belief in carnal resurrection); and (b) positively by the subsequent and emphatic assertion, apparently needed to convince the astonished and even skeptical listeners (and exegetes?), that Job himself will see God with his own eyes (vs. 27).

Now if Job expects to be "in his flesh" when he confronts the Godhead, does he think that this meeting will take place on earth before he dies, or does he refer to a post-mortem experience? At first glance the former alternative appears to be defensible and is indeed held by a number of scholars, most of whom, however, correct the text in some way which supports their interpretation. It is claimed that the poet is here antici-pating the theophany of Yahweh, through which God appears and meets Job face to face (38:1–42:6) while the sufferer is still alive upon earth. Against this view, and in favor of the post-mortem alternative, other exegetes strongly stress the fact that the sufferer's consistent prospect in the whole poetic discussion up to this point has been that of his imminent and inevitable death. In addition, the thought of the *gōʾēl,* especially when it is considered as a reiteration and development of the wish for a mediator (9:33) and of the hope in a heavenly witness (16:19), which in turn presupposes Job's murder by bloodshed (16:18), points to the conclusion that vss. 25-26*a,* whatever their exact render-ing should be, refer to the final, earthly, bloody act, which is death (Pascal). If so, Job faced a situation more paradoxical than ever: On the one hand, he was convinced that he would see God after his death; on the other hand, he knew that in Sheol human existence is no longer what might be called "life" (14:20-21) and that there is for a dead man no hope of returning to earth (7:10; 14:7-15), yet he believed that in some way

seeking faith. Was it not some whisper in the soul that led him to keep knocking on the door of grace, desiring a conference with his Maker? Never mind that sometimes he left off knocking and took to kicking: maybe it is better to be overbold than to be overcautious. When no access seemed possible, was it not that same whisper in his soul which told him there had to be access, else there was no God, no God who could have any significance for man? Was it not that whisper which had already brought him to cry out for a mediator (9:33), someone to plead his cause before God, someone to stand between him and the Eternal, a daysman Job called him, an umpire? Surely nowhere does he come nearer the N.T. than at this moment, hammered out hot on the anvil of his despair (see Expos. on 13:13-19). It is as if all at once for his leaden pain he had got him vast wings: **I know that my Redeemer liveth.** Nowhere does he come

27 Whom I shall see for myself, and mine eyes shall behold, and not another; *though* my reins be consumed within me.

27 whom I shall see on my side,^y
     and my eyes shall behold, and not another.
     My heart faints within me!

^y Or *for myself*

(probably hinted at in the now corrupt vs. 26a) he would receive new flesh for the specific purpose of the divine-human interview. This flash of expectation has nothing to do with the Greek belief in the natural immortality of the soul, nor is it to be confused with the later Jewish-Christian belief in a bodily resurrection effecting entrance into eternal life. It is merely the dying thought that he, Job, in order to be enabled to plead his defense before God, will again be made fully alive, that his personality will be endowed with the concreteness, the substantial reality, the "carnal" vitality and vigor of complete existence of a man breathing upon earth, not the shadowlike tenuousness and impassibility of the dead in Sheol. As to the way in which this transformation will be brought into effect, the present text does not allow the interpreter to say with any degree of probability. Likewise the text is silent upon the result of the encounter between Job and God, but its certain expectation is there. It shines like a beacon light over the tumult.

27. The prospect of meeting the Deity is so portentous, and at the same time so stirring to the imagination of the hero, that he feels compelled to repeat his conviction (vs. 27*ab*) ; and he cannot repress a lyrical outcry of his impatience (vs. 27*c*) . The translation **Whom I shall see on my side** (RSV, after Duhm, Budde, Driver and Gray, Kissane, *et al.*) is most unnatural. Such a rendering of the preposition and pronoun לי, **for myself,** cannot be supported from texts like Gen. 31:42; Pss. 46:2; 56:10; 118:7; 124:2, where the preposition is constructed either with the verb "to be" or with a predicate which presupposes the verbal copula. It also disregards the Masoretic accentuation (*maqqēph* and *daghesh forte conjunctivum*) . The correct rendering is the traditional one, **Whom I shall see for myself** (KJV, RSV mg.) , which recognizes in the word לי a variation of the *dativus ethicus,* well known in biblical Hebrew (see not only the many examples with the imperative, but also the close parallels of Isa. 36:9; Gen. 21:16; 22:5; Exod. 18:27; Ezek. 37:11; Hos. 8:9; Pss. 120:7; 123:5; Job 6:19; 12:11; 13:1) . Job says literally, linking vs. 27*a* to 26*b*, "Whom I, even I, shall see for myself." Indeed, Job insists, **and mine eyes shall behold, and not another** (vs. 27*b*) . He is overwhelmed by the utter novelty (should one say "modernism"?) of his conviction. As if he needed to reassure himself while new doubts harass him, or perhaps because he perceives the bewildered incredulity of his listeners, Job insists that the man who will see God will not be "a stranger" (*zār*) , some dead being "estranged" from himself and not identical with his present personality—a mere shade of his present self—but on the contrary, the very same individual who is now passing through the travails of theological parturition. Such an insistence would be superfluous, and indeed incomprehensible, were the hero thinking of an earthly

---

nearer the great high priest, touched with the feeling of our infirmities (Heb. 4:15-16). A "Yes" is beginning to thrust its way through the "No." Reconciliation, when it comes, will spring from the very heart of that contradiction. It is not by the intellect that man wins through—though he may never leave what intellect he has at home. It is the heart's logic that wins, and the heart has its own, always its own. Nothing else can ever find the jewel at the bottom of the cup of suffering (see Expos. on 6:8-13) . Nothing else will ever bring a man home trembling but trusting into his Father's arms.

27. Whom I Shall See for Myself.—We are out of the realm of theory now into the realm of persons; and the amazement of it is a shudder in the soul. Here, says Strahan, "is the everlasting individualism of faith." [3] Job will not be satisfied "with this or that attribute [of God]— wisdom, justice, or even love—[only] with a beatific vision in which all attributes are forgotten." [4] For one fleeting instant death seems no longer the end: God is the end, as he was and is the beginning, and man's fulfillment to

[3] *Job,* p. 178.
[4] *Ibid.,* p. 176.

28 But ye should say, Why persecute we him, seeing the root of the matter is found in me?

28 If you say, 'How we will pursue him!' and, 'The root of the matter is found in him';

---

and ante-mortem experience. His anticipation can hardly be contained: **Though my reins be consumed within me** (vs. 27c). According to the metaphorical use of the bodily organs which was common among the ancient Semites, the **reins** designate the most vital and intense part of the body, the seat of vigor, desire, and longing. While the verb means "to come to completion" or "to an end," and therefore may designate exhaustion and wasting away (7:8; 33:21; Ps. 73:26; etc.), it also means "to pine," "to languish with uncontrollable desire" (11:20; 17:5; cf. Jer. 14:6; Pss. 69:3; 119:82, 123; etc.). The word translated **within me** means, lit., "in my bosom" (see Akkadian *ḥîqu*, "embrace"), and is usually applied to females (Gen. 16:5; Ruth 4:16; II Sam. 12:3; etc.). Chiefly for this reason some critics wish to correct the Masoretic vocalization of כלו כליתי בחקי from *kālû kilyōthay beḥēqî* into *kālô kullēthî bheḥuqqî*, and thus translate, "I am utterly exhausted in my appointed time," a suggestion which neither fits common Hebrew usage nor yields clarity of meaning. In fact, Job uses elsewhere (23:12) the word *ḥēq* as an apparent synonym of *qérebh*, "inward being" (cf. I Kings 22:35; Eccl. 7:9). There is no compelling argument against the present form of the M.T. or against the authenticity of the line.

28-29. The strophe ends with a sudden outburst: a threat, presumably directed against the listeners, and anticipating their challenge. If the friends persist in persecuting Job (vs. 28a; cf. vs. 22), finding in the words he has just used a further pretext for their condemnation of him (vs. 28b), they should "truly be in dread of the sword" (vs. 29a), i.e., of the **wrath** [which] **brings the punishment of the sword** (vs. 29b). The text reads, lit., "because (the) iniquities (of the) sword (are) wrath." The use of the word **sword** in both vs. 29a and vs. 29b is not likely to be original, for the poet does not have the stylistic habit of identical repetition. Although commentators have proposed rendering עונות חרב by "iniquities worthy of the sword" (cf. the similarly obscure and doubtful expression in 31:11, 28, עונות פלילים, "iniquities of [for?] judges"; see Exeg. *ad loc.*), the text of vs. 29b is highly uncertain. The end of the threat is equally difficult, **that you may know there is a judgment** (vs. 29c), even if one were to assume with some of the

---

"enjoy him forever." Nothing is any longer possible but the theophany (38:1–42:6).

You say that I am dust?
Yet through my mind
Wild, unborn lightnings leap;
On my soul rolls vast, remembered music, like the
    spheres';
Deep in my pulses beats
The throb of coming sorrows,
Excess of joys long dead;
And on my ears
The tread of ghostly memories,
Frail wisps of hope that whisper as they pass,
The stealthy breathing of a fear.
I am more akin to thee
Than to the dust,
Thou God of all the past—
And this one swift hour
Which spans thy great forever! [5]

28. The Root of the Matter.—The whole approach of the friends is increasingly anthro-

[5] Paul Scherer, "Dust and Divinity." Authorship acknowledged by request. Editors.

pological, verging off toward a kind of depersonalized automatism (see Expos. on 18:2-4): Job's is increasingly theological; he understands more profoundly than they do that the ultimate issue is God (see Expos. on 19:6). The former view tends to lower the level of human responsibility (22:2-3), even as it more successfully avoids the great, simple, primal human questions: the "answers" are to be sought on the horizontal strata of existence. The latter, while it involves itself in questions that have no "answers," lifts that threshold to its very highest (ch. 31). In its quest for **the root of the matter** the one inevitably becomes self-righteous and censorious; the other may break out into blasphemy, but its face is Godward. Churches have spires that point to heaven; but so do the world's riddles and its sin.

28-29. *The Character of Job.*—(See Exeg.) It is necessary at all times to remember that at no time is Job's mind normal. We should not expect it to be. Nobody in such a state should be asked to deal with that state calmly and objectively. It is not the hour either for logic or for

29 Be ye afraid of the sword: for wrath *bringeth* the punishments of the sword, that ye may know *there is* a judgment.

29 be afraid of the sword,
    for wrath brings the punishment of the sword,
    that you may know there is a judgment."

20 Then answered Zophar the Naamathite, and said,

20 Then Zophar the Na'amathite answered:

---

ancient versions that the *Kethîbh* שדין should be read *sheddin* (although LXXᴬ probably read שׁדי, "the Almighty"). The word דין, **judgment,** is not found elsewhere in the poetic discussion, but it is a favorite of Elihu (35:14; 36:17; cf. 36:31); and this fact raises suspicion against the genuineness of the passage or against fidelity of its preservation. Nevertheless the general meaning is fairly clear.

Some interpreters find it hard to conceive that Job, "immediately after swooning at the anticipation of seeing God" (Strahan, *Job,* p. 178), should address his opponents with such vindictiveness. The fact is that Job in the poetic discussion is now neither the saint of the prologue nor yet the humbled creature of the epilogue who intercedes for his friends (42:8). Moreover, no one should expect that the hope of seeing God face to face would make Job an evangelical Christian (cf. Matt. 5:8)! In vss. 25-27 he desired to encounter the Deity in order to be able at last to defend his innocence and honor. This prospect filled him with an intense emotion, but its recital did not transform the antagonism of his friends into benevolent admiration. On the contrary, it may be presumed that the three wise men were more deeply shocked than ever before at the extravagance of Job's claims, and that possibly they threatened him with hostile gestures. If so, far from having "himself the heart of a persecutor," Job was replying to a threat by outspoken menaces. Such an attitude may or may not deserve to be called "theologically unsatisfying"; but it is psychologically true to the character of the hero (cf. 13:6-11).

5. Second Discourse of Zophar (20:1-29)

Like Eliphaz and Bildad in the second cycle (chs. 15; 18), Zophar develops only one theme: the doom of the evil man may be delayed but it is inevitable. Much of what

---

explanations. The explanation that one has brought it all on oneself (vs. 28*b*) is singularly inept. The preacher on occasion gives himself over to an analysis of the present situation. He diagnoses it up and down. The inevitable conclusion is that it is no less and no other than we deserve. But repentance is not always the upshot. Repentance comes not of understanding but of love—which last is now and then only part three of the sermon, and often the weakest part. Job is either at fever heat or lost in hopeless brooding. There is tumult in his words, as there is in his mind. Exaggeration, wrestlings unspeakable. His soul is a battleground, torn asunder by inward antagonisms, faith and hope, resentment and despair. And all the while he is harassed by the thought of his own basic integrity, the one good which for him is worse than the good of a guilty conscience; yet the very throbs of his anguish become the birth pangs of truth. Through loneliness and bitterness he falls away into a sense of utter helplessness and injustice; then the flash of an appeal to God, with the

hope that will not loosen its hold, and the fear that never allows any hope to be hope. There is no thought of renouncing God because of the loss he has suffered or the disease he has; he comes near renouncing God because God seems immoral. Like a Titan he hurls his challenge, then leaps after it with his heart in his mouth. He broods over God's cruelty, hates and loves, trembles and gibes, hides in the citadel of his own weakness and flings from it his taunts, only to be brought at last out of the maelstrom of that mad contradiction into the terror and the stillness of an eternal presence, where all his questions die stillborn. Perhaps to speak of his character is beside the point; one should rather speak of the tempest that rages in his soul, dying away, when its force is spent, into a peace that is not of this world (see Expos., pp. 905-7; also on 1:1, 20-22; 2:7-10; 3:20-21, 24; 6:8-13).

20:1-29. The Speech of Zophar.—You goad me into speaking (vs. 2*a*). I can wait no longer (vs. 2*b*), what with your insults, and the under-

| 2 Therefore do my thoughts cause me to answer, and for *this* I make haste.

3 I have heard the check of my reproach, and the spirit of my understanding causeth me to answer. | 2 "Therefore my thoughts answer me, because of my haste within me.

3 I hear censure which insults me, and out of my understanding a spirit answers me. |

he says is true and forcefully expressed, but none of his views is relevant to the situation at hand. The issues raised by Job are ignored. Yet the moving appeal of the hero to the pity of his friends (19:21) may have made a dent in Zophar's magnificent impassiveness. The opening words of this discourse indicate an element of anxiety which had not heretofore been detectable in the dogmatic assurance of any of the three wise men.

a) EXPULSION OF ANXIOUS THOUGHTS (20:1-3)

20:2-3. The word לכן, **therefore,** is unexpected at the beginning of a discourse, for it usually refers to the words which precede. If the text has been correctly preserved, Zophar is at last breaking a silence which he has maintained with utmost difficulty. He is introducing his remarks in a direct repercussion to Job's shocking statements. He confesses that he has entertained "disquieting thoughts" which easily might have led him

standing I have of the whole thing (vs. 3). From the very beginning the triumph of the wicked has been only **for a moment,** and everybody knows it. A dunghill for his pride (vss. 6-7)! He is gone like a dream (vs. 8), vanished from sight (vs. 9), only his children left to make what amends they can (vs. 10), while the **vigor** of his youth lies **down with him** like a bride in his death (vs. 11). He smacks his lips at the taste of his own wickedness, rolls it about surreptitiously under his tongue; and it turns to gall in his stomach (vss. 12-14). The wealth he has gorged God makes him to vomit up—all of it poison, and it kills him (vss. 15-16). No milk and honey in his books; never will he enjoy **the fruit of his toil** (vss. 17-18; cf. 15:31). The way he has treated the poor, the insatiable greed of his mouth—everything comes home to roost (vss. 19-22). God give him his **belly** . . . **full** (vs. 23). When he tries to get away, strike him dead (vss. 24-25). Fire from heaven, vengeance from earth (vss. 26-28), he has it coming. And as you say—it comes **from God** (vs. 29).

1-29. *Ignoring the Issue.*—Whether or not vss. 1-11, as Kissane holds, are the rebuke of the spirit which Zophar, a bit shaken by what he has heard, claims for a mentor, while vss. 12-29 constitute his own interpretation of its chiding, makes little difference. There can be no doubt that the speech as a whole is inconsequential, and therefore irrelevant and immaterial. Zophar has been unable to make heads or tails out of Job's reply to Bildad. If the words with which he launches out into his present effort mean anything at all, they mean that his mind is disturbed, and he hardly knows where to lay hold of the argument (see Exeg.). He cannot fit into

his ready-made scheme of things such undisciplined imaginings, or what would come of them if they were true. So he puts together his jigsaw puzzle with the pieces that make sense to him—the kind of sense he can belabor with all his might—and pays no attention to the others, simply lays them over to one side. The trouble is that the other pieces are the key pieces: his bewildered friend's innocence, the obvious inequities of human existence, and the incredible madness toward which the tortured soul of Job is being driven (19:25; refer to 16:18, 19, and note Zophar's reference in vs. 27).

Manifestly, the technique is ready at hand for all comparable situations. Dismiss what you cannot manage, turning a deaf ear to the very heart of the matter if you cannot still its beating. Then fight back with all the vehemence you can muster. Do it as fiercely, if need be even as coarsely (vss. 7a, 15), as you can: Eliphaz, who is himself not undisturbed (see Expos. on 15:7-16), and Bildad both find it difficult to improve on Zophar at that point. Answer insult with insult. Bite like a mad dog every chance you get. As Strahan suggests,[6] there is indeed such a thing as "dogmatic rabies," and Zophar's speech is a vivid instance of it. In no case confront the God that is. That way lies humility. Fashion him in your own image. Never re-examine a premise. How can you possibly be wrong? And never widen a view to make room for troublesome exceptions. What qualms you may have had "shall melt with fervent heat" (II Pet. 3:10).

2-5. *Haste Lays Waste.*—(See Expos. on 8:1-7.) Job is never in any great anxiety to defend himself. He is dealing with vaster issues (see Expos. on 23:2). **Not so the friends. They have**

[6] *Job,* p. 181.

4 Knowest thou *not* this of old, since man was placed upon earth,	4 Do you not know this from of old, since man was placed upon earth,

to skepticism. The word שעפי, **my thoughts,** refers to anxious reflections which prompt a man to waver in his convictions, to suspend his judgment, and to hesitate at a theological crossroad (cf. I Kings 18:21; Ps. 119:113; cf. also Job 4:13; Pss. 94:19; 139:23). Etymologically, the word suggests a branching out in two directions, a cleavage between conflicting considerations, and in some cases a double-mindedness which verges upon a dichotomy between intellectual and moral activities. Zophar implies that Job's latest discourse, with its amazing hope against hope, has penetrated deeply into his own being and has slightly unsettled his position. "Therefore my disturbing thoughts are causing me to give a retort, on account of the agitation which is within me" (vs. 2). Quickly controlling his incipient doubts, he rejects them swiftly by adding, **I have heard the check of my reproach, and the spirit of my understanding causeth me to answer.** However, the LXX appears to have read, instead of the difficult ורוח מבינתי, "and a spirit from my understanding," the words ורוח מבינה, which offer a good parallel to the preceding line and may be translated, "and a wind without intelligence." It is worth noting that Bildad and Eliphaz have begun some of their attacks by comparing Job's eloquence to an empty wind (8:2; 15:2). Zophar offers the spectacle of a dogmatic believer who dismisses disturbing thoughts as soon as they hit the well-ordered citadel of his mind. The insulting tone he adopts against the sufferer itself indicates his own insecurity.

b) EVANESCENCE OF GODLESS JOY (20:4-29)

After a brief introduction (vss. 2-3), Zophar proceeds to reaffirm the familiar belief in individual retribution (vss. 4-29). The body of this speech cannot be divided into a sequence of strophes: it is a tirade fifty-seven lines long.

4-10. Is not Job in possession of the common knowledge of mankind, according to which the triumph of the wicked is short lived? Even if the apostate (*ḥānēph;* cf. 8:13;

no time to waste, but much ground to lose. When you insinuate a doubt into the mind of a fanatic, prick the arrogant assurance with which he has been accustomed to "view the landscape o'er," he may well deliver himself into camp, bag and baggage. In his headlong rush he is likely to expose both flank and center, only to take his stand at last so far out of touch with reality that the very possibility of retreat is cut off. Zophar, with the **haste** born of wounded vanity (vs. 3*a*?) and conscious insecurity, plunges ahead of the front line of defense and renders the whole position which the friends have taken in the second cycle utterly untenable. He bitterly resents what Job has said about them (12:2; 17:4), and the scorn with which the culprit has been responding to the pious sweat of their brow (16:2; 19:2). The warnings in 13:10; 19:29 have not added to his composure. In a spirit that can scarcely be called a **spirit of understanding** (vs. 3*b*), he mistakes his hurt pride for righteous indignation—the two are easily confused—and limns out against the sky a God who is little more than Zophar in a hurry, hardly able to wait until Saturday night in order to settle accounts: it is not altogether clear whose accounts—Zophar's or God's.

Breathlessly he pulls up, and stops short with a jerk: **the joy of the godless [is] but for a moment** (vs. 5). Nothing could be more vulnerable (see Expos. on 4:8; 12:2-6). Job lays hold of it with both hands and makes rubble out of everything all three of them have said (ch. 21).

The tempo in Ps. 37:2, 10, 35-36 is very much the same, while Ps. 73 moves with considerably more deliberation, meditating in the sanctuary on the end of the wicked (vs. 17). Strahan aptly points the difference, and enriches the reference with his comment: "The great discoverers in nature and grace alike have brooded and experimented long before they have dogmatised. Had Zophar taken time to observe and reflect, he would have said, 'Some sufferers are saints'; had he taken still more time, he might even have added, 'and some are saviours.'" [7] It was the patience that wrought the transformation in Job (see Expos. on 3:24). "In quietness and in confidence . . . strength" (Isa. 30:15). "Let patience have her perfect work" (Jas. 1:4).

4-11. The Joy of the Godless.—At least Zophar understands the wicked well enough to know that they get a kind of pleasure out of their wickedness. His point is that the pleasure

[7] *Ibid.,* p. 182.

5 That the triumphing of the wicked *is* short, and the joy of the hypocrite *but* for a moment?

6 Though his excellency mount up to the heavens, and his head reach unto the clouds;

7 *Yet* he shall perish for ever like his own dung: they which have seen him shall say, Where *is* he?

8 He shall fly away as a dream, and shall not be found: yea, he shall be chased away as a vision of the night.

9 The eye also *which* saw him shall *see him* no more; neither shall his place any more behold him.

10 His children shall seek to please the poor, and his hands shall restore their goods.

11 His bones are full *of the sin* of his youth, which shall lie down with him in the dust.

12 Though wickedness be sweet in his mouth, *though* he hide it under his tongue;

---

5 that the exulting of the wicked is short,
  and the joy of the godless but for a moment?

6 Though his height mount up to the heavens,
  and his head reach to the clouds,

7 he will perish for ever like his own dung;
  those who have seen him will say, 'Where is he?'

8 He will fly away like a dream, and not be found;
  he will be chased away like a vision of the night.

9 The eye which saw him will see him no more,
  nor will his place any more behold him.

10 His children will seek the favor of the poor,
  and his hands will give back his wealth.

11 His bones are full of youthful vigor,
  but it will lie down with him in the dust.

12 "Though wickedness is sweet in his mouth,
  though he hides it under his tongue,

---

etc.) seems to be happy, he enjoys life **but for a moment** (vss. 4-5). Although he may grow proudly like a tree which touches heaven (vs. 6), **he shall perish for ever like his own dung** (vs. 7*a*) and be seen no more (vss. 7*b*-9). His sons will have to pay an indemnity or give a compensation to his victims (vs. 10*a*, cf. the meaning of the verb רצה, not to be confused with רצץ; Lev. 26: 34, 41, 43), and their hands (reading ידיהם for ידיו, *his hands*) will be compelled to restore his wealth to its rightful owner (vs. 10*b*).

11-16. The lustful vigor of youth may now fill his frame, but it [lit., "she"] **will lie down with him** like a lover, not on a couch of delight but in the **dust** of the grave (vs. 11).

---

is brief; and for the simple reason that evil devours itself and its children. Bildad laid his emphasis on the moral order (see Expos. on 18:2-4); Zophar calls attention to the fact that there is something about wrongdoing itself which turns the sweet bitter (see Expos. on vss. 12-16). Since man was placed upon earth, there has been that about the **height** which makes him dizzy. He is betrayed by his own "strength," becomes the victim of his own "virtues." Frugality has a way of turning into niggardliness, piety into sanctimoniousness, courage into foolhardiness, initiative into self-conceit, steadiness into obstinacy, conviction into intolerance, ambition into cupidity, pride into arrogance—the list is quite endless. A flight of steps leads up; but the same flight leads down (Matt. 11:21; Luke 10:15). The qualities that make for success may execute an about-face and make for failure. But Zophar, with a good idea, falls a prey to it, lets it carry him away. The dilemma of the wicked is not as inevitable as he pictures it. The denouement does not always come about so promptly. Indeed, it does not always come about! Dramatically he puts it: magnificence on a rubbish heap—it could have been said that politely if he had wanted to—a dream that vanishes, an empty place (cf. 7:8-10; 8:18), beggared children (?)—finished! The godless, where is he? A rhetorical question that may have been taken from Job's own mouth (14:10); but so desperately twisted now that Job has no difficulty supplying the answer (21: 17-18).

12-16. *Bittersweet.*—(See Exeg. on vss. 17-29; Expos. on vss. 4-11.) Zophar is of half a mind that "to enjoy the pleasures of sin for a season" (Heb. 11:25) is no enjoyment at all: the

13 *Though* he spare it, and forsake it not, but keep it still within his mouth;

14 *Yet* his meat in his bowels is turned, *it is* the gall of asps within him.

15 He hath swallowed down riches, and he shall vomit them up again: God shall cast them out of his belly.

16 He shall suck the poison of asps: the viper's tongue shall slay him.

17 He shall not see the rivers, the floods, the brooks of honey and butter.

18 That which he labored for shall he restore, and shall not swallow *it* down: according to *his* substance *shall* the restitution *be,* and he shall not rejoice *therein.*

19 Because he hath oppressed *and* hath forsaken the poor; *because* he hath violently taken away a house which he builded not;

20 Surely he shall not feel quietness in his belly, he shall not save of that which he desired.

21 There shall none of his meat be left; therefore shall no man look for his goods.

---

13 though he is loath to let it go,
   and holds it in his mouth,

14 yet his food is turned in his stomach;
   it is the gall of asps within him.

15 He swallows down riches and vomits
   them up again;
   God casts them out of his belly.

16 He will suck the poison of asps;
   the tongue of a viper will kill him.

17 He will not look upon the rivers,
   the streams flowing with honey and
   curds.

18 He will give back the fruit of his toil,
   and will not swallow it down;
   from the profit of his trading
   he will get no enjoyment.

19 For he has crushed and abandoned the
   poor,
   he has seized a house which he did not
   build.

20 "Because his greed knew no rest,
   he will not save anything in which he
   delights.

21 There was nothing left after he had
   eaten;
   therefore his prosperity will not endure.

"Though evil taste sweet in his mouth" (vs. 12*a*) and be well savored (vss. 12*b*-13), it will turn sour within him (vs. 14), and he will have to disgorge the riches he has gulped (vs. 15). "The figure of God administering the emetic is coarse and powerful" (Peake, *Job,* p. 199), and it helps Zophar to stress the conviction that ethics cannot long be flouted even under the cover of aesthetics.

17-29. The images are not altogether consistent (contrast, for example, vs. 15 with vs. 18), and the rhetorical developments suggest that Zophar is wavering ambiguously

---

"pleasures" are not pleasant, they are filled with bitterness. And one knows what he means. Fewer would like the taste if the aftertaste came first. It can be readily imagined how difficult it was for the Jews of the postexilic period to accept such doctrine as this. To be told, as the Deuteronomists would have them believe, that what had happened to them was just a spewing out into history of the evil on which they had gorged themselves, was in the poet's mind precisely as unjust a thing as the friends were doing to Job when they kept insisting that he had brought all his misery on himself. In *The Uses of the Past* Herbert J. Muller enters the lists against Arnold J. Toynbee. It is his contention that history has no meaning, in the sense of a clear pattern or determinate plot. "The problem, then, is to maintain principle and morale

in the face of ultimate uncertainty."[8] The author of Job was acutely aware of the "ultimate uncertainty." What begins as "mystery with meaning," in the phrase of Reinhold Niebuhr, ends for him as "meaning with mystery."[9] Zophar is allowed to speak truth; but his truth, oversimplified and misapplied, becomes untruth.

17-18. *The Future that Never Comes.*—Here is a man looking forward to a comfortable old age. He is laying up against the time of his retirement. But while he lives in the future, the end of all his dreams comes in the present. The lumber he is using keeps the building from completion.

18. *The Fruit of His Toil.*—(Cf. 5:5; Expos. on 15:17-35.) He has to give it back without

[8] New York: Oxford University Press, 1952, p. 43.
[9] Cf. *Discerning the Signs of the Times,* pp. 152-73.

22 In the fulness of his sufficiency he shall be in straits: every hand of the wicked shall come upon him.

23 *When* he is about to fill his belly, *God* shall cast the fury of his wrath upon him, and shall rain *it* upon him while he is eating.

24 He shall flee from the iron weapon, *and* the bow of steel shall strike him through.

25 It is drawn, and cometh out of the body; yea, the glittering sword cometh out of his gall: terrors *are* upon him.

26 All darkness *shall be* hid in his secret places: a fire not blown shall consume him; it shall go ill with him that is left in his tabernacle.

27 The heaven shall reveal his iniquity; and the earth shall rise up against him.

22 In the fulness of his sufficiency he will be in straits;
 all the force of misery will come upon him.

23 To fill his belly to the full
 God[z] will send his fierce anger into him,
 and rain it upon him as his food.[a]

24 He will flee from an iron weapon;
 a bronze arrow will strike him through.

25 It is drawn forth and comes out of his body,
 the glittering point comes out of his gall;
 terrors come upon him.

26 Utter darkness is laid up for his treasures;
 a fire not blown upon will devour him;
 what is left in his tent will be consumed.

27 The heavens will reveal his iniquity,
 and the earth will rise up against him.

[z] Heb *he*
[a] Cn: Heb *in his flesh*

between an insistence upon the brevity of a pleasure which has been wrongfully obtained (vss. 17, 21*b*) and the awareness of the fact that hedonism does not truly satisfy (vss. 20, 22). In any case, the ultimate destiny of the evil man is certain. God will indeed **fill his belly to the full** (vs. 23*a*) and rain upon him the arrows of his wrath (vss. 23*b*-25*a*). Then the "terrors of death" (*'ēmîm*) will suddenly come over him (vs. 25*b*; cf. 9:34; 13:21), and with the threefold image of **utter darkness** (vs. 26*a*), **fire** (vs. 26*bc*), and flood (vs. 28 KJV), the finality of his fate is proclaimed as **the heritage decreed for him by God** (vs. 29).

In accord with the poet's technique of delayed reaction, Zophar replies not to Job's latest speech (ch. 19), which he ignores completely, but to a statement in Job's preceding discourse. There the hero had been bold enough to address the earth as an ally (16:18) and to declare that his witness was in heaven (16:19). Zophar makes the retort that **the**

enjoying it. "Therefore . . . be ye steadfast, unmovable, always abounding in the work of the Lord, forasmuch as ye know that your labor is not in vain in the Lord" (I Cor. 15:58). Life makes its generous returns even to the wicked. God "sendeth rain on the just and on the unjust" (Matt. 5:45). Nobody disturbs the beneficent order of his creation—or avoids its hazards. The difference between the just and the unjust lies deeper; the returns are not of the same order.

22. That Which Satisfieth Not.—It has been said that sin is like a recurring decimal: three will not go into ten, no matter to what lengths the process of division is carried—tens, hundreds, thousands, tens of thousands. Lust and greed cannot slake their own thirst. Desire, satisfaction, revulsion; more desire, repeated satisfaction, increased revulsion: of all circles the most vicious. Follow through the dictionary these synonyms: satiate, sate, surfeit, cloy, glut, gorge.

23. God Requite Him!—If this is not an imprecation in form, as the RSV would indicate it to be, it certainly is in substance. Zophar's prayer is his "soul's sincere desire." Strahan notes the "indecent enthusiasm" of the whole speech.[1] The vehemence is revelatory. Zophar worships a wish (contrast Luke 15; 19:9).

24-25. The Target of Wrath.—(See Expos. on 6:4; 16:13.) Death hounds the man's very efforts to escape. He avoids the spear and is struck through with an **arrow**; he draws it forth, thinking it will be better so—and in a moment the **terrors** of death are upon him. Job is permitted, not to say compelled, to draw his own conclusions.

[1] *Op. cit.*, p. 181.

28 The increase of his house shall depart, *and his goods* shall flow away in the day of his wrath.

29 This *is* the portion of a wicked man from God, and the heritage appointed unto him by God.

21 But Job answered and said,
2 Hear diligently my speech, and let this be your consolations.

28 The possessions of his house will be carried away,
dragged off in the day of God's[b] wrath.

29 This is the wicked man's portion from God,
the heritage decreed for him by God."

21 Then Job answered:
2 "Listen carefully to my words,
and let this be your consolation.

[b] Heb *his*

---

heaven shall reveal his iniquity; and the earth shall rise up against him (vs. 27). Thus in the midst of his peroration, the third friend unmistakably links his obstinate interlocutor with the godless or profane man whose doom he has just depicted. As if anticipating a charge of irrelevant didacticism, the speaker subtly intimates that his portrait fits the case now at hand in a double way: Let Job take warning and discover his guilty self! Let him also recognize that this universe (as well as the life of the individual) is governed by the decisions of a righteous Deity!

6. Second Reply of Job to Zophar (21:1-34)

While the poet depicts Zophar and the friends generally as developing their theme in an amorphous, almost haphazard way, Job is usually shown as a meticulous speaker who respects the conventions of poetical rhetoric, formulates his arguments according to a plan, and develops them within a rather strict strophic structure: (*a*) aroused by Zophar's either willful or irresponsible distortion of the facts of experience, Job prepares himself to reply and his friends to listen (vss. 2-6); (*b*) what he has to say stands in direct contradiction to the pious affirmations which have again been rehearsed: against the stultified dogma of retribution he observes the prosperity and apparent impunity of evil men (vss. 7-13); (*c*) such a glaring display of divine injustice is not made acceptable, nor is it righted, by the subsidiary belief in the children's solidarity with the guilt of their fathers (vss. 14-21); (*d*) furthermore, death is the lot of both the just and the unjust (vss. 22-27); (*e*) even in death, however, the wicked obtain upon the earth the immortality of a fame which survives them and which they do not deserve (vss. 28-34).

(*a*) Courage of Honesty (21:1-6)

21:2-3. Job has opened one of his previous discourses by stating that his friends were "miserable comforters" (16:2), since they were rash or stupid enough to identify their own clumsy and self-righteous attempts with "the consolations of God" (15:11). He

---

29. The Image in the Glass.—So does disaster become destiny (vs. 26*a*). "A fire not blown" upon by man devours him (1:16). "The heavens . . . reveal his iniquity" (cf. 16:19), "the earth" rises "up against him" (cf. 16:18). Here is the swinging of the same dreadful pendulum that one hears in the prologue (see Expos. on 1:13). Kissane thinks the reference is rather to the Flood (vs. 28; cf. Gen. 7:11).

It is interesting and instructive to compare Zophar's approach with Nathan's (II Sam. 12:1-7*a*). Zophar proceeds from a mistaken premise: Job is not guilty, David is. Zophar's hints are ulcerous and offensive; they drive the sufferer's mind back upon itself. Even if there had been any wrong to be seen, the eyes of the wrongdoer would have been blinded with resentment. Nathan's method was completely disarming; David's conscience was given an unimpeded chance to condemn itself: then the thrust (see Expos. on 6:24-27). Zophar, with his own dogmatic ax to grind and no compassion for Job, listens at the threshold of his own spirit; Nathan, for love of David, and in the fear of God, has listened to another voice, both just and merciful.

21:1-34. The Answer of Job.—Your "consolations of God" (15:11)! Listen to me. I will show you what they really are. Then, my good friend Zophar, you may mock on (vs. 3). My contro-

3 Suffer me that I may speak; and after that I have spoken, mock on.

4 As for me, *is* my complaint to man? and if *it were so,* why should not my spirit be troubled?

5 Mark me, and be astonished, and lay *your* hand upon *your* mouth.

6 Even when I remember I am afraid, and trembling taketh hold on my flesh.

---

3 Bear with me, and I will speak, and after I have spoken, mock on.

4 As for me, is my complaint against man? Why should I not be impatient?

5 Look at me, and be appalled, and lay your hand upon your mouth.

6 When I think of it I am dismayed, and shuddering seizes my flesh.

---

now bids them, **Hear diligently my speech, and let this be your consolations** (vs. 2). According to the common interpretation of this verse, Job asks for the benevolent attention of his friends. Their silence would constitute the best kind of consolation they could offer. However, the pronoun זאת, **this,** refers to מלתי, **my speech,** rather than to the whole clause in vs. 2a. Thus it is better to understand that Job is here again speaking ironically, saying, "You offer me strange comfort when you tell me that the apostate always meets his fate, and that I am one! The words I am going to utter will show you the true nature of your consolations!" **Bear with me** for a while, **and after I have spoken, mock on** (vs. 3). The M.T. reads the last imperative in the singular, as if Job singled out one of his friends, probably Zophar. The LXX has the plural and the negative, "do not ye mock," and some critics correct the Hebrew text accordingly. Nevertheless the M.T. makes good sense and should be preserved (cf. 16:2-3).

4-6. As for me, is my complaint against man? (vs. 4a): Since Job has a quarrel with God, why should his friends be impatient with him? At least they might understand that he has the right to be angry (vs. 4b). However, what they have heard so far has been comparatively mild and harmless. Now let them brace themselves in anticipation of a thunder clap! (Note the image which lies behind the word **astonished** in vs. 5a.) They are going to be truly speechless at the intrepidity of his blasphemy (vs. 5b). He himself is already **shuddering** at the thought of his own recklessness (vs. 6).

---

versy is with God. Unlike you, I have a right to be impatient (vs. 4). Mark my word. Let the very sound of it stop your mouth. I tremble to think of it myself (vss. 5-6; so Kissane,[2] but see Exeg.). What the three of you have said is simply not true. Everything is exactly the other way about. The wicked do not die as you would like to have them die. That much is obvious. They live and prosper. And I want to know why (vs. 7). They see their children settle down, **their houses are safe,** their cattle multitudinous, the air is filled with merrymaking and music. And at the end of their days (cf. 5:26) they die in peace (vss. 8-13). What matter that they have had nothing to do with God? They leave him out (vs. 16b) and still get what they want and hold on to it (vss. 14-16). **The lamp of the wicked is put out? Does calamity** wait at their side (18:5-12)? How often? How often does God destroy them (vs. 17c; make them suffer?)? All of you have said it. How often are they "like the chaff which the wind driveth away" (Ps. 1:4; see 13:25)? No use telling me he visits the iniquities of the fathers upon the children. Let him visit the iniquities of the

fathers on the fathers! They are the ones that need to know. What earthly good is it after they are dead (vss. 19-21)? Your God who judges even the angels (15:15; see Exeg.) needs to be told how it works out down here (vs. 22). I can inform him: happy or unhappy, wicked or not, all are alike in death (vss. 23-26). I get the point of your insinuations (vss. 27-28). But just ask anybody who has ever stepped outside his own front door (vs. 29): the wicked man gets off. The evidence is all around (vs. 29b). Who charges him with what he has done, or holds him to account (vss. 30-31)? When he dies, he is buried in pomp. His grave is "in perpetual care" (vs. 32). The earth lies softly upon him. He is a shining example for multitudes to follow (vs. 33). What comfort is there in that? Take the sum of what you have said and set my facts over against it. What is then left is nothing but sheer, malicious fraud.

5-6. *Facing the Facts.*—In both the first cycle and the second, when Zophar speaks Job seems to rouse himself, like a slumbering giant out of a nightmare, to the full use of his powers. Suddenly now it dawns on him what all of them have been trying to prove. They have been say-

[2] *Job*, p. 132.

7 Wherefore do the wicked live, become old, yea, are mighty in power?	7 Why do the wicked live, reach old age, and grow mighty in power?
8 Their seed is established in their sight with them, and their offspring before their eyes.	8 Their children are established in their presence, and their offspring before their eyes.
9 Their houses *are* safe from fear, neither *is* the rod of God upon them.	9 Their houses are safe from fear, and no rod of God is upon them.

b) Impunity of Criminals (21:7-13)

7-13. Zophar has declared that the joy of the godless is soon vanished (20:5 ff.), but this declaration is contradicted by the observable facts. These are so eloquent that Job does not need to appeal to a knowledge common to the whole of mankind from the most distant antiquity. He takes for granted that his picture is obvious; indeed, nobody could miss it who takes the trouble to observe the human scene. Thus he does not need to state that **the wicked live;** he immediately accepts as evident this fact, and asks the reason why: **Wherefore do the wicked live, become old, yea, are mighty in power?** (vs. 7). Where are those so-called misfortunes which, according to Zophar, soon wipe out the profane from their tents? These sinners, far from being short lived, grow old happily, and their physical vigor is not abated but increased with their substance, wealth, influence, and authority. (Note the use of the verb *gābhar*, "to be strong," from which is derived Job's favorite appellation for man and especially for himself, i.e., *gébher*, "strong man," *vir*, almost *gibbôr*, "hero," "man of valiance"; cf. "Gabriel," the name of the archangel who transmits God's power in the Jewish and Christian literature.) Such "he-men" live long enough to see

> their seed . . . established with them in their presence,
> and their offspring before their eyes (vs. 8),

and Job insists on this cardinal aspect of happiness, since what he misses more than wealth and health is his posterity. Who dares to speak of a divine justice when, in full view for all the world to see, such individuals and **their houses are safe from fear, neither is the rod of God upon them** (vs. 9)? Not only do they and their household prosper, but their own livestock appear to be unfailingly fertile (vs. 10), and the whole

---

ing that there is "no peace to the wicked," and saying it over and over again, a kind of ridiculous metronome with its senseless ticking back and forth. Finally it gets under his skin. You can listen to such a noise almost without being conscious of it—but only for so long. Then you hurl something. Job hurls facts. He takes no pleasure in it. He is not rubbing his hands together, as Zophar did. The facts are too terrible for that. It would be far more comfortable not to know them; but who can help knowing them? These men have presumed to speak for God; and to put it mildly, they have spoken less than the truth (see Expos. on 12:2-6; 13:8; 18:21). Item by item he picks their "consolations" apart to see what is inside. The verses to which reference is made, directly or indirectly, may be listed for convenience: 15:20-21, 22-24, 27*b*, 30-35; 18:5*a*, 12*b*, 14-15, 18, 21; 20:7, 10-11, 21-22, 24-25, 26-28. He stresses three major points. First, alien facts are not to be glossed

over and brought into line with some a priori theory. They are here to be faced. No chortling over it. No glibness of speech. It is sobering business (see Expos. on 6:24-27). Second, the ultimate issue is God (see Expos. on 19:6). God was the ultimate issue on Calvary when the cry of dereliction went up from a cross. Why are things as they are, if he is worthy of worship? These two words are themselves blood kin. There is at least that about him which prefers honesty to deceitfulness (cf. 13:7-11; 42:7) and courage to cowardice (see Expos. on 6:21-27). Third, no shallow optimism will do. It is either speechless horror or speechless wonder (vs. 5*b*; 40:4*b*). And nobody can work that transformation but God himself.

7-18. The Mysteries of Godliness.—We have to accept the fact that rewards and penalties in this life are not apportioned according to desert. There is indeed a kind of "rough justice" (see Expos. on 4:8) and Job knows it; but there are

10 Their bull gendereth, and faileth not; their cow calveth, and casteth not her calf.

11 They send forth their little ones like a flock, and their children dance.

12 They take the timbrel and harp, and rejoice at the sound of the organ.

13 They spend their days in wealth, and in a moment go down to the grave.

14 Therefore they say unto God, Depart from us; for we desire not the knowledge of thy ways.

15 What *is* the Almighty, that we should serve him? and what profit should we have, if we pray unto him?

10 Their bull breeds without fail;
   their cow calves, and does not cast her
      calf.

11 They send forth their little ones like a
      flock,
   and their children dance.

12 They sing to the tambourine and the lyre,
   and rejoice to the sound of the pipe.

13 They spend their days in prosperity,
   and in peace they go down to Sheol.

14 They say to God, 'Depart from us!
   We do not desire the knowledge of thy
      ways.

15 What is the Almighty, that we should
      serve him?
   And what profit do we get if we pray to
      him?'

---

community, especially the **little ones** (עויל‍ים, the mischievous, teasing, and attractive urchins), run around barefooted "like kids," singing, dancing, and playing upon the tambourine, the lyre and the flute (vss. 11-12). In a few strokes Job sketches the traditional idyl of the patriarchal circle, where there is not only life and food in abundance, but also security; and therefore room for a gaiety and a careless freedom which some observers might call superfluous (cf. Zech. 8:5; Matt. 11:16-17). The whole passage, with its concrete charm and picturesque traits, reveals by contrast the inward pathos of the man who speaks it, a bereaved, destitute, isolated, and condemned individual. He does not lower himself to formulate his envy, his resentment, or his bitterness; but he forcefully clinches his argument by concluding that the wicked "live out their days in happiness and in peace" (cf. LXX, ἐν δέ ἀναπαύσει, confirming this special meaning of the word רגע in Jer. 6:16; cf. also Targ.); or "in an instant [i.e., without the crippling infirmities of old age and the slow disintegration of an incurable disease] they descend into the grave" (vs. 13).

c) PROFITLESSNESS OF PRAYER (21:14-18)

14-16. In these verses Job skillfully shows that the majestic monotheism of the friends, with its emphasis upon the dogma of individual retribution, is not essentially different from the practical atheism of the evil men who justify their willful ignorance of God by stating from experience that religion does not pay. Eliphaz, Bildad, and Zophar affirm that integrity always brings increase, and conversely that an ill-fate is the punishment of irreligion. In so speaking they associate themselves with "the Satan" of the prologue who asked, "Doth Job fear God for nought?" (1:9). Wealthy and unscrupulous men who wallow in their ease may not actually say,

> **Depart from us!**
> **We do not desire the knowledge of thy ways.**

---

by far too many exceptions, so many that they can scarcely be said to prove the rule (note the Exeg. for the sweep and power of the poet's canvas). Obviously, therefore, we have to accept the corollary: that religion is about something deeper. Job is being driven to it, step by step (see Expos. on 16:13; 22:21-30). That something else may involve suffering—which is precisely what the Jews could not understand about

Jesus. A good man on a cross? The Son of God there? It was blasphemy. And it must have troubled the saints. How could one reconcile the grin on the face of a lion in the arena with the smile on the face of God in heaven? It has been pointed out that a friendly and favoring universe would indeed abolish the problem, but somewhat after the manner in which death abolishes disease. Is it possible that God is still

16 Lo, their good *is* not in their hand: the counsel of the wicked is far from me.

17 How oft is the candle of the wicked put out! and *how oft* cometh their destruction upon them! *God* distributeth sorrows in his anger.

18 They are as stubble before the wind, and as chaff that the storm carrieth away.

16 Behold, is not their prosperity in their hand?
The counsel of the wicked is far from me.

17 "How often is it that the lamp of the wicked is put out?
That their calamity comes upon them?
That God[c] distributes pains in his anger?

18 That they are like straw before the wind, and like chaff that the storm carries away?

[c] Heb *he*

(Vs. 14; contrast Ps. 25:4, "Show me thy ways, O Lord.") But their behavior testifies to such a mode of thinking. They have expelled godly concerns. They have observed the poverty, the oppression, the sufferings of the pious, and have concluded that religion is useless.

What is the Almighty, that we should serve him?
And what profit do we get if we pray to him? (Vs. 15.)

By assigning these words to the prosperous, Job is indirectly making a devastating critique of the friends' position. Bildad has twice described what he believes to be ineluctably the fate of those "who do not know God" or "who forget God" (18:21; 8:13). Job replies that on the contrary there are men who ignore the Deity and yet are prosperous. Do they receive their riches from God? **Behold, is not their prosperity in their hand?** (Vs. 16a; cf. Isa. 5:18-19; Ps. 73:3-12.) Their estate is not a demonstration of the dogma of divine justice. They are the authors and the masters of their prosperity. They possess their happiness (cf. 12:10). Zophar has maintained that the prosperity (טוב) of the godless does not last (20:21). Job replies that their prosperity (טוב) is held secure within their power. Following the LXX (ἀπ' αὐτοῦ), one should probably read at the end of vs. 16b, ממנו instead of מני, and thus translate, "The counsel of the wicked is far from *him*" (i.e., God). Such a thought is more fitting to the context than the banal and irrelevant statement of the traditional versions: it admirably completes the sequence of Job's reasoning. The evil men live far from God (vs. 14) since they do not need him (vs. 15). Their earthly successes are the product of their own achievement, and they have complete control over the enjoyment of their work. Their plans do not concern God and do not take him into account. They are the proprietors of their destiny. They work out their own salvation. They are saved by their own works. And God is silent.

17-18. To Bildad's objection that "the light of the wicked shall be put out" (18:5), and that "calamity is ready for his stumbling" (18:12), Job objects that this is rarely so.

How often is it that the lamp of the wicked is put out?
That their calamity comes upon them?

(Vs. 17; cf. Prov. 13:9; 20:20; 24:20.) He implicitly concedes that such events seldom occur, but this fact cannot obscure the overwhelming and contrary observation of their

---

in his heaven in spite of the fact that all is not right in the world? Could it be that God is in his heaven to triumph over the wrong that is in the world? This is what the book of Job is actually saying. Religion is about that. A man may

have to "serve God for nought" (see Expos. on 1:6-12). What then can possibly provide an adequate motivation? Surely not the facile promises of the "peace" cults. Job himself points out the subtle atheism involved in them

19 God layeth up his iniquity for his children: he rewardeth him, and he shall know
it.

20 His eyes shall see his destruction, and
he shall drink of the wrath of the Almighty.

21 For what pleasure *hath* he in his house
after him, when the number of his months
is cut off in the midst?

22 Shall *any* teach God knowledge? seeing he judgeth those that are high.

---

19 You say, 'God stores up their iniquity for
  their sons.'
  Let him recompense it to themselves,
    that they may know it.

20 Let their own eyes see their destruction,
    and let them drink of the wrath of the
    Almighty.

21 For what do they care for their houses
    after them,
  when the number of their months is
    cut off?

22 Will any teach God knowledge,
  seeing that he judges those that are on
    high?

---

impunity. The "righteous" judge does not usually intervene. "How many times does he
[God] destroy the wicked in his anger?" (Vs. 17c.) The word חבלים, usually rendered by
pains or **sorrows**, refers to the pangs of labor in childbirth and is rather unexpected in
this context. Dhorme suggests a cognate of the Akkadian *ḫabbilu*, and understands the
verb *yeḥallēq*, ordinarily translated **distributeth**, in the light of the Akkadian idiom
muḥalliq, "one who destroys, who causes to perish." It may not be an accident that vs. 18
is strongly reminiscent of Job's description of his own fate in 13:25.

d) IMMORALITY OF HEREDITARY GUILT (21:19-27)

19-21. Undoubtedly the wise men in general and Job's friends in particular may
attempt to defend the thesis of divine justice in the government of the world by arguing
that if the wicked die in peace, **God stores up their iniquity for their sons** (vs. 19*a*), but
Job objects cogently to this line of reasoning by maintaining that such a view reveals a
strange and wholly unsatisfying conception of divine morality. **Let him [God] recompense
it to themselves, that they may know it** (vs. 19*b*). It is the guilty man himself who must
know the wrath of the Almighty (vs. 20), for when he is dead he does not really care
about the fate of his descendants (vs. 21; cf. 14:21; Jer. 31:29, 30; Ezek. 18).

22. It is difficult to relate satisfactorily this verse to its context. (*a*) Some critics
believe that Job is satirically suggesting that the friends are guilty of a grave sin of
presumption when they interpret God's actions according to the requirements of their
Procrustean dogma. Job may thus refer ironically to Zophar's pious appeal to humble
agnosticism (11:5 ff.) and to Eliphaz' opinion on the imperfections of the heavenly
beings (4:18; 15:15). Since no man can pretend to know divine motivations (cf. Isa.
45:14), why should the friends claim that they understand the meaning of Job's situation?
They cannot teach any lesson of God. (*b*) Other interpreters think that Job is here interrupting his own critique of the divine government of the world by asking whether he
has indeed the right to proceed in developing this theme. (*c*) Still other commentators
reject the verse as a marginal annotation representing the pious reaction of an early

---

(vs. 15; see Exeg.). *Dignus vindice nodus.* It
takes God to manage. Steadily we move toward
the theophany (I John 4:19).

19. The Sins of the Fathers.— (See 5:4; 8:16-
19; Expos. on 4:8; cf. Jer. 31:29-30; Ezek. 18.)
The solidarity of human existence is an empirical fact. Life channels both good and evil,
the blessing and the curse man puts into it.
Facts, however, may not be converted into
dogmas in order to bolster the theory of retributive justice, and Job will not permit it. Thank

God that the good is communicable! One
would find it difficult to suppose, under the circumstances, that the evil is not. But this is a
far cry from contending that God, in lieu of
punishing the wicked, stores up the punishment for their children. The deepest moral intuitions of the human soul, which are the
broken lights of God in us, cry out against that
(see Expos. on 3:24). Though the innocent may
suffer with the guilty, it is the guilty that need
to know their guilt; if there is suffering to be

23 One dieth in his full strength, being wholly at ease and quiet.	23 One dies in full prosperity, being wholly at ease and secure,
24 His breasts are full of milk, and his bones are moistened with marrow.	24 his body*d* full of fat and the marrow of his bones moist.
25 And another dieth in the bitterness of his soul, and never eateth with pleasure.	25 Another dies in bitterness of soul, never having tasted of good.
26 They shall lie down alike in the dust, and the worms shall cover them.	26 They lie down alike in the dust, and the worms cover them.
27 Behold, I know your thoughts, and the devices *which* ye wrongfully imagine against me.	27 "Behold, I know your thoughts, and your schemes to wrong me.
28 For ye say, Where *is* the house of the prince? and where *are* the dwelling places of the wicked?	28 For you say, 'Where is the house of the prince? Where is the tent in which the wicked dwelt?'

d The meaning of the Hebrew word is uncertain

reader who thereby intended to condemn Job's attitude. (*d*) In all probability the hero is here speaking of himself in anticipation of the subsequent part of his discourse. He grants for a moment that God indeed **judges** even **those that are on high,** and a fortiori the human creatures who are upon the earth. In a tone not of anxious humility and doubt, but on the contrary of courageous defiance, he declares that God needs to be taught a lesson. He will reveal to him what actually happens in the world of men. God must be told. Job will offer him some knowledge. According to this exegesis, vs. 22 is an introduction to vss. 23-26.

23-26. Death comes indiscriminately to all men alike. **One dieth in his full strength** (vs. 23) with his vigor still intact (vs. 24) ; **and another dieth in the bitterness of his soul,** without ever having tasted happiness (vs. 25). The same mortal fate awaits them both (vs. 26). Here is the situation which apparently God willfully ignores. The fact of death reveals less the equality of all men than the injustice of their destiny, and consequently the irresponsibility of God.

e) TESTIMONY OF THE TRAVELERS (21:28-34)

28-34. If the friends object that the wicked disappear without leaving a trace (vss. 28-29), Job appeals to the observations of world-wide travelers (vs. 29). They all know that far from being spared (vs. 30) or even confronted with their deeds (vs. 31), notorious

done, they of all others need to suffer. And they do not. So Job says. One can almost feel the problem projecting itself beyond this life into another (see Expos. on 10:8-12). The doctrine of a final judgment has to do not alone with the preservation of moral values; it has to do with the being and nature of God. Writes P. T. Forsyth:

Truly we cannot exaggerate the love of God, if we will take pains to first understand it. But we have been taught to believe only in a beneficent and not in a sovereign God, in a tender God in no sense judge, in an attractive God, more kindly than holy, more lovely than good—the God of the children, or of the evangelist, or of the honourable, successful man with the delightful home, the agreeable circle, and the generous hand—a God whose purpose of love became incredible unless it was pursued by winsome ways, and published in fine and tender discourse.

. . . Such a habit of mind, now that the lid is off hell, is suddenly struck from its only perch, feels taken in, and asks if such a world as we see can be the means to a loving end, if it could ever be made to contribute to a Divine Kingdom. . . .

I shall venture to suggest that a call has come to the Church to . . . show some deeper sense of the real moral problem—the problem within God, the problem of judgment as atonement . . . to rise above its cowardly dread of depth . . . ; to win from God's answer in Christ at least some profounder sense of the world problem and some higher sense of the one and eternal morality.[3]

26. *All Alike to All?*—In an unpublished sermon, George A. Buttrick—his text Eccl. 9:2, his subject "Good and Bad Alike?"—points out that there are areas in life where things are

[3] *The Justification of God* (London: Independent Press, 1948), pp. 36-38. Used by permission.

29 Have ye not asked them that go by the way? and do ye not know their tokens,

30 That the wicked is reserved to the day of destruction? they shall be brought forth to the day of wrath.

31 Who shall declare his way to his face? and who shall repay him *what* he hath done?

32 Yet shall he be brought to the grave, and shall remain in the tomb.

33 The clods of the valley shall be sweet unto him, and every man shall draw after him, as *there are* innumerable before him.

34 How then comfort ye me in vain, seeing in your answers there remaineth falsehood?

22 Then Eliphaz the Temanite answered and said,

29 Have you not asked those who travel the roads,
 and do you not accept their testimony
30 that the wicked man is spared in the day of calamity,
 that he is rescued in the day of wrath?
31 Who declares his way to his face,
 and who requites him for what he has done?
32 When he is borne to the grave,
 watch is kept over his tomb.
33 The clods of the valley are sweet to him;
 all men follow after him,
 and those who go before him are innumerable.
34 How then will you comfort me with empty nothings?
 There is nothing left of your answers but falsehood."

22 Then Eli′phaz the Te′manite answered:

criminals receive honorable funerals (vss. 32-33). Observe the Hebrew equivalent (vs. 33*a*) to the Latin phrase, *Sit tibi terra levis!* Job concludes that his remarks are based upon a generally accepted truth, and that consequently the opinions of his friends are vain and cannot **comfort** him. There is nothing left in their replies but deceit (rather than **falsehood,** vs. 34; cf. vs. 2).

D. THIRD CYCLE OF DISCUSSION (22:1–27:23)
1. THIRD DISCOURSE OF ELIPHAZ (22:1-30)

While Job began the discussion with the curse upon his life (ch. 3) and seems to have regained throughout the first two cycles a certain degree of emotional equilibrium,

worse for the wicked; others where they seem to be much the same for the wicked and the righteous; still others where they are worse for the righteous. They were worst for Christ! In every case it is the response that determines the issue. What Ecclesiastes sees as indifference, Jesus sees as magnanimity. God "maketh his sun to rise on the evil and on the good" (Matt. 5:45). The author of Job is himself well aware of that (38:26); cf. Gen. 42:36, "All these things are against me"; Eccl. 9:2, "All things come alike to all"; Rom. 8:28, "In everything God works for good with those who love him."

22:1–27:23. *The Third Cycle.*—The three friends have failed in their set purpose. They have not come to offer sympathy and understanding: they have come with their preconceived ideas as to how God governs the world, and on the basis of those ideas with their preconceived theory as to the only possible explanation of Job's calamities. They mean to do the best thing that can be done for him: they

mean to bring him to repentance and thereby to restoration. Review the course of the argument thus far (see Expos. on 4:1–14:22; 15:1–21:34). Now the only thing left for Eliphaz to do, as he sees it, is to gather all his powers for a final, and this time direct, assault. He will storm the central citadel of what he conceived to be Job's blind and stubborn and presumptuous self-righteousness. And this he does with something more than candor; reverting however toward the end, as if somehow he were conscious of having gone further than the facts would warrant, to that spirit of almost paternal gentleness which characterized his first speech. As for the rest of the cycle, much of it has been disturbed, it may be for the most part quite deliberately, in the way of toning down what Job has to say by the simple expedient of attributing to him a number of lines that in the original poem had almost certainly been put into the mouth of Bildad or Zophar. In the present arrangement Bildad's third speech is much too short (ch.

| 2 Can a man be profitable unto God, as he that is wise may be profitable unto himself? | 2 "Can a man be profitable to God? Surely he who is wise is profitable to himself. |

Eliphaz and his two colleagues, on the contrary, who had started in a comparatively cool and composed manner, appear to have lost in the second and especially in the third round of the rhetorical exchanges all sense of courtesy. Thus they dispense altogether with customary formulas of introduction. Eliphaz plunges into his third discourse with intemperate abruptness (vss. 2-5), and he gives substance to his new accusations with plain lies (vss. 6-10). Yet he not only hopes that Job will not follow "the ancient road" (vss. 11-20), but even invites him to make his peace with God and to be saved (vs. 21-30).

a) God Does Not Need Man (22:1-5)

22:2. Eliphaz fails to reply to the main arguments presented by Job in ch. 21, but he should not be accused of ignoring them deliberately, since the scandalous illustrations of injustice which the hero has cited present no problem to a dogmatist for whom prosperity is only an appearance whenever it adorns a godless man. Eliphaz, however, singles out one strain in his opponent's defense which outrages his own conception of the divine majesty. Job has not only said (21:22) that God needs to be told by man of the injustice of the human situation, but he has also implied all along that God owes him—an innocent man—justice and vindication. Eliphaz therefore begins the third cycle of discourses with a lofty description of God's transcendence. He maintains that the Deity dwells beyond the reaches of man's activity, and that the divine calmness is not affected by the ripples of human frenzy. **Can a man be profitable to God?** (Vs. 2a.) Can a *gébher*, the most vigorous specimen of manhood, be useful to God? Can even a thinking and reasonable, learned human being—professional in wisdom, who deserves considerably more respect than a *gébher*—be of any service to the Almighty? Eliphaz hastily brushes aside such a ludicrous possibility. He is too much a theologian of transcendence to entertain even fleetingly the idea of God's dependence upon man. **Surely he who is wise is profitable** [only] **to himself** (vs. 2b). Three ideas are here implied. (a) There is no possibility for man, a limited creature, to infringe upon the absolute freedom of God. Job's attacks against the way in which the world of men is governed amount to a practical denial of man's finitude and of God's infinity. (b) Man is wrong if he declares that God

---

25), except for anybody who may have had to listen to it. Job is represented as contradicting himself outright, notably in 24:18-24; 27:7-23, and Zophar does not come forward at all. A tentative reordering of the material is suggested in the Intro. (p. 888), and will be followed in the Expos. Consult the summaries of the individual discourses.

22:1-30. Eliphaz.—The God of heaven and earth is scarcely to be thought of as deriving any benefit from man's righteousness, or for that matter as suffering any harm from his wickedness. He has no stake in any of it. Why should he be anything but impartial? The "root of the matter" (19:28) is not in him but in you: not his inequity, but your iniquity (vss. 2-4). You have been exacting (vs. 6) and without compassion (vs. 7), tyrannous (? vs. 8; see Exeg.; the **man with power** may be Job himself) and cruel (vs. 9). No wonder calamity has overtaken you (vss. 10-11; cf. 18:8-11). I know what happened: You said in your heart that God is far, far off,

and knows nothing. The wicked have always thought that, and brought on themselves fire and flood (vss. 16, 20). Your recipe is "Leave God out if you want to make a go of it" (vss. 17-18; cf. 21:14-16; Kissane considers vss. 8, 12-14, and 18 as quotations from Job; yet see Exeg.). The kind of "go" that causes decent people to applaud and break into song (vss. 19-20; cf. Expos. on vss. 12-20). Do as we say, take warning from what has happened to you, and you can still get free of all this (vss. 21-22). Have humility enough to repent; love God, not gold, and all will be well (vss. 23-26). Your prayers will be answered, you will be under the glad necessity of redeeming your wrong to the Almighty, and everything you do will prosper (vss. 27-28), thanks to clean hands and a pure heart (vss. 29-30).

2-5. The Immutable God.—The God of Eliphaz (see Expos. on 4:20b) is so high and lifted up that he is quite out of reach. He walks in no garden in the cool of the day, calling,

3 *Is it* any pleasure to the Almighty, that thou art righteous? or *is it* gain *to him,* that thou makest thy ways perfect?

4 Will he reprove thee for fear of thee? will he enter with thee into judgment?

5 *Is* not thy wickedness great? and thine iniquities infinite?

---

3 Is it any pleasure to the Almighty if you are righteous,
  or is it gain to him if you make your ways blameless?

4 Is it for your fear of him that he reproves you,
  and enters into judgment with you?

5 Is not your wickedness great?
  There is no end to your iniquities.

---

is responsible for the punishment of the innocent or the reward of the evildoers, since God derives no advantage or profit from man's behavior. (*c*) Man is equally wrong if he believes that his religion is useless. A wise attitude toward life is profitable. "If thou art wise, it is for thyself that thou art wise!" (Prov. 9:12.) Consequently, whenever man finds life unrewarding, he must not accuse God but look within himself to discover the reason for his profitless destiny. Thus Eliphaz is stressing the gulf which separates man from God in order to achieve two goals at once: he wishes to undermine Job's worldly skepticism as it is revealed by the preceding discourse and to convince Job of sin-consciousness. By these words, however, he merely proclaims again his belief in the self-interestedness of religion, and thus unwittingly ranges himself with "the Satan" of the prologue (1:9).

3-5. In the next verses Eliphaz continues to court both truth and error at the same time (cf. Exeg. on 4:18-21). He appears to exalt the majesty of God when he asks, **Is it any pleasure to the Almighty, that thou art righteous? or is it gain to him, that thou makest thy ways perfect?** In effect, Eliphaz proposes a concept of the Deity which is utterly foreign to Hebraism and may represent an ancestral formulation of Islamic theism and philosophical deism. The idea of an impassive Deity is contradicted by the whole Bible with the exception of Ecclesiastes. To say that God does not find pleasure or gain in man's struggle toward perfection is a half-truth which turns into a flagrant error unless one remembers at the same time the testimony of the prophet, "As the bridegroom rejoiceth over the bride, so shall thy God rejoice over thee" (Isa. 62:5) and the words of Jesus, "Joy shall be in heaven over one sinner that repenteth" (Luke 15:7). The acknowledgment that men are useless and unprofitable servants (Luke 17:10) does not entail the belief that God is eternally unconcerned and immutable. Moreover, Eliphaz contradicts himself when he proceeds from his high-sounding declaration on the self-sufficiency of God (which is aimed at invalidating Job's charge that God is unjust in his dealing with men) to ask ironically, "Is it on account of thy piety that he corrects thee?" (vs 4*b*).

"Adam! Adam! Where art thou?" The exigencies of the argument have brought the aged seer to a position which is theologically quite untenable. Job's contention that God is unjust is abhorrent to him. In view of the disturbing facts marshaled against him, the only way finally to refute the charge is with one hand to rid God of all moral responsibility in the matter of rewards and punishments, while holding on with the other to the doctrine of retributive justice. It is a neat gymnastic problem, and Eliphaz attempts a solution of it by way of exalting still farther his already lofty conception of God; this time to the place where God, having nothing to gain and nothing to lose, becomes for all practical purposes totally uninvolved (see Expos. on 15:17-35) in a process which he him-

self initiates and continues. If he is not concerned, why does he concern himself? That question seems never to arise (cf. vss. 2-3 with vss. 4, 29-30). The syllogism is all that matters. The first attempt—sin incurs suffering; you suffer; therefore you have sinned—has been met by Job's vehement denial of the conclusion, and his troublesome refutation of the major premise. The second attempt—God is not to be blamed, having no ax to grind; yet this calamity has been inflicted on you; therefore you are to blame—constitutes a theodicy which succeeds in defending God to the degree in which it succeeds in eliminating him. The God of Eliphaz—is he in a vacuum where no love is, the God of Bildad in a system where no man is (see Expos. on 19:2-4)? Surely their God is Zophar's too—

6 For thou hast taken a pledge from thy brother for nought, and stripped the naked of their clothing.

7 Thou hast not given water to the weary to drink, and thou hast withholden bread from the hungry.

8 But *as for* the mighty man, he had the earth; and the honorable man dwelt in it.

9 Thou hast sent widows away empty, and the arms of the fatherless have been broken.

10 Therefore snares *are* round about thee, and sudden fear troubleth thee;

11 Or darkness, *that* thou canst not see; and abundance of waters cover thee.

6 For you have exacted pledges of your brothers for nothing,
    and stripped the naked of their clothing.

7 You have given no water to the weary to drink,
    and you have withheld bread from the hungry.

8 The man with power possessed the land,
    and the favored man dwelt in it.

9 You have sent widows away empty,
    and the arms of the fatherless were crushed.

10 Therefore snares are round about you,
    and sudden terror overwhelms you;

11 your light is darkened, so that*e* you cannot see,
    and a flood of water covers you.

e Cn Compare Gk: Heb *or darkness*

Eliphaz maintains in one breath that God is not interested in Job's efforts toward righteousness (vs. 3) while yet rebuking him for his irreligion (vs. 4). The dogmatist is unable to understand the deeper meanings of suffering either in man or in God; in his protracted attempt to explain the fate of Job, he is thrown back upon the old cliché which has been repeated by the friends throughout the poetic discussion, clothed in various garbs, **There is no end to your iniquities** (vs. 5*b*).

b) CATALOGUE OF JOB'S INIQUITIES (22:6-11)

6-11. The sufferer is harried by reason of irreligion (vs. 4). But how can Eliphaz prove the validity of this inward, negative assumption? He must postulate that Job has corrupted his heart through a series of unethical deeds. The list follows. Job has not exercised mercy toward the destitute (vss. 6-7; cf. Exod. 22:25-26; Ezek. 18:7; Isa. 58:7), and he has been the accomplice of **the man with power** (vs. 8) so that with his tacit or perhaps active approval the weak members of his community have been oppressed (vs. 9; cf. Exod. 22:21; Deut. 24:17). These are the reasons why a **sudden terror** has overwhelmed him (vs. 10; cf. 1:13 ff.).

---

in a hurry (see Expos. on 20:2*b*, 4-11). Every man's God an uneasy reflection of himself?

Job is far better off than any of them. It is not his mind that has plunged him into ambiguity, it is his heart. Let God be what God is, but a Vindicator stands somehow astride Job's poor, defeated life. The N.T. spells it out (Heb. 8:6; cf. the Patripassian controversy).

6-11. *Homemade Facts.*—No doubt much of what is here said represents current rumor. Stories spread when a man is down, and rumor is readily interpreted as fact. Everybody says such and such, and where there is so much smoke there must be fire. One needs only put two and two together. Better not speak disparagingly of the mighty; but the once mighty are anybody's field day. Everyone knows very

well that something was wrong. What happened to them was not for nothing; that much is certain (see Expos. on 19:22*b*). One is not surprised that Eliphaz indulges in more than a little exaggeration, with perhaps a dash of venom. Seriatim, before the curtain is rung down on the dialogue, Job will enter his disavowal (cf. vs. 6 with 31:19; vs. 7 with 31:16-17; vs. 9 with 29:13; 31:16). There is a way of dealing with facts that have not been manufactured. That never seems to occur to the friends. "Brethren, if a man be overtaken in a fault, ye which are spiritual, restore such a one in the spirit of meekness; considering thyself, lest thou also be tempted" (Gal. 6:1). To accuse is not to restore. Restoration involves identification. That necessity weighs upon God himself.

12 *Is* not God in the height of heaven? and behold the height of the stars, how high they are!

13 And thou sayest, How doth God know? can he judge through the dark cloud?

14 Thick clouds *are* a covering to him, that he seeth not; and he walketh in the circuit of heaven.

15 Hast thou marked the old way which wicked men have trodden?

16 Which were cut down out of time, whose foundation was overflown with a flood:

17 Which said unto God, Depart from us: and what can the Almighty do for them?

18 Yet he filled their houses with good *things:* but the counsel of the wicked is far from me.

---

12 "Is not God high in the heavens?
　　See the highest stars, how lofty they are!
13 Therefore you say, 'What does God know?
　　Can he judge through the deep darkness?
14 Thick clouds enwrap him, so that he does not see,
　　and he walks on the vault of heaven.'
15 Will you keep to the old way
　　which wicked men have trod?
16 They were snatched away before their time;
　　their foundation was washed away.
17 They said to God, 'Depart from us,'
　　and 'What can the Almighty do to us?'*f*
18 Yet he filled their houses with good things —
　　but the counsel of the wicked is far from me.

f Gk Syr: Heb *them*

---

c) The Ancient Path Trod by Wicked Men (22:12-20)

12-16. Eliphaz knows that Job agrees with him on the cardinal dogma of divine transcendence.

> Is not God high in the heavens?
> See the highest stars, how lofty they are!

But the insidious speaker misquotes his opponent in order more easily to refute him.

> Therefore you say, "What does God know?
> Can he judge through the deep darkness?"

Actually Job has used this language only when he was describing the practical atheism of the prosperous men who go unpunished in spite of their arrogance (21:14-15). Eliphaz, deliberately as it would seem, confuses his adversary by associating him with wicked men of antiquity (vss. 15 ff.), and reminds him that **they were snatched away before their time** (vs. 16*a*).

17-18. These verses are almost verbally identical with 21:14-16, and several modern commentators are led by the observation of this fact to excise them as an accidental gloss. However, Eliphaz is really misquoting this passage from the preceding development (cf.

12-20. *The Way of the Ungodly.* — (See Expos. on 4:8; 8:11-19; 15:17-35; 18:5-21.) Eliphaz does not put himself in Job's place (see Expos. on 5:8; 16:4), but he does essay to read Job's mind (Exeg.). In 21:14-16 Job was contending that the wicked feel themselves quite secure (see Expos. on 21:1-34) from God's meddling in their affairs, and prosper mightily in spite of it. The implication of course was that they were quite right: God knows nothing and cares nothing about it. One might almost think that he had taken his cue from Eliphaz' own notebook (vss. 2-3, 12). Eliphaz, however, argues from remoteness to impartiality (cf. Zophar's use of

the doctrine, 11:7-10); here he accuses Job of arguing like the wicked from remoteness to ignorance. Admitting Job's piety (vs. 4; cf. Expos. on 4:6), he suggests a quasi-religious explanation of Job's irreligion (see Expos. on 15:7-16). The inevitable results follow. As it was in the days of Noah (vs. 11*b*[?]; cf. Gen. 6–8) and in the days of Lot (vs. 20[?]; cf. 1:16; Gen. 19:24), so with Job. It shall not be with him as he thought (17:8-9). **The righteous [shall] see it and [be] glad** (Ps. 107:42). They shall raise the old familiar song of triumph (vss. 19-20).

The mind of the sinner, the issue of his sin

19 The righteous see *it*, and are glad: and the innocent laugh them to scorn.	19 The righteous see it and are glad; the innocent laugh them to scorn,
20 Whereas our substance is not cut down, but the remnant of them the fire consumeth.	20 saying, 'Surely our adversaries are cut off, and what they left the fire has consumed.'
21 Acquaint now thyself with him, and be at peace: thereby good shall come unto thee.	21 "Agree with God, and be at peace; thereby good will come to you.

vs. 13), and perhaps he continues to misquote in order to refute. This indeed he does in vs. 18, which is not a mere repetition of 21:16. (Read with LXX at the end of vs. 18*b*, "from him" instead of **from me.**) The wicked were ungrateful; they did not recognize that their happiness came from God, their counsel was far from him, and for this reason they have been cut off.

19-20. Thus when the just witness the demise of such men, they **are glad, and the innocent laugh them to scorn.**

d) A NEW CALL TO CONVERSION (22:21-30)

21-30. Eliphaz does not end on a note of condemnation. Nothing yet is irretrievably lost for Job. He can still seek reconciliation with God and **be at peace** (vs. 21*a*), and by

the response of the righteous: how wrong can a man be when he takes up the cudgels for the Almighty (see Expos. on 13:8)? If Eliphaz had entered on the first point with understanding, on the second with discretion, and on the third with the love of God in his heart, some good might have come of it. "There is joy in the presence of the angels of God over one sinner that repenteth" (Luke 15:10).

21-30. *Exhortation and Promise.*—It is extraordinary how futile exhortation is, and promise as well. When there is question of redemption, fact is what redeems, not advice; deed, not declamation. "Please" is a polite word, with its hat in its hand; it is not puissant. "Must" and "ought" and "should" are mercenaries, hired to do another's job; and they take to their heels at the first show of opposition. Eliphaz, whose theology becomes sounder as his heart grows warmer—a not unusual phenomenon—speaks now in a gentler, kindlier tone: a man must indeed be made to want what you offer. The trouble is that promises change neither the mind nor the heart nor the will. Besides, Job has heard enough of them (cf. Expos. on 5:18; 8:20-22; 11:18; 17:12). Here, ironically enough, so many of the phrases seem to be pointed phrases, complete with all "the barbs of good intention." In vs. 21 is the reconciliation which is precisely what Job longs for and cannot accomplish. God must bring it about. In vs. 22 is the suggestion that he should be a more apt pupil in the school of suffering which is God's school (Elihu will soon elaborate the point), where Eliphaz is headmaster, with Bildad and Zophar as assistant masters (cf. 15:11; 12:2-3). In vss. 24-25 is the utterly gratui-

tous assumption that he has cared more for gold than for God (cf. 31:24). In vs. 26 is the promise of rapture for present bitterness, of confidence for present shame (cf. 10:15; 11:15). In vss. 27-28 are answered prayer (19:7), security instead of ruin (as in the prologue), instead of darkness (19:8) light. No longer shall Job be reckoned among the proud, but among the lowly and innocent. By the very **cleanness** of his hands shall even the sinner be saved (vss. 29-30; cf. 42:7-9; yet see Exeg.). All of it is the deepest desire of Job's heart; none of it is in his power, and in his anguished, twisted way he knows that. Eliphaz is not within hailing distance of his tragic dilemma. Says Strahan:

Nothing could well be finer than [this] picture of a religious life in days of prosperity—the righteous man delighting himself in God, lifting a free and open face to Heaven, praying and being heard, paying his vows, laying his plans and getting them successfully executed, walking always in the sunshine. It is a religious life in the shadow that Eliphaz cannot understand; . . . and [so] does injustice to those who are most in need of sympathy.[4]

Once more (see Expos. on 20:12-16) it would be instructive to recall the situation in which the Jews found themselves after the Exile—always in the poet's mind—and to imagine the effect which these "consolations of God" from the storehouses of orthodox religion would have had on them.

21. *Acquaint Thyself with God, and Be at Peace.*—The RSV is more accurate. It is reconciliation of which Eliphaz is speaking. But the

_____
[4] *Job*, pp. 203-4; cf. Expos. on 21:7-18.

22 Receive, I pray thee, the law from his mouth, and lay up his words in thine heart.	22 Receive instruction from his mouth, and lay up his words in your heart.

22 Receive, I pray thee, the law from his mouth, and lay up his words in thine heart.

23 If thou return to the Almighty, thou shalt be built up, thou shalt put away iniquity far from thy tabernacles.

24 Then shalt thou lay up gold as dust, and the *gold* of Ophir as the stones of the brooks.

25 Yea, the Almighty shall be thy defense, and thou shalt have plenty of silver.

26 For then shalt thou have thy delight in the Almighty, and shalt lift up thy face unto God.

27 Thou shalt make thy prayer unto him, and he shall hear thee, and thou shalt pay thy vows.

28 Thou shalt also decree a thing, and it shall be established unto thee: and the light shall shine upon thy ways.

29 When *men* are cast down, then thou shalt say, *There is* lifting up; and he shall save the humble person.

30 He shall deliver the island of the innocent: and it is delivered by the pureness of thine hands.

22 Receive instruction from his mouth, and lay up his words in your heart.

23 If you return to the Almighty and humble yourself,[g] if you remove unrighteousness far from your tents,

24 if you lay gold in the dust, and gold of Ophir among the stones of the torrent bed,

25 and if the Almighty is your gold, and your precious silver;

26 then you will delight yourself in the Almighty, and lift up your face to God.

27 You will make your prayer to him, and he will hear you; and you will pay your vows.

28 You will decide on a matter, and it will be established for you, and light will shine on your ways.

29 For God abases the proud,[h] but he saves the lowly.

30 He delivers the innocent man;[i] you will be delivered through the cleanness of your hands."

g Gk: Heb *you will be built up*
h Cn: Heb *when they abased you said, Proud*
i Gk Syr Vg: Heb *him that is not innocent*

this technique obtain "a good return" (vs. 21*b*). By receiving the instruction which God gives him through correction (vs. 22), by returning and humbling himself, by removing unrighteousness from his life (vs. 23), and by loving God instead of gold (vss. 24-25), Job will find an exquisite delight in the Almighty (cf. Ps. 37:11; Isa. 55:2; 58:14; 66:11) and he will again lift up his face toward God (vs. 26), who will then answer the penitent's prayer and accept the payment of his vows (vs. 27). Job's decisions will then always bring success, and light will be bright upon his paths (vs. 28). Although Eliphaz, as is his wont, does not omit at the end a note of stern warning, **God abases the proud** (Vulg., vs. 29*a*), he stresses the positive note, and his tone is almost one of friendship and certainly one of expectation. After recalling in the third person that God **saves the lowly**, and **delivers the innocent man** (LXX; vss. 29*b*-30*a*), he offers a personal and direct promise, "Thou shalt escape [read *nimlaṭṭā* instead of *nimlaṭ*] by the purity of thy hands" (vs. 30*b*). Of course, Eliphaz still believes in salvation by works. He does not allude to the forgiving grace of God. His hope for Job is still based upon an optimistic view of human nature.

KJV has endeared itself to many generations. Certainly it is true that while the estrangement continues, there can be no deep and lasting peace for Job or for any man. "Thou hast made us for thyself, and our hearts are restless till they find their rest in thee."[5] More than for anything else Job longs for the re-establishment of the old relationship. He has taunted God with the memory of it, defied him in the ruin of it, pleaded with him for the restoration of

it—sometime, somewhere. Now he has begun to understand, as Eliphaz never will, that if anything is to be done about it, God must do it. And God does. The only thing Eliphaz had right was the deep necessity, and even that existed on levels beyond his comprehension. He might have been a channel for the great transaction; the implication that he already was, clear enough for anybody to catch, served the more to disqualify him (on vs. 21*b* see Expos. on 21:7-18).

5 Augustine *Confessions* I. 1.

23 Then Job answered and said,
2 Even to-day *is* my complaint bitter: my stroke is heavier than my groaning.

23 Then Job anwered:
2 "Today also my complaint is bitter,ⁱ hisᵏ hand is heavy in spite of my groaning.

ʲ Syr Vg Tg: Heb *rebellious*
ᵏ Gk Syr: Heb *my*

---

2. THIRD REPLY OF JOB TO ELIPHAZ (23:1–24:25)

In characteristic fashion the sufferer ignores the arguments of the discourse of Eliphaz which immediately precedes (22:1-30). Instead of replying to the false accusations which have just been put forward against him (cf. especially 22:6 ff.), he drives directly to the fundamentals of his situation. God forever thwarts his attempts to secure an encounter (23:2-17) just as he refuses to hear the prayer of the oppressed (24:1-25).

There appears to be a marked contrast between the first cycle of discussion and the third with regard to Job's conception of, and practical attitude toward, God. His theological assumptions are no longer those of hostility toward God. In aggressiveness there is a kind of rapport, however unsatisfactory; in hatred there is a mutuality of interest, a reciprocity of attention. But in God's indifference there is only the vacuum of alienation. In the first cycle Job compared God to a hunter (6:4; 10:16), a soldier (7:12), a kidnaper (9:12), a murderer (13:15), but now he intimates that God is totally unconcerned. He charges the Deity no longer with enmity, but with apathy. There the hero was convinced that God paid too much attention to him (7:17 ff.; 9:11, 18; 10:16, 20) and he indulged the dream that the old intimacy—a dialogue of love (7:21c; 14:15)—could someday be renewed and the delights of communion with the creative artist be restored; here the gulf has deepened and widened so much that no dialogue is even possible. There prayer came upon the lips of the sufferer with the ease or the survival of a happy consuetude (even though embittered and defiant, Job could not for long speak *of* God without soon speaking *to* God [6:8 ff.; 7:17-21; 10:2-22; 13:24–14:6, 13]); here the poison of physical and spiritual torture and of social isolation appears to have numbed his ability to pray. In the first cycle he prayed five times, in the second only once (17:3-4), and at that his last word of precatory utterance was probably a kind of imprecatory threat, "Thou shalt not be exalted!" (17:4b; cf. Exeg., *ad loc.*); but in the third cycle he prays not at all.

a) "OH, THAT I KNEW WHERE I MIGHT FIND HIM!" (23:1-17)

(1) A NEW PLEA FOR AN AUDIENCE (23:1-7)

23:2. Today also my complaint is bitter: This is the only place in the poetic discussion where an allusion is found to an indication of time. If the word **today** is to be taken

---

23:1–24:1-17, 22-23, 25. *Job.*—I will not humble myself (cf. 22:23a). You are right. I am a rebel still. It is of no use trying to hold it all in. I have done my best. If only I knew where I could find him. **I would lay my case before him,** and listen to all he has to say (23:5). He would no longer crush me. He would give heed. I am not guilty, and he would have to admit it. But east, west, north, south, he avoids me (23:8-9), though he knows very well that in life and heart I have kept his law (23:10-12). He has made up his mind. He does what he likes, and will go through with it (23:13-14a). Nor am I the only one. Never think it! He has other plans too, and they are much the same (23:14b)—fire and hurricane and flood. It terrifies me. Not the blight on me, the blight on

him (23:17; see Exeg.). It may be indeed that what goes on is hidden from him (24:1a; cf. Exeg., and see 22:13). Is that why there is no sign of him anywhere (24:1b)? The landed gentry go on stealing from the poor (24:2-3), depriving them of their rights (24:4a), huddling them off by themselves as if they amounted to nothing at all (24:4b), snatching infants from their mother's breast in payment of a debt (24:9). So that people with no place to eat or sleep roam about **like wild asses,** looking for work, trying to manage a little for their children living on scraps (24:6), naked, drenched to the skin (24:7-10a), hungry in the midst of plenty, thirsty while they toil in the vineyards of the rich, tramping out the wine (24:10b-11). So in the city—only worse! The wounded and the dy-

literally, the poet indicates that the discussion has been in progress for at least several days. However, the expression may simply mean "now" (cf. I Sam. 9:27; Isa. 58:4). The rendering **bitter** represents a correction of the M.T. (cf. Targ., Syriac, Vulg.) since the word מרי derives not from מרר, "to be bitter," but from מרה, "to be rebellious." Job is saying, "Even today my complaint is a revolt" (cf. Amer. Trans., "defiant"). Job is aware of the fact that his attitude has drifted into open rebellion. Far from humbling himself, as Eliphaz advised him to do (22:23a), he cannot follow any other course than that of obdurate opposition to the thesis of his guilt. In vs. 2b, the RSV follows the LXX and the Syriac, reading **His hand is heavy in spite of my groaning** although the M.T. has "My hand [ידי rather than ידו] is heavy upon [not **in spite of**] my groaning." To be sure, the text presupposed by the LXX and the Syriac makes sense; but parallelism between vs. 2a and vs. 2b favors the Hebrew text. The sequence of thought is clear enough: Job

---

ing cry for help, and God turns a deaf ear to every bit of it. Men who love darkness find prosperity: the murderer stealing along under cover of the night, the adulterer with his mantle about him and a veil over his face, the thief burrowing into houses—all of them shunning the day (24:13-17). And God? He keeps them safe and sound, delivers them out of danger, watches over all their ways (24:22-23). No? Then **prove me a liar, and show** [me] **that there is nothing in what I say** (24:25).

2. A Rebel Still.—That is manifestly what Job's friends think him to be, and he will go on being it. Whenever wrong is entrenched, and the status quo has to be challenged if there is to be life and not death, the challenger wins himself the accolade of rebel. He is subversive. He is "an enemy of the people." He undermines privilege, flies in the face of tradition, destroys the social order, upsets "our way of life, a way we are proud of, and others envy." How interminably it has happened! Luther was a rebel. Political freedom was won by rebels. Religious freedom was won by rebels. In the realm of economics, in the realm of race relations, the man in front is a revolutionary (see Expos. on 15:4).

When the book of Job was written, an old faith was dying (see Expos. on vs. 3), a new was struggling to be born (see Expos., pp. 905-7). Traditional doctrines were having to yield under the assault of bewildered minds and unrelenting facts (see Expos. on chs. 9–10; 21:5-6, 7-18, 19). The friends retreated to their Maginot Line and dug themselves in. "The old-time religion was good enough for father, and it's good enough for me." Better not ask embarrassing questions. But if the asking of embarrassing questions is precisely the opening wedge of every discovery and every revelation mankind has made or received—what then? Critics and philosophers have asked embarrassing questions about the Bible, about life and religion. Many of them have been condemned as heretics. Some of them were. But what is a heretic?

Roget's *Thesaurus* lists *s.v.* "heterodoxy" Deist, Theist, and Unitarian; Protestant and Catholic and Jew; Lutheran, Calvinist, Episcopalian, Presbyterian, Methodist, Baptist, Mohammedan and Buddhist—to mention only a few (cf. Expos. on 42:5). One of the most embarrassing questions is "When is a rebel a rebel, and when is he a pioneer?" (Cf. Expos. on 18:21.) Truth enlisted in the service of God is of all truth the most disturbing.

2. Things that Matter Most.—As has been pointed out (see Expos. on 20:2b), Job is never in any too great anxiety to defend himself against the assaults of his friends; no doubt partly because, strange as it may seem, he does not feel as insecure in his position as they do in theirs (see Expos. on 15:7-16; 20:2b); partly also because his tortured soul is not able promptly to comprehend and respond to all the implications of what is being said (see Expos. on 15:1–21:34). One thing, however, is certain: what weighs on his mind is not so much the wrong that others do him, or even the wrong God has done him; rather is it his alienation from God (cf. Expos. on vs. 15; 7:20a), and the dreadful conclusion toward which his friends and history too, individual and corporate, seem to be forcing him (see Expos. on 10:13-17). He has been accused of being a religious egoist, and to a degree that is true (see Expos. on 16:13); but whenever he gives way to brooding, he strains for a while at the leash of his own private misfortunes, then breaks out into the wider circle of all human misery everywhere (3:20 ff.; 7:1; 9:23; 10:5; 12:14-25; 21:23 ff.; 24:1 ff.; 29:12 ff.). And always, always it is God that matters most (see Expos. on 19:6).

Obsession with self is sheer, unrelieved ugliness. Ibsen's Peer Gynt visits an asylum and offers the comment that its inmates are "beside themselves." That, answers the physician, is precisely what they are not. They are instinct with self, filled with self, casks of self, with a bung of self. Peer Gynt learns from his own

3 Oh that I knew where I might find him! | 3 Oh, that I knew where I might find him,
that I might come *even* to his seat! | that I might come even to his seat!

is conscious of his revolt not only against the beliefs of his friends, but also against his own attempts to remain silent. He has tried to restrain himself from complaining, but his sighs could not be contained.

3-7. Oh, that I knew where I might find him! This sterile wish opens one of the most powerful descriptions of man's search for God in the whole Bible. There is no technique available to the finite creature whereby the infinite Absolute can be summoned and

experience what it means; and when at last he returns home, he finds the button-molder ready to melt him down as waste into raw material. Only the pure love of the maiden Solveig redeems him. Obsession with others can indeed be one of the gateways to redemption, but itself needs redemption. There is still a missing dimension, and for lack of it many a man intent upon the "good" of his fellows finds a self only to lose it again. Job's obsession is with God (vss. 13-17; 24:1; yet see Expos. on 19:22*a*). It was God who occupied the foreground. The insults (22:5-20) could wait. They always can. Jesus of Nazareth was never hurt by them. He made them take their place in a larger context. The life that does the wrong is the hurt life that needs healing (42:8-10).

3. The God Who Hides.— (Cf. vss. 8-9; see Expos. on 9:2-10; 24:1; 37:1-13; 38:1–42:6; 38:1.) It is not so much that Job cannot find God as it is that he cannot find the God he is looking for. There are times when the reason for what we call our forsakenness is very simple: the God we are looking for does not exist. The God Job was looking for was the God of the faith that was dying (see Expos. on vs. 2); in the death of that faith the God of the new faith was revealing himself. The old God seemed to be hiding on purpose, avoiding every approach that Job tried to make, knowing very well that the man was innocent, but refusing to come into court with his knowledge. He was the God who was not. The God who was broke silence at last, had in his own way been breaking it all along (see Expos. on 19:7, 25).

Yet Job's cry is the anguished cry of all troubled human life; and for reason. There is a sense in which God hides himself. Sometimes it is because we are looking for him in the wrong place (see Expos. on 11:7): back in some yesterday, while he stands here beckoning toward tomorrow; or among things that we can see, such as "answers" to prayer, until one dull morning we seem to lose him entirely because he refuses to do our bidding. Sometimes it is because we carefully avoid looking for him in the right place. Over and over again he is where we are quite sure he is not. We live in a world where our conclusions are not final and our arrange-

ments are anything but permanent. The temple is destroyed: God! The church is split wide open in the Reformation: God! The economic order breaks under a hammer called communism: God—who then breaks the hammer! Is he saying nothing, doing nothing? Read John 8: "He that is of God heareth God's words." "If a man keep my saying . . . ." "Before Abraham was, I am." Did he mean that for such folk, whatever happened or when, if they would look up, they would find his face there?

One of Tolstoy's stories is about Martin, a cobbler who lived in a tiny basement room, with one window looking out on the street; and about how a voice came to him in his sleep, "Look for me tomorrow, for I shall surely come." But from morning to night the next day no one came. There was an old soldier clearing away the snow; and a mother with a shivering child in her arms leaned for a moment against the wall. Martin opened the door and motioned for them both to come in and sit by the fire and have a cup of tea. Nothing in the afternoon. Only a poor apple woman, with a bag of chips on her back. Martin with his own eyes saw the ragged urchin from down the block run up and snatch an apple, saw her catch him, heard her screaming at him, and went out. There was little you could do about it. You could pay for the apple—that was little enough. And you could kneel in the snow with your arm around the lad until through his tears he stammered out at last that he was sorry, and please, would she like him to carry the chips for her? Martin watched them as far as the corner, then took off his shawl and sat down at his table. He always read a while in the dusk. Under the dim glow of the lamp the Gospels fell open, as they have a way of doing, to the passage he had fingered most and smoothed out so often. "I was ahungered, and ye gave me meat" (Matt. 25:35). He glanced up through his spectacles at the dark and lonely room, and smiled. "Look for me tomorrow," the voice had said, "for I shall surely come."

"Verily thou art a God that hidest thyself" (Isa. 45:15). God hidden—and revealed! Revealed in his very hiddenness.

3. God and Man in Search of One Another.— The human race has always been making pil-

4 I would order *my* cause before him, and fill my mouth with arguments.	4 I would lay my case before him and fill my mouth with arguments.
5 I would know the words *which* he would answer me, and understand what he would say unto me.	5 I would learn what he would answer me, and understand what he would say to me.
6 Will he plead against me with *his* great power? No; but he would put *strength* in me.	6 Would he contend with me in the greatness of his power? No; he would give heed to me.
7 There the righteous might dispute with him; so should I be delivered for ever from my judge.	7 There an upright man could reason with him, and I should be acquitted for ever by my judge.

compelled to appear. The poet probably knows that God does not appear because Job is not in the proper condition to meet God. The motive of the hero's search for God is not that of a humble, penitent, truly destitute son who has given up his right, his honor, and his worth, but rather that of an unbowed giant who expects that justice must be done. Job's quest is prompted by a desire for self-assertion, self-defense, and self-vindication. Job looks at God as at a human emperor and asks that he **might come even to his seat** (vs. 3*b*) in order to lay [his] **case before him and fill** [his] **mouth with arguments** (vs. 4). To be sure, Job says,

> I would learn what he would answer me,
> and understand what he would say to me (vs. 5);

yet this reveals not a true state of humility, but only a concession to the omnipotence of the divine judge. Job is so much aware of God's might that, as on previous occasions when he expressed the wish to meet his Sovereign face to face, he feels an elemental dread of annihilation (9:34; 13:21). **Would he contend with me in the greatness of his power?** (Vs. 6*a*.) Casting out this fear with a vehemence which indicates its pressure, Job replies to his own question, **No; he would give heed to me** (vs. 6*b*), or better, "he would be convinced by me" (ישם בי). Many interpreters discover in this passage evidence of the fact that Job believes now in divine clemency and hopes that a gracious God will welcome him with love, but such an exegesis is not borne out either by the words of the text or by the implications of the immediate or general context. Indeed, Job continues by musing, **There an upright man could reason with him** (vs. 7*a*), since he knows that only a godless man would fear to come before him (13:16). Job adds most significantly, **And I should be acquitted for ever by my judge** (vs. 7*b*), or better, "I would recover forever my right" (following the LXX, which reads the word משפטי as *mishpāṭî*, τὸ χρίμα μου, "my judgment of acquittal," instead of *mishshôpheṭî*, "from my judge"). In other words, Job is more than ever convinced of his own righteousness; he has such an exalted and persistent conception of it that even the unjust God who has perverted his right would in the end recognize its validity and yield to the law of ultimate justice.

grimages. Nothing is more characteristic of it. And there is hardly a sweep or flow of peoples in history but underneath it, here or there, now hiding itself away, now making itself manifest, is the impulse to reach out groping hands toward the Unseen. When men respond to it, the gesture is not a strained gesture. Those groping hands are the universal, instinctive posture of the human soul. We have no loftier heritage. True, there are times when the quest takes on strange forms, and the controlling allegiance of one's life goes out to something less than God—with the inevitable result in something less than man. If it had not been for those others whose eyes and hearts were Godward, who can say how much more poverty-stricken than it is the world would have come out of its history? The quest for God will not be safely denied—any longer than it takes human life to begin going to pieces.

But the story has another side. There is forever God's quest for man. You hear the sound of it in all the bitter complaints and even blas-

8 Behold, I go forward, but he *is* not *there;* and backward, but I cannot perceive him:

9 On the left hand, where he doth work, but I cannot behold *him:* he hideth himself on the right hand, that I cannot see *him:*

8 "Behold, I go forward, but he is not there;
  and backward, but I cannot perceive him;
9 on the left hand I seek him,[l] but I cannot behold him;
  I[m] turn to the right hand, but I cannot see him.

[l] Compare Syr: Heb *on the left hand when he works*
[m] Syr Vg: Heb *he*

(2) THE ELUSIVENESS OF GOD (23:8-14)

8-9. In his desperate effort to find the judge and obtain a hearing, Job describes himself as the lonely and wandering traveler who goes to the four corners of the earth in a vain attempt to find someone who is not there. He is the pilgrim of the horizon, for his pilgrimage has no center. In vs. 9*a*, the RSV, following the Syriac, corrects בעשׂתו, "where he works," into בקשׁתיו, **I seek him,** which offers a satisfactory sense and a good parallelism, provided a further emendation is also made in vs. 9*b*, again on the basis of the Syriac (cf. Vulg.), אעטף, **I turn,** instead of the M.T., יעטף, **he hideth himself** (KJV). Inasmuch as the four expressions of direction in vss. 8-9 refer to the four points of the compass, beginning with קדם, **forward,** i.e., "east," and since the ancient myths associated the gods' activities with the mountainous and glacial regions of the north, the text should be probably rendered as a quatrain of geographic and perhaps cosmic significance:

> If to the east I go, he is not there,
>   And to the west, I perceive him not (vs. 8).
> To the north, where he is at work, I behold him not.
> He hides himself in the south, and I see him not (vs. 9).

Job unwittingly betrays the high—perhaps extravagant—opinion in which he holds his own person. He is not only alone in the vast world, a subject of wonder for the ages to come (cf. 18:20, where Bildad describes the type of evil man at whom the west and the east are appalled), but he goes poetically across the whole terrestrial stage in an effort to reach his elusive antagonist. Job is actually implying that God is fleeing him, not merely that God is safely and transcendentally out of reach! The sufferer is on the verge of suggesting that such a God is a coward who takes advantage of his infinite power and of the puniness of his victim, and therefore succeeds in ignoring the rights of man only by evading man. God's cosmic migrations, however, constitute an oblique tribute to the gigantic quality of the hero.

phemies that fall from Job's lips. They are complaints and blasphemies that in rejecting the God-that-is-not honor the God-that-is (see Expos. on 19:25). It is in the N.T. that the two ways meet in the person of one who is here so strangely foreshadowed (see Expos. on 7:7-10; cf. 10:13-17; also Luke 19:5).

> Into the woods my Master came
> Forspent with love and shame.
> But the olives they were not blind to Him;
> The little gray leaves were kind to Him;
> The thorn-tree had a mind to Him,
> When into the woods He came.
>
> . . . .
>
> Out of the woods my Master came,

> Content with death and shame.
> When Death and Shame would woo Him last,
> From under the trees they drew Him last,
> 'Twas on a tree they slew Him—last,
> When out of the woods He came.[6]

It must be added that Job's motives were wrong (vss. 4-5), and the condition he wanted to lay down was wrong (vs. 6; cf. 9:34-35; Expos. on 38:1–42:6); but he at least desired to meet his great Adversary, and it made the friends shudder even to think of such a thing. In the very way Job begged him not to, in that way God came, and for a purpose far other, and to an end far higher.

[6] Sidney Lanier, "A Ballad of Trees and the Master."

10 But he knoweth the way that I take: *when* he hath tried me, I shall come forth as gold.

11 My foot hath held his steps, his way have I kept, and not declined.

12 Neither have I gone back from the commandment of his lips; I have esteemed the words of his mouth more than my necessary *food.*

13 But he *is* in one *mind,* and who can turn him? and *what* his soul desireth, even *that* he doeth.

10 But he knows the way that I take; when he has tried me, I shall come forth as gold.

11 My foot has held fast to his steps; I have kept his way and have not turned aside.

12 I have not departed from the commandment of his lips; I have treasured in[n] my bosom the words of his mouth.

13 But he is unchangeable and who can turn him? What he desires, that he does.

[n] Gk Vg: Heb *from*

10-12. Such a God cannot plead ignorance. He refuses to meet his pursuer, "for" (rather than **But**) **he knows the way that I take** (vs. 10*a*). When at last I shall succeed in capturing his attention, and **he has tried me, I shall come forth as gold** (vs. 10*b*). The trial I am now already enduring; he is now testing my metal. Dross, dirt, impurity? I have none! My behavior has always been without deviation from his norm. I have not been out of step (vs. 11; observe the possible irony involved in the fact that the word אשר, "step," is a cognate of אשרי, "happiness of . . ."). I have fulfilled the law (vs. 12*a*) not only in outward obedience but also **in my bosom** (vs. 12*b*; RSV, following the LXX and the Vulg., emends מחקי into בחקי), i.e., in the very core of my being (cf. 19:27*c*). The M.T., however, if correct, may be rendered, "I have preserved the words of his mouth more than my own resolves" (cf. Judg. 5:15); cf. "I have bent my own will to the words of his mouth" (Segond, Crampon, *et al.*). Here is the picture of a man who holds fast to his avowal of integrity and declares his perfect obedience to divine law. His situation is horrible, and is made more so by the fact that God appears as if he were not bound by his contract. God refuses to do his part when man has done his. Man by obedience may expect from the Deity the fulfilling of the law, the rendering of what is due (cf. Rom. 7:6 ff.; etc.). But God flouts the law. His omnipotence overshadows his justice.

13-14. The expression והוא באחד which opens vs. 13*a* is difficult since it literally means, "But he is in one," hence, **But he is in one mind** (KJV). The idea of divine immutability (cf. RSV) is neither expressed nor implied in the text. Following the paraphrasing of the LXX, εἰ δὲ καὶ αὐτὸς ἔκρινεν οὕτως, one might render, "But he has decided" or "He has fixed his resolution." Perhaps the M.T. represents a corruption from בחר, "he has chosen" (cf. 7:15; 9:14; 15:5; Ps. 132:13). No one can make him change from that decision, and **what he desires, that he does** (vs. 13*b*). The same thought

---

10. The Shield of Integrity.—It is a shield that can blunt many a weapon and ward off many an assault (see Expos. on 17:9; 27:2-6; cf. Expos. on 36:8). Few descriptions of the "righteous" can match this for sheer beauty; few breathe a loftier confidence in the ultimate righteousness of God, in spite of that taunt which provides the context (see Exeg.). There is a **gold** that comes forth from the assayer's fire; there are feet that hold to **the way** which God appoints; there are lives that, far and away beyond any prompting which comes of their will, cherish what they know of his. But to rely on any of it, when all the accounts are in and the books are opened, is to hold both life and God in debt to the self. Read II Cor. 11-12.

The Christian has fallen heir to another kind of boldness (I John 4:17).

13. The Changeless Decree.—The steadfastness of God may feel to the touch like faithfulness (I Cor. 1:9; 10:13)—or like obstinacy. Perhaps one of the most useful lessons to be learned from the book of Job is that what to one may sound like a blessing may to another sound like a curse (cf. Expos. on 5:17; 22:21). From the underside there always seems to be a kind of ambiguity about God's dealing: the interpretation is not of logic but of faith. Job in his present mood dwells only on the sovereignty of God, and the decree becomes more than changeless: it becomes dreadful (see Expos. on 10:13-17). It was of the sovereignty-in-love

14 For he performeth *the thing that is* appointed for me: and many such *things are* with him.

15 Therefore am I troubled at his presence: when I consider, I am afraid of him.

16 For God maketh my heart soft, and the Almighty troubleth me:

17 Because I was not cut off before the darkness, *neither* hath he covered the darkness from my face.

24 Why, seeing times are not hidden from the Almighty, do they that know him not see his days?

---

14 For he will complete what he appoints for me;
and many such things are in his mind.

15 Therefore I am terrified at his presence;
when I consider, I am in dread of him.

16 God has made my heart faint;
the Almighty has terrified me;

17 for I am[o] hemmed in by darkness,
and thick darkness covers my face.[p]

24 "Why are not times of judgment kept by the Almighty,
and why do those who know him never see his days?

[o] With one Ms: Heb *am not*
[p] Vg: Heb *from my face*

---

is developed in the subsequent line, enlarged in order to include the whole of the human tragedy. "He will therefore accomplish the decree which he has made over me, and he will even conceive many others like it" (vs. 14). Who knows whether the case of Job is an isolated exception? The poet introduces here a skillful anticipation of the second part of the discourse (24:1 ff.) and makes a transition from the discussion of a personal fate to that of all conditions of men.

15-16. The awareness of the unknown in God leads to an incommensurate fear. **Therefore I am terrified** [even] **at his presence** (vs. 15b). The mystery of God is so complete that Job is now again a prey to doubt. He is no longer certain that an encounter with the judge will be sufficient to establish his rights and win his acquittal (cf. vss. 4 ff.).

17. This verse is a *crux interpretum.* The negative in vs. 17a is absent in one Hebrew MS (Kennicott 48), and the RSV therefore translates, **for I am hemmed in by darkness.** However, the Niphal of צמת may mean, "to be speechless" (cf. Arabic cognate) and the sufferer probably said, "I did not keep quiet in spite of the darkness." The M.T. may yield another, and profound, meaning: "Because it is not on account of darkness that I am annihilated nor is it the shadow which covers my face." In other words, God's decree is darker to me than my fate. His inscrutable mystery is more terrifying than my misery. There is still the possibility that מפני, "from before me," in vs. 17b represents a corruption of the original text, through a scribal repetition of מפני, "by reason of," in the middle of vs. 17a. More probably, the construction of the clause in vs. 17b is elliptical, and the second מפני stands for מפני אשר, "from the fact that . . ." (cf. Exod. 19:18; Jer. 44:23; see G. R. Driver, "Problems in Job," *The American Journal of Semitic Languages and Literatures,* LII [1935-36], 161).

b) "God Pays No Heed to Prayer" (24:1-25)

From the consideration of his own destiny Job is now ready once more to broaden

---

(see Expos. on 9:2-10) that Robert Grant was thinking when he wrote:

The earth, with its store of wonders untold,
Almighty, thy power hath founded of old;
Hast stablished it fast by a changeless decree,
And round it hath cast, like a mantle, the sea.[7]

15. *Like Madness in the Brain.*—(Cf. 9:35; Expos. on 10:1-22, 1-7, 8-12, 13-17; 34:7-9; also Expos., pp. 905-7.) For Job, cowed by the thought of the majesty and power of God, be-

[7] "O worship the King, all-glorious above."

wildered by his hiddenness (see Expos. on vs. 3), tortured out of the old intimacy into a sense of alienation (see Expos. on 30:19-23), "the fear of the Lord" has turned into terror. The longer he thinks, the greater the terror grows. One thing can dispel it, and one thing only: what if there could be, somehow, a restoration of the fellowship (cf. I John 4:18)? Unless something of the sort happens, Job in winning the argument has lost his faith (see Expos. on 7:21).

24:1. *Why Does God Not Right the Wrong?*— It may be that Job is almost on the point of

2 *Some* remove the landmarks; they violently take away flocks, and feed *thereof*.

3 They drive away the ass of the fatherless, they take the widow's ox for a pledge.

4 They turn the needy out of the way: the poor of the earth hide themselves together.

2 Men remove landmarks;
   they seize flocks and pasture them.

3 They drive away the ass of the fatherless;
   they take the widow's ox for a pledge.

4 They thrust the poor off the road;
   the poor of the earth all hide themselves.

---

the field of his meditation. Developing the theme suggested by 23:14*b*, he asks the all-inclusive question of every man's suffering.

(1) BURDEN OF HUMAN PAIN (24:1-12)

24:1. The RSV brings sense out of an obscure and probably corrupt text, but its rendering remains highly hypothetical and even goes against the normal meaning of the expression נצפן מן, "to be hidden from" (Jer. 16:17; cf. Job 17:4). The main possibilities are three:

(*a*) Some critics suggest that the M.T. did not originally have the negative לא in vs. 1*a*, and they read, "Why are times [events] hidden from the Almighty?" A pious scribe, according to this conjecture, transformed the meaning of the question by inserting the word "not." However, vs. 1*b* literally means, **And why do those who know him never see his days?** The sequence of thought thus appears to require for vs. 1*a* some parallel meaning. It is possible that the hero is taking for granted the loss of belief in God's omniscience. This is the only way by which at this moment he is able to explain the power of injustice over the world of men. His statement is the equivalent of an apology for the Deity.

(*b*) Other critics respect the M.T. and suppose that vs. 1*a* is related to vs. 1*b* as a subordinate clause of restriction. Thus the whole verse might be translated, "Why is it that (although) times are not hidden from the Almighty, those who know him do not contemplate his days (of judgment)?" (Cf. ERV mg.) Such a query would provide a fitting preface to the discussion of unrequited evil which is found in vss. 2 ff.

(*c*) Another interpretation may be obtained if one considers vs. 1*a* as the main question and vs. 1*b* as a causal or consecutive subordinate. "Why are not times hidden from the Almighty, since those who know him are unable to see his days?" In other words, the hero wishes that some events were concealed from God because he could then explain the evil of this world without involving the participation of the Deity.

2-12. The categories of earthly existence seem to be utterly unrelated to a just God. The world of man is studded with acts of foul injustice. **Men remove landmarks** (vs. 2*a*), a crime which is severely condemned by the ancient codes (Deut. 19:14; 27:17; cf. Hos. 5:10; Prov. 22:28; 23:10). "They kidnap the flock and its shepherd" (vs. 2*b*, following

---

taking seriously what Eliphaz suggested in 22:13-14 (see Exeg.). At any rate, the days on which God holds his court and executes his justice seem in no hurry to put in an appearance; and Job, who undoubtedly thinks of himself as among **those who know him,** to the exclusion of the friends, wants to know why—which is precisely the question to which the whole book addresses itself (see Expos. on 1:12; 5:17; 9:2-10; 21:7-18; 23:2, 3). God deals seriously with man's freedom. What he desires is an unprejudiced relationship between himself and the human soul.

Perhaps one might now address Job and say to him: "Job, the kind of world this is does not

mean that God has no love for it. The gospel is that he loves it in spite of the kind of world it is. But you could not have known that—not fully—not as we know it. He loves the world for what his love can make of it. He loves it enough to give himself for it, not in some safe and distant sympathy for its pain, but with a love that comes in and shares. That knowledge, in its fullness, must wait until Mark takes up his pen to write; and Matthew and Luke and John. Your lights at their best are broken lights. But they are lights. In their fitful shining something momentous is getting itself done."

2-12. Man's Inhumanity to Man.—The poet draws for his generation—as for ours—not the

5 Behold, *as* wild asses in the desert, go they forth to their work; rising betimes for a prey: the wilderness *yieldeth* food for them *and* for *their* children.

6 They reap *every one* his corn in the field: and they gather the vintage of the wicked.

7 They cause the naked to lodge without clothing, that *they have* no covering in the cold.

8 They are wet with the showers of the mountains, and embrace the rock for want of a shelter.

9 They pluck the fatherless from the breast, and take a pledge of the poor.

10 They cause *him* to go naked without clothing, and they take away the sheaf *from* the hungry;

11 *Which* make oil within their walls, *and* tread *their* winepresses, and suffer thirst.

12 Men groan from out of the city, and the soul of the wounded crieth out: yet God layeth not folly *to them*.

---

5 Behold, like wild asses in the desert
    they go forth to their toil,
  seeking prey in the wilderness
    as food*q* for their children.

6 They gather their*r* fodder in the field
    and they glean the vineyard of the
      wicked man.

7 They lie all night naked, without cloth-
    ing,
  and have no covering in the cold.

8 They are wet with the rain of the moun-
    tains,
  and cling to the rock for want of
    shelter.

9 (There are those who snatch the father-
    less child from the breast,
  and take in pledge the infant of the
    poor.)

10 They go about naked, without clothing;
  hungry, they carry the sheaves;

11 among the olive rows of the wicked*s* they
    make oil;
  they tread the wine presses, but suffer
    thirst.

12 From out of the city the dying groan,
  and the soul of the wounded cries for
    help;
  yet God pays no attention to their
    prayer.

q Heb *food to him*
r Heb *his*
s Heb *their olive rows*

LXX), perhaps an allusion to 1:15, although the word עדר used here in vs. 2 refers generally to sheep and goats (cf. Gen. 29:2). Deeds of ruthlessness are especially perpetrated against the defenseless members of society, **the fatherless** and the widow (vs. 3), **the needy** and **the poor** (vs. 4), whose condition is pictured in a series of concrete and shocking scenes (vss. 5-11). In **the city** is human pain at its worst (vs. 12*ab*): there (observe the point of view of a poet who espouses the cultural outlook of a nomadic or seminomadic society) **the dying groan, and the soul of the wounded** [LXX, "little children"] **cries**

---

mind's picture alone, but the heart's picture too, of what it is that "makes countless thousands mourn." [8] In vss. 22-23 that inhumanity seems to become the project of the Almighty himself (see Expos. on 9:24). In vs. 25, on the basis of what was originally perhaps a much more severe indictment, Job defies anybody to contradict him. The facts are less one-sided than he represents them; but such as they are, only God can controvert them—by deed, not by word.

12c. How Far from Helping?—Yet God pays no attention to their prayer. Thomas Hardy in

one of his poems [9] tells about a messenger sent one day to remind God of the human race, and God cannot remember. He cannot remember a thing! More than once a man feels that he has been set down to live his life on an abandoned farm, with its weeds and broken fences, the doors of the house gaping wide open, cobwebs and great chunks of fallen plaster littered all over the place. Somebody lived there long ago— as God lived here—and the rooms then breathed. There were footsteps in the hall and on the stairs. But no more: just the creaking floor now, and echoes, and a wind stirring the

[8] Robert Burns, "Man Was Made to Mourn."

[9] "God-forgotten."

for help. And the culminating thought, which gives significance to the whole development, comes sharply and is swiftly formulated: **yet God pays no attention to their prayer** (vs. 12c; RSV, following the Syriac, reads the word תפלה as *tephillāh*, **prayer,** rather than *tiphlāh*, **folly** (KJV), or "unseemliness," "obscenity," "infamy" (cf. 1:22). Vs. 12c offers support to the third interpretation of vs. 1 (cf. Exeg., *ad loc.*). God does not answer prayer because he does not hear it. God does not pay heed to the groans of the dying and the cries of the wounded: is it not that he is unaware of what goes on? There are few queries in the whole Bible as pathetic as this one. Here the problem of theodicy is faced not by a cold formulator of creeds or a polished academician, but by a profoundly religious man who takes to heart the mystery of human suffering and, ignorant of the message of the Cross, rams his head against a closed gate in an effort to excuse the Deity from responsibility for moral evil.

---

rotted curtains. It is one of the universal moods of the human soul.

The reasons for it? Partly because life is born to a certain loneliness. In Eugene O'Neill's *Lazarus Laughed*, Tiberius Caesar sits on his throne, staring at the dead body of a woman he has poisoned and trying to tell Lazarus the tragic story of his own fear-bound life.

I know it is folly to speak—but—one gets old, one becomes talkative, one wishes to confess, to say the thing one has always kept hidden, . . . though [if] one were to cry it in the streets to multitudes, or whisper it in the kiss to one's beloved, the only ears that can ever hear one's secret are one's own! And so I talk aloud . . . ! I talk to my loneliness! [1]

Proof enough, no doubt, that man was made for God, and never will be at home anywhere else. Then there is sin, hanging on like grim death, to make people feel desolate. And misfortune. Somebody dies. Something cracks up. Life tumbles in, while the wrong out there in the world keeps piling higher and higher, until nobody can see over it, and only an optimist can think that the future is uncertain. A reporter asked a marshal of France what he would have done if he had been in Pilate's place. The answer was: "I wouldn't have waited for Jesus to infect the crowds in the capital with his seditious poison. I would have put him before the firing squad in his home province, up north in Galilee." It is exciting, is it not, to see God go down for the third time in such a welter of things as ours?

So are there times when we shut out God. But there are other times when there seems to be no particular rhyme or reason in his turning his back on us and holding his peace, pulling down the blinds of heaven and locking the door. In any case, the past always has something to say. It says, for one thing, that God is often most where he seems to be least. Ps. 22, for instance, was written during or shortly after the captivity. There they were, praying for deliverance, with

everybody laughing at them. Fear stalked around naked. Their hearts were like wax. Yet out of those bitter, bitter years came the world's most precious heritage: this human faith in the God of human history. It grew up into its own under the heel of a conqueror, marched through fire, and was clean. Against the oncoming centuries it set itself, against the ravages of war, and blazed the way to Christ. God forsaken? God controlled! He had been in front of them, and behind them, and all around them—helping them most when there was no help. Or take Jesus himself. Where was God that last week of his life? God was at home on Calvary to the whole wide world. Never anywhere so much as there. Daniel Webster said of the Great Stone Face: "Men hang out their signs indicative of their respective trades: shoemakers hang out a gigantic shoe; jewelers, a monster watch; and the dentist hangs out a gold tooth; but up in the mountains of New Hampshire, God Almighty has hung out a sign to show that there He makes men." [2] He hung out a sign on a little hill, beyond the walls of Jerusalem, to show that he would keep faith. And he does. The past has that to say. What if one had the grace to apply it every time the present turns ugly and forbidding? Bunyan in *Pilgrim's Progress* has Christian and Hopeful taken prisoner by Giant Despair, and thrown behind the bars of Doubting Castle. When all at once, a little before day, Christian, as one half amazed, broke out into passionate speech: "What a fool," quoth he, "am I, thus to lie in a stinking dungeon, when I may as well walk at liberty!" And without waiting another moment, he took from his bosom the key he had forgotten. It was called Promise, and with it he unlocked the door into the castle yard, swung back the iron gate, and they were off on the King's highway again. It can be done readily enough—with the key. God's word was not given at Versailles or at Munich. It was given on Calvary (see Expos. on 38:1).

[1] Act IV, scene 1, pp. 150-51.

[2] *The Old Man of the Mountain.*

13 They are of those that rebel against the light; they know not the ways thereof, nor abide in the paths thereof.

14 The murderer rising with the light killeth the poor and needy, and in the night is as a thief.

15 The eye also of the adulterer waiteth for the twilight, saying, No eye shall see me: and disguiseth *his* face.

16 In the dark they dig through houses, *which* they had marked for themselves in the daytime: they know not the light.

17 For the morning *is* to them even as the shadow of death: if *one* know *them, they are in* the terrors of the shadow of death.

18 He *is* swift as the waters; their portion is cursed in the earth: he beholdeth not the way of the vineyards.

19 Drought and heat consume the snow waters: *so doth* the grave *those which* have sinned.

20 The womb shall forget him; the worm shall feed sweetly on him; he shall be no more remembered; and wickedness shall be broken as a tree.

21 He evil entreateth the barren *that* beareth not: and doeth not good to the widow.

13 "There are those who rebel against the light,
    who are not acquainted with its ways,
    and do not stay in its paths.
14 The murderer rises in the dark,*t*
    that he may kill the poor and needy;
    and in the night he is as a thief.
15 The eye of the adulterer also waits for the twilight,
    saying, 'No eye will see me';
    and he disguises his face.
16 In the dark they dig through houses;
    by day they shut themselves up;
    they do not know the light.
17 For deep darkness is morning to all of them;
    for they are friends with the terrors of deep darkness.

18 "You say, 'They are swiftly carried away upon the face of the waters;
    their portion is cursed in the land;
    no treader turns toward their vineyards.
19 Drought and heat snatch away the snow waters;
    so does Sheol those who have sinned.
20 The squares of the town*u* forget them;
    their name*v* is no longer remembered;
    so wickedness is broken like a tree.'

21 "They feed on the barren childless woman,
    and do no good to the widow.

t Cn: Heb *at the light*
u Cn: Heb *obscure*
v Cn: Heb *a worm*

---

(2) TRIUMPH OF EVIL ON EARTH (24:13- [Zophar: vss. 18-24?] 25)

13-17. The mention of the city leads the poet to expatiate on the dark doings which commonly occur there. **The murderer** and **the adulterer** (vss. 14-15) are used as illustrations of those who perform the deeds of night (vss. 16-17) and therefore **rebel against the light** (vs. 13*a*).

18-24. These lines present a grave problem of interpretation, for they describe the dogma of delayed (vs. 22) but certain (vs. 23) retribution. Although the text has been poorly preserved and is obscure at many points, the general meaning is clear enough for the interpreter to conclude that Job was not the original speaker of this passage. The translators of the RSV, apparently making the same observation, surmise that we have here a quotation of the friends' opinion, and thus introduce vs. 18 with the words **You say** (which are not in the text), followed by quotation marks. Against this

---

13-17. *Denizens of the Dark.*— (Cf. John 3:19-21; Rom. 13:12; I Pet. 2:9; I John 1:5; 2:8.) The gospel is summons, not advice; revolution,

not reformation. Before the will can be touched, the desire has to be changed.

18-21, 24. See Expos. on 27:13-23.

22 He draweth also the mighty with his power: he riseth up, and no *man* is sure of life.

23 *Though* it be given him *to be* in safety, whereon he resteth; yet his eyes *are* upon their ways.

24 They are exalted for a little while, but are gone and brought low; they are taken out of the way as all *other*, and cut off as the tops of the ears of corn.

25 And if *it be* not *so* now, who will make me a liar, and make my speech nothing worth?

25 Then answered Bildad the Shuhite, and said,

2 Dominion and fear *are* with him; he maketh peace in his high places.

22 Yet God[w] prolongs the life of the mighty
   by his power;
   they rise up when they despair of life.

23 He gives them security, and they are supported;
   and his eyes are upon their ways.

24 They are exalted a little while, and then are gone;
   they wither and fade like the mallow;[x]
   they are cut off like the heads of grain.

25 If it is not so, who will prove me a liar,
   and show that there is nothing in what
   I say?"

25 Then Bildad the Shuhite answered:
2 "Dominion and fear are with God;[y]
   he makes peace in his high heaven.

[w] Heb *he*
[x] Gk: Heb *all*
[y] Heb *him*

---

conjecture there is serious objection. Job does not protest against the opinion allegedly quoted by him, but on the contrary endorses its validity with vehemence (vs. 25). It is therefore preferable to follow the hypothesis proposed by many modern critics, and to consider vss. 18-24 (with the possible exception of vss. 22-23) as editorially removed from another context and placed in the mouth of Job in order to make him appear as accepting the orthodox thesis. Indeed, it is easy to recognize in vss. 18-24 the style and ideas of the friends (cf. 15:20-35; 18:5-21; 20:4-28). It will be seen that in 27:13-23 also Job makes (for him) very strange assertions. Moreover, there is a close sequence of thought and style between the two passages. By placing them together one obtains an excellent sequence: (*a*) The fate of the evil men described in 24:18-24 is summed up in 27:13; and (*b*) there follows naturally the picture of the sons of the evil man in 27:14-23. Inasmuch as Zophar does not speak a third time, one may entertain with a great degree of probability the conjecture that parts of his original third discourse have been uprooted from their context and placed in the mouth of Job in an editorial effort to reconcile the views of the hero with the traditional dogma of individual retribution (cf. Intro., p. 888).

3. Third Discourse of Bildad and Job's Reply (25:1–27:12)

In the present M.T. the third discourse of Bildad is reduced to a doxology of a few verses (25:1-6). However, an analysis of ch. 26 shows that it contains a passage now

---

22-23. See Expos. on 19:6.

25. See Expos. on 12:2-6; 21:5-6. No doubt the conclusion of a much more bitter indictment of God than was allowed to come down to us.

25:1-6. *Bildad.*— (For the concluding verses of Bildad's third discourse see 26:5-14. Kissane assigns to Bildad 26:1-4 and 27:7-23, with Job's answer in chs. 29–30; to Zophar, 25:1-6 and 26:5-14, with Job's answer in 27:1-6 and ch. 31.) Nothing but sheer arrogance could prompt what you have said (see Exeg.). God knows and rules over all things. And you, frail nothing of a man, prate to his very face about

your integrity (cf. 23:3-7). You may well wish there were an escape (14:13), but there is none, either in hell beneath or in heaven above. "The earth, with its store of wonders untold" (see Expos. on 23:13), the vastness of all creation, the mysteries of rain and cloud, of light and darkness—from end to end they are his, the barest fringe of his glory, the merest whisper of his power.

2-6. *Right Made Wrong.*—The poet sets up no straw man to be buffeted about. Job is not engaged in shadowboxing. Some of the most stately passages of the book are set on the lips

| 3 Is there any number of his armies? and upon whom doth not his light arise? | 3 Is there any number to his armies? Upon whom does his light not arise? |

placed in the mouth of Job (vss. 5-14) which in all probability continues Bildad's discussion (see Exeg., *ad loc.*). Thus the present text may be the result of an editorial shifting in an attempt to tone down the blasphemous statements of the hero. As conjecturally reconstituted, the speeches or fragments thereof may be attributed to Bildad and to Job respectively in the following fashion: (*a*) Bildad lyrically describes the majesty of God in order to emphasize the smallness and the impurity of man (25:1-6); (*b*) Job replies that such assertions are of little help to him (26:1-4); (*c*) Bildad returns unperturbed to the theme of divine omnipotence and continues by extolling divine omniscience (26:5-14); (*d*) Job retorts by reaffirming his own integrity (27:1-12).

a) [BILDAD] GOD'S GREATNESS AND MAN'S IMPURITY (25:1-6)

25:1-3. No more than Eliphaz in 22:2 ff. does Bildad address his opponent directly. Job has just spoken of the indifference and perhaps of the ignorance of the Deity (cf. 24:1, 12). Bildad does not offer a counterargument. Instead, he proposes to raise the level of the rhetorical exchange by extolling the greatness of God. He is so reverently conscious of God's all-inclusive realm that he does not even mention the divine name. In the style of all doxologies, he refers to the Godhead with the help of a masculine singular pronoun and a series of participles. **Dominion and fear are with him; he maketh peace in his high places** (vs. 2). It is the power of the Almighty which produces fear, not only on this earth, but also in heaven. No one is able to count **his armies** (vs. 3*a*), i.e., the hosts to which Job has already alluded in full recognition of divine omnipotence (19:12). The Hebrew text of vs. 3*b* introduces an idea of great beauty and significance: **Upon whom doth not his light arise?** The light of God is more than the brightness of the sun and of the celestial bodies (cf. Heb. 4:13). It penetrates beyond the farthest recesses of the cosmos, therefore illumines all darkness and sharply reveals the impurity

---

of the friends. Bildad, far from being exhausted as Strahan suggests, gives a new and clever twist to the argument. Not only does he repeat, of what Eliphaz and Zophar have said (see Exeg. on vss. 4-6), that to which Job has himself assented, but he borrows from Job's own mouth the words which he hopes now will carry conviction with them (cf. 15:6). His theme was one of Abraham Lincoln's favorites: "Oh why should the spirit of mortal be proud?" [3] From height to depth he ranges, laying the whole universe under tribute, that the spirit before him might be struck from its lofty place and made to grovel in the dust where it belongs, rotting flesh, crawling worm (see Expos. on vs. 2). The premise is right: every conclusion drawn from it is wrong. God is great (the Moslem's *allahu akbar*). Right! Conclusion number one: therefore man is nothing and sinful to boot. Wrong! (Cf. Expos. on 1:1; 4:19-21; 9:14-19; 26:5-14.) Conclusion number two: therefore God is holy and unimpeachable. Wrong! (Cf. Expos. on 9:2-10, 8-13.) Conclusion number three: therefore Job has no reason to talk as he does. Wrong! (Cf. Expos. on 10:1-22, 1-7, 8-12, 13-17.) The whole discourse, as a result, serves but to illustrate, not only (*a*) the theological inepti-

[3] William Knox, "Mortality," st. i.

tude of the speaker, but (*b*) his moral insensitiveness as well, plus (*c*) his abysmal failure to plumb the depths of Job's real anguish (see Expos. on 23:2). So easily can right be made wrong. Recall how often the Bible has been pressed into the service of evil: to justify slavery, poverty, uncharitableness, and isolationism, both individual and national. The recipe is always the same: it was Bildad's, and he handled it expertly, with lyrical enthusiasm, after the manner of one singing a doxology.

2. Dominion and Fear.—True piety, unfortunately, is not inevitably the human response to divine majesty (see Expos. on 26:5-14). God may be able to quell all the discords of heaven (vs. 2*b*), marshal his numberless hosts (vs. 3*a*; Isa. 40:26; with us too "the heavenly host" may mean either stars or angels; yet see Exeg.), search out with his light the hidden things of darkness (see Expos. on 24:13-17); but it does not follow that a man's awe will thereby necessarily be transformed into love (cf. Expos. on 9:2-10, 8-13; 38:1).

3b. God Is Light.—The word for **arise** is scarcely to be understood of the rising sun. Here is the **light** which God speeds on its way to reveal (see Exeg.), to guide, and to infuse with warmth and life (cf. John 1:9; Expos. on 29:3).

4 How then can man be justified with God? or how can he be clean *that is* born of a woman?

5 Behold even to the moon, and it shineth not; yea, the stars are not pure in his sight.

6 How much less man, *that is* a worm? and the son of man, *which is* a worm?

4 How then can man be righteous before God?
How can he who is born of woman be clean?

5 Behold, even the moon is not bright
and the stars are not clean in his sight;

6 how much less man, who is a maggot,
and the son of man, who is a worm!"

---

even of the angels. This idea introduces the subsequent development (vss. 4-6). The LXX translates ἔνεδρα παρ' αὐτοῦ, "his ambushes" (having read perhaps instead of אורהו the word ארביו. Some critics prefer this reading for the sake of respecting a satisfactory parallelism with vs. 3a, "And against whom does not his ambush stand?" Others suggest אמרהו, "his word" (cf. Ecclus. 43:10). The traditional rendering, however, may very well be correct, for it provides a revealing glimpse into the speaker's mind and it offers an idea which fits the context. The greatness of God suggests his glory and his purity. This translation furnishes transition to the next passage.

4-6. Here Bildad is pursuing a theme which is the favorite of Eliphaz (4:17 ff.; 15:14-16) and Zophar (11:5-12), to which Job has once signified agreement (9:2; cf. 12:9-25; 14:4). But the renewal of this theme at this point is more significant than mere repetition. Job has spoken of the impunity of those "who rebel against the light" (24:13), and Bildad refuses to follow the lead, although he apparently feels the force of his opponent's argument. He shrewdly twists the thread of reasoning by concentrating his thought not on the general spectacle of injustice in the world, but on the particular case of Job's guilt. He rightly feels that here is another opportunity for him to make Job yield. **How then can man be justified with God?** (Vs. 4a.) Observe the use of the preposition עם, **with**, "beside" (rather than the prefix מן in 4:17). Can man obtain a righteousness independently of God? If even **the moon** and **the stars** are neither **bright** nor **clean in his sight** (vs. 5), no human creature should be brash enough to claim integrity, innocence, and perfection, especially when this human creature is "mortal man" (אנוש), one **born of a woman** (cf. 14:1), "the son of clay" or "of Adam" (בן־אדם; an expression found only here and perhaps in 16:21), fit to be compared only—as Job well knows—to **a maggot** (cf. 7:5; 17:14; 21:26) and to **a worm** (Ps. 22:6; Isa. 14:11; 41:14). Thus Bildad does not merely repeat the statements of his friends: he introduces a vocabulary which has already been used by Job himself and thereby attempts to maneuver Job into assent.

From the praise of God's majesty the thought runs smoothly to the acknowledgment of God's glory, effulgence, and holiness, and thus sharply underscores the insignificance of man. But is it fair to argue from man's puny limitations to man's moral and theological impurity? Bildad does not at all suspect that such a line of reasoning introduces some highly dangerous and utterly false implications. He almost stumbles into the fantastic idea that as man's finitude is the cause of his corruption, so also God's omnipotence is at the basis of God's perfection. Bildad reveals himself to be at this moment, like Eliphaz (cf. 22:2 ff.), one of the forerunners of Islamic monotheism. He ignores the categories of good and evil, he misunderstands the inner life of Job, and he fails to grasp the nature

---

6. *How Much Less!*—In the Bible man is a paradox of dust and divinity (cf. Ps. 8; Expos. on 7:17-18; 9:14-19; 16:3; 19:22a). Bildad would whittle Job down to insignificance, and argue from his limitations to his sinfulness (see Exeg.). The secret lies rather in man's rebellion against his limitations, and therefore in the dreadful potentialities of the human will: not so much in the fact that he is rigidly circum-

scribed as in the fact that he is circumscribed so little. The peril does not associate itself with size, but with stature. When God at last appears, Job's size is reduced to the vanishing point; his stature, with bowed head and mouth struck dumb, is heroic. In that moment he is both prince (31:37) and titan. Power diminishes the size; love increases the stature (see Expos. on 38:1–42:6; 38:1–40:5).

26 But Job answered and said,
2 How hast thou helped *him that is* without power? *how* savest thou the arm *that hath* no strength?

3 How hast thou counseled *him that hath* no wisdom? and *how* hast thou plentifully declared the thing as it is?

4 To whom hast thou uttered words? and whose spirit came from thee?

26 Then Job answered:
2 "How you have helped him who has no power!
How you have saved the arm that has no strength!

3 How you have counseled him who has no wisdom,
and plentifully declared sound knowledge!

4 With whose help have you uttered words, and whose spirit has come forth from you?

---

of God. In effect, albeit obliquely, he joins hands—through his theological presuppositions—with the pagan pantheists who identify the deity with a deified nature, and stops short of this ancient and modern error only by debasing man to the rank of a wormlike nonentity from which the divine image has been completely eradicated.

Far from turning in circles over the same ground, the poet subtly moves forward as he draws from his main characters the ultimate conclusions inherent in their initial positions.

b) [JOB] THE FUTILITY OF HELPING A POWERLESS MAN (26:1-4)

26:1-4. Vss. 2-4 are correctly attributed to the hero by the editor of the book (vs 1). When Bildad eloquently celebrates the divine omnipotence (25:2-6) Job readily agrees, of course, but he reflects with sad irony upon the total irrelevance of such an allocution. The help he needs is **power** and **wisdom** (vss. 2-3). Read in vs. 3b, *labbur* (לבר) instead of *lārōbh* (לרב; cf. Kennicott 82) and translate, "Practical wisdom to the ruffian [uncultivated person] thou hast revealed!" Job is on the verge of accusing his friend not only of failure but also of malicious intent. Bildad does not know what kind of man Job truly is. "With whom art thou spilling words?" (Vs. 4a.) Another interpretation, respectful of the parallelism, could be, "With whom hast thou conversed, and whose spirit hath issued forth from thee?" If this is the correct rendering of the verse, Job is suggesting satirically that Bildad, in spite of the loftiness of his sermon, has actually been moved by an evil spirit. Kissane (*Job,* p. 168) maintains the view that vss. 2-4 form a part of Bildad's third discourse, for, except in 16:2 ff., where the use of the second person singular is justified, Job never speaks to his friends separately, but always addresses them *en bloc* in the second person plural. On the contrary, the friends quite naturally address Job in the singular. If vss. 2-4 were pronounced by Bildad, the line of thought would be somewhat as follows. Bildad, like Eliphaz (cf. 4:3-4), remarks over Job's long habit of exercising pastoral responsibility over others. Has not Job succored those who had no strength (vs.

26:1-4. Cold Comfort.— (See Expos. on 27:1-12. Strahan treats these verses as the introduction of Bildad's third speech. The irony seems to fit better in the mouth of Job.) This is not the first time Job has delivered himself on the subject (see 13:12; 16:2; cf. Expos. on 6:18, 21-27; 13:1-12, 8; 19:2, 21). Perhaps it would better fit his frankly sarcastic mood, as well as his continuing self-assurance, to suppose that, far from confessing even by implication his own weakness and lack of understanding (vss. 2-3), he is taunting the friends with the air of superiority they have assumed toward him; as if to say, What do you take me to be (vs. 4a; see Exeg.)?

You have an idea that I am a puny, ignorant sort of person, uncouth and unlettered (vs. 3b; see Exeg.). What a magnificent contribution you have made! (See Expos. on 25:5-14; they have given him a stone for bread; and instead of a fish, a serpent.) There is, however, back of it all, a wistful yearning for the very **power** and **wisdom** that try to cover up their deficiencies in irony. What he so desperately needs they could have given him (see Expos. on 6:14; 19:13-19). Consolations of God indeed! (See Expos. on 15:11; cf. 21:2.) Such consolations as theirs may have had another source (see Exeg.)!

5 Dead *things* are formed from under the waters, and the inhabitants thereof.
 	
6 Hell *is* naked before him, and destruction hath no covering.
	5 The shades below tremble,
	    the waters and their inhabitants.
	6 Sheol is naked before God,
	    and Abaddon has no covering.

2*a*) ? Has not Job given advice to those who were deprived of wisdom (vs. 3*a*)? What has happened within the personality of this pastor and teacher which explains his present state of mind? Is he not animated by a spirit of evil? Has he not communed with a demon? Such an exegesis, whatever its validity may be, does not provide a satisfactory link with the Bildad context (25:2-6); it is therefore better to accept the heading of 26:1 as correct and to ascribe the passage to the hero.

c) [BILDAD] MAN'S INABILITY TO GRASP THE POWER OF GOD (26:5-14)

The theme of divine omnipotence is not foreign to Job's frame of mind. This is precisely the reason why in the first and second cycles he has accused the Deity of persecuting him without cause. But in the third cycle Job is no longer concerned primarily with the limitless power of the Deity. He charges God with indifference, aloofness, apartness, and unconcern for human justice (chs. 21; 23). Although the present section cannot be declared a priori to be an utter impossibility in the mouth of Job at this time, the exegete must recognize that there is no bond of thought between this passage and the lines which either precede (vss. 2-4) or follow (27:2 ff.). Moreover, these verses continue the theme inaugurated by Bildad in 25:2-6, and they furnish a normal, expected, and almost inevitable sequence to it. There the speaker used the motif of God's greatness in heaven in order to disparage man's mortal and moral state on earth; here the speaker uses the motif of God's sovereign control over the underworld to stress the fact that nothing in the created world escapes the power of his will; and this idea slowly builds up into his final utterance on man's inability to understand God's ways (vs. 14).

5-6. After considering heaven and earth (25:2-6), the poet turns to **hell. The shades** (lit., "the Rephaim"; cf. Isa. 14:9; 26:14; Ps. 88:10) do not survive in a state of quiet serenity (contrast Job's musing in 3:13 ff.), but they **tremble** (vs. 5*a*). The waters of the underworld and their inhabitants "are in dread" (vs. 5*b*; the verb is now missing, but the meter as well as the syntax requires its presence; it may have been יחתו, dropped by haplographic accident after the word מתחת, **below,** which belongs to the end of vs. 5*a*). No part of the universe lies beyond the eyes of the Godhead. **Sheol is naked before** him, and even **Abaddon,** the lowest hell, **has no covering** (vs. 6). Job has expressed the wish to be hidden in Sheol in order to escape the attention of his Creator (14:13; cf. Ps. 139:8*b*, 11-12), but even there he would lie open to the gaze of the eternal persecutor. Observe the parallelism of **naked** and **no covering,** as in 24:7, where the same words are found. The thought that Sheol is within the range of God's jurisdiction and interest is an unusual one for the Hebrew mind (cf. 12:22; Ps. 139:7; Prov. 15:11; Amos 9:2).

Kissane [4] takes these verses as part of Bildad's third speech, to be followed at once by 27:7-23, assigning ch. 25 and 26:5-24 to Zophar. In that case Bildad is asking Job (and the you of vs. 2 is in the singular; except for 16:2, Job always addresses the friends in the plural), very much as Eliphaz had asked him (4:3-4), how it comes that he who has consoled so many is now comfortless, implying in 26:4 that he too had been accustomed to rely on both tradition and revelation while picturing for the wicked the destiny that awaits them (27:11, 12, 7-23). A clear instance of the difficulties—and plausibilities— [4] *Job,* p. 164.	that hound the steps of the interpreter through this cycle of the poem. **5-14. *The Hem of His Garment.***—What troubles Job, of course, is that he seems unable any longer to think of God as good. Bildad has nothing to offer for remedy but the very fact which for Job renders the problem insoluble. If God can do anything he likes, how can he be good? (Cf. Exeg. and Matt. 7:9-10.) "Almighty" is a word which is flung about too casually. There are times when more downright help is to be had of dwelling on what God cannot do, if man is still to be man, and God God. He cannot settle quarrels until we are ready to

7 He stretcheth out the north over the empty place, *and* hangeth the earth upon nothing.

8 He bindeth up the waters in his thick clouds; and the cloud is not rent under them.

9 He holdeth back the face of his throne, *and* spreadeth his cloud upon it.

10 He hath compassed the waters with bounds, until the day and night come to an end.

11 The pillars of heaven tremble, and are astonished at his reproof.

12 He divideth the sea with his power, and by his understanding he smiteth through the proud.

13 By his Spirit he hath garnished the heavens; his hand hath formed the crooked serpent.

---

7 He stretches out the north over the void,
    and hangs the earth upon nothing.

8 He binds up the waters in his thick clouds,
    and the cloud is not rent under them.

9 He covers the face of the moon,[z]
    and spreads over it his cloud.

10 He has described a circle upon the face of the waters
    at the boundary between light and darkness.

11 The pillars of heaven tremble,
    and are astounded at his rebuke.

12 By his power he stilled the sea;
    by his understanding he smote Rahab.

13 By his wind the heavens were made fair;
    his hand pierced the fleeing serpent.

[z] Or *his throne*

---

7. As in 25:2*b*, and in all doxologies of the Hebrew Bible, the praise of the Creator begins and continues with the use of verbs in the participle. **He stretcheth out the north over the void** [*tōhû* as in Gen. 1:2; cf. Jer. 4:23; Isa. 34:11; 45:18] **and hangeth the earth upon nothing** (cf. the parallelism between void and nothingness in Isa. 40:17, 23). This amounts to a poetic description of *creatio ex nihilo*. The northern regions of the earth are connected in a special way with the sojourn of the gods (cf. 23:9; also Isa. 14:13; Ezek. 1:4). Possibly **the north** designates here the *Stella Polaris* on which the constellations appear to circumambulate. Although the poet's cosmogony is geocentric, he fully understands that the earth rests **upon nothing** and receives its stability only from the will of the almighty Creator.

8-13. The waters above are kept securely in reserve (vs. 8), and God's **throne** (rather than **moon**, the eclipses of which have no relevance in this context) is properly veiled from human sight (vs. 9). **He has described a circle** [read חֻק־חָג as *ḥaq-ḥugh*] **at the boundary between light and darkness** (vs. 10). As in Prov. 8:27, God has set a limit to the forces of chaos. Traces of ancient mythological belief in a cosmic fight are visible in the background of the poetic development (vss. 11-13; cf. 3:8; 7:12; 9:13), but the motifs of pagan dualism are absorbed within the overwhelming monism of the theologian. God rules unchallenged. He is truly omnipotent.

---

settle them. He cannot keep the wickedness of evil men from hurting the innocent, or bombs from bursting where little children are. "God's Weakness and Man's Might" is the tragic theme of history, brought only on Calvary and Easter to its great reversal (I Cor. 1:25). Strahan's comment [5] that "the greatest thing in the world is not greatness" reminds one inevitably of Henry Drummond's exposition of I Cor. 13.[6]

The description that Bildad gives, however, of God's majesty is almost incomparably beautiful: the trembling of the dead in Sheol (giants? Gen. 15:20; Deut. 2:11), beneath the

[5] *Job*, p. 223.
[6] "Love: The Supreme Gift: The Greatest Thing in the World," *Addresses* (New York: Fleming H. Revell Co., 1891), pp. 19-52.

waters that support the dry land; the nakedness of the abyss to his piercing sight; the heavens that rest on nothing, and the earth that hangs from it; the miracle of the filmy clouds heavy with water but not breaking; the hiddenness of his throne (vs. 9); the circle he has drawn between the light and the darkness; the trembling of the mountains; the stilling of the sea, that daily conquest of all the powers of chaos; the clearing of the skies, the rift on the horizon as the storm passes or the day dawns—and all of it hardly the edge of his royal vesture, nothing but a murmur in the ear compared to **the thunder of his power.** Granted that one may discern here some drift toward a kind of pantheism (see Exeg. on 25:4-6), note nevertheless that God is still sovereign. Neither nature nor man can

14 Lo, these *are* parts of his ways; but how little a portion is heard of him? but the thunder of his power who can understand?	14 Lo, these are but the outskirts of his ways; and how small a whisper do we hear of him! But the thunder of his power who can understand?"
27 Moreover Job continued his parable, and said,	**27** And Job again took up his discourse, and said:

14. This verse gathers the preceding doxology into a hymn to divine transcendence. Man may stand in awe at the manifestations of creative might in the realm of nature, yet what he sees of the outward universe is only an adumbration of the full display.

> **Lo, these are but the outskirts of his ways;**
> **and how small a whisper do we hear of him!**

Let no man confuse the forces of nature with the full disclosure of God himself! The universe, overpowering as its spectacle may be, is but a dim mirror of divine magnificence. Nature does not reveal God: it is merely a faint whisper of divine majesty. What does God reveal of his greatness? **The thunder of his power who can understand?** Here at last is the key to the whole discourse. With consummate skill the poet brings his discussion to a close with the soft yet swift and heart-searching impact of a query to which there can be no other answer than acquiescence.

Were this discourse spoken by Job, as vs. 1 leads the reader to believe, not only would it be sharply contradicted by the context (vss. 2-4; 27:2 ff.), but also it would be pointless and superfluous. The friends are already won to such an attitude of reverent agnosticism before the outskirts of God's ways! If on the contrary this doxology originates with one of the friends (quite naturally Bildad, since it follows the doxology of 25:2-6), then the subdued art and the perspicacious psychology of the poet appear at their best. A final effort is made by Bildad to win Job over to an acknowledgment of ignorance, but this effort is undertaken by a man who has not passed through the crucible of sorrow and who manifests no sympathy. It is therefore bound to fail.

d) [Job] Reaffirmation of Innocence (27:1-12)

27:1. And Job again took up his discourse [*wayyōṣeph 'iyyôbh se'ēth meshālô*]: The unusual character of this heading (cf. 29:1) is a further indication of the disturbed state of the text. It is superfluous if Job is the speaker of the preceding lines (26:5-14), and yields satisfactory sense only if it follows a discourse pronounced by one of the friends. Moreover, the vehemence of vss. 2 ff. is inexplicable unless they are held to be spoken not as a sequence of the hero's discourse but as a retort to the utterances of one of his opponents.

snatch the scepter from his hand. To the ears of faith Creation utters its speech (Ps. 19:1-3; see Expos. on 36:26-33); but its utterance is little other than a breath, its glory no more than the hem of his garment (Matt. 9:20; 14:36). Nature is not the Great Physician.

27:1-12. Job.— (Included here, as the introductory section of Job's reply to Bildad, is 26: 1-4; see Expos. *ad loc.*) You have been a great help to the poor benighted fellow you take me for! Where do you get such counsel as yours (26:1-4)? By the living God (27:2 ff.) —he has wronged me, but I shall swear by him still— while there is any **breath** left **in me**, I am telling

the truth: you are wrong (22:5-20), and I will not say you are right; I am innocent, I have done nothing all my life for which my conscience reproaches me. (For vss. 7-12, see also Expos. below.) I could wish nothing worse for my enemy than that he be numbered among the wicked. You count me as one of the godless. Why then do you tell me there is still hope (11:18)? Why do you keep urging me to pray (22:26)? I will tell you how God actually deals with the unrighteous man, and make no secret of it. **You have seen it yourselves:** why do you keep talking such nonsense about me? (See Exeg. on vss. 11-12.)

2 *As* God liveth, *who* hath taken away my judgment; and the Almighty, *who* hath vexed my soul;

3 All the while my breath *is* in me, and the spirit of God *is* in my nostrils;

4 My lips shall not speak wickedness, nor my tongue utter deceit.

5 God forbid that I should justify you: till I die I will not remove mine integrity from me.

6 My righteousness I hold fast, and will not let it go: my heart shall not reproach *me* so long as I live.

7 Let mine enemy be as the wicked, and

2 "As God lives, who has taken away my right,
  and the Almighty, who has made my soul bitter;

3 as long as my breath is in me,
  and the spirit of God is in my nostrils;

4 my lips will not speak falsehood,
  and my tongue will not utter deceit.

5 Far be it from me to say that you are right;
  till I die I will not put away my integrity from me.

6 I hold fast my righteousness, and will not let it go;
  my heart does not reproach me for any of my days.

7 "Let my enemy be as the wicked,

2-6. By one of the most extraordinary oaths of the Bible Job affirms once more the sincerity of his protest. God, he maintains, has disregarded his right (vs. 2*a*), and the Almighty has plunged his soul into bitterness (vs. 2*b*; cf. 3:20; 7:11; 10:1; 21:25): Job still swears by the life of this God. Nevertheless it must be recognized that the formula of oath requires the use of the name of the Deity, and that vs. 2 therefore may represent little more than colloquial habit.

Until death Job will maintain his **integrity** (*tummāh;* cf. 2:3). No compromise with his essential conviction will ever be possible. **I hold fast my righteousness, and will not let it go** (vs. 6*a*). The egocentric position of the battered giant remains entire and unshaken. Note the twelve uses of the first personal pronoun in the Hebrew text of vss. 2-6. He has once more searched his past, but he does not remember a single instance of untowardness. **My heart does not reproach me for any of my days** (vs. 6*b*).

7-10. Some commentators believe that this passage does not belong to the discourse

---

2-6. *The Last Line of Defense.*—As has already been said (see Expos. on 7:11, 19:6), Job's mind is in danger of becoming godless; his heart never is. Again and again he tries to reconcile the two (see Expos. on 9:30-35; 14:13-15; 16:19; 19:25). He swears now by the God he loves before the God who has deprived him of the peace that was his due. And to this effect: (*a*) he is not lying (vs. 4; cf. 6:28), nor will he be either cajoled or browbeaten into agreeing with them (vs. 5); (*b*) he is guiltless, so help him God (vs. 6; cf. vs. 6*a* with 2:9; Luther translates vs. 6*b*, "My conscience bites me not in respect of my whole life" [7]). True enough, as the Exeg. points out, the old self-centered confidence seems here as unshaken as ever. It is grimly, categorically, and insistently avowed: my **right**, . . . my **soul**, . . . my **breath**, . . . my **nostrils**; my **lips**, . . . my **tongue**, . . . my **integrity**, . . . my **righteousness**, . . . my **heart**, . . . my **days** (see Expos. on 23:10). Yet it must have something of what James Strahan calls heroic egoism. Says he:

[7] Quoted in Davidson and Lanchester, *Job*, p. 218.

Job is bribed by the promises, and bullied by the threats, of his friends to make confession of sin; he has the orthodox sentiment of a nation against him; and his body is wasted by disease. The temptation to see what can be done by humility is almost irresistible. But with a solemn oath—as if he required to do himself some violence—he flings it from him. . . . He will never purchase human, nor even divine, favour by forgoing his integrity, renouncing his righteousness—an act of insincerity by which he would corrupt his conscience, destroy his manhood, and—strangest thought of all—incur the wrath of God.[8]

(Cf. Expos. on 1:6-12; 8:20-22; 9:14-19; 13:1-12; 17:9.) With reference to all *quid pro quo* religion (see Expos. on 21:7-18; 31:2-4), note the words, "The temptation to see what can be done by humility."

7-12. *What Are the Facts?*—If this passage (with the exception of vss. 11-12) is attributed

[8] *The Book of Job* (2nd ed.; Edinburgh: T. & T. Clark, 1914), p. 225. Used by permission.

he that riseth up against me as the unright-eous.	and let him that rises up against me be as the unrighteous.
8 For what *is* the hope of the hypocrite, though he hath gained, when God taketh away his soul?	8 For what is the hope of the godless when God cuts him off, when God takes away his life?
9 Will God hear his cry when trouble cometh upon him?	9 Will God hear his cry, when trouble comes upon him?
10 Will he delight himself in the Al-mighty? will he always call upon God?	10 Will he take delight in the Almighty? Will he call upon God at all times?
11 I will teach you by the hand of God: *that* which *is* with the Almighty will I not conceal.	11 I will teach you concerning the hand of God; what is with the Almighty I will not conceal.
12 Behold, all ye yourselves have seen *it;* why then are ye thus altogether vain?	12 Behold, all of you have seen it yourselves; why then have you become altogether vain?

of Job, and they assign it to one of his interlocutors, preferably Zophar, who does not speak a third time according to the state in which the poem has now been preserved in the extant Hebrew MSS and versions. It is argued that these verses cannot be ascribed to Job because they imply that he is again reconciled with God and has recaptured his ancient trust, and this is held to be irreconcilable with his previous (27:2) and sub-sequent (30:20, 23; 31:35-37) pronouncements. Vss. 7-10, however, do not at all indicate such a reconciliation. Without forcing the text, the interpreter may easily consider this passage as the sequence of vss. 2-6, and especially as the transition to vss. 11-12 (which must be ascribed to the hero, since they are addressed to a plural audience). Let us trace the probable line of thought. Job once again has declared himself to be utterly innocent (vss. 5-6). In the concrete style of the ancient Near East he declares himself opposed to **the wicked, the unrighteous** (vs. 7), and especially to the *ḥānēph* or **godless** man (vs. 8a). He vigorously separates himself from such classes of men. As in 13:16, when he had said, "This will be my salvation, that a godless man [*ḥānēph*] shall not come before [God]," he declares that he cannot be accused of sin and therefore must not be confused with criminals. To be sure, there is a difference between this mood and that of utter skepticism as previously expressed (cf. especially 24:12c). He no longer states that God refuses to listen to any prayer. He now says that God does not hear the cry of the godless. The chief point of his argument seems to be this: How can the friends advise him to implore God when they maintain at the same time that he is a sinner?

11-12. These verses are probably the introduction of a development which is now lost. Job launches upon a new description of God's immoral behavior. He will **teach** his friends, he will **not conceal** a truth which they themselves know by experience: **Behold, all of you have seen it yourselves** (vs. 12a). Why do they ignore those facts of universal observation? **Why then have you become altogether vain?** (Vs. 12b.) Indeed, the reader expects to find here another of Job's discourses on the themes of God's silence, the suffering of the just, or the prosperity of the wicked. The verses which follow (vss. 13-23), however, restate the old dogma of individual and collective retribution. The only possible con-clusion is to conjecture that Job's original discourse was editorially censored and replaced

to Bildad or Zophar, as some suggest, it is to be understood as part of another straightforward delineation of the fate of the ungodly. In the mouth of Job (see Exeg.) it is another attempt to get at the real facts (see Expos. on 12:2-6; 21:5-6; cf. 18:21). After vehemently dissociating himself from the wicked (vs. 7), Job points out a glaring inconsistency in what the friends have been saying. The *non sequitur* appears in 22:5-20, 21-30. Why hope for recovery, when for his ilk there is no hope? Why pray, when God pays no heed to such as he? In the hour of death (vs. 8), in the day of **trouble** (vs. 9), all the life long of the **godless** man, there is no sanctu-

13 This *is* the portion of a wicked man with God, and the heritage of oppressors, *which* they shall receive of the Almighty.

14 If his children be multiplied, *it is* for the sword: and his offspring shall not be satisfied with bread.

15 Those that remain of him shall be buried in death: and his widows shall not weep.

16 Though he heap up silver as the dust, and prepare raiment as the clay;

17 He may prepare *it*, but the just shall put *it* on, and the innocent shall divide the silver.

18 He buildeth his house as a moth, and as a booth *that* the keeper maketh.

19 The rich man shall lie down, but he shall not be gathered: he openeth his eyes, and he *is* not.

20 Terrors take hold on him as waters, a tempest stealeth him away in the night.

21 The east wind carrieth him away, and he departeth: and as a storm hurleth him out of his place.

13 "This is the portion of a wicked man with God,
  and the heritage which oppressors receive from the Almighty:
14 If his children are multiplied, it is for the sword;
  and his offspring have not enough to eat.
15 Those who survive him the pestilence buries,
  and their widows make no lamentation.
16 Though he heap up silver like dust,
  and pile up clothing like clay;
17 he may pile it up, but the just will wear it,
  and the innocent will divide the silver.
18 The house which he builds is like a spider's web,*a*
  like a booth which a watchman makes.
19 He goes to bed rich, but will do so no more;*b*
  he opens his eyes, and his wealth is gone.
20 Terrors overtake him like a flood;
  in the night a whirlwind carries him off.
21 The east wind lifts him up and he is gone;
  it sweeps him out of his place.

a Cn Compare Gk Syr: Heb *He builds his house like the moth*
b Gk Compare Syr: Heb *shall not be gathered*

by a section borrowed from what was at first the third discourse of Zophar who, as has already been observed, does not in the present text speak a third time (see Intro., p. 888).

4. Third Discourse of Zophar and Job's Reply ([24:18-24?] 27:13-23 [?])
a) Fate of the Wicked Man's Sons (27:13-23)

13-23. The portion of a wicked man with God is not described in the immediately following verses, which deal with the fate of "his sons" (vs. 14*a*) and of **those who survive him** (vs. 15*a*). It is therefore probable that vs. 13*a* is not the introduction to this passage but rather the conclusion of another, which may very well be 24:18-24 (see

ary. Face up to it? How can anyone help facing up to it? God is—and there the editor could stomach no more (see Exeg. on vss. 11-12).

13-23. Zophar.— (For the introductory portion of Zophar's third speech see 24:18-21, 24.) Swiftly are the wicked carried off on the flood (see Expos. on 20:29); all that they possess is accursed, no man treads out their wine; as the sun burns up the freshets of the spring, so Sheol snatches them away, and they are forgotten, their "wickedness . . . broken like a tree"

(24:20)—even they that batten on the "childless" and the "widow." Here they are today, high and lifted up; tomorrow, mown down and withered (24:24; see Expos. on 20:4-11). This is their lot (cf. 20:29) and their heritage (27:13). And for their children (cf. 21:11), sword, famine, pestilence—unburied bodies in the dust (vss. 14-15). Their wealth **the innocent . . . divide**; their house is but a **spider's web**, a frail lodging in the night. Between dusk and dawn—poverty or death, cataracts of terror, whirlwinds

22 For *God* shall cast upon him, and not spare: he would fain flee out of his hand.

23 *Men* shall clap their hands at him, and shall hiss him out of his place.

28 Surely there is a vein for the silver, and a place for gold *where* they fine *it.*

22 It[c] hurls at him without pity;
    he flees from its[d] power in headlong
      flight.

23 It[c] claps its[d] hands at him,
    and hisses at him from its[d] place.

28 "Surely there is a mine for silver,
    and a place for gold which they
      refine.

c Or *he* (that is God)
d Or *his*

Exeg., *ad loc.*). Those two fragments are today commonly ascribed to Zophar, who in the present text is deprived of a third discourse. This conjecture receives strong support from the fact that not only the ideas, but also the language and style, show the same characteristics as Zophar's. Vs. 13 is closely similar to an undisputed instance of Zophar's manner (20:29), and at least two passages in the fragment now under discussion evince Zophar's rhetorical habits (cf. vs. 20 with 20:25, 28 and vs. 21 with 20:23).

b) Job's Reply to Zophar's Third Discourse [?]

Inasmuch as the poetic discussion presents a threefold cycle and the poet offers a structural pattern which reveals complete mastery and skill, it is reasonable to conjecture that Job originally made a reply to the third discourse of Zophar (see Intro., p. 888). In all likelihood the editor who has placed the latter's utterances in the mouth of the hero is also responsible for deleting Job's reply, probably because it contained statements too shocking for a pious Jewish audience. In its stead the text now includes the "Hymn on Wisdom" (ch. 28).

E. Hymn on Wisdom (28:1-28)

There can be little doubt that this magnificent poem on the inaccessibility of wisdom to man does not belong to the discourses of Job (see Intro., p. 888). It is not written in his style; it is not connected with the Joban context (either 27:2-6 or 29:1 ff.); if Job had uttered it, the rebuke of Yahweh to him (chs. 38–41) would be either considerably weakened or even completely uncalled for. Some critics incline toward the opinion that one of the friends may have been the speaker, and it must be admitted that there is some argument in favor of this view. Bildad has spoken of the omnipotence of God in heaven, on earth, and in the underworld (25:2-6; 26:5-14); and the author of the hymn likewise is making a quest in all the parts of the cosmos in an effort to find wisdom. Zophar in his first discourse has shown that man cannot "find out the deep things of God" (11:7), and he wishes that the secrets of wisdom were revealed to Job (11:6). However, the link, if it exists, is of the most tenuous nature. Actually Zophar in ch. 11 is not speaking of wisdom in the same sense as that of the poet of the hymn;

---

of calamity. Heaven has no pity. It jeers and hisses as they flee.

22-23. Cause for Rejoicing.— (See Expos. on 4:8; 8:11-19; 15:17-35; 20:1-29; 22:12-20.) Eliphaz hints at the rejoicing of the righteous (22:19), but nobody is so full of glee as Zophar. His delight in the fate of the wicked is wild and cosmic. Job has felt himself driven to think of God as evil, even as deliberately malicious (9:30-31; 10:13); Zophar's God is worse (see Expos. on 14:13; 16:19; 17:3; 19:6; Luke 15:7).

[?]. **Job.**— (See Exeg.) It is not uncommon to regard Job's "peroration" (29:1–31:40), or

parts of it, as his final reply, though it assumes the form of a monologue, after the manner of the soliloquy in ch. 3. The pattern of the cycles would seem to call for a direct answer at this point to the accusations of the friends (as in 27:1-6; 29:1-25; 31:1-40; yet see Exeg. on 29:1–31:40). In any event, what we have in ch. 28 is an insertion, possibly displaced from the original position, but more than possibly composed by the original poet himself.

28:1-28. The Place of Understanding.—It would be interesting and instructive to trace through the whole book the foregleams of that

2 Iron is taken out of the earth, and brass | 2 Iron is taken out of the earth,
is molten *out of* the stone. | and copper is smelted from the ore.

3 He setteth an end to darkness, and | 3 Men put an end to darkness,
searcheth out all perfection: the stones of | and search out to the farthest bound
darkness, and the shadow of death. | the ore in gloom and deep darkness.

for he has in mind the cognitive virtue of introspection which God may impart to some men in order to help them understand the meaning of their own situation as well as discover a sense of responsibility and, if the case need be, of guilt (11:6); whereas the poet of the hymn affirms that wisdom is possessed by God alone and is never placed at the disposal of man. One might perhaps entertain the hypothesis that one of the friends is singing an ancient hymn which does not exactly represent his own views—the words of hymns do not always fully or adequately express the singers' creed—but which might at least inspire a humble and reverent kind of agnosticism in the rebellious, proudly certain, and innocence-protesting hero. As it now stands, it provides a musical interlude between the poetic discussion properly speaking (chs. 4–27) and Job's peroration (chs. 29–31). It also foretells in some subtle way the thesis which is unfolded in the discourses of Yahweh (chs. 38–41), and it seems to signify that both Job and his friends have made vain claims to discern the ways of God with men.

It must furthermore be observed that several details of the hymn are closely paralleled in the discourses of Yahweh: (*a*) An Egyptian atmosphere is unmistakable in both pieces; the mines of 28:1-11 are in all probability those of the Sinaitic peninsula, especially those of the Wadi Maghâra and of Serabit el-Khadim, which were exploited by the Egyptians; while there is no mention of mines in chs. 38–41, we find there several Egyptian motifs, such as the descriptions of the crocodile and the hippopotamus (chs. 40–41); (*b*) the association of "the deep" and "the sea" (28:14) reappears in 38:16; (*c*) more specifically, the unusual idiom, בני־שחץ, "the sons of pride," in the sense of "proud beasts" (28:8), is found again in 41:34 (Hebrew 41:26); (*d*) the rare expression, ודרך לחזיז קלות, "and a way for the lightning of the thunder" (28:26*b, sic*) is found identically in 38:25*b*; (*e*) the peculiar phrase, תחת־כל־השמים, "under all the skies" (28:24), occurs also in 41:11 (Hebrew 41:3); (*f*) the whole passage on the control of God over the wind, the waters, the rain, and the lightning (28:25-27) finds its equivalent in 38:7 ff. (cf. Dhorme, *Le livre de Job*, p. lxxvi). In view of all these facts, one can affirm with a reasonable degree of certitude that the poet of the hymn is also the poet of the discourses of Yahweh, and probably, therefore, the author of the major part of the book (see Intro., pp. 891-92). The hymn divides itself into three parts: (*a*) man digs underground but cannot find wisdom (vss. 1-13); (*b*) the deep and the sea do not know wisdom (vss. 14-22); (*c*) God alone understands the way to wisdom (vss. 23-28).

1. Scientific Technique Fails to Find Wisdom (28:1-13)

28:1-13. The achievements of man are truly stupendous, especially in the domain of what might be called technology. He needs metals, like **silver, gold, iron,** and **copper** (vss. 1-2), and he knows where to find them. He crawls even inside the bowels of the

dawn which all along is trying to break through the black darkness of Job's soul (see Expos. on 3:23; 7:11; 9:30-35; 10:8-12; 12:13-19; 14:14; 16:19; 19:7, 25). Is he beginning to understand as never before the mysteries of godliness (see Expos. on 21:7-18; 31:2-4; Luke 19:8)? He knows now, with a dreadful knowledge, that there is a good to be had; but it is not the kind of good he thought (see Expos. on 1:6-12). If only he can have again some fellowship with the God who fashioned him! It will not be what it used to be.

It will be dissociated from much that once seemed bound up with it. It will be a queer mixture of things: sunshine and shadow, rough places and smooth, joy and sorrow, tears and laughter. They will all have their place: the tree by the rivers of water, the lamb among wolves; maybe wealth, maybe poverty; maybe peace, surely struggle; a glory somewhere, a conflict everywhere. Eugene O'Neill in *Days Without End* [9] has his hero fall down at last

[9] New York: Random House, 1934.

4 The flood breaketh out from the inhabitant; *even the waters* forgotten of the foot: they are dried up, they are gone away from men.

5 *As for* the earth, out of it cometh bread: and under it is turned up as it were fire.

6 The stones of it *are* the place of sapphires: and it hath dust of gold.

7 *There is* a path which no fowl knoweth, and which the vulture's eye hath not seen:

8 The lion's whelps have not trodden it, nor the fierce lion passed by it.

9 He putteth forth his hand upon the rock; he overturneth the mountains by the roots.

10 He cutteth out rivers among the rocks; and his eye seeth every precious thing.

4 They open shafts in a valley away from
    where men live;
  they are forgotten by travelers,
  they hang afar from men, they swing
    to and fro.

5 As for the earth, out of it comes bread;
  but underneath it is turned up as by
    fire.

6 Its stones are the place of sapphires,*e*
  and it has dust of gold.

7 "That path no bird of prey knows,
  and the falcon's eye has not seen it.

8 The proud beasts have not trodden it;
  the lion has not passed over it.

9 "Man puts his hand to the flinty rock,
  and overturns mountains by the roots.

10 He cuts out channels in the rocks,
  and his eye sees every precious thing.

e Or *lapis lazuli*

---

earth, he surmounts difficulties of all kinds, he courts mortal dangers to achieve his aim (vss. 3-4). For the sake of obtaining **sapphires** and **dust of gold,** he goes to places unknown to piercing-eyed birds or beasts (vss. 7-8). Neither the hardness of the task nor the colossal dimensions of the enterprise prevent him from reaching his goal (vss. 9-10). He is able even to divert streams to forestall the flooding of mines (vs. 11). Nothing in the material realm is impossible to him. Now the poet is ready for the first question (which will be repeated as a melancholy or satirical refrain in vs. 20), **But where shall wisdom be found? and where is the place of understanding?** (vs. 12). The two words *ḥokhmāh* and *bînāh,* **wisdom** and **understanding,** come in pairs in the sapiential literature (cf. Prov. 1:2; 4:1; etc.). They are here used synonymously, although the former probably refers more specifically to a science which is transmitted within learned circles, while the latter designates more precisely the ability to discern, weigh, judge, criticize, and therefore prepare an intelligent decision. The poet, however, is no ordinary wise man. He is a theologian who has graduated from the schools of international wisdom and has gone beyond their presuppositions or their findings. He has lost confidence in man's ability to learn how to live through a didactic or an empirical method. He contrasts man's capacity to conquer nature with man's inability to behave in accordance with his newly won power. The kind of wisdom he has in mind is not handed down through the

---

in front of a crucifix and pour out his heart in anguish for a sick wife. The peril of that prayer was that she got well. Religion is not for that. One prays desperately for some dear desire and takes the fulfillment as a token of God's love. It may well be, or may not. But Paul prayed too, and desperately, about a thorn in his flesh (II Cor. 12:7-9). And God loved him too. To stand then on the perilous edge of things, and be God's man for weal or woe—who cares, if something of the eternal splendor comes to dwell in his face?

But there is another foregleam of the dawn that is breaking. At the precise moment of his

own direst need Job is learning, as he had never known it before, the role that human compassion plays in human life. He has not been lacking in sympathy (ch. 31); but as Blake would seem to indicate (Illustration V depicts even at 30:25 a left-handed charity; see Expos. on 30:25), one has the feeling that his largess had been dealt out in the fear of the Almighty (31:23) from a kind of dais lifted above the common herd, was in very fact a giving of bounty to those with whom the giver had never sat, whose hunger had never gnawed at him, for whose tears he had shed none of his own. Not so now. His piteous cries for tenderness, for the warmth

11 He bindeth the floods from overflowing; and *the thing that is* hid bringeth he forth to light.
12 But where shall wisdom be found? and where *is* the place of understanding?
13 Man knoweth not the price thereof; neither is it found in the land of the living.
14 The depth saith, It *is* not in me: and the sea saith, It *is* not with me.
15 It cannot be gotten for gold, neither shall silver be weighed *for* the price thereof.
16 It cannot be valued with the gold of Ophir, with the precious onyx, or the sapphire.

11 He binds up the streams so that they do not trickle,
and the thing that is hid he brings forth to light.

12 "But where shall wisdom be found?
And where is the place of understanding?
13 Man does not know the way to it,*f*
and it is not found in the land of the living.
14 The deep says, 'It is not in me,'
and the sea says, 'It is not with me.'
15 It cannot be gotten for gold,
and silver cannot be weighed as its price.
16 It cannot be valued in the gold of Ophir,
in precious onyx or sapphire.*g*

f Gk: Heb *its price*
g Or *lapis lazuli*

tradition of erudite teachers. It is not obtained by observation or even experience. It is a capacity to live and to fulfill human destiny which transcends man's natural endowments.

> Man does not know the way to it,
> and it is not found in the land of the living (vs. 13).

The poet is a pessimist about man, and he separates himself deliberately from all humanist optimists. He no longer believes that the secret of living lies within man's reach, at the disposal of man on this earth, accessible to an unaided, independent, autonomous, human being. Yet his pessimism is not his last word. It is merely a step in his adventure toward the truth which he intends to impart.

2. Religious Technique Is Equally Futile (28:14-22)

14-22. Since *homo faber* is unable by himself to become *homo sapiens,* is there no method whereby to approach and unlock the secret of human existence? Where will man turn in his anxiety to find a secure, enduring, and wholly satisfying fulfillment? He will ask *tehôm,* **the deep,** and *yām,* **the sea** (vs. 14). Is this merely a poetic adornment, or does the poet refer by these words to the cultic practices of ancient Egyptian and Semitic polytheism? The exegete is unable to find in the text a clear demonstration of the latter hypothesis, but an inquiry into the purposes of the poet makes it likely. Here is universal man—not the member of the Hebrew covenant—in search of something greater and far more important than the golden fleece or the philosopher's stone. He is willing to pay an immense price for its purchase. Since the conquest of the natural world, expensive as

of a friend's presence, for the gentleness of a friend's understanding, that longing for some man who might look into his eyes and know all that was behind them (see Expos. on 6:14, 18, 28-30), that longing for God which was like thirst to parched lips—will he forget it in days to come? Will there be scars now on every gift of his hand, the print of passion on his face, as there was on that other face which looking down on Jerusalem wept over it? Life calls not

for sentiment, lofty though it may be, but for costly human compassion, making its way deliberately and with reverence into the center of another's condition, and bowing its head there. Wrongs are not righted by distant chatter, or by the finger tips of charity. They are righted by yearning hearts and steadfast journeys.

Is there even more? Is Job learning, or beginning to learn, the answer to the poet's question: **Where shall wisdom be found? and where**

17 The gold and the crystal cannot equal it: and the exchange of it *shall not be for* jewels of fine gold.

18 No mention shall be made of coral, or of pearls: for the price of wisdom *is* above rubies.

19 The topaz of Ethiopia shall not equal it, neither shall it be valued with pure gold.

20 Whence then cometh wisdom? and where *is* the place of understanding?

21 Seeing it is hid from the eyes of all living, and kept close from the fowls of the air.

22 Destruction and death say, We have heard the fame thereof with our ears.

---

17 Gold and glass cannot equal it,
   nor can it be exchanged for jewels of
      fine gold.
18 No mention shall be made of coral or of
      crystal;
   the price of wisdom is above pearls.
19 The topaz of Ethiopia cannot compare
      with it,
   nor can it be valued in pure gold.

20 "Whence then comes wisdom?
   And where is the place of understand-
      ing?
21 It is hid from the eyes of all living,
   and concealed from the birds of the air.
22 Abaddon and Death say,
   'We have heard a rumor of it with our
      ears.'

---

it is, remains of no avail, he will use that conquest, or the fruits thereof, to pursue his quest. He will turn to the cults and rites which from immemorial ages have channeled the efforts of man courting the infinite. The poet was not ignorant of the importance of religious practices in the ancient Near East. He knew what an immense amount of energy and treasure, such as **gold, silver, onyx, sapphire, coral, crystal, pearls, topaz** (vss. 15-19), was devoted to the exercise of piety, from Mesopotamia to the valley of the Nile and throughout the Fertile Crescent. It may therefore not be a literary accident that the mention of **the deep** and **the sea** (vs. 14) is followed immediately by the list of precious metals and stones (vss. 15-19). The forces of the abyss and of the primeval ocean were not only personified but also deified. Ancient man worshiped them as divine beings, and in a ceaseless effort to secure their favor and to obtain stability upon the earth he consecrated to the deities of the great abyss, under many names and circumlocutions, fabulous riches. He spent in their honor incommensurable hoards of wealth not only for the erection and ornamentation of shrines, but also for the seasonal celebrations of festive pageantry and ritual. Man paid a heavy price in order to commune with the universal forces or to be protected from them. Quite naturally man might ask of them the coveted prize—wisdom! He might seek access even to the deities of the underworld, **Abaddon** and **Death**. There may be a touch of irony in the fact that while **the deep** and **the sea** categorically reply to the seeker of wisdom, **It is not in me, ... it is not with me** (vs. 14), **Abaddon** and **Death** tantalizingly but elusively declare, **We have heard a rumor**

---

is the place of understanding? Certainly there is little in the Bible which is lovelier than this poem—far more than a grandiose nature poem —or more exquisitely wrought out. Jastrow calls it "one of the most impressive bits of literature in the entire Old Testament." [1] Wisdom, it says, that wisdom which is behind all created things, is not hidden in the earth, that men might dig for it, as they dig for silver and iron. Here is the mine where they are at work: man **setteth an end to darkness,** delving away into its farthest recesses with his shafts and his lamp. There is he **forgotten of the foot** that passes by; he hangs far from the crowd, swing-

[1] *Job*, p. 70.

ing to and fro. **He putteth forth his hand upon the rock** (vs. 9), while above him grows the harvest (vs. 5), and the birds fly (vs. 7), and the lions prowl (vs. 8; vss. 7-8 may be out of place, and mean that wisdom is beyond the ken of birds and beasts; relocate after vs. 12[?]; cf. vs. 21).

He binds up the streams so that they do not trickle, and the thing that is hid he brings forth to light.

But **wisdom?** It is back of the universe and beyond. The deep saith, **It is not in me: and the sea saith, It is not with me.** Death and Destruction say, **We have heard a rumor of it with our ears** (vs. 22). It is not to be found of those

23 God understandeth the way thereof, and he knoweth the place thereof.	23 "God understands the way to it, and he knows its place.
24 For he looketh to the ends of the earth, *and* seeth under the whole heaven;	24 For he looks to the ends of the earth, and sees everything under the heavens.
25 To make the weight for the winds; and he weigheth the waters by measure.	25 When he gave to the wind its weight, and meted out the waters by measure;
26 When he made a decree for the rain, and a way for the lightning of the thunder;	26 when he made a decree for the rain, and a way for the lightning of the thunder;
27 Then did he see it, and declare it; he prepared it, yea, and searched it out.	27 then he saw it and declared it; he established it, and searched it out.

of it with our ears (vs. 22). Religious techniques, as well as scientific achievements, are futile of themselves in the domain which matters most for human existence.

3. God Alone Understands the Way to Wisdom (28:23-28)

23-28. When all human efforts have failed, and only then, is man ready to come to himself and to acknowledge that the God who created the cosmos and remains still "the faithful Creator" (vss. 24-26), **understands the way to [wisdom] and . . . knows its place** (vs. 23). For wisdom is the supreme possession of God. The poet does not say that God created it (cf. Prov. 8:22-31; Ecclus. 1:9), but he insists in his climactic verse that God, at the moment of his creative activity, took cognizance of its reality:

> then he saw it and declared it:
> he established it, and searched it out (vs. 27).

A careful progression is observed in the succession of the verbs used here: God first perceives the existence of wisdom (ראה) and thereupon he measures it and computes its significance (ספר); then, after he has tested its value, he fixes and settles it, or sets it up, thereby ensuring its stability and its duration (הכין); finally he scrutinizes and explores it to its ultimate consequences (חקר).

Most commentators think that the hymn originally ended with vs. 27, for they maintain that here the word *ḥokhmāh* designates a metaphysical type of wisdom, hypostatized and divine, which remains forever inaccessible to finite man, whereas vs. 28 refers to practical wisdom, a way of life fully accessible to man, which is summed up in the twofold program, **the fear of the Lord,** and **to depart from evil.**

This exegetical position may very well be correct. It is true, in addition, that the word אדני, **the Lord,** is not found elsewhere in the book of Job. Nevertheless a case may be made for the thesis of the inevitability and therefore the authenticity of vs. 28. What

who pour out their treasure in the market place or to the gods (see Exeg.). **It cannot be gotten for gold** or silver, onyx or **sapphire** (lapis lazuli; its appearance is referred to in vs. 6b) or glass (a precious thing grown common, not elsewhere directly referred to in the O.T.). **God** alone **understandeth the way thereof,** it is he that **knoweth its place** (vs. 23). From the beginning of time he knoweth it, measureth it, exploreth it, God and none other. As for man, never shall he know it as God knows it. All that he may have in its stead is **the fear of the Lord.** For him, **the fear of the Lord, that is wisdom** (see Exeg.). Do these verses then belong precisely where they are? Were they written or inserted by some-	body who knew where to put them? They are not the words of Job. They are the words of one who looks on, who has listened to everything that has been said, and understands. They are set here now at the end of the long debate, face to face with the impenetrable mystery of the divine. Is Job learning that? Is he learning that there is no "answer" to what he asks, no grasp of eternal principles, not with men, only with God? Is he learning that for him the only thing which can supply the place of an "answer" is the fear of the Lord, the love and the awe— not the "simple, homely piety" of which Strahan speaks [2]—that could be like balm to his anguished soul? Is the only answer—God? [2] *Job*, p. 239.

28 And unto man he said, Behold, the fear of the Lord, that *is* wisdom; and to depart from evil *is* understanding.	28 And he said to man,
	   'Behold, the fear of the Lord, that is wisdom;
	   and to depart from evil is understanding.' "

is the fear of the Lord? Is it merely an easy and familiar obedience to the rules of piety? And what is the avoidance of evil? Is it merely an easy and familiar obedience to the rules of ethics? In other words, is man able to obtain wisdom? If so, this wisdom is not the divine knowledge which belongs only to the Creator of the cosmos, but a practical attitude of human behavior. If such is the case, there is an irreducible discrepancy between vss. 24-27 and vs. 28. Yet two observations must be made. (*a*) The hymn begins with man's quest for wisdom, and the two refrains (vss. 12, 20) stress the fact that he cannot find it by his own endeavor. This stress does not mean that the reality he is pursuing is a divine, hypostatized wisdom, but only that wisdom is the possession of God, and that God therefore is free to dispense it to whomever he pleases. (*b*) Again, the wisdom of vs. 28 is not the result of an achievement of man. It may elude his grasp as much as the wisdom of vss. 24-27. How can man truly fear his Creator and truly depart from evil? The question remains unanswered. That is precisely the motif of the whole book. The hero claims that he is able to reach human perfection precisely in terms of utter devotion to the divine and of freedom from evil (1:1). The poet, however, slowly takes his audience into his confidence and prepares them to hear Job's discovery of a need for repentance (42:6). In the light of the total theme the exegete may well maintain that **man** in vs. 28 is unable to discover wisdom precisely because its price—the perfect fulfillment of the law—remains beyond his reach.

The choral interlude bears the reader aloft and subtly prepares him for the higher level of the theophany (38:1–42:6).

28. Man's True Wisdom.—Job's was a troubled soul; and that is worse than a sick body. There was no use "going to the shore," as we might advise, with shallow mind. He was not looking for "a complete rest, with plenty of salt air, and good, wholesome food." For what ailed him, he needed wisdom. He could scrape his boils, but he could not still the tumult within or appease the deepest hunger of his being. The man who goes to the shore has to take the tumult and the hunger with him. During a week or two at high prices he discovers that the ceaseless roll of the waves comes curling in on the beach only to slither back again in a dismal sort of futility—the twentieth-century equivalent, no doubt, of that profounder futility of which the poet spoke, "The sea saith, It is not in me" (see Exeg.). Perhaps after a while he begins to wonder why people are so often passionately intent on treating sick bodies when it is the sick soul that needs treatment.

Take one or two modern "problems," modern only in the sense that so many of them have been given modern names. They are all as old as the hills, and just as real as mumps or measles, with a fatality curve that makes appendicitis and pneumonia look now like innocent bystanders. *Fear:* What was done yesterday was almost certainly the wrong thing. Something else would have been better. What has to be done tomorrow will turn out to be impossible. There is no doubt about it. And always the job. Perhaps illness. *Frustration:* The might-have-been, if it had not been for—whatever it was! Hemmed in by circumstances, and making up for it by being offensive. *Conflict:* The evil at war with the good, the real with the ideal, hopes for the future with the failures of the past—all of it slipping down into the subconscious and raising its mischief out of sight. There is little profit to be had out of trying to forget about it, or playing golf, or occupying oneself with something else.

Canst thou not minister to a mind diseased;
Pluck from the memory a rooted sorrow;
Raze out the written troubles of the brain
And with some sweet oblivious antidote
Cleanse the stuff'd bosom of that perilous stuff
Which weighs upon the heart? [3]

The author of Job, whoever he was, far back on the other side of the centuries, was sure that the process had to begin in the place which he called "the place of understanding." No psychologist has ever got any farther. As we ap-

[3] Shakespeare, *Macbeth*, Act V, scene 3.

29 Moreover Job continued his parable, and said,

29 And Job again took up his discourse, and said:

F. JOB'S PERORATION (29:1–31:40)

Some commentators maintain that Job in chs. 29–30 addresses the friends and perhaps even makes the missing reply to the third discourse of Zophar (see above, p. 1099). Such does not appear to be the case, for the hero is here summing up his past and present, and he depicts his own situation in a way not paralleled elsewhere in the extant parts of the third cycle. In fact every element of chs. 29–30, as well as each detail of ch. 31, shows that the debate is over. Job does not once speak to the friends in the second person plural, as he customarily does throughout the rhetorical exchange (see 27:5 ff.). He does not even utter one phrase for the friends' ears, or one word which might be construed as answering their arguments. Just as the discussion began with a soliloquy (ch. 3), it ends with a monologue, destined to emphasize the hero's dereliction. He rises above the level of disputation. He ignores his interlocutors as useless. He is alone.

Before Job completes his oration and returns to silence he recollects his former happiness (29:1-25), contrasts it with his present misery (30:1-31), and makes his final oath of clearance (31:1-40).

1. REMEMBERING HAPPIER THINGS (29:1-25)

With the sure touch which only a great artist possesses, the poet lets his hero reflect upon the days which are no more. Thus the nomadic ideal of quiet happiness, social

---

proach the climax of the book, God himself will move over into the picture, and the hope and despair which have been making of Job's soul a battlefield will lay down their arms. **The fear of the Lord, that is wisdom.** And over the poor, scarred life that has been lifting its face to heaven, will spread, like the dawn of a clear day, the peace of God.

Leslie Weatherhead in *Psychology in Service of the Soul* [4] has told of a young girl who came to him on the verge of a nervous breakdown. Natural love for a friend and acquired hate had set her soul in opposite camps until Christ's answer to Peter's question was whispered back, "seventy times seven" (Matt. 18:22), and the ugly chapter in her life came to an end. Knowledge of self, forgiveness, courage, strength, these are "the mighty gifts" of God—when instead of merely looking at the idea of his presence, the mind is allowed to receive it. This sounds easy. But there is nothing easy about it. Desultory prayers, idle reading between the covers of a family Bible, singing hymns, running after cults that gather in hotel ballrooms—none of it will do. Doors have to be thrown open. Who can swing them back on their rusty hinges? Nature can be conquered, but who can conquer self? Flags have to be run down. Swords have to be surrendered. **To depart from evil is understanding.** Can anyone manage, unaided and alone? A lifeboat was launched one day on pounding seas from the "Washington." It pulled toward five men who were clinging to a wrecked plane.

[4] New York: The Macmillan Co., 1930, p. 11.

There was a call for volunteers to swim the remaining distance with a line. Two of the sailors were out of the boat on the instant, plowing through the waves. In moments of high devotion, the preacher tells us—devotion of body, mind, or soul—there is little time left for

> that perilous stuff
> Which weighs upon the heart.

But are moments enough when what is at stake is lifelong? Read John 14:15-27. Then, with Calvary past, hear the risen Christ, "As my Father hath sent me, even so send I you" (John 20:21; cf. Matt. 13:46).

29:1-25. Sorrow's Crown of Sorrow.—The unrequited lover in Tennyson's "Locksley Hall" would make an interesting character study. A psychologist could hardly avoid such words as sadism, masochism, projection, egocentrism, etc. Certainly the hero is much given to sentimental brooding and self-pity. Why should "sorrow's crown of sorrow" be "remembering happier things"? Strahan [5] cites Boethius, Dante, and Chaucer. What they have to say, one by one, may be paraphrased somewhat as follows: "In every misfortune the worst is to have been happy once." "There is no greater woe than in wretchedness to recall times of felicity." "Fortune's sharpest adversity is to have the halcyon days of old keep running through the mind when all of them are gone." But why? Why not in the shadow remember the sunlight as a bless-

[5] *Job*, p. 242.

2 Oh that I were as *in* months past, as *in* the days *when* God preserved me;	2 "Oh, that I were as in the months of old, as in the days when God watched over me;

responsibility, and gracious nobility, is re-created in a page which has no equal in, or perhaps outside, the Bible. To state that Job was a model of manhood (1:1, 8) is far easier than so to describe him. Yet this is precisely what the poet has succeeded in achieving. Still more, he has made his hero offer a self-portrait which embodies the purest ideals of piety and morality, thus offering a convincing background for the final expression of pride—"Like a prince I would approach [God]" (31:37).

a) BOUNTIES OF GOD'S PRESENCE (29:1-6)

29:2-6. The days when God watched over me: At once we learn the origin of the hero's happiness. **The months of old** were filled with joy simply because a friendly God cared (vs. 2). His providence was like the shining of a lamp, the symbol and source of

ing? (Cf. Expos. on 1:20-22; 2:7-10.) A man whose son had died at twenty-one was asked one day by his minister, in the quietness of deep friendship, "As between having him for twenty-one years, or not having him at all, which would you have chosen if the choice had been offered you?" Must the storm cloud forever blot even the memory of the noon? (See Expos. on 3:20-21.)

In ch. 30, as in many other passages, some of the reasons appear: First, a misapprehension of the nature of God. Job had not lost him; nor, what is more important, had he lost Job (see Expos. on 28:1-28). Second, a preoccupation with self (see Expos. on 16:13). Third, a misinterpretation of the present as hopeless (see Expos. on 19:7; 30:1-31, 9-15; 31:1-40).

Sorrow's royal crown was worn on Calvary by "a man of sorrows, . . . acquainted with grief"; but the sorrow was not for himself, nor was the grief (Isa. 53:4). In prosperity Job was not unmindful of others (29:15-17); but in adversity the thought of them served only to deepen the gloom (7:1; 24:1-12). There have been those who have heard the cries of human life and responded. On a day when the news came that the social reforms he had so passionately championed had been defeated, Walter Rauschenbusch was found by his students in a classroom sitting at his desk with his head on his arms, sobbing. Instance the story of John Bright. Three days after his young wife died of tuberculosis, Richard Cobden called on him, and after some words of condolence said, "When the first paroxysm of your grief is past, I would advise you to come with me, and we will never rest till the Corn laws are repealed." "I accepted his invitation," added Bright, "and from that time we never ceased to labour hard on behalf of the resolution which we had made." [6] Or the story

of William Wilberforce and the slave trade; the Emancipation Bill, culmination of his lifework, was passed in August, 1833, a month after his death. Elizabeth Fry and prison reform, first at Newgate, then on the Continent. Florence Nightingale and her work at the Scutari barrack hospital: in February 1855, the death rate was 42 per cent; in June of the same year, 2 per cent. Recall the lines in F. W. H. Myers' *Saint Paul:*

> Only like souls I see the folk thereunder,
>   Bound who should conquer, slaves who should be
>   kings,
> Hearing their one hope with an empty wonder,
>   Sadly contented in a show of things;
>
> Then with a rush the intolerable craving
>   Shivers throughout me like a trumpet-call,
> Oh to save these! to perish for their saving,
>   Die for their life, be offered for them all! [7]

2-20. The Blessedness of the Righteous.—The poet pictures in detail and with exquisite beauty the ideal life of the righteous man. Some would say there is nothing loftier in literature, before or after the N.T. Many a commemorative tablet bears witness to the unforgettable loveliness of its phrasing (vss. 13, 15, 16). At the height of his fortunes, in the days of his maturity, remembered now with the infinite pathos of vs. 2 (cf. Expos. on 7:20a), vs. 3 (cf. 18:6), vs. 4 (cf. vs. 4b with Expos. on 3:23), and vs. 5 (see Expos. on vs. 3), Job would make his way to the city gate. At his approach **the young men** would withdraw, **the aged** would rise and stand, **the princes** would lay **their hand on their mouth** (cf. 40:4). Of all men he was blessed; for he had **delivered the poor . . . and the fatherless, . . . him that was ready to perish,** and had **caused the widow's heart to sing for joy.** He had been **eyes to the blind, . . . feet to**

6 Article "John Bright" in *Encyclopaedia Britannica;* 14th ed.; IV, 148.

7 Sts. xcii-xciii.

3 When his candle shined upon my head, *and when* by his light I walked *through* darkness;

4 As I was in the days of my youth, when the secret of God *was* upon my tabernacle;

5 When the Almighty *was* yet with me, *when* my children *were* about me;

6 When I washed my steps with butter, and the rock poured me out rivers of oil;

7 When I went out to the gate through the city, *when* I prepared my seat in the street!

---

3 when his lamp shone upon my head,
    and by his light I walked through darkness;

4 as I was in my autumn days,
    when the friendship of God was upon my tent;

5 when the Almighty was yet with me,
    when my children were about me;

6 when my steps were washed with milk,
    and the rock poured out for me streams of oil!

7 When I went out to the gate of the city,
    when I prepared my seat in the square,

---

felicity (cf. 18:5-6; 21:17). In the light of God's presence Job saw light (cf. Ps. 36:9), even while he **walked through darkness** (vs. 3). He lived then in the days of "fruit gathering": a season which for the ancient mind did not suggest the late maturity that ushers in the winter of old age, but rather the time when nature yields her increase and the early rains revive the parched soil and fill man with the energy of triumphant adulthood (RSV unfortunately suggests in the word **autumn** an idea which does not correspond with the intention of the poet).

Vs. 4b is difficult. **When the friendship of God was upon my tent** (RSV) is an attractive translation which disregards the difficulties of the text and the witness of the ancient versions. This construction of the word סוד, **secret,** "confidential and intimate circle," "familiar converse," hence **friendship** (cf. 15:8; 19:19), preceded by the preposition ב, "in," and followed by the preposition עלי, **upon,** is hardly possible. Moreover, the LXX, Symm., and the Syriac read בסוך instead of בסוד. Thus the rendering of the phrase easily becomes "when God protected my tent" (cf. 1:10). The joy of God's presence (vs. 5a) is increased as well as manifested by the playful gathering of the hero's **children** (vs. 5b; lit., "my youngsters") and the opulence of his living (vs. 6).

b) Satisfactions of Social Esteem (29:7-13)

7-13. Job not only lived in the blessing of God as it gave him health, posterity, and wealth (vss. 2-6); he also enjoyed the satisfaction of being approved by men because he

---

the lame, and **father to the poor,** searching out beyond all custom even **the cause of the stranger.** Little wonder that he expected "goodness and mercy" to follow him all the days of his life: counselor to the mighty (vss. 21-24) and friend to the weak (vs. 25c).

Observe that (a) his blessedness had its source in God. This was not the kind of philanthropy that comes of mere involvement in the common lot of humanity; cf. Sam Walter Foss's none-too-profound little poem, "The House by the Side of the Road":

Let me live in my house by the side of the road
  Where the race of men go by;
They are good, they are bad, they are weak, they are strong,
  Wise, foolish—so am I.
Then why should I sit in the scorner's seat,
  Or hurl the cynic's ban?
Let me live in my house by the side of the road
  And be a friend of man.

(b) His piety was a true piety, Godward and manward (vs. 14). The righteousness that was of God clothed itself with him (cf. Judg. 6:34); the justice that marked his dealing with others was the habit of his life, as native to him as **robe and . . . turban** (see ch. 31; Expos. on 1:1, 2-3). (c) His position carried with it not only the enjoyment of privilege but the weight of civic and social responsibility. He was the champion of the wronged and the helpless, even at danger to himself (vs. 17). He moved far beyond the natural area of kinship (vs. 16; [8] cf. Matt. 12:48, 50). Observe too the notes that are lacking: Matt. 5:4, 6, 10, 11; 11:6; 13:16; 16:17; Luke 6:21, 22; 10:23; 11:28; 19:38; John 20:29.

3. The Light that Never Fails.— (See Expos. on 25:3b.) Nothing is more evident throughout the book than this, that for Job the **light** of

[8] See I. Abrahams, "Family (Jewish)" in James Hastings, ed., *Encyclopaedia of Religion and Ethics* (New York: Charles Scribner's Sons, 1902-27), V, 741-42.

8 The young men saw me, and hid them- selves: and the aged arose, *and* stood up. 9 The princes refrained talking, and laid *their* hand on their mouth. 10 The nobles held their peace, and their tongue cleaved to the roof of their mouth. 11 When the ear heard *me,* then it blessed me; and when the eye saw *me,* it gave witness to me: 12 Because I delivered the poor that cried, and the fatherless, and *him that had* none to help him. 13 The blessing of him that was ready to perish came upon me: and I caused the widow's heart to sing for joy. 14 I put on righteousness, and it clothed me: my judgment *was* as a robe and a diadem. 15 I was eyes to the blind, and feet *was* to the lame. 16 I *was* a father to the poor: and the cause *which* I knew not I searched out.	8 the young men saw me and withdrew, and the aged rose and stood; 9 the princes refrained from talking, and laid their hand on their mouth; 10 the voice of the nobles was hushed, and their tongue cleaved to the roof of their mouth. 11 When the ear heard, it called me blessed, and when the eye saw, it approved; 12 because I delivered the poor who cried, and the fatherless who had none to help him. 13 The blessing of him who was about to perish came upon me, and I caused the widow's heart to sing for joy. 14 I put on righteousness, and it clothed me; my justice was like a robe and a turban. 15 I was eyes to the blind, and feet to the lame. 16 I was a father to the poor, and I searched out the cause of him whom I did not know.

fulfilled with ease and earnestness the civic duties which naturally fell upon him. As a seminomad, he lived under a tent during the grazing season (cf. vs. 4*b*) but settled down in a town in winter; and at **the gate of the city** (note the use of the Canaanite word קרת; cf. Prov. 8:3; 9:3; 11:11) not merely **young men** but even **the aged** behaved toward him with utmost respect (vss. 7-8). Incidentally, this trait indicates that the poet did not conceive of his hero as an old man, but rather represented him as a young adult in the full possession of his powers. Even **the princes** and **the nobles** in deference to the wisdom of his judgments and the high sincerity of his moves and motives were speechless in his presence (vss. 9-10). Job's happiness, however, did not elicit envy: his fame as a benefactor spread abroad and brought him nothing but congratulations and approval (vs. 11; the verb אשר, "to pronounce happy," is a cognate of the word אשרי used in the biblical beatitudes, Ps. 1:1; etc.).

c) Claims of Righteousness (29:14-20)

14-20. Job's harmonious family life and social pre-eminence were due to the fact that his **righteousness** belonged to him as genuinely as a well-fitting and well-worn vestment. He walked clothed in his justice as felicitously as in his **robe** and **turban** (vs. 14). His awareness of doing right with men was coupled with the certainty of living in a right relationship with God. His ethics was the flower of his religion (cf. Exeg. on 1:1). Not only was he **eyes to the blind, feet to the lame, a father to the poor,** but also he **searched out the cause of him whom** [he] **did not know** (vss. 15-16). His

God never had gone out (see Expos. on 3:23; Ps. 23:4-6). It is a light that does not always dispel the shadows; but it illumines them. Paul Tillich once said that the average sermon usually takes the following form: (*a*) We find ourselves at the moment in a very difficult situation; (*b*) the lights the world throws on it are broken lights; (*c*) the true light is Christ. Then he added, "It would be far better, and far	more biblical, to reverse the order" (see Expos. on 19:25). **15.** *Eyes to the Blind, Feet to the Lame.*—To help men see what they cannot see unaided, to help them achieve what they cannot achieve alone (see Expos. on vs. 24). Vision—of the world, of others, and of self—and power, these are key words in the epic of every soul that knows where it stands: at the point of intersec-

17 And I brake the jaws of the wicked, and plucked the spoil out of his teeth.

18 Then I said, I shall die in my nest, and I shall multiply *my* days as the sand.

19 My root *was* spread out by the waters, and the dew lay all night upon my branch.

20 My glory *was* fresh in me, and my bow was renewed in my hand.

21 Unto me *men* gave ear, and waited, and kept silence at my counsel.

22 After my words they spake not again; and my speech dropped upon them.

23 And they waited for me as for the rain; and they opened their mouth wide *as* for the latter rain.

24 *If* I laughed on them, they believed *it* not; and the light of my countenance they cast not down.

---

17 I broke the fangs of the unrighteous, and made him drop his prey from h teeth.

18 Then I thought, 'I shall die in my nest, and I shall multiply my days as th sand,

19 my roots spread out to the waters, with the dew all night on my branche

20 my glory fresh with me, and my bow ever new in my hand.'

21 "Men listened to me, and waited, and kept silence for my counsel.

22 After I spoke they did not speak again, and my word dropped upon them.

23 They waited for me as for the rain; and they opened their mouths as for th spring rain.

24 I smiled on them when they had no co fidence; and the light of my countenance the did not cast down.

---

social compassion led him to investigate the cases of oppression everywhere to the poir of risking trouble with the oppressors (vs. 17). Such an extraordinary pursuit of goo deeds led him to believe that he had earned the right to a long and happy life in th midst of his own descendants (vss. 18-20). The expression עִם־קִנִּי אֶגְוָע, **I shall die in m nest** (vs. 18*a*), is peculiar since the preposition עִם means "with," "in the company of. In addition, the ancient versions differ widely from the M.T. Although the exac meaning is doubtful, the general sense is clear enough. (It is possible that instead c **nest** and **sand** one should translate "reed" and "palm tree.") Job expected to live to a advanced age (vs. 18*b*). The comparison with a tree growing in a well-watered land is familiar one (vs. 19; cf. 8:16-17; 14:7-9; 18:16). Furthermore, a good case may be mad for the pointing of חוֹל, **sand**, as *ḥûl*, "phoenix," a word which brings a startling imag and fits the traditional idea of the **nest** in vs. 18*a*. In any case, Job hoped that even a the end of his years he would still be in full possession of his youthful energy (vs. 2(the **bow** is a symbol of manly strength; cf. Gen. 49:24; Jer. 49:35).

d) PRESTIGE OF INTEGRITY (29:21-25)

21-25. According to most modern interpreters, these verses are now displaced, fc they depict once again (as in vss. 7 ff.) the deference paid to the hero by the men c his community; and they are introduced not by nouns but by verbs in the masculin plural which presuppose the plural nouns of vss. 8-10, "the young men," "the aged," "th princes," "the nobles." (Observe that the versions insert the word **Men** at the beginnin

---

tion between the redemptive will of God and the rebellious life of man.

24. The Ministry of Faith.—If the RSV gives us the correct meaning of this obscure passage (see Exeg.), an interesting, though somewhat hazardous exposition suggests itself. One must not be misled by the patriarchal setting, but rather picture to oneself the condition of the postexilic Jews (cf. Expos. on 20:12-16). In days when uncertainty and fear lie like a pall

over the landscape we are to see a man who inner resources are unfailing (vs. 24*b*). He not merely an optimist who insists that ever cloud has its silver lining, and is ready at th drop of a hat to rip out the lining and thro the cloud away. Carlyle once accused Emerso of that kind of dishonesty; said he was like chatty fellow away up on a beach, throwing cheery word or two to poor souls battling in th great dark deeps, with the thundering billov

25 I chose out their way, and sat chief, and dwelt as a king in the army, as one *that* comforteth the mourners.	25 I chose their way, and sat as chief, and I dwelt like a king among his troops, like one who comforts mourners.
30 But now *they that are* younger than I have me in derision, whose fathers	30 "But now they make sport of me, men who are younger than I,

of vs. 21 in order to make the phrase intelligible.) In all probability vss. 21-25 should come between vs. 10 and vs. 11. As Job said that silence fell when he made his appearance at the city gate (vss. 9-10), he continues by recalling that silence was maintained as he spoke (vs. 21) and even after he had finished speaking (vs. 22), for his advice carried with it the weight of final authority. Indeed, his companions **waited for** [him] **as for the rain** (vs. 23a)—a powerful image in the ancient Near East, where life at the end of summer is at a standstill until the first thundershowers "renew the face of the soil." Job's opinions, however, were even more pregnant than the autumnal rain. They brought decision to maturity, as **the spring rain** in March or April brings the young shoots to fruition (vs. 23b). Born and accustomed to be a leader, Job restored with a smile the confidence of his colleagues whenever it wavered (vs. 24a). Such is at least the possible meaning of a difficult text (cf. RSV). It is true that the wording of the sentence seems to support the interpretation of the traditional Jewish commentators, "When I smiled at them, they did not even dare to believe it" (cf. 9:16). But vs. 24b means **and the light of my countenance they did not cast down,** and the parallelism requires complementary ideas in the two lines. In other words, Job was not only able to instill into the men of his community a spirit of confidence when they lacked it (vs. 24a), but his own serenity and power of decision were never undermined by their want of courage, vision, or faith (vs. 24b). The sequence of thought in vs. 25 confirms this exegesis. Job traced the course of his fellow citizens and they followed it faithfully. Thus he was for them more than a **chief** or a **king** (vs. 25ab): he was **like one who comforts mourners** (vs. 25c), i.e., he had a sense of pastoral responsibility. There is no need to correct the text on the ground that the idea of consolation for mourners is out of place here. The sense is quite plain. Job sums up his relationship with all classes of society: the public figures, the statesmen (vs. 25a), the people at large (vs. 25b), and the weak members of the community (vs. 25c).

2. THE SUFFERING OF THIS PRESENT TIME (30:1-31)

As an abrupt contrast with the idyllic picture of an irretrievable past, Job offers the concrete and circumstantial description of the calamities he now endures. The present text of ch. 30 offers many difficulties in its details. In addition, the sequence of thought is far from smooth, and it may be that the material which is gathered here is of quite heterogeneous origin; e.g., vss. 2-8 may have belonged to another poem, or they may have been displaced accidentally from another context (such as 24:5 ff.). At any rate, the threefold use of the expression וְעַתָּה, **But now,** in vss. 1, 9, 16, and that of the word

knocking the breath out of them (cf. Expos. on 3:20-21). It was not Job's temperament but his faith that would not desert him; not even in his own direst distress (see Expos. on 28:1-28). He was wroth with one he had loved. Madness, not doubt, assailed him, as the old gave way before the new. Moral and intellectual integrity may have to wrestle for a foothold at "the removing of those things that are shaken" (Heb. 12:27); but out of the wrestling, as from nothing else, comes the psalmist's assurance, "Thou hast set my feet in a larger room" (Ps. 31:8). "As

for me, my feet were almost gone; my steps had well-nigh slipped. . . . Until I went into the sanctuary of God" (Ps. 73:2, 17).

Only such a one has it in his power to restore the confidence of others (vs. 24a). There is a contagion not only of evil but of good (see Expos. on vs. 15; cf. vs. 23, the rain which refreshes, restores, and brings to maturity). For the Christian the center from which it spreads is Christ himself (Matt. 9:2; 14:27; John 16:33).

30:1-31. *How to Reckon the Sufferings of This Present Time.*— (See Expos. on 29:1-25.) To

I would have disdained to have set with the dogs of my flock.
 	
2 Yea, whereto *might* the strength of their hands *profit* me, in whom old age was perished?
 	
3 For want and famine *they were* solitary; fleeing into the wilderness in former time desolate and waste:
 	
4 Who cut up mallows by the bushes, and juniper roots *for* their meat.
 	
5 They were driven forth from among *men,* (they cried after them as *after* a thief,)
 	
6 To dwell in the cliffs of the valleys, *in* caves of the earth, and *in* the rocks.
 	
7 Among the bushes they brayed; under the nettles they were gathered together.
 	
8 *They were* children of fools, yea, children of base men: they were viler than the earth.
	whose fathers I would have disdained
	   to set with the dogs of my flock.
	2 What could I gain from the strength of
	      their hands,
	   men whose vigor is gone?
	3 Through want and hard hunger[h]
	   they gnaw the dry and desolate ground;
	4 they pick mallow and the leaves of
	      bushes,
	   and to warm themselves the roots of
	      the broom.
	5 They are driven out from among men;
	   they shout after them as after a thief.
	6 In the gullies of the torrents they must
	      dwell,
	   in holes of the earth and of the rocks.
	7 Among the bushes they bray;
	   under the nettles they huddle together.
	8 A senseless, a disreputable brood,
	   they have been whipped out of the
	      land.

[h] Heb *ground yesterday waste*

אַף, "surely," in vs. 24, indicate four main developments: (*a*) the irreverence of worthless men (vss. 1-8) ; (*b*) the hostility of society (vss. 9-15) ; (*c*) the cruelty of God (vss. 16-23) ; and (*d*) the misery of dereliction (vss. 24-31) .

a) IRREVERENCE OF WORTHLESS MEN (30:1-8)

30:1-8. Job complains that **now** the sons of men who were not even good enough to be **set with the dogs of** [his] **flock make sport of** [him] (vs. 1; cf. 19:18). The expression צְעִירִים מִמֶּנִּי לְיָמִים, "more insignificant than I in days," suggests once again that Job considered himself as a young man (cf. 29:8). The idea of vs. 2 is surprising in the mouth of a man who claims to have been "eyes to the blind, and feet to the lame" (29:15). Job is here presented as saying that he has nothing but disdain for men whose "rugged vigor" (cf. 5:26) has prematurely vanished: **the strength of their hands** would have been profitless to their employer. The thought seems to be even more strange when the subsequent context (vss. 3-4) makes clear that their physical weakness was the result of their hunger, which in turn was due to the fact that they had been expelled from society (vss. 5-7). Moreover, clear justification of their ostracism is not offered, except that they are described as בְּנֵי־נָבָל, "sons of fools," "senseless or ignoble men" in a moral and religious rather than in a purely mental sense (cf. 2:10; II Sam. 3:33; Ps. 14:1), and "sons of no name" or **base men** (KJV), **a disreputable brood** (RSV).

reckon means either to enumerate or to estimate: in both senses one encounters many an unexpected difficulty when the reckoning has to do with what Paul calls in one place "the sufferings of this present time" (Rom. 8:18). All too often the very enumeration itself is made in the mood of self-pity, with the resulting exaggerations, frustrations, and distortions (cf. the "four main developments" indicated in the Exeg.). These last may even serve to explain, in some measure at least, the contemptuous tone of vss. 2-8 (cf. 24:5-8, 10-11; 31:15; yet see Exeg.). If not in self-pity, then by way of excuse, in order to avoid responsibility. No such motive, of course, can be assigned to Job—unless indeed there is a modicum of truth, after all, in the suggestion that aside from the judicial and the punitive, human suffering has also probative (so the friends) and educative (Elihu) aspects. Sure it is, in any case, that enumeration alone, without any attempt at appraisal, is fraught with danger. When the talk is of estimating, the difficulties increase by leaps and bounds (see Expos. on vss. 9-15). Three things are note

9 And now am I their song, yea, I am their byword.	9 "And now I have become their song, I am a byword to them.
10 They abhor me, they flee far from me, and spare not to spit in my face.	10 They abhor me, they keep aloof from me; they do not hesitate to spit at the sight of me.
11 Because he hath loosed my cord, and afflicted me, they have also let loose the bridle before me.	11 Because God has loosed my cord and humbled me, they have cast off restraint in my presence.
12 Upon *my* right *hand* rise the youth; they push away my feet, and they raise up against me the ways of their destruction.	12 On my right hand the rabble rise, they drive me[i] forth, they cast up against me their ways of destruction.
13 They mar my path, they set forward my calamity, they have no helper.	13 They break up my path, they promote my calamity; no one restrains[j] them.
14 They came *upon me* as a wide breaking in *of waters:* in the desolation they rolled themselves *upon me.*	14 As through[k] a wide breach they come; amid the crash they roll on.

i Heb *my feet*
j Cn: Heb *helps*
k Cn: Heb *like*

---

b) HOSTILITY OF SOCIETY (30:9-15)

9-15. Whatever the significance of the preceding verses, there is little doubt that in the present passage Job is developing the familiar theme of his own social isolation. He explains it as a result of his physical exhaustion which even the lowest samples of humanity interpret as an act of God (vs. 11). The persecutions he endures from men (vss. 12-14) confirm the fact that he has lost his "nobility" and "salvation" (vs. 15*bc*; cf. the "spirit of nobility" and the "joy of salvation" in Ps. 51:12).

---

worthy about Paul's attempt: the pride he took in his infirmities (cf. vs. 15*bc* with II Cor. 12:9); his determination (cf. vs. 20 with II Cor. 4:8-10, 15-16; 6:4-10); and his ultimate assurance (cf. vs. 23 with II Cor. 4:17-18; Rom. 8:18). God had his own plans and they were good. To live, then, not for the goodness of the plan but for the love of the Planner and his purpose (Rom. 5:10).

9-15. *Listing Liabilities.*— (See also vss. 23, 24-31.) The trouble is, who knows what liabilities are? They may be assets, and the assets may be liabilities. On what side of the ledger to make the entry? (Cf. Expos. on 7:1-6; 21:26.)

The apostle Paul had a hale and hearty way of keeping his accounts. There was never any question as to the color of the ink when it came time to strike the final balance. It would be black, not red. No matter what happened, God would get into it and throw it all over on the credit side, he was sure of that; and because he was, he was never quite sure in which column to set down the separate items temporarily. "Thrice was I beaten with rods." In his mind, which side was that on when it happened? Credit or debit? "A night and a day I have been in the deep." What was he using that night and that day, a

plus sign or a minus sign? "There was given to me a thorn in the flesh." Was he subtracting at that point or adding? (See II Cor. 11:25; 12:7.) What would it be like to be like that? To put a finger on whatever it is that seems to stand in the way, then look up into God's face, and all at once be actually unable to tell any more where to enter it? A genius for mathematics. Where will a man enter that? It can ruin him. Ill health? In what column will he set that down? It can be the making of him.

Laotze tells of an old Chinese whose one horse strayed off and was lost. His friends in the village toiled up the hill to offer their condolences; but the old farmer looked at them and smiled. "How do you know this is bad luck?" he said. Soon the lone horse came back and brought with him a whole drove of wild horses. Whereupon the friends toiled up once more, this time to offer their congratulations. But the farmer asked them, "How do you know this is good luck?" In a week or two his son, who with so many horses about had almost learned to ride, fell and broke his leg. Again the pilgrimage, the condolences, and the question, "How do you know this is bad luck?" The next month war broke out, and his son by reason of the injury

15 Terrors are turned upon me: they pursue my soul as the wind: and my welfare passeth away as a cloud.

16 And now my soul is poured out upon me; the days of affliction have taken hold upon me.

17 My bones are pierced in me in the night season: and my sinews take no rest.

18 By the great force *of my disease* is my garment changed: it bindeth me about as the collar of my coat.

19 He hath cast me into the mire, and I am become like dust and ashes.

20 I cry unto thee, and thou dost not hear me: I stand up, and thou regardest me *not*.

21 Thou art become cruel to me: with thy strong hand thou opposest thyself against me.

15 Terrors are turned upon me;
   my honor is pursued as by the wind,
   and my prosperity has passed away like
      a cloud.

16 "And now my soul is poured out within
      me;
   days of affliction have taken hold of me.
17 The night racks my bones,
   and the pain that gnaws me takes no
      rest.
18 With violence it seizes my garment;[l]
   it binds me about like the collar of my
      tunic.
19 God has cast me into the mire,
   and I have become like dust and ashes.
20 I cry to thee and thou dost not answer
      me;
   I stand, and thou dost not[m] heed me.
21 Thou hast turned cruel to me;
   with the might of thy hand thou dost
      persecute me.

[l] Gk: Heb *my garment is disfigured*
[m] One Heb Ms and Vg: Heb lacks *not*

c) CRUELTY OF GOD (30:16-23)

16-23. The physical pains that Job endures are indeed due to the direct will of the Deity (vs. 19). So for the last time Job addresses his divine tormentor and utters his accusation against him (vss. 20-23). Not only does God refuse to answer his proud prayer (notice the possible implication of the verb **I stand up** in vs. 20*b*), but he also intensifies his strokes (vss. 21-22) until death comes (vs. 23).

was exempt.[9] It is hard to say to what lengths the story might have been extended! Besides, whatever happens, it has to pass through the alembic of the human soul (see Expos. on 3:20-21). Out of how much weakness has come strength; and vice versa (cf. Expos. on 20:4-11; see also Expos. on 29:1-25; 31:2-4; 34:9)!

Nobody has to stop anywhere and say: "That's how it is. If I'm to make the least bit of headway, I've got to use the other stuff I have and let that go." Nothing needs to be let go. If anything—this side of what?—is mere wastage that cannot be used, life is an idiotic game of chance. Psychologists talk about accepting the self. They mean that people need not fret and fume, grow peevish and resentful, because they are not Alexander the Great or Helen of Troy. They never have to accept the self and sit down beside it and eat an apple. The whole Christian gospel keeps saying over and over that nothing is refuse. No one has to brush his hands and be rid of anything before he can even start. He can

[9] See Lin Yutang, *The Importance of Living* (New York: Reynal & Hitchcock, 1938), p. 160.

start with it. There is something in this universe that makes it possible for good to come not only in spite of evil, but straight out of it. This is what came straight out of Paul's black heap of failure and disappointment: "Blessed be God, even . . . the God of all comfort; who comforteth us in all our tribulation, that we may be able to comfort them which are in any trouble, by the comfort wherewith we ourselves are comforted of God" (II Cor. 1:3-4). It is reminiscent of another desolate place, where the gentlest life the world has ever seen hung spread-eagled on its two beams of wood, halfway between the heaven he was and the hell men made to answer it. How straight out of that came the N.T. to lift up a man's head and set his feet where God's feet are, with all the broken heart of the Eternal to make him whole again! All God means is beyond. He took to changing minus signs into plus signs the day he made a cross.

19-23. *The Great Adversary.*— (Cf. Expos. on 19:6.) There is a sense in which for Job God has become satanic. He is the "adversary" par excellence, the God of retributive justice, whose

22 Thou liftest me up to the wind; thou causest me to ride *upon it,* and dissolvest my substance.

23 For I know *that* thou wilt bring me *to* death, and *to* the house appointed for all living.

24 Howbeit he will not stretch out *his* hand to the grave, though they cry in his destruction.

25 Did not I weep for him that was in trouble? was *not* my soul grieved for the poor?

22 Thou liftest me up on the wind, thou makest me ride on it,
    and thou tossest me about in the roar of the storm.
23 Yea, I know that thou wilt bring me to death,
    and to the house appointed for all living.

24 "Yet does not one in a heap of ruins stretch out his hand,
    and in his disaster cry for help?[n]
25 Did not I weep for him whose day was hard?
    Was not my soul grieved for the poor?

[n] Cn: Heb obscure

---

d) Misery of Dereliction (30:24-31)

24-31. The Hebrew of vs. 24 is most obscure, but the rendering of the RSV is not impossible. Like any other man **in a heap of ruins,** Job had cried **for help** (vs. 24) ; and he expected an answer, since he had in the past responded to the calls of men and women in distress (vs. 25; cf. 29:11-17). But nothing **came** except **evil** and **darkness** (vs. 26).

"justice" fills Job with terror (vs. 15; cf. 21:6; Expos. on 23:15). It must always be remembered, however, that the God whom he accuses is the God of the old faith, and that a new faith is being born (see Expos. on 14:13-15). For the terms of the indictment see Exeg. (cf. vs. 11 with 29:20*b*). If only the God of the old faith would write as clearly (31:35*c*). For the emergence of the new see Expos. on 16:19; 19:25, 27.

24. *The Cry for Help.*—(Cf. 19:7; 24:12; 27:9.) If this verse is to stand as in the RSV, one may comment on the pathos of that cry, and on the instinctive nature of it. It is not a cry to man but to God. Whether in profound gratitude or in deep distress there is the outstretched **hand.** Said Sir Leslie Stephen, as he wrote of his second wife after she had died, recalling all the tenderness of her love, "I thank —" and suddenly ran headlong into the tragedy of his own faith, adding lamely, "—something— that I loved her as heartily as I know how to love." [1] So with Swinburne:

> From too much love of living,
>   From hope and fear set free,
> We thank with brief thanksgiving
>   Whatever gods may be
> That no life lives for ever;
> That dead men rise up never;
> That even the weariest river
>   Winds somewhere safe to sea. [2]

[1] F. W. Maitland, ed., *The Life and Letters of Sir Leslie Stephen* (London: Duckworth & Co., 1906), p. 256.
[2] "The Garden of Proserpine," st. xi.

In a recent novel a man has leaped overboard in the night to rescue a friend. They both cling to a buoy as the yacht circles round and round unable to locate them. Finally, as their strength is ebbing, together they watch the lights disappear on the horizon. Says one to the other, when the last hope has flickered out, "I suppose, for somebody like me, who hasn't prayed for years, there's no use praying now." And the other answers, "No. Better go on as we have come." Farther down than the denial, the affirmation; under the "No" the "Yes." As for God, he is not proud. If **disaster** is the only thing that can drive us to him, it were shame to come; but greater shame not to (cf. Matt. 11:28; Luke 15:18-19; Expos. on 19:7; 24:12*c*; 35:9-16; 38:1). It is interesting to note that in Blake's Illustration I, the evening prayers in which Job's family are engaged are being read from books, while "the musical instruments of spontaneous praise hang silent upon the tree." [3]

25. *Putting God Under Obligations.*—Again there is obscurity. It is, however, quite possible that Job is thinking of the compassion which he himself has shown (see Exeg.), and suggesting that on God's side there ought to be, in all decency, something comparable. He has kept his part of the bargain, and so has given God reason enough for living up to his. This is to misunderstand not only the nature of the good (cf. 4:17-19), but also the ground of the obligation (cf. 22:3). On both counts, if Eliphaz had not pressed his premises to the wrong conclu-

[3] Damon, *Doctrine of Job, ad loc.*

26 When I looked for good, then evil came *unto me:* and when I waited for light, there came darkness.

27 My bowels boiled, and rested not: the days of affliction prevented me.

28 I went mourning without the sun: I stood up, *and* I cried in the congregation.

29 I am a brother to dragons, and a companion to owls.

30 My skin is black upon me, and my bones are burned with heat.

31 My harp also is *turned* to mourning, and my organ into the voice of them that weep.

31 I made a covenant with mine eyes; why then should I think upon a maid?

---

26 But when I looked for good, evil came;
     and when I waited for light, darkness came.

27 My heart is in turmoil, and is never still;
     days of affliction come to meet me.

28 I go about blackened, but not by the sun;
     I stand up in the assembly, and cry for help.

29 I am a brother of jackals,
     and a companion of ostriches.

30 My skin turns black and falls from me,
     and my bones burn with heat.

31 My lyre is turned to mourning,
     and my pipe to the voice of those who weep.

31 "I have made a covenant with my eyes;
     how then could I look upon a virgin?

The frustration brings a new wave of utter exasperation (vs. 27a; lit., "my bowels are made to boil"; cf. Lam. 1:20; 2:11). His disease has disfigured him (vs. 28a); and although he stands up **in the assembly**, crying **for help** (vs. 28b), he remains as far apart from man as if he were **a brother of jackals, and a companion of ostriches** (vs. 29; cf. Mic. 1:8). The wailing and the howling of the animals, which can be heard at night almost everywhere in the Near East, sound like the bitter music which soon will be heard at the time of his death. In that prospect, his **lyre** and his **pipe** turn into funeral instruments, ready to accompany the professional weepers (vs. 31). The suggestion that Job now becomes the mouthpiece of all **those who weep** is attractive, but not likely.

3. FINAL OATH OF INNOCENCE (31:1-40)

The happiness of the past (ch. 29) has been swallowed up in the sorrow and shame of the present (ch. 30). There is no future to contemplate except death, and therefore nothingness (30:23, 31). Nonetheless, Job still asserts his righteousness. So he ends his soliloquy with the most solemn and elaborate protest of innocence that he has ever tried

---

sions, he would have been nearer right than Job (cf. Expos. on 25:2-6). The obligation is not in what man does, but in what God is—and therefore does (see Expos. on vs. 24; 31:1, 2-4; 40:6–42:6). Note Blake's Illustration V, of the moment when Satan goes forth from the presence of the Lord (1:12); Damon writes of it as follows:

Job is sharing his last meal with a beggar. He does this for the same reason that he had done everything—because it is the correct thing to do, not because he naturally wishes to do it, as a man would share his last meal with a starving friend. Such charity as Job's can only be given—and taken —with the left hand; for the true sympathy is absent. . . . Yet . . . Job wants to do the best thing, even if he cannot do it in the proper spirit. Therefore angels still minister to him.

Therefore also God still keeps his seat by clinging to the book of Law; though, with a dimmed and

sinking halo, he is dragged down on the material side. It is through Job's very virtues that he sins; the flames that robe the angels are the same flames flowing into Satan's hand. . . . The margin is filled with flames and thorns, and below is the serpent, at last fully revealed, though not to Job.[4]

With reference to a man's sharing "his last meal with a starving friend," note what Schiller once said of Goethe: "I could never love him; for with all his giving, he never gives himself: he gives like a god." What god?

31:1-40. Making One's Own Memories.—To live in the past is often enough to be plagued with memories (see Expos. on 29:1-25); to live in the future is to give hostages to time (cf. Expos. on 20:17-18). Why is it that in one way

[4] *Illustrations of the Book of Job,* invented and engraved by William Blake; interpreted by S. Foster Damon, *The Doctrine of Job* (New York: United Book Guild, 1950).

to express. For this purpose he examines a series of more than sixteen concrete hypotheses of sinful acts, each one beginning with the conjunction "if" (vss. 5, 7, 9, 13, 16, 19, 20, 21, 24, 25, 26, 29, 31, 33, 38, 39), and he clears himself of any deed—or even intention—of religious or ethical turpitude, thereby revealing in exquisite terms the highest moral conscience to be found in the O.T. With a clean past and a clear mind he declares himself ready to face his judge, proud of an honor still intact and of a record unblemished (vss. 35-37).

Most commentators agree that vss. 38-40 have been accidentally inserted at the end of the chapter and that vss. 35-37 form the hero's ultimate challenge to the Deity (but see Exeg., *ad loc.*).

a) A Covenant of Inward Purity (31:1-4)

31:1-4. The lack of transition from ch. 30 is somewhat confusing, but one would not improve the literary abruptness by suggesting that vss. 1-4, which are not in the LXX, have been inserted in the Hebrew text at a later time; for the same incoherence would appear in 30:31–31:5.

> I have made a covenant with my eyes;
>   how then could I look upon a virgin? (Vs. 1.)

Cf. Ecclus. 9:5, בבתולה אל־תתבונן, "Do not look upon a virgin." There is no valid reason for correcting the word בתולה, **virgin**, into נבלה, "impiety," or בהלה, "calamity." Job is

---

or another man is so thoroughly bent on discounting the present, which is all he has? And that all is brief enough—it scarcely reaches from the *m* to the *t* as he pronounces the word "moment." Yet precisely on that knife edge between what has been and what is to come, while the second hand moves steadily around the face of the clock, we are making the memories which in hours of crisis will help either to defeat or gird us. In ch. 29 these memories, like enemy troops, march across Job's soul; then back again in reverse order, through ch. 30, leaving the landscape desolate. So is many a warrior beaten before the battle (cf. *Julius Caesar*, Act IV, scene 3; *King Richard III*, Act V, scene 3). In ch. 31 they are mustered like strong battalions for the defense (see Expos. on 23:10; 27:2-6).

1. Purity of Soul.—(Cf. also vss. 7, 9, 24, 27, 29, 33, 36.) The bold-faced heading is one of Kierkegaard's titles. By it he means "single-mindedness" (cf. Matt. 6:22-24; 18:8-9). Job knows very well that out of the heart "are the issues of life" (Prov. 4:23). By way of final response to everything Eliphaz has said in 22:2-20, and to all the imputations of guilt, implicit or explicit, in the speeches of Bildad and Zophar—these men who, in worse sense than Shakespeare meant, had taken "upon [themselves] the mystery of things, as if [they] were God's spies" [5]—he disavows not so much sin (13:26) as transgression, in thought, word, or deed. He has brought under tribute to his integrity eye (vs. 1) and heart (vs. 7b), hand (vs. 7c) and foot (vs. 5b). Nowhere else in the O.T. is there

[5] *King Lear*, Act V, scene 3.

set such a lofty standard of ethical conduct. In every case but one (vss. 8, 22, 40—note the violent emotion which is responsible for the omission after vs. 34) the imprecation calls down the self-punishment suited to the crime (see Expos. on vss. 38-40). Interestingly enough that punishment, except in vs. 11 (and in vs. 28, if that verse is to be retained), is not at man's hand but at God's (as in vss. 2 [see Exeg.], 8, 10 [where it seems to fall on the innocent, but perhaps assumes the death of the guilty, certainly the ruin of his home], 12, 14, 40). The great Ruler of the universe still rules, and for Job he is yet somehow just, with an ultimate justice (vs. 14; see Expos. on 13:1-12). Observe too the consistency with which the motivation is not only assigned but elaborated (vss. 3 [yet see Exeg.], 11 and 12, 14 and 15, 23, 28). Study these motives. Differentiate between fear of retribution and "the fear of the Lord" (vs. 23a and vs. 23b). Note especially vs. 15 (see Exeg.) and vs. 28b. What could better portray the conflict and confusion in the human soul? The N.T. understands that conflict far more profoundly (read Rom. 7). It might be said that Job's "impiety" was only relatively less heinous than the "piety" of the friends. To work out one's own salvation and yet at the same time not to be able to work it out (Phil. 2:12-13) is the paradox with which Christian faith concerns itself—the "faith which worketh by love" (Gal. 5:6), and is the gift of God (Rom. 1:5; 5:1-5; 6:2; 10:3-9). For one who has set out on the road that Job has been doing his magnificent best to travel, if there is no answer to Paul's

2 For what portion of God *is there* from above? and *what* inheritance of the Almighty from on high?

3 *Is* not destruction to the wicked? and a strange *punishment* to the workers of iniquity?

4 Doth not he see my ways, and count all my steps?

5 If I have walked with vanity, or if my foot hath hasted to deceit;

6 Let me be weighed in an even balance, that God may know mine integrity.

7 If my step hath turned out of the way, and mine heart walked after mine eyes, and if any blot hath cleaved to mine hands;

8 *Then* let me sow, and let another eat; yea, let my offspring be rooted out.

9 If mine heart have been deceived by a

2 What would be my portion from God above,
and my heritage from the Almighty on high?

3 Does not calamity befall the unrighteous, and disaster the workers of iniquity?

4 Does not he see my ways, and number all my steps?

5 "If I have walked with falsehood, and my foot has hastened to deceit;

6 (Let me be weighed in a just balance, and let God know my integrity!)

7 if my step has turned aside from the way, and my heart has gone after my eyes, and if any spot ¯has cleaved to my hands;

8 then let me sow, and another eat; and let what grows for me be rooted out.

9 "If my heart has been enticed to a woman,

selecting sensuality as the most typical form of his temptation. This trait agrees with the many allusions which he has made in the course of the discussion with his friends as to the virility of his temperament. Since he knew, centuries before Jesus, that covetousness of the eyes penetrates to the very core of sensual motives (cf. Matt. 5:28), he made a pact with himself to keep free not only from deeds of incontinence, but also from any glance which might undermine his ideal of inward purity.

Job used to believe in those days that divine retribution would have followed swiftly upon his misbehavior (vss. 2-3), and that God watched closely all his actions (vs. 4). According to another interpretation, the questions which are asked in these verses betray the present doubt of the former moralist. It is a skeptic who asks: "What should then have been my portion from God above, and my heritage on high? Should not calamity befall the unrighteous, and disaster the workers of iniquity? Is it that he does not see my ways, and fails to number my steps?" (Vss. 2-4.) The implication is that morality, even of the highest order, is futile.

b) Self-Maledictions (31:5-34)

5-8. The speaker is now ready to proceed with his last self-examination. If he has been guilty of **falsehood**, greed, and uncleanness (vss. 5-7), let him perish in hunger (vs. 8).

9-10. If he has committed adultery (vs. 9), let his own wife belong to another man (vs. 10), and let him perish in the fire (vss. 11-12).

question (Rom. 7:24) there is no answer to anything (see Expos. on 7:20a; 30:25).

2-4. *Why Be Good?*—The words **portion** and **heritage**, quoted (?) from Zophar's speech in 20:29, and indeed the whole tone of the passage, so replete with the pious phrases of the friends, incline toward the belief that what we are here dealing with is again Job's skepticism (see

Exeg.): You see what my **portion** is. What should it have been? (See Expos. on 30:25.) You say that **calamity** befalls the **unrighteous**: see for yourselves what happens to the righteous! Can it be that God is blind (vs. 4; cf. 24:1)?

It would seem then, to follow through with the argument, that there is indeed no profit in the service of God (see Expos. on 1:6-12; Luke

woman, or *if* I have laid wait at my neighbor's door;

10 *Then* let my wife grind unto another,
and let others bow down upon her.

11 For this *is* a heinous crime; yea, it *is*
an iniquity *to be punished by* the judges.

12 For it *is* a fire *that* consumeth to destruction, and would root out all mine increase.

13 If I did despise the cause of my man-
servant or of my maidservant, when they
contended with me;

14 What then shall I do when God riseth
up? and when he visiteth, what shall I
answer him?

15 Did not he that made me in the womb
make him? and did not one fashion us in
the womb?

and I have lain in wait at my neighbor's door;

10 then let my wife grind for another,
and let others bow down upon her.

11 For that would be a heinous crime;
that would be an iniquity to be punished by the judges;

12 for that would be a fire which consumes
unto Abaddon,
and it would burn to the root all my
increase.

13 "If I have rejected the cause of my man-
servant or my maidservant,
when they brought a complaint against
me;

14 what then shall I do when God rises up?
When he makes inquiry, what shall I
answer him?

15 Did not he who made me in the womb
make him?
And did not one fashion us in the
womb?

13-15. The idea that slaves have rights (vs. 13) is one of the most remarkable in this chapter, and even more astounding is the further statement that those rights are established by the Creator for all men. **Did not he who made me in the womb make him?** (Vs. 15*a*.) This awareness of the equality of birth among men is as high as the ethical level of the N.T.

19:8). If he had but known it, the very tumult in his soul was "profit" (see Expos. on 28:1-28; 30:9-15). Whatever there is of Christian virtue in the world is not for hope of reward or fear of punishment, though neither the hope nor the fear can ever be stricken from the record (see Expos. on Luke 19:17, 18, 24). Goodness is response-in-love to the goodness of God; it is God's own re-created image in the soul.

Teach us, good Lord, to serve thee as thou deservest:
To give and not to count the cost;
To fight and not to heed the wounds;
To toil and not to seek for rest;
To labor and not ask for any reward
Save that of knowing that we do thy will.[6]

13-15. The Rights of the Dispossessed.— (Cf. Expos. on 9:14-19; 16:10.) There were certain covenant ameliorations of the lot of the slave among the Hebrew people (Exod. 20:10; 21:2-11, 26-27, 32; Lev. 25:39-55); but little if any-thing in the whole scope of the O.T. can compare with this for loftiness of thought or ex-pression. God will inquire of those whom he

fashioned **in the womb** as he fashioned us (see Eph. 6:9; Col. 4:1; especially Philem. 16). Wrote Mark Rutherford:

The races to whom we owe the Bible were cruel in war; they were revengeful; their veins were filled with blood hot with lust; they knew no art, nor grace, nor dialectic, such as Greece knew, but one service they at least have rendered to the world. They have preserved in their prophets and poets this eternal verity—*He that made me in the womb made him*—and have proclaimed with divine fury a divine wrath upon all those who may be seduced into forgetfulness of it. In discernment of the real breadth and depth of social duty, nothing has gone beyond the book of Job.[7]

There is indeed an equality of birth before the God of all creation. Differences in status and endowment are for use in trust (see Expos. on Luke 19:12-27). But there is more. There is God's second creation (cf. Expos. on 14:7-12). There is the Christ in man and for him: the seal of a higher dignity and a truer brotherhood.

[7] *Notes on the Book of Job* (London: T. Fisher Unwin, n.d.), pp. 151-52.

[6] Ignatius of Loyola, "Prayer for Generosity."

16 If I have withheld the poor from *their* desire, or have caused the eyes of the widow to fail;

17 Or have eaten my morsel myself alone, and the fatherless hath not eaten thereof;

18 (For from my youth he was brought up with me, as *with* a father, and I have guided her from my mother's womb;)

19 If I have seen any perish for want of clothing, or any poor without covering;

20 If his loins have not blessed me, and *if* he were *not* warmed with the fleece of my sheep;

16 "If I have withheld anything that the poor desired,

or have caused the eyes of the widow to fail,

17 or have eaten my morsel alone,

and the fatherless has not eaten of it

18 (for from his youth I reared him*ᵒ* as a father,

and from his mother's womb I guided him) ;

19 if I have seen any one perish for lack of clothing,

or a poor man without covering;

20 if his loins have not blessed me,

and if he was not warmed with the fleece of my sheep;

ᵒ Cn: Heb *for from my youth he grew up to me as a father, and from my mother's womb I guided her*

16-23. Job now turns to sins against charity, and he indirectly sets forth the most comprehensive program of social responsibility. **If I have withheld anything that the poor desired, . . . or have eaten my morsel alone** (vss. 16-17). He has exercised more than justice in his dealings with his fellow men. He has not turned away the poor even—if the words are to be taken literally—when their demands were immoderate. He has not enjoyed advantages without sharing them with those in need. "The simplest words become revolutionary when they touch the heart or the conscience of humanity; and this line of an ancient drama, magnifying the negative virtue of self-restraint and the positive of thoughtfulness for others, has perhaps had more power to slay the sins of the epicure and the egoist than a hundred ancient sumptuary and modern socialistic laws" (Strahan, *Job,* pp. 260-61). This pregnant comment, however, with its touch of modern polemics, should be understood in the light of nomadic or seminomadic conditions of social life, which were those of Job, and not taken literally by those who would attempt to apply "biblical" ethics to a sedentary and industrial society. Yet their impact of judgment remains. In any case, Job shows by his words that his philanthropy was animated by a true understanding of the sufferings wrought on human flesh by the evils of poverty. He fed the hungry and he covered the naked, for he had experienced hunger

---

16-23. *Ye Have the Poor Always with You.*— Under the conditions of a society such as that to which Job belonged, face-to-face dealing with those in need was not only possible but doubtless a matter of daily occurrence. The very frequency and regularity of it might well have dulled the edge of his compassion. In a society highly organized and almost incredibly complex there are two grave perils that have to be faced and dealt with: the peril of remoteness, and the peril of oversimplification. The poor in the twentieth century are often **the fatherless** and the widows who have been robbed by some clever manipulation of the stock market. They are represented by bits of gilt-edged paper called bonds, readily sold, or exchanged, or transferred from one portfolio to another. There was a **widow** in New York whose eyes looked in vain (vs. 16*b*) for help, for they looked to a corporation in Detroit that had "milked" her life's savings without even knowing her name. It is not hard to withhold what the poor desire when the poor are nameless, faceless folk who live halfway across the continent. Or perhaps they are the "displaced persons" one hears of, or share croppers one has never met, or whole nations starving, while at home food products are destroyed in order to keep prices up. The conscience a modern man needs has to be infinitely more sensitive than Job's. How many are even comparably as tender? There are so many facts that have to be taken into account. It is possible to pauperize the poor, and who wants to do that? Organized charities—how are they administered, and what is their overhead? The only thing that has never changed is the will of God (Deut. 15:7-11). The horizons are broader, and the ingenuity necessary is greater;

21 If I have lifted up my hand against the fatherless, when I saw my help in the gate:

22 *Then* let mine arm fall from my shoulder blade, and mine arm be broken from the bone.

23 For destruction *from* God *was* a terror to me, and by reason of his highness I could not endure.

24 If I have made gold my hope, or have said to the fine gold, *Thou art* my confidence;

25 If I rejoiced because my wealth *was* great, and because mine hand had gotten much;

21 if I have raised my hand against the fatherless,
     because I saw help in the gate;
22 then let my shoulder blade fall from my shoulder,
     and let my arm be broken from its socket.
23 For I was in terror of calamity from God,
     and I could not have faced his majesty.

24 "If I have made gold my trust,
     or called fine gold my confidence;
25 if I have rejoiced because my wealth was great,
     or because my hand had gotten much;

---

and cold. He possessed the memory and the imagination of love. He could not enjoy the warmth of his tent if he knew that **a poor man . . . was not warmed with the fleece of** [his own] **sheep** (vss. 19-20). Always, however, at the spring of his social conscience lay his deep commitment to the will of a God who cares for all men (vs. 23; cf. vs. 15). It was religion which justified, supported, explained, and made possible his morality.

24-28. This last consideration brought him to drive deeper his introspective search from the realm of social relations to that of his own allegiance to God. Job understands the profound meaning of idolatry and polytheism. He meditates on the theological implications of **trust** and **confidence** (vs. 24). In the same breath, therefore, he repudiates his worship of **gold**. He has never desired riches in place of God. Likewise, he has resisted the subtle and alluring attraction of the astral religions. It is almost impossible for the modern mind to grasp the power exercised upon biblical men and women by the worship of **the sun** and of **the moon** (vss. 26-27) as it was practiced everywhere around them from the valley of the Nile to the plains of Mesopotamia. Quasi-material communion with the forces of life in the universe was the essential aspect of ancient Egyptian and Semitic polytheisms. The basic instincts of man for security from want and for sexual fulfillment

---

but the center is the same (vs. 18 is read by some, "For as a father he [God] brought me up from my youth, and was my guide from my mother's womb"; cf. also vs. 23b, and Expos. on vs. 1; 30:25), illuminated now by the light of the Christian gospel (Luke 18:22; I Cor. 13:3).

24-28. *No Other Gods.*—Job disavows not only the idolatry of the bended knee but the idolatry of the yearning heart (yet see Expos. on 1:4-5). "That ye present your bodies a living sacrifice" (Rom. 12:1)—to what? It is the directional drive of the mind and heart and will that is in question, the one decisive allegiance of the soul. To suppose that idol worship is the superstitious practice of a primitive mentality is to come pitifully short of Job in both insight and apprehension. The very word superstition itself implies a standing in awe by the side of something which never works. Superstition always enters at the door by which religion takes its leave. Perhaps in part for that reason the twentieth century, which prides itself on having driven out superstition in company with her

sister ignorance, is of all centuries one of the most superstitious. To say nothing of its horoscopes, its astrologers, mediums, and undisguised fortunetellers—in the United States the business runs into unbelievable millions—it has its own fifty-seven species of the genus lie (vs. 28b) to stand in the place of the God it has lost—science, power, the state. Let each one count them off on his own fingers:

> If I have made [?] my trust,
>   or called [?] my confidence;
> if I have rejoiced because my [?] was great,
>   or because my hand had gotten [?];
> if I have looked at the [?],
>   or the [?] . . . ,
> and my heart has been secretly enticed,
>   and my [hand] has kissed my [mouth—Hebrew];
> this also would be an iniquity . . . ,
>   for I should have been false to God above

(see Exeg. on 28:14-22; Expos. on 28:28).

An advertisement kept appearing in magazines during the last years of World War II. It

26 If I beheld the sun when it shined, or the moon walking *in* brightness;

27 And my heart hath been secretly enticed, or my mouth hath kissed my hand:

28 This also *were* an iniquity *to be punished by* the judge: for I should have denied the God *that is* above.

29 If I rejoiced at the destruction of him that hated me, or lifted up myself when evil found him;

30 (Neither have I suffered my mouth to sin by wishing a curse to his soul.)

26 if I have looked at the sun*p* when it
    shone,
  or the moon moving in splendor,
27 and my heart has been secretly enticed,
  and my mouth has kissed my hand;
28 this also would be an iniquity to be punished by the judges,
  for I should have been false to God
    above.

29 "If I have rejoiced at the ruin of him that
    hated me,
  or exulted when evil overtook him
30 (I have not let my mouth sin
  by asking for his life with a curse) ;

p Heb *the light*

found in the cult of the fertility forces (of which **the sun** and **the moon** were the most obvious and insistent symbols) an economic, aesthetic, and mystical satisfaction. Biblical Hebraism throughout the centuries was in constant danger of dilution and corruption, because it is more difficult for man to place himself in worship at the disposal of a Deity who transcends the forces of nature than to yield to a cultic technique which claims to enlist for human use the service of these same forces (cf. II Kings 21:3 ff.; 23:5; Jer. 8:1-2; 44:25; Ezek. 8:16; etc.; see Henri and H. A. Frankfort, *et al., The Intellectual Adventure of Ancient Man* [Chicago: University of Chicago Press, 1946], pp. 23-26). Job reveals his strength of decision and endurance when he indirectly describes the exquisite appeal which paganism exercised upon him. But there could not be any compromise between his faith and the practices of his environment, however delightful these might be to his deepest impulses; for the slightest accommodation of his fidelity to any kind of religious eclecticism would have meant a denial of **the God that is above** (vs. 28).

29-30. While other parts of the O.T. display the emotion of *Schadenfreude* or "malignant joy" before the spectacle of the punishment of the wicked or the fall of enemies (cf. Judg. 5:24-31; Isa. 14:12 ff.; the so-called imprecatory psalms), Job rejects both such a natural and cheap psychological reaction and also the desire to curse his enemy.

was the picture of a father and a son standing in a field, pointing to the sky: on the whole a hopeful posture; but the reader knew what they were really looking at. He could not see, but he knew. It was a plane turned out by an American factory: salvation on the wing, riveted by —— and Co. The future was safe! They used to make idols in Babylon, and there was a prophet who pointed to them and laughed at them. "You take an oak, and you burn part of it to warm yourself, or you bake bread with it; the rest you make into an idol. The carpenter marks it out with a line and gets his chisel. The smith hammers and molds until he is ready to drop. Then you fall down in front of it, and worship it, and say, Deliver me; for you are my god! And nobody has wit enough to pull himself up with a jolt and declare, I'm a fool. It's a lie in my hand" (Isa. 44:14-20).

29-30. *Dealing with the Enemy.*—To deal with the enemy is too often taken in the sense of making a deal with him: which is either treachery, or what is regularly called appeasement, usually by way of a bargain—which just as usually turns out for both parties to be a bad bargain, as bargains not infrequently do—and so is sneered out of court. There are ways of dealing which have nothing to do with making deals, and the Bible runs the gamut of all of them, from ruthless vengeance (I Sam. 15:2-3) to imprecation (Ps. 109), from "malignant joy over the fate of the wicked" (Exeg.; cf. Expos. on 9:20-24; 15:17-35; 20:23; 22:12-20) to Job's repudiation of it (vs. 29); and more (vs. 30; cf. Prov. 24:17), from a ministry of mercy (Prov. 25:21-22; Rom. 12:20—noting the omission) to the ministry of love (Matt. 5:43-48). Observe that in this passage Job rises to heights of which

31 If the men of my tabernacle said not, Oh that we had of his flesh! we cannot be satisfied.

32 The stranger did not lodge in the street: *but* I opened my doors to the traveler.

33 If I covered my transgressions as Adam, by hiding mine iniquity in my bosom:

34 Did I fear a great multitude, or did the contempt of families terrify me, that I kept silence, *and* went not out of the door?

31 if the men of my tent have not said,
   'Who is there that has not been filled
     with his meat?'
32 (the sojourner has not lodged in the
   street;
   I have opened my doors to the way-
     farer);
33 if I have concealed my transgressions
   from men,*q*
   by hiding my iniquity in my bosom,
34 because I stood in great fear of the multitude,
   and the contempt of families terrified
     me,
   so that I kept silence, and did not go
     out of doors —

q Cn: Heb *like men* or *like Adam*

31-32. Passing from a negative to a positive attitude, the reciter now touches upon the sacred Arab custom of hospitality (cf. 19:14-15; Exod. 22:21; etc.). When Job referred to his own fare, he spoke of "his morsel" (of bread; vs. 17), but he now says that the guests praised him for offering luxurious **meat**, a festal fare.

33-34. The hero now repudiates the sin of hypocrisy. He declares that he has never worn a mask of personal and social integrity while concealing within himself transgressions too dark for the public eye. It is generally thought that the traditional rendering, **like Adam**, is not probable, for the story of the garden represents Adam as concealing his transgressions not from men but from God himself (Gen. 3:8). The expression כאדם may mean **like Adam** or "in the manner of man," **like men** (cf. Hos. 6:7; Ps. 82:7; see Exeg. on vs. 40). Job has never needed to hide or dissimulate a sin in his **bosom** (vs. 33; the fold of the mantle above the belt, where the Arab carries his goods and just as easily a weapon), and this is the reason for which he has never developed an antisocial attitude (vs. 34c). Inasmuch as Job, however, is bringing his series of self-defensive oaths to a

apparently the friends have never dreamed; he is indeed better than the God of his own imagining (9:23)—which last is for him quite intolerable. When the N.T. takes up the refrain its eyes are not on the self (Prov. 25:22b) or on the enemy, as if love were a strategy for serving its own ends (cf. the so-called "good neighbor policy," and Dale Carnegie's extraordinarily popular book, *How to Win Friends and Influence People* [8]), but on God (Matt. 5:45).

31-32. *The Grace of Hospitality.*—In the East "grace" would scarcely be an adequate word; in the West perhaps it will have to suffice. There hospitality was not only a necessity, it was a kind of sacrament, a very covenant of friendship (cf. Ps. 41:9; Ezra 4:14, lit., "we are salted with the salt of the palace"); here it is one of the amenities of life, to be observed or not, according to taste and condition. Among the Hebrews, traditions that reached back into the mists of history were associated with it, as of the day when Abraham and Lot entertained

angels unawares (Gen. 18:1-5; 19:1-3); and memories of their own sojourn in a land of strangers, and of the Lord who had brought them out (Exod. 22:21; Ps. 146:9). In the early church, to be "given to hospitality" (Rom. 12: 13) was one of the Christian virtues (see Did. 11:3-6; the "apostle" who outstayed his time, or went about looking for better accommodations, was a false prophet), with its sanction farther down in the life of God than men had dreamed (Matt. 25:31-46; Rom. 15:7). There are but a few sad relics left of that high and ancient practice. The host now still has his obligations as the guest has his; but good manners will cover most of them. Paying off social debts is one of the degenerate scions of a noble house, *veteris vestigia flammae* (cf. Luke 14: 12-14).

33-34. *What Do People Say About You?*—There was nothing in Job's life that called for concealment, nothing he had to keep to himself, after the manner of most men (see Exeg. on vs. 33a); but the **multitude** refused to put up with

8 New York: Simon & Schuster, 1937.

35 Oh that one would hear me! behold, my desire is, that the Almighty would answer me, and that mine adversary had written a book.

35 Oh, that I had one to hear me!
　　(Here is my signature! let the Almight
　　　answer me!)
Oh, that I had the indictment writter
　　by my adversary!

---

close, and is getting ready to make his final plea for a divine hearing, he may quit understandably think of Adam running away from God in fear. By contrast, he may b reflecting on his own attitude and so decide that he would not try to hide himself among the trees of the garden, were God coming to him and asking, "Man, where ar thou?" The reference to Adam in vs. 33a may reveal a subconscious process in the mind of the hero and thus constitute a psychological prodrome of the proud and almost defian request for a divine audience (vss. 35-37). "This passage [vss. 33-34] would seem to constitute the transition from 'The Oath of Clearance' to 'The Great Challenge.' It wa probably not originally intended as a denial of the habit of secretiveness in guilt and of cowardly failure to confess sins openly because of the fear of public opinion. It wa rather a strong asseveration that there was nothing that need be kept back and nothing that Job could not lay bare with undisturbed conscience before the judgment seat of God.' (Robert A. Aytoun, "A Critical Study of Job's 'Oath of Clearance,'" The Interpreter XVI [1919-20], 297-98.)

c) The Ultimate Challenge (31:35-37)

35-37. Job has now rehearsed the events of his past. He has found nothing in hi outward deeds, in his daily attitude, or in his heart which could in the most remote fashion be related to his present tragedy. Confirmed in his certainty of innocence, he i making the last plea in the form, not of a begging for mercy (forgiveness he needs not and pity he wants not!) but of a princely challenge to meet an equal in honorable encounter.

Oh, that I had one to hear me! (vs. 35a): This is the passionate wish which has been expressed again and again throughout the discussion.

> I would speak to the Almighty,
> 　　and I desire to argue my case with God (13:3).

Man is of no avail, and there is thus no one but God, even a hostile God, whom the herc could hope to approach. "I will defend my ways to his face" (13:15b). Job proposes at alternative.

> Call, and I will answer;
> 　　or let me speak, and do thou reply to me (13:22).

But God has consistently eluded him (23:3-9; 30:20). Job now imagines that at last he is before the court of his Judge. **Here is my signature! let the Almighty answer me**

---

him, and the important people (vs. 34b) held him in contempt. The conduct of his days was an open book. Anybody could read it and welcome. Hypocrisy, which for the Hebrew was not the playing of a part, but sheer impiety or lawlessness,[9] is a modern substitute for, and a studied tribute to, conscious integrity. Job was under no such compulsion to cover up. To

[9] In the N.T. it retained much of the original meaning (faithless, wicked, crafty). See A. G. Herbert, "Hypocrite," in Richardson, ed., Theological Word Book of the Bible, p. 109.

have regard for public opinion is a mark o good sense; to be swayed by it is a mark o weakness, the seal of a hypocrite or a coward In II Cor. 6:8-10 Paul was busy opposing fac to rumor. In that there is release. In I Cor 4:3-4, to man's judgment he opposes God's. Ir that, and in the love with which God's judg ment is instinct, is "the liberty wherewith Chris hath made us free" (Gal. 5:1).

35-37. The Final Challenge.—Job has bu one last recourse (Ps. 73:25). In the uttermos depths of despair, not because of what has hap

36 Surely I would take it upon my shoulder, *and* bind it *as* a crown to me.

37 I would declare unto him the number of my steps; as a prince would I go near unto him.

36 Surely I would carry it on my shoulder;
I would bind it on me as a crown;

37 I would give him an account of all my steps;
like a prince I would approach him.

(Vs. 35b.) "My *taw*," which the RSV translates **my signature**, refers to the last letter of the Hebrew alphabet which had in the biblical period the shape of an X or cross, and which was written at the bottom of official or legal documents as a sign of approval or assent. By using this phrase, does Job refer to an actual writing? Is he not rather speaking dramatically, as if he were portraying himself at the supreme court of heaven? Then he describes in vs. 35ab his plea for a hearing, and perhaps alludes to the defense he has just now finished uttering (29:1–31:34, 38-40). This defense, however, is actually a challenge, for it requires a reply. **Let the Almighty answer me!** In vs. 35c, a new idea seems to take shape in his mind. **Oh, that I had the indictment written by my adversary!** The Hebrew word ספר, translated by the RSV as **indictment**, is, lit., a book, "a written statement," or "a letter," sometimes used in a juridical context, hence "a bill," "a deed," or "a contract" (cf. Deut. 24:1, 3; Isa. 50:1; Jer. 32:11-12; etc.). After having obtained an audience, the hero continues in imagination to anticipate the trial and now expects to hear the charges which God has made against him. The phrase איש־ריבי means, lit., "my opponent" (cf. Isa. 41:11; also Exod. 23:6; Deut. 21:5; Judg. 12:2), but does not necessarily designate a human **adversary**. In this context it obviously refers to God. Kissane, apparently uneasy over the presence of the word איש, "man," in the idiomatic expression איש־ריבי, suggests the correction of the final letter (ו instead of י), thus obtaining a pronominal suffix of the third person. The line might then be read, "His [God's] opponent has [already] written a defense," and would thus refer to Job. It would be strange, however, for the hero to speak of himself suddenly in the third person in a context which has consistently used the first person. In all probability the expression איש־ריב was idiomatic and did not refer specifically to "a man" but to "the adverse party."

Job is in perfect control of his emotions. He does not feel in the least apprehensive over the charges which are going to be officially pronounced against him. He is so certain of his innocence that he not only will have no sense of fear or shame before the public disclosure of his **indictment**, but he will also don it and wear it as a trophy or **as a crown** (vs. 36). He knows confidently that he can refute point by point "the bill of accusation," for nothing in his life needs to be dissimulated. **I would give him an account of all my steps** (vs. 37a). The poet concludes his portrait of the self-righteous man with uncommon brilliance. Job will dispute with the Almighty Judge and argue his case without any sense of moral limitation, let alone guilt (cf. 40:2). The psychological "build-up" reaches its climax in the last sentence: **like a prince I would approach him** (vs. 37b). The pronominal suffix in the phrase אקרבנו, "I would present myself to him," designates God, not the indictment, as in the parallel construction, אגידנו, "I would reveal to him" (vs. 37a). Therefore there is no ground for the common translation, "I shall present it,"

---

pened to him in mind or body or estate, but because he is forsaken of soul, betrayed by the God he had known and by the friends he had loved, he will yet refer his case, appeal it beyond all courts to the highest court, to that ultimate justice which must be in God beyond all seeming and back of every appearance (cf. Expos. on 13:1-12; 14:15). He comes in supreme confidence, **like a prince,** wearing as a trophy everything that God can possibly say about him (see Expos. on 19:4). **My desire is . . . that mine adversary had written a book** seems to be a

favorite with literary critics. To weasel words from what stateliness, to pygmies from what giants! If there is love in the heart of the Eternal it is bound to speak now. And speak it does. Out of the whirlwind it speaks, and speaks at once in the book as the poet left it. Whatever else may be thought of them, the speeches of Elihu are an intrusion. Swift upon Job's last words come the words of One who at Creation said, "Let there be light: and there was light." "And all the sons of God shouted for joy" (38:7b). That shout is trembling now in the air,

38 If my land cry against me, or that the furrows likewise thereof complain;

39 If I have eaten the fruits thereof without money, or have caused the owners thereof to lose their life:

38 "If my land has cried out against me,
    and its furrows have wept together;
39 if I have eaten its yield without payment,
    and caused the death of its owners;

---

i.e., "my bill of accusation." In addition, the Piel of the verb קרב has here an intransitive meaning (cf. Ezek. 36:8). **A prince** (נגיד) is a leader, one who is accustomed to march in front of others. The expression is commonly applied to the kings of Israel, especially to David and Solomon (I Sam. 13:14; I Kings 1:35; etc.), and it implies an ingrained sense of social responsibility, authority, and power. The poet could not have chosen a better word to suggest the inward self-confidence of his hero. Never does man in the Bible or elsewhere in the ancient literature of the Near East approach the deity **as a prince** (contrast Isa. 6:5; Mic. 6:6; etc.). The Semitic rulers called themselves "slaves" and used other self-deprecating terms in a frantic display of abjectness before their gods and goddesses. The hero, tortured by God and condemned by men, has not any sense of human finitude, or at least is not aware of the holiness of God. He faces the prospect of the divine presence with the assurance and dignity of an Arab sheik, ready to accost an equal. Thus the poet allows the unbowed sufferer to keep one possession in an outwardly destitute state: the pride of self-righteousness (cf. 32:1). Some critics do not discern here any evidence of impious audacity. Note, however, Peake's observation: "Defiant the tone may be, but why should the poet have shrunk from letting his hero brave God, in proud assurance of his integrity? It is no emasculated pietist whom he has chosen for his protagonist in this titanic struggle." (*Job*, p. 273.) In fact, the poet is thus able to introduce the theological problem of the relationship between God and man in the sharpest possible delineation. God's self-disclosure (chs. 38–41) will come as unexpectedly as a thunderbolt in the blue sky of ethical self-satisfaction.

d) ONE FURTHER SELF-IMPRECATION (31:38-40)

38-40. Most modern commentators think that these verses are now accidentally displaced and should be transferred between vss. 34 and 35. "It is disastrous," writes Peake, "that after the splendid close in verses 35-37 a dislocation of verses should have brought verses 38-40 into their present position, where they ruin the effect" (*ibid.*). Other critics likewise maintain not unreasonably that after Job has imagined the picture of his expected audience before the sovereign Judge, "to bring him down again to thistles and cockle is indeed an anti-climax" (Strahan, *Job, ad loc.*). The biblical student, however, must be extremely cautious in tampering with the text. There is no evidence whatever, either from Hebrew MSS or from those of the ancient versions, to support the thesis of a textual disorder at this point. Indeed, those scholars who agree on the conjecture of the dislocation are in wide disagreement when they suggest a reconstruction of the "original" order. N. Peters places these verses between vss. 8 and 9; Budde, between vss. 12 and 13; Hontheim, between vss. 14 and 16; Kennicott, between vss. 25 and 26; Merx, Duhm, Dhorme, and Kissane, between vss. 32 and 33; Driver and Gray, as well as many other critics, between vss. 34 and 35. One must bear in mind that Aristotelian canons of logic should not be applied to the processes of thinking which are common to Oriental (or

---

as they look down from the battlements of heaven. A life yonder on the earth, and the refuse heap is breaking into its springtime.

There is indeed a court of last appeal (Ps. 27:10). And there is a way of drawing near (Heb. 4:14-16). But the challenge is not by merit. It is for mercy (see Expos. on 7:7-10; 9:14-19; 10:8-12; 35:2-3).

38-40. *Cursed Is the Ground.*—It has been observed (see Expos. on vs. 1) that in the imprecations which Job calls down upon himself the punishment is conceived of as bearing close relation to the crime itself. Parents might learn something from reading this chapter. People who by their greed fashion dust bowls might conceivably profit. There is a strange corre-

40 Let thistles grow instead of wheat, and cockle instead of barley. The words of Job are ended.

32 So these three men ceased to answer Job, because he *was* righteous in his own eyes.

40 let thorns grow instead of wheat,
    and foul weeds instead of barley."

The words of Job are ended.

32 So these three men ceased to answer Job, because he was righteous in his

---

Occidental!) poets. Furthermore, the poet of Job himself appears to favor the device of the afterthought (cf. 3:16; 9:32; 14:13; etc.), and he also gives the impression of deliberately placing a climax not at the end but just before the end of a development (cf. 3:23; 7:20; 10:20; 14:15; etc.). He may be unconsciously following a method not unlike that of the Greek tragedians or Shakespeare, for he is wont to terminate the discourses of his characters not with a climactic display of violent emotion, but with a subdued and almost monotonic phrasing which ends and yet does not end in some unfinished suspense of quietness and melancholy (cf., e.g., 10:21-22). The result—if not the conscious intent—of such rhetoric may be a relaxing of the tension which has been produced on the auditors or readers and a subsequent return to a kind of emotional normalcy.

The "soil" (*'adhāmāh*) sown by the hero would have **cried out, . . . and its furrows** [would] **have wept together** (vs. 38), if it had been acquired illegally or murderously (vs. 39). Job may here again remember the myth of the Garden of Eden (cf. Gen. 3:17), in which the "soil" (*'adhāmāh*) is cursed on account of man (*'ādhām*). Elsewhere in the Hebrew scripture it is not the **land** but the blood shed upon it which cries out for vengeance (cf. 16:18; Gen. 4:10; also I Kings 21:1 ff.). Job knows that if he had obtained his fields in criminal fashion, he like Cain would have been "cursed from the ground" (cf. Gen. 4:11-12).

III. Discourses of Elihu (32:1–37:24)

These chapters introduce a new speaker who has not yet been mentioned either in the prologue or in the poetic discussion, and who is likewise ignored in the discourses of Yahweh and in the epilogue. Thus they raise a number of literary problems (see Intro., pp. 890-91).

The plan of the Elihu speeches is indicated in the present text by a series of introductory formulas which appear in 32:6; 34:1; 35:1; 36:1. In addition, there seems to be a

---

spondence between deed and destiny (see Expos. on 18:5-21; 20:4-11). Here the very **land** cries out against the usurper, and the **furrows** weep for thought of the slave labor that plows them (vss. 38*a*, 39*b*). Kissane locates these verses after vs. 32 [1]—though Davidson and Lanchester suggest that the poet's taste may not have coincided with ours, and they would perhaps better be left where they are [2]—and cites Deut. 24: 14-16; Jas. 5:4.

It was not unnatural that among nomadic tribes the tilling of the soil was once regarded as a hard necessity laid on man as a curse (Gen. 3:17-19; 4:12*a*). Many a time, in twisted mind, it has been made so; with results that Oliver Goldsmith, among others, once recorded:

Ill fares the land, to hastening ills a prey,
Where wealth accumulates, and men decay:
Princes and lords may flourish, or may fade;
A breath can make them, as a breath has made;
But a bold peasantry, their country's pride,
When once destroy'd, can never be supplied.[3]

Ruthless efforts to destroy, periodic attempts to conserve and reclaim, with a nature forever healing her own wounds under the beneficent hand of God (Matt. 5:45): the long story of the ages has profound implications for all human life.

32:1–37:24. The Speeches of Elihu.—These four speeches (chs. 33; 34; 35; 36–37; see Exeg. for analysis), on the whole labored and wordy, yet not without their flashes of imagination and

[1] *Job*, p. 208.
[2] *Job*, p. 255.

[3] "The Deserted Village," l. 51.

clear division in 33:1 and again in 36:26. Chs. 32–36 may accordingly be analyzed as follows: A. Preface in Prose (32:1-5) ; B. Poetic Introduction (32:6-22), in which Elihu addresses the three friends and the bystanders in an attempt to justify his intervention; C. First Part (33:1–35:16) in which Elihu refutes (1) Job's charge that God reveals his injustice by his silence (33:1-33) ; (2) Job's attack on God's retribution of good and evil (34:1-37) ; and (3) Job's conviction of innocence (35:1-16) ; D. Second Part (36:1–37:24), in which Elihu constructively ' (1) describes God's use of human suffering (36:1-25) ; (2) praises God's transcendence over the universe (36:26–37:13) ; and (3) admonishes Job to acknowledge with humility the divinity of God (37:14-24).

Whatever the literary origin of these discourses may have been, they undoubtedly offer a significant transition from the last words of the hero (31:40c) to the discourses of Yahweh (38:1–42:6). The opinion has often been expressed that they lessen the dramatic power of the book, but one may also observe that they constitute a kind of "gradual" to the divine theophany.

A. Preface in Prose (32:1-5)

1. Silence of the Friends (32:1)

32:1. The expression **these three men** indicates a stylistic departure from the habit of the poet who speaks of "three friends" (2:11 ff.; 42:10; cf. 19:21). It is found in Ezek. 14:14, 16, where it designates Noah, Job, and Daniel. The construction of the verb שבת with the preposition מן and the infinitive (**ceased to answer;** lit., "rested from answering") may be a reminiscence of the prophetic style (Jer. 31:36; Hos. 7:4). Job's confession and oath of clearance (29:1–31:40) have at last persuaded Eliphaz, Bildad, and Zophar that he is a hopeless case: **He was righteous in his own eyes** (vs. 1b). The LXX, Symm., and the Syriac read בעיניהם, "in their eyes," instead of בעיניו, **in his own eyes,** and this rendering is favored by several commentators on the ground that the friends were all along aware of Job's self-righteousness. The same view is held by other critics on the assumption that Job's passionate peroration finally convinced the friends of his innocence —a conviction which would easily explain the ire of Elihu (vs. 2). But nothing in the text allows the exegete to think that the friends have been won over to Job's side. On the contrary, it is obvious that the antagonism which separates them from Job throughout the poetic discussion has grown deeper and deeper. In addition, Elihu's anger is not aroused by the friends' avowal of Job's innocence, but rather by their silence which might easily lend itself to a wrong interpretation (see vs. 3b), and also by the belief that Job "justified himself before God" (see Exeg. on vs. 2b). It is therefore necessary to

insight (cf. 34:14-15)—repetitious and by no means an integral part of the poem, yet not without their significant contribution to the controversy—are the insertion of a later hand, and no doubt represent the clarifications, amplifications, and corrections of succeeding generations (see Intro., pp. 890-91, and Exeg.). The original poem may very well have given the impression that the case for orthodoxy was irretrievably lost (cf. 32:13, 15), and somebody, years after, felt that something had to be done about it. That "something" is Elihu, who has never been heard of before, and is dropped out of sight as soon as he leaves off speaking. Irritated by the silence of the friends (32:15-16) and their failure to justify the ways of God (vs. 12b), and outraged by the things Job has said (34:7), he is constrained to underscore two facts which thus far have not been adequately

dealt with: (a) that as far as the wicked are concerned, God bides his time, not simply to vindicate his righteousness (cf. Expos. on 21:19), but in order to provide opportunity for repentance (33:17-18) ; and (b) that everything God does is done lovingly (as in 36:15; cf. Expos. on 1:6), for a man's own highest good (33:14-30). Both of these threads have appeared in the course of the argument (see Expos. on 4:8; 5:17), but nowhere have they been woven into the pattern as Elihu, with many an interesting and not unskillful reference to what has already been said, now undertakes to weave them.

1-22. The Advantages and Disadvantages of Youth.—In vss. 1-5 the author gives his reasons for introducing Elihu. Dramatically they are presented as Elihu's reasons, which then in the rest of the chapter he is allowed in his own proper person to elaborate more fully; but back

2 Then was kindled the wrath of Elihu the son of Barachel the Buzite, of the kindred of Ram: against Job was his wrath kindled, because he justified himself rather than God.

own eyes. 2 Then Eli'hu the son of Bar'achel the Buzite, of the family of Ram, became angry. He was angry at Job because he

---

preserve the reading of the M.T. in vs. 1*b*. The statement thus accepted is not in disagreement with the poet. Indeed, Job has maintained throughout the discussion that he is certain of his own righteousness; and the poet, though in warm sympathy with the hero's plight, has never given the impression that he condoned human pride, even that which is provoked and intensified by physical and mental tortures.

2. Presentation of Elihu (32:2*a*)

2*a*. The name **Elihu** means "My God is he," and it is used for several Hebrew individuals like the grandfather of Elkanah (I Sam. 1:1), a Manasseh soldier (I Chr. 12:20), a Levite (I Chr. 26:7), and a brother of David (I Chr. 27:18). The name **Barachel** means "Bless, O God!" or "Bless God!" or more probably "God blesses" (cf. *Barikili* in the *Business Documents of Murashû Sons of Nippur,* ed. H. V. Hilprecht

---

of them is the mind of a man who is himself **angry.** The word is repeated four times in five verses. He is angry because the debate, which never should have been allowed to conclude as it does, has left Job in complete mastery of the situation (vs. 1*a*). He is angry at Job for making himself out to be in the right before the face of God, even hinting that he was better than God himself (24:12; 30:25). He is angry at the friends, because they could make no adequate reply. If "their own eyes" were to be read in vs. 1 (with the LXX and Syriac; yet see Exeg.), and "God" instead of "Job" in vs. 3*b*, his case against them would be considerably strengthened. In fact and in short, he is angry (vs. 5). And there is little ground for supposing that he was alone among those of "the younger generation" into whose hands the poem came in its earlier form. It offended them too, as the friends were offended, and with all due deference where not too much deference was due (vs. 9; cf. 12:12), they had a word to say that would illumine the matter and make it quite unnecessary to call in God (vs. 13).

Always when youth essays to play its part it begins with impatience, and often rightly so. It was not born to a mold, and much that comes down to it is warped and twisted by the past. But impatience is one thing, and true indignation another. There is room enough for righteous indignation. Luther has been called Germany's angry man. Sweeping condemnation is still another thing (vss. 9, 12). It is never necessary to clear the board and start over. The baby should only on occasion be thrown out with the bath. Said a sophomore in a woman's college: "I have heard a good many preachers, and read a good many religious books; now I have made

up my mind that all of it has to go. I must begin for myself, and begin at scratch." It would never have worked in a chemical laboratory.

Yet Elihu is no laughingstock, and would better not be treated so. Untrammeled by the traditions that bound his elders, he is in a somewhat better position to discern the truth than any of the friends, certainly than either Bildad or Zophar. If he has any affinity, it is with Eliphaz, to whom he frequently though for the most part indirectly refers. He too is a kind of seer, profoundly in earnest, heir of all that has been, and indeed prophet of things to come (cf. Exeg. on vs. 23*a*). Measure the strides he has taken. To others the spirit of God may be as "the blast of his anger" (see Expos. on 4:9-11) that consumes the wicked, or as the wind that makes the heavens fair (26:13); to him it is not only the breath that gives him life (33:4), as it gives life to all men (34:14-15), it is the **breath . . . that makes him understand** (vs. 8; cf. Prov. 20:27). To others God may be slowly disappearing in the vastness of a moral order (see Expos. on 8:4); but not to Elihu. When there are delays it is God's inexhaustible patience that waits (33:14-18; cf. 20:5); when chastening comes it is God's compassionate love that chastens (33:19-20). He understands the nature of sin better than any of the friends (cf. Exeg. on 34:5-9) and knows that in God's dealing with it justice never does tell the whole story; there is something back of justice, deep in the nature of God.

"Youth must be served." Perhaps. But to what extent? Far more pointedly, it has to be listened to (Luke 10:21).

2*b*. Can God Be Wrong?—It never occurred to Elihu or to the friends that the God of their

3 Also against his three friends was his
wrath kindled, because they had found no
answer, and *yet* had condemned Job.

4 Now Elihu had waited till Job had
spoken, because they *were* elder than he.

justified himself rather than God; **3** he was
angry also at Job's three friends because
they had found no answer, although they
had declared Job to be in the wrong. **4** Now
Eli'hu had waited to speak to Job because

---

and A. T. Clay [Philadelphia: University of Pennsylvania Press, 1898], Tablet 73, line 4,
etc.). Inasmuch as Elihu was the son of a **Buzite,** he was also a fellow countryman of Job,
because Buz was a brother of Uz (Gen. 22:21; cf. Job 1:1), and thus the new speaker was
more closely related to Job than the three friends were. Furthermore, although Buz was
a son of Nahor and thus an Aramaean (Gen. 11:26; 22:20; 24:10), the **family of Ram**
was associated with the tribe of Judah (cf. Ruth 4:19; I Chr. 2:9-10). Moreover the
appellation **Buzite** may refer to a locality mentioned in Jer. 25:23 after Dedan and Tema,
and the name "Buz" is probably the same as *Bâzu* in the Akkadian inscriptions (see
Dhorme, *Le livre de Job,* p. xx). Thus Elihu is represented as coming from the same
region as Job and the three friends, at the juncture of the territories of the Edomites,
the Aramaeans, and the Arabs, but as more directly linked with the Hebraic groups.
This latter detail may symbolize or explain the peculiar emphasis of his theological
outlook.

3. Reasons for Elihu's Intervention (32:2b-5)

2b-3. The anger of Elihu is directed against Job because **he justified himself rather
than God** (vs. 2b); lit., "he justified his *néphesh*," i.e., "his life with its desires and
ambitions." The translation **rather than,** however, is not probable, for the verb is used
here in the Piel (cf. the Hiphil in 27:5) as in Jer. 3:11; Ezek. 16:51, 52, where the
comparison is not between man and God but between Israel and Judah (cf. also Job
33:32). Moreover, in the book of Job generally the preposition מִן constructed with the
name of the Deity means not "more than" but "before," "in the presence of" (cf. 4:17;
35:2). Thus Elihu's attitude is provoked by the spectacle of Job's theological and spiritual
arrogance. It is more than an intellectual pride displayed in an argument *about* God:
Job "showed his life to be righteous *before* God." The phrase points to an existential
rather than to a purely academic situation. Actually Job by his attitude had made himself
appear even more just than God.

Elihu was irritated also by the **three friends because they had found no answer,
although they had declared Job to be in the wrong** (vs. 3). The RSV attempts to make
sense out of the traditional M.T. (cf. the **yet** of KJV), but the true rendering is elsewhere,
since the word אִיּוֹב, "Job"—as attested by the tradition itself—constitutes one of the
eighteen *Tiqqûnê Sôpherîm* (cf. Vol. I, p. 51) and represents a substitution for the
word אֱלֹהִים, "God." The scribes could not bring themselves to write as offensive a clause
as "and they condemned God." Fortunately the meaning of the original text is clear.
Elihu interpreted the silence of the friends as equivalent to a condemnation of God. This
does not mean at all that they did not hold Job to be in the wrong. But the fact remains
that they did not speak after Job's final claim to self-righteousness, and to Elihu their
silence appeared to be an acquiescence. Hence the kindling of his **wrath.**

4-5. Elihu's anger exploded the more violently because he had to contain himself
during the discussion on account of his inordinate youth. Vs. 4a is either corrupt or rather

---

faith was not necessarily the true God, and that
therefore the God they knew might be wrong.
One might well have said to the crusaders, to
the inquisitors, to many a slaveowner, "Your
God is my devil" (cf. Expos. on 13:13-19; 19:
22a); as indeed to all those who quote Scripture and distort truth. The God of a one hun-

dred per cent American may be wrong. But the
problem is not easily solved even by an appeal
to revelation. What is the Bible saying to the
man who, with all the apparatus of scholarship,
has discovered what it says? Anything? Nothing?
He is not ready to hear until he comes humbly
into the presence of Christ (see Expos. on vs.

5 When Elihu saw that *there was* no answer in the mouth of *these* three men, then his wrath was kindled.

6 And Elihu the son of Barachel the Buzite answered and said, I *am* young, and ye *are* very old; wherefore I was afraid, and durst not show you mine opinion.

7 I said, Days should speak, and multitude of years should teach wisdom.

8 But *there is* a spirit in man: and the inspiration of the Almighty giveth them understanding.

9 Great men are not *always* wise: neither do the aged understand judgment.

they were older than he. 5 And when Eli'hu saw that there was no answer in the mouth of these three men, he became angry.

6 And Eli'hu the son of Bar'achel the Buzite answered:

"I am young in years,
    and you are aged;
therefore I was timid and afraid
    to declare my opinion to you.
7 I said, 'Let days speak,
    and many years teach wisdom.'
8 But it is the spirit in a man,
    the breath of the Almighty, that makes
        him understand.
9 It is not the old*r* that are wise,
    nor the aged that understand what is
        right.

r Gk Syr Vg: Heb *many*

---

awkward, for it literally reads, "Elihu waited for [?] Job with words" (see KJV), but the meaning is not in doubt (see RSV). The observation that the three friends and Job **were older than he** does not indicate that they were advanced in age. It rather emphasizes the youthfulness of Elihu (cf. vs. 6). The prolixity of vs. 5 may be intentional.

B. POETIC INTRODUCTION (32:6-22)
1. SPIRIT, NOT AGE, IS THE SOURCE OF WISDOM (32:6-10)

6-10. The new speaker reveals a remarkable mixture of timidity and boldness. On the one hand, he acknowledges that he has kept silent because he felt the restraint of his youth (צעיר, "little," "insignificant," "puny," hence **young**; vs. 6; Gen. 43:33; etc.; cf. Judg. 6:15; Ps. 119:141); on the other hand, he was not lacking in דע (a late word), **opinion** or "knowledge," "science," "definite conviction" (vs. 6*b*; cf. vss. 10, 17), and there is an undertone of persiflage or even sarcasm when he confides,

> I said, "Let days speak,
>   and many years teach wisdom" (vs. 7).

This appears in his next statement more explicitly. Age does not in itself produce wisdom, i.e., the capacity to **understand what is right** (vs. 9; it is **the spirit** (*rûaḥ*) which **is in a man,** i.e., **the breath of the Almighty,** that gives discernment (vs. 8; cf. Ps. 119:130). Elihu alludes to divine inspiration, not to a "spiritual" element in human nature (as well recognized by Targ. which rendered רוח נבואתא, "the spirit of prophecy," and by Symm. who translated πνεῦμα θεοῦ, "the spirit of God"). Job and his friends speak of human "spirit" (6:4; 7:11; 15:13) but only in the sense of man's emotional, intellectual, or volitive faculties (as a parallel term to *néphesh*); and when they refer to the spirit of God, they hardly distinguish it from the stormy wind or the manifestation of divine judgment (4:9; 26:13). Elihu, on the contrary, thinks of the divine **spirit** or **breath** in

---

. Even then the self cannot be utterly rid of self, or of the self's distortions. What wonder that "the publican, standing afar off, would not lift up so much as his eyes unto heaven, but smote upon his breast, saying, God be merciful to me a sinner" (Luke 18:13)? Is there anything else for one who knows how it is with the human soul? Meanwhile the "impious" often are pos-

sessed of a piety denied the "pious." How often the "saint" is proved a heretic, and the "heretic" is revered as a saint!

6-8. *Arriving at a Conviction.*— (Cf. Expos. on 12:2-6; 18:21; 21:5-6.) Elihu seems to have come to his task with something more than dogmatically conceived presuppositions (cf. Expos. on 2:11-13). It is not "wisdom" of which

10 Therefore I said, Hearken to me; I also will show mine opinion.

11 Behold, I waited for your words; I gave ear to your reasons, whilst ye searched out what to say.

12 Yea, I attended unto you, and, behold, *there was* none of you that convinced Job, *or* that answered his words:

13 Lest ye should say, We have found out wisdom: God thrusteth him down, not man.

14 Now he hath not directed *his* words against me: neither will I answer him with your speeches.

10 Therefore I say, 'Listen to me;
　　let me also declare my opinion.'

11 "Behold, I waited for your words,
　　I listened for your wise sayings,
　　while you searched out what to say.

12 I gave you my attention,
　　and, behold, there was none that co
　　futed Job,
　　or that answered his words, among yo

13 Beware lest you say, 'We have four
　　wisdom;
　　God may vanquish him, not man.'

14 He has not directed his words against m
　　and I will not answer him with you
　　speeches.

---

terms of creativity (33:4; 34:12-15; cf. Gen. 1:2; 2:7) and of prophetic revelation (vs 18 ff.; cf. Num. 27:18; II Kings 2:15; Isa. 29:10; Mic. 2:11). Life, wisdom, and unde standing are the gifts of God, not the natural endowment of man. Nevertheless, Elihu not characterized by the humility and the reverent agnosticism of the prophet. He clain a possession of the divine spirit and for that reason insists on declaring his opinio (vs. 10).

2. FAILURE OF THE PROFESSIONALS (32:11-14)

11-14. In the second part of his exordium the new discourser no longer explains h previous silence on the basis of his youth. **I waited . . . while you searched out what to sa** (vs. 11). His deference has given place to definite rudeness. Those ancient worthies, s he implies, have done their best in trying to "dig" (חקר) from the treasury of the pas the wealth of experience, and—as moderns might say—the depths of the subconsciou but **behold, there was none that confuted Job . . . among you** (vs. 12). Elihu uses the sam participial form (מוכיח, "convincer," "rebuker") as Job did in 9:33, but in a differer sense which is shown by the parallel word עונה, "answerer" (vs. 12b). The sequence c thought between vs. 13a and vs. 13b is slightly elliptical. **Beware lest you say, "We hav found wisdom;** [but we must admit now that we have failed with Job. Obviously, Go alone, not any human being, can convince him of his guilt.] **God may vanquish him not man."** In other words, Elihu says to the three friends, "How can you claim to hav discovered wisdom while you admit defeat in this case?" Some commentators interpre vs. 13a as an ironical statement: "In Job we have found wisdom personified." But th words clearly refer to the friends' claims for the validity of their own position (cf. vs: 7, 9). Inasmuch as the word ידפנו, **thrusteth him down,** lit., "drives him away," appea in one Hebrew MS as ירדפנו, "persecutes him" (see Graetz *et al.*), the text of th Masoretic tradition is not certain. Dhorme therefore is willing to emend the wor ידפנו to ילפנו, "has instructed us," thus bringing vs. 13 into agreement with the precedin context. In all probability, however, the M.T. is correct, but the special nuanc of the jussive must be brought out forcefully: "Let God drive him out!" Th meaning of the verse now becomes obvious. Elihu is startled by the friends' apparen defeatism. He therefore admonishes them, "Do not say, 'We have found wisdom (an

---

he speaks (vss. 6, 10, 17), neither sentiment nor theory, but "knowledge." He has listened and set his mind to work on what he has heard (vss. 6-7, 9, 11-12). There is evidence that he has allowed his heart to speak (33:23-24, 29-30; 35:10-11; 37:13). Add to that not pride (see

Expos. on vss. 1-22) but humility (see Expos on vs. 2b), not presumption (vss. 21-22) bu courage; then give it the brooding, yearning restless love of Paul and you have a man wh has long been at home in the one Presence o this earth where the words of Elihu can com

15 They were amazed, they answered no more: they left off speaking.

16 When I had waited, (for they spake not, but stood still, *and* answered no more,)

17 *I said,* I will answer also my part; I also will show mine opinion.

18 For I am full of matter; the spirit within me constraineth me.

19 Behold, my belly *is* as wine *which* hath no vent; it is ready to burst like new bottles.

20 I will speak, that I may be refreshed: I will open my lips and answer.

21 Let me not, I pray you, accept any man's person; neither let me give flattering titles unto man.

22 For I know not to give flattering titles; *in so doing* my Maker would soon take me away.

33 Wherefore, Job, I pray thee, hear my speeches, and hearken to all my words.

---

15 "They are discomfited, they answer no more;
they have not a word to say.

16 And shall I wait, because they do not speak,
because they stand there, and answer no more?

17 I also will give my answer;
I also will declare my opinion.

18 For I am full of words,
the spirit within me constrains me.

19 Behold, my heart is like wine that has no vent;
like new wineskins, it is ready to burst.

20 I must speak, that I may find relief;
I must open my lips and answer.

21 I will not show partiality to any person
or use flattery toward any man.

22 For I do not know how to flatter,
else would my Maker soon put an end to me.

33 "But now, hear my speech, O Job,
and listen to all my words.

---

that is enough for us) . Let God drive Job away like chaff! This is not the responsibility of man!'" "Not so," retorts the youthful intruder; "I am going to show you a new line of approach." The M.T. of vs. 14*a* does not offer a satisfactory sequence of thought in the present context (cf. KJV, RSV) , but may be easily emended on the basis of the ancient versions. If one reads with the Syriac אערך instead of ערך (the scribal error is due to haplography) and with the LXX כאלה instead of אלי, vs. 14*a* may be rendered, "And I am not going to array words like these," which offers a satisfactory parallelism to vs. 14*b*, **neither will I answer him with your speeches.**

3. Inner Compulsion to Speak (32:15-22)

15-22. In the third part of his preamble Elihu continues his reflections in the style of soliloquy, perhaps in order to indicate his contempt for the impotent professionals. Of course it is because these men have found no answer to Job that he will now speak (vss. 15-16) and reveal his **opinion** (vs. 17) . He is so **full of words** that he cannot contain them, and **the spirit within** [him; lit., "his belly"] **constrains** him (vs. 18) . Like Jeremiah (20:9), this would-be prophet **is ready to burst** (vs. 19) . He **must speak** in order to **be refreshed** (a euphemistic translation; vs. 20; cf. I Sam. 16:23) . The sense of his own creatureliness will prevent him from giving titles to any man (vss. 21-22; cf. Isa. 44:5) . Elihu speaks with the tactlessness of a sincerity not mellowed by love.

C. First Part: Refutation of Job's Defense (33:1–35:16)

The speaker now attempts to succeed where the friends have failed. In order to reach his aim he will address first Job (ch. 33), then the friends (ch. 34), and again the hero (ch. 35) .

---

most deeply true: **It is . . . the breath of the Almighty, that makes him understand.**

18-20. *Under Constraint.*—The pressure has become intolerable. Elihu can hardly breathe.

He is **ready to burst** with it. The holding back (vss. 6, 11-12), the conclusion to which he has been reluctantly (?) forced (vs. 9), the impulse far away underneath it all which he is confident

2 Behold, now I have opened my mouth, my tongue hath spoken in my mouth.

3 My words *shall be of* the uprightness of my heart: and my lips shall utter knowledge clearly.

4 The Spirit of God hath made me, and the breath of the Almighty hath given me life.

5 If thou canst answer me, set *thy words* in order before me, stand up.

6 Behold, I *am* according to thy wish in God's stead: I also am formed out of the clay.

7 Behold, my terror shall not make thee afraid, neither shall my hand be heavy upon thee.

2 Behold, I open my mouth;
    the tongue in my mouth speaks.

3 My words declare the uprightness of my heart,
    and what my lips know they speak sincerely.

4 The spirit of God has made me,
    and the breath of the Almighty gives me life.

5 Answer me, if you can;
    set your words in order before me; take your stand.

6 Behold, I am toward God as you are;
    I too was formed from a piece of clay.

7 Behold, no fear of me need terrify you;
    my pressure will not be heavy upon you.

---

1. Meaning of Endurance in Suffering (33:1-33)

a) A Discussion from Man to Man (33:1-7)

33:1-7. The speaker protests his utter candor (vss. 1-3) and then invites Job to listen to him without fear and to **take** [his] **stand** (vs. 5) since they are both equals in their created humanity (vss. 6-7). **I am toward God as you are** (vs. 6a). It is not necessary to recognize here an implied criticism of the poetic discussion and especially of the theophany. Elihu merely reassures the hero who had repeatedly expressed his fear of the Deity (9:32, 34; 13:21; etc.).

---

must be assigned to a source beyond himself (vss. 8, 18b) : the time has come to speak out. So like—and yet unlike—the daily burden of another life, in debt to God (II Cor. 5:14) and man (Rom. 1:14-16; cf. Expos. on 29:1-25).

33:6-7. *I Am Toward God as You Are.*—In his first reply to what Job has been saying, Elihu, after a kind of exordium, addresses himself (a) in general to the charges of unjust treatment which Job has brought against God (vss. 8-11; see Exeg.), contending simply that no man has any right at all to judge God on the basis of his own ideas of what is right and what is wrong (vs. 12c); and (b) more particularly to Job's oft repeated assertion that God pays no attention (cf. 19:7), pointing out that it is indeed quite otherwise, as Job himself should know from his own experience: God speaks not only in dreams (cf. 7:14), to turn man away from his sin and to keep him from destruction (vss. 15-18), but also in affliction, sending his angels of instruction (vs. 23), and restoring the penitent to praise and thanksgiving (vss. 24-30).

The introduction (vss. 1-7), far less offensive to the Oriental than to the Western ear, stresses again his sincerity (vs. 3), and while perhaps once more subtly suggesting that the theophany of the original poem was wholly unnecessary (cf. 32:13b), attempts to undercut Job's insistence

that a fair trial of the case in hand was impossible (9:3, 14-16, 20, *et passim*). Elihu is a man as Job is, formed of clay (cf. 10:9), given life by the spirit of God (reading vs. 4 after vs. 6?) no need to be terrified of him (cf. 13:21; 23:15) his **pressure** [**hand**] **will not be heavy.** The **in God's stead** of the KJV is an attractive mistranslation. Job had wanted (**according to the wish**) somebody to play that role (9:33; etc.) But the point Elihu is making is rather that he stands where Job stands, on the same, created mortal footing, sharing a common lot, bearer of a common light (32:8), albeit in some uncommon measure. Except for that last intimation which runs through everything he has to say, he would have been a model for all expositors. Not once had the friends admitted in so many words that they too were subject to human frailties. They had spoken abstractly, as from a great height (cf. Expos. on 2:11-13; 4:1–5:27; 8:3 11:2-6); from that height Elihu comes at least part way down (see Expos. on 5:8)—as all men must who undertake either comfort or counsel who wish to make difficult the all too ready defense of conscious inferiority or helplessness, or to take away the refuge of uniqueness and estrangement. In the very words one draws nearer and nearer to the mystery of the Incarnation, and to what Job required that God should

8 Surely thou hast spoken in mine hearing, and I have heard the voice of *thy* words, *saying,*

9 I am clean without transgression, I *am* innocent; neither *is there* iniquity in me.

10 Behold, he findeth occasions against me, he counteth me for his enemy;

11 He putteth my feet in the stocks, he marketh all my paths.

12 Behold, *in* this thou art not just: I will answer thee, that God is greater than man.

13 Why dost thou strive against him? for he giveth not account of any of his matters.

8 "Surely, you have spoken in my hearing, and I have heard the sound of your words.

9 You say, 'I am clean, without transgression; I am pure, and there is no iniquity in me.

10 Behold, he finds occasions against me, he counts me as his enemy;

11 he puts my feet in the stocks, and watches all my paths.'

12 "Behold, in this you are not right. I will answer you. God is greater than man.

13 Why do you contend against him, saying, 'He will answer none of my[s] words'?

[s] Compare Gk: Heb *his*

---

b) IMPLICATIONS OF JOB'S CLAIMS (33:8-12)

8-12. In order to argue with Job, the new interlocutor is compelled to quote from the hero's earlier statements (vss. 8-11; cf. 9:21; 10:7; 16:17; 23:10-12; 27:5-6; 31:1 ff.; cf. especially vs. 10*b* with 13:24*b*; vs. 11 with 13:27*a*), and in some cases to attribute to Job some words which are not found in the poetic discussion (i.e., חַף, **innocent,** "immaculate," in vs. 9 and תְּנוּאוֹת, which should be read תֹּאֲנוֹת [cf. Judg. 14:4], **occasions,** in vs. 10). On the whole, however, Elihu does not misrepresent Job's repeated plea, except that he quotes words without understanding the depth of the hero's pain and sorrow. After recalling Job's claim to integrity, he merely confines himself to declaring negatively, **Behold, in this thou art not just** (rather, **right**), and positively, **I will answer thee, that God is greater than man** (vs. 12). Before pursuing this theme, however, he must raise an issue which Job has held to be fundamental.

c) SELF-DISCLOSURE OF GOD TO MAN (33:13-14)

13-14. The hero has complained that God does not answer man's questionings, and more specifically that God does not recognize man's innocence (vs. 13; cf. 9:2-3). It is not necessary to correct with the LXX דְּבָרָיו, **his words** (RSV mg.), into דְּבָרַי, **my words**

---

do and feared that he might (cf. Expos. on 7:7-10, 21*c*).

12. God Is Greater than Man.—Job is right when he expects in God at least the compassion which he finds in his own heart (30:25). The best that man knows is God's gift, and the gift must be like the giver. It is wrong to assume that God and man can have nothing in common (yet see Exeg. on 34:16-20; 35:5-8; also Expos. on 7:20*a*-21*a*; 22:2-5; 33:12; 35:5-7). There is a transvaluation of values, not a contradiction or a cancellation of them. But Elihu too is right when he insists that God cannot be judged by human standards. Job is doing precisely that, and precisely in that is Job wrong. Elihu is not primarily concerned with God's justice as the friends were, or with God's purpose, as Job has been

trying to make it out. Zophar has already spoken of how inscrutable God is (see Expos. on 11:7), but there the undertone was judgment; for Elihu here the undertone is grace (cf. Isa. 55:6-13; Rom. 11:33-36). God is beyond man's thought in this, that man cannot conceive of his lovingkindness and tender mercy. The author of these speeches understands that what has been needed all along, by the friends and Job alike, is a greater God than any they have been able to imagine. It is what is needed when evolution is suggested as a substitute for the Almighty, when men are frightened out of their dignity by interstellar space, when the world's evil piles so high that nothing human or divine seems a match for it—not another God, but a greater God. What the author of Elihu's speeches does not

14 For God speaketh once, yea twice, *yet man* perceiveth it not.

15 In a dream, in a vision of the night, when deep sleep falleth upon men, in slumberings upon the bed;

16 Then he openeth the ears of men, and sealeth their instruction,

17 That he may withdraw man *from his* purpose, and hide pride from man.

18 He keepeth back his soul from the pit, and his life from perishing by the sword.

19 He is chastened also with pain upon his bed, and the multitude of his bones with strong *pain:*

20 So that his life abhorreth bread, and his soul dainty meat.

---

14 For God speaks in one way,
     and in two, though man does not perceive it.

15 In a dream, in a vision of the night,
     when deep sleep falls upon men,
     while they slumber on their beds,

16 then he opens the ears of men,
     and terrifies them with warnings,

17 that he may turn man aside from his deed,
     and cut off*^l* pride from man;

18 he keeps back his soul from the Pit,
     his life from perishing by the sword.

19 "Man is also chastened with pain upon his bed,
     and with continual strife in his bones;

20 so that his life loathes bread,
     and his appetite dainty food.

l Cn: Heb *hide*

(RSV), since the third person pronoun refers to the אנוש, "man," in vs. 12. To the statement that God remains silent Elihu replies that **God speaks in one way, and in two** [cf. 40:5], **though man does not perceive it** (vs. 14). Job is wrong in thinking that God is deaf to his appeals, for Job thereby implies that there is no difference between infinity and finitude, creativity and creatureliness, and he forgets that "God is greater than man" (cf. vs. 12 which thus constitutes a transitional link between vss. 9-11 and vss. 14 ff.). The voice of the Almighty is clear to everyone who has ears to hear it.

d) God's Techniques and Man's Response (33:15-30)
(1) Warnings in the Night (33:15-18)

15-18. In the first place God sends his **warnings** (vs. 16) to men in night visions (cf. vs. 15b with 4:13b) **while they slumber on their beds** (vs. 15), and his purpose is always of a high ethical nature: (*a*) **that he may turn man aside from his deed** (vs. 17a); (*b*) **and cut off pride from man** (vs. 17b; read יכסח, cut off, "prune away" [cf. Isa. 33:12], instead of יכסה, hide); and thus (*c*) preserve him from untimely death (vs. 18).

(2) Chastening of Pain (33:19-22)

19-22. In the second place God chastens man by physical **pain** (vs. 19), which produces fasting (vs. 20) and thus a leanness (vs. 21) and awareness of mortality (vs.

---

understand is that only in the place of meeting between God and man can Job's anguish be resolved. An interesting series of studies could be worked out on the God of Eliphaz (see Expos. on 4:20b), of Bildad (see Expos. on 8:4), of Zophar (see Expos. on 11:7; 20:2b), of Job (see Expos. on 14:13-15), and Elihu (see Expos. on 32:6-22). "It is not the old that are wise" (32:9a).

14-30. God's Answers.—The implication is, of course, that the answers were there all the time (cf. Expos. on 17:3; 19:7; 24:12c; 35:9-16; 38:1–42:6; 38:1, 3), and Job did not perceive them (cf. 9:11; 19:7; 23:3); which is often the case.

He had made mention of his dreams, and he had bitterly complained of his afflictions; they were both God's beneficent messengers. God comes in dreams (7:14) not so much, as with Eliphaz, to reveal (see Expos. on 4:12-21), but rather to **turn man aside from his deed,** and prune away his **pride,** that **his soul** might be kept back **from the Pit,** and **his life from perishing** under the judgments of the Almighty. God comes in suffering (cf. vs. 20 with 6:6-7; vs. 21 with 19:20), that by some celestial visitant (see Exeg.) Job might be made "wise unto that which is good" (Rom. 16:19), and so, delivered and restored (cf. II Kings 5:14), come again

21 His flesh is consumed away, that it cannot be seen; and his bones *that* were not seen stick out.

22 Yea, his soul draweth near unto the grave, and his life to the destroyers.

23 If there be a messenger with him, an interpreter, one among a thousand, to show unto man his uprightness;

24 Then he is gracious unto him, and saith, Deliver him from going down to the pit: I have found a ransom.

---

21 His flesh is so wasted away that it cannot
    be seen;
  and his bones which were not seen
    stick out.

22 His soul draws near the Pit,
  and his life to those who bring death.

23 If there be for him an angel,
  a mediator, one of the thousand,
  to declare to man what is right for him;

24 and he is gracious to him, and says,
  'Deliver him from going down into the
    Pit,
  I have found a ransom;

---

22). Elihu concedes, however, that neither dreams in the lonely hours of the night nor bodily ailment carries in itself the word of God to man. Suffering is not the instrument of divine revelation but only its possible channel. It merely prepares man to listen.

(3) INTERVENTION OF A MEDIATOR (33:23-25)

23-25. Thus in the third place Elihu brings forth in a passage of great beauty and of even greater theological impact the image of the **angel** or **mediator**. This latter word, מֵלִיץ, means here "interpreter" (cf. Gen. 42:23; also Isa. 43:27), and it is quite remarkable that the Targ. translates it with the Greek word παράκλητος, i.e., פרקליטא, the "Paraclete" or "Comforter," a name which became in Hellenistic Judaism and in Christianity one of the appellations of the Holy Spirit (John 14:16; etc.). This **angel-mediator** is **one of the thousand** messengers of God's judgment and grace, who

> at his bidding speed
> And post o'er land and ocean without rest
> (Milton, "On His Blindness").

The function of this being is twofold: first, he is sent **to declare to man what is right for him** (vs. 23b), for man needs not only to interpret his suffering but also to discern where his "duty" (yōsher) lies (cf. 6:25), and to do that which makes him and keeps him "upright" (yāshār). Second, inasmuch as man is not paying heed to this disclosure of his obligations, the **angel-mediator** truly mediates not only the will of God to man but

---

with joy into the presence of God, recounting to all men **his salvation,** and singing his songs of redemption.

Elihu is not accurate in his reading: the trial in Job's case is not on God's initiative but on Satan's (see Expos. on 1:6-12; 2:7-10); its purpose, if deliberate purpose it can be said to have, was more probative (1:8-12), as Eliphaz and Bildad had at first suggested (4:6; 8:20), than disciplinary. But it must be remembered that these speeches sprang out of a deep and growing dissatisfaction with the original poem, especially with its insistence on the hero's integrity (1:8) and on the final encounter between Job, goaded by his inept comforters, and the God whom he had challenged with such impious assurance. So difficult and dangerous is it, where God's "answers" are concerned, to make any attempt at identification. The pattern of life is far too complex and ambiguous for any

man to go about lugging with him a faith which never grows up, has to be kept bundled tightly like a papoose in God's "answers" to his questions and God's "answers" to his prayers, cannot be set down to stand on its feet in the hurly-burly of a world where success may be a curse and failure a benediction. What Elihu perceives is that God does answer, answers in his own strange way, and answers in love (see Expos. on 1:6). Enough surely to justify the worship (vs. 26b) and the witness (vs. 26c; cf. II Kings 7:9), in the joy of a grateful heart (vss. 27-28), companioned (vs. 26a), secure (vss. 29-30), and **lighted with the light of life** (vs. 30b mg.).

24. *I Have Found a Ransom.*—It seems most likely that the mediator of vs. 23 is speaking: something makes it possible to satisfy God's mercy without any infringement of God's justice. Here it is the sinner's repentance, his reorienta-

25 His flesh shall be fresher than a child's: he shall return to the days of his youth:

26 He shall pray unto God, and he will be favorable unto him: and he shall see his face with joy: for he will render unto man his righteousness.

27 He looketh upon men, and *if any* say, I have sinned, and perverted *that which was* right, and it profited me not;

25 let his flesh become fresh with youth;
let him return to the days of his youthful vigor.'

26 Then man prays to God, and he accepts
him,
he comes into his presence with joy.
He recounts[u] to men his salvation,

27 and he sings before men, and says:
'I sinned, and perverted what was right,
and it was not requited to me.

[u] Cn: Heb *returns*

also the weakness of man to God: **he is gracious to** the evil-thinking, evil-doing, and thus evil-tortured creature, and he presents him before God in order to intercede on his behalf (vss. 24-25). The **mediator** is therefore also the intercessor (cf. Isa. 43:27). He not only prays for the deliverance of man from death (vs. 24*b*), but he also says, **I have found a ransom** (vs. 24*c*), i.e., the price of his atonement (כפר; cf. Exod. 21:30; etc.; also Prov. 13:8). The **ransom** is not described any further, but one can easily recognize here the language of the prophets and psalmists (cf. particularly Isa. 43:3). It is possible that Elihu belonged to a group of wise men who had been in close contact with temple singers and who, like them, spiritualized to a large extent the language and imagery which were familiar to them in the ritual of the atonement. Here the **ransom** may be obtained, perhaps, by the patient endurance of suffering (cf. 36:18).

The *hapax* of vs. 24*a*, פדעהו, is not known. Some MSS read פרעהו, "let him go," "let him alone," or "let him loose" (usually in a perjorative sense; cf. 15:4; Exod. 32:25). In all probability the original text had פדהו (cf. Targ. and Syriac as well as vs. 28), meaning "ransom him" (cf. Ps. 49:8, where the same verb is found side by side with the noun כפר, "ransom"). The intercessor prays that, through some mystery of expiation which he does not need to describe, the **flesh** of the dying man may **become fresh with youth** (vs. 25*a*; the word רטפש is a *hapax* which the RSV, following Dhorme, reads as ירטב; cf. 24:8), and that he may **return to the days of his youthful vigor** ("lustihood" [Driver and Gray]; vs. 25*b*; see 20:11).

(4) PRAYER AND CONFESSION OF THE SUFFERER (33:26-28)

26-28. In the fourth place Elihu pursues his program of theological therapeutics by setting forth the part which man in turn must undertake and fulfill. After the intercession

tion and renewed obedience (cf. Exeg. on 36:18-19); in the N.T. there is nothing less, but this much more, that Christ himself is the "ransom," producing in the hearts of men both repentance and faith (see Exeg.).

The modern attitude tends to suggest that the restoration to full fellowship [vs. 26*a*] is a direct consequence of human repentance. This is part of that . . . tendency which seeks to find rational and this-worldly reasons for the sequence of events, and so makes the restoration of fellowship automatic upon human action rather than upon the actual and personal immediate work of God. The Bible here, as elsewhere, regards God as actively busy in that he definitely and personally ["accepts"—vs. 26*a*] every penitent, and this as a deliberate and separate act.[4]

[4] N. H. Snaith, "Forgive," in Richardson, ed., *Theological Word Book of the Bible*, p. 85.

27-28. *Songs of Redemption.*—For "respectable" people in an intensely "practical" world, men and women who have only the foggiest notion of either the awful holiness of God or the unplumbed depths of human sin, the word "deliverance," which is the very theme song of the Bible from beginning to end, has precious little significance. What to Paul and those around him were "principalities" and "powers" and "rulers of the darkness" (Eph. 6:12) are to them inclinations and impulses and sudden inducements. Eat the right food, take plenty of exercise in the fresh air, and get eight hours' sleep: that should enable a man to handle most of them. For pity's sake, delivered from what? Not out of the battle, so much is certain. In it, then? Is there no whisper in the soul, "God be merciful to me a sinner" (Luke 18:13)? No clenching of the hands, no pallor on any face,

28 He will deliver his soul from going into the pit, and his life shall see the light.

29 Lo, all these *things* worketh God oftentimes with man,

30 To bring back his soul from the pit, to be enlightened with the light of the living.

---

28 He has redeemed my soul from going
    down into the Pit,
    and my life shall see the light.'

29 "Behold, God does all these things,
    twice, three times, with a man,
30 to bring back his soul from the Pit,
    that he may see the light of life.[v]

[v] Syr: Heb *to be lighted with the light of life*

---

is offered by the angel (vss. 23-25) there must be a petition made by the sufferer himself (vs. 26*ab*). **Then man prays to God** (יעתר, "supplicate," "entreat"; cf. 22:27; Gen. 25:21; Exod. 8:26) and God **will be favorable unto him** (וירצהו; cf. Isa. 42:1; Ps. 44:4; 147:11), and will let him see his face **with joy** (תרועה, not the stylized choral "shout" and orchestral "blast" of the temple ritual but the spontaneous expression of religious gladness as in 8:21). More than this, the healed individual, like most of the psalmists who have experienced a deliverance from mortal sickness, will turn to his social environment and testify before the community: **He recounts to men his salvation** (vs. 26*c*; the RSV reads ויספר or ויבשר instead of וישב). This rendering, however, is hypothetical, and the M.T. reads, lit., **for he will render unto man his righteousness** (KJV). Inasmuch as the subject of the verb appears to be God, not man (see the three clauses, obviously parallel, in vss. 26*aβbc*), it is safe and probably correct to accept here the traditional translation. Because man feels again that he is "accepted" by God and received back into his presence, he also knows that God has returned to him his righteousness. The social element, which is not absent, appears only in the next verse. It is always true to say—even apropos of a book like Job which deals mostly with religious individualism—that "the Bible knows nothing of solitary religion" (John Wesley). As soon as the sick man is healed and thus finds himself restored before God, **he sings before men** (vs. 27*a*). The song of thanksgiving is a gem of conciseness—a surprising feature in the discourses of the Buzite— and more than a psalm *in nuce*. The singer confesses not only that he has **sinned** but also that he has **perverted what was right** (the verb העויתי means, lit., "I twisted" [from עוה I], a word which suggested to the minds of auditors and readers the homonymous העויתי, "I committed iniquity" [from עוה II]; hence עון, "guilt"). Yet the enormity of the crime did not entail a mortal judgment: **And it was not requited to me** (vs. 27*c*). Thus instead of insisting on the injustice of his tortures, the sufferer emphasizes the patience and mercy of a God who might have dealt him at once the mortal blow; he praises that God for his redemption (פדה; cf. vs. 24) from **the Pit** (vs. 28*a*), and he expresses his confidence that his **life shall see the light** (vs. 28*b*).

(5) GOD'S ULTIMATE PURPOSE (33:29-30)

29-30. In the fifth and last place Elihu is thus able to conclude his picture of the redeemed sinner by saying that God acts mysteriously with men but slowly and consistently (the expression **twice, three times** does not refer to vs. 14 but signifies the duration of action; cf. Ecclus. 13:7). His intention is always to save, and there is grace in his apparently harsh treatment. His final purpose is that man may **be enlightened with the light of** [KJV] life (RSV, rather than **the living** [KJV]; cf. Pss. 27:1; 36:9).

---

as some murderer is led down the long corridor to his death, "There but for the grace of God goes Richard Baxter"?[5]

Worship is not "uplift." It is the soul's re-

[5] Attributed also to John Bradford, a century earlier, and to John Newton, a century later!

sponse to that experience of God's redeeming grace. It is not merely "the flight of the alone to the Alone": it is the fellowship of the restored (vs. 26*c*; see Exeg.). And on their lips the story is for witness (vs. 27*a*), and God's statutes for a song.

| 31 Mark well, O Job, hearken unto me: hold thy peace, and I will speak.
32 If thou hast any thing to say, answer me: speak, for I desire to justify thee.
33 If not, hearken unto me: hold thy peace, and I shall teach thee wisdom. | 31 Give heed, O Job, listen to me;
be silent, and I will speak.
32 If you have anything to say, answer me;
speak, for I desire to justify you.
33 If not, listen to me;
be silent, and I will teach you wisdom." |
| **34** Furthermore Elihu answered and said,
2 Hear my words, O ye wise *men;* and give ear unto me, ye that have knowledge. | **34** Then Eli′hu said:
2 "Hear my words, you wise men,
and give ear to me, you who know; |

e) FINAL APPEAL TO JOB (33:31-33)

31-33. Elihu is now ready to propose a direct application of his exposition to the case at hand. **Give heed, O Job** (vs. 31*a*). The words which follow (vss. 31*b*-33) were not originally translated in the LXX. Elihu offers to the patient an opportunity to speak, assuring him that his sole intention is **to justify** him (vs. 32). This is unexpected on the part of a man who began his discourse in blazing anger (cf. 32:2, 3, 5) and who was apparently intent upon "justifying" the ways of God rather than the position of Job. He may, however, be animated by the same desire as that of the three friends, for he aims at bringing the hero to confession and conversion, hence to "justification." His view of salvation is therefore not different from that of his predecessors, and his last word now is, **Hold thy peace, and I shall teach thee wisdom** (vs. 33). To be sure, he goes further than ordinary wise men by suggesting the spiritual value of endurance in suffering and by evoking the vague possibility of a mediator. But he still believes that submission brings forgiveness *and* physical restoration. He has not come to grips with the realities of darkest sorrow. The figure of the intercessor, which his imagination conjures up for a moment, belongs nevertheless to the realm of historical potentiality. Unwitting prophet —as a prophet always is—Elihu, the pedantic apprentice, calls for the necessity of a Christ. Indeed, he hails obscurely the advent of one who would "declare to man what is right for him, . . . be gracious to him," and "say, '. . . I have found a ransom!'" The exegete who reads these words in the light of the total context of the Bible is not indulging in the practice of any mystical, spiritual, or even typological interpretation. He merely observes that the poet of Job (cf. 9:33 ff.) and the Joban school (cf. 33:23 ff.), like many other members of the Old Covenant, dimly recognized the dangers of a theology of unilateral transcendence, and contemplated—however distantly and vaguely— the face of the "interpreter," a mediator who would interpret God to man and man to God; indeed, an "intercessor" who would himself be a ransom.

2. JUSTICE OF THE WAYS OF GOD (34:1-37)

Elihu now addresses the friends and perhaps also the bystanders (vs. 2) while discussing the case of Job in the third person (vss. 5, 7, etc.). After a brief exordium (vss. 2-4), he recalls the blasphemous implications of Job's protest (vss. 5-9) and there-

34:1-37. The Second Speech of Elihu.—Still in order to refute Job's claim to innocence—and therefore the charge of injustice which has been brought against God (vss. 5-6) and has been no more than touched on in 33:9-12—Elihu next undertakes to argue God's righteousness and impartiality: convincingly from his faithfulness as the creator and sustainer of all things (vss. 12-15; cf. I Pet. 4:19), far less convincingly from his sovereign rule (vss. 16-20) and om-

niscience (vss. 21-30; observe, however, the more persuasive note of benevolence and compassion in vss. 28-30). What conclusion can there be but that it is the very pinnacle of presumption, virtually amounting to nothing less than an attempt to usurp the divine prerogatives, to call into question God's handling of his own affairs (vss. 31-33; cf. vs. 7)? To enter on such a course as Job's is not only to be **without knowledge,** but to sin with a high hand, to

3 For the ear trieth words, as the mouth tasteth meat.

4 Let us choose to us judgment: let us know among ourselves what *is* good.

5 For Job hath said, I am righteous: and God hath taken away my judgment.

6 Should I lie against my right? my wound *is* incurable without transgression.

3 for the ear tests words
   as the palate tastes food.

4 Let us choose what is right;
   let us determine among ourselves what
   is good.

5 For Job has said, 'I am innocent,
   and God has taken away my right;

6 in spite of my right I am counted a liar;
   my wound is incurable, though I am
   without transgression.'

---

upon refutes them in two contentions: First, God is righteous (vss. 10-22), because he has created all men equal (vss. 10-15), he shows no partiality to the princes and the rich (vss. 16-20), and he knows all men and all things (vss. 21-28). Second, God sometimes appears to be unrighteous (vss. 29-37), but he spares the wicked only to induce them to repentance (vss. 29-33), and consequently Job by his words rises against God in monstrous judgment (vss. 34-37).

a) THE NEED TO TEST WORDS (34:1-4)

34:2-4. There is an undertone of sarcasm in the double appellation, **you wise men** and **you who know** (lit., "the learned"). Elihu does not pose as an unlearned individual, but he claims to possess—as well as his interlocutors—an innate capacity to **choose what is right** and **determine . . . what is good.** If vss. 3-4 are original (they were absent in the early MSS of LXX), Elihu seems to contradict himself as he appeals no longer to a revelation of the divine spirit (cf. 32:18) but to human "common sense." For him, "testing" the truth of the interpretative beliefs concerning life is like "tasting" a wine or a piece of cheese (cf. 12:11). It is therefore within the reach of man as man.

b) THE IRRELIGION OF JOB (34:5-9)

5-9. Elihu uses the method of quoting Job's words, as he has already done in 33:8-11. There is no question as to the accuracy of his representation of Job's attitude. The patient was certain of his innocence even when he alluded to it in conditional clauses (vs. 5*a*; cf. 9:15; 10:15; also 33:9), and he said verbatim, **God has taken away my right** (vs. 5*b*; cf. 27:2). Vs. 6 is difficult. The M.T. reads, **I lie against my right,** a statement to which the KJV attempts to give meaning by considering it as interrogative. The RSV interprets—or perhaps reads—the Piel אכזב (*'akhazzēbh*) as a Niphal (*'ekkāzēbh,* cf. Prov. 30:6) or a hypothetical Pual (*'akhuzzabh*) and renders it **I am counted a liar.** The LXX has ἐψεύσατο, which suggests the Hebrew יכזב, "he [i.e., God] is a liar." The exegete can understand without difficulty that such a reading, if original, would have been highly suspicious to the early scribes. Elihu may very well quote, here and in vs. 6*b,* an authentic statement of Job now excised from the third cycle.

---

add **rebellion** to the wrongdoing which has already laid him low (cf. 36:18). He deserves now to suffer to the bitter end.

3-4. *Prove All Things.*—Let us choose what is right, i.e., let us weigh the whole matter judiciously, free of prejudice and passion, then decide who has the better case, Elihu or Job. Consider the evidence carefully, and on the basis of sound reason and high moral and religious principles reach a verdict. Man is not so corrupt that he can no longer make a few rough-and-ready, yet on the whole reliable, distinctions between good and evil, right and wrong (see

Expos. on 17:9). **The ear** is still able to **test words as the palate tastes food.** Paul thought so too, though the gift was not "by nature" but of grace (Rom. 2:14-15; cf. 32:8). It is interesting, however, to remember that Job had said precisely the same thing (12:11), and had arrived at almost precisely the opposite result. It is ultimately the "man in Christ" who is to "prove all things," and "hold fast" to "that which is good" (I Thess. 5:21; cf. Rom. 12:1-2), the while taking "heed lest he fall" (I Cor. 10:12).

5-6. Cf. 16:17; 27:5*b;* 31:6; 27:2; 9:20*b,* 30; 6:4; 17:16.

7 What man *is* like Job, *who* drinketh up scorning like water?

8 Which goeth in company with the workers of iniquity, and walketh with wicked men.

9 For he hath said, It profiteth a man nothing that he should delight himself with God.

---

7 What man is like Job,
  who drinks up scoffing like water,
8 who goes in company with evildoers
  and walks with wicked men?
9 For he has said, 'It profits a man nothing
  that he should take delight in God.'

A man like Job who dares to pass judgment on the Deity may not be a criminal of the common ethical variety, but he certainly **goeth in company with the workers of iniquity, and walketh with wicked men** (vs. 8). He belongs to their class not on account of deeds similar to theirs, but through his outrageous blasphemies. Elihu is more subtle than his three predecessors, for he does not try to explain Job's misery by accusing him of acts or thoughts of moral turpitude, and he is on the way to discerning the theological dimension of human sinfulness. The gross sinner breaks one or more articles of the moral codes. Job does less and worse: he judges the motives and decisions of his Creator.

Vs. 9 refers to another saying of the hero which is not found verbally in the present text of the poetic dialogue. But Job has often spoken of the suffering of the innocent (9:22-24; etc.) and of the prosperity of the wicked (21:7-13; etc.), and therefore of the lack of due reward or punishment upon the earth. Such a line of reasoning is in effect equivalent to declaring, **It profiteth a man nothing that he should delight himself with God** (רצה עם־אלהים, lit., "to be willing and to have pleasure in the company of God"; vs. 9; cf. 33:26; Ps. 50:18). The Satan of the folkloric tale had already understood this idea (1:9). Elihu thus plants himself at the very center of the problem of the book. He understands that the crux of the matter lies less in the question of undeserved suffering than in the faith of profitless religion. Better than many of his subsequent commentators, he sees that religion for a profit is irreligion.

7-9. Skeptic or Sinner.—For vs. 9 cf. 9:22; 21:15 (said of the wicked, but now attributed to Job, as in 22:13, 17). This, to Elihu's mind, was not just to drink "iniquity like water" (15:16); this was to scoff, actually to pervert the truth and mock at religion, from which it was clear enough, without any further witness, what kind of **company** Job had been keeping. He had walked "in the counsel of the ungodly," had stood "in the way of sinners," and now sat "in the seat of the scornful" (Ps. 1:1). But it was not God; it was the conventional picture of God that Job hated. A college student is said to have called one day on Harry Emerson Fosdick, troubled because, as he put it, he could not believe in God. "Tell me," asked Fosdick, "what kind of God is it you cannot believe in?" Startled, the boy, after stumbling about a little, began to describe the God who was taken for granted by the Sunday school he had attended and the home he lived in. When he was through, Fosdick smiled companionably, and said very quietly, "I could never believe in him either."

Elihu understood neither the madness that was in Job's brain (cf. Expos. on 23:15), nor the love that was underneath it in Job's heart. Scoffing has deep and bitter roots too; but Job was not scoffing: he was in an agony of bewilderment. Doubting was met by Jesus on its own ground (John 20:27); but Job was not doubting: he was tormented, not so much in mind as in soul, by the very contradiction of which Elihu was aware (vss. 12-15) but could do nothing to resolve. To toss such a man over into the category of the ungodly is cruelly to miss the mark.

There are times when the skeptic—and Job is far more—owes his skepticism to his own moral delinquencies. Aldous Huxley writes of his youth and companions: there was a good deal in the Christian faith that did not suit them, and they rejected it. But to universalize on that theme is disastrous. What William James calls "the will to believe" is crucial, and Job had it. Where it is lacking, a life is far better than an argument to stir it into being; where it already exists, a life—not an argument—provides God with his most effective means of self-revelation. There Job's friends failed him, and failed him utterly (cf. Expos. on 6:14, 18). Nothing is left for it but that God shall act as his own interpreter: theophany here, one day the Incarnation (Phil. 2:5-13; cf. Browning, "Saul," st. xviii).

9. What Shall It Profit a Man?—Here again is raised the question of the prologue (see

10 Therefore hearken unto me, ye men of understanding: far be it from God, *that he should do* wickedness; and *from* the Almighty, *that he should commit* iniquity.

11 For the work of a man shall he render unto him, and cause every man to find according to *his* ways.

12 Yea, surely God will not do wickedly, neither will the Almighty pervert judgment.

13 Who hath given him a charge over the earth? or who hath disposed the whole world?

14 If he set his heart upon man, *if* he gather unto himself his spirit and his breath;

15 All flesh shall perish together, and man shall turn again unto dust.

10 "Therefore, hear me, you men of understanding,
    far be it from God that he should do wickedness,
    and from the Almighty that he should do wrong.

11 For according to the work of a man he will requite him,
    and according to his ways he will make it befall him.

12 Of a truth, God will not do wickedly,
    and the Almighty will not pervert justice.

13 Who gave him charge over the earth
    and who laid on him[w] the whole world?

14 If he should take back his spirit[x] to himself,
    and gather to himself his breath,

15 all flesh would perish together,
    and man would return to dust.

[w] Heb lacks *on him*
[x] Heb *his heart his spirit*

---

c) The Defense of Divine Justice (34:10-28)

(1) There Is No Evil in the Creator (34:10-15)

10-15. Men of understanding will agree that God does not perform **iniquity** (vs. 10), but that **the work of a man shall he render unto him** (vs. 11). Elihu sides with Bildad (8:3) in maintaining that **the Almighty will not pervert justice** (vs. 12). Such a God is God: "He is no viceroy lording it on earth!" (vs. 13 Moffatt). There is neither corruption nor caprice in his rule. He is the "faithful creator" of those whose very existence depends at every instant upon the gift of his breath (vss. 14-15; cf. Ps. 104:29-30).

Expos. on 1:6-12; 28:1-28). Elihu will discuss it in ch. 35. But Job has never said that there is no profit in being "on terms of friendship" with God (vs. 9*b*). The old friendship is what he craves more than anything else. He has simply said that too often the wicked prosper (9:24; 21:17-18) and the righteous suffer (12:4; 24:5-11) for anybody to talk glibly about God's discriminating and retributive justice. He is learning that whatever good there is in religion cannot be stated simply in terms of cash and carry (cf. Expos. on 30:9-15). Elihu knows it too. The real question, however, turns things around terribly. Christ asks it. "What shall it profit a man, if he shall gain the whole world, and lose his own soul?" (Mark 8:36.)

11. *The Law of Retribution.*—Seemingly blunt, succinct, unconditional; and to Job, as indeed to any man who insists on testing it by the facts (cf. Expos. on 12:2-6; 18:21; 21:5-6; 27:7-12), so much the more empirically vulnerable. That Elihu does not himself hold it in the form here set down becomes increasingly clear.

14. *God Is Faithful.*—Somebody who has been entrusted with responsibility by another may conceivably be guilty of partiality and injustice in order to serve his own selfish ends; but it is not so with God, argues Elihu (vs. 13) without any too great cogency. The righteousness of the Creator, indeed, as Strahan points out,[6] is scarcely to be associated with disinterestedness (cf. 22:2) by way either of motive or demonstration. It is not a quality to be lost or achieved; it is of the nature and essence of the being of God. The moment Elihu leaves the analogy behind him, however, and in the next verse shifts from anthropology to theology, he gives expression to one of the most memorable passages of the book (cf. 12:10), if not of the whole O.T. God is now creator and sustainer, not remote and uninvolved (see Expos. on 22:2-5), but moment by moment upholding and preserving (see Expos. on 10:8-12). He is the faithful God of whom Paul speaks (I Cor. 1:9), who calls us into "the fellowship of his Son," suffers none to be tempted above that he is able (I Cor. 10:13),

[6] *Job*, p. 288.

16 If now *thou hast* understanding, hear this: hearken to the voice of my words.	**16** "If you have understanding, hear this; listen to what I say.
17 Shall even he that hateth right govern? and wilt thou condemn him that is most just?	**17** Shall one who hates justice govern? Will you condemn him who is righteous and mighty,
18 *Is it fit* to say to a king, *Thou art* wicked? *and* to princes, *Ye are* ungodly?	**18** who says to a king, 'Worthless one,' and to nobles, 'Wicked man';

(2) There Is No Partiality in the Judge (34:16-20)

16-20. If Job were right, then God would be wrong, and how could an unjust God rule the universe (vs. 17)? "Shall not the Judge of all the earth do right?" (Gen. 18:25.) Elihu is standing on the edge of a cogent argument, but he confuses the issue at stake. Job has never denied the omnipotence of the Creator. Elihu seems to believe that divine might makes divine right. "That in the long run empires built on wrong fall because of it may be true. Yet we are able to say 'Rome shall perish. . . In the blood that she has spilt,' only because we are assured that the order of the world is moral. But when the previous question is raised, Is it moral? the reply, Rule and injustice cannot go together, is quite wide of the mark. Kipling's 'Lest we forget, lest we forget' is answered by Watson's 'When we forgot, when we forgot.' What retort to Watson does Elihu enable us to make?" (Peake, *Job*, pp. 289-90.) Still, Elihu discerns that the divine person is beyond human categories of justice. "God is greater than man" (33:12), even greater than man's deified idea of morality. Job accuses God of being immoral. Elihu retorts that God does not belong to the human realm, not even to the reality of ethical good which is still a part of man's conceptual world. God is not immoral but supramoral.

The argument of vss. 18-19*a* would be extremely weak if the M.T. were to be retained: **Is it fit to say to a king, Thou art wicked? . . . How much less to him that accepteth not the persons of princes.** The LXX, Vulg., and Syriac, however, read the word

---

and in the face of all the odds of human life makes "foolish the wisdom of the world" with the "weakness" which is "stronger than men" (I Cor. 1:20, 25). It is his very faithfulness which from the underside so often feels like the arbitrary indifference of some cosmic tyranny (19:7; cf. Expos. on 23:13), and is as surely to be seen in the Exile as in the return (Isa. 42:24; 41:14-15), in the Cross as in the Resurrection (cf. Expos. on 2:7-10). Of such a God, in the very midst of persecution, Peter can write, "Wherefore, let them that suffer . . . commit the keeping of their souls to him in well doing, as unto a faithful Creator" (I Pet. 4:19); and Paul, baffled by the mysteries of Providence, is brought to ask, "What shall we say then? Is there unrighteousness with God? God forbid" (Rom. 9:14; cf. Expos. on 21:7-18). The way back for Job has little to do with meditation. Says Strahan: "It is the further and deeper contemplation of the benevolence of God displayed in nature, and especially in animated nature, that ultimately brings him back from doubt to faith."[7] Is it? Granted that Job's view is partial and fragmentary (cf. Expos. on 3:1-26, 20-21), that the benevolent aspects of creation for the moment elude him, is it likely that "further and

[7] *Ibid.*

deeper contemplation" will resolve for him the terrible riddle of existence (cf. ch. 21)? The way back takes its start from a place of meeting. God encounters Job.

17. *Does Might Make Right?*—The answer to Elihu's question in the first half of this verse might very well be, "Indeed, yes!" And as instance, in the annals of human history, many a despotic tyranny could be adduced, from the Pharaoh of the oppression to Antiochus Epiphanes, from Nero to Adolf Hitler (cf. Expos. on 9:2-10). Job has been insisting all along that as a sheer matter of inescapable fact **one who hates justice [does] govern** (23:13-14). The legerdemain of vs. 17*b*, where Elihu surreptitiously couples **righteous and mighty** when nobody is looking, will not likely provide any proof to the contrary. God is mighty enough to govern, but is he righteous enough to love justice instead of hating it? Once again anthropology turns out to be a snare and a delusion (cf. Expos. on vs. 14). It may be that some measure of justice is essential to any decent and continuing order (see Exeg. on vs. 20); but how if might, instead of being relative, were absolute? In the world of the twentieth century, with mechanized power in the hands of the comparatively few, human rights are in a far more precarious position than

19 *How much less to him* that accepteth not the persons of princes, nor regardeth the rich more than the poor? for they all *are* the work of his hands.

20 In a moment shall they die, and the people shall be troubled at midnight, and pass away: and the mighty shall be taken away without hand.

21 For his eyes *are* upon the ways of man, and he seeth all his goings.

19 who shows no partiality to princes,
nor regards the rich more than the poor,
for they are all the work of his hands?
20 In a moment they die;
at midnight the people are shaken and pass away,
and the mighty are taken away by no human hand.

21 "For his eyes are upon the ways of a man,
and he sees all his steps.

האמר in vs. 18*a* not as *ha'amōr,* **Is it fit to say?** but as *hā'ōmēr,* "He who says . . ." (referring to God in vs. 17) ; the RSV correctly translates vs. 18 as a sequence of vs. 17, . . . **who says to a king, "Worthless one"** . . . , thus providing a satisfactory transition to vs. 19. According to this translation, Elihu is not using an a fortiori argument, defending the righteousness of God on the basis of a commoner's duty to revere human monarchs, but on the contrary is stating that God is just since he **shows no partiality** to the mighty of this world **for they are all the work of his hands** (vss. 18-29) .

20. As proof of the Judge's impartiality, anyone can observe that **in a moment they die,** even **at midnight** (vs. 20*a*; the ERV and ASV rightly recognize here a poetic line, against the KJV and RSV) . The text of vs. 20*b* is uncertain. The word עם, **people,** was not read by the Syriac; instead of the M.T. יגעשו עם, **the people are shaken,** one might read with Kissane, following partly a brilliant conjecture of Budde, יגע שועם, "he smiteth the rich," and then the M.T. ויעברו, **and** [they] **pass away.** Vs. 20*c* may well be rendered with the RSV, **and the mighty** [reading the plural אברים with one MS, Kennicott 248] **are taken away by no human hand.** Dhorme, however, proposes to read the verb ויסירו as ויסיר (with one MS, Kennicott 191) , and to translate, "And without effort he deposes a potentate." This rendering of vs. 20*c* permits the same critic to preserve the word **people** in vs. 20*b*, and thus to underline a fine sequence: oppressions of the masses do not last long, and dictators find a sudden end. In any case, the general meaning of the verse is clear enough. God does not make any distinction among men; rich and poor, kings and subjects, are all equal before the almighty Giver of life and death.

(3) DIVINE OMNISCIENCE IS ABSOLUTE (34:21-28)

21-28. Divine omniscience (vs. 21; cf. 24:23*b*; 31:4, 37) is so complete that no place is left—not even **gloom or deep darkness**—for the **evildoers** who would try to

---

ever before. If this were not the kind of universe where a righteous God is still sovereign, and moral not physical force is ultimately decisive, the outlook would be dark indeed. The victory belongs inherently and inalienably to the right. "The battle is the LORD's" (I Sam. 17:47; cf. II Chr. 20:15) .

19. *They Are All the Work of His Hands.*—How can there be partiality, asks Elihu, in one who fashioned all men, kings and nobles and **princes,** rich and **poor** alike **the work of his hands?** The argument would run somewhat as follows: God is the author of all; he is no respecter of persons; therefore his judgments are "true and righteous altogether." It is not the major premise Job would question, or the minor premise either—unless by it is meant that God deals out his justice with an even hand. That Job vehemently denies. God may be no respecter of persons, but demonstrably he is no respecter of a person's integrity either. Logic is not the way to faith, and begging the question is not logic. If only God's love for **the work of his hands** (10:8) could have squeezed itself in through the loopholes of the syllogism! From the very start Job had been trying to make room for it (see Expos. on 28:1-28) .

21-28. *Knowing and Doing.*—From the categories of creation and sovereignty Elihu turns to omniscience; the result is a *non sequitur* which could hardly be improved. God sees and knows all things (cf. Exeg. on 24:1) ; therefore

22 *There is* no darkness, nor shadow of death, where the workers of iniquity may hide themselves.

23 For he will not lay upon man more *than right;* that he should enter into judgment with God.

24 He shall break in pieces mighty men without number, and set others in their stead.

25 Therefore he knoweth their works, and he overturneth *them* in the night, so that they are destroyed.

26 He striketh them as wicked men in the open sight of others;

27 Because they turned back from him, and would not consider any of his ways:

28 So that they cause the cry of the poor to come unto him, and he heareth the cry of the afflicted.

29 When he giveth quietness, who then can make trouble? and when he hideth *his*

22 There is no gloom or deep darkness
     where evildoers may hide themselves.
23 For he has not appointed a time[y] for any
     man
     to go before God in judgment.
24 He shatters the mighty without investiga-
     tion,
     and sets others in their place.
25 Thus, knowing their works,
     he overturns them in the night, and
     they are crushed.
26 He strikes them for their wickedness
     in the sight of men,
27 because they turned aside from following
     him,
     and had no regard for any of his ways,
28 so that they caused the cry of the poor to
     come to him,
     and he heard the cry of the afflicted —
29 When he is quiet, who can condemn?

[y] Cn: Heb *yet*

---

hide themselves (vs. 22; cf. Ps. 139:11-12; Jer. 23:24; Amos 9:2-3). Job had complained that God refused to go to trial with him (9:32), and Elihu retorts that the Almighty **has not appointed a time** (reading with Reiske and most modern critics ישים מועד instead of ישים עוד, the letter מ having probably dropped out through haplography). God does not need to appoint any special time for a trial: he pursues his task of strict and swift justice **without investigation** (vs. 24) and **in the sight of men** (vs. 26). Thus it is not true to say that God does not hear the cry of the oppressed (vss. 27-28; cf. 24:12).

d) MEANING OF DIVINE SILENCE (34:29-37)
(1) APPARENT INACTIVITY OF GOD (34:29-33)

29-30. If God is silent, no human being has the right to condemn him (vs. 29a). In vs. 29b the parallelism may support Budde's emendation of ישורנו (**who can behold him?**) into ייסרנו ("who can blame him?"). Vs. 29c is obscure and means, lit., "and against nation and against man together." The various emendations which have been proposed are conjectural. However, one might read with Dhorme יחז, "he watches," instead of יחד, "together," and link vs. 29c with vs. 30, thus rendering, "He watches over nation and individual alike, so that he prevents a godless man from being king and ensnaring the people." Yet such a meaning is not satisfactory in a context where Elihu attempts to refute a charge against the apparent inactivity of God (vs. 29ab). It is therefore preferable to read with the Targ. (cf. Theod. and Vulg.) ממליך instead of ממלך (vs. 30a), and to render tentatively, "He watches over nation and individual alike, and

---

he never needs to hold any assize (vs. 23): **without investigation** he shatters the wicked, does it publicly for everybody to see (vs. 26), **because they . . . had no regard for any of his ways, and so caused the cry of the poor to come to him.** The whole passage is replete with references (cf. vs. 21 with 13:27; 14:16; 24:23; 31:4, 37; cf. vs. 22 with 22:13; vs. 23 with 9:16; 14:13; 24:1; vs. 27 with 21:14; 22:17; vs. 28 with 24:12); but there is nothing very persuasive about it,

except the unsupported statements of vss. 28, 30. There is a gulf between knowing and doing as everyone discovers to his sorrow. The "watcher of men" (cf. 11:11) has for Job become a spy (see Expos. on 7:20a). Neither omniscience nor omnipotence can take the place of love. Without it they are both intolerable (see Expos. on 9:2-10) —an all-knowing and all-wise celestial Gestapo!

29a. See Expos. on 19:7; 24:12c.

face, who then can behold him? whether *it be done* against a nation, or against a man only:

30 That the hypocrite reign not, lest the people be ensnared.

31 Surely it is meet to be said unto God, I have borne *chastisement,* I will not offend *any more:*

32 *That which* I see not teach thou me: if I have done iniquity, I will do no more.

33 *Should it be* according to thy mind? he will recompense it, whether thou refuse, or whether thou choose; and not I: therefore speak what thou knowest.

34 Let men of understanding tell me, and let a wise man hearken unto me.

35 Job hath spoken without knowledge, and his words *were* without wisdom.

36 My desire *is that* Job may be tried unto the end, because of *his* answers for wicked men.

37 For he addeth rebellion unto his sin, he clappeth *his hands* among us, and multiplieth his words against God.

When he hides his face, who can behold him,
    whether it be a nation or a man? —
30 that a godless man should not reign,
    that he should not ensnare the people.

31 "For has any one said to God,
    'I have borne chastisement; I will not offend any more;
32 teach me what I do not see:
    if I have done iniquity, I will do it no more'?
33 Will he then make requital to suit you, because you reject it?
    For you must choose, and not I;
    therefore declare what you know.ᶻ
34 Men of understanding will say to me,
    and the wise man who hears me will say:
35 'Job speaks without knowledge,
    his words are without insight.'
36 Would that Job were tried to the end,
    because he answers like wicked men.
37 For he adds rebellion to his sin;
    he claps his hands among us,
    and multiplies his words against God."

ᶻ The Hebrew of verses 29-33 is obscure

---

when he allows a godless man to be king, he may do so on account of the sins of the people" (cf. Theod. ἀπὸ δυσχολίας λαοῦ, and Vulg., *propter peccata populi*).

31-33. These verses are likewise difficult, but the RSV is possibly correct here. Does Job know whether the immunity of some evildoers is not due to the fact of their secret repentance (vss. 31-32)? Has Job the right to teach God how to exercise justice (vs. 33a)?

(2) The Rebelliousness of Job (34:34-37)

34-37. Skillfully Elihu returns to his initial theme (see vss. 5-9). He agrees with **men of understanding** (vs. 34) that **Job speaks without knowledge** (vs. 35) and deserves to be **tried to the end** (vs. 36) since **he adds rebellion to his sin; . . . and multiplies his words against God** (vs. 37). Once more Elihu shows that he discerns the specifically theological character of Job's guilt. His position is close to that held by the three friends in the poetic discussion because he cannot accept the validity of Job's attacks upon the righteousness of God. But unlike the three friends, he has so far been careful to argue on the basis of the sufferer's blasphemous criticism of divine rule, not on the presumption

---

31-33. The Sin of Presumption.—Elihu wants to know if Job intends to usurp the prerogatives of the Almighty and dictate what is to be done in this case or in that (see Expos. on 40:6–42:6). For his part, he will have nothing to do with such shamelessness (vs. 33c). God's judgments are absolute, and all of them in the interests of the poor and the afflicted (vs. 28), lest the godless triumph (vs. 30). He withholds the rod of his wrath, and who will condemn him (vs. 29a)? He withdraws his favor, and nobody can

make him change his mind (vs. 29b), "whether it be a nation or a man" (yet see Exeg. on vss. 29-30). If then a man should repent (vss. 31-32), must God do what Job says he must, and reject the sinner's plea because Job rejects it? That, as everybody will agree, is not merely the result of some misapprehension (vs. 35); that is unadulterated wickedness (vs. 36b), sedition (vs. 37a), and mockery (vs. 37b). Any man who mouths such abuse against the Almighty (vs. 37c) is entitled to whatever catastrophe

35 Elihu spake moreover, and said,
2 Thinkest thou this to be right, *that* thou saidst, My righteousness *is* more than God's?

35 And Eli′hu said:
2 "Do you think this to be just?
Do you say, 'It is my right before God,'

---

of the sufferer's moral guilt. He has not attempted to justify the hero's misery by charging him with ethical turpitude. He has not said that suffering is the deserved punishment of a moral violation. He has recognized an element of mystery in the government of the world, but he has been intent upon safeguarding the freedom of God from human condemnation. He now applies his attention to the central question of Job's claim of self-righteousness.

3. GIVER OF SONGS IN THE NIGHT (35:1-16)

Elihu does not deserve the unqualified severity which many modern commentators visit upon him. His attitude is admittedly aggressive, but the aggressiveness and the cocksure immodesty with which he began to talk—a probable result of youthful timidity— does not prevent him from making a distinctive contribution to the book. He reaches in this chapter a high level of poetic and religious expression.

a) RIGHTS OF MAN BEFORE GOD (35:1-4)

35:2-4. With remarkable penetration Elihu understands that Job became a blasphemer when he deemed religion and morality were unprofitable to him: **How am I**

---

overtakes him, and ought to have more (vs. 36*a*).

The attempt to usurp divine prerogatives is common enough; but Job is not guilty of it. He is not asking that everything be cut according to his cloth. What he wants is a faith that can transcend it all. Take everything he says at its face value, and he can be made to look ridiculous—and worse—without any trouble at all. Enter but a little way into his heart, as nobody did—nobody even tried—and the titanic dimensions of his struggle are at once apparent. It is not a struggle to sit on Anyone's throne; it is a struggle to kneel at Someone's feet. His knocking at the door—never mind that sometimes he kicks at it—is not that he may be lord of the house, but that he may be a guest in it— even if nothing is left within to grace the table of God's bounty but the host himself, with healing in his hands for the terrible memory of those days without.

35:2-3. Man's Perpetual Challenge to God.— It is strange to reflect that the real challenge was not Job's at all (see Expos. on 31:35-37). The unremitting challenge God has to deal with year in and year out was what Elihu and the three friends were, and what they kept saying. Perhaps one should take them, not Job, as symbols of man, always confronting the Eternal, always difficult, standing for the most part either dully or sullenly apart from his purpose, often enough striding brazenly across it or running stubbornly against it. Marc Connelly's *The Green Pastures*[8] tells the story dramatically,

[8] New York: Farrar & Rinehart, 1929.

simply, and humanly: God, with his first high hopes vaguely disturbed, looking down from his heaven, shaking his head pitifully, sending a judge, sending a prophet, sending a priest, trying to do something as the noise on earth grew louder and more rebellious; at last whispering to himself, as the curtain fell, about a sacrifice which seemed even to him appalling. "Will man ever find his way to God?" is the question men ask as they look at the dumb red horror on "the great world's altar-stairs."[9] The question that should be asked is, "Will God ever find his way to man?" That he has set himself to it is the drama of the ages.

Look at the postures these men strike. The first challenge God has to get around somehow, or break through, is the eternal challenge of the old. All four of them, each in his own measure, though Elihu least (see Expos. on 32:6-22, 6), insist on getting things hind part before. It was the old order that was God-given. And they crawled behind what had been, and hid, and grew rigid, and showed their teeth (cf. John 8). Salvation does not lie in forever beating a retreat. "Men have always resorted to war, and they always will. Talk of doing away with it is talk of the millennium." Or, "The system we have lived under all our lives, and our fathers before us, is the best of all systems. The others are damnable and corrupt." But it may be that in the changing of the order God tries to say something. The past is no fetish to frighten life back out of his future. They said: Let Job confess his sin and be restored; let him scuttle back

[9] Tennyson, *In Memoriam*, Part LV, st. iv.

| 3 For thou saidst, What advantage will it be unto thee? *and,* What profit shall I have, *if I be cleansed* from my sin? | 3 that you ask, 'What advantage have I? How am I better off than if I had sinned?' |
| 4 I will answer thee, and thy companions with thee. | 4 I will answer you and your friends with you. |

better off than if I had sinned? (vs. 3). It is this utilitarian conception which Elihu will now refute.

> **I will answer you**
> **and your friends with you.**

It is wrong to affirm, as many commentators do, that Elihu merely and wholly accepts the dogma of individual retribution and that he speaks exactly along the same lines as the three friends. Actually Elihu stands against both the friends and the hero, and shows that Job as well as they hold to a distorted view of God.

and be saved; this was nothing new they were dealing with. But it was. And life, moving, thrusting, jostling life swept by them in its solemn swing Godward. Old defeats, old victories, slip away in the wake. What is new is not necessarily true; nor what is old, false. But somewhere out in front, always ahead with his seven-league boots, is God (see Expos. on vs. 14).

The second challenge which men commonly fling out as they try to keep God at a distance is their insistence on getting things wrong side out. There is a persistent notion that the outside is what matters, not the inside. To the friends prosperity is the mark of piety; calamity, of sin. So they argue. And Elihu on the whole agrees, though with a significant change of venue (see Exeg. on 34:34-37). He accuses Job of having had an eye to the profit (vs. 3) which is to be had in God's company (cf. 34:9; Expos. on vss. 9-16), and by implication condemns it; but he has nothing whatsoever to say by way of pointing out that true religion is not about profit, nor does he hesitate, down here in the realm of mundane affairs, to lend his own support to that motive (see Expos. on vss. 5-7; cf. Expos. on vss. 5-7, 8; Exeg. on 33:31-33). He has not come—nor should we expect it, except as he represents perhaps even centuries of advance in Jewish thought—to any profound understanding of the mysteries of godliness (see Expos. on 21:7-18; yet see Exeg. on 34:9). To him might makes right (see Exeg. on 34:16-20; Expos. on 34:17) in that divine realm which is beyond man's comprehension, and though the might is instinct with mercy, it may nevertheless be expected to operate pretty much in accordance with the ancient pattern of pay as you enter and cash on delivery (cf. vs. 8). The modern world has waded out into those shallows with a vengeance. For theology: advice about relaxing and outwitting the nerves, and techniques for bolstering some way of life and undergirding democracy. For ethics: the good manners of Jesus, with a few decorative additions filched from the Sermon on the Mount, practicing this to see if it works, modifying that, substituting something else; scarcely realizing that all of life's little virtues, everything it does, can become a barrier to keep it from the vexing, harassing, prodding, uncomfortable reality of God.

The Cross was God's last bid for the whole man, laying hold of the deepest, with his face toward the farthest. There is a revealing story, pitifully inadequate as it is, told of Thomas Mott Osborne, warden of Sing Sing, so justly famous for his prison reforms. During his career he lived for a week among the convicts at Auburn, stripes and all, as if he belonged among them. One day he was engaged in carrying out some particularly revolting assignment, while a tough and unusually cold-blooded old prisoner who knew him stood by looking on with a sneer. But gradually, as the younger man kept at it unflinchingly, the sneer began to fade, and something like wonder crept into the hard face. Perhaps the world was not as ugly and selfish as it had always seemed. Maybe there was kindness in it, maybe there were people who cared, ready to get down like this under other fellows' burdens. And a lump came up in the old convict's throat, and he turned away as he felt his defenses falling, falling. In that other and far distant place, where there is no mere passing shadow of things as they are, but the deep darkness of the human soul and death, the springs of life can be clean again, setting on toward the sea: a man, free from all the tyranny of the past, and inwardly God's own.

3. *What Do You Expect of God?*—(Cf. II Pet. 3:4.) Some people expect nothing at all, and usually get it—until God comes in judgment. What they have to say is a half-smothered yawn.

| 5 Look unto the heavens, and see; and behold the clouds *which* are higher than thou. | 5 Look at the heavens, and see; and behold the clouds, which are higher than you. |

b) Freedom of God from Man (35:5-8)

5-8. With a somber but authentic awareness of divine transcendence, Elihu suggests that God, who is above the heavens and the clouds (vs. 5; cf. Eliphaz in 22:12-13), is not affected by human sin (vs. 6; cf. Job in 7:20). Much more important still, God does not need man's righteousness (vs. 7). However incomplete and unilateral such a theology may be (cf. Exeg. on 22:1-5), one has to admit that it does not necessarily lead to a

Dreams have played out. The greatest dreamer of all died for his dreaming. Why keep fooling oneself with pretty pictures from the prophets? **What advantage** have we? This would be quite intelligible if life were the cut and dried affair some folk seem to think it, and the world a dull world where nothing ever happens, and God bores people. Back in 1809, as Harry Emerson Fosdick once pointed out, Napoleon was in the news; but in that year Tennyson was born, and Darwin, and Gladstone, and Edgar Allan Poe, and Oliver Wendell Holmes, and Felix Mendelssohn. Is that sober history, or is it a fairy story? Halford Luccock writes of the world's authentic royal cities: Bethlehem; Eisleben, with its Luther; Domremy with its Joan of Arc; Dôle, with its Pasteur; Bridges Creek, Virginia, with its George Washington; Hodgenville, Kentucky, with its Abraham Lincoln.[10] What to expect? The impossible! (See Expos. on vs. 14; 38:1–42:6.)

Others look for some kind of immediate and permanent return on their investment (Matt. 19:27), something in hand to make the effort worth while. This is an exciting world; it makes no sense to assume that nothing will happen. But it is an uncertain world, and plans go awry. Jesus told Peter that it was better not to inquire too closely into what was going to happen: God would deal with everybody after his goodness, as the householder dealt with the laborers in his vineyard, giving to the last even as to the first. Better leave all that to him, and remember he would not be used. The ageless symbol of the Christian faith is a cross with a man on it, arms outstretched under a mute sky, nails in his hands; and in his heart something he has never thought to earn: the mystery of God's eternal peace. The very hardness of that is flung down like a glove in front of all the gallantry there is in the human soul. Jesus rests his whole case on it.

A world where the impossible can happen, and often does; a God who makes no practice of

holding out as an inducement anything a man might chance to like or want. One thing God does: he offers himself (see Expos. on 38:1) "She . . . spake of him to all them that looked for redemption in Jerusalem" (Luke 2:38). They had no very good definition of it. Most of them thought it meant some kind of deliverance from Rome. Simply because this was not what it meant, some of them may well have had a hand later on in that Good Friday affair. What it really meant was a deliverance they had never dreamed of, to set life on its feet again, no matter how far down it had been beaten, or how often. It meant that no highest, farthest, deepest, purest human hope had to flicker and go out any more. Those hopes were not poetry; they were God's plain prose.

Says one of the characters in Sir Philip Gibbs's *Young Anarchy,* speaking of modern youth,

They are lookers-on at this rather ridiculous game called life, trying to find some clue to its tangle of absurdities, but very doubtful whether such a clue is there. They are amused and interested at times, but generally a little bored. . . . They have no faith in human progress or human nature. All that they hope to do is to have the best time possible according to their luck, and dodge if possible the . . . unpleasantness which will probably hit them between the eyes when they least expect it.[1]

There were times when Jesus too was an on-looker. One day when the disciples felt like talking about the glories of the temple, they found him staring at a poor widow who had crept up to throw her mite in the alms box. "Look!" he said, plucking them by the sleeve and pointing, "Look at that!" (Luke 21:1-4.) Because he understood the world better than we do, he was forever peering about for the great things that happen in dark corners. And because he understood God better, he kept whispering to his friends at every turn of the road. "Listen! Maybe this is he now!"

5-7. *The Transcendent God.*— (See Expos. on 7:20a, 21a; 22:2-5; 33:12; Exeg. on vss. 5-8; 34:16-20.) What yardstick will measure the dis-

---

[10] *Preaching Values in New Translations of the New Testament* (New York and Nashville: Abingdon-Cokesbury Press, 1928), pp. 15-16.

[1] New York: George H. Doran Co., 1926, p. 42.

6 If thou sinnest, what doest thou against him? or *if* thy transgressions be multiplied, what doest thou unto him?

7 If thou be righteous, what givest thou him? or what receiveth he of thine hand?

8 Thy wickedness *may hurt* a man as thou *art;* and thy rightousness *may profit* the son of man.

9 By reason of the multitude of oppressions they make *the oppressed* to cry: they cry out by reason of the arm of the mighty.

6 If you have sinned, what do you accomplish against him?
And if your transgressions are multiplied, what do you do to him?

7 If you are righteous, what do you give to him;
or what does he receive from your hand?

8 Your wickedness concerns a man like yourself,
and your righteousness a son of man.

9 "Because of the multitude of oppressions people cry out;
they call for help because of the arm of the mighty.

Moslem distortion of monotheism. It offers an indispensable corrective to all forms of man-centered worship. At the same time, it does not fall into the fallacy of antinomianism. Man's actions are never performed in a vacuum. They affect, rightly or wrongly, the lives of other men. There is a distinction between good and evil (vs. 8).

c) GIFTS OF GOD TO MAN (35:9-12)

9-12. There is no clear transition between the preceding thought and the theme which is now developed, but the poet is pursuing a clear intention. Job has complained of his undeserved suffering. By so doing, he has merely joined the masses of humanity and

---

tance between these verses and those simple words of the Apostles' Creed, "Suffered under Pontius Pilate"? Says James Strahan:

Elihu exalts God's greatness at the cost of His grace, His transcendence at the expense of His immanence. He sets up a material instead of a spiritual standard of profit and loss. He does not realise that God does gain what He most desires by the goodness of men, and loses what He most loves by their evil. He makes God so cold, distant, apathetic, heartless, that he creates for the imagination an impassable gulf between heaven and earth, and fosters the belief that a religion worthy of the name is for ever an impossibility. This is not the God of Israel, nor the God of whom Elihu himself speaks in the next sentences.[2]

8. *What of It?*—"It profits a man nothing [34:9]. . . . What advantage have I? How am I better off?" (Vs. 3.) Supposedly the question has been asked with a shrug—and worse. "I have kept his way. I have treasured in my bosom the words of his mouth." (23:11-12.) What of it? And Elihu proceeds to answer. "God gets nothing out of it, but you do, for weal or for woe, and society does." The transaction is still on the basis of a prudential ethic and a hedonistic philosophy (yet see Expos. on vss. 9-16). The final sanction is *pro bono publico,* the greatest

[2] *The Book of Job* (2nd ed.; Edinburgh: T. & T. Clark, 1914), pp. 126-27. Used by permission.

good for the greatest number. When one asks what that may happen to be, there are few who would recommend theft or murder, unless on the titanic scale of war. For the rest, every man becomes the protagonist of his own theory. This is not wholly to invalidate Elihu's position. It points what perhaps may be called "the peril of the center." The center is not in self or in others, but in God; with a radius that is neither mind nor will, but love. To be "righteous" is to stand in the relationship of love with the God who is righteous. The O.T. understands that profoundly. Theologically there is no excuse for the friends or for Elihu. There is none for Job except that his problem is not theological but existential. So was the problem of the Jewish people. The resolution, when it comes, has to come in that area. The movement inevitably is toward the theophany and the Incarnation.

9-16. *When God Does Not Answer.*—(See Expos. on 19:7; 33:14.) Though man, unlike the beast (cf. vs. 11*a* with 6:5), can in his pain cry out to "God for God's sake" (Exeg.), he does not. He cries as an animal cries, because he is hurt (see Expos. on 30:24). It is not his spirit that yields; it is his body that by reason of **the pride of evil men** calls for help. Such vain entreaties God does not **regard.** Why complain, then, of his silence, and in some bitterness bred by God's own patience, mouth such benighted

10 But none saith, Where *is* God my maker, who giveth songs in the night;	**10** But none says, 'Where is God my Maker, who gives songs in the night,
11 Who teacheth us more than the beasts of the earth, and maketh us wiser than the fowls of heaven?	**11** who teaches us more than the beasts of the earth, and makes us wiser than the birds of the air?'
12 There they cry, but none giveth answer, because of the pride of evil men.	**12** There they cry out, but he does not answer, because of the pride of evil men.

animality which cry for relief from pain (vs. 9; 24:12). Like other men, he has not sought God for God's sake, but he has cried merely for God's help.

None says, "Where is God my Maker,
who gives songs in the night?" (Vs. 10.)

This is one of the loftiest passages of the book, and indeed of the whole Bible. The quest is not one which ignores human needs. Petition for deliverance is legitimate, provided it is offered in the full recognition of creatureliness.

First of all, prayer must be addressed to the divine **Maker;** it appeals to the feelings which a master artist always entertains for the work of his hands (cf. 10:8 ff.), and it renews within man the sense of finitude and dependence. Second, it expects that such a God will give, even in the midnight of sorrow, the **songs** which have the power of transmuting the present gloom into the hope of a morning. That man should sing praises in the deepest darkness does not explain suffering, but it negates its poison, and the ability to sing them is for God alone to give. Natural man cannot overcome suffering, but grace blunts the thorn (II Cor. 12:9). This is the way in which God makes man

and empty words? "The effectual fervent prayer of a righteous man" (Jas. 5:16) stems of course from his need; but there is a need beyond all other needs, farther and deeper than any. In such a man's eyes, beyond the self, is God. Job's prayer was like that, but Elihu assumed otherwise. Job's quest was for the God he loved, beyond the God that terrified him (23:15), upon whom his very frailty was a claim (cf. Expos. on 7:7-10; 9:14-19; 10:8-12), in whose gift alone were the **songs in the night** which his soul yearned to sing. He had long ago given up hope of recovery; something else had to put the song on his lips (29:4b-5a).

Kissane's interpretation of this passage[3] is interesting and suggestive: The oppressed cried out for redress (vs. 9), but Job did not succor them because of his respect for the wicked oppressors (vs. 12). The gratitude which he owed to God who created him and protected him in the past (vss. 10-11) should have urged him to succor the needy; but, like the impious, he assumed that God was unaware of the suffering of the distressed, and therefore of his negligence (vs. 13). In the past, when he thought that God was not aware of the sins of men, Job was silent and respectful toward him; but now, when God has intervened to punish the guilty, and has

[3] *Job,* p 237.

made no exception in his favor, he is no longer silent or respectful (vss. 14-16).

10b. Songs in the Night.—(Cf. Acts 16:25.) Paul's hymn to love (I Cor. 13) was composed in the midnight of his own distress over the church at Corinth. George Matheson's "O Love that wilt not let me go" carries with it the memory of some deep agony of soul (see Expos. on 6:4). In suffering and in sorrow, in failure and in despair, there is One whose presence is a melody in the heart, and his very will a song. There is a legend to the effect that Satan, when asked what in heaven he missed most, replied that he missed most "the sound of the trumpets in the morning." The whole ministry of God's redemption makes music out of discord. Henley writes his poem:

Out of the night that covers me,
Black as the Pit from pole to pole,
I thank whatever gods may be
For my unconquerable soul,[4]

—and gets drunk. Paul, in prison, writes to the Philippians, "Rejoice in the Lord always: and again I say, Rejoice" (Phil. 4:4), and wins an empire for Christ. Such **songs in the night** are the cradlesongs of every victory that God has wrought.

[4] "Invictus."

| 13 Surely God will not hear vanity, neither will the Almighty regard it. | 13 Surely God does not hear an empty cry, nor does the Almighty regard it. |
| 14 Although thou sayest thou shalt not see him, *yet* judgment *is* before him; therefore trust thou in him. | 14 How much less when you say that you do not see him, that the case is before him, and you are waiting for him! |

superior to the beasts (vs. 11). Such a religious attitude, however, is not widespread. **None says, "Where is God my Maker . . . ?"** (Vs. 10.) It is because men in general do not have recourse to God in true humility that **they cry out, but he does not answer** (vs. 12*a*). Job should not have accused God of silence (24:12) without at the same time having taken into consideration **the pride of evil men** (vs. 12*b*).

d) VANITY OF JOB'S ARGUMENT (35:13-16)

13-16. God does not hear an empty cry (vs. 13), and so he veils his presence and withdraws his face from Job (vs. 14). When the hero observes that the wicked appear

---

14. *Wait upon God*.—This is a difficult verse. It may be that we should translate, "Indeed, when you say that you do not see him, . . . the case is before him; therefore wait for him." Even when Job protests that he can see no sign of God anywhere (23:8-9; etc.), and that he cannot win a hearing from the Almighty (31:35; etc.), even then the hearing is on; one has only to wait (cf. Expos. on 8:20-22).

> God is His own interpreter,
> And He will make it plain.[5]

Ages upon ages have borne their witness to the truth of that. If the Bible means any one thing, it means that God is forever breaking through:

(*a*) Among the most unexpected people. W. N. Ewer put one of the earliest stages of the long story of redemption, as the O.T. records it, into one of the shortest poems which the English language boasts:

> How odd
> Of God
> To choose
> The Jews.

The great unnamed prophet of the Exile described what God had been looking for: a people gentle and unafraid, that would not cause their voice to be heard in the street (Isa. 42:2). Then he described what God got: a people deaf and blind, snared in holes, hid in prison houses, a prey and a spoil (Isa. 42:19, 22).

(*b*) In the most unexpected places: Egypt, Babylon, a remote province of the Roman Empire, Nazareth, Calvary. Four hundred years later, on the shores of North Africa, precisely where the American troops landed in World

War II, a man sat writing a book. Could he think of nothing better to do—while civilization was falling to pieces? His name was Augustine. For a thousand years his book held in thrall the history of European thought. Its title was *The City of God*. Then a German miner's hut—and Luther!

(*c*) At the most unexpected times. Read again Luke 21:25-28. Legend once had it that William Cowper wrote his poem (from which are taken the lines cited above) on a day when he had planned to put an end to his life by drowning himself, but the cabby he summoned to drive him to the river wandered round and round in a fog and set him down again at his own gate. Such strange things do not always happen. In Cowper's case there are indications that they did not. But the norm, if ever it could be discovered, would likely prove stranger than the exception—with an incalculable God at the helm! In a world like that there is no peril like the peril of settling down. God will not be put to bed—as Michal did once with her idol (I Sam. 19:13)—in any way of life, or in any system of doctrine. Too often when judgment begins, it begins "at the house of God" (I Pet. 4:17). Nor is there any futility like the futility of despair. Queer people, strange places, odd times: whose case is hopeless, what man will sneak away and hide, or because he is out of love with the present, throw up his hands and lose his zest for the future? Whenever God comes, wherever he comes, or to whom, he seems to stir a tumult. And that tumult, writes John Baillie,[6] is religion (see Expos. on vss. 2-3, 3; 36:15-17).

14. *Solutions in Parentheses*.—When you say that you do not see him, . . . the case is before him; wait for him! If this translation is correct,

[5] William Cowper, "Light Shining Out of Darkness," st. vi.

[6] *Our Knowledge of God* (New York: Charles Scribner's Sons, 1929), p. 3.

15 But now, because *it is* not *so,* he hath visited in his anger; yet he knoweth *it* not in great extremity:

16 Therefore doth Job open his mouth in vain; he multiplieth words without knowledge.

15 And now, because his anger does not punish,
  and he does not greatly heed transgression,[a]

16 Job opens his mouth in empty talk,
  he multiplies words without knowledge."

36
Elihu also proceeded, and said,
2 Suffer me a little, and I will show thee that *I have* yet to speak on God's behalf.

36
And Eli'hu continued, and said:
2 "Bear with me a little, and I will show you,
  for I have yet something to say on God's behalf.

[a] Theodotion Symmachus Compare Vg: The meaning of the Hebrew word is uncertain

to live on unpunished and then proceeds to deny the morality of God (vs. 15; cf. 21:7 ff.), he **opens his mouth in empty talk** (vs. 16). For there may be a hidden purpose in God's apparent leniency toward arrogance. Admittedly this passage is obscure and its interpretation conjectural, but if it is correct, these verses skillfully prepare for the development of ch. 36.

D. Second Part: The Hidden Mercy of God (36:1–37:24)

Elihu has now completed his refutation of Job's theological attacks. He will offer a positive contribution by describing God's purposes in the affliction of the just (36:1-25), continue with a hymnic meditation on the marvels of Providence (36:26–37:13), and conclude with a final exhortation for Job to fear his Creator (37:14-24).

1. Methods of the Divine Educator (36:1-25)
a) Further Utterances on God's Behalf (36:1-4)

36:2-4. Elihu announces that he has **yet something to say on God's behalf** (vs. 2). In the preceding part of his discourses (35:10-16) he has touched on the central theme of pure religion. He has suggested that man has no claim whatever upon the grace of God. But he must not be misconstrued: he has not proposed that God is ruled by whim

Elihu is saying that if Job patiently endures his affliction, the solution will come, as it were, in parentheses. To the friends, suffering may conceivably be probative, but the chances are overwhelming that it is punitive; to Elihu it is disciplinary, as he will explain more fully in ch. 36. For the present, then, "let patience have her perfect work" (Jas. 1:4). No head-on assault like Job's will get anywhere. It is the frontal attack that fails.

In such a view there is something significant and deep. Over and again when men set themselves deliberately to "find the answer," to achieve happiness, to build Utopia, the object of their quest turns out to be a will-o'-the-wisp. Even "goodness" refuses to be pursued. Those who take out after it, like the prodigal's elder brother, often become the reason why people leave home. There is less taken by storm than by siege. Battles may be won by forthright attack; campaigns are won by strategy. It is rather

like playing a dog-legged hole in golf: no use driving straight toward the hole; to win one aims off-side. As William James did when he was asked to write something that might help to stay the alarming increase in the rate of suicides. Instead of *A Treatise on Self-destruction,* or *The Advantages of Being Alive,* his book bore the title *The Will to Believe.*

Greatness and goodness and happiness and peace simply are not proper ends for any human soul to set up for itself. They are states of being along the road. They are the by-products of a life that has been held steadily, like a ship at sea, to some true course worth sailing.

One desolate winter day that lonely poet, Francis Thompson, walked down Chancery Lane, illy clad, carrying a kind of carpetbag full of old books, recognizing nothing, unaware of anyone, his face lifted up to the sun as it suddenly broke through the clouds; and the face was shining with ecstasy, and there were tears

3 I will fetch my knowledge from afar, and will ascribe righteousness to my Maker.

4 For truly my words *shall* not *be* false: he that is perfect in knowledge *is* with thee.

5 Behold, God *is* mighty, and despiseth not *any: he is* mighty in strength *and* wisdom.

3 I will fetch my knowledge from afar,
and ascribe righteousness to my Maker.

4 For truly my words are not false;
one who is perfect in knowledge is with you.

5 "Behold, God is mighty, and does not despise any;
he is mighty in strength of understanding.

---

and caprice. He will therefore **fetch [his] knowledge from afar** (vs. 3a), and **ascribe righteousness to [his] Maker** (vs. 3b). He is utterly confident in the truth of his convictions (vs. 4). Many critics think that he boasts extravagantly of being **perfect in knowledge** (vs. 4b), but this interpretation is unlikely, for Elihu uses elsewhere the same expression for describing the Deity (37:16). It is therefore probable that vs. 4b also refers to God and anticipates the theological development which follows.

b) PURPOSES OF AFFLICTION (36:5-15)

5-7. Divine omnipotence is not incompatible with divine justice and even kindness. **Behold, God is mighty** (כביר; vs. 5a), "but he does not despise him who is pure like milk" (vs. 5b; reading with the Syriac, בר כחלב, instead of the M.T. כביר כח לב, which is

---

in his eyes. What had done that for him—or who?

> Yea, in the night, my Soul, my daughter,
> Cry,—clinging Heaven by the hems;
> And lo, Christ walking on the water
> Not of Gennesareth, but Thames! [7]

Can it be that along the way of Christ's presence solutions appear of themselves—in parentheses? What is the theophany in Job but a foreshadow?

36:3b. To God's Defense!—(Cf. Expos. on 1:12; 13:8.) Elihu, with his doctrine of love-in-justice, comes far nearer the heart of the matter than any of the friends. The author of these speeches lived later than the original poet, perhaps by some two hundred years. The facts of human existence, to which Job had so often appealed (see Expos. on 12:2-6; 21:5-6), the sheer weight and movement of human history, had compelled certain modifications of the rigid theory of divine retribution, and had prepared the way for a much deeper and truer understanding of the nature of God's dealing. The God of Elihu is indeed a greater God (see Expos. on 33:12; 34:14). Instead of rendering the theophany unnecessary, as Elihu's speeches were no doubt intended to do, they prepare the way for it (see Exeg. on 37:23-24). God is not only the Almighty, but forever the All-just (vss. 5, 6; 37:23), the All-wise (vs. 4b), and the All-merciful (vss. 9-10). If the righteous do have

[7] "The Kingdom of God," from *Collected Works*, ed. Wilfred Meynell (Westminster, Md.: Newman Press, 1947). Used by permission.

to endure suffering (vs. 8), it does not in the least mean that he has cast them off (vs. 7a). His favor has not been withdrawn. Eliphaz indeed had hinted as much (5:17), Elihu dwells on it. To be afflicted is not to be an alien in a hostile world: it is still to be under the hand of One whose every gesture is a summons and a beckoning (vss. 9-10). True knowledge of God is theodicy enough. He is his own defense.

5-15. *The Uses of Adversity.*—Elihu of course cannot make up his mind that there is any such thing as innocent suffering. Here is precisely one of the most important points at which the later author differs from the original poet. He does not fully comprehend the "mysteries of godliness" (see Expos. on 21:7-18), and so shoots his bolt consistently wide of the mark (1:8; 2:3), yet just as consistently closer to it than the friends. How close is often subject for wonder.

The Greeks never conceived it as a problem. They were not primarily concerned, as the Hebrews were, with the nature and dealing of the Eternal. They were concerned about Nemesis and Fate, personified yet impersonal: that to them was the framework of human existence. Among the Hebrews, but especially among the Jews of the postexilic period, the holiness of the God they worshiped lifted the problem into startling prominence. To understand something at least of the vast catastrophes that overtake human life was vitally necessary; and to understand was harder for the believer than for the unbeliever. It is harder still for those whose God is not only the God of all creation but as well

6 He preserveth not the life of the wicked: but giveth right to the poor.	6 He does not keep the wicked alive, but gives the afflicted their right.

grammatically impossible and must be attributed to scribal error because it repeats the word כביר, **mighty,** from the immediately preceding clause). Heretofore Elihu has been

---

"the God and Father of our Lord Jesus Christ." With such a God, "Why?" Not once, but twice, and three times, "Why?" In the O.T. are hands without number lifted up to heaven, on how many faces an agony, on how many lips a question: not matched yet with the agony and the question on Calvary. Perhaps this is as good a place as any to ask what the book of Job as we now have it has to say on the subject. Only so can we see how near Elihu comes, and how far he falls short.

All along, from beginning to end, is the deep undertone of God's wrath against the wicked. Elihu and the friends keep insisting on it; Job himself not only takes it for granted, but constantly puts it into words. Whatever else may be said about that, it is not the rule that disturbs the thoughtful person, but the exceptions to the rule. In the vehemence of his denial that the rule applies to him and to his case, Job denies more than once that there is any such rule as everybody wants him to imagine. The whole earth, says he bitterly, is given over to the wicked (9:24). In his more sober moods, even in the midst of his suffering, he never would have said that. He knew very well that there is a rough kind of justice that does get itself done. For all the miscarriages of that justice, it is still not well with the wicked. For all the woes of the righteous, there is still a judgment, inscrutable, inexorable. But that is not the point at issue. The point at issue is that point where a man's character and the calamity which overtakes him cannot be made to balance, where the two can no longer be so equated that the one can be used to explain the other. What then? It is of design in the original poem that the friends refuse to countenance any such question. Elihu will not face it because the author of his speeches is at pains to disallow the older poet's very hypothesis.

Is it therefore by way of trial that God permits suffering? In the first cycle, especially in the first discourse of Eliphaz (4:6), some account is taken of the possibility. Certainly the thought is given shape in the mind of the original poet. There (in the prologue) is God, proud and confident of his servant; and there is Job, proving that the pride and confidence are not misplaced (cf. 42:7). In the N.T. on page after page is the boasting of apostle and martyr that they are thought worthy of the testing that has come, ships let down off the ways and set out to sea, pitting themselves against the storm, evidence of the Maker's craft and handiwork. Recall Paul's long list of hardships and perils (II Cor. 11:24-28). He calls them the unceasing pageant God has made of his life, and reviews them as a general would review a parade. Job, so to speak, is God's gladiator in the bitter arena of human life and human sorrow, vindicating the honor of the God that fashioned him —how much more than Elihu (vs. 3b); than the friends, by that much more again! He is a son sent out to battle, with a father's ineffable joy in his manhood and courage and fealty and love. Cast into the furnace like ore, emerging fine gold (23:10; cf. Expos. on 1:6). "That the trial of your faith," so comes the echo, "being much more precious than of gold that perisheth, though it be tried with fire, might be found unto praise and honor and glory at the appearing of Jesus Christ" (I Pet. 1:7). How much place will be given that in the room which every life has to make for life? Let those who have suffered answer. Yet there is nothing in it of deliberate and calculated trial (cf. vs. 16 with Expos. on 1:6-12; 19:7). It was love, nothing less and nothing other, that allowed it. No doubt a man could stand a good deal if he knew that God, who has stood a good deal too, was looking on, pointing him out to the angels in heaven and saying, "See there! That is the way my sons behave!"

If not for calculated trial then, is it for discipline that God allows the blow to fall? Elihu says it is (vss. 9-10; cf. Deut. 8:1-10). And without in the least impugning the integrity of Job's life, one can indeed find in him more than mere traces of religious egoism—as where not? It is his own self-interestedness that broods over his pain and his utter insignificance in the great universe; twists, distorts, fights back (see Expos. on 19:28-29), as if he were the special object of God's vengeance, as once he had been the very household pet of God's bounty. And that dross is burned out. One must not dismiss the fact. Read Francis Thompson's "The Hound of Heaven" and see what it was that drove him back into the arms of God. Read of "The Blind Ploughman," and the

> God, who took away my eyes,
> That my *soul* might see! [8]

[8] Marguerite Radclyffe-Hall, *Songs of Three Counties and Other Poems* (London: Chapman & Hall, 1913). Used by permission of the publishers and the agents acting for the author's estate.

| 7 He withdraweth not his eyes from the righteous: but with kings *are they* on the throne; yea, he doth establish them for ever, and they are exalted.
8 And if *they be* bound in fetters, *and* be holden in cords of affliction; | 7 He does not withdraw his eyes from the righteous,
but with kings upon the throne
he sets them for ever, and they are exalted.
8 And if they are bound in fetters
and caught in the cords of affliction, |

---

careful to avoid explicit agreement with the friends' traditional views on individual retribution. But he is now so intent upon preserving the morality of Providence that he falls into the accepted and well-worn pattern (vss. 6-7).

8-12. However, Elihu goes further than his predecessors. While they assert merely that suffering is a punishment for sin, he insists upon the disciplinary and purifying

---

Still it must be remembered that a man may come out of the fire not purged, but a cinder (vss. 13-14). Such is the risk God has to run. He ran it with Job, in the Satan's teeth. And Job stood fast, for all his wavering and beating about in the tempests that broke over him. And in Job God stood. A woman sits bound to her chair year in and year out. It would be heartless for anybody to suggest to her that her stature these sad years—in spite of them, or because of them, what difference does it make?—has grown (vs. 15), the peace on her face deepened, the smile in her eyes become radiant with an unearthly radiance, the words on her lips gayer words. But so it is. And one may not dismiss it. The trouble with Elihu is that for him too, as for the friends, love has slipped out of the picture—if not so much in theory, equally so in fact: slipped out of the figure he cuts, and out of God. His God "doth not afflict willingly, nor grieve the children of men" (cf. vss. 8-9); but neither can he "be touched with the feeling of our infirmities" (cf. 35:6-7).

Back of it all, however, more poignantly for Job than for any of the others, yet for them as well, each in his own measure (vs. 26; 11:7-9), lies the unfathomable mystery. Through it men may look, "as through a glass, darkly" (I Cor. 13:12), and argue to themselves that were the world other than it is, and did the righteous always reap the harvest and the wicked the whirlwind, then indeed the problem would be solved, but very much as death solves the problem of disease. Life could no longer have any moral significance for anybody. That much may be said. But the ultimate, at this stage of the poem, must lie in the reasons beyond human reason (see Expos. on 1:12; 2:7-10). Why else that scene at the very beginning, in the secret councils of the Almighty, the transaction of which Job is kept in ignorance? It is as if the All-wise, the All-just, the All-merciful were pursuing his own great ends beyond man's knowing, while man himself is left to grope after them in

faith. How else could they ever be apprehended by finite minds? If men understood God, they would do well to doubt him. If the finite could fathom the infinite, the infinite would be finite. Why else the poem on wisdom (ch. 28)? And why else the speeches of the Almighty, in which there is a world of mystery—made luminous with God. To march out bravely into the dark, and not to ask too closely, "Why?" On what other terms can living be triumphant?

8-25. What Price Suffering?—No wonder that the Jews, at this precise moment of all moments, found it a problem for the soul to grapple with. The sound of it runs through the psalms. In Ezekiel they keep saying, "The way of the Lord is not equal" (Ezek. 18:25, 29; 33:17); and the answer comes back, "Is not my way equal? Are not your ways unequal?" The Bible never dodges it, neither does Job. Not all that he says is true; enough of it is to make one wary of any argument about the justice of God based on the facts of human experience. There are somber realities there which seem to be the greatest of all discords in the harmony of creation, the worst contradictions imaginable to the revelation of a Father that pities his children, making it forever impossible for anybody to be comfortably optimistic, carrying his faith like an easy cloak, instead of like a shield he has done battle for.

The friends were sure that they knew what it was all about, and they were wrong. Elihu came nearer, but he too was wrong, after his kind. All of them knew that it was not an intrusion, that existence is never free from suffering; yet all of them kept talking as if it were somehow imposed from without. So did Job. Not one of them said right out what has to be said, that in some strange fashion it belongs to the texture of things. It is not supplemental, but elemental, wrought into the fabric (see Expos. on 5:6-7). All the more it must have meaning. If to banish it from the world would be to fashion a world different from this not only in

9 Then he showeth them their work, and their transgressions that they have exceeded.

9 then he declares to them their work and their transgressions, that they are behaving arrogantly.

---

significance of chastisement. By bringing men into affliction (vs. 8), God makes them aware of **their transgressions** (vs. 9), reveals to them *mûṣār*, **instruction** (vs. 10a; cf.

---

degree but in kind; if it is so closely woven into the very pattern of life that to disturb it would be to transform the quality of that life *toto caelo*, surely it must be of profounder significance than any ready "explanation" of it would suggest. What if it belongs to that Being which is the ground of all being! There is little if any hint of that in the speeches of Elihu or of the friends; in Job, nothing but the barest, broken whisper of the sorrows that have their home in the heart of God (7:21c; 14:13-15).

Add this, that as life advances from its lower to its higher forms its capabilities for suffering grow more and more acute (cf. 6:5; 35:11). A mule has sensations which a lobster very likely knows nothing about. One may be relatively sure of that without being either. See how acute Job's suffering is! The more exalted the character and the finer the nature, the higher the ideals, the quicker the wound, and the deeper. Ought it not be just the reverse? As life climbs farther up, should it not be leaving the shadow farther and farther behind, instead of getting in more deeply for every inch of ground it covers? Unless in some unaccountable way the shadow works with it toward its goal.

That the dark facts of human existence have done just that is the unfailing testimony of the ages. It is the testimony of the book of Job. That much more right Elihu and the friends were than Job himself. He thought it made demonic sense (see Expos. on 10:13-17); they thought it made God's kind of sense—only they mistook the kind. No need to insist with Elihu that God sends suffering for men to sharpen their teeth on. It is necessary only to acknowledge, as true of the realities of human experience, that when a man achieves some measure of moral greatness his triumph comes not so much in spite of suffering as through it. In some queer way out of that raw stuff his victory has been fashioned. What he has endured has gone into the warp and woof of his soul and become a part of him, as the thorn was a part of Paul, and indeed the scars a part of Jesus, so that no man now can think of God without them.

Yet there is left over what seems to be the bald and meaningless injustice of so much of the suffering there is in the world. J. Y. Simpson, in writing of it, aptly recalls the "happy little child Jesus once placed in the midst of his disciples to teach them a lesson of faith,"

and adds, "There are in the world other little children, and when we place them in our midst our faith is simply struck dumb." To watch them lifting up their pathetic faces against the crippling odds to which they have fallen heir is to make that easy phrase, "It's all for the best," stick fast in the throat. There is anguish that seems purposeless and mad—Job knew it well— a grinning mockery of God. It is quite out of the question to be sure of him at all without realizing that somehow something has gone wrong (see Expos. on 1:6-12; 16:11). The friends said it, and so did Elihu; and they were right. They said that the world is marked all over with our interference; and it is. They did not reckon on Satan's. And they all wanted to come down to cases with it, applying it to the situation in hand. It happened not to apply. When a man breaks his leg it is not always certain that he has been running after something he should have let go. Nevertheless, sin and suffering are not unrelated. "Forasmuch as it hath pleased God, of his great mercy, to take unto himself the soul of this our brother. . . ." It may not have pleased God at all. The man may have been a glutton. Life may well have been intended as a channel of mercy; but anybody can send his evil and his willfulness down its ways until it carries a very burden of woe and those who come after must stoop to the heritage that is left them (see Expos. on 21:19). How much of the pain bears that indictment written across its face? How much of the pain wears a human signature for any soul to read?

If there is any rescue for faith as it stands gazing at the spectacle of a tortured world, it must be in the passion of a God who suffers too (cf. Expos. on 12:7-25; cf. also Expos. on Heb. 12:3-11).

8. *But If, When Ye Do Well, and Suffer.*— Elihu barely hints at that problem, and solves it by dismissing it. One would suppose that in his thought the word "righteous" (vs. 7) actually did stand in quotation marks. **If they are . . . caught in the cords of affliction,** God is declaring to them "their transgressions." But no such tour de force will serve. The matter has to be taken seriously, as Job says. No man is righteous; but no man either can take advantage of that fact to hide his mind away in the doctrine of an evenhanded retribution.

Certainly what "goodness" there is cannot be

10 He openeth also their ear to discipline, and commandeth that they return from iniquity.

11 If they obey and serve *him*, they shall spend their days in prosperity, and their years in pleasures.

10 He opens their ears to instruction,
    and commands that they return from
    iniquity.
11 If they hearken and serve him,
    they complete their days in prosperity,
    and their years in pleasantness.

5:17), and bids them to **return from iniquity** (vs. 10*b*). The alternative on the one hand is **prosperity** and **pleasantness** in this life (vs. 11; cf. Ps. 16:6, 11, in which the word נעימים has probably the meaning of "religious delights"), or on the other hand an untimely and violent death (vs. 12).

---

set down as a guarantee of anybody's safety. Still there are "the slings and arrows of outrageous fortune." Indeed, the situation is worse than that: "But if, when ye do well, and suffer," i.e., from a sense of God (I Pet. 2:20, 19), knowing what he is like, and what he demands. It was precisely this that Job knew, deep in the turmoil of his soul (see Expos. on 19:6); and the knowledge itself was anguish. As the years passed, and the very goodness of God was made incarnate, men found it no shield and buckler (see Expos. on 23:10). Rather it laid them wide open, drove them out of doors into the thick of the storm, where the wind could whip their clothes about and the rain could sting their face. If anything is to be set down, it is that. When Jesus came, and was baffled and beaten and killed, not many could swallow the fantastic notion that this was God in the flesh. God could have saved himself the thorns and the reed and the nails. He could have managed differently and got along better. It should not be necessary to pay so terribly in a Father's house for being that Father's child (see Expos. on 21:7-18). What is it, a crazy world, where a man does well and suffers for it? "Aye," writes Peter, "it is that. Just so!" There is nothing in the Sermon on the Mount to the effect that the poor in spirit, the meek, the pure in heart, will have their fur stroked. No neat modicum of success, no fat surplus of well-being: just something about a kingdom sometime. And something more one day about "sheep in the midst of wolves" (Matt. 10:16). Partly no doubt because New York and London and Paris and Berlin and Tokyo are what men have made them, not what God wanted them to be.

The other fact that has to be set down is this: There is a way of meeting the world's hostility—"if ye take it patiently." Peter could not rub from his eyes that One who waited out the ribald laughter and the shouts, until life looked up amazed to find gentleness there still, and hope, and a sort of dry and tearless yearning. Does that mean a lying down under anything? Is it unconquerable might with God, but just plain,

cheap, yellow flabbiness with man? Job, with his dreadful wrestling (see Expos. on 3:24), and the faith that flatly refused to let go, came nearer God's kind of patience than any of the cowardly resignation which was commended to him. Holding on and defying the odds. Patience in the N.T. means just that. Staying with it when you are down, and everybody else has made off. A man's lonely, gallant wager that God is true (see Expos. on 8:20-22).

Franz Werfel in *Embezzled Heaven* takes an old woman and a priest into the catacombs and has them linger behind the crowd, while the priest talks of how horribly tedious everything down there seemed to him—above all else that greatest thing which nobody could see: just the incredible perseverance of the poor, simple folk by the hundreds, whose bones lay all about; their poverty, and squalor, and misery, despised by their fellows up yonder on the streets, forever facing prison and death. When at last they died, they had no idea of whether their waiting was in vain or not. Generation after generation, none of them knew. He called it "the craziest mystery in the whole history of the world . . . , the only revolution in which mankind has ever been successful." [1] Just that waiting, that awful, tremendous waiting. Job's was noisy and violent; but the noise and the violence were for God's sake.

11. *God's Kind of Security*.—Their days in prosperity, . . . their years in pleasantness (cf. Expos. on 5:17, 18, 23; 11:18; 17:12). One of the fundamental urges of human life is the urge to get through this world as safely as may be. And nobody does. More shelter for the body, less for the mind, least for the soul: there is something quite terrible about such "progress." For the Christian, paradoxically enough, there is most in that which seems to offer least (see Expos. on vs. 8; 35:14; read Eph. 4:22-28).

11-15. *Somehow Good*.—Elihu and the friends are at least never guilty of saying to Job that they are sure it will all turn out for the best.

[1] Tr. Moray Firth (New York: Viking Press, 1940), p. 326.

12 But if they obey not, they shall perish by the sword, and they shall die without knowledge.

13 But the hypocrites in heart heap up wrath: they cry not when he bindeth them.

14 They die in youth, and their life *is* among the unclean.

15 He delivereth the poor in his affliction, and openeth their ears in oppression.

16 Even so would he have removed thee out of the strait *into* a broad place, where *there is* no straitness; and that which should be set on thy table *should be* full of fatness.

12 But if they do not hearken, they perish by the sword,
    and die without knowledge.

13 "The godless in heart cherish anger;
    they do not cry for help when he binds them.
14 They die in youth,
    and their life ends in shame.*b*
15 He delivers the afflicted by their affliction,
    and opens their ear by adversity.
16 He also allured you out of distress
    into a broad place where there was no cramping,
    and what was set on your table was full of fatness.

b Heb *among the cult prostitutes*

13-15. The same thought is here repeated and amplified but in reverse order. The **godless** [vs. 13; cf. 8:13; etc.] **cherish anger** (cf. Rom. 2:5) and refuse to pray even under the strokes of distress; in their prime **they die** of premature exhaustion, lit., **among the cult prostitutes** (vs. 14 RSV mg.; cf. Deut. 23:18; I Kings 14:24; etc.). The proper acceptance of **affliction** is the way to salvation (vs. 15).

c) Let Job Beware and Praise (36:16-25)

The text of vss. 16-21 bristles with difficulties of various kinds, and the meaning is so obscure that some critics leave them untranslated. Inasmuch as the rendering of the RSV is not more conjectural than any of several others which might be proposed, and since it respects the M.T. as much as possible, it may be accepted provisionally as a basis of interpretation.

Elihu now concludes his exposition by applying it to Job's situation (vss. 16-17). He gives the hero three warnings (vss. 18-19, 20, 21-23) and ends with a solemn exhortation to turn carping against God into praise of his works (vss. 24-25).

16-17. The speaker appears to be bewildered by the fact that Job is obviously not a criminal in the usual sense of the word, and he therefore tries to find an explanation

---

Too much vapid sentimentalizing would claim for itself Tennyson's lines:

> O, yet we trust that somehow good
>   Will be the final goal of ill.[2]

There are conditions that have to be met. Elihu describes them in detail (vss. 9-11; 33:23-28; 35:10). So do the friends (5:17 ff.; 8:5-6; 11:13-17). Consistently the diagnosis was wrong, the therapy was for another ailment entirely, and the prognosis altogether beside the point (cf. modern man's approach to a world distraught).

15-17. *Round About by Way of the Wilderness.*— (Cf. Expos. on 13:17-18.) In pioneer days to leave New England and head for the West was to follow river beds and skirt moun-

[2] *In Memoriam,* Part LIV, st. i.

tains, to overcome hardships and weather privations; but those who arrived had learned something en route. An airplane flies as the crow flies, only much better; but the trip does very few travelers any good.

Elihu understands the value of the detour. The best road is not always the shortest: it may well run from *A* to *B* through *Z*. In fact, one may save a minute and lose a life. Or leap toward decency, as a whole culture tried to do in Russia, only to be caught in the toils of tyranny. The wilderness may be adversity or affliction; it may be postponement or old age—but what if the promises of God lie that way and not another? In vss. 16-17 Elihu suggests that Job's distress had its origin in

a broad place where there was no cramping,
and what was set on [the] table was full of fatness.

17 But thou hast fulfilled the judgment of the wicked: judgment and justice take hold *on thee.*	17 "But you are full of the judgment on the wicked; judgment and justice seize you.
18 Because *there is* wrath, *beware* lest he	18 Beware lest wrath entice you into scoffing;

for the hero's misery. His reasoning may have proceeded as follows. Job's past privileges and extraordinary happiness were for him an occasion of sin. God **allured** or "enticed" him (observe the pejorative meaning of the verb הסית in vs. 18 and also in 2:3; cf. I Sam. 26:19; II Sam. 24:1; Isa. 36:18) by preserving him "from the mouth of the enemy" (**out of distress**), and by establishing him in **a broad place where there was no cramping** (vs. 16*a*). Job enjoyed all that earth could offer. **What was set on [his] table was full of fatness** (vs. 16*b*). He did not suffer from the fear of insecurity which gnaws at other men. He knew neither hunger nor thirst, neither cold nor oppression. He was truly a free man.

Exceptional prosperity, however, made him soft toward himself and hard on others. His pride corrupted his sense of justice. He condemned the evildoers and in particular expressed shocked amazement that many of them never seemed to be punished. He was **full of the judgment on the wicked** (vs. 17*a*; מלאת, a verb in the perfect tense). Now **judgment and justice seize** him (vs. 17*b*; יתמכו, a verb in the imperfect tense, expressing the continuation of the past into the present and future). In other words, his own sense of justice has gone to his head, but the justice of God is catching up with him. He must now bear the penalty of his pride, but he still refuses to recognize that his plight is actually the price of his pride. Thus he increases the burden of his crime in uncommon proportion. Such may be Elihu's diagnosis in this passage. It must be emphasized that this interpretation is hypothetical. But it fits the general tenure of Elihu's thought.

18-19. Now comes the first warning: **Beware lest wrath entice you into scoffing** (vs. 18*a*). Job's resentment against God should not lead him into a more grievous sin. God

Out of his own pride (see Exeg.) and comfortable complacency had sprung his resentments at the prosperity of the wicked (vs. 17*a*); out of his surfeit **judgment and justice** had laid hold on him. It does happen. Meanwhile, the only assurance which anybody is heir to is the assurance of some crown that God has pledged himself to fashion: not to achieve something, perhaps, but to be something. That always takes time. And tears may be a part of it, and broken hopes, and bitter delays (see Expos. on 35:14).

But to make it clear, there stands One who came to a manger in Bethlehem. Thirty years he waited. Even then there was no crown to be had for a leap. In the wilderness the devil whispered to him, "Hurry!" But there was to be a cross first. And how much else to follow! He said to Simon, "Go and preach." "To the men who crucified thee, Lord?" "Yes." "To those who brought the crown of thorns?" "Yes. I still have my crown, and to him who came with the reed say that I have a scepter too." "Preach, Lord, to the men who drove the nails?" "Yes. And to those who cursed me say that I have a song for them; and to the soldier who pierced my side say that there is a nearer way to my heart than that."

It was God's road, and it was long and round

about, and it ran far away, and out of sight, toward the spires on the world's rim. In that one sentence, as also in vs. 15, is the whole story of Job; but its dimensions were far greater than Elihu dreamed.

18-25. In Life's Rough Places.—For Job three warnings (see Exeg. on vss. 18-19, 20, 21-23) and an exhortation (vss. 24-25): no mocking now, no vain hoping for release in death, no sitting in judgment on God—but praise; praise anyhow, whether under the circumstances it makes sense or not; for praise is what God wants. Besides missing the point entirely (see Expos. on vss. 18, 21), such admonition betrays on the face of it its own pitiful inadequacy: for all the beauty of the psalm that follows, these are how much more than the counsels of prudence? Come from them in one long stride to the N.T. "Tribulation . . . distress . . . persecution . . . famine . . . nakedness . . . peril . . . sword" (Rom. 8:35). Life indeed turns rough— perhaps it was never intended to run smoothly; rougher now and then than people bargain for, until they are stuck in it up to their knees: like Michelangelo's figures in the gallery at Florence, looking as if they were struggling hopelessly to be free of the marble. "What shall we then say to these things? If God be for us

take thee away with *his* stroke: then a great ransom cannot deliver thee.

19 Will he esteem thy riches? *no,* not gold, nor all the forces of strength.

20 Desire not the night, when people are cut off in their place.

21 Take heed, regard not iniquity: for this hast thou chosen rather than affliction.

22 Behold, God exalteth by his power: who teacheth like him?

23 Who hath enjoined him his way? or who can say, Thou hast wrought iniquity?

and let not the greatness of the ransom turn you aside.

19 Will your cry avail to keep you from distress,
or all the force of your strength?

20 Do not long for the night,
when peoples are cut off in their place.

21 Take heed, do not turn to iniquity,
for this you have chosen rather than affliction.

22 Behold, God is exalted in his power;
who is a teacher like him?

23 Who has prescribed for him his way,
or who can say, 'Thou hast done wrong'?

---

is not to be mocked. His **wrath** must be accepted with penitence. **Let not the greatness of the ransom turn you aside** (vs. 18*b*). Job is now bearing in his afflictions the "atonement" (כפר) of his crime. He should carry the full weight of this burden instead of being lured farther and farther from deliverance. His **cry** of distress (cf. Pss. 18:6; 66:14; etc.) will not preserve him from ultimate annihilation, not even "all the energies of [his] strength" (vs. 19). He cannot save himself by his own resources and exertions. Man's power is of no avail. The giant must surrender. Prometheus is bound.

20. The second warning seems to be quite clear, although many critics agree with Driver and Gray that it is "perhaps the most unintelligible of all these verses" (*Job,* I, 313). As a matter of fact, the literal meaning of the M.T. is not out of place in the context as we have thus far interpreted it.

> Do not long for the night,
> when peoples are cut off in their place.

Job has been tossed about between two moods: either he has desperately asked for a hearing and a vindication, or else he has begged for death. Elihu warned him in vss. 18-19 not to add rebellion to pride, and in this verse he now admonishes him that there is no hope for him in death. He probably alludes to the sufferer's initial lament (3:2) and more specifically to the line, "Like a slave who longs for the shadow" (7:2). "Do not desire the grave," says the strictly monotheistic theologian to a man possibly tempted by pagan rituals concerned with life in the underworld, "do not yearn for darkness because nothing is there but extinction."

21-23. The third warning confirms the Exeg. on vss. 16-17 and 18-19. **Take heed, do not turn to iniquity** (vs. 21*a*): Job has already chosen rebellion rather than humble acceptance of **affliction** (vs. 21). How could he dare to be the teacher of a **God** who alone is **exalted in . . . power** (vs. 22; cf. vs. 19*b*)? Will Job presume to dictate to the Almighty? There is no man who can teach God.

> Who has prescribed for him his way,
> or who can say, "Thou hast done wrong"? (Vs. 23.)

. . . ?" (Rom. 8:31.) It is worth something to start with the knowledge that however sticky the road is, he has traveled it ahead of us, and has come back to meet us (Expos. on 8:3). If he cares that much, caring may be what life is all about. If he cares that much, he soberly and honestly means, whatever happens, to make it more than worth while to go on and go through.

"Nay, in all these things" (Rom. 8:37) there is a glory beyond; beyond this grief, that failure, yonder ruined life. "For I am persuaded . . ." (Rom. 8:38-39).

18, 21. *Are Morals Enough?*—Elihu is concerned about doing; Job is concerned about being. Elihu no doubt would have been pleased with an address on "The Sufficiency of an

24 Remember that thou magnify his work, which men behold.	24 "Remember to extol his work, of which men have sung.
25 Every man may see it; man may behold *it* afar off.	25 All men have looked on it; man beholds it from afar.
26 Behold, God *is* great, and we know *him* not, neither can the number of his years be searched out.	26 Behold, God is great, and we know him not; the number of his years is unsearchable.
27 For he maketh small the drops of water: they pour down rain according to the vapor thereof;	27 For he draws up the drops of water, he distils^c his mist in rain
	^c Cn: Heb *they distil*

Job has been bold and reckless enough to pass judgment on the divine acts. He must now refrain from condemning his Maker (cf. 9:12*b*; 21:31). He must acknowledge the humanity of man and the divinity of God.

24-25. Elihu thus bids Job reverse his course and, instead of arguing against God, join the universal chorus of praise.

> Remember to extol his work,
> of which men have sung (vs. 24; cf. 33:27; 35:10).

The giant who set himself to defy the Godhead must rejoin the rank and file of mankind and gaze in gladness mixed with awe upon the toil of the Creator.

> All men have looked on it;
> man beholds it from afar (vs. 25).

Contemplation will give birth to the music of adoration. Job may be unable to comprehend the mysterious ways of God, but he can still stand above the vicissitudes of earth and even transmute the moan of his tortures into a Magnificat. His lament of self-pity can thus be turned into a hymn of praise. This is Elihu's last word of advice, "Magnify the *opus Dei!*" And, following exhortation with example, he intones a psalmodic doxology.

2. UNSEARCHABLE GLORY OF THE LORD OF NATURE (36:26–37:13)

In a style which recalls the doxologies of the prophetic literature and the hymns of praise for the Lord of nature which are found in the Psalter, Elihu extols the glory of God as it appears in the marvels of sky and storm. The themes flow one into the other like the motifs of a tone poem.

a) LORD OF AUTUMN (36:26-33)

26-33. After an overture on the greatness and eternity of the divine being, a greatness and an eternity which forever transcend the comprehension of man (vs. 26), the poet centers his meditation on two seasons of the year—autumn and winter—when meteorological portents inspire in man theological reflection.

Ethical Religion." Job would have preferred some such subject as "Morals May Be Enough If There Is No God." It was fellowship with that God which was far and away the most important item on the roster of his business (cf. Expos. on 19:4, 6; 42:5).

26-33. *The Heavens Declare the Glory of God.* — (Cf. Expos. on 11:7.) The movement in Scripture is not from nature to man to God. The Gifford Lectures were intended to travel in that direction. Modern man is still inclined to insist on it. The ambiguities of both nature and man would seem to make it difficult. Savage or kind, purposeful or meaningless? The reading depends on the reader. A man who has lost his faith cannot be brought back to it by any mere contemplation of the heavens. Because Elihu begins with God, he can see in the lightning, judgment, in the rain, mercy (vs. 31; cf. 37:13), both hidden and revealed (vss. 32-33) by them at once. The revelation is not conceived as either in nature or in history; nature and history are its footnotes (cf. Expos. on 26:5-14). When they are allowed to step into

28 Which the clouds do drop *and* distil upon man abundantly.

29 Also can *any* understand the spreadings of the clouds, *or* the noise of his tabernacle?

30 Behold, he spreadeth his light upon it, and covereth the bottom of the sea.

31 For by them judgeth he the people; he giveth meat in abundance.

32 With clouds he covereth the light; and commandeth it *not to shine* by *the cloud* that cometh betwixt.

33 The noise thereof showeth concerning it, the cattle also concerning the vapor.

37 At this also my heart trembleth, and is moved out of his place.

---

28 which the skies pour down,
    and drop upon man abundantly.

29 Can any one understand the spreading of the clouds,
    the thunderings of his pavilion?

30 Behold, he scatters his lightning about him,
    and covers the roots of the sea.

31 For by these he judges peoples;
    he gives food in abundance.

32 He covers his hands with the lightning,
    and commands it to strike the mark.

33 Its crashing declares concerning him,
    who is jealous with anger against iniquity.

37 "At this also my heart trembles,
    and leaps out of its place.

In autumn the Master of nature brings rain to the parched soil and thus renews the life of the earth with the promise of abundant food (vss. 27-31). He thereby reveals his providential bounty, but conceals at the same time the true nature of his being in the flash of lightning (vs. 32); yet **its crashing declares concerning him,** and the man of faith can discern behind the flash of light the presence of a God **who is jealous with anger against iniquity** (vs. 33; read with the Targ. מקנא, **who is jealous,** for the M.T. מקנה, **cattle,** and with Aq. and Theod. point עולה not as 'ôleh, "that which goes up," but as 'awlāh, iniquity). True to the Hebrew interpretation of nature, the poet turns a somewhat primitive view of the thunderstorm into a theology of justice and grace (cf. Ps. 29). Going beyond elemental emotions of fear, Elihu detects in the autumnal thunderstorms signs of providential fidelity and reminders of God's ethical judgment (cf. especially vs. 31).

b) Lord of Winter (37:1-13)

37:1-13. In winter the thunderstorms bring the wonders of the snow and the persistent showers of rain (vs. 6) which keep man away from his toil so that he may have leisure to consider God's wondrous works (vs. 7; with the Targ. and Syriac read אנשים

---

the text there can be little but confusion. God will not be proved by them; or disproved either. When they are allowed to stand where they belong, they are comments—and today how vast (see Expos. on 38:1-40:5)—on the majesty of that throne which he has prepared in the heavens, and on the glory of the kingdom which rules over all.

37:1-13. So Near Is God to Man.—After the autumn, winter; and after the winter, spring; and always back of it the hand of God. Writes Emerson:

> So nigh is grandeur to our dust,
>   So near is God to man,
> When Duty whispers low, *Thou must,*
>   The youth replies, *I can.*[3]

There is nothing of that here. This is the God of the Bible, transcendent, sovereign; away, but not far; above, yet in; beyond, yet near; whose splendor makes of man's proud light darkness (vs. 9), whose righteousness makes of man's vaunted wisdom conceit (vss. 23-24); hidden to how many, revealed to ears that hear and eyes that see (36:32-33).

Surely the peril of missing him is not less today (see Expos. on 23:3; read John 8). To Elihu he was the God of the familiar. In Thornton Wilder's play *Our Town*[4] there is a scene where a young girl, after death, begs to go back to the world of her home and live over again the most uneventful day of her life, but with seeing eyes. So she comes back to her home, and her mother barely lifts a tired face from

---

[3] "Voluntaries," Part III.

[4] New York: Coward-McCann, 1938, Act III.

2 Hear attentively the noise of his voice, and the sound *that* goeth out of his mouth.

3 He directeth it under the whole heaven, and his lightning unto the ends of the earth.

4 After it a voice roareth: he thundereth with the voice of his excellency; and he will not stay them when his voice is heard.

5 God thundereth marvelously with his voice; great things doeth he, which we cannot comprehend.

6 For he saith to the snow, Be thou *on* the earth; likewise to the small rain, and to the great rain of his strength.

7 He sealeth up the hand of every man; that all men may know his work.

8 Then the beasts go into dens, and remain in their places.

9 Out of the south cometh the whirlwind: and cold out of the north.

10 By the breath of God frost is given: and the breadth of the waters is straitened.

11 Also by watering he wearieth the thick cloud: he scattereth his bright cloud:

2 Hearken to the thunder of his voice
  and the rumbling that comes from his mouth.
3 Under the whole heaven he lets it go,
  and his lightning to the corners of the earth.
4 After it his voice roars;
  he thunders with his majestic voice
  and he does not restrain the lightnings*d*
  when his voice is heard.
5 God thunders wondrously with his voice;
  he does great things which we cannot comprehend.
6 For to the snow he says, 'Fall on the earth';
  and to the shower and the rain,*e* 'Be strong.'
7 He seals up the hand of every man,
  that all men may know his work.*f*
8 Then the beasts go into their lairs,
  and remain in their dens.
9 From its chamber comes the whirlwind,
  and cold from the scattering winds.
10 By the breath of God ice is given,
  and the broad waters are frozen fast.
11 He loads the thick cloud with moisture;
  the clouds scatter his lightning.

d Heb *them*
e Cn Compare Syr: Heb *shower of rain and shower of rains*
f Vg Compare Syr Tg: Heb *that all men whom he has made may know it*

---

instead of יניש‎). Here again the singer discovers a moral lesson in the phenomena of nature. God evokes the "hurricane" from the south (vs. 9*a*; the rendering **whirlwind** is unfortunate, for the word is not the same as that of 38:1) and the cold wind from the

---

the cooking. Her father hurries by absentmindedly without a word, brooding over his work. And she cannot bear it. She thinks to herself that it is really the living who are dead. In some such way do men go stumbling about blindly before the face of God's continual presence, wanting to know where he is: he who is as near as any lingering thought they have, though vast beyond it (vs. 5*b*); close as the air they breathe and the words on their lips, pressing upon them in the touch of some hand, shining into their eyes with his accustomed light. But these they pile up and say are common things, too common. Common as the steam spurting from under the lid of a kettle. Thousands had looked, but James Watt saw it. Common as the drift water on the shores of Portugal. Thousands had looked, but Columbus saw it, and it spoke to him of another world across

the sea that waited for his coming. It is recorded of Moses, "When the LORD saw that he turned aside to see, God called unto him" (Exod. 3:4).

Still harder it is for people to recognize him in the things that irk them (cf. vss. 17-18; 36:17) —unpleasant things they do not even want to look at, much less see; things that are nothing but an offense, that upset tradition, hurt pride, and trample on prejudice. Why else was it that the friends missed God, while Job with his bitterness and his longing came tremblingly near? If only Elihu had seen that—to make his heart leap out of its place. A sermon by John Timothy Stone was once published in the *Christian Century Pulpit*. The next week a reviewer cut it to pieces mercilessly, wondered why anybody ever came to hear such stuff. Promptly Dr. Stone wrote the editor, and said that he rather agreed with the criticism; he him-

12 And it is turned round about by his counsels: that they may do whatsoever he commandeth them upon the face of the world in the earth.

13 He causeth it to come, whether for correction, or for his land, or for mercy.

12 They turn round and round by his guidance,
  to accomplish all that he commands them
  on the face of the habitable world.
13 Whether for correction, or for his land,
  or for love, he causes it to happen.

---

north (vs. 9*b*), with its marvels of hoary frost and ice (vs. 10). Thus Elihu brings his lyrical meditation to a theological climax: God **causes** all these things **to happen for correction, or for his land, or for love** (vs. 13; the text is uncertain and probably overburdened).

---

self had often wondered about the crowds that came. Whereupon, in the reviewer's column this appeared: "Dr. Stone's letter is the answer to my question. They come because he is a great soul!" Pride is blind, not love. Tradition called it madness when Isaiah spoke of God's turning his sword against his own people. When pride and tradition and prejudice got together, there was a cross, and a man on it.

But the story is not yet complete. There are still the things that baffle and bewilder, the deep perplexities of life, where Elihu and the friends could never quite enter: the loss and the pain where for Job God was hidden—and revealed. It was in the mystery that Abraham met God that day he trudged up the mountain with Isaac his son. It was in the mystery of a brutally defeated life that God uttered his name at last so clearly that no one need ever miss it.

"I am persuaded . . . ," Paul's great doxology sweeps on to its close (Rom. 8:31-39). It is not the upshot of any argument. It is a gleam, caught in the web of no logic that was ever spun. It is a sudden seeing of life whole, a quick piecing together of all its sunshine and every shadow. It is a spark. It is a soul flaming away to God like the lightning. It is a man standing at salute as God passes along the lines, himself the seeker, preoccupied and intent.

13. *God: The Eternal Paradox*.—Whether for correction, . . . or for love. Elihu would not set the two in any simple antithesis. The "rod" itself is for love's sake (cf. 36:9-10), the love that carries in its hand the "rod." It is common enough to say that God's justice is tempered with mercy, and by it mean that he will tip the beam of his reckoning with the finger of his compassion. He will err a little on the side of long-suffering. But to temper does not mean to tamper. To temper steel is to make it hard and elastic like a Damascus blade, to give it tone and vigor. It is God's mercy that gives his justice its cutting edge.

It were loss indeed to lose out of the heart of the Christian gospel the rigors of that justice.

The Greeks saw the dreadful inevitableness of life and called it Fate: how one wrong brought after it a score of wrongs, until men were no longer free at all; they were bound hand and foot by a kind of tragic necessity. Shakespeare saw it, and Macbeth and Hamlet and Othello, one by one, waded in so deep that "returning were as tedious as go o'er." There are terrors in God's steadiness, and history itself is for witness. A British clergyman observed out of the midst of World War II, as he looked back over the years—it is always easier for men to see as they look back like Dives out of some hell of their own devising: We were a pleasure-loving people, dishonouring the Lord's day; now the beaches are closed, and there is a shortage of petrol. We ignored the ringing of church bells; now they are not allowed to ring except in case of invasion. The churches themselves we left half empty; now they are in ruins. The money we would not give them is taken from us in taxes. The service we would not render is conscripted by the government. The food for which we forgot to give thanks is not available any more. The nights we refused to spend in prayer we spend in air-raid shelters.

From America came a revised version: The billions we could not afford to part with for the sake of a decent world are being used to blow the world we have into bits, and our sons with it. The income we saved for stockholders during the depression by lowering wages and throwing men and women out of work is going up in smoke or rotting away at the bottom of the sea in a crusade which provides everybody with employment. The potatoes we dumped in the river to keep the prices up, the calves that were killed and buried in New England, the wheat we were warned not to plant, the cotton that was plowed under—it would all be so convenient now. The Negroes we argued about with a great show of reason, and would not house, and would not hire; the laws we passed against the Japanese with one hand while we sold them the Sixth Avenue elevated with the

14 Hearken unto this, O Job: stand still, and consider the wondrous works of God.

15 Dost thou know when God disposed them, and caused the light of his cloud to shine?

16 Dost thou know the balancings of the clouds, the wondrous works of him which is perfect in knowledge?

17 How thy garments *are* warm, when he quieteth the earth by the south *wind?*

14 "Hear this, O Job;
    stop and consider the wondrous works
      of God.
15 Do you know how God lays his command
    upon them,
    and causes the lightning of his cloud to
      shine?
16 Do you know the balancings of the
    clouds,
    the wondrous works of him who is per-
      fect in knowledge,
17 you whose garments are hot
    when the earth is still because of the
      south wind?

3. Last Admonition (37:14-24)

Elihu now turns directly to Job in final exhortation. Yet the theme of the seasons lingers on in his thought for a while, and blends appropriately with his purpose.

a) Lord of Summer (37:14-22)

14-22. Once more the poet bids the hero **consider the wondrous works of God** (vs. 14). He contemplates the Lord of nature in the stillness of the summer heat, when **the skies are spread out,** and **hard as a molten mirror** (vs. 18), and **out of the north comes golden splendor** (vs. 22*a*). Before this **God, . . . clothed with terrible majesty,** how can Job still

other—thinking perhaps they would take it over to China, but they brought it back to us, and dropped it on Pearl Harbor; the selfishness with which we got out of Europe when we had helped to make it safe for the democracy of which we washed our hands, and the willingness of some Senators to do the same thing all over again, if only they can humble the President in the process. There is something terrible on this earth, and it is not just sin: it is the way sin runs into God, and he will not move.

But even worse, it may be, than losing out of religion the rigors of God's justice is the wild guess which whole generations in the Western world are quite capable of making at the drop of a hat, that they are his agents by whom he plans to deal at last with all the others, notably with the twin demons of fascism and communism: until—God forbid it, though his forbidding seems to have very little to do with the issue—war again condemns their blind and persistent immoralities to its own suicidal insanity. Fear, men say, is not for the wise: only the ignorant tremble. Rather is it only the fools who do not. It was the "gentle Jesus, meek and mild" who said one day, "My friends, . . . I will forewarn you whom ye shall fear"—not "them that kill the body, and after that have no more that they can do," but "him, which after he hath killed hath power to cast into hell; yet, I say unto you, Fear him" (Luke 12:4-5). He

knew what there is in God that cannot be cajoled with an apple on his desk. Life is not like that. It looks instead as if a little trembling were indicated (vs. 1).

There is, however, another side of the picture. It is Elihu's badge of distinction that he saw it. A paradox is a double truth that can never be simply resolved into either one of its terms without the other. **Whether for correction, . . . or for love:** the **correction** tempered by a mercy until it cuts like a surgeon's knife to heal; a **love** that ranges this round, sad earth, and searches and pursues and tears and exposes until a man's very soul is God's (see Expos. on 5:17; 17:3; 19:25). To Isaiah God is "Like as the lion and the young lion roaring on his prey" (Isa. 31:4), with his paw stretched out over Jerusalem, never intending to give it up, unafraid of the "multitude of shepherds," or "of their voice." And then in an instant he is like a mother bird fluttering tenderly over her young (Isa. 31:5), darting down with her sharp beak at the glittering eyes of a snake. G. A. Studdert-Kennedy put the two sides of the picture together in one of his poems. A cockney soldier has gone to church and heard a sermon about that last great day of judgment. Fretting over it, he lies down in the afternoon for a nap, and has a dream which he later describes to his friends as they gather around. It was of a presence, full of "sweetness and rebuke," grim and

18 Hast thou with him spread out the sky, *which is* strong, *and* as a molten looking-glass?

19 Teach us what we shall say unto him; *for* we cannot order *our speech* by reason of darkness.

20 Shall it be told him that I speak? if a man speak, surely he shall be swallowed up.

21 And now *men* see not the bright light which *is* in the clouds: but the wind passeth, and cleanseth them.

22 Fair weather cometh out of the north: with God *is* terrible majesty.

18 Can you, like him, spread out the skies, hard as a molten mirror?

19 Teach us what we shall say to him; we cannot draw up our case because of darkness.

20 Shall it be told him that I would speak? Did a man ever wish that he would be swallowed up?

21 "And now men cannot look on the light when it is bright in the skies, when the wind has passed and cleared them.

22 Out of the north comes golden splendor; God is clothed with terrible majesty.

desire to speak (vss. 19-20*a*)? In the sultriness, when vegetal and animal life seem to come to a hellish end, would Job in his presumption court the power of death itself? **Did a man ever wish that he would be swallowed up?** (Vs. 20*b*.) With unusual poetic skill Elihu joins the motif of the seasons with the Joban crux, and from the contemplation of transcendence returns to the theme of rebellious pride.

gentle at once, staring at him to hold him fast, and with but a single word to say: "Well?"

All eyes was in 'Is eyes—all eyes,
  My wife's and a million more;
And once I thought as those two eyes
  Were the eyes of the London whore.

. . . .

There ain't no throne, and there ain't no books,
  It's 'Im you've got to see,
It's 'Im, just 'Im, that is the Judge
  Of blokes like you and me.
And, boys, I'd sooner frizzle up,
  I' the fires of a burning 'Ell,
Than stand and look into 'Is face
  And 'ear 'Is voice say—"Well?" [5]

Perhaps after all there is a tragic incongruity about the way in which the figure of Justice is commonly represented: a sword in one of her hands, a pair of scales in the other; with a bandage tied tightly over her eyes so that she cannot possibly see. Which means to say, of course, that she executes her judgments impartially; but it says more than it means to say: it says that she cannot read her own scales, never knows when they balance, and cannot tell where to strike. And that, ironically enough, is precisely the trouble with human justice. God's kind is not blindfolded. It sees with the longing, steady eyes of Jesus; and they mean to win, with God's unbroken promise in them: the God whose awful power had to be gentle, or it would never have been great; and had to be

[5] From *The Sorrows of God and Other Poems* (London: Hodder & Stoughton; New York: Harper & Bros., 1924). Used by permission.

awful, or for all his gentleness he would never have been of any use. A pity like that on Calvary did not break into human life to wander about helpless and witless, wasting its breath, unable to do anything. It broke in to probe and cut away, and so set at naught every costly fear men have—all the galling slavery of little souls, the odds that pile up, the things people ought to do and cannot—to make nothing of it, cancel it, set God in its stead. The majesty which is back of God's compassion is what makes the compassion matter.

Strange that Elihu should have seen them both more clearly than any of the others, including Job. And yet, not strange. Two long centuries, it may be, had passed, and men had had to think long, long thoughts of God. The wonder is that while throughout the original poem there are numerous and striking reminiscences of the great prophet of the Exile (Isa. 40–55), for all the similarity of subject matter there is none here. Nowhere in the O.T. is the God who "is clothed with terrible majesty" (vs. 22) seen more clearly than in Second Isaiah as the God whose boundless compassion broods forever over his own. There the prophet takes his people by the hand and leads them back with a kind of cosmic humor to the great simplicities: to the towering fact of a God who undergirds with effortless ease his huge creation. Remember how it was with them, in this flat and distant land, shut in by lofty palaces and hanging gardens. They were used to hills, and green slopes, and little freshets gurgling down through deep gullies in the springtime, spreading out

23 *Touching* the Almighty, we cannot find him out: *he is* excellent in power, and in judgment, and in plenty of justice: he will not afflict.

24 Men do therefore fear him: he respecteth not any *that are* wise of heart.

23 The Almighty — we cannot find him;
    he is great in power and justice,
      and abundant righteousness he will not violate.

24 Therefore men fear him;
    he does not regard any who are wise in their own conceit."

b) Fear of the Lord (37:23-24)

23-24. Such a God is beyond the reach of puny man. **The Almighty—we cannot find him:** This avowal of impotence, however, Elihu will not make without asserting once more and for the last time that divine omnipotence is not incompatible with divine justice:

He is great in power and justice,
and abundant righteousness he will not violate.

Or, better, "The master of righteousness will not oppress" (vs. 23; cf. KJV). For man the consequence of such a creed is ineluctable: **Therefore men fear him** (vs. 24*a*). In the fear of God is true wisdom, for **he does not regard any who are wise in their own conceit** (vs. 24*b*). If this translation is correct, Elihu thus shoots a parting arrow at the dying and prostrate, but still defiant, Job. Unsympathetic to the end, the apologist of God remains sublime in his exposition of truth, but inhuman because devoid of brotherly love or even of elementary pity. Elihu's analysis of the Joban crime is correct and his faith beyond reproach, but the hardness of his heart condemns him and thus indicts his theology.

Whatever the literary origin of the Elihu discourses (see Intro., pp. 890-91), their presence at this point of the book in its completed form is not inappropriate, for they constitute at once a negative and a positive preparation for the hearing of the voice from the whirlwind (38:1–42:6). Rhetorically, they produce dramatic suspense between the hero's oath of clearance and the intervention of the Lord. Psychologically, they show man's inability to cope with the depth of human suffering and isolation. Theologically, they condition the hero for the immediate confrontation of God. Elihu does not succeed in making Job realize the theological dimensions of sinfulness: only the voice from the whirlwind can achieve this purpose. But Elihu does succeed in raising Job's thinking from the level of egocentricity to a region at whose center God reigns in glory. In this respect the discourses of Elihu are comparable to a vestibule of the holy of holies.

---

into still waters at the bottom of the valley where the sheep were grazing; with the snows of Lebanon lifting themselves serenely on the horizon. That meant home to them—and God. But there was none of it now. Only the broad, clear sky of the East; and the stars coming out suddenly in the sharp dusk, as if they were leaping to some celestial roll call. The prophet nudges them. "Who is doing that, do you think? Look! They are the gods these befuddled men of Babylon worship, yonder in the silent heavens, beyond all this marble and this stone. And your God made them! Not bending his back to do it. There was no sweat on his face. They were just fleeting notion in his mind, a whisper on his lips, and they were there! Watch him tonight leading them forth by number, no one of them

missing. Answering when he calls, crying 'Here!' 'Here!' 'Here!' Never a star daring to quit its post at the evening summons of the Almighty.[6] That deep blue canopy itself is to him the little tent an Arab spreads in the desert at the end of the day. He gets out his smallest scales, like a jeweler's; and the mountains back home are dust in them, and the seas are a breath of moisture. Feel his muscles, dear people of mine, and laugh at this Babylon that laughs at us!" (Cf. Isa. 40.)

It is the compassion back of it that keeps the majesty of God majesty indeed. No one can say that Elihu, if only he had been there, would

[6] Cf. Paul Scherer, *Event in Eternity* (New York: Harper & Bros., 1945), pp. 35-36.

38 Then the LORD answered Job out of the whirlwind, and said,

38 Then the LORD answered Job out of the whirlwind:

IV. VOICE FROM THE WHIRLWIND (38:1–42:6)

Job has frequently requested a divine audience in order to present his claim of innocence and to hear from God himself the charges made against him so that he may show their emptiness (cf. 9:3, 14-20, 28-35; 13:22; 31:35-37). Now at last God himself speaks. He does not accuse Job of ethical transgressions, but reveals to him by ironical questioning that man has no right to judge the Deity because man cannot conceive the Deity except in terms of some human image. God's wisdom and power are truly beyond man's grasp, and man may not trespass beyond the bounds of his humanity.

The first discourse of Yahweh (38:1–39:30) depicts the wisdom of the Creator and brings Job to silence (40:1-5). The second reveals the power of the Creator over the cosmic forces, Behemoth (40:15-24) and Leviathan (40:25–41:26), and leads to Job's repentance (42:1-6).

A. FIRST DISCOURSE OF YAHWEH (38:1–40:5)

1. OPENING CHALLENGE (38:1-3)

38:1. Then the LORD answered Job out of the whirlwind: It is not possible to tell whether the poet intended to describe the event literally or symbolically. **The whirlwind**

---

not have helped to ready the mind of Job for the God whom that titan among the world's great sufferers was about to meet.

38:1–42:6. When God Appears.—It is scarcely necessary to point out that when God appears strange things happen (cf. Expos. on 23:3; 35:3). Strange things happen in these chapters. When God speaks, it is to describe his own unimaginable greatness. And to what purpose? He seems deliberately intent on overawing this Job whose rebellious sense of finitude has already contributed to that mouthing of words without knowledge (cf. Expos. on 25:6). This was the very thing Job was sure God would not do, had pleaded that he might not (9:34; 13:21; cf. Expos. on 9:2-10; 13:20-21; 23:3, "God and Man in Search of One Another"). Again God speaks, and it is to sharpen against his servant the arrows of his vast irony, calling on Job to come up and sit on the throne of the heavens and do better if he can, if he thinks it is so easy to govern the world in righteousness. There is nothing about any of it that is particularly new, nothing that can be remotely imagined to provide an answer to the struggle which has been going on in Job's soul. Nothing is explained or made clear. No reasons at all are given. Nothing is said about the wager with Satan, nothing about God's quiet confidence in Job. There is no justification of the sufferer, no acquittal, no public vindication. Nothing in short, or so it would seem, to stir any love in anybody's heart, certainly not in Job's. It is always exceedingly difficult to get a direct answer from God. The Jews rarely got one when they plied Jesus with their questions. "What

shall I do to inherit eternal life?" "How readest thou?" (Luke 10:25-26.) "Art thou he?" His friend John the Baptist asked that. "Go and show John again those things which ye do hear and see" (Matt. 11:3-4). "Art thou the King of the Jews?" Pilate asked that. "Sayest thou this thing of thyself?" (John 18:33-34.) It is very hard. God thrusts men back on themselves, as everybody must do who knows that the human spirit will not accept the answers even when they are supplied (see Expos. on Luke 22:67-69). "They have Moses and the prophets. . . . If they hear not [them], neither will they be persuaded, though one rose from the dead." (Luke 16:29, 31.) Most of them did refuse when one did rise.

In a word, the theophany is irrelevant. God appears, and what he says changes no question mark into a period. Everyone has to do that for himself. What he says has already occurred to Job, and more than once. He is full of majesty; Job knew that. He rules over all things. Job knew that. Nobody can stand up to him and win. Job had said that. None of his purposes can be defeated. Job says, "I know that." What is the meaning of it all? There are those who insist that somebody else wrote the speeches of Yahweh. Whoever else did, he was not very successful in accomplishing the end he must have had in view, viz., to solve the problem and answer the riddle. Rather, one might suppose, the author of the original poem, with his own subtle understanding of the human soul, is himself engaging to say to the reader, as clearly as may be, "There is nothing here for which you are looking, simply because you are looking for the wrong thing. You expect God to come in and untie the knot. And he never will. You expect to add *x* to *y*, two unknown quantities, and then have God speak in good intelligible Arabic numerals when he gives you the sum of them. He will speak; but when he does, you will realize that he has been speaking all the way along. That is why you hear nothing new. He has been speaking to Job ever since Job's sons died and the sores broke out" (see Expos. on 19:7; 33:14). In his heart of hearts Job has known that from the beginning, or guessed it. The friends have been speaking, and he has been speaking, and God has been speaking. Why on earth should there be anything new? The irrelevance is itself relevant. The solution will not be here. It will be somewhere else. What actually is here is magnificent in its scope and beauty. It is not instructive in its content. God is not bent on teaching Job something, he is only passing in review before him the glory he had already learned; but doing it as God would do it, with the roll of the sea in it, the vast, unmeasured sea of his own forever. Instruction, as another puts it, has become Presence, and so makes sense for the first time. God is really bent—simply on being God.

38:1–40:5. *Summons and Response.*—**Gird up now thy loins like a man. I will ask the questions. You answer them** (see Expos. on vs. 3). **Where were you when I laid the foundation of the earth? Tell me,** who measured it? Who stretched out the line along its edge? And where was it fastened?

> Who laid its cornerstone,
>   when the morning stars sang together,
>   and all the sons of God shouted for joy?
> Or who shut in the sea with doors,
>   when it burst forth from the womb;
> when I made clouds its garment,
>   and thick darkness its swaddling band?

And said to it, Hitherto shalt thou come, but no further: . . . here shall thy proud waves be stayed? Have you ever commanded the morning, and caused the dayspring to know his place? That dawn might take hold of the ends of the earth, as you would take hold of a sheet, and the wicked be shaken out of it? The dawn which changes the earth when it comes, as a man changes the clay with his seal: all things take shape in the rosy light like a coat of many colors.

> Have you entered into the springs of the sea,
>   or walked in the recesses of the deep?

Hast thou seen the doors of the shadow of death, far away there beneath them all?

> Where is the way to the dwelling of light,
>   and where is the place of darkness?

Doubtless you know, for **the number of your days is great!**

> Who has cleft a channel for the torrents of rain,
>   and a way for the thunderbolt,
> to bring rain on a land where no man is,

yonder in **the waste and desolate land,** to make the tender grass **spring forth?** Job's ideas are by way of getting themselves stretched a little. Out there in the wilderness, even there God is at work, a God who cares and tends, whose eye is on every living thing. Writes Forsyth:

We are apt to treat God as if He were only a patron saint magnified, whom we expect to attend to our affairs if He is to retain our custom and receive our worship.

There is even what we might call a racial egoism, a self-engrossment of mankind with itself, a naïve and tacit assumption that God were no God if He cared for anything more than He did for His creatures. We tend to think of God as if man were His chief end, as if He had no right to a supreme concern for His own holy name, as if His prodigals were more to Him than His only begotten Son in whom He made the worlds and has all His delight. We think and worship as if the only question was whether God loves us, instead of whether His love has absolute power to give itself eternal and righteous effect.[7]

For Job the perspective is changing, and no man readily suffers that to happen.

> Has the rain a father,
>   or who has begotten the drops of dew?

Can you lead forth the stars in their season, or **send forth lightnings,** or number the clouds? It is indeed vast, and our farthest thought runs but so little a way toward it. In that goodness which from end to end is over every one of God's works, the very bottles of heaven are laid down in a row to refresh the thirsty ground. All the beasts of the earth are in his great and keeping hands. **Who provides . . . the raven its food, when its young ones cry to God?** The hands which do that, will they not spread out for men their bounty? Is that heart a niggard's heart? Who has **sent out the wild ass free? . . . The range of the mountains is his pasture, and he** searcheth after every green thing. Harness the **wild ox to your plow,** if you can, and trust him to gather your grain. Give to the horse his might. . . . He paws in the valley, . . . he swalloweth the ground with fierceness and rage. . . . When the trumpet sounds, he says "Aha!" and smells the battle from afar, the thundering roar of command, **the shouting** of the soldiers.

Then Job answered the LORD: "Behold, I am

[7] P. T. Forsyth, *The Justification of God* (London: Independent Press, 1948), pp. 10-11. Used by permission.

in biblical usage is the medium of theophanies and designates a tempest of a specific character (סערה; cf. שערה and סערות in Nah. 1:3; Zech. 9:14; cf. also Pss. 18:7-15; 50:3; Ezek. 1:4; Hab. 3; the word is not the same as that used by Elihu in 37:9). The designation "Yahweh," the LORD, indicates beyond doubt that the poet is a Hebrew addressing a Hebrew circle of auditors or readers. God does not answer Job according to Job's expectation, but the divine silence is broken; and though the message of the revelation

---

of small account"; what shall I say? **"I lay my hand on my mouth."** I spoke once. I spoke twice. But no more. Is there any difference between this and the kind of self-abasement which is robbed of its self-respect by the immensity of creation (see Expos. on 9:2-10)? And so is ready to shrug off its responsibility? God never does that to anyone. This is humility, not self-abasement. If the ring on one's little finger were taken as the orbit of the earth around the sun, the nearest fixed star would be some twenty miles away! That was enough of itself to give one young scientist what he called a cosmic chill (see Expos. on 7:17-18; 9:14-19; 16:13; 25:6). Human life has by some been taught to think of itself as a blob of protoplasm, an itch on the epidermis of a pigmy planet, an accident of matter, the first cousin of an ape that learned how to shave. A man has a hard time thinking as highly of himself as he should (cf. Rom. 12:3; I John 3:2). There is always danger of his beginning to live down to what he has been told. Here is the bowed head of one who is beginning to enter into his dignity as a son of God, not on the point of leaving it. There had been a time when God's majesty had been of no comfort to Job, but a terror. That time is past. Sidney Lanier once sang of the marsh hen building her nest on the watery sod: "Behold I will build me a nest on the greatness of God" [8] (see Expos., pp. 905-7).

What is it that is taking place? For one thing, God is issuing his summons. Humanity does not have to look him up every once in a while. Whole generations are obsessed with techniques. How go about the business of praying? How cultivate the religious mood? How tap the reservoirs of infinite power? So was a book about the Sermon on the Mount advertised! It rarely occurs to such people that the most important step in the whole transaction has already been taken. The difficulty is not so much that they are unable to find God; the real difficulty is that they cannot manage to get rid of him. Read Francis Thompson's "The Hound of Heaven" as an interpretation of human history. Revelation is scarcely the half of it. God's is a downright stubborn pursuit. Job was sure that God was somehow on the other side of all the ruin and the loss and the pain, while he himself was in it. And here was Some-

[8] "The Marshes of Glynn."

one putting his hand through Job's arm and catching step. It was that way one day on the road from Jerusalem to Emmaus (Luke 24:13-35). A woman in a hospital reached stealthily for a pencil as the nurse went out of the room, and against orders, as she lay there, scrawled down for a minister, who had called on her without knowing her at all, the story of her life. It began in a loveless place, and stretched out wanly enough into womanhood. There were a few short years of furtive happiness during World War I, while she and her husband were being driven about from pillar to post under the foolish suspicion of being spies. When he died and she had lost all she had, she gave her high talents to the training of other women's children. Then this illness, which they said would be her last. Before it was over, she just wanted to say that God had been very good to her through it all, and she was very humble—and very grateful.

> Still with unhurrying chase,
> And unperturbèd pace
> Deliberate speed, majestic instancy,
> Came on the following Feet.[9]

Does life mean that from start to finish? People have an idea that they cannot get hold of him, and it worries some of them. What worries God is whether or not he can get hold of them.

But there is another element in religious experience, and that too is here. There is something in man that responds if he will let it. Job's response is not yet full and complete (see Exeg. on 40:3-5; Expos. on 28:1-28); but the humility and the awe that are born of God's presence are here, that spark which in a moment will flame away to God like the lightning (see Expos. on 37:1-13). **What shall I answer?** Abraham asked it, and set out from Chaldea. Israel asked it, and turned her face toward the Land of Promise. Paul asked it, and little churches sprang up all over Europe. The Pilgrims asked it, and sailed westward across the Atlantic. The world is asking it in agony, because it will not learn in any other way that God has made of one blood all the nations of the earth. The novelists and columnists who like to write of how nasty and smelly life is know nothing

[9] Francis Thompson, "The Hound of Heaven," from *Collected Works*, ed. Wilfred Meynell (Westminster, Md.: Newman Press, 1947). Used by permission.

is still unknown, Job can no longer accuse the Deity of aloofness, indifference, or apathy. Whatever the Lord will tell him, the fact which counts and which overwhelms his consciousness is that there is indeed a God who cares for him. This God loves his creature to such a measure and in such a way that he intervenes directly in an I-and-thou encounter. The bare event of the voice speaking from the whirlwind is a testimony to the love as well as to the greatness of God.

of life. They take a tiny truth and make a stupendous lie. Arthur John Gossip says somewhere that whenever Heine read Plutarch, he always wanted to jump on a fast horse and ride straight away to Berlin into the thick of things and be a great soul too. There is that in a man. God put it there. Christ of all others sees it, and is sure that life cannot keep going back to what it was before as if nothing had happened. **I am of small account.** Job was never in all his life of greater account (see Expos. on 25:6). The true **answer**, which has been struggling up from his soul through all of his bitterness and wild imaginings, is coming now to his lips, his eyes wide, his hand at his mouth.

38:1. God Behind the Scenes.—There are times when life takes such a frightful plunge into the dark that the Almighty hardly seems to be even in his accustomed hiding places (see Expos. on 23:3). Apparently he is nowhere around and has nothing to say. The vast gloom of the whole incongruous business picks out a human heart often enough, and settles down full strength. What would matter then would not be any analysis. Elihu and the friends have done enough "explaining." Say as they did that the sickening thud is never for nothing. They knew at least that history never hits bottom because the world periodically goes crazy, but simply because the world always makes sense, and nobody gets away with anything. Even Job's suffering was not for nothing—if only they and he had known for what! But none of that can possibly help. They said it was Job's fault; he said it was God's—and came farther along with it than they did because he knew what mattered (see Expos. on 23:2). Beyond events, behind the scenes, is there One whose heart is steadier than nature's own laws, intent not on rendering evil for evil but on overcoming evil with good? A God who will hear and answer and in his own way redeem (cf. Expos. on 17:3; 19:7; 24:12c; 30:24; 33:14)? Like the sound of distant footsteps in the theater, or the knocking on the door in *Macbeth*, giving notice that the world outside is trying to get in (cf. Isa. 40:1-8)? During World War II a London newspaper carried a time schedule of one day's life in the city. There in the late evening it read "Blackout: 6:37." The next item was "Moon Rises: 6:38." Famine and pestilence, concentration camps, a field of battle, great ships floundering in a

storm, starving generations, a cemetery in Honolulu, the dragging of a lake—while this is being written—for a young girl's body: try squaring any of it with an ultimate motive of love—unless God really does slip into this world when nobody much is looking. On one night of all nights he did it, coming down the stairs of heaven with a child in his arms. As Job learns to trust him with the huge pattern of things as they are, a fireside mercy steals back into life that can match any or all of his public appearances, giving to the hero's lonely, battling soul a dignity and a standing in some sort commensurate with the very cosmic purposes of God. It would be tragic were he to be unmoved by it, capable only of settling back in the old order as if nothing had happened. It is God's tomorrow which waits for the soul that will come out of its own yesterday into his presence. Recall the words spoken by Sydney Carton to the little seamstress who stood at his side as they both faced the scaffold; it is not a scaffold that life faces, but a cross: beyond it a Man who is God's pledge, saying, "Keep your eyes upon me, dear child, and mind no other object." [1]

In the quest for a theodicy what is it that you are looking for? What is it that would justify God to you? You have grown up in an age that has not yet got over the delight of having discovered in evolution the key to creation. You saw the long expanding series broadening to the perfect day. . . . The dark valleys, antres vast, and deserts horrible, you did not see. . . . But now you have been flung into one of these awful valleys. . . . You are in bloody, monstrous, and deadly dark. . . . Every aesthetic view of the world is blotted out by human wickedness and suffering. . . . You see no sense, no justice in it. . . . God has not kept His promise. . . .

What right had you to take your expectation for promise?

Where shall we get the idea of what is worthy of God? There can only be one source of such knowledge. It is the final account God gives of Himself. It is no expectation of ours, no presumption in us of what a godlike God would do [cf. Expos. on 35:3]. His account . . . , on the scale and depth of the great convulsive judgments, is in Christ and His Cross, or it is nowhere. . . . The Cross of Christ, with its judgment-grace, its tragic love, its grievous glory, . . . is God's only self-justification in such a world. . . . It is impossible even to discuss the theodicy all pine for without the theology so many deride.

[1] Charles Dickens, *A Tale of Two Cities*, ch. xv.

2 Who *is* this that darkeneth counsel by words without knowledge?

3 Gird up now thy loins like a man; for I will demand of thee, and answer thou me.

4 Where wast thou when I laid the foundations of the earth? declare, if thou hast understanding.

2 "Who is this that darkens counsel by words without knowledge?

3 Gird up your loins like a man,
  I will question you, and you shall declare to me.

4 "Where were you when I laid the foundation of the earth?
  Tell me, if you have understanding.

2-3. The poet reveals at once his attitude toward the hero. With the swift sure touch of a master of drama, he ascribes to God words which by implication exonerate the sufferer from any moral stigma and yet accuse him of self-deification. **Who is this that darkeneth counsel by words without knowledge?** (Vs. 2.) The **counsel** of the ruler of this universe operates in full light. God does not govern his world by whim or fancy but according to a well-considered plan, and Job has shown by his blasphemous judgments that he spoke **without knowledge,** i.e., without understanding the divine will. Let Job now prepare himself to fight God, if he so desires. **Gird up your loins like a man** (vs. 3a). The word גבר is a favorite designation of Job for himself, and it means "male," "valiant warrior" (cf. גבור, "hero"). Its use underlines the playful but not unkind scorn with which God invites his would-be opponent to stand his ground and answer questions (vs. 3b).

2. CREATION OF THE WORLD (38:4-15)

a) CREATION OF EARTH (38:4-7)

4-7. Job is invited to meditate first on the brevity of his own existence, and at the same time to compare his human power and wisdom with those needed for the creation

---

The only theodicy is not a system, but a salvation. . . . It is not a rational triumph but the victory of faith. Christ is the theodicy of God and the justifier both of God and the ungodly.[2]

3. The Grand Inquisitor.—(See Expos. on 13:20-27; 38:1–42:6.) When all the questions are in, God himself becomes the questioner. "I will ask; you do the answering" (see Expos. on Luke 22:67-69). Sooner or later the roles are reversed (Mark 11:29), and the really important questions are put. The ultimate dilemma of human existence lies not in God's failure to answer man (see Expos. on 19:7; 33:14; 34:9), but in man's inability of himself to answer God (cf. Expos. on 38:1–40:5) —all the way from "Where art thou?" (Gen. 3:9) to "Will ye also go away?" (John 6:67) and "Saul, Saul, why persecutest thou me?" (Acts 9:4). The Bible punctuates human history with its revelation, period. It confronts human life with its scrutiny, question mark. It records humanity's choice, exclamation point. "And they bowed the knee before him, and mocked him, saying, Hail, King of the Jews!" (Matt. 27:29.) Either that, or "O the depth of the riches both of the wis-

dom and knowledge of God! how unsearchable are his judgments, and his ways past finding out!" (Rom. 11:33). While after everything that is written stands a comma, the symbol of humanity's destiny, never fully complete, always "To be continued" (cf. Expos. on Luke 19:2).

38:4–40:5. The Mysteries of God.—(See Exeg. on 38:1–42:6.) Job is first brought face to face with unfathomable wisdom. In his wrestling with the mysteries of his own lot, he is confronted by a world instinct with mystery and illumined only by God.

Life nowadays does not take kindly to mystery. It does not like what it meets and cannot grasp. And so it has set about gaily to solve everything. It undertakes to explain itself in terms of its own lowest common denominator with whatever else it comes across, and in a vocabulary borrowed from a materialistic science. It has been taught, and it still too largely believes, that the sum total of existence, including God and the human soul, is reducible to a few general propositions, a bit complicated perhaps, but nevertheless thoroughly rational. If anything lies outside their reach, if anything suggests itself as being "beyond nature," if anything will not readily submit to the laboratory

[2] P. T. Forsyth, *The Justification of God* (London: Independent Press, 1948), pp. 158-59, 36-37, 194, 169. Used by permission.

5 Who hath laid the measures thereof, if thou knowest? or who hath stretched the line upon it?

6 Whereupon are the foundations thereof fastened? or who laid the corner stone thereof;

7 When the morning stars sang together, and all the sons of God shouted for joy?

8 Or *who* shut up the sea with doors, when it brake forth, *as if* it had issued out of the womb?

9 When I made the cloud the garment thereof, and thick darkness a swaddling band for it,

10 And brake up for it my decreed *place*, and set bars and doors,

11 And said, Hitherto shalt thou come, but no further: and here shall thy proud waves be stayed?

---

5 Who determined its measurements —
    surely you know!
  Or who stretched the line upon it?

6 On what were its bases sunk,
    or who laid its cornerstone,

7 when the morning stars sang together,
    and all the sons of God shouted for joy?

8 "Or who shut in the sea with doors,
    when it burst forth from the womb;

9 when I made clouds its garment,
    and thick darkness its swaddling band,

10 and prescribed bounds for it,
    and set bars and doors,

11 and said, 'Thus far shall you come, and
      no farther,
    and here shall your proud waves be
      stayed'?

---

of the universe. **Where wast thou when I laid the foundations of the earth?** (Vs. 4a.) Job is then subtly reminded of his position within the hierarchy of beings, since he did not even exist **when the morning stars sang together, and all the sons of God shouted for joy** (vs. 7). Observe that the cosmogony of the poet does not allow for any trace of a mythology of a fight between the Creator of order and some pre-existent forces of chaos. There is no room for a belief in the pre-existence of an uncreated evil. There is no survival of dualism in this monotheistic serenity. Even the mention of the בני אלהים, **the sons of God** (cf. 1:6), constitutes no paganistic stain, for they stand together with the constellations of dawn, singing the Jubilate of praise and adoration. The poet's monotheism is so confident that polytheistic or at least henotheistic terminology is only a literary adornment (cf. Ps. 148:2-3).

b) CREATION OF SEA (38:8-11)

8-11. Mythological language clearly appears in these verses, but no myth of a primeval ocean is accepted by the poet. The **sea** is born after the earth is founded; and while the text does not define the **womb** from which **it burst forth** (vs. 8), its origin depends entirely upon the will of the Creator who rules supreme over it (vss. 9-11). The expressions are poetical (cf. vs. 29, where the same words or similar ones are used for ice and hoarfrost).

---

method, or to the analysis of what is called logical positivism—that thing, whatever else it is, is just irritating, and not likely to be worth anybody's thought.

Some such mood may be the mood of a generation—or a century; and it has its results for religion. Whoever would speak to it of the Bible or revelation, whoever would assume the reality of the unseen, make some quite modest reference to miracle or resurrection, is stuck off before he knows it in a corner of the nursery where they are still telling fairy tales and believe in Santa Claus. His faith may be ever so strong, but he grows uneasy. He listens to the Gospels being read on Sunday, and begins to wonder if

perhaps he has not swallowed something with a string tied to it. The rise and fall of the chants; those strange stories of the Son of God. A mist forms in front of his eyes. None of it seems quite actual. It is like a landscape by Whistler, where the outlines are dim and weird. He finds himself in a sort of dream. Tomorrow around six or seven he will wake up, and start living again, with all the old solid stuff to handle once more, stuff that matters, stuff that he can understand.

And the process goes on. Not long after the Creed, the Sermon on the Mount begins to get a bit foggy around the edges; this turning of the other cheek, these lilies of the field and fowls of the air. It looks a little blurred, as if it

12 Hast thou commanded the morning since thy days; *and* caused the dayspring to know his place;	12 "Have you commanded the morning since your days began, and caused the dawn to know its place,
13 That it might take hold of the ends of the earth, that the wicked might be shaken out of it?	13 that it might take hold of the skirts of the earth, and the wicked be shaken out of it?
14 It is turned as clay *to* the seal; and they stand as a garment.	14 It is changed like clay under the seal, and it is dyed*g* like a garment.
15 And from the wicked their light is withholden, and the high arm shall be broken.	15 From the wicked their light is withheld, and their uplifted arm is broken.
16 Hast thou entered into the springs of the sea? or hast thou walked in the search of the depth?	16 "Have you entered into the springs of the sea, or walked in the recesses of the deep?
17 Have the gates of death been opened unto thee? or hast thou seen the doors of the shadow of death?	17 Have the gates of death been revealed to you, or have you seen the gates of deep darkness?
18 Hast thou perceived the breadth of the earth? declare if thou knowest it all.	18 Have you comprehended the expanse of the earth? Declare, if you know all this.

g Cn: Heb *they stand forth*

---

c) Creation of Days and Nights (38:12-15)

12-15. Just as Job was absent from the creation of earth and sea, so also he has never **commanded the morning** (vs. 12a), even within the short span of time during which he has been in existence (note the irony of vs. 12aβ). Dawn lifts up the darkness as a veil under which the earth has been asleep and shakes the wicked out of it like parasites (vs. 13). When the earth awakes, the sunrise sharply accentuates and reddens its configurations (vs. 14); and the evildoers desist from their deeds, for the light of day banishes their own false light (vs. 15).

3. Mysteries of Land and Sky (38:16-38)
a) The Deep and the Extremities of the Earth (38:16-18)

16-18. Job has not searched **the recesses of the deep** (vs. 16; *tehôm*, as in Gen. 1:2), **the gates** of the underworld (vs. 17; cf. Ps. 9:13; Isa. 38:10), or the extremities of the wide earth (vs. 18).

---

were out of focus somehow. Unfortunately that is not the kind of place he lives in, where to give means that it shall be given unto him, "good measure, pressed down, and shaken together, and running over" (Luke 6:38). He lives on hard city streets, and in a dingy office, with the fan going, and due bills fluttering across the desk. "Take no thought for your life, what ye shall eat, or what ye shall drink; nor yet for your body, what ye shall put on" (Matt. 6:25). Sounds a bit distant that, like the ghosts that chatter among the dead ruins of Pompeii, or the whispering of the ivy as it twines around the broken column of a temple. He cannot quite "get" it.

He cannot quite "get" a good deal of the talk that he hears about God, e.g., the love that leaves him out of a job and alone in the world. A surgeon lost a house and a son and a left hand, and knows now what hunger is. But what does any of it mean? The wrong marches rough-shod over the right. Nations rush blindly toward the brink of destruction. The love of God, in a century when ideals only make fools of themselves? Jacques de Lalaing, the flower of knight-hood, the pattern of chivalry for all Europe, has been called the last hero of romance. In 1453 he died an early death; not of a lover's broken heart, as we might have wished—writes another—not in any tournament with his thirty-two pennants flying, and a foeman worthy of his steel. He walked into a cannon ball fired by some shopkeepers in the little town of Ghent. So prosaic was it, like the gross facts

19 Where *is* the way *where* light dwelleth? and *as for* darkness, where *is* the place thereof,

20 That thou shouldest take it to the bound thereof, and that thou shouldest know the paths *to* the house thereof?

21 Knowest thou *it,* because thou wast then born? or *because* the number of thy days *is* great?

22 Hast thou entered into the treasures of the snow? or hast thou seen the treasures of the hail,

23 Which I have reserved against the time of trouble, against the day of battle and war?

24 By what way is the light parted, *which* scattereth the east wind upon the earth?

19 "Where is the way to the dwelling of light,
    and where is the place of darkness,
20 that you may take it to its territory
    and that you may discern the paths to its home?
21 You know, for you were born then,
    and the number of your days is great!

22 "Have you entered the storehouses of the snow,
    or have you seen the storehouses of the hail,
23 which I have reserved for the time of trouble,
    for the day of battle and war?
24 What is the way to the place where the light is distributed,
    or where the east wind is scattered upon the earth?

---

b) Light and Darkness (38:19-21)

19-21. Not only is Job circumscribed in space, but he is also pitifully limited in time. The irony becomes more incisive as he is queried over the origins of **light** and **darkness** (vss. 19-20). Yahweh prods him:

> **You know, for you were born then,**
> **and the number of your days is great!** (Vs. 21.)

c) Snow, Hail, and Lightning (38:22-24)

22-24. Hail is traditionally the weapon of God in battle (vss. 22*b*-23; cf. Josh. 10:11; Ps. 18:12-13; Isa. 30:30; Ezek. 13:11, 13). "Fog" (vs. 24*a*; read איד, "vapor," instead of אור, **light**) and the **east wind,** scorching all living things with the heat of the Arabian Desert, are of utmost importance for the inhabitants of the Fertile Crescent.

---

every dream of a better world walks into when it leaves its pew and the church door closes behind it.

Significantly, much of this disillusion has its roots deep in man's impatience with all there is about life and religion which he cannot understand and cannot quite manage. The Middle Ages looked at such things and said "God!" The modern mind looks at them and says "Nonsense!" One or the other is superstition—but which? If the whole of reality is intelligible, if all of truth is commensurate somehow with human reason, the choice is easy. Then for the man who cannot understand how God could have spoken to Moses the ready conclusion is that he did not. How could God be incarnate in Jesus of Nazareth? He was not. Wherever the meekness and the patience and the unselfishness of the N.T. cut across the common sense of mankind they are impractical. Wherever mir-

acles and creeds, this Christ with his cross, and all the woes of human history moving up like a tide toward the life of a world to come—wherever these things run counter to this world's ways of thinking they are untrue.

Certainly a more irrational approach could scarcely be devised in the name of reason. Life only succeeds in making itself ridiculous when it tries to pull over its head the hood of omniscience. Everybody in the book of Job knew that; but nobody would rest his case there. Job might have come to it if Elihu and the friends had not taken up in their hands the mystery they were all too eager to urge on him (cf. 11:7-10; 33:12; etc.) and tried to wring all the mystery out of it. The hour has now struck for the mystery to manifest itself, not as mystery, but as mystery with meaning; and the meaning is God (cf. Expos. on 36:5-15, 8-25; 38:1–42:6).

It is always well to remind oneself—or be

25 Who hath divided a watercourse for the overflowing of waters, or a way for the lightning of thunder;

26 To cause it to rain on the earth, *where no man is; on* the wilderness, wherein *there is* no man;

27 To satisfy the desolate and waste *ground;* and to cause the bud of the tender herb to spring forth?

28 Hath the rain a father? or who hath begotten the drops of dew?

29 Out of whose womb came the ice? and the hoary frost of heaven, who hath gendered it?

30 The waters are hid as *with* a stone, and the face of the deep is frozen.

31 Canst thou bind the sweet influences of Pleiades, or loose the bands of Orion?

32 Canst thou bring forth Mazzaroth in his season? or canst thou guide Arcturus with his sons?

33 Knowest thou the ordinances of heaven? canst thou set the dominion thereof in the earth?

34 Canst thou lift up thy voice to the clouds, that abundance of waters may cover thee?

35 Canst thou send lightnings, that they may go, and say unto thee, Here we *are?*

25 "Who has cleft a channel for the torrents of rain,
and a way for the thunderbolt,

26 to bring rain on a land where no man is,
on the desert in which there is no man;

27 to satisfy the waste and desolate land,
and to make the ground put forth grass?

28 "Has the rain a father,
or who has begotten the drops of dew?

29 From whose womb did the ice come forth,
and who has given birth to the hoarfrost of heaven?

30 The waters become hard like stone,
and the face of the deep is frozen.

31 "Can you bind the chains of the Plei'ades,
or loose the cords of Orion?

32 Can you lead forth the Maz'zaroth in their season,
or can you guide the Bear with its children?

33 Do you know the ordinances of the heavens?
Can you establish their rule on the earth?

34 "Can you lift up your voice to the clouds,
that a flood of waters may cover you?

35 Can you send forth lightnings, that they may go
and say to you, 'Here we are'?

---

d) RAIN, DEW, AND ICE (38:25-30)

25-30. The face of the deep is frozen: Lit., "curdled" like milk. Does the poet allude to lakes of the distant north, or even to the polar cap?

e) CONSTELLATIONS, CLOUDS, AND MIST (38:31-38)

31-38. The Pleiades and **Orion** (vs. 31) are constituted by stars which give the appearance of being held together by **chains** and **cords.** The word **Mazzaroth** (vs. 32*a*) does not designate the signs of the Zodiac (cf. II Kings 23:5) but refers to a single constellation (observe the singular Hebrew pronoun in the expression "in its time"), probably the Corona Borealis, to which **the Bear with its children** forms a natural parallel (vs. 32*b*).

The poet lends only scant attention to the **lightnings** (vs. 35; contrast Elihu in 36:26 ff.). The meaning of the words טחות, **inward parts** (vs. 36*a*; cf. Ps. 51:6[?]), and שכוי, **heart** (vs. 36*b*), is unknown, and numerous conjectures have been proposed (cf. RSV, which selects one of them). The words should probably be rendered respectively by

---

reminded—that there is much which has not yet been cleared up, e.g., being alive, to have arrived out of darkness, to be here at all, chucked into existence out of the great silence (38:4).

There is a mathematician of sorts who does not believe in a future life; while his friend, something more of a dreamer perhaps, can hardly bring himself to believe in this life! He wonders

36 Who hath put wisdom in the inward parts? or who hath given understanding to the heart?	**36** Who has put wisdom in the clouds,*h* or given understanding to the mists?*h*

36 Who hath put wisdom in the inward parts? or who hath given understanding to the heart?

37 Who can number the clouds in wisdom? or who can stay the bottles of heaven,

38 When the dust groweth into hardness, and the clods cleave fast together?

39 Wilt thou hunt the prey for the lion? or fill the appetite of the young lions,

40 When they couch in *their* dens, *and* abide in the covert to lie in wait?

41 Who provideth for the raven his food? when his young ones cry unto God, they wander for lack of meat.

39 Knowest thou the time when the wild goats of the rock bring forth? *or* canst thou mark when the hinds do calve?

2 Canst thou number the months *that* they fulfil? or knowest thou the time when they bring forth?

3 They bow themselves, they bring forth their young ones, they cast out their sorrows.

---

36 Who has put wisdom in the clouds,*h* or given understanding to the mists?*h*

37 Who can number the clouds by wisdom? Or who can tilt the waterskins of the heavens,

38 when the dust runs into a mass and the clods cleave fast together?

39 "Can you hunt the prey for the lion, or satisfy the appetite of the young lions,

40 when they crouch in their dens, or lie in wait in their covert?

41 Who provides for the raven its prey, when its young ones cry to God, and wander about for lack of food?

39 "Do you know when the mountain goats bring forth? Do you observe the calving of the hinds?

2 Can you number the months that they fulfil, and do you know the time when they bring forth,

3 when they crouch, bring forth their offspring, and are delivered of their young?

h The meaning of the Hebrew word is uncertain

"ibis" (the bird of Thot [טחות?], Egyptian god of wisdom, which announced the flood of the Nile) and "cock" (cf. the rabbinical prayer, "Blessed art thou, Adonai, our God, King of the world, who hast given to the cock [שכוי] the intelligence to discern between day and night"; cf. also First Targ. and Vulg.) . While the presence of these birds fits the context, since they are associated with meteorological prediction (cf. vs. 37), it also prepares for the long poem on the wonders of wild animals.

4. WONDERS OF WILD ANIMALS (38:39–39:30)
a) THE LION AND THE RAVEN (38:39-41)

39-41. God—not Job—feeds the lion (cf. Ps. 104:20-22) and **the raven** (cf. Ps. 147:9) .

b) MOUNTAIN GOATS AND HINDS (39:1-4)

39:1-4. God—not Job—knows the intimate life of **the mountain goats** (or "the antelopes of the rocks") and **hinds**, as well as the way in which **their young ones . . . grow up.**

---

how he remembers a name, wants to know something of the peacock's tail with its myriads of eyes, and its quills, and barbs, and barbules, and barbicels. Macneile Dixon in *The Human Situation*[3] poses some of the problems still remaining: wants to have the humble moth expounded, and the homely spider, and the doughty little cockroach that terrifies his imagi-

[3] Pp. 430, 409.

nation. Here in Job it is the morning, the rain, the clouds; the wild ox, the ostrich, the horses. Let anybody wrestle with life's magnificent simplicities for awhile, and he should not be so intolerably amazed as he starts out on a trip through the Bible (cf. Expos. on 10:1-7) .

Some of the so-called mysteries of man's being can of course be dismissed out of hand: he manufactures them himself (cf. Expos. on 3:20-

4 Their young ones are in good liking, they grow up with corn; they go forth, and return not unto them.

5 Who hath sent out the wild ass free? or who hath loosed the bands of the wild ass?

6 Whose house I have made the wilderness, and the barren land his dwellings.

7 He scorneth the multitude of the city, neither regardeth he the crying of the driver.

8 The range of the mountains is his pasture, and he searcheth after every green thing.

9 Will the unicorn be willing to serve thee, or abide by thy crib?

10 Canst thou bind the unicorn with his band in the furrow? or will he harrow the valleys after thee?

11 Wilt thou trust him, because his strength is great? or wilt thou leave thy labor to him?

12 Wilt thou believe him, that he will bring home thy seed, and gather it into thy barn?

13 Gavest thou the goodly wings unto the peacocks? or wings and feathers unto the ostrich?

14 Which leaveth her eggs in the earth, and warmeth them in the dust,

---

4 Their young ones become strong, they
    grow up in the open;
they go forth, and do not return to
    them.

5 "Who has let the wild ass go free?
    Who has loosed the bonds of the swift
    ass,
6 to whom I have given the steppe for his
    home,
    and the salt land for his dwelling place?
7 He scorns the tumult of the city;
    he hears not the shouts of the driver.
8 He ranges the mountains as his pasture,
    and he searches after every green thing.

9 "Is the wild ox willing to serve you?
    Will he spend the night at your crib?
10 Can you bind him in the furrow with
    ropes,
    or will he harrow the valleys after you?
11 Will you depend on him because his
    strength is great,
    and will you leave to him your labor?
12 Do you have faith in him that he will
    return,
    and bring your grain to your threshing
    floor?[i]

13 "The wings of the ostrich wave proudly;
    but are they the pinions and plumage
    of love?[j]
14 For she leaves her eggs to the earth,
    and lets them be warmed on the
    ground,

[i] Heb your grain and your threshing floor
[j] Heb obscure

---

c) THE WILD ASS (39:5-8)

5-8. God—not Job—has given freedom to the wild ass.

d) THE WILD OX (39:9-12)

9-12. The wild ox (רים; cf. the Akkadian rêmu, perhaps an Asiatic buffalo) is not willing to serve man, not even Job.

e) THE OSTRICH (39:13-18)

13-18. These verses were absent in the original LXX. The ostrich is ugly (vs. 13) and foolish (vss. 14-16; vs. 17 is probably a marginal comment which has crept into the main text), but it is able to outrun the horse.

---

21). As Nicodemus did that night Jesus was talking to him about being born again (John 3:1-21). He spent half an hour tacking and filling. "How can these things be?" He was more comfortable when he was puzzled. There are a good many who stick fast part way through some such Scripture as "Bless them that curse you" (Matt. 5:44). If a man sues you for your shirt, throw in the cloak too. If he compels you to go a mile, go with him two (Matt. 5:40-41).

15 And forgetteth that the foot may crush them, or that the wild beast may break them.

16 She is hardened against her young ones, as though *they were* not hers: her labor is in vain without fear;

17 Because God hath deprived her of wisdom, neither hath he imparted to her understanding.

18 What time she lifteth up herself on high, she scorneth the horse and his rider.

19 Hast thou given the horse strength? hast thou clothed his neck with thunder?

20 Canst thou make him afraid as a grasshopper? the glory of his nostrils *is* terrible.

21 He paweth in the valley, and rejoiceth in *his* strength: he goeth on to meet the armed men.

22 He mocketh at fear, and is not affrighted; neither turneth he back from the sword.

23 The quiver rattleth against him, the glittering spear and the shield.

24 He swalloweth the ground with fierceness and rage: neither believeth he that *it is* the sound of the trumpet.

15 Forgetting that a foot may crush them,
   and that the wild beast may trample
   them.

16 She deals cruelly with her young, as if
   they were not hers;
   though her labor be in vain, yet she
   has no fear;

17 because God has made her forget wisdom,
   and given her no share in understanding.

18 When she rouses herself to flee,[k]
   she laughs at the horse and his rider.

19 "Do you give the horse his might?
   Do you clothe his neck with strength?[l]

20 Do you make him leap like the locust?
   His majestic snorting is terrible.

21 He paws[m] in the valley, and exults in his
   strength;
   he goes out to meet the weapons.

22 He laughs at fear, and is not dismayed;
   he does not turn back from the sword.

23 Upon him rattle the quiver,
   the flashing spear and the javelin.

24 With fierceness and rage he swallows the
   ground;
   he cannot stand still at the sound of
   the trumpet.

[k] Heb obscure
[l] Tg: The meaning of the Hebrew word is obscure
[m] Gk Syr Vg: Heb *they dig*

f) The Horse (39:19-25)

19-25. God—not Job—gave **the horse his might** (vs. 19*a*) and "mane" (vs. 19*b*; cf. **thunder** or **strength**; the word רעמה is probably derived from the verb רעם, "to thunder" [cf. 40:9] and may mean "trembling one," hence "mane"; cf. the Greek words φόβη, "mane," and φόβος, "fear"). These verses form a distinctive poem composed of three strophes in a special meter. The poet displays an intimate knowledge and appreciation of hippology.

No use shifting about from one foot to the other and saying it makes no sense. God may not have to make that kind of sense. Mark Twain used to say that the things he could not understand about the Bible gave him very little trouble. It was the things he could understand that gave him all the trouble he was looking for.

Other "mysteries" come of insisting on the "now" and dropping out of sight the "after awhile" (cf. Expos. on 35:3). Take the promises which God has been at such pains to scatter around like flowers in a meadow. It is not always clear how he is going to make them good. Things seem to get out of hand, beyond all help. At the end of the universe is a blank wall.

The height of folly would be to quit when God is just about ready to begin. Such walls have had holes knocked in them more than once, wide enough for a regiment to march through. To keep staring out of the window when Someone is at the door—that nothing happens on such terms is no mystery at all. The trouble then is not with the Person at the door, but with the person at the window.

But when every due allowance is made for dullness and downright insincerity, there is yet the unfathomable deep. What could one make of God if he could be made out (see Expos. on 11:2-6, 7)? There is yet the problem of evil which taunted Swinburne beyond endurance

25 He saith among the trumpets, Ha, ha! and he smelleth the battle afar off, the thunder of the captains, and the shouting.

26 Doth the hawk fly by thy wisdom, *and* stretch her wings toward the south?

27 Doth the eagle mount up at thy command, and make her nest on high?

28 She dwelleth and abideth on the rock, upon the crag of the rock, and the strong place.

29 From thence she seeketh the prey, *and* her eyes behold afar off.

30 Her young ones also suck up blood: and where the slain *are*, there *is* she.

25 When the trumpet sounds, he says 'Aha!'
He smells the battle from afar,
the thunder of the captains, and the shouting.

26 "Is it by your wisdom that the hawk soars,
and spreads his wings toward the south?

27 Is it at your command that the eagle mounts up
and makes his nest on high?

28 On the rock he dwells and makes his home
in the fastness of the rocky crag.

29 Thence he spies out the prey;
his eyes behold it afar off.

30 His young ones suck up blood;
and where the slain are, there is he."

40 Moreover the Lord answered Job, and said,

2 Shall he that contendeth with the Almighty instruct *him?* he that reproveth God, let him answer it.

40 And the Lord said to Job:

2 "Shall a faultfinder contend with the Almighty?
He who argues with God, let him answer it."

g) The Hawk and the Eagle (39:26-30)

26-30. By God's intelligence and at God's command—not Job's—**the hawk soars** in the sky and **the eagle** swoops down upon its **prey.**

Now the poet has completed his gallery of vignettes on animal life—all designed to give to the hero a sense of his insignificance—and returns to the essential question as Yahweh directly challenges Job.

5. Silence of Job (40:1-5)

a) Closing Challenge (40:1-2)

40:1-2. Shall a faultfinder contend with the Almighty? This translation is based upon the Masoretic pointing which understands the word רב (*rōbh*) as an infinitive absolute of the verb ריב, "to contend," and the *hapax legomenon* יסור (*yiṣṣôr*) as a noun derived from the verb יסר (cf. 5:17) and meaning "censor," **faultfinder.** It is better to follow some of the ancient versions (Targ., Symm., Vulg.) and to consider the word רב as a participle (*rābh*) and the word יסור as an intransitive verb (*yāṣûr*) meaning "to yield," "to cease," "to desist" (cf. Isa. 11:13; Amos 6:7); thus one obtains a perfect parallelism of grammatical construction between vs. 2a and vs. 2b, as follows: "Will he who disputes with the Almighty yield? Will he who reproves God answer these things?" The question is not whether Job contends **with the Almighty** (cf. RSV), for he has done

(see Expos. on 10:1-22)—and the mystery of the good to offset it. Always somewhere the cloud and thick darkness. For those who expect it, who will not let it irritate them, or make them uneasy, or fill them with doubt, there is a kind of comfort in it. At least they are rid of the kind of God that the nineteenth century wanted to give the world (see Expos. on 33:12), with its "fifty-seven varieties" of custom-built explanations; they may even be on the way to

what the N.T., through "distress of nations, with perplexity" (Luke 21:25), goes about calling faith, in deep and awe-struck tones, ready to do the will of God where it is known, and to stop worrying about it where it is not. One who on a cross overcame the hazard of that distance which separates God from man is not likely to find an insuperable obstacle in any distance which man allows to separate him from God. In these chapters the mystery is given its

3 ¶ Then Job answered the Lord, and said,

4 Behold, I am vile; what shall I answer thee? I will lay mine hand upon my mouth.

5 Once have I spoken; but I will not answer: yea, twice; but I will proceed no further.

6 ¶ Then answered the Lord unto Job out of the whirlwind, and said,

3 Then Job answered the Lord:

4 "Behold, I am of small account; what shall I answer thee?
    I lay my hand on my mouth.

5 I have spoken once, and I will not answer;
    twice, but I will proceed no further."

6 Then the Lord answered Job out of the whirlwind:

---

just that throughout the poetic discussion with his three friends, but whether he will now desist or be able to answer the queries which Yahweh has put to him. Thus understood, this verse provides a satisfactory link with the preceding and following context.

b) Submission of the Hero (40:3-5)

3-5. Behold, I am of small account (vs. 4a; קלתי, "I am light, insignificant," perhaps with an evil connotation; cf. **vile**, KJV). Job slowly discovers his proper place in the universe, as well as the nature of his relationship to God, who created the cosmos and maintains it in order and harmony. He thus dimly becomes aware of the folly of his previous judgment of God and realizes that his presumption has been criminal. He can do so because he is now lifted into the realm of world-wide contemplation, with God as a guide, where the old questions concerning his puny self have lost their importance. He is not yet articulate about his consciousness of guilt, and may not even be conscious of it, but the way is being cleared for the inception of his sense of sin. **What shall I answer thee?** (Vs. 4aβ.) From the new vantage point afforded him by the divine intervention he is still perplexed, to be sure, by the mystery of his suffering, but he is no longer in a mood to make his claim of innocence and thus to maintain that God owes him health and wealth. His religion is undergoing a process of purification as little by little he abandons the position of paganism (idolatry of the self) and moves toward the new realm of authentic monotheism. He is gradually passing from an egocentric to a theocentric view of the world and of existence. He is not ready, however, to proceed from a confession of insignificance to a confession of repentance, because he has not yet grasped in its full import his confrontation with God (cf. 42:5-6). Therefore he says at this point merely, **I lay my hand on my mouth** (vs. 4b). His silence, however, is not one of dumbness. He could speak, but he refrains. **I have spoken once,** and I will not repeat (vs. 5a; read אשנה instead of אענה, **answer,** which is repeating vs. 4a). The negative insistence probably reveals the intensity of the inner convulsion: **Twice, but I will proceed no further** (vs. 5b). The poet admirably succeeds in suggesting that humility does not come easily to a man of Job's caliber, buffeted by pain and unbowed by the most horrible series of physical and mental tortures. If this exegesis is correct, the presence of a second discourse of Yahweh is quite justified.

B. Second Discourse of Yahweh (40:6–42:6)

Most modern commentators maintain that the second discourse of Yahweh on Behemoth (40:15-24) and Leviathan (41:1-34) represents a series of later additions, or at any rate is displaced from its original location at the end of the procession of animals

---

meaning, and its meaning is God. "Will he who disputes with the Almighty yield? Will he who reproves God answer these things?" (See Exeg. on 40:1-2.)

What shall I answer . . . ?
I lay my hand on my mouth.

40:6–42:6. *Like a Prince?*—(Cf. 31:37.) Once more now comes the challenge. I shall again ask the questions, says God. You answer them. Will you make nothing at all of my righteousness? **Will you condemn me in order to justify yourself?** Come up where I am, as you seem to wish (see Expos. on 34:31-33), and **tread down the**

7 Gird up thy loins now like a man: I will demand of thee, and declare thou unto me.

7 "Gird up your loins like a man; I will question you, and you declare to me.

(39:30). They argue that (*a*) Yahweh's purpose is already achieved when Job submits (40:3-5); (*b*) Yahweh's renewal of the challenge (40:6-14) is superfluous or even "comes perilously near nagging" (Peake, *Job,* p. 332); (*c*) the developments on Behemoth and Leviathan constitute merely a continuation of the gallery of animals (38:39–39:30); (*d*) these developments are poetically inferior to those which precede and are written in a different style, thus betraying a separate hand; (*e*) Yahweh introduces the question of Job's attacks on divine righteousness (40:8), but in his final answer (42:1-6) Job ignores this question completely and refers only to the might of the Deity; (*f*) the final confession of Job (42:1-6) is obviously an integral continuation of the first (40:4-5).

While it is probable that the developments on Behemoth and Leviathan have been expanded by another poet, and it is possible that various alterations and transpositions have been imposed on the early forms of the MS, the fact remains that the order of the present text reveals rhetorical skill, psychological perspicacity, and theological discernment. The following points should be taken into consideration: (*a*) Yahweh's purpose is not achieved when Job submits, because submission—as seen above (see Exeg. on 40:3-5)—does not mean repentance; (*b*) consequently, Yahweh's renewal of the challenge is not superfluous: it is made necessary by the purely negative character of Job's acceptance of silence; (*c*) the developments on Behemoth and Leviathan do not constitute merely a continuation of the gallery of animals, but introduce a new meditation on the nature and activity of God, with the help of mythical motifs (see Exeg. on 40:15-23; 41:1-34); (*d*) the differences of style and poetic ability may easily derive from the difference of subjects, and in any case literary heterogeneity—if demonstrated—is not at this point of direct relevance for the correctness of interpretation, since the exegete must ultimately deal with the book of Job as a finished product of the Joban school; (*e*) the fact that Job ignores Yahweh's question concerning divine righteousness is of no significance, since the hero in his final answer stands no longer on the level of intellectual discussion (see Exeg. on 40:1-5); (*f*) Job's last confession is of course an integral continuation of the first but it cannot take place at once: it needs a slow maturing which can occur only during a second discourse of Yahweh, and presumably under its impact. Thus, in addition to dramatic suspense, the separation of Job's response in two different moments suggests a depth of anguish and a breadth of bewilderment which could not otherwise be communicated to the hearer or reader, and—a most important point—implies that the spiritual phenomenon of repentance includes not only a negative act of silent submission but also a positive recognition of the presence of God; not only an avowal of guilt but also a commitment to the will of God and a dedication to his service (cf. *mutatis mutandis* the medieval distinction between attrition and contrition).

1. Renewed Challenge (40:6-14)

6-7. The introductory formulas of the second discourse of Yahweh are almost identical with those of the first (cf. 38:1, 3), an indication of a parallel pattern between the two, and a sign of the place where the second discourse actually begins.

---

wicked if you can. You think I should. Try it. **Hide them . . . in the dust.** Shut them up in the darkness of death. Then boast of **your own right hand,** and I will be the one to sing your praise! As if to say, "Suppose now that you were omnipotent, as you like to think you are, more or less; what would you do?" A physicist once spoke with chuckling amusement of some of his students, especially of those who would

come to him every now and then with their criticisms of much in particular and of almost everything in general. He said he had found a way to rock most of them back on their heels. He would let them get it all out of their system, and then ask what constructive suggestions they had to offer. Whereupon, having smashed "this Sorry Scheme of Things entire," they would begin to rebuild it "nearer to the Heart's De-

8 Wilt thou also disannul my judgment? wilt thou condemn me, that thou mayest be righteous?

9 Hast thou an arm like God? or canst thou thunder with a voice like him?

10 Deck thyself now *with* majesty and excellency; and array thyself with glory and beauty.

11 Cast abroad the rage of thy wrath: and behold every one *that is* proud, and abase him.

12 Look on every one *that is* proud, *and* bring him low; and tread down the wicked in their place.

---

8 Will you even put me in the wrong?
    Will you condemn me that you may be justified?

9 Have you an arm like God,
    and can you thunder with a voice like his?

10 "Deck yourself with majesty and dignity;
    clothe yourself with glory and splendor.

11 Pour forth the overflowings of your anger,
    and look on every one that is proud, and abase him.

12 Look on every one that is proud, and bring him low;
    and tread down the wicked where they stand.

---

8. The new questions of Yahweh penetrate to the core of the problem presented by the book of Job and delineate most clearly its configuration: the purpose of the book is not to discuss the mystery of the suffering of the innocent or the prosperity of the wicked, but to meditate on the meaning of pure religion (see Exeg. on 1:9) and therefore of justification by faith.

Wilt thou also disannul my judgment? Vs. 8*a* means, lit., "Wilt thou even reduce to nought my righteousness?" (cf. the paraphrase of RSV). Job indeed has not only asserted his innocence, he has also denied the righteousness of God (9:22; etc.). It is not necessary for Yahweh to prove his own righteousness. The poet does not believe that such a demonstration would be of any avail. Job requires more than that. Thus, subtly and devastatingly the next question will shift the argument from the plane of an academic query to the reality of an existential blow which will strike at the hero's spirit rather than at his mind. **Wilt thou condemn me, that thou mayest be righteous?** (Vs. 8*b*.) The drama is reaching its theological apex. Job, the paragon of virtue and the example of morality, had expected to receive from God his due. When frustrated, and in all appearances condemned in the eyes of his fellow men and in his own, the alternative left him was either to confess that he had no claim upon God's bounty or to declare God to be wrong in order to maintain his own self-righteousness. Thus the poet again and most eloquently exposes the sin of Job—not a sin of the horizontal type produced by ethical crimes directed against men, but a sin of the vertical type by which a creature dares to pass judgment upon his God and to indict his Creator. The vocabulary is not adequate since the poet has not yet been able to formulate a terminology which fits a doctrine of theological sinfulness. But the reality is powerfully and unambiguously suggested. If Job had the power of the Creator, then God himself would recognize the right of an equal to criticize an equal. God's further questioning is therefore infinitely sad, but its irony is not devoid of love and it half reveals compassion.

9-13. Hast thou an arm like God? (Vs. 9*a*.) Job's attacks against the righteousness of God have been expressions of his self-righteousness, and this in turn is the evidence of his delusion of self-deification. If Job were God (vs. 10), he would no doubt set the world right, abase [the] **proud, . . . and tread down the wicked in their place** (vss. 11-13).

---

sire."[4] He would listen very patiently, and then would say, "Do you know what my idea of hell is? Let me tell you. My idea of hell is for you to have to live in the kind of world you seem itching to put together." If you were omnipo-

tent, what would you do? It might at least call for less talk. And not only for humility, but for repentance. This second discourse of Yahweh has to do with power; but it is power which by implication (vss. 7-14) is set in the context of weakness (see Expos. on 9:2-10). Maybe

[4] *The Rubáiyát of Omar Khayyám*, st. xcix.

13 Hide them in the dust together; *and* bind their faces in secret.

14 Then will I also confess unto thee that thine own right hand can save thee.

15 ¶ Behold now behemoth, which I made with thee; he eateth grass as an ox.

---

13 Hide them all in the dust together;
    bind their faces in the world below.[n]

14 Then will I also acknowledge to you,
    that your own right hand can give you victory.

15 "Behold, Be'hemoth,[o]
    which I made as I made you;
    he eats grass like an ox.

[n] Heb *hidden place*
[o] Or *the hippopotamus*

---

14. Now comes a verse which may be considered as the pivot of the book, echoing the question of the Satan (1:9) and preparing the response of the hero (42:6) : "Then, I, myself, shall praise thee" (אודך) because **thine own right hand can save thee** (vs. 14; cf. Ps. 98:1). Man is aping God whenever he attempts to save himself, i.e., whenever he tries to be a man without God (cf. Gen. 3:5; cf. also Mark 15:31), the master of his own destiny, the author and fulfiller of his own salvation. The poet is anticipating here the N.T. analysis of justification by works. "The divine irony, infinitely keen and yet infinitely kind, becomes most humbling at the close of the answer from the whirlwind. It invites the doubter to array himself with honour and majesty, mount the throne of the world, seize the reins of government, and use his power to abase the proud and send the wicked to their doom. Then he will acquire the experience which will enable him to pass an intelligent judgment upon the government of the world. For he will know what it is to be God,—will realise the amazing complexity of the universe, the endless multiplicity of the divine interests and solicitudes, the relation of each self-centered human unit to the mighty sum of things. And then it will be time for God to praise a man whose own right hand hath gotten him the victory!" (James Strahan, *The Book of Job* [Edinburgh: T. & T. Clark, 1913], p. 332. Used by permission.) The expression אודך, "I would praise thee," is a technical term used in the cultic act by men who sing to God their gratitude (cf. Pss. 18:49; 30:9; etc.). The fact that the poet does not hesitate to lend it to God himself addressing a man provides the final touch of irony. The human hero is indeed offered by God the place of God! "The doubter is supposed to . . . draw the sword of justice, and bathe it in the blood of all the wicked. He makes a solitude and calls it peace. He vindicates justice by emptying the world. It is now time for God to raise a paean, either as the ancients did, 'Euge! macte virtute!' or as the moderns do, 'See, the conquering hero comes!' " (*Ibid.*, p. 335.)

2. BEHEMOTH (40:15-24)

As Job replies nothing, Yahweh continues, according to the present text, with the description of Behemoth. In all probability this section (40:15-24) has been added to the original text by a wise man of the Joban school who interpreted Leviathan (41:1-34) as a crocodile of mythical proportion and thought that its Egyptian counterpart, the mythical hippopotamus, was unfortunately absent. Both figures are found side by side or fighting together on many frescoes of the Ancient Egyptian Empire (see Adolf Erman, *Life in Ancient Egypt,* tr. H. M. Tirard [London: Macmillan & Co., 1894], pp. 239-40) and even on the late tomb of Petosiris. The Behemoth passage is not written in the style of questions as is the first discourse of Yahweh (38:2-40:5) or the section on Leviathan (41:1-34). It will be observed also that vs. 19 refers to "God" in the third person—a strange procedure in the mouth of Yahweh.

15-24. Behemoth (vs. 15*a*) has been identified with the hippopotamus, an animal of the Nile Valley, unknown in the western part of Asia Anterior. However, the poet had in mind a creature of mythical significance, not a mere representative of an animal species (see Hermann Gunkel, *Schöpfung und Chaos in Urzeit und Endzeit* [2nd ed.;

16 Lo now, his strength *is* in his loins, and his force *is* in the navel of his belly.

17 He moveth his tail like a cedar: the sinews of his stones are wrapped together.

18 His bones *are as* strong pieces of brass; his bones *are* like bars of iron.

19 He *is* the chief of the ways of God: he that made him can make his sword to approach *unto him.*

20 Surely the mountains bring him forth food, where all the beasts of the field play.

21 He lieth under the shady trees, in the covert of the reed, and fens.

22 The shady trees cover him *with* their shadow; the willows of the brook compass him about.

23 Behold, he drinketh up a river, *and* hasteth not: he trusteth that he can draw up Jordan into his mouth.

24 He taketh it with his eyes: *his* nose pierceth through snares.

16 Behold, his strength in his loins,
   and his power in the muscles of his belly.

17 He makes his tail stiff like a cedar;
   the sinews of his thighs are knit together.

18 His bones are tubes of bronze,
   his limbs like bars of iron.

19 "He is the first of the works[p] of God;
   let him who made him bring near his sword!

20 For the mountains yield food for him
   where all the wild beasts play.

21 Under the lotus plants he lies,
   in the covert of the reeds and in the marsh.

22 For his shade the lotus trees cover him;
   the willows of the brook surround him.

23 Behold, if the river is turbulent he is not frightened;
   he is confident though Jordan rushes against his mouth.

24 Can one take him with hooks,[q]
   or pierce his nose with a snare?

[p] Heb *ways*
[q] Cn: Heb *in his eyes*

Göttingen: Vandenhoeck & Ruprecht, 1921], pp. 41-69), although he conceived it largely according to a stylized image of the hippopotamus which he may well have obtained *de visu.* It has been maintained by some that the word **Behemoth** is a loan word from the Egyptian *pe-e-mu,* "water horse" (?), but the Hebrew בהמות can be explained simply as a plural of majesty of בהמה, "quadruped," meaning "the animal colossus par excellence" (cf. Ps. 73:22).

The monster in question is a creature of Yahweh, like Job (vs. 15a), and the poet's insistence upon this point may betray some polemical intent: not even a primeval beast (cf. vs. 19) originates outside of the creative act of God. The LXX omits the expression **which I made,** but the meter and syntax require its presence. The description stresses the sexual vigor of the giant (vs. 16 and probably also vs. 17ab; the word in the dual פחדו, **thighs** is euphemistic; cf. Targ., Vulg., and KJV). Behemoth is not an animal similar to those of the first discourse but a unique monster, **the chief of the ways of God** (vs. 19a; cf. Gen. 49:3; Prov. 8:22; see Gunkel, *ibid.,* p. 62; the text of vs. 19b is corrupt beyond recognition). It is not a mere hippopotamus, for, although some details suggest an Egyptian habitat (see **lotus** and **reeds** in vss. 21-22a, **the river** in vs. 23a), others point to a different geographical location (see **mountains** in vs. 20a, **beasts of the field** in vs. 20b, **willows of the brook** in vs. 22b, **Jordan rushes** in vs. 23b). Moreover, the Egyptians did capture the hippopotamus (see Erman, *op. cit.,* pp. 239-40), whereas Behemoth eludes human hunt (vs. 24); the RSV wrongly paraphrases the Hebrew **in**

---

treading down the wicked in a world like this is more even than omnipotence can accomplish. The Cross is testimony enough that God cannot do what he likes. Men can come nearer doing it than God can. Life is shudderingly nearer

what they want than it is to what he wants. "I, the Lord thy God, have a job on my hands." Hear him say that, and look at the tired lines on his face. For all his patience, centuries long; for all his sad Gethsemanes, "man won't come

41 Canst thou draw out leviathan with a hook? or his tongue with a cord *which* thou lettest down?

2 Canst thou put a hook into his nose? or bore his jaw through with a thorn?

3 Will he make many supplications unto thee? will he speak soft *words* unto thee?

4 Will he make a covenant with thee? wilt thou take him for a servant for ever?

5 Wilt thou play with him as *with* a bird? or wilt thou bind him for thy maidens?

6 Shall the companions make a banquet of him? shall they part him among the merchants?

7 Canst thou fill his skin with barbed irons? or his head with fish spears?

8 Lay thine hand upon him, remember the battle, do no more.

9 Behold, the hope of him is in vain: shall not *one* be cast down even at the sight of him?

41^r "Can you draw out Levi'athan[s] with a fishhook,
     or press down his tongue with a cord?

2 Can you put a rope in his nose,
     or pierce his jaw with a hook?

3 Will he make many supplications to you?
     Will he speak to you soft words?

4 Will he make a covenant with you
     to take him for your servant for ever?

5 Will you play with him as with a bird,
     or will you put him on leash for your maidens?

6 Will traders bargain over him?
     Will they divide him up among the merchants?

7 Can you fill his skin with harpoons,
     or his head with fishing spears?

8 Lay hands on him;
     think of the battle; you will not do it again!

9[t] Behold, the hope of a man is disappointed;
     he is laid low even at the sight of him.

[r] Ch 40. 25 in Heb
[s] Or *the crocodile*
[t] Ch 41. 1 in Heb

---

his eyes which refers to a method used for the seizure not of the hippopotamus but of the crocodile (the blinding of the animal's **eyes** with clay; Herodotus *History* II. 70); also, instead of במוקשים (plural), **with a snare** (singular, a meaning which obviously does not fit the context **pierce his nose**), read בקמשים, "with thorns" or "with harpoons."

3. LEVIATHAN (41:1-34 [=Hebrew 40:25–41:26])

As noted above (see Exeg. on 40:15-24), the second discourse of Yahweh in its original form probably passed from the unanswered challenge (40:6-14) directly to the questions on Leviathan (41:1-34).

a) MEANING OF PURE RELIGION (41:1-12)

41:1-11. Leviathan is different from an ordinary crocodile because it is a sea monster which cannot be captured (vss. 1 ff.; cf. vs. 31), produces eclipses (3:8; cf. 26:13), and is associated with the forces of the primeval chaos (Ps. 74:14; Enoch 60:7-9; II Baruch 29:4; II Esdras 6:49-52). Like the whole of mankind, Job is totally impotent before it, but Yahweh can afford to speak of it with serene detachment and even playfulness (cf. vs. 5 with Ps. 104:26). Each line of humorous interrogation leads to the final questions which give meaning to the whole passage (vss. 10-11).

Who then is he that can stand before me? (Vs. 10*b*.) Once again the poet avails himself of the opportunity to describe by inference his concept of pure religion (cf.

---

right": there are still "the sot, the fool, the tyrant, and the mob" (see Expos. on 7:20*a*, 21*a*). "I have a job on my hands. Come up yourself and take it on. You will have to go to Calvary with it."

And not for any lack of power. Witness the poems that describe **Behemoth** and **Leviathan**

(see Exeg. on 40:6–42:6; 40:15-24; 41:1-34), those mythical creatures who could not properly be allowed to associate with animals of the common or garden variety (ch. 39).

Behold now behemoth, which I made with thee, . . . his bones are like bars of iron. . . . He lieth . . . in the covert of the reed, and fens.

10 None *is so* fierce that dare stir him up: who then is able to stand before me?

11 Who hath prevented me, that I should repay *him? whatsoever is* under the whole heaven is mine.

12 I will not conceal his parts, nor his power, nor his comely proportion.

13 Who can discover the face of his garment? *or* who can come *to him* with his double bridle?

14 Who can open the doors of his face? his teeth *are* terrible round about.

10 No one is so fierce that he dares to stir him up.
Who then is he that can stand before me?

11 Who has given to me,[u] that I should repay him?
Whatever is under the whole heaven is mine.

12 "I will not keep silence concerning his limbs,
or his mighty strength, or his goodly frame.

13 Who can strip off his outer garment?
Who can penetrate his double coat of mail?[v]

14 Who can open the doors of his face?
Round about his teeth is terror.

[u] The meaning of the Hebrew is uncertain
[v] Gk: Heb *bridle*

1:9; 40:14). He therefore ascribes to God the momentous query, **Who has given to me, that I should repay him?** (vs. 11). With the Targ. and a few Hebrew MSS, some critics read הקדימו (third person suffix) instead of הקדימני (first person suffix), and therefore interpret the verse as referring to Leviathan, thus translating, "Who has ever affronted him?" The LXX, however, supports the traditional Hebrew reading of the first person suffix. The M.T. means, lit., "Who ever preceded me (with a gift)?" or "Who ever came toward me (with a gift)?" See the KJV's archaic English, **Who hath prevented me?** Such an idea fits admirably the context, **Whatever is under the whole heaven is mine** (vs. 11*b*; cf. 35:7, and especially Rom. 11:35). Here is no less than a subtle but drastic indictment of all ritualistic or moralistic attempts to force the hand of the Deity (cf. Ps. 50:10). The poet of Job takes his place among the theological singers of *sola gratia.* Man cannot bestow any gift upon God, either of his wealth or of his deeds and behavior. God does not owe Job anything and Job cannot give God anything, even less make demands upon him.

12. This verse is absent in the LXX, and its language is obscure. The RSV considers it as a reintroduction of Leviathan (vss. 13 ff.), but one may relate it to the preceding context and interpret it as an indirect reference to Job, who is already alluded to in vs. 11 (see the interrogative **who** and the personal pronoun **him**). Vs. 12 might then be rendered, "Would I keep silence [*Qerê* לו instead of *Kethibh* לא] concerning his boastings [בדיו; cf. the meaning of this word in 11:3 rather than **limbs** as in 18:13], or (his) talk of power [גבורות, plural of majesty], and his fair array (of words)!" This translation, however, is conjectural.

b) ADDITIONAL OBSERVATIONS ON LEVIATHAN (41:13-34)

13-34. A wise man of the Joban school may have been responsible for the list of wonderful details concerning Leviathan's invincibility: his scales, jaws, and back (vss.

. . . **The willows of the brook compass him about.** The rivers rage, and he fears them not. The floods swell even to his mouth, and he is not afraid. **Take him with hooks, if you can; pierce his nose with a snare.**

Or catch Leviathan for me. **Press down his** tongue with a cord. Will he make a covenant with thee, and speak soft words? Will you play **with him as with a bird?** There was an old rabbinical tradition that Yahweh spent the morning hours reading the Torah, the early afternoon attending to affairs of state, and the

15 *His* scales *are his* pride, shut up together *as with* a close seal.

16 One is so near to another, that no air can come between them.

17 They are joined one to another, they stick together, that they cannot be sundered.

18 By his sneezings a light doth shine, and his eyes *are* like the eyelids of the morning.

19 Out of his mouth go burning lamps, *and* sparks of fire leap out.

20 Out of his nostrils goeth smoke, as *out* of a seething pot or caldron.

21 His breath kindleth coals, and a flame goeth out of his mouth.

22 In his neck remaineth strength, and sorrow is turned into joy before him.

23 The flakes of his flesh are joined together: they are firm in themselves; they cannot be moved.

24 His heart is as firm as a stone; yea, as hard as a piece of the nether *millstone*.

25 When he raiseth up himself, the mighty are afraid: by reason of breakings they purify themselves.

26 The sword of him that layeth at him cannot hold: the spear, the dart, nor the habergeon.

27 He esteemeth iron as straw, *and* brass as rotten wood.

28 The arrow cannot make him flee: sling stones are turned with him into stubble.

29 Darts are counted as stubble: he laugheth at the shaking of a spear.

30 Sharp stones *are* under him: he spreadeth sharp pointed things upon the mire.

31 He maketh the deep to boil like a pot: he maketh the sea like a pot of ointment.

32 He maketh a path to shine after him; *one* would think the deep *to be* hoary.

33 Upon earth there is not his like, who is made without fear.

15 His back[w] is made of rows of shields,
    shut up closely as with a seal.

16 One is so near to another
    that no air can come between them.

17 They are joined one to another;
    they clasp each other and cannot be separated.

18 His sneezings flash forth light,
    and his eyes are like the eyelids of the dawn.

19 Out of his mouth go flaming torches;
    sparks of fire leap forth.

20 Out of his nostrils comes forth smoke,
    as from a boiling pot and burning rushes.

21 His breath kindles coals,
    and a flame comes forth from his mouth.

22 In his neck abides strength,
    and terror dances before him.

23 The folds of his flesh cleave together,
    firmly cast upon him and immovable.

24 His heart is hard as a stone,
    hard as the nether millstone.

25 When he raises himself up the mighty[x] are afraid;
    at the crashing they are beside themselves.

26 Though the sword reaches him, it does not avail;
    nor the spear, the dart, or the javelin.

27 He counts iron as straw,
    and bronze as rotten wood.

28 The arrow cannot make him flee;
    for him slingstones are turned to stubble.

29 Clubs are counted as stubble;
    he laughs at the rattle of javelins.

30 His underparts are like sharp potsherds;
    he spreads himself like a threshing sledge on the mire.

31 He makes the deep boil like a pot;
    he makes the sea like a pot of ointment.

32 Behind him he leaves a shining wake;
    one would think the deep to be hoary.

33 Upon earth there is not his like,
    a creature without fear.

[w] Cn Compare Gk Vg: Heb *pride*
[x] Or *gods*

13-17); his eyes, mouth, nostrils, breath, and neck (vss. 18-23); his might (vss. 24-30); his effect upon the deep and the sea (vss. 31-32); and—in conclusion—his uniqueness (vss. 33-34).

34 He beholdeth all high *things*: he is a king over all the children of pride.

42 Then Job answered the LORD, and said,

2 I know that thou canst do every *thing*, and *that* no thought can be withholden from thee.

3 Who *is* he that hideth counsel without knowledge? therefore have I uttered that I understood not; things too wonderful for me, which I knew not.

34 He beholds everything that is high;
    he is king over all the sons of pride."

42 Then Job answered the LORD:

2 "I know that thou canst do all things,
    and that no purpose of thine can be thwarted.

3 'Who is this that hides counsel without knowledge?'
Therefore I have uttered what I did not understand,
    things too wonderful for me, which I did not know.

---

4. REPENTANCE OF JOB (42:1-6)

42:1. Whereas the first discourse of Yahweh leads to the negative response of the hero (40:3-5), the second discourse produces Job's positive response, his confession of total humility, his acknowledgment of the immediacy of God's presence, and finally his repentance.

2-4. At last Job recognizes the omnipotence of God and at the same time discerns that the divine will is neither arbitrary nor whimsical but follows a considered and deliberate **purpose** (vs. 2). **Who is this that hides counsel without knowledge?** (Vs. 3a.) This is a quotation from the first discourse of Yahweh (38:2) which the poet may very well have ascribed to Job at this point. It is possible to imagine the hero, quietly recalling his blasphemous expostulations while quoting in a chastened mood the word of God, **Who is this that hides counsel without knowledge?** This pondering aloud might be a way in which he assimilates all the ramifications of the immense truth which is now before him as well as a preparation for the confession which follows:

> **Therefore I have uttered what I did not understand,**
>   **things too wonderful for me, which I did not know** (vs. 3*bc*).

Likewise, still in the mood of melancholy recollection and engaged in the process of

---

cool of the evening playing with Leviathan. **Will you put him on leash for your maidens? Lay hold on him, and see what happens. You will not do it again! He laughs at the rattle of javelins,** he leaves in the clay the mark of a threshing machine.

> **He counts iron as straw,**
>   **and bronze as rotten wood.**

Out of his nostrils comes forth smoke, as he blows out his hot breath with water from his mouth. **He makes the deep boil like a pot. Who then is he that can stand before me?** Who will put me in his debt? (See Expos. on 30:25.) And that is the upshot of it really; hardly calculated to warm Job's heart.

But something has changed him. Listen:

Then Job answered the LORD:
"I know that thou canst do all things,
    and that no purpose of thine can be thwarted."

Thou didst ask: **Who is this that hides counsel without knowledge?** It is I, I who

have uttered what I did not understand,
    things too wonderful for me, which I did not know.

Thou didst say, I will put the questions, you answer. What is it going to be now? Will Job argue his cause, carry his indictment on his shoulder, bind it on him as a crown, give account of all his steps, come like a prince before God (31:35-37)? Answer? Forbid it, O God, that I should! **I have heard of thee by the hearing of the ear, but now mine eye seeth thee.** I am undone! In dust and ashes I repent. What has brought about that change? Not an argument. Not anything on the surface of these chapters. Certainly God has not just overpowered him, beaten him down with majesty and the mystery of things, forced him into submission. What has happened? (See Expos. on Heb. 12:18-24.)

4 Hear, I beseech thee, and I will speak:
I will demand of thee, and declare thou
unto me.

5 I have heard of thee by the hearing of
the ear; but now mine eye seeth thee:

---

4 'Hear, and I will speak;
　　I will question you, and you declare to
　　me.'

5 I had heard of thee by the hearing of the
　　ear,
　　but now my eye sees thee;

---

intent introspection, Job may be repeating to himself the words which God has pronounced and which linger in his subconscious mind as an indicting echo:

> Hear, and I will speak;
> I will question you, and you declare to me (vs. 4; cf. 38:3).

And the word **Hear**, turning the train of thought, carries Job to the climactic discovery
expressed immediately afterward, **I had heard** . . . (vs. 5). On the other hand, these two
quotations of Yahweh's first discourse may have been originally marginal notes which an
early reader thought to be appropriate explanations of Job's statements.

5. Most commentators are inclined to discern in this verse the supreme lesson of the
book. Throughout the poetic discussion Job has displayed almost as pedantically as his
three friends an academic knowledge of the Deity. He has come closer to the truth than
they because he had been accustomed to sense the divine communion in highly personal
terms; but his certainty of God's presence has been poisoned by the seemingly unjust
fate inflicted upon him. In his frantic search for a formula which would at once preserve
the justice of God and his own righteousness, Job was led to explore some alleys of thought
down which other adventurers of faith were to follow him (see 9:33; 16:19; 19:25-26),
but even there he was hitting his head against various walls, for the God of whom he
had heard was largely the product of man's calculating imagination and a projection of
man's ideas of morality and justice upon an infinite realm. His knowledge of God proceeded from **the hearing of the ear**, the tradition of the wisdom schools, the testimony of
the ancients, the word of the fathers. His religion had been inherited: it was of the
secondhand variety. Traditional theology might well be satisfactory in times of prosperity,
but it could not survive the strokes of destitution and pain, rejection by society, and
isolation from God himself. **But now**, through an immediate confrontation of God

---

42:5. *The Meaning of the Book.*—The book
of Job is not for the casual reader. Least of all
is it for the man who thinks that religion can
be reduced to ethics, that by all odds the most
important thing is what people say and do: God
will assuredly reward them if they say and do
what is right; if not, he will assuredly punish
them (cf. Expos. on 36:18, 21).

Obviously there are three levels on which it
moves. The most superficial of them has to do
with the suffering of the innocent (see Expos.
on 36:5-15, 8-25, 8).

Deeper still is the level of the Satan's question, "Does Job fear God for nought?" (1:9;
see Expos. on 1:6-12). Peter once asked Jesus,
"Behold, we have forsaken all, and followed
thee; what shall we have therefore?" (Matt.
19:27; Mark 10:28). It was something to be
possessed, and that was bad; he put it at the
beginning, and that was worse; he thought of
what they had left for God, not of what God
had left for them, and that was worst. Jesus

answered, "A great deal; but let me tell you a
story." And he told the story of the man who
hired laborers into the vineyard; and how those
who came for only an hour got as much at the
last as those who had borne the heat and
burden of the day. It was not fair? Jesus was
scarcely interested in that. He was interested
in telling Peter that all such matters were better
left to the goodman of the house. No doubt
Peter understood and was properly ashamed
(see Expos. on Luke 19:8). When the Satan's
question finds its answer in a man who will yet
fear God—as in his heart of hearts Job did—
though it is for nought; when it is once established that the sneer of God's celestial cynic is a
lie, that there is indeed a place in this strange
world for disinterested religion, then the problem of innocent suffering has been undercut.
Job is no longer asking "Why?" (see Expos. on
3:20). There is now for him a place where
the problem is not solved; but it is beginning
to dissolve. There is still a "Why?" but the

| 6 Wherefore I abhor *myself*, and repent in dust and ashes. | 6 therefore I despise myself, and repent in dust and ashes." |

which the poet described by using the motif of the voice from the whirlwind, the hero's knowledge of religion proceeds from an entirely different source; and the only way in which he is able to express this intrinsically new reality is to say, **My eye sees thee.** The wise man has become a prophet (cf. Isa. 6:5). And like a prophet, who sees a holy God, he is thrown into the grip of self-abhorrence and the awe of self-destruction. Thus vs. 5 is indissolubly bound to the following lines. At last Job, the proud sheik, is conscious of his sinfulness and is able to confess it.

6. Wherefore I abhor myself (KJV) or **Therefore I despise myself** (RSV, Moffatt). These translations are better than "I loathe my words" (ASV mg.), "I retract" (Amer. Trans.), or "I repudiate (what I said)" (Driver and Gray), but they are probably still too weak for the difficult Hebrew word אמאס. This verb is not the transitive מאס, "to despise" but the intransitive parallel of מסס, "to flow," "to melt" (see 7:5, 16; cf. LXX, Targ., Syriac; also Ps. 58:8), meaning here, "I melt into nothingness," "I sink into the abyss of nought" (cf. the prophet's exclamation, "Woe is me! for I am undone!" Isa. 6:5). The matter is qualitatively different from one of retraction or even of self-despising. It is man's reaction to a devastating encounter with "the holy" (see Rudolf Otto, *The Idea of the Holy* [New York: Oxford University Press, 1923], pp. 74-84 *et passim*), and specifically with "the Holy One." The finiteness of the creature is crushed at the sudden onset of the Creator's infinity. Life appears at the conjuncture of being and nonbeing; and before the Being who is the source and the all-embracing mover of his own existence, man shrinks into the infinitely small. Thus Job completes his sentence saying, **I . . . repent in dust and ashes.** Repent of what? Of ethical crimes which he has not committed? Rather, of the monstrous crime of having condemned his Creator. Job does not receive the verdict of acquittal he has longed for, or the public approval which he craved from his "vindicator." But he has no longer any need of them. This does not mean at all that he now discovers the certainty of his own innocence. On the contrary, it is because he is certain of God's care for him that he is able to perceive his guilt. As in the Bible generally, his sense of sin arises at the time of his salvation.

Many exegetical comments are misleading at this point, e.g., "[Job] knows that God is righteous, he knows that, though he suffers, he is righteous also" (Peake, *Job*, p. 343). Such an observation ignores the fact that Job is no longer egocentric. His ego—and therefore his desire for righteousness—is annihilated, and thus he is able truly to repent.

His attitude, therefore, is far from being merely negative. He is redeemed from the anguish, not only or mainly of his tortures, but also of his alienation from the God of his youth. And he repents not from moral guilt, but from a reckless display of distrust. God, whom he accused of acting as a drunken foe, has taken upon himself the gracious

---

sharp outlines of it are fading. It does not disturb him any longer at the point where it first disturbed him. He is willing to leave it where the last word is not mystery at all, but faith, ineffable and triumphant.

"Say to men, *Come, suffer; you will hunger and thirst; you will, perhaps, be deceived, be betrayed, cursed; but you have a great duty to accomplish:* they will be deaf, perhaps, for a long time, to the severe voice of virtue; but on the day that they do come to you, they will come as heroes, and be invincible." [5]

[5] Giuseppe Mazzini, "Europe: Its Condition and Prospects," *Essays* (London: Walter Scott, 1887), p. 290. Quoted by Strahan, *Job*, p. 17.

Now one more step. The third and deepest level on which the book moves has to do with the ways and being and very nature of God (cf. Expos. on 1:12). It is only when Job comes face to face with him, beyond all hearsay, firsthand, that he comes to himself. There for the first time he is rid of too much self. The obsession lets go its hold. He was being weaned away from it all along. When the Almighty comes Job's last horizon disappears. His narrow little world of suffering crumbles. His mind and his heart are caught up from the pin point of his own experience and set free to roam hither and yon through the wide reaches of the majesty and friendliness of God. Where there is meeting

7 ¶ And it was *so*, that after the LORD had spoken these words unto Job, the LORD said to Eliphaz the Temanite, My wrath is kindled against thee, and against thy two friends: for ye have not spoken of me *the things that is* right, as my servant Job *hath*.

7 After the LORD had spoken these words to Job, the LORD said to Eli′phaz the Te′manite: "My wrath is kindled against you and against your two friends; for you have not spoken of me what is right, as my serv-

---

initiative of revealing himself in all the glory of the Creator and Ruler of nature. Job will not approach this God "as a prince" (31:37). He will take his place in the cosmos, trusting in God and saying in effect, "Thy will be done." His trust is the result of his immediate communion (vs. 5) and the cause of his repentance (vs. 6), a repentance which means total dedication.

To be sure, the poet's terminology is not sophisticated enough for the formulation of such a truth (cf. Ps. 73:23 ff.; Hab. 3:17-19). Yet it is hard to imagine a poet and a theologian of his caliber limited by immaturity of expression. It is therefore preferable to suppose that he respected the psychology of theological awe and knew so well the experience of holiness that he restrained himself from making his hero artificially and distastefully loquacious. It was Job, not the poet, who was laboring with a reality of tremendous newness which was fully conceived in his inner being but could not yet be brought forth into words.

V. EPILOGUE IN PROSE (42:7-17)

After the voice from the whirlwind and the response of the penitent Job (38:1–42:6), the prosaic style reappears abruptly as the storyteller, presumably the same as that of the prologue (see Intro., p. 884), describes the hero's intercession for his friends (42:7-9) and his subsequent restoration (42:10-17).

A. JOB'S INTERCESSION FOR HIS FRIENDS (42:7-9)

7. After the LORD had spoken these words to Job: This clause ignores the hero's confession (42:1-6), a fact which may indicate a discrepancy of authorship. Yahweh wrathfully accuses **Eliphaz** and his **two friends,** saying, **You have not spoken of me what is right, as my servant Job has.** Both the unqualified condemnation of the friends and the implied exculpation of the hero are unexpected; for the former have not been altogether

---

(see Expos. on 4:7) life is born and the sons of God shout together for joy. There God creates his "new creature," and the questions die on Job's lips. In the intimacies of the old relation, deepened and purified, the mists clear away into the knowledge that comes not of **the hearing of the ear** but of the **eye** with its sight restored. Could it be that there is no solution for any of the soul's anguish, the mind's fear, the heart's despair, except in the peace of that presence? "But when he was yet a great way off, his father saw him" (Luke 15:20). Why "a great way off," unless that father had been going down to the gate every evening in the twilight to see if some wayfarer on the road might indeed be his son? "When . . . his father saw him, [he] ran, and fell on his neck, and kissed him." Is that what the book of Job really means? The entering in of One whose judgments are not man's judgments. "You have not spoken of me what is right, as my servant Job has" (vs. 7). The skeptic was nearer home than the pious.

There is a religion of the irreligious. The heretic was the saint (cf. Expos. on 23:2). One whose judgments are not man's judgments, but whose coming is man's salvation. While over it all, as the arching sky, is the mystery of that mercy which rebukes him in order to gather him into the arms of its redemptive purpose.

7-17. The Epilogue.— (See Exeg.; Expos. on 5:17, 18, 23; 8:7; 11:16.) During the American economic depression of the nineteen-thirties Calvin Coolidge wrote a magazine article to the effect that in Job we have one who passed through a period of extreme deflation, and for the lessons he learned in thrift and in diet became twice as prosperous as he ever was. Perhaps it should be observed that it was not an American who wrote the book of Job. No such crudities can be imported into it and set down with a flourish. Yet the shadow of God's great hand is here, with its double bounty for every good withdrawn (see Expos. on 7:19), its peace on peace. The poet allows it to remain

8 Therefore take unto you now seven bullocks and seven rams, and go to my servant Job, and offer up for yourselves a burnt offering; and my servant Job shall pray for you: for him will I accept: lest I deal with you *after your* folly, in that ye have not spoken of me *the thing which is* right, like my servant Job.

9 So Eliphaz the Temanite and Bildad the Shuhite *and* Zophar the Naamathite went, and did according as the LORD commanded them: the LORD also accepted Job.

10 And the LORD turned the captivity of Job, when he prayed for his friends: also

ant Job has. 8 Now therefore take seven bulls and seven rams, and go to my servant Job, and offer up for yourselves a burnt offering; and my servant Job shall pray for you, for I will accept his prayer not to deal with you according to your folly; for you have not spoken of me what is right, as my servant Job has." 9 So Eli'phaz the Te'manite and Bildad the Shuhite and Zophar the Na'amathite went and did what the LORD had told them; and the LORD accepted Job's prayer.

10 And the LORD restored the fortunes of

---

wrong about God's glory and holiness, although they may not have declared about Job נכונה, "what is true" (Deut. 13:14 [Hebrew 13:15]; I Sam. 23:23; Ps. 5:11 [Hebrew 5:10]; cf. the Akkadian *kettu*, "justice," "truth"); and the latter's statements, far from being endorsed by the poet as representing **what is right,** have been thoroughly condemned by the voice from the whirlwind and by the hero himself. These two facts may constitute another indication of literary heterogeneity.

8-9. A burnt offering of **seven bulls and seven rams** for the benefit of three men was of considerable magnitude (cf. Ezekiel's prescription for the entire people, Ezek. 45:22-25), and this detail, as well as that of Job's need to intercede on the behalf of his friends, has often been interpreted as underlining the gravity of their transgressions (yet cf. Balaam's sacrifice in Num. 23:1 ff.). Furthermore, it is remarkable that the author of the story extols the intercessory power of Job exactly as Ezekiel does when he mentions Job in association with Noah and Daniel (Ezek. 14:14, 20; the fact that the prophet suggests the ineffectuality of these three ancient figures' intercessory power neither proves nor disproves that the author of the Joban epilogue was ignorant of the Ezekiel statement). Yahweh hopes that he will not be compelled to inflict upon the friends any "harsh treatment" or "disgrace" (נבלה, lit., **folly;** cf. 2:10; 30:8; cf. also Gen. 34:7; Deut. 22:21; etc.; the traditional paraphrase retained by the RSV is not supported by the Hebrew text). Job's prayer is acceptable to Yahweh, who calls him **my servant,** as in the prologue (1:8; 2:3). Observe that there is no mention of Elihu.

B. JOB'S RESTORATION (42:10-17)

10-11. The expression **restored the fortunes** (RSV) may be interpreted as **turned the captivity** (KJV; cf. Jer. 33:11; Hos. 6:11; Amos 9:14; Ps. 14:7; etc.), but this fact is

---

(see Expos., pp. 905-7) because it belongs.[6] Without it there would not only have been no artistic unity, there would not have been a rounding out of what is after all a deep religious truth. To those who think the poem is well-nigh ruined by its "happy ending," let it be said that there is restoration in this world of God; there is even reward, which in normal sequence is the result of restoration—though one must keep from attaching a too facile interpretation to them. To have said nothing of them would have been to misrepresent a fact of experience.

[6] Cf. Søren Kierkegaard, *Repetition,* tr. Walter Lowrie (Princeton: Princeton University Press, 1941), p. 132; cf. p. 100.

Two comments will be found suggestive and useful. The first is by Norman H. Snaith:

If a people has no belief in any life beyond the grave worthy of the name, then of necessity this . . . vindication of right . . . must show itself in this life, on this earth, and in the things of this life. It follows therefore that the [righteousness] which God establishes must involve the blessings of honour from men and of general prosperity. These are the things of this life by which any good favour must be judged. Even the conclusion of the Book of Job admits this. The point as to whether the Book of Job is all from one hand or not, or all from the same period or not, is of no account in this connection. The last man to touch the book left it as it is

the LORD gave Job twice as much as he had before.

11 Then came there unto him all his brethren, and all his sisters, and all they that had been of his acquaintance before, and did eat bread with him in his house: and they bemoaned him, and comforted him over all the evil that the LORD had brought upon him: every man also gave him a piece of money, and every one an earring of gold.

12 So the LORD blessed the latter end of Job more than his beginning: for he had fourteen thousand sheep, and six thousand camels, and a thousand yoke of oxen, and a thousand she asses.

Job, when he had prayed for his friends; and the LORD gave Job twice as much as he had before. 11 Then came to him all his brothers and sisters and all who had known him before, and ate bread with him in his house; and they showed him sympathy and comforted him for all the evil that the LORD had brought upon him; and each of them gave him a piece of money[y] and a ring of gold. 12 And the LORD blessed the latter days of Job more than his beginning; and he had fourteen thousand sheep, six thousand camels, a thousand yoke of oxen,

[y] Heb kesitah

---

not necessarily an indication of the exilic or postexilic date of the epilogue since the idiom may have originally meant "turned the turning." Note that Job's restoration is emphatically linked with his attitude toward his friends, for the Hebrew text means, lit., "because he prayed on the behalf of his neighbor" (vs. 10a; cf. Isa. 53:12). The return of Job to prosperity is barely stated in vs. 10b, **And the LORD gave Job twice as much as he had before** (cf. Isa. 61:7; Zech. 9:12). Then follows the social rehabilitation of the hero (vs. 11; cf. 2:11, and, for the expression **they that had been of his acquaintance** 19:19). Job's misfortunes were naturally thought to have been **the evil that the LORD had brought upon him.** A kesitah (RSV mg.) was a piece of uncoined silver (cf. Gen. 33:19; Josh. 24:32) which represented the price of a small "ewe" (cf. the Latin words *pecus* and *pecunia*). The **ring of gold** was for the nostrils (cf. Gen. 24:22, 47; Isa. 3:21). Such gifts were symbols of courtesy and friendship.

12-17. The epilogue may very well have ended originally with vs. 11, and several commentators consider vss. 12-17 to be a later elaboration destined to offer circumstantial details on Job's rehabilitation. The cattle is indeed twice as numerous as that of the prologue (cf. vs. 10 and 1:3) but the number of sons and daughters remains the same. "For us no child lost can be replaced, [but] the feeling of antiquity differed to some extent from ours" (Peake, *Job*, p. 346). The word שבענה, however, has been interpreted by the Targ. as a dual of the numeral seven, thus meaning "fourteen" (Heman, David's "seer in the words of God," is celebrated, according to I Chr. 25:5, for his "fourteen sons and three daughters"). One can hardly imagine, nevertheless, that the number of Job's daughters should not have been equally doubled, because the author appears to be exceptionally profeminist: he records the names of the girls (meaning respectively "Dove," "Cinnamon," and "Horn of Eye-shadow") but he ignores those of the boys; he stresses the girls' extraordinary beauty; and he tops his account with the unique detail, **And their father gave them inheritance among their brethren** (vs. 15; cf. Num. 27:1-11,

---

now. Presumably he was satisfied with the ending, for certainly no considerations of prior authorship, antiquity, authority, or anything else, prevented wholesale alterations. The vindication of Job is demonstrated by his increased prosperity and his new progeny in the final outcome of the story. How else was an author to demonstrate the final triumph of faithful Job, when there was no other world in which it could be demonstrated." [7]

[7] *Distinctive Ideas of the Old Testament* (London: Epworth Press, 1944), p. 89; (Philadelphia: Westminster Press, 1946, copyright by W. L. Jenkins), pp. 111-12. Used by permission.

Then in the footnote:

The literary criticism . . . of the Old Testament has often forgotten that those who pieced the Old Testament together, pieced it together as we have it now. They chose the order we have. The analysis of the sources is but the first step in literary criticism. The editors had the final say, and they used all the material from its varied sources in order to teach their particular message. This message, that of Scripture as a whole, can never be found so long as we think of the Bible only with respect to its literary sources. . . . We need both elements in

13 He had also seven sons and three daughters.

14 And he called the name of the first, Jemima; and the name of the second, Kezia; and the name of the third, Keren-happuch.

15 And in all the land were no women found *so* fair as the daughters of Job: and their father gave them inheritance among their brethren.

and a thousand she-asses. 13 He had also seven sons and three daughters. 14 And he called the name of the first Jemi'mah; and the name of the second Kezi'ah; and the name of the third Ker'en-hap'puch. 15 And in all the land there were no women so fair as Job's daughters; and their father gave them inheritance among their brothers.

---

which allowed inheritance to daughters only when there was no son). The final touch (vss. 16-17) likens the hero to the patriarchs of old (cf. Gen. 25:8; 35:29; 50:23; also Ps. 128:6; Prov. 17:6; I Chr. 29:28).

The literary discrepancies which have been observed between the epilogue and the discourses of Yahweh (see above) suggest that the poet was not responsible for the denouement of the story and thus should not be charged with upholding the traditional dogma of individual retribution. The interpreter has the right to conjecture that the poet borrowed as the setting of his theological meditation a folk tale which was already in the public domain, and that he accepted its ending because he had no alternative (see Intro., p. 888). The exegete may also consider that the poet, who was not primarily concerned with the problem of undeserved suffering, welcomed the conclusion of the ancient tale, for it provided a fitting symbol of earthly realism to his understanding of life with God. According to the biblical way of thinking, life is one, and communion with Yahweh means harmony within the self and the community, health, wealth, posterity, and death at a ripe old age. It may even have been inconceivable for the ancient Hebrews to imagine Job at peace with God and still destitute. The story of his restoration, with its stylized features, was the poetic symbol—in a prose story—of his ultimate salvation.

In any case, the biblical exegete must look at the book in its final form, and the epilogue may suggest a lesson which has not escaped the attention of theologians and thinkers (cf. Søren Kierkegaard, *Repetition,* tr. Walter Lowrie [Princeton: Princeton University Press, 1941], p. 132). Job was no longer enslaved to his self or to the egocentric aspect of happiness and enjoyment of health, wealth, and family, and therefore had given them up completely as he abdicated his claim to vindication. Totally cleansed and

---

Bible study, the message of the men who under God were responsible for the various strata, and the message of those who under God were the final editors. In both the truth of the Bible is to be found.

The other is by P. T. Forsyth:

Life begins as a problem. . . . It offers a task rather than an enjoyment. . . . The problem is disquieting, anxious, and even tragic. It is not simply interesting and amusing. . . . It touches the nerve. . . . It involves the realities of life. . . . The next step is that there is a solution to the problem. Our battle is not a sport for heaven. I am thinking of the a-theology of Thomas Hardy, and the close of *Tess of the D'Urbervilles.* Life's tragedy is not God's jest. It is working out a real issue with Him. . . . The answer is there, and is the gift of God. It is provided. And it is practical. . . . It is not . . . an answer to a riddle but a victory in a battle. . . . So, the practical solution of life by the soul is outside life. The destiny of experience is beyond itself. . . . If life is a problem, its solution is a faith. . . . We

do not see the answer; we trust the Answerer. . . . We do not gain the victory; we are united with the Victor.[8]

So the Lord turned the captivity of Job, when he prayed for his friends. It was when the ancient mariner prayed that the albatross fell from his neck:

He prayeth best who loveth best,
All things both great and small;
For the dear God who loveth us,
He made and loveth all.[9]

Could such a reconciliation as this, between man and God, and man and man, have taken place without the revelation of love as it was in Christ Jesus, without even a glimpse of the suffering which was for all men, or of the God

[8] *The Justification of God* (London: Independent Press, 1948), pp. 208-212, 220, 221. Used by permission.
[9] Coleridge, "The Ancient Mariner," Part VII, st. xxiii.

16 After this lived Job a hundred and forty years, and saw his sons, and his sons' sons, *even* four generations.

17 So Job died, *being* old and full of days.

16 And after this Job lived a hundred and forty years, and saw his sons, and his sons' sons, four generations. 17 And Job died, an old man, and full of days.

---

totally dedicated, he could receive the possessions which he had renounced. The justice of God remains entire, and religion pure (see Intro., p. 902).

---

who in him entered in where life is at its lowest, and carried the burden of it, and transformed its pain, as Job's was transformed, into a blessing and a healing thing? This book says it did happen. Long, long before that third day when the light of God's victory began to shine into the world's darkness, and the dawn of another life broke over this life's sorrow. Can it happen again?

And the Lord blessed the latter end of Job more than his beginning. And he died, being old and full of days.

I smiled to think God's greatness flowed around our
   incompleteness,—
Round our restlessness, His rest.[1]

[1] Elizabeth Barrett Browning, "The Rhyme of the Duchess May." Conclusion, st. xi.